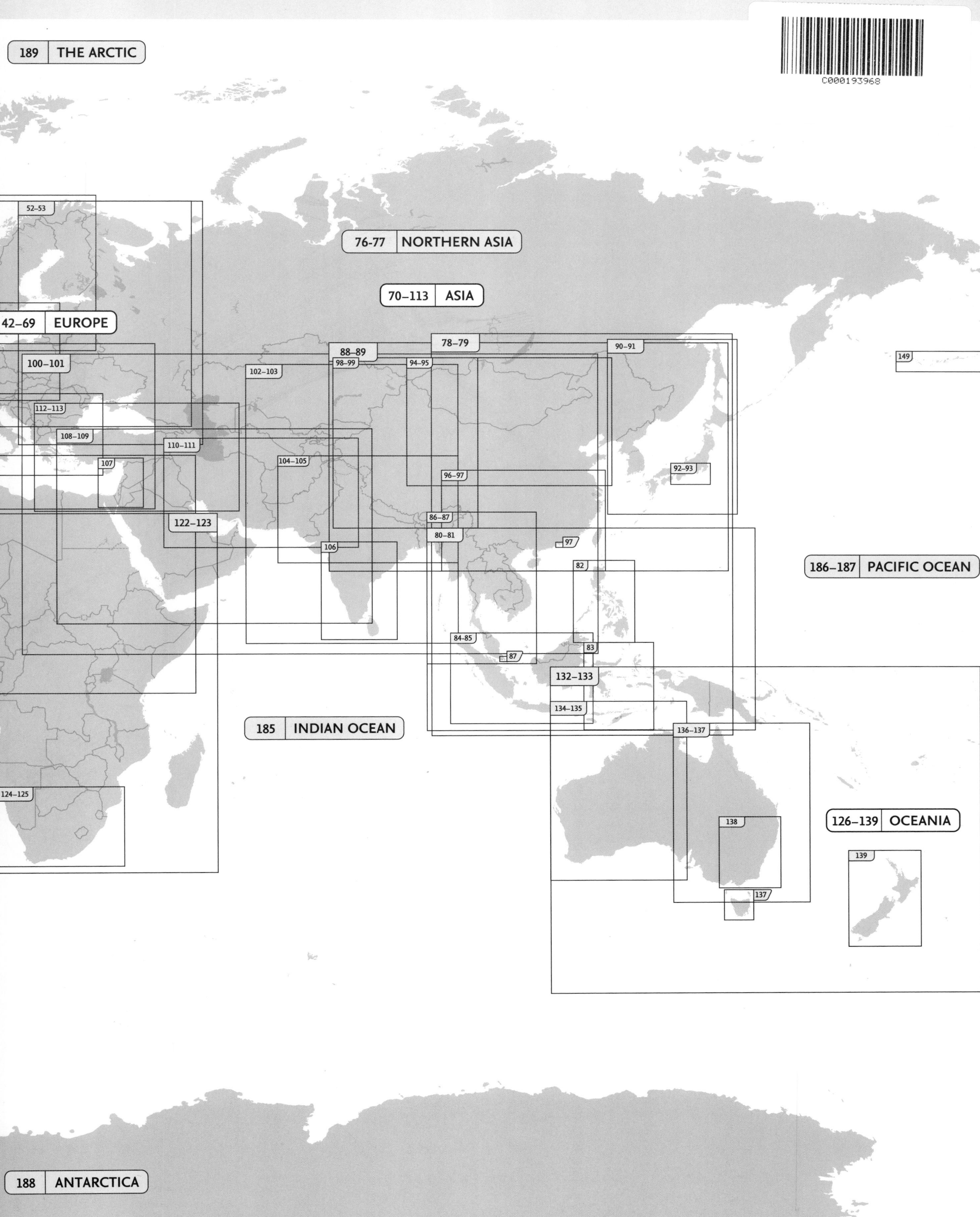

Find your map

Published by **Collins**
An imprint of HarperCollins Publishers
Westerhill Road
Bishopbriggs
Glasgow G64 2QT
www.harpercollins.co.uk

First Published 2010
Second edition 2012

Third edition 2015
Reprinted 2016

A catalogue record for this book is available from the British Library.

ISBN 978-0-00-813666-6

10 9 8 7 6 5 4 3 2

Printed in Hong Kong

All mapping in this atlas is generated from Collins Bartholomew digital databases.
Collins Bartholomew, the UK's leading independent geographical information supplier, can provide a digital, custom, and premium mapping service to a variety of markets.
For further information:
Tel: +44 (0) 208 307 4515
e-mail: collinsbartholomew@harpercollins.co.uk
or visit our website at: www.collinsbartholomew.com

If you would like to comment on any aspect of this book, please contact us at the above address or online.
e-mail: collinsmaps@harpercollins.co.uk
facebook.com/collinsmaps
@collinsmaps

Collins

WORLD ATLAS

COMPLETE EDITION

Contents

Title	Scale	Page
Map Symbols		4
World		**5–41**
Time Zones and International Organizations		5
Landscapes		6–7
Countries		8–9
Earthquakes and Volcanoes		10–11
Climate and Weather		12–13
Land Cover		14–15
Population		16–17
Urbanization and Cities		18–19
Communications		20–21
Social Indicators		22–23
Economy and Wealth		24–25
Conflict		26–27
Global Issues		28–29
Environmental Threats		30–31
Change		32–33
Satellite images		34–41
Uluṟu, Australia		34–35
Khor al Adaid, Qatar		36–37
Taylor Valley, Antarctica		38–39
Grand Coulee Dam, Washington State, U.S.A.		40–41
Europe		**42–69**
UNESCO World Heritage Sites		42–45
Landscapes		46–47
Countries		48–49
Northern Europe	1:8 600 000	50–51
Western Russian Federation	1:6 500 000	52–53
Scandinavia and the Baltic States	1:4 300 000	54–55
Inset: Iceland	1:5 200 000	
Inset: Faroe Islands	1:4 300 000	
Northwest Europe	1:4 300 000	56–57
England and Wales	1:1 700 000	58–59
Scotland	1:1 700 000	60
Inset: Shetland Islands	1:1 700 000	
Ireland	1:1 700 000	61
Belgium, Netherlands, Luxembourg and Northwest Germany	1:1 700 000	62–63
Southern Europe and the Mediterranean	1:8 600 000	64–65
France	1:4 300 000	66
Spain and Portugal	1:4 300 000	67
Italy and the Balkans	1:4 300 000	68–69
Asia		**70–113**
UNESCO World Heritage Sites		70–71
Landscapes		72–73
Countries		74–75
Northern Asia	1:17 300 000	76–77
Eastern and Southeast Asia	1:17 300 000	78–79
Southeast Asia	1:13 000 000	80–81
Philippines	1:5 600 000	82
Inset: Palau	1:1 000 000	
Central Indonesia	1:5 600 000	83
West Indonesia and Malaysia	1:5 400 000	84–85
Myanmar, Thailand, Peninsular Malaysia and Indo-China	1:6 100 000	86–87
Inset: Singapore	1:500 000	
Eastern Asia	1:13 000 000	88–89
Japan, North Korea and South Korea	1:6 100 000	90–91
Japan – Central Honshū	1:1 100 000	92–93
Northern China and Mongolia	1:6 100 000	94–95
Southeast China	1:6 100 000	96–97
Inset: Hong Kong	1:600 000	
West China	1:6 100 000	98–99
Central and Southern Asia	1:17 300 000	100–101

Contents

Asia (cont)		70–113
Southern Asia	1:11 200 000	102–103
Northern India, Nepal, Bhutan and Bangladesh	1:6 100 000	104–105
Southern India and Sri Lanka	1:6 100 000	106
Middle East	1:2 600 000	107
Southwest Asia	1:11 200 000	108–109
The Gulf, Iran, Afghanistan and Pakistan	1:6 100 000	110–111
Eastern Mediterranean, the Caucasus and Iraq	1:6 100 000	112–113

Africa		114–125
UNESCO World Heritage Sites		114–115
Landscapes		116–117
Countries		118–119
Northern Africa	1:13 800 000	120–121
Inset: Cape Verde	1:13 800 000	
Central and Southern Africa	1:13 800 000	122–123
South Africa	1:4 300 000	124–125

Oceania		126–139
UNESCO World Heritage Sites		126–127
Landscapes		128–129
Countries		130–131
Australia, New Zealand and Southwest Pacific	1:17 300 000	132–133
Western Australia	1:6 900 000	134–135
Eastern Australia	1:6 900 000	136–137
Inset: Tasmania	1:6 900 000	
Southeast Australia	1:4 300 000	138
New Zealand	1:4 500 000	139

North America		140–169
UNESCO World Heritage Sites		140–141
Landscapes		142–143
Countries		144–145
Canada	1:13 800 000	146–147
Alaska	1:6 100 000	148–149
Western Canada	1:6 100 000	150–151
Eastern Canada	1:6 100 000	152–153
United States of America	1:10 400 000	154–155
Western United States	1:6 100 000	156–157
Inset: Hawaiian Islands	1:6 100 000	
Southwest United States	1:3 000 000	158–159
Central United States	1:6 100 000	160–161
Eastern United States	1:6 100 000	162–163
Northeast United States	1:3 000 000	164–165
Mexico and Central America	1:6 200 000	166–167
Central America and the Caribbean	1:12 100 000	168–169

South America		170–179
UNESCO World Heritage Sites		170–171
Landscapes		172–173
Countries		174–175
Northern South America	1:12 100 000	176–177
Inset: Galapagos Islands	1:12 100 000	
Southern South America	1:12 100 000	178
Southeast Brazil	1:6 100 000	179

Oceans and Poles		180–189
Antarctica Satellite image		180–181
Features	1:43 200 000	182–183
Atlantic Ocean and Indian Ocean	1:43 200 000	184–185
Pacific Ocean	1:22 500 000	186–187
Antarctica	1:22 500 000	188
The Arctic		189

States and Territories	190–215
Index	216–311
Acknowledgements	312

Map Symbols

Southern Europe

Japan

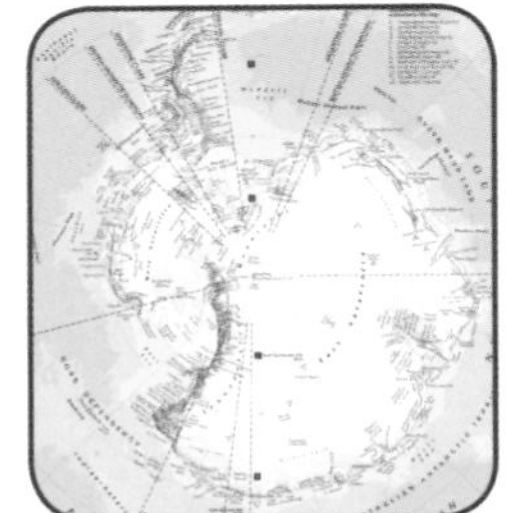

Antarctica

Population	National capital	Administrative capital	Other city or town
over 10 million	BEIJING	Karachi	New York
5 million to 10 million	JAKARTA	Tianjin	Nova Iguaçu
1 million to 5 million	KĀBUL	Sydney	Kaohsiung
500 000 to 1 million	BANGUI	Trujillo	Jeddah
100 000 to 500 000	WELLINGTON	Mansa	Apucarana
50 000 to 100 000	PORT OF SPAIN	Potenza	Arecibo
10 000 to 50 000	MALABO	Chinhoyi	Ceres
under 10 000	VALLETTA	Ati	Venta

Built-up area

Relief

Contour intervals and layer colours

Height

metres	feet
5000	16404
3000	9843
2000	6562
1000	3281
500	1640
200	656
0	0
below sea level	
0	0
200	656
2000	6562
4000	13124
6000	19686

Depth

1234 Summit
height in metres

-123 Spot height
height in metres

123 Ocean deep
depth in metres

Boundaries

International boundary

Disputed international boundary or alignment unconfirmed

Disputed territory boundary

Administrative boundary

Ceasefire line

UN Buffer zone

Miscellaneous

National park

Reserve or Regional park

Site of specific interest

Wall

Transport

Motorway (tunnel; under construction)

Main road (tunnel; under construction)

Secondary road (tunnel; under construction)

Track

Main airport

Regional airport

Main railway (tunnel; under construction)

Secondary railway (tunnel; under construction)

Other railway (tunnel; under construction)

Canal

Land and sea features

Desert

Oasis

Lava field

Marsh

1234 Volcano
height in metres

Ice cap or Glacier

Escarpment

Coral reef

1234 Pass
height in metres

Lakes and rivers

Lake

Impermanent lake

Salt lake or lagoon

Impermanent salt lake

Dry salt lake or salt pan

123 Lake height
surface height above sea level, in metres

River

Impermanent river or watercourse

Waterfall

Dam

Barrage

Time Zones

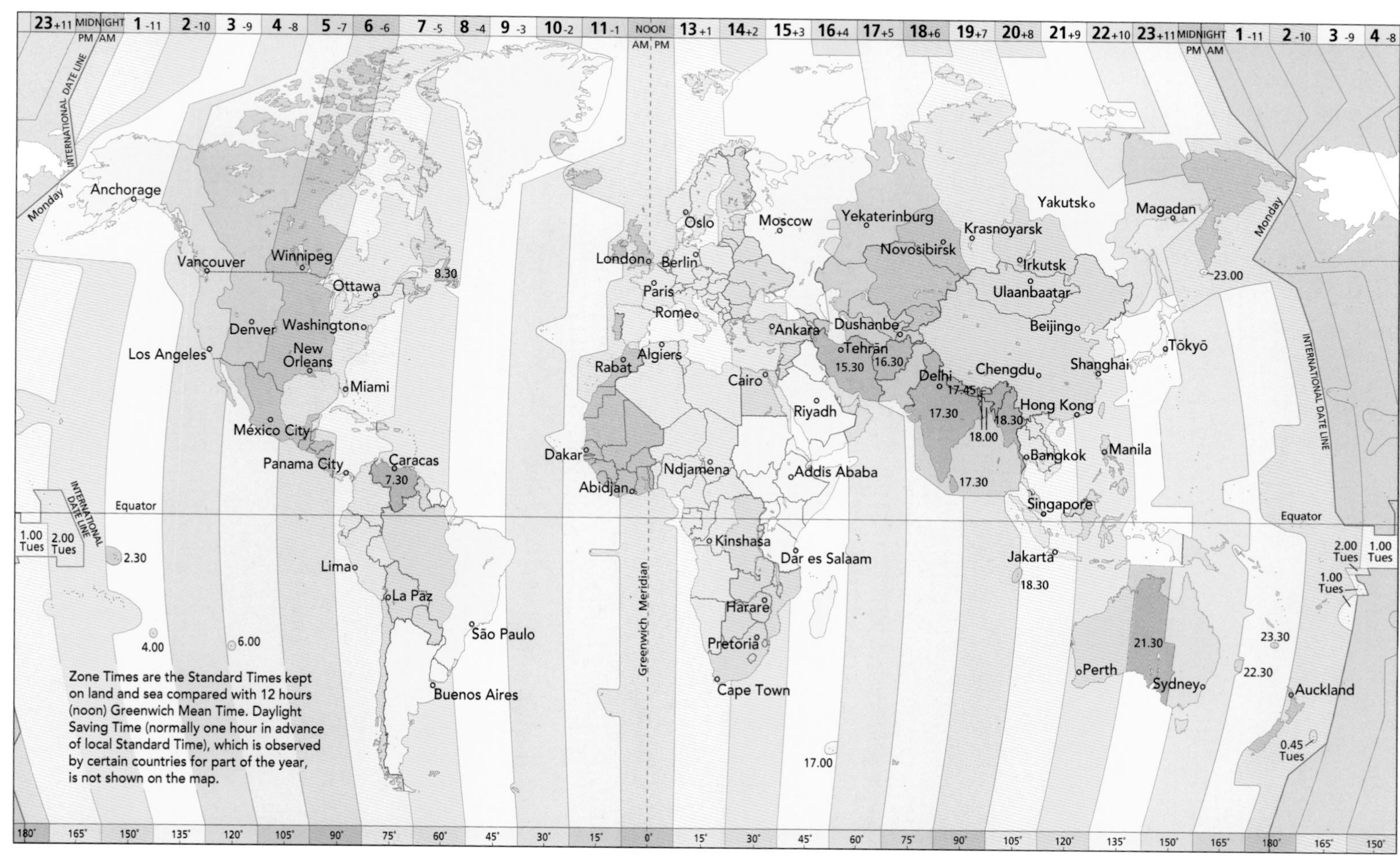

International Organizations

Andorra
Cyprus
Liechtenstein
Malta
San Marino

Antigua and Barbuda
Bahamas
Barbados
Dominica
Grenada
Jamaica
St Kitts and Nevis
St Lucia
St Vincent and the Grenadines
Trinidad and Tobago

Cape Verde
São Tomé and Príncipe

Bahrain
Qatar

Maldives

Comoros
Mauritius
Seychelles

Fiji
Kiribati
Nauru
Samoa
Solomon Islands
Tonga
Tuvalu
Vanuatu

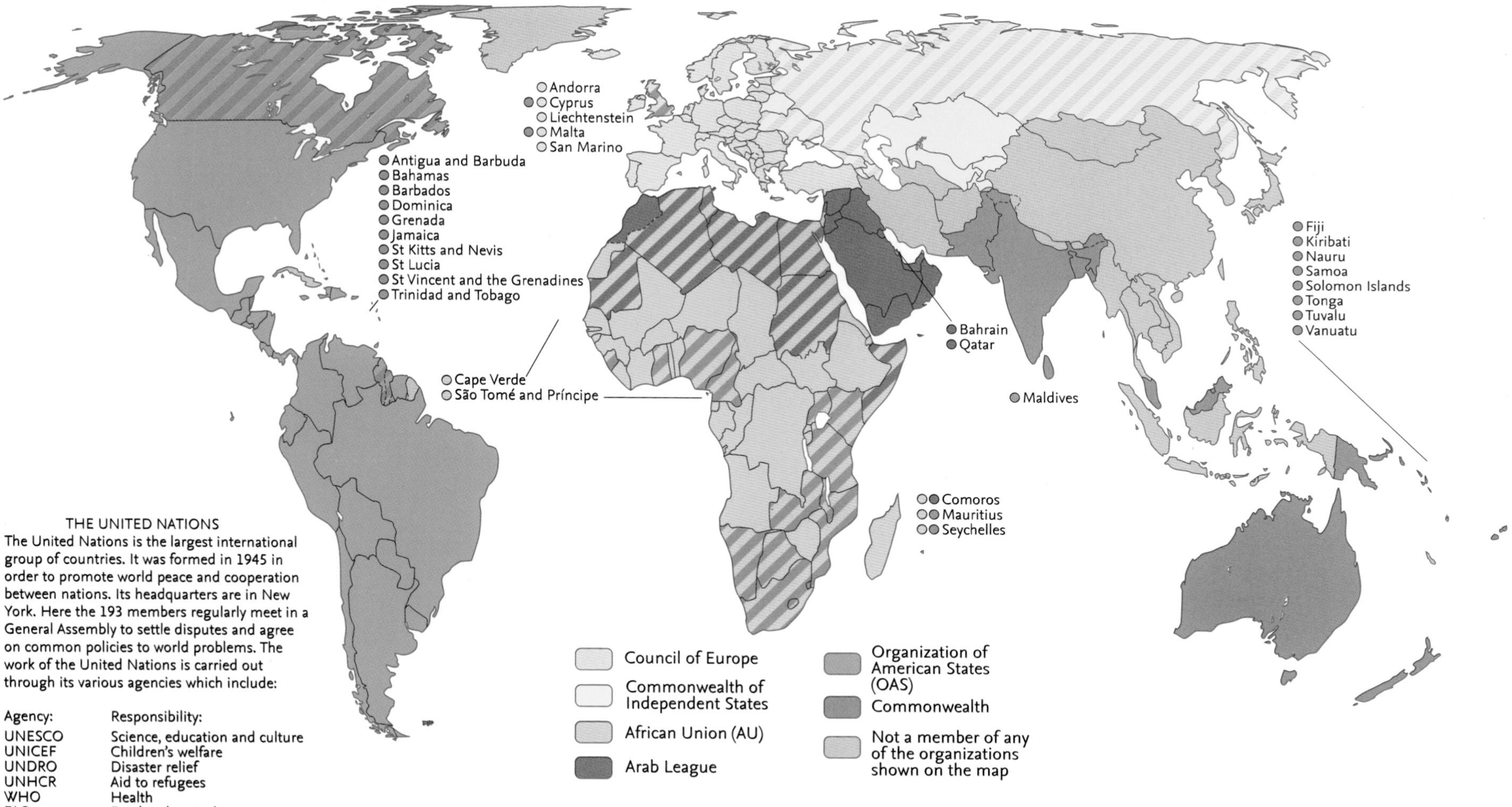

THE UNITED NATIONS

The United Nations is the largest international group of countries. It was formed in 1945 in order to promote world peace and cooperation between nations. Its headquarters are in New York. Here the 193 members regularly meet in a General Assembly to settle disputes and agree on common policies to world problems. The work of the United Nations is carried out through its various agencies which include:

Agency:	Responsibility:
UNESCO	Science, education and culture
UNICEF	Children's welfare
UNDRO	Disaster relief
UNHCR	Aid to refugees
WHO	Health
FAO	Food and agriculture
UNEP	Environment
UNDP	Development programme

Council of Europe
Commonwealth of Independent States
African Union (AU)
Arab League
Organization of American States (OAS)
Commonwealth
Not a member of any of the organizations shown on the map

Note: Countries represented by colour stripes are those which are members of more than one of the International Organizations shown on the map.

World
Landscapes

The earth's physical features, both on land and on the sea bed, closely reflect its geological structure. The current shapes of the continents and oceans have evolved over millions of years. Movements of the tectonic plates which make up the earth's crust have created some of the best-known and most spectacular features. The processes which have shaped the earth continue today with earthquakes, volcanoes, erosion, climatic variations and man's activities all affecting the earth's landscapes.

The total topographic range of the earth's surface is nearly 20 000 metres, from the highest point Mount Everest, to the lowest point in the Mariana Trench. Major mountain ranges include the Himalaya, the Andes and the Rocky Mountains, each of which give rise to some of the world's greatest rivers. In contrast, the deserts of the Sahara, Australia, the Arabian Peninsula and the Gobi cover vast areas and each provide unique landscapes.

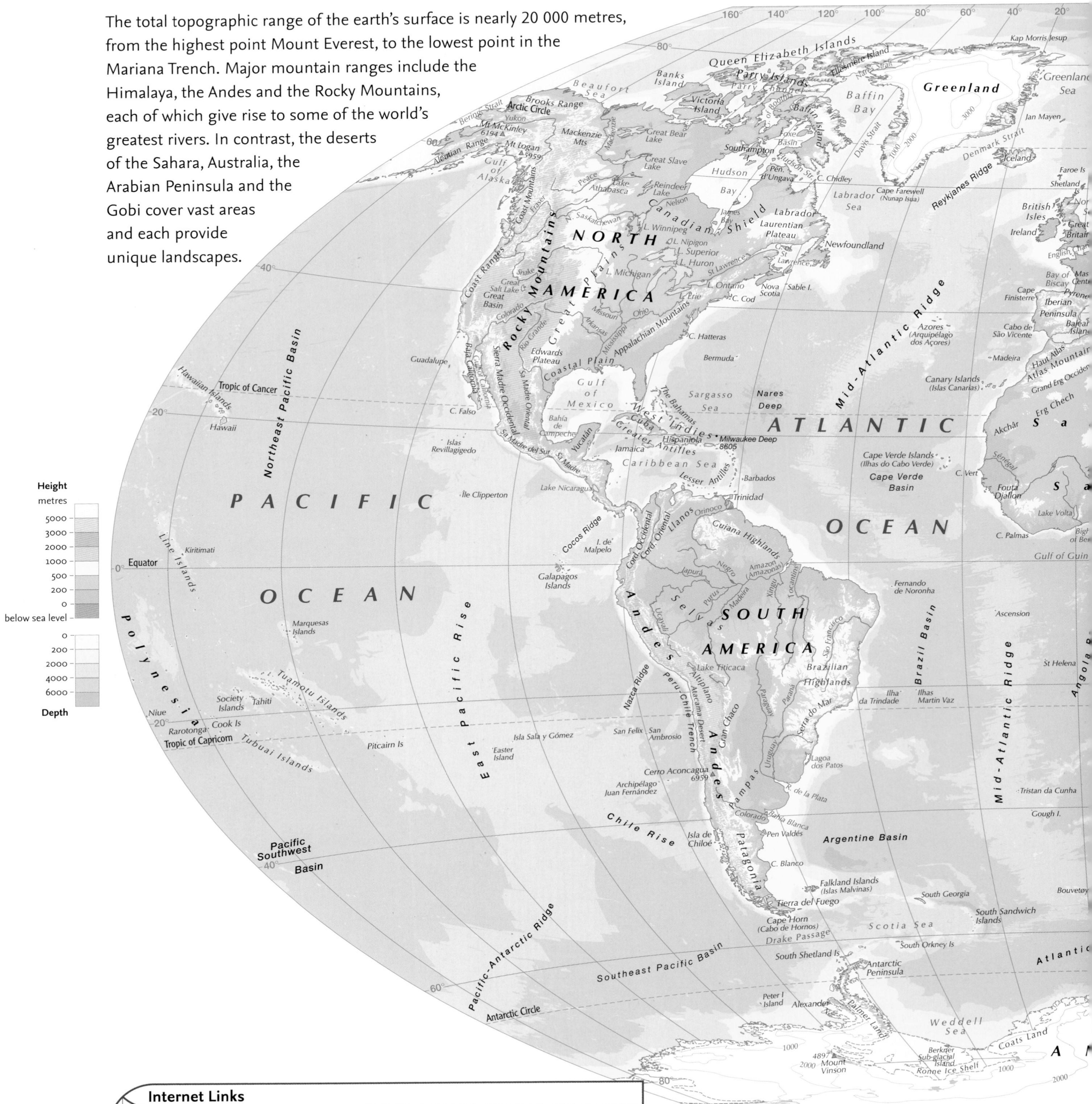

Height
metres
5000
3000
2000
1000
500
200
0
below sea level
0
200
2000
4000
6000
Depth

Internet Links	
United Nations Environment Programme	**www.unep.org**
IUCN International Union for Conservation of Nature	**www.iucn.org**
NASA Visible Earth	**visibleearth.nasa.gov**
NASA Earth Observatory	**earthobservatory.nasa.gov**
USGS Earth Resources Observation and Science	**eros.usgs.gov**

Earth's dimensions

Mass	5.974 x 10^{21} tonnes
Total area	509 450 000 sq km / 196 698 645 sq miles
Land area	149 450 000 sq km / 57 702 645 sq miles
Water area	360 000 000 sq km / 138 996 000 sq miles
Volume	1 083 207 x 10^6 cubic km / 259 911 x 10^6 cubic miles
Equatorial diameter	12 756 km / 7 927 miles
Polar diameter	12 714 km / 7 900 miles
Equatorial circumference	40 075 km / 24 903 miles
Meridional circumference	40 008 km / 24 861 miles

Facts

- Approximately 10% of the Earth's land surface is permanently covered by ice
- The Pacific Ocean is larger than all the continents' land areas combined
- The world's highest waterfall, 979 metres high, is Angel Falls, Venezuela
- 52% of the Earth's land surface is below 500 metres
- The mean elevation of the Earth's land surface is 840 metres
- Lake Baikal is the world's deepest lake with a maximum depth of 1 642 metres

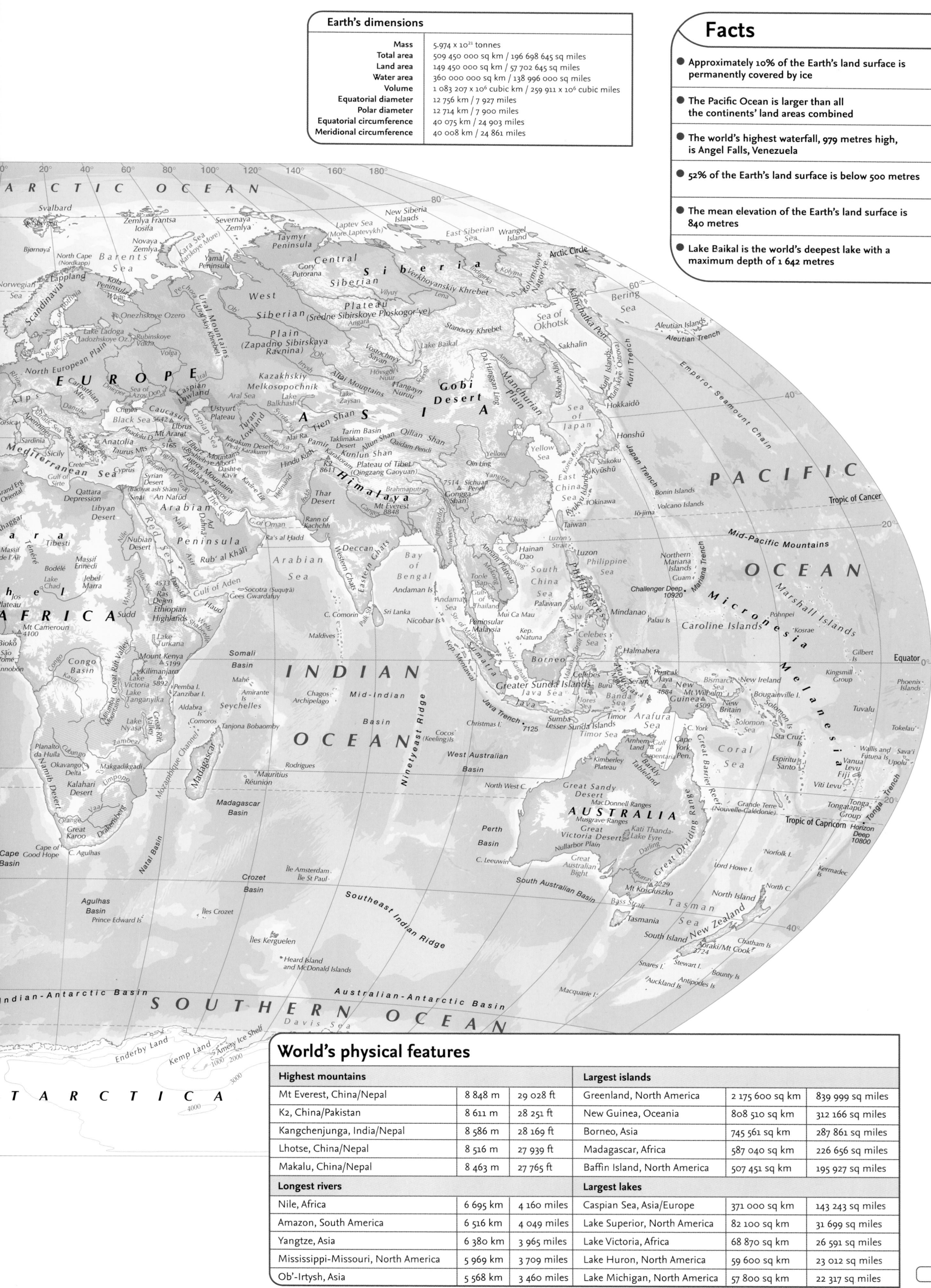

World's physical features

Highest mountains		
Mt Everest, China/Nepal	8 848 m	29 028 ft
K2, China/Pakistan	8 611 m	28 251 ft
Kangchenjunga, India/Nepal	8 586 m	28 169 ft
Lhotse, China/Nepal	8 516 m	27 939 ft
Makalu, China/Nepal	8 463 m	27 765 ft

Longest rivers		
Nile, Africa	6 695 km	4 160 miles
Amazon, South America	6 516 km	4 049 miles
Yangtze, Asia	6 380 km	3 965 miles
Mississippi-Missouri, North America	5 969 km	3 709 miles
Ob'-Irtysh, Asia	5 568 km	3 460 miles

Largest islands		
Greenland, North America	2 175 600 sq km	839 999 sq miles
New Guinea, Oceania	808 510 sq km	312 166 sq miles
Borneo, Asia	745 561 sq km	287 861 sq miles
Madagascar, Africa	587 040 sq km	226 656 sq miles
Baffin Island, North America	507 451 sq km	195 927 sq miles

Largest lakes		
Caspian Sea, Asia/Europe	371 000 sq km	143 243 sq miles
Lake Superior, North America	82 100 sq km	31 699 sq miles
Lake Victoria, Africa	68 870 sq km	26 591 sq miles
Lake Huron, North America	59 600 sq km	23 012 sq miles
Lake Michigan, North America	57 800 sq km	22 317 sq miles

World
Countries

The current pattern of the world's countries and territories is a result of a long history of exploration, colonialism, conflict and politics. The fact that there are currently 196 independent countries in the world – the most recent, South Sudan, only being created in July 2011 – illustrates the significant political changes which have occurred since 1950 when there were only eighty-two. There has been a steady progression away from colonial influences over the last fifty years, although many dependent overseas territories remain.

The shapes of countries and the pattern of international boundaries reflect both physical and political processes. Some borders follow natural features – rivers, mountain ranges, etc – others are defined according to political agreement or as a result of war. Some are still subject to dispute between two or more countries, and many remain undefined on the ground.

Facts

- **The longest single continuous land border stretches for 6 416 kilometres between Canada and the USA**
- **Both China and Russia have land borders with 14 different countries**
- **Vatican City, the smallest independent country, was created in 1929 as an enclave within Rome, the capital of Italy**
- **All countries of the world are members of the United Nations except Kosovo, Taiwan and Vatican City**

Internet Links

United Nations	**www.un.org**
Foreign and Commonwealth Office	**www.fco.gov.uk**
International Boundaries Research Unit	**www.dur.ac.uk/ibru**
Permanent Committee on Geographical Names	**www.pcgn.org.uk**
U.S. Board on Geographic Names	**geonames.usgs.gov**

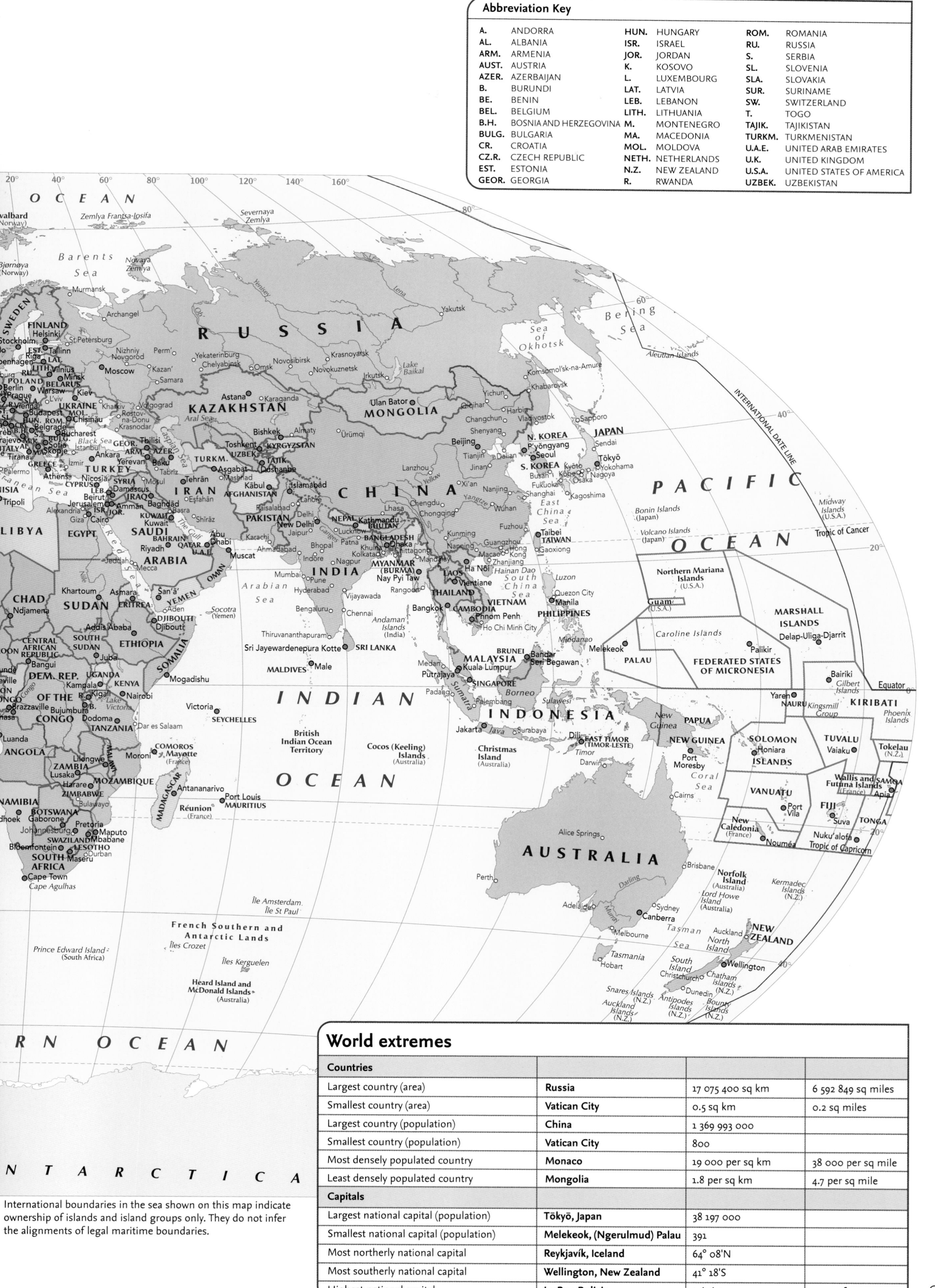

Abbreviation Key

A.	ANDORRA	HUN.	HUNGARY	ROM.	ROMANIA
AL.	ALBANIA	ISR.	ISRAEL	RU.	RUSSIA
ARM.	ARMENIA	JOR.	JORDAN	S.	SERBIA
AUST.	AUSTRIA	K.	KOSOVO	SL.	SLOVENIA
AZER.	AZERBAIJAN	L.	LUXEMBOURG	SLA.	SLOVAKIA
B.	BURUNDI	LAT.	LATVIA	SUR.	SURINAME
BE.	BENIN	LEB.	LEBANON	SW.	SWITZERLAND
BEL.	BELGIUM	LITH.	LITHUANIA	T.	TOGO
B.H.	BOSNIA AND HERZEGOVINA	M.	MONTENEGRO	TAJIK.	TAJIKISTAN
BULG.	BULGARIA	MA.	MACEDONIA	TURKM.	TURKMENISTAN
CR.	CROATIA	MOL.	MOLDOVA	U.A.E.	UNITED ARAB EMIRATES
CZ.R.	CZECH REPUBLIC	NETH.	NETHERLANDS	U.K.	UNITED KINGDOM
EST.	ESTONIA	N.Z.	NEW ZEALAND	U.S.A.	UNITED STATES OF AMERICA
GEOR.	GEORGIA	R.	RWANDA	UZBEK.	UZBEKISTAN

International boundaries in the sea shown on this map indicate ownership of islands and island groups only. They do not infer the alignments of legal maritime boundaries.

World extremes

Countries			
Largest country (area)	**Russia**	17 075 400 sq km	6 592 849 sq miles
Smallest country (area)	**Vatican City**	0.5 sq km	0.2 sq miles
Largest country (population)	**China**	1 369 993 000	
Smallest country (population)	**Vatican City**	800	
Most densely populated country	**Monaco**	19 000 per sq km	38 000 per sq mile
Least densely populated country	**Mongolia**	1.8 per sq km	4.7 per sq mile
Capitals			
Largest national capital (population)	**Tōkyō, Japan**	38 197 000	
Smallest national capital (population)	**Melekeok, (Ngerulmud) Palau**	391	
Most northerly national capital	**Reykjavík, Iceland**	64° 08'N	
Most southerly national capital	**Wellington, New Zealand**	41° 18'S	
Highest national capital	**La Paz, Bolivia**	3 636 m	11 910 ft

World

Earthquakes and Volcanoes

Earthquakes and volcanoes hold a constant fascination because of their power, their beauty, and the fact that they cannot be controlled or accurately predicted. Our understanding of these phenomena relies mainly on the theory of plate tectonics. This defines the Earth's surface as a series of 'plates' which are constantly moving relative to each other, at rates of a few centimetres per year. As plates move against each other enormous pressure builds up and when the rocks can no longer bear this pressure they fracture, and energy is released as an earthquake. The pressures involved can also melt the rock to form magma which then rises to the Earth's surface to form a volcano. The distribution of earthquakes and volcanoes therefore relates closely to plate boundaries. In particular, most active volcanoes and much of the Earth's seismic activity are centred on the 'Ring of Fire' around the Pacific Ocean.

Facts

- **Over 900 earthquakes of magnitude 5.0 or greater occur every year**
- **An earthquake of magnitude 8.0 releases energy equivalent to 1 billion tons of TNT explosive**
- **Ground shaking during an earthquake in Alaska in 1964 lasted for 3 minutes**
- **Indonesia has more than 120 volcanoes and over 30% of the world's active volcanoes**
- **Volcanoes can produce very fertile soil and important industrial materials and chemicals**

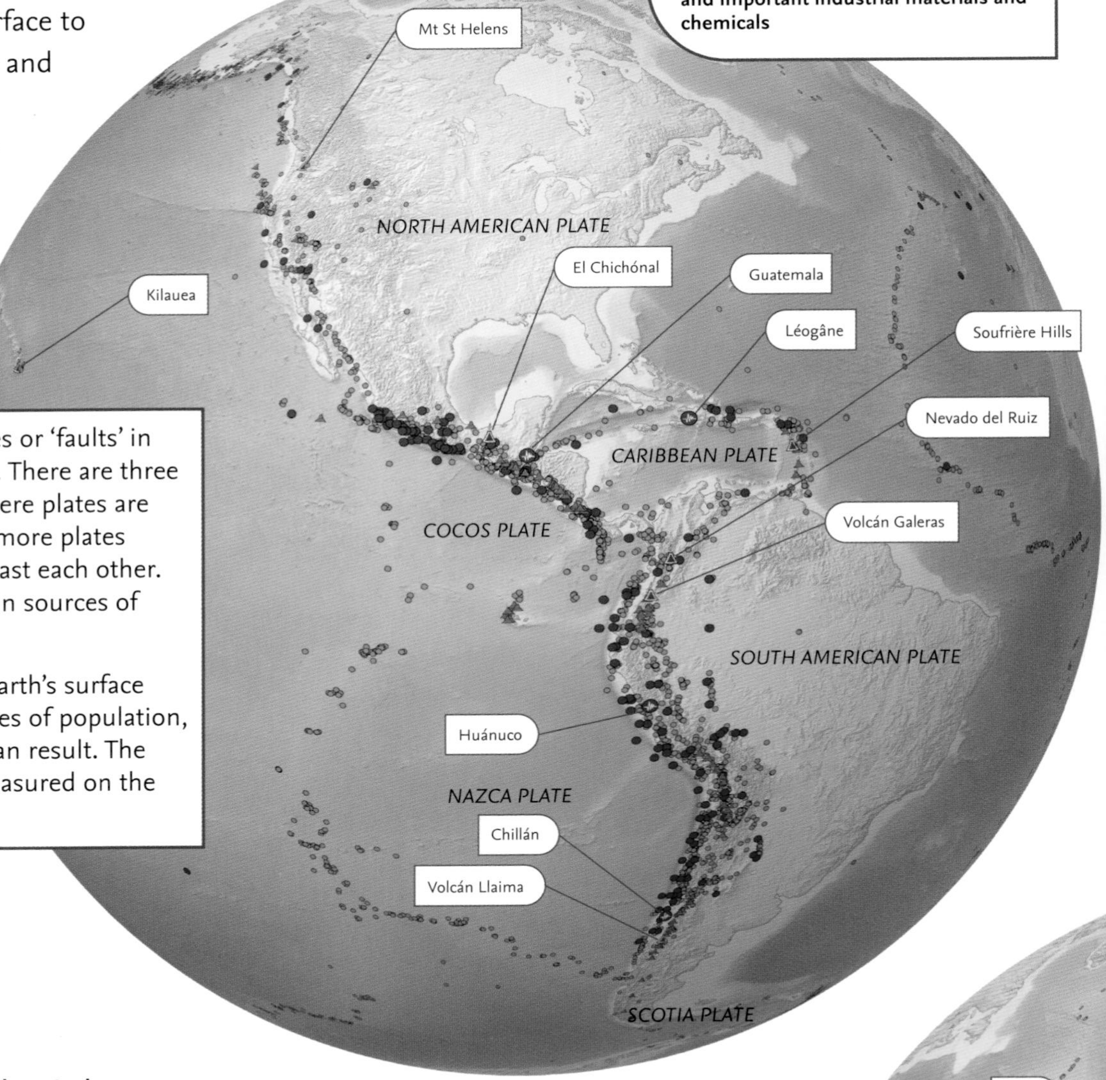

Mt St Helens
NORTH AMERICAN PLATE
Kilauea
El Chichónal
Guatemala
Léogâne
Soufrière Hills
Nevado del Ruiz
CARIBBEAN PLATE
COCOS PLATE
Volcán Galeras
SOUTH AMERICAN PLATE
Huánuco
NAZCA PLATE
Chillán
Volcán Llaima
SCOTIA PLATE
Chlef
SOUTH AMERICAN PLATE

Earthquakes

Earthquakes are caused by movement along fractures or 'faults' in the Earth's crust, particularly along plate boundaries. There are three types of plate boundary: constructive boundaries where plates are moving apart; destructive boundaries where two or more plates collide; conservative boundaries where plates slide past each other. Destructive and conservative boundaries are the main sources of earthquake activity.

The epicentre of an earthquake is the point on the Earth's surface directly above its source. If this is near to large centres of population, and the earthquake is powerful, major devastation can result. The size, or magnitude, of an earthquake is generally measured on the Richter Scale.

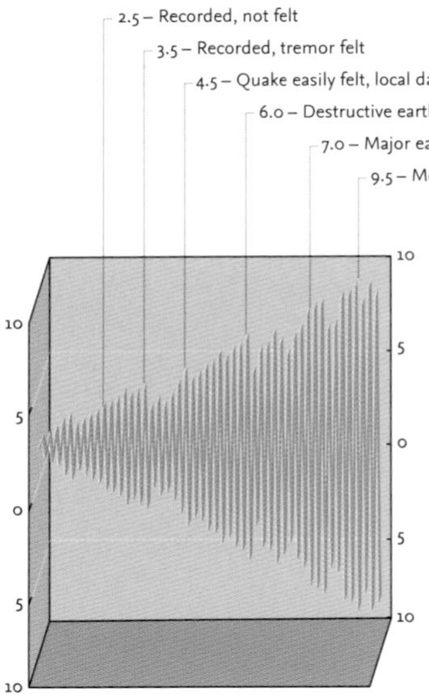

2.5 – Recorded, not felt
3.5 – Recorded, tremor felt
4.5 – Quake easily felt, local damage caused
6.0 – Destructive earthquake
7.0 – Major earthquake
9.5 – Most powerful earthquake recorded

10 5 0 5 10

Earthquake magnitude – the Richter Scale

The scale measures the energy released by an earthquake. It is a logarithmic scale: an earthquake measuring 4 is thirty times more powerful than one measuring 3, and a quake measuring 6 is 27 000 times more powerful than one measuring 3.

Plate boundaries

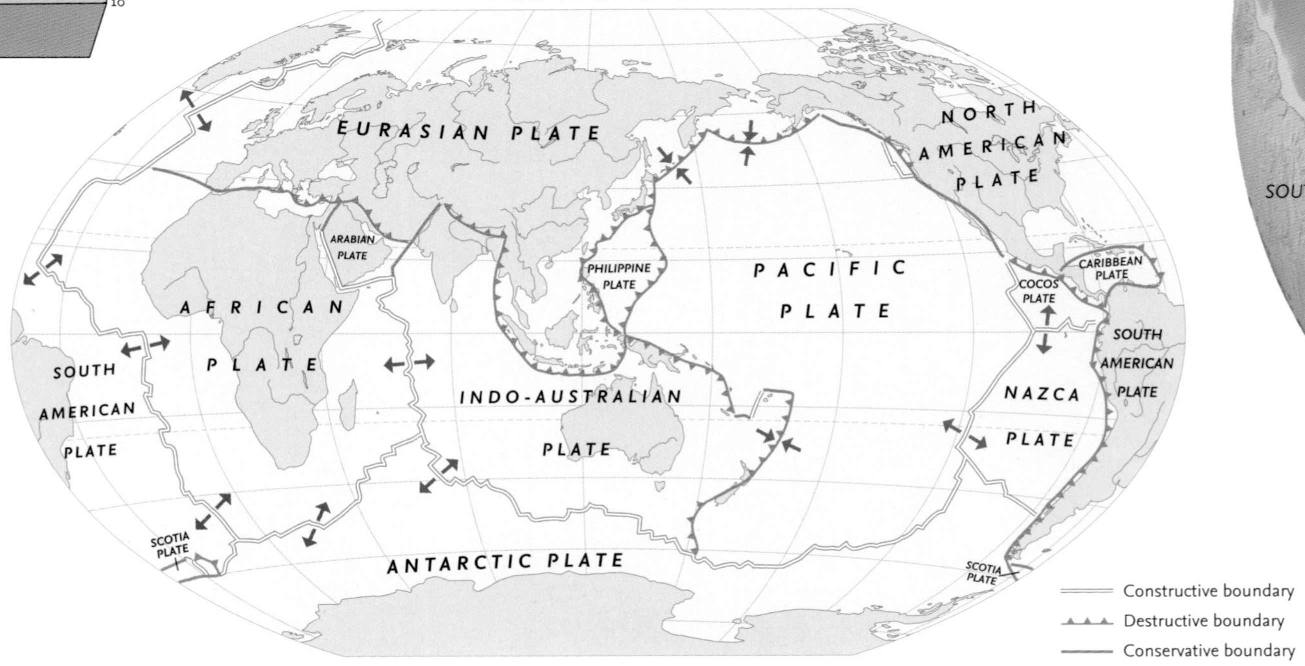

EURASIAN PLATE
NORTH AMERICAN PLATE
ARABIAN PLATE
PHILIPPINE PLATE
PACIFIC PLATE
CARIBBEAN PLATE
COCOS PLATE
AFRICAN PLATE
SOUTH AMERICAN PLATE
INDO-AUSTRALIAN PLATE
NAZCA PLATE
SCOTIA PLATE
ANTARCTIC PLATE

Constructive boundary
Destructive boundary
Conservative boundary

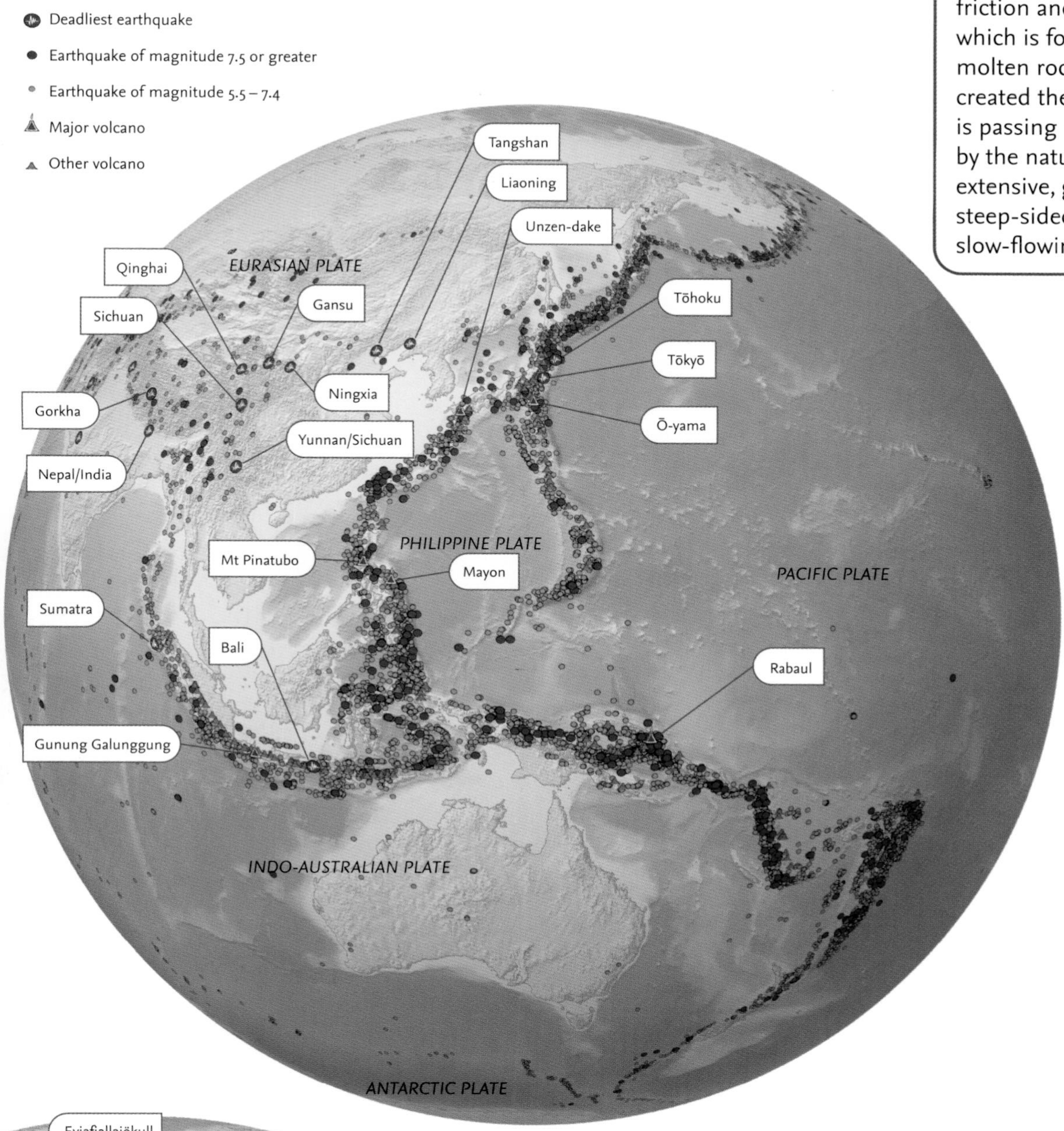

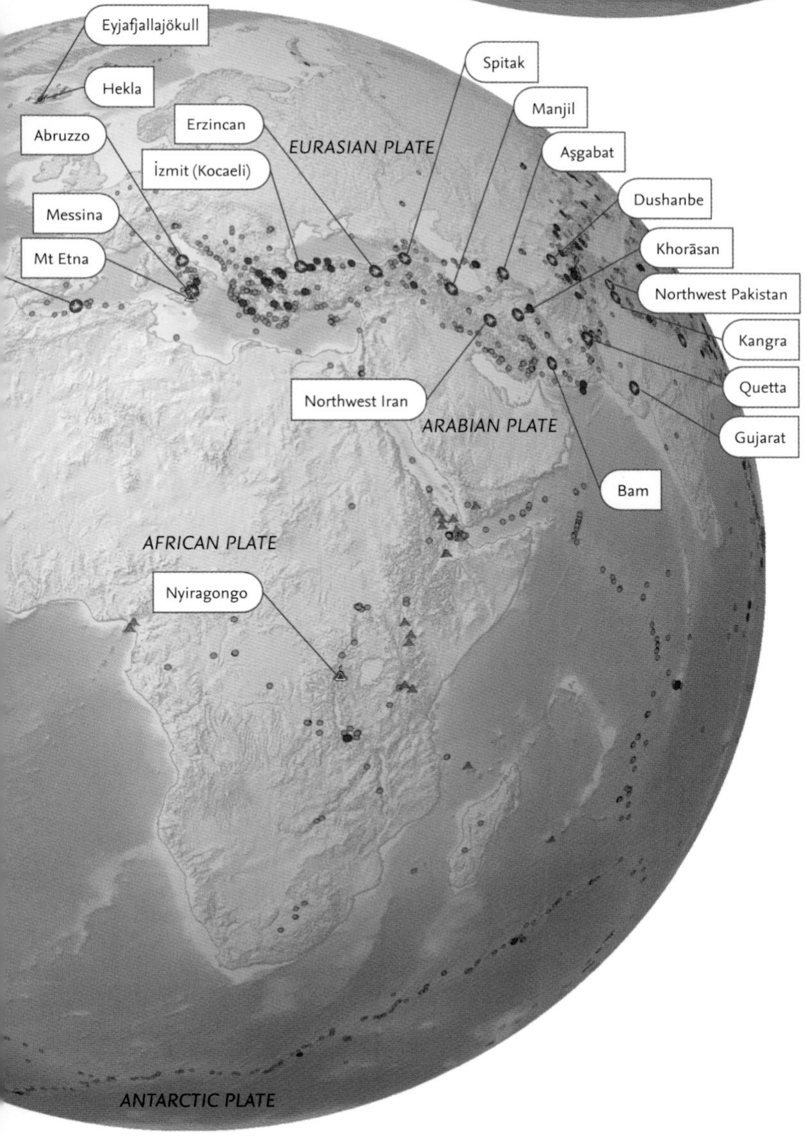

Deadliest earthquake
Earthquake of magnitude 7.5 or greater
Earthquake of magnitude 5.5 – 7.4
Major volcano
Other volcano

Volcanoes

The majority of volcanoes occur along destructive plate boundaries in the 'subduction zone' where one plate passes under another. The friction and pressure causes the rock to melt and to form magma which is forced upwards to the Earth's surface where it erupts as molten rock (lava) or as particles of ash or cinder. This process created the numerous volcanoes in the Andes, where the Nazca Plate is passing under the South American Plate. Volcanoes can be defined by the nature of the material they emit. 'Shield' volcanoes have extensive, gentle slopes formed from free-flowing lava, while steep-sided 'continental' volcanoes are created from thicker, slow-flowing lava and ash.

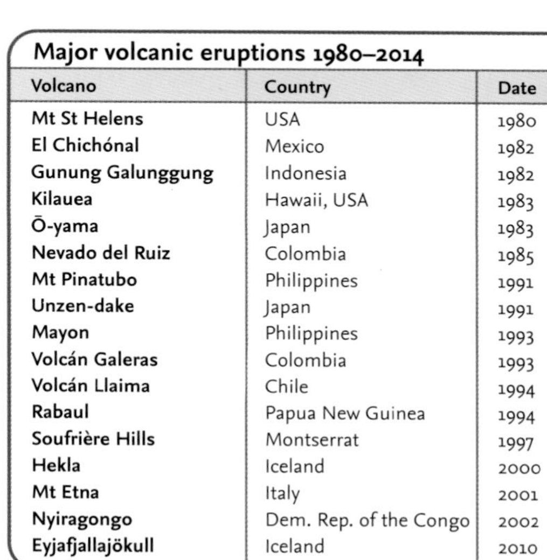

Major volcanic eruptions 1980–2014

Volcano	Country	Date
Mt St Helens	USA	1980
El Chichónal	Mexico	1982
Gunung Galunggung	Indonesia	1982
Kilauea	Hawaii, USA	1983
Ō-yama	Japan	1983
Nevado del Ruiz	Colombia	1985
Mt Pinatubo	Philippines	1991
Unzen-dake	Japan	1991
Mayon	Philippines	1993
Volcán Galeras	Colombia	1993
Volcán Llaima	Chile	1994
Rabaul	Papua New Guinea	1994
Soufrière Hills	Montserrat	1997
Hekla	Iceland	2000
Mt Etna	Italy	2001
Nyiragongo	Dem. Rep. of the Congo	2002
Eyjafjallajökull	Iceland	2010

Deadliest earthquakes since 1900

Year	Location	Deaths
1905	**Kangra,** India	19 000
1907	west of **Dushanbe,** Tajikistan	12 000
1908	**Messina,** Italy	110 000
1915	**Abruzzo,** Italy	35 000
1917	**Bali,** Indonesia	15 000
1920	**Ningxia Province,** China	200 000
1923	**Tōkyō,** Japan	142 807
1927	**Qinghai Province,** China	200 000
1932	**Gansu Province,** China	70 000
1933	**Sichuan Province,** China	10 000
1934	**Nepal/India**	10 700
1935	**Quetta,** Pakistan	30 000
1939	**Chillán,** Chile	28 000
1939	**Erzincan,** Turkey	32 700
1948	**Aşgabat,** Turkmenistan	19 800
1962	northwest **Iran**	12 225
1970	**Huánuco Province,** Peru	66 794
1974	**Yunnan** and **Sichuan Provinces,** China	20 000
1975	**Liaoning Province,** China	10 000
1976	central **Guatemala**	22 778
1976	**Tangshan,** Hebei Province, China	255 000
1978	**Khorāsan Province,** Iran	20 000
1980	**Chlef,** Algeria	11 000
1988	**Spitak,** Armenia	25 000
1990	**Manjil,** Iran	50 000
1999	**İzmit (Kocaeli),** Turkey	17 000
2001	**Gujarat,** India	20 000
2003	**Bam,** Iran	26 271
2004	off **Sumatra,** Indian Ocean	> 225 000
2005	northwest **Pakistan**	74 648
2008	**Sichuan Province,** China	> 60 000
2009	**Abruzzo** region, Italy	308
2009	**Sumatra,** Indonesia	> 1 100
2010	**Léogâne,** Haiti	222 570
2011	**Tōhoku,** Japan	> 14 500
2015	**Gorkha,** Nepal	> 7 500

Internet Links

USGS Earthquake Hazards Program	**earthquake.usgs.gov**
USGS Volcano Hazards Program	**volcanoes.usgs.gov**
British Geological Survey	**www.bgs.ac.uk**
NASA Natural Hazards	**earthobservatory.nasa.gov/NaturalHazards**
Volcano World	**volcano.oregonstate.edu**

World
Climate and Weather

The climate of a region is defined by its long-term prevailing weather conditions. Classification of Climate Types is based on the relationship between temperature and humidity and how these factors are affected by latitude, altitude, ocean currents and winds. Weather is the specific short term condition which occurs locally and consists of events such as thunderstorms, hurricanes, blizzards and heat waves. Temperature and rainfall data recorded at weather stations can be plotted graphically and the graphs shown here, typical of each climate region, illustrate the various combinations of temperature and rainfall which exist worldwide for each month of the year. Data used for climate graphs are based on average monthly figures recorded over a minimum period of thirty years.

Major climate regions, ocean currents and sea surface temperatures

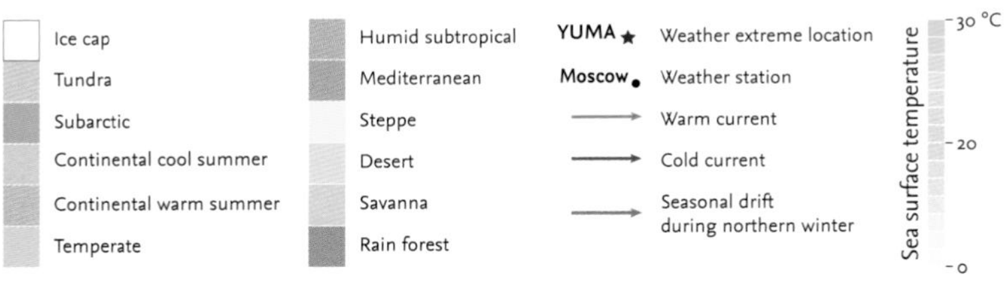

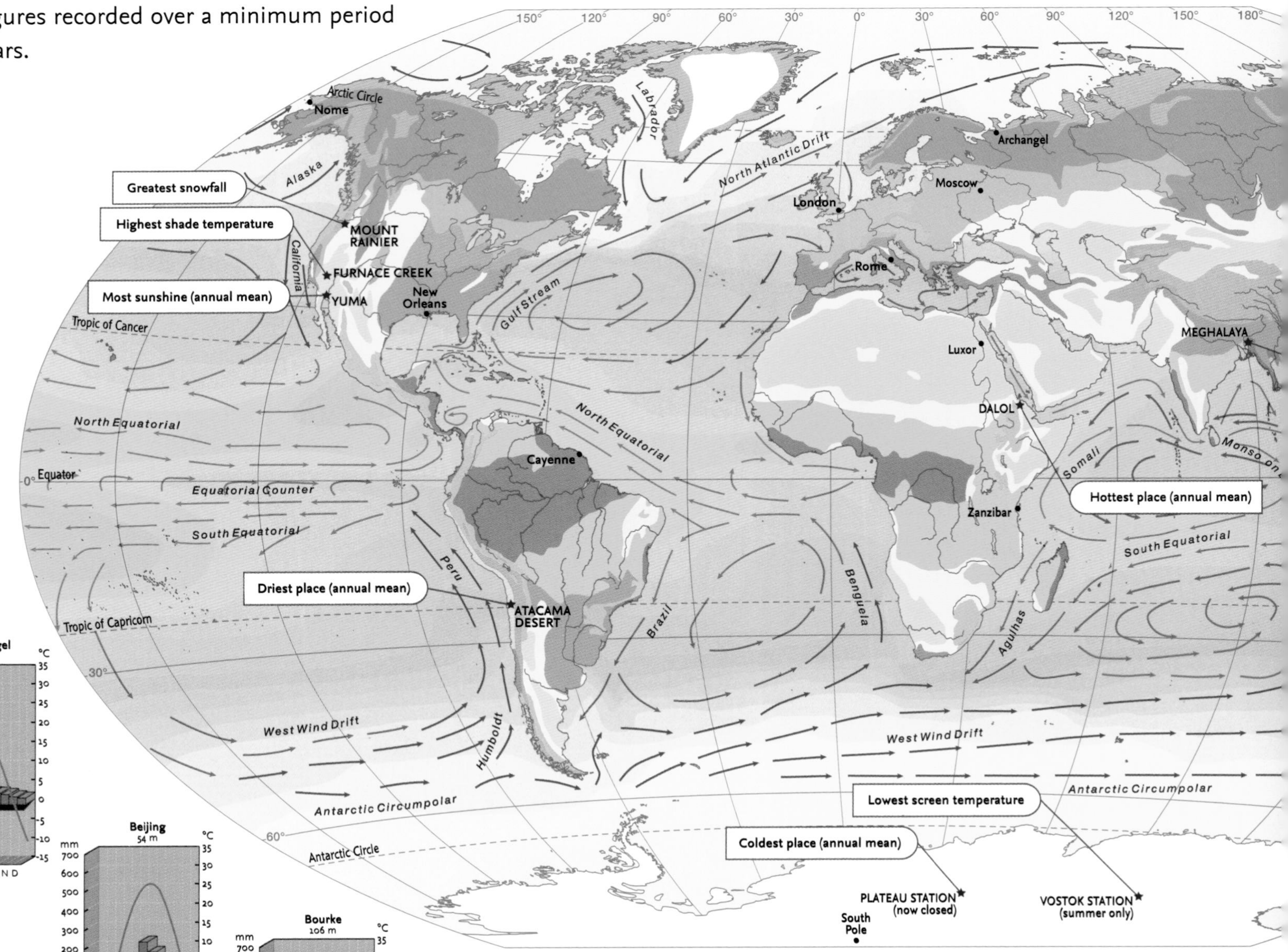

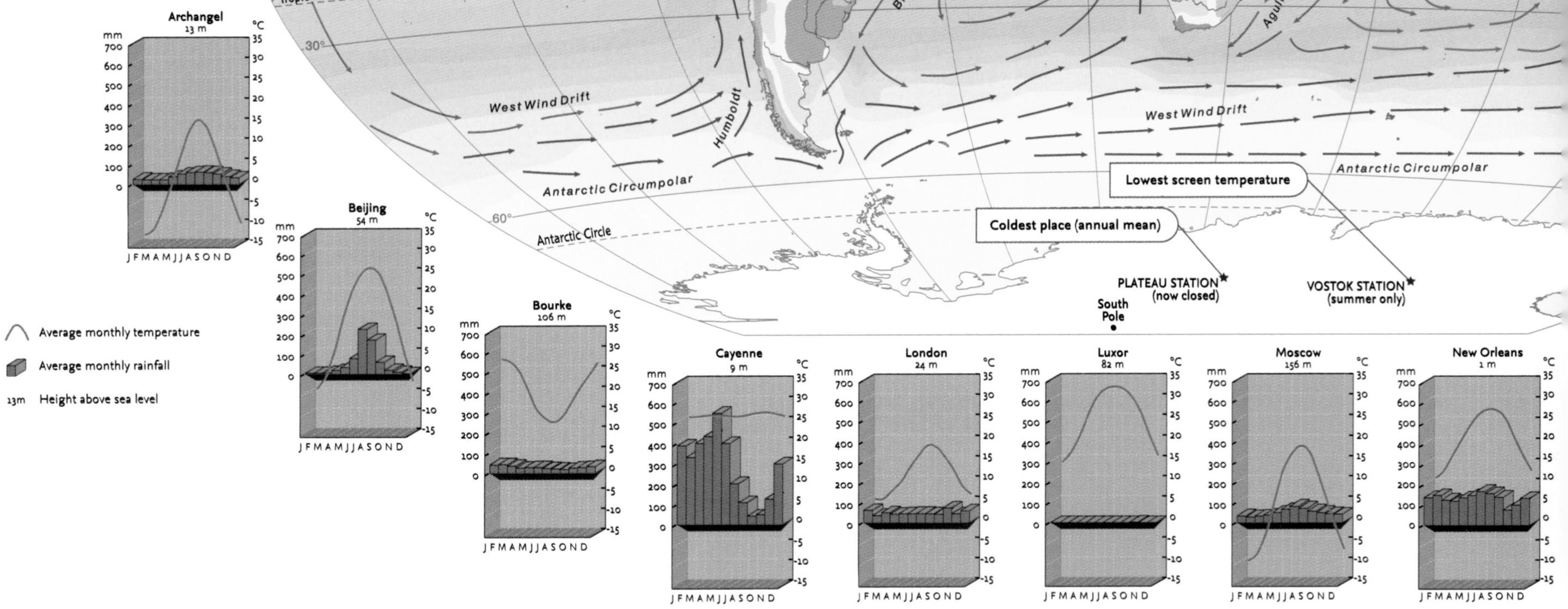

Average monthly temperature

Average monthly rainfall

13m Height above sea level

Climate change

The temperatures in 2014 were the warmest on record with a global average 0.57 °C above the 1961–90 mean. Globally fourteen of the fifteen hottest years have been recorded this century. Most of this warming is caused by human activities which result in a build-up of greenhouse gases, mainly carbon dioxide, allowing heat to be trapped within the atmosphere. Carbon dioxide emissions have increased since the beginning of the industrial revolution due to burning of fossil fuels, increased urbanization, population growth, deforestation and industrial pollution.

Annual climate indicators such as number of frost-free days, length of growing season, heat wave frequency, number of wet days, length of dry spells and frequency of weather extremes are used to monitor climate change. The map opposite shows how future changes in temperature will not be spread evenly around the world. Some regions will warm faster than the global average, while others will warm more slowly. The Arctic is warming twice as fast as other areas mainly due to ice melting and there being less to reflect sunlight to keep the surface cool.

Facts

- Arctic Sea ice thickness has declined 40% in the last 40 years
- El Niño and La Niña episodes occur at irregular intervals of 2–7 years
- Sea levels are rising by one centimetre per decade
- Precipitation in the northern hemisphere is increasing
- Droughts have increased in frequency and intensity in parts of Asia and Africa

Projection of global temperatures 2090–2099

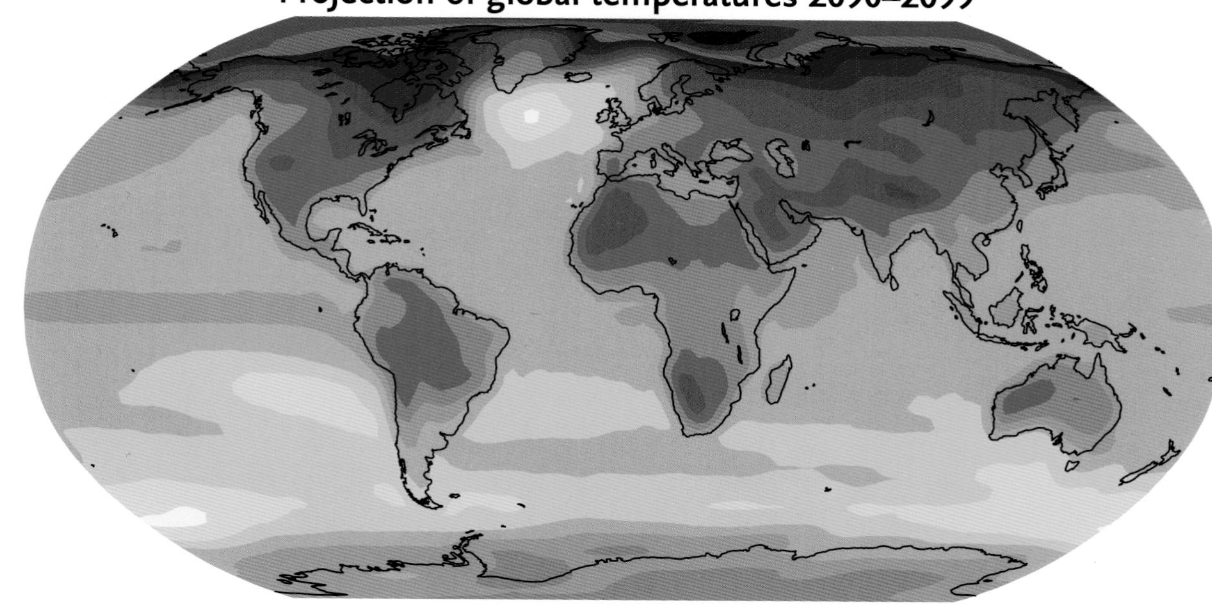

Arctic Circle
Oyashio
Beijing
Kuroshio
Tropic of Cancer
Wettest place (annual mean)
North Equatorial
Equator
Equatorial Counter
South Equatorial
Tropic of Capricorn
East Australia
Bourke
Windiest place
Antarctic Circle
COMMONWEALTH BAY

Zanzibar 15 m

Rome 2 m

Nome 11 m

Tracks of tropical storms

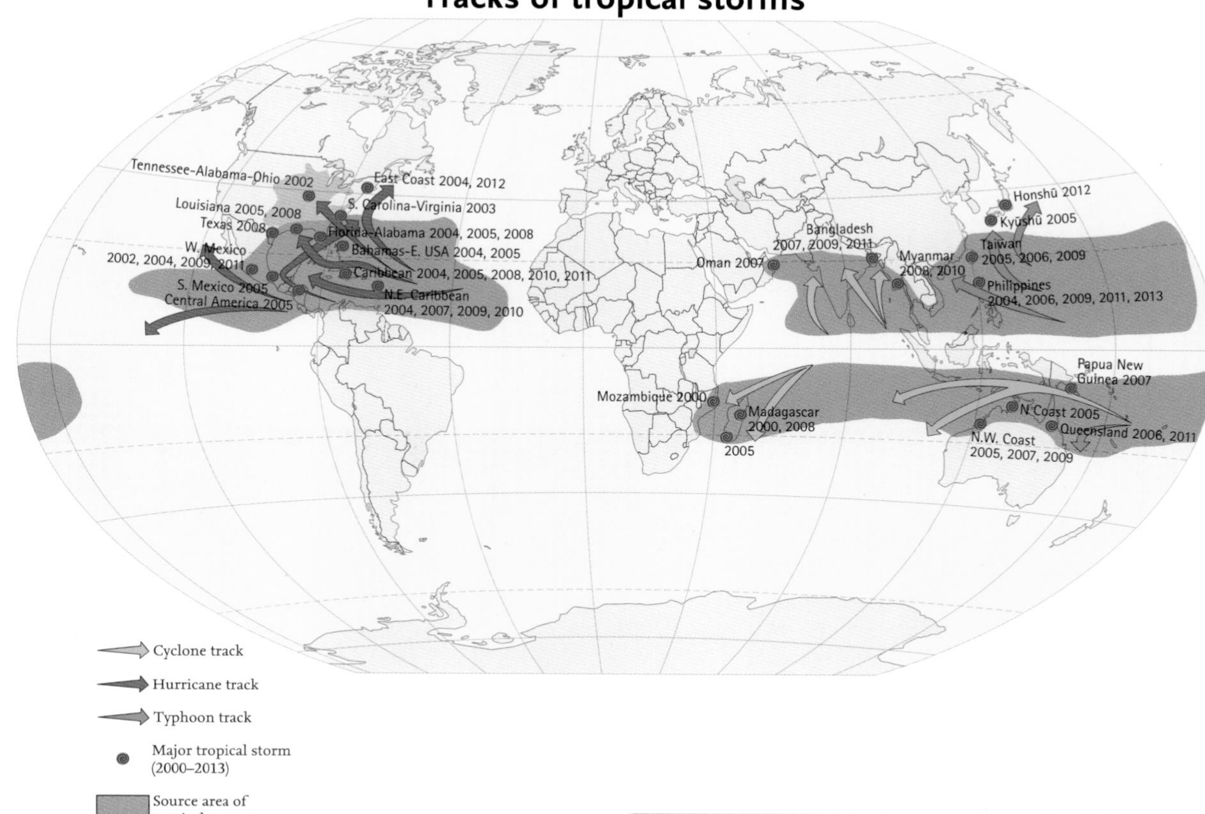

Tropical storms

Tropical storms are among the most powerful and destructive weather systems on Earth. Of the eighty to one hundred which develop annually over the tropical oceans, many make landfall and cause considerable damage to property and loss of life as a result of high winds and heavy rain. Although the number of tropical storms is projected to decrease, their intensity, and therefore their destructive power, is likely to increase.

Hurricane Sandy off the east coast of the USA, October 2012.

Weather extremes

Highest shade temperature	**56.7 °C/134 °F** Furnace Creek, Death Valley, California, USA (July 1913)
Hottest place - annual mean	**34.4 °C/93.9 °F** Dalol, Ethiopia
Driest place - annual mean	**0.1 mm/0.004 inches** Atacama Desert, Chile
Most sunshine - annual mean	**90%** Yuma, Arizona, USA (over 4000 hours)
Lowest screen temperature	**-89.2 °C/-128.6 °F** Vostok Station, Antarctica (July 1983)
Coldest place - annual mean	**-56.6 °C/-69.9 °F** Plateau Station, Antarctica
Wettest place - annual mean	**11 873 mm/467.4 inches** Meghalaya, India
Greatest snowfall	**31 102 mm/1 224.5 inches** Mount Rainier, Washington, USA (February 1971 – February 1972)
Windiest place	**322 km per hour/200 miles per hour** (in gales) Commonwealth Bay, Antarctica

Internet Links

Met Office	**www.metoffice.gov.uk**
BBC Weather Centre	**www.bbc.co.uk/weather**
National Oceanic and Atmospheric Administration	**www.noaa.gov**
National Climatic Data Center	**www.ncdc.noaa.gov**
United Nations World Meteorological Organization	**www.wmo.int**

World
Land Cover

The oxygen- and water-rich environment of the Earth has helped create a wide range of habitats. Forest and woodland ecosystems form the predominant natural land cover over most of the Earth's surface. Tropical rainforests are part of an intricate land-atmosphere relationship that is disturbed by land cover changes. Forests in the tropics are believed to hold most of the world's bird, animal, and plant species. Grassland, shrubland and deserts collectively cover most of the unwooded land surface, with tundra on frozen subsoil at high northern latitudes. These areas tend to have lower species diversity than most forests, with the notable exception of Mediterranean shrublands, which support some of the most diverse floras on the Earth. Humans have extensively altered most grassland and shrubland areas, usually through conversion to agriculture, burning and introduction of domestic livestock. They have had less immediate impact on tundra and true desert regions, although these remain vulnerable to global climate change.

World land cover

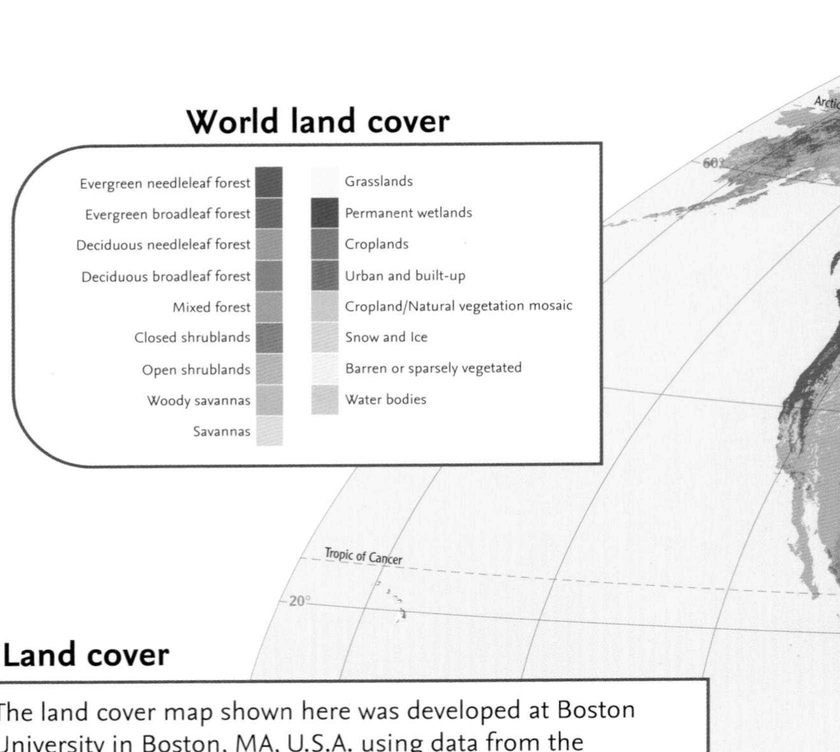

Land cover

The land cover map shown here was developed at Boston University in Boston, MA, U.S.A. using data from the Moderate-resolution Imaging-Spectroradiometer (MODIS) instrument aboard NASA's Terra satellite. The high resolution (ground resolution of 1km) of the imagery used to compile the data set and map allows detailed interpretation of land cover patterns across the world. Important uses include managing forest resources, improving estimates of the Earth's water and energy cycles, and modelling climate change.

Urban, Tōkyō, capital of Japan and the largest city in the world.

Internet Links

World Resources Institute	**www.wri.org**
World Conservation Monitoring Centre	**www.unep-wcmc.org**
United Nations Environment Programme (UNEP)	**www.unep.org**
IUCN, International Union for Conservation of Nature	**www.iucn.org**
MODIS Land Cover Group at Boston University	**www.bu.edu/lcsc**

Cropland, near Consuegra, Spain.

Barren/Shrubland, Mojave Desert, California, United States of America.

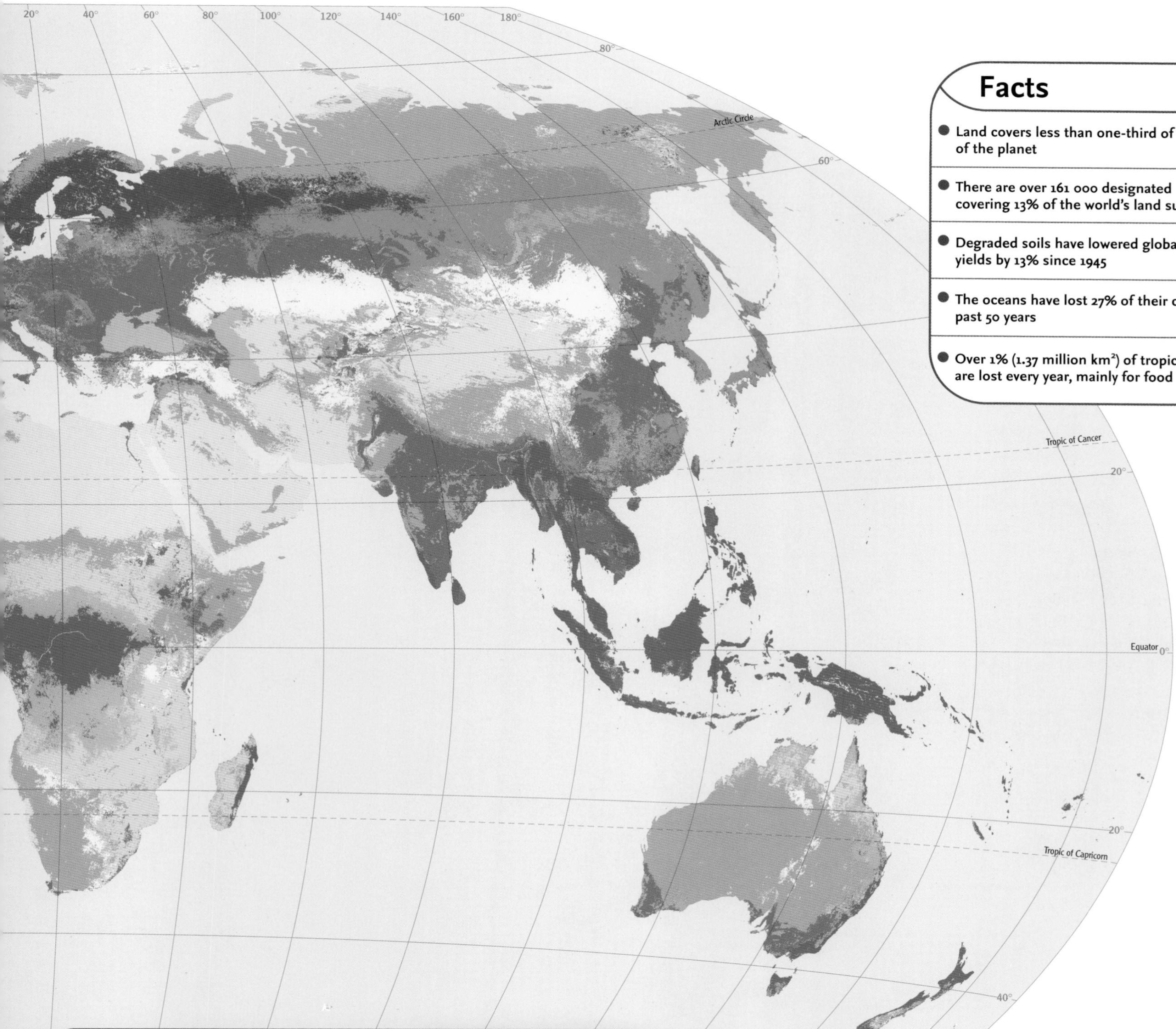

Facts

- Land covers less than one-third of the total surface of the planet
- There are over 161 000 designated Protected Areas covering 13% of the world's land surface
- Degraded soils have lowered global agricultural yields by 13% since 1945
- The oceans have lost 27% of their coral in the past 50 years
- Over 1% (1.37 million km^2) of tropical forests are lost every year, mainly for food production

Land cover composition and change

The continents all have different characteristics. There are extensive croplands in North America and eastern Europe, while south of the Sahara are belts of grass/shrubland which are at risk from desertification. Tropical forests are not pristine areas either as they show signs of human activity in deforestation of land for crops or grazing.

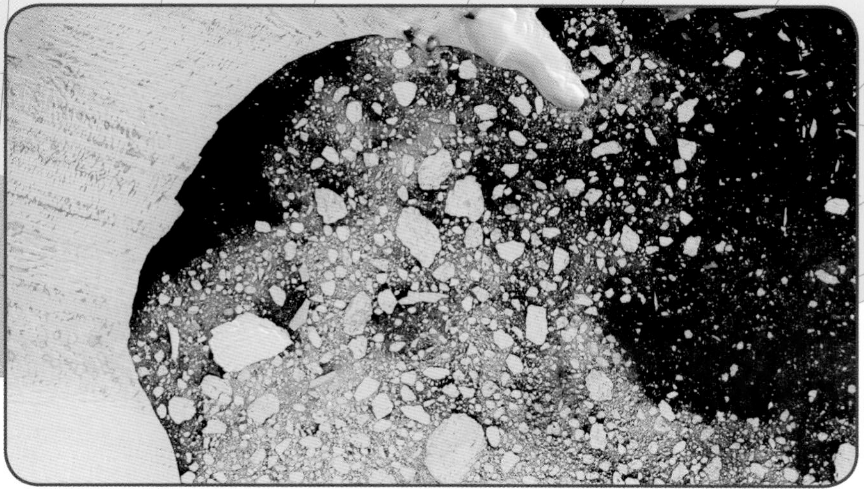

Snow and ice, Larsen Ice Shelf, Antarctica.

World

Population

After increasing very slowly for most of human history, world population more than doubled in the last half century. Whereas world population did not pass the one billion mark until 1804 and took another 123 years to reach two billion in 1927, it then added the third billion in 33 years, the fourth in 14 years and the fifth in 13 years. Just twelve years later on October 12, 1999 the United Nations announced that the global population had reached the six billion mark, with seven billion being reached only eleven years later, on October 31, 2011. It is expected that another two billion people will have been added to the world's population by 2040.

World population distribution

Population density (2005), continental populations (2013) and continental population change (2010–2015)

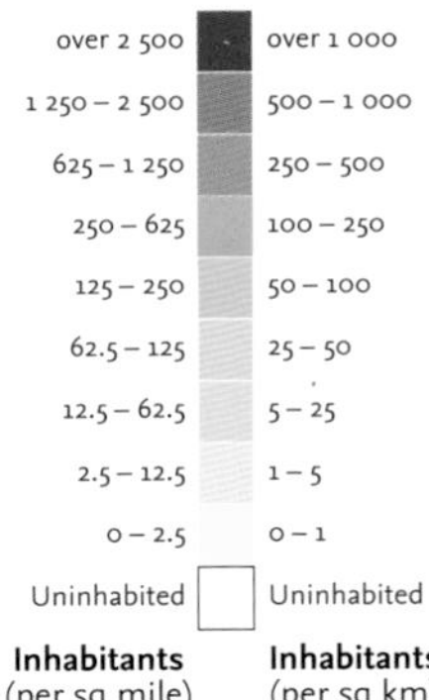

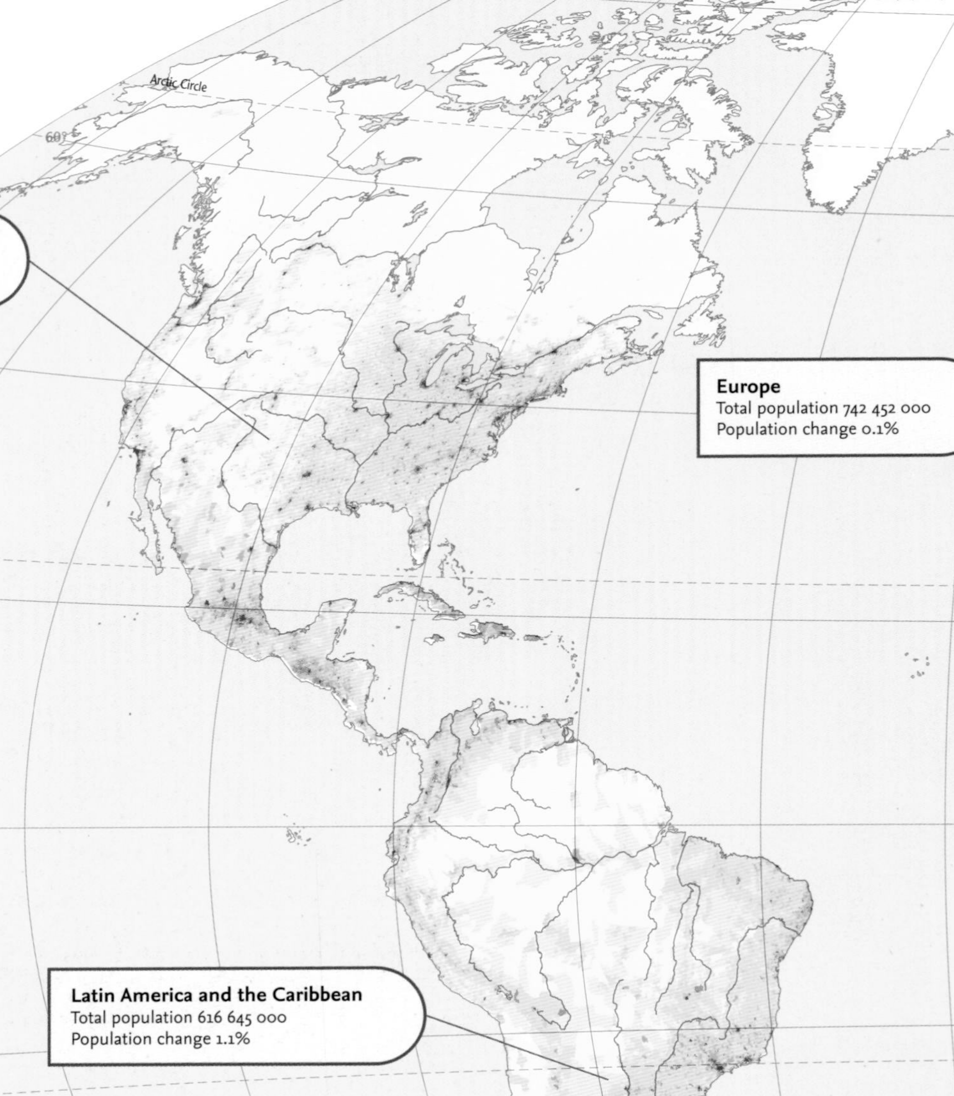

World population change

Population growth since 1950 has been spread very unevenly between the continents. While overall numbers have been growing rapidly since 1950, a massive 89 per cent increase has taken place in the less developed regions, especially southern and eastern Asia. In contrast, Europe's population level has been almost stationary and is expected to decrease in the future. India and China alone are responsible for over one-third of current growth. Most of the highest rates of growth are to be found in Sub-Saharan Africa and, until population growth is brought under tighter control, the developing world in particular will continue to face enormous problems of supporting a rising population.

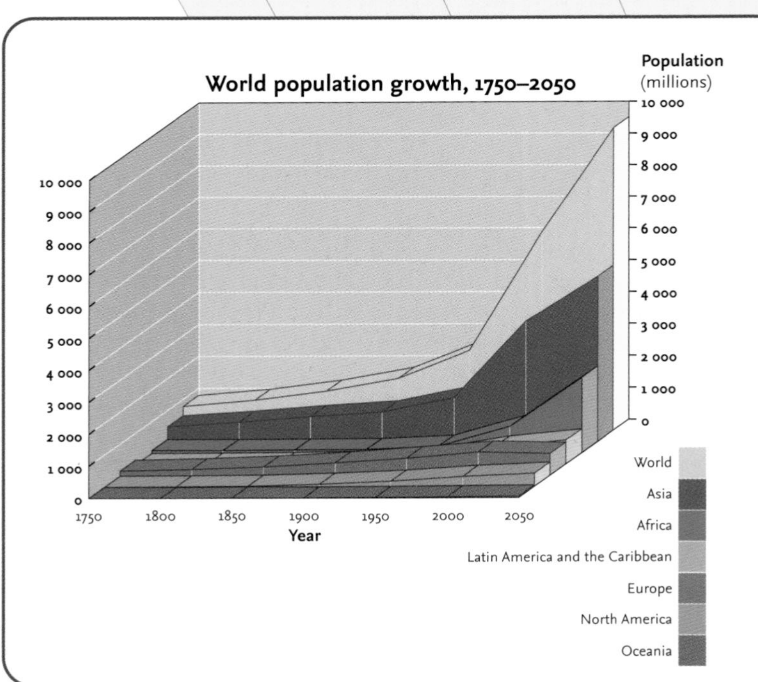

Top 10 countries by population, 2013

Rank	Country	Population
1	China	1 369 993 000
2	India	1 252 140 000
3	United States of America	320 051 000
4	Indonesia	249 866 000
5	Brazil	200 362 000
6	Pakistan	182 143 000
7	Nigeria	173 615 000
8	Bangladesh	156 595 000
9	Russia	142 834 000
10	Japan	127 144 000

The island nation of **Singapore,** the world's second most densely populated country.

Kuna Indians inhabit this congested island off the north coast of Panama.

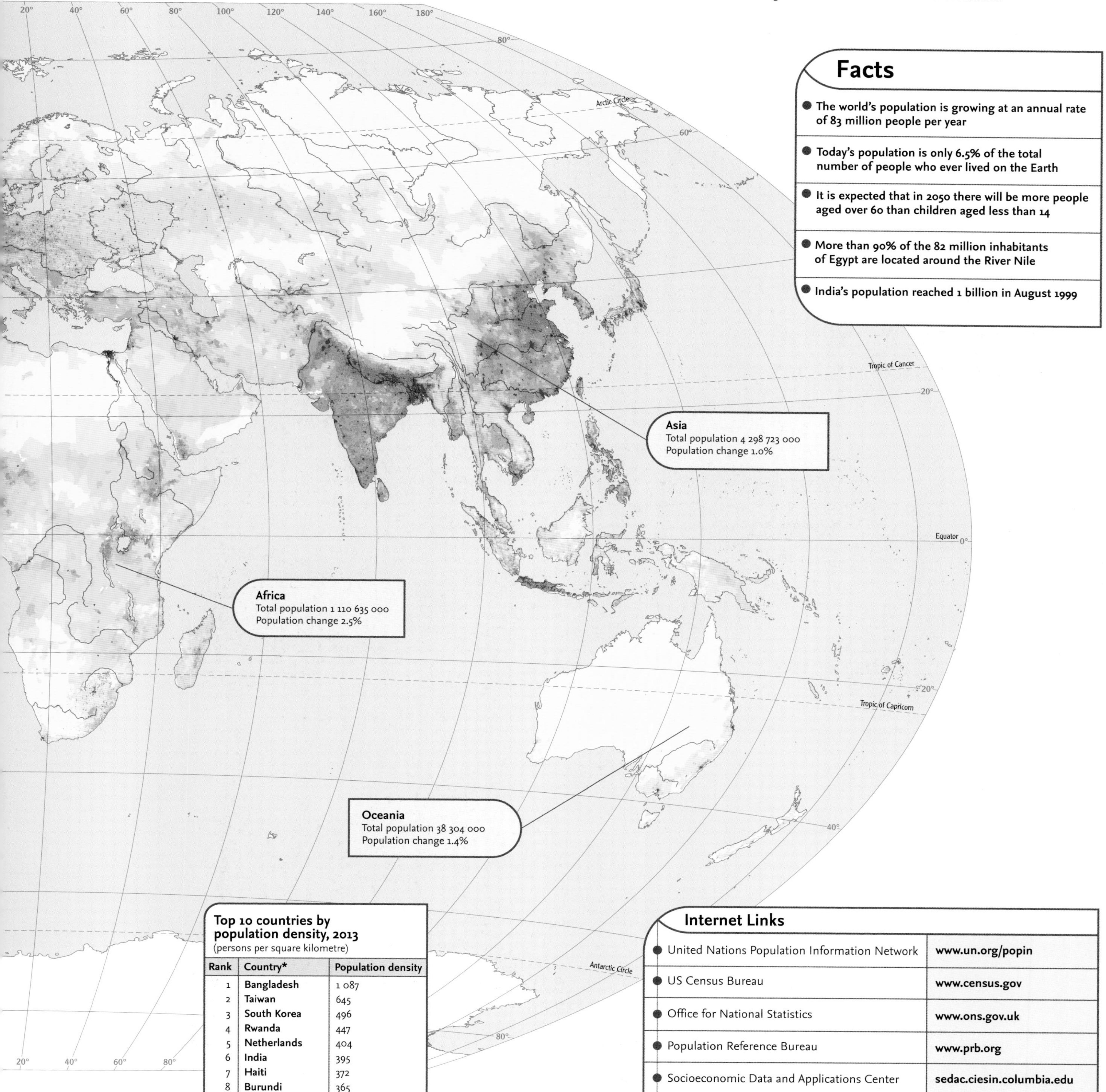

Facts

- The world's population is growing at an annual rate of 83 million people per year
- Today's population is only 6.5% of the total number of people who ever lived on the Earth
- It is expected that in 2050 there will be more people aged over 60 than children aged less than 14
- More than 90% of the 82 million inhabitants of Egypt are located around the River Nile
- India's population reached 1 billion in August 1999

Top 10 countries by population density, 2013
(persons per square kilometre)

Rank	Country*	Population density
1	Bangladesh	1 087
2	Taiwan	645
3	South Korea	496
4	Rwanda	447
5	Netherlands	404
6	India	395
7	Haiti	372
8	Burundi	365
9	Belgium	364
10	Japan	337

*Only countries with a population of over 10 million are considered

Internet Links

United Nations Population Information Network	**www.un.org/popin**
US Census Bureau	**www.census.gov**
Office for National Statistics	**www.ons.gov.uk**
Population Reference Bureau	**www.prb.org**
Socioeconomic Data and Applications Center	**sedac.ciesin.columbia.edu**

World
Urbanization and Cities

The world is becoming increasingly urban but the level of urbanization varies greatly between and within continents. At the beginning of the twentieth century only fourteen per cent of the world's population was urban and by 1950 this had increased to thirty per cent. In the more developed regions and in Latin America and the Caribbean over seventy per cent of the population is urban while in Africa and Asia the figure is around forty per cent. In recent decades urban growth has increased rapidly to over fifty per cent and in 2015 there are more than 500 cities with over 1 000 000 inhabitants. It is in the developing regions that the most rapid increases are taking place and it is expected that by 2030 over half of urban dwellers worldwide will live in Asia. Migration from the countryside to the city in the search for better job opportunities is the main factor in urban growth.

Characteristic high-rise urban development **Hong Kong,** China.

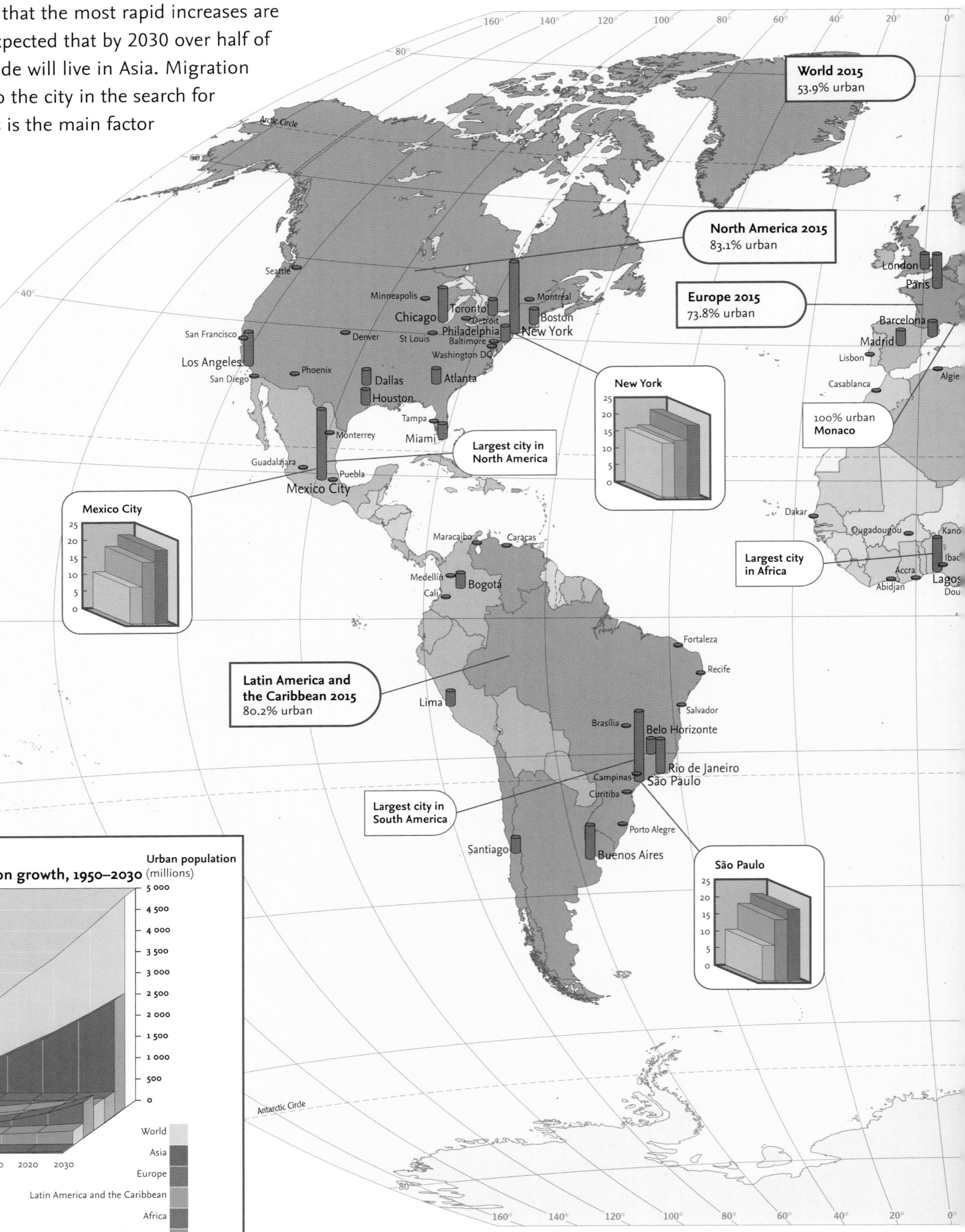

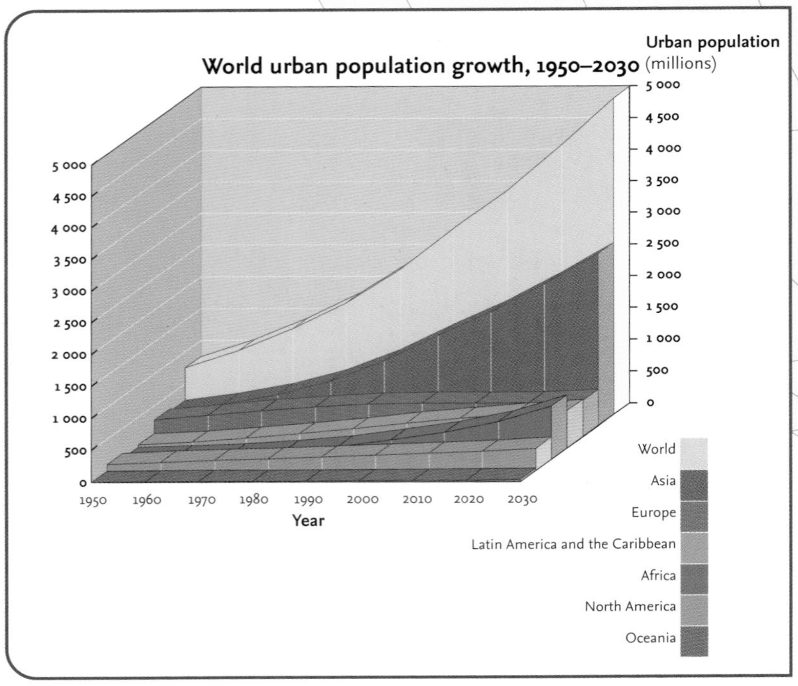

World 2015
53.9% urban

North America 2015
83.1% urban

Europe 2015
73.8% urban

Latin America and the Caribbean 2015
80.2% urban

100% urban
Monaco

Largest city in North America

Largest city in South America

Largest city in Africa

New York

Mexico City

São Paulo

Arctic Circle
Tropic of Cancer
Equator
Tropic of Capricorn
Antarctic Circle

Seattle, Minneapolis, Chicago, Toronto, Detroit, Montréal, Boston, New York, Philadelphia, Baltimore, Washington DC, San Francisco, Denver, St Louis, Los Angeles, San Diego, Phoenix, Dallas, Houston, Atlanta, Tampa, Miami, Monterrey, Guadalajara, Puebla, Mexico City, Maracaibo, Caracas, Medellín, Cali, Bogotá, Lima, Fortaleza, Recife, Salvador, Brasília, Belo Horizonte, Campinas, Rio de Janeiro, São Paulo, Curitiba, Porto Alegre, Santiago, Buenos Aires, London, Paris, Barcelona, Madrid, Lisbon, Casablanca, Algiers, Dakar, Ouagadougou, Kano, Ibadan, Accra, Abidjan, Lagos, Douala

World urban population growth, 1950–2030

Urban population (millions)

Year: 1950, 1960, 1970, 1980, 1990, 2000, 2010, 2020, 2030

World
Asia
Europe
Latin America and the Caribbean
Africa
North America
Oceania

Level of urbanization and the world's largest cities

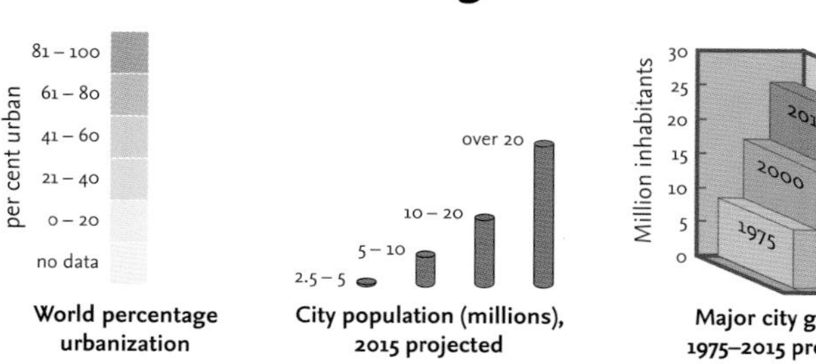

Megacities

There are currently sixty-nine cities in the world with over 5 000 000 inhabitants. Twenty-nine of these, often referred to as megacities, have over 10 000 000 inhabitants and one has over 30 000 000. Tōkyō, with 37 049 000 inhabitants, has remained the world's largest city since 1970 and is likely to remain so for the next decade. Other cities over 20 000 000 inhabitants in 2015 are Mumbai, São Paulo, Delhi, Shanghai, New York and Mexico City. Sixteen of the world's megacities are in Asia.

Facts

- **From mid-2009, cities occupying less than 2% of the Earth's land surface housed over 50% of the human population**
- **Urban growth rates in Africa are the highest in the world**
- **Antarctica is uninhabited and most settlements in the Arctic regions have less than 5 000 inhabitants**
- **In 2015 India will have 56 cities with over one million inhabitants**
- **London was the first city to reach a population of over 5 million**

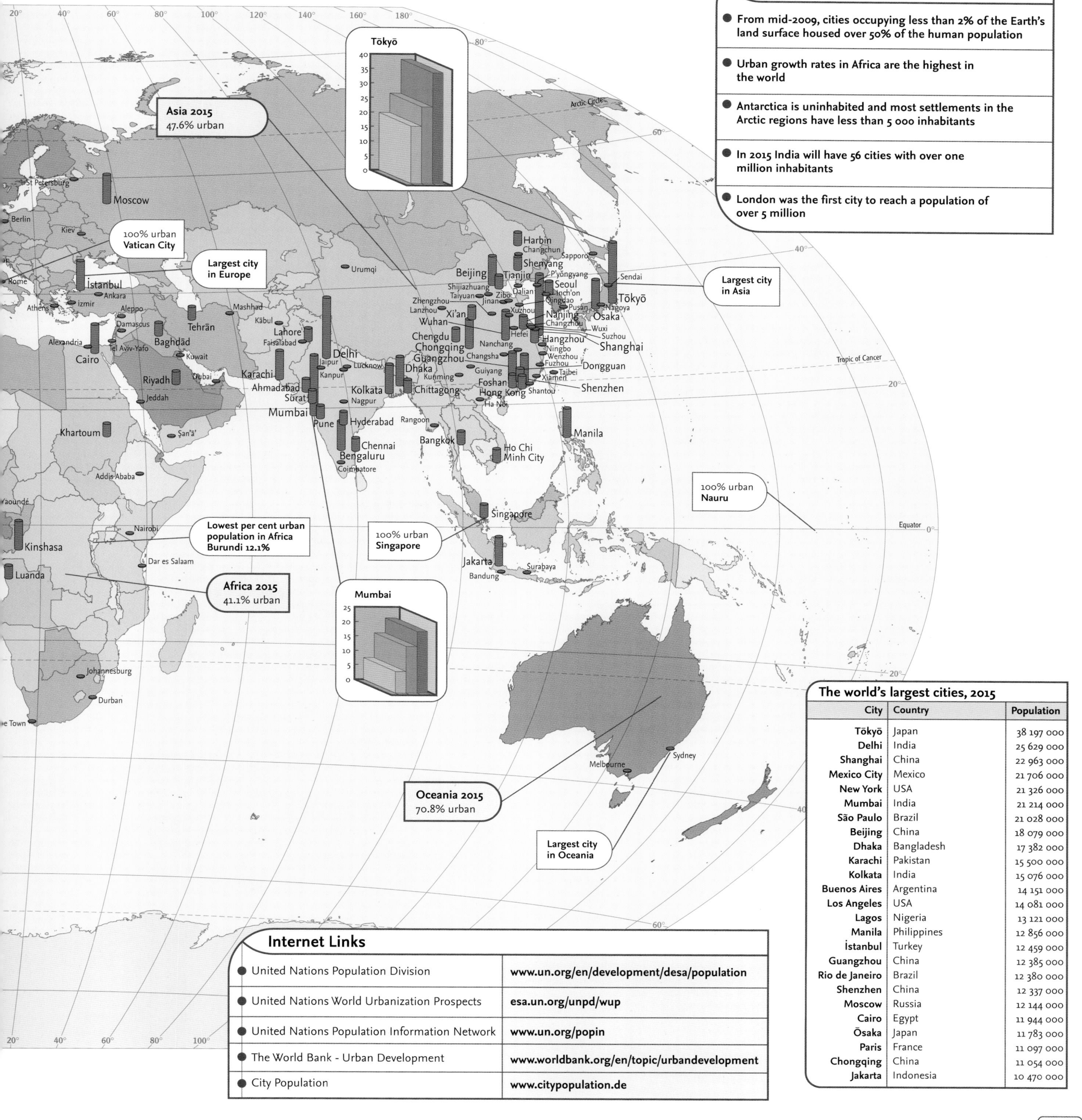

Asia 2015
47.6% urban

Africa 2015
41.1% urban

Oceania 2015
70.8% urban

100% urban Vatican City

Largest city in Europe

Largest city in Asia

Lowest per cent urban population in Africa Burundi 12.1%

100% urban Singapore

100% urban Nauru

Largest city in Oceania

The world's largest cities, 2015

City	Country	Population
Tōkyō	Japan	38 197 000
Delhi	India	25 629 000
Shanghai	China	22 963 000
Mexico City	Mexico	21 706 000
New York	USA	21 326 000
Mumbai	India	21 214 000
São Paulo	Brazil	21 028 000
Beijing	China	18 079 000
Dhaka	Bangladesh	17 382 000
Karachi	Pakistan	15 500 000
Kolkata	India	15 076 000
Buenos Aires	Argentina	14 151 000
Los Angeles	USA	14 081 000
Lagos	Nigeria	13 121 000
Manila	Philippines	12 856 000
İstanbul	Turkey	12 459 000
Guangzhou	China	12 385 000
Rio de Janeiro	Brazil	12 380 000
Shenzhen	China	12 337 000
Moscow	Russia	12 144 000
Cairo	Egypt	11 944 000
Ōsaka	Japan	11 783 000
Paris	France	11 097 000
Chongqing	China	11 054 000
Jakarta	Indonesia	10 470 000

Internet Links

United Nations Population Division	www.un.org/en/development/desa/population
United Nations World Urbanization Prospects	esa.un.org/unpd/wup
United Nations Population Information Network	www.un.org/popin
The World Bank - Urban Development	www.worldbank.org/en/topic/urbandevelopment
City Population	www.citypopulation.de

Increased availability and ownership of telecommunications equipment over the last thirty years has aided the globalization of the world economy. Over half of the world's fixed telephone lines have been installed since 1987, and the majority of the world's Internet hosts have come on line since 1997. Cellular subscribers, particularly using digital technologies, are increasing much more rapidly than fixed telephone lines as in many countries they are a more practical option. Mobile broadband subscribers have now overtaken fixed broadband subscribers in all regions.

Internet users have been increasing rapidly since 1991 when there were only 4.4 million, with many large jumps especially in the last ten years, to 2 497 million in 2012, a figure that is more than double that of 2005. However, access levels vary, with approximately twenty countries still with less than 3 per cent Internet penetration.

Facts

- The first transatlantic telegraph cable came into operation in 1858
- In 2014, forty percent of the world's population were using the Internet
- The Falkland Islands have the world's highest density of Internet subscribers
- In 2011, 45 percent of Internet users were below the age of twenty-five

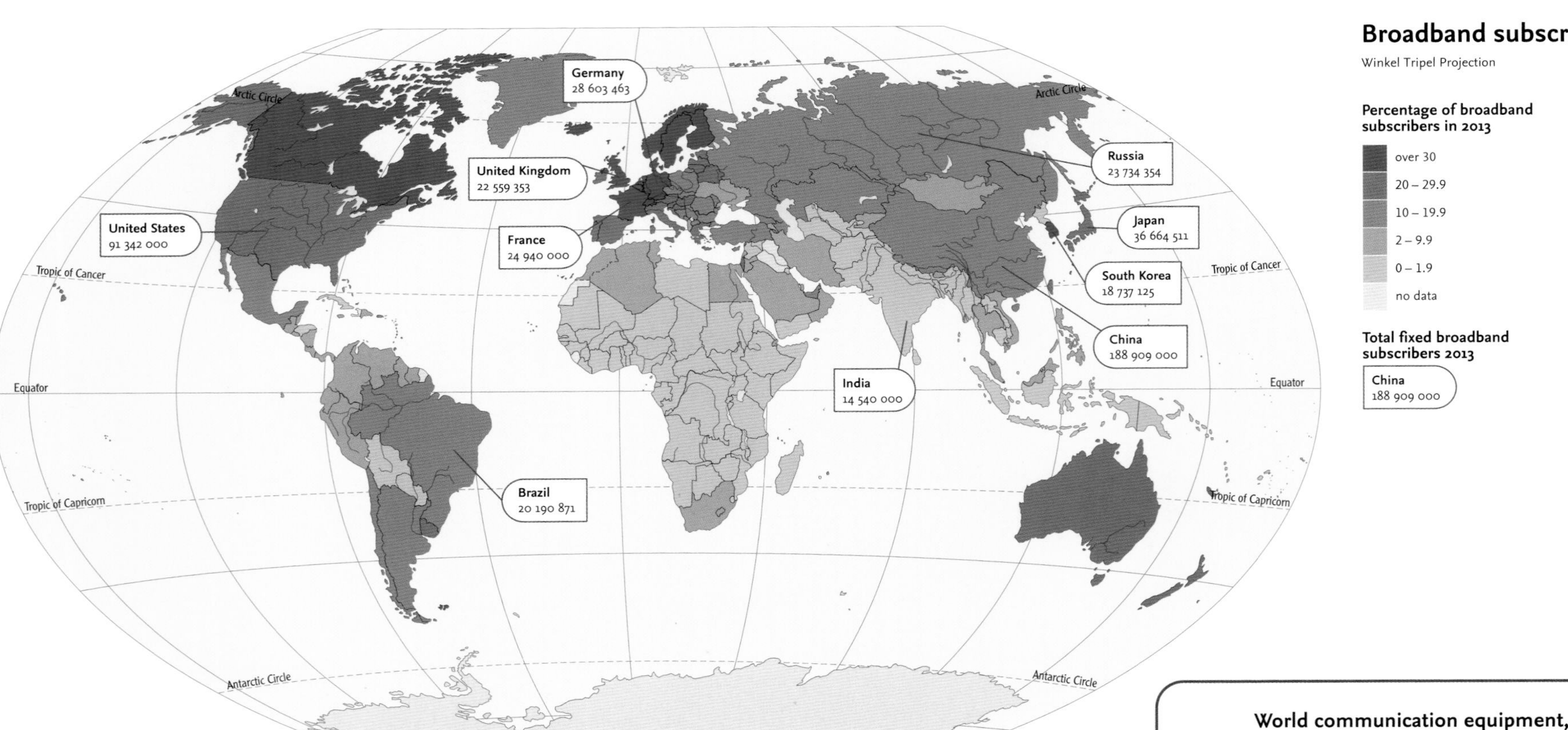

Broadband subscribers

Winkel Tripel Projection

Percentage of broadband subscribers in 2013
- over 30
- 20 – 29.9
- 10 – 19.9
- 2 – 9.9
- 0 – 1.9
- no data

Total fixed broadband subscribers 2013
China 188 909 000

The Internet

Broadband connections for access to the Internet are relatively recent, but in that short time huge developments have been made in the technology and access speeds have shown a steady rise which is still continuing. Broadband access has had an impact on the delivery of electronic services in many areas such as health, education and finance. Mobile broadband (or mobile Internet) is wireless high-speed Internet access available through a portable modem device on a laptop computer and increasingly widely on hand-held tablets and mobile cellular telephones. In 2005 all regions with broadband access showed at least 64 per cent of all subscriptions were for fixed broadband. By 2008 almost all regions showed mobile broadband subscriptions had overtaken fixed as the technology improved and users were offered more options.

Top Broadband Economies 2013
Countries with the highest broadband penetration rate – subscribers per 100 inhabitants

	Top Economies – Fixed Broadband	Rate
1	Monaco	44.7
2	Switzerland	43.0
3	Denmark	40.2
4	Netherlands	40.1
5	France	38.8
6	South Korea	38.0
7	Norway	36.4
8	United Kingdom	35.7
9	Iceland	35.1
10	Germany	34.6
	Top Economies – Mobile Broadband	**Rate**
1	Singapore	135.1
2	Finland	123.5
3	Japan	120.5
4	Australia	110.5
5	Bahrain	109.7
6	Sweden	108.7
7	Denmark	107.3
8	South Korea	105.3
9	Hong Kong, China	95.4
10	USA	92.8

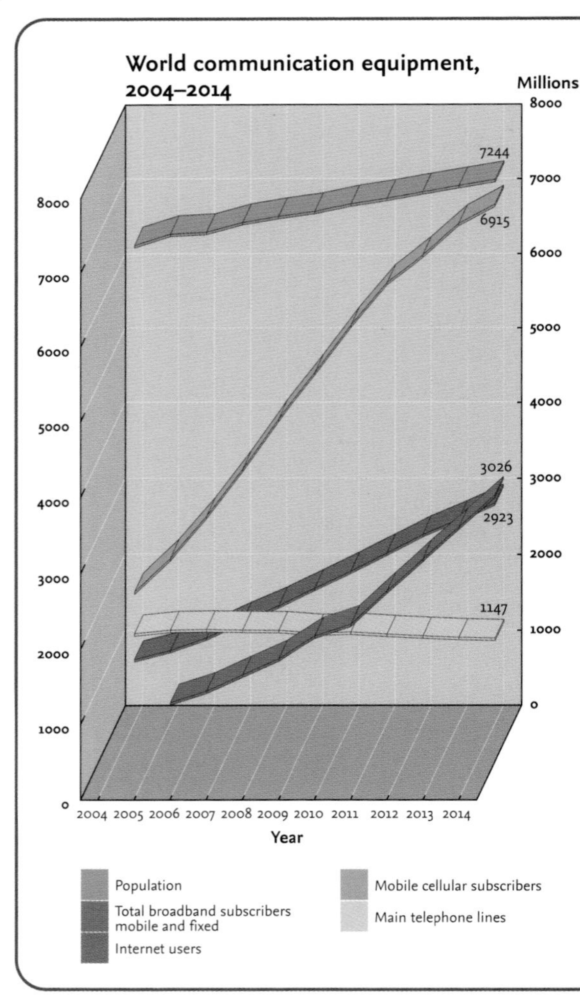

Mobile phone subscribers

Winkel Tripel Projection

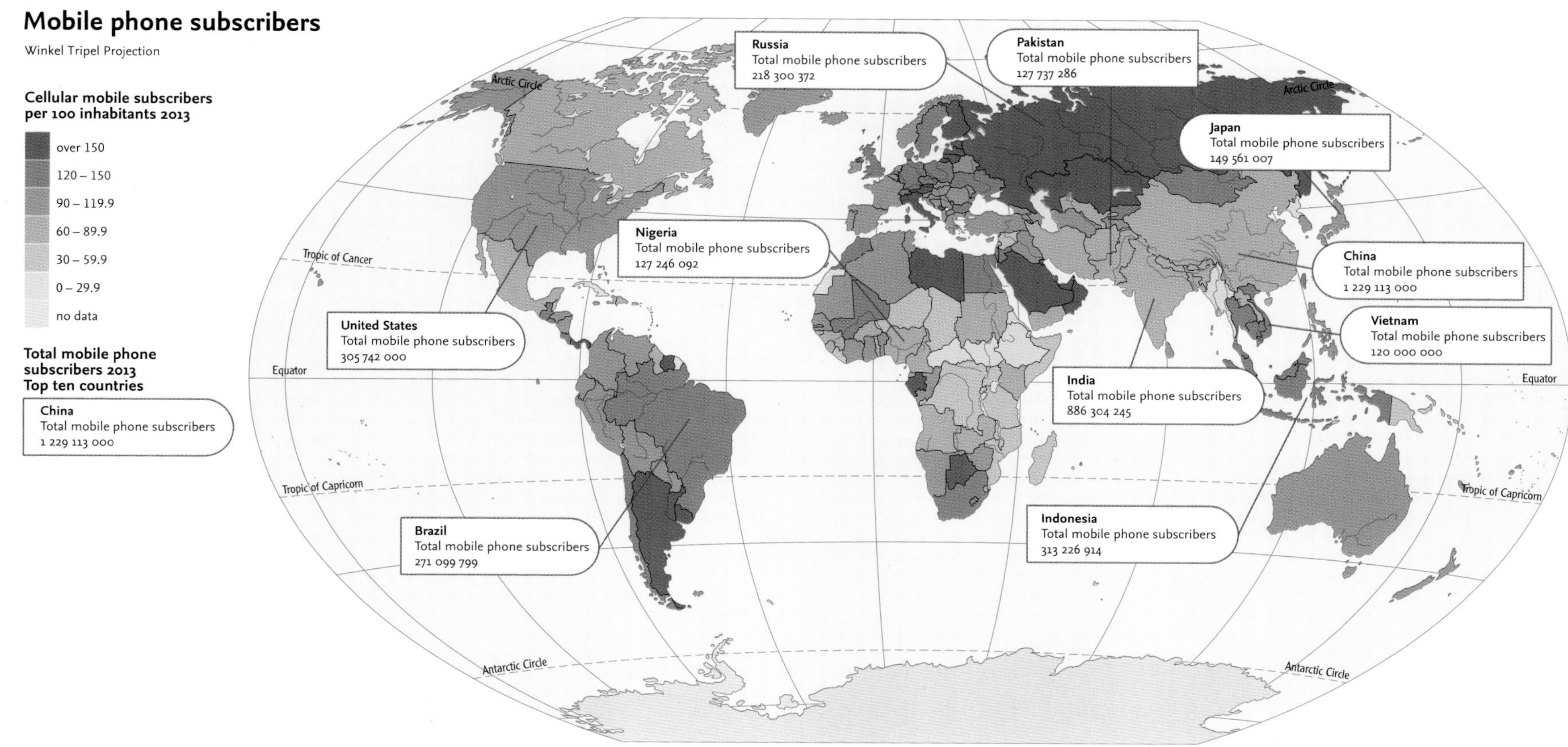

Mobile phone subscribers

In 2014, there were almost seven billion mobile cellular subscribers and it was estimated that out of every one hundred people, ninety-six of them owned a mobile. One area showing a recent change with the development of new mobile cellular technology, is mobile broadband where subscribers are now more than triple the number of fixed broadband subscribers in all regions. The total number of Short Message Service (SMS) or text messages sent globally tripled between 2007 and 2010 to over 6 trillion messages, around 200 000 every second. Many phone packages now include "unlimited" free text messages encouraging many shorter messages to be sent.

Internet Links

OECD Organisation for Economic Co-operation and Development	**www.oecd.org**
TeleGeography	**www.telegeography.com**
International Telecommunication Union	**www.itu.int**

Fixed telephone lines

Winkel Tripel Projection

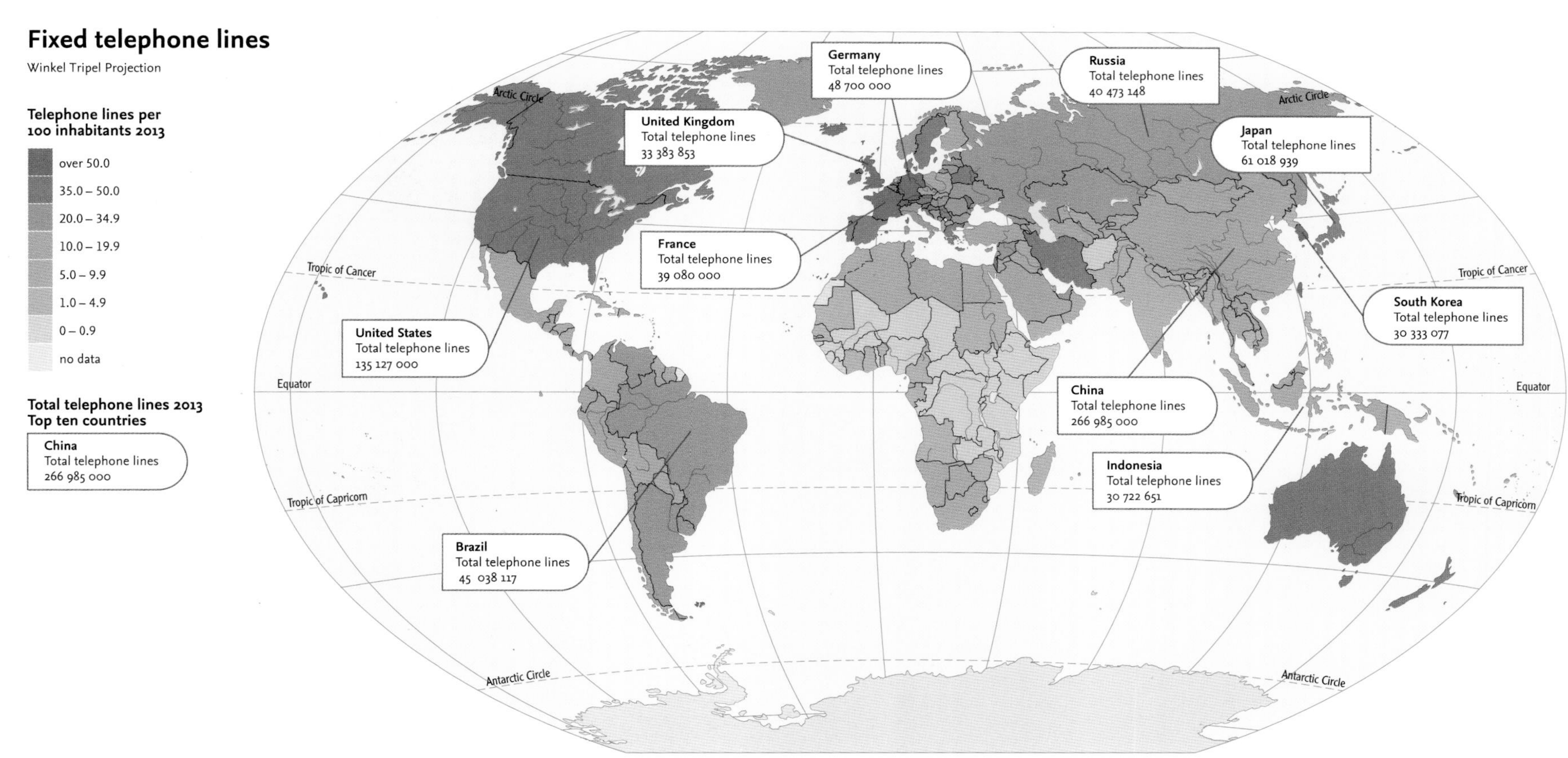

World
Social Indicators

Countries are often judged on their level of economic development, but national and personal wealth are not the only measures of a country's status. Numerous other indicators can give a better picture of the overall level of development and standard of living achieved by a country. The availability and standard of health services, levels of educational provision and attainment, levels of nutrition, water supply, life expectancy and mortality rates are just some of the factors which can be measured to assess and compare countries.

While nations strive to improve their economies, and hopefully also to improve the standard of living of their citizens, the measurement of such indicators often exposes great discrepancies between the countries of the 'developed' world and those of the 'less developed' world. They also show great variations within continents and regions and at the same time can hide great inequalities within countries.

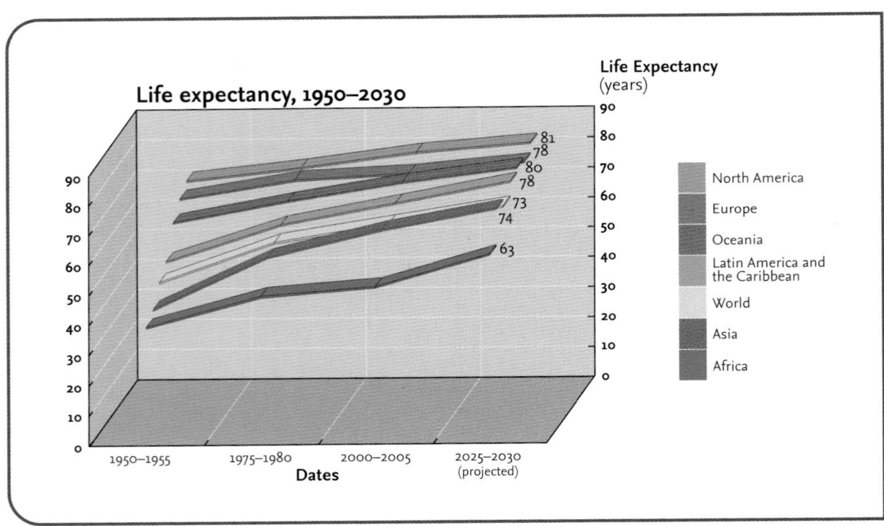

Under-five mortality rate, 2013 and life expectancy by continent, 2015–2020

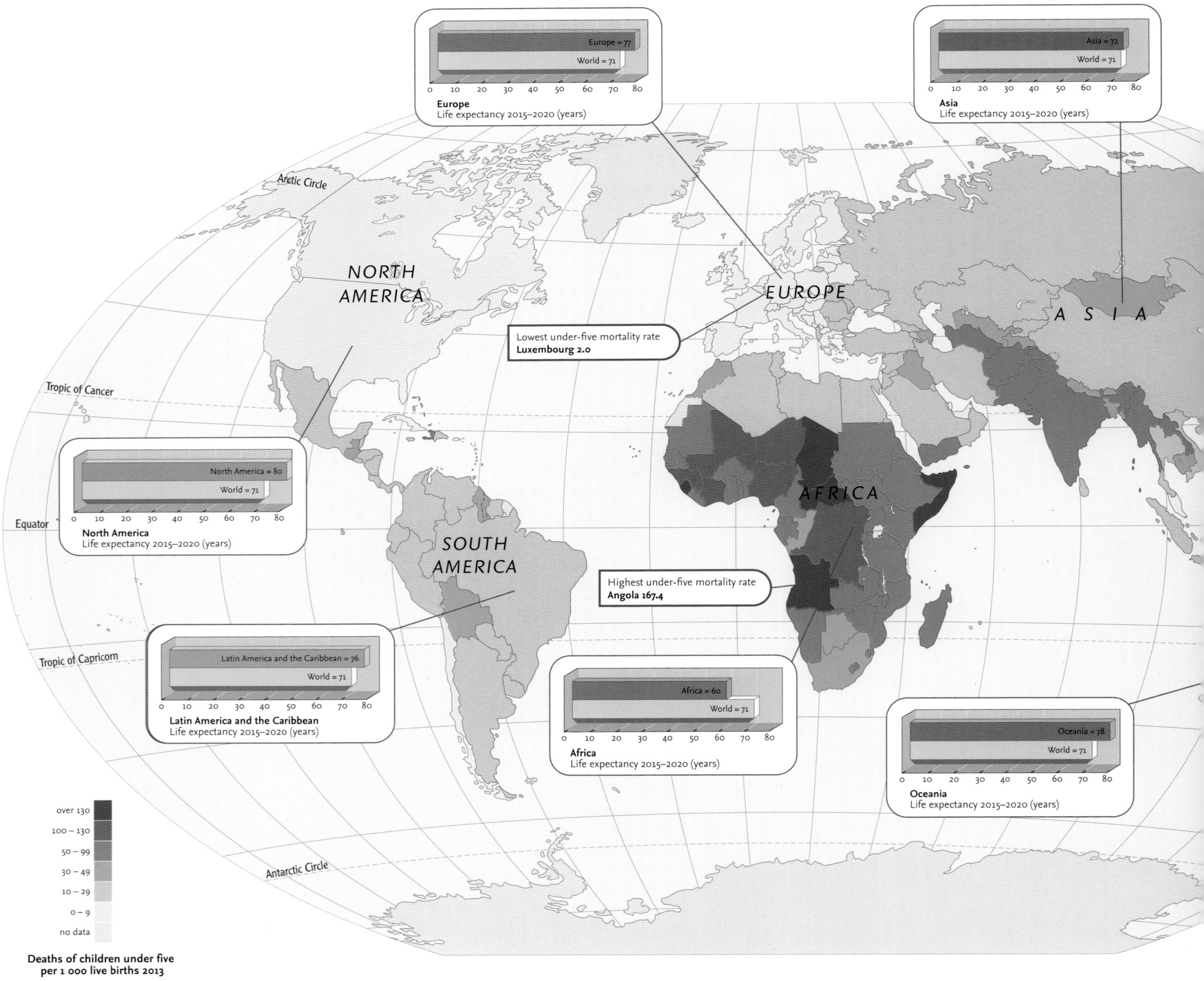

Europe = 77
World = 71
Europe
Life expectancy 2015–2020 (years)

Asia = 72
World = 71
Asia
Life expectancy 2015–2020 (years)

North America = 80
World = 71
North America
Life expectancy 2015–2020 (years)

Latin America and the Caribbean = 76
World = 71
Latin America and the Caribbean
Life expectancy 2015–2020 (years)

Africa = 60
World = 71
Africa
Life expectancy 2015–2020 (years)

Oceania = 78
World = 71
Oceania
Life expectancy 2015–2020 (years)

Lowest under-five mortality rate
Luxembourg 2.0

Highest under-five mortality rate
Angola 167.4

Arctic Circle
Tropic of Cancer
Equator
Tropic of Capricorn
Antarctic Circle
NORTH AMERICA
SOUTH AMERICA
EUROPE
AFRICA
ASIA

over 130
100 – 130
50 – 99
30 – 49
10 – 29
0 – 9
no data

Deaths of children under five per 1 000 live births 2013

Facts

- All of the 12 countries with under-5 mortality rates of more than 100 per 1000 live births, are in Africa
- Many western countries believe they have achieved satisfactory levels of education and no longer closely monitor levels of literacy
- Children born in Nepal have only a 12% chance of their birth being attended by trained health personnel; for most European countries the figure is 100%
- The illiteracy rate among young women in the Middle East and north Africa is almost twice the rate for young men

Health and education

Perhaps the most important indicators used for measuring the level of national development are those relating to health and education. Both of these key areas are vital to the future development of a country, and if there are concerns in standards attained in either (or worse, in both) of these, then they may indicate fundamental problems within the country concerned. The ability to read and write (literacy) is seen as vital in educating people and encouraging development, while easy access to appropriate health services and specialists is an important requirement in maintaining satisfactory levels of basic health.

Adult Literacy rate

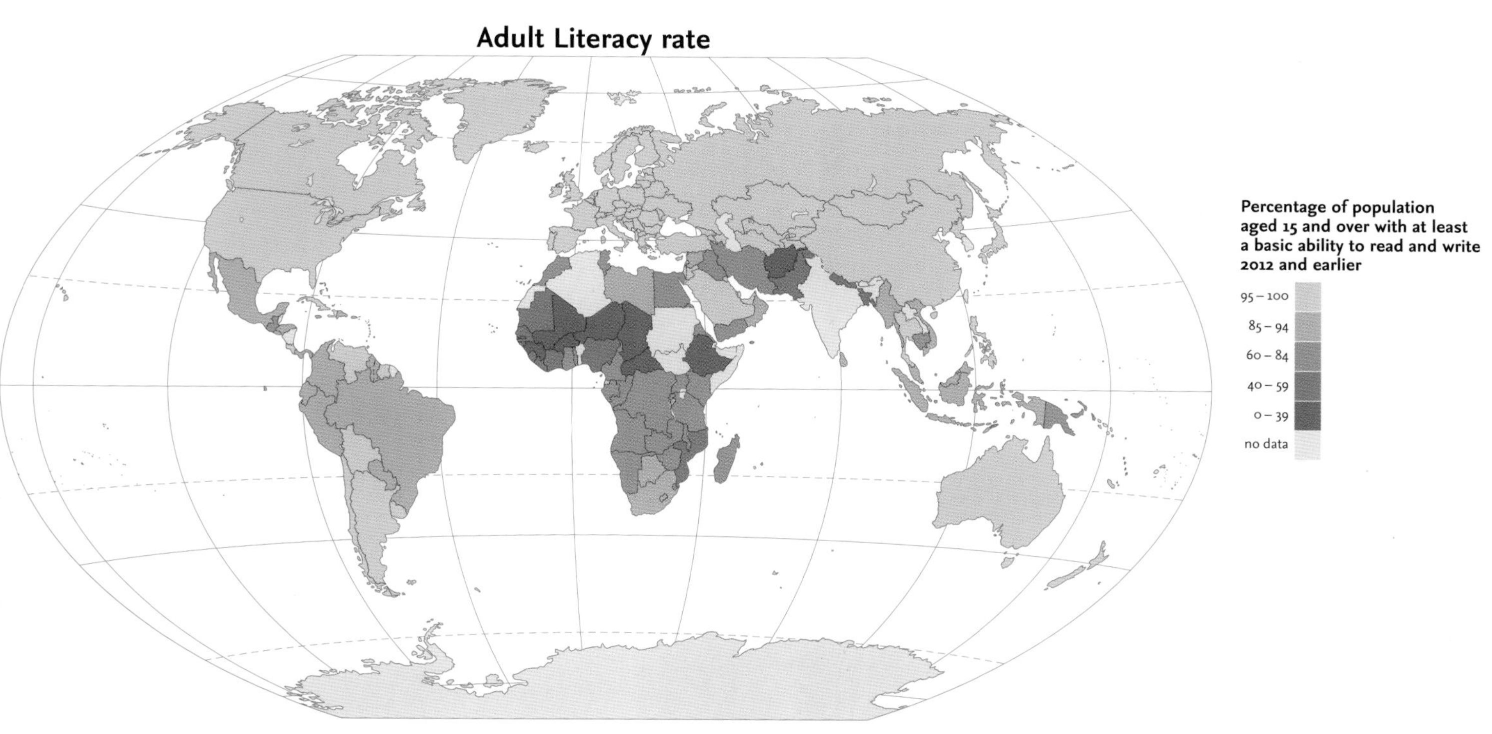

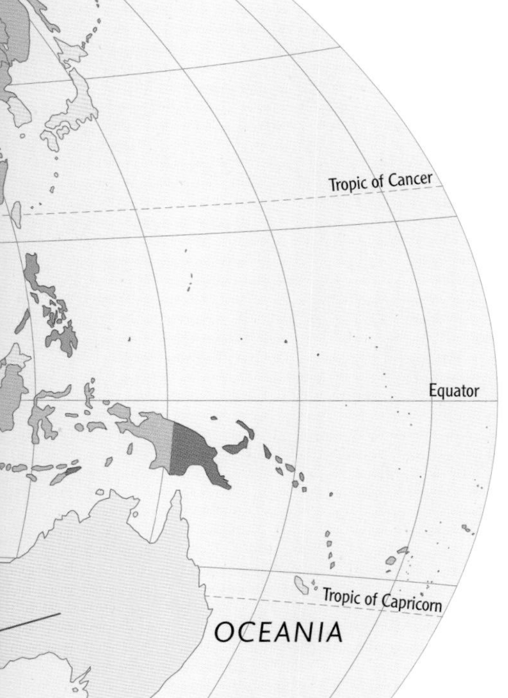

Doctors per 100 000 people

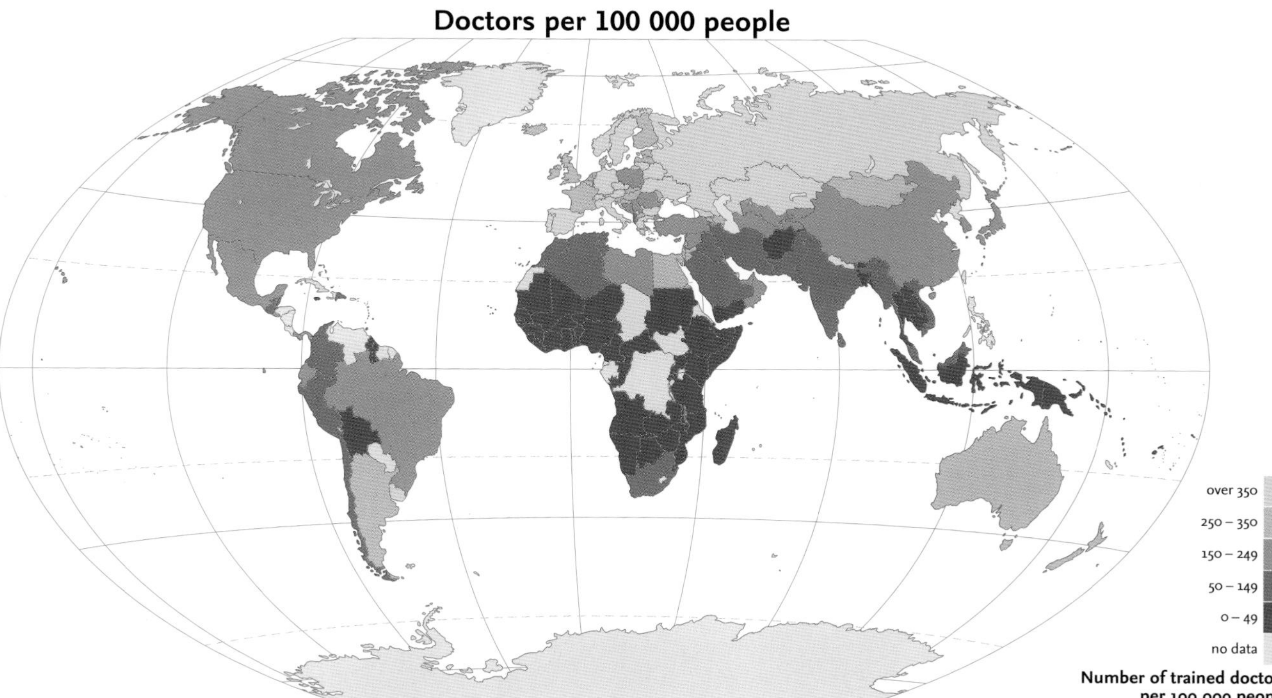

UN Millennium Development Goals

From the Millennium Declaration, 2000
Target for these to be reached is 2015

Goal 1	Eradicate extreme poverty and hunger
Goal 2	Achieve universal primary education
Goal 3	Promote gender equality and empower women
Goal 4	Reduce child mortality
Goal 5	Improve maternal health
Goal 6	Combat HIV/AIDS, malaria and other diseases
Goal 7	Ensure environmental sustainability
Goal 8	Develop a global partnership for development

Internet Links

United Nations Development Programme	www.undp.org
World Health Organization	www.who.int
United Nations Statistics Division	unstats.un.org
United Nations Millennium Development Goals Indicators	www.un.org/milleniumgoals

World

Economy and Wealth

The globalization of the economy is making the world appear a smaller place. However, this shrinkage is an uneven process. Countries are being included in and excluded from the global economy to differing degrees. The wealthy countries of the developed world, with their market-led economies, access to productive new technologies and international markets, dominate the world economic system. Great inequalities exist between and within countries. There may also be discrepancies between social groups within countries due to gender and ethnic divisions. Differences between countries are evident by looking at overall wealth on a national and individual level.

Many of the world's largest financial institutions are to be found in the City of London.

Poverty and inequality

In 2005, 25 per cent of the population of low- and middle-income economies lived in extreme poverty. With continued growth of average incomes, that number was expected to fall to less than 900 million by 2015. Even then there will be more than 2 billion people living on less than $2.00 a day or $730 a year. The greatest number of the extreme poor live in the large, lower-middle income economies of Asia – India and China – which together account for almost half of the people living in extreme poverty. But these are fast growing economies, where poverty rates have been falling rapidly. The highest rates of poverty are found in Sub-Saharan Africa, where economic growth was slowest in the 1990s and the regional poverty rate has only recently fallen below 50 per cent and was expected to reach 36 per cent by 2015. Since the mid-1990s, income inequality, as measured by the Gini index, has increased in slightly more than half of developing countries with available data.

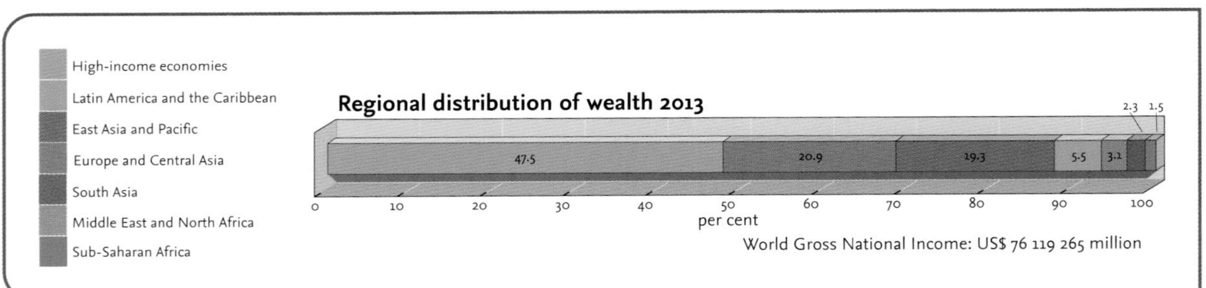

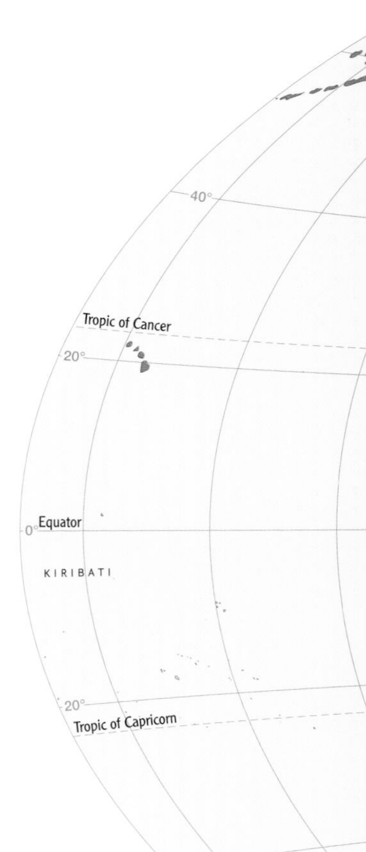

Income inequality

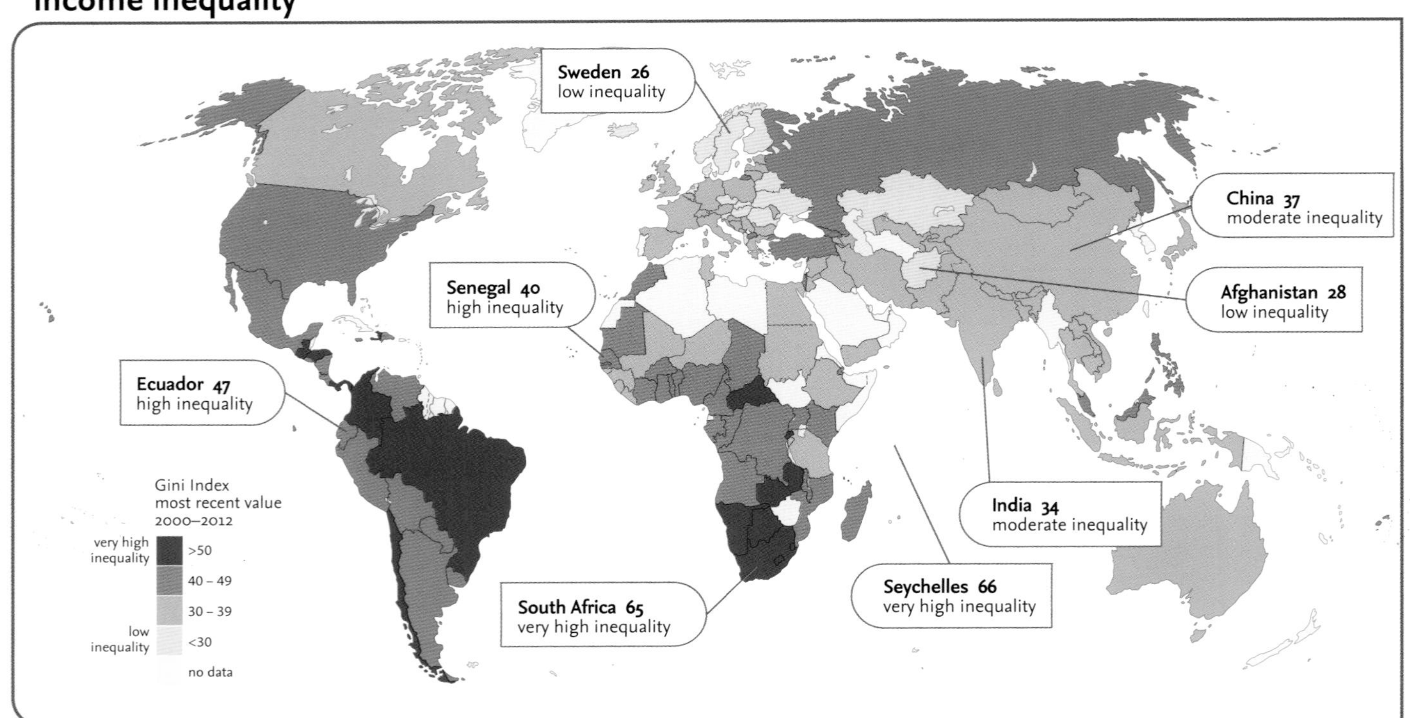

Facts

- The City, one of 33 London boroughs, is the world's largest financial centre and contains Europe's biggest stock market
- 40 percent of the world's population earns only 5% of the world's wealth
- During the second half of the 20th century rich countries gave over US$1 trillion in aid
- For every £1 in grant aid to developing countries, more than £25 comes back in debt repayments
- On average, The World Bank distributes US$40 billion each year between 100 countries

Rural village, **Malawi** – most of the world's poorest countries are in Africa.

Gross National Income per capita

Highest Gross National Income
United States US$ 16 903 045 million

Highest Gross National Income per capita
Bermuda US$ 104 610

Lowest Gross National Income
Tuvalu US$ 58 million

Lowest Gross National Income per capita
Malawi US$ 270

GNI per capita US$ 2013/2012

- over 40 000
- 20 000 – 40 000
- 10 000 – 19 999
- 2 000 – 9 999
- 1 000 – 1 999
- 0 – 999
- no data

A.	ANDORRA	LEB.	LEBANON
AL.	ALBANIA	LITH.	LITHUANIA
ARM.	ARMENIA	M.	MACEDONIA
AUST.	AUSTRIA	MO.	MONTENEGRO
AZER.	AZERBAIJAN	MOL.	MOLDOVA
B.	BURUNDI	NETH.	NETHERLANDS
BEL.	BELGIUM	R.	RWANDA
B.H.	BOSNIA AND HERZEGOVINA	ROM.	ROMANIA
BULG.	BULGARIA	RUS.	RUSSIA
CR.	CROATIA	S.	SERBIA
CZ.R.	CZECH REPUBLIC	SL.	SLOVENIA
EST.	ESTONIA	SLA.	SLOVAKIA
GEOR.	GEORGIA	SUR.	SURINAME
HUN.	HUNGARY	SW.	SWITZERLAND
ISR.	ISRAEL	TAJIK.	TAJIKISTAN
JOR.	JORDAN	TURKM.	TURKMENISTAN
K.	KOSOVO	U.A.E.	UNITED ARAB EMIRATES
L.	LUXEMBOURG	U.S.A.	UNITED STATES OF AMERICA
LAT.	LATVIA	UZBEK.	UZBEKISTAN

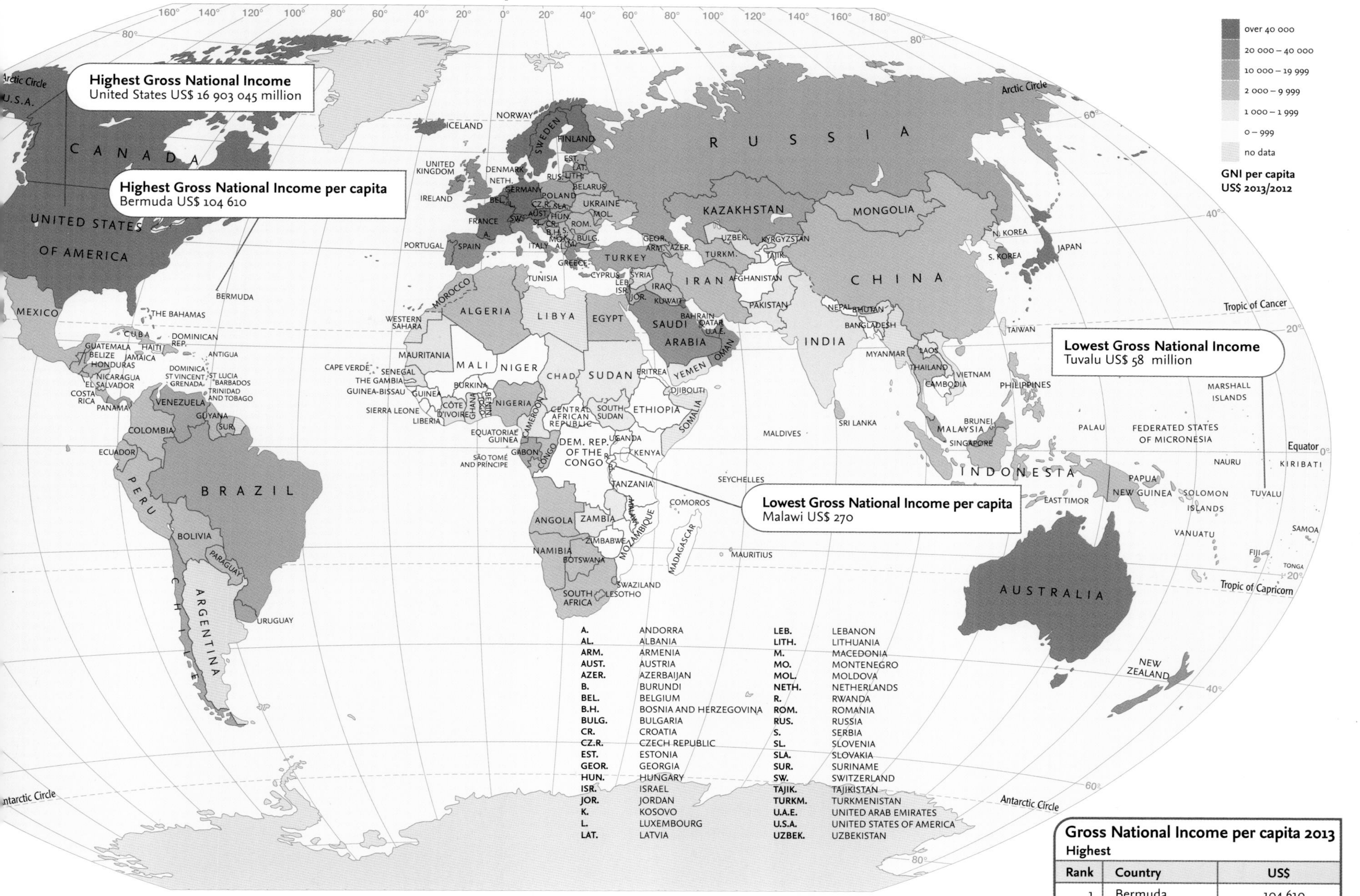

Measuring wealth

One of the indicators used to determine a country's wealth is its Gross National Income (GNI). This gives a broad measure of an economy's performance. This is the value of the final output of goods and services produced by a country plus net income from non-resident sources. The total GNI is divided by the country's population to give an average figure of the GNI per capita. From this it is evident that the developed countries dominate the world economy with the United States having the highest GNI. China is a rapidly growing world economic player with the second highest GNI figure and a relatively high GNI per capita (US$6 560) in proportion to its huge population.

Internet Links

United Nations Statistics Division	**unstats.un.org**
The World Bank	**www.worldbank.org**
International Monetary Fund	**www.imf.org**
OECD Organisation for Economic Co-operation and Development	**www.oecd.org**

Gross National Income per capita 2013

Highest

Rank	Country	US$
1	Bermuda	104 610
2	Norway	102 610
3	Qatar	85 550
4	Switzerland	80 950
5	Luxembourg	71 810
6	Australia	65 520
7	Denmark	61 110
8	Sweden	59 130
9	Singapore	54 040
10	USA	53 670

Lowest

Rank	Country	US$
178	Eritrea	490
179	Ethiopia	470
180	Guinea	460
181	Madagascar	440
182	Liberia	410
183	Niger	410
184	Dem. Rep. of the Congo	400
185	Central African Republic	320
186	Burundi	280
187	Malawi	270

World
Conflict

Geo-political issues shape the countries of the world and the current political situation in many parts of the world reflects a long history of armed conflict. Since the Second World War conflicts have been fairly localized, but there are numerous 'flash points' where factors such as territorial claims, ideology, religion, ethnicity and access to resources can cause friction between two or more countries. Such factors also lie behind the recent growth in global terrorism.

Military expenditure can take up a disproportionate amount of a country's wealth – South Sudan, with a Gross Domestic Product (GDP) per capita of US$2 030 spends over nine per cent of its total GDP on military activity. There is an encouraging trend towards wider international cooperation, mainly through the United Nations (UN) and the North Atlantic Treaty Organization (NATO), to prevent escalation of conflicts and on peacekeeping missions.

Military spending 2013, and conflicts since 1946

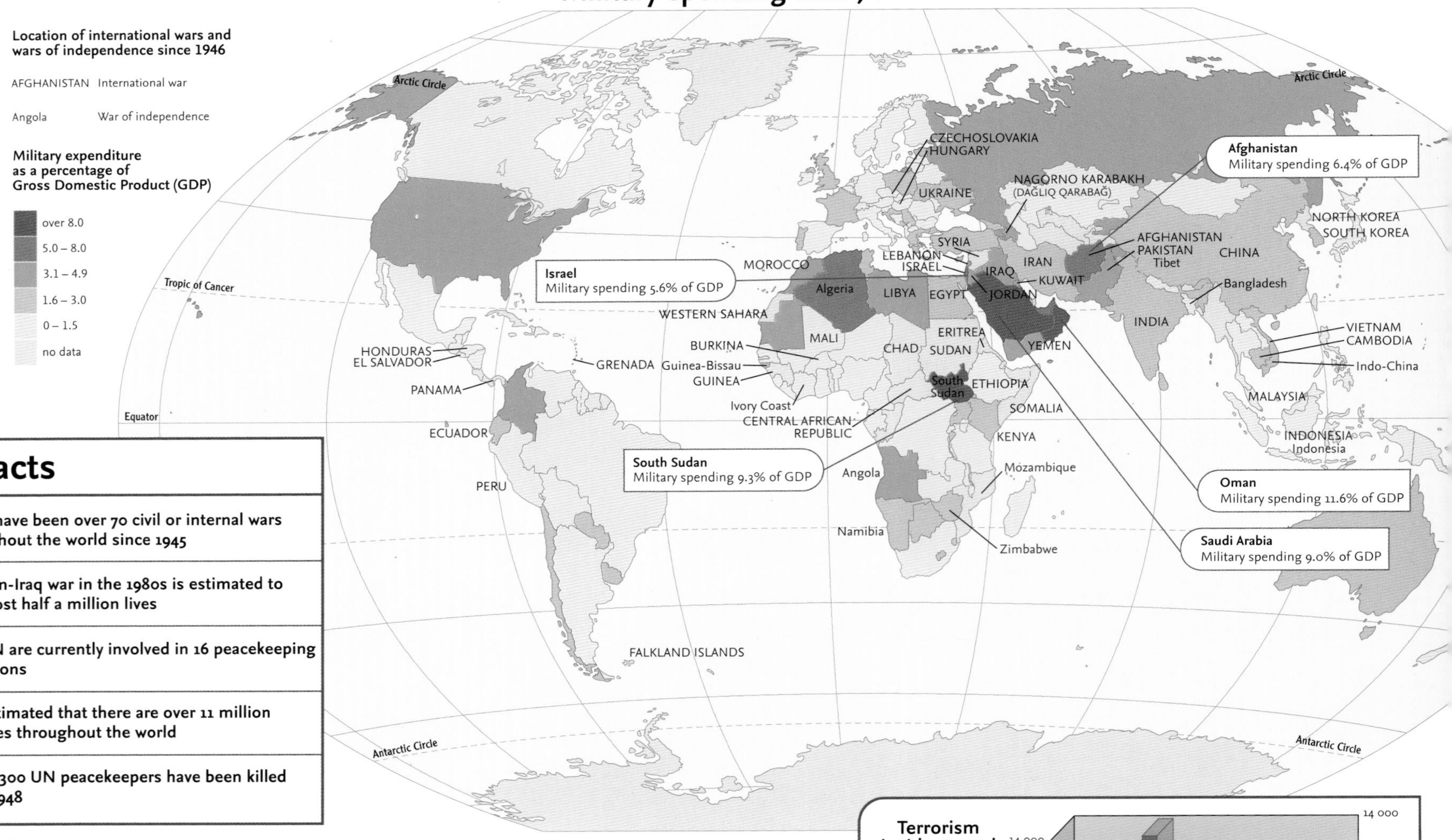

Location of international wars and wars of independence since 1946

AFGHANISTAN International war

Angola War of independence

Military expenditure as a percentage of Gross Domestic Product (GDP)

- over 8.0
- 5.0 – 8.0
- 3.1 – 4.9
- 1.6 – 3.0
- 0 – 1.5
- no data

Afghanistan Military spending 6.4% of GDP

Israel Military spending 5.6% of GDP

South Sudan Military spending 9.3% of GDP

Oman Military spending 11.6% of GDP

Saudi Arabia Military spending 9.0% of GDP

Facts

- There have been over 70 civil or internal wars throughout the world since 1945
- The Iran-Iraq war in the 1980s is estimated to have cost half a million lives
- The UN are currently involved in 16 peacekeeping operations
- It is estimated that there are over 11 million refugees throughout the world
- Over 3 300 UN peacekeepers have been killed since 1948

Global terrorism

Terrorism is defined by the United Nations as "All criminal acts directed against a State and intended or calculated to create a state of terror in the minds of particular persons or a group of persons or the general public". The world has become increasingly concerned about terrorism and the possibility that terrorists could acquire and use nuclear, chemical and biological weapons. One common form of terrorist attack is suicide bombing. Pioneered by Tamil secessionists in Sri Lanka, it has been widely used by Palestinian groups fighting against Israeli occupation of the West Bank and Gaza. In recent years it has also been used by the Al Qaida network in its attacks on the western world. Suicide bombings have also been used in Iraq and Afghanistan. The most recent terrorist organisation to be designated as such by the United Nations and many countries around the world is the Islamic State, also known as ISIS or ISIL. It is renowned for internet and social media propaganda, for the beheadings of civilians, journalists, soldiers and aid workers, and for the deliberate destruction of cultural heritage sites.

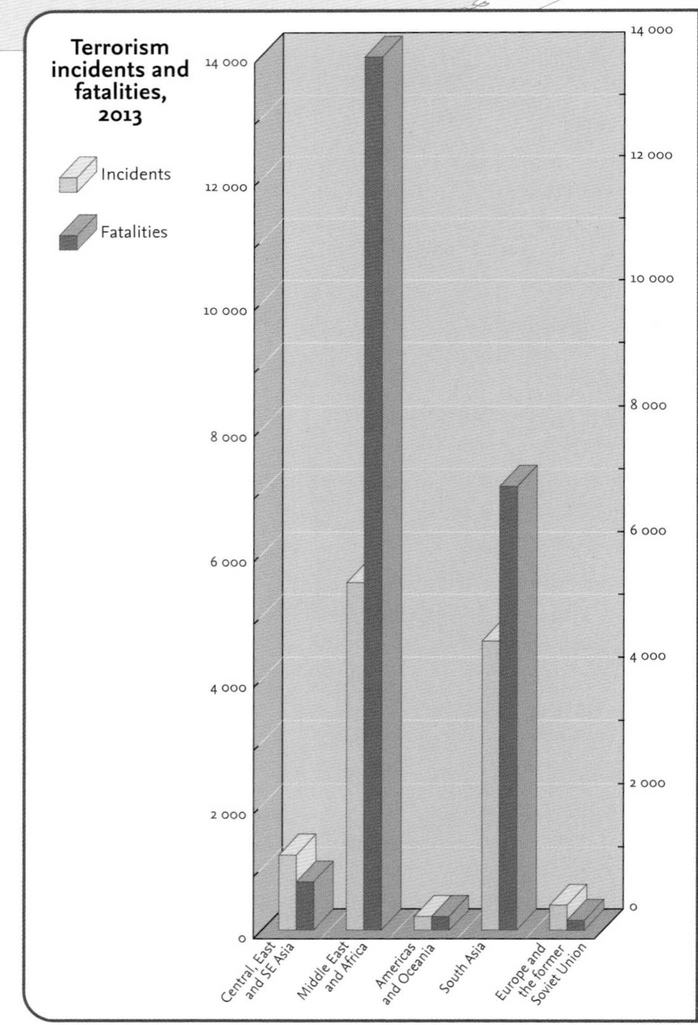

Internet Links

United Nations Peacekeeping	www.un.org/en/peacekeeping
United Nations Refugee Agency	www.unhcr.org
NATO	www.nato.int
BBC News	www.bbc.co.uk/news
International Boundaries Research Unit	www.dur.ac.uk/ibru
Peace Research Institute Oslo	www.prio.org

United Nations peacekeeping

United Nations peacekeeping was developed by the Organization as a way to help countries torn by conflict create the conditions for lasting peace. The first UN peacekeeping mission was established in 1948, when the Security Council authorized the deployment of UN military observers to the Middle East to monitor the Armistice Agreement between Israel and its Arab neighbours. Since then, there have been a total of 69 UN peacekeeping operations around the world.

UN peacekeeping goals were primarily limited to maintaining ceasefires and stabilizing situations on the ground, so that efforts could be made at the political level to resolve the conflict by peaceful means. Today's peacekeepers undertake a wide variety of complex tasks, from helping to build sustainable institutions of governance, to human rights monitoring, to security sector reform, to the disarmament, demobilization and reintegration of former combatants.

United Nations peacekeeping operations 1948–2014

Current peacekeeping operations are named on the map

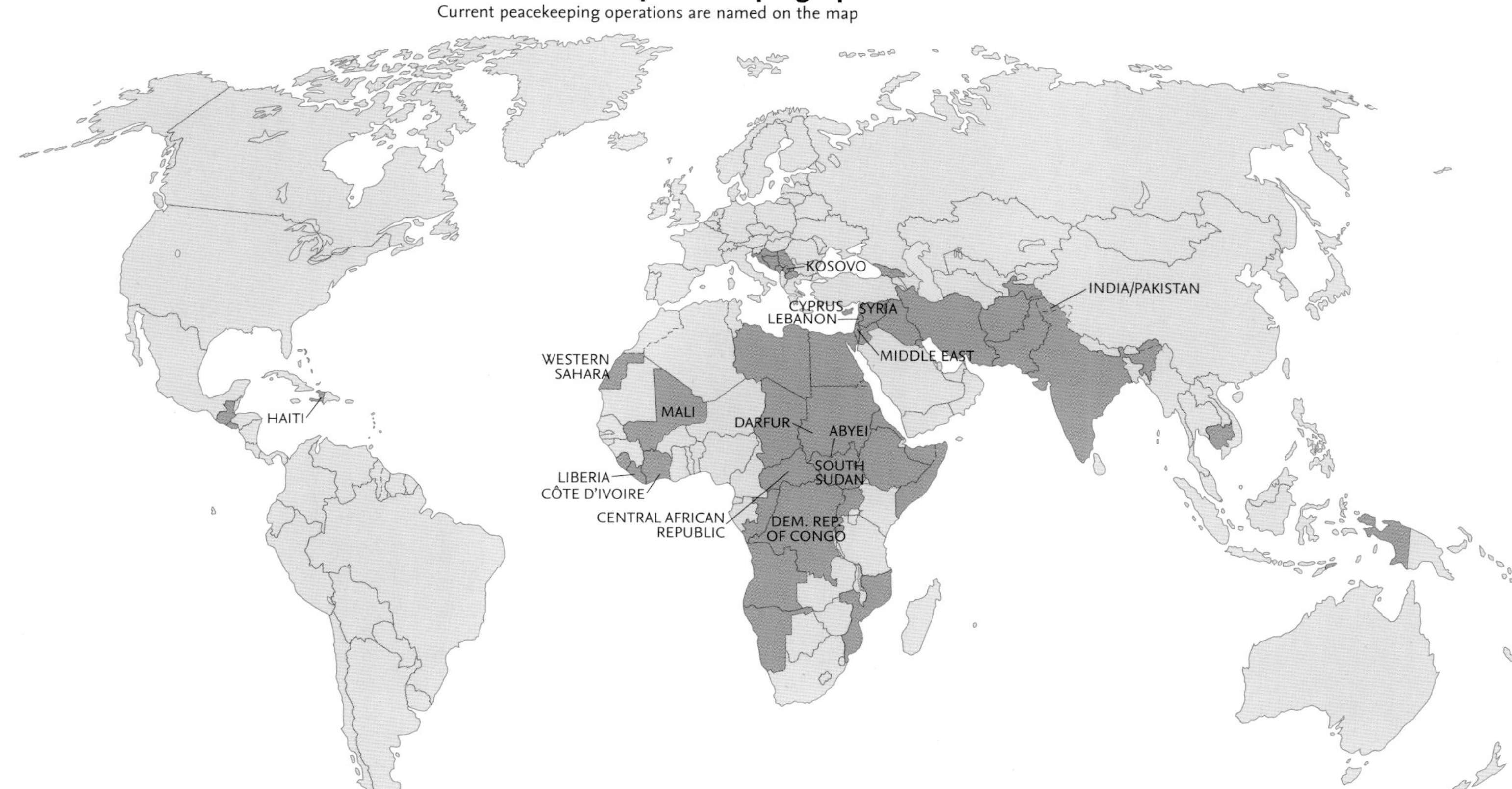

Many refugees from **Myanmar** (Burma) live in villages in Thailand.

Major terrorist incidents

Date	Location	Summary	Killed	Injured
December 1988	**Lockerbie, Scotland**	Airline bombing	270	5
March 1995	**Tōkyō, Japan**	Sarin gas attack on subway	12	5 510
April 1995	**Oklahoma City, USA**	Bomb in the Federal building	168	over 800
August 1998	**Nairobi, Kenya and Dar es Salaam, Tanzania**	US Embassy bombings	225	over 4 000
August 1998	**Omagh, Northern Ireland**	Town centre bombing	29	220
September 2001	**New York and Washington D.C., USA**	Airline hijacking and crashing	3 018	over 6 200
October 2002	**Bali, Indonesia**	Car bomb outside nightclub	202	over 200
October 2002	**Moscow, Russia**	Theatre siege	170	over 600
March 2004	**Bāghdad and Karbalā', Iraq**	Suicide bombing of pilgrims	181	over 400
March 2004	**Madrid, Spain**	Train bombings	191	1 800
September 2004	**Beslan, Russia**	School siege	385	over 700
July 2005	**London, UK**	Underground and bus bombings	56	700
July 2005	**Sharm ash Shaykh, Egypt**	Bombs at tourist sites	88	200
July 2006	**Mumbai, India**	Train bombings	209	700
August 2007	**Qahtaniya, Iraq**	Suicide bombing in town centres	796	over 1 500
November 2008	**Mumbai, India**	Coordinated shootings at eight sites	183	over 300
October 2011	**Mogadishu, Somalia**	Suicide truck bomb	139	over 90
March 2012	**Zinjibar, Yemen**	Army base attack	210	n/a
September 2013	**Nairobi, Kenya**	Shopping centre attack	72	201
May 2014	**Gamboru and Ngala, Nigeria**	Attack on market	310	n/a
April 2015	**Garissa, Kenya**	College shooting	147	79

Terrorist incidents

Number of terrorist incidents 2008-2013

- over 2000
- 1000 – 2000
- 100 – 999
- 10 – 99
- 1 – 9
- no incidents recorded

☆ Major terrorist incident location

Omagh, Lockerbie, London, Moscow, Beslan, Madrid, Oklahoma City, New York, Washington D.C., Tōkyō, Qahtaniya, Baghdād and Karbalā', Sharm ash Shaykh, Mumbai, Gamboru and Ngala, Zinjiba, Mogadishu, Nairobi, Garissa, Dar es Salaam, Bali

World
Global Issues

With the process of globalization has come an increased awareness of, and direct interest in, issues which have global implications. Social issues can now affect large parts of the world and can impact on large sections of society. Perhaps the current issues of greatest concern are those of national security, including the problem of international terrorism, health, crime and natural resources. The three social issues highlighted here reflect this and are of immediate concern.

The international drugs trade, and the crimes commonly associated with it, can impact on society and individuals in devastating ways; scarcity of water resources and lack of access to safe drinking water can have major economic implications and cause severe health problems; and the AIDS epidemic is having disastrous consequences in large parts of the world, particularly in sub-Saharan Africa.

The drugs trade

The international trade in illegal drugs is estimated to be worth over US$400 billion. While it may be a lucrative business for the criminals involved, the effects of the drugs on individual users and on society in general can be devastating. Patterns of drug production and abuse vary, but there are clear centres for the production of the most harmful drugs – the opiates (opium, morphine and heroin) and cocaine. The 'Golden Triangle' of Laos, Myanmar and Thailand, and western South America respectively are the main producing areas for these drugs. Significant efforts are expended to counter the drugs trade, and there have been signs recently of downward trends in the production of heroin and cocaine.

The **opium poppy** is the plant from which opium is extracted.

The international drugs trade

Main producers and trafficking routes for opiates (opium, morphine, heroin) and cocaine

Cocaine producer
Opiate producer
Cocaine trafficking route
Opiate trafficking route

Arctic Circle
Tropic of Cancer
Equator
Tropic of Capricorn
Antarctic Circle

UNITED STATES OF AMERICA
MEXICO
CENTRAL AMERICA
CARIBBEAN
COLOMBIA
PERU
BOLIVIA
SOUTH AMERICA
WESTERN EUROPE
EASTERN EUROPE
WEST AFRICA
SOUTH AFRICA
AFGHANISTAN
PAKISTAN
INDIA
MYANMAR
LAOS
THAILAND
VIETNAM
JAPAN
AUSTRALIA

Mexico
Opiate production 2011:
250 metric tonnes

Colombia
Cocaine production 2012:
309 metric tonnes

Peru
Cocaine production 2008:
302 metric tonnes

Bolivia
Cocaine production 2008:
113 metric tonnes

Afghanistan
Opiate production 2013:
5 500 metric tonnes

Laos
Opiate production 2013:
23 metric tonnes

Myanmar
Opiate production 2013:
870 metric tonnes

World
Opiate production 2013: 6 883 metric tonnes
Cocaine production 2008: 865 metric tonnes

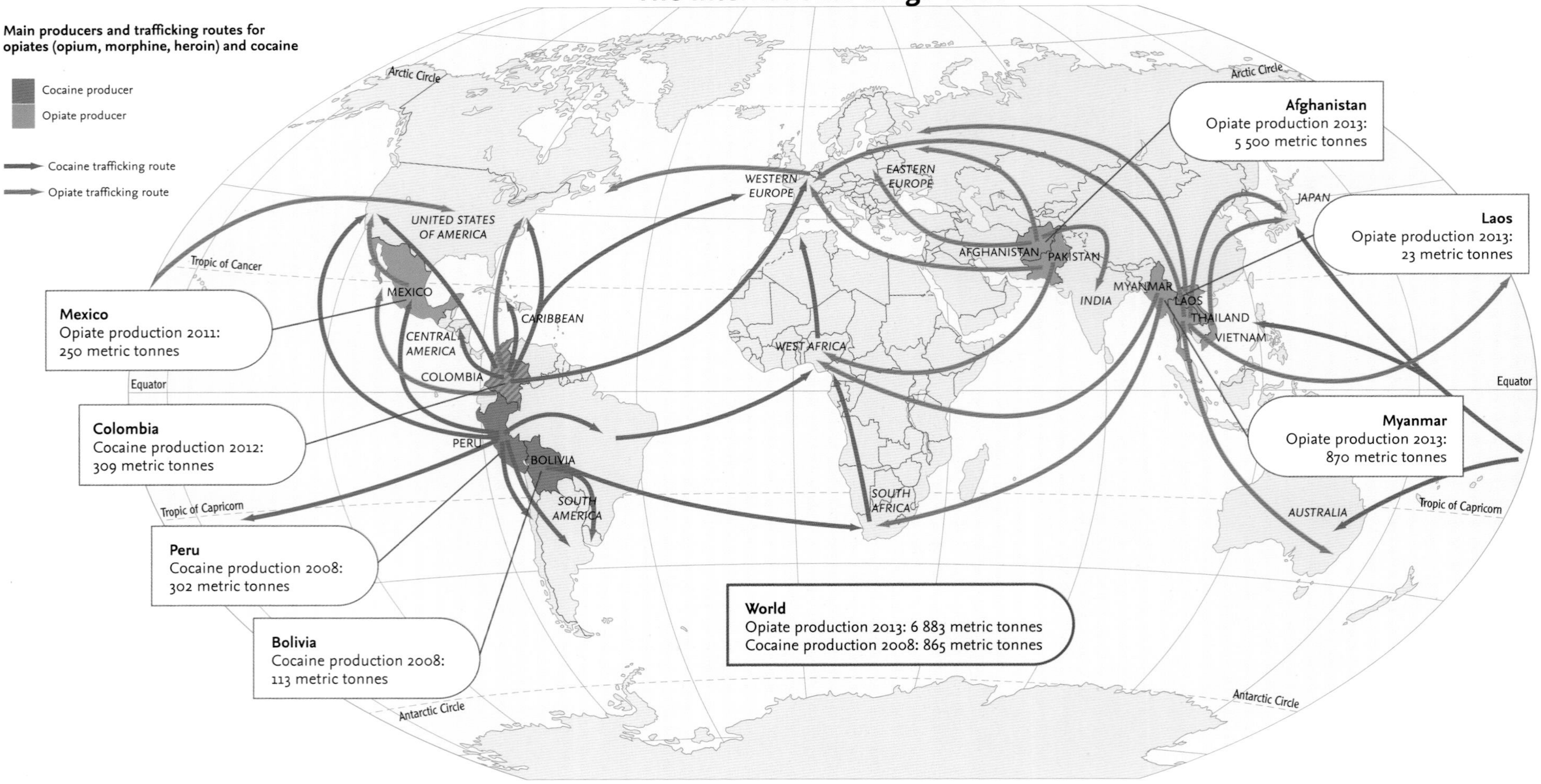

AIDS epidemic

With 35 million people living with HIV/AIDS (Human Immunodeficiency Virus/Acquired Immune Deficiency Syndrome) and more than 20 million deaths from the disease, the AIDS epidemic poses one of the biggest threats to public health. The UNAIDS project estimated that 2.1 million people were newly infected in 2013 and that 1.5 million AIDS sufferers died. This is nearly one half the number of infections than the peak of 3.2 million in 1997. As well as the death count itself, there are millions of living African children, between the ages of 10 and 17, that have been orphaned as a result of the disease. Treatment to prevent HIV transmission to babies has resulted in 33 per cent drop in infections.

Facts

- **The majority of people infected with HIV, if not treated, develop signs of AIDS within 8 to 10 years**
- **Agriculture uses 70 per cent of all the water taken from aquifers, streams and lakes**
- **Nearly 4 million people die each year from water-related diseases such as cholera and dysentery**
- **Estimates suggest that 243 million people consume illegal drugs around the world**

Population living with HIV/AIDS, 2013

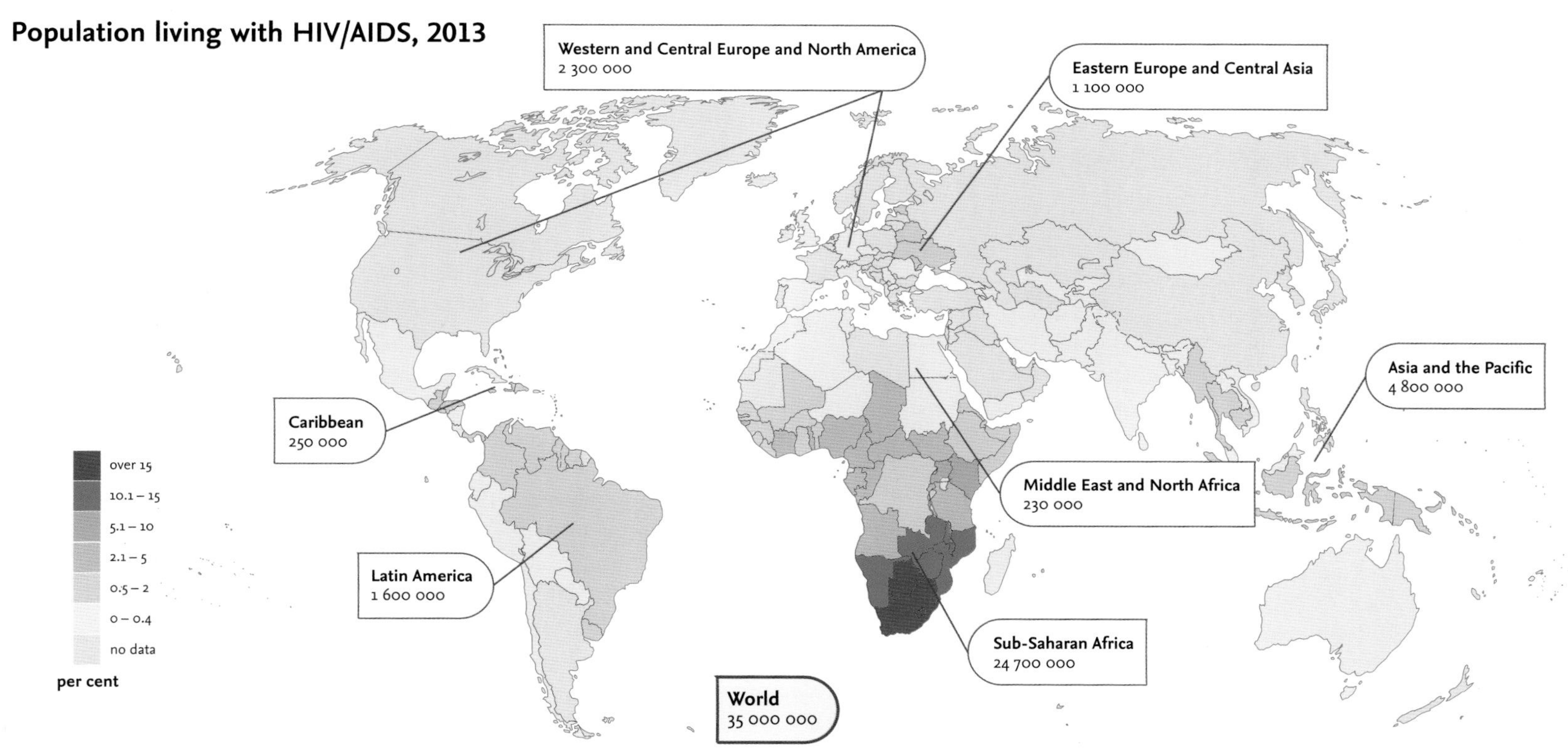

Water resources

Water is one of the fundamental requirements of life, and yet in some countries it is becoming more scarce due to increasing population and climate change. Safe drinking water, basic hygiene, health education and sanitation facilities are often virtually nonexistent for impoverished people in developing countries throughout the world. WHO/UNICEF estimate that the combination of these conditions results in over 4 000 deaths every day, most of these being children. Currently, 1.8 billion people drink untreated water and expose themselves to serious health risks, while political struggles over diminishing water resources are increasingly likely to be the cause of international conflict.

Domestic use of **untreated water** in Varanasi, India

Access to safe water, 2012

Percentage of population with access to improved drinking water

91 – 100
81 – 90
71 – 80
51 – 70
40 – 50
no data
per cent

Internet Links

UNESCO	**www.unesco.org**
UNAIDS	**www.unaids.org**
WaterAid	**www.wateraid.org.uk**
World Health Organization	**www.who.int**
UNODC United Nations Office on Drugs and Crime	**www.unodc.org**

The Earth has a rich and diverse environment which is under threat from both natural and man-induced forces. Forests and woodland form the predominant natural land cover with tropical rain forests – currently disappearing at alarming rates – believed to be home to the majority of animal and plant species. Grassland and scrub tend to have a lower natural species diversity but have suffered the most impact from man's intervention through conversion to agriculture, burning and the introduction of livestock. Wherever man interferes with existing biological and environmental processes degradation of that environment occurs to varying degrees. This interference also affects inland water and oceans where pollution, over-exploitation of marine resources and the need for fresh water has had major consequences on land and sea environments.

Facts

- The Sundarbans stretching across the Ganges delta is the largest area of mangrove forest in the world, covering 10 000 square kilometres (3 861 square miles) and forming an important ecological area, home to 260 species of birds, the Bengal tiger and other threatened species
- Over 90 000 square kilometres of precious tropical forest and wetland habitats are lost each year
- The surface level of the Dead Sea has fallen by more than 35 metres over the last 50 years
- Climate change and mismanagement of land areas can lead to soils becoming degraded and semi-arid grasslands becoming deserts – a process known as desertification

Environmental change

Whenever natural resources are exploited by man, the environment is changed. Approximately half the area of post-glacial forest has been cleared or degraded, and the amount of old-growth forest continues to decline. Desertification caused by climate change and the impact of man can turn semi-arid grasslands into arid desert. Regions bordering tropical deserts, such as the Sahel region south of the Sahara and regions around the Thar Desert in India, are most vulnerable to this process. Coral reefs are equally fragile environments, and many are under threat from coastal development, pollution and over-exploitation of marine resources.

Water resources in certain parts of the world are becoming increasingly scarce and competition for water is likely to become a common cause of conflict. The Aral Sea in central Asia was once the world's fourth largest lake but it now ranks only sixteenth after shrinking by more than 51 000 square kilometres since the 1960s. This shrinkage has been due to climatic change and to the diversion, for farming purposes, of the major rivers which feed the lake. The change has had a devastating effect on the local fishing industry and the exposure of chemicals on the lake bed has caused health problems for the local population.

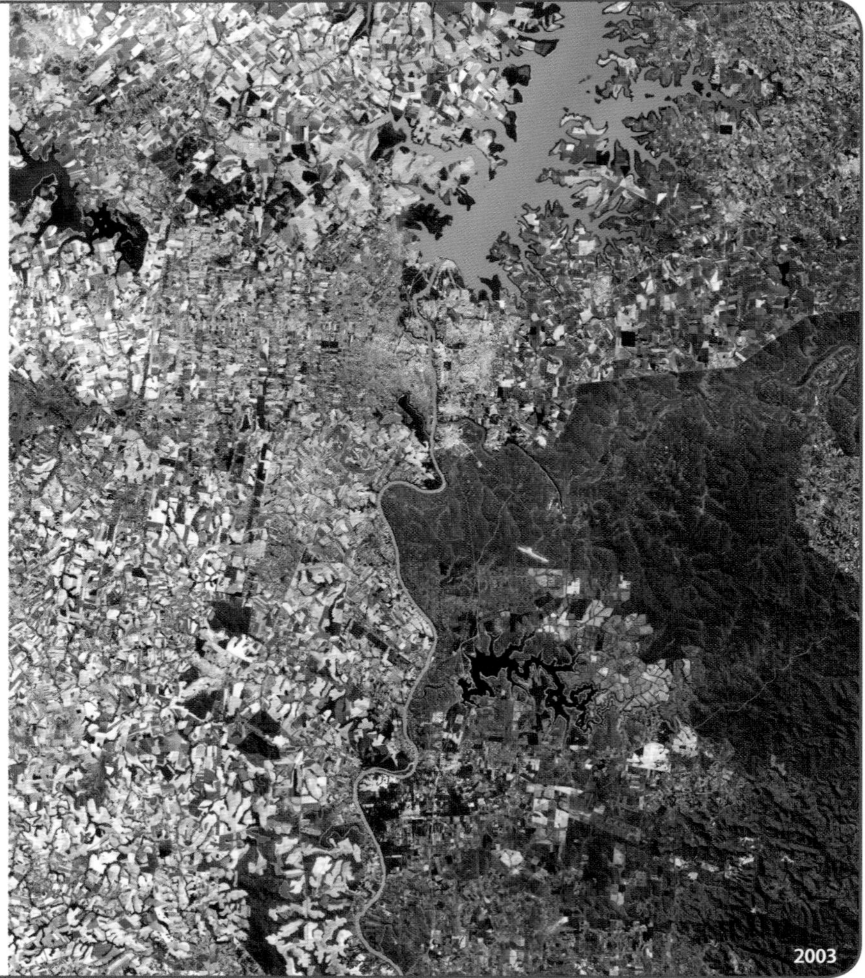

Deforestation and the creation of the **Itaipu Dam** on the Paraná river in Brazil have had a dramatic effect on the landscape and ecosystems of this part of South America. Some forest on the right of the images lies within Iguaçu National Park and has been protected from destruction.

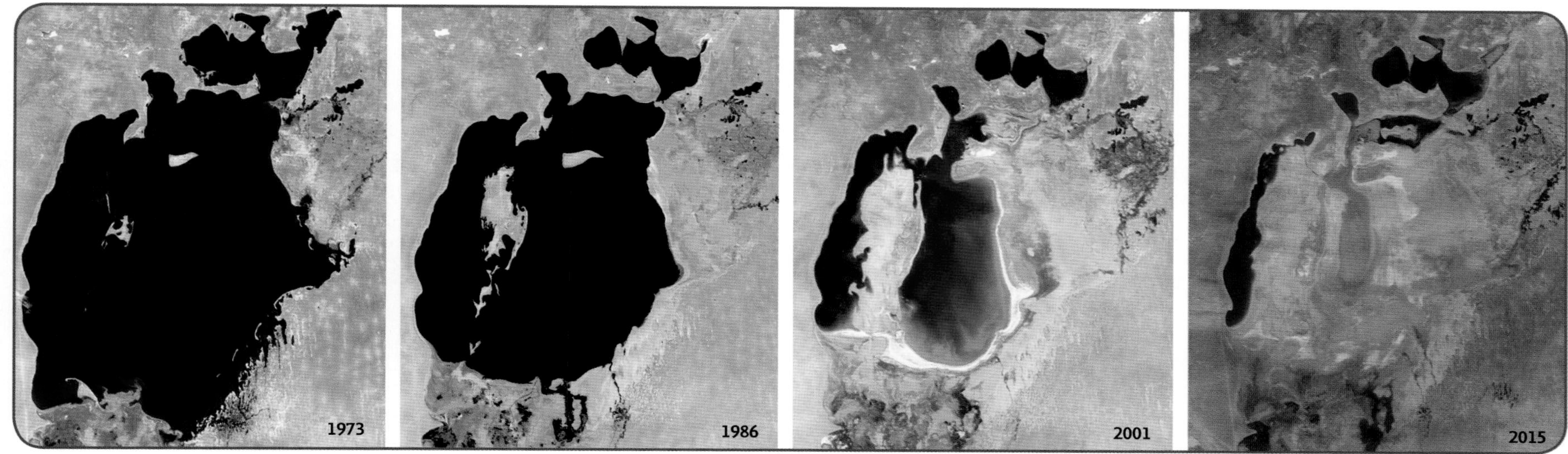

Aral Sea, Kazakhstan/Uzbekistan 1973-2015 Climate change and the diversion of rivers have caused its dramatic shrinkage.

Environmental Impacts

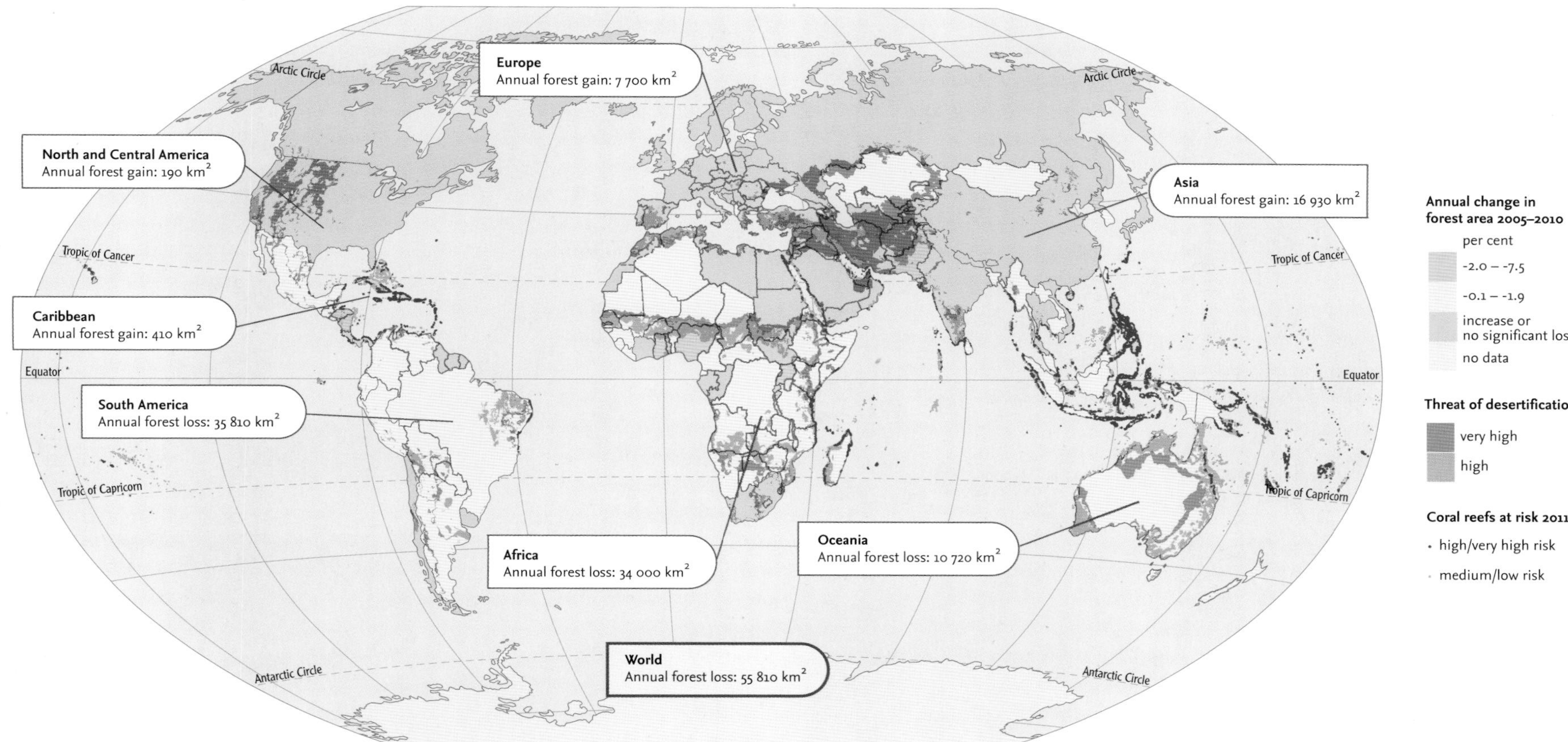

Internet links

United Nations Environment Programme (UNEP)	**www.unep.org**
IUCN International Union for Conservation of Nature	**www.iucn.org**
UNESCO World Heritage	**whc.unesco.org**

Environmental protection

Top 10 protected areas by size

Rank	Protected area	Country	Size (sq km)	Designation
1	**Natural Park of the Coral Sea**	New Caledonia, France	1 292 967	Marine Protected Area
2	**South Georgia and South Sandwich Islands Marine Protected Area**	South Georgia and South Sandwich Islands, United Kingdom	1 070 000	Marine Protected Area
3	**Coral Sea Reserve**	Australia	989 842	Marine Protected Area
4	**Northeast Greenland**	Greenland	972 000	National Park
5	**Rub' al-Khālī**	Saudi Arabia	640 000	Wildlife Management Area
6	**Chagos Marine Protected Area**	BIOT, United Kingdom	640 000	Marine Protected Area
7	**Kermadec Islands Marine Reserve**	New Zealand	469 276	Marine Protected Area
8	**Phoenix Islands Protected Area**	Kiribati	410 500	Marine Protected Area
9	**Papahānaumokuākea Marine National Monument**	United States	362 075	Marine Protected Area
10	**Great Barrier Reef Marine Park**	Australia	348 700	Marine Protected Area

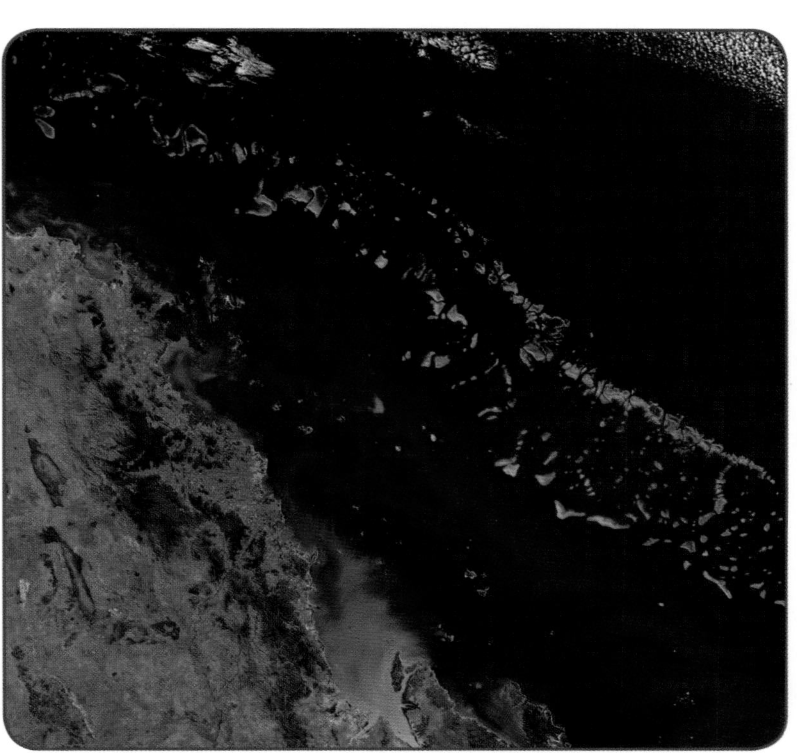

Great Barrier Reef, Australia, the world's tenth largest protected area.

Many parts of the world are undergoing significant changes which can have widespread and long-lasting effects. The principal causes of change are environmental factors – particularly climatic – and the influence of man. However, it is often difficult to separate these causes because man's activities can influence and exaggerate environmental change. Changes, whatever their cause, can have significant effects on the local population, on the wider region and even on a global scale. Major social, economic and environmental impacts can result from often irreversible changes – deforestation can affect a region's biodiversity, land reclamation can destroy fragile marine ecosystems, major dams and drainage schemes can affect whole drainage basins, and local communities can be changed beyond recognition through such projects.

Facts

- Earth-observing satellites can now detect land detail, and therefore changes in land use, of less than 1 metre extent
- Hong Kong International Airport, opened in 1998 and covering an area of over 12 square kilometres, was built almost entirely on reclaimed land
- The UN have estimated that 1800 million people will be living in places with absolute water scarcity by 2025
- Approximately 35% of cropland in Asia is irrigated

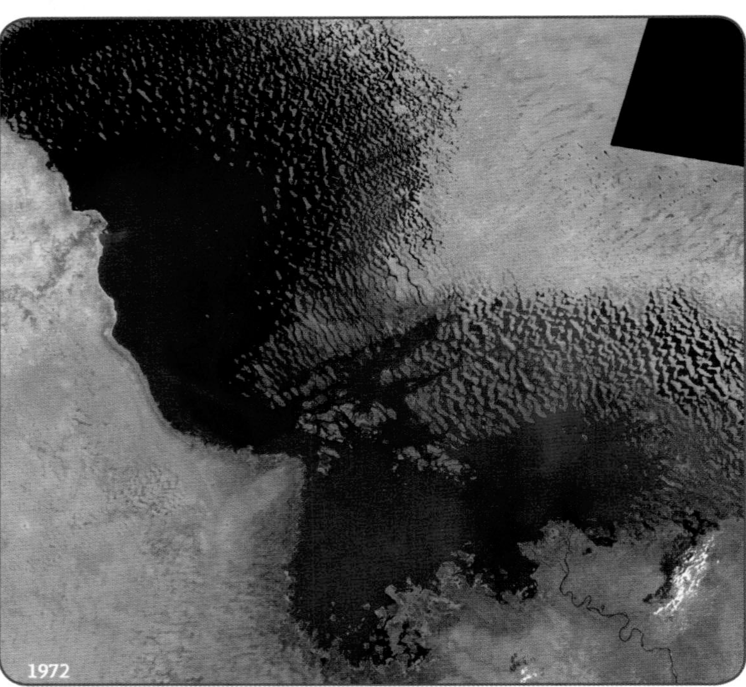

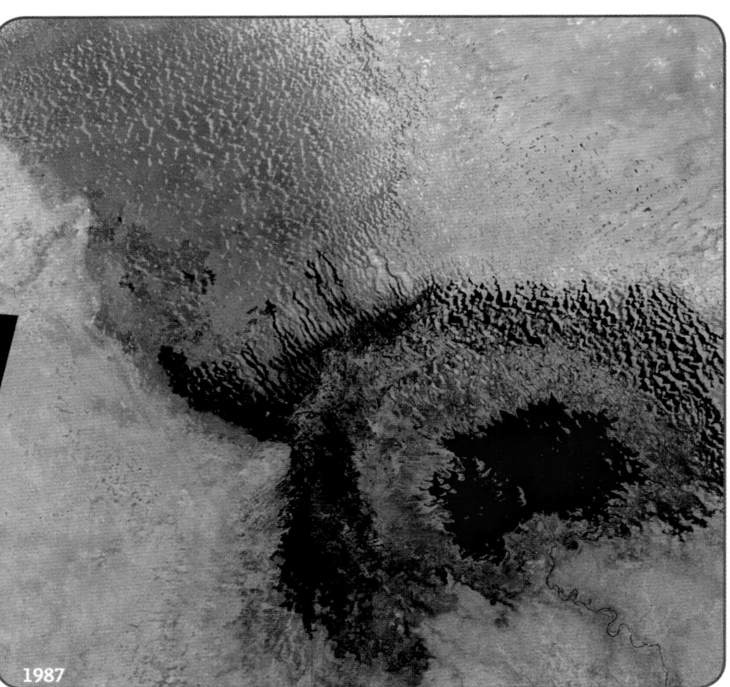

Diversion of water for irrigation and a drier climate have led to the shrinkage of **Lake Chad** in Africa.

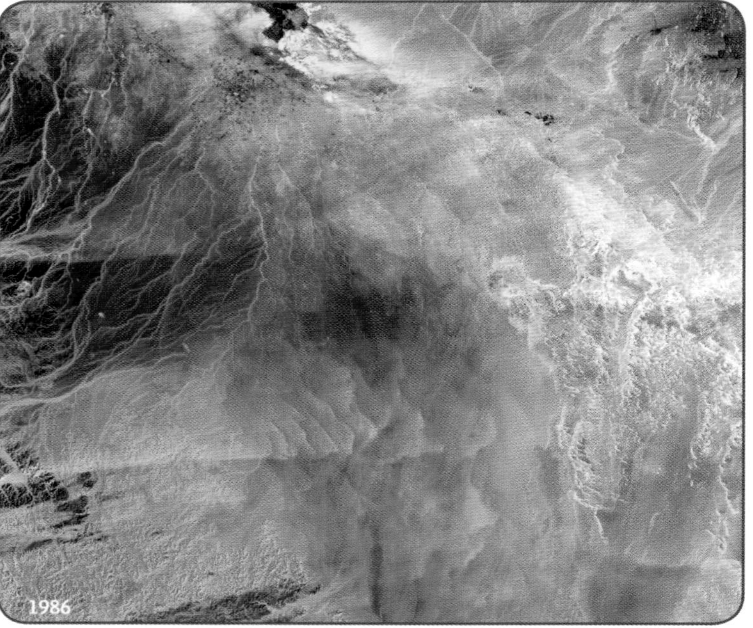

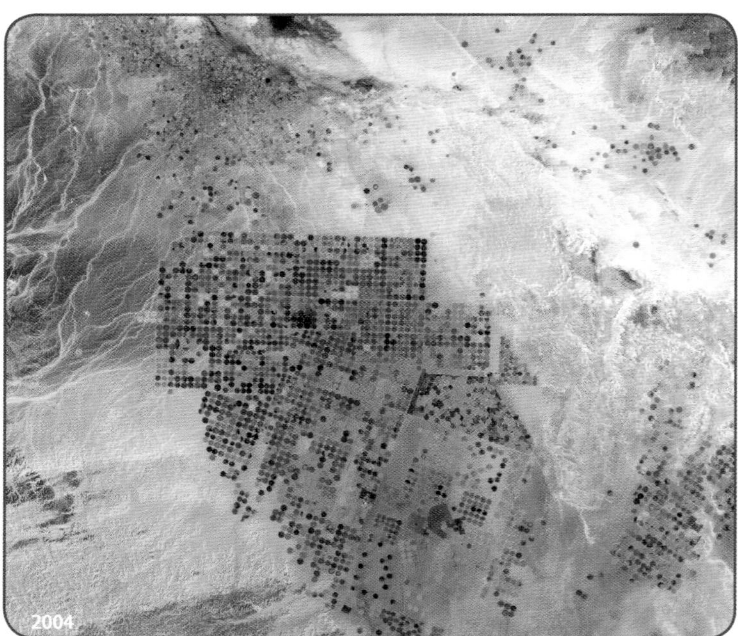

'Centre-pivot' irrigation has transformed the **Arabian Desert** near Tubarjal.

Effects of change

Both natural forces and human activity have irreversibly changed the environment in many parts of the world. Satellite images of the same area taken at different times are a powerful tool for identifying and monitoring such change. Climate change and an increasing demand for water can combine to bring about dramatic changes to lakes and rivers, while major engineering projects, reclamation of land from the sea and the expansion of towns and cities, create completely new environments. Use of water for the generation of hydro-electric power or for irrigation of otherwise infertile land leads to dramatic changes in the landscape and can also be a cause of conflict between countries. All such changes can have major social and economic impacts on the local population. However time also heals scars as regeneration of landcover gradually returns a damaged landscape to a healthier state.

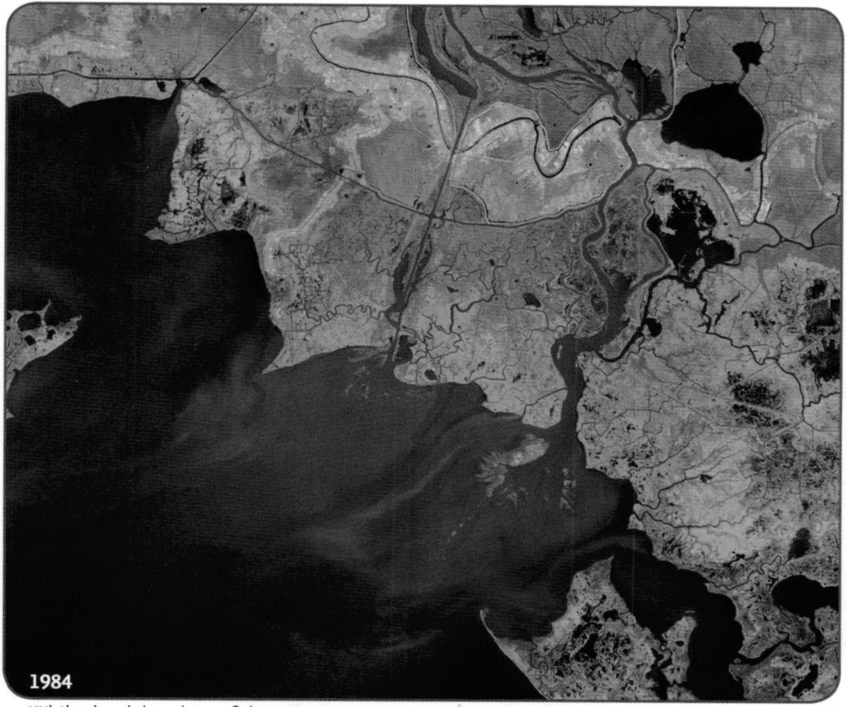

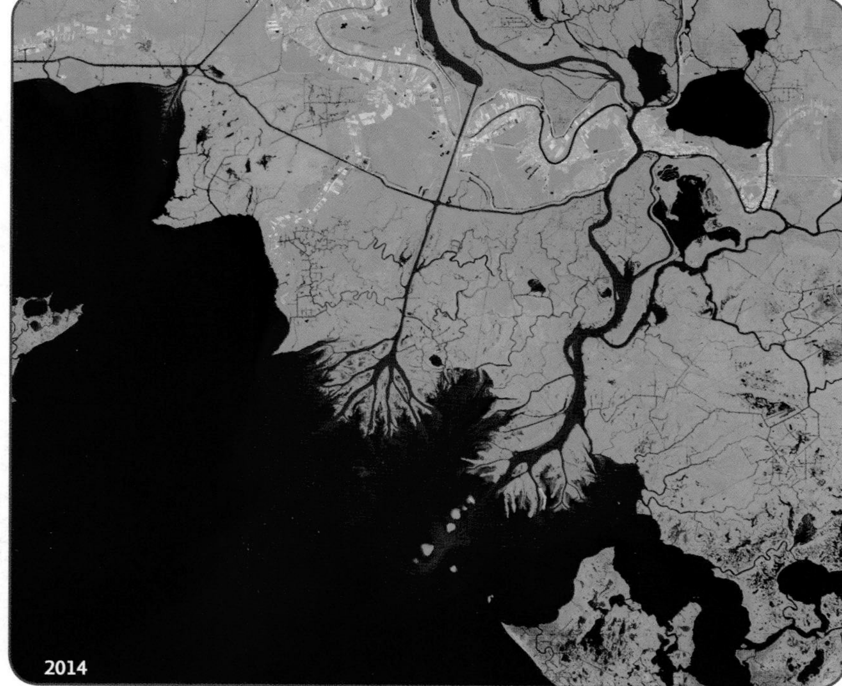

While the delta plain of the Mississippi River is disappearing in many places, up to as much as a football field every hour, Atchafalaya Bay stands out as an exception. South of Morgan City, new land is being formed at the mouths of the Wax Lake Outlet and **Atchafalaya River**, as shown in these false-colour Landsat images taken in 1984 and 2014. Water appears dark blue, vegetation is green, and bare ground is pink.

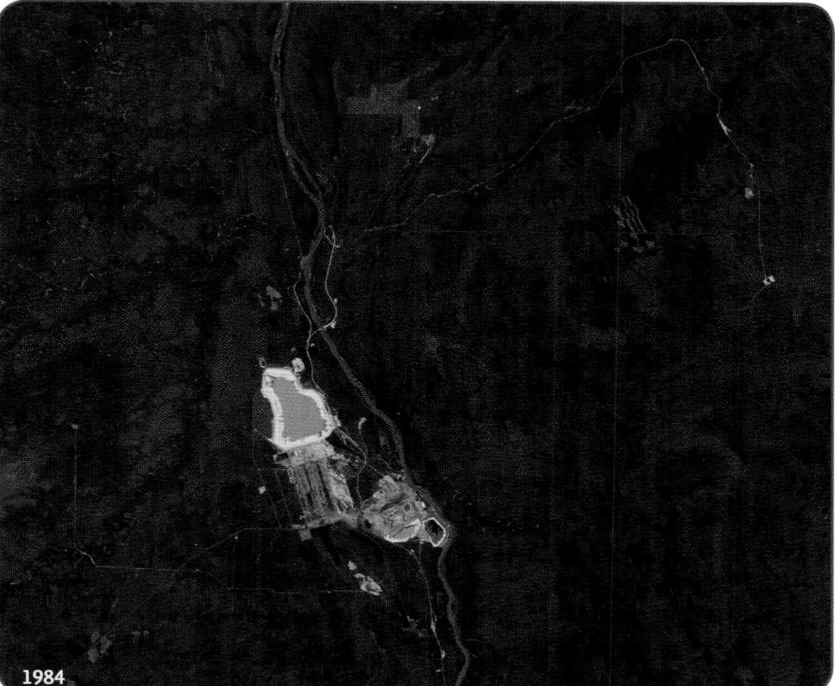

Alberta, Canada has the world's largest oil sands deposits by the **Athabasca** river. As the price of oil has risen over the past decade, mining here has become more profitable and the expansion of operations can be seen clearly. The process is toxic and releases more greenhouse gases than other oil extraction methods. However, strict Canadian environmental laws demand land restoration, and this process has been started with a restored pond.

Dubai has changed dramatically since the turn of the century, both offshore and on land. Offshore the development of the Palm Jumeirah in the bottom of the picture, "The World" and Palm Deira are clearly visible, while on the land the expansion of the urban area is extensive. Also noticeable in these infrared images are the many red areas that indicate irrigated land.

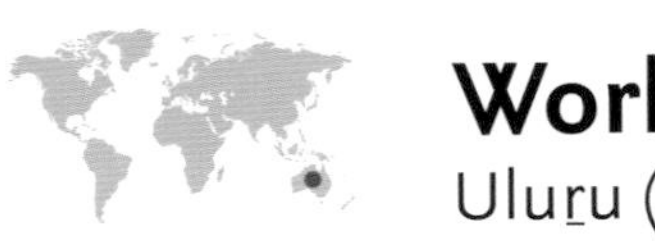

World

Uluṟu (Ayers Rock), Australia

Uluṟu, or Ayers Rock, in Australia's Northern Territory is one of Australia's most recognisable natural features. It stands 348 m above the surrounding plain as a monumental geological feature called an inselberg. It is the largest and best known feature of its kind. The sandstone it consists of is more resistant to erosion than the softer rocks, now eroded away, which used to surround it. The strata of

the sandstone are almost vertical and features on the surface of the rock, created by erosion, are clearly shown on this image. When the rock is freshly broken it has a grey colour, but weathering of iron-bearing minerals gives its surface a red-brown colour. The rock is a particularly remarkable sight at sunrise and sunset when it appears to glow red.

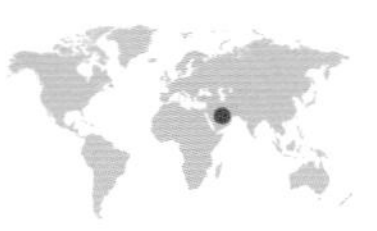

World

Khor al Adaid, Qatar

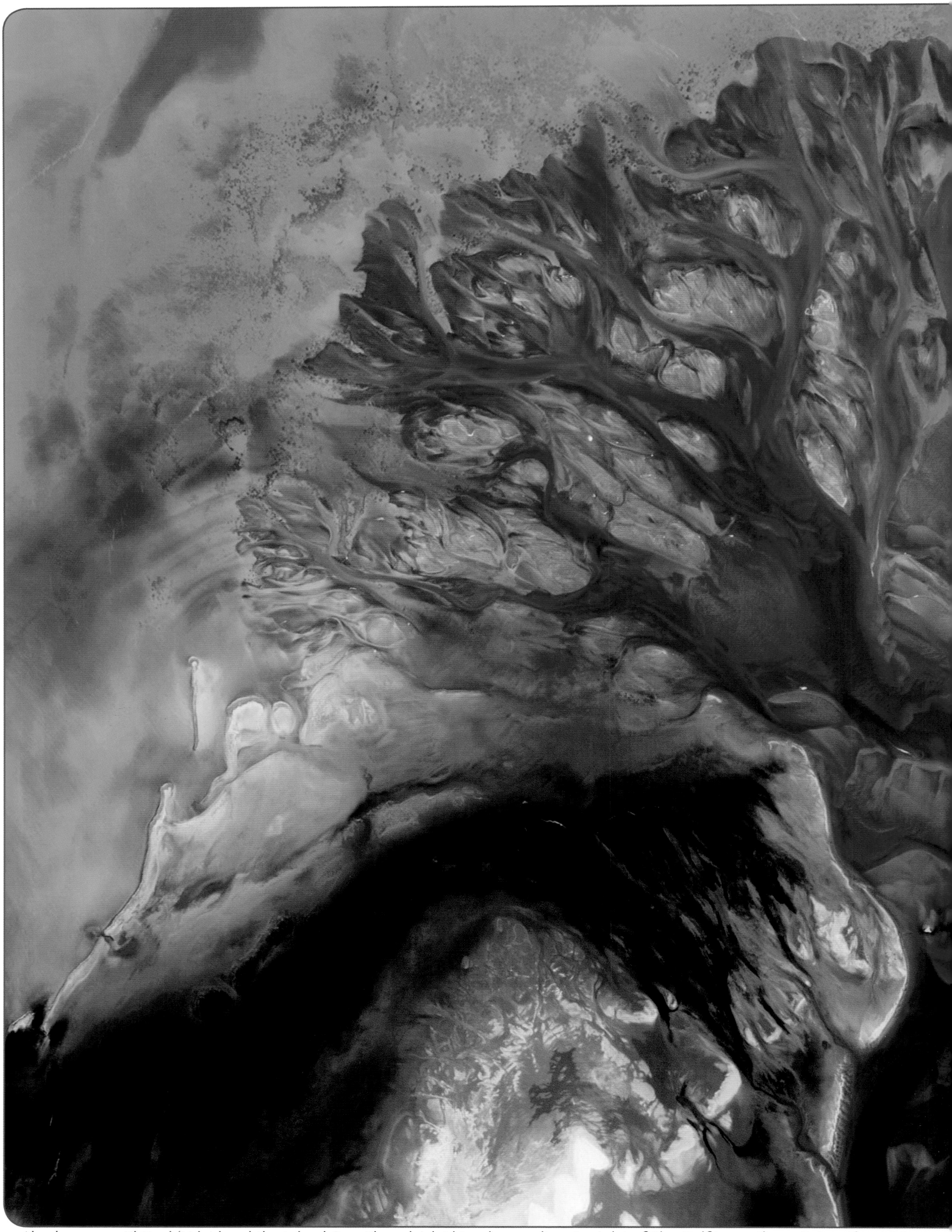

Also known as Khōr al ‘Udeid and the Inland Sea, Khor al Adaid is a large salt-water inlet of The Gulf in southern Qatar. About 15 km by 12 km in size, and surrounded by a multitude of soaring sand dunes, it is one of Qatar’s prime tourism assets, requiring experienced guides with convoys of 4x4 vehicles to access and explore. Placed on the Tentative list to become a UNESCO World

Heritage site, this globally unique area plays host to threatened marine species and diverse native flora and fauna. In this image, the flow of the tide has created a wonderfully organic tree-like shape with the sandy sediments in the channel between the northern and southern basins.

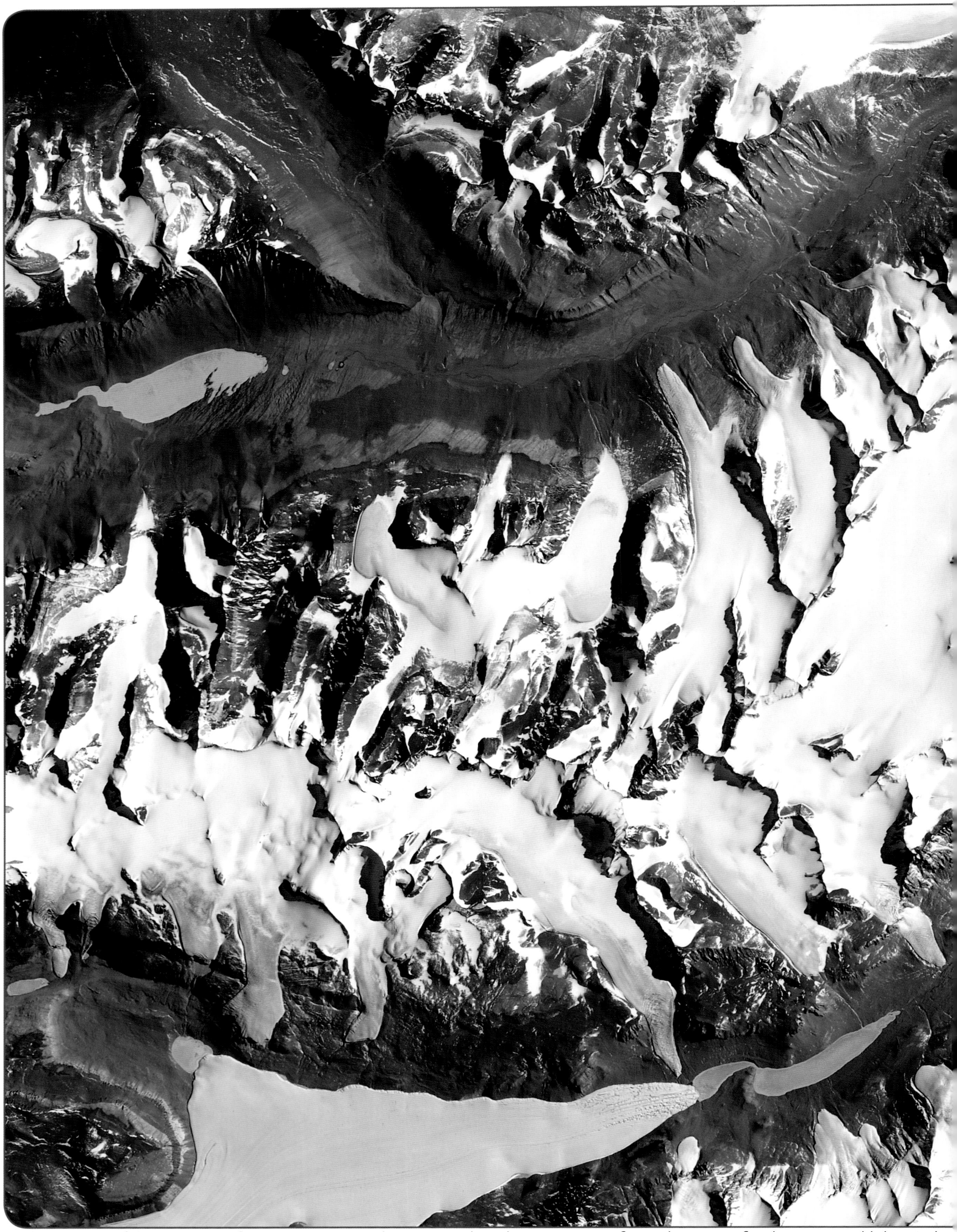

The majority of the continent of Antarctica is covered in snow and ice, however, parts of it are kept snow free by strong, cold dry winds. In this image an area known as the Dry Valleys can be seen. They are located between the Ross Sea and the East Antarctica Ice Sheet.

Taylor Valley with its ice-covered lakes and many glaciers flowing into it runs from the bottom left of the image and part of the Ferrar Glacier can also be seen at the bottom right.

Grand Coulee Dam, Washington State, U.S.A.

The Grand Coulee Dam in Washington State U.S.A. took nine years to build and was completed in 1942. A major hydroelectric gravity dam, it is located at the change of the Columbia River's course and created the Franklin D. Roosevelt Lake. The lake covers the top right part of the image, and to its south an extensive patchwork of cultivated land including pivot-point irrigation circles can be seen.

The modern channel of the Columbia River snakes off to the north and west, while the historic channel in the Grand Coulee canyon to the south west can now be seen where Banks Lake has been created.

Europe

UNESCO World Heritage Sites

In 1959, the government of Egypt decided to build the Aswan High Dam, an event that would flood a valley containing treasures of an ancient civilization such as the Abu Simbel temples. The United Nations Educational, Scientific and Cultural Organization (UNESCO) then launched an international safeguarding campaign and, as a result, Abu Simbel was moved to higher ground where it remains one of Egypt's heritage treasures. This successful project led to the creation of the World Heritage convention and formation of the List of World Heritage sites.

● Cultural site ● Natural site ● Mixed site

Belarus
1. Architectural, Residential and Cultural Complex of the Radziwill Family at Nesvizh
2. Białowieża Forest
3. Mir Castle Complex
4. Struve Geodetic Arc

Denmark
5. Jelling Mounds, Runic Stones and Church
6. Kronborg Castle
7. Roskilde Cathedral
8. Stevns Klint
9. Wadden Sea
Ilulissat Icefjord (see map on p141)

Estonia
10. Historic Centre (Old Town) of Tallinn
4. Struve Geodetic Arc

Finland
11. Bronze Age Burial Site of Sammallahdenmäki
12. Fortress of Suomenlinna
13. High Coast/Kvarken Archipelago
14. Old Rauma
15. Petäjävesi Old Church
4. Struve Geodetic Arc
16. Verla Groundwood and Board Mill

Germany
17. Aachen Cathedral
18. Abbey and Altenmünster of Lorsch
19. Bauhaus and its Sites in Weimar and Dessau
20. Bergpark Wilhelmshöhe
21. Berlin Modernism Housing Estates
22. Castles of Augustusburg and Falkenlust at Brühl
23. Carolingian Westwork and Civitas Corvey
24. Classical Weimar
25. Collegiate Church, Castle and Old Town of Quedlinburg
26. Cologne Cathedral
27. Fagus Factory in Alfeld
28. Frontiers of the Roman Empire: Upper German-Raetian Limes
29. Garden Kingdom of Dessau-Wörlitz
30. Hanseatic City of Lübeck
31. Historic Centres of Stralsund and Wismar
32. Luther Memorials in Eisleben and Wittenberg
33. Margravial Opera House, Bayreuth
34. Maulbronn Monastery Complex
35. Messel Pit Fossil Site
36. Mines of Rammelsberg, Historic Town of Goslar and Upper Harz Water Management System
37. Monastic Island of Reichenau
38. Museumsinsel (Museum Island), Berlin
39. Muskauer Park/Park Muzakowski
40. Old town of Regensburg with Stadtamhof
41. Palaces and Parks of Potsdam and Berlin
42. Pilgrimage Church of Wies
43. Prehistoric Pile dwellings around the Alps
44. Primeval Beech Forests of the Carpathians and the Ancient Beech Forests of Germany
45. Roman Monuments, Cathedral of St Peter and Church of Our Lady in Trier
46. Speyer Cathedral
47. St Mary's Cathedral and St Michael's Church at Hildesheim
48. Town Hall and Roland on the Marketplace of Bremen
49. Town of Bamberg
50. Upper Middle Rhine Valley
51. Völklingen Ironworks
9. Wadden Sea
52. Wartburg Castle
53. Würzburg Residence with the Court Gardens and Residence Square
54. Zollverein Coal Mine Industrial Complex in Essen

Iceland
55. Surtsey
56. Þingvellir National Park

Ireland
57. Brú na Bóinne – Archaeological Ensemble of the Bend of the Boyne
58. Skellig Michael Monastery

Latvia
59. Historic Centre of Riga
4. Struve Geodetic Arc

Lithuania
60. Curonian Spit
61. Kernavė Archaeological Site (Cultural Reserve of Kernavė)
4. Struve Geodetic Arc
62. Vilnius Historic Centre

Netherlands
63. Defence Line of Amsterdam
64. Droogmakerij de Beemster (Beemster Polder)
65. Ir. D.F. Woudagemaal (D.F. Wouda Steam Pumping Station)
66. Mill Network at Kinderdijk-Elshout
67. Rietveld Schröderhuis (Rietveld Schröder House)
68. Schokland and Surroundings
69. Seventeenth-century canal ring area of Amsterdam inside the Singelgracht
70. Van Nellefabriek
9. Wadden Sea
Historic Area of Willemstad, Inner City and Harbour, Netherlands Antilles (see map on p171)

Norway
71. Bryggen
72. Rock Art of Alta
73. Røros Mining Town and the Circumference
4. Struve Geodetic Arc
74. Urnes Stave Church
75. Vegaøyan – the Vega Archipelago
76. West Norwegian Fjords – Geirangerfjord and Nærøyfjord

Poland
77. Auschwitz Birkenau German Nazi Concentration and Extermination Camp (1940–1945)
78. Castle of the Teutonic Order in Malbork
79. Centennial Hall in Wroclaw
2. Białowieża Forest
80. Churches of Peace in Jawor and Swidnica
81. Historic Centre of Kraków
82. Historic Centre of Warsaw
83. Kalwaria Zebrzydowska: the Mannerist Architectural and Park Landscape Complex and Pilgrimage Park
84. Medieval Town of Toruń
39. Muskauer Park/Park Muzakowski
85. Old City of Zamość
86. Wieliczka and Bochnia Royal Salt Mines
87. Wooden Churches of Southern Małopolska
88. Wooden Tserkvas of the Carpathian Region in Poland and Ukraine

Portugal
89. Alto Douro Wine Region
90. Central Zone of the Town of Angra do Heroismo in the Azores
91. Convent of Christ in Tomar
92. Cultural Landscape of Sintra
93. Garrison Border Town of Elvas and its Fortifications
94. Historic Centre of Évora
95. Historic Centre of Guimarães
96. Historic Centre of Oporto
97. Landscape of the Pico Island Vineyard Culture
98. Laurisilva of Madeira
99. Monastery of Alcobaça
100. Monastery of Batalha
101. Monastery of the Hieronymites and Tower of Belém in Lisbon
102. Prehistoric Rock-Art Sites in the Côa Valley and Siega Verde
103. University of Coimbra – Alta and Sofia

Russia (see also p70)
104. Architectural Ensemble of the Trinity Sergius Lavra in Sergiev Posad
105. Bolgar Historical and Archaeological Complex
106. Church of the Ascension, Kolomenskoye
107. Cultural and Historic Ensemble of the Solovetsky Islands
60. Curonian Spit
108. Ensemble of the Ferrapontov Monastery
109. Ensemble of the Novodevichy Convent
110. Historic and Architectural Complex of the Kazan Kremlin
111. Historic Centre of Saint Petersburg and Related Groups of Monuments
112. Historic Monuments of Novgorod and Surroundings
113. Historical Centre of the City of Yaroslavl
114. Kizhi Pogost
115. Kremlin and Red Square, Moscow
4. Struve Geodetic Arc
116. Virgin Komi Forests
117. White Monuments of Vladimir and Suzdal

Spain
118. Alhambra, Generalife and Albayzín, Granada
119. Aranjuez Cultural Landscape
120. Archaeological Ensemble of Mérida
121. Archaeological Ensemble of Tárraco
122. Archaeological Site of Atapuerca
123. Burgos Cathedral
124. Catalan Romanesque Churches of the Vall de Boí
125. Cathedral, Alcázar and Archivo de Indias in Seville
126. Cave of Altamira and Paleolithic Cave Art of Northern Spain
127. Cultural Landscape of the Serra de Tramuntana
128. Doñana National Park
129. Garajonay National Park
130. Heritage of Mercury: Almadén and Idrija
131. Historic Centre of Cordoba
132. Historic City of Toledo
133. Historic Walled Town of Cuenca
134. Ibiza, Biodiversity and Culture
135. La Lonja de la Seda de Valencia
136. Las Médulas
137. Monastery and Site of the Escurial, Madrid
138. Monuments of Oviedo and the Kingdom of the Asturias
139. Mudéjar Architecture of Aragon
140. Old City of Salamanca
141. Old Town of Ávila with its Extra-Muros Churches
142. Old Town of Cáceres
143. Old Town of Segovia and its Aqueduct
144. Palau de la Música Catalana and Hospital de Sant Pau, Barcelona
145. Palmeral of Elche
136. Poblet Monastery
102. Prehistoric Rock-Art Sites in the Côa Valley and Siega Verde
147. Pyrénées - Mont Perdu
148. Renaissance Monumental Ensembles of Úbeda and Baeza
149. Rock Art of the Mediterranean Basin on the Iberian Peninsula
150. Roman Walls of Lugo
151. Route of Santiago de Compostela
152. Royal Monastery of Santa María de Guadalupe
153. San Cristóbal de La Laguna
154. San Millán Yuso and Suso Monasteries
155. Santiago de Compostela (Old Town)
156. Teide National Park
157. University and Historic Precinct of Alcalá de Henares
158. Tower of Hercules
159. Vizcaya Bridge
160. Works of Antoni Gaudí

Sweden
161. Agricultural Landscape of Southern Öland
162. Birka and Hovgården
163. Church Village of Gammelstad, Luleå
164. Decorated Farmhouses of Hälsingland
165. Engelsberg Ironworks
166. Hanseatic Town of Visby
13. High Coast/Kvarken Archipelago
167. Laponian Area
168. Mining Area of the Great Copper Mountain in Falun
169. Naval Port of Karlskrona
170. Rock Carvings in Tanum
171. Royal Domain of Drottningholm
172. Skogskyrkogården
4. Struve Geodetic Arc
173. Varberg Radio Station

Ukraine
174. Ancient City of Tauric Chersonese and its Chora
175. Kiev: Saint-Sophia Cathedral and Related Monastic Buildings, Kiev-Pechersk Lavra
176. L'viv – the Ensemble of the Historic Centre
44. Primeval Beech Forests of the Carpathians and the Ancient Beech Forests of Germany
177. Residence of Bukovinian and Dalmatian Metropolitans
4. Struve Geodetic Arc
88. Wooden Tserkvas of the Carpathian Region in Poland and Ukraine

United Kingdom
178. Blaenavon Industrial Landscape
179. Blenheim Palace
180. Canterbury Cathedral, St Augustine's Abbey and St Martin's Church
181. Castles and Town Walls of King Edward in Gwynedd
182. City of Bath
183. Cornwall and West Devon Mining Landscape
184. Derwent Valley Mills
185. Dorset and East Devon Coast
186. Durham Castle and Cathedral
187. Frontiers of the Roman Empire: Antonine Wall and Hadrian's Wall
188. Giant's Causeway and Causeway Coast
189. Heart of Neolithic Orkney
190. Ironbridge Gorge
191. Liverpool – Maritime Mercantile City
192. Maritime Greenwich
193. New Lanark
194. Old and New Towns of Edinburgh
195. Palace of Westminster and Westminster Abbey including Saint Margaret's Church
196. Pontcysyllte Aqueduct and Canal
197. Royal Botanic Gardens, Kew
198. Saltaire
199. St Kilda
200. Stonehenge, Avebury and Associated Sites
201. Studley Royal Park including the Ruins of Fountains Abbey
202. Tower of London

Gough and Inaccessible Islands (see map on p115)
Henderson Island (see map p127)
Historic Town of St George and Related Fortifications, Bermuda (see map on p141)

see large-scale map on pages 44–45

Europe

UNESCO World Heritage Sites

World Heritage sites in Europe are found across the continent, from the far north of Scandinavia to the extreme south of Sicily. They span the whole of Earth's human history – from Neolithic Orkney and Stonehenge, through the Acropolis and Pompeii, to twentieth century Auschwitz and the Works of Gaudi.

● Cultural site ● Natural site ● Mixed site

Albania
1. Butrint
2. Historic Centres of Berat and Gjirokastra

Andorra
3. Madriu-Perafita-Claror Valley

Austria
4. City of Graz – Historic Centre
5. Fertö/Neusiedlersee Cultural Landscape
6. Hallstatt-Dachstein/Salzkammergut Cultural Landscape
7. Historic Centre of the City of Salzburg
8. Historic Centre of Vienna
9. Palace and Gardens of Schönbrunn
10. Prehistoric Pile dwellings around the Alps
11. Semmering Railway
12. Wachau Cultural Landscape

Belgium
13. Belfries of Belgium and France
14. Flemish Béguinages
15. Historic Centre of Brugge
16. La Grand-Place, Brussels
17. Major Town Houses of the Architect Victor Horta (Brussels)
18. Major Mining Sites of Wallonia
19. Neolithic Flint Mines at Spiennes (Mons)
20. Notre-Dame Cathedral in Tournai
21. Plantin-Moretus House-Workshops-Museum Complex
22. Stoclet House
23. The Four Lifts on the Canal du Centre and their Environs, La Louvière and Le Roeulx (Hainault)

Bosnia and Herzegovina
24. Mehmed Paša Sokolović Bridge in Višegrad
25. Old Bridge Area of the Old City of Mostar

Bulgaria
26. Ancient City of Nessebar
27. Boyana Church
28. Madara Rider
29. Pirin National Park
30. Rila Monastery
31. Rock-Hewn Churches of Ivanovo
32. Srebarna Nature Reserve
33. Thracian Tomb of Kazanlak
34. Thracian Tomb of Sveshtari

Croatia
35. Cathedral of St James in Šibenik
36. Episcopal Complex of the Euphrasian Basilica in the Historic Centre of Poreč
37. Historic City of Trogir
38. Historical Complex of Split with the Palace of Diocletian
39. Old City of Dubrovnik
40. Plitvice Lakes National Park
41. Stari Grad Plain

Czech Republic
42. Gardens and Castle at Kroměříž
43. Historic Centre of Český Krumlov
44. Historic Centre of Prague
45. Historic Centre of Telč
46. Holašovice Historical Village Reservation
47. Holy Trinity Column in Olomouc
48. Jewish Quarter and St Procopius' Basilica in Třebíč
49. Kutná Hora: Historical Town Centre with the Church of St Barbara and the Cathedral of Our Lady at Sedlec
50. Lednice-Valtice Cultural Landscape
51. Litomyšl Castle
52. Pilgrimage Church of St John of Nepomuk at Zelená Hora
53. Tugendhat Villa in Brno

France
54. Abbey Church of Saint-Savin sur Gartempe
55. Amiens Cathedral
56. Arles, Roman and Romanesque Monuments
13. Belfries of Belgium and France
57. Bordeaux, Port of the Moon
58. Bourges Cathedral
59. Canal du Midi
60. Cathedral of Notre-Dame, Former Abbey of Saint-Rémi and Palace of Tau, Reims
61. Chartres Cathedral
62. Cistercian Abbey of Fontenay
63. Decorated cave of Pont d'Arc, known as Grotte Chauvet-Pont-d'Arc, Ardèche
64. Episcopal City of Albi
65. Fortifications of Vauban
66. From the Great Saltworks of Salins-les-Bains to the Royal Saltworks of Arc-et-Senans, the production of open-pan salt
67. Gulf of Porto: Calanche of Piana, Gulf of Girolata, Scandola Reserve
68. Historic Centre of Avignon: Papal Palace, Episcopal Ensemble and Avignon Bridge
69. Historic Fortified City of Carcassonne
70. Historic Site of Lyons
71. Jurisdiction of Saint-Emilion
72. Le Havre, the city rebuilt by Auguste Perret
73. Mont-Saint-Michel and its Bay
74. Palace and Park of Fontainebleau
75. Nord-Pas de Calais Mining Basin
76. Palace and Park of Versailles
77. Paris, Banks of the Seine
    Pitons, cirques and remparts of Réunion Island (see map on page 115)
78. Place Stanislas, Place de la Carrière and Place d'Alliance in Nancy
79. Pont du Gard (Roman Aqueduct)
10. Prehistoric Pile dwellings around the Alps
80. Prehistoric Sites and Decorated Caves of the Vézère Valley
81. Provins, Town of Medieval Fairs
82. Pyrénées – Mont Perdu
83. Roman Theatre and its Surroundings and the 'Triumphal Arch' of Orange
84. Routes of Santiago de Compostela in France
85. Strasbourg – Grande Île
86. The Causses and the Cévennes, Mediterranean agro-pastoral Cultural Landscape
87. The Loire Valley between Sully-sur-Loire and Chalonnes
88. Vézelay, Church and Hill
    Lagoons of New Caledonia: Reef Diversity and Associated Ecosystems (see map on page 126)

Greece
89. Acropolis, Athens
90. Archaeological Site of Aigai (modern name Vergina)
91. Archaeological Site of Delphi
92. Archaeological Site of Mystras
93. Archaeological Site of Olympia
94. Archaeological Sites of Mycenae and Tiryns
95. Delos
96. Historic Centre (Chorá) with the Monastery of Saint John, the Theologian, and the Cave of the Apocalypse on the Island of Pátmos
97. Medieval City of Rhodes
98. Meteora
99. Monasteries of Daphni, Hosios Loukas and Nea Moni of Chios
100. Mount Athos
101. Old Town of Corfu
102. Paleochristian and Byzantine Monuments of Thessalonika
103. Pythagoreion and Heraion of Samos
104. Sanctuary of Asklepios at Epidaurus
105. Temple of Apollo Epicurius at Bassae

Hungary
106. Budapest, including the Banks of the Danube, the Buda Castle Quarter and Andrássy Avenue
107. Caves of Aggtelek Karst and Slovak Karst
108. Early Christian Necropolis of Pécs (Sopianae)
5. Fertö/Neusiedlersee Cultural Landscape
109. Hortobágy National Park – the Puszta
110. Millenary Benedictine Abbey of Pannonhalma and its Natural Environment
111. Old Village of Hollókő and its Surroundings
112. Tokaj Wine Region Historic Cultural Landscape

Italy
113. Archaeological Area and the Patriarchal Basilica of Aquileia
114. Archaeological Area of Agrigento
115. Archaeological Areas of Pompei, Herculaneum and Torre Annunziata
116. Assisi, the Basilica of San Francesco and Other Franciscan Sites
117. Botanical Garden (Orto Botanico), Padua
118. Castel del Monte
119. Cathedral, Torre Civica and Piazza Grande, Modena
120. Church and Dominican Convent of Santa Maria delle Grazie with 'The Last Supper' by Leonardo da Vinci
121. Cilento and Vallo di Diano National Park with the Archeological sites of Paestum and Velia, and the Certosa di Padula
122. City of Verona
123 City of Vicenza and the Palladian Villas of the Veneto
124. Costiera Amalfitana
125. Crespi d'Adda
126. Early Christian Monuments of Ravenna
127. Eighteenth-Century Royal Palace at Caserta with the Park, the Aqueduct of Vanvitelli, and the San Leucio Complex
128. Etruscan Necropolises of Cerveteri and Tarquinia
129. Ferrara, City of the Renaissance, and its Po Delta
130. Genoa: Le Strade Nuove and the system of the Palazzi dei Rolli
131. Historic Centre of Florence
132. Historic Centre of Naples
133. Historic Centre of Rome, the Properties of the Holy See in that City Enjoying Extraterritorial Rights and San Paolo Fuori le Mura
134. Historic Centre of San Gimignano
135. Historic Centre of Siena
136. Historic Centre of the City of Pienza
137. Historic Centre of Urbino
138. Isole Eolie (Aeolian Islands)
139. Late Baroque Towns of the Val di Noto (South-Eastern Sicily)
140. Longobards in Italy. Places of the power (568–774 AD)
141. Mantua and Sabbioneta
142. Medici Villas and Gardens in Tuscany
143. Monte San Giorgio
144. Mount Etna
145. Piazza del Duomo, Pisa
146. Portovenere, Cinque Terre, and the Islands (Palmaria, Tino and Tinetto)
10. Prehistoric Pile dwellings around the Alps
147. Residences of the Royal House of Savoy
148. Rhaetian Railway in the Albula/Bernina Landscapes
149. Rock Drawings in Valcamonica
150. Sacri Monti of Piedmont and Lombardy
151. Su Nuraxi di Barumini
152. Syracuse and the Rocky Necropolis of Pantalica
153. The Dolomites
154. The Sassi and the park of the Rupestrian Churches of Matera
155. The Trulli of Alberobello
156. Val d'Orcia
157. Venice and its Lagoon
158. Villa Adriana (Tivoli)
159. Villa d'Este, Tivoli
160. Villa Romana del Casale
161. Vineyard Landscape of Piedmont: Langhe-Roero and Monferrato

Kosovo
162. Medieval Monuments in Kosovo

Luxembourg
163. City of Luxembourg: its Old Quarters and Fortifications

Macedonia (F.Y.R.O.M.)
164. Natural and Cultural Heritage of the Ohrid Region

Malta
165. City of Valletta
166. Hal Saflieni Hypogeum
167. Megalithic Temples of Malta

Moldova
168. Struve Geodetic Arc

Montenegro
169. Durmitor National Park
170. Natural and Culturo-Historical Region of Kotor

Romania
171. Churches of Moldavia
172. Dacian Fortresses of the Orastie Mountains
173. Danube Delta
174. Historic Centre of Sighişoara
175. Monastery of Horezu
176. Villages with Fortified Churches in Transylvania
177. Wooden Churches of Maramureş

San Marino
178. San Marino Historic Centre and Mount Titano

Serbia
179. Gamzigrad-Romuliana, Palace of Galerius
180. Stari Ras and Sopoćani
181. Studenica Monastery

Slovakia
182. Bardejov Town Conservation Reserve
107. Caves of Aggtelek Karst and Slovak Karst
183. Historic Town of Banská Štiavnica and the Technical Monuments in its Vicinity
184. Levoča, Spišský Hrad and the Associated Cultural Monuments
185. Primeval Beech Forests of the Carpathians and the Ancient Beech Forests of Germany
186. Vlkolínec
187. Wooden Churches of the Slovak part of the Carpathian Mountain Area

Slovenia
188. Heritage of Mercury: Almadén and Idrija
10. Prehistoric Pile dwellings around the Alps
189. Škocjan Caves

Switzerland
190. Abbey of St Gall
191. Benedictine Convent of St John at Müstair
192. La Chaux-de-Fonds/Le Locle, Watchmaking Town Planning
193. Lavaux, Vineyard Terraces
143. Monte San Giorgio
194. Old City of Berne
10. Prehistoric Pile dwellings around the Alps
148. Rhaetian Railway in the Albula/Bernina Landscapes
195. Swiss Alps Jungfrau-Aletsch
196. Swiss Tectonic Arena Sardona
197. Three Castles, Defensive Wall and Ramparts of the Market-Town of Bellinzone

Vatican City
133. Historic Centre of Rome, the Properties of the Holy See in that City Enjoying Extraterritorial Rights and San Paolo Fuori le Mura
198. Vatican City

Europe
Landscapes

Europe, the westward extension of the Asian continent and the second smallest of the world's continents, has a remarkable variety of physical features and landscapes. The continent is bounded by mountain ranges of varying character – the highlands of Scandinavia and northwest Britain, the Pyrenees, the Alps, the Carpathian Mountains, the Caucasus and the Ural Mountains. Two of these, the Caucasus and Ural Mountains, define the eastern limits of Europe, with the Black Sea and the Bosporus defining its southeastern boundary with Asia.

Across the centre of the continent stretches the North European Plain, broken by some of Europe's greatest rivers, including the Volga and the Dnieper and containing some of its largest lakes. To the south, the Mediterranean Sea divides Europe from Africa. The Mediterranean region itself has a very distinct climate and landscape.

Facts

- The Danube flows through 7 countries and has 7 different name forms
- Lakes cover almost 10% of the total land area of Finland
- The Strait of Gibraltar, separating the Atlantic Ocean from the Mediterranean Sea and Europe from Africa, is only 13 kilometres wide at its narrowest point
- The highest mountain in the Alps is Mont Blanc, 4 810 metres, on the France/Italy border

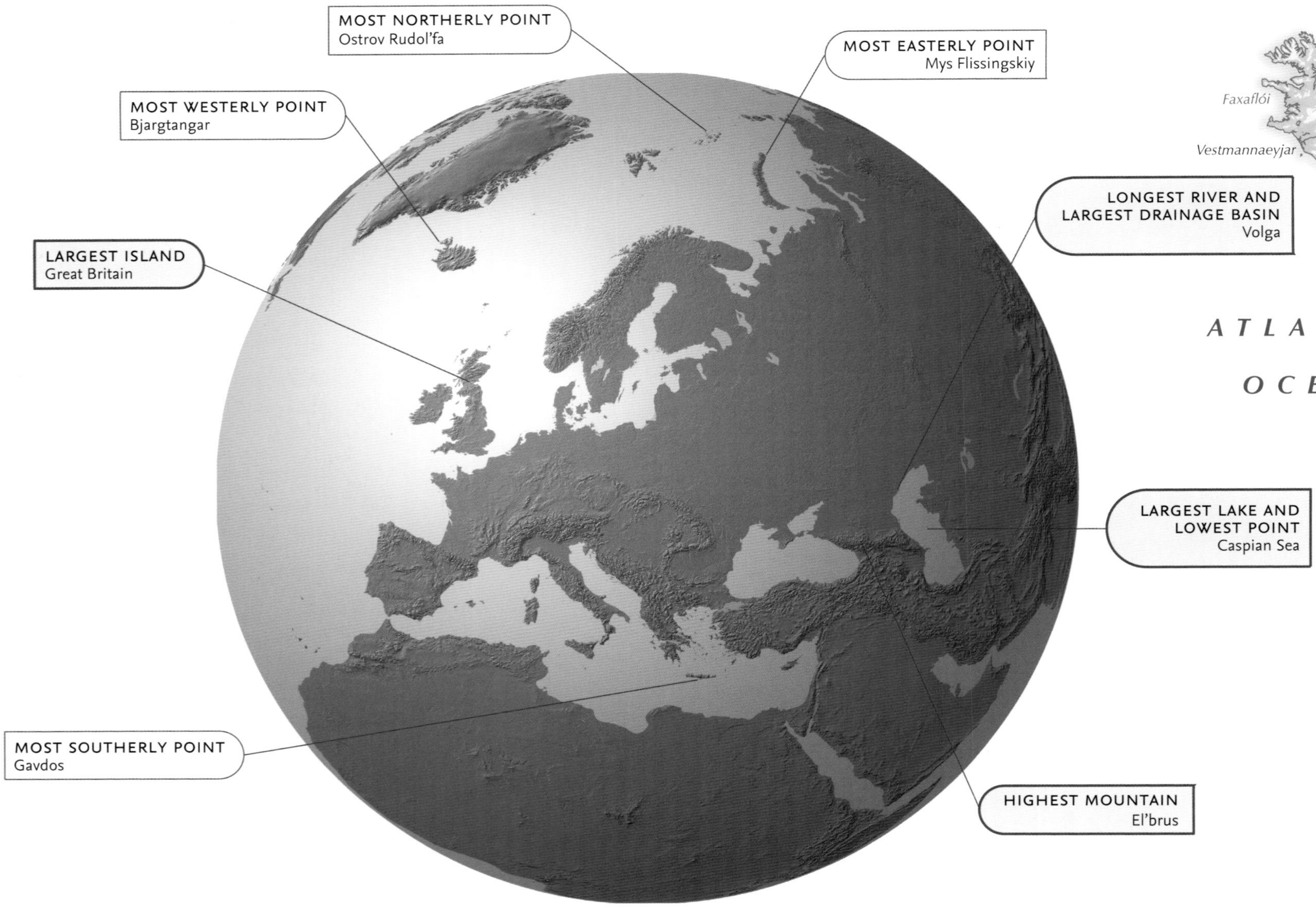

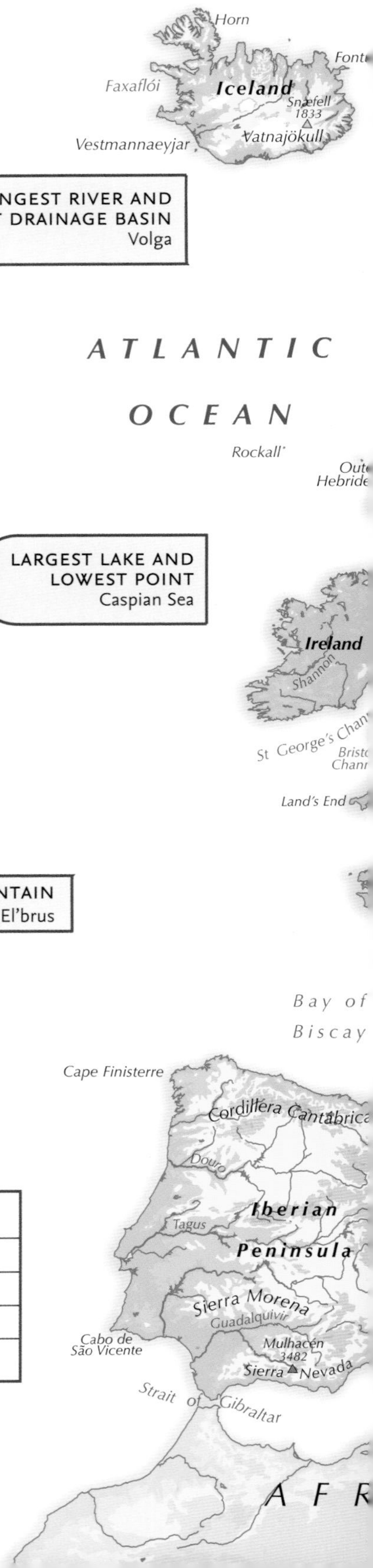

MOST NORTHERLY POINT
Ostrov Rudol'fa

MOST EASTERLY POINT
Mys Flissingskiy

MOST WESTERLY POINT
Bjargtangar

LONGEST RIVER AND LARGEST DRAINAGE BASIN
Volga

LARGEST ISLAND
Great Britain

LARGEST LAKE AND LOWEST POINT
Caspian Sea

MOST SOUTHERLY POINT
Gavdos

HIGHEST MOUNTAIN
El'brus

Horn
Faxaflói
Iceland
Snæfell 1833
Vatnajökull
Vestmannaeyjar
ATLANTIC OCEAN
Rockall
Ireland
Shannon
St George's Chan
Land's End

Europe's greatest physical features

Highest mountain	El'brus, Russia	5 642 metres	18 510 feet
Longest river	Volga, Russia	3 688 km	2 292 miles
Largest lake	Caspian Sea	371 000 sq km	143 243 sq miles
Largest island	Great Britain, United Kingdom	218 476 sq km	84 354 sq miles
Largest drainage basin	Volga, Russia	1 380 000 sq km	532 818 sq miles

Europe's extent

TOTAL LAND AREA	9 908 599 sq km / 3 825 710 sq miles
Most northerly point	Ostrov Rudol'fa, Russia
Most southerly point	Gavdos, Crete, Greece
Most westerly point	Bjargtangar, Iceland
Most easterly point	Mys Flissingskiy, Russia

Iceland in winter, one of Europe's largest islands.

Internet Links

NASA Visible Earth	**visibleearth.nasa.gov**
European Space Agency	**www.esa.int**
European Environment Agency	**www.eea.europa.eu**
Alpine mountaineering	**www.alpine-club.org.uk**

Europe
Countries

The predominantly temperate climate of Europe has led to it becoming the most densely populated of the continents. It is highly industrialized, and has exploited its great wealth of natural resources and agricultural land to become one of the most powerful economic regions in the world.

The current pattern of countries within Europe is a result of numerous and complicated changes throughout its history. Ethnic, religious and linguistic differences have often been the cause of conflict, particularly in the Balkan region which has a very complex ethnic pattern. Current boundaries reflect, to some extent, these divisions which continue to be a source of tension. The historic distinction between 'Eastern' and 'Western' Europe is no longer made, following the collapse of Communism and the break up of the Soviet Union in 1991.

Facts

- **The European Union was founded by six countries: Belgium, France, Germany, Italy, Luxembourg, and the Netherlands. It now has 28 members**
- **The newest member of the European Union, Croatia, joined in 2013**
- **Europe has the two smallest independent countries in the world – Vatican City and Monaco**
- **Vatican City is an independent country entirely within the city of Rome, and is the centre of the Roman Catholic Church**

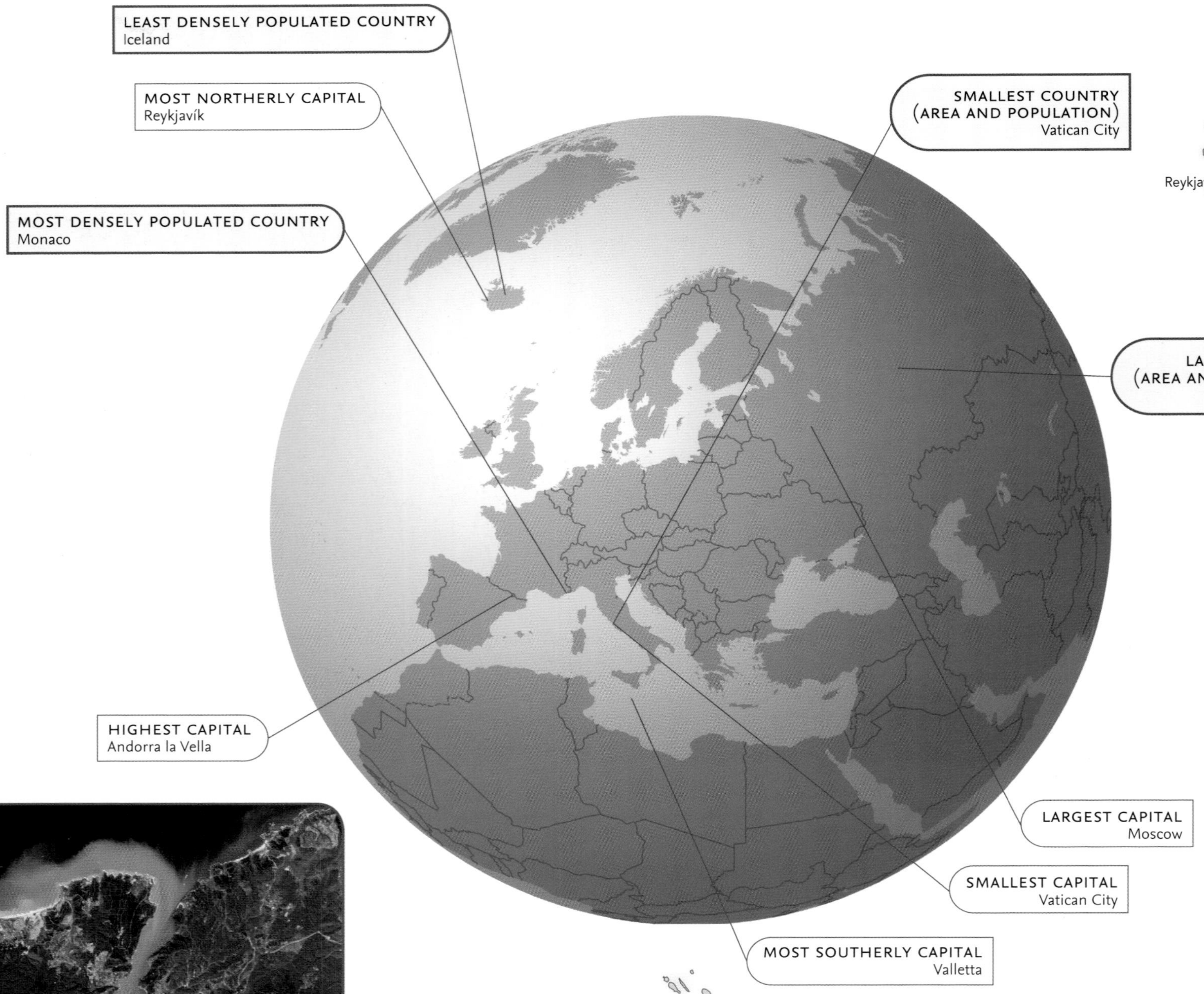

LEAST DENSELY POPULATED COUNTRY
Iceland

MOST NORTHERLY CAPITAL
Reykjavík

MOST DENSELY POPULATED COUNTRY
Monaco

SMALLEST COUNTRY (AREA AND POPULATION)
Vatican City

LARGEST COUNTRY (AREA AND POPULATION)
Russia

HIGHEST CAPITAL
Andorra la Vella

LARGEST CAPITAL
Moscow

SMALLEST CAPITAL
Vatican City

MOST SOUTHERLY CAPITAL
Valletta

Reykjavík ICELAND

ATLANTIC
Rockall (U.K.)
OCEAN

IRELAND
Dubli

Brest

Bay o
Biscay

Azores (Portugal)

Cape Finisterre
A Coruña
Bilbao
Oporto
Douro
Salamanca
Madrid
PORTUGAL
Tagus
SPAIN
Lisbon
Cabo de São Vicente
Seville
Córdoba
Cartage
Cádiz
Málaga
Str. of Gibraltar
Gibraltar
A F

Bosporus, Turkey, a narrow strait of water which separates Europe from Asia.

Europe's capitals

Largest capital (population)	Moscow, Russia	12 144 000
Smallest capital (population)	Vatican City	800
Most northerly capital	Reykjavík, Iceland	64° 39'N
Most southerly capital	Valletta, Malta	35° 54'N
Highest capital	Andorra la Vella, Andorra	1 029 metres 3 376 feet

Europe's countries

Largest country (area)	Russia	17 075 400 sq km	6 592 849 sq miles
Smallest country (area)	Vatican City	0.5 sq km	0.2 sq miles
Largest country (population)	Russia	142 834 000	
Smallest country (population)	Vatican City	800	
Most densely populated country	Monaco	19 000 per sq km	38 000 per sq mile
Least densely populated country	Iceland	3 per sq km	8 per sq mile

Internet Links

European Union	europa.eu/
UK Foreign and Commonwealth Office	www.fco.gov.uk
CIA World Factbook	www.cia.gov/library/publications/the-world-factbook/index.html

A B C D E F G H I J
65° 25° 20° 15° 10° 70° 5° 0° 5° 10° 15° 20°
Denmark Strait
Arctic Circle
ICELAND
REYKJAVÍK
Vatnajökull
Húnaflói
Faxaflói
Vestmannaeyjar
Akureyri
Norwegian Sea
ATLANTIC OCEAN
Faroe Islands (Denmark)
TÓRSHAVN
Rockall (U.K.)
Shetland Islands
Lerwick
Orkney Islands
Fair Isle
Outer Hebrides
British Isles
North Sea
UNITED KINGDOM
IRELAND
DUBLIN
Belfast
Isle of Man (U.K.)
Irish Sea
St George's Channel
Glasgow
Edinburgh
Aberdeen
Newcastle upon Tyne
Manchester
Liverpool
Leeds
Birmingham
LONDON
Cardiff
Bristol
Plymouth
Land's End
Isles of Scilly
English Channel (La Manche)
Channel Islands (U.K.)
ST PETER PORT
ST HELIER
Strait of Dover
NORWAY
SWEDEN
OSLO
STOCKHOLM
Bergen
Stavanger
Trondheim
Gothenburg
Skagerrak
Kattegat
DENMARK
COPENHAGEN
Gotland (Sweden)
Öland
Bornholm (Denmark)
Baltic Sea
NETHERLANDS
AMSTERDAM
THE HAGUE
Rotterdam
BELGIUM
BRUSSELS
LUXEMBOURG
GERMANY
BERLIN
Hamburg
Frankfurt am Main
Munich
POLAND
CZECH REPUBLIC
PRAGUE
AUSTRIA
VIENNA
BRATISLAVA
SWITZERLAND
BERN
LIECHTENSTEIN
FRANCE
PARIS
Bay of Biscay
Gulf of Gascony
Massif Central
SPAIN
ITALY
SLOVENIA
HUNGARY
BUDAPEST
↓ 64
Conic Equidistant Projection
1:8 600 000
0 100 200 300 400 miles
0 100 200 300 400 500 600 km

Barents Sea
White Sea
Kola Peninsula (Kol'skiy Poluostrov)
FINLAND
LAPPLAND
HELSINKI
St Petersburg
Gulf of Finland
Lake Ladoga (Ladozhskoye Ozero)
Onezhskoye Ozero
ESTONIA
TALLINN
Gulf of Riga
LATVIA
RIGA
LITHUANIA
VILNIUS
BELARUS
MINSK
WARSAW
MOSCOW
RUSSIA
Ural Mountains
Central Russian Upland
UKRAINE
KIEV
MOLDOVA
CHIŞINĂU
ROMANIA
Carpathian Mountains
KAZAKHSTAN
Caspian Lowland
Caspian Sea
Sea of Azov
CRIMEA
Odessa (Odesa)
Volgograd
Samara
Kazan
Nizhniy Novgorod
Archangel
Murmansk
Perm
Ufa
Kharkiv
Rostov-na-Donu
Astrakhan'
↓ 65
→ 76

Conic Equidistant Projection

1:6 500 000

0 100 200 300 miles

0 100 200 300 400 500 km

Europe
Western Russia

Conic Equidistant Projection

1:4 300 000 — 0, 50, 100, 150 miles; 0, 50, 100, 150, 200, 250 km

Europe

Scandinavia and the Baltic States

1:4 300 000

0	50	100	150	miles
0	50	100	150	200	250 km

↑ 55

NORWAY
SWEDEN
ESTONIA
LATVIA
LITHUANIA
RUSSIA
DENMARK
POLAND
GERMANY
CZECH REPUBLIC
SLOVAKIA
AUSTRIA
HUNGARY
SWITZERLAND
SLOVENIA
CROATIA
ITALY
LIECHTENSTEIN
BAVARIA
ALSACE
Skagerrak
Kattegat
Baltic Sea
Gulf of Riga
Gulf of Gdańsk
German Bight
Jutland
Zealand
Fyn
Gotland (Sweden)
Öland
Bornholm (Denmark)
Saaremaa
Vänern
Vättern
Harz
Erzgebirge
Schwäbische Alb
Black Forest
Vosges
Jura
Böhmer Wald
ODENWALD
POJEZIERZE POMORSKIE
POJEZIERZE WIELKOPOLSKIE
COPENHAGEN (København)
BERLIN
WARSAW (Warszawa)
PRAGUE (Praha)
VIENNA (Wien)
BRATISLAVA
BUDAPEST
BERN
VADUZ
LUXEMBOURG

↓ 68
→ 53

Conic Equidistant Projection

1:1 700 000

0 25 50 75 miles

0 25 50 75 100 125 km

Europe

England and Wales

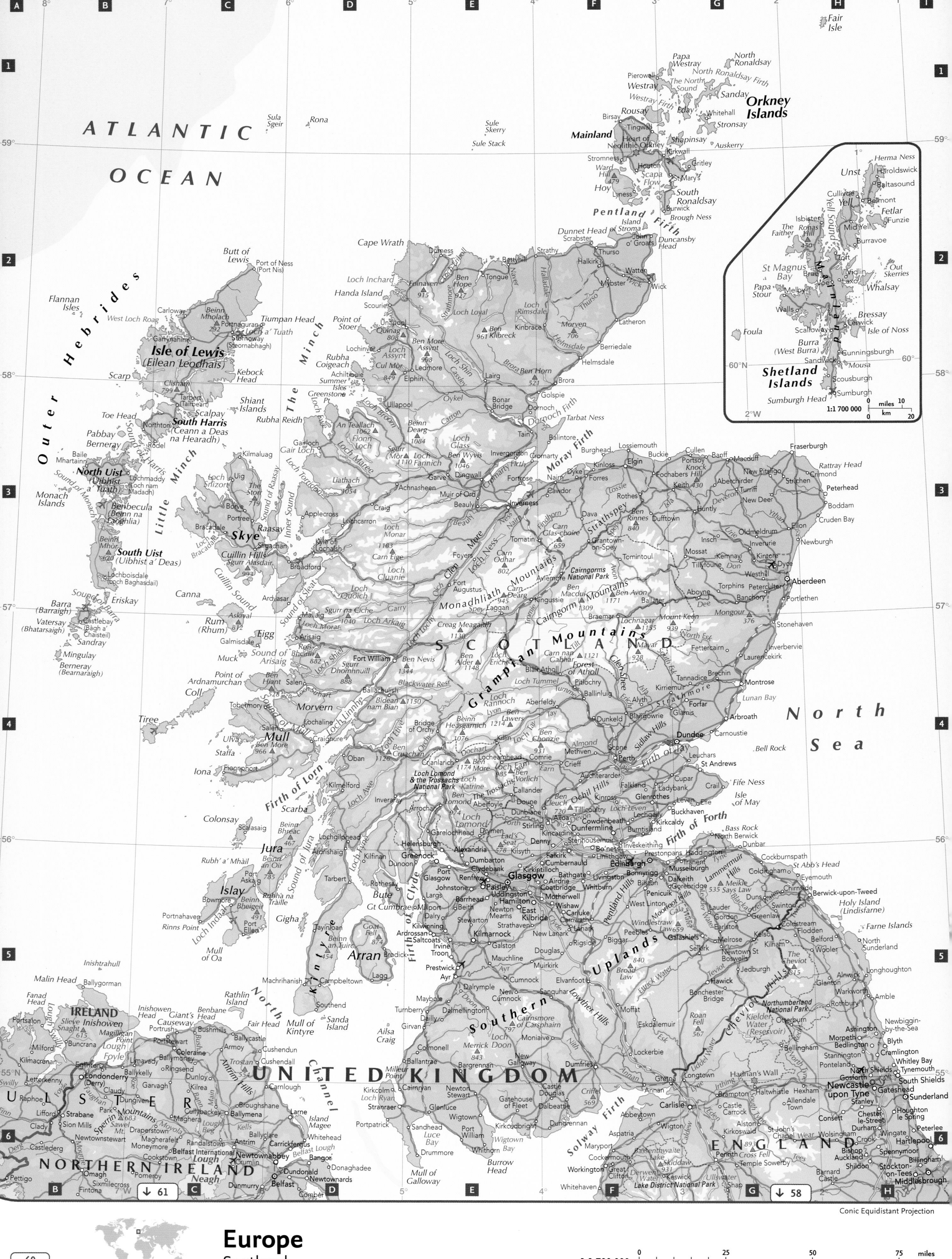

Europe
Scotland

1:1 700 000

0 25 50 75 miles

0 25 50 75 100 125 km

A B C D E F G H

11° 10° 9° 8° 7° 6°

56° 55° 54° 53° 52°N

1 2 3 4 5 6

→ 60

→ 59

A 11°W B 10° C 9° D 8° E 7° F 6° G 5° H

Conic Equidistant Projection

1:1 700 000

0 25 50 75 miles

0 25 50 75 100 125 km

Europe

Ireland

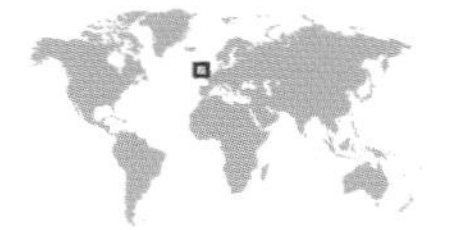

1:1 700 000 — 0, 25, 50, 75 miles; 0, 25, 50, 75, 100, 125 km

Europe

Belgium, Netherlands, Luxembourg and Northwest Germany

Conic Equidistant Projection

1:8 600 000

0 100 200 300 400 miles

0 100 200 300 400 500 600 km

↑ 51
↓ 121
→ 108
RUSSIA
BELARUS
MINSK
POLAND
WARSAW
UKRAINE
KIEV
CH REP.
PRAGUE
SLOVAKIA
VIENNA
BRATISLAVA
HUNGARY
BUDAPEST
MOLDOVA
CHIȘINĂU
ROMANIA
BUCHAREST
SLOVENIA
LJUBLJANA
CROATIA
ZAGREB
BOSNIA AND HERZEGOVINA
SARAJEVO
SERBIA
BELGRADE
MONTENEGRO
PODGORICA
KOSOVO
PRISHTINE
ALBANIA
TIRANA
MACEDONIA
SKOPJE
BULGARIA
SOFIA
GREECE
ATHENS
TURKEY
ANKARA
CYPRUS
NICOSIA
SYRIA
DAMASCUS
LEBANON
BEIRUT
ISRAEL
JERUSALEM
WEST BANK
JORDAN
'AMMAN
EGYPT
CAIRO
SAUDI ARABIA
LIBYA
MALTA
VALLETTA
CRIMEA ADMINISTERED BY RUSSIA
Black Sea
Sea of Azov
Aegean Sea
Ionian Sea
Mediterranean Sea
Red Sea
Gulf of Sirte
Carpathian Mountains
Transylvanian Alps
Balkan Mts.
Rhodope Mts
Dinaric Alps
Taurus Mountains
Anadolu Dağları
Caucasus (Bol'shoy Kavkaz)
Central Russian Upland
Pripet Marshes
Cyclades (Kykládes)
Dodecanese (Dodekanisa)
Ionian Islands
Crete (Kriti)
Rhodes (Rodos)
Sinai (Shibh Jazirat Sinā')
Eastern Desert
Qattara Depression
Libyan Plateau (Aḍ Diffah)
Istanbul
Odessa (Odesa)
Alexandria (Al Iskandarīyah)
Benghazi

Europe

France

Conic Equidistant Projection

1:4 300 000 — 0, 50, 100, 150 miles; 0, 50, 100, 150, 200, 250 km

Europe

Spain and Portugal

↑ 57
↑ 66
↓ 120
SWITZERLAND
AUSTRIA
SLOVENIA
CROATIA
BOSNIA AND HERZEGOVINA
FRANCE
ITALY
TUNISIA
ALGERIA
MALTA
SAN MARINO
MONACO
LIECHTENSTEIN
VATICAN CITY
ROME (Roma)
Milan (Milano)
Turin (Torino)
Genoa (Genova)
Venice (Venezia)
Florence (Firenze)
Naples (Napoli)
Palermo
Bologna
Bari
Messina
Catania
Cagliari
Sassari
Ajaccio
Bastia
TUNIS
VALLETTA
ZAGREB
LJUBLJANA
SARAJEVO
BERN
Trieste
Ancona
Pescara
Taranto
Reggio di Calabria
Syracuse (Siracusa)
Marseille
Lyon
Nice
Corsica (Corse) (France)
Sardinia (Sardegna) (Italy)
Sicily (Sicilia)
Ligurian Sea
Gulf of Genoa
Gulf of Venice
Adriatic Sea
Tyrrhenian Sea
Ionian Sea
Mediterranean
Sicilian Channel
Malta Channel
Strait of Bonifacio
Strait of Messina
Golfo di Taranto
Isole Lipari
Isole Egadi
Isole Pelagie (Italy)
Isola di Pantelleria (Italy)
Alps
Apennines
Dolomites
Dinaric Alps
Jura
Conic Equidistant Projection
1:4 300 000
0 50 100 150 miles
0 50 100 150 200 250 km

53
112
UKRAINE
MOLDOVA
ROMANIA
BULGARIA
SERBIA
KOSOVO
MACEDONIA (F.Y.R.O.M.)
ALBANIA
GREECE
TURKEY
CRIMEA
ADMINISTERED BY RUSSIA
VOJVODINA
DOBRUJA
THRACE
BUDAPEST
BUCHAREST (București)
BELGRADE (Beograd)
SOFIA (Sofiya)
SKOPJE
TIRANA (Tiranë)
ATHENS (Athína)
CHIȘINĂU (Kishinev)
PRISHTINË (Priština)
İstanbul
İzmir (Smyrna)
Odessa (Odesa)
Thessaloniki
Black Sea
Aegean Sea
Ionian Islands
Sea of Marmara (Marmara Denizi)
Kritiko Pelagos
Mirtoo Pelagos
Carpathian Mountains
Transylvanian Alps
Transylvanian Basin
Balkan Mountains (Stara Planina)
Rhodope Mountains
Sredna Gora
Pindus Mountains
Cyclades (Kyklades)
Dodecanese (Dodekanisa)
Peloponnese
Evvoia
Crete (Kriti)
Rhodes (Rodos)
Lesbos (Lesvos)
Chios
Samos
Corfu (Kerkyra)
Cephalonia (Kefallonia)
Zakynthos (Zante)
Danube
Bosporus (İstanbul Boğazı)

Asia
UNESCO World Heritage Sites
This vast continent contains some of the world's most spectacular sites. The Great Wall of China, the terracotta warriors in the Tomb of the First Qin Emperor, the temple of Angkor and the Taj Mahal are all well known, but smaller yet equally important sites are also on the World Heritage List.
Cultural site
Natural site
Mixed site
Afghanistan
1. Cultural Landscape and Archaeological Remains of the Bamiyan Valley
2. Minaret and Archaeological Remains of Jam
Armenia
3. Cathedral and Churches of Echmiatsin and the Archaeological Site of Zvartnots
4. Monasteries of Haghpat and Sanahin
5. Monastery of Geghard and the Upper Azat Valley
Azerbaijan
6. Gobustan Rock Art Cultural Landscape
7. Walled City of Baku with the Shirvanshah's Palace and Maiden Tower
Bahrain
8. Pearling, Testimony of an Island Economy
9. Qal'at al-Bahrain – Ancient Harbour and Capital of Dilmun
Bangladesh
10. Historic Mosque City of Bagerhat
11. Ruins of the Buddhist Vihara at Paharpur
12. The Sundarbans
Cambodia
13. Angkor
14. Temple of Preah Vihear
EUROPE
RUSSIA
KAZAKHSTAN
MONGOLIA
CHINA
UZBEKISTAN
TURKMENISTAN
KYRGYZSTAN
TAJIKISTAN
AFGHANISTAN
PAKISTAN
INDIA
NEPAL
BHUTAN
BANGLADESH
MYANMAR (BURMA)
LAOS
THAILAND
CAMBODIA
VIETNAM
MALAYSIA
BRUNEI
SINGAPORE
INDONE
SRI LANKA
MALDIVES
TURKEY
GEORGIA
ARMENIA
AZERBAIJAN
IRAN
IRAQ
KUWAIT
SAUDI ARABIA
BAHRAIN
QATAR
U.A.E.
OMAN
YEMEN
Socotra (Yemen)
Black Sea
Caspian Sea
INDIAN OCEAN
SOUTH KOREA
TAIWAN
CYPRUS
SYRIA
LEBANON
ISRAEL
JORDAN

China
15. Ancient Building Complex in the Wudang Mountains
16. Ancient City of Ping Yao
17. Ancient Villages in Southern Anhui – Xidi and Hongcun
18. Capital Cities and Tombs of the Ancient Koguryo Kingdom
19. Chengjiang Fossil Site
20. China Danxia
21. Classical Gardens of Suzhou
22. Cultural Landscape of Honghe Hani Rice Terraces
23. Dazu Rock Carvings
24. Fujian Tulou
25. Historic Centre of Macao
26. Historic Ensemble of the Potala Palace, Lhasa
27. Historic Monuments of Dengfeng in "The Centre of Heaven and Earth"
28. Huanglong Scenic and Historic Interest Area
29. Imperial Palaces of the Ming and Qing Dynasties in Beijing and Shenyang
30. Imperial Tombs of the Ming and Qing Dynasties
31. Jiuzhaigou Valley Scenic and Historic Interest Area
32. Kaiping Diaolou and Villages
33. Longmen Grottoes
34. Lushan National Park
35. Mausoleum of the First Qin Emperor
36. Mogao Caves
37. Mount Emei Scenic Area, including Leshan Giant Buddha Scenic Area
38. Mount Huangshan
39. Mount Qingcheng and the Dujiangyan Irrigation System
40. Mount Sanqingshan National Park
41. Mount Taishan
42. Mount Wutai
43. Mount Wuyi
44. Mountain Resort and its Outlying Temples, Chengde
45. Old Town of Lijiang
46. Peking Man Site at Zhoukoudian
47. Sichuan Giant Panda Sanctuaries – Wolong, Mt Siguniang and Jiajin Mountains
48. Silk Roads: the Routes Network of Chang'an – Tianshan Corridor
49. Site of Xanadu
50. South China Karst
51. Summer Palace and Imperial Garden in Beijing
52. Temple and Cemetery of Confucius and the Kong Family Mansion in Qufu
53. Temple of Heaven: an Imperial Sacrificial Altar in Beijing
54. The Grand Canal
55. The Great Wall
56. Three Parallel Rivers of Yunnan Protected Areas
57. West Lake Cultural Landscape of Hangzhou
58. Wulingyuan Scenic and Historic Interest Area
59. Xinjiang Tianshan
60. Yin Xu
61. Yungang Grottoes

Cyprus
62. Choirokoitia
63. Painted Churches in the Troodos Region
64. Paphos

Georgia
65. Bagrati Cathedral and Gelati Monastery
66. Historical Monuments of Mtskheta
67. Upper Svaneti

India
68. Agra Fort
69. Ajanta Caves
70. Buddhist Monuments at Sanchi
71. Champaner-Pavagadh Archaeological Park
72. Chhatrapati Shivaji Terminus (formerly Victoria Terminus)
73. Churches and Convents of Goa
74. Elephanta Caves
75. Ellora Caves
76. Fatehpur Sikri
77. Great Himalayan National Park Conservation Area
78. Great Living Chola Temples
79. Group of Monuments at Hampi
80. Group of Monuments at Mahabalipuram
81. Group of Monuments at Pattadakal
82. Hill Forts of Rajasthan
83. Humayun's Tomb, Delhi
84. Kaziranga National Park
85. Keoladeo National Park
86. Khajuraho Group of Monuments
87. Mahabodhi Temple Complex at Bodh Gaya
88. Manas Wildlife Sanctuary
89. Mountain Railways of India
90. Nanda Devi and Valley of Flowers National Parks
91. Qutb Minar and its Monuments, Delhi
92. Rani-Ki-Vav (the Queen's Stepwell) at Patan, Gujarat
93. Red Fort Complex
94. Rock Shelters of Bhimbetka
95. Sun Temple, Konârak
96. Sundarbans National Park
97. Taj Mahal
98. The Jantar Mantar, Jaipur
99. Western Ghats

Indonesia
100. Borobudur Temple Compounds
101. Cultural Landscape of Bali Province: the *Subak* System as a Manifestation of the *Tri Hita Karana* Philosophy
102. Komodo National Park
103. Lorentz National Park
104. Prambanan Temple Compounds
105. Sangiran Early Man Site
106. Tropical Rainforest Heritage of Sumatra
107. Ujung Kulon National Park

Iran
108. Armenian Monastic Ensembles of Iran
109. Bam and its Cultural Landscape
110. Bisotun
111. Golestan Palace
112. Gonbad-e Qābus
113. Masjed-e Jāmé of Isfahan
114. Meidan Emam, Esfahan
115. Pasargadae
116. Persepolis
117. Shahr-i Sokhta
118. Sheikh Safi al-din Khānegāh and Shrine Ensemble in Ardabil
119. Shushtar Historical Hydraulic System
120. Soltaniyeh
121. Tabriz Historic Bazaar Complex
122. Takht-e Soleyman
123. Tchogha Zanbil
124. The Persian Garden

Iraq
125. Ashur (Qal'at Sherqat)
126. Erbil Citadel
127. Hatra
128. Samarra Archaeological City

Israel
129. Bahá'í Holy Places in Haifa and the Western Galilee
130. Biblical Tels – Megiddo, Hazor, Beer Sheba
131. Caves of Maresha and Bet-Guvrin in the Judean Lowlands as a Microcosm of the Land of the Caves
132. Incense Route – Desert Cities in the Negev
133. Masada
134. Old City of Acre
135. Sites of Human Evolution at Mount Carmel: The Nahal Me'arot/ Wadi el-Mughara Caves
136. The White City of Tel-Aviv – The Modern Movement

Japan
137. Buddhist Monuments in the Horyu-ji Area
138. Fujisan, Sacred Place and Source of Artistic Inspiration
139. Gusuku Sites and Related Properties of the Kingdom of Ryukyu
140. Himeji-jo
141. Hiraizumi – Temples, Gardens and Archaeological Sites Representing the Buddhist Pure Land
142. Hiroshima Peace Memorial (Genbaku Dome)
143. Historic Monuments of Ancient Kyoto (Kyoto, Uji and Otsu Cities)
144. Historic Monuments of Ancient Nara
145. Historic Villages of Shirakawa-go and Gokayama
146. Itsukushima Shinto Shrine
147. Iwami Ginzan Silver Mine and its Cultural Landscape
148. Ogasawara Islands
149. Sacred Sites and Pilgrimage Routes in the Kii Mountain Range
150. Shirakami-Sanchi
151. Shiretoko
152. Shrines and Temples of Nikko
153. Tomioka Silk Mill and Related Sites
154. Yakushima

Jerusalem (Site proposed by Jordan)
155. Old City of Jerusalem and its Walls

Jordan
156. Petra
157. Quseir Amra
158. Um er-Rasas (Kastrom Mefa'a)
159. Wadi Rum Protected Area

Kazakhstan
160. Mausoleum of Khoja Ahmed Yasawi
161. Petroglyphs within the Archaeological Landscape of Tamgaly
162. Saryarka – Steppe and Lakes of Northern Kazakhstan
48. Silk Roads: the Routes Network of Chang'an – Tianshan Corridor

Kyrgyzstan
48. Silk Roads: the Routes Network of Chang'an – Tianshan Corridor
163. Sulaiman-Too Sacred Mountain

Laos
164. Town of Luang Prabang
165. Vat Phou and Associated Ancient Settlements within the Champasak Cultural Landscape

Lebanon
166. Anjar
167. Baalbek
168. Byblos
169. Ouadi Qadisha (the Holy Valley) and the Forest of the Cedars of God (Horsh Arz el-Rab)
170. Tyre

Malaysia
171. Archaeological Heritage of the Lenggong Valley
172. Gunung Mulu National Park
173. Kinabalu Park
174. Melaka and George Town, Historic Cities of the Straits of Malacca

Mongolia
175. Orkhon Valley Cultural Landscape
176. Petroglyphic Complexes of the Mongolian Altai
209. Uvs Nuur Basin

Myanmar
177. Pyu Ancient Cities

Nepal
178. Chitwan National Park
179. Kathmandu Valley
180. Lumbini, the Birthplace of the Lord Buddha
181. Sagarmatha National Park

North Korea
182. Complex of Koguryo Tombs
183. Historic Monuments and sites in Kaesŏng

Oman
184. Aflaj Irrigation Systems of Oman
185. Archaeological sites of Bat, Al-Khutm and Al-Ayn
186. Bahla Fort
187. Land of Frankincense

Pakistan
188. Archaeological Ruins at Moenjodaro
189. Buddhist Ruins of Takht-i-Bahi and Neighbouring City Remains at Sahr-i-Bahlol
190. Fort and Shalamar Gardens in Lahore
191. Historical Monuments at Makli, Thatta
192. Rohtas Fort
193. Taxila

Palau
194. Rock Islands Southern Lagoon

Philippines
195. Baroque Churches of the Philippines
196. Historic Town of Vigan
197. Mount Hamiguitan Range Wildlife Sanctuary
198. Puerto-Princesa Subterranean River National Park
199. Rice Terraces of the Philippine Cordilleras
200. Tubbataha Reefs Natural Park

Qatar
201. Al Zubarah Archaeological Site

Russia (see also pp42–43)
202. Central Sikhote-Alin
203. Citadel, Ancient City and Fortress Buildings of Derbent
204. Golden Mountains of Altai
205. Lake Baikal
206. Lena Pillars Nature Park
207. Natural System of Wrangel Island Reserve
208. Putorana Plateau
209. Uvs Nuur Basin
210. Volcanoes of Kamchatka
211. Western Caucasus

Saudi Arabia
112. Al-Hijr Archaeological Site (Madâin Sâlih)
113. At-Turaif District in ad-Dir'iyah
214. Historic Jeddah, the Gate to Makkah

South Korea
215. Changdeokgung Palace Complex
216. Gochang, Hwasun and Ganghwa Dolmen Sites
217. Gyeongju Historic Areas
218. Haeinsa Temple Janggyeong Panjeon, the Depositories for the Tripitaka Koreana Woodblocks
219. Historic Villages of Korea: Hahoe and Yangdong
220. Hwaseong Fortress
221. Jeju Volcanic Island and Lava Tubes
222. Jongmyo Shrine
223. Namhansanseong
224. Royal Tombs of the Joseon Dynasty
225. Seokguram Grotto and Bulguksa Temple

Sri Lanka
226. Ancient City of Polonnaruwa
227. Ancient City of Sigiriya
228. Central Highlands of Sri Lanka
229. Golden Temple of Dambulla
230. Old Town of Galle and its Fortifications
231. Sacred City of Anuradhapura
232. Sacred City of Kandy
233. Sinharaja Forest Reserve

Syria
234. Ancient City of Aleppo
235. Ancient City of Bosra
236. Ancient City of Damascus
237. Ancient Villages of Northern Syria
238. Crac des Chevaliers and Qal'at Salah El-Din
239. Site of Palmyra

Tajikistan
240. Proto-urban Site of Sarazm
241. Tajik National Park (Mountains of the Pamirs)

Thailand
242. Ban Chiang Archaeological Site
243. Dong Phayayen-Khao Yai Forest Complex
244. Historic City of Ayutthaya
245. Historic Town of Sukhothai and Associated Historic Towns
246. Thungyai-Huai Kha Khaeng Wildlife Sanctuaries

Turkey
247. Archaeological Site of Troy
248. Bursa and Cumalıkızık: the Birth of the Ottoman Empire
249. City of Safranbolu
250. Göreme National Park and the Rock Sites of Cappadocia
251. Great Mosque and Hospital of Divriği
252. Hattusha: the Hittite Capital
253. Hierapolis-Pamukkale
254. Historic Areas of Istanbul
255. Nemrut Dağ
256. Neolithic Site of Çatalhöyük
257. Pergamon and its Multi-Layered Cultural Landscape
258. Selimiye Mosque and its Social Complex
259. Xanthos-Letoon

Turkmenistan
260. Kunya-Urgench
261. Parthian Fortresses of Nisa
262. State Historical and Cultural Park 'Ancient Merv'

United Arab Emirates
263. Cultural Sites of Al Ain (Hafit, Hili, Bidaa Bint Saud and Oases Areas)

Uzbekistan
264. Historic Centre of Bukhara
265. Historic Centre of Shakhrisyabz
266. Itchan Kala
267. Samarkand – Crossroad of Cultures

Vietnam
268. Central Sector of the Imperial Citadel of Thang Long – Hanoi
269. Citadel of the Ho Dynasty
270. Complex of Hué Monuments
271. Ha Long Bay
272. Hoi An Ancient Town
273. My Son Sanctuary
274. Phong Nha-Ke Bang National Park
275. Trang An Landscape Complex

West Bank
276. Birthplace of Jesus: Church of the Nativity and the Pilgrimage Route, Bethlehem
277. Palestine: Land of Olives and Vines – Cultural Landscape of Southern Jerusalem, Battir

Yemen
278. Historic Town of Zabid
279. Old City of Sana'a
280. Old Walled City of Shibam
281. Socotra Archipelago

Asia

Landscapes

Asia is the world's largest continent and occupies almost one-third of the world's total land area. Stretching across approximately 165° of longitude from the Mediterranean Sea to the easternmost point of Russia on the Bering Strait, it contains the world's highest and lowest points and some of the world's greatest physical features. Its mountain ranges include the Himalaya, Hindu Kush, Karakoram and the Ural Mountains and its major rivers – including the Yangtze, Tigris-Euphrates, Indus, Ganges and Mekong – are equally well-known and evocative.

Asia's deserts include the Gobi, the Taklimakan, and those on the Arabian Peninsula, and significant areas of volcanic and tectonic activity are present on the Kamchatka Peninsula, in Japan, and on Indonesia's numerous islands. The continent's landscapes are greatly influenced by climatic variations, with great contrasts between the islands of the Arctic Ocean and the vast Siberian plains in the north, and the tropical islands of Indonesia.

The **Yangtze,** China, Asia's longest river, flowing into the East China Sea near Shanghai.

Internet Links

NASA Visible Earth	**visibleearth.nasa.gov**
NASA Earth Observatory	**earthobservatory.nasa.gov**
Peakware World Mountain Encyclopedia	**www.peakware.com**
Mountaineering	**www.alpine-club.org.uk**

Asia's physical features

Highest mountain	Mt Everest, China/Nepal	8 848 metres	29 028 feet
Longest river	Yangtze, China	6 380 km	3 965 miles
Largest lake	Caspian Sea	371 000 sq km	143 243 sq miles
Largest island	Borneo	745 561 sq km	287 861 sq miles
Largest drainage basin	Ob'-Irtysh, Kazakhstan/Russia	2 990 000 sq km	1 154 439 sq miles
Lowest point	Dead Sea, Israel/Jordan	-428 metres	-1 404 feet

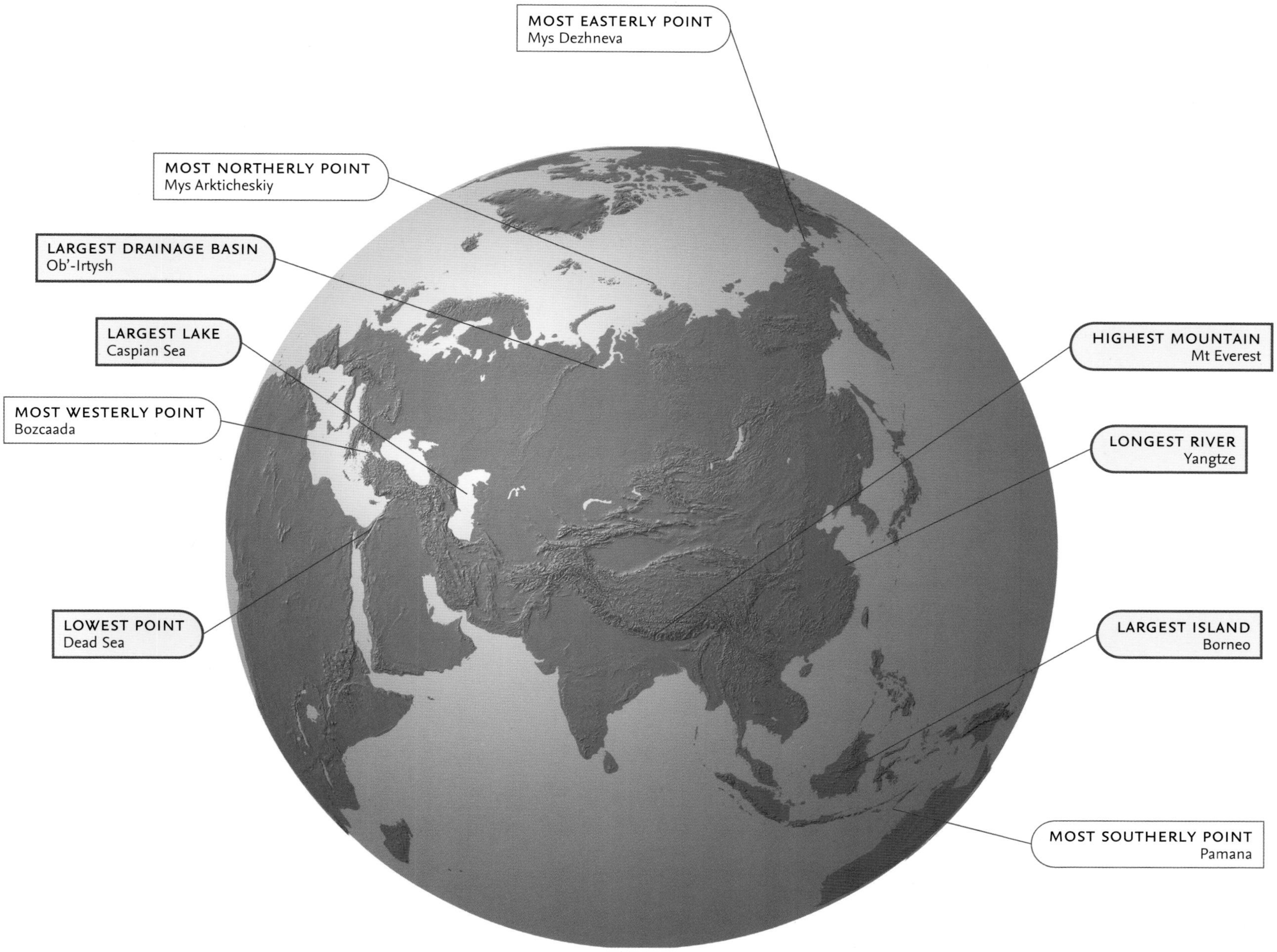

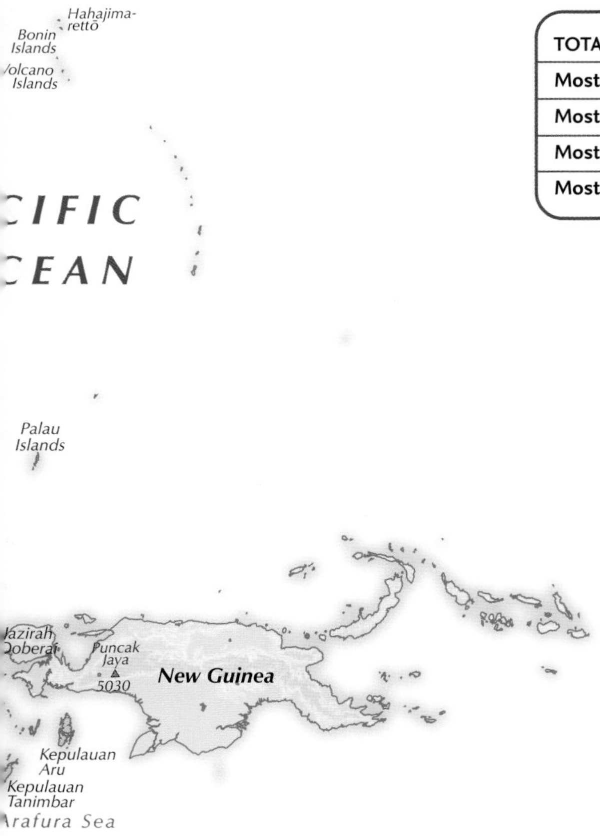

MOST EASTERLY POINT
Mys Dezhneva

MOST NORTHERLY POINT
Mys Arkticheskiy

LARGEST DRAINAGE BASIN
Ob'-Irtysh

LARGEST LAKE
Caspian Sea

MOST WESTERLY POINT
Bozcaada

LOWEST POINT
Dead Sea

HIGHEST MOUNTAIN
Mt Everest

LONGEST RIVER
Yangtze

LARGEST ISLAND
Borneo

MOST SOUTHERLY POINT
Pamana

Hahajima-rettō
Bonin Islands
Volcano Islands
PACIFIC OCEAN
Palau Islands

Asia's extent

TOTAL LAND AREA	45 036 492 sq km / 17 388 686 sq miles
Most northerly point	Mys Arkticheskiy, Russia
Most southerly point	Pamana, Indonesia
Most westerly point	Bozcaada, Turkey
Most easterly point	Mys Dezhneva, Russia

Facts

- **90 of the world's 100 highest mountains are in Asia**
- **The Indonesian archipelago is made up of over 13 500 islands**
- **The height of the land in Nepal ranges from 60 metres to 8 848 metres**
- **The deepest lake in the world is Lake Baikal, Russia, with a maximum depth of 1 642 metres**

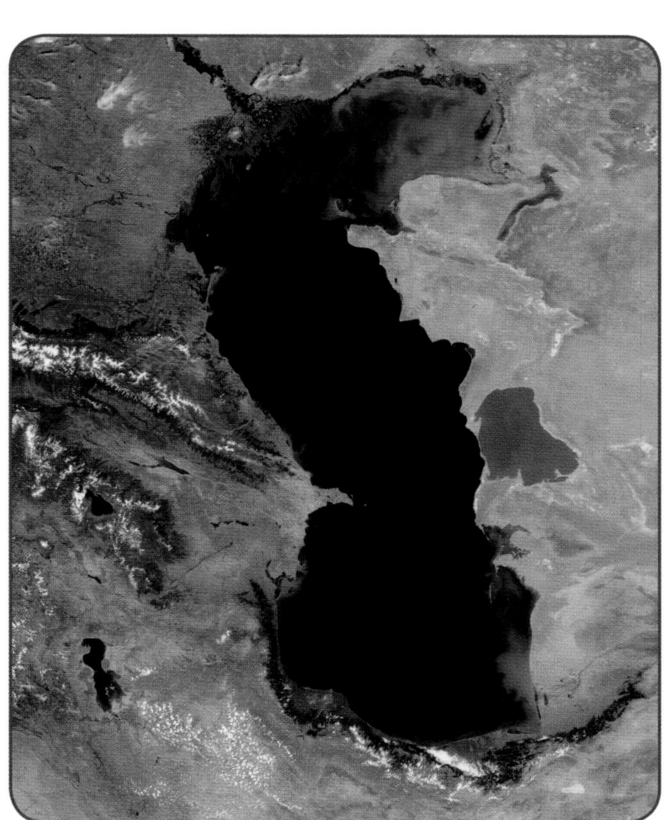

Caspian Sea, Europe/Asia, the world's largest expanse of inland water.

Asia
Countries

With approximately sixty per cent of the world's population, Asia is home to numerous cultures, people groups and lifestyles. Several of the world's earliest civilizations were established in Asia, including those of Sumeria, Babylonia and Assyria. Cultural and historical differences have led to a complex political pattern, and the continent has been, and continues to be, subject to numerous territorial and political conflicts – including the current disputes in the Middle East and in Jammu and Kashmir.

Separate regions within Asia can be defined by the cultural, economic and political systems they support. The major regions are: the arid, oil-rich, mainly Islamic southwest; southern Asia with its distinct cultures, isolated from the rest of Asia by major mountain ranges; the Indian- and Chinese-influenced monsoon region of southeast Asia; the mainly Chinese-influenced industrialized areas of eastern Asia; and Soviet Asia, made up of most of the former Soviet Union.

Timor island in southeast Asia, on which East Timor, Asia's newest independent state, is located.

ARCTIC OCEAN
Barents Sea
Laptev Sea
Bering Sea
Sea of Okhotsk
EUROPE
RUSSIA
Ural Mountains
Mediterranean Sea
Black Sea
Caspian Sea
Aral Sea
Lake Balkhash
Lake Baikal
TURKEY
CYPRUS
LEBANON
SYRIA
ISRAEL
JORDAN
GEORGIA
ARMENIA
AZERBAIJAN
IRAQ
IRAN
KUWAIT
SAUDI ARABIA
BAHRAIN
QATAR
U.A.E.
OMAN
YEMEN
KAZAKHSTAN
UZBEKISTAN
TURKMENISTAN
KYRGYZSTAN
TAJIKISTAN
AFGHANISTAN
PAKISTAN
INDIA
NEPAL
BHUTAN
BANGLADESH
MONGOLIA
Gobi Desert
CHINA
Plateau of Tibet
Tien Shan
Himalaya
Mount Everest 8848
NORTH KOREA
SOUTH KOREA
JAPAN
Sea of Japan
Yellow Sea
East China Sea
TAIWAN
PACIFIC OCEAN
MYANMAR (BURMA)
LAOS
VIETNAM
THAILAND
CAMBODIA
PHILIPPINES
South China Sea
Gulf of Thailand
Andaman Sea
Bay of Bengal
Arabian Sea
Gulf of Aden
Red Sea
The Gulf
Gulf of Oman
AFRICA
SRI LANKA
MALDIVES
MALAYSIA
BRUNEI
SINGAPORE
INDONESIA
EAST TIMOR (TIMOR-LESTE)
Borneo
Sumatra
Java
Celebes Sea
Laut Banda
Laut Jawa
Strait of Malacca
Luzon Strait
INDIAN OCEAN
Socotra (Yemen)
Laccadive Islands (India)
Andaman Islands (India)
Nicobar Islands (India)
British Indian Ocean Territory
Christmas Island (Australia)
Moscow
St Petersburg
Nizhniy Novgorod
Kazan'
Perm'
Yekaterinburg
Chelyabinsk
Samara
Ufa
Saratov
Volgograd
Orenburg
Ural'sk
Aktobe
Atyrau
Astrakhan'
Krasnodar
Tobol'sk
Omsk
Surgut
Urengoy
Noril'sk
Tomsk
Novosibirsk
Barnaul
Novokuznetsk
Krasnoyarsk
Bratsk
Irkutsk
Ust'-Kut
Ulan-Ude
Chita
Kyzyl
Tiksi
Yakutsk
Aldan
Bodaybo
Tynda
Magadan
Ugol'nyye Kopi
Petropavlovsk-Kamchatskiy
Komsomol'sk-na-Amure
Yuzhno-Sakhalinsk
Khabarovsk
Blagoveshchensk
Vladivostok
Astana
Karaganda
Semey
Ust'-Kamenogorsk
Aral'sk
Aktau
Almaty
Shymkent
Bishkek
Tashkent
Samarqand
Dushanbe
Türkmenbaşy
Aşgabat
Mashhad
Herāt
Kābul
Kandahār
Peshawar
Islamabad
Lahore
Faisalabad
Quetta
Karachi
Hyderabad
Jodhpur
Chandigarh
Delhi
New Delhi
Jaipur
Agra
Lucknow
Kota
Ahmadabad
Bhopal
Varanasi
Patna
Kathmandu
Thimphu
Darjiling
Guwahati
Dhaka
Kolkata
Chittagong
Jabalpur
Nagpur
Jamshedpur
Surat
Mumbai
Pune
Hyderabad
Cuttack
Vishakhapatnam
Dharwad
Kurnool
Bangalore
Chennai
Mangalore
Kozhikode
Madurai
Tiruchchirappalli
Jaffna
Trincomalee
Thiruvananthapuram
Colombo
Sri Jayewardenepura Kotte
Male
Bursa
İzmir
Ankara
Samsun
Sivas
Konya
Antalya
Adana
Gaziantep
Aleppo
Nicosia
Beirut
Damascus
Jerusalem
'Ammān
Tbilisi
Yerevan
Baku
Tabrīz
Mosul
Kirkūk
Kermānshāh
Baghdād
An Najaf
Basra
Ahvāz
Ābādān
Eşfahān
Tehrān
Gorgān
Shīrāz
Bīrjand
Būshehr
Zāhedān
Bandar-e 'Abbās
Dammam
Manama
Doha
Riyadh
Dubai
Abu Dhabi
Muscat
Şūr
Medina
Jeddah
Mecca
San'ā'
Hodeidah
Ta'izz
Aden
Mukalla
Şalālah
Pasni
Ürümqi
Yining
Kashi
Korla
Hotan
Golmud
Xining
Lanzhou
Yumen
Wuhai
Yinchuan
Baotou
Taiyuan
Dalandzadgad
Ulaangom
Darhan
Ulan Bator
Jargalant
Hulun Buir
Qiqihar
Harbin
Changchun
Jilin
Shenyang
Jining
Beijing
Dalian
Yantai
Jinan
Zibo
Qingdao
Zhengzhou
Xi'an
Huainan
Nanjing
Shanghai
Wuhu
Wuhan
Ningbo
Nanchong
Chengdu
Yibin
Chongqing
Changde
Hengyang
Changsha
Nanchang
Wenzhou
Fuzhou
Xiamen
Taibei
Kaohsiung
Lhasa
Panzhihua
Kunming
Guiyang
Liuzhou
Guangzhou
Shantou
Hong Kong
Macao
Nanning
Haikou
Chongjin
P'yŏngyang
Seoul
Pusan
Akita
Sendai
Hakodate
Sapporo
Kanazawa
Tōkyō
Yokohama
Kyōto
Kōbe
Ōsaka
Hiroshima
Nagasaki
Kagoshima
Myitkyina
Mandalay
Nay Pyi Taw
Sittwe
Pyè
Rangoon
Mawlamyaing
Hà Nôi
Hai Phong
Louangphabang
Vientiane
Đa Nẵng
Bangkok
Myeik
Phnom Penh
Sihanoukville
Nha Trang
Ho Chi Minh City
Nakhon Si Thammarat
George Town
Ipoh
Kota Bharu
Kuala Lumpur
Putrajaya
Singapore
Banda Aceh
Medan
Padang
Bengkulu
Palembang
Jakarta
Surabaya
Bandar Seri Begawan
Kota Kinabalu
Sandakan
Kuching
Sibu
Ketapang
Balikpapan
Palu
Parepare
Manado
Raba
Kupang
Dili
Aparri
Quezon City
Manila
Surigao
Dapitan
Davao
Zamboanga

Internet Links

UK Foreign and Commonwealth Office	www.fco.gov.uk
CIA World Factbook	www.cia.gov/library/publicaions/the-world-factbook/index.html
Asian Development Bank	www.adb.org
Association of Southeast Asian Nations (ASEAN)	www.asean.org
Asia-Pacific Economic Cooperation	www.apec.org

Asia's countries

Largest country (area)	Russia	17 075 400 sq km	6 592 849 sq miles
Smallest country (area)	Maldives	298 sq km	115 sq miles
Largest country (population)	China	1 369 993 000	
Smallest country (population)	Palau	21 000	
Most densely populated country	Singapore	8 469 per sq km	21 911 per sq mile
Least densely populated country	Mongolia	2 per sq km	5 per sq mile

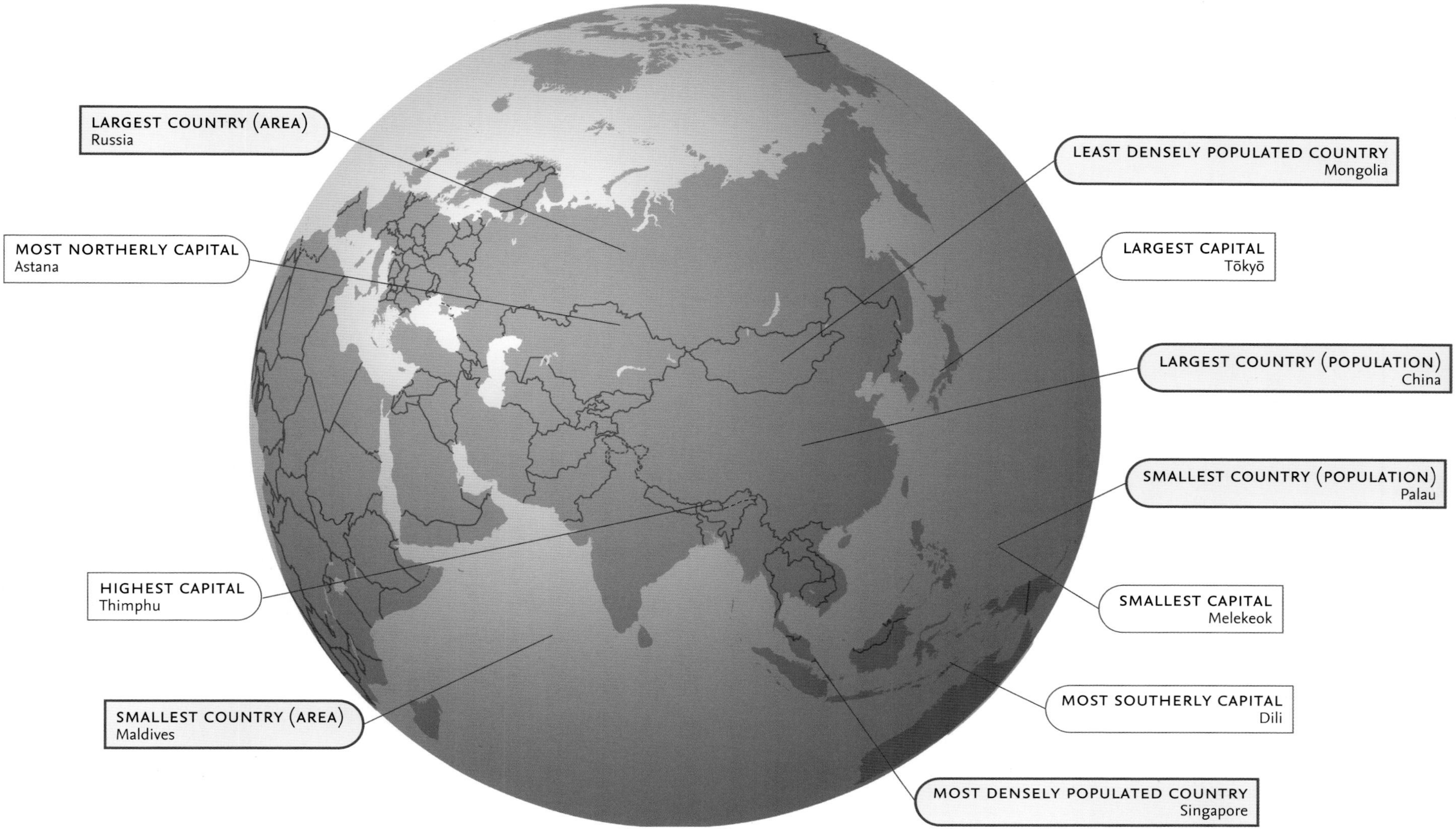

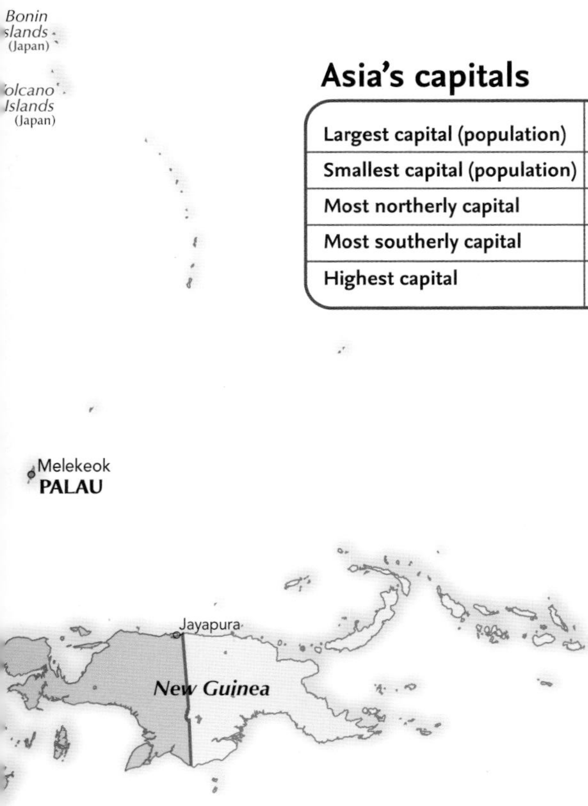

LARGEST COUNTRY (AREA)
Russia

MOST NORTHERLY CAPITAL
Astana

HIGHEST CAPITAL
Thimphu

SMALLEST COUNTRY (AREA)
Maldives

LEAST DENSELY POPULATED COUNTRY
Mongolia

LARGEST CAPITAL
Tōkyō

LARGEST COUNTRY (POPULATION)
China

SMALLEST COUNTRY (POPULATION)
Palau

SMALLEST CAPITAL
Melekeok

MOST SOUTHERLY CAPITAL
Dili

MOST DENSELY POPULATED COUNTRY
Singapore

Asia's capitals

Largest capital (population)	Tōkyō, Japan	38 197 000	
Smallest capital (population)	Melekeok, Palau	391	
Most northerly capital	Astana, Kazakhstan	51° 10'N	
Most southerly capital	Dili, East Timor	8° 35'S	
Highest capital	Thimphu, Bhutan	2 423 metres	7 949 feet

Facts

- **Over 60% of the world's population live in Asia**
- **Asia has 11 of the world's 20 largest cities**
- **The Korean peninsula was divided into North Korea and South Korea in 1948 approximately along the 38th parallel**

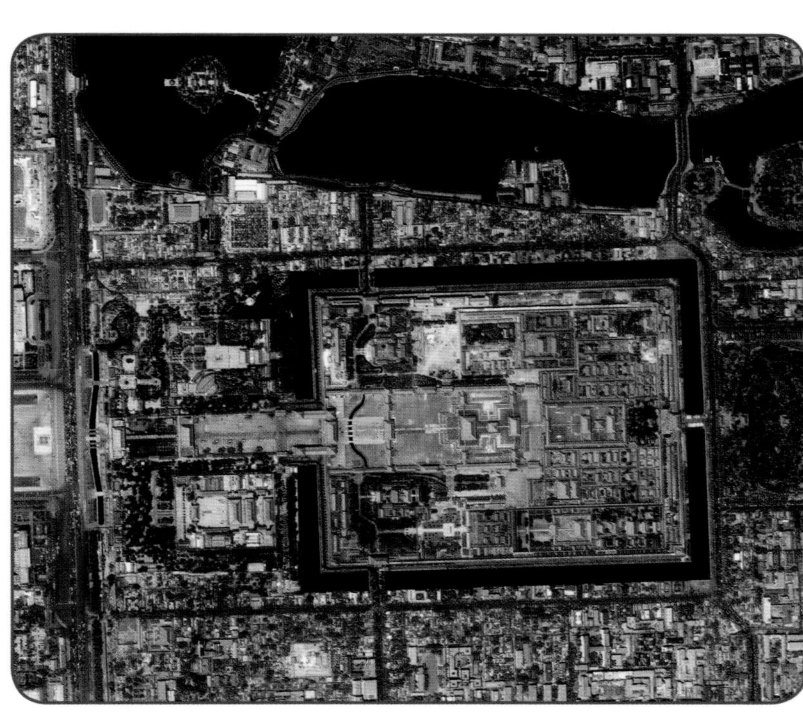

Beijing, capital of China, the most populous country in the world.

Conic Equidistant Projection

1:17 300 000 000

0	200	400	600	miles
0	200	400	600	800	1000 km

OCEAN
East Siberian Sea
(Vostochno-Sibirskoye More)
New Siberia Islands
(Novosibirskiye Ostrova)
Laptev Sea
(More Laptevykh)
Severnaya Zemlya
Chukchi Sea
Wrangel Island
(Ostrov Vrangelya)
Bering Sea
Sea of Okhotsk
(Okhotskoye More)
Kamchatka Peninsula
(Poluostrov Kamchatka)
Petropavlovsk-Kamchatskiy
Kolymskoye Nagor'ye
Koryakskoye Nagor'ye
Khrebet Cherskogo
Verkhoyanskiy Khrebet
SIBERIA
(SIBIR')
Central Siberian Plateau
(Sredne-Sibirskoye Ploskogor'ye)
Stanovoy Khrebet
Stanovoye Nagor'ye
Sakhalin
Kuril Islands
(Kuril'skiye Ostrova)
ADMINISTERED BY RUSSIA, CLAIMED BY JAPAN
Hokkaidō
PACIFIC OCEAN
Sea of Japan
(East Sea)
JAPAN
TŌKYŌ
Yokohama
Sendai
Osaka
Kyoto
Nagoya
Kobe
Hiroshima
Fukuoka
NORTH KOREA
P'YONGYANG
SOUTH KOREA
SEOUL
(Soul)
Busan
(Pusan)
Yellow Sea
(Huang Hai)
Bo Hai
BEIJING
(Peking)
Tianjin
Shenyang
Harbin
Changchun
Dalian
MANCHURIA
INNER MONGOLIA
MONGOLIA
ULAN BATOR
(Ulaanbaatar)
Gobi Desert
CHINA
Da Hinggan Ling
Xiao Hinggan Ling
Sikhote-Alin'
Khabarovsk
Vladivostok
Irkutsk
Ulan-Ude
Chita
Lake Baikal
(Ozero Baykal)
Yakutsk
Magadan
Okhotsk
Bratsk
Vostochnyy Sayan
Aleutian Islands
U.S.A.
Seward Peninsula
Arctic Circle
Bering Strait
St Lawrence Island
La Pérouse Strait
↑ 146
↓ 78

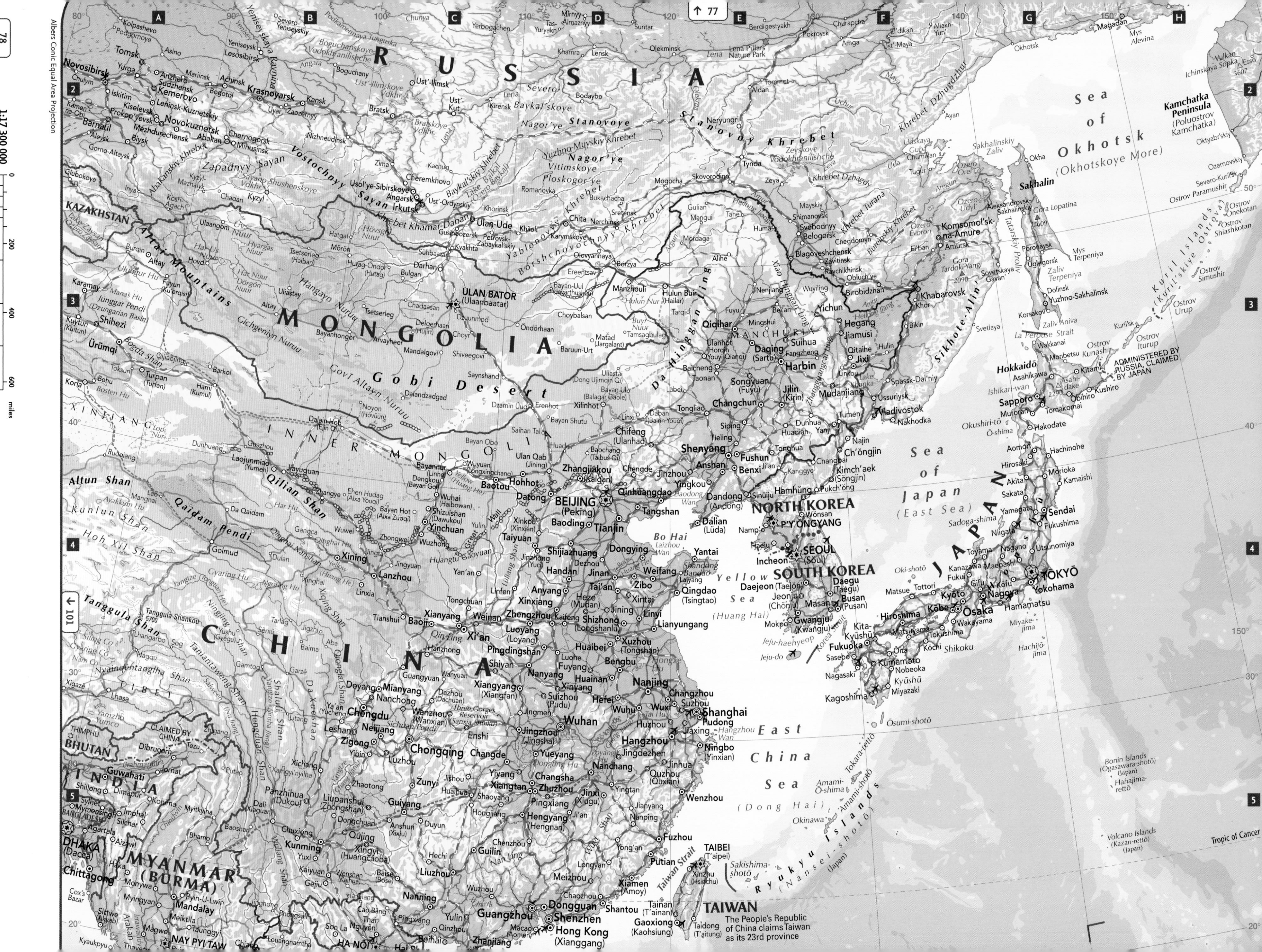

↑ 77
← 101

Albers Conic Equal Area Projection

1:17 300 000

0 200 400 600 miles

0 200 400 600 800 1000 km

PACIFIC OCEAN
PHILIPPINES
FEDERATED STATES OF MICRONESIA
PALAU
Northern Mariana Islands (U.S.A.)
Guam (U.S.A.)
PAPUA NEW GUINEA
New Guinea
VIETNAM
CAMBODIA
THAILAND
LAOS
MALAYSIA
BRUNEI
SINGAPORE
INDONESIA
EAST TIMOR (TIMOR-LESTE)
AUSTRALIA
NORTHERN TERRITORY
QUEENSLAND
WESTERN AUSTRALIA
INDIAN OCEAN
South China Sea
Celebes Sea
Sulu Sea
Arafura Sea
Timor Sea
Philippine Sea
Andaman Sea
Gulf of Thailand
Gulf of Carpentaria
Strait of Malacca
Borneo
Sumatra (Sumatera)
Java (Jawa)
Celebes (Sulawesi)
Moluccas (Maluku)
Mindanao
Luzon
Hainan Dao
MANILA
KUALA LUMPUR
JAKARTA
BANGKOK (Krung Thep)
PHNOM PENH
VIENTIANE (Viangchan)
BANDAR SERI BEGAWAN
DILI
Ho Chi Minh City (Saigon)
Rangoon (Yangon)
Great Sandy Desert
Tanami Desert
Equator
Tropic of Capricorn
Christmas Island (Australia)
Cocos (Keeling) Islands (Australia)
Ashmore and Cartier Islands (Australia)
Claimed by China, Taiwan and Vietnam
Claimed by Brunei, China, Malaysia, Philippines, Taiwan and Vietnam
↑ 132
↓ 132

1:13 000 000

0 200 400 miles

0 200 400 600 800 km

G H I J K L
125° 130° 135° 140° 145°
1 2 3 4 5 6 7 8 9

TAIBEI (T'aipei)
Jilong (Keelung)
Xinzhu
Yilan
Fengyuan
Hualian (Hualien)
Yu Shan 3950
TAIWAN
Tainan
Taidong (T'aitung)
The People's Republic of China claims Taiwan as its 23rd province
Gaoxiong (Kaohsiung)
Lan Yu
Bashi Channel
Sakishima-shotō
Ishigaki
Yaeyama-rettō
Ryukyu Islands (Nansei-shotō) (Japan)
Okino-Daitō-jima
Kita-Iō-jima
Volcano Islands (Kazan-rettō) (Japan)
Minami-Iō-jima
Tropic of Cancer
25°
Itbayat
Batan Islands
Batan
Luzon Strait
Babuyan
Calayan
Fuga
Babuyan Islands
Babuyan Channel
Okino-Tori-shima (Japan)
Farallon de Pajaros (Uracas)
Maug Islands
Asuncion
20°
Agrihan
Pagan
Alamagan
Guguan
Sarigan
Anatahan
Farallon de Medinilla
Northern Mariana Islands (U.S.A.)
CAPITOL HILL
Saipan
Tinian
Aguijan
Rota
HAGÅTÑA
Guam (U.S.A.)
15°
PACIFIC OCEAN
Philippine Sea
Laoag City
Bangued
Tuguegarao
Bontoc
Ilagan
San Fernando
Santiago
Bayombong
Baguio
Dagupan
Baler
Luzon
Cabanatuan
Polillo Islands
Quezon City
MANILA
PHILIPPINES
San Pablo
Daet
Lopez
Lucena
Calapan
Naga
Catanduanes
Virac
Iriga
2421
Mount Halcon 2585
Marinduque
Legazpi
Sorsogon
Sibuyan Sea
Burias
Mindoro
Irosin
Roxas
Romblon
Sibuyan
Laoang
Catarman
Calbayog
Catbalogan
Samar
Masbate
Looc
Semirara Is.
Roxas
Visayan Sea
Tacloban
Leyte
Cuyo Islands
Barbaza
Panay
Cadiz
Ormoc
San Jose de Buenavista
Iloilo
Bacolod
Danao
Baybay
Bago
Talisay
Cebu
Maasin
Dinagat
Negros
2450
Carcar
Bohol
Surigao
Siargao
Cauayan
Tanjay
Cebu
Bohol Sea
Dumaguete
Tandag
Cagayan de Oro
Butuan
Dipolog
Oroquieta
Ozamis
Bislig
Iligan
Lake Lanao
Malaybalay
Pagadian
Mindanao
Zamboanga
Cotabato
Mount Apo 2954
Davao
Moro Gulf
Davao Gulf
Mati
Isabela
Basilan
Jolo
Norala
Digos
Cape San Agustin
General Santos
Malita
Sulu Archipelago
Sarangani Islands
Ulithi
Colonia
Yap
Fais
FEDERATED STATES OF MICRONESIA
Gaferut
10°
Ngeruangel
PALAU
MELEKEOK
Koror
Eil Malk
Angaur
Palau Islands
Ngulu
Sorol
Faraulep
West Fayu
Pikelot
Namonuito
Olimarao
Lamotrek
Pulap
Woleai
Elato
Satawal
Puluwat
Eauripik
Ifalik
Pulusuk
Caroline Islands
Sonsorol Islands
Pulo Anna
Merir
5°
Kepulauan Nanusa
Karakelong
Kepulauan Talaud
Salibabu
Tahuna
Niampak
Kaburuang
Sangir
Celebes Sea
1784
Siau
Kepulauan Sangir
Tobi
Helen
Helen Reef
Tanjung Sopi
Morotai
Tahulandang
Susupu
Daruba
Manado
Bitung
Loloda
Tobelo
Tanjung Lelai
1635
Akelamo
Semenanjung Minahasa
Tolitoli
Tondano
Kotamobagu
Laut Maluku (Molucca Sea)
Ternate
Halmahera
Gorontalo
Taman Nasional Bogani Nani Wartabone
Moutong
Marisa
Teluk Tomini
Kepulauan Togian
Togian
Batudaka
Gebe
Waigeo
Laut Halmahera (Halmahera Sea)
Selat Dampir
Kwoka
Kaironi
Biak
Supiori
Numfoor
Equator
0°
Tanjung Pangkalsiang
Labuha
Bacan
Tg Libobo
Sorong 3000
Manokwari
Sajam
Luwuk
Ampoa
Bisa
Laiwui
Obi
Kep. Salawati Megamo
Kep. Rajaampat
Teminabuan
Jazirah Doberai
2939
Biak
Num
Pom
Yapen
Tanjung d'Urville
Rori
Teba
Ninigo Group
Aua Island
Pelleluhu Is
Wuvulu Island
St Matthias Group
Tabalo
Mussau Island
Admiralty Islands
Hermit Islands
Kabuli
Lorengau
Manus Island
Rambutyo Island
Bismarck Archipelago
Taliabu
Mangole
Kepulauan Sula
Moluccas (Maluku)
Lektobi
Kep. Boo
Atkri
Misoöl
Tg Winsop
Kep. Pisang
Laut Seram (Ceram Sea)
Rumberpon
Maswaar
Serui
Taman Nasional Teluk Cenderawasih
Teluk Cenderawasih
Sarmi
Ansudu
Demta
Jayapura
Vanimo
Sissano
Aitape
Kairiru I.
Schouten Islands
Wewak
Poso
Tentena
Kolonedale
Kepulauan Banggai
Banggai
Celebes (Sulawesi)
Bahomonte
Malili
Wahai
Seram
Taman Nasional Manusela
Arandai
Modan
Fakfak
Semenanjung Bomberai
Bomberai
Kaimana
2252
Nabire
Asori
Pegunungan Van Rees
Tariku
Taritatu
Lereh
Bewani
Lumio
Amanab
1859
Schouten Islands
Wewak
2799
Wawalalindu
Manui
Kendari
Fogi
Buru
Ambon
Ambelau
Undur
Kepulauan Gorong
Gariau
Pegunungan Maoke
3892
Puncak Jaya 4884
Mulia
Puncak Yamin 4595
Puncak Mandala 4700
Tembagapura
Green River
Ambunti
Pagwi
Maprik
Sepik
Watam
Manam I.
Mount Kanangio 1831
Karkar Island
Bismarck Sea
Witu Islands
Wowoni
Kolaka
Bone
Watampone
Raha
Buton
Nusawulan
Teluk Adi
Kepulauan Watubela
Kamrau
Taman Nasional Lorentz
4730
Amamapare
Jayawijaya
New Guinea
Central Ra.
3711
Bismarck Ra.
4509
Madang
Long I.
Umboi
Dampier Str.
Nukuhu
New Britain
Sinjai
Bulukumba
Mona
Baubau
Siumpu
Wangiwangi
Kepulauan Tukangbesi
Kepulauan Banda
Kepulauan Tayandu
Kepulauan Lucipara
Kai Besar
Kepulauan Kai
Tual
Kai Kecil
Kola
Wokam
Dobo
Benjina
Kobroör
Kepulauan Aru
Trangan
Sia
Workai
Agats
Namas
Kiunga
Kopiago
PAPUA NEW GUINEA
Tari
Mendi
Mt Hagen
Mount Wilhelm 4509
4359
Goroka
Kratke Ra.
4107
Anepmete
Wasum
Walingai
Kandrian
Lae
Finschhafen
Laut Banda (Banda Sea)
Laut Flores (Flores Sea)
Benteng
Pulau Selayar
Kepulauan Barat Daya
Pulau Romang
Damar
Kepulauan Babar
Babar
Sermata
Molu
Larat
Watmuri
Kepulauan Tanimbar
Yamdena
Selaru
Tanjung Deyong
Yomuka
Pulau Dolok
Pembre
Gatentiri
Muting
Lake Murray
Aramia
Komaio
Kikori
Kaimuru
Balimo
Bulolo
Wau
Morobe
Cape Ward Hunt
Kerema
Kep. Tonerate
Tanjung Kapondai
Komba
Kepulauan Alor
Wetar
Kalabahi
Alor
Selat Ombai
Selat Wetar
Moa
Kepulauan Leti
Ruteng
Maumere
Larantuka
Lomblen
2400
Ende
Flores
Solor
EAST TIMOR
Atambua
Selat Sumba
Laut Sawu (Savu Sea)
Waingapu
Sumba
Ngalu
Savu
Raijua
DILI
Tutuala
Foho Tatamailau
2960
EAST TIMOR (TIMOR-LESTE)
Soe
Kefamenanu
Timor
Kupang
Baa
Rote
Timor Sea
Arafura Sea
Mombum
Komoran
Kumbe
Merauke
Tanjung Vals
Weam
Morehead
Tais
Daru
Sibidiri
Bula
Boigu I.
Torres Strait
Kiwai Island
Gulf of Papua
Bereina
Hisiu
Mount Victoria 4073
Popondetta
Kokoda
Cape Nelson
Owen Stanley Ra.
3676
PORT MORESBY
Kwikila
Hood Point
Abau
10°
Badu Island
Moa Island
Prince of Wales Island
Endeavour Strait
Ashmore Reefs
Cape York
Jardine River National Park
Great Barrier Reef Marine Park (Far North Section)
Mapoon
Cape Grenville
Bramwell
Cape Van Diemen
Garig Gunak Barlu National Park
Croker Island
Cobourg Peninsula
Goulburn Is
Wessel Islands
Cape Wessel
Milikapiti
Dundas Str.
Melville I.
Bathurst Island
Mitchell Point
Maningrida
Elcho I.
AUSTRALIA
Ashmore and Cartier Islands (Australia)
ASIA

→ 132
↓ 136

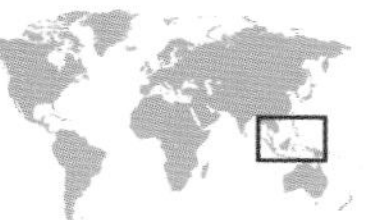

Asia
Philippines

Mercator Projection

1:5 600 000

0 50 100 150 200 miles

0 50 100 150 200 250 300 km

Asia

Central Indonesia

↑ 87
Andaman Sea
South
THAILAND
MALAYSIA
Peninsular Malaysia
KEDAH
PERAK
KELANTAN
TERENGGANU
PAHANG
SELANGOR
KUALA LUMPUR
PUTRAJAYA
NEGERI SEMBILAN
MELAKA
JOHOR
SINGAPORE
Johor Bahru
Strait of Singapore
Strait of Malacca
ACEH
SUMATERA UTARA
Medan
Danau Toba
Sumatra
RIAU
Pekanbaru
KEPULAUAN RIAU
Batam
Kepulauan Lingga
SUMATERA BARAT
Padang
JAMBI
Jambi
SUMATERA SELATAN
Palembang
BENGKULU
Bengkulu
LAMPUNG
Bandar Lampung
BANGKA
Bangka
Pangkalpinang
BANTEN
JAKARTA
Selat Sunda
Simeulue
Nias
Siberut
Selat Mentawai
Kepulauan Mentawai
Enggano
Pegunungan Barisan
Greater Sunda Islands
INDIAN OCEAN
INDO
Equator
Mercator Projection
1:5 400 000
0 50 100 150 200 miles
0 50 100 150 200 250 300 km

Asia
West Indonesia and Malaysia

↑ 96
→ 97
105 ←

Mercator Projection

1:6 100 000

miles 0 100 200

km 0 100 200 300 400

Asia

Myanmar, Thailand, Peninsular Malaysia and Indo-China

Albers Conic Equal Area Projection

1:13 000 000
0 200 400 miles
0 200 400 600 800 km

↑ 77
Sea of Okhotsk
(Okhotskoye More)
Sakhalin
Kuril Islands
(Kuril'skiye Ostrova)
ADMINISTERED BY RUSSIA, CLAIMED BY JAPAN
La Pérouse Strait
Hokkaidō
Sapporo
Khabarovsk
Komsomol'sk-na-Amure
Blagoveshchensk
Vladivostok
MANCHURIA
HEILONGJIANG
Harbin
Qiqihar
JILIN
Changchun
LIAONING
Shenyang
Dalian
NEI MONGOL ZIZHIQU
(INNER MONGOLIA)
Hohhot
Baotou
Datong
HEBEI
BEIJING
(Peking)
Tianjin
Shijiazhuang
SHANXI
Taiyuan
SHANDONG
Jinan
Qingdao
(Tsingtao)
Bo Hai
Yellow Sea
(Huang Hai)
NORTH KOREA
P'YŎNGYANG
MILITARY DEMARCATION LINE 1953
SOUTH KOREA
SEOUL
Busan (Pusan)
Daegu (Taegu)
Jeju-do
Korea Strait
Sea of Japan
(East Sea)
JAPAN
TŌKYŌ
Yokohama
Nagoya
Kyoto
Ōsaka
Kōbe
Hiroshima
Fukuoka
Nagasaki
Kagoshima
Sendai
Shikoku
Kyūshū
Honshu
HENAN
Zhengzhou
SHAANXI
Xi'an
JIANGSU
Nanjing
ANHUI
Hefei
Shanghai
SHANGHAI
HUBEI
Wuhan
ZHEJIANG
Hangzhou
Ningbo
HUNAN
Changsha
JIANGXI
Nanchang
FUJIAN
Fuzhou
Xiamen
East China Sea
(Dong Hai)
TAIBEI
(T'aipei)
TAIWAN
The People's Republic of China claims Taiwan as its 23rd province
Taiwan Strait
Gaoxiong
(Kaohsiung)
Ryukyu Islands
(Nansei-shotō)
(Japan)
Okinawa
GUANGDONG
Guangzhou
Shenzhen (Bao'an)
Hong Kong
(Xianggang)
Macao
(Aomen)
GUANGXI
ZHUANGZU ZIZHIQU
Nanning
HAINAN
Hainan Dao
Haikou
South China Sea
Bashi Channel
Luzon Strait
Babuyan Islands
PHILIPPINES
PACIFIC OCEAN
Bonin Islands
(Ogasawara-shotō)
(Japan)
Volcano Islands
(Kazan-rettō)
(Japan)
Tropic of Cancer
↓ 81

Conic Equidistant Projection

1:6 100 000

0 100 200 miles

0 100 200 300 400 km

Asia

Japan, North Korea and South Korea

1:1 100 000

0 10 20 30 40 50 60 miles

0 10 20 30 40 50 60 70 80 90 100 km

NIIGATA
GUNMA
TOCHIGI
IBARAKI
SAITAMA
TŌKYŌ
KANAGAWA
CHIBA
YAMANASHI
NAGANO
SHIZUOKA
Mikuni-sanmyaku
Kantō-sanchi
Kantō-heiya
Ashio-sanchi
Akaishi-sanmyaku
Kiso-sanmyaku
Minobu-sanchi
Abukuma-kōchi
Kashima-nada
Kujūkuri-hama
Tōkyō-wan
Sagami-wan
Sagami-nada
Suruga-wan
Uraga-suidō
Bōsō-hantō
Izu-hantō
Izu-shotō
Ō-shima
To-shima
Udone-jima
Nii-jima
Shikine-jima
Kōzu-shima
Miyake-jima
Ōnohara-jima
PACIFIC OCEAN
TŌKYŌ
Yokohama
Kawasaki
Chiba
Saitama
Maebashi
Utsunomiya
Mito
Kōfu
Nagano
Shizuoka
Sagamihara
Hachiōji
Funabashi
Narita
Tsukuba
Odawara
Numazu
Fuji
Matsumoto
Ueda
Takasaki
Hitachi
Kashima
Chōshi
Yokosuka
Hiratsuka
Atsugi
Kawagoe
Nikkō
Fujiyoshida
Gotenba
Shimizu
Fujieda
Hamakita
Omae-zaki
Irō-zaki
Nojima-zaki
138°
139°
140°
35°
36°
34°
E
F
G
1
2
3
4
5

↑ 91

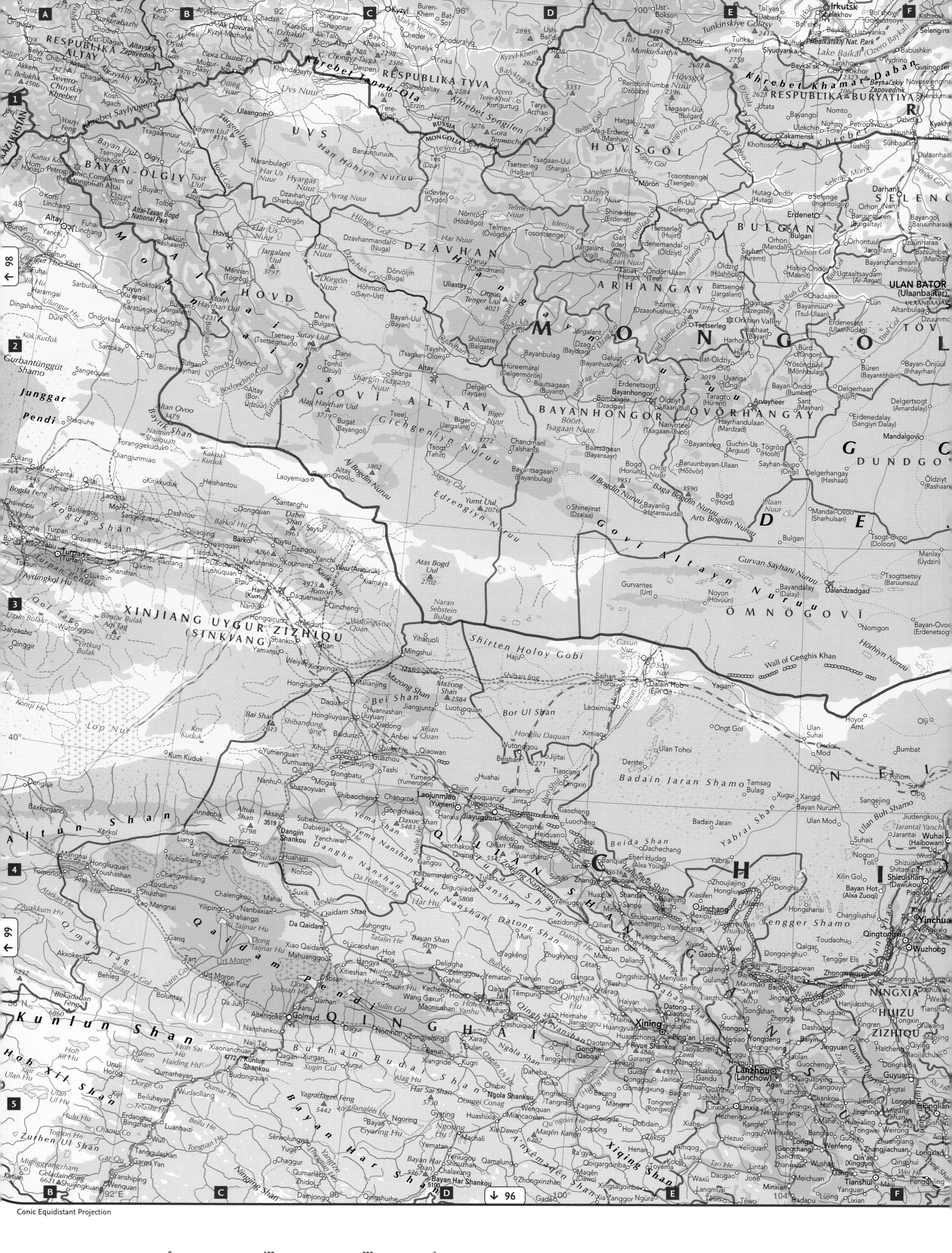

Conic Equidistant Projection

1:6 100 000

0 100 200 miles

0 100 200 300 400 km

↑ 77
→ 90
→ 91
↓ 97

Asia

Northern China and Mongolia

Conic Equidistant Projection

1:6 100 000
0 100 200 miles
0 100 200 300 400 km

Asia

Southeast China

KAZAKHSTAN
MONGOLIA
CHINA
RUSSIA
KYRGYZSTAN
XINJIANG UYGUR ZIZHIQU
(SINKIANG)
GANSU
Tarim Basin
(Tarim Pendi)
Taklimakan Desert
(Taklimakan Shamo)
Junggar Pendi
(Dzungarian Basin)
Gurbantünggüt Shamo
Altai Mountains
Lop Nur
Almaty
(Alma-Ata)
BISHKEK
(Frunze)
Ürümqi
Turpan
Kashgar
Semey (Semipalatinsk)
Ust'-Kamenogorsk
Karamay
Hami
Korla
Aksu
Ysyk-Köl
VOSTOCHNYY KAZAKHSTAN
ALMATINSKAYA OBLAST'
KARAGANDINSKAYA OBLAST'
PAVLODARSKAYA OBLAST'
ALTAYSKIY KRAY
RESPUBLIKA ALTAY
RESPUBLIKA TYVA
BAYAN-ÖLGIY
UVS
HOVD
DZAVHAN
GOVI-ALTAY
HÖVSGÖL
Conic Equidistant Projection
1:6 100 000

↑ 94
↑ 77
↓ 102

96 →
104 ↓
105 ↓
↑ 109

Asia

West China

Albers Conic Equal Area Projection

1:17 300 000

0 200 400 600 miles
0 200 400 600 800 1000 km

RUSSIA
MONGOLIA
CHINA
KYRGYZSTAN
TAJIKISTAN
NEPAL
BHUTAN
BANGLADESH
INDIA
MYANMAR (BURMA)
THAILAND
LAOS
VIETNAM
CAMBODIA
MALAYSIA
INDONESIA
SRI LANKA
MALDIVES
SINGAPORE
INNER MONGOLIA
XINJIANG
TIBET
Gobi Desert
Altai Mountains
Tien Shan
Kunlun Shan
Altun Shan
Tarim Basin (Tarim Pendi)
Taklimakan Desert (Taklimakan Shamo)
Plateau of Tibet (Qingzang Gaoyuan)
Tanggula Shan
Qaidam Pendi
Qilian Shan
Kazakh Steppe
Saryarka
Bay of Bengal
Andaman Sea
South China Sea
Gulf of Thailand
Gulf of Tongking
Strait of Malacca
Laccadive Sea
Bo Hai
Andaman Islands (India)
Nicobar Islands (India)
Hainan Dao
Mouths of the Ganges
Mouths of the Irrawaddy
Mouths of the Mekong
Ten Degree Channel
Eight Degree Channel
Nine Degree Channel
Coromandel Coast
Malabar Coast
Western Ghats
Eastern Ghats
Deccan
Equator
Tropic of Cancer
ULAN BATOR (Ulaanbaatar)
BEIJING (Peking)
ASTANA (Akmola)
BISHKEK
ISLAMABAD
NEW DELHI
KATHMANDU
THIMPHU
DHAKA (Dacca)
NAY PYI TAW
VIENTIANE (Viangchan)
HA NOI
BANGKOK (Krung Thep)
PHNOM PENH
KUALA LUMPUR
PUTRAJAYA
SRI JAYEWARDENEPURA KOTTE
Novosibirsk
Omsk
Almaty (Alma-Ata)
Ürümqi
Lanzhou
Xi'an
Chengdu
Chongqing
Wuhan
Tianjin
Kunming
Delhi
Mumbai (Bombay)
Kolkata (Calcutta)
Chennai (Madras)
Bengaluru (Bangalore)
Hyderabad
Lahore
Karachi
Rangoon (Yangon)
Mandalay
Chittagong
Colombo
Ho Chi Minh City (Saigon)
Asia
Central and Southern Asia

Albers Equal Area Conic Projection

1:11 200 000

0 100 200 300 400 500 miles

0 100 200 300 400 500 600 700 800 km

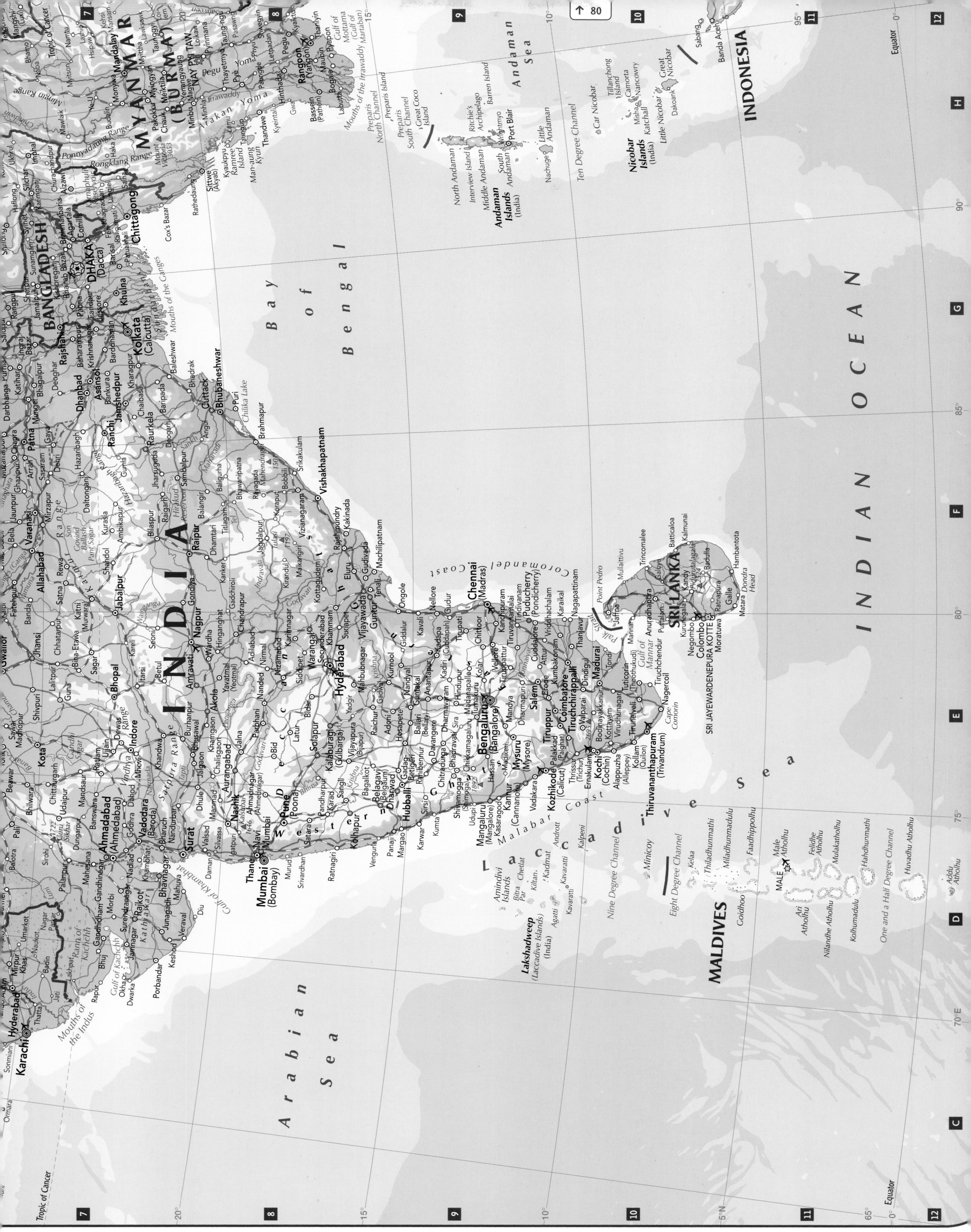

INDIA
BANGLADESH
MYANMAR (BURMA)
SRI LANKA
MALDIVES
INDONESIA
Lakshadweep (Laccadive Islands) (India)
Andaman Islands (India)
Nicobar Islands (India)
Arabian Sea
Bay of Bengal
Andaman Sea
Laccadive Sea
INDIAN OCEAN
Mumbai (Bombay)
Kolkata (Calcutta)
Chennai (Madras)
Bengaluru (Bangalore)
Hyderabad
DHAKA (Dacca)
Colombo
Rangoon (Yangon)
NAY PYI TAW
Karachi
Tropic of Cancer
Equator
↑ 80

Asia
Southern Asia

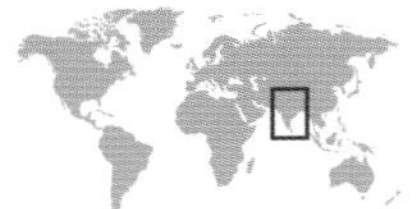

Conic Equidistant Projection

1:6 100 000
0 100 200 miles
0 100 200 300 400 km

Asia

Northern India, Nepal, Bhutan and Bangladesh

↑ 104

Arabian Sea

Bay of Bengal

INDIA

SRI LANKA

MALDIVES

LAKSHADWEEP (India)

Administrative divisions in India numbered on the map:

1. DADRA AND NAGAR HAVELI (B1)
2. DAMAN AND DIU (A1, B1)
3. PUDUCHERRY (C4)

↓ 103

Conic Equidistant Projection

Asia

Southern India and Sri Lanka

1:6 100 000

0 100 200 miles

0 100 200 300 400 km

Conic Equidistant Projection

1:2 600 000

0 25 50 75 100 miles

0 25 50 75 100 125 150 175 km

Asia
Middle East

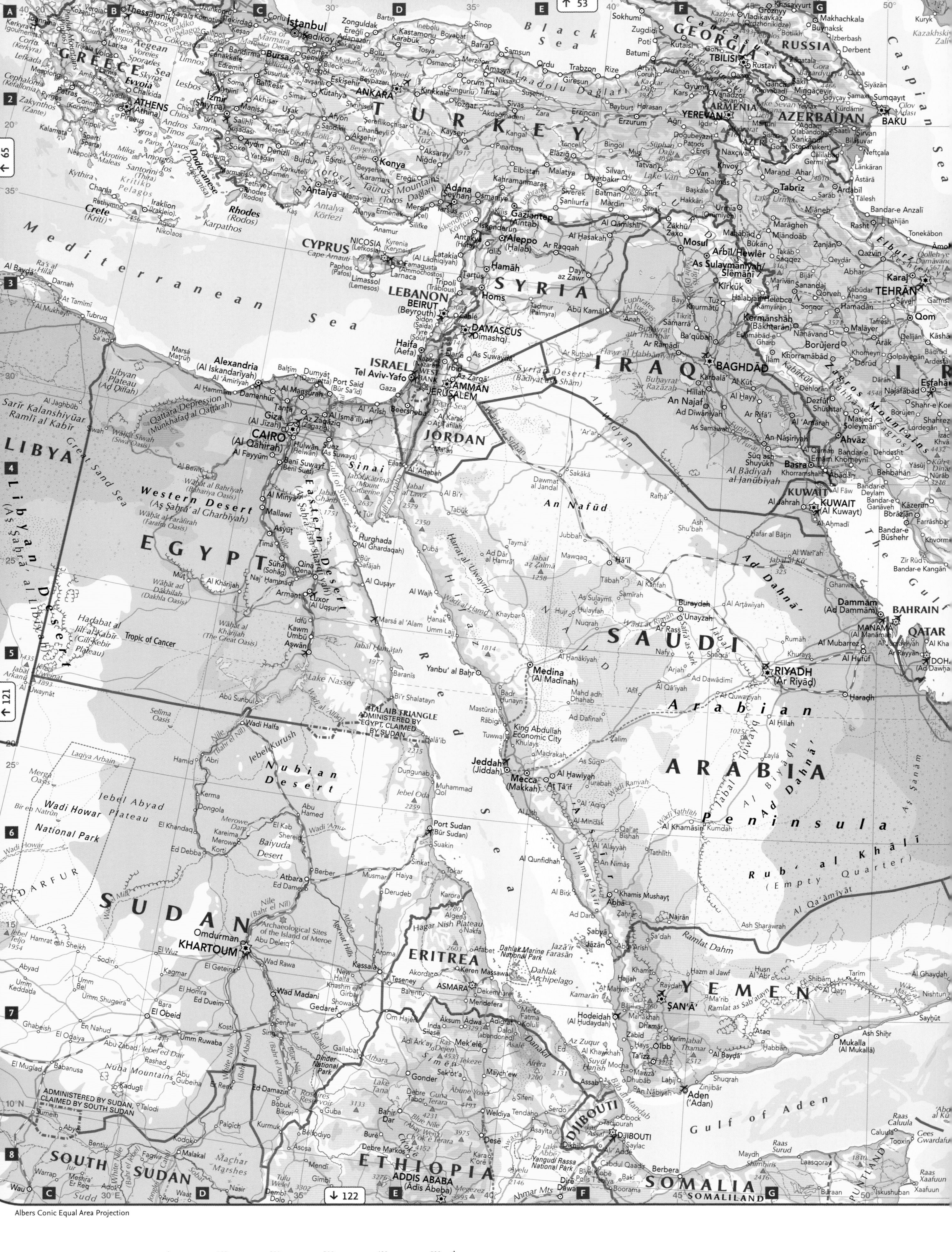

Albers Conic Equal Area Projection

1:11 200 000

0	100	200	300	400	500 miles

0	100	200	300	400	500	600	700	800 km

↑ 102
KAZAKHSTAN
KYRGYZSTAN
UZBEKISTAN
TURKMENISTAN
TAJIKISTAN
AFGHANISTAN
PAKISTAN
INDIA
CHINA
NEPAL
OMAN
UNITED ARAB EMIRATES
XINJIANG UYGUR ZIZHIQU (SINKIANG)
XIZANG ZIZHIQU (TIBET)
AKSAI CHIN UNDER CHINESE ADMINISTRATION, CLAIMED BY INDIA
ADMINISTERED BY PAKISTAN, CLAIMED BY INDIA
ADMINISTERED BY INDIA, CLAIMED BY PAKISTAN
LINE OF CONTROL
KASHMIR
Tarim Basin (Tarim Pendi)
Taklimakan Desert (Taklimakan Shamo)
Kunlun Shan
Himalaya
Hindu Kush
Karakoram Range
Pamir
Alai Range
Gissar Range
Turan Lowland
Karakum Desert (Peski Karakumy)
Kopet Dag
Dasht-e Kavīr
Dasht-e Lūt
Dasht-e Mārgo
Thar Desert
Rann of Kachchh
Satpura Range
Western Ghats
Malabar Coast
Deccan
Makran
Makran Coast Range
Central Makran Range
Toba and Kakar Ranges
Sulaiman Range
Kirthar Range
Gulf of Oman
Gulf of Kachchh
Gulf of Khambhat
Strait of Hormuz
Mouths of the Indus
Arabian Sea
Nine Degree Channel
Amindivi Islands
Lakshadweep (Laccadive Islands) (India)
Socotra (Suquṭrá) (Yemen)
Juzur al Ḩalāniyāt (Kuria Muria Islands)
Tropic of Cancer
TOSHKENT (Tashkent)
DUSHANBE
AŞGABAT (Ashkhabad)
KABUL
ISLAMABAD
NEW DELHI
MUSCAT (Masqaţ)
ABU DHABI (Abū Ẓaby)
Samarqand
Bukhara
Mashhad
Herāt
Kandahār
Quetta
Peshawar
Rawalpindi
Lahore
Faisalabad
Multan
Hyderabad
Karachi
Srinagar
Amritsar
Ludhiana
Chandigarh
Delhi
Jaipur
Agra
Lucknow
Kanpur
Jodhpur
Ahmadabad (Ahmedabad)
Vadodara (Baroda)
Surat
Rajkot
Indore
Bhopal
Nagpur
Nashik
Mumbai (Bombay)
Thane
Navi Mumbai (New Bombay)
Pune (Poona)
Solapur
Hyderabad
Kolhapur
Hubballi
Bengaluru (Bangalore)
Mangaluru (Mangalore)
Mysuru (Mysore)
Kozhikode (Calicut)
Coimbatore
Kochi (Cochin)
Thiruvananthapuram (Trivandrum)
Sharjah (Ash Shāriqah)
Dubai (Dubayy)
Zāhedān
Kermān
Bandar-e 'Abbās
Cape Comorin
Minicoy
↑ 102
↑ 103

Conic Equidistant Projection

1:6 100 000
0 100 200 miles
0 100 200 300 400 km

Asia
The Gulf, Iran, Afghanistan and Pakistan

Conic Equidistant Projection

1:6 100 000 — 0 100 200 miles; 0 100 200 300 400 km

↑ 64
↓ 108
→ 110
RUSSIA
STAVROPOL'SKIY KRAY
GEORGIA
ARMENIA
AZERBAIJAN
AZER.
KAZAKHSTAN
UZBEKISTAN
TURKMENISTAN
MANGYSTAUSKAYA OBLAST'
Ustyurt Plateau
Caspian Sea
IRAN
IRAQ
KUWAIT
SAUDI ARABIA
MESOPOTAMIA
KURDISTAN
Elburz Mountains
Zagros Mountains
Dasht-e Kavir
The Gulf
TBILISI
YEREVAN
BAKU
TEHRĀN
BAGHDĀD
KUWAIT (Al Kuwayt)
Basra
Mosul
Tabrīz
Eşfahān (Isfahan)
Shīrāz
Qom
Kermānshāh (Bākhtarān)
Hamadān
Karaj
Sumqayıt
Kirkūk
Ahvāz
An Najaf
Karbalā'
Erzurum
Lake Van (Van Gölü)
Daryācheh-ye Orūmīyeh
Garabogazköl Aylagy
Mys Peschanyy
Ostrova Tyulen'i

Africa

UNESCO World Heritage Sites

Famous archaeological sites such as the Pyramids of Giza and Abu Simbel, Egypt and the wildlife reserves of the Serengeti and Selous in Tanzania have been on the World Heritage List for a number of years. However more recently Robben Island, where Nelson Mandela was imprisoned, and the rainforests of Madagascar, their biodiversity under threat from development, have been included as representative of Africa's culture and environment.

● Cultural site ● Natural site ● Mixed site

Algeria
1. Al Qal'a of Beni Hammad
2. Djémila
3. Kasbah of Algiers
4. M'Zab Valley
5. Tassili n'Ajjer
6. Timgad
7. Tipasa

Benin
8. Royal Palaces of Abomey

Botswana
9. Okavango Delta
10. Tsodilo

Burkina Faso
11. The Ruins of Loropéni

Cameroon
12. Dja Faunal Reserve
13. Sangha Trinational

Cape Verde
14. Cidade Velha, Historic Centre of Ribeira Grande

Central African Republic
15. Manovo-Gouda St Floris National Park
13. Sangha Trinational

Chad
16. Lakes of Ounianga

Congo
13. Sangha Trinational

Congo, Democratic Republic of the
17. Garamba National Park
18. Kahuzi-Biega National Park
19. Okapi Wildlife Reserve
20. Salonga National Park
21. Virunga National Park

Côte d'Ivoire (Ivory Coast)
22. Comoé National Park
23. Historic Town of Grand-Bassam
24. Mount Nimba Strict Nature Reserve
25. Taï National Park

Egypt
26. Abu Mena
27. Ancient Thebes with its Necropolis
28. Historic Cairo
29. Memphis and its Necropolis – the Pyramid Fields from Giza to Dahshur
30. Nubian Monuments from Abu Simbel to Philae
31. Saint Catherine Area
32. Wadi Al-Hitan (Whale Valley)

Ethiopia
33. Aksum
34. Fasil Ghebbi, Gondar Region
35. Harar Jugol, the Fortified Historic Town
36. Konso Cultural Landscape
37. Lower Valley of the Awash
38. Lower Valley of the Omo
39. Rock-Hewn Churches, Lalibela
40. Simien National Park
41. Tiya

Gabon
42. Ecosystem and Relict Cultural Landscape of Lopé-Okanda

Gambia, The
43. Kunta Kinteh Island and Related Sites
44. Stone Circles of Senegambia

Ghana
45. Asante Traditional Buildings
46. Forts and Castles, Volta, Greater Accra, Central and Western Regions

Gough Island
47. Gough and Inaccessible Islands (U.K.)

Guinea
24. Mount Nimba Strict Nature Reserve

Kenya
48. Fort Jesus, Mombasa
49. Kenya Lake System in the Great Rift Valley
50. Lake Turkana National Parks
51. Lamu Old Town
52. Mount Kenya National Park/Natural Forest
53. Sacred Mijikenda Kaya Forests

Lesotho
54. Maloti-Drakensberg Park

Libya
55. Archaeological Site of Cyrene
56. Archaeological Site of Leptis Magna
57. Archaeological Site of Sabratha
58. Old Town of Ghadamès
59. Rock-Art Sites of Tadrart Acacus

Madagascar
60. Rainforests of the Atsinanana
61. The Royal Hill of Ambohimanga
62. Tsingy de Bemaraha Strict Nature Reserve

Malawi
63. Chongoni Rock-Art Area
64. Lake Malawi National Park

Mali
65. Cliff of Bandiagara (Land of the Dogons)
66. Old Towns of Djenné
67. Timbuktu
68. Tomb of Askia

Mauritania
69. Ancient Ksour of Ouadane, Chinguetti, Tichitt and Oualata
70. Banc d'Arguin National Park

Mauritius
71. Aapravasi Ghat
72. Le Morne Cultural Landscape

Morocco
73. Archaeological Site of Volubilis
74. Historic City of Meknes
75. Ksar of Ait-Ben-Haddou
76. Medina of Essaouira (formerly Mogador)
77. Medina of Fez
78. Medina of Marrakesh
79. Medina of Tétouan (formerly known as Titawin)
80. Portuguese City of Mazagan (El Jadida)
81. Rabat, Modern Capital and Historic City: a Shared Heritage

Mozambique
82. Island of Mozambique

Namibia
83. Namib Sand Sea
84. Twyfelfontein or /Ui-//aes

Niger
85. Aïr and Ténéré Natural Reserves
86. Historic Centre of Agadez
87. W National Park of Niger

Nigeria
88. Osun-Osogbo Sacred Grove
89. Sukur Cultural Landscape

Réunion
90. Pitons, cirques and remparts of Réunion Island (France)

Senegal
91. Bassari Country: Bassari, Fula and Bedik Cultural Landscapes
92. Djoudj National Bird Sanctuary
93. Island of Gorée
94. Island of Saint-Louis
95. Niokolo-Koba National Park
96. Saloum Delta
44. Stone Circles of Senegambia

Seychelles
97. Aldabra Atoll
98. Vallée de Mai Nature Reserve

South Africa
99. Cape Floral Region Protected Areas
100. Fossil Hominid Sites of South Africa
101. iSimangaliso Wetland Park
102. Mapungubwe Cultural Landscape
103. Richtersveld Cultural and Botanical Landscape
104. Robben Island
54. Maloti-Drakensberg Park
105. Vredefort Dome

Sudan
106. Archaeological Sites of the Island of Meroe
107. Gebel Barkal and the Sites of the Napatan Region

Tanzania
108. Kilimanjaro National Park
109. Kondoa Rock-Art Sites
110. Ngorongoro Conservation Area
111. Ruins of Kilwa Kisiwani and Ruins of Songo Mnara
112. Selous Game Reserve
113. Serengeti National Park
114. Stone Town of Zanzibar

Togo
115. Koutammakou, the Land of the Batammariba

Tunisia
116. Amphitheatre of El Jem
117. Dougga/Thugga
118. Ichkeul National Park
119. Kairouan
120. Medina of Sousse
121. Medina of Tunis
122. Punic Town of Kerkuane and its Necropolis
123. Site of Carthage

Uganda
124. Bwindi Impenetrable National Park
125. Rwenzori Mountains National Park
126. Tombs of Buganda Kings at Kasubi

Zambia
127. Mosi-oa-Tunya/Victoria Falls

Zimbabwe
128. Great Zimbabwe National Monument
129. Khami Ruins National Monument
130. Mana Pools National Park, Sapi and Chewore Safari Areas
131. Mosi-oa-Tunya/Victoria Falls
132. Matobo Hills

EUROPE
ASIA
Mediterranean Sea
Red Sea
ATLANTIC OCEAN
INDIAN OCEAN
MOROCCO
ALGERIA
TUNISIA
LIBYA
EGYPT
MAURITANIA
MALI
NIGER
CHAD
SUDAN
ERITREA
DJIBOUTI
ETHIOPIA
SOMALIA
SOUTH SUDAN
GUINEA
SIERRA LEONE
LIBERIA
CÔTE D'IVOIRE
BURKINA FASO
GHANA
TOGO
BENIN
NIGERIA
CENTRAL AFRICAN REPUBLIC
CAMEROON
EQUATORIAL GUINEA
SÃO TOMÉ AND PRÍNCIPE
GABON
CONGO
DEMOCRATIC REPUBLIC OF THE CONGO
CABINDA (Angola)
UGANDA
KENYA
RWANDA
BURUNDI
TANZANIA
SEYCHELLES
COMOROS
ANGOLA
ZAMBIA
MALAWI
MOZAMBIQUE
MADAGASCAR
MAURITIUS
Réunion (France)
ZIMBABWE
NAMIBIA
BOTSWANA
SWAZILAND
LESOTHO
SOUTH AFRICA
Gough Island (U.K.)

Africa

Landscapes

Some of the world's greatest physical features are in Africa, the world's second largest continent. Variations in climate and elevation give rise to the continent's great variety of landscapes. The Sahara, the world's largest desert, extends across the whole continent from west to east, and covers an area of over nine million square kilometres. Other significant African deserts are the Kalahari and the Namib. In contrast, some of the world's greatest rivers flow in Africa, including the Nile, the world's longest, and the Congo.

The Great Rift Valley is perhaps Africa's most notable geological feature. It stretches for nearly 3 000 kilometres from Jordan, through the Red Sea and south to Mozambique, and contains many of Africa's largest lakes. Significant mountain ranges on the continent are the Atlas Mountains and the Ethiopian Highlands in the north, the Ruwenzori in east central Africa, and the Drakensberg in the far southeast.

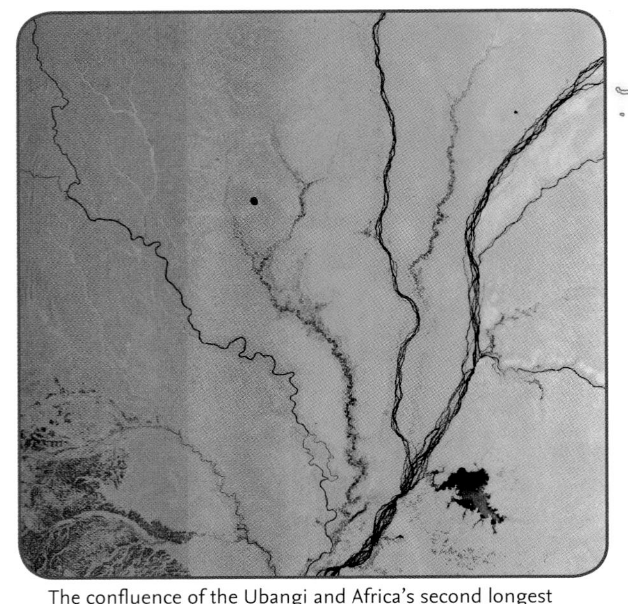

The confluence of the Ubangi and Africa's second longest river, the **Congo**.

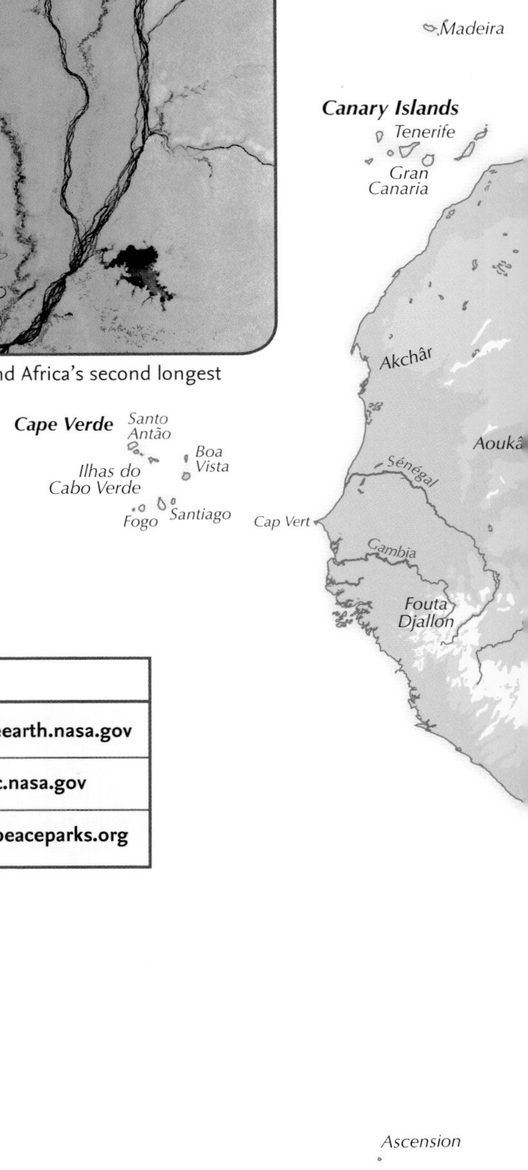

Madeira
Canary Islands
Tenerife
Gran Canaria
Akchâr
Cape Verde
Santo Antão
Boa Vista
Ilhas do Cabo Verde
Fogo
Santiago
Cap Vert
Sénégal
Aouk
Gambia
Fouta Djallon
Ascension

Africa's extent

TOTAL LAND AREA	30 343 578 sq km / 11 715 655 sq miles
Most northerly point	La Galite, Tunisia
Most southerly point	Cape Agulhas, South Africa
Most westerly point	Santo Antão, Cape Verde
Most easterly point	Raas Xaafuun, Somalia

Internet Links

NASA Visible Earth	**visibleearth.nasa.gov**
NASA Astronaut Photography	**eol.jsc.nasa.gov**
Peace Parks Foundation	**www.peaceparks.org**

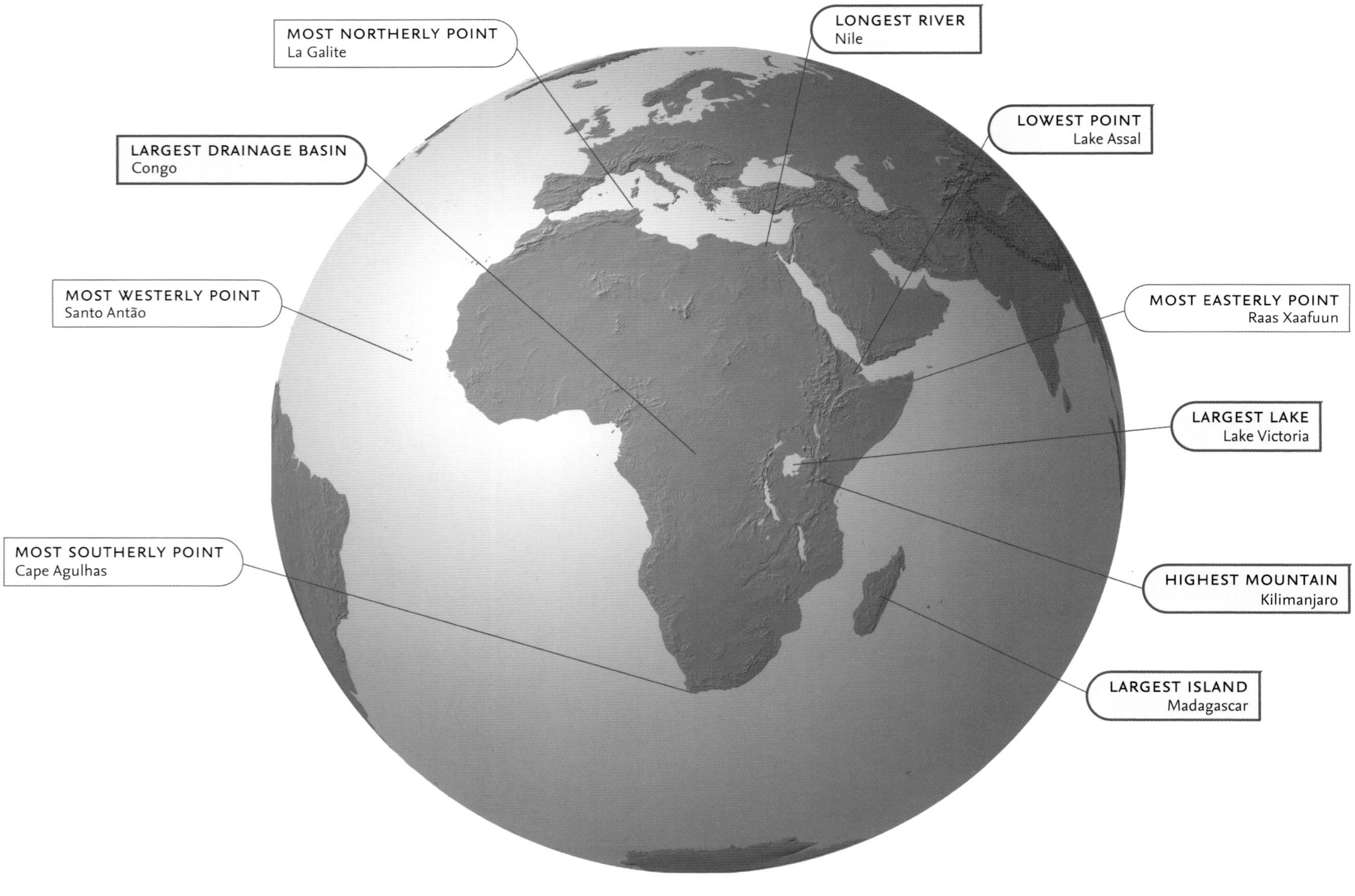

MOST NORTHERLY POINT
La Galite

LONGEST RIVER
Nile

LOWEST POINT
Lake Assal

LARGEST DRAINAGE BASIN
Congo

MOST WESTERLY POINT
Santo Antão

MOST EASTERLY POINT
Raas Xaafuun

LARGEST LAKE
Lake Victoria

MOST SOUTHERLY POINT
Cape Agulhas

HIGHEST MOUNTAIN
Kilimanjaro

LARGEST ISLAND
Madagascar

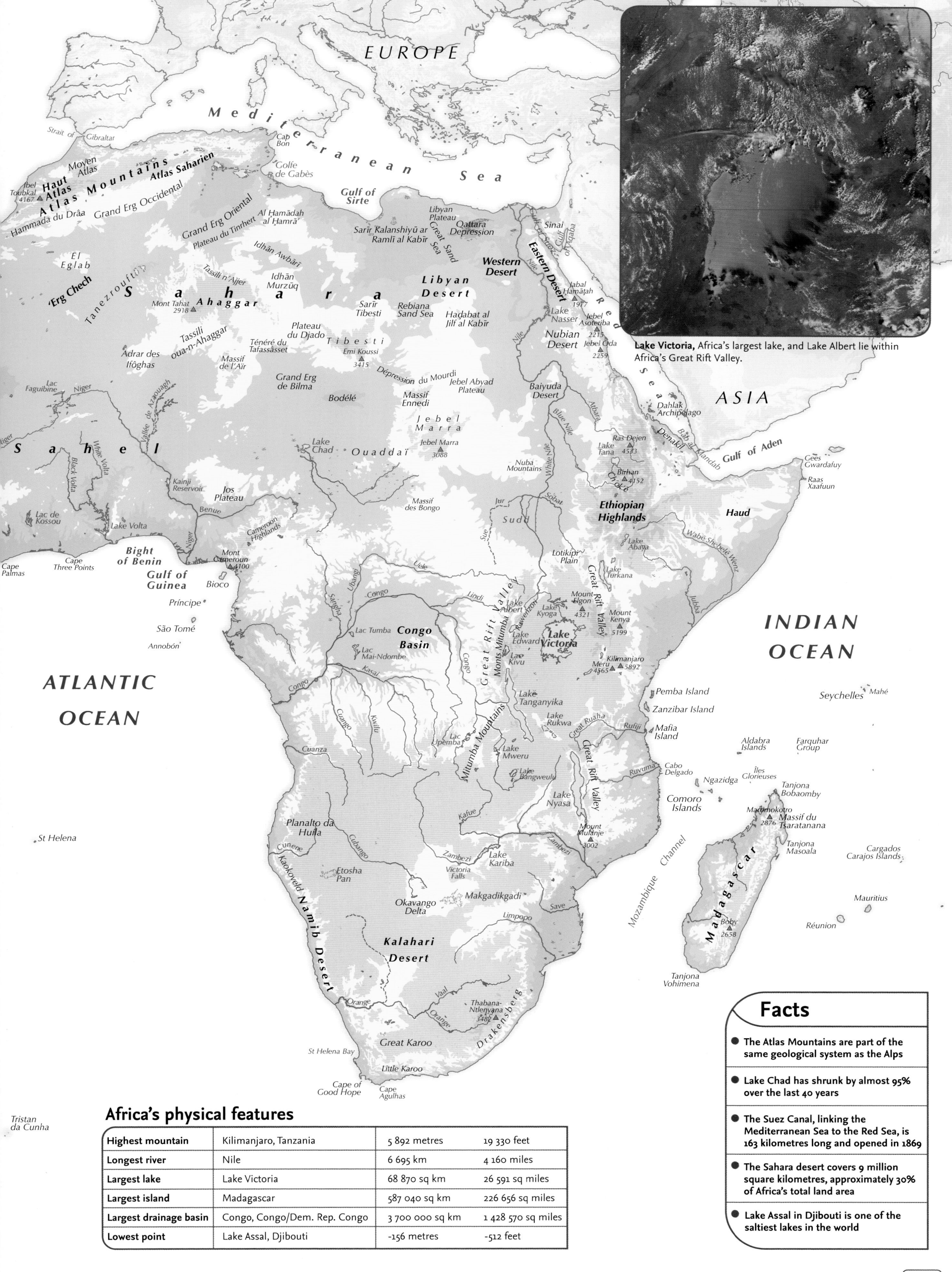

Lake Victoria, Africa's largest lake, and Lake Albert lie within Africa's Great Rift Valley.

Africa's physical features

Highest mountain	Kilimanjaro, Tanzania	5 892 metres	19 330 feet
Longest river	Nile	6 695 km	4 160 miles
Largest lake	Lake Victoria	68 870 sq km	26 591 sq miles
Largest island	Madagascar	587 040 sq km	226 656 sq miles
Largest drainage basin	Congo, Congo/Dem. Rep. Congo	3 700 000 sq km	1 428 570 sq miles
Lowest point	Lake Assal, Djibouti	-156 metres	-512 feet

Facts

- **The Atlas Mountains are part of the same geological system as the Alps**
- **Lake Chad has shrunk by almost 95% over the last 40 years**
- **The Suez Canal, linking the Mediterranean Sea to the Red Sea, is 163 kilometres long and opened in 1869**
- **The Sahara desert covers 9 million square kilometres, approximately 30% of Africa's total land area**
- **Lake Assal in Djibouti is one of the saltiest lakes in the world**

Africa
Countries

Africa is a complex continent, with over fifty independent countries and a long history of political change. It supports a great variety of ethnic groups, with the Sahara creating the major divide between Arab and Berber groups in the north and a diverse range of groups, including the Yoruba and Masai, in the south.

The current pattern of countries in Africa is a product of a long and complex history, including the colonial period, which saw European control of the vast majority of the continent from the fifteenth century until widespread moves to independence began in the 1950s. Despite its great wealth of natural resources, Africa is by far the world's poorest continent. Many of its countries are heavily dependent upon foreign aid and many are also subject to serious political instability.

Facts

- Africa has over 1 000 linguistic and cultural groups
- Only Liberia and Ethiopia have remained free from colonial rule throughout their history
- Over 30% of the world's minerals, and over 46% of the world's diamonds, come from Africa
- 9 of the 10 poorest countries in the world are in Africa

Madeira (Portugal)
Canary Islands (Spain)
Laâyoune
WESTERN SAHARA
Nouâdhibou
MAURITANIA
Nouakchott
CAPE VERDE (Cabo Verde)
Praia
St-Louis
Sénégal
Dakar
SENEGAL
Kaolack
Kayes
Banjul
THE GAMBIA
Bissau
GUINEA-BISSAU
GUINEA
Kanka
Conakry
Freetown
SIERRA LEONE
Monrovia
LIBERIA
Ascension (U.K.)

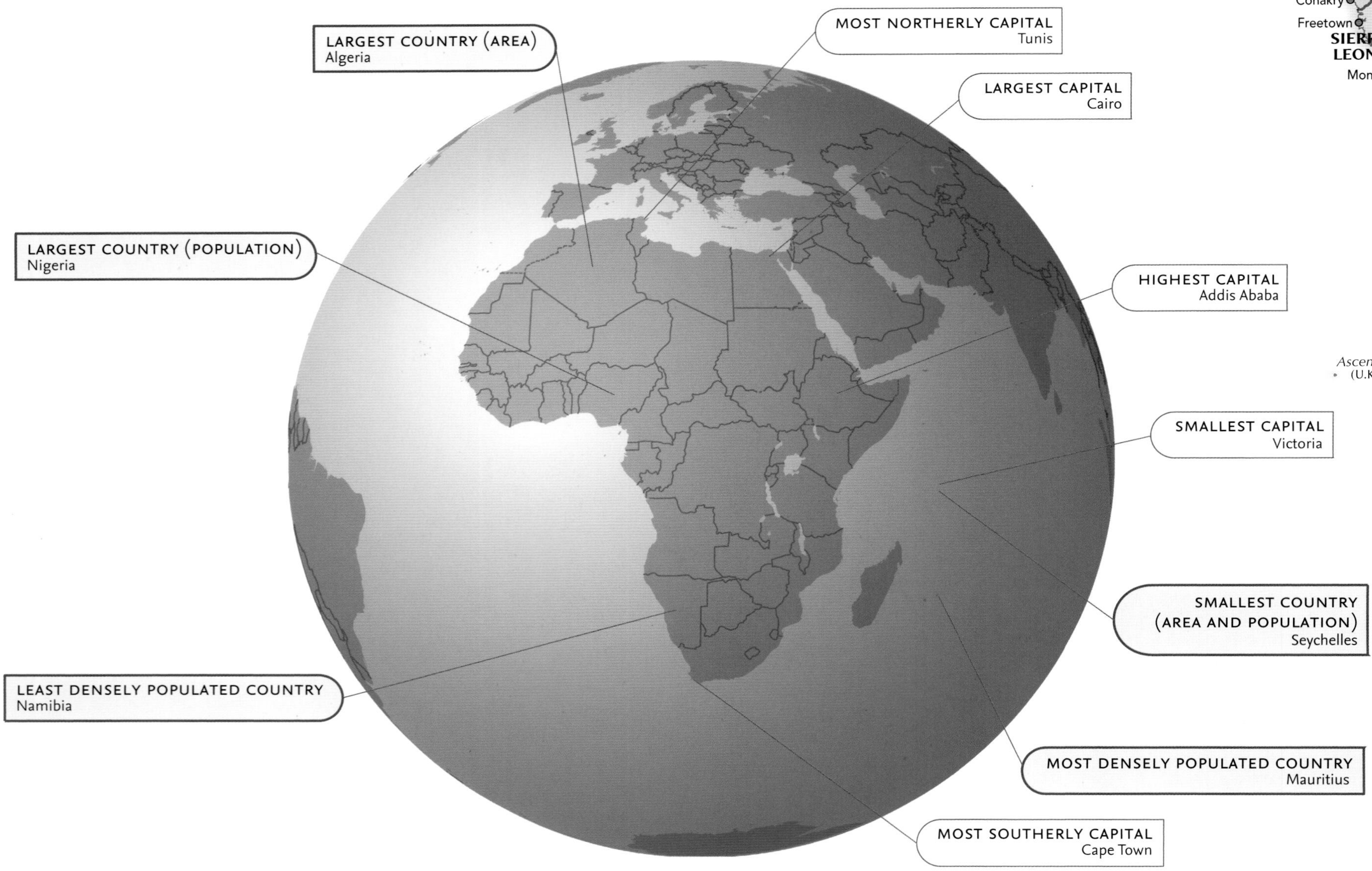

LARGEST COUNTRY (AREA)
Algeria

MOST NORTHERLY CAPITAL
Tunis

LARGEST CAPITAL
Cairo

LARGEST COUNTRY (POPULATION)
Nigeria

HIGHEST CAPITAL
Addis Ababa

SMALLEST CAPITAL
Victoria

SMALLEST COUNTRY (AREA AND POPULATION)
Seychelles

LEAST DENSELY POPULATED COUNTRY
Namibia

MOST DENSELY POPULATED COUNTRY
Mauritius

MOST SOUTHERLY CAPITAL
Cape Town

Internet Links

UK Foreign and Commonwealth Office	www.fco.gov.uk
CIA World Factbook	www.cia.gov/library/publications/the-world-factbook/index.html
Southern African Development Community	www.sadc.int
African Union (AU)	www.au.int

Cape Town, legislative capital of South Africa and the most southerly African capital city.

Africa's capitals

Largest capital (population)	Cairo, Egypt	11 944 000	
Smallest capital (population)	Victoria, Seychelles	26 000	
Most northerly capital	Tunis, Tunisia	36° 46'N	
Most southerly capital	Cape Town, South Africa	33° 57'S	
Highest capital	Addis Ababa, Ethiopia	2 408 metres	7 900 feet

Africa's countries

Largest country (area)	Algeria	2 381 741 sq km	919 595 sq miles
Smallest country (area)	Seychelles	455 sq km	176 sq miles
Largest country (population)	Nigeria	173 615 000	
Smallest country (population)	Seychelles	93 000	
Most densely populated country	Mauritius	610 per sq km	1 579 per sq mile
Least densely populated country	Namibia	3 per sq km	7 per sq mile

ATLANTIC OCEAN
Arquipélago da Madeira
Madeira (Portugal)
FUNCHAL
Canary Islands (Spain)
MOROCCO
RABAT
Casablanca
Marrakech
Agadir
Tangier (Tanger)
Gibraltar (U.K.)
SPAIN
ALGIERS (Alger)
TUNISIA
TUNIS
ALGERIA
Grand Erg Occidental
Grand Erg Oriental
Hamada du Drâa
Ahaggar (Hoggar)
Tamanrasset
WESTERN SAHARA ADMINISTERED BY MOROCCO
Tropic of Cancer
MAURITANIA
NOUAKCHOTT
Nouâdhibou
MALI
Timbuktu (Tombouctou)
BAMAKO
NIGER
NIAMEY
SENEGAL
DAKAR
THE GAMBIA
BANJUL
GUINEA-BISSAU
BISSAU
GUINEA
CONAKRY
SIERRA LEONE
FREETOWN
LIBERIA
MONROVIA
CÔTE D'IVOIRE (IVORY COAST)
YAMOUSSOUKRO
Abidjan
BURKINA FASO
OUAGADOUGOU
GHANA
ACCRA
TOGO
LOMÉ
BENIN
PORTO-NOVO
NIGERIA
ABUJA
Lagos
Kano
CAMEROON
YAOUNDÉ
Douala
EQUATORIAL GUINEA
MALABO
GABON
LIBREVILLE
SÃO TOMÉ AND PRÍNCIPE
SÃO TOMÉ
Bight of Benin
Gulf of Guinea
Equator
CAPE VERDE (CABO VERDE)
Ilhas do Cabo Verde
PRAIA
1:13 800 000
Lambert Azimuthal Equal Area Projection
1:13 800 000
0 200 400 miles
0 200 400 600 800 km

↑ 65
↓ 122
→ 108

Africa
Northern Africa

Lambert Azimuthal Equal Area Projection

1:13 800 000

0 200 400 miles

0 200 400 600 800 km

Africa

Central and Southern Africa

↑ 123
NAMIBIA
BOTSWANA
SOUTH AFRICA
ATLANTIC OCEAN
ERONGO
KHOMAS
OMAHEKE
HARDAP
!KARAS
GHANZI
KGALAGADI
KWENENG
SOUTHERN
NORTH
NORTHERN CAPE
WESTERN CAPE
GRIQUALAND WEST
GREAT NAMAQUALAND
NAMAQUALAND
Namib Desert
Kalahari Desert
Great Karoo
Little Karoo
Namib-Skeleton Coast National Park
Namib-Naukluft Park
Dorob National Park
Sperrgebiet National Park
Central Kalahari Game Reserve
Khutse Game Reserve
Mabuasehube Game Reserve
Gemsbok National Park
Kalahari Gemsbok National Park
Kgalagadi Transfrontier Park
Augrabies Falls National Park
Ai-Ais/Richtersveld Transfrontier Park
Ai-Ais Hot Springs and Fish River Canyon Park
Richtersveld Cultural and Botanical Landscape
Goegap Nature Reserve
Namaqua National Park
Mokala National Park
Tankwa-Karoo National Park
Karoo National Park
Camdeboo National Park
West Coast National Park
Table Mountain National Park
Bontebok National Park
De Hoop Nature Reserve
Garden Route National Park
Hardap Recreation Resort
Tropic of Capricorn
WINDHOEK
CAPE TOWN
OTJOZONDJUPA
Walvis Bay
Swakopmund
Rehoboth
Mariental
Keetmanshoop
Lüderitz
Karasburg
Upington
Kimberley
Springbok
Port Nolloth
Alexander Bay
Oranjemund
Calvinia
Beaufort West
Worcester
Paarl
Stellenbosch
Mossel Bay
George
Oudtshoorn
Knysna
Plettenberg Bay
Hermanus
Cape Agulhas
Cape of Good Hope
Orange
Fish
Molopo
Nossob
Auob
Kuruman
Kalkop Hills
Asbestos Mountains
Langberg
Roggeveld
Roggeveldberge
Nuweveldberge
Kamiesberge
Swartbergpas
Cango Caves
Langeberg
Kougaberge
Baviaanskloofberge
Lambert Azimuthal Equal Area Projection
1:4 300 000
0 50 100 150 miles
0 50 100 150 200 250 km

ZIMBABWE
MATABELELAND SOUTH
MASVINGO
CENTRAL
KGATLENG
GABORONE
LIMPOPO
MPUMALANGA
GAUTENG
PRETORIA (Tshwane)
Johannesburg
Soweto
GAZA
INHAMBANE
MOZAMBIQUE
MAPUTO
SWAZILAND
MBABANE
WEST
FREE STATE
BLOEMFONTEIN
KWAZULU-NATAL
LESOTHO
MASERU
Durban
Pietermaritzburg
Richards Bay
EASTERN CAPE
East London
Port Elizabeth
Drakensberg
Kruger National Park
Tropic of Capricorn
INDIAN OCEAN

Oceania

UNESCO World Heritage Sites

The sites in this continent cover a huge range in both time and type. In New Zealand the Tongariro site is of great cultural and religious significance to the Maori. There are ancient fossil sites in Australia along with the native peoples' sites such as Uluru, associated with the Anangu, one of the ancient Australian Aboriginal peoples. The world famous Great Barrier Reef is a site of great ecological significance and the iconic Sydney Opera House is a landmark feature in the city.

● Cultural site ● Natural site ● Mixed site

PALAU

FEDERATED STATES OF MICRONESIA

A S I A

PAPUA NEW GUINEA

27

8

18

Coral Sea

12

5

2

INDIAN OCEAN

A U S T R A L I A

11

17

3

14

4

9

19

6

15

1

2

13

Tasman Sea

16

Heard and McDonald Islands
(Australia)

7

10

Australia
1. Australian Convict Sites
2. Australian Fossil Mammal Sites (Riversleigh/Naracoorte)
3. Fraser Island
4. Gondwana Rainforests of Australia
5. Great Barrier Reef
6. Greater Blue Mountains Area
7. Heard and McDonald Islands
8. Kakadu National Park
9. Lord Howe Island Group
10. Macquarie Island
11. Ningaloo Coast
12. Purnululu National Park
13. Royal Exhibition Building and Carlton Gardens
14. Shark Bay, Western Australia
15. Sydney Opera House
16. Tasmanian Wilderness
17. Ulueu-Kata Tjula National Park
18. Wet Tropics of Queensland
19. Willandra Lakes Region

Fiji
20. Levuka Historical Port Town

Kiribati
21. Phoenix Islands Protected Area

Marshall Islands
22. Bikini Atoll Nuclear Test Site

New Caledonia
23. Lagoons of New Caledonia: Reef Diversity and Associated Ecosystems (France)

New Zealand
24. New Zealand Sub-Antarctic Islands
25. Te Wahipounamu – South West New Zealand
26. Tongariro National Park

Papua New Guinea
27. Kuk Early Agricultural Site

Pitcairn Islands
28. Henderson Island (U.K.)

Solomon Islands
29. East Rennell

Vanuatu
30. Chief Roi Mata's Domain

Oceania
Landscapes

Oceania comprises Australia, New Zealand, New Guinea and the islands of the Pacific Ocean. It is the smallest of the world's continents by land area. Its dominating feature is Australia, which is mainly flat and very dry. Australia's western half consists of a low plateau, broken in places by higher mountain ranges, which has very few permanent rivers or lakes. The narrow, fertile coastal plain of the east coast is separated from the interior by the Great Dividing Range, which includes the highest mountain in Australia.

The numerous Pacific islands of Oceania are generally either volcanic in origin or consist of coral. They can be divided into three main regions - Micronesia, north of the equator between Palau and the Gilbert islands; Melanesia, stretching from mountainous New Guinea to Fiji; and Polynesia, covering a vast area of the eastern and central Pacific Ocean.

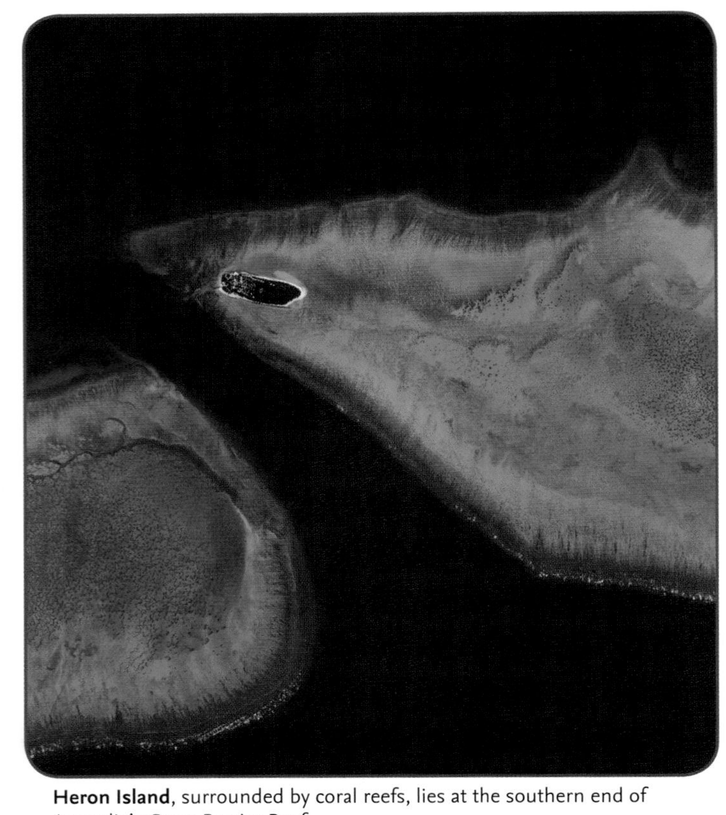

Heron Island, surrounded by coral reefs, lies at the southern end of Australia's Great Barrier Reef.

Facts

- Australia's Great Barrier Reef is the world's largest coral reef and stretches for over 2 000 kilometres
- The highest point of Tuvalu is less than 5 metres above sea level
- New Zealand lies directly on the boundary between the Pacific and Indo-Australian tectonic plates
- The Mariana Trench in the Pacific Ocean contains the earth's deepest point – Challenger Deep, 10 920 metres below sea level

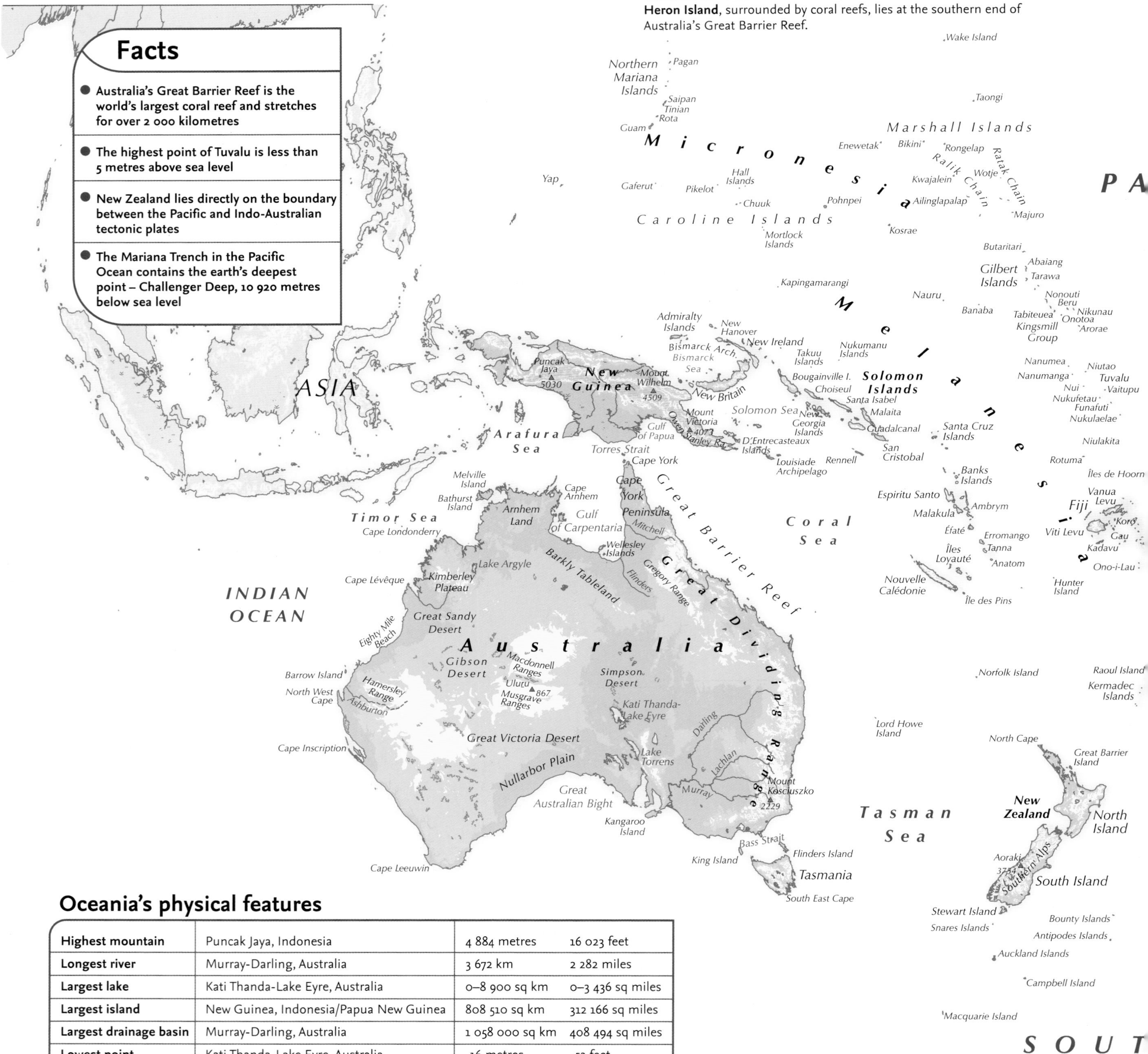

Wake Island
Northern Mariana Islands
Pagan
Saipan
Tinian
Rota
Guam
Taongi
Marshall Islands
Enewetak
Bikini
Rongelap
Ralik Chain
Ratak Chain
Wotje
Kwajalein
Ailinglapalap
Majuro
Micronesia
Yap
Gaferut
Pikelot
Hall Islands
Chuuk
Pohnpei
Kosrae
Caroline Islands
Mortlock Islands
PA
Butaritari
Abaiang
Tarawa
Gilbert Islands
Nonouti
Beru
Nikunau
Onotoa
Arorae
Tabiteuea
Kingsmill Group
Banaba
Nauru
Kapingamarangi
Melanesia
Admiralty Islands
New Hanover
New Ireland
Bismarck Arch.
Bismarck Sea
Nukumanu Islands
Takuu Islands
Bougainville I.
Choiseul
Santa Isabel
Solomon Islands
Malaita
New Georgia Islands
Guadalcanal
San Cristobal
Rennell
Solomon Sea
New Britain
Puncak Jaya 5030
New Guinea
Mount Wilhelm 4509
Mount Victoria 4073
Owen Stanley Ra.
Gulf of Papua
D'Entrecasteaux Islands
Louisiade Archipelago
ASIA
Arafura Sea
Torres Strait
Cape York
Santa Cruz Islands
Nanumea
Niutao
Nanumanga
Tuvalu
Nui
Vaitupu
Nukufetau
Funafuti
Nukulaelae
Niulakita
Rotuma
Île de Hoorn
Banks Islands
Espiritu Santo
Malakula
Ambrym
Éfaté
Erromango
Tanna
Anatom
Îles Loyauté
Nouvelle Calédonie
Île des Pins
Fiji
Vanua Levu
Viti Levu
Koro
Gau
Kadavu
Ono-i-Lau
Hunter Island
Melville Island
Bathurst Island
Cape Arnhem
Arnhem Land
Gulf of Carpentaria
Wellesley Islands
Timor Sea
Cape Londonderry
Cape York Peninsula
Mitchell
Great Barrier Reef
Coral Sea
Lake Argyle
Barkly Tableland
Flinders
Gregory Range
Great Dividing Range
Cape Lévêque
Kimberley Plateau
INDIAN OCEAN
Great Sandy Desert
Eighty Mile Beach
Australia
Gibson Desert
Macdonnell Ranges
Uluru
Musgrave Ranges 867
Simpson Desert
Barrow Island
North West Cape
Hamersley Range
Ashburton
Kati Thanda-Lake Eyre
Cape Inscription
Great Victoria Desert
Nullarbor Plain
Lake Torrens
Darling
Lachlan
Murray
Mount Kosciuszko 2229
Great Australian Bight
Kangaroo Island
Cape Leeuwin
King Island
Bass Strait
Flinders Island
Tasmania
South East Cape
Tasman Sea
Norfolk Island
Raoul Island
Kermadec Islands
Lord Howe Island
North Cape
Great Barrier Island
New Zealand
North Island
Aoraki 3754
Southern Alps
South Island
Stewart Island
Snares Islands
Bounty Islands
Antipodes Islands
Auckland Islands
Campbell Island
Macquarie Island
SOUT

Oceania's physical features

Highest mountain	Puncak Jaya, Indonesia	4 884 metres	16 023 feet
Longest river	Murray-Darling, Australia	3 672 km	2 282 miles
Largest lake	Kati Thanda-Lake Eyre, Australia	0–8 900 sq km	0–3 436 sq miles
Largest island	New Guinea, Indonesia/Papua New Guinea	808 510 sq km	312 166 sq miles
Largest drainage basin	Murray-Darling, Australia	1 058 000 sq km	408 494 sq miles
Lowest point	Kati Thanda-Lake Eyre, Australia	-16 metres	-52 feet

Internet Links

NASA Visible Earth	**visibleearth.nasa.gov**
NASA Astronaut Photography	**eol.jsc.nasa.gov**
Great Barrier Reef Marine Park Authority	**www.gbrmpa.gov.au**

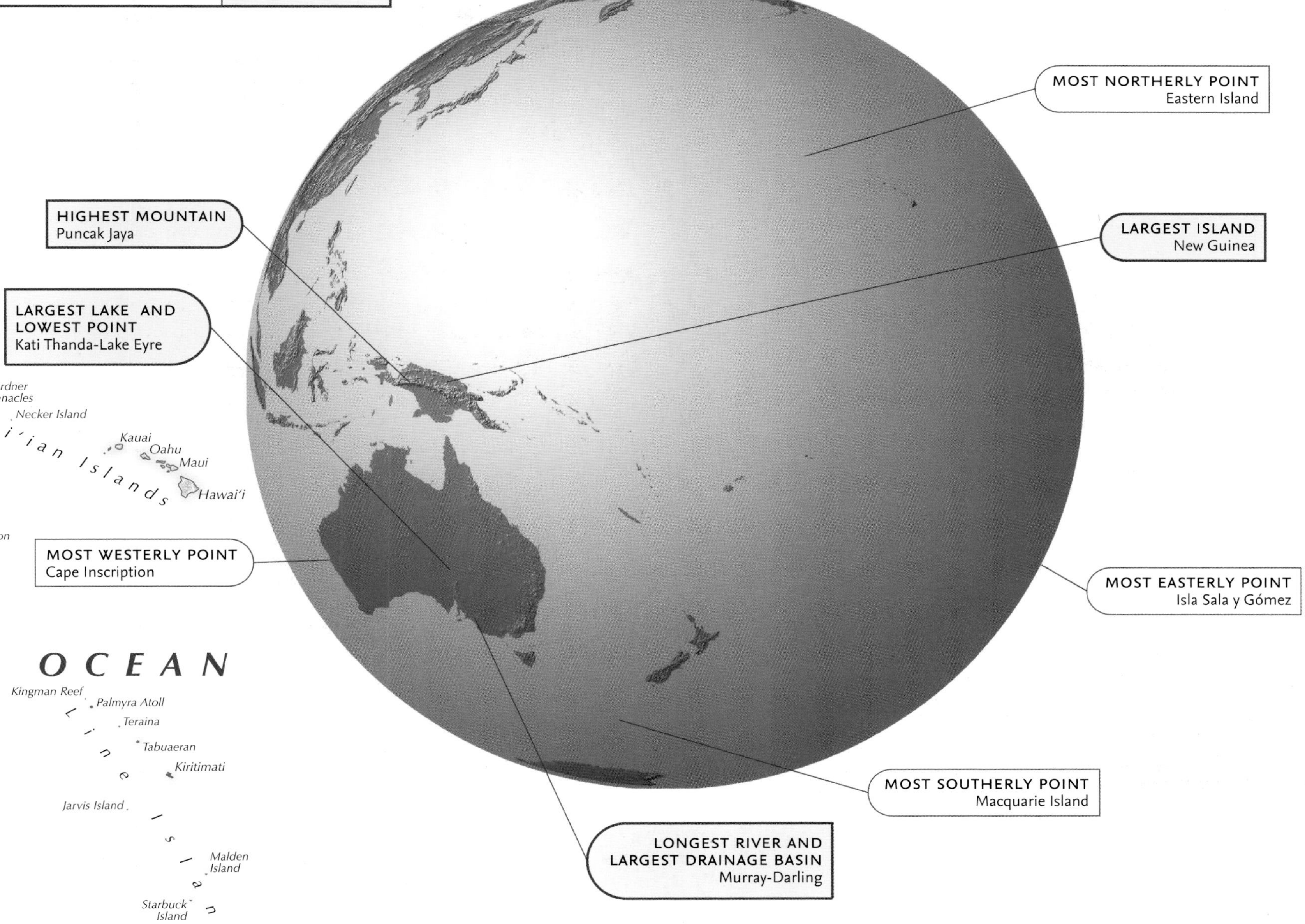

MOST NORTHERLY POINT
Eastern Island

HIGHEST MOUNTAIN
Puncak Jaya

LARGEST ISLAND
New Guinea

LARGEST LAKE AND LOWEST POINT
Kati Thanda-Lake Eyre

MOST WESTERLY POINT
Cape Inscription

MOST EASTERLY POINT
Isla Sala y Gómez

MOST SOUTHERLY POINT
Macquarie Island

LONGEST RIVER AND LARGEST DRAINAGE BASIN
Murray-Darling

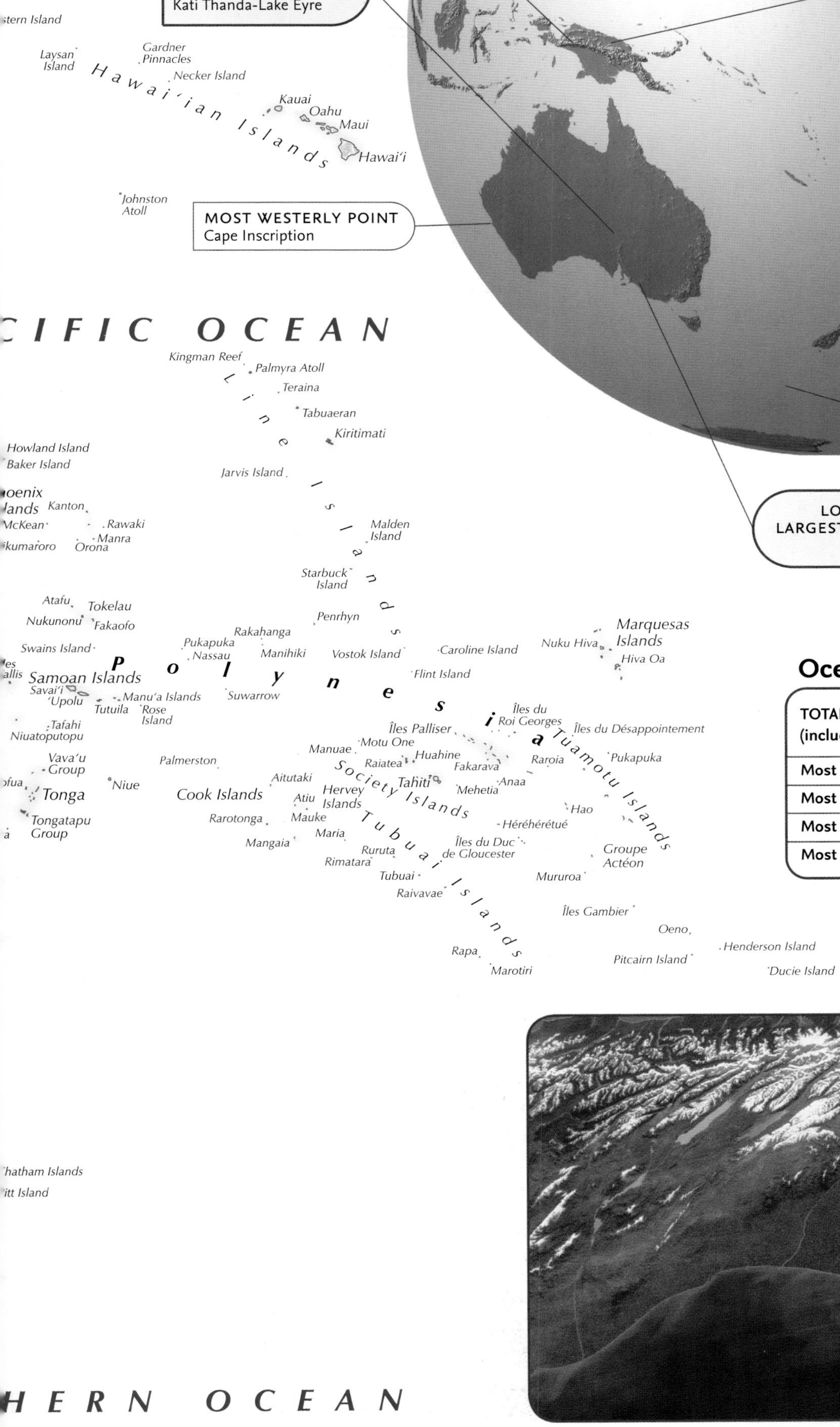

Laysan Island
Gardner Pinnacles
Necker Island
Hawai'ian Islands
Kauai
Oahu
Maui
Hawai'i
Johnston Atoll

CIFIC OCEAN

Kingman Reef
Palmyra Atoll
Teraina
Tabuaeran
Kiritimati
Line Islands
Howland Island
Baker Island
Jarvis Island
oenix
lands
Kanton
McKean
Rawaki
Manra
kumaroro
Orona
Malden Island
Starbuck Island
Penrhyn
Atafu
Tokelau
Nukunonu
Fakaofo
Swains Island
Rakahanga
Pukapuka
Nassau
Manihiki
Vostok Island
Caroline Island
Nuku Hiva
Marquesas Islands
Hiva Oa
Flint Island
Polynesia
Samoan Islands
Savai'i
'Upolu
Tutuila
Manu'a Islands
Rose Island
Suwarrow
Tafahi
Niuatoputapu
Vava'u Group
Tonga
Tongatapu Group
Niue
Palmerston
Cook Islands
Aitutaki
Atiu
Rarotonga
Mauke
Mangaia
Manuae
Motu One
Hervey Islands
Society Islands
Raiatea
Huahine
Tahiti
Mehetia
Îles Palliser
Fakarava
Anaa
Îles du Roi Georges
Îles du Désappointement
Tuamotu Islands
Raroia
Pukapuka
Hao
Hérêhérêtué
Maria
Tubuai Islands
Rurutu
Rimatara
Tubuai
Raivavae
Îles du Duc de Gloucester
Groupe Actéon
Mururoa
Îles Gambier
Oeno
Henderson Island
Pitcairn Island
Ducie Island
Rapa
Marotiri
hatham Islands
itt Island

HERN OCEAN

Oceania's extent

TOTAL LAND AREA (includes New Guinea and Pacific Island nations)	8 844 516 sq km / 3 414 868 sq miles
Most northerly point	Eastern Island, North Pacific Ocean
Most southerly point	Macquarie Island, South Pacific Ocean
Most westerly point	Cape Inscription, Australia
Most easterly point	Isla Sala y Gómez, South Pacific Ocean

Banks Peninsula, Canterbury Plains and the **Southern Alps**, South Island, New Zealand.

Oceania
Countries

Stretching across almost the whole width of the Pacific Ocean, Oceania has a great variety of cultures and an enormously diverse range of countries and territories. Australia, by far the largest and most industrialized country in the continent, contrasts with the numerous tiny Pacific island nations which have smaller, and more fragile economies based largely on agriculture, fishing and the exploitation of natural resources.

The division of the Pacific island groups into the main regions of Micronesia, Melanesia and Polynesia – often referred to as the South Sea islands – broadly reflects the ethnological differences across the continent. There is a long history of colonial influence in the region, which still contains dependent territories belonging to Australia, France, New Zealand, the UK and the USA.

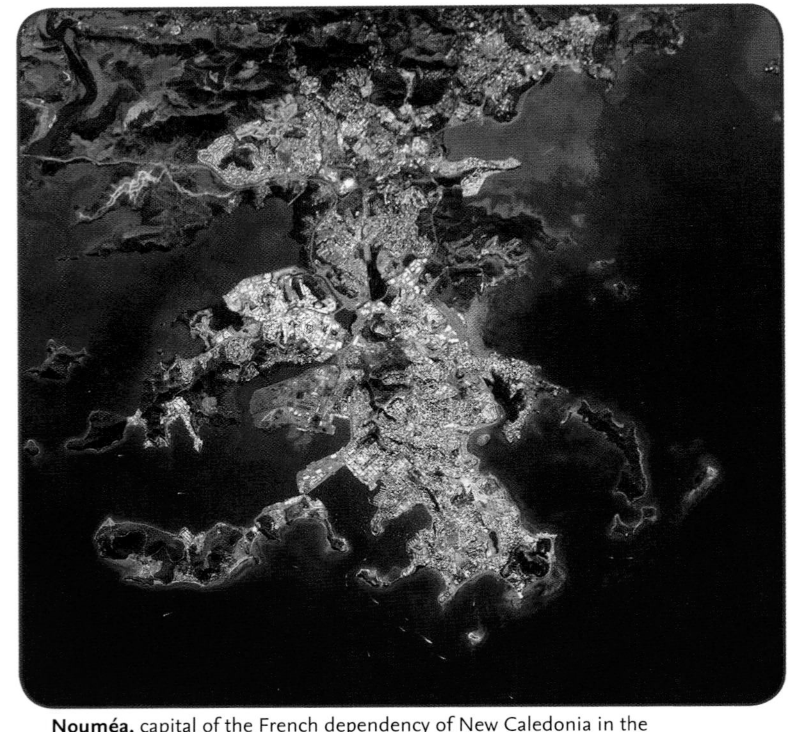

Nouméa, capital of the French dependency of New Caledonia in the southern Pacific Ocean.

Facts

- **Over 91% of Australia's population live in urban areas**
- **The Maori name for New Zealand is Aotearoa, meaning 'land of the long white cloud'**
- **Auckland, New Zealand, has the largest Polynesian population of any city in Oceania**
- **Over 800 different languages are spoken in Papua New Guinea**

ASIA
INDIAN OCEAN
P A C
S O U T H E R N
Wake Island (U.S.A.)
Pagan
Northern Mariana Islands (U.S.A.)
Saipan
Tinian
Rota
Guam (U.S.A.)
Taongi
MARSHALL ISLANDS
Enewetak
Bikini
Rongelap
Ratak Chain
Ralik Chain
Wotje
Kwajalein
Ailinglapalap
Delap-Uliga-Djarrit
Majuro
Yap
Gaferut
Pikelot
Hall Islands
Chuuk
Palikir
Pohnpei
Kosrae
Caroline Islands
Mortlock Islands
FEDERATED STATES OF MICRONESIA
Bairiki
Tarawa
Gilbert Islands
Kingsmill Group
Yaren
NAURU
Admiralty Islands
New Ireland
Rabaul
Vanimo
Wewak
Bismarck Sea
New Guinea
Mount Wilhelm 4509
Lae
New Britain
Bougainville I.
Solomon Sea
Balimo
Kerema
Gulf of Papua
Daru
Port Moresby
PAPUA NEW GUINEA
Torres Strait
Arafura Sea
SOLOMON ISLANDS
Malaita
Honiara
Guadalcanal
Santa Cruz Islands
Nanumea
Niutao
TUVALU
Vaitupu
Nukufetau
Vaiaku
Nukulaelae
Rotuma
Wallis and Futuna Is. (France)
VANUATU
Banks Islands
Espiritu Santo
Malakula
Éfaté
Port Vila
Tanna
Vanua Levu
FIJI
Viti Levu
Suva
New Caledonia (France)
Nouméa
Îles Loyauté
Coral Sea
Coral Sea Islands Territory (Australia)
Melville Island
Bathurst Island
Darwin
Timor Sea
Ashmore and Cartier Islands (Australia)
Gulf of Carpentaria
Cooktown
Cairns
Normanton
Townsville
Mackay
Wyndham
Cape Lévêque
Halls Creek
Broome
NORTHERN TERRITORY
Cloncurry
Longreach
Rockhampton
Maryborough
QUEENSLAND
Alice Springs
Charleville
Brisbane
Gold Coast
Port Hedland
Barrow Island
North West Cape
Newman
AUSTRALIA
Lake Eyre
Grafton
Tamworth
Darling
WESTERN AUSTRALIA
SOUTH AUSTRALIA
Meekatharra
Lake Torrens
Broken Hill
NEW SOUTH WALES
Orange
Newcastle
Sydney
JERVIS BAY TERR.
Canberra
A.C.T.
Port Augusta
Port Pirie
Adelaide
Murray
Albury
Kalgoorlie
Geraldton
Great Australian Bight
VICTORIA
Geelong
Melbourne
Perth
Fremantle
Esperance
Kangaroo Island
Mount Gambier
Bass Strait
Launceston
TASMANIA
Hobart
South East Cape
Cape Leeuwin
Albany
Norfolk Island (Australia)
Lord Howe Island (Australia)
Kermadec Islands (N.Z.)
Tasman Sea
North Cape
Whangarei
Auckland
Rotorua
North Island
NEW ZEALAND
Blenheim
Wellington
Greymouth
Christchurch
South Island
Invercargill
Dunedin
Stewart Island
Bounty Islands (N.Z.)
Antipodes Islands (N.Z.)
Auckland Islands (N.Z.)
Campbell Island (N.Z.)
Macquarie Island (Australia)

International boundaries in the sea shown on this map indicate ownership of islands and island groups only. They do not infer the alignment of legal maritime boundaries.

Internet Links

UK Foreign and Commonwealth Office	**www.fco.gov.uk**
CIA World Factbook	**www.cia.gov/library/publications/the-world-factbook/index.html**
Geoscience Australia	**www.ga.gov.au**

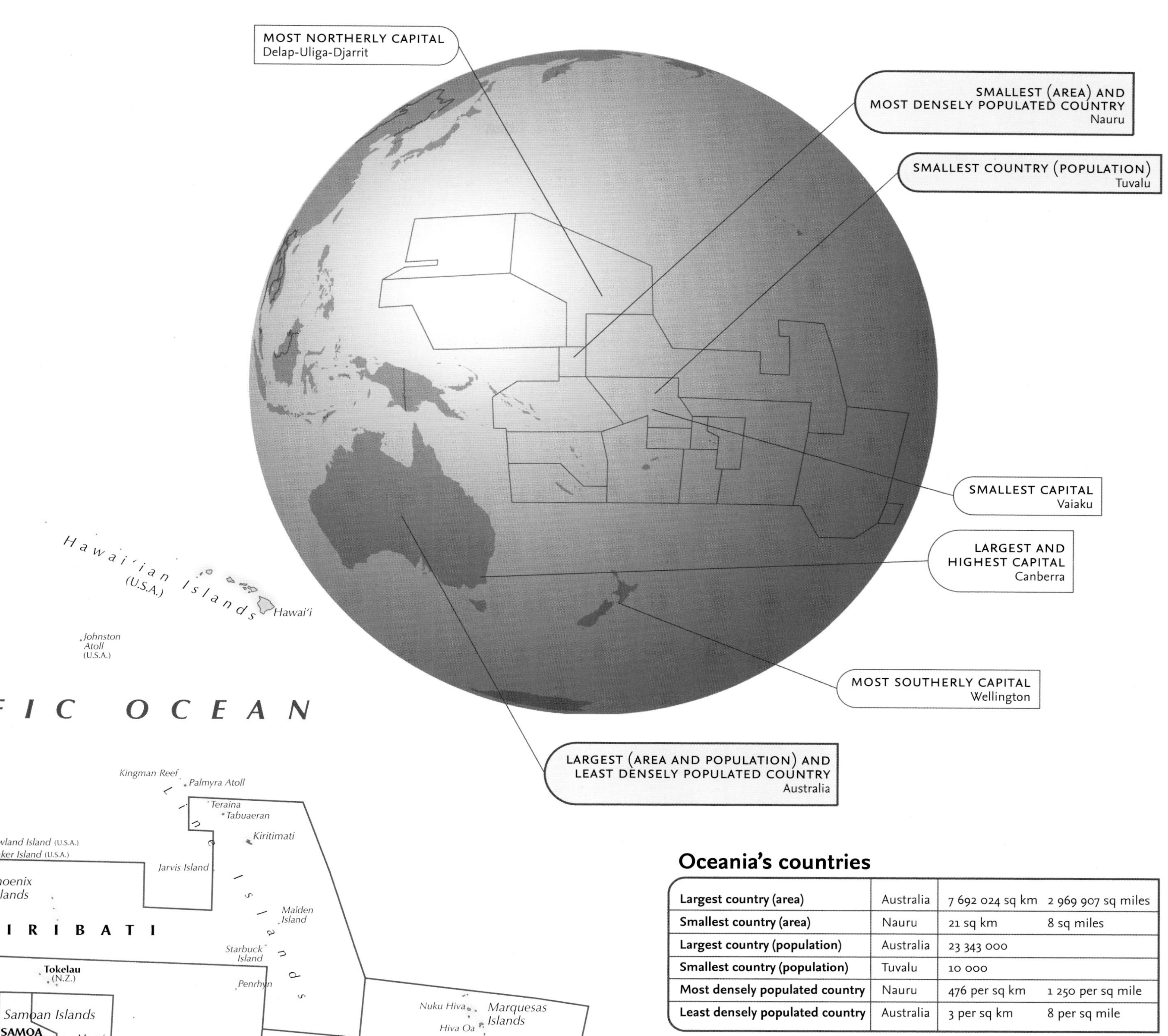

Oceania's countries

Largest country (area)	Australia	7 692 024 sq km	2 969 907 sq miles
Smallest country (area)	Nauru	21 sq km	8 sq miles
Largest country (population)	Australia	23 343 000	
Smallest country (population)	Tuvalu	10 000	
Most densely populated country	Nauru	476 per sq km	1 250 per sq mile
Least densely populated country	Australia	3 per sq km	8 per sq mile

Oceania's capitals

Largest capital (population)	Canberra, Australia	415 000	
Smallest capital (population)	Vaiaku, Tuvalu	516	
Most northerly capital	Delap-Uliga-Djarrit, Marshall Islands	7° 7'N	
Most southerly capital	Wellington, New Zealand	41° 18'S	
Highest capital	Canberra, Australia	581 metres	1 906 feet

Wellington, capital of New Zealand.

Lambert Azimuthal Equal Area Projection

1:17 300 000

0 200 400 600 miles

0 200 400 600 800 1000 km

Oceania

Australia, New Zealand and Southwest Pacific

Lambert Azimuthal Equal Area Projection

1:6 900 000 — 0 100 200 300 miles — 0 100 200 300 400 500 km

Oceania

Western Australia

PAPUA NEW GUINEA
Louisiade Archipelago
Coral Sea
Coral Sea Islands Territory (Australia)
Great Barrier Reef
Great Barrier Reef Marine Park (Far North Section)
Great Barrier Reef Marine Park (Cairns Section)
Great Barrier Reef Marine Park (Central Section)
Great Barrier Reef Marine Park (Capricorn Section)
Arafura Sea
Gulf of Carpentaria
Cape York Peninsula
Arnhem Land
Groote Eylandt
Mornington Island
Wellesley Islands
Great Dividing Range
Gregory Range
Barkly Tableland
QUEENSLAND
NORTHERN TERRITORY
Simpson Desert
Tropic of Capricorn
Cooktown
Cairns
Townsville
Mackay
Rockhampton
Gladstone
Bundaberg
Mount Isa
Cloncurry
Alice Springs
Tennant Creek
↑ 132
← 134
Lambert Azimuthal Equal Area Projection
1:6 900 000
0 100 200 300 miles
0 100 200 300 400 500 km

AUSTRALIA
SOUTH AUSTRALIA
NEW SOUTH WALES
VICTORIA
TASMANIA
AUSTRALIAN CAPITAL TERRITORY
JERVIS BAY TERRITORY
Tasman Sea
Bass Strait
Spencer Gulf
Gulf St Vincent
Kangaroo Island
Eyre Peninsula
Yorke Peninsula
Kati Thanda-Lake Eyre (North)
Lake Torrens
Lake Gairdner
Flinders Ranges
Gawler Ranges
Grey Range
Darling Downs
Sturt Stony Desert
Strzelecki Desert
Brisbane
Gold Coast
Sydney
Newcastle
Wollongong
Canberra
Melbourne
Geelong
Adelaide
Hobart
Launceston
↓ 135

Oceania
Southeast Australia

1:4 300 000

0 50 100 150 miles

0 50 100 150 200 250 km

Tasman Sea

NEW ZEALAND

North Island (Te Ika-a-Māui)

South Island (Te Waipounamu)

PACIFIC OCEAN

Three Kings Islands
Cape Maria van Diemen
North Cape
Te Paki
Ninety Mile Beach
Cape Karikari
Doubtless Bay
Ahipara Bay
Tauroa Point
Awanui
Kaitaia
Kerikeri
Broadwood
Bay of Islands
Russell
Cape Brett
Rawene
Kawakawa
Poor Knights Islands
Donnellys Crossing
Dargaville
Whangarei
Mokohinau Islands
Bream Bay
Maungaturoto
Little Barrier Island
Port Fitzroy
Great Barrier Island
North Head
Kaipara Harbour
Wellsford
Leigh
Kawau Island
Colville Channel
Hauraki Gulf
Orewa
East Coast Bays
Takapuna
Waiheke Island
Colville
Mercury Islands
Auckland
Manukau
Manukau Harbour
Whitianga
Coromandel Range
Coromandel Peninsula
The Aldermen Islands
Papakura
Pukekohe
Waiuku
Thames
Port Waikato
Waikato
Waihi
Whangamata
Mayor Island
Huntly
Matakana Island
Whakaari
1075
Cape Runaway
North Island
Hamilton
Tauranga
Motiti Island
Bay of Plenty
Hicks Bay
Te Araroa
Cambridge
Te Awamutu
Kawhia Harbour
Kawhia
Whakatane
East Cape
Otorohanga
Lake Rotorua
Kawerau
Te Teko
Opotiki
Raukumara Range
Hikurangi
1752
Ruatoria
Te Kuiti
Rotorua
Tokoroa
Piopio
Mangakino
Mount Tarawera
1111
Lake Okataina
Murupara
Te Urewera National Park
Matawai
Tokomaru Bay
Awakino
Mokau
North Taranaki Bight
Okahukura
Ohura
Waitahanui
Taupo
Huiarau Range
Tolaga Bay
New Plymouth
Taumarunui
Lake Taupo
Kaimanawa Mountains
Gisborne
Mount Taranaki (Mount Egmont)
2518
Tongariro National Park
Mount Ruapehu
2797
Whanganui National Park
Egmont National Park
Cape Egmont
Opunake
Hawera
Raetihi
Ohakune
Waiouru
Tarawera
Mohaka
Wairoa
Nuhaka
Poverty Bay
Table Cape
Mahia Peninsula
Hawke Bay
Bay View
Napier
South Taranaki Bight
Patea
Taihape
Ruahine Range
Hastings
Cape Kidnappers
Havelock North
Waimarama
Wanganui
Turakina
Marton
Rangitikei
Tikokino
Waipawa
Waipukurau
Feilding
Dannevirke
Palmerston North
Porangahau
Cape Farewell
Farewell Spit
Collingwood
Golden Bay
Kahurangi Point
Cape Stephens
Cook Strait
D'Urville Island
French Pass
Abel Tasman National Park
Tasman Bay
Tasman Mountains
Kahurangi National Park
Kapiti Island
Levin
Otaki
Tararua Range
Eketahuna
Pongaroa
Cape Turnagain
Mount Hector
1571
Masterton
Castlepoint
Karamea
Karamea Bight
Riwaka
Motueka
Richmond
Nelson
Havelock
Picton
Paraparaumu
Upper Hutt
Porirua
Featherston
Lower Hutt
Lake Wairarapa
Martinborough
WELLINGTON
Palliser Bay
Mount Ross
981
Cape Palliser
Seddonville
Hope Saddle
Wakefield
Wairau
Blenheim
Waimangaroa
Owen River
Buller
Westport
Charleston
Seddon
Cape Campbell
Mount Travers
2338
Saint Arnaud Range
2120
Awatere
Tapuae-o-Uenuku
Paparoa National Park
Reefton
Victoria Range
Nelson Lakes Nat. Park
Inland Kaikoura Range
Manakau
2608
Clarence
Greymouth
Ahaura
Springs Junction
Lewis Pass
Kaikoura
Hokitika
Lake Brunner
Rotomanu
Hope
Oaro
Ross
Otira
Arthur's Pass National Park
Lake Sumner
Culverden
Parnassus
Cheviot
Southern Alps
Abut Head
Harihari
Waikari
Westland Tai Poutini National Park
Franz Josef Glacier
Puketeraki Range
Waipara
Fox Glacier
Mount Arrowsmith
2781
Oxford
Pegasus Bay
Aoraki/Mount Cook
3724
Rangiora
Kaiapoi
Lake Paringa
Sheffield
Christchurch
Canterbury Plains
Aoraki/Mount Cook National Park
Aylesbury
Sumner
Jackson Head
Te Pirita
Tai Tapu
Banks Peninsula
Mount Ward
2645
Rakaia
Akaroa
Cascade Point
Lake Tekapo
Tekapo
Mayfield
Lake Ellesmere
Ashburton
Longbeach
Canterbury Bight
Awarua Point
Mount Aspiring National Park
Lake Pukaki
Burkes Pass
Fairlie
Geraldine
Temuka
Mount Aspiring
3033
Twizel
Pleasant Point
Timaru
Milford Sound
Mount Alta
2339
Lake Benmore
Pareora
Lake Hawea
Otematata
The Hunters Hills
Milford Sound
Mount Christina
Lake Wanaka
Wanaka
Kurow
Studholme Junction
George Sound
Kinloch
Richardson Mts
Dunstan Mts
Hawkdun Range
Waitaki
Waimate
1969
Queenstown
Duntroon
Fiordland
Lake Wakatipu
James Peak
2072
Ranfurly
Oamaru
Pukeuri Junction
Cape Wanbrow
Secretary Island
Doubtful Sound
Lake Te Anau
Alexandra
Hyde
Te Anau
Eyre Mountains
1695
Breaksea Sound
Lake Manapouri
Athol
Lammerlaw Range
Middlemarch
Moeraki Point
Shag Point
Palmerston
Resolution Island
National Park
Mossburn
Roxburgh
Waikouaiti
Kaherekoau Mts
Lumsden
Beaumont
Warrington
Port Chalmers
Otago Peninsula
Caroline Peak
1704
Ohai
Mandeville
Waitahuna
Mosgiel
Dunedin
Cape Providence
Winton
Gore
Waipahi
Milton
Henley
Puysegur Point
Te Waewae Bay
Orepuki
Edendale
Mataura
Clinton
Balclutha
Riverton
Mount Pye
720
Kaitangata
Invercargill
Nugget Point
Solander Island
Foveaux Strait
Fortrose
Bluff
Long Point
Ruapuke Island
Chaslands Mistake
Codfish Island
Mason Bay
Rakiura National Park
Halfmoon Bay
Shelter Point
Titi Islands (Muttonbird Islands)
Stewart Island
South West Cape
North Trap

Conic Equidistant Projection

1:4 500 000

0 50 100 150 miles

0 50 100 150 200 250 km

Oceania

New Zealand

North America
UNESCO World Heritage Sites

The New World has relatively few sites compared to Europe or Asia. However the sites represent significant stages in Earth's formation and human history. Ancient geological processes are preserved in Gros Morne National Park in Canada, early civilizations are represented in Central America and evidence of the slave trade and plantations is found in the islands of the Caribbean.

● Cultural site ● Natural site ● Mixed site

Barbados
1. Historic Bridgetown and its Garrison

Belize
2. Belize Barrier Reef Reserve System

Bermuda
3. Historic Town of St George and Related Fortifications (UK)

Canada
4. Canadian Rocky Mountain Parks
5. Dinosaur Provincial Park
6. Gros Morne National Park
7. Head-Smashed-In Buffalo Jump
8. Historic District of Old Québec
9. Joggins Fossil Cliffs
10. Kluane/Wrangell-St Elias/Glacier Bay/ Tatshenshini-Alsek
11. L'Anse aux Meadows National Historic Site
12. Miguasha National Park
13. Nahanni National Park
14. Old Town Lunenburg
15. Red Bay basque Whaling Station
16. Rideau Canal
17. SGang Gwaay
18. The Landscape of Grand-Pré
19. Waterton Glacier International Peace Park
20. Wood Buffalo National Park

Costa Rica
21. Area de Conservación Guanacaste
22. Cocos Island National Park
23. Precolumbian Chiefdom Settlements with Stone Spheres of the Diquís
24. Talamanca Range-La Amistad Reserves/ La Amistad National Park

Cuba
25. Alejandro de Humboldt National Park
26. Archaeological Landscape of the First Coffee Plantations in the South-East of Cuba
27. Desembarco del Granma National Park
28. Historic Centre of Camagüey
29. Old Havana and its Fortification System
30. San Pedro de la Roca Castle, Santiago de Cuba
31. Trinidad and the Valley de los Ingenios
32. Urban Historic Centre of Cienfuegos
33. Viñales Valley

Dominica
34. Morne Trois Pitons National Park

Dominican Republic
35. Colonial City of Santo Domingo

El Salvador
36. Joya de Cerén Archaeological Site

Greenland
37. Ilulissat Icefjord (Denmark)

Guatemala
38. Antigua Guatemala
39. Archaeological Park and Ruins of Quirigua
40. Tikal National Park

Honduras
41. Maya Site of Copán
42. Río Plátano Biosphere Reserve

Haiti
43. National History Park – Citadel, Sans Souci, Ramiers

Mexico
44. Agave Landscape and Ancient Industrial Facilities of Tequila
45. Ancient Maya City and Protected Tropical Forests of Calakmul, Campeche
46. Archaeological Monuments Zone of Xochicalco
47. Archeological Zone of Paquimé, Casas Grandes
48. Camino Real de Tierra Adentro
49. Central University City Campus of the Universidad Nacional Autónoma de México (UNAM)
50. Earliest 16th-Century Monasteries on the Slopes of Popocatepetl
51. El Pinacate and Gran Desierto de Altar Biosphere Reserve
52. El Tajin, Pre-Hispanic City
53. Franciscan Missions in the Sierra Gorda of Querétaro
54. Historic Centre of Mexico City and Xochimilco
55. Historic Centre of Morelia
56. Historic Centre of Oaxaca and Archaeological Site of Monte Albán
57. Historic Centre of Puebla
58. Historic Centre of Zacatecas
59. Historic Fortified Town of Campeche
60. Historic Monuments Zone of Querétaro
61. Historic Monuments Zone of Tlacotalpan
62. Historic Town of Guanajuato and Adjacent Mines
63. Hospicio Cabañas, Guadalajara
64. Islands and Protected Areas of the Gulf of California
65. Luis Barragán House and Studio
66. Monarch Butterfly Biosphere Reserve
67. Pre-Hispanic City and National Park of Palenque
68. Pre-Hispanic City of Chichen-Itza
69. Pre-Hispanic City of Teotihuacan
70. Pre-Hispanic Town of Uxmal
71. Prehistoric Caves of Yagul and Mitla in the Central Valley of Oaxaca
72. Protective town of San Miguel and the Sanctuary of Jesús Nazareno de Atotonilco
73. Rock Paintings of the Sierra de San Francisco
74. Sian Ka'an
75. Whale Sanctuary of El Vizcaino

Nicaragua
76. Léon Cathedral
77. Ruins of León Viejo

Panama
78. Archaeological Site of Panamá Viejo and Historic District of Panamá
79. Coiba National Park and its Special Zone of Marine Protection
80. Darien National Park
81. Fortifications on the Caribbean Side of Panama: Portobelo-San Lorenzo
24. Talamanca Range-La Amistad Reserves/La Amistad National Park

Saint Kitts and Nevis
82. Brimstone Hill Fortress National Park

Saint Lucia
83. Pitons Management Area

United States of America
84. Cahokia Mounds State Historic Site
85. Carlsbad Caverns National Park
86. Chaco Culture
87. Everglades National Park
88. Grand Canyon National Park
89. Great Smoky Mountains National Park
90. Hawaii Volcanoes National Park
91. Independence Hall
92. La Fortaleza and San Juan National Historic Site in Puerto Rico
10. Kluane/Wrangell-St Elias/Glacier Bay/ Tatshenshini-Alsek
93. Mammoth Cave National Park
94. Mesa Verde National Park
95. Monticello and the University of Virginia in Charlottesville
96. Monumental Earthworks of Poverty Point
97. Olympic National Park
98. Papahānaumokuākea
99. Redwood National Park
100. Statue of Liberty
101. Taos Pueblo
19. Waterton Glacier International Peace Park
102. Yellowstone National Park
103. Yosemite National Park

Greenland
(Denmark)
37
U.S.A.
10
10
10
10
13
20
C A N A D A
15
11
6
17
4
4
4
4
5
12
9
18
8
14
97
7
19
16
ATLANTIC
OCEAN
102
100
99
91
UNITED STATES
OF AMERICA
103
95
84
93
3
Bermuda
(U.K.)
94
88
86
101
89
96
85
51
64
48
64
47
73
64
75
48
75
64
THE BAHAMAS
Gulf
of Mexico
87
48
72
58
64
Hawaii
(U.S.A.)
98
90
44
62
60
53
48
49, 65
52
63
69
55
66
50
54
57
61
46
56
MEXICO
71
29
32
28
33
CUBA
31
26
25
30
27
JAMAICA
43
HAITI
DOMINICAN
REP.
35
92
Puerto
Rico
(U.S.A.)
82
ANTIGUA & BARBUDA
ST KITTS & NEVIS
34
DOMINICA
ST LUCIA
83
1
BARBADOS
ST VINCENT &
THE GRENADINES
GRENADA
TRINIDAD
& TOBAGO
Caribbean Sea
68
59
70
74
67
45
40
BELIZE
2
42
39
HONDURAS
38
41
36
GUATEMALA
EL SALVADOR
77
NICARAGUA
76
21
24
81
78
80
COSTA
RICA
24
23
PANAMA
79
SOUTH
AMERICA
PACIFIC
OCEAN
22
Isla de Coco
(Costa Rica)

North America

Landscapes

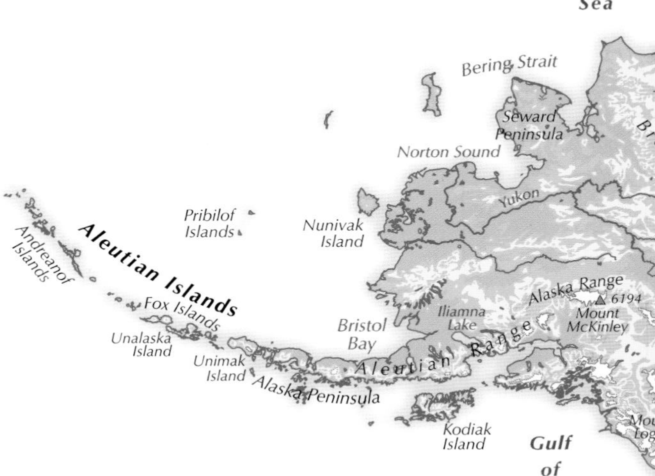

Internet Links	
NASA Visible Earth	visibleearth.nasa.gov
U.S. Geological Survey	www.usgs.gov
Natural Resources Canada	www.nrcan.gc.ca/home
Satellite imagery	www.geo-airbusds.com

North America, the world's third largest continent, supports a wide range of landscapes from the Arctic north to sub-tropical Central America. The main physiographic regions of the continent are the mountains of the west coast, stretching from Alaska in the north to Mexico and Central America in the south; the vast, relatively flat Canadian Shield; the Great Plains which make up the majority of the interior; the Appalachian Mountains in the east; and the Atlantic coastal plain.

These regions contain some significant physical features, including the Rocky Mountains, the Great Lakes – three of which are amongst the five largest lakes in the world – and the Mississippi-Missouri river system which is the world's fourth longest river. The Caribbean Sea contains a complex pattern of islands, many volcanic in origin, and the continent is joined to South America by the narrow Isthmus of Panama.

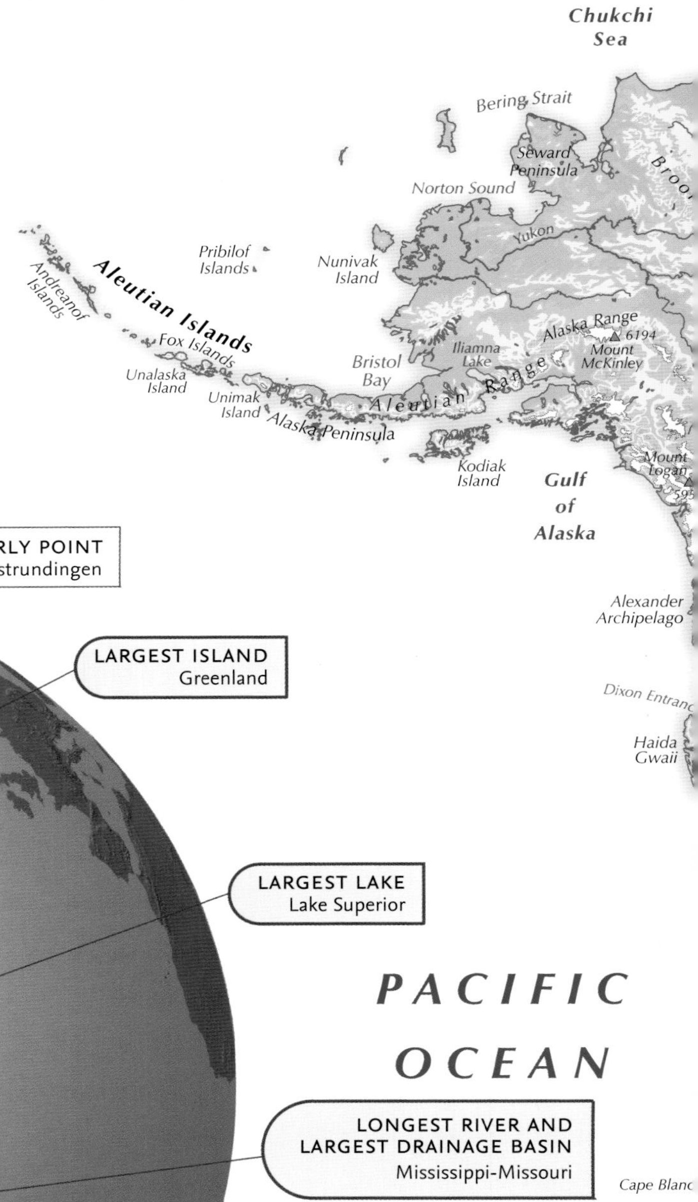

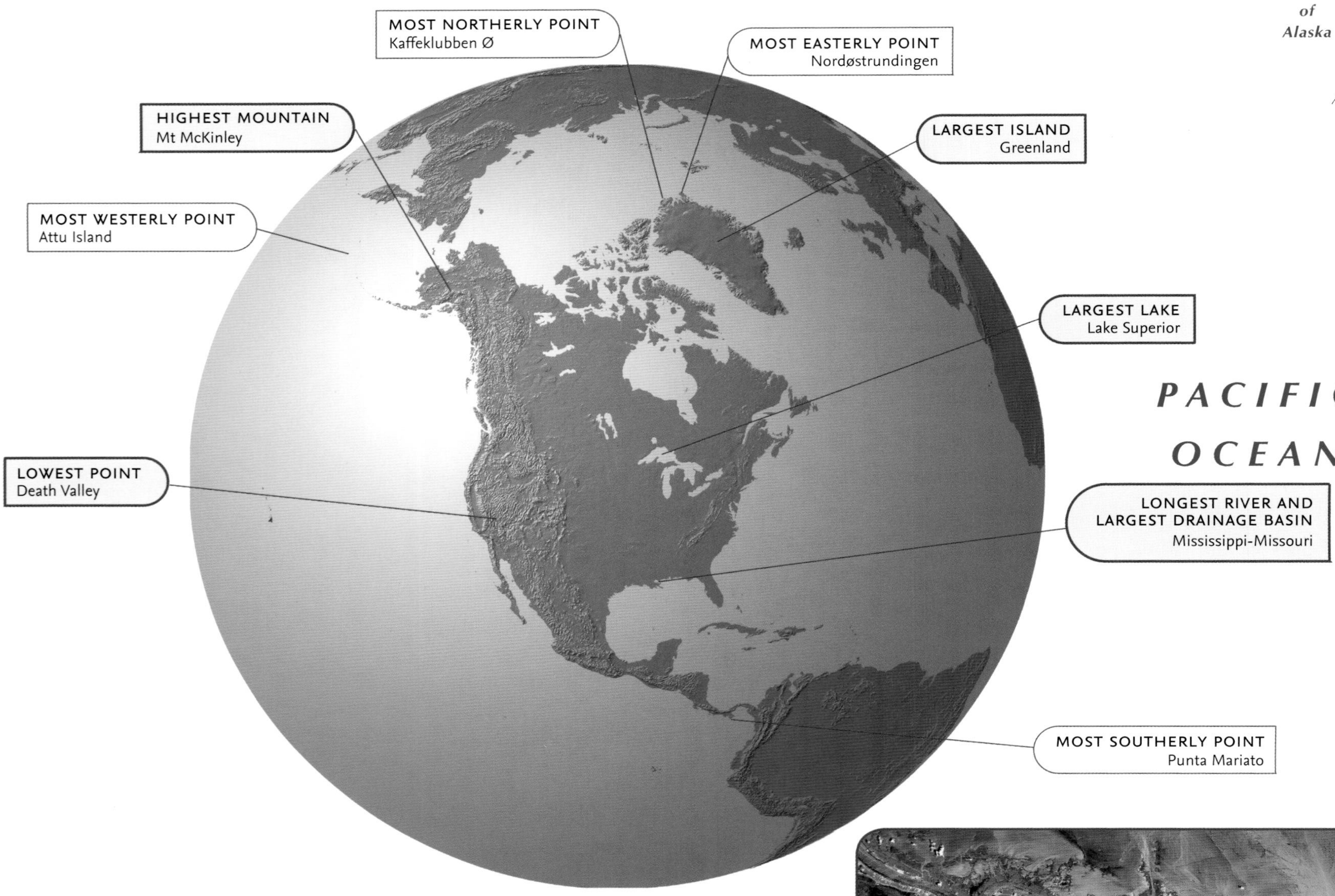

Alexander Archipelago

Dixon Entrance

Haida Gwaii

PACIFIC OCEAN

Cape Blanco

MOST NORTHERLY POINT
Kaffeklubben Ø

MOST EASTERLY POINT
Nordøstrundingen

HIGHEST MOUNTAIN
Mt McKinley

LARGEST ISLAND
Greenland

MOST WESTERLY POINT
Attu Island

LARGEST LAKE
Lake Superior

LOWEST POINT
Death Valley

LONGEST RIVER AND LARGEST DRAINAGE BASIN
Mississippi-Missouri

MOST SOUTHERLY POINT
Punta Mariato

North America's physical features

Highest mountain	Mt McKinley, USA	6 194 metres	20 321 feet
Longest river	Mississippi-Missouri, USA	5 969 km	3 709 miles
Largest lake	Lake Superior, Canada/USA	82 100 sq km	31 699 sq miles
Largest island	Greenland	2 175 600 sq km	839 999 sq miles
Largest drainage basin	Mississippi-Missouri, USA	3 250 000 sq km	1 254 825 sq miles
Lowest point	Death Valley, USA	-86 metres	-282 feet

North America's longest river system, the **Mississippi-Missouri,** flows into the Gulf of Mexico through the Mississippi Delta.

North America's extent

TOTAL LAND AREA (including Hawai'ian Islands)	24 680 331 sq km / 9 529 076 sq miles
Most northerly point	Kaffeklubben Ø, Greenland
Most southerly point	Punta Mariato, Panama
Most westerly point	Attu Island, USA
Most easterly point	Nordøstrundingen, Greenland

The **Panama Canal,** Panama, linking the Pacific Ocean to the Atlantic Ocean.

Facts

- The Panama Canal, opened in 1914, cut the journey between the Atlantic and the Pacific by over 14 000 km
- Mexico City is the highest city in North America and houses approximately 18% of Mexico's population
- The state of Alaska was bought by the USA from Russia in 1867
- The territory of Nunavut is Canada's newest administrative division, created in 1999 from the eastern part of Northwest Territories

North America

Countries

North America has been dominated economically and politically by the USA since the nineteenth century. Before that, the continent was subject to colonial influences, particularly of Spain in the south and of Britain and France in the east. The nineteenth century saw the steady development of the western half of the continent. The wealth of natural resources and the generally temperate climate were an excellent basis for settlement, agriculture and industrial development which has led to the USA being the richest nation in the world today.

Canada, Mexico and the USA have approximately eighty-five per cent of the continent's population and eighty-eight per cent of its land area. Large parts of the north remain sparsely populated, while the most densely populated areas are in the northeast USA, and the Caribbean.

North America's capitals

Largest capital (population)	Mexico City, Mexico	21 706 000	
Smallest capital (population)	Roseau, Dominica	15 000	
Most northerly capital	Ottawa, Canada	45° 25'N	
Most southerly capital	Panama City, Panama	8° 56'N	
Highest capital	Mexico City, Mexico	2 300 metres	7 546 feet

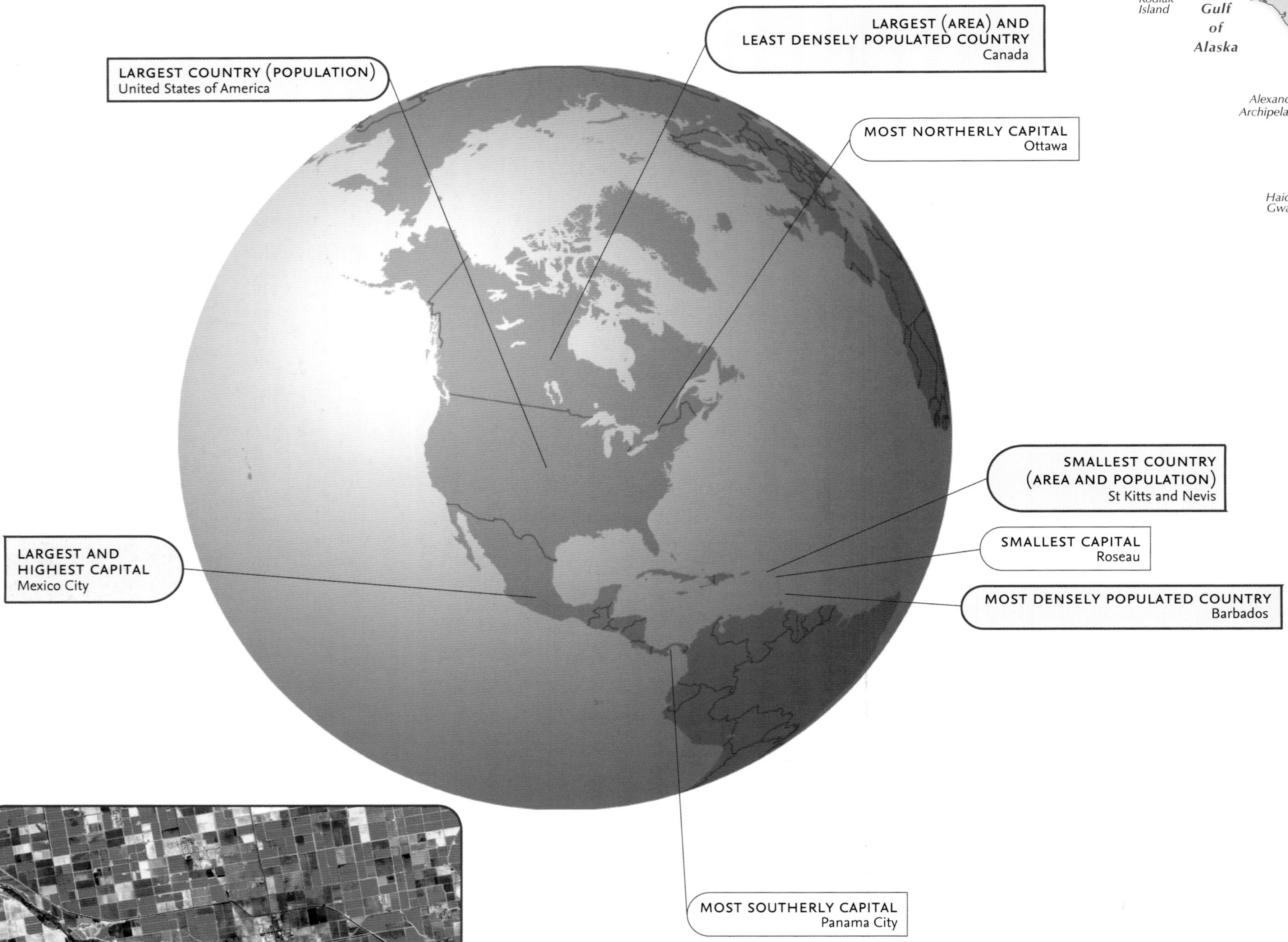

LARGEST COUNTRY (POPULATION)
United States of America

LARGEST (AREA) AND LEAST DENSELY POPULATED COUNTRY
Canada

MOST NORTHERLY CAPITAL
Ottawa

SMALLEST COUNTRY (AREA AND POPULATION)
St Kitts and Nevis

LARGEST AND HIGHEST CAPITAL
Mexico City

SMALLEST CAPITAL
Roseau

MOST DENSELY POPULATED COUNTRY
Barbados

MOST SOUTHERLY CAPITAL
Panama City

False-colour satellite image of the **Mexico-USA** boundary at Mexicali.

North America's countries

Largest country (area)	Canada	9 984 670 sq km	3 855 103 sq miles
Smallest country (area)	St Kitts and Nevis	261 sq km	101 sq miles
Largest country (population)	United States of America	320 051 000	
Smallest country (population)	St Kitts and Nevis	54 000	
Most densely populated country	Barbados	663 per sq km	1 717 per sq mile
Least densely populated country	Canada	4 per sq km	9 per sq mile

Internet Links

UK Foreign and Commonwealth Office	www.fco.gov.uk
CIA World Factbook	www.cia.gov/library/publications/the-world-factbook/index.html
U.S. Board on Geographic Names	geonames.usgs.gov
NASA Astronaut Photography	eol.jsc.nasa.gov

The Bahamas, a chain of islands in the North Atlantic Ocean, lying southeast of Florida, USA.

Facts

- The Panama Canal, opened in 1914, cut the journey between the Atlantic and the Pacific by over 14 000 km
- Mexico City is the highest city in North America and houses approximately 18% of Mexico's population
- The state of Alaska was bought by the USA from Russia in 1867
- The territory of Nunavut is Canada's newest administrative division, created in 1999 from the eastern part of Northwest Territories

Lambert Conformal Conic Projection

1:13 800 000

0 200 400 miles

0 200 400 600 800 km

North America

Canada

States in the U.S.A. numbered on the map:

1. CONNECTICUT (K5)
2. MASSACHUSETTS (K5)
3. NEW HAMPSHIRE (K5)
4. RHODE ISLAND (K5)
5. VERMONT (K5)

↓ 155

1:6 100 000 — 0, 100, 200 miles; 0, 100, 200, 300, 400 km

Beaufort Sea
Gulf of Alaska
Alexander Archipelago
ALEUTIAN ISLANDS
Alaska Maritime National Wildlife Refuge
Rat Islands
Andreanof Islands
CANADA
YUKON
NORTHWEST TERRITORIES
INUVIALUIT
NUNAVUT
BRITISH COLUMBIA
Brooks Range
Mackenzie Mountains
Selwyn Mountains
Ogilvie Mountains
Wernecke Mountains
Pelly Mountains
Cassiar Mountains
Chugach Mountains
Wrangell Mountains
St Elias Mountains
Skeena Mountains
Arctic National Wildlife Refuge
Vuntut National Park
Ivvavik National Park
Kluane National Park
Wrangell-St Elias National Park and Preserve
Glacier Bay National Park and Preserve
Tuktut Nogait National Park
Nahanni National Park Reserve
Klondike Gold Rush National Historical Park
Fairbanks
Anchorage
Whitehorse
Dawson
Inuvik
Juneau
Kenai Peninsula
Chichagof Island
Baranof Island
Prince of Wales Island
Graham Island
Haida Gwaii (Queen Charlotte Islands)
Dixon Entrance
Hecate Strait
Arctic Circle
Great Bear Lake
Mount Logan 5959
Mount St Elias 5489
Mount Vancouver 4785
Mount Cook
Mount Fairweather 4670
Mount Hubbard
Mount Wrangell 4317
Mount Sanford 4949
Mount Blackburn 4996
Mount Bona 5005
Alaska Highway
Dalton Highway
Dempster Highway
Klondike Highway
Liard Highway
Stikine Plateau
Liard Plateau
→ 150
↓ 150

1:6 100 000

0 100 200 miles

0 100 200 300 400 km

NUNAVUT
RITORIES
Hudson Bay
MANITOBA
SASKATCHEWAN
ONTARIO
ADA
U. MONTANA S. A.
NORTH DAKOTA
MINNESOTA
Southampton Island
Coats Island
Lake Winnipeg
Lake Athabasca
Lake Manitoba
Winnipeg
Regina
Saskatoon
Churchill
Wapusk National Park
Riding Mountain National Park
Prince Albert Nat. Park
Grasslands National Park
Voyageurs National Park
↑ 146
↑ 152
↓ 160

↑ 147
← 151
↓ 162
Hudson Bay
James Bay
CANADA
MANITOBA
ONTARIO
NUNAVUT
MINNESOTA
WISCONSIN
MICHIGAN
IOWA
ILLINOIS
NEW YORK
UNITED STATES OF AMERICA
Lake Superior
Lake Michigan
Lake Huron
Lake Ontario
Lake Erie
Georgian Bay
Belcher Islands
Akimiski Island
Wapusk National Park
Isle Royale National Park
Pukaskwa National Park
Voyageurs National Park
Lake Superior National Marine Conservation Area
Lake Nipigon
Lake Abitibi
Lake Nipissing
Manitoulin Island
Algonquin Park
Haliburton Highlands
Kawartha Highlands Signature Site
Adirondack Mts
Sawtooth Mountains
Gogebic Range
Mesabi Range
Churchill
Cape Churchill
Thompson
Gillam
Fort Severn
Peawanuck
Attawapiskat
Fort Albany
Moosonee
Moose Factory
Kuujjuarapik
Chisasibi
Radisson
Eastmain
Waskaganish (Fort Rupert)
Chibougamau
Thunder Bay
Duluth
Sault Sainte Marie
Marquette
Timmins
Sudbury
North Bay
Kirkland Lake
Rouyn-Noranda
Val-d'Or
OTTAWA
Montréal
Kingston
Toronto
Hamilton
Mississauga
Kitchener
London
Windsor
Detroit
Buffalo
Rochester
Syracuse
Albany
Chicago
Milwaukee
Madison
Minneapolis
St Paul
Green Bay
Grand Rapids
Lansing
Flint
Saginaw
Cedar Rapids
Davenport
Conic Equidistant Projection
1:6 100 000
0 100 200 miles
0 100 200 300 400 km

North America
Eastern Canada

↑ 146

↓ 168

1:10 400 000

0 100 200 300 400 miles

0 100 200 300 400 500 600 700 km

North America

United States of America

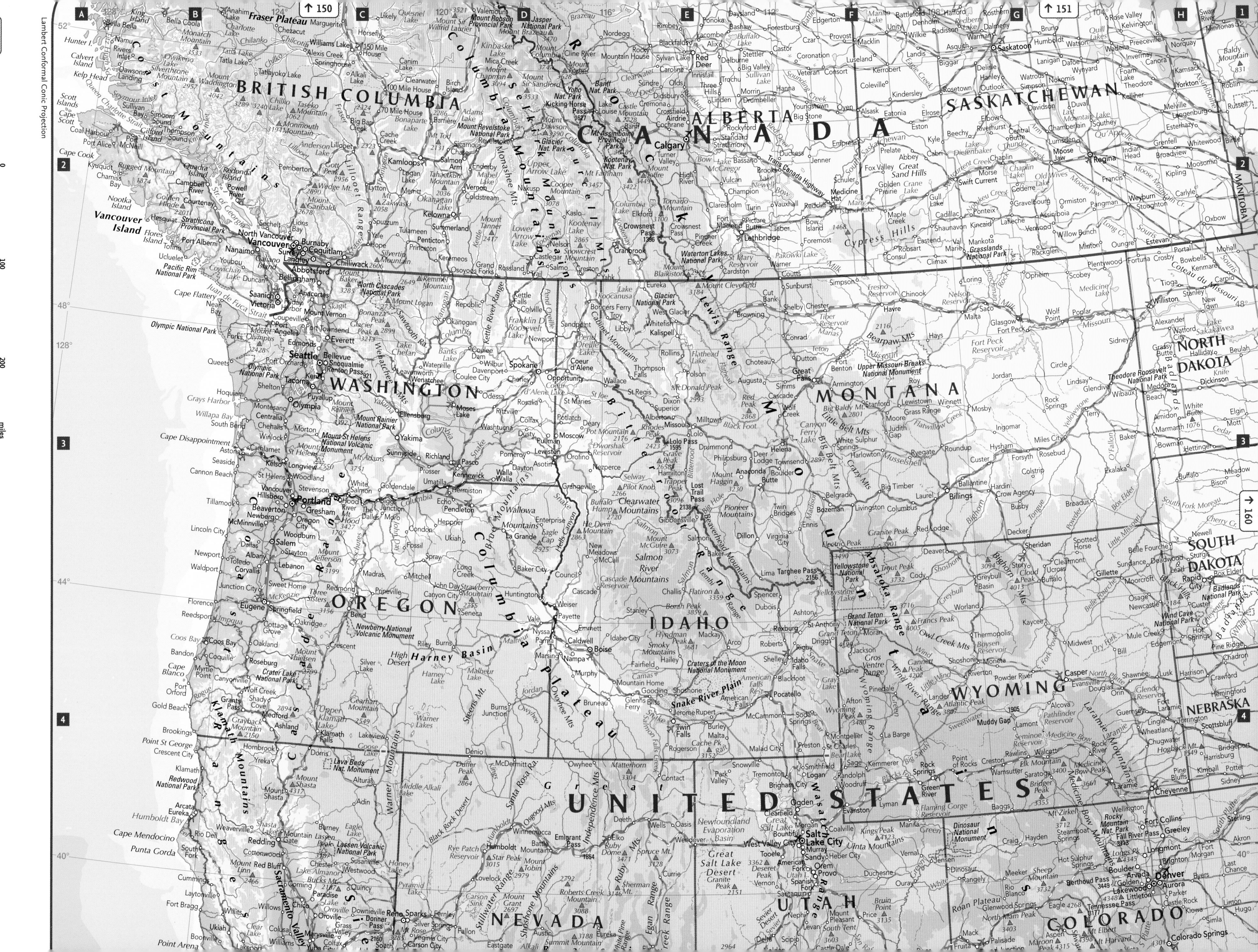

↑ 150

↑ 151

↑ 160

Lambert Conformal Conic Projection

1:6 100 000

0 100 200 miles

0 100 200 300 400 km

↑ 161

↓ 166

North America
Western United States

↑ 156

Lambert Conformal Conic Projection

1:3 000 000

0 50 100 miles

0 50 100 150 200 km

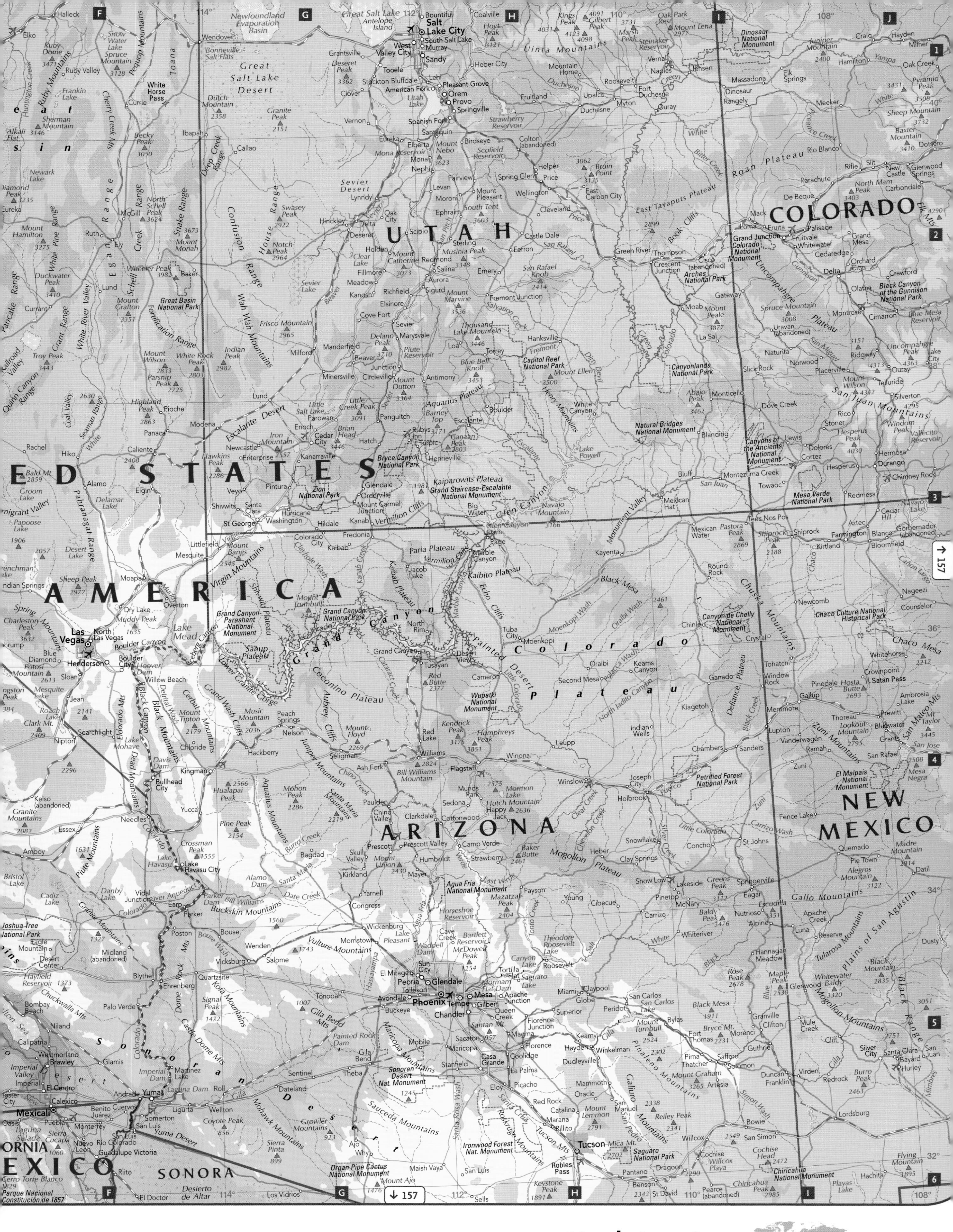

UTAH
COLORADO
ARIZONA
NEW MEXICO
UNITED STATES OF AMERICA
SONORA
Great Salt Lake Desert
Sevier Desert
Escalante Desert
Colorado Plateau
Grand Canyon
Kaibab Plateau
Coconino Plateau
Mogollon Plateau
Painted Desert
Sonoran Desert
Salt Lake City
Provo
Grand Junction
Las Vegas
Flagstaff
Phoenix
Tucson
Yuma
Mexicali
Gallup
Durango
Grand Canyon National Park
Zion National Park
Bryce Canyon National Park
Capitol Reef National Park
Canyonlands National Park
Arches National Park
Mesa Verde National Park
Petrified Forest National Park
Great Basin National Park
Saguaro National Park
↑ 157
↓ 157

↑ 151
↑ 152
↑ 162
↓ 156

Lambert Conformal Conic Projection

1:6 100 000

0	100	200	miles
0	100	200	300	400 km

↑ 163
↓ 157
↓ 166
OF AMERICA
TENNESSEE
ALABAMA
MISSISSIPPI
FLORIDA
ARKANSAS
LOUISIANA
OKLAHOMA
TEXAS
NEW MEXICO
MEXICO
CHIHUAHUA
COAHUILA
NUEVO LEÓN
TAMAULIPAS
DURANGO
ZACATECAS
Gulf of Mexico
Nashville
Memphis
Birmingham
Montgomery
Jackson
Little Rock
Shreveport
Baton Rouge
New Orleans
Oklahoma City
Tulsa
Dallas
Fort Worth
Houston
Austin
San Antonio
Corpus Christi
Laredo
Nuevo Laredo
Monterrey
Saltillo
Torreón
Chihuahua
El Paso
Ciudad Juárez
Albuquerque
Amarillo
Lubbock
Abilene
Ouachita Mountains
Edwards Plateau
Sacramento Mts
Llano Estacado
Sierra Madre Oriental
Rio Grande
Desierto de Chihuahua
Bolsón de Mapimí
Tropic of Cancer
Chandeleur Islands
Mississippi Delta
Padre Island
Matagorda Island

Lambert Conformal Conic Projection

1:6 100 000 — 0, 100, 200 miles; 0, 100, 200, 300, 400 km

North America
Eastern United States

↓ 161

↓ 169

Lambert Conformal Conic Projection

1:3 000 000

0 50 100 miles

0 50 100 150 200 km

North America

Northeast United States

Lambert Conformal Conic Projection

North America
Mexico and Central America

1:6 200 000

161
163
STATES OF AMERICA
TEXAS
LOUISIANA
MISSISSIPPI
ALABAMA
FLORIDA
COASTAL PLAIN
Edwards Plateau
Dallas
Fort Worth
Shreveport
Jackson
Montgomery
Austin
San Antonio
Houston
Baton Rouge
New Orleans
Mobile
Pensacola
Galveston
Corpus Christi
Laredo
Brownsville
Matamoros
Monterrey
Saltillo
NUEVO LEÓN
TAMAULIPAS
SAN LUIS POTOSÍ
Ciudad Victoria
Tampico
Ciudad Madero
VERACRUZ
GUANAJUATO
QUERÉTARO
HIDALGO
MEXICO CITY
Toluca
Puebla
Cuernavaca
Veracruz
Xalapa
MICHOACÁN
MORELOS
PUEBLA
GUERRERO
OAXACA
Acapulco
Oaxaca
Istmo de Tehuantepec
Sierra Madre del Sur
Sierra Madre de Chiapas
TABASCO
Villahermosa
CHIAPAS
Tuxtla Gutiérrez
CAMPECHE
Campeche
YUCATÁN
Mérida
QUINTANA ROO
Chetumal
Cancún
BELIZE
BELMOPAN
GUATEMALA
GUATEMALA CITY
EL SALVADOR
SAN SALVADOR
HONDURAS
TEGUCIGALPA
Gulf of Mexico
Bahía de Campeche
Gulf of Tehuantepec
Gulf of Honduras
Yucatan Channel
Tropic of Cancer
Mississippi Delta
Padre Island
Laguna Madre
Matagorda Island
Arrecife Alacrán
Cayo Nuevo
Cayos Arcas
OCEAN
28°
24°
20°
16°
100°
96°
92°
88°
F
G
H
I
1
2
3
4
5
6

1:12 100 000

0 200 400 miles

0 200 400 600 800 km

North America

Central America and the Caribbean

South America

UNESCO World Heritage Sites

The first World Heritage site to be listed in 1978 was the Gálapagos Islands off the coast of South America. Famous for its association with Darwin and its giant tortoises it was followed on to the List by sites representing ancient civilizations, European invaders and the continent's rich and diverse physical and natural environment.

● Cultural site ● Natural site ● Mixed site

Argentina
1. Cueva de las Manos, Río Pinturas
2. Iguazu National Park
3. Ischigualasto/Talampaya Natural Parks
4. Jesuit Block and Estancias of Córdoba
5. Jesuit Missions of the Guaranis: San Ignacio Miní, Santa Ana, Nuestra Señora de Loreto and Santa María Mayor (Argentina), Ruins of Saõ Miguel das Missões (Brazil)
6 Parque Nacional Los Glaciares
7 Península Valdés
8 Qhapaq Ñan, Andean Road System
9. Quebrada de Humahuaca

Bolivia
10. City of Potosí
11. Fuerte de Samaipata
12. Historic City of Sucre
13. Jesuit Missions of the Chiquitos
14. Noel Kempff Mercado National Park
8 Qhapaq Ñan, Andean Road System
15. Tiwanaku: Spiritual and Political Centre of the Tiwanaku Culture

Brazil
16. Atlantic Forest South-East Reserves
17. Brasilia
18. Brazilian Atlantic Islands: Fernando de Noronha and Atol das Rocas Reserves
19. Central Amazon Conservation Complex
20. Cerrado Protected Areas: Chapada dos Veadeiros and Emas National Parks
21. Discovery Coast Atlantic Forest Reserves
22. Historic Centre of Salvador de Bahia
23. Historic Centre of São Luís
24. Historic Centre of the Town of Diamantina
25. Historic Centre of the Town of Goiás
26. Historic Centre of the Town of Olinda
27. Historic Town of Ouro Preto
28. Iguaçu National Park
5. Jesuit Missions of the Guaranis: San Ignacio Miní, Santa Ana, Nuestra Señora de Loreto and Santa María Mayor (Argentina), Ruins of Saõ Miguel das Missões (Brazil)
29. Pantanal Conservation Area
30. Rio de Janeiro, Carioca Landscapes between the Mountain and the Sea
31. Sanctuary of Bom Jesus do Congonhas
32. São Francisco Square in the Town of São Cristovão
33. Serra da Capivara National Park

Chile
34. Churches of Chiloé
35. Historic Quarter of the Seaport City of Valparaíso
36. Humberstone and Santa Laura Saltpeter Works
8 Qhapaq Ñan, Andean Road System
37. Rapa Nui National Park
38. Sewell Mining Town

Colombia
39. Coffee Cultural Landscape of Colombia
40. Historic Centre of Santa Cruz de Mompox
41. Los Katíos National Park
42. Malpelo Fauna and Flora Sanctuary
43. National Archeological Park of Tierradentro
44. Port, Fortresses and Group of Monuments, Cartagena
8 Qhapaq Ñan, Andean Road System
45. San Agustín Archeological Park

Curaçao
46. Historic Area of Willemstad, Inner City and Harbour (Netherlands)

Ecuador
47. City of Quito
48. Galápagos Islands
49. Historic Centre of Santa Ana de los Ríos de Cuenca
8 Qhapaq Ñan, Andean Road System
50. Sangay National Park

Paraguay
51. Jesuit Missions of La Santísima Trinidad de Paraná and Jesús de Tavarangue

Peru
52. Chan Chan Archaeological Zone
53. Chavín (Archaeological site)
54. City of Cuzco
55. Historic Centre of Lima
56. Historic Sanctuary of Machu Picchu
57. Historical Centre of the City of Arequipa
58. Huascarán National Park
59. Lines and Geoglyphs of Nasca and Pampas de Jumana
60. Manú National Park
8 Qhapaq Ñan, Andean Road System
61. Río Abiseo National Park
62. Sacred City of Caral-Supe

Suriname
63. Central Suriname Nature Reserve
64. Historic Inner City of Paramaribo

Uruguay
65. Historic Quarter of the City of Colonia del Sacramento

Venezuela
66. Canaima National Park
67. Ciudad Universitaria de Caracas
68. Coro and its Port

37
Easter Island
(Chile)

Caribbean Sea
NORTH AMERICA
Curaçao (Netherlands)
VENEZUELA
GUYANA
SURINAME
French Guiana
COLOMBIA
ECUADOR
Galápagos Islands (Ecuador)
PERU
B R A Z I L
BOLIVIA
PARAGUAY
URUGUAY
ARGENTINA
C H I L E
PACIFIC OCEAN
ATLANTIC OCEAN

South America
Landscapes

South America is a continent of great contrasts, with landscapes varying from the tropical rainforests of the Amazon Basin, to the Atacama Desert, the driest place on earth, and the sub-Antarctic regions of southern Chile and Argentina. The dominant physical features are the Andes, stretching along the entire west coast of the continent and containing numerous mountains over 6 000 metres high, and the Amazon, which is the second longest river in the world and has the world's largest drainage basin.

The Altiplano is a high plateau lying between two of the Andes ranges. It contains Lake Titicaca, the world's highest navigable lake. By contrast, large lowland areas dominate the centre of the continent, lying between the Andes and the Guiana and Brazilian Highlands. These vast grasslands stretch from the Llanos of the north through the Selvas and the Gran Chaco to the Pampas of Argentina.

Confluence of the **Amazon** and **Negro** rivers at Manaus, northern Brazil.

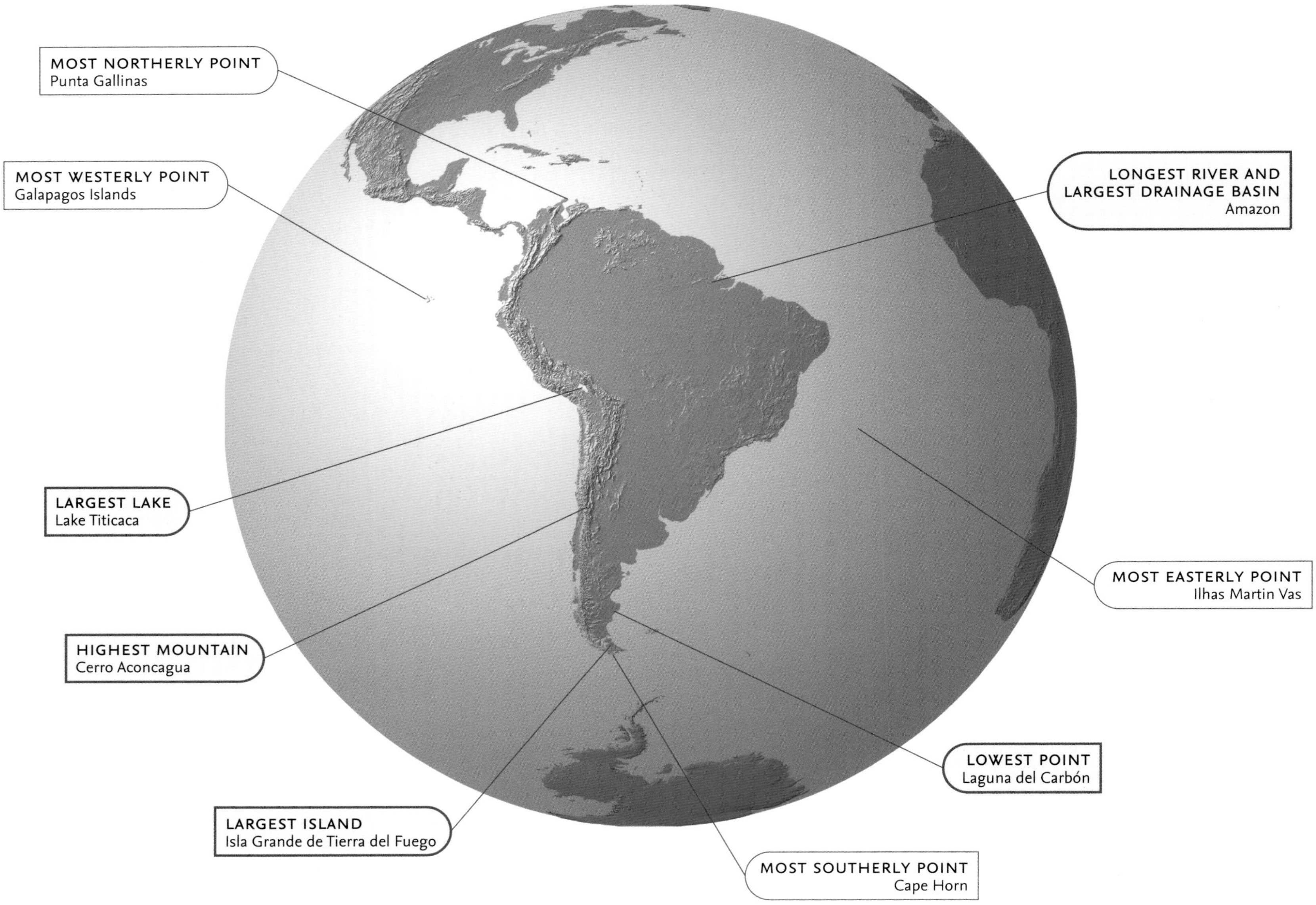

MOST NORTHERLY POINT
Punta Gallinas

MOST WESTERLY POINT
Galapagos Islands

LONGEST RIVER AND LARGEST DRAINAGE BASIN
Amazon

LARGEST LAKE
Lake Titicaca

MOST EASTERLY POINT
Ilhas Martin Vas

HIGHEST MOUNTAIN
Cerro Aconcagua

LOWEST POINT
Laguna del Carbón

LARGEST ISLAND
Isla Grande de Tierra del Fuego

MOST SOUTHERLY POINT
Cape Horn

South America's physical features

Highest mountain	Cerro Aconcagua, Argentina	6 959 metres	22 831 feet
Longest river	Amazon	6 516 km	4 049 miles
Largest lake	Lake Titicaca, Bolivia/Peru	8 340 sq km	3 220 sq miles
Largest island	Isla Grande de Tierra del Fuego, Argentina/Chile	47 000 sq km	18 147 sq miles
Largest drainage basin	Amazon	7 050 000 sq km	2 722 005 sq miles
Lowest point	Laguna del Carbón, Argentina	-105 metres	-345 feet

Internet Links

NASA Visible Earth	**visibleearth.nasa.gov**
NASA Astronaut Photography	**eol.jsc.nasa.gov**
World Rainforest Information Portal	**www.ran.org**
Peakware World Mountain Encyclopedia	**www.peakware.com**

Isla Grande de Tierra del Fuego, South America's largest island, situated at the southernmost tip of the continent.

South America's extent

TOTAL LAND AREA	17 815 420 sq km / 6 878 534 sq miles
Most northerly point	Punta Gallinas, Colombia
Most southerly point	Cape Horn, Chile
Most westerly point	Galagapos Islands, Ecuador
Most easterly point	Ilhas Martin Vas, Atlantic Ocean

Facts

- Water flow along the Amazon is over 1 500 times that of the River Thames
- Cerro Aconcagua, 6 959 metres, is the highest point in the western hemisphere
- The Amazon rainforest supports approximately half of all the world's living species
- The Pantanal in Brazil is the largest area of wetland in the world
- The world's driest desert is the Atacama, where only 1mm of rain may fall as infrequently as once every 5–20 years

South America
Countries

French Guiana, a French Department, is the only remaining territory under overseas control on a continent which has seen a long colonial history. Much of South America was colonized by Spain in the sixteenth century, with Britain, Portugal and the Netherlands each claiming territory in the northeast of the continent. This colonization led to the conquering of ancient civilizations, including the Incas in Peru. Most countries became independent from Spain and Portugal in the early nineteenth century.

The population of the continent reflects its history, being composed primarily of indigenous Indian peoples and mestizos – reflecting the long Hispanic influence. There has been a steady process of urbanization within the continent, with major movements of the population from rural to urban areas. The majority of the population now lives in the major cities and within 300 kilometres of the coast.

Galapagos Islands, an island territory of Ecuador which lies on the equator in the eastern Pacific Ocean over 900 kilometres west of the coast of Ecuador.

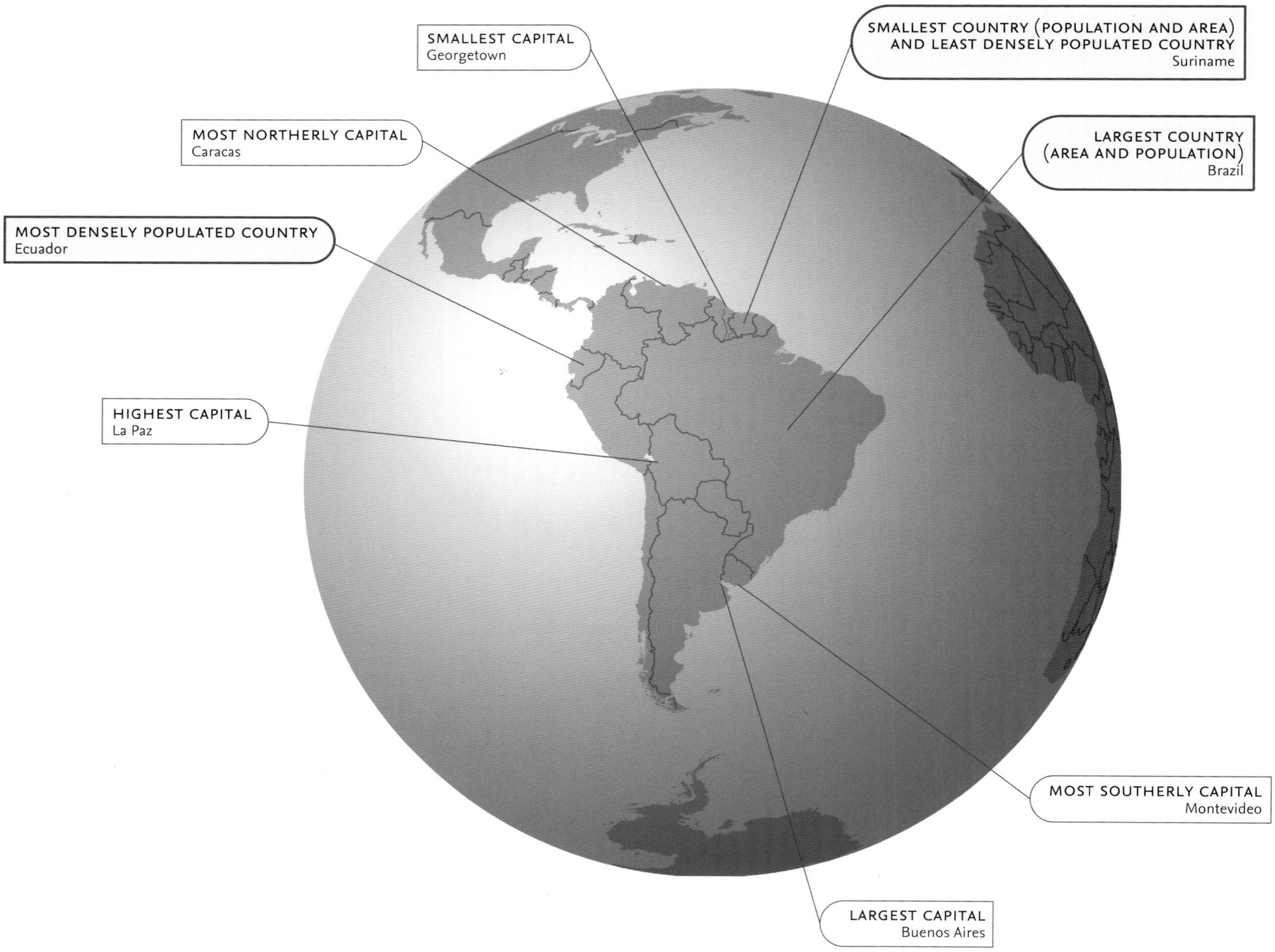

SMALLEST CAPITAL
Georgetown

SMALLEST COUNTRY (POPULATION AND AREA) AND LEAST DENSELY POPULATED COUNTRY
Suriname

MOST NORTHERLY CAPITAL
Caracas

LARGEST COUNTRY (AREA AND POPULATION)
Brazil

MOST DENSELY POPULATED COUNTRY
Ecuador

HIGHEST CAPITAL
La Paz

MOST SOUTHERLY CAPITAL
Montevideo

LARGEST CAPITAL
Buenos Aires

South America's countries

Largest country (area)	Brazil	8 514 879 sq km	3 287 613 sq miles
Smallest country (area)	Suriname	163 820 sq km	63 251 sq miles
Largest country (population)	Brazil	200 362 000	
Smallest country (population)	Suriname	539 000	
Most densely populated country	Ecuador	58 per sq km	150 per sq mile
Least densely populated country	Suriname	3 per sq km	9 per sq mile

Internet Links

UK Foreign and Commonwealth Office	**www.fco.gov.uk**
CIA World Factbook	**www.cia.gov/library/publications/the-world-factbook/index.html**
Caribbean Community (Caricom)	**www.caricom.org**
Latin American Network Information Center	**lanic.utexas.edu**

South America's capitals

Largest capital (population)	Buenos Aires, Argentina	14 151 000
Smallest capital (population)	Georgetown, Guyana	124 000
Most northerly capital	Caracas, Venezuela	10° 28'N
Most southerly capital	Montevideo, Uruguay	34° 52'S
Highest capital	La Paz, Bolivia	3 630 metres 11 909 feet

Facts

- South America is often referred to as 'Latin America', reflecting the historic influences of Spain and Portugal
- The largest city in each South American country is the capital, except in Brazil and Ecuador
- South America has only two landlocked countries – Bolivia and Paraguay
- Chile is over 4 000 kilometres long but has an average width of only 177 kilometres

Falkland Islands, an overseas UK territory in the South Atlantic Ocean.

Lambert Azimuthal Equal Area Projection

1:12 100 000 — 0, 200, 400 miles; 0, 200, 400, 600, 800 km

South America
Northern South America

South America

Southern South America

1:12 100 000 — 0, 200, 400 miles; 0, 200, 400, 600, 800 km

Lambert Azimuthal Equal Area Projection

1:6 100 000

0 100 200 miles

0 100 200 300 400 km

South America
Southeast Brazil

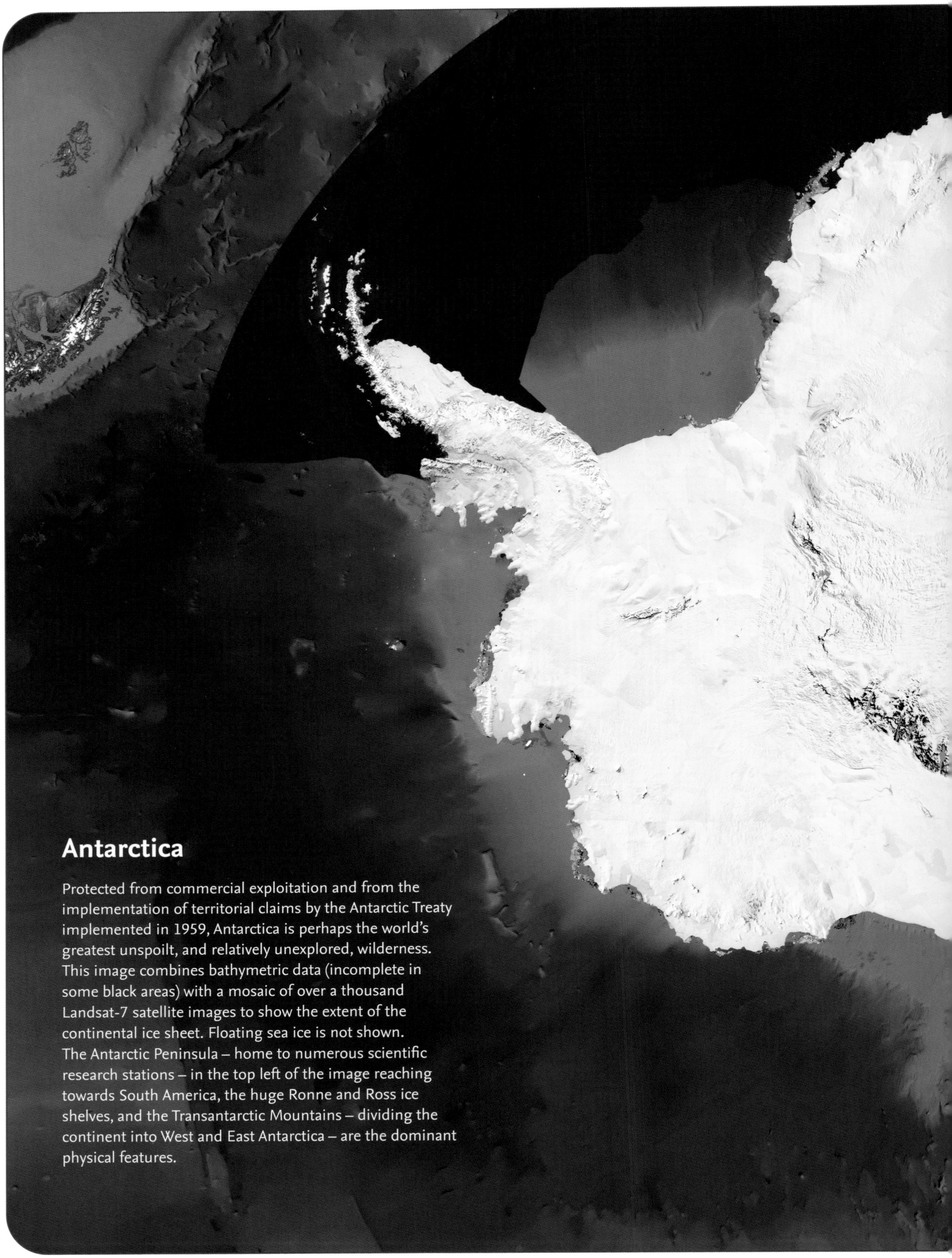

Antarctica

Protected from commercial exploitation and from the implementation of territorial claims by the Antarctic Treaty implemented in 1959, Antarctica is perhaps the world's greatest unspoilt, and relatively unexplored, wilderness. This image combines bathymetric data (incomplete in some black areas) with a mosaic of over a thousand Landsat-7 satellite images to show the extent of the continental ice sheet. Floating sea ice is not shown. The Antarctic Peninsula – home to numerous scientific research stations – in the top left of the image reaching towards South America, the huge Ronne and Ross ice shelves, and the Transantarctic Mountains – dividing the continent into West and East Antarctica – are the dominant physical features.

Oceans and Poles
Features

Between them, the world's oceans and polar regions cover approximately seventy per cent of the Earth's surface. The oceans contain ninety-six per cent of the Earth's water and a vast range of flora and fauna. They are a major influence on the world's climate, particularly through ocean currents. The Arctic and Antarctica are the coldest and most inhospitable places on the Earth. They both have vast amounts of ice which, if global warming continues, could have a major influence on sea level across the globe.

Our understanding of the oceans and polar regions has increased enormously over the last twenty years through the development of new technologies, particularly that of satellite remote sensing, which can generate vast amounts of data relating to, for example, topography (both on land and the seafloor), land cover and sea surface temperature.

Pacific Ocean
World's largest ocean: 166 241 000 sq km
Average depth: 4 200m
Challenger Deep: 10 920 metres
Mariana Trench
Deepest point
PACIFIC
OCEAN
AUSTRALIA
South Pacific Ocean
Average depth: 3 935 metres

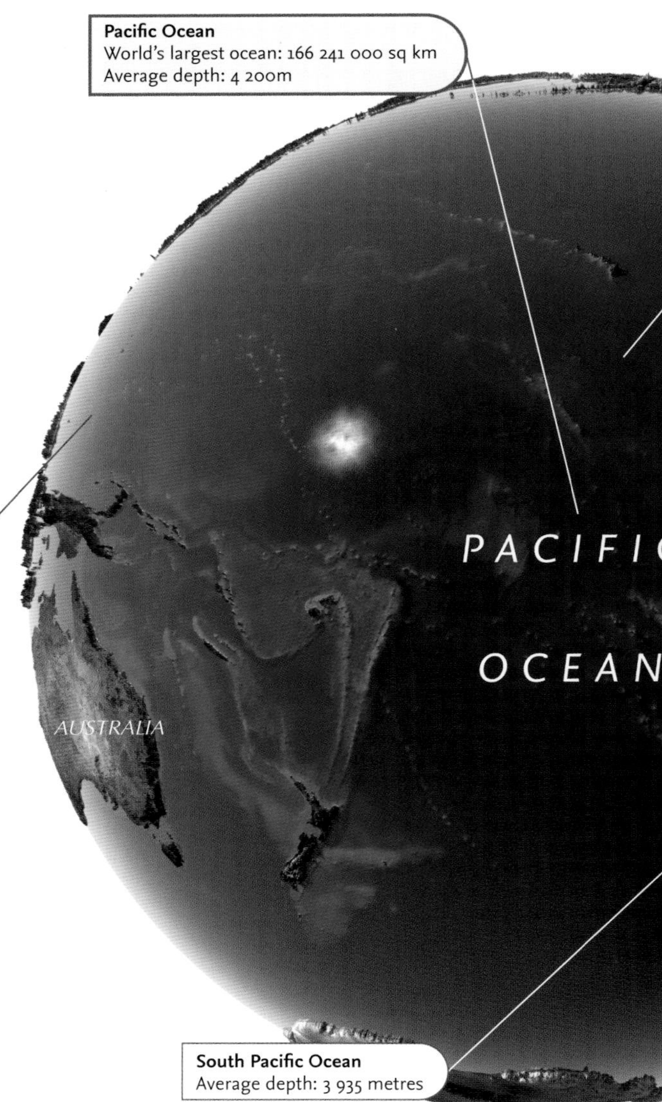

The oceans

The world's major oceans are the Pacific, the Atlantic and the Indian Oceans. The Arctic Ocean is generally considered as part of the Atlantic, and the Southern Ocean, which stretches around the whole of Antarctica is usually treated as an extension of each of the three major oceans.

One of the most important factors affecting the earth's climate is the circulation of water within and between the oceans. Differences in temperature and surface winds create ocean currents which move enormous quantities of water around the globe. These currents re-distribute heat which the oceans have absorbed from the sun, and so have a major effect on the world's climate system. El Niño is one climatic phenomenon directly influenced by these ocean processes.

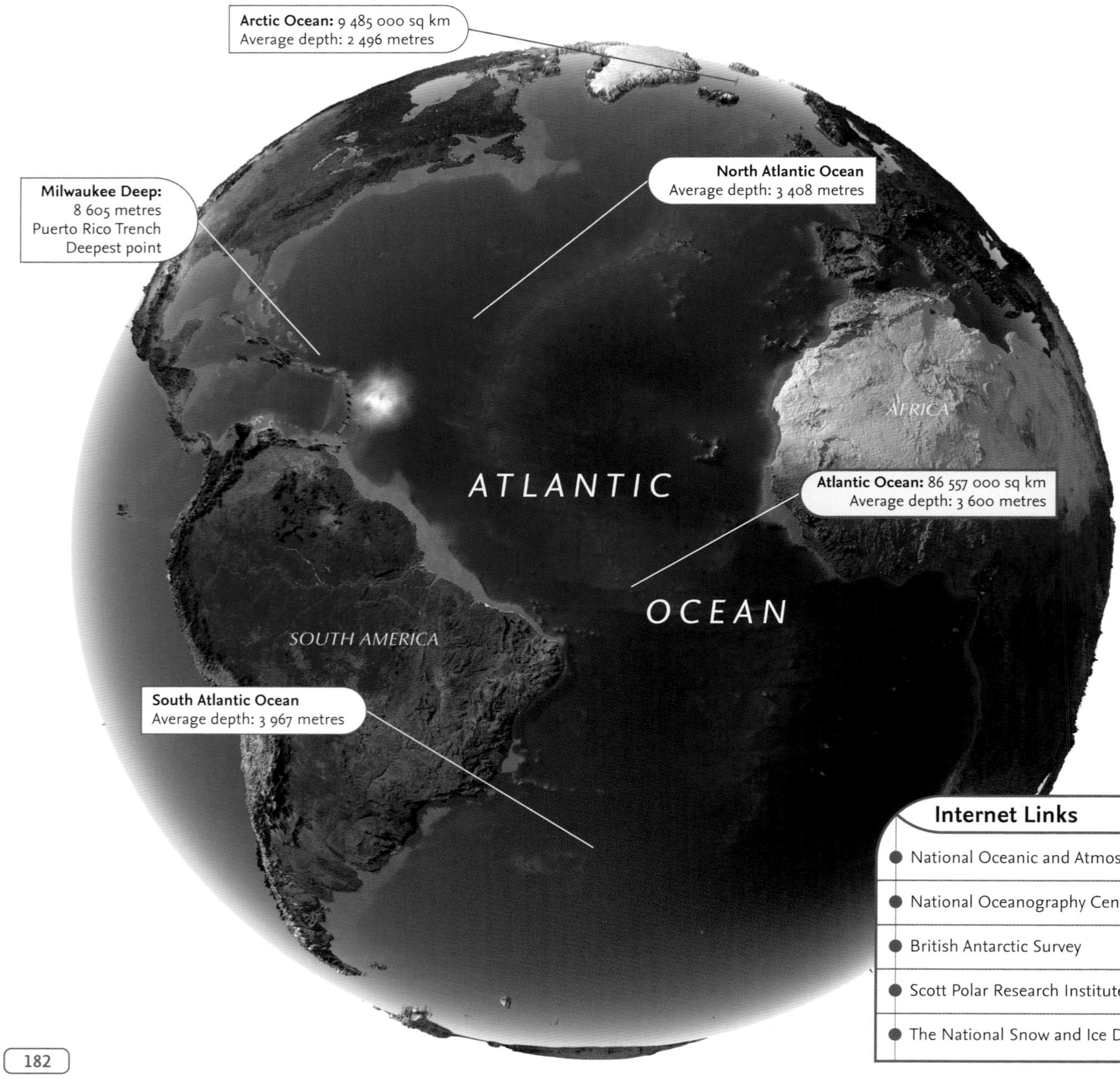
Arctic Ocean: 9 485 000 sq km
Average depth: 2 496 metres
Milwaukee Deep:
8 605 metres
Puerto Rico Trench
Deepest point
North Atlantic Ocean
Average depth: 3 408 metres
AFRICA
ATLANTIC
OCEAN
Atlantic Ocean: 86 557 000 sq km
Average depth: 3 600 metres
SOUTH AMERICA
South Atlantic Ocean
Average depth: 3 967 metres

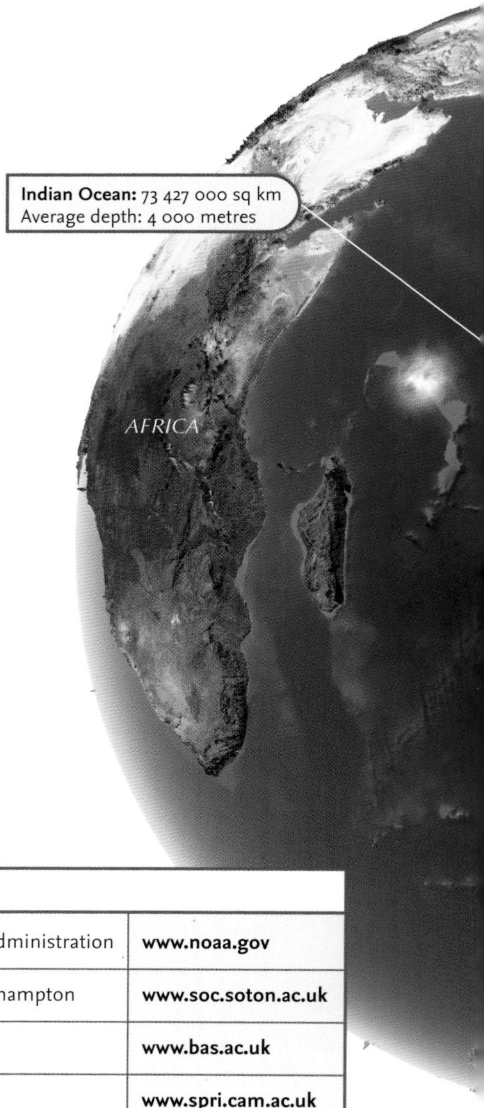
Indian Ocean: 73 427 000 sq km
Average depth: 4 000 metres
AFRICA

Internet Links

National Oceanic and Atmospheric Administration	www.noaa.gov
National Oceanography Centre, Southampton	www.soc.soton.ac.uk
British Antarctic Survey	www.bas.ac.uk
Scott Polar Research Institute (SPRI)	www.spri.cam.ac.uk
The National Snow and Ice Data Center (NSIDC)	nsidc.org

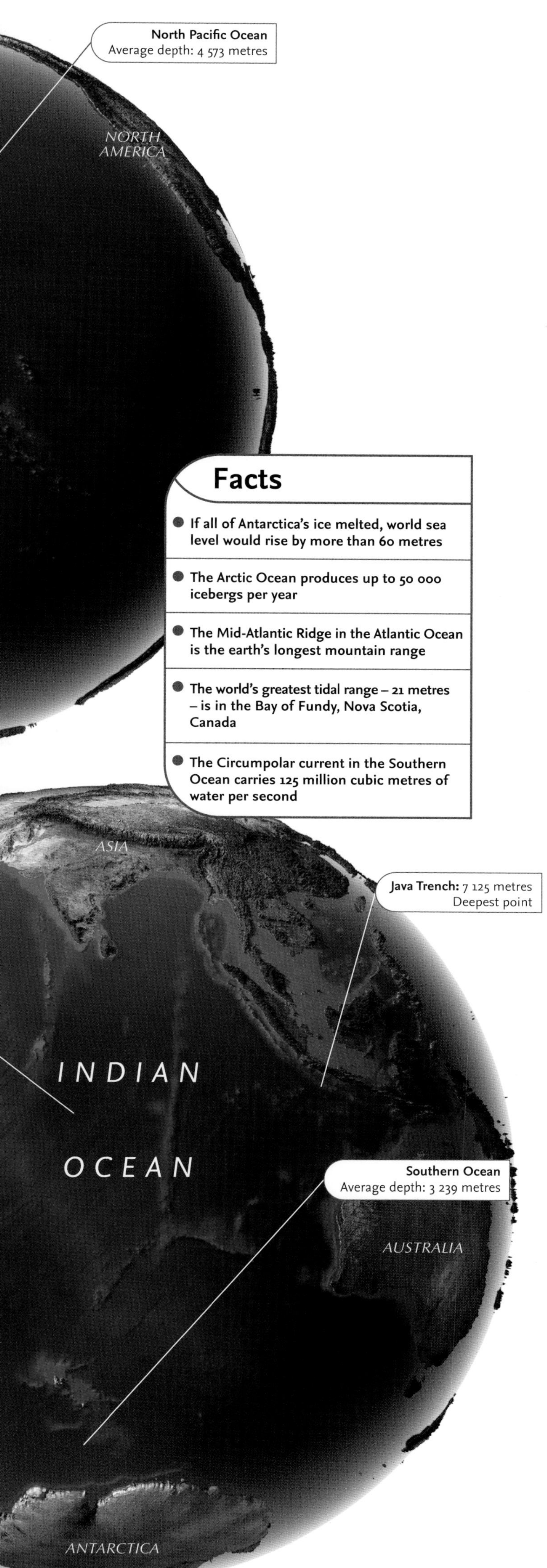

Facts

- If all of Antarctica's ice melted, world sea level would rise by more than 60 metres
- The Arctic Ocean produces up to 50 000 icebergs per year
- The Mid-Atlantic Ridge in the Atlantic Ocean is the earth's longest mountain range
- The world's greatest tidal range – 21 metres – is in the Bay of Fundy, Nova Scotia, Canada
- The Circumpolar current in the Southern Ocean carries 125 million cubic metres of water per second

Polar regions

Although a harsh climate is common to the two polar regions, there are major differences between the Arctic and Antarctica. The North Pole is surrounded by the Arctic Ocean, much of which is permanently covered by sea ice, while the South Pole lies on the huge land mass of Antarctica. This is covered by a permanent ice cap which reaches a maximum thickness of over four kilometres. Antarctica has no permanent population, but Europe, Asia and North America all stretch into the Arctic region which is populated by numerous ethnic groups. Antarctica is subject to the Antarctic Treaty of 1959 which does not recognize individual land claims and protects the continent in the interests of international scientific cooperation.

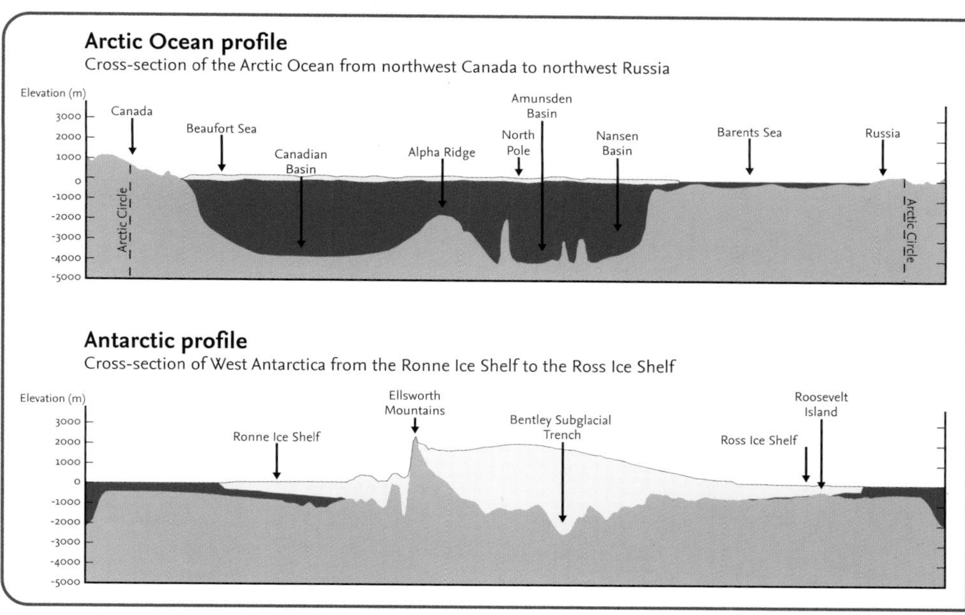

Antarctica's physical features

Highest mountain: Mt Vinson	4 897 m	16 066 ft
Total land area (excluding ice shelves)	12 093 000 sq km	4 669 107 sq miles
Ice shelves	1 559 000 sq km	601 930 sq miles
Exposed rock	49 000 sq km	18 919 sq miles
Lowest bedrock elevation (Bentley Subglacial Trench)	2 496 m below sea level	8 189 ft below sea level
Maximum ice thickness (Astrolabe Subglacial Basin)	4 776 m	15 669 ft
Mean ice thickness (including ice shelves)	1 859 m	6 099 ft
Volume of ice sheet (including ice shelves)	25 400 000 cubic km	6 094 628 cubic miles

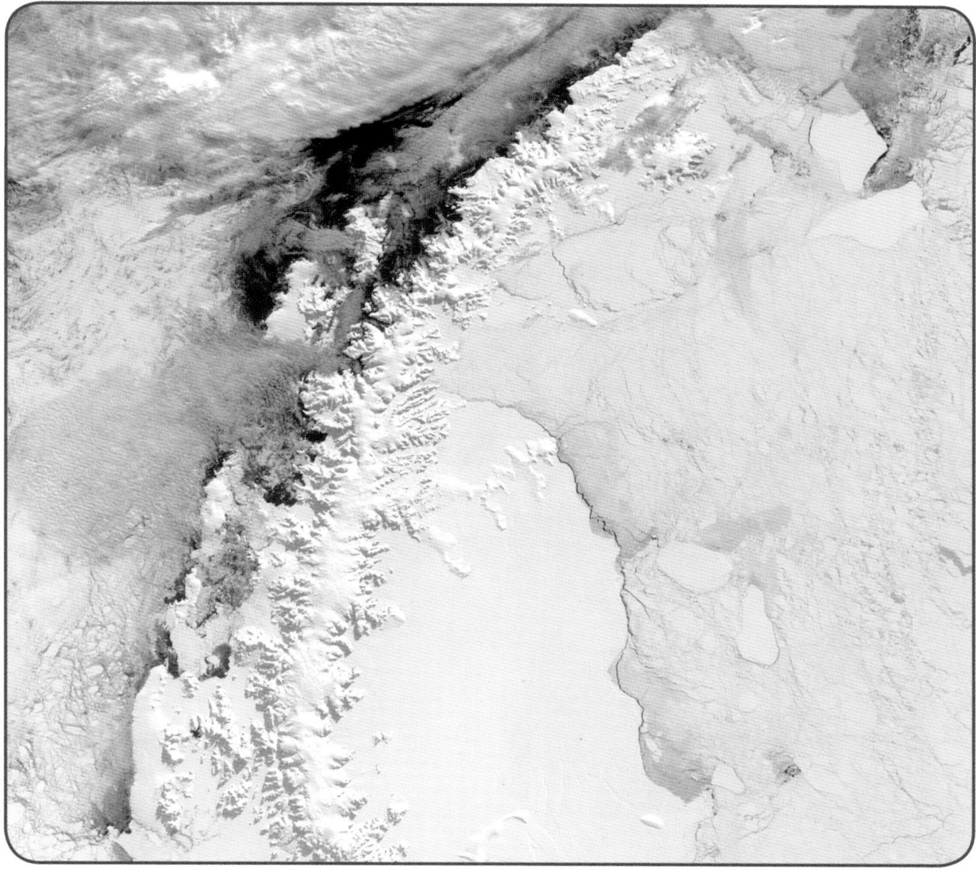

The **Antarctic Peninsula** and the **Larsen Ice Shelf** in western Antarctica.

Lambert Azimuthal Equal Area Projection

1:43 200 000

Atlantic Ocean
Indian Ocean

International boundaries in the sea shown on this map indicate ownership of islands and island groups only. They do not infer the alignments of legal maritime boundaries.
Lambert Azimuthal Equal Area Projection
1:43 200 000
0 500 1000 1500 miles
0 500 1000 1500 2000 2500 km
PAKISTAN
MONGOLIA
RUSSIA
Sea of Okhotsk
Bering Sea
Aleutian Basin
Aleutian Islands
Kamchatka Peninsula
Kuril Islands
Kuril Trench
Kuril Basin
Sakhalin
Emperor Seamount Chain
Emperor Trough
Chinook Trough
Northwest Pacific Basin
Shatsky Rise
Mapmakers Seamounts
Midway Islands
Hawaiian Ridge
Mid-Pacific Mountains
Gobi Desert
CHINA
BEIJING
Tianjin
Shenyang
Harbin
Changchun
Vladivostok
Sapporo
PYONGYANG
SEOUL
NORTH KOREA
SOUTH KOREA
Sea of Japan
Honshu
JAPAN
TŌKYŌ
Ōsaka
Nagoya
Sendai
Kyūshū
Shikoku
Kagoshima
Chengdu
Chongqing
Wuhan
Nanjing
Shanghai
Hangzhou
East China Sea
Guangzhou
Hong Kong
TAIBEI
TAIWAN
Ryukyu Islands
Ryukyu Trench
Izu-Ogasawara Trench
Bonin Islands (Japan)
Volcano Islands (Japan)
Kyushu-Palau Ridge
South Honshu Ridge
Mumbai
Pune
Hyderabad
Bengaluru
Chennai
Kolkata
Dhaka
DHAKA
Ahmadabad
Karachi
Delhi
NEW DELHI
KATHMANDU
NEPAL
Himalaya
Bay of Bengal
INDIA
Deccan
SRI LANKA
Colombo
Thiruvananthapuram
BANGKOK
THAILAND
VIETNAM
CAMBODIA
PHNOM PENH
Ho Chi Minh City
VIENTIANE
HANOI
Hainan Dao
South China Sea
Gulf of Thailand
Andaman Sea
Andaman Islands (India)
Nicobar Islands (India)
MANILA
PHILIPPINES
Quezon City
Philippine Sea
Philippine Trench
Philippine Basin
Luzon
Mindanao
Davao
Cebu
Palawan
Sulu Sea
Celebes Sea
MALAYSIA
KUALA LUMPUR
SINGAPORE
BANDAR SERI BEGAWAN
BRUNEI
Borneo
Sumatra
Java
JAKARTA
Surabaya
INDONESIA
Laut Jawa
Banda Sea
Arafura Sea
DILI
EAST TIMOR (TIMOR-LESTE)
Java Trench (Sunda Trench)
Halmahera
New Guinea
PAPUA NEW GUINEA
PORT MORESBY
Bismarck Sea
Solomon Sea
SOLOMON ISLANDS
HONIARA
Northern Mariana Islands (U.S.A.)
Guam (U.S.A.)
Mariana Trench
Mariana Ridge
West Mariana Basin
East Mariana Basin
Magellan Seamounts
Challenger Deep 10920
PALAU
MELEKEOK
Caroline Islands
FEDERATED STATES OF MICRONESIA
West Caroline Basin
East Caroline Basin
MICRONESIA
MARSHALL ISLANDS
Majuro
DELAP-ULIGA-DJARRIT
Wake Island (U.S.A.)
NAURU
YAREN
Melanesian Basin
Gilbert Islands
BAIRIKI
KIRIBATI
Central Pacific Basin
Phoenix Islands
TUVALU
Funafuti
Tokelau (N.Z.)
SAMOA
APIA
American Samoa (U.S.A.)
Wallis and Futuna Islands (France)
FIJI
SUVA
TONGA
Tonga Trench
Niue (N.Z.)
Cook Islands (N.Z.)
VANUATU
PORT VILA
New Caledonia (France)
NOUMÉA
New Hebrides Trench
Coral Sea
Coral Sea Basin
MELANESIA
POLYNESIA
PACIFIC
South Fiji Basin
Norfolk Island (Australia) KINGSTON
Kermadec Islands (N.Z.)
Kermadec Trench
Louisville Ridge
Lord Howe Rise
Lord Howe Island (Australia)
Tasman Sea
Tasman Basin
NEW ZEALAND
North Island
South Island
Auckland
WELLINGTON
Christchurch
Dunedin
Chatham Rise
Chatham Islands (N.Z.)
Campbell Plateau
AUSTRALIA
Great Sandy Desert
Great Victoria Desert
Gibson Desert
Nullarbor Plain
Great Australian Bight
Great Dividing Range
Great Barrier Reef
Cape York Peninsula
Gulf of Carpentaria
Darwin
Brisbane
Sydney
CANBERRA
Melbourne
Adelaide
Perth
Alice Springs
Tasmania
Bass Strait
Kati Thanda-Lake Eyre
Torres Strait
Timor Sea
North Australian Basin
West Australian Basin
Perth Basin
South Australian Basin
INDIAN OCEAN
Ninetyeast Ridge
Mid-Indian Basin
Cocos Basin
Cocos (Keeling) Islands (Australia)
Christmas Island (Australia)
Broken Plateau
Naturaliste Plateau
Diamantina Deep
South Tasman Rise
Macquarie Ridge
Macquarie Island (Australia)
Auckland Islands (N.Z.)
Campbell Island (N.Z.)
Antipodes Islands (N.Z.)
Bounty Islands (N.Z.)
Indian-Antarctic Ridge
Southeast Indian Ridge
Australian-Antarctic Basin
Île Amsterdam
Île St-Paul
Rodrigues Island (Mauritius)
Tropic of Capricorn
SOUTHERN
Balleny Islands
Wilkes Land
Adélie Land
George V Land
Transantarctic Mountains
Ross Ice Shelf
ANTARCTICA
Equator
Tropic of Cancer
Antarctic Circle

CANADA
UNITED STATES OF AMERICA
MEXICO
Gulf of Alaska
Rocky Mountains
Coast Mountains
Edmonton
Calgary
Winnipeg
Vancouver
Seattle
Portland
Toronto
OTTAWA
Montreal
Québec
Boston
New York
Philadelphia
WASHINGTON D.C.
Chicago
Detroit
Minneapolis
Denver
Salt Lake City
Sacramento
San Francisco
San Jose
Los Angeles
San Diego
Las Vegas
Phoenix
Dallas
Houston
San Antonio
Atlanta
Miami
New Orleans
Jacksonville
Orlando
Tampa
Great Basin
Colorado Plateau
Gulf of Mexico
ATLANTIC OCEAN
Sargasso Sea
Mid-Atlantic Ridge
Tropic of Cancer
Hatteras Abyssal Plain
Bermuda Rise
New England Seamounts
Nares Deep
THE BAHAMAS
NASSAU
HAVANA
CUBA
PORT-AU-PRINCE
SANTO DOMINGO
SAN JUAN
KINGSTON
JAMAICA
Caribbean Sea
MEXICO CITY
Guadalajara
Monterrey
Puebla
Acapulco
Tuxtla
Mérida
BELIZE
BELMOPAN
GUATEMALA CITY
SAN SALVADOR
TEGUCIGALPA
MANAGUA
SAN JOSÉ
PANAMA CITY
Caracas
Maracaibo
Barranquilla
Cartagena
Medellín
BOGOTÁ
COLOMBIA
VENEZUELA
GUYANA
GEORGETOWN
PARAMARIBO
SURINAME
CAYENNE
French Guiana
QUITO
ECUADOR
Guayaquil
PERU
LIMA
BRAZIL
Manaus
Belém
São Luís
Teresina
BOLIVIA
LA PAZ
SUCRE
PARAGUAY
ASUNCIÓN
BRASÍLIA
Goiânia
Belo Horizonte
Rio de Janeiro
São Paulo
Curitiba
Porto Alegre
URUGUAY
MONTEVIDEO
BUENOS AIRES
Córdoba
Rosario
SANTIAGO
Valparaíso
Concepción
ARGENTINA
CHILE
Tropic of Capricorn
Equator
Honolulu
Hawai'i
Northeast Pacific Basin
Tufts Abyssal Plain
East Pacific Rise
Clipperton Fracture Zone
Galapagos Islands
Galapagos Rise
Gallego Rise
Peru Basin
Nazca Ridge (Southwest Peru Ridge)
Peru-Chile Trench
Chile Basin
Roggeveen Basin
Challenger Fracture Zone
French Polynesia
PAPEETE
Marquesas Islands
Tuamotu Islands
Society Islands
Tubuai Islands
Pitcairn Islands (U.K.)
ADAMSTOWN
Tiki Basin
Easter Island (Isla de Pascua) (Chile)
Pacific-Antarctic Ridge
Southeast Pacific Basin
Amundsen Abyssal Plain
Mornington Abyssal Plain
Argentine Basin
Argentine Rise
Argentine Abyssal Plain
Falkland Islands
Drake Passage
Antarctic Circle
Amundsen Sea
Marie Byrd Land
West Antarctica
Antarctic Peninsula
Palmer Land
Bellingshausen Sea
Tierra del Fuego
Punta Arenas
Ushuaia
Cape Horn
PACIFIC OCEAN
OCEAN
K L M N O P Q R S
J K L M N O P Q R S
2 3 4 5 6 7 8 9 10 11

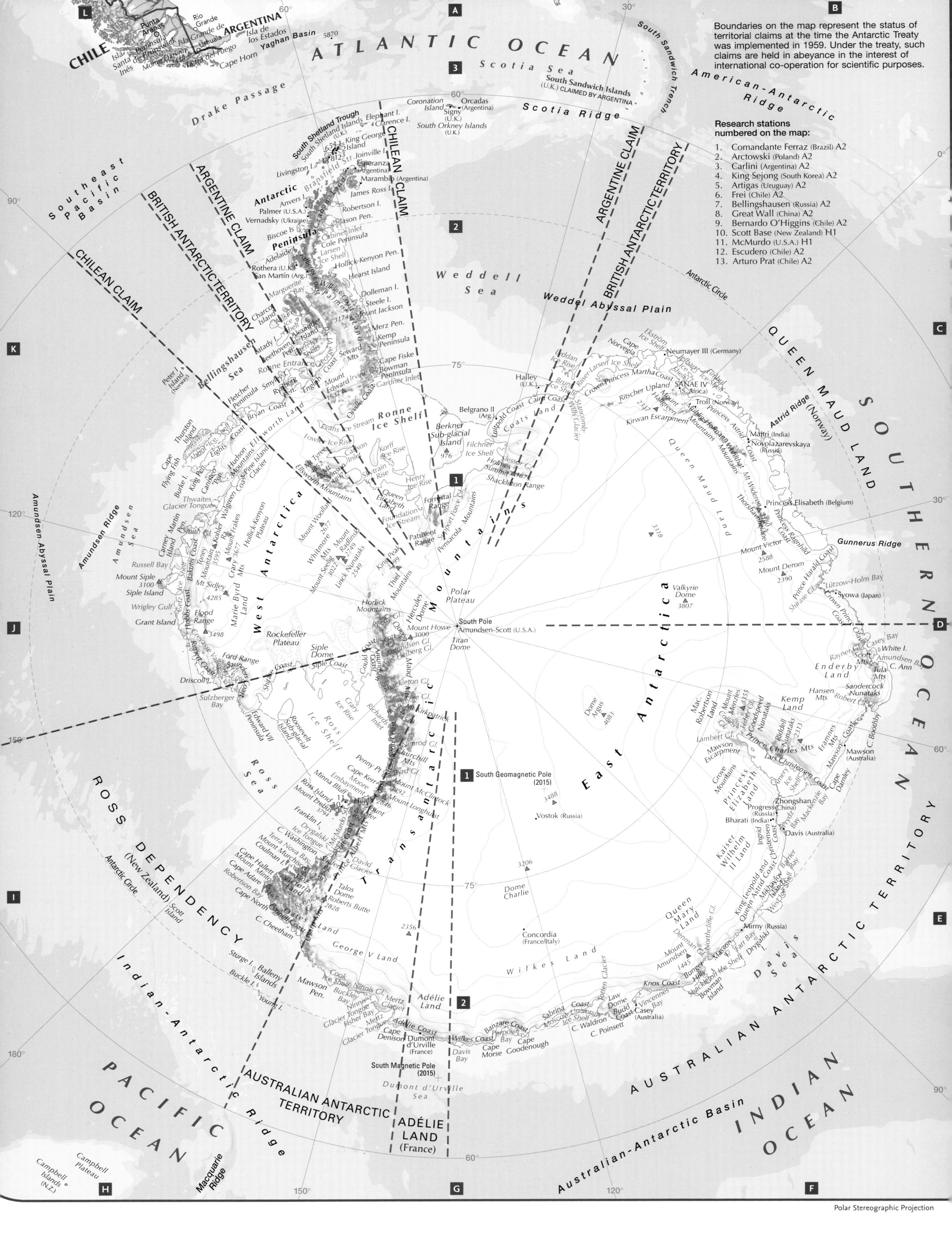

Antarctica

1:22 500 000

Scale: 0 200 400 600 800 1000 miles; 0 200 400 600 800 1000 1200 1400 1600 km

Polar Stereographic Projection

1:22 500 000

0 200 400 600 800 1000 miles

0 200 400 600 800 1000 1200 1400 1600 km

The Arctic

States and Territories

All 196 independent countries and all populated dependent and disputed territories are included in this list of the states and territories of the world; the list is arranged in alphabetical order by the conventional name form. For independent states, the full name is given below the conventional name, if this is different; for territories, the status is given. The capital city name is given in conventional English form with selected alternative, usually local, form in brackets.

Area and population statistics are the latest available and include estimates. The information on languages and religions is based on the latest information on 'de facto' speakers of the language or 'de facto' adherents of the religion. This varies greatly from country to country because some countries include questions in censuses while others do not, in which case best estimates are used. The order of the languages and religions reflects their relative importance within the country; generally, languages or religions are included when more than one per cent of the population are estimated to be speakers or adherents.

ABBREVIATIONS

CURRENCIES

CFA	Communauté Financière Africaine
CFP	Comptoirs Français du Pacifique

Membership of selected international organizations is shown by the abbreviations below; dependent territories do not normally have separate memberships of these organizations.

ORGANIZATIONS

APEC	Asia-Pacific Economic Cooperation
ASEAN	Association of Southeast Asian Nations
CARICOM	Caribbean Community
CIS	Commonwealth of Independent States
Comm.	The Commonwealth
EU	European Union
NATO	North Atlantic Treaty Organization
OECD	Organisation for Economic Co-operation and Development
OPEC	Organization of the Petroleum Exporting Countries
SADC	Southern African Development Community
UN	United Nations

Abkhazia
Disputed territory

Area Sq Km	8 700	**Languages**	Abkhaz, Russian, Georgian
Area Sq Miles	3 359	**Religions**	Abkhaz Orthodox Christianity, Sunni Muslim
Population	180 000	**Currency**	Russian rouble, Abkhaz apsar
Capital	Sokhumi (Aq"a)		

An autonomous republic within Georgia, Abkhazia has an active separatist movement seeking independence from Georgia. Although it is de jure part of Georgia, it effectively currently functions as an independent state with backing from Russia. This dispute has led to intermittent, but serious, armed conflict over the last twenty years. Abkhazia voted to separate from Georgia in 1992, a move rejected by Georgia and prompting a Georgian invasion. Abkhazian and Russian forces ousted Georgia and a cease-fire was established in 1994.

AFGHANISTAN
Islamic Republic of Afghanistan

Area Sq Km	652 225	**Languages**	Dari, Pashtu (Pushtu), Uzbek, Turkmen
Area Sq Miles	251 825	**Religions**	Sunni Muslim, Shi'a Muslim
Population	30 552 000	**Currency**	Afghani
Capital	Kābul	**Organizations**	UN

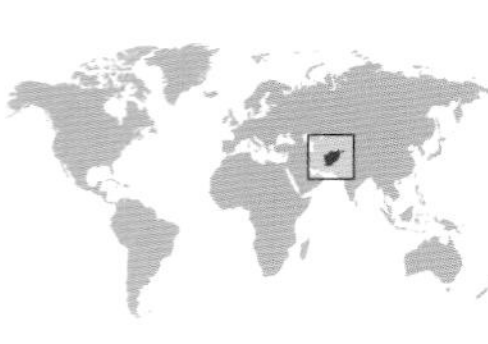

A landlocked country in central Asia with central highlands bordered by plains in the north and southwest, and by the Hindu Kush mountains in the northeast. The climate is dry continental. Over the last twenty-five years war has disrupted the economy, which is highly dependent on farming and livestock rearing. Most trade is with the former USSR, Pakistan and Iran.

ALBANIA
Republic of Albania

Area Sq Km	28 748	**Languages**	Albanian, Greek
Area Sq Miles	11 100	**Religions**	Sunni Muslim, Albanian Orthodox, Roman Catholic
Population	3 173 000	**Currency**	Lek
Capital	Tirana (Tiranë)	**Organizations**	NATO, UN

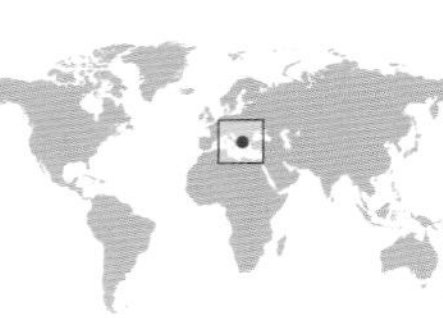

Albania lies in the western Balkan Mountains in southeastern Europe, bordering the Adriatic Sea. It is mountainous, with coastal plains where half the population lives. The economy is based on agriculture and mining. Albania is one of the poorest countries in Europe and relies heavily on foreign aid.

ALGERIA
People's Democratic Republic of Algeria

Area Sq Km	2 381 741	**Languages**	Arabic, French, Berber
Area Sq Miles	919 595	**Religions**	Sunni Muslim
Population	39 208 000	**Currency**	Algerian dinar
Capital	Algiers (Alger)	**Organizations**	OPEC, UN

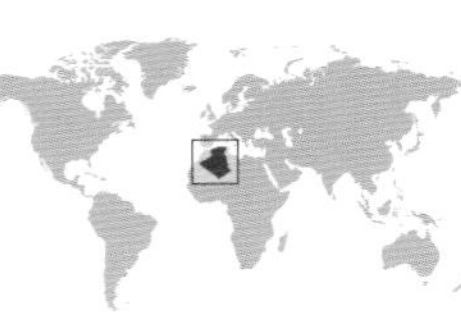

Algeria, the largest country in Africa, lies on the Mediterranean coast of northwest Africa and extends southwards to the Atlas Mountains and the dry sandstone plateau and desert of the Sahara. The climate ranges from Mediterranean on the coast to semi-arid and arid inland. The most populated areas are the coastal plains and the fertile northern slopes of the Atlas Mountains. Oil, natural gas and related products account for over ninety-five per cent of export earnings. Agriculture employs about a fifth of the workforce, producing mainly food crops. Algeria's main trading partners are Italy, France and the USA.

American Samoa
United States Unincorporated Territory

Area Sq Km	197	**Languages**	Samoan, English
Area Sq Miles	76	**Religions**	Protestant, Roman Catholic
Population	55 000	**Currency**	United States dollar
Capital	Fagatogo		

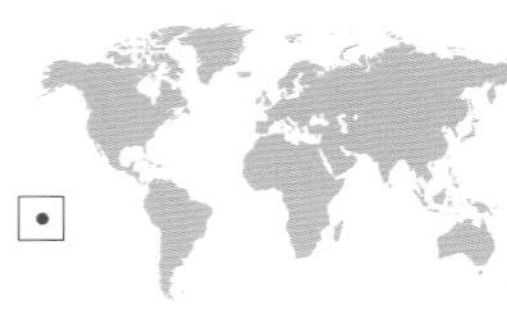

Lying in the south Pacific Ocean, American Samoa consists of five main islands and two coral atolls. The largest island is Tutuila. Tuna and tuna products are the main exports, and the main trading partner is the USA.

ANDORRA
Principality of Andorra

Area Sq Km	465	**Languages**	Catalan, Spanish, French
Area Sq Miles	180	**Religions**	Roman Catholic
Population	79 000	**Currency**	Euro
Capital	Andorra la Vella	**Organizations**	UN

A landlocked state in southwest Europe, Andorra lies in the Pyrenees mountain range between France and Spain. It consists of deep valleys and gorges, surrounded by mountains. Tourism, encouraged by the development of ski resorts, is the mainstay of the economy. Banking is also an important economic activity.

ANGOLA
Republic of Angola

Area Sq Km	1 246 700	**Languages**	Portuguese, Bantu, other local languages
Area Sq Miles	481 354	**Religions**	Roman Catholic, Protestant, traditional beliefs
Population	21 472 000	**Currency**	Kwanza
Capital	Luanda	**Organizations**	OPEC, SADC, UN

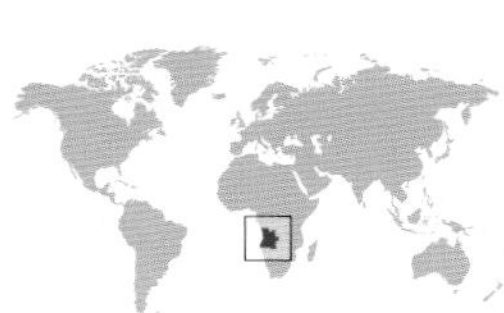

Angola lies on the Atlantic coast of south central Africa. Its small northern province, Cabinda, is separated from the rest of the country by part of the Democratic Republic of the Congo. Much of Angola is high plateau. In the west is a narrow coastal plain and in the southwest is desert. The climate is equatorial in the north but desert in the south. Around seventy per cent of the population relies on subsistence agriculture. Angola is rich in minerals (particularly diamonds), and oil accounts for approximately ninety per cent of export earnings. The USA, South Korea and Portugal are its main trading partners.

Anguilla
United Kingdom Overseas Territory

Area Sq Km	155	**Languages**	English
Area Sq Miles	60	**Religions**	Protestant, Roman Catholic
Population	14 000	**Currency**	East Caribbean dollar
Capital	The Valley		

Anguilla lies at the northern end of the Leeward Islands in the eastern Caribbean. Tourism and fishing form the basis of the economy.

ANTIGUA AND BARBUDA

Area Sq Km	442	**Languages**	English, Creole
Area Sq Miles	171	**Religions**	Protestant, Roman Catholic
Population	90 000	**Currency**	East Caribbean dollar
Capital	St John's	**Organizations**	CARICOM, Comm., UN

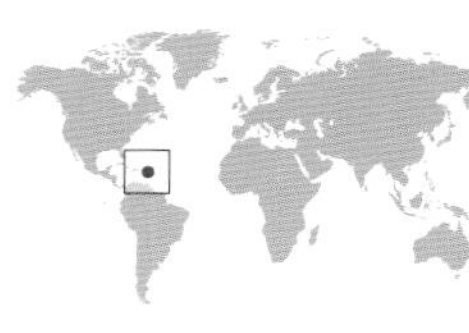

The state comprises the islands of Antigua, Barbuda and the tiny rocky outcrop of Redonda, in the Leeward Islands in the eastern Caribbean. Antigua, the largest and most populous island, is mainly hilly scrubland, with many beaches. The climate is tropical, and the economy relies heavily on tourism. Most trade is with other eastern Caribbean states and the USA.

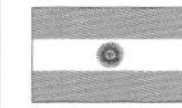

ARGENTINA
Argentine Republic

Area Sq Km	2 766 889	**Languages**	Spanish, Italian, Amerindian languages
Area Sq Miles	1 068 302	**Religions**	Roman Catholic, Protestant
Population	41 446 000	**Currency**	Argentinian peso
Capital	Buenos Aires	**Organizations**	UN

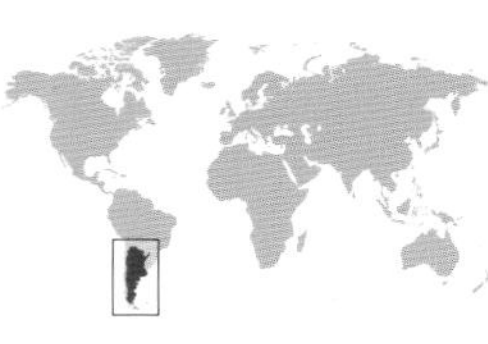

Argentina, the second largest state in South America, extends from Bolivia to Cape Horn and from the Andes mountains to the Atlantic Ocean. It has four geographical

regions: subtropical forests and swampland in the northeast; temperate fertile plains or Pampas in the centre; the wooded foothills and valleys of the Andes in the west; and the cold, semi-arid plateaus of Patagonia in the south. The highest mountain in South America, Cerro Aconcagua, is in Argentina. Over ninety per cent of the population lives in towns and cities. The country is rich in natural resources including petroleum, natural gas, ores and precious metals. Agricultural products dominate exports, which also include motor vehicles and crude oil. Most trade is with Brazil and the USA.

ARMENIA
Republic of Armenia

Area Sq Km	29 800	**Languages**	Armenian, Kurdish
Area Sq Miles	11 506	**Religions**	Armenian Orthodox
Population	2 977 000	**Currency**	Dram
Capital	Yerevan (Erevan)	**Organizations**	CIS, UN

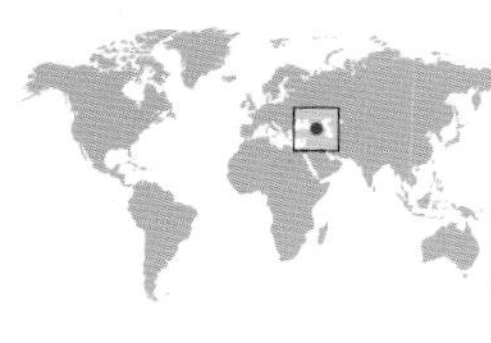

A landlocked state in southwest Asia, Armenia lies in the south of the Lesser Caucasus mountains. It is a mountainous country with a continental climate. One-third of the population lives in the capital, Yerevan. Exports include diamonds, scrap metal and machinery. Many Armenians depend on remittances from abroad.

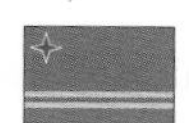

Aruba
Self-governing Netherlands Territory

Area Sq Km	193	**Languages**	Papiamento, Dutch, English
Area Sq Miles	75	**Religions**	Roman Catholic, Protestant
Population	103 000	**Currency**	Aruban florin
Capital	Oranjestad		

The most southwesterly of the islands in the Lesser Antilles in the Caribbean, Aruba lies just off the coast of Venezuela. Tourism, offshore finance and oil refining are the most important sectors of the economy. The USA is the main trading partner.

AUSTRALIA
Commonwealth of Australia

Area Sq Km	7 692 024	**Languages**	English, Italian, Greek
Area Sq Miles	2 969 907	**Religions**	Protestant, Roman Catholic, Orthodox
Population	23 343 000	**Currency**	Australian dollar
Capital	Canberra	**Organizations**	APEC, Comm., OECD, UN

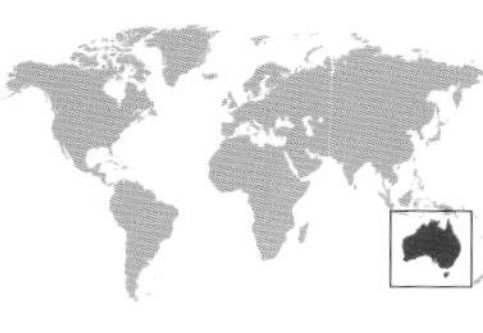

Australia, the world's sixth largest country, occupies the smallest, flattest and driest continent. The western half of the continent is mostly arid plateaus, ridges and vast deserts. The central eastern area comprises the lowlands of river systems draining into Lake Eyre, while to the east is the Great Dividing Range, a belt of ridges and plateaus running from Queensland to Tasmania. Climatically, more than two-thirds of the country is arid or semi-arid. The north is tropical monsoon, the east subtropical, and the southwest and southeast temperate. The majority of Australia's highly urbanized population lives along the east, southeast and southwest coasts. Australia has vast mineral deposits and various sources of energy. It is among the world's leading producers of iron ore, bauxite, nickel, copper and uranium. It is a major producer of coal, and oil and natural gas are also being exploited. Although accounting for under four per cent of the workforce, agriculture continues to be an important sector of the economy, with food and agricultural raw materials making up most of Australia's export earnings. Fuel, ores and metals, and manufactured goods, account for the remainder of exports. Japan and the USA are Australia's main trading partners.

Australian Capital Territory (Federal Territory)

Area Sq Km (Sq Miles)	Population	Capital
2 358 (910)	379 600	Canberra

Jervis Bay Territory (Territory)

Area Sq Km (Sq Miles)	Population
73 (28)	378

New South Wales (State)

Area Sq Km (Sq Miles)	Population	Capital
800 642 (309 130)	7 348 900	Sydney

Northern Territory (Territory)

Area Sq Km (Sq Miles)	Population	Capital
1 349 129 (520 902)	236 900	Darwin

Queensland (State)

Area Sq Km (Sq Miles)	Population	Capital
1 730 648 (668 207)	4 610 900	Brisbane

South Australia (State)

Area Sq Km (Sq Miles)	Population	Capital
983 482 (379 725)	1 662 200	Adelaide

Tasmania (State)

Area Sq Km (Sq Miles)	Population	Capital
68 401 (26 410)	512 400	Hobart

Victoria (State)

Area Sq Km (Sq Miles)	Population	Capital
227 416 (87 806)	5 679 600	Melbourne

Western Australia (State)

Area Sq Km (Sq Miles)	Population	Capital
2 529 875 (976 790)	2 472 700	Perth

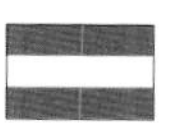

AUSTRIA
Republic of Austria

Area Sq Km	83 855	**Languages**	German, Croatian, Turkish
Area Sq Miles	32 377	**Religions**	Roman Catholic, Protestant
Population	8 495 000	**Currency**	Euro
Capital	Vienna (Wien)	**Organizations**	EU, OECD, UN

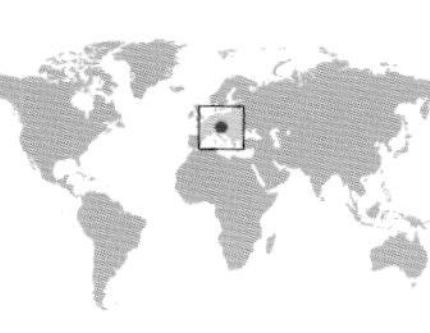

Two-thirds of Austria, a landlocked state in central Europe, lies within the Alps, with lower mountains to the north. The only lowlands are in the east. The Danube river valley in the northeast contains almost all the agricultural land and most of the population. Although the climate varies with altitude, in general summers are warm and winters cold with heavy snowfalls. Manufacturing industry and tourism are the most important sectors of the economy. Exports are dominated by manufactured goods. Germany is Austria's main trading partner.

AZERBAIJAN
Republic of Azerbaijan

Area Sq Km	86 600	**Languages**	Azeri, Armenian, Russian, Lezgian
Area Sq Miles	33 436	**Religions**	Shi'a Muslim, Sunni Muslim, Russian and Armenian Orthodox
Population	9 413 000	**Currency**	Azerbaijani manat
Capital	Baku	**Organizations**	CIS, UN

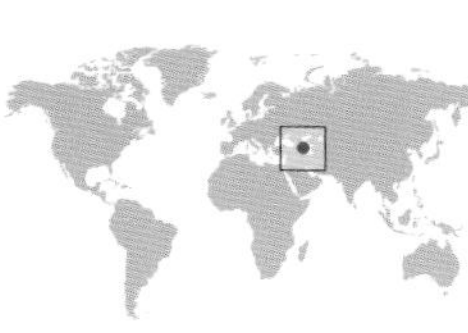

Azerbaijan lies to the southeast of the Caucasus mountains, on the Caspian Sea. Its region of Naxçıvan is separated from the rest of the country by part of Armenia. It has mountains in the northeast and west, valleys in the centre, and a low coastal plain. The climate is continental. It is rich in energy and mineral resources. Oil production, onshore and offshore, is the main industry and the basis of heavy industries. Agriculture is important, with cotton and tobacco the main cash crops.

THE BAHAMAS
Commonwealth of The Bahamas

Area Sq Km	13 939	**Languages**	English, Creole
Area Sq Miles	5 382	**Religions**	Protestant, Roman Catholic
Population	377 000	**Currency**	Bahamian dollar
Capital	Nassau	**Organizations**	CARICOM, Comm., UN

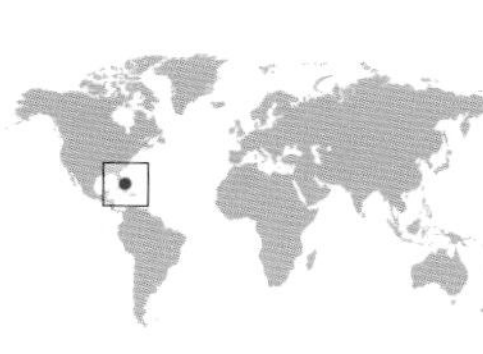

The Bahamas, an archipelago made up of approximately seven hundred islands and over two thousand cays, lies to the northeast of Cuba and east of the Florida coast of the USA. Twenty-two islands are inhabited, and seventy per cent of the population lives on the main island of New Providence. The climate is warm for much of the year, with heavy rainfall in the summer. Tourism is the islands' main industry. Offshore banking, insurance and ship registration are also major foreign exchange earners.

BAHRAIN
Kingdom of Bahrain

Area Sq Km	691	**Languages**	Arabic, English
Area Sq Miles	267	**Religions**	Shi'a Muslim, Sunni Muslim, Christian
Population	1 332 000	**Currency**	Bahraini dinar
Capital	Manama (Al Manāmah)	**Organizations**	UN

Bahrain consists of more than thirty islands lying in a bay in The Gulf, off the coasts of Saudi Arabia and Qatar. Bahrain Island, the largest island, is connected to other islands and to the mainland of Arabia by causeways. Oil production and processing are the main sectors of the economy.

BANGLADESH
People's Republic of Bangladesh

Area Sq Km	143 998	**Languages**	Bengali, English
Area Sq Miles	55 598	**Religions**	Sunni Muslim, Hindu
Population	156 595 000	**Currency**	Taka
Capital	Dhaka (Dacca)	**Organizations**	Comm., UN

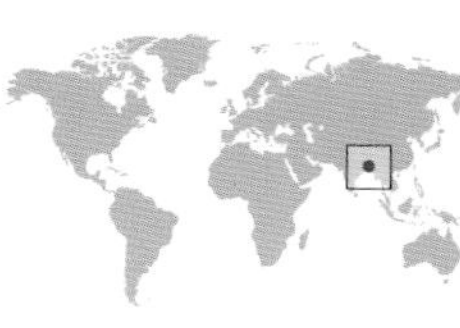

The south Asian state of Bangladesh is in the northeast of the Indian subcontinent, on the Bay of Bengal. It consists almost entirely of the low-lying alluvial plains and deltas of the Ganges and Brahmaputra rivers. The southwest is swampy, with mangrove forests in the delta area. The north, northeast and southeast have low forested hills. Bangladesh is one of the world's most densely populated and least developed countries. The economy is based on agriculture, though the garment industry is the main export sector. Storms during the summer monsoon season often cause devastating flooding and crop destruction. The country relies on large-scale foreign aid and remittances from workers abroad.

BARBADOS

Area Sq Km	430	**Languages**	English, Creole
Area Sq Miles	166	**Religions**	Protestant, Roman Catholic
Population	285 000	**Currency**	Barbadian dollar
Capital	Bridgetown	**Organizations**	CARICOM, Comm., UN

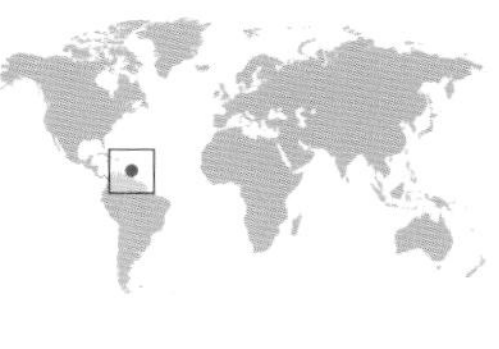

The most easterly of the Caribbean islands, Barbados is small and densely populated. It has a tropical climate and is subject to hurricanes. The economy is based on tourism, financial services, light industries and sugar production.

States and Territories

BELARUS
Republic of Belarus

Area Sq Km	207 600	Languages	Belarusian, Russian
Area Sq Miles	80 155	Religions	Belarusian Orthodox, Roman Catholic
Population	9 357 000	Currency	Belarusian rouble
Capital	Minsk	Organizations	CIS, UN

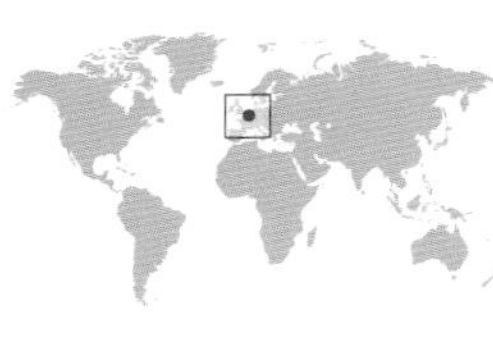

Belarus, a landlocked state in eastern Europe, consists of low hills and plains, with many lakes, rivers and, in the south, extensive marshes. Forests cover approximately one-third of the country. It has a continental climate. Agriculture contributes one-third of national income, with beef cattle and grains as the major products. Manufacturing industries produce a range of items, from construction equipment to textiles. Russia and Ukraine are the main trading partners.

BELGIUM
Kingdom of Belgium

Area Sq Km	30 520	Languages	Dutch (Flemish), French (Walloon), German
Area Sq Miles	11 784	Religions	Roman Catholic, Protestant
Population	11 104 000	Currency	Euro
Capital	Brussels (Brussel/Bruxelles)	Organizations	EU, NATO, OECD, UN

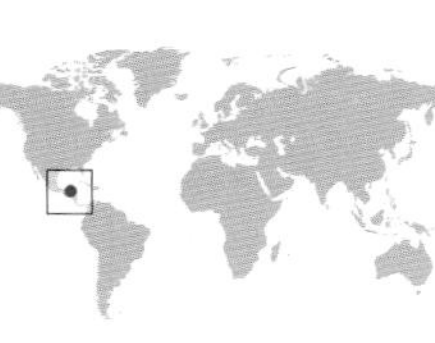

Belgium lies on the North Sea coast of western Europe. Beyond low sand dunes and a narrow belt of reclaimed land, fertile plains extend to the Sambre-Meuse river valley. The land rises to the forested Ardennes plateau in the southeast. Belgium has mild winters and cool summers. It is densely populated and has a highly urbanized population. With few mineral resources, Belgium imports raw materials for processing and manufacture. The agricultural sector is small, but provides for most food needs. A large services sector reflects Belgium's position as the home base for over eight hundred international institutions. The headquarters of the European Union are in the capital, Brussels.

BELIZE

Area Sq Km	22 965	Languages	English, Spanish, Mayan, Creole
Area Sq Miles	8 867	Religions	Roman Catholic, Protestant
Population	332 000	Currency	Belizean dollar
Capital	Belmopan	Organizations	CARICOM, Comm., UN

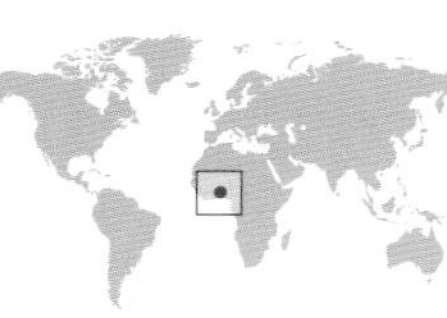

Belize lies on the Caribbean coast of central America and includes numerous cays and a large barrier reef offshore. The coastal areas are flat and swampy. To the southwest are the Maya Mountains. Tropical jungle covers much of the country and the climate is humid tropical, but tempered by sea breezes. A fifth of the population lives in the former capital Belize City. The economy is based primarily on agriculture, forestry and fishing, and exports include raw sugar, orange concentrate and bananas.

BENIN
Republic of Benin

Area Sq Km	112 620	Languages	French, Fon, Yoruba, Adja, other local languages
Area Sq Miles	43 483	Religions	Traditional beliefs, Roman Catholic, Sunni Muslim
Population	10 323 000	Currency	CFA franc
Capital	Porto-Novo	Organizations	UN

Benin is in west Africa, on the Gulf of Guinea. The climate is tropical in the north, equatorial in the south. The economy is based mainly on agriculture and transit trade. Agricultural products account for two-thirds of export earnings. Oil, produced offshore, is also a major export.

Bermuda
United Kingdom Overseas Territory

Area Sq Km	54	Languages	English
Area Sq Miles	21	Religions	Protestant, Roman Catholic
Population	65 000	Currency	Bermuda dollar
Capital	Hamilton		

In the Atlantic Ocean to the east of the USA, Bermuda comprises a group of small islands with a warm and humid climate. The economy is based on international business and tourism.

BHUTAN
Kingdom of Bhutan

Area Sq Km	46 620	Languages	Dzongkha, Nepali, Assamese
Area Sq Miles	18 000	Religions	Buddhist, Hindu
Population	754 000	Currency	Ngultrum, Indian rupee
Capital	Thimphu	Organizations	UN

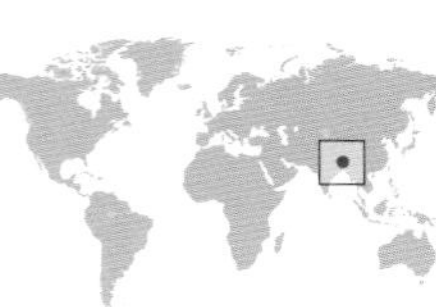

Bhutan lies in the eastern Himalaya mountains, between China and India. It is mountainous in the north, with fertile valleys. The climate ranges between permanently cold in the far north and subtropical in the south. Most of the population is involved in livestock rearing and subsistence farming. Bhutan is a producer of cardamom. Tourism is an increasingly important foreign currency earner and hydro electric power is also sold to India from the Tala site in the south-west.

BOLIVIA
Plurinational State of Bolivia

Area Sq Km	1 098 581	Languages	Spanish, Quechua, Aymara
Area Sq Miles	424 164	Religions	Roman Catholic, Protestant, Baha'i
Population	10 671 000	Currency	Boliviano
Capital	La Paz/Sucre	Organizations	UN

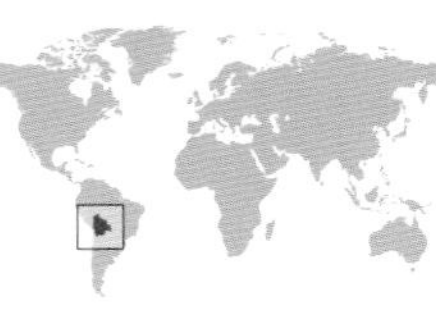

Bolivia is a landlocked state in central South America. Most Bolivians live on the high plateau within the Andes mountains. The lowlands range between dense rainforest in the northeast and semi-arid grasslands in the southeast. Bolivia is rich in minerals (zinc, tin and gold), and sales generate approximately half of export income. Natural gas, timber and soya beans are also exported. The USA is the main trading partner.

BOSNIA AND HERZEGOVINA

Area Sq Km	51 130	Languages	Bosnian, Serbian, Croatian
Area Sq Miles	19 741	Religions	Sunni Muslim, Serbian Orthodox, Roman Catholic, Protestant
Population	3 829 000	Currency	Convertible mark
Capital	Sarajevo	Organizations	UN

Bosnia and Herzegovina lies in the western Balkan Mountains of southern Europe, on the Adriatic Sea. It is mountainous, with ridges running northwest-southeast. The main lowlands are around the Sava valley in the north. Summers are warm, but winters can be very cold. The economy relies heavily on overseas aid.

BOTSWANA
Republic of Botswana

Area Sq Km	581 370	Languages	English, Setswana, Shona, other local languages
Area Sq Miles	224 468	Religions	Traditional beliefs, Protestant, Roman Catholic
Population	2 021 000	Currency	Pula
Capital	Gaborone	Organizations	Comm., SADC, UN

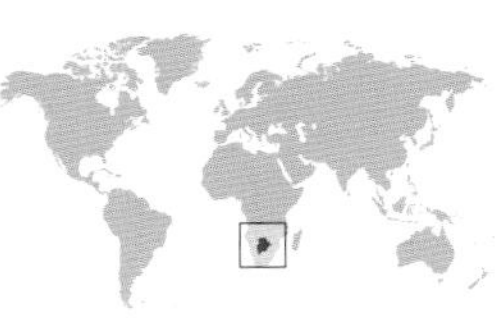

Botswana is a landlocked state in southern Africa. Over half of the country lies within the Kalahari Desert, with swamps to the north and salt-pans to the northeast. Most of the population lives near the eastern border. The climate is subtropical, but drought-prone. The economy was founded on cattle rearing, and although beef remains an important export, the economy is now based on mining. Diamonds account for seventy per cent of export earnings. Copper-nickel matte is also exported. The main trading partners are the UK and South Africa.

BRAZIL
Federative Republic of Brazil

Area Sq Km	8 514 879	Languages	Portuguese
Area Sq Miles	3 287 613	Religions	Roman Catholic, Protestant
Population	200 362 000	Currency	Real
Capital	Brasília	Organizations	UN

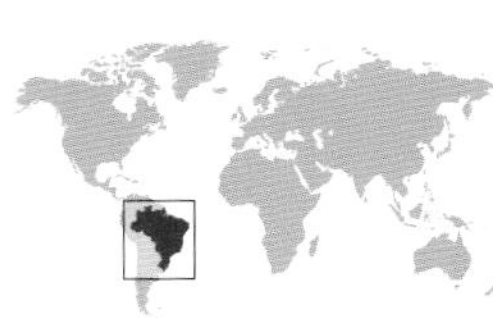

Brazil, in eastern South America, covers almost half of the continent, and is the world's fifth largest country. The northwest contains the vast basin of the Amazon, while the centre-west is largely a vast plateau of savanna and rock escarpments. The northeast is mostly semi-arid plateaus, while to the east and south are rugged mountains, fertile valleys and narrow, fertile coastal plains. The Amazon basin is hot, humid and wet; the rest of the country is cooler and drier, with seasonal variations. The northeast is drought-prone. Most Brazilians live in urban areas along the coast and on the central plateau. Brazil has well-developed agricultural, mining and service sectors, and the economy is larger than that of all other South American countries combined. Brazil is the world's biggest producer of coffee, and other agricultural crops include grains and sugar cane. Mineral production includes iron, aluminium and gold. Manufactured goods include food products, transport equipment, machinery and industrial chemicals. The main trading partners are the USA and Argentina. Economic reforms in Brazil have turned it into one of the fastest growing economies.

BRUNEI
Brunei Darussalam

Area Sq Km	5 765	Languages	Malay, English, Chinese
Area Sq Miles	2 226	Religions	Sunni Muslim, Buddhist, Christian
Population	418 000	Currency	Bruneian dollar
Capital	Bandar Seri Begawan	Organizations	APEC, ASEAN, Comm., UN

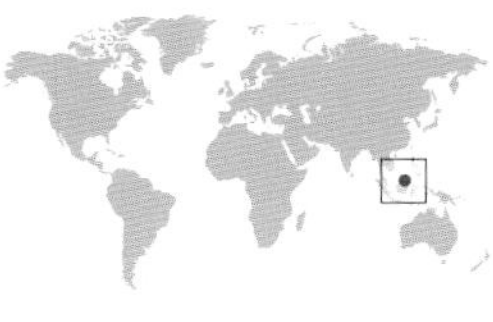

The southeast Asian oil-rich state of Brunei lies on the northwest coast of the island of Borneo, on the South China Sea. Its two enclaves are surrounded by the Malaysian state of Sarawak. Tropical rainforest covers over two-thirds of the country. The economy is dominated by the oil and gas industries.

BULGARIA
Republic of Bulgaria

Area Sq Km	110 994	Languages	Bulgarian, Turkish, Romany, Macedonian
Area Sq Miles	42 855	Religions	Bulgarian Orthodox, Sunni Muslim
Population	7 223 000	Currency	Lev
Capital	Sofia	Organizations	EU, NATO, UN

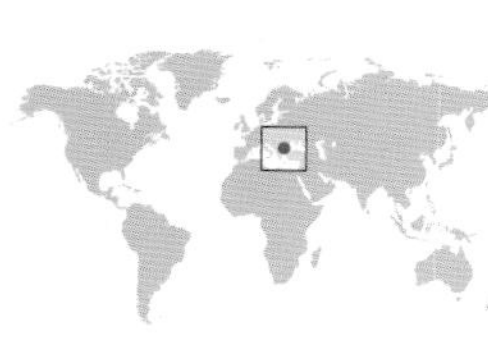

Bulgaria, in southern Europe, borders the western shore of the Black Sea. The Balkan Mountains separate the Danube plains in the north from the Rhodope Mountains and the lowlands in the south. The economy has a strong agricultural base. Manufacturing industries include machinery, consumer goods, chemicals and metals. Most trade is with Russia, Italy and Germany.

BURKINA FASO

Area Sq Km	274 200	Languages	French, Moore (Mossi), Fulani, other local languages
Area Sq Miles	105 869	Religions	Sunni Muslim, traditional beliefs, Roman Catholic
Population	16 935 000	Currency	CFA franc
Capital	Ouagadougou	Organizations	UN

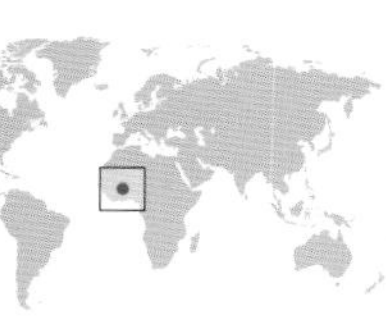

Burkina, a landlocked country in west Africa, lies within the Sahara desert to the north and semi-arid savanna to the south. Rainfall is erratic, and droughts are common. Livestock rearing and farming are the main activities, and cotton, livestock, groundnuts and some minerals are exported. Burkina relies heavily on foreign aid, and is one of the poorest and least developed countries in the world.

BURUNDI
Republic of Burundi

Area Sq Km	27 835	Languages	Kirundi (Hutu, Tutsi), French
Area Sq Miles	10 747	Religions	Roman Catholic, traditional beliefs, Protestant
Population	10 163 000	Currency	Burundian franc
Capital	Bujumbura	Organizations	UN

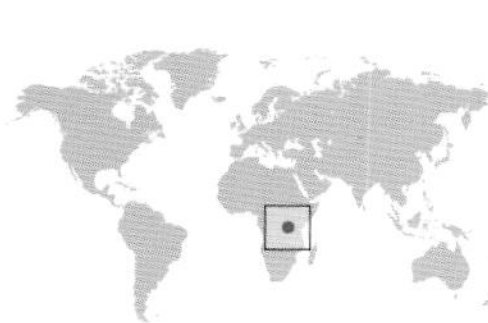

The densely populated east African state of Burundi consists of high plateaus rising from the shores of Lake Tanganyika in the southwest. It has a tropical climate and depends on subsistence farming. Coffee is its main export, and its main trading partners are Germany and Belgium. The country has been badly affected by internal conflict since the early 1990s.

CAMBODIA
Kingdom of Cambodia

Area Sq Km	181 000	Languages	Khmer
Area Sq Miles	69 884	Religions	Buddhist, Roman Catholic, Sunni Muslim
Population	15 135 000	Currency	Riel
Capital	Phnom Penh (Phnum Pénh)	Organizations	ASEAN, UN

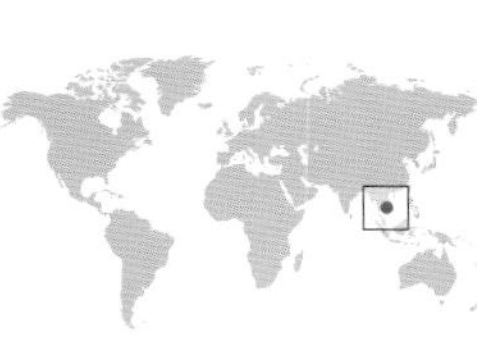

Cambodia lies in southeast Asia on the Gulf of Thailand, and occupies the Mekong river basin, with the Tônlé Sap (Great Lake) at its centre. The climate is tropical monsoon. Forests cover half the country. Most of the population lives on the plains and is engaged in farming (chiefly rice growing), fishing and forestry. The economy is recovering following the devastation of civil war in the 1970s with rapid progress since 2000. Mineral resources are starting to be indentified for development.

CAMEROON
Republic of Cameroon

Area Sq Km	475 442	Languages	French, English, Fang, Bamileke, other local languages
Area Sq Miles	183 569	Religions	Roman Catholic, traditional beliefs, Sunni Muslim, Protestant
Population	22 254 000	Currency	CFA franc
Capital	Yaoundé	Organizations	Comm., UN

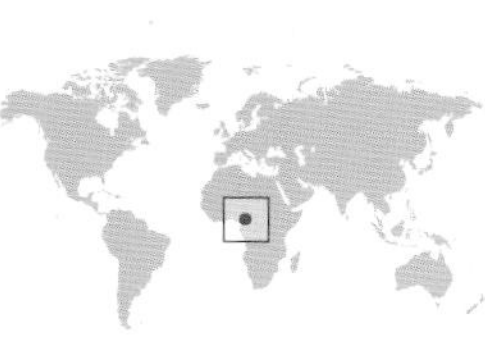

Cameroon is in west Africa, on the Gulf of Guinea. The coastal plains and southern and central plateaus are covered with tropical forest. Despite oil resources and favourable agricultural conditions Cameroon still faces problems of underdevelopment. Oil, timber and cocoa are the main exports. France is the main trading partner.

CANADA

Area Sq Km	9 984 670	Languages	English, French
Area Sq Miles	3 855 103	Religions	Roman Catholic, Protestant, Eastern Orthodox, Jewish
Population	35 182 000	Currency	Canadian dollar
Capital	Ottawa	Organizations	APEC, Comm., NATO, OECD, UN

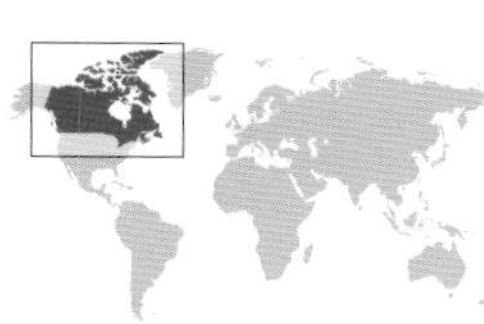

The world's second largest country, Canada covers the northern two-fifths of North America and has coastlines on the Atlantic, Arctic and Pacific Oceans. In the west are the Coast Mountains, the Rocky Mountains and interior plateaus. In the centre lie the fertile Prairies. Further east, covering about half the total land area, is the Canadian Shield, a relatively flat area of infertile lowlands around Hudson Bay, extending to Labrador on the east coast. The Shield is bordered to the south by the fertile Great Lakes-St Lawrence lowlands. In the far north climatic conditions are polar, while the rest has a continental climate. Most Canadians live in the urban areas of the Great Lakes-St Lawrence basin. Canada is rich in mineral and energy resources. Only five per cent of land is arable. Canada is among the world's leading producers of wheat, of wood from its vast coniferous forests, and of fish and seafood from its Atlantic and Pacific fishing grounds. It is a major producer of nickel, uranium, copper, iron ore, zinc and other minerals, as well as oil and natural gas. Its abundant raw materials are the basis for many manufacturing industries. Main exports are machinery, motor vehicles, oil, timber, newsprint and paper, wood pulp and wheat. Since the 1989 free trade agreement with the USA and the 1994 North America Free Trade Agreement, trade with the USA has grown and now accounts for around fifty per cent of imports and around seventy-five per cent of exports.

Alberta (Province)

Area Sq Km (Sq Miles)	Population	Capital
661 848 (255 541)	3 965 339	Edmonton

British Columbia (Province)

Area Sq Km (Sq Miles)	Population	Capital
944 735 (364 764)	4 650 004	Victoria

Manitoba (Province)

Area Sq Km (Sq Miles)	Population	Capital
647 797 (250 116)	1 277 339	Winnipeg

New Brunswick (Province)

Area Sq Km (Sq Miles)	Population	Capital
72 908 (28 150)	754 039	Fredericton

Newfoundland and Labrador (Province)

Area Sq Km (Sq Miles)	Population	Capital
405 212 (156 453)	513 568	St John's

Northwest Territories (Territory)

Area Sq Km (Sq Miles)	Population	Capital
1 346 106 (519 734)	43 349	Yellowknife

Nova Scotia (Province)

Area Sq Km (Sq Miles)	Population	Capital
55 284 (21 345)	945 015	Halifax

Nunavut (Territory)

Area Sq Km (Sq Miles)	Population	Capital
2 093 190 (808 185)	34 023	Iqaluit

Ontario (Province)

Area Sq Km (Sq Miles)	Population	Capital
1 076 395 (415 598)	13 583 710	Toronto

Prince Edward Island (Province)

Area Sq Km (Sq Miles)	Population	Capital
5 660 (2 185)	145 763	Charlottetown

Québec (Province)

Area Sq Km (Sq Miles)	Population	Capital
1 542 056 (595 391)	8 099 095	Québec

Saskatchewan (Province)

Area Sq Km (Sq Miles)	Population	Capital
651 036 (251 366)	1 093 880	Regina

Yukon (Territory)

Area Sq Km (Sq Miles)	Population	Capital
482 443 (186 272)	36 418	Whitehorse

CAPE VERDE (Cabo Verde)
Republic of Cabo Verde

Area Sq Km	4 033	Languages	Portuguese, Creole
Area Sq Miles	1 557	Religions	Roman Catholic, Protestant
Population	499 000	Currency	Cape Verdean escudo
Capital	Praia	Organizations	UN

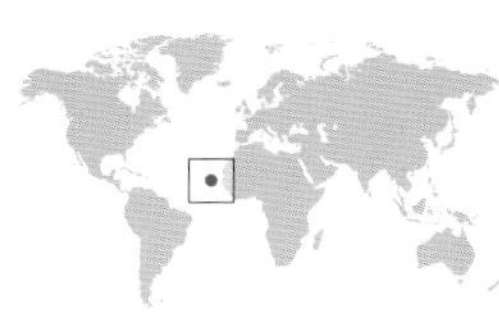

Cape Verde is a group of semi-arid volcanic islands lying off the coast of west Africa. The economy is based on fishing, subsistence farming and service industries. Windfarms on four islands supply around a quarter of all electricity.

Cayman Islands
United Kingdom Overseas Territory

Area Sq Km	259	Languages	English
Area Sq Miles	100	Religions	Protestant, Roman Catholic
Population	58 000	Currency	Cayman Islands dollar
Capital	George Town		

A group of islands in the Caribbean, northwest of Jamaica. There are three main islands: Grand Cayman, Little Cayman and Cayman Brac. The Cayman Islands are one of the world's major offshore financial centres. Tourism is also important to the economy.

CENTRAL AFRICAN REPUBLIC

Area Sq Km	622 436	Languages	French, Sango, Banda, Baya, other local languages
Area Sq Miles	240 324	Religions	Protestant, Roman Catholic, traditional beliefs, Sunni Muslim
Population	4 616 000	Currency	CFA franc
Capital	Bangui	Organizations	UN

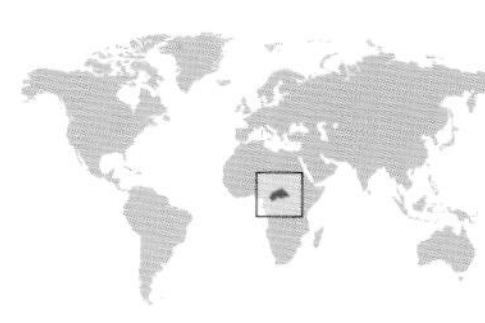

A landlocked country in central Africa, the Central African Republic is mainly savanna plateau, drained by the Ubangi and Chari river systems, with mountains to the east and west. The climate is tropical, with high rainfall. Most of the population lives in the south and west, and a majority of the workforce is involved in subsistence farming. Some cotton, coffee, tobacco and timber are exported, but diamonds account for around half of export earnings.

States and Territories

CHAD
Republic of Chad

Area Sq Km	1 284 000	Languages	Arabic, French, Sara, other local languages
Area Sq Miles	495 755	Religions	Sunni Muslim, Roman Catholic, Protestant, traditional beliefs
Population	12 825 000	Currency	CFA franc
Capital	Ndjamena	Organizations	UN

Chad is a landlocked state of north-central Africa. It consists of plateaus, the Tibesti mountains in the north and the Lake Chad basin in the west. Climatic conditions range between desert in the north and tropical forest in the southwest. With few natural resources, Chad relies on subsistence farming, exports of raw cotton, and foreign aid. The main trading partners are France, Portugal and Cameroon.

CHILE
Republic of Chile

Area Sq Km	756 945	Languages	Spanish, Amerindian languages
Area Sq Miles	292 258	Religions	Roman Catholic, Protestant
Population	17 620 000	Currency	Chilean peso
Capital	Santiago	Organizations	APEC, OECD, UN

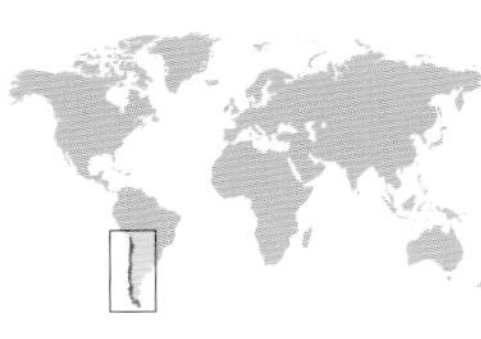

Chile lies along the Pacific coast of the southern half of South America. Between the Andes in the east and the lower coastal ranges is a central valley, with a mild climate, where most Chileans live. To the north is the arid Atacama Desert and to the south is cold, wet forested grassland. Chile has considerable mineral resources and is the world's leading exporter of copper. Nitrates, molybdenum, gold and iron ore are also mined. Agriculture (particularly viticulture), forestry and fishing are also important to the economy.

CHINA
People's Republic of China

Area Sq Km	9 606 802	Languages	Mandarin (Putonghua), Wu, Cantonese, Hsiang, regional languages
Area Sq Miles	3 709 186	Religions	Confucian, Taoist, Buddhist, Christian, Sunni Muslim
Population	1 369 993 000	Currency	Yuan, Hong Kong dollar, Macao pataca
Capital	Beijing (Peking)	Organizations	APEC, UN

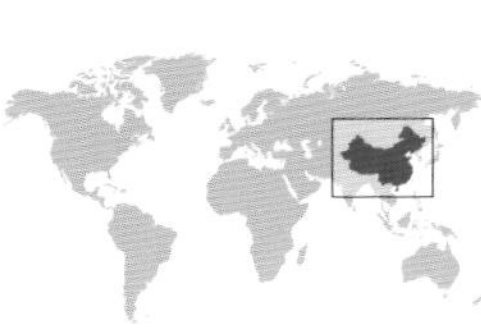

China, the world's most populous and fourth largest country, occupies a large part of east Asia, borders fourteen states and has coastlines on the Yellow, East China and South China Seas. It has a huge variety of landscapes. The southwest contains the high Plateau of Tibet, flanked by the Himalaya and Kunlun Shan mountains. The north is mountainous with arid basins and extends from the Tien Shan and Altai Mountains and the vast Taklimakan Desert in the west to the plateau and Gobi Desert in the centre-east. Eastern China is predominantly lowland and is divided broadly into the basins of the Yellow River (Huang He) in the north, the Yangtze (Chang Jiang) in the centre and the Pearl River (Xi Jiang) in the southeast. Climatic conditions and vegetation are as diverse as the topography: much of the country experiences temperate conditions, while the southwest has an extreme mountain climate and the southeast enjoys a moist, warm subtropical climate. Just under fifty per cent of China's huge population lives in rural areas, and agriculture employs around thirty-five per cent of the working population. The main crops are rice, wheat, soya beans, peanuts, cotton, tobacco and hemp. China is rich in coal, oil and natural gas and has the world's largest potential in hydroelectric power. It is a major world producer of iron ore, molybdenum, copper, asbestos and gold. Economic reforms from the early 1980's led to an explosion in manufacturing development concentrated on the 'coastal economic open region'. The main exports are machinery, textiles, footwear, toys and sports goods. Japan and the USA are China's main trading partners.

	Area Sq Km (Sq Miles)	Population	Capital
Anhui (Province)	139 000 (53 900)	59 680 000	Hefei
Beijing (Municipality)	16 411 (6 336)	20 186 000	Beijing (Peking)
Chongqing (Municipality)	82 400 (31 815)	29 190 000	Chongqing
Fujian (Province)	124 000 (47 876)	37 200 000	Fuzhou
Gansu (Province)	425 800 (164 401)	25 642 000	Lanzhou
Guangdong (Province)	179 800 (69 421)	105 048 000	Guangzhou (Canton)
Guangxi Zhuangzu Zizhiqu (Autonomous Region)	237 600 (91 737)	46 450 000	Nanning
Guizhou (Province)	176 000 (67 954)	34 687 000	Guiyang
Hainan (Province)	35 000 (13 514)	8 773 000	Haikou
Hebei (Province)	188 000 (72 587)	72 405 000	Shijiazhuang
Heilongjiang (Province)	473 000 (182 625)	38 340 000	Harbin
Henan (Province)	167 000 (64 479)	93 880 000	Zhengzhou
Hong Kong (Xianggang) (Special Administrative Region)	1 104 (426)	7 112 000	Hong Kong (Xianggang)
Hubei (Province)	185 900 (71 776)	57 575 000	Wuhan
Hunan (Province)	211 800 (81 776)	65 956 000	Changsha
Jiangsu (Province)	102 600 (39 614)	78 988 000	Nanjing
Jiangxi (Province)	166 900 (64 440)	44 884 000	Nanchang
Jilin (Province)	187 400 (72 355)	27 494 000	Changchun
Liaoning (Province)	148 000 (57 143)	43 830 000	Shenyang
Macao (Special Administrative Region)	30 (12)	557 000	Macao
Nei Mongol Zizhiqu Inner Mongolia (Autonomous Region)	1 183 000 (456 756)	24 817 000	Hohhot
Ningxia Huizu Zizhiqu (Autonomous Region)	66 400 (25 637)	6 395 000	Yinchuan
Qinghai (Province)	722 300 (278 880)	5 682 000	Xining
Shaanxi (Province)	205 800 (79 459)	37 426 000	Xi'an
Shandong (Province)	157 100 (60 656)	96 370 000	Jinan
Shanghai (Municipality)	6 340 (2 448)	23 475 000	Shanghai
Shanxi (Province)	156 700 (60 502)	35 930 000	Taiyuan
Sichuan (Province)	486 000 (187 645)	80 500 000	Chengdu
Tianjin (Municipality)	11 917 (4 601)	13 550 000	Tianjin
Xinjiang Uygur Zizhiqu Sinkiang (Autonomous Region)	1 664 900 (642 818)	22 087 000	Ürümqi
Xizang Zizhiqu Tibet (Autonomous Region)	1 202 200 (464 169)	3 033 000	Lhasa
Yunnan (Province)	394 000 (152 123)	46 308 000	Kunming
Zhejiang (Province)	101 800 (39 305)	54 630 000	Hangzhou

Taiwan: The People's Republic of China claims Taiwan as its 23rd Province

Christmas Island
Australian External Territory

Area Sq Km	135	Languages	English
Area Sq Miles	52	Religions	Buddhist, Sunni Muslim, Protestant, Roman Catholic
Population	2 072	Currency	Australian dollar
Capital	The Settlement (Flying Fish Cove)		

The island is situated in the east of the Indian Ocean, to the south of Indonesia. The economy was formerly based on phosphate extraction, although the mine is now closed. Tourism is developing and is a major employer.

Cocos (Keeling) Islands
Australian External Territory

Area Sq Km	14	Languages	English
Area Sq Miles	5	Religions	Sunni Muslim, Christian
Population	550	Currency	Australian dollar
Capital	West Island		

The Cocos Islands consist of numerous islands on two coral atolls in the eastern Indian Ocean between Sri Lanka and Australia. Most of the population lives on West Island or Home Island. Coconuts are the only cash crop, and the main export.

COLOMBIA
Republic of Colombia

Area Sq Km	1 141 748	Languages	Spanish, Amerindian languages
Area Sq Miles	440 831	Religions	Roman Catholic, Protestant
Population	48 321 000	Currency	Colombian peso
Capital	Bogotá	Organizations	UN

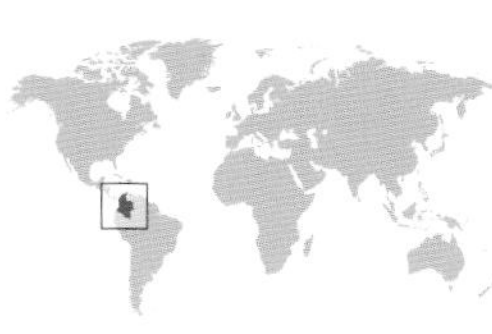

A state in northwest South America, Colombia has coastlines on the Pacific Ocean and the Caribbean Sea. Behind coastal plains lie three ranges of the Andes mountains, separated by high valleys and plateaus where most Colombians live. To the southeast are grasslands and the forests of the Amazon. The climate is tropical, although temperatures vary with altitude. Only five per cent of land is cultivable. Coffee (Colombia is the world's second largest producer), sugar, bananas, cotton and flowers are exported. Coal, nickel,

gold, silver, platinum and emeralds (Colombia is the world's largest producer) are mined. Oil and its products are the main export. Industries include the processing of minerals and crops. The main trade partner is the USA. Internal violence – both politically motivated and relating to Colombia's leading role in the international trade in illegal drugs – continues to hinder development.

COMOROS
Union of the Comoros

Area Sq Km	1 862	Languages	Shikomor (Comorian), French, Arabic
Area Sq Miles	719	Religions	Sunni Muslim, Roman Catholic
Population	735 000	Currency	Comorian franc
Capital	Moroni	Organizations	UN

This state, in the Indian Ocean off the east African coast, comprises three volcanic islands of Ngazidja (Grande Comore), Nzwani (Anjouan) and Mwali (Mohéli), and some coral atolls. These tropical islands are mountainous, with poor soil and few natural resources. Subsistence farming predominates. Vanilla, cloves and ylang-ylang (an essential oil) are exported, and the economy relies heavily on workers' remittances from abroad.

CONGO
Republic of the Congo

Area Sq Km	342 000	Languages	French, Kongo, Monokutuba, other local languages
Area Sq Miles	132 047	Religions	Roman Catholic, Protestant, traditional beliefs, Sunni Muslim
Population	4 448 000	Currency	CFA franc
Capital	Brazzaville	Organizations	UN

Congo, in central Africa, is mostly a forest or savanna-covered plateau drained by the Ubangi-Congo river systems. Sand dunes and lagoons line the short Atlantic coast. The climate is hot and tropical. Most Congolese live in the southern third of the country. Half of the workforce are farmers, growing food and cash crops including sugar, coffee, cocoa and oil palms. Oil and timber are the mainstays of the economy, and oil generates over fifty per cent of the country's export revenues.

CONGO, DEMOCRATIC REPUBLIC OF THE

Area Sq Km	2 345 410	Languages	French, Lingala, Swahili, Kongo, other local languages
Area Sq Miles	905 568	Religions	Christian, Sunni Muslim
Population	67 514 000	Currency	Congolese franc
Capital	Kinshasa	Organizations	SADC, UN

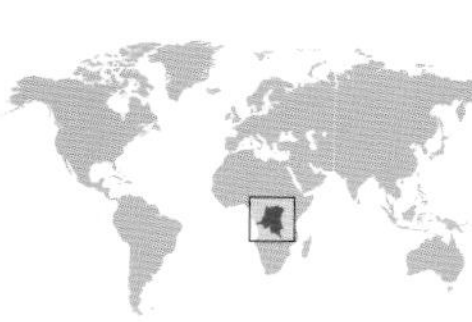

This central African state, formerly Zaire, consists of the basin of the Congo river flanked by plateaus, with high mountain ranges to the east and a short Atlantic coastline to the west. The climate is tropical, with rainforest close to the Equator and savanna to the north and south. Fertile land allows a range of food and cash crops to be grown, chiefly coffee. The country has vast mineral resources, with copper, cobalt and diamonds being the most important.

Cook Islands
Self-governing New Zealand Overseas Territory

Area Sq Km	293	Languages	English, Maori
Area Sq Miles	113	Religions	Protestant, Roman Catholic
Population	21 000	Currency	New Zealand dollar
Capital	Avarua		

These consist of groups of coral atolls and volcanic islands in the southwest Pacific Ocean. The main island is Rarotonga. Distance from foreign markets and restricted natural resources hinder development.

COSTA RICA
Republic of Costa Rica

Area Sq Km	51 100	Languages	Spanish
Area Sq Miles	19 730	Religions	Roman Catholic, Protestant
Population	4 872 000	Currency	Costa Rican colón
Capital	San José	Organizations	UN

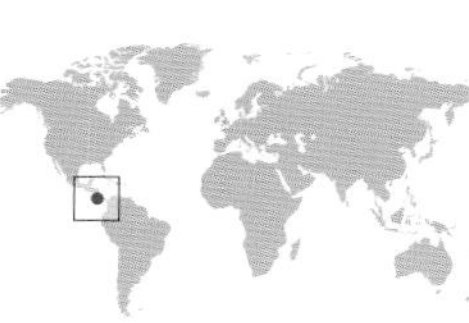

Costa Rica, in central America, has coastlines on the Caribbean Sea and Pacific Ocean. From tropical coastal plains, the land rises to mountains and a temperate central plateau, where most of the population lives. The economy depends on agriculture and tourism, with ecotourism becoming increasingly important. Main exports are textiles, coffee and bananas, and the USA is the main trading partner.

CÔTE D'IVOIRE (Ivory Coast)
Republic of Côte d'Ivoire

Area Sq Km	322 463	Languages	French, Creole, Akan, other local languages
Area Sq Miles	124 504	Religions	Sunni Muslim, Roman Catholic, traditional beliefs, Protestant
Population	20 316 000	Currency	CFA franc
Capital	Yamoussoukro	Organizations	UN

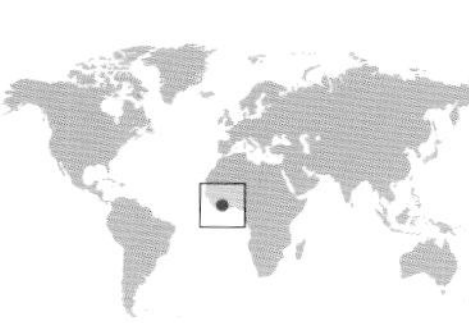

Côte d'Ivoire (Ivory Coast) is in west Africa, on the Gulf of Guinea. In the north are plateaus and savanna; in the south are low undulating plains and rainforest, with sand-bars and lagoons on the coast. Temperatures are warm, and rainfall is heavier in the south. Most of the workforce is engaged in farming. Côte d'Ivoire is a major producer of cocoa and coffee, and agricultural products (also including cotton and timber) are the main exports. Oil and gas have begun to be exploited.

Crimea
Disputed territory

Area Sq Km	27 000	Languages	Ukrainian, Russian
Area Sq Miles	10 400	Religions	Russian Orthodox, Sunni Muslim
Population	2 348 600	Currency	Russian rouble
Capital	Simferopol'		

Following internal unrest in Ukraine in 2014, Russian-supported separatists in Crimea in southern Ukraine seized power in that region and a quickly arranged referendum resulted in the two administrative divisions in Crimea – the Autonomous Republic of Crimea (Respublika Krym) and the municipality of Sevastopol' – declaring independence from Ukraine as the Republic of Crimea. The referendum and its outcome were not recognized by the majority of the international community. Russia then passed a law in March 2014 annexing the Republic of Crimea, declaring it to be part of Russia – a move similarly not recognized, and strongly condemned by the majority of the international community. Ukrainian forces withdrew from Crimea soon after this annexation.

CROATIA
Republic of Croatia

Area Sq Km	56 538	Languages	Croatian, Serbian
Area Sq Miles	21 829	Religions	Roman Catholic, Serbian Orthodox, Sunni Muslim
Population	4 290 000	Currency	Kuna
Capital	Zagreb	Organizations	EU, NATO, UN

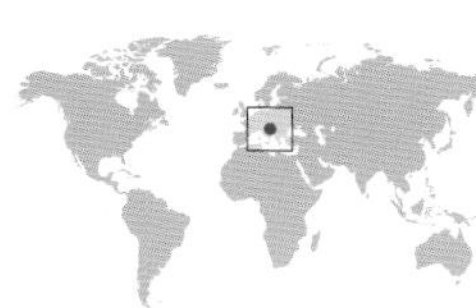

The southern European state of Croatia has a long coastline on the Adriatic Sea, with many offshore islands. Coastal areas have a Mediterranean climate; inland is cooler and wetter. Croatia was once strong agriculturally and industrially, but conflict in the early 1990s, and associated loss of markets and a fall in tourist revenue, caused economic difficulties from which recovery has been slow.

CUBA
Republic of Cuba

Area Sq Km	110 860	Languages	Spanish
Area Sq Miles	42 803	Religions	Roman Catholic, Protestant
Population	11 266 000	Currency	Cuban peso
Capital	Havana (La Habana)	Organizations	UN

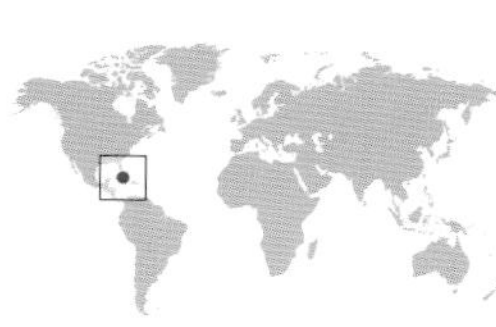

The country comprises the island of Cuba (the largest island in the Caribbean), and many islets and cays. A fifth of Cubans live in and around Havana. Cuba is slowly recovering from the withdrawal of aid and subsidies from the former USSR. Sugar remains the basis of the economy, although tourism is developing and is, together with remittances from workers abroad, an important source of revenue.

Curaçao
Self-governing Netherlands territory

Area Sq Km	444	Languages	Dutch, Papiamento
Area Sq Miles	171	Religions	Roman Catholic, Protestant
Population	159 000	Currency	Caribbean guilder
Capital	Willemstad		

Situated in the Caribbean Sea off the north coast of Venezuela, Curaçao was previously part of the Netherlands Antilles until they were dissolved in October 2010. It consists of the main island and the smaller uninhabited Klein Curaçao and is the largest and most populous of the Lesser Antilles. Oil refining and tourism form the basis of the economy.

CYPRUS
Republic of Cyprus

Area Sq Km	9 251	Languages	Greek, Turkish, English
Area Sq Miles	3 572	Religions	Greek Orthodox, Sunni Muslim
Population	1 141 000	Currency	Euro
Capital	Nicosia (Lefkosia)	Organizations	Comm., EU, UN

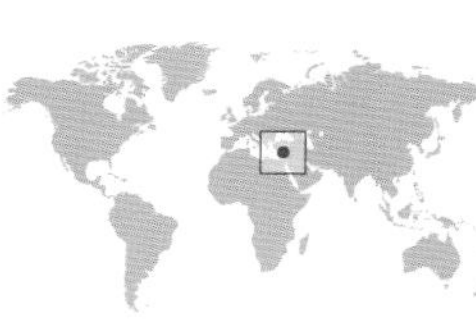

The eastern Mediterranean island of Cyprus has effectively been divided into two since 1974. The economy of the Greek-speaking south is based mainly on specialist agriculture and tourism, with shipping and offshore banking. The ethnically Turkish north depends on agriculture, tourism and aid from Turkey. The island has hot dry summers and mild winters. Cyprus joined the European Union in May 2004.

CZECH REPUBLIC

Area Sq Km	78 864	Languages	Czech, Moravian, Slovakian
Area Sq Miles	30 450	Religions	Roman Catholic, Protestant
Population	10 702 000	Currency	Koruna
Capital	Prague (Praha)	Organizations	EU, NATO, OECD, UN

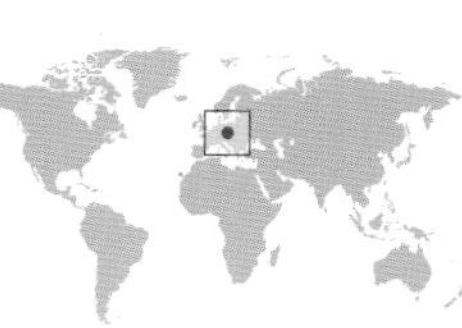

The landlocked Czech Republic in central Europe consists of rolling countryside, wooded hills and fertile valleys. The climate is continental. The country has substantial reserves of coal and lignite, timber and some minerals, chiefly iron ore. It is highly industrialized, and major manufactured goods include industrial machinery, consumer goods, cars, iron and steel, chemicals and glass. Germany is the main trading partner. The Czech Republic joined the European Union in May 2004.

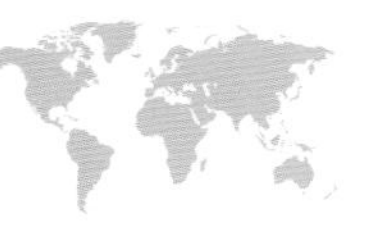

States and Territories

DENMARK
Kingdom of Denmark

Area Sq Km	43 075	Languages	Danish
Area Sq Miles	16 631	Religions	Protestant
Population	5 619 000	Currency	Danish krone
Capital	Copenhagen (København)	Organizations	EU, NATO, OECD, UN

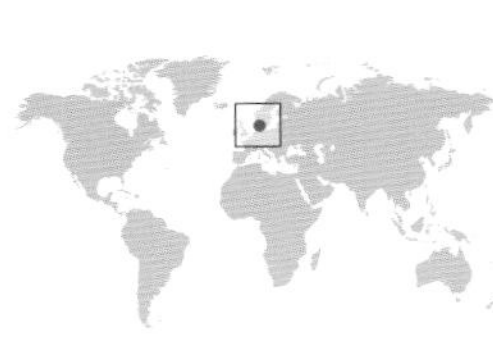

In northern Europe, Denmark occupies the Jutland (Jylland) peninsula and nearly five hundred islands in and between the North and Baltic Seas. The country is low-lying, with long, indented coastlines. The climate is cool and temperate, with rainfall throughout the year. A fifth of the population lives in and around the capital, Copenhagen (København), on the largest of the islands, Zealand (Sjælland). The country's main natural resource is its agricultural potential: two-thirds of the total area is fertile farmland or pasture. Agriculture is high-tech, and with forestry and fishing employs only around six per cent of the workforce. Denmark is self-sufficient in oil and natural gas, produced from fields in the North Sea. Manufacturing, largely based on imported raw materials, accounts for over half of all exports, which include machinery, food, furniture and pharmaceuticals. The main trading partners are Germany and Sweden.

DJIBOUTI
Republic of Djibouti

Area Sq Km	23 200	Languages	Somali, Afar, French, Arabic
Area Sq Miles	8 958	Religions	Sunni Muslim, Christian
Population	873 000	Currency	Djiboutian franc
Capital	Djibouti	Organizations	UN

Djibouti lies in northeast Africa, on the Gulf of Aden at the entrance to the Red Sea. Most of the country is semi-arid desert with high temperatures and low rainfall. More than two-thirds of the population live in the capital. There is some camel, sheep and goat herding, but with few natural resources the economy is based on services and trade. Djibouti serves as a free trade zone for northern Africa, and the capital's port is a major transhipment and refuelling destination. It is linked by rail to Addis Ababa in Ethiopia.

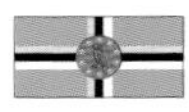

DOMINICA
Commonwealth of Dominica

Area Sq Km	750	Languages	English, Creole
Area Sq Miles	290	Religions	Roman Catholic, Protestant
Population	72 000	Currency	East Caribbean dollar
Capital	Roseau	Organizations	CARICOM, Comm., UN

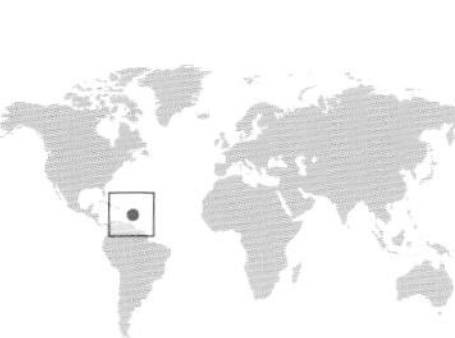

Dominica is the most northerly of the Windward Islands, in the eastern Caribbean. It is very mountainous and forested, with a coastline of steep cliffs. The climate is tropical and rainfall is abundant. Approximately a quarter of Dominicans live in the capital. The economy is based on agriculture, with bananas (the major export), coconuts and citrus fruits the most important crops. Tourism is a developing industry.

DOMINICAN REPUBLIC

Area Sq Km	48 442	Languages	Spanish, Creole
Area Sq Miles	18 704	Religions	Roman Catholic, Protestant
Population	10 404 000	Currency	Dominican peso
Capital	Santo Domingo	Organizations	UN

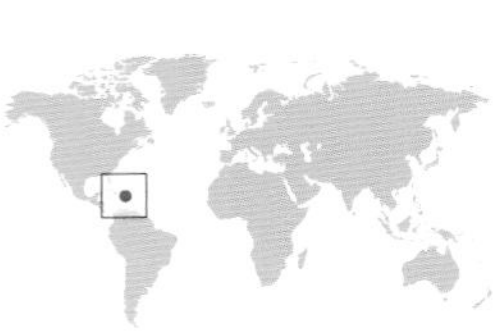

The state occupies the eastern two-thirds of the Caribbean island of Hispaniola (the western third is Haiti). It has a series of mountain ranges, fertile valleys and a large coastal plain in the east. The climate is hot tropical, with heavy rainfall. Sugar, coffee and cocoa are the main cash crops. Nickel (the main export), and gold are mined, and there is some light industry. The USA is the main trading partner. Tourism is the main foreign exchange earner.

EAST TIMOR (Timor-Leste)
Democratic Republic of Timor-Leste

Area Sq Km	14 874	Languages	Portuguese, Tetun, English
Area Sq Miles	5 743	Religions	Roman Catholic
Population	1 133 000	Currency	United States dollar
Capital	Dili	Organizations	UN

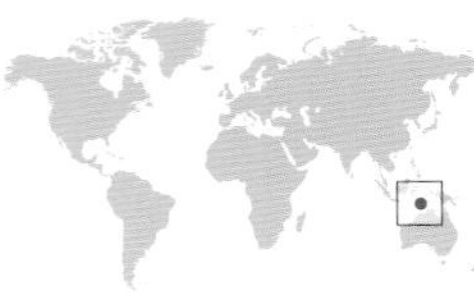

The island of Timor is part of the Indonesian archipelago, to the north of western Australia. East Timor occupies the eastern section of the island, and a small coastal enclave (Ocussi) to the west. A referendum in 1999 ended Indonesia's occupation, after which the country was under UN transitional administration until full independence was achieved in 2002. The economy is in a poor state and East Timor is heavily dependent on foreign aid.

ECUADOR
Republic of Ecuador

Area Sq Km	272 045	Languages	Spanish, Quechua, and other Amerindian languages
Area Sq Miles	105 037	Religions	Roman Catholic
Population	15 738 000	Currency	United States dollar
Capital	Quito	Organizations	OPEC, UN

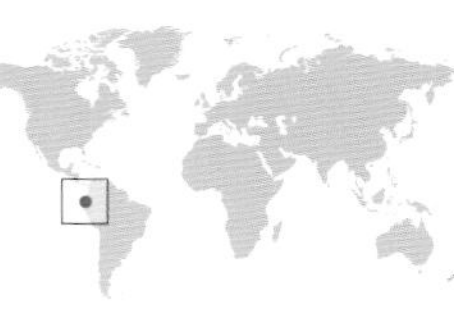

Ecuador is in northwest South America, on the Pacific coast. It consists of a broad coastal plain, high mountain ranges in the Andes, and part of the forested upper Amazon basin to the east. The climate is tropical, moderated by altitude. Most people live on the coast or in the mountain valleys. Ecuador is one of South America's main oil producers, and mineral reserves include gold. Most of the workforce depends on agriculture. Petroleum, bananas, shrimps, coffee and cocoa are exported. The USA is the main trading partner.

EGYPT
Arab Republic of Egypt

Area Sq Km	1 101 450	Languages	Arabic
Area Sq Miles	386 660	Religions	Sunni Muslim, Coptic Christian
Population	82 056 000	Currency	Egyptian pound
Capital	Cairo (Al Qāhirah)	Organizations	UN

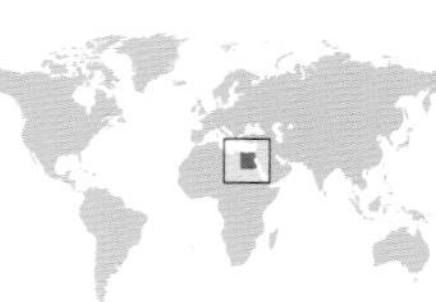

Egypt, on the eastern Mediterranean coast of north Africa, is low-lying, with areas below sea level in the Qattara depression. It is a land of desert and semi-desert, except for the Nile valley, where ninety-nine per cent of Egyptians live. The Sinai peninsula in the northeast of the country forms the only land bridge between Africa and Asia. The summers are hot, the winters mild and rainfall is negligible. Less than four per cent of land (chiefly around the Nile floodplain and delta) is cultivated. Farming employs about one-third of the workforce; cotton is the main cash crop. Egypt imports over half its food needs. There are oil and natural gas reserves, although nearly a quarter of electricity comes from hydroelectric power. Main exports are oil and oil products, cotton, textiles and clothing.

EL SALVADOR
Republic of El Salvador

Area Sq Km	21 041	Languages	Spanish
Area Sq Miles	8 124	Religions	Roman Catholic, Protestant
Population	6 340 000	Currency	United States dollar
Capital	San Salvador	Organizations	UN

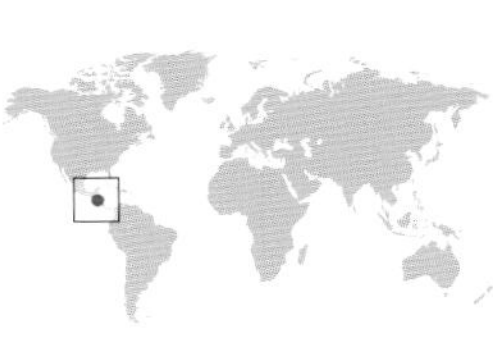

Located on the Pacific coast of central America, El Salvador consists of a coastal plain and volcanic mountain ranges which enclose a densely populated plateau area. The coast is hot, with heavy summer rainfall; the highlands are cooler. Coffee (the chief export), sugar and cotton are the main cash crops. The main trading partners are the USA and Guatemala.

EQUATORIAL GUINEA
Republic of Equatorial Guinea

Area Sq Km	28 051	Languages	Spanish, French, Fang
Area Sq Miles	10 831	Religions	Roman Catholic, traditional beliefs
Population	757 000	Currency	CFA franc
Capital	Malabo	Organizations	UN

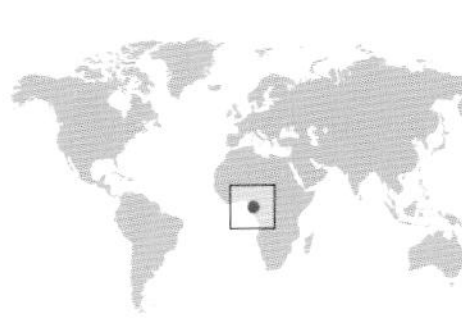

The state consists of Río Muni, an enclave on the Atlantic coast of central Africa, and the islands of Bioco, Annobón and the Corisco group. Most of the population lives on the coastal plain and upland plateau of Río Muni. The capital city, Malabo, is on the fertile volcanic island of Bioco. The climate is hot, humid and wet. Oil production started in 1992, and oil is now the main export, along with timber. The economy depends heavily on foreign aid.

ERITREA
State of Eritrea

Area Sq Km	117 400	Languages	Tigrinya, Tigre
Area Sq Miles	45 328	Religions	Sunni Muslim, Coptic Christian
Population	6 333 000	Currency	Nakfa
Capital	Asmara	Organizations	UN

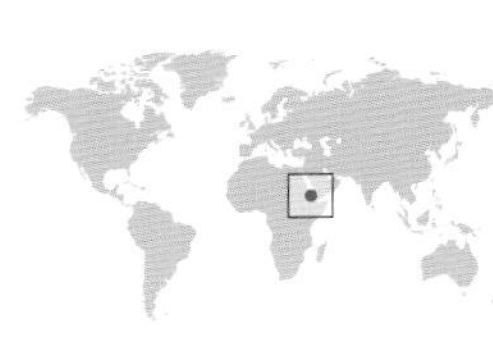

Eritrea, on the Red Sea coast of northeast Africa, consists of a high plateau in the north with a coastal plain which widens to the south. The coast is hot; inland is cooler. Rainfall is unreliable. The agriculture-based economy has suffered from over thirty years of war and occasional poor rains. Eritrea is one of the least developed countries in the world.

ESTONIA
Republic of Estonia

Area Sq Km	45 200	Languages	Estonian, Russian
Area Sq Miles	17 452	Religions	Protestant, Estonian and Russian Orthodox
Population	1 287 000	Currency	Kroon
Capital	Tallinn	Organizations	EU, NATO, OECD, UN

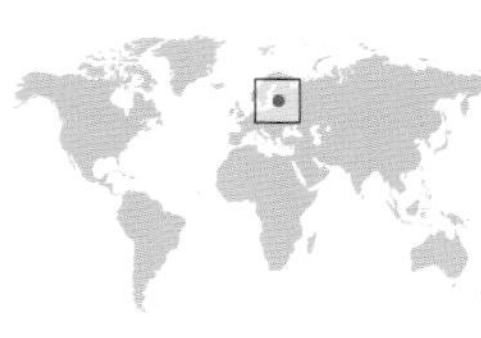

Estonia is in northern Europe, on the Gulf of Finland and the Baltic Sea. The land, over one-third of which is forested, is generally low-lying with many lakes. Approximately one-third of Estonians live in the capital, Tallinn. Exported goods include machinery, wood products, textiles and food products. The main trading partners are Russia, Finland and Sweden. Estonia joined the European Union in May 2004.

ETHIOPIA
Federal Democratic Republic of Ethiopia

Area Sq Km	1 133 880	**Languages**	Oromo, Amharic, Tigrinya, other local languages
Area Sq Miles	437 794	**Religions**	Ethiopian Orthodox, Sunni Muslim, traditional beliefs
Population	94 101 000	**Currency**	Birr
Capital	Addis Ababa (Ādīs Ābeba)	**Organizations**	UN

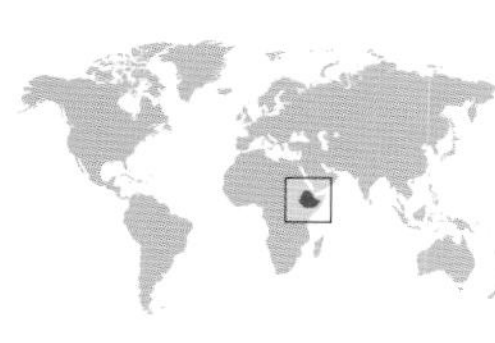

A landlocked country in northeast Africa, Ethiopia comprises a mountainous region in the west which is traversed by the Great Rift Valley. The east is mostly arid plateau land. The highlands are warm with summer rainfall. Most people live in the central–northern area. In recent years civil war, conflict with Eritrea and poor infrastructure have hampered economic development. Subsistence farming is the main activity, although droughts have led to frequent famines. Coffee is the main export and there is some light industry. Ethiopia is one of the least developed countries in the world.

Falkland Islands (Islas Malvinas)
United Kingdom Overseas Territory

Area Sq Km	12 170	**Languages**	English
Area Sq Miles	4 699	**Religions**	Protestant, Roman Catholic
Population	2 931	**Currency**	Falkland Islands pound
Capital	Stanley		

Lying in the southwest Atlantic Ocean, northeast of Cape Horn, two main islands, West Falkland and East Falkland and many smaller islands, form the territory of the Falkland Islands. The economy is based on sheep farming and the sale of fishing licences.

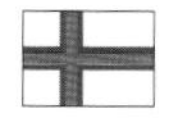

Faroe Islands
Self-governing Danish Territory

Area Sq Km	1 399	**Languages**	Faroese, Danish
Area Sq Miles	540	**Religions**	Protestant
Population	49 000	**Currency**	Danish krone
Capital	Thorshavn (Tórshavn)		

A self-governing territory, the Faroe Islands lie in the north Atlantic Ocean between the UK and Iceland. The islands benefit from the North Atlantic Drift ocean current, which has a moderating effect on the climate. The economy is based on deep-sea fishing.

FIJI
Republic of Fiji

Area Sq Km	18 330	**Languages**	English, Fijian, Hindi
Area Sq Miles	7 077	**Religions**	Christian, Hindu, Sunni Muslim
Population	881 000	**Currency**	Fijian dollar
Capital	Suva	**Organizations**	Comm., UN

The southwest Pacific republic of Fiji comprises two mountainous and volcanic islands, Vanua Levu and Viti Levu, and over three hundred smaller islands. The climate is tropical and the economy is based on agriculture (chiefly sugar, the main export), fishing, forestry, gold mining and tourism.

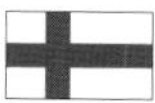

FINLAND
Republic of Finland

Area Sq Km	338 145	**Languages**	Finnish, Swedish, Sami languages
Area Sq Miles	130 559	**Religions**	Protestant, Greek Orthodox
Population	5 426 000	**Currency**	Euro
Capital	Helsinki (Helsingfors)	**Organizations**	EU, OECD, UN

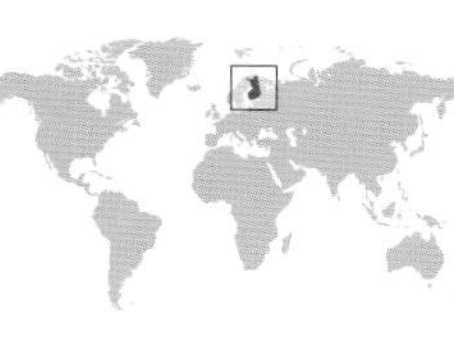

Finland is in northern Europe, and nearly one-third of the country lies north of the Arctic Circle. Forests cover over seventy per cent of the land area, and ten per cent is covered by lakes. Summers are short and warm, and winters are long and severe, particularly in the north. Most of the population lives in the southern third of the country, along the coast or near the lakes. Timber is a major resource and there are important minerals, chiefly chromium. Main industries include metal working, electronics, paper and paper products, and chemicals. The main trading partners are Germany, Sweden and the UK.

FRANCE
French Republic

Area Sq Km	543 965	**Languages**	French, German dialects, Italian, Arabic, Breton
Area Sq Miles	210 026	**Religions**	Roman Catholic, Protestant, Sunni Muslim
Population	64 291 000	**Currency**	Euro
Capital	Paris	**Organizations**	EU, NATO, OECD, UN

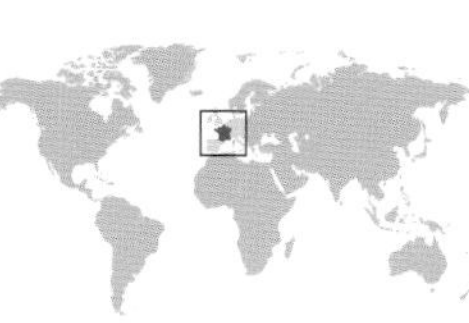

France lies in western Europe and has coastlines on the Atlantic Ocean and the Mediterranean Sea. It includes the Mediterranean island of Corsica. Northern and western regions consist mostly of flat or rolling countryside, and include the major lowlands of the Paris basin, the Loire valley and the Aquitaine basin, drained by the Seine, Loire and Garonne river systems respectively. The centre-south is dominated by the hill region of the Massif Central. To the east are the Vosges and Jura mountains and the Alps. In the southwest, the Pyrenees form a natural border with Spain. The climate is temperate with warm summers and cool winters, although the Mediterranean coast has hot, dry summers and mild winters. Over seventy per cent of the population lives in towns, with almost a sixth of the population living in the Paris area. The French economy has a substantial and varied agricultural base. It is a major producer of both fresh and processed food. There are relatively few mineral resources; it has coal reserves, and some oil and natural gas, but it relies heavily on nuclear and hydroelectric power and imported fuels. France is one of the world's major industrial countries. Main industries include food processing, iron, steel and aluminium production, chemicals, cars, electronics and oil refining. The main exports are transport equipment, plastics and chemicals. Tourism is a major source of revenue and employment. Trade is predominantly with other European Union countries.

French Guiana
French Overseas Department

Area Sq Km	90 000	**Languages**	French, Creole
Area Sq Miles	34 749	**Religions**	Roman Catholic
Population	249 000	**Currency**	Euro
Capital	Cayenne		

French Guiana, on the north coast of South America, is densely forested. The climate is tropical, with high rainfall. Most people live in the coastal strip, and agriculture is mostly subsistence farming. Forestry and fishing are important, but mineral resources are largely unexploited and industry is limited. French Guiana depends on French aid. The main trading partners are France and the USA.

French Polynesia
French Overseas Collectivity

Area Sq Km	3 265	**Languages**	French, Tahitian, other Polynesian languages
Area Sq Miles	1 261	**Religions**	Protestant, Roman Catholic
Population	277 000	**Currency**	CFP franc
Capital	Papeete		

Extending over a vast area of the southeast Pacific Ocean, French Polynesia comprises more than one hundred and thirty islands and coral atolls. The main island groups are the Marquesas Islands, the Tuamotu Archipelago and the Society Islands. The capital, Papeete, is on Tahiti in the Society Islands. The climate is subtropical, and the economy is based on tourism. The main export is cultured pearls.

GABON
Gabonese Republic

Area Sq Km	267 667	**Languages**	French, Fang, other local languages
Area Sq Miles	103 347	**Religions**	Roman Catholic, Protestant, traditional beliefs
Population	1 672 000	**Currency**	CFA franc
Capital	Libreville	**Organizations**	UN

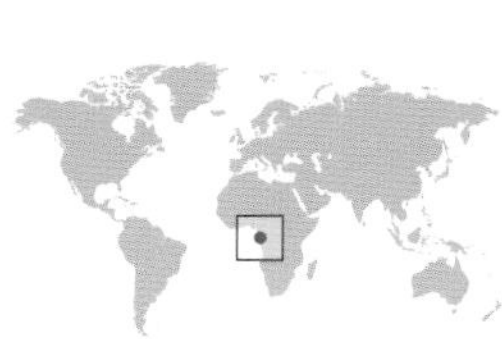

Gabon, on the Atlantic coast of central Africa, consists of low plateaus and a coastal plain lined by lagoons and mangrove swamps. The climate is tropical and rainforests cover over three-quarters of the land area. Nearly ninety per cent of the population lives in towns. The economy is heavily dependent on oil, which accounts for around seventy-five per cent of exports; manganese, uranium and timber are the other main exports. Agriculture is mainly at subsistence level.

THE GAMBIA
Republic of The Gambia

Area Sq Km	11 295	**Languages**	English, Malinke, Fulani, Wolof
Area Sq Miles	4 361	**Religions**	Sunni Muslim, Protestant
Population	1 849 000	**Currency**	Dalasi
Capital	Banjul	**Organizations**	UN

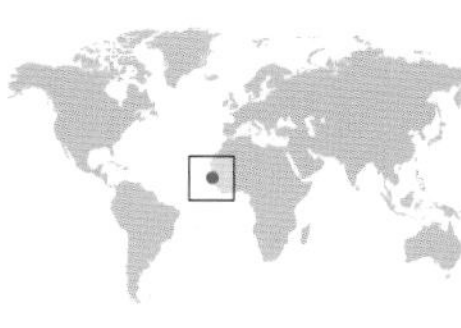

The Gambia, on the coast of west Africa, occupies a strip of land along the lower Gambia river. Sandy beaches are backed by mangrove swamps, beyond which is savanna. The climate is tropical, with most rainfall in the summer. Over seventy per cent of Gambians are farmers, growing chiefly groundnuts (the main export), cotton, oil palms and food crops. Livestock rearing and fishing are important, while manufacturing is limited. Re-exports, mainly from Senegal, and tourism are major sources of income.

Gaza
Disputed territory

Area Sq Km	363	**Languages**	Arabic
Area Sq Miles	140	**Religions**	Sunni Muslim, Shi'a Muslim
Population	1 701 437	**Currency**	Israeli shekel
Capital	Gaza		

Gaza is a narrow strip of land on the southeast corner of the Mediterranean Sea, between Egypt and Israel. This Palestinian territory has limited autonomy from Israel, but hostilities between Israel and the indigenous Arab population continue to restrict its economic development.

States and Territories

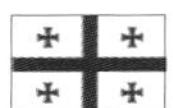

GEORGIA

Area Sq Km	69 700	Languages	Georgian, Russian, Armenian, Azeri, Ossetian, Abkhaz
Area Sq Miles	26 911	Religions	Georgian Orthodox, Russian Orthodox, Sunni Muslim
Population	4 341 000	Currency	Lari
Capital	Tbilisi	Organizations	UN

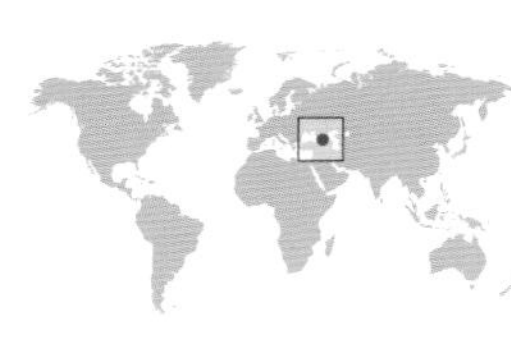

Georgia is in the northwest Caucasus area of southwest Asia, on the eastern coast of the Black Sea. Mountain ranges in the north and south flank the Kura and Rioni valleys. The climate is generally mild, and along the coast it is subtropical. Agriculture is important, with tea, grapes, and citrus fruits the main crops. Mineral resources include manganese ore and oil, and the main industries are steel, oil refining and machine building. The main trading partners are and Turkey, Ukraine and Azerbaijan.

GERMANY

Federal Republic of Germany

Area Sq Km	357 022	Languages	German, Turkish
Area Sq Miles	137 847	Religions	Protestant, Roman Catholic
Population	82 727 000	Currency	Euro
Capital	Berlin	Organizations	EU, NATO, OECD, UN

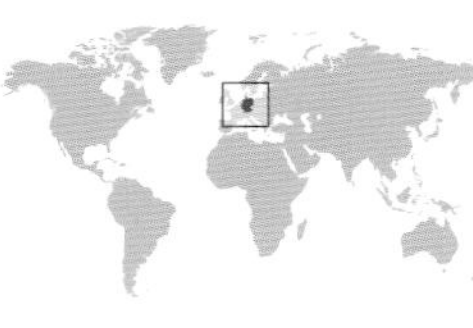

The central European state of Germany borders nine countries and has coastlines on the North and Baltic Seas. Behind the indented coastline, and covering about one-third of the country, is the north German plain, a region of fertile farmland and sandy heaths drained by the country's major rivers. The central highlands are a belt of forested hills and plateaus which stretch from the Eifel region in the west to the Erzgebirge mountains along the border with the Czech Republic. Farther south the land rises to the Swabian Alps (Schwäbische Alb), with the high rugged and forested Black Forest (Schwarzwald) in the southwest. In the far south the Bavarian Alps form the border with Austria. The climate is temperate, with continental conditions in eastern areas. The population is highly urbanized, with over seventy-five per cent living in cities and towns. With the exception of coal, lignite, potash and baryte, Germany lacks minerals and other industrial raw materials. It has a small agricultural base, although a few products (chiefly wines and beers) enjoy an international reputation. Germany is the world's fourth ranking economy after the USA, China and Japan. Its industries are amongst the world's most technologically advanced. Exports include machinery, vehicles and chemicals. The majority of trade is with other countries in the European Union, the USA and Japan.

Baden-Württemberg (State)

Area Sq Km (Sq Miles)	Population	Capital
35 752 (13 804)	10 842 000	Stuttgart

Bayern (State)

Area Sq Km (Sq Miles)	Population	Capital
70 550 (27 240)	12 670 000	Munich (München)

Berlin (State)

Area Sq Km (Sq Miles)	Population	Capital
892 (344)	3 544 000	Berlin

Brandenburg (State)

Area Sq Km (Sq Miles)	Population	Capital
29 476 (11 381)	2 492 000	Potsdam

Bremen

Area Sq Km (Sq Miles)	Population	Capital
404 (156)	663 000	Bremen

Hamburg (State)

Area Sq Km (Sq Miles)	Population	Capital
755 (292)	1 814 000	Hamburg

Hessen (State)

Area Sq Km (Sq Miles)	Population	Capital
21 114 (8 152)	6 116 000	Wiesbaden

Mecklenburg-Vorpommern (State)

Area Sq Km (Sq Miles)	Population	Capital
23 173 (8 947)	1 629 000	Schwerin

Niedersachsen (State)

Area Sq Km (Sq Miles)	Population	Capital
47 616 (18 385)	7 919 000	Hannover

Nordrhein-Westfalen (State)

Area Sq Km (Sq Miles)	Population	Capital
34 082 (13 159)	17 853 000	Düsseldorf

Rheinland-Pfalz (State)

Area Sq Km (Sq Miles)	Population	Capital
19 847 (7 663)	4 000 000	Mainz

Saarland (State)

Area Sq Km (Sq Miles)	Population	Capital
2 568 (992)	1 010 000	Saarbrücken

Sachsen (State)

Area Sq Km (Sq Miles)	Population	Capital
18 413 (7 109)	4 134 000	Dresden

Sachsen-Anhalt (State)

Area Sq Km (Sq Miles)	Population	Capital
20 447 (7 895)	2 297 000	Magdeburg

Schleswig-Holstein (State)

Area Sq Km (Sq Miles)	Population	Capital
15 761 (6 085)	2 842 000	Kiel

Thüringen (State)

Area Sq Km (Sq Miles)	Population	Capital
16 172 (6 244)	2 211 000	Erfurt

GHANA

Republic of Ghana

Area Sq Km	238 537	Languages	English, Hausa, Akan, other local languages
Area Sq Miles	92 100	Religions	Christian, Sunni Muslim, traditional beliefs
Population	25 905 000	Currency	Cedi
Capital	Accra	Organizations	Comm., UN

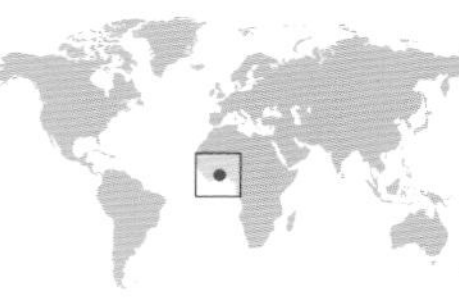

A west African state on the Gulf of Guinea, Ghana is a land of plains and low plateaus covered with savanna and rainforest. In the east is the Volta basin and Lake Volta. The climate is tropical, with the highest rainfall in the south, where most of the population lives. Agriculture employs over fifty per cent of the workforce. Main exports are gold, timber, cocoa, bauxite and manganese ore.

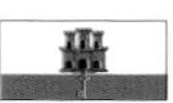

Gibraltar

United Kingdom Overseas Territory

Area Sq Km	7	Languages	English, Spanish
Area Sq Miles	3	Religions	Roman Catholic, Protestant, Sunni Muslim
Population	29 000	Currency	Gibraltar pound
Capital	Gibraltar		

Gibraltar lies on the south coast of Spain at the western entrance to the Mediterranean Sea. The economy depends on tourism, offshore banking and shipping services.

GREECE

Hellenic Republic

Area Sq Km	131 957	Languages	Greek
Area Sq Miles	50 949	Religions	Greek Orthodox, Sunni Muslim
Population	11 128 000	Currency	Euro
Capital	Athens (Athina)	Organizations	EU, NATO, OECD, UN

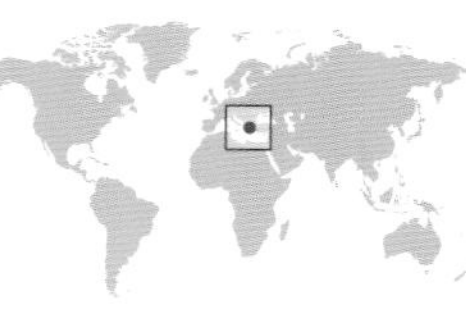

Greece comprises a mountainous peninsula in the Balkan region of southeastern Europe and many islands in the Ionian, Aegean and Mediterranean Seas. The islands make up over one-fifth of its area. Mountains and hills cover much of the country. The main lowland areas are the plains of Thessaly in the centre and around Thessaloniki in the northeast. Summers are hot and dry while winters are mild and wet, but colder in the north with heavy snowfalls in the mountains. One-third of Greeks live in the Athens area. Employment in agriculture accounts for approximately twenty per cent of the workforce, and exports include citrus fruits, raisins, wine, olives and olive oil. Aluminium and nickel are mined and a wide range of manufactures are produced, including food products and tobacco, textiles, clothing, and chemicals. Tourism is an important industry and there is a large services sector. Most trade is with other European Union countries.

Greenland

Self-governing Danish Territory

Area Sq Km	2 175 600	Languages	Greenlandic, Danish
Area Sq Miles	840 004	Religions	Protestant
Population	57 000	Currency	Danish krone
Capital	Nuuk (Godthåb)		

Situated to the northeast of North America between the Atlantic and Arctic Oceans, Greenland is the largest island in the world. It has a polar climate and over eighty per cent of the land area is covered by permanent ice cap. The economy is based on fishing and fish processing.

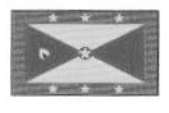

GRENADA

Area Sq Km	378	Languages	English, Creole
Area Sq Miles	146	Religions	Roman Catholic, Protestant
Population	106 000	Currency	East Caribbean dollar
Capital	St George's	Organizations	CARICOM, Comm., UN

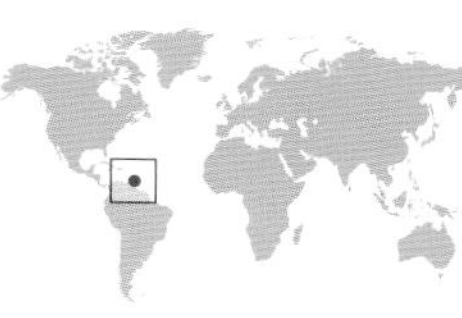

The Caribbean state comprises Grenada, the most southerly of the Windward Islands, and the southern islands of the Grenadines. Grenada has wooded hills, with beaches in the southwest. The climate is warm and wet. Agriculture is the main activity, with bananas, nutmeg and cocoa the main exports. Tourism is the main foreign exchange earner.

Guadeloupe

French Overseas Department

Area Sq Km	1 780	Languages	French, Creole
Area Sq Miles	687	Religions	Roman Catholic
Population	466 000	Currency	Euro
Capital	Basse-Terre		

Guadeloupe, in the Leeward Islands in the Caribbean, consists of two main islands (Basse-Terre and Grande-Terre, connected by a bridge), Marie-Galante, and a few outer islands. The climate is tropical, but moderated by trade winds. Bananas, sugar and rum are the main exports and tourism is a major source of income.

Guam

United States Unincorporated Territory

Area Sq Km	541	Languages	Chamorro, English, Tagalog
Area Sq Miles	209	Religions	Roman Catholic
Population	165 000	Currency	United States dollar
Capital	Hagåtña		

Lying at the south end of the Northern Mariana Islands in the western Pacific Ocean, Guam has a humid tropical climate. The island has a large US military base and the economy relies on that and on tourism.

GUATEMALA
Republic of Guatemala

Area Sq Km	108 890	**Languages**	Spanish, Mayan languages
Area Sq Miles	42 043	**Religions**	Roman Catholic, Protestant
Population	15 468 000	**Currency**	Quetzal
Capital	Guatemala City (Guatemala)	**Organizations**	UN

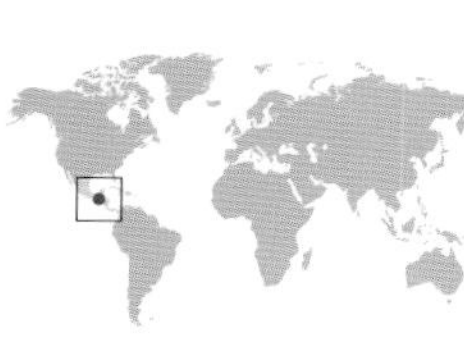

The most populous country in Central America after Mexico, Guatemala has long Pacific and short Caribbean coasts separated by a mountain chain which includes several active volcanoes. The climate is hot tropical in the lowlands and cooler in the highlands, where most of the population lives. Farming is the main activity and coffee, sugar and bananas are the main exports. There is some manufacturing of clothing and textiles. The main trading partner is the USA.

Guernsey
United Kingdom Crown Dependency

Area Sq Km	78	**Languages**	English, French
Area Sq Miles	30	**Religions**	Protestant, Roman Catholic
Population	65 578	**Currency**	Pound sterling
Capital	St Peter Port		

Guernsey is one of the Channel Islands, lying off northern France. The dependency also includes the nearby islands of Alderney, Sark and Herm. Financial services are an important part of the island's economy.

GUINEA
Republic of Guinea

Area Sq Km	245 857	**Languages**	French, Fulani, Malinke, other local languages
Area Sq Miles	94 926	**Religions**	Sunni Muslim, traditional beliefs, Christian
Population	11 745 000	**Currency**	Guinean franc
Capital	Conakry	**Organizations**	UN

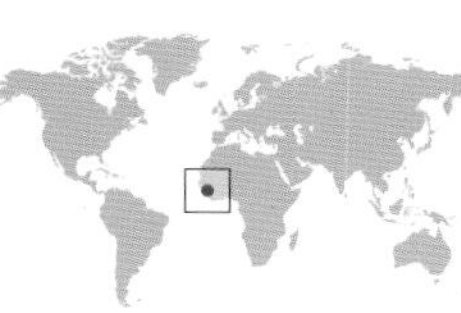

Guinea is in west Africa, on the Atlantic Ocean. There are mangrove swamps along the coast, while inland are lowlands and the Fouta Djallon mountains and plateaus. To the east are savanna plains drained by the upper Niger river system. The southeast is hilly. The climate is tropical, with high coastal rainfall. Agriculture is the main activity, employing nearly eighty per cent of the workforce, with coffee, bananas and pineapples the chief cash crops. There are huge reserves of bauxite, which accounts for more than seventy per cent of exports. Other exports include aluminium oxide, gold, coffee and diamonds.

GUINEA-BISSAU
Republic of Guinea-Bissau

Area Sq Km	36 125	**Languages**	Portuguese, Crioulo, other local languages
Area Sq Miles	13 948	**Religions**	Traditional beliefs, Sunni Muslim, Christian
Population	1 704 000	**Currency**	CFA franc
Capital	Bissau	**Organizations**	UN

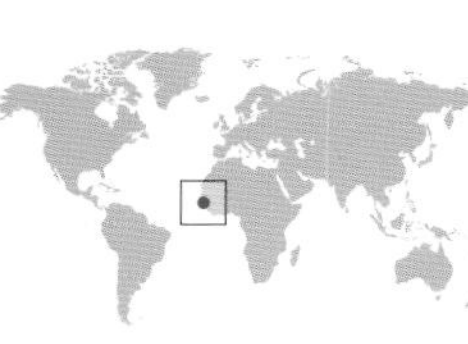

Guinea-Bissau is on the Atlantic coast of west Africa. The mainland coast is swampy and contains many estuaries. Inland are forested plains, and to the east are savanna plateaus. The climate is tropical. The economy is based mainly on subsistence farming. There is little industry, and timber and mineral resources are largely unexploited. Cashews account for seventy per cent of exports. Guinea-Bissau is one of the least developed countries in the world.

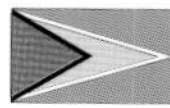

GUYANA
Co-operative Republic of Guyana

Area Sq Km	214 969	**Languages**	English, Creole, Amerindian languages
Area Sq Miles	83 000	**Religions**	Protestant, Hindu, Roman Catholic, Sunni Muslim
Population	800 000	**Currency**	Guyanese dollar
Capital	Georgetown	**Organizations**	CARICOM, Comm., UN

Guyana, on the northeast coast of South America, consists of highlands in the west and savanna uplands in the southwest. Most of the country is densely forested. A lowland coastal belt supports crops and most of the population. The generally hot, humid and wet conditions are modified along the coast by sea breezes. The economy is based on agriculture, bauxite, and forestry. Sugar, bauxite, gold, rice and timber are the main exports.

HAITI
Republic of Haiti

Area Sq Km	27 750	**Languages**	French, Creole
Area Sq Miles	10 714	**Religions**	Roman Catholic, Protestant, Voodoo
Population	10 317 000	**Currency**	Gourde
Capital	Port-au-Prince	**Organizations**	CARICOM, UN

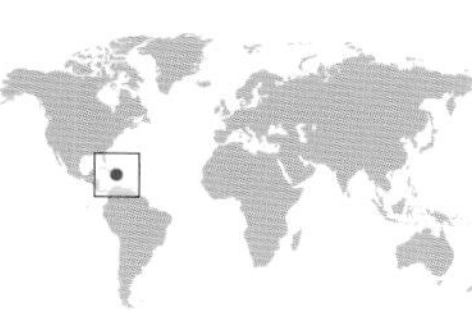

Haiti, occupying the western third of the Caribbean island of Hispaniola, is a mountainous state with small coastal plains and a central valley. The Dominican Republic occupies the rest of the island. The climate is tropical, and is hottest in coastal areas. Haiti has few natural resources, is densely populated and relies on exports of local crafts and coffee, and remittances from workers abroad. The country has not yet recovered from the 2010 earthquake.

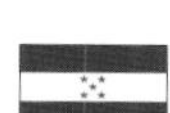

HONDURAS
Republic of Honduras

Area Sq Km	112 088	**Languages**	Spanish, Amerindian languages
Area Sq Miles	43 277	**Religions**	Roman Catholic, Protestant
Population	8 098 000	**Currency**	Lempira
Capital	Tegucigalpa	**Organizations**	UN

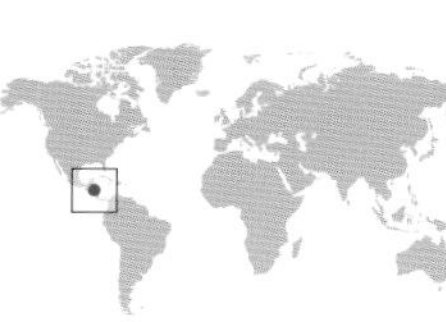

Honduras, in central America, is a mountainous and forested country with lowland areas along its long Caribbean and short Pacific coasts. Coastal areas are hot and humid with heavy summer rainfall; inland is cooler and drier. Most of the population lives in the central valleys. Coffee and bananas are the main exports, along with shellfish and zinc. Industry involves mainly agricultural processing.

HUNGARY

Area Sq Km	93 030	**Languages**	Hungarian
Area Sq Miles	35 919	**Religions**	Roman Catholic, Protestant
Population	9 955 000	**Currency**	Forint
Capital	Budapest	**Organizations**	EU, NATO, OECD, UN

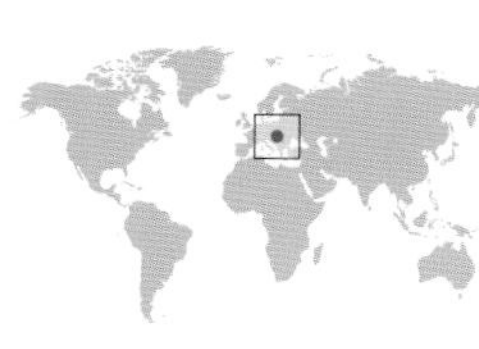

The Danube river flows north-south through central Hungary, a landlocked country in eastern Europe. In the east lies a great plain, flanked by highlands in the north. In the west low mountains and Lake Balaton separate a smaller plain and southern uplands. The climate is continental. Seventy per cent of the population lives in urban areas, and one-sixth lives in the capital, Budapest. Some minerals and energy resources are exploited, chiefly bauxite, coal and natural gas. Hungary has an industrial economy based on metals, machinery, transport equipment, chemicals and food products. The main trading partners are Germany and Austria. Hungary joined the European Union in May 2004.

ICELAND
Republic of Iceland

Area Sq Km	102 820	**Languages**	Icelandic
Area Sq Miles	39 699	**Religions**	Protestant
Population	330 000	**Currency**	Icelandic króna
Capital	Reykjavík	**Organizations**	NATO, OECD, UN

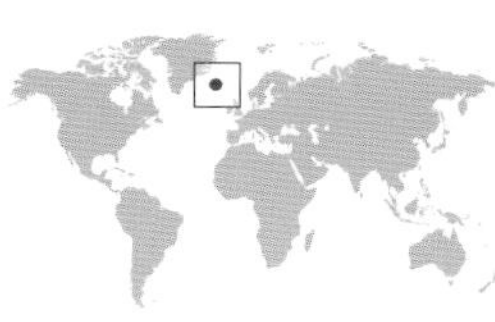

Iceland lies in the north Atlantic Ocean near the Arctic Circle, to the northwest of Scandinavia. The landscape is volcanic, with numerous hot springs, geysers, and approximately two hundred volcanoes. One-tenth of the country is covered by ice caps. Only coastal lowlands are cultivated and settled, and over half the population lives in the Reykjavík area. The climate is mild, moderated by the North Atlantic Drift ocean current and by southwesterly winds. The mainstays of the economy are fishing and fish processing, which account for seventy per cent of exports. Agriculture involves mainly sheep and dairy farming. Hydroelectric and geothermal energy resources are considerable. The main industries produce aluminium, ferro-silicon and fertilizers. Tourism, including ecotourism, is growing in importance.

INDIA
Republic of India

Area Sq Km	3 166 620	**Languages**	Hindi, English, many regional languages
Area Sq Miles	1 222 632	**Religions**	Hindu, Sunni Muslim, Shi'a Muslim, Sikh, Christian
Population	1 252 140 000	**Currency**	Indian rupee
Capital	New Delhi	**Organizations**	Comm., UN

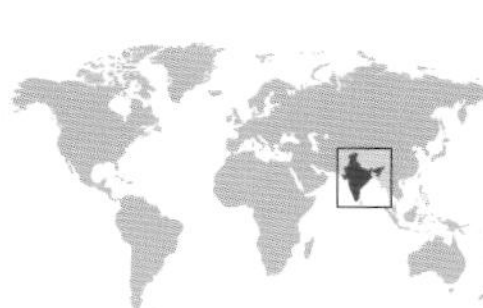

The south Asian country of India occupies a peninsula that juts out into the Indian Ocean between the Arabian Sea and Bay of Bengal. The heart of the peninsula is the Deccan plateau, bordered on either side by ranges of hills, the western Ghats and the lower eastern Ghats, which fall away to narrow coastal plains. To the north is a broad plain, drained by the Indus, Ganges and Brahmaputra rivers and their tributaries. The plain is intensively farmed and is the most populous region. In the west is the Thar Desert. The mountains of the Himalaya form India's northern border, together with parts of the Karakoram and Hindu Kush ranges in the northwest. The climate shows marked seasonal variation: a hot season from March to June; a monsoon season from June to October; and a cold season from November to February. Rainfall ranges between very high in the northeast Assam region to negligible in the Thar Desert. Temperatures range from very cold in the Himalaya to tropical heat over much of the south. Over sixty-seven per cent of the huge population – the second largest in the world – is rural, although Delhi, Mumbai (Bombay) and Kolkata (Calcutta) all rank among the ten largest cities in the world. Agriculture, forestry and fishing account for a quarter of national output and two-thirds of employment. Much of the farming is on a subsistence basis and involves mainly rice and wheat. India is a major world producer of tea, sugar, jute, cotton and tobacco. Livestock is reared mainly for dairy products and hides. There are major reserves of coal, reserves of oil and natural gas, and many minerals, including iron, manganese, bauxite, diamonds and gold. The manufacturing sector is large and diverse – mainly chemicals and chemical products, textiles, iron and steel, food products, electrical goods and transport equipment; software and pharmaceuticals are also important. All the main manufactured products are exported, together with diamonds and jewellery. The USA, Germany, Japan and the UK are the main trading partners.

States and Territories

INDONESIA
Republic of Indonesia

Area Sq Km	1 919 445	Languages	Indonesian, other local languages
Area Sq Miles	741 102	Religions	Sunni Muslim, Protestant, Roman Catholic, Hindu, Buddhist
Population	249 866 000	Currency	Rupiah
Capital	Jakarta	Organizations	APEC, ASEAN, OPEC, UN

Indonesia, the largest and most populous country in southeast Asia, consists of over thirteen thousand islands extending between the Pacific and Indian Oceans. Sumatra, Java, Sulawesi (Celebes), Kalimantan (two-thirds of Borneo) and Papua (formerly Irian Jaya, western New Guinea) make up ninety per cent of the land area. Most of Indonesia is mountainous and covered with rainforest or mangrove swamps, and there are over three hundred volcanoes, many active. Two-thirds of the population lives in the lowland areas of the islands of Java and Madura. The climate is tropical monsoon. Agriculture is the largest sector of the economy and Indonesia is among the world's top producers of rice, palm oil, tea, coffee, rubber and tobacco. Many goods are produced, including textiles, clothing, cement, tin, fertilizers and vehicles. Main exports are oil, natural gas, timber products and clothing. Main trading partners are Japan, the USA and Singapore. Indonesia is a relatively poor country, and ethnic tensions and civil unrest often hinder economic development.

IRAN
Islamic Republic of Iran

Area Sq Km	1 648 000	Languages	Farsi, Azeri, Kurdish, regional languages
Area Sq Miles	636 296	Religions	Shi'a Muslim, Sunni Muslim
Population	77 447 000	Currency	Iranian rial
Capital	Tehrān	Organizations	OPEC, UN

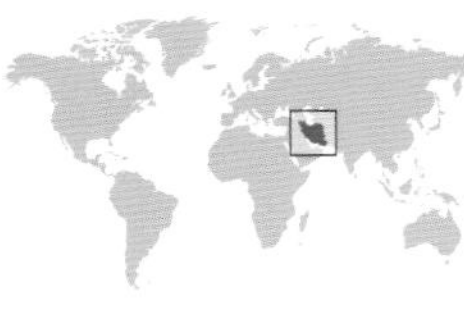

Iran is in southwest Asia, and has coasts on The Gulf, the Caspian Sea and the Gulf of Oman. In the east is a high plateau, with large salt pans and a vast sand desert. In the west the Zagros Mountains form a series of ridges, and to the north lie the Elburz Mountains. Most farming and settlement is on the narrow plain along the Caspian Sea and in the foothills of the north and west. The climate is one of extremes, with hot summers and very cold winters. Most of the light rainfall is in the winter months. Agriculture involves approximately one-fifth of the workforce. Wheat is the main crop, but fruit (especially dates) and pistachio nuts are grown for export. Petroleum (the main export) and natural gas are Iran's leading natural resources. Manufactured goods include carpets, clothing, food products and construction materials.

IRAQ
Republic of Iraq

Area Sq Km	438 317	Languages	Arabic, Kurdish, Turkmen
Area Sq Miles	169 235	Religions	Shi'a Muslim, Sunni Muslim, Christian
Population	33 765 000	Currency	Iraqi dinar
Capital	Baghdād	Organizations	OPEC, UN

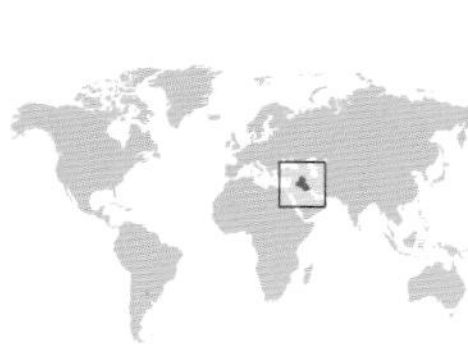

Iraq, in southwest Asia, has at its heart the lowland valley of the Tigris and Euphrates rivers. In the southeast, where the two rivers join, are the Mesopotamian marshes and the Shaṭṭ al 'Arab waterway leading to The Gulf. The north is hilly, while the west is mostly desert. Summers are hot and dry, and winters are mild with light, unreliable rainfall. The Tigris-Euphrates valley contains most of the country's arable land. One in five of the population lives in the capital, Baghdad. The economy has suffered following the 1991 Gulf War and the invasion of US-led coalition forces in 2005. The latter resulted in the overthrow of the dictator Saddam Hussein, but there is continuing internal instability. Oil is normally the main export.

IRELAND

Area Sq Km	70 282	Languages	English, Irish
Area Sq Miles	27 136	Religions	Roman Catholic, Protestant
Population	4 627 000	Currency	Euro
Capital	Dublin (Baile Átha Cliath)	Organizations	EU, OECD, UN

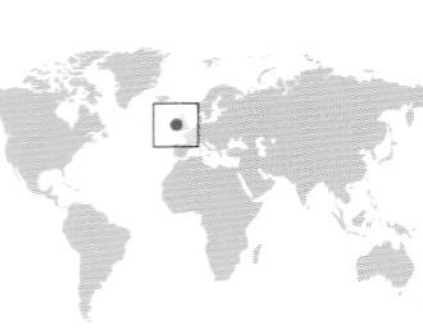

The Irish Republic occupies some eighty per cent of the island of Ireland, in northwest Europe. It is a lowland country of wide valleys, lakes and peat bogs, with isolated mountain ranges around the coast. The west coast is rugged and indented with many bays. The climate is mild due to the modifying effect of the North Atlantic Drift ocean current and rainfall is plentiful, although highest in the west. Over sixty per cent of the population lives in urban areas, Dublin and Cork being the main cities. Resources include natural gas, peat, lead and zinc. Agriculture, the traditional mainstay, now employs less than six per cent of the workforce, while industry employs nearly thirty per cent. The main industries are electronics, pharmaceuticals and engineering as well as food processing, brewing and textiles. Service industries are expanding, with tourism a major earner. The UK is the main trading partner.

Isle of Man
United Kingdom Crown Dependency

Area Sq Km	572	Languages	English
Area Sq Miles	221	Religions	Protestant, Roman Catholic
Population	86 000	Currency	Pound sterling
Capital	Douglas		

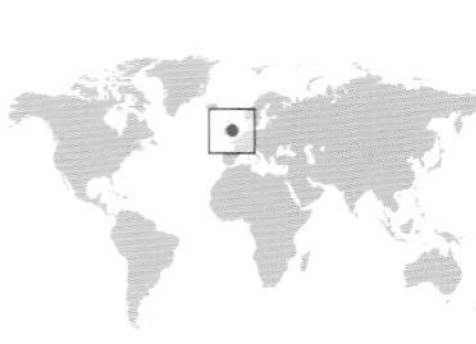

The Isle of Man lies in the Irish Sea between England and Northern Ireland. The island is self-governing, although the UK is responsible for its defence and foreign affairs. It is not part of the European Union, but has a special relationship with the EU which allows for free trade. Eighty per cent of the economy is based on the service sector, particularly financial services.

ISRAEL
State of Israel

Area Sq Km	22 072	Languages	Hebrew, Arabic
Area Sq Miles	8 522	Religions	Jewish, Sunni Muslim, Christian, Druze
Population	7 733 000	Currency	Shekel
Capital	Jerusalem (Yerushalayim) (El Quds) De facto capital. Disputed.	Organizations	OECD, UN

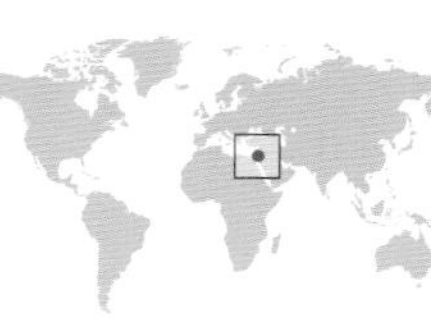

Israel lies on the Mediterranean coast of southwest Asia. Beyond the coastal Plain of Sharon are the hills and valleys of Samaria, with the Galilee highlands to the north. In the east is a rift valley, which extends from Lake Tiberias (Sea of Galilee) to the Gulf of Aqaba and contains the Jordan river and the Dead Sea. In the south is the Negev, a triangular semi-desert plateau. Most of the population lives on the coastal plain or in northern and central areas. Much of Israel has warm summers and mild, wet winters. The south is hot and dry. Agricultural production was boosted by the occupation of the West Bank in 1967. Manufacturing makes the largest contribution to the economy, and tourism is also important. Israel's main exports are machinery and transport equipment, software, diamonds, clothing, fruit and vegetables. The country relies heavily on foreign aid. Security issues relating to territorial disputes over the West Bank and Gaza have still to be resolved.

ITALY
Italian Republic

Area Sq Km	301 245	Languages	Italian
Area Sq Miles	116 311	Religions	Roman Catholic
Population	60 990 000	Currency	Euro
Capital	Rome (Roma)	Organizations	EU, NATO, OECD, UN

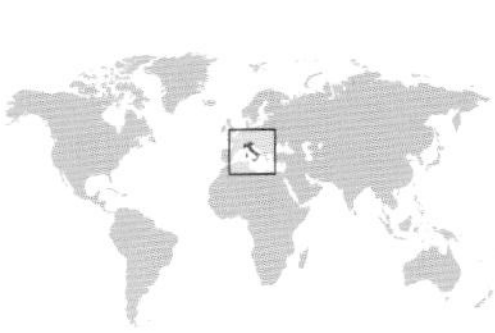

Most of the southern European state of Italy occupies a peninsula that juts out into the Mediterranean Sea. It includes the islands of Sicily and Sardinia and approximately seventy much smaller islands in the surrounding seas. Italy is mountainous, dominated by the Alps, which form its northern border, and the various ranges of the Apennines, which run almost the full length of the peninsula. Many of Italy's mountains are of volcanic origin, and its active volcanoes are Vesuvius, near Naples, Etna and Stromboli. The main lowland area, the Po river valley in the northeast, is the main agricultural and industrial area and is the most populous region. Italy has a Mediterranean climate, although the north experiences colder, wetter winters, with heavy snow in the Alps. Natural resources are limited, and only about twenty per cent of the land is suitable for cultivation. The economy is fairly diversified. Some oil, natural gas and coal are produced, but most fuels and minerals used by industry are imported. Agriculture is important, with cereals, vines, fruit and vegetables the main crops. Italy is the world's largest wine producer. The north is the centre of Italian industry, especially around Turin, Milan and Genoa. Leading manufactures include industrial and office equipment, domestic appliances, cars, textiles, clothing, leather goods, chemicals and metal products. There is a strong service sector, and with over forty-six million visitors a year, tourism is a major employer and accounts for ten per cent of the national income. Finance and banking are also important. Most trade is with other European Union countries.

JAMAICA

Area Sq Km	10 991	Languages	English, Creole
Area Sq Miles	4 244	Religions	Protestant, Roman Catholic
Population	2 784 000	Currency	Jamaican dollar
Capital	Kingston	Organizations	CARICOM, Comm., UN

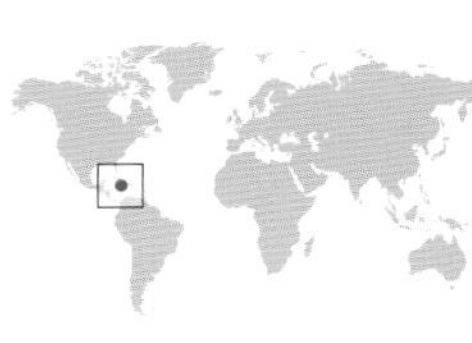

Jamaica, the third largest Caribbean island, has beaches and densely populated coastal plains traversed by hills and plateaus rising to the forested Blue Mountains in the east. The climate is tropical, but cooler and wetter on high ground. The economy is based on tourism, agriculture, mining and light manufacturing. Bauxite, aluminium oxide, sugar and bananas are the main exports. The USA is the main trading partner. Foreign aid is also significant.

JAPAN

Area Sq Km	377 727	Languages	Japanese
Area Sq Miles	145 841	Religions	Shintoist, Buddhist, Christian
Population	127 144 000	Currency	Yen
Capital	Tōkyō	Organizations	APEC, OECD, UN

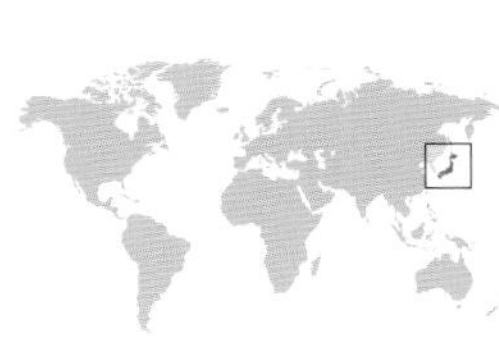

Japan lies in the Pacific Ocean off the coast of eastern Asia and consists of four main islands – Hokkaidō, Honshū, Shikoku and Kyūshū – and more than three thousand smaller islands in the surrounding Sea of Japan, East China Sea and Pacific Ocean. The central island of Honshū accounts for sixty per cent of the total land area and contains eighty per cent of the population. Behind the long and deeply indented coastline, nearly three-quarters of the country is mountainous and heavily forested. Japan has over sixty active volcanoes, and is subject to frequent earthquakes and typhoons. The climate is generally temperate

maritime, with warm summers and mild winters, except in western Hokkaidō and northwest Honshū, where the winters are very cold with heavy snow. Only fourteen per cent of the land area is suitable for cultivation, and its few raw materials (coal, oil, natural gas, lead, zinc and copper) are insufficient for its industry. Most materials must be imported, including about ninety per cent of energy requirements. Yet Japan has the world's third largest industrial economy, with a range of modern heavy and light industries centred mainly around the major ports of Yokohama, Ōsaka and Tōkyō. It is the world's largest manufacturer of cars, motorcycles and merchant ships, and a major producer of steel, textiles, chemicals and cement. It is also a leading producer of many consumer durables, such as washing machines, and electronic equipment, chiefly office equipment and computers. Japan has a strong service sector, banking and finance being particularly important, and Tōkyō has one of the world's major stock exchanges. Owing to intensive agricultural production, Japan is seventy per cent self-sufficient in food. The main food crops are rice, barley, fruit, wheat and soya beans. Livestock rearing (chiefly cattle, pigs and chickens) and fishing are also important, and Japan has one of the largest fishing fleets in the world. A major trading nation, Japan has trade links with many countries in southeast Asia and in Europe, although its main trading partner is the USA.

Jersey
United Kingdom Crown Dependency

Area Sq Km	116	**Languages**	English, French
Area Sq Miles	45	**Religions**	Protestant, Roman Catholic
Population	99 000	**Currency**	Pound sterling
Capital	St Helier		

One of the Channel Islands lying off the west coast of the Cherbourg peninsula in northern France. Financial services are the most important part of the economy.

JORDAN
Hashemite Kingdom of Jordan

Area Sq Km	89 206	**Languages**	Arabic
Area Sq Miles	34 443	**Religions**	Sunni Muslim, Christian
Population	7 274 000	**Currency**	Jordanian dinar
Capital	'Ammān	**Organizations**	UN

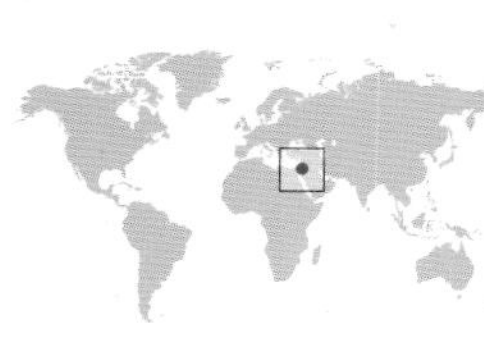

Jordan, in southwest Asia, is landlocked apart from a short coastline on the Gulf of Aqaba. Much of the country is rocky desert plateau. To the west of the mountains, the land falls below sea level to the Dead Sea and the Jordan river. The climate is hot and dry. Most people live in the northwest. Phosphates, potash, pharmaceuticals, fruit and vegetables are the main exports. The tourist industry is important, and the economy relies on workers' remittances from abroad and foreign aid.

KAZAKHSTAN
Republic of Kazakhstan

Area Sq Km	2 717 300	**Languages**	Kazakh, Russian, Ukrainian, German, Uzbek, Tatar
Area Sq Miles	1 049 155		
Population	16 441 000	**Religions**	Sunni Muslim, Russian Orthodox, Protestant
Capital	Astana (Akmola)	**Currency**	Tenge
		Organizations	CIS, UN

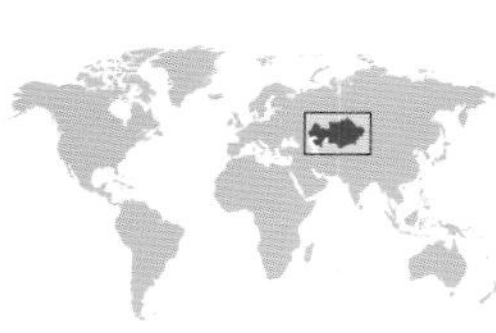

Stretching across central Asia, Kazakhstan covers a vast area of steppe land and semi-desert. The land is flat in the west, with large lowlands around the Caspian Sea, rising to mountains in the southeast. The climate is continental. Agriculture and livestock rearing are important, and cotton and tobacco are the main cash crops. Kazakhstan is very rich in minerals, including coal, chromium, gold, molybdenum, lead and zinc, and has substantial reserves of oil and gas. Mining, metallurgy, machine building and food processing are major industries. Oil, gas and minerals are the main exports, and Russia is the dominant trading partner.

KENYA
Republic of Kenya

Area Sq Km	582 646	**Languages**	Swahili, English, other local languages
Area Sq Miles	224 961		
Population	44 354 000	**Religions**	Christian, traditional beliefs
Capital	Nairobi	**Currency**	Kenyan shilling
		Organizations	Comm., UN

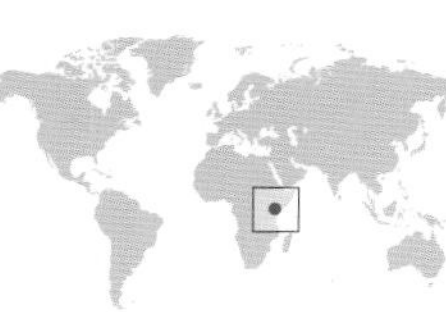

Kenya is in east Africa, on the Indian Ocean. Inland beyond the coastal plains the land rises to plateaus interrupted by volcanic mountains. The Great Rift Valley runs north-south to the west of the capital, Nairobi. Most of the population lives in the central area. Conditions are tropical on the coast, semi-desert in the north and savanna in the south. Hydroelectric power from the Upper Tana river provides most of the country's electricity. Agricultural products, mainly tea, coffee, fruit and vegetables, are the main exports. Light industry is important, and tourism, oil refining and re-exports for landlocked neighbours are major foreign exchange earners.

KIRIBATI
Republic of Kiribati

Area Sq Km	717	**Languages**	Gilbertese, English
Area Sq Miles	277	**Religions**	Roman Catholic, Protestant
Population	102 000	**Currency**	Australian dollar
Capital	Bairiki	**Organizations**	Comm., UN

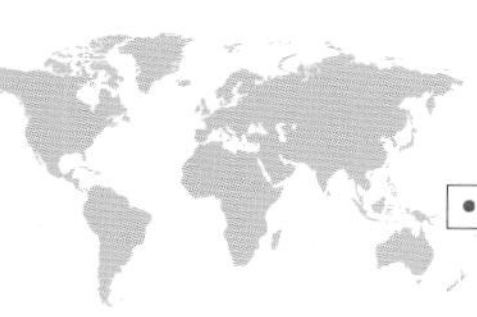

Kiribati, in the Pacific Ocean, straddles the Equator and comprises coral islands in the Gilbert, Phoenix and Line Island groups and the volcanic island of Banaba. Most people live on the Gilbert Islands, and the capital, Bairiki, is on Tarawa island in this group. The climate is hot, and wetter in the north. Copra and fish are exported. Kiribati relies on remittances from workers abroad and foreign aid.

KOSOVO
Republic of Kosovo

Area Sq Km	10 908	**Languages**	Albanian, Serbian
Area Sq Miles	4 212	**Religions**	Sunni Muslim, Serbian Orthodox
Population	1 815 606		
Capital	Prishtinë (Priština)	**Currency**	Euro

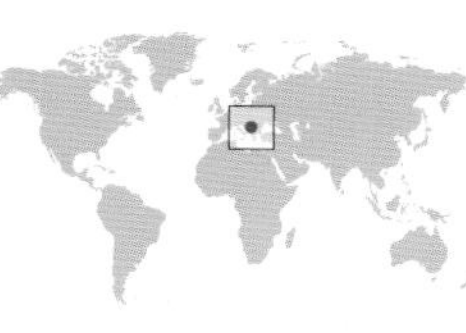

Kosovo, traditionally an autonomous southern province of Serbia, was the focus of ethnic conflict between Serbs and the majority ethnic Albanians in the 1990s until international intervention in 1999, after which it was administered by the UN. Kosovo declared its independence from Serbia in February 2008. The landscape is largely hilly or mountainous, especially along the southern and western borders.

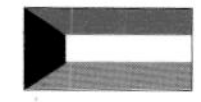

KUWAIT
State of Kuwait

Area Sq Km	17 818	**Languages**	Arabic
Area Sq Miles	6 880	**Religions**	Sunni Muslim, Shi'a Muslim, Christian, Hindu
Population	3 369 000		
Capital	Kuwait (Al Kuwayt)	**Currency**	Kuwaiti dinar
		Organizations	OPEC, UN

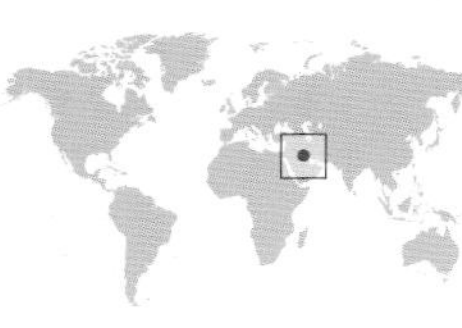

Kuwait lies on the northwest shores of The Gulf in southwest Asia. It is mainly low-lying desert, with irrigated areas along the bay, Kuwait Jun, where most people live. Summers are hot and dry, and winters are cool with some rainfall. The oil industry, which accounts for over ninety per cent of exports, has recovered from the damage caused by the Gulf War in 1991. Income is also derived from extensive overseas investments. Japan and the USA are the main trading partners.

KYRGYZSTAN
Kyrgyz Republic

Area Sq Km	198 500	**Languages**	Kyrgyz, Russian, Uzbek
Area Sq Miles	76 641	**Religions**	Sunni Muslim, Russian Orthodox
Population	5 548 000		
Capital	Bishkek (Frunze)	**Currency**	Kyrgyz som
		Organizations	CIS, UN

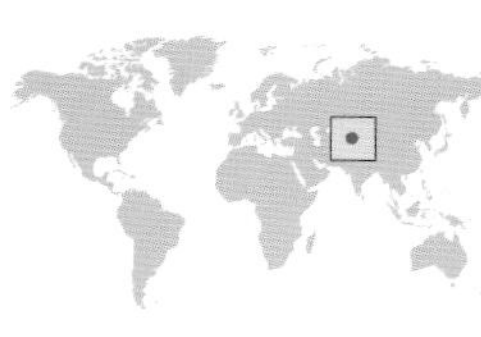

A landlocked central Asian state, Kyrgyzstan is rugged and mountainous, lying to the west of the Tien Shan mountain range. Most of the population lives in the valleys of the north and west. Summers are hot and winters cold. Agriculture (chiefly livestock farming) is the main activity. Some oil and gas, coal, gold, antimony and mercury are produced. Manufactured goods include machinery, metals and metal products, which are the main exports. Most trade is with Germany, Russia, Kazakhstan and Uzbekistan.

LAOS
Lao People's Democratic Republic

Area Sq Km	236 800	**Languages**	Lao, other local languages
Area Sq Miles	91 429	**Religions**	Buddhist, traditional beliefs
Population	6 770 000	**Currency**	Kip
Capital	Vientiane (Viangchan)	**Organizations**	ASEAN, UN

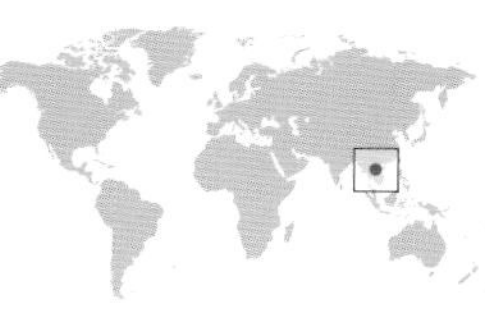

A landlocked country in southeast Asia, Laos is a land of mostly forested mountains and plateaus. The climate is tropical monsoon. Most of the population lives in the Mekong valley and the low plateau in the south, where food crops, chiefly rice, are grown. Hydroelectricity from a plant on the Mekong river, timber, coffee and tin are exported. Laos relies heavily on foreign aid.

LATVIA
Republic of Latvia

Area Sq Km	64 589	**Languages**	Latvian, Russian
Area Sq Miles	24 938	**Religions**	Protestant, Roman Catholic, Russian Orthodox
Population	2 050 000		
Capital	Rīga	**Currency**	Euro
		Organizations	EU, NATO, UN

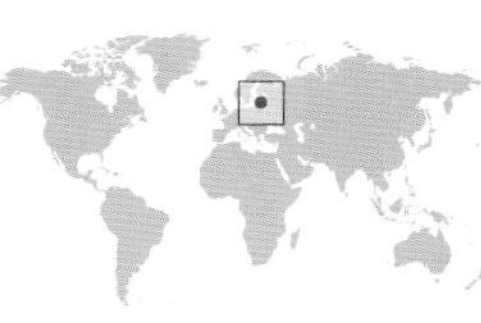

Latvia is in northern Europe, on the Baltic Sea and the Gulf of Riga. The land is flat near the coast but hilly with woods and lakes inland. The country has a modified continental climate. Over a quarter of the people live in the capital, Rīga. Crop and livestock farming are important. There are few natural resources. Industries and main exports include food products, transport equipment, wood and wood products and textiles. The main trading partners are Russia and Germany. Latvia joined the European Union in May 2004.

LEBANON
Lebanese Republic

Area Sq Km	10 452	**Languages**	Arabic, Armenian, French
Area Sq Miles	4 036	**Religions**	Shi'a Muslim, Sunni Muslim, Christian
Population	4 822 000		
Capital	Beirut (Beyrouth)	**Currency**	Lebanese pound
		Organizations	UN

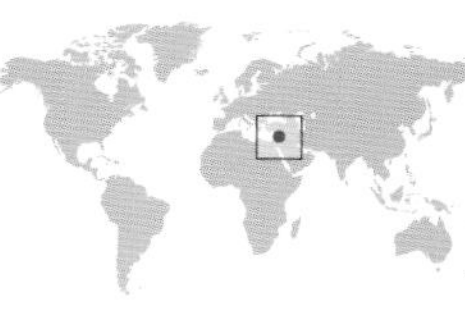

Lebanon lies on the Mediterranean coast of southwest Asia. Beyond the coastal strip, where most of the population lives, are two parallel mountain ranges, separated by the Bekaa Valley (El Beq'a). The economy and infrastructure have been recovering since the 1975–1991 civil war crippled the traditional sectors of financial services and tourism. Switzerland, the USA, France and the UAE are the main trading partners.

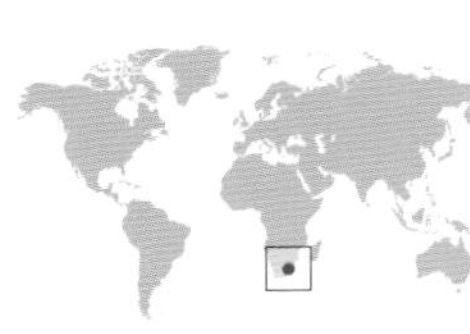

LESOTHO
Kingdom of Lesotho

Area Sq Km	30 355	Languages	Sesotho, English, Zulu
Area Sq Miles	11 720	Religions	Christian, traditional beliefs
Population	2 074 000	Currency	Loti, South African rand
Capital	Maseru	Organizations	Comm., SADC, UN

Lesotho is a landlocked state surrounded by South Africa. It is a mountainous country lying within the Drakensberg mountain range. Farming and herding are the main activities. The economy depends heavily on South Africa for transport links and employment. A major hydroelectric plant completed in 1998 allows the sale of water to South Africa. Exports include manufactured goods (mainly clothing and road vehicles), food, live animals, wool and mohair.

LIBERIA
Republic of Liberia

Area Sq Km	111 369	Languages	English, Creole, other local languages
Area Sq Miles	43 000	Religions	Traditional beliefs, Christian, Sunni Muslim
Population	4 294 000	Currency	Liberian dollar
Capital	Monrovia	Organizations	UN

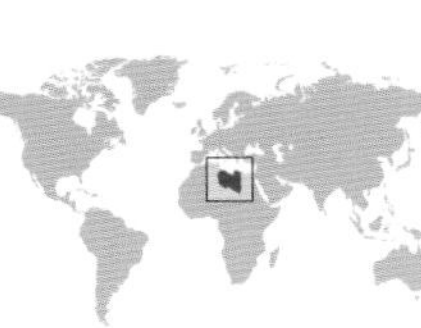

Liberia is on the Atlantic coast of west Africa. Beyond the coastal belt of sandy beaches and mangrove swamps the land rises to a forested plateau and highlands along the Guinea border. A quarter of the population lives along the coast. The climate is hot with heavy rainfall. Liberia is rich in mineral resources and forests. The economy is based on the production and export of basic products. Exports include diamonds, iron ore, rubber and timber. Liberia has a huge international debt and relies heavily on foreign aid.

LIBYA
State of Libya

Area Sq Km	1 759 540	Languages	Arabic, Berber
Area Sq Miles	679 362	Religions	Sunni Muslim
Population	6 202 000	Currency	Libyan dinar
Capital	Tripoli (Ṭarābulus)	Organizations	OPEC, UN

Libya lies on the Mediterranean coast of north Africa. The desert plains and hills of the Sahara dominate the landscape and the climate is hot and dry. Most of the population lives in cities near the coast, where the climate is cooler with moderate rainfall. Farming and herding, chiefly in the northwest, are important but the main industry is oil. Libya is a major producer, and oil accounts for virtually all of its export earnings. Italy and Germany are the main trading partners. As a result of the civil war in 2011 oil exports were disrupted and there was severe damage to the infrastructure of the country.

LIECHTENSTEIN
Principality of Liechtenstein

Area Sq Km	160	Languages	German
Area Sq Miles	62	Religions	Roman Catholic, Protestant
Population	37 000	Currency	Swiss franc
Capital	Vaduz	Organizations	UN

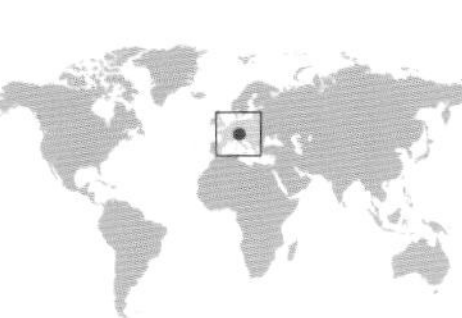

A landlocked state between Switzerland and Austria, Liechtenstein has an industrialized, free-enterprise economy. Low business taxes have attracted companies to establish offices which provide approximately one-third of state revenues. Banking is also important. Major products include precision instruments, ceramics and textiles.

LITHUANIA
Republic of Lithuania

Area Sq Km	65 200	Languages	Lithuanian, Russian, Polish
Area Sq Miles	25 174	Religions	Roman Catholic, Protestant, Russian Orthodox
Population	3 017 000	Currency	Euro
Capital	Vilnius	Organizations	EU, NATO, UN

Lithuania is in northern Europe on the eastern shores of the Baltic Sea. It is mainly lowland with many lakes, rivers and marshes. Agriculture, fishing and forestry are important, but manufacturing dominates the economy. The main exports are machinery, mineral products and chemicals. Russia and Germany are the main trading partners. Lithuania joined the European Union in May 2004.

LUXEMBOURG
Grand Duchy of Luxembourg

Area Sq Km	2 586	Languages	Letzeburgish, German, French
Area Sq Miles	998	Religions	Roman Catholic
Population	530 000	Currency	Euro
Capital	Luxembourg	Organizations	EU, NATO, OECD, UN

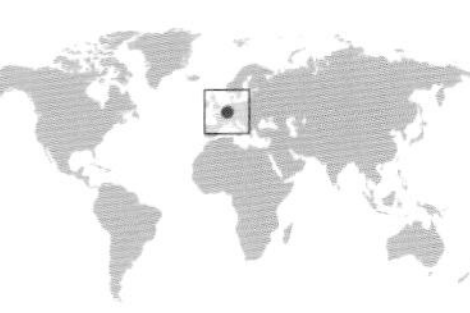

Luxembourg, a small landlocked country in western Europe, borders Belgium, France and Germany. The hills and forests of the Ardennes dominate the north, with rolling pasture to the south, where the main towns, farms and industries are found. The iron and steel industry is still important, but light industries (including textiles, chemicals and food products) are growing. Luxembourg is a major banking centre. Main trading partners are Belgium, Germany and France.

MACEDONIA (F.Y.R.O.M.)
Republic of Macedonia

Area Sq Km	25 713	Languages	Macedonian, Albanian, Turkish
Area Sq Miles	9 928	Religions	Macedonian Orthodox, Sunni Muslim
Population	2 107 000	Currency	Macedonian denar
Capital	Skopje	Organizations	NATO, UN

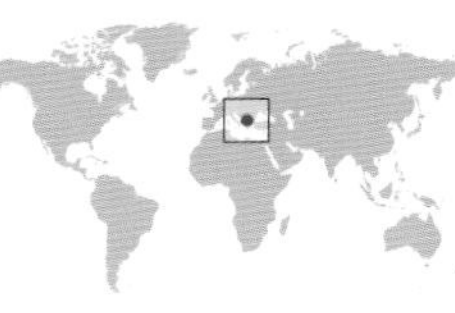

The Former Yugoslav Republic of Macedonia is a landlocked state in southern Europe. Lying within the southern Balkan Mountains, it is traversed northwest-southeast by the Vardar valley. The climate is continental. The economy is based on industry, mining and agriculture, but conflicts in the region have reduced trade and caused economic difficulties. Foreign aid and loans are now assisting in modernization and development of the country.

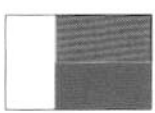

MADAGASCAR
Republic of Madagascar

Area Sq Km	587 041	Languages	Malagasy, French
Area Sq Miles	226 658	Religions	Traditional beliefs, Christian, Sunni Muslim
Population	22 925 000	Currency	Ariary
Capital	Antananarivo	Organizations	SADC, UN

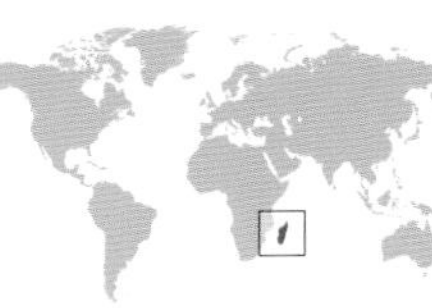

Madagascar lies off the east coast of southern Africa. The world's fourth largest island, it is mainly a high plateau, with a coastal strip to the east and scrubby plain to the west. The climate is tropical, with heavy rainfall in the north and east. Most of the population lives on the plateau. Although the amount of arable land is limited, the economy is based on agriculture. The main industries are agricultural processing, textile manufacturing and oil refining. Foreign aid is important. Exports include coffee, vanilla, cotton cloth, sugar and shrimps. France is the main trading partner.

MALAWI
Republic of Malawi

Area Sq Km	118 484	Languages	Chichewa, English, other local languages
Area Sq Miles	45 747	Religions	Christian, traditional beliefs, Sunni Muslim
Population	16 363 000	Currency	Malawian kwacha
Capital	Lilongwe	Organizations	Comm., SADC, UN

Landlocked Malawi in central Africa is a narrow hilly country at the southern end of the Great Rift Valley. One-fifth is covered by Lake Nyasa. Most of the population lives in rural areas in the southern regions. The climate is mainly subtropical, with varying rainfall. The economy is predominantly agricultural, with tobacco, tea and sugar the main exports. Malawi is one of the world's least developed countries and relies heavily on foreign aid. South Africa is the main trading partner.

MALAYSIA

Area Sq Km	332 965	Languages	Malay, English, Chinese, Tamil, other local languages
Area Sq Miles	128 559	Religions	Sunni Muslim, Buddhist, Hindu, Christian, traditional beliefs
Population	29 717 000	Currency	Ringgit
Capital	Kuala Lumpur/ Putrajaya	Organizations	APEC, ASEAN, Comm., UN

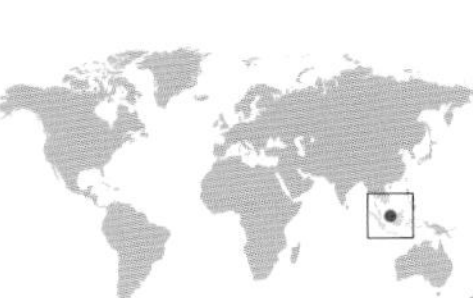

Malaysia, in southeast Asia, comprises two regions, separated by the South China Sea. The western region occupies the southern Malay Peninsula, which has a chain of mountains dividing the eastern coastal strip from wider plains to the west. East Malaysia, consisting of the states of Sabah and Sarawak in the north of the island of Borneo, is mainly rainforest-covered hills and mountains with mangrove swamps along the coast. Both regions have a tropical climate with heavy rainfall. About eighty per cent of the population lives in Peninsular Malaysia. The country is rich in natural resources and has reserves of minerals and fuels. It is an important producer of tin, oil, natural gas and tropical hardwoods. Agriculture remains a substantial part of the economy, but industry is the most important sector. The main exports are transport and electronic equipment, oil, chemicals, palm oil, wood and rubber. The main trading partners are Japan, the USA and Singapore.

MALDIVES
Republic of the Maldives

Area Sq Km	298	Languages	Divehi (Maldivian)
Area Sq Miles	115	Religions	Sunni Muslim
Population	345 000	Currency	Rufiyaa
Capital	Male	Organizations	Comm., UN

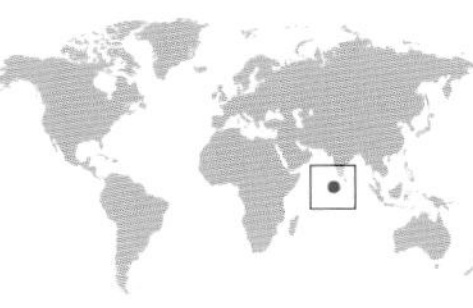

The Maldive archipelago comprises over a thousand coral atolls (around two hundred of which are inhabited), in the Indian Ocean, southwest of India. Over eighty per cent of the land area is less than one metre above sea level. The main atolls are North and South Male and Addu. The climate is hot, humid and monsoonal. There is little cultivation and almost all food is imported. Tourism has expanded rapidly and is the most important sector of the economy.

MALI

Republic of Mali

Area Sq Km	1 240 140	**Languages**	French, Bambara, other local languages
Area Sq Miles	478 821	**Religions**	Sunni Muslim, traditional beliefs, Christian
Population	15 302 000	**Currency**	CFA franc
Capital	Bamako	**Organizations**	UN

A landlocked state in west Africa, Mali is low-lying, with a few rugged hills in the northeast. Northern regions lie within the Sahara desert. To the south, around the Niger river, are marshes and savanna grassland. Rainfall is unreliable. Most of the population lives along the Niger and Falémé rivers. Exports include cotton, livestock and gold. Mali is one of the least developed countries in the world and relies heavily on foreign aid.

MALTA

Republic of Malta

Area Sq Km	316	**Languages**	Maltese, English
Area Sq Miles	122	**Religions**	Roman Catholic
Population	429 000	**Currency**	Euro
Capital	Valletta	**Organizations**	Comm., EU, UN

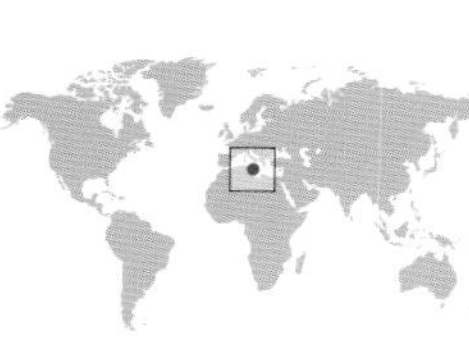

The islands of Malta and Gozo lie in the Mediterranean Sea, off the coast of southern Italy. The islands have hot, dry summers and mild winters. The economy depends on foreign trade, tourism and the manufacture of electronics and textiles. Main trading partners are the USA, France and Italy. Malta joined the European Union in May 2004.

MARSHALL ISLANDS

Republic of the Marshall Islands

Area Sq Km	181	**Languages**	English, Marshallese
Area Sq Miles	70	**Religions**	Protestant, Roman Catholic
Population	53 000	**Currency**	United States dollar
Capital	Delap-Uliga-Djarrit	**Organizations**	UN

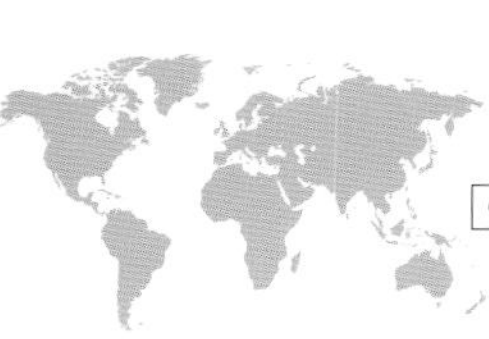

The Marshall Islands consist of over a thousand atolls, islands and islets, within two chains in the north Pacific Ocean. The main atolls are Majuro (home to half the population), Kwajalein, Jaluit, Enewetak and Bikini. The climate is tropical, with heavy autumn rainfall. About half the workforce is employed in farming or fishing. Tourism is a small source of foreign exchange and the islands depend heavily on aid from the USA.

Martinique

French Overseas Department

Area Sq Km	1 079	**Languages**	French, Creole
Area Sq Miles	417	**Religions**	Roman Catholic, traditional beliefs
Population	404 000	**Currency**	Euro
Capital	Fort-de-France		

Martinique, one of the Caribbean Windward Islands, has volcanic peaks in the north, a populous central plain, and hills and beaches in the south. Tourism is a major source of foreign exchange, and substantial aid is received from France. The main trading partners are France and Guadeloupe.

MAURITANIA

Islamic Republic of Mauritania

Area Sq Km	1 030 700	**Languages**	Arabic, French, other local languages
Area Sq Miles	397 955	**Religions**	Sunni Muslim
Population	3 890 000	**Currency**	Ouguiya
Capital	Nouakchott	**Organizations**	UN

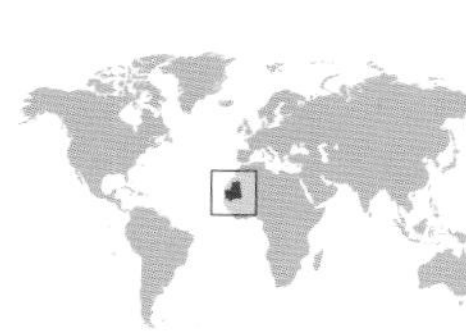

Mauritania is on the Atlantic coast of northwest Africa and lies almost entirely within the Sahara desert. Oases and a fertile strip along the Senegal river to the south are the only areas suitable for cultivation. The climate is generally hot and dry. About a quarter of Mauritanians live in the capital, Nouakchott. Most of the workforce depends on livestock rearing and subsistence farming. There are large deposits of iron ore which account for more than half of total exports. Mauritania's coastal waters are among the richest fishing grounds in the world. The main trading partners are France, Japan, China and Italy.

MAURITIUS

Republic of Mauritius

Area Sq Km	2 040	**Languages**	English, Creole, Hindi, Bhojpurī, French
Area Sq Miles	788	**Religions**	Hindu, Roman Catholic, Sunni Muslim
Population	1 244 000	**Currency**	Mauritian rupee
Capital	Port Louis	**Organizations**	Comm., SADC, UN

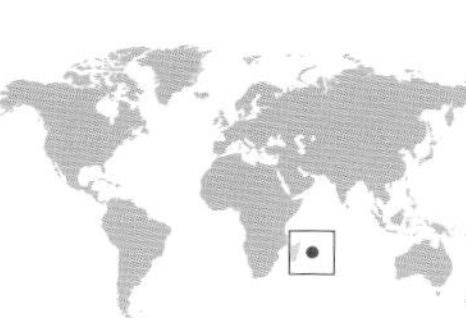

The state comprises Mauritius, Rodrigues and some twenty small islands in the Indian Ocean, east of Madagascar. The main island of Mauritius is volcanic in origin and has a coral coast, rising to a central plateau. Most of the population lives on the north and west sides of the island. The climate is warm and humid. The economy is based on sugar production, light manufacturing (chiefly clothing) and tourism.

Mayotte

French Overseas Department

Area Sq Km	373	**Languages**	French, Mahorian (Shimaore), Kibushi
Area Sq Miles	144	**Religions**	Sunni Muslim, Christian
Population	222 000	**Currency**	Euro
Capital	Dzaoudzi		

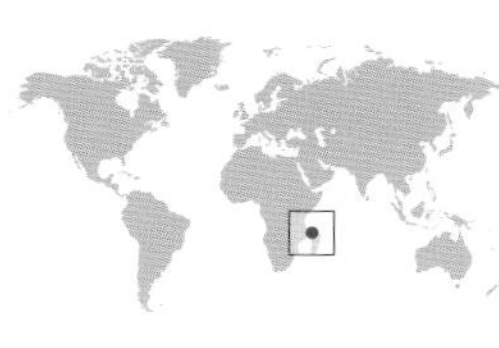

Lying in the Indian Ocean off the east coast of central Africa, Mayotte is geographically part of the Comoro archipelago. The economy is based on agriculture, but Mayotte depends heavily on aid from France.

MEXICO

United Mexican States

Area Sq Km	1 972 545	**Languages**	Spanish, Amerindian languages
Area Sq Miles	761 604	**Religions**	Roman Catholic, Protestant
Population	122 332 000	**Currency**	Mexican peso
Capital	México City (Mexico)	**Organizations**	APEC, OECD, UN

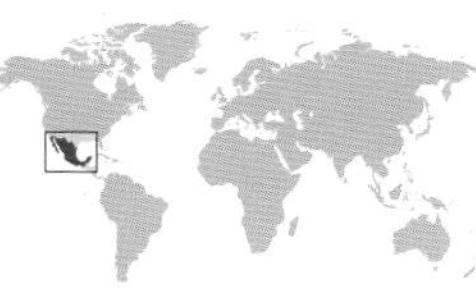

The largest country in Central America, Mexico extends south from the USA to Guatemala and Belize, and from the Pacific Ocean to the Gulf of Mexico. The greater part of the country is high plateau flanked by the western and eastern ranges of the Sierra Madre mountains. The principal lowland is the Yucatán peninsula in the southeast. The climate varies with latitude and altitude: hot and humid in the lowlands, warm on the plateau and cool with cold winters in the mountains. The north is arid, while the far south has heavy rainfall. Mexico City is the fourth largest conurbation in the world and the country's centre of trade and industry. Agriculture involves a sixth of the workforce; crops include grains, coffee, cotton and vegetables. Mexico is rich in minerals, including copper, zinc, lead, tin, sulphur, and silver. It is one of the world's largest producers of oil, from vast reserves in the Gulf of Mexico. The oil and petrochemical industries still dominate the economy, but a variety of manufactured goods are produced, including iron and steel, motor vehicles, textiles, chemicals and food and tobacco products. Tourism is growing in importance. Over three-quarters of all trade is with the USA.

MICRONESIA, FEDERATED STATES OF

Area Sq Km	701	**Languages**	English, Chuukese, Pohnpeian, other local languages
Area Sq Miles	271	**Religions**	Roman Catholic, Protestant
Population	104 000	**Currency**	United States dollar
Capital	Palikir	**Organizations**	UN

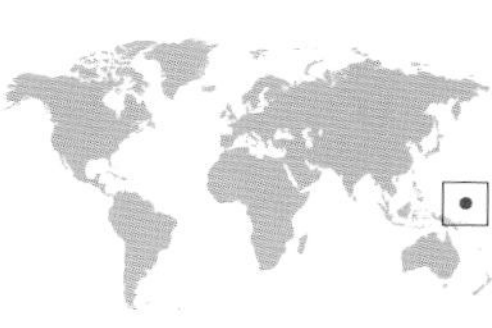

Micronesia comprises over six hundred atolls and islands of the Caroline Islands in the north Pacific Ocean. A third of the population lives on Pohnpei. The climate is tropical, with heavy rainfall. Fishing and subsistence farming are the main activities. Fish, garments and bananas are the main exports. Income is also derived from tourism and the licensing of foreign fishing fleets. The islands depend heavily on aid from the USA.

MOLDOVA

Republic of Moldova

Area Sq Km	33 700	**Languages**	Romanian, Ukrainian, Gagauz, Russian
Area Sq Miles	13 012	**Religions**	Romanian Orthodox, Russian Orthodox
Population	3 487 000	**Currency**	Moldovan leu
Capital	Chişinău (Kishinev)	**Organizations**	CIS, UN

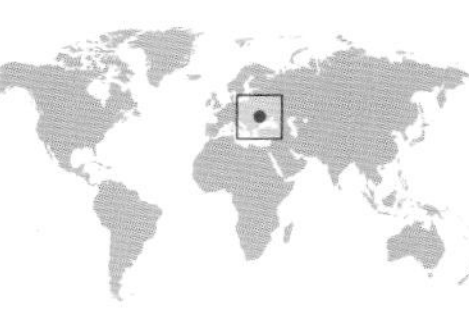

Moldova lies between Romania and Ukraine in eastern Europe. It consists of hilly steppe land, drained by the Prut and Dniester rivers. Moldova has no mineral resources, and the economy is mainly agricultural, with sugar beet, tobacco, wine and fruit the chief products. Food processing, machinery and textiles are the main industries. Russia is the main trading partner.

MONACO

Principality of Monaco

Area Sq Km	2	**Languages**	French, Monégasque, Italian
Area Sq Miles	1	**Religions**	Roman Catholic
Population	38 000	**Currency**	Euro
Capital	Monaco-Ville	**Organizations**	UN

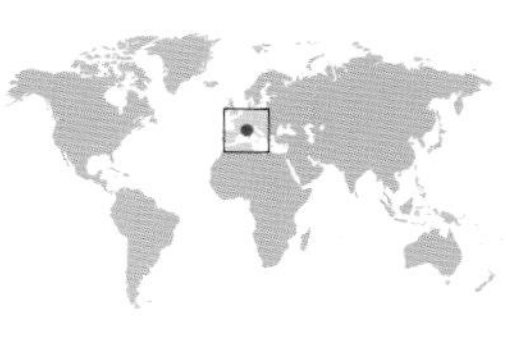

The principality occupies a rocky peninsula and a strip of land on France's Mediterranean coast. Monaco's economy depends on service industries (chiefly tourism, banking and finance) and light industry.

MONGOLIA

Area Sq Km	1 565 000	Languages	Khalka (Mongolian), Kazakh, other local languages
Area Sq Miles	604 250	Religions	Buddhist, Sunni Muslim
Population	2 839 000	Currency	Tugrik (tögrög)
Capital	Ulan Bator (Ulaanbaatar)	Organizations	UN

Mongolia is a landlocked country in eastern Asia between Russia and China. Much of it is high steppe land, with mountains and lakes in the west and north. In the south is the Gobi desert. Mongolia has long, cold winters and short, mild summers. A quarter of the population lives in the capital, Ulaanbaatar. Livestock breeding and agricultural processing are important. There are substantial mineral resources. Copper and textiles are the main exports. China and Russia are the main trading partners.

MONTENEGRO

Area Sq Km	13 812	Languages	Serbian (Montenegrin), Albanian
Area Sq Miles	5 333	Religions	Montenegrin Orthodox, Sunni Muslim
Population	621 000	Currency	Euro
Capital	Podgorica	Organizations	UN

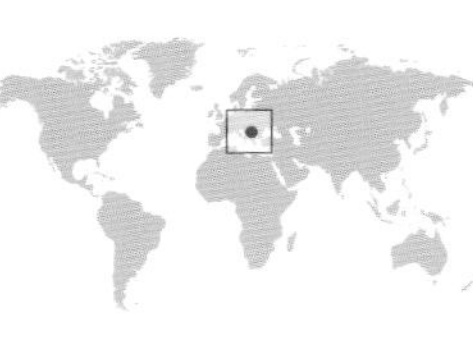

Montenegro, previously a constituent republic of the former Yugoslavia, became an independent nation in June 2006 when it opted to split from the state union of Serbia and Montenegro. Montenegro separates the much larger Serbia from the Adriatic coast. The landscape is rugged and mountainous, and the climate Mediterranean.

Montserrat
United Kingdom Overseas Territory

Area Sq Km	100	Languages	English
Area Sq Miles	39	Religions	Protestant, Roman Catholic
Population	4 922	Currency	East Caribbean dollar
Capital	Brades (Temporary Capital)	Organizations	CARICOM

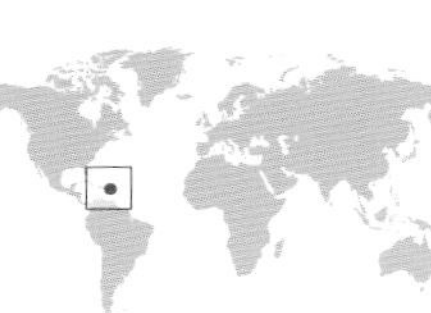

An island in the Leeward Islands group in the Lesser Antilles, in the Caribbean. From 1995 to 1997 the volcanoes in the Soufrière Hills erupted for the first time since 1630. Over sixty per cent of the island was covered in volcanic ash and Plymouth, the capital, was virtually destroyed. Many people emigrated, and the remaining population moved to the north of the island. Brades has replaced Plymouth as the temporary capital. Reconstruction is being funded by aid from the UK.

MOROCCO
Kingdom of Morocco

Area Sq Km	446 550	Languages	Arabic, Berber, French
Area Sq Miles	172 414	Religions	Sunni Muslim
Population	33 008 000	Currency	Moroccan dirham
Capital	Rabat	Organizations	UN

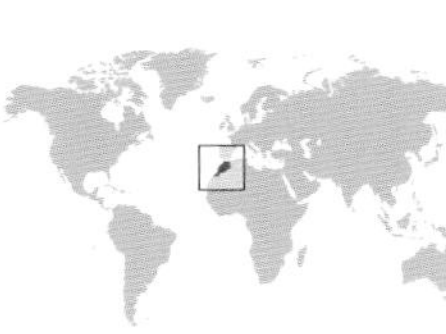

Lying in the northwest of Africa, Morocco has both Atlantic and Mediterranean coasts. The Atlas Mountains separate the arid south and disputed region of western Sahara from the fertile west and north, which have a milder climate. Most Moroccans live on the Atlantic coastal plain. The economy is based on agriculture, phosphate mining and tourism; the most important industries are food processing, textiles and chemicals.

MOZAMBIQUE
Republic of Mozambique

Area Sq Km	799 380	Languages	Portuguese, Makua, Tsonga, other local languages
Area Sq Miles	308 642	Religions	Traditional beliefs, Roman Catholic, Sunni Muslim
Population	25 834 000	Currency	Metical
Capital	Maputo	Organizations	Comm., SADC, UN

Mozambique lies on the east coast of southern Africa. The land is mainly a savanna plateau drained by the Zambezi and Limpopo rivers, with highlands to the north. Most of the population lives on the coast or in the river valleys. In general the climate is tropical with winter rainfall, but droughts occur. The economy is based on subsistence agriculture. Exports include shrimps, cashews, cotton and sugar, but Mozambique relies heavily on aid, and remains one of the least developed countries in the world.

MYANMAR (Burma)
Republic of the Union of Myanmar

Area Sq Km	676 577	Languages	Burmese, Shan, Karen, other local languages
Area Sq Miles	261 228	Religions	Buddhist, Christian, Sunni Muslim
Population	53 259 000	Currency	Kyat
Capital	Nay Pyi Taw	Organizations	ASEAN, UN

Myanmar (Burma) is in southeast Asia, bordering the Bay of Bengal and the Andaman Sea. Most of the population lives in the valley and delta of the Irrawaddy river, which is flanked by mountains and high plateaus. The climate is hot and monsoonal, and rainforest covers much of the land. Most of the workforce is employed in agriculture. Myanmar is rich in minerals, including zinc, lead, copper and silver. Political and social unrest and lack of foreign investment have affected economic development.

Nagorno-Karabakh
Disputed territory

Area Sq Km	6 000	Languages	Armenian
Area Sq Miles	2 317	Religions	Armenian Orthodox
Population	146 600	Currency	Armenian dram
Capital	Xankändi (Stepanakert)		

Established as an Autonomous Region within Azerbaijan in 1923, Nagorno-Karabakh is a disputed enclave of Azerbaijan. It is legally part of Azerbaijan, but is populated largely by ethnic Armenians who have established what amounts to a separatist de facto republic operating with support from Armenia. In 1991, the local Armenian population declared independence and Azerbaijan abolished the area's autonomous status. As a result of conflict, Nagorno-Karabakh/Armenia occupies approximately twenty per cent of Azerbaijan. A Russian-brokered cease-fire has been in place since 1994, with the cease-fire line enclosing the territory of Nagorno-Karabakh and the additional parts of Azerbaijan, up to the Armenian border, seized by Karabakh Armenians during the fighting. The area between the cease-fire line and the boundary of Nagorno-Karabakh is effectively a 'no-go' area.

NAMIBIA
Republic of Namibia

Area Sq Km	824 292	Languages	English, Afrikaans, German, Ovambo, other local languages
Area Sq Miles	318 261	Religions	Protestant, Roman Catholic
Population	2 303 000	Currency	Namibian dollar
Capital	Windhoek	Organizations	Comm., SADC, UN

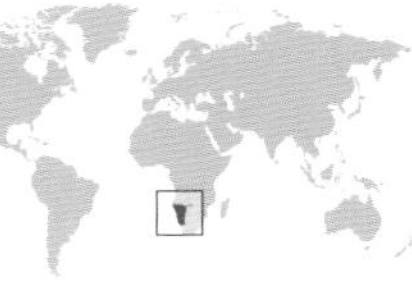

Namibia lies on the southern Atlantic coast of Africa. Mountain ranges separate the coastal Namib Desert from the interior plateau, bordered to the south and east by the Kalahari Desert. The country is hot and dry, but some summer rain in the north supports crops and livestock. Employment is in agriculture and fishing, although the economy is based on mineral extraction – diamonds, uranium, lead, zinc and silver. The economy is closely linked to South Africa.

NAURU
Republic of Nauru

Area Sq Km	21	Languages	Nauruan, English
Area Sq Miles	8	Religions	Protestant, Roman Catholic
Population	10 000	Currency	Australian dollar
Capital	Yaren	Organizations	Comm., UN

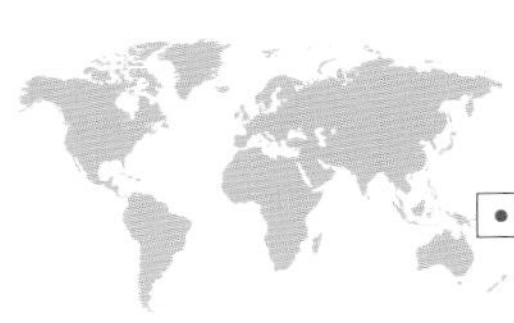

Nauru is a coral island near the Equator in the Pacific Ocean. It has a fertile coastal strip and a barren central plateau. The climate is tropical. The economy was based on phosphate mining, but reserves are exhausted and replacement of this income is a serious long-term problem.

NEPAL
Federal Democratic Republic of Nepal

Area Sq Km	147 181	Languages	Nepali, Maithili, Bhojpuri, English, other local languages
Area Sq Miles	56 827	Religions	Hindu, Buddhist, Sunni Muslim
Population	27 797 000	Currency	Nepalese rupee
Capital	Kathmandu	Organizations	UN

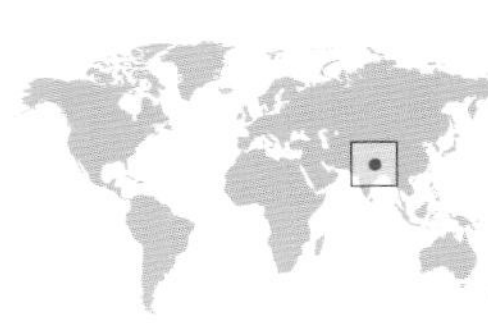

Nepal lies in the eastern Himalaya mountains between India and China. High mountains (including Everest) dominate the north. Most people live in the temperate central valleys and subtropical southern plains. The economy is based largely on agriculture and forestry. There is some manufacturing, chiefly of textiles and carpets, and tourism is important. Nepal relies heavily on foreign aid.

NETHERLANDS
Kingdom of the Netherlands

Area Sq Km	41 526	Languages	Dutch, Frisian
Area Sq Miles	16 033	Religions	Roman Catholic, Protestant, Sunni Muslim
Population	16 759 000	Currency	Euro
Capital	Amsterdam/ 's-Gravenhage (The Hague)	Organizations	EU, NATO, OECD, UN

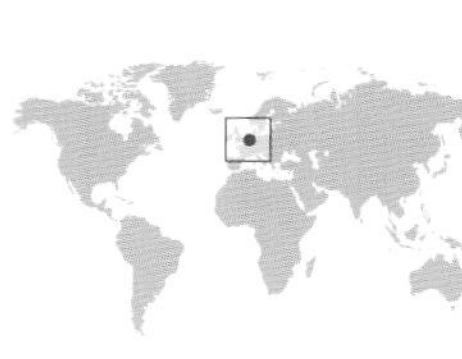

The Netherlands lies on the North Sea coast of western Europe. Apart from low hills in the far southeast, the land is flat and low-lying, much of it below sea level. The coastal region includes the delta of five rivers and polders (reclaimed land), protected by sand dunes, dykes and canals. The climate is temperate, with cool summers and mild winters. Rainfall is spread evenly throughout the year. The Netherlands is a densely populated and highly urbanized country, with the majority of the population living in the cities of Amsterdam, Rotterdam and The Hague. Horticulture and dairy farming are important activities, although they employ less than three per cent of the workforce. The Netherlands is an important agricultural exporter, and is a leading producer and exporter of natural gas from reserves in the North Sea. The economy is based mainly on international trade and manufacturing industry. The main industries produce food products, chemicals, machinery, electrical and electronic goods and transport equipment. Germany is the main trading partner, followed by other European Union countries.

New Caledonia
French Overseas Collectivity

Area Sq Km	19 058	Languages	French, other local languages
Area Sq Miles	7 358	Religions	Roman Catholic, Protestant, Sunni Muslim
Population	256 000		
Capital	Nouméa	Currency	CFP franc

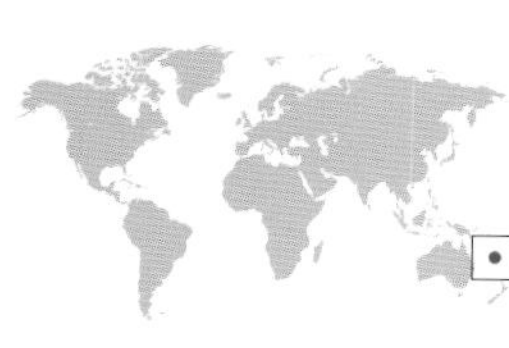

An island group lying in the southwest Pacific, with a sub-tropical climate. New Caledonia has over one-fifth of the world's nickel reserves, and the main economic activity is metal mining. Tourism is also important. New Caledonia relies on aid from France.

NEW ZEALAND

Area Sq Km	270 534	Languages	English, Maori
Area Sq Miles	104 454	Religions	Protestant, Roman Catholic
Population	4 506 000	Currency	New Zealand dollar
Capital	Wellington	Organizations	APEC, Comm., OECD, UN

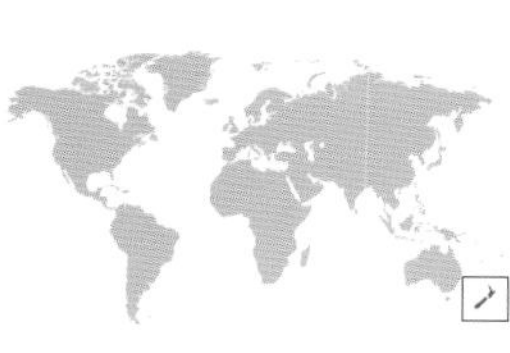

New Zealand comprises two main islands separated by the narrow Cook Strait, and a number of smaller islands. North Island, where three-quarters of the population lives, has mountain ranges, broad fertile valleys and a central plateau with hot springs and active volcanoes. South Island is also mountainous, with the Southern Alps running its entire length. The only major lowland area is the Canterbury Plains in the centre-east. The climate is generally temperate, although South Island has colder winters. Farming is the mainstay of the economy. New Zealand is one of the world's leading producers of meat (beef, lamb and mutton), wool and dairy products; fruit and fish are also important. Hydroelectric and geothermal power provide much of the country's energy needs. Other industries produce timber, wood pulp, iron, aluminium, machinery and chemicals. Tourism is the fastest growing sector of the economy. The main trading partners are Australia, the USA, China, the UK and Japan.

NICARAGUA
Republic of Nicaragua

Area Sq Km	130 000	Languages	Spanish, Amerindian languages
Area Sq Miles	50 193		
Population	6 080 000	Religions	Roman Catholic, Protestant
Capital	Managua	Currency	Córdoba
		Organizations	UN

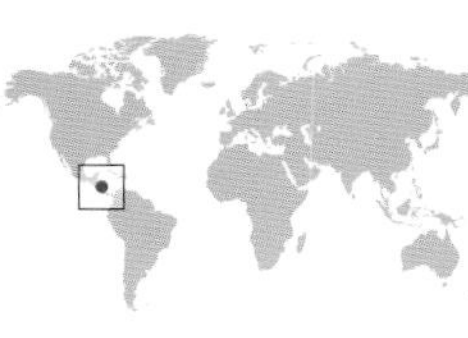

Nicaragua lies at the heart of Central America, with both Pacific and Caribbean coasts. Mountain ranges separate the east, which is largely rainforest, from the more developed western regions, which include Lake Nicaragua and some active volcanoes. The highest land is in the north. The climate is tropical. Nicaragua is one of the western hemisphere's poorest countries, and the economy is largely agricultural but growth in tourism is having a positive effect on other areas. Exports include coffee, seafood, cotton and bananas. The USA is the main trading partner. Nicaragua has a huge national debt, and relies heavily on foreign aid.

NIGER
Republic of Niger

Area Sq Km	1 267 000	Languages	French, Hausa, Fulani, other local languages
Area Sq Miles	489 191		
Population	17 831 000	Religions	Sunni Muslim, traditional beliefs
Capital	Niamey	Currency	CFA franc
		Organizations	UN

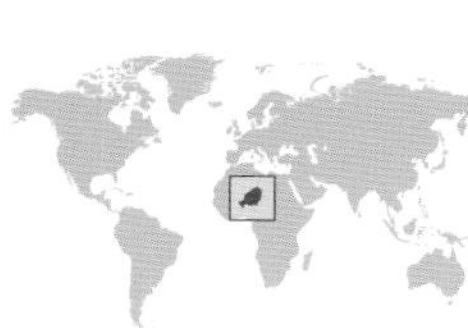

A landlocked state of west Africa, Niger lies mostly within the Sahara desert, but with savanna in the south and in the Niger valley area. The mountains of the Massif de l'Aïr dominate central regions. Much of the country is hot and dry. The south has some summer rainfall, although droughts occur. The economy depends on subsistence farming and herding, and uranium exports, but Niger is one of the world's least developed countries and relies heavily on foreign aid. France is the main trading partner.

NIGERIA
Federal Republic of Nigeria

Area Sq Km	923 768	Languages	English, Hausa, Yoruba, Ibo, Fulani, other local languages
Area Sq Miles	356 669		
Population	173 615 000	Religions	Sunni Muslim, Christian, traditional beliefs
Capital	Abuja	Currency	Naira
		Organizations	Comm., OPEC, UN

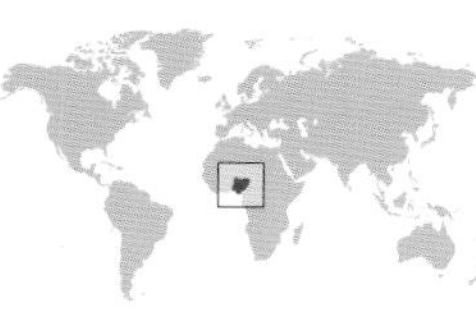

Nigeria is in west Africa, on the Gulf of Guinea, and is the most populous country in Africa. The Niger delta dominates coastal areas, fringed with sandy beaches, mangrove swamps and lagoons. Inland is a belt of rainforest which gives way to woodland or savanna on high plateaus. The far north is the semi-desert edge of the Sahara. The climate is tropical, with heavy summer rainfall in the south but low rainfall in the north. Most of the population lives in the coastal lowlands or in the west. About half the workforce is involved in agriculture, mainly growing subsistence crops. Agricultural production, however, has failed to keep up with demand, and Nigeria is now a net importer of food. Cocoa and rubber are the only significant export crops. The economy is heavily dependent on vast oil resources in the Niger delta and in shallow offshore waters, and oil accounts for over ninety per cent of export earnings. Nigeria also has natural gas reserves and some mineral deposits, but these are largely undeveloped. Industry involves mainly oil refining, chemicals (chiefly fertilizers), agricultural processing, textiles, steel manufacture and vehicle assembly. Political instability in the past has left Nigeria with heavy debts, poverty and unemployment, but it is now the largest economy in Africa.

Niue
Self-governing New Zealand Overseas Territory

Area Sq Km	258	Languages	English, Nivean
Area Sq Miles	100	Religions	Christian
Population	1 460	Currency	New Zealand dollar
Capital	Alofi		

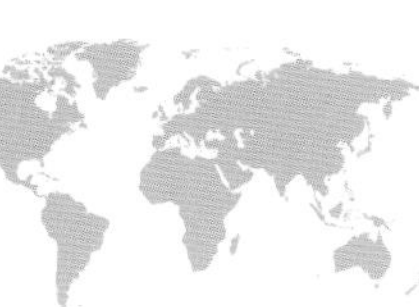

Niue, one of the largest coral islands in the world, lies in the south Pacific Ocean about 500 kilometres (300 miles) east of Tonga. The economy depends on aid and remittances from New Zealand. The population is declining because of migration to New Zealand.

Norfolk Island
Australian External Territory

Area Sq Km	35	Languages	English
Area Sq Miles	14	Religions	Protestant, Roman Catholic
Population	2 302	Currency	Australian dollar
Capital	Kingston		

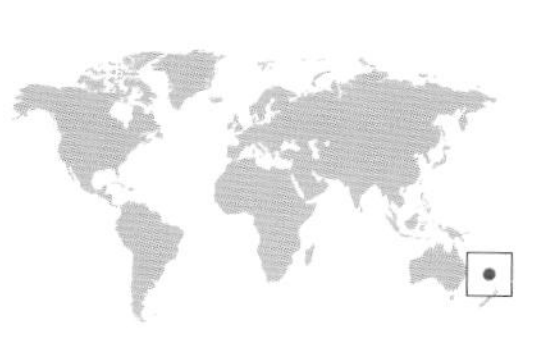

In the south Pacific Ocean, Norfolk Island lies between Vanuatu and New Zealand. Tourism has increased steadily and is the mainstay of the economy and provides revenues for agricultural development.

Northern Mariana Islands
United States Commonwealth

Area Sq Km	477	Languages	English, Chamorro, other local languages
Area Sq Miles	184		
Population	54 000	Religions	Roman Catholic
Capital	Capitol Hill	Currency	United States dollar

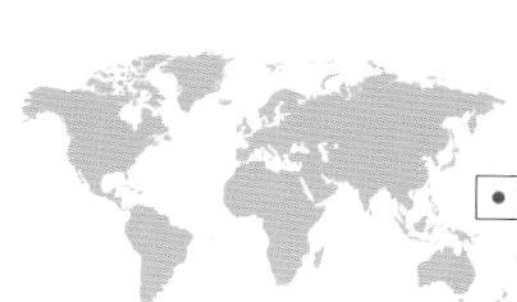

A chain of islands in the northwest Pacific Ocean, extending over 550 kilometres (350 miles) north to south. The main island is Saipan. Tourism is a major industry, employing approximately half the workforce.

NORTH KOREA
Democratic People's Republic of Korea

Area Sq Km	120 538	Languages	Korean
Area Sq Miles	46 540	Religions	Traditional beliefs, Chondoist, Buddhist
Population	24 895 000		
Capital	P'yŏngyang	Currency	North Korean won
		Organizations	UN

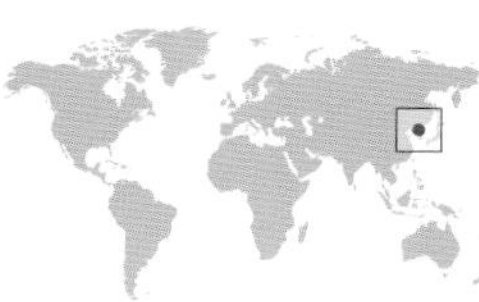

Occupying the northern half of the Korean peninsula in eastern Asia, North Korea is a rugged and mountainous country. The principal lowlands and the main agricultural areas are the plains in the southwest. Over sixty per cent the population lives in urban areas, mainly on the coastal plains. North Korea has a continental climate, with cold, dry winters and hot, wet summers. Approximately one-third of the workforce is involved in agriculture, mainly growing food crops on cooperative farms. Various minerals, notably iron ore, are mined and are the basis of the country's heavy industries. Exports include minerals (lead, magnesite and zinc) and metal products (chiefly iron and steel). The economy declined after 1991, when ties to the former USSR and eastern bloc collapsed, and there have been serious food shortages.

NORWAY
Kingdom of Norway

Area Sq Km	323 878	Languages	Norwegian, Sami languages
Area Sq Miles	125 050	Religions	Protestant, Roman Catholic
Population	5 043 000		
Capital	Oslo	Currency	Norwegian krone
		Organizations	NATO, OECD, UN

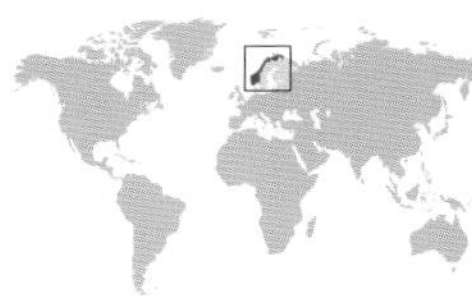

Norway stretches along the north and west coasts of Scandinavia, from the Arctic Ocean to the North Sea. Its extensive coastline is indented with fjords and fringed with many islands. Inland, the terrain is mountainous, with coniferous forests and lakes in the south. The only major lowland areas are along the southern North Sea and Skagerrak coasts, where most of the population lives. The climate is modified by the effect of the North Atlantic Drift ocean current. Norway has vast petroleum and natural gas resources

in the North Sea. It is one of western Europe's leading producers of oil and gas, and exports of oil account for approximately half of total export earnings. Related industries include engineering (oil and gas platforms) and petrochemicals. More traditional industries process local raw materials, particularly fish, timber and minerals. Agriculture is limited, but fishing and fish farming are important. Norway is the world's leading exporter of farmed salmon. Merchant shipping and tourism are major sources of foreign exchange.

OMAN
Sultanate of Oman

Area Sq Km	309 500	Languages	Arabic, Baluchi, Indian languages
Area Sq Miles	119 499	Religions	Ibadhi Muslim, Sunni Muslim
Population	3 632 000	Currency	Omani rial
Capital	Muscat (Masqat)	Organizations	UN

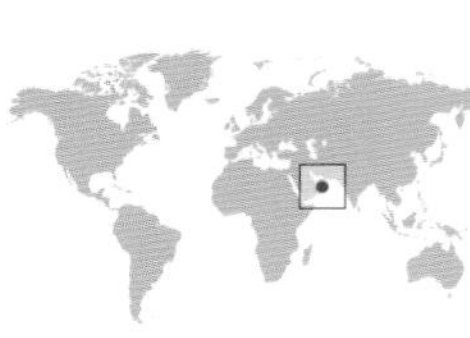

In southwest Asia, Oman occupies the east and southeast coasts of the Arabian Peninsula and an enclave north of the United Arab Emirates. Most of the land is desert, with mountains in the north and south. The climate is hot and mainly dry. Most of the population lives on the coastal strip on the Gulf of Oman. The majority depend on farming and fishing, but the oil and gas industries dominate the economy with around eighty per cent of export revenues coming from oil.

PAKISTAN
Islamic Republic of Pakistan

Area Sq Km	881 888	Languages	Urdu, Punjabi, Sindhi, Pashtu (Pushtu), English, Balochi
Area Sq Miles	340 497	Religions	Sunni Muslim, Shi'a Muslim, Christian, Hindu
Population	182 143 000	Currency	Pakistani rupee
Capital	Islamabad	Organizations	Comm., UN

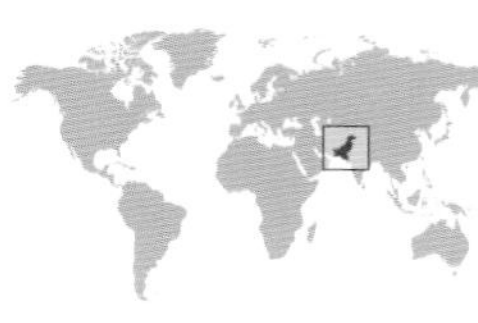

Pakistan is in the northwest part of the Indian subcontinent in south Asia, on the Arabian Sea. The east and south are dominated by the great basin of the Indus river system. This is the main agricultural area and contains most of the predominantly rural population. To the north the land rises to the mountains of the Karakoram, Hindu Kush and Himalaya mountains. The west is semi-desert plateaus and mountain ranges. The climate ranges between dry desert, and arctic tundra on the mountain tops. Temperatures are generally warm and rainfall is monsoonal. Agriculture is the main sector of the economy, employing over a third of the workforce, and is based on extensive irrigation schemes. Pakistan is one of the world's leading producers of cotton and a major exporter of rice. Pakistan produces natural gas and has a variety of mineral deposits including coal and gold, but they are little developed. The main industries are textiles and clothing manufacture and food processing, with fabrics and ready-made clothing the leading exports. Pakistan also produces leather goods, fertilizers, chemicals, paper and precision instruments. The country depends heavily on foreign aid and remittances from workers abroad.

PALAU
Republic of Palau

Area Sq Km	497	Languages	Palauan, English
Area Sq Miles	192	Religions	Roman Catholic, Protestant, traditional beliefs
Population	21 000	Currency	United States dollar
Capital	Melekeok (Ngerulmud)	Organizations	UN

Palau comprises over three hundred islands in the western Caroline Islands, in the west Pacific Ocean. The climate is tropical. The economy is based on farming, fishing and tourism, but Palau is heavily dependent on aid from the USA.

PANAMA
Republic of Panama

Area Sq Km	77 082	Languages	Spanish, English, Amerindian languages
Area Sq Miles	29 762	Religions	Roman Catholic, Protestant, Sunni Muslim
Population	3 864 000	Currency	Balboa
Capital	Panama City (Panamá)	Organizations	UN

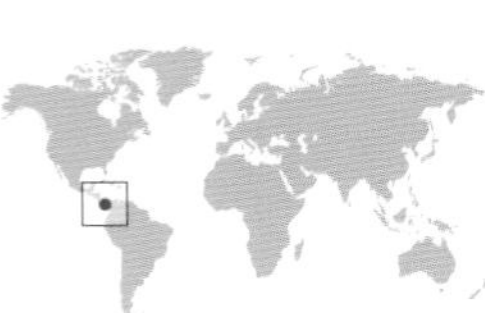

Panama is the most southerly state in central America and has Pacific and Caribbean coasts. It is hilly, with mountains in the west and jungle near the Colombian border. The climate is tropical. Most of the population lives on the drier Pacific side. The economy is based mainly on services related to the Panama Canal: shipping, banking and tourism. Exports include bananas, shrimps, coffee, clothing and fish products. The USA is the main trading partner.

PAPUA NEW GUINEA
Independent State of Papua New Guinea

Area Sq Km	462 840	Languages	English, Tok Pisin (Creole), other local languages
Area Sq Miles	178 704	Religions	Protestant, Roman Catholic, traditional beliefs
Population	7 321 000	Currency	Kina
Capital	Port Moresby	Organizations	APEC, Comm., UN

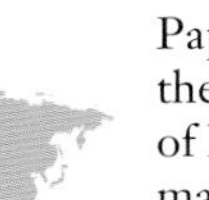

Papua New Guinea occupies the eastern half of the island of New Guinea and includes many island groups. It has a forested and mountainous interior, bordered by swampy plains, and a tropical monsoon climate. Most of the workforce are farmers. Timber, copra, coffee and cocoa are important, but exports are dominated by minerals, chiefly gold and copper. The country depends on foreign aid. Australia, Japan and Singapore are the main trading partners.

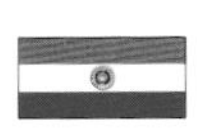

PARAGUAY
Republic of Paraguay

Area Sq Km	406 752	Languages	Spanish, Guaraní
Area Sq Miles	157 048	Religions	Roman Catholic, Protestant
Population	6 802 000	Currency	Guaraní
Capital	Asunción	Organizations	UN

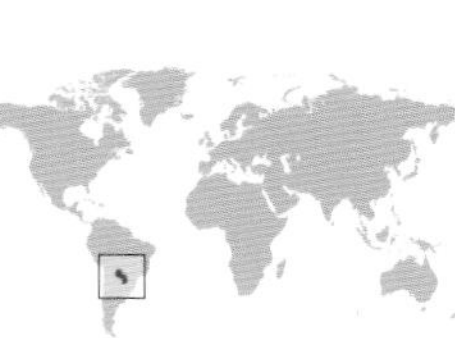

Paraguay is a landlocked country in central South America, bordering Bolivia, Brazil and Argentina. The Paraguay river separates a sparsely populated western zone of marsh and flat alluvial plains from a more developed, hilly and forested region to the east and south. The climate is subtropical. Virtually all electricity is produced by hydroelectric plants, and surplus power is exported to Brazil and Argentina. The hydroelectric dam at Itaipú is one of the largest in the world. The mainstay of the economy is agriculture and related industries. Exports include cotton, soya bean and edible oil products, timber and meat. Brazil and Argentina are the main trading partners.

PERU
Republic of Peru

Area Sq Km	1 285 216	Languages	Spanish, Quechua, Aymara
Area Sq Miles	496 225	Religions	Roman Catholic, Protestant
Population	30 376 000	Currency	Sol
Capital	Lima	Organizations	APEC, UN

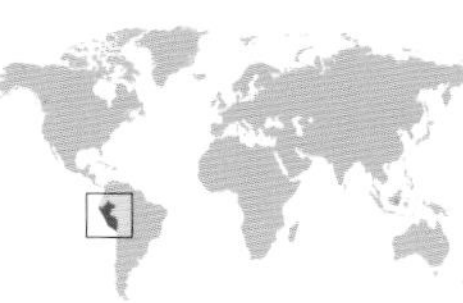

Peru lies on the Pacific coast of South America. Most Peruvians live on the coastal strip and on the plateaus of the high Andes mountains. East of the Andes is the Amazon rainforest. The coast is temperate with low rainfall while the east is hot, humid and wet. Agriculture involves one-third of the workforce and fishing is also important. Agriculture and fishing have both been disrupted by the El Niño climatic effect in recent years. Sugar, cotton, coffee and, illegally, coca are the main cash crops. Copper and copper products, fishmeal, zinc products, coffee, petroleum and its products, and textiles are the main exports. The USA and the European Union are the main trading partners.

PHILIPPINES
Republic of the Philippines

Area Sq Km	300 000	Languages	English, Filipino, Tagalog, Cebuano, other local languages
Area Sq Miles	115 831	Religions	Roman Catholic, Protestant, Sunni Muslim, Aglipayan
Population	98 394 000	Currency	Philippine peso
Capital	Manila	Organizations	APEC, ASEAN, UN

The Philippines, in southeast Asia, consists of over seven thousand islands and atolls lying between the South China Sea and the Pacific Ocean. The islands of Luzon and Mindanao account for two-thirds of the land area. They and nine other fairly large islands are mountainous and forested. There are active volcanoes, and earthquakes and tropical storms are common. Most of the population lives in the plains on the larger islands or on the coastal strips. The climate is hot and humid with heavy monsoonal rainfall. Rice, coconuts, sugar cane, pineapples and bananas are the main agricultural crops, and fishing is also important. Main exports are electronic equipment, machinery and transport equipment, garments and coconut products. Foreign aid and remittances from workers abroad are important to the economy, which faces problems of high population growth rate and high unemployment. The USA and Japan are the main trading partners.

Pitcairn Islands
United Kingdom Overseas Territory

Area Sq Km	45	Languages	English
Area Sq Miles	17	Religions	Protestant
Population	50	Currency	New Zealand dollar
Capital	Adamstown		

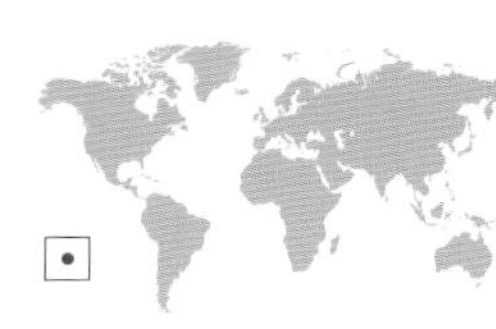

An island group in the southeast Pacific Ocean consisting of Pitcairn Island and three uninhabited islands, Henderson, Ducie and Oeno Islands. It was originally settled by mutineers from HMS *Bounty* in 1790.

POLAND
Republic of Poland

Area Sq Km	312 683	Languages	Polish, German
Area Sq Miles	120 728	Religions	Roman Catholic, Polish Orthodox
Population	38 217 000	Currency	Złoty
Capital	Warsaw (Warszawa)	Organizations	EU, NATO, OECD, UN

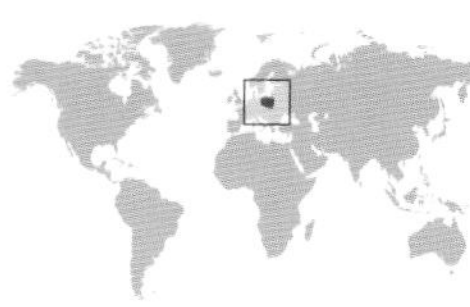

Poland lies on the Baltic coast of eastern Europe. The Oder (Odra) and Vistula (Wisła) river deltas dominate the coast. Inland, much of the country is low-lying, with woods and lakes. In the south the land rises to the Sudeten Mountains and the western part of the Carpathian Mountains, which form the borders with the Czech Republic and Slovakia respectively. The climate is continental. Around a sixth of the workforce is involved in agriculture, and exports include livestock products and sugar. The economy is heavily industrialized, with mining and manufacturing accounting for forty per cent

of national income. Poland is one of the world's major producers of coal, and also produces copper, zinc, lead, sulphur and natural gas. The main industries are machinery and transport equipment, shipbuilding, and metal and chemical production. Exports include machinery and transport equipment, manufactured goods, food and live animals. Germany is the main trading partner. Poland joined the European Union in May 2004.

PORTUGAL
Portuguese Republic

Area Sq Km	88 940	Languages	Portuguese
Area Sq Miles	34 340	Religions	Roman Catholic, Protestant
Population	10 608 000	Currency	Euro
Capital	Lisbon (Lisboa)	Organizations	EU, NATO, OECD, UN

Portugal lies in the western part of the Iberian peninsula in southwest Europe, has an Atlantic coastline and is bordered by Spain to the north and east. The island groups of the Azores and Madeira are parts of Portugal. On the mainland, the land north of the river Tagus (Tejo) is mostly highland, with extensive forests of pine and cork. South of the river is undulating lowland. The climate in the north is cool and moist; the south is warmer, with dry, mild winters. Most Portuguese live near the coast, and more than one-third of the total population lives around the capital, Lisbon (Lisboa). Agriculture, fishing and forestry involve approximately ten per cent of the workforce. Mining and manufacturing are the main sectors of the economy. Portugal produces kaolin, copper, tin, zinc, tungsten and salt. Exports include textiles, clothing and footwear, electrical machinery and transport equipment, cork and wood products, and chemicals. Service industries, chiefly tourism and banking, are important to the economy, as are remittances from workers abroad. Most trade is with other European Union countries.

Puerto Rico
United States Commonwealth

Area Sq Km	9 104	Languages	Spanish, English
Area Sq Miles	3 515	Religions	Roman Catholic, Protestant
Population	3 688 000	Currency	United States dollar
Capital	San Juan		

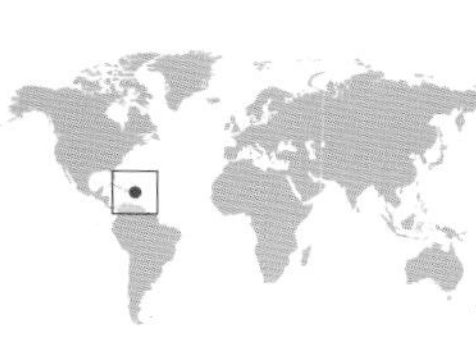

The Caribbean island of Puerto Rico has a forested, hilly interior, coastal plains and a tropical climate. Half of the population lives in the San Juan area. The economy is based on manufacturing (chiefly chemicals, electronics and food), tourism and agriculture. The USA is the main trading partner.

QATAR
State of Qatar

Area Sq Km	11 437	Languages	Arabic
Area Sq Miles	4 416	Religions	Sunni Muslim
Population	2 169 000	Currency	Qatari riyal
Capital	Doha (Ad Dawḩah)	Organizations	OPEC, UN

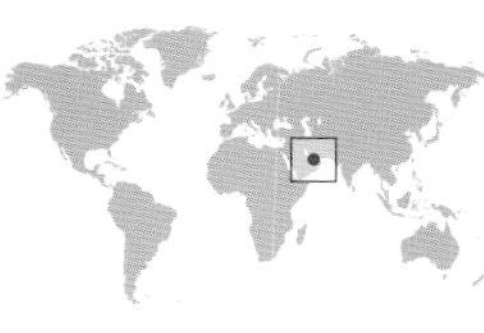

Qatar occupies a peninsula in southwest Asia that extends northwards from east-central Saudi Arabia into The Gulf. The land is flat and barren with sand dunes and salt pans. The climate is hot and mainly dry. Most people live in the area of the capital, Doha. The economy is heavily dependent on oil and natural gas production and the oil-refining industry. Income also comes from overseas investment. Japan is the largest trading partner.

Réunion
French Overseas Department

Area Sq Km	2 551	Languages	French, Creole
Area Sq Miles	985	Religions	Roman Catholic
Population	875 000	Currency	Euro
Capital	St-Denis		

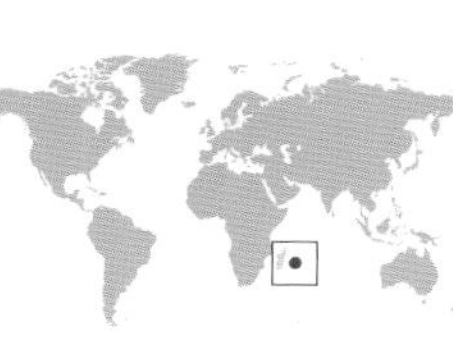

The Indian Ocean island of Réunion is mountainous, with coastal lowlands and a warm climate. The economy depends on tourism, French aid, and exports of sugar. In 2005 France transferred the administration of various small uninhabited islands in the seas around Madagascar from Réunion to the French Southern and Antarctic Lands.

ROMANIA

Area Sq Km	237 500	Languages	Romanian, Hungarian
Area Sq Miles	91 699	Religions	Romanian Orthodox, Protestant, Roman Catholic
Population	21 699 000	Currency	Romanian leu
Capital	Bucharest (București)	Organizations	EU, NATO, UN

Romania lies in eastern Europe, on the northwest coast of the Black Sea. Mountains separate the Transylvanian Basin in the centre of the country from the populous plains of the east and south and from the Danube delta. The climate is continental. Romania has mineral resources (zinc, lead, silver and gold) and oil and natural gas reserves. Economic development has been slow and sporadic, but measures to accelerate change were introduced in 1999. Agricultural employment has since declined. The main exports are textiles, mineral products, chemicals, machinery and footwear. The main trading partners are Germany and Italy.

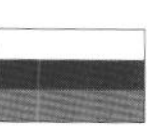

RUSSIA

Area Sq Km	17 075 400	Languages	Russian, Tatar, Ukrainian, other local languages
Area Sq Miles	6 592 849	Religions	Russian Orthodox, Sunni Muslim, Protestant
Population	142 834 000	Currency	Russian rouble
Capital	Moscow (Moskva)	Organizations	APEC, CIS, UN

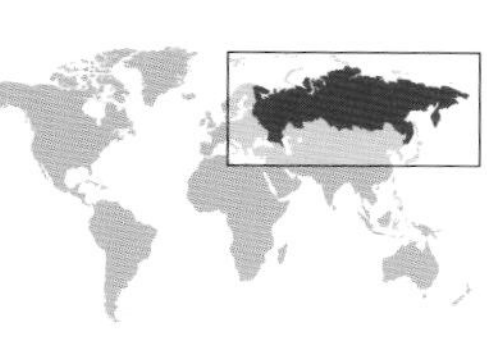

Russia occupies much of eastern Europe and all of northern Asia, and is the world's largest country. It borders fourteen countries to the west and south and has long coastlines on the Arctic and Pacific Oceans to the north and east. European Russia lies west of the Ural Mountains. To the south the land rises to uplands and the Caucasus mountains on the border with Georgia and Azerbaijan. East of the Urals lies the flat West Siberian Plain and the Central Siberian Plateau. In the south-east is Lake Baikal, the world's deepest lake, and the Sayan ranges on the border with Kazakhstan and Mongolia. Eastern Siberia is rugged and mountainous, with many active volcanoes in the Kamchatka Peninsula. The country's major rivers are the Volga in the west and the Ob', Irtysh, Yenisey, Lena and Amur in Siberia. The climate and vegetation range between arctic tundra in the north and semi-arid steppe towards the Black and Caspian Sea coasts in the south. In general, the climate is continental with extreme temperatures. The majority of the population (the tenth largest in the world), and industry and agriculture are concentrated in European Russia. The economy is dependent on exploitation of raw materials and on heavy industry. Russia has a wealth of mineral resources, although they are often difficult to exploit because of climate and remote locations. It is one of the world's leading producers of petroleum, natural gas and coal as well as iron ore, nickel, copper, bauxite, and many precious and rare metals. Forests cover over forty per cent of the land area and supply an important timber, paper and pulp industry. Approximately eight per cent of the land is suitable for cultivation. Agriculture has shown steady growth since 1999, with grain now exported. Fishing is important and Russia has a large fleet operating around the world. The transition to a market economy has been slow and difficult, with considerable underemployment. As well as mining and extractive industries there is a wide range of manufacturing industry, from steel mills to aircraft and space vehicles, shipbuilding, synthetic fabrics, plastics, cotton fabrics, consumer durables, chemicals and fertilizers. Exports include fuels, metals, machinery, chemicals and forest products. The most important trading partners include Germany, the USA and Belarus.

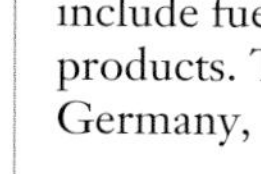

RWANDA
Republic of Rwanda

Area Sq Km	26 338	Languages	Kinyarwanda, French, English
Area Sq Miles	10 169	Religions	Roman Catholic, traditional beliefs, Protestant
Population	11 777 000	Currency	Rwandan franc
Capital	Kigali	Organizations	Comm., UN

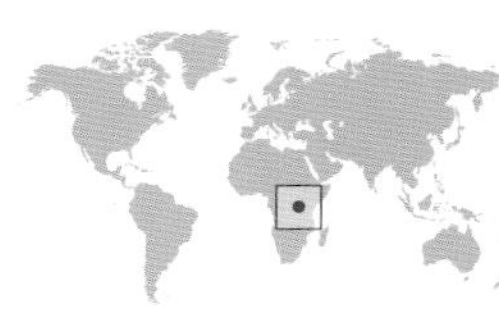

Rwanda, the most densely populated country in continental Africa, is situated in the mountains and plateaus to the east of the western branch of the Great Rift Valley in east Africa. The climate is warm with a summer dry season. Rwanda depends on subsistence farming, coffee and tea exports, light industry and foreign aid. The country is slowly recovering from serious internal conflict which caused devastation in the early 1990s.

St-Barthélemy
French Overseas Collectivity

Area Sq Km	21	Languages	French
Area Sq Miles	8	Religions	Roman Catholic
Population	9 072	Currency	Euro
Capital	Gustavia		

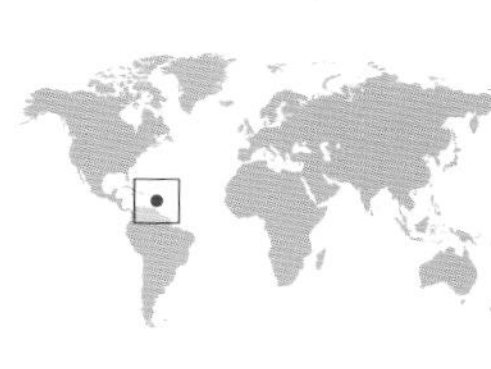

An island in the Leeward Islands in the Lesser Antilles, in the Caribbean south of St-Martin. It was separated from Guadeloupe politically in 2007. Tourism is the main economic activity.

St Helena Ascension and Tristan da Cunha
United Kingdom Overseas Territory

Area Sq Km	410	Languages	English
Area Sq Miles	158	Religions	Protestant, Roman Catholic
Population	5 366	Currency	St Helena pound, Pound sterling
Capital	Jamestown		

Known until 2009 as St Helena and Dependencies, this UK territory lies in the south Atlantic Ocean. The islands, all of volcanic origin, are very remote from each other and from Africa and South America. The economy varies from island to island, but depends also on UK aid. Main trading partners are the UK and South Africa.

ST KITTS AND NEVIS
Federation of Saint Kitts and Nevis

Area Sq Km	261	Languages	English, Creole
Area Sq Miles	101	Religions	Protestant, Roman Catholic
Population	54 000	Currency	East Caribbean dollar
Capital	Basseterre	Organizations	CARICOM, Comm., UN

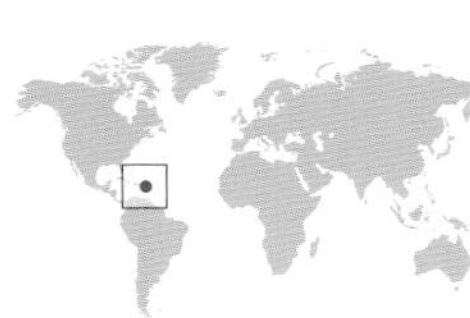

St Kitts and Nevis are in the Leeward Islands, in the Caribbean. Both volcanic islands are mountainous and forested, with sandy beaches and a warm, wet climate. About three-quarters of the population lives on St Kitts. Agriculture is the main activity, with sugar the main product. Tourism and manufacturing (chiefly garments and electronic components) and offshore banking are important activities.

ST LUCIA
Saint Lucia

Area Sq Km	616	Languages	English, Creole
Area Sq Miles	238	Religions	Roman Catholic, Protestant
Population	182 000	Currency	East Caribbean dollar
Capital	Castries	Organizations	CARICOM, Comm., UN

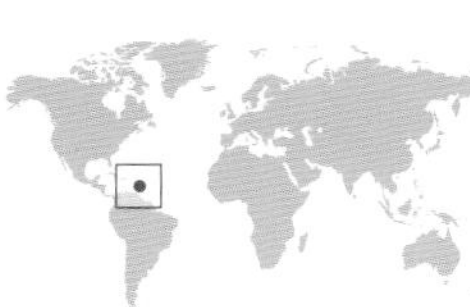

St Lucia, one of the Windward Islands in the Caribbean Sea, is a volcanic island with forested mountains, hot springs, sandy beaches and a wet tropical climate. Agriculture is the main activity, with bananas accounting for approximately forty per cent of export earnings. Tourism, agricultural processing and light manufacturing are increasingly important.

St-Martin
French Overseas Collectivity

Area Sq Km	54	Languages	French
Area Sq Miles	21	Religions	Roman Catholic
Population	37 630	Currency	Euro
Capital	Marigot		

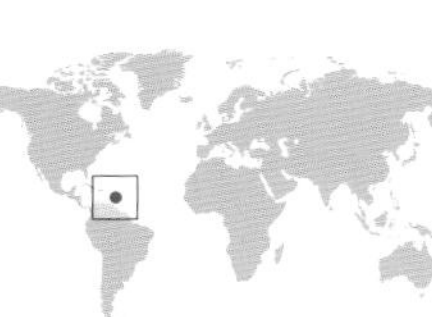

The northern part of St-Martin, one of the Leeward Islands, in the Caribbean. The other part of the island is a self-governing Netherlands territory (Sint Maarten). It was separated from Guadeloupe politically in 2007. Tourism is the main source of income.

St Pierre and Miquelon
French Territorial Collectivity

Area Sq Km	242	Languages	French
Area Sq Miles	93	Religions	Roman Catholic
Population	6 312	Currency	Euro
Capital	St-Pierre		

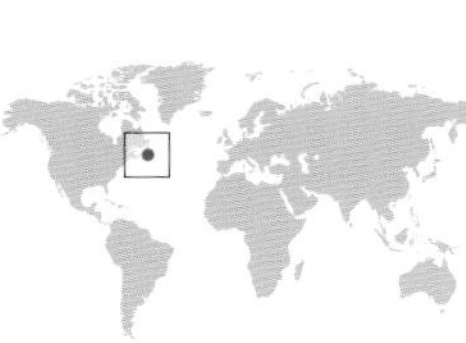

A group of islands off the south coast of Newfoundland in eastern Canada. The islands are largely unsuitable for agriculture, and fishing and fish processing are the most important activities. The islands rely heavily on financial assistance from France.

ST VINCENT AND THE GRENADINES
Saint Vincent and the Grenadines

Area Sq Km	389	Languages	English, Creole
Area Sq Miles	150	Religions	Protestant, Roman Catholic
Population	109 000	Currency	East Caribbean dollar
Capital	Kingstown	Organizations	CARICOM, Comm., UN

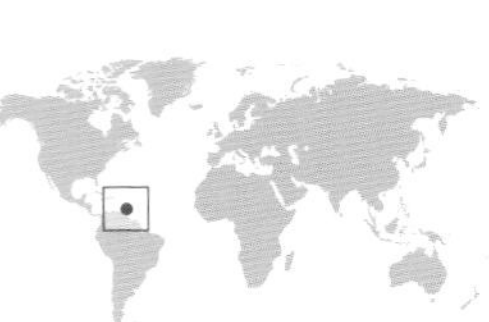

St Vincent, whose territory includes islets and cays in the Grenadines, is in the Windward Islands, in the Caribbean. St Vincent itself is forested and mountainous, with an active volcano, Soufrière. The climate is tropical and wet. The economy is based mainly on agriculture and tourism. Bananas account for approximately one-third of export earnings and arrowroot is also important. Most trade is with the USA and other CARICOM countries.

SAMOA
Independent State of Samoa

Area Sq Km	2 831	Languages	Samoan, English
Area Sq Miles	1 093	Religions	Protestant, Roman Catholic
Population	190 000	Currency	Tala
Capital	Apia	Organizations	Comm., UN

Samoa consists of two larger mountainous and forested islands, Savai'i and Upolu, and seven smaller islands, in the south Pacific Ocean. Over half the population lives on Upolu. The climate is tropical. The economy is based on agriculture, with some fishing and light manufacturing. Traditional exports are coconut products, fish and beer. Tourism is increasing, but the islands depend on workers' remittances and foreign aid.

SAN MARINO
Republic of San Marino

Area Sq Km	61	Languages	Italian
Area Sq Miles	24	Religions	Roman Catholic
Population	31 000	Currency	Euro
Capital	San Marino	Organizations	UN

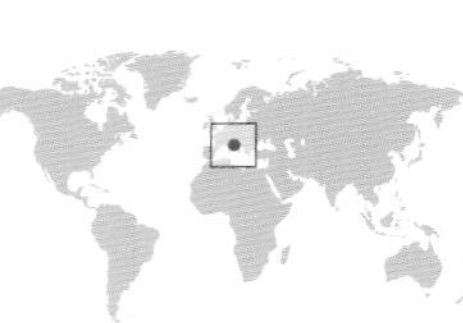

Landlocked San Marino lies in northeast Italy. A third of the people live in the capital. There is some agriculture and light industry, but most income comes from tourism. Italy is the main trading partner.

SÃO TOMÉ AND PRÍNCIPE
Democratic Republic of São Tomé and Príncipe

Area Sq Km	964	Languages	Portuguese, Creole
Area Sq Miles	372	Religions	Roman Catholic, Protestant
Population	193 000	Currency	Dobra
Capital	São Tomé	Organizations	UN

The two main islands and adjacent islets lie off the coast of west Africa in the Gulf of Guinea. São Tomé is the larger island, with over ninety per cent of the population. Both São Tomé and Príncipe are mountainous and tree-covered, and have a hot and humid climate. The economy is heavily dependent on cocoa, which accounts for around ninety per cent of export earnings.

SAUDI ARABIA
Kingdom of Saudi Arabia

Area Sq Km	2 200 000	Languages	Arabic
Area Sq Miles	849 425	Religions	Sunni Muslim, Shi'a Muslim
Population	28 829 000	Currency	Saudi Arabian riyal
Capital	Riyadh (Ar Riyāḍ)	Organizations	OPEC, UN

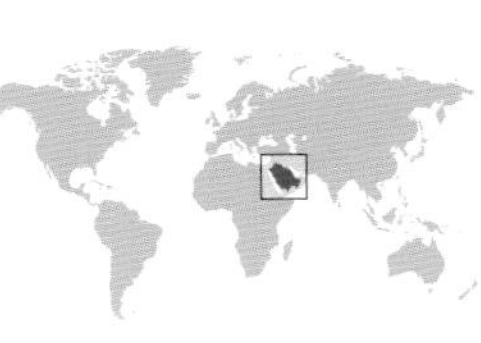

Saudi Arabia occupies most of the Arabian Peninsula in southwest Asia. The terrain is desert or semi-desert plateaus, which rise to mountains running parallel to the Red Sea in the west and slope down to plains in the southeast and along The Gulf in the east. Over eighty per cent of the population lives in urban areas. There are around four million foreign workers in Saudi Arabia, employed mainly in the oil and service industries. Summers are hot, winters are warm and rainfall is low. Saudi Arabia has the world's largest reserves of oil and significant natural gas reserves, both onshore and in The Gulf. Crude oil and refined products account for over ninety per cent of export earnings. Other industries and irrigated agriculture are being encouraged, but most food and raw materials are imported. Saudi Arabia has important banking and commercial interests. Japan and the USA are the main trading partners.

SENEGAL
Republic of Senegal

Area Sq Km	196 720	Languages	French, Wolof, Fulani, other local languages
Area Sq Miles	75 954	Religions	Sunni Muslim, Roman Catholic, traditional beliefs
Population	14 133 000	Currency	CFA franc
Capital	Dakar	Organizations	UN

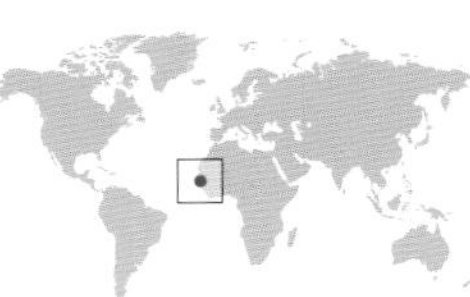

Senegal lies on the Atlantic coast of west Africa. The north is arid semi-desert, while the south is mainly fertile savanna bushland. The climate is tropical with summer rains, although droughts occur. One-fifth of the population lives in and around Dakar, the capital and main port. Fish, groundnuts and phosphates are the main exports. France is the main trading partner.

SERBIA
Republic of Serbia

Area Sq Km	77 453	Languages	Serbian, Hungarian
Area Sq Miles	29 904	Religions	Serbian Orthodox, Roman Catholic, Sunni Muslim
Population	7 181 505	Currency	Serbian dinar
Capital	Belgrade (Beograd)	Organizations	UN

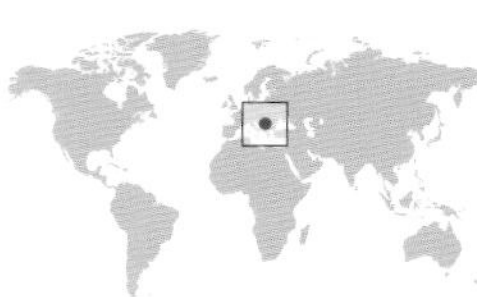

Following ethnic conflict and the break-up of Yugoslavia through the 1990s, the state union of Serbia and Montenegro retained the name Yugoslavia until 2003. The two then became separate independent countries in 2006. The southern Serbian province of Kosovo declared its independence from Serbia in February 2008. The landscape is rugged, mountainous and forested in the south, while the north is low-lying and drained by the Danube river system.

SEYCHELLES
Republic of Seychelles

Area Sq Km	455	Languages	English, French, Creole
Area Sq Miles	176	Religions	Roman Catholic, Protestant
Population	93 000	Currency	Seychelles rupee
Capital	Victoria	Organizations	Comm., SADC, UN

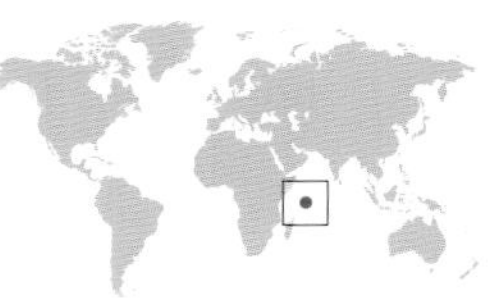

The Seychelles comprises an archipelago of over one hundred granitic and coral islands in the western Indian Ocean. Over ninety per cent of the population lives on the main island, Mahé. The climate is hot and humid with heavy rainfall. The economy is based mainly on tourism, fishing and light manufacturing.

SIERRA LEONE
Republic of Sierra Leone

Area Sq Km	71 740	Languages	English, Creole, Mende, Temne, other local languages
Area Sq Miles	27 699	Religions	Sunni Muslim, traditional beliefs
Population	6 092 000	Currency	Leone
Capital	Freetown	Organizations	Comm., UN

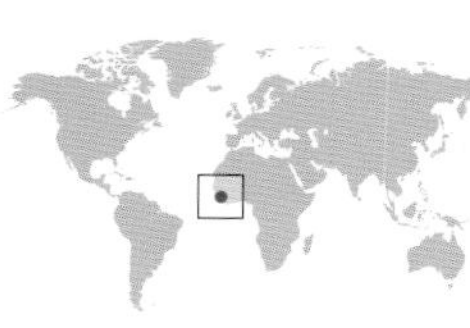

Sierra Leone lies on the Atlantic coast of west Africa. Its coastline is heavily indented and is lined with mangrove swamps. Inland is a forested area rising to savanna plateaus, with mountains to the northeast. The climate is tropical and rainfall is heavy. Most of the workforce is involved in subsistence farming. Cocoa and coffee are the main cash crops. Diamonds and rutile (titanium ore) are the main exports. Sierra Leone is one of the world's poorest countries, and the economy relies on substantial foreign aid.

SINGAPORE
Republic of Singapore

Area Sq Km	639	Languages	Chinese, English, Malay, Tamil
Area Sq Miles	247	Religions	Buddhist, Taoist, Sunni Muslim, Christian, Hindu
Population	5 412 000	Currency	Singapore dollar
Capital	Singapore	Organizations	APEC, ASEAN, Comm., UN

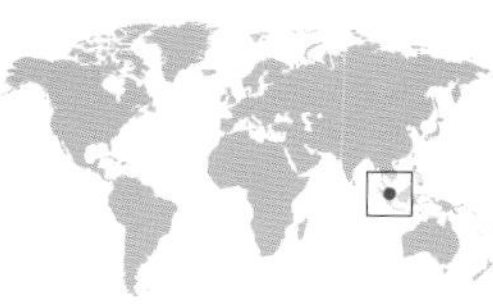

The state comprises the main island of Singapore and over fifty other islands, lying off the southern tip of the Malay Peninsula in southeast Asia. Singapore is generally low-lying and includes land reclaimed from swamps and the sea. It is hot and humid, with heavy rainfall throughout the year. There are fish farms and vegetable gardens in the north and east of the island, but most food is imported. Singapore also lacks mineral and energy resources. Manufacturing industries and services are the main sectors of the economy. Their rapid development has fuelled the nation's impressive economic growth during recent decades. Main industries include electronics, oil refining, chemicals, pharmaceuticals, ship repair, food processing and textiles. Singapore is also a major financial centre. Its port is one of the world's largest and busiest and acts as an entrepôt for neighbouring states. Tourism is also important. Japan, the USA and Malaysia are the main trading partners.

Sint Maarten
Self-governing Netherlands territory

Area Sq Km	34	Languages	Dutch, English
Area Sq Miles	13	Religions	Roman Catholic, Protestant
Population	45 000	Currency	Caribbean guilder
Capital	Philipsburg		

The southern part of one of the Leeward Islands, in the Caribbean; the other part of the island is a dependency of France. Sint Maarten was previously part of the Netherlands Antilles until they were dissolved in October 2010. Tourism and fishing are the most important industries.

SLOVAKIA
Slovak Republic

Area Sq Km	49 035	Languages	Slovak, Hungarian, Czech
Area Sq Miles	18 933	Religions	Roman Catholic, Protestant, Orthodox
Population	5 450 000	Currency	Euro
Capital	Bratislava	Organizations	EU, NATO, OECD, UN

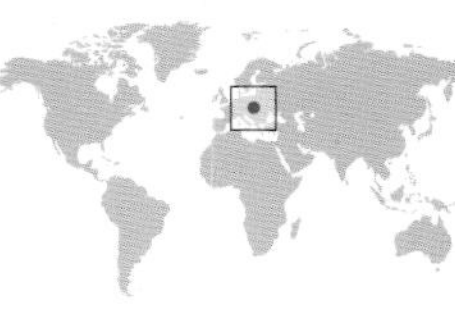

A landlocked country in central Europe, Slovakia is mountainous in the north, but low-lying in the southwest. The climate is continental. There is a range of manufacturing industries, and the main exports are machinery and transport equipment, but in recent years there have been economic difficulties and growth has been slow. Slovakia joined the European Union in May 2004. Most trade is with other EU countries, especially the Czech Republic and Germany.

SLOVENIA
Republic of Slovenia

Area Sq Km	20 251	Languages	Slovene, Croatian, Serbian
Area Sq Miles	7 819	Religions	Roman Catholic, Protestant
Population	2 072 000	Currency	Euro
Capital	Ljubljana	Organizations	EU, NATO, OECD, UN

Slovenia lies in the northwest Balkan Mountains of southern Europe and has a short coastline on the Adriatic Sea. It is mountainous and hilly, with lowlands on the coast and in the Sava and Drava river valleys. The climate is generally continental inland and Mediterranean nearer the coast. The main agricultural products are potatoes, grain and sugar beet; the main industries include metal processing, electronics and consumer goods. Trade has been re-orientated towards western markets and the main trading partners are Germany and Italy. Slovenia joined the European Union in May 2004.

SOLOMON ISLANDS

Area Sq Km	28 370	Languages	English, Creole, other local languages
Area Sq Miles	10 954	Religions	Protestant, Roman Catholic
Population	561 000	Currency	Solomon Islands dollar
Capital	Honiara	Organizations	Comm., UN

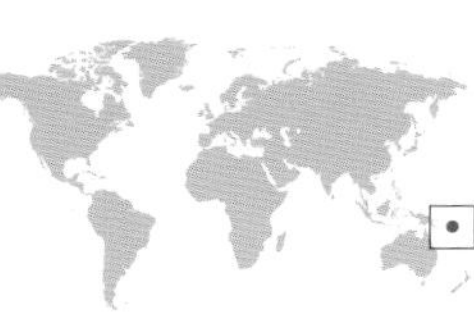

The state consists of the Solomon, Santa Cruz and Shortland Islands in the southwest Pacific Ocean. The six main islands are volcanic, mountainous and forested, although Guadalcanal, the most populous, has a large lowland area. The climate is generally hot and humid. Subsistence farming, forestry and fishing predominate. Exports include timber products, fish, copra and palm oil. The islands depend on foreign aid.

SOMALIA
Federal Republic of Somalia

Area Sq Km	637 657	Languages	Somali, Arabic
Area Sq Miles	246 201	Religions	Sunni Muslim
Population	10 496 000	Currency	Somali shilling
Capital	Mogadishu (Muqdisho)	Organizations	UN

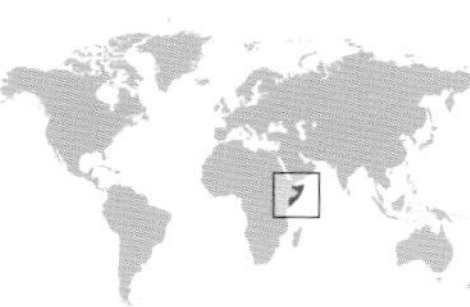

Somalia is in northeast Africa, on the Gulf of Aden and Indian Ocean. It consists of a dry scrubby plateau, rising to highlands in the north. The climate is hot and dry, but coastal areas and the Jubba and Webi Shabeelle river valleys support crops and most of the population. Subsistence farming and livestock rearing are the main activities. Exports include livestock and bananas. Frequent drought and civil war have prevented economic development. Somalia is one of the poorest, most unstable and least developed countries in the world.

Somaliland
Disputed territory

Area Sq Km	140 000	Languages	Somali, Arabic, English
Area Sq Miles	54 054	Religions	Sunni Muslim
Population	3 500 000	Currency	Somaliland shilling
Capital	Hargeysa		

After the collapse of the central Somali government in 1991 and at the start of the civil war, Somaliland, in the northwest of the country, covering the area of the former British Protectorate of Somaliland, declared its independence from Somalia as the Republic of Somaliland. A referendum in 2001 saw a majority vote for secession, and Somaliland currently operates as a de facto independent country, with fairly close relations with Ethiopia. The Transitional Federal Government of Somalia does not recognize its independence and conflicts still arise between Somaliland and the neighbouring region of Puntland over ownership of the administrative regions of Sanaag and Sool.

SOUTH AFRICA

Area Sq Km	1 219 090	Languages	Afrikaans, English, nine other official languages
Area Sq Miles	470 693	Religions	Protestant, Roman Catholic, Sunni Muslim, Hindu
Population	52 776 000	Currency	Rand
Capital	Bloemfontein/ Cape Town/ Pretoria (Tshwane)	Organizations	Comm., SADC, UN

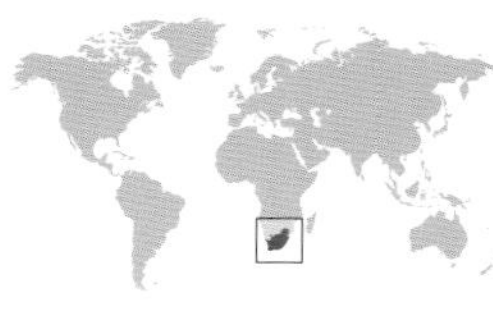

South Africa occupies most of the southern part of Africa. It surrounds Lesotho and has a long coastline on the Atlantic and Indian Oceans. Much of the land is a vast plateau, covered with grassland or bush and drained by the Orange and Limpopo river systems. A fertile coastal plain rises to mountain ridges in the south and east, including Table Mountain near Cape Town and the Drakensberg range in the east. Gauteng is the most populous province, with Johannesburg and Pretoria its main cities. South Africa has warm summers and mild winters. Most of the country has the majority of its rainfall in summer, but the coast around Cape Town has winter rains. South Africa has the largest economy in Africa, although wealth is unevenly distributed and unemployment is very high. Agriculture employs about six per cent of the workforce, and produce includes fruit, wine, wool and maize. The country is the world's leading producer of gold and chromium and an important producer of diamonds. Many other minerals are also mined. The main industries are mineral and food processing, chemicals, electrical equipment, textiles and motor vehicles. Financial services are also important.

SOUTH KOREA
Republic of Korea

Area Sq Km	99 274	Languages	Korean
Area Sq Miles	38 330	Religions	Buddhist, Protestant, Roman Catholic
Population	49 263 000	Currency	South Korean won
Capital	Seoul (Sŏul)	Organizations	APEC, OECD, UN

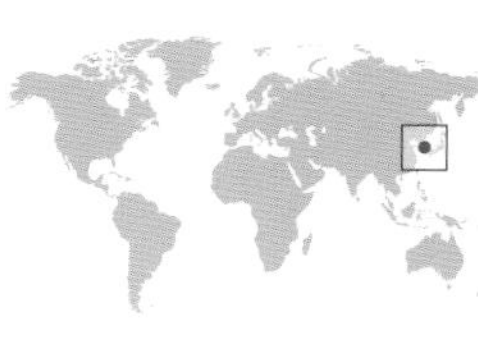

The state consists of the southern half of the Korean Peninsula in eastern Asia and many islands lying off the western and southern coasts in the Yellow Sea. The terrain is mountainous, although less rugged than that of North Korea. Population density is high and the country is highly urbanized; most of the population lives on the western coastal plains and in the river basins of the Han-gang in the northwest and the Naktong-gang in the southeast. The climate is continental, with hot, wet summers and dry, cold winters. Arable land is limited by the mountainous terrain, but because of intensive farming South Korea is nearly self-sufficient in food. Sericulture (silk) is important, as is fishing, which contributes to exports. South Korea has few mineral resources, except for coal and tungsten. It has achieved high economic growth based mainly on export manufacturing. The main manufactured goods are cars, electronic and electrical goods, ships, steel, chemicals and toys, as well as textiles, clothing, footwear and food products. The USA and Japan are the main trading partners.

South Ossetia
Disputed territory

Area Sq Km	4 000	Languages	Ossetian, Russian, Georgian
Area Sq Miles	1 544	Religions	Eastern Orthodox
Population	70 000	Currency	Russian rouble
Capital	Tskhinvali		

The formerly autonomous region of South Ossetia seeks independence from Georgia and looks to Russia, which recognizes its independence, as its principal ally. South Ossetia's autonomous status was removed in 1990. Violent conflicts followed between Georgia and the separatists, supported by Russia, who wished to unite with Russian North Ossetia. A cease-fire was agreed in 1992. Elections in 1996 were not recognized by Georgia, nor were elections and an independence referendum, voting in favour of independence, in 2006. Russian interference and interest in the area has continued to cause tensions with the Georgian government, the most recent conflict was in 2008 when Georgian troops attacked separatists. Russia responded and a week of fighting was ended by a cease-fire and resulted in Russia recognising South Ossetia's independence.

SOUTH SUDAN
Republic of South Sudan

Area Sq Km	644 329	Languages	English, Arabic, Dinka, Nuer, other local languages
Area Sq Miles	248 775	Religions	Traditional beliefs, Christian
Population	11 296 000	Currency	South Sudanese pound
Capital	Juba	Organizations	UN

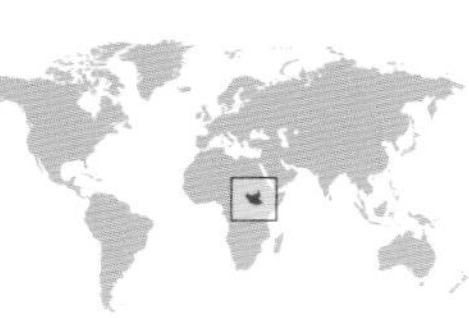

South Sudan in northeast Africa has grasslands, tropical forests and swamps in the north with higher lands in the south. The equatorial climate has moderate temperatures, high humidity and heavy rainfall. Independence from Sudan was gained in July 2011 as a result of a referendum held as part of the agreement which ended decades of civil war between north and south. The government plan to move the capital from Juba to Ramciel in the centre of the country. The economy is mostly agricultural, but the vast natural resources, including huge oil-reserves, are now being increasingly exploited. South Sudan is one of the world's least developed countries.

SPAIN
Kingdom of Spain

Area Sq Km	504 782	Languages	Spanish (Castilian), Catalan, Galician, Basque
Area Sq Miles	194 897	Religions	Roman Catholic
Population	46 927 000	Currency	Euro
Capital	Madrid	Organizations	EU, NATO, OECD, UN

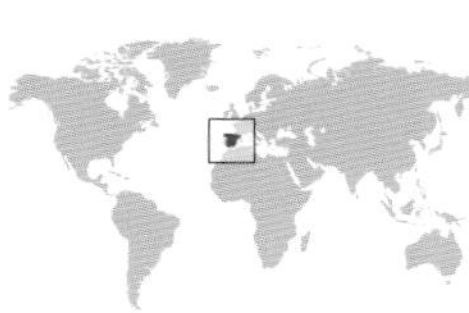

Spain occupies the greater part of the Iberian peninsula in southwest Europe, with coastlines on the Atlantic Ocean and Mediterranean Sea. It includes the Balearic Islands in the Mediterranean, the Canary Islands in the Atlantic, and two enclaves in north Africa (Ceuta and Melilla). Much of the mainland is a high plateau drained by the Douro (Duero), Tagus (Tajo) and Guadiana rivers. The plateau is interrupted by a low mountain range and bounded to the east and north also by mountains, including the Pyrenees, which form the border with France and Andorra. The main lowland areas are the Ebro basin in the northeast, the eastern coastal plains and the Guadalquivir basin in the southwest. Over three-quarters of the population lives in urban areas. The plateau experiences hot summers and cold winters. Conditions are cooler and wetter to the north, and warmer and drier to the south. Agriculture involves under five per cent of the workforce, and fruit, vegetables and wine are exported. Fishing is an important industry, and Spain has a large fishing fleet. Mineral resources include lead, copper, mercury and fluorspar. Some oil is produced, but Spain has to import most energy needs. The economy is based mainly on manufacturing and services. The principal products are machinery, transport equipment, motor vehicles and food products, with a wide variety of other manufactured goods. With over fifty-five million visitors a year, tourism is a major industry. Banking and commerce are also important. Approximately seventy per cent of trade is with other European Union countries.

SRI LANKA
Democratic Socialist Republic of Sri Lanka

Area Sq Km	65 610	Languages	Sinhalese, Tamil, English
Area Sq Miles	25 332	Religions	Buddhist, Hindu, Sunni Muslim, Roman Catholic
Population	21 273 000	Currency	Sri Lankan rupee
Capital	Sri Jayewardenepura Kotte	Organizations	Comm., UN

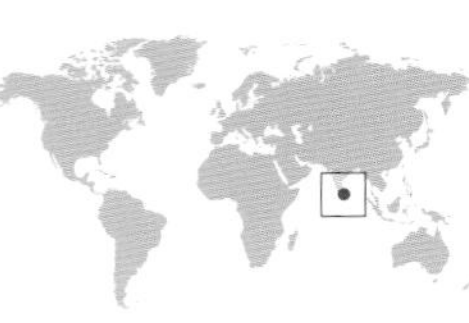

Sri Lanka lies in the Indian Ocean off the southeast coast of India in south Asia. It has rolling coastal plains, with mountains in the centre-south. The climate is hot and monsoonal. Most people live on the west coast. Manufactures (chiefly textiles and clothing), tea, rubber, copra and gems are exported. The economy relies on foreign aid and workers' remittances. The USA and the UK are the main trading partners.

SUDAN
Republic of the Sudan

Area Sq Km	1 861 484	Languages	Arabic, English, Nubian, Beja, Fur, other local languages
Area Sq Miles	718 725	Religions	Sunni Muslim, traditional beliefs, Christian
Population	37 964 000	Currency	Sudanese pound (Sudani)
Capital	Khartoum	Organizations	UN

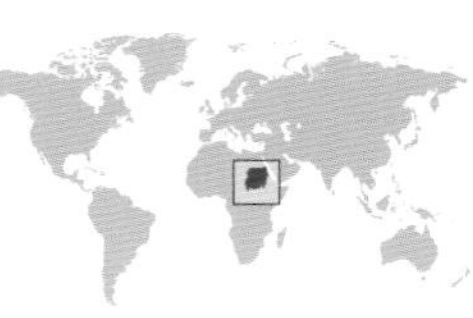

The Sudan is in the northeast of the continent of Africa, on the Red Sea. It lies within the upper Nile basin, much of which is arid plain but with swamps to the south. Mountains lie to the northeast, west and south. The climate is hot and arid with light summer rainfall, and droughts occur. Most people live along the Nile and are farmers and herders. Cotton, gum arabic, livestock and other agricultural products are exported. The government is working with foreign investors to develop oil resources, but the independence of South Sudan in July 2011 after civil war, and ethnic cleansing in Darfur continue to restrict the economy. Main trading partners are Saudi Arabia, China and UAE.

SURINAME
Republic of Suriname

Area Sq Km	163 820	Languages	Dutch, Surinamese, English, Hindi
Area Sq Miles	63 251	Religions	Hindu, Roman Catholic, Protestant, Sunni Muslim
Population	539 000	Currency	Surinamese dollar
Capital	Paramaribo	Organizations	CARICOM, UN

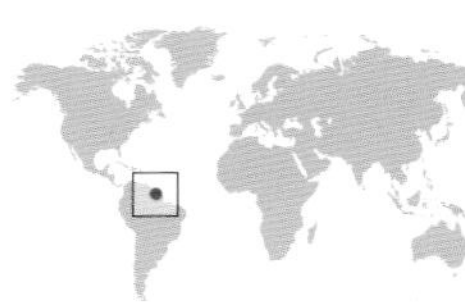

Suriname, on the Atlantic coast of northern South America, consists of a swampy coastal plain (where most of the population lives), central plateaus, and highlands in the south. The climate is tropical, and rainforest covers much of the land. Bauxite mining is the main industry, and alumina and aluminium are the chief exports, with shrimps, rice, bananas and timber also exported. The main trading partners are the Netherlands, Norway and the USA.

SWAZILAND
Kingdom of Swaziland

Area Sq Km	17 364	Languages	Swazi, English
Area Sq Miles	6 704	Religions	Christian, traditional beliefs
Population	1 250 000	Currency	Lilangeni, South African rand
Capital	Mbabane	Organizations	Comm., SADC, UN

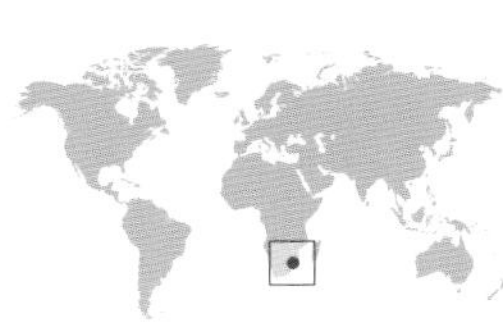

Landlocked Swaziland in southern Africa lies between Mozambique and South Africa. Savanna plateaus descend from mountains in the west towards hill country in the east. The climate is subtropical, but temperate in the mountains. Subsistence farming predominates. Asbestos and diamonds are mined. Exports include sugar, fruit and wood pulp. Tourism and workers' remittances are important to the economy. Most trade is with South Africa.

SWEDEN
Kingdom of Sweden

Area Sq Km	449 964	Languages	Swedish, Sami languages
Area Sq Miles	173 732	Religions	Protestant, Roman Catholic
Population	9 571 000	Currency	Swedish krona
Capital	Stockholm	Organizations	EU, OECD, UN

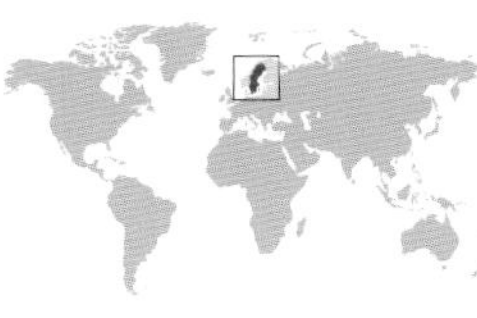

Sweden occupies the eastern part of the Scandinavian peninsula in northern Europe and borders the Baltic Sea, the Gulf of Bothnia, and the Kattegat and Skagerrak, connecting with the North Sea. Forested mountains cover the northern half, part of which lies within the Arctic Circle. The southern part of the country is a lowland lake region where most of the population lives. Sweden has warm summers and cold winters, which are more severe in the north. Natural resources include coniferous forests, mineral deposits and water resources. Some dairy products, meat, cereals and vegetables are produced in the south. The forests supply timber for export and for the important pulp, paper and furniture industries. Sweden is an important producer of iron ore and copper. Zinc, lead, silver and gold are also mined. Machinery and transport equipment, chemicals, pulp and wood, and telecommunications equipment are the main exports. The majority of trade is with other European Union countries.

SWITZERLAND
Swiss Confederation

Area Sq Km	41 293	Languages	German, French, Italian, Romansch
Area Sq Miles	15 943	Religions	Roman Catholic, Protestant
Population	8 078 000	Currency	Swiss franc
Capital	Bern	Organizations	OECD, UN

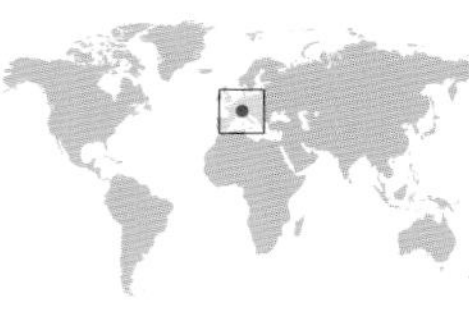

Switzerland is a mountainous landlocked country in west central Europe. The southern regions lie within the Alps, while the northwest is dominated by the Jura mountains. The rest of the land is a high plateau, where most of the population lives. The climate varies greatly, depending on altitude and relief, but in general summers are mild and winters are cold with heavy snowfalls. Switzerland has one of the highest standards of living in the world, yet it has few mineral resources, and most food and industrial raw materials are imported. Manufacturing makes the largest contribution to the economy. Engineering is the most important industry, producing precision instruments and heavy machinery. Other important industries are chemicals and pharmaceuticals. Banking and financial services are very important, and Zürich is one of the world's leading banking cities. Tourism, and international organizations based in Switzerland, are also major foreign currency earners. Germany is the main trading partner.

SYRIA
Syrian Arab Republic

Area Sq Km	184 026	**Languages**	Arabic, Kurdish, Armenian
Area Sq Miles	71 052	**Religions**	Sunni Muslim, Shi'a Muslim, Christian
Population	21 898 000	**Currency**	Syrian pound
Capital	Damascus (Dimashq)	**Organizations**	UN

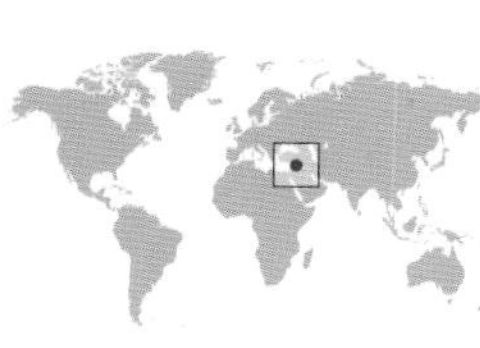

Syria is in southwest Asia, has a short coastline on the Mediterranean Sea, and stretches inland to a plateau traversed northwest-southeast by the Euphrates river. Mountains flank the southwest borders with Lebanon and Israel. The climate is Mediterranean in coastal regions, hotter and drier inland. Most Syrians live on the coast or in the river valleys. Syria's economy has been struggling since the start of the civil unrest in 2011 and the oil and gas industry has collapsed.

TAIWAN
Republic of China

Area Sq Km	36 179	**Languages**	Mandarin (Putonghua), Min, Hakka, other local languages
Area Sq Miles	13 969	**Religions**	Buddhist, Taoist, Confucian, Christian
Population	23 344 000	**Currency**	New Taiwan dollar
Capital	Taibei (T'aipei)	**Organizations**	APEC

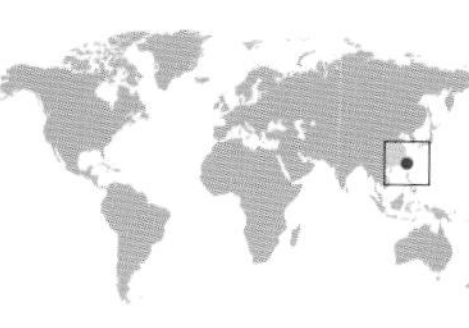

The east Asian state consists of the island of Taiwan, separated from mainland China by the Taiwan Strait, and several much smaller islands. Much of Taiwan is mountainous and forested. Densely populated coastal plains in the west contain the bulk of the population and most economic activity. Taiwan has a tropical monsoon climate, with warm, wet summers and mild winters. Agriculture is highly productive. The country is virtually self-sufficient in food and exports some products. Coal, oil and natural gas are produced and a few minerals are mined, but none of them are of great significance to the economy. Taiwan depends heavily on imports of raw materials and exports of manufactured goods. The main manufactures are electrical and electronic goods, including television sets, personal computers and calculators, textiles, fertilizers, clothing, footwear and toys. The main trading partners are the USA, Japan and Germany. The People's Republic of China claims Taiwan as its 23rd Province.

TAJIKISTAN
Republic of Tajikistan

Area Sq Km	143 100	**Languages**	Tajik, Uzbek, Russian
Area Sq Miles	55 251	**Religions**	Sunni Muslim
Population	8 208 000	**Currency**	Somoni
Capital	Dushanbe	**Organizations**	CIS, UN

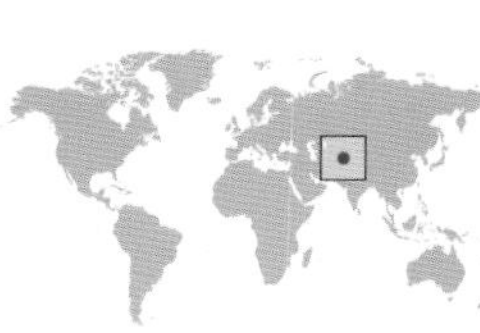

Landlocked Tajikistan in central Asia is a mountainous country, dominated by the mountains of the Alai Range and the Pamir. In the less mountainous western areas summers are warm, although winters are cold. Agriculture is the main sector of the economy, chiefly cotton growing and cattle breeding. Mineral deposits include lead, zinc, and uranium. Processed metals, textiles and clothing are the main manufactured goods; the main exports are aluminium and cotton. Uzbekistan, Kazakhstan and Russia are the main trading partners.

TANZANIA
United Republic of Tanzania

Area Sq Km	945 087	**Languages**	Swahili, English, Nyamwezi, other local languages
Area Sq Miles	364 900	**Religions**	Shi'a Muslim, Sunni Muslim, traditional beliefs, Christian
Population	49 253 000	**Currency**	Tanzanian shilling
Capital	Dodoma	**Organizations**	Comm., SADC, UN

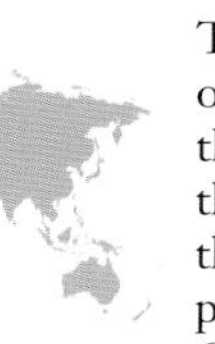

Tanzania lies on the coast of east Africa and includes the island of Zanzibar in the Indian Ocean. Most of the mainland is a savanna plateau lying east of the Great Rift Valley. In the north, near the border with Kenya, is Kilimanjaro, the highest mountain in Africa. The climate is tropical. The economy is predominantly based on agriculture, which employs an estimated ninety per cent of the workforce. Agricultural processing and gold and diamond mining are the main industries, although tourism is growing. Coffee, cotton, cashew nuts and tobacco are the main exports, with cloves from Zanzibar. Most export trade is with India China and Switzerland. Tanzania depends heavily on foreign aid.

THAILAND
Kingdom of Thailand

Area Sq Km	513 115	**Languages**	Thai, Lao, Chinese, Malay, Mon-Khmer languages
Area Sq Miles	198 115	**Religions**	Buddhist, Sunni Muslim
Population	67 011 000	**Currency**	Baht
Capital	Bangkok (Krung Thep)	**Organizations**	APEC, ASEAN, UN

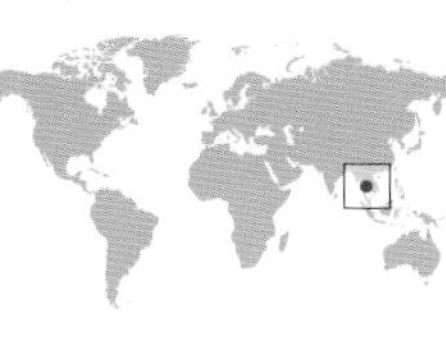

The largest country in the Indo-China peninsula, Thailand has coastlines on the Gulf of Thailand and Andaman Sea. Central Thailand is dominated by the Chao Phraya river basin, which contains Bangkok, the capital city and centre of most economic activity. To the east is a dry plateau drained by tributaries of the Mekong river, while to the north, west and south, extending down most of the Malay peninsula, are forested hills and mountains. Many small islands line the coast. The climate is hot, humid and monsoonal. About half the workforce is involved in agriculture. Fishing and fish processing are important. Thailand produces natural gas, some oil and lignite, minerals (chiefly tin, tungsten and baryte) and gemstones. Manufacturing is the largest contributor to national income, with electronics, textiles, clothing and footwear, and food processing the main industries. With around seven million visitors a year, tourism is the major source of foreign exchange. Thailand is one of the world's leading exporters of rice, rubber, palm oil and cassava. Japan, China and the USA are the main trading partners.

TOGO
Togolese Republic

Area Sq Km	56 785	**Languages**	French, Ewe, Kabre, other local languages
Area Sq Miles	21 925	**Religions**	Traditional beliefs, Christian, Sunni Muslim
Population	6 817 000	**Currency**	CFA franc
Capital	Lomé	**Organizations**	UN

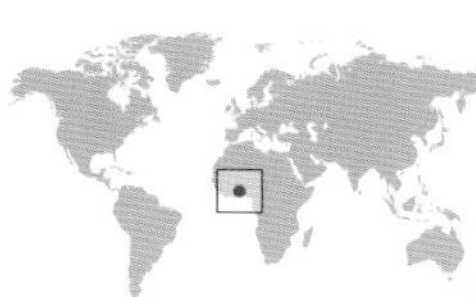

Togo is a long narrow country in west Africa with a short coastline on the Gulf of Guinea. The interior consists of plateaus rising to mountainous areas. The climate is tropical, and is drier inland. Agriculture is the mainstay of the economy. Phosphate mining and food processing are the main industries. Cotton, phosphates, coffee and cocoa are the main exports. Lomé, the capital, is an entrepôt trade centre.

Tokelau
New Zealand Overseas Territory

Area Sq Km	10	**Languages**	English, Tokelauan
Area Sq Miles	4	**Religions**	Christian
Population	1 411	**Currency**	New Zealand dollar

Tokelau consists of three atolls, Atafu, Nukunonu and Fakaofa, lying in the Pacific Ocean north of Samoa. Subsistence agriculture is the main activity, and the islands rely on aid from New Zealand and remittances from workers overseas.

TONGA
Kingdom of Tonga

Area Sq Km	748	**Languages**	Tongan, English
Area Sq Miles	289	**Religions**	Protestant, Roman Catholic
Population	105 000	**Currency**	Pa'anga
Capital	Nuku'alofa	**Organizations**	Comm., UN

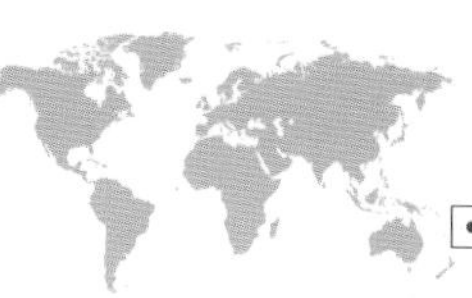

Tonga comprises some one hundred and seventy islands in the south Pacific Ocean, northeast of New Zealand. The three main groups are Tongatapu (where sixty per cent of Tongans live), Ha'apai and Vava'u. The climate is warm and wet, and the economy relies heavily on agriculture. Tourism and light industry are also important to the economy. Exports include squash, fish, vanilla beans and root crops. Most trade is with New Zealand, Japan and Australia.

Transnistria
Disputed territory

Area Sq Km	4 200	**Languages**	Russian, Ukrainian, Moldovan
Area Sq Miles	1 622	**Religions**	Eastern Orthodox, Roman Catholic
Population	520 000	**Currency**	Transnistrian rouble, Moldovan leu
Capital	Tiraspol		

Transnistria, the area of Moldova mainly between the Dniester river and the Ukrainian border, is a predominantly ethnic Russian, and Russian-speaking region. Campaigns for Transnistrian autonomy and independence led to civil war between Moldovan forces and separatists who had proclaimed the self-styled 'Dniester Republic', aligned to Russia, in 1990. A peace agreement with Russia in 1992 ended this war, granted Transnistria special status and established a security zone along its border with Moldova, controlled by Russian, Moldovan and Transnistrian troops. An agreement between Moldova and Transnistria in 1996 stated that Transnistria would remain a part of Moldova, but the campaign for independence continues and the status of the region remains to be resolved. It currently functions as a (predominantly Russian) de facto autonomous republic, separate from Moldova – the Pridnestrovian Moldavian Republic.

TRINIDAD AND TOBAGO
Republic of Trinidad and Tobago

Area Sq Km	5 130	**Languages**	English, Creole, Hindi
Area Sq Miles	1 981	**Religions**	Roman Catholic, Hindu, Protestant, Sunni Muslim
Population	1 341 000	**Currency**	Trinidad and Tobago dollar
Capital	Port of Spain	**Organizations**	CARICOM, Comm., UN

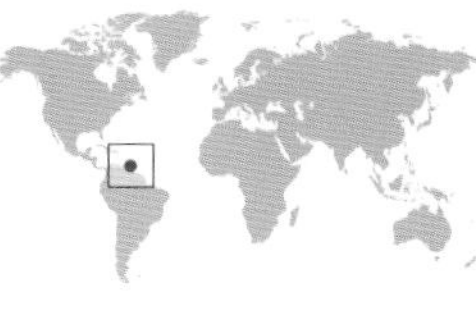

Trinidad, the most southerly Caribbean island, lies off the Venezuelan coast. It is hilly in the north, with a central plain. Tobago, to the northeast, is smaller, more mountainous and less developed. The climate is tropical. The main crops are cocoa, sugar cane, coffee, fruit and vegetables. Oil and petrochemical industries dominate the economy. Tourism is also important. The USA is the main trading partner.

States and Territories

TUNISIA
Republic of Tunisia

Area Sq Km	164 150	Languages	Arabic, French
Area Sq Miles	63 379	Religions	Sunni Muslim
Population	10 997 000	Currency	Tunisian dinar
Capital	Tunis	Organizations	UN

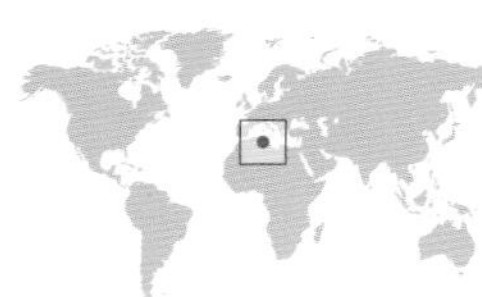

Tunisia is on the Mediterranean coast of north Africa. The north is mountainous with valleys and coastal plains, has a Mediterranean climate and is the most populous area. The south is hot and arid. Oil and phosphates are the main resources, and the main crops are olives and citrus fruit. Tourism is an important industry. Exports include petroleum products, textiles, fruit and phosphorus. Most trade is with European Union countries.

TURKEY
Republic of Turkey

Area Sq Km	779 452	Languages	Turkish, Kurdish
Area Sq Miles	300 948	Religions	Sunni Muslim, Shi'a Muslim
Population	74 933 000	Currency	Lira
Capital	Ankara	Organizations	NATO, OECD, UN

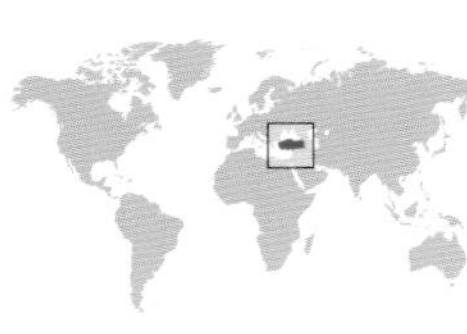

Turkey occupies a large peninsula of southwest Asia and has coastlines on the Black, Mediterranean and Aegean Seas. It includes eastern Thrace, which is in southeastern Europe and is separated from the rest of the country by the Bosporus, the Sea of Marmara and the Dardanelles. The Asian mainland consists of the semi-arid Anatolian plateau, flanked to the north, south and east by mountains. Over forty per cent of Turks live in central Anatolia and on the Marmara and Aegean coastal plains. The coast has a Mediterranean climate, but inland conditions are more extreme with hot, dry summers and cold, snowy winters. Agriculture involves about thirty per cent of the workforce, and products include cotton, grain, tobacco, fruit, nuts and livestock. Turkey is a leading producer of chromium, iron ore, lead, tin, borate, and baryte while coal is also mined. The main manufactured goods are clothing, textiles, food products, steel and vehicles. Tourism is a major industry, around forty million visitors a year. Germany and the USA are the main trading partners. Remittances from workers abroad are important to the economy.

TURKMENISTAN

Area Sq Km	488 100	Languages	Turkmen, Uzbek, Russian
Area Sq Miles	188 456	Religions	Sunni Muslim, Russian Orthodox
Population	5 240 000	Currency	Turkmen manat
Capital	Aşgabat (Ashkhabad)	Organizations	UN

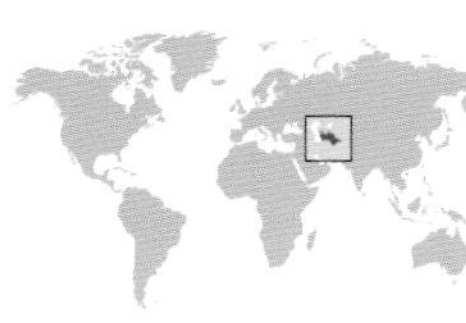

Turkmenistan, in central Asia, comprises the plains of the Karakum Desert, the foothills of the Kopet Dag mountains in the south, the Amudar'ya valley in the north and the Caspian Sea plains in the west. The climate is dry, with extreme temperatures. The economy is based mainly on irrigated agriculture (chiefly cotton growing), and natural gas and oil. Main exports are natural gas, oil and cotton fibre. Ukraine, Iran, Turkey and Russia are the main trading partners.

Turks and Caicos Islands
United Kingdom Overseas Territory

Area Sq Km	430	Languages	English
Area Sq Miles	166	Religions	Protestant
Population	33 000	Currency	United States dollar
Capital	Grand Turk (Cockburn Town)		

The state consists of over forty low-lying islands and cays in the northern Caribbean. Only eight islands are inhabited, and two-fifths of the people live on Grand Turk and Salt Cay. The climate is tropical, and the economy is based on tourism, fishing and offshore banking.

TUVALU

Area Sq Km	25	Languages	Tuvaluan, English
Area Sq Miles	10	Religions	Protestant
Population	10 000	Currency	Australian dollar
Capital	Vaiaku	Organizations	Comm., UN

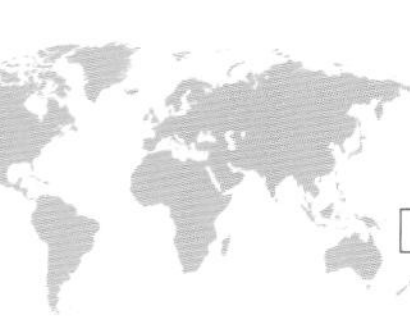

Tuvalu comprises nine low-lying coral atolls in the south Pacific Ocean. One-third of the population lives on Funafuti, and most people depend on subsistence farming and fishing. The islands export copra, stamps and clothing, but rely heavily on foreign aid. Most trade is with Fiji, Australia and New Zealand.

UGANDA
Republic of Uganda

Area Sq Km	241 038	Languages	English, Swahili, Luganda, other local languages
Area Sq Miles	93 065	Religions	Roman Catholic, Protestant, Sunni Muslim, traditional beliefs
Population	37 579 000	Currency	Ugandan shilling
Capital	Kampala	Organizations	Comm., UN

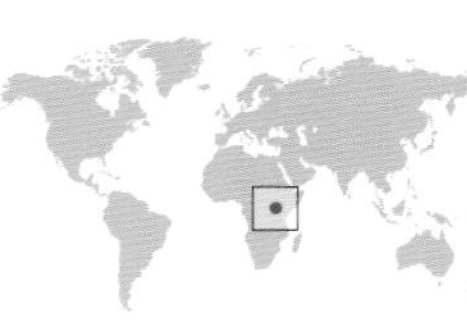

A landlocked country in east Africa, Uganda consists of a savanna plateau with mountains and lakes. The climate is warm and wet. Most people live in the southern half of the country. Agriculture employs around eighty per cent of the workforce and dominates the economy. Coffee, tea, fish and fish products are the main exports. Uganda relies heavily on aid.

UKRAINE

Area Sq Km	603 700	Languages	Ukrainian, Russian
Area Sq Miles	233 090	Religions	Ukrainian Orthodox, Ukrainian Catholic, Roman Catholic
Population	45 239 000	Currency	Hryvnia
Capital	Kiev (Kyiv)	Organizations	UN

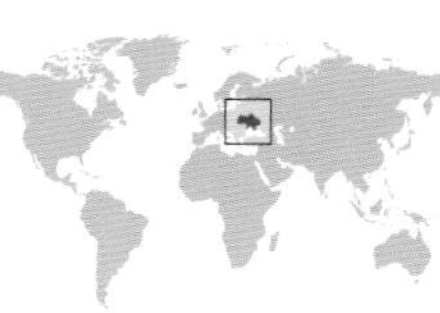

The country lies on the Black Sea coast of eastern Europe. Much of the land is steppe, generally flat and treeless, but with rich black soil, and it is drained by the river Dnieper. Along the border with Belarus are forested, marshy plains. The only uplands are the Carpathian Mountains in the west and smaller ranges on the Crimean peninsula. Summers are warm and winters are cold, with milder conditions in the Crimea. About a quarter of the population lives in the mainly industrial areas around Donets'k, Kiev and Dnipropetrovs'k. The Ukraine is rich in natural resources: fertile soil, substantial mineral and natural gas deposits, and forests. Agriculture and livestock rearing are important, but mining and manufacturing are the dominant sectors of the economy. Coal, iron and manganese mining, steel and metal production, machinery, chemicals and food processing are the main industries. The EU and Russia are the main trading partners but the economy is struggling.

UNITED ARAB EMIRATES
Federation of Emirates

Area Sq Km	77 700	Languages	Arabic, English
Area Sq Miles	30 000	Religions	Sunni Muslim, Shi'a Muslim
Population	9 346 000	Currency	United Arab Emirates dirham
Capital	Abu Dhabi (Abū Ẓaby)	Organizations	OPEC, UN

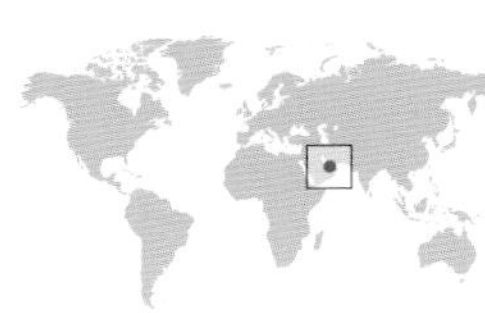

The UAE lies on the Gulf coast of the Arabian Peninsula. Six emirates are on The Gulf, while the seventh, Fujairah, is on the Gulf of Oman. Most of the land is flat desert with sand dunes and salt pans. The only hilly area is in the northeast. Over eighty per cent of the population lives in three of the emirates - Abu Dhabi, Dubai and Sharjah. Summers are hot and winters are mild, with occasional rainfall in coastal areas. Fruit and vegetables are grown in oases and irrigated areas, but the Emirates' wealth is based on hydrocarbons found in Abu Dhabi, Dubai, Sharjah and Ras al Khaimah. The UAE is one of the major oil producers in the Middle East. Dubai is an important entrepôt trade centre The main trading partners are India, Iran, Iraq and China.

Abu Dhabi (Abū Ẓaby) (Emirate)

Area Sq Km (Sq Miles)	Population	Capital
67 340 (26 000)	1 628 000	Abu Dhabi (Abū Ẓaby)

Ajman (Emirate)

Area Sq Km (Sq Miles)	Population	Capital
259 (100)	250 000	Ajman

Dubai (Emirate)

Area Sq Km (Sq Miles)	Population	Capital
3 885 (1 500)	1 722 000	Dubai

Fujairah (Emirate)

Area Sq Km (Sq Miles)	Population	Capital
1 165 (450)	152 000	Fujairah

Ra's al Khaymah (Emirate)

Area Sq Km (Sq Miles)	Population	Capital
1 684 (650)	241 000	Ra's al Khaymah

Sharjah (Emirate)

Area Sq Km (Sq Miles)	Population	Capital
2 590 (1 000)	1 017 000	Sharjah

Umm al Qaywayn (Emirate)

Area Sq Km (Sq Miles)	Population	Capital
777 (300)	56 000	Umm al Qaywayn

UNITED KINGDOM
United Kingdom of Great Britain and Northern Ireland

Area Sq Km	243 609	Languages	English, Welsh, Gaelic
Area Sq Miles	94 058	Religions	Protestant, Roman Catholic, Muslim
Population	63 136 000	Currency	Pound sterling
Capital	London	Organizations	Comm., EU, NATO, OECD, UN

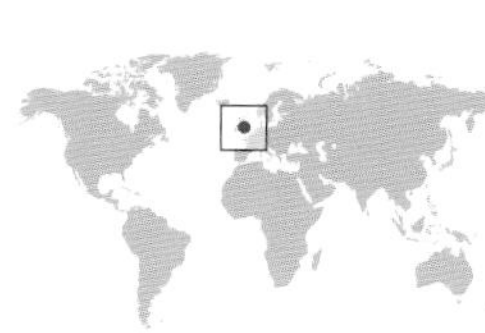

The United Kingdom, in northwest Europe, occupies the island of Great Britain, part of Ireland, and many small adjacent islands. Great Britain comprises England, Scotland and Wales. England covers over half the land area and supports over four-fifths of the population, at its densest in the southeast. The English landscape is flat or rolling with some uplands, notably the Cheviot Hills on the Scottish border, the Pennines in the centre-north, and the hills of the Lake District in the northwest. Scotland consists of southern uplands, central lowlands, the Highlands (which include the UK's

highest peak) and many islands. Wales is a land of hills, mountains and river valleys. Northern Ireland contains uplands, plains and the UK's largest lake, Lough Neagh. The climate of the UK is mild, wet and variable. There are few mineral deposits, but important energy resources. Agricultural activities involve sheep and cattle rearing, dairy farming, and crop and fruit growing in the east and southeast. Productivity is high, but approximately one-third of food is imported. The UK produces petroleum and natural gas from reserves in the North Sea and is self-sufficient in energy in net terms. Major manufactures are food and drinks, motor vehicles and parts, aerospace equipment, machinery, electronic and electrical equipment, and chemicals and chemical products. However, the economy is dominated by service industries, including banking, insurance, finance and business services. London, the capital, is one of the world's major financial centres. Tourism is also a major industry, with approximately thirty-two million visitors a year. International trade is also important, around forty per cent of national income. Main trading partners and the USA and other European Union countries.

England (Constituent country)

Area Sq Km (Sq Miles)	Population	Capital
130 433 (50 360)	53 493 700	London

Northern Ireland (Province)

Area Sq Km (Sq Miles)	Population	Capital
13 576 (5 242)	1 823 600	Belfast

Scotland (Constituent country)

Area Sq Km (Sq Miles)	Population	Capital
78 822 (30 433)	5 313 600	Edinburgh

Wales (Principality)

Area Sq Km (Sq Miles)	Population	Capital
20 778 (8 022)	3 074 100	Cardiff

UNITED STATES OF AMERICA

Area Sq Km	9 826 635	Languages	English, Spanish
Area Sq Miles	3 794 085	Religions	Protestant, Roman Catholic, Sunni Muslim, Jewish
Population	320 051 000	Currency	United States dollar
Capital	Washington D.C.	Organizations	APEC, NATO, OECD, UN

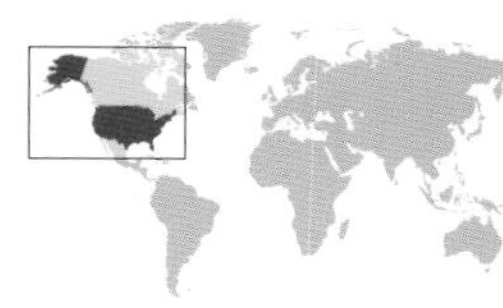

The USA comprises forty-eight contiguous states in North America, bounded by Canada and Mexico, plus the states of Alaska, to the northwest of Canada, and Hawaii, in the north Pacific Ocean. The populous eastern states cover the Atlantic coastal plain (which includes the Florida peninsula and the Gulf of Mexico coast) and the Appalachian Mountains. The central states occupy a vast interior plain drained by the Mississippi-Missouri river system. To the west lie the Rocky Mountains, separated from the Pacific coastal ranges by intermontane plateaus. The Pacific coastal zone is also mountainous, and prone to earthquakes. Hawaii is a group of some twenty volcanic islands. Climatic conditions range between arctic in Alaska to desert in the intermontane plateaus. Most of the USA has a temperate climate, although the interior has continental conditions. There are abundant natural resources, including major reserves of minerals and energy resources. The USA has the largest and most technologically advanced economy in the world, based on manufacturing and services. Although agriculture accounts for approximately two per cent of national income, productivity is high and the USA is a net exporter of food, chiefly grains and fruit. Cotton is the major industrial crop. The USA produces iron ore, copper, lead, zinc, and many other minerals. It is a major producer of coal, petroleum and natural gas, although being the world's biggest energy user it imports significant quantities of petroleum and its products. Manufacturing is diverse. The main industries are petroleum, steel, motor vehicles, aerospace, telecommunications, electronics, food processing, chemicals and consumer goods. Tourism is a major foreign currency earner, with approximately seventy-four million visitors a year. Other important service industries are banking and finance, Wall Street in New York being one of the world's major stock exchanges. Canada and Mexico are the main trading partners.

Alabama (State)

Area Sq Km (Sq Miles)	Population	Capital
135 765 (52 419)	4 822 023	Montgomery

Alaska (State)

Area Sq Km (Sq Miles)	Population	Capital
1 717 854 (663 267)	731 449	Juneau

Arizona (State)

Area Sq Km (Sq Miles)	Population	Capital
295 253 (113 998)	6 553 255	Phoenix

Arkansas (State)

Area Sq Km (Sq Miles)	Population	Capital
137 733 (53 179)	2 949 131	Little Rock

California (State)

Area Sq Km (Sq Miles)	Population	Capital
423 971 (163 696)	38 041 430	Sacramento

Colorado (State)

Area Sq Km (Sq Miles)	Population	Capital
269 602 (104 094)	5 187 582	Denver

Connecticut (State)

Area Sq Km (Sq Miles)	Population	Capital
14 356 (5 543)	3 590 347	Hartford

Delaware (State)

Area Sq Km (Sq Miles)	Population	Capital
6 446 (2 489)	917 092	Dover

District of Columbia (District)

Area Sq Km (Sq Miles)	Population	Capital
176 (68)	632 323	Washington

Florida (State)

Area Sq Km (Sq Miles)	Population	Capital
170 305 (65 755)	19 317 568	Tallahassee

Georgia (State)

Area Sq Km (Sq Miles)	Population	Capital
153 910 (59 425)	9 919 945	Atlanta

Hawaii (State)

Area Sq Km (Sq Miles)	Population	Capital
28 311 (10 931)	1 392 313	Honolulu

Idaho (State)

Area Sq Km (Sq Miles)	Population	Capital
216 445 (83 570)	1 595 728	Boise

Illinois (State)

Area Sq Km (Sq Miles)	Population	Capital
149 997 (57 914)	12 875 255	Springfield

Indiana (State)

Area Sq Km (Sq Miles)	Population	Capital
94 322 (36 418)	6 537 334	Indianapolis

Iowa (State)

Area Sq Km (Sq Miles)	Population	Capital
145 744 (56 272)	3 074 186	Des Moines

Kansas (State)

Area Sq Km (Sq Miles)	Population	Capital
213 096 (82 277)	2 885 905	Topeka

Kentucky (State)

Area Sq Km (Sq Miles)	Population	Capital
104 659 (40 409)	4 380 415	Frankfort

Louisiana (State)

Area Sq Km (Sq Miles)	Population	Capital
134 265 (51 840)	4 601 893	Baton Rouge

Maine (State)

Area Sq Km (Sq Miles)	Population	Capital
91 647 (35 385)	1 329 192	Augusta

Maryland (State)

Area Sq Km (Sq Miles)	Population	Capital
32 134 (12 407)	5 884 563	Annapolis

Massachusetts (State)

Area Sq Km (Sq Miles)	Population	Capital
27 337 (10 555)	6 646 144	Boston

Michigan (State)

Area Sq Km (Sq Miles)	Population	Capital
250 493 (96 716)	9 883 360	Lansing

Minnesota (State)

Area Sq Km (Sq Miles)	Population	Capital
225 171 (86 939)	5 379 139	St Paul

Mississippi (State)

Area Sq Km (Sq Miles)	Population	Capital
125 433 (48 430)	2 984 926	Jackson

Missouri (State)

Area Sq Km (Sq Miles)	Population	Capital
180 533 (69 704)	6 021 988	Jefferson City

Montana (State)

Area Sq Km (Sq Miles)	Population	Capital
380 837 (147 042)	1 005 141	Helena

Nebraska (State)

Area Sq Km (Sq Miles)	Population	Capital
200 346 (77 354)	1 855 525	Lincoln

Nevada (State)

Area Sq Km (Sq Miles)	Population	Capital
286 352 (110 561)	2 758 931	Carson City

New Hampshire (State)

Area Sq Km (Sq Miles)	Population	Capital
24 216 (9 350)	1 320 718	Concord

States and Territories

New Jersey (State)

Area Sq Km (Sq Miles)	Population	Capital
22 587 (8 721)	8 864 590	Trenton

New Mexico (State)

Area Sq Km (Sq Miles)	Population	Capital
314 914 (121 589)	2 085 538	Santa Fe

New York (State)

Area Sq Km (Sq Miles)	Population	Capital
141 299 (54 556)	19 570 261	Albany

North Carolina (State)

Area Sq Km (Sq Miles)	Population	Capital
139 391 (53 819)	9 752 073	Raleigh

North Dakota (State)

Area Sq Km (Sq Miles)	Population	Capital
183 112 (70 700)	699 628	Bismarck

Ohio (State)

Area Sq Km (Sq Miles)	Population	Capital
116 096 (44 825)	11 544 225	Columbus

Oklahoma (State)

Area Sq Km (Sq Miles)	Population	Capital
181 035 (69 898)	3 814 820	Oklahoma City

Oregon (State)

Area Sq Km (Sq Miles)	Population	Capital
254 806 (98 381)	3 899 353	Salem

Pennsylvania (State)

Area Sq Km (Sq Miles)	Population	Capital
119 282 (46 055)	12 763 536	Harrisburg

Rhode Island (State)

Area Sq Km (Sq Miles)	Population	Capital
4 002 (1 545)	1 050 292	Providence

South Carolina (State)

Area Sq Km (Sq Miles)	Population	Capital
82 931 (32 020)	4 723 723	Columbia

South Dakota (State)

Area Sq Km (Sq Miles)	Population	Capital
199 730 (77 116)	833 354	Pierre

Tennessee (State)

Area Sq Km (Sq Miles)	Population	Capital
109 150 (42 143)	6 456 243	Nashville

Texas (State)

Area Sq Km (Sq Miles)	Population	Capital
695 622 (268 581)	26 059 203	Austin

Utah (State)

Area Sq Km (Sq Miles)	Population	Capital
219 887 (84 899)	2 855 287	Salt Lake City

Vermont (State)

Area Sq Km (Sq Miles)	Population	Capital
24 900 (9 614)	626 011	Montpelier

Virginia (State)

Area Sq Km (Sq Miles)	Population	Capital
110 784 (42 774)	8 185 867	Richmond

Washington (State)

Area Sq Km (Sq Miles)	Population	Capital
184 666 (71 300)	6 897 012	Olympia

West Virginia (State)

Area Sq Km (Sq Miles)	Population	Capital
62 755 (24 230)	1 855 413	Charleston

Wisconsin (State)

Area Sq Km (Sq Miles)	Population	Capital
169 639 (65 498)	5 726 398	Madison

Wyoming (State)

Area Sq Km (Sq Miles)	Population	Capital
253 337 (97 814)	576 412	Cheyenne

URUGUAY
Oriental Republic of Uruguay

Area Sq Km	176 215	Languages	Spanish
Area Sq Miles	68 037	Religions	Roman Catholic, Protestant, Jewish
Population	3 407 000	Currency	Uruguayan peso
Capital	Montevideo	Organizations	UN

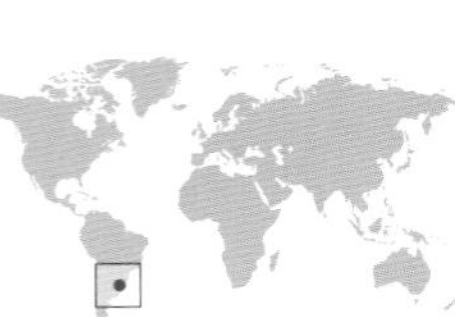

Uruguay, on the Atlantic coast of central South America, is a low-lying land of prairies. The coast and the River Plate estuary in the south are fringed with lagoons and sand dunes. Almost half the population lives in the capital, Montevideo. Uruguay has warm summers and mild winters. The economy is based on cattle and sheep ranching, and the main industries produce food products, textiles, and petroleum products. Meat, wool, hides, textiles and agricultural products are the main exports. Brazil and Argentina are the main trading partners.

UZBEKISTAN
Republic of Uzbekistan

Area Sq Km	447 400	Languages	Uzbek, Russian, Tajik, Kazakh
Area Sq Miles	172 742	Religions	Sunni Muslim, Russian Orthodox
Population	28 934 000	Currency	Uzbek som
Capital	Toshkent (Tashkent)	Organizations	CIS, UN

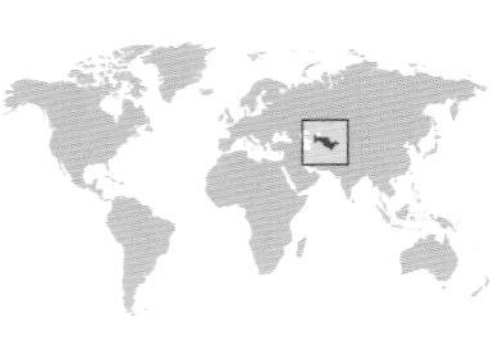

A landlocked country of central Asia, Uzbekistan consists mainly of the flat Kyzylkum Desert. High mountains and valleys are found towards the southeast borders with Kyrgyzstan and Tajikistan. Most settlement is in the Fergana basin. The climate is hot and dry. The economy is based mainly on irrigated agriculture, chiefly cotton production. Uzbekistan is rich in minerals, including gold, copper, lead, zinc and uranium, and it has one of the largest gold mines in the world. Industry specializes in fertilizers and machinery for cotton harvesting and textile manufacture. Russia is the main trading partner.

VANUATU
Republic of Vanuatu

Area Sq Km	12 190	Languages	English, Bislama (Creole), French
Area Sq Miles	4 707	Religions	Protestant, Roman Catholic, traditional beliefs
Population	253 000	Currency	Vatu
Capital	Port Vila	Organizations	Comm., UN

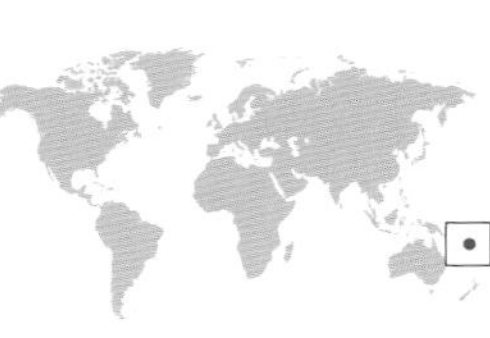

Vanuatu occupies an archipelago of approximately eighty islands in the southwest Pacific. Many of the islands are mountainous, of volcanic origin and densely forested. The climate is tropical, with heavy rainfall. Half of the population lives on the main islands of Éfaté and Espíritu Santo, and the majority of people are employed in agriculture. Copra, beef, timber, vegetables, and cocoa are the main exports. In March 2015 Cyclone Pam caused catastrophic damage to the islands.

VATICAN CITY
Vatican City State or Holy See

Area Sq Km	0.5	Languages	Italian
Area Sq Miles	0.2	Religions	Roman Catholic
Population	800	Currency	Euro
Capital	Vatican City		

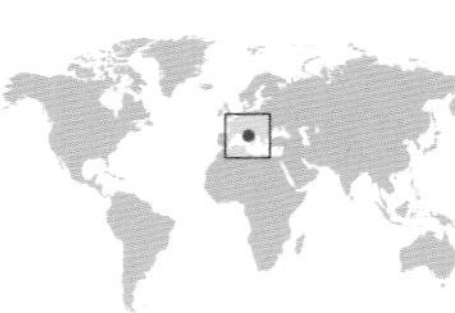

The world's smallest sovereign state, the Vatican City occupies a hill to the west of the river Tiber within the Italian capital, Rome. It is the headquarters of the Roman Catholic church, and income comes from investments, voluntary contributions and tourism.

VENEZUELA
Bolivarian Republic of Venezuela

Area Sq Km	912 050	Languages	Spanish, Amerindian languages
Area Sq Miles	352 144	Religions	Roman Catholic, Protestant
Population	30 405 000	Currency	Bolívar
Capital	Caracas	Organizations	OPEC, UN

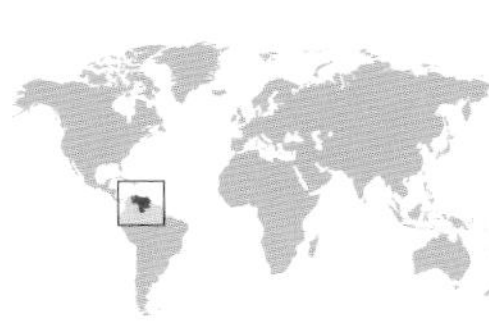

Venezuela is in northern South America, on the Caribbean. Its coast is much indented, with the oil-rich area of Lake Maracaibo at the western end, and the swampy Orinoco Delta to the east. Mountain ranges run parallel to the coast, and turn southwestwards to form a northern extension of the Andes. Central Venezuela is an area of lowland grasslands drained by the Orinoco river system. To the south are the Guiana Highlands, which contain the Angel Falls, the world's highest waterfall. Almost ninety per cent of the population lives in towns, mostly in the coastal mountain areas. The climate is tropical, with most rainfall in summer. Farming is important, particularly cattle ranching and dairy farming; coffee, maize, rice and sugar cane are the main crops. Venezuela is a major oil producer, and oil accounts for about seventy-five per cent of export earnings. Aluminium, iron ore, copper and gold are also mined, and manufactures include petrochemicals, aluminium, steel, textiles and food products. The USA, China and Brazil are the main trading partners.

VIETNAM
Socialist Republic of Vietnam

Area Sq Km	329 565	Languages	Vietnamese, Thai, Khmer, Chinese, other local languages
Area Sq Miles	127 246	Religions	Buddhist, Taoist, Roman Catholic, Cao Dai, Hoa Hao
Population	91 680 000	Currency	Dong
Capital	Ha Nôi (Hanoi)	Organizations	APEC, ASEAN, UN

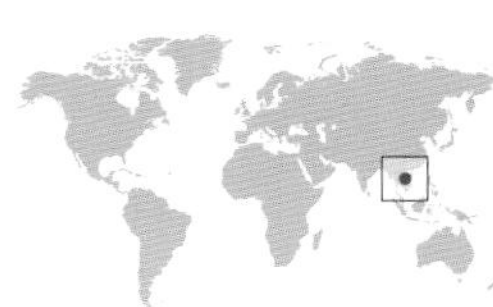

Vietnam lies in southeast Asia on the west coast of the South China Sea. The Red River delta lowlands in the north are separated from the huge Mekong delta in the south by long, narrow coastal plains backed by the mountainous and forested terrain of the Annam Highlands. Most of the population lives in the river deltas. The climate is tropical, with summer monsoon rains. Over three-quarters of the workforce is involved in agriculture, forestry and fishing. Coffee, tea and rubber are important cash crops, but Vietnam is the world's second largest rice exporter. Oil, coal and copper are produced, and other main industries are food processing, clothing and footwear, cement and fertilizers. Exports include oil, coffee, rice, clothing, fish and fish products. Japan and Singapore are the main trading partners.

Virgin Islands (U.K.)
United Kingdom Overseas Territory

Area Sq Km	153	Languages	English
Area Sq Miles	59	Religions	Protestant, Roman Catholic
Population	28 000	Currency	United States dollar
Capital	Road Town		

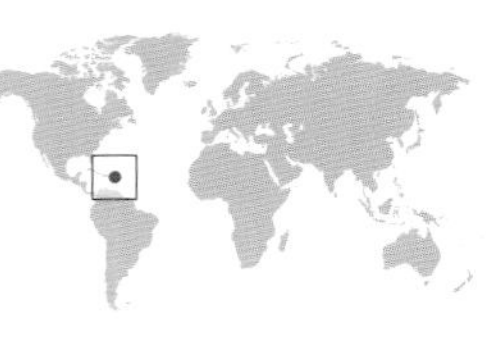

The Caribbean territory comprises four main islands and over thirty islets at the eastern end of the Virgin Islands group. Apart from the flat coral atoll of Anegada, the islands are volcanic in origin and hilly. The climate is subtropical, and tourism is the main industry.

Virgin Islands (U.S.A.)

United States Unincorporated Territory

Area Sq Km	352	**Languages**	English, Spanish
Area Sq Miles	136	**Religions**	Protestant, Roman Catholic
Population	107 000	**Currency**	United States dollar
Capital	Charlotte Amalie		

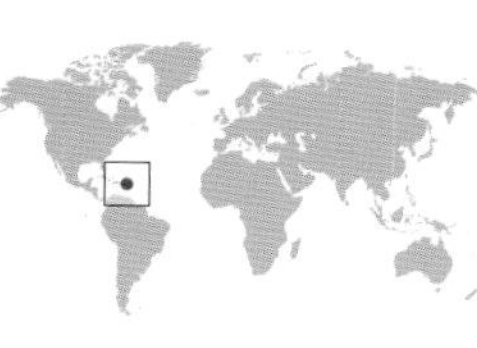

The territory consists of three main islands and over fifty islets in the Caribbean's western Virgin Islands. The islands are hilly, of volcanic origin, and the climate is subtropical. The economy is based on tourism, with some manufacturing, including a major oil refinery on St Croix.

Wallis and Futuna Islands

French Overseas Collectivity

Area Sq Km	274	**Languages**	French, Wallisian, Futunian
Area Sq Miles	106	**Religions**	Roman Catholic
Population	13 000	**Currency**	CFP franc
Capital	Matā'utu		

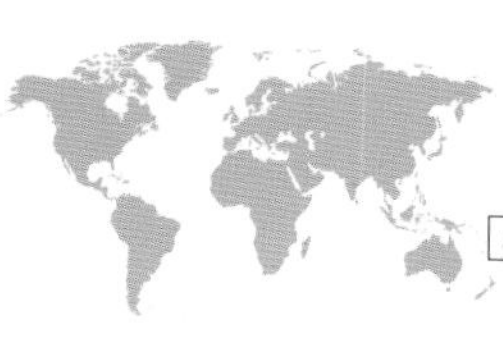

The south Pacific territory comprises the volcanic islands of the Wallis archipelago and the Hoorn Islands. The climate is tropical. The islands depend on subsistence farming, the sale of licences to foreign fishing fleets, workers' remittances from abroad and French aid.

West Bank

Disputed territory

Area Sq Km	5 860	**Languages**	Arabic, Hebrew
Area Sq Miles	2 263	**Religions**	Sunni Muslim, Jewish, Shi'a Muslim, Christian
Population	2 719 112	**Currency**	Jordanian dinar, Israeli shekel

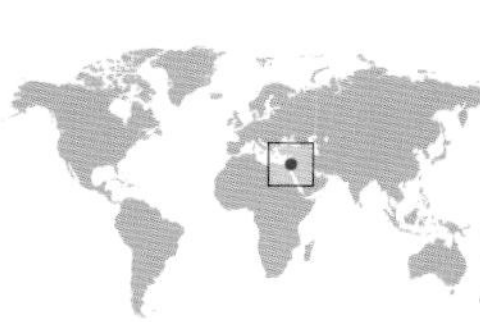

The territory consists of the west bank of the river Jordan and parts of Judea and Samaria. The land was annexed by Israel in 1967, but some areas have been granted autonomy under agreements between Israel and the Palestinian Authority. Conflict between the Israelis and the Palestinians continues to restrict economic development.

Western Sahara

Disputed territory (Morocco)

Area Sq Km	266 000	**Languages**	Arabic
Area Sq Miles	102 703	**Religions**	Sunni Muslim
Population	567 000	**Currency**	Moroccan dirham
Capital	Laâyoune		

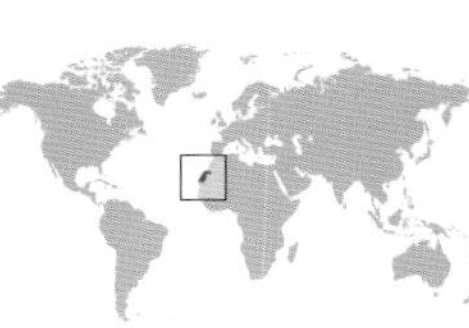

Situated on the northwest coast of Africa, the territory of the Western Sahara is now effectively controlled by Morocco. The land is low, flat desert with higher land in the northeast. There is little cultivation and only about twenty per cent of the land is pasture. Livestock herding, fishing and phosphate mining are the main activities. All trade is controlled by Morocco.

YEMEN

Republic of Yemen

Area Sq Km	527 968	**Languages**	Arabic
Area Sq Miles	203 850	**Religions**	Sunni Muslim, Shi'a Muslim
Population	24 407 000	**Currency**	Yemeni riyal
Capital	Şan'ā'	**Organizations**	UN

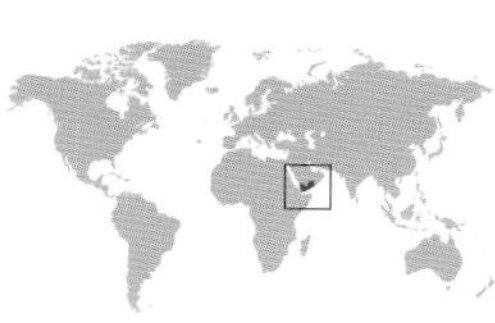

Yemen occupies the southwestern part of the Arabian Peninsula, on the Red Sea and the Gulf of Aden. Beyond the Red Sea coastal plain the land rises to a mountain range and then descends to desert plateaus. Much of the country is hot and arid, but there is more rainfall in the west, where most of the population lives. Farming and fishing are the main activities, with cotton the main cash crop. The main exports are crude oil, fish, coffee and dried fruit. Despite some oil resources Yemen is one of the poorest countries in the Arab world. Main trading partners are Thailand, China, South Korea and Saudi Arabia.

ZAMBIA

Republic of Zambia

Area Sq Km	752 614	**Languages**	English, Bemba, Nyanja, Tonga, other local languages
Area Sq Miles	290 586	**Religions**	Christian, traditional beliefs
Population	14 539 000	**Currency**	Zambian kwacha
Capital	Lusaka	**Organizations**	Comm., SADC, UN

A landlocked state in south central Africa, Zambia consists principally of high savanna plateaus and is bordered by the Zambezi river in the south. Most people live in the Copperbelt area in the centre-north. The climate is tropical, with a rainy season from November to May. Agriculture employs over sixty per cent of the workforce, but is mainly at subsistence level. Copper mining is the mainstay of the economy, although reserves are declining. Copper and cobalt are the main exports. Most trade is with South Africa.

ZIMBABWE

Republic of Zimbabwe

Area Sq Km	390 759	**Languages**	English, Shona, Ndebele
Area Sq Miles	150 873	**Religions**	Christian, traditional beliefs
Population	14 150 000	**Currency**	US dollar and other currencies
Capital	Harare	**Organizations**	SADC, UN

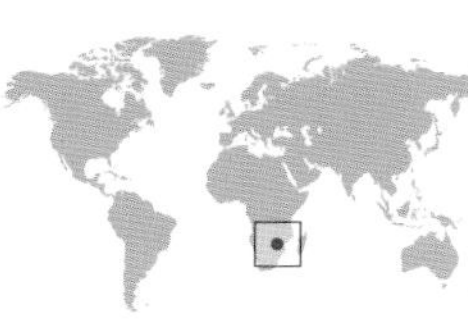

Zimbabwe, a landlocked state in south-central Africa, consists of high plateaus flanked by the Zambezi river valley and Lake Kariba in the north and the Limpopo river in the south. Most of the population lives in the centre of the country. There are significant mineral resources, including gold, nickel, copper, asbestos, platinum and chromium. Agriculture is a major sector of the economy, with crops including tobacco, maize, sugar cane and cotton. Beef cattle are also important. Exports include tobacco, gold, ferroalloys, nickel and cotton. South Africa is the main trading partner. The economy has suffered recently through significant political unrest and instability.

Index

Introduction to the index

The index includes all names shown on the reference maps in the atlas. Each entry includes the country or geographical area in which the feature is located, a page number and an alphanumeric reference. Additional entry details and aspects of the index are explained below.

Name forms

The names policy in this atlas is generally to use local name forms which are officially recognized by the governments of the countries concerned. Rules established by the Permanent Committee on Geographical Names for British Official Use (PCGN) are applied to the conversion of non-roman alphabet names, for example in Russia, into the roman alphabet used in English.

However, English conventional name forms are used for the most well-known places for which such a form is in common use. In these cases, the local form is included in brackets on the map and appears as a cross-reference in the index. Other alternative names, such as well-known historical names or those in other languages, may also be included in brackets on the map and as cross-references in the index. All country names and those for international physical features appear in their English forms. Names appear in full in the index, although they may appear in abbreviated form on the maps.

Referencing

Names are referenced by page number and by grid reference. The grid reference relates to the alphanumeric values which appear on the edges of each map. These reflect the graticule on the map – the letter relates to longitude divisions, the number to latitude divisions.

Names are generally referenced to the largest scale map page on which they appear. For large geographical features, including countries, the reference is to the largest scale map on which the feature appears in its entirety, or on which the majority of it appears.

Rivers are referenced to their lowest downstream point – either their mouth or their confluence with another river. The river name will generally be positioned as close to this point as possible.

Alternative names

Alternative names appear as cross-references and refer the user to the index entry for the form of the name used on the map.

For rivers with multiple names - for example those which flow through several countries - all alternative name forms are included within the main index entries, with details of the countries in which each form applies.

Administrative qualifiers

Administrative divisions are included in entries to differentiate duplicate names - entries of exactly the same name and feature type within the one country - where these division names are shown on the maps. In such cases, duplicate names are alphabetized in the order of the administrative division names.

Additional qualifiers are included for names within selected geographical areas, to indicate more clearly their location.

Descriptors

Entries, other than those for towns and cities, include a descriptor indicating the type of geographical feature. Descriptors are not included where the type of feature is implicit in the name itself, unless there is a town or city of exactly the same name.

Insets

Where relevant, the index clearly indicates [inset] if a feature appears on an inset map.

Alphabetical order

The Icelandic characters Þ and þ are transliterated and alphabetized as 'Th' and 'th'. The German character ß is alphabetized as 'ss'. Names beginning with Mac or Mc are alphabetized exactly as they appear. The terms Saint, Sainte, etc, are abbreviated to St, Ste, etc, but alphabetized as if in the full form.

Numerical entries

Entries beginning with numerals appear at the beginning of the index, in numerical order. Elsewhere, numerals are alphabetized before 'a'.

Permuted terms

Names beginning with generic geographical terms are permuted - the descriptive term is placed after, and the index alphabetized by, the main part of the name. For example, Mount Everest is indexed as Everest, Mount; Lake Superior as Superior, Lake. This policy is applied to all languages. Permuting has not been applied to names of towns, cities or administrative divisions beginning with such geographical terms. These remain in their full form, for example, Lake Isabella, USA.

Abbreviations

admin. dist.	administrative district	i.	island	OR	Oregon
admin. div.	administrative division	IA	Iowa	PA	Pennsylvania
admin. reg.	administrative region	ID	Idaho	Pak.	Pakistan
Afgh.	Afghanistan	IL	Illinois	Para.	Paraguay
AK	Alaska	imp. l.	impermanent lake	P.E.I.	Prince Edward Island
AL	Alabama	IN	Indiana	pen.	peninsula
Alg.	Algeria	Indon.	Indonesia	Phil.	Philippines
AR	Arkansas	is	islands	plat.	plateau
Arg.	Argentina	Kazakh.	Kazakhstan	P.N.G.	Papua New Guinea
aut. comm.	autonomous community	KS	Kansas	Port.	Portugal
aut. reg.	autonomous region	KY	Kentucky	pref.	prefecture
aut. rep.	autonomous republic	Kyrg.	Kyrgyzstan	prov.	province
AZ	Arizona	l.	lake	pt	point
Azer.	Azerbaijan	LA	Louisiana	Qld	Queensland
b.	bay	lag.	lagoon	Que.	Québec
Bangl.	Bangladesh	Lith.	Lithuania	r.	river
B.C.	British Columbia	Lux.	Luxembourg	reg.	region
B.I.O.T.	British Indian Ocean Territory	MA	Massachusetts	res.	reserve
Bol.	Bolivia	Madh. Prad.	Madhya Pradesh	resr	reservoir
Bos. & Herz.	Bosnia and Herzegovina	Mahar.	Maharashtra	RI	Rhode Island
Bulg.	Bulgaria	Madag.	Madagascar	S.	South, Southern
c.	cape	Man.	Manitoba	S.A.	South Australia
CA	California	MD	Maryland	Sask.	Saskatchewan
Cent. Afr. Rep.	Central African Republic	ME	Maine	SC	South Carolina
chan.	channel	Mex.	Mexico	SD	South Dakota
CO	Colorado	MI	Michigan	Sing.	Singapore
Col.	Colombia	MN	Minnesota	Switz.	Switzerland
CT	Connecticut	MO	Missouri	Tajik.	Tajikistan
Czech Rep.	Czech Republic	Moz.	Mozambique	Tanz.	Tanzania
DC	District of Columbia	MS	Mississippi	Tas.	Tasmania
DE	Delaware	MT	Montana	terr.	territory
Dem. Rep. Congo	Democratic Republic of the Congo	mt.	mountain	Thai.	Thailand
depr.	depression	mts	mountains	TN	Tennessee
des.	desert	mun.	municipality	Trin. and Tob.	Trinidad and Tobago
disp. terr.	disputed territory	N.	North, Northern	Turkm.	Turkmenistan
Dom. Rep.	Dominican Republic	nat. park	national park	TX	Texas
E.	East, Eastern	N.B.	New Brunswick	U.A.E.	United Arab Emirates
Equat. Guinea	Equatorial Guinea	NC	North Carolina	U.K.	United Kingdom
esc.	escarpment	ND	North Dakota	Ukr.	Ukraine
est.	estuary	NE	Nebraska	U.S.A.	United States of America
Eth.	Ethiopia	Neth.	Netherlands	UT	Utah
Fin.	Finland	Nfld. and Lab.	Newfoundland and Labrador	Uttar Prad.	Uttar Pradesh
FL	Florida	NH	New Hampshire	Uzbek.	Uzbekistan
for.	forest	NJ	New Jersey	VA	Virginia
Fr. Guiana	French Guiana	NM	New Mexico	Venez.	Venezuela
Fr. Polynesia	French Polynesia	N.S.	Nova Scotia	Vic.	Victoria
F.Y.R.O.M.	Former Yugoslav Republic of Macedonia	N.S.W.	New South Wales	vol.	volcano
g.	gulf	N.T.	Northern Territory	VT	Vermont
GA	Georgia	NV	Nevada	W.	West, Western
Guat.	Guatemala	N.W.T.	Northwest Territories	WA	Washington
hd	headland	NY	New York	W.A.	Western Australia
HI	Hawaii	N.Z.	New Zealand	WI	Wisconsin
Hima. Prad.	Himachal Pradesh	OH	Ohio	WV	West Virginia
H.K.	Hong Kong	OK	Oklahoma	WY	Wyoming
Hond.	Honduras	Ont.	Ontario	Y.T.	Yukon

1st Three Mile Opening sea chan. Australia **136** D2
2nd Three Mile Opening sea chan. Australia **136** C2
5 de Outubro Angola see **Xá-Muteba**
9 de Julio Arg. **178** D5
25 de Mayo Buenos Aires Arg. **178** D5
25 de Mayo La Pampa Arg. **178** C5
70 Mile House Canada **150** F5
100 Mile House Canada **150** F5
150 Mile House Canada **150** F4

Aabenraa Denmark **55** F9
Aachen Germany **62** G4
Aalborg Denmark **55** F8
Aalborg Bugt b. Denmark **55** G8
Aalen Germany **63** K6
Aalesund Norway see **Ålesund**
Aaley Lebanon see **Aley**
Aalo India **105** H3
Aalst Belgium **62** E4
Aanaar Fin. see **Inari**
Aarhus Denmark **55** G8
Aarlen Belgium see **Arlon**
Aars Denmark **55** F8
Aarschot Belgium **62** E4
Aasiaat Greenland **147** M3
Aath Belgium see **Ath**
Aba China **96** D1
Aba Dem. Rep. Congo **122** D3
Aba Nigeria **120** D4
Abacaxis r. Brazil **177** G4
Ābādān Iran **110** C4
Abadan Turkm. **110** E2
Ābādeh Iran **110** D4
Ābādeh Ţashk Iran **110** D4
Abadla Alg. **64** D5
Abaeté Brazil **179** B2
Abaetetuba Brazil **177** I4
Abagaytuy Russia **95** I1
Abagnar Qi China see **Xilinhot**
Abag Qi China see **Xin Hot**
Abaiang atoll Kiribati **186** H5
Abajo Peak UT U.S.A. **159** I3
Abakaliki Nigeria **120** D4
Abakan Russia **88** G2
Abakanskiy Khrebet mts Russia **88** F2
Abalak Niger **120** D3
Abana Turkey **112** D2
Abancay Peru **176** D6
Abariringa atoll Kiribati see **Kanton**
Abarkūh Iran **110** D4
Abarkūh, Kavīr-e des. Iran **110** D4
Abarshahr Iran see **Neyshābūr**
Abashiri Japan **90** G3
Abashiri-wan b. Japan **90** G3
Abasolo Mex. **161** D7
Abau P.N.G. **136** E1
Abaya, Lake Eth. **122** D3
Ābaya Hāyk' l. Eth. see **Abaya, Lake**
Ābay Wenz r. Eth./Sudan **108** E2 see **Blue Nile**
Abaza Russia **88** G2
Abba Cent. Afr. Rep. **122** B3
'Abbāsābād Eşfahān Iran **110** D3
'Abbāsābād Semnān Iran **110** E2
Abbasanta Sardinia Italy **68** C4
Abbatis Villa France see **Abbeville**
Abbe, Lake Djibouti/Eth. **108** F7
Abbeville France **62** B4
Abbeville AL U.S.A. **163** C6
Abbeville GA U.S.A. **163** D6
Abbeville LA U.S.A. **161** E6
Abbeville SC U.S.A. **163** D5
Abbey Canada **151** I5
Abbeyfeale Ireland **61** C5
Abbeytown U.K. **58** D4
Abborrträsk Sweden **54** K4
Abbot, Mount Australia **136** D4
Abbot Ice Shelf Antarctica **188** K2
Abbotsford Canada **150** F5
Abbott NM U.S.A. **157** G5
Abbott VA U.S.A. **164** E5
Abbottabad Pak. **111** I3
'Abd al 'Azīz hill Syria **113** F3
'Abd al Kūrī i. Yemen **108** H7
'Abd Allah, Khawr sea chan. Iraq/Kuwait **110** C4
Abd al Ma'asīr well Saudi Arabia **107** D4
Ābdānān Iran **110** B3
'Abdollāhābād Iran **110** D3
Abdulino Russia **51** Q5
Abéché Chad **121** F3
Ab-e Garm, Chashmeh-ye spring Iran **110** E3
Abe-gawa r. Japan **93** E4
Abellinum Italy see **Avellino**
Abel Tasman National Park N.Z. **139** D5
Abengourou Côte d'Ivoire **120** C4
Åbenrå Denmark see **Aabenraa**
Abensberg Germany **63** L6
Abeokuta Nigeria **120** D4
Aberaeron U.K. **59** C6
Aberchirder U.K. **60** G3
Abercorn Zambia see **Mbala**
Abercrombie r. Australia **138** D4
Aberdare U.K. **59** D7
Aberdaron U.K. **59** C6
Aberdaugleddau U.K. see **Milford Haven**
Aberdeen Australia **138** E4
Aberdeen H.K. China **97** [inset]
Aberdeen S. Africa **124** G7
Aberdeen U.K. **60** G3
Aberdeen SD U.S.A. **160** D2
Aberdeen Lake Canada **151** L1
Aberdovey U.K. **59** C6
Aberdyfi U.K. see **Aberdovey**
Aberfeldy U.K. **60** F4
Aberford U.K. **58** F5
Aberfoyle U.K. **60** E4
Abergavenny U.K. **59** D7
Abergwaun U.K. see **Fishguard**
Aberhonddu U.K. see **Brecon**
Abermaw U.K. see **Barmouth**
Abernathy TX U.S.A. **161** C5
Aberporth U.K. **59** C6
Abersoch U.K. **59** C6
Abertawe U.K. see **Swansea**
Aberteifi U.K. see **Cardigan**
Aberystwyth U.K. **59** C6
Abeshr Chad see **Abéché**
Abez' Russia **51** S2
Ābgāh Iran **111** E5
Abhā Saudi Arabia **108** F6
Abhar Iran **110** C2
Abiad, Bahr el r. Africa **108** D6 see **White Nile**

►Abidjan Côte d'Ivoire **120** C4
Former capital of Côte d'Ivoire (Ivory Coast).

Abijatta-Shalla National Park Eth. **122** D3
Ab-i-Kavīr salt flat Iran **110** E3
Abiko Japan **93** G3
Abilene KS U.S.A. **160** D4
Abilene TX U.S.A. **161** D5
Abingdon U.K. **59** F7
Abingdon VA U.S.A. **164** D5
Abington Reef Australia **136** E3
Abinsk Russia **112** E1
Abitau Lake Canada **151** J2
Abitibi, Lake Canada **152** E4
Abkhazia disp. terr. Georgia **113** F2
Āb Khūrak Iran **110** E3
Abminga Australia **135** F6
Abnūb Egypt **112** C6
Åbo Fin. see **Turku**
Abohar India **104** C3
Aboisso Côte d'Ivoire **120** C4
Aboite IN U.S.A. **164** C3
Abomey Benin **120** D4
Abongabong, Gunung mt. Indon. **84** B1
Abong Mbang Cameroon **120** E4
Aborlan Palawan Phil. **82** B4
Abō-tōge pass Japan **92** D2
Abou Déia Chad **121** E3
Abovyan Armenia **113** G2
Aboyne U.K. **60** G3
Abqaiq Saudi Arabia **110** C5
Abraham's Bay Bahamas **163** F8
Abramovskiy, Mys pt Russia **52** I2
Abrantes Port. **67** B4
Abra Pampa Arg. **178** C2
Abreojos, Punta pt Mex. **166** B3
'Abri Sudan **108** D5
Abrolhos Bank sea feature S. Atlantic Ocean **184** F7
Abruzzo, Lazio e Molise, Parco Nazionale d' nat. park Italy **68** E4
Absaroka Range mts WY U.S.A. **156** F3
Abtar, Jabal al hills Syria **107** C2
Abtsgmünd Germany **63** J6
Abū aḑ Ḑuhūr Syria **107** C2
Abū al Abyaḑ i. U.A.E. **110** D5
Abū al Ḩusayn, Qā' imp. l. Jordan **107** D3
Abū 'Alī i. Saudi Arabia **110** C5
Abū 'Āmūd, Wādī watercourse Jordan **107** C4
Abū 'Arīsh Saudi Arabia **108** F6
Abu 'Aweigîla well Egypt see **Abū 'Uwayqilah**
Abu Deleiq Sudan **108** D6

►Abu Dhabi U.A.E. **110** D5
Capital of the United Arab Emirates.

Abū Du'ān Syria **107** D1
Abu Gubeiha Sudan **108** D7
Abū Ḩafnah, Wādī watercourse Jordan **107** D3
Abu Haggag Egypt see **Ra's al Ḩikmah**
Abū Ḩallūfah, Jabal hill Jordan **107** C4
Abu Hamed Sudan **108** D6

►Abuja Nigeria **120** D4
Capital of Nigeria.

Abū Jifān well Saudi Arabia **110** B5
Abū Jurdhān Jordan **107** B4
Abū Kamāl Syria **113** F4
Abukuma-gawa r. Japan **93** G1
Abukuma-kōchi plat. Japan **93** G2
Abu Matariq Sudan **121** F3
Abumombazi Dem. Rep. Congo **122** C3
Abu Musa i. The Gulf see **Abū Mūsá, Jazīreh-ye**
Abū Mūsá, Jazīreh-ye i. The Gulf **110** D5
Abunã r. Bol. **176** E5
Abunã Brazil **176** E5
Ābune Yosēf mt. Eth. **108** E7
Abū Nujaym Libya **121** E1
Abū Qa'ţūr Syria **107** C2
Abū Rawthah, Jabal mt. Egypt **107** B5
Aburazaka-tōge pass Japan **92** C3
Aburo mt. Dem. Rep. Congo **122** D3
Abu Road India **101** G4
Abū Rujmayn, Jabal mts Syria **107** D2
Abū Rûtha, Gebel mt. Egypt see **Abū Rawthah, Jabal**
Abū Sawādah well Saudi Arabia **110** C5
Abu Simbil Egypt see **Abū Sunbul**
Abū Sunbul Egypt **108** D5
Abū Ţarfā', Wādī watercourse Egypt **107** A5
Abut Head hd N.Z. **139** C6
Abū 'Uwayqilah well Egypt **107** B4
Abuyog Leyte Phil. **82** D4
Abu Zabad Sudan **108** C7
Abū Ẓaby U.A.E. see **Abu Dhabi**
Abūzam Iran **110** C4
Abū Zanīmah Egypt **112** D5
Abu Zenîma Egypt see **Abū Zanīmah**
Abyad Sudan **108** C7
Abyaḑ, Jabal al mts Syria **107** C2
Abyār al Ḩakīm well Libya **112** A5
Abydos Australia **134** B5
Abyei Sudan **108** C8
Abyssinia country Africa see **Ethiopia**
Academician Vernadskiy research station Antarctica see **Vernadsky**
Academy Bay Russia see **Akademii, Zaliv**
Acadia prov. Canada see **Nova Scotia**
Acadia National Park ME U.S.A. **162** G2
Açailândia Brazil **177** I5
Acajutla El Salvador **167** H6
Acamarachi mt. Chile see **Pili, Cerro**
Acambaro Mex. **167** E4
Acampamento de Caça do Mucusso Angola **123** C5
Acancéh Mex. **167** H4
Acandí Col. **176** C2
A Cañiza Spain **67** B2
Acaponeta Mex. **168** C4
Acapulco Mex. **168** E5
Acapulco de Juárez Mex. see **Acapulco**
Acará Brazil **177** I4
Acarai Mountains hills Brazil/Guyana **177** G3
Acaraú Brazil **177** J4
Acaray, Represa de resr Para. **178** E3
Acarigua Venez. **176** E2
Acatlán Mex. **168** E5
Acatzingo Mex. **167** F5
Acayucán Mex. **167** G5
Accho Israel see **'Akko**
Accomac VA U.S.A. **165** H5
Accomack VA U.S.A. see **Accomac**

►Accra Ghana **120** C4
Capital of Ghana.

Accrington U.K. **58** E5
Aceh admin. dist. Indon. **84** B1
Ach r. Germany **63** L6
Achacachi Bol. **176** E7
Achaguas Venez. **176** E2
Achalpur India **104** D5
Achampet India **106** C2
Achan Russia see **Bolon'**
Achayvayam Russia **77** S3
Achchen Russia **148** D2
Acheh admin. dist. Indon. see **Aceh**
Acheng China **90** B3
Achhota India **106** D1
Achi Japan **92** D3
Achicourt France **62** C4
Achill Ireland **61** C4
Achillbeg Island Ireland **61** C4
Achill Island Ireland **61** B4
Achiltibuie U.K. **60** D2
Achim Germany **63** J1
Achin admin. dist. Indon. see **Aceh**
Achinsk Russia **76** K4
Achit Russia **51** R4
Achit Nuur l. Mongolia **94** B1
Achkhoy-Martan Russia **113** G2
Achna Cyprus **107** A2
Achnasheen U.K. **60** D3
Acıgöl l. Turkey **69** M6
Acıpayam Turkey **69** M6
Acireale Sicily Italy **68** F6
Ackerman MS U.S.A. **161** F5
Ackley IA U.S.A. **160** E3
Acklins Island Bahamas **163** F8
Acle U.K. **59** I6

►Aconcagua, Cerro mt. Arg. **178** B4
Highest mountain in South America.

Acopiara Brazil **177** K5
A Coruña Spain **67** B2
Acoyapa Nicaragua **166** [inset] I7
Acquaviva delle Fonti Italy **68** G4
Acqui Terme Italy **68** C2
Acra NY U.S.A. **165** H2
Acragas Sicily Italy see **Agrigento**
Acraman, Lake salt flat Australia **137** A7
Acre r. Brazil **176** E6
Acre Israel see **'Akko**
Acre, Bay of Israel see **Haifa, Bay of**
Acri Italy **68** G5
Ács Hungary **57** Q7
Actaeon Group is Fr. Polynesia see **Actéon, Groupe**
Actéon, Groupe is Fr. Polynesia **187** K7
Acton Canada **164** E2
Acton CA U.S.A. **158** D4
Actopán Mex. **167** F4
Açungui Brazil **179** A4
Acunum Acusio France see **Montélimar**
Ada MN U.S.A. **160** D2
Ada OH U.S.A. **164** D3
Ada OK U.S.A. **161** D5
Ada WI U.S.A. **164** B2
Adabazar Turkey see **Adapazarı**
Adaja r. Spain **67** D3
Adak AK U.S.A. **148** [inset] C6
Adak Island AK U.S.A. **148** [inset] C6
Adalia Turkey see **Antalya**
Adam Oman **109** I5
Adam, Mount hill Falkland Is **178** E8
Adamantina Brazil **179** A3
Adams IN U.S.A. **164** C4
Adams KY U.S.A. **164** D4
Adams MA U.S.A. **165** I2
Adams NY U.S.A. **165** G2
Adams, Mount WA U.S.A. **156** C3
Adams Center NY U.S.A. **165** G2
Adams Lake Canada **150** G5
Adams Mountain AK U.S.A. **149** O5
Adam's Peak Sri Lanka **106** D5
Adams Peak CA U.S.A. **158** C2

►Adamstown Pitcairn Is **187** L7
Capital of the Pitcairn Islands.

'Adan Yemen see **Aden**
Adana Turkey **107** B1
Adana prov. Turkey **107** B1
Adana Yemen see **Aden**
Adang, Teluk b. Indon. **85** G3
Adapazarı Turkey **69** N4
Adare Ireland **61** D5
Adare, Cape Antarctica **188** H2
Adavale Australia **137** D5
Ad Dabbah Sudan see **Ed Debba**
Ad Ḑabbīyah well Saudi Arabia **110** C5
Ad Dafīnah Saudi Arabia **108** F5
Ad Dahnā' des. Saudi Arabia **108** G5
Ad Dakhla W. Sahara see **Dakhla**
Ad Damir Sudan see **Ed Damer**
Ad Dammām Saudi Arabia see **Dammam**
Addanki India **106** C3
Ad Dār al Ḩamrā' Saudi Arabia **108** E4
Ad Darb Saudi Arabia **108** F6
Ad Dawādimī Saudi Arabia **108** F5
Ad Dawḩah Qatar see **Doha**
Ad Dawr Iraq **113** F4
Ad Daww plain Syria **107** C2
Ad Dayr Iraq **113** G5
Ad Dibdibah plain Saudi Arabia **110** B5
Ad Ḑiffah plat. Egypt see **Libyan Plateau**
Ad Dir'īyah Saudi Arabia **121** H2

►Addis Ababa Eth. **122** D3
Capital of Ethiopia.

Addison NY U.S.A. **165** G2
Ad Dīwānīyah Iraq **113** G5
Addlestone U.K. **59** G7
Addo Elephant National Park S. Africa **125** G7
Addoo Atoll Maldives see **Addu Atholhu**
Addu Atholhu Maldives **103** D12
Ad Duqm Oman **109** I6
Ad Duwayd well Saudi Arabia **113** F5
Ad Duwaym Sudan see **Ed Dueim**
Ad Duwayris well Saudi Arabia **110** C6
Adegaon India **104** D5
Adel GA U.S.A. **163** D6
Adel IA U.S.A. **160** E3

►Adelaide Australia **137** B7
Capital of South Australia.

Adelaide r. Australia **134** E3
Adelaide Bahamas **163** E7
Adelaide Island Antarctica **188** L2
Adelaide River Australia **134** E3
Adele Island Australia **134** C3
Adélie Coast Antarctica **188** G2
Adélie Land reg. Antarctica **188** G2
Adelong Australia **138** D5
Aden Yemen **108** F7
Aden, Gulf of Somalia/Yemen **108** G7
Adena OH U.S.A. **164** E3
Adenau Germany **62** G4
Adendorf Germany **63** K1
Aderbissinat Niger **120** D3
Aderno Sicily Italy see **Adrano**
Adesar India **104** B5
Adhan, Jabal mt. U.A.E. **110** E5
Adh Dhāyūf well Saudi Arabia **113** G6
'Adhfā' well Saudi Arabia **113** F5
'Ādhirīyāt, Jibāl al mts Jordan **107** C4
Adi i. Indon. **81** I7
Ādī Ārk'ay Eth. **108** E7
Adige r. Italy **68** E2
Ādīgrat Eth. **122** D2
Adilabad India **106** C2
Adilcevaz Turkey **113** F3
Adin CA U.S.A. **156** C4
Adīrī Libya **121** E2
Adirondack Mountains NY U.S.A. **165** H1
Ādīs Ābeba Eth. see **Addis Ababa**
Adi Ugri Eritrea see **Mendefera**
Adıyaman Turkey **112** E3
Adjud Romania **69** L1
Adjuntas, Presa de las resr Mex. **161** D8
Adlavik Islands Canada **153** K3
Admiralty Island Canada **147** H3
Admiralty Island AK U.S.A. **149** N4
Admiralty Island National Monument-Kootznoowoo Wilderness nat. park AK U.S.A. **150** C3
Admiralty Islands P.N.G. **81** L7
Ado-Ekiti Nigeria **120** D4
Adogawa Japan **92** C3
Ado-gawa r. Japan **92** C3
Adok South Sudan **108** D8
Adolfo L. Mateos Mex. **157** E8
Adolphus KY U.S.A. **164** B5
Adonara i. Indon. **83** B5
Adoni India **106** C3
Adorf (Diemelsee) Germany **63** I3
Adorf/Vogtland Germany **63** M4
Ado-Tymovo Russia **90** F2
Adour r. France **66** D5
Adra Spain **67** E5
Adramyttium Turkey see **Edremit**
Adramyttium, Gulf of Turkey see **Edremit Körfezi**
Adrano Sicily Italy **68** F6
Adrar Alg. **120** C2
Adrar hills Mali see **Ifôghas, Adrar des**
Adrar, Ḑahr hills Mauritania **120** B3
Adré Chad **121** F3
Adrian MI U.S.A. **164** C3
Adrian TX U.S.A. **161** C5
Adrianople Turkey see **Edirne**
Adrianopolis Turkey see **Edirne**
Adriatic Sea Europe **68** E2
Adua Eth. see **Ādwa**
Adunara i. Indon. see **Adonara**
Adusa Dem. Rep. Congo **122** C3
Aduwa Eth. see **Ādwa**
Adverse Well Australia **134** C5
Ādwa Eth. **108** E7
Adycha r. Russia **77** O3
Adyk Russia **53** J7
Adzopé Côte d'Ivoire **120** C4
Aegean Sea Greece/Turkey **69** K5
Aegina i. Greece see **Aigina**
Aegyptus country Africa see **Egypt**
Aela Jordan see **Al 'Aqabah**
Aelana Jordan see **Al 'Aqabah**
Aelia Capitolina Israel/West Bank see **Jerusalem**
Aelōnlaplap atoll Marshall Is see **Ailinglaplap**
Aenus Turkey see **Enez**
Aerzen Germany **63** J2
Aesernia Italy see **Isernia**
A Estrada Spain **67** B2
Afabet Eritrea **108** E6
Afanas'yevo Russia **52** L4
Affreville Alg. see **Khemis Miliana**
Afghānestān country Asia see **Afghanistan**
Afghanistan country Asia **111** G3
Afgooye Somalia **122** E3
'Afīf Saudi Arabia **108** F5
Afiun Karahissar Turkey see **Afyon**
Åfjord Norway **54** G5
Aflou Alg. **64** E5
Afmadow Somalia **122** E3
Afogados da Ingazeira Brazil **177** K5
Afognak AK U.S.A. **148** I4
Afognak Island AK U.S.A. **148** I4
A Fonsagrada Spain **67** C2
Afonso Cláudio Brazil **179** C3
Āfrēra vol. Eth. **108** F7
Africa Nova country Africa see **Tunisia**
'Afrīn Syria **107** C1
'Afrīn, Nahr r. Syria/Turkey **107** C1
Afşin Turkey **112** E3
Afsluitdijk barrage Neth. **62** F2
Afton WY U.S.A. **156** F4
Afuá Brazil **177** H4
'Afula Israel **107** B3
Afyon Turkey **69** N5
Afyonkarahisar Turkey see **Afyon**
Aga Germany **63** M4
Aga Russia **95** H1
Aga r. Russia **95** H1
Agadès Niger see **Agadez**
Agadez Niger **120** D3
Agadir Morocco **120** C1
Agalega Islands Mauritius **185** L6
Agalta, Sierra de mts Hond. **166** [inset] I6
Agan China **94** E5
Agana Guam see **Hagåtña**
Agara Georgia **113** F2
Agartala India **105** G5
Agashi India **106** B2
Agate Canada **152** E4
Agathe France see **Agde**
Agathonisi i. Greece **69** L6
Agats Indon. **81** J8
Agatsuma-gawa r. Japan **93** F2
Agatti i. India **106** B4
Agattu Island AK U.S.A. **148** [inset] A5
Agattu Strait AK U.S.A. **148** [inset] A5
Agboville Côte d'Ivoire **120** C4
Ağcabädi Azer. **113** G2
Ağdam (abandoned) Azer. **113** G3
Ağdaş Azer. **113** G2
Agdash Azer. see **Ağdaş**
Agde France **66** F5
Agdzhabedi Azer. see **Ağcabädi**
Agedabia Libya see **Ajdābiyā**
Agematsu Japan **92** D3
Agen France **66** E4
Ageo Japan **93** F3
Aggeneys S. Africa **124** D5
Aggteleki nat. park Hungary **57** R6
Aghil Dawan China **104** D1
Agiabampo Mex. **166** C3
Agiguan i. N. Mariana Is see **Aguijan**
Ağın Turkey **112** E3
Aginskoye Krasnoyarskiy Kray Russia **88** G1
Aginskoye Zabaykal'skiy Kray Russia **95** H1
Aginum France see **Agen**
Agios Dimitrios Greece **69** J6
Agios Efstratios i. Greece **69** K5
Agios Georgios i. Greece **69** J6
Agios Nikolaos Greece **69** K7
Agios Theodoros Cyprus **107** B2
Agiou Orous, Kolpos b. Greece **69** J4
Agirwat Hills Sudan **108** E6
Agisanang S. Africa **125** G4
Agnes, Mount hill Australia **135** E6
Agnew Australia **135** C6
Agnibilékrou Côte d'Ivoire **120** C4
Agnita Romania **69** K2
Agniye-Afanas'yevsk Russia **90** E2
Ago Japan see **Shima**
Agose Japan **93** F3
Ago-wan b. Japan **92** C4
Agra India **104** D4
Agrakhanskiy Poluostrov pen. Russia **113** G2
Agram Croatia see **Zagreb**
Ağrı Turkey **113** F3
Agria Gramvousa i. Greece **69** J7
Ağrı Dağı mt. Turkey see **Ararat, Mount**
Agrigan i. N. Mariana Is see **Agrihan**
Agrigento Sicily Italy **68** E6
Agrigentum Sicily Italy see **Agrigento**
Agrihan i. N. Mariana Is **81** L3
Agrinio Greece **69** I5
Agropoli Italy **68** F4
Agryz Russia **51** Q4
Ağsu Azer. **113** H2
Agta Point Phil. **82** C3
Agua, Volcán de vol. Guat. **168** F6
Agua Brava, Laguna lag. Mex. **166** D4
Água Clara Brazil **178** F2
Aguada Mex. **167** H5
Agua de Correra Mex. **167** E5
Aguadilla Puerto Rico **169** K5
Aguadulce Panama **166** [inset] J7
Agua Escondida Arg. **178** C5
Agua Fria r. AZ U.S.A. **159** G5
Agua Fria National Monument nat. park AZ U.S.A. **159** G4
Aguamilpa, Presa l. Mex. **166** D4
Aguanaval r. Mex. **161** C7
Aguanga CA U.S.A. **158** E5
Aguanish r. Canada **153** J4
Aguanqueterique Hond. **166** [inset] I6
Agua Nueva Mex. **166** D3
Aguapeí r. Brazil **179** A3
Agua Prieta Mex. **166** C2
Aguaro-Guariquito, Parque Nacional nat. park Venez. **176** E2
Aguaruto Mex. **166** D3
Aguascalientes Mex. **168** D4
Aguascalientes state Mex. **166** E4
Águas Lindas de Goiás Brazil **179** A1
Agudos Brazil **179** A3
Águeda Port. **67** B3
Aguemour reg. Alg. **120** D2
Agui Japan **92** C4
Aguié Niger **120** D3
Aguijan i. N. Mariana Is **81** L4
Aguilar CO U.S.A. **157** G5
Aguilar de Campoo Spain **67** D2
Águilas Spain **67** F5
Aguililla Mex. **166** E5

►Agulhas, Cape S. Africa **124** E8
Most southerly point of Africa.

Agulhas Basin sea feature Southern Ocean **185** J9
Agulhas Negras mt. Brazil **179** B3
Agulhas Plateau sea feature Southern Ocean **185** J8
Agulhas Ridge sea feature S. Atlantic Ocean **184** I8
Agusan r. Mindanao Phil. **82** D4
Agutaya Phil. **82** C4
Agutaya i. Phil. **82** C4
Ağva Turkey **69** M4
Agvali Russia **113** G2
Ahaggar plat. Alg. **120** D2
Ahaggar, Tassili oua-n- plat. Alg. **120** D2
Āhangarān Iran **111** F3
Ahar Iran **110** B2
Ahaura N.Z. **139** C6
Ahaus Germany **62** H2
Ahipara Bay N.Z. **139** D2
Ahiri India **106** D2
Ahklun Mountains AK U.S.A. **148** G4
Ahlen Germany **63** H3
Ahmadabad India **104** C5
Aḩmadābād Iran **111** E3
Aḩmad al Bāqir, Jabal mt. Jordan **107** B5
Ahmadī Iran **110** E5
Ahmadnagar India **106** B2
Ahmadpur East Pak. **111** H4
Ahmar Mountains mts Eth. **122** E3
Ahmedabad India see **Ahmadabad**
Ahmednagar India see **Ahmadnagar**
Ahome Mex. **166** C3
Ahorn Germany **63** K4
Ahr r. Germany **62** H4
Ahram Iran **110** C4
Ahrensburg Germany **63** K1
Āhtāri Fin. **54** N5
Ahtme Estonia **55** O7
Ahu China **97** H1
Āhū Iran **110** C4
Ahuacatlán Mex. **166** D4
Ahuachapán El Salvador **167** H6
Ahualulco Jalisco Mex. **166** E4
Ahualulco San Luis Potosí Mex. **167** E4
Ahun France **66** F3
Ahuzhen China see **Ahu**
Ahvāz Iran **110** C4
Ahwa India **106** B1
Ahwāz Iran see **Ahvāz**
Ai i. Moluccas Indon. **83** D4
Ai-Ais Namibia **124** C4
Ai-Ais Hot Springs and Fish River Canyon Park nature res. Namibia **124** C4
Aibag He r. China **95** G3
Aībak Afgh. **111** H2
Aichi pref. Japan **92** D4
Aichi-kōgen Kokutei-kōen park Japan **92** D3
Aichilik r. AK U.S.A. **149** L1
Aichwara India **104** D4
Aid OH U.S.A. **164** D4
Aigialousa Cyprus **107** B2
Aigina i. Greece **69** J6
Aigio Greece **69** J5
Aigle de Chambeyron mt. France **66** H4
Aigüestortes i Estany de Sant Maurici, Parc Nacional d' nat. park Spain **67** G2
Ai He r. China **90** B4
Aihua China see **Yunxian**
Aihui China see **Heihe**
Aijal India see **Aizawl**
Aikawa Kanagawa Japan **93** F3
Aikawa Niigata Japan **91** E5
Aiken SC U.S.A. **163** D5
Ailao Shan mts China **96** D3
Aileron Australia **134** F5
Aileu East Timor **83** C5
Ailigandi Panama **166** [inset] K7
Ailinglabelab atoll Marshall Is see **Ailinglaplap**
Ailinglaplap atoll Marshall Is **186** H5
Ailly-sur-Noye France **62** C5
Ailsa Craig Canada **164** E2
Ailsa Craig i. U.K. **60** D5
Ailt an Chorráin Ireland **61** D3
Aimere Flores Indon. **83** B5
Aimorés, Serra dos hills Brazil **179** C2
Aïn Beïda Alg. **68** B7
'Aïn Ben Tili Mauritania **120** C2
'Aïn Dâlla spring Egypt see **'Ayn Dāllah**
Aïn Defla Alg. **67** H5
Aïn Deheb Alg. **67** G6
Aïn el Hadjel Alg. **67** H6

'Ain el Maqfi *spring* Egypt *see* 'Ayn al Maqfī
Aïn el Melh Alg. 67 I6
Aïn Mdila *well* Alg. 68 B7
Aïn-M'Lila Alg. 64 F4
Aïn Oussera Alg. 67 H6
Ain Salah Alg. *see* In Salah
Aïn Sefra Alg. 64 D5
Ainsworth *NE* U.S.A. 160 D3
Aintab Turkey *see* Gaziantep
Aïn Taya Alg. 67 H5
Aïn Tédélès Alg. 67 G6
Aïn Temouchent Alg. 67 F6
'Ain Tibaghbagh *spring* Egypt *see* 'Ayn Tabaghbugh
'Ain Timeira *spring* Egypt *see* 'Ayn Tumayrah
'Ain Zeitûn Egypt *see* 'Ayn az Zaytūn
Aiquile Bol. 176 E7
Air *i.* Indon. 84 D2
Aïr, Massif de l' *mts* Niger 120 D3
Airai Palau 82 [inset]
Airaines France 62 B5
Airbangis *Sumatra* Indon. 84 B2
Airdrie Canada 150 H5
Airdrie U.K. 60 F5
Aire *r.* France 62 E5
Aire, Canal d' France 62 C4
Aire-sur-l'Adour France 66 D5
Air Force Island Canada 147 K3
Airgin Sum China 95 G3
Airhitam *r.* Indon. 85 E3
Airhitam, Teluk *b.* Indon. 85 E3
Air Muda, Tasik *l.* Malaysia 84 C1
Airpanas *Moluccas* Indon. 83 C4
Air Pedu, Tasik *l.* Malaysia 84 C1
Aisai Japan 92 C3
Aisatung Mountain Myanmar 86 A2
Aisch *r.* Germany 63 L5
Ai Shan *hill* China 95 J4
Aishihik Canada 149 M3
Aishihik Lake Canada 149 M3
Aishō Japan 92 C3
Aisne *r.* France 62 D5
Aïssa, Djebel *mt.* Alg. 64 D5
Aitamännikkö Fin. 54 N3
Aitana *mt.* Spain 67 F4
Aït Benhaddou *tourist site* Morocco 64 C5
Aiterach *r.* Germany 63 M6
Aitkin *MN* U.S.A. 160 E2
Aitō Japan 92 C3
Aiud Romania 69 J1
Aiwokako Passage Palau 82 [inset]
Aix France *see* Aix-en-Provence
Aix-en-Provence France 66 G5
Aix-la-Chapelle Germany *see* Aachen
Aix-les-Bains France 66 G4
Aiyina *i.* Greece *see* Aigina
Aiyion Greece *see* Aigio
Aizawl India 105 H5
Aizkraukle Latvia 55 N8
Aizpute Latvia 55 L8
Aizuwakamatsu Japan 91 E5
Ajaccio *Corsica* France 66 I6
Ajalpán Mex. 167 F5
Ajanta India 106 B1
Ajanta Range *hills* India *see* Sahyadriparvat Range
Ajaureforsen Sweden 54 I4
Ajax Canada 164 F2
Ajayameru India *see* Ajmer
Ajban U.A.E. 110 D5
Aj Bogdīn Nuruu *mts* Mongolia 94 C2
Ajdābiyā Libya 121 F1
a-Jiddét *des.* Oman *see* Ḥarāsīs, Jiddat al
Ajiro Japan 93 F3
Ajjer, Tassili n' *plat.* Alg. 120 D2
'Ajlūn Jordan 107 B3
'Ajman U.A.E. 110 D5
Ajmer India 104 C4
Ajmer-Merwara India *see* Ajmer
Ajnala India 104 C3
Ajo *AZ* U.S.A. 159 G5
Ajo, Mount *AZ* U.S.A. 159 G5
Ajrestān Afgh. 111 G3
Ajuchitlán Mex. 167 E5
Ajuy *Panay* Phil. 82 C4
Ajyyap Turkm. 110 D2
Akabane Japan 92 D4
Akabori Japan 93 F2
Akademii, Zaliv *b.* Russia 90 E1
Akademii Nauk, Khrebet *mt.* Tajik. *see* Akademiyai Fanho, Qatorkŭhi
Akademiyai Fanho, Qatorkŭhi *mt.* Tajik. 111 H2
Akadyr Kazakh. 102 D2
Akagera National Park Rwanda 122 D4
Akagi Japan 93 F2
Akagi-yama *vol.* Japan 93 F2
Akaishi-dake *mt.* Japan 93 E3
Akaishi-sanmyaku *mts* Japan 93 D4
Akalkot India 106 C2
Akama, Akra *c.* Cyprus *see* Arnauti, Cape
Akamagaseki Japan *see* Shimonoseki
Akan Kokuritsu-kōen Japan 90 G4
Akaroa N.Z. 139 D6
Akas *reg.* India 96 B3
'Akāshāt Iraq 113 E4
Akashi Japan 92 A4
Akashi-kaikyō *str.* Japan 92 A4
Akashina Japan 93 D2
Akbalyk Kazakh. 98 B3
Akbarābād Iran 113 I5
Akbarpur *Uttar Prad.* India 104 E4
Akbarpur *Uttar Prad.* India 105 E4
Akbaur Kazakh. 98 A2
Akbaytal, Pereval *pass* Tajik. 111 I2
Akbaytal Pass Tajik. *see* Akbaytal, Pereval
Akbez Turkey 107 C1
Akbulak *Vostochnyy Kazakhstan* Kazakh. 98 B2
Akbulak *Vostochnyy Kazakhstan* Kazakh. 98 D2
Akçadağ Turkey 112 E3
Akçakale Turkey 107 D1
Akçakoca Turkey 69 N4
Akçakoca Dağları *mts* Turkey 69 N4
Akçakoyunlu Turkey 107 C1
Akçalı Dağları *mts* Turkey 107 A1
Akchâr *reg.* Mauritania 120 B3
Akchi Kazakh. *see* Akshi
Akdağlar *mts* Turkey 69 M6
Akdağmadeni Turkey 112 D3
Akdere Turkey 107 A1
Akechi Japan 92 D3
Akelamo *Halmahera* Indon. 83 C3
Akelamo *Halmahera* Indon. 83 D2
Akeno *Ibaraki* Japan 93 G2
Akeno *Yamanashi* Japan 93 E3
Åkersberga Sweden 55 K7
Akersloot Neth. 62 E2
Aketi Dem. Rep. Congo 122 C3
Akgyr Erezi *hills* Turkm. 110 D1
Akhali-Afoni Georgia *see* Akhali Atoni
Akhali Atoni Georgia 113 F2
Akhḍar, Al Jabal al *mts* Libya 121 F1
Akhḍar, Jabal *mts* Oman 110 E6
Akhiok *AK* U.S.A. 148 I4
Akhisar Turkey 69 L5
Akhnoor India 104 C2
Akhsu Azer. *see* Ağsu
Akhta Armenia *see* Hrazdan
Akhtarīn Syria 107 C1
Akhtubinsk Russia 53 J6
Akhty Russia 113 G2
Akhtyrka Ukr. *see* Okhtyrka
Aki Japan 91 D6
Akiachak *AK* U.S.A. 148 G3
Akiéni Gabon 122 B4
Akimiski Island Canada 152 E3
Akiruno Japan 93 F3
Akishma *r.* Russia 90 D1
Akita Japan 91 F5
Akiyama-gawa *r.* Japan 93 F2
Akjoujt Mauritania 120 B3
Akkajaure *l.* Sweden 54 J3
Akkani Russia 148 E2
Akkem Russia 98 D2
Akkerman Ukr. *see* Bilhorod-Dnistrovs'kyy
Akkeshi Japan 90 G4
'Akko Israel 107 B3
Akkol' *Akmolinskaya Oblast'* Kazakh. 102 D1
Akkol' *Almatinskaya Oblast'* Kazakh. 98 A3
Akkol' *Atyrauskaya Oblast'* Kazakh. 53 K7
Akku Kazakh. 102 E1
Akkul' Kazakh. *see* Akkol'
Akkuş Turkey 112 E2
Akkyr, Gory *hills* Turkm. *see* Akgyr Erezi
Aklavik Canada 149 N1
Aklera India 104 D4
Ak-Mechet Kazakh. *see* Kyzylorda
Akmeņrags *pt* Latvia 55 L8
Akmeqit China 99 B5
Akmola Kazakh. *see* Astana
Akmolinsk Kazakh. *see* Astana
Ak-Moyun Kyrg. 98 B4
Akobo South Sudan 121 G4
Akobo Wenz *r.* Eth./South Sudan 122 D3
Akokan Niger 120 D3
Akola India 106 C1
Akom II Cameroon 120 E4
Akongkür China 98 B4
Akonolinga Cameroon 120 E4
Akordat Eritrea 108 E6
Akören Turkey 112 D3
Akot India 104 D5
Akpatok Island Canada 153 I1
Akqi China 98 B4
Akra, Jabal *mt.* Syria/Turkey *see* Aqra', Jabal al
Akranes Iceland 54 [inset 1]
Åkrehamn Norway 55 D7
Akréréb Niger 120 D3
Akron *CO* U.S.A. 160 C3
Akron *IN* U.S.A. 164 B3
Akron *OH* U.S.A. 164 E3
Akrotiri Bay Cyprus 107 A2
Akrotirion Bay Cyprus *see* Akrotiri Bay
Akrotiriou, Kolpos *b.* Cyprus *see* Akrotiri Bay
Akrotiri Sovereign Base Area *military base* Cyprus 107 A2
Aksai Chin *terr.* Asia 104 D2
Aksaray Turkey 112 D3
Aksay China 98 F5
Aksay Kazakh. 51 Q5
Ak-Say *r.* Kyrg. 109 M1
Aksay Russia 53 H7
Aksayqin Hu *l.* China 99 B6
Akşehir Turkey 69 N5
Akşehir Gölü *l.* Turkey 69 N5
Akseki Turkey 112 C3
Aksha Russia 95 H1
Akshatau Kazakh. 98 A3
Akshi Kazakh. 102 E3
Akshiganak Kazakh. 102 B2
Akshukyr Kazakh. 113 H2
Aksu *Xinjiang* China 98 C4
Aksu *Xinjiang* China 98 C4
Aksu *Almatinskaya Oblast'* Kazakh. 98 B3
Aksu *Pavlodarskaya Oblast'* Kazakh. 102 E1
Aksu *r.* Kazakh. 98 B3
Aksu *r.* Tajik. *see* Oqsu
Aksu *r.* Turkey 69 N6
Aksuat Kazakh. 102 F2
Aksu-Ayuly Kazakh. 102 D2
Aksubayevo Russia 53 K5
Aksu He *r.* China 98 C4
Āksum Eth. 108 E7
Aksuyek Kazakh. 98 A3
Aktag *mt.* China 99 D5
Aktam China 98 B5
Aktas Dağı *mt.* Turkey 113 G3
Aktash Russia 98 D2
Aktau *Karagandinskaya Oblast'* Kazakh. 98 A2
Aktau *Mangystauskaya Oblast'* Kazakh. 100 E2
Akto China 98 B5
Aktobe Kazakh. 100 E1
Aktogay *Karagandinskaya Oblast'* Kazakh. 102 E2
Aktogay *Vostochnyy Kazakhstan* Kazakh. 102 E2
Aktsyabrski Belarus 53 F5
Ak-Tüz Kyrg. 98 A4
Aktyubinsk Kazakh. *see* Aktobe
Akulivik Canada 147 K3
Akune Japan 91 C6
Akun Island *AK* U.S.A. 148 F5
Akure Nigeria 120 D4
Akuressa Sri Lanka 106 D5
Akureyri Iceland 54 [inset 1]
Akusha Russia 53 J8
Akutan *AK* U.S.A. 148 F5
Akutan Island *AK* U.S.A. 148 F5
Akutan Pass *sea chan. AK* U.S.A. 148 F5
Akwanga Nigeria 120 D4
Akxokesay China 99 E5
Akyab Myanmar *see* Sittwe
Akyatan Gölü *salt l.* Turkey 107 B1
Akyazı Turkey 69 N4
Akzhal *Karagandinskaya Oblast'* Kazakh. 98 A3
Akzhal *Vostochnyy Kazakhstan* Kazakh. 98 C2
Akzhar Kazakh. 98 C3
Akzhartas Kazakh. 98 A3
Akzhaykyn, Ozero *salt l.* Kazakh. 102 C3
Ål Norway 55 F6
'Alā, Jabal al *hills* Syria 107 C2
Alabama *r. AL* U.S.A. 163 C6
Alabama *state* U.S.A. 163 C5
Alabaster *AL* U.S.A. 163 C5
Alabaster *MI* U.S.A. 164 D1
Alabel Phil. 82 D5
Al 'Abṭīyah *well* Iraq 113 G5
Alaca Turkey 112 D2
Alacahan Turkey 112 E3
Alaçam Turkey 112 D2
Alaçam Dağları *mts* Turkey 69 M5
Alacant Spain *see* Alicante
Alaçatı Turkey 69 L5
Alacrán, Arrecife *reef* Mex. 167 H4
Aladağ Turkey 112 D3
Ala Dağlar *mts* Turkey 113 F3
Ala Dağları *mts* Turkey 112 D3
Al 'Adam Libya 112 A5
Al Aflāj *reg.* Saudi Arabia 110 B6
Alaganik *AK* U.S.A. 149 K3
Alag-Erdene Mongolia 94 D1
Alag Hayrhan Uul *mt.* Mongolia 94 C2
Alag Hu *l.* China 94 D5
Alagir Russia 113 G2
Alagnak *r. AK* U.S.A. 148 H4
Alagoinhas Brazil 179 D1
Ala Gou *r.* China 98 E4
Alah *r. Mindanao* Phil. 82 D5
Alahanpanjang *Sumatra* Indon. 84 C3
Alahärmä Fin. 54 M5
Al Aḥmadī Kuwait 110 C4
Alai Range *mts* Asia 111 H2
Ālaivān Iran 110 D3
Ālājah Syria 107 B2
Alajärvi Fin. 54 M5
Al 'Ajrūd *well* Egypt 107 B4
Alajuela Costa Rica 166 [inset] I7
Alakanuk *AK* U.S.A. 148 F3
Al Akhḍar Saudi Arabia 112 E5
Alakol', Ozero *salt l.* Kazakh. 102 F2
Alaktak *AK* U.S.A. 148 I1
Ala Kul *salt l.* Kazakh. *see* Alakol', Ozero
Alakurtti Russia 54 Q3
Al 'Alamayn Egypt 112 C5
Al 'Alayyah Saudi Arabia 108 F6
Alama Somalia 122 E3
Alamagan *i.* N. Mariana Is 81 L3
Alamaguan *i.* N. Mariana Is *see* Alamagan
Al 'Amārah Iraq 113 G5
'Alam ar Rūm, Ra's *pt* Egypt 112 B5
'Alāmarvdasht *watercourse* Iran 110 D4
Alameda *CA* U.S.A. 158 B3
'Alam el Rûm, Râs *pt* Egypt *see* 'Alam ar Rūm, Ra's
Al Amghar *waterhole* Iraq 113 G5
Alamikamba Nicaragua 166 [inset] I6
Alaminos *Luzon* Phil. 82 B2
Al 'Āmirīyah Egypt 112 C5
Alamítos, Sierra de los *mt.* Mex. 166 E3
Alamo *GA* U.S.A. 163 D5
Alamo *NV* U.S.A. 159 F3
Alamo Dam *AZ* U.S.A. 159 G4
Alamogordo *NM* U.S.A. 157 G6
Alamo Heights *TX* U.S.A. 161 D6
Alamos *Sonora* Mex. 166 C2
Alamos *Sonora* Mex. 166 C3
Alamos *r.* Mex. 167 E3
Alamos, Sierra *mts* Mex. 166 C3
Alamosa *CO* U.S.A. 157 G5
Alamos de Peña Mex. 166 D2
Alampur India 106 C3
Alan Myanmar *see* Aunglan
Alanäs Sweden 54 I4
Åland *is* Fin. *see* Åland Islands
Aland *r.* Germany 63 L1
Aland India 106 C2
Al Andarīn Syria 107 C2
Åland Islands Fin. 55 K6
Alando China 99 F7
Alandur India 106 D3
Alang *Kalimantan* Indon. 85 G1
Alangalang, Tanjung *pt* Indon. 85 G3
Alang Besar *i. Sumatra* Indon. 84 C2
Alanggantang *i.* Indon. 84 D3
Alanson *MI* U.S.A. 164 C1
Alanya Turkey 112 D3
Alaplı Turkey 69 N4
Alappuzha India 106 C4
Alapuzha India *see* Alappuzha
Al 'Aqabah Jordan 107 B5
'Alāqahdārī Gēlān Afgh. 111 G3
'Alāqahdārī Gulistān Afgh. 111 F3
'Alāqahdārī Shāh Jōy Afgh. 111 G3
'Alāqahdārī Shumūlzaī Afgh. 111 G4
'Alāqahdārī-ye Kirān wa Munjān Afgh. 111 H2
Al 'Aqīq Saudi Arabia 108 F5
Al 'Arabīyah as Sa'ūdīyah *country* Asia *see* Saudi Arabia
Alarcón, Embalse de *resr* Spain 67 E4
Al 'Arīsh Egypt 107 A4
Al Arṭāwīyah Saudi Arabia 108 G4
Alas *Sumbawa* Indon. 85 G5
Alas, Selat *sea chan.* Indon. 85 G5
Alaşehir Turkey 69 M5
Alashiya *country* Asia *see* Cyprus
Al Ashmūnayn Egypt 112 C6
Alaska *state* U.S.A. 149 L3
Alaska, Gulf of *AK* U.S.A. 149 K4
Alaska Highway Canada/U.S.A. 149 L3
Alaska Maritime National Wildlife Refuge *nature res. AK* U.S.A. 148 [inset] B5
Alaska Peninsula *AK* U.S.A. 148 G5
Alaska Peninsula National Wildlife Refuge *nature res. AK* U.S.A. 148 H4
Alaska Range *mts AK* U.S.A. 149 J3
Alas Purwo, Taman Nasional *nat. park* Indon. 85 F5
Ālät Azer. 113 H3
Alat Uzbek. *see* Olot
Alataw Shankou *pass* China/Kazakh. *see* Dzungarian Gate
Alatna *AK* U.S.A. 148 I2
Alatna *r. AK* U.S.A. 148 I2
Al Atwā' *well* Saudi Arabia 113 F5
Alatyr' Russia 53 J5
Alatyr' *r.* Russia 53 J5
Alausí Ecuador 176 C4
Alaverdi Armenia 113 G2
Alavieska Fin. 54 N4
'Alavījeh Iran 110 C3
Alavus Fin. 54 M5
Alawbum Myanmar 86 B1
Alawoona Australia 137 C7
Alay Kyrka Toosu *mts* Asia *see* Alai Range
Al 'Ayn Oman 110 E6
Al 'Ayn U.A.E. 110 D5
Alayskiy Khrebet *mts* Asia *see* Alai Range
Al 'Azīzīyah Iraq 113 G4
Al 'Azīzīyah Libya 65 G5
Al Azraq al Janūbī Jordan 107 C4
Alba Italy 68 C2
Alba *MI* U.S.A. 164 C1
Al Bāb Syria 107 C1
Albacete Spain 67 F4
Al Badī' Saudi Arabia 110 B6
Al Bādiyah al Janūbīyah *hill* Iraq 113 G5
Al Bahrayn *country* Asia *see* Bahrain
Alba Iulia Romania 69 J1
Al Bajā' *well* U.A.E. 110 C5
Albājī Iran 110 C4
Al Bakhrā *well* Saudi Arabia 110 B5
Albanel, Lac *l.* Canada 153 G4
Albania *country* Europe 69 H4
Albany Australia 135 B8
Albany *r.* Canada 152 E3
Albany *GA* U.S.A. 163 C6
Albany *IN* U.S.A. 164 C3
Albany *KY* U.S.A. 164 C5
Albany *MO* U.S.A. 160 E3

▶Albany *NY* U.S.A. 165 I2
Capital of New York state.

Albany *OH* U.S.A. 164 D4
Albany *OR* U.S.A. 156 C3
Albany *TX* U.S.A. 161 D5
Albany Downs Australia 138 D1
Al Bāridah *hills* Saudi Arabia 107 D5
Al Başrah Iraq *see* Basra
Al Baṭḥa' *marsh* Iraq 113 G5
Al Bāṭinah *reg.* Oman 110 E5
Albatross Bay Australia 136 C2
Albatross Island Australia 137 [inset]
Al Bawītī Egypt 112 C5
Al Bayḍā' Libya 108 B3
Al Bayḍā' Yemen 108 G7
Albay Gulf *Luzon* Phil. 82 C3
Albemarle *NC* U.S.A. 163 D5
Albemarle Island *Galápagos* Ecuador *see* Isabela, Isla
Albemarle Sound *sea chan. NC* U.S.A. 162 E5
Albenga Italy 68 C2
Alberche *r.* Spain 67 D4
Alberga Australia 137 A5
Alberga *watercourse* Australia 137 A5
Albergaria-a-Velha Port. 67 B3
Albert Australia 138 C4
Albert France 62 C5
Albert, Lake Dem. Rep. Congo/Uganda 122 D3
Albert, Parc National *nat. park* Dem. Rep. Congo *see* Virunga, Parc National des
Alberta *prov.* Canada 150 H4
Alberta *VA* U.S.A. 165 G5
Albert Kanaal *canal* Belgium 62 F4
Albert Lea *MN* U.S.A. 160 E3
Albert Nile *r.* South Sudan/Uganda 121 G4
Alberto de Agostini, Parque Nacional *nat. park* Chile 178 B8
Alberton S. Africa 125 I4
Alberton *MT* U.S.A. 156 E3
Albert Town Bahamas 163 F8
Albertville Dem. Rep. Congo *see* Kalemie
Albertville France 66 H4
Albertville *AL* U.S.A. 163 C5
Albestroff France 62 G6
Albi France 66 F5
Albia *IA* U.S.A. 160 E3
Al Biḍah *des.* Saudi Arabia 110 C5
Albina Suriname 177 H2
Albino Italy 68 C2
Albion *CA* U.S.A. 158 B2
Albion *IL* U.S.A. 160 F4
Albion *IN* U.S.A. 164 C3
Albion *MI* U.S.A. 164 C2
Albion *NE* U.S.A. 160 D3
Albion *NY* U.S.A. 165 F2
Albion *PA* U.S.A. 164 E3
Al Biqā' *valley* Lebanon *see* El Béqaa
Al Bi'r Saudi Arabia 112 E5
Al Birk Saudi Arabia 108 F6
Al Biyāḍh *reg.* Saudi Arabia 108 G5
Alborán, Isla de *i.* Spain 67 E6
Alboran Sea *sea* Europe 67 E5
Ålborg Denmark *see* Aalborg
Ålborg Bugt *b.* Denmark *see* Aalborg Bugt
Albro Australia 136 D4
Al Budayyi' Bahrain 110 C5
Albufeira Port. 67 B5
Al Buḥayrāt al Murrah *lakes* Egypt *see* Bitter Lakes
Albuquerque *NM* U.S.A. 157 G6
Albuquerque, Cayos de *is* Caribbean Sea 166 [inset] J6
Al Burayj Syria 107 C2
Al Buraymī Oman 110 D5
Al Burdī Libya 112 B5
Al Burj Jordan 107 B5
Alburquerque Spain 67 C4
Albury Australia 138 C6
Al Buşayrah Syria 113 F4
Al Buşayṭā' *plain* Saudi Arabia 107 D4
Al Bushūk *well* Saudi Arabia 110 B4
Alcácer do Sal Port. 67 B4
Alcalá de Henares Spain 67 E3
Alcalá la Real Spain 67 E5
Alcamo *Sicily* Italy 68 E6
Alcañiz Spain 67 F3
Alcántara Spain 67 C4
Alcantara Lake Canada 151 I2
Alcaraz Spain 67 E4
Alcázar de San Juan Spain 67 E4
Alcazarquivir Morocco *see* Ksar el Kebir
Alchevs'k Ukr. 53 H6
Alcobaça Brazil 179 D2
Alcoi Spain *see* Alcoy-Alcoi
Alcoota Australia 134 F5
Alcova *WY* U.S.A. 156 G4
Alcoy Spain *see* Alcoy-Alcoi
Alcoy-Alcoi Spain 67 F4
Alcúdia Spain 67 H4
Aldabra Islands Seychelles 123 E4
Aldama *Chihuahua* Mex. 166 D2
Aldama *Tamaulipas* Mex. 167 F4
Aldan Russia 77 N4
Aldan *r.* Russia 77 N3
Al Dayyen *town* Qatar 110 C5
Alde *r.* U.K. 59 I6
Aldeboarn Neth. 62 F1
Aldeburgh U.K. 59 I6
Alder Creek *NY* U.S.A. 165 H2
Alderney *i.* Channel Is 59 E9
Alder Peak *CA* U.S.A. 158 C4
Aldershot U.K. 59 G7
Al Dhafrah *reg.* U.A.E. 110 D6
Aldingham U.K. 58 D4
Aldridge U.K. 59 F6
Aleg Mauritania 120 B3
Alegre *Espírito Santo* Brazil 179 C3
Alegre *Minas Gerais* Brazil 179 B2
Alegrete Brazil 178 E3
Alegros Mountain *NM* U.S.A. 159 I4
Aleknagik *AK* U.S.A. 148 H4
Aleknagik, Lake *AK* U.S.A. 148 H4
Aleksandra, Mys *hd* Russia 90 E1
Aleksandriya Ukr. *see* Oleksandriya
Aleksandro-Nevskiy Russia 53 I5
Aleksandrovsk Armenia *see* Gyumri
Aleksandrov Russia 52 H4
Aleksandrov Gay Russia 53 K6
Aleksandrovsk Russia 51 R4
Aleksandrovsk Ukr. *see* Zaporizhzhya
Aleksandrovsky Russia *see* Aleksandrovsk
Aleksandrovskoye Russia 113 F1
Aleksandrovsk-Sakhalinskiy Russia 90 F2
Aleksandry, Zemlya *i.* Russia 76 F1
Alekseyevka *Akmolinskaya Oblast'* Kazakh. *see* Akkol'
Alekseyevka *Vostochnyy Kazakhstan* Kazakh. *see* Terekty
Alekseyevka *Amurskaya Oblast'* Russia 90 B1
Alekseyevka *Belgorodskaya Oblast'* Russia 53 H6
Alekseyevka *Belgorodskaya Oblast'* Russia 53 H6
Alekseyevskaya Russia 53 I6
Alekseyevskoye Russia 52 K5
Aleksin Russia 53 H5
Aleksinac Serbia 69 I3
Alèmbé Gabon 122 B4
Ålen Norway 54 G5
Alençon France 66 E2
Alenquer Brazil 177 H4
'Alenuihāhā Channel *HI* U.S.A. 157 [inset]
Alep Syria *see* Aleppo
Aleppo Syria 107 C1
Alert Canada 147 L1
Alerta Peru 176 D6
Alès France 66 G4
Aleşd Romania 69 J1
Aleshki Ukr. *see* Tsyurupyns'k
Aleşkirt Turkey *see* Eleşkirt
Alessandria Italy 68 C2
Alessio Albania *see* Lezhë
Ålesund Norway 54 E5
Aleutian Basin *sea feature* Bering Sea 186 H2
Aleutian Islands *AK* U.S.A. 146 A4
Aleutian Range *mts AK* U.S.A. 148 H4
Aleutian Trench *sea feature* N. Pacific Ocean 186 I2
Alevina, Mys *c.* Russia 77 Q4
Alevişik Turkey *see* Samandağı
Alexander *ND* U.S.A. 160 C2
Alexander, Kap *c.* Greenland *see* Ullersuaq
Alexander, Mount *hill* Australia 136 B2
Alexander Archipelago *is AK* U.S.A. 149 M4
Alexander Bay *b.* Namibia/S. Africa 124 C5
Alexander Bay S. Africa 124 C5
Alexander City *AL* U.S.A. 163 C5
Alexander Island Antarctica 188 L2
Alexandra Australia 138 B6
Alexandra N.Z. 139 B7
Alexandra, Cape S. Georgia 178 I8
Alexandra Channel India 87 A4
Alexandra Land *i.* Russia *see* Aleksandry, Zemlya
Alexandreia Greece 69 J4
Alexandretta Turkey *see* İskenderun
Alexandria Afgh. *see* Ghaznī
Alexandria Canada 165 H1
Alexandria Egypt 112 C5
Alexandria Romania 69 K3
Alexandria S. Africa 125 H7
Alexandria Turkm. *see* Mary
Alexandria U.K. 60 E5
Alexandria *IN* U.S.A. 164 C3
Alexandria *KY* U.S.A. 164 C4
Alexandria *LA* U.S.A. 161 E6
Alexandria *VA* U.S.A. 165 G4
Alexandria Arachoton Afgh. *see* Kandahār
Alexandria Areion Afgh. *see* Herāt
Alexandria Bay *NY* U.S.A. 165 H1
Alexandria Prophthasia Afgh. *see* Farāh
Alexandrina, Lake Australia 137 B7
Alexandroupoli Greece 69 K4
Alexis *r.* Canada 153 K3
Alexis Creek Canada 150 F4
Aley Lebanon 107 B3
Aleyak Iran 110 E2
Aleysk Russia 88 E2
Alf Germany 62 H4
Al Farwānīyah Kuwait 110 B4
Al Fas Morocco *see* Fès
Al Fatḥah Iraq 113 F4
Al Fāw Iraq 113 H5
Al Fayyūm Egypt 112 C5
Alfeld (Leine) Germany 63 J3
Alfenas Brazil 179 B3
Alford U.K. 58 H5
Alfred *ME* U.S.A. 165 J2
Alfred *NY* U.S.A. 165 G2
Alfred and Marie Range *hills* Australia 135 D6
Alfred M. Terrazas Mex. 167 F4
Al Fujayrah U.A.E. *see* Fujairah
Al Fuqahā' Libya 121 E2
Al Furāt *r.* Asia 107 D2 *see* Euphrates
Alga Kazakh. 102 A2
Ålgård Norway 55 D7
Algarrobo del Aguilla Arg. 178 C5
Algarve *reg.* Port. 67 B5
Algeciras Spain 67 D5
Algemesí Spain 67 F4
Algena Eritrea 108 E6
Alger Alg. *see* Algiers
Alger *MI* U.S.A. 164 C1

▶Algeria *country* Africa 120 C2
Largest country in Africa and 10th largest in the world.

Algérie *country* Africa *see* Algeria
Algermissen Germany 63 J2
Algha Kazakh. *see* Alga
Al Ghāfāt Oman 110 E6
Al Ghammās Iraq 113 G5
Al Ghardaqah Egypt *see* Hurghada
Al Ghawr *plain* Jordan/West Bank 107 B4
Al Ghayḍah Yemen 108 H6
Alghero *Sardinia* Italy 68 C4
Al Ghurdaqah Egypt *see* Hurghada
Al Ghuwayr *well* Qatar 110 C5

▶Algiers Alg. 67 H5
Capital of Algeria.

Algoa Bay S. Africa 125 G7
Algoma *WI* U.S.A. 164 B1
Algona *IA* U.S.A. 160 E3
Algonac *MI* U.S.A. 164 D2
Algonquin Park Canada 165 F1
Algonquin Provincial Park Canada 165 F1
Algorta Spain 67 E2
Algueirao Moz. *see* Hacufera
Al Habakah *well* Saudi Arabia 113 F5
Al Ḥabbānīyah Iraq 113 F4
Al Ḥadaqah *well* Saudi Arabia 110 B4
Al Ḥadd Bahrain 110 C5
Al Hadhālīl *plat.* Saudi Arabia 113 F5
Al Ḥadīthah Iraq 113 F4
Al Ḥadīthah Saudi Arabia 107 C4
Al Ḥaḍr Iraq *see* Hatra
Al Ḥafār *well* Saudi Arabia 113 F5
Al Ḥaffah Syria 107 C2
Al Ḥajar al Gharbī *mts* Oman 110 E5
Al Ḥajar ash Sharqī *mts* Oman 110 E6
Al Ḥamād *plain* Asia 112 E5
Alhama de Murcia Spain 67 F5
Al Ḥamar Saudi Arabia 110 B6
Al Ḥamdānīyah Syria 107 C2
Al Ḥamīdīyah Syria 107 B2
Al Ḥammām Egypt 112 C5
Al Ḥanākīyah Saudi Arabia 108 F5
Al Haniyah *esc.* Iraq 113 G5
Al Hariq Saudi Arabia 110 B6
Al Ḥarrah Egypt 112 C5
Al Harūj al Aswad *hills* Libya 121 E2
Al Hasa *reg.* Saudi Arabia 110 C5
Al Ḥasakah Syria 113 F3
Al Hawi *salt pan* Saudi Arabia 107 D5
Al Ḥawīyah Saudi Arabia 108 F5
Al Hawjā' Saudi Arabia 112 E5
Al Ḥawṭah *reg.* Saudi Arabia 110 B6

Al Ḩayy Iraq 113 G4
Al Ḩayz Egypt 112 C5
Al Hazīm Jordan 107 C4
Al Ḩazm Saudi Arabia 112 E5
Al Ḩibāk des. Saudi Arabia 109 H6
Al Hījānah Syria 107 C3
Al Ḩillah Iraq see Hillah
Al Ḩillah Saudi Arabia 108 G5
Al Ḩinnāh Saudi Arabia 122 E1
Al Ḩinw mt. Saudi Arabia 107 D4
Al Hirrah well Saudi Arabia 110 C6
Al Hīshah Syria 107 D1
Al Ḩismā plain Saudi Arabia 112 D5
Al Ḩişn Jordan 107 B3
Al Hoceima Morocco 67 E6
Al Hoceima, Baie d' b. Morocco 67 E6
Al Ḩudaydah Yemen see Hodeidah
Al Ḩufrah reg. Saudi Arabia 112 E5
Al Hufūf Saudi Arabia 108 G4
Al Hūj hills Saudi Arabia 112 E5
Al Husayfin Oman 110 E5
Al Huwwah Saudi Arabia 110 B6
Ali China 99 B6
'Alīābād Afgh. 111 H2
'Alīābād Golestān Iran 110 D2
'Alīābād Hormozgān Iran 110 D4
'Alīābād Khorāsān-e Jonūbī Iran 111 F4
'Alīābād, Kūh-e mt. Iran 110 C3
'Alīābād-e Marān Iran 110 B2
'Ali'Addé Djibouti 108 F7
Aliağa Turkey 69 L5
Aliakmonas r. Greece 69 J4
Aliambata East Timor 83 C5
Alibag India 106 B2
Alicante Spain 67 F4
Alice r. Australia 136 C2
Alice watercourse Australia 136 D5
Alice TX U.S.A. 161 D7
Alice, Punta pt Italy 68 G5
Alice Arm (abandoned) Canada 149 O5
Alice Springs Australia 135 F5
Alice Town Bahamas 163 E7
Aliceville AL U.S.A. 161 F5
Alichur Tajik. 111 I2
Alichur r. Tajik. 111 I2
Alicia Mindanao Phil. 82 C5
Alick Creek r. Australia 136 C4
Alifu Atoll Maldives see Ari Atholhu
Al Ifzi'iyyah i. U.A.E. 110 C5
Aliganj India 104 D4
Aligarh Rajasthan India 104 D4
Aligarh Uttar Prad. India 104 D4
Alīgūdarz Iran 110 C3
Alihe China 95 J1
'Alījūq, Kūh-e mt. Iran 110 C4
'Alī Khēl Afgh. 111 H3
Al Imārāt al 'Arabīyah at Muttaḩidah country Asia see United Arab Emirates
Alimia i. Greece 69 L6
Alimpaya Point Mindanao Phil. 82 C5
Alindao Cent. Afr. Rep. 122 C3
Alindau Celebes Indon. 83 A3
Alingsås Sweden 55 H8
Aliova r. Turkey 69 M5
Alipura India 104 D4
Alipur Duar India 105 G4
Alirajpur India 104 C5
Al 'Irāq country Asia see Iraq
Al 'Īsāwīyah Saudi Arabia 107 C4
Al Iskandarīyah Egypt see Alexandria
Al Iskandarīyah Iraq 113 G4
Al Ismā'īlīyah Egypt 112 D5
Al Ismā'īlīyah governorate Egypt 107 A4
Alitak Bay AK U.S.A. 148 I4
Aliveri Greece 69 K5
Aliwal North S. Africa 125 H6
Alix Canada 150 H4
Al Jafr Jordan 107 C4
Al Jāfūrah des. Saudi Arabia 110 C5
Al Jaghbūb Libya 112 B5
Al Jahrah Kuwait 110 B4
Al Jarāwī well Saudi Arabia 107 D4
Al Jauf Saudi Arabia see Dawmat al Jandal
Al Jawb reg. Saudi Arabia 110 C6
Al Jawf Libya 121 F2
Al Jawsh Libya 120 E1
Al Jaza'ir country Africa see Algeria
Al Jaza'ir Alg. see Algiers
Aljezur Port. 67 B5
Al Jībān reg. Saudi Arabia 110 C5
Al Jil well Iraq 113 F5
Al Jilh esc. Saudi Arabia 110 B5
Al Jithāmīyah Saudi Arabia 113 F6
Al Jīzah Egypt see Giza
Al Jīzah Jordan 107 B4
Al Jubayl hills Saudi Arabia 110 B5
Al Jubaylah Saudi Arabia 110 B5
Al Jufrah Libya 121 E2
Al Julayqah well Saudi Arabia 110 C5
Al Jumaylīyah Qatar 110 C5
Aljustrel Port. 67 B5
Al Juwayf depr. Syria 107 C3
Al Kahfah Ash Sharqīyah Saudi Arabia 110 C5
Al Kahfah Ḩā'il Saudi Arabia 108 F4
Alkali Lake Canada 150 F5
Al Karak Jordan 107 B4
Al'katvaam Russia 148 B3
Al Kāẓimīyah Iraq 113 G4
Al Khābūrah Oman 110 E6
Al Khalīl West Bank see Hebron
Al Khāliş Iraq 113 G4
Al Khamāsīn Saudi Arabia 108 F5
Al Khārijah Egypt 108 D4
Al Kharj reg. Saudi Arabia 110 B6
Al Kharrārah Qatar 110 C5
Al Kharrūbah Egypt 107 A4
Al Khaşab Oman 110 E5
Al Khatam reg. U.A.E. 110 D5
Al Khawkhah Yemen 108 F7
Al Khawr Qatar 110 C5
Al Khizāmī well Saudi Arabia 110 C5
Al Khums Libya 121 E1
Al Khunfah sand area Saudi Arabia 112 E5
Al Khunn Saudi Arabia 122 E1
Al Kifl Iraq 113 G4
Al Kir'ānah Qatar 110 C5
Al Kiswah Syria 107 C3
Alkmaar Neth. 62 E2
Al Kūbrī Egypt 107 A4
Al Kūfah Iraq 113 G4
Al Kumayt Iraq 113 G4
Al Kuntillah Egypt 107 B5
Al Kusūr hills Saudi Arabia 107 D4
Al Kūt Iraq 113 G4
Al Kuwayt country Asia see Kuwait
Al Kuwayt Kuwait see Kuwait
Al Labbah plain Saudi Arabia 113 F5
Al Lādhiqīyah Syria see Latakia
Allagadda India 106 C3
Allahabad India 105 E4
Al Lajā lava field Syria 107 C3
Allakaket AK U.S.A. 148 I2
Allakh-Yun' Russia 77 O3
Allanmyo Myanmar see Aunglan
Allanridge S. Africa 125 H4
Allapalli India 106 D2
'Allāqī, Wādī al watercourse Egypt 108 D5
'Allâqi, Wâdi el watercourse Egypt see 'Allāqī, Wādī al
Allardville Canada 153 I5
Alldays S. Africa 125 I2
Allegan MI U.S.A. 164 C2
Allegheny r. PA U.S.A. 164 F3
Allegheny Mountains U.S.A. 164 D5
Allegheny Reservoir PA U.S.A. 165 F3
Allen, Lough l. Ireland 61 D3
Allen, Mount AK U.S.A. 149 L3
Allendale SC U.S.A. 163 D5
Allendale Town U.K. 58 E4
Allende Coahuila Mex. 167 E2
Allende Nuevo León Mex. 167 E3
Allendorf (Lumda) Germany 63 I4
Allenford Canada 164 E1
Allenstein Poland see Olsztyn
Allensville KY U.S.A. 164 B5
Allentown PA U.S.A. 165 H3
Alleppey India see Alappuzha
Aller r. Germany 63 J2
Alliance NE U.S.A. 160 C3
Alliance OH U.S.A. 164 E3
Al Lībīyah country Africa see Libya
Allier r. France 66 F3
Al Liḩābah well Saudi Arabia 110 B5
Allinge-Sandvig Denmark 55 I9
Al Lişāfah well Saudi Arabia 110 B5
Al Lisān pen. Jordan 107 B4
Alliston Canada 164 F1
Al Līth Saudi Arabia 108 F5
Al Liwā' oasis U.A.E. 110 D6
Alloa U.K. 60 F4
Allons TN U.S.A. 164 C5
Allora Australia 138 F2
Allu Celebes Indon. 83 A4
Allur India 106 D3
Alluru Kottapatnam India 106 D3
Al Lussuf well Iraq 113 F5
Alma Canada 153 H4
Alma MI U.S.A. 164 C2
Alma NE U.S.A. 160 D3
Alma WI U.S.A. 160 F2
Al Ma'ānīyah Iraq 113 F5
Alma-Ata Kazakh. see Almaty
Almada Port. 67 B4
Al Madāfi' plat. Saudi Arabia 112 E5
Al Ma'danīyāt well Iraq 113 G5
Almaden Australia 136 D3
Almadén Spain 67 D4
Al Madīnah Saudi Arabia see Medina
Al Mafraq Jordan 107 C3
Al Maghrib country Africa see Morocco
Al Maghrib reg. U.A.E. 110 D6
Al Maḩajjah depr. Saudi Arabia 112 E6
Al Mahākik reg. Saudi Arabia 110 C6
Al Maḩwīt Yemen 108 F6
Al Malsūnīyah reg. Saudi Arabia 110 C5
Almalyk Uzbek. see Olmaliq
Al Manadir reg. Oman 110 D6
Al Manāmah Bahrain see Manama
Al Manjūr well Saudi Arabia 110 B6
Almanor, Lake CA U.S.A. 158 C1
Almansa Spain 67 F4
Al Manşūrah Egypt 112 C5
Almanzor mt. Spain 67 D3
Al Mariyyah U.A.E. 110 D6
Al Marj Libya 121 F1
Almas, Rio das r. Brazil 179 A1
Al Maţarīyah Egypt 112 D5
Almatinskaya Oblast' admin. div. Kazakh. 98 B3

▶Almaty Kazakh. 102 E3
Former capital of Kazakhstan.

Al Mawşil Iraq see Mosul
Al Mayādīn Syria 113 F4
Al Mazār Egypt 107 A4
Almaznyy Russia 77 M3
Almeirim Brazil 177 H4
Almeirim Port. 67 B4
Almelo Neth. 62 G2
Almenara Brazil 179 C2
Almendra, Embalse de resr Spain 67 C3
Almendralejo Spain 67 C4
Almere Neth. 62 F2
Almería Spain 67 E5
Almería, Golfo de b. Spain 67 E5
Al'metievsk Russia see Al'met'yevsk
Al'met'yevsk Russia 51 Q5
Älmhult Sweden 55 I8
Almina, Punta pt Spain 67 D6
Al Mindak Saudi Arabia 108 F5
Al Minyā Egypt 112 C5
Almirós Greece see Almyros
Al Mish'āb Saudi Arabia 110 C4
Almodôvar Port. 67 B5
Almoloya Mex. 167 E5
Almond r. U.K. 60 F4
Almont MI U.S.A. 164 D2
Almonte Spain 67 C5
Almora India 104 D3
Al Mu'ayzīlah hill Saudi Arabia 107 D5
Al Mubarrez Saudi Arabia 108 G4
Al Muḑaibī Oman 109 I5
Al Muḑairib Oman 110 E6
Al Muḩarraq Bahrain 110 C5
Al Mukallā Yemen see Mukalla
Al Mukhā Yemen see Mocha
Al Mukhaylī Libya 108 B3
Al Munbaţiḩ des. Saudi Arabia 110 C6
Almuñécar Spain 67 E5
Al Muqdādīyah Iraq 113 G4
Al Mūrītānīyah country Africa see Mauritania
Al Murūt well Saudi Arabia 113 E5
Almus Turkey 112 E2
Al Musannāh ridge Saudi Arabia 110 B4
Al Musayyib Iraq 110 B3
Al Muwaqqar Jordan 107 C4
Almyros Greece 69 J5
Almyrou, Ormos b. Greece 69 K7
Alnwick U.K. 58 F3

▶Alofi Niue 133 J3
Capital of Niue.

Aloja Latvia 55 N8
Alon Myanmar 86 A2
Alongshan China 90 A2
Alonnisos i. Greece 69 J5
Alor i. Indon. 83 C5
Alor, Kepulauan is Indon. 83 C5
Alor, Selat sea chan. Indon. 83 B5
Alor Setar Malaysia see Alor Star
Alor Star Malaysia 84 C1
Alost Belgium see Aalst
Aloysius, Mount Australia 135 E6
Alozero (abandoned) Russia 54 Q4
Alpen Germany 62 G3
Alpena MI U.S.A. 164 D1
Alpercatas, Serra das hills Brazil 177 J5
Alpha Australia 136 D4
Alpha Ridge sea feature Arctic Ocean 189 A1
Alpine AZ U.S.A. 159 I5
Alpine NY U.S.A. 165 G2
Alpine TX U.S.A. 161 C6
Alpine WY U.S.A. 156 F4
Alpine National Park Australia 138 C6
Alps mts Europe 66 H4
Al Qa'āmīyāt reg. Saudi Arabia 108 G6
Al Qaddāḩīyah Libya 121 E1
Al Qadmūs Syria 107 C2
Al Qaffāy i. U.A.E. 110 D5
Al Qāhirah Egypt see Cairo
Al Qā'īyah Saudi Arabia 108 F5
Al Qā'īyah well Saudi Arabia 110 B5
Al Qalībah Saudi Arabia 112 E5
Al Qāmishlī Syria 113 F3
Al Qar'ah Libya 112 B5
Al Qar'ah well Saudi Arabia 110 B5
Al Qar'ah lava field Syria 107 C3
Al Qardāḩah Syria 107 C2
Al Qarqar Saudi Arabia 107 C4
Al Qaryatayn Syria 107 C2
Al Qaşab Ar Riyāḑ Saudi Arabia 110 B5
Al Qaşab Ash Sharqīyah Saudi Arabia 110 C6
Al Qaţīf Saudi Arabia 110 C5
Al Qaţn Yemen 108 G6
Al Qaţrānah Jordan 107 C4
Al Qaţrūn Libya 121 E2
Al Qayşūmah well Saudi Arabia 113 F5
Alqueva, Barragem de resr Port. 67 C4
Al Qumur country Africa see Comoros
Al Qunayţirah (abandoned) Syria 107 B3
Al Qunfidhah Saudi Arabia 108 F6
Al Qurayyāt Saudi Arabia 107 C4
Al Qurnah Iraq 113 G5
Al Quşaymah Egypt 107 B4
Al Quşayr Egypt 108 D4
Al Quşayr Syria 107 C2
Al Qūşīyah Egypt 112 C6
Al Qūşūrīyah Saudi Arabia 110 B6
Al Quţayfah Syria 107 C3
Al Quwayi' Saudi Arabia 110 B6
Al Quwayīyah Saudi Arabia 108 G5
Al Quwayrah Jordan 107 B5
Al Rabbād reg. U.A.E. 110 D6
Alroy Downs Australia 136 B3
Alsace admin. reg. France 63 H6
Alsace reg. France 66 H2
Alsager U.K. 59 E5
Al Samīt well Iraq 113 F5
Alsask Canada 151 I5
Alsatia reg. France see Alsace
Alsek r. AK U.S.A. 149 M4
Alsfeld Germany 63 J4
Alsleben (Saale) Germany 63 L3
Alston U.K. 58 E4
Alstonville Australia 138 F2
Alsunga Latvia 55 L8
Alta Norway 54 M2
Alta, Mount N.Z. 139 B7
Altaelva r. Norway 54 M2
Altafjorden sea chan. Norway 54 M1
Alta Floresta Brazil 177 G5
Altagracia Nicaragua 166 [inset] I7
Altai Mountains Asia 88 F3
Altai Tavan Bogd National Park Mongolia 98 E2
Altamaha r. GA U.S.A. 163 D6
Altamira Brazil 177 H4
Altamira Costa Rica 166 [inset] I7
Altamira Mex. 167 F4
Altamirano Mex. 167 G5
Altamura Italy 68 G4
Altan Zabaykal'skiy Kray Russia 95 G1
Altan Zabaykal'skiy Kray Russia 95 G1
Altanbulag Mongolia 94 F2
Altan Emel China 95 I1
Altan Ovoo mt. China/Mongolia 94 B2
Altan Xiret China 95 G4
Altar Mex. 166 C2
Altar r. Mex. 157 F7
Altar, Desierto de des. Mex. 166 B1
Altata Mex. 166 D3
Altavista VA U.S.A. 164 F5
Altay China 98 E3
Altay Govĭ-Altay Mongolia 94 C2
Altay Govĭ-Altay Mongolia 94 D2
Altay Hovd Mongolia 94 C2
Altay, Respublika aut. rep. Russia 94 A1
Altayskiy Khrebet mts Asia see Altai Mountains
Altayskiy Zapovednik nature res. Russia 94 B1
Altayskoye Russia 102 G1
Altdorf Switz. 66 I3
Altea Spain 67 F4
Alteidet Norway 54 M1
Altenahr Germany 62 G4
Altenberge Germany 63 H2
Altenburg Germany 63 M4
Altenkirchen (Westerwald) Germany 63 H4
Altenqoke China 94 C4
Altin Köprü Iraq 113 G4
Altınoluk Turkey 69 L5
Altınözü Turkey 107 C1
Altıntaş Turkey 69 N5
Altiplano plain Bol. 176 E7
Altmark reg. Germany 63 L2
Altmühl r. Germany 63 L6
Alto, Monte hill Italy 68 D2
Alto Chicapa Angola 123 B5
Alto Garças Brazil 177 H7
Alto Madidi, Parque Nacional nat. park Bol. 176 E6
Alton CA U.S.A. 158 A1
Alton IL U.S.A. 160 F4
Alton MO U.S.A. 161 F4
Alton NH U.S.A. 165 J2
Altona Canada 150 F3
Altoona PA U.S.A. 165 F3
Alto Paraíso de Goiás Brazil 179 B1
Alto Parnaíba Brazil 177 I5
Alto Taquari Brazil 177 H7
Altotonga Mex. 167 F5
Altötting Germany 57 N6
Altrincham U.K. 58 E5
Alt Schwerin Germany 63 M1
Altūn Kūbrī Iraq see Altin Köprü
Altun Shan mt. China 98 F5
Altun Shan mts China 99 D5
Alturas CA U.S.A. 156 C4
Altus OK U.S.A. 161 D5
Al 'Ubaylah Saudi Arabia 122 F1
Alucra Turkey 112 E2
Alūksne Latvia 55 O8
Alūm Iran 110 C3
Alum Bridge WV U.S.A. 164 E4
Al 'Uqaylah Libya 121 E1
Al 'Uqaylah Saudi Arabia see An Nabk
Al Uqşur Egypt see Luxor
Alur India 106 C3
Al 'Urayq des. Saudi Arabia 112 E5
Al 'Urdun country Asia see Jordan
Alur Setar Malaysia see Alor Star
Ālūt Iran 110 B3
Aluva India 106 C4
Al 'Uwayjā' well Saudi Arabia 110 C6
Al 'Uwaynāt Libya 108 B5
Al 'Uwayqīlah Saudi Arabia 113 F5
Al 'Uzayr Iraq 113 G5
Alva OK U.S.A. 161 D4
Alvand, Kūh-e mt. Iran 110 C3
Alvarado Mex. 167 G5
Alvarado TX U.S.A. 167 F1
Alvarães Brazil 176 F4
Alvaton KY U.S.A. 164 B5
Alvdal Norway 54 G5
Älvdalen Sweden 55 I6
Alvesta Sweden 55 I8
Ålvik Norway 55 E6
Alvik Sweden 54 J5
Alvin TX U.S.A. 161 E6
Alvorada do Norte Brazil 179 B1
Älvsbyn Sweden 54 L4
Al Wafrah Kuwait 110 B4
Al Wajh Saudi Arabia 108 E4
Al Wakrah Qatar 110 C5
Al Waqbá well Saudi Arabia 110 B4
Alwar India 104 D4
Al Wari'ah Saudi Arabia 108 G4
Al Wāţīyah well Egypt 112 B5
Alwaye India see Aluva
Al Widyān plat. Iraq/Saudi Arabia 113 F4
Al Wusayţ well Saudi Arabia 110 B4
Alxa Youqi China see Ehen Hudag
Alxa Zuoqi China see Bayan Hot
Al Yamāmah Saudi Arabia 110 B5
Al Yaman country Asia see Yemen
Alyangula Australia 136 B2
Al Ya'rūbīyah Syria 113 F3
Al Yāsāt i. U.A.E. 110 C5
Alyth U.K. 60 F4
Alytus Lith. 55 N9
Alzette r. Lux. 62 G5
Alzey Germany 63 I5
Ama Japan 92 C3
Amacayacu, Parque Nacional nat. park Col. 176 D4
Amadeus, Lake salt flat Australia 135 E6
'Amādīyah/Amêdî Iraq 113 F3
Amadjuak Lake Canada 147 K3
Amadora Port. 67 B4
Amaga-dake mt. Japan 93 E3
Amagasaki Japan 92 B4
Amagi-san vol. Japan 93 E4
Amagi-tōge pass Japan 93 E4
Amagiyugashima Japan 93 E4
Amagoi-dake mt. Japan 92 C3
Amahai Seram Indon. 83 D3
Amakazari-yama mt. Japan 93 D2
Amakusa-nada b. Japan 91 C6
Åmål Sweden 55 H7
Amalia S. Africa 125 G4
Amaliada Greece 69 I6
Amalner India 104 C5
Amamapare Indon. 81 J7
Amambaí Brazil 178 E2
Amambaí, Serra de hills Brazil/Para. 178 E2
Amami-Ō-shima i. Japan 91 C7
Amami-shotō is Japan 91 C8
Amamula Dem. Rep. Congo 122 C4
Amanab P.N.G. 81 K7
Amankeldi Kazakh. see Amankel'dy
Amankel'dy Kazakh. 102 C1
Amantea Italy 68 G5
Amapá Brazil 177 H3
Amapala Hond. 166 [inset] I6
Amarante Brazil 177 J5
Amarapura Myanmar 86 B2
Amardalay Mongolia see Delgertsogt
Amareleja Port. 67 C4
Amargosa Brazil 179 D1
Amargosa watercourse CA U.S.A. 158 E3
Amargosa Desert NV U.S.A. 158 E3
Amargosa Range mts CA U.S.A. 158 E3
Amargosa Valley NV U.S.A. 158 E3
Amarillo TX U.S.A. 161 C5
Amarillo, Cerro mt. Arg. 178 C4
Amarkantak India 105 E5
Amarpur India 104 E5
Amasia Turkey see Amasya
Amasra Turkey 112 D2
Amassine W. Sahara 120 B2
Amasya Turkey 112 D2
Amata Australia 135 E6
Amatenango Mex. 167 G5
Amatique, Bahía de b. Guat. 166 [inset] H6
Amatitán Mex. 166 E4
Amatlán de Cañas Mex. 166 D4
Amatsu-Kominato Japan 93 G3
Amatulla India 105 H4
Amau P.N.G. 136 E1
Amay Belgium 62 F4
Amazar Russia 90 A1
Amazar r. Russia 90 A1

▶Amazon r. S. America 176 F4
Longest river and largest drainage basin in South America and 2nd longest river in the world.
Also known as Amazonas or Solimões

Amazon, Mouths of the Brazil 177 I3
Amazonas r. S. America 176 F4 see Amazon
Amazon Cone sea feature S. Atlantic Ocean 184 E5
Amazônia, Parque Nacional nat. park Brazil 177 G4
Ambajogai India 106 C2
Ambala India 104 D3
Ambalangoda Sri Lanka 106 D5
Ambalavao Madag. 123 E6
Ambam Cameroon 122 B3
Ambar Iran 110 E4
Ambarchik Russia 77 R3
Ambarnyy Russia 54 R4
Ambasa India see Ambassa
Ambasamudram India 106 C4
Ambassa India 105 G5
Ambathala Australia 137 D5
Ambato Ecuador 176 C4
Ambato Boeny Madag. 123 E5
Ambato Finandrahana Madag. 123 E6
Ambatolampy Madag. 123 E5
Ambatomainty Madag. 123 E5
Ambatondrazaka Madag. 123 E5
Ambejogai India see Ambajogai
Ambelau i. Moluccas Indon. 83 C3
Ambeno enclave East Timor see Ocussi
Amberg Germany 63 L5
Ambergris Caye i. Belize 167 I5
Ambérieu-en-Bugey France 66 G4
Amberley Canada 164 E1
Ambgaon India 106 D1
Ambianum France see Amiens
Ambikapur India 105 E5
Ambil i. Phil. 82 C3
Ambilobe Madag. 123 E5
Ambition, Mount Canada 149 O4
Amble U.K. 58 F3
Ambler AK U.S.A. 148 H2
Ambler r. AK U.S.A. 148 H2
Ambleside U.K. 58 E4
Amblève r. Belgium 62 F4
Ambo India 105 F5
Amboasary Madag. 123 E6
Ambodifotatra Madag. 123 E5
Ambohimahasoa Madag. 123 E6
Ambohitra mt. Madag. 123 E5
Amboina Moluccas Indon. see Ambon
Ambon Moluccas Indon. 83 D3
Ambon i. Moluccas Indon. 83 C3
Amboró, Parque Nacional nat. park Bol. 176 F7
Ambositra Madag. 123 E6
Ambovombe Madag. 123 E6
Amboy CA U.S.A. 159 F4
Ambre, Cap d' c. Madag. see Bobaomby, Tanjona
Ambrim i. Vanuatu see Ambrym
Ambriz Angola 123 B4
Ambrizete Angola see N'zeto
Ambrosia Lake NM U.S.A. 159 J4
Ambrym i. Vanuatu 133 G3
Ambunten Java Indon. 85 F4
Ambunti P.N.G. 81 K7
Ambur India 106 C3
Amchitka Island AK U.S.A. 148 [inset] B6
Amchitka Pass sea chan. AK U.S.A. 148 [inset] C5
Am-Dam Chad 121 F3
Amded, Oued watercourse Alg. 120 D2
Am-Djarass Chad 121 F3
Amdo China 99 E6
Ameca Mex. 166 D4
Amecameca Mex. 167 F5
Ameland i. Neth. 62 F1
Amelia Court House VA U.S.A. 165 G5
Amellu India 99 C8
Amenia NY U.S.A. 165 I3
Amer, Erg d' des. Alg. 122 A1
Amereli India see Amreli
American, North Fork r. CA U.S.A. 158 C2
Americana Brazil 179 B3
American-Antarctic Ridge sea feature S. Atlantic Ocean 184 G9
American Falls ID U.S.A. 156 E4
American Falls Reservoir ID U.S.A. 156 E4
American Fork UT U.S.A. 159 H1

▶American Samoa terr. S. Pacific Ocean 133 J3
United States Unincorporated Territory.

Americus GA U.S.A. 163 C5
Amersfoort Neth. 62 F2
Amersfoort S. Africa 125 I4
Amersham U.K. 59 G7
Amery Canada 151 M3
Amery Ice Shelf Antarctica 188 E2
Ames IA U.S.A. 160 E3
Amesbury U.K. 59 F7
Amesbury MA U.S.A. 165 J2
Amet India 104 C4
Amethi India 105 E4
Amfissa Greece 69 J5
Amga Russia 77 O3
Amgalang China 95 I1
Amgu Russia 90 E3
Amguema Russia 148 C2
Amguema r. Russia 148 C1
Amguid Alg. 120 D2
Amgun' r. Russia 90 E1
Amherst Canada 153 I5
Amherst Myanmar see Kyaikkami
Amherst MA U.S.A. 165 I2
Amherst OH U.S.A. 164 D3
Amherst VA U.S.A. 164 F5
Amherstburg Canada 164 D2
Amherst Island Canada 165 G1
Ami Japan 93 G2
Amiata, Monte mt. Italy 68 D3
Amida Turkey see Diyarbakır
Amidon ND U.S.A. 160 C2
Amiens France 62 C5
'Amīj, Wādī watercourse Iraq 113 F4
Amik Ovası marsh Turkey 107 C1
Amīnābād Iran 110 D4
Amindivi atoll India see Amini
Amindivi Islands India 106 B4
Amini atoll India 106 B4
Amino Eth. 122 E3
Amino Japan 92 B3
Aminuis Namibia 124 D2
Amīr, Band-e l. Afgh. 111 G3
Amīrābād Īlām Iran 110 B3
Amīrābād Yazd Iran 110 E3
Amirante Islands Seychelles 185 L6
Amirante Trench sea feature Indian Ocean 185 L6
Amisk Lake Canada 151 K4
Amistad, Represa de resr Mex./U.S.A. see Amistad Reservoir
Amistad Reservoir Mex./U.S.A. 167 E2
Amisus Turkey see Samsun
Amite LA U.S.A. 161 F6
Amity Point Australia 138 F1
Amla India 104 D5
Amlash Iran 110 C2
Amlekhganj Nepal 105 F4
Åmli Norway 55 F7
Amlia Island AK U.S.A. 148 [inset] D5
Amlwch U.K. 58 C5

▶'Ammān Jordan 107 B4
Capital of Jordan.

Ammanazar Turkm. 110 D2
Ammanford U.K. 59 D7
Ämmänsaari Fin. 54 P4
'Ammar, Tall hill Syria 107 C3
Ammarnäs Sweden 54 J4
Ammaroo Australia 136 A4
Ammassalik Greenland see Tasiilaq
Ammerland reg. Germany 63 H1
Ammern Germany 63 K3
Ammochostos Cyprus see Famagusta
Ammochostos Bay Cyprus 107 B2
Amne Machin Range mts China see A'nyêmaqên Shan
Amnok-kang r. China/N. Korea see Yalu Jiang
Amo Jiang r. China 96 D4
Āmol Iran 110 D2
Amorbach Germany 63 J5
Amorgos i. Greece 69 K6
Amory MS U.S.A. 161 F5
Amos Canada 152 F4
Amourj Mauritania 120 C3
Amoy China see Xiamen
Ampah Kalimantan Indon. 85 F3
Ampana Celebes Indon. 83 B3
Ampani India 106 D2
Ampanihy Madag. 123 E6
Ampara Sri Lanka 106 D5
Amparo Brazil 179 B3
Ampasimanolotra Madag. 123 E5
Ampenan Lombok Indon. 85 G5
Amphitheatre Australia 138 A6
Amphitrite Group is Paracel Is 80 E3
Ampibaku Celebes Indon. 83 B3
Ampoa Celebes Indon. 83 B3
Amqog China 94 E5
'Amrah, Qaşr tourist site Jordan 107 C4
Amraoti India see Amravati
Amravati India 106 C1
Amrawad India 104 D5
Amreli India 104 B5
Amri Pak. 111 H5

Amring India 105 H4
'Amrīt Syria 107 B2
Amritsar India 104 C3
Amroha India 104 D3
Amsden OH U.S.A. 164 D3
Åmsele Sweden 54 K4
Amstelveen Neth. 62 E2

▶Amsterdam Neth. 62 E2
Official capital of the Netherlands.

Amsterdam S. Africa 125 J4
Amsterdam NY U.S.A. 165 H2
Amsterdam, Île i. Indian Ocean 185 N8
Amstetten Austria 57 O6
Am Timan Chad 121 F3
Amu Co l. China 99 E6
Amudar'ya r. Asia 111 F2
Amudaryo r. Asia see Amudar'ya
Amukta Island AK U.S.A. 148 E5
Amukta Pass sea chan. AK U.S.A. 148 D5
Amund Ringnes Island Canada 147 I2
Amundsen, Mount Antarctica 188 F2
Amundsen Abyssal Plain sea feature Southern Ocean 188 J2
Amundsen Basin sea feature Arctic Ocean 189 H1
Amundsen Bay Antarctica 188 D2
Amundsen Coast Antarctica 188 J1
Amundsen Glacier Antarctica 188 I1
Amundsen Gulf Canada 146 F2
Amundsen Ridges sea feature Southern Ocean 188 J2
Amundsen-Scott research station Antarctica 188 C1
Amundsen Sea Antarctica 188 K2
Amuntai Kalimantan Indon. 85 F3
Amur r. China/Russia 90 D2
also known as Heilong Jiang (China)
Amur r. Russia 90 F1
'Amur, Wadi watercourse Sudan 108 D6
Amurang Celebes Indon. 83 C2
Amuro-Baltiysk Russia 90 B1
Amur Oblast admin. div. Russia see Amurskaya Oblast'
Amursk Russia 90 E2
Amurskaya Oblast' admin. div. Russia 90 C1
Amurskiy Liman strait Russia 90 F1
Amurzet Russia 90 C3
Amvrosiyivka Ukr. 53 H7
Amyderya r. Asia see Amudar'ya
Am-Zoer Chad 121 F3
An Myanmar 86 A3
Anaa atoll Fr. Polynesia 187 K7
Anabanua Celebes Indon. 83 B3
Anabar r. Russia 77 M2
Anacapa Island CA U.S.A. 158 D4
Anaconda MT U.S.A. 156 E3
Anacortes WA U.S.A. 156 C2
Anacuao, Mount Phil. 82 C2
Anadarko OK U.S.A. 161 D5
Anadolu reg. Turkey 112 D3
Anadolu Dağları mts Turkey 112 E2
Anadyr' Russia 148 B2
Anadyrskaya Nizmennost' lowland Russia 148 B2
Anadyrskiy Liman b. Russia 148 B2
Anadyrskiy Zaliv b. Russia 148 C3
Anafi i. Greece 69 K6
Anagé Brazil 179 C1
'Ānah Iraq 113 F4
Anaheim CA U.S.A. 158 E5
Anahim Lake Canada 150 E4
Anáhuac Mex. 167 E3
Anahuac TX U.S.A. 161 E6
Anaimalai Hills India 106 C4
Anai Mudi mt. India 106 C4
Anaiteum i. Vanuatu see Anatom
Anajás Brazil 177 I4
Anakie Australia 136 D4
Anaktuvuk r. AK U.S.A. 149 J1
Anaktuvuk Pass AK U.S.A. 149 J1
Analalava Madag. 123 E5
Anamã Brazil 176 F4
Anambas, Kepulauan is Indon. 84 D2
Anamosa IA U.S.A. 160 F3
Anamur Turkey 107 A1
Anan Nagano Japan 93 D3
Anan Tokushima Japan 91 D6
Anand India 104 C5
Anandapur India 105 F5
Anan'ev Kyrg. 98 B4
Anano i. Indon. 83 C4
Anantapur India 106 C3
Ananthapur India see Anantapur
Anantnag India 104 C2
Anant Peth India 104 D4
Anantpur India see Anantapur
Ananyev Ukr. see Anan'yiv
Anan'yiv Ukr. 53 F7
Anapa Russia 112 E1
Anápolis Brazil 179 A2
Anār Fin. see Inari
Anār Iran 110 D4
Anār Darah Afgh. 111 F3
Anatahan i. N. Mariana Is 81 L3
Anatajan i. N. Mariana Is see Anatahan
Anatom i. Vanuatu 133 G4
Añatuya Arg. 178 D3
Anaypazari Turkey see Gülnar
An Baile Breac Ireland 61 B6
Anbei China 94 D3
An Bun Beag Ireland 61 D2
Anbūr-e Kālārī Iran 110 D5
Anbyon N. Korea 91 B5
Ancenis France 66 D3
Anchorage AK U.S.A. 149 J3
Anchorage Island atoll Cook Is see Suwarrow
Anchor Bay MI U.S.A. 164 D2
Anchor Point AK U.S.A. 149 J4
Anchuthengu India 106 C4
Anci China see Langfang
Ancient City of Tauric Chersonese tourist site Ukr. 53 G7
Ancient Villages of Northern Syria tourist site Syria 107 C1
An Clochán Liath Ireland 61 D3
An Cóbh Ireland see Cobh
Ancona Italy 68 E3
Ancón de Sardinas, Bahía de b. Col. 176 C3
Ancud, Golfo de g. Chile 178 B6
Ancyra Turkey see Ankara
Anda Heilong. China see Daqing
Anda Heilong. China 90 B3
Anda i. Indon. 83 C1
Andacollo Chile 178 B4
Andado Australia 136 A5
Andahuaylas Peru 176 D6
Andal India 105 F5
Åndalsnes Norway 54 E5
Andalucía aut. comm. Spain 67 D5
Andalusia aut. comm. Spain see Andalucía
Andalusia AL U.S.A. 163 C6
Andaman Basin sea feature Indian Ocean 185 O5
Andaman Islands India 87 A4
Andaman Sea Indian Ocean 87 A5
Andaman Strait India 87 A4
Andamooka Australia 137 B6
Andapa Madag. 123 E5
Andarāb, Darah-ye reg. Afgh. 111 H3
Ande China 96 E4
Andegavum France see Angers
Andelle r. France 62 B5
Andenes Norway 54 J2
Andenne Belgium 62 F4
Andéramboukane Mali 120 D3
Anderlecht Belgium 62 E4
Andermatt Switz. 66 I3
Andernos-les-Bains France 66 D4
Anderson r. Canada 149 O1
Anderson AK U.S.A. 149 J2
Anderson IN U.S.A. 164 C3
Anderson SC U.S.A. 163 D5
Anderson TX U.S.A. 161 E6
Anderson Bay Australia 137 [inset]
Anderson Lake Canada 150 F5
Andes mts S. America 178 C4
Andfjorden sea chan. Norway 54 J2
Andhíparos i. Greece see Antiparos
Andhra Lake India 106 B2
Andhra Pradesh state India 106 C2
Andijon Uzbek. 102 D3
Andikíthira i. Greece see Antikythira
Andilamena Madag. 123 E5
Andilanatoby Madag. 123 E5
Andīmeshk Iran 110 C3
Andímilos i. Greece see Antimilos
Andípsara i. Greece see Antipsara
Andırın Turkey 112 E3
Andirlangar China 99 C5
Andizhan Uzbek. see Andijon
Andkhōy Afgh. 111 G2
Andoany Madag. 123 E5
Andoas Peru 176 C4
Andogskaya Gryada hills Russia 52 H4
Andol India 106 C2
Andong China see Dandong
Andong S. Korea 91 C5
Andongwei China 95 I5
Andoom Australia 136 C2
Andorra country Europe 67 G2

▶Andorra la Vella Andorra 67 G2
Capital of Andorra.

Andorra la Vieja Andorra see Andorra la Vella
Andover U.K. 59 F7
Andover NY U.S.A. 165 G2
Andover OH U.S.A. 164 E3
Andøya i. Norway 54 I2
Andrade CA U.S.A. 159 F5
Andradina Brazil 179 A3
Andranomavo Madag. 123 E5
Andranopasy Madag. 123 E6
Andreafsky r. AK U.S.A. 148 G3
Andreafsky, East Fork r. AK U.S.A. 148 G3
Andreanof Islands AK U.S.A. 186 I2
Andreapol' Russia 52 G4
Andreas Isle of Man 58 C4
André Félix, Parc National nat. park Cent. Afr. Rep. 122 C3
Andrelândia Brazil 179 B3
Andrew Canada 151 H4
Andrew Bay Myanmar 86 A3
Andrews SC U.S.A. 163 E5
Andrews TX U.S.A. 161 C5
Andria Italy 68 G4
Androka Madag. 123 E6
Andropov Russia see Rybinsk
Andros i. Bahamas 163 E7
Andros i. Greece 69 K6
Androscoggin r. Maine/New Hampshire U.S.A. 165 K2
Andros Town Bahamas 163 E7
Andrott i. India 106 B4
Andselv Norway 54 K2
Andújar Spain 67 D4
Andulo Angola 123 B5
Anec, Lake salt flat Australia 135 E5
Āneen-Kio terr. N. Pacific Ocean see Wake Island
Anéfis Mali 120 D3
Anegada, Bahía b. Arg. 178 D6
Anegada Passage Virgin Is (U.K.) 169 L5
Aného Togo 120 D4
Aneityum i. Vanuatu see Anatom
'Aneiza, Jabal hill Iraq see 'Unayzah, Jabal
Anemourion tourist site Turkey 107 A1
Anepmete P.N.G. 81 L8
Anet France 62 B6
Anetchom, Île i. Vanuatu see Anatom
Aneto mt. Spain 67 G2
Ānewetak atoll Marshall Is see Enewetak
Aney Niger 120 E3
Aneytioum, Île i. Vanuatu see Anatom
Anfu China 97 G3
Angalarri r. Australia 134 E3
Angamos, Punta pt Chile 178 B2
Ang'angxi China 95 J2

▶Angara r. Russia 88 G1
Part of the Yenisey-Angara-Selenga, 3rd longest river in Asia.

Angarsk Russia 88 I2
Angas Downs Australia 135 F6
Angat Luzon Phil. 82 C3
Angatuba Brazil 179 A3
Angaur i. Palau 81 I5
Ånge Sweden 54 I5
Angel, Salto waterfall Venez. see Angel Falls
Ángel de la Guarda, Isla i. Mex. 166 B2
Angeles Luzon Phil. 82 C3

▶Angel Falls waterfall Venez. 176 F2
Highest waterfall in the world.

Ängelholm Sweden 55 H8
Angellala Creek r. Australia 138 C1
Angels Camp CA U.S.A. 158 C2
Ångermanälven r. Sweden 54 J5
Angers France 66 D3
Anggana Kalimantan Indon. 85 G3
Angikuni Lake Canada 151 L2
Angiola CA U.S.A. 158 D4
Angkor tourist site Cambodia 87 C4
Angledool Australia 138 C2
Anglesea Australia 138 B7
Anglesey i. U.K. 58 C5
Angleton TX U.S.A. 161 E6
Anglo-Egyptian Sudan country Africa see Sudan
Angmagssalik Greenland see Tasiilaq
Ang Mo Kio Sing. 87 [inset]
Ango Dem. Rep. Congo 122 C3
Angoche Moz. 123 D5
Angol Chile 178 B5
Angola country Africa 123 B5
Angola IN U.S.A. 164 C3
Angola NY U.S.A. 164 F2
Angola Basin sea feature S. Atlantic Ocean 184 H7
Angora Turkey see Ankara
Angostura Mex. 157 F8
Angoulême France 66 E4
Angra dos Reis Brazil 179 B3
Angren Uzbek. 102 D3
Ang Thong Thai. 87 C4
Anguang China 95 J2

▶Anguilla terr. West Indies 169 L5
United Kingdom Overseas Territory.

Anguilla Cays is Bahamas 163 E8
Anguille, Cape Canada 153 K5
Angul India 106 E1
Anguli Nur l. China 95 H3
Anguo China 95 H4
Angus Canada 164 F1
Angutia Char i. Bangl. 105 G5
Angutikada Peak AK U.S.A. 148 H2
Anholt i. Denmark 55 G8
Anhua China 97 F2
Anhui prov. China 97 H1
Anhumas Brazil 177 H7
Anhwei prov. China see Anhui
Aniak AK U.S.A. 148 H3
Aniak r. AK U.S.A. 148 H3
Aniakchak National Monument and Preserve nat. park AK U.S.A. 146 C4
Animaki-san hill Japan 93 G2
Anin Myanmar 86 B4
Anini India 99 F7
Anitaguipan Point Samar Phil. 82 D4
Anitápolis Brazil 179 A4
Anıtlı Turkey 107 A1
Aniva Russia 90 F3
Aniva, Mys c. Russia 90 F3
Aniva, Zaliv b. Russia 90 F3
Anizy-le-Château France 62 D5
Anjadip i. India 106 B3
Anjengo India see Anchuthengu
Anji China 97 H2
Anjihai China 98 D3
Anjīr Āvand Iran 110 D3
Anjō Japan 92 D4
Anjoman Iran 110 E3
Anjou reg. France 66 D3
Anjouan i. Comoros see Ndzuani
Anjozorobe Madag. 123 E5
Anjuman reg. Afgh. 111 H3
Anjuthengu India see Anchuthengu
Ankang China 97 F1

▶Ankara Turkey 112 D3
Capital of Turkey.

Ankaratra mt. Madag. 123 E5
Ankazoabo Madag. 123 E6
Ankeny IA U.S.A. 160 E3
An Khê Vietnam 87 E4
Ankleshwar India 104 C5
Anklesvar India see Ankleshwar
Ankola India 106 B3
Ankou China 94 F5
Anling China see Yanling
An Lôc Vietnam 87 D5
Anlong China 96 E3
Anlu China 97 G2
Anmoore WV U.S.A. 164 E4
An Muileann gCearr Ireland see Mullingar
Anmyeon-do i. S. Korea 91 B5
Ann, Cape Antarctica 188 D2
Ann, Cape MA U.S.A. 165 J2
Anna Russia 53 I6
Anna, Lake VA U.S.A. 165 G4
Anna, Pulo i. Palau 81 I6
Annaba Alg. 68 B6
Annaberg-Buchholz Germany 63 N4
An Nābiyah Yemen 108 F7
An Nabk Saudi Arabia 107 C4
An Nabk Syria 107 C2
An Nafūd des. Saudi Arabia 113 F5
An Najaf Iraq 113 G5
Annaka Japan 93 E2
Annalee r. Ireland 61 E3
Annalong U.K. 61 G3
Annam reg. Vietnam 80 D3
Annam Highlands mts Laos/Vietnam 86 D3
Annan U.K. 60 F6
Annan r. U.K. 60 F6
'Annān, Wādī al watercourse Syria 107 D2
Annanba China 94 C4
Annandale VA U.S.A. 165 G4
Anna Plains Australia 134 C4

▶Annapolis MD U.S.A. 165 G4
Capital of Maryland.

Annapurna Conservation Area nature res. Nepal 105 F3

▶Annapurna I mt. Nepal 105 E3
10th highest mountain in Asia and the world.

Ann Arbor MI U.S.A. 164 D2
Anna Regina Guyana 177 G2
An Nás Ireland see Naas
An Nāşirīyah Iraq 113 G5
Annean, Lake salt flat Australia 135 B6
Anne Arundel Town MD U.S.A. see Annapolis
Annecy France 66 H4
Anne Marie Lake Canada 153 J3
Annen Neth. 62 G1
Annette Island AK U.S.A. 149 O5
An Nimārah Syria 107 C3
An Nimāş Saudi Arabia 108 F6
Anning China 96 D3
Anniston AL U.S.A. 163 C5
Annobón i. Equat. Guinea 120 D5
Annonay France 66 G4
An Nu'mānīyah Iraq 113 G4
Anō Japan 92 C4
Anonima atoll Micronesia see Namonuito
Anorontany, Tanjona hd Madag. 123 E5
Ano Viannos Greece see Viannos
Anpu Gang b. China 97 F4
Anqing China 97 H2
Anqiu China 95 I4
Anren China 97 G3
Ans Belgium 62 F4
Ansai China 95 G4
Ansbach Germany 63 K5
Anser Group is Australia 138 C7
Anshan China 95 J3
Anshun Guizhou China 96 E3
Anshun Sichuan China 96 D2
Ansley NE U.S.A. 160 D3
Anson TX U.S.A. 161 D5
Anson Bay Australia 134 E3
Ansongo Mali 120 D3
Ansonville Canada 152 E4
Ansted WV U.S.A. 164 E4
Ansu China see Xushui
Ansudu Indon. 81 J7
Antabamba Peru 176 D6
Antakya Turkey 107 C1
Antalaha Madag. 123 F5
Antalya Turkey 69 N6
Antalya prov. Turkey 107 A1
Antalya Körfezi g. Turkey 69 N6

▶Antananarivo Madag. 123 E5
Capital of Madagascar.

An tAonach Ireland see Nenagh

▶Antarctica 188
Most southerly and coldest continent, and the continent with the highest average elevation.

Antarctic Peninsula Antarctica 188 L2
Antas r. Brazil 179 A5
An Teallach mt. U.K. 60 D3
Antelope Island UT U.S.A. 159 G1
Antelope Range mts NV U.S.A. 158 E2
Antequera Spain 67 D5
Anthony NM U.S.A. 166 D1
Anthony Lagoon Australia 136 A3
Anti-Atlas mts Morocco 64 C6
Antibes France 66 H5
Anticosti, Île d' i. Canada 153 J4
Anticosti Island Canada see Anticosti, Île d'
Antifer, Cap d' c. France 59 H9
Antigo WI U.S.A. 160 F2
Antigonish Canada 153 J5
Antigua i. Antigua and Barbuda 169 L5
Antigua Guat. see Antigua Guatemala
Antigua country West Indies see Antigua and Barbuda
Antigua and Barbuda country West Indies 169 L5
Antigua Guatemala Guat. 167 H6
Antiguo-Morelos Mex. 167 F4
Antikythira i. Greece 69 J7
Antikythiro, Steno sea chan. Greece 69 J7
Anti Lebanon mts Lebanon/Syria see Sharqī, Jabal ash
Antimilos i. Greece 69 K6
Antimony UT U.S.A. 159 H2
An tInbhear Mór Ireland see Arklow
Antioch Turkey see Antakya
Antioch CA U.S.A. 158 C2
Antiocheia ad Cragum tourist site Turkey 107 A1
Antiochia Turkey see Antakya
Antiparos i. Greece 69 K6
Antipodes Islands N.Z. 133 H6
Antipsara i. Greece 69 K5
Antium Italy see Anzio
Antlers OK U.S.A. 161 E5
Antofagasta Chile 178 B2
Antofagasta de la Sierra Arg. 178 C3
Antofalla, Volcán vol. Arg. 178 C3
Antoing Belgium 62 D4
Antonine Wall tourist site U.K. 60 E5
António Enes Moz. see Angoche
Antri India 104 D4
Antrim U.K. 61 F3
Antrim Hills U.K. 61 F2
Antrim Plateau Australia 134 E4
Antropovo Russia 52 I4
Antsalova Madag. 123 E5
Antseranana Madag. see Antsirañana
Antsirabe Madag. 123 E5
Antsirañana Madag. 123 E5
Antsla Estonia 55 O8
Antsohihy Madag. 123 E5
Anttis Sweden 54 M3
Anttola Fin. 55 O6
An Tuc Vietnam see An Khê
Antwerp Belgium 62 E3
Antwerp NY U.S.A. 165 H1
Antwerpen Belgium see Antwerp
An Uaimh Ireland see Navan
Anuc, Lac l. Canada 152 G2
Anuchino Russia 90 D4
Anugul India see Angul
Anupgarh India 104 C3
Anuradhapura Sri Lanka 106 D4
Anveh Iran 110 D5
Anvers Island Antarctica 188 L2
Anvik AK U.S.A. 148 G3
Anvik r. AK U.S.A. 148 G3
Anvil Range mts Canada 149 N3
Anxi China 97 H3
Anxiang China 97 G2
Anxin China 95 H4
Anxious Bay Australia 135 F8
Anyang Guangxi China see Du'an
Anyang Henan China 95 H4
Anyang S. Korea 91 B5
Anyar Java Indon. 84 D4
A'nyêmaqên Shan mts China 94 D5
Anyuan Jiangxi China 97 G3
Anyuan Jiangxi China 97 G3
Anyue China 96 E2
Anyuy r. Russia 90 E2
Anyuysk Russia 77 R3
Anzac Alta Canada 151 I3
Anzac B.C. Canada 150 F4
Anze China 95 H4
Anzhero-Sudzhensk Russia 76 J4
Anzi Dem. Rep. Congo 122 C4
Anzio Italy 68 E4
Aoba Japan 93 F3
Aoba i. Vanuatu 133 G3
Aoba-yama hill Japan 92 B3
Aogaki Japan 92 B3
Aoga-shima i. Japan 91 E6
Aohan Qi China see Xinhui
Ao Kham, Laem pt Thai. 87 B5
Aoki Japan 93 E2
Aomen China see Macao
Aomen aut. reg. China see Macao
Aomen Tebie Xingzhengqu aut. reg. China see Macao
Aomori Japan 90 F4
A'ong Co l. China 99 C6
Ao Phang Nga National Park Thai. 87 B5

▶Aoraki/Mount Cook mt. N.Z. 139 C6
Highest mountain in New Zealand.

Aoraki/Mount Cook National Park N.Z. 139 C6
Aôral, Phnum mt. Cambodia 87 D4
Aorangi mt. N.Z. see Aoraki/Mount Cook
Aosta Italy 68 B2
Aotearoa country Oceania see New Zealand
Aouk, Bahr r. Cent. Afr. Rep./Chad 121 E4
Aoukâr reg. Mali/Mauritania 120 C2
Aoulef Alg. 120 D2
Aoussard W. Sahara 120 B2
Aoyama Japan 92 C4
Aozou Chad 121 E2
Apa r. Brazil 178 E2
Apache Creek NM U.S.A. 159 I5
Apache Junction AZ U.S.A. 159 H5
Apaiang atoll Kiribati see Abaiang
Apalachee Bay FL U.S.A. 163 C6
Apalachicola FL U.S.A. 163 C6
Apalachicola r. FL U.S.A. 163 C6
Apalachin NY U.S.A. 165 G2
Apamea Turkey see Dinar
Apan Mex. 167 F5
Apaporis r. Col. 176 E4
Apar, Teluk b. Indon. 85 G3
Aparecida do Tabuado Brazil 179 A3
Aparima N.Z. see Riverton
Aparri Luzon Phil. 82 C2
Apatity Russia 54 R3
Apatzingán Mex. 168 D5
Apavawook Cape AK U.S.A. 148 E3
Ape Latvia 55 O8
Apeldoorn Neth. 62 F2
Apelern Germany 63 J2
Apennines mts Italy 68 C2
Apensen Germany 63 J1
Apex Mountain Canada 149 M3
Aphrewn r. AK U.S.A. 148 F3
Api mt. Nepal 104 E3
Api i. Vanuatu see Épi
Api, Tanjung pt Indon. 83 B3
Apia atoll Kiribati see Abaiang

▶Apia Samoa 133 I3
Capital of Samoa.

Apiacas, Serra dos hills Brazil 177 G6
Apiaí Brazil 179 A4
Apipilulco Mex. 167 F5
Apishapa r. CO U.S.A. 160 C4
Apiti N.Z. 139 E4
Apizaco Mex. 167 F5
Apizolaya Mex. 166 E3
Apkhazeti disp. terr. Georgia see Abkhazia
Aplao Peru 176 D7
Apo, Mount vol. Mindanao Phil. 82 D5
Apo East Passage Phil. 82 C3
Apoera Suriname 177 G2
Apolda Germany 63 L3
Apollo Bay Australia 138 A7
Apollonia Bulg. see Sozopol
Apolo Bol. 176 E6
Aporé Brazil 179 A2
Aporé r. Brazil 179 A2
Apostelens Tommelfinger mt. Greenland 147 N3
Apostle Islands WI U.S.A. 160 F2
Apostolos Andreas, Cape Cyprus 107 B2
Apoteri Guyana 177 G3
Apo West Passage Phil. 82 C3
Apozai Pak. 111 H4
Appalachian Mountains U.S.A. 164 D5
Appalla i. Fiji see Kabara
Appennino mts Italy see Apennines
Appennino Abruzzese mts Italy 68 E3
Appennino Tosco-Emiliano mts Italy 68 D3
Appennino Umbro-Marchigiano mts Italy 68 E3
Appingedam Neth. 62 G1
Applecross U.K. 60 D3
Appleton MN U.S.A. 160 D2
Appleton WI U.S.A. 164 A1
Apple Valley CA U.S.A. 158 E4
Appomattox VA U.S.A. 165 F5
Aprilia Italy 68 E4
Aprunyi India 96 B2
Apsheronsk Russia 113 E1
Apsheronskaya Russia see Apsheronsk
Apsley Canada 165 F1
Apt France 66 G5
Apucarana Brazil 179 A3
Apucarana, Serra da hills Brazil 179 A3
Apuka Russia 77 R3
Apulum Romania see Alba Iulia
Apurahuan Palawan Phil. 82 B4
Apurashokoru i. Palau 82 [inset]
Aq''a Georgia see Sokhumi
'Aqaba Jordan see Al 'Aqabah
Aqaba, Gulf of Asia 112 D5
'Aqaba, Wādī el watercourse Egypt see 'Aqabah, Wādī al
'Aqabah, Birkat al well Iraq 110 A4
'Aqabah, Wādī al watercourse Egypt 107 A4
Aqadyr Kazakh. see Akadyr
Aqal China 98 B4
Aqdoghmish r. Iran 110 B2
Aqi Tag mt. China 94 B3
Aqköl Akmolinskaya Oblast' Kazakh. see Akkol'
Aqköl Atyrauskaya Oblast' Kazakh. see Akkol'
Aqmola Kazakh. see Astana
Aqqan Xinjiang China 99 C5
Aqqan Xinjiang China 99 D5
Aqqikkol Hu salt l. China 99 E5
Aqra', Jabal al mt. Syria/Turkey 107 B2
'Aqran hill Saudi Arabia 107 D4
Aqsay Kazakh. see Aksay
Aqshī Kazakh. see Akshi
Aqshuqyr Kazakh. see Akshukyr
Aqsū Kazakh. see Aksu
Aqsüat Kazakh. see Aksuat
Aqsū-Ayuly Kazakh. see Aksu-Ayuly
Aqtaū Kazakh. see Aktau
Aqtöbe Kazakh. see Aktobe
Aqtoghay Kazakh. see Aktogay
Aquae Grani Germany see Aachen
Aquae Gratianae France see Aix-les-Bains
Aquae Sextiae France see Aix-en-Provence
Aquae Statiellae Italy see Acqui Terme
Aquarius Mountains AZ U.S.A. 159 G4
Aquarius Plateau UT U.S.A. 159 H3
Aquidauana Brazil 178 E2
Aquila Mex. 166 E5
Aquiles Mex. 166 D2
Aquincum Hungary see Budapest
Aquiry r. Brazil see Acre
Aquisgranum Germany see Aachen
Aquitaine reg. France 66 D5
Aquitania reg. France see Aquitaine
Aqzhayqyn Köli salt l. Kazakh. see Akzhaykyn, Ozero
Ara India see Arrah
Āra Ārba Eth. 122 E3
'Arab Afgh. 111 G4
Arab, Bahr el watercourse Sudan 121 F4
'Arab, Khalīg el b. Egypt see 'Arab, Khalīj al
'Arab, Khalīj al b. Egypt 112 C5
'Arabah, Wādī al watercourse Israel/Jordan 107 B5
Arabian Basin sea feature Indian Ocean 185 M5
Arabian Gulf Asia see The Gulf
Arabian Peninsula Asia 108 G5
Arabian Sea Indian Ocean 109 K6
Araç Turkey 112 D2
Araça r. Brazil 176 F4
Aracaju Brazil 177 K6
Aracati Brazil 177 K4
Aracatu Brazil 179 C1
Araçatuba Brazil 179 A3
Aracena Spain 67 C5
Aracruz Brazil 179 C2
Araçuaí Brazil 179 C2
Araçuaí r. Brazil 179 C2
'Arad Israel 107 B4
Arad Romania 69 I1

'Arādah U.A.E. 110 D6
Arafune-yama mt. Japan 93 E2
Arafura Sea Australia/Indon. 132 D2
Arafura Shelf sea feature Australia/Indon. 186 E6
Aragarças Brazil 177 H7
Ara-gawa r. Japan 93 E1
Ara-gawa r. Japan 93 F3
Aragón r. Spain 67 F2
Araguaçu Brazil 179 A1
Araguaia r. Brazil 179 A1
Araguaia, Parque Nacional do nat. park Brazil 177 H6
Araguaiana Brazil 179 A1
Araguaína Brazil 177 I5
Araguari Brazil 179 A2
Araguari r. Brazil 177 H3
Araguatins Brazil 177 I5
Araí Brazil 179 B1
Arai Niigata Japan see Myōkō
Arai Shizuoka Japan 92 D4
'Arâif el Naga, Gebel hill Egypt see 'Urayf an Nāqah, Jabal
Araioses Brazil 177 J4
Arak Alg. 120 D2
Arāk Iran 110 C3
Arak Syria 107 D2
Arakai-yama mt. Japan 93 F1
Arakamchechen, Ostrov i. Russia 148 D2
Arakan reg. Myanmar 86 A2
Arakan Yoma mts Myanmar 86 A2
Araki-gawa r. Japan 92 D2
Arakkonam India 106 C3
Araks r. Azer. see Araz
Araku India 106 D2
Aral Qinghai China 99 E5
Aral Xinjiang China 98 C4
Aral Kazakh. see Aral'sk
Aral Tajik. see Vose'

▶Aral Sea salt l. Kazakh./Uzbek. 102 B2
4th largest lake in Asia.

Aral'sk Kazakh. 102 B2
Aral'skoye More salt l. Kazakh./Uzbek. see Aral Sea
Aralsor, Ozero l. Kazakh. 53 K6
Aral Tengizi salt l. Kazakh./Uzbek. see Aral Sea
Araltobe China 94 B2
Aramac Australia 136 D4
Aramac Creek watercourse Australia 136 D4
Aramah plat. Saudi Arabia 110 B5
Aramberri Mex. 161 D7
Aramia r. P.N.G. 81 K8
Aran r. India 106 C2
Aranda de Duero Spain 67 E3
Arandai Indon. 81 I7
Aranđelovac Serbia 69 I2
Arandis Namibia 124 B2
Arang India 105 E5
Arani India 106 C3
Aran Islands Ireland 61 C4
Aranjuez Spain 67 E3
Aranos Namibia 124 D3
Aransas Pass TX U.S.A. 161 D7
Arantangi India 106 C4
Aranuka atoll Kiribati 133 H1
Aranyaprathet Thai. 87 C4
Arao Japan 91 C6
Araouane Mali 120 C3
Arapaho OK U.S.A. 161 D5
Arapgir Turkey 112 E3
Arapiraca Brazil 177 K5
Arapis, Akra pt Greece see Arapis, Akrotirio
Arapis, Akrotirio pt Greece 69 K4
Arapkir Turkey see Arapgir
Arapongas Brazil 179 A3
Araquari Brazil 179 A4
'Ar'ar Saudi Arabia 113 F5
Araraj India 99 D8
Araranguá Brazil 179 A5
Araraquara Brazil 179 A3
Araras Brazil 177 H5
Ararat Armenia 113 G3
Ararat Australia 138 A6
Ararat, Mount Turkey 113 G3
Araria India 105 F4
Araripina Brazil 177 J5
Aras r. Azer. see Araz
Aras Turkey 113 F3
Ar-Asgat Mongolia see Ugtaaltsaydam
Arashima-dake mt. Japan 92 C3
Arataca Brazil 179 D1
Aratürük China see Yiwu
Arauca Col. 176 D2
Arauca r. Venez. 176 E2
Aravalli Range mts India 104 C4
Aravete Estonia 55 N7
Arawa P.N.G. 132 F2
Araxá Brazil 179 B2
Araxes r. Azer. see Araz
Arayıt Dağı mt. Turkey 69 N5
Araz r. Azer. 113 H2
also spelt Araks (Armenia), Aras (Turkey), formerly known as Araxes
Arbailu Iraq see Arbīl/Hewlêr
Arbela Iraq see Arbīl/Hewlêr
Arberth U.K. see Narberth
Arbīl/Hewlêr Iraq 113 G3
Arboga Sweden 55 I7
Arborfield Canada 151 K4
Arborg Canada 151 L5
Arbroath U.K. 60 G4
Arbuckle CA U.S.A. 158 B2
Arbū-ye Shamālī, Dasht-e des. Afgh. 111 F4
Arcachon France 66 D4
Arcade NY U.S.A. 165 F2
Arcadia FL U.S.A. 163 D7
Arcadia LA U.S.A. 161 E5
Arcadia MI U.S.A. 164 B1
Arcanum OH U.S.A. 164 C4
Arcas, Cayos is Mex. 167 H4
Arcata CA U.S.A. 156 B4
Arc Dome mt. NV U.S.A. 158 E2
Arcelia Mex. 168 D5
Archaeological Sites of the Island of Meroe tourist site Sudan 121 G3
Archangel Russia 52 I2
Archer r. Australia 79 G9
Archer Bend National Park Australia 136 C2
Archer City TX U.S.A. 161 D5
Arches National Park UT U.S.A. 159 I2
Archipel-de-Mingan, Réserve du Parc National de l' nat. park Canada 153 J4
Archipiélago Los Roques, Parque Nacional nat. park Venez. 176 E1
Ärçivan Azer. 113 H3
Arckaringa watercourse Australia 137 A6
Arco ID U.S.A. 156 E4
Arcos Brazil 179 B3
Arcos de la Frontera Spain 67 D5
Arctic Bay Canada 147 J2
Arctic Institute Islands Russia see Arkticheskogo Instituta, Ostrova
Arctic Lagoon AK U.S.A. 148 F2
Arctic Mid-Ocean Ridge sea feature Arctic Ocean 189 H1
Arctic National Wildlife Refuge nature res. AK U.S.A. 149 K1
Arctic Ocean 189 B1
Arctic Red r. Canada 149 N2
Arctic Red River Canada see Tsiigehtchic
Arctic Village AK U.S.A. 149 K1
Arctowski research station Antarctica 188 A2
Arda r. Bulg. 69 L4
also known as Ardas (Greece)
Ardabīl Iran 110 C2
Ardahan Turkey 113 F2
Ardakān Iran 110 D3
Årdalstangen Norway 55 E6
Ardara Ireland 61 D3
Ardas r. Bulg. see Arda
Arḍ aṣ Ṣawwān plain Jordan 107 C4
Ardatov Nizhegorodskaya Oblast' Russia 53 I5
Ardatov Respublika Mordoviya Russia 53 J5
Ardee Ireland 61 F4
Ardennes plat. Belgium 62 E5
Ardennes, Canal des France 62 E5
Arden Town CA U.S.A. 158 C2
Arderin hill Ireland 61 E4
Ardestān Iran 110 D3
Ardglass U.K. 61 G3
Ardila r. Port. 67 C4
Ardlethan Australia 138 C5
Ardmore OK U.S.A. 161 D5
Ardnamurchan, Point of U.K. 60 C4
Ardon Russia 113 G2
Ardrishaig U.K. 60 D4
Ardrossan U.K. 60 E5
Ardvasar U.K. 60 D3
Areia Branca Brazil 177 K4
Arekalong Peninsula Palau 82 [inset]
Arel Belgium see Arlon
Arelas France see Arles
Arelate France see Arles
Aremberg hill Germany 62 G4
Arena reef Phil. 82 C4
Arena, Point CA U.S.A. 158 B2
Arena, Punta pt Mex. 166 C4
Arena de la Ventana, Punta pt Mex. 166 C3
Arenal, Volcán vol. Costa Rica 166 [inset] I7
Arena Point Luzon Phil. 82 C3
Arenas de San Pedro Spain 67 D3
Arendal Norway 55 F7
Arendsee (Altmark) Germany 63 L2
Areopoli Greece 69 J6
Areponapuchi Mex. 166 D3
Arequipa Peru 176 D7
Arere Brazil 177 H4
Arévalo Spain 67 D3
Arezzo Italy 68 D3
'Arfajah well Saudi Arabia 107 D4
Argadargada Australia 136 B4
Argalant Mongolia 95 G2
Argan China 98 E4
Arganda del Rey Spain 67 E3
Argao Cebu Phil. 82 C4
Argatay Mongolia see Bayanjargalan
Argel Alg. see Algiers
Argentan France 66 D2
Argentario, Monte hill Italy 68 D3
Argentera, Cima dell' mt. Italy 68 B2
Argenthal Germany 63 H5

▶Argentina country S. America 178 C5
2nd largest and 3rd most populous country in South America and 8th largest in the world.

Argentine Abyssal Plain sea feature S. Atlantic Ocean 184 E9
Argentine Basin sea feature S. Atlantic Ocean 184 F8
Argentine Republic country S. America see Argentina
Argentine Rise sea feature S. Atlantic Ocean 184 E8
Argentino, Lago l. Arg. 178 B8
Argenton-sur-Creuse France 66 E3
Argentoratum France see Strasbourg
Argeș r. Romania 69 L2
Arg-e Zārī Afgh. 111 G3
Arghandāb Rōd r. Afgh. 111 G4
Argi r. Russia 90 C1
Argolikos Kolpos b. Greece 69 J6
Argos Greece 69 J6
Argos IN U.S.A. 164 B3
Argostoli Greece 69 I5
Arguis Spain 67 F2
Argun' r. China/Russia 89 M2
Argun Russia 113 G2
Argungu Nigeria 120 D3
Argunskiy Khrebet mts Russia 95 I1
Argus, Dome ice feature Antarctica 188 E1
Argus Range mts CA U.S.A. 158 E4
Arguut Mongolia see Guchin-Us
Argyle Canada 153 I6
Argyle, Lake Australia 134 E4
Argyrokastron Albania see Gjirokastër
Arhangay prov. Mongolia 94 E2
Ar Horqin Qi China see Tianshan
Århus Denmark see Aarhus
Arhymot Lake AK U.S.A. 148 G3
Ariaga i. Indon. 83 C1
Ariah Park Australia 138 C5
Ariamsvlei Namibia 124 D5
Ariana Tunisia see L'Ariana
Ariano Irpino Italy 68 F4
Ari Atholhu Maldives 103 D11
Aribinda Burkina Faso 120 C3
Arica Chile 176 D7
Arid, Cape Australia 135 C8
Arida Japan 92 B4
Aridagawa Japan 92 B4
Arida-gawa r. Japan 92 B4
Arigiyn Gol r. Mongolia 94 E1
Arigza China 96 C1
Arīḥā Syria 107 C2
Arīḥā West Bank see Jericho
Arikaree r. CO U.S.A. 160 C3
Arima Trin. and Tob. 169 L6
Arimine-ko resr Japan 92 D2
Ariminum Italy see Rimini
Arinos Brazil 179 B1
Ario de Rosáles Mex. 167 E5
Aripuanã Brazil 177 G6
Aripuanã r. Brazil 176 F5
Ariquemes Brazil 176 F5
Aris Namibia 124 C2
Arisaig U.K. 60 D4
Arisaig, Sound of sea chan. U.K. 60 D4
'Arīsh, Wādī al watercourse Egypt 107 A4
Aristazabal Island Canada 150 D4
Arixang China see Wenquan
Ariyalur India 106 C4
Arizaro, Salar de salt flat Arg. 178 C2
Arizona Arg. 178 C5
Arizona state U.S.A. 157 F6
Arizpe Mex. 166 C2
'Arjah Saudi Arabia 108 F5
Arjasa Java Indon. 85 F4
Arjeplog Sweden 54 J3
Arjuni Chhattisgarh India 106 D1
Arjuni Mahar. India 104 E5
Arkadak Russia 53 I6
Arkadelphia AR U.S.A. 161 E5
Arkaig, Loch l. U.K. 60 D4
Arkalyk Kazakh. 102 C1
Arkansas r. AR U.S.A. 161 F5
Arkansas state U.S.A. 161 E5
Arkansas City AR U.S.A. 161 F5
Arkansas City KS U.S.A. 161 D4
Arkanū, Jabal mt. Libya 108 B5
Arka Tag mts China 99 E5
Arkell, Mount Canada 149 N3
Arkhangel'sk Russia see Archangel
Arkhara Russia 90 C2
Arkhipovka Russia 90 D4
Árki i. Greece see Arkoi
Arklow Ireland 61 F5
Arkoi i. Greece 69 L6
Arkona Canada 164 E2
Arkona, Kap c. Germany 57 N3
Arkonam India see Arakkonam
Arkport NY U.S.A. 165 G2

▶Arkticheskiy, Mys c. Russia 189 E1
Most northerly point of Asia.

Arkticheskogo Instituta, Ostrova is Russia 76 J2
Arkul' Russia 52 K4
Arlandag mt. Turkm. 110 D2
Arles France 66 G5
Arli, Parc National de l' nat. park Burkina Faso 120 D3
Arlington S. Africa 125 H5
Arlington NY U.S.A. 165 I3
Arlington OH U.S.A. 164 D3
Arlington SD U.S.A. 160 D2
Arlington VA U.S.A. 165 G4
Arlington Heights IL U.S.A. 164 A2
Arlit Niger 120 D3
Arlon Belgium 62 F5
Arm r. Canada 151 J5
Armadale Australia 135 A8
Armadores i. Indon. 83 C1
Armagh U.K. 61 F3
Arma Konda mt. India 106 D2
Armant Egypt 108 D4
Armavir Armenia 113 G2
Armavir Russia 113 F1
Armenia country Asia 113 G2
Armenia Col. 176 C3
Armenopolis Romania see Gherla
Armeria Mex. 168 D5
Armidale Australia 138 E3
Armington MT U.S.A. 156 F3
Armit Lake Canada 151 N1
Armori India 106 D1
Armour SD U.S.A. 160 D3
Armoy U.K. 61 F2
Armstrong r. Australia 134 E4
Armstrong Canada 152 C4
Armstrong, Mount Canada 149 N3
Armstrong Island Cook Is see Rarotonga
Armu r. Russia 90 E3
Armur India 106 C2
Armutçuk Dağı mts Turkey 69 L5
Armyanskaya S.S.R. country Asia see Armenia
Arnaoutis, Cape Cyprus see Arnauti, Cape
Arnaud r. Canada 153 H2
Arnauti, Cape Cyprus 107 A2
Årnes Norway 55 G6
Arnett OK U.S.A. 161 D4
Arnhem Neth. 62 F3
Arnhem, Cape Australia 136 B2
Arnhem Land reg. Australia 134 F3
Arniston S. Africa 124 E8
Arno r. Italy 68 D3
Arno Bay Australia 137 B7
Arnold U.K. 59 F5
Arnold's Cove Canada 153 L5
Arnon r. Jordan see Mawjib, Wādī al
Arnprior Canada 165 G1
Arnsberg Germany 63 I3
Arnstadt Germany 63 K4
Arnstein Germany 63 J5
Arnstorf Germany 63 M6
Aroab Namibia 124 D4
Aroland Canada 152 D4
Arolsen Germany 63 J3
Aroma Sudan 108 E6
Arona Italy 68 C2
Aropuk Lake AK U.S.A. 148 G3
Arorae i. Kiribati 133 H2
Arore i. Kiribati see Arorae
Aroroy Masbate Phil. 82 C3
Aros r. Mex. 166 C2
Arossi i. Solomon Is see Makira
Arpa Kyrg. 98 A4
Arqalyq Kazakh. see Arkalyk
Arquipélago da Madeira aut. reg. Port. 120 B1
Arrabury Australia 137 C5
Arrah India 105 F4
Arraias Brazil 179 B1
Arraias, Serra de hills Brazil 179 B1
Ar Ramādī Iraq 113 F4
Ar Ramlah Jordan 107 B5
Ar Ramthā Jordan 107 C3
Arran i. U.K. 60 D5
Arranmore Island Ireland 61 D3
Ar Raqqah Syria 107 D2
Arras France 62 C4
Ar Rass Saudi Arabia 108 F4
Ar Rastan Syria 107 C2
Ar Rayyān Qatar 110 C5
Arrecife Canary Is 120 B2
Arretium Italy see Arezzo
Arriagá Mex. 168 F5
Arriaga Mex. 167 E4
Ar Rifā'ī Iraq 113 G5
Ar Rihāb salt flat Iraq 113 G5
Ar Rimāl reg. Saudi Arabia 122 F1
Arrington VA U.S.A. 165 F5
Ar Riyāḍ Saudi Arabia see Riyadh
Arrochar U.K. 60 E4
Arrojado r. Brazil 179 B1
Arrow, Lough l. Ireland 61 D3
Arrowsmith, Mount N.Z. 139 C6
Arroyo Grande CA U.S.A. 158 C4
Arroyo Seco Mex. 167 F4
Ar Rubay'iyah Saudi Arabia 110 B5
Ar Rummān Jordan 107 B3
Ar Ruq'ī well Saudi Arabia 110 B4
Ar Ruṣayfah Jordan 107 C3
Ar Rustāq Oman 110 E6
Ar Ruṭbah Iraq 113 F4
Ar Ruwaydah Saudi Arabia 110 B5
Ar Ruwaydah Saudi Arabia 110 B6
Ar Ruwayḍah Syria 107 C2
Års Denmark see Aars
Ars Iran 110 B2
Arseno Lake Canada 150 H1
Arsen'yev Russia 90 D3
Arshaly Kazakh. 98 C2
Arsk Russia 52 K4
Arta Greece 69 I5
Arteaga Coahuila Mex. 167 E3
Arteaga Michoacán Mex. 166 E5
Artem Russia 90 D4
Artemisa Cuba 163 D8
Artemivs'k Ukr. 53 H6
Artemovsk Ukr. see Artemivs'k
Artenay France 66 E2
Artesia AZ U.S.A. 159 I5
Artesia NM U.S.A. 157 G6
Arthur Canada 164 E2
Arthur NE U.S.A. 160 C3
Arthur TN U.S.A. 164 D5
Arthur, Lake PA U.S.A. 164 E3
Arthur's Pass National Park N.Z. 139 C6
Arthur's Town Bahamas 163 F7
Arti Russia 51 R4
Artigas research station Antarctica 188 A2
Artigas Uruguay 178 E4
Art'ik Armenia 113 F2
Artillery Lake Canada 151 I2
Artisia Botswana 125 H3
Artois reg. France 62 B4
Artois, Collines d' hills France 62 B4
Artos Dağı mt. Turkey 113 F3
Artova Turkey 112 E2
Artsakh disp. terr. Azer. see Nagorno-Karabakh
Arts Bogdīn Nuruu mts Mongolia 94 E2
Artsiz Ukr. see Artsyz
Artsyz Ukr. 69 M2
Artur de Paiva Angola see Kuvango
Arturo Prat research station Antarctica 188 A2
Artux China 98 B5
Artvin Turkey 113 F2
Artyk Turkm. 110 E2
Aru, Kepulauan is Moluccas Indon. 134 F1
Arua Uganda 122 D3
Aruanã Brazil 179 A1

▶Aruba terr. West Indies 169 K6
Self-governing Netherlands territory.

Arumã Brazil 176 F4
Arunachal Pradesh state India 105 H4
Arundel U.K. 59 G8
Arun He r. China 95 K2
Arun Qi China see Naji
Aruppukkottai India 106 C4
Arus, Tanjung pt Indon. 83 B2
Arusha Tanz. 122 D4
Arut r. Indon. 85 E3
Aruwimi r. Dem. Rep. Congo 122 C3
Arvada CO U.S.A. 156 G5
Arvagh Ireland 61 E4
Arvayheer Mongolia 94 E2
Arviat Canada 151 M2
Arvidsjaur Sweden 54 K4
Arvika Sweden 55 H7
Arvonia VA U.S.A. 165 F5
Arwā' Saudi Arabia 110 B6
Arwād, Jazīrat i. Syria 107 B2
Arwala Moluccas Indon. 83 C4
Arxan Nei Mongol China 95 I2
Arxan Xinjiang China 98 D4
Aryanah Tunisia see L'Ariana
Āryanshahr Iran 110 E3
Arys Kazakh. 102 C3
Arzamas Russia 53 I5
Arzanah i. U.A.E. 110 D5
Arzberg Germany 63 M4
Arzew Alg. 67 F6
Arzgir Russia 113 G1
Arzila Morocco see Asilah
Aš Czech Rep. 63 M4
Asaba Japan 93 D4
Asaba Nigeria 120 D4
Asad, Buḥayrat al resr Syria 107 D1
Asadābād Afgh. 111 H3
Asadābād Iran 110 C3
Asago Hyōgo Japan 92 A3
Asago Hyōgo Japan 92 A3
Asahan r. Indon. 84 B2
Asahi Aichi Japan 92 D3
Asahi Chiba Japan 93 G3
Asahi Gifu Japan 92 D2
Asahi Ibaraki Japan 93 G2
Asahi Kanagawa Japan 93 F3
Asahi Mie Japan 92 C3
Asahi Nagano Japan 93 D2
Asahi Toyama Japan 92 D2
Asahi-dake vol. Japan 90 F4
Asahikawa Japan 90 F4
Asaka Japan 93 F3
Asakawa Japan 93 G1
Asake-gawa r. Japan 92 C3
'Asal Egypt 107 A5
Āsalē l. Eth. 122 E2
Asālem Iran 110 C2
'Asalūyeh Iran 110 D5
Asamaga-take hill Japan 92 C4
Asama-yama vol. Japan 93 E2
Asan-man b. S. Korea 91 B5
Asansol India 105 F5
Asao Japan 93 F3
Asar China 95 I2
Asashina Japan 93 E2
Āsayita Eth. 122 E2
Asbach Germany 63 H4
Asbestos Mountains S. Africa 124 F5
Asbury Park NJ U.S.A. 165 H3
Ascalon Israel see Ashqelon
Ascea Italy 68 F4
Ascensión Bol. 176 F7
Ascensión Chihuahua Mex. 166 D2
Ascensión Nuevo León Mex. 167 F3
Ascension atoll Micronesia see Pohnpei

▶Ascension i. S. Atlantic Ocean 184 H6
Part of St Helena, Ascension and Tristan da Cunha.

Ascensión, Bahía de la b. Mex. 169 G5
Aschaffenburg Germany 63 J5
Ascheberg Germany 63 H3
Aschersleben Germany 63 L3
Ascoli Piceno Italy 68 E3
Asculum Italy see Ascoli Piceno
Asculum Picenum Italy see Ascoli Piceno
Ascutney VT U.S.A. 165 I2
Āseb Eritrea see Assab
Åseda Sweden 55 I8
Åsele Sweden 54 J4
Asenovgrad Bulg. 69 K3
Aşfar, Jabal al mt. Jordan 107 C3
Aşfar, Tall al hill Syria 107 C3

▶Aşgabat Turkm. 110 E2
Capital of Turkmenistan.

Asha Russia 51 R5
Ashahi-dake mt. Japan 92 D2
Ashāwī, Mishāsh al well Saudi Arabia 110 C5
Ashburn GA U.S.A. 163 D6
Ashburton watercourse Australia 134 A5
Ashburton N.Z. 139 C6
Ashburton Range hills Australia 134 F4
Ashdod Israel 107 B4
Ashdown AR U.S.A. 161 E5
Asheboro NC U.S.A. 162 E5
Asher OK U.S.A. 161 D5
Ashern Canada 151 L5
Asheville NC U.S.A. 162 D5
Asheweig r. Canada 152 D3
Ashford Australia 138 E2
Ashford U.K. 59 H7
Ash Fork AZ U.S.A. 159 G4
Ashgabat Turkm. see Aşgabat
Ashibetsu Japan 90 F4
Ashigawa Japan 93 E3
Ashikaga Japan 93 F2
Ashington U.K. 58 F3
Ashino-ko l. Japan 93 F3
Ashio Japan 93 F2
Ashio-sanchi mts Japan 93 F2
Ashiwada Japan 93 E3
Ashiya Japan 92 B4
Ashizuri-misaki pt Japan 91 D6
Ashkelon Israel see Ashqelon
Ashkhabad Turkm. see Aşgabat
Ashkum IL U.S.A. 164 B3
Ashkun reg. Afgh. 111 H3
Ashland AL U.S.A. 163 C5
Ashland ME U.S.A. 162 G2
Ashland NH U.S.A. 165 J2
Ashland OH U.S.A. 164 D3
Ashland OR U.S.A. 156 C4
Ashland VA U.S.A. 165 G5
Ashland WI U.S.A. 160 F2
Ashland City TN U.S.A. 164 B5
Ashley Australia 138 D2
Ashley MI U.S.A. 164 C2
Ashley ND U.S.A. 160 D2

▶Ashmore and Cartier Islands terr. Australia 134 C3
Australian External Territory.

Ashmore Reef Australia 134 C3
Ashmore Reefs Australia 136 D1
Ashmyany Belarus 55 N9
Ashqelon Israel 107 B4
Ash Shabakah Iraq 113 F5
Ash Shaddādah Syria 113 F3
Ash Shallūfah Egypt 107 A4
Ash Sham Syria see Damascus
Ash Shanāfīyah Iraq 113 G5
Ash Shaqīq well Saudi Arabia 113 F5
Ash Sharāh mts Jordan 107 B4
Ash Sharawrah Saudi Arabia 108 G6
Ash Shāriqah U.A.E. see Sharjah
Ash Sharqāṭ Iraq 113 F4
Ash Shaṭrah Iraq 113 G5
Ash Shaṭṭ Egypt 107 A5
Ash Shawbak Jordan 107 B4
Ash Shaybānī well Saudi Arabia 113 F5
Ash Shaykh Ibrāhīm Syria 107 D2
Ash Shiblīyāt hill Saudi Arabia 107 C5
Ash Shiḥr Yemen 108 G7
Ash Shu'āybah Saudi Arabia 113 F6
Ash Shu'bah Saudi Arabia 108 F4
Ash Shurayf Saudi Arabia see Khaybar
Ashta India 104 D5
Ashtabula OH U.S.A. 164 E3
Ashtarak Armenia 113 G2
Ashti Mahar. India 104 D5
Ashti Mahar. India 106 B2
Ashti Mahar. India 106 C2
Āshtīān Iran 110 C3
Ashton S. Africa 124 E7
Ashton ID U.S.A. 156 F3
Ashton-under-Lyne U.K. 58 E5
Ashuanipi r. Canada 153 I3
Ashuanipi Lake Canada 153 I3
Ashur Iraq see Ash Sharqāṭ
Ashville AL U.S.A. 163 C5
Ashwaubenon WI U.S.A. 164 A1
Asi r. Asia 112 E3 see 'Āṣī, Nahr al
'Āṣī r. Lebanon/Syria see Orontes
'Āṣī, Nahr al r. Asia 112 E3
also known as Asi or Orontes
Āsīā Bak Iran 110 C3
Asid Gulf Masbate Phil. 82 C3
Asientos Mex. 166 E4
Asifabad India 106 C2
Asika India 106 E2
Asilah Morocco 67 C6
Asinara, Golfo dell' b. Sardinia Italy 68 C4
Asino Russia 76 J4
Asipovichy Belarus 53 F5
Asīr Iran 110 D5
'Asīr reg. Saudi Arabia 108 F5
Asisium Italy see Assisi
Askale Pak. 104 C2
Aşkale Turkey 113 F3
Asker Norway 55 G7
Askersund Sweden 55 I7
Askim Norway 55 G7
Askī Mawşil Iraq 113 F3
Askino Russia 51 R4
Askival hill U.K. 60 C4
Asl Egypt see 'Asal
Aslanköy r. Turkey 107 B1
Āsmār reg. Afgh. 111 H3

▶Asmara Eritrea 108 E6
Capital of Eritrea.

Āsmera Eritrea see Asmara
Åsnen l. Sweden 55 I8
Aso-Kuju Kokuritsu-kōen Japan 91 C6
Asonli India 96 B2
Asop India 104 C4
Asori Indon. 81 J7
Āsosa Eth. 122 D2
Asotin WA U.S.A. 156 D3
Aspang-Markt Austria 57 P7
Aspara Kazakh. 98 A4
Aspatria U.K. 58 D4
Aspen CO U.S.A. 156 G5
Asperg Germany 63 J6
Aspermont TX U.S.A. 161 C5
Aspiring, Mount N.Z. 139 B7
Aspro, Cape Cyprus 107 A2
Aspromonte, Parco Nazionale dell' nat. park Italy 68 F5
Aspron, Cape Cyprus see Aspro, Cape
Aspur India 111 I6
Asquith Canada 151 J4
As Sa'an Syria 107 C2
Assab Eritrea 108 F7
As Sabsab well Saudi Arabia 110 C5
Assad, Lake resr Syria see Asad, Buḥayrat al
Aş Şadr U.A.E. 110 D5
Aş Şafā lava field Syria 107 C3
Aş Şafāqīs Tunisia see Sfax
Aş Şaff Egypt 112 C5
As Safirah Syria 107 C1
Aş Şaḥrā' al Gharbīyah des. Egypt see Western Desert
Aş Şaḥrā' ash Sharqīyah des. Egypt see Eastern Desert
Assake-Audan, Vpadina depr. Kazakh./Uzbek. 113 J2
'Assal, Lac l. Djibouti see 'Assal, Lac

▶'Assal, Lac Djibouti 108 F7
Lowest point in Africa.

Aş Şāliḩīyah Syria 113 F4
As Sallūm Egypt 112 B5
As Salmān Iraq 113 G5
As Salţ Jordan 107 B3
Assam *state* India 105 G4
Assamakka Niger 120 D3
As Samāwah Iraq 113 G5
As Samrā' Jordan 107 C3
Aş Şanām *reg.* Saudi Arabia 108 H5
As Sarīr *reg.* Libya 121 F2
Assateague Island *MD* U.S.A. 165 H4
As Sawādah *reg.* Saudi Arabia 110 B6
Assayeta Eth. *see* Āsayita
As Sayḩ Saudi Arabia 110 B6
Assen Neth. 62 G1
Assenede Belgium 62 D3
Assesse Belgium 62 F4
As Sidrah Libya 121 E1
As Sīfah Oman 110 E6
Assigny, Lac *l.* Canada 153 I3
As Sikak Saudi Arabia 110 C5
Assiniboia Canada 151 J5
Assiniboine *r.* Canada 151 L5
Assiniboine, Mount Canada 146 G4
Assis Brazil 179 A3
Assisi Italy 68 E3
Aßlar Germany 63 I4
Aş Şubayḩīyah Kuwait 110 B4
Aş Şufayrī *well* Saudi Arabia 110 B4
As Sukhnah Syria 107 D2
As Sulaymānīyah/Slêmānî Iraq 113 G4
As Sulaymī Saudi Arabia 108 F4
Aş Şulb *reg.* Saudi Arabia 110 C5
Aş Şummān *plat.* Saudi Arabia 110 B5
Aş Şummān *plat.* Saudi Arabia 110 C6
As Sūq Saudi Arabia 108 F5
As Sūrīyah *country* Asia *see* Syria
Aş Şuwar Syria 113 F4
As Suwaydā' Syria 107 C3
As Suways Egypt *see* Suez
As Suways *governorate* Egypt 107 A4
Assynt, Loch *l.* U.K. 60 D2
Astacus Turkey *see* İzmit
Astakida *i.* Greece 69 L7
Astakos Greece 69 I5
Astalu Island Pak. *see* Astola Island

▶Astana Kazakh. 102 D1
Capital of Kazakhstan.

Āstāneh-ye Ashrafīyeh Iran 110 C2
Astara Azer. 113 H3
Āstārā Iran 108 G2
Asterābād Iran *see* Gorgān
Asti Italy 68 C2
Astillero Peru 176 E6
Astin Tag *mts* China *see* Altun Shan
Astipálaia *i.* Greece *see* Astypalaia
Astola Island Pak. 111 F5
Astor Pak. 99 A6
Astor *r.* Pak. 111 I3
Astorga Spain 67 C2
Astoria *OR* U.S.A. 156 C3
Åstorp Sweden 55 H8
Astrabad Iran *see* Gorgān
Astrakhan' Russia 53 K7
Astrakhan' Bazar Azer. *see* Cälilabad
Astravyets Belarus 55 N9
Astrida Rwanda *see* Butare
Asturias *aut. comm.* Spain 67 C2
Asturias, Principado de *aut. comm.* Spain *see* Asturias
Asturica Augusta Spain *see* Astorga
Astypalaia *i.* Greece 69 L6
Asubulak Kazakh. 98 C2
Asuka Japan 92 B4
Asuke Japan 92 D3
Asuncion *i.* N. Mariana Is 81 L3

▶Asunción Para. 178 E3
Capital of Paraguay.

'Āşūr, Tall *mt.* West Bank 107 B4
Asuwa-gawa *r.* Japan 92 C2
Aswad Oman 110 E5
Aswân Egypt *see* Aswān
Aswān Egypt 108 D5
Asyāḩ, Safrā' al *esc.* Saudi Arabia 110 A5
Asyûţ Egypt *see* Asyūţ
Asyūţ Egypt 112 C6
Ata *i.* Tonga 133 I4
Atacama, Desierto de *des.* Chile *see* Atacama Desert
Atacama, Salar de *salt flat* Chile 178 C2

▶Atacama Desert Chile 178 C3
Driest place in the world.

Atafu *atoll* Tokelau 133 I2
Atafu *i.* Tokelau 186 I6
Atago-san *hill* Japan 92 B3
Atago-yama *hill* Japan 93 F3
'Aţā'iţah, Jabal al *mt.* Jordan 107 B4
Atakent Turkey 107 B1
Atakpamé Togo 120 D4
Atalándi Greece *see* Atalanti
Atalanti Greece 69 J5
Atalaya Panama 166 [inset] J7
Atalaya Peru 176 D6
Ataléia Brazil 179 C2
Atambua Indon. 134 D2
Atami Japan 93 F3
Atamyrat Turkm. 111 G2
Ataniya Turkey *see* Adana
Atanur India 106 C2
Atapupu *Timor* Indon. 83 C5
'Ataq Yemen 108 G7
Atâr Mauritania 120 B2
Atari Pak. 111 I4
Atas Bogd Uul *mt.* Mongolia 94 D3
Atascadero *CA* U.S.A. 158 C4
Ātashān Iran 110 D3
Atasu Kazakh. 102 D2
Atatkan He *r.* China 99 E5
Ataúro, Ilha de *i.* East Timor 83 C5
Atáviros *mt.* Greece *see* Atavyros
Atavyros *mt.* Greece 69 L6
Atayurt Turkey 107 A1
Atbara Sudan 108 D6
Atbara *r.* Sudan 108 D6
Atbasar Kazakh. 102 C1
At-Bashy Kyrg. 98 A4
Atchafalaya Bay *LA* U.S.A. 167 H2
Atchison *KS* U.S.A. 160 E4
Atchueelinguk *r. AK* U.S.A. 148 G3
Atebubu Ghana 120 C4
Atema-yama *mt.* Japan 93 E1
Ateransk Kazakh. *see* Atyrau
Atessa Italy 68 F3
Ath Belgium 62 D4
Athabasca *r.* Canada 151 I3
Athabasca, Lake Canada 151 I3
Athalia *OH* U.S.A. 164 D4
'Athāmīn, Birkat al *well* Iraq 110 A4
Atharan Hazari Pak. 111 I4
Athboy Ireland 61 F4
Athenae Greece *see* Athens
Athenry Ireland 61 D4
Athens Canada 165 H1

▶Athens Greece 69 J6
Capital of Greece.

Athens *AL* U.S.A. 163 C5
Athens *GA* U.S.A. 163 D5
Athens *MI* U.S.A. 164 C2
Athens *OH* U.S.A. 164 D4
Athens *PA* U.S.A. 165 G3
Athens *TN* U.S.A. 162 C5
Athens *TX* U.S.A. 161 E5
Atherstone U.K. 59 F6
Atherton Australia 136 D3
Athies France 62 C5
Athina Greece *see* Athens
Athínai Greece *see* Athens
Athleague Ireland 61 D4
Athlone Ireland 61 E4
Athnā', Wādī al *watercourse* Jordan 107 D3
Athni India 106 B2
Athol N.Z. 139 B7
Athol *MA* U.S.A. 165 I2
Atholl, Forest of *reg.* U.K. 60 E4
Athos *mt.* Greece 69 K4
Ath Thamad Egypt 107 B5
Ath Thawrah Syria 107 D2
Ath Thāyat *mt.* Saudi Arabia 107 C5
Ath Thumāmī *well* Saudi Arabia 110 B5
Athy Ireland 61 F5
Ati Chad 121 E3
Aţiābād Iran 110 E3
Atico Peru 176 D7
Atigun Pass *AK* U.S.A. 149 J1
Atikameg Canada 150 H4
Atikameg *r.* Canada 152 E3
Atik Lake Canada 151 M4
Atikokan Canada 147 I5
Atikonak Lake Canada 153 I3
Atimonan *Luzon* Phil. 82 C3
Atiquizaya El Salvador 167 H6
Ātish Khānah, Kōh-e *hill* Afgh. 111 F3
Atitlán Guat. 167 H6
Atitlán, Parque Nacional *nat. park* Guat. 167 H6
Atjeh *admin. dist.* Indon. *see* Aceh
Atka Russia 77 Q3
Atka *AK* U.S.A. 148 [inset] D5
Atka Island *AK* U.S.A. 148 [inset] D5
Atkarsk Russia 53 J6
Atkinson Point *pt* Canada 149 O1
Atkri *Papua* Indon. 83 D3

▶Atlanta *GA* U.S.A. 163 C5
Capital of Georgia.

Atlanta *IN* U.S.A. 164 B3
Atlanta *MI* U.S.A. 164 C1
Atlantic *IA* U.S.A. 160 E3
Atlantic *NC* U.S.A. 163 E5
Atlantic City *NJ* U.S.A. 165 H4
Atlantic-Indian-Antarctic Basin *sea feature* S. Atlantic Ocean 184 H10
Atlantic-Indian Ridge *sea feature* Southern Ocean 184 H9

▶Atlantic Ocean 184
2nd largest ocean in the world.

Atlantic Peak *WY* U.S.A. 156 F4
Atlantis S. Africa 124 D7
Atlas Méditerranéen *mts* Alg. *see* Atlas Tellien
Atlas Mountains Africa 64 C5
Atlas Saharien *mts* Alg. 64 E5
Atlas Tellien *mts* Alg. 67 H6
Atlin Lake Canada 149 N4
Atlixco Mex. 167 F5
Atmakur India 106 C3
Atmautluak *AK* U.S.A. 148 G3
Atmore *AL* U.S.A. 163 C6
Atocha Bol. 176 E8
Atoka *OK* U.S.A. 161 D5
Atotonilco el Alto Mex. 166 E4
Atouat *mt.* Laos 86 D3
Atouila, Erg *des.* Mali 120 C2
Atoyac de Álvarez Mex. 167 E5
Atqan China *see* Aqqan
Atqasuk *AK* U.S.A. 148 H1
Atrak *r.* Iran/Turkm. *see* Atrek
Atrato *r.* Col. 176 C2
Atrek *r.* Iran/Turkm. 110 D2
also known as Atrak, *alt.* Etrek
Atropatene *country* Asia *see* Azerbaijan
Atsonupuri, Vulkan *vol.* Russia 90 G3
Atsugi Japan 93 F3
Atsumi Japan 92 D4
Atsumi-hantō *pen.* Japan 92 D4
Aţ Ţafīlah Jordan 107 B4
Aţ Ţā'if Saudi Arabia 108 F5
Attalea Turkey *see* Antalya
Attalia Turkey *see* Antalya
At Tamīmī Libya 112 A4
Attapu Laos 86 D4
Attawapiskat Canada 152 E3
Attawapiskat *r.* Canada 152 E3
Attawapiskat Lake Canada 152 D3
Aţ Ţawīl *mts* Saudi Arabia 113 E5
At Taysīyah *plat.* Saudi Arabia 113 F5
Attendorn Germany 63 H3
Attersee *l.* Austria 57 N7
Attica *IN* U.S.A. 164 B3
Attica *NY* U.S.A. 165 F2
Attica *OH* U.S.A. 164 D3
Attigny France 62 E5
Attikamagen Lake Canada 153 I3
Attleborough U.K. 59 I6
Attopeu Laos *see* Attapu
Attu Greenland 147 M3
Aţ Ţubayq *reg.* Saudi Arabia 107 C5

▶Attu Island *AK* U.S.A. 148 [inset] A5
Most westerly point of North America.

At Tūnisīyah *country* Africa *see* Tunisia
Aţ Ţūr Egypt 112 D5
Attur India 106 C4
Attu Station *AK* U.S.A. 148 [inset] A5
Aţ Ţuwayyah *well* Saudi Arabia 113 F6
Atuk Mountain *hill AK* U.S.A. 148 E3
Åtvidaberg Sweden 55 I7
Atwari Bangl. 99 E8
Atwater *CA* U.S.A. 158 C3
Atwood *KS* U.S.A. 160 C4
Atwood Lake *OH* U.S.A. 164 E3
Atyashevo Russia 53 J5
Atyrau Kazakh. 100 E2
Atyraū *admin. div.* Kazakh. *see* Atyrauskaya Oblast'
Atyrau Oblast *admin. div.* Kazakh. *see* Atyrauskaya Oblast'
Atyrauskaya Oblast' *admin. div.* Kazakh. 51 Q6
Aua Island P.N.G. 81 K7
Aub Germany 63 K5
Aubagne France 66 G5
Aubange Belgium 62 F5
Aubarede Point *Luzon* Phil. 82 C2
Aubenas France 66 G4
Aubergenville France 62 B6
Auboué France 62 F5
Aubrey Cliffs *mts AZ* U.S.A. 159 G4
Aubry Lake Canada 149 P2
Auburn *r.* Australia 137 E5
Auburn Canada 164 E2
Auburn *AL* U.S.A. 163 C5
Auburn *CA* U.S.A. 158 C2
Auburn *IN* U.S.A. 164 C3
Auburn *KY* U.S.A. 164 B5
Auburn *ME* U.S.A. 165 J1
Auburn *NE* U.S.A. 160 E3
Auburn *NY* U.S.A. 165 G2
Auburn Range *hills* Australia 136 E5
Aubusson France 66 F4
Auch France 66 E5
Auche Myanmar 86 B1
Auchterarder U.K. 60 F4

▶Auckland N.Z. 139 E3
5th most populous city in Oceania.

Auckland Islands N.Z. 133 G7
Auden Canada 152 D4
Audenarde Belgium *see* Oudenaarde
Audo Range *mts* Eth. 122 E3
Audruicq France 62 C4
Audubon *IA* U.S.A. 160 E3
Aue Germany 63 M4
Auerbach Germany 63 M4
Auerbach in der Oberpfalz Germany 63 L5
Auersberg *mt.* Germany 63 M4
Auezov Kazakh. 98 C2
Augathella Australia 137 D5
Augher U.K. 61 E3
Aughnacloy U.K. 61 F3
Aughrim Ireland 61 F5
Augrabies S. Africa 124 E5
Augrabies Falls S. Africa 124 E5
Augrabies Falls National Park S. Africa 124 E5
Au Gres *MI* U.S.A. 164 D1
Augsburg Germany 57 M6
Augusta Australia 135 A8
Augusta *Sicily* Italy 68 F6
Augusta *AR* U.S.A. 161 F5
Augusta *GA* U.S.A. 163 D5
Augusta *KY* U.S.A. 164 C4

▶Augusta *ME* U.S.A. 165 K1
Capital of Maine.

Augusta *MT* U.S.A. 156 E3
Augusta Auscorum France *see* Auch
Augusta Taurinorum Italy *see* Turin
Augusta Treverorum Germany *see* Trier
Augusta Vindelicorum Germany *see* Augsburg
Augustine Island *AK* U.S.A. 148 I4
Augusto de Lima Brazil 179 B2
Augustus, Mount Australia 135 B6
Auke Bay *AK* U.S.A. 149 N4
Aukštaitijos nacionalinis parkas *nat. park* Lith. 55 O9
Aulavik National Park Canada 146 G2
Auld, Lake *salt flat* Australia 134 C5
Auliye Ata Kazakh. *see* Taraz
Aulnoye-Aymeries France 62 D4
Aulon Albania *see* Vlorë
Aulong *i.* Palau 82 [inset]
Ault France 62 B4
Auluptagel *i.* Palau 82 [inset]
Aumale Alg. *see* Sour el Ghozlane
Aumale France 62 B5
Aundh India 106 B2
Aundhi India 106 D1
Aunglan Myanmar 86 A3
Auob *watercourse* Namibia/S. Africa 124 E4
Aupaluk Canada 153 H2
Auponhia *Moluccas* Indon. 83 C3
Aur *i.* Malaysia 84 D2
Aura Fin. 55 M6
Auraiya India 104 D4
Aurangabad *Bihar* India 105 F4
Aurangabad *Mahar.* India 106 B2
Aure *r.* France 59 F9
Aurich Germany 63 H1
Aurigny *i.* Channel Is *see* Alderney
Aurilândia Brazil 179 A2
Aurillac France 66 F4
Aurkuning *Kalimantan* Indon. 85 E3
Aurora *Mindanao* Phil. 82 C5
Aurora *CO* U.S.A. 156 G5
Aurora *IL* U.S.A. 164 A3
Aurora *MO* U.S.A. 161 E4
Aurora *NE* U.S.A. 160 D3
Aurora *UT* U.S.A. 159 H2
Aurora Island Vanuatu *see* Maéwo
Aurukun Australia 136 C2
Aus Namibia 124 C4
Au Sable *MI* U.S.A. 164 D1
Au Sable Point *MI* U.S.A. 164 D1
Auskerry *i.* U.K. 60 G1
Austin *IN* U.S.A. 164 C4
Austin *MN* U.S.A. 160 E3
Austin *NV* U.S.A. 158 E2

▶Austin *TX* U.S.A. 161 D6
Capital of Texas.

Austin, Lake *salt flat* Australia 135 B6
Austintown *OH* U.S.A. 164 E3
Austral Downs Australia 136 B4
Australes, Îles *is* Fr. Polynesia *see* Tubuai Islands

▶Australia *country* Oceania 132 C4
Largest and most populous country in Oceania and 6th largest in the world.

Australian-Antarctic Basin *sea feature* S. Atlantic Ocean 186 C9
Australian Antarctic Territory *reg.* Antarctica 188 G2
Australian Capital Territory *admin. div.* Australia 138 D5
Australian Convict Sites *tourist site* Australia 137 D9
Austria *country* Europe 57 N7
Austvågøy *i.* Norway 54 I2
Autazes Brazil 177 G4
Autesiodorum France *see* Auxerre
Authie *r.* France 62 B4
Autlán Mex. 166 D5
Autti Fin. 54 O3
Auvergne *reg.* France 66 F4
Auvergne, Monts d' *mts* France 66 F4
Auxerre France 66 F3
Auxi-le-Château France 62 C4
Auxonne France 66 G3
Auyuittuq National Park Canada 147 L3
Auzangate, Nevado *mt.* Peru 176 D6
Ava *MO* U.S.A. 161 E4
Ava *NY* U.S.A. 165 H2
Āvaj Iran 110 C3
Avalik *r. AK* U.S.A. 148 H1
Avallon France 66 F3
Avalon *CA* U.S.A. 158 D5
Avalon Peninsula Canada 153 L5
Ávalos Mex. 167 E3
Avān Iran 113 G3
Avarau *atoll* Cook Is *see* Palmerston
Avaré Brazil 179 A3
Avaricum France *see* Bourges

▶Avarua Cook Is 187 J7
Capital of the Cook Islands, on Rarotonga.

Avawam *KY* U.S.A. 164 D5
Āvāz Iran 111 F3
Aveiro Port. 67 B3
Aveiro, Ria de *est.* Port. 67 B3
Avellino Italy 68 F4
Avenal *CA* U.S.A. 158 C3
Avenio France *see* Avignon
Aversa Italy 68 F4
Avesnes-sur-Helpe France 62 D4
Avesta Sweden 55 J6
Aveyron *r.* France 66 E4
Avezzano Italy 68 E3
Aviemore U.K. 60 F3
Avignon France 66 G5
Ávila Spain 67 D3
Avilés Spain 67 D2
Avion France 62 C4
Avis *PA* U.S.A. 165 G3
Avlama Dağı *mt.* Turkey 107 A1
Avlona Albania *see* Vlorë
Avnyugskiy Russia 52 J3
Avoca Australia 138 A6
Avoca *r.* Australia 138 A5
Avoca Ireland 61 F5
Avoca *IA* U.S.A. 160 E3
Avoca *NY* U.S.A. 165 G2
Avola *Sicily* Italy 68 F6
Avon *r. England* U.K. 59 E6
Avon *r. England* U.K. 59 E7
Avon *r. England* U.K. 59 F8
Avon *r. Scotland* U.K. 60 F3
Avon *NY* U.S.A. 165 G2
Avondale *AZ* U.S.A. 159 G5
Avonmore *r.* Ireland 61 F5
Avonmore *PA* U.S.A. 164 F3
Avonmouth U.K. 59 E7
Avranches France 66 D2
Avre *r.* France 62 C5
Avsuyu Turkey 107 C1
Avuavu Solomon Is 133 G2
Avveel Fin. *see* Ivalo
Avvil Fin. *see* Ivalo
A'waj, Nahr al *r.* Syria 107 B3
Awaji *Hyōgo* Japan 92 A4
Awaji *Hyōgo* Japan 92 B4
Awaji-shima *i.* Japan 92 A4
Awakino N.Z. 139 E4
'Awālī Bahrain 110 C5
Awang *Lombok* Indon. 85 G5
Awano Japan 93 F2
Awanui N.Z. 139 D2
Awara *Fukui* Japan 92 C2
Awara *Fukui* Japan 92 C2
Awarawar, Tanjung *pt* Indon. 85 F4
Āwarē Eth. 122 E3
'Awāriḑ, Wādī al *watercourse* Syria 107 D2
Awarua Point N.Z. 139 B7
Āwash Eth. 122 E3
Āwash *r.* Eth. 122 E2
Awa-shima *i.* Japan 91 E5
Āwash National Park Eth. 122 D3
Awasib Mountains Namibia 124 B3
Awat *Xinjiang* China 98 B5
Awat *Xinjiang* China 98 C4
Awatere *r.* N.Z. 139 E5
Awbārī Libya 120 E2
Awbārī, Idhān *des.* Libya 120 E2
Awbeg *r.* Ireland 61 D5
'Awdah *well* Saudi Arabia 110 C6
'Awdah, Hawr al *imp. l.* Iraq 113 G5
Aw Dheegle Somalia 121 H4
Awe, Loch *l.* U.K. 60 D4
Aweil South Sudan 121 F4
Awka Nigeria 120 D4
Awkal Afgh. 111 F3
Awo *r.* Indon. 83 B3
Awu *vol.* Indon. 83 C2
Awuna *r. AK* U.S.A. 148 I1
Axe *r. England* U.K. 59 D8
Axe *r. England* U.K. 59 E7
Axedale Australia 138 B6
Axel Heiberg Glacier Antarctica 188 I1
Axel Heiberg Island Canada 147 I2
Axim Ghana 120 C4
Axminster U.K. 59 E8
Axum Eth. *see* Āksum
Ay France 62 E5
Ay Kazakh. 98 C3
Ayabe Japan 92 B3
Ayachi, Jbel *mt.* Morocco 64 D5
Ayacucho Arg. 178 E5
Ayacucho Peru 176 D6
Ayadaw Myanmar 86 A2
Ayagoz Kazakh. 102 F2
Ayagoz *watercourse* Kazakh. 98 B3
Ayaguz Kazakh. *see* Ayagoz
Ayakkum Hu *salt l.* China 99 E5
Ayaköz Kazakh. *see* Ayagoz
Ayakulik *AK* U.S.A. 148 I4
Ayama Japan 92 C4
Ayan Russia 77 O4
Ayancık Turkey 112 D2
Ayang N. Korea 91 B5
Ayaş Turkey 112 D2
Ayase Japan 93 F3
Aybas Kazakh. 53 K7
Aydar *r.* Ukr. 53 H6
Aydarko'l ko'li *l.* Uzbek. 102 C3
Aydere Turkm. 110 E2
Aydın Turkey 69 L6
Aydıncık Turkey 107 A1
Aydın Dağları *mts* Turkey 69 L5
Aydingkol Hu *marsh* China 98 E4
Aýdyň Turkm. 110 D2
Āyelu *vol.* Eth. 108 F7
Ayer *MA* U.S.A. 165 J2
Ayers Rock *hill* Australia *see* Uluṟu
Ayeyarwady *r.* Myanmar *see* Irrawaddy
Aygulakskiy Khrebet *mts* Russia 98 D2
Aygyrzhal Kazakh. 98 C2
Ayila Ri'gyü *mts* China 99 B6
Áyios Dhimítrios Greece *see* Agios Dimitrios
Áyios Evstrátios *i.* Greece *see* Agios Efstratios
Áyios Nikólaos Greece *see* Agios Nikolaos
Áyios Yeóryios *i.* Greece *see* Agios Georgios
Aykol China 98 C4
Aylesbury N.Z. 139 D6
Aylesbury U.K. 59 G7
Aylett *VA* U.S.A. 165 G5
Ayllón Spain 67 E3
Aylmer *Ont.* Canada 164 E2
Aylmer *Que.* Canada 165 H1
Aylmer Lake Canada 151 I1
Aymangala India 106 C3
Aynabulak Kazakh. 98 B3
'Ayn al 'Abd *well* Saudi Arabia 110 C4
'Ayn al 'Arab Syria 107 D1
'Ayn al Baidā' Saudi Arabia 107 C4
'Ayn al Bayḑā' *well* Syria 107 C2
'Ayn al Ghazalah *well* Libya 112 A4
'Ayn al Maqfī *spring* Egypt 112 C6
'Ayn az Zaytūn Egypt 112 B5
'Ayn Dāllah *spring* Egypt 112 B6
Ayní Tajik. 111 H2
'Ayn 'Īsá Syria 107 D1
'Ayn Tabaghbugh *spring* Egypt 112 B5
'Ayn Tumayrah *spring* Egypt 112 B5
Ayod South Sudan 108 D8
Ayon, Ostrov *i.* Russia 77 R3
'Ayoûn el 'Atroûs Mauritania 120 C3
Ayr Australia 136 D3
Ayr Canada 164 E2
Ayr U.K. 60 E5
Ayr *r.* U.K. 60 E5
Ayr, Point of U.K. 58 D5
Ayrag Nuur *salt l.* Mongolia 94 C1
Ayrancı Turkey 112 D3
Ayre, Point of Isle of Man 58 C4
Aytos Bulg. 69 L3
Ayu *i. Papua* Indon. 83 D2
Ayu, Kepulauan *atoll Papua* Indon. 83 D2
A Yun Pa Vietnam 87 E4
Ayuthia Thai. *see* Ayutthaya
Ayutla *Guerrero* Mex. 167 F5
Ayutla *Jalisco* Mex. 166 D4
Ayutthaya Thai. 87 C4
Ayvacık Turkey 69 L5
Ayvalı Turkey 112 E3
Ayvalık Turkey 69 L5
Azad Kashmir *admin. div.* Pak. 111 I3
Azai Japan 92 C3
Azak Russia *see* Azov
Azalia *IN* U.S.A. 164 C4
Azamgarh India 105 E4
Azania *area* Somalia 122 E3
Azaouâd *reg.* Mali 120 C3
Azaouagh, Vallée de *watercourse* Mali/Niger 120 D3
Azaran Iran *see* Hashtrūd
Azärbaycan *country* Asia *see* Azerbaijan
Azärbayjan *country* Asia *see* Azerbaijan
Azare Nigeria 120 E3
Azawad *reg.* Mali 120 C3
A'zāz Syria 107 C1
Azbine *mts* Niger *see* Aïr, Massif de l'
Azdavay Turkey 112 D2
Azerbaijan *country* Asia 113 G2
Azerbaydzhanskaya S.S.R. *country* Asia *see* Azerbaijan
Azhibeksor, Ozero *salt l.* Kazakh. 101 F1
Azhikode India 106 B4
Aziscohos Lake *ME* U.S.A. 165 J1
'Azīzābād Iran 110 E4
Aziziye Turkey *see* Pınarbaşı
Azogues Ecuador 176 C4

▶Azores *terr.* N. Atlantic Ocean 184 G3
Autonomous Region of Portugal.

Azores-Biscay Rise *sea feature* N. Atlantic Ocean 184 G3
Azotus Israel *see* Ashdod
Azov Russia 53 H7
Azov, Sea of Russia/Ukr. 53 H7
Azovs'ke More *sea* Russia/Ukr. *see* Azov, Sea of
Azovskoye More *sea* Russia/Ukr. *see* Azov, Sea of
Azraq, Bahr el *r.* Eth./Sudan 108 D6 *see* Blue Nile
Azraq, Qaşr al Jordan 107 C4
Azraq ash Shīshān Jordan 107 C4
Azrou Morocco 64 C5
Aztec *NM* U.S.A. 159 I3
Azuaga Spain 67 D4
Azuchi Japan 92 C3
Azuero, Península de *pen.* Panama 166 [inset] J8
Azul *r.* Mex. 167 H5
Azul, Cordillera *mts* Peru 176 C5
Azul Meambar, Parque Nacional *nat. park* Hond. 166 [inset] I6
Azuma *Gunma* Japan 93 F2
Azuma *Gunma* Japan 93 F2
Azuma *Ibaraki* Japan 93 G3
Azuma-san *vol.* Japan 91 F5
Azumaya-san *mt.* Japan 93 E2
Azumi Japan 93 D2
Azumino Japan 93 D2
Azur, Côte d' *coastal area* France 66 H5
Azusa-ko *resr* Japan 92 D2
'Azza Gaza *see* Gaza
Azzaba Alg. 68 B6
Az Ẓāhirīyah West Bank 107 B4
Az Ẓahrān Saudi Arabia *see* Dhahran
Az Zaqāzīq Egypt 112 C5
Az Zarbah Syria 107 C1
Az Zarqā' Jordan 107 C3
Az Za'tarī Jordan 107 C3
Az Ẓa'yin *town* Qatar *see* Al Dayyen
Azzeffâl *hills* Mauritania/W. Sahara 120 B2
Az Zubayr Iraq 113 G5
Az Zuqur *i.* Yemen 108 F7

Ba, Sông *r.* Vietnam 87 E4
Baa Indon. 83 B5
Baabda Lebanon 107 B3
Baai *r.* Indon. 85 G2
Ba'albek Lebanon 107 C2
Baan Baa Australia 138 D3
Baardheere Somalia 122 E3
Baatsagaan Mongolia 94 D2
Bab India 104 D4
Bābā, Kōh-e *mts* Afgh. 111 H3
Baba Burnu *pt* Turkey 69 L5
Babadağ *mt.* Azer. 113 H2
Babadag Romania 69 M2
Babadurmaz Turkm. 110 E2
Babaeski Turkey 69 L4
Babahoyo Ecuador 176 C4
Babai India 104 D5
Babai *r.* Nepal 105 E3
Babak Phil. 82 D5
Bābā Kalān Iran 110 C4
Bāb al Mandab *strait* Africa/Asia 108 F7
Babana *Celebes* Indon. 83 A3
Babanusa Sudan 108 C7
Babao *Qinghai* China *see* Qilian
Babao *Yunnan* China 96 E4
Babar *i. Moluccas* Indon. 83 D4
Babar, Kepulauan *is Moluccas* Indon. 83 D4
Babati Tanz. 123 D4
Babau *Timor* Indon. 83 B5
Babayevo Russia 52 G4
Babayurt Russia 113 G2
Babbage *r.* Canada 149 M1
B'abdā Lebanon *see* Baabda

Babeldaob i. Palau 82 [inset]
Bab el Mandeb, Straits of Africa/Asia see Bāb al Mandab
Babelthuap i. Palau see Babeldaob
Babi, Pulau i. Indon. 84 B2
Babian Jiang r. China 96 D4
Babine r. Canada 150 E4
Babine Lake Canada 150 E4
Babine Range mts Canada 150 E4
Bābol Iran 110 D2
Bābolsar Iran 110 D2
Babongo Cameroon 121 E4
Baboon Point S. Africa 124 D7
Baboua Cent. Afr. Rep. 122 B3
Babruysk Belarus 53 F5
Babstovo Russia 90 D2
Babu China see Hezhou
Babuhri India 104 B4
Babusar Pass Pak. 111 I3
Babushkina, imeni Russia 52 I4
Babuyan Palawan Phil. 82 B4
Babuyan i. Phil. 82 C2
Babuyan Channel Phil. 82 C2
Babuyan Islands Phil. 82 C2
Bacaadweyn Somalia 122 E3
Bacabáchi Mex. 166 C3
Bacabal Brazil 177 J4
Bacalar Mex. 167 H5
Bacalar Chico, Boca sea chan. Mex. 167 I5
Bacan i. Moluccas Indon. 83 C3
Bacang China 94 E5
Bacanora Mex. 166 C2
Bacarra Luzon Phil. 82 C2
Bacău Romania 69 L1
Baccaro Point Canada 153 I6
Bắc Giang Vietnam 86 D2
Bacha China 90 D2
Bach Ice Shelf Antarctica 188 L2
Bach Long Vi, Đao i. Vietnam 86 D2
Bachu China 98 B5
Bachuan China see Tongliang
Back r. Australia 136 C3
Back r. Canada 151 M1
Bačka Palanka Serbia 69 H2
Backbone Mountain MD U.S.A. 164 F4
Backbone Ranges mts Canada 149 O3
Backe Sweden 54 J5
Backstairs Passage Australia 137 B7
Bac Liêu Vietnam 87 D5
Bắc Ninh Vietnam 86 D2
Bacnotan Luzon Phil. 82 C2
Baco, Mount Mindoro Phil. 82 C3
Bacoachi Mex. 166 C2
Bacoachi watercourse Mex. 157 F7
Bacobampo Mex. 166 C3
Bacolod Negros Phil. 82 C4
Bacqueville, Lac l. Canada 152 G2
Bacqueville-en-Caux France 59 H9
Bacubirito Mex. 166 D3
Baculin Bay Mindanao Phil. 82 D5
Bada China see Xilin
Bada mt. Eth. 122 D3
Bada i. Myanmar 87 B5
Badabayhan Turkm. 111 F2
Bad Abbach Germany 63 M6
Badain Jaran China 94 E4
Badain Jaran Shamo des. China 94 E3
Badajoz Spain 67 C4
Badami India 106 B3
Badampaharh India 105 F5
Badamsha Kazakh. 102 A1
Badanah Saudi Arabia 113 F5
Badaojiang China see Baishan
Badarpur India 105 H4
Badas Brunei 85 F1
Badas, Kepulauan is Indon. 84 D2
Badaun India see Budaun
Bad Axe MI U.S.A. 164 D2
Bad Bederkesa Germany 63 I1
Bad Belzig Germany 63 M2
Bad Bergzabern Germany 63 H5
Bad Berleburg Germany 63 I3
Bad Bevensen Germany 63 K1
Bad Blankenburg Germany 63 L4
Bad Camberg Germany 63 I4
Badderen Norway 54 M2
Bad Driburg Germany 63 J3
Bad Düben Germany 63 M3
Bad Dürkheim Germany 63 I5
Bad Dürrenberg Germany 63 M3
Bademli Turkey see Aladağ
Bademli Geçidi pass Turkey 112 C3
Bad Ems Germany 63 H4
Baden Austria 57 P6
Baden Switz. 66 I3
Baden-Baden Germany 63 I6
Baden-Württemberg land Germany 63 I6
Bad Essen Germany 63 I2
Bad Fallingbostel Germany 63 J2
Bad Grund (Harz) Germany 63 K3
Bad Harzburg Germany 63 K3
Bad Hersfeld Germany 63 J4
Bad Hofgastein Austria 57 N7
Bad Homburg vor der Höhe Germany 63 I4
Badia Polesine Italy 68 D2
Badin Pak. 111 H5
Bad Ischl Austria 57 N7
Bādiyat ash Shām des. Asia see Syrian Desert
Bad Kissingen Germany 63 K4
Bad Königsdorff Poland see Jastrzębie-Zdrój
Bad Kösen Germany 63 L3
Bad Kötzting Germany 63 M5
Bad Kreuznach Germany 63 H5
Bad Laasphe Germany 63 I4
Badlands reg. ND U.S.A. 160 C2
Badlands reg. SD U.S.A. 160 C3
Badlands National Park SD U.S.A. 160 C3
Bad Langensalza Germany 63 K3
Bad Lauterberg im Harz Germany 63 K3
Bad Liebenwerda Germany 63 N3
Bad Lippspringe Germany 63 I3
Bad Marienberg (Westerwald) Germany 63 H4
Bad Mergentheim Germany 63 J5
Bad Nauheim Germany 63 I4
Badnawar India 104 C5
Badnera India 106 C1
Bad Neuenahr-Ahrweiler Germany 62 H4
Bad Neustadt an der Saale Germany 63 K4
Badnor India 104 C4
Badong China 97 F2
Ba Đông Vietnam 87 D5
Badou China 95 I4
Badou Togo 120 D4
Bad Pyrmont Germany 63 J3
Badrah Iraq 113 G4
Badreh Iran 110 B3
Bad Reichenhall Germany 57 N7
Badr Ḥunayn Saudi Arabia 108 E5
Bādrūd Iran 110 D3
Bad Sachsa Germany 63 K3
Bad Salzdetfurth Germany 63 K2
Bad Salzuflen Germany 63 I2
Bad Salzungen Germany 63 K4
Bad Schwalbach Germany 63 I4
Bad Schwartau Germany 57 M4
Bad Segeberg Germany 57 M4
Bad Sobernheim Germany 63 H5
Bad Staffelstein Germany 63 K4
Badu Island Australia 136 C1
Badulla Sri Lanka 106 D5
Bad Vilbel Germany 63 I4
Bad Wilsnack Germany 63 L2
Bad Windsheim Germany 63 K5
Badzhal Russia 90 D2
Badzhal'skiy Khrebet mts Russia 90 D2
Bad Zwischenahn Germany 63 I1
Bae Colwyn U.K. see Colwyn Bay
Baengnyeong-do i. S. Korea 91 B5
Baesweiler Germany 62 G4
Baeza Spain 67 E5
Bafatá Guinea-Bissau 120 B3
Baffa Pak. 111 I3
Baffin Bay sea Canada/Greenland 147 L2

▶Baffin Island Canada 147 L3
2nd largest island in North America and 5th in the world.

Bafia Cameroon 120 E4
Bafilo Togo 120 D4
Bafing r. Africa 120 B3
Bafoulabé Mali 120 B3
Bafoussam Cameroon 120 E4
Bāfq Iran 110 D4
Bafra Turkey 112 D2
Bafra Burnu pt Turkey 112 D2
Bāft Iran 110 E4
Bafwaboli Dem. Rep. Congo 122 C3
Bafwasende Dem. Rep. Congo 122 C3
Baga Bogdin Nuruu mts Mongolia 94 E2
Bagac Bay Luzon Phil. 82 C3
Bagaha India 105 F4
Bagahak, Gunung hill Malaysia 85 G1
Bagalkot India 106 B2
Bagalkote India see Bagalkot
Bagamoyo Tanz. 123 D4
Bagan China 96 C1
Bagan Datoh Malaysia see Bagan Datuk
Bagan Datuk Malaysia 84 C2
Baganga Mindanao Phil. 82 D5
Baganian Peninsula Mindanao Phil. 82 C5
Bagan Serai Malaysia 84 C1
Bagansiapiapi Sumatra Indon. 84 C2
Baganuur Mongolia 95 G2
Bagar China 99 F7
Bagata Dem. Rep. Congo 122 B4
Bagdad AZ U.S.A. 159 G4
Bagdarin Russia 89 K2
Bagé Brazil 178 F4
Bagenalstown Ireland 61 F5
Bagerhat Bangl. 105 G5
Bageshwar India 104 D3
Baggs WY U.S.A. 156 G4
Baggy Point U.K. 59 C7
Bagh India 104 C5
Bāgh, Chāh-e well Iran 110 D4
Bàgh a'Chaisteil U.K. see Castlebay
Baghak Pak. 111 G4
Baghbaghū Iran 111 F2

▶Baghdād Iraq 113 G4
Capital of Iraq.

Bāgh-e Malek Iran 110 C4
Bagherhat Bangl. see Bagerhat
Bāghīn Iran 110 E4
Baghlān Afgh. 111 H2
Baghrān Afgh. 111 G3
Baginda, Tanjung pt Indon. 84 D3
Bağirsak r. Turkey 107 C1
Bağirsak Deresi r. Syria/Turkey see Sājūr, Nahr
Bagley MN U.S.A. 160 E2
Bagley Icefield AK U.S.A. 149 J4
Baglung Nepal 105 E3
Bagnères-de-Luchon France 66 E5
Bagnuiti r. Nepal 99 D8
Bago Myanmar see Pegu
Bago Negros Phil. 82 C4
Bagong China see Sansui
Bagor India 111 I5
Bagrationovsk Russia 55 L9
Bagrax China see Bohu
Bagrax Hu l. China see Bosten Hu
Baguio Luzon Phil. 82 C2
Baguio Mindanao Phil. 82 D5
Baguio Point Luzon Phil. 82 C2
Bagur, Cabo c. Spain see Begur, Cap de
Bagzane, Monts mts Niger 120 D3
Bahādorābād Iran 110 E4
Bahadurganj Nepal 99 C8
Bahalda India 105 F5
Bahamas, The country West Indies 163 E7
Bahara Pak. 111 G5
Baharampur India 105 G4
Bahardipur Pak. 111 H5
Bahariya Oasis oasis Egypt see Bahrīyah, Wāḥāt al
Bahau r. Indon. 85 G2
Bahau Malaysia 84 C2
Bahaur Kalimantan Indon. 85 F3
Bahawalnagar Pak. 111 I4
Bahawalpur Pak. 111 H4
Bahçe Adana Turkey 107 B1
Bahçe Osmaniye Turkey 112 E3
Baher Dar Eth. see Bahir Dar
Baheri India 104 D3
Bahia Brazil see Salvador
Bahia state Brazil 179 C1
Bahía, Islas de la is Hond. 166 [inset] I5
Bahía Asunción Mex. 157 E8
Bahía Blanca Arg. 178 D5
Bahía Honda Point Palawan Phil. 82 B4
Bahía Kino Mex. 166 C2
Bahía Laura Arg. 178 C7
Bahía Negra Para. 178 E2
Bahía Tortugas Mex. 166 B3
Bahir Dar Eth. 122 D2
Bahl India 104 C3
Bahlā Oman 110 E6
Bahomonte Celebes Indon. 83 B3
Bahraich India 105 E4
Bahrain country Asia 110 C5
Bahrain, Gulf of Asia 110 C5
Bahrāmābād Iran see Rafsanjān
Bahrām Beyg Iran 110 C2
Bahrāmjerd Iran 110 E4
Bahrīyah, Wāḥāt al oasis Egypt 112 C6
Bahuaja-Sonene, Parque Nacional nat. park Peru 176 E6
Bahubulu i. Indon. 83 B3
Baia Mare Romania 69 J1
Baicang China 105 G3
Baicheng Jilin China 95 J2
Baicheng Xinjiang China 98 C4
Baidoa Somalia see Baydhabo
Baidoi Co l. China 99 D6
Baidu China 97 H3
Baidunzi Gansu China 94 F4
Baidunzi Gansu China 98 F4
Baie-aux-Feuilles Canada see Tasiujaq
Baie-Comeau Canada 153 H4
Baie-du-Poste Canada see Mistissini
Baie-St-Paul Canada 153 H5
Baie-Trinité Canada 153 I4
Baie Verte Canada 153 K4
Baiguo He r. China 95 I4
Baiguan China see Shangyu
Baiguo Hubei China 97 G2
Baiguo Hunan China 97 G3
Baihar India 104 E5
Baihe Jilin China 90 C4
Baihe Shaanxi China 97 F1
Bai He r. China 95 I3
Baiji Iraq see Bayjī
Baijiantan China 98 D3

▶Baikal, Lake Russia 94 F1
Deepest lake in Asia and the world, and 2nd largest lake in Asia and 8th in the world.

Baikalu Shan mt. China 90 A1
Baikouquan China 98 D3
Baikunthpur India 105 E5
Bailang China 95 J2
Baile Átha Cliath Ireland see Dublin
Baile Átha Luain Ireland see Athlone
Baile Mhartainn U.K. 60 B3
Baile na Finne Ireland 61 D3
Băileşti Romania 69 J2
Bailey Range hills Australia 135 C7
Bailianhe Shuiku resr China 97 G2
Bailieborough Ireland 61 F4
Bailingmiao China 95 G3
Bailleul France 62 C4
Baillie r. Canada 151 J1
Baillie Islands Canada 149 O1
Bailong China see Hadapu
Bailong Jiang r. China 96 E1
Baima Qinghai China 96 D1
Baima Xizang China see Baxoi
Baima Jian mt. China 97 H2
Baimuru P.N.G. 81 K8
Bain r. U.K. 58 G5
Bainang China see Norkyung
Bainbridge GA U.S.A. 163 C6
Bainbridge IN U.S.A. 164 B4
Bainbridge NY U.S.A. 165 H2
Bainduru India 106 B3
Baingoin China 99 E7
Baini China see Yuqing
Baiona Spain 67 B2
Baiqên China 96 D1
Baiquan China 90 B3
Bā'ir Jordan 107 C4
Bā'ir, Wādī watercourse Jordan/Saudi Arabia 107 C4
Bairab Co l. China 99 C6
Bairat India 104 D4
Baird TX U.S.A. 161 D5
Baird, Mount Canada 149 N2
Baird Inlet AK U.S.A. 148 F3
Baird Mountains AK U.S.A. 148 H2

▶Bairiki Kiribati 186 H5
Capital of Kiribati, on Tarawa atoll.

Bairin Qiao China 95 I3
Bairin Youqi China see Daban
Bairin Zuoqi China see Lindong
Bairnsdale Australia 138 C6
Bais Negros Phil. 82 C4
Baise China 96 E4
Baisha Chongqing China 96 E2
Baisha Hainan China 97 F5
Baisha Sichuan China 97 F2
Baishan Guangxi China see Mashan
Baishan Jilin China 90 B4
Bai Shan mt. China 98 F4
Baishanzhen China see Baishan
Baishi Shuiku resr China 95 J3
Baishui Shaanxi China 95 G5
Baishui Sichuan China 96 E1
Baishui Jiang r. China 96 E1
Baisogala Lith. 55 M9
Baitadi Nepal 104 E3
Baitang China 96 C1
Bai Thương Vietnam 86 D3
Baitou Shan mt. China/N. Korea 90 C4
Baixi China see Yibin
Baixiang China 95 H4
Baixingt China 95 J3
Baiyanghe China 98 E4
Baiyashi China see Dong'an
Baiyin China 94 F4
Baiyü China 96 C2
Baiyuda Desert Sudan 108 D6
Baiyu Shan mts China 95 F4
Baja Hungary 68 H1
Baja, Punta pt Mex. 166 B2
Baja California pen. Mex. 166 B2
Baja California state Mex. 166 B2
Baja California Sur state Mex. 166 B3
Bajan Mex. 167 E3
Bajau i. Indon. 84 D2
Bajaur reg. Pak. 111 H3
Bajawa Flores Indon. 83 B5
Baj Baj India 105 G5
Bājgīrān Iran 110 E2
Bajiang China 97 F3
Bājil Yemen 108 F7
Bajo Boquete Panama 166 [inset] J7
Bajo Caracoles Arg. 178 B7
Bajoga Nigeria 120 E3
Bajoi China 96 D2
Bajrakot India 105 F5
Baka, Bukit mt. Indon. 85 F3
Bakala Cent. Afr. Rep. 121 F4
Bakanas Kazakh. 102 E3
Bakanas watercourse Kazakh. 98 B3
Bakar Pak. 111 H5
Bakaucengal Kalimantan Indon. 85 G3
Bakayan, Gunung mt. Indon. 85 G2
Bakel Senegal 120 B3
Baker CA U.S.A. 158 E4
Baker ID U.S.A. 156 E3
Baker LA U.S.A. 161 F6
Baker MT U.S.A. 156 G3
Baker NV U.S.A. 159 F2
Baker WV U.S.A. 165 F4
Baker, Mount vol. WA U.S.A. 156 C2
Baker Butte mt. AZ U.S.A. 159 H4
Baker City OR U.S.A. 156 D3

▶Baker Island terr. N. Pacific Ocean 133 I1
United States Unincorporated Territory.

Baker Island AK U.S.A. 149 N5
Baker Lake salt flat Australia 135 D6
Baker Lake Canada 151 M1
Baker Lake l. Canada 151 M1
Baker's Dozen Islands Canada 152 F2
Bakersfield CA U.S.A. 158 D4
Bakersville NC U.S.A. 162 D4
Bâ Kêv Cambodia 87 D4
Bakhardok Turkm. see Bokurdak
Bākharz, Kūhhā-ye mts Iran 111 F3
Bakhasar India 104 B4
Bakhirevo Russia 90 C2
Bakhmach Ukr. 53 G6
Bakhma Dam Iraq see Bēkma, Sadd
Bakhmut Ukr. see Artemivs'k
Bākhtarān Iran see Kermānshāh
Bakhtegan, Daryācheh-ye l. Iran 110 D4
Bakhtiari Country reg. Iran 110 C3
Bakı Azer. see Baku
Baki Somalia 122 E2
Bakırköy Turkey 69 M4
Bakkejord Norway 54 K2
Bakloh India 104 C2
Bako Eth. 122 D3
Bako National Park Malaysia 85 E2
Bakongan Sumatra Indon. 84 B2
Bakouma Cent. Afr. Rep. 122 C3
Baksan Russia 113 F2
Bakty Kazakh. 98 C3

▶Baku Azer. 113 H2
Capital of Azerbaijan.

Baku Dem. Rep. Congo 122 D3
Bakulin Point Mindanao Phil. 82 D4
Bakung i. Sumatra Indon. 84 D2
Bakutis Coast Antarctica 188 J2
Baky Azer. see Baku
Balâ Turkey 112 D3
Bala U.K. 59 D6
Bala, Cerros de mts Bol. 176 E6
Balabac Phil. 82 B4
Balabac i. Phil. 82 B4
Balabac Strait Malaysia/Phil. 80 F5
Balabalangan, Kepulauan atolls Indon. 85 G3
Baladeh Māzandarān Iran 110 C2
Baladeh Māzandarān Iran 110 C2
Baladek Russia 90 D1
Balagar Gaole China see Bayan Ul
Balaghat India 104 E5
Balaghat Range hills India 106 B2
Bālā Ḥowẓ Iran 110 E4
Balaiberkuak Kalimantan Indon. 85 E3
Balaikarangan Kalimantan Indon. 85 E2
Balaipungut Sumatra Indon. 84 C2
Balairiam Kalimantan Indon. 85 E3
Balaka Malawi 123 D5
Balakän Azer. 113 G2
Balakhna Russia 52 I4
Balakhta Russia 88 G1
Balaklava Australia 137 B7
Balaklava Crimea 112 D1
Balakleya Ukr. see Balakliya
Balakliya Ukr. 53 H6
Balakovo Russia 53 J5
Bala Lake l. U.K. 59 D6
Balaman India 104 E4
Balambangan i. Malaysia 82 B5
Balan India 104 B4
Balancán Mex. 167 H5
Balanda Russia see Kalininsk
Balanda r. Russia 53 J6
Balan Dağı hill Turkey 69 M6
Balanga Luzon Phil. 82 C3
Ba Lang An, Mui pt Vietnam 86 E4
Balangir India 106 D1
Balantak Celebes Indon. 83 B3
Balaözen r. Kazakh./Russia see Saryozen
Balarampur India see Balrampur
Balase r. Indon. 83 B3
Bālā Shahr Iran 110 E5
Balashov Russia 53 I6
Balasore India see Baleshwar
Balaton, Lake Hungary 68 G1
Balatonboglár Hungary 68 G1
Balatonfüred Hungary 68 G1
Balauring Indon. 83 B5
Balbina Brazil 177 G4
Balbina, Represa de resr Brazil 177 G4
Balbriggan Ireland 61 F4
Balchik Bulg. 69 M3
Bal Chirāgh Afgh. 111 G3
Balclutha N.Z. 139 B8
Balcones Escarpment TX U.S.A. 161 C6
Bald Knob WV U.S.A. 164 E5
Bald Mountain NV U.S.A. 159 F3
Baldock Lake Canada 151 L3
Baldwin Canada 164 F1
Baldwin FL U.S.A. 163 D6
Baldwin MI U.S.A. 164 C2
Baldwin PA U.S.A. 164 F3
Baldwin Peninsula AK U.S.A. 148 G2
Baldy Mount Canada 156 D2
Baldy Mountain hill Canada 151 K5
Baldy Peak AZ U.S.A. 159 I5
Bal'dzhikan Russia 95 G1
Bale Sumatra Indon. 84 C3
Bâle Switz. see Basel
Baléa Mali 120 B3
Baleares is Spain see Balearic Islands
Baleares, Islas is Spain see Balearic Islands
Baleares Insulae is Spain see Balearic Islands
Balearic Islands is Spain 67 G4
Balears is Spain see Balearic Islands
Balears, Illes is Spain see Balearic Islands
Baleh r. Malaysia 85 F2
Baleia, Ponta da pt Brazil 179 D2
Baleine, Grande Rivière de la r. Canada 152 F3
Baleine, Petite Rivière de la r. Canada 152 F3
Baleine, Rivière à la r. Canada 153 I2
Bale Mountains National Park Eth. 122 D3
Baleno Masbate Phil. 82 C3
Baler Luzon Phil. 82 C3
Baler Bay Luzon Phil. 82 C3
Baleshwar India 105 F5
Balestrand Norway 55 E6
Balestrieri, Punta mt. Italy 68 C4
Baléyara Niger 120 D3
Balezino Russia 51 Q4
Balfate Hond. 166 [inset] I6
Balfes Creek Australia 136 D4
Balfour Downs Australia 134 C5
Balgatay Mongolia see Shilüüstey
Balgo Australia 134 D5
Balguntay China 98 D4
Bali India 104 C4
Bali i. Indon. 85 F5
Bali prov. Indon. 85 F5
Bali, Laut sea Indon. 85 F4
Bali, Selat sea chan. Indon. 85 F5
Balia India see Ballia
Baliangao Mindanao Phil. 82 C4
Baliapal India 105 F5
Bali Barat, Taman Nasional nat. park Bali Indon. 85 F5
Balige Sumatra Indon. 84 B2
Baliguda India 106 D1
Balihan China 95 I3
Balıkesir Turkey 69 L5
Balīkh r. Syria/Turkey 107 D2
Balikpapan Kalimantan Indon. 85 G3
Balikpapan, Teluk b. Indon. 85 G3
Balimila Reservoir India 106 D2
Balimo P.N.G. 81 K8
Balin China 95 J1
Baling Malaysia 84 C1
Balingen Germany 57 L6
Balingian Sarawak Malaysia 85 F2
Balingian r. Malaysia 85 F2
Balinqiao China see Bairin Qiao
Balintang Channel Phil. 82 C2
Balintore U.K. 60 F3
Bali Sea Indon. see Bali, Laut
Baliungan i. Phil. 82 C5
Balk Neth. 62 F2
Balkanabat Turkm. 110 D2
Balkan Mountains Bulg./Serbia 69 J3
Balkash Kazakh. 102 D2
Balkassar Pak. 111 I3
Balkh r. Afgh. 111 G2

▶Balkhash, Lake Kazakh. 102 D2
3rd largest lake in Asia.

Balkhash, Ozero l. Kazakh. see Balkhash, Lake
Balkuduk Kazakh. 53 J7
Ballachulish U.K. 60 D4
Balladonia Australia 135 C8
Balladoran Australia 138 D3
Ballaghaderreen Ireland 61 D4
Ballan Australia 138 B6
Ballangen Norway 54 J2
Ballantine MT U.S.A. 156 F3
Ballantrae U.K. 60 E5
Ballarat Australia 138 A6
Ballard, Lake salt flat Australia 135 C7
Ballari India 106 C3
Ballarpur India 106 C2
Ballater U.K. 60 F3
Ballé Mali 120 C3
Ballena, Punta pt Chile 178 B3
Balleny Islands Antarctica 188 H2
Ballia India 105 F4
Ballina Australia 138 F2
Ballina Ireland 61 C3
Ballinafad Ireland 61 D3
Ballinalack Ireland 61 E4
Ballinamore Ireland 61 E3
Ballinasloe Ireland 61 D4
Ballindine Ireland 61 D4
Ballinger TX U.S.A. 161 D6
Ballinluig U.K. 60 F4
Ballinrobe Ireland 61 C4
Ballston Spa NY U.S.A. 165 I2
Ballybay Ireland 61 F3
Ballybunion Ireland 61 C5
Ballycanew Ireland 61 F5
Ballycastle Ireland 61 C3
Ballycastle U.K. 61 F2
Ballyclare U.K. 61 G3
Ballyconnell Ireland 61 E3
Ballygar Ireland 61 D4
Ballygawley U.K. 61 E3
Ballygorman Ireland 61 E2
Ballyhaunis Ireland 61 D4
Ballyheigue Ireland 61 C5
Ballykelly U.K. 61 E2
Ballylynan Ireland 61 E5
Ballymacmague Ireland 61 E5
Ballymahon Ireland 61 E4
Ballymena U.K. 61 F3
Ballymoney U.K. 61 F2
Ballymote Ireland 61 D3
Ballynahinch U.K. 61 G3
Ballyshannon Ireland 61 D3
Ballyteige Bay Ireland 61 F5
Ballyvaughan Ireland 61 C4
Ballyward U.K. 61 F3
Balmartin U.K. see Baile Mhartainn
Balmer India see Barmer
Balmertown Canada 151 M5
Balmorhea TX U.S.A. 161 C6
Baloa Celebes Indon. 83 B3
Balochistan prov. Pak. 111 G4
Balok, Teluk b. Indon. 85 D3
Balombo Angola 123 B5
Balonne r. Australia 138 D2
Balontohe i. Indon. 83 C2
Balotra India 104 C4
Balpyk Bi Kazakh. 98 B3
Balqash Kazakh. see Balkash
Balqash Köli l. Kazakh. see Balkhash, Lake
Balrampur India 105 E4
Balranald Australia 138 A5
Balş Romania 69 K2
Balsam Lake Canada 165 F1
Balsas Brazil 177 I5
Balsas Mex. 167 F5
Balsas r. Mex. 166 E5
Balta Ukr. 53 F7
Baltasound U.K. 60 [inset]
Baltay Russia 53 J5
Bălţi Moldova 53 E7
Baltic OH U.S.A. 164 E3
Baltic Sea g. Europe 55 J9
Balṭīm Egypt see Balṭīm
Balṭīm Egypt 112 C5
Baltimore S. Africa 125 I2
Baltimore MD U.S.A. 165 G4
Baltimore OH U.S.A. 164 D4
Baltinglass Ireland 61 F5
Baltistan reg. Pak. 104 C2
Baltiysk Russia 55 K9
Balu India 96 B3
Baluarte, Arroyo watercourse TX U.S.A. 161 D7
Baluch Ab well Iran 110 E4
Balui r. Malaysia 85 F2
Balumundam Sumatra Indon. 84 B2
Baluran, Gunung mt. Indon. 85 F3
Baluran, Taman Nasional nat. park Indon. 85 F4
Balurghat India 105 G4
Balut i. Phil. 82 D5
Balve Germany 63 H3
Balvi Latvia 55 O8
Balya Turkey 69 L5
Balyaga Russia 95 G1
Balykchy Kyrg. 102 E3
Balykshi Kazakh. 100 E2
Balyktyg-Khem r. Russia 94 D1
Balyqshy Kazakh. see Balykshi
Bam Iran 110 E4
Bām Iran 110 E2
Bama China 96 E3

▶Bamako Mali 120 C3
Capital of Mali.

Bamba Mali 120 C3
Bambang Luzon Phil. 82 C2
Bambannan i. Phil. 82 C5
Bambari Cent. Afr. Rep. 122 C3
Bambel Sumatra Indon. 84 B2
Bamberg Germany 63 K5
Bamberg SC U.S.A. 163 D5
Bambili Dem. Rep. Congo 122 C3
Bambio Cent. Afr. Rep. 122 B3
Bamboesberg mts S. Africa 125 H6
Bamboo Creek Australia 134 C5
Bambouti Cent. Afr. Rep. 122 C3
Bambuí Brazil 179 B3
Bambulung Kalimantan Indon. 85 F3

Bamda China 96 C2
Bamenda Cameroon 120 E4
Bamiancheng China 95 K3
Bamiantong China see Muling
Bamingui Cent. Afr. Rep. 122 C3
Bamingui-Bangoran, Parc National du nat. park Cent. Afr. Rep. 122 B3
Bamkeri Papua Indon. 83 D3
Bâmnák Cambodia 87 D4
Bamnet Narong Thai. 86 C4
Bamoa Mex. 166 C3
Bamor India 104 D4
Bamori India 106 C1
Bamposht reg. Iran 111 F5
Bampton U.K. 59 D8
Bampūr Iran 111 F5
Bampūr watercourse Iran 111 E5
Bamrūd Iran 111 F3
Bāmyān Afgh. 111 G3
Bamyili Australia 134 F3
Banaba i. Kiribati 133 G2
Banabuiu, Açude resr Brazil 177 K5
Banagher Ireland 61 E4
Banahao, Mount vol. Luzon Phil. 82 C3
Banalia Dem. Rep. Congo 122 C3
Banamana, Lagoa l. Moz. 125 K2
Banamba Mali 120 C3
Banámichi Mex. 166 C2
Banana Australia 136 E5
Bananal, Ilha do i. Brazil 177 H6
Bananga India 87 A6
Banapur India 106 E2
Banas r. India 104 D4
Banawaya i. Indon. 83 A4
Banaz Turkey 69 M5
Ban Ban Laos 86 C3
Banbān, 'Irq des. Saudi Arabia 110 B5
Banbar China 99 F7
Ban Bo Laos 86 C3
Banbridge U.K. 61 F3
Ban Bua Chum Thai. 86 C4
Ban Bua Yai Thai. 86 C4
Ban Bungxai Laos 86 D4
Banbury U.K. 59 F6
Ban Cang Vietnam 86 C2
Banc d'Arguin, Parc National du nat. park Mauritania 120 B2
Ban Channabot Thai. 86 C3
Banchory U.K. 60 G3
Bancoran i. Phil. 82 B5
Bancroft Canada 165 G1
Bancroft Zambia see Chililabombwe
Banda Dem. Rep. Congo 122 C3
Banda India 104 E4
Banda, Kepulauan is Moluccas Indon. 83 D4
Banda, Laut sea Indon. 83 D4
Banda Aceh Sumatra Indon. 84 A1
Banda Banda, Mount Australia 138 F3
Banda Daud Shah Pak. 111 H3
Bandahara, Gunung mt. Indon. 84 B2
Bandama r. Côte d'Ivoire 120 C4
Bandaneira Moluccas Indon. 83 D4
Bandān Kūh mts Iran 111 F4
Bandar India see Machilipatnam
Bandar Moz. 123 D5
Bandar Abbas Iran see Bandar-e 'Abbās
Bandaragung Sumatra Indon. 84 D4
Bandarban Bangl. 105 H5
Bandar-e 'Abbās Iran 110 E5
Bandar-e Anzalī Iran 110 C2
Bandar-e Būshehr Iran 110 C4
Bandar-e Dayyer Iran 110 C5
Bandar-e Deylam Iran 110 C4
Bandar-e Emām Khomeynī Iran 110 C4
Bandar-e Ganāveh Iran 110 C4
Bandar-e Ḥeydarābād Iran 110 B2
Bandar-e Jāsk Iran 110 E5
Bandar-e Kangān Iran 110 D5
Bandar-e Lengeh Iran 110 D5
Bandar-e Māhshahr Iran 110 C4
Bandar-e Nakhīlū Iran 110 D5
Bandar-e Pahlavī Iran see Bandar-e Anzalī
Bandar-e Shāh Iran see Bandar-e Torkaman
Bandar-e Torkaman Iran 110 D2
Bandar Lampung Sumatra Indon. 84 D4
Bandarpunch mt. India 104 D3

▶Bandar Seri Begawan Brunei 85 F1
Capital of Brunei.

Banda Sea Indon. see Banda, Laut
Band-e Bābā, Silsilah-ye Kōh-e mts Afgh. 111 F3
Band-e Bamposht, Kūh-e mts Iran 111 F5
Bandeira Brazil 179 C1
Bandeirante Brazil 179 A1
Bandeiras, Pico de mt. Brazil 179 C3
Bandelierkop S. Africa 125 I2
Banderas Mex. 166 D2
Banderas, Bahía de b. Mex. 168 C4
Band-e Sar Qom Iran 110 D3
Bandhi Pak. 111 H5
Bandhogarh India 104 E5
Bandi r. India 104 C4
Bandiagara Mali 120 C3
Bandikui India 104 D4
Bandingilo National Park South Sudan 121 G4
Bandipur National Park India 106 C4
Bandırma Turkey 69 L4
Bandjarmasin Kalimantan Indon. see Banjarmasin
Bandō Japan 93 F2
Bandon Ireland 61 D6
Bandon r. Ireland 61 D6
Ban Don Thai. see Surat Thani
Bandon OR U.S.A. 156 B4
Band Qīr Iran 110 C4
Bandra India 106 B2
Bandundu Dem. Rep. Congo 122 B4
Bandung Java Indon. 85 D4
Bandya Australia 135 C6
Bāneh Iran 110 B3
Banemo Halmahera Indon. 83 D2
Banera India 104 C4
Banes Cuba 169 I4
Banff Canada 150 H5
Banff U.K. 60 G3
Banff National Park Canada 150 G5
Banfora Burkina Faso 120 C3
Bang, Gunung mt. Indon. 85 F2
Banga Dem. Rep. Congo 123 C4
Banga Mindanao Phil. 82 D5
Banga r. Mindanao Phil. 82 D5
Bangai Point Mindanao Phil. 82 D5
Bangalore India see Bengaluru
Bangalow Australia 138 F2
Banganga r. India 99 B8
Bangaon India 105 G5
Bangar Brunei 85 F1
Bangar Luzon Phil. 82 C2
Bangassou Cent. Afr. Rep. 122 C3
Bangdag Co salt l. China 99 C6
Banggai Celebes Indon. 83 B3
Banggai i. Indon. 83 B3
Banggai, Kepulauan is Indon. 81 G7
Banggai, Kepulauan is Indon. 83 B3
Banggi i. Malaysia 85 G1
Banghāzī Libya see Benghazi
Banghiang, Xé r. Laos 86 D3
Bangil Java Indon. 85 F4
Bangka i. Indon. 83 C2
Bangka i. Indon. 84 D3
Bangka, Selat sea chan. Indon. 83 C2
Bangka, Selat sea chan. Indon. 84 D3
Bangka-Belitung prov. Indon. 84 D3
Bangkal Kalimantan Indon. 85 F3
Bangkala, Teluk b. Indon. 83 A4
Bangkalan Java Indon. 85 F4
Bangkalan i. Indon. 83 B3
Bangkaru i. Indon. 84 B2
Bangkinang Sumatra Indon. 84 C2
Bangkir Celebes Indon. 83 B2
Bangko Sumatra Indon. 84 C3

▶Bangkok Thai. 87 C4
Capital of Thailand.

Bangkok, Bight of b. Thai. 87 C4
Bangkor China 99 D7
Bangkuang Kalimantan Indon. 85 F3
Bangkulu i. Indon. 83 B3
Bangkulua Sumbawa Indon. 85 G5
Bangla state India see West Bengal

▶Bangladesh country Asia 105 G4
5th most populous country in Asia and 8th in the world.

Bang Lang, Ang Kep Nam Thai. 84 C1
Bangluo China 94 F5
Bangma Shan mts China 96 C4
Bang Mun Nak Thai. 86 C3
Ba Ngoi Vietnam 87 E5
Bangolo Côte d'Ivoire 120 C4
Bangong Co salt l. China/India 104 D2
Bangor Northern Ireland U.K. 61 G3
Bangor Wales U.K. 58 C5
Bangor ME U.S.A. 162 G2
Bangor MI U.S.A. 164 B2
Bangor PA U.S.A. 165 H3
Bangor Erris Ireland 61 C3
Bangs, Mount AZ U.S.A. 159 G3
Bangsalsepulun Kalimantan Indon. 85 G3
Bang Saphan Yai Thai. 87 B5
Bangsund Norway 54 G4
Bangued Luzon Phil. 82 C2

▶Bangui Cent. Afr. Rep. 122 B3
Capital of the Central African Republic.

Bangui Luzon Phil. 82 C2
Bangunpurba Sumatra Indon. 84 B2
Bangweulu, Lake Zambia 123 C5
Banhā Egypt 112 C5
Banhine, Parque Nacional de nat. park Moz. 125 K2
Ban Hin Heup Laos 86 C3
Ban Houei Sai Laos see Houayxay
Ban Huai Khon Thai. 86 C3
Ban Huai Yang Thai. 87 B5
Bani Luzon Phil. 82 B2
Bani, Jebel ridge Morocco 64 C6
Bania Cent. Afr. Rep. 122 B3
Bani-Bangou Niger 120 D3
Banifing r. Mali 120 C3
Banihal Pass and Tunnel India 104 C2
Bani Point Luzon Phil. 82 C2
Banister r. VA U.S.A. 164 F5
Banī Suwayf Egypt 112 C5
Banī Walīd Libya 121 E1
Banī Wuṭayfān well Saudi Arabia 110 C5
Bāniyās Israel 107 B3
Bāniyās Syria 107 B2
Bani Yas reg. U.A.E. 110 D6
Banja Luka Bos. & Herz. 68 G2
Banjarmasin Kalimantan Indon. 85 F3
Banjës, Liqeni i resr Albania 69 I4
Banjiegou China 98 E4
Banjieta China 95 I3

▶Banjul Gambia 120 B3
Capital of The Gambia.

Banka India 105 F4
Banka Banka Australia 134 F4
Bankapur India 106 B3
Bankass Mali 120 C3
Ban Kèngkabao Laos 86 D3
Ban Khao Yoi Thai. 87 B4
Ban Khok Kloi Thai. 87 B5
Bankilaré Niger 120 D3
Bankobankoang i. Indon. 85 G4
Banks Island B.C. Canada 149 O5
Banks Island N.W.T. Canada 146 F2
Banks Islands Vanuatu 133 G3
Banks Lake Canada 151 M2
Banks Lake WA U.S.A. 156 D3
Banks Peninsula N.Z. 139 D6
Banks Strait Australia 137 [inset]
Bankura India 105 F5
Ban Lamduan Thai. 87 C4
Banlan China 97 F3
Ban Mae La Luang Thai. 86 B3
Banmaw Myanmar see Bhamo
Banmo Myanmar see Bhamo
Bann r. Ireland 61 F5
Bann r. U.K. 61 F2
Ban Nakham Laos 86 D3
Bannerman Town Bahamas 163 E7
Banning CA U.S.A. 158 E5
Banningville Dem. Rep. Congo see Bandundu
Ban Noi Myanmar 86 B3
Ban Nonghèt Laos 86 D3
Ban Nong Kung Thai. 86 D3
Bannu Pak. 111 H3
Bano India 105 F5
Bañolas Spain see Banyoles
Ban Phai Thai. 86 C3
Ban Phôn Laos see Xékong
Ban Phôn-Hông Laos 86 C3
Banqiao Gansu China 94 E4
Banqiao Yunnan China 96 C3
Banqiao Yunnan China 96 E3
Ban Sanam Chai Thai. 84 C1
Bansgaon India 99 C8
Bansi Bihar India 105 F4
Bansi Rajasthan India 104 C4
Bansi Uttar Prad. India 104 D4
Bansi Uttar Prad. India 105 E4
Bansihari India 105 G4
Banská Bystrica Slovakia 57 Q6
Banspani India 105 F5
Bansur India 104 D4
Ban Sut Ta Thai. 86 B3
Ban Suwan Wari Thai. 86 D4
Banswara India 104 C5
Banta i. Indon. 83 A5
Bantaeng Celebes Indon. 83 A4
Bantayan i. Phil. 82 C4
Banteer Ireland 61 D5
Banten prov. Indon. 84 D4
Ban Tha Song Yang Thai. 86 B3
Banthat mts Cambodia/Thai. see Cardamom Range
Ban Tha Tum Thai. 86 C4
Ban Thepha Thai. 84 C1
Ban Tôp Laos 86 D3
Bantry Ireland 61 C6
Bantry Bay Ireland 61 C6
Bantul Java Indon. 85 E4
Bantval India 106 B3
Ban Wang Chao Thai. 86 B3
Ban Woen Laos 86 C3
Ban Xepian Laos 86 D4
Banyak, Pulau-pulau is Indon. 84 B2
Ban Yang Yong Thai. 87 B4
Banyo Cameroon 120 E4
Banyoles Spain 67 H2
Banyuasin r. Indon. 84 D3
Banyuwangi Java Indon. 85 F5
Banzare Coast Antarctica 188 G2
Banzare Seamount sea feature Indian Ocean 185 N9
Banzart Tunisia see Bizerte
Banzkow Germany 63 L1
Banzyville Dem. Rep. Congo see Mobayi-Mbongo
Bao'an Guangdong China see Shenzhen
Bao'an Qinghai China 94 E5
Bao'an Shaanxi China see Zhidan
Baochang China 95 H3
Baocheng China 96 E1
Baodi China 95 I4
Baoding China 95 H4
Baofeng China 97 G1
Baohe China see Weixi
Baoji China 95 F5
Baokang Hubei China 97 F2
Baokang Nei Mongol China 95 J2
Bao Lac Vietnam 86 D2
Baolin China 90 C3
Bao Lôc Vietnam 87 D5
Baoqing China 90 D3
Baoro Cent. Afr. Rep. 122 B3
Baoshan China 96 C3
Baotou China 95 G3
Baoulé r. Mali 120 C3
Baoxing China 96 D2
Baoying China 97 H1
Baoyou China see Ledong
Bap India 104 C4
Bapatla India 106 D3
Bapaume France 62 C4
Baptiste Lake Canada 165 F1
Bapu China see Meigu
Baq'ā' oasis Saudi Arabia 113 F6
Baqbaq Egypt see Buqbuq
Baqên Xizang China 99 F6
Baqên Xizang China 99 F7
Baqiu China 97 G3
Ba'qūbah Iraq 113 G4
Bar Montenegro 69 H3
Bar Russia 95 F1
Bara Buru Indon. 83 C3
Bara Sudan 108 D7
Baraawe Somalia 122 E3
Barabai Kalimantan Indon. 85 F3
Bara Banki India see Barabanki
Barabanki India 104 E4
Baraboo WI U.S.A. 160 F3
Baracaju r. Brazil 179 A1
Baracaldo Spain see Barakaldo
Baracoa Cuba 169 J4
Baradá, Nahr r. Syria 107 C3
Baradine Australia 138 D3
Baradine r. Australia 138 D3
Baragarh India see Bargarh
Barahona Dom. Rep. 169 J5
Barahoti India 99 B7
Barail Range mts India 105 H4
Baraka watercourse Eritrea/Sudan 121 G3
Barakaldo Spain 67 E2
Barakī Barak Afgh. 111 H3
Baralaba Australia 136 E5
Bara Lacha La India 104 D2
Baralzon Lake Canada 151 L3
Baram India 105 F5
Baram r. Malaysia 85 F1
Baram, Tanjung pt Malaysia 85 F1
Baramati India 106 B2
Baramula India see Baramulla
Baramulla India 104 C2
Baran India 104 D4
Baran r. Pak. 111 H5
Bārān, Kūh-e mts Iran 111 F3
Barana Pak. 111 I4
Baranavichy Belarus 55 O10
Barang, Dasht-e des. Afgh. 111 F3
Baranikha Russia 77 R3
Baranīs Egypt 108 E5
Baranîs Egypt see Baranīs
Barannda India 104 E4
Baranof AK U.S.A. 149 N4
Baranof Island AK U.S.A. 149 N4
Baranovichi Belarus see Baranavichy
Baranowicze Belarus see Baranavichy
Baraouéli Mali 120 C3
Baraque de Fraiture hill Belgium 62 F4
Barasat India 105 G5
Barat Daya, Kepulauan is Moluccas Indon. 83 C4
Barati Timor Indon. 83 B5
Baraut India 104 D3
Barbacena Brazil 179 C3
Barbados country West Indies 169 M6
Barbar, Gebel el mt. Egypt see Barbar, Jabal
Barbar, Jabal mt. Egypt 107 A5
Barbara Lake Canada 152 D4
Barbastro Spain 67 G2
Barbate Spain 67 D5
Barbaza Panay Phil. 82 C4
Barbechitos Mex. 166 D3
Barberton S. Africa 125 J3
Barberton OH U.S.A. 164 E3
Barbezieux-St-Hilaire France 66 D4
Barbour Bay Canada 151 M2
Barbourville KY U.S.A. 164 D5
Barbuda i. Antigua and Barbuda 169 L5
Barby Germany 63 L3
Barcaldine Australia 136 D4
Barce Libya see Al Marj
Barcelona Spain 67 H3
Barcelona Venez. 176 F1
Barcelonnette France 66 H4
Barcelos Brazil 176 F4
Barchfeld Germany 63 K4
Barcino Spain see Barcelona
Barclay de Tolly atoll Fr. Polynesia see Raroia
Barclayville Liberia 120 C4
Barcoo watercourse Australia 136 C5
Barcoo Creek watercourse Australia see Cooper Creek
Barcoo National Park Australia see Welford National Park
Barcs Hungary 68 G2
Bärdä Azer. 113 G2
Bardaï Chad 121 E2
Bárðarbunga mt. Iceland 54 [inset 1]
Bardawīl, Khabrat al salt pan Saudi Arabia 107 D4
Bardawīl, Sabkhat al lag. Egypt 107 A4
Barddhaman India 105 F5
Bardejov Slovakia 53 D6
Bardera Somalia see Baardheere
Bardeskan Iran 110 E3
Bardhaman India see Barddhaman
Bardsey Island U.K. 59 C6
Bardsīr Iran 110 E4
Barðsneshorn pt Iceland 50 D2
Bardstown KY U.S.A. 164 C5
Barduli Italy see Barletta
Bardwell KY U.S.A. 161 F4
Bareilly India 104 D3
Barellan Australia 138 C5
Barentin France 59 H9
Barentsburg Svalbard 76 C2
Barents Sea Arctic Ocean 52 I1
Barentu Eritrea 108 E6
Bareo Sarawak Malaysia 85 F2
Barfleur, Pointe de pt France 59 F9
Barga China 99 C7
Bārgāh Iran 110 E5
Bargarh India 105 E5
Barghamad Iran 110 E2
Bargrennan U.K. 60 E5
Bargteheide Germany 63 K1
Barguna Bangl. 105 G5
Barhaj India 105 E4
Barham Australia 138 B5
Bari Italy 68 G4
Bariadi Tanz. 122 D4
Bari Doab lowland Pak. 111 I4
Barika Alg. 64 F4
Barinas Venez. 176 D2
Baripada India 105 F5
Bariri Brazil 179 A3
Bari Sadri India 104 C4
Barisal Bangl. 105 G5
Barisan, Pegunungan mts Indon. 84 C3
Barito r. Indon. 85 F3
Barium Italy see Bari
Barkal Bangl. 105 H5
Barkam China 96 D2
Barkan, Ra's-e pt Iran 110 C4
Barkava Latvia 55 O8
Bark Lake Canada 165 G1
Barkly East S. Africa 125 H6
Barkly Homestead Australia 136 A3
Barkly-Oos S. Africa see Barkly East
Barkly Tableland reg. Australia 136 A3
Barkly-Wes S. Africa see Barkly West
Barkly West S. Africa 124 G5
Barkol China 94 C3
Barkol Hu salt l. China 94 C3
Barla Turkey 69 N5
Bârlad Romania 69 L1
Barlag Gol watercourse Mongolia 94 C2
Bar-le-Duc France 62 F6
Barlee, Lake salt flat Australia 135 B7
Barlee Range hills Australia 135 A5
Barletta Italy 68 G4
Barlow Canada 149 M3
Barlow Lake Canada 151 K2
Barmah Forest Australia 138 B5
Barmedman Australia 138 C5
Barmen-Elberfeld Germany see Wuppertal
Barmer India 104 B4
Barm Fīrūz, Kūh-e mt. Iran 110 C4
Barmouth U.K. 59 C6
Barnala India 104 C3
Barnard, Mount Canada/U.S.A. 149 M4
Barnard Castle U.K. 58 F4
Barnato Australia 138 B3
Barnaul Russia 88 E2
Barnegat Bay NJ U.S.A. 165 H4
Barnes Icecap Canada 147 K2
Barnesville GA U.S.A. 163 D5
Barnesville MN U.S.A. 160 D2
Barneveld Neth. 62 F2
Barneville-Carteret France 59 F9
Barneys Lake imp. l. Australia 138 B4
Barney Top mt. UT U.S.A. 159 H3
Barnhart TX U.S.A. 167 E2
Barnsley U.K. 58 F5
Barnstable MA U.S.A. 165 J3
Barnstaple U.K. 59 C7
Barnstaple Bay U.K. 59 C7
Barnstorf Germany 63 I2
Barnum Bay Palau 82 [inset]
Baro Nigeria 120 D4
Baroda Gujarat India see Vadodara
Baroda Madh. Prad. India 104 D4
Barong China 96 C2
Barons Range hills Australia 135 D6
Barpathar India 96 B3
Barpeta India 105 G4
Bar Pla Soi Thai. see Chon Buri
Barques, Point Aux MI U.S.A. 164 D1
Barquisimeto Venez. 176 E1
Barra Brazil 177 J6
Barra i. U.K. 60 B4
Barra, Ponta da pt Moz. 125 L2
Barra, Sound of sea chan. U.K. 60 B3
Barraba Australia 138 E3
Barra Bonita Brazil 179 A3
Barracão do Barreto Brazil 177 G5
Barra de Navidad Mex. 166 D5
Barra do Bugres Brazil 177 G7
Barra do Corda Brazil 177 I5
Barra do Cuieté Brazil 179 C2
Barra do Garças Brazil 177 H7
Barra do Piraí Brazil 179 C3
Barra do São Manuel Brazil 177 G5
Barra do Turvo Brazil 179 A4
Barra Falsa, Ponta da pt Moz. 125 L2
Barraigh i. U.K. see Barra
Barra Kruta Hond. 166 [inset] J6
Barra Mansa Brazil 179 B3
Barranca Peru 176 C4
Barranca del Cobre, Parque Natural nature res. Mex. 166 D3
Barranqueras Arg. 178 E3
Barranquilla Col. 176 D1
Barre MA U.S.A. 165 I2
Barre VT U.S.A. 165 I1
Barre des Écrins mt. France 66 H4
Barreiras Brazil 177 J6
Barreirinha Brazil 177 G4
Barreirinhas Brazil 177 J4
Barreiro Port. 67 B4
Barreiros Brazil 177 K5
Barren Island India 87 A4
Barren Island Kiribati see Starbuck Island
Barren Islands AK U.S.A. 148 I4
Barren River Lake KY U.S.A. 164 B5
Barretos Brazil 179 A3
Barrett, Mount hill Australia 134 D4
Barrhead Canada 150 H4
Barrhead U.K. 60 E5
Barrie Canada 164 F1
Barrier Bay Antarctica 188 E2
Barrière Canada 150 F5
Barrier Range hills Australia 137 C6
Barrier Reef Belize 167 H5
Barrington Canada 153 I6
Barrington, Mount Australia 138 E4
Barrington Tops National Park Australia 138 E4
Barringun Australia 138 B2
Barro Alto Brazil 179 A1
Barrocão Brazil 179 C2
Barron WI U.S.A. 160 F2
Barroterán Mex. 167 E3
Barrow r. Ireland 61 F5
Barrow AK U.S.A. 148 H1
Barrow, Point pt AK U.S.A. 148 H1
Barrow Creek Australia 134 F5
Barrow-in-Furness U.K. 58 D4
Barrow Island Australia 134 A5
Barrow Range hills Australia 135 D6
Barrow Strait Canada 147 I2
Barr Smith Range hills Australia 135 C6
Barry U.K. 59 D7
Barrydale S. Africa 124 E7
Barry Mountains Australia 138 C6
Barrys Bay Canada 165 G1
Barryville NY U.S.A. 165 H3
Barsalpur India 104 C3
Barshatas Kazakh. 102 E2
Barshi India see Barsi
Barsi India 106 B2
Barsinghausen Germany 63 J2
Barstow CA U.S.A. 158 E4
Barsur India 106 D2
Bar-sur-Aube France 66 G2
Bartang Tajik. 111 H2
Barter Island AK U.S.A. 149 L1
Barth Germany 57 N3
Bartica Guyana 177 G2
Bartın Turkey 112 D2
Bartle Frere, Mount Australia 136 D3
Bartlett NE U.S.A. 160 D3
Bartlett Reservoir AZ U.S.A. 159 H5
Barton VT U.S.A. 165 I1
Barton, Port b. Palawan Phil. 82 B4
Barton-upon-Humber U.K. 58 G5
Bartoszyce Poland 57 R3
Bartow FL U.S.A. 163 D7
Barú, Volcán vol. Panama 169 H7
Barumun r. Indon. 84 C2
Barun China 94 D4
Barung i. Indon. 85 F5
Barunga Australia see Bamyili
Barun-Torey, Ozero l. Russia 95 H1
Barus Sumatra Indon. 84 B2
Baruunbayan-Ulaan Mongolia 94 E2
Baruunbüren Mongolia 94 F1
Baruunharaa Mongolia see Bayangol
Baruunsuu Mongolia see Tsogttsetsiy
Baruunturuun Mongolia 94 C1
Baruun-Urt Mongolia 95 H2
Baruva India 106 E2
Barwani India 104 C5
Barwéli Mali see Baraouéli
Barwon r. Australia 138 C3
Barygaza India see Bharuch
Barykova, Mys hd Russia 148 B3
Barysaw Belarus 55 P9
Barysh Russia 53 J5
Basaga Turkm. 111 G2
Basăk, Tônlé r. Cambodia 87 D5
Basalt r. Australia 136 D3
Basalt Island H.K. China 97 [inset]
Basankusu Dem. Rep. Congo 122 B3
Basar India 106 C2
Basarabi Romania 69 M2
Basargechar Armenia see Vardenis
Basaseachic, Parque Nacional Cascada de nat. park Mex. 166 C2
Basay Negros Phil. 82 C4
Basco Phil. 82 C1
Bascuñán, Cabo c. Chile 178 B3
Basel Switz. 66 H3
Basey Samar Phil. 82 D4
Bāsh Ābdān Afgh. 111 H2
Bashäkerd, Kūhhā-ye mts Iran 110 E5
Bashanta Russia see Gorodovikovsk
Bashaw Canada 150 H4
Bāshī Iran 110 C4
Bashi Channel Phil./Taiwan 81 G2
Bashkaus r. Russia 98 D2
Bashmakovo Russia 53 I5
Bāsht Iran 110 C4
Bashtanka Ukr. 53 G7
Basi Punjab India 104 D3
Basi Rajasthan India 104 D4
Basia India 105 F5
Basilan i. Phil. 82 C5
Basilan Strait Phil. 82 C5
Basildon U.K. 59 H7
Basile, Pico mt. Equat. Guinea 120 D4
Basin WY U.S.A. 156 F3
Basingstoke U.K. 59 F7
Basin Lake Canada 151 J4
Basirhat India 105 G5
Basīṭ, Ra's al pt Syria 107 B2
Başkale Turkey 113 G3
Baskatong, Réservoir resr Canada 152 G5
Baskerville, Cape Australia 134 C4
Başkomutan Tarıhı Milli Parkı nat. park Turkey 112 C3
Başköy Turkey 107 A1
Baskunchak, Ozero l. Russia 53 J6
Basle Switz. see Basel
Basmat India 106 C2
Baso i. Indon. 84 C3
Basoko Dem. Rep. Congo 122 C3
Basol r. Pak. 111 G5
Basra Iraq 113 G5
Bassano Canada 151 H5
Bassano del Grappa Italy 68 D2
Bassar Togo 120 D4
Bassas da India reef Indian Ocean 123 D6
Bassas de Pedro Padua Bank sea feature India 106 B3
Bassein Myanmar 86 A3
Bassein r. Myanmar 86 A3
Basse-Normandie admin. reg. France 59 F9
Bassenthwaite Lake U.K. 58 D4
Basse Santa Su Gambia 120 B3

▶Basse-Terre Guadeloupe 169 L5
Capital of Guadeloupe.

▶Basseterre St Kitts and Nevis 169 L5
Capital of St Kitts and Nevis.

Bassett NE U.S.A. 160 D3
Bassett VA U.S.A. 164 F5
Bassikounou Mauritania 120 C3
Bass Rock i. U.K. 60 G4
Bass Strait Australia 137 D8
Bassum Germany 63 I2
Basswood Lake Canada 152 C4
Båstad Sweden 55 H8
Bastheim Germany 63 K4
Basti India 105 E4
Bastia Corsica France 66 I5
Bastioes r. Brazil 177 K5
Bastogne Belgium 62 F4
Bastrop LA U.S.A. 161 F5
Bastrop TX U.S.A. 161 D6
Basu, Tanjung pt Indon. 84 C3
Basuo China see Dongfang
Basutoland country Africa see Lesotho
Başyayla Turkey 107 A1
Bata Equat. Guinea 120 D4
Bataan Peninsula Luzon Phil. 82 C3
Batabanó, Golfo de b. Cuba 169 H4

Batac Luzon Phil. 82 C2
Batagay Russia 77 O3
Batakan Kalimantan Indon. 85 F4
Batala India 104 C3
Batalha Port. 67 B4
Batam Indon. 84 D2
Batam i. Sumatra Indon. 84 D2
Batamay Russia 77 N3
Batamshy Kazakh. see Badamsha
Batan Jiangsu China 97 I1
Batan Qinghai China 96 D1
Batan i. Phil. 82 C1
Batan i. Phil. 82 D3
Batang China 96 C2
Batang Java Indon. 85 E4
Batangafo Cent. Afr. Rep. 122 B3
Batang Ai National Park Malaysia 85 F2
Batangas Luzon Phil. 82 C3
Batanghari r. Indon. 84 D3
Batangpele i. Papua Indon. 83 D3
Batangtarang Kalimantan Indon. 85 E2
Batangtoru Sumatra Indon. 84 B2
Batan Islands Phil. 82 C1
Batanta i. Papua Indon. 83 D3
Batavia Java Indon. see Jakarta
Batavia NY U.S.A. 165 F2
Batavia OH U.S.A. 164 C4
Bataysk Russia 53 H7
Batbatan i. Phil. 82 C4
Batchawana Mountain hill Canada 152 D5
Bătdâmbâng Cambodia 87 C4
Bateemeucica, Gunung mt. Indon. 84 A1
Batéké, Plateaux Congo 122 B4
Batemans Bay Australia 138 E5
Bates Range hills Australia 135 C6
Batesville AR U.S.A. 161 F5
Batesville IN U.S.A. 164 C4
Batesville MS U.S.A. 161 F5
Batetskiy Russia 52 F4
Bath N.B. Canada 153 I5
Bath Ont. Canada 165 G1
Bath U.K. 59 E7
Bath ME U.S.A. 165 K2
Bath NY U.S.A. 165 G2
Bath PA U.S.A. 165 H3
Batha watercourse Chad 121 E3
Bathéay Cambodia 87 D5
Bathgate U.K. 60 F5
Bathinda India 104 C3
Bathurst Australia 138 D4
Bathurst Canada 153 I5
Bathurst Gambia see Banjul
Bathurst S. Africa 125 H7
Bathurst, Cape Canada 149 P1
Bathurst, Lake Australia 138 D5
Bathurst Inlet inlet Canada 146 H3
Bathurst Inlet (abandoned) Canada 146 H3
Bathurst Island Australia 134 E2
Bathurst Island Canada 147 I2
Bathyz Döwlet Gorugy nature res. Turkm. 111 F3
Batié Burkina Faso 120 C4
Batikala, Tanjung pt Indon. 83 B3
Batı Menteşe Dağları mts Turkey 69 L6
Batı Toroslar mts Turkey 69 N6
Batken Kyrg. 102 D4
Batkes Moluccas Indon. 134 E1
Bāţlāq-e Gavkhūnī marsh Iran 110 D3
Batley U.K. 58 F5
Batlow Australia 138 D5
Batman Turkey 113 F3
Batna Alg. 64 F4
Batnorov Mongolia 95 G2
Batok, Bukit hill Sing. 87 [inset]
Bat-Öldziy Mongolia 94 E2
Batong, Ko i. Thai. 84 B1

▶Baton Rouge LA U.S.A. 161 F6
Capital of Louisiana.

Batopilas Mex. 166 D3
Batouri Cameroon 121 E4
Batrā' tourist site Jordan see Petra
Batrā', Jabal al mt. Jordan 107 B5
Batroûn Lebanon 107 B2
Båtsfjord Norway 54 P1
Batshireet Mongolia 95 G1
Batsümber Mongolia 94 F1
Battambang Cambodia see Bătdâmbâng
Batticaloa Sri Lanka 106 D5
Batti Malv i. India 87 A5
Battipaglia Italy 68 F4
Battle r. Canada 151 I4
Battle Creek MI U.S.A. 164 C2
Battleford Canada 151 I4
Battle Mountain NV U.S.A. 158 E1
Battle Mountain mt. NV U.S.A. 158 E1
Battsengel Mongolia 94 E2
Battura Glacier Pak. 104 C1
Batu mt. Eth. 122 D3
Batu, Bukit mt. Malaysia 85 F2
Batu, Pulau-pulau is Indon. 84 B3
Batu, Tanjung pt Indon. 85 G2
Batuata i. Indon. 83 B4
Batubetumbang Indon. 84 D3
Batu Bora, Bukit mt. Malaysia 85 F2
Batudaka i. Indon. 83 B3
Batu Gajah Malaysia 84 C1
Batuhitam, Tanjung pt Indon. 83 B3
Batui Celebes Indon. 83 B3
Batulaki Mindanao Phil. 82 D5
Batulicin Kalimantan Indon. 85 G3
Batulilangmebang, Gunung mt. Indon. 85 F2
Batum Georgia see Bat'umi
Bat'umi Georgia 113 F2
Batumonga Sumatra Indon. 84 C3
Batu Pahat Malaysia 84 C2
Batu Putih, Gunung mt. Malaysia 84 C1
Baturaja Sumatra Indon. 84 D4
Baturetno Java Indon. 85 E5
Baturité Brazil 177 K4
Batusangkar Sumatra Indon. 84 C3
Batyrevo Russia 53 J5
Batys Qazaqstan admin. div. Kazakh. see Zapadnyy Kazakhstan
Bau Sarawak Malaysia 85 E2
Baubau Celebes Indon. 83 B4
Baucau East Timor 83 C5
Bauchi Nigeria 120 D3
Bauda India 106 E1
Baudette MN U.S.A. 160 E1
Baudh India see Bauda
Baugé-en-Anjou France 66 D3
Bauhinia Australia 136 E5
Baukau East Timor see Baucau
Baula Celebes Indon. 83 B4
Bauld, Cape Canada 153 L4
Baume-les-Dames France 66 H3
Baunach r. Germany 63 K5
Baura Bangl. 105 G4
Bauru Brazil 179 A3
Bausendorf Germany 62 G4
Bauska Latvia 55 N8
Bautino Kazakh. 113 H1
Bautzen Germany 57 O5
Bavānāt Iran 110 D4
Bavaria land Germany see Bayern
Bavaria reg. Germany 63 L6
Bavda India 106 B2
Baviaanskloofberge mts S. Africa 124 F7
Bavispe Mex. 166 C2
Bavispe r. Mex. 166 C2
Bavla India 104 C5
Bavly Russia 51 Q5
Baw Myanmar 86 A2
Bawal India 104 D3
Bawal i. Indon. 85 E3
Bawan Kalimantan Indon. 85 F3
Bawang, Tanjung pt Indon. 85 E3
Baw Baw National Park Australia 138 C6
Bawdeswell U.K. 59 I6
Bawdwin Myanmar 86 B2
Bawean i. Indon. 85 F4
Bawinkel Germany 63 H2
Bawlake Myanmar 86 B3
Bawolung China 96 D2
Baxi China 96 D1
Baxian China see Bazhou
Baxkorgan China 98 E5
Baxley GA U.S.A. 163 D6
Baxoi China 96 C2
Baxter Mountain CO U.S.A. 159 J2
Bay China see Baicheng
Bay, Laguna de lag. Luzon Phil. 82 C3
Bayamo Cuba 169 I4
Bayan Heilong. China 90 B3
Bayan Qinghai China 94 D5
Bayan Qinghai China see Hualong
Bayan Lombok Indon. 85 G5
Bayan Arhangay Mongolia see Hashaat
Bayan Govĭ-Altay Mongolia see Bayan-Uul
Bayan Töv Mongolia 95 F2
Bayana India 104 D4
Bayan-Adarga Mongolia 95 G1
Bayanauyl Kazakh. 102 E1
Bayanbulag Bayanhongor Mongolia see Bayantsagaan
Bayanbulag Bayanhongor Mongolia 94 D2
Bayanbulag Hentiy Mongolia see Ömnödelger
Bayanbulak Xinjiang China 98 D3
Bayanbulak Xinjiang China 98 D4
Bayanchandmanĭ Mongolia 94 F1
Bayandalay Mongolia 94 E3
Bayanday Russia 88 J2
Bayandelger Sühbaatar Mongolia 95 H2
Bayandelger Töv Mongolia 95 G2
Bayandun Mongolia 95 H1
Bayang, Pegunungan mts Indon. 85 E2
Bayan Gol China see Dengkou
Bayangol Govĭ-Altay Mongolia see Bugat
Bayangol Selenge Mongolia 94 F1
Bayangol Russia 94 E1
Bayan Har Shan mts China 94 C5
Bayan Har Shankou pass China 94 D5
Bayanhongor Mongolia 94 E2
Bayanhongor prov. Mongolia 94 D2
Bayan Hot China 94 F4
Bayanhushuu Mongolia see Galuut
Bayanjargalan Mongolia 95 F2
Bayan-Kol Russia 94 D1
Bayanlig Mongolia 94 E2
Bayanlü Iran 110 B3
Bayanmönh Mongolia 95 G2
Bayannur China 95 F3
Bayan Nurun China 94 F3
Bayannuur Mongolia 94 F2
Bayan Obo China 95 G3
Bayan-Ölgiy prov. Mongolia 94 B1
Bayan-Öndör Mongolia 94 F2
Bayan-Önjüül Mongolia 94 F2
Bayan-Ovoo Govĭ-Altay Mongolia see Altay
Bayan-Ovoo Hentiy Mongolia see Dadal
Bayan-Ovoo Hentiy Mongolia 95 H2
Bayan-Ovoo Ömnögovĭ Mongolia 94 F3
Bayan Qagan Nei Mongol China 95 I1
Bayan Qagan Nei Mongol China 95 J2
Bayansayr Mongolia see Baatsagaan
Bayan Shan mt. China 94 D4
Bayan Shutu China 95 H3
Bayansumküre China 98 D4
Bayan Tal China 95 I1
Bayanteeg Mongolia 94 E2
Bayan Tohoi China 95 I1
Bayantöhöm Mongolia see Büren
Bayantsagaan Bayanhongor Mongolia 94 D2
Bayantsagaan Töv Mongolia 95 F2
Bayan Ul China 95 I2
Bayan Us China 95 G3
Bayan-Uul Dornod Mongolia 95 H1
Bayan-Uul Govĭ-Altay Mongolia 94 C2
Bayan Uul mts Mongolia 94 B1
Bayard NM U.S.A. 159 I5
Bayasgalant Mongolia see Mönhhaan
Bayat Turkey 69 N5
Bayawan Negros Phil. 82 C4
Bayāẕ Iran 110 E4
Bayāẕīyeh Iran 110 D3
Baybay Leyte Phil. 82 D4
Bayboro NC U.S.A. 163 E5
Bayburt Turkey 113 F2
Bay Canh, Hon i. Vietnam 87 D5
Bay City MI U.S.A. 164 D2
Bay City TX U.S.A. 161 D6
Baydaratskaya Guba Russia 76 H3
Baydhabo Somalia 122 E3
Baydrag Mongolia see Dzag
Baydrag Gol r. Mongolia 94 D2
Bayerischer Wald mts Germany 57 N6
Bayerischer Wald, Nationalpark nat. park Germany 57 N6
Bayern land Germany 63 L6
Bayeux France 59 G9
Bayfield Canada 164 E2
Bayiji China 95 I5
Bayındır Turkey 69 L5
Bay Islands is Hond. see Bahía, Islas de la
Bayizhen China see Nyingchi
Bayjī Iraq 113 F4
Baykal-Amur Magistral Russia 90 C1
Baykal Range mts Russia see Baykal'skiy Khrebet
Baykal'sk Russia 94 F1
Baykal'skiy Khrebet mts Russia 89 J2
Baykal'skiy Zapovednik nature res. Russia 94 F1
Baykan Turkey 113 F3
Bay-Khaak Russia 102 H1
Baykibashevo Russia 51 R4
Baykonur Kazakh. see Baykonyr
Baykonyr Kazakh. 102 B2
Baymak Russia 76 G4
Bay Minette AL U.S.A. 163 C6
Baynūna'h reg. U.A.E. 110 D6
Bayombong Luzon Phil. 82 C2
Bayona Spain see Baiona
Bayonne France 66 D5
Bayonne NJ U.S.A. 165 H3
Bayo Point Panay Phil. 82 C4
Bay Point Phil. 82 B4
Bay Port MI U.S.A. 164 D2
Bayqongyr Kazakh. see Baykonyr
Bayram-Ali Turkm. see Baýramaly
Baýramaly Turkm. 111 F2
Bayramiç Turkey 69 L5
Bayreuth Germany 63 L5
Bayrūt Lebanon see Beirut
Bays, Lake of Canada 164 F1
Bay Shore MI U.S.A. 164 C1
Bay Shore NY U.S.A. 165 I3
Bay Springs MS U.S.A. 161 F6
Bayston Hill U.K. 59 E6
Baysun Uzbek. see Boysun
Baytik Shan mts China 94 B2
Bayt Jālā West Bank 107 B4
Bayt Lahm West Bank see Bethlehem
Baytown TX U.S.A. 161 E6
Bayu Celebes Indon. 83 B3
Bayunglincir Sumatra Indon. 84 C3
Bay View N.Z. 139 F4
Bayy al Kabīr, Wādī watercourse Libya 121 E1
Baza Spain 67 E5
Baza, Sierra de mts Spain 67 E5
Bazar watercourse Kazakh. 98 C2
Bāzārak Afgh. 111 G3
Bazardüzü Dağı mt. Azer./Russia see Bazardyuzyu, Gora
Bazardyuzyu, Gora mt. Azer./Russia 113 G2
Bāzār-e Māsāl Iran 110 C2
Bazarnyy Karabulak Russia 53 J5
Bazaruto, Ilha do i. Moz. 123 D6
Bazdar Pak. 111 G5
Bazhong China 96 E2
Bazhou Hebei China 95 I4
Bazhou Sichuan China see Bazhong
Bazin r. Canada 152 G5
Bazmān Iran 111 F5
Bazmān, Kūh-e mt. Iran 111 F4
Bcharré Lebanon 107 C2
Be, Sông r. Vietnam 87 D5
Beach ND U.S.A. 160 C2
Beachy Head hd U.K. 59 H8
Beacon NY U.S.A. 165 I3
Beacon Bay S. Africa 125 H7
Beaconsfield U.K. 59 G7
Beagle, Canal sea chan. Arg. 178 C8
Beagle Bank reef Australia 134 C3
Beagle Bay Australia 134 C4
Beagle Gulf Australia 134 E3
Bealanana Madag. 123 E5
Béal an Átha Ireland see Ballina
Béal an Mhuirthead Ireland 61 C3
Béal Átha na Sluaighe Ireland see Ballinasloe
Beale, Lake India 106 B2
Beaminster U.K. 59 E8
Bear r. ID U.S.A. 156 E4
Bearalváhki Norway see Berlevåg
Bear Cove Point Canada 151 O2
Beardmore Canada 152 D4
Beardmore Glacier Antarctica 188 H1
Bear Island Arctic Ocean see Bjørnøya
Bear Island Canada 152 E3
Bear Lake l. Canada 152 A3
Bear Lake MI U.S.A. 164 B1
Bear Lake l. ID U.S.A. 156 F4
Bearma r. India 104 D4
Bear Mountain SD U.S.A. 160 C3
Bearnaraigh i. U.K. see Berneray
Bear Paw Mountain MT U.S.A. 156 F2
Bearpaw Mountains MT U.S.A. 156 F2
Bearskin Lake Canada 151 N4
Beas Dam India 104 C3
Beata, Cabo c. Dom. Rep. 169 J5
Beatrice NE U.S.A. 160 D3
Beatrice, Cape Australia 136 B2
Beatton r. Canada 150 F3
Beatton River Canada 150 F3
Beatty NV U.S.A. 158 E3
Beattyville Canada 152 F4
Beattyville KY U.S.A. 164 D5
Beaucaire France 66 G5
Beauchene Island Falkland Is 178 E8
Beaufort Australia 138 A6
Beaufort Sabah Malaysia 85 F1
Beaufort NC U.S.A. 163 E5
Beaufort SC U.S.A. 163 D5
Beaufort Island H.K. China 97 [inset]
Beaufort Lagoon AK U.S.A. 149 L1
Beaufort Sea Canada/U.S.A. 146 D2
Beaufort West S. Africa 124 F7
Beaulieu r. Canada 151 H2
Beauly U.K. 60 E3
Beauly r. U.K. 60 E3
Beaumaris U.K. 58 C5
Beaumont Belgium 62 E4
Beaumont N.Z. 139 B7
Beaumont MS U.S.A. 161 F6
Beaumont TX U.S.A. 161 E6
Beaune France 66 G3
Beaupréau France 66 D3
Beauquesne France 62 C4
Beauraing Belgium 62 E4
Beauséjour Canada 151 L5
Beauvais France 62 C5
Beauval France 62 C4
Beaver r. Alba/Sask. Canada 151 J4
Beaver r. Ont. Canada 152 D3
Beaver r. Y.T. Canada 149 N3
Beaver r. Y.T. Canada 150 E3
Beaver AK U.S.A. 149 K2
Beaver OK U.S.A. 161 C4
Beaver PA U.S.A. 164 E3
Beaver UT U.S.A. 159 G2
Beaver r. UT U.S.A. 159 G2
Beaver Creek Canada 149 L3
Beavercreek OH U.S.A. 164 C4
Beaver Creek r. AK U.S.A. 149 K2
Beaver Creek r. MT U.S.A. 160 B1
Beaver Creek r. ND U.S.A. 160 C2
Beaver Dam KY U.S.A. 164 B5
Beaver Dam WI U.S.A. 160 F3
Beaver Falls PA U.S.A. 164 E3
Beaverhead Mountains MT U.S.A. 156 E3
Beaverhill Lake Alta Canada 151 H4
Beaver Hill Lake Canada 151 M4
Beaverhill Lake N.W.T. Canada 151 J2
Beaver Island MI U.S.A. 162 C2
Beaverlodge Canada 150 G4
Beaver Mountains AK U.S.A. 148 H3
Beaverton Canada 164 F1
Beaverton MI U.S.A. 164 C2
Beaverton OR U.S.A. 156 C3
Beawar India 104 C4
Beazley Arg. 178 C4
Bebedouro Brazil 179 A3
Bebington U.K. 58 D5
Bebra Germany 63 J4
Bêca China 96 C2
Bécard, Lac l. Canada 153 G1
Beccles U.K. 59 I6
Bečej Serbia 69 I2
Becerreá Spain 67 C2
Béchar Alg. 64 D5
Becharof Lake AK U.S.A. 148 H4
Becharof National Wildlife Refuge nature res. AK U.S.A. 148 H4
Bechevin Bay AK U.S.A. 148 G5
Bechhofen Germany 63 K5
Bechuanaland country Africa see Botswana
Beckley WV U.S.A. 164 E5
Beckum Germany 63 I3
Becky Peak NV U.S.A. 159 F2
Beco East Timor 83 C5
Bečov nad Teplou Czech Rep. 63 M4
Bedale U.K. 58 F4
Bedburg Germany 62 G4
Bedel', Pereval pass China/Kyrg. see Bedel Pass
Bedelē Eth. 122 D3
Bedel Pass China/Kyrg. 98 B4
Bedford N.S. Canada 153 J5
Bedford Que. Canada 165 I1
Bedford E. Cape S. Africa 125 H7
Bedford KwaZulu-Natal S. Africa 125 J5
Bedford U.K. 59 G6
Bedford IN U.S.A. 164 B4
Bedford KY U.S.A. 164 C4
Bedford PA U.S.A. 165 F3
Bedford VA U.S.A. 164 F5
Bedford, Cape Australia 136 D2
Bedford Downs Australia 134 D4
Bedgerebong Australia 138 C4
Bedi India 104 B5
Bedinggong Indon. 84 D3
Bedla India 104 C4
Bedlington U.K. 58 F3
Bedok Sing. 87 [inset]
Bedok Jetty Sing. 87 [inset]
Bedok Reservoir Sing. 87 [inset]
Bedourie Australia 136 B5
Bedum Neth. 62 G1
Bedworth U.K. 59 F6
Beechworth Australia 138 C6
Beechy Canada 151 J5
Beecroft Peninsula Australia 138 E5
Beed India see Bid
Beelitz Germany 63 M2
Beenleigh Australia 138 F1
Beernem Belgium 62 D3
Beersheba Israel 107 B4
Be'ér Sheva' Israel see Beersheba
Be'ér Sheva', Naḥal watercourse Israel 107 B4
Beervlei Dam S. Africa 124 F7
Beerwah Australia 138 F1
Beetaloo Australia 134 F4
Beethoven Peninsula Antarctica 188 L2
Beeville TX U.S.A. 161 D6
Befori Dem. Rep. Congo 122 C3
Beg, Lough l. U.K. 61 F3
Bega Australia 138 D6
Bega Moluccas Indon. 83 C3
Begari r. Pak. 111 H4
Begicheva, Ostrov i. Russia see Bol'shoy Begichev, Ostrov
Begur, Cap de c. Spain 67 H3
Begusarai India 105 F4
Behābād Iran 110 D4
Béhague, Pointe pt Fr. Guiana 177 H3
Behbahān Iran 110 C4
Behchokǫ̀ Canada 150 G2
Behleg China 99 E5
Behrūsī Iran 110 D4
Behshahr Iran 110 D2
Bei'an China 90 B2
Bei'ao China see Dongtou
Beibei China 96 E2
Beichuan China see Qushan
Beida Libya see Al Bayḍā'
Beida Shan mts China 94 E4
Beigang Taiwan 97 I4
Beihai China 97 F4
Bei Hulsan Hu salt l. China 99 F5

▶Beijing China 95 I4
Capital of China. 5th most populous city in Asia and 8th in the world.

Beijing mun. China 95 I3
Beik Myanmar see Myeik
Beilen Neth. 62 G2
Beiliu China 97 F4
Beilngries Germany 63 L5
Beilu He r. China 99 F6
Beiluheyan China 94 C5
Beining China see Beizhen
Beinn an Oir hill U.K. 60 D5
Beinn an Tuirc hill U.K. 60 D5
Beinn Bheigeir hill U.K. 60 C5
Beinn Bhreac hill U.K. 60 D4
Beinn Dearg mt. U.K. 60 E3
Beinn Heasgarnich mt. U.K. 60 E4
Beinn Mholach hill U.K. 60 C2
Beinn Mhòr hill U.K. 60 B3
Beinn na Faoghlia i. U.K. see Benbecula
Beipan Jiang r. China 96 E3
Beipiao China 95 J3
Beira Moz. 123 D5
Beiru He r. China 95 H5

▶Beirut Lebanon 107 B3
Capital of Lebanon.

Beishan China 94 D3
Bei Shan mts China 94 C3
Beitbridge Zimbabwe 123 C6
Beith U.K. 60 E5
Beitun China 98 D3
Beizhen China 95 J3
Beja Port. 67 C4
Béja Tunisia 68 C6
Bejaïa Alg. 67 I5
Béjar Spain 67 D3
Beji r. Pak. 102 C6
Bejucos Mex. 167 E5
Bekaa valley Lebanon see El Béqaa
Bekasi Java Indon. 84 D4
Békés Hungary 69 I1
Békéscsaba Hungary 69 I1
Bekily Madag. 123 E6
Bēkma, Sadd dam Iraq 113 G3
Bekovo Russia 53 I5
Bekwai Ghana 120 C4
Bela India 105 E4
Bela Pak. 111 G5
Belab r. Pak. 111 H4
Bela-Bela S. Africa 125 I3
Bélabo Cameroon 120 E4
Bela Crkva Serbia 69 I2
Belaga Sarawak Malaysia 85 F2
Bel'agash Kazakh. 98 C2
Belagavi India 106 B3
Bel Air MD U.S.A. 165 G4
Belalcázar Spain 67 D4
Bělá nad Radbuzou Czech Rep. 63 M5
Belang Celebes Indon. 83 C2
Belangbelang i. Moluccas Indon. 83 C3
Belapur India 106 B2
Belarus country Europe 53 E5
Belau country N. Pacific Ocean see Palau
Bela Vista Brazil 178 E2
Bela Vista Moz. 125 K4
Bela Vista de Goiás Brazil 179 A2
Belawan Sumatra Indon. 84 B2
Belaya r. Russia 77 S3
also known as Bila
Belaya, Gora mt. Russia 148 A2
Belaya Glina Russia 53 I7
Belaya Kalitva Russia 53 I6
Belaya Kholunitsa Russia 52 K4
Belayan r. Indon. 85 G3
Belayan, Gunung mt. Indon. 85 F2
Belaya Tserkva Ukr. see Bila Tserkva
Belbédji Niger 120 D3
Bełchatów Poland 57 Q5
Belcher KY U.S.A. 164 D5
Belcher Islands Canada 152 F2
Belcoo U.K. 61 E3
Belden CA U.S.A. 158 C1
Belding MI U.S.A. 164 C2
Beleapani reef India see Cherbaniani Reef
Belebey Russia 51 Q5
Beledweyne Somalia 122 E3
Belém Brazil 177 I4
Belém Novo Brazil 179 A5
Belén Arg. 178 C3
Belen Antalya Turkey 107 A1
Belen Hatay Turkey 107 C1
Belen NM U.S.A. 157 G6
Belep, Îles is New Caledonia 133 G3
Belev Russia 53 H5

▶Belfast U.K. 61 G3
Capital of Northern Ireland.

Belfast ME U.S.A. 162 G2
Belfast Lough inlet U.K. 61 G3
Bēlfodiyo Eth. 122 D2
Belford U.K. 58 F3
Belfort France 66 H3
Belgaum India see Belagavi
Belgern Germany 63 N3
Belgian Congo country Africa see Congo, Democratic Republic of the
België country Europe see Belgium
Belgique country Europe see Belgium
Belgium country Europe 62 E4
Belgorod Russia 53 H6
Belgorod-Dnestrovskyy Ukr. see Bilhorod-Dnistrovs'kyy

▶Belgrade Serbia 69 I2
Capital of Serbia.

Belgrade ME U.S.A. 165 K1
Belgrade MT U.S.A. 156 F3
Belgrano II research station Antarctica 188 A1
Belice r. Sicily Italy 68 E6
Beliliou i. Palau see Peleliu
Belimbing Sumatra Indon. 84 D4
Belinskiy Russia 53 I5
Belinyu Indon. 84 D3
Belitung i. Indon. 85 E3
Belize Angola 123 B4

▶Belize Belize 167 H5
Former capital of Belize.

Belize country Central America 167 H5
Beljak Austria see Villach
Belkina, Mys pt Russia 90 E3
Belkofski (abandoned) AK U.S.A. 148 G5
Bel'kovskiy, Ostrov i. Russia 77 O2
Bell Australia 138 E1
Bell r. Australia 138 D4
Bell r. Que. Canada 152 F4
Bell r. Y.T. Canada 149 M2
Bella Bella Canada 150 D4
Bellac France 66 E3
Bella Coola Canada 150 E4
Bellaire MI U.S.A. 164 C1
Bellaire TX U.S.A. 167 G2
Bellary India see Ballari
Bellata Australia 138 D2
Bella Unión Uruguay 178 E4
Bella Vista CA U.S.A. 158 B1
Bellbrook Australia 138 F3
Bell Cay reef Australia 136 E4
Belledonne mts France 66 G4
Bellefontaine OH U.S.A. 164 D3
Bellefonte PA U.S.A. 165 G3
Belle Fourche SD U.S.A. 160 C2
Belle Fourche r. SD U.S.A. 160 C2
Belle Glade FL U.S.A. 163 D7
Belle-Île i. France 66 C3
Belle Isle i. Canada 153 L4
Belle Isle, Strait of Canada 153 K4
Belleville Canada 165 G1
Belleville IL U.S.A. 160 F4
Belleville KS U.S.A. 160 D4
Bellevue IA U.S.A. 160 F3
Bellevue MI U.S.A. 164 C2
Bellevue OH U.S.A. 164 D3
Bellevue WA U.S.A. 156 C3
Bellin Canada see Kangirsuk
Bellingham U.K. 58 E3
Bellingham WA U.S.A. 156 C2
Bellingshausen research station Antarctica 188 A2
Bellingshausen Sea Antarctica 188 L2
Bellinzona Switz. 66 I3
Bellows Falls VT U.S.A. 165 I2
Bellpat Pak. 111 H4
Belluno Italy 68 E1
Bell Ville Arg. 178 D4
Bellville S. Africa 124 D7
Belm Germany 63 I2
Belmont Australia 138 E4
Belmont U.K. 60 [inset]
Belmont NY U.S.A. 165 F2
Belmonte Brazil 179 D1

▶Belmopan Belize 167 H5
Capital of Belize.

Belmore, Mount hill Australia 138 F2
Belo Madag. 123 E6
Belo Campo Brazil 179 C1
Belœil Belgium 62 D4
Belogorsk Crimea see Bilohirs'k
Belogorsk Russia 90 C2
Beloha Madag. 123 E6
Belo Horizonte Brazil 179 C2
Beloit KS U.S.A. 160 D4
Beloit WI U.S.A. 160 F3
Belokurikha Russia 102 F1
Belo Monte Brazil 177 H4
Belomorsk Russia 52 G2
Belonia India 105 G5
Belopa Celebes Indon. 83 B3
Belorechensk Russia 113 E1
Belorechenskaya Russia see Belorechensk
Belören Turkey 112 D3
Beloretsk Russia 76 G4
Belorussia country Europe see Belarus
Belorusskaya S.S.R. country Europe see Belarus
Belostok Poland see Białystok
Belot, Lac l. Canada 149 P2
Belo Tsiribihina Madag. 123 E5
Belousovka Kazakh. 98 C2
Belovo Russia 88 F2
Beloyarskiy Russia 51 T3
Beloye, Ozero l. Russia 52 H3

Beloye More sea Russia see White Sea
Belozersk Russia 52 H3
Belpre OH U.S.A. 164 E4
Beltana Australia 137 B6
Belted Range mts NV U.S.A. 158 E3
Beltes Gol r. Mongolia 94 D1
Belton TX U.S.A. 161 D6
Bel'ts' Moldova see Bălţi
Bel'tsy Moldova see Bălţi
Beluga Lake AK U.S.A. 149 J3
Belukha, Gora mt. Kazakh./Russia 102 G2
Beluran Sabah Malaysia 85 G1
Belush'ye Russia 52 J2
Belvidere IL U.S.A. 160 F3
Belvidere NJ U.S.A. 165 H3
Belyaka, Kosa spit Russia 148 D2
Belyando r. Australia 136 D4
Belyayevka Ukr. see Bilyayivka
Belyy Russia 52 G5
Belyy, Ostrov i. Russia 76 I2
Belyy Bom Russia 98 D2
Belzoni MS U.S.A. 161 F5
Bemaraha, Plateau du Madag. 123 E5
Bembe Angola 123 B4
Bemidji MN U.S.A. 160 E2
Béna Burkina Faso 120 C3
Bena Dibele Dem. Rep. Congo 122 C4
Benagin Kalimantan Indon. 85 F3
Ben Alder mt. U.K. 60 E4
Benalla Australia 138 B6
Benares India see Varanasi
Ben Arous Tunisia 68 D6
Benavente Spain 67 D2
Ben Avon mt. U.K. 60 F3
Benbane Head hd U.K. 61 F2
Benbecula i. U.K. 60 B3
Ben Boyd National Park Australia 138 E6
Benburb U.K. 61 F3
Bencha China 97 I1
Bencheng China see Luannan
Ben Chonzie hill U.K. 60 F4
Ben Cleuch hill U.K. 60 F4
Ben Cruachan mt. U.K. 60 D4
Bend OR U.S.A. 156 C3
Bendearg mt. S. Africa 125 H6
Bendeleben, Mount AK U.S.A. 148 F2
Bendeleben Mountains AK U.S.A. 148 F2
Bender Moldova 69 M1
Bender-Bayla Somalia 122 F3
Bendery Moldova see Bender
Bendigo Australia 138 B6
Bendoc Australia 138 D6
Bene Moz. 123 D5
Benedict, Mount hill Canada 153 K3
Benenitra Madag. 123 E6
Benešov Czech Rep. 57 O6
Bénestroff France 62 G6
Benevento Italy 68 F4
Beneventum Italy see Benevento
Benezette PA U.S.A. 165 F3
Beng, Nâm r. Laos 86 C3
Bengal, Bay of sea Indian Ocean 103 G8
Bengaluru India 106 C3
Bengamisa Dem. Rep. Congo 122 C3
Bengbu China 97 H1
Benghazi Libya 121 F1
Beng He r. China 95 I5
Bengkalis Sumatra Indon. 84 C2
Bengkalis i. Sumatra Indon. 84 C2
Bengkayang Kalimantan Indon. 85 E2
Bengkulu Sumatra Indon. 84 C3
Bengkulu prov. Indon. 84 C3
Bengkung Kalimantan Indon. 85 G3
Bengoi Seram Indon. 83 D3
Bengtsfors Sweden 55 H7
Benguela Angola 123 B5
Benha Egypt see Banhā
Ben Hiant hill U.K. 60 C4
Ben Hope hill U.K. 60 E2
Ben Horn hill U.K. 60 E2
Beni r. Bol. 176 E6
Beni Dem. Rep. Congo 122 C3
Beni Nepal 105 E3
Beni Abbès Alg. 64 D5
Beniah Lake Canada 151 H2
Benidorm Spain 67 F4
Beni Hammad, Al Qal'a tourist site Alg. 67 I6
Beni Mellal Morocco 64 C5
Benin country Africa 120 D4
Benin, Bight of g. Africa 120 D4
Benin City Nigeria 120 D4
Beni Saf Alg. 67 F6
Beni Snassen, Monts des mts Morocco 67 E6
Beni Suef Egypt see Banī Suwayf
Benito, Islas is Mex. 166 B2
Benito Juárez Arg. 178 E5
Benito Juárez Mex. 159 F5
Benito Soliven Luzon Phil. 82 C2
Benjamin TX U.S.A. 161 D5
Benjamin Constant Brazil 176 E4
Benjamin Hill Mex. 166 C2
Benjina Moluccas Indon. 81 I8
Benkelman NE U.S.A. 160 C3
Ben Klibreck hill U.K. 60 E2
Ben Lavin Nature Reserve S. Africa 125 I2
Ben Lawers mt. U.K. 60 E4
Ben Lomond mt. Australia 138 E3
Ben Lomond hill U.K. 60 E4
Ben Lomond National Park Australia 137 [inset]
Ben Macdui mt. U.K. 60 F3
Benmara Australia 136 B3
Ben More hill U.K. 60 C4
Ben More mt. U.K. 60 E4
Benmore, Lake N.Z. 139 C7
Ben More Assynt hill U.K. 60 E2
Bennäs Fin. 54 M5
Bennetta, Ostrov i. Russia 77 P2
Bennett Island Russia see Bennetta, Ostrov
Bennett Lake Canada 149 N4
Bennettsville SC U.S.A. 163 E5
Ben Nevis mt. U.K. 60 D4
Bennington NH U.S.A. 165 J2
Bennington VT U.S.A. 165 I2
Benoni S. Africa 125 I4
Bénoué, Parc National de la nat. park Cameroon 121 E4
Ben Rinnes hill U.K. 60 F3
Bensheim Germany 63 I5
Benson AZ U.S.A. 159 H6
Benson MN U.S.A. 160 E2
Benta Seberang Malaysia 84 C1
Benteng Celebes Indon. 83 B4
Bentinck Island Myanmar 87 B5
Bentiu South Sudan 108 C8
Bent Jbaïl Lebanon 107 B3
Bentley U.K. 58 F5
Bento Gonçalves Brazil 179 A5
Benton AR U.S.A. 161 E5
Benton CA U.S.A. 158 D3
Benton IL U.S.A. 160 F4
Benton KY U.S.A. 161 F4
Benton LA U.S.A. 161 E5
Benton MO U.S.A. 161 F4
Benton PA U.S.A. 165 G3
Bentong Malaysia see Bentung
Benton Harbor MI U.S.A. 164 B2
Bentonville AR U.S.A. 161 E4
Bên Tre Vietnam 87 D5
Bentung Malaysia 84 C2
Benua Celebes Indon. 83 B4
Benua i. Indon. 84 D2
Benuamartinus Kalimantan Indon. 85 F2
Benue r. Nigeria 120 D4
Benum, Gunung mt. Malaysia 84 C2
Ben Vorlich hill U.K. 60 E4
Benwee Head hd Ireland 61 C3
Benwood WV U.S.A. 164 E3
Ben Wyvis mt. U.K. 60 E3
Benxi Liaoning China 90 B4
Benxi Liaoning China 95 J3
Beo Celebes Indon. 83 C1
Beograd Serbia see Belgrade
Béoumi Côte d'Ivoire 120 C4
Bepagut, Gunung mt. Indon. 84 C4
Beppu Japan 91 C6
Béqaa valley Lebanon see El Béqaa
Bera, Tasik l. Malaysia 84 C2
Berach r. India 104 C4
Beraketa Madag. 123 E6
Berangas Kalimantan Indon. 85 G3
Bérard, Lac l. Canada 153 H2
Berasia India 104 D5
Berastagi Sumatra Indon. 84 B2
Berat Albania 69 H4
Beratus, Gunung mt. Indon. 85 G3
Berau r. Indon. 85 G2
Beravina Madag. 123 E5
Berbak, Taman Nasional nat. park Indon. 84 D3
Berber Sudan 108 D6
Berbera Somalia 122 E2
Berbérati Cent. Afr. Rep. 122 B3
Berchtesgaden, Nationalpark nat. park Germany 57 N7
Berck France 62 B4
Berdichev Ukr. see Berdychiv
Berdigestyakh Russia 77 N3
Berdyans'k Ukr. 53 H7
Berdychiv Ukr. 53 F6
Berea KY U.S.A. 164 C5
Berea OH U.S.A. 164 E3
Berebere Moluccas Indon. 83 D2
Beregovo Ukr. see Berehove
Beregovoy Russia 90 B1
Berehove Ukr. 53 D6
Bereina P.N.G. 81 L8
Bere Island Ireland 61 C6
Bereket Turkm. 110 D2
Berekum Ghana 120 C4
Berel' Kazakh. 98 D2
Berenice Egypt see Baranīs
Berenice Libya see Benghazi
Berens r. Canada 151 L4
Berens Island Canada 151 L4
Berens River Canada 151 L4
Beresford SD U.S.A. 160 D3
Bereza Belarus see Byaroza
Berezino Belarus see Byerazino
Berezivka Ukr. 53 F7
Berezne Ukr. 53 E6
Bereznik Russia 52 I3
Berezniki Russia 51 R4
Berezov Russia see Berezovo
Berezovka Russia 90 B2
Berezovka Ukr. see Berezivka
Berezovo Russia 51 T3
Berezovyy Russia 90 D2
Berga Germany 63 L3
Berga Spain 67 G2
Bergama Turkey 69 L5
Bergamo Italy 68 C2
Bergby Sweden 55 J6
Bergen Germany 63 J2
Bergen Norway 55 D6
Bergen NY U.S.A. 165 G2
Bergen auf Rügen Germany 57 N3
Bergen op Zoom Neth. 62 E3
Bergerac France 66 E4
Bergères-lès-Vertus France 62 E6
Bergheim Germany 62 G4
Bergisches Land reg. Germany 63 H4
Bergisch Gladbach Germany 62 H4
Bergland Namibia 124 C2
Bergomum Italy see Bergamo
Bergoo WV U.S.A. 164 E4
Bergpark Wilhelmshöhe tourist site Germany 57 L5
Bergsjö Sweden 55 J6
Bergsviken Sweden 54 L4
Bergtheim Germany 63 K5
Bergues France 62 C4
Bergum Neth. see Burgum
Bergville S. Africa 125 I5
Berh Mongolia 95 G2
Berhala, Selat sea chan. Indon. 84 C3
Berhampur India see Baharampur
Berikat, Tanjung pt Indon. 84 D3
Beringa, Ostrov i. Russia 77 R4
Beringen Belgium 62 F3
Bering Glacier AK U.S.A. 148 H4
Bering Glacier AK U.S.A. 149 L3
Bering Lake AK U.S.A. 149 K3
Bering Land Bridge National Preserve nature res. AK U.S.A. 148 F2
Beringovskiy Russia 77 S3
Bering Sea N. Pacific Ocean 77 S4
Bering Strait Russia/U.S.A. 148 E2
Beris, Ra's pt Iran 111 F5
Berislav Ukr. see Beryslav
Berkåk Norway 54 G5
Berkane Morocco 67 E6
Berkel r. Neth. 62 G2
Berkeley CA U.S.A. 158 B3
Berkeley Springs WV U.S.A. 165 F4
Berkhout Neth. 62 F2
Berkner Sub-glacial Island Antarctica 188 A1
Berkovitsa Bulg. 69 J3
Berkshire Downs hills U.K. 59 F7
Berkshire Hills MA U.S.A. 165 I2
Berland r. Canada 150 G4
Berlare Belgium 62 E3
Berlevåg Norway 54 P1

►**Berlin** Germany 63 N2
Capital of Germany.

Berlin land Germany 63 N2
Berlin MD U.S.A. 165 H4
Berlin NH U.S.A. 165 J1
Berlin PA U.S.A. 165 F4
Berlin Lake OH U.S.A. 164 E3
Bermagui Australia 138 E6
Bermejíllo Mex. 166 E3
Bermejo r. Arg./Bol. 178 E3
Bermejo Bol. 176 F8
Bermen, Lac l. Canada 153 H3

►**Bermuda** terr. N. Atlantic Ocean 169 L2
United Kingdom Overseas Territory.

Bermuda Rise sea feature N. Atlantic Ocean 184 D4

►**Bern** Switz. 66 H3
Capital of Switzerland.

Bernalillo NM U.S.A. 157 G6
Bernardino de Campos Brazil 179 A3
Bernardo O'Higgins research station Antarctica 188 A2
Bernardo O'Higgins, Parque Nacional nat. park Chile 178 B7
Bernasconi Arg. 178 D5
Bernau bei Berlin Germany 63 N2
Bernburg (Saale) Germany 63 L3
Berne Germany 63 I1
Berne Switz. see Bern
Berne IN U.S.A. 164 C3
Berner Alpen mts Switz. 66 H3
Berneray i. Scotland U.K. 60 B3
Berneray i. Scotland U.K. 60 B4
Bernier Island Australia 135 A6
Bernina, Piz mt. Italy/Switz. 68 C1
Bernina Pass Switz. 66 J3
Bernkastel-Kues Germany 62 H5
Beroea Greece see Veroia
Beroea Syria see Aleppo
Beroroha Madag. 123 E6
Beroun Czech Rep. 57 O6
Berounka r. Czech Rep. 57 O6
Berovina Madag. see Beravina
Berri Australia 137 C7
Berriane Alg. 64 E5
Berridale Australia 138 D6
Berriedale U.K. 60 F2
Berrigan Australia 138 B5
Berrima Australia 138 E5
Berrouaghia Alg. 67 H5
Berry Australia 138 E5
Berry KY U.S.A. 164 C4
Berryessa, Lake CA U.S.A. 158 B2
Berry Head hd U.K. 59 D8
Berry Islands Bahamas 163 E7
Berryville VA U.S.A. 165 G4
Berseba Namibia 124 C4
Bersenbrück Germany 63 H2
Bertam Malaysia 84 C1
Berté, Lac l. Canada 153 H4
Berthoud Pass CO U.S.A. 156 G5
Bertolínia Brazil 177 J5
Bertoua Cameroon 120 E4
Bertraghboy Bay Ireland 61 C4
Beru atoll Kiribati 133 H2
Beruri Brazil 176 F4
Beruwala Sri Lanka 106 C5
Berwick Australia 138 B7
Berwick PA U.S.A. 165 G3
Berwick-upon-Tweed U.K. 58 E3
Berwyn hills U.K. 59 D6
Beryslav Ukr. 69 O1
Berytus Lebanon see Beirut
Besah Kalimantan Indon. 85 G2
Besalampy Madag. 123 E5
Besançon France 66 H3
Besar i. Indon. 83 B5
Besar, Gunung mt. Indon. 85 F3
Besar, Gunung mt. Malaysia 87 C7
Besbay Kazakh. 102 A2
Besboro Island AK U.S.A. 148 G2
Beserah Malaysia 84 C2
Beshkent Uzbek. 111 G2
Besheh Iran 110 D4
Besikama Timor Indon. 83 C5
Besitang Sumatra Indon. 84 B1
Beskra Alg. see Biskra
Beslan Russia 113 G2
Besnard Lake Canada 151 J4
Besni Turkey 112 E3
Besoba Kazakh. 98 A2
Besor, Naḥal watercourse Israel 107 B4
Beşparmak Dağları mts Cyprus see Pentadaktylos Range
Bessbrook U.K. 61 F3
Bessemer AL U.S.A. 163 C5
Besshoky, Gora hill Kazakh. 113 I1
Besskorbnaya Russia 53 I7
Bessonovka Russia 53 J5
Bestamak Kazakh. 98 B2
Betalongchhip mt. India 105 H5
Betanzos Spain 67 B2
Betet i. Indon. 84 D3
Bet Guvrin Israel 107 B4
Bethal S. Africa 125 I4
Bethanie Namibia 124 C4
Bethany MO U.S.A. 160 E3
Bethari Nepal 99 C8
Bethel AK U.S.A. 148 G3
Bethel ME U.S.A. 153 H5
Bethel Park PA U.S.A. 164 E3
Bethesda U.K. 58 C5
Bethesda MD U.S.A. 165 G4
Bethesda OH U.S.A. 164 E3
Bethlehem S. Africa 125 I5
Bethlehem PA U.S.A. 165 H3
Bethlehem West Bank 107 B4
Bethulie S. Africa 125 G6
Béthune France 62 C4
Beti Pak. 111 H4
Betim Brazil 179 B2
Betiri, Gunung mt. Indon. 85 F5
Bet Lehem West Bank see Bethlehem
Betma India 104 C5
Betong Sarawak Malaysia 85 E2
Betong Thai. 87 C6
Betoota (abandoned) Australia 136 C5
Betpakdala plain Kazakh. 102 D2
Betroka Madag. 123 E6
Bet She'an Israel 107 B3
Betsiamites Canada 153 H4
Betsiamites r. Canada 153 H4
Betsukai Japan 90 G4
Betsu-zan mt. Japan 92 C2
Bettiah India 105 F4
Bettles AK U.S.A. 149 J2
Bettyhill U.K. 60 E2
Bettystown Ireland 61 F4
Betul India 104 D5
Betun Timor Indon. 83 C5
Betung Kerihun, Taman Nasional Indon. 85 F2
Betwa r. India 104 D4
Betws-y-coed U.K. 59 D5
Betzdorf Germany 63 H4
Beulah Australia 137 C7
Beulah MI U.S.A. 164 B1
Beulah ND U.S.A. 160 C2
Beult r. U.K. 59 H7
Beuthen Poland see Bytom
Bever r. Germany 63 H2
Beverley U.K. 58 G5
Beverley, Lake AK U.S.A. 148 H4
Beverly MA U.S.A. 165 J2
Beverly OH U.S.A. 164 E4
Beverly Hills CA U.S.A. 158 D4
Beverly Lake Canada 151 K1
Beverstedt Germany 63 I1
Beverungen Germany 63 J3
Beverwijk Neth. 62 E2
Bewani P.N.G. 81 K7
Bexbach Germany 63 H5
Bexhill U.K. 59 H8
Bexley, Cape Canada 146 G3
Beyce Turkey see Orhaneli
Bey Dağları mts Turkey 69 N6
Beykoz Turkey 69 M4
Beyla Guinea 120 C4
Beylagan Azer. see Beyläqan
Beyläqan Azer. 113 G3
Beyneu Kazakh. 100 E2
Beypazarı Turkey 69 N4
Beypınarı Turkey 112 E3
Beypore India 106 B4
Beyrouth Lebanon see Beirut
Beyşehir Turkey 112 C3
Beyşehir Gölü l. Turkey 112 C3
Beytonovo Russia 90 B1
Beytüşşebap Turkey 113 F3
Bezameh Iran 110 E3
Bezbozhnik Russia 52 K4
Bezhanitsy Russia 52 F4
Bezhetsk Russia 52 H4
Béziers France 66 F5
Bezmein Turkm. see Abadan
Bezwada India see Vijayawada
Bhabha India see Bhabua
Bhabhar India 104 B4
Bhabhua India see Bhabua
Bhabua India 105 E4
Bhachau India 104 B5
Bhachbhar India 104 B4
Bhadarwah India 99 A6
Bhadgaon Nepal see Bhaktapur
Bhadohi India 105 E4
Bhadra India 104 C3
Bhadrachalam Road Station India see Kottagudem
Bhadrak India 105 F5
Bhadrakh India see Bhadrak
Bhadravati India 106 B3
Bhag Pak. 111 G4
Bhaga r. India 99 B6
Bhagalpur India 105 F4
Bhainsa India 106 C2
Bhainsdehi India 104 D5
Bhairab Bazar Bangl. 105 G4
Bhairi Hol mt. Pak. 111 G5
Bhaktapur Nepal 105 F4
Bhalki India 106 C2
Bhamo Myanmar 86 B1
Bhamragarh India 106 D2
Bhandal India 104 C2
Bhandara India 104 D5
Bhanjanagar India 106 E2
Bhanrer Range hills India 104 D5
Bhaptiahi India 105 F4
Bharat country Asia see India
Bharati research station Antarctica 188 E2
Bharatpur India 104 D4
Bhareli r. India 105 H4
Bharuch India 104 C5
Bhatapara India 105 E5
Bhatarsaigh i. U.K. see Vatersay
Bhatghar Lake India 106 B2
Bhatinda India see Bathinda
Bhatnair India see Hanumangarh
Bhatpara India 105 G5
Bhaunagar India see Bhavnagar
Bhavani r. India 106 C4
Bhavani Sagar l. India 106 C4
Bhavnagar India 104 C5
Bhawana Pak. 111 I4
Bhawanipatna India 106 D2
Bhearnaraigh, Eilean i. U.K. see Berneray
Bheemavaram India see Bhimavaram
Bhekuzulu S. Africa 125 J4
Bhera Pak. 111 I3
Bheri r. Nepal 99 C7
Bhigvan India 106 B2
Bhikhna Thori Nepal 105 F4
Bhilai India 104 E5
Bhildi India 104 C4
Bhilwara India 104 C4
Bhima r. India 106 C2
Bhimar India 104 B4
Bhimavaram India 106 D2
Bhimlath India 104 E5
Bhimphedi Nepal 99 D8
Bhind India 104 D4
Bhinga India 105 E4
Bhisho S. Africa 125 H7
Bhiwandi India 106 B2
Bhiwani India 104 D3
Bhogaipur India 104 D4
Bhojpur Nepal 105 F4
Bhola Bangl. 105 G5
Bhongweni S. Africa 125 I6
Bhopal India 104 D5
Bhopalpatnam India 106 D2
Bhrigukaccha India see Bharuch
Bhuban India 106 E1
Bhubaneshwar India 106 E1
Bhubaneswar India see Bhubaneshwar
Bhuj India 104 B5
Bhusawal India 104 C5
Bhutan country Asia 105 G4
Bhuttewala India 104 B4
Bia r. Ghana 120 C4
Biābān mts Iran 110 E5
Biafo Glacier Pak. 104 C2
Biak Celebes Indon. 83 B3
Biak Papua Indon. 81 J7
Biak i. Indon. 81 J7
Biała Podlaska Poland 53 D5
Białogard Poland 57 O4
Białystok Poland 53 D5
Bianco, Monte mt. France/Italy see Blanc, Mont
Biandan Gang r. mouth China 95 J5
Bianzhao China 95 J2
Bianzhuang China see Cangshan
Biao Mindanao Phil. 82 D5
Biaora India 104 D5
Biaro i. Indon. 83 C2
Biarritz France 66 D5
Bi'ār Tabrāk well Saudi Arabia 110 B5
Bibai Japan 90 F4
Bibbenluke Australia 138 D6
Bibbiena Italy 68 D3
Bibby Island Canada 151 M2
Biberach an der Riß Germany 57 L6
Bibile Sri Lanka 106 D5
Biblis Germany 63 I5
Biblos Lebanon see Jbail
Bicas Brazil 179 C3
Biçer Turkey 69 N5
Bicester U.K. 59 F7
Bichabhera India 104 C4
Bicheng China see Bishan
Bichevaya Russia 90 D3
Bichi r. Russia 90 E1
Bichraltar Nepal 99 D8
Bichura Russia 95 F1
Bickerton Island Australia 136 B2
Bickleigh U.K. 59 D8
Bicknell IN U.S.A. 164 B4
Bicoli Halmahera Indon. 83 D2
Bicuari, Parque Nacional do nat. park Angola 123 B5
Bid India 106 B2
Bida Nigeria 120 D4
Bidadari, Tanjung pt Malaysia 85 G1
Bidar India 106 C2
Biddeford ME U.S.A. 165 J2
Biddinghuizen Neth. 62 F2
Bidean nam Bian mt. U.K. 60 D4
Bideford U.K. 59 C7
Bideford Bay U.K. see Barnstaple Bay
Bīdokht Iran 110 E3
Bidzhan Russia 90 C3
Bié Angola see Kuito
Bié, Planalto do Angola 123 B5
Biebrzański Park Narodowy nat. park Poland 55 M10
Biedenkopf Germany 63 I4
Bielawa Poland 57 P5
Biel/Bienne Switz. 66 H3
Bielefeld Germany 63 I2
Bielitz Poland see Bielsko-Biała
Biella Italy 68 C2
Bielsko-Biała Poland 57 Q6
Bielstein hill Germany 63 J3
Bienenbüttel Germany 63 K1
Biên Hoa Vietnam 87 D5
Bienne Switz. see Biel/Bienne
Bienville, Lac l. Canada 153 G3
Bierbank Australia 138 B1
Biesiesvlei S. Africa 125 G4
Bietigheim-Bissingen Germany 63 J6
Bièvre Belgium 62 F5
Bifoun Gabon 122 B4
Big r. Canada 153 K3
Big r. AK U.S.A. 148 I3
Biga Turkey 69 L4
Bigadiç Turkey 69 M5
Biga Yarımadası pen. Turkey 69 L5
Big Baldy Mountain MT U.S.A. 156 F3
Big Bar Creek Canada 150 F5
Big Bear Lake CA U.S.A. 158 E4
Big Belt Mountains MT U.S.A. 156 F3
Big Bend Swaziland 125 J4
Big Bend National Park TX U.S.A. 161 C6
Big Black r. MS U.S.A. 167 H1
Bigbury-on-Sea U.K. 59 D8
Big Canyon watercourse TX U.S.A. 161 C6
Big Delta AK U.S.A. 149 K2
Biger Mongolia 94 D2
Biger Nuur salt l. Mongolia 94 D2
Big Falls MN U.S.A. 160 E1
Big Fork r. MN U.S.A. 160 E1
Biggar Canada 151 J4
Biggar U.K. 60 F5
Biggar, Lac l. Canada 152 G4
Bigge Island Australia 134 D3
Biggenden Australia 137 F5
Bigger, Mount Canada 149 M4
Biggesee l. Germany 63 H3
Biggleswade U.K. 59 G6
Biggs CA U.S.A. 158 C2
Biggs Junction OR U.S.A. 156 C3
Big Hole r. MT U.S.A. 156 E3
Bighorn r. Montana/Wyoming U.S.A. 156 G3
Bighorn Mountains WY U.S.A. 156 G3
Big Island Nunavut Canada 147 K3
Big Island N.W.T. Canada 150 G2
Big Island Ont. Canada 151 M5
Big Kalzas Lake Canada 149 N3
Big Koniuji Island AK U.S.A. 148 H5
Big Lake l. Canada 151 H1
Big Lake AK U.S.A. 149 J3
Big Lake TX U.S.A. 161 C6
Big Pine CA U.S.A. 158 D3
Big Pine Peak CA U.S.A. 158 D4
Big Raccoon r. IN U.S.A. 164 B4
Big Rapids MI U.S.A. 164 C2
Big River Canada 151 J4
Big Sable Point MI U.S.A. 164 B1
Big Salmon r. Canada 149 N3
Big Salmon (abandoned) Canada 149 N3
Big Sand Lake Canada 151 L3
Big Sandy r. WY U.S.A. 156 F4
Big Sandy Lake Canada 151 J4
Big Smokey Valley NV U.S.A. 158 E2
Big South Fork National River and Recreation Area park Kentucky/Tennessee U.S.A. 164 C5
Big Spring TX U.S.A. 161 C5
Big Stone Canada 151 I5
Big Stone Gap VA U.S.A. 164 D5
Bigstone Lake Canada 151 M4
Big Timber MT U.S.A. 156 F3
Big Trout Lake Canada 151 N4
Big Trout Lake l. Canada 151 N4
Big Valley Canada 151 H4
Big Water UT U.S.A. 159 H3
Bihać Bos. & Herz. 68 F2
Bihar state India 105 F4
Bihariganj India 105 F4
Bihar Sharif India 105 F4
Bihor, Vârful mt. Romania 69 J1
Bihoro Japan 90 G4
Bijagós, Arquipélago dos is Guinea-Bissau 120 B3
Bijapur India 104 D4
Bijapur India see Vijayapura
Bijār Iran 110 B3
Bijbehara India 104 C2
Bijeljina Bos. & Herz. 69 H2
Bijelo Polje Montenegro 69 H3
Bijiang China see Zhiziluo
Bijie China 96 E3
Bijji India 106 D2
Bijnor India 104 D3
Bijnore India see Bijnor
Bijnot Pak. 111 H4
Bijrān well Saudi Arabia 110 C5
Bijrān, Khashm hill Saudi Arabia 110 C5
Bikampur India 104 C4
Bikaner India 104 C3
Bīkhūyeh Iran 110 D5
Bikin Russia 90 D3
Bikin r. Russia 90 D3
Bikini atoll Marshall Is 186 H5
Bikori Sudan 108 D7
Bikoro Dem. Rep. Congo 122 B4
Bikou China 96 E1
Bikramganj India 105 F4
Bilaa Point Mindanao Phil. 82 D4
Bilād Banī Bū 'Alī Oman 109 I5
Bilaigarh India 106 D1
Bilangbilangan i. Indon. 85 G2
Bilara India 104 C4
Bilaspur Chhattisgarh India 105 E5
Bilaspur Hima. Prad. India 104 D3
Biläsuvar Azer. 113 H3
Bila Tserkva Ukr. 53 F6
Bilauktaung Range mts Myanmar/Thai. 87 B4
Bilbao Spain 67 E2
Bilbays Egypt 112 C5
Bilbeis Egypt see Bilbays
Bilbo Spain see Bilbao
Bil'chir Russia 95 G1
Bilecik Turkey 69 M4
Biłgoraj Poland 53 D6
Bilharamulo Tanz. 122 D4
Bilhaur India 104 E4
Bilhorod-Dnistrovs'kyy Ukr. 69 N1
Bili Dem. Rep. Congo 122 C3
Bilibino Russia 77 R3
Bilin Myanmar 86 B3
Biliran i. Phil. 82 D4
Bilit Sabah Malaysia 85 G1
Bill WY U.S.A. 156 G4

Billabalong Australia 135 A6
Billabong Creek r. Australia see Moulamein Creek
Billericay U.K. 59 H7
Billiluna Australia 134 D4
Billingham U.K. 58 F4
Billings MT U.S.A. 156 F3
Billiton i. Indon. see Belitung
Bill Moores AK U.S.A. 148 G3
Bill of Portland hd U.K. 59 E8
Bill Williams r. AZ U.S.A. 159 F4
Bill Williams Mountain AZ U.S.A. 159 G4
Bilma Niger 120 E3
Bilma, Grand Erg de des. Niger 120 E3
Biloela Australia 136 E5
Bilohirs'k Crimea 112 D1
Bilohir''ya Ukr. 53 E6
Biloku Guyana 177 G3
Biloli India 106 C2
Bilovods'k Ukr. 53 H6
Biloxi MS U.S.A. 161 F6
Bilpa Morea Claypan salt flat Australia 136 B5
Bilston U.K. 60 F5
Biltine Chad 121 F3
Bilto Norway 54 L2
Bilugyun Island Myanmar 86 B3
Bilungala Celebes Indon. 83 B2
Bilwascarma Nicaragua 166 [inset] J6
Bilyayivka Ukr. 69 N1
Bilzen Belgium 62 F4
Bima Sumbawa Indon. 85 G5
Bima, Teluk b. Sumbawa Indon. 85 G5
Bimberi, Mount Australia 138 D5
Bimbo Cent. Afr. Rep. 121 E4
Bimini Islands Bahamas 163 E7
Bimlipatam India 106 D2
Bina-Etawa India 104 D4
Binaija, Gunung mt. Seram Indon. 83 D3
Binalbagan Negros Phil. 82 C4
Bīnālūd, Reshteh Kūh-e mts Iran 110 E2
Binatang Sarawak Malaysia 85 E2
Binbei China 95 I4
Binboğa Daği mt. Turkey 112 E3
Bincheng China see Binzhou
Binchuan China 96 D3
Bindebango Australia 138 C1
Binder Mongolia 95 G1
Bindle Australia 138 D1
Bindu Dem. Rep. Congo 123 B4
Bindura Zimbabwe 123 D5
Binéfar Spain 67 G3
Binga Zimbabwe 123 C5
Binga, Monte mt. Moz. 123 D5
Bingara Australia 138 E2
Bingaram i. India 106 B4
Bing Bong Australia 136 B2
Bingcaowan China 94 E4
Bingen am Rhein Germany 63 H5
Bingham ME U.S.A. 165 K1
Binghamton NY U.S.A. 165 H2
Bingmei China see Congjiang
Bingöl Turkey 113 F3
Bingol Dağı mt. Turkey 113 F3
Bingxi China see Yushan
Bingzhongluo China 96 C2
Binh Gia Vietnam 86 D2
Binicuil Negros Phil. 82 C4
Binika India 105 E5
Binjai Sumatra Indon. 84 B2
Bin Mürkhan well U.A.E. 110 D5
Binnaway Australia 138 D3
Binongko i. Indon. 83 C4
Binpur India 105 F5
Bintan i. Sumatra Indon. 84 D2
Bintang, Bukit mts Malaysia 84 C1
Bint Jbeil Lebanon see Bent Jbaïl
Bintuan Phil. 82 C3
Bintuhan Sumatra Indon. 84 C4
Bintulu Sarawak Malaysia 85 F2
Binubusan Luzon Phil. 82 C3
Binxian Heilong. China 90 B3
Binxian Shaanxi China 95 G5
Binxian Shandong China see Binbei
Binya Australia 138 C5
Binyang China 97 F4
Bin-Yauri Nigeria 120 D3
Binzhou Guangxi China see Binyang
Binzhou Heilong. China see Binxian
Binzhou Shandong China 95 I4
Bioco i. Equat. Guinea see Bioko
Biograd na Moru Croatia 68 F3
Bioko i. Equat. Guinea 120 D4
Biokovo mts Croatia 68 G3
Bi Qu r. China 99 F6
Biquinhas Brazil 179 B2
Bir India see Bid
Bira Russia 90 D2
Bi'r Abū Jady oasis Syria 107 D1
Birāk Libya 121 E2
Birakan Russia 90 C2
Bi'r al 'Abd Egypt 107 A4
Bi'r al Ḥalbā well Syria 107 D2
Bi'r al Jifjāfah well Egypt 107 A4
Bi'r al Khamsah well Egypt 112 B5
Bi'r al Māliḥah well Egypt 107 A5
Bi'r al Mulūsi Iraq 113 F4
Bi'r al Munbaṭiḥ well Syria 107 D2
Bi'r al Qaṭrānī well Egypt 112 B5
Bi'r al Ubbayiḍ well Egypt 112 B6
Bi'r an Nuṣf well Egypt see Bi'r an Nuṣṣ
Bi'r an Nuṣṣ well Egypt 112 B5
Bir Anzarane W. Sahara 120 B2
Birao Cent. Afr. Rep. 122 C2
Bi'r ar Rābiyah well Egypt 112 B5
Birata Turkm. 111 F1
Biratar Bulak spring China 98 E4
Biratnagar Nepal 105 F4
Bi'r aṭ Ṭarfāwī well Libya 112 B5
Bi'r Başīrī well Syria 107 C2
Bi'r Bayḍā' well Egypt 107 B4
Bi'r Baylī well Egypt 112 B5
Bîr Beîḍa well Egypt see Bi'r Bayḍā'
Bi'r Buṭaymān Syria 113 E3
Birch r. Canada 151 H3
Birch Creek AK U.S.A. 149 K2
Birch Creek r. AK U.S.A. 149 K2
Birches AK U.S.A. 148 I2
Birch Hills Canada 151 J4
Birch Island Canada 150 G5
Birch Lake N.W.T. Canada 150 G2
Birch Lake Ont. Canada 151 M5
Birch Lake Sask. Canada 151 I4
Birch Mountains Canada 150 H3
Birch River WV U.S.A. 164 E4
Birch Run MI U.S.A. 164 D2
Bircot Eth. 122 E3
Birdaard Neth. see Burdaard
Bîr Diqnâsh well Egypt see Bi'r Diqnāsh
Bi'r Diqnāsh well Egypt 112 B5
Bird Island N. Mariana Is see Farallon de Medinilla
Birdseye UT U.S.A. 159 H2
Birdsville Australia 137 B5
Birecik Turkey 112 E3
Bîr el 'Abd Egypt see Bi'r al 'Abd
Bir el Arbi well Alg. 67 I6
Bîr el Iṣṭabl well Egypt see Bi'r Iṣṭabl
Bîr el Khamsa well Egypt see Bi'r al Khamsah
Bîr el Nuṣṣ well Egypt see Bi'r an Nuṣṣ
Bîr el Obeiyiḍ well Egypt see Bi'r al Ubbayiḍ
Bîr el Qatrâni well Egypt see Bi'r al Qaṭrānī
Bîr el Rābia well Egypt see Bi'r ar Rābiyah
Birendranagar Nepal see Surkhet
Bir en Natrûn well Sudan 108 C6
Bireun Sumatra Indon. 84 B1
Bi'r Fāḍil well Saudi Arabia 110 C6
Bi'r Fajr well Saudi Arabia 112 E5
Bi'r Fu'ād well Egypt 112 B5
Bīrg, Kūh-e mts Iran 111 F5
Birganj Nepal 99 D8
Bîr Gifgâfa well Egypt see Bi'r al Jifjāfah
Bi'r Ḥajal well Syria 107 D2
Bi'r Ḥasanah well Egypt 107 A4
Bi'r Ḥayzān well Saudi Arabia 112 E6
Biri i. Phil. 82 D3
Bi'r Ibn Hirmās Saudi Arabia see Al Bi'r
Bir Ibn Juhayyim Saudi Arabia 110 C6
Birigui Brazil 179 A3
Bīrīn Syria 107 C2
Bi'r Iṣṭabl well Egypt 112 B5
Bīrjand Iran 110 E3
Bi'r Jubnī well Libya 112 B5
Birkát Hamad well Iraq 113 G5
Birkenfeld Germany 63 H5
Birkenhead U.K. 58 D5
Birkirkara Malta 68 F7
Birksgate Range hills Australia 135 E6
Bîrlad Romania see Bârlad
Bi'r Lahfān well Egypt 107 A4
Bir Lahlou W. Sahara 120 C2
Birlik Zhambylskaya Oblast' Kazakh. 98 A3
Birlik Zhambylskaya Oblast' Kazakh. 102 D3
Birmal reg. Afgh. 111 H3
Birmingham U.K. 59 F6
Birmingham AL U.S.A. 163 C5
Bîr Mogreïn Mauritania 120 B2
Bi'r Muḥaymid al Wazwaz well Syria 107 D2
Bi'r Nāḥid oasis Egypt 112 C5
Birnin-Gwari Nigeria 120 D3
Birnin-Kebbi Nigeria 120 D3
Birnin Konni Niger 120 D3
Birobidzhan Russia 90 D2
Birong Palawan Phil. 82 B4
Bi'r Qaṣīr as Sirr well Egypt 112 B5
Birr Ireland 61 E4
Bi'r Rawḍ Sālim well Egypt 107 A4
Birrie r. Australia 138 C2
Birrindudu Australia 134 E4
Bîr Rôḍ Sâlim well Egypt see Bi'r Rawḍ Sālim
Birsay U.K. 60 F1
Bi'r Shalatayn Egypt 108 E5
Bîr Shalatein Egypt see Bi'r Shalatayn
Birsk Russia 51 R4
Birstall U.K. 59 F6
Birstein Germany 63 J4
Bir Ṭalḥah well Saudi Arabia 110 B6
Birthday Mountain hill Australia 136 C2
Birtle Canada 151 K5
Biru China 99 F7
Birur India 106 B3
Bi'r Usaylīlah well Saudi Arabia 110 B6
Biržai Lith. 55 N8
Bisa India 86 A1
Bisa i. Moluccas Indon. 83 C3
Bisai Japan 92 C3
Bisalpur India 104 D3
Bisau India 104 C3
Bisbee AZ U.S.A. 157 F7
Biscay, Bay of sea France/Spain 66 B4
Biscay Abyssal Plain sea feature N. Atlantic Ocean 184 H3
Biscayne National Park FL U.S.A. 163 D7
Biscoe Islands Antarctica 188 L2
Biscotasi Lake Canada 152 E5
Biscotasing Canada 152 E5
Bisezhai China 96 D4
Bishan China 96 E2
Bishbek Kyrg. see Bishkek
Bishenpur India see Bishnupur
▶Bishkek Kyrg. 102 D3
Capital of Kyrgyzstan.
Bishnupur Manipur India 105 H4
Bishnupur W. Bengal India 105 F5
Bishop CA U.S.A. 158 D3
Bishop Auckland U.K. 58 F4
Bishop Lake Canada 150 G1
Bishop's Stortford U.K. 59 H7
Bishopville SC U.S.A. 163 D5
Bishrī, Jabal hills Syria 107 D2
Bishui Heilong. China 90 A1
Bishui Henan China see Biyang
Biskra Alg. 64 F5
Bislig Mindanao Phil. 82 D4
Bislig Bay Mindanao Phil. 82 D4
▶Bismarck ND U.S.A. 160 C2
Capital of North Dakota.
Bismarck Archipelago is P.N.G. 81 L7
Bismarck Range mts P.N.G. 81 K7
Bismarck Sea P.N.G. 81 L7
Bismark (Altmark) Germany 63 L2
Bismil Turkey 113 F3
Bismo Norway 54 F6
Bison SD U.S.A. 160 C2
Bispgården Sweden 54 J5
Bispingen Germany 63 K1
Bissa, Djebel mt. Alg. 67 G5
Bissagos Islands Guinea-Bissau see Bijagós, Arquipélago dos
Bissamcuttak India 106 D2
▶Bissau Guinea-Bissau 120 B3
Capital of Guinea-Bissau.
Bissaula Nigeria 120 E4
Bissett Canada 151 M5
Bistcho Lake Canada 150 G3
Bistrița Romania 69 K1
Bistrița r. Romania 69 L1
Bisucay i. Phil. 82 C4
Bitburg Germany 62 G5
Bitche France 63 H5
Bithur India 104 E4
Bithynia reg. Turkey 69 M4
Bitkine Chad 121 E3
Bitlis Turkey 113 F3
Bitola Macedonia 69 I4
Bitolj Macedonia see Bitola
Bitonto Italy 68 G4
Bitrān, Jabal hill Saudi Arabia 110 B6
Bitra Par reef India 106 B4
Bitter Creek r. UT U.S.A. 159 I2
Bitterfeld Germany 63 M3
Bitterfontein S. Africa 124 D6
Bitter Lakes Egypt 112 D5
Bitterroot r. MT U.S.A. 156 E3
Bitterroot Range mts ID U.S.A. 156 E3
Bitterwater CA U.S.A. 158 C3
Bittkau Germany 63 L2
Bitung Celebes Indon. 83 C2
Biu Nigeria 120 E3
Biwa-ko l. Japan 92 B3
Biwa-ko Kokutei-kōen park Japan 92 C3
Biwmaris U.K. see Beaumaris
Biyang China 97 G1
Bīye K'obē Polīs T'abīya Eth. 122 E2
Biysk Russia 88 F2
Bizana S. Africa 125 I6
Bizerta Tunisia see Bizerte
Bizerte Tunisia 68 C6
▶Bjargtangar hd Iceland 54 [inset]
Most westerly point of Europe.
Bjästa Sweden 54 K5
Bjelovar Croatia 68 G2
Bjerkvik Norway 54 J2
Bjerringbro Denmark 55 F8
Bjørgan Norway 54 G5
Björkliden Sweden 54 K2
Björklinge Sweden 55 J6
Bjorli Norway 54 F5
Björna Sweden 54 K5
Björneborg Fin. see Pori
▶Bjørnøya i. Arctic Ocean 76 C2
Part of Norway.
Bjurholm Sweden 54 K5
Bla Mali 120 C3
Black r. Man. Canada 151 L5
Black r. Ont. Canada 152 E4
Black r. Canada/U.S.A. 149 K2
Black AK U.S.A. 148 F3
Black r. AR U.S.A. 161 F5
Black r. AZ U.S.A. 159 H5
Black r. Vietnam 86 D2
Blackadder Water r. U.K. 60 G5
Blackall Australia 136 D5
Blackbear r. Canada 151 N4
Black Birch Lake Canada 151 J3
Black Bourton U.K. 59 F7
Blackbull Australia 136 C3
Blackburn U.K. 58 E5
Blackburn, Mount AK U.S.A. 149 L3
Blackbutt Australia 138 F1
Black Butte mt. CA U.S.A. 158 B2
Black Butte Lake CA U.S.A. 158 B2
Black Canyon gorge AZ U.S.A. 159 F4
Black Canyon of the Gunnison National Park CO U.S.A. 159 J2
Black Combe hill U.K. 58 D4
Black Creek watercourse AZ U.S.A. 159 I4
Black Donald Lake Canada 165 G1
Blackdown Tableland National Park Australia 136 E4
Blackduck MN U.S.A. 160 E2
Blackfalds Canada 150 H4
Blackfoot ID U.S.A. 156 E4
Black Foot r. MT U.S.A. 156 E3
Black Forest mts Germany 57 L7
Black Hill hill U.K. 58 F5
Black Hills SD U.S.A. 154 G3
Black Hills SD U.S.A. 156 G3
Black Island Canada 151 L5
Black Lake Canada 151 J3
Black Lake l. Canada 151 J3
Black Lake l. MI U.S.A. 164 C1
Black Mesa mt. AZ U.S.A. 159 I5
Black Mesa ridge AZ U.S.A. 159 H3
Black Mountain Pak. 111 I3
Black Mountain hill U.K. 59 D7
Black Mountain AK U.S.A. 148 G1
Black Mountain CA U.S.A. 158 E4
Black Mountain KY U.S.A. 164 D5
Black Mountain NM U.S.A. 159 I5
Black Mountains hills U.K. 59 D7
Black Mountains AZ U.S.A. 159 F4
Black Nossob watercourse Namibia 124 D2
Black Pagoda India see Konarka
Blackpool U.K. 58 D5
Black Range mts NM U.S.A. 159 I5
Black Rapids AK U.S.A. 149 K3
Black River MI U.S.A. 164 D1
Black River NY U.S.A. 165 H1
Black River Falls WI U.S.A. 160 F2
Black Rock hill Jordan see 'Unāb, Jabal al
Black Rock Desert NV U.S.A. 156 D4
Blacksburg VA U.S.A. 164 E5
Black Sea Asia/Europe 53 H8
Blacks Fork r. WY U.S.A. 156 F4
Blackshear GA U.S.A. 163 D6
Blacksod Bay Ireland 61 B3
Black Springs NV U.S.A. 158 D2
Blackstairs Mountains hills Ireland 61 F5
Blackstone r. Canada 149 M2
Blackstone VA U.S.A. 165 F5
Black Sugarloaf mt. Australia 138 E3
Black Tickle Canada 153 L3
Blackville Australia 138 E3
Blackwater Australia 136 E4
Blackwater Ireland 61 F5
Blackwater r. Ireland 61 E5
Blackwater r. Ireland/U.K. 61 F3
Blackwater watercourse New Mexico/Texas U.S.A. 161 C5
Blackwater Lake Canada 149 Q3
Blackwater Reservoir U.K. 60 E4
Blackwood r. Australia 135 A8
Blackwood National Park Australia 136 D4
Bladensburg National Park Australia 136 C4
Blaenavon U.K. 59 D7
Blagodarnyy Russia 113 F1
Blagoevgrad Bulg. 69 J3
Blagoveshchensk Amurskaya Oblast' Russia 90 B2
Blagoveshchensk Respublika Bashkortostan Russia 51 R4
Blaikiston, Mount Canada 150 H5
Blaine Lake Canada 151 J4
Blair NE U.S.A. 160 D3
Blair Athol Australia 136 D4
Blair Atholl U.K. 60 F4
Blairgowrie U.K. 60 F4
Blairsden CA U.S.A. 158 C2
Blairsville GA U.S.A. 163 D5
Blakang Mati, Pulau i. Sing. see Sentosa
Blakely GA U.S.A. 163 C6
Blakeney U.K. 59 I6
Blambangan, Semenanjung pen. Indon. 85 F5
▶Blanc, Mont mt. France/Italy 66 H4
5th highest mountain in Europe.
Blanca, Bahía b. Arg. 178 D5
Blanca, Sierra mt. NM U.S.A. 157 G6
Blanca Peak CO U.S.A. 157 G5
Blanche, Lake salt flat S.A. Australia 137 B6
Blanche, Lake salt flat W.A. Australia 134 C5
Blanchester OH U.S.A. 164 D4
Blanc Nez, Cap c. France 62 B4
Blanco r. Bol. 176 F6
Blanco NM U.S.A. 159 J3
Blanco, Cabo c. Costa Rica 166 [inset] I7
Blanco, Cape OR U.S.A. 156 B4
Blanc-Sablon Canada 153 K4
Bland r. Australia 138 C4
Bland VA U.S.A. 164 E5
Blanda r. Iceland 54 [inset 1]
Blandford Forum U.K. 59 E8
Blanding UT U.S.A. 159 I3
Blanes Spain 67 H3
Blangah, Telok Sing. 87 [inset]
Blangkejeren Sumatra Indon. 84 B2
Blangpidie Sumatra Indon. 84 B2
Blankenberge Belgium 62 D3
Blankenheim Germany 62 G4
Blanquilla, Isla i. Venez. 176 F1
Blansko Czech Rep. 57 P6
Blantyre Malawi 123 D5
Blarney Ireland 61 D6
Blau Celebes Indon. 83 B2
Blaufelden Germany 63 J5
Blåviksjön Sweden 54 K4
Blaye France 66 D4
Blayney Australia 138 D4
Blaze, Point Australia 134 E3
Bleckede Germany 63 K1
Blega Java Indon. 85 F4
Bleilochtalsperre resr Germany 63 L4
Blenheim Canada 164 E2
Blenheim N.Z. 139 D5
Blenheim Palace tourist site U.K. 59 F7
Blerick Neth. 62 G3
Blessington Lakes Ireland 61 F4
Bletchley U.K. 59 G6
Blida Alg. 67 H5
Blies r. Germany 63 H5
Bligh Water b. Fiji 133 H3
Blind River Canada 152 E5
Bliss ID U.S.A. 156 E4
Blissfield MI U.S.A. 164 D3
Blitar Java Indon. 85 F5
Blitta Togo 120 D4
Blocher IN U.S.A. 164 C4
Block Island RI U.S.A. 165 J3
Block Island Sound sea chan. RI U.S.A. 165 J3
Bloemfontein S. Africa 125 H5
Bloemhof S. Africa 125 G4
Bloemhof Dam S. Africa 125 G4
Bloemhof Dam Nature Reserve S. Africa 125 G4
Blomberg Germany 63 J3
Blönduós Iceland 54 [inset 1]
Blongas Lombok Indon. 85 G5
Bloods Range mts Australia 135 E6
Bloodsworth Island MD U.S.A. 165 G4
Bloodvein r. Canada 151 L5
Bloody r. Canada 149 Q2
Bloody Foreland pt Ireland 61 D2
Bloomer WI U.S.A. 160 F2
Bloomfield Canada 165 G2
Bloomfield IA U.S.A. 160 E3
Bloomfield IN U.S.A. 164 B4
Bloomfield MO U.S.A. 161 F4
Bloomfield NM U.S.A. 159 J3
Blooming Prairie MN U.S.A. 160 E3
Bloomington IL U.S.A. 160 F3
Bloomington IN U.S.A. 164 B4
Bloomington MN U.S.A. 160 E2
Bloomsburg PA U.S.A. 165 G3
Blora Java Indon. 85 E4
Blossburg PA U.S.A. 165 G3
Blosseville Kyst coastal area Greenland 147 P3
Blouberg S. Africa 125 I2
Blouberg Nature Reserve S. Africa 125 I2
Blountstown FL U.S.A. 163 C6
Blountville TN U.S.A. 164 D5
Blow r. Canada 149 M1
Bloxham U.K. 59 F6
Blue r. Canada 149 O4
Blue watercourse AZ U.S.A. 159 I5
Blue Bell Knoll mt. UT U.S.A. 159 H2
Blueberry r. Canada 150 F3
Blue Creek r. Mex. see Azul
Blue Diamond NV U.S.A. 159 F3
Blue Earth MN U.S.A. 160 E3
Bluefield VA U.S.A. 162 D4
Bluefield WV U.S.A. 164 E5
Bluefields Nicaragua 166 [inset] J6
Blue Hills Turks and Caicos Is 163 F8
Blue Knob hill PA U.S.A. 165 F3
Blue Mesa Reservoir CO U.S.A. 159 J2
Blue Mountain hill Canada 153 K4
Blue Mountain Lake NY U.S.A. 165 H2
Blue Mountain Pass Lesotho 125 H5
Blue Mountains Australia 138 D4
Blue Mountains OR U.S.A. 156 D3
Blue Mountains National Park Australia 138 E4
Blue Nile r. Eth./Sudan 108 D6
also known as Ābay Wenz (Ethiopia), Bahr el Azraq (Sudan)
Bluenose Lake Canada 149 R1
Blue Ridge GA U.S.A. 163 C5
Blue Ridge VA U.S.A. 164 F5
Blue Ridge mts VA U.S.A. 164 E5
Blue Stack hill Ireland 61 D3
Blue Stack Mountains hills Ireland 61 D3
Bluestone Lake WV U.S.A. 164 E5
Bluewater NM U.S.A. 159 J4
Bluff N.Z. 139 B8
Bluff UT U.S.A. 159 I3
Bluffdale UT U.S.A. 159 H1
Bluff Island H.K. China 97 [inset]
Bluff Knoll mt. Australia 135 B8
Bluffton IN U.S.A. 164 C3
Bluffton OH U.S.A. 164 D3
Blumenau Brazil 179 A4
Blustry Mountain Canada 156 C2
Blyde River Canyon Nature Reserve S. Africa 125 J3
Blying Sound sea chan. AK U.S.A. 149 J4
Blyth Canada 164 E2
Blyth England U.K. 58 F3
Blyth England U.K. 58 F5
Blythe CA U.S.A. 159 F5
Blytheville AR U.S.A. 161 F5
Bø Norway 55 F7
Bo Sierra Leone 120 B4
Boac Phil. 82 C3
Boaco Nicaragua 166 [inset] I6
Boa Esperança Brazil 179 B3
Bo'ai Henan China 95 H5
Bo'ai Yunnan China 96 E4
Boali Cent. Afr. Rep. 122 B3
Boalsert Neth. see Bolsward
Boane Moz. 125 K4
Boano i. Moluccas Indon. 83 C3
Boano, Selat sea chan. Moluccas Indon. 83 C3
Boa Nova Brazil 179 C1
Boardman OH U.S.A. 164 E3
Boatlaname Botswana 125 G2
Boa Viagem Brazil 177 K5
Boa Vista Brazil 176 F3
Boa Vista i. Cape Verde 120 [inset]
Bobadah Australia 138 C4
Bobai China 97 F4
Bobaomby, Tanjona c. Madag. 123 E5
Bobbili India 106 D2
Bobcaygeon Canada 165 F1
Bobo-Dioulasso Burkina Faso 120 C3
Bobon Samar Phil. 82 D3
Bobotov Kuk mt. Montenegro see Durmitor
Bobriki Russia see Novomoskovsk
Bobrinets Ukr. see Bobrynets'
Bobrov Russia 53 I6
Bobrovitsa Ukr. see Bobrovytsya
Bobrovytsya Ukr. 53 F6
Bobruysk Belarus see Babruysk
Bobrynets' Ukr. 53 G6
Bobs Lake Canada 165 G1
Bobuk Sudan 108 D7
Bobures Venez. 176 D2
Boby mt. Madag. 123 E6
Boca del Río Mex. 167 F5
Boca de Macareo Venez. 176 F2
Boca do Acre Brazil 176 E5
Boca do Jari Brazil 177 H4
Bocaiúva Brazil 179 C2
Bocaranga Cent. Afr. Rep. 122 B3
Boca Raton FL U.S.A. 163 D7
Bocas del Toro Panama 166 [inset] J7
Bocas del Toro, Archipiélago de is Panama 166 [inset] J7
Bochnia Poland 57 R6
Bocholt Germany 62 G3
Bochum Germany 63 H3
Bockenem Germany 63 K2
Bocoio Angola 123 B5
Bocoyna Mex. 166 D3
Boda Cent. Afr. Rep. 122 B3
Bodalla Australia 138 E6
Bodallin Australia 135 B7
Bodaybo Russia 77 M4
Boddam U.K. 60 H3
Bode r. Germany 63 L3
Bodega Head hd CA U.S.A. 158 B2
Bodélé reg. Chad 121 E3
Boden Sweden 54 L4
Bodenham U.K. 59 E6
Bodensee l. Germany/Switz. see Constance, Lake
Bodenteich Germany 63 K2
Bodenwerder Germany 63 J3
Bodie (abandoned) CA U.S.A. 158 D2
Bodinayakkanur India 106 C4
Bodmin U.K. 59 C8
Bodmin Moor moorland U.K. 59 C8
Bodø Norway 54 I3
Bodonchiyn Gol watercourse Mongolia 94 C2
Bodoquena Brazil 177 G7
Bodoquena, Serra da hills Brazil 178 E2
Bodrum Turkey 69 L6
Bodträskfors Sweden 54 L3
Boechout Belgium 62 E3
Boende Dem. Rep. Congo 121 F5
Bœng Méaléa Cambodia 87 D4
Bo Epinang Celebes Indon. 83 B4
Boerne TX U.S.A. 161 D6
Boeuf r. LA U.S.A. 161 F6
Boffa Guinea 120 B3
Bogalay Myanmar see Bogale
Bogale Myanmar 86 A3
Bogale r. Myanmar 86 A4
Bogalusa LA U.S.A. 161 F6
Bogan r. Australia 138 C2
Bogandé Burkina Faso 120 C3
Bogan Gate Australia 138 C4
Bogani Nani Wartabone, Taman Nasional nat. park Indon. 83 B2
Boğazlıyan Turkey 112 D3
Bogcang Zangbo r. China 99 D7
Bogd Bayanhongor Mongolia 94 E2
Bogd Övörhangay Mongolia 94 E2
Bogda Feng mt. China 98 E4
Bogda Shan mts China 94 B3
Bogen Kazakh. 102 B2
Boggabilla Australia 138 E2
Boggabri Australia 138 E3
Boggeragh Mountains hills Ireland 61 C5
Boghar Alg. 67 H6
Boghari Alg. see Ksar el Boukhari
Bognor Regis U.K. 59 G8
Bogo Cebu Phil. 82 D4
Bogodukhov Ukr. see Bohodukhiv
Bog of Allen reg. Ireland 61 E4
Bogong, Mount Australia 138 C6
Bogopol' Russia 90 D3
Bogor Java Indon. 84 D4
Bogoroditsk Russia 53 H5
Bogorodsk Russia 52 I4
Bogorodskoye Khabarovskiy Kray Russia 90 F1
Bogorodskoye Kirovskaya Oblast' Russia 52 K4
Bogoslof Island AK U.S.A. 148 E5
▶Bogotá Col. 176 D3
Capital of Colombia. 5th most populous city in South America.
Bogotol Russia 76 J4
Bogoyavlenskoye Russia see Pervomayskiy
Bogra Bangl. 105 G4
Boguchanskoye Vodokhranilishche resr Russia 77 L4
Boguchanskoye Vodokhranilishche resr Russia 78 C2
Boguchany Russia 77 K4
Boguchar Russia 53 I6
Bogué Mauritania 120 B3
Boh r. Indon. 85 F2
Bo Hai g. China 95 I4
Bohai Haixia sea chan. China 95 J4
Bohain-en-Vermandois France 62 D5
Bohai Wan b. China 78 D4
Bohemian Forest mts Germany see Böhmer Wald
Böhlen Germany 63 M3
Bohlokong S. Africa 125 I5
Böhme r. Germany 63 J2
Böhmer Wald mts Germany 63 M5
Bohmte Germany 63 I2
Bohodukhiv Ukr. 53 G6
Bohol i. Phil. 82 D4
Bohol Sea Phil. 82 D4
Bohol Strait Phil. 82 C4
Bohu China 98 D4
Boiaçu Brazil 176 F4
Boiba China 96 C1
Boichoko S. Africa 124 F5
Boigu Island Australia 81 K8
Boikhutso S. Africa 125 H4
Boileau, Cape Australia 134 C4
Boim Brazil 177 G4
Boipeba, Ilha i. Brazil 179 D1
Bois r. Brazil 179 A2
Bois, Lac des l. Canada 149 P2
Bois Blanc Island MI U.S.A. 162 C2
▶Boise ID U.S.A. 156 D4
Capital of Idaho.
Boise City OK U.S.A. 161 C4
Boissevain Canada 151 K5
Boitumelong S. Africa 125 G4
Boizenburg/Elbe Germany 63 K1

Bojd Iran 110 E3
Bojeador, Cape Luzon Phil. 82 C2
Bojnūrd Iran 110 E2
Bojonegoro Java Indon. 85 E4
Bojong Java Indon. 84 D4
Bokaak atoll Marshall Is see Taongi
Bokajan India 105 H4
Bokaro India 105 F5
Bokaro Reservoir India 105 F5
Bokat Celebes Indon. 83 B2
Bokatola Dem. Rep. Congo 122 B4
Boké Guinea 120 B3
Boke Kazakh. 98 C2
Bokele Dem. Rep. Congo 122 C4
Bokhara r. Australia 138 C2
Bo Kheo Cambodia see Bâ Kêv
Boknafjorden sea chan. Norway 55 D7
Bokoko Dem. Rep. Congo 122 C3
Bökönbaev Kyrg. 98 B4
Bokoro Chad 121 E3
Bokovskaya Russia 53 I6
Bokspits S. Africa 124 E4
Boktor Russia 90 E2
Bokurdak Turkm. 110 E2
Bol Chad 121 E3
Bolaang Celebes Indon. 83 B3
Bolaiti Dem. Rep. Congo 121 F5
Bolama Guinea-Bissau 120 B3
Bolangir India see Balangir
Bolan Pass Pak. 111 G4
Bolavén, Phouphiang plat. Laos 86 D4
Bolbec France 66 E2
Bole China 98 C3
Bole Ghana 120 C4
Boleko Dem. Rep. Congo 122 B4
Bolen Russia 90 D2
Bolgar Russia 53 K5
Bolgatanga Ghana 120 C3
Bolgrad Ukr. see Bolhrad
Bolhrad Ukr. 69 M2
Boli China 90 C3
Bolia Dem. Rep. Congo 122 B4
Boliden Sweden 54 L4
Bolikhamxai Laos 86 C3
Bolinao Luzon Phil. 82 B2
Bolingbrook IL U.S.A. 164 A3
Bolintin-Vale Romania 69 K2
Bolívar Peru 176 C5
Bolivar NY U.S.A. 165 F2
Bolivar TN U.S.A. 161 F5
Bolívar, Pico mt. Venez. 176 D2
Bolivia Cuba 163 E8

▶Bolivia country S. America 176 E7
5th largest country in South America.

Bolkhov Russia 53 H5
Bollène France 66 G4
Bollnäs Sweden 55 J6
Bollon Australia 138 C2
Bollstabruk Sweden 54 J5
Bolmen l. Sweden 55 H8
Bolo Panay Phil. 82 C4
Bolobo Dem. Rep. Congo 122 B4
Bolod Islands Phil. 82 C5
Bologna Italy 68 D2
Bolognesi Peru 176 D5
Bologoye Russia 52 G4
Bolokanang S. Africa 125 G5
Bolomba Dem. Rep. Congo 122 B3
Bolon' Russia 90 E2
Bolong Mindanao Phil. 82 C5
Bolpur India 105 F5
Bolsena, Lago di l. Italy 68 D3
Bol'shakovo Russia 55 L9
Bol'shaya Chernigovka Russia 51 Q5
Bol'shaya Glushitsa Russia 53 K5
Bol'shaya Imandra, Ozero l. Russia 54 R3
Bol'shaya Kovriga, Gora hill Russia 52 K2
Bol'shaya Martynovka Russia 53 I7
Bol'shaya Osinovaya r. Russia 148 A2
Bol'shaya Tsarevshchina Russia see Volzhskiy
Bol'shaya Vladimirovka Kazakh. 98 B2
Bol'shevik, Ostrov i. Russia 77 L2
Bol'shezemel'skaya Tundra lowland Russia 52 L2
Bol'shiye Barsuki, Peski des. Kazakh. 102 A2
Bol'shiye Chirki Russia 52 J3
Bol'shoy Begichev, Ostrov i. Russia 189 E2
Bol'shoye Murashkino Russia 52 J5
Bol'shoy Irgiz r. Russia 53 J6
Bol'shoy Kamen' Russia 90 D4
Bol'shoy Kavkaz mts Asia/Europe see Caucasus
Bol'shoy Kundysh r. Russia 52 J4
Bol'shoy Lyakhovskiy, Ostrov i. Russia 77 P2
Bol'shoy Tokmak Ukr. see Tokmak
Bolsward Neth. 62 F1
Bolton Canada 164 F2
Bolton Mindanao Phil. 82 D5
Bolton U.K. 58 E5
Bolu Turkey 69 N4
Boluntay China 99 F5
Boluo China 97 G4
Bolus Head hd Ireland 61 B6
Bolvadin Turkey 69 N5
Bolzano Italy 68 D1
Boma Dem. Rep. Congo 123 B4
Bomaderry Australia 138 E5
Bombala Australia 138 D6
Bombay India see Mumbai
Bombay Beach CA U.S.A. 159 F5
Bomberai, Semenanjung pen. Indon. 81 I7
Bömbögör Mongolia 94 D2
Bomboma Dem. Rep. Congo 122 B3
Bom Comércio Brazil 176 E5
Bomdila India 105 H4
Bomi China 99 F7
Bomili Dem. Rep. Congo 122 C3
Bom Jardim de Goiás Brazil 179 A2
Bom Jesus Brazil 179 A5
Bom Jesus da Gurgueia, Serra do hills Brazil 177 J5
Bom Jesus da Lapa Brazil 179 C1
Bom Jesus do Norte Brazil 179 C3
Bømlo i. Norway 55 D7
Bomokandi r. Dem. Rep. Congo 122 C3
Bom Retiro Brazil 179 A4
Bom Sucesso Brazil 179 B3
Bon, Cap c. Tunisia 68 D6
Bon, Ko i. Thai. 87 B5
Bona Alg. see Annaba
Bona, Mount AK U.S.A. 149 L3
Bonāb Āzarbāyjān-e Sharqī Iran 110 B2
Bonāb Zanjān Iran 110 C2
Bon Air VA U.S.A. 165 G5
Bonaire mun. West Indies 169 K6
Bonandolok Sumatra Indon. 84 B2
Bonanza Nicaragua 166 [inset] I6
Bonanza Peak WA U.S.A. 156 C2
Bonaparte Archipelago is Australia 134 D3
Bonaparte Lake Canada 150 F5
Bonar Bridge U.K. 60 E3
Bonasila Dome hill AK U.S.A. 148 G3
Bonavista Canada 153 L4
Bonavista Bay Canada 153 L4
Bonchester Bridge U.K. 60 G5
Bondo Dem. Rep. Congo 122 C3
Bondoc Peninsula Luzon Phil. 82 C3
Bondokodi Sumba Indon. 83 A5
Bondoukou Côte d'Ivoire 120 C4
Bondowoso Java Indon. 85 F4
Bonduel WI U.S.A. 164 A1
Bondyuzhskiy Russia see Mendeleyevsk
Bône Alg. see Annaba
Bone Celebes Indon. 83 B4
Bone, Teluk b. Indon. 83 B4
Bonelipu Celebes Indon. 83 B4
Bönen Germany 63 H3
Bonerate Celebes Indon. 83 B4
Bonerate i. Indon. 83 B4
Bonerate, Kepulauan is Indon. 83 B4
Bo'ness U.K. 60 F4

▶Bonete, Cerro mt. Arg. 178 C3
3rd highest mountain in South America.

Bonga Eth. 122 D3
Bongabong Mindoro Phil. 82 C3
Bongaigaon India 105 G4
Bongandanga Dem. Rep. Congo 122 C3
Bongani S. Africa 124 F5
Bongao Phil. 82 B5
Bongba China 99 C6
Bong Co l. China 99 E7
Bongka r. Indon. 83 B3
Bongo i. Phil. 82 D5
Bongo, Massif des mts Cent. Afr. Rep. 122 C3
Bongo, Serra do mts Angola 123 B4
Bongolava mts Madag. 123 E5
Bongor Chad 121 E3
Bông Sơn Vietnam 87 E4
Bonham TX U.S.A. 161 D5
Bonheiden Belgium 62 E3
Boni Mali 120 C3
Bonifacio Corsica France 66 I6
Bonifacio, Bocche di strait France/Italy see Bonifacio, Strait of
Bonifacio, Bouches de strait France/Italy see Bonifacio, Strait of
Bonifacio, Strait of France/Italy 66 I6

▶Bonin Islands Japan 91 F8
Part of Japan.

Bonjol Sumatra Indon. 84 C2

▶Bonn Germany 62 H4
Former capital of Germany.

Bonna Germany see Bonn
Bonnåsjøen Norway 54 I3
Bonners Ferry ID U.S.A. 156 D2
Bonnet, Lac du resr Canada 151 M5
Bonnet Plume r. Canada 149 N2
Bonneville France 66 H3
Bonneville Salt Flats UT U.S.A. 159 G1
Bonnières-sur-Seine France 62 B5
Bonnie Rock Australia 135 B7
Bonnieville KY U.S.A. 164 C5
Bonnyrigg U.K. 60 F5
Bonnyville Canada 151 I4
Bonobono Palawan Phil. 82 B4
Bononia Italy see Bologna
Bonorva Sardinia Italy 68 C4
Bonshaw Australia 138 E2
Bontang Kalimantan Indon. 85 G2
Bontebok National Park S. Africa 124 E8
Bonthe Sierra Leone 120 B4
Bontoc Luzon Phil. 82 C2
Bontomatane Celebes Indon. 83 B4
Bontosunggu Celebes Indon. 83 A4
Bontrug S. Africa 125 G7
Bonvouloir Islands P.N.G. 136 E1
Bonwapitse Botswana 125 H2
Boo, Kepulauan is Papua Indon. 83 D3
Book Cliffs ridge UT U.S.A. 159 I2
Booker TX U.S.A. 161 C4
Boolba Australia 138 D2
Booligal Australia 138 B4
Boomer WV U.S.A. 164 E4
Boomi Australia 138 D2
Boon MI U.S.A. 164 C1
Boonah Australia 138 F1
Boone CO U.S.A. 157 G5
Boone IA U.S.A. 160 E3
Boone NC U.S.A. 162 D4
Boone Lake TN U.S.A. 164 D5
Boones Mill VA U.S.A. 164 F5
Booneville AR U.S.A. 161 E5
Booneville KY U.S.A. 164 D5
Booneville MS U.S.A. 161 F5
Böön Tsagaan Nuur salt l. Mongolia 94 D2
Boonville CA U.S.A. 158 B2
Boonville IN U.S.A. 164 B4
Boonville MO U.S.A. 160 E4
Boonville NY U.S.A. 165 H2
Boorabin National Park Australia 135 C7
Boorama Somalia 122 E3
Booroorban Australia 138 B5
Boorowa Australia 138 D5
Boort Australia 138 A6
Boothby, Cape Antarctica 188 D2
Boothia, Gulf of Canada 147 J3
Boothia Peninsula Canada 147 I2
Bootle U.K. 58 E5
Booué Gabon 122 B4
Boppard Germany 63 H4
Boqê China 99 E7
Boqueirão, Serra do hills Brazil 177 J6
Boquilla, Presa de la resr Mex. 166 D3
Boquillas del Carmen Mex. 166 E2
Bor Czech Rep. 63 M5
Bor Russia 52 J4
Bor Serbia 69 J2
Bor South Sudan 121 G4
Bor Turkey 112 D3
Bor, Lagh watercourse Kenya/Somalia 122 E3
Boraha, Nosy i. Madag. 123 F5
Borah Peak ID U.S.A. 156 E3
Borai India 106 D1
Borakalalo Nature Reserve S. Africa 125 H3
Boran Kazakh. 102 G2
Boraphet, Bung l. Thai. 86 C4
Boraphet, Nong l. Thai. see Boraphet, Bung
Borås Sweden 55 H8
Borasambar India 106 D1
Borāzjān Iran 110 C4
Borba Brazil 177 G4
Borbon Cebu Phil. 82 D4
Borborema, Planalto da plat. Brazil 177 K5
Borchen Germany 63 I3
Borçka Turkey 113 F2
Bor Dağı mt. Turkey 69 M6
Bordeaux France 66 D4
Borden Island Canada 147 G2
Borden Peninsula Canada 147 J2
Border Ranges National Park Australia 138 F2
Borðeyri Iceland 54 [inset 1]
Bordj Bou Arréridj Alg. 67 I5
Bordj Bounaama Alg. 67 G6
Bordj Flye Ste-Marie Alg. 120 C2
Bordj Messaouda Alg. 64 F5
Bordj Mokhtar Alg. 120 D2
Bordj Omar Driss Alg. see Bordj Omer Driss
Bordj Omer Driss Alg. 120 D2
Bordu Kyrg. 98 A4
Boreas Abyssal Plain sea feature Arctic Ocean 189 H1
Borel r. Canada 153 H2
Borgå Fin. see Porvoo
Borgarfjörður Iceland 54 [inset 1]
Borgarnes Iceland 54 [inset 1]
Børgefjell Nasjonalpark nat. park Norway 54 H4
Borger TX U.S.A. 161 C5
Borgholm Sweden 55 J8
Borgne, Lake b. LA U.S.A. 161 F6
Borgo San Lorenzo Italy 68 D3
Bori India 106 C1
Bori r. India 104 C5
Borislav Ukr. see Boryslav
Borisoglebsk Russia 53 I6
Borisov Belarus see Barysaw
Borisovka Russia 53 H6
Borispol' Ukr. see Boryspil'
Bo River South Sudan 121 F4
Borja Peru 176 C4
Borken Germany 62 G3
Borkenes Norway 54 J2
Borkovskaya Russia 52 K2
Borkum Germany 62 G1
Borkum i. Germany 62 G1
Borlänge Sweden 55 I6
Borlaug Norway 55 E6
Borlu Turkey 69 M5
Borna Germany 63 M3
Born-Berge hill Germany 63 K3
Borndiep sea chan. Neth. 62 F1
Borne Neth. 62 G2

▶Borneo i. Asia 80 E6
Largest island in Asia and 3rd in the world.

Bornholm i. Denmark 55 I9
Bornova Turkey 69 L5
Borobudur tourist site Indon. 85 E4
Borodino Russia 76 J3
Borodinskoye Russia 55 P6
Borogontsy Russia 77 O3
Borohoro Shan mts China 98 C3
Boroko Celebes Indon. 83 B2
Borok-Sulezhskiy Russia 52 H4
Boromo Burkina Faso 120 C3
Boron CA U.S.A. 158 E4
Borondi India 106 D2
Borongan Samar Phil. 82 D4
Boroughbridge U.K. 58 F4
Borovichi Russia 52 G4
Borovoy Kirovskaya Oblast' Russia 52 K4
Borovoy Respublika Kareliya Russia 54 R4
Borovoy Respublika Komi Russia 52 L3
Borpeta India see Barpeta
Borrisokane Ireland 61 D5
Borroloola Australia 136 B3
Børsa Norway 54 G5
Borşa Romania 53 E7
Borsakelmas sho'rxogi salt marsh Uzbek. 113 J2
Borshchiv Ukr. 53 E6
Borshchovochnyy Khrebet mts Russia 95 G1
Bortala China see Bole
Bortala He r. China 98 C3
Borton IL U.S.A. 164 B4
Bor-Üdzüür Mongolia see Altay
Borūjen Iran 110 C4
Borūjerd Iran 110 C3
Bor Ul Shan mts China 94 D3
Borūn Iran 110 E3
Borve U.K. 60 C3
Boryslav Ukr. 53 D6
Boryspil' Ukr. 53 F6
Borzna Ukr. 53 G6
Borzya Russia 95 I1
Borzya r. Russia 95 H1
Bosaga Kazakh. 98 A3
Bosanska Dubica Bos. & Herz. 68 G2
Bosanska Gradiška Bos. & Herz. 68 G2
Bosanska Krupa Bos. & Herz. 68 G2
Bosanski Novi Bos. & Herz. 68 G2
Bosansko Grahovo Bos. & Herz. 68 G2
Boscawen Island Tonga see Niuatoputopu
Bose China see Baise
Bosencheve, Parque Nacional nat. park Mex. 167 E5
Boseong S. Korea 91 B6
Boshof S. Africa 125 G5
Boshrū'īyeh Iran 110 E3
Bosna i Hercegovina country Europe see Bosnia and Herzegovina
Bosna Saray Bos. & Herz. see Sarajevo
Bosnia and Herzegovina country Europe 68 G2
Bosobogolo Pan salt pan Botswana 124 F3
Bosobolo Dem. Rep. Congo 122 B3
Bōsō-hantō pen. Japan 93 G3
Bosporus strait Turkey 69 M4
Bossaga Turkm. see Basaga
Bossangoa Cent. Afr. Rep. 122 B3
Bossembélé Cent. Afr. Rep. 122 B3
Bossier City LA U.S.A. 161 E5
Bossiesvlei Namibia 124 C3
Bossut, Cape Australia 134 C4
Bostān Iran 110 B4
Bostan Pak. 111 G4
Bostānābād Iran 110 B2
Bostāneh, Ra's-e pt Iran 110 D5
Bostan Tograk He r. China 99 C5
Bosten Hu l. China 98 D4
Boston U.K. 59 G6

▶Boston MA U.S.A. 165 J2
Capital of Massachusetts.

Boston Mountains AR U.S.A. 161 E5
Boston Spa U.K. 58 F5
Boswell IN U.S.A. 164 B3
Botad India 104 B5
Botakara Kazakh. 102 D1
Botany Bay Australia 138 E4
Botev mt. Bulg. 69 K3
Botevgrad Bulg. 69 J3
Bothaville S. Africa 125 H4
Bothnia, Gulf of Fin./Sweden 55 K6
Bothwell Canada 164 E2
Botkins OH U.S.A. 164 C3
Botlikh Russia 113 G2
Botoşani Romania 53 E7
Botou China 95 I4
Bô Trach Vietnam 86 D3
Botshabelo S. Africa 125 H5
Botswana country Africa 123 C6
Botte Donato, Monte mt. Italy 68 G5
Bottesford U.K. 58 G5
Bottrop Germany 62 G3
Botucatu Brazil 179 A3
Botuporã Brazil 179 C1
Botwood Canada 153 L4
Bouaflé Côte d'Ivoire 120 C4
Bouaké Côte d'Ivoire 120 C4
Bouar Cent. Afr. Rep. 122 B3
Bou Arfa Morocco 64 D5
Bouba Ndjida, Parc National de nat. park Cameroon 121 E4
Bouca Cent. Afr. Rep. 122 B3
Boucaut Bay Australia 134 F3
Bouchain France 62 D4
Boucle du Baoulé, Parc National de la nat. park Mali 120 C3
Bouctouche Canada 153 I5
Boudh India see Bauda
Bougaa Alg. 67 I5
Bougainville, Cape Australia 134 D3
Bougainville, Selat sea chan. Papua Indon. 83 D3
Bougainville Island P.N.G. 132 F2
Bougainville Reef Australia 136 D2
Boughessa Mali 120 D3
Bougie Alg. see Bejaïa
Bougouni Mali 120 C3
Bougtob Alg. 64 E5
Bouillon Belgium 62 F5
Bouira Alg. 67 H5
Bou Izakarn Morocco 120 C2
Boujdour W. Sahara 120 B2
Boulder Australia 135 C7
Boulder CO U.S.A. 156 G4
Boulder MT U.S.A. 156 E3
Boulder UT U.S.A. 159 H3
Boulder Canyon gorge NV U.S.A. 159 F3
Boulder City NV U.S.A. 159 F4
Boulevard CA U.S.A. 158 E5
Boulia Australia 136 B4
Boulogne France see Boulogne-sur-Mer
Boulogne-Billancourt France 62 C6
Boulogne-sur-Mer France 62 B4
Boumerdès Alg. 67 H5
Bouna Côte d'Ivoire 120 C4
Bou Naceur, Jbel mt. Morocco 64 D5
Boû Nâga Mauritania 120 B3
Boundary AK U.S.A. 149 L2
Boundary Mountains ME U.S.A. 165 J1
Boundary Peak NV U.S.A. 158 D3
Boundiali Côte d'Ivoire 120 C4
Boundji Congo 122 B4
Boun Nua Laos 86 C2
Bountiful UT U.S.A. 159 H1
Bounty Islands N.Z. 133 H6
Bounty Trough sea feature S. Pacific Ocean 186 H9
Bourail New Caledonia 133 G4
Bourbon reg. France see Bourbonnais
Bourbon terr. Indian Ocean see Réunion
Bourbon IN U.S.A. 164 B3
Bourbonnais reg. France 66 F3
Bourem Mali 120 C3
Bouressa Mali see Boughessa
Bourg-Achard France 59 H9
Bourganeuf France 66 E4
Bourg-en-Bresse France 66 G3
Bourges France 66 F3
Bourget Canada 165 H1
Bourgogne reg. France see Burgundy
Bourgogne, Canal de France 66 G3
Bourke Australia 138 B3
Bourne U.K. 59 G6
Bournemouth U.K. 59 F8
Bourtoutou Chad 121 F3
Bou Saâda Alg. 67 I6
Bou Salem Tunisia 68 C6
Bouse AZ U.S.A. 159 F5
Bouse Wash watercourse AZ U.S.A. 159 F4
Boussu Belgium 62 D4
Boutilimit Mauritania 120 B3
Bouvet Island terr. S. Atlantic Ocean see Bouvetøya

▶Bouvetøya terr. S. Atlantic Ocean 184 I9
Dependency of Norway.

Bouy France 62 E5
Bova Marina Italy 68 F6
Bovenden Germany 63 J3
Boven Kapuas Mountains Indon./Malaysia see Kapuas Hulu, Pegunungan
Bow r. Alta Canada 151 I5
Bow r. Alta Canada 156 F2
Bowa China see Muli
Bowbells ND U.S.A. 160 C1
Bowden WV U.S.A. 164 F4
Bowditch atoll Tokelau see Fakaofo
Bowen Australia 136 E4
Bowen, Mount Australia 138 D6
Bowenville Australia 138 E1
Bowers Ridge sea feature Bering Sea 186 H2
Bowie Australia 136 D4
Bowie AZ U.S.A. 159 I5
Bowie TX U.S.A. 161 D5
Bow Island Canada 151 I5
Bowling Green KY U.S.A. 164 B5
Bowling Green MO U.S.A. 160 F4
Bowling Green OH U.S.A. 164 D3
Bowling Green VA U.S.A. 165 G4
Bowling Green Bay National Park Australia 136 D3
Bowman ND U.S.A. 160 C2
Bowman, Mount Canada 156 C2
Bowman Island Antarctica 188 F2
Bowman Peninsula Antarctica 188 L2
Bowmore U.K. 60 C5
Bowo China see Bomi
Bowral Australia 138 E5
Bowser Lake Canada 149 O4
Boxberg Germany 63 J5
Box Elder SD U.S.A. 160 C2
Box Elder r. SD U.S.A. 160 C2
Boxing China 95 I4
Boxtel Neth. 62 F3
Boyabat Turkey 112 D2
Boyana tourist site Bulg. 69 J3
Boyang China see Poyang
Boyd r. Australia 138 F2
Boyd Lagoon salt flat Australia 135 D6
Boyd Lake Canada 151 K2
Boydton VA U.S.A. 165 F5
Boyers PA U.S.A. 164 F3
Boykins VA U.S.A. 165 G5
Boyle Canada 151 H4
Boyle Ireland 61 D4
Boyne r. Ireland 61 F4
Boyne City MI U.S.A. 164 C1
Boysen Reservoir WY U.S.A. 156 F4
Boysun Uzbek. 111 G2
Boyuibe Bol. 176 F8
Böyük Qafqaz mts Asia/Europe see Caucasus

▶Bozcaada i. Turkey 69 L5
Most westerly point of Asia.

Bozdağ mt. Turkey 69 L5
Bozdağ mt. Turkey 107 C1
Boz Dağları mts Turkey 69 L5
Bozdoğan Turkey 69 M6
Bozeat U.K. 59 G6
Bozeman MT U.S.A. 156 F3
Bozen Italy see Bolzano
Bozhou China 97 G1
Bozoum Cent. Afr. Rep. 122 B3
Bozova Turkey 112 E3
Bozqūsh, Kūh-e mts Iran 110 B2
Bozüyük Turkey 69 N5
Bozyazı Turkey 107 A1
Bozymbay Kazakh. 98 C2
Bra Italy 68 B2
Brač i. Croatia 68 G3
Bracadale U.K. 60 C3
Bracadale, Loch b. U.K. 60 C3
Bracara Port. see Braga
Bracciano, Lago di l. Italy 68 E3
Bracebridge Canada 164 F1
Bräcke Sweden 54 I5
Brackenheim Germany 63 J5
Brackettville TX U.S.A. 161 C6
Bracknell U.K. 59 G7
Bradano r. Italy 68 G4
Bradenton FL U.S.A. 163 D7

▶Brades Montserrat 169 L5
Temporary capital of Montserrat. Plymouth was abandoned in 1997 owing to volcanic activity.

Bradford Canada 164 F1
Bradford U.K. 58 F5
Bradford OH U.S.A. 164 C3
Bradford PA U.S.A. 165 F3
Bradley IL U.S.A. 164 B3
Brady TX U.S.A. 161 D6
Brady Glacier AK U.S.A. 150 B3
Brae U.K. 60 [inset]
Braemar U.K. 60 F3
Braga Port. 67 B3
Bragado Arg. 178 D5
Bragança Brazil 177 I4
Bragança Port. 67 C3
Bragança Paulista Brazil 179 B3
Brahin Belarus 53 F6
Brahlstorf Germany 63 K1
Brahmanbaria Bangl. 105 G5
Brahmapur India 106 E2
Brahmaputra r. India 105 H4 see Dihang
Brahmaur India 104 D2
Brăila Romania 69 L2
Braine France 62 D5
Braine-le-Comte Belgium 62 E4
Brainerd MN U.S.A. 160 E2
Braintree U.K. 59 H7
Braithwaite Point Australia 134 F2
Brak r. S. Africa 125 I2
Brake (Unterweser) Germany 63 I1
Brakel Belgium 62 D4
Brakel Germany 63 J3
Brakwater Namibia 124 C2
Bramfield Australia 135 F8
Bramming Denmark 55 F9
Brämön i. Sweden 54 J5
Brampton Canada 164 F2
Brampton England U.K. 58 E4
Brampton England U.K. 59 I6
Bramsche Germany 63 I2
Bramwell Australia 136 C2
Brancaster U.K. 59 H6
Branch Canada 153 L5
Branco r. Brazil 176 F4
Brandberg mt. Namibia 123 B6
Brandbu Norway 55 G6
Brande Denmark 55 F9
Brandenburg land Germany 63 N2
Brandenburg KY U.S.A. 164 B5
Brandenburg an der Havel Germany 63 M2
Brandfort S. Africa 125 H5
Brandis Germany 63 N3
Brandon Canada 151 L5
Brandon U.K. 59 H6
Brandon MS U.S.A. 161 F5
Brandon VT U.S.A. 165 I2
Brandon Head hd Ireland 61 B5
Brandon Mountain hill Ireland 61 B5
Brandvlei S. Africa 124 E6
Braniewo Poland 57 Q3
Bransfield Strait Antarctica 188 L2
Branson CO U.S.A. 161 C4
Brantas r. Indon. 85 F4
Brantford Canada 164 E2
Branxton Australia 138 E4
Bras d'Or Lake Canada 153 J5
Brasil country S. America see Brazil
Brasil, Planalto do plat. Brazil 177 J7
Brasiléia Brazil 176 E6

▶Brasília Brazil 179 B1
Capital of Brazil.

Brasília de Minas Brazil 179 B2
Braslav Belarus see Braslaw
Braslaw Belarus 55 O9
Braşov Romania 69 K2
Brassey, Banjaran mts Malaysia 85 G1
Brassey, Mount Australia 135 F5
Brassey Range hills Australia 135 C6
Brasstown Bald mt. GA U.S.A. 163 D5

▶Bratislava Slovakia 57 P6
Capital of Slovakia.

Bratsk Russia 88 I1
Bratskoye Vodokhranilishche resr Russia 88 I1
Brattleboro VT U.S.A. 165 I2
Braulio Carrillo, Parque Nacional nat. park Costa Rica 166 [inset] J7
Braunau am Inn Austria 57 N6
Braunfels Germany 63 I4
Braunlage Germany 63 K3
Braunsbedra Germany 63 L3
Braunschweig Germany 63 K2
Brava i. Cape Verde 120 [inset]
Brave PA U.S.A. 164 E4
Bråviken inlet Sweden 55 J7
Bravo, Cerro mt. Bol. 176 F7
Bravo del Norte, Río r. Mex. 154 H6
Bravo del Norte, Río r. Mex./U.S.A. 157 G7 see Rio Grande
Bravo del Norte, Río r. Mex./U.S.A. 167 F3
Brawley CA U.S.A. 159 F5
Bray Ireland 61 F4
Bray, Pays de reg. France 62 B5
Bray Island Canada 147 K3
Brazeau r. Canada 150 H4
Brazeau, Mount Canada 150 G4

▶Brazil country S. America 177 G5
Largest and most populous country in South America and 5th largest and 5th most populous in the world.

Brazil IN U.S.A. 164 B4
Brazil Basin sea feature S. Atlantic Ocean 184 G7
Brazos r. TX U.S.A. 161 E6
▶Brazzaville Congo 123 B4
Capital of Congo.
Brčko Bos. & Herz. 68 H2
Bré Ireland see Bray
Breadalbane Australia 136 B4
Breaksea Sound inlet N.Z. 139 A7
Bream Bay N.Z. 139 E2
Brebes Java Indon. 85 E4
Brebes, Tanjung pt Indon. 85 E4
Brechfa U.K. 59 C7
Brechin U.K. 60 G4
Brecht Belgium 62 E3
Breckenridge MI U.S.A. 164 C2
Breckenridge MN U.S.A. 160 D2
Breckenridge TX U.S.A. 161 D5
Břeclav Czech Rep. 57 P6
Brecon U.K. 59 D7
Brecon Beacons reg. U.K. 59 D7
Brecon Beacons National Park U.K. 59 D7
Breda Neth. 62 E3
Bredasdorp S. Africa 124 E8
Bredbo Australia 138 D5
Breddin Germany 63 M2
Bredevoort Neth. 62 G3
Bredviken Sweden 54 I3
Bree Belgium 62 F3
Breed WI U.S.A. 164 A1
Bregenz Austria 57 L7
Breiðafjörður b. Iceland 54 [inset 1]
Breiðdalsvík Iceland 54 [inset 1]
Breidenbach Germany 63 I4
Breien ND U.S.A. 160 C2
Breitenfelde Germany 63 K1
Breitengüßbach Germany 63 K5
Breiter Luzinsee l. Germany 63 N1
Breivikbotn Norway 54 M1
Breizh reg. France see Brittany
Brejo Velho Brazil 179 C1
Brekstad Norway 54 F5
Bremen Germany 63 I1
Bremen land Germany 63 I1
Bremen IN U.S.A. 164 B3
Bremen OH U.S.A. 164 D4
Bremer Bay Australia 135 B8
Bremerhaven Germany 63 I1
Bremer Range hills Australia 135 C8
Bremersdorp Swaziland see Manzini
Bremervörde Germany 63 J1
Bremm Germany 62 H4
Bremner r. AK U.S.A. 149 K3
Brenham TX U.S.A. 161 D6
Brenna Norway 54 H4
Brennero, Passo di pass Austria/Italy see Brenner Pass
Brenner Pass Austria/Italy 68 D1
Brennerpaß pass Austria/Italy see Brenner Pass
Brentwood U.K. 59 H7
Brescia Italy 68 D2
Breslau Poland see Wrocław
Bresle r. France 62 B4
Brésolles, Lac l. Canada 153 H3
Bressanone Italy 68 D1
Bressay i. U.K. 60 [inset]
Bressuire France 66 D3
Brest Belarus 55 M10
Brest France 66 B2
Brest-Litovsk Belarus see Brest
Bretagne reg. France see Brittany
Breteuil France 62 C5
Brétigny-sur-Orge France 62 C6
Breton Canada 150 H4
Breton Sound b. LA U.S.A. 161 F6
Brett, Cape N.Z. 139 E2
Bretten Germany 63 I5
Bretton U.K. 58 E5
Breueh, Pulau i. Indon. 84 A1
Brevard NC U.S.A. 163 D5
Breves Brazil 177 H4
Brevig Mission AK U.S.A. 148 F2
Brewarrina Australia 138 C2
Brewer ME U.S.A. 162 G2
Brewster NE U.S.A. 160 D3
Brewster OH U.S.A. 164 E3
Brewster, Kap c. Greenland see Kangikajik
Brewster, Lake imp. l. Australia 138 B4
Brewton AL U.S.A. 163 C6
Breyten S. Africa 125 I4
Breytovo Russia 52 H4
Brezhnev Russia see Naberezhnyye Chelny
Brezno Slovakia 57 Q6
Brezovo Bulg. 69 K3
Brezovo Polje hill Croatia 68 G2
Bria Cent. Afr. Rep. 122 C3
Briançon France 66 H4
Brian Head mt. UT U.S.A. 159 G3
Bribbaree Australia 138 C5
Bribie Island Australia 138 F1
Briceni Moldova 53 E6
Brichany Moldova see Briceni
Brichen' Moldova see Briceni
Bridgend U.K. 59 D7
Bridge of Orchy U.K. 60 E4
Bridgeport CA U.S.A. 158 D2
Bridgeport CT U.S.A. 165 I3
Bridgeport IL U.S.A. 164 B4
Bridgeport NE U.S.A. 160 C3
Bridgeport TX U.S.A. 167 F1
Bridger Peak WY U.S.A. 156 G4
Bridgeton NJ U.S.A. 165 H4
Bridgetown Australia 135 B8
▶Bridgetown Barbados 169 M6
Capital of Barbados.
Bridgetown Canada 153 I5
Bridgeville DE U.S.A. 165 H4
Bridgewater Canada 153 I5
Bridgewater NY U.S.A. 165 H2
Bridgnorth U.K. 59 E6
Bridgton ME U.S.A. 165 J1
Bridgwater U.K. 59 D7
Bridgwater Bay U.K. 59 D7
Bridlington U.K. 58 G4
Bridlington Bay U.K. 58 G4
Bridport Australia 137 [inset]
Bridport U.K. 59 E8
Brie reg. France 66 F2
Brie-Comte-Robert France 62 C6
Brieg Poland see Brzeg
Briery Knob mt. WV U.S.A. 164 E4
Brig Switz. 66 H3
Brigg U.K. 58 G5
Brigham City UT U.S.A. 156 E4
Brightlingsea U.K. 59 I7
Brighton Canada 165 G1
Brighton U.K. 59 G8
Brighton CO U.S.A. 156 G5
Brighton MI U.S.A. 164 D2
Brighton NY U.S.A. 165 G2
Brighton WV U.S.A. 164 D4
Brignoles France 66 H5
Brikama Gambia 120 B3
Brillion WI U.S.A. 164 A1
Brilon Germany 63 I3
Brindisi Italy 68 G4
Brinkley AR U.S.A. 161 F5
Brion, Île i. Canada 153 J5
Brioude France 66 F4
Brisay Canada 153 H3
▶Brisbane Australia 138 F1
Capital of Queensland. 3rd most populous city in Oceania.
Brisbane Ranges National Park Australia 138 B6
Bristol U.K. 59 E7
Bristol CT U.S.A. 165 I3
Bristol FL U.S.A. 163 C6
Bristol NH U.S.A. 165 J2
Bristol RI U.S.A. 165 J3
Bristol TN U.S.A. 164 D5
Bristol VT U.S.A. 165 I1
Bristol Bay AK U.S.A. 148 G4
Bristol Channel est. U.K. 59 C7
Bristol Lake CA U.S.A. 159 F4
Britannia Island New Caledonia see Maré
British Antarctic Territory reg. Antarctica 188 L2
British Columbia prov. Canada 150 F5
British Empire Range mts Canada 147 J1
British Guiana country S. America see Guyana
British Honduras country Central America see Belize
▶British Indian Ocean Territory terr. Indian Ocean 185 M6
United Kingdom Overseas Territory.
British Mountains Canada/U.S.A. 149 L1
British Solomon Islands country S. Pacific Ocean see Solomon Islands
Brito Godins Angola see Kiwaba N'zogi
Brits S. Africa 125 H3
Britstown S. Africa 124 F6
Brittany reg. France 66 C2
Britton SD U.S.A. 160 D2
Brive-la-Gaillarde France 66 E4
Briviesca Spain 67 E2
Brixham U.K. 59 D8
Brixia Italy see Brescia
Brlik Kazakh. see Birlik
Brno Czech Rep. 57 P6
Broach India see Bharuch
Broad r. SC U.S.A. 163 D5
Broadalbin NY U.S.A. 165 H2
Broad Arrow (abandoned) Australia 135 C7
Broadback r. Canada 152 F4
Broad Bay U.K. see Tuath, Loch a'
Broadford Australia 138 B6
Broadford Ireland 61 D5
Broadford U.K. 60 D3
Broad Law hill U.K. 60 F5
Broadmere Australia 136 A3
Broad Pass AK U.S.A. 149 J3
Broad Peak China/Pak. 111 J3
Broad Sound sea chan. Australia 136 E4
Broadstairs U.K. 59 I7
Broadus MT U.S.A. 156 G3
Broadview Canada 151 K5
Broadway VA U.S.A. 165 F4
Broadwood N.Z. 139 D2
Brochet Canada 151 K3
Brochet, Lac l. Canada 151 K3
Brochet, Lac au l. Canada 153 H4
Brock r. Canada 149 Q1
Brocken mt. Germany 63 K3
Brockman, Mount Australia 134 B5
Brockport NY U.S.A. 165 G2
Brockport PA U.S.A. 165 F3
Brockton MA U.S.A. 165 J2
Brockville Canada 165 H1
Brockway PA U.S.A. 165 F3
Brodeur Peninsula Canada 147 J2
Brodhead KY U.S.A. 164 C5
Brodick U.K. 60 D5
Brodnica Poland 57 Q4
Brody Ukr. 53 E6
Broghil, Kōtal-e Afgh. 111 I2
Broken Arrow OK U.S.A. 161 E4
Broken Bay Australia 138 E4
Broken Bow NE U.S.A. 160 D3
Broken Bow OK U.S.A. 161 E5
Brokenhead r. Canada 151 L5
Broken Hill Australia 137 C6
Broken Hill Zambia see Kabwe
Broken Plateau sea feature Indian Ocean 185 O8
Brokopondo Suriname 177 G2
Brokopondo Stuwmeer resr Suriname see Professor van Blommestein Meer
Bromberg Poland see Bydgoszcz
Brome Germany 63 K2
Bromo Tengger Semeru, Taman Nasional nat. park Indon. 85 F4
Bromsgrove U.K. 59 E6
Brønderslev Denmark 55 F8
Brønnøysund Norway 54 H4
Bronson FL U.S.A. 163 D6
Bronson MI U.S.A. 164 C3
Brooke U.K. 59 I6
Brooke's Point Palawan Phil. 82 B4
Brookfield WI U.S.A. 164 A2
Brookhaven MS U.S.A. 161 F6
Brookings OR U.S.A. 156 B4
Brookings SD U.S.A. 160 D2
Brookline MA U.S.A. 165 J2
Brooklyn MI U.S.A. 164 C2
Brooklyn Park MN U.S.A. 160 E2
Brookneal VA U.S.A. 165 F5
Brooks Canada 151 I5
Brooks Brook Canada 149 N3
Brooks Mountain hill AK U.S.A. 148 F2
Brooks Range mts AK U.S.A. 149 K1
Brookston IN U.S.A. 164 B3
Brooksville FL U.S.A. 163 D6
Brooksville KY U.S.A. 164 C4
Brookton Australia 135 B8
Brookville IN U.S.A. 164 C4
Brookville PA U.S.A. 164 F3
Brookville Lake IN U.S.A. 164 C4
Broom, Loch inlet U.K. 60 D3
Broome Australia 134 C4
Brora U.K. 60 F2
Brora r. U.K. 60 F2
Brösarp Sweden 55 I9
Brosna r. Ireland 61 E4
Brosville VA U.S.A. 164 F5
Brothers is India 87 A5
Brough U.K. 58 E4
Brough Ness pt U.K. 60 G2
Broughshane U.K. 61 F3
Broughton Island Canada see Qikiqtarjuaq
Broughton Islands Australia 138 F4
Brovary Ukr. 53 F6
Brovinia Australia 137 E5
Brovst Denmark 55 F8
Brown City MI U.S.A. 164 D2
Brown Deer WI U.S.A. 164 B2
Browne Range hills Australia 135 D6
Brownfield TX U.S.A. 161 C5
Browning MT U.S.A. 156 E2
Brown Mountain CA U.S.A. 158 E4
Brownstown IN U.S.A. 164 B4
Brownsville KY U.S.A. 164 B5
Brownsville PA U.S.A. 164 F3
Brownsville TN U.S.A. 161 F5
Brownsville TX U.S.A. 161 D7
Brownwood TX U.S.A. 161 D6
Brownwood, Lake TX U.S.A. 167 F2
Browse Island Australia 134 C3
Bruay-la-Buissière France 62 C4
Bruce Peninsula Canada 164 E1
Bruce Peninsula National Park Canada 164 E1
Bruce Rock Australia 135 B7
Bruchsal Germany 63 I5
Brück Germany 63 M2
Bruck an der Mur Austria 57 O7
Brue r. U.K. 59 E7
Bruges Belgium see Brugge
Brugge Belgium 62 D3
Brühl Baden-Württemberg Germany 63 I5
Brühl Nordrhein-Westfalen Germany 62 G4
Bruin KY U.S.A. 164 D4
Bruin PA U.S.A. 164 F3
Bruini India 105 I3
Bruin Point mt. UT U.S.A. 159 H2
Brûk, Wâdi el watercourse Egypt see Burūk, Wādī al
Brukkaros Namibia 124 D3
Brûlé Canada 150 G4
Brûlé, Lac l. Canada 153 J3
Brûly Belgium 62 E5
Brumado Brazil 179 C1
Brumath France 63 H6
Brumunddal Norway 55 G6
Brunau Germany 63 L2
Brundisium Italy see Brindisi
Bruneau ID U.S.A. 156 E4
Brunei country Asia 85 F1
Brunei Brunei see Bandar Seri Begawan
Brunei Bay Malaysia 85 F1
Brunette Downs Australia 136 A3
Brunflo Sweden 54 I5
Brunico Italy 68 D1
Brünn Czech Rep. see Brno
Brunner, Lake N.Z. 139 C6
Bruno Canada 151 J4
Brunswick Germany see Braunschweig
Brunswick GA U.S.A. 163 D6
Brunswick MD U.S.A. 165 G4
Brunswick ME U.S.A. 165 K2
Brunswick, Península de pen. Chile 178 B8
Brunswick Bay Australia 134 D3
Brunswick Lake Canada 152 E4
Bruntál Czech Rep. 57 P6
Brunt Ice Shelf Antarctica 188 B2
Bruntville S. Africa 125 J5
Bruny Island Australia 137 [inset]
Brusa Turkey see Bursa
Brusenets Russia 52 I3
Brushton NY U.S.A. 165 H1
Brusque Brazil 179 A4
Brussel Belgium see Brussels
▶Brussels Belgium 62 E4
Capital of Belgium.
Bruthen Australia 138 C6
Bruxelles Belgium see Brussels
Bruzual Venez. 176 E2
Bryan OH U.S.A. 164 C3
Bryan TX U.S.A. 161 D6
Bryan, Mount hill Australia 137 B7
Bryan Coast Antarctica 188 L2
Bryansk Bryanskaya Oblast' Russia 53 G5
Bryansk Respublika Dagestan Russia 113 G1
Bryant Pond ME U.S.A. 165 J1
Bryantsburg IN U.S.A. 164 C4
Bryce Canyon National Park UT U.S.A. 159 G3
Bryce Mountain AZ U.S.A. 159 I5
Brynbuga U.K. see Usk
Bryne Norway 55 D7
Bryukhovetskaya Russia 53 H7
Brzeg Poland 57 P5
Brześć nad Bugiem Belarus see Brest
Bua r. Malawi 123 D5
Bu'aale Somalia 122 E3
Buala Solomon Is 133 F2
Buan S. Korea 91 B6
Buang i. Indon. 83 C2
Buatan Sumatra Indon. 84 C2
Bu'ayj well Saudi Arabia 110 C5
Būbīyān, Jazīrat Kuwait 110 C4
Bubuan i. Phil. 82 C5
Bucak Turkey 69 N6
Bucaramanga Col. 176 D2
Bucas Grande i. Phil. 82 D4
Buccaneer Archipelago is Australia 134 C4
Buchanan Liberia 120 B4
Buchanan MI U.S.A. 164 B3
Buchanan VA U.S.A. 164 F5
Buchanan, Lake salt flat Australia 136 D4
Buchanan, Lake TX U.S.A. 167 F2
Buchan Gulf Canada 147 K2
▶Bucharest Romania 69 L2
Capital of Romania.
Büchen Germany 63 K1
Buchen (Odenwald) Germany 63 J5
Bucheon S. Korea 91 B5
Buchholz Germany 63 M1
Buchholz in der Nordheide Germany 63 J1
Buchon, Point CA U.S.A. 158 C4
Buchy France 62 B5
Bucin, Pasul pass Romania 69 K1
Buckambool Mountain hill Australia 138 B3
Bückeburg Germany 63 J2
Bücken Germany 63 J2
Buckeye AZ U.S.A. 159 G5
Buckhannon WV U.S.A. 164 E4
Buckhaven U.K. 60 F4
Buckhorn Lake Canada 165 F1
Buckie U.K. 60 G3
Buckingham U.K. 59 G6
Buckingham VA U.S.A. 165 F5
Buckingham Bay Australia 79 F9
Buckland AK U.S.A. 148 G2
Buckland r. AK U.S.A. 148 G2
Buckland Tableland reg. Australia 136 E5
Buckleboo Australia 135 G8
Buckle Island Antarctica 188 H2
Buckley watercourse Australia 136 B4
Buckley Bay Antarctica 188 G2
Bucklin KS U.S.A. 160 D4
Buckskin Mountains AZ U.S.A. 159 G4
Bucks Mountain CA U.S.A. 158 C2
Bucksport ME U.S.A. 153 H5
Bückwitz Germany 63 M2
Bucureşti Romania see Bucharest
Bucyrus OH U.S.A. 164 D3
Buda-Kashalyova Belarus 53 F5
Budalin Myanmar 86 A2
▶Budapest Hungary 69 H1
Capital of Hungary.
Budaun India 104 D3
Budawang National Park Australia 138 E5
Budda Australia 138 B3
Budd Coast Antarctica 188 F2
Buddusò Sardinia Italy 68 C4
Bude U.K. 59 C8
Bude MS U.S.A. 161 F6
Budennovsk Russia 113 G1
Buderim Australia 138 F1
Būding Iran 110 E5
Büdingen Germany 63 J4
Budīyah, Jabal hills Egypt 107 A5
Budongquan China 94 C5
Budoni Sardinia Italy 68 C4
Budū, Ḩadabat al plain Saudi Arabia 110 C6
Budū', Sabkhat al salt pan Saudi Arabia 110 C6
Budweis Czech Rep. see České Budějovice
Buenaventura Col. 176 C3
Buenaventura Mex. 166 D2
Buena Vista i. N. Mariana Is see Tinian
Buenavista Mindanao Phil. 82 D4
Buenavista Phil. 82 C3
Buena Vista CO U.S.A. 156 G5
Buena Vista VA U.S.A. 164 F5
Buendía, Embalse de resr Spain 67 E3
▶Buenos Aires Arg. 178 E4
Capital of Argentina. 2nd most populous city in South America.
Buenos Aires Costa Rica 166 [inset] J7
Buenos Aires, Lago l. Arg./Chile 178 B7
Buenos Aires National Wildlife Refuge nature res. AZ U.S.A. 166 C2
Buerarema Brazil 179 D1
Buet r. Canada 153 H1
Búfalo Mex. 166 D3
Buffalo r. Canada 150 H2
Buffalo KY U.S.A. 164 C5
Buffalo MO U.S.A. 160 E4
Buffalo NY U.S.A. 165 F2
Buffalo OK U.S.A. 161 D4
Buffalo SD U.S.A. 160 C2
Buffalo TX U.S.A. 161 D6
Buffalo WY U.S.A. 156 G3
Buffalo Head Hills Canada 150 G3
Buffalo Head Prairie Canada 150 G3
Buffalo Hump mt. ID U.S.A. 156 E3
Buffalo Lake Alta Canada 151 H4
Buffalo Lake N.W.T. Canada 150 H2
Buffalo Narrows Canada 151 I4
Buffels watercourse S. Africa 124 C5
Buffels Drift S. Africa 125 H2
Buftea Romania 69 K2
Bug r. Poland 57 S5
Buga Col. 176 C3
Buga Mongolia see Dörvöljin
Bugaldie Australia 138 D3
Bugant Mongolia 95 F1
Bugat Mongolia 94 C2
Bugdaýly Turkm. 110 D2
Bugel, Tanjung pt Indon. 85 E4
Buggenhout Belgium 62 E3
Bugojno Bos. & Herz. 68 G2
Bugrino Russia 52 K1
Bugsuk i. Phil. 82 B4
Bugt China 95 J1
Buguey Luzon Phil. 82 C2
Bugul'ma Russia 51 Q5
Bügür China see Luntai
Buguruslan Russia 51 Q5
Buhera Zimbabwe 123 D5
Buh He r. China 94 D4
Buhi Luzon Phil. 82 C3
Bühl Germany 63 I6
Buhuşi Romania 69 L1
Buick Canada 150 F3
Builth Wells U.K. 59 D6
Buin, Piz mt. Austria/Switz. 57 M7
Bui National Park Ghana 120 C4
Buinsk Russia 53 K5
Bū'īn Zahrā Iran 110 C3
Buitepos Namibia 124 D2
Bujanovac Serbia 69 I3
▶Bujumbura Burundi 122 C4
Capital of Burundi.
Bukachacha Russia 89 L2
Bukadaban Feng mt. China 99 E5
Buka Island P.N.G. 132 F2
Būkān Iran 110 B2
Būkand Iran 110 D4
Bukavu Dem. Rep. Congo 122 C4
Bukhara Uzbek. see Buxoro
Bukhoro Uzbek. see Buxoro
Bukide i. Indon. 83 C2
Bukit Baka-Bukit Raya, Taman Nasional nat. park Indon. 85 F3
Bukitlidi Kalimantan Indon. 85 F3
Bukittinggi Sumatra Indon. 84 C3
Bukkapatnam India 106 C3
Bukoba Tanz. 122 D4
Bükreş Romania see Bucharest
Buktyrma, Vodokhranilishche resr Kazakh. 98 D2
Buku, Tanjung pt Sumatra Indon. 84 D3
Bukukun Russia 95 G1
Būl, Kūh-e mt. Iran 110 D4
Bula Seram Indon. 83 D3
Bula P.N.G. 81 K8
Bülach Switz. 66 I3
Bulag Mongolia see Möngönmorīt
Bulagtay Mongolia see Hüder
Bulalacao Mindoro Phil. 82 C3
Bulan i. Sumatra Indon. 84 C2
Bulan Luzon Phil. 82 C3
Bulan i. Phil. 82 C5
Bulancak Turkey 112 E2
Bulandshahr India 104 D3
Bulanık Turkey 113 F3
Bulava Russia 90 F2
Bulawa, Gunung mt. Indon. 83 B2
Bulawayo Zimbabwe 123 C6
Buldan Turkey 69 M5
Buldana India 106 C1
Buldhana India see Buldana
Buldir Island AK U.S.A. 148 [inset] A5
Buldur India 99 B7
Buleda reg. Pak. 111 F5
Bulembu Swaziland 125 J3
Bulgan Bayan-Ölgiy Mongolia 94 B2
Bulgan Bulgan Mongolia 94 E1
Bulgan Dornod Mongolia 95 H1
Bulgan Hovd Mongolia 94 B2
Bulgan Hovd Mongolia see Darvi
Bulgan Hövsgöl Mongolia see Tsagaan-Üür
Bulgan Ömnögovĭ Mongolia 94 E2
Bulgan prov. Mongolia 94 E1
Bulgan Gol r. Mongolia 94 B2
Bulgar Russia see Bolgar
Bulgaria country Europe 69 K3
Bŭlgariya country Europe see Bulgaria
Buli Halmahera Indon. 83 D2
Buli, Teluk b. Halmahera Indon. 83 D2
Buliluyan, Cape Palawan Phil. 82 B4
Bulkley Ranges mts Canada 149 O5
Bullawarra, Lake salt flat Australia 138 A1
Bullen r. Canada 151 K1
Bullen AK U.S.A. 149 K1
Buller r. N.Z. 139 C5
Buller, Mount Australia 138 C6
Bulleringa National Park Australia 136 C3
Bullfinch Australia 135 B7
Bullhead City AZ U.S.A. 159 F4
Bulli Australia 138 E5
Bullion Mountains CA U.S.A. 158 E4
Bullo r. Australia 134 E3
Bulloo Downs Australia 137 C6
Bulloo Lake salt flat Australia 137 C6
Büllsport Namibia 124 C3
Bully Choop Mountain CA U.S.A. 158 B1
Bulman Australia 134 F3
Bulman Gorge Australia 134 F3
Bulmer Lake Canada 150 F2
Buloh, Pulau i. Sing. 87 [inset]
Buloke, Lake dry lake Australia 138 A6
Bulolo P.N.G. 81 L8
Bulsar India see Valsad
Bultfontein S. Africa 125 H5
Bulu, Gunung mt. Indon. 85 G2
Buluan Mindanao Phil. 82 D5
Bulubulu Celebes Indon. 83 B4
Bulukumba Celebes Indon. 83 B4
Bulun Russia 77 N2
Bulungu Dem. Rep. Congo 123 C4
Bulung'ur Uzbek. 111 G2
Bumba Dem. Rep. Congo 122 C3
Būmbah Libya 112 A4
Bumbah, Khalīj al b. Libya 112 A4
Bumbat China 94 F3
Bumbat Mongolia see Bayan-Öndör
Bumhkang Myanmar 86 B1
Bumhpa Bum mt. Myanmar 86 B1
Buna Dem. Rep. Congo 122 B4
Buna Kenya 122 D3
Bunayyān well Saudi Arabia 110 C6
Bunazi Tanz. 122 D4
Bunbury Australia 135 A8
Bunclody Ireland 61 F5
Buncrana Ireland 61 E2
Bunda Tanz. 122 D4
Bundaberg Australia 136 F5
Bundaleer Australia 138 C2
Bundarra Australia 138 E3
Bundi India 104 C4
Bundjalung National Park Australia 138 F2
Bundoran Ireland 61 D3
Bundukia South Sudan 121 G4
Buner reg. Pak. 111 I3
Bunga-dake mt. Japan 92 B3
Bungalaut, Selat sea chan. Indon. 84 B3
Bungay U.K. 59 I6
Bungendore Australia 138 D5
Bunger Hills Antarctica 188 F2
Bungi Celebes Indon. 83 B4
Bungku Celebes Indon. 83 B3
Bungle Bungle National Park Australia see Purnululu National Park
Bungona'gy China 99 E6
Bungo-suidō sea chan. Japan 91 D6
Bunguran, Kepulauan is Indon. see Natuna, Kepulauan
Bunguran, Pulau i. Indon. see Natuna Besar
Buni, Ci r. Indon. 84 D4
Bunia Dem. Rep. Congo 122 D3
Bunianga Dem. Rep. Congo 122 C4
Buningonia well Australia 135 C7
Bunji Pak. 104 C2
Bunker Group atolls Australia 136 F4
Bunker Hill AK U.S.A. 148 F2
Bunkeya Dem. Rep. Congo 123 C5
Bunkie LA U.S.A. 167 G2
Bunnell FL U.S.A. 163 D6
Bünsum China 99 C7
Buntok Kalimantan Indon. 85 F3
Buntokecil Kalimantan Indon. 85 F3
Bunya Mountains National Park Australia 138 E1
Bünyan Turkey 112 D3
Bunyu i. Indon. 85 G2
Buôn Đôn Vietnam 87 D4
Buôn Ma Thuột Vietnam 87 E4
Buor-Khaya, Guba b. Russia 77 O2
Bup r. China 99 D7
Buqayq Saudi Arabia see Abqaiq
Buqbuq Egypt 112 B5
Bura Kenya 122 D4
Buraan Somalia 122 E2
Buram Sudan 121 F3
Buran Kazakh. see Boran
Burang China 99 C7
Buranhaém r. Brazil 179 D2
Buranhém Brazil 179 C2
Burāq Syria 107 C3
Burauen Leyte Phil. 82 D4
Buray r. India 104 C5
Buraydah Saudi Arabia 108 F4
Burbach Germany 63 I4
Burbank CA U.S.A. 158 D4
Burcher Australia 138 C4
Burco Somalia 122 E3
Bürd Mongolia 94 E2
Burdaard Neth. 62 F1
Burdalyk Turkm. 111 G2
Burdigala France see Bordeaux
Burdur Turkey 69 N6
Burdur Gölü l. Turkey 69 N6
Burdwan India see Barddhaman
Burē Eth. 122 D2
Bure r. U.K. 59 I6
Bureå Sweden 54 L4
Bureinskiy Khrebet mts Russia 90 D2
Bureinskiy Zapovednik nature res. Russia 90 D2
Büren Mongolia 94 F2
Bürentsogt Mongolia 95 G2
Burewala Pak. 111 I4
Bureya r. Russia 90 C2
Bureya Range mts Russia see Bureinskiy Khrebet
Burford Canada 164 E2
Burg Germany 63 L2
Burgaltay Mongolia see Baruunbüren
Burgas Bulg. 69 L3
Burgaw NC U.S.A. 163 E5
Burgbernheim Germany 63 K5
Burgdorf Germany 63 K2
Burgeo Canada 153 K5
Burgersdorp S. Africa 125 H6
Burgersfort S. Africa 125 J3
Burges, Mount hill Australia 135 C7
Burgess, Mount Canada 149 M2
Burgess Hill U.K. 59 G8

Burghaun Germany 63 J4
Burghausen Germany 57 N6
Burghead U.K. 60 F3
Burgh-Haamstede Neth. 62 D3
Burgio, Serra di hill Sicily Italy 68 F6
Burglengenfeld Germany 63 M5
Burgos Mex. 167 F3
Burgos Spain 67 E2
Burgstädt Germany 63 M4
Burgsvik Sweden 55 K8
Burgum Neth. 62 G1
Burgundy reg. France 66 G3
Burhan Budai Shan mts China 94 C5
Burhaniye Turkey 69 L5
Burhanpur India 104 D5
Burhar-Dhanpuri India 105 E5
Burhi Gandak r. India 99 D8
Buri Brazil 179 A3
Buriai Sumatra Indon. 84 C3
Burias i. Phil. 82 C3
Buriat-Mongol Republic aut. rep. Russia see Buryatiya, Respublika
Burica, Punta pt Costa Rica 166 [inset] J7
Buri Gandak r. Nepal 99 C8
Burin Canada 153 L5
Burin Peninsula Canada 153 L5
Buriram Thai. 86 C4
Buritama Brazil 179 A3
Buriti Alegre Brazil 179 A2
Buriti Bravo Brazil 177 J5
Buritirama Brazil 177 J6
Buritis Brazil 179 B1
Burjay China 98 E4
Burj Aziz Khan Pak. 111 G4
Burkan-Suu r. Kyrg. 98 B4
Burke SD U.S.A. 160 D3
Burke Island Antarctica 188 K2
Burke Pass N.Z. see Burkes Pass
Burkes Pass N.Z. 139 C7
Burkesville KY U.S.A. 164 C5
Burketown Australia 136 B3
Burkeville VA U.S.A. 165 F5
Burkina country Africa see Burkina Faso
Burkina Faso country Africa 120 C3
Burkitty Kazakh. 98 B2
Burk's Falls Canada 152 F5
Burley ID U.S.A. 156 E4
Burlington Canada 164 F2
Burlington CO U.S.A. 160 C4
Burlington IA U.S.A. 160 F3
Burlington KS U.S.A. 160 E4
Burlington KY U.S.A. 164 C4
Burlington VT U.S.A. 165 I1
Burlington WI U.S.A. 164 A2
Burmantovo Russia 51 S3
Burnaby Canada 150 F5
Burnet TX U.S.A. 161 D6
Burney CA U.S.A. 158 C1
Burney, Monte vol. Chile 178 B8
Burnham PA U.S.A. 165 G3
Burnie Australia 137 [inset]
Burniston U.K. 58 G4
Burnley U.K. 58 E5
Burns OR U.S.A. 156 D4
Burnside r. Canada 146 H3
Burnside KY U.S.A. 164 C5
Burnside, Lake salt flat Australia 135 C6
Burns Junction OR U.S.A. 156 D4
Burns Lake Canada 150 E4
Burntisland U.K. 60 F4
Burnt Lake Canada see Brûlé, Lac
Burntwood r. Canada 151 L4
Burog Co l. China 99 D6
Buron r. Canada 153 H2
Burovoy Uzbek. 111 F1
Burqin China 98 D3
Burqin He r. China 98 D3
Burqu' Jordan 107 D3
Burqu', Qaşr tourist site Jordan 107 C3
Burra Australia 137 B7
Burra i. U.K. 60 [inset]
Burravoe U.K. 60 [inset]
Burrel Albania 69 I4
Burrel CA U.S.A. 158 D3
Burren reg. Ireland 61 C4
Burrendong, Lake Australia 138 D4
Burren Junction Australia 138 D3
Burrewarra Point Australia 138 E5
Burrinjuck Australia 138 D5
Burrinjuck Reservoir Australia 138 D5
Burro, Serranías del mts Mex. 167 E2
Burr Oak Reservoir OH U.S.A. 164 D4
Burro Creek watercourse AZ U.S.A. 159 G4
Burro Peak NM U.S.A. 159 I5
Burrowa Pine Mountain National Park Australia 138 C6
Burrow Head hd U.K. 60 E6
Burrows IN U.S.A. 164 B3
Burrundie Australia 134 E3
Bursa Turkey 69 M4
Būr Safāga Egypt see Būr Safājah
Būr Safājah Egypt 108 D4
Būr Sa'īd Egypt see Port Said
Būr Sa'īd Egypt see Port Said
Būr Sa'īd governorate Egypt see Būr Sa'īd
Būr Sa'īd governorate Egypt 107 A4
Bürstadt Germany 63 I5
Būr Sudan Sudan see Port Sudan
Burt Lake MI U.S.A. 162 C2
Burton MI U.S.A. 164 D2
Burton, Lac l. Canada 152 F3
Burton upon Trent U.K. 59 F6
Burträsk Sweden 54 L4
Burt Well Australia 135 F5
Buru i. Moluccas Indon. 83 C3
Burūk, Wādī al watercourse Egypt 107 A4
Burullus, Baḥra el lag. Egypt see Burullus, Lake
Burullus, Buḥayrat al lag. Egypt see Burullus, Lake
Burullus, Lake lag. Egypt 112 C5
Burultokay China see Fuhai
Burūn, Ra's pt Egypt 107 A4
Burundi country Africa 122 C4
Burunniy Russia see Tsagan Aman
Bururi Burundi 122 C4
Burwash Landing Canada 149 M3
Burwick U.K. 60 G2
Buryatia aut. rep. Russia see Buryatiya, Respublika
Buryatiya, Respublika aut. rep. Russia 94 E1
Buryatskaya Mongolskaya A.S.S.R. aut. rep. Russia see Buryatiya, Respublika
Burylbaytal Kazakh. 98 A3
Buryn' Ukr. 53 G6
Bury St Edmunds U.K. 59 H6
Burzil Pass Pak. 104 C2
Busambra, Rocca mt. Sicily Italy 68 E6
Busan S. Korea 91 C6
Busan Bay Mindanao Phil. 82 C5
Busanga Dem. Rep. Congo 122 C4
Busby MT U.S.A. 156 G3
Buseire Syria see Al Buşayrah
Bush r. U.K. 61 F2
Bushêngcaka China 105 E2
Bushenyi Uganda 122 D4
Bushire Iran see Bandar-e Būshehr
Bushmills U.K. 61 F2
Bushnell FL U.S.A. 163 D6
Businga Dem. Rep. Congo 122 C3
Busobuso Moluccas Indon. 83 D2
Buşrá ash Shām Syria 107 C3
Busse Russia 90 B2
Busselton Australia 135 A8
Bussum Neth. 62 F2
Bustamante Mex. 167 E3
Bustillos, Lago l. Mex. 166 D2
Busto Arsizio Italy 68 C2
Busuanga i. Phil. 82 B3
Buta Dem. Rep. Congo 122 C3
Butare Rwanda 122 C4
Butaritari atoll Kiribati 186 H5
Bute Australia 137 B7
Bute i. U.K. 60 D5
Butedale (abandoned) Canada 150 D4
Butha-Buthe Lesotho 125 I5
Butha Qi China see Zalantun
Buthidaung Myanmar 86 A2
Butler AL U.S.A. 161 F5
Butler GA U.S.A. 163 C5
Butler IN U.S.A. 164 C3
Butler KY U.S.A. 164 C4
Butler MO U.S.A. 160 E4
Butler PA U.S.A. 164 F3
Butlers Bridge Ireland 61 E3
Buton i. Indon. 83 B4
Buton, Selat sea chan. Indon. 83 B4
Bütow Germany 63 M1
Butte MT U.S.A. 156 E3
Butte NE U.S.A. 160 D3
Buttelstedt Germany 63 L3
Butterworth Malaysia 84 C1
Butterworth S. Africa see Gcuwa
Buttes, Sierra mt. CA U.S.A. 158 C2
Buttevant Ireland 61 D5
Butt of Lewis hd U.K. 60 C2
Button Bay Canada 151 M3
Butuan Mindanao Phil. 82 D4
Butuan Bay Mindanao Phil. 82 D4
Butuo China 96 D3
Buturlinovka Russia 53 I6
Butwal Nepal 105 E4
Butzbach Germany 63 I4
Buulobarde Somalia 122 E3
Buur Gaabo Somalia 122 E4
Buurhabaka Somalia 122 E3
Buutsagaan Mongolia 94 D2
Buxar India 105 F4
Buxoro Uzbek. 111 G2
Buxtehude Germany 63 J1
Buxton U.K. 58 F5
Buy Russia 52 I4
Buyant Bayanhongor Mongolia see Buutsagaan
Buyant Bayan-Ölgiy Mongolia 94 B1
Buyant Dundgovĭ Mongolia 95 F2
Buyant Hentiy Mongolia see Galshar
Buyant Gol r. Mongolia 94 D2
Buyant Gol r. Mongolia 98 E2
Buyant-Uhaa Mongolia 95 G2
Buynaksk Russia 113 G2
Buyr Nuur l. Mongolia 95 I2
Büyükçekmece Turkey 112 C2
Büyük Egri Dağ mt. Turkey 107 A1
Büyükmenderes r. Turkey 69 L6
Buyun Shan mt. China 95 J3
Buzancy France 62 E5
Buzău Romania 69 L2
Buzdyak Russia 51 Q5
Búzi Moz. 123 D5
Büzmeýin Turkm. see Abadan
Buzuluk Russia 51 Q5
Buzuluk r. Russia 53 I6
Buzzards Bay MA U.S.A. 165 J3
Byakar Bhutan see Jakar
Byala Bulg. 69 K3
Byala Slatina Bulg. 69 J3
Byalynichy Belarus 53 F5
Byarezina r. Belarus 53 F5
Byaroza Belarus 55 N10
Byblos tourist site Lebanon 107 B2
Bydgoszcz Poland 57 Q4
Byelorussia country Europe see Belarus
Byerazino Belarus 53 F5
Byers CO U.S.A. 156 G5
Byeshankovichy Belarus 53 F5
Byesville OH U.S.A. 164 E4
Bygland Norway 55 E7
Bykhaw Belarus 53 F5
Bykhov Belarus see Bykhaw
Bykle Norway 55 E7
Bykovo Russia 53 J6
Bylas AZ U.S.A. 159 H5
Bylkyldak Kazakh. 98 A2
Bylot Island Canada 147 K2
Byramgore Reef India 106 A4
Byrd Glacier Antarctica 188 H1
Byrdstown TN U.S.A. 164 C5
Byrka Russia 95 I1
Byrkjelo Norway 55 E6
Byrock Australia 138 C3
Byron ME U.S.A. 165 J1
Byron, Cape Australia 138 F2
Byron Bay Australia 138 F2
Byron Island Kiribati see Nikunau
Byrranga, Gory mts Russia 77 K2
Byske Sweden 54 L4
Byssa Russia 90 C1
Byssa r. Russia 90 C1
Bystrinskiy Golets, Gora mt. Russia 95 G1
Bytom Poland 57 Q5
Bytów Poland 57 P3
Byurgyutli Turkm. 110 D2
Byzantium Turkey see İstanbul

Ca, Sông r. Vietnam 86 D3
Caacupé Para. 178 E3
Caatinga Brazil 179 B2
Caazapá Para. 178 E3
Cabaiguán Cuba 163 E8
Caballas Peru 176 C6
Caballococha Peru 176 D4
Caballo Reservoir NM U.S.A. 166 D1
Caballos Mesteños, Llano de los plain Mex. 166 D2
Cabanaconde Peru 176 D7
Cabanatuan Luzon Phil. 82 C3
Cabano Canada 153 H5
Cabarroguis Phil. 82 C2
Cabdul Qaadir Somalia 122 E2
Cabeceira Rio Manso Brazil 177 G7
Cabeceiras Brazil 179 B1
Cabeza del Buey Spain 67 D4
Cabeza Prieta National Wildlife Refuge nature res. AZ U.S.A. 166 B1
Cabezas Bol. 176 F7
Cabimas Venez. 176 D1
Cabinda Angola 123 B4
Cabinda prov. Angola 123 B5
Cabinet Inlet Antarctica 188 L2
Cabinet Mountains MT U.S.A. 156 E2
Cabingaan i. Phil. 82 C5
Cabistra Turkey see Ereğli
Cabo Frio Brazil 179 C3
Cabo Frio, Ilha do i. Brazil 179 C3
Cabonga, Réservoir resr Canada 152 F5
Cabool MO U.S.A. 161 E4
Caboolture Australia 138 F1
Cabo Orange, Parque Nacional de nat. park Brazil 177 H3
Cabo Pantoja Peru 176 C4
Cabora Bassa, Lake resr Moz. 123 D5
Cabo Raso Arg. 178 C6
Caborca Mex. 166 B2
Cabo San Lucas Mex. 166 C4
Cabot Head hd Canada 164 E1
Cabot Strait Canada 153 J5
Cabourg France 59 G9
Cabo Verde country Africa see Cape Verde
Cabo Verde, Ilhas do is N. Atlantic Ocean 120 [inset]
Cabo Yubi Morocco see Tarfaya
Cabra i. Phil. 82 C3
Cabral, Serra do mts Brazil 179 B2
Cäbrayıl Azer. 113 G3
Cabrera, Illa de i. Spain 67 H4
Cabrera, Sierra de la mts Spain 67 C2
Cabri Canada 151 I5
Cabugao Luzon Phil. 82 C2
Cabulauan i. Phil. 82 C4
Cabullona Mex. 166 C2
Cabutunan Point Luzon Phil. 82 C2
Caçador Brazil 179 A4
Cacagoin China see Qagca
Cacahuatepec Mex. 167 F5
Čačak Serbia 69 I3
Caccia, Capo c. Sardinia Italy 68 C4
Çäçe Turkm. 111 F2
Cacequi Brazil 178 F3
Cáceres Brazil 177 G7
Cáceres Spain 67 C4
Cache Creek Canada 150 F5
Cache Peak ID U.S.A. 156 E4
Cacheu Guinea-Bissau 120 B3
Cachi, Nevados de mts Arg. 178 C2
Cachimbo, Serra do hills Brazil 177 H5
Cachoeira Brazil 179 D1
Cachoeira Alta Brazil 179 A2
Cachoeira de Goiás Brazil 179 A2
Cachoeira do Arari Brazil 177 I4
Cachoeiro de Itapemirim Brazil 179 C3
Cacine Guinea-Bissau 120 B3
Caciporé, Cabo c. Brazil 177 H3
Cacolo Angola 123 B5
Caconda Angola 123 B4
Cactus TX U.S.A. 161 C4
Caçu Brazil 179 A2
Caculé Brazil 179 C1
Čadca Slovakia 57 Q6
Caddo Lake TX U.S.A. 167 G1
Cadereyta Mex. 167 E3
Cadibarrawirracanna, Lake salt flat Australia 137 A6
Cadig Mountains Luzon Phil. 82 C3
Cadillac Canada 151 J5
Cadillac MI U.S.A. 164 C1
Cadiz Negros Phil. 82 C4
Cádiz Spain 67 C5
Cadiz IN U.S.A. 164 C4
Cadiz KY U.S.A. 162 C4
Cadiz OH U.S.A. 164 E3
Cádiz, Golfo de g. Spain 67 C5
Cadiz Lake CA U.S.A. 159 F4
Cadomin Canada 150 G4
Cadotte r. Canada 150 G3
Cadotte Lake Canada 150 G3
Caen France 66 D2
Caerdydd U.K. see Cardiff
Caerffili U.K. see Caerphilly
Caerfyrddin U.K. see Carmarthen
Caergybi U.K. see Holyhead
Caernarfon U.K. 59 C5
Caernarfon Bay U.K. 59 C5
Caernarvon U.K. see Caernarfon
Caerphilly U.K. 59 D7
Caesaraugusta Spain see Zaragoza
Caesarea Alg. see Cherchell
Caesarea Cappadociae Turkey see Kayseri
Caesarea Philippi Syria see Bāniyās
Caesarodunum France see Tours
Caesaromagus U.K. see Chelmsford
Caetité Brazil 179 C1
Cafayate Arg. 178 C3
Cafelândia Brazil 179 A3
Caffa Crimea see Feodosiya
Cagayan i. Phil. 82 C4
Cagayan r. Luzon Phil. 82 C2
Cagayan de Oro Mindanao Phil. 82 D4
Cagayan de Tawi-Tawi i. Phil. 82 B5
Cagayan Islands Phil. 82 C4
Cagles Mill Lake IN U.S.A. 164 B4
Cagli Italy 68 E3
Cagliari Sardinia Italy 68 C5
Cagliari, Golfo di b. Sardinia Italy 68 C5
Cagua, Mount vol. Phil. 82 C2
Çagyl Turkm. 113 I2
Cahama Angola 123 B5
Caha Mountains hills Ireland 61 C6
Cahermore Ireland 61 B6
Cahersiveen Ireland see Cahirsiveen
Cahir Ireland 61 E5
Cahirsiveen Ireland 61 B6
Cahora Bassa, Lago de resr Moz. see Cabora Bassa, Lake
Cahore Point Ireland 61 F5
Cahors France 66 E4
Cahuapanas Peru 176 C5
Cahuita, Punta pt Costa Rica 166 [inset] J7
Cahul Moldova 69 M2
Caia Moz. 123 D5
Caiabis, Serra dos hills Brazil 177 G6
Caianda Angola 123 C5
Caiapó r. Brazil 179 A1
Caiapó, Serra do mts Brazil 179 A2
Caiapônia Brazil 179 A2
Caibarién Cuba 163 E8
Cai Bâu, Đao i. Vietnam 86 D2
Caicara Venez. 176 E2
Caicos Islands Turks and Caicos Is 169 J4
Caicos Passage Bahamas/Turks and Caicos Is 163 F8
Caidian China 97 G2
Caiguna Australia 135 D8
Caimanero, Laguna del lag. Mex. 166 D4
Caiman Point Luzon Phil. 82 B3
Caimodorro mt. Spain 67 F3
Cainnyigoin China 96 D1
Cains Store KY U.S.A. 164 C5
Caipe Arg. 178 C2
Caird Coast Antarctica 188 B1
Cairngorm Mountains U.K. 60 F3
Cairngorms National Park U.K. 60 F3
Cairn Mountain AK U.S.A. 148 I3
Cairnryan U.K. 60 D6
Cairns Australia 136 D3
Cairnsmore of Carsphairn hill U.K. 60 E5

►Cairo Egypt 112 C5
Capital of Egypt. 2nd most populous city in Africa.

Cairo GA U.S.A. 163 C6
Caisleán an Bharraigh Ireland see Castlebar
Caiundo Angola 123 B5
Caiwarro (abandoned) Australia 138 B2
Caiyuanzhen China see Shengsi
Caizi Hu l. China 97 H2
Cajamarca Peru 176 C5
Cajati Brazil 179 A4
Cajidiocan Phil. 82 C3
Cajuru Brazil 179 B3
Caka Qinghai China 94 D4
Caka Xizang China 99 C6
Čakovec Croatia 68 G1
Çal Denizli Turkey 69 M5
Çal Hakkâri Turkey see Çukurca
Cala S. Africa 125 H6
Calabar Nigeria 120 D4
Calabogie Canada 165 G1
Calabria, Parco Nazionale della nat. park Italy 68 G5
Calafat Romania 69 J3
Calagnaan i. Phil. 82 C4
Calagua Mex. 166 C3
Calagua Islands Phil. 82 C3
Calagurris Spain see Calahorra
Calahorra Spain 67 F2
Calai Angola 123 B5
Calais France 62 B4
Calais ME U.S.A. 153 I5
Calakmus tourist site Mex. 167 H5
Calalasteo, Sierra de mts Arg. 178 C3
Calama Brazil 176 F5
Calama Chile 178 C2
Calamajué Mex. 157 E7
Calamar Col. 176 D1
Calamian Group is Phil. 82 B4
Calamocha Spain 67 F3
Calandagan i. Phil. 82 C4
Calandula Angola 123 B4
Calang Sumatra Indon. 84 A1
Calanques, Parc National des nat. park France 66 G5
Calapan Mindoro Phil. 82 C3
Călărași Romania 69 L2
Calatayud Spain 67 F3
Calauag Luzon Phil. 82 C3
Calauit i. Phil. 82 B3
Calavite Passage Phil. 82 C3
Calayan i. Phil. 82 C2
Calbayog Samar Phil. 82 D3
Calbe (Saale) Germany 63 L3
Calbiga Samar Phil. 82 D4
Calcasieu r. LA U.S.A. 167 G2
Calcasieu Lake LA U.S.A. 167 G2
Calçoene Brazil 177 H3
Calcutta India see Kolkata
Caldas da Rainha Port. 67 B4
Caldas Novas Brazil 177 I7
Calden Germany 63 J3
Calder r. Canada 150 G1
Caldera Chile 178 B3
Calderitas Mex. 167 H5
Caldervale Australia 136 D5
Caldew r. U.K. 58 E4
Caldwell ID U.S.A. 156 D4
Caldwell KS U.S.A. 161 D4
Caldwell OH U.S.A. 164 E4
Caldwell TX U.S.A. 161 D6
Caledon r. Lesotho/S. Africa 125 H6
Caledon S. Africa 124 D8
Caledon Bay Australia 136 B2
Caledonia Canada 164 F2
Caledonia admin. div. U.K. see Scotland
Caledonia NY U.S.A. 165 G2
Caleta el Cobre Chile 178 B2
Calexico CA U.S.A. 159 F5
Calf of Man i. Isle of Man 58 C4
Calgary Canada 150 H5
Calhoun KY U.S.A. 164 B5
Cali Col. 176 C3
Calicoan i. Phil. 82 D4
Calicut India see Kozhikode
Caliente NV U.S.A. 159 F3
California PA U.S.A. 164 F3
California state U.S.A. 157 C4
California, Gulf of g. Mex. 166 B2
California Aqueduct canal CA U.S.A. 158 C3
Cälilabad Azer. 113 H3
Calingasta Arg. 178 C4
Calipatria CA U.S.A. 159 F5
Calistoga CA U.S.A. 158 B2
Calkiní Mex. 167 H4
Callabonna, Lake salt flat Australia 137 C6
Callaghan, Mount NV U.S.A. 158 E2
Callan Ireland 61 E5
Callan r. U.K. 61 F3
Callander Canada 152 F5
Callander U.K. 60 E4
Callao Peru 176 C6
Callao UT U.S.A. 159 G2
Calles Mex. 167 F4
Callicoon NY U.S.A. 165 H3
Calling Lake Canada 150 H4
Callington U.K. 59 C8
Calliope Australia 136 E5
Callipolis Turkey see Gallipoli
Calmar IA U.S.A. 160 F3
Calobre Panama 166 [inset] J7
Caloosahatchee r. FL U.S.A. 163 D7
Calotmul Mex. 167 H4
Caloundra Australia 138 F1
Calpulálpan Mex. 167 F5
Caltagirone Sicily Italy 68 F6
Caltanissetta Sicily Italy 68 F6
Calucinga Angola 123 B5
Calulo Angola 123 B4
Calunga Angola 123 B5
Caluquembe Angola 123 B5
Calusa i. Phil. 82 C4
Caluula Somalia 122 F2
Caluula, Raas pt Somalia 122 F2
Caluya i. Phil. 82 C4
Calvados Chain is P.N.G. 136 F1
Calvert Hills Australia 136 B3
Calvert Island Canada 150 D5
Calvi Corsica France 66 I5
Calvià Spain 67 H4
Calvinia S. Africa 124 D6
Calvo, Monte mt. Italy 68 F4
Cam r. U.K. 59 H6
Camaçari Brazil 179 D1
Camache Reservoir CA U.S.A. 158 C2
Camachigama r. Canada 152 F5
Camacho Mex. 161 C7
Camacuio Angola 123 B5
Camacupa Angola 123 B5
Camagüey Cuba 169 I4
Camagüey, Archipiélago de is Cuba 169 I4
Camamu Brazil 179 D1
Camaná Peru 176 D7
Camanongue Angola 123 C5
Camapuã Brazil 177 H7
Camaquã Brazil 178 F4
Çamardı Turkey 112 D3
Camargo Bol. 176 E8
Camargo Mex. 167 F3
Camargo, Parque Natural nature res. Mex. 167 F3
Camargue reg. France 66 G5
Camarillo CA U.S.A. 158 D4
Camarón, Cabo c. Hond. 166 [inset] I6
Camarones Arg. 178 C6
Camarones, Bahía b. Arg. 178 C6
Camas r. ID U.S.A. 156 E4
Ca Mau Vietnam 87 D5
Ca Mau, Mui c. Vietnam 87 D5
Cambay India see Khambhat
Cambay, Gulf of India see Khambhat, Gulf of
Camberley U.K. 59 G7
Cambodia country Asia 87 D4
Camboriú Brazil 179 A4
Camborne U.K. 59 B8
Cambrai France 62 D4
Cambria admin. div. U.K. see Wales
Cambrian Mountains hills U.K. 59 D6
Cambridge Canada 164 E2
Cambridge N.Z. 139 E3
Cambridge U.K. 59 H6
Cambridge MA U.S.A. 165 J2
Cambridge MD U.S.A. 165 G4
Cambridge MN U.S.A. 160 E2
Cambridge NY U.S.A. 165 I2
Cambridge OH U.S.A. 164 E3
Cambridge Bay Canada 147 H3
Cambridge City IN U.S.A. 164 C4
Cambridge Springs PA U.S.A. 164 E3
Cambrien, Lac l. Canada 153 H2
Cambulo Angola 123 C4
Cambundi-Catembo Angola 123 B5
Cambuquira Brazil 179 B3
Cam Co l. China 99 C6
Camdeboo National Park S. Africa 124 G7
Camden AL U.S.A. 163 C5
Camden AR U.S.A. 161 E5
Camden NJ U.S.A. 165 H4
Camden NY U.S.A. 165 H2
Camden SC U.S.A. 163 D5
Camden Bay AK U.S.A. 149 K1
Camdenton MO U.S.A. 160 E4
Cameia Angola 123 C5
Cameia, Parque Nacional da nat. park Angola 123 C5
Cameron AZ U.S.A. 159 H4
Cameron LA U.S.A. 161 E6
Cameron MO U.S.A. 160 E4
Cameron TX U.S.A. 161 D6
Cameron Highlands mts Malaysia 84 C1
Cameron Hills Canada 150 G3
Cameron Island Canada 147 H2
Cameron Park CA U.S.A. 158 C2
Cameroon country Africa 120 E4
Cameroon, Mount vol. Cameroon see Cameroun, Mont
Cameroon Highlands slope Cameroon/Nigeria 120 E4
Caméroun country Africa see Cameroon
Cameroun, Mont vol. Cameroon 120 D4
Cametá Brazil 177 I4
Camiguin i. Phil. 82 C2
Camiguin i. Phil. 82 D4
Camiling Luzon Phil. 82 C3
Camiña Chile 176 E7
Camino Real de Tierra Adentro tourist site Mex. 161 B6
Camiri Bol. 176 F8
Camisea Peru 176 D6
Camocim Brazil 177 J4
Camooweal Australia 136 B3
Camooweal Caves National Park Australia 136 B4
Camorta i. India 103 H10
Camotes Sea g. Phil. 82 D4
Campamento Hond. 166 [inset] I6
Campana Mex. 166 E3
Campana, Isla i. Chile 178 A7
Campania Island Canada 150 D4
Campbell S. Africa 124 F5
Campbell, Cape N.Z. 139 E5
Campbell, Mount hill Australia 134 E5
Campbellford Canada 165 G1
Campbell Hill hill OH U.S.A. 164 D3
Campbell Island N.Z. 186 H9
Campbell Lake N.W.T. Canada 149 N1
Campbell Lake N.W.T. Canada 151 J2
Campbell Plateau sea feature S. Pacific Ocean 186 H9
Campbell Range hills Australia 134 D3
Campbell River Canada 150 E5
Campbellsville KY U.S.A. 164 C5
Campbellton Canada 153 I5
Campbelltown Australia 138 E5
Campbeltown U.K. 60 D5
Campeche Mex. 167 H5
Campeche state Mex. 167 H5
Campeche, Bahía de g. Mex. 168 F5
Camperdown Australia 138 A7
Câmpina Romania 69 K2
Campina Grande Brazil 177 K5
Campinas Brazil 179 B3
Campina Verde Brazil 179 A2
Camplong Timor Indon. 83 B5
Campo Cameroon 120 D4
Campobasso Italy 68 F4
Campo Belo Brazil 179 B3
Campo Belo do Sul Brazil 179 A4
Campo de Diauarum Brazil 177 H6
Campo Florido Brazil 179 A2
Campo Gallo Arg. 178 D3
Campo Grande Brazil 178 F2
Campo Largo Brazil 179 A4
Campo Maior Brazil 177 J4
Campo Maior Port. 67 C4
Campo Mourão Brazil 178 F2
Campos Brazil 179 C3
Campos Altos Brazil 179 B2
Campos dos Goytacazes Brazil 179 C3
Campos Novos Brazil 179 A4
Campos Sales Brazil 177 J5
Campton KY U.S.A. 164 D5
Câmpulung Romania 69 K2
Câmpulung Moldovenesc Romania 69 K1
Camp Verde AZ U.S.A. 159 H4
Camrose Canada 151 H4
Camrose U.K. 59 B7
Camsell Lake Canada 151 I2
Camsell Portage Canada 151 I3
Camsell Range mts Canada 150 F2
Camulodunum U.K. see Colchester
Çan Turkey 69 L4
Ca Na, Mui hd Vietnam 87 E5
Canaã dos Carajás Brazil 177 H5
Canaan r. Canada 153 I5
Canaan CT U.S.A. 165 I2
Canaan Peak UT U.S.A. 159 H3
Canabrava Brazil 179 B2
Canabungan i. Phil. 82 B4
Canacona India 106 B3

►Canada country N. America 146 H4
Largest country in North America and 2nd in the world. 3rd most populous country in North America.

Canada Basin sea feature Arctic Ocean 189 A1
Canadian TX U.S.A. 161 C5
Canadian r. U.S.A. 161 E5
Canadian Abyssal Plain sea feature Antarctica 189 A1
Cañadón Grande, Sierra mts Arg. 178 C7
Canaima, Parque Nacional nat. park Venez. 176 F2
Çanakkale Turkey 69 L4
Çanakkale Boğazı strait Turkey see **Dardanelles**
Canalejas Arg. 178 C5
Canal-Supe, Sacred City of tourist site Peru 176 C6
Cañamares Spain 67 E3
Canandaigua NY U.S.A. 165 G2
Cananea Mex. 166 C2
Cananéia Brazil 179 B4
Canápolis Brazil 179 A2
Cañar Ecuador 176 C4
Canarias terr. N. Atlantic Ocean see **Canary Islands**
Canárias, Ilha das i. Brazil 177 J4
Canarias, Islas terr. N. Atlantic Ocean see **Canary Islands**
Canarreos, Archipiélago de los is Cuba 169 H4

►**Canary Islands** terr. N. Atlantic Ocean 120 B2
Autonomous Community of Spain.

Canasayab Mex. 167 H5
Canaseraga NY U.S.A. 165 G2
Canastota NY U.S.A. 165 H2
Canastra, Serra da mts Goiás Brazil 179 A1
Canastra, Serra da mts Minas Gerais Brazil 179 B2
Canatiba Brazil 179 C1
Canatlán Mex. 161 B7
Canaveral, Cape FL U.S.A. 163 D6
Cañaveras Spain 67 E3
Canavieiras Brazil 179 D1
Cañazas Panama 166 [inset] J7
Canbelego Australia 138 C3

►**Canberra** Australia 138 D5
Capital of Australia and Australian Capital Territory.

Cancún Mex. 167 I4
Çandar Turkey see **Kastamonu**
Çandarlı Turkey 69 L5
Candela Mex. 167 E3
Candela r. Mex. 161 C7
Candelaria Campeche Mex. 167 H5
Candelaria Chihuahua Mex. 166 D2
Candia Greece see **Iraklion**
Cândido de Abreu Brazil 179 A4
Çandır Turkey 112 D2
Candle AK U.S.A. 148 G2
Candle Lake Canada 151 J4
Candlewood, Lake CT U.S.A. 165 I3
Cando ND U.S.A. 160 D1
Candon Luzon Phil. 82 C2
Candon Point Luzon Phil. 82 C2
Cane r. Australia 134 A5
Canea Greece see **Chania**
Canela Brazil 179 A5
Canelones Uruguay 178 E4
Cane Valley KY U.S.A. 164 C5
Cangallo Peru 176 D6
Cangamba Angola 123 B5
Cangandala, Parque Nacional de nat. park Angola 123 B4
Canglun Malaysia see **Changlun**
Cango Caves S. Africa 124 F7
Cangola Angola 123 B4
Cangshan China 95 I5
Canguaretama Brazil 177 K5
Canguçu Brazil 178 F4
Canguçu, Serra do hills Brazil 178 F4
Cangwu China 97 F4
Cangzhou China 95 I4
Caniapiscau Canada 153 H3
Caniapiscau r. Canada 153 H2
Caniapiscau, Réservoir de l. Canada 153 H3
Caniçado Moz. see **Guija**
Canicattì Sicily Italy 68 E6
Canigao Channel Phil. 82 D4
Canim Lake Canada 150 F5
Canindé Brazil 177 K4
Canisteo NY U.S.A. 165 G2
Canisteo r. NY U.S.A. 165 G2
Canisteo Peninsula Antarctica 188 K2
Cañitas de Felipe Pescador Mex. 161 C8
Çankırı Turkey 112 D2
Canlaon Negros Phil. 82 C4
Canna Australia 135 A7
Canna i. U.K. 60 C3
Cannanore India see **Kannur**
Cannanore Islands India 106 B4
Cannelton IN U.S.A. 164 B5
Cannes France 66 H5
Canning r. AK U.S.A. 149 K1
Cannock U.K. 59 E6
Cannon Beach OR U.S.A. 156 C3
Cann River Australia 138 D6
Canoas Brazil 179 A5
Canõas, Rio das r. Brazil 179 A4
Canoeiros Brazil 179 B2
Canoe Lake Canada 151 I4
Canoe Lake l. Canada 151 I4
Canoinhas Brazil 179 A4
Canon City CO U.S.A. 157 G5
Cañón del Sumidero, Parque Nacional nat. park Mex. 167 G5
Cañon Largo watercourse NM U.S.A. 159 J3
Canoona Australia 136 E4
Canora Canada 151 K5
Canowindra Australia 138 D4
Canso Canada 153 J5
Canso, Cape Canada 153 J5
Cantabrian Mountains Spain see **Cantábrica, Cordillera**
Cantábrica, Cordillera mts Spain 67 D2
Cantábrico, Mar sea Spain 67 C2
Cantagalo Brazil 179 C3
Canterbury U.K. 59 I7
Canterbury Bight b. N.Z. 139 C7
Canterbury Plains N.Z. 139 C6
Cần Thơ Vietnam 87 D5
Cantil CA U.S.A. 158 E4
Cantilan Mindanao Phil. 82 D4
Canton GA U.S.A. 163 C5
Canton IL U.S.A. 160 F3
Canton MO U.S.A. 160 F3
Canton MS U.S.A. 161 F5
Canton NY U.S.A. 165 H1
Canton OH U.S.A. 164 E3
Canton PA U.S.A. 165 G3
Canton SD U.S.A. 160 D3
Canton TX U.S.A. 161 E5
Canton Island atoll Kiribati see **Kanton**
Cantuaria U.K. see **Canterbury**
Cantwell AK U.S.A. 149 J3
Canunda National Park Australia 137 C8
Canutama Brazil 176 F5
Canutillo Mex. 161 B7
Canvey Island U.K. 59 H7
Canwood Canada 151 J4
Cany-Barville France 59 H9
Canyon TX U.S.A. 161 C5
Canyon City OR U.S.A. 156 D3
Canyon City (abandoned) Canada 149 M3
Canyondam CA U.S.A. 158 C1
Canyon de Chelly National Monument nat. park AZ U.S.A. 159 I3
Canyon Ferry Lake MT U.S.A. 156 F3
Canyon Lake AZ U.S.A. 159 H5
Canyonlands National Park UT U.S.A. 159 I2
Canyon Ranges mts Canada 149 P3
Canyons of the Ancients National Monument nat. park CO U.S.A. 159 I3
Canyonville OR U.S.A. 156 C4
Cao Bằng Vietnam 86 D2
Caocheng China see **Caoxian**
Cao Daban China 94 E4
Caohai China see **Weining**
Caohe China see **Qichun**
Caohu Xinjiang China 98 D4
Caohu Xinjiang China 98 D4
Caojiahe China see **Qichun**
Caojian China 96 C3
Caoshi China 90 B4
Caoxian China 95 H5
Caozhou China see **Heze**
Cap i. Phil. 82 C5
Capac MI U.S.A. 164 D2
Çapakçur Turkey see **Bingöl**
Capalulu, Selat sea chan. Indon. 83 C3
Capanaparo r. Venez. 176 E2
Capanema Brazil 177 I4
Capão Bonito Brazil 179 A4
Caparaó, Serra do mts Brazil 179 C3
Capas Luzon Phil. 82 C3
Cap-aux-Meules Canada 153 J5
Cap-de-la-Madeleine Canada 153 G5
Cape r. Australia 136 D4
Cape Arid National Park Australia 135 C8
Cape Barren Island Australia 137 [inset]
Cape Basin sea feature S. Atlantic Ocean 184 I8
Cape Breton Highlands National Park Canada 153 J5
Cape Breton Island Canada 153 J5
Cape Charles Canada 153 L3
Cape Charles VA U.S.A. 165 G5
Cape Coast Ghana 120 C4
Cape Coast Castle Ghana see **Cape Coast**
Cape Cod Bay MA U.S.A. 165 J3
Cape Cod National Seashore nature res. MA U.S.A. 165 K3
Cape Coral FL U.S.A. 163 D7
Cape Crawford Australia 136 A3
Cape Dorset Canada 147 K3
Cape Fanshaw AK U.S.A. 149 N4
Cape Fear r. NC U.S.A. 163 E5
Cape Girdeau at Fort Glenn AK U.S.A. 148 F5
Cape George Canada 153 J5
Cape Girardeau MO U.S.A. 161 F4
Cape Johnson Depth sea feature N. Pacific Ocean 186 E5
Cape Juby Morocco see **Tarfaya**
Cape Krusenstern National Monument nat. park AK U.S.A. 148 G2
Capel Australia 135 A8
Cape Le Grand National Park Australia 135 C8
Capelinha Brazil 179 C2
Capella Australia 136 E4
Capelle aan den IJssel Neth. 62 E3
Capelongo Angola see **Kuvango**
Cape May NJ U.S.A. 165 H4
Cape May Court House NJ U.S.A. 165 H4
Cape May Point NJ U.S.A. 165 H4
Cape Melville National Park Australia 136 D2
Capenda-Camulemba Angola 123 B4
Cape Palmerston National Park Australia 136 E4
Cape Range National Park Australia 134 A5
Cape St George Canada 153 K4

►**Cape Town** S. Africa 124 D7
Legislative capital of South Africa.

Cape Tribulation National Park Australia 136 D2
Cape Upstart National Park Australia 136 D3
Cape Verde country Africa 120 [inset]
Cape Verde Basin sea feature N. Atlantic Ocean 184 F5
Cape Verde Plateau sea feature N. Atlantic Ocean 184 F4
Cape Vincent NY U.S.A. 165 G1
Cape Yakataga AK U.S.A. 149 L3
Cape York Peninsula Australia 136 C2
Cap-Haïtien Haiti 169 J5
Capim r. Brazil 177 I4

►**Capitol Hill** N. Mariana Is 81 L3
Capital of the Northern Mariana Islands, on Saipan.

Capitol Reef National Park UT U.S.A. 159 H2
Capivara, Represa resr Brazil 179 A3
Čapljina Bos. & Herz. 68 G3
Cappadocia reg. Turkey 112 D3
Cappoquin Ireland 61 E5
Capraia, Isola di i. Italy 68 C3
Caprara, Punta pt Sardinia Italy 68 C4
Capri, Isola di i. Italy 68 F4
Capricorn Channel Australia 136 E4
Capricorn Group atolls Australia 136 F4
Caprivi Strip reg. Namibia 123 C5
Cap Rock Escarpment TX U.S.A. 161 C5
Capsa Tunisia see **Gafsa**
Captain Cook HI U.S.A. 157 [inset]
Captina r. OH U.S.A. 164 E4
Capuava Brazil 179 B4
Caquetá r. Col. 176 E4
Carabao i. Phil. 82 C3
Caracal Romania 69 K2

►**Caracas** Venez. 176 E1
Capital of Venezuela.

Caraga Mindanao Phil. 82 D5
Caraguatatuba Brazil 179 B3
Caraí Brazil 179 C2
Carajás, Serra dos hills Brazil 177 H5
Carales Sardinia Italy see **Cagliari**
Caralis Sardinia Italy see **Cagliari**
Caramoan Peninsula Luzon Phil. 82 C3
Carandaí Brazil 179 C3
Caransebeş Romania 69 J2
Caraquet Canada 153 I5
Carat, Tanjung pt Indon. 84 D3
Caratasca Hond. 166 [inset] J6
Caratasca, Laguna de lag. Hond. 166 [inset] J6
Caratinga Brazil 179 C2
Carauari Brazil 176 E4
Caravaca de la Cruz Spain 67 F4
Caravelas Brazil 179 D2
Carberry Canada 151 L5
Carbó Mex. 166 C2
Carbon, Cap hd Alg. 67 F6

►**Carbón, Laguna del** l. Arg. 178 C7
Lowest point in South America.

Carbonara, Capo c. Sardinia Italy 68 C5
Carbondale CO U.S.A. 159 J2
Carbondale PA U.S.A. 165 H3
Carboneras Mex. 161 D7
Carbonia Sardinia Italy 68 C5
Carbonita Brazil 179 C2
Carcaixent Spain 67 F4
Carcajou Canada 150 G3
Carcajou r. Canada 149 O2
Carcar Cebu Phil. 82 C4
Carcassonne France 66 F5
Carcross Canada 149 N3
Cardamomes, Chaîne des mts Cambodia/Thai. see **Cardamom Range**
Cardamom Hills India 106 C4
Cardamom Range mts Cambodia/Thai. 87 C4
Cárdenas Cuba 169 H4
Cárdenas San Luis Potosí Mex. 168 E4
Cárdenas Tabasco Mex. 167 G5
Cardenyabba watercourse Australia 138 A2
Çardi Turkey see **Harmancık**
Cardiel, Lago l. Arg. 178 B7

►**Cardiff** U.K. 59 D7
Capital of Wales.

Cardiff MD U.S.A. 165 G4
Cardigan U.K. 59 C6
Cardigan Bay U.K. 59 C6
Cardinal Lake Canada 150 G3
Cardington OH U.S.A. 164 D3
Cardón, Cerro hill Mex. 166 B3
Cardoso Brazil 179 A3
Cardoso, Ilha do i. Brazil 179 B4
Cardston Canada 150 H5
Careen Lake Canada 151 I3
Carei Romania 69 J1
Carentan France 66 D2
Carey OH U.S.A. 164 D3
Carey, Lake salt flat Australia 135 C7
Carey Lake Canada 151 K2
Cargados Carajos Islands Mauritius 185 L7
Carhaix-Plouguer France 66 C2
Cariacica Brazil 179 C3
Cariamanga Ecuador 176 C4
Caribbean Sea N. Atlantic Ocean 169 H5
Cariboo Mountains Canada 150 F4
Caribou r. Man. Canada 151 M3
Caribou r. N.W.T. Canada 149 P3
Caribou r. Y.T. Canada 149 N2
Caribou AK U.S.A. 149 K2
Caribou ME U.S.A. 162 G2
Caribou Lake Canada 147 J4
Caribou Mountains Canada 150 H3
Carichic Mex. 166 D3
Carigara Leyte Phil. 82 D4
Carignan France 62 F5
Carinda Australia 138 C3
Cariñena Spain 67 F3
Carinhanha r. Brazil 179 C1
Carlabhagh U.K. see **Carloway**
Carleton MI U.S.A. 164 D2
Carleton, Mount hill Canada 153 I5
Carletonville S. Africa 125 H4
Carlin NV U.S.A. 158 E1
Carlingford Lough inlet Ireland/U.K. 61 F3
Carlini research station Antarctica 188 A2
Carlinville IL U.S.A. 160 F4
Carlisle U.K. 58 E4
Carlisle IN U.S.A. 164 B4
Carlisle KY U.S.A. 164 C4
Carlisle NY U.S.A. 165 H2
Carlisle PA U.S.A. 165 G3
Carlisle Lakes salt flat Australia 135 D7
Carlit, Pic mt. France 66 E5
Carlos Chagas Brazil 179 C2
Carlow Ireland 61 F5
Carloway U.K. 60 C2
Carlsbad Czech Rep. see **Karlovy Vary**
Carlsbad CA U.S.A. 158 E5
Carlsbad NM U.S.A. 157 G6
Carlsbad TX U.S.A. 167 E2
Carlsbad Caverns National Park NM U.S.A. 157 G6
Carlsberg Ridge sea feature Indian Ocean 185 L5
Carlson Inlet Antarctica 188 L1
Carlton MN U.S.A. 160 E2
Carlton Hill Australia 134 E3
Carluke U.K. 60 F5
Carlyle Canada 151 K5
Carmacks Canada 149 M3
Carmagnola Italy 68 B2
Carman Canada 151 L5
Carmana Iran see **Kermān**
Carmarthen U.K. 59 C7
Carmarthen Bay U.K. 59 C7
Carmaux France 66 F4
Carmel IN U.S.A. 164 B4
Carmel NY U.S.A. 165 I3
Carmel, Mount hill Israel 107 B3
Carmel Head hd U.K. 58 C5
Carmelita Guat. 167 H5
Carmel Valley CA U.S.A. 158 C3
Carmen Mex. 167 E3
Carmen r. Mex. 166 D2
Carmen Bohol Phil. 82 D4
Carmen AZ U.S.A. 157 F7
Carmen, Isla i. Mex. 166 C3
Carmen, Isla del i. Mex. 167 H5
Carmen de Patagones Arg. 178 D6
Carmi IL U.S.A. 160 F4
Carmichael CA U.S.A. 158 C2
Carmo da Cachoeira Brazil 179 B3
Carmo do Paranaíba Brazil 179 B2
Carmona Angola see **Uíge**
Carmona Hond. 166 [inset] I7
Carmona Spain 67 D5
Carnac France 66 C3
Carnamah Australia 135 A7
Carnarvon Australia 135 A6
Carnarvon S. Africa 124 F6
Carnarvon National Park Australia 136 D5
Carnarvon Range hills Australia 135 C6
Carnarvon Range mts Australia 136 E5
Carn Dearg hill U.K. 60 E3
Carndonagh Ireland 61 E2
Carnegie Australia 135 C6
Carnegie, Lake salt flat Australia 135 C6
Carn Eige mt. U.K. 60 D3
Carnes Australia 135 F7
Carney Island Antarctica 188 J2
Carnforth U.K. 58 E4
Carn Glas-choire hill U.K. 60 F3
Car Nicobar i. India 87 A5
Carnlough U.K. 61 G3
Carn nan Gabhar mt. U.K. 60 F4
Carn Odhar hill U.K. 60 E3
Carnot Cent. Afr. Rep. 122 B3
Carnoustie U.K. 60 G4
Carnsore Point Ireland 61 F5
Carnwath r. Canada 149 O1
Carnwath U.K. 60 F5
Caro AK U.S.A. 149 J2
Caro MI U.S.A. 164 D2
Carola Cay reef Australia 136 F3
Carol City FL U.S.A. 163 D7
Carolina Brazil 177 I5
Carolina S. Africa 125 J4
Carolina Beach NC U.S.A. 163 E5
Caroline Canada 150 H4
Caroline Island atoll Kiribati 187 J6
Caroline Islands N. Pacific Ocean 81 K5
Caroline Peak N.Z. 139 A7
Caroline Range hills Australia 134 D4
Carolingian Westwork and Civitas Corvey tourist site Germany 63 J3
Caroní r. Venez. 176 F2
Carp Canada 165 G1
Carpathian Mountains Europe 53 C6
Carpaţii mts Europe see **Carpathian Mountains**
Carpaţii Meridionali mts Romania see **Transylvanian Alps**
Carpaţii Occidentali mts Romania 69 J2
Carpentaria, Gulf of Australia 136 B2
Carpentras France 66 G4
Carpi Italy 68 D2
Carpinteria CA U.S.A. 158 D4
Carpio ND U.S.A. 160 C1
Carra, Lough l. Ireland 61 C4
Carraig na Siuire Ireland see **Carrick-on-Suir**
Carrantuohill mt. Ireland 61 C6
Carrara Italy 68 D2
Carrasco, Parque Nacional nat. park Bol. 176 F7
Carrathool Australia 138 B5
Carrhae Turkey see **Harran**
Carrickfergus U.K. 61 G3
Carrickmacross Ireland 61 F4
Carrick-on-Shannon Ireland 61 D4
Carrick-on-Suir Ireland 61 E5
Carrigallen Ireland 61 E4
Carrigtohill Ireland 61 D6
Carrillo Mex. 166 E3
Carrington ND U.S.A. 160 D2
Carrizal Mex. 166 D2
Carrizal Bajo Chile 178 B3
Carrizo AZ U.S.A. 159 H4
Carrizo Creek r. TX U.S.A. 161 C4
Carrizos Mex. 167 F3
Carrizo Springs TX U.S.A. 161 D6
Carrizo Wash watercourse Arizona/New Mexico U.S.A. 159 I4
Carrizozo NM U.S.A. 157 G6
Carroll IA U.S.A. 160 E3
Carrollton AL U.S.A. 161 F5
Carrollton GA U.S.A. 163 C5
Carrollton IL U.S.A. 160 F4
Carrollton KY U.S.A. 164 C4
Carrollton MO U.S.A. 160 E4
Carrollton OH U.S.A. 164 E3
Carrolltown PA U.S.A. 165 F3
Carron r. U.K. 60 E3
Carrot r. Canada 151 K4
Carrothers OH U.S.A. 164 D3
Carrot River Canada 151 K4
Carrowmore Lake Ireland 61 C3
Carrsville VA U.S.A. 165 G5
Carruthers Lake Canada 151 K2
Carry Falls Reservoir NY U.S.A. 165 H1
Çarşamba Turkey 112 E2
Carson r. NV U.S.A. 158 D2
Carson City MI U.S.A. 164 C2

►**Carson City** NV U.S.A. 158 D2
Capital of Nevada.

Carson Escarpment Australia 134 D3
Carson Lake NV U.S.A. 158 D2
Carson Sink l. NV U.S.A. 158 D2
Carstensz Pyramid mt. Indon. see **Jaya, Puncak**
Carstensz-top mt. Indon. see **Jaya, Puncak**
Carswell Lake Canada 151 I3
Cartagena Col. 176 C1
Cartagena Spain 67 F5
Cartago Costa Rica 166 [inset] J7
Carteret Group is P.N.G. see **Kilinailau Islands**
Carteret Island Solomon Is see **Malaita**
Cartersville GA U.S.A. 163 C5
Carthage tourist site Tunisia 68 D6
Carthage MO U.S.A. 161 E4
Carthage NC U.S.A. 163 E5
Carthage NY U.S.A. 165 H2
Carthage TX U.S.A. 161 E5
Carthago tourist site Tunisia see **Carthage**
Carthago Nova Spain see **Cartagena**
Cartier Island Australia 134 C3
Cartmel U.K. 58 E4
Cartwright Man. Canada 151 L5
Cartwright Nfld. and Lab. Canada 153 K3
Caruarú Brazil 177 K5
Carúpano Venez. 176 F1
Caruthersville MO U.S.A. 161 F4
Carver KY U.S.A. 164 D5
Carvin France 62 C4
Cary NC U.S.A. 162 E5
Caryapundy Swamp Australia 137 C6
Casablanca Morocco 64 C5
Casa Branca Brazil 179 B3
Casa de Janos Mex. 166 C2
Casadepaga AK U.S.A. 148 F2
Casa de Piedra, Embalse resr Arg. 178 C5
Casa Grande AZ U.S.A. 159 H5
Casale Monferrato Italy 68 C2
Casalmaggiore Italy 68 D2
Casares Nicaragua 166 [inset] I7
Casas Grandes Mex. 166 D2
Casas Grandes r. Mex. 166 D2
Casca Brazil 179 A5
Cascade Australia 135 C8
Cascade r. N.Z. 139 B7
Cascade ID U.S.A. 156 D3
Cascade MT U.S.A. 156 F3
Cascade Point N.Z. 139 B7
Cascade Range mts Canada/U.S.A. 156 C4
Cascade Reservoir ID U.S.A. 156 D3
Cascais Port. 67 B4
Cascal, Paso del pass Nicaragua 166 [inset] I7
Cascavel Brazil 178 F2
Casco Bay ME U.S.A. 165 K2
Caserta Italy 68 F4
Casey research station Antarctica 188 F2
Casey Bay Antarctica 188 D2
Caseyr, Raas c. Somalia see **Gwardafuy, Gees**
Cashel Ireland 61 E5
Cashmere Australia 138 D1
Casiguran Luzon Phil. 82 C2
Casiguran Sound sea chan. Luzon Phil. 82 C2
Casino Australia 138 F2
Casiquiare, Canal r. Venez. 176 E3
Casita Mex. 157 F7
Casnewydd U.K. see **Newport**
Casogoran Bay Phil. 82 D4
Caspe Spain 67 F3
Casper WY U.S.A. 156 G4
Caspian Lowland Kazakh./Russia 100 D2

►**Caspian Sea** l. Asia/Europe 113 H1
Largest lake in Asia/Europe and the world, and lowest point in Europe.

Cass WV U.S.A. 164 F4
Cass r. MI U.S.A. 164 D2
Cassacatiza Moz. 123 D5
Cassadaga NY U.S.A. 164 F2
Cassaigne Alg. see **Sidi Ali**
Cassamba Angola 123 C5
Cass City MI U.S.A. 164 D2
Cassel France 62 C4
Casselman Canada 165 H1
Cássia Brazil 179 B3
Cassiar (abandoned) Canada 149 O4
Cassiar Mountains Canada 149 O4
Cassilândia Brazil 179 A2
Cassilis Australia 138 D4
Cassino Italy 68 E4
Cassley r. U.K. 60 E3
Cassongue Angola 123 B5
Cassopolis MI U.S.A. 164 B3
Cassville MO U.S.A. 161 E4
Castanhal Brazil 177 I4
Castanho Brazil 176 F5
Castaños Mex. 167 E3
Castelfranco Veneto Italy 68 D2
Castell-nedd U.K. see **Neath**
Castell Newydd Emlyn U.K. see **Newcastle Emlyn**
Castellón Spain see **Castellón de la Plana**
Castellón de la Plana Spain 67 F4
Castelo Branco Port. 67 C4
Castelo de Vide Port. 67 C4
Casteltermini Sicily Italy 68 E6
Castelvetrano Sicily Italy 68 E6
Castiglione della Pescaia Italy 68 D3
Castignon, Lac l. Canada 153 H2
Castilla y León reg. Spain 66 B6
Castlebar Ireland 61 C4
Castlebay U.K. 60 B4
Castlebellingham Ireland 61 F4
Castleblayney Ireland 61 F3
Castlebridge Ireland 61 F5
Castle Carrock U.K. 58 E4
Castle Cary U.K. 59 E7
Castle Dale UT U.S.A. 159 H2
Castlederg U.K. 61 E3
Castledermot Ireland 61 F5
Castle Dome Mountains AZ U.S.A. 159 F5
Castle Donington U.K. 59 F6
Castle Douglas U.K. 60 F6
Castleford U.K. 58 F5
Castlegar Canada 150 G5
Castlegregory Ireland 61 B5
Castle Island Bahamas 163 F8
Castleisland Ireland 61 C5
Castlemaine Australia 138 B6
Castlemaine Ireland 61 C5
Castlemartyr Ireland 61 D6
Castle Mountain Alta Canada 150 H5
Castle Mountain Y.T. Canada 149 N2
Castle Mountain CA U.S.A. 158 C4
Castle Peak hill H.K. China 97 [inset]
Castle Peak Bay H.K. China 97 [inset]
Castlepoint N.Z. 139 F5
Castlepollard Ireland 61 E4
Castlerea Ireland 61 D4
Castlereagh r. Australia 138 C3
Castle Rock CO U.S.A. 156 G5
Castletown Ireland 61 E5
Castletown Isle of Man 58 C4
Castor Canada 151 I4
Castor r. MO U.S.A. 161 F4
Castor, Rivière du r. Canada 152 F3
Castra Regina Germany see **Regensburg**
Castres France 66 F5
Castricum Neth. 62 E2

►**Castries** St Lucia 169 L6
Capital of St Lucia.

Castro Brazil 179 A4
Castro Chile 178 B6
Castro Alves Brazil 179 D1
Castro Verde Port. 67 B5
Castroville CA U.S.A. 158 C3
Caswell AK U.S.A. 149 J3
Çat Turkey 113 F3
Catacamas Hond. 166 [inset] I6
Catacaos Peru 176 B5
Cataguases Brazil 179 C3
Catahoula Lake LA U.S.A. 161 E6
Cataingan Masbate Phil. 82 C3
Çatak Turkey 113 F3
Catalão Brazil 179 B2
Çatalca Yarımadası pen. Turkey 69 M4
Çatal Hüyük tourist site Turkey 112 D3
Catalina AZ U.S.A. 159 H5
Catalonia aut. comm. Spain see **Cataluña**
Cataluña aut. comm. Spain 67 G3
Catalunya aut. comm. Spain see **Cataluña**
Catamarca Arg. 178 C3
Catana Sicily Italy see **Catania**
Catanauan Luzon Phil. 82 C3
Catanduanes i. Phil. 82 D3
Catanduva Brazil 179 A3
Catania Sicily Italy 68 F6
Catanzaro Italy 68 G5
Cataract Creek watercourse AZ U.S.A. 159 G3
Catarina TX U.S.A. 161 D6
Catarina, Raso da hills Brazil 177 K5
Catarino Rodríguez Mex. 167 E3
Catarman Samar Phil. 82 D3
Catarman Point Mindanao Phil. 82 D5
Catastrophe, Cape Australia 137 A7
Catawba r. SC U.S.A. 163 D5
Cataxa Moz. 123 D5
Cat Ba, Đao i. Vietnam 86 D2
Catbalogan Samar Phil. 82 D4
Cateel Mindanao Phil. 82 D5
Cateel Bay Mindanao Phil. 82 D5
Catemaco Mex. 167 G5
Catembe Moz. 125 K4
Catengue Angola 123 B5
Catete Angola 123 B4
Cathair Dónall Ireland 61 B6
Cathcart Australia 138 D6
Cathcart S. Africa 125 H7
Cathedral Peak S. Africa 125 I5
Cathedral Rock National Park Australia 138 F3
Catherine, Mount UT U.S.A. 159 G2

Catheys Valley CA U.S.A. 158 C3
Cathlamet WA U.S.A. 156 C3
Catió Guinea-Bissau 120 B3
Catisimiña Venez. 176 F3
Cat Island Bahamas 163 F7
Cat Lake Canada 151 N5
Catlettsburg KY U.S.A. 164 D4
Catoche, Cabo c. Mex. 167 I4
Cato Island and Bank reef Australia 136 F4
Catorce Mex. 167 E4
Catriló Arg. 178 D5
Cats, Mont des hill France 62 C4
Catskill NY U.S.A. 165 I2
Catskill Mountains NY U.S.A. 165 H2
Catuane Moz. 125 K4
Cauayan Negros Phil. 82 C4
Caubvick, Mount Canada 153 J2
Cauca r. Col. 169 J7
Caucaia Brazil 177 K4
Caucasia Col. 176 C2
Caucasus mts Asia/Europe 113 F2
Cauchon Lake Canada 151 L4
Caudry France 62 D4
Câu Giat Vietnam 86 D3
Cauit Point Mindanao Phil. 82 D4
Caulonia Italy 68 G5
Caungula Angola 123 B4
Cauquenes Chile 178 B5
Causapscal Canada 153 I4
Cavaglià Italy 68 C2
Cavalcante, Serra do hills Brazil 179 B1
Cavalier ND U.S.A. 160 D1
Cavan Ireland 61 E4
Çavdır Turkey 69 M6
Cave City KY U.S.A. 164 C5
Cave Creek AZ U.S.A. 159 H5
Caveira r. Brazil 179 C1
Cavern Island Myanmar 87 B5
Cave Run Lake KY U.S.A. 164 D4
Caviana, Ilha i. Brazil 177 H3
Cavili reef Phil. 82 C4
Cavite Luzon Phil. 82 C3
Cawdor U.K. 60 F3
Cawnpore India see Kanpur
Cawston U.K. 59 I6
Caxias Brazil 177 J4
Caxias do Sul Brazil 179 A5
Caxito Angola 123 B4
Çay Turkey 69 N5
Cayambe, Volcán vol. Ecuador 176 C3
Çaybaşı Turkey see Çayeli
Çaycuma Turkey 69 O4
Çayeli Turkey 113 F2

▶Cayenne Fr. Guiana 177 H3
Capital of French Guiana.

Cayeux-sur-Mer France 62 B4
Çayırhan Turkey 69 N4
Cayman Brac i. Cayman Is 169 I5

▶Cayman Islands terr. West Indies 169 H5
United Kingdom Overseas Territory.

Cayman Trench sea feature Caribbean Sea 184 C4
Caynaba Somalia 122 E3
Cay Sal i. Bahamas 163 D8
Cay Sal Bank sea feature Bahamas 163 D8
Cay Santa Domingo i. Bahamas 163 F8
Cayucos CA U.S.A. 158 C4
Cayuga Canada 164 F2
Cayuga Lake NY U.S.A. 165 G2
Cay Verde i. Bahamas 163 F8
Cazê China 99 D7
Cazenovia NY U.S.A. 165 H2
Cazombo Angola 123 C5
Ceadâr-Lunga Moldova see Ciadîr-Lunga
Ceanannus Mór Ireland see Kells
Ceará Brazil see Fortaleza
Ceara Abyssal Plain sea feature S. Atlantic Ocean 184 F6
Ceatharlach Ireland see Carlow
Ceballos Mex. 166 D3
Ceboruco, Volcán vol. Mex. 166 D4
Cebu Cebu Phil. 82 C4
Cebu i. Phil. 82 C4
Čechy reg. Czech Rep. 57 N6
Cecil Plains Australia 138 E1
Cecil Rhodes, Mount hill Australia 135 C6
Cecina Italy 68 D3
Cedar r. ND U.S.A. 160 C2
Cedar r. NE U.S.A. 160 D3
Cedar City UT U.S.A. 159 G3
Cedar Creek Reservoir TX U.S.A. 167 F1
Cedaredge CO U.S.A. 159 J2
Cedar Falls IA U.S.A. 160 E3
Cedar Grove WI U.S.A. 164 B2
Cedar Hill NM U.S.A. 159 J3
Cedar Hill TN U.S.A. 164 B5
Cedar Island VA U.S.A. 165 H5
Cedar Lake Canada 151 K4
Cedar Point OH U.S.A. 164 D3
Cedar Rapids IA U.S.A. 160 F3
Cedar Run NJ U.S.A. 165 H4
Cedar Springs MI U.S.A. 164 C2
Cedartown GA U.S.A. 163 C5
Cedarville S. Africa 125 I6
Cedeño Hond. 166 [inset] I6
Cedral Quintana Roo Mex. 167 I4
Cedral San Luis Potosí Mex. 167 E4
Cedros Hond. 166 [inset] I6
Cedros Sonora Mex. 166 C3
Cedros Zacatecas Mex. 167 E3
Cedros, Cerro mt. Mex. 157 E7
Cedros, Isla i. Mex. 166 B2
Ceduna Australia 135 F8
Ceeldheere Somalia 122 E3
Ceerigaabo Somalia 122 E2
Cefalù Sicily Italy 68 F5
Cegléd Hungary 69 H1
Cêgnê China 99 F6
Ceheng China 96 E3
Çekerek Turkey 112 D2
Çekiçler Turkm. 110 D2
Celah, Gunung mt. Malaysia see Mandi Angin, Gunung
Celaque, Parque Nacional nat. park Hond. 167 H6
Celaya Mex. 168 D4
Celbridge Ireland 61 F4

▶Celebes i. Indon. 83 B3
4th largest island in Asia.

Celebes Basin sea feature Pacific Ocean 186 E5
Celebes Sea Indon./Phil. 81 G6
Celestún Mex. 167 H4
Celina OH U.S.A. 164 C3
Celina TN U.S.A. 164 C5
Celje Slovenia 68 F1
Celle Germany 63 K2
Celovec Austria see Klagenfurt am Wörthersee
Celtic Sea Ireland/U.K. 56 D5
Celtic Shelf sea feature N. Atlantic Ocean 184 H2
Cemaru, Gunung mt. Indon. 85 F2
Çemenibit Turkm. 111 F3
Cempi, Teluk b. Sumbawa Indon. 85 G5
Cenderawasih, Teluk b. Indon. 81 J7
Çendir r. Turkm. 110 D2
Cenrana Celebes Indon. 83 A3
Centane S. Africa 125 I7
Centenary Zimbabwe 123 D5
Center NE U.S.A. 160 D3
Center TX U.S.A. 161 E6
Centereach NY U.S.A. 165 I3
Center Point AL U.S.A. 163 C5
Centerville IA U.S.A. 160 E3
Centerville MO U.S.A. 161 F4
Centerville TX U.S.A. 161 E6
Centerville WV U.S.A. 164 E4
Centrafricaine, République country Africa see Central African Republic
Central admin. dist. Botswana 125 H2
Central AK U.S.A. 149 K2
Central, Cordillera mts Col. 176 C3
Central, Cordillera mts Panama 166 [inset] J7
Central, Cordillera mts Peru 176 C6
Central, Cordillera mts Luzon Phil. 82 C2
Central African Empire country Africa see Central African Republic
Central African Republic country Africa 122 B3
Central Brahui Range mts Pak. 111 G4
Central Butte Canada 156 G2
Central City NE U.S.A. 160 D3
Centralia IL U.S.A. 160 F4
Centralia WA U.S.A. 156 C3
Central Kalahari Game Reserve nature res. Botswana 124 F2
Central Kara Rise sea feature Arctic Ocean 189 F1
Central Makran Range mts Pak. 111 G5
Central Mount Stuart hill Australia 134 F5
Central Pacific Basin sea feature Pacific Ocean 186 H5
Central Provinces state India see Madhya Pradesh
Central Range mts P.N.G. 81 K7
Central Russian Upland hills Russia 53 H5
Central Siberian Plateau Russia 77 M3
Central Square NY U.S.A. 165 G2
Centre AL U.S.A. 163 C5
Centreville AL U.S.A. 163 C5
Centreville MD U.S.A. 165 G4
Cenxi China 97 F4
Cenyang China see Hengfeng
Ceos i. Greece see Tzia
Cephaloedium Sicily Italy see Cefalù
Cephalonia i. Greece 69 I5
Cepu Java Indon. 85 E4
Ceram i. Moluccas Indon. see Seram
Ceram Sea Indon. see Seram, Laut
Cerbat Mountains AZ U.S.A. 159 F4
Čerchov mt. Czech Rep. 63 M5
Ceres Arg. 178 D3
Ceres Brazil 179 A1
Ceres S. Africa 124 D7
Ceres CA U.S.A. 158 C3
Céret France 66 F5
Cerezo de Abajo Spain 67 E3
Cêri China 99 D7
Cerignola Italy 68 F4
Cerigo i. Greece see Kythira
Cêringgolêb China see Dongco
Çerkeş Turkey 112 D2
Çerkeşli Turkey 69 M4
Çermik Turkey 113 E3
Cernăuţi Ukr. see Chernivtsi
Cernavodă Romania 69 M2
Cerralvo Mex. 167 F3
Cerralvo, Isla i. Mex. 166 C3
Cërrik Albania 69 H4
Cerritos Mex. 168 D4
Cerro Azul Brazil 179 A4
Cerro Azul Mex. 167 F4
Cerro de Pasco Peru 176 C6
Cerro Hoya, Parque Nacional nat. park Panama 166 [inset] J8
Cerro Prieto Mex. 166 D3
Cerros Colorados, Embalse resr Arg. 178 C5
Cervantes, Cerro mt. Arg. 178 B8
Cervati, Monte mt. Italy 68 F4
Cervione Corsica France 66 I5
Cervo Spain 67 C2
Cesena Italy 68 E2
Cēsis Latvia 55 N8
Česká Republika country Europe see Czech Republic
České Budějovice Czech Rep. 57 O6
Českomoravská vysočina hills Czech Rep. 57 O6
Český Krumlov Czech Rep. 57 O6
Český les mts Czech Rep./Germany 63 M5
Çeşme Turkey 69 L5
Cessnock Australia 138 E4
Cetaceo, Mount Luzon Phil. 82 C2
Cêtar China 94 E4
Cetatea Albă Ukr. see Bilhorod-Dnistrovs'kyy
Cetinje Montenegro 68 H3
Cetraro Italy 68 F5

▶Ceuta N. Africa 67 D6
Autonomous Community of Spain.

Ceva-i-Ra reef Fiji 133 H4
Cévennes mts France 66 F5
Cévennes, Parc National des nat. park France 66 F4
Cevizli Turkey 107 C1
Cevizlik Turkey see Maçka
Ceyhan Turkey 112 D3
Ceyhan r. Turkey 107 B1
Ceyhan Boğazı r. mouth Turkey 107 B1
Ceylanpınar Turkey 113 F3
Ceylon country Asia see Sri Lanka
Chābahār Iran 111 F5
Chablé Mex. 167 H5
Chabrol i. New Caledonia see Lifou
Chabug China 99 C6
Chabyêr Caka salt l. China 99 D7
Chachapoyas Peru 176 C5
Chacharan Pak. 111 H4
Chäche Turkm. see Çäçe
Chachoengsao Thai. 87 C4
Chachro Pak. 111 H5
Chaco r. NM U.S.A. 159 I3
Chaco Boreal reg. Para. 178 E2
Chaco Culture National Historical Park nat. park NM U.S.A. 159 J3
Chaco Mesa plat. NM U.S.A. 159 J4

▶Chad country Africa 121 E3
5th largest country in Africa.

Chad, Lake Africa 121 E3
Chadaasan Mongolia 94 E2
Chadan Russia 102 H1
Chadibe Botswana 125 H2
Chadron NE U.S.A. 160 C3
Chadyr-Lunga Moldova see Ciadîr-Lunga
Chae Hom Thai. 86 B3
Chaek Kyrg. 98 A4
Chaeryŏng N. Korea 91 B5
Chae Son National Park Thai. 86 B3
Chagai Pak. 111 G4
Chagai Hills Afgh./Pak. 111 F4
Chaganuzun Russia 98 E2
Chagdo Kangri mt. China 105 F2
Chaggur China 99 F6
Chaghcharān Afgh. 111 G3
Chagny France 66 G3
Chagoda Russia 52 G4
Chagos Archipelago is B.I.O.T. 185 M6
Chagos-Laccadive Ridge sea feature Indian Ocean 185 M6
Chagos Trench sea feature Indian Ocean 185 M6
Chagoyan Russia 90 C1
Chagrayskoye Plato plat. Kazakh. see Shagyray, Plato
Chagres, Parque Nacional nat. park Panama 166 [inset] K7
Chagyoi China 96 C2
Chāh Āb Afgh. 111 H2
Chāh Ākhvor Iran 111 E3
Chāh 'Alī Akbar Iran 110 E3
Chahār Borj Iran 110 E2
Chahār Kent Afgh. 111 G2
Chahbounia Alg. 67 H6
Chahchaheh Turkm. 111 F2
Chāh-e Bāzargānī Iran 110 D4
Chāh-e Dow Chāhī Iran 110 D4
Chāh-e Khoshāb Iran 110 E3
Chāh-e Rāh Iran 110 D4
Chāh Kūh Iran 110 D4
Chāh Lak Iran 110 E5
Chah Sandan Pak. 111 F4
Chahuites Mex. 167 G5
Chaibasa India 105 F5
Chaigneau, Lac l. Canada 153 I3
Chaigoubu China see Huai'an
Chaihe China 95 J2
Chainat Thai. 86 C4
Chainjoin Co l. China 99 D6
Chai Prakan Thai. 86 B3
Chaitén Chile 178 B6
Chai Wan H.K. China 97 [inset]
Chaiwopu China 98 D4
Chaiya Thai. 87 B5
Chaiyaphum Thai. 86 C4
Chajarí Arg. 178 E4
Chakachamna Lake AK U.S.A. 148 I3
Chakai India 105 F4
Chak Amru Pak. 111 I3
Chakar r. Pak. 111 H4
Chakaria Bangl. 105 H5
Chakdarra Pak. 111 I3
Chakku Pak. 111 G5
Chakonipau, Lac l. Canada 153 H2
Chakoria Bangl. see Chakaria
Chakvi Georgia 113 F2
Chala Peru 176 D7
Chalatenango El Salvador 166 [inset] H6
Chaláua Moz. 123 D5
Chalaxung China 94 D5
Chalcedon Turkey see Kadıköy
Chalengkou China 99 F5
Chaleur Bay inlet Canada 153 I4
Chaleurs, Baie des inlet Canada see Chaleur Bay
Chali China 96 C2
Chaling China 97 G3
Chalisgaon India 106 B1
Chalki i. Greece 69 L6
Chalkida Greece 69 J5
Chalkyitsik AK U.S.A. 149 L2
Challakere India 106 C3
Challans France 66 D3
Challapata Bol. 176 E7

▶Challenger Deep sea feature N. Pacific Ocean 186 F5
Deepest point in the world (Mariana Trench).

Challenger Fracture Zone sea feature S. Pacific Ocean 186 M8
Challis ID U.S.A. 156 E3
Chalmette LA U.S.A. 161 F6
Châlons-en-Champagne France 62 E6
Châlons-sur-Marne France see Châlons-en-Champagne
Chalon-sur-Saône France 66 G3
Chālūs Iran 110 C2
Cham Germany 63 M5
Cham, Cu Lao i. Vietnam 86 E4
Cham, Kūh-e hill Iran 110 C3
Chamah, Gunung mt. Malaysia 84 C1
Chamaico Arg. 178 D5
Chamais Bay Namibia 124 B4
Chaman Pak. 100 F3
Chaman Bīd Iran 110 E2
Chamao, Khao mt. Thai. 87 C4
Chamarajanagar India 106 C4
Chamba India 104 D2
Chamba Tanz. 123 D5
Chambal r. India 104 D4
Chambas Cuba 163 E8
Chambeaux, Lac l. Canada 153 H3
Chamberlain r. Australia 134 D4
Chamberlain Canada 151 J5
Chamberlain SD U.S.A. 160 D3
Chamberlain Lake ME U.S.A. 162 G2
Chamberlin, Mount AK U.S.A. 149 K1
Chambers AZ U.S.A. 159 I4
Chambersburg PA U.S.A. 165 G4
Chambers Island WI U.S.A. 164 B1
Chambéry France 66 G4
Chambeshi r. Zambia 123 C5
Chambi, Jebel mt. Tunisia 68 C7
Chambūk Iran 110 E3
Chamda China 99 E7
Chamdo China see Qamdo
Chame Panama 166 [inset] K7
Chamechaude mt. France 66 G4
Chamela Mex. 166 D5
Chamiss Bay Canada 150 E5
Chamoli India see Gopeshwar
Chamonix-Mont-Blanc France 66 H4
Champa India 105 E5
Champagne Canada 149 M3
Champagne-Ardenne admin. reg. France 62 E6
Champagne Castle mt. S. Africa 125 I5
Champagne Humide reg. France 66 G2
Champagne Pouilleuse reg. France 66 F2
Champagnole France 66 G3
Champagny Islands Australia 134 D3
Champaign IL U.S.A. 160 F3
Champasak Laos 86 D4
Champdoré, Lac l. Canada 153 I3
Champhai India 105 H5
Champion Canada 150 H5
Champlain VA U.S.A. 165 G4
Champlain, Lake Canada/U.S.A. 165 I1
Champotón Mex. 167 H5
Chamu Co l. China 99 E6
Chamzinka Russia 53 J5
Chana Thai. 87 C6
Chanak Turkey see Çanakkale
Chanal Mex. 167 G5
Chañaral Chile 178 B3
Chanchén Mex. 167 H5
Chanda India see Chandrapur
Chandalar AK U.S.A. 149 J2
Chandalar r. AK U.S.A. 149 K2
Chandalar, East Fork r. AK U.S.A. 149 K2
Chandalar, Middle Fork r. AK U.S.A. 149 J2
Chandalar, North Fork r. AK U.S.A. 149 J2
Chandalar Lake AK U.S.A. 149 J2
Chandausi India 104 D3
Chandbali India 105 F5
Chandeleur Islands LA U.S.A. 161 F6
Chanderi India 104 D4
Chandigarh India 104 D3
Chandil India 105 F5
Chandir Uzbek. 111 G2
Chandler Canada 153 I4
Chandler AZ U.S.A. 159 H5
Chandler IN U.S.A. 164 B4
Chandler OK U.S.A. 161 D5
Chandler r. AK U.S.A. 149 J1
Chandler Lake AK U.S.A. 148 I1
Chandmanī Dzavhan Mongolia see Yaruu
Chandmanī Govĭ-Altay Mongolia 94 D2
Chandod India 104 C5
Chandos Lake Canada 165 G1
Chandpur Bangl. 105 G5
Chandpur India 104 D3
Chandragiri India 106 C3
Chandrapur India 106 C2
Chandvad India 106 B1
Chang, Ko i. Thai. 87 C4
Chang'an China 95 G5
Changane r. Moz. 125 K3
Changbai China 90 C4
Changbai Shan mts China/N. Korea 90 B4
Chang Cheng research station Antarctica see Great Wall
Changcheng China 97 F5
Changchow Fujian China see Zhangzhou
Changchow Jiangsu China see Changzhou
Changchun China 90 B4
Changchunling China 90 B3
Changdao China 95 J4
Changde China 97 F2
Changgang China 97 G3
Changge China 95 H5
Changgo China 99 D7
Chang Hu l. China 97 G2
Changhua Taiwan see Zhanghua
Changhwa Taiwan see Zhanghua
Changi Sing. 87 [inset]
Changji China 98 D4
Changjiang China 97 F5
Chang Jiang r. China 97 I2 see Yangtze
Changjiang Kou China see Mouth of the Yangtze
Changjin-ho resr N. Korea 91 B4
Changkiang China see Zhanjiang
Changlang India 105 H4
Changleng China see Xinjian
Changli China 95 I4
Changling China 95 J2
Changliushui China 94 F4
Changlun Malaysia 84 C1
Changlung India 109 M3
Changma China 94 D4
Changmar China 99 C6
Changna China 99 D7
Changning Jiangxi China see Xunwu
Changning Sichuan China 96 E2
Changnyŏn N. Korea 91 B5
Ch'ang-pai Shan mts China/N. Korea see Changbai Shan
Changping China 95 I3
Changpu China see Suining
Changsan-got pt N. Korea 91 B5
Changsha China 97 G2
Changshan China 97 H2
Changshan Qundao is China 95 J4
Changshi China 96 E3
Changshou China 97 G2
Changshoujie China see Changshou
Changshu China 97 I2
Changtai China 97 H3
Changteh China see Changde
Changting Fujian China 97 H3
Changting Heilong. China 90 C3
Changuinola Panama 166 [inset] J7
Changweiliang China 99 F5
Changwon S. Korea 91 C6
Changwu China 95 F5
Changxing China 97 H2
Changxing Dao i. China 95 J4
Changyang China 97 F2
Changyi China 95 I4
Changyŏn N. Korea 91 B5
Changyuan China 95 H5
Changzhi Shanxi China 95 H4
Changzhi Shanxi China 95 H5
Changzhou China 97 H2
Chañi, Nevado de mt. Arg. 178 C2
Chania Greece 69 K7
Chanion, Kolpos b. Greece 69 J7
Chankou China 94 F5
Channahon IL U.S.A. 164 A3
Channapatna India 106 C3
Channel Islands English Chan. 59 E9
Channel Islands CA U.S.A. 158 D5
Channel Islands National Park CA U.S.A. 158 D4
Channel-Port-aux-Basques Canada 153 K5
Channel Rock i. Bahamas 163 E8
Channel Tunnel France/U.K. 59 I7
Channing TX U.S.A. 161 C5
Chantada Spain 67 C2
Chantal'skiy mt. Russia 148 B2
Chantal'vergyrgyn r. Russia 148 C2
Chanthaburi Thai. 87 C4
Chantilly France 62 C5
Chanumla India 87 A5
Chanute KS U.S.A. 160 E4
Chanuwala Pak. 111 I3
Chany, Ozero salt l. Russia 76 I4
Chaohu China 97 H2
Chao Hu l. China 97 H2
Chaor China 95 J1
Chaor He r. China 95 J2
Chaowula Shan mt. China 96 C1
Chaoyang Guangdong China 97 H4
Chaoyang Heilong. China see Jiayin
Chaoyang Liaoning China 95 J3
Chaoyang Nei Mongol China 95 K1
Chaoyang Hu l. China 99 D6
Chaozhong China 95 J1
Chaozhou China 97 H4
Chapada Diamantina, Parque Nacional nat. park Brazil 179 C1
Chapada dos Veadeiros, Parque Nacional da nat. park Brazil 179 B1
Chapais Canada 152 G4
Chapak Gozār Afgh. 111 G2
Chapala Mex. 166 E4
Chapala, Laguna de l. Mex. 168 D4
Chāpārī, Kōtal-e Afgh. 111 G3
Chapayeva, imeni Turkm. see S. A. Nyýazow Adyndaky
Chapayevo Kazakh. 100 E1
Chapayevsk Russia 53 K5
Chapecó Brazil 178 F3
Chapecó r. Brazil 178 F3
Chapel-en-le-Frith U.K. 58 F5
Chapelle-lez-Herlaimont Belgium 62 E4
Chapeltown U.K. 58 F5
Chapleau Canada 152 E5
Chaplin Canada 151 J5
Chaplin Lake Canada 151 J5
Chaplino Russia 148 D2
Chaplygin Russia 53 H5
Chapman, Mount Canada 150 G5
Chapmanville WV U.S.A. 164 D5
Chappell NE U.S.A. 160 C3
Chappell Islands Australia 137 [inset]
Chapra Bihar India 105 F4
Chapra Jharkhand India see Chatra
Chaqmaqtīn, Kōl-e Afgh. 111 I2
Charagua Bol. 176 F7
Charay Mex. 166 C3
Charcas Mex. 168 D4
Charcot Island Antarctica 188 L2
Chard Canada 151 I4
Chard U.K. 59 E8
Chardara Kazakh. see Shardara
Chardara, Step' plain Kazakh. see Shardara, Step'
Chardon OH U.S.A. 164 E3
Chardzhev Turkm. see Türkmenabat
Chardzhou Turkm. see Türkmenabat
Charef Alg. 67 H6
Charef, Oued watercourse Morocco 64 D5
Charente r. France 66 D4
Chari r. Cameroon/Chad 121 E3
Chārī Iran 110 E4
Chārīkār Afgh. 111 H3
Chariot AK U.S.A. 148 F1
Chariton IA U.S.A. 160 E3
Chärjew Turkm. see Türkmenabat
Charkayuvom Russia 52 L2
Charkhlik China see Ruoqiang
Charleroi Belgium 62 E4
Charles, Cape VA U.S.A. 165 H5
Charlesbourg Canada 153 H5
Charles City IA U.S.A. 160 E3
Charles City VA U.S.A. 165 G5
Charles Hill Botswana 124 E2
Charles Island Galápagos Ecuador see Floreana, Isla
Charles Lake Canada 151 I3
Charles Point Australia 134 E3
Charleston N.Z. 139 C5
Charleston IL U.S.A. 160 F4
Charleston MO U.S.A. 161 F4
Charleston SC U.S.A. 163 E5

▶Charleston WV U.S.A. 164 E4
Capital of West Virginia.

Charleston Peak NV U.S.A. 159 F3
Charlestown Ireland 61 D4
Charlestown IN U.S.A. 164 C4
Charlestown NH U.S.A. 165 I2
Charlestown RI U.S.A. 165 J3
Charles Town WV U.S.A. 165 G4
Charleville Australia 137 D5
Charleville Ireland 61 D5
Charleville-Mézières France 62 E5
Charlevoix MI U.S.A. 164 C1
Charley r. AK U.S.A. 149 L2
Charlie, Dome ice feature Antarctica 188 F2
Charlie Lake Canada 150 F3
Charlotte MI U.S.A. 164 C2
Charlotte NC U.S.A. 163 D5
Charlotte TN U.S.A. 164 B5

▶Charlotte Amalie Virgin Is (U.S.A.) 169 L5
Capital of the U.S. Virgin Islands.

Charlotte Bank sea feature S. China Sea 85 D1
Charlotte Harbor b. FL U.S.A. 163 D7
Charlotte Lake Canada 150 E4
Charlottesville VA U.S.A. 165 F4

▶Charlottetown Canada 153 J5
Capital of Prince Edward Island.

Charlton Australia 138 A6
Charlton Island Canada 152 F3
Charron Lake Canada 151 M4
Charsadda Pak. 111 H3
Charshanga Turkm. see Köýtendag
Charshangngy Turkm. see Köýtendag
Charters Towers Australia 136 D4
Chartres France 66 E2
Chas India 105 F5
Chase Canada 150 G5
Chase MI U.S.A. 164 C2
Chase City VA U.S.A. 165 F5
Chashmeh Nūrī Iran 110 E3
Chashmeh-ye Palasi Iran 110 D3
Chashniki Belarus 53 F5
Chaska MN U.S.A. 160 E2
Chaslands Mistake c. N.Z. 139 B8
Chasŏng N. Korea 90 B4
Chasseral mt. Switz. 57 K7
Chassiron, Pointe de pt France 66 D3
Chastab, Kūh-e mts Iran 110 D3
Chāt Iran 110 D2
Chatanika AK U.S.A. 149 K2
Chatanika r. AK U.S.A. 149 J2
Châteaubriant France 66 D3
Château-du-Loir France 66 E3
Châteaudun France 66 E2
Chateaugay NY U.S.A. 165 H1
Châteauguay Canada 165 I1
Châteauguay r. Canada 153 H2
Châteauguay, Lac l. Canada 153 H2
Châteaulin France 66 B2
Châteaumeillant France 66 F3
Châteauneuf-en-Thymerais France 62 B6
Châteauneuf-sur-Loire France 66 F3
Chateau Pond l. Canada 153 K3
Châteauroux France 66 E3
Château-Salins France 62 G6
Château-Thierry France 62 D5
Chateh Canada 150 G3
Châtelet Belgium 62 E4
Châtellerault France 66 E3
Chatfield MN U.S.A. 152 B6
Chatham Canada 164 D2
Chatham U.K. 59 H7
Chatham AK U.S.A. 149 N4
Chatham MA U.S.A. 165 K3
Chatham NY U.S.A. 165 I2
Chatham PA U.S.A. 165 H4
Chatham VA U.S.A. 164 F5
Chatham, Isla i. Chile 178 B8
Chatham Island Galápagos Ecuador see San Cristóbal, Isla

Chatham Island N.Z. 133 I6
Chatham Island Samoa see Savai'i
Chatham Islands N.Z. 133 I6
Chatham Rise sea feature S. Pacific Ocean 186 I8
Chatham Sound sea chan. Canada 149 O5
Chatham Strait AK U.S.A. 149 N4
Châtillon-sur-Seine France 66 G3
Chatkal Range mts Kyrg./Uzbek. 102 D3
Chatom AL U.S.A. 161 F6
Chatra India 105 F4
Chatra Nepal 105 F4
Chatsworth Canada 164 E1
Chatsworth NJ U.S.A. 165 H4
Chattagam Bangl. see Chittagong
Chattanooga TN U.S.A. 163 C5
Chattarpur India see Chhatarpur
Chatteris U.K. 59 H6
Chattisgarh state India see Chhattisgarh
Chatturat Thai. 86 C4
Chatyr-Köl l. Kyrg. 98 A4
Chatyr-Tash Kyrg. 102 E3
Châu Đôc Vietnam 87 D5
Chauhtan India 104 B4
Chauk Myanmar 86 A2
Chauka r. India 99 C8
Chaukhamba mts India 99 B7
Chaumont France 66 G2
Chauncey OH U.S.A. 164 D4
Chaungzon Myanmar 86 B3
Chaunskaya Guba b. Russia 77 R3
Chauny France 62 D5
Châu Phu Vietnam see Châu Đôc
Chausu-yama mt. Japan 92 D3
Chausy Belarus see Chavusy
Chautauqua, Lake NY U.S.A. 164 F2
Chauter Pak. 111 G4
Chauvin Canada 151 I4
Chavakachcheri Sri Lanka 106 D4
Chavakkad India 106 B4
Chaves Port. 67 C3
Chavigny, Lac l. Canada 152 G2
Chavusy Belarus 53 F5
Chawal r. Pak. 111 G4
Chay, Sông r. Vietnam 86 D2
Chayatyn, Khrebet ridge Russia 90 E1
Chayevo Russia 52 H4
Chaykovskiy Russia 51 Q4
Chäyul China see Qayü
Chazhegovo Russia 52 L3
Chazy NY U.S.A. 165 I1
Cheadle U.K. 59 F6
Cheaha Mountain hill AL U.S.A. 163 C5
Cheat r. WV U.S.A. 164 F4
Cheatham Lake TN U.S.A. 164 B5
Cheb Czech Rep. 63 M4
Chebba Tunisia 68 D7
Cheboksarskoye Vodokhranilishche resr Russia 52 J5
Cheboksary Russia 52 J4
Cheboygan MI U.S.A. 162 C2
Chechen Russia 148 D2
Chechen', Ostrov i. Russia 113 G2
Chedabucto Bay Canada 153 J5
Chedao China 95 J4
Cheddar U.K. 59 E7
Cheduba Myanmar see Man-aung
Cheduba Island i. Myanmar see Man-aung Kyun
Chée r. France 62 E6
Cheektowaga NY U.S.A. 165 F2
Cheepie Australia 138 B1
Cheetham, Cape Antarctica 188 H2
Chefchaouene Morocco 67 D6
Chefoo China see Yantai
Chefornak AK U.S.A. 148 F3
Chefu Moz. 125 K2
Chegdomyn Russia 90 D2
Chegga Mauritania 120 C2
Chegitun' Russia 148 E2
Chegitun' r. Russia 148 E2
Chegutu Zimbabwe 123 D5
Chehalis WA U.S.A. 156 C3
Chehardeh Iran 110 E3
Chehel Chashmeh, Kūh-e hill Iran 110 B3
Chehel Dokhtarān, Kūh-e mt. Iran 111 F4
Chehel Pāyeh Iran 110 E4
Cheju S. Korea see Jeju
Cheju-do i. S. Korea 91 B6
Chek Chue H.K. China see Stanley
Chekhov Moskovskaya Oblast' Russia 53 H5
Chekhov Sakhalinskaya Oblast' Russia 90 F3
Chekiang prov. China see Zhejiang
Chekichler Turkm. see Çekiçler
Chek Lap Kok reg. H.K. China 97 [inset]
Chek Mun Hoi Hap H.K. China see Tolo Channel
Chekunda Russia 90 D2
Chela, Serra da mts Angola 123 B5
Chelan, Lake WA U.S.A. 156 C2
Chelatna Lake AK U.S.A. 149 J3
Cheleken Turkm. see Hazar
Cheline Moz. 125 L2
Chelkar Kazakh. see Shalkar
Chełm Poland 53 D6
Chelmer r. U.K. 59 H7
Chełmno Poland 57 Q4
Chelmsford U.K. 59 H7
Chelsea MI U.S.A. 164 C2
Chelsea VT U.S.A. 165 I2
Cheltenham U.K. 59 E7
Chelva Spain 67 F4
Chelyabinsk Russia 76 H4
Chemax Mex. 167 I4
Chemba Moz. 123 D5
Chêm Co l. China 99 B6
Chemnitz Germany 63 M4
Chemulpo S. Korea see Incheon
Chemyndy Kyrg. 98 A4
Chena r. AK U.S.A. 149 K2
Chenab r. India/Pak. 104 B3
Chenachane, Oued watercourse Alg. 120 C2
Chena Hot Springs AK U.S.A. 149 K2
Chenārān Iran 110 E2
Chencang China 95 F5
Chenderoh, Tasik resr Malaysia 84 C1
Chendir r. Turkm. see Çendir
Chenega (abandoned) AK U.S.A. 149 J3
Cheney WA U.S.A. 156 D3
Cheney Reservoir KS U.S.A. 160 D4
Chengalpattu India 106 D3
Cheng'an China 95 H4
Chengbu China 97 F3
Chengcheng China 95 G5
Chengchow China see Zhengzhou
Chengde Hebei China 95 I3
Chengde Hebei China 95 I3
Chengdu China 96 E2
Chengele India 96 C2
Chenggong China 96 D3
Chenghai China 97 H4
Cheng Hai l. China 96 D3
Chengjiang China see Taihe
Chengjiang Fossil Site tourist site China 96 D3
Chengmai China 97 F5
Chengqian China 95 I5
Chengshan China 95 J4
Chengtu China see Chengdu
Chengwu China 95 H5
Chengxian China 96 E1
Chengxiang Chongqing China see Wuxi
Chengxiang Jiangxi China see Quannan
Chengyang China see Juxian
Chengzhong China see Ningming
Cheniu Shan i. China 95 I5
Chenkaladi Sri Lanka 106 D5
Chennai India 106 D3
Chenqing China 90 B2
Chenqingqiao China see Chenqing
Chenstokhov Poland see Częstochowa
Chenxi China 97 F3
Chenyang China see Chenxi
Chenying China see Wannian
Chenzhou China 97 G3
Chenzhuang China 95 H4
Cheonan S. Korea 91 B5
Cheongdo S. Korea 91 C6
Cheongju S. Korea 91 B5
Chepén Peru 176 C5
Chepes Arg. 178 C4
Chepo Panama 166 [inset] K7
Chepstow U.K. 59 E7
Cheptsa r. Russia 52 K4
Chequamegon Bay WI U.S.A. 160 F2
Cher r. France 66 E3
Chera state India see Kerala
Cherán Mex. 167 E5
Cheraw SC U.S.A. 163 E5
Cherbaniani Reef India 106 A3
Cherbourg-Octeville France 66 D2
Cherchell Alg. 67 H5
Cherchen China see Qiemo
Cherdakly Russia 53 K5
Cherdyn' Russia 51 R3
Chereapani reef India see Byramgore Reef
Cheremkhovo Russia 88 I2
Cheremshany Russia 90 D3
Cheremukhovka Russia 52 K4
Cherepanovo Russia 88 E2
Cherepovets Russia 52 H4
Cherevkovo Russia 52 J3
Chergui, Chott ech imp. l. Alg. 64 D5
Chéria Alg. 68 B7
Cheriton VA U.S.A. 165 H5
Cheriyakara, Suheli India 106 B4
Cheriyam atoll India 106 B4
Cherkassy Ukr. see Cherkasy
Cherkasy Ukr. 53 G6
Cherkessk Russia 113 F1
Cherla India 106 D2
Chernabura Island AK U.S.A. 148 H5
Chernaya Russia 52 M1
Chernaya r. Russia 52 M1
Chernigov Ukr. see Chernihiv
Chernigovka Russia 90 D3
Chernihiv Ukr. 53 F6
Cherninivka Ukr. 53 H7
Chernivtsi Ukr. 53 E6
Chernobyl' Ukr. see Chornobyl'
Chernogorsk Russia 88 G2
Chernovtsy Ukr. see Chernivtsi
Chernoye More sea Asia/Europe see Black Sea
Chernushka Russia 51 R4
Chernyakhiv Ukr. 53 F6
Chernyakhovsk Russia 55 L9
Chernyanka Russia 53 H6
Chernyayevo Russia 90 B1
Chernyshevsk Russia 89 L2
Chernyshevskiy Russia 77 M3
Chernyshkovskiy Russia 53 I6
Chernyye Zemli reg. Russia 53 J7
Chernyy Irtysh r. China/Kazakh. see Ertix He
Chernyy Porog Russia 52 G3
Chernyy Yar Russia 53 J6
Cherokee IA U.S.A. 160 E3
Cherokee Sound Bahamas 163 E7

▶Cherrapunji India 105 G4
Highest recorded annual rainfall in the world.

Cherry Creek r. SD U.S.A. 160 C2
Cherry Creek Mountains NV U.S.A. 159 F1
Cherry Hill NJ U.S.A. 165 H4
Cherry Island Solomon Is 133 G3
Cherry Lake CA U.S.A. 158 D2
Cherskiy Russia 189 C2
Cherskiy Range mts Russia see Cherskogo, Khrebet
Cherskogo, Khrebet mts Zabaykal'skiy Kray Russia 95 G1
Cherskogo, Khrebet mts Russia 77 P3
Chertkov Ukr. see Chortkiv
Chertkovo Russia 53 I6
Cherven Bryag Bulg. 69 K3
Chervonoarmeyskoye Ukr. see Vil'nyans'k
Chervonoarmiys'k Donets'ka Oblast' Ukr. see Krasnoarmiys'k
Chervonoarmiys'k Rivnens'ka Oblast' Ukr. see Radyvyliv
Chervonograd Ukr. see Chervonohrad
Chervonohrad Ukr. 53 E6
Chervyen' Belarus 53 F5
Cherwell r. U.K. 59 F7
Cherykaw Belarus 53 F5
Chesapeake VA U.S.A. 165 G5
Chesapeake Bay Maryland/Virginia U.S.A. 165 G4
Chesham U.K. 59 G7
Cheshire Plain U.K. 58 E5
Cheshme Vtoroy Turkm. 111 F2
Cheshskaya Guba b. Russia 52 J2
Cheshtebe Tajik. 111 I2
Cheshunt U.K. 59 G7
Chesnokovka Russia see Novoaltaysk
Chester Canada 153 I5
Chester U.K. 58 E5
Chester CA U.S.A. 158 C1
Chester IL U.S.A. 160 F4
Chester MT U.S.A. 156 F2
Chester OH U.S.A. 164 E4
Chester SC U.S.A. 163 D5
Chester r. MD U.S.A. 165 G4
Chesterfield U.K. 58 F5
Chesterfield VA U.S.A. 165 G5
Chesterfield, Îles is New Caledonia 133 F3
Chesterfield Inlet Canada 151 N2
Chesterfield Inlet inlet Canada 151 M2
Chester-le-Street U.K. 58 F4
Chestertown MD U.S.A. 165 G4
Chestertown NY U.S.A. 165 I2
Chesterville Canada 165 H1
Chestnut Ridge PA U.S.A. 164 F3
Chesuncook Lake ME U.S.A. 162 G2
Chetaïbi Alg. 68 B6
Chéticamp Canada 153 J5
Chetlat i. India 106 B4
Chetumal Mex. 167 H5
Chetwynd Canada 150 F4
Cheung Chau H.K. China 97 [inset]
Chevak AK U.S.A. 148 F3
Chevelon Creek r. AZ U.S.A. 159 H4
Cheviot N.Z. 139 D6
Cheviot Hills U.K. 58 E3
Cheviot Range hills Australia 136 C5
Chevreulx r. Canada 152 G3
Cheyenne OK U.S.A. 161 D5

▶Cheyenne WY U.S.A. 156 G4
Capital of Wyoming.

Cheyenne r. SD U.S.A. 160 C2
Cheyenne Wells CO U.S.A. 160 C4
Cheyne Bay Australia 135 B8
Cheyur India 106 D3
Chezacut Canada 150 E4
Chhapra India see Chapra
Chhata India 104 D4
Chhatak Bangl. 105 G4
Chhatarpur Jharkhand India 105 F4
Chhatarpur Madh. Prad. India 104 D4
Chhatr Pak. 111 H4
Chhatrapur India 106 E2
Chhattisgarh state India 105 E5
Chhay Arêng, Stœng r. Cambodia 87 C5
Chhindwara India 104 D5
Chhitkul India see Chitkul
Chhlong Cambodia 87 D4
Chhukha Bhutan 105 G4
Chi, Lam r. Thai. 87 C4
Chi, Mae Nam r. Thai. 86 D4
Chiai Taiwan see Jiayi
Chiamboni Somalia 122 E4
Chiange Angola 123 B5
Chiang Kham Thai. 86 C3
Chiang Khan Thai. 86 C3
Chiang Mai Thai. 86 B3
Chiang Rai Thai. 86 B3
Chiang Saen Thai. 86 C2
Chiapa Mex. 167 G5
Chiapas state Mex. 167 G5
Chiapilla Mex. 167 G5
Chiari Italy 68 C2
Chiautla Mex. 168 E5
Chiavenna Italy 68 C1
Chiayi Taiwan see Jiayi
Chiba Japan 93 G3
Chiba pref. Japan 93 G3
Chibi China 97 G2
Chibia Angola 123 B5
Chibit Russia 98 D2
Chibizovka Russia see Zherdevka
Chiboma Moz. 123 D6
Chibougamau Canada 152 G4
Chibougamau, Lac l. Canada 152 G4
Chibuto Moz. 125 K3
Chibuzhang Co l. China 99 E6
Chicacole India see Srikakulam

▶Chicago IL U.S.A. 164 B3
4th most populous city in North America.

Chic-Chocs, Monts mts Canada 153 I4
Chichagof AK U.S.A. 149 M4
Chichagof Island AK U.S.A. 149 N4
Chichak r. Pak. 111 G5
Chichaoua Morocco 64 C5
Chichatka Russia 90 A1
Chicheng Hebei China 95 H3
Chicheng Sichuan China see Pengxi
Chichén Itzá tourist site Mex. 167 H4
Chichester U.K. 59 G8
Chichester Range mts Australia 134 B5
Chichgarh India 106 D1
Chichibu Japan 93 F3
Chichibu-gawa r. Japan 93 F2
Chichibu-Tama Kokuritsu-kōen nat. park Japan 93 E3
Chichijima-rettō is Japan 91 F8
Chickaloon AK U.S.A. 149 J3
Chickasawhay r. MS U.S.A. 167 H2
Chickasha OK U.S.A. 161 D5
Chicken AK U.S.A. 149 L2
Chiclana de la Frontera Spain 67 C5
Chiclayo Peru 176 C5
Chico r. Arg. 178 C6
Chico CA U.S.A. 158 C2
Chicomo Moz. 125 L3
Chicomucelo Mex. 167 G6
Chicopee MA U.S.A. 165 I2
Chico Sapocoy, Mount Luzon Phil. 82 C2
Chicoutimi Canada 153 H4
Chicualacuala Moz. 125 J2
Chidambaram India 106 C4
Chidenguele Moz. 125 L3
Chidley, Cape Canada 147 L3
Chido China see Sêndo
Chiducuane Moz. 125 L3
Chiefland FL U.S.A. 163 D6
Chiemsee l. Germany 57 N7
Chiengmai Thai. see Chiang Mai
Chiers r. France 62 F5
Chieti Italy 68 F3
Chifeng China 95 I3
Chifre, Serra do mts Brazil 179 C2
Chigasaki Japan 93 F3
Chiginagak Volcano, Mount AK U.S.A. 146 C4
Chigmit Mountains AK U.S.A. 148 I3
Chignik AK U.S.A. 148 H4
Chignik Bay AK U.S.A. 148 H4
Chignik Lagoon AK U.S.A. 148 H4
Chignik Lake AK U.S.A. 148 H4
Chigu China 99 E7
Chigubo Moz. 125 K2
Chigu Co l. China 99 E7
Chihil Abdālān, Kōh-e mts Afgh. 111 G3
Chihuahua Mex. 166 D2
Chihuahua state Mex. 166 D2
Chijin China 94 D3
Chikalda India 104 D5
Chikan China 97 F4
Chikaskia r. KS U.S.A. 161 D4
Chikhli India 106 C1
Chikishlyar Turkm. see Çekiçler
Chikkamagaluru India 106 B3
Chikodi India 106 B2
Chikoy Russia 94 F1
Chikoy r. Russia 95 F1
Chikuhoku Japan 93 E2
Chikuma Japan 93 E2
Chikuma-gawa r. Japan 93 E1
Chikuminuk Lake AK U.S.A. 148 H3
Chikura Japan 93 F4
Chikusei Japan 93 F2
Chilanko r. Canada 150 F4
Chilapa Mex. 167 F5
Chilas Pak. 104 C2
Chilaw Sri Lanka 106 C5
Chilcotin r. Canada 150 F5
Childers Australia 136 F5
Childress TX U.S.A. 161 C5
Chile country S. America 178 B4
Chile Basin sea feature S. Pacific Ocean 187 O8
Chile Chico Chile 178 B7
Chile Rise sea feature S. Pacific Ocean 187 O8
Chilgir Russia 53 J7
Chilhowie VA U.S.A. 164 E5
Chilia-Nouă Ukr. see Kiliya
Chilika Lake India 106 E2
Chililabombwe Zambia 123 C5
Chilko r. Canada 150 F4
Chilko Lake Canada 150 E5
Chilkoot Pass Canada/U.S.A. 149 N4
Chilkoot Trail National Historic Site nat. park Canada 149 N4
Chillán Chile 178 B5
Chillicothe MO U.S.A. 160 E4
Chillicothe OH U.S.A. 164 D4
Chilliwack Canada 150 F5
Chilo India 104 C4
Chiloé, Isla de i. Chile 178 B6
Chiloé, Isla Grande de i. Chile see Chiloé, Isla de
Chilpancingo Mex. 168 E5
Chilpancingo de los Bravos Mex. see Chilpancingo
Chilpi Pak. 104 C1
Chiltern Hills U.K. 59 G7
Chilton WI U.S.A. 164 A1
Chiluage Angola 123 C4
Chilubi Zambia 123 C5
Chilung Taiwan see Jilong
Chilwa, Lake Malawi 123 D5
Chimala Tanz. 123 D4
Chimalapa Mex. 167 G5
Chimaltenango Guat. 167 H6
Chimán Panama 166 [inset] K7
Chi Ma Wan H.K. China 97 [inset]
Chimay Belgium 62 E4
Chimbas Arg. 178 C4
Chimbay Uzbek. see Chimboy
Chimborazo mt. Ecuador 176 C4
Chimbote Peru 176 C5
Chimboy Uzbek. 102 A3
Chimchineykuyim, Laguna lag. Russia 148 B3
Chimishliya Moldova see Cimişlia
Chimkent Kazakh. see Shymkent
Chimney Rock CO U.S.A. 159 J3
Chimoio Moz. 123 D5
Chimtargha, Qullai mt. Tajik. 111 H2
Chimtorga, Gora mt. Tajik. see Chimtargha, Qullai

▶China country Asia 88 H5
Most populous country in Asia and the world. 2nd largest country in Asia and 4th largest in the world.

China Mex. 167 F3
China, Republic of country Asia see Taiwan
China Bakir r. Myanmar see To
Chinacates Mex. 166 D3
Chinajá Guat. 167 H5
China Lake CA U.S.A. 158 E4
China Lake ME U.S.A. 165 K1
Chinandega Nicaragua 166 [inset] I6
China Point CA U.S.A. 158 D5
Chinati Peak TX U.S.A. 161 B6
Chincha Alta Peru 176 C6
Chinchaga r. Canada 150 G3
Chinchilla Australia 138 E1
Chincholi India 106 C2
Chinchorro, Banco sea feature Mex. 167 I5
Chincoteague Bay Maryland/Virginia U.S.A. 165 H5
Chinde Moz. 123 D5
Chindwin r. Myanmar 86 A2
Chinese Turkestan aut. reg. China see Xinjiang Uygur Zizhiqu
Chinghai prov. China see Qinghai
Chingleput India see Chengalpattu
Chingola Zambia 123 C5
Chinguar Angola 123 B5
Chinguețți Mauritania 120 B2
Chinhoyi Zimbabwe 123 D5
Chini India see Kalpa
Chiniak AK U.S.A. 148 I4
Chiniak, Cape AK U.S.A. 148 I4
Chining China see Jining
Chiniot Pak. 111 I4
Chinipas Mex. 166 C3
Chinĭt, Stœng r. Cambodia 87 D4
Chinju S. Korea 91 C6
Chinle AZ U.S.A. 159 I3
Chinmen Taiwan see Jinmen
Chinmen Tao i. Taiwan see Jinmen Dao
Chinnamp'o N. Korea see Namp'o
Chinnur India 106 C2
Chino Japan 93 E3
Chino Creek watercourse AZ U.S.A. 159 G4
Chinon France 66 E3
Chinook MT U.S.A. 156 F2
Chinook Trough sea feature N. Pacific Ocean 186 I3
Chino Valley AZ U.S.A. 159 G4
Chinsali Zambia 123 D5
Chin-shan China see Zhujing
Chintamani India 106 C3
Chioggia Italy 68 E2
Chios Greece 69 L5
Chios i. Greece 69 K5
Chipam Guat. 167 H6
Chipata Zambia 123 D5
Chip Chap r. China/India 99 B6
Chipchihua, Sierra de mts Arg. 178 C6
Chiphu Cambodia 87 D5
Chipindo Angola 123 B5
Chiping China 95 I4
Chipinga Zimbabwe see Chipinge
Chipinge Zimbabwe 123 D6
Chipley FL U.S.A. 163 C6
Chipman Canada 153 I5
Chippenham U.K. 59 E7
Chippewa, Lake WI U.S.A. 160 F2
Chippewa Falls WI U.S.A. 160 F2
Chipping Norton U.K. 59 F7
Chipping Sodbury U.K. 59 E7
Chipurupalle Andhra Prad. India 106 D2
Chipurupalle Andhra Prad. India 106 D2
Chiquibul National Park Belize 167 H5
Chiquilá Mex. 167 I4
Chiquimula Guat. 167 H6
Chiquinquirá Col. 176 D2
Chir r. Russia 53 I6
Chirada India 106 D3
Chirala India 106 D3
Chīras Afgh. 111 G3
Chirchiq Uzbek. 102 C3
Chiredzi Zimbabwe 123 D6
Chirfa Niger 120 E2
Chiricahua National Monument nat. park AZ U.S.A. 159 I5
Chiricahua Peak AZ U.S.A. 159 I6
Chirikof Island AK U.S.A. 148 I5
Chiriquí, Golfo de b. Panama 166 [inset] J7
Chiriquí, Laguna de b. Panama 166 [inset] J7
Chiriquí, Volcán de vol. Panama see Barú, Volcán
Chiriquí Grande Panama 166 [inset] J7
Chirk U.K. 59 D6
Chirnside U.K. 60 G5
Chirripó mt. Costa Rica 169 H7
Chirripó, Parque Nacional nat. park Costa Rica 166 [inset] J7
Chiryū Japan 92 D3
Chisamba Zambia 123 C5
Chisana r. AK U.S.A. 149 L3
Chisana (abandoned) AK U.S.A. 149 L3
Chisana Glacier AK U.S.A. 149 J3
Chisasibi Canada 152 F3
Chisec Guat. 167 H6
Chishima-retto is Russia see Kuril Islands
Chisholm Canada 150 H4
Chishtian Pak. 111 I4
Chishui Guizhou China 96 E2
Chishui Sichuan China 96 E3
Chisimaio Somalia see Kismaayo

▶Chişinău Moldova 69 M1
Capital of Moldova.

Chistochina AK U.S.A. 149 K3
Chistopol' Russia 52 K5
Chita Japan 92 C4
Chita Russia 89 K2
Chitado Angola 123 B5
Chita-hantō pen. Japan 92 C4
Chitaldrug India see Chitradurga
Chitalwana India 104 B4
Chitambo Zambia 123 D5
Chitanana r. AK U.S.A. 149 J2
Chitanga Russia 95 G1
Chitato Angola 123 C4
Chita-wan b. Japan 92 C4
Chitek Lake Canada 151 J4
Chitek Lake l. Canada 151 L4
Chitembo Angola 123 B5
Chitina AK U.S.A. 149 K3
Chitina r. AK U.S.A. 149 K3
Chitipa Malawi 123 D4
Chitkul India 104 D3
Chitobe Moz. 123 D6
Chitoor India see Chittoor
Chitor India see Chittaurgarh
Chitose Japan 90 F4
Chitradurga India 106 C3
Chitrakoot India 104 E4
Chitrakut India see Chitrakoot
Chitral Pak. 111 H3
Chitral r. Pak. 111 H3
Chitravati r. India 106 C3
Chitré Panama 166 [inset] J8
Chitrod India 104 B5
Chittagong Bangl. 105 G5
Chittaurgarh India 104 C4
Chittoor India 106 C3
Chittor India see Chittoor
Chittorgarh India see Chittaurgarh
Chittur India 106 C4
Chitungwiza Zimbabwe 123 D5
Chiu Lung H.K. China see Kowloon
Chiume Angola 123 C5
Chivasso Italy 68 B2
Chívato, Punta pt Mex. 166 C3
Chivela Mex. 167 G5
Chivhu Zimbabwe 123 D5
Chixixu China 97 G4
Chiyoda Gunma Japan 93 F2
Chiyoda Ibaraki Japan see Kasumigaura
Chiyogawa Japan 93 F2
Chizarira National Park Zimbabwe 123 C5
Chizhou China 97 H2
Chizu Japan 91 D6
Chkalov Russia see Orenburg
Chkalovsk Russia 52 I4
Chkalovskoye Russia 90 D3
Chlef Alg. 67 G5
Chlef, Oued r. Alg. 67 G5
Chloride AZ U.S.A. 159 F4
Chlya, Ozero l. Russia 90 F1
Choa Chu Kang Sing. 87 [inset]
Choa Chu Kang hill Sing. 87 [inset]
Chobe National Park Botswana 123 C5
Chodov Czech Rep. 63 M4
Chodro Russia 98 E2
Choele Choel Arg. 178 C5
Chōfu Japan 93 F3
Chogar r. Russia 90 D1
Chogo Lungma Glacier Pak. 99 A6
Chogori Feng mt. China/Pak. see K2
Chograyskoye Vodokhranilishche resr Russia 53 J7
Choiseul i. Solomon Is 133 F2
Choix Mex. 166 C3
Chojnice Poland 57 P4
Chōkai-san vol. Japan 91 F5
Ch'ok'ē mts Eth. 122 D2
Ch'ok'ē Mountains Eth. see Ch'ok'ē
Ch'ok'ē Terara mt. Eth. 122 D2
Chokola mt. China 104 E3
Choksum China 105 F3
Chok-Tal Kyrg. 98 B4
Chokue Moz. see Chókwè
Chokurdakh Russia 77 P2
Chókwè Moz. 125 K3
Cho La pass China 96 C2
Cholame CA U.S.A. 158 C4
Cholet France 66 D3
Choloma Hond. 166 [inset] I6
Cholpon Kyrg. 98 A4
Cholpon-Ata Kyrg. 102 E3
Cholula Mex. 167 F5
Choluteca Hond. 166 [inset] I6
Choma Zambia 123 C5
Chomo Ganggar mt. China 99 E7
Chơ Moi Vietnam 86 D2
Chomo Lhari mt. Bhutan/China 105 G4
Chom Thong Thai. 86 B3
Chomun India 99 A8
Chomutov Czech Rep. 57 N5
Chōnan Japan 93 G3
Chon Buri Thai. 87 C4
Ch'ŏnch'ŏn N. Korea 90 B4
Chone Ecuador 176 B4
Ch'ŏngch'ŏn-gang r. N. Korea 91 B5
Chŏnggye China see Qonggyai
Ch'ŏngjin N. Korea 90 C4
Ch'ŏngju S. Korea see Cheongju
Chŏng Kal Cambodia 87 C4
Chongkŭ China 96 C2
Chongli China 95 H3
Chonglong China see Zizhong
Chongming Dao i. China 97 I2
Chongoroi Angola 123 B5
Chŏngp'yŏng N. Korea 91 B5
Chongqing China 96 E2
Chongqing mun. China 96 E2
Chonguene Moz. 125 K3
Chongyang China 97 G2
Chongyi China 97 G3
Chongzuo China 96 E4
Chŏnju S. Korea see Jeonju
Chonogol Mongolia see Erdenetsagaan
Chonos, Archipiélago de los is Chile 178 A6
Chontalpa Mex. 167 G5

▶Cho Oyu mt. China/Nepal 105 F3
6th highest mountain in Asia and the world.

Chopda India 104 C5
Chor Pak. 111 H5
Chora Sfakion Greece 69 K7
Chorley U.K. 58 E5
Chornobyl' Ukr. 53 F6
Chornomors'ke Crimea 69 O2
Chortkiv Ukr. 53 E6
Ch'osan N. Korea 90 B4
Chōshi Japan 93 G3
Chosŏn country Asia see South Korea
Chosŏn-minjujuŭi-inmin-konghwaguk country Asia see North Korea
Choszczno Poland 57 O4
Chota Peru 176 C5
Chota Sinchula hill India 105 G4
Choteau MT U.S.A. 156 E3
Choti Pak. 111 H4
Choûm Mauritania 120 B2
Chowchilla CA U.S.A. 158 C3
Chown, Mount Canada 150 G4
Choybalsan Mongolia 95 H2
Choyr Mongolia 95 G2
Chrétiens, Île aux i. Canada see Christian Island
Chřiby hills Czech Rep. 57 P6
Chrisman IL U.S.A. 164 B4
Chrissiesmeer S. Africa 125 J4
Christchurch N.Z. 139 D6
Christchurch U.K. 59 F8
Christian AK U.S.A. 149 K2
Christian r. AK U.S.A. 149 K2
Christian, Cape Canada 147 L2
Christiana S. Africa 125 G4
Christiania Norway see Oslo
Christian Island Canada 164 E1
Christiansburg VA U.S.A. 164 E5
Christianshåb Greenland see Qasigiannguit
Christie Bay Canada 151 I2
Christie Island Myanmar 87 B5
Christina r. Canada 151 I3
Christina, Mount N.Z. 139 B7

▶Christmas Island terr. Indian Ocean 80 D9
Australian External Territory.

Christopher, Lake salt flat Australia 135 D6
Chrudim Czech Rep. 57 O6
Chrysi i. Greece see Gaïdouronisi
Chrysochou Bay Cyprus 107 A2
Chrysochous, Kolpos b. Cyprus see Chrysochou Bay
Chu Kazakh. see Shu
Chuadanga Bangl. 105 G5
Chuali, Lago l. Moz. 125 K3
Chuanhui China see Zhoukou
Chuanjing China 95 G3
Chuansha China 97 I2
Chuathbaluk AK U.S.A. 148 H3
Chubalung China 96 C2
Chubarovka Ukr. see Polohy
Chubartau Kazakh. see Barshatas
Chūbu airport Japan 92 C4
Chūbu-Sangaku Kokuritsu-kōen nat. park Japan 92 D2
Chubxi China 94 D5
Chu-ching China see Zhujing
Chuchkovo Russia 53 I5
Chuckwalla Mountains CA U.S.A. 159 F5
Chucunaque r. Panama 166 [inset] K7
Chudniv Ukr. 53 F6
Chudovo Russia 52 F4
Chudskoye, Ozero l. Estonia/Russia see Peipus, Lake
Chugach Mountains AK U.S.A. 149 K3
Chuginadak Island AK U.S.A. 148 E5
Chūgoku-sanchi mts Japan 91 D6
Chugqênsumdo China see Jigzhi
Chuguchak China see Tacheng
Chuguyev Ukr. see Chuhuyiv
Chuguyevka Russia 90 D3
Chugwater WY U.S.A. 156 G4
Chuhai China see Zhuhai
Chuhuyiv Ukr. 53 H6
Chuimatan China see Jishishan
Chujiang China see Shimen
Chukai Malaysia see Cukai
Chukchagirskoye, Ozero l. Russia 90 E1
Chukchi Abyssal Plain sea feature Arctic Ocean 189 B1
Chukchi Plateau sea feature Arctic Ocean 189 B1
Chukchi Range mts Russia see Chukotskoye Nagor'ye
Chukchi Sea Russia/U.S.A. 148 E1
Chukhloma Russia 52 I4
Chukotskiy, Mys c. Russia 148 D2
Chukotskiy Khrebet mts Russia see Chukotskoye Nagor'ye
Chukotskiy Poluostrov pen. Russia 148 D2
Chukotskoye Nagor'ye mts Russia 148 B2
Chulakkurgan Kazakh. see Sholakkorgan
Chulaktau Kazakh. see Karatau
Chulasa Russia 52 J2
Chula Vista CA U.S.A. 158 E5
Chulitna AK U.S.A. 149 J3
Chulloonawick AK U.S.A. 148 F3
Chulucanas Peru 176 B5
Chulung Pass Pak. 104 D2
Chuluut Gol r. Mongolia 94 E1
Chulym Russia 76 J4
Chulyshman r. Russia 98 D2
Chumar India 104 D2
Chumbicha Arg. 178 C3
Chumda China 96 C1
Chumek Kazakh. 98 D2
Chumikan Russia 77 O4
Chum Phae Thai. 86 C3
Chumphon Thai. 87 B5
Chum Saeng Thai. 86 C4
Chunar India 105 E4
Chuncheon S. Korea 91 B5
Chunga Zambia 123 C5
Chung-hua Jen-min Kung-ho-kuo country Asia see China
Chung-hua Min-kuo country Asia see Taiwan
Chungju S. Korea 91 B5
Chungking China see Chongqing
Ch'ungmu S. Korea see Tongyeong
Chŭngsan N. Korea 91 B5
Chunhua China 95 G5
Chunhuhux Mex. 167 H5
Chunian Pak. 111 I4
Chunskiy Russia 88 H1
Chunya r. Russia 77 K3
Chūō Japan 93 E3
Chuôi, Hon i. Vietnam 87 D5
Chuosijia China see Guanyinqiao
Chupa Russia 54 R3
Chūplū Iran 110 B2
Chuquicamata Chile 178 C2
Chur Switz. 66 I3
Churachandpur India 105 H4
Chūrān Iran 110 D4
Churapcha Russia 77 O3
Churchill Canada 151 M3
Churchill r. Man. Canada 151 M3
Churchill r. Nfld. and Lab. Canada 153 J3
Churchill, Cape Canada 151 M3
Churchill Falls Canada 153 J3
Churchill Lake Canada 151 I4
Churchill Mountains Antarctica 188 H1
Churchill Sound sea chan. Canada 152 F2
Churchs Ferry ND U.S.A. 160 D1
Churchville VA U.S.A. 164 F4
Churek-Dag, Gora mt. Russia 94 B1
Churia Ghati Hills Nepal 105 F4
Churu India 104 C3
Churubusco IN U.S.A. 164 C3
Churumuco Mex. 167 E5
Churún-Merú waterfall Venez. see Angel Falls
Chushul India 104 D2
Chuska Mountains NM U.S.A. 159 I3
Chusovaya r. Russia 51 R4
Chusovoy Russia 51 R4
Chust Ukr. see Khust
Chute-des-Passes Canada 153 H4
Chutia Assam India 105 H4
Chutia Jharkhand India 105 F5
Chutung Taiwan see Zhudong
Chuuk is Micronesia 186 G5
Chuxiong China 96 D3
Chüy r. Kazakh./Kyrg. see Shu
Chüy admin. div. Kyrg. 98 A4
Chūzenji-ko l. Japan 93 F2
Chuzhou Anhui China 97 H1
Chuzhou Jiangsu China 97 H1
Chūzu Japan 92 C3
Chymyshliya Moldova see Cimişlia
Chyulu Hills National Park Kenya 122 D4
Ciadâr-Lunga Moldova see Ciadîr-Lunga
Ciadîr-Lunga Moldova 69 M1
Ciamis Java Indon. 85 E4
Cianjur Java Indon. 84 D4
Cianorte Brazil 178 F2
Cibadak Java Indon. 84 D4
Cibatu Java Indon. 85 E4
Cibecue AZ U.S.A. 159 H4
Cibinong Java Indon. 84 D4
Cibolo Creek r. TX U.S.A. 161 D6
Cibuta Mex. 166 C2
Cibuta, Sierra mt. Mex. 166 C2
Čićarija mts Croatia 68 E2
Cicero IL U.S.A. 164 B3
Cidade Velha Cape Verde 120 [inset]
Cidaun Java Indon. 84 D4
Cide Turkey 112 D2
Ciechanów Poland 57 R4
Ciego de Ávila Cuba 169 I4
Ciénaga Col. 176 D1
Ciénega Mex. 167 E3
Ciénega de Flores Mex. 161 C7
Cieneguillas Mex. 166 D3
Cienfuegos Cuba 169 H4
Cieza Spain 67 F4
Çiftlik Turkey see Kelkit
Cifuentes Spain 67 E3
Cigeulis Java Indon. 84 D4
Cigüela r. Spain 67 E4
Cihanbeyli Turkey 112 D3
Cihuatlán Mex. 166 D5
Cíjara, Embalse de resr Spain 67 D4
Cikalong Java Indon. 85 E4
Cilacap Java Indon. 85 E4
Cilangkahan Java Indon. 84 D4
Çıldır Turkey 113 F2
Çıldır Gölü l. Turkey 113 F2
Çıldıroba Turkey 107 C1
Ciledug Java Indon. 85 E4
Cilento, Vallo di Diano e Alburni, Parco Nazionale del nat. park Italy 68 F4
Cili China 97 F2
Cilician Gates pass Turkey see Gülek Boğazı
Cill Airne Ireland see Killarney
Cill Chainnigh Ireland see Kilkenny
Cill Mhantáin Ireland see Wicklow
Çilmämmetgum des. Turkm. 110 D1
Cilo Dağı mt. Turkey 113 G3
Çilov Adası i. Azer. 113 H2
Cimahi Java Indon. 84 D4
Cimarron CO U.S.A. 159 J2
Cimarron KS U.S.A. 160 C4
Cimarron NM U.S.A. 157 G5
Cimarron r. OK U.S.A. 161 D4
Cimişlia Moldova 69 M1
Cimone, Monte mt. Italy 68 D2
Cîmpina Romania see Câmpina
Cîmpulung Romania see Câmpulung
Cîmpulung Moldovenesc Romania see Câmpulung Moldovenesc
Cina, Tanjung c. Indon. 84 D4
Çınar Turkey 113 F3
Cinca r. Spain 67 G3
Cincinnati OH U.S.A. 164 C4
Cinco de Outubro Angola see Xá-Muteba
Cinderford U.K. 59 E7
Çine Turkey 69 M6
Ciney Belgium 62 F4
Cintalapa Mex. 168 F5
Cinto, Monte mt. France 66 I5
Cipatuja Java Indon. 85 E4
Ciping China 97 G3
Cirata, Waduk resr Java Indon. 84 D4
Circeo, Parco Nazionale del nat. park Italy 68 E4
Circle AK U.S.A. 149 K2
Circle MT U.S.A. 156 G3
Circle Hot Springs AK U.S.A. 149 K2
Circleville OH U.S.A. 164 D4
Circleville UT U.S.A. 159 G2
Cirebon Java Indon. 85 E4
Cirencester U.K. 59 F7
Cirenti Sumatra Indon. 84 C3
Cirò Marina Italy 68 G5
Cirta Alg. see Constantine
Cisco (abandoned) UT U.S.A. 159 I2
Cisne, Islas del is Caribbean Sea 169 H5
Citlaltépetl vol. Mex. see Orizaba, Pico de
Čitluk Bos. & Herz. 68 G3
Citronelle AL U.S.A. 161 F6
Citrus Heights CA U.S.A. 158 C2
Città di Castello Italy 68 E3
Ciucaş, Vârful mt. Romania 69 K2
Ciudad Acuña Mex. 167 E2
Ciudad Altamirano Mex. 168 D5
Ciudad Bolívar Venez. 176 F2
Ciudad Camargo Mex. 166 D3
Ciudad Constitución Mex. 166 C3
Ciudad Cortés Costa Rica 166 [inset] J7
Ciudad Cuauhtémoc Mex. 167 H6
Ciudad Darío Nicaragua 166 [inset] I6
Ciudad del Carmen Mex. 167 H5
Ciudad Delicias Mex. 166 D2
Ciudad del Maíz Mex. 167 F4
Ciudad de Panamá Panama see Panama City
Ciudad de Valles Mex. 168 E4
Ciudad Guayana Venez. 176 F2
Ciudad Guerrero Mex. 157 G7
Ciudad Guzmán Mex. 168 D5
Ciudad Hidalgo Mex. 167 E5
Ciudad Ixtepec Mex. 167 G5
Ciudad Juárez Mex. 166 D2
Ciudad Lerdo Mex. 166 E3
Ciudad Madero Mex. 167 F4
Ciudad Mante Mex. 168 E4
Ciudad Manuel Doblado Mex. 167 E4
Ciudad Mendoza Mex. 167 F5
Ciudad Mier Mex. 167 F3
Ciudad Obregón Mex. 166 C3
Ciudad Real Spain 67 E4
Ciudad Río Bravo Mex. 167 F3
Ciudad Rodrigo Spain 67 C3
Ciudad Tecún Uman Guat. 167 G6
Ciudad Trujillo Dom. Rep. see Santo Domingo
Ciudad Victoria Mex. 161 D8
Ciutadella Spain 67 H3
Çıva Burnu pt Turkey 112 E2
Cividale del Friuli Italy 68 E1
Civitanova Marche Italy 68 E3
Civitavecchia Italy 68 D3
Çivril Turkey 69 M5
Cixi China 97 I2
Cixian China 95 H4
Ciyao China 95 I5
Cizhou China see Cixian
Cizre Turkey 113 F3
Clacton-on-Sea U.K. 59 I7
Clady U.K. 61 E3
Claire, Lake Canada 151 H3
Clairfontaine Alg. see El Aouinet
Clamecy France 66 F3
Clam Gulch AK U.S.A. 149 J3
Clane Ireland 61 F4
Clanton AL U.S.A. 163 C5
Clanwilliam Dam S. Africa 124 D7
Clara Ireland 61 E4
Clara Island Myanmar 87 B5
Claraville Australia 136 C3
Clare N.S.W. Australia 138 A4
Clare S.A. Australia 137 B7
Clare r. Ireland 61 C4
Clare MI U.S.A. 164 C2
Clarecastle Ireland 61 D5
Clare Island Ireland 61 B4
Claremont NH U.S.A. 165 I2
Claremore OK U.S.A. 161 E4
Claremorris Ireland 61 D4
Clarence r. Australia 138 F2
Clarence N.Z. 139 D6
Clarence Island Antarctica 188 A2
Clarence Strait Iran see Khūran
Clarence Strait AK U.S.A. 149 N4
Clarence Town Bahamas 163 F8
Clarendon AR U.S.A. 161 F5
Clarendon PA U.S.A. 164 F3
Clarendon TX U.S.A. 161 C5
Clarenville Canada 153 L4
Claresholm Canada 150 H5
Clarie Coast Antarctica see Wilkes Coast
Clarinda IA U.S.A. 160 E3
Clarington OH U.S.A. 164 E4
Clarion IA U.S.A. 160 E3
Clarion PA U.S.A. 164 F3
Clarion r. PA U.S.A. 164 F3
Clarión, Isla i. Mex. 168 B5
Clark SD U.S.A. 160 D2
Clark, Lake AK U.S.A. 148 I3
Clark, Mount Canada 149 Q2
Clarkdale AZ U.S.A. 159 G4
Clarkebury S. Africa 125 I6
Clarke Range mts Australia 136 D4
Clarke River Australia 136 D3
Clarke's Head Canada 153 L4
Clark Mountain CA U.S.A. 159 F4
Clark Point Canada 164 E1
Clarksburg WV U.S.A. 164 E4
Clarksdale MS U.S.A. 161 F5
Clarks Hill IN U.S.A. 164 B3
Clarks Point AK U.S.A. 148 H4
Clarksville AR U.S.A. 161 E5
Clarksville TN U.S.A. 164 B5
Clarksville TX U.S.A. 161 E5
Clarksville VA U.S.A. 165 F5
Claro r. Goiás Brazil 179 A2
Claro r. Mato Grosso Brazil 179 A1
Clashmore Ireland 61 E5
Claude TX U.S.A. 161 C5
Claudy U.K. 61 E3
Claveria Luzon Phil. 82 C2
Clavier Belgium 62 F4
Claxton GA U.S.A. 163 D5
Clay WV U.S.A. 164 E4
Clayburg NY U.S.A. 165 I1
Clay Center KS U.S.A. 160 D4
Clay Center NE U.S.A. 160 D3
Clay City IN U.S.A. 164 B4
Clay City KY U.S.A. 164 D5
Clayhole Wash watercourse AZ U.S.A. 159 G3
Claypool AZ U.S.A. 159 H5
Clay Springs AZ U.S.A. 159 H4
Clayton DE U.S.A. 165 H4
Clayton GA U.S.A. 163 D5
Clayton MI U.S.A. 164 C3
Clayton MO U.S.A. 160 F4
Clayton NM U.S.A. 161 C4
Clayton NY U.S.A. 165 G1
Claytor Lake VA U.S.A. 164 E5
Clay Village KY U.S.A. 164 C4
Clear, Cape Ireland 61 C6
Clearco WV U.S.A. 164 E4
Clear Creek Canada 164 E2
Clear Creek r. AZ U.S.A. 159 H4
Cleare, Cape AK U.S.A. 146 D4
Clearfield PA U.S.A. 165 F3
Clearfield UT U.S.A. 156 E4
Clear Fork Brazos r. TX U.S.A. 161 D5
Clear Hills Canada 150 G3
Clear Island Ireland 61 C6
Clear Lake IA U.S.A. 160 E3
Clear Lake SD U.S.A. 160 D2
Clear Lake l. CA U.S.A. 158 B2
Clear Lake l. UT U.S.A. 159 G2
Clearmont WY U.S.A. 156 G3
Clearwater Canada 150 G5
Clearwater r. Alta/Sask. Canada 151 I3
Clearwater r. Alta Canada 150 H4
Clearwater FL U.S.A. 163 D7
Clearwater Lake Canada 151 K4
Clearwater Mountains ID U.S.A. 156 E3
Cleaton KY U.S.A. 164 B5
Cleburne TX U.S.A. 161 D5
Cleethorpes U.K. 58 G5
Clementi Sing. 87 [inset]
Clendenin WV U.S.A. 164 E4
Clendening Lake OH U.S.A. 164 E3
Cleopatra Needle mt. Palawan Phil. 82 B4
Clères France 62 B5
Clerf Lux. see Clervaux
Clerke Reef Australia 134 B4
Clermont Australia 136 D4
Clermont France 62 C5
Clermont-en-Argonne France 62 F5
Clermont-Ferrand France 66 F4
Clervaux Lux. 62 G4
Cles Italy 68 D1
Clevedon U.K. 59 E7
Cleveland MS U.S.A. 161 F5
Cleveland OH U.S.A. 164 E3
Cleveland TN U.S.A. 163 C5
Cleveland TX U.S.A. 167 G2
Cleveland UT U.S.A. 159 H2
Cleveland WI U.S.A. 164 B2
Cleveland, Cape Australia 136 D3
Cleveland, Mount MT U.S.A. 156 E2
Cleveland Heights OH U.S.A. 164 E3
Cleveland Hills U.K. 58 F4
Cleveleys U.K. 58 D5
Cleves Germany see Kleve
Clew Bay Ireland 61 C4
Clifden Ireland 61 B4
Cliff NM U.S.A. 159 I5
Cliffoney Ireland 61 D3
Clifton Australia 138 E1
Clifton AZ U.S.A. 159 I5
Clifton Beach Australia 136 D3
Clifton Forge VA U.S.A. 164 F5
Clifton Park NY U.S.A. 165 I2
Climax Canada 151 I5
Climax MI U.S.A. 164 C2
Clinch Mountain mts Tennessee/Virginia U.S.A. 164 D5
Cline River Canada 150 G4
Clinton B.C. Canada 150 F5
Clinton Ont. Canada 164 E2
Clinton IA U.S.A. 160 F3
Clinton IL U.S.A. 160 F3
Clinton IN U.S.A. 164 B4
Clinton KY U.S.A. 161 F4
Clinton MI U.S.A. 164 D2
Clinton MO U.S.A. 160 E4
Clinton MS U.S.A. 161 F5
Clinton NC U.S.A. 163 E5
Clinton U.S.A. 165 H3
Clinton OK U.S.A. 161 D5
Clinton-Colden Lake Canada 151 J1
Clinton Creek (abandoned) Canada 149 L2
Clintwood VA U.S.A. 164 D5

▶Clipperton, Île terr. N. Pacific Ocean 187 M5
Part of France. Most easterly point of Oceania.

Clisham hill U.K. 60 C3
Clitheroe U.K. 58 E5
Clive Lake Canada 150 G2
Cliza Bol. 176 E7
Clocolan S. Africa 125 H5
Cloghan Ireland 61 E4
Clonakilty Ireland 61 D6
Clonbern Ireland 61 D4
Cloncurry Australia 136 C4
Cloncurry r. Australia 136 C3
Clones Ireland 61 E3
Clonmel Ireland 61 E5
Clonygowan Ireland 61 E4
Cloonbannin Ireland 61 C5
Clooneagh Ireland 61 E4
Cloppenburg Germany 63 I2
Cloquet MN U.S.A. 160 E2
Cloquet r. MN U.S.A. 160 E2
Cloud Peak WY U.S.A. 154 F3
Cloud Peak WY U.S.A. 156 G3
Clova Canada 152 G4
Clover UT U.S.A. 159 G1
Cloverdale CA U.S.A. 158 B2
Cloverdale IN U.S.A. 164 B4
Cloverport KY U.S.A. 164 B5
Clovis CA U.S.A. 158 D3
Clovis NM U.S.A. 161 C5
Cloyne Canada 165 G1
Cluain Meala Ireland see Clonmel
Cluanie, Loch l. U.K. 60 D3
Cluff Lake Mine Canada 151 I3
Cluj-Napoca Romania 69 J1
Clun U.K. 59 D6
Clunes Australia 138 A6
Cluny Australia 136 B5
Cluses France 66 H3
Cluster Springs VA U.S.A. 165 F5
Clut Lake Canada 150 G1
Clutterbuck Head hd Canada 153 H1
Clutterbuck Hills hill Australia 135 D6
Clwydian Range hills U.K. 58 D5
Clyde Canada 150 H4
Clyde r. U.K. 60 E5
Clyde NY U.S.A. 165 G2
Clyde OH U.S.A. 164 D3
Clyde, Firth of est. U.K. 60 E5
Clydebank U.K. 60 E5
Clyde River Canada 147 L2
Côa r. Port. 67 C3
Coachella CA U.S.A. 158 E5
Coahuayutla de Guerrero Mex. 167 E5
Coahuila state Mex. 166 E3
Coal r. Canada 149 P4
Coal City IL U.S.A. 164 A3
Coalcomán Mex. 166 E5
Coaldale (abandoned) NV U.S.A. 158 E2
Coalgate OK U.S.A. 161 D5
Coal Harbour Canada 150 E5
Coalinga CA U.S.A. 158 C3
Coalport PA U.S.A. 165 F3
Coal River Canada 149 P4
Coal Valley NV U.S.A. 159 F3
Coalville U.K. 59 F6
Coalville UT U.S.A. 159 H1
Coari Brazil 176 F4
Coari r. Brazil 176 F4
Coarsegold CA U.S.A. 158 D3
Coastal Plain U.S.A. 161 E6
Coast Mountains Canada 150 E4
Coast Range hills Australia 137 E5
Coast Ranges mts CA U.S.A. 158 B1
Coatbridge U.K. 60 E5
Coatepec Mex. 167 F5
Coatepeque Guat. 167 H6
Coatesville PA U.S.A. 165 H4
Coaticook Canada 165 J1
Coatlán Mex. 167 F5
Coats Island Canada 147 J3
Coats Land reg. Antarctica 188 A1
Coatzacoalcos Mex. 168 F5
Cobán Guat. 167 H6
Cobar Australia 138 B3
Cobargo Australia 138 D6
Cobden Australia 138 A7
Cobh Ireland 61 D6
Cobham r. Canada 151 M4
Cobija Bol. 176 E6
Coblenz Germany see Koblenz
Cobleskill NY U.S.A. 165 H2
Cobos Mex. 167 F4
Cobourg Peninsula Australia 134 F2
Cobra Australia 135 B6
Cobram Australia 138 B5
Coburg Germany 63 K4
Coburg Island Canada 147 K2
Coca Ecuador 176 C4
Coca Spain 67 D3
Cocalinho Brazil 179 A1
Cocanada India see Kakinada
Cochabamba Bol. 176 E7
Cochem Germany 63 H4
Cochin India see Kochi
Cochin reg. Vietnam 87 D5
Cochinos, Bahía de b. Cuba see Pigs, Bay of
Cochise AZ U.S.A. 159 I5
Cochise Head mt. AZ U.S.A. 159 I5
Cochrane Alta Canada 150 H5
Cochrane Ont. Canada 152 E4
Cochrane r. Canada 151 K3
Cockburn Australia 137 C7
Cockburnspath U.K. 60 G5
Cockburn Town Bahamas 163 F7
Cockburn Town Turks and Caicos Is see Grand Turk
Cockermouth U.K. 58 D4
Cocklebiddy Australia 135 D8
Cockscomb mt. S. Africa 124 G7
Coclé del Norte Panama 166 [inset] J7
Coco r. Hond./Nicaragua 166 [inset] J6
Coco, Cayo i. Cuba 163 E8
Coco, Isla de i. N. Pacific Ocean 169 G7
Cocobeach Gabon 122 A3
Coco Channel India 87 A4
Cocomórachic Mex. 166 D2
Coconino Plateau AZ U.S.A. 159 G4
Cocopara National Park Australia 138 C5
Cocoro i. Phil. 82 C4
Cocos Brazil 179 B1

▶Cocos (Keeling) Islands terr. Indian Ocean 80 B9
Australian External Territory.

Cocos Basin sea feature Indian Ocean 185 O5
Cocos Ridge sea feature N. Pacific Ocean 187 O5
Cocula Mex. 166 E4
Cocuy, Sierra Nevada del mt. Col. 176 D2
Cod, Cape MA U.S.A. 165 J3
Codajás Brazil 176 F4
Coderre Canada 151 J5
Codfish Island N.Z. 139 A8
Codigoro Italy 68 E2
Cod Island Canada 153 J2
Codlea Romania 69 K2
Codó Brazil 177 J4
Codsall U.K. 59 E6
Cod's Head hd Ireland 61 B6
Cody WY U.S.A. 156 F3
Coeburn VA U.S.A. 164 D5
Coen Australia 136 C2
Coesfeld Germany 63 H3
Coeur d'Alene ID U.S.A. 156 D3
Coeur d'Alene Lake ID U.S.A. 156 D3
Coevorden Neth. 62 G2
Coffee Bay S. Africa 125 I6
Coffee Cultural Landscape of Colombia tourist site Col. 176 C2
Coffeyville KS U.S.A. 161 E4
Coffin Bay Australia 137 A7
Coffin Bay National Park Australia 137 A7
Coffs Harbour Australia 138 F3
Cofimvaba S. Africa 125 H7
Cofradía Hond. 166 [inset] H6
Cofre de Perote, Parque Nacional nat. park Mex. 167 F5
Cognac France 66 D4
Cogo Equat. Guinea 120 D4
Coguno Moz. 125 L3
Cohoes NY U.S.A. 165 I2
Cohuna Australia 138 B5
Coiba, Isla de i. Panama 166 [inset] J8
Coigeach, Rubha pt U.K. 60 D2
Coihaique Chile 178 B7
Coimbatore India 106 C4
Coimbra Port. 67 B3
Coipasa, Salar de salt flat Bol. 176 E7
Coire Switz. see Chur
Colac Australia 138 A7
Colair Lake India see Kolleru Lake
Colatina Brazil 179 C2
Colbitz Germany 63 L2
Colborne Canada 165 G2
Colby KS U.S.A. 160 C4
Colchester U.K. 59 H7
Colchester CT U.S.A. 165 I3
Cold Bay AK U.S.A. 148 G5
Cold Bay AK U.S.A. 148 G5
Coldfoot AK U.S.A. 149 J2
Coldingham U.K. 60 G5
Colditz Germany 63 M3
Cold Lake Canada 151 I4
Cold Lake l. Canada 151 I4
Coldspring TX U.S.A. 161 E6
Coldstream Canada 150 G5
Coldstream U.K. 60 G5
Coldwater Canada 164 F1
Coldwater KS U.S.A. 161 D4
Coldwater MI U.S.A. 164 C3
Coldwater r. MS U.S.A. 161 F5
Coleambally Australia 138 B5
Colebrook NH U.S.A. 165 J1
Coleen r. AK U.S.A. 149 L2
Coleman r. Australia 136 C2
Coleman TX U.S.A. 161 D6
Çölemerik Turkey see Hakkâri
Colenso S. Africa 125 I5
Cole Peninsula Antarctica 188 L2
Coleraine Australia 137 C8
Coleraine U.K. 61 F2
Coles, Punta de pt Peru 176 D7
Coles Bay Australia 137 [inset]
Colesberg S. Africa 125 G6
Coleville Canada 151 I5
Colfax CA U.S.A. 158 C2
Colfax LA U.S.A. 161 E6
Colfax WA U.S.A. 156 D3
Colhué Huapí, Lago l. Arg. 178 C7
Coligny S. Africa 125 H4
Colima Mex. 168 D5
Colima state Mex. 166 E5
Colima, Nevado de vol. Mex. 168 D5
Coll i. U.K. 60 C4
Collado Villalba Spain 67 E3
Collarenebri Australia 138 D2
College AK U.S.A. 149 K2
College Station TX U.S.A. 161 D6
Collerina Australia 138 C2
Collie N.S.W. Australia 138 D3
Collie W.A. Australia 135 B8
Collier Bay Australia 134 D4
Collier Range National Park Australia 135 B6
Collingwood Canada 164 E1
Collingwood N.Z. 139 D5
Collins MS U.S.A. 161 F6
Collins Glacier Antarctica 188 E2
Collinson Peninsula Canada 147 H2
Collipulli Chile 178 B5
Collmberg hill Germany 63 N3
Collooney Ireland 61 D3
Colmar France 66 H2
Colmenar Viejo Spain 67 E3
Colmonell U.K. 60 E5
Colne r. U.K. 59 H7
Cologne Germany 62 G4

Coloma MI U.S.A. 164 B2
Colomb-Béchar Alg. see Béchar
Colômbia Brazil 179 A3
Colombia Mex. 167 F3

▶Colombia country S. America 176 D3
2nd most populous and 4th largest country in South America.

Colombian Basin sea feature S. Atlantic Ocean 184 C5

▶Colombo Sri Lanka 106 C5
Former capital of Sri Lanka.

Colomiers France 66 E5
Colón Buenos Aires Arg. 178 D4
Colón Entre Ríos Arg. 178 E4
Colón Cuba 163 D8
Colón Panama 166 [inset] K7
Colon MI U.S.A. 164 C3
Colón, Archipiélago de is Ecuador see Galapagos Islands
Colón, Isla i. Panama 166 [inset] J7
Colón, Montañas de mts Hond. 166 [inset] I6
Colona Australia 135 F7
Colonelganj India 105 E4
Colonel Hill Bahamas 163 F8
Colonet, Cabo c. Mex. 166 A2
Colônia r. Brazil 179 D1
Colonia Micronesia 81 J5
Colonia Agrippina Germany see Cologne
Colonia Díaz Mex. 166 C2
Colonia Julia Fenestris Italy see Fano
Colonial Heights VA U.S.A. 165 G5
Colonna, Capo c. Italy 68 G5
Colonsay i. U.K. 60 C4
Colorado r. Arg. 178 D5
Colorado r. Mex./U.S.A. 157 E7
Colorado r. TX U.S.A. 161 D6
Colorado state U.S.A. 156 G5
Colorado City AZ U.S.A. 159 G3
Colorado City TX U.S.A. 161 C5
Colorado Desert CA U.S.A. 158 E5
Colorado National Monument nat. park CO U.S.A. 159 I2
Colorado Plateau CO U.S.A. 159 I3
Colorado River Aqueduct canal CA U.S.A. 159 F4
Colorado Springs CO U.S.A. 156 G5
Colossae Turkey see Honaz
Colotlán Mex. 168 D4
Cölpin Germany 63 N1
Colquiri Bol. 176 E7
Colquitt GA U.S.A. 163 C6
Colson KY U.S.A. 164 D5
Colsterworth U.K. 59 G6
Colstrip MT U.S.A. 156 G3
Coltishall U.K. 59 I6
Colton CA U.S.A. 158 E4
Colton NY U.S.A. 165 H1
Colton (abandoned) UT U.S.A. 159 H2
Columbia KY U.S.A. 164 C5
Columbia LA U.S.A. 161 E5
Columbia MD U.S.A. 165 G4
Columbia MO U.S.A. 160 E4
Columbia MS U.S.A. 161 F6
Columbia NC U.S.A. 162 E5
Columbia PA U.S.A. 165 G3

▶Columbia SC U.S.A. 163 D5
Capital of South Carolina.

Columbia TN U.S.A. 162 C5
Columbia r. WA U.S.A. 156 C3
Columbia, District of admin. dist. U.S.A. 165 G4
Columbia, Mount Canada 150 G4
Columbia, Sierra mts Mex. 166 B2
Columbia City IN U.S.A. 164 C3
Columbia Lake Canada 150 H5
Columbia Mountains Canada 150 F4
Columbia Plateau U.S.A. 156 D3
Columbine, Cape S. Africa 124 C7
Columbus GA U.S.A. 163 C5
Columbus IN U.S.A. 164 C4
Columbus MS U.S.A. 161 F5
Columbus MT U.S.A. 156 F3
Columbus NC U.S.A. 163 D5
Columbus NE U.S.A. 160 D3
Columbus NM U.S.A. 157 G7

▶Columbus OH U.S.A. 164 D4
Capital of Ohio.

Columbus TX U.S.A. 161 D6
Columbus Grove OH U.S.A. 164 C3
Columbus Salt Marsh NV U.S.A. 158 D2
Colusa CA U.S.A. 158 B2
Colville N.Z. 139 E3
Colville WA U.S.A. 156 D2
Colville r. AK U.S.A. 149 J1
Colville Channel N.Z. 139 E3
Colville Lake Canada 149 P2
Colville Lake l. Canada 149 P2
Colwyn Bay U.K. 58 D5
Comacchio Italy 68 E2
Comacchio, Valli di lag. Italy 68 E2
Comai China 99 E7
Comalcalco Mex. 167 G5
Comanche TX U.S.A. 161 D6
Comandante Ferraz research station Antarctica 188 A2
Comandante Salas Arg. 178 C4
Comănești Romania 69 L1
Comayagua Hond. 166 [inset] I6
Combahee r. SC U.S.A. 163 D5
Combarbalá Chile 178 B4
Comber U.K. 61 G3
Combermere Bay Myanmar 86 A3
Combles France 62 C4
Combol i. Sumatra Indon. 84 C2
Combomune Moz. 125 K2
Comboyne Australia 138 F3
Comencho, Lac l. Canada 152 G4
Comendador Dom. Rep. see Elías Piña
Comendador Gomes Brazil 179 A2
Comeragh Mountains hills Ireland 61 E5
Comercinho Brazil 179 C2
Cometela Moz. 125 L1
Comfort TX U.S.A. 161 D6
Comilla Bangl. 105 G5
Comines Belgium 62 C4
Comino, Capo c. Sardinia Italy 68 C4
Comitán de Domínguez Mex. 167 G5
Commack NY U.S.A. 165 I3
Commentry France 66 F3
Committee Bay Canada 147 J3
Commonwealth Territory admin. div. Australia see Jervis Bay Territory
Como Italy 68 C2
Como, Lago di Italy see Como, Lake
Como, Lake Italy 68 C2
Como Chamling l. China 99 E7
Comodoro Rivadavia Arg. 178 C7
Comoé, Parc National de la nat. park Côte d'Ivoire 120 C4
Comonfort Mex. 167 E4
Comores country Africa see Comoros
Comorin, Cape India 106 C4
Comoro Islands country Africa see Comoros
Comoros country Africa 123 E5
Compiègne France 62 C5
Compostela Mex. 166 D4
Compostela Mindanao Phil. 82 D5
Comprida, Ilha i. Brazil 179 B4
Comrat Moldova 69 M1
Comrie U.K. 60 F4
Comstock TX U.S.A. 161 C6
Côn, Sông r. Vietnam 87 E4
Cona China 99 E8

▶Conakry Guinea 120 B4
Capital of Guinea.

Cona Niyeo Arg. 178 C6
Conceição r. Brazil 179 B2
Conceição da Barra Brazil 179 D2
Conceição do Araguaia Brazil 177 I5
Conceição do Mato Dentro Brazil 179 C2
Concepción Chile 178 B5
Concepción Mex. 161 C7
Concepción r. Mex. 166 B2
Concepción Para. 178 E2
Concepción, Punta pt Mex. 166 C3
Concepción de la Vega Dom. Rep. see La Vega
Conception, Point CA U.S.A. 158 C4
Conception Island Bahamas 163 F8
Concha Mex. 166 D4
Conchas NM U.S.A. 157 G6
Conchas Lake NM U.S.A. 157 G6
Concho Mex. 166 D3
Concho AZ U.S.A. 159 I4
Conchos r. Chihuahua Mex. 166 D2
Conchos r. Nuevo León/Tamaulipas Mex. 167 F3
Concord CA U.S.A. 158 B3
Concord NC U.S.A. 163 D5

▶Concord NH U.S.A. 165 J2
Capital of New Hampshire.

Concord VT U.S.A. 165 J1
Concordia research station Antarctica 188 G2
Concordia Arg. 178 E4
Concordiá Mex. 161 B8
Concordia Peru 176 D4
Concordia S. Africa 124 C5
Concordia KS U.S.A. 160 D4
Concordia KY U.S.A. 164 B4
Concord Peak Afgh. 111 I2
Con Cuông Vietnam 86 D3
Condamine Australia 138 E1
Condamine r. Australia 138 D1
Côn Đao Vietnam 87 D5
Condega Nicaragua 166 [inset] I6
Condeúba Brazil 179 C1
Condobolin Australia 138 C4
Condom France 66 E5
Condon OR U.S.A. 156 C3
Cóndor, Cordillera del mts Ecuador/Peru 176 C4
Condroz reg. Belgium 62 E4
Conecuh r. AL U.S.A. 163 C6
Conegliano Italy 68 E2
Conejos Mex. 166 E3
Conejos CO U.S.A. 157 G5
Conemaugh r. PA U.S.A. 164 F3
Cone Mountain AK U.S.A. 148 H2
Conestogo Lake Canada 164 E2
Conesus Lake NY U.S.A. 165 G2
Conflict Group is P.N.G. 136 E1
Confoederatio Helvetica country Europe see Switzerland
Confusion Range mts UT U.S.A. 159 G2
Congdü China 99 D7
Conghua China 97 G4
Congjiang China 97 F3
Congleton U.K. 58 E5
Congo country Africa 122 B4

▶Congo r. Congo/Dem. Rep. Congo 122 B4
2nd longest river in Africa and 8th in the world. Formerly known as Zaïre.

Congo (Brazzaville) country Africa see Congo
Congo (Kinshasa) country Africa see Congo, Democratic Republic of the

▶Congo, Democratic Republic of the country Africa 122 C4
2nd largest and 4th most populous country in Africa.

Congo, Republic of the country Africa see Congo
Congo Basin Dem. Rep. Congo 122 C4
Congo Cone sea feature S. Atlantic Ocean 184 I6
Congo Free State country Africa see Congo, Democratic Republic of the
Congonhas Brazil 179 C3
Congress AZ U.S.A. 159 G4
Conhuas Mex. 167 H5
Conimbla National Park Australia 138 D4
Coningsby U.K. 59 G5
Coniston Canada 152 E5
Coniston U.K. 58 D4
Conjuboy Australia 136 D3
Conkal Mex. 167 H4
Conklin Canada 151 I4
Conn r. Canada 152 F3
Conn, Lough l. Ireland 61 C3
Connacht reg. Ireland 61 C4
Connaught reg. Ireland see Connacht
Conneaut OH U.S.A. 164 E3
Connecticut state U.S.A. 165 I3
Connemara reg. Ireland 61 C4
Connemara National Park Ireland 61 C4
Connersville IN U.S.A. 164 C4
Connolly, Mount Canada 149 N3
Connors Range hills Australia 136 E4
Conoble Australia 138 B4
Conquista Brazil 179 B2
Conrad MT U.S.A. 156 F2
Conrad Rise sea feature Southern Ocean 185 K9
Conroe TX U.S.A. 161 E6
Conroe, Lake TX U.S.A. 167 G2
Consejo Belize 167 H5
Conselheiro Lafaiete Brazil 179 C3
Consett U.K. 58 F4
Consolación del Sur Cuba 163 D8
Côn Sơn, Đao i. Vietnam 87 D5
Consort Canada 151 I4
Constance Germany see Konstanz
Constance, Lake Germany/Switz. 57 L7
Constância dos Baetas Brazil 176 F5
Constanța Romania 69 M2
Constantia tourist site Cyprus see Salamis
Constantia Germany see Konstanz
Constantina Spain 67 D5
Constantine Alg. 64 F4
Constantine, Cape AK U.S.A. 148 H4
Constantine Harbor AK U.S.A. 148 [inset] B6
Constantinople Turkey see İstanbul
Constitución de 1857, Parque Nacional nat. park Mex. 166 B1
Consul Canada 151 I5
Contact NV U.S.A. 156 E4
Contamana Peru 176 C5
Contas r. Brazil 179 D1
Contoy, Isla i. Mex. 167 I4
Contria Brazil 179 B2
Contwoyto Lake Canada 151 I1
Convención Col. 176 D2
Convent LA U.S.A. 161 F6
Conway U.K. see Conwy
Conway AR U.S.A. 161 E5
Conway ND U.S.A. 160 D1
Conway NH U.S.A. 165 J2
Conway SC U.S.A. 163 E5
Conway, Cape Australia 136 E4
Conway, Lake salt flat Australia 137 A6
Conway National Park Australia 136 E4
Conway Reef Fiji see Ceva-i-Ra
Conwy U.K. 58 D5
Conwy r. U.K. 59 D5
Coober Pedy Australia 135 F7
Cooch Behar India see Koch Bihar
Coochbehar India see Koch Bihar
Cook Australia 135 E7
Cook, Cape Canada 150 E5
Cook, Grand Récif de reef New Caledonia 133 G3
Cook, Mount Canada/U.S.A. 149 M3
Cook, Mount N.Z. see Aoraki/Mount Cook
Cookes Peak NM U.S.A. 157 G6
Cookeville TN U.S.A. 162 C4
Cookhouse S. Africa 125 G7
Cook Ice Shelf Antarctica 188 H2
Cook Inlet sea chan. AK U.S.A. 148 I3

▶Cook Islands terr. S. Pacific Ocean 186 J7
Self-governing New Zealand overseas territory.

Cooksburg NY U.S.A. 165 H2
Cooks Passage Australia 136 D2
Cookstown U.K. 61 F3
Cook Strait N.Z. 139 E5
Cooktown Australia 136 D2
Coolabah Australia 138 C3
Cooladdi Australia 138 B1
Coolah Australia 138 D3
Coolamon Australia 138 C5
Coolgardie Australia 135 C7
Coolibah Australia 134 E3
Coolidge AZ U.S.A. 159 H5
Coolum Beach Australia 137 F5
Cooma Australia 138 D6
Coombah Australia 137 C7
Coonabarabran Australia 138 D3
Coonamble Australia 138 D3
Coondambo Australia 137 A6
Coondapoor India see Kundapura
Coongoola Australia 138 B1
Coon Rapids MN U.S.A. 160 E2
Cooper Creek watercourse Australia 137 B6
Cooper Mountain Canada 150 G5
Coopernook Australia 138 F3
Cooper's Town Bahamas 163 E7
Cooperstown ND U.S.A. 160 D2
Cooperstown NY U.S.A. 165 H2
Coopracambra National Park Australia 138 D6
Coorabie Australia 135 F7
Coorong National Park Australia 137 B8
Coorow Australia 135 B7
Coosa r. AL U.S.A. 163 C5
Coos Bay OR U.S.A. 156 B4
Coos Bay b. OR U.S.A. 156 B4
Cootamundra Australia 138 D5
Cootehill Ireland 61 E3
Cooyar Australia 138 E1
Copainalá Mex. 167 G5
Copala Mex. 168 E5
Copán tourist site Hond. 166 [inset] H6
Cope CO U.S.A. 160 C4
Copemish MI U.S.A. 164 C1

▶Copenhagen Denmark 55 H9
Capital of Denmark.

Copenhagen NY U.S.A. 165 H2
Copertino Italy 68 H4
Copeton Reservoir Australia 138 E2
Cô Pi, Phou mt. Laos/Vietnam 86 D3
Copiapó Chile 178 B3
Copley Australia 137 B6
Copparo Italy 68 D2
Copper r. AK U.S.A. 149 K3
Copper Cliff Canada 152 E5
Copper Harbor MI U.S.A. 162 C2
Coppermine Canada see Kugluktuk
Coppermine r. Canada 150 H1
Coppermine Point Canada 152 D5
Copperton S. Africa 124 F5
Copp Lake Canada 150 H2
Coqên Xizang China 99 D7
Coqên Xizang China 99 D7
Coquilhatville Dem. Rep. Congo see Mbandaka
Coquille i. Micronesia see Pikelot
Coquille OR U.S.A. 156 B4
Coquimbo Chile 178 B3
Coquitlam Canada 150 F5
Corabia Romania 69 K3
Coração de Jesus Brazil 179 B2
Coracesium Turkey see Alanya
Coraki Australia 138 F2
Coral Bay Australia 135 A5
Coral Bay Palawan Phil. 82 B4
Coral Harbour Canada 147 J3
Coral Sea S. Pacific Ocean 132 F3
Coral Sea Basin S. Pacific Ocean 186 G6

▶Coral Sea Islands Territory terr. Australia 132 F3
Australian External Territory.

Corangamite, Lake Australia 138 A7
Corat Azer. 113 H2
Corbeny France 62 D5
Corbett Inlet Canada 151 M2
Corbett National Park India 104 D3
Corbie France 62 C5
Corbin KY U.S.A. 164 C5
Corby U.K. 59 G6
Corcaigh Ireland see Cork
Corcoran CA U.S.A. 158 D3
Corcovado, Golfo de sea chan. Chile 178 B6
Corcovado, Parque Nacional nat. park Costa Rica 166 [inset] J7
Corcyra i. Greece see Corfu
Cordele GA U.S.A. 163 D6
Cordelia CA U.S.A. 158 B2
Cordell OK U.S.A. 161 D5
Cordilheiras, Serra das hills Brazil 177 I5
Cordillera Azul, Parque Nacional nat. park Peru 176 C5
Cordillera de los Picachos, Parque Nacional nat. park Col. 176 D3
Cordilleras Range mts Panay Phil. 82 C4
Cordillo Downs Australia 137 C5
Cordisburgo Brazil 179 B2
Córdoba Arg. 178 D4
Córdoba Durango Mex. 166 E3
Córdoba Veracruz Mex. 168 E5
Córdoba Spain 67 D5
Córdoba, Sierras de mts Arg. 178 D4
Cordova Spain see Córdoba
Cordova AK U.S.A. 149 K3
Cordova Peak AK U.S.A. 149 K3
Corduba Spain see Córdoba
Corfu i. Greece 69 H5
Coria Spain 67 C4
Coribe Brazil 179 B1
Coricudgy mt. Australia 138 E4
Corigliano Calabro Italy 68 G5
Coringa Islands Australia 136 E3
Corinium U.K. see Cirencester
Corinth Greece 69 J6
Corinth KY U.S.A. 164 C4
Corinth MS U.S.A. 161 F5
Corinth NY U.S.A. 165 I2
Corinth, Gulf of sea chan. Greece 69 J5
Corinthus Greece see Corinth
Corinto Brazil 179 B2
Corinto Nicaragua 166 [inset] I6
Cork Ireland 61 D6
Corleone Sicily Italy 68 E6
Çorlu Turkey 69 L4
Cormeilles France 59 H9
Cormoran Reef Palau 82 [inset]
Cornelia S. Africa 125 I4
Cornélio Procópio Brazil 179 A3
Cornélios Brazil 179 A5
Cornell WI U.S.A. 160 F2
Corner Brook Canada 153 K4
Corner Inlet b. Australia 138 C7
Corner Seamounts sea feature N. Atlantic Ocean 184 E3
Corneto Italy see Tarquinia
Cornillet, Mont hill France 62 E5
Corning AR U.S.A. 161 F4
Corning CA U.S.A. 158 B2
Corning NY U.S.A. 165 G2
Cornish watercourse Australia 136 D4
Corn Islands is Nicaragua see Maíz, Islas del
Corno di Campo mt. Italy/Switz. 66 J3
Corno Grande mt. Italy 68 E3
Cornwall Canada 165 H1
Cornwallis Island Canada 147 I2
Cornwall Island Canada 147 I2
Coro Venez. 176 E1
Coroaci Brazil 179 C2
Coroatá Brazil 177 J4
Corofin Ireland 61 C5
Coromandel Brazil 179 B2
Coromandel Coast India 106 D4
Coromandel Peninsula N.Z. 139 E3
Coromandel Range hills N.Z. 139 E3
Coron Phil. 82 C3
Corona CA U.S.A. 158 E5
Corona NM U.S.A. 157 G6
Coronado CA U.S.A. 158 E5
Coronado, Bahía de b. Costa Rica 166 [inset] J7
Coronado Bay Mindanao Phil. 82 C5
Coronation Canada 151 I4
Coronation Gulf Canada 146 G3
Coronation Island S. Atlantic Ocean 188 A2
Coronation Island AK U.S.A. 149 N5
Coron Bay Phil. 82 C4
Coronda Arg. 178 D4
Coronel Fabriciano Brazil 179 C2
Coronel Oviedo Para. 178 E3
Coronel Pringles Arg. 178 D5
Coronel Suárez Arg. 178 D5
Coropuna, Nudo mt. Peru 176 D7
Çorovodë Albania 69 I4
Corowa Australia 138 C5
Corozal Belize 167 H5
Corpus Christi TX U.S.A. 161 D7
Corpus Christi, Lake TX U.S.A. 167 F2
Corque Bol. 176 E7
Corral de Cantos mt. Spain 67 D4
Corrales Mex. 161 B7
Corralilla Cuba 163 D8
Corrandibby Range hills Australia 135 A6
Corrente Brazil 177 I6
Corrente r. Bahia Brazil 179 C1
Corrente r. Minas Gerais Brazil 179 A2
Correntes Brazil 177 H7
Correntina Brazil 179 B1
Correntina r. Brazil see Éguas
Corrib, Lough l. Ireland 61 C4
Corrientes Arg. 178 E3
Corrientes, Cabo c. Col. 176 C2
Corrientes, Cabo c. Cuba 163 C8
Corrientes, Cabo c. Mex. 168 C4
Corrigan TX U.S.A. 167 G2
Corrigin Australia 135 B8
Corris U.K. 59 D6
Corry PA U.S.A. 164 F3
Corse i. France see Corsica
Corse, Cap c. Corsica France 66 I5
Corsham U.K. 59 E7
Corsica i. France 66 I5
Corsicana TX U.S.A. 161 D5
Corte Corsica France 66 I5
Cortegana Spain 67 C5
Cortes, Sea of g. Mex. see California, Gulf of
Cortez CO U.S.A. 159 I3
Cortina d'Ampezzo Italy 68 E1
Cortland NY U.S.A. 165 G2
Corton U.K. 59 I6
Cortona Italy 68 D3
Coruche Port. 67 B4
Çoruh Turkey see Artvin
Çoruh r. Turkey 113 F2
Çorum Turkey 112 D2
Corumbá Brazil 177 G7
Corumbá r. Brazil 179 A2
Corumbá de Goiás Brazil 179 A1
Corumbaíba Brazil 179 A2
Corumbaú, Ponta pt Brazil 179 D2
Corunna Spain see A Coruña
Corunna MI U.S.A. 164 C2
Corvallis OR U.S.A. 156 C3
Corvette, Lac de la l. Canada 152 G3
Corwen U.K. 59 D6
Corydon IA U.S.A. 160 E3
Corydon IN U.S.A. 164 B4
Coryville PA U.S.A. 165 F3
Cos i. Greece see Kos
Cosalá Mex. 166 D3
Cosamaloapan Mex. 167 G5
Cosentia Italy see Cosenza
Cosenza Italy 68 G5
Coshocton OH U.S.A. 164 E3
Cosne-Cours-sur-Loire France 66 F3
Costa Blanca coastal area Spain 67 F4
Costa Brava coastal area Spain 67 H3
Costa de la Luz coastal area Spain 67 C5
Costa del Sol coastal area Spain 67 D5
Costa Marques Brazil 176 F6
Costa Rica Brazil 177 H7
Costa Rica country Central America 169 H6
Costa Rica Mex. 166 D3
Costa Verde coastal area Spain 67 C2
Costermansville Dem. Rep. Congo see Bukavu
Costești Romania 69 K2
Costigan Lake Canada 151 J3
Coswig (Anhalt) Germany 63 M3
Cotabato Mindanao Phil. 82 D5
Cotagaita Bol. 176 E8
Cotahuasi Peru 176 D7
Cote, Mount AK U.S.A. 149 O4
Coteau des Prairies slope SD U.S.A. 160 D2
Coteau du Missouri slope ND U.S.A. 160 C1
Coteau du Missouri slope SD U.S.A. 160 C2
Côte d'Ivoire country Africa 120 C4
Côte Française de Somalis country Africa see Djibouti
Cotentin pen. France 59 F9
Cothi r. U.K. 59 C7
Cotiaeum Turkey see Kütahya
Cotiella mt. Spain 67 G2
Cotonou Benin 120 D4
Cotopaxi, Volcán vol. Ecuador 176 C4
Cotswold Hills U.K. 59 E7
Cottage Grove OR U.S.A. 156 C4
Cottbus Germany 57 O5
Cottenham U.K. 59 H6
Cottian Alps mts France/Italy 66 H4
Cottica Suriname 177 H3
Cottiennes, Alpes mts France/Italy see Cottian Alps
Cottonwood AZ U.S.A. 159 G4
Cottonwood CA U.S.A. 158 B1
Cottonwood r. KS U.S.A. 160 D4
Cottonwood Falls KS U.S.A. 160 D4
Cotulla TX U.S.A. 161 D6
Coubre, Pointe de la pt France 66 D4
Coudersport PA U.S.A. 165 F3
Couedic, Cape du Australia 137 B8
Coulee City WA U.S.A. 156 D3
Coulee Dam WA U.S.A. 156 D3
Coulman Island Antarctica 188 H2
Coulogne France 62 B4
Coulommiers France 62 D6
Coulonge r. Canada 152 F5
Coulterville CA U.S.A. 158 C3
Council AK U.S.A. 148 G2
Council ID U.S.A. 156 D3
Council Bluffs IA U.S.A. 160 E3
Council Grove KS U.S.A. 160 D4
Councillor Island Australia 137 [inset]
Counselor NM U.S.A. 159 J3
Coupeville WA U.S.A. 156 C2
Courageous Lake Canada 151 I1
Courland Lagoon b. Lith./Russia 55 L9
Courtenay Canada 150 E5
Courtland VA U.S.A. 165 G5
Courtmacsherry Ireland 61 D6
Courtmacsherry Bay Ireland 61 D6
Courtown Ireland 61 F5
Courtrai Belgium see Kortrijk
Coushatta LA U.S.A. 161 E5
Coutances France 66 D2
Coutts Canada 151 I5
Couture, Lac l. Canada 152 G2
Couvin Belgium 62 E4
Cove Fort UT U.S.A. 159 G2
Cove Island Canada 164 E1
Cove Mountains hills PA U.S.A. 165 F4
Coventry U.K. 59 F6
Covesville VA U.S.A. 165 F5
Covilhã Port. 67 C3
Coville, Lake AK U.S.A. 148 I4
Covington GA U.S.A. 163 D5
Covington IN U.S.A. 164 B3
Covington KY U.S.A. 164 C4
Covington LA U.S.A. 161 F6
Covington MI U.S.A. 160 F2
Covington TN U.S.A. 161 F5
Covington VA U.S.A. 164 E5
Cowal, Lake dry lake Australia 138 C4
Cowan, Lake salt flat Australia 135 C7
Cowansville Canada 165 I1
Cowargarzê China 96 C1
Cowcowing Lakes salt flat Australia 135 B7
Cowdenbeath U.K. 60 F4
Cowell Australia 137 B7
Cowes U.K. 59 F8
Cowichan Lake Canada 150 E5
Cowley Australia 138 B1
Cowper Point Canada 147 G2
Cowra Australia 138 D4
Cox r. Australia 136 A2
Coxá r. Brazil 179 B1
Coxen Hole Hond. see Roatán
Coxilha de Santana hills Brazil/Uruguay 178 E4
Coxilha Grande hills Brazil 178 F3
Coxim Brazil 177 H7
Cox's Bazar Bangl. 105 G5
Coyame Mex. 161 B6
Coyhaique Chile see Coihaique
Coyote, Punta pt Mex. 166 C3
Coyote Lake CA U.S.A. 158 E4
Coyote Peak hill AZ U.S.A. 159 F5
Coyotitán Mex. 166 D4
Coyuca de Benítez Mex. 167 E5
Cozhê Xizang China 99 D7
Cozie, Alpi mts France/Italy see Cottian Alps
Cozumel Mex. 167 I4
Cozumel, Isla de i. Mex. 167 I4
Craboon Australia 138 D4
Cracovia Poland see Kraków
Cracow Australia 136 E5
Cracow Poland see Kraków
Cradle Mountain Lake St Clair National Park Australia 137 [inset]
Cradock S. Africa 125 G7
Craig U.K. 60 D3
Craig AK U.S.A. 149 N5
Craig CO U.S.A. 159 J1
Craigavon U.K. 61 F3
Craigieburn Australia 138 B6
Craig Island Taiwan see Mianhua Yu
Craignure U.K. 60 D4
Craigsville WV U.S.A. 164 E4
Crail U.K. 60 G4
Crailsheim Germany 63 K5
Craiova Romania 69 J2
Cramlington U.K. 58 F3
Cranberry Junction Canada 149 O5
Cranberry Lake NY U.S.A. 165 H1
Cranberry Portage Canada 151 K4
Cranborne Chase for. U.K. 59 E8
Cranbourne Australia 138 B7
Cranbrook Canada 150 H5
Crandon WI U.S.A. 160 F2
Crane TX U.S.A. 166 E2
Crane Lake Canada 151 I5
Cranston KY U.S.A. 164 D4

Cranston *RI* U.S.A. **165** J3
Cranz Russia *see* **Zelenogradsk**
Crary Ice Rise Antarctica **188** I1
Crary Mountains Antarctica **188** J1
Crater Lake National Park *OR* U.S.A. **156** C4
Crater Peak *CA* U.S.A. **158** C1
Craters of the Moon National Monument *nat. park ID* U.S.A. **156** E4
Crateús Brazil **177** J5
Crato Brazil **177** K5
Crawford *CO* U.S.A. **159** J2
Crawford *NE* U.S.A. **160** C3
Crawford Point *Palawan* Phil. **82** B4
Crawfordsville *IN* U.S.A. **164** B3
Crawfordville *FL* U.S.A. **163** C6
Crawfordville *GA* U.S.A. **163** D5
Crawley U.K. **59** G7
Crazy Mountains *AK* U.S.A. **149** K2
Crazy Mountains *MT* U.S.A. **156** F3
Creag Meagaidh *mt.* U.K. **60** E4
Crécy-en-Ponthieu France **62** B4
Credenhill U.K. **59** E6
Crediton U.K. **59** D8
Cree *r.* Canada **151** J3
Creel Mex. **157** G8
Cree Lake Canada **151** J3
Creemore Canada **164** E1
Creighton Canada **151** K4
Creil France **62** C5
Creil Neth. **62** F2
Crema Italy **68** C2
Cremlingen Germany **63** K2
Cremona Canada **150** H5
Cremona Italy **68** D2
Crépy-en-Valois France **62** C5
Cres *i.* Croatia **68** F2
Crescent *OR* U.S.A. **156** C4
Crescent City *CA* U.S.A. **156** B4
Crescent City *FL* U.S.A. **163** D6
Crescent Group *is* Paracel Is **80** E3
Crescent Head Australia **138** F3
Crescent Junction *UT* U.S.A. **159** I2
Crescent Valley *NV* U.S.A. **158** E1
Cressy Australia **138** A7
Cresta, Mount Phil. **82** C2
Crestline *OH* U.S.A. **164** D3
Creston Canada **150** G5
Creston *IA* U.S.A. **160** E3
Creston *WY* U.S.A. **156** G4
Crestview *FL* U.S.A. **163** C6
Creswick Australia **138** A6
Creta *i.* Greece *see* **Crete**
Crete *i.* Greece **69** K7
Crete *NE* U.S.A. **160** D3
Creus, Cap de *c.* Spain **67** H2
Creuse *r.* France **66** E3
Creußen Germany **63** L5
Creutzwald France **62** G5
Creuzburg Germany **63** K3
Crevasse Valley Glacier Antarctica **188** J1
Crewe U.K. **59** E5
Crewe *VA* U.S.A. **165** F5
Crewkerne U.K. **59** E8
Crianlarich U.K. **60** E4
Criccieth U.K. **59** C6
Criciúma Brazil **179** A5
Crieff U.K. **60** F4
Crifell *hill* U.K. *see* **Criffel**
Criffel *hill* U.K. **60** F6
Crikvenica Croatia **68** F2
Crillon, Mount *AK* U.S.A. **149** M4
Crimea *disp. terr.* Europe **65** K2
Crimmitschau Germany **63** M4
Crimond U.K. **60** H3
Cripple Landing *AK* U.S.A. **148** H3
Crisfield *MD* U.S.A. **165** H5
Cristalândia Brazil **177** I6
Cristalina Brazil **179** B2
Cristalino *r.* Brazil *see* **Mariembero**
Cristóbal Colón, Pico *mt.* Col. **176** D1
Crixás Brazil **179** A1
Crixás Açu *r.* Brazil **179** A1
Crixás Mirim *r.* Brazil **179** A1
Crna Gora *country* Europe *see* **Montenegro**
Crni Vrh *mt.* Serbia **69** J2
Črnomelj Slovenia **68** F2
Croagh Patrick *hill* Ireland **61** C4
Croajingolong National Park Australia **138** D6
Croatia *country* Europe **68** G2
Crocker, Banjaran *mts* Malaysia **85** F1
Crocker Range National Park Malaysia **85** G1
Crockett *TX* U.S.A. **161** E6
Crofton *KY* U.S.A. **164** B5
Crofton *NE* U.S.A. **160** D3
Croghan *NY* U.S.A. **165** H2
Croisilles France **62** C4
Croker *r.* Canada **149** R1
Croker, Cape Canada **164** E1
Croker Island Australia **134** F2
Cromarty U.K. **60** E3
Cromarty Firth *est.* U.K. **60** E3
Cromer U.K. **59** I6
Crook U.K. **58** F4
Crooked Creek *AK* U.S.A. **148** H3
Crooked Creek *AK* U.S.A. **149** L2
Crooked Harbour *b. H.K.* China **97** [inset]
Crooked Island Bahamas **163** F8
Crooked Island *H.K.* China **97** [inset]
Crooked Island Passage Bahamas **163** F8
Crookston *MN* U.S.A. **160** D2
Crooksville *OH* U.S.A. **164** D4
Crookwell Australia **138** D5
Croom Ireland **61** D5
Croppa Creek Australia **138** E2
Crosby U.K. **58** D5
Crosby *MN* U.S.A. **160** E2
Crosby *ND* U.S.A. **160** C1
Crosbyton *TX* U.S.A. **161** C5
Cross Bay Canada **151** M2
Cross City *FL* U.S.A. **163** D6
Cross Fell *hill* U.K. **58** E4
Crossfield Canada **150** H5
Crossgar U.K. **61** G3
Crosshaven Ireland **61** D6
Cross Inn U.K. **59** C6
Cross Lake Canada **151** L4
Cross Lake *l.* Canada **151** L4
Cross Lake *l. NY* U.S.A. **165** G2
Crossley Lakes Canada **149** O1
Crossmaglen U.K. **61** F3
Crossman Peak *AZ* U.S.A. **159** F4
Cross Sound *sea chan. AK* U.S.A. **149** M4
Crossville *TN* U.S.A. **162** C5
Crotch Lake Canada **165** G1
Croton Italy *see* **Crotone**
Crotone Italy **68** G5
Crouch *r.* U.K. **59** H7
Crow *r.* Canada **150** E3
Crow Agency *MT* U.S.A. **156** G3
Crowal *watercourse* Australia **138** C3
Crowborough U.K. **59** H7
Crowdy Bay National Park Australia **138** F3
Crowell *TX* U.S.A. **161** D5
Crowland U.K. **59** G6
Crowley *LA* U.S.A. **161** E6
Crowley, Lake *CA* U.S.A. **158** D3
Crown Point *IN* U.S.A. **164** B3
Crownpoint *NM* U.S.A. **159** I4
Crown Point *NY* U.S.A. **165** I2
Crown Prince Olav Coast Antarctica **188** D2
Crown Princess Martha Coast Antarctica **188** B1
Crows Nest Australia **138** F1
Crowsnest Pass Canada **150** H5
Crowsnest Pass *pass* Canada **150** H5
Crow Wing *r. MN* U.S.A. **160** E2
Croydon Australia **136** C3
Crozet *VA* U.S.A. **165** F4
Crozet, Îles *is* Indian Ocean **185** L9
Crozet Basin *sea feature* Indian Ocean **185** M8
Crozet Plateau *sea feature* Indian Ocean **185** K8
Crozon France **66** B2
Cruces Cuba **163** D8
Cruden Bay U.K. **60** H3
Cruillas Mex. **161** D7
Crum *WV* U.S.A. **164** D5
Crumlin U.K. **61** F3
Crusheen Ireland **61** D5
Cruz Alta Brazil **178** F3
Cruz del Eje Arg. **178** D4
Cruzeiro Brazil **179** B3
Cruzeiro do Sul Brazil **176** D5
Cruz Grande Mex. **167** F5
Cry Lake Canada **149** O4
Crysdale, Mount Canada **150** F4
Crystal *NM* U.S.A. **159** I3
Crystal City Canada **151** L5
Crystal City *TX* U.S.A. **161** D6
Crystal Falls *MI* U.S.A. **160** F2
Crystal Lake *IL* U.S.A. **164** A2
Crystal River *FL* U.S.A. **163** D6
Csongrád Hungary **69** I1
Cửa Lớn, Sông *r.* Vietnam **87** D5
Cuamba Moz. **123** D5
Cuando *r.* Angola/Zambia **123** C5
Cuangar Angola **123** B5
Cuango Angola **123** B4
Cuanza *r.* Angola **123** B4
Cuatro Ciénegas Mex. **166** E3
Cuauhtémoc Mex. **166** D2
Cuautla Mex. **167** F5
Cuba *NM* U.S.A. **157** G5
Cuba *NY* U.S.A. **165** F2

▶**Cuba** *country* West Indies **169** H4
5th largest island and 5th most populous country in North America.

Cubal Angola **123** B5
Cubango *r.* Angola/Namibia **123** C5
Cubatão Brazil **179** B3
Cub Hills Canada **151** J4
Çubuk Turkey **112** D2
Cubulco Guat. **167** H6
Cucapa, Sierra *mts* Mex. **159** F5
Cuchi Angola **123** B5
Cuchilla Grande *hills* Uruguay **178** E4
Cuchumatanes, Alto *mts* Guat. **167** H6
Cucuí Brazil **176** E3
Cucurpe Mex. **166** C2
Cúcuta Col. **176** D2
Cudal Australia **138** D4
Cuddalore India **106** C4
Cuddapah India *see* **Kadapa**
Cuddeback Lake *CA* U.S.A. **158** E4
Cue Australia **135** B6
Cuéllar Spain **67** D3
Cuemba Angola **123** B5
Cuenca Ecuador **176** C4
Cuenca *Luzon* Phil. **82** C3
Cuenca Spain **67** E3
Cuenca, Serranía de *mts* Spain **67** E3
Cuencamé Mex. **166** E3
Cuernavaca Mex. **168** E5
Cuero *TX* U.S.A. **161** D6
Cuervos Mex. **159** F5
Cugir Romania **69** J2
Cuiabá *Amazonas* Brazil **177** G5
Cuiabá *Mato Grosso* Brazil **177** G7
Cuiabá *r.* Brazil **177** G7
Cuicatlan Mex. **167** F5
Cuihua China *see* **Daguan**
Cuijiang China *see* **Ninghua**
Cuijk Neth. **62** F3
Cuilapa Guat. **167** H6
Cuilcagh *hill* Ireland/U.K. **61** E3
Cuillin Hills U.K. **60** C3
Cuillin Sound *sea chan.* U.K. **60** C3
Cuilo Angola **123** B4
Cuiluan China **90** C3
Cuité *r.* Brazil **179** C2
Cuitláhuac Mex. **167** F5
Cuito *r.* Angola **123** C5
Cuito Cuanavale Angola **123** B5
Cuitzeo, Laguna de *l.* Mex. **167** E5
Cujangan *i.* Phil. **82** C5
Cukai Malaysia **84** C1
Çukurca Turkey **110** A2
Çukurova *plat.* Turkey **107** B1
Culasi *Panay* Phil. **82** C4
Culcairn Australia **138** C5
Culebra, Sierra de la *mts* Spain **67** C3
Culfa Azer. **113** G3
Culgoa *r.* Australia **138** C2
Culiacán Mex. **166** D3
Culion Phil. **82** B4
Culion *i.* Phil. **82** B4
Cullen U.K. **60** G3
Cullen Point Australia **136** C1
Cullera Spain **67** F4
Cullivoe U.K. **60** [inset]
Cullman *AL* U.S.A. **163** C5
Cullybackey U.K. **61** F3
Cul Mòr *hill* U.K. **60** D2
Culpeper *VA* U.S.A. **165** G4
Cultural Landscape of the Serra de Tramuntana *tourist site* Spain **67** H4
Cultural Sites of Al Ain *tourist site* U.A.E. **109** I5
Culuene *r.* Brazil **177** H6
Culver, Point Australia **135** D8
Culverden N.Z. **139** D6
Cumaná Venez. **176** F1
Cumari Brazil **179** A2
Cumbal, Nevado de *vol.* Col. **176** C3
Cumberland *KY* U.S.A. **164** D5
Cumberland *MD* U.S.A. **165** F4
Cumberland *VA* U.S.A. **165** F5
Cumberland *r. KY* U.S.A. **162** C4
Cumberland, Lake *KY* U.S.A. **164** C5
Cumberland Lake Canada **151** K4
Cumberland Mountains *Kentucky/Tennessee* U.S.A. **164** D5
Cumberland Peninsula Canada **147** L3
Cumberland Plateau *Kentucky/Tennessee* U.S.A. **162** C5
Cumberland Point *MI* U.S.A. **160** F2
Cumberland Sound *sea chan.* Canada **147** L3
Cumbernauld U.K. **60** F5
Cumbres de Majalca, Parque Nacional *nat. park* Mex. **166** D2
Cumbres de Monterey, Parque Nacional *nat. park* Mex. **167** E3
Cumbum India **106** C3
Cumlosen Germany **63** L1
Cummings *CA* U.S.A. **158** B2
Cummins Australia **137** A7
Cummins Range *hills* Australia **134** D4
Cumnock Australia **138** D4
Cumnock U.K. **60** E5
Cumpas Mex. **166** C2
Çumra Turkey **112** D3
Cumuripa Mex. **166** C2
Cumuruxatiba Brazil **179** D2
Cunagua Cuba *see* **Bolivia**
Cunderdin Australia **135** B7
Cunén Guat. **167** H6
Cunene *r.* Angola **123** B5
also known as Kunene
Cuneo Italy **68** B2
Cung Sơn Vietnam **87** E4
Cunnamulla Australia **138** B2
Cunningsburgh U.K. **60** [inset]
Cupar U.K. **60** F4
Cupica, Golfo de *b.* Col. **176** C2
Cupula, Pico *mt.* Mex. **166** C3
Curaçá Brazil **177** K5
Curaçá *r.* Brazil **176** D4

▶**Curaçao** *terr.* West Indies **169** K6
Self-governing Netherlands territory.

Curaray *r.* Ecuador **176** D4
Curdlawidny Lagoon *salt flat* Australia **137** B6
Curia Switz. *see* **Chur**
Curicó Chile **178** B4
Curitiba Brazil **179** A4
Curitibanos Brazil **179** A4
Curlewis Australia **138** E3
Curlew Lake *AK* U.S.A. **148** G3
Curnamona Australia **137** B6
Currabubula Australia **138** E3
Currais Novos Brazil **177** K5
Curran *MI* U.S.A. **164** D1
Currane, Lough *l.* Ireland **61** B6
Currant *NV* U.S.A. **159** F2
Curranyalpa Australia **138** B3
Currawilla Australia **136** C5
Currawinya National Park Australia **138** B2
Currie Australia **132** E5
Currie *NV* U.S.A. **159** F1
Currituck *NC* U.S.A. **165** G5
Currockbilly, Mount Australia **138** E5
Curry *AK* U.S.A. **149** J3
Curtis Channel Australia **136** F5
Curtis Island Australia **136** E4
Curtis Island N.Z. **133** I5
Curuá *r.* Brazil **177** H5
Curup *Sumatra* Indon. **84** C3
Curupira, Serra *mts* Brazil/Venez. **176** F3
Cururupu Brazil **177** J4
Curvelo Brazil **179** B2
Curwood, Mount *hill MI* U.S.A. **160** F2
Cusco Peru **176** D6
Cushendall U.K. **61** F2
Cushendun U.K. **61** F2
Cushing *OK* U.S.A. **161** D4
Cusseta *GA* U.S.A. **163** C5
Custer *MT* U.S.A. **156** G3
Custer *SD* U.S.A. **160** C3
Cut Bank *MT* U.S.A. **156** E2
Cuthbert *GA* U.S.A. **163** C6
Cuthbertson Falls Australia **134** F3
Cut Knife Canada **151** I4
Cutler Ridge *FL* U.S.A. **163** D7
Cut Off *LA* U.S.A. **167** H2
Cuttaburra Creek *r.* Australia **138** B2
Cuttack India **106** E1
Cuvelai Angola **123** B5
Cuxhaven Germany **57** L4
Cuya Chile **176** D7
Cuyahoga Falls *OH* U.S.A. **164** E3
Cuyama *CA* U.S.A. **158** D4
Cuyama *r. CA* U.S.A. **158** C4
Cuyapo *Luzon* Phil. **82** C3
Cuyo Phil. **82** C4
Cuyo *i.* Phil. **82** C4
Cuyo East Passage Phil. **82** C4
Cuyo Islands Phil. **82** C4
Cuyo West Passage Phil. **82** C4
Cuyuni *r.* Guyana **177** G2
Cuyutingni Nicaragua *see* **Kuyu Tingni**
Cuzco Peru *see* **Cusco**
Cwmbrân U.K. **59** D7
Cyangugu Rwanda **122** C4
Cyclades *is* Greece **69** K6
Cydonia Greece *see* **Chania**
Cygnet *OH* U.S.A. **164** D3
Cymru *admin. div.* U.K. *see* **Wales**
Cynthiana *KY* U.S.A. **164** C4
Cypress Hills Canada **151** I5
Cyprus *country* Asia **107** A2
Cyrenaica *reg.* Libya **121** F2
Cythera *i.* Greece *see* **Kythira**
Czar Canada **151** I4
Czechia *country* Europe *see* **Czech Republic**

▶**Czechoslovakia**
Divided in 1993 into the Czech Republic and Slovakia.

Czech Republic *country* Europe **57** O6
Czernowitz Ukr. *see* **Chernivtsi**
Czersk Poland **57** P4
Częstochowa Poland **57** Q5

Đa, Sông *r.* Vietnam *see* **Black**
Da'an China **95** K2
Daanbantayan Phil. **82** C4
Daba China **99** B7
Ḍabāb, Jabal aḍ *mt.* Jordan **107** B4
Dabakala Côte d'Ivoire **120** C4
Daban China **95** I3
Daban Shan *mts* China **94** E4
Dabao China **96** D2
Daba Shan *mts* China **97** F1
Dabba China *see* **Daocheng**
Dabein Myanmar **86** B3
Dabhoi India **104** C5
Ḍab'i, Wādī aḍ *watercourse* Jordan **107** C4
Dabiegai China **94** C4
Dabie Shan *mts* China **97** G2
Dablana India **104** C4
Dabola Guinea **120** B3
Dabqig China **95** G4
Dąbrowa Górnicza Poland **57** Q5
Dabsan China **94** C4
Dabs Nur *l.* China **90** A3
Dabu *Guangdong* China **97** H3
Dabu *Guangxi* China *see* **Liucheng**
Dabusu Pao *l.* China *see* **Dabs Nur**
Dacca Bangl. *see* **Dhaka**
Dachau Germany **57** M6
Dachechang China **94** E4
Dachengzi China *see* **Harqin**
Dachuan China *see* **Dazhou**
Dacre Canada **165** G1
Dadaab Kenya **122** E3
Dadal Mongolia **95** G1
Daday Turkey **112** D2
Dade City *FL* U.S.A. **163** D6
Dadeville *AL* U.S.A. **163** C5
Dādkān Iran **111** F5
Dadohae Haesang National Park S. Korea **91** B6
Dadong China *see* **Donggang**
Dadra India *see* **Achalpur**
Dadu Pak. **111** G5
Daecheong-do *i.* S. Korea **91** B5
Daegu S. Korea **91** C6
Daeheuksan-gundo *is* S. Korea **91** B6
Daejeon S. Korea **91** B5
Daejeong S. Korea **91** B6
Daet *Luzon* Phil. **82** C3
Dafang China **96** E3
Dafeng China **97** I1
Dafla Hills India **105** H4
Dafoe Canada **151** J5
Dafoe *r.* Canada **151** M4
Dagana Senegal **120** B3
Dagasuli *i. Moluccas* Indon. **83** C2
Dagcagoin China *see* **Zoigê**
Dagcanglhamo China *see* **Langmusi**
Dage China *see* **Fengning**
Dagezhen China *see* **Fengning**
Daghmar Oman **110** E6
Dağlıq Qarabağ *disp. terr.* Azer. *see* **Nagorno-Karabakh**
Daglung China **99** E7
Dagma China **99** F7
Dagö *i.* Estonia *see* **Hiiumaa**
Dagon Myanmar *see* **Rangoon**
Dagrag Zangbo *r.* China **99** D7
Dagu China **95** I4
Daguan China **96** D3
Daguokui Shan *hill* China **90** C3
Dagupan *Luzon* Phil. **82** C2
Dagur China **94** C4
Dagxoi *Sichuan* China *see* **Yidun**
Dagxoi *Sichuan* China *see* **Sowa**
Dagzê China **99** E7
Dagzê Co *salt l.* China **99** D7
Dagzhuka China **99** E7
Dahadinni *r.* Canada **149** P3
Dahalach, Isole *is* Eritrea *see* **Dahlak Archipelago**
Da Haltang He *r.* China **94** C4
Dahana *des.* Saudi Arabia *see* **Ad Dahnā'**
Dahe *Guangxi* China *see* **Ziyuan**
Dahe *Heilong.* China **90** D3
Daheba China **94** D5
Daheiding Shan *mt.* China **90** C3
Dahei Shan *mt.* China **94** C3
Dahei Shan *mts* China **90** B4
Dahej India **104** C5
Daheyan China *see* **Turpan Zhan**
Da Hinggan Ling *mts* China **95** I3
Daḥl, Nafūd ad *des.* Saudi Arabia **110** B6
Dahlak Archipelago *is* Eritrea **108** F6
Dahlak Marine National Park Eritrea **108** F6
Daḥl al Furayy *well* Saudi Arabia **110** B5
Dahlem Germany **62** G4
Dahlenburg Germany **63** K1
Dahm, Ramlat *des.* Saudi Arabia/Yemen **108** G6
Dahmani Tunisia **68** C7
Dahme/Mark Germany **63** N3
Dahn Germany **63** H5
Dahnā' *plain* Saudi Arabia **110** B5
Dahod India **104** C5
Dahomey *country* Africa *see* **Benin**
Dahongliutan China **99** B6
Dahra Senegal *see* **Dara**
Dähre Germany **63** K2
Dahūk/Dihok Iraq **113** F3
Dai *i. Moluccas* Indon. **83** D4
Daian Japan **92** C3
Daibosatsu-rei *mt.* Japan **93** E3
Daicheng China **95** I4
Daigo Japan **93** G2
Daik *Sumatra* Indon. **84** D3
Daik-U Myanmar **86** B3
Đai Lanh, Mui *pt* Vietnam **87** E4
Dailekh Nepal **105** E3
Dailly U.K. **60** E5
Daimiel Spain **67** E4
Daimon Japan **92** D2
Daimon-tōge *pass* Japan **93** E2
Daimugen-zan *mt.* Japan **93** E3
Daingean Uí Chúis Ireland **61** B5
Dainichiga-take *vol.* Japan **92** C2
Dainichi-gawa *r.* Japan **92** C2
Dainichi-zan *mt.* Japan **92** C2
Dainkognubma China **96** C1
Daintree National Park Australia **136** D3
Daiō Japan **92** C4
Daiō-zaki *pt* Japan **92** C4
Dair, Jebel ed *mt.* Sudan **108** D7
Dairen China *see* **Dalian**
Dai-sen *vol.* Japan **91** D6
Daisetsu-zan Kokuritsu-kōen Japan **90** F4
Daishan China **97** I2
Daitō *Ōsaka* Japan **92** B4
Daitō *Shizuoka* Japan **93** E4
Daiya-gawa *r.* Japan **93** F2
Daiyue China *see* **Shanyin**
Daiyun Shan *mts* China **97** H3
Dajarra Australia **136** B4
Dajin Chuan *r.* China **96** D2
Dajing China **94** E4
Da Juh China **94** C4

▶**Dakar** Senegal **120** B3
Capital of Senegal.

Dākhilah, Wāḥāt ad *oasis* Egypt **108** C4
Dakhla W. Sahara **120** B2
Dakhla Oasis *oasis* Egypt *see* **Dākhilah, Wāḥāt ad**
Dakituy Russia **95** G1
Đăk Lăk, Cao Nguyên *plat.* Vietnam **87** E4
Dakoank India **87** A6
Dakol'ka *r.* Belarus **53** F5
Dakor India **104** C5
Dakoro Niger **120** D3
Dakota City *IA* U.S.A. **160** E3
Dakota City *NE* U.S.A. **160** D3
Đakovica Kosovo *see* **Gjakovë**
Đakovo Croatia **68** H2
Daktuy Russia **90** B1
Dala Angola **123** C5
Dalaba Guinea **120** B3
Dalad Qi China *see* **Shulinzhao**
Dalai China *see* **Da'an**
Dalain Hob China **94** E3
Dalai Nur *l.* China **95** I3
Dālakī Iran **110** C4
Dalälven *r.* Sweden **55** J6
Dalamamiao China **95** H3
Dalaman Turkey **69** M6
Dalandzadgad Mongolia **94** F3
Dalanganem Islands Phil. **82** C4
Dalap-Uliga-Darrit Marshall Is *see* **Delap-Uliga-Djarrit**
Dalat *Sarawak* Malaysia **85** E2
Đa Lat Vietnam **87** E5
Dalatando Angola *see* **N'dalatando**
Dalaud India **104** C5
Dalauda India **104** C5
Dalay Mongolia *see* **Bayandalay**
Dalbandin Pak. **111** G4
Dalbeattie U.K. **60** F6
Dalbeg Australia **136** D4
Dalby Australia **138** E1
Dalby Isle of Man **58** C4
Dale *Hordaland* Norway **55** D6
Dale *Sogn og Fjordane* Norway **55** D6
Dale City *VA* U.S.A. **165** G4
Dale Hollow Lake *TN* U.S.A. **164** C5
Dalen Neth. **62** G2
Dalet Myanmar **86** A3
Daletme Myanmar **86** A2
Dalfors Sweden **55** I6
Dalgān Iran **110** E5
Dalgety Australia **138** D6
Dalgety *r.* Australia **135** A6
Dalhart *TX* U.S.A. **161** C4
Dalhousie Canada **153** I4
Dalhousie, Cape Canada **149** O1
Dali *Shaanxi* China **97** F1
Dali *Yunnan* China **96** D3
Dalian China **95** J4
Daliang *Guangdong* China *see* **Shunde**
Daliang *Qinghai* China **94** E4
Daliang Shan *mts* China **96** D2
Dalian Wan *b.* China **95** J4
Dali He *r.* China **95** G4
Dalin China **95** J3
Dalinghe China *see* **Linghai**
Daling He *r.* China **95** J3
Dalizi China **90** B4
Dalkeith U.K. **60** F5
Dall, Mount *AK* U.S.A. **148** I3
Dallas *OR* U.S.A. **156** C3
Dallas *TX* U.S.A. **161** D5
Dalles City *OR* U.S.A. *see* **The Dalles**
Dall Island *AK* U.S.A. **149** N5
Dall Lake *AK* U.S.A. **148** G3
Dall Mountain *AK* U.S.A. **149** J2
Dalmā *i.* U.A.E. **110** D5
Dalmacija *reg.* Bos. & Herz./Croatia *see* **Dalmatia**
Dalmas, Lac *l.* Canada **153** H3
Dalmatia *reg.* Bos. & Herz./Croatia **100** A2
Dalmau India **104** E4
Dalmellington U.K. **60** E5
Dalmeny Canada **151** J4
Dalmi India **105** F5
Dal'negorsk Russia **90** D3
Dal'nerechensk Russia **90** D3
Dal'niye Zelentsy Russia **52** H1
Dalny China *see* **Dalian**
Daloa Côte d'Ivoire **120** C4

▶**Dalol (abandoned)** Eth. **108** F7
Highest recorded annual mean temperature in the world.

Daloloia Group *is* P.N.G. **136** E1
Dalou Shan *mts* China **96** E3
Dalqān *well* Saudi Arabia **110** B5
Dalry U.K. **60** E5
Dalrymple U.K. **60** E5
Dalrymple, Lake Australia **136** D4
Daltenganj India *see* **Daltonganj**
Dalton Canada **152** D4
Dalton S. Africa **125** J5
Dalton *GA* U.S.A. **163** C5
Dalton *MA* U.S.A. **165** I2
Dalton *PA* U.S.A. **165** H3
Daltonganj India **105** F4
Dalton-in-Furness U.K. **58** D4
Daludalu *Sumatra* Indon. **84** C2
Daluo China **96** D4
Dalupiri *i.* Phil. **82** C2
Daly *r.* Australia **134** E3
Daly City *CA* U.S.A. **158** B3
Daly River Australia **134** E3
Daly Waters Australia **134** F4
Damagaram Takaya Niger **120** D3
Daman India **106** B1
Daman and Diu *union terr.* India **106** A1
Damanhūr Egypt **112** C5
Damanhûr Egypt *see* **Damanhūr**
Damant Lake Canada **151** J2
Damão India *see* **Daman**
Damaqun Shan *mts* China **95** H3
Damar *Celebes* Indon. **83** C2
Damar *i. Moluccas* Indon. **83** D3
Damar *i. Moluccas* Indon. **83** D4
Damara Cent. Afr. Rep. **122** B3
Damaraland *reg.* Namibia **123** B6
Damas Syria *see* **Damascus**

▶**Damascus** Syria **107** C3
Capital of Syria.

Damascus *VA* U.S.A. **164** E5
Damaturu Nigeria **120** E3
Damāvand Iran **110** D3
Damāvand, Qolleh-ye *mt.* Iran **110** D3
Dambulla Sri Lanka **106** D5
Damdy Kazakh. **102** B1
Dāmghān Iran **110** D2
Damianópolis Brazil **179** B1
Damietta Egypt *see* **Dumyāṭ**
Daming China **95** H4
Daming Shan *mt.* China **97** F4
Dāmiyā Jordan **107** B3
Damjong China **96** B1
Damlasu Turkey **107** D1
Dammam Saudi Arabia **108** H4
Damme Belgium **62** D3
Damme Germany **63** I2
Damoh India **104** D5
Damour Lebanon **107** B3
Dampar, Tasik *l.* Malaysia **84** C2
Dampelas, Tanjung *pt* Indon. **83** A2
Dampier Archipelago *is* Australia **134** B5
Dampier Island P.N.G. *see* **Karkar Island**
Dampier Land *reg.* Australia **134** C4
Dampier Strait P.N.G. **81** L8
Dampir, Selat *sea chan. Papua* Indon. **83** D3
Damqoq Zangbo *r.* China **99** D7
Dam Qu *r.* China **99** F6
Dâmrei, Chuŏr Phnum *mts* Cambodia **87** D5
Damroh India **96** B2
Damwâld Neth. **62** G1
Damwoude Neth. *see* **Damwâld**
Damxoi China *see* **Comai**
Dana *i.* Indon. **83** B5
Ḍānā Jordan **107** B4
Dana Nepal **105** E3
Danakil *reg.* Africa **122** E2
Danané Côte d'Ivoire **120** C4
Đa Năng Vietnam **86** E3
Đa Năng, Vung *b.* Vietnam **86** E3
Danao *Cebu* Phil. **82** D4

Danata Turkm. 110 D2
Danau Sentarum, Taman Nasional nature res. Kalimantan Indon. 85 F2
Danba Shaanxi China 95 G4
Danba Sichuan China 96 D2
Danbury CT U.S.A. 165 I3
Danbury NC U.S.A. 162 D4
Danby VT U.S.A. 165 I2
Danby Lake CA U.S.A. 159 F4
Dancheng China 95 H5
Dandaragan Australia 135 A7
Dande Eth. 122 D3
Dandeldhura Nepal 104 E3
Dandeli India 106 B3
Dandong China 91 B4
Dando-san mt. Japan 92 D3
Dandot Pak. 111 I3
Dandridge TN U.S.A. 162 D4
Dane r. U.K. 58 E5
Daneborg Greenland 189 I2
Danese WV U.S.A. 164 E5
Danfeng China see Shizong
Dangan Liedao i. China 97 G4
Dangara Tajik. see Danghara
Dangbi China 90 C3
Dangchang China 94 F5
Dangchengwan China see Subei
Danger Islands atoll Cook Is see Pukapuka
Danger Point S. Africa 124 D8
Danghara Tajik. 111 H2
Dang He r. China 94 C3
Danghe Nanshan mts China 94 C4
Dangjin Shankou pass China 98 F5
Dangla Shan mts China see Tanggula Shan
Dangqên China 99 E7
Dângrêk, Chuŏr Phnum mts Cambodia/Thai. see Phanom Dong Rak, Thiu Khao
Dangriga Belize 167 H5
Dangshan China 95 I5
Dangtu China 97 H2
Daniel's Harbour Canada 153 K4
Daniëlskuil S. Africa 124 F5
Danilov Russia 52 I4
Danilovka Russia 53 J6
Danilovskaya Vozvyshennost' hills Russia 52 H4
Daning China 95 G4
Danjiang China see Leishan
Danjiangkou China 97 F1
Danjiangkou Shuiku resr China 97 F1
Danjo-guntō is Japan 91 C6
Ḍank Oman 110 E6
Dankhar India 104 D2
Dankov Russia 53 H5
Dan'kova, Pik mt. Kyrg. 98 B4
Danlí Hond. 166 [inset] I6
Danmark country Europe see Denmark
Dannebrog Ø i. Greenland see Qillak
Dannenberg (Elbe) Germany 63 L1
Dannenwalde Germany 63 N1
Dannevirke N.Z. 139 F5
Dannhauser S. Africa 125 J5
Dano Burkina Faso 120 C3
Danshui Taiwan 97 I3
Dansville NY U.S.A. 165 G2
Danta India 104 C4
Dantan India 105 F5
Dantevada India see Dantewada
Dantewada India 106 D2
Dantewara India see Dantewada
Dantu China see Zhenjiang

▶Danube r. Europe 57 P6
2nd longest river in Europe. Also spelt Donau (Austria/Germany) or Duna (Hungary) or Dunaj (Slovakia) or Dunărea (Romania) or Dunav (Bulgaria/Croatia/Yugoslavia) or Dunay (Ukraine).

Danube Delta Romania/Ukr. 69 M2
Danubyu Myanmar 86 A3
Danumparai Kalimantan Indon. 85 F2
Danum Valley Conservation Area nature res. Malaysia 85 G1
Danville IL U.S.A. 164 B3
Danville IN U.S.A. 164 B4
Danville KY U.S.A. 164 C5
Danville OH U.S.A. 164 D3
Danville PA U.S.A. 165 G3
Danville VA U.S.A. 164 F5
Danville VT U.S.A. 165 I1
Danxian China see Danzhou
Danzhai China 96 E3
Danzhou Guangxi China 97 F3
Danzhou Hainan China 97 F5
Danzhou Shaanxi China see Yichuan
Danzig Poland see Gdańsk
Danzig, Gulf of Poland/Russia see Gdańsk, Gulf of
Daocheng China 96 D2
Daogao China 94 E5
Daokou China see Huaxian
Daotanghe China 94 E4
Dao Tay Sa is S. China Sea see Paracel Islands
Daoud Alg. see Aïn Beïda
Daoukro Côte d'Ivoire 120 C4
Daozhen China 96 E2
Dapa Phil. 82 D4
Dapaong Togo 120 D3
Dapeng Wan b. H.K. China see Mirs Bay
Dapha Bum mt. India 105 I4
Dapiak, Mount Mindanao Phil. 82 C4
Dapitan Mindanao Phil. 82 C4
Daporijo India 105 H4
Đâp Sơn La resr Vietnam 86 C2
Dapu China see Liucheng
Da Qaidam China 99 F5
Daqiao China 96 D3
Daqing China 90 B3
Daqinghe China 95 I4
Daqing Shan mts China 95 G3
Daqin Tal China 95 J3
Daqiu China 97 H3
Dāq Mashī Iran 110 E3
Daquan China 98 F4
Daquanwan China 94 C3
Daqu Shan i. China 97 I2
Dara Senegal 120 B3
Dar'ā Syria 107 C3
Dâra, Gebel mt. Egypt see Dārah, Jabal
Dārāb Iran 110 D4
Daraga Luzon Phil. 82 C3
Darāgāh Iran 110 D4
Dārah, Jabal mt. Egypt 112 D6
Dārākūyeh Iran 110 D4
Dārān Iran 110 C3
Daraut-Korgon Kyrg. 111 I2
Darazo Nigeria 120 E3
Darband Tajik. 111 H2
Darband, Kūh-e mt. Iran 110 E4
Darband-e Hajjī Boland Turkm. 111 F2
Darbhanga India 105 F4
Darby, Cape AK U.S.A. 148 G2
Darby Mountains AK U.S.A. 148 G2
Darcang China 96 C1
Dardanelle AR U.S.A. 161 E5
Dardanelles strait Turkey 69 L4
Dardania prov. Europe see Kosovo
Dardesheim Germany 63 K3
Dardo China see Kangding
Dar el Beida Morocco see Casablanca
Darende Turkey 112 E3

▶Dar es Salaam Tanz. 123 D4
Former capital of Tanzania.

Dāreyn, Kūh-e mt. Iran 110 E3
Darfo Boario Terme Italy 68 D2
Dargai Pak. 111 H3
Dargaville N.Z. 139 D2
Dargo Australia 138 C6
Dargo Zangbo r. China 105 F3
Darhan Mongolia 94 F1
Darhan Muminggan Lianheqi China see Bailingmiao
Darhan Ul China 95 H2
Darien GA U.S.A. 163 D6
Darién, Golfo del g. Col. 176 C2
Darién, Parque Nacional de nat. park Panama 166 [inset] K8
Darién, Serranía del mts Panama 166 [inset] K7
Dariga Pak. 111 G5
Darīganga Mongolia 95 H2
Dariya Kazakh. 98 A2
Darjeeling India see Darjiling
Darjiling India 105 G4
Darkhazīneh Iran 110 C4

▶Darling r. Australia 138 B3
2nd longest river in Oceania, and a major part of the longest (Murray-Darling).

Darling Downs hills Australia 138 D1
Darling Range hills Australia 135 A8
Darlington U.K. 58 F4
Darlington WI U.S.A. 160 F3
Darlington Point Australia 138 C5
Darlot, Lake salt flat Australia 135 C6
Darłowo Poland 57 P3
Darma Pass China/India 99 C7
Darmstadt Germany 63 I5
Darnah Libya 112 A4
Darnall S. Africa 125 J5
Darnick Australia 138 A4
Darnley, Cape Antarctica 188 E2
Darnley Bay Canada 149 P1
Daroca Spain 67 F3
Darong China 97 H3
Daroot-Korgon Kyrg. see Daraut-Korgon
Darovskoy Russia 52 J4
Darr watercourse Australia 136 C4
Darreh Bīd Iran 110 E3
Darreh-ye Bāhābād Iran 110 D4
Darsi India 106 C3
Dart r. U.K. 59 D8
Dartford U.K. 59 H7
Dartmoor Australia 137 C8
Dartmoor hills U.K. 59 C8
Dartmoor National Park U.K. 59 D8
Dartmouth Canada 153 J5
Dartmouth U.K. 59 D8
Dartmouth, Lake salt flat Australia 137 D5
Dartmouth Reservoir Australia 138 C6
Darton U.K. 58 F5
Daru P.N.G. 81 K8
Daru Sierra Leone 120 B4
Daruba Moluccas Indon. 83 D2
Daruga-mine mt. Japan 92 A3
Darvaza Turkm. see Içoguz
Darvi Govĭ-Altay Mongolia 94 C2
Darvi Hovd Mongolia 94 C2
Darvoz, Qatorkŭhi mts Tajik. 111 H2
Darwāzagêy Afgh. 111 G4
Darwen U.K. 58 E5

▶Darwin Australia 134 E3
Capital of Northern Territory.

Darwin, Monte mt. Chile 178 C8
Daryaboyi China 98 C5
Daryācheh-ye Orūmīyeh salt l. Iran see Urmia, Lake
Dar'yalyktakyr, Ravnina plain Kazakh. 102 B2
Dar"yoi Amu r. Asia see Amudar'ya
Darzāb Afgh. 111 G3
Darzhuo China 99 E6
Dārzīn Iran 110 E4
Dās i. U.A.E. 110 D5
Dasada India 104 B5
Dashbalbar Mongolia 95 H1
Dashetai China 95 G3
Dashhowuz Turkm. see Daşoguz
Dashiqiao China 95 J3
Dashitou China 94 B3
Dashizhai China 95 J2
Dashkesan Azer. see Daşkäsän
Dashkhovuz Turkm. see Daşoguz
Dashkŏpri Turkm. see Daşköpri
Dashoguz Turkm. see Daşoguz
Dasht Iran 110 E2
Dashtiari Iran 111 F5
Dashuikeng China 94 F4
Dashuiqiao China 94 D4
Dashuitou China 94 F4
Daska Pak. 111 I3
Daşkäsän Azer. 113 G2
Daşköpri Turkm. 111 F2
Daşoguz Turkm. 109 I1
Daspar mt. Pak. 111 I2
Dassalan i. Phil. 82 C5
Dassel Germany 63 J3
Dastgerdān Iran 110 E3
Datadian Kalimantan Indon. 85 F2
Datça Turkey 69 L6
Date Japan 90 F4
Date Creek watercourse AZ U.S.A. 159 G4
Dateland AZ U.S.A. 159 G5
Datha India 104 C5
Datia India 104 D4
Datian China 97 H3
Datian Ding mt. China 97 F4
Datil NM U.S.A. 159 J4
Datong Anhui China 97 H2
Datong Heilong. China 90 B3
Datong Qinghai China 94 E4
Datong Shanxi China 95 H3
Datong He r. China 94 E4
Datong Shan mts China 94 D4
Dattapur India 106 C1
Datu i. Indon. 85 E2
Datu, Tanjung c. Indon./Malaysia 85 E2
Datuk, Tanjung pt Indon. 84 C3
Datu Piang Mindanao Phil. 82 D5
Daudkandi Bangl. 105 G5
Daugava r. Latvia 55 N8
Daugavpils Latvia 55 O9
Daulatabad India 106 B2
Daulatabad Iran see Malāyer
Daulatpur Bangl. 105 G5
Daun Germany 62 G4
Daungyu r. Myanmar 86 A2
Dauphin Canada 151 K5
Dauphiné reg. France 66 G4
Dauphiné, Alpes du mts France 66 G4
Dauphin Island AL U.S.A. 167 H2
Dauphin Lake Canada 151 L5
Daurie Creek r. Australia 135 A6
Dauriya Russia 95 I1
Daurskiy Khrebet mts Russia 95 G1
Dausa India 104 D4
Dâu Tiêng, Hô resr Vietnam 87 D5
Dava U.K. 60 F3
Davanagere India see Davangere
Davangere India 106 B3
Davao Mindanao Phil. 82 D5
Davao Gulf Mindanao Phil. 82 D5
Dāvarī Iran 110 E5
Dāvarzan Iran 110 E2
Davel S. Africa 125 I4
Davenport IA U.S.A. 160 F3
Davenport WA U.S.A. 156 D3
Davenport Downs Australia 136 C5
Davenport Range hills Australia 134 F5
Daventry U.K. 59 F6
Daveyton S. Africa 125 I4
David Panama 166 [inset] J7
David City NE U.S.A. 160 D3
David Glacier Antarctica 188 H1
Davidson Canada 151 J5
Davidson, Mount hill Australia 134 E5
Davidson Mountains AK U.S.A. 149 L1
Davis research station Antarctica 188 E2
Davis r. Australia 134 C5
Davis CA U.S.A. 158 C2
Davis WV U.S.A. 164 F4
Davis, Mount hill PA U.S.A. 164 F4
Davis Bay Antarctica 188 G2
Davis Dam AZ U.S.A. 159 F4
Davis Inlet (abandoned) Canada 153 J3
Davis Island i. Myanmar see Than Kyun
Davis Sea Antarctica 188 F2
Davis Strait Canada/Greenland 147 M3
Davlekanovo Russia 51 Q5
Davos Switz. 66 I3
Davy Lake Canada 151 I3
Dawa China 95 J3
Dawa Co l. China 99 D7
Dawa Wenz r. Eth. 122 E3
Dawaxung China 99 D7
Dawê China 96 D2
Dawei Myanmar 87 B4
Dawei r. mouth Myanmar see Tavoy
Daweloor i. Moluccas Indon. 83 D4
Dawera i. Moluccas Indon. 83 D4
Dawmat al Jandal Saudi Arabia 113 E5
Dawna Range mts Myanmar/Thai. 86 B3
Dawna Taungdan mts Myanmar/Thai. see Dawna Range
Dawo China see Maqên
Dawqah Oman 109 H6
Dawson r. Australia 136 E4
Dawson Canada 149 M2
Dawson GA U.S.A. 163 C6
Dawson ND U.S.A. 160 D2
Dawson, Mount Canada 150 G5
Dawson Bay Canada 151 K4
Dawson Creek Canada 150 F4
Dawson Inlet Canada 151 M2
Dawson Range mts Canada 149 L3
Dawsons Landing Canada 150 E5
Dawu China 97 G2
Dawu Taiwan 97 I4
Dawukou China see Shizuishan
Dawu Shan hill China 97 G2
Dawusi China 99 E5
Dax France 66 D5
Daxian China see Dazhou
Daxiang Ling mts China 96 D2
Daxihaizi Shuiku resr China 98 D4
Daxin China 96 E4
Daxing Yunnan China see Ninglang
Daxing Yunnan China see Lüchun
Daxue Shan mt. China 94 D4
Da Xueshan mts China 96 D2
Dayan China see Lijiang
Dayang r. India 99 F8
Dayangshu China 95 K1
Dayan Nuur l. Mongolia 94 B1
Dayao China 96 D3
Dayao Shan mts China 97 F4
Daye China 97 G2
Daying China 96 E2
Daying Jiang r. China 96 C3
Dayishan China see Guanyun
Daylesford Australia 138 B6
Daylight Pass NV U.S.A. 158 E3
Dayong China see Zhangjiajie
Dayr Abū Sa'īd Jordan 107 B3
Dayr az Zawr Syria 113 F4
Dayr Ḥāfir Syria 107 C1
Dayrī, Wādī watercourse Saudi Arabia 113 F6
Daysland Canada 151 H4
Dayton OH U.S.A. 164 C4
Dayton TN U.S.A. 162 C5
Dayton TX U.S.A. 167 G2
Dayton VA U.S.A. 165 F4
Dayton WA U.S.A. 156 D3
Daytona Beach FL U.S.A. 163 D6
Dayu Kalimantan Indon. 85 F3
Dayu Ling mts China 97 G3
Da Yunhe canal China 95 I5
Dayyīna i. U.A.E. 110 D5
Dazhai China 95 H4
Dazhongji China see Dafeng
Dazhou China 96 E2
Dazhou Dao i. China 97 F5
Dazhu China 96 E2
Dazigou China 94 C3
Dazu China 96 E2
Dazu Rock Carvings tourist site China 96 E2
Ddhaw Gro Habitat Protection Area nature res. Canada 149 N3
De Aar S. Africa 124 G6
Dead r. Ireland 61 D5
Deadhorse AK U.S.A. 149 J1
Deadman Lake CA U.S.A. 158 E4
Deadman's Cay Bahamas 163 F8
Dead Mountains NV U.S.A. 159 F4

▶Dead Sea salt l. Asia 107 B4
Lowest point in Asia and the world.

Deadwood SD U.S.A. 160 C2
Deakin Australia 135 E7
Deal U.K. 59 I7
Dealesville S. Africa 125 G5
De'an China 97 G2
Dean, Forest of U.K. 59 E7
Deán Funes Arg. 178 D4
Deanuvuotna inlet Norway see Tanafjorden
Dearborn MI U.S.A. 164 D2
Dearne r. U.K. 58 F5
Deary ID U.S.A. 156 D3
Dease r. Canada 149 O4
Dease Arm b. Canada 149 Q2
Dease Inlet AK U.S.A. 148 I1
Dease Lake Canada 149 O4
Dease Lake Canada 149 O4
Dease Strait Canada 146 H3

▶Death Valley depr. CA U.S.A. 158 E3
Lowest point in the Americas.

Death Valley Junction CA U.S.A. 158 E3
Death Valley National Park CA U.S.A. 158 E3
Deauville France 66 E2
Deaver WY U.S.A. 156 F3
De Baai S. Africa see Port Elizabeth
Debak Sarawak Malaysia 85 E2
Debao China 96 E4
Debar Macedonia 69 I4
Debauch Mountain AK U.S.A. 148 H2
Debden Canada 151 J4
Debenham U.K. 59 I6
De Beque CO U.S.A. 159 I2
De Biesbosch, Nationaal Park nat. park Neth. 62 E3
Débo, Lac l. Mali 120 C3
Deborah, Mount AK U.S.A. 149 K3
Deborah East, Lake salt flat Australia 135 B7
Deborah West, Lake salt flat Australia 135 B7
Debrecen Hungary 69 I1
Debre Markos Eth. 108 E7
Debre Tabor Eth. 108 E7
Debre Zeyit Eth. 122 D3
Decatur AL U.S.A. 163 C5
Decatur GA U.S.A. 163 C5
Decatur IL U.S.A. 160 F4
Decatur IN U.S.A. 164 C3
Decatur MI U.S.A. 164 C2
Decatur MS U.S.A. 161 F5
Decatur TX U.S.A. 161 D5

▶Deccan plat. India 106 C2
Plateau making up most of southern and central India.

Deception Bay Australia 138 F1
Dechang China 96 D3
Děčín Czech Rep. 57 O5
Decker MT U.S.A. 156 G3
Decorah IA U.S.A. 160 F3
Dedap i. Indon. see Penasi, Pulau
Dedaye Myanmar 86 A3
Deddington U.K. 59 F7
Dedegöl Dağları mts Turkey 69 N6
Dedeleben Germany 63 K2
Dedelstorf Germany 63 K2
Dedemsvaart Neth. 62 G2
Dedo de Deus mt. Brazil 179 B4
Dédougou Burkina Faso 120 C3
Dedovichi Russia 52 F4
Dedu China see Wudalianchi
Dee r. Ireland 61 F4
Dee est. U.K. 58 D5
Dee r. England/Wales U.K. 59 D5
Dee r. Scotland U.K. 60 G3
Deel r. Cork/Limerick Ireland 61 D5
Deel r. Meath/Westmeath Ireland 61 F4
Deep Bay H.K. China 97 [inset]
Deep Creek Lake MD U.S.A. 164 F4
Deep Creek Range mts UT U.S.A. 159 G2
Deep River Canada 152 F5
Deepwater Australia 138 E2
Deeri Somalia 122 E3
Deering AK U.S.A. 148 G2
Deering, Mount Australia 135 E6
Deer Island AK U.S.A. 148 G5
Deer Lake Canada 151 M4
Deer Lake l. Canada 151 M4
Deer Lodge MT U.S.A. 156 E3
Deerpass Bay Canada 149 Q2
Deesa India see Disa
Deeth NV U.S.A. 156 E4
Defeng China see Liping
Defensores del Chaco, Parque Nacional nat. park Para. 178 D2
Defiance OH U.S.A. 164 C3
Defiance Plateau AZ U.S.A. 159 I4
De Funiak Springs FL U.S.A. 167 I2
Degana India 104 C4
Degeh Bur Eth. 122 E3
Degema Nigeria 120 D4
Deggendorf Germany 63 M6
Degh r. Pak. 111 I4
De Goorn Neth. 62 E2
De Grey r. Australia 134 B5
De Groote Peel, Nationaal Park nat. park Neth. 62 F3
Degtevo Russia 53 I6
De Haan Belgium 62 D3
Dê Hadē Ghar Afgh. 111 G4
Dehak Seydābād Iran 111 F4
Dehaq Iran 110 C3
Dehdasht Iran 110 C4
Deh-e Shū Afgh. 111 F4
Dehestān-e Bālā Iran 110 D4
Dehgolān Iran 110 B3
Dehgon Afgh. 111 F3
Dehī Afgh. 111 G3
Dehkūyeh Iran 110 D5
Dehlorān Iran 110 B3
De Hoge Veluwe, Nationaal Park nat. park Neth. 62 F2
De Hoop Nature Reserve S. Africa 124 E8
Dehqonobod Uzbek. 111 G2
Dehra Dun India 104 D3
Dehradun India see Dehra Dun
Dehram Iran 110 D4
Dehri India 105 F4
Deim Zubeir South Sudan 121 F4
Deinze Belgium 62 D4
Deir-ez-Zor Syria see Dayr az Zawr
Dej Romania 69 J1
Deji China see Rinbung
Dejiang China 97 F2
De Jouwer Neth. see Joure
DeKalb IL U.S.A. 160 F3
De Kalb MS U.S.A. 161 F5
De Kalb TX U.S.A. 161 E5
De Kalb Junction NY U.S.A. 165 H1
De-Kastri Russia 90 F2
Dekemhare Eritrea 108 E6
Dekhkanabad Uzbek. see Dehqonobod
Dekina Nigeria 120 D4
Dékoa Cent. Afr. Rep. 122 B3
De Koog Neth. 62 E1
De Kooy Neth. 62 E2
Delaki Indon. 83 C5
Delamar Lake NV U.S.A. 159 F3
DeLand FL U.S.A. 163 D6
Delano CA U.S.A. 158 D4
Delano Peak UT U.S.A. 159 G2

▶Delap-Uliga-Djarrit Marshall Is 186 H5
Capital of the Marshall Islands, on Majuro atoll.

Delareyville S. Africa 125 G4
Delarof Islands AK U.S.A. 148 [inset] C6
Delaronde Lake Canada 151 J4
Delavan WI U.S.A. 152 C6
Delaware OH U.S.A. 164 D3
Delaware r. New Jersey/Pennsylvania U.S.A. 165 H4
Delaware state U.S.A. 165 H4
Delaware, East Branch r. NY U.S.A. 165 H3
Delaware Bay Delaware/New Jersey U.S.A. 165 H4
Delaware Lake OH U.S.A. 164 D3
Delaware Water Gap National Recreational Area park New Jersey/Pennsylvania U.S.A. 165 H3
Delay r. Canada 153 H2
Delbarton WV U.S.A. 164 D5
Delbrück Germany 63 I3
Delburne Canada 150 H4
Delegate Australia 138 D6
De Lemmer Neth. see Lemmer
Delémont Switz. 66 H3
Delevan CA U.S.A. 158 B2
Delevan NY U.S.A. 165 F2
Delfinópolis Brazil 179 B3
Delft Neth. 62 E2
Delfzijl Neth. 62 G1
Delgada, Point CA U.S.A. 158 A1
Delgado, Cabo c. Moz. 123 E5
Delger Mongolia 94 D2
Delgerhaan Mongolia 94 F2
Delgerhangay Mongolia 94 F2
Delgermörön Mongolia see Hüreemaral
Delger Mörön r. Mongolia 94 E1
Delgertsogt Mongolia 94 F2
Delhi Canada 164 E2
Delhi China see Delingha

▶Delhi India 104 D3
2nd most populous city in Asia and the world.

Delhi admin. div. India 99 B7
Delhi CO U.S.A. 157 G5
Delhi LA U.S.A. 161 F5
Delhi NY U.S.A. 165 H2
Deli i. Indon. 84 D4
Delice Turkey 112 D3
Delice r. Turkey 112 D2
Delījān Iran 110 C3
Déline Canada 149 Q2
Delingha China 94 D4
Delisle Canada 151 J5
Delitua Sumatra Indon. 84 B2
Delitzsch Germany 63 M3
Delligsen Germany 63 J3
Dell Rapids SD U.S.A. 160 D3
Dellys Alg. 67 H5
Del Mar CA U.S.A. 158 E5
Delmenhorst Germany 63 I1
Delnice Croatia 68 F2
Del Norte CO U.S.A. 157 G5
De-Longa, Ostrova is Russia 77 Q2
De Long Islands Russia see De-Longa, Ostrova
De Long Mountains AK U.S.A. 148 G1
De Long Strait Russia see Longa, Proliv
Deloraine Canada 151 K5
Delphi IN U.S.A. 164 B3
Delphos OH U.S.A. 164 C3
Delportshoop S. Africa 124 G5
Delray Beach FL U.S.A. 163 D7
Delrey IL U.S.A. 164 A3
Del Río Mex. 166 C2
Del Rio TX U.S.A. 161 C6
Delsbo Sweden 55 J6
Delta CO U.S.A. 159 I2
Delta OH U.S.A. 164 C3
Delta UT U.S.A. 159 G2
Delta r. AK U.S.A. 149 K2
Delta Downs Australia 136 C3
Delta Junction AK U.S.A. 149 K2
Deltona FL U.S.A. 163 D6
Delungra Australia 138 E2
Delüün Mongolia 94 B2
Delvin Ireland 61 E4
Delvinë Albania 69 I5
Delwara India 104 C4
De Maasduinen, Nationaal Park nat. park Neth. 62 G3
Demak Java Indon. 85 E4
Demanda, Sierra de la mts Spain 67 E2
Demarcation Point pt AK U.S.A. 149 L1
Demavend mt. Iran see Damāvand, Qolleh-ye
Demba Dem. Rep. Congo 123 C4
Dembī Dolo Eth. 108 D8
Demerara Guyana see Georgetown
Demerara Abyssal Plain sea feature S. Atlantic Ocean 184 E5
Demidov Russia 53 F5
Deming NM U.S.A. 157 G6
Demirci Turkey 69 M5
Demirköy Turkey 69 L4
Demirtaş Turkey 107 A1
Demmin Germany 57 N4
Demopolis AL U.S.A. 163 C5
DeMotte IN U.S.A. 164 B3
Dempo, Gunung vol. Indon. 84 C4
Dempster Highway Canada 149 M2
Dêmqog China 104 D2
Demta Indon. 81 K7
Dê Mūsá Qal'ah Rōd r. Afgh. 111 G3
Dem'yanovo Russia 52 J3
De Naawte S. Africa 124 E6
Denakil reg. Africa see Danakil
Denali AK U.S.A. 149 K3
Denali AK U.S.A. see McKinley, Mount
Denali Highway AK U.S.A. 149 K3
Denali National Park and Preserve AK U.S.A. 149 J3
Denan Eth. 122 E3
Denbigh Canada 165 G1
Denbigh U.K. 58 D5
Denbigh, Cape AK U.S.A. 148 G2
Den Bosch Neth. see 's-Hertogenbosch
Den Burg Neth. 62 E1
Den Chai Thai. 86 C3
Dendang Indon. 85 D3
Dendâra Mauritania 120 C3
Dendermonde Belgium 62 E3
Dendi mt. Eth. 122 D3
Dendre r. Belgium 62 E3
Dendron S. Africa see Mogwadi
Denezhkin Kamen', Gora mt. Russia 51 R3
Denges Passage Palau 82 [inset]
Dengfeng China 95 H5
Dênggar China 99 D7
Dêngka China see Têwo
Dêngkagoin China see Têwo
Dengkou China 95 F3
Dêngqên China 99 F7
Dengta China 97 G4
Dengxian China see Dengzhou
Dêngzê China 99 C6
Dengzhou Henan China 97 G1
Dengzhou Shandong China see Penglai
Den Haag Neth. see The Hague
Denham Australia 135 A6
Denham r. Australia 134 E3
Den Ham Neth. 62 G2
Denham Range mts Australia 136 E4
Den Helder Neth. 62 E2
Denholm Canada 151 I4
Dénia Spain 67 G4
Denial Bay Australia 137 A7
Deniliquin Australia 138 B5

Denio NV U.S.A. 156 D4
Denison IA U.S.A. 160 E3
Denison TX U.S.A. 161 D5
Denison, Cape Antarctica 188 G2
Denison Plains Australia 134 E4
Deniyaya Sri Lanka 106 D5
Denizli Turkey 69 M6
Denman Australia 138 E4
Denman Glacier Antarctica 188 F2
Denmark Australia 132 B5
Denmark country Europe 55 G8
Denmark WI U.S.A. 164 B1
Denmark Strait Greenland/Iceland 50 A2
Dennis, Lake salt flat Australia 134 E5
Dennison IL U.S.A. 164 B4
Dennison OH U.S.A. 164 E3
Denny U.K. 60 F4
Denov Uzbek. 111 G2
Denow Uzbek. see Denov
Denpasar Bali Indon. 85 F5
Densongi Celebes Indon. 83 B3
Denton MD U.S.A. 165 H4
Denton TX U.S.A. 161 D5
D'Entrecasteaux, Point Australia 135 A8
D'Entrecasteaux, Récifs reef New Caledonia 133 G3
D'Entrecasteaux Islands P.N.G. 132 F2
D'Entrecasteaux National Park Australia 135 A8

▶Denver CO U.S.A. 156 G5
Capital of Colorado.

Denver PA U.S.A. 165 G3
Denys r. Canada 152 F3
Deo India 105 F4
Deoband India 104 D3
Deogarh Jharkhand India see Deoghar
Deogarh Odisha India 105 F5
Deogarh Rajasthan India 104 C4
Deogarh Uttar Prad. India 104 D4
Deogarh mt. India 105 E5
Deoghar India 105 F4
Deolali India 106 B2
Deoli India 105 F5
Deomali mt. India 106 D2
Deori India 104 D5
Deoria India 105 E4
Deosai, Plains of Pak. 104 C2
Deosil India 105 E5
Deothang Bhutan 105 G4
De Panne Belgium 62 C3
De Pere WI U.S.A. 164 A1
Deposit NY U.S.A. 165 H2
Deputatskiy Russia 77 O3
Dêqên Xizang China 99 E7
Dêqên Xizang China see Dagzê
Dêqên Xizang China 99 E7
De Queen AR U.S.A. 161 E5
DeQuincy LA U.S.A. 167 G2
Dera Ghazi Khan Pak. 111 H4
Dera Ismail Khan Pak. 111 H4
Derajat reg. Pak. 111 H4
Derawar Fort Pak. 111 H4
Derbent Russia 113 H2
Derbesiye Turkey see Şenyurt
Derbur China 90 A2
Derby Australia 134 C4
Derby U.K. 59 F6
Derby CT U.S.A. 165 I3
Derby KS U.S.A. 161 D4
Derby NY U.S.A. 165 F2
Đerdap, Nacionalni Park nat. park Serbia 69 J2
Dereham U.K. 59 H6
Derg r. Ireland/U.K. 61 E3
Derg, Lough l. Ireland 61 D5
Dergachi Russia 53 K6
Dergachi Ukr. see Derhachi
Derhachi Ukr. 53 H6
DeRidder LA U.S.A. 161 E6
Derik Turkey 113 F3
Derm Namibia 124 D2
Derna Libya see Darnah
Dernberg, Cape Namibia 124 B4
Derom, Mount Antarctica 188 D2
Dêrong China 96 C2
Déroute, Passage de la strait Channel Is/France 59 E9
Derravaragh, Lough l. Ireland 61 E4
Derry U.K. see Londonderry
Derry NH U.S.A. 165 J2
Derryveagh Mountains hills Ireland 61 D3
Derst China 95 H3
Derstei China 94 E3
Dêrub China 99 B6
Derudeb Sudan 108 E6
De Rust S. Africa 124 F7
Derventa Bos. & Herz. 68 G2
Derwent r. England U.K. 58 F6
Derwent r. England U.K. 58 G5
Derwent Water l. U.K. 58 D4
Derzhavinsk Kazakh. 102 C1
Derzhavinskiy Kazakh. see Derzhavinsk
Desaguadero r. Arg. 178 C4
Désappointement, Îles du is Fr. Polynesia 187 K6
Desatoya Mountains NV U.S.A. 158 E2
Deschambault Lake Canada 151 K4
Deschutes r. OR U.S.A. 156 C3
Desē Eth. 122 D2
Deseado r. Arg. 178 C7
Desemboque Mex. 166 B2
Desengaño, Punta pt Arg. 178 C7
Deseret UT U.S.A. 159 G2
Deseret Peak UT U.S.A. 159 G1
Deseronto Canada 165 G1
Desert Canal Pak. 111 H4
Desert Center CA U.S.A. 159 F5
Desert Lake NV U.S.A. 159 F3
Desert View AZ U.S.A. 159 H3
Deshler OH U.S.A. 164 D3
Desierto Central de Baja California, Parque Natural del nature res. Mex. 166 B2
De Smet SD U.S.A. 160 D2

▶Des Moines IA U.S.A. 160 E3
Capital of Iowa.

Des Moines NM U.S.A. 161 C4
Des Moines r. IA U.S.A. 160 F3
Desna r. Russia/Ukr. 53 F6
Desnogorsk Russia 53 G5
Desolación, Isla i. Chile 178 B8
Desolation Point Phil. 82 D4
Despen Russia 94 C1
Des Plaines IL U.S.A. 164 B2
Dessau-Roßlau Germany 63 M3
Dessye Eth. see Desē
Destelbergen Belgium 62 D3
Destruction Bay Canada 189 A2
Desventuradas, Islas is S. Pacific Ocean 187 O7
Desvres France 62 B4
Detah Canada 150 H2
Dete Zimbabwe 123 C5
Detmold Germany 63 I3
Detrital Wash watercourse AZ U.S.A. 159 F3
Detroit MI U.S.A. 164 D2
Detroit Lakes MN U.S.A. 160 E2
Dett Zimbabwe see Dete
Deua National Park Australia 138 D5
Deuben Germany 63 M3
Deurne Neth. 62 F3
Deutschland country Europe see Germany
Deutschlandsberg Austria 57 O7
Deutzen Germany 63 M3
Deva Romania 69 J2
Deva U.K. see Chester
Devana U.K. see Aberdeen
Devangere India see Davangere
Devanhalli India 106 C3
Deve Bair pass Bulg./Macedonia see Velbŭzhdki Prokhod
Develi Turkey 112 D3
Deventer Neth. 62 G2
Deveron r. U.K. 60 G3
Devét skal hill Czech Rep. 57 P6
Devgarh India 106 B2
Devghar India see Deoghar
Devikot India 104 B4
Devil Mountain hill AK U.S.A. 148 F2
Devil's Bridge U.K. 59 D6
Devils Gate pass CA U.S.A. 158 D2
Devils Lake ND U.S.A. 160 D1
Devils Lake l. TX U.S.A. 167 E2
Devils Paw mt. AK U.S.A. 149 N4
Devils Peak CA U.S.A. 158 D3
Devil's Point Bahamas 163 F7
Devil's Thumb mt. Canada/U.S.A. 149 N4
Devine TX U.S.A. 161 D6
Devizes U.K. 59 F7
Devli India 104 C4
Devnya Bulg. 69 L3
Devon r. U.K. 60 F4
Devon Island Canada 147 I2
Devonport Australia 137 [inset]
Devrek Turkey 69 N4
Devrukh India 106 B2
Dewa, Tanjung pt Indon. 84 A2
Dewakang Besar i. Indon. 85 G4
Dewas India 104 D5
De Weerribben-Wieden, Nationaal Park nat. park Neth. 62 G2
Dewetsdorp S. Africa 125 H5
De Witt AR U.S.A. 161 F5
De Witt IA U.S.A. 160 F3
Dewsbury U.K. 58 F5
Dexing China 97 H2
Dêxing China 99 F7
Dexter ME U.S.A. 165 K1
Dexter MI U.S.A. 164 D2
Dexter MO U.S.A. 161 F4
Dexter NM U.S.A. 157 G6
Dexter NY U.S.A. 165 G1
Deyang China 96 E2
Dey-Dey Lake salt flat Australia 135 E7
Deyhūk Iran 110 E3
Deyong, Tanjung pt Indon. 81 J8
Dez r. Iran 108 G3
Dezadeash Lake Canada 149 M3
Dezfūl Iran 110 C3

▶Dezhneva, Mys c. Russia 148 E2
Most easterly point of Asia.

Dezhou Shandong China 95 I4
Dezhou Sichuan China see Dechang
Dezh Shāhpūr Iran see Marīvān
Dhabarau India 105 E4
Dhahab, Wādī adh r. Syria 107 B3
Dhahran Saudi Arabia 110 C5

▶Dhaka Bangl. 105 G5
Capital of Bangladesh. 9th most populous city in the world.

Dhalbhum reg. India 105 F5
Dhalgaon India 106 B2
Dhamār Yemen 108 F7
Dhamoni India 104 D4
Dhamtari India 106 D1
Dhana Pak. 111 H5
Dhana Sar Pak. 111 H4
Dhanbad India 105 F5
Dhanera India 104 C4
Dhang Range mts Nepal 105 E3
Dhankuta Nepal 105 F4
Dhansia India 104 C3
Dhar India 104 C5
Dharampur India 106 B1
Dharamsala India 104 D2
Dharan Nepal 105 F4
Dharashiv India see Osmanabad
Dhari India 104 B5
Dharmapuri India 106 C3
Dharmavaram India 106 C3
Dharmsala Hima. Prad. India see Dharamsala
Dharmsala Odisha India 105 F5
Dharnaoda India 104 D4
Dharug National Park Australia 138 E4
Dharur India 106 C2
Dharwad India 106 B3
Dharwar India see Dharwad
Dharwas India 104 D2
Dhasan r. India 104 D4
Dhāt al Ḥājj Saudi Arabia 112 E5

▶Dhaulagiri I mt. Nepal 105 E3
7th highest mountain in Asia and the world.

Dhaulpur India see Dholpur
Dhaura India 104 D4
Dhaurahra India 104 E4
Dhawlagiri mt. Nepal see Dhaulagiri I
Dhebar Lake India see Jaisamand Lake
Dhekelia Sovereign Base Area military base Cyprus 107 A2
Dhemaji India 105 H4
Dhenkanal India 106 E1
Dhībān Jordan 107 B4
Dhidhimótikhon Greece see Didymoteicho
Dhing India 105 H4
Dhirwah, Wādī adh watercourse Jordan 107 C4
Dhodhekánisos is Greece see Dodecanese
Dhola India 104 B5
Dholera India 104 C5
Dholpur India 104 D4
Dhomokós Greece see Domokos
Dhone India 106 C3
Dhoraji India 104 B5
Dhori India 104 B5
Dhrangadhra India 104 B5
Dhubāb Yemen 108 F7
Dhubri India 105 G4
Dhuburi India see Dhubri
Dhudial Pak. 111 I3
Dhule India 106 B1
Dhulia India see Dhule
Dhulian India 105 F4
Dhulian Pak. 111 I3
Dhuma India 104 D5
Dhund r. India 104 D4
Dhupgarh mt. India 104 D5
Dhurwai India 104 D4
Dhuusa Marreeb Somalia 122 E3
Dia i. Greece 69 K7
Diablo, Mount CA U.S.A. 158 C3
Diablo, Picacho del mt. Mex. 166 B2
Diablo Range mts CA U.S.A. 158 C3
Diagbe Dem. Rep. Congo 122 C3
Diamante Arg. 178 D4
Diamantina watercourse Australia 136 B5
Diamantina Brazil 179 C2
Diamantina, Chapada plat. Brazil 179 C1
Diamantina Deep sea feature Indian Ocean 185 O8
Diamantina Gates National Park Australia 136 C4
Diamantino Brazil 177 G6
Diamond Islets Australia 136 E3
Diamond Peak NV U.S.A. 159 F2
Dianbai China 97 F4
Diancang Shan mt. China 96 D3
Dian Chi l. China 96 D3
Diandioumé Mali 120 C3
Diane Bank sea feature Australia 136 E2
Dianjiang China 96 E2
Dianópolis Brazil 177 I6
Dianyang China see Shidian
Diaobingshan China 95 J3
Diaokou China 95 I4
Diaoling China 90 C3
Diapaga Burkina Faso 120 D3
Diarizos r. Cyprus 107 A2
Diavolo, Mount hill India 87 A4
Diaz Point Namibia 124 B4
Dibaya Dem. Rep. Congo 123 C4
Dibella well Niger 120 E3
Dibeng S. Africa 124 F4
Dibete Botswana 125 H2
Dibrugarh India 105 H4
Dibse Syria see Dibsī
Dibsī Syria 107 D2
Dickens TX U.S.A. 161 C5
Dickinson ND U.S.A. 160 C2
Dicle r. Asia 113 F3 see Tigris
Dīdēsa Wenz r. Eth. 122 D3
Didicas i. Phil. 82 C2
Didiéni Mali 120 C3
Didsbury Canada 150 H5
Didwana India 104 C4
Didymoteicho Greece 69 L4
Die France 66 G4
Dieblich Germany 63 H4
Diébougou Burkina Faso 120 C3
Dieburg Germany 63 I5
Diedenhofen France see Thionville
Diefenbaker, Lake Canada 151 I5
Diego de Almagro, Isla i. Chile 178 A8
Diégo Suarez Madag. see Antsirañana
Diekirch Lux. 62 G5
Diéma Mali 120 C3
Diemel r. Germany 63 J3
Điện Biên Vietnam see Điện Biên Phu
Điện Biên Phu Vietnam 86 C2
Diên Châu Vietnam 86 D3
Diên Khanh Vietnam 87 E4
Diepholz Germany 63 I2
Dieppe France 62 B5
Dierks AR U.S.A. 161 E5
Di'er Songhua Jiang r. China see Songhua Jiang
Diessen Neth. 62 F3
Diest Belgium 62 F4
Dietikon Switz. 66 I3
Dietrich Camp AK U.S.A. 149 J2
Diez Germany 63 I4
Diffa Niger 120 E3
Digby Canada 153 I5
Diggi India 104 C4
Diglur India 106 C2
Digne France see Digne-les-Bains
Digne-les-Bains France 66 H4
Digoin France 66 F3
Digollorin Point Luzon Phil. 82 C2
Digos Mindanao Phil. 82 D5
Digras India 106 C1
Digri Pak. 111 H5
Digul r. Indon. 81 K8
Diguojiadan China 94 D4
Digya National Park Ghana 120 C4
Dihang r. Asia 105 H4
also known as Dihang (India) or Jamuna (Bangladesh) or Siang (India) or Yarlung Zangbo (China)
Dihok Iraq see Dahūk/Dihok
Dihourse, Lac l. Canada 153 I2
Diinsoor Somalia 122 E3
Dijon France 66 G3
Dik Chad 121 E4
Diken India 104 C4
Dikhil Djibouti 108 F7
Dikhu r. India 99 F8
Dikili Turkey 69 L5
Dik'losmta mt. Russia 53 J8
Diksmuide Belgium 62 C3
Dikson Russia 76 J2
Dīla Eth. 122 D3
Dilārām Afgh. 111 F3
Dilaram Iran 110 E4

▶Dili East Timor 83 C5
Capital of East Timor (Timor-Leste).

Di Linh Vietnam 87 E5
Dillenburg Germany 63 I4
Dilley TX U.S.A. 161 D6
Dillingen an der Donau Germany 57 M6
Dillingen/Saar Germany 62 G5
Dillingham AK U.S.A. 148 H4
Dillon r. Canada 151 I4
Dillon MT U.S.A. 156 E3
Dillon SC U.S.A. 163 E5
Dillwyn VA U.S.A. 165 F5
Dilolo Dem. Rep. Congo 123 C5
Dilsen Belgium 62 F3
Dimapur India 105 H4
Dimas Mex. 166 D4
Dimashq Syria see Damascus
Dimbokro Côte d'Ivoire 120 C4
Dimboola Australia 137 C8
Dime Landing AK U.S.A. 148 G2
Dimitrov Ukr. see Dymytrov
Dimitrovgrad Bulg. 69 K3
Dimitrovgrad Russia 53 K5
Dimitrovo Bulg. see Pernik
Dimmitt TX U.S.A. 161 C5
Dimona Israel 107 B4
Dimpho Pan salt pan Botswana 124 E3
Dinagat i. Phil. 82 D4
Dinajpur Bangl. 105 G4
Dinan France 66 C2
Dinant Belgium 62 E4
Dinapur India 105 F4
Dinar Turkey 69 N5
Dīnār, Kūh-e mt. Iran 110 C4
Dinara Planina mts Bos. & Herz./Croatia see Dinaric Alps
Dinaric Alps mts Bos. & Herz./Croatia 68 G2
Dinbych U.K. see Denbigh
Dinbych-y-pysgod U.K. see Tenby
Dinder National Park Sudan 121 G3
Dindi r. India 106 C2
Dindigul India 106 C4
Dindima Nigeria 120 E3
Dindiza Moz. 125 K2
Dindori India 104 E5
Dingalan Bay Luzon Phil. 82 C3
Dingbian China 95 F4
Dingcheng China see Dingyuan
Dingelstädt Germany 63 K3
Dinggo China 99 D6
Dinggyê China 99 D7
Dingin, Bukit mt. Indon. 84 C3
Dingla Nepal 105 F4
Dingle Ireland see Daingean Uí Chúis
Dingle Bay Ireland 61 B5
Dingnan China 97 G3
Dingo Australia 136 E4
Dingolfing Germany 63 M6
Dingping China see Linshui
Dingras Luzon Phil. 82 C2
Dingshan China 98 D3
Dingtao China 95 H5
Dinguiraye Guinea 120 B3
Dingwall U.K. 60 E3
Dingxi China 94 F5
Dingxian China see Dingzhou
Dingxin China 94 D3
Dingxing China 95 H4
Dingyuan China 97 H1
Dingzhou China 95 H4
Dingzi Gang b. China 95 J4
Dingzikou China 98 F5
Dinh Lâp Vietnam 86 D2
Dinkelsbühl Germany 63 K5
Dinokwe Botswana 125 H2
Dinosaur CO U.S.A. 159 I1
Dinosaur National Monument nat. park CO U.S.A. 159 I1
Dinslaken Germany 62 G3
Dintiteladas Sumatra Indon. 84 D4
Dinwiddie VA U.S.A. 165 G5
Dioïla Mali 120 C3
Diomede AK U.S.A. 148 E2
Diomede Islands Russia/U.S.A. 148 E2
Dionísio Cerqueira Brazil 178 F3
Diorama Brazil 179 A2
Dioscurias Georgia see Sokhumi
Diouloulou Senegal 120 B3
Diourbel Senegal 120 B3
Dipayal Nepal 104 E3
Diphu India 105 H4
Dipkarpaz Cyprus see Rizokarpason
Diplo Pak. 111 H5
Dipolog Mindanao Phil. 82 C4
Dipperu National Park Australia 136 E4
Dipu China see Anji
Dir reg. Pak. 111 I3
Dirang India 105 H4
Diré Mali 120 C3
Direction, Cape Australia 136 C2
Dirē Dawa Eth. 122 E3
Diriamba Nicaragua 166 [inset] I7
Dirico Angola 123 C5
Dirj Libya 120 E1
Dirk Hartog Island Australia 135 A6
Dirranbandi Australia 138 D2
Ḍirs Saudi Arabia 122 E2
Dirschau Poland see Tczew
Dirty Devil r. UT U.S.A. 159 H3
Disa India 104 C4
Disang r. India 105 H4
Disappointment, Cape S. Georgia 178 I8
Disappointment, Cape WA U.S.A. 156 B3
Disappointment, Lake salt flat Australia 135 C5
Disappointment Islands Fr. Polynesia see Désappointement, Îles du
Disappointment Lake Canada 153 J3
Disaster Bay Australia 138 D6
Discovery Bay Australia 137 C8
Dishna r. AK U.S.A. 148 H3
Disko i. Greenland see Qeqertarsuaq
Disko Bugt b. Greenland see Qeqertarsuup Tunua
Dismal Swamp VA U.S.A. 162 E4
Dispur India 105 G4
Disputanta VA U.S.A. 165 G5
Disraeli Canada 153 H5
Diss U.K. 59 I6
Distrito Federal admin. dist. Brazil 179 B1
Distrito Federal admin. dist. Mex. 167 F5
Disūq Egypt 112 C5
Dit i. Phil. 82 C4
Ditloung S. Africa 124 F5
Dittaino r. Sicily Italy 68 F6
Diu India 106 A1
Diuata Mountains Mindanao Phil. 82 D4
Diuata Point Mindanao Phil. 82 D4
Dīvāndarreh Iran 110 B3
Divehi country Indian Ocean see Maldives
Divi, Point India 106 D3
Divichi Azer. see Şabran
Divide Mountain AK U.S.A. 149 L3
Divilican Bay Luzon Phil. 82 C2
Divinópolis Brazil 179 B3
Divnoye Russia 53 I7
Divo Côte d'Ivoire 120 C4
Divriği Turkey 112 E3
Diwana Pak. 111 G5
Diwaniyah Iraq see Ad Dīwānīyah
Dixfield ME U.S.A. 165 J1
Dixon CA U.S.A. 158 C2
Dixon IL U.S.A. 160 F3
Dixon KY U.S.A. 164 B5
Dixon MT U.S.A. 156 E3
Dixon Entrance sea chan. Canada/U.S.A. 149 N5
Dixonville Canada 150 G3
Dixville Canada 165 J1
Diyadin Turkey 113 F3
Diyarbakır Turkey 113 F3
Diz Pak. 111 F5
Diz Chah Iran 110 D3
Dize Turkey see Yüksekova
Dizney KY U.S.A. 164 D5
Djado Niger 120 E2
Djado, Plateau du Niger 120 E2
Djaja, Puntjak mt. Indon. see Jaya, Puncak
Djakarta Java Indon. see Jakarta
Djakovica Kosovo see Gjakovë
Djakovo Croatia see Đakovo
Djambala Congo 122 B4
Djanet Alg. 120 D2
Djarrit-Uliga-Dalap Marshall Is see Delap-Uliga-Djarrit
Djelfa Alg. 67 H6
Djéma Cent. Afr. Rep. 122 C3
Djenné Mali 120 C3
Djenoun, Garet el mt. Alg. 120 D2
Djibloho Equat. Guinea 120 E4
Djibo Burkina Faso 120 C3
Djibouti country Africa 108 F7

▶Djibouti Djibouti 108 F7
Capital of Djibouti.

Djidjelli Alg. see Jijel
Djizak Uzbek. see Jizzax
Djougou Benin 120 D4
Djoum Cameroon 120 E4
Djourab, Erg du des. Chad 121 E3
Djúpivogur Iceland 54 [inset 1]
Djurås Sweden 55 I6
Djurdjura, Parc National du Alg. 67 I5
Dmitriya Lapteva, Proliv sea chan. Russia 77 P2
Dmitriyev-L'govskiy Russia 53 G5
Dmitriyevsk Ukr. see Makiyivka
Dmitrov Russia 52 H4
Dmytriyevs'k Ukr. see Makiyivka
Dnepr r. Europe 53 F5 see Dnieper
Dneprodzerzhinsk Ukr. see Dniprodzerzhyns'k
Dnepropetrovsk Ukr. see Dnipropetrovs'k

▶Dnieper r. Europe 53 G7
3rd longest river in Europe. Also spelt Dnepr (Rus. Fed.) or Dnipro (Ukraine) or Dnyapro (Belarus).

Dniester r. Ukr. 53 F6
also spelt Dnister (Ukraine) or Nistru (Moldova)
Dnipro r. Europe 53 G7 see Dnieper
Dniprodzerzhyns'k Ukr. 53 G6
Dnipropetrovs'k Ukr. 53 G6
Dnister r. Ukr. 53 F6 see Dniester
Dno Russia 52 F4
Dnyapro r. Europe 53 F6 see Dnieper
Doaba Pak. 111 H3
Doangdoangan Besar i. Indon. 85 G4
Doangdoangan Kecil i. Indon. 85 G4
Đoan Hung Vietnam 86 D2
Doba Chad 121 E4
Dobdain China 94 E5
Dobele Latvia 55 M8
Döbeln Germany 63 N3
Doberai, Jazirah pen. Indon. 81 I7
Doberai Peninsula Indon. see Doberai, Jazirah
Dobo Moluccas Indon. 81 I8
Doboj Bos. & Herz. 68 H2
Doborjī Iran 110 D4
Döbraberg hill Germany 63 L4
Dobrich Bulg. 69 L3
Dobrinka Russia 53 I5
Dobroye Russia 53 H5
Dobrudja reg. Romania see Dobruja
Dobruja reg. Romania 69 L3
Dobrush Belarus 53 F5
Dobryanka Russia 51 R4
Dobyn Kazakh. 98 C4
Dobzha China 99 E7
Đốc, Mui pt Vietnam 86 D3
Doc Can reef Phil. 82 B5
Doce r. Brazil 179 D2
Dochart r. U.K. 60 E4
Docking U.K. 59 H6
Doctor Arroyo Mex. 167 E4
Doctor Belisario Domínguez Mex. 166 D2
Doctor Hicks Range hills Australia 135 D7
Doctor Pedro P. Peña Para. 178 D2
Doda India 104 C2
Doda Betta mt. India 106 C4
Dod Ballapur India 106 C3
Dodê China 99 E7
Dodecanese is Greece 69 L7
Dodekanisa is Greece see Dodecanese
Dodekanisos is Greece see Dodecanese
Dodge City KS U.S.A. 160 C4
Dodgeville WI U.S.A. 160 F3
Dodman Point U.K. 59 C8

▶Dodoma Tanz. 123 D4
Capital of Tanzania.

Dodsonville OH U.S.A. 164 D4
Doetinchem Neth. 62 G3
Dofa Moluccas Indon. 83 C3
Dog r. Canada 152 C4
Dogai Coring salt l. China 99 E6
Dogaicoring Qangco salt l. China 99 E6
Doğanşehir Turkey 112 E3
Dogên Co l. China 99 E7
Dōgen-ko l. Japan 93 F2
Doghārūn Iran 111 F3
Dog Island Canada 153 J2
Dog Lake Man. Canada 151 L5
Dog Lake Ont. Canada 152 C4
Dog Lake Ont. Canada 152 D4
Dōgo i. Japan 91 D5
Dogondoutchi Niger 120 D3
Dog Rocks is Bahamas 163 E7
Doğubeyazıt Turkey 113 G3
Doğu Menteşe Dağları mts Turkey 69 M6
Dogxung Zangbo r. China 99 D7
Do'gyaling China 105 G3

▶Doha Qatar 110 C5
Capital of Qatar.

Dohad India see Dahod
Dohazari Bangl. 105 H5
Dohrighat India 99 C8
Doi i. Fiji 133 I4
Doi i. Moluccas Indon. 83 C2
Doi Inthanon National Park Thai. 86 B3
Doijang China 99 E7
Doi Luang National Park Thai. 86 B3
Doilungdêqên China 99 E7
Doire U.K. see Londonderry
Doi Saket Thai. 86 B3
Dois Irmãos, Serra dos hills Brazil 177 J5
Dokan, Sadd Iraq 113 G4
Dok-do i. N. Pacific Ocean see Liancourt Rocks
Dokhara, Dunes de des. Alg. 64 F5
Dokka Norway 55 G6
Dokkum Neth. 62 F1
Dokog He r. China 96 D2
Dokri Pak. 111 H5
Dokshukino Russia see Nartkala
Dokshytsy Belarus 55 O9
Dokuchayeva, Mys c. Russia 90 G3
Dokuchayevka Kazakh. see Karamendy
Dokuchayevs'k Ukr. 53 H7
Dolbenmaen U.K. 59 C6
Dol-de-Bretagne France 66 D2
Dole France 66 G3
Dolgellau U.K. 59 D6
Dolgen Germany 63 N1
Dolgiy, Ostrov i. Russia 52 L1
Dolgorukovo Russia 53 H5
Dolina Ukr. see Dolyna
Dolinsk Russia 90 F3
Dolisie Congo 123 B4

Dolit Halmahera Indon. 83 C3
Dolleman Island Antarctica 188 L2
Dollnstein Germany 63 L6
Dolo Celebes Indon. 83 A3
Dolok, Pulau i. Indon. 81 J8
Dolomites mts Italy 68 D2
Dolomiti mts Italy see Dolomites
Dolomiti Bellunesi, Parco Nazionale delle nat. park Italy 68 D1
Dolomitiche, Alpi mts Italy see Dolomites
Dolon Ashuusu pass Kyrg. 98 A4
Dolonnur China see Duolun
Dolo Odo Eth. 122 E3
Doloon Mongolia see Tsogt-Ovoo
Dolores Arg. 178 E5
Dolores Guat. 167 H5
Dolores Mex. 166 C3
Dolores Uruguay 178 E4
Dolores CO U.S.A. 159 I3
Dolores Hidalgo Mex. 167 E4
Dolphin and Union Strait Canada 146 G3
Dolphin Head hd Namibia 124 B3
Đô Lương Vietnam 86 D3
Dolyna Ukr. 53 D6
Domaila India 104 D3
Domaniç Turkey 69 M5
Domar Bangl. 99 E8
Domar China 99 C6
Domartang China 99 F7
Domažlice Czech Rep. 63 M5
Domba China 99 F6
Dom Bākh Iran 110 B3
Dombås Norway 54 F5
Dombóvár Hungary 68 H1
Dombrau Poland see Dąbrowa Górnicza
Dombrovitsa Ukr. see Dubrovytsya
Dombrowa Poland see Dąbrowa Górnicza
Domda China see Qingshuihe
Dome Creek Canada 150 F4
Dome Rock Mountains AZ U.S.A. 159 F5
Domeyko Chile 178 B3
Domfront France 66 D2
Dominica country West Indies 169 L5
Dominicana, República country West Indies see Dominican Republic
Dominican Republic country West Indies 169 J5
Dominion, Cape Canada 147 K3
Dominique i. Fr. Polynesia see Hiva Oa
Dömitz Germany 63 L1
Dom Joaquim Brazil 179 C2
Dommel r. Neth. 62 F3
Domo Eth. 122 E3
Domokos Greece 69 J5
Dompu Sumbawa Indon. 85 G5
Domuyo, Volcán vol. Arg. 178 B5
Domville, Mount hill Australia 138 E2
Don Mex. 166 C3

▶Don r. Russia 53 H7
5th longest river in Europe.

Don r. U.K. 60 G3
Don, Xé r. Laos 86 D4
Donaghadee U.K. 61 G3
Donaghmore U.K. 61 F3
Donald Australia 138 A6
Donaldsonville LA U.S.A. 161 F6
Donalsonville GA U.S.A. 163 C6
Doñana, Parque Nacional de nat. park Spain 67 C5
Donau r. Europe 57 P6 see Danube
Donauwörth Germany 63 K6
Don Benito Spain 67 D4
Doncaster U.K. 58 F5
Dondo Angola 123 B4
Dondo Moz. 123 D5
Dondo, Tanjung pt Indon. 83 B2
Dondo, Teluk b. Indon. 83 B2
Dondonay i. Phil. 82 C4
Dondra Head hd Sri Lanka 106 D5
Donegal Ireland 61 D3
Donegal Bay Ireland 61 D3
Donenbay Kazakh. 98 C2
Donets'k Ukr. 53 H7
Donetsko-Amrovsiyevka Ukr. see Amvrosiyivka
Donets'kyy Kryazh hills Russia/Ukr. 53 H6
Donga r. Cameroon/Nigeria 120 D4
Dong'an China 97 F3
Dongane, Lagoa lag. Moz. 125 L3
Dongara Australia 135 A7
Dongbatu China 98 F4
Dongbei Pingyuan plain China 95 J3
Dongbo China see Mêdog
Dongchuan Yunnan China see Tangdan
Dongchuan Yunnan China see Yao'an
Dongchuan Yunnan China 96 D3
Dongco China 99 D6
Dong Co l. China 99 D6
Dongcun Shandong China see Haiyang
Dongcun Shanxi China see Lanxian
Dong Dabsan Hu salt l. China 99 F5
Dongducheon S. Korea 91 B5
Dong'e China 95 I4
Dongfang China 97 F5
Dongfanghong China 90 D3
Donggala Celebes Indon. 83 A3
Donggang Liaoning China 91 B5
Donggang Shandong China 95 I5
Donggar China see Doilungdêqên
Donggi Conag l. China 94 D5
Donggou Liaoning China see Donggang
Donggou Qinghai China 94 E5
Donggu China 97 G3
Dongguan China 97 G4
Donghae S. Korea 91 C5
Donghai China 95 I5
Dong Hai sea N. Pacific Ocean see East China Sea
Donghaiba China 94 F4
Dong Haxat China 90 B3
Đông Hơi Vietnam 86 D3
Donghu China 94 E4
Donghuachi China 95 G4
Donghuang China see Xishui
Dongjiang Shuiku resr China 97 G3
Dongjug China 96 B2
Dongkait, Tanjung pt Indon. 83 A3
Dongkar China 99 E7
Dongkou China 97 F3
Donglan China 96 E3
Dongle China 94 E4
Dongliao He r. China 95 J3
Donglük China 98 E5
Dongmen China see Luocheng
Dongming China 95 H5
Dongminzhutun China 90 A3
Dongning China 90 C3
Dongo Angola 123 B5
Dongo Dem. Rep. Congo 122 B3
Dongola Sudan 108 D6
Dongou Congo 122 B3
Dong Phraya Yen esc. Thai. 86 C4
Dongping Guangdong China 97 G4
Dongping Hunan China see Anhua
Dongping Hu l. China 95 I4
Dongpo China see Meishan
Dongqiao China 99 E7
Dongqinghu China 94 F4
Dongqu r. China 99 F6
Dongquan China 94 C3
Dongshan Fujian China 97 H4
Dongshan Jiangsu China 97 I2
Dongshan Jiangxi China see Shangyou
Dongshao China 97 G3
Dongsha Qundao is China see Pratas Islands
Dongsheng Nei Mongol China 95 G4
Dongsheng Sichuan China see Shuangliu
Dongtai China 97 I1
Dong Taijnar Hu l. China 99 F5
Dongting Hu l. China 97 G2
Dongtou China 97 I3
Đông Triêu Vietnam 86 D2
Dong Ujimqin Qi China see Uliastai
Đông Văn Vietnam 86 D2
Dongxiang Gansu China 94 E5
Dongxiang Jiangxi China 97 H2
Dongxi Liandao i. China 97 H1
Dongxing Guangxi China 96 E4
Dongxing Heilong. China 90 B3
Dongyang China 97 I2
Dongying China 95 I4
Dongzhi China 97 H2
Donkerbroek Neth. 62 G1
Don Kêv Cambodia 87 D5
Donnacona Canada 153 H5
Donnelly AK U.S.A. 149 K3
Donnellys Crossing N.Z. 139 D2
Donner Pass CA U.S.A. 158 C2
Donnersberg hill Germany 63 H5
Donostia Spain see San Sebastián
Donousa i. Greece 69 K6
Donoussa i. Greece see Donousa
Donskoye Russia 53 I7
Donsol Luzon Phil. 82 C3
Donyztau, Sor dry lake Kazakh. 102 A2
Dooagh Ireland 61 B4
Doomadgee Australia 136 B3
Doon r. U.K. 60 E5
Doon, Loch l. U.K. 60 E5
Doonbeg r. Ireland 61 C5
Doonerak, Mount AK U.S.A. 149 J2
Doorn Neth. 62 F2
Door Peninsula WI U.S.A. 164 B1
Doorwerth Neth. 62 F3
Doqêmo China 99 F7
Doqên Co l. China 105 G3
Doqoi China 99 E7
Do Qu r. China 94 D5
Dor Israel 107 B3
Dora NM U.S.A. 161 C5
Dora, Lake salt flat Australia 134 C5
Dorado Mex. 166 D3
Dorah Pass Pak. 111 H2
Doran Lake Canada 151 I2
Dorbiljin China see Emin
Dorbod China 95 K2
Dorbod Qi China see Ulan Hua
Dorchester U.K. 59 E8
Dordabis Namibia 124 C2
Dordogne r. France 66 D4
Dordrecht Neth. 62 E3
Dordrecht S. Africa 125 H6
Doreenville Namibia 124 D2
Doré Lake Canada 151 J4
Doré Lake l. Canada 151 J4
Dores do Indaiá Brazil 179 B2
Dorgê Co l. China 94 C5
Dörgön Mongolia 94 C1
Dörgön Nuur salt l. Mongolia 94 C2
Dori Burkina Faso 120 C3
Doring r. S. Africa 124 D6
Dorisvale Australia 134 E3
Dorking U.K. 59 G7
Dormagen Germany 62 G3
Dormans France 62 D5
Dormidontovka Russia 90 D3
Dornoch U.K. 60 E3
Dornoch Firth est. U.K. 60 E3
Dornod prov. Mongolia 95 H1
Dornogovĭ prov. Mongolia 95 G2
Dornum Germany 63 H1
Doro Mali 120 C3
Dorob National Park park Namibia 124 B2
Dorogobuzh Russia 53 G5
Dorogorskoye Russia 52 J2
Doroḩ Iran 111 F3
Dorohoi Romania 53 E7
Doroninskoye Russia 95 H1
Dorostol Bulg. see Silistra
Dorotea Sweden 54 J4
Dorpat Estonia see Tartu
Dorre Island Australia 135 A6
Dorrigo Australia 138 F3
Dorris CA U.S.A. 156 C4
Dorset Canada 165 F1
Dorset and East Devon Coast (Jurassic Coast) tourist site U.K. 59 D8
Dorsoidong Co l. China 99 E6
Dortmund Germany 63 H3
Dörtyol Turkey 107 C1
Dorūd Iran 110 C3
Dorum Germany 63 I1
Doruma Dem. Rep. Congo 122 C3
Dorüneh, Kūh-e mts Iran 110 E3
Dörverden Germany 63 J2
Dörvöljin Mongolia 94 C2
Dorylaeum Turkey see Eskişehir
Dos Bahías, Cabo c. Arg. 178 C6
Dos de Mayo Peru 176 C5
Doshakh, Koh-i- mt. Afgh. see Dū Shākh, Kōh-e
Dōshi Japan 93 F3
Dos Lagunos Guat. 167 H5
Đô Sơn Vietnam 86 D2
Dos Palos CA U.S.A. 158 C3
Dosse r. Germany 63 M2
Dosso Niger 120 D3
Dostyk Kazakh. 98 C3
Dothan AL U.S.A. 163 C6
Dot Lake AK U.S.A. 149 K3
Dotsero CO U.S.A. 159 J2
Douai France 62 D4
Douala Cameroon 120 D4
Douarnenez France 66 B2
Double Headed Shot Cays is Bahamas 163 D8
Double Island H.K. China 97 [inset]
Double Island Point Australia 137 F5
Double Mountain Fork r. TX U.S.A. 161 C5
Double Peak AK U.S.A. 148 I3
Double Peak CA U.S.A. 158 D4
Double Point Australia 136 D3
Double Springs AL U.S.A. 163 C5
Doubs r. France/Switz. 66 G3
Doubtful Sound inlet N.Z. 139 A7
Doubtless Bay N.Z. 139 D2
Doucan China see Fuping
Douentza Mali 120 C3
Dougga tourist site Tunisia 68 C6

▶Douglas Isle of Man 58 C4
Capital of the Isle of Man.

Douglas S. Africa 124 F5
Douglas U.K. 60 F5
Douglas AZ U.S.A. 157 F7
Douglas GA U.S.A. 163 D6
Douglas WY U.S.A. 156 G4
Douglas, Cape AK U.S.A. 148 I4
Douglas Reef i. Japan see Okino-Tori-shima
Douglasville GA U.S.A. 163 C5
Douhudi China see Gong'an
Doulatpur Bangl. see Daulatpur
Douliu Taiwan 97 I4
Doullens France 62 C4
Douna Mali 120 C3
Doune U.K. 60 E4
Doupovské hory mts Czech Rep. 63 N4
Dourada, Serra hills Brazil 179 A2
Dourada, Serra mts Brazil 179 A1
Dourados Brazil 178 F2
Douro r. Port. 67 B3
also known as Duero (Spain)
Doushi China see Gong'an
Doushui Shuiku resr China 97 G3
Douve r. France 59 F9
Douzy France 62 F5
Dove r. U.K. 59 F6
Dove Brook Canada 153 K3
Dove Creek CO U.S.A. 159 I3
Dover U.K. 59 I7

▶Dover DE U.S.A. 165 H4
Capital of Delaware.

Dover NH U.S.A. 165 J2
Dover NJ U.S.A. 165 H3
Dover OH U.S.A. 164 E3
Dover TN U.S.A. 162 C4
Dover, Strait of France/U.K. 66 E1
Dover-Foxcroft ME U.S.A. 165 K1
Dovey r. U.K. 59 D6
Dovrefjell Nasjonalpark nat. park Norway 54 F5
Dowagiac MI U.S.A. 164 B3
Dowi, Tanjung pt Indon. 84 B2
Dowlaiswaram India 106 D2
Dowlatābād Afgh. 111 F3
Dowlatābād Fārs Iran 110 C4
Dowlatābād Fārs Iran 110 D4
Dowlatābād Khorāsān-e Raẕavī Iran 110 E2
Dowlatābād Khorāsān-e Raẕavī Iran 111 F2
Dowlat Khān Afgh. 111 H3
Dowlatyār Afgh. 111 G3
Downieville CA U.S.A. 158 C2
Downpatrick U.K. 61 G3
Downsville NY U.S.A. 165 H2
Doxong China 99 F7
Doyle CA U.S.A. 158 C1
Doylestown PA U.S.A. 165 H3
Dozdān r. Iran 110 E5
Dōzen is Japan 91 D5
Dozois, Réservoir resr Canada 152 F5
Dozulé France 59 G9
Drâa, Hamada du plat. Alg. 64 C6
Dracena Brazil 179 A3
Drachten Neth. 62 G1
Drăgănești-Olt Romania 69 K2
Drăgășani Romania 69 K2
Dragonera, Isla i. Spain see Sa Dragonera
Dragoon AZ U.S.A. 159 H5
Dragsfjärd Fin. 55 M6
Draguignan France 66 H5
Drahichyn Belarus 55 N10
Drake Australia 138 F2
Drake ND U.S.A. 160 C2
Drakensberg mts S. Africa 125 I3
Drake Passage S. Atlantic Ocean 184 D9
Drakes Bay CA U.S.A. 158 B3
Drama Greece 69 K4
Drammen Norway 55 G7
Drang, Ia r. Cambodia 87 D4
Drangedal Norway 55 F7
Drangme Chhu r. Bhutan 99 E8
Dransfeld Germany 63 J3
Draper, Mount AK U.S.A. 149 M4
Draperstown U.K. 61 F3
Drapsaca Afgh. see Kunduz
Dras India 104 C2
Drasan Pak. 111 I2
Drau r. Europe 57 O7 see Drava
Dráva r. Europe see Drava
Drava r. Europe 68 H2
also known as Drau (Austria), Drave or Drava (Slovenia and Croatia), Dráva (Hungary)
Drave r. Europe see Drava
Drayton Valley Canada 150 H4
Drazinda Pak. 111 H4
Dréan Alg. 68 B6
Dreistelzberge hill Germany 63 J4
Drentse Hoofdvaart canal Neth. 62 G2
Drepano, Akra pt Greece see Laimos, Akrotirio
Dresden Canada 164 D2
Dresden Germany 57 N5
Dreux France 62 B6
Drevsjø Norway 55 H6
Drewryville VA U.S.A. 165 G5
Dri China 96 C2
Driffield U.K. 58 G4
Driftwood PA U.S.A. 165 F3
Driggs ID U.S.A. 156 F4
Drillham Australia 138 E1
Drimoleague Ireland 61 C6
Drina r. Bos. & Herz./Serbia 69 H2
Driscoll Island Antarctica 188 J1
Drissa Belarus see Vyerkhnyadzvinsk
Drniš Croatia 68 G3
Drobeta-Turnu Severin Romania 69 J2
Drochtersen Germany 63 J1
Drogheda Ireland 61 F4
Drogichin Belarus see Drahichyn
Drogobych Ukr. see Drohobych
Drohobych Ukr. 53 D6
Droichead Átha Ireland see Drogheda
Droichead Nua Ireland see Newbridge
Droitwich U.K. see Droitwich Spa
Droitwich Spa U.K. 59 E6
Dromedary, Cape Australia 138 E6
Dromod Ireland 61 E4
Dromore Northern Ireland U.K. 61 E3
Dromore Northern Ireland U.K. 61 F3
Dronfield U.K. 58 F5
Dronning Louise Land reg. Greenland 189 I1
Dronning Maud Land reg. Antarctica see Queen Maud Land
Dronten Neth. 62 F2
Drovyanaya Russia 95 H1
Druk-Yul country Asia see Bhutan
Drumheller Canada 151 H5
Drummond atoll Kiribati see Tabiteuea
Drummond MT U.S.A. 156 E3
Drummond, Lake VA U.S.A. 165 G5
Drummond Island Kiribati see McKean
Drummond Range hills Australia 136 D5
Drummondville Canada 153 G5
Drummore U.K. 60 E6
Drury Lake Canada 150 C2
Druskieniki Lith. see Druskininkai
Druskininkai Lith. 55 N10
Druzhina Russia 77 P3
Druzhnaya Gorka Russia 55 Q7
Dry r. Australia 134 F3
Dryanovo Bulg. 69 K3
Dryberry Lake Canada 151 M5
Dry Creek AK U.S.A. 149 K3
Dryden Canada 151 M5
Dryden NY U.S.A. 165 G2
Dry Fork r. WY U.S.A. 156 G4
Drygalski Ice Tongue Antarctica 188 H1
Drygalski Island Antarctica 188 F2
Dry Lake NV U.S.A. 159 F3
Dry Lake l. ND U.S.A. 160 D1
Drymen U.K. 60 E4
Dry Ridge KY U.S.A. 164 C4
Drysdale r. Australia 134 D3
Drysdale River National Park Australia 134 D3
Dry Tortugas is FL U.S.A. 163 D7
Du'an China 97 F4
Duancun China see Wuxiang
Duaringa Australia 136 E4
Duars reg. India 99 E8
Duarte, Pico mt. Dom. Rep. 169 J5
Duartina Brazil 179 A3
Ḑubā Saudi Arabia 108 E4
Dubai U.A.E. 110 D5
Dubakella Mountain CA U.S.A. 158 B1
Dubawnt r. Canada 151 L2
Dubawnt Lake Canada 151 K2
Dubayy U.A.E. see Dubai
Dubbo Australia 138 D4
Dublán Mex. 166 D2

▶Dublin Ireland 61 F4
Capital of Ireland.

Dublin GA U.S.A. 163 D5
Dubna Russia 52 H4
Dubno Ukr. 53 E6
Dubois ID U.S.A. 156 E3
Dubois IN U.S.A. 164 B4
Du Bois PA U.S.A. 165 F3
Dubovka Russia 53 J6
Dubovskoye Russia 53 I7
Dubréka Guinea 120 B4
Dubris U.K. see Dover
Dubrovnik Croatia 68 H3
Dubrovytsya Ukr. 53 E6
Dubuque IA U.S.A. 160 F3
Dubysa r. Lith. 55 M9
Đưc Bôn Vietnam 87 D5
Duc de Gloucester, Îles du is Fr. Polynesia 187 K7
Duchang China 97 H2
Ducheng China see Yunan
Duchesne UT U.S.A. 159 H1
Duchesne r. UT U.S.A. 159 I1
Duchess Canada 151 I5
Duchess (abandoned) Australia 136 B4
Ducie Island atoll Pitcairn Is 187 L7
Duck Bay Canada 151 K4
Duck Creek r. Australia 134 B5
Duck Lake Canada 151 J4
Duckwater Peak NV U.S.A. 159 F2
Duc Tho Vietnam 86 D3
Ducun China see Fuping
Dudelange Lux. 62 G5
Duderstadt Germany 63 K3
Dudhi India 105 E4
Dudhwa India 104 E3
Dudinka Russia 76 J3
Dudley U.K. 59 E6
Dudleyville AZ U.S.A. 159 H5
Dudna r. India 106 C2
Dudu India 104 C4
Duékoué Côte d'Ivoire 120 C4
Duen, Bukit vol. Indon. 84 C3
Duero r. Spain 67 C3
also known as Douro (Portugal)
Duffel Belgium 62 E3
Dufferin, Cape Canada 152 F2
Duffer Peak NV U.S.A. 156 D4
Duff Islands Solomon Is 133 G2
Duffreboy, Lac l. Canada 153 H2
Dufftown U.K. 60 F3
Dufourspitze mt. Italy/Switz. 66 H4
Dufrost, Pointe pt Canada 152 F1
Dugi Otok i. Croatia 68 F2
Dugi Rat Croatia 68 G3
Du He r. China 97 F1
Dúiche Sheoigheach reg. Ireland see Joyce Country
Duida-Marahuaca, Parque Nacional nat. park Venez. 176 E3
Duisburg Germany 62 G3
Dujiangyan China 96 D2
Dukathole S. Africa 125 H6
Duke Island AK U.S.A. 149 O5
Duke of Clarence atoll Tokelau see Nukunonu
Duke of Gloucester Islands Fr. Polynesia see Duc de Gloucester, Îles du
Duke of York atoll Tokelau see Atafu
Duk Fadiat South Sudan 121 G4
Dukhovnitskoye Russia 53 K5
Duki Pak. 111 H4
Duki Russia 90 D2
Duki r. Russia 90 D2
Dukou China see Panzhihua
Dūkštas Lith. 55 O9
Dulaanhaan Mongolia 94 F1
Dulac LA U.S.A. 161 F6
Dulan China 94 D4
Dulawan Mindanao Phil. see Datu Piang
Dulbi r. AK U.S.A. 148 H2
Dulce r. Arg. 178 D4
Dulce NM U.S.A. 157 G5
Dulce, Golfo b. Costa Rica 166 [inset] J7
Dulce Nombre de Culmí Hond. 166 [inset] I6
Dul'durga Russia 95 H1
Dulhunty r. Australia 136 C1
Dulishi Hu salt l. China 99 C6
Dulit, Pegunungan mts Malaysia 85 F2
Duliu Jiang r. China 97 F3
Dullewala Pak. 111 H4
Dullstroom S. Africa 125 J3
Dülmen Germany 63 H3
Dulmera India 104 C3
Dulovo Bulg. 69 L3
Duluth MN U.S.A. 160 E2
Dulverton U.K. 59 D7
Dūmā Syria 107 C3
Dumaguete Negros Phil. 82 C4
Dumai Sumatra Indon. 84 C2
Dumanquilas Bay Mindanao Phil. 82 C5
Dumaran i. Phil. 82 C4
Dumarchen i. Indon. 83 C1
Dumaresq r. Australia 138 E2
Dumas TX U.S.A. 161 C5
Ḑumayr Syria 107 C3
Ḑumayr, Jabal mts Syria 107 C3
Dumbakh Iran see Dom Bākh
Dumbarton U.K. 60 E5
Dumbe S. Africa 125 J4
Ďumbier mt. Slovakia 57 Q6
Dumchele India 104 D2
Dumdum i. Indon. 84 D2
Dum Duma India 105 H4
Dumfries U.K. 60 F5
Dumka India 105 F4
Dumoga Celebes Indon. 83 C2
Dumont d'Urville research station Antarctica 188 G2
Dumont d'Urville Sea Antarctica 188 G2
Dümpelfeld Germany 62 G4
Dumyâṭ Egypt see Dumyāṭ
Dumyāṭ Egypt 112 C5
Duna r. Europe 68 H2 see Danube
Dünaburg Latvia see Daugavpils
Dunaj r. Europe see Danube
Dunajská Streda Slovakia 57 P7
Dunakeszi Hungary 69 H1
Dunany Point Ireland 61 F4
Dunărea r. Europe see Danube
Dunării, Delta Romania/Ukr. see Danube Delta
Dunaújváros Hungary 68 H1
Dunav r. Europe 68 L2 see Danube
Dunay r. Europe see Danube
Dunayivtsi Ukr. 53 E6
Dunbar Australia 136 C3
Dunbar U.K. 60 G4
Dunbar AK U.S.A. 149 J2
Dunblane U.K. 60 F4
Dunboyne Ireland 61 F4
Duncan Canada 150 F5
Duncan AZ U.S.A. 159 I5
Duncan OK U.S.A. 161 D5
Duncan, Cape Canada 152 E3
Duncan, Lac l. Canada 152 F3
Duncan Lake Canada 150 H2
Duncan Passage India 87 A5
Duncansby Head hd U.K. 60 F2
Duncan Town Bahamas 163 F8
Duncormick Ireland 61 F5
Dundaga Latvia 55 M8
Dundalk Ireland 61 F3
Dundalk MD U.S.A. 165 G4
Dundalk Bay Ireland 61 F4
Dundas Canada 164 F2
Dundas, Lake salt flat Australia 135 C8
Dundas Island Canada 149 O5
Dundas Strait Australia 134 E2
Dundbürd Mongolia see Batnorov
Dún Dealgan Ireland see Dundalk
Dundee S. Africa 125 J5
Dundee U.K. 60 G4
Dundee MI U.S.A. 164 D3
Dundee NY U.S.A. 165 G2
Dundgovĭ prov. Mongolia 94 F2
Dundonald U.K. 61 G3
Dundoo Australia 138 B1
Dundrennan U.K. 60 F6
Dundrum U.K. 61 G3
Dundrum Bay U.K. 61 G3
Dundwa Range mts India/Nepal 105 E4
Dune, Lac l. Canada 152 G2
Dunedin N.Z. 139 C7
Dunedin FL U.S.A. 163 D6
Dunfermline U.K. 60 F4
Dungannon U.K. 61 F3
Dún Garbhán Ireland see Dungarvan
Dungarpur India 104 C5
Dungarvan Ireland 61 E5
Dung Co l. China 99 E7
Dungeness hd U.K. 59 H8
Dungeness, Punta pt Arg. 178 C8
Düngenheim Germany 63 H4
Dungiven U.K. 61 F3
Dungog Australia 138 E4
Dungu Dem. Rep. Congo 122 C3
Dungun Malaysia 84 C1
Dungunab Sudan 108 E5
Dunhua China 90 C4
Dunhuang China 98 F4
Dunkeld Australia 138 D1
Dunkeld U.K. 60 F4
Dunkellin r. Ireland 61 D4
Dunkerque France see Dunkirk
Dunkery Hill hill U.K. 59 D7
Dunkirk France 62 C3
Dunkirk NY U.S.A. 164 F2
Dún Laoghaire Ireland 61 F4
Dunlap IA U.S.A. 160 E3
Dunlap TN U.S.A. 162 C5
Dunlavin Ireland 61 F4
Dunleer Ireland 61 F4
Dunloy U.K. 61 F2
Dunmanway Ireland 61 C6
Dunmarra Australia 134 F4
Dunmor KY U.S.A. 164 B5
Dunmore Ireland 61 D4
Dunmore PA U.S.A. 165 H3
Dunmore Town Bahamas 163 E7
Dunmurry U.K. 61 G3
Dunnet Head hd U.K. 60 F2
Dunnigan CA U.S.A. 158 C2
Dunning NE U.S.A. 160 C3
Dunnville Canada 164 F2
Dunnville KY U.S.A. 164 C5
Dunolly Australia 138 A6
Dunoon U.K. 60 E5
Dunphy NV U.S.A. 158 E1
Duns U.K. 60 G5
Dunseith ND U.S.A. 160 C1
Dunstable U.K. 59 G7
Dunstan Mountains N.Z. 139 B7
Dun-sur-Meuse France 62 F5
Duntroon N.Z. 139 C7
Dunvegan Lake Canada 151 J2
Dunyapur Pak. 111 H4
Duobukur He r. China 95 K1
Duolun China 95 I3
Duomula China 99 C6
Dupang Ling mts China 97 F3
Duperré Alg. see Aïn Defla
Dupnitsa Bulg. 69 J3
Dupree SD U.S.A. 160 C2
Duque de Bragança Angola see Calandula
Dūrā West Bank 107 B4
Durack r. Australia 134 D3
Durack Range hills Australia 134 D4
Dura Europos Syria see Aş Şāliḩīyah
Durağan Turkey 112 D2
Durance r. France 66 G5
Durand WI U.S.A. 160 F2
Durango Mex. 161 B7
Durango state Mex. 161 B7
Durango Spain 67 E2
Durango CO U.S.A. 159 J3
Durānī reg. Afgh. 111 G4
Durant OK U.S.A. 161 D5
Durazno Uruguay 178 E4
Durazzo Albania see Durrës
Durban S. Africa 125 J5
Durban-Corbières France 66 F5
Durbanville S. Africa 124 D7
Durbin WV U.S.A. 164 F4
Durbun Pak. 111 G4
Durbuy Belgium 62 F4
Düre China 98 E3
Düren Germany 62 G4
Düren Iran 110 E3
Durg India 104 E5
Durgapur Bangl. 105 G4
Durgapur India 105 F5

Durham Canada 164 E1
Durham U.K. 58 F4
Durham NC U.S.A. 162 E5
Durham Downs Australia 137 C5
Duri Sumatra Indon. 84 C2
Duriansebatang Kalimantan Indon. 85 E3
Durlas Ireland see Thurles
Durleşti Moldova 69 M1
Durmersheim Germany 63 I6
Durmitor mt. Montenegro 69 H3
Durmitor, Nacionalni Park nat. park Montenegro 68 H3
Durness U.K. 60 E2
Durocortorum France see Reims
Durong South Australia 137 E5
Durostorum Bulg. see Silistra
Durour Island P.N.G. see Aua Island
Durovernum U.K. see Canterbury
Durrës Albania 69 H4
Durrie Australia 136 C5
Durrington U.K. 59 F7
Dursey Island Ireland 61 B6
Dursunbey Turkey 69 M5
Duru China see Wuchuan
Durukhsi Somalia 122 E3
Durusu Gölü l. Turkey 69 M4
Durūz, Jabal ad mt. Syria 107 C3
D'Urville, Tanjung pt Indon. 81 J7
D'Urville Island N.Z. 139 D5
Duşak Turkm. 111 E2
Dushai Pak. 111 G4
Dū Shākh, Kōh-e mt. Afgh. 111 F3
Dushan China 96 E3

▶Dushanbe Tajik. 111 H2
Capital of Tajikistan.

Dushanzi China 98 D3
Dusheti Georgia 113 G2
Dushikou China 95 H3
Dushore PA U.S.A. 165 G3
Dusse-Alin', Khrebet mts Russia 90 D2
Düsseldorf Germany 62 G3
Dusty NM U.S.A. 159 J5
Dusty WA U.S.A. 156 D3
Dutch East Indies country Asia see Indonesia
Dutch Guiana country S. America see Suriname
Dutch Mountain UT U.S.A. 159 G1
Dutlwe Botswana 124 F2
Dutse Nigeria 120 D3
Dutsin-Ma Nigeria 120 D3
Dutton r. Australia 136 C4
Dutton Canada 164 E2
Dutton MT U.S.A. 156 F3
Dutton, Lake salt flat Australia 137 B6
Dutton, Mount UT U.S.A. 159 G2
Dutywa S. Africa 125 I7
Duudka, Taagga reg. Somalia 122 E3
Duval Canada 151 J5
Duvert, Lac l. Canada 153 H2
Duvno Bos. & Herz. see Tomislavgrad
Duwa China 99 B5
Duyun China 96 E3
Duzab Pak. 111 F5
Düzce Turkey 69 N4
Duzdab Iran see Zāhedān
Dvina r. Europe see Zapadnaya Dvina
Dvina r. Russia see Severnaya Dvina
Dvinsk Latvia see Daugavpils
Dvinskaya Guba g. Russia 52 H2
Dwarka India 104 B5
Dwarsberg S. Africa 125 H3
Dwên Iraq 113 G3
Dwingelderveld, Nationaal Park nat. park Neth. 62 G2
Dworshak Reservoir ID U.S.A. 156 E3
Dwyka S. Africa 124 E7
Dyat'kovo Russia 53 G5
Dyce U.K. 60 G3
Dyer, Cape Canada 147 L3
Dyer Bay Canada 164 E1
Dyersburg TN U.S.A. 161 F4
Dyfi r. U.K. see Dovey
Dyfrdwy r. U.K. see Dee
Dyje r. Austria/Czech Rep. 57 P6
Dyke U.K. 60 F3

▶Dykh-Tau, Gora mt. Russia 113 F2
2nd highest mountain in Europe.

Dyle r. Belgium 62 E4
Dyleň hill Czech Rep. 63 M5
Dylewska Góra hill Poland 57 Q4
Dymytrov Ukr. 53 H6
Dynevor Downs Australia 138 B2
Dyoki S. Africa 125 I6
Dyrrhachium Albania see Durrës
Dysart Australia 136 E4
Dysselsdorp S. Africa 124 F7
Dyurtyuli Russia 51 Q4
Dzaanhushuu Mongolia see Ihtamir
Dzadgay Mongolia see Bömbögör
Dzadrān reg. Afgh. 111 H3
Dzag Mongolia 94 D2
Dzag Gol r. Mongolia 94 D2
Dzalaa Mongolia see Shinejinst
Dzamīn Üüd Mongolia 95 G3
Dzanga-Ndoki, Parc National de nat. park Cent. Afr. Rep. 122 B3

▶Dzaoudzi Mayotte 123 E5
Capital of Mayotte.

Dzaudzhikau Russia see Vladikavkaz
Dzavhan Mongolia 94 C1
Dzavhan prov. Mongolia 94 C1
Dzavhan Gol r. Mongolia 94 C1
Dzavhanmandal Mongolia 94 C1
Dzegstey Mongolia see Ögiynuur
Dzerzhinsk Belarus see Dzyarzhynsk
Dzerzhinsk Russia 52 I4
Dzhagdy, Khrebet mts Russia 90 C1
Dzhaki-Unakhta Yakbyyana, Khrebet mts Russia 90 D2
Dzhalal-Abad Kyrg. see Jalal-Abad
Dzhalil' Russia 51 Q4
Dzhalilabad Azer. see Cälilabad
Dzhalinda Russia 90 A1
Dzhaltyr Kazakh. see Zhaltyr
Dzhambeyty Kazakh. see Zhympity
Dzhambul Kazakh. see Taraz
Dzhankoy Crimea 53 G7
Dzhanybek Kazakh. see Zhanibek
Dzharkent Kazakh. see Zharkent
Dzhava Georgia see Java
Dzhetygara Kazakh. see Zhitikara
Dzhezkazgan Kazakh. see Zhezkazgan
Dzhida Russia 94 F1
Dzhida r. Russia 94 F1
Dzhidinskiy Khrebet mts Mongolia/Russia 94 E1
Dzhirgatal' Tajik. see Jirghatol
Dzhizak Uzbek. see Jizzax
Dzhokhar Ghala Russia see Groznyy
Dzhubga Russia 112 E1
Dzhugdzhur, Khrebet mts Russia 77 O4
Dzhul'fa Azer. see Culfa
Dzhuma Uzbek. see Juma
Dzhungarskiye Vorota valley Kazakh. 98 C3
Dzhusaly Kyzylordinskaya Oblast' Kazakh. see Zhosaly
Dzhusaly Pavlodarskaya Oblast' Kazakh. 98 B2
Działdowo Poland 57 R4
Dzibalchén Mex. 167 H5
Dzilam de Bravo Mex. 167 H4
Dzitás Mex. 167 H4
Dzogsool Mongolia see Bayantsagaan
Dzöölön Mongolia see Renchinlhümbe
Dzūkijos nacionalinis parkas nat. park Lith. 55 N9
Dzungarian Basin China see Junggar Pendi
Dzungarian Gate pass China/Kazakh. 102 F2
Dzur Mongolia see Tes
Dzüünbayan Mongolia 95 G2
Dzüünharaa Mongolia 94 F1
Dzuunmod Mongolia 94 F2
Dzüyl Mongolia see Tonhil
Dzyaniskavichy Belarus 55 O10
Dzyarzhynsk Belarus 55 O10
Dzyatlavichy Belarus 55 O10

E

Eabamet Lake Canada 152 D4
Eads CO U.S.A. 160 C4
Eagar AZ U.S.A. 159 I4
Eagle r. Nfld. and Lab. Canada 153 K3
Eagle r. Y.T. Canada 149 M2
Eagle AK U.S.A. 146 D3
Eagle CO U.S.A. 156 G5
Eagle Cap mt. OR U.S.A. 156 D3
Eagle Crags mt. CA U.S.A. 158 E4
Eagle Creek r. Canada 151 J4
Eagle Lake Canada 151 M5
Eagle Lake CA U.S.A. 158 C1
Eagle Lake ME U.S.A. 162 G2
Eagle Mountain CA U.S.A. 159 F5
Eagle Mountain hill MN U.S.A. 160 F2
Eagle Mountain Lake TX U.S.A. 167 F1
Eagle Pass TX U.S.A. 161 C6
Eagle Peak TX U.S.A. 157 G7
Eagle Plain Canada 149 M2
Eagle Plains Canada 149 M2
Eagle River AK U.S.A. 149 J3
Eagle River WI U.S.A. 160 F2
Eagle Rock VA U.S.A. 164 F5
Eaglesham Canada 150 G4
Eagle Summit pass AK U.S.A. 149 K2
Eagle Village AK U.S.A. 149 L2
Eap i. Micronesia see Yap
Ear Falls Canada 151 M5
Earlimart CA U.S.A. 158 D4
Earl's Seat hill U.K. 60 E4
Earlston U.K. 60 G5
Earn r. U.K. 60 F4
Earn, Loch l. U.K. 60 E4
Earn Lake Canada 149 N3
Earp CA U.S.A. 159 F4
Earth TX U.S.A. 161 C5
Easington U.K. 58 H5
Easley SC U.S.A. 163 D5
East Alligator r. Australia 134 F3
East Antarctica reg. Antarctica 188 F1
East Ararat PA U.S.A. 165 H3
East Aurora NY U.S.A. 165 F2
East Bay LA U.S.A. 167 H2
East Bay inlet FL U.S.A. 163 C6
East Bengal country Asia see Bangladesh
Eastbourne U.K. 59 H8
East Branch Clarion River Reservoir PA U.S.A. 165 F3
East Caicos i. Turks and Caicos Is 163 G8
East Cape N.Z. 139 G3
East Cape AK U.S.A. 148 [inset] B6
East Carbon City UT U.S.A. 159 H2
East Caroline Basin sea feature N. Pacific Ocean 186 F5
East Channel watercourse Canada 149 N1
East China Sea N. Pacific Ocean 89 N6
East Coast Bays N.Z. 139 E3
East Dereham U.K. see Dereham
Eastend Canada 151 I5
East Entrance sea chan. Palau 82 [inset]

▶Easter Island S. Pacific Ocean 187 M7
Part of Chile.

Eastern Cape prov. S. Africa 125 H6
Eastern Desert Egypt 108 D4
Eastern Fields reef Australia 136 D1
Eastern Ghats mts India 106 C4

▶Eastern Island HI U.S.A. 186 I4
Most northerly point of Oceania.

Eastern Nara canal Pak. 111 H5
Eastern Samoa terr. S. Pacific Ocean see American Samoa
Eastern Sayan Mountains Russia see Vostochnyy Sayan
Eastern Taurus plat. Turkey see Güneydoğu Toroslar
Eastern Transvaal prov. S. Africa see Mpumalanga
Easterville Canada 151 L4
Easterwâlde Neth. see Oosterwolde
East Falkland i. Falkland Is 178 E8
East Falmouth MA U.S.A. 165 J3
East Frisian Islands Germany 57 K4
Eastgate NV U.S.A. 158 E2
East Greenwich RI U.S.A. 165 J3
East Grinstead U.K. 59 G7
Easthampton MA U.S.A. 165 I2
East Hampton NY U.S.A. 165 I3
East Hartford CT U.S.A. 165 I3
East Indiaman Ridge sea feature Indian Ocean 185 O7
East Jordan MI U.S.A. 164 C1
East Kilbride U.K. 60 E5
Eastlake OH U.S.A. 164 E3
East Lamma Channel H.K. China 97 [inset]
Eastland TX U.S.A. 161 D5
East Lansing MI U.S.A. 164 C2
Eastleigh U.K. 59 F8
East Liverpool OH U.S.A. 164 E3
East London S. Africa 125 H7
East Lynn Lake WV U.S.A. 164 D4
Eastmain Canada 152 F3
Eastmain r. Canada 152 F3
Eastman GA U.S.A. 163 D5
East Mariana Basin sea feature N. Pacific Ocean 186 G5
Eastmere Australia 136 D4
East Naples FL U.S.A. 163 D7
Easton MD U.S.A. 165 G4
Easton PA U.S.A. 165 H3
East Orange NJ U.S.A. 165 H3
East Pacific Rise sea feature N. Pacific Ocean 187 M4
East Pakistan country Asia see Bangladesh
East Palestine OH U.S.A. 164 E3
East Park Reservoir CA U.S.A. 158 B2
East Point Canada 153 J5
East Porcupine r. Canada 149 M2
Eastport ME U.S.A. 162 H2
East Providence RI U.S.A. 165 J3
East Range mts NV U.S.A. 158 E1
East Retford U.K. see Retford
East St Louis IL U.S.A. 160 F4
East Sea N. Pacific Ocean see Japan, Sea of
East Shoal Lake Canada 151 L5
East Siberian Sea Russia 77 P2
East Side Canal r. CA U.S.A. 158 D4
East Stroudsburg PA U.S.A. 165 H3
East Tavaputs Plateau UT U.S.A. 159 I2

▶East Timor country Asia 83 C5
Former Portuguese territory. Gained independence from Indonesia in 2002.

East Tons r. India 99 D8
East Toorale Australia 138 B3
East Troy WI U.S.A. 164 A2
East Verde r. AZ U.S.A. 159 H4
Eastville VA U.S.A. 165 H5
East-Vlylân Neth. see Oost-Vlieland
East York Canada 164 F2
Eaton OH U.S.A. 164 C4
Eatonia Canada 151 I5
Eaton Rapids MI U.S.A. 164 C2
Eatonton GA U.S.A. 163 D5
Eau Claire WI U.S.A. 160 F2
Eau Claire, Lac à l' l. Canada 152 G2
Eau Claire, Rivière à l' r. Canada 152 G2
Eauripik atoll Micronesia 81 K5
Eauripik Rise-New Guinea Rise sea feature N. Pacific Ocean 186 F5
Eaurypyg atoll Micronesia see Eauripik
Ebano Mex. 167 F4
Ebbw Vale U.K. 59 D7
Ebebiyin Equat. Guinea 120 E4
Ebenerde Namibia 124 C3
Ebensburg PA U.S.A. 165 F3
Eber Gölü l. Turkey 69 N5
Ebergötzen Germany 63 K3
Eberswalde Germany 57 N4
Ebetsu Japan 90 F4
Ebian China 96 D2
Ebina Japan 93 F3
Ebi Nor salt l. China see Ebinur Hu
Ebinur Hu salt l. China 98 C3
Eboli Italy 68 F4
Ebolowa Cameroon 120 E4
Ebony Namibia 124 B2
Ebre r. Spain see Ebro
Ebro r. Spain 67 G3
Ebstorf Germany 63 K1
Eburacum U.K. see York
Ebusus i. Spain see Ibiza
Ecbatana Iran see Hamadān
Eceabat Turkey 69 L4
Echague Luzon Phil. 82 C2
Ech Chélif Alg. see Chlef
Echegárate, Puerto pass Spain 67 E2
Echeng China see Ezhou
Echeverria, Pico mt. Mex. 166 B2
Echigo-Sanzan-Tadami Kokutei-kōen park Japan 93 F1
Echizen Fukui Japan 92 C3
Echizen Fukui Japan 92 C3
Echizen Fukui Japan 92 C3
Echizen-dake mt. Japan 93 E3
Echizen-Kaga-kaigan Kokutei-kōen park Japan 92 C2
Echizen-misaki pt Japan 92 B3
Echmiadzin Armenia see Vagharshapat
Echo OR U.S.A. 156 D3
Echo Bay N.W.T. Canada 150 G1
Echo Bay Ont. Canada 152 D5
Echo Cliffs AZ U.S.A. 159 H3
Echoing r. Canada 151 M4
Echt Neth. 62 F3
Echternach Lux. 62 G5
Echuca Australia 138 B6
Echzell Germany 63 I4
Écija Spain 67 D5
Eckental Germany 63 L5
Eckernförde Germany 57 L3
Eclipse Sound sea chan. Canada 147 J2
Écrins, Parc National des nat. park France 66 H4
Ecuador country S. America 176 C4
Écueils, Pointe aux pt Canada 152 F2
Ed Eritrea 108 F7
Ed Sweden 55 G7
Edam Neth. 62 F2
Eday i. U.K. 60 G1
Ed Da'ein Sudan 121 F3
Ed Damazin Sudan 108 D7
Ed Damer Sudan 108 D6
Ed Debba Sudan 108 D6
Eddies Cove Canada 153 K4
Ed Dueim Sudan 108 D7
Eddystone Point Australia 137 [inset]
Eddyville KY U.S.A. 161 F4
Ede Neth. 62 F2
Edéa Cameroon 120 E4
Edehon Lake Canada 151 L2
Edéia Brazil 179 A2
Eden Australia 138 D6
Eden r. U.K. 58 D4
Eden NC U.S.A. 164 F5
Eden TX U.S.A. 161 D6
Eden, Tanjung pt Moluccas Indon. 83 C4
Edenburg S. Africa 125 G5
Edendale N.Z. 139 B8
Edenderry Ireland 61 E4
Edenton NC U.S.A. 162 E4
Edenville S. Africa 125 H4
Eder r. Germany 63 J3
Eder-Stausee resr Germany 63 I3
Edessa Greece 69 J4
Edessa Turkey see Şanlıurfa
Edewecht Germany 63 H1
Edfu Egypt see Idfū
Edgar Ranges hills Australia 134 C4
Edgartown MA U.S.A. 165 J3
Edgecumbe Island Solomon Is see Utupua
Edgefield SC U.S.A. 163 D5
Edge Island Svalbard see Edgeøya
Edgemont SD U.S.A. 160 C3
Edgeøya i. Svalbard 76 D2
Edgerton Canada 151 I4
Edgerton OH U.S.A. 164 C3
Edgeworthstown Ireland 61 E4
Édhessa Greece see Edessa
Edina MO U.S.A. 160 E3
Edinboro PA U.S.A. 164 E3
Edinburg TX U.S.A. 161 D7
Edinburg VA U.S.A. 165 F4

▶Edinburgh U.K. 60 F5
Capital of Scotland.

Edirne Turkey 69 L4
Edith, Mount MT U.S.A. 156 F3
Edith Cavell, Mount Canada 150 G4
Edith Ronne Land ice feature Antarctica see Ronne Ice Shelf
Edjeleh Libya 120 D2
Edjudina Australia 135 C7
Edku Egypt see Idkū
Edmond OK U.S.A. 161 D5
Edmonds WA U.S.A. 156 C3

▶Edmonton Canada 150 H4
Capital of Alberta.

Edmonton KY U.S.A. 164 C5
Edmore MI U.S.A. 164 C2
Edmore ND U.S.A. 160 D1
Edmund Lake Canada 151 M4
Edmundston Canada 153 H5
Edna TX U.S.A. 161 D6
Edna Bay AK U.S.A. 149 N5
Edo Japan see Tōkyō
Edo-gawa r. Japan 93 F3
Edom reg. Israel/Jordan 107 B4
Édouard, Lac l. Dem. Rep. Congo/Uganda see Edward, Lake
Edremit Turkey 69 L5
Edremit Körfezi b. Turkey 69 L5
Edrengiyn Nuruu mts Mongolia 94 D2
Edsbyn Sweden 55 I6
Edson Canada 150 G4
Eduni, Mount Canada 149 O2
Edward r. N.S.W. Australia 138 B5
Edward r. Qld Australia 136 C2
Edward, Lake Dem. Rep. Congo/Uganda 122 C4
Edward, Mount Antarctica 188 L1
Edwardesabad Pak. see Bannu
Edwards NY U.S.A. 165 H1
Edward's Creek Australia 137 A6
Edwards Plateau TX U.S.A. 161 C6
Edwardsville IL U.S.A. 160 F4
Edward VII Peninsula Antarctica 188 I1
Edziza, Mount Canada 149 O4
Eek AK U.S.A. 148 G3
Eek r. AK U.S.A. 148 G3
Eeklo Belgium 62 D3
Eel r. CA U.S.A. 158 A1
Eel, South Fork r. CA U.S.A. 158 B1
Eem r. Neth. 62 F2
Eemshaven pt Neth. 62 G1
Eenrum Neth. 62 G1
Eenzamheid Pan salt pan S. Africa 124 E4
Eesti country Europe see Estonia
Éfaté i. Vanuatu 133 G3
Effingham IL U.S.A. 160 F4
Efsus Turkey see Afşin
Eg Mongolia see Batshireet
Egadi, Isole is Sicily Italy 68 D5
Egan Range mts NV U.S.A. 159 F2
Eganville Canada 165 G1
Egavik AK U.S.A. 148 G2
Egedesminde Greenland see Aasiaat
Egegik Bay AK U.S.A. 148 H4
Eger r. Germany 63 M4
Eger Hungary 57 R7
Egersund Norway 55 E7
Egerton, Mount hill Australia 135 B6
Eggegebirge hills Germany 63 I3
Egg Island AK U.S.A. 148 G3
Egg Lake Canada 151 J4
Eggolsheim Germany 63 L5
Eghezée Belgium 62 E4
Egilsstaðir Iceland 54 [inset 1]
Eğin Turkey see Kemaliye
Eğirdir Turkey 69 N6
Eğirdir Gölü l. Turkey 69 N6
Egiyn Gol r. Mongolia 94 E1
Eglinton U.K. 61 E2
Egmond aan Zee Neth. 62 E2
Egmont, Cape N.Z. 139 D4
Egmont, Mount vol. N.Z. see Taranaki, Mount
Egmont National Park N.Z. 139 E4
eGoli S. Africa see Johannesburg
Eğrigöz Dağı mts Turkey 69 M5
Egton U.K. 58 G4
Éguas r. Brazil 179 B1
Egvekinot Russia 148 C2

▶Egypt country Africa 108 C4
3rd most populous country in Africa.

Ehden Lebanon 107 B2
Ehen Hudag China 94 E4
Ehingen (Donau) Germany 57 L6
Ehle r. Germany 63 L2
Ehra-Lessien Germany 63 K2
Ehrenberg AZ U.S.A. 159 F5
Ehrenberg Range hills Australia 135 E5
Eibelstadt Germany 63 K5
Eibergen Neth. 62 G2
Eichenzell Germany 63 J4
Eichstätt Germany 63 L6
Eidfjord Norway 55 E6
Eidsvold Australia 136 E5
Eidsvoll Norway 55 G6
Eifel hills Germany 62 G4
Eigenji Japan 92 C3
Eigg i. U.K. 60 C4
Eight Degree Channel India/Maldives 106 B5
Eights Coast Antarctica 188 K2
Eighty Mile Beach Australia 134 C4
Eiheiji Fukui Japan 92 C2
Eiheiji Fukui Japan 92 C2
Eilat Israel 107 B5
Eildon Australia 138 B6
Eildon, Lake Australia 138 C6
Eileen Lake Canada 151 J2
Eilenburg Germany 63 M3
Eil Malk i. Palau 82 [inset]
Eimke Germany 63 K2
Einasleigh Australia 136 D3
Einasleigh r. Australia 136 C3
Einbeck Germany 63 J3
Eindhoven Neth. 62 F3
Einme Myanmar 86 A3
Einsiedeln Switz. 66 I3
Éire country Europe see Ireland
Eirik Ridge sea feature N. Atlantic Ocean 184 F2
Eiriosgaigh i. U.K. see Eriskay
Eirunepé Brazil 176 E5
Eisberg hill Germany 63 J3
Eiseb watercourse Namibia 123 C5
Eisenach Germany 63 K4
Eisenberg Germany 63 L4
Eisenhower, Mount Canada see Castle Mountain
Eisenhüttenstadt Germany 57 O4
Eisenstadt Austria 57 P7
Eisfeld Germany 63 K4
Eisleben, Lutherstadt Germany 63 L3
Eite, Loch inlet U.K. see Etive, Loch
Eiterfeld Germany 63 J4
Eivissa Spain see Ibiza
Eivissa i. Spain see Ibiza
Ejea de los Caballeros Spain 67 F2
Ejeda Madag. 123 E6
Ejin Horo Qi China see Altan Xiret
Ejin Qi China see Dalain Hob
Ejmiadzin Armenia see Vagharshapat
Ejutla Mex. 167 F5
Ekalaka MT U.S.A. 156 G3
Ekenäs Fin. 55 M7
Ekerem Turkm. 110 D2
Ekeren Belgium 62 E3
Eketahuna N.Z. 139 E5
Ekimchan Russia 90 D1
Ekinyazı Turkey 107 D1
Ekityki, Ozero l. Russia 148 B2
Ekka Island Canada 149 Q2
Ekonda Russia 77 L3
Ekostrovskaya Imandra, Ozero l. Russia 54 R3
Ekshärad Sweden 55 H6
Eksjö Sweden 55 I8
Eksteenfontein S. Africa 124 C5
Ekström Ice Shelf Antarctica 188 B2
Ekuk AK U.S.A. 148 H4
Ekwan r. Canada 152 E3
Ekwan Point Canada 152 E3
Ekwok AK U.S.A. 148 H4
Ela Myanmar 86 B3
El Aaiún W. Sahara see Laâyoune
Elafonisou, Steno sea chan. Greece 69 J6
El 'Agrûd well Egypt see Al 'Ajrūd
Elaia, Cape Cyprus 107 B2
El 'Alamein Egypt see Al 'Alamayn
El Alamo Mex. 166 A2
El 'Âmirîya Egypt see Al 'Āmirīyah
Elands r. S. Africa 125 I3
Elandsdoorn S. Africa 125 I3
El Aouinet Alg. 68 B7
Elar Armenia see Abovyan
El Araïche Morocco see Larache
El Arba, Tizi hill Alg. 67 H5
El Arco Mex. 166 B2
El Ariana Tunisia see L'Ariana
El Aricha Alg. 64 D5
El 'Arîsh Egypt see Al 'Arīsh
El Arrouch Alg. 68 B6
El Ashmûnein Egypt see Al Ashmūnayn
El Asnam Alg. see Chlef
Elassona Greece 69 J5
Elat Israel see Eilat
Elato atoll Micronesia 81 L5
Elazığ Turkey 113 E3
Elba AL U.S.A. 163 C6
Elba, Isola d' i. Italy 68 D3
El'ban Russia 90 E2
El Barco de Valdeorras Spain see O Barco
El Barreal salt l. Mex. 166 D2
Elbasan Albania 69 I4
El Batroun Lebanon see Batroûn
El Baúl Venez. 176 E2
El Bawîti Egypt see Al Bawīṭī
El Bayadh Alg. 64 E5
Elbe r. Germany 63 J1
also known as Labe (Czech Republic)
Elbe-Havel-Kanal canal Germany 63 L2
El Béqaa valley Lebanon 107 C2
Elbert, Mount CO U.S.A. 156 G5
Elberta UT U.S.A. 159 H2
Elberton GA U.S.A. 163 D5
Elbeuf France 66 E2
Elbeyli Turkey 107 C1
El Billete, Cerro mt. Mex. 167 E5
Elbing Poland see Elbląg
Elbistan Turkey 112 E3
Elbląg Poland 57 Q3
El Bluff Nicaragua 166 [inset] J6
El Boulaïda Alg. see Blida
Elbow Canada 151 J5
Elbow Lake MN U.S.A. 160 D2
El Bozal Mex. 161 C8
El Brasil Mex. 167 E3

▶El'brus mt. Russia 113 F2
Highest mountain in Europe.

Elburg Neth. 62 F2
El Burgo de Osma Spain 67 E3
Elburz Mountains Iran 110 C2
El Cajon CA U.S.A. 158 E5
El Cajón, Represa dam Hond. 166 [inset] I6
El Callao Venez. 176 F2
El Campo TX U.S.A. 161 D6
El Capitan Mountain NM U.S.A. 157 G6
El Capulín r. Mex. 161 C7
El Casco Mex. 166 D3
El Cebú, Cerro mt. Mex. 167 G6
El Centro CA U.S.A. 159 F5
El Cerro Bol. 176 F7
Elche Spain see Elche-Elx
Elche-Elx Spain 67 F4
El Chichónal vol. Mex. 167 G5
El Chilicote Mex. 166 D2
Elcho Island Australia 136 A1
El Coca Ecuador see Coca
El Cocuy, Parque Nacional nat. park Col. 176 D2
El Cuyo Mex. 167 I4
Elda Spain 67 F4
El Dátil Mex. 166 B2
El Desemboque Mex. 157 E7
El Diamante Mex. 166 E2
El'dikan Russia 77 O3
El Djezair country Africa see Algeria
El Djezair Alg. see Algiers
El Doctor Mex. 166 B2
Eldon MO U.S.A. 160 E4
Eldorado Arg. 178 F3
Eldorado Brazil 179 A4
El Dorado Col. 176 D3
El Dorado Mex. 166 D3
El Dorado AR U.S.A. 161 E5
El Dorado KS U.S.A. 160 D4
Eldorado TX U.S.A. 161 C6
El Dorado Venez. 176 F2
Eldorado Mountains NV U.S.A. 159 F4
Eldoret Kenya 122 D3
Eldridge, Mount AK U.S.A. 149 L2
Elea, Cape Cyprus see Elaia, Cape
Eleanor WV U.S.A. 164 E4
Electric Peak MT U.S.A. 156 F3
Elefantes r. Moz./S. Africa see Olifants
El Eglab plat. Alg. 120 C2
El Ejido Spain 67 E5
El Encanto Col. 176 D4
Elend Germany 63 K3
Elephanta Caves tourist site India 106 B2
Elephant Butte Reservoir NM U.S.A. 157 G6
Elephant Island Antarctica 188 A2
Elephant Pass Sri Lanka 106 D4
Elephant Point Bangl. 105 H5
Elephant Point AK U.S.A. 148 G2
Eleşkirt Turkey 113 F3
El Estor Guat. 167 H6
El Eulma Alg. 64 F4
Eleuthera i. Bahamas 163 E7
Eleven Point r. MO U.S.A. 161 F4
El Fahs Tunisia 68 C6
El Faiyûm Egypt see Al Fayyūm
El Fasher Sudan 121 F3
El Ferrol Spain see Ferrol
El Ferrol del Caudillo Spain see Ferrol
Elfershausen Germany 63 J4
El Fud Eth. 122 E3

El Fuerte Mex. 166 C3
El Fula Sudan 122 C2
El Gara Egypt see Qārah
El Geneina Sudan 121 F3
El Geteina Sudan 108 D7
El Ghardaqa Egypt see Hurghada
El Ghor plain Jordan/West Bank see Al Ghawr
Elgin U.K. 60 F3
Elgin IL U.S.A. 160 F3
Elgin ND U.S.A. 160 C2
Elgin NV U.S.A. 159 F3
Elgin TX U.S.A. 161 D6
El'ginskiy Russia 77 P3
El Gîza Egypt see Giza
El Goléa Alg. 64 E5
El Golfo de Santa Clara Mex. 166 B2
Elgon, Mount Kenya/Uganda 100 C6
El Grullo Mex. 167 F3
El Guante Mex. 166 D2
El Hadjar Alg. 68 B6
El-Hagounia W. Sahara 120 B2
El Ḥammâm Egypt see Al Ḥammām
El Ḥammâmi reg. Mauritania 120 B2
El Ḥank esc. Mali/Mauritania 120 C2
El Ḥarra Egypt see Al Ḥarrah
El Hazim Jordan see Al Hazīm
El Ḥeiz Egypt see Al Ḥayz
El Hierro i. Canary Is 120 B2
El Higo Mex. 167 F4
El Homr Alg. 64 E6
El Homra Sudan 108 D7
Elhovo Bulg. 69 L3
Eliase Moluccas Indon. 83 D5
Elías Piña Dom. Rep. 169 J5
Elichpur India see Achalpur
Elida OH U.S.A. 164 C3
Elie U.K. 60 G4
Elila r. Dem. Rep. Congo 122 C4
Elim AK U.S.A. 148 G2
Elimberrum France see Auch
Eling China see Yinjiang
Elingampangu Dem. Rep. Congo 122 C4
Eliot, Mount Canada 153 J2
Élisabethville Dem. Rep. Congo see Lubumbashi
Eliseu Martins Brazil 177 J5
El Iskandarîya Egypt see Alexandria
Elista Russia 53 J7
Elixku China 98 B5
Elizabeth NJ U.S.A. 165 H3
Elizabeth WV U.S.A. 164 E4
Elizabeth, Mount hill Australia 134 D4
Elizabeth Bay Namibia 124 B4
Elizabeth City NC U.S.A. 162 E4
Elizabeth Island Pitcairn Is see Henderson Island
Elizabeth Point Namibia 124 B4
Elizabethton TN U.S.A. 162 D4
Elizabethtown IL U.S.A. 160 F4
Elizabethtown KY U.S.A. 164 C5
Elizabethtown NC U.S.A. 163 E5
Elizabethtown NY U.S.A. 165 I1
El Jadida Morocco 64 C5
El Jaralito Mex. 166 D3
El Jem Tunisia 68 D7
El Jícaro Nicaragua 166 [inset] I6
El Juile Mex. 167 G5
Elk r. Canada 150 H5
Ełk Poland 57 S4
Elk r. MD U.S.A. 165 H4
El Kaa Lebanon see Qaa
El Kab Sudan 108 D6
Elkader IA U.S.A. 160 F3
El Kala Alg. 68 C6
Elk City OK U.S.A. 161 D5
Elkedra Australia 136 A4
Elkedra watercourse Australia 136 B4
El Kef Tunisia see Le Kef
El Kelaâ des Srarhna Morocco 64 C5
Elkford Canada 150 H5
Elk Grove CA U.S.A. 158 C2
El Khalil West Bank see Hebron
El Khandaq Sudan 108 D6
El Khârga Egypt see Al Khārijah
El Kharrûba Egypt see Al Kharrūbah
Elkhart IN U.S.A. 164 C3
Elkhart KS U.S.A. 161 C4
El Khartûm Sudan see Khartoum
El Khenachich esc. Mali see El Khnâchîch
El Khnâchîch esc. Mali 120 C2
Elkhorn WI U.S.A. 160 F3
Elkhorn City KY U.S.A. 164 D5
Elki Turkey see Beytüşşebap
Elkin NC U.S.A. 162 D4
Elkins WV U.S.A. 164 F4
Elk Island National Park Canada 151 H4
Elk Lake Canada 152 E5
Elk Lake l. MI U.S.A. 164 C1
Elkland PA U.S.A. 165 G3
Elk Mountain WY U.S.A. 156 G4
Elk Mountains CO U.S.A. 159 J2
Elko Canada 150 H5
Elko NV U.S.A. 159 F1
Elk Point Canada 151 I4
Elk Point SD U.S.A. 160 D3
Elk Springs CO U.S.A. 159 I1
Elkton MD U.S.A. 165 H4
Elkton VA U.S.A. 165 F4
El Kûbri Egypt see Al Kūbrī
El Kuntilla Egypt see Al Kuntillah
Elkview WV U.S.A. 164 E4
Ellas country Europe see Greece
Ellaville GA U.S.A. 163 C5
Ell Bay Canada 151 O1
Ellef Ringnes Island Canada 147 H2
Ellen, Mount UT U.S.A. 159 H2
Ellenburg Depot NY U.S.A. 165 I1
Ellendale ND U.S.A. 160 D2
Ellensburg WA U.S.A. 156 C3
Ellenville NY U.S.A. 165 H3
El León, Cerro mt. Mex. 161 B7
Ellesmere, Lake N.Z. 139 D6

▶Ellesmere Island Canada 147 J2
4th largest island in North America and 10th in the world.

Ellesmere Island National Park Reserve Canada see Quttinirpaaq National Park
Ellesmere Port U.K. 58 E5
Ellettsville IN U.S.A. 164 B4
Ellice r. Canada 151 K1
Ellice Island Canada 149 N1
Ellice Island atoll Tuvalu see Funafuti
Ellice Islands country S. Pacific Ocean see Tuvalu
Ellicott City MD U.S.A. 165 G4
Ellijay GA U.S.A. 163 C5
El Limón Mex. 167 F4
Ellingen Germany 63 K5
Elliot S. Africa 125 H6
Elliot, Mount Australia 136 D3
Elliotdale S. Africa 125 I6
Elliot Knob mt. VA U.S.A. 164 F4
Elliot Lake Canada 152 E5
Elliott Australia 134 F4
Elliott Highway AK U.S.A. 149 J2
Elliston VA U.S.A. 164 E5
Ellon U.K. 60 G3
Ellora Caves tourist site India 106 B1
Ellsworth KS U.S.A. 160 D4
Ellsworth ME U.S.A. 162 G2
Ellsworth NE U.S.A. 160 C3
Ellsworth WI U.S.A. 160 E2
Ellsworth Land reg. Antarctica 188 K1
Ellsworth Mountains Antarctica 188 L1
Ellwangen (Jagst) Germany 63 K6
El Maghreb country Africa see Morocco
Elmakuz Dağı mt. Turkey 107 A1
Elmalı Turkey 69 M6
El Malpais National Monument nat. park NM U.S.A. 159 J4
El Manṣûra Egypt see Al Manṣūrah
El Maṭarîya Egypt see Al Maṭarīyah
El Mazâr Egypt see Al Mazār
El Médano Mex. 166 C3
El Meghaïer Alg. 64 F5
El Milia Alg. 64 F4
El Minya Egypt see Al Minyā
Elmira Ont. Canada 164 E2
Elmira P.E.I. Canada 153 J5
Elmira MI U.S.A. 164 C1
Elmira NY U.S.A. 165 G2
El Mirage AZ U.S.A. 159 G5
El Moral Mex. 167 E2
El Moral Spain 67 E5
Elmore Australia 138 B6
El Mreyyé reg. Mauritania 120 C3
Elmshorn Germany 63 J1
El Muglad Sudan 108 C7
Elmvale Canada 164 F1
Elnesvågen Norway 54 E5
El Nevado, Cerro mt. Col. 176 D3
El Nido Palawan Phil. 82 B4
El Oasis Mex. 159 F5
El Obeid Sudan 108 D7
El Ocote, Parque Natural nature res. Mex. 167 G5
El Odaiya Sudan 108 C7
El Oro Mex. 166 E3
Elorza Venez. 176 E2
Elota Mex. 166 D4
El Oued Alg. 64 F5
Eloy AZ U.S.A. 159 H5
El Palmito Mex. 166 D3
Elpaputih, Teluk b. Seram Indon. 83 D3
El Paso IL U.S.A. 160 F3
El Paso KS U.S.A. see Derby
El Paso TX U.S.A. 157 G7
El Peñasco Mex. 167 E4
Elphin U.K. 60 D2
Elphinstone Island i. Myanmar see Thayawthadangyi Kyun
El Pino, Sierra mts Mex. 166 E2
El Portal CA U.S.A. 158 D3
El Porvenir Mex. 166 D2
El Porvenir Panama 166 [inset] K7
El Prat de Llobregat Spain 67 H3
El Progreso Guat. see Guastatoya
El Progreso Hond. 166 [inset] I6
El Puente Nicaragua 166 [inset] I6
El Puerto de Santa María Spain 67 C5
El Qâhira Egypt see Cairo
El Qasimiye r. Lebanon 107 B3
El Quds Israel/West Bank see Jerusalem
El Quṣeima Egypt see Al Quṣaymah
El Quṣeir Egypt see Al Quṣayr
El Qûṣîya Egypt see Al Qūṣīyah
El Real de Santa María Panama 166 [inset] K7
El Regocijo Mex. 161 B8
El Reno OK U.S.A. 161 D5
El Retorno Mex. 167 E4
Elrose Canada 151 I5
El Rucio Mex. 166 E4
Elsa Canada 149 N3
El Sabinal, Parque Nacional nat. park Mex. 167 F3
El Ṣaff Egypt see Aṣ Ṣaff
El Sahuaro Mex. 166 B2
El Salado Mex. 161 C7
El Salto Mex. 161 B8
El Salvador country Central America 167 H6
El Salvador Chile 178 C3
El Salvador Mex. 161 C7
Elsass reg. France see Alsace
El Sauz Mex. 166 D2
Else r. Germany 63 I2
El Sellûm Egypt see As Sallūm
Elsey Australia 134 F3
El Shallûfa Egypt see Ash Shallūfah
El Sharana Australia 134 F3
El Shaṭṭ Egypt see Ash Shaṭṭ
Elsie MI U.S.A. 164 C2
Elsinore Denmark see Helsingør
Elsinore UT U.S.A. 159 G2
Elsinore Lake CA U.S.A. 158 E5
El Socorro Mex. 166 E3
Elson Lagoon AK U.S.A. 148 H1
El Sueco Mex. 166 D2
El Suweis Egypt see Suez
El Suweis governorate Egypt see As Suways
El Tajín tourist site Mex. 167 F4
El Tama, Parque Nacional nat. park Venez. 176 D2
El Tarf Alg. 68 C6
El Teleno mt. Spain 67 C2
El Temascal Mex. 161 D7
El Thamad Egypt see Ath Thamad
El Tigre Venez. 176 F2
El Tigre, Parque Nacional nat. park Guat. 167 H5
Eltmann Germany 63 K5
El'ton Russia 53 J6
El'ton, Ozero l. Russia 53 J6
El Tren Mex. 166 B2
El Triunfo Hond. 166 [inset] I6
El Triunfo Mex. 166 C4
El Tuparro, Parque Nacional nat. park Col. 176 E2
El Ṭûr Egypt see Aṭ Ṭūr
El Turbio Arg. 178 B8
El Uqṣur Egypt see Luxor
Eluru India 106 D2
Elva Estonia 55 O7
El Vallecillo Mex. 166 C2
Elvanfoot U.K. 60 F5
Elvas Port. 67 C4
Elverum Norway 55 G6
El Vigía, Cerro mt. Mex. 166 D4
Elvira Brazil 176 D5
El Wak Kenya 122 E3
El Wâtya well Egypt see Al Wāṭiyah
Elwood IN U.S.A. 164 C3
Elwood NE U.S.A. 160 D3
El Wuz Sudan 108 D7
Elx Spain see Elche-Elx
Elxleben Germany 63 K3
Ely U.K. 59 H6
Ely MN U.S.A. 160 F2
Ely NV U.S.A. 159 F2
Elyria OH U.S.A. 164 D3
Elz Germany 63 I4
El Zacatón, Cerro mt. Mex. 167 F5
El Zagâzîg Egypt see Az Zaqāzīq
El Zape Mex. 166 D3
Elze Germany 63 J2
Émaé i. Vanuatu 133 G3
eMakhazeni S. Africa 125 J3
eMalahleni S. Africa 125 I3
Emām Taqī Iran 110 E2
Emån r. Sweden 55 J8
eManzimtoti S. Africa 125 J6
E. Martínez Mex. see Emiliano Martínez
Emas, Parque Nacional das nat. park Brazil 177 H7
Emazar Kazakh. 98 C3
Emba Kazakh. 102 A2
Embalenhle S. Africa 125 I4
Embarcación Arg. 178 D2
Embarras Portage Canada 151 I3
Embi Kazakh. see Emba
Embira r. Brazil see Envira
Emborcação, Represa de resr Brazil 179 B2
Embrun Canada 165 H1
Embu Kenya 122 D4
Emden Germany 63 H1
Emden Deep sea feature N. Pacific Ocean see Cape Johnson Depth
Emei China see Emeishan
Emeishan China 96 D2
Emei Shan mt. China 96 D2
Emerald Australia 136 E4
Emeril Canada 153 I3
Emerita Augusta Spain see Mérida
Emerson Canada 151 L5
Emerson KY U.S.A. 164 D4
Emery UT U.S.A. 159 H2
Emesa Syria see Homs
Emet Turkey 69 M5
eMgwenya S. Africa 125 J3
Emgwenya S. Africa 125 J3
Emigrant Pass NV U.S.A. 158 E1
Emigrant Valley NV U.S.A. 159 F3
Emi Koussi mt. Chad 121 E3
Emile r. Canada 150 G2
Emiliano Martínez Mex. 166 D3
Emiliano Zapata Mex. 167 H5
Emin China 98 C3
Emine, Nos pt Bulg. 69 L3
Eminence KY U.S.A. 164 C4
Emin He r. China 98 C3
Eminska Planina hills Bulg. 69 L3
Emirdağ Turkey 69 N5
Emir Dağı mt. Turkey 69 N5
Emir Dağları mts Turkey 69 N5
Emissi, Tarso mt. Chad 121 E2
eMjindini S. Africa 125 J3
eMkhondo S. Africa 125 J4
Emmaboda Sweden 55 I8
Emmahaven Sumatra Indon. see Telukbayur
Emmaste Estonia 55 M7
Emmaville Australia 138 E2
Emmeloord Neth. 62 F2
Emmelshausen Germany 63 H4
Emmen Neth. 62 G2
Emmen Switz. 66 I3
Emmerich am Rhein Germany 62 G3
Emmet Australia 136 D5
Emmetsburg IA U.S.A. 160 E3
Emmett ID U.S.A. 156 D4
Emmiganuru India 106 C3
Emmonak AK U.S.A. 148 F3
Emo Canada 151 M5
Emona Slovenia see Ljubljana
eMondlo S. Africa 125 J4
Emory Peak TX U.S.A. 161 C6
Empalme Mex. 166 C3
Empangeni S. Africa 125 J5
Emperor Seamount Chain sea feature N. Pacific Ocean 186 H2
Emperor Trough sea feature N. Pacific Ocean 186 H2
Empingham Reservoir U.K. see Rutland Water
Emplawas Moluccas Indon. 83 D5
Empoli Italy 68 D3
Emporia KS U.S.A. 160 D4
Emporia VA U.S.A. 165 G5
Emporium PA U.S.A. 165 F3
Empress Canada 151 I5
Empty Quarter des. Saudi Arabia see Rub' al Khālī
Ems r. Germany 63 H1
Emsdale Canada 164 F1
Emsdetten Germany 63 H2
Ems-Jade-Kanal canal Germany 63 H1
eMzinoni S. Africa 125 I4
Ena Japan 92 D3
Enafors Sweden 54 H5
Ena-san mt. Japan 92 D3
Encantadas, Serra das hills Brazil 178 F4
Encanto, Cape Luzon Phil. 82 C3
Encarnación Mex. 166 E4
Encarnación Para. 178 E3
Enchi Ghana 120 C4
Encinal TX U.S.A. 161 D6
Encinitas CA U.S.A. 158 E5
Encino NM U.S.A. 157 G6
Encruzilhada Brazil 179 C1
Endako Canada 150 E4
Endau r. Malaysia 84 C2
Endau-Rompin National Park nat. park Malaysia 87 C7
Ende Flores Indon. 83 B5
Ende i. Indon. 83 B5
Endeavour Strait Australia 136 C1
Enderby Canada 150 G5
Enderby atoll Micronesia see Puluwat
Enderby Land reg. Antarctica 188 D2
Endicott NY U.S.A. 165 G2
Endicott Mountains AK U.S.A. 148 I2
EnenKio terr. N. Pacific Ocean see Wake Island
Energodar Ukr. see Enerhodar
Enerhodar Ukr. 53 G7
Enewetak atoll Marshall Is 186 G5
Enez Turkey 69 L4
Enfe Lebanon 107 B2
Enfião, Ponta do pt Angola 123 B5
Enfidaville Tunisia 68 D6
Enfield NC U.S.A. 162 E4
Engan Norway 54 F5
Engaru Japan 90 F3
En Gedi Israel 107 B4
Engelhard NC U.S.A. 162 F5
Engel's Russia 53 J6
Engelschmangat sea chan. Neth. 62 E1
Enggano i. Sumatra Indon. 84 C4
Enghien Belgium 62 E4
England admin. div. U.K. 59 E6
Englee Canada 153 L4
Englehart Canada 152 F5
Englewood FL U.S.A. 163 D7
Englewood OH U.S.A. 164 C4
English r. Canada 151 M5
English IN U.S.A. 164 B4
English Bazar India see Ingraj Bazar
English Channel France/U.K. 59 F9
English Coast Antarctica 188 L2
Engozero Russia 52 G2
Enhlalakahle S. Africa 125 J5
Enid OK U.S.A. 161 D4
Eniwa Japan 90 F4
Eniwetok atoll Marshall Is see Enewetak
Enjiang China see Yongfeng
Enkeldoorn Zimbabwe see Chivhu
Enkhuizen Neth. 62 F2
Enköping Sweden 55 J7
Enmelen Russia 148 D2
Enna Sicily Italy 68 F6
Ennadai Lake Canada 151 K2
En Nahud Sudan 108 C7
Ennedi, Massif mts Chad 121 F3
Ennell, Lough l. Ireland 61 E4
Engonia Australia 138 B2
Enning SD U.S.A. 160 C2
Ennis Ireland 61 D5
Ennis MT U.S.A. 156 F3
Ennis TX U.S.A. 161 D5
Enniscorthy Ireland 61 F5
Enniskillen U.K. 61 E3
Ennistymon Ireland 61 C5
Enn Nâqoûra Lebanon 107 B3
Enns r. Austria 57 O6
Eno Fin. 54 Q5
Enoch UT U.S.A. 159 G3
Enok Sumatra Indon. 84 C3
Enontekiö Fin. 54 M2
Enosburg Falls VT U.S.A. 165 I1
Enos Corner IN U.S.A. 164 B4
Enping China 97 G4
Enrekang Celebes Indon. 83 A3
Enrile Luzon Phil. 82 C2
Ens Neth. 62 F2
Ensay Australia 138 C6
Enschede Neth. 62 G2
Ense Germany 63 I3
Ensenada Baja California Mex. 166 A2
Ensenada Baja California Sur Mex. 166 C4
Enshi China 97 F2
Enshū-nada g. Japan 92 D4
Ensley FL U.S.A. 163 C6
Entebbe Uganda 122 D3
Enterprise Canada 150 G2
Enterprise AL U.S.A. 163 C6
Enterprise OR U.S.A. 156 D3
Enterprise UT U.S.A. 159 G3
Enterprise Point Palawan Phil. 82 B4
Entimau, Bukit hill Malaysia 85 F2
Entre Ríos Bol. 176 F8
Entre Rios Brazil 177 H5
Entre Rios de Minas Brazil 179 B3
Entroncamento Port. 67 B4
Enugu Nigeria 120 D4
Enurmino Russia 148 E2
Envira Brazil 176 D5
Envira r. Brazil 176 D5
'En Yahav Israel 107 B4
Enyamba Dem. Rep. Congo 122 C4
Eochaill Ireland see Youghal
Epe Neth. 62 F2
Epéna Congo 122 B3
Épernay France 62 D5
Ephraim UT U.S.A. 159 H2
Ephrata PA U.S.A. 165 G3
Épi i. Vanuatu 133 G3
Epidamnus Albania see Durrës
Épinal France 66 H2
Episkopi Bay Cyprus 107 A2
Episkopis, Kolpos b. Cyprus see Episkopi Bay
ePitoli S. Africa see Pretoria
Epomeo, Monte hill Italy 68 E4
Epping U.K. 59 H7
Epping Forest National Park Australia 136 D4
Eppstein Germany 63 I4
Eppynt, Mynydd hills U.K. 59 D6
Epsom U.K. 59 G7
Epte r. France 62 B5
Eqlīd Iran 110 D4
Equatorial Guinea country Africa 120 D4
Équeurdreville-Hainneville France 59 F9
Erac Creek watercourse Australia 138 B1
Eran Bay Palawan Phil. 82 B4
Erandol India 106 B1
Erawadi r. Myanmar see Irrawaddy
Erawan National Park Thai. 87 B4
Erbaa Turkey 112 E2
Erbendorf Germany 63 M5
Erbeskopf hill Germany 62 H5
Erbet Iraq 113 G4
Ercan airport Cyprus 107 A2
Erciş Turkey 113 F3
Erciyes Dağı mt. Turkey 112 D3
Érd Hungary 68 H1
Erdaobaihe China see Baihe
Erdaogou Bingzhan China 94 C5
Erdao Jiang r. China 90 B4
Erdek Turkey 69 L4
Erdemli Turkey 107 B1
Erdene Mongolia 95 G2
Erdenedalay Mongolia 94 F2
Erdenemandal Mongolia 94 E1
Erdenesant Mongolia 94 F2
Erdenet Hövsgöl Mongolia see Shine-Ider
Erdenet Orhon Mongolia 94 F1
Erdenetsagaan Mongolia 95 H2
Erdenetsogt Bayanhongor Mongolia 94 E2
Erdenetsogt Ömnögovĭ Mongolia see Bayan-Ovoo
Erdi reg. Chad 121 F3
Erdniyevskiy Russia 53 J7

▶Erebus, Mount vol. Antarctica 188 H1
Highest active volcano in Antarctica.

Erechim Brazil 178 F3
Ereentsav Mongolia 95 H1
Ereğli Konya Turkey 112 D3
Ereğli Zonguldak Turkey 69 N4
Erego Moz. see Errego
Erei, Monti mts Sicily Italy 68 F6
Ereke Celebes Indon. 83 B4
Erementaū Kazakh. see Yereymentau
Eréndira Mex. 167 E5
Eren Gobi China 95 I2
Erenhabirga Shan mts China 98 D4
Erenhot China 95 H3
Erepucu, Lago de l. Brazil 177 G4
Erevan Armenia see Yerevan
Erfurt Germany 63 L4
Erfurt airport Germany 63 K4
Ergani Turkey 113 E3
'Erg Chech des. Alg./Mali 120 C2
Ergel Mongolia see Hatanbulag
Ergene r. Turkey 69 L4
Ērgļi Latvia 55 N8
Ergu China 90 C3
Ergun China 95 J1
Ergun He r. China/Russia see Argun'
Ergun Youqi China see Ergun
Ergun Zuoqi China see Gegen Gol
Erguveyem r. Russia 148 C2
Er Hai l. China 96 D3
Erhulai China 90 B4
Eriboll, Loch inlet U.K. 60 E2
Ericht r. U.K. 60 F4
Ericht, Loch l. U.K. 60 E4
Erickson Canada 151 L5
Erie KS U.S.A. 161 E4
Erie PA U.S.A. 164 E2
Erie, Lake Canada/U.S.A. 164 E2
'Erîgât des. Mali 120 C3
Erik Eriksenstretet sea chan. Svalbard 76 D2
Eriksdale Canada 151 L5
Erimo-misaki c. Japan 90 F4
Erin Canada 164 E2
Erinpura Road India 104 C4
Eriskay i. U.K. 60 B3
Eritrea country Africa 108 E6
Erlangen Germany 63 L5
Erlangping China 97 F1
Erldunda Australia 135 F6
Erlistoun watercourse Australia 135 C6
Erlong Shan mt. China 90 C4
Erlongshan Shuiku resr China 90 B4
Ermak Kazakh. see Aksu
Ermana, Khrebet mts Russia 95 H1
Ermelo Neth. 62 F2
Ermelo S. Africa 125 I4
Ermenek Turkey 107 A1
Ermenek r. Turkey 107 A1
Ermont Egypt see Armant
Ermoupoli Greece 69 K6
Ernakulam India 106 C4
Erne r. Ireland/U.K. 61 D3
Ernest Giles Range hills Australia 135 C6
Erode India 106 C4
Eromanga Australia 137 C5
Erongo admin. reg. Namibia 124 B1
Erp Neth. 62 F3
Erpu China 94 C3
Erqu China see Zhouzhi
Errabiddy Hills Australia 135 A6
Er Rachidia Morocco 64 D5
Errego Moz. 123 D5
Er Remla Tunisia 68 D7
Er Renk South Sudan 108 D7
Errigal hill Ireland 61 D2
Errinundra National Park Australia 138 D6
Erris Head hd Ireland 61 B3
Errol NH U.S.A. 165 J1
Erromango i. Vanuatu 133 G3
Erronan i. Vanuatu see Futuna
Erseka Albania see Ersekë
Ersekë Albania 69 I4
Erskine MN U.S.A. 160 D2
Ersmark Sweden 54 L5
Ertai China 94 B2
Ertil' Russia 53 I6
Ertis r. Kazakh./Russia see Irtysh
Ertix He r. China/Kazakh. 102 G2
Ērtra country Africa see Eritrea
Eruh Turkey 113 F3
Erwin TN U.S.A. 162 D4
Erwitte Germany 63 I3
Erxleben Sachsen-Anhalt Germany 63 L2
Erxleben Sachsen-Anhalt Germany 63 L2
Eryuan China 96 C3
Erzerum Turkey see Erzurum
Erzgebirge mts Czech Rep./Germany 63 N4
Erzhan China 90 B2
Erzin Russia 94 C1
Erzin Turkey 107 C1
Erzincan Turkey 113 E3
Erzurum Turkey 113 F3
Esa-ala P.N.G. 136 E1
Esan-misaki pt Japan 90 F4
Esashi Japan 90 F3
Esbjerg Denmark 55 F9
Esbo Fin. see Espoo
Escalante Negros Phil. 82 C4
Escalante UT U.S.A. 159 H3
Escalante r. UT U.S.A. 159 H3
Escalante Desert UT U.S.A. 159 G3
Escalón Mex. 166 D3
Escambia r. FL U.S.A. 163 C6
Escanaba MI U.S.A. 162 C2
Escárcega Mex. 167 H5
Escarpada Point Luzon Phil. 82 C2
Escatrón Spain 67 F3
Escaut r. Belgium 62 D4
Esch Neth. 62 F3
Eschede Germany 63 K2
Eschscholtz atoll Marshall Is see Bikini
Eschscholtz Bay AK U.S.A. 148 G2
Esch-sur-Alzette Lux. 62 F5
Eschwege Germany 63 K3
Eschweiler Germany 62 G4
Escondido r. Mex. 161 C6
Escondido r. Nicaragua 166 [inset] J6
Escondido CA U.S.A. 158 E5
Escudilla mt. AZ U.S.A. 159 I5
Escuinapa Mex. 168 C4
Escuintla Guat. 167 H6
Escuintla Mex. 167 G6
Eséka Cameroon 120 E4
Eşen Turkey 69 M6
Esenguly Turkm. 110 D2
Esenguly Döwlet Gorugy nature res. Turkm. 110 D2
Esens Germany 63 H1
Eşfahān Iran 110 C3
Esfarayen, Reshteh-ye mts Iran 110 E2
Esfedān Iran 111 E3
Eshan China 96 D3
Eshkanān Iran 110 D5
Eshowe S. Africa 125 J5
'Eshqābād Iran 110 E3
eSikhaleni S. Africa 125 J5
eSikhawini S. Africa see eSikhaleni
Esil Kazakh. see Yesil'
Esil r. Kazakh./Russia see Yesil'
Esk Australia 138 F1
Esk r. Australia 137 [inset]
Esk r. U.K. 58 D4
Eskdalemuir U.K. 60 F5
Esker Canada 153 I3
Eskifjörður Iceland 54 [inset 1]
Eski Gediz Turkey 69 M5
Eskilstuna Sweden 55 J7
Eskimo Lakes Canada 149 O1
Eskimo Point Canada see Arviat
Eskipazar Turkey 112 D2
Eskişehir Turkey 69 N5
Eski-Yakkabog' Uzbek. 111 G2
Esla r. Spain 67 C3
Eslāmābād-e Gharb Iran 110 B3
Esler Dağı mt. Turkey 69 M6
Eslohe (Sauerland) Germany 63 I3
Eslöv Sweden 55 H9
Esmā'īlī-ye Pā'īn Iran 110 E4
Eşme Turkey 69 M5
Esmeraldas Ecuador 176 C3
Esmont VA U.S.A. 165 F5
Esnagami Lake Canada 152 D4
Esnes France 62 D4
Espakeh Iran 111 F5
Espalion France 66 F4
España country Europe see Spain
Espanola Canada 152 E5
Espanola NM U.S.A. 161 B4
Esparta Hond. 166 [inset] I6
Espelkamp Germany 63 I2
Espenberg, Cape AK U.S.A. 148 G2
Esperance Australia 135 C8

Esperance Bay Australia 135 C8
Esperanza research station Antarctica 188 A2
Esperanza Arg. 178 B8
Esperanza Mex. 166 C3
Esperanza Masbate Phil. 82 D4
Esperanza, Sierra de la mts Hond. 166 [inset] I6
Espichel, Cabo c. Port. 67 B4
Espigão, Serra do mts Brazil 179 A4
Espigüete mt. Spain 67 D2
Espinazo Mex. 167 E3
Espinhaço, Serra do mts Brazil 179 C2
Espinosa Brazil 179 C1
Espírito Santo Brazil see **Vila Velha**
Espírito Santo state Brazil 179 C2
Espírito Santo do Pinhal Brazil 179 B3
Espiritu Luzon Phil. 82 C2
Espiritu Santo i. Vanuatu 133 G3
Espíritu Santo, Isla i. Mex. 166 C3
Espita Mex. 167 H4
Espoo Fin. 55 N6
Espuña mt. Spain 67 F5
Esqueda Mex. 166 C2
Esquel Arg. 178 B6
Esquimalt Canada 150 F5
Essang Celebes Indon. 83 C1
Essaouira Morocco 120 C1
Essen Belgium 62 E3
Essen Germany 62 H3
Essen (Oldenburg) Germany 63 H2
Essequibo r. Guyana 177 G2
Essex Canada 164 D2
Essex CA U.S.A. 159 F4
Essex MD U.S.A. 165 G4
Essex NY U.S.A. 165 I1
Essexville MI U.S.A. 164 D2
Esslingen am Neckar Germany 63 J6
Es-Smara W. Sahara 120 B2
Esso Russia 77 Q4
Essoyla Russia 52 G3
Est, Canal de l' France 62 G6
Est, Île de l' i. Canada 153 J5
Est, Pointe de l' pt Canada 153 J4
Estación Marítima Antárctica research station Chile 188 A2
Estados, Isla de los i. Arg. 178 D8
Estagno Point Luzon Phil. 82 C2
Eşţahbān Iran 110 D4
Estância Brazil 177 K6
Estancia NM U.S.A. 157 G6
Estand, Kūh-e mt. Iran 111 F4
Estats, Pic d' mt. France/Spain 66 E5
Estcourt S. Africa 125 I5
Este r. Germany 63 J1
Estelí Nicaragua 166 [inset] I6
Estella Spain 67 E2
Estepa Spain 67 D5
Estepona Spain 67 D5
Ester AK U.S.A. 149 K2
Esteras de Medinaceli Spain 67 E3
Esterhazy Canada 151 K5
Estero Bay CA U.S.A. 158 C4
Esteros Mex. 167 F4
Esteros Para. 178 D2
Este Sudeste, Cayos del is Col. 166 [inset] J6
Estevan Canada 151 K5
Estevan Group is Canada 150 D4
Estherville IA U.S.A. 160 E3
Estill SC U.S.A. 163 D5
Eston Canada 151 I5
Estonia country Europe 55 N7
Estonskaya S.S.R. country Europe see **Estonia**
Estrées-St-Denis France 62 C5
Estrela Brazil 179 A5
Estrela, Serra da mts Port. 67 C3
Estrela do Sul Brazil 179 B2
Estrella mt. Spain 67 E4
Estrella, Punta pt Mex. 166 B2
Estremoz Port. 67 C4
Estrondo, Serra hills Brazil 177 I5
Etadunna Australia 137 B6
Etah India 104 D4
Étain France 62 F5
Étamamiou Canada 153 K4
Étampes France 66 F2
Étaples France 62 B4
Etawah Rajasthan India 104 D4
Etawah Uttar Prad. India 104 D4
Etchojoa Mex. 166 C3
Ethandakukhanya S. Africa 125 J4
Ethelbert Canada 151 K5
Ethel Creek Australia 135 C5
E'Thembini S. Africa 124 F5

▶**Ethiopia** country Africa 122 D3
2nd most populous country in Africa.

Etimesgut Turkey 112 D3
Etive, Loch inlet U.K. 60 D4
Etivluk r. AK U.S.A. 148 H1

▶**Etna, Mount** vol. Sicily Italy 68 F6
Highest active volcano in Europe.

Etne Norway 55 D7
Etobicoke Canada 164 F2
Etolin Strait AK U.S.A. 148 F3
Etorofu-tō i. Russia see **Iturup, Ostrov**
Etosha National Park Namibia 123 B5
Etosha Pan salt pan Namibia 123 B5
Etoumbi Congo 122 B3
Etrek r. Iran/Turkm. see **Atrek**
Etrek Turkm. 110 D2
Étrépagny France 62 B5
Étretat France 59 H9
Ettelbruck Lux. 62 G5
Etten-Leur Neth. 62 E3
Ettlingen Germany 63 I6
Ettrick Water r. U.K. 60 F5
Etzatlán Mex. 166 D4
Euabalong Australia 138 C4
Euboea i. Greece see **Evvoia**
Eucla Australia 135 E7
Euclid OH U.S.A. 164 E3
Euclides da Cunha Brazil 177 K6
Eucumbene, Lake Australia 138 D6
Eudistes, Lac des l. Canada 153 I4
Eudora AR U.S.A. 161 F5
Eudunda Australia 137 B7
Eufaula AL U.S.A. 163 C6
Eufaula OK U.S.A. 161 E5
Eufaula Lake resr OK U.S.A. 161 E5
Eugene OR U.S.A. 156 C3
Eugenia, Punta pt Mex. 166 B3
Eugowra Australia 138 D4
Eulo Australia 138 B2
Eumungerie Australia 138 D3
Eungella Australia 136 E4
Eungella National Park Australia 136 E4
Eunice LA U.S.A. 161 E6
Eunice NM U.S.A. 161 C5
Eupen Belgium 62 G4

▶**Euphrates** r. Asia 113 G5
Longest river in western Asia. Also known as Al Furāt (Iraq/Syria) or Fırat (Turkey).

Eura Fin. 55 M6
Eure r. France 62 B5
Eureka AK U.S.A. 149 J2
Eureka CA U.S.A. 156 B4
Eureka KS U.S.A. 160 D4
Eureka MT U.S.A. 156 E2
Eureka NV U.S.A. 159 F2
Eureka OH U.S.A. 164 D4
Eureka SD U.S.A. 160 D2
Eureka UT U.S.A. 159 G2
Eureka Roadhouse AK U.S.A. 149 K3
Eureka Sound sea chan. Canada 147 J2
Eureka Springs AR U.S.A. 161 E4
Eureka Valley CA U.S.A. 158 E3
Euriowie Australia 137 C6
Euroa Australia 138 B6
Eurombah Australia 137 E5
Eurombah Creek r. Australia 137 E5
Europa, Île i. Indian Ocean 123 E6
Europa, Punta de pt Gibraltar see **Europa Point**
Europa Point Gibraltar 67 D5
Euskirchen Germany 62 G4
Eutaw AL U.S.A. 163 C5
Eutsuk Lake Canada 150 E4
Eutzsch Germany 63 M3
Eva Downs Australia 134 F4
Evans, Lac l. Canada 152 F4
Evans, Mount CO U.S.A. 156 G5
Evansburg Canada 150 H4
Evans City PA U.S.A. 164 E3
Evans Head Australia 138 F2
Evans Head hd Australia 138 F2
Evans Ice Stream Antarctica 188 L1
Evans Strait Canada 151 P2
Evanston IL U.S.A. 164 B2
Evanston WY U.S.A. 156 F4
Evansville Canada 152 E5
Evansville AK U.S.A. 149 J2
Evansville IN U.S.A. 164 B5
Evansville WY U.S.A. 156 G4
Evant TX U.S.A. 161 D6
Eva Perón Arg. see **La Plata**
Evart MI U.S.A. 164 C2
Evaton S. Africa 125 H4
Evaz Iran 110 D5
Evening Shade AR U.S.A. 161 F4
Evensk Russia 77 Q3
Everard, Lake salt flat Australia 137 A6
Everard, Mount Australia 135 F5
Everard Range hills Australia 135 F6
Everdingen Neth. 62 F3
Everek Turkey see **Develi**

▶**Everest, Mount** China/Nepal 105 F4
Highest mountain in Asia and the world.

Everett PA U.S.A. 165 F3
Everett WA U.S.A. 156 C3
Evergem Belgium 62 D3
Everglades swamp FL U.S.A. 163 D7
Everglades National Park FL U.S.A. 163 D7
Evergreen AL U.S.A. 163 C6
Evesham Australia 136 C4
Evesham U.K. 59 F6
Evesham, Vale of valley U.K. 59 F6
Evijärvi Fin. 54 M5
Evje Norway 55 E7
Évora Port. 67 C4
Evoron, Ozero l. Russia 90 E2
Évreux France 62 B5
Evros r. Bulg. see **Maritsa**
Evros r. Turkey see **Meriç**
Evrotas r. Greece 69 J6
Évry France 62 C6
Evrychou Cyprus 107 A2
Evrykhou Cyprus see **Evrychou**
Evvoia i. Greece 69 K5
Ewan Australia 136 D3
Ewaso Ngiro r. Kenya 122 E3
Ewe, Loch b. U.K. 60 D3
Ewenkizu Zizhiqi China see **Bayan Tohoi**
Ewing VA U.S.A. 164 D5
Ewirgol China 98 D4
Ewo Congo 122 B4
Exaltación Bol. 176 E6
Excelsior S. Africa 125 H5
Excelsior Mountain CA U.S.A. 158 D2
Excelsior Mountains NV U.S.A. 158 D2
Exe r. U.K. 59 D8
Exeter Australia 138 E5
Exeter Canada 164 E2
Exeter U.K. 59 D8
Exeter CA U.S.A. 158 D3
Exeter NH U.S.A. 165 J2
Exeter Lake Canada 151 I1
Exloo Neth. 62 G2
Exminster U.K. 59 D8
Exmoor hills U.K. 59 D7
Exmoor National Park U.K. 59 D7
Exmore VA U.S.A. 165 H5
Exmouth Australia 134 A5
Exmouth U.K. 59 D8
Exmouth, Mount Australia 138 D3
Exmouth Gulf Australia 134 A5
Exmouth Lake Canada 150 H1
Exmouth Plateau sea feature Indian Ocean 185 P7
Expedition National Park Australia 136 E5
Expedition Range mts Australia 136 E5
Exploits r. Canada 153 L4
Exton PA U.S.A. 165 H3
Extremadura aut. comm. Spain 67 D4
Exuma Cays is Bahamas 163 E7
Exuma Sound sea chan. Bahamas 163 F7
Eyasi, Lake salt l. Tanz. 122 D4
Eyawadi r. Myanmar see **Irrawaddy**
Eye U.K. 59 I6
Eyeberry Lake Canada 151 J2
Eyelenoborsk Russia 51 S3
Eyemouth U.K. 60 G5
Eyjafjörður inlet Iceland 54 [inset 1]
Eyl Somalia 122 E3
Eylau Russia see **Bagrationovsk**
Eynsham U.K. 59 F7
Eyre Creek watercourse Australia 136 B5
Eyre Mountains N.Z. 139 B7
Eyre Peninsula Australia 137 A7
Eystrup Germany 63 J2
Eysturoy i. Faroe Is 54 [inset 2]
Ezakheni S. Africa 125 J5
Ezel KY U.S.A. 164 D5
Ezenzeleni S. Africa 125 I4
Ezequiel Ramos Mexía, Embalse resr Arg. 178 C5
Ezhou China 97 G2
Ezhva Russia 52 K3
Ezine Turkey 69 L5
Ezo i. Japan see **Hokkaidō**
Ezousa r. Cyprus 107 A2

Faaborg Denmark 55 G9
Faadhippolhu Maldives 106 B5
Faafxadhuun Somalia 122 E3
Fabens TX U.S.A. 157 G7
Faber, Mount hill Sing. 87 [inset]
Faber Lake Canada 150 G2
Fåborg Denmark see **Faaborg**
Fabriano Italy 68 E3
Faches-Thumesnil France 62 D4
Fachi Niger 120 E3
Fada Chad 121 F3
Fada-N'Gourma Burkina Faso 120 D3
Fadghāmī Syria 113 F4
Fadiffolu Atoll Maldives see **Faadhippolhu**
Fadippolu Atoll Maldives see **Faadhippolhu**
Faenza Italy 68 D2
Færoerne terr. N. Atlantic Ocean see **Faroe Islands**
Faeroes terr. N. Atlantic Ocean see **Faroe Islands**
Fafanlap Papua Indon. 83 D3
Făgăraş Romania 69 K2

▶**Fagatogo** American Samoa 133 I3
Capital of American Samoa.

Fagersta Sweden 55 I7
Fagita Papua Indon. 83 D3
Fagne reg. Belgium 62 E4
Fagurhólsmýri Iceland 54 [inset 1]
Fagwir South Sudan 108 D8
Fahraj Iran 110 D4
Fā'id Egypt 112 D5
Fairbanks AK U.S.A. 149 K2
Fairborn OH U.S.A. 164 C4
Fairbury NE U.S.A. 160 D3
Fairchance PA U.S.A. 164 F4
Fairfax VA U.S.A. 165 G4
Fairfield CA U.S.A. 158 B2
Fairfield IA U.S.A. 160 F3
Fairfield ID U.S.A. 156 E4
Fairfield IL U.S.A. 160 F4
Fairfield OH U.S.A. 164 C4
Fairfield TX U.S.A. 161 D6
Fair Haven VT U.S.A. 165 I2
Fair Head hd U.K. 61 F2
Fairie Queen Shoal sea feature Phil. 82 B4
Fair Isle i. U.K. 60 H1
Fairlee VT U.S.A. 165 I2
Fairlie N.Z. 139 C7
Fairmont MN U.S.A. 160 E3
Fairmont WV U.S.A. 164 E4
Fair Oaks IN U.S.A. 164 B3
Fairplay, Mount AK U.S.A. 149 L3
Fairview Australia 136 D2
Fairview Canada 150 G3
Fairview MI U.S.A. 164 C1
Fairview OK U.S.A. 161 D4
Fairview PA U.S.A. 164 E2
Fairview UT U.S.A. 159 H2
Fairview Park H.K. China 97 [inset]
Fairweather, Cape AK U.S.A. 149 M4
Fairweather, Mount Canada/U.S.A. 149 M4
Fais i. Micronesia 81 K5
Faisalabad Pak. 111 I4
Faissault France 62 E5
Faith SD U.S.A. 160 C2
Faīzābād Afgh. 111 H2
Faizabad Afgh. see **Faīzābād**
Faizabad India 105 E4
Fakaofo atoll Tokelau 133 I2
Fakaofu atoll Tokelau see **Fakaofo**
Fakenham U.K. 59 H6
Fåker Sweden 54 I5
Fakfak Indon. 81 I7
Fakhrābād Iran 110 D4
Fakiragram India 105 G4
Fako vol. Cameroon see **Cameroun, Mont**
Faku China 95 J3
Fal r. U.K. 59 C8
Falaba Sierra Leone 120 B4
Falaise Lake Canada 150 G2
Falam Myanmar 86 A2
Falāvarjān Iran 110 C3
Falcon Lake Canada 151 M5
Falcon Lake l. Mex./U.S.A. 167 F3
Falenki Russia 52 K4
Falfurrias TX U.S.A. 161 D7
Falher Canada 150 G4
Falkenberg Sweden 55 H8
Falkenberg/Elster Germany 63 N3
Falkenhagen Germany 63 M1
Falkenhain Germany 63 M3
Falkensee Germany 63 N2
Falkenstein Germany 63 M5
Falkirk U.K. 60 F5
Falkland U.K. 60 F4
Falkland Escarpment sea feature S. Atlantic Ocean 184 E9

▶**Falkland Islands** terr. S. Atlantic Ocean 178 E8
United Kingdom Overseas Territory.

Falkland Plateau sea feature S. Atlantic Ocean 184 E9
Falkland Sound sea chan. Falkland Is 178 D8
Falköping Sweden 55 H7
Fallbrook CA U.S.A. 158 E5
Fallieres Coast Antarctica 188 L2
Falling Spring WV U.S.A. 164 E5
Fallon NV U.S.A. 158 D2
Fall River MA U.S.A. 165 J3
Fall River Pass CO U.S.A. 156 G4
Falls City NE U.S.A. 160 E3
Falmouth U.K. 59 B8
Falmouth KY U.S.A. 164 C4
Falmouth VA U.S.A. 165 G4
False r. Canada 153 H2
False Bay S. Africa 124 D8
False Pass AK U.S.A. 148 G5
False Point India 105 F5
Falso, Cabo c. Hond. 166 [inset] J6
Falster i. Denmark 55 G9
Fălticeni Romania 53 E7
Falun Sweden 55 I6
Fam, Kepulauan is Papua Indon. 83 D3
Famagusta Cyprus 107 A2
Famagusta Bay Cyprus see **Ammochostos Bay**
Fameck France 62 G5
Fāmenīn Iran 110 C3
Fame Range hills Australia 135 C6
Family Lake Canada 151 M5
Family Well Australia 134 D5
Fāmūr, Daryācheh-ye l. Iran 110 C4
Fana Mali 120 C3
Fanad Head hd Ireland 61 E2
Fandriana Madag. 123 E6
Fane r. Ireland 61 F4
Fang Thai. 86 B3
Fangcheng Guangxi China 97 F4
Fangcheng Henan China 97 G1
Fangchenggang China see **Fangcheng**
Fangdou Shan mts China 97 F2
Fangliao Taiwan 97 I4
Fangshan Taiwan 97 I4
Fangxian China 97 F1
Fangzheng China 90 C3
Fankuai China 97 F2
Fankuaidian China see **Fankuai**
Fanling H.K. China 97 [inset]
Fannich, Loch l. U.K. 60 D3
Fannūj Iran 111 E5
Fano Italy 68 E3
Fanshan Anhui China 97 H2
Fanshan Zhejiang China 97 I3
Fanshi China 95 H4
Fanum Fortunae Italy see **Fano**
Faqīh Aḥmadān Iran 110 C4
Farab Turkm. see **Farap**
Faraba Mali 120 B3
Faradofay Madag. see **Tôlañaro**
Farafangana Madag. 123 E6
Farāfirah, Wāḥāt al oasis Egypt 108 C4
Farafra Oasis oasis Egypt see **Farāfirah, Wāḥāt al**
Farāh Afgh. 111 F3
Farahābād Iran see **Khezerābād**
Farallon de Medinilla i. N. Mariana Is 81 L3
Farallon de Pajaros vol. N. Mariana Is 81 K2
Farallones de Cali, Parque Nacional nat. park Col. 176 C3
Faranah Guinea 120 B3
Farap Turkm. 111 F2
Fararah Oman 109 I6
Farasān, Jazā'ir is Saudi Arabia 108 F6
Faraulep atoll Micronesia 81 K5
Fareham U.K. 59 F8
Farewell AK U.S.A. 148 I3
Farewell, Cape Greenland 147 N3
Farewell, Cape N.Z. 139 D5
Farewell Spit N.Z. 139 D5
Färgelanda Sweden 55 H7
Farghona Uzbek. see **Farg'ona**
Fargo ND U.S.A. 160 D2
Farg'ona Uzbek. 109 L1
Faribault MN U.S.A. 160 E2
Faribault, Lac l. Canada 153 H2
Faridabad India 104 D3
Faridkot India 104 C3
Faridpur Bangl. 105 G5
Farīmān Iran 111 E3
Farkhār Afgh. 111 H2
Farkhor Tajik. 111 H2
Farmahīn Iran 110 C3
Farmer Island Canada 152 E2
Farmerville LA U.S.A. 161 E5
Farmington Canada 150 F4
Farmington ME U.S.A. 165 J1
Farmington MO U.S.A. 160 F4
Farmington NH U.S.A. 165 J2
Farmington NM U.S.A. 159 I3
Farmington Hills MI U.S.A. 164 D2
Far Mountain Canada 150 E4
Farmville VA U.S.A. 165 F5
Farnborough U.K. 59 G7
Farne Islands U.K. 58 F3
Farnham U.K. 59 G7
Farnham, Lake salt flat Australia 135 D6
Farnham, Mount Canada 150 G5
Faro Brazil 177 G4
Faro Canada 149 N3
Faro Port. 67 C5
Fårö i. Sweden 55 K8
Faroe - Iceland Ridge sea feature Arctic Ocean 189 I2

▶**Faroe Islands** terr. N. Atlantic Ocean 54 [inset]
Self-governing Danish territory.

Fårösund Sweden 55 K8
Farquhar, Atoll de is Seychelles 123 F5
Farquharson Tableland hills Australia 135 C6
Farrāshband Iran 110 D4
Farr Bay Antarctica 188 F2
Farristown KY U.S.A. 164 C5
Farsund Norway 55 E7
Fārūj Iran 110 E2
Farwell MI U.S.A. 164 C2
Farwell TX U.S.A. 161 C5
Fasā Iran 110 D4
Fasano Italy 68 G4
Faşikan Geçidi pass Turkey 107 A1
Faßberg Germany 63 K2
Fastiv Ukr. 53 F6
Fastov Ukr. see **Fastiv**
Fatehabad India 104 C3
Fatehgarh India 104 D4
Fatehpur Rajasthan India 104 C4
Fatehpur Uttar Prad. India 104 E4
Fatick Senegal 120 B3
Fattoilep atoll Micronesia see **Faraulep**
Faughan r. U.K. 61 E2
Faulkton SD U.S.A. 160 D2
Faulquemont France 62 G5
Fauresmith S. Africa 125 G5
Fauske Norway 54 I3
Faust Canada 150 H4
Fawcett Canada 150 H4
Fawley U.K. 59 F8
Fawn r. Canada 151 N4
Faxaflói b. Iceland 54 [inset 1]
Faxälven r. Sweden 54 J5
Faya Chad 121 E3
Fayette AL U.S.A. 163 C5
Fayette MO U.S.A. 160 E4
Fayette MS U.S.A. 161 F6
Fayette OH U.S.A. 164 C3
Fayetteville AR U.S.A. 161 E4
Fayetteville NC U.S.A. 163 E5
Fayetteville TN U.S.A. 163 C5
Fayetteville WV U.S.A. 164 E4
Fâyid Egypt see **Fā'id**
Faylakah i. Kuwait 110 C4
Fazao Malfakassa, Parc National de nat. park Togo 120 D4
Fazilka India 104 C3
Fazrān, Jabal hill Saudi Arabia 110 C5
Fdérik Mauritania 120 B2
Fead Group is P.N.G. see **Nuguria Islands**
Feale r. Ireland 61 C5
Fear, Cape NC U.S.A. 163 E5
Featherston N.Z. 139 E5
Feathertop, Mount Australia 138 C6
Fécamp France 66 E2
Federal District admin. dist. Brazil see **Distrito Federal**
Federalsburg MD U.S.A. 165 H4
Federated Malay States country Asia see **Malaysia**
Fedusar India 104 C4
Fehet Lake Canada 151 M1
Fehmarn i. Germany 57 M3
Fehrbellin Germany 63 M2
Feia, Lagoa lag. Brazil 179 C3
Feicheng China see **Feixian**
Feijó Brazil 176 D5
Feilding N.Z. 139 E5
Fei Ngo Shan hill H.K. China see **Kowloon Peak**
Feio r. Brazil see **Aguapeí**
Feira de Santana Brazil 179 D1
Feixi China 97 H2
Feixian China 95 I5
Feixiang China 95 H4
Fejd el Abiod pass Alg. 68 B6
Feke Turkey 112 D3
Felanitx Spain 67 H4
Feldberg Germany 63 N1
Feldberg mt. Germany 57 L7
Feldkirch Austria 57 L7
Feldkirchen in Kärnten Austria 57 O7
Felidhe Atholhu Maldives 103 D11
Felidu Atoll Maldives see **Felidhe Atholhu**
Felipe C. Puerto Mex. 167 H5
Felixlândia Brazil 179 B2
Felixstowe U.K. 59 I7
Felixton S. Africa 125 J5
Fellowsville WV U.S.A. 164 F4
Felsina Italy see **Bologna**
Felton DE U.S.A. 165 H4
Feltre Italy 68 D1
Femunden l. Norway 54 G5
Femundsmarka Nasjonalpark nat. park Norway 54 H5
Fenaio, Punta del pt Italy 68 D3
Fence Lake NM U.S.A. 159 I4
Fener Burnu hd Turkey 107 B1
Fénérive Madag. see **Fenoarivo Atsinanana**
Fengari mt. Greece 69 K4
Fengcheng Fujian China see **Anxi**
Fengcheng Fujian China see **Lianjiang**
Fengcheng Fujian China see **Yongding**
Fengcheng Guangdong China see **Xinfeng**
Fengcheng Guangxi China see **Fengshan**
Fengcheng Guizhou China see **Tianzhu**
Fengcheng Jiangxi China 97 G2
Fenggang Fujian China see **Shaxian**
Fenggang Guizhou China 96 E3
Fenggang Jiangxi China see **Yihuang**
Fenggeling China 94 F5
Fengguang China 90 B3
Fenghuang China 97 F3
Fengjiaba China see **Wangcang**
Fengjie China 97 F2
Fengkai China 97 F4
Fenglin Taiwan 97 I4
Fengman China 90 B4
Fengming Shaanxi China see **Qishan**
Fengming Sichuan China see **Pengshan**
Fengnan China 95 I4
Fengning China 95 I3
Fengqi China see **Luochuan**
Fengqing China 96 C3
Fengqiu China 95 H5
Fengrun China 95 I4
Fengshan Fujian China see **Luoyuan**
Fengshan Guangxi China 96 E3
Fengshan Hubei China see **Luotian**
Fengshan Yunnan China see **Fengqing**
Fengshuba Shuiku resr China 97 G3
Fengtongzhai Nature Reserve nature res. China 96 D2
Fengxian Jiangsu China 95 I5
Fengxian Shaanxi China 96 E1
Fengxiang Heilong. China see **Luobei**
Fengxiang Shaanxi China 95 F5
Fengxiang Yunnan China see **Lincang**
Fengyang China 97 H1
Fengyuan China 95 G5
Fengyuan Taiwan 97 I3
Fengzhen China 95 H3
Feni Bangl. 105 G5
Feniak Lake AK U.S.A. 148 H1
Feni Islands P.N.G. 132 F2
Fenimore Pass sea chan. AK U.S.A. 148 [inset] D5
Fennville MI U.S.A. 164 B2
Feno, Capo di c. Corsica France 66 I6
Fenoarivo Atsinanana Madag. 123 E5
Fenshui Guan pass China 97 H3
Fenton MI U.S.A. 164 D2
Fenua Ura atoll Fr. Polynesia see **Manuae**
Fenyang China 95 G4
Fenyi China 97 G3
Feodosiya Crimea 112 D1
Fer, Cap de c. Alg. 68 B6
Férai Greece see **Feres**
Ferdows Iran 110 E3
Fère-Champenoise France 62 D6
Feres Greece 69 L4
Fergus Canada 164 E2
Fergus Falls MN U.S.A. 160 D2
Ferguson Lake Canada 151 L2
Fergusson Island P.N.G. 132 F2
Fériana Tunisia 68 C7
Ferizaj Kosovo 69 I3
Ferkessédougou Côte d'Ivoire 120 C4
Fermo Italy 68 E3
Fermont Canada 153 I3
Fermoselle Spain 67 C3
Fermoy Ireland 61 D5
Fernandina, Isla i. Galápagos Ecuador 176 [inset]
Fernandina Beach FL U.S.A. 163 D6
Fernando de Magallanes, Parque Nacional nat. park Chile 178 B8
Fernando de Noronha i. Brazil 184 F6
Fernandópolis Brazil 179 A3
Fernando Poó i. Equat. Guinea see **Bioko**
Fernão Dias Brazil 179 B2
Ferndale CA U.S.A. 158 A1
Ferndown U.K. 59 F8
Fernlee Australia 138 C2
Fernley NV U.S.A. 158 D2
Ferns Ireland 61 F5
Ferozepore India see **Firozpur**
Ferrara Italy 68 D2
Ferreira Gomes Brazil 177 H3
Ferriday LA U.S.A. 167 H2
Ferro, Capo c. Sardinia Italy 68 C4
Ferrol Spain 67 B2
Ferron UT U.S.A. 159 H2
Ferros Brazil 179 C2
Ferry AK U.S.A. 149 J2
Ferryland Canada 153 L5
Ferryville Tunisia see **Menzel Bourguiba**
Fert-tavi nat. park Hungary 68 G1
Ferwerd Neth. 62 F1
Ferwert Neth. see **Ferwerd**
Fès Morocco 64 D5
Feshi Dem. Rep. Congo 123 B4
Fessenden ND U.S.A. 160 D2
Festus MO U.S.A. 160 F4
Fet Dom, Tanjung pt Papua Indon. 83 D3
Fété Bowé Senegal 120 B3
Fethard Ireland 61 E5
Fethiye Malatya Turkey see **Yazıhan**
Fethiye Muğla Turkey 69 M6
Fethiye Körfezi b. Turkey 69 M6
Fetisovo Kazakh. 113 I2
Fetlar i. U.K. 60 [inset]
Fettercairn U.K. 60 G4
Feucht Germany 63 L5
Feuchtwangen Germany 63 K5
Feuilles, Rivière aux r. Canada 153 H2
Fevral'sk Russia 90 C1
Fevzipaşa Turkey 112 E3
Feyzābād Kermān Iran 110 D4

Feyzābād Khorāsān-e Razavī Iran 110 E3
Fez Morocco see Fès
Fezzan reg. Libya 120 E2
Ffestiniog U.K. 59 D6
Fianarantsoa Madag. 123 E6
Fichē Eth. 122 D3
Fichtelgebirge hills Germany 63 M4
Field KY U.S.A. 164 D5
Fier Albania 69 H4
Fiery Creek r. Australia 136 B3
Fife Lake MI U.S.A. 164 C1
Fife Ness pt U.K. 60 G4
Fifield Australia 138 C4
Fifth Meridian Canada 150 H3
Figeac France 66 F4
Figueira da Foz Port. 67 B3
Figueras Spain see Figueres
Figueres Spain 67 H2
Figuig Morocco 64 D5
Figuil Cameroon 121 E4

▶Fiji country S. Pacific Ocean 133 H3
4th most populous and 5th largest country in Oceania.

Fīk' Eth. 122 E3
Filadelfia Para. 178 D2
Filchner Ice Shelf Antarctica 188 A1
Filey U.K. 58 G4
Filibe Bulg. see Plovdiv
Filingué Niger 120 D3
Filipinas country Asia see Philippines
Filippiada Greece 69 I5
Filipstad Sweden 55 I7
Fillan Norway 54 F5
Fillmore CA U.S.A. 158 D4
Fillmore UT U.S.A. 159 G2
Fils r. Germany 63 J6
Fītu Eth. 122 E3
Fimbul Ice Shelf Antarctica 188 C2
Finch Canada 165 H1
Findhorn r. U.K. 60 F3
Fındık Turkey 110 A2
Findlay OH U.S.A. 164 D3
Fine NY U.S.A. 165 H1
Fīn-e 'Olyā Iran 110 C3
Finger Lake Canada 151 M4
Finger Lakes NY U.S.A. 165 G2
Finike Turkey 69 N6
Finike Körfezi b. Turkey 69 N6
Finisterre Spain see Fisterra
Finisterre, Cabo c. Spain see Finisterre, Cape
Finisterre, Cape Spain 67 B2
Fink Creek AK U.S.A. 148 G2
Finke watercourse Australia 136 A5
Finke, Mount hill Australia 135 F7
Finke Bay Australia 134 E3
Finke Gorge National Park Australia 135 F6
Finland country Europe 54 O5
Finland, Gulf of Europe 55 M7

▶Finlay r. Canada 150 E3
Part of the Mackenzie-Peace-Finlay, the 2nd longest river in North America.

Finlay, Mount Canada 150 E3
Finlay Forks Canada 150 F4
Finley ND U.S.A. 160 D2
Finn r. Ireland 61 E3
Finne ridge Germany 63 L3
Finnigan, Mount Australia 136 D2
Finniss, Cape Australia 135 F8
Finnmarksvidda reg. Norway 54 H2
Finnsnes Norway 54 J2
Fins Oman 110 E6
Finschhafen P.N.G. 81 L8
Finspång Sweden 55 I7
Fintona U.K. 61 E3
Finucane Range hills Australia 136 C4
Fionn Loch l. U.K. 60 D3
Fionnphort U.K. 60 C4
Fiordland National Park N.Z. 139 A7
Fir reg. Saudi Arabia 110 B4
Fırat r. Asia 112 E3 see Euphrates
Firebaugh CA U.S.A. 158 C3
Firedrake Lake Canada 151 J2
Fire Island AK U.S.A. 149 J3
Firenze Italy see Florence
Fireside Canada 149 P4
Firk, Sha'īb watercourse Iraq 113 G5
Firmat Arg. 178 D4
Firminy France 66 G4
Firmum Italy see Fermo
Firmum Picenum Italy see Fermo
Firovo Russia 52 G4
Firozabad India 104 D4
Firozkoh reg. Afgh. 111 G3
Firozpur Haryana India 99 B8
Firozpur Punjab India 104 C3
Firth r. Canada 149 M1
Fīrūzābād Iran 110 D4
Fīrūzkūh Iran 110 D3
Firyuza Turkm. see Pöwrize
Fischbach Germany 63 H5
Fischersbrunn Namibia 124 B3
Fish watercourse Namibia 124 C5
Fisher (abandoned) Australia 135 E7
Fisher Bay Antarctica 188 G2
Fisher Glacier Antarctica 188 E2
Fisher River Canada 151 L5
Fishers IN U.S.A. 164 B4
Fishers Island NY U.S.A. 165 J3
Fisher Strait Canada 147 J3
Fishguard U.K. 59 C7
Fishing Branch Game Reserve nature res. Canada 149 M2
Fishing Creek MD U.S.A. 165 G4
Fishing Lake Canada 151 M4
Fish Lake Canada 150 F2
Fish Lake AK U.S.A. 149 J2
Fish Point MI U.S.A. 164 D2
Fish Ponds H.K. China 97 [inset]
Fiske, Cape Antarctica 188 L2
Fiskenæsset Greenland see Qeqertarsuatsiaat
Fismes France 62 D5
Fisterra Spain 67 B2
Fisterra, Cabo c. Spain see Finisterre, Cape
Fitchburg WI U.S.A. 160 F3
Fitri, Lac l. Chad 121 E3
Fitton, Mount Canada 149 M1
Fitzgerald Canada 151 I3
Fitzgerald GA U.S.A. 163 D6
Fitzgerald River National Park Australia 135 B8
Fitz Hugh Sound sea chan. Canada 150 D5
Fitz Roy Arg. 178 C7
Fitzroy r. Australia 134 C4
Fitz Roy, Cerro mt. Arg. 178 B7
Fitzroy Crossing Australia 134 D4
Fitzwilliam Island Canada 164 E1
Fiume Croatia see Rijeka
Fivemiletown U.K. 61 E3
Five Points CA U.S.A. 158 C3
Fizi Dem. Rep. Congo 123 C4
Fizuli Azer. see Füzuli
Flå Norway 55 F6
Flagstaff S. Africa 125 I6
Flagstaff AZ U.S.A. 159 H4
Flagstaff Lake ME U.S.A. 162 G2
Flaherty Island Canada 152 F2
Flambeau r. WI U.S.A. 160 F2
Flamborough Head hd U.K. 58 G4
Fläming hills Germany 63 M2
Flaming Gorge Reservoir WY U.S.A. 156 F4
Flaminksvlei salt pan S. Africa 124 E6
Flanagan r. Canada 151 M4
Flandre reg. France 62 C4
Flannagan Lake VA U.S.A. 164 D5
Flannan Isles U.K. 60 B2
Flåsjön l. Sweden 54 I4
Flat r. Canada 149 P3
Flat r. MI U.S.A. 164 C2
Flat (abandoned) AK U.S.A. 148 H3
Flat Creek Canada 149 M3
Flathead r. MT U.S.A. 154 E2
Flathead Lake MT U.S.A. 156 E3
Flatiron mt. ID U.S.A. 156 E3
Flat Island S. China Sea 80 F4
Flat Lick KY U.S.A. 164 D5
Flattery, Cape Australia 136 D2
Flattery, Cape WA U.S.A. 156 B2
Flat Top mt. Canada 149 M3
Flatwillow Creek r. MT U.S.A. 156 G3
Flatwoods WV U.S.A. 164 E4
Fleetmark Germany 63 L2
Fleetwood Australia 136 D4
Fleetwood U.K. 58 D5
Fleetwood PA U.S.A. 165 H3
Flekkefjord Norway 55 E7
Flemingsburg KY U.S.A. 164 D4
Flemington NJ U.S.A. 165 H3
Flen Sweden 55 J7
Flensburg Germany 57 L3
Flers France 66 D2
Flesherton Canada 164 E1
Flesko, Tanjung pt Indon. 83 C2
Fletcher Lake Canada 151 I2
Fletcher Peninsula Antarctica 188 L2
Fleur de Lys Canada 153 K4
Fleur-de-May, Lac l. Canada 153 I4
Flinders r. Australia 136 C3
Flinders Chase National Park Australia 137 B7
Flinders Group National Park Australia 136 D2
Flinders Island Australia 137 [inset]
Flinders Passage Australia 136 E3
Flinders Ranges mts Australia 137 B7
Flinders Ranges National Park Australia 137 B6
Flinders Reefs Australia 136 E3
Flin Flon Canada 151 K4
Flint U.K. 58 D5
Flint MI U.S.A. 164 D2
Flint r. GA U.S.A. 163 C6
Flint Island Kiribati 187 J6
Flinton Australia 138 D1
Flisa Norway 55 H6

▶Flissingskiy, Mys c. Russia 76 H2
Most easterly point of Europe.

Flixecourt France 62 C4
Flodden U.K. 58 E3
Flöha Germany 63 N4
Flood Range mts Antarctica 188 J1
Flora r. Australia 134 E3
Flora IN U.S.A. 164 B3
Florac France 66 F4
Florala AL U.S.A. 163 C6
Florange France 62 G5
Flora Reef Australia 136 D3
Floreana, Isla i. Galápagos Ecuador 176 [inset]
Florence Italy 68 D3
Florence AL U.S.A. 163 C5
Florence AZ U.S.A. 159 H5
Florence CO U.S.A. 157 G5
Florence OR U.S.A. 156 B4
Florence SC U.S.A. 163 E5
Florence WI U.S.A. 160 F2
Florence Junction AZ U.S.A. 159 H5
Florencia Col. 176 C3
Florennes Belgium 62 E4
Florentia Italy see Florence
Florentino Ameghino, Embalse resr Arg. 178 C6
Flores r. Arg. 178 E5
Flores Guat. 167 H5
Flores i. Indon. 83 B5
Flores, Laut sea Indon. 83 A4
Flores Island Canada 150 E5
Flores Sea Indon. see Flores, Laut
Floresta Brazil 177 K5
Floresville TX U.S.A. 161 D6
Floriano Brazil 177 J5
Florianópolis Brazil 179 A4
Florida Uruguay 178 E4
Florida state U.S.A. 163 D6
Florida, Straits of Bahamas/U.S.A. 163 D8
Florida Bay FL U.S.A. 163 D7
Florida City FL U.S.A. 163 D7
Florida Islands Solomon Is 133 G2
Florida Keys is FL U.S.A. 163 D7
Florin CA U.S.A. 158 C2
Florina Greece 69 I4
Florissant MO U.S.A. 160 F4
Florø Norway 55 D6
Flour Lake Canada 153 I3
Floyd VA U.S.A. 164 E5
Floyd, Mount AZ U.S.A. 159 G4
Floydada TX U.S.A. 161 C5
Fluessen l. Neth. 62 F2
Fluk Moluccas Indon. 83 C3
Flushing Neth. see Vlissingen
Fly r. P.N.G. 81 K8
Flying Fish, Cape Antarctica 188 K2
Flying Mountain NM U.S.A. 159 I6
Flylân i. Neth. see Vlieland
Foam Lake Canada 151 K5
Foča Bos. & Herz. 68 H3
Foça Turkey 69 L5
Fochabers U.K. 60 F3
Focşani Romania 69 L2
Fogang China 97 G4
Foggia Italy 68 F4
Fogi Buru Indon. 83 C3
Fogo i. Cape Verde 120 [inset]
Fogo Island Canada 153 L4
Foinaven hill U.K. 60 E2
Foix France 66 E5
Folda sea chan. Norway 54 I3
Foldereid Norway 54 H4
Foldfjorden sea chan. Norway 54 G4
Folegandros i. Greece 69 K6
Foleyet Canada 152 E4
Foley Island Canada 147 K3
Folger AK U.S.A. 148 H3
Foligno Italy 68 E3
Folkestone U.K. 59 I7
Folkingham U.K. 59 G6
Folkston GA U.S.A. 163 D6
Folldal Norway 54 G5
Follonica Italy 68 D3
Folsom Lake CA U.S.A. 158 C2
Fomboni Comoros 123 E5
Fomento Cuba 163 E8
Fomin Russia 53 I7
Fominskaya Russia 52 K2
Fominskoye Russia 52 I4
Fonda NY U.S.A. 165 H2
Fond-du-Lac Canada 151 J3
Fond du Lac r. Canada 151 J3
Fond du Lac WI U.S.A. 164 A2
Fondevila Spain 67 B3
Fondi Italy 68 E4
Fonni Sardinia Italy 68 C4
Fonsagrada Spain see A Fonsagrada
Fonseca, Golfo do b. Central America 168 G6
Fontaine Lake Canada 151 J3
Fontanges Canada 153 H3
Fontas Canada 150 F3
Fontas r. Canada 150 F3
Fonte Boa Brazil 176 E4
Fonteneau, Lac l. Canada 153 J4
Fontur pt Iceland 54 [inset 1]
Foochow China see Fuzhou
Foot's Bay Canada 164 F1
Foping China 97 F1
Foraker, Mount AK U.S.A. 149 J3
Foraulep atoll Micronesia see Faraulep
Forbes Australia 138 D4
Forbes, Mount Canada 150 G4
Forchheim Germany 63 L5
Ford r. MI U.S.A. 162 C2
Ford City CA U.S.A. 158 D4
Førde Norway 55 D6
Forde Lake Canada 151 L2
Fordham U.K. 59 H6
Fordingbridge U.K. 59 F8
Ford Range mts Antarctica 188 J1
Fords Bridge Australia 138 B2
Fordsville KY U.S.A. 164 B5
Fordyce AR U.S.A. 161 E5
Forécariah Guinea 120 B4
Forel, Mont mt. Greenland 147 O3
Foreland hd U.K. 59 F8
Foreland Point U.K. 59 D7
Foremost Canada 156 F2
Foresight Mountain Canada 150 E4
Forest Canada 164 E2
Forest MS U.S.A. 161 F5
Forest OH U.S.A. 164 D3
Forestburg Canada 151 H4
Forest Creek r. Australia 136 C3
Foreste Casentinesi, Monte Falterona e Campigna, Parco Nazionale delle nat. park Italy 68 D3
Forest Hill Australia 138 C5
Forest Ranch CA U.S.A. 158 C2
Forestville Canada 153 H4
Forestville CA U.S.A. 158 B2
Forestville MI U.S.A. 164 D2
Forfar U.K. 60 G4
Forgan OK U.S.A. 161 C4
Forges-les-Eaux France 62 B5
Forillon, Parc National de nat. park Canada 153 I4
Forked River NJ U.S.A. 165 H4
Forks WA U.S.A. 156 B3
Fork Union VA U.S.A. 165 F5
Forlì Italy 68 E2
Forman ND U.S.A. 160 D2
Formby U.K. 58 D5
Formentera i. Spain 67 G4
Formentor, Cap de c. Spain 67 H4
Formerie France 62 B5
Former Yugoslav Republic of Macedonia country Europe see Macedonia
Formiga Brazil 179 B3
Formosa Arg. 178 E3
Formosa country Asia see Taiwan
Formosa Brazil 179 B1
Formosa, Serra hills Brazil 177 G6
Formosa Bay Kenya see Ungwana Bay
Formosa Strait China/Taiwan see Taiwan Strait
Formoso r. Bahia Brazil 179 B1
Formoso r. Tocantins Brazil 179 A1
Fornos Moz. 125 L2
Forres U.K. 60 F3
Forrest Vic. Australia 138 A7
Forrest W.A. Australia 135 E7
Forrestal Range mts Antarctica 188 A1
Forrest City AR U.S.A. 161 F5
Forrester Island AK U.S.A. 149 N5
Forrest Lake Canada 151 I3
Forrest Lakes salt flat Australia 135 E7
Fors Sweden 54 J5
Forsayth Australia 136 C3
Forsnäs Sweden 54 M3
Forssa Fin. 55 M6
Forster Australia 138 F4
Forsyth GA U.S.A. 163 D5
Forsyth MT U.S.A. 156 G3
Forsyth Range hills Australia 136 C4
Fort Abbas Pak. 111 I4
Fort Albany Canada 152 E3
Fortaleza Brazil 177 K4
Fort Amsterdam NY U.S.A. see New York
Fort Archambault Chad see Sarh
Fort Ashby WV U.S.A. 165 F4
Fort Assiniboine Canada 150 H4
Fort Augustus U.K. 60 E3
Fort Beaufort S. Africa 125 H7
Fort Benton MT U.S.A. 156 F3
Fort Bragg CA U.S.A. 158 B2
Fort Branch IN U.S.A. 164 B4
Fort Carillon NY U.S.A. see Ticonderoga
Fort Charlet Alg. see Djanet
Fort Chimo Canada see Kuujjuaq
Fort Chipewyan Canada 151 I3
Fort Collins CO U.S.A. 156 G4
Fort-Coulonge Canada 152 F5
Fort Crampel Cent. Afr. Rep. see Kaga Bandoro
Fort-Dauphin Madag. see Tôlañaro
Fort Davis TX U.S.A. 161 C6

▶Fort-de-France Martinique 169 L6
Capital of Martinique.

Fort de Kock Sumatra Indon. see Bukittinggi
Fort de Polignac Alg. see Illizi
Fort Deposit AL U.S.A. 167 I1
Fort Dodge IA U.S.A. 160 E3
Fort Duchesne UT U.S.A. 159 I1
Fort Edward NY U.S.A. 165 I2
Fortescue r. Australia 134 B5
Forte Veneza Brazil 177 H5
Fort Flatters Alg. see Bordj Omer Driss
Fort Foureau Cameroon see Kousséri
Fort Franklin Canada see Déline
Fort Gardel Alg. see Zaouatallaz
Fort Gay WV U.S.A. 164 D4
Fort George Canada see Chisasibi
Fort Good Hope Canada 149 O2
Fort Gouraud Mauritania see Fdérik
Forth r. U.K. 60 F4
Forth, Firth of est. U.K. 60 F4
Fort Hancock TX U.S.A. 166 D2
Fort Hertz Myanmar see Putao
Fortification Range mts NV U.S.A. 159 F2
Fortín General Mendoza Para. 178 D2
Fortín Leonida Escobar Para. 178 D2
Fortín Madrejón Para. 178 E2
Fortín Pilcomayo Arg. 178 D2
Fortín Ravelo Bol. 176 F7
Fortín Sargento Primero Leyes Arg. 178 E2
Fortín Suárez Arana Bol. 176 F7
Fortín Teniente Juan Echauri López Para. 178 D2
Fort Jameson Zambia see Chipata
Fort Johnston Malawi see Mangochi
Fort Kent ME U.S.A. 162 G2
Fort Lamy Chad see Ndjamena
Fort Laperrine Alg. see Tamanrasset
Fort Laramie WY U.S.A. 156 G4
Fort Lauderdale FL U.S.A. 163 D7
Fort Liard Canada 150 F2
Fort Mackay Canada 151 I3
Fort Macleod Canada 150 H5
Fort Madison IA U.S.A. 160 F3
Fort Manning Malawi see Mchinji
Fort McMurray Canada 151 I3
Fort McPherson Canada 149 N2
Fort Morgan CO U.S.A. 160 C3
Fort Munro Pak. 111 H4
Fort Myers FL U.S.A. 163 D7
Fort Myers Beach FL U.S.A. 163 D7
Fort Nelson Canada 150 F3
Fort Nelson r. Canada 150 F3
Fort Norman Canada see Tulita
Fort Orange NY U.S.A. see Albany
Fort Payne AL U.S.A. 163 C5
Fort Peck MT U.S.A. 156 G2
Fort Peck Reservoir MT U.S.A. 156 G3
Fort Pierce FL U.S.A. 163 D7
Fort Portal Uganda 122 D3
Fort Providence Canada 150 G2
Fort Resolution Canada 150 H2
Fortrose N.Z. 139 B8
Fortrose U.K. 60 E3
Fort Rosebery Zambia see Mansa
Fort Rousset Congo see Owando
Fort Rupert Canada see Waskaganish
Fort St James Canada 150 E4
Fort St John Canada 150 F3
Fort Sandeman Pak. see Zhob
Fort Saskatchewan Canada 150 H4
Fort Scott KS U.S.A. 160 E4
Fort Severn Canada 152 D2
Fort-Shevchenko Kazakh. 100 E2
Fort Simpson Canada 150 F2
Fort Smith Canada 151 H2
Fort Smith AR U.S.A. 161 E5
Fort Stockton TX U.S.A. 161 C6
Fort Sumeshwar mt. India 105 F4
Fort Sumner NM U.S.A. 157 G6
Fort Supply OK U.S.A. 161 D4
Fort Thomas AZ U.S.A. 159 I5
Fort Trinquet Mauritania see Bîr Mogreïn
Fortuna ND U.S.A. 160 C1
Fortune Bay Canada 153 L5
Fort Valley GA U.S.A. 163 D5
Fort Vermilion Canada 150 G3
Fort Victoria Zimbabwe see Masvingo
Fort Walton Beach FL U.S.A. 167 I2
Fort Ware Canada see Ware
Fort Wayne IN U.S.A. 164 C3
Fort William U.K. 60 D4
Fort Worth TX U.S.A. 161 D5
Fort Yates ND U.S.A. 160 C2
Fortymile r. Canada/U.S.A. 149 L2
Fortymile, Middle Fork r. AK U.S.A. 149 L2
Fortymile, West Fork r. AK U.S.A. 149 L2
Fort Yukon AK U.S.A. 149 K2
Forum Iulii France see Fréjus
Forūr-e Bozorg, Jazīreh-ye i. Iran 110 D5
Forūr-e Kūchek, Jazīreh-ye i. Iran 110 D5
Forvik Norway 54 H4
Foshan China 97 G4
Fo Shek Chau H.K. China see Basalt Island
Fossano Italy 68 B2
Fossil OR U.S.A. 156 C3
Fossil Downs Australia 134 D4
Foster Australia 138 C7
Foster KY U.S.A. 164 C4
Foster, Mount Canada/U.S.A. 149 N4
Foster Lakes Canada 151 J3
Fostoria OH U.S.A. 164 D3
Fotadrevo Madag. 123 E6
Fotherby U.K. 58 G5
Fotokol Cameroon 121 E3
Fotuna i. Vanuatu see Futuna
Fougères France 66 D2
Foula i. U.K. 60 [inset]
Foul Island Myanmar 86 A3
Foulness Point U.K. 59 H7
Foul Point Sri Lanka 106 D4
Foumban Cameroon 120 E4
Foundation Ice Stream glacier Antarctica 188 L1
Fount KY U.S.A. 164 D5
Fountains Abbey and Studley Royal Water Garden (NT) tourist site U.K. 58 F4
Fourches, Mont des hill France 66 G2
Four Corners CA U.S.A. 158 E4
Fouriesburg S. Africa 125 I5
Fourmies France 62 E4
Four Mountains, Islands of the AK U.S.A. 148 E5
Fournier, Lac l. Canada 153 I4
Fournoi i. Greece 69 L6
Fourpeaked Mountain AK U.S.A. 148 I4
Fouta Djallon reg. Guinea 120 B3
Foveaux Strait N.Z. 139 A8
Fowey r. U.K. 59 C8
Fowler CO U.S.A. 157 G5
Fowler IN U.S.A. 164 B3
Fowler Ice Rise Antarctica 188 L1
Fowlers Bay Australia 135 F7
Fowlers Bay b. Australia 135 F8
Fowlerville MI U.S.A. 164 C2
Fox r. B.C. Canada 150 E3
Fox r. Man. Canada 151 M3
Fox r. WI U.S.A. 160 F3
Fox Creek Canada 150 G4
Fox Creek KY U.S.A. 164 C5
Foxdale Isle of Man 58 C4
Foxe Basin g. Canada 147 K3
Foxe Channel Canada 147 J3
Foxe Peninsula Canada 147 K3
Fox Glacier N.Z. 139 C6
Fox Islands AK U.S.A. 148 E5
Fox Lake Canada 150 H3
Fox Mountain Canada 149 N3
Fox Valley Canada 151 I5
Foyers U.K. 60 E3
Foyle r. Ireland/U.K. 61 E3
Foyle, Lough b. Ireland/U.K. 61 E2
Foynes Ireland 61 C5
Foz de Areia, Represa de resr Brazil 179 A4
Foz do Cunene Angola 123 B5
Foz do Iguaçu Brazil 178 F3
Fraga Spain 67 G3
Frakes, Mount Antarctica 188 K1
Framingham MA U.S.A. 165 J2
Framnes Mountains Antarctica 188 E2
Franca Brazil 179 B3
Français, Récif des reef New Caledonia 133 G3
Francavilla Fontana Italy 68 G4

▶France country Europe 66 F3
3rd largest and 3rd most populous country in Europe.

Frances Australia 137 C8
Frances r. Canada 149 O3
Frances Lake Canada 150 D2
Frances Lake Canada 149 O3
Franceville Gabon 122 B4
Francis Canada 151 K5
Francis atoll Kiribati see Beru
Francis, Lake NH U.S.A. 165 J1
Francisco de Orellana Ecuador see Coca
Francisco I. Madero Coahuila Mex. 166 E3
Francisco I. Madero Durango Mex. 161 B7
Francisco Zarco Mex. 166 A1
Francistown Botswana 123 C6
Francois Canada 153 K5
François Lake Canada 150 E4
Francois Peron National Park Australia 135 A6
Francs Peak WY U.S.A. 156 F4
Franeker Neth. 62 F1
Frankenberg (Eder) Germany 63 I3
Frankenberg/Sachsen Germany 63 N4
Frankenhöhe hills Germany 57 M6
Frankenmuth MI U.S.A. 164 D2
Frankenthal (Pfalz) Germany 63 I5
Frankenwald mts Germany 63 L4
Frankford Canada 165 G1
Frankfort IN U.S.A. 164 B3

▶Frankfort KY U.S.A. 164 C4
Capital of Kentucky.

Frankfort MI U.S.A. 164 B1
Frankfort OH U.S.A. 164 D4
Frankfurt Germany see Frankfurt am Main
Frankfurt (Oder) Germany 57 O4
Frankfurt am Main Germany 63 I4
Frank Hann National Park Australia 135 C8
Frankin Lake NV U.S.A. 159 F1
Fränkische Alb hills Germany 63 K6
Fränkische Schweiz reg. Germany 63 L5
Frankland, Cape Australia 137 [inset]
Franklin AZ U.S.A. 159 I5
Franklin GA U.S.A. 163 C5
Franklin IN U.S.A. 164 B4
Franklin KY U.S.A. 164 B5
Franklin LA U.S.A. 161 F6
Franklin MA U.S.A. 165 J2
Franklin NC U.S.A. 163 D5
Franklin NE U.S.A. 160 D3
Franklin NH U.S.A. 165 J2
Franklin PA U.S.A. 164 F3
Franklin TN U.S.A. 162 C5
Franklin TX U.S.A. 161 D6
Franklin VA U.S.A. 165 G5
Franklin WV U.S.A. 164 F4
Franklin, Point pt AK U.S.A. 148 H1
Franklin Bay Canada 149 P1
Franklin D. Roosevelt Lake resr WA U.S.A. 156 D2
Franklin Furnace OH U.S.A. 164 D4
Franklin-Gordon National Park Australia 137 [inset]
Franklin Island Antarctica 188 H1
Franklin Mountains Canada 149 Q3
Franklin Mountains AK U.S.A. 149 K1
Franklin Strait Canada 147 I2
Franklinton LA U.S.A. 161 F6
Franklinville NY U.S.A. 165 F2
Frankston Australia 138 B7
Fränsta Sweden 54 J5
Frantsa-Iosifa, Zemlya is Russia 76 G2
Franz Canada 152 D4
Franz Josef Glacier N.Z. 139 C6
Frasca, Capo della c. Sardinia Italy 68 C5
Frascati Italy 68 E4
Fraser r. Australia 134 C4
Fraser r. B.C. Canada 150 F5
Fraser r. Nfld. and Lab. Canada 153 J2
Fraser, Mount hill Australia 135 B6
Fraserburg S. Africa 124 E6
Fraserburgh U.K. 60 G3
Fraserdale Canada 152 E4
Fraser Island Australia 136 F5
Fraser Lake Canada 150 E4
Fraser Plateau Canada 150 E4
Fraser Range hills Australia 135 C8
Frauenfeld Switz. 66 I3
Fray Bentos Uruguay 178 E4
Frazeysburg OH U.S.A. 164 D3
Frechen Germany 62 G4
Freckleton U.K. 58 E5
Frederic MI U.S.A. 164 C1
Frederica DE U.S.A. 165 H4
Fredericia Denmark 55 F9
Frederick MD U.S.A. 165 G4
Frederick OK U.S.A. 161 D5
Frederick Reef Australia 136 F4
Fredericksburg TX U.S.A. 161 D6
Fredericksburg VA U.S.A. 165 G4
Frederick Sound sea chan. AK U.S.A. 149 N4
Fredericktown MO U.S.A. 160 F4

▶Fredericton Canada 153 I5
Capital of New Brunswick.

Frederikshåb Greenland see Paamiut
Frederikshavn Denmark 55 G8
Frederiksværk Denmark 55 H9
Fredonia AZ U.S.A. 159 G3
Fredonia KS U.S.A. 161 E4
Fredonia NY U.S.A. 164 F2
Fredonia WI U.S.A. 164 B2
Fredrika Sweden 54 K4
Fredrikshamn Fin. see Hamina
Fredrikstad Norway 55 G7
Freedonyer Peak CA U.S.A. 158 C1
Freehold NJ U.S.A. 165 H3
Freeland PA U.S.A. 165 H3
Freeling Heights hill Australia 137 B6
Freel Peak CA U.S.A. 158 D2
Freels, Cape Canada 153 L4
Freeman SD U.S.A. 160 D3
Freeman, Lake IN U.S.A. 164 B3
Freeport Bahamas 163 E7
Freeport FL U.S.A. 163 C6
Freeport IL U.S.A. 160 F3
Freeport TX U.S.A. 161 E6
Freer TX U.S.A. 161 D7
Free Soil MI U.S.A. 164 B1
Free State prov. S. Africa 125 H5

▶Freetown Sierra Leone 120 B4
Capital of Sierra Leone.

Frégate, Lac de la *l.* Canada 152 G3
Fregenal de la Sierra Spain 67 C4
Fregon Australia 135 F6
Fréhel, Cap *c.* France 66 C2
Frei (Chile) *research station* Antarctica 188 A2
Freiberg Germany 63 N4
Freiburg Switz. *see* Fribourg
Freiburg im Breisgau Germany 57 K6
Freisen Germany 63 H5
Freising Germany 57 M6
Freistadt Austria 57 O6
Fréjus France 66 H5
Fremantle Australia 135 A8
Fremont *CA* U.S.A. 158 C3
Fremont *IN* U.S.A. 164 C3
Fremont *MI* U.S.A. 164 C2
Fremont *NE* U.S.A. 160 D3
Fremont *OH* U.S.A. 164 D3
Fremont *r. UT* U.S.A. 159 H2
Fremont Junction *UT* U.S.A. 159 H2
Frenchburg *KY* U.S.A. 164 D5
French Cay *i.* Turks and Caicos Is 163 F8
French Congo *country* Africa *see* Congo

▶French Guiana *terr.* S. America 177 H3
French Overseas Department.

French Guinea *country* Africa *see* Guinea
French Island Australia 138 B7
French Lick *IN* U.S.A. 164 B4
Frenchman *r. MT* U.S.A. 156 G2
Frenchman Lake *CA* U.S.A. 158 C2
Frenchman Lake *NV* U.S.A. 159 F3
Frenchpark Ireland 61 D4
French Pass N.Z. 139 D5

▶French Polynesia *terr.* S. Pacific Ocean 187 K7
French Overseas Country.

French Somaliland *country* Africa *see* Djibouti

▶French Southern and Antarctic Lands *terr.* Indian Ocean 185 M8
French Overseas Territory.

French Sudan *country* Africa *see* Mali
French Territory of the Afars and Issas *country* Africa *see* Djibouti
Frenda Alg. 67 G6
Frentsjer Neth. *see* Franeker
Freren Germany 63 H2
Fresco *r.* Brazil 177 H5
Freshford Ireland 61 E5
Fresnillo Mex. 168 D4
Fresno *CA* U.S.A. 158 D3
Fresno *r. CA* U.S.A. 158 C3
Fresno Reservoir *MT* U.S.A. 156 F2
Fressel, Lac *l.* Canada 152 G3
Freu, Cap des *c.* Spain 67 H4
Freudenberg Germany 63 H4
Freudenstadt Germany 57 L6
Frévent France 62 C4
Frew *watercourse* Australia 136 A4
Frewena Australia 136 A3
Freycinet Estuary *inlet* Australia 135 A6
Freycinet Peninsula Australia 137 [inset]
Freyenstein Germany 63 M1
Freyming-Merlebach France 62 G5
Fria Guinea 120 B3
Fria, Cape Namibia 123 B5
Friant *CA* U.S.A. 158 D3
Frías Arg. 178 C3
Fribourg Switz. 66 H3
Friday Harbor *WA* U.S.A. 156 C2
Friedeburg Germany 63 H1
Friedens *PA* U.S.A. 165 F3
Friedland Russia *see* Pravdinsk
Friedrichshafen Germany 57 L7
Friedrichskanal *canal* Germany 63 L2
Friend *NE* U.S.A. 160 D3
Friendly Islands *country* S. Pacific Ocean *see* Tonga
Friendship *WI* U.S.A. 160 F3
Friesack Germany 63 M2
Friese Wad *tidal flat* Neth. 62 F1
Friesoythe Germany 63 H1
Frinton-on-Sea U.K. 59 I7
Frio *r. TX* U.S.A. 161 D6
Frio *watercourse New Mexico/Texas* U.S.A. 161 C5
Frisco Mountain *UT* U.S.A. 159 G2
Frissell, Mount *hill CT* U.S.A. 165 I2
Fritzlar Germany 63 J3
Frjentsjer Neth. *see* Franeker
Frobisher Bay Canada *see* Iqaluit
Frobisher Bay *b.* Canada 147 L3
Frobisher Lake Canada 151 I3
Frohavet *b.* Norway 54 F5
Frohburg Germany 63 M3
Froissy France 62 C5
Frolovo Russia 53 I6
Frome *watercourse* Australia 137 B6
Frome U.K. 59 E7
Frome *r.* U.K. 59 E8
Frome, Lake *salt flat* Australia 137 B6
Frome Downs Australia 137 B6
Fröndenberg/Ruhr Germany 63 H3
Frontera *Coahuila* Mex. 167 E3
Frontera *Tabasco* Mex. 167 G5
Frontera, Punta *pt* Mex. 167 G5
Fronteras Mex. 166 C2
Front Royal *VA* U.S.A. 165 F4
Frosinone Italy 68 E4
Frostburg *MD* U.S.A. 165 F4
Frøya *i.* Norway 54 F5
Fruges France 62 C4
Fruita *CO* U.S.A. 159 I2
Fruitland *UT* U.S.A. 159 H1
Fruitvale *CO* U.S.A. 159 I2
Frunze Kyrg. *see* Bishkek
Frusino Italy *see* Frosinone
Fruška Gora, Nacionalni Park *nat. park* Serbia 69 H2
Frýdek-Místek Czech Rep. 57 Q6
Fu'an China 97 H3
Fucheng *Anhui* China *see* Fengyang
Fucheng *Shaanxi* China *see* Fuxian
Fuchū *Tōkyō* Japan 93 F3
Fuchū *Toyama* Japan 92 D2
Fuchuan China 97 F3
Fuchun Jiang *r.* China 97 I2
Fude China 97 H3
Fuding China 97 I3
Fudul *reg.* Saudi Arabia 110 B6
Fuefuki Japan 93 E3
Fuenlabrada Spain 67 E3
Fuerte *r.* Mex. 157 F8
Fuerte Olimpo Para. 178 E2
Fuerteventura *i.* Canary Is 120 B2
Fufeng China 96 E1
Fuga *i.* Phil. 82 C2
Fugong China 96 C3
Fugou China 97 G1
Fugu China 95 G4
Fuguo China *see* Zhanhua
Fuhai China 98 D3
Fuhai Linchang China 98 E3
Fuḩaymī Iraq 113 F4
Fujairah U.A.E. 110 E5
Fujeira U.A.E. *see* Fujairah
Fuji Japan 93 E3
Fujian *prov.* China 97 H3
Fujieda Japan 93 E4
Fuji-Hakone-Izu Kokuritsu-kōen *nat. park* Japan 93 F4
Fujihashi Japan 92 C3
Fujiidera Japan 92 B4
Fujikawa *Shizuoka* Japan 93 E3
Fujikawa *Yamanashi* Japan 93 E3
Fuji-kawa *r.* Japan 93 E3
Fujikawaguchiko Japan 93 E3
Fujimi *Nagano* Japan 93 E3
Fujimi *Saitama* Japan 93 F3
Fujimino Japan 93 F3
Fujin China 90 C3
Fujino Japan 93 F3
Fujinomiya Japan 93 E3
Fujioka *Aichi* Japan 92 D3
Fujioka *Gunma* Japan 93 F2
Fujioka *Tochigi* Japan 93 F2
Fuji-san *vol.* Japan 93 E3
Fujisawa Japan 93 F3
Fujishiro Japan 93 G3
Fujiwara *Mie* Japan 92 C3
Fujiwara *Tochigi* Japan 93 F2
Fujiyoshida Japan 93 E3
Fûka Egypt *see* Fūkah
Fūkah Egypt 112 B5
Fukang China 98 D3
Fukaya Japan 93 F2
Fukiage Japan 93 F2
Fukien *prov.* China *see* Fujian
Fukuchiyama Japan 92 B3
Fukude Japan 93 D4
Fukue-jima *i.* Japan 91 C6
Fukui Japan 92 C2
Fukui *pref.* Japan 92 C3
Fukumitsu Japan 92 C2
Fukuoka *Fukuoka* Japan 91 C6
Fukuoka *Gifu* Japan 92 D3
Fukuoka *Toyama* Japan 92 C2
Fukuroi Japan 93 D4
Fukusaki Japan 92 A4
Fukushima Japan 91 F5
Fukuyama Japan 91 C7
Fûl, Gebel *hill* Egypt *see* Fūl, Jabal
Fūl, Jabal *hill* Egypt 107 A5
Fulchhari Bangl. 105 G4
Fulda Germany 63 J4
Fulda *r.* Germany 63 J3
Fulham U.K. 59 G7
Fuli *Anhui* China 97 H1
Fuli *Heilong.* China *see* Jixian
Fuling China 96 E2
Fulitun China *see* Jixian
Fullerton *CA* U.S.A. 158 E5
Fullerton *NE* U.S.A. 160 D3
Fullerton, Cape Canada 151 N2
Fulton *IN* U.S.A. 164 B3
Fulton *MO* U.S.A. 160 F4
Fulton *MS* U.S.A. 161 F5
Fulton *NY* U.S.A. 165 G2
Fumane Moz. 125 K3
Fumay France 62 E5
Fumin China 96 D3
Funabashi Japan 93 F3
Funafuti *atoll* Tuvalu 133 H2
Funahashi Japan 92 D2
Funan China 97 G1

▶Funchal Madeira 120 B1
Capital of Madeira.

Fundão Brazil 179 C2
Fundão Port. 67 C3
Fundi Italy *see* Fondi
Fundición Mex. 166 C3
Fundy, Bay of *g.* Canada 153 I5
Fundy National Park Canada 153 I5
Fünen *i.* Denmark *see* Fyn
Funeral Peak *CA* U.S.A. 158 E3
Fünfkirchen Hungary *see* Pécs
Fung Wong Shan *hill* H.K. China *see* Lantau Peak
Funhalouro Moz. 125 L2
Funing *Jiangsu* China 97 H1
Funing *Yunnan* China 96 E4
Funiu Shan *mts* China 97 F1
Funtua Nigeria 120 D3
Funzie U.K. 60 [inset]
Fuping *Hebei* China 95 H4
Fuping *Shaanxi* China 95 G5
Fuqing China 97 H3
Fürgun, Kūh-e *mt.* Iran 110 E5
Furmanov Russia 52 I4
Furmanovka Kazakh. *see* Moyynkum
Furmanovo Kazakh. *see* Zhalpaktal
Furnás *hill* Spain 67 G4
Furnas, Represa *resr* Brazil 179 B3
Furneaux Group *is* Australia 137 [inset]
Furnes Belgium *see* Veurne
Furong China *see* Wan'an
Fürstenau Germany 63 H2
Fürstenberg/Havel Germany 63 N1
Fürstenwalde/Spree Germany 57 O4
Fürth Germany 63 K5
Furth im Wald Germany 63 M5
Furudono Japan 93 G1
Fury and Hecla Strait Canada 147 J3
Fusan S. Korea *see* Busan
Fushan *Shandong* China 95 J4
Fushan *Shanxi* China 95 G5
Fushimi Japan 92 B4
Fushun China 95 J3
Fushuncheng China *see* Shuncheng
Fusō Japan 92 C3
Fusong China 90 B4
Fussa Japan 93 F3
Futaba Japan 93 E3
Futagawa Japan 92 D4
Futago-yama *mt.* Japan 93 E2
Futami Japan 92 C4
Fu Tau Pun Chau *i.* H.K. China 97 [inset]
Futtsu Japan 93 F3
Futtsu-misaki *pt* Japan 93 F3
Futuna *i.* Vanuatu 133 H3
Futuna Islands Wallis and Futuna Is *see* Horn, Îles de
Fuxian *Liaoning* China *see* Wafangdian
Fuxian *Shaanxi* China 95 G5
Fuxian Hu *l.* China 96 D3
Fuxin *Liaoning* China 95 J3
Fuxin *Liaoning* China 95 J3
Fuxing China *see* Wangmo
Fuxinzhen China *see* Fuxin
Fuyang *Anhui* China 97 G1
Fuyang *Guangxi* China *see* Fuchuan
Fuyang *Zhejiang* China 97 H2
Fuyang He *r.* China 95 I4
Fuying Dao *i.* China 97 I3
Fuyu *Anhui* China *see* Susong
Fuyu *Heilong.* China 95 K2
Fuyu *Jilin* China 90 B3
Fuyu *Jilin* China *see* Songyuan
Fuyuan *Heilong.* China 90 D2
Fuyuan *Yunnan* China 96 E3
Fuyun China 94 B2
Fuzhou *Fujian* China 97 H3
Fuzhou *Jiangxi* China 97 H3
Füzuli Azer. 113 G3
Fyn *i.* Denmark 55 G9
Fyne, Loch *inlet* U.K. 60 D5
F.Y.R.O.M *country* Europe *see* Macedonia

G

Gaâfour Tunisia 68 C6
Gaafu Atoll Maldives *see* Huvadhu Atholhu
Gaalkacyo Somalia 122 E3
Gaat *r.* Malaysia 85 F2
Gabakly Turkm. 111 F2
Gabasumdo China *see* Tongde
Gabbs *NV* U.S.A. 158 E2
Gabbs Valley Range *mts NV* U.S.A. 158 D2
Gabd Pak. 111 F5
Gabela Angola 123 B5
Gaberones Botswana *see* Gaborone
Gabès Tunisia 64 G5
Gabès, Golfe de *g.* Tunisia 64 G5
Gabiden Mustafin Kazakh. 98 A2
Gabo Island Australia 138 D6
Gabon *country* Africa 122 B4

▶Gaborone Botswana 125 G3
Capital of Botswana.

Gābrīk Iran 110 E5
Gabrovo Bulg. 69 K3
Gabú Guinea-Bissau 120 B3
Gadag-Betigeri India 106 B3
Gadaisu P.N.G. 136 E1
Gadap Pak. 111 G5
Gadchiroli India 106 D1
Gäddede Sweden 54 I4
Gadê China 96 C1
Gades Spain *see* Cádiz
Gadhda India 104 B5
Gadhka India 111 H6
Gadra Pak. 111 H5
Gadsden *AL* U.S.A. 163 C5
Gadsden *AZ* U.S.A. 166 B1
Gadwal India 106 C2
Gadyach Ukr. *see* Hadyach
Gaer U.K. 59 D7
Găeşti Romania 69 K2
Gaeta Italy 68 E4
Gaeta, Golfo di *g.* Italy 68 E4
Gaferut *i.* Micronesia 81 L5
Gaffney *SC* U.S.A. 163 D5
Gafsa Tunisia 68 C7
Gag *i. Papua* Indon. 83 D3
Gagarin Russia 53 G5
Gagnoa Côte d'Ivoire 120 C4
Gagnon Canada 153 H4
Gago Coutinho Angola *see* Lumbala N'guimbo
Gagra Georgia 53 I8
Gahai China 94 D4
Gaiab *watercourse* Namibia 124 D5
Gaibanda Bangl. *see* Gaibandha
Gaibandha Bangl. 105 G4
Gaïdouronisi *i.* Greece 69 K7
Gaifi, Wâdi el *watercourse* Egypt *see* Jayfī, Wādī al
Gail *TX* U.S.A. 161 C5
Gaildorf Germany 63 J6
Gaillac France 66 E5
Gaillimh Ireland *see* Galway
Gaillon France 62 B5
Gainesboro *TN* U.S.A. 164 C5
Gainesville *FL* U.S.A. 163 D6
Gainesville *GA* U.S.A. 163 D5
Gainesville *MO* U.S.A. 161 E4
Gainesville *TX* U.S.A. 161 D5
Gainsborough U.K. 58 G5
Gairdner, Lake *salt flat* Australia 137 A6
Gairloch U.K. 60 D3
Gair Loch *b.* U.K. 60 D3
Gaixian China *see* Gaizhou
Gaizhou China 95 J3
Gajah Hutan, Bukit *hill* Malaysia 84 C1
Gajipur India *see* Ghazipur
Gajol India 105 G4
Gakarosa *mt.* S. Africa 124 F4
Gakona *AK* U.S.A. 149 K3
Gala China 99 E7
Galaasiya Uzbek. *see* Galaosiyo
Gala Co *l.* China 99 E7
Galâla el Baḥarîya, Gebel el *plat.* Egypt *see* Jalālah al Baḥrīyah, Jabal
Galana *r.* Kenya 122 E4
Galang Besar *i. Sumatra* Indon. 84 D2
Galanta Slovakia 57 P6
Galaosiyo Uzbek. 111 G2
Galápagos, Parque Nacional *nat. park* Ecuador 176 [inset]

▶Galapagos Islands *is* Ecuador 187 O6
Part of Ecuador. Most westerly point of South America.

Galapagos Rise *sea feature* Pacific Ocean 187 N6
Galashiels U.K. 60 G5
Galaţi Romania 69 M2
Galatina Italy 68 H4
Gala Water *r.* U.K. 60 G5
Galax *VA* U.S.A. 164 E5
Galaýmor Turkm. 111 F3
Galbally Ireland 61 D5
Galdhøpiggen *mt.* Norway 55 F6
Galeana *Chihuahua* Mex. 166 D2
Galeana *Nuevo León* Mex. 167 E3
Galela *Halmahera* Indon. 83 C2
Galena *AK* U.S.A. 148 H2
Galena *IL* U.S.A. 160 F3
Galena *MD* U.S.A. 165 H4
Galena *MO* U.S.A. 161 E4
Galera, Punta *pt* Chile 178 B6
Galera, Punta *pt* Mex. 167 F6
Galesburg *IL* U.S.A. 160 F3
Galesburg *MI* U.S.A. 164 C2
Galeshewe S. Africa 124 G5
Galeton *PA* U.S.A. 165 G3
Galey *r.* Ireland 61 C5
Galheirão *r.* Brazil 179 B1
Galiano Island Canada 150 F5
Galich Russia 52 I4
Galichskaya Vozvyshennost' *hills* Russia 52 I4
Galicia *aut. comm.* Spain 67 C2
Galičica *nat. park* Macedonia 69 I4
Galilee, Lake *salt flat* Australia 136 D4
Galilee, Sea of *l.* Israel 107 B3
Galion *OH* U.S.A. 164 D3
Galite, Canal de la *sea chan.* Tunisia 68 C6
Galiuro Mountains *AZ* U.S.A. 159 H5
Galizia *aut. comm.* Spain *see* Galicia
Gallabat Sudan 108 E7
G'allaorol Uzbek. 111 G1
Gallatin *MO* U.S.A. 160 E4
Gallatin *TN* U.S.A. 164 B5
Galle Sri Lanka 106 D5
Gallego Rise *sea feature* Pacific Ocean 187 M6
Gallegos *r.* Arg. 178 C8
Gallia *country* Europe *see* France

▶Gallinas, Punta *pt* Col. 176 D1
Most northerly point of South America.

Gallipoli Italy 68 H4
Gallipoli Turkey 69 L4
Gallipolis *OH* U.S.A. 164 D4
Gällivare Sweden 54 L3
Gällö Sweden 54 I5
Gallo Island *NY* U.S.A. 165 G2
Gallo Mountains *NM* U.S.A. 159 I4
Gallup *NM* U.S.A. 159 I4
Galmisdale U.K. 60 C4
Galmudug *reg.* Somalia 122 E3
Galong Australia 138 D5
Galoya Sri Lanka 106 D4
Gal Oya National Park Sri Lanka 106 D5
Galshar Mongolia 95 G2
Galston U.K. 60 E5
Galt Mongolia 94 D1
Galt *CA* U.S.A. 158 C2
Galtat-Zemmour W. Sahara 120 B2
Galtee Mountains *hills* Ireland 61 D5
Galtymore *hill* Ireland 56 C4
Galūgāh, Kūh-e *mts* Iran 110 D4
Galuut Mongolia 94 E2
Galveston *IN* U.S.A. 164 B3
Galveston *TX* U.S.A. 161 E6
Galveston Bay *TX* U.S.A. 161 E6
Galwa Nepal 105 E3
Galway Ireland 61 C4
Galway Bay Ireland 61 C4
Gam *i. Papua* Indon. 83 D3
Gam *i. Papua* Indon. 83 D3
Gâm, Sông *r.* Vietnam 86 D2
Gamagōri Japan 92 D4
Gamalakhe S. Africa 125 J6
Gamalama *vol. Moluccas* Indon. 83 C2
Gamay Bay *Samar* Phil. 82 D3
Gamba China 99 E7
Gamba Gabon 122 A4
Gambēla Eth. 122 D3
Gambēla National Park Eth. 122 D3
Gambell *AK* U.S.A. 148 E3
Gambella Eth. *see* Gambēla
Gambia, The *country* Africa 120 B3
Gambier, Îles *is* Fr. Polynesia 187 L7
Gambier Islands Australia 137 B7
Gambier Islands Fr. Polynesia *see* Gambier, Îles
Gambo Canada 153 L4
Gamboma Congo 122 B4
Gamboola Australia 136 C3
Gamboula Cent. Afr. Rep. 122 B3
Gamda China *see* Zamtang
Gamêtî Canada 149 R2
Gamkunoro, Gunung *vol. Halmahera* Indon. 83 C2
Gamlakarleby Fin. *see* Kokkola
Gamleby Sweden 55 J8
Gammelstaden Sweden 54 M4
Gamō Japan 92 C3
Gamova, Mys *pt* Russia 90 C4
Gamshadzai Kūh *mts* Iran 111 F4
Gamtog China 96 C2
Gamud *mt.* Eth. 122 D3
Gana China 96 D1
Ganado *AZ* U.S.A. 159 I4
Ga-Nala S. Africa 125 I4
Gananoque Canada 165 G1
Gäncä Azer. 113 G2
Gancaohu China 98 E4
Gancheng China 97 F5
Ganda Angola 123 B5
Ganda China 99 F7
Gandadiwata, Bukit *mt.* Indon. 83 A3
Gandaingoin China 105 G3
Gandajika Dem. Rep. Congo 123 C4
Gandak Barrage Nepal 105 E4
Gandari Mountain Pak. 111 H4
Gandava Pak. 111 G4
Gander Canada 153 L4
Ganderkesee Germany 63 I1
Gandesa Spain 67 G3
Gandhidham India 104 B5
Gandhinagar India 104 C5
Gandhi Sagar *resr* India 104 C4
Gandia Spain 67 F4
Gandu China 94 E5
Gandzha Azer. *see* Gäncä
Ganes Creek *AK* U.S.A. 148 H3
Ganga *r.* Bangl./India 105 G5 *see* Ganges
Ganga Cone *sea feature* Indian Ocean *see* Ganges Cone
Gangán Arg. 178 C6
Ganganagar India 104 C3
Gangapur India 104 D4
Ganga Sera India 104 B4
Gangaw Myanmar 86 A2
Gangawati India 106 C3
Gangaw Range *mts* Myanmar 86 B2
Gangca China 94 E4
Gangdisê Shan *mts* China 99 C7
Ganges *r.* Bangl./India 105 G5
also known as Ganga
Ganges France 66 F5
Ganges, Mouths of the Bangl./India 105 G5
Ganges Cone *sea feature* Indian Ocean 185 N4
Ganghwa S. Korea 91 B5
Gangneung S. Korea 91 C5
Gangou China 94 D4
Gangouyi China 94 F5
Gangra Turkey *see* Çankırı
Gangtok India 105 G4
Gangu China 94 F5
Gangziyao China 95 H4
Gan He *r.* China 95 K1
Ganhezi China 98 E3
Gani *Halmahera* Indon. 83 D3
Gan Jiang *r.* China 97 H2
Ganjig China 95 J3
Ganjing China 95 G5
Ganjur Sum China 95 H2
Ganluo China 96 D2
Ganmain Australia 138 C5
Gannan China 95 J2
Gannat France 66 F3
Gannett Peak *WY* U.S.A. 156 F4
Ganq China 99 F5
Ganquan China 95 G4
Ganshui China 96 E2
Gansu *prov.* China 94 D3
Gantang China 94 F4
Gantheaume Point Australia 134 C4
Ganting China *see* Huxian
Gantsevichi Belarus *see* Hantsavichy
Gantung Indon. 85 E3
Ganxian China 97 G3
Ganye Nigeria 120 E4
Ganyu China 95 I5
Ganyushkino Kazakh. 51 P6
Ganzhou China 97 G3
Ganzi South Sudan 121 G4
Gao Mali 120 C3
Gaoba China 94 E4
Gaocheng *Hebei* China 95 H4
Gaocheng *Sichuan* China *see* Litang
Gaocun China *see* Mayang
Gaohe China *see* Huaining
Gaohebu China *see* Huaining
Gaolan China 94 E4
Gaoleshan China *see* Xianfeng
Gaoliangjian China *see* Hongze
Gaoling China 95 G5
Gaomi China 95 I4
Gaomudang China 97 F3
Gaoping China 95 H5
Gaoqing China 95 I4
Gaotai China 94 D4
Gaotang China 95 I4
Gaoth Dobhair Ireland 61 D2
Gaoting China *see* Daishan
Gaotingzhen China *see* Daishan
Gaotouyao China 95 G4
Gaoua Burkina Faso 120 C3
Gaoual Guinea 120 B3
Gaoxiong Taiwan 97 I4
Gaoyang China 95 H4
Gaoyao China *see* Zhaoqing
Gaoyi China 95 H4
Gaoyou China 97 H1
Gaoyou Hu *l.* China 97 H1
Gap France 66 H4
Gapan *Luzon* Phil. 82 C3
Gapuwiyak Australia 136 A2
Gaqoi China 99 C7
Gaqung China 99 D7
Gar China 104 E2
Gar Pak. 111 F5
Gar' *r.* Russia 90 C1
Gara, Lough *l.* Ireland 61 D4
Garabekevyul Turkm. *see* Garabekewül
Garabekewül Turkm. 111 G2
Garabil Belentligi *hills* Turkm. 111 F2
Garabogaz Turkm. 113 I2
Garabogaz Aylagy *b.* Turkm. *see* Garabogazköl Aýlagy
Garabogazköl Aylagy *b.* Turkm. *see* Garabogazköl Aýlagy
Garabogazköl Aýlagy *b.* Turkm. 113 I2
Garabogazköl Bogazy *sea chan.* Turkm. 113 I2
Garachiné Panama 166 [inset] K7
Garachiné, Punta *pt* Panama 166 [inset] K7
Garāgheh Iran 111 F4
Garagum *des.* Turkm. *see* Karakum Desert
Garagum Kanaly *canal* Turkm. 111 F2
Garah Australia 138 D2
Garalo Mali 120 C3
Garamätnyýaz Turkm. 111 G2
Garamba *r.* Dem. Rep. Congo 122 C3
Garamba, Parc National de la *nat. park* Dem. Rep. Congo 122 C3
Garang China 94 E4
Garanhuns Brazil 177 K5
Ga-Rankuwa S. Africa 125 H3
Garapuava Brazil 179 B2
Gárasavvon Sweden *see* Karesuando
Garautha India 104 D4
Garba China *see* Jiulong
Garbahaarrey Somalia 122 E3
Garba Tula Kenya 122 D3
Garberville *CA* U.S.A. 158 B1
Garbsen Germany 63 J2
Garça Brazil 179 A3
Garco China 105 G2
Garda, Lago di Italy *see* Garda, Lake
Garda, Lake Italy 68 D2
Garde, Cap de *c.* Alg. 68 B6
Gardelegen Germany 63 L2
Garden City *KS* U.S.A. 160 C4
Garden Hill Canada 151 M4
Garden Mountain *VA* U.S.A. 164 E5
Garden Route National Park *nat. park* S. Africa 124 F7
Gardeyz Afgh. *see* Gardēz
Gardēz Afgh. 111 H3
Gardinas Belarus *see* Hrodna
Gardiner *ME* U.S.A. 165 K1
Gardiner, Mount Australia 134 F5
Gardiner Range *hills* Australia 134 E4
Gardiners Island *NY* U.S.A. 165 I3
Gardīz Afgh. *see* Gardēz
Gardner *atoll* Micronesia *see* Faraulep
Gardner *MA* U.S.A. 165 J2
Gardner Inlet Antarctica 188 L1
Gardner Island *atoll* Kiribati *see* Nikumaroro
Gardner Pinnacles *is HI* U.S.A. 186 I4
Gáregasnjárga Fin. *see* Karigasniemi
Garelochhead U.K. 60 E4
Gareloi Island *AK* U.S.A. 148 [inset] C6
Gargano, Parco Nazionale del *nat. park* Italy 68 F4
Gargantua, Cape Canada 152 D5
Gargünsa China *see* Gar
Gargždai Lith. 55 L9
Garhchiroli India *see* Gadchiroli
Garhi *Madh. Prad.* India 106 C1
Garhi *Rajasthan* India 104 C5
Garhi Khairo Pak. 111 G4
Garhmuktesar India 99 B7
Garhwa India 105 E4
Gari Russia 51 S4
Gariau Indon. 81 I7
Garibaldi, Mount Canada 150 F5
Gariep Dam *resr* S. Africa 125 G6
Garies S. Africa 124 C6
Garig Gunak Barlu National Park Australia 134 F2
Garigliano *r.* Italy 68 E4
Garissa Kenya 122 D4
Garkalne Latvia 55 N8
Garkung Caka *l.* China 99 D6
Garland *TX* U.S.A. 161 D5
Garm Tajik. *see* Gharm
Garmāb *Khorāsān-e Jonūbī* Iran 111 E3
Garmāb *Semnān* Iran 110 E3
Garm Āb, Chashmeh-ye *spring* Iran 110 E3
Garmsār Iran 110 D3
Garm Sēr *reg.* Afgh. 111 F4
Garner *IA* U.S.A. 160 E3
Garner *KY* U.S.A. 164 D5
Garnett *KS* U.S.A. 160 E4
Garnpung Lake *imp. l.* Australia 138 A4
Garo Hills India 105 G4
Garonne *r.* France 66 D4
Garoowe Somalia 122 E3
Garopaba Brazil 179 A5
Garoua Cameroon 120 E4
Garoua Boulai Cameroon 121 E4
Gar Qu *r.* China 99 F6
Garqu Yan China 99 F6
Garré Arg. 178 D5
Garrett *IN* U.S.A. 164 C3
Garrison *MN* U.S.A. 160 E2

Garruk Pak. 111 G4
Garry r. U.K. 60 E3
Garrychyrla Turkm. see Garryçyrla
Garryçyrla Turkm. 111 F2
Garry Island Canada 149 N1
Garry Lake Canada 151 K1
Garrynahine U.K. 60 C2
Garsen Kenya 122 E4
Garshy Turkm. see Garşy
Garsila Sudan 121 F3
Garşy Turkm. 113 I2
Gartar China see Pamai
Garth U.K. 59 D6
Gartog China see Markam
Gartok China see Garyarsa
Gartow Germany 63 L1
Garub Namibia 124 C4
Garusuun Palau 82 [inset]
Garut Java Indon. 85 D4
Garvagh U.K. 61 F3
Garve U.K. 60 E3
Garwa India see Garhwa
Garwha India see Garhwa
Gar Xincun China 99 C6
Gary IN U.S.A. 164 B3
Gary WV U.S.A. 164 E5
Garyarsa China 99 C7
Garyi China 96 C2
Garyū-zan mt. Japan 91 D6
Garza García Mex. 161 C7
Gar Zangbo r. China 99 B6
Garzê China 96 C2
Gasan-Kuli Turkm. see Esenguly
Gas City IN U.S.A. 164 C3
Gascogne reg. France see Gascony
Gascogne, Golfe de g. France see Gascony, Gulf of
Gascony reg. France 66 D5
Gascony, Gulf of France 66 C5
Gascoyne r. Australia 135 A6
Gascoyne Junction Australia 135 A6
Gase China 99 D7
Gasherbrum I mt. China/Pak. 104 D2
Gas Hu salt l. China 99 E5
Gashua Nigeria 120 E3
Gask Iran 111 E3
Gaspar Cuba 163 E8
Gaspar, Selat sea chan. Indon. 84 D3
Gaspé Canada 153 I4
Gaspé, Cap c. Canada 153 I4
Gaspésie, Péninsule de la pen. Canada 153 I4
Gassan vol. Japan 91 F5
Gassaway WV U.S.A. 164 E4
Gasselte Neth. 62 G2
Gasteiz Spain see Vitoria-Gasteiz
Gastello Russia 90 F2
Gaston NC U.S.A. 165 G5
Gaston, Lake NC U.S.A. 165 G5
Gastonia NC U.S.A. 163 D5
Gata, Cabo de c. Spain 67 E5
Gata, Cape Cyprus 107 A2
Gata, Sierra de mts Spain 67 C3
Gataga r. Canada 149 P4
Gatas, Akra c. Cyprus see Gata, Cape
Gatchina Russia 55 Q7
Gate City VA U.S.A. 164 D5
Gatehouse of Fleet U.K. 60 E6
Gatentiri Indon. 81 K8
Gateshead U.K. 58 F4
Gates of the Arctic National Park and Preserve AK U.S.A. 148 I2
Gatesville TX U.S.A. 161 D6
Gateway CO U.S.A. 159 I2
Gatīj Iran 110 E5
Gatineau Canada 165 H1
Gatineau r. Canada 152 G5
Gatong China see Jomda
Gatooma Zimbabwe see Kadoma
Gatton Australia 138 F1
Gatvand Iran 110 C3
Gatyana S. Africa see Willowvale
Gau i. Fiji 133 H3
Gauer Lake Canada 151 L3
Gauhati India see Guwahati
Gaujas nacionālais parks nat. park Latvia 55 N8
Gaul country Europe see France
Gaula r. Norway 54 G5
Gaume reg. Belgium 62 F5
Gaurama Brazil 179 A4
Gauribidanur India 106 C3
Gauteng prov. S. Africa 125 I4
Gavarr Armenia 113 G2
Gāvbūs, Kūh-e mts Iran 110 D5

▶Gavdos i. Greece 69 K7
Most southerly point of Europe.

Gaven Reefs Spratly Is 80 E4
Gavião r. Brazil 179 C1
Gavīleh Iran 110 B3
Gav Khūnī Iran 110 D3
Gävle Sweden 55 J6
Gavrilovka Vtoraya Russia 53 I5
Gavrilov-Yam Russia 52 H4
Gawachab Namibia 124 C4
Gawai Myanmar 96 C3
Gawan India 105 F4
Gawilgarh Hills India 104 D5
Gawler Australia 137 B7
Gawler Ranges hills Australia 137 A7
Gaxun Nur salt l. China 94 E3
Gaya India 105 F4
Gaya i. Malaysia 85 G1
Gaya i. Malaysia 85 G1
Gaya Niger 120 D3
Gaya He r. China 90 C4
Gayam Java Indon. 85 F4
Gayéri Burkina Faso 120 D3
Gaylord MI U.S.A. 164 C1
Gayndah Australia 137 E5
Gayny Russia 52 L3
Gaysin Ukr. see Haysyn
Gayutino Russia 52 H4
Gaza disp. terr. Asia 107 B4

▶Gaza Gaza 107 B4
Capital of Gaza.

Gaza prov. Moz. 125 K2
Gazan Pak. 111 G4
Gazandzhyk Turkm. see Bereket
Gazanjyk Turkm. see Bereket
Gaza Strip disp. terr. Asia see Gaza
Gaz-e Barkhūār Iran 110 C3
Gaziantep Turkey 112 E3
Gaziantep prov. Turkey 107 C1
Gazibenli Turkey see Yahyalı
Gazīk Iran 111 F3
Gazimağusa Cyprus see Famagusta
Gazimuro-Ononskiy Khrebet mts Russia 95 G1
Gazimurskiy Khrebet mts Russia 89 L2
Gazimurskiy Zavod Russia 89 L2
Gazipaşa Turkey 107 A1
Gazli Uzbek. 111 F1
Gaz Māhū Iran 110 E5
Gbarnga Liberia 120 C4
Gboko Nigeria 120 D4
Gcuwa S. Africa 125 I7
Gdańsk Poland 57 Q3
Gdańsk, Gulf of Poland/Russia 57 Q3
Gdańska, Zatoka g. Poland/Russia see Gdańsk, Gulf of
Gdingen Poland see Gdynia
Gdov Russia 55 O7
Gdynia Poland 57 Q3
Geaidnovuohppi Norway 54 M2
Gearhart Mountain OR U.S.A. 156 C4
Gearraidh na h-Aibhne U.K. see Garrynahine
Gebe i. Moluccas Indon. 83 D2
Gebesee Germany 63 K3
Geçitkale Cyprus see Lefkonikon
Gedang, Gunung mt. Indon. 84 C3
Gedaref Sudan 108 E7
Gedern Germany 63 J4
Gedinne Belgium 62 E5
Gediz r. Turkey 69 L5
Gedney Drove End U.K. 59 H6
Gedong Sarawak Malaysia 85 E2
Gedong, Tanjong pt Sing. 87 [inset]
Gedser Denmark 55 G9
Gedungpakuan Sumatra Indon. 84 D4
Geel Belgium 62 F3
Geelong Australia 138 B7
Geelvink Channel Australia 135 A7
Geel Vloer salt pan S. Africa 124 E5
Gees Gwardafuy c. Somalia see Gwardafuy, Gees
Geeste Germany 63 H2
Geesthacht Germany 63 K1
Gegen Gol China 90 A2
Gegen He r. China 95 I1
Gê'gyai China 99 C6
Ge Hu l. China 97 H2
Geidam Nigeria 120 E3
Geiersberg hill Germany 63 J5
Geikie r. Canada 151 K3
Geilenkirchen Germany 62 G4
Geilo Norway 55 F6
Geinō Japan 92 C4
Geiranger Norway 54 E5
Geislingen an der Steige Germany 63 J6
Geisūm, Gezâ'ir is Egypt see Qaysūm, Juzur
Geita Tanz. 122 D4
Geithain Germany 63 M3
Gejiu China 96 D4
Geka, Mys hd Russia 148 B2
Gēkdepe Turkm. 110 E2
Gela Sicily Italy 68 F6
Gêladaindong mt. China 99 E6
Geladī Eth. 122 E3
Gelam i. Indon. 85 E3
Gelang, Tanjung pt Malaysia 87 C7
Geldern Germany 62 G3
Gelendzhik Russia 112 E1
Gelibolu Turkey see Gallipoli
Gelidonya Burnu pt Turkey see Yardımcı Burnu
Gelincik Dağı mt. Turkey 69 N5
Gelnhausen Germany 63 J4
Gelsenkirchen Germany 62 H3
Gelumbang Sumatra Indon. 84 D3
Gemas Malaysia 84 C2
Gemena Dem. Rep. Congo 122 B3
Geminokağı Cyprus see Karavostasi
Gemlik Turkey 69 M4
Gemona del Friuli Italy 68 E1
Gemsa Egypt see Jamsah
Gemsbok National Park Botswana 124 E3
Gemsbokplein well S. Africa 124 E4
Gemuk Mountain AK U.S.A. 148 H3
Genalē Wenz r. Eth. 122 E3
Genappe Belgium 62 E4
General Acha Arg. 178 D5
General Alvear Arg. 178 C5
General Belgrano II research station Antarctica see Belgrano II
General Bravo Mex. 161 D7

▶General Carrera, Lago l. Arg./Chile 178 B7
Deepest lake in South America.

General Conesa Arg. 178 D6
General Escobeda Mex. 167 E3
General Freire Angola see Muxaluando
General Juan Madariaga Arg. 178 E5
General La Madrid Arg. 178 D5
General Luna Phil. 82 D4
General MacArthur Samar Phil. 82 D4
General Machado Angola see Camacupa
General Pico Arg. 178 D5
General Pinedo Arg. 178 D3
General Roca Arg. 178 C5
General Salgado Brazil 179 A3
General San Martín research station Antarctica see San Martín
General Santos Mindanao Phil. 82 D5
General Simón Bolívar Mex. 161 C7
General Terán Mex. 167 F3
General Trías Mex. 166 D2
General Villegas Arg. 178 D5
Genesee PA U.S.A. 165 G3
Geneseo NY U.S.A. 165 G2
Geneva S. Africa 125 H4
Geneva Switz. 66 H3
Geneva AL U.S.A. 163 C6
Geneva IL U.S.A. 164 A3
Geneva NE U.S.A. 160 D3
Geneva NY U.S.A. 165 G2
Geneva OH U.S.A. 164 E3
Geneva, Lake France/Switz. 66 H3
Genève Switz. see Geneva
Genf Switz. see Geneva
Gengda China see Gana
Genglou China 97 H2
Gengma China 96 C4
Gengxuan China see Gengma
Genhe China see Gegen Gol
Genichesk Ukr. see Heniches'k
Genji India 104 C5
Genk Belgium 62 F4
Genkanyy, Khrebet ridge Russia 148 D2
Gennargentu, Parco Nazionale del nat. park Sardinia Italy 68 C4
Gennep Neth. 62 F3
Genoa Australia 138 D6
Genoa Italy 68 C2
Genoa, Gulf of Italy 68 C2
Genova Italy see Genoa
Genova, Golfo di Italy see Genoa, Gulf of
Gent Belgium see Ghent
Genteng Java Indon. 84 D4
Genteng i. Indon. 85 F4
Genthin Germany 63 M2
Genting Highlands Malaysia 84 C2
Gentioux, Plateau de France 66 F4
Genua Italy see Genoa
Geographe Bay Australia 135 A8
Geographical Society Ø i. Greenland 147 P2
Geoje-do i. S. Korea 91 C6
Geok-Tepe Turkm. see Gëkdepe
Geongju S. Korea 91 C6
Georga, Zemlya i. Russia 76 F1
George r. Canada 153 I2
George S. Africa 124 F7
George, Lake Australia 138 D5
George, Lake AK U.S.A. 149 K3
George, Lake FL U.S.A. 163 D6
George, Lake NY U.S.A. 165 I2
George Land i. Russia see Georga, Zemlya
Georges Mills NH U.S.A. 165 I2
George Sound inlet N.Z. 139 A7
Georgetown Australia 136 C3

▶George Town Cayman Is 169 H5
Capital of the Cayman Islands.

▶Georgetown Guyana 177 G2
Capital of Guyana.

George Town Malaysia 84 C1
Georgetown AK U.S.A. 148 H3
Georgetown DE U.S.A. 165 H4
Georgetown GA U.S.A. 163 C6
Georgetown IL U.S.A. 164 B4
Georgetown KY U.S.A. 164 C4
Georgetown OH U.S.A. 164 D4
Georgetown SC U.S.A. 163 E5
Georgetown TX U.S.A. 161 D6
George VI Sound sea chan. Antarctica 188 L2
George V Land reg. Antarctica 188 G2
George West TX U.S.A. 161 D6
Georgia country Asia 113 F2
Georgia state U.S.A. 163 D5
Georgia, Strait of Canada 150 E5
Georgiana AL U.S.A. 161 G6
Georgian Bay Canada 164 E1
Georgian Bay Islands National Park Canada 164 F1
Georgienne, Baie b. Canada see Georgian Bay
Georgina watercourse Australia 136 B5
Georgiu-Dezh Russia see Liski
Georgiyevka Vostochnyy Kazakhstan Kazakh. 102 F2
Georgiyevka Zhambylskaya Oblast' Kazakh. see Korday
Georgiyevsk Russia 113 F1
Georgiyevskoye Russia 52 J4
Georg von Neumayer research station Antarctica see Neumayer III
Gera Germany 63 M4
Geraardsbergen Belgium 62 D4
Geral, Serra mts Brazil 179 A4
Geral de Goiás, Serra hills Brazil 179 B1
Geraldine N.Z. 139 C7
Geral do Paraná, Serra hills Brazil 179 B1
Geraldton Australia 135 A7
Gerama i. Indon. 83 C1
Gerar, Naḥal watercourse Israel 107 B4
Gerber CA U.S.A. 158 B1
Gercüş Turkey 113 F3
Gerdine, Mount AK U.S.A. 148 I3
Gerede Turkey 112 D2
Gerik Malaysia 84 C1
Gerlach NV U.S.A. 158 D1
Germain, Grand Lac l. Canada 153 I4
Germaine, Lac l. Canada 153 I3
Germania country Europe see Germany
Germanicea Turkey see Kahramanmaraş
Germansen Landing Canada 150 E4
German South-West Africa country Africa see Namibia
Germantown OH U.S.A. 164 C4
Germantown WI U.S.A. 164 A2

▶Germany country Europe 57 L5
2nd most populous country in Europe.

Germersheim Germany 63 I5
Germī Iran 110 C2
Gernsheim Germany 63 I5
Gero Japan 92 D3
Gerolstein Germany 62 G4
Gerolzhofen Germany 63 K5
Gerona Spain see Girona
Gerrit Denys is P.N.G. see Lihir Group
Gers r. France 66 E4
Gersfeld (Rhön) Germany 63 J4
Gersoppa India 106 B3
Gerstungen Germany 63 K4
Gerwisch Germany 63 L2
Géryville Alg. see El Bayadh
Gêrzê China 99 D6
Gerze Turkey 112 D2
Gescher Germany 62 H3
Gesoriacum France see Boulogne-sur-Mer
Gessie IN U.S.A. 164 B3
Gestro Wenz, Wabē r. Eth. 100 D6
Getai China 95 G5
Gete r. Belgium 62 F4
Gettysburg PA U.S.A. 165 G4
Gettysburg SD U.S.A. 160 D2
Gettysburg National Military Park nat. park PA U.S.A. 165 G4
Getz Ice Shelf Antarctica 188 J2
Geumapang r. Indon. 84 B2
Geumeo-do i. S. Korea 91 B6
Geumpang Sumatra Indon. 84 B1
Geureudong, Gunung vol. Indon. 84 B1
Geurie Australia 138 D4
Gevaş Turkey 113 F3
Gevgelija Macedonia 69 J4
Gêwārām Band Afgh. 111 G4
Gexianzhuang China see Qinghe
Gexto Spain see Algorta
Gey Iran see Nīkshahr
Geyikli Turkey 69 L5
Geylegphug Bhutan 105 G4
Geysdorp S. Africa 125 G4
Geyserville CA U.S.A. 158 B2
Geyve Turkey 69 N4
Gezidong China 94 E4
Gezīr Iran 110 D5
Ghaap Plateau S. Africa 124 F4
Ghāb, Wādī al r. Syria 107 C2
Ghabāghib Syria 107 C3
Ghabeish Sudan 108 C7
Ghadaf, Wādī al watercourse Jordan 107 C4
Ghadamés Libya see Ghadāmis
Ghadāmis Libya 120 D1
Ghaghara r. India 105 F4
Ghaibi Dero Pak. 111 G5
Ghalend Iran 111 F4
Ghallaorol Uzbek. see G'allaorol
Ghana country Africa 120 C4
Ghanādah, Rās pt U.A.E. 110 D5
Ghantila India 104 B5
Ghanwā Saudi Arabia 108 G4
Ghanzi Botswana 123 C6
Ghanzi admin. dist. Botswana 124 F2
Ghap'an Armenia see Kapan
Ghār, Ras al pt Saudi Arabia 110 C5
Ghardaïa Alg. 64 E5
Gharghoda India 106 D1
Ghârib, Gebel mt. Egypt see Ghārib, Jabal
Ghārib, Jabal mt. Egypt 112 D5
Gharm Tajik. 111 H2
Gharqābād Iran 110 C3
Gharwa India see Garhwa
Gharyān Libya 121 E1
Ghāt Libya 120 E2
Ghatgaon India 105 F5
Ghatol India 104 C5
Ghawdex i. Malta see Gozo
Ghazal, Bahr el watercourse Chad 121 E3
Ghazaouet Alg. 67 F6
Ghaziabad India 104 D3
Ghazi Ghat Pak. 111 H4
Ghazipur India 105 E4
Ghazna Afgh. see Ghaznī
Ghaznī Afgh. 111 H3
Ghaznī Rōd r. Afgh. 111 G3
Ghazzah Gaza see Gaza
Ghebar Gumbad Iran 110 E3
Ghent Belgium 62 D3
Gheorghe Gheorghiu-Dej Romania see Onești
Gheorgheni Romania 69 K1
Gherla Romania 69 J1
Ghijduwon Uzbek. see G'ijduvon
Ghilzaī reg. Afgh. 111 G4
Ghīnah, Wādī al watercourse Saudi Arabia 107 D4
Ghisonaccia Corsica France 66 I5
Ghōrak Afgh. 111 G3
Ghōriyān Afgh. 111 F3
Ghost Lake Canada 150 H2
Ghotaru India 104 B4
Ghotki Pak. 111 H5
Ghudamis Libya see Ghadāmis
Ghugri r. India 105 F4
Ghurayfah hill Saudi Arabia 107 C4
Ghūrī Iran 110 D4
Ghurrab, Jabal hill Saudi Arabia 110 B5
Ghuwayṭah, Nafūd al des. Saudi Arabia 107 D5
Ghuzor Uzbek. see G'uzor
Ghyvelde France 62 C3
Giaginskaya Russia 113 F1
Gialias r. Cyprus 107 A2
Gia Nghia Vietnam 87 D4
Gianisada i. Greece 69 L7
Giannitsa Greece 69 J4
Giant's Castle mt. S. Africa 125 I5
Giant's Causeway lava field U.K. 61 F2
Gianysada i. Greece see Gianisada
Gia Rai Vietnam 87 D5
Giarre Sicily Italy 68 F6
Gibb r. Australia 134 D3
Gibbonsville ID U.S.A. 156 E3
Gibeon Namibia 124 C3
Gibraltar terr. Europe 67 D5

▶Gibraltar Gibraltar 184 H3
United Kingdom Overseas Territory.

Gibraltar, Strait of Morocco/Spain 67 C6
Gibraltar Range National Park Australia 138 F2
Gibson Australia 135 C8
Gibson City IL U.S.A. 164 A3
Gibson Desert Australia 135 C6
Gichgeniyn Nuruu mts Mongolia 94 C2
Gidar Pak. 111 G4
Giddalur India 106 C3
Gîddi, Gebel el hill Egypt see Jiddī, Jabal al
Giddings TX U.S.A. 161 D6
Gīdolē Eth. 121 G4
Gien France 66 F3
Gießen Germany 63 I4
Gīfān-e 'Olyā Iran 110 E2
Gifford r. Canada 147 J2
Gifhorn Germany 63 K2
Gift Lake Canada 150 H4
Gifu Japan 92 C3
Gifu pref. Japan 92 C3
Giganta, Cerro mt. Mex. 166 C3
Gigha i. U.K. 60 D5
Gīgiga Eth. see Jijiga
G'ijduvon Uzbek. 111 G1
Gijón Spain see Gijón/Xixón
Gijón/Xixón Spain 67 D2
Gila r. AZ U.S.A. 159 F5
Gila, Tanjung pt Moluccas Indon. 83 D2
Gila Bend AZ U.S.A. 159 G5
Gila Bend Mountains AZ U.S.A. 159 G5
Gīlān-e Gharb Iran 110 B3
Gilbert r. Australia 136 C3
Gilbert AZ U.S.A. 159 H5
Gilbert WV U.S.A. 164 E5
Gilbert, Mount AK U.S.A. 149 J3
Gilbert Islands Kiribati 186 H5
Gilbert Islands country Pacific Ocean see Kiribati
Gilbert Peak UT U.S.A. 159 H1
Gilbert Ridge sea feature Pacific Ocean 186 H6
Gilbert River Australia 136 C3
Gilbués Brazil 177 I5
Gil Chashmeh Iran 110 E3
Gilé Moz. 123 D5
Giles Creek r. Australia 134 E4
Gilford Island Canada 150 E5
Gilgai Australia 138 E2
Gilgandra Australia 138 D3
Gil Gil Creek r. Australia 138 D2
Gilgit Pak. 104 C2
Gilgit r. Pak. 109 L2
Gilgit-Baltistan admin. div. Pak. 111 I2
Gilgunnia Australia 138 C4
Gili Iyang i. Indon. 85 F4
Gilimanuk Bali Indon. 85 F5
Gılındire Turkey see Aydıncık
Gillam Canada 151 M3
Gillen, Lake salt flat Australia 135 D6
Gilles, Lake salt flat Australia 137 B7
Gillett PA U.S.A. 165 G3
Gillette WY U.S.A. 156 G3
Gilliat Australia 136 C4
Gillingham England U.K. 59 E7
Gillingham England U.K. 59 H7
Gilling West U.K. 58 F4
Gillon Point pt AK U.S.A. 148 [inset] A5
Gilman IL U.S.A. 164 B3
Gilmer TX U.S.A. 161 E5
Gilmour Island Canada 152 F2
Gilroy CA U.S.A. 158 C3
Gīmbī Eth. 122 D3
Gimcheon S. Korea 91 C5
Gimhae S. Korea 91 C6
Gimhwa S. Korea 91 B5
Gimli Canada 151 L5
Gimol'skoye, Ozero l. Russia 52 G3
Ginebra, Laguna l. Bol. 176 E6
Gineifa Egypt see Junayfah
Gin Gin Australia 136 E5
Gingin Australia 135 A7
Gingolx Canada 150 D4
Gingoog Mindanao Phil. 82 D4
Gīnīr Eth. 122 E3
Ginosa Italy 68 G4
Ginzo de Limia Spain see Xinzo de Limia
Gioia del Colle Italy 68 G4
Gipouloux r. Canada 152 G3
Gippsland reg. Australia 138 B7
Girā, Wādī watercourse Egypt see Jirā', Wādī
Gīrān Rīg mt. Iran 110 E4
Girard PA U.S.A. 164 E2
Girardin, Lac l. Canada 153 I2
Girdab Iran 110 E3
Girdwood AK U.S.A. 149 J3
Giresun Turkey 112 E2
Girgenti Sicily Italy see Agrigento
Giridih India see Giridih
Giridih India 105 F4
Girilambone Australia 138 C3
Girishk Afgh. 111 G4
Girna r. India 104 C5
Gir National Park India 104 B5
Girne Cyprus see Kyrenia
Girón Ecuador 176 C4
Giron Sweden see Kiruna
Girona Spain 67 H3
Gironde est. France 66 D4
Girot Pak. 111 I3
Girral Australia 138 C4
Girraween National Park Australia 138 E2
Girvan U.K. 60 E5
Girvas Russia 52 G3
Gisasa r. AK U.S.A. 148 H2
Gisborne N.Z. 139 G4
Giscome Canada 150 F4
Gislaved Sweden 55 H8
Gisors France 62 B5
Gissar Tajik. see Hisor
Gissar Range mts Tajik./Uzbek. 111 G2
Gissarskiy Khrebet mts Tajik./Uzbek. see Gissar Range
Gitarama Rwanda 122 C4
Gitega Burundi 122 C4
Giuba r. Somalia see Jubba
Giulianova Italy 68 E3
Giurgiu Romania 69 K3
Giuvala, Pasul pass Romania 69 K2
Gīvar Iran 110 E2
Givet France 62 E4
Givors France 66 G4
Givry-en-Argonne France 62 E6
Giyani S. Africa 125 J2
Giza Egypt 112 C5
Gizhiga Russia 77 R3
Gjakovë Kosovo 69 I3
Gjilan Kosovo 69 I3
Gjirokastër Albania 69 I4
Gjirokastra Albania see Gjirokastër
Gjoa Haven Canada 147 I3
Gjøra Norway 54 F5
Gjøvik Norway 55 G6
Gkinas, Akrotirio pt Greece 69 M6
Glace Bay Canada 153 K5
Glacier Bay AK U.S.A. 149 N4
Glacier Bay National Park and Preserve AK U.S.A. 149 M4
Glacier National Park Canada 150 G5
Glacier National Park MT U.S.A. 156 E2
Glacier Peak vol. WA U.S.A. 156 C2
Gladstad Norway 54 G4
Gladstone Australia 136 E4
Gladstone Canada 151 L5
Gladwin MI U.S.A. 164 C2
Gladys VA U.S.A. 164 F5
Gladys Lake Canada 150 C3
Glamis U.K. 60 F4
Glamis CA U.S.A. 159 F5
Glamoč Bos. & Herz. 68 G2
Glan r. Germany 63 H5
Glan Mindanao Phil. 82 D5
Glandorf Germany 63 I2
Glanton U.K. 58 F3
Glasgow U.K. 60 E5
Glasgow KY U.S.A. 164 C5
Glasgow MT U.S.A. 156 G2
Glasgow VA U.S.A. 164 F5
Glaslyn Canada 151 I4
Glass, Loch l. U.K. 60 E3
Glass Mountain CA U.S.A. 158 D3
Glass Peninsula AK U.S.A. 149 N4
Glastonbury U.K. 59 E7
Glauchau Germany 63 M4
Glazov Russia 52 L4
Gleiwitz Poland see Gliwice
Glen NH U.S.A. 165 J1
Glen Allen VA U.S.A. 165 G5
Glen Alpine Dam S. Africa 125 I2
Glenamaddy Ireland 61 D4
Glenamoy r. Ireland 61 C3
Glen Arbor MI U.S.A. 164 C1
Glenbawn, Lake Australia 138 E4
Glenboro Canada 151 L5
Glen Canyon gorge UT U.S.A. 159 H3
Glen Canyon Dam AZ U.S.A. 159 H3
Glencoe Canada 164 E2
Glencoe S. Africa 125 J5
Glencoe MN U.S.A. 160 E2
Glendale AZ U.S.A. 159 G5
Glendale CA U.S.A. 158 D4
Glendale UT U.S.A. 159 G3
Glendale Lake PA U.S.A. 165 F3
Glen Davis Australia 138 E4
Glenden Australia 136 E4
Glendive MT U.S.A. 156 G3
Glendon Canada 151 I4
Glendo Reservoir WY U.S.A. 156 G4
Glenfield NY U.S.A. 165 H2
Glengavlen Ireland 61 E3
Glengyle Australia 136 B5
Glen Innes Australia 138 E2
Glenluce U.K. 60 E6
Glen Lyon PA U.S.A. 165 G3
Glenlyon Peak Canada 149 N3
Glen More valley U.K. 60 E3
Glenmorgan Australia 138 D1
Glenn CA U.S.A. 158 B2
Glennallen AK U.S.A. 149 K3
Glenn Highway AK U.S.A. 149 K3
Glennie MI U.S.A. 164 D1
Glenns Ferry ID U.S.A. 156 E4
Glenora Canada 149 O4
Glenore Australia 136 C3
Glenormiston Australia 136 B4
Glenreagh Australia 138 F3
Glen Rose TX U.S.A. 161 D5
Glenrothes U.K. 60 F4
Glens Falls NY U.S.A. 165 I2
Glen Shee valley U.K. 60 F4
Glenties Ireland 61 D3
Glenveagh National Park Ireland 61 E2
Glenville WV U.S.A. 164 E4
Glenwood AR U.S.A. 161 E5
Glenwood IA U.S.A. 160 E3
Glenwood MN U.S.A. 160 E2
Glenwood NM U.S.A. 159 I5
Glenwood Springs CO U.S.A. 159 J2
Glevum U.K. see Gloucester
Glinde Germany 63 K1
Glittertinden mt. Norway 55 F6
Gliwice Poland 57 Q5
Globe AZ U.S.A. 159 H5
Glogau Poland see Głogów
Głogów Poland 57 P5
Glomfjord Norway 54 H3
Glomma r. Norway 54 G7
Glommersträsk Sweden 54 K4
Glorieuses, Îles is Indian Ocean 123 E5

Glorioso Islands Indian Ocean see Glorieuses, Îles
Glory of Russia Cape AK U.S.A. 148 D3
Gloster MS U.S.A. 161 F6
Gloucester Australia 138 E3
Gloucester U.K. 59 E7
Gloucester MA U.S.A. 165 J2
Gloucester VA U.S.A. 165 G5
Glover Reef Belize 167 I5
Gloversville NY U.S.A. 165 H2
Glovertown Canada 153 L4
Glöwen Germany 63 M2
Glubinnoye Russia 90 D3
Glubokiy Krasnoyarskiy Kray Russia 88 H2
Glubokiy Rostovskaya Oblast' Russia 53 I6
Glubokoye Belarus see Hlybokaye
Glubokoye Kazakh. 102 F1
Gluggarnir hill Faroe Is 54 [inset 2]
Glukhov Ukr. see Hlukhiv
Glusburn U.K. 58 F5
Glynebwy U.K. see Ebbw Vale
Gmelinka Russia 53 J6
Gmünd Austria 57 O6
Gmunden Austria 57 N7
Gnarp Sweden 55 J5
Gnarrenburg Germany 63 J1
Gnesen Poland see Gniezno
Gniezno Poland 57 P4
Gnjilane Kosovo see Gjilan
Gnowangerup Australia 135 B8
Gnows Nest Range hills Australia 135 B7
Goa India 106 B3
Goa state India 106 B3
Goageb Namibia 124 C4
Goalen Head hd Australia 138 E6
Goalpara India 105 G4
Goang Flores Indon. 83 A5
Goat Fell hill U.K. 60 D5
Goba Eth. 122 E3
Gobabis Namibia 124 D2
Gobannium U.K. see Abergavenny
Gobas Namibia 124 D4
Gobernador (abandoned) NM U.S.A. 159 J3
Gobi Desert des. China/Mongolia 88 J4
Gobindpur India 105 F5
Gobles MI U.S.A. 164 C2
Gobō Japan 92 B5
Goch Germany 62 G3
Gochas Namibia 124 D3
Go Công Vietnam 87 D5
Godalming U.K. 59 G7
Godavari r. India 106 D2
Godavari, Cape India 106 D2
Godda India 105 F4
Godē Eth. 122 E3
Godere Eth. 122 E3
Goderich Canada 164 E2
Goderville France 59 H9
Godhavn Greenland see Qeqertarsuaq
Godhra India 104 C5
Godia Creek b. India 111 H6
Gōdo Japan 92 C3
Godo, Gunung mt. Indon. 83 C3
Gods r. Canada 151 M3
Gods Lake Canada 151 M4
God's Mercy, Bay of Canada 151 O2
Godthåb Greenland see Nuuk
Godwin-Austen, Mount China/Pak. see K2
Goedereede Neth. 62 D3
Goedgegun Swaziland see Nhlangano
Goegap Nature Reserve S. Africa 124 D5
Goélands, Lac aux l. Canada 153 J3
Goes Neth. 62 D3
Gogama Canada 152 E5
Gogebic Range hills MI U.S.A. 160 F2
Gogra r. India see Ghaghara
Goheung S. Korea 91 B6
Goiana Brazil 177 L5
Goiandira Brazil 179 A2
Goianésia Brazil 179 A1
Goiânia Brazil 179 A2
Goiás Brazil 179 A1
Goiás state Brazil 179 A2
Goicangmai China 99 C6
Goidhoo Maldives 106 B5
Goifulha Fehendhu Atoll Maldives see Goidhoo
Goikul Palau 82 [inset]
Goincang China 94 E5
Goinsargoin China 96 C2
Goioerê Brazil 178 F2
Gojō Japan 92 B4
Gojra Pak. 111 I4
Goka Japan 93 F2
Gokak India 106 B2
Gokarn India 106 B3
Gök Çay r. Turkey 107 A1
Gökçeada i. Turkey 69 K4
Gökdepe Turkm. see Gëkdepe
Gökdere r. Turkey 107 A1
Goklenkuy, Solonchak salt l. Turkm. 110 E1
Gökova Körfezi b. Turkey 69 L6
Gokprosh Hills Pak. 111 F5
Göksun Turkey 112 E3
Göksu Parkı Turkey 107 A1
Gokteik Myanmar 86 B2
Gokwe Zimbabwe 123 C5
Gol Norway 55 F6
Golaghat India 105 H4
Golbāf Iran 110 E4
Gölbaşı Turkey 112 E3
Golconda NV U.S.A. 158 E1
Gölcük Turkey 69 M4
Gold PA U.S.A. 165 G3
Goldap Poland 57 S3
Gold Beach OR U.S.A. 156 B4
Goldberg Germany 63 M1
Gold Coast country Africa see Ghana
Gold Coast Australia 138 F2
Gold Creek AK U.S.A. 149 J3
Golden CO U.S.A. 156 G5
Golden Bay N.Z. 139 D5
Goldendale WA U.S.A. 156 C3
Goldene Aue reg. Germany 63 K3
Golden Gate Highlands National Park S. Africa 125 I5
Golden Hinde mt. Canada 150 E5
Golden Lake Canada 165 G1
Golden Meadow LA U.S.A. 167 H2
Golden Prairie Canada 151 I5
Goldenstedt Germany 63 I2
Goldfield NV U.S.A. 158 E3
Goldsand Lake Canada 151 K3
Goldsboro NC U.S.A. 163 E5
Goldstone Lake CA U.S.A. 158 E4
Goldsworthy (abandoned) Australia 134 B5
Goldthwaite TX U.S.A. 161 D6
Goldvein VA U.S.A. 165 G4
Göle Turkey 113 F2
Goleta CA U.S.A. 158 D4
Golets-Davydov, Gora mt. Russia 89 J2
Golfito Costa Rica 166 [inset] J7
Gölgeli Dağları mts Turkey 69 M6
Goliad TX U.S.A. 161 D6
Golin Baixing China 95 J2
Gölköy Turkey 112 E2
Gollel Swaziland see Lavumisa
Golm Germany 63 M2
Golmberg hill Germany 63 N2
Golmud China 94 C4
Golmud He r. China 94 C4
Golovin AK U.S.A. 148 G2
Golovin Bay AK U.S.A. 148 G2
Golovnino Russia 90 G4
Golpāyegān Iran 110 C3
Gölpazarı Turkey 69 N4
Golsovia AK U.S.A. 148 G3
Golspie U.K. 60 F3
Gol Vardeh Iran 111 F3
Golyama Syutkya mt. Bulg. 69 K4
Golyam Persenk mt. Bulg. 69 K4
Golyshi Russia see Vetluzhskiy
Golzow Germany 63 M2
Goma Dem. Rep. Congo 122 C4
Gōmal Kēlay Afgh. 111 H3
Gomang Co salt l. China 99 E7
Gomangxung China 94 E5
Gomanodan-zan mt. Japan 92 B4
Gomati r. India 109 N4
Gombak, Bukit hill Sing. 87 [inset]
Gombe Nigeria 120 E3
Gombe r. Tanz. 123 D4
Gombi Nigeria 120 E3
Gombroon Iran see Bandar-e 'Abbās
Gomel' Belarus see Homyel'
Gómez Palacio Mex. 166 E3
Gomīsh Tappeh Iran 110 D2
Gommern Germany 63 L2
Gomo China 99 D6
Gomo Co salt l. China 99 D6
Gomumu i. Moluccas Indon. 83 C3
Gonābād Iran 110 E2
Gonaïves Haiti 169 J5
Gonarezhou National Park Zimbabwe 123 D6
Gonâve, Île de la i. Haiti 169 J5
Gonbad, Chāh-e well Iran 110 D3
Gonbad-e Kāvūs Iran 110 D2
Gonda India 105 E4
Gondal India 104 B5
Gondar Eth. see Gonder
Gonder Eth. 122 D2
Gondia India see Gondiya
Gondiya India 104 E5
Gönen Turkey 69 L4
Gonfreville-l'Orcher France 59 H9
Gong'an China 97 G2
Gongbalou China see Gamba
Gongbo'gyamda China 99 F7
Gongchakou China 94 D4
Gongchang China see Longxi
Gongcheng China 97 F3
Gonggar China 99 E7
Gongga Shan mt. China 96 D2
Gonghe Qinghai China 94 E4
Gonghe Yunnan China see Mouding
Gonghui China 95 H3
Gongjiang China see Yudu
Gongliu China 98 C4
Gongogi r. Brazil 179 D1
Gongolgon Australia 138 C3
Gongquan China 96 E2
Gongtang China 99 E7
Gongwang Shan mts China 96 D3
Gongxian Henan China see Gongyi
Gongxian Sichuan China see Gongquan
Gongyi China 95 H5
Gonjo China see Kasha
Gonzáles Mex. 167 F4
Gonzales CA U.S.A. 158 C3
Gonzales TX U.S.A. 161 D6
Gonzha Russia 90 B1
Goochland VA U.S.A. 165 G5
Goodenough, Cape Antarctica 188 G2
Goodenough, Mount hill Canada 149 N2
Goodenough Island P.N.G. 132 F2
Gooderham Canada 165 F1
Good Hope, Cape of S. Africa 124 D8
Goodhope Bay AK U.S.A. 148 G2
Good Hope Mountain Canada 156 B2
Gooding ID U.S.A. 156 E4
Goodland IN U.S.A. 164 B3
Goodland KS U.S.A. 160 C4
Goodlettsville TN U.S.A. 164 B5
Goodnews Bay AK U.S.A. 148 G4
Goodnews Bay b. AK U.S.A. 148 G4
Goodooga Australia 138 C2
Goodpaster r. AK U.S.A. 149 K2
Goodspeed Nunataks Antarctica 188 E2
Goole U.K. 58 G5
Goolgowi Australia 138 B5
Goolma Australia 138 D4
Gooloogong Australia 138 D4
Goomalling Australia 135 B7
Goombalie Australia 138 B2
Goondiwindi Australia 138 E2
Goongarrie, Lake salt flat Australia 135 C7
Goongarrie National Park Australia 135 C7
Goonyella Australia 136 D4
Goorly, Lake salt flat Australia 135 B7
Goose Bay Canada see Happy Valley-Goose Bay
Goose Creek SC U.S.A. 163 D5
Goose Lake CA U.S.A. 156 C4
Gooty India 106 C3
Gopalganj Bangl. 105 G5
Gopalganj India 105 F4
Gopeshwar India 104 D3
Göppingen Germany 63 J6
Gorakhnath mt. India 104 B5
Gorakhpur India 105 E4
Goražde Bos. & Herz. 68 H3
Gorczański Park Narodowy nat. park Poland 57 R6
Gorda, Punta pt Nicaragua 166 [inset] J6
Gorda, Punta pt CA U.S.A. 158 A1
Gördes Turkey 69 M5
Gordil Cent. Afr. Rep. 122 C3
Gordon r. Canada 151 O1
Gordon U.K. 60 G5
Gordon AK U.S.A. 149 L1
Gordon NE U.S.A. 160 C3
Gordon, Lake Australia 137 [inset]
Gordon Downs Australia 134 E4
Gordon Lake Canada 151 I3
Gordon Lake PA U.S.A. 165 F4
Gordonsville VA U.S.A. 165 F4
Goré Chad 121 E4
Gorē Eth. 122 D3
Gore N.Z. 139 B8
Gore VA U.S.A. 165 F4
Gorebridge U.K. 60 F5
Gore Point pt AK U.S.A. 149 J4
Gorey Ireland 61 F5
Gorg Iran 111 E4
Gorgān Iran 110 D2
Gorgān, Khalīj-e Iran 110 D2
Gorge Range hills Australia 134 B5
Gorgona, Isla i. Col. 176 C3
Gorham NH U.S.A. 165 J1
Gori Georgia 108 F1
Gorinchem Neth. 62 E3
Goris Armenia 113 G3
Gorizia Italy 68 E2
Gorki Belarus see Horki
Gor'kiy Russia see Nizhniy Novgorod
Gor'kovskoye Vodokhranilishche resr Russia 52 I4
Gorlice Poland 53 D6
Görlitz Germany 57 O5
Gorlovka Ukr. see Horlivka
Gorna Dzhumaya Bulg. see Blagoevgrad
Gorna Oryahovitsa Bulg. 69 K3
Gornji Milanovac Serbia 69 I2
Gornji Vakuf Bos. & Herz. 68 G3
Gorno-Altaysk Russia 102 G1
Gorno-Altayskaya Avtonomnaya Oblast' aut. rep. Russia see Altay, Respublika
Gornotrakiyska Nizina lowland Bulg. 69 K3
Gornozavodsk Permskiy Kray Russia 51 R4
Gornozavodsk Sakhalinskaya Oblast' Russia 90 F3
Gornyak Russia 98 C2
Gornyy Russia 53 K6
Gornyy Altay aut. rep. Russia see Altay, Respublika
Gornyye Klyuchi Russia 90 D3
Goro i. Fiji see Koro
Gorodenka Ukr. see Horodenka
Gorodets Russia 52 I4
Gorodishche Penzenskaya Oblast' Russia 53 J5
Gorodishche Volgogradskaya Oblast' Russia 53 J6
Gorodok Belarus see Haradok
Gorodok Russia see Zakamensk
Gorodok Khmel'nyts'ka Oblast' Ukr. see Horodok
Gorodok L'vivs'ka Oblast' Ukr. see Horodok
Gorodovikovsk Russia 53 I7
Goroka P.N.G. 81 L8
Gorokhovets Russia 52 I4
Gorom Gorom Burkina Faso 120 C3
Gorong, Kepulauan is Moluccas Indon. 81 I7
Gorongosa mt. Moz. 123 D5
Gorongosa, Parque Nacional da nat. park Moz. 123 D5
Gorontalo Celebes Indon. 83 B2
Gorontalo prov. Indon. 83 B2
Gorshechnoye Russia 53 H6
Gort Ireland 61 D4
Gort an Choirce Ireland 61 D2
Gorūh Iran 110 E4
Gorutuba r. Brazil 179 C1
Goryachiy Klyuch Russia 113 E1
Goryeong S. Korea 91 C6
Görzke Germany 63 M2
Gorzów Wielkopolski Poland 57 O4
Gosainthan mt. China see Xixabangma Feng
Gose Japan 92 B4
Gosforth U.K. 58 F3
Goshen CA U.S.A. 158 D3
Goshen IN U.S.A. 164 C3
Goshen NH U.S.A. 165 I2
Goshen NY U.S.A. 165 H3
Goshen VA U.S.A. 164 F5
Goshiki Japan 92 A4
Goshoba Turkm. see Goşoba
Goslar Germany 63 K3
Goşoba Turkm. 113 I2
Gospić Croatia 68 F2
Gosport U.K. 59 F8
Gossi Mali 120 C3
Gostivar Macedonia 69 I4
Gosu China 96 C1
Göteborg Sweden see Gothenburg
Gotemba Japan see Gotenba
Gotenba Japan 93 E3
Götene Sweden 55 H7
Gotenhafen Poland see Gdynia
Gotha Germany 63 K4
Gothenburg Sweden 55 G8
Gothenburg NE U.S.A. 160 C3
Gotland i. Sweden 55 K8
Gotō-rettō is Japan 91 C6
Gotse Delchev Bulg. 69 J4
Gotska Sandön i. Sweden 55 K7
Gōtsu Japan 91 D6
Göttingen Germany 63 J3
Gott Peak Canada 150 F5
Gottwaldow Czech Rep. see Zlín
Gouda Neth. 62 E2
Goudiri Senegal 120 B3
Goudoumaria Niger 120 E3
Goûgaram Niger 120 D3

▶Gough Island S. Atlantic Ocean 184 H8
Dependency of Tristan da Cunha.

Gouin, Réservoir resr Canada 152 G4
Goulburn Australia 138 D5
Goulburn r. N.S.W. Australia 138 E4
Goulburn r. Vic. Australia 138 B6
Goulburn Islands Australia 134 F2
Goulburn River National Park Australia 138 E4
Gould Coast Antarctica 188 J1
Goulou atoll Micronesia see Ngulu
Goundam Mali 120 C3
Goundi Chad 121 E4
Goupil, Lac l. Canada 153 H3
Gouraya Alg. 67 G5
Gourcy Burkina Faso 120 C3
Gourdon France 66 E4
Gouré Niger 120 E3
Gouripur Bangl. 105 G4
Gourits r. S. Africa 124 E8
Gourma-Rharous Mali 120 C3
Gournay-en-Bray France 62 B5
Goussainville France 62 C5
Gouverneur NY U.S.A. 165 H1
Governador Valadares Brazil 179 C2
Governor Generoso Mindanao Phil. 82 D5
Governor's Harbour Bahamas 163 E7
Govĭ-Altay prov. Mongolia 94 C2
Govĭ Altayn Nuruu mts Mongolia 94 D2
Govind Ballash Pant Sagar resr India 105 E4
Govind Sagar resr India 99 B7
Govĭ-Ugtaal Mongolia 95 F2
Gowanda NY U.S.A. 165 F2
Gowan Range hills Australia 136 D5
Gowaqungo China 99 D7
Gowna, Lough l. Ireland 61 E4
Goya Arg. 178 E3
Göyçay Azer. 113 G2
Goyder watercourse Australia 135 F6
Göygöl Azer. 113 G2
Goýmatdag hills Turkm. 110 D1
Göynük Turkey 69 N4
Goyoum Cameroon 120 E4
Goz-Beïda Chad 121 F3
Gozen-yama Japan 93 G2
Gozha Co salt l. China 99 C6
Gözkaya Turkey 107 C1
Gozo i. Malta 68 F6
Graaff-Reinet S. Africa 124 G7
Grabfeld plain Germany 63 K4
Grabo Côte d'Ivoire 120 C4
Grabouw S. Africa 124 D8
Grabow Germany 63 L1
Gračac Croatia 68 F2
Gracefield Canada 152 F5
Gracey KY U.S.A. 164 B5
Grachi (abandoned) Kazakh. 98 B2
Gracias Hond. 166 [inset] H6
Gradaús, Serra dos hills Brazil 177 H5
Gradiška Bos. & Herz. see Bosanska Gradiška
Grady NM U.S.A. 161 C5
Gräfenhainichen Germany 63 M3
Grafenwöhr Germany 63 L5
Grafton Australia 138 F2
Grafton ND U.S.A. 160 D1
Grafton WI U.S.A. 164 B2
Grafton WV U.S.A. 164 E4
Grafton, Cape Australia 136 D3
Grafton, Mount NV U.S.A. 159 F2
Grafton Passage Australia 136 D3
Graham NC U.S.A. 162 E4
Graham TX U.S.A. 161 D5
Graham, Mount AZ U.S.A. 159 I5
Graham Bell Island Russia see Greem-Bell, Ostrov
Graham Island B.C. Canada 149 N5
Graham Island Nunavut Canada 147 I2
Graham Land reg. Antarctica 188 L2
Grahamstown S. Africa 125 H7
Grahovo Bos. & Herz. see Bosansko Grahovo
Graigue Ireland 61 F5
Grajagan Java Indon. 85 F5
Grajaú Brazil 177 I5
Grajaú r. Brazil 177 J4
Grammont Belgium see Geraardsbergen
Grammos mt. Greece 69 I4
Grampian Mountains U.K. 60 E4
Grampians National Park Australia 137 C8
Granada Nicaragua 166 [inset] I7
Granada Spain 67 E5
Granada CO U.S.A. 160 C4
Granard Ireland 61 E4
Granbury TX U.S.A. 161 D5
Granby Canada 153 G5
Gran Canaria i. Canary Is 120 B2
Gran Chaco reg. Arg./Para. 178 D3
Grand r. MO U.S.A. 164 B2
Grand r. SD U.S.A. 160 C2
Grand Atlas mts Morocco see Haut Atlas
Grand Bahama i. Bahamas 163 E7
Grand Ballon mt. France 57 K7
Grand Bank Canada 153 L5
Grand Banks of Newfoundland sea feature N. Atlantic Ocean 184 E3
Grand-Bassam Côte d'Ivoire 120 C4
Grand Bay-Westfield Canada 153 I5
Grand Bend Canada 164 E2
Grand Blanc MI U.S.A. 164 D2
Grand Canal Ireland 61 E4
Grand Canary i. Canary Is see Gran Canaria
Grand Canyon AZ U.S.A. 159 G3
Grand Canyon gorge AZ U.S.A. 159 G3
Grand Canyon National Park AZ U.S.A. 159 G3
Grand Canyon-Parashant National Monument nat. park AZ U.S.A. 159 G3
Grand Cayman i. Cayman Is 169 H5
Grand Drumont mt. France 57 K7
Grande r. Bahia Brazil 179 B1
Grande r. São Paulo Brazil 179 A3
Grande, Bahía b. Arg. 178 C8
Grande, Cerro mt. Mex. 167 F5
Grande, Ilha i. Brazil 179 B3
Grande Cache Canada 150 G4
Grande Comore i. Comoros see Ngazidja
Grande de Matagalpa r. Nicaragua 166 [inset] J6
Grande Prairie Canada 150 G4
Grand Erg Occidental des. Alg. 64 D5
Grand Erg Oriental des. Alg. 64 F6
Grande-Rivière Canada 153 I4
Grandes, Salinas salt marsh Arg. 178 C4
Gran Desierto del Pinacate, Parque Natural del nature res. Mex. 166 B2
Grande-Vallée Canada 153 I4
Grand Falls Canada 153 I5
Grand Falls-Windsor Canada 153 L4
Grand Forks Canada 150 G5
Grand Forks ND U.S.A. 160 D2
Grand Gorge NY U.S.A. 165 H2
Grand Haven MI U.S.A. 164 B2
Grandin, Lac l. Canada 150 G1
Grandioznyy, Pik mt. Russia 88 H2
Grand Island NE U.S.A. 160 D3
Grand Isle LA U.S.A. 161 F6
Grand Junction CO U.S.A. 159 I2
Grand-Lahou Côte d'Ivoire 120 C4
Grand Lake N.B. Canada 153 I5
Grand Lake Nfld. and Lab. Canada 153 J3
Grand Lake Nfld. and Lab. Canada 153 K4
Grand Lake LA U.S.A. 161 E6
Grand Lake MI U.S.A. 164 D1
Grand Lake St Marys OH U.S.A. 164 C3
Grand Ledge MI U.S.A. 164 C2
Grand Manan Island Canada 153 I5
Grand Marais MI U.S.A. 162 C2
Grand Marais MN U.S.A. 160 F2
Grand-Mère Canada 153 G5
Grand Mesa CO U.S.A. 159 J2
Grândola Port. 67 B4
Grand Passage New Caledonia 133 G3
Grand Pré, Landscape of tourist site Canada 153 I5
Grand Rapids Canada 151 L4
Grand Rapids MI U.S.A. 164 C2
Grand Rapids MN U.S.A. 160 E2
Grand-Sault Canada see Grand Falls
Grand St-Bernard, Col du pass Italy/Switz. see Great St Bernard Pass
Grand Teton mt. WY U.S.A. 156 F4
Grand Teton National Park WY U.S.A. 156 F4
Grand Traverse Bay MI U.S.A. 164 C1

▶Grand Turk Turks and Caicos Is 169 J4
Capital of the Turks and Caicos Islands.

Grandville MI U.S.A. 164 C2
Grandvilliers France 62 B5
Grand Wash Cliffs mts AZ U.S.A. 159 F4
Grange Ireland 61 E6
Grängesberg Sweden 55 I6
Grangeville ID U.S.A. 156 D3
Granisle Canada 150 E4
Granite Falls MN U.S.A. 160 E2
Granite Mountain hill AK U.S.A. 148 G2
Granite Mountain hill AK U.S.A. 148 H3
Granite Mountain NV U.S.A. 158 E1
Granite Mountains CA U.S.A. 159 F4
Granite Mountains CA U.S.A. 159 F5
Granite Peak MT U.S.A. 156 F3
Granite Peak UT U.S.A. 159 G1
Granite Range mts AK U.S.A. 149 K4
Granite Range mts NV U.S.A. 158 D1
Granitola, Capo c. Sicily Italy 68 E6
Granja Brazil 177 J4
Gran Laguna Salada l. Arg. 178 C6
Gränna Sweden 55 I7
Gran Paradiso mt. Italy 68 B2
Gran Paradiso, Parco Nazionale del nat. park Italy 68 B2
Gran Pilastro mt. Austria/Italy 57 M7
Gran San Bernardo, Colle del pass Italy/Switz. see Great St Bernard Pass
Gran Sasso e Monti della Laga, Parco Nazionale del nat. park Italy 68 E3
Granschütz Germany 63 M3
Gransee Germany 63 N1
Grant NE U.S.A. 160 C3
Grant, Mount NV U.S.A. 158 E2
Grant Creek AK U.S.A. 148 I2
Grantham U.K. 59 G6
Grant Island Antarctica 188 J2
Grant Lake Canada 150 G1
Grantown-on-Spey U.K. 60 F3
Grant Range mts NV U.S.A. 159 F2
Grants NM U.S.A. 159 J4
Grants Pass OR U.S.A. 156 C4
Grantsville UT U.S.A. 159 G1
Grantsville WV U.S.A. 164 E4
Granville France 66 D2
Granville AZ U.S.A. 159 I5
Granville NY U.S.A. 165 I2
Granville TN U.S.A. 164 C5
Granville (abandoned) Canada 149 M3
Granville Lake Canada 151 K3
Grão Mogol Brazil 179 C2
Grapevine Mountains NV U.S.A. 158 E3
Gras, Lac de l. Canada 151 I1
Graskop S. Africa 125 J3
Grasplatz Namibia 124 B4
Grass r. Canada 151 L3
Grass r. NY U.S.A. 165 H1
Grasse France 66 H5
Grassflat PA U.S.A. 165 F3
Grassington U.K. 58 F4
Grasslands National Park Canada 151 J5
Grass Range MT U.S.A. 156 F3
Grass Valley CA U.S.A. 158 C2
Grassy Butte ND U.S.A. 160 C2
Grästorp Sweden 55 H7
Gratz KY U.S.A. 164 C4
Graudenz Poland see Grudziądz
Graus Spain 67 G2
Gravataí Brazil 179 A5
Grave, Pointe de pt France 66 D4
Gravelbourg Canada 151 J5
Gravel Hill Lake Canada 151 K2
Gravelines France 62 C4
Gravelotte S. Africa 125 J2
Gravenhurst Canada 164 F1
Grave Peak ID U.S.A. 156 E3
Gravesend Australia 138 E2
Gravesend U.K. 59 H7
Gravina in Puglia Italy 68 G4
Grawn MI U.S.A. 164 C1
Gray France 66 G3
Gray GA U.S.A. 163 D5
Gray KY U.S.A. 164 C5
Gray ME U.S.A. 165 J2
Grayback Mountain OR U.S.A. 156 C4
Gray Lake Canada 151 I2
Grayling r. Canada 150 E3
Grayling AK U.S.A. 148 G3
Grayling MI U.S.A. 164 C1
Grayling Fork r. Canada/U.S.A. 149 L2
Grays U.K. 59 H7
Grays Harbor inlet WA U.S.A. 156 B3
Grays Lake ID U.S.A. 156 F4
Grayson KY U.S.A. 164 D4
Graz Austria 57 O7
Greasy Lake Canada 150 F2
Great Abaco i. Bahamas 163 E7
Great Australian Bight g. Australia 135 E8
Great Baddow U.K. 59 H7
Great Bahama Bank sea feature Bahamas 163 E7
Great Barrier Island N.Z. 139 E3
Great Barrier Reef Australia 136 D1
Great Barrier Reef Marine Park (Cairns Section) Australia 136 D3
Great Barrier Reef Marine Park (Capricorn Section) Australia 136 E4
Great Barrier Reef Marine Park (Central Section) Australia 136 E3
Great Barrier Reef Marine Park (Far North Section) Australia 136 D2
Great Barrington MA U.S.A. 165 I2
Great Basalt Wall National Park Australia 136 D3
Great Basin NV U.S.A. 158 E2
Great Basin National Park NV U.S.A. 159 F2
Great Bear r. Canada 149 P2

▶Great Bear Lake Canada 150 G1
4th largest lake in North America and 7th in the world.

Great Belt sea chan. Denmark 55 G9
Great Bend KS U.S.A. 160 D4
Great Bitter Lake Egypt 107 A4
Great Blasket Island Ireland 61 B5

▶Great Britain i. U.K. 56 G4
Largest island in Europe and 8th in the world.

Great Clifton U.K. 58 D4
Great Coco Island Cocos Is 80 A4
Great Cumbrae i. U.K. 60 E5
Great Dismal Swamp National Wildlife Refuge nature res. VA U.S.A. 165 G5
Great Dividing Range mts Australia 138 B6
Great Eastern Erg des. Alg. see Grand Erg Oriental
Greater Antarctica reg. Antarctica see East Antarctica
Greater Antilles is Caribbean Sea 169 H4
Greater Khingan Mountains China see Da Hinggan Ling
Greater Tunb i. The Gulf see Tonb-e Bozorg, Jazīreh-ye
Great Exuma i. Bahamas 163 F8
Great Falls MT U.S.A. 156 F3
Great Fish r. S. Africa 125 H7
Great Fish Point S. Africa 125 H7
Great Fish River Reserve Complex nature res. S. Africa 125 H7
Great Gandak r. India 105 F4
Great Ganges atoll Cook Is see Manihiki
Great Guana Cay i. Bahamas 163 E7
Great Himalayan National Park India 104 D3
Great Inagua i. Bahamas 169 J4
Great Karoo plat. S. Africa 124 F7
Great Kei r. S. Africa 125 I7
Great Lake Australia 137 [inset]
Great Limpopo Transfrontier Park Africa 125 J2
Great Malvern U.K. 59 E6
Great Meteor Tablemount sea feature N. Atlantic Ocean 184 G4
Great Namaqualand reg. Namibia 124 C4
Great Nicobar i. India 87 A6

Great Ormes Head hd U.K. 58 D5
Great Ouse r. U.K. 59 H6
Great Oyster Bay Australia 137 [inset]
Great Palm Islands Australia 136 D3
Great Plains NE U.S.A. 160 C3
Great Point MA U.S.A. 165 J3
Great Rift Valley Africa 122 D4
Great Ruaha r. Tanz. 123 D4
Great Sacandaga Lake NY U.S.A. 165 H2
Great St Bernard Pass Italy/Switz. 68 B2
Great Salt Lake UT U.S.A. 159 G1
Great Salt Lake Desert UT U.S.A. 159 G1
Great Sand Hills Canada 151 I5
Great Sand Sea des. Egypt/Libya 112 B5
Great Sandy Desert Australia 134 C5
Great Sandy Island Australia see Fraser Island
Great Sandy National Park Australia 136 F5
Great Sea Reef Fiji 133 H3
Great Sitkin Island AK U.S.A. 148 [inset] C5

▶Great Slave Lake Canada 150 H2
Deepest and 5th largest lake in North America and 10th largest in the world.

Great Smoky Mountains N. Carolina/Tennessee U.S.A. 163 C5
Great Smoky Mountains National Park N. Carolina/Tennessee U.S.A. 162 D5
Great Snow Mountain Canada 150 E3
Greatstone-on-Sea U.K. 59 H8
Great Stour r. U.K. 59 I7
Great Torrington U.K. 59 C8
Great Victoria Desert Australia 135 E7
Great Wall research station Antarctica 188 A2
Great Wall tourist site China 95 I3
Great Waltham U.K. 59 H7
Great Western Erg des. Alg. see Grand Erg Occidental
Great Western Torres Islands Myanmar 87 B5
Great Whernside hill U.K. 58 F4
Great Yarmouth U.K. 59 I6
Grebenkovskiy Ukr. see Hrebinka
Grebyonka Ukr. see Hrebinka
Greco, Cape Cyprus see Greko, Cape
Gredos, Sierra de mts Spain 67 D3
Greece country Europe 69 I5
Greece NY U.S.A. 165 G2
Greeley CO U.S.A. 156 G4
Greeley NE U.S.A. 160 D3
Greem-Bell, Ostrov i. Russia 76 H1
Green r. KY U.S.A. 164 B5
Green r. WY U.S.A. 159 I2
Green Bay WI U.S.A. 164 A1
Green Bay b. WI U.S.A. 164 B1
Greenbrier TN U.S.A. 164 B5
Greenbrier r. WV U.S.A. 164 E5
Green Cape Australia 138 E6
Greencastle Bahamas 163 E7
Greencastle U.K. 61 F3
Greencastle IN U.S.A. 164 B4
Green Cove Springs FL U.S.A. 163 D6
Greene ME U.S.A. 165 J1
Greene NY U.S.A. 165 H2
Greeneville TN U.S.A. 162 D4
Greenfield CA U.S.A. 158 C3
Greenfield IN U.S.A. 164 C4
Greenfield MA U.S.A. 165 I2
Greenfield OH U.S.A. 164 D4
Green Head hd Australia 135 A7
Greenhill Island Australia 134 F2
Green Island Taiwan see Lü Dao
Green Island Bay Palawan Phil. 82 B4
Green Lake Canada 151 J4

▶Greenland terr. N. America 147 N3
Self-governing Danish territory. Largest island in North America and the world, and 3rd largest political entity in North America.

Greenland Basin sea feature Arctic Ocean 189 I2
Greenland Fracture Zone sea feature Arctic Ocean 189 I1
Greenland Sea Greenland/Svalbard 76 A2
Greenlaw U.K. 60 G5
Green Mountains VT U.S.A. 165 I1
Greenock U.K. 60 E5
Greenore Ireland 61 F3
Greenough, Mount AK U.S.A. 149 L1
Greenport NY U.S.A. 165 I3
Green River P.N.G. 81 K7
Green River UT U.S.A. 159 H2
Green River WY U.S.A. 156 F4
Green River Lake KY U.S.A. 164 C5
Greensboro GA U.S.A. 163 D5
Greensburg IN U.S.A. 164 C4
Greensburg KS U.S.A. 160 D4
Greensburg KY U.S.A. 164 C5
Greensburg LA U.S.A. 161 F6
Greensburg PA U.S.A. 164 F3
Greens Peak NM U.S.A. 159 I4
Greenstone Point U.K. 60 D3
Green Swamp NC U.S.A. 163 E5
Greentown IN U.S.A. 164 C3
Greenup IL U.S.A. 160 F4
Greenup KY U.S.A. 164 D4
Green Valley Canada 165 H1
Green Valley AZ U.S.A. 159 H6
Greenville Canada see Laxgalts'ap
Greenville Liberia 120 C4
Greenville AL U.S.A. 163 C6
Greenville IL U.S.A. 160 F4
Greenville KY U.S.A. 164 B5
Greenville ME U.S.A. 162 G2
Greenville MI U.S.A. 164 C2
Greenville MS U.S.A. 161 F5
Greenville NC U.S.A. 162 E5
Greenville NH U.S.A. 165 J2
Greenville OH U.S.A. 164 C3
Greenville PA U.S.A. 164 E3
Greenville SC U.S.A. 163 D5
Greenville TX U.S.A. 161 D5
Greenwich atoll Micronesia see Kapingamarangi
Greenwich CT U.S.A. 165 I3
Greenwich OH U.S.A. 164 D3
Greenwood AR U.S.A. 161 E5
Greenwood IN U.S.A. 164 B4
Greenwood MS U.S.A. 161 F5
Greenwood SC U.S.A. 163 D5
Gregory r. Australia 136 B3
Gregory, Lake salt flat S.A. Australia 137 B6
Gregory, Lake salt flat W.A. Australia 134 D5
Gregory, Lake salt flat W.A. Australia 135 B6
Gregory Downs Australia 136 B3
Gregory National Park Australia 134 E4
Gregory Range hills Qld Australia 136 C3
Gregory Range hills W.A. Australia 134 C5
Greifswald Germany 57 N3
Greiz Germany 63 M4
Greko, Cape Cyprus 107 B2
Gremyachinsk Russia 51 R4
Grenå Denmark see Grenaa
Grenaa Denmark 55 G8
Grenada MS U.S.A. 161 F5
Grenada country West Indies 169 L6
Grenade France 66 E5
Grenen spit Denmark 55 G8
Grenfell Australia 138 D4
Grenfell Canada 151 K5
Grenoble France 66 G4
Grense-Jakobselv Norway 54 Q2
Grenville, Cape Australia 136 C1
Grenville Island Fiji see Rotuma
Greshak Pak. 111 G5
Gresham OR U.S.A. 156 C3
Gresik Java Indon. 85 F4
Gressåmoen Nasjonalpark nat. park Norway 54 H4
Greta r. U.K. 58 E4
Gretna U.K. 60 F6
Gretna LA U.S.A. 161 F6
Gretna VA U.S.A. 164 F5
Greußen Germany 63 K3
Grevelingen sea chan. Neth. 62 D3
Greven Germany 63 H2
Grevena Greece 69 I4
Grevenbicht Neth. 62 F3
Grevenbroich Germany 62 G3
Grevenmacher Lux. 62 G5
Grevesmühlen Germany 57 M4
Grey, Cape Australia 136 B2
Greybull WY U.S.A. 156 F3
Greybull r. WY U.S.A. 156 F3
Grey Hunter Peak Canada 149 N3
Grey Islands Canada 153 L4
Greylock, Mount MA U.S.A. 165 I2
Greymouth N.Z. 139 C6
Grey Range hills Australia 138 A2
Grey's Plains Australia 135 A6
Greytown S. Africa 125 J5
Grez-Doiceau Belgium 62 E4
Gribanovskiy Russia 53 I6
Gridley CA U.S.A. 158 C2
Griffin GA U.S.A. 163 C5
Griffin Point pt AK U.S.A. 149 L1
Griffith Australia 138 C5
Grigan i. N. Mariana Is see Agrihan
Grik Malaysia see Gerik
Grim, Cape Australia 137 [inset]
Grimari Cent. Afr. Rep. 122 C3
Grimma Germany 63 M3
Grimmen Germany 57 N3
Grimnitzsee l. Germany 63 N2
Grimsby U.K. 58 G5
Grímsey i. Iceland 54 [inset 1]
Grimshaw Canada 150 G3
Grímsstaðir Iceland 54 [inset 1]
Grimstad Norway 55 F7
Grindavík Iceland 54 [inset 1]
Grindsted Denmark 55 F9
Grind Stone City MI U.S.A. 164 D1
Grindul Chituc spit Romania 69 M2
Grinnell Peninsula Canada 147 I2
Griqualand East reg. S. Africa 125 I6
Griqualand West reg. S. Africa 124 F5
Griquatown S. Africa 124 F5
Grise Fiord Canada 147 J2
Grishino Ukr. see Krasnoarmiys'k
Grisik Sumatra Indon. 84 C3
Gris Nez, Cap c. France 62 B4
Gritley U.K. 60 G2
Grizzly Bear Mountain hill Canada 150 F1
Grmeč mts Bos. & Herz. 68 G2
Grobbendonk Belgium 62 E3
Groblersdal S. Africa 125 I3
Groblershoop S. Africa 124 F5
Grodno Belarus see Hrodna
Groen watercourse N. Cape S. Africa 124 F6
Groen watercourse Northern Cape/Western Cape S. Africa 124 C6
Groix, Île de i. France 66 C3
Grombalia Tunisia 68 D6
Gronau (Westfalen) Germany 62 H2
Grong Norway 54 H4
Groningen Neth. 62 G1
Groninger Wad tidal flat Neth. 62 G1
Grønland terr. N. America see Greenland
Groom Lake NV U.S.A. 159 F3
Groot-Aar Pan salt pan S. Africa 124 E4
Groot Berg r. S. Africa 124 D7
Groot Brakrivier S. Africa 124 F8
Grootdraaidam dam S. Africa 125 I4
Grootdrink S. Africa 124 E5
Groote Eylandt i. Australia 136 B2
Grootfontein Namibia 123 B5
Groot Karas Berg plat. Namibia 124 D4
Groot Letaba r. S. Africa 125 J2
Groot Marico S. Africa 125 H3
Groot Swartberge mts S. Africa 124 E7
Grootvloer salt pan S. Africa 124 E5
Groot Winterberg mt. S. Africa 125 H7
Gros Morne National Park Canada 153 K4
Gross Barmen Namibia 124 C2
Große Aue r. Germany 63 J2
Große Laaber r. Germany 63 M6
Großengottern Germany 63 K3
Großenkneten Germany 63 I2
Großenlüder Germany 63 J4
Großer Arber mt. Germany 63 N5
Großer Beerberg hill Germany 63 K4
Großer Eyberg hill Germany 63 H5
Großer Gleichberg hill Germany 63 K4
Großer Kornberg hill Germany 63 M4
Großer Osser mt. Czech Rep./Germany 63 N5
Großer Rachel mt. Germany 57 N6
Grosser Speikkogel mt. Austria 57 O7
Grosseto Italy 68 D3
Grossevichi Russia 90 E3
Groß-Gerau Germany 63 I5
Großglockner mt. Austria 57 N7
Groß Oesingen Germany 63 K2
Großrudestedt Germany 63 L3
Groß Schönebeck Germany 63 N2
Gross Ums Namibia 124 D2
Großvenediger mt. Austria 57 N7
Gros Ventre Range mts WY U.S.A. 156 F4
Groswater Bay Canada 153 K3
Groton SD U.S.A. 160 D2
Grottoes VA U.S.A. 165 F4
Grou Neth. 62 F1
Groundhog r. Canada 152 E4
Grouw Neth. see Grou
Grove OK U.S.A. 161 E4
Grove City OH U.S.A. 164 D4
Grove Hill AL U.S.A. 163 C6
Grove Mountains Antarctica 188 E2
Grover Beach CA U.S.A. 158 C4
Grovertown IN U.S.A. 164 B3
Groveton NH U.S.A. 165 J1
Groveton TX U.S.A. 161 E6
Growler Mountains AZ U.S.A. 159 G5
Groznyy Russia 113 G2
Grubišno Polje Croatia 68 G2
Grudovo Bulg. see Sredets
Grudziądz Poland 57 Q4
Grünau Namibia 124 D4
Grünberg Poland see Zielona Góra
Grundarfjörður Iceland 54 [inset 1]
Grundy VA U.S.A. 164 D5
Gruñidora Mex. 161 C7
Grünstadt Germany 63 I5
Gruver TX U.S.A. 161 C4
Gruzinskaya S.S.R. country Asia see Georgia
Gryazi Russia 53 H5
Gryazovets Russia 52 I4
Gryfice Poland 57 O4
Gryfino Poland 57 O4
Gryfów Śląski Poland 57 O5
Gryllefjord Norway 54 J2
Grytviken S. Georgia 178 I8
Gua India 105 F5
Guacanayabo, Golfo de b. Cuba 169 I4
Guachochi Mex. 157 G8
Guadajoz r. Spain 67 D5
Guadalajara Mex. 168 D4
Guadalajara Spain 67 E3
Guadalcanal i. Solomon Is 133 G2
Guadalete r. Spain 67 C5
Guadalope r. Spain 67 F3
Guadalquivir r. Spain 67 C5
Guadalupe Nuevo León Mex. 167 E3
Guadalupe Zacatecas Mex. 166 E4
Guadalupe i. Mex. 166 A2
Guadalupe watercourse Mex. 158 E5
Guadalupe CA U.S.A. 158 C4
Guadalupe r. TX U.S.A. 167 F2
Guadalupe, Sierra de mts Spain 67 D4
Guadalupe Aguilera Mex. 161 B7
Guadalupe Bravos Mex. 157 G7
Guadalupe Mountains National Park TX U.S.A. 157 G7
Guadalupe Peak TX U.S.A. 157 G7
Guadalupe Victoria Baja California Mex. 159 F5
Guadalupe Victoria Durango Mex. 161 B7
Guadalupe y Calvo Mex. 166 D3
Guadarrama, Sierra de mts Spain 67 D3

▶Guadeloupe terr. West Indies 169 L5
French Overseas Department.

Guadeloupe Passage Caribbean Sea 169 L5
Guadiana r. Port./Spain 67 C5
Guadix Spain 67 E5
Guafo, Isla i. Chile 178 B6
Guagua Luzon Phil. 82 C3
Guaíba Brazil 179 A5
Guaiçuí Brazil 179 B2
Guaíra Brazil 178 F2
Guajaba, Cayo i. Cuba 163 E8
Guaje, Laguna de l. Mex. 166 E2
Guaje, Llano de plain Mex. 166 E3
Guajira, Península de la pen. Col. 176 D1
Gualala CA U.S.A. 158 B2
Gualán Guat. 167 H6
Gualeguay Arg. 178 E4
Gualeguaychu Arg. 178 E4
Gualicho, Salina salt flat Arg. 178 C6

▶Guam terr. N. Pacific Ocean 81 K4
United States Unincorporated Territory.

Guamblin, Isla i. Chile 178 A6
Guampí, Sierra de mts Venez. 176 E2
Guamúchil Mex. 166 C3
Gua Musang Malaysia 84 C1
Gu'an China 95 I4
Guanabacoa Cuba 163 D8
Guanacaste, Cordillera de mts Costa Rica 166 [inset] I7
Guanacaste, Parque Nacional nat. park Costa Rica 166 [inset] I7
Guanacevi Mex. 166 D3
Guanahacabibes, Península de pen. Cuba 163 C8
Guanaja Hond. 166 [inset] I5
Guanajay Cuba 163 D8
Guanajuato Mex. 168 D4
Guanajuato state Mex. 167 E4
Guanambi Brazil 179 C1
Guanare Venez. 176 E2
Guandaokou China 95 G5
Guandi Shan mt. China 95 G4
Guandu China 97 G3
Guane Cuba 169 H4
Guang'an China 96 E2
Guangchang China 97 H3
Guangdong prov. China 97 [inset]
Guanghai China 97 G4
Guanghan China 96 E2
Guanghua China see Laohekou
Guangling China 95 H4
Guangming China see Xide
Guangming Ding mt. China 97 H2
Guangnan China 96 E3
Guangning China see Beizhen
Guangrao China 95 I4
Guangshan China 97 G2
Guangxi aut. reg. China see Guangxi Zhuangzu Zizhiqu
Guangxi Zhuangzu Zizhiqu aut. reg. China 96 F4
Guangyuan China 96 E1
Guangze China 97 H3
Guangzhou China 97 G4
Guangzong China 95 H4
Guanhães Brazil 179 C2
Guan He r. China 95 I5
Guanhe Kou r. mouth China 95 I5
Guanipa r. Venez. 176 F2
Guanling China 96 E3
Guanmian Shan mts China 97 F2
Guannan China 97 H1
Guanpo China 97 F1
Guanshui China 90 B4
Guansuo China see Guanling
Guantánamo Cuba 169 I4
Guantao China 95 H4
Guanting China 94 E5
Guanxian China see Dujiangyan
Guanyang China 97 F3
Guanyinqiao China 96 D2
Guanyun China 95 I5
Guapé Brazil 179 B3
Guapí Col. 176 C3
Guápiles Costa Rica 166 [inset] J7
Guaporé r. Bol./Brazil 176 E6
Guaporé Brazil 179 A5
Guaqui Bol. 176 E7
Guará r. Brazil 179 B1
Guarabira Brazil 177 K5
Guaranda Ecuador 176 C4
Guarapari Brazil 179 C3
Guarapuava Brazil 179 A4
Guararapes Brazil 179 A3
Guaratinguetá Brazil 179 B3
Guaratuba Brazil 179 A4
Guaratuba, Baía de b. Brazil 179 A4
Guarda Port. 67 C3
Guardafui, Cape Somalia see Gwardafuy, Gees
Guardiagrele Italy 68 F3
Guardo Spain 67 D2
Guárico, del Embalse resr Venez. 176 E2
Guarujá Brazil 179 B3
Guasave Mex. 166 C3
Guasdualito Venez. 176 D2
Guastatoya Guat. 167 H6

▶Guatemala country Central America 167 H6
4th most populous country in North America.

Guatemala Guat. see Guatemala City

▶Guatemala City Guat. 167 H6
Capital of Guatemala.

Guaviare r. Col. 176 E3
Guaxupé Brazil 179 B3
Guayaquil Ecuador 176 C4
Guayaquil, Golfo de g. Ecuador 176 B4
Guaymas Mex. 166 C3
Guazacapán Guat. 167 H6
Guazhou Gansu China 94 C3
Guazhou Gansu China 94 C3
Guba Eth. 122 D2
Gubakha Russia 51 R4
Gubat Luzon Phil. 82 D3
Gubbi India 106 C3
Gubeikou China 95 I3
Gubio Nigeria 120 E3
Gubkin Russia 53 H6
Gucheng Gansu China 94 D3
Gucheng Gansu China 94 E4
Gucheng Hebei China 95 H4
Gucheng Hubei China 97 F1
Gucheng Shanxi China 95 G5
Gucheng Yunnan China 96 D3
Guchin-Us Mongolia 94 E2
Gudari India 106 D2
Gudbrandsdalen valley Norway 55 F6
Gudermes Russia 113 G2
Gudivada India 106 D2
Gudiyattam India 106 C3
Gudur Andhra Prad. India 106 C3
Gudur Andhra Prad. India 106 C3
Gudvangen Norway 55 E6
Gudzhal r. Russia 90 D2
Gué, Rivière du r. Canada 153 H2
Guecho Spain see Algorta
Guéckédou Guinea 120 B4
Guelma Alg. 68 B6
Guelmim Morocco 120 B2
Guelph Canada 164 E2
Guémez Mex. 161 D8
Guénange France 62 G5
Guerara Alg. 64 E5
Guérard, Lac l. Canada 153 I2
Guercif Morocco 64 D5
Guéret France 66 E3

▶Guernsey terr. Channel Is 59 E9
United Kingdom Crown Dependency.

Guernsey WY U.S.A. 156 G4
Guérou Mauritania 120 B3
Guerrah Et-Tarf salt pan Alg. 68 B7
Guerrero Mex. 167 F3
Guerrero state Mex. 167 E5
Guerrero Negro Mex. 166 B3
Guers, Lac l. Canada 153 I2
Gueugnon France 66 G3
Gufeng China see Pingnan
Gufu China see Xingshan
Gugē mt. Eth. 122 D3
Gūgerd, Kūh-e mts Iran 110 D3
Guguan i. N. Mariana Is 81 L3
Guhakolak, Tanjung pt Indon. 84 D4
Guhe China 97 H2
Gūh Kūh mt. Iran 110 E5
Guhrān Iran 110 E5
Guhuai China see Pingyu
Guiana Basin sea feature N. Atlantic Ocean 184 E5
Guiana Highlands mts S. America 176 E2
Guichi China see Chizhou
Guichicovi Mex. 167 G5
Guidan-Roumji Niger 120 D3
Guide China 94 E5
Guider Cameroon 121 E4
Guiding China 96 E3
Guidong China 97 G3
Guidonia Montecelio Italy 68 E4
Guigang China 97 F4
Guiglo Côte d'Ivoire 120 C4
Guignicourt France 62 D5
Guija Moz. 125 K3
Guiji Shan mts China 97 I2
Guildford U.K. 59 G7
Guilford ME U.S.A. 162 G2
Guilherme Capelo Angola see Cacongo
Guilin China 97 F3
Guillaume-Delisle, Lac l. Canada 152 F2
Guimarães Brazil 177 J4
Guimarães Port. 67 B3
Guimaras i. Phil. 82 C4
Guimaras Strait Phil. 82 C4
Guimeng Ding mt. China 95 I5
Guinan China see Mangra
Guindulman Bohol Phil. 82 D4
Guinea country Africa 120 B3
Guinea, Gulf of Africa 120 D4
Guinea Basin sea feature N. Atlantic Ocean 184 H5
Guinea-Bissau country Africa 120 B3
Guinea-Conakry country Africa see Guinea
Guinea Ecuatorial country Africa see Equatorial Guinea
Guiné-Bissau country Africa see Guinea-Bissau
Guinée country Africa see Guinea
Güines Cuba 169 H4
Guînes France 62 B4
Guines, Lac l. Canada 153 J3
Guingamp France 66 C2
Guiones, Punta pt Costa Rica 166 [inset] I7
Guipavas France 66 B2
Guiping China 97 F4
Güira de Melena Cuba 163 D8
Guiratinga Brazil 177 H7
Guiscard France 62 D5
Guise France 62 D5
Guishan China see Xinping
Guishan Dao i. Taiwan 97 I3
Guishun China 96 E3
Guiuan Samar Phil. 82 D4
Guixi Chongqing China see Dianjiang
Guixi Jiangxi China 97 H2
Guiyang Guizhou China 96 E3
Guiyang Hunan China 97 G3
Guizhou prov. China 96 E3
Guizi China 97 F4
Gujarat state India 104 C5
Gujar Khan Pak. 111 I3
Gujerat state India see Gujarat
Gujiao China 95 H4
Gujō Japan 92 C3
Gujranwala Pak. 111 I3
Gujrat Pak. 111 I3
Gukovo Russia 53 H6
Gulabgarh India 104 D2
Gulang China 94 E4
Gulbarga India see Kalaburagi
Gulbene Latvia 55 O8
Gul'cha Kyrg. see Gülchö
Gülchö Kyrg. 102 D3
Gülcihan Turkey 107 B1
Gülek Boğazı pass Turkey 112 D3
Gulf of Chihli China see Bo Hai
Gulfport MS U.S.A. 161 F6
Gulgong Australia 138 D4
Gulian China 90 A1
Gulin China 96 E3
Gulistan Uzbek. see Guliston
Guliston Uzbek. 102 C3
Gulitel hill Palau 82 [inset]
Gülitz Germany 63 L1
Guliya Shan mt. China 95 J1
Gulja China see Yining
Gul Kach Pak. 111 H4
Gulkana AK U.S.A. 149 K3
Gul'kevichi Russia 113 F1
Gull Lake Canada 151 I5
Gullrock Lake Canada 151 M5
Gullträsk Sweden 54 L3
Güllük Körfezi b. Turkey 69 L6
Gülnar Turkey 107 A1
Gul'shat Kazakh. 98 A3
Gulü China see Xincai
Gulu Uganda 122 D3
Guluwuru Island Australia 136 B1
Gulyayevskiye Koshki, Ostrova is Russia 52 L1
Guma China see Pishan
Gumal r. Pak. 111 H4
Gumare Botswana 123 C5
Gumbaz Pak. 111 H4
Gumbinnen Russia see Gusev
Gumdag Turkm. 110 D2
Gumel Nigeria 120 D3
Gümgüm Turkey see Varto
Gumi S. Korea 91 C5
Gumla India 105 F5
Gumma Japan see Gunma
Gumma pref. Japan see Gunma
Gummersbach Germany 63 H3
Gumpang r. Indon. 84 B1
Gümüşhacıköy Turkey 112 D2
Gümüşhane Turkey 113 E2
Guna India 104 D4
Gunan China see Qijiang
Guna Terara mt. Eth. 108 E7
Gunbar Australia 138 B5
Gunbower Australia 138 B5
Güncang China 96 B2
Gund r. Tajik. see Gunt
Gundabooka National Park nat. park Australia 137 D6
Gundagai Australia 138 D5
Gundelsheim Germany 63 J5
Güney Turkey 69 M5
Güneydoğu Toroslar plat. Turkey 112 F3
Gunglilap Myanmar 86 B1
Gungu Dem. Rep. Congo 123 B4
Gunib Russia 113 G2
Gunisao r. Canada 151 L4
Gunisao Lake Canada 151 L4
Gunma Japan 93 F2
Gunma pref. Japan 93 E2
Gunnaur India 104 D3
Gunnbjørn Fjeld nunatak Greenland 147 P3
Gunnedah Australia 138 E3
Gunning Australia 138 D5
Gunnison CO U.S.A. 157 G5
Gunnison r. CO U.S.A. 159 I2
Gunong Ayer Sarawak Malaysia see Gunung Ayer
Güns Hungary see Kszeg
Gunsan S. Korea 91 B6
Gunt r. Tajik. 111 H2
Guntakal India 106 C3
Güntersberge Germany 63 K3
Guntur India 106 D2
Gunungapi i. Moluccas Indon. 83 C4
Gunung Ayer Sarawak Malaysia 85 E2
Gunungbatubesar Kalimantan Indon. 85 G3
Gunung Gading National Park Malaysia 85 E2
Gunung Gede Pangrango, Taman Nasional nat. park Indon. 84 D4
Gunung Halimun, Taman Nasional nat. park Indon. 84 D4
Gunung Leuser, Taman Nasional nat. park Indon. 84 B2
Gunung Mulu National Park Malaysia 85 F1
Gunung Niyut, Suaka Margasatwa nature res. Indon. 85 E2
Gunung Palung, Taman Nasional nat. park Indon. 85 E3
Gunung Rinjani, Taman Nasional nat. park Lombok Indon. 85 G5
Gunungsitoli Sumatra Indon. 84 B2
Gunungsugih Sumatra Indon. 84 D4
Gunungtua Sumatra Indon. 84 B2
Günyüzü Turkey 112 C3
Gunza Angola see Porto Amboim
Günzburg Germany 57 M6
Gunzenhausen Germany 63 K5
Guochengyi China 94 F4
Guo He r. China 95 H5
Guo He r. China 97 H1
Guojia China 94 F5
Guojiatun China 95 I3
Guoluezhen China see Lingbao
Guovdageaidnu Norway see Kautokeino
Guoyang China 95 I5
Guozhen China see Chencang
Gupis Pak. 104 C1
Gurban Obo China 95 H3
Gurbantünggüt Shamo des. China 98 D3
Gurdaspur India 104 C2
Gurdon AR U.S.A. 161 E5
Gurdzhaani Georgia see Gurjaani
Güre Turkey 69 M5
Gurgan Iran see Gorgān
Gurgaon India 104 D3
Gurgei, Jebel mt. Sudan 121 F3
Gurha India 104 B4
Guri, Embalse de resr Venez. 176 F2
Gurinhatã Brazil 179 A2
Gurjaani Georgia 113 G2
Gur Khar Iran 111 E4
Guro Moz. 123 D5
Gurşunmagdan Kärhanasy Turkm. 111 G2
Guru China 105 G3
Gürün Turkey 112 E3
Gurupá Brazil 177 H4
Gurupi Brazil 177 I6
Gurupi r. Brazil 177 I4
Gurupi, Serra do hills Brazil 177 I4
Guru Sikhar mt. India 104 C4
Guruzala India 106 C2
Gurvandzagal Mongolia 95 H1
Gurvansayhan Mongolia 95 F2

Gurvan Sayhan Nuruu mts Mongolia 94 E3
Gurvantes Mongolia 94 E3
Gur'yev Kazakh. see Atyrau
Gur'yevsk Russia 55 L9
Gur'yevskaya Oblast' admin. div. Kazakh. see Atyrauskaya Oblast'
Gusau Nigeria 120 D3
Güsen Germany 63 L2
Gusev Russia 55 M9
Gushan China 91 A5
Gushgy Turkm. see Serhetabat
Gushi China 97 G1
Gusino Russia 53 F5
Gusinoozersk Russia 94 F1
Gusinoye, Ozero l. Russia 94 F1
Gus'-Khrustal'nyy Russia 52 I5
Guspini Sardinia Italy 68 C5
Gustav Holm, Kap c. Greenland see Tasiilap Karra
Gustavo Sotelo Mex. 166 B2
Gustavus AK U.S.A. 149 N4
Güsten Germany 63 L3
Gustine CA U.S.A. 158 C3
Güstrow Germany 57 N4
Gutang China 99 F7
Güterfelde Germany 63 N2
Gütersloh Germany 63 I3
Guthrie AZ U.S.A. 159 I5
Guthrie KY U.S.A. 164 B5
Guthrie OK U.S.A. 161 D5
Guthrie TX U.S.A. 161 C5
Gutian Fujian China 97 H3
Gutian Fujian China 97 H3
Gutian Shuiku resr China 97 H3
Guting China see Yutai
Gutsuo China 105 F3
Guwahati India 105 G4
Guwlumaýak Turkm. 110 D1
Guxhagen Germany 63 J3
Guxian China 97 G3
Guyana country S. America 177 G2
Guyane Française terr. S. America see French Guiana
Guyang Hunan China see Guzhang
Guyang Nei Mongol China 95 G3
Guyenne reg. France 66 D4
Guy Fawkes River National Park Australia 138 F3
Guyi China see Sanjiang
Guymon OK U.S.A. 161 C4
Guyot Glacier Canada/U.S.A. 149 L3
Guyra Australia 138 E3
Guysborough Canada 153 J5
Guyuan Hebei China 95 H3
Guyuan Ningxia China 94 F5
Gužarah Afgh. 111 F3
Güzeloluk Turkey 107 B1
Güzelyurt Cyprus see Morfou
Guzhang China 97 F2
Guzhen China 97 H1
Guzhou China see Rongjiang
Guzmán Mex. 166 D2
Guzmán, Lago de l. Mex. 166 D2
G'uzor Uzbek. 111 G2
Gvardeysk Russia 55 L9
Gvasyugi Russia 90 E3
Gwa Myanmar 86 A3
Gwabegar Australia 138 D3
Gwadar West Bay Pak. 111 F5
Gwaii Haanas Canada 149 N5
Gwaii Haanas National Park Reserve and Haida Heritage Site Canada 150 D4
Gwaldam India 99 B7
Gwal Haidarzai Pak. 111 H4
Gwalior India 104 D4
Gwanda Zimbabwe 123 C6
Gwane Dem. Rep. Congo 122 C3
Gwangcheon S. Korea 91 B5
Gwangju S. Korea 91 B6
Gwardafuy, Gees c. Somalia 122 F2
Gwash Pak. 111 G4
Gwatar Bay Pak. 111 F5
Gwedaukkon Myanmar 86 A1
Gweebarra Bay Ireland 61 D3
Gwelo Zimbabwe see Gweru
Gwêr Iraq 113 F3
Gweru Zimbabwe 123 C5
Gweta Botswana 123 C6
Gwinner ND U.S.A. 160 D2
Gwoza Nigeria 120 E3
Gwydir r. Australia 138 D2
Gyablung China 99 F7
Gyaca China 99 F7
Gyaco China 99 C6
Gyagartang China 96 D1
Gyaijêpozhanggê China see Zhidoi
Gyai Qu r. China 99 F7
Gyaisi China see Jiulong
Gyali i. Greece 69 L6
Gyamug China 99 C6
Gyandzha Azer. see Gäncä
Gyangnyi Caka salt l. China 99 D6
Gyangrang China 99 D7
Gyangtse China see Gyangzê
Gyangzê China 99 E7
Gya'nyima China 99 C7
Gyaring China 94 D5
Gyaring Co l. China 99 E7
Gyaring Hu l. China 94 D5
Gyarishing India 96 B2
Gyaros i. Greece 69 K6
Gyarubtang China 96 B2
Gydan, Khrebet mts Russia see Kolymskoye Nagor'ye
Gydan Peninsula Russia 76 I2
Gydanskiy Poluostrov pen. Russia see Gydan Peninsula
Gyêgu China see Yushu
Gyêmdong China 99 F7
Gyêsar Co l. China 99 D7
Gyêwa China see Zabqung
Gyimda China 99 F7
Gyipug China 99 C6
Gyirong Xizang China 99 D7
Gyirong Xizang China 99 D7
Gyitang China 99 F7
Gyixong China see Gonggar
Gyiza China 99 F6
Gyldenløve Fjord inlet Greenland see Umiiviip Kangertiva
Gympie Australia 137 F5
Gyobingauk Myanmar 86 A3
Gyōda Japan 93 F2
Gyöngyös Hungary 57 Q7
Győr Hungary 68 G1
Gypsum Point Canada 150 H2
Gypsumville Canada 151 L5
Gyrfalcon Islands Canada 153 H2
Gytheio Greece 69 J6
Gyula Hungary 69 I1
Gyulafehérvár Romania see Alba Iulia
Gyümai China see Tarlag
Gyumri Armenia 113 F2
Gyungcang China 99 B6
Gyzylarbat Turkm. see Serdar
Gyzylbaýdak Turkm. 111 F2
Gzhatsk Russia see Gagarin

Haa Bhutan 105 G4
Haa-Alif Atoll Maldives see Ihavandhippolhu
Ha'apai Group is Tonga 133 I3
Haapajärvi Fin. 54 N5
Haapavesi Fin. 54 N4
Haapsalu Estonia 55 M7
Ha 'Arava watercourse Israel/Jordan see 'Arabah, Wādī al
Ha'Arava, Naḥal watercourse Israel/Jordan see Jayb, Wādī al
Haarlem Neth. 62 E2
Haarlem S. Africa 124 F7
Haarstrang ridge Germany 63 H3
Hab r. Pak. 111 G5
Habahe China 98 D2
Habana Cuba see Havana
Habarane Sri Lanka 106 D4
Habarōn well Saudi Arabia 110 C6
Habaswein Kenya 122 D3
Habay Canada 150 G3
Ḥabbān Yemen 108 G7
Ḥabbānīyah, Hawr al l. Iraq 113 F4
Hab Chauki Pak. 111 G5
Habiganj Bangl. 105 G4
Habikino Japan 92 B4
Habirag China 95 H3
Habra India 105 G5
Hachibuse-yama mt. Japan 93 E2
Hachijō-jima i. Japan 91 E6
Hachikai Japan 92 C3
Hachiman-misaki c. Japan 93 G3
Hachimori-yama mt. Japan 92 D2
Hachinohe Japan 90 F4
Hachiōji Japan 93 F3
Hachita NM U.S.A. 159 I6
Hacıköy Turkey see Çekerek
Hacıqabul Azer. 113 H2
Hack, Mount Australia 137 B6
Hackberry AZ U.S.A. 159 G4
Hackensack NJ U.S.A. 165 H3
Hacufera Moz. 123 D6
Ḥaḍabat al Jilf al Kabīr plat. Egypt see Jilf al Kabīr, Haḍabat al
Hadadong China 98 C4
Hadagalli India 106 B3
Hadano Japan 93 F3
Hadapu China 94 F5
Hadat China 95 I1
Hadayang China 95 K1
Ḥadd, Ra's al pt Oman 111 E6
Haddington U.K. 60 G5
Haddumati Atoll Maldives see Hahdhunmathi
Haddunmahti Atoll Maldives see Hahdhunmathi
Hadejia Nigeria 120 E3
Hadera Israel 107 B3
Ḥadera, Naḥal r. Israel 107 B3
Haderslev Denmark 55 F9
Hadhramaut reg. Yemen see Ḥaḍramawt
Hādī, Jabal al mts Jordan 107 C4
Hadilik China 99 D5
Hadım Turkey 112 D3
Hadjer Hadid Chad 121 F3
Hadleigh U.K. 59 H6
Hadong S. Korea 91 B6
Ḥaḍraj, Wādī watercourse Saudi Arabia 107 C4
Ḥaḍramawt reg. Yemen 122 E2
Hadranum Sicily Italy see Adrano
Hadrian's Wall tourist site U.K. 58 E3
Hadrumetum Tunisia see Sousse
Hadsund Denmark 55 G8
Hadweenzic r. AK U.S.A. 149 K2
Hadyach Ukr. 53 G6
Haeju N. Korea 91 B5
Haeju-man b. N. Korea 91 B5
Haenam S. Korea 91 B6
Haenertsburg S. Africa 125 I2
Ha'erbin China see Harbin
Ha'ertao China 95 J3
Ḥafar al 'Atk well Saudi Arabia 110 B5
Ḥafar al Bāṭin Saudi Arabia 108 G4
Hafford Canada 151 J4
Hafik Turkey 112 E3
Ḥafīrah, Qā' al salt pan Jordan 107 C4
Hafirat Nasah Saudi Arabia 110 B5
Hafizabad Pak. 111 I3
Haflong India 105 H4
Hafnarfjörður Iceland 54 [inset 1]
Haftgel Iran 110 C4
Hafursfjörður b. Iceland 54 [inset 1]
Haga Myanmar see Haka
Hagachi-zaki pt Japan 93 E4
Hagar Nish Plateau Eritrea 108 E6

▶Hagåtña Guam 81 K4
Capital of Guam.

Hagelberg hill Germany 63 M2
Hagemeister Island AK U.S.A. 148 G4
Hagemeister Strait AK U.S.A. 148 G4
Hagen Germany 63 H3
Hagenow Germany 63 L1
Hagerhill KY U.S.A. 164 D5
Hagerstown MD U.S.A. 165 G4
Hagfors Sweden 55 H6
Haggin, Mount MT U.S.A. 156 E3
Hagi Japan 91 C6
Ha Giang Vietnam 86 D2
Hagiwara Japan 92 D3
Hagley U.K. 59 E6
Hag's Head hd Ireland 61 C5
Hague NY U.S.A. 165 I2
Hague, Cap de la c. France 66 D2
Haguenau France 63 H6
Hahajima-rettō is Japan 91 F8
Hahdhunmathi Maldives 103 D11
Hahoe tourist site S. Korea 91 C5
Hai Tanz. 121 G5
Hai, Ko i. Thai. 84 B1
Hai'an China 97 F4
Haib watercourse Namibia 124 C5
Haibowan China see Wuhai
Haicheng Guangdong China see Haifeng
Haicheng Liaoning China 95 J3
Haicheng Ningxia China 94 F4
Haida Gwaii Canada 149 N5
Haiding Hu salt l. China 94 C5
Hai Dương Vietnam 86 D2
Haifa Israel 107 B3
Haifa, Bay of Israel 107 B3
Haifeng China 97 G4
Haig Australia 135 D7
Haiger Germany 63 I4
Haihu China 94 E4
Haikakan country Asia see Armenia
Haikang China see Leizhou
Haikou China 97 F4
Ḥā'il Saudi Arabia 113 F6
Hai-la-erh China see Hulun Buir
Hailar China see Hulun Buir
Hailey ID U.S.A. 156 E4
Haileybury Canada 152 F5
Hailin China 90 C3
Hailong China see Meihekou
Hails China 95 I3
Hailsham U.K. 59 H8
Hailun China 90 B3
Hailuoto Fin. 54 N4
Hainan prov. China 97 F5
Hainan Dao i. China 97 F5
Hai-nang Myanmar 86 B2
Hainan Strait China 97 F5
Hainaut reg. France 62 D4
Haines AK U.S.A. 149 N4
Haines Junction Canada 149 M3
Haines Road Canada/U.S.A. 149 M3
Hainichen Germany 63 N4
Hainleite ridge Germany 63 K3
Hai Phong Vietnam 86 D2
Haiphong Vietnam see Hai Phong
Haiqing China 90 D3
Hairag China 94 E4
Haitan Dao i. China 97 H3
Haitangwan China 97 F5
Haiti country West Indies 169 J5
Haitou China 97 F5
Hai Triều Vietnam 87 E4
Haiwee Reservoir CA U.S.A. 158 E3
Haiya Sudan 108 E6
Haiyan Qinghai China 94 E4
Haiyan Zhejiang China 97 I2
Haiyang Anhui China see Xiuning
Haiyang Shandong China 95 J4
Haiyang Dao i. China 91 A5
Haiyou China see Sanmen
Haiyuan China see Haicheng
Haizhou Wan b. China 95 I5
Hajdúböszörmény Hungary 69 I1
Hajeb El Ayoun Tunisia 68 C7
Hajhir mt. Yemen 109 H7
Haji Mahesar Pak. 111 G4
Hajipur India 105 F4
Hajir reg. Saudi Arabia 110 C5
Ḥajjah Yemen 108 F6
Ḥājj 'Alī Qolī, Kavīr-e salt l. Iran 110 D3
Ḥājjīābād Fārs Iran 110 D4
Ḥājjīābād Hormozgān Iran 110 D4
Ḥājjīābād Yazd Iran 110 D3
Haju China 94 D3
Hajuu-Us Mongolia see Govĭ-Ugtaal
Haka Myanmar 86 A2
Hakha Myanmar see Haka
Hakkâri Turkey 113 F3
Hakkas Sweden 54 L3
Hakken-zan mt. Japan 92 B4
Hakkō-san hill Japan 93 E4
Hako-dake mt. Japan 90 F3
Hakodate Japan 90 F4
Hakone Japan 93 F3
Hakone-tōge pass Japan 93 F3
Hakos Mountains Namibia 124 C2
Hakseen Pan salt pan S. Africa 124 E4
Hakuba Japan 93 D2
Hakui Japan 92 C2
Hakusan Ishikawa Japan 92 C2
Hakusan Mie Japan 92 C4
Haku-san vol. Japan 92 C2
Haku-san Kokuritsu-kōen nat. park Japan 92 C2
Hakushū Japan 93 E3
Hal Belgium see Halle
Hala Pak. 111 H5
Ḥalab Syria see Aleppo
Ḥalabjah/Helebce Iraq 113 G4
Halaç Turkm. 111 G2
Halachó Mex. 167 H4
Halahai China 90 B3
Ḥalā'ib Sudan 108 E5
Halaib Triangle terr. Egypt 108 E5
Halâl, Gebel hill Egypt see Hilāl, Jabal
Ha Lam Vietnam 86 E4
Ḥalāniyāt, Juzur al is Oman 109 I6
Hālawa HI U.S.A. 157 [inset]
Halba Lebanon 107 C2
Halban Mongolia see Tsetserleg
Halberstadt Germany 63 L3
Halcon, Mount Mindoro Phil. 82 C3
Haldane r. Canada 149 Q2
Halden Norway 55 G7
Haldensleben Germany 63 L2
Haldwani India 104 D3
Hale watercourse Australia 136 A5
Hale China 95 G3
Hale MI U.S.A. 164 D1
Hāleh Iran 110 D5
Haleparki Deresi r. Syria/Turkey see Quwayq, Nahr
Halesowen U.K. 59 E6
Halesworth U.K. 59 I6
Half Assini Ghana 120 C4
Halfmoon Bay N.Z. 139 B8
Halfway r. Canada 150 F3
Halfway Ireland 61 D6
Halfway Mountain hill AK U.S.A. 148 I3
Halfweg Neth. 62 E2
Halhgol Dornod Mongolia 95 I2
Halhgol Dornod Mongolia 95 I2
Halia India 105 E4
Ḥalībīyah Syria 113 E4
Haliburton Canada 165 F1
Haliburton Highlands hills Canada 165 F1
Halicarnassus Turkey see Bodrum

▶Halifax Canada 153 J5
Capital of Nova Scotia.

Halifax U.K. 58 F5
Halifax NC U.S.A. 162 E4
Halifax VA U.S.A. 165 F5
Halifax, Mount Australia 136 D3
Halik Shan mts China 98 C4
Halilulik Timor Indon. 83 C5
Ḥalīmah mt. Lebanon/Syria 107 C2
Haliut China 95 G3
Halkett, Cape AK U.S.A. 148 I1
Halkirk U.K. 60 F2
Hall KY U.S.A. 164 C5
Hälla Sweden 54 J5
Halladale r. U.K. 60 F2
Halla-san National Park S. Korea 91 B6
Hall Beach Canada 147 J3
Halle Belgium 62 E4
Halle Neth. 62 G3
Halle (Saale) Germany 63 L3
Halleck NV U.S.A. 159 F1
Hällefors Sweden 55 I7
Hallein Austria 57 N7
Halle-Neustadt Germany 63 L3
Hallett, Cape Antarctica 188 H2
Hallettsville TX U.S.A. 161 D6
Halley research station Antarctica 188 B1
Hallgreen, Mount Antarctica 188 B2
Halliday ND U.S.A. 160 C2
Halliday Lake Canada 151 I2
Hall Island AK U.S.A. 148 D3
Hall Islands Micronesia 186 G5
Hällnäs Sweden 54 K4
Hallock MN U.S.A. 160 D1
Hall Peninsula Canada 147 L3
Hallsberg Sweden 55 I7
Halls Creek Australia 134 D4
Halls Gap KY U.S.A. 164 C5
Halls Lake Canada 165 F1
Hallstead PA U.S.A. 165 H3
Halluin Belgium 62 D4
Hallviken Sweden 54 I5
Halmahera i. Moluccas Indon. 83 D2
Halmahera, Laut sea Moluccas Indon. 83 D3
Halmahera Sea Moluccas Indon. see Halmahera, Laut
Halmstad Sweden 55 H8
Ha Long Vietnam 86 D2
Hals Denmark 55 G8
Hälsingborg Sweden see Helsingborg
Halsua Fin. 54 N5
Haltern am See Germany 63 H3
Haltunchén Mex. 167 H5
Haltwhistle U.K. 58 E4
Ḥālūl i. Qatar 110 D5
Halura i. Indon. 83 B5
Ḥalvān Iran 110 E3
Halver Germany 63 H3
Haly, Mount hill Australia 138 E1
Ham France 62 D5
Hamada Japan 91 D6
Hamadān Iran 110 C3
Ḥamāh Syria 107 C2
Hamajima Japan 92 C4
Hamakita Japan 93 D4
Hamam Turkey 107 C1
Hamamatsu Japan 92 D4
Hamana-ko l. Japan 92 D4
Hamaoka Japan 93 E4
Hamar Norway 55 G6
Ḥamâṭa, Gebel mt. Egypt see Ḥamāṭah, Jabal
Ḥamāṭah, Jabal mt. Egypt 108 D5
Hamatonbetsu Japan 90 F3
Hambantota Sri Lanka 106 D5
Hambergen Germany 63 I1
Hambleton Hills U.K. 58 F4
Hamburg Germany 63 J1
Hamburg land Germany 63 J1
Hamburg S. Africa 125 H7
Hamburg AR U.S.A. 161 F5
Hamburg NY U.S.A. 165 F2
Hamburgisches Wattenmeer, Nationalpark nat. park Germany 57 L4
Ḥamḍ, Wādī al watercourse Saudi Arabia 108 E4
Hamden CT U.S.A. 165 I3
Hämeenlinna Fin. 55 N6
HaMelaḥ, Yam salt l. Asia see Dead Sea
Hamelin Australia 135 A6
Hameln Germany 63 J2
Hamersley Lakes salt flat Australia 135 B7
Hamersley Range mts Australia 134 B5
Hamhŭng N. Korea 91 B5
Hami China 94 C3
Hamid Sudan 108 D5
Hamilton Qld Australia 136 C4
Hamilton S.A. Australia 137 A5
Hamilton Vic. Australia 137 C8
Hamilton watercourse Qld Australia 136 B4
Hamilton watercourse S.A. Australia 137 A5

▶Hamilton Bermuda 169 L2
Capital of Bermuda.

Hamilton Canada 164 F2
Hamilton r. Canada see Churchill
Hamilton N.Z. 139 E3
Hamilton U.K. 60 E5
Hamilton AK U.S.A. 148 G3
Hamilton AL U.S.A. 163 C5
Hamilton CO U.S.A. 159 J1
Hamilton MI U.S.A. 164 B2
Hamilton MT U.S.A. 156 E3
Hamilton NY U.S.A. 165 H2
Hamilton OH U.S.A. 164 C4
Hamilton TX U.S.A. 161 D6
Hamilton, Mount AK U.S.A. 148 H3
Hamilton, Mount CA U.S.A. 158 C3
Hamilton, Mount NV U.S.A. 159 F2
Hamilton City CA U.S.A. 158 B2
Hamilton Inlet Canada 153 K3
Hamilton Mountain hill NY U.S.A. 165 H2
Hamīm, Wādī al watercourse Libya 65 I5
Hamina Fin. 55 O6
Hamirpur Hima. Prad. India 104 D3
Hamirpur Uttar Prad. India 104 E4
Hamitabat Turkey see Isparta
Hamju N. Korea 91 B5
Hamlet NC U.S.A. 163 E5
Hamlin TX U.S.A. 161 C5
Hamlin WV U.S.A. 164 D4
Hamm Germany 63 H3
Ḥammām al 'Alīl Iraq 113 F3
Hammam Boughrara Alg. 67 F6
Hammamet Tunisia 68 D6
Hammamet, Golfe de g. Tunisia 68 D6
Ḥammār, Hawr al imp. l. Iraq 113 G5
Hammarstrand Sweden 54 J5
Hammelburg Germany 63 J4
Hammerdal Sweden 54 I5
Hammerfest Norway 54 M1
Hamminkeln Germany 62 G3
Hammond IN U.S.A. 164 B3
Hammond LA U.S.A. 167 H2
Hammone, Lac l. Canada 153 K4
Hammonton NJ U.S.A. 165 H4
Ham Ninh Vietnam 87 D5
Hamoir Belgium 62 F4
Hampden Sydney VA U.S.A. 165 F5
Hampshire Downs hills U.K. 59 F7
Hampton AR U.S.A. 161 E5
Hampton IA U.S.A. 160 E3
Hampton NH U.S.A. 165 J2
Hampton SC U.S.A. 163 D5
Hampton VA U.S.A. 165 G5
Hampton Tableland reg. Australia 135 D8
Ḥamrā', Al Ḥamādah al plat. Libya 120 E2
Ḥamrā, Birkat al well Saudi Arabia 113 F5
Hamra, Vâdii watercourse Syria/Turkey see Ḥimār, Wādī al
Hamrā Jūdah plat. Saudi Arabia 110 C5
Hamrat esh Sheikh Sudan 108 C7
Ham Tân Vietnam 87 D5
Hamta Pass India 104 D2
Hāmūn Ṣāberī, Daryācheh-ye marsh Afgh./Iran 111 F4
Hamunt Kūh hill Iran 111 F5
Hamur Turkey 113 F3
Hamura Japan 93 F3
Hamwic U.K. see Southampton
Hāna HI U.S.A. 157 [inset]
Hanábana r. Cuba 163 D8
Hanahai watercourse Botswana/Namibia 124 F2
Ḥanak Saudi Arabia 108 E4
Hanakpınar Turkey see Çınar
Hanalei HI U.S.A. 157 [inset]
Hanamaki Japan 91 F5
Hanamigawa Japan 93 G3
Hanang mt. Tanz. 123 D4
Hanau Germany 63 I4
Hanawa Japan 93 G2
Hanbin China see Ankang
Hanbogd Mongolia 95 F3
Hanchang China see Pingjiang
Hancheng China 95 G5
Hanchuan China 97 G2
Hancock MD U.S.A. 165 F4
Hancock NY U.S.A. 165 H3
Handa Japan 92 C4
Handa Island U.K. 60 D2
Handan China 95 H4
Handeni Tanz. 123 D4
Handian China see Changzhi
Haneda airport Japan 93 F3
HaNegev des. Israel see Negev
HaNeqarot, Naḥal watercourse Israel 107 B4
Hanfeng China see Kaixian
Hanford CA U.S.A. 158 D3
Hangan Myanmar 86 B4
Hangayn Nuruu mts Mongolia 94 D1
Hangchow China see Hangzhou
Hangchuan China see Guangze
Hanggin Houqi China see Xamba
Hanggin Qi China see Xin
Hangö Fin. see Hanko
Hangu China see Qianshangjie
Hanguang China 97 G3
Hangya China 94 D4
Hangzhou China 97 I2
Hangzhou Wan b. China 97 I2
Han Hōhiyn Nuruu mts Mongolia 94 C1
Hani Turkey 113 F3
Hanish Kabir i. Yemen see Suyūl Ḥanīsh
Hanji China see Linxia
Hanjia China see Pengshui
Hanjiaoshui China 94 F4
Hankensbüttel Germany 63 K2
Hankey S. Africa 124 G7
Hanko Fin. 55 M7
Hanksville UT U.S.A. 159 H2
Hanle India 104 D2
Hanley Canada 151 J5
Hann, Mount hill Australia 134 D3
Hanna Canada 151 I5
Hannagan Meadow AZ U.S.A. 159 I5
Hannah Bay Canada 152 E4
Hannibal MO U.S.A. 160 F4
Hannibal NY U.S.A. 165 G2
Hannō Japan 93 F3
Hannover Germany 63 J2
Hannoversch Münden Germany 63 J3
Hann Range mts Australia 135 F5
Hannut Belgium 62 F4
Hanöbukten b. Sweden 55 I9
Hanoi Vietnam see Ha Nôi

▶Ha Nôi Vietnam 86 D2
Capital of Vietnam.

Hanover Canada 164 E1
Hanover Germany see Hannover
Hanover S. Africa 124 G6
Hanover NH U.S.A. 165 I2
Hanover PA U.S.A. 165 G4
Hanover VA U.S.A. 165 G5
Hansen Mountains Antarctica 188 D2
Hanshou China 97 F2
Han Shui r. China 97 G2
Hansi India 104 D3
Hansnes Norway 54 K2
Hanstholm Denmark 55 F8
Han Sum China 95 I2
Han-sur-Nied France 62 G6
Hantsavichy Belarus 55 O10
Hanumangarh India 104 C3
Hanuy Gol r. Mongolia 94 E1
Hanwood Australia 138 C5
Hanxia China 94 D4
Hanyang China see Caidian
Hanyang Feng mt. China 97 G2
Hanyin China 97 F1
Hanyū Japan 93 F2
Hanzhong China 96 E1
Hao atoll Fr. Polynesia 187 K7
Haomen China see Menyuan
Haora India 105 G5
Haparanda Sweden 54 N4
Happy Jack AZ U.S.A. 159 H4
Happy Valley-Goose Bay Canada 153 J3
Hapur India 99 B7
Ḥaql Saudi Arabia 107 B5
Haqshah well Saudi Arabia 110 C6
Hara Japan 93 E3
Ḥaraḍ well Saudi Arabia 110 C5
Ḥarad, Jabal al mt. Jordan 107 B5
Ḥaraḍh Saudi Arabia 108 G5
Haradok Belarus 53 F5
Haramachi Japan 91 F5
Haramgai China 98 D3
Haramukh mt. India 104 C2
Haran Turkey see Harran
Harappa Road Pak. 111 I4
Harar Eth. see Hārer

▶Harare Zimbabwe 123 D5
Capital of Zimbabwe.

Ḥarāsīs, Jiddat al des. Oman 109 I6
Harāt Iran 110 D4
Haraze-Mangueigne Chad 121 F3
Harb, Jabal mt. Saudi Arabia 112 D6
Harbin China 90 B3
Harboi Hills Pak. 111 G4
Harbor Beach MI U.S.A. 164 D2
Har Buh Gol r. Mongolia 94 F1
Harchoka India 105 E5
Harda India 104 D5
Harda Khas India see Harda
Hardangerfjorden sea chan. Norway 55 D7
Hardangervidda plat. Norway 55 E6
Hardangervidda Nasjonalpark nat. park Norway 55 E6
Hardap admin. reg. Namibia 124 C3
Hardap Dam Namibia 124 C3
Hardap Recreation Resort nature res. Namibia 124 C3
Harden, Bukit mt. Indon. 85 F1
Hardenberg Neth. 62 G2
Harderwijk Neth. 62 F2
Hardeveld mts S. Africa 124 D6
Hardheim Germany 63 J5
Hardin MT U.S.A. 156 G3
Harding r. Canada 149 R1
Harding S. Africa 125 I6
Harding Ice Field AK U.S.A. 149 J3
Harding Range hills Australia 135 B6
Hardinsburg IN U.S.A. 164 B4
Hardinsburg KY U.S.A. 164 B5
Hardoi India 104 E4
Hardwar India see Haridwar
Hardwick VT U.S.A. 165 I1
Hardy AR U.S.A. 161 F4
Hardy Reservoir MI U.S.A. 164 C2
Hare Bay Canada 153 L4
Ḥareiḍīn, Wâdi watercourse Egypt see Ḥuraydīn, Wādī

Hare Indian r. Canada 149 O2
Harelbeke Belgium 62 D4
Haren Neth. 62 G1
Haren (Ems) Germany 63 H2
Hārer Eth. 122 E3
Harf el Mreffi mt. Lebanon 107 B3
Hargant China 95 I1
Hargeisa Somalia see Hargeysa
Hargele Eth. 122 E3

▶Hargeysa Somalia 122 E3
Capital of Somaliland.

Harghita-Mădăraş, Vârful mt. Romania 69 K1
Harhatan China 95 F4
Harhorin Mongolia 94 E2
Har Hu l. China 94 D4
Ḥaricha, Ḥamâda El des. Mali 120 C2
Haridwar India 104 D3
Ḥarif, Har mt. Israel 107 B4
Harihar India 106 B3
Harihari N.Z. 139 C6
Hariharpur India 106 B3
Ḥārim Syria 107 C1
Ḥarīm, Jabal al mt. Oman 110 E5
Harima Japan 92 A4
Harima-nada b. Japan 92 A4
Haringhat r. Bangl. 105 G5
Haringvliet est. Neth. 62 E3
Harinoki-dake mt. Japan 92 D2
Ḥarīr, Wādī al r. Syria 107 C3
Harī Rōd r. Afgh./Iran 111 F2
Harjavalta Fin. 55 M6
Harlan IA U.S.A. 160 E3
Harlan KY U.S.A. 164 D5
Harlan County Lake NE U.S.A. 160 D3
Harlech U.K. 59 C6
Harleston U.K. 59 I6
Harlingen Neth. 62 F1
Harlingen TX U.S.A. 161 D7
Harlow U.K. 59 H7
Harlowton MT U.S.A. 156 F3
Harly France 62 D5
Harman WV U.S.A. 164 F4
Harmancık Turkey 69 M5
Harmanli Bulg. 69 K4
Harmony ME U.S.A. 165 K1
Harmsdorf Germany 63 K1
Harnai India 106 B2
Harnai Pak. 111 G4
Harnes France 62 C4
Harney Basin OR U.S.A. 156 D4
Harney Lake OR U.S.A. 156 D4
Härnösand Sweden 54 J5
Harns Neth. see Harlingen
Har Nuden China 95 I1
Har Nuur l. Mongolia 94 C1
Har Nuur l. Mongolia 94 D1
Haroldswick U.K. 60 [inset]
Harper Liberia 120 C4
Harper KS U.S.A. 161 D4
Harper, Mount Canada 149 M2
Harper, Mount AK U.S.A. 149 L2
Harper Bend reg. AK U.S.A. 149 J2
Harper Creek r. Canada 150 H3
Harper Lake CA U.S.A. 158 E4
Harp Lake Canada 153 J3
Harpstedt Germany 63 I2
Harqin China 95 I3
Harqin Qi China see Jinshan
Harquahala Mountains AZ U.S.A. 157 E6
Harrai India 104 D5
Harran Turkey 107 D1
Harrand Pak. 111 H4
Harricana, Rivière d' r. Canada 152 F4
Harrington Australia 138 F3
Harrington DE U.S.A. 165 H4
Harris, Lake salt flat Australia 137 A6
Harris, Mount Australia 135 E6
Harris, Sound of sea chan. U.K. 60 B3
Harrisburg AR U.S.A. 161 F5
Harrisburg IL U.S.A. 160 F4
Harrisburg NE U.S.A. 160 C3

▶Harrisburg PA U.S.A. 165 G3
Capital of Pennsylvania.

Harrismith Australia 135 B8
Harrison AR U.S.A. 161 E4
Harrison MI U.S.A. 164 C1
Harrison NE U.S.A. 160 C3
Harrison OH U.S.A. 164 C4
Harrison, Cape Canada 153 K3
Harrison Bay AK U.S.A. 149 J1
Harrisonburg LA U.S.A. 161 F6
Harrisonburg VA U.S.A. 165 F4
Harrisonville MO U.S.A. 160 E4
Harriston Canada 164 E2
Harrisville MI U.S.A. 164 D1
Harrisville NY U.S.A. 165 H1
Harrisville PA U.S.A. 164 E3
Harrisville WV U.S.A. 164 E4
Harrodsburg IN U.S.A. 164 B4
Harrodsburg KY U.S.A. 164 C5
Harrodsville N.Z. see Otorohanga
Harrogate U.K. 58 F5
Harrowsmith Canada 165 G1
Harry S. Truman Reservoir MO U.S.A. 160 E4
Har Sai Shan mt. China 94 D5
Harsefeld Germany 63 J1
Harsīn Iran 110 B3
Harşit r. Turkey 112 E2
Hârşova Romania 69 L2
Harstad Norway 54 J2
Harsud India 104 D5
Harsum Germany 63 J2
Hart r. Canada 146 E3
Hart MI U.S.A. 164 B2
Hartbees watercourse S. Africa 124 E5
Hartberg Austria 57 O7
Harteigan mt. Norway 55 E6
Harter Fell hill U.K. 58 E4

▶Hartford CT U.S.A. 165 I3
Capital of Connecticut.

Hartford KY U.S.A. 164 B5
Hartford MI U.S.A. 164 B2
Hartford City IN U.S.A. 164 C3
Hartland U.K. 59 C8
Hartland ME U.S.A. 165 K1
Hartland Point U.K. 59 C7
Hartlepool U.K. 58 F4
Hartley TX U.S.A. 161 C5
Hartley Zimbabwe see Chegutu
Hartley Bay Canada 150 D4
Hartola Fin. 55 O6
Harts r. S. Africa 125 G5
Härtsfeld hills Germany 63 K6
Harts Range mts Australia 135 F5
Hartsville TN U.S.A. 164 B5
Hartswater S. Africa 124 G4
Hartville MO U.S.A. 161 E4
Hartwell GA U.S.A. 163 D5
Harue Japan 92 C2
Haruku i. Moluccas Indon. 83 D3
Haruna Japan 93 E2
Haruno Japan 93 D3
Ḥarūrī, 'Irq al des. Saudi Arabia 110 B5
Har Us Nuur l. Mongolia 94 C2
Har Us Nuur salt l. Mongolia 94 C1
Hārūt r. Afgh. 111 F3
Harūz Iran 110 E4
Harvard, Mount CO U.S.A. 156 G5
Harvey Australia 135 A8
Harvey ND U.S.A. 160 C2
Harvey Mountain CA U.S.A. 158 C1
Harwich U.K. 59 I7
Haryana state India 104 D3
Harz hills Germany 57 M5
Har Zin Israel 107 B4
Ḥaşāh, Wādī al watercourse Jordan 107 B4
Ḥaşāh, Wādī al watercourse Jordan/Saudi Arabia 107 C4
Hasalbag China 99 B5
Häsänabad Azer. 113 H3
Ḥasanah, Wādī watercourse Egypt 107 A4
Hasan Dağı mts Turkey 112 D3
Hasan Guli Turkm. see Esenguly
Hasankeyf Turkey 113 F3
Ḥasan Kūlah Afgh. 111 F3
Hasanur India 106 C4
Hasardag mt. Turkm. 110 E2
Hasbaïya Lebanon 107 B3
Hasbaya Lebanon see Hasbaïya
Hase r. Germany 63 H2
Hase Japan 93 E3
Haselünne Germany 63 H2
Hashaat Arhangay Mongolia 94 E2
Hashaat Dundgovĭ Mongolia see Delgerhangay
HaSharon plain Israel 107 B3
Hashima Japan 92 C3
Hashimoto Japan 92 B4
Hashtgerd Iran 110 C3
Hashtpar Iran see Tālesh
Hashtrūd Iran 110 B2
Haskell TX U.S.A. 161 D5
Haskovo Bulg. 69 K4
Haslemere U.K. 59 G7
Hăşmaşul Mare mt. Romania 69 K1
Ḥaşş, Jabal al hills Syria 107 C1
Hassan India 106 C3
Hassayampa watercourse AZ U.S.A. 159 G5
Haßberge hills Germany 63 K4
Hasselt Belgium 62 F4
Hasselt Neth. 62 G2
Hassi Bel Guebbour Alg. 120 D2
Hassi Messaoud Alg. 64 F5
Hässleholm Sweden 55 H8
Hastings Australia 138 B7
Hastings r. Australia 138 F3
Hastings Canada 165 G1
Hastings N.Z. 139 F4
Hastings U.K. 59 H8
Hastings MI U.S.A. 164 C2
Hastings MN U.S.A. 160 E2
Hastings NE U.S.A. 160 D3
Hasuda Japan 93 F3
Hasunuma Japan 93 G3
Hata India 105 E4
Hata Japan 93 D2
Hatanbulag Mongolia 95 G3
Hatansuudal Mongolia see Bayanlig
Hatashō Japan 92 C3
Hatay Turkey see Antakya
Hatay prov. Turkey 107 C1
Hatch UT U.S.A. 159 G3
Hatches Creek (abandoned) Australia 136 A4
Hatchet Lake Canada 151 K3
Hatfield Australia 138 A4
Hatfield U.K. 58 G5
Hatgal Mongolia 94 E1
Hath India 106 D1
Hat Head National Park Australia 138 F3
Hathras India 104 D4
Ha Tiên Vietnam 87 D5
Ha Tinh Vietnam 86 D3
Hatisar Bhutan see Geylegphug
Hatod India 104 C5
Hato Hud East Timor see Hatudo
Hatra Iraq 113 F4
Hatsu-shima i. Japan 93 F3
Hattah Australia 137 C7
Hattah Kulkyne National Park Australia 137 C7
Hatteras, Cape NC U.S.A. 163 F5
Hatteras Abyssal Plain sea feature S. Atlantic Ocean 184 D4
Hattfjelldal Norway 54 H4
Hattiesburg MS U.S.A. 161 F6
Hattingen Germany 63 H3
Hatton, Gunung hill Malaysia 85 G1
Hattori-gawa r. Japan 92 C4
Hattras Passage Myanmar 87 B4
Hatudo East Timor 83 C5
Hat Yai Thai. 87 C6
Hau Bon Vietnam see A Yun Pa
Haubstadt IN U.S.A. 164 B4
Haud reg. Eth. 122 E3
Hauge Norway 55 E7
Haugesund Norway 55 D7
Haukeligrend Norway 55 E7
Haukipudas Fin. 54 N4
Haukivesi l. Fin. 54 P5
Haultain r. Canada 151 J4
Hauraki Gulf N.Z. 139 E3
Haut Atlas mts Morocco 64 C5
Haute-Normandie admin. reg. France 62 B5
Haute-Volta country Africa see Burkina Faso
Haut-Folin hill France 66 G3
Hauts Plateaux Alg. 64 D5

▶Havana Cuba 169 H4
Capital of Cuba.

Havana IL U.S.A. 160 F3
Havant U.K. 59 G8
Havasu, Lake Arizona/California U.S.A. 159 F4
Havel r. Germany 63 L2
Havelange Belgium 62 F4
Havelberg Germany 63 M2
Havelock Canada 165 G1
Havelock N.Z. 139 D5
Havelock Swaziland see Bulembu
Havelock NC U.S.A. 163 E5
Havelock Falls Australia 134 F3
Havelock Island India 87 A5
Havelock North N.Z. 139 F4
Haverfordwest U.K. 59 C7
Haverhill MA U.S.A. 165 J2
Haveri India 106 B3
Haversin Belgium 62 F4
Havixbeck Germany 63 H3
Havlíčkův Brod Czech Rep. 57 O6
Havøysund Norway 54 N1
Havran Turkey 69 L5
Havre MT U.S.A. 156 F2
Havre Aubert, Île du i. Canada 153 J5
Havre Rock i. Kermadec Is 133 I5
Havre-St-Pierre Canada 153 J4
Havza Turkey 112 D2
Hawadax Island AK U.S.A. 148 [inset] B6
Hawai'i i. HI U.S.A. 157 [inset]
Hawai'ian Islands N. Pacific Ocean 186 I4
Hawaiian Ridge sea feature N. Pacific Ocean 186 I4
Hawai'i Volcanoes National Park HI U.S.A. 157 [inset]
Ḥawallī Kuwait 110 C4
Hawar i. Bahrain see Ḥuwār
Hawarden U.K. 58 D5
Hawea, Lake N.Z. 139 B7
Hawera N.Z. 139 E4
Hawes U.K. 58 E4
Hawesville KY U.S.A. 164 B5
Hāwī HI U.S.A. 157 [inset]
Hawick U.K. 60 G5
Ḥawīzah, Hawr al imp. l. Iraq 113 G5
Hawkdun Range mts N.Z. 139 B7
Hawke Bay N.Z. 139 F4
Hawkes Bay Canada 153 K4
Hawkins Peak UT U.S.A. 159 G3
Hawlēr Iraq see Arbīl/Hewlêr
Hawley PA U.S.A. 165 H3
Hawng Luk Myanmar 86 B2
Ḥawrān, Wādī watercourse Iraq 113 F4
Ḥawshah, Jibāl al mts Saudi Arabia 110 B6
Hawston S. Africa 124 D8
Hawthorne NV U.S.A. 158 D2
Haxat Hudag China 95 H2
Haxby U.K. 58 F4
Hay Australia 138 B5
Hay watercourse Australia 136 B5
Hay r. Canada 150 H2
Haya Seram Indon. 83 D3
Hayachine-san mt. Japan 91 F5
Haya-gawa r. Japan 93 D1
Hayakawa Japan 93 E3
Haya-kawa r. Japan 93 E3
Hayama Japan 93 F3
Hayastan country Asia see Armenia
Haycock AK U.S.A. 148 G2
Haydān, Wādī al r. Jordan 107 B4
Hayden AZ U.S.A. 159 H5
Hayden CO U.S.A. 159 J1
Hayden IN U.S.A. 164 C4
Hayes r. Man. Canada 151 M3
Hayes r. Nunavut Canada 147 I3
Hayes, Mount AK U.S.A. 149 K3
Hayes Halvø pen. Greenland 147 L2
Hayfield Reservoir CA U.S.A. 159 F5
Hayfork CA U.S.A. 158 B1
Hayl, Wādī watercourse Syria 107 C3
Hayl, Wādī al watercourse Syria 107 D2
Haylaastay Mongolia see Sühbaatar
Hayle U.K. 59 B8
Haymā' Oman 109 I6
Haymana Turkey 112 D3
Haymarket VA U.S.A. 165 G4
Hay-on-Wye U.K. 59 D6
Hayrabolu Turkey 69 L4
Hayrhandulaan Mongolia 94 E2
Hay River Canada 146 G3
Hay River Reserve Canada 150 H2
Hays KS U.S.A. 160 D4
Hays MT U.S.A. 156 F2
Ḥays Yemen 108 F7
Haysville KS U.S.A. 161 D4
Haysyn Ukr. 53 F6
Ḥaytān, Jabal hill Egypt 107 A4
Hayward CA U.S.A. 158 B3
Hayward WI U.S.A. 160 F2
Haywards Heath U.K. 59 G8
Hazar Turkm. 110 D2
Hazārah Jāt reg. Afgh. 111 G3
Hazard KY U.S.A. 164 D5
Hazaribag India see Hazaribagh
Hazaribagh India 105 F5
Hazaribagh Range mts India 105 E5
Hazār Masjed, Kūh-e mts Iran 110 E2
Hazebrouck France 62 C4
Hazelton Canada 150 E4
Hazen Bay AK U.S.A. 148 F3
Hazen Strait Canada 147 G2
Hazerswoude-Rijndijk Neth. 62 E2
Hazhdanahr reg. Afgh. 111 G2
Hazira India 104 C5
Hazlehurst MS U.S.A. 167 H2
Hazleton IN U.S.A. 164 B4
Hazleton PA U.S.A. 165 H3
Hazlett, Lake salt flat Australia 134 E5
Ḥazm al Jawf Yemen 108 F6
Ḥaẓrat-e Sulṭān Afgh. 111 G2
Hazu Japan 92 D4
Hazumi-saki pt Japan 92 C4
H. Bouchard Arg. 178 D4
Headford Ireland 61 C4
Headingly Australia 136 B4
Head of Bight b. Australia 135 E7
Healdsburg CA U.S.A. 158 B2
Healesville Australia 138 B6
Healy AK U.S.A. 149 J3
Healy Lake AK U.S.A. 149 K3
Heanor U.K. 59 F5
Hearadh, Ceann a Deas na pen. U.K. see South Harris
Heard Island Indian Ocean 185 M9

▶Heard Island and McDonald Islands terr. Indian Ocean 185 M9
Australian External Territory.

Hearne TX U.S.A. 161 D6
Hearne Lake Canada 151 H2
Hearrenfean Neth. see Heerenveen
Hearst Canada 152 E4
Hearst Island Antarctica 188 L2
Heart r. ND U.S.A. 160 C2
Heart of Neolithic Orkney tourist site U.K. 60 F1
Heathcote Australia 138 B6
Heathfield U.K. 59 H8
Heathsville VA U.S.A. 165 G5
Hebbardsville KY U.S.A. 164 B5
Hebbronville TX U.S.A. 161 D7
Hebei prov. China 95 H4
Hebel Australia 138 C2
Heber AZ U.S.A. 159 H4
Heber City UT U.S.A. 159 H1
Heber Springs AR U.S.A. 161 E5
Hebi China see Shancheng
Hebian China 95 H4
Hebron Canada 153 J2
Hebron NE U.S.A. 160 D3
Hebron West Bank 107 B4
Hecate Strait Canada 149 O5
Hecelchakán Mex. 167 H4
Hecheng Jiangxi China see Zixi
Hecheng Zhejiang China see Qingtian
Hechi China 97 F3
Hechuan Chongqing China 96 E2
Hechuan Jiangxi China see Yongxin
Hecla Island Canada 151 L5
Heda Japan 93 E4
Hede China see Sheyang
Hede Sweden 54 H5
Hedemora Sweden 55 I6
He Devil Mountain ID U.S.A. 156 D3
Hedionda Grande Mex. 167 E3
Hedi Shuiku resr China 97 F4
Heech Neth. see Heeg
Heeg Neth. 62 F2
Heek Germany 62 H2
Heer Belgium 62 E4
Heerde Neth. 62 G2
Heerenveen Neth. 62 F2
Heerhugowaard Neth. 62 E2
Heerlen Neth. 62 F4
Ḥefa Israel see Haifa
Ḥefa, Mifraz Israel see Haifa, Bay of
Hefei China 97 H2
Hefeng China 97 F2
Heflin AL U.S.A. 163 C5
Hegang China 90 C3
Heho Myanmar 86 B2
Heidan r. Jordan see Haydān, Wādī al
Heidberg hill Germany 63 L3
Heide Germany 57 L3
Heide Namibia 124 C2
Heidelberg Germany 63 I5
Heidelberg S. Africa 125 I4
Heidenheim an der Brenz Germany 63 K6
Heihe China 90 B2
Heilbron S. Africa 125 H4
Heilbronn Germany 63 J5
Heiligenhafen Germany 57 M3
Hei Ling Chau i. H.K. China 97 [inset]
Heilongjiang prov. China 95 J2
Heilong Jiang r. China/Russia 90 D2
also known as Amur (Russia)
Heilsbronn Germany 63 K5
Heilungkiang prov. China see Heilongjiang
Heimahe China 94 D4
Heinola Fin. 55 O6
Heinze Islands Myanmar 87 B4
Heiquan China 94 D4
Heirnkut Myanmar 86 A1
Heishan China 95 J3
Heishantou Nei Mongol China 95 I1
Heishantou Xinjiang China 94 B2
Heishi Beihu l. China 99 C6
Heishui China 96 D1
Heisker Islands U.K. see Monach Islands
Heist-op-den-Berg Belgium 62 E3
Ḥeiṭān, Gebel hill Egypt see Ḥayṭān, Jabal
Heituo Shan mt. China 95 H4
Hejaz reg. Saudi Arabia see Hijaz
Hejian China 95 I4
Hejiang China 96 E2
He Jiang r. China 97 F4
Hejiao China 95 G3
Hejin China 95 G5
Hejing China 98 D4
Hekimhan Turkey 112 E3
Hekinan Japan 92 C4
Hekla vol. Iceland 54 [inset 1]
Heko-san mt. Japan 92 C3
Hekou Gansu China 94 E4
Hekou Hubei China 97 G2
Hekou Jiangxi China see Yanshan
Hekou Sichuan China see Yajiang
Hekou Yunnan China 96 D4
Helagsfjället mt. Sweden 54 H5
Helam India 96 B3
Helan Shan mts China 94 F4
Helbra Germany 63 L3
Helen atoll Palau 81 I6
Helena AR U.S.A. 161 F5

▶Helena MT U.S.A. 156 E3
Capital of Montana.

Helen Reef Palau 81 I6
Helensburgh U.K. 60 E4
Helen Springs Australia 134 F4
Ḥelez Israel 107 B4
Helgoland i. Germany 57 K3
Helgoländer Bucht g. Germany 57 L3
Heligoland i. Germany see Helgoland
Heligoland Bight g. Germany see Helgoländer Bucht
Heliopolis Lebanon see Ba'albek
Helixi China see Ningguo
Hella Iceland 54 [inset 1]
Helland Norway 54 J2
Hellas country Europe see Greece
Helleh r. Iran 110 C4
Hellespont strait Turkey see Dardanelles
Hellevoetsluis Neth. 62 E3
Hellhole Gorge National Park Australia 136 D5
Hellín Spain 67 F4
Hellinikon tourist site Greece 112 A3
Hells Canyon gorge Idaho/Oregon U.S.A. 156 D3
Hell-Ville Madag. see Andoany
Helmand r. Afgh. 111 F4
Helmand, Hāmūn salt flat Afgh./Iran 111 F4
Helmantica Spain see Salamanca
Helmbrechts Germany 63 L4
Helme r. Germany 63 L3
Helmeringhausen Namibia 124 C3
Helmet Mountain AK U.S.A. 149 K2
Helmond Neth. 62 F3
Helmsdale U.K. 60 F2
Helmsdale r. U.K. 60 F2
Helmstedt Germany 63 L2
Helong China 90 C4
Helper UT U.S.A. 159 H2
Helpter Berge hills Germany 63 N1
Helsingborg Sweden 55 H8
Helsingfors Fin. see Helsinki
Helsingør Denmark 55 H8

▶Helsinki Fin. 55 N6
Capital of Finland.

Helston U.K. 59 B8
Helvécia Brazil 179 D2
Helvetic Republic country Europe see Switzerland
Ḥelwân Egypt see Ḥulwān
Hemel Hempstead U.K. 59 G7
Hemet CA U.S.A. 158 E5
Hemingford NE U.S.A. 160 C3
Hemlock Lake NY U.S.A. 165 G2
Hemmingen Germany 63 J2
Hemmingford Canada 165 I1
Hemmoor Germany 63 J1
Hempstead TX U.S.A. 161 D6
Hemsby U.K. 59 I6
Hemse Sweden 55 K8
Henan China 94 E5
Henan prov. China 97 G1
Henares r. Spain 67 E3
Henashi-zaki pt Japan 91 E4
Henbury Australia 135 F6
Hendek Turkey 69 N4
Henderson KY U.S.A. 164 B5
Henderson NC U.S.A. 162 E4
Henderson NV U.S.A. 159 F3
Henderson NY U.S.A. 165 G2
Henderson TN U.S.A. 161 F5
Henderson TX U.S.A. 161 E5
Henderson Island Pitcairn Is 187 L7
Hendersonville NC U.S.A. 163 D5
Hendersonville TN U.S.A. 164 B5
Henderville atoll Kiribati see Aranuka
Hendon U.K. 59 G7
Hendorābī, Jazīreh-ye i. Iran 110 D5
Hendy-Gwyn U.K. see Whitland
Hengām Iran 111 E5
Hengduan Shan mts China 96 C2
Hengelo Neth. 62 G2
Hengfeng China 97 H2
Hengnan China see Hengyang
Hengshan Heilong. China 90 C3
Hengshan Shaanxi China 95 G4
Heng Shan mt. China 97 G3
Heng Shan mts China 95 H4
Hengshui Hebei China 95 H4
Hengshui Jiangxi China see Chongyi
Hengxian China 97 F4
Hengyang Hunan China 97 G3
Hengyang Hunan China 97 G3
Hengzhou China see Hengxian
Heniches'k Ukr. 53 G7
Henley N.Z. 139 C7
Henley-on-Thames U.K. 59 G7
Henlopen, Cape DE U.S.A. 165 H4
Hennef (Sieg) Germany 63 H4
Hennenman S. Africa 125 H4
Hennepin IL U.S.A. 160 F3
Hennessey OK U.S.A. 161 D4
Hennigsdorf Germany 63 N2
Henniker NH U.S.A. 165 J2
Henning IL U.S.A. 164 B3
Henrietta TX U.S.A. 161 D5
Henrietta Maria, Cape Canada 152 E3
Henrieville UT U.S.A. 159 H3
Henrique de Carvalho Angola see Saurimo
Henry, Cape NC U.S.A. 165 G5
Henry Ice Rise Antarctica 188 A1
Henryk Arctowski research station Antarctica see Arctowski
Henry Kater, Cape Canada 147 L3
Henry Mountains UT U.S.A. 159 H2
Hensall Canada 164 E2
Henshaw, Lake CA U.S.A. 158 E5
Henteyn Nuruu mts Mongolia 95 F1
Hentiesbaai Namibia 124 B2
Hentiy prov. Mongolia 95 G2
Henty Australia 138 C5
Henzada Myanmar see Hinthada
Heping Guangdong China 97 G3
Heping Guizhou China see Huishui
Heping Guizhou China see Yanhe
Hepo China see Jiexi
Heppner OR U.S.A. 156 D3
Heptanesus is Greece see Ionian Islands
Hepu China 97 F4
Heqiao China 94 E4
Heqing China 96 D3
Hequ China 95 G4
Heraclea Turkey see Ereğli
Heraclea Pontica Turkey see Ereğli
Heraklion Greece see Iraklion
Herald Cays atolls Australia 136 E3
Herāt Afgh. 111 F3
Hérault r. France 66 F5
Herbertabad India 87 A5
Herbert Downs Australia 136 B4
Herbert Island AK U.S.A. 148 E5
Herbert River Falls National Park Australia 136 D3
Herbert Wash salt flat Australia 135 D6
Herborn Germany 63 I4
Herbstein Germany 63 J4
Hercules Dome ice feature Antarctica 188 K1
Herdecke Germany 63 H3
Herdorf Germany 63 H4
Heredia Costa Rica 166 [inset] I7
Hereford U.K. 59 E6
Hereford TX U.S.A. 161 C5
Hereheretue atoll Fr. Polynesia 187 K7
Herent Belgium 62 E4
Herford Germany 63 I2
Heringen (Werra) Germany 63 K4
Herington KS U.S.A. 160 D4
Herīs Iran 110 B2
Herisau Switz. 66 I3
Herkimer NY U.S.A. 165 H2
Herlen Mongolia 95 G2
Herlen Gol r. China/Mongolia 89 L3
Herlen He r. China/Mongolia see Herlen Gol
Herleshausen Germany 63 K3
Herlong CA U.S.A. 158 C1
Herm i. Channel Is 59 E9
Hermanas Mex. 167 E3
Herma Ness hd U.K. 60 [inset]
Hermann MO U.S.A. 160 F4
Hermannsburg Germany 63 K2
Hermanus S. Africa 124 D8
Hermel Lebanon 107 C2
Hermes, Cape S. Africa 125 I6
Hermidale Australia 138 C3
Hermiston OR U.S.A. 156 D3
Hermitage MO U.S.A. 160 E4
Hermitage PA U.S.A. 164 E3
Hermitage Bay Canada 153 K5
Hermite, Islas is Chile 178 C9
Hermit Islands P.N.G. 81 L7
Hermon, Mount Lebanon/Syria 107 B3
Hermonthis Egypt see Armant
Hermopolis Magna Egypt see Al Ashmūnayn
Hermosa CO U.S.A. 159 J3
Hermosillo Mex. 166 C2
Hernandarias Para. 178 F3
Hernando MS U.S.A. 161 F5
Herndon CA U.S.A. 158 D3
Herndon PA U.S.A. 165 G3
Herndon WV U.S.A. 164 E5
Herne Germany 63 H3
Herne Bay U.K. 59 I7
Herning Denmark 55 F8
Heroica Nogales Mex. see Nogales
Heroica Puebla de Zaragoza Mex. see Puebla
Hérouville-St-Clair France 59 G9
Herowābād Iran see Khalkhāl
Herradura Mex. 167 E4
Herrera del Duque Spain 67 D4
Herrero, Punta pt Mex. 167 I5
Herrieden Germany 63 K5
Herschel Canada 149 M1
Herschel Island Canada 149 M1
Hershey PA U.S.A. 165 G3
Hertford U.K. 59 G7
Hertzogville S. Africa 125 G5
Herve Belgium 62 F4
Hervé, Lac l. Canada 153 H3
Hervey Islands Cook Is 187 J7
Herzberg Germany 63 M2
Herzberg (Elster) Germany 63 N3
Herzlake Germany 63 H2
Herzliyya Israel 107 B3
Herzogenaurach Germany 63 K5
Herzsprung Germany 63 M1
Ḥeşār Būshehr Iran 110 C4
Ḥeşār Hormozgān Iran 110 E5
Ḥeşār Zanjān Iran 110 C2

Hesdin France 62 C4
Hesel Germany 63 H1
Heshan China 97 F4
Heshengqiao China 97 G2
Heshui China 95 G5
Heshun China 95 H4
Hesperia CA U.S.A. 158 E4
Hesperus CO U.S.A. 159 I3
Hesperus, Mount AK U.S.A. 148 I3
Hesperus Peak CO U.S.A. 159 I3
Hesquiat Canada 150 E5
Hess r. Canada 149 N3
Hess Creek r. AK U.S.A. 149 J2
Heßdorf Germany 63 K5
Hesse land Germany see Hessen
Hesselberg hill Germany 63 K5
Hessen land Germany 63 J4
Hessisch Lichtenau Germany 63 J3
Hess Mountains Canada 149 N3
Het r. Laos 86 D2
Hetauda town Nepal 105 F4
Heteren Neth. 62 F3
Hetou China 97 F4
Hettinger ND U.S.A. 160 C2
Hetton U.K. 58 E4
Hettstedt Germany 63 L3
Heung Kong Tsai H.K. China see Aberdeen
Hève, Cap de la c. France 59 H9
Hevron West Bank see Hebron
Hexham U.K. 58 E4
Hexian Anhui China 97 H2
Hexian Guangxi China see Hezhou
Hexigten Qi China see Jingpeng
Hexipu China 94 E4
Heyang China 95 G5
Ḩeydarābād Iran 111 F4
Heydebreck Poland see Kędzierzyn-Koźle
Heyin China see Guide
Heysham U.K. 58 E4
Heyshope Dam S. Africa 125 J4
Heyuan China 97 G4
Heywood U.K. 58 E5
Heze China 95 H5
Hezhang China 96 E3
Hezheng China 94 E5
Hezhou China 97 F3
Hezuo China 94 E5
Hialeah FL U.S.A. 163 D7
Hiawassee GA U.S.A. 163 D5
Hiawatha KS U.S.A. 160 E4
Hibbing MN U.S.A. 160 E2
Hibbs, Point Australia 137 [inset]
Hibernia Reef Australia 134 C3
Hīchān Iran 111 F5
Hichisō Japan 92 D3
Hicks, Point Australia 138 D6
Hicks Bay N.Z. 139 G3
Hicks Cayes is Belize 167 H5
Hicks Lake Canada 151 K2
Hicksville OH U.S.A. 164 C3
Hico TX U.S.A. 161 D5
Hida Japan 92 D2
Hida-gawa r. Japan 92 D3
Hidaka Hokkaidō Japan 90 F4
Hidaka Hyōgo Japan 92 A3
Hidaka Saitama Japan 93 F3
Hidaka Wakayama Japan 92 B5
Hidakagawa Japan 92 B5
Hidaka-gawa r. Japan 92 B5
Hidaka-sanmyaku mts Japan 90 F4
Hida-Kiso-gawa Kokutei-kōen park Japan 92 D3
Hida-kōchi plat. Japan 92 C2
Hidalgo Coahuila Mex. 167 E3
Hidalgo Tamaulipas Mex. 161 D7
Hidalgo state Mex. 167 F4
Hidalgo del Parral Mex. 166 D3
Hidalgotitlán Mex. 167 G5
Hida-sanmyaku mts Japan 92 D2
Hidrolândia Brazil 179 A2
Hierosolyma Israel/West Bank see Jerusalem
Higashi Japan 93 G1
Higashiagatsuma Japan 93 E2
Higashiizu Japan 93 F4
Higashi-Matsuyama Japan 93 F2
Higashimurayama Japan 93 F3
Higashiōmi Japan 92 C3
Higashi-Ōsaka Japan 92 B4
Higashishirakawa Japan 92 D3
Higashi-suidō sea chan. Japan 91 C6
Higashiura Aichi Japan 92 C4
Higashiura Hyōgo Japan 92 A4
Higashi-yama mt. Japan 93 D2
Higgins TX U.S.A. 161 C4
Higgins Bay NY U.S.A. 165 H2
Higgins Lake MI U.S.A. 164 C1
High Atlas mts Morocco see Haut Atlas
High Desert OR U.S.A. 156 C4
High Island i. H.K. China 97 [inset]
High Island TX U.S.A. 161 E6
High Island Reservoir H.K. China 97 [inset]
Highland Peak CA U.S.A. 158 D2
Highland Peak NV U.S.A. 159 F3
Highlands NJ U.S.A. 165 I3
Highland Springs VA U.S.A. 165 G5
High Level Canada 150 G3
Highmore SD U.S.A. 160 D2
High Point NC U.S.A. 162 E5
High Point hill NJ U.S.A. 165 H3
High Prairie Canada 150 G4
High River Canada 150 H5
Highrock Lake Man. Canada 151 K4
Highrock Lake Sask. Canada 151 J3
High Springs FL U.S.A. 163 D6
High Tatras mts Poland/Slovakia see Tatra Mountains
High Wycombe U.K. 59 G7
Higuera de Abuya Mex. 166 D3
Higuera de Zaragoza Mex. 166 C3
Higüey Dom. Rep. 169 K5
Higuri-gawa r. Japan 93 F3
Hiiumaa i. Estonia 55 M7
Hijānah, Buḩayrat al imp. l. Syria 107 C3
Hijau, Gunung mt. Indon. 84 C3
Hijaz reg. Saudi Arabia 108 E4
Hijiri-dake mt. Japan 93 E3
Hikabo-yama mt. Japan 93 E2
Hikata Japan 93 G3
Hiki-gawa r. Japan 92 B5
Ḩikmah, Ra's al pt Egypt 112 B5
Hiko NV U.S.A. 159 F3
Hikone Japan 92 C3
Hikurangi mt. N.Z. 139 G3
Hila Moluccas Indon. 83 C4
Hilahila Celebes Indon. 83 B4
Hilāl, Jabal hill Egypt 107 A4
Hilāl, Ra's al pt Libya 108 B3
Hilary Coast Antarctica 188 H1
Hildale UT U.S.A. 159 G3
Hildburghausen Germany 63 K4
Hilders Germany 63 K4
Hildesheim Germany 63 J2
Hillah Iraq 113 G4
Hill Bank Belize 167 H5
Hill City KS U.S.A. 160 D4
Hillegom Neth. 62 E2
Hill End Australia 138 D4
Hillerød Denmark 55 H9
Hillgrove Australia 136 D3
Hill Island Lake Canada 151 I2
Hillman MI U.S.A. 164 D1
Hillsboro ND U.S.A. 160 D2
Hillsboro NM U.S.A. 157 G6
Hillsboro OH U.S.A. 164 D4
Hillsboro OR U.S.A. 156 C3
Hillsboro TX U.S.A. 161 D5
Hillsdale IN U.S.A. 164 B4
Hillsdale MI U.S.A. 164 C3
Hillside Australia 134 B5
Hillston Australia 138 B4
Hillsville VA U.S.A. 164 E5
Hilo HI U.S.A. 157 [inset]
Hilton Australia 136 B4
Hilton S. Africa 125 J5
Hilton NY U.S.A. 165 G2
Hilton Head Island SC U.S.A. 163 D5
Hilvan Turkey 112 E3
Hilversum Neth. 62 F2
Himachal Pradesh state India 104 D3
Himaga-shima i. Japan 92 D4
Himalaya mts Asia 104 D2
Himalchul mt. Nepal 105 F3
Himanka Fin. 54 M4
Ḩimār, Wādī al watercourse Syria/Turkey 107 D1
Himarë Albania 69 H4
Himatnagar India 104 C5
Hime-gawa r. Japan 93 D1
Himeji Japan 92 A4
Himi Japan 92 C2
Ḩimş Syria see Homs
Ḩimş, Baḩrat resr Syria see Qaţţīnah, Buḩayrat
Hinako i. Indon. 84 B2
Hinatuan Mindanao Phil. 82 D4
Hinatuan Passage Phil. 82 D4
Hinchinbrook Entrance sea chan. AK U.S.A. 149 K3
Hinchinbrook Island Australia 136 D3
Hinchinbrook Island AK U.S.A. 149 K3
Hinckley U.K. 59 F6
Hinckley MN U.S.A. 160 E2
Hinckley UT U.S.A. 159 G2
Hinckley Reservoir NY U.S.A. 165 H2
Hindan r. India 99 B7
Hindaun India 104 D4
Hinderwell U.K. 58 G4
Hindley U.K. 58 E5
Hindman KY U.S.A. 164 D5
Hindmarsh, Lake dry lake Australia 137 C8
Hindu Kush mts Afgh./Pak. 111 G3
Hindupur India 106 C3
Hines Creek Canada 150 G3
Hinesville GA U.S.A. 163 D6
Hinganghat India 106 C1
Hingoli India 106 C2
Hınıs Turkey 113 F3
Hinnøya i. Norway 54 I2
Hino Shiga Japan 92 C3
Hino Tōkyō Japan 93 F3
Hinoba-an Negros Phil. 82 C4
Hinoemata Japan 93 F1
Hino-gawa r. Japan 92 C2
Hino-gawa r. Japan 92 C3
Hinojosa del Duque Spain 67 D4
Hino-misaki pt Japan 92 B5
Hinsdale NH U.S.A. 165 I2
Hinte Germany 63 H1
Hinthada Myanmar 86 A3
Hinton Canada 150 G4
Hinton WV U.S.A. 164 E5
Hi-numa l. Japan 93 G2
Hiort i. U.K. see St Kilda
Hippolytushoef Neth. 62 E2
Hipponium Italy see Vibo Valentia
Hippo Regius Alg. see Annaba
Hippo Zarytus Tunisia see Bizerte
Hirabit Dağ mt. Turkey 113 G3
Hiraga-take mt. Japan 93 F1
Hiraizumi tourist site Japan 91 F5
Hirakata Japan 92 B4
Hirakud Dam India 105 E5
Hirakud Reservoir India 105 E5
Hirapur India 104 D4
Hiratsuka Japan 93 F3
Hiraya Japan 92 D3
Hiriyur India 106 C3
Hirogawa Japan 92 B4
Hirosaki Japan 90 F4
Hiroshima Japan 91 D6
Hirschaid Germany 63 L5
Hirschberg Germany 63 L4
Hirschberg mt. Germany 57 M7
Hirschberg Poland see Jelenia Góra
Hirschenstein mt. Germany 63 M6
Hirson France 62 E5
Hîrşova Romania see Hârşova
Hirtshals Denmark 55 F8
Hiruga-take mt. Japan 93 F3
Hirukawa Japan 92 D3
Hisai Japan 92 C4
Hisar India 104 C3
Hisarköy Turkey see Domaniç
Hisarönü Turkey 69 O4
Ḩisb, Sha'īb watercourse Iraq 113 G5
Ḩisbān Jordan 107 B4
Hishig-Öndör Mongolia 94 E1
Hisiu P.N.G. 81 L8
Hisor Tajik. 111 H2
Hisor tizmasi mts Tajik./Uzbek. see Gissar Range
Hispalis Spain see Seville
Hispania country Europe see Spain

▶Hispaniola i. Caribbean Sea 169 J4
Consists of the Dominican Republic and Haiti.

Hispur Glacier Pak. 104 C1
Hissar India see Hisar
Hisua India 105 F4
Ḩisyah Syria 107 C2
Hīt Iraq 113 F4
Hitachi Japan 93 G2
Hitachinaka Japan 93 G2
Hitachiōmiya Japan 93 G2
Hitachiōta Japan 93 G2
Hitra i. Norway 54 F5
Hitzacker (Elbe) Germany 63 L1
Hiuchiga-take vol. Japan 93 F2
Hiva Oa i. Fr. Polynesia 187 K6
Hixon Canada 150 F4
Hixson Cay reef Australia 136 F4
Hiyoshi Kyōto Japan 92 B3
Hiyoshi Nagano Japan 92 D3
Hiyyon, Naḩal watercourse Israel 107 B4
Hizan Turkey 113 F3
Hjälmaren l. Sweden 55 I7
Hjerkinn Norway 54 F5
Hjo Sweden 55 I7
Hjørring Denmark 55 G8
Hkakabo Razi mt. China/Myanmar 96 C2
Hlaingdet Myanmar 86 B2
Hlane Royal National Park Swaziland 125 J4
Hlatikulu Swaziland 125 J4
Hlegu Myanmar 86 B3
Hlohlowane S. Africa 125 H5
Hlotse Lesotho 125 I5
Hluhluwe-Umfolozi Park nature res. S. Africa 125 J5
Hlukhiv Ukr. 53 G6
Hlung-Tan Myanmar 86 B2
Hlusha Belarus 53 F5
Hlybokaye Belarus 55 O9
Ho Ghana 120 D4
Hoa Binh Hoa Binh Vietnam 86 D2
Hoa Binh Nghê An Vietnam 86 D3
Hoachanas Namibia 124 D2
Hoagland IN U.S.A. 164 C3
Hoang Liên Sơn mts Vietnam 86 C2
Hoang Sa is S. China Sea see Paracel Islands

▶Hobart Australia 137 [inset]
Capital of Tasmania.

Hobart OK U.S.A. 161 D5
Hobbs NM U.S.A. 161 C5
Hobbs Coast Antarctica 188 J1
Hobe Sound FL U.S.A. 163 D7
Hobiganj Bangl. see Habiganj
Hoboksar China 98 D3
Hobor China 95 H3
Hobro Denmark 55 F8
Hobyo Somalia 122 E3
Hochandochtla Mountain hill AK U.S.A. 148 I2
Höchberg Germany 63 J5
Hochfeiler mt. Austria/Italy see Gran Pilastro
Hochfeld Namibia 123 B6
Hochharz, Nationalpark nat. park Germany 63 K3
Hô Chi Minh Vietnam see Ho Chi Minh City
Ho Chi Minh City Vietnam 87 D5
Hochschwab mt. Austria 57 O7
Hochschwab mts Austria 57 O7
Hockenheim Germany 63 I5
Ḩôḑ reg. Mauritania 120 C3
Hodal India 99 B8
Hōdatsu-san hill Japan 92 C2
Hōdatsushimizu Japan 92 C2
Hoddesdon U.K. 59 G7
Hodeidah Yemen 108 F7
Hodgenville KY U.S.A. 164 C5
Hodgson Downs Australia 134 F3
Hódmezővásárhely Hungary 69 I1
Hodna, Chott el salt l. Alg. 67 I6
Hodo-dan pt N. Korea 91 B5
Hödrögö Mongolia see Nömrög
Ho Dynasty Citadel tourist site Vietnam 86 D2
Hodzana r. AK U.S.A. 149 K2
Hoek van Holland Neth. see Hook of Holland
Hoensbroek Neth. 62 F4
Hoeryŏng N. Korea 90 C4
Hof Germany 63 L4
Hoffman Mountain NY U.S.A. 165 I2
Hofheim in Unterfranken Germany 63 K4
Hofmeyr S. Africa 125 G6
Höfn Iceland 54 [inset 1]
Hofors Sweden 55 J6
Hofsjökull ice cap Iceland 54 [inset 1]
Hofsós Iceland 54 [inset 1]
Hōfu Japan 91 C6
Höganäs Sweden 55 H8
Hogan Group is Australia 138 C7
Hogansburg NY U.S.A. 165 H1
Hogatza AK U.S.A. 148 I2
Hogatza r. AK U.S.A. 148 I2
Hogback Mountain NE U.S.A. 160 C3
Hoge Vaart canal Neth. 62 F2
Hogg, Mount Canada 149 N3
Hoggar plat. Alg. see Ahaggar
Hog Island VA U.S.A. 165 H5
Högsby Sweden 55 J8
Hohenloher Ebene plain Germany 63 J5
Hohenmölsen Germany 63 M3
Hohennauen Germany 63 M2
Hohensalza Poland see Inowrocław
Hohenwald TN U.S.A. 162 C5
Hohenwartetalsperre resr Germany 63 L4
Hoher Dachstein mt. Austria 57 N7
Hoh Ereg China see Wuchuan
Hohe Rhön mts Germany 63 J4
Hohe Tauern mts Austria 57 N7
Hohe Venn moorland Belgium 62 G4
Hohhot China 95 G3
Höhmorīt Mongolia 94 C2
Hohneck mt. France 66 H2
Hoholitna r. AK U.S.A. 148 H3
Hoh Sai Hu l. China 94 C5
Hoh Xil Hu salt l. China 99 E6
Hoh Xil Shan mts China 99 E6
Hoh Yanhu salt l. China 94 D4
Hôi An Vietnam 86 E4
Hoika China 94 D5
Hoima Uganda 122 D3
Hoit Taria China 94 D4
Hojagala Turkm. 110 E2
Hojai India 105 H4
Hojambaz Turkm. 111 G2
Højryggen mts Greenland 147 M2
Hōki-gawa r. Japan 93 G2
Hokitika N.Z. 139 C6
Hokkaidō i. Japan 90 F4
Hokksund Norway 55 F7
Hokota Japan 93 G2
Hokudan Japan 92 A4
Hokunō Japan 92 C3
Hokusei Japan 92 C3
Hokuto Japan 93 E3
Hol Norway 55 F6
Holbæk Denmark 55 G9
Holbeach U.K. 59 H6
Holbrook Australia 138 C5
Holbrook AZ U.S.A. 159 H4
Holden UT U.S.A. 159 G2
Holdenville OK U.S.A. 161 D5
Holdrege NE U.S.A. 160 D3
Holgate OH U.S.A. 164 C3
Holguín Cuba 169 I4
Holikachuk AK U.S.A. 148 H3
Holin He r. China 90 B3
Holitna r. AK U.S.A. 148 H3
Höljes Sweden 55 H6
Holland country Europe see Netherlands
Holland MI U.S.A. 164 B2
Holland NY U.S.A. 165 F2
Hollandia Indon. see Jayapura
Hollick-Kenyon Peninsula Antarctica 188 L2
Hollick-Kenyon Plateau Antarctica 188 K1
Hollidaysburg PA U.S.A. 165 F3
Hollis AK U.S.A. 149 N5
Hollis OK U.S.A. 161 D5
Hollister CA U.S.A. 158 C3
Holly MI U.S.A. 164 D2
Hollyhill KY U.S.A. 164 C5
Holly Springs MS U.S.A. 161 F5
Hollywood CA U.S.A. 159 D4
Hollywood FL U.S.A. 163 D7
Holm Norway 54 H4
Holmes Reef Australia 136 D3
Holmes Summit Antarctica 188 B1
Holmestrand Norway 55 G7
Holmgard Russia see Velikiy Novgorod
Holm Ø i. Greenland see Kiatassuaq
Holmön i. Sweden 54 L5
Holmsund Sweden 54 L5
Holokuk Mountain hill AK U.S.A. 148 H3
Ḩolon Israel 107 B3
Holoog Namibia 124 C4
Holothuria Banks reef Australia 134 D3
Holroyd r. Australia 136 C2
Holstebro Denmark 55 F8
Holstein IA U.S.A. 160 E3
Holsteinsborg Greenland see Sisimiut
Holston r. TN U.S.A. 162 D4
Holsworthy U.K. 59 C8
Holt U.K. 59 I6
Holt MI U.S.A. 164 C2
Holton MI U.S.A. 164 B2
Holwerd Neth. 62 F1
Holwert Neth. see Holwerd
Holycross Ireland 61 E5
Holy Cross AK U.S.A. 148 H3
Holy Cross, Mount of the CO U.S.A. 156 G5
Holyhead U.K. 58 C5
Holyhead Bay U.K. 58 C5
Holy Island England U.K. 58 F3
Holy Island Wales U.K. 58 C5
Holyoke CO U.S.A. 160 C3
Holy See Europe see Vatican City
Holywell U.K. 58 D5
Holzhausen Germany 63 M3
Holzkirchen Germany 57 M7
Holzminden Germany 63 J3
Homand Iran 111 E3
Homāyūnshahr Iran see Khomeynīshahr
Homberg (Efze) Germany 63 J3
Hombori Mali 120 C3
Homburg Germany 63 H5
Home Bay Canada 147 L3
Homécourt France 62 F5
Homer AK U.S.A. 149 J4
Homer GA U.S.A. 163 D5
Homer LA U.S.A. 161 E5
Homer MI U.S.A. 164 C2
Homer NY U.S.A. 165 G2
Homerville GA U.S.A. 163 D6
Homestead Australia 136 D4
Hom Hanas China 98 D2
Homnabad India 106 C2
Homoine Moz. 125 L2
Homs Libya see Al Khums
Homs Syria 107 C2
Homyel' Belarus 53 F5
Honan prov. China see Henan
Honavar India 106 B3
Honawad India 106 B2
Honaz Turkey 69 M6
Hon Chông Vietnam 87 D5
Honda Bay Palawan Phil. 82 B4
Hondeklipbaai S. Africa 124 C6
Hondo r. Belize/Mex. 167 H5
Hondo TX U.S.A. 161 D6
Hondsrug reg. Neth. 62 G1

▶Honduras country Central America 169 G6
5th largest country in North America.

Honduras, Gulf of Belize/Hond. 166 [inset] I5
Hønefoss Norway 55 G6
Honesdale PA U.S.A. 165 H3
Honey Mex. 167 F4
Honey Lake salt l. CA U.S.A. 158 C1
Honeyoye Lake NY U.S.A. 165 G2
Honfleur France 66 E2
Hong, Mouths of the Vietnam see Red River, Mouths of the
Hông, Sông r. Vietnam see Red
Hongcheng China 94 E4
Hongchuan China see Hongya
Hongde China 95 F4
Honggor China 95 H2
Honggouzi China 98 E5
Honggu China 94 E4
Hongguo China see Panxian
Honghai Wan b. China 97 G4
Honghe China 96 D4
Hong He r. China 97 G1
Honghe Hani Rice Terraces tourist site China 96 D4
Honghu China 97 G2
Hongjialou China see Licheng
Hongjiang Hunan China 97 F3
Hongjiang Sichuan China see Wangcang
Hong Kong H.K. China 97 [inset]
Hong Kong aut. reg. China 97 [inset]
Hong Kong Harbour sea chan. H.K. China 97 [inset]
Hong Kong Island H.K. China 97 [inset]
Hongliu Daquan well China 94 D3
Hongliuhe China 94 C3
Hongliu He r. China 95 G4
Hongliuquan China 98 E5
Hongliuwan China see Aksay
Hongliuyuan Gansu China 94 E4
Hongliuyuan Gansu China 98 F4
Hongor Mongolia see Naran
Hongqiao China see Qidong
Hongqicun China 94 C3
Hongqizhen China see Wuzhishan
Hongshan China 97 G2
Hongshansi China 94 F4
Hongshilazi China 90 B4
Hongshui He r. China 96 F4
Hongtong China 95 G4
Hongueedo, Détroit d' sea chan. Canada 153 I4
Hongwansi China see Sunan
Hongwŏn N. Korea 91 B4
Hongxing China 95 J2
Hongya China 96 D2
Hongyashan Shuiku resr China 94 E4
Hongyuan China 96 D1
Hongze China 97 H1
Hongze Hu l. China 97 H1

▶Honiara Solomon Is 133 F2
Capital of the Solomon Islands.

Honiton U.K. 59 D8
Honjō Nagano Japan 93 D2
Honjō Saitama Japan 93 F2
Honkajoki Fin. 55 M6
Honkawane Japan 93 E3
Honningsvåg Norway 54 N1
Honoka'a HI U.S.A. 157 [inset]

▶Honolulu HI U.S.A. 157 [inset]
Capital of Hawaii.

▶Honshū i. Japan 91 E6
Largest island in Japan, 3rd largest in Asia and 7th in the world.

Hood, Mount vol. OR U.S.A. 156 C3
Hood Bay AK U.S.A. 149 N4
Hood Point Australia 135 B8
Hood Point P.N.G. 136 D1
Hood River OR U.S.A. 156 C3
Hoogeveen Neth. 62 G2
Hoogezand-Sappemeer Neth. 62 G1
Hooghly r. mouth India see Hugli
Hooker OK U.S.A. 161 C4
Hook Head hd Ireland 61 F5
Hook of Holland Neth. 62 E3
Hook Reef Australia 136 E3
Hoolt Mongolia see Tögrög
Hoonah AK U.S.A. 149 N4
Hooper Bay AK U.S.A. 148 F3
Hooper Bay AK U.S.A. 148 F3
Hooper Island MD U.S.A. 165 G4
Hoopeston IL U.S.A. 164 B3
Hoopstad S. Africa 125 G4
Höör Sweden 55 H9
Hoorn Neth. 62 F2
Hōō-san mt. Japan 93 E3
Hoosick NY U.S.A. 165 I2
Hoover Dam Arizona/Nevada U.S.A. 159 F3
Hoover Memorial Reservoir OH U.S.A. 164 D3
Höövör Mongolia see Baruunbayan-Ulaan
Hopa Turkey 113 F2
Hope Canada 150 F5
Hope r. N.Z. 139 D6
Hope AK U.S.A. 149 J3
Hope AR U.S.A. 161 E5
Hope IN U.S.A. 164 C4
Hope, Lake salt flat Australia 135 C8
Hope, Point pt AK U.S.A. 148 F1
Hopedale Canada 153 J3
Hopefield S. Africa 124 D7
Hopei prov. China see Hebei
Hopelchén Mex. 167 H5
Hope Mountains Canada 153 J3
Hope Saddle pass N.Z. 139 D5
Hopes Advance, Baie b. Canada 153 H2
Hopes Advance, Cap c. Canada 147 L3
Hopes Advance Bay Canada see Aupaluk
Hopetoun Australia 137 C7
Hopetown S. Africa 124 G5
Hopewell VA U.S.A. 165 G5
Hopewell Islands Canada 152 F2
Hopin Myanmar 86 B1
Hopkins r. Australia 137 C8
Hopkins, Lake salt flat Australia 135 E6
Hopkinsville KY U.S.A. 164 B5
Hopland CA U.S.A. 158 B2
Hoquiam WA U.S.A. 156 C3
Hor Qinghai China 94 E5
Hor Xizang China 99 C7
Horace Mountain AK U.S.A. 149 J2
Horado Japan 92 C3
Hōrai Japan 92 D4
Hōraiji-san hill Japan 92 D4
Horasan Turkey 113 F2
Hörby Sweden 55 H9
Horcasitas Mex. 166 D2
Horgo Mongolia see Tariat
Horgos Kou'an China 98 C3
Hörhiyn Nuruu mts Mongolia 94 F3
Horigane Japan 93 D2
Horinger China 95 G3
Horiult Mongolia see Bogd

▶Horizon Deep sea feature S. Pacific Ocean 186 I7
Deepest point in the Tonga Trench, and 2nd in the world.

Horki Belarus 53 F5
Horlick Mountains Antarctica 188 K1
Horlivka Ukr. 53 H6
Hormoz, Jazīreh-ye i. Iran 110 E5
Hormoz, Kūh-e mt. Iran 110 D5
Hormuz, Strait of Iran/Oman 110 E5
Horn Austria 57 O6
Horn r. Canada 150 G2
Horn c. Iceland 54 [inset 1]

▶Horn, Cape Chile 178 C9
Most southerly point of South America.

Horn, Îles de is Wallis and Futuna Is 133 I3
Hornaday r. Canada 149 Q1
Hornavan l. Sweden 54 J3
Hornbeck LA U.S.A. 167 G2
Hornbrook CA U.S.A. 156 C4
Hornburg Germany 63 K2
Horncastle U.K. 58 G5
Horndal Sweden 55 J6
Horne, Îles de is Wallis and Futuna Is see Horn, Îles de
Horneburg Germany 63 J1
Hörnefors Sweden 54 K5
Hornell NY U.S.A. 165 G2
Hornepayne Canada 152 D4
Hornillos Mex. 166 C3
Hornisgrinde mt. Germany 57 L6
Horn Island MS U.S.A. 167 H2
Hornkranz Namibia 124 C2
Horn Mountains Canada 150 F2
Horn Mountains AK U.S.A. 148 H3
Hornos, Cabo de Chile see Horn, Cape
Hornoy-le-Bourg France 62 B5
Horn Peak Canada 149 O3
Hornsby Australia 138 E4
Hornsea U.K. 58 G5
Hornslandet pen. Sweden 55 J6
Horodenka Ukr. 53 E6
Horodnya Ukr. 53 F6
Horodok Khmel'nyts'ka Oblast' Ukr. 53 E6
Horodok L'vivs'ka Oblast' Ukr. 53 D6
Horokanai Japan 90 F3
Horo Shan mts China 98 C4
Horoshiri-dake mt. Japan 90 F4
Horqin Shadi reg. China 95 J3
Horqin Youyi Qianqi China see Ulanhot
Horqin Zuoyi Houqi China see Ganjig
Horqin Zuoyi Zhongqi China see Baokang
Horrabridge U.K. 59 C8
Horrocks Australia 135 A7
Horru China 99 E7
Horse Cave KY U.S.A. 164 C5
Horsefly Canada 150 F4
Horseheads NY U.S.A. 165 G2
Horse Islands Canada 153 L4
Horseleap Ireland 61 D4
Horsens Denmark 55 F9
Horseshoe Bend Australia 135 F6
Horseshoe Reservoir AZ U.S.A. 159 H4
Horseshoe Seamounts sea feature N. Atlantic Ocean 184 G3
Horsham Australia 137 C8
Horsham U.K. 59 G7
Horšovský Týn Czech Rep. 63 M5
Horst hill Germany 63 J4
Hörstel Germany 63 H2
Horten Norway 55 G7

Hortobágyi nat. park Hungary 69 I1
Horton r. Canada 149 P1
Horwood Lake Canada 152 E4
Hōryūji tourist site Japan 92 B4
Hosapete India 106 C3
Hösbach Germany 63 J4
Hose, Pegunungan mts Malaysia 85 F2
Ḩoseynābād Iran 110 B3
Ḩoseynīyeh Iran 110 C4
Hoshab Pak. 111 F5
Hoshangabad India 104 D5
Hoshiarpur India 104 C3
Höshööt Arhangay Mongolia see Öldziyt
Höshööt Bayan-Ölgiy Mongolia see Tsengel
Hosoe Japan 92 D4
Hospital Ireland 61 D5
Hosta Butte mt. NM U.S.A. 159 I4
Hotagen r. Sweden 54 I5
Hotahudo East Timor see Hatudo
Hotaka Japan 93 D2
Hotaka-dake mt. Japan 92 D2
Hotaka-yama mt. Japan 93 F2
Hotan China 99 C5
Hotan He watercourse China 98 C4
Hotazel S. Africa 124 F4
Hot Creek Range mts NV U.S.A. 158 E2
Hotgi India 106 C2
Hotham r. Australia 135 B8
Hotham Inlet AK U.S.A. 148 G2
Hoti Seram Indon. 83 D3
Hoting Sweden 54 J4
Hot Springs AR U.S.A. 161 E5
Hot Springs NM U.S.A. see Truth or Consequences
Hot Springs SD U.S.A. 160 C3
Hot Sulphur Springs CO U.S.A. 156 G4
Hottah Lake Canada 150 G1
Hottentots Bay Namibia 124 B4
Hottentots Point Namibia 124 B4
Houayxay Laos 86 C2
Houdan France 62 B6
Houffalize Belgium 62 F4
Hougang Sing. 87 [inset]
Houghton MI U.S.A. 160 F2
Houghton NY U.S.A. 165 F2
Houghton Lake MI U.S.A. 164 C1
Houghton Lake l. MI U.S.A. 164 C1
Houghton le Spring U.K. 58 F4
Houie Moc, Phou mt. Laos 86 C2
Houlton ME U.S.A. 162 H2
Houma China 95 G5
Houma LA U.S.A. 161 F6
Houmen China 97 G4
Houri China 94 D4
House Range mts UT U.S.A. 159 G2
Houston Canada 150 E4
Houston AK U.S.A. 149 J3
Houston MO U.S.A. 161 F4
Houston MS U.S.A. 161 F5
Houston TX U.S.A. 161 E6
Houtman Abrolhos is Australia 135 A7
Houton U.K. 60 F2
Houwater S. Africa 124 F6
Houxia China 98 D4
Houzihe China 94 E4
Hovd Hovd Mongolia 94 B2
Hovd Övörhangay Mongolia see Bogd
Hovd prov. Mongolia 94 C2
Hovd Gol r. Mongolia 94 C1
Hove U.K. 59 G8
Hoveton U.K. 59 I6
Hovmantorp Sweden 55 I8
Hövsgöl Mongolia 95 G3
Hövsgöl prov. Mongolia 94 E1
Hövsgöl Nuur l. Mongolia 94 E1
Hövüün Mongolia see Noyon
Howar, Wadi watercourse Sudan 108 C6
Howard Australia 136 F5
Howard PA U.S.A. 165 G3
Howard SD U.S.A. 160 D2
Howard WI U.S.A. 164 A1
Howard City MI U.S.A. 164 C2
Howard Lake Canada 151 J2
Howard Pass AK U.S.A. 148 H1
Howden U.K. 58 G5
Howe, Cape Australia 138 D6
Howe, Mount Antarctica 188 J1
Howell MI U.S.A. 164 D2
Howick Canada 165 I1
Howick S. Africa 125 J5
Howland ME U.S.A. 162 G2

▶Howland Island terr. N. Pacific Ocean 133 I1
United States Unincorporated Territory.

Howlong Australia 138 C5
Howrah India see Haora
Howth Ireland 61 F4
Ḩowz well Iran 110 E3
Ḩowz-e Khān well Iran 110 E3
Ḩowz-e Panj Iran 110 E4
Ḩowz-e Panj waterhole Iran 110 D3
Howz i-Mian i-Tak Iran 110 D3
Hô Xa Vietnam 86 D3
Höxter Germany 63 J3
Hoxtolgay China 98 D3
Hoxud China 98 D4
Hoy i. U.K. 60 F2
Hoya Germany 63 J2
Hōya Japan 93 F3
Høyanger Norway 55 E6
Hoyerswerda Germany 57 O5
Høylandet Norway 54 H4
Hoym Germany 63 L3
Hoyor Amt China 94 F3
Höytiäinen l. Fin. 54 P5
Hoyt Peak UT U.S.A. 159 H1
Hozu-gawa r. Japan 92 B3
Hpa-an Myanmar 86 B3
Hpapun Myanmar 86 B3
Hpungan Pass India/Myanmar 86 B1
Hradec Králové Czech Rep. 57 O5
Hradiště hill Czech Rep. 63 N4
Hrasnica Bos. & Herz. 68 H3
Hrazdan Armenia 113 G2
Hrebinka Ukr. 53 G6
Hrodna Belarus 55 M10
Hrvatska country Europe see Croatia
Hrvatsko Grahovo Bos. & Herz. see Bosansko Grahovo
Hsenwi Myanmar 86 B2
Hsiang Chang i. H.K. China see Hong Kong Island
Hsiang Kang H.K. China see Hong Kong
Hsi-hseng Myanmar 86 B2
Hsin-chia-p'o country Asia see Singapore
Hsin-chia-p'o Sing. see Singapore
Hsinchu Taiwan see Xinzhu
Hsinking China see Changchun
Hsinying Taiwan see Xinying
Hsipaw Myanmar 86 B2
Hsi-sha Ch'ün-tao is S. China Sea see Paracel Islands
Huab watercourse Namibia 123 B6
Huabei Pingyuan plain China 95 H4
Huachi China 95 G4
Huachinera Mex. 166 C2
Huacho Peru 176 C6
Huachuan China 90 C3
Huade China 95 H3
Huadian China 90 B4
Huadu China 97 G4
Huahai China 94 D3
Huahaizi China 98 F5
Hua Hin Thai. 87 B4
Huai'an Hebei China 95 H3
Huai'an Jiangsu China see Chuzhou
Huai'an Jiangsu China 97 H1
Huaibei China 97 H1
Huaibin China 97 G1
Huaicheng Guangdong China see Huaiji
Huaicheng Jiangsu China see Chuzhou
Huaide China 90 B4
Huaidian China see Shenqiu
Huai Had National Park Thai. 86 D3
Huaihua China 97 F3
Huaiji China 97 G4
Huai Kha Khaeng Wildlife Reserve nature res. Thai. 86 B4
Huailai China 95 H3
Huaillas mt. Peru 176 C5
Huainan China 97 H1
Huaining Anhui China 97 H2
Huaining Anhui China see Shipai
Huairen China 95 H4
Huairou China 95 I3
Huaiyang China 97 G1
Huaiyin Jiangsu China 97 H1
Huaiyin Jiangsu China see Huai'an
Huaiyuan China 97 H1
Huajialing China 94 F5
Huajuápan de León Mex. 168 E5
Huaki Moluccas Indon. 83 C4
Hualahuises Mex. 167 F3
Hualapai Peak AZ U.S.A. 159 G4
Hualian Taiwan 97 I3
Hualien Taiwan see Hualian
Huallaga r. Peru 176 C5
Hualong China 94 E4
Huambo Angola 123 B5
Huanan China 90 C3
Huancane Peru 176 E7
Huancavelica Peru 176 C6
Huancayo Peru 176 C6
Huancheng China see Huanxian
Huangbei China 97 G3
Huangcaoba China see Xingyi
Huangcheng China 94 E4
Huang-chou China see Huanggang
Huangchuan China 97 G1
Huanggang China 97 G2
Huang Hai sea N. Pacific Ocean see Yellow Sea
Huang He r. China see Yellow River
Huanghekou China 95 I4
Huanghe Kou r. mouth China 95 I4
Huanghua China 95 I4
Huangjian China 97 I1
Huang-kang China see Huanggang
Huangling China 95 G5
Huangliu China 97 F5
Huanglong China 95 G5
Huanglongsi China see Kaifeng
Huangmao Jian mt. China 97 H3
Huangmei China 97 G2
Huangpu China 97 G4
Huangqi China 97 H3
Huangshan China 97 H2
Huangshi China 97 G2
Huangtu Gaoyuan plat. China 95 F4
Huangxian China see Longkou
Huangyan China 97 I2
Huangyang China 94 E4
Huangyuan China 94 E4
Huangzhong China 94 E4
Huangzhou China see Huanggang
Huaning China 96 D3
Huaniushan China 94 C3
Huanjiang China 97 F3
Huanren China 90 B4
Huanshan China see Yuhuan
Huantai China 95 I4
Huánuco Peru 176 C5
Huanxian China 95 F4
Huaping China 96 D3
Huaping Yu i. Taiwan 97 I3
Huaqiao China 96 E2
Huaqiaozhen China see Huaqiao
Huaraz Peru 176 C5
Huarmey Peru 176 C6
Huarong China 97 G2
Huascarán, Nevado de mt. Peru 176 C5
Huasco Chile 178 B3
Hua Shan mt. China 95 G5
Huashaoying China 95 H3
Huashixia China 94 D5
Huashulinzi China 90 B4
Huatabampo Mex. 166 C3
Huatong China 95 J3
Huatusco Mex. 167 F5
Huauchinango Mex. 167 F4
Huaxian Guangdong China see Huadu
Huaxian Henan China 95 H5
Huaxian Shaanxi China 95 G5
Huayacocotla Mex. 167 F4
Huayang China see Jixi
Huayin China 97 F1
Huayuan China 97 F2
Huazangsi China see Tianzhu
Huazhai China 94 E4
Hubballi India 106 B3
Hubbard, Mount Canada/U.S.A. 149 M3
Hubbard, Pointe pt Canada 153 I2
Hubbard Lake MI U.S.A. 164 D1
Hubbart Point Canada 151 M3
Hubei prov. China 97 G2
Hubli India see Hubballi
Hückelhoven Germany 62 G3
Hucknall U.K. 59 F5
Huddersfield U.K. 58 F5
Huder China 95 J1
Hüder Mongolia 95 F1
Hudiksvall Sweden 55 J6
Hudson MA U.S.A. 165 J2
Hudson MD U.S.A. 165 G4
Hudson MI U.S.A. 164 C3
Hudson NH U.S.A. 165 J2
Hudson NY U.S.A. 165 I2
Hudson r. NY U.S.A. 165 I3
Hudson, Baie d' sea Canada see Hudson Bay
Hudson, Détroit d' strait Canada see Hudson Strait
Hudson Bay Canada 151 K4
Hudson Bay sea Canada 147 J4
Hudson Falls NY U.S.A. 165 I2
Hudson Island Tuvalu see Nanumanga
Hudson Mountains Antarctica 188 K2
Hudson's Hope Canada 150 F3
Hudson Strait Canada 147 K3
Huê Vietnam 86 D3
Huehuetán Mex. 167 G6
Huehuetenango Guat. 167 H6
Huehueto, Cerro mt. Mex. 161 B7
Huejuqilla Mex. 166 E4
Huejutla Mex. 167 F4
Huelva Spain 67 C5
Huentelauquén Chile 178 B4
Huépac Mex. 166 C2
Huércal-Overa Spain 67 F5
Huertecillas Mex. 161 C7
Huesca Spain 67 F2
Huéscar Spain 67 E5
Huétamo Mex. 167 E5
Huggins Island AK U.S.A. 148 I2
Hughenden Australia 136 D4
Hughes r. Canada 151 K3
Hughes AK U.S.A. 148 I2
Hughes (abandoned) Australia 135 E7
Hughson CA U.S.A. 158 C3
Hugli r. mouth India 105 F5
Hugli-Chinsurah India 105 G5
Hugo CO U.S.A. 160 C4
Hugo OK U.S.A. 161 E5
Hugo Lake OK U.S.A. 161 E5
Hugoton KS U.S.A. 161 C4
Huhehot China see Hohhot
Huhhot China see Hohhot
Huhudi S. Africa 124 G4
Hui'an China 97 H3
Hui'anpu China 94 F4
Huiarau Range mts N.Z. 139 F4
Huib-Hoch Plateau Namibia 124 C4
Huichang China 97 G3
Huicheng Anhui China see Shexian
Huicheng Guangdong China see Huilai
Huicholes, Sierra de los mts Mex. 166 D4
Huidong China 96 D3
Huihe China 95 I1
Huijbergen Neth. 62 E3
Huiji He r. China 95 H5
Huila, Nevado de vol. Col. 176 C3
Huíla, Planalto da Angola 123 B5
Huilai China 97 H4
Huili China 96 D3
Huimanguillo Mex. 167 G5
Huimin China 95 I4
Huinan China see Nanhui
Huining China 94 F5
Huinong China see Majiawan
Huishi China see Huining
Huishui China 96 E3
Huiten Nur l. China 94 B5
Huitong China 97 F3
Huittinen Fin. 55 M6
Huitupan Mex. 167 G5
Huixian Gansu China 96 E1
Huixian Henan China 95 H5
Huixtla Mex. 167 G6
Huiyang China see Huizhou
Huize China 96 D3
Huizhou China 97 G4
Hujirt Arhangay Mongolia see Tsetserleg
Hujirt Övörhangay Mongolia 94 E2
Hujirt Töv Mongolia see Delgerhaan
Hujr Saudi Arabia 108 F4
Hukawng Valley Myanmar 86 B1
Hukuntsi Botswana 124 E2
Hulahula r. AK U.S.A. 149 K1
Hulan China 90 B3
Hulan Ergi China 95 J2
Ḩulayfah Saudi Arabia 108 F4
Ḩulayḩilah well Syria 107 D2
Huliao China see Dabu
Hulilan Iran 110 B3
Hulin China 90 D3
Hulingol China 95 J3
Hull Canada 165 H1
Hull U.K. see Kingston upon Hull
Hull Island atoll Kiribati see Orona
Hultsfred Sweden 55 I8
Huludao China 95 J3
Hulu Hu salt l. China 99 E6
Hulun Buir China 95 I1
Hulun Nur l. China 95 I1
Ḩulwān Egypt 112 C5
Huma China 90 B2
Humahuaca Arg. 178 C2
Humaitá Brazil 176 F5
Humaya r. Mex. 157 G8
Humaym well U.A.E. 110 D6
Humayyān, Jabal hill Saudi Arabia 110 B5
Humber, Mouth of the U.K. 58 H5
Humboldt Canada 151 J4
Humboldt AZ U.S.A. 159 G4
Humboldt NE U.S.A. 160 E3
Humboldt NV U.S.A. 158 D1
Humboldt r. NV U.S.A. 158 D1
Humboldt Bay CA U.S.A. 156 B4
Humboldt Range mts NV U.S.A. 158 D1
Humbolt Salt Marsh NV U.S.A. 158 E2
Hume r. Canada 149 O2
Humeburn Australia 138 B1
Hu Men sea chan. China 97 G4
Hume Reservoir Australia 138 C5
Humphrey Island atoll Cook Is see Manihiki
Humphreys, Mount CA U.S.A. 158 D3
Humphreys Peak AZ U.S.A. 159 H4
Hūn Libya 121 E2
Húnaflói b. Iceland 54 [inset 1]
Hunan prov. China 97 F3
Hundeluft Germany 63 M3
Hunedoara Romania 69 J2
Hünfeld Germany 63 J4
Hungary country Europe 65 H2
Hungerford Australia 138 B2
Hung Fa Leng hill H.K. China see Robin's Nest
Hüngiy Gol r. Mongolia 94 C1
Hŭngnam N. Korea 91 B5
Hung Shui Kiu H.K. China 97 [inset]
Hưng Yên Vietnam 86 D2
Hun He r. China 95 J3
Hunjiang China see Baishan
Huns Mountains Namibia 124 C4
Hunstanton U.K. 59 H6
Hunte r. Germany 63 I1
Hunter r. Australia 138 E4
Hunter, Mount AK U.S.A. 149 J3
Hunter Island Australia 137 [inset]
Hunter Island Canada 150 D5
Hunter Island S. Pacific Ocean 133 H4
Hunter Islands Australia 137 [inset]
Huntingburg IN U.S.A. 164 B4
Huntingdon Canada 165 H1
Huntingdon U.K. 59 G6
Huntingdon PA U.S.A. 165 G3
Huntingdon TN U.S.A. 161 F4
Huntington IN U.S.A. 164 C3
Huntington OR U.S.A. 156 D3
Huntington WV U.S.A. 164 D4
Huntington Beach CA U.S.A. 158 D5
Huntington Creek r. NV U.S.A. 159 F1
Huntly N.Z. 139 E3
Huntly U.K. 60 G3
Hunt Mountain WY U.S.A. 156 G3
Huntsville Canada 164 F1
Huntsville AL U.S.A. 163 C5
Huntsville AR U.S.A. 161 E4
Huntsville TN U.S.A. 164 C5
Huntsville TX U.S.A. 161 E6
Hunucmá Mex. 167 H4
Hunyuan China 95 H4
Hunza r. Pak. 99 A6
Hunza reg. Pak. 104 C1
Huocheng China 98 C3
Huoer China see Hor
Huojia China 95 H5
Huolin He r. China see Holin He
Huolongmen China 90 B2
Huolu China see Luquan
Hương Khê Vietnam 86 D3
Huonville Australia 137 [inset]
Huoqiu China 97 H1
Huoshan China 97 H2
Huoshao Tao i. Taiwan see Lü Dao
Huoxian China see Huozhou
Huozhou China 95 G4
Hupeh prov. China see Hubei
Hupnik r. Turkey 107 C1
Hupu India 96 B2
Ḩūr Iran 110 E4
Hurault, Lac l. Canada 153 H3
Ḩuraydīn, Wādī watercourse Egypt 107 A4
Huraysān reg. Saudi Arabia 110 B6
Hurd, Cape Canada 164 E1
Hurd Island Kiribati see Arorae
Hure China 95 J3
Hüreemaral Mongolia 94 D2
Hüremt Bulgan Mongolia see Sayhan
Hüremt Övörhangay Mongolia see Taragt
Hüren Tovon Uul mt. Mongolia 102 I3
Hure Qi China see Hure
Hurghada Egypt 108 D4
Hurleg China 94 D4
Hurleg Hu l. China 94 D4
Hurler's Cross Ireland 61 D5
Hurley NM U.S.A. 159 I5
Hurley WI U.S.A. 160 F2
Hurmagai Pak. 111 G4
Huron CA U.S.A. 158 C3
Huron SD U.S.A. 160 D2

▶Huron, Lake Canada/U.S.A. 164 D1
2nd largest lake in North America and 4th in the world.

Hurricane UT U.S.A. 159 G3
Hursley U.K. 59 F7
Hurst Green U.K. 59 H7
Hurung, Gunung mt. Indon. 85 F2
Husain Nika Pak. 111 H4
Húsavík Norðurland eystra Iceland 54 [inset 1]
Húsavík Vestfirðir Iceland 54 [inset 1]
Huseyinabat Turkey see Alaca
Huseyinli Turkey see Kızılırmak
Hūshak Iran 111 F5
Hushan Zhejiang China 97 H2
Hushan Zhejiang China see Wuyi
Hushan Zhejiang China see Cixi
Huşi Romania 69 M1
Huskvarna Sweden 55 I8
Huslia AK U.S.A. 148 H2
Huslia r. AK U.S.A. 148 H2
Husn Jordan see Al Ḩiṣn
Ḩuṣn Āl 'Abr Yemen 108 G6
Husnes Norway 55 D7
Husum Germany 57 L3
Husum Sweden 54 K5
Hutag Mongolia see Hutag-Öndör
Hutag-Öndör Mongolia 94 E1
Hutanopan Sumatra Indon. 84 B2
Hutchinson KS U.S.A. 160 D4
Hutchinson MN U.S.A. 160 E2
Hutch Mountain AZ U.S.A. 159 H4
Hutou China 90 D3
Hutsonville IL U.S.A. 164 B4
Hutton, Mount hill Australia 137 E5
Hutton Range hills Australia 135 C6
Hutubi China 98 D3
Hutubi He r. China 98 D3
Hutuo He r. China 95 I4
Huvadhu Atholhu Maldives 103 D11
Hüvek Turkey see Bozova
Hūvīān, Kūh-e mts Iran 111 E5
Ḩuwār i. Bahrain 110 C5
Huwaytat reg. Saudi Arabia 107 C5
Huxi China 97 G3
Huxian China 95 G5
Huzhong China 90 A2
Huzhou China 97 I2
Huzhu China 94 E4
Hvannadalshnúkur vol. Iceland 54 [inset 1]
Hvar i. Croatia 68 G3
Hvide Sande Denmark 55 F8
Hvíta r. Iceland 54 [inset 1]
Hwange Zimbabwe 123 C5
Hwange National Park Zimbabwe 123 C5
Hwang Ho r. China see Yellow River
Hwedza Zimbabwe 123 D5
Hwlffordd U.K. see Haverfordwest
Hyakuriga-take hill Japan 92 B3
Hyannis MA U.S.A. 165 J3
Hyannis NE U.S.A. 160 C3
Hyargas Nuur salt l. Mongolia 94 C1
Hyco Lake NC U.S.A. 164 F5
Hyde N.Z. 139 C7
Hyden Australia 135 B8
Hyden KY U.S.A. 164 D5
Hyde Park VT U.S.A. 165 I1
Hyder AK U.S.A. 149 O5
Hyderabad India 106 C2
Hyderabad Pak. 111 H5
Hydra i. Greece see Ydra
Hyères France 66 H5
Hyères, Îles d' is France 66 H5
Hyesan N. Korea 90 C4
Hyland r. Canada 149 O4
Hyland, Mount Australia 138 F3
Hyland Post Canada 150 D3
Hyllestad Norway 55 D6
Hyltebruk Sweden 55 H8
Hyndman Peak ID U.S.A. 156 E4
Hyōgo pref. Japan 92 A3
Hyōno-sen mt. Japan 91 D6
Hyrynsalmi Fin. 54 P4
Hysham MT U.S.A. 156 G3
Hythe Canada 150 G4
Hythe U.K. 59 I7
Hyūga Japan 91 C6
Hyvinkää Fin. 55 N6

I

Iaciara Brazil 179 B1
Iaco r. Brazil 176 E5
Iaçu Brazil 179 C1
Iadera Croatia see Zadar
Iaeger WV U.S.A. 164 E5
Iakora Madag. 123 E6
Ialomiţa r. Romania 69 L2
Ianca Romania 69 L2
Iaşi Romania 69 L1
Iba Luzon Phil. 82 B3
Ibadan Nigeria 120 D4
Ibagué Col. 176 C3
Ibaiti Brazil 179 A3
Ibapah UT U.S.A. 159 G1
Ibaraki Ibaraki Japan 93 G2
Ibaraki Ōsaka Japan 92 B4
Ibaraki pref. Japan 93 G2
Ibarra Ecuador 176 C3
Ibb Yemen 108 F7
Ibbenbüren Germany 63 H2
Iberá, Esteros del marsh Arg. 178 E3
Iberia Peru 176 E6

▶Iberian Peninsula Europe 67
Consists of Portugal, Spain and Gibraltar.

Iberville, Lac d' l. Canada 153 G3
Ibeto Nigeria 120 D3
iBhayi S. Africa see Port Elizabeth
Ibi Sumatra Indon. 84 B1
Ibi Nigeria 120 D4
Ibiá Brazil 179 B2
Ibiaí Brazil 179 B2
Ibiapaba, Serra da hills Brazil 177 J4
Ibiassucê Brazil 179 C1
Ibicaraí Brazil 179 D1
Ibigawa Japan 92 C3
Ibi-gawa r. Japan 92 C3
Ibiquera Brazil 179 C1
Ibirama Brazil 179 A4
Ibiranhém Brazil 179 C2
Ibi-Sekigahara-Yōrō Kokutei-kōen park Japan 92 C3
Ibitinga Brazil 179 A3
Ibiza Spain 67 G4
Ibiza i. Spain 67 G4
Iblei, Monti mts Sicily Italy 68 F6
Ibn Buşayyiş well Saudi Arabia 110 B5
Ibotirama Brazil 177 J6
Iboundji, Mont hill Gabon 122 B4
Ibrā' Oman 110 E6
İbradı Turkey 112 C3
Ibrī Oman 110 E6
Ibu Halmahera Indon. 83 C2
Ibuhos i. Phil. 82 C1
Ibuki Japan 92 C3
Ibuki-sanchi mts Japan 92 C3
Ibuki-yama mt. Japan 92 C3
Ica r. Col. see Putumayo
Ica Peru 176 C6
Icaiché Mex. 167 H5
Içana Brazil 176 E3
Içana r. Brazil 176 E3
Icaria i. Greece see Ikaria
Icatu Brazil 177 J4
Iceberg Canyon gorge NV U.S.A. 159 F3
İçel Turkey see Mersin

▶Iceland country Europe 54 [inset]
2nd largest island in Europe.

Iceland Basin sea feature N. Atlantic Ocean 184 G2
Icelandic Plateau sea feature N. Atlantic Ocean 189 I2
Ichalkaranji India 106 B2
Ichifusa-yama mt. Japan 91 C6
Ichihara Japan 93 G3
Ichikai Japan 93 G2
Ichikawa Chiba Japan 93 F3
Ichikawa Hyōgo Japan 92 A3
Ichi-kawa r. Japan 92 A4
Ichikawamisato Japan 93 E3
Ichinomiya Aichi Japan 92 C3
Ichinomiya Aichi Japan 92 D4
Ichinomiya Chiba Japan 93 G3
Ichinomiya Hyōgo Japan 92 A4
Ichinomiya Yamanashi Japan 93 E3
Ichinoseki Japan 91 F5
Ichinskaya Sopka, Vulkan vol. Russia 77 Q4
Ichishi Japan 92 C4
Ichkeul, Parc National de l' Tunisia 68 C6
Ichnya Ukr. 53 G6
Ichtegem Belgium 62 D3
Ichtershausen Germany 63 K4
Icó Brazil 177 K5
Içoguz Turkm. 110 E1
Iconha Brazil 179 C3
Iconium Turkey see Konya
Icosium Alg. see Algiers
Iculisma France see Angoulême
Icy Bay AK U.S.A. 149 K4
Icy Bay AK U.S.A. 149 L4
Icy Cape AK U.S.A. 148 G1
Icy Strait AK U.S.A. 149 N4
İd Turkey see Narman
Idabel OK U.S.A. 161 E5
Ida Grove IA U.S.A. 160 E3
Idah Nigeria 120 D4
Idaho state U.S.A. 156 E3
Idaho City ID U.S.A. 156 E4
Idaho Falls ID U.S.A. 156 E4
Idalia National Park Australia 136 D5
Idar India 104 C5
Idar-Oberstein Germany 63 H5
Ide Japan 92 B4
Ider Mongolia see Galt
Ideriyn Gol r. Mongolia 94 E1
Idfū Egypt 108 D5
Idhra i. Greece see Ydra
Idi Amin Dada, Lake Dem. Rep. Congo/Uganda see Edward, Lake
Idiofa Dem. Rep. Congo 123 B4
Iditarod r. AK U.S.A. 148 H3
Iditarod (abandoned) AK U.S.A. 148 H3
Idivuoma Sweden 54 M2
Idkū Egypt 112 C5
Idle r. U.K. 58 G5
Idlewild airport NY U.S.A. see John F. Kennedy
Idlib Syria 107 C2
Idra i. Greece see Ydra
Idre Sweden 55 H6
Idrija Slovenia 68 E1
Idstein Germany 63 I4
Idutywa S. Africa see Dutywa
Idzhevan Armenia see Ijevan
Iecava Latvia 55 N8
Iepê Brazil 179 A3
Ieper Belgium 62 C4
Ierapetra Greece 69 K7
Ierissou, Kolpos b. Greece 69 J4
Iešjávri l. Norway 54 N2
Ifakara Tanz. 123 D4
Ifalik atoll Micronesia 81 K5
Ifaluk atoll Micronesia see Ifalik
Ifanadiana Madag. 123 E6
Ife Nigeria 120 D4
Ifenat Chad 121 E3
Iferouâne Niger 120 D3
Iffley Australia 136 C3
Ifjord Norway 54 O1
Ifôghas, Adrar des hills Mali 120 D3
Iforas, Adrar des hills Mali see Ifôghas, Adrar des
Iga Mie Japan 92 C4
Iga Mie Japan 92 C4
Igan Sarawak Malaysia 85 E2
Igan r. Malaysia 85 E2
Iganga Uganda 121 G4
Igarapava Brazil 179 B3
Igarka Russia 76 J3
Igatpuri India 106 B2
Igbeti Nigeria see Igbetti
Igbetti Nigeria 120 D4
Igdir Iran 110 B2
Iğdır Turkey 113 G3

Igel'veyem r. Russia 148 D2
Iggesund Sweden 55 J6
Igikpak, Mount AK U.S.A. 148 I2
Igiugig AK U.S.A. 148 I4
Igizyar China 111 J2
Iglesias Sardinia Italy 68 C5
Iglesiente reg. Sardinia Italy 68 C5
Igloolik Canada 147 J3
Igluligaarjuk Canada see Chesterfield Inlet
Ignace Canada 151 N5
Ignacio Zaragoza Chihuahua Mex. 166 D2
Ignacio Zaragoza Tamaulipas Mex. 167 F4
Ignacio Zaragoza Zacatecas Mex. 161 C8
Ignalina Lith. 55 O9
İğneada Turkey 69 L4
İğneada Burnu pt Turkey 69 M4
Ignoitijala India 87 A5
iGoli S. Africa see Johannesburg
Igom Papua Indon. 83 D3
Igoumenitsa Greece 69 I5
Igra Russia 51 Q4
Igrim Russia 51 S3
Iguaçu r. Brazil 179 A4
Iguaçu, Saltos do waterfall Arg./Brazil see Iguaçu Falls
Iguaçu Falls Arg./Brazil 178 F3
Iguaí Brazil 179 C1
Iguala Mex. 168 E5
Igualada Spain 67 G3
Iguape Brazil 179 B4
Iguaraçu Brazil 179 A3
Iguatama Brazil 179 B3
Iguatemi Brazil 178 F2
Iguatu Brazil 177 K5
Iguazú, Cataratas do waterfall Arg./Brazil see Iguaçu Falls
Iguéla Gabon 122 A4
Iguidi, Erg des. Alg./Mauritania 120 C2
Igunga Tanz. 123 D4
Iharaña Madag. 123 E5
Ihavandhippolhu Maldives 106 B5
Ihavandiffulu Atoll Maldives see Ihavandhippolhu
Ihbulag Mongolia see Hanbogd
Ihhayrhan Mongolia see Bayan-Önjüül
Ihosy Madag. 123 E6
Ih Tal China 95 J3
Ihtamir Mongolia 94 E2
Ihtiman Bulg. 69 J3
Ih Tol Gol China 95 J1
Ih-Uul Mongolia 94 E1
Iida Japan 93 D3
Iide-san mt. Japan 91 E5
Iijärvi l. Fin. 54 O2
Iijima Japan 93 D3
Iijoki r. Fin. 54 N4
Iinan Japan 92 C4
Iioka Japan 93 G3
Iisalmi Fin. 54 O5
Iitaka Japan 92 C4
Iiyama Japan 93 E2
Iizuka Japan 91 C6
Iizuna Japan 93 E2
Ijebu-Ode Nigeria 120 D4
Ijen-Merapi-Maelang, Cagar Alam nature res. Java Indon. 85 F5
Ijevan Armenia 113 G2
IJmuiden Neth. 62 E2
IJssel r. Neth. 62 F2
IJsselmeer l. Neth. 62 F2
IJzer r. France see Yser
Ikaahuk Canada see Sachs Harbour
Ikaalinen Fin. 55 M6
Ikageleng S. Africa 125 H3
Ikageng S. Africa 125 H4
Ikaho Japan 93 E2
iKapa S. Africa see Cape Town
Ikare Nigeria 120 D4
Ikaria i. Greece 69 L6
Ikaruga Japan 92 B4
Ikast Denmark 55 F8
Ikawa Japan 93 E3
Ikeda Fukui Japan 92 C3
Ikeda Hokkaidō Japan 90 F4
Ikeda Nagano Japan 93 D2
Ikeda Ōsaka Japan 92 B3
Ikegoya-yama mt. Japan 92 C4
Ikela Dem. Rep. Congo 122 C4
Ikhutseng S. Africa 124 G5
Iki-Burul Russia 53 J7
Ikom Nigeria 120 D4
Ikoma Japan 92 B4
Ikpikpuk r. AK U.S.A. 148 I1
Iksan S. Korea 91 B6
Ikuji-hana pt Japan 92 D2
Ikungu Tanz. 123 D4
Ikuno Japan 92 A3
Ikusaka Japan 93 D2
Ilagan Luzon Phil. 82 C2
Ilaisamis Kenya 122 D3
Īlām Iran 110 B3
Ilam Nepal 105 F4
Ilan Taiwan see Yilan
Ilave Peru 176 E7
Iława Poland 57 Q4
Ilazārān, Kūh-e mt. Iran 110 E4
Il Bogd'in Nuruu mts Mongolia 94 D2
Île-à-la-Crosse Canada 151 J4
Île-à-la-Crosse, Lac l. Canada 151 J4
Ilebo Dem. Rep. Congo 123 C4
Île-de-France admin. reg. France 62 C6
Île Europa i. Indian Ocean see Europa, Île
Ilek Kazakh. 51 Q5
Ilemi Triangle terr. Africa 122 D3
Ilen r. Ireland 61 C6
Ileret Kenya 122 D3
Ileza Russia 52 I3
Ilfeld Germany 63 K3
Ilford Canada 151 M3
Ilford U.K. 59 H7
Ilfracombe Australia 136 D4
Ilfracombe U.K. 59 C7
Ilgaz Turkey 112 D2
Ilgın Turkey 112 C3
Ilha Grande resr Brazil 178 F2
Ilha Solteíra, Represa resr Brazil 179 A3
Ílhavo Port. 67 B3
Ilhéus Brazil 179 D1
Ili r. China/Kazakh. 98 B3
Ili Kazakh. see Kapshagay
Iliamna AK U.S.A. 148 I4
Iliamna Lake AK U.S.A. 148 I4
Iliamna Volcano AK U.S.A. 148 I3
İliç Turkey 112 E3
Il'ichevsk Azer. see Şärur
Il'ichevsk Ukr. see Illichivs'k
Ilici Spain see Elche-Elx
Iligan Mindanao Phil. 82 D4
Iligan Bay Mindanao Phil. 82 D4
Iligan Point Luzon Phil. 82 C2
Ilimananngip Nunaa i. Greenland 147 P2
Il'inka Astrakhanskaya Oblast' Russia 53 J7
Il'inka Respublika Tyva Russia 94 C1
Il'inskiy Permskiy Kray Russia 51 R4
Il'inskiy Sakhalinskaya Oblast' Russia 90 F3
Il'insko-Podomskoye Russia 52 J3
Ilin Strait Phil. 82 C3
Iliomar East Timor 83 C5
Ilion NY U.S.A. 165 H2
Ilium tourist site Turkey see Troy
Ilivit Mountains AK U.S.A. 148 G3
Iliysk Kazakh. see Kapshagay
Ilkal India 106 C3
Ilkeston U.K. 59 F6
Ilkley U.K. 58 F5
Illana Bay Mindanao Phil. 82 C5
Illapel Chile 178 B4
Illéla Niger 120 D3
Iller r. Germany 57 L6
Illichivs'k Ukr. 69 N1
Illimani, Nevado de mt. Bol. 176 E7
Illinois r. IL U.S.A. 160 F4
Illinois state U.S.A. 164 A3
Illizi Alg. 120 D2
Illogwa watercourse Australia 136 A5
Ilm r. Germany 63 L3
Ilmajoki Fin. 54 M5
Il'men', Ozero l. Russia 52 F4
Ilmenau Germany 63 K4
Ilmenau r. Germany 63 K1
Ilminster U.K. 59 E8
Ilnik AK U.S.A. 148 H4
Ilo Peru 176 D7
Iloc i. Phil. 82 B4
Iloilo Panay Phil. 82 C4
Iloilo Strait Phil. 82 C4
Ilomantsi Fin. 54 Q5
Ilong India 96 B3
Ilorin Nigeria 120 D4
Ilovlya Russia 53 I6
Ilsede Germany 63 K2
Iluka Australia 138 F2
Ilulissat Greenland 147 M3
Iluppur India 106 C4
Ilva i. Italy see Elba, Isola d'
Imabari Japan 91 D6
Imadate Japan 92 C3
Imaichi Japan see Nikkō
Imajō Japan 92 C3
Imala Moz. 123 D5
Imam-baba Turkm. 111 F2
İmamoğlu Turkey 112 D3
Imām Şāḥib Afgh. 111 H2
Iman Russia see Dal'nerechensk
Iman r. Russia 90 D3
Imari Japan 91 C6
Imaruí Brazil 179 A5
Imataca, Serranía de mts Venez. 176 F2
Imatra Fin. 55 P6
Imazu Japan 92 C3
Imba-numa l. Japan see Inba-numa
Imbituva Brazil 179 A4
imeni 26 Bakinskikh Komissarov Azer. see Häsänabad
imeni Petra Stuchki Latvia see Aizkraukle
Īmī Eth. 122 E3
Imishli Azer. see İmişli
İmişli Azer. 113 H3
Imit Pak. 104 C1
Imizu Japan 92 D2
Imja-do i. S. Korea 91 B6
Imlay NV U.S.A. 158 D1
Imlay City MI U.S.A. 164 D2
Imola Italy 68 D2
iMonti S. Africa see East London
Impendle S. Africa 125 I5
Imperatriz Brazil 177 I5
Imperia Italy 68 C3
Imperial CA U.S.A. 159 F5
Imperial NE U.S.A. 160 C3
Imperial Beach CA U.S.A. 158 E5
Imperial Dam Arizona/California U.S.A. 159 F5
Imperial Valley plain CA U.S.A. 159 F5
Imperieuse Reef Australia 134 B4
Impfondo Congo 122 B3
Imphal India 105 H4
İmralı Adası i. Turkey 69 M4
İmroz Turkey 69 K4
İmroz i. Turkey see Gökçeada
Imtān Syria 107 C3
Imuris Mex. 166 C2
Imuruan Bay Palawan Phil. 82 B4
Imuruk Basin l. AK U.S.A. 148 F2
Imuruk Lake AK U.S.A. 148 G2
In r. Russia 90 D2
Ina Japan 93 D3
Inabe Japan 92 C3
Inabu Japan 92 D3
Inae Japan 92 C3
Inagauan Palawan Phil. 82 B4
Inagawa Japan 92 B4
Ina-gawa r. Japan 92 B4
Inage Japan 93 G3
Inagi Japan 93 F3
Inalik AK U.S.A. see Diomede
Inambari r. Peru 176 E6
Inami Hyōgo Japan 92 A4
Inami Toyama Japan 92 C2
Inanam Sabah Malaysia 85 G1
Inanudak Bay AK U.S.A. 148 E5
Inari Fin. 54 O2
Inarijärvi l. Fin. 54 O2
Inarijoki r. Fin./Norway 54 N2
Inasa Japan 92 D4
Inashiki Japan 93 G3
Inazawa Japan 92 C3
Inba Japan 93 G3
Inba-numa l. Japan 93 G3
Inca Spain 67 H4
İnce Burnu pt Turkey 69 L4
İnce Burun pt Turkey 112 D2
Inch Ireland 61 F5
Inchard, Loch b. U.K. 60 D2
Incheon S. Korea 91 B5
Inchicronan Lough l. Ireland 61 D5
Inch'ŏn S. Korea see Incheon
Inchoun Russia 148 E2
Incirli Turkey see Karasu
Indaal, Loch b. U.K. 60 C5
Indalsälven r. Sweden 54 J5
Indalstø Norway 55 D6
Inda Silasē Eth. 122 D2
Indaw Myanmar 86 A2
Indawgyi Lake Myanmar 96 C3
Indé Mex. 166 D3
Indefatigable Island Galápagos Ecuador see Santa Cruz, Isla
Independence CA U.S.A. 158 D3
Independence IA U.S.A. 160 F3
Independence KS U.S.A. 161 E4
Independence KY U.S.A. 164 C4
Independence MO U.S.A. 160 E4
Independence VA U.S.A. 164 E5
Independence Mountains NV U.S.A. 156 D4
Inder China 95 J2
Inderbor Kazakh. 100 E2
Indi India 106 C2

▶India country Asia 103 E7
2nd most populous country in Asia and the world. 3rd largest country in Asia and 7th in the world.

Indian r. Canada 149 M3
Indiana PA U.S.A. 164 F3
Indiana state U.S.A. 164 B3
Indian-Antarctic Ridge sea feature Southern Ocean 186 D9

▶Indianapolis IN U.S.A. 164 B4
Capital of Indiana.

Indian Cabins Canada 150 G3
Indian Desert India/Pak. see Thar Desert
Indian Harbour Canada 153 K3
Indian Head Canada 151 K5
Indian Lake NY U.S.A. 165 H2
Indian Lake l. NY U.S.A. 165 H2
Indian Lake l. OH U.S.A. 164 D3
Indian Lake l. PA U.S.A. 165 F3
Indian Mountain AK U.S.A. 148 I2

▶Indian Ocean 185
3rd largest ocean in the world.

Indianola IA U.S.A. 160 E3
Indianola MS U.S.A. 161 F5
Indian Peak UT U.S.A. 159 G2
Indian Springs IN U.S.A. 164 B4
Indian Springs NV U.S.A. 159 F3
Indian Wells AZ U.S.A. 159 H4
Indiga Russia 52 K2
Indigirka r. Russia 77 P2
Indigskaya Guba b. Russia 52 K2
Inđija Serbia 69 I2
Indin Lake Canada 150 H1
Indio r. Nicaragua 166 [inset] J7
Indio CA U.S.A. 158 E5
Indira Point India 87 A6
Indira Priyadarshini Pench National Park India 104 D5
Indispensable Reefs Solomon Is 133 G3
Indjija Serbia see Inđija
Indo-China reg. Asia 86 D3

▶Indonesia country Asia 80 E7
3rd most populous country in Asia and 4th in the world.

Indore India 104 C5
Indragiri r. Indon. 84 C3
Indramayu Java Indon. 85 E4
Indramayu, Tanjung pt Indon. 85 E4
Indrapura Sumatra Indon. 84 C3
Indrapura, Gunung vol. Indon. see Kerinci, Gunung
Indrapura, Tanjung pt Indon. 84 C3
Indravati r. India 106 D2
Indre r. France 66 E3
Indulkana Australia 135 F6
Indur India see Nizamabad
Indus r. China/Pak. 111 G6
also known as Sênggê Zangbo or Shiquan He
Indus, Mouths of the Pak. 111 G5
Indus Cone sea feature Indian Ocean 185 M4
Indwe S. Africa 125 H6
Ine Japan 92 B3
İnebolu Turkey 112 D2
İnegöl Turkey 69 M4
Inerie vol. Flores Indon. 83 B5
Inevi Turkey see Cihanbeyli
Inez KY U.S.A. 164 D5
Infantes Spain see Villanueva de los Infantes
Infiernillo, Presa resr Mex. 168 D5
Ing, Nam Mae r. Thai. 86 C2
Inga Russia 54 S3
Ingalls, Mount CA U.S.A. 158 C2
Ingelmunster Belgium 62 D4
Ingenika r. Canada 150 E3
Ingersoll Canada 164 E2
Ingettolgoy Mongolia see Selenge
Inggelang i. Moluccas Indon. 83 D2
Ingham Australia 136 D3
Ingichka Uzbek. 111 G2
Ingleborough hill U.K. 58 E4
Inglefield Land reg. Greenland 147 K2
Ingleton U.K. 58 E4
Inglewood Qld Australia 138 E2
Inglewood Vic. Australia 138 A6
Inglewood CA U.S.A. 158 D5
Ingoda r. Russia 95 H1
Ingoka Pum mt. Myanmar 86 B1
Ingoldmells U.K. 58 H5
Ingolstadt Germany 63 L6
Ingomar Australia 135 F7
Ingomar MT U.S.A. 156 G3
Ingonish Canada 153 J5
Ingraj Bazar India 105 G4
Ingram VA U.S.A. 164 F5
Ingray Lake Canada 150 G1
Ingrid Christensen Coast Antarctica 188 E2
Ingwavuma S. Africa 125 K4
Ingwavuma r. S. Africa/Swaziland see Ngwavuma
Ingwiller France 63 H6
Inhaca Moz. 125 K3
Inhaca, Península pen. Moz. 125 K4
Inhambane Moz. 125 L2
Inhambane prov. Moz. 125 L2
Inhaminga Moz. 123 D5
Inharrime Moz. 125 L3
Inhassoro Moz. 123 D6
Inhaúmas Brazil 179 B1
Inhobim Brazil 179 C1
Inhumas Brazil 179 A2
Inielika vol. Flores Indon. 83 B5
Inírida Col. 176 E3
Inis Ireland see Ennis
Inis Córthaidh Ireland see Enniscorthy
Inishark i. Ireland 61 B4
Inishbofin i. Ireland 61 B4
Inisheer i. Ireland 61 C4
Inishkea North i. Ireland 61 B3
Inishkea South i. Ireland 61 B3
Inishmaan i. Ireland 61 C4
Inishmore i. Ireland 61 C4
Inishmurray i. Ireland 61 D3
Inishowen pen. Ireland 61 E2
Inishowen Head hd Ireland 61 F2
Inishtrahull i. Ireland 61 E2
Inishturk i. Ireland 61 B4
Injgan Sum China 95 I2
Injune Australia 137 E5
Inkerman Australia 136 C3
Inkeroinen Fin. 55 O6
Inklin Canada 150 C3
Inklin r. Canada 149 N4
Inkylap Turkm. 111 F2
Inland Kaikoura Range mts N.Z. 139 D6
Inland Lake AK U.S.A. 148 H2
Inland Sea Japan see Seto-naikai
Inlet NY U.S.A. 165 H2
Inman r. Canada 149 R1
Inn r. Europe 57 M7
Innaanganeq c. Greenland 147 L2
Innamincka Australia 137 C5
Innamincka Regional Reserve nature res. Australia 137 C5
Inndyr Norway 54 I3
Inner Mongolia aut. reg. China see Nei Mongol Zizhiqu
Inner Sound sea chan. U.K. 60 D3
Innes National Park Australia 137 B7
Innisfail Australia 136 D3
Innisfail Canada 150 H4
Innokent'yevka Russia 90 C2
Innoko r. AK U.S.A. 148 H3
Innoko National Wildlife Refuge nature res. AK U.S.A. 148 H3
Innsbruck Austria 57 M7
Innuksuak r. Canada 152 F2
Inny r. Ireland 61 E4
Inobonto Celebes Indon. 83 C2
Inocência Brazil 179 A2
Inokuchi Japan 92 C2
Inongo Dem. Rep. Congo 122 B4
İnönü Turkey 69 N5
Inoucdjouac Canada see Inukjuak
Inowrocław Poland 57 Q4
In Salah Alg. 120 D2
Insch U.K. 60 G3

▶Inscription, Cape Australia 135 A6
Most westerly point of Oceania.

Insein Myanmar 86 B3
Insterburg Russia see Chernyakhovsk
Inta Russia 51 S2
Interamna Italy see Teramo
Interlaken Switz. 66 H3
International Falls MN U.S.A. 160 E1
Interview Island India 87 A4
Intracoastal Waterway canal TX U.S.A. 161 E6
Intutu Peru 176 D4
Inubō-zaki pt Japan 91 F6
Inukjuak Canada 152 F2
Inuvialuit area Canada 146 E3
Inuvik Canada 149 N1
Inuyama Japan 92 C3
Inveraray U.K. 60 D4
Inverbervie U.K. 60 G4
Invercargill N.Z. 139 B8
Inverell Australia 138 E2
Invergordon U.K. 60 E3
Inverkeithing U.K. 60 F4
Inverleigh Australia 136 C3
Invermay Canada 151 K5
Inverness Canada 153 J5
Inverness U.K. 60 E3
Inverness CA U.S.A. 158 B2
Inverness FL U.S.A. 163 D6
Inverurie U.K. 60 G3
Investigator Channel Myanmar 87 B4
Investigator Group is Australia 135 F8
Investigator Ridge sea feature Indian Ocean 185 O6
Investigator Strait Australia 137 B7
Inwood WV U.S.A. 165 F4
Inya Russia 98 D2
Inyanga Zimbabwe see Nyanga
Inyokern CA U.S.A. 158 E4
Inyo Mountains CA U.S.A. 158 D3
Inyonga Tanz. 123 D4
Inza Russia 53 J5
Inzai Japan 93 G3
Inzhavino Russia 53 I5
Ioannina Greece 69 I5
Iokan'ga r. Russia 52 H2
Iola KS U.S.A. 160 E4
Iolgo, Khrebet mts Russia 102 G1
Iolotan' Turkm. see Ýolöten
Iona Canada 153 J5
Iona i. U.K. 60 C4
Iona, Parque Nacional do nat. park Angola 123 B5
Ione NV U.S.A. 158 E2
Iongo Angola 123 B4
Ionia MI U.S.A. 164 C2
Ionian Islands Greece 69 H5
Ionian Sea Greece/Italy 68 H5
Ionioi Nisoi is Greece see Ionian Islands
Ioniveyem r. Russia 148 D2
Iōno Japan 93 G2
Ios i. Greece 69 K6
Iowa state U.S.A. 160 E3
Iowa City IA U.S.A. 160 F3
Iowa Falls IA U.S.A. 160 E3
Iō-zan hill Japan 92 C2
Ipameri Brazil 179 A2
Ipanema Brazil 179 C2
Iparía Peru 176 D5
Ipatinga Brazil 179 C2
Ipatovo Russia 53 I7
Ipelegeng S. Africa 125 G4
Ipewik r. AK U.S.A. 148 F1
Ipiales Col. 176 C3
Ipiaú Brazil 179 D1
Ipil Phil. 82 C5
Ipirá Brazil 179 D1
Ipiranga Brazil 179 A4
iPitoli S. Africa see Pretoria
Ipixuna r. Brazil 176 F5
Ipoh Malaysia 84 C1
Iporá Brazil 179 A2
Ippy Cent. Afr. Rep. 122 C3
İpsala Turkey 69 L4
Ipswich Australia 138 F1
Ipswich U.K. 59 I6
Ipswich SD U.S.A. 160 D2
Ipu Brazil 177 J4
Ipuh Sumatra Indon. 84 C3

▶Iqaluit Canada 147 L3
Capital of Nunavut.

Iqe China 94 C4
Iqe He r. China 99 F5
Iquique Chile 178 B2
Iquiri r. Brazil see Ituxi
Iquitos Peru 176 D4
Iraan Palawan Phil. 82 B4
Īrafshān reg. Iran 111 F5
Irago-misaki pt Japan 92 D4
Irago-suidō str. Japan 92 C4
Iraí Brazil 178 F3
Irakleio Greece see Iraklion
Iraklion Greece 69 K7
Iramaia Brazil 179 C1
Iran country Asia 110 D3
Iran, Pegunungan mts Indon. 85 F2
Īrānshahr Iran 111 F5
Irapuato Mex. 168 D4
Iraq country Asia 113 F4
Irará Brazil 179 D1
Irati Brazil 179 A4
Irayel' Russia 52 L2
Irazú, Volcán vol. Costa Rica 166 [inset] J7
Irbid Jordan 107 B3
Irbil Iraq see Arbīl/Hewlêr
Irbit Russia 76 H4
Irecê Brazil 177 J6
Ireland country Europe 61 E4

▶Ireland i. Ireland/U.K. 61
3rd largest island in Europe.

Irema Dem. Rep. Congo 122 C4
Iri S. Korea see Iksan
Irian, Teluk b. Indon. see Cenderawasih, Teluk
Iriba Chad 121 F3
Īrī Dāgh mt. Iran 110 B2
Iriga Luzon Phil. 82 C3
Irîgui reg. Mali/Mauritania 120 C3
Iringa Tanz. 123 D4
Iriri r. Brazil 177 H4
Irish Free State country Europe see Ireland
Irish Sea Ireland/U.K. 61 G4
Irituia Brazil 177 I4
'Irj well Saudi Arabia 110 C5
Irkutsk Russia 88 I2
Irma Canada 151 I4
Irmak Turkey 112 D3
Irminger Basin sea feature N. Atlantic Ocean 184 F2
Iron Baron Australia 137 B7
Iron Creek AK U.S.A. 148 F2
Irondequoit NY U.S.A. 165 G2
Iron Mountain MI U.S.A. 160 F2
Iron Mountain mt. UT U.S.A. 159 G3
Iron Range National Park Australia 136 C2
Iron River MI U.S.A. 160 F2
Ironton MO U.S.A. 160 F4
Ironton OH U.S.A. 164 D4
Ironwood Forest National Monument nat. park AZ U.S.A. 159 H5
Iroquois r. Canada 149 O1
Iroquois r. IN U.S.A. 164 B3
Iroquois Falls Canada 152 E4
Irosin Luzon Phil. 82 D3
Irō-zaki pt Japan 93 E4
Irpen' Ukr. see Irpin'
Irpin' Ukr. 53 F6
Irrawaddy r. Myanmar 86 A4
Irrawaddy, Mouths of the Myanmar 86 A4
Irshad Pass Afgh./Pak. 111 I2
Irta Russia 52 K3
Irthing r. U.K. 58 E4

▶Irtysh r. Kazakh./Russia 102 E1
5th longest river in Asia and 10th in the world, and a major part of the 2nd longest in Asia (Ob'-Irtysh).

Iruma Japan 93 F3
Iruma-gawa r. Japan 93 F3
Irun Spain 67 F2
Iruña Spain see Pamplona
Iruñea Spain see Pamplona
Irvine U.K. 60 E5
Irvine CA U.S.A. 158 E5
Irvine KY U.S.A. 164 D5
Irvine Glacier Antarctica 188 L2
Irving TX U.S.A. 161 D5
Irvington KY U.S.A. 164 B5
Irwin r. Australia 135 A7
Irwinton GA U.S.A. 163 D5
Isa Nigeria 120 D3
Isaac r. Australia 136 E4
Isabel SD U.S.A. 160 C2
Isabela Negros Phil. 82 C4
Isabela Phil. 82 C5
Isabela, Isla i. Galápagos Ecuador 176 [inset]
Isabelia, Cordillera mts Nicaragua 166 [inset] I6
Isabella Lake CA U.S.A. 158 D4
Isachsen, Cape Canada 147 H2
Ísafjarðardjúp est. Iceland 54 [inset 1]
Ísafjörður Iceland 54 [inset 1]
Isa Khel Pak. 111 H3
Isalo, Massif de l' mts Madag. 123 E6
Isalo, Parc National de l' nat. park Madag. 123 E6
Isar r. Germany 63 M6
Isarog, Mount Phil. 82 C3
Isbister U.K. 60 [inset]
Ischia, Isola d' i. Italy 68 E4
Ise Japan 92 C4
Isehara Japan 93 F3
Isère r. France 66 G4
Isère, Pointe pt Fr. Guiana 177 H2
Iserlohn Germany 63 H3
Isernhagen Germany 63 J2
Isernia Italy 68 F4
Isesaki Japan 93 F2
Ise-shima Kokuritsu-kōen nat. park Japan 92 C4
Ise-wan b. Japan 92 C4
Iseyin Nigeria 120 D4
Isfahan Iran see Eşfahān
Isfana Kyrg. 111 H2
Isheyevka Russia 53 K5
Ishibe Japan 92 C3
Ishigaki Japan 89 M8
Ishige Japan 93 F2
Ishikari-wan b. Japan 90 F4
Ishikawa pref. Japan 92 C2
Ishinomaki Japan 91 F5
Ishinomaki-wan b. Japan 89 Q5
Ishioka Japan 93 G2
Ishkamish Afgh. 111 H2
Ishpeming MI U.S.A. 162 C2
Ishqoshim Tajik. 111 H2
Ishtikhon Uzbek. see Ishtixon
Ishtixon Uzbek. 111 G2
Ishurdi Bangl. 105 G4
Ishwardi Bangl. see Ishurdi
Isiboro Sécure, Parque Nacional nat. park Bol. 176 E7
Isigny-sur-Mer France 59 F9
Işıklar Dağı mts Turkey 69 L4
Işıklı Turkey 69 M5
Isil'kul' Russia 76 I4
iSimangaliso Wetland Park nature res. S. Africa 125 K4
Isimu Celebes Indon. 83 B2
Isipingo S. Africa 125 J5
Isiro Dem. Rep. Congo 122 C3
Isisford Australia 136 D5
Iskar r. Bulg. 69 K3
Iskateley Russia 52 L2
İskenderun Turkey 107 C1
İskenderun Körfezi b. Turkey 107 B1
İskilip Turkey 112 D2
Iskitim Russia 76 J4
Iskushuban Somalia 122 F2
Iskut r. Canada 149 O4
Isla r. Scotland U.K. 60 F4
Isla r. Scotland U.K. 60 G3
Isla Gorge National Park Australia 136 E5
İslahiye Turkey 112 E3
Islamabad India see Anantnag

▶Islamabad Pak. 111 I3
Capital of Pakistan.

Islamgarh Pak. 111 H5
Islamkot Pak. 111 H5
Island r. Canada 150 F2
Ísland country Europe see Iceland
Island KY U.S.A. 164 B5
Island Bay Palawan Phil. 82 B4
Island Falls ME U.S.A. 162 G2
Island Lagoon salt flat Australia 137 B6
Island Lake Canada 151 M4

Island Lake l. Canada 151 M4
Island of Meroe, Archaeological Sites of the tourist site Sudan 121 G3
Island Pond VT U.S.A. 165 J1
Islands, Bay of N.Z. 139 E2
Islas de Bahá, Parque Nacional nat. park Hond. 166 [inset] I5
Islay i. U.K. 60 C5

▶Isle of Man terr. Irish Sea 58 C4
United Kingdom Crown Dependency.

Isle of Wight VA U.S.A. 165 G5
Isle Royale National Park MI U.S.A. 160 F2
Ismail Ukr. see Izmayil
Ismâ'ilîya Egypt see Al Ismā'īlīyah
Ismâ'ilîya governorate Egypt see Al Ismā'īlīyah
Ismailly Azer. see İsmayıllı
İsmayıllı Azer. 113 H2
Isobe Japan 92 C4
Isogo Japan 93 F3
Isojoki Fin. 54 L5
Isoka Zambia 123 D5
Isokylä Fin. 54 O3
Isokyrö Fin. 54 M5
Isola di Capo Rizzuto Italy 68 G5
Ispahan Iran see Eşfahān
Isparta Turkey 69 N6
Isperih Bulg. 69 L3
Ispikan Pak. 111 F5
İspir Turkey 113 F2
Ispisar Tajik. see Khŭjand
Isplinji Pak. 111 G4
Israel country Asia 107 B4
Israelite Bay Australia 135 C8
Isra'il country Asia see Israel
Isselburg Germany 62 G3
Isshiki Japan 92 D4
Issia Côte d'Ivoire 120 C4
Issoire France 66 F4
Issyk-Kul' Kyrg. see Balykchy
Issyk-Kul', Ozero salt l. Kyrg. see Ysyk-Köl
Istālif Afgh. 111 H3

▶İstanbul Turkey 69 M4
Most populous city in Europe.

İstanbul Boğazı strait Turkey see Bosporus
Istaravshan Tajik. 111 H2
Īstgāh-e Eznā Iran 110 C3
Istiaia Greece 69 J5
Istik r. Tajik. 111 I2
Istočni Drvar Bos. & Herz. 68 G2
Istra pen. Croatia see Istria
Istres France 66 G5
Istria pen. Croatia 68 E2
Isulan Phil. 82 D5
Isumi Chiba Japan 93 G3
Isumi Chiba Japan 93 G3
Isumi-gawa r. Japan 93 G3
Isüüj Mongolia see Bayanchandmanī
Iswardi Bangl. see Ishurdi
Itabapoana r. Brazil 179 C3
Itaberá Brazil 179 A3
Itaberaba Brazil 179 C1
Itaberaí Brazil 179 A2
Itabira Brazil 179 C2
Itabirito Brazil 179 C3
Itabuna Brazil 179 D1
Itacajá Brazil 177 I5
Itacarambi Brazil 179 B1
Itacoatiara Brazil 177 G4
Itadori Japan 92 C3
Itaeté Brazil 179 C1
Itagmatana Iran see Hamadān
Itaguaçu Brazil 179 C2
Itaí Brazil 179 A3
Itaiópolis Brazil 179 A4
Itäisen Suomenlahden kansallispuisto nat. park Fin. 55 O6
Itaituba Brazil 177 G4
Itajaí Brazil 179 A4
Itajubá Brazil 179 B3
Itajuípe Brazil 179 D1
Itako Japan 93 G3
Itakura Gunma Japan 93 F2
Itakura Niigata Japan 93 E1
Italia country Europe see Italy
Italia, Laguna l. Bol. 176 F6

▶Italy country Europe 68 E3
5th most populous country in Europe.

Itamarandiba Brazil 179 C2
Itambé Brazil 179 C1
Itambé, Pico de mt. Brazil 179 C2
It Amelân i. Neth. see Ameland
Itami Japan 92 B4
Itami airport Japan 92 B4
Itampolo Madag. 123 E6
Itanagar India 105 H4
Itanguari r. Brazil 179 B1
Itanhaém Brazil 179 B4
Itanhém Brazil 179 C2
Itanhém r. Brazil 179 D2
Itaobim Brazil 179 C2
Itapaci Brazil 179 A1
Itapajipe Brazil 179 A2
Itapebi Brazil 179 D1
Itapecerica Brazil 179 B3
Itapecuru Mirim Brazil 177 J4
Itapemirim Brazil 179 C3
Itaperuna Brazil 179 C3
Itapetinga Brazil 179 C1
Itapetininga Brazil 179 A3
Itapeva Brazil 179 A3
Itapeva, Lago l. Brazil 179 A5
Itapicuru Brazil 177 J6
Itapicuru, Serra de hills Brazil 177 I5
Itapipoca Brazil 177 K4
Itapira Brazil 179 B3
Itaporanga Brazil 179 A3
Itapuã Brazil 179 A5
Itaqui Brazil 178 E3
Itararé Brazil 179 A4
Itarsi India 104 D5
Itarumã Brazil 179 A2
Itatiba Brazil 179 B3
Itatuba Brazil 176 F5
Itaúna Brazil 179 B3
Itaúnas Brazil 179 D2
Itbayat i. Phil. 82 C1
Itchen Lake Canada 151 H1
Itea Greece 69 J5
Ithaca MI U.S.A. 164 C2
Ithaca NY U.S.A. 165 G2
It Hearrenfean Neth. see Heerenveen
iThekweni S. Africa see Durban
Ith Hils ridge Germany 63 J2
Ithrah Saudi Arabia 107 C4
Itilleq Greenland 147 M3
Itimbiri r. Dem. Rep. Congo 122 C3
Itinga Brazil 179 C2
Itiquira Brazil 177 H7
Itiruçu Brazil 179 C1
Itiúba, Serra de hills Brazil 177 K6
Itkillik r. AK U.S.A. 149 J1
Itō Japan 93 F4
Itoigawa Japan 93 D1
Itonuki Japan 92 C3
iTswane S. Africa see Pretoria
Ittiri Sardinia Italy 68 C4
Ittoqqortoormiit Greenland 147 P2
Itu Brazil 179 B3
Itu Aba Island Spratly Is 80 E4
Ituaçu Brazil 179 C1
Ituberá Brazil 179 D1
Ituí r. Brazil 176 D4
Ituiutaba Brazil 179 A2
Itumbiara Brazil 179 A2
Itumbiara, Barragem resr Brazil 179 A2
Ituni Guyana 177 G2
Itupiranga Brazil 177 I5
Ituporanga Brazil 179 A4
Iturama Brazil 179 A2
Iturbide Campeche Mex. 167 H5
Iturbide Nuevo León Mex. 161 D7
Ituri r. Dem. Rep. Congo 122 C3
Iturup, Ostrov i. Russia 90 G3
Itutinga Brazil 179 B3
Ituxi r. Brazil 176 F5
Ītyop'ia country Africa see Ethiopia
Itz r. Germany 63 K5
Itzehoe Germany 57 L4
Iuka MS U.S.A. 161 F5
Iul'tin Russia 148 C2
Ivalo Fin. 54 O2
Ivalojoki r. Fin. 54 O2
Ivanava Belarus 55 N10
Ivanhoe Australia 138 B4
Ivanhoe MN U.S.A. 160 D2
Ivanhoe Lake Canada 151 J2
Ivankiv Ukr. 53 F6
Ivankovtsy Russia 90 D2
Ivanof Bay AK U.S.A. 148 H5
Ivano-Frankivs'k Ukr. 53 E6
Ivano-Frankovsk Ukr. see Ivano-Frankivs'k
Ivanovka Russia 90 B2
Ivanovo Belarus see Ivanava
Ivanovo tourist site Bulg. 69 K3
Ivanovo Russia 52 I4
Ivanovskiy Khrebet mts Kazakh. 98 C2
Ivanteyevka Russia 53 K5
Ivantsevichi Belarus see Ivatsevichy
Ivatsevichy Belarus 55 N10
Ivaylovgrad Bulg. 69 L4
Ivdel' Russia 51 S3
Ivishak r. AK U.S.A. 149 J1
Ivittuut Greenland 147 N3
Iviza i. Spain see Ibiza
Ivory Coast country Africa see Côte d'Ivoire
Ivrea Italy 68 B2
İvrindi Turkey 69 L5
Ivris Ughelt'ekhili pass Georgia 113 G2
Ivry-la-Bataille France 62 B6
Ivugivik Canada see Ivujivik
Ivujivik Canada 147 K3
Ivvavik National Park Canada 149 M1
Ivyanyets Belarus 55 O10
Ivydale WV U.S.A. 164 E4
Iwade Japan 92 B4
Iwafune Japan 93 F2
Iwaki Japan 93 G1
Iwaki-san vol. Japan 90 F4
Iwakuni Japan 91 D6
Iwakura Japan 92 C3
Iwama Japan 93 G2
Iwamizawa Japan 90 F4
Iwamura Japan 92 D3
Iwamurada Japan 93 E2
Iwan r. Indon. 85 F2
Iwase Japan 93 G2
Iwasehama Japan 92 D2
Iwasuge-yama vol. Japan 93 E2
Iwata Japan 93 D4
Iwatsuki Japan 93 F3
Iwo Nigeria 120 D4
Iwye Belarus 55 N10
Ixcamilpa Mex. 167 F5
Ixelles Belgium 62 E4
Ixhuatlán Mex. 167 F4
Ixiamas Bol. 176 E6
Ixmiquilpán Mex. 168 E4
Ixopo S. Africa 125 J6
Ixtacomitán Mex. 167 G5
Ixtapa, Punta pt Mex. 167 E5
Ixtlán Nayarit Mex. 168 D4
Ixtlán Oaxaca Mex. 167 F5
Ixworth U.K. 59 H6
Iya i. Indon. 83 B5
İyirmi Altı Bakı Komissarı Azer. see Hāsānabad
Izabal Guat. 166 [inset] H6
Izabal, Lago de l. Guat. 167 H6
Īzadkhāst Iran see Shāhīn Dezh
Īzad Khvāst Iran 110 D4
Izamal Mex. 167 H4
Izapa tourist site Mex. 167 G6
Izberbash Russia 113 G2
Izegem Belgium 62 D4
Īzeh Iran 110 C4
Izembek National Wildlife Refuge nature res. AK U.S.A. 148 G5
Izgal Pak. 111 I3
Izhevsk Russia 51 Q4
Izhma Respublika Komi Russia 52 L2
Izhma Respublika Komi Russia see Sosnogorsk
Izhma r. Russia 52 L2
Izigan, Cape AK U.S.A. 148 F5
Izmail Ukr. see Izmayil
Izmayil Ukr. 69 M2
İzmir Turkey 69 L5
İzmir Körfezi g. Turkey 69 L5
İzmit Turkey 69 M4
İzmit Körfezi b. Turkey 69 M4
Izozog Bol. 176 F7
Izozog, Bañados del swamp Bol. 176 F7
Izra' Syria 107 C3
Iztochni Rodopi mts Bulg. 69 K4
Izu Japan 93 E4
Izúcar de Matamoros Mex. 167 F5
Izu-hantō pen. Japan 93 E4
Izumi Fukui Japan 92 C3
Izumi Fukushima Japan 93 G2
Izumi Kanagawa Japan 93 F3
Izumi Ōsaka Japan 92 B4
Izumiōtsu Japan 92 B4
Izumisano Japan 92 B4
Izumo Japan 91 D6
Izunokuni Japan 93 E3

▶Izu-Ogasawara Trench sea feature N. Pacific Ocean 186 F3
5th deepest trench in the world.

Izushi Japan 92 A3
Izu-shotō is Japan 93 F4
Izyaslav Ukr. 53 E6
Iz"yayu Russia 52 M2
Izyum Ukr. 53 H6

Jabal Dab Saudi Arabia 110 C6
Jabalón r. Spain 67 D4
Jabalpur India 104 D5
Jabbūl, Sabkhat al salt flat Syria 107 C2
Jabir reg. Oman 110 E6
Jabiru Australia 134 F3
Jablah Syria 107 B2
Jablanica Bos. & Herz. 68 G3
Jaboatão dos Guararapes Brazil 177 L5
Jaboticabal Brazil 179 A3
Jabung, Tanjung pt Indon. 84 D3
Jacala Mex. 167 F4
Jacaltenango Guat. 167 H6
Jacaraci Brazil 179 C1
Jacareacanga Brazil 177 G5
Jacareí Brazil 179 B3
Jacarezinho Brazil 179 A3
Jáchymov Czech Rep. 63 M4
Jacinto Brazil 179 C2
Jack r. Australia 136 D2
Jack Lake Canada 165 F1
Jackman ME U.S.A. 162 G2
Jacksboro TX U.S.A. 161 D5
Jackson Australia 138 D1
Jackson AL U.S.A. 163 C6
Jackson CA U.S.A. 158 C2
Jackson GA U.S.A. 163 D5
Jackson KY U.S.A. 164 D5
Jackson MI U.S.A. 164 C2
Jackson MN U.S.A. 160 E3

▶Jackson MS U.S.A. 161 F5
Capital of Mississippi.

Jackson NC U.S.A. 162 E4
Jackson OH U.S.A. 164 D4
Jackson TN U.S.A. 161 F5
Jackson WY U.S.A. 156 F4
Jackson, Mount Antarctica 188 L2
Jackson Head hd N.Z. 139 B6
Jacksonville AR U.S.A. 161 E5
Jacksonville FL U.S.A. 163 D6
Jacksonville IL U.S.A. 160 F4
Jacksonville NC U.S.A. 163 E5
Jacksonville OH U.S.A. 164 D4
Jacksonville TX U.S.A. 161 E6
Jacksonville Beach FL U.S.A. 163 D6
Jack Wade AK U.S.A. 146 D3
Jacmel Haiti 169 J5
Jaco i. East Timor 83 C5
Jacobabad Pak. 111 H4
Jacobina Brazil 177 J6
Jacob Lake AZ U.S.A. 159 G3
Jacobsdal S. Africa 124 G5
Jacques-Cartier, Détroit de sea chan. Canada 153 I4
Jacques-Cartier, Mont mt. Canada 153 I4
Jacques Cartier Passage Canada see Jacques-Cartier, Détroit de
Jacuí Brazil 179 B3
Jacuípe r. Brazil 177 K6
Jacundá Brazil 177 I4
Jaddangi India 106 D2
Jaddi, Ras pt Pak. 111 F5
Jadebusen b. Germany 63 I1
J. A. D. Jensen Nunatakker nunataks Greenland 147 N3
Jadotville Dem. Rep. Congo see Likasi
Jādū Libya 120 E1
Jaen Luzon Phil. 82 C3
Jaén Spain 67 E5
Ja'farābād Iran 110 E2
Jaffa, Cape Australia 137 B8
Jaffna Sri Lanka 106 C4
Jafr, Qā' al imp. l. Jordan 107 C4
Jagadhri India 104 D3
Jagalur India 106 C3
Jagatsinghapur India see Jagatsinghpur
Jagatsinghpur India 105 F5
Jagdalpur India 106 D2
Jagdaqi China 95 K1
Jagersfontein S. Africa 125 G5
Jaggang China 99 B6
Jaggayyapeta India 106 D2
Jagsamka China see Luding
Jagst r. Germany 63 J5
Jagtial India 106 C2
Jaguariaíva Brazil 179 A4
Jaguaripe Brazil 179 D1
Jagüey Grande Cuba 163 D8
Jahām, 'Irq des. Saudi Arabia 110 B5
Jahanabad India see Jehanabad
Jahmah well Iraq 113 G5
Jahrom Iran 110 D4
Jaicós Brazil 177 J5
Jaigarh India 106 B2
Jailolo Halmahera Indon. 83 C2
Jailolo, Selat sea chan. Moluccas Indon. 83 D3
Jailolo Gilolo i. Moluccas Indon. see Halmahera
Jainca China 94 E5
Jainpur India 105 E4
Jaintapur Bangl. see Jaintiapur
Jaintiapur Bangl. 105 H4
Jainzhug China see Gutang
Jaipur India 104 C4
Jaipurhat Bangl. see Joypurhat
Jais India 105 E4
Jaisalmer India 104 B4
Jaisamand Lake India 104 C4
Jaitaran India 104 C4
Jaitgarh hill India 106 C1
Jajapur India see Jajpur
Jajarkot Nepal 109 N4
Jajce Bos. & Herz. 68 G2
Jajnagar state India see Odisha
Jajpur India 105 F5
Jakān mt. Afgh. 111 G4
Jakar Bhutan 105 G4

▶Jakarta Java Indon. 84 D4
Capital of Indonesia.

Jakes Corner Canada 149 N3
Jakhau India 104 B5
Jäkkvik Sweden 54 J3
Jakliat India 104 C3
Jako i. East Timor see Jaco
Jakobshavn Greenland see Ilulissat
Jakobstad Fin. 54 M5
Jal NM U.S.A. 161 C5
Jalaid China see Inder
Jalājil Saudi Arabia 110 B5
Jalālābād Afgh. 111 H3
Jalalabad India 99 B8
Jalal-Abad Kyrg. 102 D3
Jalal-Abad admin. div. Kyrg. 98 A4
Jalālah al Baḩrīyah, Jabal plat. Egypt 112 C5
Jalalpur Pirwala Pak. 111 H4
Jalāmid, Ḩazm al ridge Saudi Arabia 113 E5
Jalandhar India 104 C3
Jalapa Guat. 167 H6
Jalapa Tabasco Mex. 167 G5
Jalapa Veracruz Mex. see Xalapa
Jalapa Nicaragua 166 [inset] I6
Jalapa Enríquez Mex. see Xalapa
Jālaq Iran 111 F5
Jalasjärvi Fin. 54 M5
Jalaun India 104 D4
Jalawlā' Iraq 113 G4
Jaldhaka r. Bangl. 99 E8
Jaldrug India 106 C2
Jales Brazil 179 A3
Jalesar India 104 D4
Jalgaon India 104 C5
Jalībah Iraq 113 G5
Jalingo Nigeria 120 E4
Jalisco state Mex. 166 D5
Jallābī Iran 110 E5
Jalna India 106 B2
Jalón r. Spain 67 F3
Jalor India see Jalore
Jalore India 104 C4
Jalostotitlán Mex. 166 E4
Jalpa Guanajuato Mex. 167 E4
Jalpa Zacatecas Mex. 168 D4
Jalpaiguri India 105 G4
Jalpan Mex. 167 F4
Jālū Libya 121 F2
Jalūlā Iraq see Jalawlā'
Jam China 98 C4
Jām reg. Iran 111 F3
Jam, Minaret of tourist site Afgh. 111 G3
Jamaica country West Indies 169 I5
Jamaica Channel Haiti/Jamaica 169 I5
Jamalpur Bangl. 105 G4
Jamalpur India 105 F4
Jamanxim r. Brazil 177 G4
Jamati China 98 C3
Jambi Sumatra Indon. 84 C3
Jambi prov. Indon. 84 C3
Jambin Australia 136 E5
Jambo India 104 C4
Jamboaye r. Indon. 84 B1
Jambongan i. Malaysia 85 G1
Jambu Kalimantan Indon. 85 G3
Jambuair, Tanjung pt Indon. 84 B1
Jamda India 105 F5
Jamekunte India 106 C2
James r. N. Dakota/S. Dakota U.S.A. 160 D3
James r. VA U.S.A. 165 G5
James, Baie b. Canada see James Bay
Jamesabad Pak. 111 H5
James Bay Canada 152 E3
Jamesburg NJ U.S.A. 165 H3
James Island Galápagos Ecuador see Santiago, Isla
Jameson Land reg. Greenland 147 P2
James Peak N.Z. 139 B7
James Ranges mts Australia 135 F6
James Ross Island Antarctica 188 A2
James Ross Strait Canada 147 I3
Jamestown Australia 137 B7
Jamestown Canada see Wawa
Jamestown S. Africa 125 H6

▶Jamestown St Helena 184 H7
Capital of St Helena.

Jamestown ND U.S.A. 160 D2
Jamestown NY U.S.A. 164 F2
Jamestown TN U.S.A. 164 C5
Jamkhed India 106 B2
Jammu India 104 C2
Jammu and Kashmir reg. Asia see Kashmir
Jammu and Kashmir admin. dist. India 104 D2
Jamnagar India 104 B5
Jampang Kulon Java Indon. 84 D4
Jampur Pak. 111 H4
Jamrud Pak. 111 H3
Jämsä Fin. 55 N6
Jamsah Egypt 112 D6
Jämsänkoski Fin. 54 N6
Jamshedpur India 105 F5
Jamtari Nigeria 120 E4
Jamui India 105 F4
Jamuk, Gunung mt. Indon. 85 G2
Jamuna r. Bangl. see Raimangal
Jamuna r. India 99 F8
Jamuna r. India see Yamuna
Janā i. Saudi Arabia 110 C5
Janāb, Wādī al watercourse Jordan 107 C4
Janakpur India 105 E5
Janaúba Brazil 179 C1
Jand Pak. 111 I3
Jandaia Brazil 179 A2
Jandaq Iran 110 D3
Jandola Pak. 111 H3
Jandowae Australia 138 E1
Janesville CA U.S.A. 158 C1
Janesville WI U.S.A. 160 F3
Jang, Tanjung pt Sumatra Indon. 84 D3
Jangada do Sul Brazil 179 A4
Jangal Iran 110 E3
Jangamo Moz. 125 L3
Jangaon India 106 C2
Jangco China 99 E7
Janggi-gap pt S. Korea 91 C5
Jangheung S. Korea 91 B6
Jangipur India 105 G4
Jangnga Turkm. see Jaňňa
Jangngai Ri mts China 99 D6
Jangngai Zangbo r. China 99 D6
Jangpyeong S. Korea 91 C5
Jänickendorf Germany 63 N2
Jani Khel Pak. 111 H3
Janīn West Bank 107 B3
Janjanbureh Gambia 120 B3

▶Jan Mayen terr. Arctic Ocean 189 I2
Part of Norway.

Jan Mayen Fracture Zone sea feature Arctic Ocean 189 I2
Jaňňa Turkm. 110 D1
Janos Mex. 166 C2
Jans Bay Canada 151 I4
Jansenville S. Africa 124 G7
Januária Brazil 179 B1
Janūb Sīnā' governorate Egypt see Janūb Sīnā'
Janūb Sīnā' governorate Egypt 107 A5
Janzar mt. Pak. 111 F5
Jaodar Pak. 111 F5

▶Japan country Asia 91 D5
10th most populous country in the world.

Japan, Sea of N. Pacific Ocean 91 D5
Japan Alps National Park Japan see Chūbu-Sangaku Kokuritsu-kōen
Japan Trench sea feature N. Pacific Ocean 186 F3
Japiim Brazil 176 D5
Japón Hond. 166 [inset] I6
Japurá r. Brazil 176 F4
Jaqué Panama 166 [inset] K8
Jarābulus Syria 107 D1
Jaraguá Brazil 179 A1
Jaraguá, Serra mts Brazil 179 A4
Jaraguá do Sul Brazil 179 A4
Jarantai China 94 F4
Jarantai Yanchi salt l. China 94 F4
Jarash Jordan 107 B3
Jarboesville MD U.S.A. see Lexington Park
Jardine River National Park Australia 136 C1
Jardines de la Reina, Archipiélago de los is Cuba 169 I4
Jardinésia Brazil 179 A2
Jardinópolis Brazil 179 B3
Jargalang China 90 A4
Jargalant Arhangay Mongolia see Battsengel
Jargalant Bayanhongor Mongolia 94 D2
Jargalant Bayan-Ölgiy Mongolia see Bulgan
Jargalant Dornod Mongolia see Matad
Jargalant Govĭ-Altay Mongolia see Biger
Jargalant Hovd Mongolia see Hovd
Jargalant Hövsgöl Mongolia 94 D1
Jargalant Töv Mongolia 94 F1
Jargalant Uul mt. Mongolia 94 C2
Jargalthaan Mongolia 95 G2
Jari r. Brazil 177 H4
Järna Sweden 55 J7
Jarocin Poland 57 P5
Jarosław Poland 53 D6
Järpen Sweden 54 H5
Jarqo'rg'o'n Uzbek. 111 G2
Jarqŭrghon Uzbek. see Jarqo'rg'o'n
Jarrettsville MD U.S.A. 165 G4
Jaru Brazil 176 F6
Jarud China see Lubei
Järvakandi Estonia 55 N7
Järvenpää Fin. 55 N6

▶Jarvis Island terr. S. Pacific Ocean 186 J6
United States Unincorporated Territory.

Jarwa India 105 E4
Jashpur India 105 F5
Jāsk-e Kohneh Iran 110 E5
Jasliq Uzbek. 113 J2
Jasło Poland 53 D6
Jasol India 104 C4
Jason Islands Falkland Is 178 D8
Jason Peninsula Antarctica 188 L2
Jasonville IN U.S.A. 164 B4
Jasper Canada 150 G4
Jasper AL U.S.A. 163 C5
Jasper FL U.S.A. 163 D6
Jasper GA U.S.A. 163 C5
Jasper IN U.S.A. 164 B4
Jasper NY U.S.A. 165 G2
Jasper TN U.S.A. 163 C5
Jasper TX U.S.A. 161 E6
Jasper National Park Canada 150 G4
Jasrasar India 104 C4
Jaşşān Iraq 113 G4
Jassy Romania see Iaşi
Jastrzębie-Zdrój Poland 57 Q6
Jaswantpura India 104 C4
Jászberény Hungary 69 H1
Jataí Brazil 179 A2
Jatapu r. Brazil 177 G4
Jath India 106 B2
Jati Pak. 111 H5
Jatibarang Java Indon. 85 E4
Jatibonico Cuba 163 E8
Jatiluhur, Waduk resr Java Indon. 84 D4
Játiva Spain see Xàtiva
Jatiwangi Java Indon. 85 E4
Jatoi Janubi Pak. 111 H4
Jaú Brazil 179 A3
Jaú r. Brazil 176 F4
Jaú, Parque Nacional do nat. park Brazil 176 F4
Jaua-Sarisariñama, Parque Nacional nat. park Venez. 176 F3
Jauja Peru 176 C6
Jaumave Mex. 167 F4
Jaunlutriņi Latvia 55 M8
Jaunpiebalga Latvia 55 O8
Jaunpur India 105 E4
Jauri Iran 111 F4
Java Georgia 113 F2

▶Java i. Indon. 85 E4
5th largest island in Asia.

Javaés r. Brazil see Formoso
Javari r. Brazil/Peru see Yavarí
Java Ridge sea feature Indian Ocean 185 P6
Javarthushuu Mongolia see Bayan-Uul
Java Sea Indon. see Jawa, Laut

▶Java Trench sea feature Indian Ocean 185 P6
Deepest point in the Indian Ocean.

Jävenitz Germany 63 L2
Jävre Sweden 54 L4
Jawa i. Indon. see Java
Jawa, Laut sea Indon. 85 E4
Jawa Barat prov. Indon. 84 D4
Jawa Tengah prov. Indon. 85 E4
Jawa Timur prov. Indon. 85 F4
Jawhar India 106 B2
Jawhar Somalia 122 E3
Jawor Poland 57 P5
Jay OK U.S.A. 161 E4

▶Jaya, Puncak mt. Indon. 81 J7
Highest mountain in Oceania.

Jayakusumu mt. Indon. see Jaya, Puncak
Jayakwadi Sagar l. India 106 B2
Jayantiapur Bangl. see Jaintiapur
Jayapura Indon. 81 K7
Jayawijaya, Pegunungan mts Indon. 81 J7
Jayb, Wādī al watercourse Israel/Jordan 107 B4
Jayfī, Wādī al watercourse Egypt 107 B4
Jaypur India 106 D2
Jayrūd Syria 107 C3
Jayton TX U.S.A. 161 C5
Jāzān Saudi Arabia 108 F6
Jazminal Mex. 167 E3
Jaz Mūrīān, Hāmūn-e salt marsh Iran 110 E5
Jbail Lebanon 107 B2
J. C. Murphey Lake IN U.S.A. 164 B3
Jean NV U.S.A. 159 F4
Jean Marie River Canada 150 F2
Jeannin, Lac l. Canada 153 I2
Jebāl Bārez, Kūh-e mts Iran 110 E4
Jebel, Bahr el r. Africa see White Nile
Jebel Abyad Plateau Sudan 108 C6
Jebus Indon. 84 D3
Jech Doab lowland Pak. 111 I4
Jecheon S. Korea 91 C5
Jedburgh U.K. 60 G5
Jeddah Saudi Arabia 108 E5
Jedeida Tunisia 68 C6
Jeetze r. Germany 63 L1
Jefferson IA U.S.A. 160 E3
Jefferson NC U.S.A. 162 D4
Jefferson OH U.S.A. 164 E3

Jefferson TX U.S.A. 161 E5
Jefferson, Mount NV U.S.A. 158 E2
Jefferson, Mount vol. OR U.S.A. 156 C3

▶Jefferson City MO U.S.A. 160 E4
Capital of Missouri.

Jeffersonville GA U.S.A. 163 D5
Jeffersonville IN U.S.A. 164 C4
Jeffersonville OH U.S.A. 164 D4
Jeffreys Bay S. Africa 124 G8
Jehanabad India 105 F4
Jeju S. Korea 91 B6
Jeju-haehyeop sea chan. S. Korea 91 B6
Jejuí Guazú r. Para. 178 E2
Jēkabpils Latvia 55 N8
Jekegūr Iran 111 F5
Jelbart Ice Shelf Antarctica 188 B2
Jelenia Góra Poland 57 O5
Jelep La pass China/India 99 E8
Jelgava Latvia 55 M8
Jellico TN U.S.A. 164 C5
Jellicoe Canada 152 D4
Jelloway OH U.S.A. 164 D3
Jemaja i. Indon. 84 D2
Jember Java Indon. 85 F5
Jeminay China 98 D3
Jeminay Kazakh. 98 D3
Jempang, Danau l. Indon. 85 G3
Jena Germany 63 L4
Jena LA U.S.A. 161 E6
Jendouba Tunisia 68 C6
Jengish Chokusu mt. China/Kyrg. see Pobeda Peak
Jenkins KY U.S.A. 164 D5
Jênlung China 99 D7
Jenne Mali see Djenné
Jenner Canada 151 I5
Jennings r. Canada 149 N4
Jennings LA U.S.A. 161 E6
Jenolan Caves Australia 138 E4
Jenpeg Canada 151 L4
Jensen UT U.S.A. 159 I1
Jens Munk Island Canada 147 K3
Jeongeup S. Korea 91 B6
Jeonju S. Korea 91 B6
Jepara Java Indon. 85 E4
Jeparit Australia 137 C8
Jequié Brazil 179 C1
Jequitaí r. Brazil 179 B2
Jequitinhonha Brazil 179 C2
Jequitinhonha r. Brazil 179 D1
Jerantut Malaysia 84 C2
Jerba, Île de i. Tunisia 64 G5
Jerbar South Sudan 121 G4
Jereh Iran 110 C4
Jérémie Haiti 169 J5
Jerez Mex. 168 D4
Jerez de la Frontera Spain 67 C5
Jergol Norway 54 N2
Jergucat Albania 69 I5
Jericho Australia 136 D4
Jericho West Bank 107 B4
Jerichow Germany 63 M2
Jerid, Chott el salt l. Tunisia 64 F5
Jerijeh, Tanjung pt Malaysia 85 E2
Jerilderie Australia 138 B5
Jerimoth Hill hill RI U.S.A. 165 J3
Jeroaquara Brazil 179 A1
Jerome ID U.S.A. 156 E4
Jerruck Pak. 111 H5

▶Jersey terr. Channel Is 59 E9
United Kingdom Crown Dependency.

Jersey City NJ U.S.A. 165 H3
Jersey Shore PA U.S.A. 165 G3
Jerseyville IL U.S.A. 160 F4
Jerumenha Brazil 177 J5

▶Jerusalem Israel/West Bank 107 B4
De facto capital of Israel, disputed.

Jervis Bay Australia 138 E5
Jervis Bay b. Australia 138 E5
Jervis Bay Territory admin. div. Australia 138 E5
Jesenice Slovenia 68 F1
Jesenice, Vodní nádrž resr Czech Rep. 63 M4
Jesi Italy 68 E3
Jesselton Sabah Malaysia see Kota Kinabalu
Jessen (Elster) Germany 63 M3
Jessheim Norway 55 G6
Jessore Bangl. 105 G5
Jesteburg Germany 63 J1
Jesu Maria Island P.N.G. see Rambutyo Island
Jesup GA U.S.A. 163 D6
Jesús Carranza Mex. 167 G5
Jesús María, Barra spit Mex. 161 D7
Jeti-Ögüz Kyrg. 98 B4
Jetmore KS U.S.A. 160 D4
Jetpur India 104 B5
Jever Germany 63 H1
Jewell Ridge VA U.S.A. 164 E5
Jewish Autonomous Oblast admin. div. Russia see Yevreyskaya Avtonomnaya Oblast'
Jeypur India see Jaypur
Jezercë, Maja mt. Albania 69 H3
Jezzine Lebanon 107 B3
Jhabua India 104 C5
Jhajhar India see Jhajjar
Jhajjar India 104 D3
Jhal Pak. 111 G4
Jhalawar India 104 D4
Jhal Jhao Pak. 111 G5
Jhang Pak. 111 I4
Jhansi India 104 D4
Jhanzi r. India 86 A1
Jhapa Nepal 105 F4
Jharia India 105 F5
Jharkhand state India 105 F5
Jharsuguda India 105 F5
Jhawani Nepal 105 F4
Jhelum r. India/Pak. 111 I4
Jhelum Pak. 111 I3
Jhenaidah Bangl. 105 G5
Jhenaidaha Bangl. see Jhenaidah
Jhenida Bangl. see Jhenaidah
Jhimpir Pak. 111 H5
Jhingtubum mt. India 96 B3
Jhudo Pak. 111 H5
Jhumritilaiya India 105 F4
Jhund India 104 B5
Jhunjhunun India 104 C3
Jiachuan China 96 E1
Jiachuanzhen China see Jiachuan
Jiading Jiangxi China see Xinfeng
Jiading Shanghai China 97 I2
Jiahe China 97 G3
Jiajiang China 96 D2
Jialing Jiang r. China 94 F6
Jialu China see Jiaxian
Jialu He r. China 95 H5
Jiamusi China 90 C3
Ji'an Jiangxi China 97 G3
Ji'an Jilin China 90 B4
Jianchang China 95 I3
Jianchuan China 96 C3
Jiande China 97 H2
Jiangbei China see Yubei
Jiangbiancun China 97 G3
Jiangcheng China 96 D4
Jiangcun China 97 F3
Jiangdu China 97 H1
Jiange China see Pu'an
Jianghong China 97 F4
Jiangjiapo China 95 J4
Jiangjin China 96 E2
Jiangjunmiao China 94 B2
Jiangjunmu China 95 H4
Jiangjuntai China 94 D3
Jiangkou Guangdong China see Fengkai
Jiangkou Guizhou China 97 F3
Jiangkou Shaanxi China 96 E1
Jiangling China see Jingzhou
Jiangluo China 96 E1
Jiangmen China 97 G4
Jiangna China see Yanshan
Jiangshan China 97 H2
Jiangsi China see Dejiang
Jiangsu prov. China 97 H1
Jiangtai China 94 F5
Jiangxi prov. China 97 G3
Jiangxia China 97 G2
Jiangxian China 95 G5
Jiangxigou China 94 E4
Jiangyan China 97 I1
Jiangyin China 97 I2
Jiangyou China 96 E2
Jiangyu China 95 I4
Jiangzhesongrong China 99 D7
Jianhu China 95 I5
Jianjun China see Yongshou
Jiankang China 96 D3
Jianli China 97 G2
Jian'ou China 97 H3
Jianping Anhui China see Langxi
Jianping Liaoning China 95 I3
Jianping Liaoning China 95 I3
Jianqiao China 95 I4
Jianshe Qinghai China 94 D5
Jianshe Sichuan China see Baiyü
Jianshi China 97 F2
Jianshui China 96 D4
Jianshui Hu l. China 99 C6
Jianxing China 96 E2
Jianyang Fujian China 97 H3
Jianyang Sichuan China 96 E2
Jiaochang China 96 D1
Jiaochangba China see Jiaochang
Jiaocheng Guangdong China see Jiaoling
Jiaocheng Shanxi China 95 H4
Jiaohe Hebei China 95 I4
Jiaohe Jilin China 90 B4
Jiaojiang China see Taizhou
Jiaokou China 95 G4
Jiaokui China see Yiliang
Jiaolai He r. China 95 J3
Jiaoling China 97 H3
Jiaonan China 95 I5
Jiaopingdu China 96 D3
Jiaowei China 97 H3
Jiaozhou China 95 J4
Jiaozuo China 95 H5
Jiarsu China 94 C4
Jiasa China 96 D3
Jiashan China see Mingguang
Jiashi China 98 B5
Jia Tsuo La pass China 99 D7
Jiawang China 97 H1
Jiaxian Henan China 97 G1
Jiaxian Shaanxi China 95 G4
Jiaxing China 97 I2
Jiayi Taiwan 97 I4
Jiayin China 90 C2
Jiayuguan China 94 D4
Jiazi China 97 H4
Jībūtī country Africa see Djibouti
Jibuti Djibouti see Djibouti
Jiddah Saudi Arabia see Jeddah
Jiddī, Jabal al hill Egypt 107 A4
Jido S. Korea 91 B6
Jidong China 90 C3
Jiehkkevárri mt. Norway 54 K2
Jiehu China see Yinan
Jieshi China 97 G4
Jieshipu China 94 F5
Jieshi Wan b. China 97 G4
Jiexi China 97 G4
Jiexiu China 95 G4
Jieyang China 97 H4
Jieznas Lith. 55 N9
Jigzhi China 96 D1
Jiḩār, Wādī al watercourse Syria 107 C2
Jih-chao China see Donggang
Jihlava Czech Rep. 57 O6
Jījah Afgh. 111 F3
Jijel Alg. 64 F4
Jijiga Eth. 122 E3
Jījīrud Iran 110 C3
Jijitai China 94 D3
Jijū China 96 D2
Jil'ād reg. Jordan 107 B3
Jilf al Kabīr, Haḑabat al plat. Egypt 108 C5
Jilh al 'Ishār plain Saudi Arabia 110 B5
Jilib Somalia 122 E3
Jili Hu l. China 98 D3
Jilin China 90 B4
Jilin prov. China 95 K3
Jiling China 94 E4
Jilin Hada Ling mts China 90 B4
Jiliu He r. China 90 A2
Jilo India 104 C4
Jilong Taiwan 97 I3
Jīma Eth. 122 D3
Jiménez Chihuahua Mex. 166 D3
Jiménez Coahuila Mex. 167 E2
Jiménez Tamaulipas Mex. 161 D7
Jimía, Cerro mt. Hond. 168 G5
Jimo China 95 J4
Jimokuji Japan 92 C3
Jimsar China 98 E4
Jim Thorpe PA U.S.A. 165 H3
Jinan China 95 I4
Jin'an China see Songpan
Jinbi China see Dayao
Jinchang China 94 E4
Jincheng Shanxi China 95 H5
Jincheng Sichuan China 96 E2
Jincheng Yunnan China see Wuding
Jinchengjiang China see Hechi
Jinchuan Gansu China see Jinchang
Jinchuan Jiangxi China see Xingan
Jind India 104 D3
Jinding China see Lanping
Jindo S. Korea 91 B6
Jin-do i. S. Korea 91 B6
Jindřichův Hradec Czech Rep. 57 O6
Jin'e China see Longchang
Jinfosi China 94 D4
Jing China see Jinghe
Jingbian China 95 G4
Jingchuan China 95 F5
Jingde China 97 H2
Jingdezhen China 97 H2
Jingellic Australia 138 C5
Jinggangshan China see Ciping
Jinggang Shan hill China 97 G3
Jinggongqiao China 97 H2
Jinggu Gansu China 94 E5
Jinggu Yunnan China 96 D4
Jinghai China 95 I4
Jinghai Wan b. China 95 J4
Jinghe China 98 C3
Jing He r. China 95 G5
Jinghong China 96 D4
Jingle China 95 H4
Jingmen China 97 G2
Jingning China 94 F5
Jingpeng China 95 I3
Jingpo China 90 C4
Jingpo Hu resr China 90 C4
Jingsha China see Jingzhou
Jingtai China 94 F4
Jingxi China 96 E4
Jingxian Anhui China 97 H2
Jingxian Hunan China see Jingzhou
Jingyang China see Jingde
Jingyu China 90 B4
Jingyuan China 94 F4
Jingzhou Hubei China 97 G2
Jingzhou Hubei China 97 G2
Jingzhou Hunan China 97 F3
Jinhae S. Korea 91 C6
Jinhe Nei Mongol China 90 A2
Jinhe Yunnan China see Jinping
Jinhu China 97 H1
Jinhua Yunnan China see Jianchuan
Jinhua Zhejiang China 97 H2
Jining Nei Mongol China see Ulan Qab
Jining Shandong China 95 I5
Jinja Uganda 122 D3
Jinjiang Hainan China see Chengmai
Jinjiang Yunnan China 96 D3
Jin Jiang r. China 97 G2
Jinka Eth. 122 D3
Jinmen Taiwan 97 H3
Jinmen Dao i. Taiwan 97 H3
Jinmu Jiao pt China 97 F5
Jinning China 96 D3
Jinotega Nicaragua 166 [inset] I6
Jinotepe Nicaragua 166 [inset] I7
Jinping Guizhou China 97 F3
Jinping Yunnan China 96 D4
Jinping Yunnan China see Qiubei
Jinping Shan mts China 96 D3
Jinsen S. Korea see Incheon
Jinsha China 96 E3
Jinsha Jiang r. China 96 C2 see Yangtze
Jinshan Nei Mongol China see Guyang
Jinshan Nei Mongol China 95 I3
Jinshan Shanghai China see Zhujing
Jinshan Yunnan China see Lufeng
Jinshi Hunan China 97 F2
Jinshi Hunan China see Xinning
Jinta China 94 D4
Jintotolo i. Phil. 82 C4
Jintotolo Channel Phil. 82 C4
Jintur India 106 C2
Jinxi Anhui China see Taihu
Jinxi Jiangxi China 97 H3
Jinxi Liaoning China see Lianshan
Jin Xi r. China 97 H3
Jinxian Jiangxi China 97 H2
Jinxian Liaoning China see Linghai
Jinxiang China 95 I5
Jinyun China 97 I2
Jinz, Qā' al salt flat Jordan 107 C4
Jinzhai China 97 G2
Jinzhong China 95 H4
Jinzhou Liaoning China 95 J3
Jinzhou Liaoning China 95 J4
Jinzhou Wan b. China 95 J4
Jinzhu China see Daocheng
Jinzū-gawa r. Japan 92 D2
Ji-Paraná Brazil 176 F6
Jipijapa Ecuador 176 B4
Ji Qu r. China 99 G7
Jiquilisco El Salvador 166 [inset] H6
Jiquiriçá Brazil 179 D1
Jiquitaia Brazil 179 D2
Jirā', Wādī watercourse Egypt 107 A5
Jirānīyāt, Shi'bān al watercourse Saudi Arabia 107 D4
Jirghatol Tajik. 111 H2
Jiri r. India 86 A1
Jirin Gol China 95 I2
Jiri-san mt. S. Korea 91 B6
Jirmeng China 94 D4
Jīroft Iran 110 E4
Jirriiban Somalia 122 E3
Jirwān Saudi Arabia 110 C6
Jirwan well Saudi Arabia 110 C6
Jishan China 95 G5
Jishi China see Xunhua
Jishishan China 94 E5
Jishou China 97 F2
Jisr ash Shughūr Syria 107 C2
Jitian China see Lianshan
Jitotol Mex. 167 G5
Jitra Malaysia 84 C1
Jiu r. Romania 69 J3
Jiuchenggong China see Linyou
Jiudengkou China 94 F4
Jiuding Shan mt. China 96 D2
Jiuhe China 96 C3
Jiujiang Jiangxi China 97 G2
Jiujiang Jiangxi China 97 H2
Jiulian China see Mojiang
Jiuling Shan mts China 97 G2
Jiulong H.K. China see Kowloon
Jiulong Sichuan China 96 D2
Jiumiao China 95 J3
Jiuqian China 97 F3
Jiuquan China 94 D4
Jiuxian China 95 G4
Jiuxu China 96 E3
Jiuzhou Jiang r. China 97 F4
Jiwani Pak. 111 F5
Jiwen China 95 J1
Jixi Anhui China 97 H2
Jixi Heilong. China 90 C3
Jixian Hebei China see Jizhou
Jixian Heilong. China 90 C3
Jixian Henan China see Weihui
Jixian Shanxi China 95 G4
Jiyuan China 95 H5
Jīzah, Ahrāmāt al tourist site Egypt see Pyramids of Giza
Jizhou China 95 H4
Jizō-dake mt. Japan 93 F2
Jizzakh Uzbek. see Jizzax
Jizzax Uzbek. 111 G1
Joaçaba Brazil 179 A4
Joaíma Brazil 179 C2
João Belo Moz. see Xai-Xai
João de Almeida Angola see Chibia
João Maria, Albardão do coastal area Brazil 178 F4
João Pessoa Brazil 177 L5
João Pinheiro Brazil 179 B2
Joaquín V. González Arg. 178 D3
Jōban Japan 93 G2
Jobo Point Mindanao Phil. 82 D4
Job Peak NV U.S.A. 158 D2
Jocketa Germany 63 M4
Jocotán Guat. 167 H6
Joda India 105 F5
Jodhpur India 104 C4
Jodiya India 104 B5
Joensuu Fin. 54 P5
Jōetsu Japan 93 E1
Jofane Moz. 123 D6
Joffre, Mount Canada 150 H5
Jōganji-gawa r. Japan 92 D2
Jōga-shima i. Japan 93 F3
Jogbura Nepal 104 E3
Jõgeva Estonia 55 O7
Jogjakarta Java Indon. see Yogyakarta
Jōhana Japan 92 C2
Johannesburg S. Africa 125 H4
Johannesburg CA U.S.A. 158 E4
Johan Peninsula Canada 147 K2
Johi Pak. 111 G5
John r. AK U.S.A. 149 J2
John Day OR U.S.A. 156 D3
John Day r. OR U.S.A. 156 C3
John D'Or Prairie Canada 150 H3
John F. Kennedy airport NY U.S.A. 165 I3
John H. Kerr Reservoir VA U.S.A. 165 F5
John Jay, Mount Canada/U.S.A. 149 O4
John o' Groats U.K. 60 F2
Johnson KS U.S.A. 160 C4
Johnsonburg PA U.S.A. 165 F3
Johnson City NY U.S.A. 165 H2
Johnson City TN U.S.A. 162 D4
Johnson City TX U.S.A. 161 D6
Johnsondale CA U.S.A. 158 D4
Johnson Draw watercourse TX U.S.A. 161 C6
Johnson's Crossing Canada 149 N3
Johnston, Lake salt flat Australia 135 C8
Johnston and Sand Islands terr. N. Pacific Ocean see Johnston Atoll

▶Johnston Atoll terr. N. Pacific Ocean 186 I4
United States Unincorporated Territory.

Johnstone U.K. 60 E5
Johnstone Lake Canada see Old Wives Lake
Johnston Range hills Australia 135 B7
Johnstown Ireland 61 E5
Johnstown NY U.S.A. 165 H2
Johnstown PA U.S.A. 165 F3
Johor state Malaysia 84 C2
Johor, Selat strait Malaysia/Sing. 87 [inset]
Johor, Sungai r. Malaysia 87 [inset]
Johor Bahru Malaysia 84 C2
Jõhvi Estonia 55 O7
Joinville Brazil 179 A4
Joinville France 66 G2
Joinville Island Antarctica 188 A2
Jojutla Mex. 167 F5
Jokkmokk Sweden 54 K3
Jökulsá r. Iceland 54 [inset 1]
Jökulsá á Fjöllum r. Iceland 54 [inset 1]
Jökulsá í Fljótsdal r. Iceland 54 [inset 1]
Jolfā Iran 110 B2
Joliet IL U.S.A. 164 A3
Joliet, Lac l. Canada 152 F4
Joliette Canada 153 G5
Jolly Lake Canada 151 H1
Jolo Phil. 82 C5
Jolo i. Phil. 82 C5
Jomalig i. Phil. 82 C3
Jombang Java Indon. 85 F4
Jomda China 96 C2
Jōmine-san mt. Japan 93 F2
Jonancy KY U.S.A. 164 D5
Jonathan Point Belize 167 H5
Jonava Lith. 55 N9
Jonê China 94 E5
Jōnen-dake mt. Japan 92 D2
Jonesboro AR U.S.A. 161 F5
Jonesboro LA U.S.A. 161 E5
Jones Islands AK U.S.A. 149 J1
Jones Sound sea chan. Canada 147 J2
Jonesville MI U.S.A. 164 C3
Jonesville VA U.S.A. 164 D5
Jonglei Canal South Sudan 108 D8
Jönköping Sweden 55 I8
Jonquière Canada 153 H4
Jonuta Mex. 167 G5
Joplin MO U.S.A. 161 E4
Joppa Israel see Tel Aviv-Yafo
Jora India 104 D4
Jordan country Asia 107 C4
Jordan r. Asia 107 B4
Jordan MT U.S.A. 156 G3
Jordan r. OR U.S.A. 156 D4
Jordânia Brazil 179 C1
Jordet Norway 55 H6
Jorhat India 105 H4
Jor Hu l. China 98 B5
Jork Germany 63 J1
Jörn Sweden 54 L4
Joroinen Fin. 54 O5
Jorong Kalimantan Indon. 85 F3
Jørpeland Norway 55 E7
Jos Nigeria 120 D4
Jose Abad Santos Mindanao Phil. 82 D5
José Cardel Mex. 167 F5
José de San Martín Arg. 178 B6
Jose Panganiban Luzon Phil. 82 C3
Joseph, Lac l. Canada 153 I3
Joseph Bonaparte Gulf Australia 134 E3
Joseph City AZ U.S.A. 159 H4
Joshimath India 104 D3
Jōshinetsu-kōgen Kokuritsu-kōen nat. park Japan 93 E2
Joshipur India 106 E1
Joshua Tree National Park CA U.S.A. 159 F5
Jōsō Japan 93 F2
Jos Plateau Nigeria 120 D4
Jostedalsbreen Nasjonalpark nat. park Norway 55 E6
Jotunheimen Nasjonalpark nat. park Norway 55 F6
Jouaiya Lebanon 107 B3
Joubertina S. Africa 124 F7
Jouberton S. Africa 125 H4
Jōuga Estonia 55 O7
Joûnié Lebanon 107 B3
Joure Neth. 62 F2
Joutsa Fin. 55 O6
Joutseno Fin. 55 P6
Jouy-aux-Arches France 62 G5
Jovellanos Cuba 163 D8
Jowai India 105 H4
Jowand Afgh. 111 G3
Jowr Deh Iran 110 C2
Joy, Mount Canada 149 N3
Joya de Cerén tourist site El Salvador 167 H6
Joyce Country reg. Ireland 61 C4
Jōyō Japan 92 B4
Joypurhat Bangl. 105 G4
Juan Aldama Mex. 161 C7
Juancheng China 95 H5
Juan de Fuca Strait Canada/U.S.A. 154 C2
Juan Escutia Mex. 166 D4
Juan Fernández, Archipiélago is S. Pacific Ocean 187 O8
Juan Fernández Islands S. Pacific Ocean see Juan Fernández, Archipiélago
Juanjuí Peru 176 C5
Juankoski Fin. 54 P5
Juan Mata Ortíz Mex. 166 C2
Juárez Mex. 167 E3
Juárez, Sierra de mts Mex. 166 A1
Juazeiro Brazil 177 J5
Juazeiro do Norte Brazil 177 K5
Juba r. Somalia see Jubba

▶Juba South Sudan 121 G4
Capital of South Sudan.

Jubba r. Somalia 122 E4
Jubbah Saudi Arabia 113 F5
Jubbulpore India see Jabalpur
Jubilee Lake salt flat Australia 135 D7
Juby, Cap c. Morocco 120 B2
Juchatengo Mex. 167 F5
Juchitán Mex. 168 E5
Jucuruçu Brazil 179 D2
Jucuruçu r. Brazil 179 D2
Judaberg Norway 55 D7
Judaidat al Hamir Iraq 113 F5
Judayyidat 'Ar'ar well Iraq 113 F5
Judenburg Austria 57 O7
Judian China 96 C3
Judith Gap MT U.S.A. 156 F3
Juegang China see Rudong
Juelsminde Denmark 55 G9
Juerana Brazil 179 D2
Jugar China see Sêrxü
Juh China 95 G4
Juhongtu China 94 D4
Juigalpa Nicaragua 166 [inset] I6
Juillet, Lac l. Canada 153 J3
Juína Brazil 177 G6
Juist i. Germany 62 H1
Juiz de Fora Brazil 179 C3
Jujuhan r. Indon. 84 C3
Ju Ju Klu Turkm. 111 F2
Jukkoku-tōge pass Japan 93 E2
Julaca Bol. 176 E8
Julesburg CO U.S.A. 160 C3
Julia Brazil 176 E4
Juliaca Peru 176 D7
Julia Creek Australia 136 C4
Julian CA U.S.A. 158 E5
Julian, Lac l. Canada 152 F3
Julianadorp Neth. 62 E2
Julian Alps mts Slovenia see Julijske Alpe
Julianatop mt. Indon. see Mandala, Puncak
Juliana Top mt. Suriname 177 G3
Julianehåb Greenland see Qaqortoq
Jülich Germany 62 G4
Julijske Alpe mts Slovenia 68 E1
Julimes Mex. 166 D2
Juliomagus France see Angers
Julius, Lake Australia 136 B4
Jullundur India see Jalandhar
Juma Uzbek. 111 G2
Jumbilla Peru 176 C5
Jumilla Spain 67 F4
Jumla Nepal 105 E3
Jümme r. Germany 63 H1
Jumna r. India see Yamuna
Jump r. WI U.S.A. 160 F2
Junagadh India 104 B5
Junagarh India 106 D2
Junan China 95 I5
Junayfah Egypt 107 A4
Jun Bulen China 95 I2
Junction TX U.S.A. 161 D6
Junction UT U.S.A. 159 G2
Junction City KS U.S.A. 160 D4
Junction City KY U.S.A. 164 C5
Junction City OR U.S.A. 156 C3
Jundiaí Brazil 179 B3
Jundian China 97 F1

▶Juneau AK U.S.A. 149 N4
Capital of Alaska.

Juneau WI U.S.A. 160 F3
Juneau Icefield Canada 149 N4
Junee Australia 138 C5
Jûn el Khudr b. Lebanon 107 B3
Jungar Qi China see Xuejiawan
Jungfrau mt. Switz. 66 H3
Junggar Pendi basin China 102 G2
Jungsi China 99 E6
Juniata r. PA U.S.A. 165 G3
Junín Arg. 178 D4
Junín Peru 176 C6
Junior WV U.S.A. 164 F4
Juniper Mountain CO U.S.A. 159 I1
Juniper Mountains AZ U.S.A. 159 G4
Junipero Serro Peak CA U.S.A. 158 C3
Junlian China 96 E2
Junmenling China 97 G3
Juno TX U.S.A. 161 C6
Junsele Sweden 54 J5
Junshan Hu l. China 97 H2
Junxi China see Datian
Junxian China see Danjiangkou
Ju'nyung China 96 C1
Ju'nyunggoin China see Ju'nyung
Jūō Japan 93 G2
Juodup Lith. 55 N8
Jupiá Brazil 179 A3
Jupiá, Represa resr Brazil 179 A3
Jupiter FL U.S.A. 163 D7
Juquiá r. Brazil 179 B4
Jur r. South Sudan 108 C8
Jura mts France/Switz. 66 G4
Jura i. U.K. 60 D4
Jur'ā, Nafūd al des. Saudi Arabia 110 B5
Jura, Sound of sea chan. U.K. 60 D5
Juraci Brazil 179 C1
Juradó Col. 166 [inset] K8
Jurbarkas Lith. 55 M9
Jurf ad Darāwīsh Jordan 107 B4
Jürgenstorf Germany 63 M1
Jurh Nei Mongol China 95 J2
Jurh Nei Mongol China 95 J2
Jurhen Ul mts China 99 E6
Jurm Afgh. 111 H2
Jūrmala Latvia 55 M8
Jurmu Fin. 54 O4
Jurong Sing. 87 [inset]
Jurong, Sungai r. Sing. 87 [inset]
Jurong Island reg. Sing. 87 [inset]
Juruá r. Brazil 176 E4
Juruena r. Brazil 177 G5
Juruti Brazil 177 G4
Jurva Fin. 54 L5
Jūshiyama Japan 92 C3
Jūshqān Iran 110 E2
Jūsīyah Syria 107 C2
Jussara Brazil 179 A1
Justice WV U.S.A. 164 E5
Jutaí Brazil 176 E5
Jutaí r. Brazil 176 E4
Jüterbog Germany 63 N3
Jutiapa Guat. 167 H6
Jutiapa Hond. 166 [inset] I6

Juticalpa Hond. 166 [inset] I6
Jutis Sweden 54 J3
Jutland pen. Denmark 55 F8
Juuka Fin. 54 P5
Juva Fin. 54 O6
Juventud, Isla de la i. Cuba 169 H4
Juwana Java Indon. 85 E4
Juxian China 95 I5
Juye China 95 I5
Jūyom Iran 110 D4
Jūzak Iran 111 F4
Južnoukrajinsk Ukr. see Yuzhnoukrayins'k
Jwaneng Botswana 124 G3
Jylland pen. Denmark see Jutland
Jyrgalang Kyrg. 98 B4
Jyväskylä Fin. 54 N5

K

▶K2 mt. China/Pak. 104 D2
2nd highest mountain in Asia and the world.

Ka r. Nigeria 120 D3
Kaa-Iya del Gran Chaco, Parque Nacional nat. park Bol. 176 F7
Kaakhka Turkm. see Kaka
Ka'ala mt. HI U.S.A. 157 [inset]
Kaapstad S. Africa see Cape Town
Kaarina Fin. 55 M6
Kaarßen Germany 63 L1
Kaarst Germany 62 G3
Kaavi Fin. 54 P5
Kaba China see Habahe
Kaba r. China/Kazakh. 98 D3
Kabaena i. Indon. 83 B4
Kabakly Turkm. see Gabakly
Kabala Sierra Leone 120 B4
Kabale Uganda 122 C4
Kabalega Falls National Park Uganda see Murchison Falls National Park
Kabalo Dem. Rep. Congo 123 C4
Kabambare Dem. Rep. Congo 123 C4
Kabanbay Kazakh. 102 F2
Kabangu Dem. Rep. Congo 123 C5
Kabanjahe Sumatra Indon. 84 B2
Kabara i. Fiji 133 I3
Kabarai Papua Indon. 83 D3
Kabarega National Park Uganda see Murchison Falls National Park
Kabasalan Mindanao Phil. 82 C5
Kaba-san hill Japan 93 G2
Kabaw Valley Myanmar 86 A2
Kabbani r. India 106 C3
Kåbdalis Sweden 54 L3
Kabetan i. Indon. 83 B2
Kabīd, Mushāsh al well Jordan 107 C5
Kabinakagami r. Canada 152 D4
Kabinakagami Lake Canada 152 D4
Kabinda Dem. Rep. Congo 123 C4
Kabir Indon. 83 C5
Kabīr, Nahr al r. Syria 107 B2
Kabīrkūh mts Iran 110 B3
Kabo Cent. Afr. Rep. 122 B3
Kābol Afgh. see Kābul
Kabompo r. Zambia 123 C5
Kabong Sarawak Malaysia 85 E2
Kabongo Dem. Rep. Congo 123 C4
Kaboré Tambi, Parc National de nat. park Burkina Faso 120 C3
Kabūdar Āhang Iran 110 C3
Kabūd Gonbad Iran see Kalāt
Kabugao Luzon Phil. 82 C2

▶Kābul Afgh. 111 H3
Capital of Afghanistan.

Kābul r. Afgh. 111 I3
Kabuli P.N.G. 81 L7
Kabunda Dem. Rep. Congo 123 C5
Kabunduk Sumba Indon. 83 A5
Kabuntalan Mindanao Phil. 82 D5
Kabura-gawa r. Japan 93 F2
Kaburuang i. Indon. 83 C2
Kabūtar Khān Iran 110 E4
Kabwe Zambia 123 C5
Kacepi Moluccas Indon. 83 D3
Kāchā Kūh mts Iran/Pak. 111 F4
Kachalinskaya Russia 53 J6
Kachchh, Great Rann of marsh India see Kachchh, Rann of
Kachchh, Gulf of India 104 B5
Kachchh, Little Rann of marsh India 104 B5
Kachchh, Rann of marsh India 104 B4
Kachemak Bay AK U.S.A. 149 J4
Kachia Nigeria 120 D4
Kachkanar Russia 51 R4
K'ach'reti Georgia 113 G2
Kachug Russia 88 J2
Kaçkar Dağı mt. Turkey 113 F2
Kada Japan 92 B4
Kadaingti Myanmar 86 B3
Kadaiyanallur India 106 C4
Kadanai r. Afgh./Pak. 111 G4
Kadan Kyun i. Myanmar 87 B4
Kadapa India 106 C3
Kadapongan i. Indon. 85 F4
Kadatuang i. Indon. 83 B4
Kadavu i. Fiji 133 H3
Kadavu Passage Fiji 133 H3
Kadaya Russia 95 I1
Kaddam l. India 106 C2
Kade Ghana 120 C4
Kadi India 104 C5
Kadıköy Turkey 69 M4
Kadınhanı Turkey 112 D3
Kadiolo Mali 120 C3
Kadiri India 106 C3
Kadirli Turkey 112 E3
Kadiyevka Ukr. see Stakhanov
Kadmat atoll India 106 B4
Ka-do i. N. Korea 91 B5
Kadok Malaysia 84 C1
Kadoka SD U.S.A. 160 C3
Kadoma Zimbabwe 123 C5
Kadonkani Myanmar 86 A4
Kadu Myanmar 86 B1
Kadugli Sudan 108 C7
Kaduna Nigeria 120 D3
Kaduna r. Nigeria 120 D4
Kadusam mt. China/India 105 I3
Kaduy Russia 52 H4
Kadyy Russia 52 I4
Kadzherom Russia 52 L2
Kaédi Mauritania 120 B3
Kaélé Cameroon 121 E3
Kaeng Krachan National Park Thai. 87 B4
Kaesŏng N. Korea 91 B5
Kāf Saudi Arabia 107 C4
Kafa Crimea see Feodosiya
Kafakumba Dem. Rep. Congo 123 C4
Kafan Armenia see Kapan
Kafanchan Nigeria 120 D4

▶Kaffeklubben Ø i. Greenland 189 I1
Most northerly point of North America.

Kaffrine Senegal 120 B3
Kafiau i. Papua Indon. 83 D3
Kafireas, Akra pt Greece see Ntoro, Kavo
Kafiristan reg. Pak. 111 H3
Kafr ash Shaykh Egypt 112 C5
Kafr el Sheikh Egypt see Kafr ash Shaykh
Kafue Zambia 123 C5
Kafue r. Zambia 123 C5
Kafue National Park Zambia 123 C5
Kaga Japan 92 C2
Kaga Bandoro Cent. Afr. Rep. 122 B3
Kagan Pak. 111 I3
Kagan Uzbek. see Kogon
Kagang China 94 E5
Kaganovichabad Tajik. see Kolkhozobod
Kaganovichi Pervyye Ukr. see Polis'ke (abandoned)
Kagarlyk Ukr. see Kaharlyk
Kåge Sweden 54 L4
Kağızman Turkey 113 F2
Kaglik Lake Canada 149 O1
Kagmar Sudan 108 D7
Kagologolo Sumatra Indon. 84 B3
Kagosaka-tōge pass Japan 93 E3
Kagoshima Japan 91 C7
Kagoshima pref. Japan 91 C7
Kagul Moldova see Cahul
Kaguyak AK U.S.A. 148 I4
Kahama Tanz. 122 D4
Kaharlyk Ukr. 53 F6
Kahatola i. Moluccas Indon. 83 C2
Kahayan r. Indon. 85 F3
Kaherekoau Mountains N.Z. 139 A7
Kahīrī Iran 111 F5
Kahla Germany 63 L4
Kahmard reg. Afgh. 111 G3
Kahnūj-e Pā'īn Iran 110 E4
Kahoka MO U.S.A. 160 F3
Kahoku Japan 92 C2
Kahoku-gata l. Japan 92 C2
Kaho'olawe i. HI U.S.A. 157 [inset]
Kahperusvaarat mts Fin. 54 L2
Kahramanmaraş Turkey 112 E3
Kahror Pakka Pak. 111 H4
Kahta Turkey 112 E3
Kahuku HI U.S.A. 157 [inset]
Kahuku Point HI U.S.A. 157 [inset]
Kahulaui i. HI U.S.A. see Kaho'olawe
Kahurangi National Park N.Z. 139 D5
Kahurangi Point N.Z. 139 D5
Kahuta Pak. 111 I3
Kahuzi-Biega, Parc National du nat. park Dem. Rep. Congo 122 C4
Kai Japan 93 E3
Kai, Kepulauan is Moluccas Indon. 81 I8
Kaiapoi N.Z. 139 D6
Kaibab AZ U.S.A. 159 G3
Kaibab Plateau AZ U.S.A. 159 G3
Kaibamardang China 94 D4
Kaibara Japan 92 B3
Kai Besar i. Moluccas Indon. 81 I8
Kaibito Plateau AZ U.S.A. 159 H3
Kaida Japan 92 D3
Kaidu He r. China 98 D4
Kaifeng Henan China 95 H5
Kaifeng Henan China 95 H5
Kaihua Yunnan China see Wenshan
Kaihua Zhejiang China 97 H2
Kaiingveld reg. S. Africa 124 E5
Kaijiang China 96 E2
Kai Kecil i. Moluccas Indon. 81 I8
Kai Keung Leng H.K. China 97 [inset]
Kaikoura N.Z. 139 D6
Kailas mt. China see Kangrinboqê Feng
Kailasahar India see Kailashahar
Kailashahar India 105 H4
Kailas Range mts China see Gangdisê Shan
Kaili China 96 E3
Kailu China 95 J3
Kailua HI U.S.A. 157 [inset]
Kailua-Kona HI U.S.A. 157 [inset]
Kaimana Indon. 81 I7
Kaimanawa Mountains N.Z. 139 E4
Kaimar China 96 B1
Kaimganj India 99 B8
Kaimur Range hills India 104 E4
Käina Estonia 55 M7
Kainan Japan 92 B4
Kainda Kyrg. see Kayyngdy
Kaindy Kyrg. see Kayyngdy
Kainji Lake National Park Nigeria 120 D4
Kaipara Harbour N.Z. 139 E3
Kaiparowits Plateau UT U.S.A. 159 H3
Kaiping China 97 G4
Kaipokok Bay Canada 153 K3
Kairana India 104 D3
Kairatu Seram Indon. 83 D3
Kairiru Island P.N.G. 81 K7
Kaironi Indon. 81 I7
Kairouan Tunisia 68 D7
Kaiserslautern Germany 63 H5
Kaiser Wilhelm II Land reg. Antarctica 188 E2
Kait, Tanjung pt Indon. 84 D3
Kaitaia N.Z. 139 D2
Kaitangata N.Z. 139 B8
Kaitawa N.Z. 139 F4
Kaithal India 104 D3
Kaitong China see Tongyu
Kaitum Sweden 54 L3
Kaiwatu Moluccas Indon. 83 C5
Kaiwi Channel HI U.S.A. 157 [inset]
Kaixian China 97 F2
Kaiyang China 96 E3
Kaiyuan Liaoning China 95 K3
Kaiyuan Yunnan China 96 D4
Kaiyuh Mountains AK U.S.A. 148 H3
Kaizu Japan 92 C3
Kaizuka Japan 92 B4
Kajaani Fin. 54 O4
Kajabbi Australia 136 C4
Kajakī Suflá Afgh. 111 G3
Kajang Malaysia 84 C2
Kajarabie, Lake Australia 138 D1
Kajikazawa Japan 93 E3
Kajīrān Afgh. 111 G3
Kajy-Say Kyrg. 98 B4
Kaka Turkm. 111 E2
Kakaban i. Indon. 85 G2
Kakabeka Falls Canada 152 C4
Kakabia i. Indon. 83 B4
Kakadu National Park Australia 134 F3
Kakagi Lake Canada 151 M5
Kakal r. Mindanao Phil. 82 D5
Kakali Celebes Indon. 83 A3
Kakamas S. Africa 124 E5
Kakamega Kenya 122 D3
Kakamigahara Japan 92 C3
Kakana India 87 A5
Kakar Pak. 111 G5
Kakata Liberia 120 B4
Kake AK U.S.A. 149 N4
Kakegawa Japan 93 E4
Kakenge Dem. Rep. Congo 123 C4
Kakerbeck Germany 63 L2
Kakhi Azer. see Qax
Kakhovka Ukr. 69 O1
Kakhovs'ke Vodoskhovyshche resr Ukr. 53 G7
Kakhul Moldova see Cahul
Kākī Iran 110 C4
Kakinada India 106 D2
Kakisa Canada 150 G2
Kakisa r. Canada 150 G2
Kakisa Lake Canada 150 G2
Kakogawa Japan 92 A4
Kako-gawa r. Japan 92 A4
Kakori India 104 E4
Kakpak Kuduk well China 94 B2
Kakshaal-Too mts China/Kyrg. 102 E3
Kaktovik AK U.S.A. 149 L1
Kakul Pak. 111 I3
Kakus r. Malaysia 85 F2
Kakwa r. Canada 150 G4
Kala Pak. 111 H4
Kala Tanz. 123 D4
Kalaâ Kebira Tunisia 68 D7
Kalaallit Nunaat terr. N. America see Greenland
Kalabahi Indon. 83 C5
Kalabáka Greece see Kalampaka
Kalabakan Sabah Malaysia 85 G1
Kalabgur India 106 C2
Kalabo Zambia 123 C5
Kalaburagi India 106 C2
Kalābust Afgh. 111 G4
Kalach Russia 53 I6
Kalacha Dida Kenya 122 D3
Kalach-na-Donu Russia 53 I6
Kaladan r. India/Myanmar 86 A2
Kaladar Canada 165 G1
Ka Lae pt HI U.S.A. 157 [inset]
Kalaena r. Indon. 83 B3
Kalagwe Myanmar 86 B2
Kalahari Desert Africa 124 F2
Kalahari Gemsbok National Park S. Africa 124 E3
Kalaikhum Tajik. see Qalaikhumb
Kalai-Khumb Tajik. see Qalaikhumb
Kalajoki Fin. 54 M4
Kalaliok Celebes Indon. 83 B3
Kalalusu i. Indon. 83 C1
Kalam India 106 C1
Kalam Pak. 111 I3
Kalámai Greece see Kalamata
Kalamare Botswana 125 H2
Kalamaria Greece 69 J4
Kalamata Greece 69 J6
Kalamazoo MI U.S.A. 164 C2
Kalambau i. Indon. 85 F4
Kalampaka Greece 69 I5
Kalanchak Ukr. 69 O1
Kalandi Pak. 111 F4
Kalandula Angola see Calandula
Kalanguy Russia 95 I1
Kalannie Australia 135 B7
Kalanshiyū ar Ramlī al Kabīr, Sarīr des. Libya 108 B3
Kālān Zīād Iran 111 E5
Kalao i. Indon. 83 B4
Kalaong Mindanao Phil. 82 D5
Kalaotoa i. Indon. 83 B4
Kalapa Indon. 84 D3
Kalapana (abandoned) HI U.S.A. 157 [inset]
Kalār, Kūh-e mt. Iran 110 C4
Kalār/Kelar Iraq 113 G4
Kalasin Thai. 86 C3
Kalāt Afgh. see Qalāt
Kalāt Khorāsān-e Razavī Iran 111 E2
Kalāt Sīstān va Balūchestān Iran 111 E5
Kalat Balochistan Pak. 111 G4
Kalat Balochistan Pak. 111 G5
Kalāt, Kūh-e mt. Iran 110 E3
Kalāteh Kabūdeh Iran 111 F3
Kalaupapa HI U.S.A. 157 [inset]
Kalaus r. Russia 53 J7
Kalaw Myanmar 86 B2
Kalba, Khrebet mts Kazakh. 98 C2
Kälbäcär Azer. 113 G2
Kalbarri Australia 135 A6
Kalbarri National Park Australia 135 A6
Kalbe (Milde) Germany 63 L2
Kale Turkey 69 M6
Kalecik Turkey 112 D2
Kaledupa i. Indon. 83 B4
Kalefeld Germany 63 K3
Kaleindaung inlet Myanmar 86 A3
Kalélé Benin 120 D3
Kalemie Dem. Rep. Congo 123 C4
Kalemyo Myanmar 86 A2
Kāl-e Namak Iran 110 D3
Kalevala Russia 54 Q4
Kalewa Myanmar 86 A2
Kaleybar Iran 110 B2
Kalga Russia 95 I1
Kalgan China see Zhangjiakou
Kalghatgi India 106 B3
Kalgoorlie Australia 135 C7
Kāl Gūsheh Iran 110 E4
Kali Croatia 68 F2
Kali r. India/Nepal 104 E3
Kaliakra, Nos pt Bulg. 69 M3
Kalianda Sumatra Indon. 84 D4
Kalibo Panay Phil. 82 C4
Kaliet Sumatra Indon. 84 B3
Kali Gandaki r. Nepal 105 F4
Kaligiri India 106 C3
Kalikata India see Kolkata
Kalima Dem. Rep. Congo 122 C4
Kalimantan reg. Indon. 85 E3
Kalimantan Barat prov. Indon. 85 E2
Kalimantan Selatan prov. Indon. 85 F3
Kalimantan Tengah prov. Indon. 85 F3
Kalimantan Timur prov. Indon. 85 G2
Kalimantan Utara prov. Indon. 85 G2
Kálimnos i. Greece see Kalymnos
Kali Nadi r. India 99 C8
Kalinin Russia see Tver'
Kalinina, imeni Tajik. see Cheshtebe
Kalinin Adyndaky Tajik. see Cheshtebe
Kaliningrad Russia 55 L9
Kalinino Armenia see Tashir
Kalinino Russia 52 I4
Kalininsk Russia 53 J6
Kalininskaya Russia 53 H7
Kalinjara India 104 C5
Kalinkavichy Belarus 53 F5
Kalinkovichi Belarus see Kalinkavichy
Kalisat Java Indon. 85 F5
Kalisch Poland see Kalisz
Kalispell MT U.S.A. 156 E2
Kalisz Poland 57 Q5
Kalitva r. Russia 53 I6
Kaliua Tanz. 123 D4
Kaliujar India 104 E4
Kalix Sweden 54 M4
Kalkalighat India 105 H4
Kalkalpen, Nationalpark nat. park Austria 57 O7
Kalkan Turkey 69 M6
Kalkaska MI U.S.A. 164 C1
Kalkfeld Namibia 123 B6
Kalkfonteindam dam S. Africa 125 G5
Kalkhochalpen, Nationalpark nat. park Austria 57 N7
Kalkudah Sri Lanka 106 D5
Kall Germany 62 G4
Kallang r. Sing. 87 [inset]
Kallaste Estonia 55 O7
Kallavesi l. Fin. 54 O5
Kallsedet Sweden 54 H5
Kallsjön l. Sweden 54 H5
Kallur India 106 C2
Kalmar Sweden 55 J8
Kalmard Iran 110 E3
Kalmarsund sea chan. Sweden 55 J8
Kalmit hill Germany 63 I5
Kalmūkh Qal'eh Iran 110 E2
Kalmunai Sri Lanka 106 D5
Kalmykia aut. rep. Russia see Kalmykiya-Khalm'g-Tangch, Respublika
Kalmykiya-Khalm'g-Tangch, Respublika aut. rep. Russia 113 G1
Kalmykovo Kazakh. see Taypak
Kalmytskaya Avtonomnaya Oblast' aut. rep. Russia see Kalmykiya-Khalm'g-Tangch, Respublika
Kalnai India 105 E5
Kalodnaye Belarus 55 O11
Kalol India 104 C5
Kaloma i. Indon. 83 C2
Kalomo Zambia 123 C5
Kalone Peak Canada 150 E4
Kalongan Celebes Indon. 83 C1
Kalpa India 104 D3
Kalpeni atoll India 106 B4
Kalpetta India 106 C4
Kalpi India 104 D4
Kalpin China 98 B4
Kalsi India 99 B7
Kalsubai mt. India 104 C6
Kaltag AK U.S.A. 148 H2
Kaltensundheim Germany 63 K4
Kaltukatjara Australia 135 E6
Kalu India 111 I4
Kaluga Russia 53 H5
Kalukalukuang i. Indon. 85 G4
Kaluku Celebes Indon. 83 A3
Kalulong, Bukit mt. Malaysia 85 F2
Kalundborg Denmark 55 G9
Kalupis Falls Malaysia 85 G1
Kalush Ukr. 53 E6
Kalvakol India 106 C2
Kälviä Fin. 54 M5
Kal'ya Russia 51 R3
Kalyan India 106 B2
Kalyandurg India 109 M7
Kalyansingapuram India 106 D2
Kalyazin Russia 52 H4
Kalymnos i. Greece 69 L6
Kalzhat Kazakh. 98 C4
Kama Dem. Rep. Congo 122 C4
Kama Myanmar 86 A3

▶Kama r. Russia 52 L4
4th longest river in Europe.

Kamagaya Japan 93 F3
Kamaishi Japan 91 F5
Kamakura Japan 93 F3
Kamalamai Nepal 105 F4
Kamalia Pak. 111 I4
Kaman India 99 B8
Kaman Turkey 112 D3
Kamanashi-gawa r. Japan 93 E3
Kamanashi-yama mt. Japan 93 E3
Kamaniskeg Lake Canada 165 G1
Kamanjab Namibia 123 B5
Kamarān i. Yemen 108 F6
Kamaran Island Yemen see Kamarān
Kamarod Pak. 111 F5
Kamaron Sierra Leone 120 B4
Kamashi Uzbek. see Qamashi
Kamasin India 104 E4
Kambaiti Myanmar 86 B1
Kambalda Australia 135 C7
Kambam India 106 C4
Kambang Sumatra Indon. 84 C3
Kambangan i. Indon. 85 E5
Kambara i. Fiji see Kabara
Kambara Japan see Kanbara
Kambardi China 98 C4
Kambia Sierra Leone 120 B4
Kambing, Pulau i. East Timor see Ataúro, Ilha de
Kambo-san mt. N. Korea see Kwanmo-bong
Kambove Dem. Rep. Congo 123 C5
Kambuno, Bukit mt. Indon. 83 B3
Kambūt Libya 112 B5
Kamchatka, Poluostrov pen. Russia see Kamchatka Peninsula
Kamchatka Basin sea feature Bering Sea 186 H2
Kamchatka Peninsula Russia 77 Q4
Kamchia r. Bulg. 69 L3
Kameia, Parque Nacional de nat. park Angola see Cameia, Parque Nacional da
Kamelik r. Russia 53 K5
Kamen Germany 63 H3
Kamen', Gory mt. Russia 76 K3
Kamenets-Podol'skiy Ukr. see Kam"yanets'-Podil's'kyy
Kamenitsa mt. Bulg. 69 J4
Kamenjak, Rt pt Croatia 68 E2
Kamenka Arkhangel'skaya Oblast' Russia 52 J2
Kamenka Penzenskaya Oblast' Russia 53 J5
Kamenka Primorskiy Kray Russia 90 E3
Kamenka-Bugskaya Ukr. see Kam"yanka-Buz'ka
Kamenka-Strumilovskaya Ukr. see Kam"yanka-Buz'ka
Kamen'-na-Obi Russia 88 E2
Kamennogorsk Russia 55 P6
Kamennomostskiy Russia 113 F1
Kamenolomni Russia 53 I7
Kamenongue Angola see Camanongue
Kamen'-Rybolov Russia 90 D3
Kamenskoye Russia 77 R3
Kamenskoye Ukr. see Dniprodzerzhyns'k
Kamensk-Shakhtinskiy Russia 53 I6
Kamensk-Ural'skiy Russia 76 H4
Kameoka Japan 92 B3
Kamet mt. China 99 B7
Kameyama Japan 92 C4
Kami Hyōgo Japan 92 A3
Kami Nagano Japan 93 D3
Kamiesberge mts S. Africa 124 D6
Kamieskroon S. Africa 124 C6
Kamiichi Japan 92 D2
Kami-ishizu Japan 92 C3
Kami-jima i. Japan 92 C4
Kamikawa Hyōgo Japan 92 A3
Kamikawa Saitama Japan 93 F2
Kamikawachi Japan 93 F2
Kamikitayama Japan 92 B4
Kamikuishiki Japan 93 E3
Kamileroi Australia 136 C3
Kamilukuak Lake Canada 151 K2
Kamina Dem. Rep. Congo 123 C4
Kaminaka Japan 92 B3
Kaminak Lake Canada 151 M2
Kaminoho Japan 92 D3
Kaminokawa Japan 93 F2
Kaminuriak Lake Canada see Qamanirjuaq Lake
Kamioka Japan 92 D2
Kamishak Bay AK U.S.A. 148 I4
Kamishihi Japan 92 C2
Kamishihoro Japan 90 F4
Kamisu Japan 93 G3
Kami-taira Japan 92 C2
Kami-takara Japan 92 D2
Kami-yahagi Japan 92 D3
Kamiyamada Japan 93 E2
Kamla r. India 99 F8
Kamloops Canada 150 F5
Kamlung China 96 C1
Kammuri-jima i. Japan see Kanmuri-jima
Kammuri-yama mt. Japan see Kanmuri-yama
Kamo Armenia see Gavarr
Kamo Kyōto Japan 92 B4
Kamo Shizuoka Japan 93 E4
Kamogawa Japan 93 G3
Kamoke Pak. 111 I4
Kamonia Dem. Rep. Congo 123 C4
Kampa Indon. 84 D3

▶Kampala Uganda 122 D3
Capital of Uganda.

Kampar r. Indon. 84 C2
Kampar Malaysia 84 C1
Kampara India 106 D1
Kamparkiri r. Indon. 84 C2
Kampen Neth. 62 F2
Kampene Dem. Rep. Congo 122 C4
Kamphaeng Phet Thai. 86 B3
Kampinoski Park Narodowy nat. park Poland 57 R4
Kâmpóng Cham Cambodia 87 D5
Kâmpóng Chhnăng Cambodia 87 D4
Kâmpóng Khleăng Cambodia 87 D4
Kâmpóng Saôm Cambodia see Sihanoukville
Kâmpóng Spœ Cambodia 87 D5
Kâmpóng Thum Cambodia 87 D4
Kâmpóng Trâbêk Cambodia 87 D5
Kâmpôt Cambodia 87 D5
Kampuchea country Asia see Cambodia
Kamrau, Teluk b. Indon. 81 I7
Kamsack Canada 151 K5
Kamskoye Vodokhranilishche resr Russia 51 R4
Kamsuuma Somalia 122 E3
Kamuchawie Lake Canada 151 K3
Kamuli Uganda 122 D3
Kam"yanets'-Podil's'kyy Ukr. 53 E6
Kam"yanka-Buz'ka Ukr. 53 E6
Kamyanyets Belarus 55 M10
Kāmyārān Iran 110 B3
Kamyshin Russia 53 J6
Kamystybas, Ozero l. Kazakh. 102 B2
Kamyzyak Russia 53 K7
Kamzar Oman 110 E5
Kanaaupscow r. Canada 152 F3
Kanab UT U.S.A. 159 G3
Kanab Creek r. AZ U.S.A. 159 G3
Kanae Japan 93 D3
Kanaga Island AK U.S.A. 148 [inset] C6
Kanagawa pref. Japan 93 F3
Kanairiktok r. Canada 153 K3
Kanak Pak. 111 G4
Kanakanak AK U.S.A. 148 H4
Kananga Dem. Rep. Congo 123 C4
Kanangio, Mount vol. P.N.G. 81 L7
Kanangra-Boyd National Park Australia 138 E4
Kanarak India see Konarka
Kanarraville UT U.S.A. 159 G3
Kanas watercourse Namibia 124 C4
Kanasagō Japan 93 G2
Kanash Russia 52 J5
Kanas Köl l. China 98 D2
Kanatak AK U.S.A. 148 H4
Kanauj India see Kannauj
Kanaya Shizuoka Japan 93 E4
Kanaya Wakayama Japan 92 B4
Kanayama Japan 92 D3
Kanazawa Ishikawa Japan 92 C2
Kanazawa Kanagawa Japan 93 F3
Kanazu Japan see Awara
Kanbalu Myanmar 86 A2
Kanbara Japan 93 E3
Kanchalan Russia 148 B2
Kanchalan r. Russia 148 B2
Kanchanaburi Thai. 87 B4
Kanchanjanga mt. India/Nepal see Kangchenjunga
Kanchipuram India 106 C3
Kand mt. Pak. 111 G4
Kanda Pak. 111 G4
Kandahār Afgh. 111 G4
Kandalaksha Russia 54 R3
Kandalakshskiy Zaliv g. Russia 54 R3
Kandang Sumatra Indon. 84 B2
Kandangan Kalimantan Indon. 85 F3
Kandar Moluccas Indon. 134 E2
Kandavu i. Fiji see Kadavu
Kandavu Passage Fiji see Kadavu Passage
Kandé Togo 120 D4
Kandenmarai mt. India 106 C2
Kandh Kot Pak. 111 H4
Kandi Benin 120 D3
Kandi India 106 C2
Kandi, Tanjung pt Indon. 83 B2
Kandiaro Pak. 111 H5
Kandik r. Canada/U.S.A. 149 L2
Kandıra Turkey 69 N4
Kandos Australia 138 D4
Kandreho Madag. 123 E5
Kandrian P.N.G. 81 L8
Kandukur India 106 C3
Kandy Sri Lanka 106 D5
Kandyagash Kazakh. 102 A2
Kane PA U.S.A. 165 F3
Kane Bassin b. Greenland 189 K1
Kaneh watercourse Iran 110 D5
Kanektok r. AK U.S.A. 148 G4
Kāne'ohe HI U.S.A. 157 [inset]
Kaneti Pak. 111 G4
Kanevskaya Russia 53 H7
Kaneyama Japan 92 D3
Kang Botswana 124 F2
Kang (abandoned) Afgh. 111 F4
Kangaamiut Greenland 147 M3
Kangaarsussuaq c. Greenland 147 K2
Kangaba Mali 120 C3
Kangal Turkey 112 E3
Kangān Iran 110 E5
Kangandala, Parque Nacional de nat. park Angola see Cangandala, Parque Nacional de
Kangar Malaysia 84 C1
Kangaroo Island Australia 137 B7
Kangaroo Point Australia 136 B3
Kangaslampi Fin. 54 P5
Kangasniemi Fin. 54 O6
Kangāvar Iran 110 B3
Kangbao China 95 H3

▶Kangchenjunga mt. India/Nepal 105 G4
3rd highest mountain in Asia and the world.

Kangding China 96 D2
Kangean, Kepulauan is Indon. 85 F4
Kangen r. South Sudan 121 G4
Kangerlussuaq Greenland 147 M3
Kangerlussuaq inlet Greenland 147 M3
Kangerlussuaq inlet Greenland 189 J2
Kangersuatsiaq Greenland 147 M2
Kangertittivaq sea chan. Greenland 147 P2
Kanggye N. Korea 90 B4
Kangikajik c. Greenland 147 P2
Kangiqsualujjuaq Canada 153 I2
Kangirsuk Canada 153 H1
Kang Krung National Park Thai. 87 B5
Kangle Gansu China 94 E5
Kangle Jiangxi China see Wanzai
Kangmar Xizang China 99 E7
Kangmar Xizang China 105 F3
Kango Gabon 122 B3
Kangping China 95 J3
Kangri Karpo La China/India 105 I3
Kangrinboqê Feng mt. China 99 C7
Kangro China 99 D6
Kangsangdobdê China see Xainza
Kangto mt. China/India 99 F8
Kangtog China 99 D6
Kangxian China 96 E1
Kangxiwar China 99 B5
Kani Japan 92 D3
Kanibongan Sabah Malaysia 85 G1
Kanie Japan 92 C3
Kanigiri India 106 C3
Kanin, Poluostrov pen. Russia 52 J2
Kanin Nos Russia 189 G2
Kanin Nos, Mys c. Russia 52 I1
Kaninskiy Bereg coastal area Russia 52 I2
Kanjiroba mt. Nepal 105 E3
Kankaanpää Fin. 55 M6
Kankakee IL U.S.A. 164 B3
Kankan Guinea 120 C3
Kanker India 106 D1
Kankesanturai Sri Lanka 106 D4
Kankossa Mauritania 120 B3
Kanlaon, Mount vol. Phil. 82 C4
Kanmaw Kyun i. Myanmar 87 B5
Kanmuri-jima i. Japan 92 B3
Kanmuri-yama mt. Japan 92 C3
Kanna Japan 93 E2
Kanna-gawa r. Japan 93 F2
Kannami Japan 93 E3
Kannauj India 104 D4
Kanniya Kumari c. India see Comorin, Cape
Kannonkoski Fin. 54 N5
Kannon-zaki pt Japan 92 D1
Kannur India 106 B4
Kannus Fin. 54 M5
Kano i. Indon. 83 C3
Kano Nigeria 120 D3
Kano-gawa r. Japan 93 E3
Kanonerka Kazakh. 98 B2
Kanonpunt pt S. Africa 124 E8
Kanosh UT U.S.A. 159 G2
Kanovlei Namibia 123 B5
Kanowit Sarawak Malaysia 85 F2
Kanoya Japan 91 C7
Kanpur Odisha India 106 E1
Kanpur Uttar Prad. India 104 E4
Kanra Japan 93 E2
Kanrach reg. Pak. 111 G5
Kansai airport Japan 92 B4
Kansas IL U.S.A. 164 B4
Kansas r. KS U.S.A. 160 E4
Kansas state U.S.A. 160 D4
Kansas City KS U.S.A. 160 E4
Kansas City MO U.S.A. 160 E4
Kansk Russia 77 K4
Kansu China 98 A5
Kansu prov. China see Gansu
Kantang Thai. 87 B6
Kantara hill Cyprus 107 A2
Kantaralak Thai. 87 D4
Kantavu i. Fiji see Kadavu
Kantchari Burkina Faso 120 D3
Kantemirovka Russia 53 H6
Kanthi India 105 F5
Kantishna AK U.S.A. 149 J3
Kantishna r. AK U.S.A. 149 J2
Kantli r. India 99 A7
Kantō-heiya plain Japan 93 F3
Kanton atoll Kiribati 133 I2
Kanto-sanchi mts Japan 93 E3
Kantulong Myanmar 86 B3
Kanturk Ireland 61 D5
Kanuku Mountains Guyana 177 G3
Kanuma Japan 93 F2
Kanur India 106 C3
Kanus Namibia 124 D4
Kanuti r. AK U.S.A. 148 I2
Kanuti National Wildlife Refuge nature res. AK U.S.A. 149 J2
Kanyakubja India see Kannauj
Kanyamazane S. Africa 125 J3
Kanye Botswana 125 G3
Kanzaki Japan 92 A3
Kao Halmahera Indon. 83 C2
Kao, Teluk b. Halmahera Indon. 83 C2
Kaôh Kŏng Cambodia 87 C5
Kaôh Kŏng Cambodia 87 C5
Kaohsiung Taiwan see Gaoxiong
Kaokoveld plat. Namibia 123 B5
Kaolack Senegal 120 B3
Kaoma Zambia 123 C5
Kaouadja Cent. Afr. Rep. 122 C3
Kapa S. Africa see Cape Town
Kapa'a HI U.S.A. 157 [inset]
Kapa'au HI U.S.A. 157 [inset]
Kapal Kazakh. 98 B3
Kapalabuaya Moluccas Indon. 83 C3
Kapan Armenia 113 G3
Kapanga Dem. Rep. Congo 123 C4
Kaparhā Iran 110 C4
Kapatu Zambia 123 D4
Kap Dan Greenland see Kulusuk
Kapellen Belgium 62 E3
Kapello, Akra pt Greece see Kapello, Akrotirio
Kapello, Akrotirio pt Greece 69 J6
Kapellskär Sweden 55 K7
Kapelskär Sweden see Kapellskär
Kapingamarangi atoll Micronesia 186 G5
Kapingamarangi Rise sea feature N. Pacific Ocean 186 G5
Kapıorman Dağları mts Turkey 69 N4
Kapip Pak. 111 H4
Kapiri Mposhi Zambia 123 C5
Kapisillit Greenland 147 M3
Kapiskau r. Canada 152 E3
Kapit Sarawak Malaysia 85 F2
Kapiti Island N.Z. 139 E5
Kaplamada, Gunung mt. Buru Indon. 83 C3
Kaplankyr, Chink hills Asia 113 I2
Kaplankyr Döwlet Gorugy nature res. Turkm. 110 E1
Kapoeta South Sudan 121 G4
Kapondai, Tanjung pt Flores Indon. 83 B5
Kaposvár Hungary 68 G1
Kappel Germany 63 H5
Kappeln Germany 57 L3
Kapshagay Kazakh. 102 E3
Kapshagay, Vodokhranilishche resr Kazakh. 102 E3
Kapsukas Lith. see Marijampol
Kaptai Bangl. 105 H5
Kaptsegaytuy Russia 95 I1
Kapuas r. Indon. 85 E3
Kapuas r. Indon. 85 F3
Kapuas Hulu, Pegunungan mts Indon./Malaysia 85 F2
Kapuriya India 104 C4
Kapurthala India 104 C3
Kapuskasing Canada 152 E4
Kapustin Yar Russia 53 J6
Kaputar mt. Australia 138 E3
Kaputir Kenya 122 D3
Kapuvár Hungary 68 G1
Kapydzhik, Gora mt. Armenia/Azer. see Qazangöldağ
Kapyl' Belarus 55 O10
Ka Qu r. China 99 F7
Kaqung China 111 J2
Kara India 104 E4
Kara Togo 120 D4
Kara r. Turkey 113 F3
Kara Art Pass China 98 A5
Karaauyl Kazakh. 98 B2
Kara-Balta Kyrg. 102 D3
Karabalyk Kazakh. 100 F1
Karabas Kazakh. 98 A2
Karabaur, Uval hills Kazakh./Uzbek. 113 I2
Karabekaul' Turkm. see Garabekewül
Karabiga Turkey 69 L4
Karabil', Vozvyshennost' hills Turkm. see Garabil Belentligi
Kara-Bogaz-Gol, Proliv sea chan. Turkm. see Garabogazköl Bogazy
Kara-Bogaz-Gol'skiy Zaliv b. Turkm. see Garabogazköl Aýlagy
Karabük Turkey 112 D2
Karabulak Almatinskaya Oblast' Kazakh. 98 B3
Karabulak Vostochnyy Kazakhstan Kazakh. 98 D3
Karabulakskaya (abandoned) Kazakh. 98 A2
Karabura China see Yumin
Karaburun Turkey 69 L5
Karabutak Kazakh. 102 B2
Karacabey Turkey 69 M4
Karacaköy Turkey 69 M4
Karacalı Dağ mt. Turkey 113 E3
Karaçal Tepe mt. Turkey 107 A1
Karacasu Turkey 69 M6
Karaca Yarımadası pen. Turkey 69 N6
Karachayevsk Russia 113 F2
Karachev Russia 53 G5

▶Karachi Pak. 111 G5
10th most populous city in the world.

Karacurun Turkey see Hilvan
Karad India 106 B2
Kara Dağ hill Turkey 107 D1
Kara Dağ mt. Turkey 112 D3
Kara-Dar'ya Uzbek. see Payshanba
Kara Deniz sea Asia/Europe see Black Sea
Karagan Russia 90 A1
Karagandinskaya Oblast' admin. div. Kazakh. 98 A2
Karagandy Kazakh. 102 D2
Karagash Kazakh. 98 B3
Karagayly Kazakh. 102 E2
Karagaylybulak Kazakh. 98 D2
Karaginskiy Zaliv b. Russia 77 R4
Karagiye, Vpadina depr. Kazakh. 113 H2
Karagola India 105 F4
Karahallı Turkey 69 M5
Karahasanlı Turkey 112 D3
Karaikal India 106 C4
Karaikkudi India 106 C4
Karaisalı Turkey 112 D3
Karaitan Kalimantan Indon. 85 G2
Karaitivu i. Sri Lanka 106 C4
Karaj Iran 110 C3
Karak Jordan see Al Karak
Karakalli Turkey see Özalp
Kara Kara National Park Australia 138 A6
Karakax China see Moyu
Karakax He r. China 99 C5
Karakelong i. Indon. 83 C1
Karakitang i. Indon. 83 C2
Karaklis Armenia see Vanadzor
Karakoçan Turkey 113 F3
Kara-Köl Kyrg. 101 G2
Karakol Ysyk-Köl Kyrg. 98 B4
Karakol Ysyk-Köl Kyrg. 102 E3
Karakoram Pass China/India 104 D2
Karakoram Range mts Asia 101 G3
Kara K'orē Eth. 122 D2
Karakorum Range mts Asia see Karakoram Range
Karaköse Turkey see Ağrı
Karakozha Kazakh. 98 C2
Kara Kul' Kyrg. see Kara-Köl
Karakul', Ozero l. Tajik. see Qarokŭl
Karakum Kazakh. 98 B3
Kara Kum des. Turkm. see Karakum Desert
Karakum, Peski Kazakh. see Karakum Desert
Karakum Desert Kazakh. 100 E2
Karakum Desert Turkm. 110 F2
Karakumskiy Kanal canal Turkm. see Garagum Kanaly
Karakurt Turkey 113 F2
Karakuş Dağı ridge Turkey 69 N5
Karal Chad 121 E3
Karala Estonia 55 L7
Karalundi Australia 135 B6
Karaman, Bone r. Indon. 83 A3
Karamagay China see Haramgai
Karaman Turkey 112 D3
Karaman prov. Turkey 107 A1
Karamanlı Turkey 69 M6
Karamay China 98 D3
Karambar Pass Afgh./Pak. 111 I2
Karambu Kalimantan Indon. 85 G3
Karamea N.Z. 139 D5
Karamea Bight b. N.Z. 139 C5
Karamendy Kazakh. 102 B1
Karamian i. Indon. 85 F4
Karamiran China 99 D5
Karamiran He r. China 99 D5
Karamiran Shankou pass China 99 D5
Karamürsel Turkey 69 M4
Karamyshevo Russia 55 P8
Karān i. Saudi Arabia 110 C5
Karang, Tanjung pt Indon. 83 A3
Karangagung Sumatra Indon. 84 D3
Karangan Sumatra Indon. 84 D4
Karangasem Bali Indon. 85 F5
Karangbolong, Tanjung pt Indon. 85 E5
Karangetang vol. Indon. 83 C2
Karanja India 106 C1
Karanjia India 104 E5
Karaoy (abandoned) Kazakh. 98 A3
Karapınar Gaziantep Turkey 107 C1
Karapınar Konya Turkey 112 D3
Karaqi China 98 B4
!Karas admin. reg. Namibia 124 C4
Karasay China 99 C5
Kara-Say Kyrg. 98 B4
Karasburg Namibia 124 D5
Kara Sea Russia 76 I2
Kárášjohka Norway see Karasjok
Karasjok Norway 54 N2
Karasor, Ozero salt l. Kazakh. 98 A2
Kara Strait Russia see Karskiye Vorota, Proliv
Karasu Japan 92 C4
Karasu Kazakh. 98 A3
Karasu r. Syria/Turkey 107 C1
Karasu Bitlis Turkey see Hizan
Karasu Sakarya Turkey 69 N4
Karasu r. Turkey 113 F3
Karasubazar Crimea see Bilohirs'k
Karasu-gawa r. Japan 93 F2
Karasuk Russia 76 I4
Karāt Iran 111 F3
Karatal Kazakh. 98 D3
Karataş Turkey 107 B1
Karataş Burnu hd Turkey see Fener Burnu
Karatau Kazakh. 102 D3
Karatau, Khrebet mts Kazakh. 102 C3
Karatax Shan mts China 99 C6
Karatepe Turkey 107 A1
Karathuri Myanmar 87 B5
Karatol r. Kazakh. 98 B3
Karatsu Japan 91 C6
Karatung i. Indon. 83 C1
Karatüngke China 94 B2
Karaudanawa Guyana 177 G3
Karauli India 104 D4
Karavan Kyrg. see Kerben
Karavostasi Cyprus 107 A2
Karawang Java Indon. 84 D4
Karaxahar He r. China see Kaidu He
Kara Yertis r. Kazakh. 98 D3
Karayılan Turkey 107 C1
Karayulgun China 98 C4
Karazhal Kazakh. 102 D2
Karazhingil (abandoned) Kazakh. 98 A3
Karbalā' Iraq 113 G4
Karben Germany 63 I4
Karcag Hungary 69 I1
Karden Germany 63 H4
Kardhítsa Greece see Karditsa
Karditsa Greece 69 I5
Kärdla Estonia 55 M7
Kardzhali Bulg. 69 K4
Karee S. Africa 125 H5
Kareeberge mts S. Africa 124 E6
Kareima Sudan 108 D6
Kareli India 104 D5
Karelia aut. rep. Russia see Kareliya, Respublika
Kareliya, Respublika aut. rep. Russia 54 R5
Karel'skaya A.S.S.R. aut. rep. Russia see Kareliya, Respublika
Karel'skiy Bereg coastal area Russia 54 R3
Karema Tanz. 123 D4
Karera India 104 D4
Karesuando Sweden 54 M2
Kārevāndar Iran 111 F5
Kārēz Afgh. 111 F3
Kārēz Ilyās Afgh. 111 F3
Kargalinskaya Russia 113 G2
Kargalinski Russia see Kargalinskaya
Kargaly Kazakh. 98 A2
Kargapazarı Dağları mts Turkey 113 F3
Karghalik China see Yecheng
Kargı Turkey 112 D2
Kargil India 104 D2
Kargilik China see Yecheng
Kargıpınarı Turkey 107 B1
Kargopol' Russia 52 H3
Kari Nigeria 120 E3
Karīān Iran 110 E5
Kariba Zimbabwe 123 C5
Kariba, Lake resr Zambia/Zimbabwe 123 C5
Kariba Dam Zambia/Zimbabwe 123 C5
Kariba-yama vol. Japan 90 E4
Karibib Namibia 124 B1
Karigasniemi Fin. 54 N2
Karijini National Park Australia 135 B5
Karijoki Fin. 54 L5
Karikachi-tōge pass Japan 90 F4
Karikari, Cape N.Z. 139 D2
Karimata i. Indon. 85 E3
Karimata, Pulau-pulau is Indon. 85 E3
Karimata, Selat str. Indon. 85 E3
Karimganj India 105 H4
Karimnagar India 106 C2
Karimun Besar i. Sumatra Indon. 84 C2
Karimunjawa i. Indon. 85 E4
Karimunjawa, Pulau-pulau is Indon. 85 E4
Káristos Greece see Karystos
Kariya Japan 92 C4
Karjat Mahar. India 106 B2
Karjat Mahar. India 106 B2
Karkaralong, Kepulauan is Indon. 82 D5
Karkaraly Kazakh. 102 E2
Karkar Island P.N.G. 81 L7
Karkh Pak. 111 G5
Karkinits'ka Zatoka g. Crimea 69 O2
Kärkölä Fin. 55 N6
Karkonoski Park Narodowy nat. park Czech Rep./Poland see Krkonošský národní park
Karksi-Nuia Estonia 55 N7
Kärkük Iraq see Kirkūk
Karlachi Pak. 111 H3
Karlholmsbruk Sweden 55 J6
Karlik Shan mts China 94 C3
Karlıova Turkey 113 F3
Karlivka Ukr. 53 G6
Karl Marks, Qullai mt. Tajik. 111 I2
Karl-Marx-Stadt Germany see Chemnitz
Karlovac Croatia 68 F2
Karlovka Ukr. see Karlivka
Karlovo Bulg. 69 K3
Karlovy Vary Czech Rep. 63 M4
Karlsbad Germany 63 I6
Karlsborg Sweden 55 I7
Karlsburg Romania see Alba Iulia
Karlshamn Sweden 55 I8
Karlskoga Sweden 55 I7
Karlskrona Sweden 55 I8
Karlsruhe Germany 63 I5
Karlstad Sweden 55 H7
Karlstad MN U.S.A. 160 D1
Karlstadt Germany 63 J5
Karluk AK U.S.A. 148 I4
Karlyk Turkm. 111 G2
Karmala India 106 B2
Karmel, Har hill Israel see Carmel, Mount
Karmona Spain see Córdoba
Karmøy i. Norway 55 D7
Karmpur Pak. 111 I4
Karnal India 104 D3
Karnali r. Nepal 99 C7
Karnaphuli Reservoir Bangl. 105 H5
Karnataka state India 106 B3
Karnavati India see Ahmadabad
Karnes City TX U.S.A. 161 D6
Karnobat Bulg. 69 L3
Karodi Pak. 111 G5
Karoi Zimbabwe 123 C5
Karokpi Myanmar 86 B4
Karo La pass China 99 E7
Karompalompo i. Indon. 83 B4
Karong India 105 H4
Karonga Malawi 123 D4
Karonie Australia 135 C7
Karool-Döbö Kyrg. 98 B4
Karoo National Park S. Africa 124 F7
Karoonda Australia 137 B7
Karora Eritrea 108 E6
Káros i. Greece see Keross
Karossa Celebes Indon. 83 A3
Karossa, Tanjung pt Sumba Indon. 85 G5
Karow Germany 63 M1
Karpasia pen. Cyprus 107 B2
Karpas Peninsula Cyprus see Karpasia
Karpathos i. Greece 69 L7
Karpathou, Steno sea chan. Greece 69 L6
Karpaty mts Europe see Carpathian Mountains
Karpenisi Greece 69 I5
Karpilovka Belarus see Aktsyabrski
Karpinsk Russia 51 S4
Karpogory Russia 52 J2
Karpuz r. Turkey 107 A1
Karratha Australia 134 B5
Karroo plat. S. Africa see Great Karoo
Karrychirla Turkm. see Garryçyrla
Kars Turkey 113 F2
Kärsämäki Fin. 54 N5
Kārsava Latvia 55 O8
Karshi Uzbek. see Qarshi
Karskiye Vorota, Proliv strait Russia 76 G3
Karskoye More sea Russia see Kara Sea
Karstädt Germany 63 L1
Karstula Fin. 54 N5
Karsu Turkey 107 C1
Karsun Russia 53 J5
Kartal Turkey 69 M4
Kartaly Russia 76 H4
Kartayel' Russia 52 L2
Karttula Fin. 54 O5
Karuizawa Japan 93 E2
Karumba Australia 136 C3
Karumbhar Island India 104 B5
Kārūn, Kūh-e hill Iran 110 C4
Kārūn, Rūd-e r. Iran 110 C4
Karuni Sumba Indon. 83 A5
Karur India 106 C4
Karvia Fin. 54 M5
Karviná Czech Rep. 57 Q6
Karwar India 106 B3
Karyagino Azer. see Füzuli
Karymskoye Russia 89 K2
Karynzharyk, Peski des. Kazakh. 113 I2
Karystos Greece 69 K5
Kaş Turkey 69 M6
Kasa India 106 B2
Kasaba Turkey see Turgutlu
Kasabonika Canada 152 C3
Kasabonika Lake Canada 152 C3
Kasaga-dake mt. Japan 92 D2
Kasagi Japan 92 B4
Kasagi-yama mt. Japan 92 D3
Kasahara Japan 92 D3
Kāsah Murgh mts Afgh. 111 F3
Kasaï r. Dem. Rep. Congo 122 B4 *also known as Kwa*
Kasai Japan 92 A4
Kasaï, Plateau du Dem. Rep. Congo 123 C4
Kasaji Dem. Rep. Congo 123 C5
Kasama Ibaraki Japan 93 G2
Kasama Ibaraki Japan 93 G2
Kasama Zambia 123 D5
Kasamatsu Japan 92 C3
Kasan Uzbek. see Koson
Kasane Botswana 123 C5
Kasano-misaki pt Japan 92 C2
Kasaragod India 106 B3
Kasargod India see Kasaragod
Kasargode India see Kasaragod
Kasatkino Russia 90 C2
Kasatori-yama hill Japan 92 C4
Kasba Lake Canada 151 K2
Kasba Tadla Morocco 64 C5
Kasegaluk Lagoon AK U.S.A. 148 G1
Kasenga Dem. Rep. Congo 123 C5
Kasengu Dem. Rep. Congo 123 C4
Kasese Dem. Rep. Congo 122 C4
Kasese Uganda 122 D3
Kasevo Russia see Neftekamsk
Kasganj India 104 D4
Kasha China 96 C2
Kashabowie Canada 152 C4
Kāshān Iran 110 C3
Kashary Russia 53 I6
Kashechewan Canada 152 E3
Kashega AK U.S.A. 148 F5
Kashegelok AK U.S.A. 148 H3
Kashgar China see Kashi
Kashi China 98 B5
Kashiba Japan 92 B4
Kashihara Japan 92 B4
Kashima Ibaraki Japan 93 G3
Kashima Ishikawa Japan 92 C2
Kashima-nada b. Japan 93 G2
Kashimayaria-dake mt. Japan 92 D2
Kashimo Japan 92 D3
Kashin Russia 52 H4
Kashipur India 104 D3
Kashira Russia 53 H5
Kashiwa Japan 93 F3
Kashiwara Japan 92 B4
Kashiwazaki Japan 91 E5
Kashkanteniz Kazakh. 98 A3
Kashkarantsy Russia 52 H2
Kashkū'iyeh Iran 110 D4
Kāshmar Iran 110 E3
Kashmir reg. Asia 104 D2
Kashmir, Vale of reg. India 104 C2
Kashunuk r. AK U.S.A. 148 F3
Kashyr Kazakh. 88 D2
Kashyukulu Dem. Rep. Congo 123 C4
Kasi India see Varanasi
Kāsīgar Afgh. 111 H3
Kasigluk AK U.S.A. 148 G3
Kasimbar Celebes Indon. 83 A3
Kasimov Russia 53 I5
Kasiruta i. Moluccas Indon. 83 C3
Kaskattama r. Canada 151 N3
Kaskelen Kazakh. 98 B4
Kaskinen Fin. 54 L5
Kas Klong i. Cambodia see Kŏng, Kaôh
Kaskö Fin. see Kaskinen
Kaslo Canada 150 G5
Kasmere Lake Canada 151 K3
Kasongan Kalimantan Indon. 85 F3
Kasongo Dem. Rep. Congo 123 C4
Kasongo-Lunda Dem. Rep. Congo 123 B4
Kasos i. Greece 69 L7
Kaspīy Mangy Oypaty lowland Kazakh./Russia see Caspian Lowland
Kaspiysk Russia 113 G2
Kaspiyskiy Russia see Lagan'
Kaspiyskoye More l. Asia/Europe see Caspian Sea
Kassa Slovakia see Košice
Kassala Sudan 108 E6
Kassandras, Akra pt Greece see Kassandras, Akrotirio
Kassandras, Akrotirio pt Greece 69 J5
Kassandras, Kolpos b. Greece 69 J4
Kassel Germany 63 J3
Kasserine Tunisia 68 C7
Kastag Pak. 111 F5
Kastamonu Turkey 112 D2
Kastellaun Germany 63 H4
Kastelli Greece see Kissamos
Kastéllion Greece see Kissamos
Kastellorizon i. Greece see Megisti
Kasterlee Belgium 62 E3
Kastoria Greece 69 I4
Kastornoye Russia 53 H6
Kastsyukovichy Belarus 53 G5
Kasuga Gifu Japan 92 C3
Kasuga Hyōgo Japan 92 B3
Kasugai Japan 92 C3
Kasukabe Japan 93 F3
Kasukawa Japan 93 F2
Kasulu Tanz. 123 D4
Kasumigaura Ibaraki Japan 93 G2
Kasumigaura Ibaraki Japan 93 G2
Kasumiga-ura l. Japan 93 G2
Kasumkent Russia 113 H2
Kasungu Malawi 123 D5
Kasungu National Park Malawi 123 D5
Kasur Pak. 111 I4
Katâdtlit Nunât terr. N. America see Greenland
Katahdin, Mount ME U.S.A. 162 G2
Katah Sang Srah Afgh. 111 G3
Kataklik India 104 D2
Katako-Kombe Dem. Rep. Congo 122 C4
Katakwi Uganda 122 D3
Katalla AK U.S.A. 149 K3
Katana India 104 C5
Katangi India 104 D5
Katanning Australia 135 B8
Katano Japan 92 B4
Katashina Japan 93 F2
Katashina-gawa r. Japan 93 F2
Katata Japan 92 B3
Katavi National Park Tanz. 123 D4
Katāwāz reg. Afgh. 111 G3
Katchall i. India 87 A6
Katea Dem. Rep. Congo 123 C4
Kateel r. AK U.S.A. 148 H2
Katerini Greece 69 J4
Katesh Tanz. 123 D4
Kate's Needle mt. Canada/U.S.A. 149 N4
Katete Zambia 123 D5
Katherîna, Gebel mt. Egypt see Kātrīnā, Jabal
Katherine Australia 134 F3
Katherine Gorge National Park Australia see Nitmiluk National Park
Kathi India 111 I6
Kathiawar pen. India 104 B5
Kathihar India see Katihar
Kathiraveli Sri Lanka 106 D4
Kathiwara India 104 C5
Kathleen Falls Australia 134 E3

▶Kathmandu Nepal 105 F4
Capital of Nepal.

Kathu S. Africa 124 F4
Kathua India 104 C2
Kati Mali 120 C3
Katibas r. Malaysia 85 F2
Katihar India 105 F4
Katikati S. Africa 125 H7
Katima Mulilo Namibia 123 C5
Katimik Lake Canada 151 L4
Katiola Côte d'Ivoire 120 C4
Kā Tiritiri o te Moana mts N.Z. see Southern Alps

▶Kati Thanda-Lake Eyre Australia 137 B6
Largest lake in Oceania and lowest point.

Kati Thanda-Lake Eyre (North) Australia 137 B6
Kati Thanda-Lake Eyre (South) Australia 137 B6
Kati Thanda-Lake Eyre National Park Australia 137 B6
Katkop Hills S. Africa 124 E6
Katlehong S. Africa 125 I4
Katma China 99 D5
Katmai National Park and Preserve AK U.S.A. 146 C4
Katmandu Nepal see Kathmandu
Katni India 104 E5
Katō Japan 92 A4
Kato Achaïa Greece 69 I5
Kat O Chau H.K. China see Crooked Island
Kat O Hoi b. H.K. China see Crooked Harbour
Katonkaragay Kazakh. 98 D2
Katoomba Australia 138 E4
Katoposa, Gunung mt. Indon. 83 B3
Katori Japan 93 G3
Katowice Poland 57 Q5
Katoya India 105 G5
Katrancık Dağı mts Turkey 69 M6
Kātrīnā, Jabal mt. Egypt 112 D5
Katrine, Loch l. U.K. 60 E4
Katrineholm Sweden 55 J7
Katse Dam Lesotho 125 I5
Katsina Nigeria 120 D3
Katsina-Ala Nigeria 120 D4
Katsunuma Japan 93 E3
Katsura-gawa r. Japan 93 F3
Katsuragi-san hill Japan 92 B4
Katsuura Japan 93 G3
Katsuyama Japan 92 C2
Kattaktoc, Cap c. Canada 153 I2
Kattamudda Well Australia 134 D5
Kattaqo'rg'on Uzbek. 111 G2
Kattaqŭrghon Uzbek. see Kattaqo'rg'on
Kattegat strait Denmark/Sweden 55 G8
Kattowitz Poland see Katowice
Katumbar India 104 D4
Katun' r. Russia 98 D1
Katunino Russia 52 J4
Katunskiy Khrebet mts Russia 98 D2
Katuri Pak. 111 H4
Katwa India see Katoya
Katwijk aan Zee Neth. 62 E2
Katzenbuckel hill Germany 63 J5
Kaua'i i. HI U.S.A. 157 [inset]
Kaua'i Channel HI U.S.A. 157 [inset]
Kaub Germany 63 H4
Kaufungen Germany 63 J3
Kauhajoki Fin. 54 M5

Kauhava Fin. 54 M5
Kaukauna WI U.S.A. 164 A1
Kaukkwè Hills Myanmar 86 B1
Kaukonen Fin. 54 N3
Ka'ula i. HI U.S.A. 157 [inset]
Kaulakahi Channel HI U.S.A. 157 [inset]
Kaumajet Mountains Canada 153 J2
Kaunakakai HI U.S.A. 157 [inset]
Kaunas Lith. 55 M9
Kaunata Latvia 55 O8
Kaundy, Vpadina depr. Kazakh. 113 I2
Kaunia Bangl. 105 G4
Kaura-Namoda Nigeria 120 D3
Kau Sai Chau i. H.K. China 97 [inset]
Kaustinen Fin. 54 M5
Kautokeino Norway 54 M2
Kau-ye Kyun i. Myanmar 87 B5
Kavadarci Macedonia 69 J4
Kavak Turkey 112 E2
Kavaklıdere Turkey 69 M6
Kavala Greece 69 K4
Kavalas, Kolpos b. Greece 69 K4
Kavalerovo Russia 90 D3
Kavali India 106 D3
Kavango Zambezi Transfrontier Conservation Area res. Africa 123 C5
Kavār Iran 110 D4
Kavaratti India 106 B4
Kavaratti atoll India 106 B4
Kavarna Bulg. 69 M3
Kavendou, Mont mt. Guinea 120 B3
Kaveri r. India 106 C4
Kavīr Iran 110 C3
Kavīr, Chāh-e well Iran 110 E3
Kavīr, Dasht-e des. Iran 110 D3
Kavīr Kūshk well Iran 110 E3
Kavkasioni mts Asia/Europe see Caucasus
Kawa Seram Indon. 83 D3
Kawa Myanmar 86 B3
Kawabe Japan 92 D3
Kawachi Ibaraki Japan 93 G3
Kawachi Ishikawa Japan 92 C2
Kawachi Tochigi Japan 93 F2
Kawachi-Nagano Japan 92 D4
Kawagama Lake Canada 165 F1
Kawage Japan 92 C4
Kawagoe Japan 93 F3
Kawaguchi Japan 93 F3
Kawaguchi-ko l. Japan 93 E3
Kawai Japan 92 D2
Kawaihae HI U.S.A. 157 [inset]
Kawaikini HI U.S.A. 157 [inset]
Kawakami Nagano Japan 93 E3
Kawakami Nara Japan 92 B4
Kawakawa N.Z. 139 E2
Kawakita Japan 92 C2
Kawambwa Zambia 123 C4
Kawamoto Japan 93 F2
Kawana Zambia 123 C5
Kawanakajima Japan 93 E2
Kawana-zaki pt Japan 93 F4
Kawane Japan 93 E4
Kawanehon Japan 93 E3
Kawangkoan Celebes Indon. 83 C2
Kawanishi Japan 92 B3
Kawarazawa-gawa r. Japan 93 F2
Kawardha India 104 E5
Kawartha Highlands Signature Site park Canada 165 F1
Kawartha Lakes Canada 165 F1
Kawasaki Japan 93 F3
Kawashima Japan 92 C3
Kawato Celebes Indon. 83 B3
Kawaue Japan 92 D3
Kawau Island N.Z. 139 E3
Kawawachikamach Canada 153 I3
Kawazu Japan 93 E4
Kawdut Myanmar 86 B4
Kawe i. Papua Indon. 83 D2
Kawerau N.Z. 139 F4
Kawhia N.Z. 139 E4
Kawhia Harbour N.Z. 139 E4
Kawich Peak NV U.S.A. 158 E3
Kawich Range mts NV U.S.A. 158 E3
Kawinaw Lake Canada 151 L4
Kawinda Sumbawa Indon. 85 G5
Kawio i. Indon. 83 C1
Kaw Lake OK U.S.A. 161 D4
Kawlin Myanmar 86 A2
Kawm Umbū Egypt 108 D5
Kawngmeum Myanmar 86 B2
Kawthaung Myanmar 87 B5
Kaxgar China see Kashi
Kaxgar He r. China 98 B5
Kax He r. China 98 C4
Kaxtexi China 99 B5
Kaxtexi Shan mts China 99 C5
Kaya Burkina Faso 120 C3
Kaya Japan 92 B3
Kayadibi Turkey 112 E3
Kayaga-take mt. Japan 93 E3
Kayak Island AK U.S.A. 149 K4
Kayan r. Indon. 85 E3
Kayan r. Indon. 85 G2
Kayangel Atoll Palau 82 [inset]
Kayangel Passage Palau 82 [inset]
Kayankulam India 106 C4
Kayan Mentarang, Taman Nasional nat. park Indon. 85 F2
Kayar India 106 C2
Kayasa Halmahera Indon. 83 C2
Kaycee WY U.S.A. 156 G4
Kaydak, Sor dry lake Kazakh. 113 I1
Kaydanovo Belarus see Dzyarzhynsk
Kayembe-Mukulu Dem. Rep. Congo 123 C4
Kayenta AZ U.S.A. 159 H3
Kayes Mali 120 B3
Kayigyalik Lake AK U.S.A. 148 G3
Kaylahgay (abandoned) Afgh. 111 H3
Kaymaz Turkey 69 N5
Kaynar Vostochnyy Kazakhstan Kazakh. 102 E2
Kaynar Zhambylskaya Oblast' Kazakh. 98 A4
Kaynar Turkey 112 E3
Kayoa i. Moluccas Indon. 83 C2
Kay Point pt Canada 149 M1
Kayseri Turkey 112 D3
Kayuadi i. Indon. 83 B4
Kayuagung Sumatra Indon. 84 D3
Kayuyu Dem. Rep. Congo 122 C4
Kayyngdy Kyrg. 102 D3
Kazach'ye Russia 77 O2
Kazakh Azer. see Qazax
Kazakhskaya S.S.R. country Asia see Kazakhstan
Kazakhskiy Zaliv b. Kazakh. 113 I2

▶Kazakhstan country Asia 100 F2
4th largest country in Asia and 9th in the world.

Kazakhstan Kazakh. see Aksay
Kazakh Steppe plain Kazakh. see Saryarka
Kazakstan country Asia see Kazakhstan
Kazan r. Canada 151 M2
Kazan' Russia 52 K5
Kazandzhik Turkm. see Bereket
Kazanka r. Russia 52 K5
Kazanlak Bulg. 69 K3
Kazanlı Turkey 107 B1
Kazan-rettō is Japan see Volcano Islands
Kazanshunkyr Kazakh. 98 C2
Kazatin Ukr. see Kozyatyn

▶Kazbek mt. Georgia/Russia 53 J8
4th highest mountain in Europe.

Kaz Dağı mts Turkey 69 L5
Kāzerūn Iran 110 C4
Kazhym Russia 52 K3
Kazidi Tajik. see Qozide
Kazi Magomed Azer. see Hacıqabul
Kazincbarcika Hungary 53 D6
Kaziranga National Park India 105 H4
Kazo Japan 93 F2
K'azreti Georgia 113 G2
Kaztalovka Kazakh. 51 P6
Kazusa Japan 93 G3
Kazy Turkm. 110 E2
Kazym r. Russia 51 T3
Kazym-Mys Russia 51 T3
Kea i. Greece see Tzia
Keady U.K. 61 F3
Keams Canyon AZ U.S.A. 159 H4
Kéamu i. Vanuatu see Anatom
Kearney NE U.S.A. 160 D3
Kearny AZ U.S.A. 159 H5
Keban Turkey 112 E3
Keban Barajı resr Turkey 112 E3
Kebatu i. Indon. 85 E3
Kébémèr Senegal 120 B3
Kebili Tunisia 64 F5
Kebīr, Nahr al r. Lebanon/Syria 107 B2
Kebkabiya Sudan 121 F3
Kebnekaise mt. Sweden 54 K3
Kebock Head hd U.K. 60 C2
K'ebrī Dehar Eth. 122 E3
Kebumen Java Indon. 85 E4
Kebur Sumatra Indon. 84 C3
Kech reg. Pak. 111 F5
Kecheng China 94 D4
Kechika r. Canada 149 P4
Keçiborlu Turkey 69 N6
Kecskemét Hungary 69 H1
Keda Georgia 113 F2
Kedah state Malaysia 84 C1
Kdainiai Lith. 55 M9
Kedairu Passage Fiji see Kadavu Passage
Kedarnath Peak India 99 B7
Kedgwick Canada 153 I5
Kedian China 97 G2
Kediri Java Indon. 85 F4
Kedong China 90 B3
Kédougou Senegal 120 B3
Kedva r. Russia 52 L2
Kędzierzyn-Koźle Poland 57 Q5
Keele r. Canada 149 P2
Keele Peak Canada 149 O3
Keeler CA U.S.A. 158 E3
Keeley Lake Canada 151 I4
Keeling Islands terr. Indian Ocean see Cocos (Keeling) Islands
Keelung Taiwan see Jilong
Keen, Mount hill U.K. 60 G4
Keenapusan i. Phil. 82 B5
Keene CA U.S.A. 158 D4
Keene KY U.S.A. 164 C5
Keene NH U.S.A. 165 I2
Keene OH U.S.A. 164 E3
Keeper Hill hill Ireland 61 D5
Keepit, Lake resr Australia 138 E3
Keep River National Park Australia 134 E3
Keerbergen Belgium 62 E3
Keer-weer, Cape Australia 136 C2
Keetmanshoop Namibia 124 D4
Keewatin Canada 151 M5
Kefallinía i. Greece see Cephalonia
Kefallonia i. Greece see Cephalonia
Kefamenanu Timor Indon. 83 C5
Kefe Crimea see Feodosiya
Keffi Nigeria 120 D4
Keflavík Iceland 54 [inset 1]
Kê Ga, Mui pt Vietnam 87 E5
Kegalla Sri Lanka 106 D5
Kegen Kazakh. 102 E3
Kegeti Kyrg. 98 A4
Keglo, Baie de b. Canada 153 I2
Keg River Canada 150 G3
Kegul'ta Russia 53 J7
Kehra Estonia 55 N7
Kehsi Mansam Myanmar 86 B2
Keighley U.K. 58 F5
Keihoku Japan 92 B3
Keila Estonia 55 N7
Keimoes S. Africa 124 E5
Keitele Fin. 54 O5
Keitele l. Fin. 54 O5
Keith Australia 137 C8
Keith U.K. 60 G3
Keith Arm b. Canada 149 Q2
Kejimkujik National Park Canada 153 I5
Kekachi-yama mt. Japan 92 D2
Kekaha HI U.S.A. 157 [inset]
Kékes mt. Hungary 57 R7
Kekik i. Moluccas Indon. 83 D3
Keklau Palau 82 [inset]
Kekri India 104 C4
Kelaa i. Maldives 106 B5
K'elafo Eth. 122 E3
Kelan China 95 G4
Kelang i. Moluccas Indon. 83 C3
Kelang Malaysia see Klang
Kelantan r. Malaysia 84 C1
Kelantan state Malaysia 84 C1
Kelapa i. Moluccas Indon. 83 D5
Kelara r. Indon. 83 A4
Kelawar i. Indon. 85 E3
Kelberg Germany 62 G4
Kel'dermurat Kazakh. 98 C3
Kelheim Germany 63 L6
Kelibia Tunisia 68 D6
Kelif Uzboýy marsh Turkm. 111 F2
Kelīrī Iran 110 E5
Kelkheim (Taunus) Germany 63 I4
Kelkit Turkey 113 E2
Kelkit r. Turkey 112 E2
Kéllé Congo 122 B4
Keller Lake Canada 150 F2
Kellett, Cape Canada 146 F2
Kelleys Island OH U.S.A. 164 D3
Kelliher Canada 151 K5
Kelloselkä Fin. 54 P3
Kells Ireland 61 F4
Kells r. U.K. 61 F3
Kelly KY U.S.A. 164 B5
Kelly r. AK U.S.A. 148 G2
Kelly, Mount hill AK U.S.A. 148 G1
Kelly Lake Canada 149 P2
Kelly Range hills Australia 135 C6
Kelm Lith. 55 M9
Kelmis Belgium 62 G4
Kélo Chad 121 E4
Kelowna Canada 150 G5
Kelp Head hd Canada 150 E5
Kelseyville CA U.S.A. 158 B2
Kelso U.K. 60 G5
Kelso WA U.S.A. 156 C3
Kelso (abandoned) CA U.S.A. 159 F4
Keluang Malaysia 84 C2
Kelvington Canada 151 K4
Kem' Russia 52 G2
Kem' r. Russia 52 G2
Kemabung Sabah Malaysia 85 F1
Ke Macina Mali see Macina
Kemah Turkey 112 E3
Kemaliye Turkey 112 E3
Kemalpaşa Turkey 69 L5
Kemano (abandoned) Canada 150 E4
Kemasik Malaysia 84 C1
Kembayan Kalimantan Indon. 85 E2
Kembé Cent. Afr. Rep. 122 C3
Kemeneshát hills Hungary 68 G1
Kemer Antalya Turkey 69 N6
Kemer Muğla Turkey 69 M6
Kemer Barajı resr Turkey 69 M6
Kemerovo Russia 76 J4
Kemi Fin. 54 N4
Kemijärvi Fin. 54 O3
Kemijärvi l. Fin. 54 O3
Kemijoki r. Fin. 54 N4
Kemin Kyrg. 98 A4
Kemiö Fin. see Kimito
Kemir Turkm. see Keymir
Kemmerer WY U.S.A. 156 F4
Kemnath Germany 63 L5
Kemnay U.K. 60 G3
Kemp Coast reg. Antarctica see Kemp Land
Kempele Fin. 54 N4
Kempen Germany 62 G3
Kempisch Kanaal canal Belgium 62 F3
Kemp Land reg. Antarctica 188 D2
Kemp Peninsula Antarctica 188 A2
Kemp's Bay Bahamas 163 E7
Kempsey Australia 138 F3
Kempt, Lac l. Canada 152 G5
Kempten (Allgäu) Germany 57 M7
Kempton IN U.S.A. 164 B3
Kempton Park S. Africa 125 I4
Kemptville Canada 165 H1
Kemujan i. Indon. 85 E4
Ken r. India 104 E4
Kenai AK U.S.A. 149 J3
Kenai Fiords National Park AK U.S.A. 149 J4
Kenai Lake AK U.S.A. 149 J3
Kenai Mountains AK U.S.A. 149 J4
Kenai National Wildlife Refuge nature res. AK U.S.A. 149 J3
Kenai Peninsula AK U.S.A. 149 J3
Kenam, Tanjung pt Indon. 84 D4
Kenamu r. Canada 153 K3
Kenansville NC U.S.A. 163 E5
Kenâyis, Râs el pt Egypt see Ḥikmah, Ra's al
Kenbridge VA U.S.A. 165 F5
Kencong Java Indon. 85 F5
Kendal Java Indon. 85 E4
Kendal U.K. 58 E4
Kendall Australia 138 F3
Kendall, Cape Canada 147 J3
Kendall Island Bird Sanctuary nature res. Canada 149 N1
Kendallville IN U.S.A. 164 C3
Kendari Celebes Indon. 83 B3
Kendawangan Kalimantan Indon. 85 E3
Kendawangan r. Indon. 85 E3
Kendégué Chad 121 E3
Kendirli-Kiyasan, Plato plat. Kazakh. 113 I2
Kendrapara India 105 F5
Kendraparha India see Kendrapara
Kendrick Peak AZ U.S.A. 159 H4
Kendujhar India see Kendujhargarh
Kendujhargarh India 105 F5
Kendyktas mts Kazakh. 98 A4
Kendyrlisor, Solonchak salt l. Kazakh. 113 I2
Kenebri Australia 138 D3
Kenedy TX U.S.A. 161 D6
Kenema Sierra Leone 120 B4
Kenepai, Gunung mt. Indon. 85 E2
Kenge Dem. Rep. Congo 123 B4
Keng Lap Myanmar 86 C2
Kengtung Myanmar 86 B2
Kenhardt S. Africa 124 E5
Kéniéba Mali 120 B3
Kenitra Morocco 64 C5
Kenli China 95 I4
Kenmare Ireland 61 C6
Kenmare ND U.S.A. 160 C1
Kenmare River inlet Ireland 61 B6
Kenmore NY U.S.A. 165 F2
Kenn Germany 62 G5
Kenna NM U.S.A. 161 C5
Kennebec SD U.S.A. 160 D3
Kennebec r. ME U.S.A. 162 G2
Kennebunkport ME U.S.A. 165 J2
Kennedy, Cape FL U.S.A. see Canaveral, Cape
Kennedy Entrance sea chan. AK U.S.A. 148 I4
Kennedy Range National Park Australia 135 A6
Kennedy Town H.K. China 97 [inset]
Kenner LA U.S.A. 161 F6
Kennet r. U.K. 59 G7
Kenneth Range hills Australia 135 B5
Kennett MO U.S.A. 161 F4
Kennewick WA U.S.A. 156 D3
Kennicott AK U.S.A. 149 L3
Kenn Reef Australia 136 F4
Kenny Lake AK U.S.A. 149 K3
Kenogami r. Canada 152 D4
Keno Hill Canada 149 N3
Kenora Canada 151 M5
Kenosha WI U.S.A. 164 B2
Kenozero, Ozero l. Russia 52 H3
Kent r. U.K. 58 E4
Kent OH U.S.A. 164 E3
Kent TX U.S.A. 161 B6
Kent VA U.S.A. 164 E5
Kent WA U.S.A. 156 C3
Kentani S. Africa see Centane
Kent Group is Australia 137 [inset]
Kentland IN U.S.A. 164 B3
Kenton OH U.S.A. 164 D3
Kent Peninsula Canada 146 H3
Kentucky state U.S.A. 164 C5
Kentucky Lake KY U.S.A. 161 F4
Kentwood LA U.S.A. 167 H2
Kenya country Africa 122 D3

▶Kenya, Mount Kenya 122 D4
2nd highest mountain in Africa.

Kenyir, Tasik resr Malaysia 84 C1
Ken-zaki pt Japan 93 F3
Keokuk IA U.S.A. 160 F3
Keoladeo National Park India 104 D4
Keonjhar India see Kendujhargarh
Keonjhargarh India see Kendujhargarh
Keosauqua IA U.S.A. 160 F3
Keowee, Lake resr SC U.S.A. 163 D5
Kepahiang Sumatra Indon. 84 C3
Kepina r. Russia 52 I2
Keppel Bay Australia 136 E4
Kepsut Turkey 69 M5
Kepulauan Bangka-Belitung prov. Indon. see Bangka-Belitung
Kera India 105 F5
Kerāh Iran 110 E4
Kerala state India 106 B4
Kerang Australia 138 A5
Kerava Fin. 55 N6
Kerba Alg. 67 G5
Kerbau, Tanjung pt Indon. 84 C3
Kerbela Iraq see Karbalā'
Kerben Kyrg. 102 D3
Kerbi r. Russia 90 E1
Kerbodot, Lac l. Canada 153 I3
Kerch Crimea 112 E1
Kerchom''ya Russia 52 L3
Kerema P.N.G. 81 L8
Keremeos Canada 150 G5
Kerempe Burun pt Turkey 112 D2
Keren Eritrea 108 E6
Kerepakupai Merú waterfall Venez. see Angel Falls
Kerewan Gambia 120 B3
Kergeli Turkm. 110 E2
Kerguélen, Îles is Indian Ocean 185 M9
Kerguelen Islands Indian Ocean see Kerguélen, Îles
Kerguelen Plateau sea feature Indian Ocean 185 M9
Kericho Kenya 122 D4
Kerihun mt. Indon. 85 F2
Kerikeri N.Z. 139 D2
Kerimäki Fin. 54 P6
Kerinci, Danau l. Indon. 84 C3
Kerinci, Gunung vol. Indon. 84 C3
Kerinci Seblat, Taman Nasional nat. park Indon. 84 C3
Kerintji vol. Indon. see Kerinci, Gunung
Keriya China see Yutian
Keriya He watercourse China 99 C5
Keriya Shankou pass China 99 C6
Kerken Germany 62 G3
Kerkennah, Îles is Tunisia 68 D7
Kerkiçi Turkm. 111 G2
Kerkini, Limni l. Greece 69 J4
Kerkinitis, Limni l. Greece see Kerkini, Limni
Kérkira i. Greece see Corfu
Kerkouane tourist site Tunisia 68 D6
Kerkyra Greece 69 H5
Kerkyra i. Greece see Corfu
Kerma Sudan 108 D6
Kermadec Islands S. Pacific Ocean 133 I5

▶Kermadec Trench sea feature S. Pacific Ocean 186 I8
4th deepest trench in the world.

Kermān Iran 110 E4
Kerman CA U.S.A. 158 C3
Kermān, Bīābān-e Iran 110 E4
Kermānshāh Kermānshāh Iran 110 B3
Kermānshāh Yazd Iran 110 D4
Kermine Uzbek. see Navoiy
Kermit TX U.S.A. 161 C6
Kern r. CA U.S.A. 158 D4
Kernertut, Cap c. Canada 153 I2
Keroh Malaysia see Pengkalan Hulu
Keros Russia 52 L3
Keross i. Greece 69 K6
Kérouané Guinea 120 C4
Kerpen Germany 62 G4
Kerr, Cape Antarctica 188 H1
Kerrobert Canada 151 I5
Kerrville TX U.S.A. 161 D6
Kerry Head hd Ireland 61 C5
Kerteh Malaysia 84 C1
Kerteminde Denmark 55 G9
Kertosono Java Indon. 85 F4
Keruak Lombok Indon. 85 G5
Kerulen r. China/Mongolia see Herlen Gol
Kerumutan, Suaka Margasatwa nature res. Indon. 84 C3
Kerur India 106 B2
Keryneia Cyprus see Kyrenia
Kerzaz Alg. 120 C2
Kerzhenets r. Russia 52 J4
Kesagami Lake Canada 152 E4
Kesälahti Fin. 54 P6
Keşan Turkey 69 L4
Keşap Turkey 53 H8
Kesariya India 105 F4
Kesennuma Japan 91 F5
Keshan China 90 B2
Keshena WI U.S.A. 164 A1
Keshod India 104 B5
Keshvar Iran 110 C3
Keskin Turkey 112 D3
Keskozero Russia 52 G3
Kesova Gora Russia 52 H4
Kessel Neth. 62 G3
Kestell S. Africa 125 I5
Kesten'ga Russia 54 Q4
Kestilä Fin. 54 O4
Keswick Canada 164 F1
Keswick U.K. 58 D4
Keszthely Hungary 68 G1
Ketahun Sumatra Indon. 84 C3
Ketapang Java Indon. 85 F4
Ketapang Kalimantan Indon. 85 E3
Ketchikan AK U.S.A. 149 O5
Ketian China 99 E6
Keti Bandar Pak. 111 G5
Ketik r. AK U.S.A. 148 H1
Ketlkede Mountain hill AK U.S.A. 148 H2
Ketmen', Khrebet mts China/Kazakh. 102 F3
Kettering U.K. 59 G6
Kettering OH U.S.A. 164 C4
Kettle r. Canada 150 G5
Kettle Creek r. PA U.S.A. 165 G3
Kettle Falls WA U.S.A. 156 D2
Kettleman City CA U.S.A. 158 D3
Kettle River Range mts WA U.S.A. 156 D2
Ketungau r. Indon. 85 E2
Keuka NY U.S.A. 165 G2
Keuka Lake NY U.S.A. 165 G2
Keumgang, Mount N. Korea see Kumgang-san
Keumsang, Mount N. Korea see Kumgang-san
Keuruu Fin. 54 N5
Kew Turks and Caicos Is 163 F8
Kewanee IL U.S.A. 160 F3
Kewapante Flores Indon. 83 B5
Kewaunee WI U.S.A. 164 B1
Keweenaw Bay MI U.S.A. 160 F2
Keweenaw Peninsula MI U.S.A. 160 F2
Keweenaw Point MI U.S.A. 162 C2
Key, Lough l. Ireland 61 D3
Keyala South Sudan 121 G4
Keyano Canada 153 G3
Keya Paha r. NE U.S.A. 160 D3
Key Harbour Canada 152 E5
Keyi China 98 C4
Keyihe China 95 J1
Key Largo FL U.S.A. 163 D7
Keymir Turkm. 110 D2
Keynsham U.K. 59 E7
Keyser WV U.S.A. 165 F4
Keystone Lake OK U.S.A. 161 D4
Keystone Peak AZ U.S.A. 159 H6
Keysville VA U.S.A. 165 F5
Keytesville MO U.S.A. 160 E4
Keyvy, Vozvyshennost' hills Russia 52 H2
Key West FL U.S.A. 163 D7
Kez Russia 51 Q4
Kezi Zimbabwe 123 C6
Kgalagadi admin. dist. Botswana 124 E3
Kgalagadi Transfrontier Park Botswana/S. Africa 125 D2
Kgalazadi admin. dist. Botswana see Kgalagadi
Kgatlen admin. dist. Botswana see Kgatleng
Kgatleng admin. dist. Botswana 125 H3
Kgomofatshe Pan salt pan Botswana 124 E2
Kgoro Pan salt pan Botswana 124 G3
Kgotsong S. Africa 125 H4
Kgun Lake AK U.S.A. 148 G3
Khabab Syria 107 C3
Khabar Iran 110 D4
Khabarikha Russia 52 L2
Khabarovsk Russia 90 D2
Khabarovskiy Kray admin. div. Russia 90 D2
Khabarovsk Kray admin. div. Russia see Khabarovskiy Kray
Khabary Russia 88 D2
Khabis Iran see Shahdād
Khachmas Azer. see Xaçmaz
Khadar, Jabal mt. Oman 110 E6
Khadīr Afgh. 111 G3
Khadro Pak. 111 H5
Khadzhiolen Turkm. 110 E2
Khafs Banbān well Saudi Arabia 110 B5
Khagaria India 105 F4
Khagrachari Bangl. 105 G5
Khagrachhari Bangl. see Khagrachari
Khairgarh Pak. 111 H4
Khairpur Punjab Pak. 111 I4
Khairpur Sindh Pak. 111 H5
Khāīz, Kūh-e mt. Iran 110 C4
Khajuha India 104 E4
Khāk-e Jabār-e Bālā Afgh. 111 H3
Khakhea Botswana 124 F3
Khākrēz Afgh. 111 G4
Khākrēz reg. Afgh. 111 G4
Khalajestan reg. Iran 110 C3
Khalatse India 104 D2
Khalifat mt. Pak. 111 G4
Khalīj Surt g. Libya see Sirte, Gulf of
Khalilabad India 105 E4
Khalīlī Iran 110 D5
Khalkabad Turkm. 111 F1
Khalkhāl Iran 110 C2
Khálki i. Greece see Chalki
Khalkís Greece see Chalkida
Khallikot India 106 E2
Khalturin Russia see Orlov
Khamar-Daban, Khrebet mts Russia 94 E1
Khamaria India 106 D1
Khambhat India 104 C5
Khambhat, Gulf of India 106 A2
Khamgaon India 106 C1
Khamis Mushayṭ Saudi Arabia 108 F6
Khamkeut Laos 86 D3
Khamma well Saudi Arabia 110 B5
Khammam India 106 D2
Khammouan Laos see Thakhèk
Khamr Yemen 108 F6
Khamra Russia 77 M3
Khamseh reg. Iran 110 C3
Khan, Nâm r. Laos 86 C3
Khānābād Afgh. 111 H2
Khān al Baghdādī Iraq 113 F4
Khān al Mashāhidah Iraq 113 G4
Khān al Muṣallá Iraq 113 G4
Khanapur India 106 B2
Khān ar Raḥbah Iraq 113 G5
Khanasur Pass Iran/Turkey 113 G3
Khanbalik China see Beijing
Khānch Iran 110 B2
Khandagayty Russia 94 C1
Khandu India 111 I6
Khandwa India 104 D5
Khandyga Russia 77 O3
Khanewal Pak. 111 H4
Khanh Hung Vietnam see Soc Trăng
Khaniá Greece see Chania
Khānī Yek Iran 110 D4
Khanka, Lake China/Russia 90 D3
Khanka, Ozero l. China/Russia see Khanka, Lake
Khankendi Azer. see Xankändi
Khanna India 104 D3
Khannā, Qā' salt pan Jordan 107 C3
Khanpur Balochistan Pak. 111 H4
Khanpur Punjab Pak. 111 H4
Khān Ruḥābah Iraq see Khān ar Raḥbah
Khansar Pak. 111 H4
Khān Shaykhūn Syria 107 C2
Khantau Kazakh. 98 A3
Khantayskoye, Ozero l. Russia 76 K3
Khan-Tengri, Pik mt. Kazakh./Kyrg. 98 C4
Khanthabouli Laos see Savannakhét
Khanty-Mansiysk Russia 76 H3
Khān Yūnus Gaza 107 B4
Khanzi admin. dist. Botswana see Ghanzi
Khao Ang Rua Nai Wildlife Reserve nature res. Thai. 87 C4
Khao Banthat Wildlife Reserve nature res. Thai. 87 B6
Khao Chum Thong Thai. 87 B5
Khaoen Si Nakarin National Park Thai. 87 B4
Khao Laem, Ang Kep Nam Thai. 86 B4
Khao Laem National Park Thai. 86 B4
Khao Luang National Park Thai. 87 B5
Khao Pu-Khao Ya National Park Thai. 87 B6
Khao Soi Dao Wildlife Reserve nature res. Thai. 87 C4
Khao Sok National Park Thai. 87 B5
Khao Yai National Park Thai. 87 C4
Khapcheranga Russia 95 H1
Khaplu Pak. 102 E4
Khaptad National Park Nepal 104 E3
Kharabali Russia 53 J7
Kharagpur Bihar India 105 F4
Kharagpur W. Bengal India 105 F5
Kharāmeh Iran 110 D4
Khārān r. Iran 109 I4
Kharānaq, Kūh-e mt. Iran 110 D3
Kharanor Russia 95 I1
Kharari India see Abu Road
Kharda India 106 B2
Khardi India 104 C6
Khardong La pass India see Khardung La
Khardung La pass India 104 D2
Kharfiyah Iraq 113 G5
Kharga Egypt see Al Khārijah
Kharga r. Russia 90 D1
Khârga, El Wâhât el oasis Egypt see Khārijah, Wāḥāt al
Kharga Oasis Egypt see Khārijah, Wāḥāt al

Kharg Islands Iran 110 C4
Khargone India 104 C5
Khari r. Rajasthan India 104 C4
Khari r. Rajasthan India 104 C4
Kharian Pak. 111 I3
Khariar India 106 D1
Khārijah, Wāḥāt al oasis Egypt 108 D5
Kharīm, Gebel hill Egypt see Kharīm, Jabal
Kharīm, Jabal hill Egypt 107 A4
Kharkhara r. India 104 E5
Kharkhauda India 99 B7
Kharkiv Ukr. 53 H6
Khar'kov Ukr. see Kharkiv
Kharlovka Russia 52 H1
Kharlu Russia 54 Q6
Kharōṭī reg. Afgh. 111 H3
Kharovsk Russia 52 I4
Kharsia India 105 E5

▶Khartoum Sudan 108 D6
Capital of Sudan. 5th most populous city in Africa.

Kharwār reg. Afgh. 111 H3
Khasavyurt Russia 113 G2
Khāsh Iran 111 F4
Khāsh, Dasht-e Afgh. 111 F4
Khashm el Girba Sudan 108 E7
Khashm Ṣanaʻ Saudi Arabia 112 E6
Khāsh Rōd Afgh. 111 F4
Khāsh Rōd r. Afgh. 111 F4
Khashuri Georgia 113 F2
Khasi Hills India 105 G4
Khatanga Russia 77 L2
Khatanga, Gulf of Russia see Khatangskiy Zaliv
Khatangskiy Zaliv b. Russia 77 L2
Khatayakha Russia 52 M2
Khatinza Pass Pak. 111 H2
Khatmat al Malāha Oman 110 E5
Khatyrka Russia 77 S3
Khaur Pak. 111 I3
Khavda India 104 B5
Khāwāk, Kōtal-e Afgh. 111 H3
Khayamnandi S. Africa 125 G6
Khayang mt. India 105 H4
Khaybar Saudi Arabia 108 E4
Khayelitsha S. Africa 124 D8
Khayrān, Ra's al pt Oman 110 E6
Khefa Israel see Haifa
Khehuene, Ponta pt Moz. 125 L2
Khemis Miliana Alg. 67 H5
Khemmarat Thai. 86 D3
Khenchela Alg. 68 B7
Khenifra Morocco 64 C5
Kherrata Alg. 67 I5
Kherreh Iran 110 D5
Khersan r. Iran 110 C4
Kherson Ukr. 69 O1
Kheta r. Russia 77 L2
Kheyrābād Iran 110 D4
Khezerābād Iran 110 D2
Khezrī Dasht-e Bayāẓ Iran 110 E3
Khiching India 105 F5
Khilok Russia 95 G1
Khilok r. Russia 95 F1
Khinganskiy Zapovednik nature res. Russia 90 C2
Khinsar Pak. 111 H5
Khíos i. Greece see Chios
Khipro Pak. 111 H5
Khirbat Isrīyah Syria 107 C2
Khisrow Afgh. 111 G3
Khitai Dawan pass China 99 B6
Khīyāv Iran 110 B2
Khiytola Russia 55 P6
Khlevnoye Russia 53 H5
Khlong, Mae r. Thai. 87 C4
Khlong Saeng Wildlife Reserve nature res. Thai. 87 B5
Khlong Wang Chao National Park Thai. 86 B3
Khlung Thai. 87 C4
Khmel'nik Ukr. see Khmil'nyk
Khmel'nitskiy Ukr. see Khmel'nyts'kyy
Khmel'nyts'kyy Ukr. 53 E6
Khmer Republic country Asia see Cambodia
Khmil'nyk Ukr. 53 E6
Khoai, Hon i. Vietnam 87 D5
Khobi Georgia 113 F2
Khodā Āfarīd spring Iran 110 E3
Khodzha-Kala Turkm. see Hojagala
Khodzhambaz Turkm. see Hojambaz
Khodzhent Tajik. see Khŭjand
Khodzheyli Uzbek. see Xoʻjayli
Khojand Tajik. see Khŭjand
Khokhowe Pan salt pan Botswana 124 E3
Khokhropar Pak. 111 H5
Khoksar India 104 D2
Kholm Poland see Chełm
Kholm Russia 52 F4
Kholmsk Russia 90 F3
Kholon Israel see Ḥolon
Kholtoson Russia 94 E1
Kholzun, Khrebet mts Kazakh./Russia 98 D2
Khomas admin. reg. Namibia 124 C2
Khomas Highland hills Namibia 124 B2
Khomeyn Iran 110 C3
Khomeynīshahr Iran 110 C3
Khong, Mae Nam r. Asia 86 D4 see Mekong
Khonj Iran 110 D5
Khonj, Kūh-e mts Iran 110 D5
Khon Kaen Thai. 86 C3
Khon Kriel Cambodia see Kon Kriel
Khonsa India 105 H4
Khonuu Russia 77 P3
Khoper r. Russia 53 I6
Khor Russia 90 D3
Khor r. Russia 90 D3
Khorāsān, Chāh-e well Iran 110 D3
Khorat Plateau Thai. 86 C3
Khorda India see Khordha
Khordha India 106 E1
Khorey-Ver Russia 52 M2
Khorinsk Russia 89 J2
Khorixas Namibia 123 B6
Khormūj, Kūh-e mt. Iran 110 C4
Khorog Tajik. see Khorugh
Khorol Russia 90 D3
Khorol Ukr. 53 G6
Khoroslū Dāgh hills Iran 110 B2
Khorramābād Iran 110 C3
Khorramshahr Iran 110 C4
Khorugh Tajik. 111 H2
Khosheutovo Russia 53 J7
Khoshgort Russia 51 T2
Khōst Afgh. 111 H3
Khōst reg. Afgh./Pak. 111 H3
Khosūyeh Iran 110 D4
Khotan China see Hotan
Khotang Nepal 99 D8
Khotol Mountain hill AK U.S.A. 148 H2
Khouribga Morocco 64 C5
Khovaling Tajik. 111 H2
Khowrjān Iran 110 D4
Khreum Myanmar 86 A2
Khri r. India 99 E8
Khroma r. Russia 77 P2
Khromtau Kazakh. 102 A1
Khru r. India 99 F8
Khrushchev Ukr. see Svitlovods'k
Khrysokhou Bay Cyprus see Chrysochou Bay
Khrystynivka Ukr. 53 F6
Khudumelapye Botswana 124 G2
Khudzhand Tajik. see Khŭjand
Khufaysah, Khashm al hill Saudi Arabia 110 B6
Khugiana Afgh. see Pīr Zādah
Khuis Botswana 124 E4
Khŭjand Tajik. 102 C3
Khŭjayli Uzbek. see Xoʻjayli
Khu Khan Thai. 87 D4
Khulays Saudi Arabia 108 E5
Khulkhuta Russia 53 J7
Khulm Afgh. 111 G2
Khulm, Daryā-ye r. Afgh. 111 G2
Khulna Bangl. 105 G5
Khulo Georgia 113 F2
Khuma S. Africa 125 H4
Khunayzīr, Jabal al mts Syria 107 C2
Khūnīk Iran 110 E3
Khūnīnshahr Iran see Khorramshahr
Khunjerab Pass China/Pak. 104 C1
Khun Yuam Thai. 86 B3
Khūr Iran 110 E3
Khūran sea chan. Iran 110 D5
Khurayṣ Saudi Arabia 108 G4
Khurda India see Khordha
Khurdha India see Khordha
Khurja India 104 D3
Khurmāliq Afgh. 111 F3
Khurmuli Russia 90 E2
Khushab Pak. 111 I3
Khushalgarh Pak. 111 H3
Khushshah, Wādī al watercourse Jordan/Saudi Arabia 107 C5
Khust Ukr. 53 D6
Khutse Game Reserve nature res. Botswana 124 G2
Khutsong S. Africa 125 H4
Khutu r. Russia 90 E2
Khuzdar Pak. 111 G5
Khvāf Iran 111 F3
Khvāf reg. Iran 111 F3
Khvājeh Iran 110 B2
Khvalynsk Russia 53 K5
Khvānsār Iran 110 C3
Khvodrān Iran 110 D4
Khvormūj Iran 110 C4
Khvors Iran 110 D3
Khvoy Iran 110 B2
Khvoynaya Russia 52 G4
Khwaja Amran mt. Pak. 111 G4
Khwājah Dū Kōh hill Afgh. 111 G2
Khwājah Muḥammad, Kōh-e mts Afgh. 111 H2
Khyber Pakhtunkhwa prov. Pak. 111 H3
Khyber Pass Afgh./Pak. 111 H3
Kiama Australia 138 E5
Kiamba Mindanao Phil. 82 D5
Kiamichi r. OK U.S.A. 161 E5
Kiana AK U.S.A. 148 G2
Kiangsi prov. China see Jiangxi
Kiangsu prov. China see Jiangsu
Kiantajärvi l. Fin. 54 P4
Kiari India 99 B6
Kīāsar Iran 110 D2
Kiatassuaq i. Greenland 147 M2
Kibaha Tanz. 123 D4
Kibali r. Dem. Rep. Congo 122 C3
Kibangou Congo 122 B4
Kibawe Mindanao Phil. 82 D5
Kibaya Tanz. 123 D4
Kiboga Uganda 122 D3
Kibombo Dem. Rep. Congo 122 C4
Kibondo Tanz. 122 D4
Kibre Mengist Eth. 121 G4
Kıbrıs country Asia see Cyprus
Kibungo Rwanda 122 D4
Kičevo Macedonia 69 I4
Kichmengskiy Gorodok Russia 52 J4
Kiçik Qafqaz mts Asia see Lesser Caucasus
Kicking Horse Pass Canada 150 G5
Kidal Mali 120 D3
Kidapawan Phil. 82 D5
Kidderminster U.K. 59 E6
Kidepo Valley National Park Uganda 122 D3
Kidira Senegal 120 B3
Kidmang India 104 D2
Kidnappers, Cape N.Z. 139 F4
Kidsgrove U.K. 59 E5
Kidurong, Tanjung pt Malaysia 85 F2
Kiel Germany 57 M3
Kiel WI U.S.A. 164 A2
Kiel Canal Germany 57 L3
Kielce Poland 57 R5
Kielder Water resr U.K. 58 E3
Kieler Bucht b. Germany 57 M3
Kienge Dem. Rep. Congo 123 C5
Kierspe Germany 63 H3

▶Kiev Ukr. 53 F6
Capital of Ukraine.

Kiffa Mauritania 120 B3
Kifisia Greece 69 J5
Kifrī Iraq 113 G4

▶Kigali Rwanda 122 D4
Capital of Rwanda.

Kigalik r. AK U.S.A. 148 I1
Kiğı Turkey 113 F3
Kiglapait Mountains Canada 153 J2
Kigluaik Mountains AK U.S.A. 148 F2
Kigoma Tanz. 123 C4
Kihambatang Kalimantan Indon. 85 F3
Kihlanki Fin. 54 M3
Kihniö Fin. 54 M5
Kihoku Japan 92 C4
Kīholo HI U.S.A. 157 [inset]
Kii-hantō pen. Japan 92 B5
Kiik Kazakh. 98 A3
Kiiminki Fin. 54 N4
Kii-Nagashima Japan 92 C4
Kii-sanchi mts Japan 92 B5
Kii-suidō sea chan. Japan 91 D6
Kijimadaira Japan 93 E2
Kikerino Russia 55 P7
Kikiakrorak r. AK U.S.A. 149 J1
Kikinda Serbia 69 I2
Kikki Pak. 111 F5
Kikládhes is Greece see Cyclades
Kikmiktalikamiut AK U.S.A. 148 F3
Kiknur Russia 52 J4
Kikonai Japan 90 F4
Kikori P.N.G. 81 K8
Kikori r. P.N.G. 81 K8
Kikugawa Japan 93 E4
Kikwit Dem. Rep. Congo 123 B4
Kilafors Sweden 55 J6
Kilar India 104 D2
Kīlauea HI U.S.A. 157 [inset]
Kīlauea Volcano HI U.S.A. 157 [inset]
Kilbon Seram Indon. 83 D3
Kilbuck Mountains AK U.S.A. 148 H3
Kilchu N. Korea 90 C4
Kilcoole Ireland 61 F4
Kilcormac Ireland 61 E4
Kilcoy Australia 138 F1
Kildare Ireland 61 F4
Kil'dinstroy Russia 54 R2
Kilekale Lake Canada 149 Q2
Kilemary Russia 52 J4
Kilembe Dem. Rep. Congo 123 B4
Kilfinan U.K. 60 D5
Kilgore TX U.S.A. 161 E5
Kilham U.K. 58 E3
Kilia Ukr. see Kiliya
Kılıç Dağı mt. Syria/Turkey see Aqraʻ, Jabal al
Kilifi Kenya 122 D4
Kilik Pass China 99 A5

▶Kilimanjaro vol. Tanz. 122 D4
Highest mountain in Africa.

Kilimanjaro National Park Tanz. 122 D4
Kilinailau Islands P.N.G. 132 F2
Kilindoni Tanz. 123 D4
Kilingi-Nõmme Estonia 55 N7
Kilis Turkey 107 C1
Kilis prov. Turkey 107 C1
Kiliuda Bay AK U.S.A. 148 I4
Kiliya Ukr. 69 M2
Kilkee Ireland 61 C5
Kilkeel U.K. 61 G3
Kilkenny Ireland 61 E5
Kilkhampton U.K. 59 C8
Kilkis Greece 69 J4
Killala Ireland 61 C3
Killala Bay Ireland 61 C3
Killaloe Ireland 61 D5
Killam Canada 151 I4
Killarney N.T. Australia 134 E4
Killarney Qld Australia 138 F2
Killarney Canada 152 E5
Killarney Ireland 61 C5
Killarney National Park Ireland 61 C6
Killary Harbour b. Ireland 61 C4
Killbuck OH U.S.A. 164 E3
Killeen TX U.S.A. 161 D6
Killenaule Ireland 61 E5
Killik r. AK U.S.A. 148 I1
Killimor Ireland 61 D4
Killin U.K. 60 E4
Killinchy U.K. 61 G3
Killíni mt. Greece see Kyllini
Killinick Ireland 61 F5
Killorglin Ireland 61 C5
Killurin Ireland 61 F5
Killybegs Ireland 61 D3
Kilmacrenan Ireland 61 E2
Kilmaine Ireland 61 C4
Kilmallock Ireland 61 D5
Kilmaluag U.K. 60 C3
Kilmarnock U.K. 60 E5
Kilmelford U.K. 60 D4
Kil'mez' Russia 52 K4
Kil'mez' r. Russia 52 K4
Kilmona Ireland 61 D6
Kilmore Australia 138 B6
Kilmore Quay Ireland 61 F5
Kilosa Tanz. 123 D4
Kilpisjärvi Fin. 54 L2
Kilrea U.K. 61 F3
Kilrush Ireland 61 C5
Kilsyth U.K. 60 E5
Kiltan atoll India 106 B4
Kiltullagh Ireland 61 D4
Kilwa Masoko Tanz. 123 D4
Kilwinning U.K. 60 E5
Kim CO U.S.A. 161 C4
Kimanis, Teluk b. Malaysia 85 F1
Kimba Australia 135 G8
Kimba Congo 122 B4
Kimball NE U.S.A. 160 C3
Kimball, Mount AK U.S.A. 149 K3
Kimbe P.N.G. 132 F2
Kimberley S. Africa 124 G5
Kimberley Plateau Australia 134 D4
Kimberley Range hills Australia 135 B6
Kimch'aek N. Korea 91 C4
Kimhae S. Korea see Gimhae
Kimhandu mt. Tanz. 123 D4
Kimi Greece see Kymi
Kimino Japan 92 B4
Kimito Fin. 55 M6
Kimitsu Japan 93 F3
Kimjŏngsuk N. Korea 90 B4
Kimmirut Canada 147 L3
Kimolos i. Greece 69 K6
Kimovsk Russia 53 H5
Kimpese Dem. Rep. Congo 123 B4
Kimpoku-san mt. Japan see Kinpoku-san
Kimry Russia 52 H4
Kimsquit Canada 150 E4
Kimvula Dem. Rep. Congo 123 B4
Kinabalu, Gunung mt. Sabah Malaysia 85 G1
Kinabalu National Park Malaysia 85 G1
Kinabatangan r. Malaysia 85 G1
Kinabatangan, Kuala r. mouth Malaysia 85 G1
Kinango Kenya 123 D4
Kinasa Japan 93 E2
Kinaskan Lake Canada 149 O4
Kinbasket Lake Canada 150 G4
Kinbrace U.K. 60 F2
Kincaid Canada 151 J5
Kincardine Canada 164 E1
Kincardine U.K. 60 F4
Kinchega National Park Australia 137 C7
Kincolith Canada see Gingolx
Kinda Dem. Rep. Congo 123 C4
Kindat Myanmar 86 A2
Kinde MI U.S.A. 164 D2
Kinder LA U.S.A. 167 G2
Kinder Scout hill U.K. 58 F5
Kindersley Canada 151 I5
Kindia Guinea 120 B3
Kindu Dem. Rep. Congo 122 C4
Kinegnak AK U.S.A. 148 G4
Kinel' Russia 53 K5
Kineshma Russia 52 I4
King Abdullah Economic City Saudi Arabia 100 C4
Kingaroy Australia 138 E1
King Christian Island Canada 147 H2
King City CA U.S.A. 158 C3
King Cove AK U.S.A. 148 G5
King Edward VII Land pen. Antarctica see Edward VII Peninsula
Kingfield ME U.S.A. 165 J1
Kingfisher OK U.S.A. 161 D5
King George VA U.S.A. 165 G4
King George, Mount Canada 156 E2
King George Island Antarctica 188 A2
King George Islands Canada 152 F2
King George Islands Fr. Polynesia see Roi Georges, Îles du
King Hill hill Australia 134 C5
Kingisepp Russia 55 P7
King Island Australia 137 [inset]
King Island Canada 150 E4
King Island Myanmar see Kadan Kyun
King Island AK U.S.A. 148 E2
Kingisseppa Estonia see Kuressaare
Kinglake National Park Australia 138 B6
King Leopold and Queen Astrid Coast Antarctica 188 E2
King Leopold Range National Park Australia 134 D4
King Leopold Ranges hills Australia 134 D4
Kingman AZ U.S.A. 159 F4

▶Kingman Reef terr. N. Pacific Ocean 186 J5
United States Unincorporated Territory.

King Mountain Canada 149 O4
King Mountain hill TX U.S.A. 161 C6
Kingoonya Australia 137 A6
King Peak Antarctica 188 L1
King Peninsula Antarctica 188 K2
Kingri Pak. 111 H4
Kings r. Ireland 61 E5
Kings r. CA U.S.A. 158 C3
Kings r. NV U.S.A. 156 D4
King Salmon AK U.S.A. 148 H4
King Salmon r. AK U.S.A. 148 H4
Kingsbridge U.K. 59 D8
Kingsburg CA U.S.A. 158 D3
Kings Canyon National Park CA U.S.A. 158 D3
Kingscliff Australia 138 F2
Kingscote Australia 137 B7
Kingscourt Ireland 61 F4
King Sejong research station Antarctica 188 A2
King's Lynn U.K. 59 H6
Kingsmill Group is Kiribati 133 H2
Kingsnorth U.K. 59 H7
King Sound b. Australia 134 C4
Kings Peak UT U.S.A. 159 H1
Kingsport TN U.S.A. 162 D4
Kingston Australia 137 [inset]
Kingston Canada 165 G1

▶Kingston Jamaica 169 I5
Capital of Jamaica.

▶Kingston Norfolk I. 133 G4
Capital of Norfolk Island.

Kingston MO U.S.A. 160 E4
Kingston NY U.S.A. 165 H3
Kingston OH U.S.A. 164 D4
Kingston PA U.S.A. 165 H3
Kingston Peak CA U.S.A. 159 F4
Kingston South East Australia 137 B8
Kingston upon Hull U.K. 58 G5

▶Kingstown St Vincent 169 L6
Capital of St Vincent.

Kingstree SC U.S.A. 163 E5
Kingsville TX U.S.A. 161 D7
Kingswood U.K. 59 E7
Kington U.K. 59 D6
Kingungi Dem. Rep. Congo 123 B4
Kingurutik r. Canada 153 J2
Kingussie U.K. 60 E3
King William VA U.S.A. 165 G5
King William Island Canada 147 I3
King William's Town S. Africa 125 H7
Kingwood TX U.S.A. 161 E6
Kingwood WV U.S.A. 164 F4
Kinloch N.Z. 139 B7
Kinloss U.K. 60 F3
Kinmen Taiwan see Jinmen
Kinmen i. Taiwan see Jinmen Dao
Kinmount Canada 165 F1
Kinna Sweden 55 H8
Kinnegad Ireland 61 E4
Kinneret, Yam l. Israel see Galilee, Sea of
Kinniyai Sri Lanka 106 D4
Kinnula Fin. 54 N5
Kinoje r. Canada 152 E3
Kinokawa Japan 92 B4
Kino-kawa r. Japan 92 B4
Kinomoto Japan 92 C3
Kinoosao Canada 151 K3
Kinosaki Japan 92 A3
Kinpoku-san mt. Japan 91 E5
Kinross U.K. 60 F4
Kinsale Ireland 61 D6
Kinsale VA U.S.A. 165 G4

▶Kinshasa Dem. Rep. Congo 123 B4
Capital of the Democratic Republic of the Congo. 3rd most populous city in Africa.

Kinsley KS U.S.A. 160 D4
Kinsman OH U.S.A. 164 E3
Kinston NC U.S.A. 163 E5
Kintom Celebes Indon. 83 B3
Kintop Kalimantan Indon. 85 F3
Kintore U.K. 60 G3
Kintyre pen. U.K. 60 D5
Kin-U Myanmar 86 A2
Kinu-gawa r. Japan 93 G3
Kinunuma-yama mt. Japan 93 F2
Kinushseo r. Canada 152 E3
Kinyeti mt. South Sudan 121 G4
Kinzig r. Germany 63 I4
Kiowa CO U.S.A. 156 G5
Kiowa KS U.S.A. 161 D4
Kipahigan Lake Canada 151 K4
Kiparissía Greece see Kyparissia
Kipawa, Lac l. Canada 152 F5
Kipchak Pass China 98 B4
Kipling Canada 151 K5
Kipling Station Canada see Kipling
Kipnuk AK U.S.A. 148 F4
Kiptopeke VA U.S.A. 165 H5
Kipungo Angola see Quipungo
Kipushi Dem. Rep. Congo 123 C5
Kira Japan 92 D4
Kirakira Solomon Is 133 G3
Kirandul India 106 D2
Kirchdorf Germany 63 I2
Kirchheimbolanden Germany 63 I5
Kirchheim unter Teck Germany 63 J6
Kircubbin U.K. 61 G3
Kirdimi Chad 121 E3
Kirenga r. Russia 89 J1
Kirensk Russia 77 L4
Kireyevsk Russia 53 H5
Kirghizia country Asia see Kyrgyzstan
Kirghiz Range mts Kazakh./Kyrg. 102 D3
Kirgizskaya S.S.R. country Asia see Kyrgyzstan
Kirgizskiy Khrebet mts Kazakh./Kyrg. see Kirghiz Range
Kirgizstan country Asia see Kyrgyzstan
Kiri Dem. Rep. Congo 122 B4
Kiribati country Pacific Ocean 186 I6
Kiriga-mine mt. Japan 93 E2
Kırıkhan Turkey 107 C1
Kırıkkale Turkey 112 D3
Kirikkuduk China 94 B2
Kirillov Russia 52 H4
Kirillovo (abandoned) Russia 90 F3
Kirin China see Jilin
Kirin prov. China see Jilin
Kirinda Sri Lanka 106 D5
Kirinyaga mt. Kenya see Kenya, Mount
Kirishi Russia 52 G4
Kirishima-Yaku Kokuritsu-kōen Japan 91 C7
Kirishima-yama vol. Japan 91 C7
Kiritimati atoll Kiribati 187 J5
Kiriwina Islands P.N.G. see Trobriand Islands
Kırkağaç Turkey 69 L5
Kirk Bulāg Dāgi mt. Iran 110 B2
Kirkby U.K. 58 E5
Kirkby in Ashfield U.K. 59 F5
Kirkby Lonsdale U.K. 58 E4
Kirkby Stephen U.K. 58 E4
Kirkcaldy U.K. 60 F4
Kirkcolm U.K. 60 D6
Kirkcudbright U.K. 60 E6
Kirkenær Norway 55 H6
Kirkenes Norway 54 Q2
Kirkfield Canada 165 F1
Kirkintilloch U.K. 60 E5
Kirkkonummi Fin. 55 N6
Kirkland AZ U.S.A. 159 G4
Kirkland Lake Canada 152 E4
Kırklareli Turkey 69 L4
Kirklin IN U.S.A. 164 B3
Kirk Michael Isle of Man 58 C4
Kirkoswald U.K. 58 E4
Kirkpatrick, Mount Antarctica 188 H1
Kirksville MO U.S.A. 160 E3
Kirkūk Iraq 113 G4
Kirkwall U.K. 60 G2
Kirkwood S. Africa 125 G7
Kirman Iran see Kermān
Kirn Germany 63 H5
Kirov Kaluzhskaya Oblast' Russia 53 G5
Kirov Kirovskaya Oblast' Russia 52 K4
Kirova, imeni Kazakh. see Kopbirlik
Kirova, Zaliv b. Azer. see Qızılağac Körfäzi
Kirovabad Azer. see Gäncä
Kirovabad Tajik. see Panj
Kirovakan Armenia see Vanadzor
Kirovo Ukr. see Kirovohrad
Kirovo-Chepetsk Russia 52 K4
Kirovo-Chepetskiy Russia see Kirovo-Chepetsk
Kirovograd Ukr. see Kirovohrad
Kirovohrad Ukr. 53 G6
Kirovsk Leningradskaya Oblast' Russia 52 F4
Kirovsk Murmanskaya Oblast' Russia 54 R3
Kirovsk Turkm. see Badabaýhan
Kirovs'ke Crimea 112 D1
Kirovskiy Amurskaya Oblast' Russia 90 B1
Kirovskiy Primorskiy Kray Russia 90 D3
Kirovskoye Crimea see Kirovs'ke
Kırpaşa pen. Cyprus see Karpasia
Kirpili Turkm. 110 E2
Kirriemuir U.K. 60 F4
Kirs Russia 52 L4
Kirsanov Russia 53 I5
Kırşehir Turkey 112 D3
Kirthar National Park Pak. 111 G5
Kirthar Range mts Pak. 111 G5
Kirtland NM U.S.A. 159 I3
Kirtorf Germany 63 J4
Kiruna Sweden 54 L3
Kirundu Dem. Rep. Congo 122 C4
Kirwan Escarpment Antarctica 188 B2
Kiryū Japan 93 F2
Kisa Sweden 55 I8
Kisama, Parque Nacional de nat. park Angola see Quiçama, Parque Nacional do
Kisandji Dem. Rep. Congo 123 B4
Kisangani Dem. Rep. Congo 122 C3
Kisantu Dem. Rep. Congo 123 B4
Kisar i. Moluccas Indon. 83 C5
Kisaralik r. AK U.S.A. 148 G3
Kisaran Sumatra Indon. 84 B2
Kisarazu Japan 93 F3
Kisei Japan 92 C4
Kiselevka Russia 90 E2
Kiselevsk Russia 88 F2
Kīsh, Jazīreh-ye i. Iran 110 D5
Kishanganj India 105 F4
Kishangarh Madh. Prad. India 104 D4
Kishangarh Rajasthan India 104 B4
Kishangarh Rajasthan India 104 C4
Kishangarh Rajasthan India 104 D4
Kishi Nigeria 120 D4
Kishigawa Japan 92 B4
Kishi-gawa r. Japan 92 B4
Kishim Afgh. 111 H2
Kishindih-ye Bālā Afgh. 111 G2
Kishinev Moldova see Chişinău
Kishiwada Japan 92 B4
Kishkenekol' Kazakh. 101 G1
Kishoreganj Bangl. 105 G4
Kishorganj Bangl. see Kishoreganj
Kisi Nigeria see Kishi
Kisii Kenya 122 D4
Kiska Island AK U.S.A. 148 [inset] B6
Kiskittogisu Lake Canada 151 L4
Kiskitto Lake Canada 151 L4
Kiskunfélegyháza Hungary 69 H1
Kiskunhalas Hungary 69 H1
Kiskunsági nat. park Hungary 69 H1
Kislovodsk Russia 113 F2
Kismaayo Somalia 122 E4
Kismayu Somalia see Kismaayo
Kiso Nagano Japan 92 D3
Kiso Nagano Japan 93 D3
Kisofukushima Japan see Kiso
Kisogawa Japan 92 C3
Kiso-gawa r. Japan 92 C3
Kiso-gawa r. Japan 93 E3
Kisoro Uganda 121 F5
Kisosaki Japan 92 C3
Kiso-sanmyaku mts Japan 93 D3
Kispiox Canada 150 E4
Kispiox r. Canada 150 E4
Kissamos Greece 69 J7
Kisseraing Island Myanmar see Kanmaw Kyun
Kissidougou Guinea 120 B4
Kissimmee FL U.S.A. 163 D6
Kissimmee, Lake FL U.S.A. 163 D7
Kississing Lake Canada 151 K4
Kistendey Russia 53 I5
Kistigan Lake Canada 151 M4
Kistna r. India see Krishna
Kisumu Kenya 122 D4
Kisykkamys Kazakh. see Zhanakala
Kita Hyōgo Japan 92 B4
Kita Kyōto Japan 92 B3
Kita Mali 120 C3
Kitab Uzbek. see Kitob
Kita-Daitō-jima i. Japan 89 O7
Kitagata Japan 92 C3
Kitaibaraki Japan 93 G2
Kita-Iō-jima vol. Japan 81 K1
Kitakami Japan 91 F5

Kita-Kyūshū Japan 91 C6
Kitale Kenya 122 D3
Kitami Japan 90 F4
Kitamimaki Japan 93 E2
Kitamoto Japan 93 F3
Kitanagoya Japan 92 C3
Kitatachibana Japan 93 F2
Kitaura Japan 93 G2
Kita-ura *l.* Japan 93 G3
Kitayama Japan 92 B5
Kit Carson *CO* U.S.A. 160 C4
Kitchener Canada 164 E2
Kitchigama *r.* Canada 152 F4
Kitee Fin. 54 Q5
Kitgum Uganda 122 D3
Kíthira *i.* Greece *see* Kythira
Kíthnos *i.* Greece *see* Kythnos
Kiti, Cape Cyprus *see* Kition, Cape
Kitimat Canada 150 D4
Kitinen *r.* Fin. 54 O3
Kition, Cape Cyprus 107 A2
Kitiou, Akra *c.* Cyprus *see* Kition, Cape
Kitkatla Canada 149 O5
Kitob Uzbek. 111 G2
Kitsault Canada 149 O5
Kitsuregawa Japan 93 G2
Kittanning *PA* U.S.A. 164 F3
Kittatinny Mountains *hills NJ* U.S.A. 165 H3
Kittery *ME* U.S.A. 165 J2
Kittilä Fin. 54 N3
Kittur India 106 B3
Kitty Hawk *NC* U.S.A. 162 F4
Kitui Kenya 122 D4
Kitwanga Canada 150 D4
Kitwe Zambia 123 C5
Kitzbüheler Alpen *mts* Austria 57 N7
Kitzingen Germany 63 K5
Kitzscher Germany 63 M3
Kiukpalik Island *AK* U.S.A. 148 I4
Kiu Lom, Ang Kep Nam Thai. 86 B3
Kiunga P.N.G. 81 K8
Kiuruvesi Fin. 54 O5
Kivak Russia 148 D2
Kivalina *AK* U.S.A. 148 F2
Kividlo *AK* U.S.A. 148 F2
Kivijärvi Fin. 54 N5
Kiviõli Estonia 55 O7
Kivu, Lac Dem. Rep. Congo/Rwanda 122 C4
Kiwaba N'zogi Angola 123 B4
Kiwai Island P.N.G. 81 K8
Kiwalik *AK* U.S.A. 148 G2
Kiwalik *r. AK* U.S.A. 148 G2
Kiyev Ukr. *see* Kiev
Kiyevskoye Vodokhranilishche *resr* Ukr. *see* Kyivs'ke Vodoskhovyshche
Kıyıköy Turkey 69 M4
Kiyomi Japan 92 D2
Kiyosato Japan 93 E1
Kiyosumi-yama *hill* Japan 93 G3
Kiyotsu-gawa *r.* Japan 93 E1
Kizel Russia 51 R4
Kizema Russia 52 J3
Kizha Russia 95 G1
Kizil China 98 C4
Kızılcadağ Turkey 69 M6
Kızılca Dağ *mt.* Turkey 112 C3
Kızılcahamam Turkey 112 D2
Kızıldağ *mt.* Turkey 107 A1
Kızıldağ *mt.* Turkey 107 B1
Kızıl Dağı *mt.* Turkey 112 E3
Kızılırmak Turkey 112 D2
Kızılırmak *r.* Turkey 112 D2
Kızıltepe Turkey 113 F3
Kizilyurt Russia 113 G2
Kızkalesi Turkey 107 B1
Kizlyar Russia 113 G2
Kizlyarskiy Zaliv *b.* Russia 113 G1
Kizner Russia 52 K4
Kizugawa Japan 92 B4
Kizu-gawa *r.* Japan 92 B4
Kizyl-Arbat Turkm. *see* Serdar
Kizyl-Atrek Turkm. *see* Etrek
Kizyl Jilga China 99 B6
Kjøllefjord Norway 54 O1
Kjøpsvik Norway 54 J2
Kladno Czech Rep. 57 O5
Klagan *Sabah* Malaysia 85 G1
Klagenfurt am Wörthersee Austria 57 O7
Klagetoh *AZ* U.S.A. 159 I4
Klaipėda Lith. 55 L9
Klaksvík Faroe Is 54 [inset 2]
Klamath *CA* U.S.A. 156 B4
Klamath *r. CA* U.S.A. 146 F5
Klamath Falls *OR* U.S.A. 156 C4
Klamath Mountains *CA* U.S.A. 156 C4
Klampo *Kalimantan* Indon. 85 G2
Klang Malaysia 84 C2
Klappan *r.* Canada 149 O4
Klarälven *r.* Sweden 55 H7
Klaten *Java* Indon. 85 E4
Klatovy Czech Rep. 57 N6
Klawer S. Africa 124 D6
Klawock *AK* U.S.A. 149 N5
Klazienaveen Neth. 62 G2
Kleides Islands Cyprus 107 B2
Kleinbegin S. Africa 124 E5
Klein Karas Namibia 124 D4
Klein Nama Land *reg.* S. Africa *see* Namaqualand
Klein Roggeveldberge *mts* S. Africa 124 E7
Kleinsee S. Africa 124 C5
Klemtu Canada 150 D4
Klerksdorp S. Africa 125 H4
Klery Creek *AK* U.S.A. 148 G2
Kletnya Russia 53 G5
Kletsk Belarus *see* Klyetsk
Kletskaya Russia 53 I6
Kletskiy Russia *see* Kletskaya
Kleve Germany 62 G3
Klichka Russia 95 I1
Klidhes Islands Cyprus *see* Kleides Islands
Klimkovka Russia 52 K4
Klimovo Russia 53 G5
Klin Russia 52 H4
Kling *Mindanao* Phil. 82 D5
Klingenberg am Main Germany 63 J5
Klingenthal Germany 63 M4
Klingkang, Banjaran *mts* Indon./Malaysia 85 E2
Klink Germany 63 M1
Klínovec *mt.* Czech Rep. 63 N4
Klintehamn Sweden 55 K8
Klintsy Russia 53 G5
Ključ Bos. & Herz. 68 G2
Kłodzko Poland 57 P5
Klondike *r.* Canada 149 M2
Klondike Gold Rush National Historical Park *nat. park AK* U.S.A. 149 N4
Kloosterhaar Neth. 62 G2
Klosterneuburg Austria 57 P6
Klotz, Mount Canada 149 L2
Klötze (Altmark) Germany 63 L2
Kluane Game Sanctuary *nature res.* Canada 149 L3
Kluane Lake Canada 149 M3
Kluane National Park Canada 149 M3
Kluang Malaysia *see* Keluang
Kluang, Tanjung *pt* Indon. 85 E3
Kluczbork Poland 57 Q5
Klukhori Russia *see* Karachayevsk
Klukhorskiy, Pereval Georgia/Russia 113 F2
Klukwan *AK* U.S.A. 149 N4
Klumpang, Teluk *b.* Indon. 85 G3
Klungkung *Bali* Indon. 85 F5
Klutina Lake *AK* U.S.A. 149 K3
Klyetsk Belarus 55 O10
Klyuchevskaya Sopka, Vulkan *vol.* Russia 77 R4
Klyuchi Russia 90 B2
Knåda Sweden 55 I6
Knaresborough U.K. 58 F4
Knee Lake *Man.* Canada 151 M4
Knee Lake *Sask.* Canada 151 J4
Knetzgau Germany 63 K5
Knife *r. ND* U.S.A. 160 C2
Knight Inlet Canada 150 E5
Knighton U.K. 59 D6
Knights Landing *CA* U.S.A. 158 C2
Knightstown *IN* U.S.A. 164 C4
Knin Croatia 68 G2
Knittelfeld Austria 57 O7
Knjaževac Serbia 69 J3
Knob Lake Canada *see* Schefferville
Knob Lick *KY* U.S.A. 164 C5
Knob Peak *hill* Australia 134 E3
Knock Ireland 61 D4
Knockalongy *hill* Ireland 61 D3
Knockalough Ireland 61 C5
Knockanaffrin *hill* Ireland 61 E5
Knockboy *hill* Ireland 61 C6
Knock Hill *hill* U.K. 60 G3
Knockmealdown Mountains *hills* Ireland 61 D5
Knocknaskagh *hill* Ireland 61 D5
Knokke-Heist Belgium 62 D3
Knorrendorf Germany 63 N1
Knowle U.K. 59 F6
Knowlton Canada 165 I1
Knox *IN* U.S.A. 164 B3
Knox *PA* U.S.A. 164 F3
Knox, Cape Canada 149 N5
Knox Coast Antarctica 188 F2
Knoxville *GA* U.S.A. 163 D5
Knoxville *TN* U.S.A. 162 D5
Knud Rasmussen Land *reg.* Greenland 147 L2
Knysna S. Africa 124 F8
Ko, Gora *mt.* Russia 90 E3
Koartac Canada *see* Quaqtaq
Koba Indon. 84 D3
Kobanê Syria *see* 'Ayn al 'Arab
Kobbfoss Norway 54 P2
Kobda Kazakh. 102 A1
Kobe *Halmahera* Indon. 83 C2
Kōbe Japan 92 B4
København Denmark *see* Copenhagen
Kobenni Mauritania 120 C3
Kobi *Seram* Indon. 83 D3
Koblenz Germany 63 H4
Koboldo Russia 90 D1
Kobrin Belarus *see* Kobryn
Kobroör *i. Moluccas* Indon. 81 I8
Kobryn Belarus 55 N10
Kobuchizawa Japan 93 E3
Kobuk *AK* U.S.A. 148 H2
Kobuk *r. AK* U.S.A. 148 G2
Kobuk Valley National Park *AK* U.S.A. 148 H2
Kobuleti Georgia 113 F2
Kobushiga-take *mt.* Japan 93 E3
Kocaeli Turkey *see* İzmit
Kocaeli Yarımadası *pen.* Turkey 69 M4
Kočani Macedonia 69 J4
Kocasu *r.* Turkey 69 M4
Kocê China 94 E5
Kočevje Slovenia 68 F2
Koch Bihar India 105 G4
Kocher *r.* Germany 63 J5
Kochevo Russia 51 Q4
Kochi India 106 C4
Kōchi Japan 91 D6
Koçhisar Turkey *see* Kızıltepe
Koch Island Canada 147 K3
Kochkor Kyrg. 102 E3
Kochkorka Kyrg. *see* Kochkor
Kochkurovo Russia 53 J5
Kochubeyevskoye Russia 113 F1
Kod India 106 B3
Kodaira Japan 93 F3
Kodala India 106 E2
Kodama Japan 93 F2
Kodarma India 105 F4
Kōdera Japan 92 A4
Koderma India *see* Kodarma
Kodiak *AK* U.S.A. 148 I4
Kodiak Island *AK* U.S.A. 148 I4
Kodiak National Wildlife Refuge *nature res. AK* U.S.A. 148 I4
Kodibeleng Botswana 125 H2
Kodino Russia 52 H3
Kodiyakkarai India 106 C4
Kodok South Sudan 108 D8
Kodyma Ukr. 53 F6
Kodzhaele *mt.* Bulg./Greece 69 K4
Koedoesberg *mts* S. Africa 124 E7
Koegrabie S. Africa 124 E5
Koekenaap S. Africa 124 D6
Koersel Belgium 62 F3
Koës Namibia 124 D3
Kofa Mountains *AZ* U.S.A. 159 G5
Koffiefontein S. Africa 124 G5
Koforidua Ghana 120 C4
Kōfu Japan 93 E3
Koga Japan 93 F2
Kogaluc *r.* Canada 152 F2
Kogaluc, Baie de *b.* Canada 152 F2
Kogaluk *r.* Canada 153 J2
Kogaly Kazakh. 98 B3
Kogan Australia 138 E1
Køge Denmark 55 H9
Kogon *r.* Guinea 120 B3
Kogon Uzbek. 111 G2
Kohan Pak. 111 G5
Kohat Pak. 111 H3
Koh-e Şayyād Afgh. 111 G2
Kohestān *reg.* Afgh. 111 H3
Kohila Estonia 55 N7
Kohima India 105 H4
Kohistan *reg.* Pak. 111 I3
Kohistānāt Afgh. 111 G3
Kohler Range *mts* Antarctica 188 K2
Kohlu Pak. 111 H4
Kohoku Japan 92 C3
Kohtla-Järve Estonia 55 O7
Koidern Canada 149 L3
Koidern Mountain Canada 149 L3
Koidu Sierra Leone *see* Koidu-Sefadu
Koidu-Sefadu Sierra Leone 120 B4
Koihoa India 87 A5
Koikyim Qu *r.* China 99 F6
Koilkonda India 106 C2
Koin N. Korea 91 B4
Koin *r.* Russia 52 K3
Koito-gawa *r.* Japan 93 F3
Kojonup Australia 135 B8
Kōka *Shiga* Japan 92 C4
Kōka *Shiga* Japan 92 C4
Kokai-gawa *r.* Japan 93 G3
Kokand Uzbek. *see* Qo'qon
Kökar Fin. 55 L7
Kök-Art Kyrg. 98 A4
Kokawa Japan 92 B4
Kök-Aygyr Kyrg. 98 A4
Kokchetav Kazakh. *see* Kokshetau
Kokemäenjoki *r.* Fin. 55 L6
Kokerboom Namibia 124 D5
Ko Kha Thai. 86 B3
Kokhanok *AK* U.S.A. 148 I4
Kokkilai Sri Lanka 106 D4
Kokkola Fin. 54 M5
Kok Kuduk *well* China 98 D3
Koko Nigeria 120 D3
Kokolik *r. AK* U.S.A. 148 G1
Kokomo *IN* U.S.A. 164 B3
Kokong Botswana 124 F3
Kokos *i.* Indon. 87 A7
Kokosi S. Africa 125 H4
Kokpekty Kazakh. 102 F2
Kokrines *AK* U.S.A. 148 I2
Kokrines Hills *AK* U.S.A. 148 I2
Kokruagarok *AK* U.S.A. 148 I1
Koksan N. Korea 91 B5
Kokshaal-Tau, Khrebet *mts* China/Kyrg. *see* Kakshaal-Too
Koksharka Russia 52 J4
Kokshetau Kazakh. 101 F1
Koksoak *r.* Canada 153 H2
Kokstad S. Africa 125 I6
Koksu *Almatinskaya Oblast'* Kazakh. 98 B3
Koksu *Almatinskaya Oblast'* Kazakh. 98 B3
Koktal Kazakh. 102 E3
Koktas Kazakh. 98 A2
Kokterek *Almatinskaya Oblast'* Kazakh. 98 B3
Kokterek *Zapadnyy Kazakhstan* Kazakh. 53 K6
Koktokay China 94 B2
Koktuma Kazakh. 98 C3
Koku, Tanjung *pt* Indon. 83 B4
Kokufu Japan 92 D2
Kokushiga-take *mt.* Japan 93 E3
Koküy China 94 B2
Kokyar China 99 B5
Kokzhayyk Kazakh. 98 C2
Kola *i. Moluccas* Indon. 81 I8
Kola Russia 54 R2
Kolachi *r.* Pak. 111 G5
Kolahoi *mt.* India 104 C2
Kolaka *Celebes* Indon. 83 B4
Kolambugan *Mindanao* Phil. 82 C4
Kolana Indon. 83 C5
Ko Lanta Thai. 87 B6
Kola Peninsula Russia 52 H2
Kolar *Chhattisgarh* India 106 D2
Kolar *Karnataka* India 106 C3
Kolār, Kūh-e *hill* Iran 110 C4
Kolaras India 104 D4
Kolar Gold Fields India 106 C3
Kolari Fin. 54 M3
Kolarovgrad Bulg. *see* Shumen
Kolasib India 105 H4
Kolayat India 104 C4
Kolbano *Timor* Indon. 83 C5
Kolberg Poland *see* Kołobrzeg
Kol'chugino Russia 52 H4
Kolda Senegal 120 B3
Kolding Denmark 55 F9
Kole *Kasaï-Oriental* Dem. Rep. Congo 122 C4
Kole *Orientale* Dem. Rep. Congo 122 C3
Koléa Alg. 67 H5
Koler Sweden 54 L4
Kolguyev, Ostrov *i.* Russia 52 K1
Kolhan *reg.* India 105 F5
Kolhapur India 106 B2
Kolhumadulu Maldives 103 D11
Koliganek *AK* U.S.A. 148 H4
Kolikata India *see* Kolkata
Kõljala Estonia 55 M7
Kolkasrags *pt* Latvia 55 M8
Kolkata India 105 G5
Kolkhozabad *Khatlon* Tajik. *see* Vose'
Kolkhozabad *Khatlon* Tajik. *see* Kolkhozobod
Kolkhozobod Tajik. 111 H2
Kollam India 106 C4
Kolleru Lake India 106 D2
Kollum Neth. 62 G1
Kolmanskop (abandoned) Namibia 124 B4
Köln Germany *see* Cologne
Köln-Bonn *airport* Germany 63 H4
Kołobrzeg Poland 57 O3
Kologriv Russia 52 J4
Kolokani Mali 120 C3
Kolombangara *i.* Solomon Is 133 F2
Kolomea Ukr. *see* Kolomyya
Kolomna Russia 53 H5
Kołomyja Ukr. *see* Kolomyya
Kolomyya Ukr. 53 E6
Kolondiéba Mali 120 C3
Kolonedale *Celebes* Indon. 83 B3
Koloni Cyprus 107 A2
Kolonkwaneng Botswana 124 E4
Kolono *Celebes* Indon. 83 B4
Kolowana Watobo, Teluk *b.* Indon. 83 B4
Kolozsvár Romania *see* Cluj-Napoca
Kolpashevo Russia 76 J4
Kol'skiy Poluostrov *pen.* Russia *see* Kola Peninsula
Kölük Turkey *see* Kahta
Koluli Eritrea 108 F7
Kolumadulu Atoll Maldives *see* Kolhumadulu
Kolva *r.* Russia 52 M2
Kolvan India 106 B2
Kolvereid Norway 54 G4
Kolvik Norway 54 N1
Kolvitskoye, Ozero *l.* Russia 54 R3
Kolwa *reg.* Pak. 111 G5
Kolwezi Dem. Rep. Congo 123 C5
Kolyma *r.* Russia 77 R3
Kolyma Lowland Russia *see* Kolymskaya Nizmennost'
Kolyma Range *mts* Russia *see* Kolymskoye Nagor'ye
Kolymskaya Nizmennost' *lowland* Russia 77 Q3
Kolymskoye Nagor'ye *mts* Russia 77 R3
Kolyshley Russia 53 J5
Kolyuchaya, Gora *mt.* Russia 148 A2
Kolyuchin, Ostrov *i.* Russia 148 D2
Kolyuchinskaya Guba *b.* Russia 148 D2
Kom *mt.* Bulg. 69 J3
Komadugu-Gana *watercourse* Nigeria 120 E3
Komae Japan 93 F3
Komaga-dake *mt.* Japan 93 D3
Komagane Japan 93 D3
Komaga-take *mt.* Japan 93 F1
Komaggas S. Africa 124 C5
Komaio P.N.G. 81 K8
Komaki Japan 92 C3
Komandnaya, Gora *mt.* Russia 90 E2
Komandorskiye Ostrova *is* Russia 77 R4
Komárno Slovakia 57 Q7
Komati *r.* Swaziland 125 J3
Komatipoort S. Africa 125 J3
Komatsu Japan 92 C2
Komba *i.* Indon. 83 B4
Kombakomba *Celebes* Indon. 83 B3
Komebail Lagoon Palau 82 [inset]
Komering *r.* Indon. 84 D3
Komga S. Africa 125 H7
Komintern Ukr. *see* Marhanets'
Kominternivs'ke Ukr. 69 N1
Komiža Croatia 68 G3
Komló Hungary 68 H1
Kommunarsk Ukr. *see* Alchevs'k
Komodo *i.* Indon. 83 A5
Komodo, Taman Nasional *nat. park* Indon. 83 A5
Kôm Ombo Egypt *see* Kawm Umbū
Komono Congo 122 B4
Komono Japan 92 C3
Komoran *i.* Indon. 81 J8
Komoro Japan 93 E2
Komotini Greece 69 K4
Kompong Cham Cambodia *see* Kâmpóng Cham
Kompong Chhnang Cambodia *see* Kâmpóng Chhnăng
Kompong Kleang Cambodia *see* Kâmpóng Khleăng
Kompong Som Cambodia *see* Sihanoukville
Kompong Speu Cambodia *see* Kâmpóng Spœ
Kompong Thom Cambodia *see* Kâmpóng Thum
Komrat Moldova *see* Comrat
Komsberg *mts* S. Africa 124 E7
Komsomol Kazakh. *see* Karabalyk
Komsomolabad Tajik. *see* Darband
Komsomolets Kazakh. *see* Karabalyk
Komsomolets, Ostrov *i.* Russia 76 K1
Komsomol's'k Ukr. 53 G6
Komsomol'skiy *Chukotskiy Avtonomnyy Okrug* Russia 189 C2
Komsomol'skiy *Khanty-Mansiyskiy Avtonomnyy Okrug-Yugra* Russia *see* Yugorsk
Komsomol'skiy *Respublika Kalmykiya-Khalm'g-Tangch* Russia 53 J7
Komsomol'sk-na-Amure Russia 90 E2
Komsomol'skoye Kazakh. 102 B1
Komsomol'skoye Russia 53 J6
Kömürlü Turkey 113 F2
Kon India 105 E4
Konacık Turkey 107 B1
Konada India 106 D2
Kōnan *Aichi* Japan 92 C3
Konan Japan 92 C3
Kōnan *Shiga* Japan 92 C4
Konarak India *see* Konarka
Konarka India 105 F6
Konch India 104 D4
Konda Japan 92 B3
Kondagaon India 106 D2
Kondinin Australia 135 B8
Kondinskoye Russia *see* Oktyabr'skoye
Kondoa Tanz. 123 D4
Kondol' Russia 53 J5
Kondopoga Russia 52 G3
Kondoz Afgh. *see* Kunduz
Kondrovo Russia 53 G5
Konergino Russia 148 C2
Köneürgenç Turkm. 109 I1
Kong Cameroon 120 E4
Kông, Kaôh *i.* Cambodia 87 C5
Kông, Tônlé *r.* Cambodia 87 D4
Kong, Xé *r.* Laos 86 D4
Kongakut *r. AK* U.S.A. 149 L1
Kongauru *i.* Palau 82 [inset]
Kong Christian IX Land *reg.* Greenland 147 O3
Kong Christian X Land *reg.* Greenland 147 P2
Kongelab *atoll* Marshall Is *see* Rongelap
Kong Frederik IX Land *reg.* Greenland 147 M3
Kong Frederik VI Kyst *coastal area* Greenland 147 N3
Kongiganak *AK* U.S.A. 148 G4
Kong Kat *hill* Indon. 85 G2
Kongkemul *mt.* Indon. 85 G2
Kongōdo-san *mt.* Japan 92 D2
Kongō-Ikoma Kokutei-kōen *park* Japan 92 B4
Kongolo Dem. Rep. Congo 123 C4
Kongor South Sudan 121 G4
Kong Oscars Fjord *inlet* Greenland 147 P2
Kongoussi Burkina Faso 120 C3
Kongsberg Norway 55 F7
Kongsvinger Norway 55 H6
Kongur Shan *mt.* China 98 A5
Königsberg Russia *see* Kaliningrad
Königsee Germany 63 L4
Königswinter Germany 63 H4
Königs Wusterhausen Germany 63 N2
Konimekh Uzbek. *see* Konimex
Konimex Uzbek. 111 G1
Konin Poland 57 Q4
Konjic Bos. & Herz. 68 G3
Konkiep *watercourse* Namibia 124 C5
Kon Kriel Cambodia 87 C4
Könnern Germany 63 L3
Konnevesi Fin. 54 O5
Kōno Japan 92 C3
Konosha Russia 52 I3
Kōnosu Japan 93 F2
Konotop Ukr. 53 G6
Konpara India 105 E5
Kon Plông Vietnam 87 D4
Konqi He *r.* China 98 E4
Konrei Palau 82 [inset]
Konsei-tōge *pass* Japan 93 F2
Konso Eth. 122 D3
Konso Cultural Landscape *tourist site* Eth. 121 G4
Konstantinograd Ukr. *see* Krasnohrad
Konstantinovka Russia 90 B2
Konstantinovka Ukr. *see* Kostyantynivka
Konstantinovy Lázně Czech Rep. 63 M5
Konstanz Germany 57 L7
Kontha Myanmar 86 B2
Kontiolahti Fin. 54 P5
Konttila Fin. 54 O4
Kon Tum Vietnam 87 D4
Kon Tum, Cao Nguyên Vietnam 87 E4
Könugard Ukr. *see* Kiev
Konus *mt.* Russia 148 B2
Konushin, Mys *pt* Russia 52 I2
Konya Turkey 112 D3
Konyrat *Karagandinskaya Oblast'* Kazakh. 98 A3
Konyrat *Karagandinskaya Oblast'* Kazakh. 98 A3
Konyrolen Kazakh. 98 B3
Konz Germany 62 G5
Konzhakovskiy Kamen', Gora *mt.* Russia 51 R4
Koocanusa, Lake *resr* Canada/U.S.A. 150 H5
Kooch Bihar India *see* Koch Bihar
Kookynie Australia 135 C7
Koolyanobbing Australia 135 B7
Koondrook Australia 138 B5
Koorawatha Australia 138 D5
Koordarrie Australia 134 A5
Kootenay *r.* Canada 150 G5
Kootenay Lake Canada 150 G5
Kootenay National Park Canada 150 G5
Kootjieskolk S. Africa 124 E6
Koozata Lagoon *AK* U.S.A. 148 E3
Kopa *Almatinskaya Oblast'* Kazakh. 98 A4
Kopa *Vostochnyy Kazakhstan* Kazakh. 98 B3
Kópasker Iceland 54 [inset 1]
Kopbirlik Kazakh. 102 E2
Koper Slovenia 68 E2
Kopet Dag *mts* Iran/Turkm. 110 E2
Kopet-Dag, Khrebet *mts* Iran/Turkm. *see* Kopet Dag
Köpetdag Gershi *mts* Iran/Turkm. *see* Kopet Dag
Kopili *r.* India 105 G4
Köping Sweden 55 J7
Köpmanholmen Sweden 54 K5
Kopong Botswana 125 G3
Koppal India 106 C3
Koppang Norway 55 G6
Kopparberg Sweden 55 I7
Koppeh Dāgh *mts* Iran/Turkm. *see* Kopet Dag
Köppel *hill* Germany 63 H4
Koppi *r.* Russia 90 F2
Koppies S. Africa 125 H4
Koppieskraal Pan *salt pan* S. Africa 124 E4
Koprivnica Croatia 68 G1
Köprülü Turkey 107 A1
Köprülü Kanyon Milli Parkı *nat. park* Turkey 69 N6
Kopyl' Belarus *see* Kapyl'
Kora India 104 E4
Kōra Japan 92 C3
Korablino Russia 53 I5
K'orahē Eth. 122 E3
Korak Pak. 111 G5
Koramlik China 99 D5
Korangal India 106 C2
Korangi Pak. 111 G5
Koraput India 106 D2
Korat Thai. *see* Nakhon Ratchasima
Koratla India 106 C2
Korba India 105 E5
Korbach Germany 63 I3
Korbu, Gunung *mt.* Malaysia 84 C1
Korçë Albania 69 I4
Korčula Croatia 68 G3
Korčula *i.* Croatia 68 G3
Korčulanski Kanal *sea chan.* Croatia 68 G3
Korday Kazakh. 102 D3
Kord Küy Iran 110 D2
Kords *reg.* Iran 111 F5
Korea, North *country* Asia 91 B5
Korea, South *country* Asia 91 B5
Korea Bay *g.* China/N. Korea 91 B5
Korea Strait Japan/S. Korea 91 C6
Koregaon India 106 B2
Korenovsk Russia 113 E1
Korenovskaya Russia *see* Korenovsk
Korepino Russia 51 R3
Korets' Ukr. 53 E6
Körfez Turkey 69 M4
Korff Ice Rise Antarctica 188 L1
Korfovskiy Russia 90 D2
Korgalzhyn Kazakh. 102 D1
Korgen Norway 54 H3
Korhogo Côte d'Ivoire 120 C4
Koribundu Sierra Leone 120 B4
Kori Creek *inlet* India 104 B5
Korinthiakos Kolpos *sea chan.* Greece *see* Corinth, Gulf of
Korinthos Greece *see* Corinth
Kris-hegy *hill* Hungary 68 G1
Koritnik *mt.* Albania 69 I3
Koritsa Albania *see* Korçë
Kōriyama Japan 91 F5
Korkuteli Turkey 69 N6
Korla China 98 D4
Kormakitis, Cape Cyprus 107 A2
Körmend Hungary 68 G1
Kornati, Nacionalni Park *nat. park* Croatia 68 F3
Korneyevka Kazakh. 98 A2
Korneyevka Russia 53 K6
Koro Côte d'Ivoire 120 C4
Koro *i.* Fiji 133 H3
Koro *r.* Indon. 83 B3
Koro Mali 120 C3
Koroc *r.* Canada 153 I2
Köroğlu Dağları *mts* Turkey 69 O4
Köroğlu Tepesi *mt.* Turkey 112 D2
Korogwe Tanz. 123 D4
Koronadal Phil. 82 D5
Koroneia, Limni *l.* Greece 69 J4
Korong Vale Australia 138 A6
Koronia, Limni *l.* Greece *see* Koroneia, Limni

▶Koror Palau 82 [inset]
Former capital of Palau.

Koror *i.* Palau 82 [inset]
Koro Sea *b.* Fiji 133 H3
Korosten' Ukr. 53 F6
Korostyshiv Ukr. 53 F6
Koro Toro Chad 121 E3
Korovin Bay *AK* U.S.A. 148 [inset] D5
Korovin Volcano *AK* U.S.A. 148 [inset] D5
Korpilahti Fin. 54 N5
Korpo Fin. 55 L6
Korppoo Fin. *see* Korpo
Korsakov Russia 90 F3
Korsnäs Fin. 54 L5
Korsør Denmark 55 G9
Korsun'-Shevchenkivs'kyy Ukr. 53 F6
Korsun'-Shevchenkovskiy Ukr. *see* Korsun'-Shevchenkivs'kyy
Korsze Poland 57 R3
Kortesjärvi Fin. 54 M5
Korti Sudan 108 D6
Kortkeros Russia 52 K3
Kortrijk Belgium 62 D4
Korvala Fin. 54 O3
Koryakskaya Sopka, Vulkan *vol.* Russia 77 Q4
Koryakskoye Nagor'ye *mts* Russia 77 S3
Koryazhma Russia 52 J3
Kōryō Japan 92 B4
Kos *i.* Greece 69 L6
Kosa Russia 51 Q4
Kosai Japan 92 D4
Kosam India 104 E4

Kosan N. Korea 91 B5
Kościan Poland 57 P4
Kosciusko, Mount Australia see Kosciuszko, Mount
Kosciuszko, Mount Australia 138 D6
Kosciuszko National Park Australia 138 D6
Köse Turkey 113 E2
Köseçobanlı Turkey 107 A1
Kōsei Japan see Konan
Kosgi India 106 C2
Kosh-Agach Russia 94 B1
Kosh-Döbö Kyrg. 98 A4
Koshigaya Japan 93 F3
Koshikijima-rettō is Japan 91 C7
Koshino Japan 92 C2
Koshk Afgh. 111 F3
Koshkarkol', Ozero l. Kazakh. 98 C3
Koshki Russia 53 K5
Kōshū Japan 93 E3
Kosi r. India 99 B7
Kosi Bay S. Africa 125 K4
Košice Slovakia 53 D6
Kosigi India 106 C3
Kosi Reservoir Nepal 99 D8
Koskudyk Kazakh. 98 B3
Koskullskulle Sweden 54 L3
Köslin Poland see Koszalin
Kosma r. Russia 52 K2
Koson Uzbek. 111 G2
Kosŏng N. Korea 91 C5
Kosova prov. Europe see Kosovo

▶Kosovo country Europe 69 I3
Gained independence from Serbia in February 2008.

Kosovo-Metohija prov. Europe see Kosovo
Kosovska Mitrovica Kosovo see Mitrovicë
Kosrae atoll Micronesia 186 G5
Kösseine hill Germany 63 L5
Kossol Passage Palau 82 [inset]
Kossol Reef Palau 82 [inset]
Kosta-Khetagurovo Russia see Nazran'
Kostanay Kazakh. 100 F1
Kostenets Bulg. 69 J3
Kosti Sudan 108 D7
Kostinbrod Bulg. 69 J3
Kostino Russia 76 J3
Kostomuksha Russia 54 Q4
Kostopil' Ukr. 53 E6
Kostopol' Ukr. see Kostopil'
Kostroma Russia 52 I4
Kostrzyn nad Odrą Poland 57 O4
Kostyantynivka Ukr. 53 H6
Kostyukovichi Belarus see Kastsyukovichy
Kosuge Japan 93 E3
Kos'yu Russia 51 R2
Koszalin Poland 57 P3
Kszeg Hungary 68 G1
Kota Andhra Prad. India 106 D3
Kota Chhattisgarh India 105 E5
Kota Rajasthan India 104 C4
Kōta Japan 92 D4
Kotaagung Sumatra Indon. 84 D4
Kota Baharu Malaysia see Kota Bharu
Kotabaru Kalimantan Indon. 85 E3
Kotabaru Kalimantan Indon. 85 G3
Kotabaru Sumatra Indon. 84 B2
Kota Belud Sabah Malaysia 85 G1
Kotabesi Kalimantan Indon. 85 F3
Kota Bharu Malaysia 84 C1
Kotabumi Sumatra Indon. 84 D4
Kotabunan Celebes Indon. 83 C2
Kot Addu Pak. 111 H4
Kota Kinabalu Sabah Malaysia 85 G1
Kotamobagu Celebes Indon. 83 C2
Kotaneelee Range mts Canada 150 E2
Kotanemel', Gora mt. Kazakh. 98 B3
Kotaparh India 106 D2
Kotapinang Sumatra Indon. 84 C2
Kota Samarahan Sarawak Malaysia 85 E2
Kotatengah Sumatra Indon. 84 C2
Kota Tinggi Malaysia 84 C2
Kotawaringin Kalimantan Indon. 85 E3
Kotcho r. Canada 150 F3
Kotcho Lake Canada 150 F3
Kot Diji Pak. 111 H5
Kotdwara India 99 B7
Kotel'nich Russia 52 K4
Kotel'nikovo Russia 53 I7
Kotel'nyy, Ostrov i. Russia 77 O2
Kotgar India 106 D2
Kotgarh India 104 D3
Kothagudem India see Kottagudem
Köthen (Anhalt) Germany 63 L3
Kotido Uganda 121 G4
Kotikovo Russia 90 D3
Kot Imamgarh Pak. 111 H5
Kotka Fin. 55 O6
Kot Kapura India 104 C3
Kotkino Russia 52 K2
Kotlas Russia 52 J3
Kotli Pak. 111 I3
Kotlik AK U.S.A. 148 G3
Kötlutangi pt Iceland 54 [inset 1]
Kotly Russia 55 P7
Kotō Japan 92 C3
Kotovo Russia 53 J6
Kotovsk Russia 53 I5
Kotra India 104 C4
Kotra Pak. 111 G4
Kotri r. India 106 D2
Kot Sarae Pak. 111 G6
Kottagudem India 106 D2
Kottarakara India 106 C4
Kottayam India 106 C4
Kotte Sri Lanka see Sri Jayewardenepura Kotte
Kotto r. Cent. Afr. Rep. 122 C3
Kotturu India 106 C3
Kotuy r. Russia 77 L2
Kotzebue AK U.S.A. 148 G2
Kotzebue Sound sea chan. AK U.S.A. 148 G2
Kouango Cent. Afr. Rep. 122 C3
Koubia Guinea 120 B3
Kouchibouguac National Park Canada 153 I5
Koudougou Burkina Faso 120 C3
Kouebokkeveld mts S. Africa 124 D7
Koufey Niger 120 E3
Koufonisi i. Greece 69 L7
Kougaberge mts S. Africa 124 F7
Koukdjuak, Great Plain of the Canada 147 K3
Koukourou r. Cent. Afr. Rep. 122 B3
Koulen Cambodia see Kulên
Koulikoro Mali 120 C3
Koumac New Caledonia 133 G4
Koumenzi China 94 C3
Koumi Japan 93 E2
Koumpentoum Senegal 120 B3
Koumra Chad 121 E4
Koundâra Guinea 120 B3
Kountze TX U.S.A. 161 E6
Koupéla Burkina Faso 120 C3
Kourou Fr. Guiana 177 H2
Kouroussa Guinea 120 C3
Kousséri Cameroon 121 E3
Koutiala Mali 120 C3
Kouvola Fin. 55 O6
Kovallberget Sweden 54 J4
Kovdor Russia 54 Q3
Kovel' Ukr. 53 E6
Kovernino Russia 52 I4
Kovilpatti India 106 C4
Kovno Lith. see Kaunas
Kovrov Russia 52 I4
Kovylkino Russia 53 I5
Kovzhskoye, Ozero l. Russia 52 H3
Kowangge Sumbawa Indon. 85 G5
Kowanyama Australia 136 C2
Kowloon H.K. China 97 [inset]
Kowloon Peak hill H.K. China 97 [inset]
Kowloon Peninsula H.K. China 97 [inset]
Kowŏn N. Korea 91 B5
Kox Kuduk well China 94 C3
Koxrap China 99 B5
Koxtag China 99 B5
Kōya Japan 92 B4
Kōyaguchi Japan 92 B4
Kōyama-misaki pt Japan 91 C6
Koyamutthoor India see Coimbatore
Kōya-Ryūjin Kokutei-kōen park Japan 92 B4
Köyceğiz Turkey 69 M6
Koyginveyem r. Russia 148 A2
Koygorodok Russia 52 K3
Koyna Reservoir India 106 B2
Köytendag Turkm. 111 G2
Koyuk AK U.S.A. 148 G2
Koyuk r. AK U.S.A. 148 G2
Koyukuk AK U.S.A. 148 H2
Koyukuk r. AK U.S.A. 148 H2
Koyukuk, Middle Fork r. AK U.S.A. 149 J2
Koyukuk, North Fork r. AK U.S.A. 149 J2
Koyukuk, South Fork r. AK U.S.A. 149 J2
Koyukuk Island AK U.S.A. 148 H2
Koyukuk National Wildlife Refuge nature res. AK U.S.A. 148 H2
Koyulhisar Turkey 112 E2
Kozağacı Turkey see Günyüzü
Kozakai Japan 92 D4
Kōzaki Japan 93 G3
Kō-zaki pt Japan 91 C6
Kozan Turkey 112 D3
Kozani Greece 69 I4
Kozara mts Bos. & Herz. 68 G2
Kozara, Nacionalni Park nat. park Bos. & Herz. 68 G2
Kozarska Dubica Bos. & Herz. see Bosanska Dubica
Kozelets' Ukr. 53 F6
Kozel'sk Russia 53 G5
Kozhikode India 106 B4
Kozhva Russia 52 M2
Kozlu Turkey 69 N4
Kozly Russia 52 H2
Koz'modem'yansk Russia 52 J4
Kožuf mts Greece/Macedonia 69 J4
Kōzu-shima i. Japan 93 F4
Kozyatyn Ukr. 53 F6
Kpandae Ghana 120 C4
Kra, Isthmus of Thai. 87 B5
Krabi Thai. 87 B5
Kra Buri Thai. 87 B5
Krâchéh Cambodia 87 D4
Kraddsele Sweden 54 J4
Kragan Java Indon. 85 E4
Kragerø Norway 55 F7
Kraggenburg Neth. 62 F2
Kragujevac Serbia 69 I2

▶Krakatau i. Indon. 84 D4
2nd deadliest recorded volcanic eruption (1883).

Krakatau vol. Indon. 80 D8
Krakatau, Taman Nasional nat. park Indon. 84 D4
Krakau Poland see Kraków
Kraków Poland 57 Q5
Krakower See l. Germany 63 M1
Krâlănh Cambodia 87 C4
Kralendijk Bonaire 169 K6
Kramators'k Ukr. 53 H6
Kramfors Sweden 54 J5
Krammer est. Neth. 62 E3
Kranidi Greece 69 J6
Kranj Slovenia 68 F1
Kranji Reservoir Sing. 87 [inset]
Kranskop S. Africa 125 J5
Krasavino Russia 52 J3
Krasilov Ukr. see Krasyliv
Krasino Russia 76 G2
Kraskino Russia 90 C4
Krāslava Latvia 55 O9
Kraslice Czech Rep. 63 M4
Krasnaya Gorbatka Russia 52 I5
Krasnaya Polyana Kazakh. 98 A2
Krasnaya Yaranga Russia 148 D2
Krasnoarmeysk Russia 53 J6
Krasnoarmeysk Ukr. see Krasnoarmiys'k
Krasnoarmiys'k Ukr. 53 H6
Krasnoborsk Russia 52 J3
Krasnodar Russia 112 E1
Krasnodar Kray admin. div. Russia see Krasnodarskiy Kray
Krasnodarskiy Kray admin. div. Russia 112 E1
Krasnodon Ukr. 53 H6
Krasnogorodsk Russia 55 P8
Krasnogorsk Russia 90 F2
Krasnogorskoye Russia 52 L4
Krasnograd Ukr. see Krasnohrad
Krasnogvardeysk Uzbek. see Bulung'ur
Krasnogvardeyskoye Russia 53 I7
Krasnohrad Ukr. 53 G6
Krasnohvardiys'ke Crimea 53 G7
Krasnokamensk Russia 95 I1
Krasnokamsk Russia 51 R4
Krasnoperekops'k Crimea 53 G7
Krasnopol'ye Russia 90 F2
Krasnorechenskiy Russia 90 D3
Krasnoslobodsk Russia 53 I5
Krasnotur'insk Russia 51 S4
Krasnoufimsk Russia 51 R4
Krasnovishersk Russia 51 R3
Krasnovodsk Turkm. see Türkmenbaşy
Krasnovodsk, Mys pt Turkm. 110 D2
Krasnovodskoye Plato plat. Turkm. 113 I2
Krasnowodsk Aylagy b. Turkm. see Türkmenbaşy Aýlagy
Krasnoyarovo Russia 90 C2
Krasnoyarsk Russia 76 K4
Krasnoyarskoye Vodokhranilishche resr Russia 88 G2
Krasnoye Lipetskaya Oblast' Russia 53 H5
Krasnoye Respublika Kalmykiya-Khalm'g-Tangch Russia see Ulan Erge
Krasnoznamenskiy Kazakh. see Yegindykol'
Krasnoznamenskoye Kazakh. see Yegindykol'
Krasnyy Russia 53 F5
Krasnyy Chikoy Russia 95 G1
Krasnyye Baki Russia 52 J4
Krasnyy Kamyshanik Russia see Komsomol'skiy
Krasnyy Kholm Russia 52 H4
Krasnyy Kut Russia 53 J6
Krasnyy Luch Ukr. 53 H6
Krasnyy Lyman Ukr. 53 H6
Krasnyy Oktyabr' Kazakh. 98 B3
Krasnyy Yar Russia 53 K7
Krasyliv Ukr. 53 E6
Kratie Cambodia see Krâchéh
Kratke Range mts P.N.G. 81 L8
Kraulshavn Greenland see Nuussuaq
Krâvanh, Chuŏr Phnum mts Cambodia/Thai. see Cardamom Range
Kraynovka Russia 113 G2
Krefeld Germany 62 G3
Krekatok Island AK U.S.A. 148 F3
Kremenchug Ukr. see Kremenchuk
Kremenchugskoye Vodokhranilishche resr Ukr. see Kremenchuts'ke Vodoskhovyshche
Kremenchuk Ukr. 53 G6
Kremenchuts'ke Vodoskhovyshche resr Ukr. 53 G6
Křemešník hill Czech Rep. 57 O6
Kremges Ukr. see Svitlovods'k
Kremmidi, Akra pt Greece see Kremmydi, Akrotirio
Kremmydi, Akrotirio pt Greece 69 J6
Krems Austria see Krems an der Donau
Krems an der Donau Austria 57 O6
Krenitzin Islands AK U.S.A. 148 F5
Kresta, Zaliv g. Russia 148 C2
Kresttsy Russia 52 G4
Kretinga Lith. 55 L9
Kreuzau Germany 62 G4
Kreuztal Germany 63 H4
Kreva Belarus 55 O9
Kribi Cameroon 120 D4
Krichev Belarus see Krychaw
Kriel S. Africa see Ga-Nala
Krikellos Greece 69 I5
Kril'on, Mys c. Russia 90 F3
Krishna India 106 C2
Krishna r. India 106 D2
Krishnanagar India 105 G5
Krishnarajanagara India 106 C3
Krishnaraja Sagara l. India 106 C3
Kristiania Norway see Oslo
Kristiansand Norway 55 E7
Kristianstad Sweden 55 I8
Kristiansund Norway 54 E5
Kristiinankaupunki Fin. see Kristinestad
Kristinehamn Sweden 55 I7
Kristinestad Fin. 54 L5
Kristinopol' Ukr. see Chervonohrad
Kriti i. Greece see Crete
Kritiko Pelagos sea Greece 69 K6
Krivoy Rog Ukr. see Kryvyy Rih
Križevci Croatia 68 G1
Krk i. Croatia 68 F2
Krka, Nacionalni Park nat. park Croatia 68 F3
Krkonošský národní park nat. park Czech Rep./Poland 57 O5
Krokom Sweden 54 I5
Krokstadøra Norway 54 F5
Krokstranda Norway 54 I3
Krolevets' Ukr. 53 G6
Kronach Germany 63 L4
Kronoby Fin. 54 M5
Kronprins Christian Land reg. Greenland 189 I1
Kronprins Frederik Bjerge nunataks Greenland 147 O3
Kronshtadt Russia 55 P7
Kronstadt Romania see Braşov
Kronstadt Russia see Kronshtadt
Kronwa Myanmar 86 B4
Kroonstad S. Africa 125 H4
Kropotkin Russia 113 F1
Kropstädt Germany 63 M3
Krosno Poland 53 D6
Krotoszyn Poland 57 P5
Kroya Java Indon. 85 E4
Kruger National Park S. Africa 125 J2
Kruglikovo Russia 90 D2
Krugloi Point pt AK U.S.A. 148 [inset]
Kruglyakov Russia see Oktyabr'skiy
Krui Sumatra Indon. 84 C4
Kruisfontein S. Africa 124 G8
Kruja Albania see Krujë
Krujë Albania 69 H4
Krumovgrad Bulg. 69 K4
Krungkao Thai. see Ayutthaya
Krung Thep Thai. see Bangkok
Krupa Bos. & Herz. see Bosanska Krupa
Krupa na Uni Bos. & Herz. see Bosanska Krupa
Krupki Belarus 53 F5
Krusenstern, Cape AK U.S.A. 148 G2
Kruševac Serbia 69 I3
Krušné hory mts Czech Rep. 63 M4
Kruzof Island AK U.S.A. 149 N4
Krychaw Belarus 53 F5
Krylov Seamount sea feature N. Atlantic Ocean 184 G4
Krymsk Russia 112 E1
Krymskaya Russia see Krymsk
Krypsalo (abandoned) Kazakh. 98 A3
Krystynopol Ukr. see Chervonohrad
Krytiko Pelagos sea Greece see Kritiko Pelagos
Kryvyy Rih Ukr. 53 G7
Ksabi Alg. 64 D6
Ksar Chellala Alg. 67 H6
Ksar el Boukhari Alg. 67 H6
Ksar el Kebir Morocco 67 D6
Ksar-es-Souk Morocco see Er Rachidia
Ksenofontova Russia 51 R3
Kshirpai India 105 F5
Ksour Essaf Tunisia 68 D7
Kstovo Russia 52 J4
Kū', Jabal al hill Saudi Arabia 108 G4
Kuah Malaysia 84 B1
Kuaidamao China see Tonghua
Kuala Belait Brunei 85 F1
Kuala Dungun Malaysia see Dungun
Kualajelai Kalimantan Indon. 85 E3
Kuala Kangsar Malaysia 84 C1
Kualakapuas Kalimantan Indon. 85 F3
Kuala Kerai Malaysia 84 C1
Kualakuayan Kalimantan Indon. 85 F3
Kuala Kubu Baharu Malaysia 84 C2
Kualakurun Kalimantan Indon. 85 F3
Kualalangsa Sumatra Indon. 84 B1
Kuala Lipis Malaysia 84 C1

▶Kuala Lumpur Malaysia 84 C2
Joint capital (with Putrajaya) of Malaysia.

Kuala Nerang Malaysia 84 C1
Kualapembuang Kalimantan Indon. 85 F3
Kuala Penyu Sabah Malaysia 85 F1
Kuala Pilah Malaysia 84 C2
Kuala Rompin Malaysia 84 C2
Kualasampit Kalimantan Indon. 85 F3
Kuala Selangor Malaysia 84 C2
Kualasimpang Sumatra Indon. 84 B1
Kuala Terengganu Malaysia 84 C1
Kualatungal Sumatra Indon. 84 C3
Kuamut Sabah Malaysia 85 G1
Kuamut r. Malaysia 85 G1
Kuancheng China 95 I3
Kuandian China 90 B4
Kuantan Malaysia 84 C2
Kuba Azer. see Quba
Kuban' r. Russia 53 H7
Kubār Syria 113 E4
Kubaybāt Syria 107 C2
Kubaysah Iraq 113 F4
Kubenskoye, Ozero l. Russia 52 H4
Kubrat Bulg. 69 L3
Kubu Bali Indon. 85 F5
Kubu Kalimantan Indon. 85 E3
Kubuang Kalimantan Indon. 85 F2
Kubukhay Russia 95 H1
Kubumesaäi Kalimantan Indon. 85 F2
Kuchaman Road India 111 I5
Kuchema Russia 52 I2
Kuching Sarawak Malaysia 85 E2
Küchnay Darwēshān Afgh. 111 G4
Kucing Sarawak Malaysia see Kuching
Kuçovë Albania 69 H4
Kuda India 104 B5
Kudal India 106 B3
Kudangan Kalimantan Indon. 85 E3
Kudap Sumatra Indon. 84 C2
Kudara-Somon Russia 95 F1
Kudat Sabah Malaysia 85 G1
Kudiakof Islands AK U.S.A. 148 G5
Kudligi India 106 C3
Kudobin Islands AK U.S.A. 148 G4
Kudoyama Japan 92 B4
Kudremukh mt. India 106 B3
Kudus Java Indon. 85 E4
Kudymkar Russia 51 Q4
Ku'erqisi China see Fuyun
Kufar Seram Indon. 83 D3
Kufstein Austria 57 N7
Kugaaruk Canada 147 J3
Kugaluk r. Canada 149 O1
Kugesi Russia 52 J4
Kugka Lhai China 99 E7
Kugluktuk Canada 146 G3
Kugmallit Bay Canada 149 N1
Kugri China 94 D5
Kuguno Japan 92 D2
Kūh, Khār mt. Iran 110 D4
Kūh, Ra's-al- pt Iran 110 E5
Kūh, Shīr mt. Iran 110 D4
Kūhak Iran 111 F5
Kuhanbokano mt. China 105 E3
Kuhbier Germany 63 M1
Kūhdasht Iran 110 B3
Kūhīn Iran 110 C2
Kuhmo Fin. 54 P4
Kuhmoinen Fin. 55 N6
Kūhpāyeh mt. Iran 110 E4
Kūhrān, Kūh-e mt. Iran 110 E5
Kühren Germany 63 M3
Kuhsān Afgh. 111 F3
Kui Buri Thai. 87 B4
Kuile He r. China 95 K1
Kuis Namibia 124 C3
Kuiseb watercourse Namibia 124 B2
Kuitan China 97 G4
Kuito Angola 123 B5
Kuitun China see Kuytun
Kuiu Island AK U.S.A. 149 N4
Kuivaniemi Fin. 54 N4
Kujang N. Korea 91 B5
Kuji Japan 91 F4
Kuji-gawa r. Japan 93 G2
Kujūkuri Japan 93 G3
Kujūkuri-hama coastal area Japan 93 G3
Kujū-san vol. Japan 91 C6
Kuk r. AK U.S.A. 148 G1
Kukaklek Lake AK U.S.A. 148 I4
Kukan Russia 90 D2
Kukës Albania 69 I3
Kukesi Albania see Kukës
Kuki Japan 93 F2
Kukizaki Japan 93 G3
Kuki-zaki pt Japan 92 C4
Kukmor Russia 52 K4
Kukpowruk r. AK U.S.A. 148 G1
Kukpuk r. AK U.S.A. 148 F1
Kukshi India 104 C5
Kukunuru India 106 D2
Kukup Malaysia 84 C2
Kükürtli Turkm. 110 E2
Kukusan, Gunung hill Indon. 85 F3
Kūl r. Iran 110 D5
Kula Turkey 69 M5
Kulabu, Gunung mt. Indon. 84 B2
Kulaisila India 105 F5
Kula Kangri mt. Bhutan/China 105 G3
Kulanak Kyrg. 98 A4
Kulanch reg. Pak. 111 F5
Kulandy Kazakh. 102 A2
Kular Russia 77 O2
Kulassein i. Phil. 82 C5
Kulat, Gunung mt. Indon. 85 G2
Kulawi Celebes Indon. 83 A3
Kuldīga Latvia 55 L8
Kuldja China see Yining
Kul'dur Russia 90 C2
Kule Botswana 124 E2
Kulebaki Russia 53 I5
Kulên Cambodia 87 D4
Kulgera Australia 135 F6
Kulikovka Kazakh. 98 B4
Kulikovo Russia 52 J3
Kulim Malaysia 84 C1
Kulin Australia 135 B8
Kulja Australia 135 B7
Kulkyne watercourse Australia 138 B3
Kullu India 104 D3
Kulmbach Germany 63 L4
Kŭlob Tajik. 111 H2
Kuloy Russia 52 I3
Kuloy r. Russia 52 I2
Kulp Turkey 113 F3
Kul'sary Kazakh. 100 E2
Külsheim Germany 63 J5
Kulu India see Kullu
Kulu Turkey 112 D3
Kulunda Russia 88 D2
Kulundinskaya Ravnina plain Kazakh./Russia 88 D2
Kulundinskoye, Ozero salt l. Russia 88 D2
Kulusuk Greenland 147 O3
Kulusutay Russia 95 H1
Kulwin Australia 137 C7
Kulyab Tajik. see Kŭlob
Kuma r. Russia 53 J7
Kumagaya Japan 93 F2
Kumai Kalimantan Indon. 85 E3
Kumai, Teluk b. Indon. 85 E3
Kumakhta Russia 95 H1
Kumalar Dağı mts Turkey 69 N5
Kumamoto Japan 91 C6
Kumano Japan 92 E6
Kumanovo Macedonia 69 I3
Kumara Russia 90 B2
Kumasi Ghana 120 C4
Kumayri Armenia see Gyumri
Kumba Cameroon 120 D4
Kumbakonam India 106 C4
Kumbe Indon. 81 K8
Kümbet Turkey 69 N5
Kumbharli Ghat mt. India 106 B2
Kumbher Nepal 99 C7
Kumbla India 106 B3
Kumchuru Botswana 124 F2
Kum-Dag Turkm. see Gumdag
Kumdah Saudi Arabia 108 G5
Kumel well Iran 110 D3
Kumeny Russia 52 K4
Kumertau Russia 76 G4
Kumgang-san mt. N. Korea 91 C5
Kumguri India 105 G4
Kumi Uganda 121 G4
Kumihama Japan 92 A3
Kumihama-wan l. Japan 92 A3
Kumiyama Japan 92 B4
Kum Kuduk well China 98 E4
Kumla Sweden 55 I7
Kumlu Turkey 107 C1
Kummersdorf-Alexanderdorf Germany 63 N2
Kumo Nigeria 120 E3
Kumon Range mts Myanmar 86 B1
Kumotori-yama mt. Japan 93 E3
Kumozu-gawa r. Japan 92 C4
Kumphawapi Thai. 86 C3
Kums Namibia 124 D5
Kumta India 106 B3
Kumu Dem. Rep. Congo 122 C3
Kumukh Russia 113 G2
Kumul China see Hami
Kumund India 106 D1
Kümüx China 98 E4
Kumylzhenskaya Russia see Kumylzhenskiy
Kumylzhenskiy Russia 53 I6
Kun r. Myanmar 86 B3
Kuna r. AK U.S.A. 148 H1
Kunar Sīnd r. Afgh. 111 H3
Kunashir, Ostrov i. Russia 90 G3
Kunashirskiy Proliv sea chan. Japan/Russia see Nemuro-kaikyō
Kunchaung Myanmar 86 B2
Kunchuk Tso salt l. China 105 E2
Kunda Estonia 55 O7
Kunda India 105 E4
Kundapura India 106 B3
Kundelungu, Parc National de nat. park Dem. Rep. Congo 123 C5
Kundelungu Ouest, Parc National de nat. park Dem. Rep. Congo 123 C5
Kundia India 104 C4
Kundur i. Sumatra Indon. 84 C2
Kunduz Afgh. 111 H2
Kundykol' Kazakh. 98 A2
Kunene r. Angola see Cunene
Kuneneng admin. dist. Botswana see Kweneng
Künes China see Xinyuan
Künes Chang China 98 C4
Künes He r. China 98 C4
Künes Linchang China 98 D4
Kungälv Sweden 55 G8
Kungei Alatau mts Kazakh./Kyrg. 98 B4
Kunggar China see Maizhokunggar
Kunghit Island Canada 149 O5
Kungsbacka Sweden 55 H8
Kungshamn Sweden 55 G7
Kungu Dem. Rep. Congo 122 B3
Kungur mt. China see Kongur Shan
Kungur Russia 51 R4
Kungurtug Russia 94 D1
Kunhing Myanmar 86 B2
Kuni r. India 106 C2
Kuni Japan 93 E2
Kunié i. New Caledonia see Pins, Île des
Kunigal India 106 C3
Kunimi-dake hill Japan 92 C2
Kunimi-dake mt. Japan 91 C6
Kuningan Java Indon. 85 E4
Kunkavav India 104 B5
Kunlong Myanmar 86 B2
Kunlui r. India/Nepal 99 E8

▶Kunlun Shan mts China 94 B5
Location of highest active volcano in Asia.

Kunlun Shankou pass China 94 C5
Kunming China 96 D3
Kuno r. India 99 B8
Kunshan China 97 I2
Kununurra Australia 134 E3
Kunwak r. Canada 151 L2
Kunwari r. India 99 B8
Kun'ya Russia 52 F4
Kunyang Yunnan China see Jinning
Kunyang Zhejiang China see Pingyang
Kunya-Urgench Turkm. see Köneürgenç
Kunyu Shan mts China 95 J4
Künzelsau Germany 63 J5
Künzels-Berg hill Germany 63 L3
Kuocang Shan mts China 97 I2
Kuohijärvi l. Fin. 55 N6
Kuoloyarvi Russia 54 P3
Kuopio Fin. 54 O5
Kuortane Fin. 54 M5
Kupa r. Croatia/Slovenia 68 G2
Kupang Timor Indon. 83 B5
Kupang, Teluk b. Timor Indon. 83 B5
Kupari India 105 F5
Kuparuk r. AK U.S.A. 149 J1
Kupiškis Lith. 55 N9
Kupreanof Island AK U.S.A. 149 N4
Kupreanof Point pt AK U.S.A. 148 H5
Kupreanof Strait AK U.S.A. 148 I4
Kupwara India 104 C2
Kup"yans'k Ukr. 53 H6
Kuqa China 98 C4
Kur r. Russia 90 D2
Kura r. Asia 113 G2
also known as Kur (Armenia), Kür (Azerbaijan), Mt'k'vari (Georgia)
Kuragino Russia 88 G2
Kurai-yama mt. Japan 92 D2
Kurakh Russia 53 J8
Kurama Range mts Asia 109 K1
Kurama-yama hill Japan 92 B3
Kuraminskiy Khrebet mts Asia see Kurama Range
Kūrān Dap Iran 111 E5
Kurashiki Japan 91 D6
Kurasia India 105 E5
Kurayn i. Saudi Arabia 110 C5
Kurayoshi Japan 91 D6
Kurayskiy Khrebet mts Russia 94 B1
Kurchatov Russia 53 G6
Kūrd, Kōh-e mt. Afgh. 111 G3
Kürdämir Azer. 113 H2
Kurday (abandoned) Kazakh. 98 A4
Kurdistan reg. Asia 113 F3
Kure Japan 91 D6
Küre Turkey 112 D2
Kure Atoll HI U.S.A. 186 I4
Kuressaare Estonia 55 M7
Kurgal'dzhino Kazakh. see Korgalzhyn
Kurgal'dzhinskiy Kazakh. see Korgalzhyn

Kurgan Russia 76 H4
Kurganinsk Russia 113 F1
Kurgannaya Russia see Kurganinsk
Kurgantyube Tajik. see Qŭrghonteppa
Kūrī Afgh. 111 H2
Kuri India 104 B4
Kuria Muria Islands Oman see Ḥalāniyāt, Juzur al
Kuridala (abandoned) Australia 136 C4
Kurigram Bangl. 105 G4
Kurihama Japan 93 F3
Kurihashi Japan 93 F2
Kurikka Fin. 54 M5
Kuril Basin sea feature Sea of Okhotsk 186 F2
Kuril Islands Russia 90 H3
Kurilovka Russia 53 K6
Kuril'sk Russia 90 G3
Kuril'skiye Ostrova is Russia see Kuril Islands
Kuril Trench sea feature N. Pacific Ocean 186 F3
Kurimoto Japan 93 G3
Kuriyama Japan 93 F2
Kurkino Russia 53 H5
Kurmashkino Kazakh. see Kurshim
Kurmuk Sudan 108 D7
Kurnool India 106 C3
Kurobane Japan 93 G2
Kurobe Japan 92 D2
Kurobe-gawa r. Japan 92 D2
Kurobe-ko resr Japan 92 D2
Kurodashō Japan 92 B3
Kurohime-yama mt. Japan 93 D2
Kurohone Japan 93 F2
Kuro-shima i. Japan 92 B4
Kuroso-yama mt. Japan 92 C4
Kurow N.Z. 139 C7
Kurram Pak. 111 H3
Kurri Kurri Australia 138 E4
Kursavka Russia 113 F1
Kurshim Kazakh. 102 F2
Kürshim Kazakh. see Kurshim
Kurshim r. Kazakh. 98 C2
Kurshskiy Zaliv b. Lith./Russia see Courland Lagoon
Kuršių marios b. Lith./Russia see Courland Lagoon
Kursk Russia 53 H6
Kurskaya Russia 113 G1
Kurskiy Zaliv b. Lith./Russia see Courland Lagoon
Kurşunlu Turkey 112 D2
Kurtalan Turkey 113 F3
Kurtoğlu Burnu pt Turkey 69 M6
Kurtpınar Turkey 107 B1
Kurtty r. Kazakh. 98 B3
Kurucaşile Turkey 112 D2
Kuruçay Turkey 112 E3
Kurukshetra India 104 D3
Kuruk Tag mts China 98 D4
Kuruman S. Africa 124 F4
Kuruman watercourse S. Africa 124 E4
Kurume Japan 91 C6
Kurumkan Russia 89 K2
Kurunegala Sri Lanka 106 D5
Kurunzulay Russia 95 I1
Kurupa r. AK U.S.A. 148 I1
Kurupam India 106 D2
Kurupkan Russia 148 D2
Kurush, Jebel hills Sudan 108 D5
Kur'ya Russia 51 R3
Kuryk Kazakh. 113 H2
Kuşadası Turkey 69 L6
Kuşadası, Gulf of b. Turkey 69 L6
Kusaie atoll Micronesia see Kosrae
Kusary Azer. see Qusar
Kusatsu Gunma Japan 93 E2
Kusatsu Shiga Japan 92 B3
Kuşcenneti nature res. Turkey 107 B1
Kuschke Nature Reserve S. Africa 125 I3
Kusel Germany 63 H5
Kuş Gölü l. Turkey 69 L4
Kushalgarh India 104 C5
Kushchëvskaya Russia 53 H7
Kushida-gawa r. Japan 92 C4
Kushihara Japan 92 D3
Kushimoto Japan 91 D6
Kushiro Japan 90 G4
Kushka Turkm. see Serhetabat
Kushk-e Kuhnah Afgh. 111 F3
Kushkopala Russia 52 J3
Kushtagi India 106 C3
Kushtia Bangl. 105 G5
Kushtih Iran 111 E4
Kuskan Turkey 107 A1
Kuskokwim r. AK U.S.A. 148 G3
Kuskokwim, North Fork r. AK U.S.A. 148 I3
Kuskokwim, South Fork r. AK U.S.A. 148 I3
Kuskokwim Bay AK U.S.A. 148 F4
Kuskokwim Mountains AK U.S.A. 148 I2
Kuşluyan Turkey see Gölköy
Kusmuryn Kazakh. 100 F1
Kusŏng N. Korea 91 B5
Kustanay Kazakh. see Kostanay
Kustatan AK U.S.A. 149 J3
Küstence Romania see Constanţa
Küstenkanal canal Germany 63 H1
Kustia Bangl. see Kushtia
Kusu Halmahera Indon. 83 C2
Kusu Japan 92 C4
Kut, Ko i. Thai. 87 C5
Kuta Bali Indon. 85 F5
Kutabagok Sumatra Indon. 84 B1
Kūt 'Abdollāh Iran 110 C4
Kutacane Sumatra Indon. 84 B2
Kütahya Turkey 69 M5
Kutai, Taman Nasional nat. park Indon. 85 G2
Kutaisi Georgia 113 F2
Kut-al-Imara Iraq see Al Kūt
Kutan Russia 113 G1
Kutanibong Sumatra Indon. 87 B7
Kutaraja Sumatra Indon. see Banda Aceh
Kutch, Gulf of India see Kachchh, Gulf of
Kutch, Rann of marsh India see Kachchh, Rann of
Kutchan Japan 90 F4
Kutina Croatia 68 G2
Kutjevo Croatia 68 G2
Kutkai Myanmar 86 B2
Kutno Poland 57 Q4
Kutru India 106 D2
Kūt Seyyed Na'īm Iran 110 C4
Kutsuki Japan 92 B3
Kutu Dem. Rep. Congo 122 B4
Kutubdia Island Bangl. 105 G5
Kutum Sudan 121 F3
Kutztown PA U.S.A. 165 H3
Kuujjua r. Canada 146 G2
Kuujjuaq Canada 153 H2
Kuujjuarapik Canada 152 F3
Kuusamo Fin. 54 P4
Kuusankoski Fin. 55 O6
Kuvango Angola 123 B5
Kuvshinovo Russia 52 G4
Kuwait country Asia 110 B4

▶Kuwait Kuwait 110 B4
Capital of Kuwait.

Kuwajleen atoll Marshall Is see Kwajalein
Kuwana Japan 92 C3
Kūyah/Koye Iraq 113 G3
Kuybyshev Novosibirskaya Oblast' Russia 76 I4
Kuybyshev Respublika Tatarstan Russia see Bolgar
Kuybyshev Samarskaya Oblast' Russia see Samara
Kuybysheve Ukr. 53 H7
Kuybyshevka-Vostochnaya Russia see Belogorsk
Kuybyshevskoye Vodokhranilishche resr Russia 53 K5
Kuyeda Russia 51 R4
Kuye He r. China 95 G4
Kuygan Kazakh. 102 D2
Küysu China 94 C3
Kuytun China 98 D3
Kuytun Russia 88 I2
Kuytun He r. China 98 C3
Kuyucak Turkey 69 M6
Kuyus Russia 98 D2
Kuyu Tingni Nicaragua 166 [inset] J6
Kuze Japan 92 C3
Kuzino Russia 51 R4
Kuzitrin r. AK U.S.A. 148 F2
Kuznechnoye Russia 55 P6
Kuznetsk Russia 53 J5
Kuznetsovo Russia 90 E3
Kuznetsovs'k Ukr. 53 E6
Kuzovatovo Russia 53 J5
Kuzuryū-gawa r. Japan 92 C2
Kuzuryū-ko resr Japan 92 C3
Kuzuu Japan 93 F2
Kvænangen sea chan. Norway 54 L1
Kvaløya i. Norway 54 K2
Kvalsund Norway 54 M1
Kvarnerić sea chan. Croatia 68 F2
Kvichak AK U.S.A. 148 H4
Kvichak r. AK U.S.A. 148 H4
Kvichak Bay AK U.S.A. 148 H4
Kvitøya ice feature Svalbard 76 E2
Kwa r. Dem. Rep. Congo see Kasaï
Kwabhaca S. Africa see Mount Frere
Kwadelen atoll Marshall Is see Kwajalein
KwaDukuza S. Africa 125 J5
Kwajalein atoll Marshall Is 186 H5
Kwajok South Sudan 121 F4
Kwala Sumatra Indon. 84 B2
Kwale Nigeria 120 D4
KwaMashu S. Africa 125 J5
KwaMhlanga S. Africa 125 I3
Kwa Mtoro Tanz. 123 D4
Kwandang Celebes Indon. 83 B2
Kwangchow China see Guangzhou
Kwangju S. Korea see Gwangju
Kwangsi Chuang Autonomous Region aut. reg. China see Guangxi Zhuangzu Zizhiqu
Kwangtung prov. China see Guangdong
Kwanmo-bong mt. N. Korea 90 C4
KwaNobuhle S. Africa 125 G7
KwaNojoli S. Africa 125 G7
Kwanonqubela S. Africa 125 H7
KwaNonzame S. Africa 124 G6
Kwanza r. Angola see Cuanza
Kwatarkwashi Nigeria 120 D3
Kwatinidubu S. Africa 125 H7
KwaZamokuhle S. Africa 125 I4
KwaZamukucinga S. Africa 124 G7
Kwazamuxolo S. Africa 124 G6
KwaZanele S. Africa 125 I4
KwaZulu-Natal prov. S. Africa 125 J5
Kweichow prov. China see Guizhou
Kweiyang China see Guiyang
Kwekwe Zimbabwe 123 C5
Kweneng admin. dist. Botswana 124 G2
Kwenge r. Dem. Rep. Congo 123 B4
Kwetabohigan r. Canada 152 E4
Kwethluk AK U.S.A. 148 G3
Kwethluk r. AK U.S.A. 148 G3
Kwezi-Naledi S. Africa 125 H6
Kwidzyn Poland 57 Q4
Kwigillingok AK U.S.A. 148 G4
Kwiguk AK U.S.A. 148 F3
Kwikila P.N.G. 81 L8
Kwilu r. Angola/Dem. Rep. Congo 123 B4
Kwo Chau Kwan To is H.K. China see Ninepin Group
Kwoka mt. Indon. 81 I7
Kyabra Australia 137 C5
Kyabram Australia 138 B6
Kyadet Myanmar 86 A2
Kyaikkami Myanmar 86 B3
Kyaiklat Myanmar 86 A3
Kyaikto Myanmar 86 B3
Kyakhta Russia 94 F1
Kyalite Australia 138 A5
Kyancutta Australia 135 F8
Kyangin Myanmar 86 B3
Kyangngoin China 99 F7
Kyaukhnyat Myanmar 86 B3
Kyaukkyi Myanmar 86 B3
Kyaukme Myanmar 86 B2
Kyaukpadaung Myanmar 86 A2
Kyaukpyu Myanmar 86 A3
Kyaukse Myanmar 86 B2
Kyauktaw Myanmar 86 A2
Kyaunggon Myanmar 86 A3
Kybartai Lith. 55 M9
Kyebogyi Myanmar 86 B3
Kyêbxang Co l. China 105 G2
Kyeikdon Myanmar 86 B3
Kyeikywa Myanmar 86 B3
Kyeintali Myanmar 86 A3
Kyela Tanz. 123 D4
Kyelang India 104 D2
Kyidaunggan Myanmar 86 B3
Kyikug China 94 E4
Kyiv Ukr. see Kiev
Kyivs'ke Vodoskhovyshche resr Ukr. 53 F6
Kyklades is Greece see Cyclades
Kyle Canada 151 I5
Kyle of Lochalsh U.K. 60 D3
Kyll r. Germany 62 G5
Kyllini mt. Greece 69 J6
Kymi Greece 69 K5
Kymis, Akra pt Greece see Kymis, Akrotirio
Kymis, Akrotirio pt Greece 69 K5
Kynazhegubskoye Vodokhranilishche l. Russia 54 R3
Kyneton Australia 138 B6
Kynuna Australia 136 C4
Kyoga, Lake Uganda 122 D3
Kyōga-dake mt. Japan 92 C2
Kyōga-dake mt. Japan 93 D3
Kyōga-misaki pt Japan 92 B3
Kyogle Australia 138 F2
Kyonan Japan 93 F3
Kyong Myanmar 86 B2
Kyonpyaw Myanmar 86 A3
Kyōtanabe Japan 92 B4
Kyōtanba Japan 92 B3
Kyōtango Japan 92 B3
Kyōto Japan 92 B4
Kyōto pref. Japan 92 B3
Kyōwa Japan 93 G2
Kyparissia Greece 69 I6
Kypros country Asia see Cyprus
Kyra Russia 95 H1
Kyra Panagia i. Greece 69 K5
Kyrenia Cyprus 107 A2
Kyrenia Mountains Cyprus see Pentadaktylos Range
Kyrgyz Ala-Too mts Kazakh./Kyrg. see Kirghiz Range
Kyrgyzstan country Asia 102 D3
Kyritz Germany 63 M2
Kyrksæterøra Norway 54 F5
Kyrta Russia 51 R3
Kyssa Russia 52 J2
Kytalyktakh Russia 77 O3
Kythira i. Greece 69 J6
Kythnos i. Greece 69 K6
Kyunglung China 99 C7
Kyunhla Myanmar 86 A2
Kyuquot Canada 150 E5
Kyurdamir Azer. see Kürdämir
Kyūshū i. Japan 91 C7
Kyushu-Palau Ridge sea feature N. Pacific Ocean 186 F4
Kyustendil Bulg. 69 J3
Kywebwe Myanmar 86 B3
Kywong Australia 138 C5
Kyyev Ukr. see Kiev
Kyyiv Ukr. see Kiev
Kyyjärvi Fin. 54 N5
Kyzyl Russia 102 H1
Kyzylagash Kazakh. 98 B3
Kyzyl-Art, Pereval pass Kyrg./Tajik. see Kyzylart Pass
Kyzylart Pass Kyrg./Tajik. 111 I2
Kyzyl-Burun Azer. see Siyäzän
Kyzylkesek Kazakh. 98 C3
Kyzyl-Khaya Russia 94 B1
Kyzyl-Kiya Kyrg. see Kyzyl-Kyya
Kyzylkum, Peski des. Kazakh./Uzbek. see Kyzylkum Desert
Kyzylkum Desert Kazakh./Uzbek. 102 B3
Kyzyl-Kyya Kyrg. 102 D3
Kyzyl-Mazhalyk Russia 102 H1
Kyzylorda Kazakh. 102 C3
Kyzylrabot Tajik. see Qizilrabot
Kyzylsay Kazakh. 113 I2
Kyzyl-Suu Kyrg. 98 B4
Kyzylysor Kazakh. 113 H1
Kyzylzhar Kazakh. 102 C2
Kzyl-Dzhar Kazakh. see Kyzylzhar
Kzyl-Orda Kazakh. see Kyzylorda
Kzyltu Kazakh. see Kishkenekol'

L

Laagri Estonia 55 N7
La Aguja Mex. 166 C4
La Amistad, Parque Internacional nat. park Costa Rica/Panama 166 [inset] J7
Laamu Atoll Maldives see Hahdhunmathi
La Angostura, Presa de resr Mex. 167 G6
Laanila Fin. 54 O2
La Ardilla, Cerro mt. Mex. 166 E4
Laascaanood Somalia 122 E3
Laasqoray Somalia 122 E2

▶Laâyoune W. Sahara 120 B2
Capital of Western Sahara.

La Babia Mex. 166 E2
La Baie Canada 153 H4
Labala Indon. 83 B5
La Banda Arg. 178 D3
Labang Sarawak Malaysia 85 F2
La Barge WY U.S.A. 156 F4
Labasa Fiji 133 H3
La Baule-Escoublac France 66 C3
Labe r. Germany see Elbe
Labé Guinea 120 B3
La Belle FL U.S.A. 163 D7
Labengke i. Indon. 83 B3
Laberge, Lake Canada 149 N3
Labi Brunei 85 F1
Labian, Tanjung pt Malaysia 85 G1
La Biche, Lac l. Canada 151 H4
Labinsk Russia 113 F1
Labis Malaysia 84 C2
La Biznaga Mex. 166 C2
Labo Luzon Phil. 82 C3
Labobo i. Indon. 83 B3
La Boquilla Mex. 166 D3
Labouheyre France 66 D4
Laboulaye Arg. 178 D4
Labozhskoye Russia 52 L2
Labrador reg. Canada 153 J3
Labrador City Canada 153 I3
Labrador Sea Canada/Greenland 147 M3
Labrang China see Xiahe
Lábrea Brazil 176 F5
Labuan Malaysia 85 F1
Labuan i. Malaysia 85 F1
Labuan state Malaysia 85 F1
Labuanbajo Celebes Indon. 83 B3
Labudalin China see Ergun
La Bufa, Cerro mt. Mex. 166 E5
Labuhan Java Indon. 84 D4
Labuhanbajo Flores Indon. 83 A5
Labuhanbilik Sumatra Indon. 84 C2
Labuhanhaji Sumatra Indon. 84 B2
Labuhanmeringgai Sumatra Indon. 84 D4
Labuhanruku Sumatra Indon. 84 B2
Labuk r. Malaysia 85 G1
Labuk, Teluk b. Malaysia 85 G1
Labuna Moluccas Indon. 83 C3
Labutta Myanmar 86 A3
Labyrinth, Lake salt flat Australia 137 A6
Labytnangi Russia 76 H3
Laç Albania 69 H4
La Cadena Mex. 166 D3
Lac-Allard Canada 153 J4
La Calle Alg. see El Kala
Lacandón, Parque Nacional nat. park Guat. 167 H5
La Cañiza Spain see A Cañiza
Lacantún r. Mex. 167 H5
La Capelle France 62 D5
La Carlota Arg. 178 D4
La Carlota Negros Phil. 82 C4
La Carolina Spain 67 E4
Lăcăuţi, Vârful mt. Romania 69 L2
Laccadive, Minicoy and Amindivi Islands union terr. India see Lakshadweep
Laccadive Islands is India see Lakshadweep
Laccadive Sea Indian Ocean 103 D9
Lac du Bonnet Canada 151 L5
Lacedaemon Greece see Sparti
La Ceiba Hond. 166 [inset] I6
Lacepede Bay Australia 137 B8
Lacepede Islands Australia 134 C4
Lacha, Ozero l. Russia 52 H3
La Chaux-de-Fonds Switz. 66 H3
Lachendorf Germany 63 K2
Lachine MI U.S.A. 164 D1

▶Lachlan r. Australia 138 A5
5th longest river in Oceania.

La Chorrera Panama 166 [inset] K7
Lachute Canada 152 G5
Laçın Azer. 113 G3
La Ciotat France 66 G5
La Ciudad Mex. 166 D4
Lac La Biche Canada 151 I4
Lac la Martre Canada see Whatî
Lacolle Canada 165 I1
La Colorada Sonora Mex. 166 C2
La Colorada Zacatecas Mex. 161 C8
Lacombe Canada 150 H4
La Concepción Panama 166 [inset] J7
La Concordia Mex. 167 G5
Laconi Sardinia Italy 68 C5
Laconia NH U.S.A. 165 J2
La Corey Canada 151 I4
La Coruña Spain see A Coruña
La Crete Canada 150 G3
La Crosse KS U.S.A. 160 D4
La Crosse VA U.S.A. 165 F5
La Crosse WI U.S.A. 160 F3
La Cruz Costa Rica 166 [inset] I7
La Cruz Chihuahua Mex. 166 D3
La Cruz Sinaloa Mex. 166 D4
La Cruz Tamaulipas Mex. 167 F3
La Cruz, Cerro mt. Mex. 167 E5
La Cruz de Río Grande Nicaragua 166 [inset] I6
La Cuesta Mex. 166 E2
La Cygne KS U.S.A. 160 E4
Lada, Teluk b. Indon. 84 D4
Ladainha Brazil 179 C2
Ladakh reg. India/Pak. 104 D2
Ladakh Range mts India 104 D2
Ladang, Ko i. Thai. 87 B6
La Demajagua Cuba 163 D8
La Democracia Guat. 167 H6
Ladik Turkey 112 D2
Lādīz Iran 111 F4
Ladnun India 104 C4

▶Ladoga, Lake Russia 52 F3
2nd largest lake in Europe.

Ladong China 97 F3
Ladozhskoye Ozero l. Russia see Ladoga, Lake
Ladrone Islands China see Wanshan Qundao
Ladrones terr. N. Pacific Ocean see Northern Mariana Islands
Ladrones, Islas is Panama 166 [inset] J8
Ladu mt. India 105 H4
Ladue r. Canada/U.S.A. 149 L3
La Dura Mex. 166 C2
Ladva-Vetka Russia 52 G3
Ladybank U.K. 60 F4
Ladybrand S. Africa 125 H5
Lady Frere S. Africa 125 H6
Lady Grey S. Africa 125 H6
Ladysmith S. Africa 125 I5
Ladysmith WI U.S.A. 160 F2
Ladzhanurges Georgia see Lajanurp'ekhi
Lae P.N.G. 81 L8
Laem Ngop Thai. 87 C4
Lærdalsøyri Norway 55 E6
La Esmeralda Bol. 176 F8
Læsø i. Denmark 55 G8
La Esperanza Hond. 166 [inset] H6
Lafayette Alg. see Bougaa
La Fayette AL U.S.A. 163 C5
Lafayette IN U.S.A. 164 B3
Lafayette LA U.S.A. 161 E6
Lafayette TN U.S.A. 164 B5
Lafé Cuba 163 C8
La Fère France 62 D5
Laferte r. Canada 150 G2
La Ferté-Gaucher France 62 D6
La Ferté-Milon France 62 D5
La Ferté-sous-Jouarre France 62 D6
Lafia Nigeria 120 D4
Lafiagi Nigeria 120 D4
Laflamme r. Canada 152 F4
Lafleche Canada 151 J5
La Flèche France 66 D3
LaFollette TN U.S.A. 164 C5
La Forest, Lac l. Canada 153 H3
Laforge Canada 153 G3
Laforge r. Canada 153 G3
Lāft Iran 110 D5
Laful India 87 A6
La Galissonnière, Lac l. Canada 153 J4

▶La Galite i. Tunisia 68 C6
Most northerly point of Africa.

La Gallega Mex. 166 D3
Lagan' Russia 53 J7
Lagan r. U.K. 61 G3
Lagarto Brazil 177 K6
Lage Germany 63 I3
Lågen r. Norway 55 G7
Lages Brazil 179 A4
Lage Vaart canal Neth. 62 F2
Lagg U.K. 60 D5
Laggan U.K. 60 E3
Laghouat Alg. 64 E5
Lagkor Co salt l. China 99 D6
La Gloria Mex. 161 D7
Lago Agrio Ecuador see Nueva Loja
Lagoa Santa Brazil 179 C2
Lagoa Vermelha Brazil 179 A5
Lagodekhi Georgia 113 G2
Lagolândia Brazil 179 A1
La Gomera i. Canary Is 120 B2
La Gomera Guat. 167 H6
Lagong i. Indon. 85 E2
Lagonoy Gulf Luzon Phil. 82 C3

▶Lagos Nigeria 120 D4
Former capital of Nigeria. Most populous city in Africa.

Lagos Port. 67 B5
Lagosa Tanz. 123 C4
Lagos de Moreno Mex. 167 E4
La Grande r. Canada 152 F3
La Grande OR U.S.A. 156 D3
La Grande 3, Réservoir resr Canada 152 G3
La Grande 4, Réservoir resr Canada 153 G3
La Grange Australia 134 C4
La Grange CA U.S.A. 158 C3
La Grange GA U.S.A. 163 C5
Lagrange IN U.S.A. 164 C3
La Grange KY U.S.A. 162 C4
La Grange TX U.S.A. 161 D6
La Gran Sabana plat. Venez. 176 F2
La Grita Venez. 176 D2
Laguna Brazil 179 A5
Laguna, Picacho de la mt. Mex. 166 C4
Laguna Dam Arizona/California U.S.A. 159 F5
Laguna de Perlas Nicaragua 166 [inset] J6
Laguna de Temascal, Parque Natural nature res. Mex. 167 F5
Laguna Lachua, Parque Nacional nat. park Guat. 167 H6
Laguna Mountains CA U.S.A. 158 E5
Laguna Ojo de Liebre, Parque Natural de la nature res. Mex. 166 B3
Lagunas Chile 178 C2
Laguna San Rafael, Parque Nacional nat. park Chile 178 B7
Lagunas de Catemaco, Parque Natural nature res. Mex. 167 G5
Lagunas de Chacahua, Parque Nacional nat. park Mex. 167 F6
Lagunas de Montebello, Parque Nacional nat. park Mex. 167 H5
Laha China 95 K1
La Habana Cuba see Havana
La Habra CA U.S.A. 158 E5
Lahad Datu Sabah Malaysia 85 G1
Lahad Datu, Teluk b. Malaysia 85 G1
Lahar India 99 B8
Laharpur India 104 E4
Lahat Sumatra Indon. 84 C3
Lahe Myanmar 86 A1
Lahemaa rahvuspark nat. park Estonia 55 N7
Lahewa Sumatra Indon. 84 B2
Laḥij Yemen 108 F7
Lāhījān Iran 110 C2
Lahn r. Germany 63 H4
Lahnstein Germany 63 H4
Laholm Sweden 55 H8
Lahontan Reservoir NV U.S.A. 158 D2
Lahore Pak. 111 I4
Lahri Pak. 111 H4
Lāhrūd Iran 110 B2
Lahti Fin. 55 N6
La Huerta Mex. 166 D5
Laï Chad 121 E4
Lai'an China 97 H1
Laibach Slovenia see Ljubljana
Laibin China 97 F4
Laidley Australia 138 F1
Laifeng China 97 F2
L'Aigle France 66 E2
Laihia Fin. 54 M5
Lai-hka Myanmar 86 B2
Lai-Hsak Myanmar 86 B2
Laimakuri India 105 H4
Laimos, Akrotirio pt Greece 69 J5
Laingsburg S. Africa 124 E7
Laingsburg MI U.S.A. 164 C2
Lainioälven r. Sweden 54 M3
Lair KY U.S.A. 164 C4
Lairg U.K. 60 E2
Lais Sumatra Indon. 84 C3
Lais Mindanao Phil. 82 D5
La Isabela Cuba 163 D8
Laishevo Russia 52 K5
Laishui China 95 H4
Laitila Fin. 55 L6
Laives Italy 68 D1
Laiwu China 95 I4
Laiwui Moluccas Indon. 83 C3
Laixi China 95 J4
Laiyang China 95 J4
Laiyuan China 95 H4
Laizhou China 95 I4
Laizhou Wan b. China 95 I4
Lajamanu Australia 134 E4
Lajanurp'ekhi Georgia 113 F2
Lajeado Brazil 179 A5
Lajes Brazil 177 K5
La Joya Mex. 166 D3
La Junta Mex. 166 D2
La Junta CO U.S.A. 160 C4
Lakadiya India 104 B5
La Kagera, Parc National de nat. park Rwanda see Akagera National Park
L'Akagera, Parc National de nat. park Rwanda see Akagera National Park
Lake KY U.S.A. 164 D5
Lake Andes SD U.S.A. 160 D3
Lakeba i. Fiji 133 I3
Lake Bardawil Reserve nature res. Egypt 107 A4
Lake Bolac Australia 138 A6
Lake Butler FL U.S.A. 163 D6
Lake Cargelligo Australia 138 C4
Lake Cathie Australia 138 F3
Lake Charles LA U.S.A. 161 E6
Lake City CO U.S.A. 159 J3
Lake City FL U.S.A. 163 D6
Lake City MI U.S.A. 164 C1
Lake Clark National Park and Preserve AK U.S.A. 148 I3
Lake Clear NY U.S.A. 165 H1
Lake District National Park U.K. 58 D4
Lake Eildon National Park Australia 138 B6
Lake Elsinore CA U.S.A. 158 E5
Lakefield Australia 136 D2
Lakefield Canada 165 F1
Lake Forest IL U.S.A. 164 B2
Lake Gairdner National Park Australia 137 B7
Lake Geneva WI U.S.A. 160 F3
Lake George MI U.S.A. 164 C2
Lake George NY U.S.A. 165 I2
Lake Grace Australia 135 B8
Lake Harbour Canada see Kimmirut
Lake Havasu City AZ U.S.A. 159 F4
Lakehurst NJ U.S.A. 165 H3
Lake Isabella CA U.S.A. 158 D4
Lake Jackson TX U.S.A. 161 E6
Lake King Australia 135 B8
Lake Kopiago P.N.G. 81 K8
Lakeland FL U.S.A. 163 D7
Lakeland GA U.S.A. 163 D6
Lake Louise Canada 150 G5
Lakemba i. Fiji see Lakeba
Lake Mills IA U.S.A. 160 E3
Lake Minchumina AK U.S.A. 148 I3
Lake Nash Australia 136 B4
Lake Odessa MI U.S.A. 164 C2
Lake Paringa N.Z. 139 B6
Lake Placid FL U.S.A. 163 D7
Lake Placid NY U.S.A. 165 I1
Lake Pleasant NY U.S.A. 165 H2
Lakeport CA U.S.A. 158 B2
Lakeport MI U.S.A. 164 D2
Lake Providence LA U.S.A. 161 F5
Lake Range mts NV U.S.A. 158 D1
Lake River Canada 152 E3
Lakes Entrance Australia 138 D6
Lakeside AZ U.S.A. 159 I4
Lakeside VA U.S.A. 165 G5
Lakes of Ounianga tourist site Chad 121 F3
Lake Superior National Marine Conservation Area park Canada 152 D4
Lake Tabourie Australia 138 E5
Lake Tekapo N.Z. 139 C7
Lake Torrens National Park Australia 137 B6
Lakeview MI U.S.A. 164 C2
Lakeview OH U.S.A. 164 D3
Lakeview OR U.S.A. 156 C4

Lake Village *AR* U.S.A. **161** F5
Lake Wales *FL* U.S.A. **163** D7
Lakewood *CO* U.S.A. **156** G5
Lakewood *NJ* U.S.A. **165** H3
Lakewood *NY* U.S.A. **164** F2
Lakewood *OH* U.S.A. **164** E3
Lake Worth *FL* U.S.A. **163** D7
Lakha India **104** B4
Lakhdenpokh'ya Russia **54** Q6
Lakhimpur *Assam* India *see* **North Lakhimpur**
Lakhimpur *Uttar Prad.* India **104** E4
Lakhisarai India **105** F4
Lakhish, Naḥal *r.* Israel **107** B4
Lakhnadon India **104** D5
Lakhpat India **104** B5
Lakhtar India **104** B5
Lakin *KS* U.S.A. **160** C4
Lakitusaki *r.* Canada **152** E3
Lakki Marwat Pak. **111** H3
Lakohembi *Sumba* Indon. **83** B5
Lakonikos Kolpos *b.* Greece **69** J6
Lakor *i. Moluccas* Indon. **83** D5
Lakota Côte d'Ivoire **120** C4
Lakota *ND* U.S.A. **160** D1
Laksefjorden *sea chan.* Norway **54** O1
Lakselv Norway **54** N1
Lakshadweep India **106** B4
Lakshadweep *union terr.* India **106** B4
Lakshettipet India **106** C2
Lakshmipur Bangl. **105** G5
Laksmipur Bangl. *see* **Lakshmipur**
Lala *Mindanao* Phil. **82** C5
Lalaghat India **105** H4
Lalbara India **106** D1
L'Alcora Spain **67** F3
Lāleh Zār, Kūh-e *mt.* Iran **110** E4
Lalganj India **105** F4
Lālī Iran **110** C3
La Libertad El Salvador **167** H6
La Libertad Guat. **167** H5
La Libertad Nicaragua **166** [inset] I6
La Ligua Chile **178** B4
Laliki *Moluccas* Indon. **83** C4
Lalimboee *Celebes* Indon. **83** B3
Lalin China **90** B3
Lalín Spain **67** B2
La Línea de la Concepción Spain **67** D5
Lalin He *r.* China **90** B3
Lalitpur India **104** D4
Lalitpur Nepal *see* **Patan**
Lal-Lo *Luzon* Phil. **82** C2
Lalmanirhat Bangl. *see* **Lalmonirhat**
Lalmonirhat Bangl. **105** G4
Laloa *Celebes* Indon. **83** B3
La Loche Canada **151** I3
La Loche, Lac *l.* Canada **151** I3
La Louvière Belgium **62** E4
Lal'sk Russia **52** J3
Laluin *i. Moluccas* Indon. **83** C3
Lalung La *pass* China **99** D7
Lama Bangl. **105** H5
La Macarena, Parque Nacional *nat. park* Col. **176** D3
La Maddalena *Sardinia* Italy **68** C4
Lamadian China **95** K2
Lamadianzi China *see* **Lamadian**
Lamag *Sabah* Malaysia **85** G1
Lamakera Indon. **83** B5
La Malbaie Canada **153** H5
La Malinche, Parque Nacional *nat. park* Mex. **167** F5
La Mancha Mex. **166** E3
La Mancha *reg.* Spain **67** E4
La Manche *strait* France/U.K. *see* **English Channel**
La Máquina Mex. **166** D2
Lamar *CO* U.S.A. **160** C4
Lamar *MO* U.S.A. **161** E4
La Marmora, Punta *mt. Sardinia* Italy **68** C5
La Marque *TX* U.S.A. **161** E6
La Martre, Lac *l.* Canada **150** G2
Lamas *r.* Turkey **107** B1
La Masica Hond. **166** [inset] I6
La Mauricie, Parc National de *nat. park* Canada **153** G5
Lamawan China **95** G3
Lambaréné Gabon **122** B4
Lambasa Fiji *see* **Labasa**
Lambasina *i.* Indon. **83** B4
Lambayeque Peru **176** C5
Lambay Island Ireland **61** G4
Lambeng *Kalimantan* Indon. **85** F3
Lambert *atoll* Marshall Is *see* **Ailinglaplap**

▶**Lambert Glacier** Antarctica **188** E2
Largest glacier in the world.

Lambert's Bay S. Africa **124** D7
Lambeth Canada **164** E2
Lambi India **104** C3
Lambourn Downs *hills* U.K. **59** F7
Lame *Sumatra* Indon. **84** B2
Lamego Port. **67** C3
Lamèque, Île *i.* Canada **153** I5
La Merced Arg. **178** C3
La Merced Peru **176** C6
Lāmerd Iran **110** D5
Lameroo Australia **137** C7
La Mesa *CA* U.S.A. **158** E5
Lamesa *TX* U.S.A. **161** C5
Lamia Greece **69** J5
Lamigan Point *Mindanao* Phil. **82** D5
Lamington National Park Australia **138** F2
La Misa Mex. **166** C2
La Misión Mex. **158** E5
Lamitan Phil. **82** C5
Lamlam *Papua* Indon. **83** D3
Lamma Island *H.K.* China **97** [inset]
Lammerlaw Range *mts* N.Z. **139** B7
Lammermuir Hills U.K. **60** G5
Lammhult Sweden **55** I8
Lammi Fin. **55** N6
Lamon Bay Phil. **82** C3
Lamongan *Java* Indon. **85** F4
Lamont *CA* U.S.A. **158** D4
Lamont *WY* U.S.A. **156** G4
La Montaña de Covadonga, Parque Nacional de *nat. park* Spain *see* **Picos de Europa, Parque Nacional de los**
La Mora Mex. **166** E3
La Morita *Chihuahua* Mex. **166** D2
La Morita *Coahuila* Mex. **166** E2
Lamotrek *atoll* Micronesia **81** L5
LaMoure *ND* U.S.A. **160** D2
Lampang Thai. **86** B3
Lam Pao, Ang Kep Nam Thai. **86** C3
Lampasas *TX* U.S.A. **161** D6
Lampazos Mex. **167** E3
Lampedusa, Isola di *i. Sicily* Italy **68** E7
Lampeter U.K. **59** C6
Lamphun Thai. **86** B3
Lampsacus Turkey *see* **Lâpseki**
Lampung *prov.* Indon. **84** D4
Lampung, Teluk *b.* Indon. **84** D4
Lam Tin *H.K.* China **97** [inset]
Lamu Kenya **122** E4
Lamu Myanmar **86** A3
Lan, Loi *mt.* Myanmar/Thai. **86** B3
Lāna'i *i. HI* U.S.A. **157** [inset]
Lāna'i City *HI* U.S.A. **157** [inset]
Lanao, Lake *Mindanao* Phil. **82** D5
Lanark Canada **165** G1
Lanark U.K. **60** F5
Lanas *Sabah* Malaysia **85** G1
Lanbi Kyun *i.* Myanmar **87** B5
Lanboyan Point *Mindanao* Phil. **82** C4
Lancang China **96** C4
Lancang Jiang *r.* China *see* **Mekong**
Lancaster Canada **165** H1
Lancaster U.K. **58** E4
Lancaster *CA* U.S.A. **158** D4
Lancaster *KY* U.S.A. **164** C5
Lancaster *MO* U.S.A. **160** E3
Lancaster *NH* U.S.A. **165** J1
Lancaster *OH* U.S.A. **164** D4
Lancaster *PA* U.S.A. **165** G3
Lancaster *SC* U.S.A. **163** D5
Lancaster *VA* U.S.A. **165** G5
Lancaster *WI* U.S.A. **160** F3
Lancaster Canal U.K. **58** E5
Lancaster Sound *strait* Canada **147** J2
Lancun China **95** J4
Landak *r.* Indon. **85** E3
Landana Angola *see* **Cacongo**
Landau an der Isar Germany **63** M6
Landau in der Pfalz Germany **63** I5
Landeck Austria **57** M7
Landeh Iran **110** C4
Lander *watercourse* Australia **134** E5
Lander *WY* U.S.A. **156** F4
Landesbergen Germany **63** J2
Landfall Island India **87** A4
Landhi Pak. **111** G5
Landik, Gunung *mt.* Indon. **84** C3
Landis Canada **151** I4
Landor Australia **135** B6
Landsberg Poland *see* **Gorzów Wielkopolski**
Landsberg am Lech Germany **57** M6
Land's End *pt* U.K. **59** B8
Landshut Germany **63** M6
Landskrona Sweden **55** H9
Landstuhl Germany **63** H5
Land Wursten *reg.* Germany **63** I1
Lanesborough Ireland **61** E4
Lanfeng China *see* **Lankao**
Lang, Nam *r.* Myanmar **86** B2
La'nga Co *l.* China **99** C7
Langao China **97** F1
Langar Afgh. **111** H3
Langara *Celebes* Indon. **83** B4
Langberg *mts* S. Africa **124** F5
Langdon *ND* U.S.A. **160** D1
Langeac France **66** F4
Langeberg *mts* S. Africa **124** D7
Langeland *i.* Denmark **55** G9
Längelmäki Fin. **55** N6
Langelsheim Germany **63** K3
Langen Germany **63** I1
Langenburg Canada **151** K5
Langenhagen Germany **63** J2
Langenhahn Germany **63** H4
Langenlonsheim Germany **63** H5
Langenthal Switz. **66** H3
Langenweddingen Germany **63** L2
Langeoog Germany **63** H1
Langesund Norway **55** F7
Langfang China **95** I4
Langgam *Sumatra* Indon. **84** C2
Langgapayung *Sumatra* Indon. **84** C2
Langgar China **99** F7
Langgöns Germany **63** I4
Langholm U.K. **60** G5
Langjan Nature Reserve S. Africa **125** I2
Langjökull *ice cap* Iceland **54** [inset 1]
Langka *Sumatra* Indon. **84** B1
Langkawi *i.* Malaysia **84** B1
Langkesi, Kepulauan *is* Indon. **83** C4
Lang Kha Toek, Khao *mt.* Thai. **87** B5
Langklip S. Africa **124** E5
Langkon *Sabah* Malaysia **85** G1
Langley Canada **150** F5
Langley *KY* U.S.A. **164** D5
Langlo Crossing Australia **137** D5
Langmusi China **94** E5
Langong, Xé *r.* Laos **86** D3
Langøya *i.* Norway **54** I2
Langphu *mt.* China **105** F3
Langport U.K. **59** E7
Langqên Zangbo *r.* China **99** B7
Langqi China **97** H3
Langres France **66** G3
Langres, Plateau de France **66** G3
Langru China **99** B5
Langsa *Sumatra* Indon. **84** B1
Langsa, Teluk *b.* Indon. **84** B1
Långsele Sweden **54** J5
Langshan China **95** F3
Lang Shan *mts* China **95** F3
Lang Sơn Vietnam **86** D2
Langtang National Park Nepal **105** F3
Langtao Myanmar **86** B1
Langting India **105** H4
Langtoft U.K. **58** G4
Langtoutun China **95** J2
Langtry *TX* U.S.A. **161** C6
Languan China *see* **Lantian**
Languedoc *reg.* France **66** E5
Langundu, Tanjung *pt Sumbawa* Indon. **85** G5
Långvattnet Sweden **54** L4
Langwedel Germany **63** J2
Langxi China **97** H2
Langya Shan *mt.* China **95** H4
Langzhong China **96** E2
Lanigan Canada **151** J5
Lanín, Parque Nacional *nat. park* Arg. **178** B5
Lanín, Volcán *vol.* Arg./Chile **178** B5
Lanjak, Bukit *mt.* Malaysia **85** E2
Lanji India **104** E5
Lanka *country* Asia *see* **Sri Lanka**
Lankao China **95** H5
Länkäran Azer. **113** H3
Lannion France **66** C2
La Noria Mex. **166** D4
Lanping China **96** C3
Lansån Sweden **54** M3
L'Anse *MI* U.S.A. **160** F2
Lanshan China **97** G3

▶**Lansing** *MI* U.S.A. **164** C2
Capital of Michigan.

Lanta, Ko *i.* Thai. **87** B6
Lantau Island *H.K.* China **97** [inset]
Lantau Peak *hill H.K.* China **97** [inset]
Lantian China **95** G5
Lantoto National Park South Sudan **122** D3
Lanuza Bay *Mindanao* Phil. **82** D4
Lanxi *Heilong.* China **90** B3
Lanxi *Zhejiang* China **97** H2
Lanxian China **95** G4
Lan Yu *i.* Taiwan **97** I4
Lanzarote *i.* Canary Is **120** B2
Lanzhou China **94** E4
Lanzi China **95** J2
Laoag City *Luzon* Phil. **82** C2
Laoang Phil. **82** D3
Laobie Shan *mts* China **96** C4
Laobu China **97** F3
Lao Cai Vietnam **86** C2
Laodicea Syria *see* **Latakia**
Laodicea Turkey *see* **Denizli**
Laodicea ad Lycum Turkey *see* **Denizli**
Laodicea ad Mare Syria *see* **Latakia**
Laofengkou China **98** C3
Laoha He *r.* China **95** J3
Laohekou China **97** F1
Laohutun China **95** J4
Laojie China *see* **Yongping**
Laojunmiao China **94** D4
Lao Ling *mts* China **90** B4
Lao Mangnai China **99** E5
Laon France **62** D5
Laoqitai China **94** B3
La Oroya Peru **176** C6
Laos *country* Asia **86** C3
Laoshan China **95** J4
Laoshawan China **98** D3
Laotieshan Shuidao *sea chan.* China *see* **Bohai Haixia**
Laotougou China **90** C4
Laotu Dingzi *hill* China **90** B4
Laowohi *pass* India *see* **Khardung La**
Laoximiao China **94** E3
Laoyacheng China **94** E4
Laoye Ling *mts Heilongjiang/Jilin* China **90** C4
Laoye Ling *mts Jilin* China **90** B3
Laoyemiao China **94** C2
Lapa Brazil **179** A4
Lapac *i.* Phil. **82** C5
La Palma *i.* Canary Is **120** B2
La Palma Guat. **167** H5
La Palma Panama **166** [inset] K7
La Palma *AZ* U.S.A. **159** H5
La Palma del Condado Spain **67** C5
La Panza Range *mts CA* U.S.A. **158** C4
La Paragua Venez. **176** F2
Laparan *i.* Phil. **82** B5
La Parilla Mex. **161** B8
La Paya, Parque Nacional *nat. park* Col. **176** D3
La Paz Arg. **178** E4

▶**La Paz** Bol. **176** E7
Joint capital (with Sucre) of Bolivia.

La Paz Hond. **166** [inset] I6
La Paz Mex. **166** C3
La Paz, Bahía *b.* Mex. **166** C3
La Paz Centro Nicaragua **166** [inset] I6
La Pedrera Col. **176** E4
Lapeer *MI* U.S.A. **164** D2
La Perla Mex. **166** D2
La Pérouse Strait Japan/Russia **90** F3
La Pesca Mex. **161** D8
La Piedad Mex. **166** E4
Lapinig *Samar* Phil. **82** D3
Lapinlahti Fin. **54** O5
La Pintada Panama **166** [inset] J7
Lapithos Cyprus **107** A2
Laplace *LA* U.S.A. **167** H2
Lap Lae Thai. **86** C3
La Plant *SD* U.S.A. **160** C2
La Plata Arg. **178** E4
La Plata *MD* U.S.A. **165** G4
La Plata *MO* U.S.A. **160** E3
La Plata, Isla *i.* Ecuador **176** B4

▶**La Plata, Río de** *sea chan.* Arg./Uruguay **178** E4
Part of the Río de la Plata - Paraná, 2nd longest river in South America and 9th in the world.

La Plonge, Lac *l.* Canada **151** J4
Lapmežciems Latvia **55** M8
La Pola Spain **67** D2
La Pola Siero Spain **67** D2
Lapominka Russia **52** I2
La Porte *IN* U.S.A. **164** B3
Laporte *PA* U.S.A. **165** G3
Laporte, Mount Canada **149** P3
Laposo, Bukit *mt.* Indon. **83** A4
La Potherie, Lac *l.* Canada **153** G2
La Poza Grande Mex. **166** B3
Lappajärvi Fin. **54** M5
Lappajärvi *l.* Fin. **54** M5
Lappeenranta Fin. **55** P6
Lappersdorf Germany **63** M5
Lappi Fin. **55** L6
Lappland *reg.* Europe **54** K3
La Pryor *TX* U.S.A. **161** D6
Lâpseki Turkey **69** L4
Laptevo Russia *see* **Yasnogorsk**
Laptev Sea Russia **77** N2
Lapua Fin. **54** M5
Lapuko *Celebes* Indon. **83** B4
Lapu-Lapu Phil. **82** C4
Lapurdum France *see* **Bayonne**
La Purísima Mex. **166** B3
Laqiya Arbain *well* Sudan **108** C5
La Quiaca Arg. **178** C2
L'Aquila Italy **68** E3
La Quinta *CA* U.S.A. **158** E5
Lār Iran **110** D5
Larache Morocco **67** C6
Lārak, Jazīreh-ye *i.* Iran **110** E5
Laramie *WY* U.S.A. **156** G4
Laramie *r. WY* U.S.A. **156** G4
Laramie Mountains *WY* U.S.A. **156** G4
Laranda Turkey *see* **Karaman**
Laranjal Paulista Brazil **179** B3
Laranjeiras do Sul Brazil **178** F3
Laranjinha *r.* Brazil **179** A3
Larantuka *Flores* Indon. **83** B5
Larat *Moluccas* Indon. **134** E1
Larat *i. Moluccas* Indon. **134** E1
Larba Alg. **67** H5
Lärbro Sweden **55** K8
L'Ardenne, Plateau de *plat.* Belgium *see* **Ardennes**
Laredo Spain **67** E2
Laredo *TX* U.S.A. **161** D7
La Reforma Mex. **167** F4
La Reina Adelaida, Archipiélago de *is* Chile **178** B8
Largeau Chad *see* **Faya**
Largo *FL* U.S.A. **163** D7
Largs U.K. **60** E5
L'Ariana Tunisia **68** D6
Lariang *Celebes* Indon. **83** A3
Lariang *r.* Indon. **83** A3
Larimore *ND* U.S.A. **160** D2
La Rioja Arg. **178** C3
La Rioja *aut. comm.* Spain **67** E2
Larisa Greece **69** J5
Larissa Greece *see* **Larisa**
Laristan *reg.* Iran **110** E5
Larkana Pak. **111** H5
Lark Harbour Canada **153** K4
Lark Passage Australia **136** D2
Larnaca Cyprus **107** A2
Larnaka Cyprus *see* **Larnaca**
Larnaka Bay Cyprus **107** A2
Larnakos, Kolpos *b.* Cyprus *see* **Larnaka Bay**
Larne U.K. **61** G3
Larned *KS* U.S.A. **160** D4
La Robla Spain **67** D2
La Roche-en-Ardenne Belgium **62** F4
La Rochelle France **66** D3
La Roche-sur-Yon France **66** D3
La Roda Spain **67** E4
La Romana Dom. Rep. **169** K5
La Ronge Canada **151** J4
La Ronge, Lac *l.* Canada **151** J4
La Rosa Mex. **167** E3
La Rosita Mex. **167** E2
Larrey Point Australia **134** B4
Larrimah Australia **134** F3
Lars Christensen Coast Antarctica **188** E2
Larsen Bay *AK* U.S.A. **148** I4
Larsen Ice Shelf Antarctica **188** L2
Larsmo Fin. **54** M5
Larvik Norway **55** G7
Lasahau *Celebes* Indon. **83** B4
La Sal *UT* U.S.A. **159** I2
LaSalle Canada **165** I1
La Salle *IL* U.S.A. **152** C6
Lasan *Kalimantan* Indon. **85** F2
Las Animas *CO* U.S.A. **160** C4
Las Ánimas, Punta *pt* Mex. **166** B2
Las Anod Somalia *see* **Laascaanood**
La Sarre Canada **152** F4
Las Avispas Mex. **166** C2
La Savonnière, Lac *l.* Canada **153** G3
Lascano Uruguay **178** F4
La Scie Canada **153** L4
Las Cruces Mex. **166** D2
Las Cruces *CA* U.S.A. **158** C4
Las Cruces *NM* U.S.A. **157** G6
La Selle, Pic *mt.* Haiti **169** J5
La Serena Chile **178** B3
Las Esperanças Mex. **167** E3
La Seu d'Urgell Spain **67** G2
Las Flores Arg. **178** E5
Las Guacamatas, Cerro *mt.* Mex. **157** F7
Lāshār, Rūd-e *r.* Iran **111** F5
Lashburn Canada **151** I4
Lāsh-e Juwayn Afgh. **111** F4
Las Heras *Mendoza* Arg. **178** C4
Las Heras *Santa Cruz* Arg. **178** C7
Las Herreras Mex. **166** D3
Lashio Myanmar **86** B2
Lashkar India **104** D4
Lashkar Gāh Afgh. **111** G4
Las Juntas Chile **178** C3
Las Lavaderos Mex. **167** F4
Las Lomitas Arg. **178** D2
Las Marismas *marsh* Spain **67** C5
Las Martinetas Arg. **178** C7
Las Mesteñas Mex. **166** D2
Las Minas, Cerro de *mt.* Hond. **167** H6
Las Mulatas *is* Panama *see* **San Blas, Archipiélago de**
Las Nieves Mex. **166** D3
Las Nopaleras, Cerro *mt.* Mex. **166** E3
La Société, Archipel de *is* Fr. Polynesia *see* **Society Islands**
Lasolo, Teluk *b.* Indon. **83** B3
Las Palmas *watercourse* Mex. **158** E5
Las Palmas Panama **166** [inset] J7

▶**Las Palmas de Gran Canaria** Canary Is **120** B2
Joint capital (with Santa Cruz de Tenerife) of the Canary Islands.

Las Petas Bol. **177** G7
La Spezia Italy **68** C2
Las Planchas Hond. **166** [inset] I6
Las Plumas Arg. **178** C6
Laspur Pak. **111** I2
Lassance Brazil **179** B2
Lassen Peak *vol. CA* U.S.A. **158** C1
Lassen Volcanic National Park *CA* U.S.A. **158** C1
Las Tablas Mex. **167** F4
Las Tablas Panama **166** [inset] J8
Last Chance *CO* U.S.A. **160** C4
Last Mountain Lake Canada **151** J5
Las Tórtolas, Cerro *mt.* Chile **178** C3
Lastoursville Gabon **122** B4
Lastovo *i.* Croatia **68** G3
Las Tres Vírgenes, Volcán *vol.* Mex. **166** B3
Lastrup Germany **63** H2
Las Tunas Cuba **169** I4
Las Varas *Chihuahua* Mex. **166** D2
Las Varas *Nayarit* Mex. **168** C4
Las Varillas Arg. **178** D4
Las Vegas *NM* U.S.A. **157** G6
Las Vegas *NV* U.S.A. **159** F3
Las Villuercas *mt.* Spain **67** D4
La Tabatière Canada **153** K4
Latacunga Ecuador **176** C4
Latady Island Antarctica **188** L2
Latakia Syria **107** B2
Latalata *i. Moluccas* Indon. **83** C3
La Teste-de-Buch France **66** D4
La Tetilla, Cerro *mt.* Mex. **166** D4
Latham Australia **135** B7
Lathen Germany **63** H2
Latheron U.K. **60** F2
Lathi India **104** B4
Latho India **104** D2
Lathrop *CA* U.S.A. **158** C3
Latina Italy **68** E4
La Tortuga, Isla *i.* Venez. **176** E1
Latouche *AK* U.S.A. **149** K3
Latouche Island *AK* U.S.A. **149** K3
La Trinidad Nicaragua **166** [inset] I6
La Trinidad *Luzon* Phil. **82** C2
La Trinitaria Mex. **167** G5
Latrobe *PA* U.S.A. **164** F3
Laṭrūn West Bank **107** B4
Lattaquié Syria *see* **Latakia**
Lattrop Neth. **62** G2
La Tuque Canada **153** G5
Latur India **106** C2
Latvia *country* Europe **55** N8
Latvija *country* Europe *see* **Latvia**
Latviyskaya S.S.R. *country* Europe *see* **Latvia**
Lauca, Parque Nacional *nat. park* Chile **176** E7
Lauchhammer Germany **57** N5
Lauder U.K. **60** G5
Laudio Spain **67** E2
Lauenbrück Germany **63** J1
Lauenburg (Elbe) Germany **63** K1
Lauf an der Pegnitz Germany **63** L5
Laufen Switz. **66** H3
Lauge Koch Kyst *reg.* Greenland **147** L2
Laughlen, Mount Australia **135** F5
Laughlin Peak *NM* U.S.A. **157** G5
Lauka Estonia **55** M7
Launceston Australia **137** [inset]
Launceston U.K. **59** C8
Laune *r.* Ireland **61** C5
Launggyaung Myanmar **86** B1
Launglon Myanmar **87** B4
Launglon Bok Islands Myanmar **87** B4
La Unidad Mex. **167** G6
La Unión Bol. **176** F7
La Unión El Salvador **166** [inset] I6
La Unión Hond. **166** [inset] I6
La Unión Mex. **167** E5
Laur *Luzon* Phil. **82** C3
Laura Australia **136** D2
Laurel *DE* U.S.A. **165** H4
Laurel *MS* U.S.A. **161** F6
Laurel *MT* U.S.A. **156** F3
Laureldale *PA* U.S.A. **165** H3
Laurel Hill *hills PA* U.S.A. **164** F4
Laurencekirk U.K. **60** G4
Laurieton Australia **138** F3
Laurinburg *NC* U.S.A. **163** E5
Lauru *i.* Solomon Is *see* **Choiseul**
Lausanne Switz. **66** H3
Laut *i.* Indon. **85** E1
Laut *i.* Indon. **85** E3
Laut *i.* Indon. **85** G3
Laut, Selat *sea chan.* Indon. **85** F3
Lautem East Timor **83** C5
Lauterbach (Hessen) Germany **63** J4
Laut Kecil, Kepulauan *is* Indon. **85** F4
Lautoka Fiji **133** H3
Lauttawar, Danau *l.* Indon. **84** B1
Lauvuskylä Fin. **54** P5
Lauwersmeer *l.* Neth. **62** G1
Lava Beds National Monument *nat. park CA* U.S.A. **156** C4
Laval Canada **152** G5
Laval France **66** D2
La Vall d'Uixó Spain **67** F4
Lāvān, Jazīreh-ye *i.* Iran **110** D5
Lavapié, Punta *pt* Chile **178** B5
Lāvar Iran **110** C4
Laveaga Peak *CA* U.S.A. **158** C3
La Vega Dom. Rep. **169** J5
La Venta Hond. **166** [inset] I6
Laverne *OK* U.S.A. **161** D4
Laverton Australia **135** C7
La Víbora Mex. **166** E3
La Vila Joíosa Spain *see* **Villajoyosa-La Vila Joiosa**
La Viña Peru **176** C5
Lavongal *i.* P.N.G. *see* **New Hanover**
Lavras Brazil **179** B3
Lavrentiya Russia **148** E2
Lavumisa Swaziland **125** J4
Lavushi-Manda National Park Zambia **123** D5
Lawa India **104** C4
Lawa Myanmar **86** B1
Lawa Pak. **111** H3
Lawang *i.* Indon. **85** G5
Lawas *Sarawak* Malaysia **85** F1
Lawashi *r.* Canada **152** E3
Law Dome *ice feature* Antarctica **188** F2
Lawele *Celebes* Indon. **83** B4
Lawin *i. Moluccas* Indon. **83** D3
Lawit, Gunung *mt.* Indon./Malaysia **85** F2
Lawit, Gunung *mt.* Malaysia **84** C1
Lawksawk Myanmar **86** B2
Lawn Hill National Park Australia **136** B3
Lawra Ghana **120** C3
Lawrence *IN* U.S.A. **164** B4
Lawrence *KS* U.S.A. **160** E4
Lawrence *MA* U.S.A. **165** J2
Lawrenceburg *IN* U.S.A. **164** C4
Lawrenceburg *KY* U.S.A. **164** C4
Lawrenceburg *TN* U.S.A. **162** C5
Lawrenceville *GA* U.S.A. **163** D5
Lawrenceville *IL* U.S.A. **164** B4
Lawrenceville *VA* U.S.A. **165** G5
Lawrence Wells, Mount *hill* Australia **135** C6
Lawton *OK* U.S.A. **161** D5
Lawu, Gunung *vol.* Indon. **85** E4
Lawz, Jabal al *mt.* Saudi Arabia **112** D5
Laxå Sweden **55** I7
Laxey Isle of Man **58** C4
Laxgalts'ap Canada **149** O5
Lax Kw'alaams Canada **149** O5
Laxo U.K. **60** [inset]
Laxong Co *l.* China **99** D6
Laya *r.* Russia **52** M2
Layar, Tanjung *pt* Indon. **85** G4
Laydennyy, Mys *c.* Russia **52** J1
Layeni *Moluccas* Indon. **83** D4
Laylá Saudi Arabia **108** G5
Laylá *salt pan* Saudi Arabia **107** D4
Laysan Island *HI* U.S.A. **186** I4
Laysu China **98** C4
Laytonville *CA* U.S.A. **158** B2
Layyah Pak. **111** H4
Laza Myanmar **86** B1
La Zacatosa, Picacho *mt.* Mex. **166** C4
Lazarev Russia **90** F1
Lazarevac Serbia **69** I2
Lázaro Cárdenas *Baja California* Mex. **166** B2
Lázaro Cárdenas *Baja California* Mex. **166** B2
Lázaro Cárdenas *Michoacán* Mex. **168** D5
Lazdijai Lith. **55** M9
Lazhuglung China **99** C6
Lazikou China **96** D1
Lazo *Primorskiy Kray* Russia **90** D4
Lazo *Respublika Sakha (Yakutiya)* Russia **77** O3
Lead *SD* U.S.A. **160** C2
Leader Water *r.* U.K. **60** G5
Leadville Australia **138** D4
Leaf *r. MS* U.S.A. **161** F6
Leaf Bay Canada *see* **Tasiujaq**
Leaf Rapids Canada **151** K3
Leakey *TX* U.S.A. **161** D6
Leaksville *NC* U.S.A. *see* **Eden**
Leamington Canada **164** D2
Leane, Lough *l.* Ireland **61** C5
Leap Ireland **61** C6
Leatherhead U.K. **59** G7
L'Eau d'Heure *l.* Belgium **62** E4
Leavenworth *IN* U.S.A. **164** B4
Leavenworth *KS* U.S.A. **160** E4
Leavenworth *WA* U.S.A. **156** C3
Leavitt Peak *CA* U.S.A. **158** D2
Lebach Germany **62** G5
Lebak *Mindanao* Phil. **82** D5
Lebanon *country* Asia **107** B2
Lebanon *IN* U.S.A. **164** B3
Lebanon *KY* U.S.A. **164** C5
Lebanon *MO* U.S.A. **160** E4
Lebanon *NH* U.S.A. **165** I2
Lebanon *OH* U.S.A. **164** C4
Lebanon *OR* U.S.A. **156** C3
Lebanon *PA* U.S.A. **165** G3
Lebanon *TN* U.S.A. **162** C4
Lebanon *VA* U.S.A. **164** D5
Lebanon Junction *KY* U.S.A. **164** C5
Lebanon Mountains Lebanon *see* **Liban, Jebel**
Lebbeke Belgium **62** E3
Lebec *CA* U.S.A. **158** D4
Lebedyan' Russia **53** H5
Lebel-sur-Quévillon Canada **152** F4
Le Blanc France **66** E3
Lebo *Celebes* Indon. **83** B4
Lębork Poland **57** P3

Lebowakgomo S. Africa 125 I3
Lebrija Spain 67 C5
Łebsko, Jezioro lag. Poland 57 P3
Lebu Chile 178 B5
Lebyazh'ye Kazakh. see **Akku**
Lebyazh'ye Russia 52 K4
Le Caire Egypt see **Cairo**
Le Cateau-Cambrésis France 62 D4
Le Catelet France 62 D4
Lecce Italy 68 H4
Lecco Italy 68 C2
Lech r. Austria/Germany 57 M7
Lechaina Greece 69 I6
Lechang China 97 G3
Le Chasseron mt. Switz. 66 H3
Le Chesne France 62 E5
Lechtaler Alpen mts Austria 57 M7
Leck Germany 57 L3
Lecompte LA U.S.A. 161 E6
Le Creusot France 66 G3
Le Crotoy France 62 B4
Lectoure France 66 E5
Ledang, Gunung mt. Malaysia 84 C2
Ledbury U.K. 59 E6
Ledesma Spain 67 D3
Ledmore U.K. 60 E2
Ledmozero Russia 54 R4
Ledo Kalimantan Indon. 85 E2
Ledong Hainan China 86 E3
Ledong Hainan China 97 F5
Le Dorat France 66 E3
Ledu China 94 E4
Leduc Canada 150 H4
Lee r. Ireland 61 D6
Lee IN U.S.A. 164 B3
Lee MA U.S.A. 165 I2
Leech Lake MN U.S.A. 160 E2
Leeds U.K. 58 F5
Leedstown U.K. 59 B8
Leek Neth. 62 G1
Leek U.K. 59 E5
Leende Neth. 62 F3
Leer (Ostfriesland) Germany 63 H1
Leesburg FL U.S.A. 163 D6
Leesburg GA U.S.A. 163 C6
Leesburg OH U.S.A. 164 D4
Leesburg VA U.S.A. 165 G4
Leese Germany 63 J2
Lee Steere Range hills Australia 135 C6
Leesville LA U.S.A. 161 E6
Leesville Lake OH U.S.A. 164 E3
Leesville Lake VA U.S.A. 164 F5
Leeton Australia 138 C5
Leeu-Gamka S. Africa 124 E7
Leeuwarden Neth. 62 F1
Leeuwin, Cape Australia 135 A8
Leeuwin-Naturaliste National Park Australia 135 A8
Lee Vining CA U.S.A. 158 D3
Leeward Islands Caribbean Sea 169 L5
Lefka Cyprus 107 A2
Lefkada Greece 69 I5
Lefkada i. Greece 69 I5
Lefkás Greece see **Lefkada**
Lefke Cyprus see **Lefka**
Lefkimmi Greece 69 I5
Lefkoniko Cyprus see **Lefkonikon**
Lefkonikon Cyprus 107 A2
Lefkoşa Cyprus see **Nicosia**
Lefkosia Cyprus see **Nicosia**
Lefroy r. Canada 153 H2
Lefroy, Lake salt flat Australia 135 C7
Legarde r. Canada 152 D4
Legazpi Luzon Phil. 82 C3
Legden Germany 62 H2
Legges Tor mt. Australia 137 [inset]
Leghorn Italy see **Livorno**
Legnago Italy 68 D2
Legnica Poland 57 P5
Legohli Canada see **Norman Wells**
Le Grand CA U.S.A. 158 C3
Legune Australia 134 E3
Leh India 104 D2
Le Havre France 66 E2
Lehi UT U.S.A. 159 H1
Lehighton PA U.S.A. 165 H3
Lehmo Fin. 54 P5
Lehre Germany 63 K2
Lehrte Germany 63 J2
Lehtimäki Fin. 54 M5
Lehututu Botswana 124 E2
Leibnitz Austria 57 O7
Leicester U.K. 59 F6
Leichhardt r. Australia 132 B3
Leichhardt Falls Australia 136 B3
Leichhardt Range mts Australia 136 D4
Leiden Neth. 62 E2
Leie r. Belgium 62 D3
Leigh N.Z. 139 E3
Leigh U.K. 58 E5
Leighton Buzzard U.K. 59 G7
Leiktho Myanmar 86 B3
Leimen Germany 63 I5
Leine r. Germany 63 J2
Leinefelde Germany 63 K3
Leinster Australia 135 C6
Leinster reg. Ireland 61 F4
Leinster, Mount hill Ireland 61 F5
Leipsic OH U.S.A. 164 D3
Leipsoi i. Greece 69 L6
Leipzig Germany 63 M3
Leipzig-Halle airport Germany 63 M3
Leiranger Norway 54 I3
Leiria Port. 67 B4
Leirvik Norway 55 D7
Leishan China 97 F3
Leisler, Mount hill Australia 135 E5
Leisnig Germany 63 M3
Leitchfield KY U.S.A. 164 B5
Leith Hill hill U.K. 59 G7
Leiva, Cerro mt. Col. 176 D3
Leixlip Ireland 61 F4
Leiyang China 97 G3
Leizhou China 97 F4
Leizhou Bandao pen. China 97 F4
Leizhou Wan b. China 97 F4
Lek r. Neth. 62 E3
Leka Norway 54 G4
Lékana Congo 122 B4
Le Kef Tunisia 68 C6
Lekhainá Greece see **Lechaina**
Lekitobi Moluccas Indon. 83 C3
Lekkersing S. Africa 124 C5
Lékoni Gabon 122 B4
Leksand Sweden 55 I6
Leksozero, Ozero l. Russia 54 Q5
Leksula Buru Indon. 83 C3
Lelai, Tanjung pt Halmahera Indon. 83 D2
Leland MI U.S.A. 164 C1
Leli China see **Tianlin**
Leling China 95 I4
Lelinta Papua Indon. 83 D3
Lelogama Timor Indon. 83 B5
Lélouma Guinea 120 B3
Lelystad Neth. 62 F2
Le Maire, Estrecho de sea chan. Arg. 178 C9
Léman, Lac l. France/Switz. see **Geneva, Lake**
Le Mans France 66 E2
Le Mars IA U.S.A. 160 D3
Lembeh i. Indon. 83 C2
Lemberg France 63 H5
Lemberg Ukr. see **L'viv**
Lembruch Germany 63 I2
Lembu Kalimantan Indon. 85 G2
Lembu, Gunung mt. Indon. 84 B1
Lembubut Kalimantan Indon. 85 G1
Lemdiyya Alg. see **Médéa**
Leme Brazil 179 B3
Lemele Neth. 62 G2
Lemesos Cyprus see **Limassol**
Lemgo Germany 63 I2
Lemhi Range mts ID U.S.A. 156 E3
Lemi Fin. 55 O6
Lemieux Islands Canada 147 L3
Lemmenjoen kansallispuisto nat. park Fin. 54 N2
Lemmer Neth. 62 F2
Lemmon SD U.S.A. 160 C2
Lemmon, Mount AZ U.S.A. 159 H5
Lemnos i. Greece see **Limnos**
Lemoncove CA U.S.A. 158 D3
Lemoore CA U.S.A. 158 D3
Le Moyne, Lac l. Canada 153 H2
Lemro r. Myanmar 86 A2
Lemtybozh Russia 51 R3
Lemukutan i. Indon. 85 E2
Le Murge hills Italy 68 G4
Lemvig Denmark 55 F8
Lem"yu r. Russia 52 M3
Lena r. Russia 88 J1
Lena WI U.S.A. 164 A1
Lena, Mount UT U.S.A. 159 I1
Lenadoon Point Ireland 61 C3
Lenangguar Sumbawa Indon. 85 G5
Lena Pillars Nature Park tourist site Russia 77 N3
Lenchung Tso salt l. China 105 E2
Lençóis Brazil 179 C1
Lençóis Maranhenses, Parque Nacional dos nat. park Brazil 177 J4
Lendery Russia 54 Q5
Le Neubourg France 59 H9
Lengerich Germany 63 H2
Lenghu China 98 F5
Lenglong Ling mts China 94 E4
Lengshuijiang China 97 F3
Lenham U.K. 59 H7
Lenhovda Sweden 55 I8
Lenin, Qullai mt. Kyrg./Tajik. see **Lenin Peak**
Lenina, Pik mt. Kyrg./Tajik. see **Lenin Peak**
Leninabad Tajik. see **Khŭjand**
Leninakan Armenia see **Gyumri**
Lenin Atyndagy Choku mt. Kyrg./Tajik. see **Lenin Peak**
Lenine Crimea 112 D1
Leningrad Russia see **St Petersburg**
Leningrad Tajik. 111 H2
Leningrad Oblast admin. div. Russia see **Leningradskaya Oblast'**
Leningradskaya Russia 53 H7
Leningradskaya Oblast' admin. div. Russia 55 R7
Leningradskiy Russia 77 S3
Leningradskiy Tajik. see **Leningrad**
Lenino Crimea see **Lenine**
Leninobod Tajik. see **Khŭjand**
Lenin Peak Kyrg./Tajik. 111 I2
Leninsk Kazakh. see **Baykonyr**
Leninsk Russia 53 J6
Leninskiy Russia 53 H5
Leninsk-Kuznetskiy Russia 76 J4
Leninskoye Kirovskaya Oblast' Russia 52 J4
Leninskoye Yevreyskaya Avtonomnaya Oblast' Russia 90 D3
Lenkoran' Azer. see **Länkäran**
Lenne r. Germany 63 H3
Lennoxville Canada 165 J1
Lenoir NC U.S.A. 162 D5
Lenore WV U.S.A. 164 D5
Lenore Lake Canada 151 J4
Lenox MA U.S.A. 165 I2
Lens France 62 C4
Lensk Russia 77 M3
Lenti Hungary 68 G1
Lentini Sicily Italy 68 F6
Lenya Myanmar 87 B5
Lenzen (Elbe) Germany 63 L1
Léo Burkina Faso 120 C3
Leoben Austria 57 O7
Leodhais, Eilean i. U.K. see **Lewis, Isle of**
Leok Celebes Indon. 83 B2
Leominster U.K. 59 E6
Leominster MA U.S.A. 165 J2
León Mex. 168 D4
León Nicaragua 166 [inset] I6
León Spain 67 D2
Leon r. TX U.S.A. 161 D6
Leonardtown MD U.S.A. 165 G4
Leonardville Namibia 124 D2
Leona Vicario Mex. 167 I4
Leongatha Australia 138 B7
Leonidi Greece see **Leonidio**
Leonidio Greece 69 J6
Leonidovo Russia 90 F2
Leonora Australia 135 C7
Leontovich, Cape AK U.S.A. 148 G5
Leopold WV U.S.A. 164 E4
Leopold and Astrid Coast Antarctica see **King Leopold and Queen Astrid Coast**
Léopold II, Lac l. Dem. Rep. Congo see **Mai-Ndombe, Lac**
Leopoldina Brazil 179 C3
Leopoldo de Bulhões Brazil 179 A2
Léopoldville Dem. Rep. Congo see **Kinshasa**
Leoti KS U.S.A. 160 C4
Leoville Canada 151 J4
Lepalale S. Africa see **Lephalale**
Lepar i. Indon. 84 D3
Lepaya Latvia see **Liepāja**
Lepel' Belarus see **Lyepyel'**
Lepellé r. Canada 153 H1
Lephalala r. S. Africa 125 H2
Lephalale S. Africa 125 H2
Lephepe Botswana 125 G2
Lephoi S. Africa 125 G6
Leping China 97 H2
Lepontine Alps mts Italy/Switz. 68 C1
Leppävirta Fin. 54 O5
Lepreau, Point Canada 153 I5
Lepsa Kazakh. see **Lepsi**
Lepsi Almatinskaya Oblast' Kazakh. 98 C3
Lepsi Almatinskaya Oblast' Kazakh. 102 E2
Lepsi r. Kazakh. 98 B3
Le Puy France see **Le Puy-en-Velay**
Le Puy-en-Velay France 66 F4
Le Quesnoy France 62 D4
Lerala Botswana 125 H2
Leratswana S. Africa 125 H5
Léré Mali 120 C3
Lereh Indon. 81 J7
Leribe Lesotho see **Hlotse**
Lérida Col. 176 D4
Lérida Spain see **Lleida**
Lerik Azer. 113 H3
Lerma Mex. 167 H5
Lerma Spain 67 E2
Lermontov Russia 113 F1
Lermontovka Russia 90 D3
Lermontovskiy Russia see **Lermontov**
Leros i. Greece 69 L6
Le Roy NY U.S.A. 165 G2
Le Roy, Lac l. Canada 152 G2
Lerum Sweden 55 H8
Lerwick U.K. 60 [inset]
Les Amirantes is Seychelles see **Amirante Islands**
Lesbos i. Greece 69 K5
Les Cayes Haiti 169 J5
Leshan China 96 D2
Leshou China see **Xianxian**
Leshukonskoye Russia 52 J2
Lesi watercourse South Sudan 121 F4
Leskhimstroy Ukr. see **Syeverodonets'k**
Leskovac Serbia 69 I3
Leslie MI U.S.A. 164 C2
Lesneven France 66 B2
Lesnoy Kirovskaya Oblast' Russia 52 L4
Lesnoy Murmanskaya Oblast' Russia see **Umba**
Lesnoye Russia 52 G4
Lesogorskoye Russia 90 F2
Lesopil'noye Russia 90 D3
Lesosibirsk Russia 76 K4
Lesotho country Africa 125 I5
Lesozavodsk Russia 90 D3
L'Espérance Rock i. Kermadec Is 133 I5
Les Pieux France 59 F9
Les Sables-d'Olonne France 66 D3
Lesse r. Belgium 62 E4
Lesser Antarctica reg. Antarctica see **West Antarctica**
Lesser Antilles is Caribbean Sea 169 K6
Lesser Caucasus mts Asia 113 F2
Lesser Himalaya mts India/Nepal 104 D3
Lesser Khingan Mountains China see **Xiao Hinggan Ling**
Lesser Slave Lake Canada 150 H4
Lesser Tunb i. The Gulf see **Tonb-e Küchek, Jazīreh-ye**
Lessines Belgium 62 D4
Lester WV U.S.A. 164 E5
Lestijärvi Fin. 54 N5
Lesung, Bukit mt. Indon. 85 F2
Les Vans France 66 G4
Lesvos i. Greece see **Lesbos**
Leszno Poland 57 P5
Letaba S. Africa 125 J2
Letchworth Garden City U.K. 59 G7
Le Télégraphe hill France 66 G3
Leteri India 104 D4
Letha Range mts Myanmar 86 A2
Lethbridge Alta Canada 151 H5
Lethbridge Nfld. and Lab. Canada 153 L4
Leti i. Moluccas Indon. 83 C5
Leti, Kepulauan is Moluccas Indon. 83 C5
Leticia Col. 176 E4
Leting China 95 I4
Letlhakeng Botswana 125 G3
Letnerechenskiy Russia 52 G2
Letniy Navolok Russia 52 H2
Letoda Moluccas Indon. 83 D5
Le Touquet-Paris-Plage France 62 B4
Letpadan Myanmar 86 A3
Le Tréport France 62 B4
Letsitele S. Africa 125 J2
Letsopa S. Africa 125 G4
Letterkenny Ireland 61 E3
Letung Sumatra Indon. 84 D2
Letwurung Moluccas Indon. 83 D4
Lëtzebuerg country Europe see **Luxembourg**
Letzlingen Germany 63 L2
Léua Angola 123 C5
Leucas Greece see **Lefkada**
Leucate, Étang de l. France 66 F5
Leuchars U.K. 60 G4
Leukas Greece see **Lefkada**
Leung Shuen Wan Chau i. H.K. China see **High Island**
Leunovo Russia 52 I2
Leupp AZ U.S.A. 159 H4
Leupung Sumatra Indon. 87 A6
Leura Australia 136 E4
Leusden Neth. 62 F2
Leuser, Gunung mt. Indon. 84 B2
Leutershausen Germany 63 K5
Leuven Belgium 62 E4
Levadeia Greece see **Livadeia**
Levan UT U.S.A. 159 H2
Levanger Norway 54 G5
Levante, Riviera di coastal area Italy 68 C2
Levanto Italy 68 C2
Levashi Russia 113 G2
Levelland TX U.S.A. 161 C5
Levelock AK U.S.A. 148 H4
Leven England U.K. 58 G5
Leven Scotland U.K. 60 G4
Leven, Loch l. U.K. 60 F4
Lévêque, Cape Australia 134 C4
Leverkusen Germany 62 G3
Lévézou mts France 66 F4
Levice Slovakia 57 Q6
Levin N.Z. 139 E5
Lévis Canada 153 H5
Levitha i. Greece 69 L6
Levittown NY U.S.A. 165 I3
Levittown PA U.S.A. 165 H3
Levkás i. Greece see **Lefkada**
Levkímmi Greece see **Lefkimmi**
Levskigrad Bulg. see **Karlovo**
Lev Tolstoy Russia 53 H5
Levuka Fiji 133 H3
Lévy, Cap c. France 59 F9
Lewa Sumba Indon. 83 A5
Lewe Myanmar 86 B3
Lewerberg mt. S. Africa 124 C5
Lewes U.K. 59 H8
Lewes DE U.S.A. 165 H4
Lewis CO U.S.A. 159 I3
Lewis IN U.S.A. 164 B4
Lewis KS U.S.A. 160 D4
Lewis, Isle of i. U.K. 60 C2
Lewis, Lake salt flat Australia 134 F5
Lewisburg KY U.S.A. 164 B5
Lewisburg PA U.S.A. 165 G3
Lewisburg WV U.S.A. 164 E5
Lewis Cass, Mount Canada/U.S.A. 149 O4
Lewis Hills hill Canada 153 K4
Lewis Pass N.Z. 139 D6
Lewis Range hills Australia 134 E5
Lewis Range mts MT U.S.A. 156 E2
Lewis Smith, Lake AL U.S.A. 163 C5
Lewiston ID U.S.A. 156 D3
Lewiston ME U.S.A. 165 J1
Lewistown IL U.S.A. 160 F3
Lewistown MT U.S.A. 156 F3
Lewistown PA U.S.A. 165 G3
Lewisville AR U.S.A. 161 E5
Lewoleba Indon. 83 B5
Lewotobi, Gunung vol. Flores Indon. 83 B5
Lexington KY U.S.A. 164 C4
Lexington MI U.S.A. 164 D2
Lexington NC U.S.A. 162 D5
Lexington NE U.S.A. 160 D3
Lexington TN U.S.A. 161 F5
Lexington VA U.S.A. 164 F5
Lexington Park MD U.S.A. 165 G4
Leyden Neth. see **Leiden**
Leye China 96 E3
Leyla Dāgh mt. Iran 110 B2
Leyte i. Phil. 82 D4
Leyte Gulf Phil. 82 D4
Lezha Albania see **Lezhë**
Lezhë Albania 69 H4
Lezhi China 96 E2
Lezhu China 97 G4
L'gov Russia 53 G6
Lhari Xizang China 99 F7
Lhari Xizang China see **Si'erdingka**
Lharigarbo China 99 E6
Lhasa China 99 E7
Lhasa He r. China 99 E7
Lhasoi China 99 F7
Lhatog China 96 C2
Lhaviyani Atoll Maldives see **Faadhippolhu**
Lhazê Xizang China 99 D7
Lhazê Xizang China 99 F7
Lhazhong China 105 F3
Lhokkruet Sumatra Indon. 84 A1
Lhokseumawe Sumatra Indon. 84 B1
Lhoksukon Sumatra Indon. 84 B1
Lhoma China 99 E7
Lhorong China 99 F7

▶**Lhotse** mt. China/Nepal 105 F4
4th highest mountain in Asia and the world.

Lhozhag China 99 E7
Lhuentse Bhutan 105 G4
Lhünzê Xizang China 99 F7
Liakoura mt. Greece 69 J5
Liancheng China see **Guangnan**
Liancourt France 62 C5
Liancourt Rocks i. N. Pacific Ocean 91 C5
Liandu China see **Lishui**
Liang Celebes Indon. 83 B3
Lianga Mindanao Phil. 82 D4
Lianga Bay Mindanao Phil. 82 D4
Liangcheng China 95 H3
Liangdang China 96 E1
Lianghe Chongqing China 97 F2
Lianghe Sichuan China 96 D2
Lianghe Yunnan China 96 C3
Lianghekou Chongqing China see **Lianghe**
Lianghekou Gansu China 96 E1
Liangping China 96 E2
Liangpran, Bukit mt. Indon. 85 F2
Liangshan China see **Liangping**
Liang Shan mt. Myanmar 86 B1
Liangshi China see **Shaodong**
Liangtian China 97 F4
Liang Timur, Gunung mt. Malaysia 84 C2
Liangzhen China 95 G4
Liangzhou China see **Wuwei**
Liangzi Hu l. China 97 G2
Lianhe China see **Qianjiang**
Lianhua China 97 G3
Lianhua Shan mts China 97 G4
Lianjiang Fujian China 97 H3
Lianjiang Jiangxi China see **Xingguo**
Liannan China 97 G3
Lianping China 97 G3
Lianran China see **Anning**
Lianshan Guangdong China 97 G3
Lianshan Liaoning China 95 J3
Lianshui China 97 H1
Liant, Cape i. Thai. see **Samae San, Ko**
Liantang China see **Nanchang**
Lianxian China see **Lianzhou**
Lianyin China 90 A1
Lianyun China 95 I5
Lianyungang China 95 I5
Lianzhou Guangdong China 97 G3
Lianzhou Guangxi China see **Hepu**
Liaocheng China 95 H4
Liaodong Bandao pen. China 95 J3
Liaodong Wan b. China 95 J3
Liaodun China 94 C3
Liaodunzhan China 94 C3
Liaogao China see **Songtao**
Liao He r. China 95 J3
Liaoning prov. China 95 J3
Liaoyang China 95 J3
Liaoyuan China 90 B4
Liaozhong China 95 J3
Liapades Greece 69 H5
Liard r. Canada 150 F2
Liard Highway Canada 150 F2
Liard Plateau Canada 149 P3
Liard River Canada 149 P4
Liari Pak. 111 G5
Liat i. Indon. 84 D3
Liathach mt. U.K. 60 D3
Liban country Asia see **Lebanon**
Liban, Jebel mts Lebanon 107 C2
Libau Latvia see **Liepāja**
Libby MT U.S.A. 156 E2
Libenge Dem. Rep. Congo 122 B3
Liberal KS U.S.A. 161 C4
Liberdade Brazil 179 B3
Liberec Czech Rep. 57 O5
Liberia country Africa 120 C4
Liberia Costa Rica 166 [inset] I7
Liberty AK U.S.A. 149 L2
Liberty IN U.S.A. 164 C4
Liberty KY U.S.A. 164 C5
Liberty ME U.S.A. 165 K1
Liberty MO U.S.A. 160 E4
Liberty MS U.S.A. 161 F6
Liberty NY U.S.A. 165 H3
Liberty TX U.S.A. 161 E6
Liberty Lake MD U.S.A. 165 G4
Libin Belgium 62 F5
Libmanan Luzon Phil. 82 C3
Libni, Gebel hill Egypt see **Libnī, Jabal**
Libnī, Jabal hill Egypt 107 A4
Libo China 96 E3
Libobo, Tanjung pt Halmahera Indon. 83 D3
Libode S. Africa 125 I6
Libong, Ko i. Thai. 87 B6
Libourne France 66 D4
Libral Well Australia 134 D5
Libre, Sierra mts Mex. 166 C2

▶**Libreville** Gabon 122 A3
Capital of Gabon.

Libuganon r. Mindanao Phil. 82 D5

▶**Libya** country Africa 121 E2
4th largest country in Africa.

Libyan Desert Egypt/Libya 108 C5
Libyan Plateau Egypt 112 B5
Licantén Chile 178 B4
Licata Sicily Italy 68 E6
Lice Turkey 113 F3
Lich Germany 63 I4
Lichas pen. Greece 69 J5
Licheng Guangxi China see **Lipu**
Licheng Jiangsu China see **Jinhu**
Licheng Shandong China 95 I4
Licheng Shanxi China 95 H4
Lichfield U.K. 59 F6
Lichinga Moz. 123 D5
Lichte Germany 63 L4
Lichtenau Germany 63 I3
Lichtenburg S. Africa 125 H4
Lichtenfels Germany 63 L4
Lichtenvoorde Neth. 62 G3
Lichuan Hubei China 97 F2
Lichuan Jiangxi China 97 H3
Licun China see **Laoshan**
Lida Belarus 55 N10
Liddel Water r. U.K. 60 G5
Lidfontein Namibia 124 D3
Lidköping Sweden 55 H7
Lidsjöberg Sweden 54 I4
Liebenau Germany 63 J2
Liebenburg Germany 63 K2
Liebenwalde Germany 63 N2
Liebig, Mount Australia 135 E5
Liechtenstein country Europe 66 I3
Liège Belgium 62 F4
Liegnitz Poland see **Legnica**
Lieksa Fin. 54 Q5
Lielupe r. Latvia 55 N8
Lielvārde Latvia 55 N8
Lienart Dem. Rep. Congo 122 C3
Lienchung i. Taiwan see **Mazu Dao**
Liên Nghia Vietnam 87 E5
Liên Sơn Vietnam 87 E4
Lienz Austria 57 N7
Liepāja Latvia 55 L8
Liepaya Latvia see **Liepāja**
Lier Belgium 62 E3
Lierre Belgium see **Lier**
Lieshout Neth. 62 F3
Lietuva country Europe see **Lithuania**
Liévin France 62 C4
Lièvre, Rivière du r. Canada 152 G5
Liezen Austria 57 O7
Lifamatola i. Indon. 83 C3
Liffey r. Ireland 61 F4
Lifford Ireland 61 E3
Lifi Mahuida mt. Arg. 178 C6
Lifou i. New Caledonia 133 G4
Lifu i. New Caledonia see **Lifou**
Ligao Luzon Phil. 82 C3
Līgatne Latvia 55 N8
Lighthouse Reef Belize 167 I5
Lightning Ridge Australia 138 C2
Ligny-en-Barrois France 62 F6
Ligonha r. Moz. 123 D5
Ligonier IN U.S.A. 164 C3
Ligui Mex. 166 C3
Ligure, Mar sea France/Italy see **Ligurian Sea**
Ligurian Sea France/Italy 68 C3
Ligurienne, Mer sea France/Italy see **Ligurian Sea**
Ligurta AZ U.S.A. 159 F5
Lihir Group is P.N.G. 132 F2
Lihou Reef and Cays Australia 136 E3
Lihua China 97 F3
Liivi laht b. Estonia/Latvia see **Riga, Gulf of**
Liji China 97 H1
Lijiang Yunnan China 96 D3
Lijiang Yunnan China see **Yuanjiang**
Lijiazhai China 97 G2
Lika reg. Croatia 68 F2
Likasi Dem. Rep. Congo 123 C5
Likati Dem. Rep. Congo 122 C3
Likely Canada 150 F4
Likhachevo Ukr. see **Pervomays'kyy**
Likhachyovo Ukr. see **Pervomays'kyy**
Likhapani India 105 H4
Likhás pen. Greece see **Lichas**
Likhoslavl' Russia 52 G4
Likisia East Timor see **Liquiçá**
Liku Kalimantan Indon. 85 E2
Liku Sarawak Malaysia 85 F1
Likupang Celebes Indon. 83 C2
Likurga Russia 52 I4
L'Île-Rousse Corsica France 66 I5
Lilienthal Germany 63 I1
Liling China 97 G3
Lilla Pak. 111 I3
Lilla Edet Sweden 55 H7
Lille Belgium 62 E3
Lille France 62 D4
Lille (Lesquin) airport France 62 D4
Lille Bælt sea chan. Denmark see **Little Belt**
Lillebonne France 59 H9
Lillehammer Norway 55 G6
Lillers France 62 C4
Lillesand Norway 55 F7
Lillestrøm Norway 55 G7
Lilley MI U.S.A. 164 C2
Lillholmsjö Sweden 54 I5
Lillian, Point hill Australia 135 D6
Lillington NC U.S.A. 163 E5
Lillooet Canada 150 F5
Lillooet r. Canada 150 F5
Lillooet Range mts Canada 150 F5

▶**Lilongwe** Malawi 123 D5
Capital of Malawi.

Liloy Mindanao Phil. 82 C4
Lilydale Australia 137 B7

▶**Lima** Peru 176 C6
Capital of Peru. 4th most populous city in South America.

Lima MT U.S.A. 156 E3
Lima NY U.S.A. 165 G2
Lima OH U.S.A. 164 C3
Lima Duarte Brazil 179 C3
Liman Russia 53 J7
Limar Moluccas Indon. 83 C4
Limas Sumatra Indon. 84 D2
Limassol Cyprus 107 A2
Limavady U.K. 61 F2
Limay r. Arg. 178 C5
Limbang Sarawak Malaysia 85 F1
Limbaži Latvia 55 N8
Limboto Celebes Indon. 83 B2
Limboto, Danau l. Indon. 83 B2
Limbung Celebes Indon. 83 A4
Limbungan Kalimantan Indon. 85 F3
Limbunya Australia 134 E4
Limburg an der Lahn Germany 63 I4
Lim Chu Kang hill Sing. 87 [inset]
Lime Acres S. Africa 124 F5
Lime Hills AK U.S.A. 148 I3
Limeira Brazil 179 B3
Limerick Ireland 61 D5
Limestone Point Canada 151 L4
Lime Village AK U.S.A. 148 I3
Limingen Norway 54 H4
Limingen l. Norway 54 H4
Limington ME U.S.A. 165 J2

Liminka Fin. 54 N4
Limmen Bight *b.* Australia 136 B2
Limmen National Park Australia 134 F3
Limnos *i.* Greece 69 K5
Limoeiro Brazil 177 K5
Limoges Canada 165 H1
Limoges France 66 E4
Limón Hond. 166 [inset] I6
Limon *CO* U.S.A. 160 C4
Limonlu Turkey 107 B1
Limonum France *see* **Poitiers**
Limousin *reg.* France 66 E4
Limoux France 66 F5
Limpopo *prov.* S. Africa 125 I2
Limpopo *r.* S. Africa/Zimbabwe 125 K3
Limu China 97 F3
Līnah *well* Saudi Arabia 113 F5
Linakhamari Russia 54 Q2
Lin'an China *see* **Jianshui**
Linao Bay *Mindanao* Phil. 82 D5
Linapacan *i.* Phil. 82 B4
Linapacan Strait Phil. 82 B4
Linares Chile 178 B5
Linares Mex. 167 F3
Linares Spain 67 E4
Linau Balui *plat.* Malaysia 85 F2
Lincang China 96 D4
Lincheng *Hainan* China *see* **Lingao**
Lincheng *Hunan* China *see* **Huitong**
Linchuan China *see* **Fuzhou**
Linck Nunataks *nunataks* Antarctica 188 K1
Lincoln Arg. 178 D4
Lincoln U.K. 58 G5
Lincoln *CA* U.S.A. 158 C2
Lincoln *IL* U.S.A. 160 F3
Lincoln *MI* U.S.A. 164 D1

▶**Lincoln** *NE* U.S.A. 160 D3
Capital of Nebraska.

Lincoln City *IN* U.S.A. 164 B4
Lincoln City *OR* U.S.A. 156 B3
Lincoln Island Paracel Is 80 E3
Lincoln National Park Australia 137 A7
Lincoln Sea Canada/Greenland 189 J1
Lincolnshire Wolds *hills* U.K. 58 G5
Lincolnton *GA* U.S.A. 163 D5
Linda, Serra *hills* Brazil 179 C1
Linda Creek *watercourse* Australia 136 B4
Lindau Germany 63 M2
Lindau (Bodensee) Germany 57 L7
Lindeman Group *is* Australia 136 E4
Linden Canada 150 H5
Linden Germany 63 I4
Linden Guyana 177 G2
Linden *AL* U.S.A. 163 C5
Linden *MI* U.S.A. 164 D2
Linden *TN* U.S.A. 162 C5
Linden *TX* U.S.A. 161 E5
Linden Grove *MN* U.S.A. 160 E2
Lindern (Oldenburg) Germany 63 H2
Lindesnes *c.* Norway 55 E7
Líndhos Greece *see* **Lindos**
Lindi *r.* Dem. Rep. Congo 122 C3
Lindi Tanz. 123 D4
Lindian China 95 K2
Lindisfarne *i.* U.K. *see* **Holy Island**
Lindley S. Africa 125 H4
Lindong China 95 I3
Lindos Greece 65 J4
Lindos, Akra *pt* Greece *see* **Gkinas, Akrotirio**
Lindsay Canada 165 F1
Lindsay *CA* U.S.A. 158 D3
Lindsay *MT* U.S.A. 156 G3
Lindsborg *KS* U.S.A. 160 D4
Lindside *WV* U.S.A. 164 E5
Lindum U.K. *see* **Lincoln**
Line Islands Kiribati 187 J5
Linesville *PA* U.S.A. 164 E3
Linfen China 95 G4
Lingampet India 106 C2
Linganamakki Reservoir India 106 B3
Lingao China 97 F5
Lingayen *Luzon* Phil. 82 C2
Lingayen Gulf *Luzon* Phil. 82 C2
Lingbao China 95 G5
Lingbi China 97 H1
Lingcheng *Anhui* China *see* **Lingbi**
Lingcheng *Guangxi* China *see* **Lingshan**
Lingcheng *Hainan* China *see* **Lingshui**
Lingcheng *Shandong* China *see* **Lingxian**
Lingchuan *Guangxi* China 97 F3
Lingchuan *Shanxi* China 95 H5
Lingelethu S. Africa 125 H7
Lingen (Ems) Germany 63 H2
Lingga *i. Sumatra* Indon. 84 D3
Lingga *Sarawak* Malaysia 85 E2
Lingga, Kepulauan *is Sumatra* Indon. 84 D3
Linggo Co *l.* China 99 E6
Linghai China 95 J3
Lingig *Mindanao* Phil. 82 D5
Lingkabau *Sabah* Malaysia 85 G1
Lingkas *Kalimantan* Indon. 85 G2
Lingle *WY* U.S.A. 156 G4
Lingling China 97 F3
Lingomo Dem. Rep. Congo 122 C3
Lingqiu China 95 H4
Lingshan China 97 F4
Lingshan Wan *b.* China 95 J5
Lingshi China 95 G4
Lingshui China 97 F5
Lingshui Wan *b.* China 97 F5
Lingsugur India 106 C2
Lingtai China 95 F5
Linguère Senegal 120 B3
Lingui China 97 F3
Lingxi China *see* **Yongshun**
Lingxia China 95 J2
Lingxian *Hunan* China *see* **Yanling**
Lingxian *Shandong* China 95 I4
Lingxiang China 97 G2
Lingyang China *see* **Cili**
Lingyuan China 95 I3
Lingyun China 96 E3
Lingzi Tang *reg.* China 99 B6
Linh, Ngok *mt.* Vietnam 86 D4
Linhai China 97 I2
Linhares Brazil 179 C2
Linhe China *see* **Bayannur**
Linhpa Myanmar 86 A1
Linjiang China 90 B4
Linjin China 97 F1
Linköping Sweden 55 I7
Linkou China 90 C3
Linli China 97 F2
Linlithgow U.K. 60 F5
Linlü Shan *mt.* China 95 H4
Linmingguan China *see* **Yongnian**
Linn *MO* U.S.A. 160 F4
Linn *TX* U.S.A. 161 D7
Linn, Mount *CA* U.S.A. 158 B1
Linnansaaren kansallispuisto *nat. park* Fin. 54 P5
Linnhe, Loch *inlet* U.K. 60 D4
Linnich Germany 62 G4
Linosa, Isola di *i. Sicily* Italy 68 E7
Linqing China 95 H4
Linquan China 97 G1
Linru *Henan* China *see* **Ruzhou**
Linru *Henan* China 95 H5
Lins Brazil 179 A3
Linshu China 97 H1
Linshui China 96 E2
Lintah, Selat *sea chan.* Indon. 83 A5
Lintan China 94 E5
Lintao China 94 E5
Linton *IN* U.S.A. 164 B4
Linton *ND* U.S.A. 160 C2
Lintong China 95 G5
Linwu China 97 G3
Linxi China 95 I3
Linxia *Gansu* China 94 E5
Linxia *Gansu* China 94 E5
Linxian *Henan* China *see* **Linzhou**
Linxian *Shanxi* China 95 G4
Linxiang China 97 G2
Linyi *Shandong* China 95 I4
Linyi *Shandong* China 95 I5
Linyi *Shanxi* China 95 G5
Linying China 97 G1
Linyou China 95 F5
Linz Austria 57 O6
Linze China 94 E4
Linzhou China 95 H4
Lio Matoh *Sarawak* Malaysia 85 F2
Lion, Golfe du *g.* France 66 F5
Lions, Gulf of France *see* **Lion, Golfe du**
Lions Bay Canada 150 F5
Lioppa *Moluccas* Indon. 83 C4
Lioua Chad 121 E3
Lipa *Luzon* Phil. 82 C3
Lipang *i.* Indon. 83 C2
Lipari *Sicily* Italy 68 F5
Lipari, Isole *is* Italy 68 F5
Lipatkain *Sumatra* Indon. 84 C2
Lipetsk Russia 53 H5
Lipin Bor Russia 52 H3
Liping China 97 F3
Lipova Romania 69 I1
Lipovtsy Russia 90 C3
Lippe *r.* Germany 63 G3
Lippstadt Germany 63 I3
Lipsoi *i.* Greece *see* **Leipsoi**
Lipti Lekh *pass* Nepal 104 E3
Liptrap, Cape Australia 138 B7
Lipu China 97 F3
Liquiçá East Timor 83 C5
Liquissa East Timor *see* **Liquiçá**
Lira Uganda 122 D3
Liran *i. Moluccas* Indon. 83 C4
Liranga Congo 122 B4
Lircay Peru 176 D6
Lirung *Celebes* Indon. 83 C2
Lisala Dem. Rep. Congo 122 C3
Lisbellaw U.K. 61 E3
Lisboa Port. *see* **Lisbon**

▶**Lisbon** Port. 67 B4
Capital of Portugal.

Lisbon *ME* U.S.A. 165 J1
Lisbon *NH* U.S.A. 165 J1
Lisbon *OH* U.S.A. 164 E3
Lisburn U.K. 61 F3
Lisburne, Cape *AK* U.S.A. 148 F1
Liscannor Bay Ireland 61 C5
Lisdoonvarna Ireland 61 C4
Lishan China *see* **Lintong**
Lishan Taiwan 97 I3
Lishe Jiang *r.* China 96 D3
Lishi China *see* **Dingnan**
Lishu China 90 B4
Lishui China 97 H2
Li Shui *r.* China 97 F2
Lisichansk Ukr. *see* **Lysychans'k**
Lisieux France 66 E2
Liskeard U.K. 59 C8
Liski Russia 53 H6
L'Isle-Adam France 62 C5
Lismore Australia 138 F2
Lismore Ireland 61 E5
Lisnarrick U.K. 61 E3
Lisnaskea U.K. 61 E3
Liss *mt.* Saudi Arabia 107 D4
Lissa Poland *see* **Leszno**
Lister, Mount Antarctica 188 H1
Listowel Canada 164 E2
Listowel Ireland 61 C5
Listvyaga, Khrebet *mts* Kazakh./Russia 98 D2
Lit Sweden 54 I5
Litang *Guangxi* China 97 F4
Litang *Sichuan* China 96 D2
Līṭānī, Nahr el *r.* Lebanon 107 B3
Litchfield *CA* U.S.A. 158 C1
Litchfield *CT* U.S.A. 165 I3
Litchfield *IL* U.S.A. 160 F4
Litchfield *MI* U.S.A. 164 C2
Litchfield *MN* U.S.A. 160 E2
Lit-et-Mixe France 66 D4
Lithgow Australia 138 E4
Lithino, Akra *pt* Greece *see* **Lithino, Akrotirio**
Lithino, Akrotirio *pt* Greece 69 K7
Lithuania *country* Europe 55 M9
Lititz *PA* U.S.A. 165 G3
Litoměřice Czech Rep. 57 O5
Litovko Russia 90 D2
Litovskaya S.S.R. *country* Europe *see* **Lithuania**
Little *r. LA* U.S.A. 161 E6
Little Abaco *i.* Bahamas 163 E7
Little Abitibi *r.* Canada 152 E4
Little Abitibi Lake Canada 152 E4
Little Andaman *i.* India 87 A5
Little Bahama Bank *sea feature* Bahamas 163 E7
Little Barrier Island *i.* N.Z. 139 E3
Little Belt *sea chan.* Denmark 55 F9
Little Belt Mountains *MT* U.S.A. 156 F3
Little Bitter Lake Egypt 107 A4
Little Black *r. AK* U.S.A. 149 K2
Little Cayman *i.* Cayman Is 169 H5
Little Churchill *r.* Canada 151 M3
Little Chute *WI* U.S.A. 164 A1
Little Coco Island Cocos Is 87 A4
Little Colorado *r. AZ* U.S.A. 159 H3
Little Creek Peak *UT* U.S.A. 159 G3
Little Current Canada 152 E5
Little Current *r.* Canada 152 D4
Little Desert National Park Australia 137 C8
Little Diomede *i. AK* U.S.A. 148 E2
Little Egg Harbor *inlet NJ* U.S.A. 165 H4
Little Exuma *i.* Bahamas 163 F8
Little Falls *MN* U.S.A. 160 E2
Littlefield *AZ* U.S.A. 159 G3
Littlefield *TX* U.S.A. 161 C5
Little Fork *r. MN* U.S.A. 160 E1
Little Grand Rapids Canada 151 M4
Littlehampton U.K. 59 G8
Little Inagua Island Bahamas 163 F8
Little Karas Berg *plat.* Namibia 124 D4
Little Karoo *plat.* S. Africa 124 E7
Little Lake *CA* U.S.A. 158 E4
Little Mecatina *r.* Canada *see* **Petit Mécatina**
Little Mecatina Island Canada *see* **Petit Mécatina, Île du**
Little Minch *sea chan.* U.K. 60 B3
Little Missouri *r. ND* U.S.A. 160 C2
Little Namaqualand *reg.* S. Africa *see* **Namaqualand**
Little Nicobar *i.* India 87 A6
Little Ouse *r.* U.K. 59 H6
Little Pamir *mts* Asia 111 I2
Little Rancheria *r.* Canada 150 D2
Little Red River Canada 150 H3

▶**Little Rock** *AR* U.S.A. 161 E5
Capital of Arkansas.

Littlerock *CA* U.S.A. 158 E4
Little Sable Point *MI* U.S.A. 164 B2
Little Salmon Lake Canada 149 N3
Little Salt Lake *UT* U.S.A. 159 G3
Little Sandy Desert Australia 135 B5
Little San Salvador *i.* Bahamas 163 F7
Little Sitkin Island *AK* U.S.A. 148 [inset] B6
Little Smoky Canada 150 G4
Little Tibet *reg.* India/Pak. *see* **Ladakh**
Littleton *CO* U.S.A. 156 G5
Little Valley *NY* U.S.A. 165 F2
Little Wind *r. WY* U.S.A. 156 F4
Litunde Moz. 123 D5
Liu'an China *see* **Lu'an**
Liuba China 96 E1
Liucheng China 97 F3
Liuchong He *r.* China 96 E3
Liuchow China *see* **Liuzhou**
Liugong Dao *i.* China 95 J4
Liuhe China 90 B4
Liuheng Dao *i.* China 97 I2
Liujiachang China 97 F2
Liujiaxia China *see* **Yongjing**
Liujiaxia Shuiku *resr* China 96 D1
Liukesong China 90 B3
Liulin *Gansu* China *see* **Jonê**
Liulin *Shanxi* China 95 G4
Liupan Shan *mts* China 94 F5
Liupanshui China 96 E3
Liuqiu Yu *i.* Taiwan 97 I4
Liuquan China 95 I5
Liure Hond. 166 [inset] I6
Liushuquan China 94 C3
Liuwa Plain National Park Zambia 123 C5
Liuyang China 97 G2
Liuyuan China 98 F4
Liuzhan China 95 K1
Liuzhangzhen China *see* **Yuanqu**
Liuzhi China 96 E3
Liuzhou China 97 F3
Livadeia Greece 69 J5
Līvāni Latvia 55 O8
Livengood *AK* U.S.A. 149 J2
Live Oak *FL* U.S.A. 163 D6
Liveringa Australia 132 C3
Livermore *CA* U.S.A. 158 C3
Livermore *KY* U.S.A. 164 B5
Livermore, Mount *TX* U.S.A. 161 B6
Livermore Falls *ME* U.S.A. 165 J1
Liverpool Australia 138 E4
Liverpool Canada 153 I5
Liverpool U.K. 58 E5
Liverpool Bay Canada 149 O1
Liverpool Plains Australia 138 E3
Liverpool Range *mts* Australia 138 D3
Livia *KY* U.S.A. 164 B5
Livingston Guat. 167 H6
Livingston U.K. 60 F5
Livingston *AL* U.S.A. 161 F5
Livingston *KY* U.S.A. 164 C5
Livingston *MT* U.S.A. 156 F3
Livingston *TN* U.S.A. 164 C5
Livingston *TX* U.S.A. 161 E6
Livingston, Lake *TX* U.S.A. 161 E6
Livingstone Zambia 123 C5
Livingston Island Antarctica 188 L2
Livingston Manor *NY* U.S.A. 165 H3
Livno Bos. & Herz. 68 G3
Livny Russia 53 H5
Livojoki *r.* Fin. 54 O4
Livonia *MI* U.S.A. 164 D2
Livonia *NY* U.S.A. 165 G2
Livorno Italy 68 D3
Livramento de Nossa Senhora Brazil 179 C1
Liwā Oman 110 E5
Liwā', Wādī al *watercourse* Syria 107 C3
Liwale Tanz. 123 D4
Liwu China *see* **Lixian**
Lixian *Gansu* China 94 F5
Lixian *Hebei* China 95 H4
Lixian *Sichuan* China 96 D2
Lixus Morocco *see* **Larache**
Liyang China *see* **Hexian**
Liyuan China *see* **Sangzhi**
Lizard U.K. 59 B9
Lizarda Brazil 177 I5
Lizard Point U.K. 59 B9
Lizarra Spain *see* **Estella**
Lizemores *WV* U.S.A. 164 E4
Liziping China 96 D2
Lizy-sur-Ourcq France 62 D5
Ljouwert Neth. *see* **Leeuwarden**

▶**Ljubljana** Slovenia 68 F1
Capital of Slovenia.

Ljugarn Sweden 55 K8
Ljungan *r.* Sweden 54 J5
Ljungaverk Sweden 54 J5
Ljungby Sweden 55 H8
Ljusdal Sweden 55 J6
Ljusnan *r.* Sweden 55 J6
Ljusne Sweden 55 J6
Llaima, Volcán *vol.* Chile 178 B5
Llanandras U.K. *see* **Presteigne**
Llanbadarn Fawr U.K. 59 C6
Llanbedr Pont Steffan U.K. *see* **Lampeter**
Llanbister U.K. 59 D6
Llandeilo U.K. 59 D7
Llandissilio U.K. 59 C7
Llandovery U.K. 59 D7
Llandrindod Wells U.K. 59 D6
Llandudno U.K. 58 D5
Llandysul U.K. 59 C6
Llanegwad U.K. 59 C7
Llanelli U.K. 59 C7
Llanfair Caereinion U.K. 59 D6
Llanfair-ym-Muallt U.K. *see* **Builth Wells**
Llangefni U.K. 58 C5
Llangollen U.K. 59 D6
Llangurig U.K. 59 D6
Llanllyfni U.K. 59 C5
Llannerch-y-medd U.K. 58 C5
Llannor U.K. 59 C6
Llano Mex. 166 C2
Llano *TX* U.S.A. 161 D6
Llano *r. TX* U.S.A. 161 D6
Llano Estacado *plain New Mexico/Texas* U.S.A. 161 C5
Llano Grande Mex. 166 D4
Llanos *plain* Col./Venez. 176 E2
Llanquihue, Lago *l.* Chile 178 B6
Llanrhystud U.K. 59 C6
Llantrisant U.K. 59 D7
Llanuwchllyn U.K. 59 D6
Llanwnog U.K. 59 D6
Llanymddyfri U.K. *see* **Llandovery**
Llay U.K. 59 D5
Lleida Spain 67 G3
Llerena Spain 67 C4
Llíria Spain 67 F4
Llodio Spain *see* **Laudio**
Lloyd George, Mount Canada 150 E3
Lloyd Lake Canada 151 I3
Lloydminster Canada 151 I4
Lluchmayor Spain *see* **Llucmajor**
Llucmajor Spain 67 H4

▶**Llullaillaco, Volcán** *vol.* Chile 178 C2
Highest active volcano in South America and the world.

Lô, Sông *r.* China/Vietnam 86 D2
Loa *r.* Chile 178 B2
Loa *UT* U.S.A. 159 H2
Loagan Bunut National Park Malaysia 85 F2
Loakulu *Kalimantan* Indon. 85 G3
Loango Congo 123 B4
Loay *Bohol* Phil. 82 D4
Loban' *r.* Russia 52 K4
Lobata *Celebes* Indon. 83 B3
Lobatejo *mt.* Spain 67 D5
Lobatse Botswana 125 G3
Lobaye *r.* Cent. Afr. Rep. 122 B3
Löbejün Germany 63 L3
Löbenberg *hill* Germany 63 M3
Loberia Arg. 178 E5
Lobi, Mount *vol.* Phil. 82 D4
Lobito Angola 123 B5
Lobos Arg. 178 E5
Lobos, Cabo *c.* Mex. 166 B2
Lobos, Isla *i.* Mex. 166 C3
Lobos, Isla de *i.* Mex. 167 F4
Lobos de Tierra, Isla *i.* Peru 176 B5
Loburg Germany 63 M2
Lôc Binh Vietnam 86 D2
Lochaline U.K. 60 D4
Lo Chau *H.K.* China *see* **Beaufort Island**
Loch Baghasdail U.K. *see* **Lochboisdale**
Lochboisdale U.K. 60 B3
Lochcarron U.K. 60 D3
Lochearnhead U.K. 60 E4
Lochem Neth. 62 G2
Lochern National Park Australia 136 C5
Loches France 66 E3
Loch Garman Ireland *see* **Wexford**
Lochgelly U.K. 60 F4
Lochgilphead U.K. 60 D4
Lochinver U.K. 60 D2
Loch Lomond and the Trossachs National Park U.K. 60 E4
Lochmaddy U.K. 60 B3
Lochnagar *mt.* U.K. 60 F4
Loch na Madadh U.K. *see* **Lochmaddy**
Loch Raven Reservoir *MD* U.S.A. 165 G4
Lochy, Loch *l.* U.K. 60 E4
Lock Australia 137 A7
Lockerbie U.K. 60 F5
Lockhart Australia 138 C5
Lockhart *TX* U.S.A. 161 D6
Lock Haven *PA* U.S.A. 165 G3
Löcknitz *r.* Germany 63 L1
Lockport *NY* U.S.A. 165 F2
Lockwood Hills *AK* U.S.A. 148 H2
Lôc Ninh Vietnam 87 D5
Lod Israel 107 B4
Loddon *r.* Australia 138 A5
Lodève France 66 F5
Lodeynoye Pole Russia 52 G3
Lodge, Mount Canada/U.S.A. 149 M4
Lodhikheda India 104 D5
Lodhran Pak. 111 H4
Lodi Italy 68 C2
Lodi *CA* U.S.A. 158 C2
Lodi *OH* U.S.A. 164 D3
Lødingen Norway 54 I2
Lodja Dem. Rep. Congo 122 C4
Lodomeria Russia *see* **Vladimir**
Lodrani India 104 B5
Lodwar Kenya 122 D3
Łódź Poland 57 Q5
Loei Thai. 86 C3
Loeriesfontein S. Africa 124 D6
Lofoten *is* Norway 54 H2
Lofusa South Sudan 121 G4
Log Russia 53 I6
Loga Niger 120 D3
Logan *IA* U.S.A. 160 E3
Logan *OH* U.S.A. 164 D4
Logan *UT* U.S.A. 156 F4
Logan *WV* U.S.A. 164 E5

▶**Logan, Mount** Canada 149 L3
2nd highest mountain in North America.

Logan, Mount *WA* U.S.A. 156 C2
Logan Creek *r.* Australia 136 D4
Logan Lake Canada 150 F5
Logan Mountains Canada 149 O3
Logansport *IN* U.S.A. 164 B3
Logansport *LA* U.S.A. 161 E6
Logatec Slovenia 68 F2
Logpung China 94 E5
Logroño Spain 67 E2
Lohardaga India 105 F5
Loharu India 104 C3
Lohatlha S. Africa 124 F5
Lohawat India 104 C4
Lohfelden Germany 63 J3
Lohil *r.* China/India *see* **Zayü Qu**
Lohiniva Fin. 54 N3
Lohit *r.* India 105 H4
Lohjanjärvi *l.* Fin. 55 M6
Löhne Germany 63 I2
Lohne (Oldenburg) Germany 63 I2
Lohtaja Fin. 54 M4
Loi, Nam *r.* Myanmar 86 C2
Loikaw Myanmar 86 B3
Loi-lem Myanmar 86 B2
Loi Lun Myanmar 86 B2
Loimaa Fin. 55 M6
Loipyet Hills Myanmar 86 B1
Loire *r.* France 66 C3
Loja Ecuador 176 C4
Loja Spain 67 D5
Lokan *r.* Malaysia 85 G1
Lokan tekojärvi *l.* Fin. 54 O3
Lokchim *r.* Russia 52 K3
Lokeren Belgium 62 E3
Lokgwabe Botswana 124 E3
Lokichar Kenya 100 C6
Lokichokio Kenya 122 D3
Lokilalaki, Gunung *mt.* Indon. 83 B3
Løkken Denmark 55 F8
Løkken Norway 54 F5
Loknya Russia 52 F4
Lokoja Nigeria 120 D4
Lokolama Dem. Rep. Congo 122 B4
Lokossa Benin 120 D4
Lokot' Russia 53 G5
Loktak Lake India 105 H4
Lol South Sudan 121 F4
Lola Guinea 120 C4
Lola, Mount *CA* U.S.A. 158 C2
Loleta *CA* U.S.A. 158 A1
Loliondo Tanz. 122 D4
Lolland *i.* Denmark 55 G9
Lolo *MT* U.S.A. 156 E3
Lolobata *Halmahera* Indon. 83 D2
Loloda *Halmahera* Indon. 83 C2
Loloda Utara, Kepulauan *is Moluccas* Indon. 83 C2
Lolo Pass *MT* U.S.A. 156 E3
Lolotoi East Timor 83 C5
Lolowau *Sumatra* Indon. 84 B2
Lolwane S. Africa 124 F4
Lom Bulg. 69 J3
Lom Norway 55 F6
Loma *CO* U.S.A. 159 I2
Lomami *r.* Dem. Rep. Congo 122 C3
Lomar Pass Afgh. 111 G3
Lomas, Bahía de *b.* Chile 178 C8
Lomas de Zamora Arg. 178 E4
Lombarda, Serra *hills* Brazil 177 H3
Lomblen *i.* Indon. 83 B5
Lombok *Lombok* Indon. 85 G5
Lombok *i.* Indon. 85 G5
Lombok, Selat *sea chan.* Indon. 85 F5

▶**Lomé** Togo 120 D4
Capital of Togo.

Lomela Dem. Rep. Congo 122 C4
Lomela *r.* Dem. Rep. Congo 121 F5
Lomira *WI* U.S.A. 164 A2
Lomme France 62 C4
Lommel Belgium 62 F3
Lomond Canada 153 K4
Lomond, Loch *l.* U.K. 60 E4
Lomonosov Russia 55 P7
Lomonosov Ridge *sea feature* Arctic Ocean 189 B1
Lomovoye Russia 52 I2
Lomphat Cambodia *see* **Lumphăt**
Lompobatang, Hutan Lindung *nature res. Celebes* Indon. 85 G4
Lompobattang, Gunung *mt.* Indon. 83 A4
Lompoc *CA* U.S.A. 158 C4
Lom Sak Thai. 86 C3
Łomża Poland 57 S4
Lơn, Hon *i.* Vietnam 87 E4
Lonar India 106 C2
Londa Bangl. 105 G5
Londa India 106 B3
Londinières France 62 B5
Londinium U.K. *see* **London**
Londoko Russia 90 D2
London Canada 164 E2

▶**London** U.K. 59 G7
Capital of the United Kingdom and of England. 4th most populous city in Europe.

London *KY* U.S.A. 164 C5
London *OH* U.S.A. 164 D4
Londonderry U.K. 61 E3
Londonderry *OH* U.S.A. 164 D4
Londonderry *VT* U.S.A. 165 I2
Londonderry, Cape Australia 134 D3
Londrina Brazil 179 A3
Lone Pine *CA* U.S.A. 158 D3
Long Thai. 86 B3
Long *AK* U.S.A. 148 I2
Longa Angola 123 B5
Longa, Proliv *sea chan.* Russia 77 S2
Longagung *Kalimantan* Indon. 85 F2
Long Akah *Sarawak* Malaysia 85 F2
Long'an China 96 E4
Long'anqiao China 95 K2
Long Ashton U.K. 59 E7
Longbao China 96 C1
Longbawan *Kalimantan* Indon. 85 F2
Long Bay *NC* U.S.A. 163 E5
Longbeach N.Z. 139 C7
Long Beach *CA* U.S.A. 158 D5
Longberini *Kalimantan* Indon. 85 F2
Longbia *Kalimantan* Indon. 85 G2
Longbo China *see* **Shuangpai**
Longboh *Kalimantan* Indon. 85 F2
Long Branch *NJ* U.S.A. 165 I3
Longchang China 96 E2
Longcheng *Anhui* China *see* **Xiaoxian**
Longcheng *Guangdong* China *see* **Longmen**
Longcheng *Yunnan* China *see* **Chenggong**
Longchuan China *see* **Nanhua**
Longchuan Jiang *r.* China 96 C4
Long Creek *r.* Canada 151 K5
Long Creek *OR* U.S.A. 156 D3
Longde China 94 F5
Long Eaton U.K. 59 F6
Longford Ireland 61 E4
Longgang *Chongqing* China *see* **Dazu**
Longgang *Guangdong* China 97 G4
Longgang *Shandong* China 95 J4
Longgi *r.* Indon. 85 G2
Longhoughton U.K. 58 F3
Longhua China 95 I3
Longhui China 97 F3
Longhurst, Mount Antarctica 188 H1
Longibau *Kalimantan* Indon. 85 G2
Longikis *Kalimantan* Indon. 85 G3
Longiram *Kalimantan* Indon. 85 F3
Long Island Bahamas 163 F8
Long Island *N.S.* Canada 153 I5
Long Island *Nunavut* Canada 152 F3
Long Island India 87 A4
Long Island P.N.G. 81 L8
Long Island *NY* U.S.A. 165 I3
Long Island Sound *sea chan. Connecticut/New York* U.S.A. 165 I3
Longjiang China 95 J2
Longjin China *see* **Qingliu**
Longju China 96 B2
Longkou China 95 J4
Longlac Canada 152 D4
Long Lake *l.* Canada 152 D4
Long Lake *NY* U.S.A. 165 H2
Long Lake *l. ME* U.S.A. 162 G2
Long Lake *l. MI* U.S.A. 164 D1
Long Lake *l. ND* U.S.A. 160 C2
Long Lake *l. NY* U.S.A. 165 H1
Long Lama *Sarawak* Malaysia 85 F2
Longli China 96 E3
Longlin China 96 E3
Longling China 96 C3
Longmeadow *MA* U.S.A. 165 I2
Long Melford U.K. 59 H6
Longmen *Guangdong* China 97 G4
Longmen *Heilong.* China 90 B2
Longmen Shan *hill* China 97 F1
Longmen Shan *mts* China 96 E1
Longming China 96 E4
Longmont *CO* U.S.A. 156 G4
Long Murum *Sarawak* Malaysia 85 F2
Longnan *Gansu* China 96 E1
Longnan *Jiangxi* China 97 G3
Longnawan *Kalimantan* Indon. 85 F2

Longpahangai Kalimantan Indon. 85 F2
Long Phu Vietnam 87 D5
Longping China see Luodian
Long Point Canada 164 E2
Long Point Man. Canada 151 L4
Long Point Ont. Canada 164 E2
Long Point N.Z. 139 B8
Long Point Bay Canada 164 E2
Long Prairie MN U.S.A. 160 E2
Long Preston U.K. 58 E4
Longpujungan Kalimantan Indon. 85 F2
Longquan Guizhou China see Fenggang
Longquan Guizhou China see Danzhai
Longquan Hunan China see Xintian
Longquan Xi r. China 97 I2
Long Range Mountains Nfld. and Lab. Canada 153 K4
Long Range Mountains Nfld. and Lab. Canada 153 K5
Longreach Australia 136 D4
Longriba China 96 D1
Longshan Guizhou China see Longli
Longshan Hunan China 97 F2
Longshan Yunnan China see Longling
Long Shan mts China 94 F5
Longshanlu China see Shizhong
Longsheng China 97 F3
Longshou Shan mts China 94 E4
Longs Peak CO U.S.A. 156 G4
Long Stratton U.K. 59 I6
Long Teru Sarawak Malaysia 85 F2
Longtom Lake Canada 150 G1
Longtou China 95 J1
Longtown U.K. 58 E3
Longue-Pointe-de-Mingan Canada 153 I4
Longueuil Canada 152 G5
Longuyon France 62 F5
Longvale CA U.S.A. 158 B2
Longview TX U.S.A. 161 E5
Longview WA U.S.A. 156 C3
Longwai Kalimantan Indon. 85 G2
Longwangmiao China 90 D3
Longwei Co l. China 99 E6
Longxi China 94 F5
Longxian Guangdong China see Wengyuan
Longxian Shaanxi China 94 F5
Longxingchang China see Wuyuan
Longxi Shan mt. China 97 H3
Longxu China see Cangwu
Long Xuyên Vietnam 87 D5
Longyan China 97 H3
Longyao China 95 H4

▶Longyearbyen Svalbard 76 C2
Capital of Svalbard.

Longzhen China 90 B2
Longzhou China 96 E4
Longzhouping China see Changyang
Löningen Germany 63 H2
Lonoke AR U.S.A. 161 F5
Lonpo Myanmar 86 B2
Lönsboda Sweden 55 I8
Lons-le-Saunier France 66 G3
Lontar i. Moluccas Indon. 83 D4
Lonton Myanmar 86 B1
Looc Phil. 82 C3
Loochoo Islands Japan see Ryukyu Islands
Loogootee IN U.S.A. 164 B4
Lookout, Cape Canada 152 E3
Lookout, Cape NC U.S.A. 163 E5
Lookout, Point Australia 138 F1
Lookout, Point MI U.S.A. 164 D1
Lookout Mountain NM U.S.A. 159 I4
Lookout Point Australia 135 B8
Lookout Ridge AK U.S.A. 148 H1
Loolmalasin vol. crater Tanz. 122 D4
Loon Canada 152 C4
Loon r. Canada 150 H3
Loongana Australia 135 D7
Loon Lake Canada 151 I4
Loop Head hd Ireland 61 C5
Lop China 99 C5
Lopasnya Russia see Chekhov
Lopatina, Gora mt. Russia 90 F2
Lop Buri Thai. 86 C4
Lopez Luzon Phil. 82 C3
Lopez, Cap c. Gabon 122 A4
Lopnur China see Yuli
Lop Nur salt flat China 98 E4
Lopphavet b. Norway 54 L1
Loptyuga Russia 52 K3
Loqung China 96 C1
Lora Pak. 111 G5
Lora r. Venez. 176 D2
Lora, Hāmūn-i- dry lake Afgh./Pak. 111 G4
Lora del Río Spain 67 D5
Lorain OH U.S.A. 164 D3
Loralai Pak. 111 H4
Loralai r. Pak. 111 H4
Loramie, Lake OH U.S.A. 164 C3
Lorana Celebes Indon. 83 B3
Lorca Spain 67 F5
Lorch Germany 63 H4
Lord Auckland Shoal sea feature Phil. 82 B4
Lordegān Iran 110 C4
Lord Howe Atoll Solomon Is see Ontong Java Atoll
Lord Howe Island Australia 133 F5
Lord Howe Rise sea feature S. Pacific Ocean 186 G7
Lord Loughborough Island Myanmar 87 B5
Lordsburg NM U.S.A. 159 I5
Lore East Timor 83 C5
Lore Lindu, Taman Nasional nat. park Indon. 83 B3
Lorena Brazil 179 B3
Lorengau P.N.G. 81 L7
Lorentz, Taman Nasional nat. park Indon. 81 J7
Lorenzo del Real Mex. 167 F4
Loreto Arg. 178 D3
Loreto Brazil 177 I5
Loreto Mex. 166 C3
Loreto Phil. 82 D4
Lorient France 66 C3
Lorillard r. Canada 151 N1
Loring MT U.S.A. 156 G2
Lorino Russia 148 E2
Lorn, Firth of est. U.K. 60 D4
Lorne Australia 136 D5
Lorne watercourse Australia 136 B3
Loro r. China 99 F7
Loropéni Burkina Faso 120 C3
Lorrain, Plateau France 63 G6
Lorraine Australia 136 B3
Lorraine admin. reg. France 62 G6
Lorraine reg. France 62 F5
Lorsch Germany 63 I5
Lorup Germany 63 H2
Losal India 104 C4
Los Alamos CA U.S.A. 158 C4
Los Alamos NM U.S.A. 157 G6
Los Aldamas Mex. 167 F3
Los Alerces, Parque Nacional nat. park Arg. 178 B6
Los Ángeles Chile 178 B5

▶Los Angeles CA U.S.A. 158 D4
3rd most populous city in North America.

Los Angeles Aqueduct canal CA U.S.A. 158 D4
Los Arabos Cuba 163 D8
Los Baños Mex. 166 D3
Los Banos CA U.S.A. 158 C3
Los Blancos Arg. 178 D2
Los Cerritos watercourse Mex. 157 F8
Los Chiles Costa Rica 166 [inset] I7
Los Coronados, Islas is Mex. 158 E5
Los Gigantes, Llanos de plain Mex. 161 B6
Los Glaciares, Parque Nacional nat. park Arg. 178 B8
Losheim am See Germany 62 G5
Los Hoyos Mex. 166 C2
Lošinj i. Croatia 68 F2
Los Juríes Arg. 178 D3
Los Katios, Parque Nacional nat. park Col. 169 I7
Loskop Dam S. Africa 125 I3
Los Leones Mex. 166 D2
Los Lunas NM U.S.A. 157 G6
Los Mármoles, Parque Nacional nat. park Mex. 167 F4
Los Menucos Arg. 178 C6
Los Mochis Mex. 166 C3
Los Molinos CA U.S.A. 158 B1
Losombo Dem. Rep. Congo 122 B3
Los Palacios Cuba 163 D8
Lospalos East Timor 83 C5
Los Remedios r. Mex. 161 B7
Los Reyes Mex. 166 E5
Los Roques, Islas is Venez. 176 E1
Losser Neth. 62 G2
Lossie r. U.K. 60 F3
Lossiemouth U.K. 60 F3
Lößnitz Germany 63 M4
Lost Creek KY U.S.A. 164 D5
Lost Creek WV U.S.A. 164 E4
Los Teques Venez. 176 E1
Los Testigos is Venez. 176 F1
Lost Hills CA U.S.A. 158 D4
Lost Trail Pass ID U.S.A. 156 E3
Lostwithiel U.K. 59 C8
Los Vidrios Mex. 159 G6
Los Vilos Chile 178 B4
Lot r. France 66 E4
Lota Chile 178 B5
Loṭfābād Turkm. 110 E2
Lothringen reg. France see Lorraine
Lotikipi Plain Kenya/South Sudan 122 D3
Loto Dem. Rep. Congo 122 C4
Lotsane r. Botswana 125 I2
Lot's Wife i. Japan see Sōfu-gan
Lotta r. Fin./Russia 54 Q2
also known as Lutto
Lotte Germany 63 H2
Louangnamtha Laos 86 C2
Louangphabang Laos 86 C3
Loubomo Congo see Dolisie
Loudéac France 66 C2
Loudi China 97 F3
Loufan China 95 G4
Louga Senegal 120 B3
Loughborough U.K. 59 F6
Lougheed Island Canada 147 H2
Loughor r. U.K. 59 C7
Loughrea Ireland 61 D4
Loughton U.K. 59 H7
Louhans France 66 G3
Louisa KY U.S.A. 164 D4
Louisa VA U.S.A. 165 G4
Louisbourg Canada 153 K5
Louisburg Canada see Louisbourg
Louisburgh Ireland 61 C4
Louise, Lake AK U.S.A. 149 K3
Louise Falls Canada 150 G2
Louis-Gentil Morocco see Youssoufia
Louisiade Archipelago is P.N.G. 136 F1
Louisiana MO U.S.A. 160 F4
Louisiana state U.S.A. 161 F6
Louis Trichardt S. Africa see Makhado
Louisville GA U.S.A. 163 D5
Louisville IL U.S.A. 160 F4
Louisville KY U.S.A. 164 C4
Louisville MS U.S.A. 161 F5
Louisville Ridge sea feature S. Pacific Ocean 186 I8
Louis-XIV, Pointe pt Canada 152 F3
Loukhi Russia 54 R3
Loukoléla Congo 122 B4
Loukouo Congo 121 E5
Loulé Port. 67 B5
Loum Cameroon 120 D4
Louny Czech Rep. 57 N5
Loup r. NE U.S.A. 160 D3
Loups Marins, Lacs des lakes Canada 152 G2
Loups Marins, Petit lac des l. Canada 153 G2
Lourdes Canada 153 K4
Lourdes France 66 D5
Lourenço Marques Moz. see Maputo
Lousã Port. 67 B3
Loushan China 90 C3
Loushanguan China see Tongzi
Louth Australia 138 B3
Louth U.K. 58 G5
Loutra Aidipsou Greece 69 J5
Louvain Belgium see Leuven
Louviers France 62 B5
Louwater-Suid Namibia 124 C2
Louwsburg S. Africa 125 J4
Lövånger Sweden 54 L4
Lovat' r. Russia 52 F4
Lovech Bulg. 69 K3
Lovell ME U.S.A. 165 J1
Lovelock NV U.S.A. 158 D1
Lovendegem Belgium 62 D3
Lovers Leap mt. VA U.S.A. 164 E5
Loviisa Fin. 55 O6
Lovington NM U.S.A. 161 C5
Lovozero Russia 52 G1
Lóvua Lunda Norte Angola 123 C4
Lóvua Moxico Angola 123 C5
Low, Cape Canada 147 J3
Lowa Dem. Rep. Congo 122 C4
Lowa r. Dem. Rep. Congo 122 C4
Lowarai Pass Pak. 111 H3
Lowell IN U.S.A. 164 B3
Lowell MA U.S.A. 165 J2
Lower Arrow Lake Canada 150 G5
Lower California pen. Mex. see Baja California
Lower Glenelg National Park Australia 137 C8
Lower Granite Gorge AZ U.S.A. 159 G4
Lower Hutt N.Z. 139 E5
Lower Laberge Canada 149 N3
Lower Lake CA U.S.A. 158 B2
Lower Lough Erne l. U.K. 61 E3
Lower Post Canada 149 O4
Lower Red Lake MN U.S.A. 160 E2
Lower Saxony land Germany see Niedersachsen
Lower Tunguska r. Russia see Nizhnyaya Tunguska
Lower Zambezi National Park Zambia 123 C5
Lowestoft U.K. 59 I6
Łowicz Poland 57 Q4
Low Island Kiribati see Starbuck Island
Lowrah, Hāmūn-e dry lake Afgh./Pak. see Lora, Hāmūn-i-
Lowther Hills U.K. 60 F5
Lowville NY U.S.A. 165 H2
Loxicha Mex. 167 F5
Loxstedt Germany 63 I1
Loxton Australia 137 C7
Loyal, Loch l. U.K. 60 E2
Loyalsock Creek r. PA U.S.A. 165 G3
Loyalton CA U.S.A. 158 C2
Loyalty Islands New Caledonia see Loyauté, Îles
Loyang China see Luoyang
Loyauté, Îles is New Caledonia 133 G4
Loyev Belarus see Loyew
Loyew Belarus 53 F6
Lozère, Mont mt. France 66 F4
Loznica Serbia 69 H2
Lozova Ukr. 53 H6
Lozovaya Ukr. see Lozova
Lua r. Dem. Rep. Congo 122 B3
Luacano Angola 123 C5
Lu'an China 97 H2
Luân Châu Vietnam 86 C2
Luanchuan China 97 F1

▶Luanda Angola 123 B4
Capital of Angola. 4th most populous city in Africa.

Luang i. Moluccas Indon. 83 D5
Luang, Khao mt. Thai. 87 B5
Luang, Thale lag. Thai. 87 C6
Luang Namtha Laos see Louangnamtha
Luang Phrabang, Thiu Khao mts Laos/Thai. 86 C3
Luang Prabang Laos see Louangphabang
Luanhaizi China 94 C5
Luan He r. China 95 I4
Luannan China 95 I4
Luanping China 95 I3
Luanshya Zambia 123 C5
Luanxian China 95 I4
Luanza Dem. Rep. Congo 123 C4
Luanzhou China see Luanxian
Luao Angola see Luau
Luar, Danau l. Indon. 85 F2
Luarca Spain 67 C2
Luashi Dem. Rep. Congo 123 C5
Luau Angola 123 C5
Luba Equat. Guinea 120 D4
Lubaczów Poland 53 D6
Lubalo Angola 123 B4
Lubānas ezers l. Latvia 55 O8
Lubang Phil. 82 C3
Lubang i. Phil. 82 C3
Lubang Islands Phil. 82 B3
Lubango Angola 123 B5
Lubao Dem. Rep. Congo 123 C4
Lubartów Poland 53 D6
Lübbecke Germany 63 I2
Lubbeskolk salt pan S. Africa 124 D5
Lubbock TX U.S.A. 161 C5
Lübbow Germany 63 L2
Lübeck Germany 57 M4
Lubeck WV U.S.A. 164 E4
Lubefu Dem. Rep. Congo 123 C4
Lubei China 95 J2
Lüben Poland see Lubin
Lubersac France 66 E4
Lubin Poland 57 P5
Lublin Poland 53 D6
Lubnān country Asia see Lebanon
Lubnān, Jabal mts Lebanon see Liban, Jebel
Lubny Ukr. 53 G6
Lubok Antu Sarawak Malaysia 85 E2
Lübtheen Germany 63 L1
Lubuagan Luzon Phil. 82 C2
Lubudi Dem. Rep. Congo 123 C4
Lubukbalang Sumatra Indon. 84 D3
Lubuklinggau Sumatra Indon. 84 C3
Lubukpakam Sumatra Indon. 84 B2
Lubuksikaping Sumatra Indon. 84 C2
Lubumbashi Dem. Rep. Congo 123 C5
Lubutu Dem. Rep. Congo 122 C4
Lübz Germany 63 M1
Lucala Angola 123 B4
Lucan Canada 164 E2
Lucan Ireland 61 F4
Lucania, Mount Canada 149 L3
Lücaoshan China 99 F5
Lucapa Angola 123 C4
Lucas KY U.S.A. 164 B5
Lucasville OH U.S.A. 164 D4
Lucca Italy 68 D3
Luce Bay U.K. 60 E6
Lucedale MS U.S.A. 161 F6
Lucélia Brazil 179 A3
Lucena Luzon Phil. 82 C3
Lucena Spain 67 D5
Lučenec Slovakia 57 Q6
Lucera Italy 68 F4
Lucerne Switz. 66 I3
Lucerne Valley CA U.S.A. 158 E4
Lucero Mex. 166 D2
Luchegorsk Russia 90 D3
Lucheng Guangxi China see Luchuan
Lucheng Shanxi China 95 H4
Lucheng Sichuan China see Kangding
Luchuan China 97 F4
Lüchun China 96 D4
Lucipara, Kepulauan is Moluccas Indon. 83 C4
Łuck Ukr. see Luts'k
Luckeesarai India see Lakhisarai
Luckenwalde Germany 63 N2
Luckhoff S. Africa 124 G5
Lucknow Canada 164 E2
Lucknow India 104 E4
Lücongpo China 97 F2
Lucrecia, Cabo c. Cuba 169 I4
Lucusse Angola 123 C5
Lucy Creek Australia 136 B4
Lüda China see Dalian
Lü Dao i. Taiwan 97 I4
Lüdenscheid Germany 63 H3
Lüderitz Namibia 124 B4
Ludewa Tanz. 123 D5
Ludhiana India 104 C3
Ludian China 96 D3
Luding China 96 D2
Ludington MI U.S.A. 164 B2
Ludlow U.K. 59 E6
Ludlow CA U.S.A. 158 E4
Ludogorie reg. Bulg. 69 L3
Ludowici GA U.S.A. 163 D6
Ludvika Sweden 55 I6
Ludwigsburg Germany 63 J6
Ludwigsfelde Germany 63 N2
Ludwigshafen am Rhein Germany 63 I5
Ludwigslust Germany 63 L1
Ludza Latvia 55 O8
Luebo Dem. Rep. Congo 123 C4
Luena Angola 123 B5
Luena Flats plain Zambia 123 C5
Lüeyang China 96 E1
Lufeng Guangdong China 97 G4
Lufeng Yunnan China 96 D3
Lufkin TX U.S.A. 161 E6
Lufu China see Shilin
Luga Russia 55 P7
Luga r. Russia 55 P7
Lugano Switz. 66 I3
Lugansk Ukr. see Luhans'k
Lugau/Erzgebirge Germany 63 M4
Lügde Germany 63 J3
Lugdunum France see Lyon
Lugg r. U.K. 59 E6
Lugnaquilla hill Ireland 61 F5
Lugo Italy 68 D2
Lugo Spain 67 C2
Lugoj Romania 69 I2
Lugu China 99 D6
Lugus i. Phil. 82 C5
Luhans'k Ukr. 53 H6
Luhe China 97 H1
Lu He r. China 95 G4
Luhe r. Germany 63 K1
Luḩfī, Wādī watercourse Jordan 107 C3
Luhin Sum China 95 I2
Luhit r. China/India see Zayü Qu
Luhua China see Heishui
Luhuo China 96 D2
Luhyny Ukr. 53 F6
Luia Angola 123 C4
Luiana Angola 123 C5
Luichow Peninsula China see Leizhou Bandao
Luik Belgium see Liège
Luimneach Ireland see Limerick
Luiro r. Fin. 54 O3
Luis Echeverría Álvarez Mex. 158 E5
Luis L. León, Presa resr Mex. 166 D2
Luis Moya Mex. 166 E4
Luitpold Coast Antarctica 188 A1
Luiza Dem. Rep. Congo 123 C4
Lujiang China 97 H2
Lüjing China 94 F5
Lukachek Russia 90 D1
Lukapa Angola see Lucapa
Lukavac Bos. & Herz. 68 H2
Lukenga, Lac l. Dem. Rep. Congo 123 C4
Lukenie r. Dem. Rep. Congo 122 B4
Lukeville AZ U.S.A. 166 B2
Lukh r. Russia 52 I4
Lukhī Afgh. 111 F4
Lukhovitsy Russia 53 H5
Luk Keng H.K. China 97 [inset]
Lukou China see Zhuzhou
Lukovit Bulg. 69 K3
Łuków Poland 53 D6
Lukoyanov Russia 53 J5
Lükqün China 98 E4
Luksagu Celebes Indon. 83 B3
Lukusuzi National Park Zambia 123 D5
Luleå Sweden 54 M4
Luleälven r. Sweden 54 M4
Lüleburgaz Turkey 69 L4
Lüliang China 95 G4
Luliang China 96 D3
Lüliang Shan mts China 95 G4
Lulimba Dem. Rep. Congo 123 C4
Luling TX U.S.A. 161 D6
Lulong China 95 I4
Lulonga r. Dem. Rep. Congo 122 B3
Luluabourg Dem. Rep. Congo see Kananga
Lumachomo China 99 D7
Lumajang Java Indon. 85 F5
Lumajangdong Co salt l. China 99 C6
Lumbala Moxico Angola see Lumbala N'guimbo
Lumbala Moxico Angola see Lumbala Kaquengue
Lumbala Kaquengue Angola 123 C5
Lumbala N'guimbo Angola 123 C5
Lumberton NC U.S.A. 163 E5
Lumbini Nepal 105 E4
Lumbis Kalimantan Indon. 85 G1
Lumbrales Spain 67 C3
Lumezzane Italy 68 D2
Lumi P.N.G. 81 K7
Lumphăt Cambodia 87 D4
Lumpkin GA U.S.A. 163 C5
Lumsden Canada 151 J5
Lumsden N.Z. 139 B7
Lumut Malaysia 84 C1
Lumut, Gunung mt. Indon. 85 F3
Lumut, Tanjung pt Indon. 84 D3
Lün Mongolia 94 F2
Luna Luzon Phil. 82 C2
Luna NM U.S.A. 159 I5
Lunan China see Shilin
Lunan Bay U.K. 60 G4
Lunan Lake Canada 151 M1
Lunan Shan mts China 96 D3
Luna Pier MI U.S.A. 164 D3
Lund Pak. 111 H5
Lund Sweden 55 H9
Lund NV U.S.A. 159 F2
Lund UT U.S.A. 159 G2
Lundar Canada 151 L5
Lundu Sarawak Malaysia 85 E2
Lundy U.K. 59 C7
Lune r. Germany 63 I1
Lune r. U.K. 58 E4
Lüneburg Germany 63 K1
Lüneburger Heide reg. Germany 63 K1
Lünen Germany 63 H3
Lunenburg VA U.S.A. 165 F5
Lunéville France 66 H2
Lunga r. Zambia 123 C5
Lungdo China 105 E2
Lunggar China 99 C7
Lunggar Shan mts China 99 C7
Lung Kwu Chau i. H.K. China 97 [inset]
Lungleh India see Lunglei
Lunglei India 105 H5
Lungmari mt. China 99 D7
Lungmu Co salt l. China 99 C6
Lung-tzu China see Lhünzê
Lungwebungu r. Zambia 123 C5
Lunh Nepal 105 E3
Luni India 104 C4
Luni r. India 104 B4
Luni r. Pak. 111 H4
Luninets Belarus see Luninyets
Luning NV U.S.A. 158 D2
Luninyets Belarus 55 O10
Lunkaransar India 104 C3
Lunkha India 104 C3
Lünne Germany 63 H2
Lunsar Sierra Leone 120 B4
Lunsklip S. Africa 125 I3
Luntai China 98 D4
Lunyuk Sumbawa Indon. 85 G5
Luobei China 90 C3
Luobuzhuang China 98 E5
Luocheng Fujian China see Hui'an
Luocheng Gansu China 94 D4
Luocheng Guangxi China 97 F3
Luochuan China 95 G5
Luodian China 96 E3
Luoding China 97 F4
Luodou Sha i. China 97 F4
Luohe China 97 G1
Luo He r. Henan China 95 H5
Luo He r. Shaanxi China 95 G5
Luoma Hu l. China 95 I5
Luonan China 95 G5
Luoning China 95 G5
Luoping China 96 E3
Luotian China 97 G2
Luoto Fin. see Larsmo
Luotuoquan China 94 D3
Luoxiao Shan mts China 97 G3
Luoxiong China see Luoping
Luoyang Guangdong China see Boluo
Luoyang Henan China 95 H5
Luoyang Zhejiang China see Taishun
Luoyuan China 97 H3
Luozigou China 90 C4
Lupane Zimbabwe 123 C5
Lupanshui China see Liupanshui
Lupar r. Malaysia 85 E2
Lupeni Romania 69 J2
Lupilichi Moz. 123 D5
Lupon Mindanao Phil. 82 D5
Lupton AZ U.S.A. 159 I4
Luqiao China see Luding
Luqu China 94 E5
Lu Qu r. China see Tao He
Luquan Hebei China 95 H4
Luquan Yunnan China 86 C1
Luray VA U.S.A. 165 F4
Luremo Angola 123 B4
Lurgan U.K. 61 F3
Lúrio Moz. 123 E5
Lurio r. Moz. 123 E5
Lūr Kōh mt. Afgh. 111 F3

▶Lusaka Zambia 123 C5
Capital of Zambia.

Lusambo Dem. Rep. Congo 123 C4
Lusancay Islands and Reefs P.N.G. 132 F2
Lusangi Dem. Rep. Congo 123 C4
Luseland Canada 151 I4
Lush, Mount hill Australia 134 D4
Lushar China see Huangzhong
Lushi China 95 G5
Lushnja Albania see Lushnjë
Lushnjë Albania 69 H4
Lushui China see Luzhang
Lushuihe China 90 B4
Lüshunkou China 95 J4
Lusi r. Indon. 85 E4
Lüsigang China 97 I1
Lusikisiki S. Africa 125 I6
Lusk WY U.S.A. 156 G4
Luso Angola see Luena
Lussvale Australia 138 C1
Lut, Bahrat salt l. Asia see Dead Sea
Lūt, Dasht-e des. Iran see Lūt, Kavīr-e
Lūt, Kavīr-e des. Iran 110 E4
Lutai China see Ninghe
Lutetia France see Paris
Lūt-e Zangī Aḩmad des. Iran 110 E4
Luther MI U.S.A. 164 C1
Luther Lake Canada 164 E2
Luton U.K. 59 G7
Lutong Sarawak Malaysia 85 F1
Łutselk'e Canada 151 I2
Luts'k Ukr. 53 E6
Luttelgeest Neth. 62 F2
Luttenberg Neth. 62 G2
Lutto r. Fin./Russia see Lotta
Lutz FL U.S.A. 163 D6
Lützelbach Germany 63 J5
Lützow-Holm Bay Antarctica 188 D2
Lutzputs S. Africa 124 E5
Lutzville S. Africa 124 D6
Luuk Phil. 82 C5
Luumäki Fin. 55 O6
Luuq Somalia 122 E3
Luverne AL U.S.A. 163 C6
Luverne MN U.S.A. 160 D3
Luvuei Angola 123 C5
Luvuvhu r. S. Africa 125 J2
Luwero Uganda 122 D3
Luwingu Zambia 123 C5
Luwuhuyu Kalimantan Indon. 85 E3
Luwuk Celebes Indon. 83 B3
Luxembourg country Europe 62 G5

▶Luxembourg Lux. 62 G5
Capital of Luxembourg.

Luxemburg country Europe see Luxembourg
Luxeuil-les-Bains France 66 H3
Luxi Hunan China see Wuxi
Luxi Yunnan China see Mangshi
Luxi Yunnan China 96 D3
Luxolweni S. Africa 125 G6
Luxor Egypt 108 D4
Luya Shan mts China 95 G4
Luyi China 97 G1
Luyksgestel Neth. 62 F3
Luyuan China see Gaoling
Luza Russia 52 J3
Luza r. Russia 52 J3
Luza r. Russia 52 M2
Luzern Switz. see Lucerne
Luzhai China 97 F3
Luzhang China 96 C3
Luzhou China 96 E2
Luzhskaya Russia 55 P7
Luziânia Brazil 179 B2
Luzon i. Phil. 82 C3
Luzon Strait Phil. 82 C1
Luzy France 66 F3
L'viv Ukr. 53 E6
L'vov Ukr. see L'viv
Lwów Ukr. see L'viv
Lyady Russia 55 P7
Lyakhavichy Belarus 55 O10
Lyakhovichi Belarus see Lyakhavichy
Lyallpur Pak. see Faisalabad
Lyamtsa Russia 52 H2
Lycia reg. Turkey 69 M6
Lyck Poland see Ełk
Lycksele Sweden 54 K4
Lycopolis Egypt see Asyūṭ
Lydd U.K. 59 H8
Lydda Israel see Lod
Lyddan Ice Rise Antarctica 188 B2
Lydia reg. Turkey 69 L5
Lydney U.K. 59 E7
Lyel'chytsy Belarus 53 F6
Lyell, Mount CA U.S.A. 158 D3
Lyell Brown, Mount hill Australia 135 E5
Lyell Island Canada 149 O5
Lyepyel' Belarus 55 P9
Lykens PA U.S.A. 165 G3
Lyman WY U.S.A. 156 F4
Lyme Bay U.K. 59 E8
Lyme Regis U.K. 59 E8

M

Malabuñgan Palawan Phil. 82 B4
Malaca Spain see Málaga
Malacca Malaysia see Melaka
Malacca state Malaysia see Melaka
Malacca, Strait of Indon./Malaysia 84 B1
Malad City ID U.S.A. 156 E4
Maladzyechna Belarus 55 O9
Malá Fatra, Národný park nat. park Slovakia 57 Q6
Málaga Spain 67 D5
Malaga NM U.S.A. 161 B5
Malagasy Republic country Africa see Madagascar
Malahar Sumba Indon. 83 B5
Málainn Mhóir Ireland 61 D3
Malaita i. Solomon Is 133 G2
Malaka mt. Sumbawa Indon. 85 G5
Malakal Palau 82 [inset]
Malakal South Sudan 108 D8
Malakal Passage Palau 82 [inset]
Malakanagiri India see Malkangiri
Malakheti Nepal 104 E3
Malakula i. Vanuatu 133 G3
Malamala Celebes Indon. 83 B3
Malampaya Sound sea chan. Palawan Phil. 82 B4
Malan, Ras pt Pak. 111 G5
Malang Java Indon. 85 F4
Malangana Nepal see Malangwa
Malange Angola see Malanje
Malangwa Nepal 105 F4
Malanje Angola 123 B4
Malappuram India 106 C4
Mälaren l. Sweden 55 J7
Malargüe Arg. 178 C5
Malartic Canada 152 F4
Malasoro, Teluk b. Indon. 83 A4
Malaspina Glacier AK U.S.A. 149 L4
Malatayur, Tanjung pt Indon. 85 F3
Malatya Turkey 112 E3
Malavalli India 106 C3
Malawali i. Malaysia 85 G1
Malawi country Africa 123 D5
Malawi, Lake Africa see Nyasa, Lake
Malawi National Park Zambia see Nyika National Park
Malaya pen. Malaysia see Peninsular Malaysia
Malaya Pera Russia 52 L2
Malaya Vishera Russia 52 G4
Malaybalay Mindanao Phil. 82 D4
Malāyer Iran 110 C3
Malay Peninsula Asia 87 B4
Malay Reef Australia 136 E3
Malaysary Kazakh. 98 B3
Malaysia country Asia 80 D5
Malaysia, Semenanjung pen. Malaysia see Peninsular Malaysia
Malazgirt Turkey 113 F3
Malbon Australia 136 C4
Malbork Poland 57 Q3
Malborn Germany 62 G5
Malchin Germany 57 N4
Malcolm (abandoned) Australia 135 C7
Malcolm, Point Australia 135 C8
Malcolm Island Myanmar 87 B5
Maldegem Belgium 62 D3
Malden MO U.S.A. 161 F4
Malden Island Kiribati 187 J6
Maldives country Indian Ocean 103 D10
Maldon Australia 138 B6
Maldon U.K. 59 H7
Maldonado Uruguay 178 F4
Maldonado, Punta pt Mex. 167 F5

▶Male Maldives 103 D11
Capital of the Maldives.

Maleas, Akra pt Greece see Maleas, Akrotirio
Maleas, Akrotirio pt Greece 69 J6
Male Atholhu Maldives 103 D11
Male Atoll Maldives see Male Atholhu
Malebogo S. Africa 125 G5
Malegaon Mahar. India 106 B1
Malegaon Mahar. India 106 C2
Malek, Chāh-e well Iran 110 D3
Malé Karpaty hills Slovakia 57 P6
Malek Mīrzā, Chāh-e well Iran 110 D4
Malek Sīāh Kōh mt. Afgh. 111 F4
Malele Dem. Rep. Congo 123 B4
Maler Kotla India 104 C3
Maleševski Planini mts Bulg./Macedonia 69 J4
Maleta Russia 95 G1
Malgobek Russia 113 G2
Malgomaj l. Sweden 54 J4
Malḥa, Naqb mt. Egypt see Māliḥah, Naqb
Malhada Brazil 179 C1
Malheur r. OR U.S.A. 156 D3
Malheur Lake OR U.S.A. 156 D4
Mali country Africa 120 C3
Mali Dem. Rep. Congo 122 C4
Mali Guinea 120 B3
Maliana East Timor 83 C5
Malianjing Gansu China 94 C3
Malianjing Gansu China 94 E4
Maligay Bay Mindanao Phil. 82 C5
Malihabad India 99 C8
Māliḥah, Naqb mt. Egypt 107 A5
Malik Naro mt. Pak. 111 F4
Maliku Celebes Indon. 83 B3
Mali Kyun i. Myanmar 87 B4
Malili Celebes Indon. 83 B3
Malin Ukr. see Malyn
Malindi Kenya 122 E4
Malines Belgium see Mechelen
Maling China 95 F4
Malin Head hd Ireland 61 E2
Malino Celebes Indon. 83 A4
Malino, Gunung mt. Indon. 83 B2
Malipo China 96 E4
Mali Raginac mt. Croatia 68 F2
Malita Mindanao Phil. 82 D5
Malitbog Leyte Phil. 82 D4
Malka r. Russia 113 G2
Malkangiri India 106 D2
Malkapur India 106 B2
Malkara Turkey 69 L4
Mal'kavichy Belarus 55 O10
Malkhanskiy Khrebet mts Russia 95 G1
Malko Tarnovo Bulg. 69 L4
Mallacoota Australia 138 D6
Mallacoota Inlet b. Australia 138 D6
Mallaig U.K. 60 D4
Mallani reg. India 111 H5
Mallawī Egypt 112 C6
Mallee Cliffs National Park Australia 137 C7
Mallery Lake Canada 151 L1
Mallet Brazil 179 A4
Mallorca i. Spain see Majorca
Mallow Ireland 61 D5
Mallowa Well Australia 134 D5
Mallwyd U.K. 59 D6
Malm Norway 54 G4
Malmberget Sweden 54 L3
Malmedy Belgium 62 G4
Malmesbury S. Africa 124 D7
Malmesbury U.K. 59 E7
Malmö Sweden 55 H9
Malmyzh Russia 52 K4
Malo i. Indon. 83 C1
Maloca Brazil 177 G3
Malolos Luzon Phil. 82 C3
Malone NY U.S.A. 165 H1
Malonje mt. Tanz. 123 D4
Maloshuyka Russia 52 H3
Malovodnoye Kazakh. 98 B4
Måløy Norway 54 D6
Maloyaroslavets Russia 53 H5
Malozemel'skaya Tundra lowland Russia 52 K2
Malpaso Mex. 166 E4
Malpelo, Isla de i. N. Pacific Ocean 169 H8
Malprabha r. India 106 C2
Malta country Europe 68 F7
Malta Latvia 55 O8
Malta ID U.S.A. 156 E4
Malta MT U.S.A. 156 G2
Malta Channel Italy/Malta 68 F6
Maltahöhe Namibia 124 C3
Maltby U.K. 58 F5
Maltby le Marsh U.K. 58 H5
Malton U.K. 58 G4
Maluku is Indon. 83 C2
Maluku is Indon. see Moluccas
Maluku prov. Indon. 83 D3
Maluku, Laut sea Indon. 83 C3
Maluku Utara prov. Indon. 83 C2
Ma'lūlā, Jabal mts Syria 107 C3
Malung Sweden 55 H6
Maluti Mountains Lesotho 125 I5
Malu'u Solomon Is 133 G2
Malvan India 106 B2
Malvasia Greece see Monemvasia
Malvern U.K. see Great Malvern
Malvern AR U.S.A. 161 E5
Malvérnia Moz. see Chicualacuala
Malvinas, Islas terr. S. Atlantic Ocean see Falkland Islands
Malyn Ukr. 53 F6
Malyy Anyuy r. Russia 77 R3
Malyye Derbety Russia 53 J7
Malyy Kavkaz mts Asia see Lesser Caucasus
Malyy Kunaley Russia 95 F1
Malyy Lyakhovskiy, Ostrov i. Russia 77 P2
Mamadysh Russia 52 K5
Mamafubedu S. Africa 125 I4
Mamasa Celebes Indon. 83 A3
Mamatān Nāwēr l. Afgh. 111 G4
Mamba China 99 F7
Mamba Japan see Kanna
Mambahenauhan i. Phil. 82 B5
Mambaí Brazil 179 B1
Mambajao Phil. 82 D4
Mambasa Dem. Rep. Congo 122 C3
Mambi Celebes Indon. 83 A3
Mamburao Mindoro Phil. 82 C3
Mamelodi S. Africa 125 I3
Mamfe Cameroon 120 D4
Mamit India 105 H5
Mammoth AZ U.S.A. 159 H5
Mammoth Cave National Park KY U.S.A. 164 B5
Mammoth Reservoir CA U.S.A. 158 D3
Mamonas Brazil 179 C1
Mamoré r. Bol./Brazil 176 E6
Mamou Guinea 120 B3
Mampikony Madag. 123 E5
Mampong Ghana 120 C4
Mamuju Celebes Indon. 83 A3
Mamuno Botswana 124 E2
Man Côte d'Ivoire 120 C4
Man India 106 B2
Man r. India 106 B2
Man WV U.S.A. 164 E5

▶Man, Isle of terr. Irish Sea 58 C4
United Kingdom Crown Dependency.

Manacapuru Brazil 176 F4
Manacor Spain 67 H4
Manado Celebes Indon. 83 C2
Manadotua i. Indon. 83 C2

▶Managua Nicaragua 166 [inset] I6
Capital of Nicaragua.

Managua, Lago de l. Nicaragua 166 [inset] I6
Manakara Madag. 123 E6
Manakau mt. N.Z. 139 D6
Manākhah Yemen 108 F6

▶Manama Bahrain 110 C5
Capital of Bahrain.

Manamadurai India 106 C4
Mana Maroka National Park S. Africa 125 H5
Manamelkudi India 106 C4
Manam Island P.N.G. 81 L7
Mananara Avaratra Madag. 123 E5
Manangoora Australia 136 B3
Mananjary Madag. 123 E6
Manantali, Lac de l. Mali 120 B3
Manantenina Madag. 123 E6
Mana Pass China/India 99 B7
Mana Pools National Park Zimbabwe 123 C5

▶Manapouri, Lake N.Z. 139 A7
Deepest lake in Oceania.

Manas China 98 D3
Manasa India 104 C4
Manas He r. China 98 D3
Manas Hu l. China 98 D3
Manāşīr reg. U.A.E. 110 D6

▶Manaslu mt. Nepal 105 F3
8th highest mountain in Asia and the world.

Manas National Park nature res. Bhutan 105 G4
Manassas VA U.S.A. 165 G4
Manastir Macedonia see Bitola
Manatang Indon. 83 C5
Manatuto East Timor 83 C5
Man-aung Myanmar 86 A3
Man-aung Kyun i. Myanmar 86 A3
Manaus Brazil 176 F4
Manavgat Turkey 112 C3
Manay Mindanao Phil. 82 D5
Manazuru Japan 93 F3
Manazuru-misaki pt Japan 93 F3
Manbazar India 105 F5
Manbij Syria 107 C1
Manby U.K. 58 H5
Mancelona MI U.S.A. 164 C1
Manchar India 106 B2
Manchester U.K. 58 E5
Manchester CT U.S.A. 165 I3
Manchester IA U.S.A. 160 F3
Manchester KY U.S.A. 164 D5
Manchester MD U.S.A. 165 G4
Manchester MI U.S.A. 164 C2
Manchester NH U.S.A. 165 J2
Manchester OH U.S.A. 164 D4
Manchester TN U.S.A. 162 C5
Manchester VT U.S.A. 165 I2
Mancılık Turkey 112 E3
Mand Pak. 111 F5
Mand, Rūd-e r. Iran 110 C4
Manda Tanz. 123 D4
Manda, Jabal mt. South Sudan 121 F4
Manda, Parc National de nat. park Chad 121 E4
Mandabe Madag. 123 E6
Mandah Sumatra Indon. 84 C3
Mandah Mongolia 95 G2
Mandai Sing. 87 [inset]
Mandal Bulgan Mongolia see Orhon
Mandal Töv Mongolia see Batsümber
Mandal Norway 55 E7

▶Mandala, Puncak mt. Indon. 81 K7
3rd highest mountain in Oceania.

Mandalay Myanmar 86 B2
Mandale Myanmar see Mandalay
Mandalgovi Mongolia 94 F2
Mandalī Iraq 113 G4
Mandal-Ovoo Mongolia 94 F2
Mandalt China 95 H3
Mandan ND U.S.A. 160 C2
Mandaon Masbate Phil. 82 C3
Mandar, Teluk b. Indon. 83 A3
Mandas Sardinia Italy 68 C5
Mandasa India 106 E2
Mandasor India see Mandsaur
Mandav Hills India 104 B5
Mandera Kenya 122 E3
Manderfield UT U.S.A. 159 G2
Manderscheid Germany 62 G4
Mandeville Jamaica 169 I5
Mandeville N.Z. 139 B7
Mandha India 104 B4
Mandhoúdhíon Greece see Mantoudi
Mandi India 104 D3
Mandiana Guinea 120 C3
Mandi Angin, Gunung mt. Malaysia 84 C1
Mandié Moz. 123 D5
Mandini S. Africa 125 J5
Mandioli i. Moluccas Indon. 83 C3
Mandira Dam India 105 F5
Mandla India 104 E5
Mandleshwar India 104 C5
Mandor Kalimantan Indon. 85 E2
Mandor, Cagar Alam nature res. Indon. 85 E2
Mandrael India 104 D4
Mandritsara Madag. 123 E5
Mandsaur India 104 C4
Mandul i. Indon. 85 G2
Mandurah Australia 135 A8
Manduria Italy 68 G4
Mandvi India 104 B5
Mandya India 106 C3
Manerbio Italy 68 D2
Manevychi Ukr. 53 E6
Manfalūţ Egypt 112 C6
Manfredonia Italy 68 F4
Manfredonia, Golfo di g. Italy 68 G4
Manga Brazil 179 C1
Manga Burkina Faso 120 C3
Mangabeiras, Serra das hills Brazil 177 I6
Mangai Dem. Rep. Congo 122 B4
Mangaia i. Cook Is 187 J7
Mangakino N.Z. 139 E4
Mangalagiri India 106 D2
Mangaldai India see Mangaldoi
Mangaldoi India 105 H4
Mangalia Romania 69 M3
Mangalmé Chad 121 E3
Mangalore India see Mangaluru
Mangaluru India 106 B3
Mangaon India 106 B2
Mangareva Islands Fr. Polynesia see Gambier, Îles
Mangaung Free State S. Africa 125 H5
Mangaung Free State S. Africa see Bloemfontein
Mangawan India 105 E4
Ma'ngê China see Luqu
Mangea i. Cook Is see Mangaia
Manggar Indon. 85 E3
Mangghyshlaq Kazakh. see Mangistau
Mangghystaū Kazakh. see Mangistau
Mangghystaū admin. div. Kazakh. see Mangystauskaya Oblast'
Mangghyt Uzbek. see Mang'it
Manghāl Afgh. 111 F3
Manghit Uzbek. see Mang'it
Mangin Range mts Myanmar see Mingin Range
Mangistau Kazakh. 113 H2
Mang'it Uzbek. 102 B3
Mangkalihat, Tanjung pt Indon. 85 G2
Mangkutup r. Indon. 85 F3
Mangla Bangl. see Mongla
Mangla Pak. 111 I3
Mangnai China 99 E5
Mangochi Malawi 123 D5
Mangoky r. Madag. 123 E6
Mangole i. Indon. 83 C3
Mangole, Selat sea chan. Indon. 83 C3
Mangoli India 106 B2
Mangotsfield U.K. 59 E7
Mangqystaū Shyghanaghy b. Kazakh. see Mangystau, Zaliv
Mangra China 94 E5
Mangrol India 104 B5
Mangrul India 106 C1
Mangshi China 96 C3
Mangualde Port. 67 C3
Manguéni, Plateau du Niger 120 E2
Mangui China 90 A2
Mangula Zimbabwe see Mhangura
Mangulile Hond. 166 [inset] I6
Mangum OK U.S.A. 161 D5
Mangupung i. Indon. 83 C1
Manguri Australia 135 F7
Mangut Russia 95 H1
Mangyshlak Kazakh. see Mangistau
Mangyshlak Oblast admin. div. Kazakh. see Mangystauskaya Oblast'
Mangyshlakskaya Oblast' admin. div. Kazakh. see Mangystauskaya Oblast'
Mangystau Kazakh. see Mangistau
Mangystau, Poluostrov pen. Kazakh. 113 H1
Mangystau, Zaliv b. Kazakh. 113 H1
Mangystauskaya Oblast' admin. div. Kazakh. 113 I2
Manhã Brazil 179 B1
Manhan Hovd Mongolia 94 C2
Manhan Hövsgöl Mongolia see Alag-Erdene
Manhattan KS U.S.A. 160 D4
Manhica Moz. 125 K3
Manhoca Moz. 125 K4
Manhuaçu Brazil 179 C3
Manhuaçu r. Brazil 179 C2
Mani China 99 D6
Mania r. Madag. 123 E5
Maniago Italy 68 E1
Manicouagan Canada 153 H4
Manicouagan r. Canada 153 H4
Manicouagan, Petit Lac l. Canada 153 I3
Manicouagan, Réservoir resr Canada 153 H4
Manic Trois, Réservoir resr Canada 153 H4
Manīfah Saudi Arabia 110 C5
Maniganggo China 96 C2
Manigotagan Canada 151 L5
Manihiki atoll Cook Is 186 J6
Maniitsoq Greenland 147 M3
Manikchhari Bangl. 105 H5
Manikgarh India see Rajura

▶Manila Luzon Phil. 82 C3
Capital of the Philippines.

Manila UT U.S.A. 156 F4
Manila Bay Luzon Phil. 82 C3
Manildra Australia 138 D4
Manilla Australia 138 E3
Manimbaya, Tanjung pt Indon. 83 A3
Maningrida Australia 134 F3
Maninjau, Danau l. Indon. 84 C3
Manipa i. Moluccas Indon. 83 C3
Manipa, Selat sea chan. Moluccas Indon. 83 C3
Manipur India see Imphal
Manipur state India 105 H4
Manisa Turkey 69 L5
Manismata Kalimantan Indon. 85 E3
Manistee MI U.S.A. 164 B1
Manistee r. MI U.S.A. 164 B1
Manistique MI U.S.A. 162 C2
Manitoba prov. Canada 151 L4
Manitoba, Lake Canada 151 L5
Manito Lake Canada 151 I4
Manitou Canada 151 L5
Manitou, Lake IN U.S.A. 164 B3
Manitou Beach NY U.S.A. 165 G2
Manitou Falls Canada 151 M5
Manitou Islands MI U.S.A. 164 B1
Manitoulin Island Canada 152 E5
Manitouwadge Canada 152 D4
Manitowoc WI U.S.A. 164 B1
Maniwaki Canada 152 G5
Manizales Col. 176 C2
Manja Madag. 123 E6
Manjarabad India 106 B3
Manjeri India 106 C4
Manjhand Pak. 111 H5
Manjhi India 105 F4
Manjra r. India 106 C2
Man Kabat Myanmar 86 B1
Mankaiana Swaziland see Mankayane
Mankato KS U.S.A. 160 D4
Mankato MN U.S.A. 160 E2
Mankayane Swaziland 125 J4
Mankera Pak. 111 H4
Mankono Côte d'Ivoire 120 C4
Mankota Canada 151 J5
Manlay Mongolia 94 F2
Manley Hot Springs AK U.S.A. 149 J2
Manmad India 106 B1
Mann r. Australia 134 F3
Mann, Mount Australia 135 E6
Manna Sumatra Indon. 84 C4
Man Na Myanmar 86 B2
Mannahill Australia 137 B7
Mannar Sri Lanka 106 C4
Mannar, Gulf of India/Sri Lanka 106 C4
Manneru r. India 106 D3
Mannessier, Lac l. Canada 153 H3
Mannheim Germany 63 I5
Mannicolo Islands Solomon Is see Vanikoro Islands
Manning r. Australia 138 F3
Manning Canada 150 G3
Manning SC U.S.A. 163 D5
Mannington WV U.S.A. 164 E4
Manningtree U.K. 59 I7
Mann Ranges mts Australia 135 E6
Mannsville KY U.S.A. 164 C5
Mannsville NY U.S.A. 165 G2
Mannu, Capo c. Sardinia Italy 68 C4
Manville Canada 151 I4
Manoel Ribas Brazil 179 A4
Manoel Vitorino Brazil 179 C1
Man-of-War Rocks is HI U.S.A. see Gardner Pinnacles
Manoharpur India 99 B8
Manohar Thana India 104 D4
Manokotak AK U.S.A. 148 H4
Manokwari Indon. 81 I7
Manoron Myanmar 87 B5
Manosque France 66 G5
Manouane r. Canada 153 H4
Manouane, Lac l. Canada 153 H4
Manouba town Tunisia 68 D6
Manovo-Gounda Saint Floris, Parc National du nat. park Cent. Afr. Rep. 122 C3
Man Pan Myanmar 86 B2
Manp'o N. Korea 90 B4
Manra i. Kiribati 133 I2
Manresa Spain 67 G3
Mansa Gujarat India 104 C5
Mansa Punjab India 104 C3
Mansa Zambia 123 C5
Mansalean Celebes Indon. 83 B3
Man Sam Myanmar 86 B2
Mansehra Pak. 109 L3
Mansel Island Canada 147 K3
Mansfield Australia 138 C6
Mansfield U.K. 59 F5
Mansfield LA U.S.A. 161 E5
Mansfield OH U.S.A. 164 D3
Mansfield PA U.S.A. 165 G3
Mansfield, Mount VT U.S.A. 165 I1
Man Si Myanmar 86 B1
Mansi Myanmar 86 A1
Manso r. Brazil see Mortes, Rio das
Mansuela Seram Indon. 83 D3
Manta Ecuador 176 B4
Mantalingajan, Mount Palawan Phil. 82 B4
Mantarara Moluccas Indon. 83 C3
Mantaro r. Peru 176 D6
Manteca CA U.S.A. 158 C3
Mantehage i. Indon. 83 C2
Mantena Brazil 179 C2
Manteo NC U.S.A. 162 F5
Mantes-la-Jolie France 62 B6
Mantiqueira, Serra da mts Brazil 179 B3
Manto Hond. 166 [inset] I6
Manton MI U.S.A. 164 C1
Mantoudi Greece 69 J5
Mantova Italy see Mantua
Mäntsälä Fin. 55 N6
Mänttä Fin. 54 N5
Mantua Cuba 163 C8
Mantua Italy 68 D2
Mantuan Downs Australia 136 D5
Manturovo Russia 52 J4
Mäntyharju Fin. 55 O6
Mäntyjärvi Fin. 54 O3
Manú Peru 176 D6
Manu, Parque Nacional del nat. park Peru 176 D6
Manuae atoll Fr. Polynesia 187 J7
Manu'a Islands American Samoa 133 I3
Manuelzinho Brazil 177 H5
Manui i. Indon. 83 B3
Manuk i. Moluccas Indon. 83 D4
Manukan Mindanao Phil. 82 C4
Manukau N.Z. 139 E3
Manukau Harbour N.Z. 139 E3
Manuk Manka i. Phil. 82 B5
Manunda watercourse Australia 137 B7
Manusela, Taman Nasional nat. park Seram Indon. 83 D3
Manus Island P.N.G. 81 L7
Manvi India 106 C3
Many LA U.S.A. 161 E6
Manyakatana S. Africa 125 J3
Manyana Botswana 125 G3
Manyas Turkey 69 L4
Manyas Gölü l. Turkey see Kuş Gölü
Many Island Lake Canada 151 I5
Manyoni Tanz. 123 D4
Manzai Pak. 111 H3
Manzanares Spain 67 E4
Manzanillo Cuba 169 I4
Manzanillo Mex. 168 D5
Manzanillo, Punta pt Panama 166 [inset] K7
Manzhouli China 95 I1
Manzini Swaziland 125 J4
Mao Chad 121 E3
Maó Spain 67 I4
Maoba Guizhou China 96 E3
Maoba Hubei China 97 F2
Maobi Tou c. Taiwan 97 I4
Mao'ergai China 96 D1
Maojiachuan China 94 F4
Maojing China 94 F4
Maoke, Pegunungan mts Indon. 81 J7
Maokeng S. Africa 125 H4
Maokui Shan mt. China 90 A4
Maolin China 95 J3
Maomao Shan mt. China 94 E4
Maoming China 97 F4
Maoniupo China 99 D6
Maoniushan China 94 D4
Ma On Shan hill H.K. China 97 [inset]
Maopi T'ou c. Taiwan see Maobi Tou
Maopora i. Moluccas Indon. 83 C4
Maotou Shan mt. China 96 D3
Mapai Moz. 125 J2
Mapam Yumco l. China 99 C7
Mapane Celebes Indon. 83 B3
Mapanza Zambia 123 C5
Mapastepec Mex. 167 G6
Maphodi S. Africa 125 G6
Mapimí Mex. 166 E3
Mapimí, Bolsón de des. Mex. 166 D3
Mapinhane Moz. 125 L2
Mapiri Bol. 176 E7
Maple r. MI U.S.A. 164 C2
Maple r. ND U.S.A. 160 D2
Maple Creek Canada 151 I5
Maple Heights OH U.S.A. 164 E3
Maple Peak AZ U.S.A. 159 I5
Mapmaker Seamounts sea feature N. Pacific Ocean 186 H4
Mapoon Australia 136 C1
Mapor i. Sumatra Indon. 84 D2
Mapoteng Lesotho 125 H5
Maprik P.N.G. 81 K7
Mapuera r. Brazil 177 G4
Mapulanguene Moz. 125 K3
Mapungubwe National Park S. Africa 125 I2

▶Maputo Moz. 125 K3
Capital of Mozambique.

Maputo prov. Moz. 125 K3
Maputo r. Moz./S. Africa 125 K4
Maputo, Baía de b. Moz. 125 K4
Maputsoe Lesotho 125 H5
Maqanshy Kazakh. see Makanshy
Maqar an Na'am well Iraq 113 F5
Maqat Kazakh. see Makat
Maqên Qinghai China 94 E5
Maqên Xizang China 99 E7
Maqên Kangri mt. China 94 D5
Maqiao China 98 D3
Maqnā Saudi Arabia 112 D5
Maqteïr reg. Mauritania 120 B2
Maqu China 96 D1
Ma Qu r. China see Yellow River
Maquan He r. China see Damqog Zangbo
Maqueda Channel Phil. 82 C3
Maquela do Zombo Angola 123 B4
Maquinchao Arg. 178 C6
Mar r. Pak. 111 G5
Mar, Serra do mts Rio de Janeiro/São Paulo Brazil 179 B3
Mar, Serra do mts Rio Grande do Sul/Santa Catarina Brazil 179 A5
Mara r. Canada 151 I1
Mara India 105 E5
Mara S. Africa 125 I2
Maraã Brazil 176 E4
Marabá Brazil 177 I5
Marabahan Kalimantan Indon. 85 F3
Marabatua i. Indon. 85 F4
Maraboon, Lake resr Australia 136 E4
Maracá, Ilha de i. Brazil 177 H3
Maracaibo Venez. 176 D1
Maracaibo, Lago de Venez. see Maracaibo, Lake
Maracaibo, Lake Venez. 176 D2
Maracaju Brazil 178 E2
Maracaju, Serra de hills Brazil 178 E2
Maracanda Uzbek. see Samarqand
Maracás Brazil 179 C1
Maracás, Chapada de hills Brazil 179 C1
Maracay Venez. 176 E1
Marādah Libya 121 E2
Maradi Niger 120 D3
Marāgheh Iran 110 B2
Maragondon Luzon Phil. 82 C3
Marahuaca, Cerro mt. Venez. 176 E3
Marajó, Baía de est. Brazil 177 I4
Marajó, Ilha de i. Brazil 177 H4
Marakele National Park S. Africa 125 H3
Maralal Kenya 122 D3
Maralbashi China see Bachu
Maralinga Australia 135 E7
Maralwexi China see Bachu
Maramasike i. Solomon Is 133 G2
Maramba Zambia see Livingstone
Marambio research station Antarctica 188 A2
Marampit i. Indon. 83 C1
Maran Malaysia 84 C2
Marana AZ U.S.A. 159 H5
Marand Iran 110 B2
Marandellas Zimbabwe see Marondera
Marang Malaysia 84 C1

Marang Myanmar 87 B5
Maranhão r. Brazil 179 A1
Maranoa r. Australia 138 D1
Marañón r. Peru 176 D4
Marão Moz. 125 L3
Marão mt. Port. 67 C3
Marapi, Gunung vol. Sumatra Indon. 84 C3
Mara Rosa Brazil 179 A1
Maraş Turkey see Kahramanmaraş
Marasende i. Indon. 85 G4
Marathon Canada 152 D4
Marathon FL U.S.A. 163 D7
Marathon NY U.S.A. 165 G2
Marathon TX U.S.A. 161 C6
Maratua i. Indon. 85 G2
Maraú Brazil 179 D1
Marau Kalimantan Indon. 85 E3
Maravillas Creek watercourse TX U.S.A. 161 C6
Marawi Mindanao Phil. 82 D4
Marbella Spain 67 D5
Marble Bar Australia 134 B5
Marble Canyon AZ U.S.A. 159 H3
Marble Canyon gorge AZ U.S.A. 159 H3
Marble Hall S. Africa 125 I3
Marble Hill MO U.S.A. 161 F4
Marble Island Canada 151 N2
Marbul Pass India 104 C2
Marburg Germany 63 I4
Marburg S. Africa 125 J6
Marburg Slovenia see Maribor
Marca, Ponta do pt Angola 123 B5
Marcala Hond. 166 [inset] H6
Marcali Hungary 68 G1
Marcelino Ramos Brazil 179 A4
March U.K. 59 H6
Marche reg. France 66 E3
Marche-en-Famenne Belgium 62 F4
Marchena Spain 67 D5
Marchinbar Island Australia 136 B1
Mar Chiquita, Laguna l. Arg. 178 D4
Marchtrenk Austria 57 O6
Marco FL U.S.A. 163 D7
Marcoing France 62 D4
Marcona Peru 176 C7
Marcopeet Islands Canada 152 F2
Marcus Baker, Mount AK U.S.A. 149 K3
Marcy, Mount NY U.S.A. 165 I1
Mardan Pak. 111 I3
Mar del Plata Arg. 178 E5
Mardīan Afgh. 111 G2
Mardin Turkey 113 F3
Mardzad Mongolia see Hayrhandulaan
Maré i. New Caledonia 133 G4
Maree, Loch l. U.K. 60 D3
Mareh Ḩoseynābād Iran 111 E5
Marengo IA U.S.A. 160 E3
Marengo IN U.S.A. 164 B4
Marengo OH U.S.A. 164 D3
Marevo Russia 52 G4
Marfa TX U.S.A. 161 B6
Margai Caka l. China 99 D6
Margam Ri mts China 99 D6
Marganets Ukr. see Marhanets'
Margao India 106 B3
Margaret r. Australia 134 D4
Margaret watercourse Australia 137 B6
Margaret, Mount hill Australia 134 B5
Margaret Lake Alta Canada 150 H3
Margaret Lake N.W.T. Canada 150 G1
Margaret River Australia 135 A8
Margaretville NY U.S.A. 165 H2
Margarita, Isla de i. Venez. 176 F1
Margaritovo Russia 90 D4
Margate U.K. 59 I7
Margeride, Monts de la mts France 66 F4
Margherita, Lake Eth. see Abaya, Lake

▶Margherita Peak Dem. Rep. Congo/Uganda 122 C3
3rd highest mountain in Africa.

Marghilon Uzbek. see Marg'ilon
Marg'ilon Uzbek. 102 D3
Mārgō, Dasht-e des. Afgh. 111 F4
Mārgo, Dasht-i- des. Afgh. see Mārgō, Dasht-e
Margog Caka l. China 99 D6
Margosatubig Mindanao Phil. 82 C5
Margraten Neth. 62 F4
Marguerite Canada 150 F4
Marguerite, Pic mt. Dem. Rep. Congo/Uganda see Margherita Peak
Marguerite Bay Antarctica 188 L2
Margyang China 99 E7
Marhaj Khalīl Iraq 113 G4
Marhanets' Ukr. 53 G7
Marhoum Alg. 64 D5
Mari Myanmar 86 B1
Maria atoll Fr. Polynesia 187 J7
María Cleofas, Isla i. Mex. 166 D4
María Elena Chile 178 C2
Maria Island Australia 136 A2
Maria Island Myanmar 87 B5
Maria Island National Park Australia 137 [inset]
Mariala National Park Australia 137 D5
María Madre, Isla i. Mex. 166 D4
María Magdelena, Isla i. Mex. 166 D4
Mariana Brazil 179 C3
Marianao Cuba 163 D8
Mariana Ridge sea feature N. Pacific Ocean 186 F4

▶Mariana Trench sea feature N. Pacific Ocean 186 F5
Deepest trench in the world.

Mariani India 105 H4
Mariánica, Cordillera mts Spain see Morena, Sierra
Marian Lake Canada 150 G2
Marianna AR U.S.A. 161 F5
Marianna FL U.S.A. 163 C6
Mariano Machado Angola see Ganda
Mariánské Lázně Czech Rep. 63 M5
Marias r. MT U.S.A. 156 F3
Marías, Islas is Mex. 168 C4

▶Mariato, Punta pt Panama 166 [inset] J8
Most southerly point of North America.

Maria van Diemen, Cape N.Z. 139 D2
Ma'rib Yemen 108 G6
Maribor Slovenia 68 F1
Marica r. Bulg. see Maritsa
Maricopa AZ U.S.A. 159 G5
Maricopa CA U.S.A. 158 D4
Maricopa Mountains AZ U.S.A. 159 G5
Maridi South Sudan 121 F4
Marie Byrd Land reg. Antarctica 188 J1
Marie-Galante i. Guadeloupe 169 L5
Mariehamn Fin. 55 K6
Mariembero r. Brazil 179 A1
Marienbad Czech Rep. see Mariánské Lázně
Marienberg Germany 63 N4
Marienburg Poland see Malbork
Marienhafe Germany 63 H1
Mariental Namibia 124 C3
Marienwerder Poland see Kwidzyn
Mariestad Sweden 55 H7
Mariet r. Canada 152 F2
Marietta GA U.S.A. 163 C5
Marietta OH U.S.A. 164 E4
Marietta OK U.S.A. 161 D5
Marignane France 66 G5
Marii, Mys pt Russia 78 G2
Mariinsk Russia 76 J4
Mariinskiy Posad Russia 52 J4
Marijampol Lith. 55 M9
Marília Brazil 179 A3
Marillana Australia 134 B5
Marimba Angola 123 B4
Marimun Kalimantan Indon. 85 F3
Marín Mex. 167 E3
Marin mt. Pak. 111 G4
Marín Spain 67 B2
Marina CA U.S.A. 158 C3
Marina di Gioiosa Ionica Italy 68 G5
Mar'ina Gorka Belarus see Mar"ina Horka
Mar"ina Horka Belarus 55 P10
Marinduque i. Phil. 82 C3
Marinette WI U.S.A. 164 B1
Maringá Brazil 179 A3
Maringa r. Dem. Rep. Congo 122 B3
Marinha Grande Port. 67 B4
Marion AL U.S.A. 163 C5
Marion AR U.S.A. 161 F5
Marion IL U.S.A. 160 F4
Marion IN U.S.A. 164 C3
Marion KS U.S.A. 160 D4
Marion MI U.S.A. 164 C1
Marion NY U.S.A. 165 G2
Marion OH U.S.A. 164 D3
Marion SC U.S.A. 163 E5
Marion VA U.S.A. 164 E5
Marion, Lake SC U.S.A. 163 D5
Marion Reef Australia 136 F3
Maripa Venez. 176 E2
Mariposa CA U.S.A. 158 D3
Marisa Celebes Indon. 83 B2
Mariscala Mex. 167 F5
Mariscal José Félix Estigarribia Para. 178 D2
Maritime Alps mts France/Italy 66 H4
Maritime Kray admin. div. Russia see Primorskiy Kray
Maritimes, Alpes mts France/Italy see Maritime Alps
Maritsa r. Bulg. 69 L4
also known as Evros (Greece), Marica (Bulgaria), Meriç (Turkey)
Marittime, Alpi mts France/Italy see Maritime Alps
Mariupol' Ukr. 53 H7
Mariusa, Parque Nacional nat. park Venez. 176 F2
Marīvān Iran 110 B3
Marjan Afgh. see Mashōrêy
Marjayoûn Lebanon 107 B3
Marka Somalia 122 E3
Markakol', Ozero l. Kazakh. 98 D2
Markala Mali 120 C3
Markam China 96 C2
Markaryd Sweden 55 H8
Markaz-e Sayyidābād Afgh. 111 H3
Markdale Canada 164 E1
Marken S. Africa 125 I2
Markermeer l. Neth. 62 F2
Market Deeping U.K. 59 G6
Market Drayton U.K. 59 E6
Market Harborough U.K. 59 G6
Markethill U.K. 61 F3
Market Weighton U.K. 58 G5
Markha r. Russia 77 M3
Markham Canada 164 F2
Markit China 98 B5
Markkleeberg Germany 63 M3
Markleeville CA U.S.A. 158 D2
Marklohe Germany 63 J2
Markog Qu r. China 96 D1
Markounda Cent. Afr. Rep. 122 B3
Markovo Russia 77 S3
Markranstädt Germany 63 M3
Marks Russia 53 J6
Marks MS U.S.A. 161 F5
Marksville LA U.S.A. 161 E6
Marktheidenfeld Germany 63 J5
Marktredwitz Germany 63 M4
Marl Germany 62 H3
Marla Australia 135 F6
Marlborough Downs hills U.K. 59 F7
Marle France 62 D5
Marlette MI U.S.A. 164 D2
Marlin TX U.S.A. 161 D6
Marlinton WV U.S.A. 164 E4
Marlo Australia 138 D6
Marmagao India 106 B3
Marmande France 66 E4
Marmara, Sea of g. Turkey 69 M4
Marmara Denizi g. Turkey see Marmara, Sea of
Marmara Gölü l. Turkey 69 M5
Marmarica reg. Libya 112 B5
Marmaris Turkey 69 M6
Marmarth ND U.S.A. 160 C2
Marmê China 99 C6
Marmet WV U.S.A. 164 E4
Marmion, Lake salt l. Australia 135 C7
Marmion Lake Canada 151 N5
Marmolada mt. Italy 68 D1
Marmot Bay AK U.S.A. 148 I4
Marmot Island AK U.S.A. 149 J4
Marne r. France 62 C6
Marne au Rhin, Canal de la France 62 G6
Marne-la-Vallée France 62 C6
Marnitz Germany 63 L1
Maroantsetra Madag. 123 E5
Maroc country Africa see Morocco
Marol Pak. 104 D2
Maroldsweisach Germany 63 K4
Maromokotro mt. Madag. 123 E5
Marondera Zimbabwe 123 D5
Maroochydore Australia 138 F1
Maroonah Australia 135 A5
Maroon Peak CO U.S.A. 156 G5
Maros Celebes Indon. 83 A4
Maros r. Indon. 83 A4
Marosvásárhely Romania see Târgu Mureş
Marot Pak. 111 I4
Maroua Cameroon 121 E3
Marovoay Madag. 123 E5
Marowali Celebes Indon. 83 B3
Marqadah Syria 113 F4
Mar Qu r. China see Markog Qu
Marquard S. Africa 125 H5
Marquesas Islands Fr. Polynesia 187 K6
Marquesas Keys is FL U.S.A. 163 D7
Marquette MI U.S.A. 162 C2
Marquez TX U.S.A. 161 D6
Marquion France 62 D4
Marquise France 62 B4
Marquises, Îles is Fr. Polynesia see Marquesas Islands
Marra Australia 138 A3
Marra r. Australia 138 C3
Marra, Jebel mt. Sudan 121 F3
Marra, Jebel plat. Sudan 121 F3
Marracuene Moz. 125 K3
Marrakech Morocco 64 C5
Marrakesh Morocco see Marrakech
Marrangua, Lagoa l. Moz. 125 L3
Marrar Australia 138 C5
Marrawah Australia 137 [inset]
Marree Australia 137 B6
Marrowbone KY U.S.A. 164 C5
Marruecos country Africa see Morocco
Marrupa Moz. 123 D5
Marryat Australia 135 F6
Marsá al 'Alam Egypt 108 D4
Marsa 'Alam Egypt see Marsá al 'Alam
Marsá al Burayqah Libya 121 E1
Marsabit Kenya 122 D3
Marsala Sicily Italy 68 E6
Marsá Maṭrūḩ Egypt 112 B5
Marsberg Germany 63 I3
Marsciano Italy 68 E3
Marsden Australia 138 C4
Marsden Canada 151 I4
Marsdiep sea chan. Neth. 62 E2
Marseille France 66 G5
Marseilles France see Marseille
Marsfjället mt. Sweden 54 I4
Marshall watercourse Australia 136 B4
Marshall AK U.S.A. 148 G3
Marshall AR U.S.A. 161 E5
Marshall IL U.S.A. 164 B4
Marshall MI U.S.A. 164 C2
Marshall MN U.S.A. 160 E2
Marshall MO U.S.A. 160 E4
Marshall TX U.S.A. 161 E5
Marshall Islands country N. Pacific Ocean 186 H5
Marshalltown IA U.S.A. 160 E3
Marshfield MO U.S.A. 161 E4
Marshfield WI U.S.A. 160 F2
Marsh Harbour Bahamas 163 E7
Mars Hill ME U.S.A. 162 H2
Marsh Island LA U.S.A. 161 F6
Marsh Lake Canada 149 N3
Marsh Lake l. Canada 149 N3
Marsh Peak UT U.S.A. 159 I1
Marsh Point Canada 151 M3
Marsing ID U.S.A. 156 D4
Märsta Sweden 55 J7
Marsyaty Russia 51 S3
Martaban, Gulf of Myanmar see Mottama, Gulf of
Martanai Besar i. Malaysia 85 G1
Martapura Kalimantan Indon. 85 F3
Martapura Sumatra Indon. 84 D4
Marten River Canada 152 F5
Marte R. Gómez, Presa resr Mex. 167 F3
Martha's Vineyard i. MA U.S.A. 165 J3
Martigny Switz. 66 H3
Martim Vaz, Ilhas is S. Atlantic Ocean see Martin Vas, Ilhas
Martin r. Canada 150 F2
Martin Slovakia 57 Q6
Martin MI U.S.A. 164 C2
Martin SD U.S.A. 160 C3
Martínez Mex. 167 F4
Martinez Lake AZ U.S.A. 159 F5
Martinho Campos Brazil 179 B2

▶Martinique terr. West Indies 169 L6
French Overseas Department.

Martinique Passage Dominica/Martinique 169 L5
Martin Peninsula Antarctica 188 K2
Martin Point pt AK U.S.A. 149 L1
Martinsburg WV U.S.A. 165 G4
Martins Ferry OH U.S.A. 164 E3
Martinsville IL U.S.A. 164 B4
Martinsville IN U.S.A. 164 B4
Martinsville VA U.S.A. 164 F5

▶Martin Vas, Ilhas is S. Atlantic Ocean 184 G7
Most easterly point of South America.

Martin Vaz Islands S. Atlantic Ocean see Martin Vas, Ilhas
Martok Kazakh. 100 E1
Martök Kazakh. see Martok
Marton N.Z. 139 E5
Martorell Spain 67 G3
Martos Spain 67 E5
Martuni Armenia 113 G2
Marudi Sarawak Malaysia 85 F1
Marudu, Teluk b. Malaysia 85 G1
Ma'rūf Afgh. 111 G4
Maruim Brazil 177 K6
Marukhis Ugheltekhili pass Georgia/Russia 113 F2
Maruko Japan 93 E2
Marulan Australia 138 D5
Maruoka Japan 92 C2
Marusthali reg. India 111 H5
Maruyama Japan 93 F3
Maruyama-gawa r. Japan 92 A3
Marvast Iran 110 D4
Marvdasht Iran 110 D4
Marvejols France 66 F4
Marvine, Mount UT U.S.A. 159 H2
Marwayne Canada 151 I4
Mary r. Australia 134 E3
Mary Turkm. 111 F2
Maryborough Qld Australia 137 F5
Maryborough Vic. Australia 138 A6
Marydale S. Africa 124 F5
Mary Frances Lake Canada 151 J2
Mary Lake Canada 151 K2
Maryland state U.S.A. 165 G4
Maryport U.K. 58 D4
Mary's Harbour Canada 153 L3
Marys Igloo AK U.S.A. 148 F2
Marysvale UT U.S.A. 159 G2
Marysville CA U.S.A. 158 C2
Marysville KS U.S.A. 160 D4
Marysville OH U.S.A. 164 D3
Maryvale N.T. Australia 135 F6
Maryvale Qld Australia 136 D3
Maryville MO U.S.A. 160 E3
Maryville TN U.S.A. 162 D5
Marzagão Brazil 179 A2
Marzahna Germany 63 M2
Masachapa Nicaragua 166 [inset] I7
Masada tourist site Israel 107 B4
Masagua Guat. 167 H6
Masāhūn, Kūh-e mt. Iran 110 D4
Masai Steppe plain Tanz. 123 D4
Masaka Uganda 122 D4
Masakhane S. Africa 125 H6
Masalembu Besar i. Indon. 85 F4
Masalembu Kecil i. Indon. 85 F4
Masallı Azer. 113 H3
Masamba Celebes Indon. 83 B3
Masamba mt. Indon. 83 B3
Masan S. Korea 91 C6
Masapun Moluccas Indon. 83 C4
Masasi Tanz. 123 D5
Masavi Bol. 176 F7
Masaya Nicaragua 166 [inset] I7
Masaya, Volcán vol. Nicaragua 166 [inset] I7
Masbate Masbate Phil. 82 C3
Masbate i. Phil. 82 C3
Mascara Alg. 67 G6
Mascarene Basin sea feature Indian Ocean 185 L7
Mascarene Plain sea feature Indian Ocean 185 L7
Mascarene Ridge sea feature Indian Ocean 185 L6
Mascota Mex. 166 D4
Mascote Brazil 179 D1
Masein Myanmar 86 A2
Ma Sekatok b. Indon. 85 G2
Masela Moluccas Indon. 83 D5
Masela i. Moluccas Indon. 83 D5
Masepe i. Indon. 83 B3

▶Maseru Lesotho 125 H5
Capital of Lesotho.

Mashai Lesotho 125 I5
Mashan China 97 F4
Masherbrum mt. Pak. 104 D2
Mashhad Iran 111 E2
Mashiko Japan 93 G2
Mashishing S. Africa 125 J3
Mashkel, Hamun-i- salt flat Pak. 111 F4
Mashkel, Rudi-i r. Pak. 111 F5
Mashki Chah Pak. 111 F4
Mashōrêy Afgh. 111 H3
Masi Norway 54 M2
Masiáca Mex. 166 C3
Masibambane S. Africa 125 H6
Masīlah, Wādī al watercourse Yemen 108 H6
Masilo S. Africa 125 H5
Masi-Manimba Dem. Rep. Congo 123 B4
Masimbu Celebes Indon. 83 A3
Masindi Uganda 122 D3
Masinloc Luzon Phil. 82 B3
Masinyusane S. Africa 124 F6
Masira, Gulf of Oman see Maşīrah, Khalīj
Maşīrah, Jazīrat i. Oman 109 I5
Maşīrah, Khalīj b. Oman 109 I6
Masira Island Oman see Maşīrah, Jazīrat
Masiwang r. Seram Indon. 83 D3
Masjed Soleymān Iran 110 C4
Mask, Lough l. Ireland 61 C4
Maskūtān Iran 111 E5
Maslovo Russia 51 S3
Masoala, Tanjona c. Madag. 123 F5
Masohi Seram Indon. 83 D3
Mason MI U.S.A. 164 C2
Mason OH U.S.A. 164 C4
Mason TX U.S.A. 161 D6
Mason, Lake salt flat Australia 135 B6
Mason Bay N.Z. 139 A8
Mason City IA U.S.A. 160 E3
Masoni i. Indon. 83 C3
Masontown PA U.S.A. 164 F4
Masqaţ Oman see Muscat
Masqaţ reg. Oman see Muscat
'Masrūg well Oman 110 D6
Massa Italy 68 D2
Massachusetts state U.S.A. 165 I2
Massachusetts Bay MA U.S.A. 165 J2
Massadona CO U.S.A. 159 I1
Massafra Italy 68 G4
Massakory Chad 121 E3
Massa Marittima Italy 68 D3
Massangena Moz. 123 D6
Massango Angola 123 B4
Massawa Eritrea 108 E6
Massawippi, Lac l. Canada 165 I1
Massena NY U.S.A. 165 H1
Massenya Chad 121 E3
Masset Canada 149 N5
Massieville OH U.S.A. 164 D4
Massif Central mts France 66 F4
Massilia France see Marseille
Massillon OH U.S.A. 164 E3
Massinga Moz. 125 L2
Massingir Moz. 125 K2
Massingir, Barragem de resr Moz. 125 K2
Masson Island Antarctica 188 F2
Mastchoh Tajik. 111 H2
Masteksay Kazakh. 53 K6
Masterton N.Z. 139 E5
Masticho, Akra pt Greece see Oura, Akrotirio
Mastung Pak. 100 F4
Mastūrah Saudi Arabia 108 E5
Masty Belarus 55 N10
Masuda Japan 91 C6
Masuku Gabon see Franceville
Masulipatam India see Machilipatnam
Masulipatnam India see Machilipatnam
Masuna i. American Samoa see Tutuila
Masurai, Bukit mt. Indon. 84 C3
Masvingo Zimbabwe 123 D6
Masvingo prov. Zimbabwe 125 J1
Maswa Tanz. 122 D4
Maswaar i. Indon. 81 I7
Maşyāf Syria 107 C2
Mat, Nam r. Laos 86 D3
Mata Myanmar 86 B1
Matabeleland South prov. Zimbabwe 125 I1
Matachewan Canada 152 E5
Matachic Mex. 166 D2
Matad Mongolia 95 H2
Matadi Dem. Rep. Congo 123 B4
Matador TX U.S.A. 161 C5
Matagalpa Nicaragua 166 [inset] I6
Matagami Canada 152 F4
Matagami, Lac l. Canada 152 F4
Matagorda TX U.S.A. 167 F2
Matagorda Island TX U.S.A. 161 D6
Mataigou China 94 F4
Matak i. Indon. 84 D2
Matak Kazakh. 98 A2
Matakana Island N.Z. 139 F3
Matala Angola 123 B5
Maţāli', Jabal hill Saudi Arabia 113 F6
Matam Senegal 120 B3
Matamey Niger 120 D3
Matamoras PA U.S.A. 165 H3
Matamoros Coahuila Mex. 166 E3
Matamoros Tamaulipas Mex. 167 F3
Matana, Danau l. Indon. 83 B3
Matanal Point Phil. 82 C5
Matandu r. Tanz. 123 D4
Matane Canada 153 I4
Matanuska AK U.S.A. 149 J3
Matanzas Cuba 169 H4
Matapalo, Cabo c. Costa Rica 166 [inset] J7
Matapan, Cape pt Greece see Tainaro, Akrotirio
Matapédia, Lac l. Canada 153 I4
Maţār well Saudi Arabia 110 B5
Matara Sri Lanka 106 D5
Mataram Lombok Indon. 85 G5
Matarani Peru 176 D7
Mataranka Australia 134 F3
Matarape, Teluk b. Indon. 83 B3
Matarinao Bay Samar Phil. 82 D4
Mataripe Brazil 179 D1
Mataró Spain 67 H3
Matarombea r. Indon. 83 B3
Matasiri i. Indon. 85 F4
Matatiele S. Africa 125 I6
Matatila Reservoir India 104 D4
Mataura N.Z. 139 B8

▶Matā'utu Wallis and Futuna Is 133 I3
Capital of Wallis and Futuna Islands.

Mata-Utu Wallis and Futuna Is see Matā'utu
Matawai N.Z. 139 F4
Matay Kazakh. 102 E2
Matcha Tajik. see Mastchoh
Mat Con, Hon i. Vietnam 86 D3
Mategua Bol. 176 F6
Matehuala Mex. 161 C8
Matemanga Tanz. 123 D5
Matera Italy 68 G4
Mateur Tunisia 68 C6
Mathaji India 104 B4
Matheson Canada 152 E4
Mathews VA U.S.A. 165 G5
Mathis TX U.S.A. 161 D6
Mathoura Australia 138 B5
Mathura India 104 D4
Mati Mindanao Phil. 82 D5
Matiali India 105 G4
Matias Cardoso Brazil 179 C1
Matías Romero Mex. 168 E5
Matimekosh Canada 153 I3
Matin India 105 E5
Matina Costa Rica 166 [inset] J7
Matinenda Lake Canada 152 E5
Matizi China 96 D1
Matla r. India 105 G5
Matlabas r. S. Africa 125 H2
Matli Pak. 111 H5
Matlock U.K. 59 F5
Mato, Cerro mt. Venez. 176 E2
Matobo Hills Zimbabwe 123 C6
Mato Grosso state Brazil 179 A1
Mato Grosso, Planalto do plat. Brazil 177 H7
Matola Moz. 125 K3
Matopo Hills Zimbabwe see Matobo Hills
Matos Costa Brazil 179 A4
Matosinhos Port. 67 B3
Mato Verde Brazil 179 C1
Maţraḩ Oman 110 E6
Matroosberg mt. S. Africa 124 D7
Matsubara Japan 92 B4
Matsuda Japan 93 F3
Matsudai Japan 93 E1
Matsudo Japan 93 F3
Matsue Japan 91 D6
Matsuida Japan 93 E2
Matsukawa Nagano Japan 93 D2
Matsukawa Nagano Japan 93 D3
Matsumoto Japan 93 D2
Matsunoyama Japan 93 E1
Matsuo Japan 93 G3
Matsuoka Japan see Eiheiji
Matsusaka Japan 92 C4
Matsushiro Japan 93 E2
Matsu Tao i. Taiwan see Mazu Dao
Matsuyama Japan 91 D6
Matsuzaki Japan 93 E4
Mattagami r. Canada 152 E4
Mattamuskeet, Lake NC U.S.A. 162 E5
Mattawa Canada 152 F5
Matterhorn mt. Italy/Switz. 68 B2
Matterhorn mt. NV U.S.A. 156 E4
Matthew Town Bahamas 169 J4
Maţţī, Sabkhat salt pan Saudi Arabia 110 D6
Mattoon IL U.S.A. 160 F4
Matturai Sri Lanka see Matara
Matu Sarawak Malaysia 85 E2
Matuku i. Fiji 133 H3
Matumbo Angola 123 B5
Maturín Venez. 176 F2
Matusadona National Park Zimbabwe 123 C5
Matutuang i. Indon. 83 C1
Matutum, Mount vol. Phil. 82 D5
Matwabeng S. Africa 125 H5
Maty Island P.N.G. see Wuvulu Island
Mau India see Maunath Bhanjan
Maúa Moz. 123 D5
Maubeuge France 62 D4
Maubin Myanmar 86 A3
Ma-ubin Myanmar 86 B1
Maubourguet France 66 E5
Mauchline U.K. 60 E5
Maudaha India 104 E4
Maude Australia 137 D7
Maud Seamount sea feature S. Atlantic Ocean 184 I10
Mau-é-ele Moz. see Marão
Maués Brazil 177 G4
Maughold Head hd Isle of Man 58 C4
Maug Islands N. Mariana Is 81 L2
Maui i. HI U.S.A. 157 [inset]
Maukkadaw Myanmar 86 A2
Maulbronn Germany 63 I6
Maule r. Chile 178 B5
Maulvi Bazar Bangl. see Moulvibazar
Maumee OH U.S.A. 164 D3
Maumee Bay Michigan/Ohio U.S.A. 164 D3
Maumere Flores Indon. 83 B5
Maumturk Mountains hills Ireland 61 C4
Maun Botswana 123 C5
Mauna Kea vol. HI U.S.A. 157 [inset]
Mauna Loa vol. HI U.S.A. 157 [inset]
Maunath Bhanjan India 105 E4
Maunatlala Botswana 125 H2
Mauneluk r. AK U.S.A. 148 H2
Maungaturoto N.Z. 139 E3
Maungdaw Myanmar 86 A2
Maungmagan Islands Myanmar 87 B4
Maunoir, Lac l. Canada 149 P2
Maurepas, Lake LA U.S.A. 161 F6
Mauriac France 66 F4
Maurice country Indian Ocean see Mauritius
Maurice, Lake salt flat Australia 135 E7
Maurik Neth. 62 F3
Mauritania country Africa 120 B3
Mauritanie country Africa see Mauritania
Mauritius country Indian Ocean 185 L7
Maurs France 66 F4
Mauston WI U.S.A. 160 F3
Mava Dem. Rep. Congo 122 C3
Mavago Moz. 123 D5
Mavan, Kūh-e hill Iran 110 E3
Mavanza Moz. 125 L2
Mavinga Angola 123 C5
Mavrovo nat. park Macedonia 69 I4
Mavume Moz. 125 L2
Mavuya S. Africa 125 H6
Mawa, Bukit mt. Indon. 85 F2
Ma Wan i. H.K. China 97 [inset]
Māwān, Khashm hill Saudi Arabia 110 B6
Mawana India 104 D3

Mawanga Dem. Rep. Congo 123 B4
Ma Wang Dui tourist site China 97 G2
Mawasangka Celebes Indon. 83 B4
Mawei China 97 H3
Mawjib, Wādī al r. Jordan 107 B4
Mawkmai Myanmar 86 B2
Mawlaik Myanmar 86 A2
Mawlamyaing Myanmar 86 B3
Mawlamyine Myanmar see Mawlamyaing
Mawqaq Saudi Arabia 113 F6
Mawson research station Antarctica 188 E2
Mawson Coast Antarctica 188 E2
Mawson Escarpment Antarctica 188 E2
Mawson Peninsula Antarctica 188 H2
Maw Taung mt. Myanmar 87 B5
Mawza' Yemen 108 F7
Maxán Arg. 178 C3
Maxcanú Mex. 167 H4
Maxhamish Lake Canada 150 F3
Maxia, Punta mt. Sardinia Italy 68 C5
Maxixe Moz. 125 L2
Maxmo Fin. 54 M5
Maxüt China 99 C5
May, Isle of i. U.K. 60 G4
Maya i. Indon. 85 E3
Maya r. Russia 77 O3
Mayaguana i. Bahamas 163 F8
Mayaguana Passage Bahamas 163 F8
Mayagüez Puerto Rico 169 K5
Mayahi Niger 120 D3
Mayak Russia 90 E2
Mayakovskiy, Qullai mt. Tajik. 111 H2
Mayakovskogo, Pik mt. Tajik. see Mayakovskiy, Qullai
Mayalibit, Teluk b. Papua Indon. 83 D3
Mayama Congo 122 B4
Maya Mountains Belize/Guat. 167 H5
Mayan China see Mayanhe
Mayang China 97 F3
Mayanhe China 94 F5
Mayar hill U.K. 60 F4
Maya-san hill Japan 92 B4
Maybeury WV U.S.A. 164 E5
Maybole U.K. 60 E5
Maych'ew Eth. 122 D2
Maydān Shahr Afgh. see Maīdān Shahr
Maydh Somalia 108 G7
Maydos Turkey see Eceabat
Mayen Germany 63 H4
Mayenne France 66 D2
Mayenne r. France 66 D3
Mayer AZ U.S.A. 159 G4
Mayêr Kangri mt. China 99 D6
Mayersville MS U.S.A. 161 F5
Mayerthorpe Canada 150 H4
Mayfield N.Z. 139 C6
Mayhan Mongolia see Sant
Mayhill NM U.S.A. 166 D1
Mayi He r. China 90 C3
Maykamys Kazakh. 98 B3
Maykop Russia 113 F1
Mayna Respublika Khakasiya Russia 76 K4
Mayna Ul'yanovskaya Oblast' Russia 53 J5
Mayni India 106 B2
Maynooth Canada 165 G1
Mayo Canada 149 N3
Mayo r. Mex. 166 C3
Mayo FL U.S.A. 163 D6
Mayo Alim Cameroon 120 E4
Mayoko Congo 122 B4
Mayo Lake Canada 149 N3
Mayon vol. Luzon Phil. 82 C3
Mayor, Puig mt. Spain see Major, Puig
Mayor Island N.Z. 139 F3
Mayor Pablo Lagerenza Para. 178 D1

▶Mayotte terr. Africa 123 E5
French Overseas Department.

Mayraira Point Luzon Phil. 82 C2
Mayskiy Amurskaya Oblast' Russia 90 C1
Mayskiy Kabardino-Balkarskaya Respublika Russia 113 G2
Mays Landing NJ U.S.A. 165 H4
Mayson Lake Canada 151 J3
Maysville KY U.S.A. 164 D4
Maytag China see Dushanzi
Mayu i. Moluccas Indon. 83 C2
Mayumba Gabon 122 B4
Mayum La pass China 99 C7
Mayuram India 106 C4
Mayville MI U.S.A. 164 D2
Mayville ND U.S.A. 160 D2
Mayville NY U.S.A. 164 F2
Mayville WI U.S.A. 164 A2
Mazabuka Zambia 123 C5
Mazaca Turkey see Kayseri
Mazagan Morocco see El Jadida
Mazapil Mex. 167 E3
Mazar China 99 B5
Mazār, Kōh-e mt. Afgh. 111 G3
Mazara, Val di valley Sicily Italy 68 E6
Mazara del Vallo Sicily Italy 68 E6
Mazār-e Sharīf Afgh. 111 G2
Mazārī' reg. U.A.E. 110 D6
Mazartag China 98 C5
Mazar Tag mt. China 98 B5
Mazatán Mex. 166 C2
Mazatenango Guat. 167 H6
Mazatlán Mex. 168 C4
Mazatzal Peak AZ U.S.A. 159 H4
Mazdaj Iran 113 H4
Mazdāvand Iran 111 F2
Maze Japan 92 D3
Maze-gawa r. Japan 92 D3
Mažeikiai Lith. 55 M8
Mazhūr, 'Irq al des. Saudi Arabia 110 A5
Mazīm Oman 110 E6
Mazocahui Mex. 166 C2
Mazocruz Peru 176 E7
Mazomora Tanz. 123 D4
Mazongshan China 94 D3
Mazong Shan mt. China 94 D3
Mazong Shan mts China 94 C3
Mazowiecka, Nizina reg. Poland 57 R4
Mazu Dao i. Taiwan 97 I3
Mazunga Zimbabwe 123 C6
Mazyr Belarus 53 F5
Mazzouna Tunisia 68 C7

▶Mbabane Swaziland 125 J4
Capital of Swaziland.

Mbabo, Tchabal mt. Cameroon 120 E4
Mbahiakro Côte d'Ivoire 120 C4
Mbaïki Cent. Afr. Rep. 122 B3
Mbakaou, Lac de l. Cameroon 120 E4
Mbala Zambia 123 D4
Mbale Uganda 122 D3
Mbalmayo Cameroon 120 E4
Mbam r. Cameroon 120 E4
Mbandaka Dem. Rep. Congo 122 B4
M'banza Congo Angola 123 B4
Mbarara Uganda 121 G5
Mbari r. Cent. Afr. Rep. 122 C3
Mbaswana S. Africa 125 K4
Mbemkuru r. Tanz. 123 D4
Mbeya Tanz. 123 D4
Mbhashe r. S. Africa 125 I7
Mbinga Tanz. 123 D5
Mbini Equat. Guinea 120 D4
Mbizi Zimbabwe 123 D6
Mboki Cent. Afr. Rep. 122 C3
Mbombela S. Africa 125 J3
Mbomo Congo 122 B3
Mbouda Cameroon 120 E4
Mbour Senegal 120 B3
Mbout Mauritania 120 B3
Mbozi Tanz. 123 D4
Mbrès Cent. Afr. Rep. 122 B3
Mbuji-Mayi Dem. Rep. Congo 123 C4
Mbulu Tanz. 122 D4
Mburucuyá Arg. 178 E3
McAdam Canada 153 I5
McAlester OK U.S.A. 161 E5
McAlister mt. Australia 138 D5
McAllen TX U.S.A. 161 D7
McArthur r. Australia 136 B2
McArthur OH U.S.A. 164 D4
McArthur Mills Canada 165 G1
McBain MI U.S.A. 164 C1
McBride Canada 150 F4
McCall ID U.S.A. 156 D3
McCamey TX U.S.A. 161 C6
McCammon ID U.S.A. 156 E4
McCarthy AK U.S.A. 149 L3
McCauley Island Canada 149 O5
McClintock, Mount Antarctica 188 H1
McClintock Channel Canada 147 H2
McClintock Range hills Australia 134 D4
McClure, Lake CA U.S.A. 158 C3
McClure Strait Canada 146 G2
McClusky ND U.S.A. 160 C2
McComb MS U.S.A. 161 F6
McConaughy, Lake NE U.S.A. 160 C3
McConnell Range mts Canada 149 P2
McConnellsburg PA U.S.A. 165 G4
McConnelsville OH U.S.A. 164 E4
McCook NE U.S.A. 160 C3
McCormick SC U.S.A. 163 D5
McCrea r. Canada 150 H2
McCreary Canada 151 L5
McCullum, Mount Canada 149 M2
McDame (abandoned) Canada 150 D3
McDermitt NV U.S.A. 156 D4
McDonald Islands Indian Ocean 185 M9
McDonald Peak MT U.S.A. 156 E3
McDonough GA U.S.A. 163 C5
McDougall AK U.S.A. 149 J3
McDougall's Bay S. Africa 124 C5
McDowell Peak AZ U.S.A. 159 H5
McFarland CA U.S.A. 158 D4
McGill NV U.S.A. 159 F2
McGivney Canada 153 I5
McGrath AK U.S.A. 148 I3
McGrath MN U.S.A. 160 E2
McGraw NY U.S.A. 165 G2
McGregor r. Canada 150 F4
McGregor S. Africa 124 D7
McGregor, Lake Canada 150 H5
McGregor Range hills Australia 137 C5
McGuire, Mount ID U.S.A. 156 E3
Mchinga Tanz. 123 D4
Mchinji Malawi 123 D5
McIlwraith Range hills Australia 136 C2
McInnes Lake Canada 151 M4
McIntosh SD U.S.A. 160 C2
McKay Range hills Australia 134 C5
McKean i. Kiribati 133 I2
McKee KY U.S.A. 164 C5
McKenzie r. OR U.S.A. 156 C3
McKinlay r. Australia 136 C4

▶McKinley, Mount AK U.S.A. 149 J3
Highest mountain in North America.

McKinley Park AK U.S.A. 149 J3
McKinney TX U.S.A. 161 D5
McKittrick CA U.S.A. 158 D4
McLaughlin SD U.S.A. 160 C2
McLeansboro IL U.S.A. 160 F4
McLennan Canada 150 G4
McLeod r. Canada 150 H4
McLeod Bay Canada 151 I2
McLeod Lake Canada 150 F4
McLoughlin, Mount OR U.S.A. 156 C4
McMillan, Lake NM U.S.A. 161 B5
McMinnville OR U.S.A. 156 C3
McMinnville TN U.S.A. 162 C5
McMurdo research station Antarctica 188 H1
McMurdo Sound b. Antarctica 188 H1
McNary AZ U.S.A. 159 I4
McNaughton Lake Canada see Kinbasket Lake
McPherson KS U.S.A. 160 D4
McQuesten r. Canada 149 M3
McRae GA U.S.A. 163 D5
McTavish Arm b. Canada 150 G1
McVeytown PA U.S.A. 165 G3
McVicar Arm b. Canada 150 F1
Mdantsane S. Africa 125 H7
M'Daourouch Alg. 68 B6
M'Đrăk Vietnam 87 E4
Mê, Hon i. Vietnam 86 D3
Mead, Lake resr NV U.S.A. 159 F3
Meade KS U.S.A. 161 C4
Meade r. AK U.S.A. 148 H1
Meadow Australia 135 A6
Meadow SD U.S.A. 160 C2
Meadow UT U.S.A. 159 G2
Meadow Lake Canada 151 I4
Meadville MS U.S.A. 161 F6
Meadville PA U.S.A. 164 E3
Meaford Canada 164 E1
Meaken-dake vol. Japan 90 G4
Mealhada Port. 67 B3
Mealy Mountains Canada 153 K3
Meandarra Australia 138 D1
Meander River Canada 150 G3
Meares i. Indon. 83 C1
Meaux France 62 C6
Mebulu, Tanjung pt Bali Indon. 85 F5
Mecca Saudi Arabia 108 E5
Mecca CA U.S.A. 158 E5
Mecca OH U.S.A. 164 E3
Mechanic Falls ME U.S.A. 165 J1
Mechanicsville VA U.S.A. 165 G5
Mechelen Belgium 62 E3
Mechelen Neth. 62 F4
Mecherchar i. Palau see Eil Malk
Mecheria Alg. 64 D5
Mechernich Germany 62 G4
Mechigmen Russia 148 D2
Mecitözü Turkey 112 D2
Meckenheim Germany 62 H4
Mecklenburger Bucht b. Germany 57 M3
Mecklenburg-Vorpommern land Germany 63 M1
Mecklenburg-West Pomerania land Germany see Mecklenburg-Vorpommern
Meda r. Australia 134 C4
Meda Port. 67 C3
Medak India 106 C2
Medan Sumatra Indon. 84 B2
Medang i. Indon. 85 G5
Medanosa, Punta pt Arg. 178 C7
Médanos de Coro, Parque Nacional nat. park Venez. 176 E1
Medawachchiya Sri Lanka 106 D4
Médéa Alg. 67 H5
Medebach Germany 63 I3
Medellín Col. 176 C2
Meden r. U.K. 58 G5
Medenine Tunisia 64 G5
Mederdra Mauritania 120 B3
Medford NY U.S.A. 165 I3
Medford OK U.S.A. 161 D4
Medford OR U.S.A. 156 C4
Medford WI U.S.A. 160 F2
Medfra AK U.S.A. 148 I3
Medgidia Romania 69 M2
Media PA U.S.A. 165 H4
Mediaş Romania 69 K1
Medicine Bow r. WY U.S.A. 156 G4
Medicine Bow Mountains WY U.S.A. 156 G4
Medicine Bow Peak WY U.S.A. 156 G4
Medicine Hat Canada 151 I5
Medicine Lake MT U.S.A. 156 G2
Medicine Lodge KS U.S.A. 161 D4
Medina Brazil 179 C2
Medina Saudi Arabia 108 E5
Medina ND U.S.A. 160 D2
Medina NY U.S.A. 165 F2
Medina OH U.S.A. 164 E3
Medinaceli Spain 67 E3
Medina del Campo Spain 67 D3
Medina de Rioseco Spain 67 D3
Medina Lake TX U.S.A. 161 D6
Medinipur India 105 F5
Mediolanum Italy see Milan
Mediterranean Sea 64 K5
Medjerda, Monts de la mts Alg. 68 B6
Mednyy, Ostrov i. Russia 186 H2
Médoc reg. France 66 D4
Mêdog China 99 F7
Medora ND U.S.A. 160 C2
Medstead Canada 151 I4
Medu Kongkar China see Maizhokunggar
Meduro atoll Marshall Is see Majuro
Medvedevo Russia 52 J4
Medveditsa r. Russia 53 I6
Medvednica mts Croatia 68 F2
Medvezh'i, Ostrova is Russia 77 R2
Medvezh'ya, Gora mt. Russia 90 E3
Medvezh'ya, Gora vol. Russia 90 H3
Medvezh'yegorsk Russia 52 G3
Medway r. U.K. 59 H7
Meekatharra Australia 135 B6
Meeker CO U.S.A. 159 J1
Meeker OH U.S.A. 164 D3
Meelpaeg Reservoir Canada 153 K4
Meemu Atoll Maldives see Mulakatholhu
Meerane Germany 63 M4
Meerlo Neth. 62 G3
Meerut India 104 D3
Mega i. Indon. 84 C3
Mega Escarpment Eth./Kenya 122 D3
Megalopoli Greece 69 J6
Megamo Indon. 81 I7
Mégantic, Lac l. Canada 153 H5
Megara Greece 69 J5
Megezez mt. Eth. 122 D3

▶Meghalaya state India 105 G4
Highest mean annual rainfall in the world.

Meghasani mt. India 105 F5
Meghri Armenia 113 G3
Megin Turkm. 110 E2
Megisti i. Greece 69 M6
Megri Armenia see Meghri
Mehamn Norway 54 O1
Mehar Pak. 111 G5
Meharry, Mount Australia 135 B5
Mehbubnagar India see Mahbubnagar
Mehdia Tunisia see Mahdia
Meherpur Bangl. 105 G5
Meherrin VA U.S.A. 165 F5
Meherrin r. VA U.S.A. 165 G5
Mehlville MO U.S.A. 160 F4
Mehrakān salt marsh Iran 110 D5
Mehrān Hormozgān Iran 110 D5
Mehrān Īlām Iran 110 B3
Mehren Germany 62 G4
Mehrestān Iran 111 F4
Mehrīz Iran 110 D4
Mehsana India see Mahesana
Mehtar Lām Afgh. 111 H3
Meia Ponte r. Brazil 179 A2
Meicheng China see Minqing
Meichuan China 94 F5
Meiganga Cameroon 121 E4
Meighen Island Canada 147 I2
Meigu China 96 D2
Meihekou China 90 B4
Meihō Japan 92 D3
Meikeng China 97 G3
Meikle r. Canada 150 G3
Meikle Says Law hill U.K. 60 G5
Meiktila Myanmar 86 A2
Meilin China see Ganxian
Meilleur r. Canada 150 E2
Meilü China see Wuchuan
Meine Germany 63 K2
Meinersen Germany 63 K2
Meiningen Germany 63 K4
Meishan Anhui China see Jinzhai
Meishan Sichuan China 96 D2
Meishan Shuiku resr China 97 G2
Meißen Germany 57 N5
Meister r. Canada 149 O3
Meitan China 96 E3
Meiwa Gunma Japan 93 F2
Meiwa Mie Japan 92 C4
Meixi China 90 C3
Meixian Guangdong China see Meizhou
Meixian Shaanxi China 95 F5
Meixing China see Xiaojin
Meizhou China 97 H3
Mej r. India 104 D4
Mejicana mt. Arg. 178 C3
Mejillones Chile 178 B2
Mékambo Gabon 122 B3
Mek'elē Eth. 122 D2
Mekele Eth. see Mek'elē
Mékhé Senegal 120 B3
Mekhtar Pak. 111 H4
Meknassy Tunisia 68 C7
Meknès Morocco 64 C5
Mekong r. Asia 86 D4
also known as Lancang Jiang (China), Mae Nam Khong (Laos/Thailand)
Mekong, Mouths of the Vietnam 87 D5
Mekoryuk AK U.S.A. 148 F3
Melaka Malaysia 84 C2
Melaka state Malaysia 84 C2
Melalap Sabah Malaysia 85 F1
Melalo, Tanjung pt Indon. 84 D3
Melanau, Gunung hill Indon. 87 E7
Melanesia is Pacific Ocean 186 G6
Melanesian Basin sea feature Pacific Ocean 186 G5
Melawi r. Indon. 85 E2

▶Melbourne Australia 138 B6
Capital of Victoria. 2nd most populous city in Oceania.

Melbourne FL U.S.A. 163 D6
Melby U.K. 60 [inset]
Melchor de Mencos Guat. 167 H5
Melchor Ocampo Mex. 167 E3
Meldorf Germany 57 L3

▶Melekeok Palau 82 [inset]
Capital of Palau.

Melekess Russia see Dimitrovgrad
Melenki Russia 53 I5
Melet Turkey see Mesudiye
Mélèzes, Rivière aux r. Canada 153 H2
Melfa VA U.S.A. 165 H5
Melfi Chad 121 E3
Melfi Italy 68 F4
Melfort Canada 151 J4
Melhus Norway 54 G5
Meliadine Lake Canada 151 M2
Meliau Kalimantan Indon. 85 E3
Melide Spain 67 C2
Melilis i. Indon. 83 B3

▶Melilla N. Africa 67 E6
Autonomous Community of Spain.

Melimoyu, Monte mt. Chile 178 B6
Melintang, Danau l. Indon. 85 G3
Meliskerke Neth. 62 D3
Melita Canada 151 K5
Melitene Turkey see Malatya
Melitopol' Ukr. 53 G7
Melk Austria 57 O6
Melka Guba Eth. 122 D3
Melksham U.K. 59 E7
Mellakoski Fin. 54 N3
Mellansel Sweden 54 K5
Melle Germany 63 I2
Mellerud Sweden 55 H7
Mellette SD U.S.A. 160 D2
Mellid Spain see Melide
Mellilia N. Africa see Melilla
Mellrichstadt Germany 63 K4
Mellum i. Germany 63 I1
Melmoth S. Africa 125 J5
Mel'nichoye Russia 90 D3
Melo Uruguay 178 F4
Meloco Moz. 123 D5
Melolo Sumba Indon. 83 B5
Melozitna r. AK U.S.A. 148 I2
Melrhir, Chott salt l. Alg. 64 F5
Melrose Australia 135 C6
Melrose U.K. 60 G5
Melrose MN U.S.A. 160 E2
Melsungen Germany 63 J3
Melta, Mount Malaysia see Tawai, Bukit
Melton Australia 138 B6
Melton Mowbray U.K. 59 G6
Meluan Sarawak Malaysia 85 E2
Melun France 66 F2
Melville Canada 151 K5
Melville, Cape Australia 136 D2
Melville, Cape Phil. 82 B5
Melville, Lake Canada 153 K3
Melville Bugt b. Greenland see Qimusseriarsuaq
Melville Hills Canada 149 Q1
Melville Island Australia 134 E2
Melville Island Canada 147 H2
Melville Peninsula Canada 147 J3
Melvin IL U.S.A. 164 A3
Melvin, Lough l. Ireland/U.K. 61 D3
Mêmar Co salt l. China 99 C6
Memba Moz. 123 E5
Memberamo r. Indon. 81 J7
Memboro Sumba Indon. 83 A5
Memel Lith. see Klaipėda
Memel S. Africa 125 I4
Memmelsdorf Germany 63 K5
Memmingen Germany 57 M7
Mempawah Kalimantan Indon. 85 E2
Memphis tourist site Egypt 112 C5
Memphis MI U.S.A. 164 D2
Memphis TN U.S.A. 161 F5
Memphis TX U.S.A. 161 C5
Memphrémagog, Lac l. Canada 165 I1
Mena Timor Indon. 83 C5
Mena Ukr. 53 G6
Mena AR U.S.A. 161 E5
Ménaka Mali 120 D3
Menanga Moluccas Indon. 83 C3
Menard TX U.S.A. 161 D6
Menasha WI U.S.A. 164 A1
Mendanau i. Indon. 84 D3
Mendanha Brazil 179 C2
Mendarik i. Indon. 84 D2
Mendawai Kalimantan Indon. 85 F3
Mendawai r. Indon. 85 F3
Mende France 66 F4
Mendefera Eritrea 108 E7
Mendeleyev Ridge sea feature Arctic Ocean 189 B1
Mendeleyevsk Russia 52 L5
Mendenhall MS U.S.A. 161 F6
Mendenhall, Cape AK U.S.A. 148 F4
Mendenhall Glacier AK U.S.A. 149 N4
Méndez Mex. 167 F3
Mendī Eth. 122 D3
Mendi P.N.G. 81 K8
Mendip Hills U.K. 59 E7
Mendocino CA U.S.A. 158 B2
Mendocino, Cape CA U.S.A. 158 A1
Mendocino, Lake CA U.S.A. 158 B2
Mendooran Australia 138 D3
Mendota CA U.S.A. 158 C3
Mendota IL U.S.A. 160 F3
Mendoza Arg. 178 C4
Menemen Turkey 69 L5
Ménerville Alg. see Thenia
Mengalum i. Malaysia 85 F1
Mengba China 95 F5
Mengban China 96 D4
Mengcheng China 97 H1
Menggala Sumatra Indon. 84 D4
Menghai China 96 D4
Mengjin China 97 G1
Mengkatip Kalimantan Indon. 85 F3
Mengkiang r. Indon. 85 E2
Mengkoka, Gunung mt. Indon. 83 B3
Mengla China 96 D4
Menglang China see Lancang
Menglie China see Jiangcheng
Mengxian China see Mengzhou
Mengyang China see Mingshan
Mengyin China 95 I5
Mengzhou China 95 H5
Mengzi China 96 D4
Menihek Canada 153 I3
Menihek Lakes Canada 153 I3
Menindee Australia 137 C7
Menindee, Lake Australia 137 C7
Ménistouc, Lac l. Canada 153 I3
Menkere Russia 77 N3
Mennecy France 62 C6
Menominee MI U.S.A. 164 B1
Menomonee Falls WI U.S.A. 164 A2
Menomonie WI U.S.A. 160 F2
Menongue Angola 123 B5
Menorca i. Spain see Minorca
Mensalong Kalimantan Indon. 85 G2
Mentakab Malaysia 84 C2
Mentarang r. Indon. 85 G2
Mentasta Lake AK U.S.A. 149 L3
Mentasta Mountains AK U.S.A. 149 K3
Mentawai, Kepulauan is Indon. 84 B3
Mentawai, Selat sea chan. Indon. 84 C3
Mentaya r. Indon. 85 F3
Menteroda Germany 63 K3
Mentmore NM U.S.A. 159 I4
Mentok Indon. 84 D3
Menton France 66 H5
Mentone TX U.S.A. 161 C6
Mentuba r. Indon. 85 F3
Menuf Egypt see Minūf
Menukung Kalimantan Indon. 85 F3
Menuma Japan 93 F2
Menunu Celebes Indon. 83 B2
Menyapa, Gunung mt. Indon. 85 G2
Menyuan China 94 E4
Menza Russia 95 G1
Menza r. Russia 95 G1
Menzel Bourguiba Tunisia 68 C6
Menzelet Barajı resr Turkey 112 E3
Menzelinsk Russia 51 Q4
Menzel Temime Tunisia 68 D6
Menzies Australia 135 C7
Menzies, Mount Antarctica 188 E2
Meobbaai b. Namibia 124 B3
Meoqui Mex. 166 D2
Meppel Neth. 62 G2
Meppen Germany 63 H2
Mepuze Moz. 125 K2
Meqheleng S. Africa 125 H5
Mequon WI U.S.A. 164 B2
Merah Kalimantan Indon. 85 G2
Merak Java Indon. 84 D4
Meråker Norway 54 G5
Merano Italy 68 D1
Merapi, Gunung vol. Java Indon. 85 E4
Meratswe r. Botswana 124 G2
Meratus, Pegunungan mts Indon. 85 F3
Merauke Indon. 81 K8
Merbau Sumatra Indon. 84 C2
Merca Somalia see Marka
Mercantour, Parc National du nat. park France 66 H4
Merced CA U.S.A. 158 C3
Merced r. CA U.S.A. 158 C3
Mercedes Arg. 178 E3
Mercedes Uruguay 178 E4
Mercer ME U.S.A. 165 K1
Mercer PA U.S.A. 164 E3
Mercer WI U.S.A. 160 F2
Mercês Brazil 179 C3
Mercury Islands N.Z. 139 E3
Mercy, Cape Canada 147 L3
Merdenik Turkey see Göle
Mere Belgium 62 D4
Mere U.K. 59 E7
Meredith NH U.S.A. 165 J2
Meredith, Lake TX U.S.A. 161 C5
Merefa Ukr. 53 H6
Merga Oasis Sudan 108 C6
Mergui Myanmar see Myeik
Mergui Archipelago is Myanmar 87 B5
Meriç r. Turkey 69 L4
also known as Evros (Greece), Marica, Maritsa (Bulgaria)
Mérida Mex. 167 H4
Mérida Spain 67 C4
Mérida Venez. 176 D2
Mérida, Cordillera de mts Venez. 176 D2
Meriden CT U.S.A. 165 I3
Meridian MS U.S.A. 161 F5
Meridian TX U.S.A. 161 D6
Mérignac France 66 D4
Merijärvi Fin. 54 N4
Merikarvia Fin. 55 L6
Merimbula Australia 138 D6
Merín, Laguna l. Brazil/Uruguay see Mirim, Lagoa
Meringur Australia 137 C7
Merir i. Palau 81 I6
Merit Sarawak Malaysia 85 F2
Merjayoun Lebanon see Marjayoûn
Merkel TX U.S.A. 161 C5
Merluna Australia 136 C2
Mermaid Reef Australia 134 B4
Meron, Har mt. Israel 107 B3
Merowe Sudan 108 D6
Merowe Dam Sudan 108 D6
Mêrqung Co l. China 105 F3
Merredin Australia 135 B7
Merrick hill U.K. 60 E5
Merrickville Canada 165 H1
Merrill MI U.S.A. 164 C2
Merrill WI U.S.A. 160 F2
Merrill, Mount Canada 150 E2
Merrillville IN U.S.A. 164 B3
Merriman NE U.S.A. 160 C3
Merritt Canada 150 F5
Merritt Island FL U.S.A. 163 D6
Merriwa Australia 138 E4
Merrygoen Australia 138 D3
Mersa Fatma Eritrea 108 F7
Mersa Maṭrûḥ Egypt see Marsá Maṭrūḥ
Mersch Lux. 62 G5
Merseburg Germany 63 L3
Mersey est. U.K. 58 E5
Mersin Turkey 107 B1
Mersin prov. Turkey 107 A1
Mersing Malaysia 84 C2
Mersing, Bukit mt. Malaysia 85 F2
Mērsrags Latvia 55 M8
Merta India 104 C4
Merthyr Tydfil U.K. 59 D7
Mértola Port. 67 C5
Mertz Glacier Antarctica 188 G2
Mertz Glacier Tongue Antarctica 188 G2
Mertzon TX U.S.A. 161 C6
Méru France 62 C5

▶Meru vol. Tanz. 122 D4
4th highest mountain, and highest active volcano in Africa.

Meru Betiri, Taman Nasional nat. park Indon. 85 F5
Merui Pak. 111 F4
Merutai Sabah Malaysia 85 G1
Merv Turkm. see Mary
Merweville S. Africa 124 E7
Merzifon Turkey 112 D2
Merzig Germany 62 G5
Merz Peninsula Antarctica 188 L2
Mesa Halmahera Indon. 83 D2
Mesa AZ U.S.A. 159 H5
Mesa NM U.S.A. 157 G6
Mesabi Range hills MN U.S.A. 160 E2
Mesagne Italy 68 G4
Mesa Mountain hill AK U.S.A. 148 I3
Mesanak i. Sumatra Indon. 84 D2
Mesa Negra mt. NM U.S.A. 159 J4
Mesara, Ormos b. Greece see Messaras, Kolpos
Mesa Verde National Park CO U.S.A. 159 I3

Mescalero Apache Indian Reservation res. NM U.S.A. 166 D1
Meschede Germany 63 I3
Mese Myanmar 86 B3
Meselefors Sweden 54 J4
Mesgouez, Lac Canada 152 G4
Meshed Iran see Mashhad
Meshkān Iran 110 E2
Meshra' Er Req South Sudan 108 C8
Mesick MI U.S.A. 164 C1
Mesimeri Greece 69 J4
Mesolongi Greece 69 I5
Mesolóngion Greece see Mesolongi
Mesopotamia reg. Iraq 113 F4
Mesopotamia Marshlands National Park Iraq 113 G5
Mesquita Brazil 179 C2
Mesquite NV U.S.A. 159 F3
Mesquite TX U.S.A. 161 D5
Mesquite Lake CA U.S.A. 159 F4
Messaad Alg. 64 E5
Messana Sicily Italy see Messina
Messaras, Kolpos b. Greece 69 K7
Messina Sicily Italy 68 F5
Messina, Strait of Italy 68 F5
Messina, Stretta di Italy see Messina, Strait of
Messini Greece 69 J6
Messiniakos Kolpos b. Greece 69 J6
Mesta r. Bulg. 69 K4
Mesta r. Greece see Nestos
Mesta, Akrotirio pt Greece 69 K5
Mestghanem Alg. see Mostaganem
Mestlin Germany 63 L1
Meston, Akra pt Greece see Mesta, Akrotirio
Mestre Italy 68 E2
Mesudiye Turkey 112 E2
Mesuji r. Indon. 84 D4
Meta r. Col./Venez. 176 E2
Métabetchouan Canada 153 H4
Meta Incognita Peninsula Canada 147 L3
Metairie LA U.S.A. 161 F6
Metallifere, Colline mts Italy 68 D3
Metán Arg. 178 C3
Metangai Kalimantan Indon. 85 F3
Metapán El Salvador 167 H6
Meteghan Canada 153 I5
Meteor Depth sea feature S. Atlantic Ocean 184 G9
Methoni Greece 69 I6
Methuen MA U.S.A. 165 J2
Methven U.K. 60 F4
Metionga Lake Canada 152 C4
Metković Croatia 68 G3
Metlaoui Tunisia 64 F5
Metoro Moz. 123 D5
Metro Sumatra Indon. 84 D4
Metropolis IL U.S.A. 161 F4
Metsada tourist site Israel see Masada
Metter GA U.S.A. 163 D5
Mettet Belgium 62 E4
Mettingen Germany 63 H2
Mettler CA U.S.A. 158 D4
Mettur India 106 C4
Metu Eth. 122 D3
Metz France 62 G5
Metz IN U.S.A. 164 C3
Meulaboh Sumatra Indon. 84 B1
Meureudu Sumatra Indon. 84 B1
Meuse r. Belgium/France 62 F3 also known as Maas (Netherlands)
Meuse, Côtes de ridge France 62 E5
Meuselwitz Germany 63 M3
Mevagissey U.K. 59 C8
Mêwa China 96 D1
Mexcala Mex. 167 F5
Mexia TX U.S.A. 161 D6
Mexiana, Ilha i. Brazil 177 I3
Mexicali Mex. 166 B1
Mexican Hat UT U.S.A. 159 I3
Mexicanos, Lago de los l. Mex. 166 D2
Mexican Water AZ U.S.A. 159 I3

▶Mexico country Central America 166 D4 2nd most populous and 3rd largest country in North America.

México Mex. see Mexico City
México state Mex. 167 F5
Mexico ME U.S.A. 165 J1
Mexico MO U.S.A. 160 F4
Mexico NY U.S.A. 165 G2
Mexico, Gulf of Mex./U.S.A. 155 H6

▶Mexico City Mex. 168 E5 Capital of Mexico. Most populous city in North America and 4th in the world.

Meybod Iran 110 D3
Meydanī, Ra's-e pt Iran 110 E5
Meyenburg Germany 63 M1
Meyersdale PA U.S.A. 164 F4
Meymeh Iran 110 C3
Meynypil'gyno Russia 189 C2
Mezada tourist site Israel see Masada
Mezcalapa Mex. 167 G5
Mezcalapa r. Mex. 167 G5
Mezdra Bulg. 69 J3
Mezen' Russia 52 J2
Mezen' r. Russia 52 J2
Mézenc, Mont mt. France 66 G4
Mezenskaya Guba b. Russia 52 I2
Mezhdurechensk Kemerovskaya Oblast' Russia 88 F2
Mezhdurechensk Respublika Komi Russia 52 K3
Mezhdurech'ye Russia see Shali
Mezhdusharskiy, Ostrov i. Russia 76 G2
Mezitli Turkey 107 B1
Meztúr Hungary 69 I1
Mezquital Mex. 166 D4
Mezquital r. Mex. 166 D4
Mezquitic Mex. 166 E4
Mežvidi Latvia 55 O8
Mfolozi r. S. Africa 125 K5
Mhàil, Rubh' a' pt U.K. 60 C5
Mhangura Zimbabwe 123 D5
Mhlume Swaziland 125 J4
Mhow India 104 C5
Mi r. Myanmar 105 H5
Miahuatlán Mex. 168 E5
Miajadas Spain 67 D4
Miaméré Cent. Afr. Rep. 122 B3
Miami AZ U.S.A. 159 H5

▶Miami FL U.S.A. 163 D7 5th most populous city in North America.

Miami OK U.S.A. 161 E4
Miami Beach FL U.S.A. 163 D7
Miancaowan China 94 D5
Mianchi China 95 G5
Miāndehī Iran 110 E3
Miāndoāb Iran 110 B2
Miandrivazo Madag. 123 E5
Mianduhe China 95 J1
Mīāneh Iran 110 B2
Miang, Phu mt. Thai. 86 C3
Miangas i. Phil. 82 D5
Mianhua Yu i. Taiwan 97 I3
Miani India 111 I4
Miani Hor b. Pak. 111 G5
Mīān Jōy Afgh. 111 G3
Mianning China 96 D2
Mianwali Pak. 111 H3
Mianxian China 96 E1
Mianyang Hubei China see Xiantao
Mianyang Shaanxi China see Mianxian
Mianyang Sichuan China 96 E2
Mianzhu China 96 E2
Miaodao Qundao is China 95 J4
Miao'ergou China 98 C3
Miaoli Taiwan 97 I3
Miarinarivo Madag. 123 E5
Miarritze France see Biarritz
Miasa Japan 93 D2
Miass Russia 76 H4
Miboro-ko l. Japan 92 C2
Mibu Japan 93 F2
Mibu-gawa r. Japan 93 D3
Mica Creek Canada 150 G4
Mica Mountain AZ U.S.A. 159 H5
Micang Shan mts China 96 E1
Michalovce Slovakia 53 D6
Michel Canada 151 I4
Michelau in Oberfranken Germany 63 L4
Michelson, Mount AK U.S.A. 149 K1
Michelstadt Germany 63 J5
Michendorf Germany 63 N2
Micheng China see Midu
Michigan state U.S.A. 164 C2

▶Michigan, Lake Michigan/Wisconsin U.S.A. 164 B2 3rd largest lake in North America and 5th in the world.

Michigan City IN U.S.A. 164 B3
Michinberi India 106 D2
Michipicoten Bay Canada 152 D5
Michipicoten Island Canada 152 D5
Michipicoten River Canada 152 D5
Michoacán state Mex. 167 E5
Michurin Bulg. see Tsarevo
Michurinsk Russia 53 I5
Mico r. Nicaragua 166 [inset] I6
Micronesia country N. Pacific Ocean see Micronesia, Federated States of
Micronesia is Pacific Ocean 186 F5
Micronesia, Federated States of country N. Pacific Ocean 186 G5
Midai i. Indon. 85 D2
Mid-Atlantic Ridge sea feature Atlantic Ocean 184 E4
Mid-Atlantic Ridge sea feature Atlantic Ocean 184 G7
Middelburg Neth. 62 D3
Middelburg E. Cape S. Africa 125 G6
Middelburg Mpumalanga S. Africa 125 I3
Middelfart Denmark 55 F9
Middelharnis Neth. 62 E3
Middelwit S. Africa 125 H3
Middle Alkali Lake CA U.S.A. 156 C4
Middle America Trench sea feature N. Pacific Ocean 187 N5
Middle Andaman i. India 87 A4
Middle Atlas mts Morocco see Moyen Atlas
Middle Bay Canada 153 K4
Middlebourne WV U.S.A. 164 E4
Middleburg PA U.S.A. 165 G3
Middleburgh NY U.S.A. 165 H2
Middlebury IN U.S.A. 164 C3
Middlebury VT U.S.A. 165 I1
Middle Caicos i. Turks and Caicos Is 163 G8
Middle Channel watercourse Canada 149 N1
Middle Concho r. TX U.S.A. 161 C6
Middle Congo country Africa see Congo
Middle Island Thai. see Tasai, Ko
Middle Loup r. NE U.S.A. 160 D3
Middlemarch N.Z. 139 C7
Middlemount Australia 136 E4
Middle River MD U.S.A. 165 G4
Middlesbrough U.K. 58 F4
Middle Strait India see Andaman Strait
Middleton Australia 136 C4
Middleton Canada 153 I5
Middleton Island atoll American Samoa see Rose Island
Middleton Island AK U.S.A. 149 K4
Middletown CA U.S.A. 158 B2
Middletown CT U.S.A. 165 I3
Middletown NY U.S.A. 165 H3
Middletown VA U.S.A. 165 F4
Midelt Morocco 64 D5
Midhurst U.K. 59 G8
Midi, Canal du France 66 F5
Mid-Indian Basin sea feature Indian Ocean 185 N6
Mid-Indian Ridge sea feature Indian Ocean 185 M7
Midland Canada 165 F1
Midland IN U.S.A. 164 B4
Midland MI U.S.A. 164 C2
Midland SD U.S.A. 160 C2
Midland TX U.S.A. 161 C5
Midland (abandoned) CA U.S.A. 159 F5
Midleton Ireland 61 D6
Midnapore India see Medinipur
Midnapur India see Medinipur
Midongy Atsimo Madag. 123 E6
Midori Japan 93 F3
Mid-Pacific Mountains sea feature N. Pacific Ocean 186 G4
Midu China 96 D3
Miðvágur Faroe Is 54 [inset 2]
Midway Oman see Thamarīt

▶Midway Islands terr. N. Pacific Ocean 186 I4 United States Unincorporated Territory.

Midway Islands AK U.S.A. 149 J1
Midway Well Australia 135 C5
Midwest WY U.S.A. 156 G4
Midwest City OK U.S.A. 161 D5
Midwoud Neth. 62 F2
Midyat Turkey 113 F3
Midye Turkey see Kıyıköy
Mid Yell U.K. 60 [inset]
Midzhur mt. Bulg./Serbia 112 A2
Mie pref. Japan 92 C4
Miehikkälä Fin. 55 O6
Miekojärvi l. Fin. 54 N3
Mielec Poland 53 D6
Mieraslompola Fin. 54 O2
Mierašluoppal Fin. see Mieraslompola
Miercurea Ciuc Romania 69 K1
Mieres Spain see Mieres del Camín
Mieres del Camín Spain 67 D2
Mī'ēso Eth. 122 E3
Mieste Germany 63 L2
Mifflinburg PA U.S.A. 165 G3
Mifflintown PA U.S.A. 165 G3
Migang Shan mt. China 94 F5
Migdol S. Africa 125 G4
Miging India 96 B2
Miguel Alemán, Presa resr Mex. 167 F5
Miguel Auza Mex. 161 C7
Miguel de la Borda Panama 166 [inset] J7
Miguel Hidalgo, Presa resr Mex. 166 C3
Mihalıççık Turkey 69 N5
Mihama Aichi Japan 92 C4
Mihama Fukui Japan 92 B3
Mihama Wakayama Japan 92 B5
Mihara Japan 91 D6
Mihara-yama vol. Japan 93 F4
Mihintale Sri Lanka 106 D4
Mihmandar Turkey 107 B1
Miho Japan 93 G3
Mijares r. Spain see Millárs
Mijdrecht Neth. 62 E2
Mikata-ko l. Japan 92 B3
Mikawa Japan 92 C2
Mikawa-wan b. Japan 92 D4
Mikawa-wan Kokutei-kōen park Japan 92 D4
Mikhaylov Russia 53 H5
Mikhaylovgrad Bulg. see Montana
Mikhaylov Island Antarctica 188 E2
Mikhaylovka Amurskaya Oblast' Russia 90 C2
Mikhaylovka Primorskiy Kray Russia 90 D4
Mikhaylovka Tul'skaya Oblast' Russia see Kimovsk
Mikhaylovka Volgogradskaya Oblast' Russia 53 I6
Mikhaylovsk Russia 113 F1
Mikhaylovskoye Altayskiy Kray Russia 102 E1
Mikhaylovskoye Stavropol'skiy Kray Russia see Mikhaylovsk
Mikhrot Timna Israel 107 B5
Miki Japan 92 A4
Mikir Hills India 105 H4
Miki-zaki pt Japan 92 C5
Mikkabi Japan 92 D4
Mikkeli Fin. 55 O6
Mikkelin mlk Fin. 55 O6
Mikkwa r. Canada 150 H3
Míkonos i. Greece see Mykonos
Mikoyan Armenia see Yeghegnadzor
Mikulkin, Mys c. Russia 52 J2
Mikumi National Park Tanz. 123 D4
Mikumo Japan 92 C4
Mikun' Russia 52 K3
Mikuni Japan 92 C2
Mikuni-sanmyaku mts Japan 93 E2
Mikuni-yama mt. Japan 93 E3
Mikura-jima i. Japan 91 E6
Milaca MN U.S.A. 160 E2
Miladhunmadulu Maldives 106 B5
Miladummadulu Atoll Maldives see Miladhunmadulu
Milan Italy 68 C2
Milan MI U.S.A. 164 D2
Milan MO U.S.A. 160 E3
Milan OH U.S.A. 164 D3
Milange Moz. 123 D5
Milano Italy see Milan
Milas Turkey 69 L6
Milazzo Sicily Italy 68 F5
Milazzo, Capo di c. Sicily Italy 68 F5
Milbank SD U.S.A. 160 D2
Milbridge ME U.S.A. 162 H2
Milde r. Germany 63 L2
Mildenhall U.K. 59 H6
Mildura Australia 137 C7
Mile China 96 D3
Mileiz, Wâdi el watercourse Egypt see Mulayz, Wādī al
Miles Australia 138 E1
Miles City MT U.S.A. 156 G3
Milestone Ireland 61 D5
Miletto, Monte mt. Italy 68 F4
Mileura Australia 135 B6
Milford Ireland 61 E2
Milford DE U.S.A. 165 H4
Milford IL U.S.A. 164 B3
Milford MA U.S.A. 165 J2
Milford MI U.S.A. 164 D2
Milford NE U.S.A. 160 D3
Milford NH U.S.A. 165 J2
Milford PA U.S.A. 165 H3
Milford UT U.S.A. 159 G2
Milford VA U.S.A. 165 G4
Milford Haven U.K. 59 B7
Milford Sound N.Z. 139 A7
Milford Sound inlet N.Z. 139 A7
Milgarra Australia 136 C3
Milḥ, Baḥr al l. Iraq see Razāzah, Buḥayrat ar
Milḥ, Qurayyāt al l. Jordan 107 C4
Miliana Alg. 67 H5
Milid Turkey see Malatya
Milikapiti Australia 134 E2
Miling Australia 135 B7
Milk r. MT U.S.A. 156 G2
Milk, Wadi el watercourse Sudan 108 D6
Mil'kovo Russia 77 Q4
Millaa Millaa Australia 136 D3
Millárs r. Spain 67 F4
Millau France 66 F4
Millbrook Canada 165 F1
Mill Creek r. CA U.S.A. 158 B1
Milledgeville GA U.S.A. 163 D5
Mille Lacs lakes MN U.S.A. 160 E2
Mille Lacs, Lac des l. Canada 147 I5
Millen GA U.S.A. 163 D5
Millennium Island atoll Kiribati see Caroline Island
Miller SD U.S.A. 160 D2
Miller, Mount AK U.S.A. 149 L3
Miller Lake Canada 164 E1
Millerovo Russia 53 I6
Millersburg OH U.S.A. 164 E3
Millersburg PA U.S.A. 165 G3
Millers Creek KY U.S.A. 164 D5
Millersville PA U.S.A. 165 G4
Millerton Lake CA U.S.A. 158 D3
Millet Canada 150 H4
Milleur Point U.K. 60 D5
Mill Hall PA U.S.A. 165 G3
Millicent Australia 137 C8
Millington MI U.S.A. 164 D2
Millington TN U.S.A. 161 F5
Millinocket ME U.S.A. 162 G2
Mill Island Canada 147 K3
Millmerran Australia 138 E1
Millom U.K. 58 D4
Millport U.K. 60 E5
Millsboro DE U.S.A. 165 H4
Mills Creek watercourse Australia 136 C4
Mills Lake Canada 150 G2
Millstone KY U.S.A. 164 D5
Millstone WV U.S.A. 164 E4
Millstream-Chichester National Park Australia 134 B5
Millthorpe Australia 138 D4
Milltown Canada 153 I5
Milltown MT U.S.A. 156 E3
Millungera Australia 136 C3
Millville NJ U.S.A. 165 H4
Millwood KY U.S.A. 164 B5
Millwood Lake AR U.S.A. 161 E5
Milly Milly Australia 135 B6
Milne Land i. Greenland see Ilimananngip Nunaa
Milner CO U.S.A. 159 J1
Milo r. Guinea 120 C3
Milogradovo Russia 90 D4
Miloli'i HI U.S.A. 157 [inset]
Milos i. Greece 69 K6
Milparinka Australia 137 C6
Milpitas CA U.S.A. 158 C3
Milroy PA U.S.A. 165 G3
Milton N.Z. 139 B8
Milton DE U.S.A. 165 H4
Milton FL U.S.A. 167 I2
Milton NH U.S.A. 165 J2
Milton WV U.S.A. 164 D4
Milton Keynes U.K. 59 G6
Miltown Malbay Ireland 61 C5
Miluo China 97 G2
Milverton Canada 164 E2
Milwaukee WI U.S.A. 164 B2

▶Milwaukee Deep sea feature Caribbean Sea 184 D4 Deepest point in the Puerto Rico Trench (deepest in the Atlantic).

Milybulak Kazakh. 98 A2
Mimbres watercourse NM U.S.A. 159 J5
Mimili Australia 135 F6
Mimisal India 106 C4
Mimizan France 66 D4
Mimongo Gabon 122 B4
Mimosa Rocks National Park Australia 138 E6
Mina Mex. 167 E3
Mina NV U.S.A. 158 D2
Mīnāb Iran 110 E5
Minaçu Brazil 179 A1
Minahasa, Semenanjung pen. Indon. 83 B2
Minahassa Peninsula Indon. see Minahasa, Semenanjung
Minakami Gunma Japan 93 E2
Minakami Gunma Japan 93 E2
Minaker Canada see Prophet River
Mīnakh Syria 107 C1
Minaki Canada 151 M5
Minakuchi Japan see Kōka
Minami Japan 92 C3
Minamia Australia 134 F3
Minami-Alps Japan 93 E3
Minami-arupusu Kokuritsu-kōen nat. park Japan 93 E3
Minamiashigara Japan 93 F3
Minamiawaji Japan 92 A4
Minamibōsō Japan 93 F3
Minami-Bōsō Kokutei-kōen park Japan 93 F4
Minamichita Japan 92 C4
Minami-Daitō-jima i. Japan 89 O7
Minamiechizen Japan 92 C3
Minami-gawa r. Japan 92 B3
Minami-Iō-jima vol. Japan 81 K2
Minamiise Japan 92 C4
Minamiizu Japan 93 E4
Minami-kawara Japan 93 F2
Minamimaki Japan 93 E2
Minamiminowa Japan 93 D3
Minaminasu Japan 93 G2
Minamishinano Japan 93 D3
Minamiuonuma Japan 93 E1
Min'an China see Longshan
Minano Japan 93 F2
Minas Sumatra Indon. 84 C2
Minas Uruguay 178 E4
Minas, Sierra de las mts Guat. 167 H6
Minas de Matahambre Cuba 163 D8
Minas Gerais state Brazil 179 B2
Minas Novas Brazil 179 C2
Minatitlán Mex. 168 F5
Minbu Myanmar 86 A2
Minbya Myanmar 86 A2
Minchinmávida vol. Chile 178 B6
Minchumina, Lake AK U.S.A. 148 I3
Mindanao i. Phil. 82 D5
Mindanao r. Mindanao Phil. 82 D5
Mindanao Trench sea feature N. Pacific Ocean see Philippine Trench
Mindelo Cape Verde 120 [inset]
Minden Canada 165 F1
Minden Germany 63 I2
Minden LA U.S.A. 161 E5
Minden NE U.S.A. 154 H3
Minden NV U.S.A. 158 D2
Mindon Myanmar 86 A3
Mindoro i. Phil. 82 C3
Mindoro Strait Phil. 82 B3
Mindouli Congo 122 B4
Mine Head hd Ireland 61 E6
Minehead U.K. 59 D7
Mineola NY U.S.A. 165 I3
Mineola TX U.S.A. 167 G1
Miner r. N.W.T. Canada 149 O1
Miner r. Y.T. Canada 149 M2
Mineral VA U.S.A. 165 G4
Mineral'nye Vody Russia 113 F1
Mineral Wells TX U.S.A. 161 D5
Mineral Wells WV U.S.A. 164 E4
Minersville PA U.S.A. 165 G3
Minersville UT U.S.A. 159 G2
Minerva OH U.S.A. 164 E3
Minerva Reefs Fiji 133 I4
Minfeng China 99 C5
Minga Dem. Rep. Congo 123 C5
Mingäçevir Azer. 113 G2
Mingäçevir Su Anbarı resr Azer. 113 G2
Mingala Cent. Afr. Rep. 122 C3
Mingan, Îles de is Canada 153 J4
Mingan Archipelago National Park Reserve Canada see Archipel-de-Mingan, Réserve du Parc National de l'
Ming'antu China 95 H3
Mingbuloq Uzbek. 102 B3
Mingechaur Azer. see Mingäçevir
Mingechaurskoye Vodokhranilishche resr Azer. see Mingäçevir Su Anbarı
Mingenew Australia 135 A7
Mingfeng China see Yuan'an
Minggang China 97 G1
Mingguang China 97 H1
Mingin Range mts Myanmar 86 A2
Ming-Kush Kyrg. 98 A4
Minglanilla Spain 67 F4
Mingoyo Tanz. 123 D5
Mingshan China 96 D2
Mingshui Gansu China 94 D3
Mingshui Heilong. China 90 B3
Mingulay i. U.K. 60 B4
Mingxi China 97 H3
Mingzhou Hebei China see Weixian
Mingzhou Shaanxi China see Suide
Minhe China see Jinxian
Minhla Bago Myanmar 86 A3
Minhla Magway Myanmar 86 A3
Minho r. Port./Spain see Miño
Minicoy atoll India 106 B4
Minigwal, Lake salt flat Australia 135 C7
Minilya Australia 135 A5
Minilya r. Australia 135 A5
Minipi Lake Canada 153 J3
Miniss Lake Canada 151 N5
Minitonas Canada 151 K4
Minjian China see Mabian
Min Jiang r. Fujian China 97 H3
Min Jiang r. Sichuan China 96 E2
Minle China 94 E4
Minna Nigeria 120 D4
Minna Bluff pt Antarctica 188 H1
Minne Sweden 54 I5
Minneapolis KS U.S.A. 160 D4
Minneapolis MN U.S.A. 160 E2
Minnedosa Canada 151 L5
Minnehaha Springs WV U.S.A. 164 F4
Minneola KS U.S.A. 161 C4
Minnesota r. MN U.S.A. 160 E2
Minnesota state U.S.A. 160 E2
Minnewaukan ND U.S.A. 160 D1
Minnitaki Lake Canada 151 N5
Mino Japan 92 C3
Miño r. Port./Spain 67 B3 also known as Minho
Minobu Yamanashi Japan 93 E3
Minobu Yamanashi Japan 93 E3
Minobu-san mt. Japan 93 E3
Minobu-sanchi mts Japan 93 E4
Minokamo Japan 92 D3
Mino-Mikawa-kōgen reg. Japan 92 D3
Minoo Japan 92 B4
Minorca i. Spain 67 H3
Minot ND U.S.A. 160 C1
Minowa Japan 93 D3
Minqin China 94 E4
Minqing China 97 H3
Minquan China 95 H5
Min Shan mts China 96 D1
Minsin Myanmar 86 A1

▶Minsk Belarus 55 O10 Capital of Belarus.

Mińsk Mazowiecki Poland 57 R4
Minsterley U.K. 59 E6
Mintaka Pass China/Pak. 104 C1
Mintang China 94 E5
Minto AK U.S.A. 149 J2
Minto, Lac l. Canada 152 G2
Minto, Mount Antarctica 188 H2
Minto Inlet Canada 146 G2
Minton Canada 151 J5
Mīnūdasht Iran 110 D2
Minūf Egypt 112 C5
Minusinsk Russia 88 G2
Minvoul Gabon 122 B3
Minxian China 94 F5
Minya Konka mt. China see Gongga Shan
Minywa Myanmar 86 A2
Minzong India 105 I4
Mio MI U.S.A. 164 C1
Miquan China 98 D4
Miquelon Canada 152 F4
Miquelon i. St Pierre and Miquelon 153 K5
Mīrābād Afgh. 111 F4
Mirabela Brazil 179 B2
Mirador, Parque Nacional de nat. park Brazil 177 I5
Mirador-Dos Lagunos-Río Azul, Parque Nacional nat. park Guat. 167 H5
Miraflores Mex. 166 C4
Mīrah, Wādī al watercourse Iraq/Saudi Arabia 113 F4
Miraí Brazil 179 C3
Miraj India 106 B2
Miramar Arg. 178 E5
Miramar, Lago l. Mex. 167 H5
Miramichi Canada 153 I5
Miramichi Bay Canada 153 I5
Mirampellou, Kolpos b. Greece 69 K7
Mirampelou, Kolpos b. Greece see Mirampellou, Kolpos
Miran China 98 E5
Miranda Brazil 178 E2
Miranda Moz. see Macaloge
Miranda CA U.S.A. 158 B1
Miranda, Lake salt flat Australia 135 C6
Miranda de Ebro Spain 67 E2
Mirandela Port. 67 C3
Mirandola Italy 68 D2
Mirante Brazil 179 C1
Mirante, Serra do hills Brazil 179 A3
Mirassol Brazil 179 A3
Mir-Bashir Azer. see Tärtär
Mirbāṭ Oman 109 H6
Mirboo North Australia 138 C7
Mirepoix France 66 E5
Mirgarh Pak. 111 I4
Mirgorod Ukr. see Myrhorod
Miri Sarawak Malaysia 85 F1
Miri mt. Pak. 111 F4
Mirialguda India 106 C2
Miri Hills India 105 H4
Mirim, Lagoa l. Brazil/Uruguay 178 F4
Mirim, Lagoa do l. Brazil 179 A5
Mirintu watercourse Australia 138 A2
Mirjan India 106 B3
Mirny research station Antarctica 188 F2
Mirnyy Arkhangel'skaya Oblast' Russia 52 I3
Mirnyy Respublika Sakha (Yakutiya) Russia 77 M3
Mirond Lake Canada 151 K4
Mironovka Ukr. see Myronivka
Mirow Germany 63 M1
Mirpur Khas Pak. 111 H5
Mirpur Sakro Pak. 111 G5
Mirsali China 98 D4
Mirs Bay H.K. China 97 [inset]
Mirtoan Sea Greece see Myrtoo Pelagos
Miryalaguda India see Mirialguda
Miryang S. Korea 91 C6
Mirzachirla Turkm. see Murzechirla
Mirzachul Uzbek. see Guliston
Mirzapur India 105 E4
Mirzawal India 104 C3
Misaka Japan 93 E3
Misaki Chiba Japan 93 G3
Misaki Ōsaka Japan 92 B4
Misakubo Japan 93 D3
Misalay China 99 C5
Misantla Mex. 167 F5
Misato Gunma Japan 93 E2
Misato Mie Japan 92 C4
Misato Nagano Japan 93 D2
Misato Saitama Japan 93 F2
Misato Saitama Japan 93 F3
Misato Wakayama Japan 92 B4
Misaw Lake Canada 151 K3
Miscou Island Canada 153 I5
Misehkow r. Canada 152 C4
Mīsh, Kūh-e hill Iran 110 E3
Misha India 87 A6
Mishawaka IN U.S.A. 164 B3
Misheguk Mountain AK U.S.A. 148 G1
Mishicot WI U.S.A. 164 B1
Mishima Japan 93 E3
Mi-shima i. Japan 91 C6
Mishmi Hills India 105 H3
Mishvan' Russia 52 L2
Misima Island P.N.G. 136 F1

Misis Dağ hills Turkey 107 B1
Miskin Oman 110 E6
Miskitos, Cayos is Nicaragua 166 [inset] J6
Miskitos, Costa de coastal area Nicaragua see Mosquitos, Costa de
Miskolc Hungary 53 D6
Mismā, Tall al hill Jordan 107 C3
Misoöl i. Papua Indon. 83 D3
Misquah Hills MN U.S.A. 160 F2
Misr country Africa see Egypt
Misraç Turkey see Kurtalan
Mişrātah Libya 121 E1
Missinaibi r. Canada 152 E4
Mission TX U.S.A. 167 F3
Mission Beach Australia 136 D3
Mission Viejo CA U.S.A. 158 E5
Missisa r. Canada 152 D3
Missisa Lake Canada 152 D3
Missisicabi r. Canada 152 F4
Mississauga Canada 164 F2
Mississinewa Lake IN U.S.A. 164 C3

▶Mississippi r. U.S.A. 161 F6
4th longest river in North America, and a major part of the longest (Mississippi-Missouri).

Mississippi state U.S.A. 161 F5
Mississippi Delta LA U.S.A. 161 F6
Mississippi Lake Canada 165 G1

▶Mississippi-Missouri r. U.S.A. 155 I4
Longest river in North America and 4th in the world.

Mississippi Sound sea chan. MS U.S.A. 161 F6
Missolonghi Greece see Mesolongi
Missoula MT U.S.A. 156 E3

▶Missouri r. U.S.A. 160 F4
3rd longest river in North America, and a major part of the longest (Mississippi-Missouri).

Missouri state U.S.A. 160 E4
Mistanipisipou r. Canada 153 J4
Mistassibi r. Canada 147 K5
Mistassini Canada 153 G4
Mistassini r. Canada 153 G4
Mistassini, Lac l. Canada 152 G4
Mistastin Lake Canada 153 J3
Mistelbach Austria 57 P6
Mistinibi, Lac l. Canada 153 J2
Mistissini Canada 152 G4
Misty Fiords National Monument Wilderness nat. park AK U.S.A. 150 D4
Misugi Japan 92 C4
Misumba Dem. Rep. Congo 123 C4
Misuratah Libya see Mişrātah
Mita, Punta de pt Mex. 166 D4
Mitaka Japan 93 F3
Mitake Gifu Japan 92 D3
Mitake Nagano Japan 92 D3
Mitchell Australia 137 D5
Mitchell r. N.S.W. Australia 138 F2
Mitchell r. Qld Australia 136 C2
Mitchell r. Vic. Australia 138 C6
Mitchell Canada 164 E2
Mitchell IN U.S.A. 164 B4
Mitchell OR U.S.A. 156 C3
Mitchell SD U.S.A. 160 D3
Mitchell, Lake Australia 136 D3
Mitchell, Mount NC U.S.A. 162 D5
Mitchell and Alice Rivers National Park Australia 136 C2
Mitchell Island Cook Is see Nassau
Mitchell Island atoll Tuvalu see Nukulaelae
Mitchell Point Australia 134 E2
Mitchelstown Ireland 61 D5
Mīt Ghamr Egypt 112 C5
Mit Ghamr Egypt see Mīt Ghamr
Mithi Pak. 111 H5
Mithrau Pak. 111 H5
Mithri Pak. 111 G4
Miti i. Moluccas Indon. 83 D2
Mitilíni Greece see Mytilini
Mitkof Island AK U.S.A. 149 N4
Mito Aichi Japan 92 D4
Mito Ibaraki Japan 93 G2
Mitole Tanz. 123 D4
Mitomi Japan 93 E3
Mitre mt. N.Z. 139 E5
Mitre Island Solomon Is 133 H3
Mitrofania Island AK U.S.A. 148 H5
Mitrofanovka Russia 53 H6
Mitrovica Kosovo see Mitrovicë
Mitrovicë Kosovo 69 I3
Mitsinjo Madag. 123 E5
Mits'iwa Eritrea see Massawa
Mitsue Japan 92 C4
Mitsumatarenge-dake mt. Japan 92 D2
Mitsutōge-yama mt. Japan 93 E3
Mitta Mitta Australia 138 C6
Mittellandkanal canal Germany 63 I2
Mitterteich Germany 63 M5
Mittimatalik Canada see Pond Inlet
Mittweida Germany 63 M4
Mitú Col. 176 D3
Mitumba, Chaîne des mts Dem. Rep. Congo 123 C5
Mitzic Gabon 122 B3
Miughalaigh i. U.K. see Mingulay
Miura Japan 93 F3
Miura-hantō pen. Japan 93 F3
Miwa Fukushima Japan 93 G1
Miwa Ibaraki Japan 93 G2
Miwa Kyōto Japan 92 B3
Mixian China see Xinmi
Miya Japan 92 D2
Miyada Japan 93 D3
Miyagase-ko resr Japan 93 F3
Miyagawa Gifu Japan 92 D2
Miyagawa Mie Japan 92 C4
Miya-gawa r. Japan 92 C4
Miya-gawa r. Japan 92 D2
Miyake-jima i. Japan 93 F4
Miyako Japan 91 F5
Miyakonojō Japan 91 C7
Miyama Fukui Japan 92 C2
Miyama Gifu Japan 92 C3
Miyama Kyōto Japan 92 B3
Miyama Wakayama Japan 92 B5
Miyamae Japan 93 F3
Miyang China see Mile
Miyani India 104 B5
Miyazaki Fukui Japan 92 C3
Miyazaki Miyazaki Japan 91 C7
Miyazu Japan 92 B3
Miyazu-wan b. Japan 92 B3
Miyi China 96 D3
Miyoshi Aichi Japan 92 D3
Miyoshi Chiba Japan 93 F3
Miyoshi Hiroshima Japan 91 D6
Miyota Japan 93 E2
Miyun China 95 I3
Miyun Shuiku resr China 95 I3
Mizān 'Alāqahdārī Afgh. 111 G3
Mīzan Teferī Eth. 122 D3
Mizdah Libya 121 E1
Mizen Head hd Ireland 61 C6
Mizhhir"ya Ukr. 53 D6
Mizhi China 95 G4
Mizo Hills state India see Mizoram
Mizoram state India 105 H5
Mizpe Ramon Israel 107 B4
Mizugaki-yama mt. Japan 93 E3
Mizuhashi Japan 92 D2
Mizuho Kyōto Japan 92 B3
Mizuho Tōkyō Japan 93 F3
Mizunami Japan 92 D3
Mizuno-gawa r. Japan 93 F2
Mjölby Sweden 55 I7
Mkata Tanz. 123 D4
Mkushi Zambia 123 C5
Mladá Boleslav Czech Rep. 57 O5
Mladenovac Serbia 69 I2
Mława Poland 57 R4
Mlilwane Nature Reserve Swaziland 125 J4
Mljet i. Croatia 68 G3
Mlungisi S. Africa 125 H6
Mlu Prey Cambodia 87 D4
Mmabatho S. Africa 125 G3
Mmamabula Botswana 125 H2
Mmathethe Botswana 125 G3
Mo Norway 55 D6
Moa i. Moluccas Indon. 83 D5
Moab reg. Jordan 107 B4
Moab UT U.S.A. 159 I2
Moa Island Australia 136 C1
Moala i. Fiji 133 H3
Mo'allā Iran 110 D3
Moamba Moz. 125 K3
Moanda Gabon 122 B4
Moapa NV U.S.A. 159 F3
Moate Ireland 61 E4
Mobara Japan 93 G3
Mobārakeh Iran 110 C3
Mobayembongo Dem. Rep. Congo see Mobayi-Mbongo
Mobayi-Mbongo Dem. Rep. Congo 122 C3
Moberly MO U.S.A. 160 E4
Moberly Lake Canada 150 F4
Mobha India 104 C5
Mobile AL U.S.A. 161 F6
Mobile AZ U.S.A. 159 G5
Mobile Bay AL U.S.A. 161 F6
Mobile Point AL U.S.A. 167 I2
Moble watercourse Australia 138 B1
Mobo Masbate Phil. 82 C3
Mobridge SD U.S.A. 160 C2
Mobutu, Lake Dem. Rep. Congo/Uganda see Albert, Lake
Mobutu Sese Seko, Lake Dem. Rep. Congo/Uganda see Albert, Lake
Moca Geçidi pass Turkey 107 A1
Moçambique country Africa see Mozambique
Moçambique Moz. 123 E5
Moçâmedes Angola see Namibe
Môc Châu Vietnam 86 D2
Mocha Yemen 108 F7
Mocha, Isla i. Chile 178 B5
Mochicahui Mex. 166 C3
Mochirma, Parque Nacional nat. park Venez. 176 F1
Mochudi Botswana 125 H3
Mochudi admin. dist. Botswana see Kgatleng
Mocimboa da Praia Moz. 123 E5
Möckern Germany 63 L2
Möckmühl Germany 63 J5
Mockträsk Sweden 54 L4
Mocoa Col. 176 C3
Mococa Brazil 179 B3
Mocoduene Moz. 125 L2
Mocorito Mex. 166 D3
Moctezuma Chihuahua Mex. 166 D2
Moctezuma San Luis Potosí Mex. 168 D4
Moctezuma Sonora Mex. 166 C2
Mocuba Moz. 123 D5
Mocun China 97 G4
Modan Indon. 81 I7
Modane France 66 H4
Modder r. S. Africa 125 G5
Modena Italy 68 D2
Modena UT U.S.A. 159 G3
Modesto CA U.S.A. 158 C3
Modesto Lake CA U.S.A. 158 C3
Modimolle S. Africa 125 I3
Modjadjiskloof S. Africa 125 J2
Modot Mongolia see Tsenhermandal
Modung China 96 C2
Moe Australia 138 C7
Moel Sych hill U.K. 59 D6
Moelv Norway 55 G6
Moen Norway 54 K2
Moenkopi AZ U.S.A. 159 H3
Moenkopi Wash r. AZ U.S.A. 159 H4
Moeraki Point N.Z. 139 C7
Moero, Lake Dem. Rep. Congo/Zambia see Mweru, Lake
Moers Germany 62 G3
Moffat U.K. 60 F5
Moga India 104 C3

▶Mogadishu Somalia 122 E3
Capital of Somalia.

Mogador Morocco see Essaouira
Mogadore Reservoir OH U.S.A. 164 E3
Moganyaka S. Africa 125 I3
Mogao China 98 F5
Mogaung Myanmar 86 B1
Mogdy Russia 90 D2
Mögelin Germany 63 M2
Mogi das Cruzes Brazil 179 B3
Mogilev Belarus see Mahilyow
Mogilev Podol'skiy Ukr. see Mohyliv-Podil's'kyy
Mogi Mirim Brazil 179 B3
Mogiquiçaba Brazil 179 D2
Mogocha Russia 89 L2
Mogod mts Tunisia 68 C6
Mogoditshane Botswana 125 G3
Mogollon Mountains NM U.S.A. 159 I5
Mogollon Plateau AZ U.S.A. 159 H4
Mogontiacum Germany see Mainz
Mogoytuy Russia 95 H1
Mogroum Chad 121 E3
Moguqi China 95 J2
Mogwadi S. Africa 125 I2
Mogwadi r. S. Africa 125 I2
Mogwase S. Africa 125 H3
Mogzon Russia 89 K2
Mohács Hungary 68 H2
Mohaka r. N.Z. 139 F4
Mohala India 106 D1
Mohale Dam Lesotho 125 I5
Mohale's Hoek Lesotho 125 H6
Mohali town India 104 D3
Mohall ND U.S.A. 160 C1
Moḩammad Iran 110 E3
Moḩammadābād Iran 110 E4
Mohammadia Alg. 67 G6
Mohan r. India/Nepal 104 E3
Mohana India 104 D4
Mohave, Lake NV U.S.A. 159 F4
Mohawk r. NY U.S.A. 165 I2
Mohawk Mountains AZ U.S.A. 159 G5
Mohenjo Daro tourist site Pak. 111 H5
Moher, Cliffs of Ireland 61 C5
Mohican, Cape AK U.S.A. 148 F3
Mohill Ireland 61 E4
Möhne r. Germany 63 H3
Möhnetalsperre resr Germany 63 I3
Mohon Peak AZ U.S.A. 159 G4
Mohoro Tanz. 123 D4
Mohyliv-Podil's'kyy Ukr. 53 E6
Moi Norway 55 E7
Moijabana Botswana 125 H2
Moincêr China 99 C7
Moindawang India 99 E8
Moine Moz. 125 K3
Moinești Romania 69 L1
Mointy Kazakh. see Moyynty
Mo i Rana Norway 54 I3
Moirang India 96 B3
Mõisaküla Estonia 55 N7
Moisie Canada 153 I4
Moisie r. Canada 153 I4
Moissac France 66 E4
Mojave CA U.S.A. 158 D4
Mojave r. CA U.S.A. 158 E4
Mojave Desert CA U.S.A. 158 E4
Mojiang China 96 D4
Mojokerto Java Indon. 85 F4
Mojos, Llanos de plain Bol. 176 E6
Moju r. Brazil 177 I4
Mōka Japan 93 G2
Mokala National Park S. Africa 124 G5
Mokama India 105 F4
Mokau N.Z. 139 E4
Mokau r. N.Z. 139 E4
Mokelumne r. CA U.S.A. 158 C2
Mokelumne Aqueduct canal CA U.S.A. 158 C2
Mokh, Gowd-e l. Iran 110 D4
Mokhoabong Pass Lesotho 125 I5
Mokhotlong Lesotho 125 I5
Mokhtārān Iran 110 E3
Moknine Tunisia 68 D7
Mokohinau Islands N.Z. 139 E2
Mokokchung India 105 H4
Mokolo Cameroon 121 E3
Mokolo r. S. Africa 125 H2
Mokopane S. Africa 125 I3
Mokpo S. Korea 91 B6
Mokrous Russia 53 J6
Moksha r. Russia 53 I5
Mokshan Russia 53 J5
Möksy Fin. 54 N5
Môktama Myanmar see Mottama
Môktama, Gulf of Myanmar see Mottama, Gulf of
Mokundurra India see Mukandwara
Mokwa Nigeria 120 D4
Molaly Kazakh. 98 B3
Molango Mex. 167 F4
Molatón mt. Spain 67 F4
Moldavia country Europe see Moldova
Moldavskaya S.S.R. country Europe see Moldova
Molde Norway 54 E5
Moldjord Norway 54 I3
Moldova country Europe 53 F7
Moldoveanu, Vârful mt. Romania 69 K2
Moldovei de Sud, Cîmpia plain Moldova 69 M1
Mol'dyr Kazakh. 98 B2
Molega Lake Canada 153 I5
Molen r. S. Africa 125 I4
Mole National Park Ghana 120 C4
Molepolole Botswana 125 G3
Moltai Lith. 55 N9
Molfetta Italy 68 G4
Molière Alg. see Bordj Bounaama
Molihong Shan mt. China see Morihong Shan
Molina de Aragón Spain 67 F3
Moline KS U.S.A. 161 D4
Moling mt. India 105 H3
Molkom Sweden 55 H7
Mollagara Turkm. 110 D2
Mollakara Turkm. see Mollagara
Mol Len mt. India 105 H4
Möllenbeck Germany 63 N1
Mollendo Peru 176 D7
Mölln Germany 63 K1
Mölnlycke Sweden 55 H8
Molochnyy Russia 54 R2
Molodechno Belarus see Maladzyechna
Moloka'i i. HI U.S.A. 157 [inset]
Moloma r. Russia 52 K4
Molong Australia 138 D4
Molopo watercourse Botswana/S. Africa 124 E5
Molotov Russia see Perm'
Molotovsk Kyrg. see Kayyngdy
Molotovsk Arkhangel'skaya Oblast' Russia see Severodvinsk
Molotovsk Kirovskaya Oblast' Russia see Nolinsk
Moloundou Cameroon 121 E4
Molson Lake Canada 151 L4
Molu i. Moluccas Indon. 81 I8
Moluccas is Indon. 83 C3
Molucca Sea Indon. see Maluku, Laut
Molukken is Indon. see Moluccas
Moma Moz. 123 D5
Moma r. Russia 77 P3
Momba Australia 138 A3
Mombaça Brazil 177 K5
Mombasa Kenya 122 D4
Mombetsu Hokkaidō Japan see Monbetsu
Mombetsu Hokkaidō Japan see Hidaka
Mombi New India 105 H4
Mombum Indon. 81 J8
Momchilgrad Bulg. 69 K4
Momence IL U.S.A. 164 B3
Momī, Rhiy di- pt Yemen 109 H7
Momotombo, Volcán vol. Nicaragua 166 [inset] I6
Momoyama Japan 92 B4
Mompog Pass Phil. 82 C3
Mompós Col. 176 D2
Møn i. Denmark 55 H9
Mon India 105 H4
Mona UT U.S.A. 159 H2
Monaca PA U.S.A. 164 E3
Monach, Sound of sea chan. U.K. 60 B3
Monach Islands U.K. 60 B3
Monaco country Europe 66 H5
Monaco Basin sea feature N. Atlantic Ocean 184 G4
Monadhliath Mountains U.K. 60 E3
Monaghan Ireland 61 F3
Monahans TX U.S.A. 161 C6
Mona Passage Dom. Rep./Puerto Rico 169 K5
Monapo Moz. 123 E5
Monar, Loch l. U.K. 60 D3
Monarch Mountain Canada 150 E5
Monarch Pass CO U.S.A. 157 G5
Mona Reservoir UT U.S.A. 159 H2
Monashee Mountains Canada 150 G5
Monastir Macedonia see Bitola
Monastir Tunisia 68 D7
Monastyrishche Ukr. see Monastyryshche
Monastyryshche Ukr. 53 F6
Monbetsu Japan 90 F3
Moncalieri Italy 68 B2
Moncayo mt. Spain 67 F3
Monchegorsk Russia 54 R3
Mönchengladbach Germany 62 G3
Monchique Port. 67 B5
Moncks Corner SC U.S.A. 163 D5
Monclova Mex. 167 E3
Moncouche, Lac l. Canada 153 H4
Moncton Canada 153 I5
Mondego r. Port. 67 B3
Mondo Chad 121 E3
Mondovì Italy 68 B2
Mondragone Italy 68 E4
Mondy Russia 88 I2
Monemvasia Greece 69 J6
Monessen PA U.S.A. 164 F3
Moneta WY U.S.A. 156 G4
Moneygall Ireland 61 E5
Moneymore U.K. 61 F3
Monfalcone Italy 68 E2
Monfalut Egypt see Manfalūţ
Monforte de Lemos Spain 67 C2
Monga Dem. Rep. Congo 122 C3
Mongala r. Dem. Rep. Congo 122 B3
Mongar Bhutan 105 G4
Mongbwalu Dem. Rep. Congo 122 D3
Mông Cai Vietnam 86 D2
Mongers Lake salt flat Australia 135 B7
Monggon Qulu China 95 I1
Mong Hang Myanmar 86 B2
Mong Hkan Myanmar 86 C2
Mong Hpayak Myanmar 86 B2
Mong Hsat Myanmar 86 B2
Mong Hsawk Myanmar 86 B2
Mong Hsu Myanmar 86 B2
Monghyr India see Munger
Mong Kung Myanmar 86 B2
Mong Kyawt Myanmar 86 B3
Mongla Bangl. 105 G5
Mong Lin Myanmar 86 C2
Mong Loi Myanmar 86 C2
Mong Long Myanmar 86 B2
Mong Nai Myanmar 86 B2
Mong Nawng Myanmar 86 B2
Mongo Chad 121 E3
Mongolia country Asia 88 I3
Mongolian Altai, Petroglyphic Complexes of the 98 E2
Mongolküre China see Zhaosu
Mongol Uls country Asia see Mongolia
Möngönmorīt Mongolia 95 G1
Mongora Pak. 111 I3
Mongour hill U.K. 60 G4
Mong Pan Myanmar 86 B2
Mong Ping Myanmar 86 B2
Mong Pu Myanmar 86 B2
Mong Pu-awn Myanmar 86 B2
Mongrove, Punta pt Mex. 166 E5
Mong Si Myanmar 86 B2
Mongu Zambia 123 C5
Mong Un Myanmar 86 C2
Monguno Nigeria 120 E3
Mong Yai Myanmar 86 B2
Mong Yang Myanmar 86 B2
Mong Yawn Myanmar 86 B2
Mong Yawng Myanmar 86 C2
Mönhbulag Mongolia see Yösöndzüyl
Mönhhaan Mongolia 95 H2
Mönh Hayrhan Uul mt. Mongolia 94 B2
Moniaive U.K. 60 F5
Monitor Mountain NV U.S.A. 158 E2
Monitor Range mts NV U.S.A. 158 E2
Monivea Ireland 61 D4
Monkey Bay Malawi 123 D5
Monkira Australia 136 C5
Monkton Canada 164 E2
Monmouth U.K. 59 E7
Monmouth IL U.S.A. 160 F3
Monmouth Mountain Canada 150 F5
Monnow r. U.K. 59 E7
Mono, Punta pt Nicaragua 166 [inset] J7
Mono Lake CA U.S.A. 158 D2
Monolithos Greece 69 L6
Monomoy Point MA U.S.A. 165 J3
Monon IN U.S.A. 164 B3
Monopoli Italy 68 G4
Monreal del Campo Spain 67 F3
Monreale Sicily Italy 68 E5
Monroe IN U.S.A. 164 C3
Monroe LA U.S.A. 161 E5
Monroe MI U.S.A. 164 D3
Monroe NC U.S.A. 163 D5
Monroe WI U.S.A. 160 F3
Monroe Center WI U.S.A. 160 F2
Monroe Lake IN U.S.A. 164 B4
Monroeton PA U.S.A. 165 G3
Monroeville AL U.S.A. 167 I2

▶Monrovia Liberia 120 B4
Capital of Liberia.

Mons Belgium 62 D4
Monschau Germany 62 G4
Monselice Italy 68 D2
Montabaur Germany 63 H4
Montagne d'Ambre, Parc National de nat. park Madag. 123 E5
Montagu S. Africa 124 E7
Montague Canada 153 J5
Montague MI U.S.A. 164 B2
Montague TX U.S.A. 161 D5
Montague Island AK U.S.A. 149 K3
Montague Range hills Australia 135 B6
Montague Strait AK U.S.A. 149 J4
Montalat r. Indon. 85 F3
Montalto mt. Italy 68 F5
Montalto Uffugo Italy 68 G5
Montana Bulg. 69 J3
Montana AK U.S.A. 149 J3
Montana state U.S.A. 156 F3
Montaña de Comayagua, Parque Nacional nat. park Hond. 166 [inset] I6
Montaña de Cusuco, Parque Nacional nat. park Hond. 167 H6
Montaña de Yoro, Parque Nacional nat. park Hond. 166 [inset] I6
Montanhas do Tumucumaque, Parque Nacional nat. park Brazil 177 H3
Montargis France 66 F3
Montauban France 66 E4
Montauk NY U.S.A. 165 J3
Montauk Point NY U.S.A. 165 J3
Mont-aux-Sources mt. Lesotho 125 I5
Montbard France 66 G3
Montblanc Spain 67 G3
Montblanch Spain see Montblanc
Montbrison France 66 G4
Montceau-les-Mines France 66 G3
Montcornet France 62 E5
Mont-de-Marsan France 66 D5
Montdidier France 62 C5
Monte Alban tourist site Mex. 167 F5
Monte Alegre Brazil 177 H4
Monte Alegre de Goiás Brazil 179 B1
Monte Alegre de Minas Brazil 179 A2
Monte Azul Brazil 179 C1
Monte Azul Paulista Brazil 179 A3
Montebello Canada 152 G5
Montebello Islands Australia 134 A5
Montebelluna Italy 68 E2
Monte-Carlo Monaco 66 H5
Monte Cristi Dom. Rep. 169 J5
Monte Cristo S. Africa 125 H2
Monte Dourado Brazil 177 H4
Monte Escobedo Mex. 166 E4
Montego Bay Jamaica 169 I5
Montélimar France 66 G4
Monte Lindo r. Para. 178 E2
Montello WI U.S.A. 160 F3
Montemorelos Mex. 167 F3
Montemor-o-Novo Port. 67 B4

▶Montenegro country Europe 68 H3
Gained independence from Serbia in June 2006.

Montepulciano Italy 68 D3
Monte Quemado Arg. 178 D3
Montereau-Fault-Yonne France 66 F2
Monterey Mex. see Monterrey
Monterey CA U.S.A. 158 C3
Monterey VA U.S.A. 164 F4
Monterey Bay CA U.S.A. 158 B3
Montería Col. 176 C2
Monteros Arg. 178 C3
Monterrey Baja California Mex. 159 F5
Monterrey Nuevo León Mex. 167 E3
Montesano WA U.S.A. 156 C3
Montesano sulla Marcellana Italy 68 F4
Monte Santo Brazil 177 K6
Monte Santu, Capo di c. Sardinia Italy 68 C4
Montes Claros Brazil 179 C2
Montesilvano Italy 68 F3
Montevarchi Italy 68 D3

▶Montevideo Uruguay 178 E4
Capital of Uruguay.

Montevideo MN U.S.A. 160 E2
Montezuma IA U.S.A. 160 E3
Montezuma Creek UT U.S.A. 159 I3
Montezuma Peak NV U.S.A. 158 E3
Montfort Neth. 62 F3
Montgomery U.K. 59 D6

▶Montgomery AL U.S.A. 163 C5
Capital of Alabama.

Montgomery WV U.S.A. 164 E4
Montgomery Islands Australia 134 C3
Monthey Switz. 66 H3
Monticello AR U.S.A. 161 F5
Monticello FL U.S.A. 163 D6
Monticello IN U.S.A. 164 B3
Monticello KY U.S.A. 164 C5
Monticello MO U.S.A. 160 F3
Monticello NY U.S.A. 165 H3
Monticello UT U.S.A. 159 I3
Montieri, Poggio di mt. Italy 68 D3
Montignac France 66 E4
Montignies-le-Tilleul Belgium 62 E4
Montigny-lès-Metz France 62 G5
Montilla Spain 67 D5
Monti Sibillini, Parco Nazionale dei nat. park Italy 68 E3
Montividiu Brazil 179 A2
Montivilliers France 59 H9
Mont-Joli Canada 153 H4
Mont-Laurier Canada 152 G5
Montluçon France 66 F3
Montmagny Canada 153 H5
Montmédy France 62 F5
Montmirail France 62 D6
Montmorillon France 66 E3
Montmort-Lucy France 62 D6
Monto Australia 136 E5
Montour Falls NY U.S.A. 165 G2
Montoursville PA U.S.A. 165 G3
Montpelier ID U.S.A. 156 F4

▶Montpelier VT U.S.A. 165 I1
Capital of Vermont.

Montpellier France 66 F5
Montréal Canada 152 G5
Montreal r. Ont. Canada 152 D5
Montreal r. Ont. Canada 152 F5
Montreal Lake Canada 151 J4
Montreal Lake l. Canada 151 J4
Montréal-Mirabel airport Canada 152 G5
Montreal River Canada 152 D5
Montréal-Trudeau airport Canada 152 G5
Montreuil France 62 B4
Montreux Switz. 66 H3
Montrose well S. Africa 124 E4
Montrose U.K. 60 G4
Montrose CO U.S.A. 159 J2
Montrose PA U.S.A. 165 H3
Montross VA U.S.A. 165 G4
Monts, Pointe des pt Canada 153 I4
Mont-St-Aignan France 59 I9

▶Montserrat terr. West Indies 169 L5
United Kingdom Overseas Territory.

Montuosa, Isla i. Panama 166 [inset] J8
Montviel, Lac l. Canada 153 H3
Monument Mountain hill AK U.S.A. 148 G2
Monument Valley reg. AZ U.S.A. 159 H3
Monywa Myanmar 86 A2
Monza Italy 68 C2
Monze, Cape pt Pak. see Muari, Ras
Monzón Spain 67 G3
Mooi r. S. Africa 125 J5
Mooifontein Namibia 124 C4
Mookane Botswana 125 H2
Mookgophong S. Africa 125 I3
Mookgopong S. Africa see Mookgophong
Moolawatana Australia 137 B6
Moomba Australia 137 C6
Moomin Creek r. Australia 138 D2
Moonaree Australia 137 A6
Moonbi Range mts Australia 138 E3
Moonda Lake salt flat Australia 137 C5
Moonie Australia 138 E1
Moonie r. Australia 138 D2
Moora Australia 135 B7
Mooraberree Australia 136 C5
Moorcroft WY U.S.A. 156 G3
Moore r. Australia 135 A7
Moore MT U.S.A. 156 F3
Moore, Lake salt flat Australia 135 B7
Moore Creek AK U.S.A. 148 H3
Moore Embayment b. Antarctica 188 H1
Moorefield WV U.S.A. 165 F4
Moore Haven FL U.S.A. 163 D7
Moore Reef Australia 136 E3
Moore Reservoir New Hampshire/Vermont U.S.A. 165 J1

Moore River National Park Australia 135 A7
Moores Island Bahamas 163 E7
Moorfoot Hills U.K. 60 F5
Moorhead MN U.S.A. 160 D2
Moorman KY U.S.A. 164 B5
Moornanyah Lake imp. l. Australia 138 A4
Mooroopna Australia 138 B6
Moorreesburg S. Africa 124 D7
Moorrinya National Park Australia 136 D4
Moose r. Canada 152 E4
Moose Creek AK U.S.A. 149 K2
Moose Factory Canada 152 E4
Moosehead Lake ME U.S.A. 162 G2
Moose Jaw Canada 151 J5
Moose Jaw r. Canada 151 J5
Moose Lake MN U.S.A. 160 E2
Mooselookmeguntic Lake ME U.S.A. 165 J1
Moose Mountain Creek r. Canada 151 K5
Moose Pass AK U.S.A. 149 J3
Moosilauke, Mount NH U.S.A. 165 J1
Moosomin Canada 151 K5
Moosonee Canada 152 E4
Mootwingee National Park Australia 137 C6
Mopane S. Africa 125 I2
Mopeia Moz. 123 D5
Mopipi Botswana 123 C6
Mopti Mali 120 C3
Moquegua Peru 176 D7
Mora Cameroon 121 E3
Mora Spain 67 E4
Mora Sweden 55 I6
Mora MN U.S.A. 160 E2
Mora NM U.S.A. 157 G6
Mora r. NM U.S.A. 157 G6
Moradabad India 104 D3
Morada Nova Brazil 177 K5
Moraine Lake Canada 151 J1
Moraleda, Canal sea chan. Chile 178 B6
Morales Guat. 166 [inset] H6
Moram India 106 C2
Moramanga Madag. 123 E5
Moran WY U.S.A. 156 F4
Moranbah Australia 136 E4
Morang Nepal see Biratnagar
Morar, Loch l. U.K. 60 D4
Morari, Tso l. India 104 D2
Moratuwa Sri Lanka 106 C5
Morava reg. Czech Rep. 57 P6
Moravia NY U.S.A. 165 G2
Morawa Australia 135 A7
Moray Firth b. U.K. 60 E3
Moray Range hills Australia 134 E3
Morbach Germany 62 H5
Morbeng S. Africa see Morebeng
Morbi India 104 B5
Morcenx France 66 D4
Morcillo Mex. 161 B7
Mordaga China 89 M2
Mor Dağı mt. Turkey 113 G3
Morden Canada 151 L5
Mordovo Russia 53 I5
Mordvinof, Cape AK U.S.A. 148 F5
Moreau r. SD U.S.A. 160 C2
Moreau, South Fork r. SD U.S.A. 160 C2
Morebeng S. Africa 125 I2
Morecambe U.K. 58 E4
Morecambe Bay U.K. 58 D4
Moree Australia 138 D2
Morehead P.N.G. 81 K8
Morehead KY U.S.A. 164 D4
Morehead City NC U.S.A. 169 I2
Morel r. India 99 B8
Moreland KY U.S.A. 164 C5
More Laptevykh sea Russia see Laptev Sea
Morelia Mex. 168 D5
Morella Australia 136 C4
Morella Spain 67 F3
Morelos Mex. 157 G8
Morelos state Mex. 167 F5
Morena India 104 D4
Morena, Sierra mts Spain 67 C5
Morenci AZ U.S.A. 159 I5
Morenci MI U.S.A. 164 C3
Moreni Romania 69 K2
Moreno Mex. 166 C2
Moreno Valley CA U.S.A. 158 E5
Moresby, Mount Canada 149 N5
Moresby Island Canada see Gwaii Haanas
Moreswe Pan salt pan Botswana 124 G2
Moreton Bay Australia 138 F1
Moreton-in-Marsh U.K. 59 F7
Moreton Island Australia 138 F1
Moreton Island National Park Australia 138 F1
Moreuil France 62 C5
Morez France 66 H3
Morfou Cyprus 107 A2
Morfou Bay Cyprus 107 A2
Morgan UT U.S.A. 156 F4
Morgan City LA U.S.A. 161 F6
Morgan Hill CA U.S.A. 158 C3
Morganton NC U.S.A. 162 D5
Morgantown KY U.S.A. 164 B5
Morgantown WV U.S.A. 164 F4
Morgenzon S. Africa 125 I4
Morges Switz. 66 H3
Morghāb, Daryā-ye r. Afgh. 111 F3
Morhar r. India 105 F4
Mori China 94 B3
Mori Hokkaidō Japan 90 F4
Mori Shizuoka Japan 93 D4
Moriah, Mount NV U.S.A. 159 F2
Moriarty's Range hills Australia 138 B2
Morice Lake Canada 150 E4
Morichal Col. 176 D3
Moriguchi Japan 92 B4
Morihong Shan mt. China 90 B4
Morija Lesotho 125 H5
Morin Dawa China see Nirji
Moringen Germany 63 J3
Morioka Japan 91 F5
Moris Mex. 166 C2
Morisset Australia 138 E4
Moriya Japan 93 F3
Moriyama Japan 92 C3
Moriyoshi-zan vol. Japan 91 F5
Morjärv Sweden 54 M3
Morjen r. Pak. 111 F4
Morki Russia 52 K4
Morlaix France 66 C2
Morley U.K. 58 F5
Mormam Flat Dam AZ U.S.A. 159 H5
Mormant France 62 C6
Mormon Lake AZ U.S.A. 159 H4
Mormugao India see Marmagao
Morne Diablotins vol. Dominica 169 L5
Morney watercourse Australia 136 C5
Mornington, Isla i. Chile 178 A7
Mornington Abyssal Plain sea feature S. Atlantic Ocean 184 C9
Mornington Island Australia 136 B3
Mornington Peninsula National Park Australia 138 B7
Moro Pak. 111 G5
Moro OR U.S.A. 156 C3
Morobe P.N.G. 81 L8
Morocco country Africa 120 C1
Morocco IN U.S.A. 164 B3
Morococala mt. Bol. 176 E7
Morogoro Tanz. 123 D4
Moro Gulf Phil. 82 C5
Morojaneng S. Africa 125 H5
Morokweng S. Africa 124 F4
Moroleón Mex. 167 E4
Moromaho i. Indon. 83 C4
Morombe Madag. 123 E6
Morón Cuba 163 E8
Mörön Mongolia 94 E1
Morondava Madag. 123 E6
Morón de la Frontera Spain 67 D5
Moron Gol watercourse China 94 E3

▶Moroni Comoros 123 E5
Capital of the Comoros.

Moroni UT U.S.A. 159 H2
Moron Us He r. China see Tongtian He
Morotai i. Moluccas Indon. 83 D2
Morotai, Selat sea chan. Moluccas Indon. 83 C2
Moroto Uganda 122 D3
Morowali, Cagar Alam nature res. Indon. 83 B3
Morozovsk Russia 53 I6
Morpeth Canada 164 E2
Morpeth U.K. 58 F3
Morphou Cyprus see Morfou
Morrill KY U.S.A. 164 C5
Morrilton AR U.S.A. 161 E5
Morrin Canada 151 H5
Morrinhos Brazil 179 A2
Morris Canada 151 L5
Morris IL U.S.A. 160 F3
Morris MN U.S.A. 160 E2
Morris PA U.S.A. 165 G3
Morrison IL U.S.A. 160 F3
Morristown AZ U.S.A. 159 G5
Morristown NJ U.S.A. 165 H3
Morristown NY U.S.A. 165 H1
Morristown TN U.S.A. 162 D4
Morrisville NY U.S.A. 165 H2
Morro Brazil 179 B2
Morro Bay CA U.S.A. 158 C4
Morro de Petatlán hd Mex. 167 E5
Morro do Chapéu Brazil 177 J6
Morro Grande hill Brazil 177 H4
Morrosquillo, Golfo de b. Col. 176 C2
Morrumbene Moz. 125 L2
Morschen Germany 63 J3
Morse Canada 151 J5
Morse TX U.S.A. 161 C4
Morse, Cape Antarctica 188 G2
Morse Reservoir IN U.S.A. 164 B3
Morshanka Russia see Morshansk
Morshansk Russia 53 I5
Morsott Alg. 68 C7
Mort watercourse Australia 136 C4
Mortagne-au-Perche France 66 E2
Mortagne-sur-Sèvre France 66 D3
Mortara Italy 68 C2
Mortehoe U.K. 59 C7
Morteros Arg. 178 D4
Mortes, Rio das r. Brazil 179 A1
Mortimer's Bahamas 163 F8
Mortlake Australia 138 A7
Mortlock Islands Micronesia 186 G5
Mortlock Islands P.N.G. see Takuu Islands
Morton U.K. 59 G6
Morton TX U.S.A. 161 C5
Morton WA U.S.A. 156 C3
Morton National Park Australia 138 E5
Morundah Australia 138 C5
Morupule Botswana 125 H2
Moruroa atoll Fr. Polynesia see Mururoa
Moruya Australia 138 E5
Morven Australia 137 D5
Morven hill U.K. 60 F2
Morvern reg. U.K. 60 D4
Morvi India see Morbi
Morwell Australia 138 C7
Morzhovets, Ostrov i. Russia 52 I2
Morzhovoi Bay AK U.S.A. 148 G5
Mosbach Germany 63 J5
Mosborough U.K. 58 F5
Mosby MT U.S.A. 156 G3

▶Moscow Russia 52 H5
Capital of Russia. 2nd most populous city in Europe.

Moscow ID U.S.A. 156 D3
Moscow PA U.S.A. 165 H3
Moscow University Ice Shelf Antarctica 188 G2
Mosel r. Germany 63 H4
Moselebe watercourse Botswana 124 F3
Moselle r. France 62 G5
Möser Germany 63 L2
Moses, Mount NV U.S.A. 158 E1
Moses Lake WA U.S.A. 156 D3
Moses Point AK U.S.A. 148 G2
Mosgiel N.Z. 139 C7
Moshaweng watercourse S. Africa 124 F4
Moshchnyy, Ostrov i. Russia 55 O7
Moshi Tanz. 122 D4
Mosh'yuga Russia 52 L2
Mosi-oa-Tunya waterfall Zambia/Zimbabwe see Victoria Falls
Mosjøen Norway 54 H4
Moskal'vo Russia 90 F1
Moskenesøy i. Norway 54 H3
Moskva Russia see Moscow
Moskva Tajik. 111 H2
Mosonmagyaróvár Hungary 57 P7
Mosquera Col. 176 C3
Mosquero NM U.S.A. 157 G6
Mosquitia reg. Hond. 166 [inset] J6
Mosquito r. Brazil 179 C1
Mosquito Creek Lake OH U.S.A. 164 E3
Mosquito Lake Canada 151 K2
Mosquito Mountain hill AK U.S.A. 148 H3
Mosquitos, Costa de coastal area Nicaragua 166 [inset] J6
Mosquitos, Golfo de los b. Panama 166 [inset] J7
Moss Norway 55 G7
Mossâmedes Angola see Namibe
Mossat U.K. 60 G3
Mossburn N.Z. 139 B7
Mosselbaai S. Africa see Mossel Bay
Mossel Bay S. Africa 124 F8
Mossel Bay b. S. Africa 124 F8
Mossgiel Australia 138 B4
Mossman Australia 136 D3
Mossoró Brazil 177 K5
Moss Vale Australia 138 E5
Mossy r. Canada 151 K4
Most Czech Rep. 57 N5
Mostaganem Alg. 67 G6
Mostar Bos. & Herz. 68 G3
Mostoos Hills Canada 151 I4
Mostovskoy Russia 113 F1
Mosty Belarus see Masty
Mostyn Sabah Malaysia 85 G1
Mosul Iraq 113 F3
Mosuowan China 98 D3
Møsvatnet l. Norway 55 F7
Motagua r. Guat. 167 H6
Motala Sweden 55 I7
Motaze Moz. 125 K3
Motegi Japan 93 G2
Motetema S. Africa 125 I3
Moth India 104 D4
Motherwell U.K. 60 F5
Moti i. Moluccas Indon. 83 C2
Motian Ling hill China 90 A4
Motihari India 105 F4
Motilla del Palancar Spain 67 F4
Motiti Island N.Z. 139 F3
Motokwe Botswana 124 F3
Motono Japan 93 G3
Motosu Japan 92 C3
Motosu-ko l. Japan 93 E3
Motozintla Mex. 167 G6
Motril Spain 67 E5
Motru Romania 69 J2
Mott ND U.S.A. 160 C2
Mottama Myanmar 86 B3
Mottama, Gulf of Myanmar 86 B3
Motu Ihupuku i. N.Z. see Campbell Island
Motul Mex. 167 H4
Mouaskar Alg. see Mascara
Mouding China 96 D3
Moudjéria Mauritania 120 B3
Moudros Greece 69 K5
Mouhijärvi Fin. 55 M6
Mouila Gabon 122 B4
Moulamein Australia 138 B5
Moulamein Creek r. Australia 138 A5
Moulavibazar Bangl. see Moulvibazar
Mould Bay (abandoned) Canada 146 G2
Moulèngui Binza Gabon 122 B4
Moulins France 66 F3
Moulmein Myanmar see Mawlamyaing
Moulouya r. Morocco 64 D4
Moultrie GA U.S.A. 163 D6
Moultrie, Lake SC U.S.A. 163 E5
Moulvibazar Bangl. 105 G4
Mound City KS U.S.A. 160 E4
Mound City SD U.S.A. 160 C2
Moundou Chad 121 E4
Moundsville WV U.S.A. 164 E4
Moŭng Cambodia 87 C4
Moŭng Rœssei Cambodia 87 C4
Mount Abu India 104 C4
Mountain r. Canada 149 O2
Mountainair NM U.S.A. 157 G6
Mountain Brook AL U.S.A. 163 C5
Mountain City TN U.S.A. 164 E5
Mountain Gate CA U.S.A. 156 C4
Mountain Home AR U.S.A. 161 E4
Mountain Home ID U.S.A. 156 E4
Mountain Home UT U.S.A. 159 H1
Mountain Lake Park MD U.S.A. 164 F4
Mountain View AR U.S.A. 161 E5
Mountain Village AK U.S.A. 148 G3
Mountain Zebra National Park S. Africa 125 G7
Mount Airy NC U.S.A. 164 E5
Mount Aspiring National Park N.Z. 139 B7
Mount Assiniboine Provincial Park Canada 150 H5
Mount Ayliff S. Africa 125 I6
Mount Ayr IA U.S.A. 160 E3
Mountbellew Ireland 61 D4
Mount Buffalo National Park Australia 138 C6
Mount Carmel IL U.S.A. 164 B4
Mount Carmel Junction UT U.S.A. 159 G3
Mount Coolon Australia 136 D4
Mount Darwin Zimbabwe 123 D5
Mount Denison Australia 134 F5
Mount Desert Island ME U.S.A. 162 G2
Mount Dutton Australia 137 A5
Mount Eba Australia 137 A6
Mount Elgon National Park Uganda 122 D3
Mount Fletcher S. Africa 125 I6
Mount Forest Canada 164 E2
Mount Frankland National Park Australia 135 B8
Mount Frere S. Africa 125 I6
Mount Gambier Australia 137 C8
Mount Gilead OH U.S.A. 164 D3
Mount Hagen P.N.G. 81 K8
Mount Hamiguitan Range Wildlife Sanctuary tourist site Phil. 82 D5
Mount Holly NJ U.S.A. 165 H4
Mount Hope Australia 138 B4
Mount Hope WV U.S.A. 164 E5
Mount Howitt Australia 137 C5
Mount Isa Australia 136 B4
Mount Jackson VA U.S.A. 165 F4
Mount Jewett PA U.S.A. 165 F3
Mount Joy PA U.S.A. 165 G3
Mount Kaputar National Park Australia 138 E3
Mount Keith Australia 135 C6
Mount Lofty Range mts Australia 137 B7
Mount Magnet Australia 135 B7
Mount Manara Australia 138 A4
Mount McKinley National Park AK U.S.A. see Denali National Park and Preserve
Mount Meadows Reservoir CA U.S.A. 158 C1
Mountmellick Ireland 61 E4
Mount Moorosi Lesotho 125 H6
Mount Morgan Australia 136 E4
Mount Morris MI U.S.A. 164 D2
Mount Morris NY U.S.A. 165 G2
Mount Murchison Australia 138 A3
Mount Nebo WV U.S.A. 164 E4
Mount Olivet KY U.S.A. 164 C4
Mount Pearl Canada 153 L5
Mount Pleasant Canada 153 I5
Mount Pleasant IA U.S.A. 160 F3
Mount Pleasant MI U.S.A. 164 C2
Mount Pleasant TX U.S.A. 161 E5
Mount Pleasant UT U.S.A. 159 H2
Mount Rainier National Park WA U.S.A. 156 C3
Mount Remarkable National Park Australia 137 B7
Mount Revelstoke National Park Canada 150 G5
Mount Robson Provincial Park Canada 150 G4
Mount Rogers National Recreation Area park VA U.S.A. 164 E5
Mount St Helens National Volcanic Monument nat. park WA U.S.A. 156 C3
Mount Sanford Australia 134 E4
Mount's Bay U.K. 59 B8
Mount Shasta CA U.S.A. 156 C4
Mountsorrel U.K. 59 F6
Mount Sterling KY U.S.A. 164 D4
Mount Swan Australia 136 A4
Mount Union PA U.S.A. 165 G3
Mount Vernon Australia 135 B6
Mount Vernon AL U.S.A. 167 H2
Mount Vernon IL U.S.A. 160 F4
Mount Vernon IN U.S.A. 162 C4
Mount Vernon KY U.S.A. 164 C5
Mount Vernon MO U.S.A. 161 E4
Mount Vernon OH U.S.A. 164 D3
Mount Vernon TX U.S.A. 161 E5
Mount Vernon WA U.S.A. 156 C2
Mount William National Park Australia 137 [inset]
Mount Willoughby Australia 135 F6
Moura Australia 136 E5
Moura Brazil 176 F4
Moura Port. 67 C4
Mourdi, Dépression du depr. Chad 121 F3
Mourdiah Mali 120 C3
Mourne r. U.K. 61 E3
Mourne Mountains hills U.K. 61 F3
Mousa i. U.K. 60 [inset]
Mouscron Belgium 62 D4
Mousgougou Chad 122 B2
Moussafoyo Chad 121 E4
Moussoro Chad 121 E3
Moutamba Congo 122 B4
Mouth of the Yangtze China 97 I2
Moutong Celebes Indon. 83 B2
Mouy France 62 C5
Mouydir, Monts du plat. Alg. 120 D2
Mouzon France 62 F5
Movas Mex. 166 C2
Mowbullan, Mount Australia 138 E1
Moxey Town Bahamas 163 E7
Moy r. Ireland 61 C3
Moyahua Mex. 166 E4
Moyale Eth. 122 D3
Moyen Atlas mts Morocco 64 C5
Moyen-Congo country Africa see Congo
Moyeni Lesotho 125 H6
Moynalyk Russia 102 I1
Moynaq Uzbek. see Mo'ynoq
Mo'ynoq Uzbek. 102 A3
Moyo i. Indon. 85 G5
Moyobamba Peru 176 C5
Moyock NC U.S.A. 165 G5
Moyola r. U.K. 61 F3
Moyu China 99 B5
Moyynkum Kazakh. 102 D3
Moyynkum, Peski des. Kazakh. 102 C3
Moyynty Kazakh. 102 D2
Mozambique country Africa 123 D6
Mozambique Channel Africa 123 E6
Mozambique Ridge sea feature Indian Ocean 185 K7
Mozdok Russia 113 G2
Mozhaysk Russia 53 H5
Mozhga Russia 52 L4
Mozo Myanmar 96 B4
Mozyr' Belarus see Mazyr
Mpaathutlwa Pan salt pan Botswana 124 E3
Mpanda Tanz. 123 D4
Mpen India 105 I4
Mpika Zambia 123 D5
Mpolweni S. Africa 125 J5
Mporokoso Zambia 123 D4
Mpulungu Zambia 123 D4
Mpumalanga prov. S. Africa 125 I4
Mpunde mt. Tanz. 123 D4
Mpwapwa Tanz. 123 D4
Mqanduli S. Africa 125 I6
Mqinvartsveri mt. Georgia/Russia see Kazbek
Mrauk-U Myanmar 86 A2
Mrewa Zimbabwe see Murehwa
Mrkonjić-Grad Bos. & Herz. 68 G2
M'Saken Tunisia 68 D7
Mshinskaya Russia 55 P7
M'Sila Alg. 67 I6
Msta r. Russia 52 F4
Mstislavl' Belarus see Mstsislaw
Mstsislaw Belarus 53 F5
Mtelo Kenya 122 D3
Mthatha S. Africa 125 I6
Mtoko Zimbabwe see Mutoko
Mtorwi Tanz. 123 D4
Mtsensk Russia 53 H5
Mts'ire Kavkasioni Asia see Lesser Caucasus
Mtubatuba S. Africa 125 K5
Mtunzini S. Africa 125 J5
Mtwara Tanz. 123 E5
Mu r. Myanmar 86 A2
Mu'āb, Jibāl reg. Jordan see Moab
Muanda Dem. Rep. Congo 123 B4
Muang Ham Laos 86 D2
Muang Hiam Laos 86 C2
Muang Hinboun Laos 86 D3
Muang Hôngsa Laos 86 C3
Muang Khi Laos 86 C3
Muang Không Laos 87 D4
Muang Khoua Laos 86 C2
Muang Lamam Laos see Xékong
Muang Mok Laos 86 D3
Muang Ngoy Laos 86 C2
Muang Ou Nua Laos 86 C2
Muang Pakbeng Laos 86 C3
Muang Paktha Laos 86 C2
Muang Pakxan Laos see Pakxan
Muang Phalan Laos 80 D3
Muang Phin Laos 86 D3
Muang Sam Sip Thai. 86 D4
Muang Sing Laos 86 C2
Muang Soum Laos 86 C3
Muang Souy Laos 86 C3
Muang Thadua Laos 86 C3
Muang Thai country Asia see Thailand
Muang Va Laos 86 C2
Muang Vangviang Laos 86 C3
Muang Xon Laos 86 C2
Muar Malaysia 84 C2
Muar r. Malaysia 84 C2
Muara Brunei 85 F1
Muaraancalong Kalimantan Indon. 85 G2
Muaraatap Kalimantan Indon. 85 G2
Muarabeliti Sumatra Indon. 84 C3
Muarabulian Sumatra Indon. 84 C3
Muarabungo Sumatra Indon. 84 C3
Muaradua Sumatra Indon. 84 D4
Muaraenim Sumatra Indon. 84 C3
Muarainu Kalimantan Indon. 85 F3
Muarajawa Kalimantan Indon. 85 G3
Muarakaman Kalimantan Indon. 85 G3
Muara Kaman Sedulang, Cagar Alam nature res. Kalimantan Indon. 85 G2
Muaralabuh Sumatra Indon. 84 C3
Muaralakitan Sumatra Indon. 84 C3
Muaralaung Kalimantan Indon. 85 F3
Muaralesan Kalimantan Indon. 85 G2
Muaramayang Kalimantan Indon. 85 G2
Muaranawai Kalimantan Indon. 85 G2
Muararupit Sumatra Indon. 84 C3
Muarasabak Sumatra Indon. 84 C3
Muarasiberut Sumatra Indon. 84 B3
Muarasipongi Sumatra Indon. 84 B2
Muarasoma Sumatra Indon. 84 B2
Muaras Reef Indon. 85 G2
Muaratebo Sumatra Indon. 84 C3
Muaratembesi Sumatra Indon. 84 C3
Muarateweh Kalimantan Indon. 85 F3
Muara Tuang Sarawak Malaysia see Kota Samarahan
Muarawahau Kalimantan Indon. 85 G2
Muari i. Moluccas Indon. 83 C3
Muari, Ras pt Pak. 111 G5
Mu'ayqil, Khashm al hill Saudi Arabia 110 C5
Mubarek Uzbek. see Muborak
Mubarraz well Saudi Arabia 113 F5
Mubende Uganda 122 D3
Mubi Nigeria 120 E3
Muborak Uzbek. 111 G2
Mubur i. Indon. 84 D2
Mucajaí, Serra do mts Brazil 176 F3
Mucalic r. Canada 153 I2
Muccan Australia 134 C5
Much Germany 63 H4
Mucheng China see Wuzhi
Muchinga Escarpment Zambia 123 D5
Muchuan China 96 D2
Muck i. U.K. 60 C4
Mucojo Moz. 123 E5
Muconda Angola 123 C5
Mucubela Moz. 123 D5
Mucugê Brazil 179 C1
Mucur Turkey 112 D3
Mucuri Brazil 179 D2
Mucuri r. Brazil 179 D2
Mūd Iran 110 E3
Muda r. Malaysia 84 C1
Mudabidri India 106 B3
Mudan China see Heze
Mudanjiang China 90 C3
Mudan Jiang r. China 90 C3
Mudan Ling mts China 90 B4
Mudanya Turkey 69 M4
Mudaybī Oman 110 E6
Mudaysīsāt, Jabal al hill Jordan 107 C4
Muddus nationalpark nat. park Sweden 54 K3
Muddy r. NV U.S.A. 159 F3
Muddy Gap WY U.S.A. 156 G4
Muddy Peak NV U.S.A. 159 F3
Mudersbach Germany 63 H4
Mudgal India 106 C3
Mudgee Australia 138 D4
Mudhol India 106 B2
Mudigere India 106 B3
Mudjatik r. Canada 151 J3
Mud Lake NV U.S.A. 158 E3
Mudraya country Africa see Egypt
Mudurnu Turkey 69 N4
Mud'yuga Russia 52 H3
Mueda Moz. 123 D5
Mueller Range hills Australia 134 D4
Muerto, Mar lag. Mex. 167 G5
Muertos Cays is Bahamas 163 D7
Muftyuga Russia 52 J2
Mufulira Zambia 123 C5
Mufumbwe Zambia 123 C5
Mufu Shan mts China 97 G2
Muğan Düzü lowland Azer. 113 H3
Mugarripug China 105 F2
Mugegawa Japan 92 C3
Mughalbhin Pak. see Jati
Mughal Kot Pak. 111 H4
Mughal Sarai India 105 E4
Mūghār Iran 110 D3
Mughayrā' Saudi Arabia 107 C5
Mughayrā' well Saudi Arabia 110 B5
Mugi Japan 92 D3
Muğla Turkey 69 M6
Mugodzhary, Gory mts Kazakh. 102 A2
Mug Qu r. China 94 C5
Mugu Karnali r. Nepal 99 C7
Mugur-Aksy Russia 94 B1
Mugxung China 99 F6
Mūḩ, Sabkhat al imp. l. Syria 107 D2
Muhala China see Yutian
Muhammad Ashraf Pak. 111 H5
Muhammad Qol Sudan 108 E5
Muhammarah Iran see Khorramshahr
Muhar China 94 D4
Muhashsham, Wādī al watercourse Egypt 107 B4
Muḩaysh, Wādī al watercourse Jordan 107 C5
Muḩaysinīyah Syria 107 D1
Mühlanger Germany 63 M3
Mühlberg/Elbe Germany 63 N3
Mühlhausen/Thüringen Germany 63 K3
Mühlig-Hofmann Mountains Antarctica 188 C2
Muhos Fin. 54 N4
Muḩradah Syria 107 C2
Mui Bai Bung c. Vietnam see Ca Mau, Mui
Muié Angola 123 C5
Muiliyk i. Moluccas Indon. 83 D3
Muineachán Ireland see Monaghan
Muir MI U.S.A. 164 C2
Muirkirk U.K. 60 E5
Muir of Ord U.K. 60 E3
Muite Moz. 123 D5
Mūjān, Chāh-e well Iran 110 D3
Mujeres, Isla i. Mex. 167 I4
Muji China 99 B5
Mujong r. Malaysia 85 F2
Muju S. Korea 91 B5
Mukacheve Ukr. 53 D6
Mukachevo Ukr. see Mukacheve
Mukah Sarawak Malaysia 85 F2
Mukah r. Malaysia 85 F2
Mukalla Yemen 108 G7
Mukandwara India 104 D4
Mukawa Japan 93 E3
Mukdahan Thai. 86 D3
Mukden China see Shenyang
Mukeru Palau 82 [inset]
Muketei r. Canada 152 D3
Mukhen Russia 90 E2
Mukhino Russia 90 B1
Mukhorshibir' Russia 95 G1
Mukhtuya Russia see Lensk
Mūkīk, Chashmeh-ye spring Iran 110 E3
Mukinbudin Australia 135 B7
Mukō Japan 92 B4
Mu Ko Chang Marine National Park Thai. 87 C5
Mukojima-rettō is Japan 91 F8
Mukomuko Sumatra Indon. 84 C3
Mukry Turkm. 111 G2
Muktsar India 104 C3
Mukutawa r. Canada 151 L4
Mukwonago WI U.S.A. 164 A2
Mukyr Kazakh. 98 C2
Mula r. India 106 B2
Mulainagiri mt. India 106 B3
Mulakatholhu Maldives 103 D11
Mulaku Atoll atoll Maldives see Mulakatholhu
Mulan China 90 C3
Mulanay Luzon Phil. 82 C3
Mulanje, Mount Malawi 123 D5
Mulapula, Lake salt flat Australia 137 B6
Mulatos Mex. 166 C2
Mula-tupo Panama 166 [inset] K7
Mulayḩ Saudi Arabia 110 B5
Mulayḩah, Jabal hill U.A.E. 110 D5

Mulayz, Wādī al *watercourse* Egypt 107 A4
Mulchatna *r.* *AK* U.S.A. 148 H3
Mulde *r.* Germany 63 M3
Mule Creek *NM* U.S.A. 159 I5
Mule Creek *WY* U.S.A. 156 G4
Mulegé Mex. 166 B3
Mules *i.* Indon. 83 B5
Muleshoe *TX* U.S.A. 161 C5
Mulga Park Australia 135 E6
Mulgathing Australia 135 F7
Mulgrave Hills *AK* U.S.A. 148 G2
Mulhacén *mt.* Spain 67 E5
Mülhausen France *see* Mulhouse
Mülheim an der Ruhr Germany 62 G3
Mulhouse France 66 H3
Muli China 96 D3
Muli Russia *see* Vysokogorniy
Mulia Indon. 81 J7
Muling *Heilong.* China 90 C3
Muling *Heilong.* China 90 C3
Muling He *r.* China 90 D3
Mull *i.* U.K. 60 D4
Mull, Sound of *sea chan.* U.K. 60 C4
Mullaghcleevaun *hill* Ireland 61 F4
Mullaittivu Sri Lanka 106 D4
Mullaley Australia 138 D3
Mullengudgery Australia 138 C3
Mullens *WV* U.S.A. 164 E5
Muller *watercourse* Australia 134 F5
Muller, Pegunungan *mts* Indon. 85 F2
Mullett Lake *MI* U.S.A. 164 C1
Mullewa Australia 135 A7
Mullica *r.* *NJ* U.S.A. 165 H4
Mullingar Ireland 61 E4
Mullion Creek Australia 138 D4
Mull of Galloway *c.* U.K. 60 E6
Mull of Kintyre *hd* U.K. 60 D5
Mull of Oa *hd* U.K. 60 C5
Mullumbimby Australia 138 F2
Mulobezi Zambia 123 C5
Mulshi Lake India 106 B2
Multai India 104 D5
Multan Pak. 111 H4
Multia Fin. 54 N5
Multien *reg.* France 62 C6
Mulu, Gunung *mt.* Malaysia 85 F1
Mulug India 106 C2

▶Mumbai India 106 B2
4th most populous city in Asia and 6th the world.

Mumbil Australia 138 D4
Mumbwa Zambia 123 C5
Muminabad Tajik. *see* Leningrad
Mŭ'minobod Tajik. *see* Leningrad
Mun, Mae Nam *r.* Thai. 86 D4
Muna *i.* Indon. 83 B4
Muna Mex. 167 H4
Muna *r.* Russia 77 N3
Munabao Pak. 111 H5
Munaðarnes Iceland 54 [inset 1]
Münchberg Germany 63 L4
München Germany *see* Munich
München-Gladbach Germany *see* Mönchengladbach
Münchhausen Germany 63 I4
Muncho Lake Canada 150 E3
Muncie *IN* U.S.A. 164 C3
Muncoonie West, Lake *salt flat* Australia 136 B5
Muncy *PA* U.S.A. 165 G3
Munda Pak. 111 H4
Mundel Lake Sri Lanka 106 C5
Mundesley U.K. 59 I6
Mundford U.K. 59 H6
Mundiwindi (abandoned) Australia 135 C5
Mundra India 104 B5
Mundrabilla Australia 132 C5
Munds Park *AZ* U.S.A. 159 H4
Mundubbera Australia 137 E5
Mundwa India 104 C4
Munfordville *KY* U.S.A. 164 C5
Mungallala Australia 137 D5
Mungana Australia 136 D3
Mungap-do *i.* S. Korea 91 B5
Mungári Moz. 123 D5
Mungbere Dem. Rep. Congo 122 C3
Mungeli India 105 E5
Munger India 105 F4
Mu Nggava *i.* Solomon Is *see* Rennell
Munggaresak, Tanjung *pt* Indon. 85 E2
Mungindi Australia 138 D2
Mungla Bangl. *see* Mongla
Mungo Angola 123 B5
Mungo, Lake Australia 138 A4
Mungo National Park Australia 138 A4
Munich Germany 57 M6
Munising *MI* U.S.A. 162 C2
Munjpur India 104 B5
Munkács Ukr. *see* Mukacheve
Munkebakken Norway 54 P2
Munkedal Sweden 55 G7
Munkfors Sweden 55 H7
Munkhafaḍ al Qaṭṭārah *depr.* Egypt *see* Qattara Depression
Munku-Sardyk, Gora *mt.* Mongolia/Russia 94 E1
Münnerstadt Germany 63 K4
Munnik S. Africa 125 I2
Munroe Lake Canada 151 L3
Munsan S. Korea 91 B5
Munse *Celebes* Indon. 83 B4
Münster *Hessen* Germany 63 I5
Munster Germany 63 K2
Münster *Nordrhein-Westfalen* Germany 63 H3
Munster *reg.* Ireland 61 D5
Münsterland *reg.* Germany 63 H3
Muntadgin Australia 135 B7
Munte *Celebes* Indon. 83 A2
Muntervary *hd* Ireland 61 C6
Munyal-Par *sea feature* India *see* Bassas de Pedro Padua Bank
Munzur Vadisi Milli Parkı *nat. park* Turkey 65 L4
Muojärvi *l.* Fin. 54 P4
Mương Nhe Vietnam 86 C2
Muong Sai Laos *see* Oudômxai
Muonio Fin. 54 M3
Muonioälven *r.* Fin./Sweden 54 M3
Muonionjoki *r.* Fin./Sweden *see* Muonioälven
Muor *i.* *Moluccas* Indon. 83 D2
Mupa, Parque Nacional da *nat. park* Angola 123 B5
Muping *Shandong* China 95 J4
Muping *Sichuan* China *see* Baoxing
Muqaynimah *well* Saudi Arabia 110 C6
Muqdisho Somalia *see* Mogadishu
Muqêr Afgh. 111 G3
Muquém Brazil 179 A1
Muqui Brazil 179 C3
Muqur Afgh. 111 F3
Mur *r.* Austria 57 P7
also known as Mura (Croatia/Slovenia)
Mura *r.* Croatia/Slovenia *see* Mur
Murai, Tanjong *pt* Sing. 87 [inset]
Murai Reservoir Sing. 87 [inset]
Murakami Japan 91 E5
Murallón, Cerro *mt.* Chile 178 B7
Muramvya Burundi 122 C4
Murashi Russia 52 K4
Murat *r.* Turkey 113 E3
Muratlı Turkey 69 L4
Muraysah, Ra's al *pt* Libya 112 B5
Murchison *watercourse* Australia 135 A6
Murchison, Mount Antarctica 188 H2
Murchison, Mount *hill* Australia 135 B6
Murchison Falls National Park Uganda 122 D3
Murcia Spain 67 F5
Murcia *aut. comm.* Spain 67 F5
Murcielagos Bay *Mindanao* Phil. 82 C4
Murdo *SD* U.S.A. 160 C3
Murehwa Zimbabwe 123 D5
Mureşul *r.* Romania 69 I1
Muret France 66 E5
Murewa Zimbabwe *see* Murehwa
Murfreesboro *AR* U.S.A. 161 E5
Murfreesboro *TN* U.S.A. 162 C5
Murg *r.* Germany 63 I6
Murgab Tajik. *see* Murghob
Murgab Turkm. *see* Murgap
Murgab *r.* Turkm. *see* Murgap
Murgap Turkm. 111 F2
Murgap *r.* Turkm. 109 J2
Murgh, Kōtal-e Afgh. 111 H3
Murghāb *reg.* Afgh. 111 F3
Murgha Kibzai Pak. 111 H4
Murghob Tajik. 111 I2
Murgon Australia 137 E5
Murgoo Australia 135 B6
Muri *Qinghai* China 94 D4
Muri *Qinghai* China 94 E4
Muri India 105 F5
Muria, Gunung *mt.* Indon. 85 E4
Muriaé Brazil 179 C3
Murid Pak. 111 G4
Muriege Angola 123 C4
Murih, Pulau *i.* Indon. 85 E2
Müritz *l.* Germany 63 M1
Müritz, Nationalpark *nat. park* Germany 63 N1
Murmansk Russia 54 R2
Murmanskaya Oblast' *admin. div.* Russia 54 S2
Murmanskiy Bereg *coastal area* Russia 52 G1
Murmansk Oblast *admin. div.* Russia *see* Murmanskaya Oblast'
Murō Japan 92 C4
Muro, Capo di *c.* *Corsica* France 66 I6
Murō-Akame-Aoyama Kokutei-kōen *park* Japan 92 C4
Murom Russia 52 I5
Muromagi-gawa *r.* Japan 92 D2
Muroran Japan 90 F4
Muros Spain 67 B2
Muroto Japan 91 D6
Muroto-zaki *pt* Japan 91 D6
Murphy *ID* U.S.A. 156 D4
Murphy *NC* U.S.A. 163 D5
Murphysboro *IL* U.S.A. 160 F4
Murrah *reg.* Saudi Arabia 110 C6
Murrah al Kubrá, Al Buḥayrah al *l.* Egypt *see* Great Bitter Lake
Murrah aş Şughrá, Al Buḥayrah al *l.* Egypt *see* Little Bitter Lake
Murramarang National Park *nat. park* Australia 138 I5
Murra Murra Australia 138 C2
Murrat el Kubra, Buheirat *l.* Egypt *see* Great Bitter Lake
Murrat el Sughra, Buheirat *l.* Egypt *see* Little Bitter Lake

▶Murray *r.* S.A. Australia 137 B7
3rd longest river in Oceania, and a major part of the longest (Murray-Darling).

Murray *r.* W.A. Australia 135 A8
Murray *KY* U.S.A. 161 F4
Murray *UT* U.S.A. 159 H1
Murray, Lake P.N.G. 81 K8
Murray, Lake *SC* U.S.A. 163 D5
Murray, Mount Canada 149 O3
Murray Bridge Australia 137 B7

▶Murray-Darling *r.* Australia 132 E5
Longest river in Oceania.

Murray Downs Australia 134 F5
Murray Range *hills* Australia 135 E6
Murraysburg S. Africa 124 F6
Murray Sunset National Park Australia 137 C7
Murrhardt Germany 63 J6
Murrieta *CA* U.S.A. 158 E5
Murringo Australia 138 D5
Murrisk *reg.* Ireland 61 C4
Murroogh Ireland 61 C4

▶Murrumbidgee *r.* Australia 138 A5
4th longest river in Oceania.

Murrumburrah Australia 138 D5
Murrurundi Australia 138 E3
Mursan India 104 D4
Murshidabad India 105 G4
Murska Sobota Slovenia 68 G1
Mūrt Iran 111 F5
Murtoa Australia 137 C8
Murua *i.* P.N.G. *see* Woodlark Island
Murud India 106 B2
Murud, Gunung *mt.* Indon. 85 F2
Murui *r.* Indon. 85 F3
Muruin Sum Shuiku *resr* China 95 J3
Murujuga National Park Australia 134 B5
Murung *r.* Indon. 85 F3
Murung *r.* Indon. 85 F3
Murunkan Sri Lanka 106 D4
Murupara N.Z. 139 F4
Mururoa *atoll* Fr. Polynesia 187 K7
Murviedro Spain *see* Sagunto
Murwara India *see* Katni
Murwillumbah Australia 138 F2
Murzechirla Turkm. 111 F2
Murzūq Libya 121 E2
Murzuq, Ḥamādat *plat.* Libya 122 B1
Murzuq, Idhān *des.* Libya 120 E2
Mürzzuschlag Austria 57 O7
Muş Turkey 113 F3
Mūsā, Khowr-e *b.* Iran 110 C4
Mūsá, Ţal'at *mt.* Lebanon/Syria 107 C2
Musakhel Pak. 111 H4
Musala *mt.* Bulg. 69 J3
Musala *i.* Indon. 84 B2
Musan N. Korea 90 C4
Musandam Peninsula Oman/U.A.E. 110 E5
Musashino Japan 93 F3
Musay'īd Qatar *see* Umm Sa'id

▶Muscat Oman 110 E6
Capital of Oman.

Muscat *reg.* Oman 110 E5
Muscat and Oman *country* Asia *see* Oman
Muscatine *IA* U.S.A. 160 F3
Musgrave Australia 136 C2
Musgrave Harbour Canada 153 L4
Musgrave Ranges *mts* Australia 135 E6
Mushayyish, Wādī al *watercourse* Jordan 107 C4
Mushie Dem. Rep. Congo 122 B4
Mushkaf Pak. 111 G4
Musi *r.* Indon. 84 D3
Music Mountain *AZ* U.S.A. 159 G4
Musina S. Africa 125 J2
Musinia Peak *UT* U.S.A. 159 H2
Muskeg *r.* Canada 150 F2
Muskeget Channel *MA* U.S.A. 165 J3
Muskegon *MI* U.S.A. 164 B2
Muskegon *r.* *MI* U.S.A. 164 B2
Muskegon Heights *MI* U.S.A. 164 B2
Muskeg River Canada 150 G4
Muskogee *OK* U.S.A. 161 E5
Muskoka, Lake Canada 164 F1
Muskrat Dam Lake Canada 151 N4
Musmar Sudan 108 E6
Musoma Tanz. 122 D4
Musquanousse, Lac *l.* Canada 153 J4
Musquaro, Lac *l.* Canada 153 J4
Mussau Island P.N.G. 81 L7
Musselburgh U.K. 60 F5
Musselkanaal Neth. 62 H2
Musselshell *r.* *MT* U.S.A. 156 G3
Mussende Angola 123 B5
Mustafabad India 99 C8
Mustafakemalpaşa Turkey 69 M4
Mustau, Gora *mt.* China 98 D3
Mustjala Estonia 55 M7
Mustvee Estonia 55 O7
Musu-dan *pt* N. Korea 90 C4
Muswellbrook Australia 138 E4
Mūţ Egypt 108 C4
Mut Turkey 107 A1
Mutá, Ponta do *pt* Brazil 179 D1
Mutare Zimbabwe 123 D5
Mutayr *reg.* Saudi Arabia 110 B5
Mutina Italy *see* Modena
Muting Indon. 81 K8
Mutis Col. 176 C2
Mutis, Gunung *mt.* *Timor* Indon. 83 C5
Mutnyy Materik Russia 52 L2
Mutoko Zimbabwe 123 D5
Mutsamudu Comoros 123 E5
Mutsu Japan 90 F4
Mutsuzawa Japan 93 G3
Muttaburra Australia 136 D4
Mutton Island Ireland 61 C5
Muttukuru India 106 D3
Muttupet India 106 C4
Mutum Brazil 179 C2
Mutunópolis Brazil 179 A1
Mutur Sri Lanka 106 D4
Mutusjärvi *r.* Fin. 54 O2
Muurola Fin. 54 N3
Mu Us Shadi *des.* China 95 G4
Muxaluando Angola 123 B4
Muxi China *see* Muchuan
Muxima Angola 123 B4
Muyezerskiy Russia 54 R5
Muyinga Burundi 122 D4
Mŭynoq Uzbek. *see* Mo'ynoq
Muyu China 97 F2
Muyumba Dem. Rep. Congo 123 C4
Muyunkum, Peski *des.* Kazakh. *see* Moyynkum, Peski
Muzaffarabad Pak. 111 I3
Muzaffargarh Pak. 111 H4
Muzaffarnagar India 104 D3
Muzaffarpur India 105 F4
Muzamane Moz. 125 K2
Muzat He *r.* China 98 C4
Muzbel', Uval *hills* Kazakh. 113 I2
Muzhi Russia 51 S2
Mūzin Iran 111 F5
Muzon, Cape *AK* U.S.A. 149 N5
Múzquiz Mex. 167 E3
Muz Shan *mt.* China 99 C6
Muz Tag *mt.* China 99 D5
Muztagata *mt.* China 98 A5
Muztor Kyrg. *see* Toktogul
Mvadi Gabon 122 B3
Mvolo South Sudan 121 F4
Mvuma Zimbabwe 123 D5
Mwanza Malawi 123 D5
Mwanza Tanz. 122 D4
Mweelrea *hill* Ireland 61 C4
Mweka Dem. Rep. Congo 123 C4
Mwene-Ditu Dem. Rep. Congo 123 C4
Mwenezi Zimbabwe 123 D6
Mwenga Dem. Rep. Congo 122 C4
Mweru, Lake Dem. Rep. Congo/Zambia 123 C4
Mweru Wantipa National Park Zambia 123 C4
Mwimba Dem. Rep. Congo 123 C4
Mwinilunga Zambia 123 C5
Myadaung Myanmar 86 B2
Myadzyel Belarus 55 O9
Myajlar India 104 B4
Myall Lakes National Park Australia 138 F4
Myanaung Myanmar 86 A3
Myanmar *country* Asia 86 A2
Myauk-Oo Myanmar *see* Mrauk-U
Myaungmya Myanmar 86 A3
Myawadi Thai. 86 B3
Mybster U.K. 60 F2
Myebon Myanmar 86 A2
Myede Myanmar *see* Aunglan
Myeik Myanmar 87 B4
Myingyan Myanmar 86 A2
Myinkyado Myanmar 86 B2
Myinmoletkat *mt.* Myanmar 87 B4
Myitkyina Myanmar 86 B1
Myitson Myanmar 86 B2
Myitta Myanmar 87 B4
Myittha Myanmar 86 B2
Mykolayiv Ukr. 69 O1
Mykonos *i.* Greece 69 K6
Myla Russia 52 K2
Myla *r.* Russia 52 K2
Mylae *Sicily* Italy *see* Milazzo
Mylasa Turkey *see* Milas
Mymensing Bangl. *see* Mymensingh
Mymensingh Bangl. 105 G4
Mynämäki Fin. 55 M6
Mynaral Kazakh. 98 A3
Myōgi Japan 93 E2
Myōgi-Arafune-Saku-kōgen Kokutei-kōen *park* Japan 93 E2
Myōgi-san *mt.* Japan 93 E2
Myōken-yama *hill* Japan 92 A4
Myōkō *Niigata* Japan 93 E2
Myōkō *Niigata* Japan 93 E2
Myōkō-kōgen Japan 93 E2
Myŏnggan N. Korea 90 C4
Myory Belarus 55 O9
My Phước Vietnam 87 D5
Mýrdalsjökull *ice cap* Iceland 54 [inset 1]
Myre Norway 54 I2
Myrheden Sweden 54 L4
Myrhorod Ukr. 53 G6
Myrnam Canada 151 I4
Myronivka Ukr. 53 F6
Myrtle Beach *SC* U.S.A. 163 E5
Myrtleford Australia 138 C6
Myrtle Point *OR* U.S.A. 156 B4
Myrtoo Pelagos *sea* Greece 69 J6
Mys Chelyuskin Russia 189 E1
Mysia *reg.* Turkey 69 L5
Mys Lazareva Russia *see* Lazarev
Myślibórz Poland 57 O4
My Sơn Sanctuary *tourist site* Vietnam 86 E4
Mysore India *see* Mysuru
Mysore *state* India *see* Karnataka
Mys Shmidta Russia 77 T3
Mysuru India 106 C3
Mysy Russia 52 L3
My Tho Vietnam 87 D5
Mytikas *mt.* Greece *see* Olympus, Mount
Mytilene *i.* Greece *see* Lesbos
Mytilini Greece 69 L5
Mytilini Strait Greece/Turkey 69 L5
Mytishchi Russia 52 H5
Myton *UT* U.S.A. 159 H1
Myyeldino Russia 52 L3
Mzamomhle S. Africa 125 H6
Mže *r.* Czech Rep. 63 M5
Mzimba Malawi 123 D5
Mzuzu Malawi 123 D5

N

Naab *r.* Germany 63 M5
Nā'ālehu *HI* U.S.A. 157 [inset]
Naantali Fin. 55 M6
Naas Ireland 61 F4
Náàts'ihch'oh National Park Reserve *nat. park* Canada 149 P3
Naba Myanmar 86 B1
Nababeep S. Africa 124 C5
Nababganj Bangl. *see* Nawabganj
Nabadwip India *see* Navadwip
Nabarangapur India 106 D2
Nabarangpur India *see* Nabarangapur
Nabari Japan 92 C4
Nabari-gawa *r.* Japan 92 C4
Nabas *Panay* Phil. 82 C4
Nabatîyé et Tahta Lebanon 107 B3
Nabatiyet et Tahta Lebanon *see* Nabatîyé et Tahta
Nabberu, Lake *salt flat* Australia 135 C6
Nabburg Germany 63 M5
Naberera Tanz. 123 D4
Naberezhnyye Chelny Russia 51 Q4
Nabesna *AK* U.S.A. 149 L3
Nabesna *r.* *AK* U.S.A. 149 L3
Nabesna Glacier *AK* U.S.A. 148 I3
Nabesna Village *AK* U.S.A. 149 L3
Nabeul Tunisia 68 D6
Nabha India 104 D3
Nabil'skiy Zaliv *lag.* Russia 90 F2
Nabire Indon. 81 J7
Nabi Younés, Ras en *pt* Lebanon 107 B3
Nāblus West Bank 107 B3
Nabq Protected Area *nature res.* Egypt 112 D5
Nābulus West Bank *see* Nāblus
Nabunturan Phil. 82 D5
Nacajuca Mex. 167 G5
Nacala Moz. 123 E5
Nacaome Hond. 166 [inset] I6
Nachalovo Russia 53 K7
Nachicapau, Lac *l.* Canada 153 I2
Nachingwea Tanz. 123 D5
Nachna India 104 B4
Nachuge India 87 A5
Nacimiento Reservoir *CA* U.S.A. 158 C4
Naco *AZ* U.S.A. 157 F7
Nacogdoches *TX* U.S.A. 161 E6
Nacozari de García Mex. 166 C2
Nada China *see* Danzhou
Nadachi Japan 93 E1
Nadaleen *r.* Canada 150 C2
Nadbai India 99 B8
Nådendal Fin. *see* Naantali
Nadezhdinskoye Russia 90 D2
Nadiad India 104 C5
Nadol India 104 C4
Nador Morocco 67 E6
Nadqān, Qalamat *well* Saudi Arabia 110 C6
Nadūshan Iran 110 D3
Nadvirna Ukr. 53 E6
Nadvoitsy Russia 52 G3
Nadvornaya Ukr. *see* Nadvirna
Nadym Russia 76 I3
Næstved Denmark 55 G9
Nafarroa *aut. comm.* Spain *see* Navarra
Nafas, Ra's an *mt.* Egypt 107 B5
Nafḥa, Har *hill* Israel 107 B4
Nafpaktos Greece 69 I5
Nafplio Greece 69 J6
Naftalan Azer. 113 G2
Naft-e Safīd Iran 110 C4
Naft-e Shāh Iran *see* Naft Shahr
Naft Shahr Iran 110 B3
Nafūsah, Jabal *hills* Libya 120 E1
Nafy Saudi Arabia 108 F4
Nag, Co *l.* China 99 E6
Naga Japan 92 B4
Naga *Luzon* Phil. 82 C3
Nagagami *r.* Canada 152 D4
Nagagami Lake Canada 152 D4
Nagahama *Ehime* Japan 91 D6
Nagahama *Shiga* Japan 92 C3
Naga Hills India 105 H4
Naga Hills *state* India *see* Nagaland
Nagai Island *AK* U.S.A. 148 G5
Nagaizumi Japan 93 E3
Nagakute Japan 92 D3
Nagaland *state* India 105 H4
Nagamangala India 106 C3
Nagambie Australia 138 B6
Nagano Japan 93 E2
Nagano *pref.* Japan 93 D2
Naganohara Japan 93 E2
Nagaoka Japan 91 E5
Nagaokakyō Japan 92 B4
Nagaon India 105 H4
Nagapatam India *see* Nagapattinam
Nagapattinam India 106 C4
Nagar *r.* Bangl./India 99 E8
Nagar *Hima. Prad.* India 109 M3
Nagar *Karnataka* India 106 B3
Nagara Japan 93 G3
Nagara-gawa *r.* Japan 92 C3
Nagaram India 106 D2
Nagareyama Japan 93 F3
Nagari Hills India 106 C3
Nagarjuna Sagar Reservoir India 106 C2
Nagar Parkar Pak. 111 H5
Nagar Untari India 105 E4
Nagarzê China 99 E7
Nagasaka Japan 93 E3
Nagasaki Japan 91 C6
Nagashima Japan 92 C3
Nagato Japan 91 C6
Nagatoro Japan 93 F2
Nagaur India 104 C4
Nagawa *Nagano* Japan 92 D2
Nagawa *Nagano* Japan 93 E2
Nagbhir India 106 C1
Nagda India 104 C5
Nageezi *NM* U.S.A. 159 J3
Nagercoil India 106 C4
Nagha Kalat Pak. 111 G5
Nag' Ḥammâdî Egypt *see* Naj' Ḥammādī
Nagina India 104 D3
Nagiso Japan 92 D3
Nagjog China 99 G7
Nagold *r.* Germany 63 I6
Nagong Chu *r.* China *see* Parlung Zangbo
Nagorno-Karabakh *disp. terr.* Azer. 113 G3
Nagornyy Russia 148 B3
Nagornyy Karabakh *disp. terr.* Azer. *see* Nagorno-Karabakh
Nagorsk Russia 52 K4
Nagoya Japan 92 C3
Nagpur India 104 D5
Nagqu China 99 F7
Nag Qu *r.* China 99 F7
Nagurskoye Russia 76 F1
Nagyatád Hungary 68 G1
Nagybecskerek Serbia *see* Zrenjanin
Nagyenyed Romania *see* Aiud
Nagykanizsa Hungary 68 G1
Nagyvárad Romania *see* Oradea
Naha Japan 89 N7
Nahan India 104 D3
Nahanni Butte Canada 150 F2
Nahanni National Park Reserve Canada 149 P3
Nahanni Range *mts* Canada 150 F2
Naharāyim Jordan 107 B3
Nahariyya Israel 107 B3
Nahāvand Iran 110 C3
Nahr Dijlah *r.* Asia 113 G5 *see* Tigris
Nahrīn Afgh. 111 H2
Nahrīn *reg.* Afgh. 111 H2
Nahuel Huapí, Parque Nacional *nat. park* Arg. 178 B6
Nahunta *GA* U.S.A. 163 D6
Naic *Luzon* Phil. 82 C3
Naica Mex. 166 D3
Nai Ga Myanmar 96 C3
Naij Tal China 94 C5
Naikliu *Timor* Indon. 83 B5
Nailung China 99 F7
Naiman Qi China *see* Daqin Tal
Naimin Shuiquan *well* China 94 B2
Nain Canada 153 J2
Nā'īn Iran 110 D3
Naini Tal India *see* Nainital
Nainital India 104 D3
Nairn U.K. 60 F3
Nairn *r.* U.K. 60 F3

▶Nairobi Kenya 122 D4
Capital of Kenya.

Naissus Serbia *see* Niš
Naivasha Kenya 122 D4
Najafābād Iran 110 C3
Na'jān Saudi Arabia 110 B5
Najd *reg.* Saudi Arabia 108 F4
Nájera Spain 67 E2
Naj' Ḥammādī Egypt 108 D4
Naji China 95 J1
Najibabad India 104 D3
Najin N. Korea 90 C4
Najitun China *see* Naji
Najrān Saudi Arabia 108 F6
Naka Japan 93 G2
Nakadōri-shima *i.* Japan 91 C6
Na Kae Thai. 86 D3
Nakagawa *Nagano* Japan 93 D3
Nakagawa *Tochigi* Japan 93 G2
Naka-gawa *r.* Japan 93 G2
Nakagō Japan 93 E2
Nakai Japan 93 F3
Nakaizu Japan 93 F4
Nakajima *Fukushima* Japan 93 G1
Nakajima *Ishikawa* Japan 92 C1
Nakajō Japan 93 E2
Nakambé *r.* Burkina Faso/Ghana *see* White Volta
Nakamichi Japan 93 E3
Nakaminato Japan 93 G2
Nakanbe *r.* Burkina Faso/Ghana *see* White Volta
Nakanno Russia 77 L3
Nakano Japan 93 E2
Nakanojō Japan 93 E2
Nakano-shima *i.* Japan 91 D5
Nakano-take *mt.* Japan 93 F1
Nakanoto Japan 92 C2
Nakasato *Gunma* Japan 93 E2
Nakasato *Niigata* Japan 93 E1
Nakasongola Uganda 121 G4
Nakatomi Japan *see* Minobu
Nakatsu *Ōita* Japan 91 C6
Nakatsu *Wakayama* Japan 92 B5
Nakatsugawa Japan 92 D3
Nakatsu-gawa *r.* Japan 93 E2
Nakdong-gang *r.* S. Korea 91 C6
Nakfa Eritrea 108 E6
Nakhichevan' Azer. *see* Naxçıvan
Nakhl Egypt 107 A5
Nakhodka Russia 90 D4
Nakhola India 105 H4
Nakhon Nayok Thai. 87 C4
Nakhon Pathom Thai. 87 C4
Nakhon Phanom Thai. 86 D3
Nakhon Ratchasima Thai. 86 C4
Nakhon Sawan Thai. 86 C4
Nakhon Si Thammarat Thai. 87 B5
Nakhtarana India 104 B5
Nakina Canada 152 D4
Nakina *r.* Canada 149 N4
Naknek *AK* U.S.A. 148 H4
Naknek Lake *AK* U.S.A. 148 H4
Nakodar India 99 A7
Nakonde Zambia 123 D4
Nakoso Japan 93 G2
Nakskov Denmark 55 G9
Nakuru Kenya 122 D4
Nakusp Canada 150 G5
Nal Pak. 111 G5
Nal *r.* Pak. 111 G5
Na-lang Myanmar 86 B2
Nalayh Mongolia 95 F2
Nalázi Moz. 125 K3
Nalbari India 105 G4
Nal'chik Russia 113 F2
Naldurg India 106 C2
Nalgonda India 106 C2
Naliya India 104 B5
Nallamala Hills India 106 C3
Nallıhan Turkey 69 N4
Nālūt Libya 120 E1
Namaa, Tanjung *pt* *Seram* Indon. 83 D3
Namaacha Moz. 125 K3
Namacurra Moz. 123 D5
Namadgi National Park Australia 138 D5
Namahadi S. Africa 125 I4
Namai Bay Palau 82 [inset]

Namak, Daryācheh-ye *salt flat* Iran 110 C3
Namak, Kavīr-e *salt flat* Iran 110 E3
Namakkal India 106 C4
Namakwaland *reg.* Namibia *see* **Great Namaqualand**
Namakzar-e Shadad *salt flat* Iran 110 E4
Namaland *reg.* Namibia *see* **Great Namaqualand**
Namang Indon. 84 D3
Namangan Uzbek. 102 D3
Namaqualand *reg.* Namibia *see* **Great Namaqualand**
Namaqualand *reg.* S. Africa 124 C5
Namaqua National Park S. Africa 124 C6
Namas Indon. 81 K8
Namatanai P.N.G. 132 F2
Nambour Australia 138 F1
Nambu Japan *see* **Nanbu**
Nambucca Heads Australia 138 F3
Nambung National Park Australia 135 A7
Năm Căn Vietnam 87 D5
Namcha Barwa *mt.* China *see* **Namjagbarwa Feng**
Namche Bazar Nepal 105 F4
Namco China 99 E7
Nam Co *salt l.* China 99 E7
Namdalen *valley* Norway 54 H4
Namdalseid Norway 54 G4
Nam Đinh Vietnam 86 D2
Nam Du, Quân Đao *i.* Vietnam 87 D5
Namegata Japan 93 G3
Namegawa Japan 93 F2
Namelakl Passage Palau 82 [inset]
Namen Belgium *see* **Namur**
Namerikawa Japan 92 D2
Nam-gang *r.* N. Korea 91 B5
Namhae-do *i.* S. Korea 91 B6
Namhsan Myanmar 86 B2
Namiai Japan 92 D3
Namib Desert Namibia 124 B3
Namibe Angola 123 B5
Namibia *country* Africa 123 B6
Namibia Abyssal Plain *sea feature* N. Atlantic Ocean 184 I8
Namib-Naukluft Park *nature res.* Namibia 124 B3
Namie (abandoned) Japan 91 F5
Namīn Iran 113 H3
Namjagbarwa Feng *mt.* China 99 F7
Namlan Myanmar 86 B2
Namlea *Buru* Indon. 83 C3
Namling China 99 E7
Nam Nao National Park Thai. 86 C3
Namoding China 99 D7
Namoi *r.* Australia 138 D3
Namonuito *atoll* Micronesia 81 L5
Nampa *mt.* Nepal 104 E3
Nampa *ID* U.S.A. 156 D4
Nampala Mali 120 C3
Nam Phong Thai. 86 C3
Namp'o N. Korea 91 B5
Nampula Moz. 123 D5
Namrole *Buru* Indon. 83 C3
Namsai Myanmar 86 B1
Namsang Myanmar 86 B2
Namsen *r.* Norway 54 G4
Nam She Tsim *hill* H.K. China *see* **Sharp Peak**
Namsos Norway 54 G4
Nam Theun 2 *resr* Laos 86 D3
Namti Myanmar 86 B1
Namtok Myanmar 86 B3
Nam Tok Chattakan National Park Thai. 86 C3
Namton Myanmar 86 B2
Namtsy Russia 77 N3
Namtu Myanmar 86 B2
Namu Canada 150 E5
Namuli, Monte *mt.* Moz. 123 D5
Namuno Moz. 123 D5
Namur Belgium 62 E4
Namutoni Namibia 123 B5
Namwon S. Korea 91 B6
Namya Ra Myanmar 86 B1
Namyit Island S. China Sea 80 E4
Nan Thai. 86 C3
Nana Bakassa Cent. Afr. Rep. 122 B3
Nanaimo Canada 150 F5
Nanakai Japan 93 G2
Nanam N. Korea 90 C4
Nan'an China 97 H3
Nanango Australia 138 F1
Nananib Plateau Namibia 124 C3
Nanao Japan 92 C1
Nanatsuka Japan 92 C2
Nanatsu-shima *i.* Japan 91 E5
Nanbai China *see* **Zunyi**
Nanbaxian China 99 F5
Nanbin China *see* **Shizhu**
Nanbu China 96 E2
Nanbu *Yamanashi* Japan 93 E3
Nanbu *Yamanashi* Japan 93 E3
Nancha China 90 C3
Nanchang *Jiangxi* China 97 G2
Nanchang *Jiangxi* China 97 G2
Nanchangshan China *see* **Changdao**
Nanchong China 96 E2
Nanchuan China 96 E2
Nancowry *i.* India 87 A6
Nancun *Henan* China 95 H5
Nancun *Shanxi* China *see* **Zezhou**
Nancy France 62 G6
Nancy (Essey) *airport* France 62 G6
Nanda Devi *mt.* India 104 E3
Nanda Kot *mt.* India 104 E3
Nandan China 96 E3
Nandapur India 106 D2
Nanded India 106 C2
Nander India *see* **Nanded**
Nandewar Range *mts* Australia 138 E3
Nandod India 106 B1
Nandurbar India 104 C5
Nandyal India 106 C3
Nanfeng *Guangdong* China 97 F4
Nanfeng *Jiangxi* China 97 H3
Nang China 99 F7
Nanga Eboko Cameroon 120 E4
Nangah Dedai *Kalimantan* Indon. 85 E3
Nangahembaloh *Kalimantan* Indon. 85 F2
Nangahkemangai *Kalimantan* Indon. 85 F3
Nangahketungau *Kalimantan* Indon. 85 E2
Nangahmau *Kalimantan* Indon. 85 E3
Nangah Merakai *Kalimantan* Indon. 85 E2
Nangahpinoh *Kalimantan* Indon. 85 E3
Nangahsuruk *Kalimantan* Indon. 85 F2
Nangahtempuai *Kalimantan* Indon. 85 F2
Nangalao *i.* Phil. 82 C4

▶**Nanga Parbat** *mt.* Pak. 104 C2
9th highest mountain in Asia and the world.

Nangar National Park Australia 138 D4
Nangataman *Kalimantan* Indon. 85 E3
Nangatayap *Kalimantan* Indon. 85 E3
Nangdoi China 94 E4
Nangin Myanmar 87 B5
Nangnim-sanmaek *mts* N. Korea 91 B4
Nangong China 95 H4
Nangqên China 96 C1
Nangsin Sum China 95 G4
Nangulangwa Tanz. 123 D4
Nanguneri India 106 C4
Nanhu *Gansu* China 98 F5
Nanhu *Xinjiang* China 94 C3
Nanhua *Gansu* China 94 D4
Nanhua *Yunnan* China 96 D3
Nanhui China 97 I2
Nanjian China 96 D3
Nanjiang China 96 E1
Nanjing China 97 H1
Nanji Shan *i.* China 97 I3
Nanka Jiang *r.* China 96 C4
Nankang China 97 G3
Nanking China *see* **Nanjing**
Nankova Angola 123 B5
Nanle China 95 H4
Nanlei He *r.* China 96 C4
also known as Nam Loi (Myanmar)
Nanling China 97 H2
Nan Ling *mts* China 97 F3
Nanliu Jiang *r.* China 97 F4
Nanlong China *see* **Nanbu**
Nanma China *see* **Yiyuan**
Nanmoku Japan 93 E2
Nanmulinxue China *see* **Namling**
Nannilam India 106 C4
Nannine (abandoned) Australia 135 B6
Nanning China 97 F4
Nanniwan China 95 G4
Nannō Japan 92 C3
Nannup Australia 135 A8
Na Noi Thai. 86 C3
Nanortalik Greenland 147 N3
Nanouki *atoll* Kiribati *see* **Nonouti**
Nanouti *atoll* Kiribati *see* **Nonouti**
Nanpan Jiang *r.* China 96 E3
Nanpi China 95 I4
Nanpiao China 95 J3
Nanping China 97 H3
Nanpu China *see* **Pucheng**
Nanri Dao *i.* China 97 H3
Nansei-shotō *is* Japan *see* **Ryukyu Islands**
Nansei-shotō Trench *sea feature* N. Pacific Ocean *see* **Ryukyu Trench**
Nansen Basin *sea feature* Arctic Ocean 189 H1
Nansen Sound *sea chan.* Canada 147 I1
Nan-sha Ch'ün-tao *is* S. China Sea *see* **Spratly Islands**
Nanshan China 97 [inset]
Nanshan Island S. China Sea 80 F4
Nanshankou *Qinghai* China 94 C4
Nanshankou *Xinjiang* China 94 C3
Nansha Qundao *is* S. China Sea *see* **Spratly Islands**
Nansio Tanz. 122 D4
Nantai-san *hill* Japan 93 G2
Nantai-san *mt.* Japan 93 F2
Nantan Japan 92 B3
Nantes France 66 D3
Nantes à Brest, Canal de France 66 C3
Nanteuil-le-Haudouin France 62 C5
Nanthi Kadal Lagoon *lag.* Sri Lanka 106 D4
Nanticoke Canada 164 E2
Nanticoke *MD* U.S.A. 165 H4
Nantō Japan 92 C4
Nanto Japan 92 C2
Nantong China 97 I2
Nantou Taiwan 97 I4
Nantucket *MA* U.S.A. 165 J3
Nantucket Island *MA* U.S.A. 165 K3
Nantucket Sound *g. MA* U.S.A. 165 J3
Nantwich U.K. 59 E5
Nanumaga *i.* Tuvalu *see* **Nanumanga**
Nanumanga *i.* Tuvalu 133 H2
Nanumea *atoll* Tuvalu 133 H2
Nanuque Brazil 179 C2
Nanusa, Kepulauan *is* Indon. 83 C1
Nanushuk *r. AK* U.S.A. 149 J1
Nanxi China 96 E2
Nanxian China 97 G2
Nanxiong China 97 G3
Nanyang China 97 G1
Nanyuki Kenya 122 D4
Nanzamu China 95 K3
Nanzhang China 97 F2
Nanzhao China *see* **Zhao'an**
Nanzhou China *see* **Nanxian**
Nao, Cabo de la *c.* Spain 67 G4
Naococane, Lac *l.* Canada 153 H3
Naoero *country* S. Pacific Ocean *see* **Nauru**
Naogaon Bangl. 105 G4
Naoli He *r.* China 90 D3
Nāomīd, Dasht-e *des.* Afgh./Iran 111 F3
Naong, Bukit *mt.* Malaysia 85 F2
Naoshera India 104 C2
Napa *CA* U.S.A. 158 B2
Napaimiut *AK* U.S.A. 148 H3
Napakiak *AK* U.S.A. 148 G3
Napaktulik Lake Canada 151 H1
Napanee Canada 165 G1
Napaskiak *AK* U.S.A. 148 G3
Napasoq Greenland 147 M3
Naperville *IL* U.S.A. 164 A3
Napier N.Z. 139 F4
Napier Range *hills* Australia 134 D4
Napierville Canada 165 I1
Naples Italy 68 F4
Naples *FL* U.S.A. 163 D7
Naples *ME* U.S.A. 165 J2
Naples *TX* U.S.A. 161 E5
Naples *UT* U.S.A. 159 I1
Napo China 96 E4
Napoleon *IN* U.S.A. 164 C4
Napoleon *ND* U.S.A. 160 D2
Napoleon *OH* U.S.A. 164 C3
Napoli Italy *see* **Naples**
Naqadeh Iran 110 B2
Nara India 104 B5
Nara Japan 92 B4
Nara *pref.* Japan 92 B4
Nara Mali 120 C3
Narach Belarus 55 O9
Naracoorte Australia 137 C8
Naradhan Australia 138 C4
Narai-gawa *r.* Japan 93 D2
Narakawa Japan 93 D3
Naralua India 105 F4
Naran Mongolia 95 H2
Naranbulag *Dornod* Mongolia *see* **Bayandun**
Naranbulag *Uvs* Mongolia 94 C1
Naranjal Ecuador 176 C4
Naranjo Mex. 157 F8
Naranjos Mex. 167 F4
Naran Sebstein Bulag *spring* China 94 D3
Narasapur India 106 D2
Narasaraopet India 106 D2
Narashino Japan 93 G3
Narasinghapur India 106 E1
Narasun Russia 95 H1
Narat China 98 D4
Narathiwat Thai. 87 C6
Narat Shan *mts* China 98 C4
Nara Visa *NM* U.S.A. 161 C5
Narayanganj Bangl. 105 G5
Narayanganj India 104 E5
Narayangarh India 104 C4
Narayanpur India 106 D2
Narbada *r.* India *see* **Narmada**
Narberth U.K. 59 C7
Narbo France *see* **Narbonne**
Narbonne France 66 F5
Narborough Island *Galápagos* Ecuador *see* **Fernandina, Isla**
Narcea *r.* Spain 67 C2
Narcondam Island India 87 A4
Nardò Italy 68 H4
Narechi *r.* Pak. 111 H4
Narembeen Australia 135 B8
Nares Abyssal Plain *sea feature* S. Atlantic Ocean 184 D4
Nares Deep *sea feature* N. Atlantic Ocean 184 D4
Nares Strait Canada/Greenland 147 K2
Naretha Australia 135 D7
Narew *r.* Poland 57 R4
Narib Namibia 124 C3
Narikel Jinjira *i.* Bangl. *see* **St Martin's Island**
Narimanov Russia 53 J7
Narimskiy Khrebet *mts* Kazakh. *see* **Naryn, Khrebet**
Narin China 95 G4
Narince Turkey 112 E3
Narin Gol *watercourse* China 99 F5
Narita Japan 93 G3
Narita *airport* Japan 93 G3
Nariu-misaki *pt* Japan 92 B3
Nariynteel Mongolia 94 E2
Narizon, Punta *pt* Mex. 166 C3
Narkher India 104 D5
Narmada *r.* India 104 C5
Narman Turkey 113 F2
Narnaul India 104 D3
Narni Italy 68 E3
Narnia Italy *see* **Narni**
Narodnaya, Gora *mt.* Russia 51 S3
Naro-Fominsk Russia 53 H5
Narok Kenya 122 D4
Narooma Australia 138 E6
Narovchat Russia 53 I5
Narowlya Belarus 53 F6
Närpes Fin. 54 L5
Narrabri Australia 138 D3
Narragansett Bay *RI* U.S.A. 165 J3
Narran *r.* Australia 138 C2
Narrandera Australia 138 C5
Narran Lake Australia 138 C2
Narrogin Australia 135 B8
Narromine Australia 138 D4
Narrows *VA* U.S.A. 164 E5
Narrowsburg *NY* U.S.A. 165 H3
Narsapur India 106 C2
Narsaq Greenland 147 N3
Narshingdi Bangl. *see* **Narsingdi**
Narsimhapur India 104 D5
Narsingdi Bangl. 105 G5
Narsinghpur India *see* **Narsimhapur**
Narsipatnam India 106 D2
Nart China 95 H3
Nart Mongolia *see* **Orhon**
Nartkala Russia 113 F2
Narusawa Japan 93 E3
Naruto Japan 91 D6
Narva Estonia 55 P7
Narva Bay Estonia/Russia 55 O7
Narvacan *Luzon* Phil. 82 C2
Narva laht *b.* Estonia/Russia *see* **Narva Bay**
Narva Reservoir *resr* Estonia/Russia 55 P7
Narva veehoidla *resr* Estonia/Russia *see* **Narva Reservoir**
Narvik Norway 54 J2
Narvskiy Zaliv *b.* Estonia/Russia *see* **Narva Bay**
Narvskoye Vodokhranilishche *resr* Estonia/Russia *see* **Narva Reservoir**
Narwana India 104 D3
Nar'yan-Mar Russia 52 L2
Naryn Kyrg. 102 E3
Naryn *admin. div.* Kyrg. 98 A4
Naryn *r.* Kyrg./Uzbek. 98 A4
Naryn Russia 94 C1
Naryn, Khrebet *mts* Kazakh. 102 F2
Narynkol Kazakh. 98 C4
Näsåker Sweden 54 J5
Nash Harbor *AK* U.S.A. 148 F3
Nashik India 106 B1
Nashua *NH* U.S.A. 165 J2
Nashville *AR* U.S.A. 161 E5
Nashville *GA* U.S.A. 163 D6
Nashville *IN* U.S.A. 164 B4
Nashville *NC* U.S.A. 162 E5
Nashville *OH* U.S.A. 164 D3

▶**Nashville** *TN* U.S.A. 162 C4
Capital of Tennessee.

Naşīb Syria 107 C3
Näsijärvi *l.* Fin. 55 M6
Nasik India *see* **Nashik**
Nasilat *Kalimantan* Indon. 85 E2
Nasinu Fiji 133 H3
Nasir Pak. 111 H4
Nasir South Sudan 108 D8
Nasirabad Bangl. *see* **Mymensingh**
Nasirabad India 104 C4
Naskaupi *r.* Canada 153 J3
Naşr Egypt 112 C5
Naşrānī, Jabal an *mts* Syria 107 C3
Naşrīān Iran 110 B3
Nass *r.* Canada 149 O5
Nassau *r.* Australia 136 C2

▶**Nassau** Bahamas 163 E7
Capital of the Bahamas.

Nassau *i.* Cook Is 133 J3
Nassau *NY* U.S.A. 165 I2
Nassawadox *VA* U.S.A. 165 H5
Nasser, Lake *resr* Egypt 108 D5
Nässjö Sweden 55 I8
Nassuttooq *inlet* Greenland 147 M3
Nastapoca *r.* Canada 152 F2
Nastapoka Islands Canada 152 F2
Nasu Japan 93 G1
Nasu-dake *vol.* Japan 93 F1
Nasugbu *Luzon* Phil. 82 C3
Nasukarasuyama Japan 93 G2
Nasushiobara Japan 93 G2
Nasva Russia 52 F4
Nata Botswana 123 C6
Nataboti *Buru* Indon. 83 C3
Natal Brazil 177 K5
Natal *Sumatra* Indon. 84 B2
Natal *prov.* S. Africa *see* **KwaZulu-Natal**
Natal Basin *sea feature* Indian Ocean 185 K8
Naţanz Iran 110 C3
Natashō Japan 92 B3
Natashquan Canada 153 J4
Natashquan *r.* Canada 153 J4
Natazhat, Mount *AK* U.S.A. 149 L3
Natchez *MS* U.S.A. 161 F6
Natchitoches *LA* U.S.A. 161 E6
Nathalia Australia 138 B6
Nathia Gali Pak. 111 I3
Nati, Punta *pt* Spain 67 H3
Natillas Mex. 167 E3
Nation *AK* U.S.A. 149 L2
National City *CA* U.S.A. 158 E5
Natitingou Benin 120 D3
Natividad, Isla *i.* Mex. 166 B3
Natividade Brazil 177 I6
Natkyizin Myanmar 86 B4
Natla *r.* Canada 149 O3
Natmauk Myanmar 86 A2
Nator Bangl. *see* **Natore**
Nátora Mex. 157 F7
Natore Bangl. 105 G4
Natori Japan 91 F5
Natron, Lake *salt l.* Tanz. 122 D4
Nattai National Park Australia 138 E5
Nattalin Myanmar 86 A3
Nattaung *mt.* Myanmar 86 B3
Na'tū Iran 111 F3
Natuashish Canada 153 J3
Natuna, Kepulauan *is* Indon. 85 D1
Natuna Besar *i.* Indon. 85 E1
Natural Bridges National Monument *nat. park UT* U.S.A. 159 H3
Naturaliste, Cape Australia 135 A8
Naturaliste Plateau *sea feature* Indian Ocean 185 P8
Naturita *CO* U.S.A. 159 I2
Nauchas Namibia 124 C2
Nau Co *l.* China 99 C6
Nauen Germany 63 M2
Naufragados, Ponta dos *pt* Brazil 179 A4
Naujan *Mindoro* Phil. 82 C3
Naujoji Akmen Lith. 55 M8
Naukh India 104 C4
Naukot Pak. 111 H5
Naumburg (Hessen) Germany 63 J3
Naumburg (Saale) Germany 63 L3
Naunglon Myanmar 86 B3
Naungpale Myanmar 86 B3
Naupada India 106 E2
Na'ūr Jordan 107 B4
Nauroz Kalat Pak. 111 G4
Naurskaya Russia 113 G2
Nauru *i.* Nauru 133 G2
Nauru *country* S. Pacific Ocean 133 G2
Naushki Russia 94 F1
Naustdal Norway 55 D6
Nauta Peru 176 D4
Nautaca Uzbek. *see* **Qarshi**
Nautanwa India 99 C8
Naute Dam Namibia 124 C4
Nautla Mex. 167 F4
Nava Mex. 167 E2
Navadwip India 105 G5
Navahrudak Belarus 55 N10
Navajo Lake *NM* U.S.A. 159 J3
Navajo Mountain *UT* U.S.A. 159 H3
Naval Phil. 82 D4
Navalmoral de la Mata Spain 67 D4
Navalvillar de Pela Spain 67 D4
Navan Ireland 61 F4
Navangar India *see* **Jamnagar**
Navapolatsk Belarus 55 P9
Navarin, Mys *c.* Russia 77 S3
Navarra *aut. comm.* Spain 67 F2
Navarra, Comunidad Foral de *aut. comm.* Spain *see* **Navarra**
Navarre Australia 138 A6
Navarre *aut. comm.* Spain *see* **Navarra**
Navarro *r. CA* U.S.A. 158 B2
Navashino Russia 52 I5
Navasota *TX* U.S.A. 161 D6
Navasota *r. TX* U.S.A. 167 F2

▶**Navassa Island** *terr.* West Indies 169 I5
United States Unincorporated Territory.

Naver *r.* U.K. 60 E2
Näverede Sweden 54 I5
Navi Mumbai India 109 L6
Navlakhi India 104 B5
Navlya Russia 53 G5
Năvodari Romania 69 M2
Navoi Uzbek. *see* **Navoiy**
Navoiy Uzbek. 111 G1
Navojoa Mex. 166 C3
Navolato Mex. 166 D3
Návpaktos Greece *see* **Nafpaktos**
Návplion Greece *see* **Nafplio**
Navşar Turkey *see* **Şemdinli**
Navsari India 106 B1
Navy Town *AK* U.S.A. 148 [inset] A5
Nawá Syria 107 C3
Nawabganj Bangl. 105 G4
Nawabshah Pak. 111 H5
Nawada India 105 F4
Nāwah Afgh. 111 G3
Nāwah-ye Gurz Afgh. 111 G3
Nawalgarh India 104 C4
Nawanshahr India 104 D3
Nawan Shehar India *see* **Nawanshahr**
Nawar, Dasht-i- *depr.* Afgh. *see* **Nāwer, Dasht-e**
Nawarangpur India *see* **Nabarangapur**
Nāwer, Dasht-e *depr.* Afgh. 111 G3
Nawngcho Myanmar *see* **Nawnghkio**
Nawnghkio Myanmar 86 B2
Nawng Hpa Myanmar 86 B2
Nawngleng Myanmar 86 B2
Nawoiy Uzbek. *see* **Navoiy**
Naxçıvan Azer. 113 G3
Naxos *i.* Greece 69 K6
Nayag China 99 E7
Nayagarh India 106 E1
Nayak Afgh. 111 G3
Nayar Mex. 168 D4
Nayarit *state* Mex. 166 D4
Nāy Band, Kūh-e *mt.* Iran 110 E3
Nayong China 96 E3
Nayoro Japan 90 F3

▶**Nay Pyi Taw** Myanmar 86 B3
Capital of Myanmar.

Nazaré Brazil 179 D1
Nazareno Mex. 166 E3
Nazareth Israel *see* **Naẓerat**
Nazário Brazil 179 A2
Nazas Mex. 166 D3
Nazas *r.* Mex. 166 D3
Nazca Peru 176 D6
Nazca Ridge *sea feature* S. Pacific Ocean 187 O7
Naẓerat Israel 107 B3
Nāzīl Iran 111 F4
Nazilli Turkey 69 M6
Nazimabad Pak. 111 G5
Nazımiye Turkey 113 E3
Nazir Hat Bangl. 105 G5
Nazko Canada 150 F4
Nazran' Russia 113 G2
Nazrēt Eth. 122 D3
Nazwá Oman 110 E6
Ncojane Botswana 124 E2
N'dalatando Angola 123 B4
Ndao *i.* Indon. 83 B5
Ndélé Cent. Afr. Rep. 122 C3
Ndendé Gabon 122 B4
Ndende *i.* Solomon Is *see* **Nendo**
N'Djamena Chad *see* **Ndjamena**

▶**Ndjamena** Chad 121 E3
Capital of Chad.

Ndjouani *i.* Comoros *see* **Ndzuani**
Ndoi *i.* Fiji *see* **Doi**
Ndola Zambia 123 C5
Nduke *i.* Solomon Is *see* **Kolombangara**
Ndwedwe S. Africa 125 J5
Ndzuani *i.* Comoros 123 E5
Ne, Hon *i.* Vietnam 86 D3
Neabul Creek *r.* Australia 138 C1
Neagari Japan 92 C2
Neagh, Lough *l.* U.K. 61 F3
Neah Bay *WA* U.S.A. 156 B2
Neale, Lake *salt flat* Australia 135 E6
Nea Liosia Greece 69 J5
Neapoli Greece 69 J6
Neapolis Italy *see* **Naples**
Near Islands *AK* U.S.A. 148 [inset]5
Nea Roda Greece 69 J4
Neath U.K. 59 D7
Neath *r.* U.K. 59 D7
Neba Japan 92 D3
Nebbi Uganda 122 D3
Nebesnaya, Gora *mt.* China 98 C4
Nebine Creek *r.* Australia 138 C2
Neblina, Pico da *mt.* Brazil 176 E3
Nebo Australia 136 E4
Nebo, Mount *UT* U.S.A. 159 H2
Nebolchi Russia 52 G4
Nebraska *state* U.S.A. 160 C3
Nebraska City *NE* U.S.A. 160 E3
Nebrodi, Monti *mts Sicily* Italy 68 F6
Neches *r. TX* U.S.A. 161 E6
Nechisar National Park Eth. 122 D3
Nechranice, Vodní nádrž *resr* Czech Rep. 63 N4
Neckar *r.* Germany 63 I5
Neckarsulm Germany 63 J5
Necker Island *HI* U.S.A. 186 J4
Necochea Arg. 178 E5
Nederland *country* Europe *see* **Netherlands**
Neder Rijn *r.* Neth. 62 F3
Nedlouc, Lac *l.* Canada 153 G2
Nedluk Lake Canada *see* **Nedlouc, Lac**
Nêdong China 99 E7
Nedre Soppero Sweden 54 L2
Nédroma Alg. 67 F6
Neeba-san *mt.* Japan 93 E2
Needle Mountain *WY* U.S.A. 156 F3
Needles *CA* U.S.A. 159 F4
Neemach India *see* **Neemuch**
Neemuch India 104 C4
Neenah *WI* U.S.A. 164 A1
Neepawa Canada 151 L5
Neergaard Lake Canada 147 J2
Neerijnen Neth. 62 F3
Neerpelt Belgium 62 F3
Neftçala Azer. 113 H3
Neftechala Azer. *see* **Neftçala**
Neftechala Azer. *see* **Häsänabad**
Neftegorsk Russia 53 K5
Neftegorsk (abandoned) Russia 90 F1
Neftekamsk Russia 51 Q4
Neftekumsk Russia 113 G1
Nefteyugansk Russia 76 I3
Neftezavodsk Turkm. *see* **Seýdi**
Neftezavodsk Turkm. *see* **Seýdi**
Nefyn U.K. 59 C6
Nefza Tunisia 68 C6
Negage Angola 123 B4
Negār Iran 110 E4
Negara *Bali* Indon. 85 F5
Negara *Kalimantan* Indon. 85 F3
Negara *r.* Indon. 85 F3
Negēlē Eth. 122 D3
Negeri Sembilan *state* Malaysia 84 C2
Negev *des.* Israel 107 B4
Negomane Moz. 123 D5
Negombo Sri Lanka 106 C5
Negotino Macedonia 69 J4
Negra, Cordillera *mts* Peru 176 C5
Negra, Punta *pt* Peru 176 B5
Negra, Serra *mts* Brazil 179 C2
Negrais, Cape Myanmar 86 A4
Négrine Alg. 68 B7
Negri Sembilan *state* Malaysia *see* **Negeri Sembilan**
Negro *r.* Arg. 178 D6
Negro *r. Mato Grosso do Sul* Brazil 177 G7
Negro *r. Paraná/Santa Catarina* Brazil 179 A4
Negro *r.* S. America 176 G4
Negro, Cabo *c.* Morocco 67 D6
Negroponte *i.* Greece *see* **Evvoia**
Negros *i.* Phil. 82 C4
Negru Vodă, Podişul *plat.* Romania 69 M3
Nehbandān Iran 111 F4
Nehe China 95 K1
Neiguanying China 94 F5
Neijiang China 96 E2
Neilburg Canada 151 I4
Neimenggu *aut. reg.* China *see* **Nei Mongol Zizhiqu**
Nei Mongol Zizhiqu *aut. reg.* China 95 E3
Neinstedt Germany 63 L3
Neiqiu China 95 H4
Neiva Col. 176 C3
Neixiang China 97 F1
Nejanilini Lake Canada 151 L3
Nejapa Mex. 167 G5
Nejd *reg.* Saudi Arabia *see* **Najd**
Nekā Iran 110 D2
Nek'emtē Eth. 122 D3
Neko-zaki *pt* Japan 92 A3
Nekrasovskoye Russia 52 I4
Nelang India 104 D3
Nelia Australia 136 C4
Nelidovo Russia 52 G4
Neligh *NE* U.S.A. 160 D3
Nel'kan Russia 77 P3
Nelligere India 106 C3
Nellore India 106 C3
Nelluz *watercourse* Turkey 107 D1
Nel'ma Russia 90 E3
Nelson Canada 150 G5
Nelson *r.* Canada 151 M3
Nelson N.Z. 139 D5
Nelson U.K. 58 E5
Nelson *AZ* U.S.A. 159 G4
Nelson, Cape Australia 137 C8
Nelson, Cape P.N.G. 81 L8
Nelson, Estrecho *strait* Chile 178 A8
Nelson Bay Australia 138 F4
Nelson Forks Canada 150 F3
Nelsonia *VA* U.S.A. 165 H5
Nelson Island *AK* U.S.A. 148 F3

Nelson Lagoon AK U.S.A. 148 G5
Nelson Lakes National Park N.Z. 139 D6
Nelson Reservoir MT U.S.A. 156 G2
Nelspruit S. Africa see Mbombela
Néma Mauritania 120 C3
Nema Russia 52 K4
Neman r. Belarus/Lith. see Nyoman
Neman Russia 55 M9
Nemausus France see Nîmes
Nemawar India 104 D5
Nemed Russia 52 L3
Nementcha, Monts des mts Alg. 68 B7
Nemetocenna France see Arras
Nemetskiy, Mys c. Russia 54 Q2
Nemirov Ukr. see Nemyriv
Nemiscau r. Canada 152 F4
Nemiscau, Lac l. Canada 152 F4
Nemor He r. China 95 K1
Nemours Alg. see Ghazaouet
Nemours France 66 F2
Nemrut Dağı mt. Turkey 113 F3
Nemunas r. Belarus/Lith. see Nyoman
Nemuro Japan 90 G4
Nemuro-kaikyō sea chan. Japan/Russia 90 G4
Nemyriv Ukr. 53 F6
Nenagh Ireland 61 D5
Nenan China 95 K1
Nenana AK U.S.A. 149 J2
Nenana r. AK U.S.A. 149 J2
Nendo i. Solomon Is 133 G3
Nene r. U.K. 59 H6
Nenjiang China 95 K1
Nen Jiang r. China 95 K2
Neo Japan 92 C3
Neo-gawa r. Japan 92 C3
Neosho MO U.S.A. 161 E4
Nepal country Asia 105 E3
Nepalganj Nepal 105 E3
Nepean Canada 165 H1
Nepean, Point Australia 138 B7
Nephi UT U.S.A. 159 H2
Nephin hill Ireland 61 C3
Nephin Beg Range hills Ireland 61 C3
Nepisiguit r. Canada 153 I5
Nepoko r. Dem. Rep. Congo 122 C3
Nérac France 66 E4
Neragon Island AK U.S.A. 148 F3
Nerang Australia 138 F1
Nera Tso l. China 105 H3
Nerchinsk Russia 89 L2
Nerekhta Russia 52 I4
Néret, Lac l. Canada 153 H3
Neretva r. Bos. & Herz./Croatia 68 G3
Nêri Pünco l. China 99 E7
Neriquinha Angola 123 C5
Neris r. Lith. 55 M9
also known as Viliya (Belarus/Lithuania)
Nerl' r. Russia 52 H4
Nerópolis Brazil 179 A2
Neryungri Russia 77 N4
Nes Neth. 62 F1
Nes Norway 55 F6
Nes' Russia 52 J2
Nesbyen Norway 55 F6
Neshkan Russia 148 D2
Neshkenpil'khyn, Laguna lag. Russia 148 D2
Neskaupstaður Iceland 54 [inset 1]
Nesle France 62 C5
Nesna Norway 54 H3
Nesri India 106 B2
Ness r. U.K. 60 E3
Ness, Loch l. U.K. 60 E3
Ness City KS U.S.A. 160 D4
Nesse r. Germany 63 K4
Nesselrode, Mount Canada/U.S.A. 149 N4
Nestor Falls Canada 151 M5
Nestos r. Greece 69 K4
also known as Mesta
Nesvizh Belarus see Nyasvizh
Netanya Israel 107 B3
Netherlands country Europe 62 F2
▶Netherlands Antilles West Indies 169 K6
The Netherlands Antilles was dissolved into 5 contsituent dependencies of the Netherlands in Oct 2010.
Netphen Germany 63 I4
Netrakona Bangl. 105 G4
Netrokona Bangl. see Netrakona
Nettilling Lake Canada 147 K3
Neubrandenburg Germany 63 N1
Neuburg an der Donau Germany 63 L6
Neuchâtel Switz. 66 H3
Neuchâtel, Lac de l. Switz. 66 H3
Neuendettelsau Germany 63 K5
Neuenhaus Germany 62 G2
Neuenkirchen Germany 63 J1
Neuenkirchen (Oldenburg) Germany 63 I2
Neufchâteau Belgium 62 F5
Neufchâteau France 66 G2
Neufchâtel-en-Bray France 62 B5
Neufchâtel-Hardelot France 62 B4
Neuharlingersiel Germany 63 H1
Neuhausen Russia see Gur'yevsk
Neuhof Germany 63 J4
Neu Kaliß Germany 63 L1
Neukirchen Germany 63 J4
Neukirchen/Erzgebirge Germany 63 M4
Neukuhren Russia see Pionerskiy
Neum Bos. & Herz. 68 G3
Neumarkt in der Oberpfalz Germany 63 L5
Neumayer III research station Antarctica 188 B2
Neumünster Germany 57 L3
Neunburg vorm Wald Germany 63 M5
Neunkirchen Austria 57 P7
Neunkirchen Germany 63 H5
Neuquén Arg. 178 C5
Neuruppin Germany 63 M2
Neu Sandez Poland see Nowy Sącz
Neuse r. NC U.S.A. 163 E5
Neusiedler See l. Austria/Hungary 57 P7
Neusiedler See Seewinkel, Nationalpark nat. park Austria 57 P7
Neuss Germany 62 G3
Neustadt (Wied) Germany 63 H4
Neustadt am Rübenberge Germany 63 J2
Neustadt an der Aisch Germany 63 K5
Neustadt an der Hardt Germany see Neustadt an der Weinstraße
Neustadt an der Waldnaab Germany 63 M5
Neustadt an der Weinstraße Germany 63 I5
Neustadt bei Coburg Germany 63 L4
Neustadt-Glewe Germany 63 L1
Neustrelitz Germany 63 N1
Neutraubling Germany 63 M6
Neuville-lès-Dieppe France 62 B5
Neuwied Germany 63 H4
Neu Wulmstorf Germany 63 J1
Nevada IA U.S.A. 160 E3
Nevada MO U.S.A. 160 E4
Nevada state U.S.A. 156 D5
Nevada, Sierra mts Spain 67 E5
Nevada, Sierra mts CA U.S.A. 158 C1
Nevada City CA U.S.A. 158 C2
Nevado, Cerro mt. Arg. 178 C5
Nevado, Sierra del mts Arg. 178 C5
Nevado de Colima, Parque Nacional nat. park Mex. 166 E5
Nevasa India 106 B2
Nevatim Israel 107 B4
Nevdubstroy Russia see Kirovsk
Nevel' Russia 52 F4
Nevel'sk Russia 90 F3
Never Russia 90 B1
Nevers France 66 F3
Nevertire Australia 138 C3
Nevesinje Bos. & Herz. 68 H3
Nevinnomyssk Russia 113 F1
Nevşehir Turkey 112 D3
Nevskoye Russia 90 D3
New r. CA U.S.A. 159 F5
New r. WV U.S.A. 164 E5
Newala Tanz. 123 D5
New Albany IN U.S.A. 164 C4
New Albany MS U.S.A. 161 F5
New Amsterdam Guyana 177 G2
New Amsterdam NY U.S.A. see New York
Newark DE U.S.A. 165 H4
Newark NJ U.S.A. 165 H3
Newark NY U.S.A. 165 G2
Newark OH U.S.A. 164 D3
Newark Lake NV U.S.A. 159 F2
Newark Liberty airport NJ U.S.A. 162 F3
Newark-on-Trent U.K. 59 G5
New Bedford MA U.S.A. 165 J3
Newberg OR U.S.A. 156 C3
New Berlin NY U.S.A. 165 H2
New Bern NC U.S.A. 163 E5
Newberry IN U.S.A. 164 B4
Newberry MI U.S.A. 162 C2
Newberry SC U.S.A. 163 D5
Newberry National Volcanic Monument nat. park OR U.S.A. 156 C4
Newberry Springs CA U.S.A. 158 E4
New Bethlehem PA U.S.A. 164 F3
Newbiggin-by-the-Sea U.K. 58 F3
New Bight Bahamas 163 F7
New Bloomfield PA U.S.A. 165 G3
Newboro Canada 165 G1
New Boston OH U.S.A. 164 D4
New Boston TX U.S.A. 161 E5
New Braunfels TX U.S.A. 161 D6
Newbridge Ireland 61 F4
New Britain i. P.N.G. 81 L8
New Britain CT U.S.A. 165 I3
New Britain Trench sea feature S. Pacific Ocean 186 G6
New Brunswick prov. Canada 153 I5
New Brunswick NJ U.S.A. 165 H3
New Buffalo MI U.S.A. 164 B3
Newburgh Canada 165 G1
Newburgh U.K. 60 G3
Newburgh NY U.S.A. 165 H3
Newbury U.K. 59 F7
Newburyport MA U.S.A. 165 J2
New Busuanga Phil. 82 B3
Newby Bridge U.K. 58 E4
▶New Caledonia terr. S. Pacific Ocean 133 G4
French Overseas Collectivity.
New Caledonia Trough sea feature Tasman Sea 186 G7
New Carlisle Canada 153 I4
Newcastle Australia 138 E4
Newcastle Canada 165 F2
Newcastle Ireland 61 F4
Newcastle S. Africa 125 I4
Newcastle U.K. 61 G3
New Castle CO U.S.A. 159 J2
New Castle IN U.S.A. 164 C4
New Castle KY U.S.A. 164 C4
New Castle PA U.S.A. 164 E3
Newcastle UT U.S.A. 159 G3
New Castle VA U.S.A. 164 E5
Newcastle WY U.S.A. 156 G4
Newcastle Emlyn U.K. 59 C6
Newcastle-under-Lyme U.K. 59 E5
Newcastle upon Tyne U.K. 58 F4
Newcastle Waters Australia 134 F4
Newcastle West Ireland 61 C5
Newchwang China see Yingkou
New City NY U.S.A. 165 I3
Newcomb NM U.S.A. 159 I3
New Concord OH U.S.A. 164 E4
New Cumberland WV U.S.A. 164 E3
New Cumnock U.K. 60 E5
New Deer U.K. 60 G3
▶New Delhi India 104 D3
Capital of India.
New Don Pedro Reservoir CA U.S.A. 158 C3
Newell SD U.S.A. 160 C2
Newell, Lake salt flat Australia 135 D6
Newell, Lake Canada 151 I5
New England National Park Australia 138 F3
New England Range mts Australia 138 E3
New England Seamounts sea feature N. Atlantic Ocean 184 E3
Newenham, Cape AK U.S.A. 148 G4
Newent U.K. 59 E7
New Era MI U.S.A. 164 B2
Newfane NY U.S.A. 165 F2
Newfane VT U.S.A. 165 I2
New Forest National Park nat. park U.K. 59 F8
Newfoundland i. Canada 153 K4
Newfoundland prov. Canada see Newfoundland and Labrador
Newfoundland and Labrador prov. Canada 153 K3
Newfoundland Evaporation Basin salt l. UT U.S.A. 159 G1
New Galloway U.K. 60 E5
New Georgia i. Solomon Is 133 F2
New Georgia Islands Solomon Is 133 F2
New Georgia Sound sea chan. Solomon Is 133 F2
New Glasgow Canada 153 J5
▶New Guinea i. Indon./P.N.G. 81 K8
Largest island in Oceania and 2nd in the world.
Newhalen AK U.S.A. 148 I4
New Halfa Sudan 108 E6
New Hamilton AK U.S.A. 148 G3
New Hampshire state U.S.A. 165 J1
New Hampton IA U.S.A. 160 E3
New Hanover i. P.N.G. 132 F2
Newhaven town U.K. 59 H8
New Haven CT U.S.A. 165 I3
New Haven IN U.S.A. 164 C3
New Haven WV U.S.A. 164 E4
New Hebrides country S. Pacific Ocean see Vanuatu
New Hebrides Trench sea feature S. Pacific Ocean 186 H7
New Holstein WI U.S.A. 164 A2
New Iberia LA U.S.A. 161 F6
Newinn Ireland 61 E5
New Ireland i. P.N.G. 132 F2
New Jersey state U.S.A. 165 H4
New Kensington PA U.S.A. 164 F3
New Kent VA U.S.A. 165 G5
Newkirk OK U.S.A. 161 D4
New Lanark U.K. 60 F5
Newland Range hills Australia 135 C7
New Lexington OH U.S.A. 164 D4
New Liskeard Canada 152 F5
New London CT U.S.A. 165 I3
New London MO U.S.A. 160 F4
New Madrid MO U.S.A. 161 F4
Newman Australia 135 B5
Newman CA U.S.A. 158 C3
Newmarket Canada 164 F1
Newmarket Ireland 61 C5
Newmarket U.K. 59 H6
New Market VA U.S.A. 165 F4
Newmarket-on-Fergus Ireland 61 D5
New Martinsville WV U.S.A. 164 E4
New Meadows ID U.S.A. 156 D3
New Mexico state U.S.A. 157 G6
New Miami OH U.S.A. 164 C4
New Milford PA U.S.A. 165 H3
Newnan GA U.S.A. 163 C5
New Orleans LA U.S.A. 161 F6
New Paris IN U.S.A. 164 C3
New Paris OH U.S.A. 164 C4
New Philadelphia OH U.S.A. 164 E3
New Pitsligo U.K. 60 G3
New Plymouth N.Z. 139 E4
Newport Mayo Ireland 61 C4
Newport Tipperary Ireland 61 D5
Newport England U.K. 59 E6
Newport England U.K. 59 F8
Newport Wales U.K. 59 D7
Newport AR U.S.A. 161 F5
Newport IN U.S.A. 164 B4
Newport KY U.S.A. 164 C4
Newport MI U.S.A. 164 D3
Newport NH U.S.A. 165 I2
Newport NJ U.S.A. 165 H4
Newport OR U.S.A. 156 B3
Newport RI U.S.A. 165 J3
Newport VT U.S.A. 165 I1
Newport WA U.S.A. 156 D2
Newport Beach CA U.S.A. 158 E5
Newport News VA U.S.A. 165 G5
Newport Pagnell U.K. 59 G6
New Port Richey FL U.S.A. 163 D6
New Providence i. Bahamas 163 E7
Newquay U.K. 59 B8
New Roads LA U.S.A. 161 F6
New Rochelle NY U.S.A. 165 I3
New Rockford ND U.S.A. 160 D2
New Romney U.K. 59 H8
New Ross Ireland 61 F5
Newry Australia 134 E4
Newry U.K. 61 F3
New Siberia Islands Russia 77 P2
New Smyrna Beach FL U.S.A. 163 D6
New South Wales state Australia 138 C4
New Stanton PA U.S.A. 164 F3
New Stuyahok AK U.S.A. 148 H4
Newtok AK U.S.A. 148 F3
Newton U.K. 58 E5
Newton GA U.S.A. 163 C6
Newton IA U.S.A. 160 E3
Newton IL U.S.A. 160 F4
Newton KS U.S.A. 160 D4
Newton MA U.S.A. 165 J2
Newton MS U.S.A. 161 F5
Newton NC U.S.A. 162 D5
Newton NJ U.S.A. 165 H3
Newton TX U.S.A. 161 E6
Newton Abbot U.K. 59 D8
Newton Mearns U.K. 60 E5
Newton Stewart U.K. 60 E6
Newtown Ireland 61 D5
Newtown England U.K. 59 E6
Newtown Wales U.K. 59 D6
Newtown KY U.S.A. 164 C4
New Town ND U.S.A. 160 C1
Newtownabbey U.K. 61 G3
Newtownards U.K. 61 G3
Newtownbarry Ireland see Bunclody
Newtownbutler U.K. 61 E3
Newtown Mount Kennedy Ireland 61 F4
Newtown St Boswells U.K. 60 G5
Newtownstewart U.K. 61 E3
New Ulm MN U.S.A. 160 E2
Newville PA U.S.A. 165 G3
New World Island Canada 153 L4
▶New York NY U.S.A. 165 I3
2nd most populous city in North America and 5th in the world.
New York state U.S.A. 165 H2
▶New Zealand country Oceania 139 D5
3rd largest and 3rd most populated country in Oceania.
Nexø Denmark 55 I9
Neya Russia 52 I4
Neyagawa Japan 92 B4
Ney Bīd Iran 110 E4
Neyrīz Iran 110 D4
Neyshābūr Iran 110 E2
Nezahualcóyotl, Presa resr Mex. 167 G5
Nezhin Ukr. see Nizhyn
Nezperce ID U.S.A. 156 D3
Ngabang Kalimantan Indon. 85 E2
Ngabé Congo 122 B4
Nga Chong, Khao mt. Myanmar/Thai. 86 B4
Ngadubolu Sumba Indon. 83 A5
Ngagahtawng Myanmar 96 C3
Ngagau mt. Tanz. 123 D4
Ngajangel i. Palau 82 [inset]
Ngalipaëng Celebes Indon. 83 C2
Ngalu Sumba Indon. 83 B5
Ngamegei Passage Palau 82 [inset]
Ngamring China 99 D7
Ngangla Ringco salt l. China 99 C7
Nganglong Kangri mt. China 99 C6
Nganglong Kangri mts China 99 C6
Ngangzê Co salt l. China 99 D7
Ngangzê Shan mts China 99 D7
Nganjuk Java Indon. 85 E4
Ngân Sơn Vietnam 86 D2
Ngaoundal Cameroon 120 E4
Ngaoundéré Cameroon 121 E4
Ngape Myanmar 86 A2
Ngaputaw Myanmar 86 A3
Ngaras Sumatra Indon. 84 D4
Ngardmau Palau 82 [inset]
Ngardmau Bay Palau 82 [inset]
Ngaregur i. Palau 82 [inset]
Ngariungs i. Palau 82 [inset]
Ngateguil, Point Palau 82 [inset]
Ngathainggyaung Myanmar 86 A3
Ngau i. Fiji see Gau
Ngawa China see Aba
Ngawi Java Indon. 85 E4
Ngazidja i. Comoros 123 E5
Ngcheangel atoll Palau see Kayangel Atoll
Ngcobo S. Africa 125 H6
Ngeaur i. Palau see Angaur
Ngemelachel Palau see Malakal
Ngemelis Islands Palau 82 [inset]
Ngergoi i. Palau 82 [inset]
Ngeruangel i. Palau 81 I5
Ngerulmud Palau 82 [inset]
Ngesebus i. Palau 82 [inset]
Ngga Pulu mt. Indon. see Jaya, Puncak
Ngiap r. Laos 86 C3
Ngilmina Timor Indon. 83 C5
Ngimbang Java Indon. 85 F4
Ngiva Angola see Ondjiva
Ngo Congo 122 B4
Ngoako Ramalepe S. Africa see Modjadjiskloof
Ngobasangel i. Palau 82 [inset]
Ngofakiaha Moluccas Indon. 83 C2
Ngoichogê China 99 F7
Ngoin, Co salt l. China 99 E7
Ngoko r. Cameroon/Congo 121 E4
Ngola Shan mts China 94 D4
Ngola Shankou pass China 94 D5
Ngom Qu r. China 99 G7
Ngong Shuen Chau pen. H.K. China see Stonecutters' Island
Ngoqumaima China 99 D6
Ngoring China 94 D5
Ngoring Hu l. China 94 D5
Ngourti Niger 120 E3
Ngqamakhwe S. Africa 125 H7
Nguigmi Niger 120 E3
Nguiu Australia 134 E2
Ngükang China 99 F7
Ngukurr Australia 134 F3
Ngulu atoll Micronesia 81 J5
Ngum, Ang Kep Nam Laos 86 C3
Ngunju, Tanjung pt Sumba Indon. 83 B5
Ngunza Angola see Sumbe
Ngunza-Kabolu Angola see Sumbe
Ngüra China 94 E5
Nguru Nigeria 120 E3
Ngwaketse admin. dist. Botswana see Southern
Ngwane country Africa see Swaziland
Ngwathe S. Africa 125 H4
Ngwavuma r. S. Africa/Swaziland 125 K4
Ngwelezana S. Africa 125 J5
Nhachengue Moz. 125 L2
Nhamalabué Moz. 123 D5
Nha Trang Vietnam 87 E4
Nhecolândia Brazil 177 G7
Nhill Australia 137 C8
Nhlangano Swaziland 125 J4
Nho Quan Vietnam 86 D2
Nhow i. Fiji see Gau
Nhulunbuy Australia 136 B2
Niacam Canada 151 J4
Niafounké Mali 120 C3
Niagara WI U.S.A. 162 C2
Niagara Falls Canada 164 F2
Niagara Falls NY U.S.A. 164 F2
Niagara-on-the-Lake Canada 164 F2
Niagzu China 99 B6
Niah Sarawak Malaysia 85 F2
Niakaramandougou Côte d'Ivoire 120 C4
▶Niamey Niger 120 D3
Capital of Niger.
Nīām Kand Iran 110 E5
Niampak Celebes Indon. 81 H6
Nianbai China see Ledu
Niangara Dem. Rep. Congo 122 C3
Niangay, Lac l. Mali 120 C3
Nianyuwan China see Xingang
Nianzishan China 95 J2
Nias i. Indon. 84 B2
Niassa, Lago l. Africa see Nyasa, Lake
Niaur i. Palau see Angaur
Nīāzābād Iran 111 F3
Nibil Well Australia 134 D5
Nīca Latvia 55 L8
▶Nicaragua country Central America 169 G6
4th largest country in North America.
Nicaragua, Lago de Nicaragua see Nicaragua, Lake
Nicaragua, Lake l. Nicaragua 166 [inset] I7
Nicastro Italy 68 G5
Nice France 66 H5
Nice CA U.S.A. 158 B2
Nicephorium Syria see Ar Raqqah
Niceville FL U.S.A. 163 C6
Nichicun, Lac l. Canada 153 H3
Nicholas Channel Bahamas/Cuba 163 D8
Nicholasville KY U.S.A. 164 C5
Nichols WI U.S.A. 164 A1
Nicholson r. Australia 136 B3
Nicholson Lake Canada 151 K2
Nicholson Range hills Australia 135 B6
Nicholville NY U.S.A. 165 H1
Nicobar Islands India 87 A5
Nicolás Bravo Mex. 167 H5
Nicolaus CA U.S.A. 158 C2
Nicomedia Turkey see İzmit
▶Nicosia Cyprus 107 A2
Capital of Cyprus.
Nicoya Costa Rica 166 [inset] I7
Nicoya, Golfo de b. Costa Rica 166 [inset] I7
Nicoya, Península de pen. Costa Rica 166 [inset] I7
Nida Lith. 55 L9
Nidagunda India 106 C2
Nidd r. U.K. 58 F4
Nidda Germany 63 J4
Nidder r. Germany 63 I4
Nidzica Poland 57 R4
Niebüll Germany 57 L3
Nied r. France 62 G5
Niederanven Lux. 62 G5
Niederaula Germany 63 J4
Niedere Tauern mts Austria 57 N7
Niedersachsen land Germany 63 I2
Niedersächsisches Wattenmeer, Nationalpark nat. park Germany 62 G1
Niefang Equat. Guinea 120 E4
Niellé Côte d'Ivoire 120 C3
Nienburg (Weser) Germany 63 J2
Niers r. Germany 62 F3
Nierstein Germany 63 I5
Nieuwe Niedorp Neth. 62 E2
Nieuwerkerk aan den IJssel Neth. 62 E3
Nieuw Nickerie Suriname 177 G2
Nieuwolda Neth. 62 G1
Nieuwoudtville S. Africa 124 D6
Nieuwpoort Belgium 62 C3
Nieuw-Vossemeer Neth. 62 E3
Nif Seram Indon. 83 D3
Niğde Turkey 112 D3
Niger country Africa 120 D3
▶Niger r. Africa 120 D4
3rd longest river in Africa.
Niger, Mouths of the Nigeria 120 D4
Niger Cone sea feature S. Atlantic Ocean 184 I5
▶Nigeria country Africa 120 D4
Most populous country in Africa and 7th in the world.
Nighthawk Lake Canada 152 E4
Nightmute AK U.S.A. 148 F3
Nigrita Greece 69 J4
Nihing Pak. 111 G4
Nihon country Asia see Japan
Niigata Japan 91 E5
Niigata pref. Japan 93 E1
Niigata-yake-yama vol. Japan 93 E2
Niihama Japan 91 D6
Niiharu Japan 93 E2
Ni'ihau i. HI U.S.A. 157 [inset]
Nii-jima i. Japan 93 F4
Niimi Japan 91 D6
Niitsu Japan 91 E5
Niiza Japan 93 F3
Nijil, Wādī watercourse Jordan 107 B4
Nijkerk Neth. 62 F2
Nijmegen Neth. 62 F3
Nijverdal Neth. 62 G2
Nikel' Russia 54 Q2
Nikiniki Timor Indon. 83 C5
Nikiski AK U.S.A. 149 J3
Nikki Benin 120 D4
Nikkō Tochigi Japan 93 F2
Nikkō Tochigi Japan 93 F2
Nikkō Kokuritsu-kōen nat. park Japan 93 F2
Nikolaevsk AK U.S.A. 149 J4
Nikolai AK U.S.A. 148 I3
Nikolayev Ukr. see Mykolayiv
Nikolayevka Russia 53 J5
Nikolayevsk Russia 53 J6
Nikolayevskiy Russia see Nikolayevsk
Nikolayevsk-na-Amure Russia 90 F1
Nikol'sk Russia 52 J4
Nikolski AK U.S.A. 148 E5
Nikol'skiy Kazakh. see Satpayev
Nikol'skoye Kamchatskiy Kray Russia 77 R4
Nikol'skoye Vologod. Obl. Russia see Sheksna
Nikopol' Ukr. 53 G7
Niksar Turkey 112 E2
Nīkshahr Iran 111 F5
Nikšić Montenegro 68 H3
Nīkū Jahān Iran 111 F5
Nikumaroro atoll Kiribati 133 I2
Nikunau i. Kiribati 133 H2
Nīl, Bahr el r. Africa see Nile
Nila vol. Moluccas Indon. 83 D4
Nilagiri India 105 F5
Niland CA U.S.A. 159 F5
Nilande Atoll Maldives see Nilandhe Atholhu
Nilandhe Atholhu Maldives 103 D11
Nilandhe Atoll Maldives see Nilandhe Atholhu
Nilang India see Nelang
Nilanga India 106 C2
Nilaveli Sri Lanka 106 D4
▶Nile r. Africa 112 C5
Longest river in Africa and the world.
Niles MI U.S.A. 164 B3
Niles OH U.S.A. 164 E3
Nilgiri Hills India 106 C4
Nīlī Afgh. 111 G3
Nilka China 98 C4
Nīl Kōtal Afgh. 111 G3
Nilphamari Bangl. 105 G4
Nilsiä Fin. 54 P5
Nimach India see Neemuch
Niman r. Russia 90 D2
Nimba, Mont mts Africa see Richard-Molard, Mont
Nimbal India 106 B2
Nimberra Well Australia 135 C5
Nimelen r. Russia 90 E1
Nîmes France 66 G5
Nimmitabel Australia 137 E8
Nimrod Glacier Antarctica 188 H1
Nimu India 104 D2
Nimule South Sudan 121 G4
Nimwegen Neth. see Nijmegen
Nindigully Australia 138 D2
Nine Degree Channel India 106 B4
Nine Islands P.N.G. see Kilinailau Islands
Ninepin Group is H.K. China 97 [inset]
Ninetyeast Ridge sea feature Indian Ocean 185 N8
Ninety Mile Beach Australia 138 C7
Ninety Mile Beach N.Z. 139 D2
Nineveh NY U.S.A. 165 H2
Ningaloo Coast tourist site Australia 135 A5
Ningaloo Coast tourist site Australia 134 A5
Ning'an China 90 C3
Ningbo China 97 I2
Ningcheng China 95 I3
Ningde China 97 H3
Ning'er China 96 D4
Ningguo China 97 H2
Ninghai China 97 I2
Ninghe China 95 I4
Ninghsia Hui Autonomous Region aut. reg. China see Ningxia Huizu Zizhiqu
Ninghua China 97 H3
Ningjiang China see Songyuan
Ningjing Shan mts China 96 C2
Ninglang China 96 D3
Ningling China 95 H5
Ningming China 96 E4
Ningnan China 96 D3
Ningqiang China 96 E1
Ningwu China 95 H4
Ningxia aut. reg. China see Ningxia Huizu Zizhiqu
Ningxia Huizu Zizhiqu aut. reg. China 94 F4
Ningxian China 95 F5
Ningxiang China 97 G2
Ningyang China 95 I5
Ningzhou China see Huaning
Ninh Binh Vietnam 86 D2
Ninh Hoa Vietnam 87 E4
Ninigo Group atolls P.N.G. 81 K7
Ninilchik AK U.S.A. 149 J3
Ninnis Glacier Antarctica 188 G2
Ninnis Glacier Tongue Antarctica 188 H2
Ninohe Japan 91 F4
Ninomiya Kanagawa Japan 93 F3
Ninomiya Tochigi Japan 93 F2
Niobrara r. NE U.S.A. 160 D3

Niokolo Koba, Parc National du nat. park Senegal 120 B3
Nioku India 99 F8
Niono Mali 120 C3
Nioro Mali 120 C3
Niort France 66 D3
Nipani India 106 B2
Nipanipa, Tanjung pt Indon. 83 B3
Nipawin Canada 151 J4
Niphad India 106 B1
Nipigon Canada 147 J5
Nipigon, Lake Canada 147 J5
Nipishish Lake Canada 153 J3
Nipissing, Lake Canada 152 F5
Nippon country Asia see Japan
Nippon Hai sea N. Pacific Ocean see Japan, Sea of
Nipton CA U.S.A. 159 F4
Niquelândia Brazil 179 A1
Nīr Iran 110 B2
Nir Iran 110 D4
Nira r. India 106 B2
Nirasaki Japan 93 E3
Nirayama Japan 93 E3
Nirji China 95 K1
Nirmal India 106 C2
Nirmali India 105 F4
Nirmal Range hills India 106 C2
Niš Serbia 69 I3
Nisa Port. 67 C4
Nisarpur India 106 B1
Niscemi Sicily Italy 68 F6
Nishan China 99 D6
Nīshāpūr Iran see Neyshābūr
Nishiazai Japan 92 C3
Nishiizu Japan 93 E4
Nishikata Japan 93 F2
Nishikatsura Japan 93 E3
Nishi-maizuru Japan 92 B3
Nishinasuno Japan 93 F2
Nishinomiya Japan 92 B4
Nishino-shima vol. Japan 91 F8
Nishio Japan 92 D4
Nishi-Sonogi-hantō pen. Japan 91 C6
Nishiwaki Japan 92 A4
Nishiyoshino Japan 92 B4
Nisibis Turkey see Nusaybin
Nísiros i. Greece see Nisyros
Niskibi r. Canada 151 N3
Nisling r. Canada 149 M3
Nispen Neth. 62 E3
Nissan r. Sweden 55 H8
Nisshin Japan 92 D3
Nistru r. Ukr. 69 N1 see Dniester
Nisutlin r. Canada 149 N3
Nisyros i. Greece 69 L6
Niṭā Saudi Arabia 110 C5
Nitchequon (abandoned) Canada 153 H3
Nitendi i. Solomon Is see Nendo
Niterói Brazil 179 C3
Nith r. U.K. 60 F5
Nitibe East Timor 83 C5
Niti Pass China/India 104 D3
Niti Shankou pass China/India see Niti Pass
Nitmiluk National Park Australia 134 F3
Nitra Slovakia 57 Q6
Nitro WV U.S.A. 164 E4
Nitta Japan 93 F2
Niuafo'ou i. Tonga 133 I3
Niuatoputopu i. Tonga 133 I3
Niubiziliang China 98 F5

▶Niue terr. S. Pacific Ocean 133 J3
Self-governing New Zealand Overseas Territory.

Niujing China see Binchuan
Niulakita i. Tuvalu 133 H3
Niur, Pulau i. Indon. 84 C3
Niushan China see Donghai
Niutao i. Tuvalu 133 H2
Niutoushan China 97 H2
Niuzhuang China 95 J3
Nivala Fin. 54 N5
Nive watercourse Australia 136 D5
Nivelles Belgium 62 E4
Niwai India 104 C4
Niwas India 104 E5
Nixia China see Sêrxü
Nixon NV U.S.A. 158 D2
Niya China see Minfeng
Niya He r. China 99 C5
Niyut, Gunung mt. Indon. 85 E2
Nizamabad India 106 C2
Nizam Sagar l. India 106 C2
Nizhnedevitsk Russia 53 H6
Nizhnekamsk Russia 52 K5
Nizhnekamskoye Vodokhranilishche resr Russia 51 Q4
Nizhnekolymsk Russia 77 R3
Nizhnetambovskoye Russia 90 E2
Nizhneudinsk Russia 88 H2
Nizhnevartovsk Russia 76 I3
Nizhnevolzhsk Russia see Narimanov
Nizhneyansk Russia 77 O2
Nizhneye Giryunino Russia 95 I1
Nizhniy Baskunchak Russia 53 J6
Nizhniye Kresty Russia see Cherskiy
Nizhniy Lomov Russia 53 I5
Nizhniy Novgorod Russia 52 I4
Nizhniy Odes Russia 52 L3
Nizhniy Pyandzh Tajik. see Panji Poyon
Nizhniy Tagil Russia 51 R4
Nizhniy Torey Russia 94 F1
Nizhniy Tsasuchey Russia 95 H1
Nizhnyaya Mola Russia 52 J2
Nizhnyaya Omra Russia 52 L3
Nizhnyaya Pirenga, Ozero l. Russia 54 R3
Nizhnyaya Tunguska r. Russia 76 J3
Nizhnyaya Tura Russia 51 R4
Nizhyn Ukr. 53 F6
Nizina r. AK U.S.A. 150 A2
Nizip Turkey 107 C1
Nízke Tatry, Národný park nat. park Slovakia 57 Q6
Nizkiy, Mys hd Russia 148 B2
Nizwā Oman see Nazwá
Nizza France see Nice
Njallavarri mt. Norway 54 L2
Njavve Sweden 54 K3
Njombe Tanz. 123 D4
Njurundabommen Sweden 54 J5
Nkambe Cameroon 120 E4
Nkandla S. Africa 125 J5
Nkawkaw Ghana 120 C4
Nkhata Bay Malawi 123 D5
Nkhotakota Malawi 123 D5
Nkondwe Tanz. 123 D4
Nkongsamba Cameroon 120 D4
N'Koulal, Tizi pass Alg. 67 I5
Nkululeko S. Africa 125 H6
Nkurenkuru Namibia 123 B5
Nkwenkwezi S. Africa 125 H7
Noakhali Bangl. 105 G5
Noatak AK U.S.A. 148 G2
Noatak r. AK U.S.A. 148 G2
Noatak National Preserve nature res. AK U.S.A. 148 H1
Nobber Ireland 61 F4
Nobeoka Japan 91 C6
Noblesville IN U.S.A. 164 B3
Noboribetsu Japan 90 F4
Noccundra Australia 137 C5
Nochistlán Mex. 166 E4
Nochixtlán Mex. 167 F5
Nockatunga Australia 137 C5
Nocona TX U.S.A. 161 D5
Noda Japan 93 F3
Nodagawa Japan 92 B3
Noel Kempff Mercado, Parque Nacional nat. park Bol. 176 F6
Noelville Canada 152 E5
Nogales Mex. 166 C2
Nogales AZ U.S.A. 157 F7
Nōgata Japan 91 C6
Nogent-le-Rotrou France 66 E2
Nogent-sur-Oise France 62 C5
Nogi Japan 93 F2
Noginsk Russia 52 H5
Nogliki Russia 90 F2
Nogoa r. Australia 136 E4
Nōgōhaku-san mt. Japan 92 C3
Nogon Toli China 94 F4
Noguchigorō-dake mt. Japan 92 D2
Nohalal Mex. 167 H5
Nohar India 104 C3
Noheji Japan 90 F4
Nohfelden Germany 62 H5
Nohoit China 94 C4
Noida India 104 D3
Noirmoutier, Île de i. France 66 C3
Noirmoutier-en-l'Île France 66 C3
Noisseville France 62 G5
Nojima-zaki c. Japan 93 F4
Nojiri-ko l. Japan 93 E2
Nokhowch, Kūh-e mt. Iran 111 F5
Nōkis Uzbek. see Nukus
Nok Kundi Pak. 111 F4
Nokomis Canada 151 J5
Nokomis Lake Canada 151 K3
Nokou Chad 121 E3
Nokrek Peak India 105 G4
Nola Cent. Afr. Rep. 122 B3
Nolin River Lake KY U.S.A. 164 B5
Nolinsk Russia 52 K4
No Mans Land i. MA U.S.A. 165 J3
Nome AK U.S.A. 148 F2
Nome, Cape AK U.S.A. 148 F2
Nomgon Mongolia 94 F3
Nomhon China 94 D4
Nomhon He r. China 94 C4
Nomi Japan 92 C2
Nomoi Islands Micronesia see Mortlock Islands
Nomonde S. Africa 125 H6
Nōmrōg Mongolia 94 D1
Nomto Russia 94 F1
Nomugi-tōge pass Japan 92 D2
Nomzha Russia 52 I4
Nonacho Lake Canada 151 I2
Nondalton AK U.S.A. 148 I4
Nondweni S. Africa 125 J5
Nong'an China 90 B3
Nonghui China see Guang'an
Nong Khai Thai. 86 C3
Nongoma S. Africa 125 J4
Nongstoin India 105 G4
Nonidas Namibia 124 B2
Nonni r. China see Nen Jiang
Nonning Australia 137 B7
Nonnweiler Germany 62 G5
Nonoava Mex. 166 D3
Nonoichi Japan 92 C2
Nonouti atoll Kiribati 133 H2
Nonthaburi Thai. 87 C4
Nonvianuk Lake AK U.S.A. 148 I4
Nonzwakazi S. Africa 124 G6
Noolyeanna Lake salt flat Australia 137 B5
Noondie, Lake salt flat Australia 135 B7
Noonkanbah Australia 134 D4
Noonthorangee Range hills Australia 137 C6
Noorama Creek watercourse Australia 138 B1
Noordbeveland i. Neth. 62 D3
Noorderhaaks i. Neth. 62 E2
Noordoost Polder Neth. 62 F2
Noordwijk Neth. 62 E2
Noorvik AK U.S.A. 148 G2
Nootka Island Canada 150 E5
Nora r. Russia 90 C2
Norak Tajik. 111 H2
Norak, Obanbori resr Tajik. 111 H2
Norala Mindanao Phil. 82 D5
Noranda Canada 152 F4
Nor-Bayazet Armenia see Gavarr
Norberg Sweden 55 I6
Norcang China 99 D7
Nord Greenland see Station Nord
Nord, Canal du France 62 D4
Nordaustlandet i. Svalbard 76 D2
Nordegg Canada 150 G4
Norden Germany 63 H1
Nordenshel'da, Arkhipelag is Russia 76 K2
Nordenskjold Archipelago is Russia see Nordenshel'da, Arkhipelag
Norderney Germany 63 H1
Norderstedt Germany 63 K1
Nordfjordeid Norway 54 D6
Nordfold Norway 54 I3
Nordfriesische Inseln Germany see North Frisian Islands
Nordhausen Germany 63 K3
Nordholz Germany 63 I1
Nordhorn Germany 62 H2
Nordkapp c. Norway see North Cape
Nordkinnhalvøya i. Norway 54 O1
Nordkjosbotn Norway 54 K2
Nordli Norway 54 H4
Nördlingen Germany 63 K6
Nordmaling Sweden 54 K5
Nord- og Østgrønland, Nationalparken i nat. park Greenland 147 O2

▶Nordostrundingen c. Greenland 189 I1
Most easterly point of North America.

Nord-Ostsee-Kanal Germany see Kiel Canal
Norðoyar i. Faroe Is 50 E3
Nord-Pas-de-Calais admin. reg. France 62 C4
Nord-Pas de Calais Mining Basin tourist site France 62 D4
Nordpfälzer Bergland reg. Germany 63 H5
Nordre Strømfjord inlet Greenland see Nassuttooq
Nordrhein-Westfalen land Germany 63 H3
Nordvik Russia 77 M2
Nore r. Ireland 61 F5
Nore, Pic de mt. France 66 F5
Noreg country Europe see Norway
Norfolk NE U.S.A. 160 D3
Norfolk NY U.S.A. 165 H1
Norfolk VA U.S.A. 165 G5

▶Norfolk Island terr. S. Pacific Ocean 133 G4
Australian External Territory.

Norfolk Island Ridge sea feature Tasman Sea 186 H7
Norfork Lake AR U.S.A. 161 E4
Norg Neth. 62 G1
Norge country Europe see Norway
Norheimsund Norway 55 E6
Norikura-dake vol. Japan 92 D2
Noril'sk Russia 76 J3
Norkyung China 99 E7
Norland Canada 165 F1
Norma Co l. China 99 E6
Norman OK U.S.A. 161 D5
Norman, Lake resr NC U.S.A. 162 D5
Normanby Island P.N.G. 136 E1
Normandes, Îles is English Chan. see Channel Islands
Normandia Brazil 177 G3
Normandie reg. France see Normandy
Normandie, Collines de hills France 66 D2
Normandy reg. France 66 D2
Normanton Australia 136 C3
Norman Wells Canada 149 P2
Norogachic Mex. 166 D3
Norovlin Mongolia 95 G1
Norquay Canada 151 K5
Ñorquinco Arg. 178 B6
Norra Kvarken strait Fin./Sweden 54 L5
Norra Storfjället mts Sweden 54 I4
Norrent-Fontes France 62 C4
Norris Lake TN U.S.A. 164 D5
Norristown PA U.S.A. 165 H3
Norrköping Sweden 55 J7
Norrtälje Sweden 55 K7
Norseman Australia 135 C8
Norsjö Sweden 54 K4
Norsk Russia 90 C1
Norsup Vanuatu 133 G3
Norte, Punta pt Arg. 178 E5
Norte, Serra do hills Brazil 177 G6
Nortelândia Brazil 177 G6
Nörten-Hardenberg Germany 63 J3
North, Cape Antarctica 188 H2
North, Cape Canada 153 J5
Northallerton U.K. 58 F4
Northam Australia 135 B7
Northampton Australia 132 B4
Northampton U.K. 59 G6
Northampton MA U.S.A. 165 I2
Northampton PA U.S.A. 165 H3
North Andaman i. India 87 A4
North Anna r. VA U.S.A. 165 G5
North Arm b. Canada 150 H2
North Atlantic Ocean Atlantic Ocean 155 O4
North Augusta SC U.S.A. 163 D5
North Aulatsivik Island Canada 153 J2
North Australian Basin sea feature Indian Ocean 185 P6
North Balabac Strait Phil. 82 B4
North Baltimore OH U.S.A. 164 D3
North Battleford Canada 151 I4
North Bay Canada 152 F5
North Belcher Islands Canada 152 F2
North Berwick U.K. 60 G4
North Berwick ME U.S.A. 165 J2
North Borneo state Malaysia see Sabah
North Bourke Australia 138 B3
North Branch MN U.S.A. 160 E2
North Caicos i. Turks and Caicos Is 163 G8
North Canton OH U.S.A. 164 E3
North Cape Canada 153 I5
North Cape Norway 54 N1
North Cape N.Z. 139 D2
North Cape AK U.S.A. 148 [inset] D5
North Caribou Lake Canada 151 N4
North Carolina state U.S.A. 162 E4
North Cascades National Park WA U.S.A. 156 C2
North Channel lake channel Canada 152 E5
North Channel U.K. 61 G2
North Charleston SC U.S.A. 163 E5
North Chicago IL U.S.A. 164 B2
North China Plain plain China see Huabei Pingyuan
Northcliffe Glacier Antarctica 188 F2
North Collins NY U.S.A. 165 F2
North Concho r. TX U.S.A. 161 C6
North Conway NH U.S.A. 165 J1
North Dakota state U.S.A. 160 C2
North Downs hills U.K. 59 G7
North East PA U.S.A. 164 F2
Northeast Cape AK U.S.A. 148 E3
Northeast Foreland c. Greenland see Nordostrundingen
North-East Frontier Agency state India see Arunachal Pradesh
Northeast Pacific Basin sea feature N. Pacific Ocean 187 J4
Northeast Point Bahamas 163 F8
Northeast Providence Channel Bahamas 163 E7
North Edwards CA U.S.A. 158 E4
Northeim Germany 63 J3
North Entrance sea chan. Palau 82 [inset]
Northern prov. S. Africa see Limpopo
Northern Areas admin. div. Pak. see Gilgit-Baltistan
Northern Cape prov. S. Africa 124 D5
Northern Cyprus disp. terr. Asia 107 A2
Northern Donets r. Russia/Ukr. 53 I7 also known as Northern Donets, Sivers'kyy Donets'
Northern Dvina r. Russia see Severnaya Dvina
Northern Indian Lake Canada 151 L3
Northern Ireland prov. U.K. 61 F3
Northern Lau Group is Fiji 133 I3
Northern Light Lake Canada 152 C4

▶Northern Mariana Islands terr. N. Pacific Ocean 81 K3
United States Commonwealth.

Northern Rhodesia country Africa see Zambia
Northern Sporades is Greece see Voreies Sporades
Northern Territory admin. div. Australia 132 D3
Northern Transvaal prov. S. Africa see Limpopo
North Esk r. U.K. 60 G4
Northfield MN U.S.A. 160 E2
Northfield VT U.S.A. 165 I1
North Foreland c. U.K. 59 I7
North Fork CA U.S.A. 158 D3
North Fork Pass Canada 149 M2
North French r. Canada 152 E4
North Frisian Islands Germany 57 L3
North Geomagnetic Pole (2015) Arctic Ocean 147 K1
North Grimston U.K. 58 G4
North Haven CT U.S.A. 165 I3
North Head hd N.Z. 139 E3
North Henik Lake Canada 151 L2
North Hero VT U.S.A. 165 I1
North Horr Kenya 122 D3

▶North Island N.Z. 139 D4
3rd largest island in Oceania.

North Island Phil. 82 C1
North Islet reef Phil. 82 C4
North Jadito Canyon gorge AZ U.S.A. 159 H4
North Judson IN U.S.A. 164 B3
North Kingsville OH U.S.A. 164 E3
North Knife r. Canada 151 M3
North Knife Lake Canada 151 L3
North Korea country Asia 91 B5
North Lakhimpur India 105 H4
North Las Vegas NV U.S.A. 159 F3
North Little Rock AR U.S.A. 161 E5
North Loup r. NE U.S.A. 160 D3
North Luangwa National Park Zambia 123 D5
North Magnetic Pole (2015) Canada 189 B1
North Malosmadulu Atoll Maldives see Maalhosmadulu Uthuruburi
North Mam Peak CO U.S.A. 159 J2
North Muskegon MI U.S.A. 164 B2
North Palisade mt. CA U.S.A. 158 D3
North Perry OH U.S.A. 164 E3
North Platte NE U.S.A. 160 C3
North Platte r. NE U.S.A. 160 C3
North Pole Arctic Ocean 189 I1
North Pole AK U.S.A. 149 K2
North Port FL U.S.A. 163 D7
North Reef Island India 87 A4
North Rhine-Westphalia land Germany see Nordrhein-Westfalen
North Rim AZ U.S.A. 159 G3
North Rona i. U.K. see Rona
North Ronaldsay i. U.K. 60 G1
North Ronaldsay Firth sea chan. U.K. 60 G1
North Saskatchewan r. Canada 151 J4
North Schell Peak NV U.S.A. 159 F2
North Sea Europe 56 H2
North Seal r. Canada 151 L3
North Sentinel Island India 87 A5
North Shields U.K. 58 F3
North Shoal Lake Canada 151 L5
North Shoshone Peak NV U.S.A. 158 E2
North Siberian Lowland Russia 76 L2
North Sinai governorate Egypt see Shamāl Sīnā'
North Slope plain AK U.S.A. 149 J1
North Somercotes U.K. 58 H5
North Spirit Lake Canada 151 M4
North Stradbroke Island Australia 138 F1
North Sunderland U.K. 58 F3
North Syracuse NY U.S.A. 165 G2
North Taranaki Bight b. N.Z. 139 E4
North Terre Haute IN U.S.A. 164 B4
Northton U.K. 60 B3
North Tonawanda NY U.S.A. 165 F2
North Trap reef N.Z. 139 A8
North Troy VT U.S.A. 165 I1
North Tyne r. U.K. 58 E4
North Ubian i. Phil. 82 C5
North Uist i. U.K. 60 B3
Northumberland National Park U.K. 58 E3
Northumberland Strait Canada 153 I5
North Vancouver Canada 150 F5
North Verde i. Phil. 82 B4
North Vernon IN U.S.A. 164 C4
Northville NY U.S.A. 165 H2
North Wabasca Lake Canada 150 H3
North Walsham U.K. 59 I6
Northway Junction AK U.S.A. 149 L3
North West prov. S. Africa 124 G4
Northwest Atlantic Mid-Ocean Channel N. Atlantic Ocean 184 E1
North West Cape Australia 134 A5
Northwest Cape AK U.S.A. 148 E3
North West Frontier prov. Pak. see Khyber Pakhtunkhwa
North West Nelson Forest Park nat. park N.Z. see Kahurangi National Park
Northwest Pacific Basin sea feature N. Pacific Ocean 186 G3
Northwest Providence Channel Bahamas 163 E7
North West River Canada 153 K3
Northwest Territories admin. div. Canada 150 J2
Northwich U.K. 58 E5
North Wildwood NJ U.S.A. 165 H4
North Windham ME U.S.A. 165 J2
Northwind Ridge sea feature Arctic Ocean 189 B1
Northwood NH U.S.A. 165 J2
North York Canada 164 F2
North York Moors moorland U.K. 58 G4
North York Moors National Park U.K. 58 G4
Norton U.K. 58 G4
Norton KS U.S.A. 160 D4
Norton VA U.S.A. 164 D5
Norton VT U.S.A. 165 J1
Norton Bay AK U.S.A. 148 G2
Norton de Matos Angola see Balombo
Norton Shores MI U.S.A. 164 B2
Norton Sound sea chan. AK U.S.A. 148 G3
Nortonville KY U.S.A. 164 B5
Norutak Lake AK U.S.A. 148 I2
Norvegia, Cape Antarctica 188 B2
Norwalk CT U.S.A. 165 I3
Norwalk OH U.S.A. 164 D3
Norway country Europe 54 E6
Norway ME U.S.A. 165 J1
Norway House Canada 151 L4
Norwegian Basin sea feature N. Atlantic Ocean 184 H1
Norwegian Bay Canada 147 I2
Norwegian Sea N. Atlantic Ocean 189 H2
Norwich Canada 164 E2
Norwich U.K. 59 I6
Norwich CT U.S.A. 165 I3
Norwich NY U.S.A. 165 H2
Norwood CO U.S.A. 159 I2
Norwood NY U.S.A. 165 H1
Norwood OH U.S.A. 164 C4
Norzagaray Luzon Phil. 82 C3
Nosaka Japan 93 G3
Nose Japan 92 B4
Nosegawa Japan 92 B4
Nose Lake Canada 151 I1
Noshiro Japan 91 F4
Nosovaya Russia 52 L1
Noṣratābād Iran 111 E4
Noss, Isle of i. U.K. 60 [inset]
Nossebro Sweden 55 H7
Nossen Germany 63 N3
Nossob watercourse Africa 124 D2 also known as Nosop
Notakwanon r. Canada 153 J2
Notch Peak UT U.S.A. 159 G2
Noteć r. Poland 57 O4
Notikewin r. Canada 150 G3
Noto, Golfo di g. Sicily Italy 68 F6
Notodden Norway 55 F7
Notogawa Japan 92 C3
Noto-hantō pen. Japan 91 E5
Notojima Japan 92 D1
Noto-jima i. Japan 92 D1
Notre-Dame, Monts mts Canada 153 H5
Notre Dame Bay Canada 153 L4
Notre-Dame-de-Koartac Canada see Quaqtaq
Nottawasaga Bay Canada 164 E1
Nottaway r. Canada 152 F4
Nottingham U.K. 59 F6
Nottingham Island Canada 147 K3
Nottoway r. VA U.S.A. 165 G5
Nottuln Germany 63 H3
Notukeu Creek r. Canada 151 J5
Nou Japan 93 D1
Nouabalé-Ndoki, Parc National de nat. park Congo 122 B3
Nouâdhibou Mauritania 120 B2
Nouâdhibou, Râs c. Mauritania 120 B2

▶Nouakchott Mauritania 120 B3
Capital of Mauritania.

Nouâmghâr Mauritania 120 B3
Nouei Vietnam 86 D4

▶Nouméa New Caledonia 133 G4
Capital of New Caledonia.

Nouna Burkina Faso 120 C3
Noupoort S. Africa 124 G6
Nousu Fin. 54 P3
Nouveau-Brunswick prov. Canada see New Brunswick
Nouveau-Comptoir Canada see Wemindji
Nouvelle Calédonie i. S. Pacific Ocean 133 G4
Nouvelle Calédonie terr. S. Pacific Ocean see New Caledonia
Nouvelle-France, Cap de c. Canada 147 K3
Nouvelles Hébrides country S. Pacific Ocean see Vanuatu
Nova América Brazil 179 A1
Nova Chaves Angola see Muconda
Nova Freixa Moz. see Cuamba
Nova Friburgo Brazil 179 C3
Nova Gaia Angola see Cambundi-Catembo
Nova Goa India see Panaji
Nova Gradiška Croatia 68 G2
Nova Iguaçu Brazil 179 C3
Nova Kakhovka Ukr. 69 O1
Nova Lima Brazil 179 C2
Nova Lisboa Angola see Huambo
Novalukoml' Belarus 53 F5
Nova Mambone Moz. 123 D6
Nova Nabúri Moz. 123 D5
Nova Odesa Ukr. 53 F7
Nova Ponte Brazil 179 B2
Nova Ponte, Represa resr Brazil 179 B2
Novara Italy 68 C2
Nova Roma Brazil 179 B1
Nova Scotia prov. Canada 153 I6
Novato CA U.S.A. 158 B2
Nova Trento Brazil 179 A4
Nova Venécia Brazil 179 C2
Nova Xavantina Brazil 177 H6
Novaya Kakhovka Ukr. see Nova Kakhovka
Novaya Ladoga Russia 52 G3
Novaya Lyalya Russia 51 S4
Novaya Matsesta Russia 113 E2
Novaya Odessa Ukr. see Nova Odesa
Novaya Sibir', Ostrov i. Russia 77 P2
Novaya Zemlya is Russia 76 G2
Nova Zagora Bulg. 69 L3
Novelda Spain 67 F4
Nové Zámky Slovakia 57 Q7
Novgorod Russia see Velikiy Novgorod
Novgorod-Severskiy Ukr. see Novhorod-Sivers'kyy
Novgorod-Volynskiy Ukr. see Novohrad-Volyns'kyy
Novhorod-Sivers'kyy Ukr. 53 G6
Novi Grad Bos. & Herz. see Bosanski Novi
Novi Iskar Bulg. 69 J3
Novikovo Russia 90 F3
Novi Kritsim Bulg. see Stamboliyski
Novi Ligure Italy 68 C2
Novillero Mex. 166 D4
Novi Pazar Bulg. 69 L3
Novi Pazar Serbia 69 I3
Novi Sad Serbia 69 H2
Novo Acre Brazil 179 C1
Novoalekseyevka Kazakh. see Kobda
Novoaltaysk Russia 88 E2
Novoanninskiy Russia 53 I6
Novo Aripuanã Brazil 176 F5
Novoazovs'k Ukr. 53 H7
Novocheboksarsk Russia 52 J4
Novocherkassk Russia 53 I7
Novo Cruzeiro Brazil 179 C2
Novodugino Russia 52 G5
Novodvinsk Russia 52 I2
Novoekonomicheskoye Ukr. see Dymytrov
Novogeorgiyevka Russia 90 B2
Novogrudok Belarus see Navahrudak
Novo Hamburgo Brazil 179 A5
Novohradské hory mts Czech Rep. 57 O6
Novohrad-Volyns'kyy Ukr. 53 E6
Novokhopersk Russia 53 I6
Novokiyevskiy Uval Russia 90 C2
Novokubansk Russia 113 F1
Novokubanskiy Russia see Novokubansk
Novokuybyshevsk Russia 53 K5
Novokuznetsk Russia 88 F2
Novolazarevskaya research station Antarctica 188 C2
Novolukoml' Belarus see Novalukoml'
Novo mesto Slovenia 68 F2
Novomikhaylovskiy Russia 112 E1
Novomoskovsk Russia 53 H5
Novomoskovs'k Ukr. 53 G6
Novonikolayevsk Russia see Novosibirsk
Novonikolayevskiy Russia 53 I6
Novooleksiyivka Ukr. 53 G7
Novo Paraíso Brazil 176 F3
Novopashiyskiy Russia see Gornozavodsk
Novopavlovka Russia 95 G1
Novopokrovka Kazakh. 98 C2
Novopokrovka Russia 90 D3
Novopokrovskaya Russia 53 I7
Novopolotsk Belarus see Navapolatsk
Novopskov Ukr. 53 H6
Novo Redondo Angola see Sumbe
Novorossiya Russia 90 C1
Novorossiysk Russia 112 E1
Novorybnaya Russia 77 L2
Novorzhev Russia 52 F4
Novoselenginsk Russia 94 F1

Novoselovo Russia 88 G1
Novoselskoye Russia see Achkhoy-Martan
Novosel'ye Russia 55 P7
Novosergiyevka Russia 51 Q5
Novoshakhtinsk Russia 53 H7
Novosheshminsk Russia 52 K5
Novosibirsk Russia 76 J4
Novosibirskiye Ostrova is Russia see New Siberia Islands
Novosil' Russia 53 H5
Novosokol'niki Russia 52 F4
Novospasskoye Russia 53 J5
Novotroyits'ke Ukr. 53 G7
Novoukrainka Ukr. see Novoukrayinka
Novoukrayinka Ukr. 53 F6
Novoussuri (abandoned) Russia 90 E2
Novouzensk Russia 53 K6
Novovolyns'k Ukr. 53 E6
Novovoronezh Russia 53 H6
Novovoronezhskiy Russia see Novovoronezh
Novovoskresenovka Russia 90 B1
Novovoznesenovka Kyrg. 98 B4
Novoye Chaplino Russia 148 D2
Novozybkov Russia 53 F5
Nový Jičín Czech Rep. 57 P6
Novyy Afon Georgia see Akhali Atoni
Novyy Bor Russia 52 L2
Novyy Donbass Ukr. see Dymytrov
Novyye Petushki Russia see Petushki
Novyy Kholmogory Russia see Archangel
Novyy Margelan Uzbek. see Farg'ona
Novyy Nekouz Russia 52 H4
Novyy Oskol Russia 53 H6
Novyy Port Russia 76 I3
Novyy Urengoy Russia 76 I3
Novyy Urgal Russia 90 D2
Novyy Uzen' Kazakh. see Zhanaozen
Novyy Zay Russia see Zainsk
Now Iran 110 D4
Nowabganj Bangl. see Nawabganj
Nowata OK U.S.A. 161 E4
Nowdī Iran 110 C2
Nowgong India see Nagaon
Nowitna r. AK U.S.A. 148 I2
Nowitna National Wildlife Refuge nature res. AK U.S.A. 148 I2
Now Kharegan Iran 110 D2
Nowleye Lake Canada 151 K2
Nowogard Poland 57 O4
Noworadomsk Poland see Radomsko
Nowra Australia 138 E5
Nowrangapur India see Nabarangapur
Nowshera Pak. 111 I3
Nowyak Lake Canada 151 L2
Nowy Sącz Poland 57 R6
Nowy Targ Poland 57 R6
Now Zād Afgh. 111 G3
Noxen PA U.S.A. 165 G3
Noy, Xé r. Laos 86 D3
Noyabr'sk Russia 76 I3
Noyes Island AK U.S.A. 149 N5
Noyon France 62 C5
Noyon Mongolia 94 E3
Nozawaonsen Japan 93 E2
Nozizwe S. Africa 125 G6
Nqutu S. Africa 125 J5
Nsanje Malawi 123 D5
Nsombo Zambia 123 C5
Nsukka Nigeria 120 D4
Nsumbu National Park Zambia see Sumbu National Park
Ntabankulu S. Africa 125 I6
Ntambu Zambia 123 C5
Ntha S. Africa 125 H4
Ntoro, Kavo pt Greece 69 K5
Ntoum Gabon 122 A3
Ntungamo Uganda 122 D4
Nuanetsi Zimbabwe see Mwenezi
Nuangan Celebes Indon. 83 C2
Nu'aym reg. Oman 110 D6
Nuba Mountains Sudan 108 D7
Nubian Desert Sudan 108 D5
Nubra r. India 99 B6
Nüden Mongolia see Ulaanbadrah
Nueces r. TX U.S.A. 161 D7
Nueltin Lake Canada 151 L2
Nueva Arcadia Hond. 166 [inset] H6
Nueva Ciudad Guerrero Mex. 161 D7
Nueva Gerona Cuba 169 H4
Nueva Harberton Arg. 178 C8
Nueva Imperial Chile 178 B5
Nueva Loja Ecuador 176 C3
Nueva Ocotepeque Hond. 166 [inset] H6
Nueva Rosita Mex. 167 E3
Nueva San Salvador El Salvador see Santa Tecla
Nueva Villa de Padilla Mex. 161 D7
Nueve de Julio Arg. see 9 de Julio
Nuevitas Cuba 169 I4
Nuevo, Cayo i. Mex. 167 H4
Nuevo, Golfo g. Arg. 178 D6
Nuevo Casas Grandes Mex. 166 D2
Nuevo Ideal Mex. 166 D3
Nuevo Laredo Mex. 167 F3
Nuevo León Mex. 159 F5
Nuevo León state Mex. 161 D7
Nuevo Rocafuerte Ecuador 176 C4
Nuga Mongolia see Dzavhanmandal
Nugaal watercourse Somalia 122 E3
Nugaaleed, Dooxo valley Somalia 122 E3
Nugget Point N.Z. 139 B8
Nugur India 106 D2
Nuguria Islands P.N.G. 132 F2
Nuh, Ras pt Pak. 111 F5
Nuhaka N.Z. 139 F4
Nui atoll Tuvalu 133 H2
Nui Con Voi r. Vietnam see Red
Nuiqsut AK U.S.A. 149 J1
Nui Thanh Vietnam 86 E4
Nujiang China 96 C2
Nu Jiang r. China/Myanmar see Salween
Nukata Japan 92 D4
Nukey Bluff hill Australia 137 A7
Nukha Azer. see Şäki

▶Nuku'alofa Tonga 133 I4
Capital of Tonga.

Nukufetau atoll Tuvalu 133 H2
Nukuhiva i. Fr. Polynesia see Nuku Hiva
Nuku Hiva i. Fr. Polynesia 187 K6
Nukuhu P.N.G. 81 L8
Nukulaelae atoll Tuvalu 133 H2
Nukulailai atoll Tuvalu see Nukulaelae
Nukumanu Islands P.N.G. 133 F2
Nukunau i. Kiribati see Nikunau
Nukunono atoll Tokelau see Nukunonu
Nukunonu atoll Tokelau 133 I2
Nukus Uzbek. 102 A3
Nulato AK U.S.A. 148 H2
Nullagine Australia 134 C5
Nullarbor Australia 135 E7
Nullarbor National Park Australia 135 E7
Nullarbor Plain Australia 135 E7
Nullarbor Regional Reserve park Australia 135 E7
Nuluarniavik, Lac l. Canada 152 F2
Nulu'erhu Shan mts China 95 I3
Num i. Indon. 81 J7
Num Nepal 99 D8
Numalla, Lake salt flat Australia 138 B2
Numan Nigeria 122 B3
Numanuma P.N.G. 136 E1
Numata Japan 93 F2
Numazu Japan 93 E3
Numbulwar Australia 136 A2
Numedal valley Norway 55 F6
Numfoor i. Indon. 81 I7
Numin He r. China 90 B3
Numurkah Australia 138 B6
Nunachuak AK U.S.A. 148 H4
Nunaksaluk Island Canada 153 J3
Nunakuluut i. Greenland 147 N3
Nunam Iqua AK U.S.A. 148 F3
Nunap Isua c. Greenland see Farewell, Cape
Nunapitchuk AK U.S.A. 148 G3
Nunarsuit i. Greenland see Nunakuluut
Nunavakpak Lake AK U.S.A. 148 G3
Nunavaugaluk, Lake AK U.S.A. 148 H4
Nunavik reg. Canada 152 G1
Nunavut admin. div. Canada 151 L2
Nunda NY U.S.A. 165 G2
Nundle Australia 138 E3
Nuneaton U.K. 59 F6
Nungba India 105 H4
Nungesser Lake Canada 151 M5
Nungnain Sum China 95 I2
Nunivak Island AK U.S.A. 148 F4
Nunkapasi India 106 E1
Nunkun mt. India 104 D2
Nunligran Russia 148 D2
Nuñomoral Spain 67 C3
Nunspeet Neth. 62 F2
Nunukan i. Indon. 85 G2
Nunyamo Russia 148 E2
Nuojiang China see Tongjiang
Nuomin He r. China 95 K1
Nuoro Sardinia Italy 68 C4
Nupani i. Solomon Is 133 G3
Nuqrah Saudi Arabia 108 F4
Nur China 99 C5
Nūr Iran 110 C2
Nura Almatinskaya Oblast' Kazakh. 98 B4
Nura Karagandinskaya Oblast' Kazakh. 98 A2
Nura r. Kazakh. 98 A2
Nūrābād Iran 110 C4
Nurakita i. Tuvalu see Niulakita
Nurata Uzbek. see Nurota
Nur Dağları mts Turkey 107 B1
Nurek Tajik. see Norak
Nurek Reservoir Tajik. see Norak, Obanbori
Nurekskoye Vodokhranilishche resr Tajik. see Norak, Obanbori
Nuremberg Germany 63 L5
Nuri Mex. 166 C2
Nuri, Teluk b. Indon. 85 E3
Nūristān reg. 111 H3
Nurla India 104 D2
Nurlat Russia 53 K5
Nurmes Fin. 54 P5
Nurmo Fin. 54 M5
Nürnberg Germany see Nuremberg
Nurota Uzbek. 102 C3
Nurri, Mount hill Australia 138 C3
Nūr Rūd r. Iran 110 D2
Nur Turu China 99 F5
Nusa Kambangan, Cagar Alam nature res. Java Indon. 85 E4
Nusa Laut i. Moluccas Indon. 83 D3
Nusa Tenggara Barat prov. Indon. 85 G5
Nusawulan Indon. 81 I7
Nusaybin Turkey 113 F3
Nuşayrīyah, Jabal an mts Syria 107 C2
Nusela, Kepulauan is Papua Indon. 83 D3
Nushagak r. AK U.S.A. 148 H4
Nushagak Bay AK U.S.A. 148 H4
Nushagak Peninsula AK U.S.A. 148 H4
Nu Shan mts China 96 C3
Nu-shima i. Japan 92 A4
Nushki Pak. 111 G4
Nusratiye Turkey 107 D1
Nutak Canada 153 J2
Nutarawit Lake Canada 151 L2
Nutauge, Laguna lag. Russia 148 C2
Nutepel'men Russia 148 D2
Nutrioso AZ U.S.A. 159 I5
Nuttal Pak. 111 H4
Nutwood Downs Australia 134 F3
Nutzotin Mountains AK U.S.A. 149 K2

▶Nuuk Greenland 147 M3
Capital of Greenland.

Nuupas Fin. 54 O3
Nuussuaq Greenland 147 M2
Nuussuaq pen. Greenland 147 M2
Nuwaybi' al Muzayyinah Egypt 112 D5
Nuweiba el Muzeina Egypt see Nuwaybi' al Muzayyinah
Nuwerus S. Africa 124 D6
Nuweveldberge mts S. Africa 124 E7
Nuwuk AK U.S.A. 148 H1
Nuyakuk r. AK U.S.A. 148 H4
Nuyakuk Lake AK U.S.A. 148 H4
Nuyts, Point Australia 135 B8
Nuyts Archipelago is Australia 135 F8
Nuzvid India 106 D2
Nwanedi Nature Reserve S. Africa 125 J2
Nxai Pan National Park Botswana 123 C5
Nyaän, Bukit hill Indon. 85 F2
Nyac AK U.S.A. 148 H3
Nyagan' Russia 51 T3
Nyagquka China see Yajiang
Nyagrong China see Xinlong
Nyahururu Kenya 122 D3
Nyah West Australia 138 A5
Nyaimai China 99 F7
Nyainqêntanglha Feng mt. China 99 E7
Nyainqêntanglha Shan mts China 99 E7
Nyainrong China 99 F6
Nyåker Sweden 54 K5
Nyakh Russia see Nyagan'
Nyaksimvol' Russia 51 S3
Nyala Sudan 121 F3
Nyalam China see Congdü
Nyalikungu Tanz. see Maswa
Nyamandhlovu Zimbabwe 123 C5
Nyamtumbo Tanz. 123 D5
Nyande Zimbabwe see Masvingo
Nyandoma Russia 52 I3
Nyandomskaya Vozvyshennost' hills Russia 52 H3
Nyanga Congo 122 B4
Nyanga Zimbabwe 123 D5
Nyangani mt. Zimbabwe 123 D5
Nyangbo China 99 F7
Nyang Qu r. China 99 F7
Nyapa, Gunung mt. Indon. 85 G2
Nyar r. India 99 B7
Nyarling r. Canada 150 H2

▶Nyasa, Lake Africa 123 D4
3rd largest lake in Africa and 9th in the world.

Nyasaland country Africa see Malawi
Nyashabozh Russia 52 L2
Nyasvizh Belarus 55 O10
Nyaungdon Myanmar see Yandoon
Nyaunglebin Myanmar 86 B3
Nyborg Denmark 55 G9
Nyborg Norway 54 P1
Nybro Sweden 55 I8
Nyeboe Land reg. Greenland 147 M1
Nyêmo China 99 E7
Nyenchen Tanglha Range mts China see Nyainqêntanglha Shan
Nyeri Kenya 122 D4
Nygchigen, Mys c. Russia 148 D2
Nyi, Co l. China 99 D6
Nyika National Park Zambia 123 D5
Nyima China 99 F7
Nyimba Zambia 123 D5
Nyingchi Xizang China 99 F7
Nyingchi Xizang China 99 F7
Nyingzhong China 99 E7
Nyinma China see Maqu
Nyíregyháza Hungary 53 D7
Nyiru, Mount Kenya 122 D3
Nykarleby Fin. 54 M5
Nykøbing Falster Denmark 55 G9
Nykøbing Sjælland Denmark 55 G9
Nyköping Sweden 55 J7
Nyland Sweden 54 J5
Nylsvley nature res. S. Africa 125 I3
Nymagee Australia 138 C4
Nymboida National Park Australia 138 F2
Nynäshamn Sweden 55 J7
Nyngan Australia 138 C3
Nyogzê China 99 C7
Nyohō-san mt. Japan 93 F2
Nyoman r. Belarus/Lith. 55 M10
also known as Neman or Nemunas
Nyon Switz. 66 H3
Nyons France 66 G4
Nýřany Czech Rep. 63 N5
Nyrob Russia 51 R3
Nysa Poland 57 P5
Nysh Russia 90 F2
Nyssa OR U.S.A. 156 D4
Nystad Fin. see Uusikaupunki
Nytva Russia 51 R4
Nyūgasa-yama mt. Japan 93 E3
Nyūkawa Japan 92 D2
Nyuksenitsa Russia 52 J3
Nyunzu Dem. Rep. Congo 123 C4
Nyurba Russia 77 M3
Nyūzen Japan 92 D2
Nyyskiy Zaliv lag. Russia 90 F1
Nzambi Congo 122 B4
Nzega Tanz. 123 D4
Nzérékoré Guinea 120 C4
N'zeto Angola 123 B4

O

Oahe, Lake SD U.S.A. 160 C2
O'ahu i. HI U.S.A. 157 [inset]
Oaitupu i. Tuvalu see Vaitupu
Oak Bluffs MA U.S.A. 165 J3
Oak City UT U.S.A. 159 G2
Oak Creek CO U.S.A. 159 J1
Oakdale LA U.S.A. 161 E6
Oakes ND U.S.A. 160 D2
Oakey Australia 138 E1
Oak Grove KY U.S.A. 164 B5
Oak Grove LA U.S.A. 161 F5
Oak Grove MI U.S.A. 164 C1
Oakham U.K. 59 G6
Oak Harbor OH U.S.A. 164 D3
Oak Hill OH U.S.A. 164 D4
Oak Hill WV U.S.A. 164 E5
Oakhurst CA U.S.A. 158 D3
Oak Lake Canada 151 K5
Oakland CA U.S.A. 158 B3
Oakland MD U.S.A. 164 F4
Oakland ME U.S.A. 165 K1
Oakland NE U.S.A. 160 D3
Oakland OR U.S.A. 156 C4
Oakland airport CA U.S.A. 158 B3
Oakland City IN U.S.A. 164 B4
Oaklands Australia 138 C5
Oak Lawn IL U.S.A. 164 B3
Oakley KS U.S.A. 160 C4
Oakover r. Australia 134 C5
Oak Park IL U.S.A. 164 B3
Oak Park MI U.S.A. 164 C2
Oak Park Reservoir UT U.S.A. 159 I1
Oakridge OR U.S.A. 156 C4
Oak Ridge TN U.S.A. 162 C4
Oakvale Australia 137 C7
Oak View CA U.S.A. 158 D4
Oakville Canada 164 F2
Oakwood OH U.S.A. 164 C3
Oakwood TN U.S.A. 164 B5
Oamaru N.Z. 139 C7
Ōamishirasato Japan 93 G3
Ōarai Japan 93 G2
Oaro N.Z. 139 D6
Ōashi-gawa r. Japan 93 F2
Oasis CA U.S.A. 158 E3
Oasis NV U.S.A. 156 E4
Oates Coast reg. Antarctica see Oates Land
Oates Land reg. Antarctica 188 H2
Oaxaca Mex. 168 E5
Oaxaca state Mex. 167 F5
Oaxaca de Juárez Mex. see Oaxaca

▶Ob' r. Russia 88 E2
Part of the Ob'-Irtysh, the 2nd longest river in Asia.

Ob, Gulf of sea chan. Russia see Obskaya Guba
Oba Canada 152 D4
Oba r. Kazakh. 98 C2
Oba i. Vanuatu see Aoba
Obako-dake mt. Japan 92 B4
Obala Cameroon 120 E4
Obama Japan 92 B3
Obama-wan b. Japan 92 B3
Oban U.K. 60 D4
Obara Japan 92 D3
O Barco Spain 67 C2
Obata Japan 92 C4
Obbia Somalia see Hobyo
Obdorsk Russia see Salekhard
Óbecse Serbia see Bečej
Obed Canada 150 G4
Ōbêh Afgh. 111 F3
Oberaula Germany 63 J4
Oberdorla Germany 63 K3
Oberhausen Germany 62 G3
Oberlin KS U.S.A. 160 C4
Oberlin LA U.S.A. 161 E6
Oberlin OH U.S.A. 164 D3
Obermoschel Germany 63 H5
Oberon Australia 138 D4
Oberpfälzer Wald mts Germany 63 M5
Obersinn Germany 63 J4
Oberthulba Germany 63 J4
Obertshausen Germany 63 I4
Oberwälder Land reg. Germany 63 J3
Obi i. Moluccas Indon. 83 C3
Obi, Kepulauan is Moluccas Indon. 83 C3
Obi, Selat sea chan. Moluccas Indon. 83 C3
Óbidos Brazil 177 G4
Obihiro Japan 90 F4
Obilatu i. Moluccas Indon. 83 C3
Obil'noye Russia 53 J7

▶Ob'-Irtysh r. Russia 76 H3
2nd longest river in Asia and 5th in the world.

Obitsu-gawa r. Japan 93 F3
Obluch'ye Russia 90 C2
Obninsk Russia 53 H5
Obo Cent. Afr. Rep. 122 C3
Obo China 94 E4
Obock Djibouti 108 F7
Ŏbŏk N. Korea 90 C4
Obokote Dem. Rep. Congo 122 C4
Obo Liang China 98 F5
Obong, Gunung mt. Malaysia 85 F1
Obouya Congo 122 B4
Oboyan' Russia 53 H6
Obozerskiy Russia 52 I3
Obregón, Presa resr Mex. 166 C3
Obrenovac Serbia 69 I2
Obruk Turkey 112 D3
Observatory Hill hill Australia 135 F7
Obshchiy Syrt hills Russia 51 Q5
Obskaya Guba sea chan. Russia 76 I3
Ōbu Japan 92 C3
Obuasi Ghana 120 C4
Obuse Japan 93 E2
Ob''yachevo Russia 52 K3
Ocala FL U.S.A. 163 D6
Ocampo Chihuahua Mex. 166 C2
Ocampo Coahuila Mex. 166 E3
Ocaña Col. 176 D2
Ocaña Spain 67 E4
Occidental, Cordillera mts Chile 176 E7
Occidental, Cordillera mts Col. 176 C3
Occidental, Cordillera mts Peru 176 D7
Oceana WV U.S.A. 164 E5
Ocean Cape AK U.S.A. 149 M4
Ocean Cay i. Bahamas 163 E7
Ocean City MD U.S.A. 165 H4
Ocean City NJ U.S.A. 165 H4
Ocean Falls Canada 150 E4
Ocean Island Kiribati see Banaba
Ocean Island atoll HI U.S.A. see Kure Atoll
Oceanside CA U.S.A. 158 E5
Ocean Springs MS U.S.A. 161 F6
Ochakiv Ukr. 69 N1
Ochamchire Georgia 113 F2
Ocher Russia 51 Q4
Ochiishi-misaki pt Japan 90 G4
Ochil Hills U.K. 60 F4
Ochito r. Pak. 111 G5
Ochrida, Lake Albania/Macedonia see Ohrid, Lake
Ochsenfurt Germany 63 K5
Ochtrup Germany 63 H2
Ocilla GA U.S.A. 163 D6
Ockelbo Sweden 55 J6
Ocolaşul Mare, Vârful mt. Romania 69 K1
Oconomowoc WI U.S.A. 164 A2
Oconto WI U.S.A. 164 B1
Ocoroni Mex. 166 C3
Ocos Guat. 167 G6
Ocosingo Mex. 167 G5
Ocotal Nicaragua 166 [inset] I6
Ocotlán Mex. 167 F5
Ocozocoautla Mex. 167 G5
Octeville-sur-Mer France 59 H9
October Revolution Island Russia see Oktyabr'skoy Revolyutsii, Ostrov
Ocú Panama 166 [inset] J8
Ocussi enclave East Timor 134 D2
Ocussi-Ambeno enclave East Timor see Ocussi
Oda, Jebel mt. Sudan 108 E5
Ódáðahraun lava field Iceland 54 [inset 1]
Ŏdaejin N. Korea 90 C4
Odae-san National Park S. Korea 91 C5
Ōdai Japan 92 C4
Ōdaigahara-zan mt. Japan 92 C4
Odaira-tōge pass Japan 92 D3
Ōdate Japan 91 F4
Odawara Japan 93 F3
Odda Norway 55 E6
Odei r. Canada 151 L3
Odell IN U.S.A. 164 B3
Odem TX U.S.A. 161 D7
Odemira Port. 67 B5
Ödemiş Turkey 69 L5
Ödenburg Hungary see Sopron
Odense Denmark 55 G9
Odenwald reg. Germany 63 I5
Oder r. Germany 63 J3
also known as Odra (Poland)
Oderbucht b. Germany 57 O3
Oder-Havel-Kanal canal Germany 63 N2
Ödeshög Sweden 55 I7
Odessa Ukr. 69 N1
Odessa TX U.S.A. 161 C6
Odessa WA U.S.A. 156 D3
Odessus Bulg. see Varna
Odiel r. Spain 67 C5
Odienné Côte d'Ivoire 120 C4
Odintsovo Russia 52 H5
Odisha state India 106 E1
Ŏdŏngk Cambodia 87 D5
Odra r. Germany/Poland 57 Q6
also known as Oder (Germany)
Odzala-Kokoua, Parc National d' nat. park Congo 122 B3
Ōe Japan 92 B3
Oea Libya see Tripoli
Oé-Cusse enclave East Timor see Ocussi
Oecussi enclave East Timor see Ocussi
Oeiras Brazil 177 J5
Oekussi enclave East Timor see Ocussi
Oelsnitz/Vogtland Germany 63 M4
Oenkerk Neth. 62 F1
Oenpelli Australia 134 F3
Oesel i. Estonia see Hiiumaa
Oeufs, Lac des l. Canada 153 G3
Ōe-yama hill Japan 92 B3
Of Turkey 113 F2
O'Fallon r. MT U.S.A. 156 G3
Ofanto r. Italy 68 G4
Ofaqim Israel 107 B4
Offa Nigeria 120 D4
Offenbach am Main Germany 63 I4
Offenburg Germany 57 K6
Oga r. Indon. 85 F2
Oga Japan 91 E5
Oga-dake mt. Japan 93 F1
Ogadēn reg. Eth. 122 E3
Oga-hantō pen. Japan 91 E5
Ōgaki Japan 92 C3
Ogallala NE U.S.A. 160 C3
Ogan r. Indon. 84 D3
Ogano Japan 93 F2
Ogasa Japan 93 E4
Ogasawara-shotō is Japan see Bonin Islands
Ōga-tō mt. Japan 93 E2
Ogawa Ibaraki Japan 93 G2
Ogawa Ibaraki Japan 93 G2
Ogawa Nagano Japan 93 D2
Ogawa Saitama Japan 93 F2
Ogawa Tochigi Japan 93 G2
Ogbomosho Nigeria see Ogbomoso
Ogbomoso Nigeria 120 D4
Ogden IA U.S.A. 160 E3
Ogden UT U.S.A. 156 F4
Ogden, Mount Canada 149 N4
Ogdensburg NY U.S.A. 165 H1
Ogidaki Canada 152 D5
Ogilvie r. Canada 149 M2
Ogilvie Mountains Canada 149 L2
Ögiynuur Mongolia 94 E2
Oglala Pass sea chan. AK U.S.A. 148 [inset] B6
Oglethorpe, Mount GA U.S.A. 163 C5
Oglio r. Italy 68 D2
Oglongi Russia 90 E1
Ogmore Australia 136 E4
Ōgo Japan 93 F2
Ogoamas, Gunung mt. Indon. 83 B2
Ogōchi-damu dam Japan 93 F3
Ogodzha Russia 90 D1
Ogoja Nigeria 120 D4
Ogoki r. Canada 152 D4
Ogoki Lake Canada 160 G1
Ogoki Reservoir Canada 152 C4
Ogoron Russia 90 C1
Ogose Japan 93 F3
Ogosta r. Bulg. 69 J3
Ogre Latvia 55 N8
Ōguchi Japan 92 C3
Oguchi Japan 92 C2
Ogulin Croatia 68 F2
Ogurchinskiy, Ostrov i. Turkm. see Ogurjaly Adasy
Ogurjaly Adasy i. Turkm. 110 D2
Oğuzeli Turkey 107 C1
Ohai N.Z. 139 A7
Ohakune N.Z. 139 E4
Ohanet Alg. 120 D2
Ōhara Japan see Isumi
Ōhata Japan 90 F4
Ohcejohka Fin. see Utsjoki
O'Higgins, Lago l. Chile 178 B7
Ohio r. Ohio/West Virginia U.S.A. 164 A5
Ohio state U.S.A. 164 D3
Ōhira Japan 93 F2
Ōhito Japan 93 E3
Ohm r. Germany 63 I4
Ohogamiut AK U.S.A. 148 G3
Ohrdruf Germany 63 K4
Ohře r. Czech Rep. 63 N4
Ohre r. Germany 63 L2
Ohrid Macedonia 69 I4
Ohrid, Lake Albania/Macedonia 69 I4
Ohridsko Ezero l. Albania/Macedonia see Ohrid, Lake
Ohrigstad S. Africa 125 J3
Öhringen Germany 63 J5
Ohrit, Liqeni i l. Albania/Macedonia see Ohrid, Lake
Ohura N.Z. 139 E4
Ōi Japan 92 B3
Oich r. U.K. 60 E3
Oiga China 99 F7
Ōigawa Japan 93 E4
Ōi-gawa r. Japan 92 B3
Ōi-gawa r. Japan 93 E4
Oignies France 62 C4
Oil City PA U.S.A. 164 F3
Oise r. France 62 C6
Oise à l'Aisne, Canal de l' France 62 D5
Ōiso Japan 93 F3
Ōita Japan 91 C6
Oiti mt. Greece 69 J5
Ōizumi Japan 93 E3
Oizuruga-dake mt. Japan 92 C2
Ojai CA U.S.A. 158 D4
Ojalava i. Samoa see 'Upolu
Ōji Japan 92 B4
Ojinaga Mex. 166 D2
Ojitlán Mex. 167 F5
Ojiya Japan 91 E5
Ojo Caliente NM U.S.A. 157 G5
Ojo de Laguna Mex. 166 D2
Ojo de Liebre, Lago b. Mex. 166 B3

▶Ojos del Salado, Nevado mt. Arg./Chile 178 C3
2nd highest mountain in South America.

Ojuelos de Jalisco Mex. 167 E4
Oka r. Russia 53 I4
Oka r. Russia 88 I1
Okabe Saitama Japan 93 F2
Okabe Shizuoka Japan 93 E4
Okahandja Namibia 124 C1
Okahukura N.Z. 139 E4
Okakarara Namibia 123 B6
Okak Islands Canada 153 J2
Okanagan Lake Canada 150 G5
Okanda Sri Lanka 106 D5
Okano r. Gabon 122 B4
Okanogan WA U.S.A. 156 D2
Okanogan r. WA U.S.A. 156 D2
Okapi, Parc National de la nat. park Dem. Rep. Congo 122 C3
Okara Pak. 111 I4
Okarem Turkm. see Ekerem
Okataina vol. N.Z. see Tarawera, Mount
Okaukuejo Namibia 123 B5
Okavango r. Africa 123 C5

▶Okavango Delta swamp Botswana 123 C5
Largest oasis in the world.

Okavango Swamps Botswana see Okavango Delta
Okaya Japan 93 E2
Okayama Japan 91 D6
Okazaki Japan 92 D4
Okeechobee FL U.S.A. 163 D7
Okeechobee, Lake FL U.S.A. 163 D7
Okeene OK U.S.A. 161 D4
Okefenokee Swamp GA U.S.A. 163 D6
Okegawa Japan 93 F2
Okehampton U.K. 59 C8
Okemah OK U.S.A. 161 D5
Oker r. Germany 63 K2
Okha India 104 B5
Okha Russia 90 F1
Okha Rann marsh India 104 B5
Okhotsk Russia 77 P4
Okhotsk, Sea of Japan/Russia 90 G3
Okhotskoye More sea Japan/Russia see Okhotsk, Sea of
Okhtyrka Ukr. 53 G6
Okinawa i. Japan 91 B8
Okinawa-guntō is Japan see Okinawa-shotō
Okinawa-shotō is Japan 91 B8
Okino-Daitō-jima i. Japan 89 O8
Okino-shima i. Japan 92 B4

Okino-Tori-shima i. Japan 89 P8
Oki-shotō is Japan 91 D5
Okkan Myanmar 86 A3
Oklahoma state U.S.A. 161 D5
▶Oklahoma City OK U.S.A. 161 D5
Capital of Oklahoma.
Okmok sea feature N. Pacific Ocean 148 E5
Okmulgee OK U.S.A. 161 D5
Okolona KY U.S.A. 164 C4
Okolona MS U.S.A. 161 F5
Okondja Gabon 122 B4
Okovskiy Les for. Russia 52 G5
Okoyo Congo 122 B4
Okpan, Gora hill Kazakh. 113 H1
Okpekty, Gora mt. Kazakh. 98 C3
Øksfjord Norway 54 M1
Oktemberyan Armenia see Armavir
Oktwin Myanmar 86 B3
Oktyabr' Kazakh. see Kandyagash
Oktyabr'sk Kazakh. see Kandyagash
Oktyabr'skiy Belarus see Aktsyabrski
Oktyabr'skiy Amurskaya Oblast' Russia 90 C1
Oktyabr'skiy Arkhangel'skaya Oblast' Russia 52 I3
Oktyabr'skiy Kamchatskiy Kray Russia 77 Q4
Oktyabr'skiy Respublika Bashkortostan Russia 51 Q5
Oktyabr'skiy Volgogradskaya Oblast' Russia 53 I7
Oktyabr'skoye Russia 51 T3
Oktyabr'skoy Revolyutsii, Ostrov i. Russia 77 K2
Okulovka Russia 52 G4
Oku-sangai-dake mt. Japan 92 D3
Okushiri-tō i. Japan 90 E4
Okusi enclave East Timor see Ocussi
Okuta Nigeria 120 D4
Okutadami-ko resr Japan 93 F1
Okutama Japan 93 F3
Okutama-ko l. Japan 93 F3
Okutango-hantō pen. Japan 92 B3
Okutone-ko resr Japan 93 F2
Ōkuwa Japan 92 D3
Okwa watercourse Botswana 124 G1
Ólafsvík Iceland 54 [inset 1]
Olakkur India 106 C3
Olancha CA U.S.A. 158 D3
Olancha Peak CA U.S.A. 158 D3
Olanchito Hond. 166 [inset] I6
Öland i. Sweden 55 J8
Olary Australia 137 C7
Olathe CO U.S.A. 159 J2
Olathe KS U.S.A. 160 E4
Olavarría Arg. 178 D5
Oława Poland 57 P5
Olbernhau Germany 63 N4
Olbia Sardinia Italy 68 C4
Old Bahama Channel Bahamas/Cuba 163 E8
Old Bastar India 106 D2
Oldcastle Ireland 61 E4
Old Cork Australia 136 C4
Old Crow Canada 149 M2
Old Crow r. Canada 149 M2
Oldeboorn Neth. see Aldeboarn
Oldenburg Germany 63 I1
Oldenburg in Holstein Germany 57 M3
Oldenzaal Neth. 62 G2
Olderdalen Norway 54 L2
Old Forge NY U.S.A. 165 H2
Old Gidgee Australia 135 B6
Oldham U.K. 58 E5
Old Harbor AK U.S.A. 148 I4
Old Head of Kinsale hd Ireland 61 D6
Old John Lake AK U.S.A. 149 K1
Oldman r. Canada 150 I5
Oldmeldrum U.K. 60 G3
Old Perlican Canada 153 L5
Old Rampart AK U.S.A. 149 L2
Old River CA U.S.A. 158 D4
Olds Canada 150 H5
Old Speck Mountain ME U.S.A. 165 J1
Old Station CA U.S.A. 158 C1
Old Wives Lake Canada 151 J5
Öldziyt Arhangay Mongolia see Erdenemandal
Öldziyt Arhangay Mongolia 94 E1
Öldziyt Bayanhongor Mongolia 94 E2
Öldziyt Dornogovĭ Mongolia see Sayhandulaan
Öldziyt Dundgovĭ Mongolia 94 F2
Olean NY U.S.A. 165 F2
Olecko Poland 57 S3
Olekma r. Russia 77 N3
Olekminsk Russia 77 N3
Olekminskiy Stanovik mts Russia 89 M2
Oleksandrivs'k Ukr. see Zaporizhzhya
Oleksandriya Ukr. 53 G6
Ølen Norway 55 D7
Olenegorsk Russia 54 R2
Olenek Russia 77 M3
Olenek r. Russia 77 M2
Olenek Bay Russia see Olenekskiy Zaliv
Olenekskiy Zaliv b. Russia 77 N2
Olenino Russia 52 G4
Olenitsa Russia 52 G2
Olenivs'ki Kar"yery Ukr. see Dokuchayevs'k
Olentuy Russia 95 H1
Olenya Russia see Olenegorsk
Oleshky Ukr. see Tsyurupyns'k
Olet Tongo mt. Sumbawa Indon. 85 G5
Olevs'k Ukr. 53 E6
Ol'ga Russia 90 D4
Olga, Lac l. Canada 152 F4
Olga, Mount Australia 135 E6
Ol'ginsk Russia 90 D1
Olginskoye Russia see Kochubeyevskoye
Ölgiy Mongolia 94 B1
Olhão Port. 67 C5
Olia Chain mts Australia 135 E6
Olifants r. Moz./S. Africa 125 J3
also known as Elefantes
Olifants watercourse Namibia 124 D3
Olifants S. Africa 125 J2
Olifants r. W. Cape S. Africa 124 D6
Olifants r. W. Cape S. Africa 124 E7
Olifantshoek S. Africa 124 F4
Olifantsrivierberge mts S. Africa 124 D7
Olimarao atoll Micronesia 81 L5
Olimbos hill Cyprus see Olympos
Olimbos mt. Greece see Olympus, Mount
Olimpos Beydağları Milli Parkı nat. park Turkey 69 N6
Olinalá Mex. 167 F5
Olinda Brazil 177 L5
Olinga Moz. 123 D5
Olio Australia 136 C4
Oliphants Drift S. Africa 125 H3
Olisipo Port. see Lisbon
Oliva Spain 67 F4
Oliva, Cordillera de mts Arg./Chile 178 C3
Olivares, Cerro de mt. Arg./Chile 178 C4
Olive Hill KY U.S.A. 164 D4
Olivehurst CA U.S.A. 158 C2
Oliveira dos Brejinhos Brazil 179 C1
Olivença Moz. see Lupilichi
Olivenza Spain 67 C4
Oliver Lake Canada 151 K3
Olivet MI U.S.A. 164 C2
Olivet SD U.S.A. 160 D3
Olivia MN U.S.A. 160 E2
Olji Nei Mongol China 94 F3
Olji Nei Mongol China 94 F3
Oljoq China 95 F4
Ol'khovka Russia 53 J6
Ollagüe Chile 178 C2
Ollombo Congo 122 B4
Olmaliq Uzbek. 102 C3
Olmos Peru 176 C5
Olmütz Czech Rep. see Olomouc
Olney U.K. 59 G6
Olney IL U.S.A. 160 F4
Olney MD U.S.A. 165 G4
Olney TX U.S.A. 161 D5
Olofström Sweden 55 I8
Olomane r. Canada 153 J4
Olomouc Czech Rep. 57 P6
Olonets Russia 52 G3
Olongapo Luzon Phil. 82 C3
Olongliko Kalimantan Indon. 85 F3
Oloron-Ste-Marie France 66 D5
Olosenga atoll American Samoa see Swains Island
Olot Spain 67 H2
Olot Uzbek. 111 F2
Olovyannaya Chukotskiy Avtonomnyy Okrug Russia 148 C2
Olovyannaya Zabaykal'skiy Kray Russia 95 H1
Oloy r. Russia 77 Q3
Oloy, Qatorkŭhi mts Asia see Alai Range
Olpe Germany 63 H3
Olsztyn Poland 57 R4
Olt r. Romania 69 K3
Olten Switz. 66 H3
Oltenița Romania 69 L2
Oltu Turkey 113 F2
Oluan Bi c. Taiwan 97 I4
Olutanga i. Phil. 82 C5
Ol'viopol' Ukr. see Pervomays'k
Olymbos hill Cyprus see Olympos
▶Olympia WA U.S.A. 156 C3
Capital of Washington state.
Olympic National Park WA U.S.A. 156 C3
Olympos hill Cyprus 107 A2
Olympos Greece see Olympus, Mount
Olympos nat. park Greece see Olympou, Ethnikos Drymos
Olympou, Ethnikos Drymos nat. park Greece 69 J4
Olympus, Mount Cyprus 107 A2
Olympus, Mount Greece 69 J4
Olympus, Mount WA U.S.A. 156 C3
Olyutorskiy, Mys c. Russia 77 S4
Olyutorskiy Zaliv b. Russia 77 R4
Olzheras Russia see Mezhdurechensk
Oma China 99 C6
Oma r. Russia 52 J2
Ōmachi Japan 93 D2
Omaezaki Japan 93 E4
Omae-zaki pt Japan 93 E4
Omagh U.K. 61 E3
Omaha NE U.S.A. 160 E3
Omaheke admin. reg. Namibia 124 D2
Omal'skiy Khrebet mts Russia 90 E1
Ōmama Japan 93 F2
Oman country Asia 109 I6
Oman, Gulf of Asia 110 E5
Omaruru Namibia 123 B6
Omate Peru 176 D7
Omaweneno Botswana 124 F3
Omba i. Vanuatu see Aoba
Ombai, Selat sea chan. Indon. 83 C5
Ombalantu Namibia see Outapi
Ombolata Sumatra Indon. 84 B2
Omboué Gabon 122 A4
Ombu China 99 D7
Omdraaisvlei S. Africa 124 F6
Omdurman Sudan 108 D6
Ōme Japan 93 F3
Omeo Australia 138 C6
Omer MI U.S.A. 164 D1
Ometepe, Isla de i. Nicaragua 166 [inset] I7
Ometepec Mex. 168 E5
Omgoy Wildlife Reserve nature res. Thai. 86 B3
Om Hajēr Eritrea 108 E7
Ōmi Japan 93 E2
Ōmi Niigata Japan 93 D1
Ōmi Shiga Japan 92 C3
Omīdīyeh Iran 110 C4
Omigawa Japan 93 G3
Ōmihachiman Japan 92 C3
Omineca Mountains Canada 150 E3
Omitara Namibia 124 C2
Omitama Japan 93 G2
Ōmiya Kyōto Japan 92 B3
Ōmiya Saitama Japan 93 F3
Ommaney, Cape AK U.S.A. 149 N4
Ommen Neth. 62 G2
Ömnödelger Mongolia 95 G2
Ömnögovĭ prov. Mongolia 94 F3
Omōi-gawa r. Japan 93 F2
Omolon Russia 77 R3
Omo National Park Eth. 122 D3
Omon Gol watercourse China 94 E3
Omotegō Japan 93 G1
Omsk Russia 76 I4
Omsukchan Russia 77 Q3
Ōmu Japan 90 F3
O-mu Myanmar 86 B2
Omu, Vârful mt. Romania 69 K2
Ōmura Japan 91 C6
Ōmuro-yama hill Japan 93 F4
Ōmuro-yama mt. Japan 93 E3
Ōmuro-yama mt. Japan 93 F3
Omutninsk Russia 52 L4
Onaman Lake Canada 152 D4
Onamia MN U.S.A. 160 E2
Onancock VA U.S.A. 165 H5
Onang Celebes Indon. 83 A3
Onangué, Lac l. Gabon 122 B4
Onaping Lake Canada 152 E5
Onatchiway, Lac l. Canada 153 H4
Onavas Mex. 166 C2
Onawa IA U.S.A. 160 D3
Onaway MI U.S.A. 164 C1
Önay, Kōtal-e Afgh. 111 H3
Onbingwin Myanmar 87 B4
Oncativo Arg. 178 D4
Onchan Isle of Man 58 C4
Oncócua Angola 123 B5
Öncül Turkey 107 D1
Ondal India see Andal
Ondangwa Namibia 123 B5
Onderstedorings S. Africa 124 E6
Ondjiva Angola 123 B5
Ondo Nigeria 120 D4
Öndörhaan Mongolia 95 G2
Ondor Had China 95 J2
Öndörhushuu Mongolia see Bulgan
Ondorkara China 94 B2
Ondor Mod China 94 F3
Öndörshil Mongolia 95 G2
Ondor Sum China 95 H3
Öndör-Ulaan Mongolia 94 E1
Ondozero Russia 52 G3
One Botswana 124 E2
One and a Half Degree Channel Maldives 103 D11
Onega Russia 52 H3
Onega r. Russia 52 H3
▶Onega, Lake Russia 52 G3
3rd largest lake in Europe.
Onega Bay g. Russia see Onezhskaya Guba
One Hundred and Fifty Mile House Canada see 150 Mile House
One Hundred Mile House Canada see 100 Mile House
Oneida NY U.S.A. 165 H2
Oneida TN U.S.A. 164 C5
Oneida Lake NY U.S.A. 165 H2
O'Neill NE U.S.A. 160 D3
Onekama MI U.S.A. 164 B1
Onekotan, Ostrov i. Russia 77 Q5
Oneonta AL U.S.A. 163 C5
Oneonta NY U.S.A. 165 H2
Onești Romania 69 L1
Onezhskaya Guba g. Russia 52 G2
Onezhskoye Ozero l. Russia see Onega, Lake
Ong r. India 106 D1
Onga Gabon 122 B4
Ongers watercourse S. Africa 124 F5
Onggot China 95 J1
Ongi Dundgovĭ Mongolia see Sayhan-Ovoo
Ongi Övörhangay Mongolia see Uyanga
Ongiyn Gol r. Mongolia 94 E2
Ongjin N. Korea 91 B5
Ongniud Qi China see Wudan
Ongole India 106 D3
Ongon Mongolia see Bürd
Ongt Gol China 94 E3
Onguday Russia 98 D2
Onida SD U.S.A. 160 C2
Onilahy r. Madag. 123 E6
Onishi Japan 93 F2
Onistagane, Lac l. Canada 153 H4
Onitsha Nigeria 120 D4
Onjati Mountain Namibia 124 C2
Onjiva Angola see Ondjiva
Onjuku Japan 93 G3
Ōno Fukui Japan 92 C3
Ōno Gifu Japan 92 C3
Ono Japan 92 A4
Ōnohara-jima i. Japan 93 F4
Ono-i-Lau i. Fiji 133 I4
Onomichi Japan 91 D6
Onon atoll Micronesia see Namonuito
Onon Mongolia see Binder
Onon r. Russia 95 H1
Onon Gol r. Mongolia 95 H1
Onor, Gora mt. Russia 90 F2
Onotoa atoll Kiribati 133 H2
Onseepkans S. Africa 124 D5
Onslow Australia 134 A5
Onslow Bay NC U.S.A. 163 E5
Onstwedde Neth. 62 H1
Ontake-san vol. Japan 92 D3
Ontaratue r. Canada 149 O2
Ontario prov. Canada 164 E1
Ontario CA U.S.A. 158 E4
Ontario, Lake Canada/U.S.A. 165 G2
Ontong Java Atoll Solomon Is 133 F2
Onutu atoll Kiribati see Onotoa
Onverwacht Suriname 177 G2
Onyx CA U.S.A. 158 D4
Oodnadatta Australia 137 A5
Oodweyne Somalia 122 E3
Ōoka Japan 93 D2
Oolambeyan National Park Australia 137 D7
Ooldea Australia 135 E7
Ooldea Range hills Australia 135 E7
Oologah Lake resr OK U.S.A. 161 E4
Ooratippra r. Australia 136 B4
Oos-Londen S. Africa see East London
Oostburg Neth. 62 D3
Oostende Belgium see Ostend
Oostendorp Neth. 62 F2
Oosterhout Neth. 62 E3
Oosterschelde est. Neth. 62 D3
Oosterwolde Neth. 62 G2
Oostvleteren Belgium 62 C4
Oost-Vlieland Neth. 62 F1
Ootacamund India see Udagamandalam
Ootsa Lake Canada 150 E4
Ootsa Lake l. Canada 150 E4
Opal Mex. 161 C7
Opala Dem. Rep. Congo 122 C4
Oparino Russia 52 K4
Oparo i. Fr. Polynesia see Rapa
Opasatika r. Canada 152 E4
Opasatika Lake Canada 152 E4
Opasquia Canada 151 M4
Opataca, Lac l. Canada 152 G4
Opava Czech Rep. 57 P6
Opel hill Germany 63 H5
Opelika AL U.S.A. 163 C5
Opelousas LA U.S.A. 161 E6
Opeongo Lake Canada 152 F5
Opheim MT U.S.A. 156 G2
Ophir, Gunung vol. Indon. 84 C2
Opienge Dem. Rep. Congo 122 C3
Opin Seram Indon. 83 D3
Opinaca r. Canada 152 F3
Opinaca, Réservoir resr Canada 152 F3
Opinnagau r. Canada 152 E3
Opiscotéo, Lac l. Canada 153 H3
Op Luang National Park Thai. 86 B3
Opmeer Neth. 62 E2
Opochka Russia 55 P8
Opocopa, Lac l. Canada 153 I3
Opodepe Mex. 166 C2
Opole Poland 57 P5
Oporto Port. 67 B3
Opotiki N.Z. 139 F4
Opp AL U.S.A. 163 C6
Oppdal Norway 54 F5
Oppeid Norway 54 I2
Oppeln Poland see Opole
Opportunity WA U.S.A. 156 D3
Opunake N.Z. 139 D4
Opuwo Namibia 123 B5
Oqsu r. Tajik. 111 I2
Oquitoa Mex. 166 C2
Ōra Japan 93 F2
Oracle AZ U.S.A. 159 H5
Oradea Romania 69 I1
Orahovac Kosovo see Rahovec
Orai India 104 D4
Oraibi AZ U.S.A. 159 H4
Oraibi Wash watercourse AZ U.S.A. 159 H4
Oral Kazakh. see Ural'sk
Oran Alg. 67 F6
Orán Arg. 178 D2
Orang India 105 H4
Ŏrang N. Korea 90 C4
Orange Australia 138 D4
Orange France 66 G4
Orange r. Namibia/S. Africa 124 C5
Orange CA U.S.A. 158 E5
Orange MA U.S.A. 165 I2
Orange TX U.S.A. 161 E6
Orange VA U.S.A. 165 F4
Orange, Cabo c. Brazil 177 H3
Orangeburg SC U.S.A. 163 D5
Orange City IA U.S.A. 160 D3
Orange Cone sea feature S. Atlantic Ocean 184 I8
Orange Free State prov. S. Africa see Free State
Orangeville Canada 164 E2
Orange Walk Belize 167 H5
Orani Luzon Phil. 82 C3
Oranienburg Germany 63 N2
Oranje r. Namibia/S. Africa see Orange
Oranje Gebergte hills Suriname 177 G3
Oranjemund Namibia 124 C5
▶Oranjestad Aruba 169 J6
Capital of Aruba.
Oranmore Ireland 61 D4
Orapa Botswana 123 C6
Oras Samar Phil. 82 D3
Oras Bay Samar Phil. 82 D3
Orăștie Romania 69 J2
Orașul Stalin Romania see Brașov
Oratia, Mount AK U.S.A. 148 G4
Oravais Fin. 54 M5
Orba Co l. China 99 C6
Orbetello Italy 68 D3
Orbost Australia 138 D6
Orca Bay AK U.S.A. 149 K3
Orcadas research station S. Atlantic Ocean 188 A2
Orchard City CO U.S.A. 159 J2
Orchha India 104 D4
Orchila, Isla i. Venez. 176 E1
Orchy r. U.K. 60 D4
Orcutt CA U.S.A. 158 C4
Ord r. Australia 134 E3
Ord NE U.S.A. 160 D3
Ord, Mount hill Australia 134 D4
Órdenes Spain see Ordes
Orderville UT U.S.A. 159 G3
Ordes Spain 67 B2
Ordesa y Monte Perdido, Parque Nacional de nat. park Spain 67 G2
Ord Mountain CA U.S.A. 158 E4
Ordos Nei Mongol China see Dongsheng
Ordos China 95 G4
Ord River Dam Australia 134 E4
Ordu Hatay Turkey see Yayladağı
Ordu Ordu Turkey 112 E2
Ordubad Azer. 113 G3
Ordway CO U.S.A. 160 C4
Ordzhonikidze Russia see Vladikavkaz
Ore Nigeria 120 D4
Oreana NV U.S.A. 158 D1
O Reăng Cambodia 87 D4
Örebro Sweden 55 I7
Oregon IL U.S.A. 160 F3
Oregon OH U.S.A. 164 D3
Oregon state U.S.A. 156 C4
Oregon City OR U.S.A. 156 C3
Orekhov Ukr. see Orikhiv
Orekhovo-Zuyevo Russia 52 H5
Orel' Kazakh. 102 G2
Orel Russia 53 H5
Orel, Gora mt. Russia 90 E1
Orel', Ozero l. Russia 90 E1
Orem UT U.S.A. 159 H1
Ore Mountains Czech Rep./Germany see Erzgebirge
Orenburg Russia 76 G4
Orense Spain see Ourense
Oreor Palau see Koror
Oreor i. Palau see Koror
Orepuki N.Z. 139 A8
Öresund strait Denmark/Sweden 55 H9
Oretana, Cordillera mts Spain see Toledo, Montes de
Orewa N.Z. 139 E3
Oreye Belgium 62 F4
Orfanou, Kolpos b. Greece 69 J4
Orford Australia 137 [inset]
Orford U.K. 59 I6
Orford Ness hd U.K. 59 I6
Organabo Fr. Guiana 177 H2
Organ Pipe Cactus National Monument nat. park AZ U.S.A. 159 G5
Orge r. France 62 C6
Orgil Mongolia see Jargalant
Orgon Tal China 95 H3
Orhaneli Turkey 69 M5
Orhangazi Turkey 69 M4
Orhon Bulgan Mongolia 94 E1
Orhon Selenge Mongolia 94 F1
Orhon Gol r. Mongolia 94 F1
Orhontuul Mongolia 94 F1
Orichi Russia 52 K4
Oriental, Cordillera mts Bol. 176 E7
Oriental, Cordillera mts Col. 176 D2
Oriental, Cordillera mts Peru 176 E6
Orihuela Spain 67 F4
Orikhiv Ukr. 53 G7
Orillia Canada 164 F1
Orimattila Fin. 55 N6
Orin WY U.S.A. 156 G4
Orinoco r. Col./Venez. 176 F2
Orinoco, Delta del Venez. 176 F2
Orissa state India see Odisha
Orissaare Estonia 55 M7
Oristano Sardinia Italy 68 C5
Orivesi Fin. 55 N6
Orivesi l. Fin. 54 P5
Oriximiná Brazil 177 G4
Orizaba Mex. 168 E5
▶Orizaba, Pico de vol. Mex. 168 E5
Highest active volcano and 3rd highest mountain in North America.
Orizona Brazil 179 A2
Orkanger Norway 54 F5
Örkelljunga Sweden 55 H8
Orkhon Valley tourist site Mongolia 94 E2
Orkla r. Norway 54 F5
Orkney S. Africa 125 H4
Orkney Islands is U.K. 60 F1
Orla TX U.S.A. 161 C6
Orland CA U.S.A. 158 B2
Orlândia Brazil 179 B3
Orlando FL U.S.A. 163 D6
Orland Park IL U.S.A. 164 B3
Orleans Brazil 179 A5
Orléans France 66 E3
Orleans IN U.S.A. 164 B4
Orleans VT U.S.A. 165 I1
Orléans, Île d' i. Canada 153 H5
Orléansville Alg. see Chlef
Orlik Russia 88 H2
Orlov Russia 52 K4
Orlov Gay Russia 53 K6
Orlovskiy Russia 53 I7
Ormara Pak. 111 G5
Ormara, Ras hd Pak. 111 G5
Ormiston Canada 151 J5
Ormoc Leyte Phil. 82 D4
Ormskirk U.K. 58 E5
Ormstown Canada 165 I1
Ornach Pak. 111 G5
Ornain r. France 62 E6
Orne r. France 66 D2
Ørnes Norway 54 H3
Örnsköldsvik Sweden 54 K5
Orobie, Alpi mts Italy 68 C1
Orobo, Serra do hills Brazil 179 C1
Orodara Burkina Faso 120 C3
Orofino ID U.S.A. 156 D3
Orog Nuur salt l. Mongolia 94 E2
Oro Grande CA U.S.A. 158 E4
Orogrande NM U.S.A. 157 G6
Orol Dengizi salt l. Kazakh./Uzbek. see Aral Sea
Oromocto Canada 153 I5
Oromocto Lake Canada 153 I5
Oron Israel 107 B4
Orona atoll Kiribati 133 I2
Orono ME U.S.A. 162 G2
Orontes r. Asia 112 E3 see 'Āṣī, Nahr al
Orontes r. Lebanon/Syria 107 C2
Oroqen Zizhiqi China see Alihe
Oroquieta Mindanao Phil. 82 C4
Orós, Açude resr Brazil 177 K5
Orosei, Golfo di b. Sardinia Italy 68 C4
Orosháza Hungary 69 I1
Oroville CA U.S.A. 158 C2
Oroville, Lake CA U.S.A. 158 C2
Orqohan China 95 J1
Orr MN U.S.A. 160 E1
Orsa Sweden 55 I6
Orsha Belarus 53 F5
Orshanka Russia 52 J4
Orsk Russia 76 G4
Ørsta Norway 54 E5
Orta Toroslar plat. Turkey 107 A1
Ortegal, Cabo c. Spain 67 C2
Orthez France 66 D5
Ortigueira Spain 67 C2
Ortíz Mex. 166 C2
Ortles mt. Italy 68 D1
Orton U.K. 58 E4
Ortona Italy 68 F3
Ortonville MN U.S.A. 160 D2
Ortospana Afgh. see Kābul
Orto-Tokoy Kyrg. 98 A4
Orukuizu i. Palau 82 [inset]
Orulgan, Khrebet mts Russia 77 N3
Orumbo Namibia 124 C2
Orūmīyeh Iran see Urmia
Oruro Bol. 176 E7
Orvieto Italy 68 E3
Orville Coast Antarctica 188 L1
Orwell OH U.S.A. 164 E3
Orwell VT U.S.A. 165 I2
Orxon He r. China 95 I1
Oryol Russia see Orel
Os Norway 54 G5
Osa Russia 51 R4
Osa, Península de pen. Costa Rica 166 [inset] J7
Osage IA U.S.A. 160 E3
Osage WV U.S.A. 164 E4
Osage WY U.S.A. 156 G3
Osaka Japan 92 D3
Ōsaka Japan 92 B4
Ōsaka pref. Japan 92 B4
Osakarovka Kazakh. 102 D1
Ōsakasayama Japan 92 B4
Ōsaka-wan b. Japan 92 B4
Ōsaki Japan 91 F5
Osam r. Bulg. 69 K3
Ōsawano Japan 92 D2
Osawatomie KS U.S.A. 160 E4
Osborn, Mount AK U.S.A. 148 F2
Osborne KS U.S.A. 160 D4
Osby Sweden 55 H8
Osceola IA U.S.A. 160 E3
Osceola MO U.S.A. 160 E4
Osceola NE U.S.A. 160 D3
Oschatz Germany 63 N3
Oschersleben (Bode) Germany 63 L2
Oschiri Sardinia Italy 68 C4
Ösel i. Estonia see Hiiumaa
Osetr r. Russia 53 H5
Ōse-zaki pt Japan 91 C6
Ōse-zaki pt Japan 93 E3
Osgoode Canada 165 H1
Osgood Mountains NV U.S.A. 156 D4
Osh Kyrg. 102 D3
Oshakati Namibia 123 B5
Oshawa Canada 165 F2
Ōshika Japan 93 E3
Oshika-hantō pen. Japan 91 F5
Ōshima Niigata Japan 93 E1
Ōshima Tōkyō Japan 93 F4
Ōshima Toyama Japan 92 D2
Ō-shima i. Japan 90 E4
Ō-shima i. Japan 92 C2
Ō-shima i. Japan 93 F4
Oshimizu Japan 92 C2
Oshino Japan 93 E3
Oshkosh NE U.S.A. 160 C3
Oshkosh WI U.S.A. 164 A1
Oshmyany Belarus see Ashmyany
Oshnavīyeh Iran 110 B2
Oshogbo Nigeria see Osogbo
Oshtorān Kūh mt. Iran 110 C3
Ōshū Japan 91 F5
Oshwe Dem. Rep. Congo 122 B4
Osijek Croatia 68 H2
Osilinka r. Canada 150 E3
Osimo Italy 68 E3
Osinovka Russia 95 G1
Osipenko Ukr. see Berdyans'k
Osipovichi Belarus see Asipovichy
Osiyan India 104 C4
oSizweni S. Africa 125 J4
Osječenica mts Bos. & Herz. 68 G2
Ösjön l. Sweden 54 I5
Oskaloosa IA U.S.A. 160 E3
Oskarshamn Sweden 55 J8
Öskemen Kazakh. see Ust'-Kamenogorsk
▶Oslo Norway 55 G7
Capital of Norway.
Oslob Cebu Phil. 82 C4
Oslofjorden sea chan. Norway 55 G7
Osmanabad India 106 C2
Osmancık Turkey 112 D2
Osmaneli Turkey 69 M4
Osmaniye Turkey 112 E3
Osmannagar India 106 C2
Os'mino Russia 55 P7
Osnabrück Germany 63 I2
Osnaburg atoll Fr. Polynesia see Mururoa
Osogbo Nigeria 120 D4
Osogovska Planina mts Bulg./Macedonia 69 J3

Osogovske Planine mts Bulg./Macedonia see Osogovska Planina
Osogovski Planini mts Bulg./Macedonia see Osogovska Planina
Osorno Chile 178 B6
Osorno Spain 67 D2
Osoyoos Canada 150 G5
Osøyro Norway 55 D6
Osprey Reef Australia 136 D2
Oss Neth. 62 F3
Ossa, Mount Australia 137 [inset]
Osseo WI U.S.A. 152 C5
Ossineke MI U.S.A. 164 D1
Ossining NY U.S.A. 165 I3
Ossipee NH U.S.A. 165 J2
Ossipee Lake NH U.S.A. 165 J2
Oßmannstedt Germany 63 L3
Ossokmanuan Lake Canada 153 I3
Ossora Russia 77 R4
Ossu East Timor 83 C5
Ostashkov Russia 52 G4
Ostbevern Germany 63 H2
Oste r. Germany 63 J1
Ostend Belgium 62 C3
Ostende Belgium see Ostend
Osterburg (Altmark) Germany 63 L2
Österbymo Sweden 55 I8
Österdalälven l. Sweden 55 H6
Østerdalen valley Norway 55 G5
Osterfeld Germany 63 L3
Osterholz-Scharmbeck Germany 63 I1
Osterode am Harz Germany 63 K3
Österreich country Europe see Austria
Östersund Sweden 54 I5
Osterwieck Germany 63 K3
Ostfriesische Inseln Germany see East Frisian Islands
Ostfriesland reg. Germany 63 H1
Östhammar Sweden 55 K6
Ostrava Czech Rep. 57 Q6
Ostróda Poland 57 Q4
Ostrogozhsk Russia 53 H6
Ostrov Czech Rep. 63 M4
Ostrov Russia 55 P8
Ostrovets Poland see Ostrowiec Świętokrzyski
Ostrovnoy Russia 189 G2
Ostrovskoye Russia 52 I4
Ostrov Vrangelya i. Russia see Wrangel Island
Ostrów Poland see Ostrów Wielkopolski
Ostrowiec Poland see Ostrowiec Świętokrzyski
Ostrowiec Świętokrzyski Poland 53 D6
Ostrów Mazowiecka Poland 57 R4
Ostrowo Poland see Ostrów Wielkopolski
Ostrów Wielkopolski Poland 57 P5
Ōsuka Japan 93 D4
O'Sullivan Lake Canada 152 D4
Ōsumi-shotō is Japan 91 C7
Osuna Spain 67 D5
Oswego KS U.S.A. 161 E4
Oswego NY U.S.A. 165 G2
Oswestry U.K. 59 D6
Ota Japan 92 C3
Ōta Japan 93 F2
Otago Peninsula N.Z. 139 C7
Otahiti i. Fr. Polynesia see Tahiti
Ōtake-san mt. Japan 93 F3
Ōtaki Chiba Japan 93 G3
Ōtaki Nagano Japan 92 D3
Ōtaki Saitama Japan 93 E3
Otaki N.Z. 139 E5
Otanmäki Fin. 54 O4
Otar Kazakh. 98 A4
Otari Japan 93 D2
Otaru Japan 90 F4
Otavi Namibia 123 B5
Ōtawara Japan 93 G2
Otdia atoll Marshall Is see Wotje
Otegen Batyr Kazakh. 98 B4
Otelnuc, Lac l. Canada 153 H2
Otematata N.Z. 139 C7
Otepää Estonia 55 O7
Oteros r. Mex. 166 C3
Otgon Tenger Uul mt. Mongolia 94 D2
oThongathi S. Africa 125 J5
Oti Celebes Indon. 83 A3
Otinapa Mex. 161 B7
Otira N.Z. 139 C6
Otis CO U.S.A. 160 C3
Otish, Monts hills Canada 153 H4
Otjinene Namibia 123 B6
Otjiwarongo Namibia 123 B6
Otjozondjupa admin. reg. Namibia 124 C1
Otley U.K. 58 F5
Ōtō Japan 92 B4
Otog Qi China see Ulan
Otorohanga N.Z. 139 E4
Otoskwin r. Canada 151 N5
Otowa Japan 92 D4
Otpor Russia see Zabaykal'sk
Otradnoye Russia see Otradnyy
Otradnyy Russia 53 K5
Otranto Italy 68 H4
Otranto, Strait of Albania/Italy 68 H4
Otrogovo Russia see Stepnoye
Otrozhnyy Russia 77 S3
Otsego Lake NY U.S.A. 165 H2
Ōtsu Ibaraki Japan 93 G2
Ōtsu Shiga Japan 92 B3
Ōtsuki Japan 93 E3
Otta Norway 55 F6
▶Ottawa Canada 165 H1
Capital of Canada.
Ottawa r. Canada 152 G5
also known as Rivière des Outaouais
Ottawa IL U.S.A. 160 F3
Ottawa KS U.S.A. 160 E4
Ottawa OH U.S.A. 164 C3
Ottawa Islands Canada 152 E2
Otter r. U.K. 59 D8
Otterbein IN U.S.A. 164 B3
Otterburn U.K. 58 E3
Otter Island AK U.S.A. 148 E4
Otter Rapids Canada 152 E4
Ottersberg Germany 63 J1
Ottignies Belgium 62 E4
Ottuk Kyrg. 98 A4
Ottumwa IA U.S.A. 160 E3
Ottweiler Germany 63 H5
Otukpo Nigeria 120 D4
Oturkpo Nigeria see Otukpo
Otuzco Peru 176 C5
Otway, Cape Australia 138 A7
Otway National Park Australia 138 A7
Ouachita r. AR U.S.A. 161 F6
Ouachita, Lake AR U.S.A. 161 E5
Ouachita Mountains Arkansas/Oklahoma U.S.A. 161 E5
Ouadda Cent. Afr. Rep. 122 C3
Ouaddaï reg. Chad 121 F3
▶Ouagadougou Burkina Faso 120 C3
Capital of Burkina Faso.
Ouahigouya Burkina Faso 120 C3
Ouahran Alg. see Oran
Ouaka r. Cent. Afr. Rep. 122 B3
Oualâta Mauritania 120 C3
Oualâta, Dahr hills Mauritania 120 C3
Ouallam Niger 120 D3
Ouanda Djallé Cent. Afr. Rep. 122 C3
Ouando Cent. Afr. Rep. 122 C3
Ouango Cent. Afr. Rep. 122 C3
Ouara r. Cent. Afr. Rep. 122 C3
Ouarâne reg. Mauritania 120 C2
Ouargaye Burkina Faso 120 D3
Ouargla Alg. 64 F5
Ouarogou Burkina Faso see Ouargaye
Ouarzazate Morocco 64 C5
Ouasiemsca r. Canada 153 G4
Oubangui r. Cent. Afr. Rep./Dem. Rep. Congo see Ubangi
Oubergpas pass S. Africa 124 G7
Ōuchiyama Japan 92 C4
Ōuda Japan 92 B4
Oudenaarde Belgium 62 D4
Oudômxai Laos 86 C2
Oudtshoorn S. Africa 124 F7
Oud-Turnhout Belgium 62 E3
Oued Tlélat Alg. 67 F6
Oued Zem Morocco 64 C5
Oued Zénati Alg. 68 B6
Ouessant, Île d' i. France 66 B2
Ouesso Congo 122 B3
Ouest, Pointe de l' pt Canada 153 I4
Ouezzane Morocco 67 D6
Oughter, Lough l. Ireland 61 E3
Ougo-gawa r. Japan 92 A4
Ouguati Namibia 124 B1
Ougura-yama mt. Japan 93 E2
Ouiriego Mex. 166 C3
Ouistreham France 59 G9
Oujda Morocco 67 E6
Oujeft Mauritania 120 B3
Oulainen Fin. 54 N4
Oulangan kansallispuisto nat. park Fin. 54 P3
Ouled Djellal Alg. 67 I6
Ouled Farès Alg. 67 G5
Ouled Naïl, Monts des mts Alg. 67 H6
Oulu Fin. 54 N4
Oulujärvi l. Fin. 54 O4
Oulujoki r. Fin. 54 N4
Oulunsalo Fin. 54 N4
Oulx Italy 68 B2
Oum-Chalouba Chad 121 F3
Oum el Bouaghi Alg. 68 B7
Oum-Hadjer Chad 121 E3
Ounasjoki r. Fin. 54 N3
Oundle U.K. 59 G6
Oungre Canada 151 K5
Ounianga Kébir Chad 121 F3
Oupeye Belgium 62 F4
Our r. Lux. 62 G5
Our, Vallée de l' valley Germany/Lux. 62 G5
Oura, Akrotirio pt Greece 69 L5
Ouray CO U.S.A. 159 J2
Ouray UT U.S.A. 159 I1
Ourcq r. France 62 D5
Ourense Spain 67 C2
Ouricuri Brazil 177 J5
Ourinhos Brazil 179 A3
Ouro r. Brazil 179 A1
Ouro Preto Brazil 179 C3
Ourthe r. Belgium 62 F4
Ous Russia 51 S3
Ouse r. England U.K. 58 G5
Ouse r. England U.K. 59 H8
Outaouais, Rivière des r. Canada 152 G5 see Ottawa
Outapi Namibia 123 B5
Outardes, Rivière aux r. Canada 153 H4
Outardes Quatre, Réservoir resr Canada 153 H4
Outer Hebrides is U.K. 60 B3
Outer Mongolia country Asia see Mongolia
Outer Santa Barbara Channel CA U.S.A. 158 D5
Outjo Namibia 123 B6
Outlook Canada 151 J5
Outokumpu Fin. 54 P5
Out Skerries is U.K. 60 [inset]
Ouvéa atoll New Caledonia 133 G4
Ouyanghai Shuiku resr China 97 G3
Ouyen Australia 137 C7
Ouzel r. U.K. 59 G6
Ouzinkie AK U.S.A. 148 I4
Ovace, Punta d' mt. Corsica France 66 I6
Ovacık Turkey 107 A1
Ovada Italy 68 C2
Ovalle Chile 178 B4
Ovamboland reg. Namibia 123 B5
Ovan Gabon 122 B3
Ovar Port. 67 B3
Overath Germany 63 H4
Överkalix Sweden 54 M3
Overlander Roadhouse Australia 135 A6
Overland Park KS U.S.A. 160 E4
Overton NV U.S.A. 159 F3
Övertorneå Sweden 54 M3
Överum Sweden 55 J8
Overveen Neth. 62 E2
Övgödiy Mongolia see Telmen
Ovid CO U.S.A. 160 C3
Ovid NY U.S.A. 165 G2
Oviedo Spain 67 D2
Ovoot Mongolia see Darïganga
Övörhangay prov. Mongolia 94 E2
Øvre Anárjohka Nasjonalpark nat. park Norway 54 N2
Øvre Dividal Nasjonalpark nat. park Norway 54 K2
Øvre Rendal Norway 55 G6
Ovruch Ukr. 53 F6
Ovsyanka Russia 90 B1
Övt Mongolia see Bat-Öldziy
Owando Congo 122 B4
Owa Rafa i. Solomon Is see Santa Ana
Owasco Lake NY U.S.A. 165 G2
Owase Japan 92 C4
Owase-wan b. Japan 92 C4
Owatonna MN U.S.A. 160 E2
Owego NY U.S.A. 165 G2
Owel, Lough l. Ireland 61 E4
Owen Island Myanmar 87 B5
Owenmore r. Mayo Ireland 61 C3
Owenmore r. Sligo Ireland 61 D3
Owenreagh r. U.K. 61 E3
Owen River N.Z. 139 D5
Owens r. CA U.S.A. 158 E3
Owensboro KY U.S.A. 164 B5
Owen Sound Canada 164 E1
Owen Sound inlet Canada 164 E1
Owen Stanley Range mts P.N.G. 81 L8
Owenton KY U.S.A. 164 C4
Owerri Nigeria 120 D4
Owikeno Lake Canada 150 E5
Owingsville KY U.S.A. 164 D4
Owl r. Canada 151 M3
Owl Creek Mountains WY U.S.A. 156 F4
Owo Nigeria 120 D4
Owosso MI U.S.A. 164 C2
Owyhee NV U.S.A. 156 D4
Owyhee r. OR U.S.A. 156 D4
Owyhee Mountains ID U.S.A. 156 D4
Öxarfjörður b. Iceland 54 [inset 1]
Oxbow Canada 151 K5
Ox Creek r. ND U.S.A. 160 C1
Oxelösund Sweden 55 J7
Oxford N.Z. 139 D6
Oxford U.K. 59 F7
Oxford IN U.S.A. 164 B3
Oxford MA U.S.A. 165 J2
Oxford MD U.S.A. 165 G4
Oxford MS U.S.A. 161 F5
Oxford NC U.S.A. 162 E4
Oxford NY U.S.A. 165 H2
Oxford OH U.S.A. 164 C4
Oxford House Canada 151 M4
Oxford Lake Canada 151 M4
Oxkutzcab Mex. 167 H4
Oxley Australia 138 B5
Oxleys Peak Australia 138 E3
Oxley Wild Rivers National Park Australia 138 F3
Ox Mountains hills Ireland 61 C4
Oxnard CA U.S.A. 158 D4
Oxtongue Lake Canada 165 F1
Oxus r. Asia see Amudar'ya
Oya Sarawak Malaysia 85 E2
Øya Norway 54 H3
Oyabe Japan 92 C2
Oyabe-gawa r. Japan 92 D2
Oyama Shizuoka Japan 93 E3
Oyama Tochigi Japan 93 F2
Ōyama Japan 92 D2
Ō-yama mt. Japan 93 F3
Ō-yama vol. Japan 93 F4
Ōyamada Japan 92 C4
Ōyamazaki Japan 92 B4
Oyapock r. Brazil/Fr. Guiana 177 H3
Oyem Gabon 122 B3
Oyen Canada 151 I5
Oygon Mongolia see Tüdevtey
Oykel r. U.K. 60 E3
Oyo Nigeria 120 D4
Ōyodo Japan 92 B4
Oyonnax France 66 G3
Oyshilik Kazakh. 98 C3
Oyster Rocks is India 106 B3
Oy-Tal Kyrg. 98 A4
Oyten Germany 63 J1
Oytograk China 99 C5
Oyukludağı mt. Turkey 107 A1
Oyyaylak China 99 D5
Özalp Turkey 113 G3
Ozamis Mindanao Phil. 82 C4
Ozark AL U.S.A. 163 C6
Ozark AR U.S.A. 161 E5
Ozark MO U.S.A. 161 E4
Ozark Plateau MO U.S.A. 161 E4
Ozarks, Lake of the MO U.S.A. 160 E4
O'zbekiston country Asia see Uzbekistan
Özen Kazakh. see Kyzylsay
Ozernovskiy Russia 77 Q4
Ozernyy Chukotskiy Avtonomnyy Okrug Russia 148 C2
Ozernyy Smolenskaya Oblast' Russia 53 G5
Ozerpakh Russia 90 F1
Ozersk Russia 55 M9
Ozerskiy Russia 90 F3
Ozery Russia 53 H5
Ozeryane Russia 90 C2
Ozieri Sardinia Italy 68 C4
Ozinki Russia 53 K6
Oznachennoye Russia see Sayanogorsk
Ozona TX U.S.A. 161 C6
Ozuki Japan 91 C6
Ozuluama Mex. 167 F4

Paamiut Greenland 147 N3
Pa-an Myanmar see Hpa-an
Paanayarvi Natsional'nyy Park nat. park Russia 54 Q3
Paanopa i. Kiribati see Banaba
Paarl S. Africa 124 D7
Paatsjoki r. Europe see Patsoyoki
Paballelo S. Africa 124 E5
P'abal-li N. Korea 90 C4
Pabbay i. U.K. 60 B3
Pabianice Poland 57 Q5
Pabianitz Poland see Pabianice
Pabna Bangl. 105 G4
Pabrade Lith. 55 N9
Pab Range mts Pak. 111 G5
Pacaás Novos, Parque Nacional nat. park Brazil 176 F6
Pacaraimã, Serra mts S. America see Pakaraima Mountains
Pacasmayo Peru 176 C5
Pacaya, Volcán de vol. Guat. 167 H6
Pachagarh Bangl. see Panchagarh
Pachala South Sudan 121 G4
Pacheco Chihuahua Mex. 166 C2
Pacheco Zacatecas Mex. 161 C7
Pachikha Russia 52 J3
Pachino Sicily Italy 68 F6
Pachmarhi India 104 D5
Pachor India 104 D5
Pachora India 106 B1
Pachpadra India 104 C4
Pachuca Mex. 168 E4
Pachuca de Soto Mex. see Pachuca
Pacific-Antarctic Ridge sea feature S. Pacific Ocean 187 J9
Pacific Grove CA U.S.A. 158 C3
▶Pacific Ocean 186
Largest ocean in the world.
Pacific Rim National Park Canada 150 E5
Pacijan i. Phil. 82 D4
Pacinan, Tanjung pt Indon. 85 F4
Pacitan Java Indon. 85 E5
Packsaddle Australia 137 C6
Pacoval Brazil 177 H4
Pacuí r. Brazil 179 B2
Paczków Poland 57 P5
Padada Mindanao Phil. 82 D5
Padalere Celebes Indon. 83 B3
Padali Russia see Amursk
Padamarang i. Indon. 83 B4
Padampur India 104 C3
Padang Celebes Indon. 83 B4
Padang Kalimantan Indon. 85 E3
Padang Sumatra Indon. 84 C3
Padang i. Sumatra Indon. 84 C2
Padang Endau Malaysia 84 C2
Padang Luwai, Cagar Alam nature res. Kalimantan Indon. 85 G3
Padangpanjang Sumatra Indon. 84 C3
Padangsidimpuan Sumatra Indon. 84 B2
Padangtikar Kalimantan Indon. 85 E3
Padangtikar i. Indon. 85 E3
Padany Russia 52 G3
Padas r. Malaysia 85 F1
Padatha, Kūh-e mt. Iran 110 C3
Padaung Myanmar 86 A3
Padcaya Bol. 176 F8
Paddington Australia 138 B4
Padeabesar i. Indon. 83 B3
Paden City WV U.S.A. 164 E4
Paderborn Germany 63 I3
Paderborn/Lippstadt airport Germany 63 I3
Padeşu, Vârful mt. Romania 69 J2
Padibyu Myanmar 86 B2
Padilla Bol. 176 F7
Padjelanta nationalpark nat. park Sweden 54 J3
Padova Italy see Padua
Padrão, Ponta pt Angola 123 B4
Padrauna India 105 F4
Padre Island TX U.S.A. 161 D7
Padstow U.K. 59 C8
Padsvillye Belarus 55 O9
Padua India 106 D2
Padua Italy 68 D2
Paducah KY U.S.A. 161 F4
Paducah TX U.S.A. 161 C5
Padum India 104 D2
Paegam N. Korea 90 C4
Paektu-san mt. China/N. Korea see Baitou Shan
Paete Luzon Phil. 82 C3
Pafos Cyprus see Paphos
Pafuri Moz. 125 J2
Pag Croatia 68 F2
Pag i. Croatia 68 F2
Paga Flores Indon. 83 B5
Pagadenbaru Java Indon. 85 D4
Pagadian Mindanao Phil. 82 C5
Pagai Selatan i. Indon. 84 C3
Pagai Utara i. Indon. 84 C3
Pagalu i. Equat. Guinea see Annobón
Pagan i. N. Mariana Is 81 L3
Pagaralam Sumatra Indon. 84 C4
Pagasitikos Kolpos b. Greece 69 J5
Pagatan Kalimantan Indon. 85 F3
Pagatan Kalimantan Indon. 85 F3
Page AZ U.S.A. 159 H3
Page, Mount Canada 149 L1
Pagerdewa Sumatra Indon. 84 D3
Paget, Mount S. Georgia 178 I8
Paget Cay reef Australia 136 F3
Pagon i. N. Mariana Is see Pagan
Pagosa Springs CO U.S.A. 157 G5
Pagqên China see Gadê
Pagri China 99 E8
Pagwa River Canada 152 D4
Pagwi P.N.G. 81 K7
Pah r. AK U.S.A. 148 H2
Pāhala HI U.S.A. 157 [inset]
Pahang r. Malaysia 84 C2
Pahang state Malaysia 84 C2
Pahauman Kalimantan Indon. 85 E2
Pahlgam India 104 C2
Pāhoa HI U.S.A. 157 [inset]
Pahokee FL U.S.A. 163 D7
Pahranagat Range mts NV U.S.A. 159 F3
Pahrump NV U.S.A. 159 F3
Pahuj r. India 104 D4
Pahute Mesa plat. NV U.S.A. 158 E3
Pai Thai. 86 B3
Paicines CA U.S.A. 158 C3
Paide Estonia 55 N7
Paignton U.K. 59 D8
Päijänne l. Fin. 55 N6
Paikü Co l. China 99 D7
Pailĭn Cambodia 87 C4
Pailolo Channel HI U.S.A. 157 [inset]
Paimio Fin. 55 M6
Paimiut AK U.S.A. 148 F3
Paimiut AK U.S.A. 148 G3
Painan Sumatra Indon. 84 C3
Painel Brazil 179 A4
Painesville OH U.S.A. 164 E3
Pains Brazil 179 B3
Painted Desert AZ U.S.A. 159 H3
Painted Rock Dam AZ U.S.A. 159 G5
Paint Hills Canada see Wemindji
Paint Rock TX U.S.A. 161 D6
Paintsville KY U.S.A. 164 D5
Paisley U.K. 60 E5
Paita Peru 176 B5
Paitan, Teluk b. Malaysia 85 G1
Paitou China 97 I2
Paiva Couceiro Angola see Quipungo
Paixban Mex. 167 H5
Paizhouwan China 97 G2
Pajala Sweden 54 M3
Paka Malaysia 84 C1
Pakal i. Moluccas Indon. 83 D2
Pakala India 106 C3
Pakanbaru Sumatra Indon. see Pekanbaru
Pakangyi Myanmar 86 A2
Pakaraima Mountains S. America 176 F3
Pakaur India see Pakur
Pakesley (abandoned) Canada 152 E5
Pakhachi Russia 77 R3
Pakhoi China see Beihai
Paki Nigeria 120 D3
▶Pakistan country Asia 111 H4
4th most populous country in Asia and 6th in the world.
Pakkat Sumatra Indon. 84 B2
Paknampho Thai. see Nakhon Sawan
Pakokku Myanmar 86 A2
Pakowki Lake imp. l. Canada 151 I5
Pakpattan Pak. 111 I4
Pak Phanang Thai. 87 C5
Pak Phayun Thai. 87 C6
Pakruojis Lith. 55 M9
Paks Hungary 68 H1
Pakse Laos see Pakxé
Pak Tam Chung H.K. China 97 [inset]
Pak Thong Chai Thai. 86 C4
Paku r. Malaysia 85 F2
Paku, Tanjung pt Indon. 84 D3
Pakue Celebes Indon. 83 B3
Pakur India 105 F4
Pakxan Laos 86 C3
Pakxé Laos 86 D4
Pakxeng Laos 86 C2
Pala Chad 121 E4
Pala Myanmar 87 B4
Palabuhanratu Java Indon. 84 D4
Palabuhanratu, Teluk b. Indon. 84 D4
Palaestinia reg. Asia see Palestine
Palaiochora Greece 69 J7
Palaiseau France 62 C6
Palakkad India 106 C4
Palakkat India see Palakkad
Palamakoloi Botswana 124 F2
Palamau India see Palamu
Palamea Moluccas Indon. 83 C3
Palamós Spain 67 H3
Palamu India 105 F5
Palana Russia 77 Q4
Palanan Luzon Phil. 82 C2
Palanan Point Luzon Phil. 82 C2
Palandur India 106 D1
Palangān, Kūh-e mts Iran 111 F4
Palangkaraya Kalimantan Indon. 85 F3
Palani India 106 C4
Palanpur India 104 C4
Palanro Celebes Indon. 83 A4
Palantak Pak. 111 G5
Palapag Samar Phil. 82 D3
Palapye Botswana 125 H2
Palasa Celebes Indon. 83 B2
Palatka Russia 77 Q3
Palatka FL U.S.A. 163 D6
Palau country N. Pacific Ocean 82 [inset]
Palau Hatta i. Moluccas Indon. 83 D4
Palaui i. Phil. 82 C2
Palauig Luzon Phil. 82 B3
Palau Islands Palau 81 I5
Palauk Myanmar 87 B4
Palausekopong, Tanjung pt Indon. 84 D4
Palaw Myanmar 87 B4
Palawan i. Phil. 82 B4
Palawan Passage str. Phil. 82 B4
Palawan Trough sea feature N. Pacific Ocean 186 D5
Palayan Luzon Phil. 82 C3
Palayankottai India 106 C4
Palchal Lake India 106 D2
Paldiski Estonia 55 N7
Palekh Russia 52 I4
Paleleh Celebes Indon. 83 B2
Palembang Sumatra Indon. 84 D3
Palena Chile 178 B6
Palencia Spain 67 D2
Palermo Sicily Italy 68 E5
Palestine disp. terr. Asia see West Bank
Palestine disp. terr. Asia see Gaza
Palestine reg. Asia 107 B3
Palestine TX U.S.A. 161 E6
Paletwa Myanmar 86 A2
Palezgir Chauki Pak. 111 H4
Palghat India see Palakkad
Palgrave, Mount hill Australia 135 A5
Palhoça Brazil 179 A4
Pali Chhattisgarh India 106 D1
Pali Mahar. India 106 B2
Pali Rajasthan India 104 C4
Paliat i. Indon. 85 F4
▶Palikir Micronesia 186 G5
Capital of Micronesia.
Palimbang Mindanao Phil. 82 D5
Palimé Togo 120 D4
Palinuro, Capo c. Italy 68 F4
Paliouri, Akra pt Greece see Paliouri, Akrotirio
Paliouri, Akrotirio pt Greece 69 J5
Palisade CO U.S.A. 159 I2
Paliseul Belgium 62 F5
Palitana India 104 B5
Palivere Estonia 55 M7
Palk Bay Sri Lanka 106 C4
Palkino Russia 55 P8
Palkonda Range mts India 106 C3
Palk Strait India/Sri Lanka 106 C4
Palla Bianca mt. Austria/Italy see Weißkugel
Pallamallawa Australia 138 E2
Pallas Grean New Ireland 61 D5
Pallasovka Russia 53 J6
Pallas-Yllästunturin kansallispuisto nat. park Fin. 54 M2
Pallavaram India 106 D3
Palliser, Cape N.Z. 139 E5
Palliser, Îles is Fr. Polynesia 187 K7
Palliser Bay N.Z. 139 E5
Pallu India 104 C3
Palma r. Brazil 179 B1
Palma del Río Spain 67 D5
Palma de Mallorca Spain 67 H4
Palmaner India 106 C3
Palmares Brazil 177 K5
Palmares do Sul Brazil 179 A5
Palmas Paraná Brazil 179 A4
Palmas Tocantins Brazil 176 I6
Palmas, Cape Liberia 120 C4
Palm Bay FL U.S.A. 163 D7
Palmdale CA U.S.A. 158 D4
Palmeira Brazil 179 A4
Palmeira das Missões Brazil 178 F3
Palmeira dos Índios Brazil 177 K5
Palmeirais Brazil 177 J5
Palmeiras Brazil 179 C1
Palmeirinhas, Ponta das pt Angola 123 B4
Palmer research station Antarctica 188 L2
Palmer r. Australia 136 C3
Palmer watercourse Australia 135 F6
Palmer AK U.S.A. 149 J3
Palmer Land reg. Antarctica 188 L2
Palmerston N.T. Australia see Darwin
Palmerston N.T. Australia 134 E3
Palmerston Canada 164 E2
Palmerston atoll Cook Is 133 J3
Palmerston N.Z. 139 C7
Palmerston North N.Z. 139 E5
Palmerton PA U.S.A. 165 H3
Palmerville Australia 136 D2
Palmetto Point Bahamas 163 E7
Palmi Italy 68 F5
Palmillas Mex. 167 F4
Palmira Col. 176 C3
Palmira Cuba 163 D8
Palm Springs CA U.S.A. 158 E5
Palmyra Syria see Tadmur
Palmyra MO U.S.A. 160 F4
Palmyra PA U.S.A. 165 G3
Palmyra VA U.S.A. 165 F5
▶Palmyra Atoll terr. N. Pacific Ocean 186 J5
United States Unincorporated Territory.
Palmyras Point India 105 F5
Palni Hills India 106 C4
Palo Alto CA U.S.A. 158 B3
Palo Blanco Mex. 167 E3
Palo Chino watercourse Mex. 157 E7
Palo de las Letras Col. 166 [inset] K8
Palo Duro watercourse TX U.S.A. 161 C5
Paloh Sarawak Malaysia 85 E2
Paloich South Sudan 108 D7
Palojärvi Fin. 54 M2
Palojoensuu Fin. 54 M2
Palomaa Fin. 54 O2
Palomares Mex. 167 G5
Palomar Mountain CA U.S.A. 158 E5
Paloncha India 106 D2
Palo Pinto TX U.S.A. 161 D5
Palopo Celebes Indon. 83 B3
Palos, Cabo de c. Spain 67 F5
Palo Verde CA U.S.A. 159 F5
Palo Verde, Parque Nacional nat. park Costa Rica 166 [inset] I7
Palpetu, Tanjung pt Buru Indon. 83 C3
Paltamo Fin. 54 O4
Palu Celebes Indon. 83 A3
Palu i. Indon. 83 B5
Palu r. Indon. 83 A3
Palu Turkey 113 E3
Paluan Mindoro Phil. 82 C3
Paluan Bay Mindoro Phil. 82 C3
Pal'vart Turkm. 111 G2
Palwal India 104 D3
Palwancha India see Paloncha

Palyeskaya Nizina marsh Belarus/Ukr. see Pripet Marshes
Pamai China 96 D2

▶Pamana i. Indon. 83 B5
Most southerly point of Asia.

Pamana Besar i. Indon. 83 B5
Pamanukan Java Indon. 85 D4
Pambarra Moz. 125 L1
Pambero Celebes Indon. 83 A2
Pambula Australia 138 D6
Pamekasan Java Indon. 85 F4
Pameungpeuk Java Indon. 85 D4
Pamidi India 106 C3
Pamiers France 66 E5
Pamir mts Asia 111 I2
Pamlico Sound sea chan. NC U.S.A. 163 E5
Pamouscachiou, Lac l. Canada 153 H4
Pampa TX U.S.A. 161 C5
Pampa de Infierno Arg. 178 D3
Pampas reg. Arg. 178 D5
Pampeluna Spain see Pamplona
Pamphylia reg. Turkey 69 N6
Pamplin VA U.S.A. 165 F5
Pamplona Col. 176 D2
Pamplona Negros Phil. 82 C4
Pamplona Spain 67 F2
Pampow Germany 63 L1
Pamukan, Teluk b. Indon. 85 G3
Pamukova Turkey 69 N4
Pamzal India 104 D2
Pana IL U.S.A. 160 F4
Panabá Mex. 167 H4
Panabo Mindanao Phil. 82 D5
Panabutan Bay Mindanao Phil. 82 C5
Panaca NV U.S.A. 159 F3
Panache, Lake Canada 152 E5
Panagtaran Point Palawan Phil. 82 B4
Panagyurishte Bulg. 69 K3
Panaitan i. Indon. 84 D4
Panaji India 106 B3
Panama country Central America 169 H7
Panamá Panama see Panama City
Panamá, Bahía de b. Panama 166 [inset] K7
Panamá, Canal de Panama 166 [inset] K7
Panamá, Golfo de Panama see Panama, Gulf of
Panama, Gulf of g. Panama 166 [inset] K8
Panama, Isthmus of Panama see Panamá, Istmo de
Panamá, Istmo de Panama 169 I7

▶Panama City Panama 166 K7
Capital of Panama.

Panama City FL U.S.A. 163 C6
Panamint Range mts CA U.S.A. 158 E3
Panamint Valley CA U.S.A. 158 E3
Pananjung Pangandaran, Taman Wisata nat. park Indon. 85 E4
Panao Peru 176 C5
Panar r. India 99 E8
Panarea, Isola i. Italy 68 F5
Panarik Sumatra Indon. 85 E2
Panarukan Java Indon. 85 F4
Panay i. Phil. 82 C4
Panay Gulf Phil. 82 C4
Pancake Range mts NV U.S.A. 159 F2
Pančevo Serbia 69 I2
Panchagarh Bangl. 105 G4
Pancingapan, Bukit mt. Indon. 85 F2
Pancsova Serbia see Pančevo
Pancurbatu Sumatra Indon. 84 B2
Panda Moz. 125 L3
Pandan Phil. 82 D3
Pandan, Selat strait Sing. 87 [inset]
Pandan Bay Panay Phil. 82 C4
Pandang Kalimantan Indon. 85 F3
Pandan Reservoir Sing. 87 [inset]
Pandeglang Java Indon. 84 D4
Pandeiros r. Brazil 179 B1
Pandharpur India 106 B2
Pandora Costa Rica 166 [inset] J7
Pandy U.K. 59 E7
Paneas Syria see Bāniyās
Panevėžys Lith. 55 N9
Panfilov Kazakh. see Zharkent
Pang, Nam r. Myanmar 86 B2
Pangandaran Java Indon. 85 E4
Panganiban Phil. 82 D3
Pangean Celebes Indon. 83 A3
Panghsang Myanmar 86 B2
Pangi Range mts Pak. 111 I3
Pangjiabu China 95 H3
Pangkah, Tanjung pt Indon. 85 F4
Pangkajene Celebes Indon. 83 A4
Pangkalanbuun Kalimantan Indon. 85 E3
Pangkalanlunang Sumatra Indon. 84 B2
Pangkalansusu Sumatra Indon. 84 B1
Pangkal Kalong Malaysia 84 C1
Pangkalpinang Indon. 84 D3
Pangkalsiang, Tanjung pt Indon. 83 B3
Pangkog Co salt l. China 99 E7
Panglang Myanmar 86 B1
Panglao i. Phil. 82 C4
Panglima Sugala Phil. 82 B5
Pangman Canada 151 J5
Pangnirtung Canada 147 L3
Pangody Russia 76 I3
Pangong Tso salt l. China/India see Bangong Co
Pangrango vol. Indon. 84 D4
Pangrengrean, Buttu mt. Indon. 83 A3
Pang Sida National Park Thai. 87 C4
Pang Sua, Sungai r. Sing. 87 [inset]
Pangtara Myanmar 96 C4
Pangu He r. China 90 B1
Panguitch UT U.S.A. 159 G3
Pangujon, Tanjung pt Indon. 85 E3
Pangururan Sumatra Indon. 84 B2
Pangutaran i. Phil. 82 C5
Pangutaran Group is Phil. 82 C5
Panhandle TX U.S.A. 161 C5
Panipat India 104 D3
Panir Pak. 111 G4
Panitian Palawan Phil. 82 B4
Panj Tajik. 111 H2
Panjāb Afgh. 111 G3
Panjakent Tajik. 111 G2
Panjang Sumatra Indon. 84 D4
Panjang i. Indon. 85 E2
Panjang i. Indon. 85 G2
Panjang, Bukit Sing. 87 [inset]
Panjang, Selat sea chan. Indon. 84 C2
Panjgur Pak. 111 G5
Panjim India see Panaji
Panjin China see Panshan
Panji Poyon Tajik. 111 H2
Panjnad r. Pak. 111 H4
Panjshayr reg. Afgh. 111 H3
Pankakoski Fin. 54 Q5
Pankof, Cape AK U.S.A. 148 G5
Panlian China see Miyi
Panna India 104 E4
Panna reg. India 104 D4
Pannawonica Australia 134 B5
Pano Lefkara Cyprus 107 A2
Panopah Kalimantan Indon. 85 E3
Panorama Brazil 179 A3
Panormus Sicily Italy see Palermo
Panshan China 95 J3
Panshi China 90 B4
Panshui China see Pu'an
Pantai Kalimantan Indon. 85 G3
Pantaicermin, Gunung mt. Indon. 84 C3

▶Pantanal marsh Brazil 177 G7
Largest area of wetlands in the world.

Pantanal Matogrossense, Parque Nacional do nat. park Brazil 177 G7
Pantano AZ U.S.A. 159 H6
Pantar i. Indon. 83 C5
Pantelaria Sicily Italy see Pantelleria
Pantelleria Sicily Italy 68 D6
Pantelleria, Isola di i. Sicily Italy 68 E6
Pante Macassar East Timor 83 C5
Pantemakassar East Timor see Pante Macassar
Pantha Myanmar 86 A2
Panther r. KY U.S.A. 164 B5
Panth Piploda India 104 C5
Panticapaeum Crimea see Kerch
Pantonlabu Sumatra Indon. 84 B1
Pantukan Mindanao Phil. 82 D5
Panua, Cagar Alam nature res. Indon. 83 B2
Pánuco Sinaloa Mex. 161 B8
Pánuco Veracruz Mex. 168 E4
Pánuco r. Mex. 167 F4
Panwari India 104 D4
Panxian China 96 E3
Panyu China 97 G4
Panzhihua China 96 D3
Panzi Dem. Rep. Congo 123 B4
Panzos Guat. 167 H6
Paola Italy 68 G5
Paola KS U.S.A. 160 E4
Paoli IN U.S.A. 164 B4
Paoni Seram Indon. 83 D3
Paoua Cent. Afr. Rep. 122 B3
Paôy Pêt Cambodia 87 C4
Pápa Hungary 68 G1
Papa, Monte del mt. Italy 68 F4
Papagni r. India 106 C3
Papahānaumokuākea tourist site U.S.A. 186 I4
Pāpa'ikou HI U.S.A. 157 [inset]
Papakura N.Z. 139 E3
Papanasam India 106 C4
Papanoa Mex. 167 E5
Papanoa, Morro de hd Mex. 167 E5
Papantla Mex. 168 E4
Papar Sabah Malaysia 85 F1
Paparoa National Park N.Z. 139 C6
Papa Stour i. U.K. 60 [inset]
Papa Westray i. U.K. 60 G1
Papay i. U.K. see Papa Westray

▶Papeete Fr. Polynesia 187 K7
Capital of French Polynesia.

Papenburg Germany 63 H1
Paphos Cyprus 107 A2
Paphus Cyprus see Paphos
Papillion NE U.S.A. 160 D3
Papoose Lake NV U.S.A. 159 F3
Pappenheim Germany 63 K6
Papua, Gulf of P.N.G. 81 K8
Papua Barat prov. Indon. 83 D3

▶Papua New Guinea country Oceania 132 E2
2nd largest and 2nd most populous country in Oceania.

Pā Qal'eh Iran 110 D4
Par U.K. 59 C8
Pará r. Brazil 179 B2
Para i. Indon. 83 C2
Pará, Rio do r. Brazil 177 I4
Paraburdoo Australia 135 B5
Paracale Luzon Phil. 82 C3
Paracatu Brazil 179 B2
Paracatu r. Brazil 179 B2
Paracel Islands S. China Sea 80 E3
Parachilna Australia 137 B6
Parachute CO U.S.A. 159 I2
Paraćin Serbia 69 I3
Paracuru Brazil 177 K4
Pará de Minas Brazil 179 B2
Paradis Canada 152 F4
Paradise r. Canada 153 K3
Paradise AK U.S.A. 148 G3
Paradise CA U.S.A. 158 C2
Paradise Hill Canada 151 I4
Paradise Peak NV U.S.A. 158 E2
Paradise River Canada 153 K3
Parado Sumbawa Indon. 85 G5
Paradwip India 105 F5
Paraetonium Egypt see Marsá Maṭrūḥ
Paragominas Brazil 177 I4
Paragould AR U.S.A. 161 F4
Paragua i. Phil. see Palawan
Paraguaçu Paulista Brazil 179 A3
Paraguay r. Arg./Para. 178 E3
Paraguay country S. America 178 E2
Paraíba do Sul r. Brazil 179 C3
Parainen Fin. see Pargas
Paraíso Tabasco Mex. 167 G5
Paraíso Tabasco Mex. 167 G5
Paraíso do Tocantins Brazil 177 I6
Paraisópolis Brazil 179 B3
Parak Iran 110 D5
Pārak Hūtān Iran 111 F5
Parakou Benin 120 D4
Paralakhemundi India 106 E2
Paralkot India 106 D2
Paramagudi India see Paramakkudi
Paramakkudi India 106 C4

▶Paramaribo Suriname 177 G2
Capital of Suriname.

Paramillo, Parque Nacional nat. park Col. 176 C2
Paramirim Brazil 179 C1
Paramo Frontino mt. Col. 176 C2
Paramus NJ U.S.A. 165 H3
Paramushir, Ostrov i. Russia 77 Q4
Paran, Naḥal watercourse Israel 107 B4
Paraná Arg. 178 D4
Paranã Brazil 179 B1
Paraná r. Brazil 179 A1
Paraná state Brazil 179 A4

▶Paraná r. S. America 178 E4
Part of the Río de la Plata - Paraná, 2nd longest river in South America.

Paraná, Serra do hills Brazil 179 B1
Paranaguá Brazil 179 A4
Paranaíba Brazil 179 A2
Paranaíba r. Brazil 179 A3
Paranapiacaba, Serra mts Brazil 179 A4
Paranas Samar Phil. 82 D4
Paranavaí Brazil 178 F2
Parang i. Indon. 85 E4
Parang Phil. 82 C5
Parangi Aru r. Sri Lanka 106 D4
Parang Pass India 104 D2
Parângul Mare, Vârful mt. Romania 69 J2
Parantan Sri Lanka 106 D4
Paraopeba Brazil 179 B2
Parapara Halmahera Indon. 83 C2
Pārapāra Iraq 113 G4
Paraparaumu N.Z. 139 E5
Paras Mex. 161 D7
Paras Pak. 111 I3
Parasia India 104 D5
Parasnath mt. India 105 F5
Paraspori, Akra pt Greece see Paraspori, Akrotirio
Paraspori, Akrotirio pt Greece 69 L7
Parateca Brazil 179 C1
Paratinga Brazil 179 C1
Parāū, Kūh-e mt. Iraq 113 G4
Paraúna Brazil 179 A2
Parbhani India 106 C2
Parchim Germany 63 L1
Parc National de Lobéké nat. park Cameroon 121 E4
Parding China 105 G2
Pardo r. Bahia Brazil 179 D1
Pardo r. Mato Grosso do Sul Brazil 178 F2
Pardo r. São Paulo Brazil 179 A3
Pardoo Australia 134 B5
Pardubice Czech Rep. 57 O5
Parece Vela i. Japan see Okino-Tori-shima
Pare Chu r. China 99 B6
Parecis, Serra dos hills Brazil 176 F6
Paredón Mex. 167 E3
Pareh Iran 110 B2
Parenda India 106 B2
Parenggean Kalimantan Indon. 85 F3
Parent Canada 152 G5
Parent, Lac l. Canada 152 F4
Pareora N.Z. 139 C7
Parepare Celebes Indon. 83 A4
Parga Greece 69 I5
Pargas Fin. 55 M6
Parghelia Italy 68 F5
Pargi India 106 C2
Paria, Gulf of Trin. and Tob./Venez. 169 L6
Paria, Península de pen. Venez. 176 F1
Pariaman Sumatra Indon. 84 C3
Paria Plateau AZ U.S.A. 159 G3
Parida, Isla i. Panama 166 [inset] J7
Parigi Celebes Indon. 83 B3
Parikkala Fin. 55 P6
Parikud Islands India 106 E2
Parima, Serra mts Brazil 176 F3
Parima-Tapirapecó, Parque Nacional nat. park Venez. 176 F3
Parintins Brazil 177 G4
Paris Canada 164 E2

▶Paris France 62 C6
Capital of France. 3rd most populous city in Europe.

Paris IL U.S.A. 164 B4
Paris KY U.S.A. 164 C4
Paris MO U.S.A. 160 E4
Paris TN U.S.A. 161 F4
Paris TX U.S.A. 161 E5
Paris (Charles de Gaulle) airport France 62 C5
Paris (Orly) airport France 62 C6
Paris Crossing IN U.S.A. 164 C4
Parit Buntar Malaysia 84 C1
Pārīz Iran 110 D4
Park U.K. 61 E3
Parkano Fin. 55 M5
Park City KY U.S.A. 164 B5
Parke Lake Canada 153 K3
Parker AZ U.S.A. 159 F4
Parker CO U.S.A. 156 G5
Parker Dam CA U.S.A. 159 F4
Parker Lake Canada 151 M2
Parker Range hills Australia 135 B8
Parkersburg WV U.S.A. 164 E4
Parkers Lake KY U.S.A. 164 C5
Parkes Australia 138 D4
Park Falls WI U.S.A. 160 F2
Park Forest IL U.S.A. 164 B3
Parkhar Tajik. see Farkhor
Parkhill Canada 164 E2
Park Rapids MN U.S.A. 160 E2
Parkutta Pak. 104 D2
Park Valley UT U.S.A. 156 E4
Parla Kimedi India see Paralakhemundi
Parlakimidi India see Paralakhemundi
Parli Vaijnath India 106 C2
Parlung Zangbo r. China 96 B2
Parma Italy 68 D2
Parma ID U.S.A. 156 D4
Parma OH U.S.A. 164 E3
Parnaíba Brazil 177 J4
Parnaíba r. Brazil 177 J4
Parnassos mt. Greece see Liakoura
Parnassus N.Z. 139 D6
Parner India 106 B2
Parnon mts Greece see Parnonas
Parnonas mts Greece 69 J6
Pärnu Estonia 55 N7
Pärnu-Jaagupi Estonia 55 N7
Paro Bhutan 105 G4
Paroikia Greece 69 K6
Parona Turkey see Fındık
Paroo watercourse Australia 138 A3
Paroo Channel watercourse Australia 138 A3
Paroo-Darling National Park Australia 137 C6
Paropamisus mts Afgh. see Safēd Kōh, Silsilah-ye
Paros Greece see Paroikia
Paros i. Greece 69 K6
Parowan UT U.S.A. 159 G3
Parque Nacional do Limpopo nat. park S. Africa 125 J2
Parque Natural del Gran Desierto del Pinacate tourist site Mex. 168 B2
Parral Chile 178 B5
Parramatta Australia 138 E4
Parramore Island VA U.S.A. 165 H5
Parras Mex. 166 E3
Parrett r. U.K. 59 D7
Parrita Costa Rica 166 [inset] I7
Parry, Cape Canada 149 P1
Parry, Kap c. Greenland see Kangaarsussuaq
Parry, Lac l. Canada 152 G2
Parry Bay Canada 147 J3
Parry Channel Canada 147 G2
Parry Islands Canada 147 G2
Parry Peninsula Canada 149 P1
Parry Range hills Australia 134 A5
Parry Sound Canada 164 E1
Pārsīān Iran 110 D5
Parsnip Peak NV U.S.A. 159 F2
Parsons KS U.S.A. 161 E4
Parsons WV U.S.A. 164 F4
Parsons Lake Canada 149 N1
Parsons Range hills Australia 134 F3
Parta China 99 E7
Partabgarh India 106 B2
Partabpur India 105 E5
Partenstein Germany 63 J4
Parthenay France 66 D3
Partida, Isla i. Mex. 166 C3
Partizansk Russia 90 D4
Partney U.K. 58 H5
Partridge r. Canada 152 E4
Partry Ireland 61 C4
Partry Mountains hills Ireland 61 C4
Paru r. Brazil 177 H4
Pārūd Iran 111 F5
Paryang China 99 C7
Parygino Kazakh. 98 D2
Parys S. Africa 125 H4
Pās, Chāh well Iran 110 D3
Pasa Dağı mt. Turkey 112 D3
Pasadena Canada 153 K4
Pasadena CA U.S.A. 158 D4
Pasadena TX U.S.A. 161 E6
Pasado, Cabo c. Ecuador 176 B4
Pa Sang Thai. 86 B3
Pasangkayu Celebes Indon. 83 A3
Pasarbantal Sumatra Indon. 84 C3
Pasarseblat Sumatra Indon. 84 C3
Pasarseluma Sumatra Indon. 84 C4
Pasarwajo Celebes Indon. 83 B4
Pasawng Myanmar 86 B3
Pascagama r. Canada 152 G4
Pascagoula MS U.S.A. 161 F6
Pascagoula r. MS U.S.A. 161 F6
Paşcani Romania 69 L1
Pasco WA U.S.A. 156 D3
Pascoal, Monte hill Brazil 179 D2
Pascua, Isla de i. S. Pacific Ocean see Easter Island
Pas de Calais strait France/U.K. see Dover, Strait of
Pasewalk Germany 57 O4
Pasfield Lake Canada 151 J3
Pasha Russia 52 G3
Pashih Haihsia sea chan. Phil./Taiwan see Bashi Channel
Pashkovo Russia 90 C2
Pashkovskiy Russia 53 H7
Pashū'īyeh Iran 110 E4
Pasig Luzon Phil. 82 C3
Pasi Ga Myanmar 86 B1
Pasige i. Indon. 83 C2
Pasighat India 105 H3
Pasinler Turkey 113 F3
Pasir Gudang Malaysia 87 [inset]
Pasirian Java Indon. 85 F5
Pasir Mas Malaysia 84 C1
Pasirpangarayan Sumatra Indon. 84 C2
Pasir Putih Malaysia 84 C1
Pasitelu, Pulau-pulau is Indon. 83 B4
Paskūh Iran 111 F5
Pasni Pak. 185 M4
Paso Caballos Guat. 167 H5
Paso de los Toros Uruguay 178 E4
Paso de San Antonio Mex. 161 C6
Pasok Myanmar 86 A2
Paso Real Hond. 166 [inset] I6
Paso Robles CA U.S.A. 158 C4
Pasqua Hills Canada 151 K4
Passaic NJ U.S.A. 165 H3
Passa Tempo Brazil 179 B3
Passau Germany 57 N6
Passi Panay Phil. 82 C4
Passo del San Gottardo Switz. see St Gotthard Pass
Passo Fundo Brazil 178 F3
Passos Brazil 179 B3
Passur r. Bangl. see Pusur
Passuri Nadi r. Bangl. see Pusur
Pastavy Belarus 55 O9
Pastaza r. Peru 176 C4
Pasto Col. 176 C3
Pastol Bay AK U.S.A. 148 G3
Pastora Peak AZ U.S.A. 159 I3
Pastos Bons Brazil 177 J5
Pasu Pak. 104 C1
Pasuquin Luzon Phil. 82 C2
Pasur Turkey see Kulp
Pasuruan Java Indon. 85 F4
Pasvalys Lith. 55 N8
Pasvikelva r. Europe see Patsoyoki
Pata i. Phil. 82 C5
Patache, Punta pt Chile 178 B2
Patagonia reg. Arg. 178 B8
Pataliputra India see Patna
Patan Gujarat India see Somnath
Patan Gujarat India 104 C5
Patan Mahar. India 106 B2
Patan Nepal 105 F4
Patan Pak. 111 I3
Patandar, Koh-i- mt. Pak. 111 G5
Patani Halmahera Indon. 83 D2
Patargān, Daqq-e salt flat Iran 111 F3
Patavium Italy see Padua
Patea N.Z. 139 E4
Patea inlet N.Z. see Doubtful Sound
Pate Island Kenya 122 E4
Pateley Bridge U.K. 58 F4
Patensie S. Africa 124 G7
Patera India 104 D4
Paterson Australia 138 E4
Paterson r. Australia 138 C2
Paterson NJ U.S.A. 165 H3
Paterson Range hills Australia 134 C5
Pathanamthitta India 106 C4
Pathankot India 104 C2
Pathari India 104 D5
Pathein Myanmar see Bassein
Pathfinder Reservoir WY U.S.A. 156 G4
Pathiu Thai. 87 B5
Pathum Thani Thai. 87 C4
Pati Java Indon. 85 E4
Patía r. Col. 176 C3
Patiala India 104 D3
Patinti, Selat sea chan. Moluccas Indon. 83 C3
Patkai Bum mts India/Myanmar 105 H4
Patkaklik China 99 D5
Patmos i. Greece 69 L6
Patna Bihar India 105 F4
Patna Odisha India 105 F5
Patnagarh India 105 E5
Patnanongan i. Phil. 82 C3
Patnos Turkey 113 F3
Pato Branco Brazil 178 F3
Patoda India 106 B2
Patoka r. IN U.S.A. 164 B4
Patoka Lake IN U.S.A. 164 B4
Patos Albania 69 H4
Patos Brazil 177 K5
Patos, Lagoa dos l. Brazil 178 F4
Patos de Minas Brazil 179 B2
Patquía Arg. 178 C4
Patra Greece see Patras
Patrae Greece see Patras
Pátrai Greece see Patras
Patras Greece 69 I5
Patreksfjörður Iceland 54 [inset 1]
Patricio Lynch, Isla i. Chile 178 A7
Patrick Creek watercourse Australia 136 D4
Patrimônio Brazil 179 A2
Patrocínio Brazil 179 B2
Paṭrū Iran 111 E3
Patsoyoki r. Europe 54 Q2
Pattadakal tourist site India 106 B2
Pattani Thai. 87 C6
Pattani, Mae Nam r. Thai. 84 C1
Pattaya Thai. 87 C4
Pattensen Germany 63 J2
Patterson CA U.S.A. 158 C3
Patterson LA U.S.A. 161 F6
Patterson, Mount Canada 149 N2
Patti India 105 E4
Patti Moluccas Indon. 83 C5
Pattijoki Fin. 54 N4
Pättikkä Fin. 54 L2
Pattiro, Tanjung pt Indon. 83 B4
Patton PA U.S.A. 165 F3
Pattullo, Mount Canada 149 O4
Patu Brazil 177 K5
Patuakhali Bangl. 105 G5
Patuanak Canada 151 J4
Patuca r. Hond. 166 [inset] I6
Patuca, Punta pt Hond. 166 [inset] I6
Patucas, Parque Nacional nat. park Hond. 166 [inset] I6
Patur India 106 C1
Patuxent r. MD U.S.A. 165 G4
Patuxent Range mts Antarctica 188 L1
Patvinsuon kansallispuisto nat. park Fin. 54 Q5
Pátzcuaro Mex. 167 E5
Pau France 66 D5
Pauhunri mt. China/India 105 G4
Pauillac France 66 D4
Pauini Brazil 176 E5
Pauini r. Brazil 176 E5
Pauk Myanmar 86 A2
Paukkaung Myanmar 86 A3
Paulatuk Canada 149 Q1
Paulatuuq Canada see Paulatuk
Paulden AZ U.S.A. 159 G4
Paulding OH U.S.A. 164 C3
Paulicéia Brazil 179 A3
Paulis Dem. Rep. Congo see Isiro
Paul Island Canada 153 J2
Paulo Afonso Brazil 177 K5
Paulo de Faria Brazil 179 A3
Pauloff Harbor AK U.S.A. 148 G5
Paulpietersburg S. Africa 125 J4
Paul Roux S. Africa 125 H5
Paulstown Ireland 61 E5
Pauls Valley OK U.S.A. 161 D5
Paumotu, Îles is Fr. Polynesia see Tuamotu Islands
Paung Myanmar 86 B3
Paungbyin Myanmar 86 A1
Paungde Myanmar 86 A3
Pauni India 106 C1
Pauri India 104 D3
Pavagada India 106 C3
Pavão Brazil 179 C2
Pāveh Iran 110 B3
Pavia Italy 68 C2
Pāvilosta Latvia 55 L8
Pavino Russia 52 J4
Pavlikeni Bulg. 69 K3
Pavlodar Kazakh. 102 E1
Pavlodarskaya Oblast' admin. div. Kazakh. 98 B1
Pavlof Bay AK U.S.A. 148 G5
Pavlof Islands AK U.S.A. 148 G5
Pavlof Volcano AK U.S.A. 148 [inset]5
Pavlograd Ukr. see Pavlohrad
Pavlohrad Ukr. 53 G6
Pavlovka Russia 53 J5
Pavlovo Russia 52 I5
Pavlovsk Altayskiy Kray Russia 88 E2
Pavlovsk Voronezhskaya Oblast' Russia 53 I6
Pavlovskaya Russia 53 H7
Pawahku Myanmar 86 B1
Pawai India 104 E4
Pawan r. Indon. 85 E3
Pawayan India 99 C7
Pawnee OK U.S.A. 161 D4
Pawnee r. KS U.S.A. 160 D4
Pawnee City NE U.S.A. 160 D3
Paw Paw MI U.S.A. 164 C2
Paw Paw WV U.S.A. 165 F4
Pawtucket RI U.S.A. 165 J3
Pawut Myanmar 87 B4
Paxson AK U.S.A. 149 K3
Paxton IL U.S.A. 164 A3
Payahe Halmahera Indon. 83 C2
Payakumbuh Sumatra Indon. 84 C3
Paya Lebar Sing. 87 [inset]
Pāy Bōldak Ghar mt. Afgh. 111 G4
Payette ID U.S.A. 156 D3
Pay-Khoy, Khrebet hills Russia 76 H3
Payne Canada see Kangirsuk
Payne, Lac l. Canada 152 G2
Paynes Creek CA U.S.A. 158 C1
Paynes Find Australia 135 B7
Paynesville MN U.S.A. 160 E2
Paysandú Uruguay 178 E4
Payshanba Uzbek. 111 G1
Payson AZ U.S.A. 159 H4
Payung, Tanjung pt Malaysia 85 F2
Payzawat China see Jiashi
Pazar Turkey 113 F2
Pazarcık Turkey 112 E3
Pazardzhik Bulg. 69 K3
Pazin Croatia 68 E2
Pe Myanmar 87 B4
Peabody KS U.S.A. 160 D4
Peabody MA U.S.A. 165 J2

▶Peace r. Canada 150 I3
Part of the Mackenzie-Peace-Finlay, the 2nd longest river in North America.

Peace Point Canada 151 H3
Peace River Canada 150 G3
Peach Creek WV U.S.A. 164 E5
Peach Springs AZ U.S.A. 159 G4
Peacock Hills Canada 151 I1
Peak Charles hill Australia 135 C8
Peak Charles National Park Australia 135 C8
Peak District National Park U.K. 58 F5
Peake watercourse Australia 137 B6
Peaked Mountain hill ME U.S.A. 162 G2
Peak Hill Australia 138 D4
Peak Hill (abandoned) Australia 135 B6
Peale, Mount UT U.S.A. 159 I2
Peanut CA U.S.A. 158 B1
Pearce (abandoned) AZ U.S.A. 159 I6
Pearce Point Australia 134 E3
Peard Bay AK U.S.A. 148 H1
Pearisburg VA U.S.A. 164 E5
Pearl r. MS U.S.A. 161 F6
Pearl Harbor inlet HI U.S.A. 157 [inset]
Pearsall TX U.S.A. 161 D6
Pearson GA U.S.A. 163 D6
Pearston S. Africa 125 G7
Peary Channel Canada 147 I2
Peary Land reg. Greenland 189 J1
Pease r. TX U.S.A. 161 D5
Peawanuck Canada 152 D3
Pebane Moz. 123 D5

Pebas Peru 176 D4
Pebengko Celebes Indon. 83 B3
Peć Kosovo see Pejë
Peçanha Brazil 179 C2
Pecan Island LA U.S.A. 167 G2
Peças, Ilha das i. Brazil 179 A4
Pechenga Russia 54 Q2
Pechora Russia 52 M2
Pechora r. Russia 52 L1
Pechora Sea Russia see Pechorskoye More
Pechorskaya Guba b. Russia 52 L1
Pechorskoye More sea Russia 189 G2
Pechory Russia 55 O8
Peck MI U.S.A. 164 D2
Pecos TX U.S.A. 161 C6
Pecos r. New Mexico/Texas U.S.A. 161 C6
Pécs Hungary 68 H1
Pedasí Panama 166 [inset] J8
Pedda Vagu r. India 106 C2
Pedder, Lake Australia 137 [inset]
Peddie S. Africa 125 H7
Pedernales Dom. Rep. 169 J5
Pedieos r. Cyprus 107 A2
Pediva Angola 123 B5
Pediwang Halmahera Indon. 83 C2
Pedra Azul Brazil 179 C1
Pedra Preta, Serra da mts Brazil 179 A1
Pedras de Maria da Cruz Brazil 179 B1
Pedregal Panama 166 [inset] J7
Pedregulho Brazil 179 B3
Pedreiras Brazil 177 J4
Pedriceña Mex. 166 E3
Pedro, Point Sri Lanka 106 D4
Pedro Bay AK U.S.A. 148 I4
Pedro Betancourt Cuba 163 D8
Pedro Canário Brazil 179 D2
Pedro II, Ilha reg. Brazil/Venez. 176 E3
Pedro Juan Caballero Para. 178 E2
Peebles U.K. 60 F5
Peebles OH U.S.A. 164 D4
Pee Dee r. SC U.S.A. 163 E5
Peekskill NY U.S.A. 165 I3
Peel r. Australia 138 E3
Peel r. Canada 149 N1
Peel Isle of Man 58 C4
Peel River Game Preserve nature res. Canada 149 N2
Peer Belgium 62 F3
Peera Peera Poolanna Lake salt flat Australia 137 B5
Peerless Lake Canada 150 H3
Peerless Lake l. Canada 150 H3
Peers Canada 150 G4
Peery Lake salt flat Australia 138 A3
Pegasus Bay N.Z. 139 D6
Pegnitz Germany 63 L5
Pegu Myanmar 86 B3
Pegunungan Latimojong nature res. Indon. 83 B3
Pegunungan Peruhumpenai nature res. Indon. 83 B3
Pegu Yoma mts Myanmar 86 A3
Pegysh Russia 52 K3
Pehuajó Arg. 178 D5
Peikang Taiwan see Beigang
Peine Chile 178 C2
Peine Germany 63 K2
Peint India 106 B1
Peipsi järv l. Estonia/Russia see Peipus, Lake
Peipus, Lake Estonia/Russia 55 O7
Peiraias Greece see Piraeus
Pei Shan mts China see Bei Shan
Peißen Germany 63 L3
Peixe Brazil 177 I6
Peixe r. Brazil 179 A1
Peixian Jiangsu China see Pizhou
Peixian Jiangsu China 95 I5
Peixoto de Azevedo Brazil 177 H6
Pejantan i. Indon. 84 D2
Pejë Kosovo 69 I3
Pèk Laos see Phônsavan
Peka Lesotho 125 H5
Pekabata Celebes Indon. 83 A3
Pekalongan Java Indon. 85 E4
Pekan Malaysia 84 C2
Pekanbaru Sumatra Indon. 84 C2
Pekin IL U.S.A. 160 F3
Peking China see Beijing
Pekinga Benin 120 D3
Pelabuhan Klang Malaysia 84 C2
Pelagie, Isole is Sicily Italy 68 E7
Pelaihari Kalimantan Indon. 85 F3
Pelalawan Sumatra Indon. 84 C2
Pelapis i. Indon. 85 E3
Pelawanbesar Kalimantan Indon. 85 G2
Peleaga, Vârful mt. Romania 69 J2
Pelee Island Canada 164 D3
Pelee Point Canada 164 D3
Peleliu i. Palau 82 [inset]
Peleng i. Indon. 83 B3
Peleng, Selat sea chan. Indon. 83 B3
Peleng, Teluk b. Indon. 83 B3
Peles Russia 52 K3
Pélican, Lac du l. Canada 153 G2
Pelican Lake Canada 151 K4
Pelican Lake MN U.S.A. 160 E1
Pelican Narrows Canada 151 K4
Pelkosenniemi Fin. 54 O3
Pella S. Africa 124 D5
Pellatt Lake Canada 151 I1
Pelleluhu Islands P.N.G. 81 K7
Pello Fin. 54 M3
Pelly r. Canada 150 C2
Pelly Crossing Canada 149 M3
Pelly Island Canada 149 N1
Pelly Lake Canada 151 K1
Pelly Mountains Canada 149 N3
Pelokang is Indon. 85 G4
Pelotas Brazil 178 F4
Pelotas, Rio das r. Brazil 179 A4
Pelusium tourist site Egypt 107 A4
Pelusium, Bay of Egypt see Ţīnah, Khalīj aţ
Pemalang Java Indon. 85 E4
Pemangkat Kalimantan Indon. 85 E2
Pemarung, Pulau i. Indon. 85 G3
Pematangsiantar Sumatra Indon. 84 B2
Pemba Moz. 123 E5
Pemba Island Tanz. 123 D4
Pemberton Canada 150 F5
Pembina r. Canada 150 H4
Pembina r. ND U.S.A. 160 D1
Pembine WI U.S.A. 162 C2
Pembre Indon. 81 J8
Pembroke Canada 152 F5
Pembroke U.K. 59 C7
Pembroke GA U.S.A. 163 D5
Pembrokeshire Coast National Park U.K. 59 B7
Pembuanghulu Kalimantan Indon. 85 F3
Pemuar Kalimantan Indon. 85 E3
Pen India 106 B2
Peña Cerredo mt. Spain see Torrecerredo
Peñalara mt. Spain 67 E3
Penamar Brazil 179 C1
Penambo Range mts Malaysia see Tama Abu, Banjaran
Penampang Sabah Malaysia 85 G1
Peña Nevada, Cerro mt. Mex. 168 E4
Penang state Malaysia see Pinang
Penápolis Brazil 179 A3
Peñaranda de Bracamonte Spain 67 D3
Penarie Australia 138 A5
Penarlâg U.K. see Hawarden
Peñarroya mt. Spain 67 F3
Peñarroya-Pueblonuevo Spain 67 D4
Penarth U.K. 59 D7
Peñas, Cabo de c. Spain 67 D2
Penas, Golfo de g. Chile 178 A7
Peñas Blancas Nicaragua 166 [inset] I7
Penasi, Pulau i. Indon. 87 A6
Pencoso, Alto de hills Arg. 178 C4
Pender NE U.S.A. 160 D3
Pendjari, Parc National de la nat. park Benin 120 D3
Pendle Hill hill U.K. 58 E5
Pendleton OR U.S.A. 156 D3
Pendleton Bay Canada 150 E4
Pendopo Sumatra Indon. 84 C3
Pend Oreille r. WA U.S.A. 156 D2
Pend Oreille Lake ID U.S.A. 156 D2
Pendra India 105 E5
Penduv India 106 B2
Pendzhikent Tajik. see Panjakent
Penebangan i. Indon. 85 E3
Peneda Gerês, Parque Nacional da nat. park Port. 67 B3
Penetanguishene Canada 164 F1
Penfro U.K. see Pembroke
Peng'an China 96 E2
Penganga r. India 106 C2
Peng Chau i. H.K. China 97 [inset]
Penge Dem. Rep. Congo 123 C4
Penge S. Africa 125 J3
Penghu Dao i. Taiwan 97 H4
P'enghu Lieh-tao is Taiwan see Penghu Qundao
Penghu Qundao is Taiwan 97 H4
Pengiki i. Indon. 85 E2
Pengjia Yu i. Taiwan 97 I3
Pengkalan Hulu Malaysia 84 C1
Peng Kang hill Sing. 87 [inset]
Penglai China 95 J4
Penglaizhen China see Daying
Pengshan China 96 D2
Pengshui China 97 F2
Pengwa Myanmar 86 A2
Pengxi China 96 E2
Penha Brazil 179 A4
Penhoek Pass S. Africa 125 H6
Penhook VA U.S.A. 164 F5
Peniche Port. 67 B4
Penicuik U.K. 60 F5
Penida i. Indon. 85 F5
Penig Germany 63 M4
Peninga Russia 54 R5
Peninsular Malaysia Malaysia 84 C2
Penitente, Serra do hills Brazil 177 I5
Penn PA U.S.A. see Penn Hills
Pennell Coast Antarctica 188 H2
Penn Hills PA U.S.A. 164 F3
Pennine, Alpi mts Italy/Switz. 68 B2
Pennine Alps mts Italy/Switz. see Pennine, Alpi
Pennines hills U.K. 58 E4
Pennington Gap VA U.S.A. 164 D5
Pennsburg PA U.S.A. 165 H3
Penns Grove NJ U.S.A. 165 H4
Pennsville NJ U.S.A. 165 H4
Pennsylvania state U.S.A. 164 F3
Pennville IN U.S.A. 164 C3
Penn Yan NY U.S.A. 165 G2
Penny Icecap Canada 147 L3
Penny Point Antarctica 188 H1
Penola Australia 137 C8
Peñón Blanco Mex. 166 D3
Penong Australia 135 F7
Penonomé Panama 166 [inset] J7
Penrhyn atoll Cook Is 187 J6
Penrhyn Basin sea feature S. Pacific Ocean 187 J6
Penrith Australia 138 E4
Penrith U.K. 58 E4
Pensacola FL U.S.A. 163 C6
Pensacola Mountains Antarctica 188 L1
Pensiangan Sabah Malaysia 85 G1
Pensi La pass India 104 D2
Pentadaktylos Range mts Cyprus 107 A2
Pentakota India 106 D2
Pentecost Island Vanuatu 133 G3
Pentecôte, Île i. Vanuatu see Pentecost Island
Penticton Canada 150 G5
Pentire Point U.K. 59 B8
Pentland Australia 136 D4
Pentland Firth sea chan. U.K. 60 F2
Pentland Hills U.K. 60 F5
Pentwater MI U.S.A. 164 B2
Penuba Sumatra Indon. 84 D3
Penuguan Sumatra Indon. 84 D3
Penunjuk, Tanjung pt Malaysia 84 C1
Penwegon Myanmar 86 B3
Pen-y-bont ar Ogwr U.K. see Bridgend
Penygadair hill U.K. 59 D6
Penylan Lake Canada 151 J2
Penyu, Kepulauan is Moluccas Indon. 83 C4
Penza Russia 53 J5
Penzance U.K. 59 B8
Penzhinskaya Guba b. Russia 77 R3
Peoria AZ U.S.A. 159 G5
Peoria IL U.S.A. 160 F3
Peotone IL U.S.A. 164 B3
Peper, Teluk b. Indon. see Lada, Teluk
Pequeña, Punta pt Mex. 166 B3
Pequop Mountains NV U.S.A. 159 F1
Peradeniya Sri Lanka 106 D5
Pera Head hd Australia 136 C2
Perak i. Malaysia 84 B1
Perak r. Malaysia 84 C1
Perak state Malaysia 84 C1
Perales del Alfambra Spain 67 F3
Perambalur India 106 C4
Perämeren kansallispuisto nat. park Fin. 54 N4
Peranap Sumatra Indon. 84 C3
Peräseinäjoki Fin. 54 M5
Percé Canada 153 I4
Percival Lakes salt flat Australia 134 D5
Percy NH U.S.A. 165 J1
Percy Isles Australia 136 E4
Percy Reach l. Canada 165 G1
Perdizes Brazil 179 B2
Perdu, Lac l. Canada 153 H4
Peregrebnoye Russia 51 T3
Pereira Col. 176 C3
Pereira Barreto Brazil 179 A3
Pereira de Eça Angola see Ondjiva
Pere Marquette r. MI U.S.A. 164 B2
Peremul Par reef India 106 B4
Peremyshlyany Ukr. 53 E6
Perenjori Australia 135 B7
Pereslavl'-Zalesskiy Russia 52 H4
Pereslavskiy Natsional'nyy Park nat. park Russia 52 H4
Pereyaslavka Russia 90 D3
Pereyaslav-Khmel'nitskiy Ukr. see Pereyaslav-Khmel'nyts'kyy
Pereyaslav-Khmel'nyts'kyy Ukr. 53 F6
Perforated Island Thai. see Bon, Ko
Pergamino Arg. 178 D4
Perhentian Besar, Pulau i. Malaysia 84 C1
Perho Fin. 54 N5
Péribonka, Lac l. Canada 153 H4
Perico Arg. 178 C2
Pericos Mex. 166 D3
Peridot AZ U.S.A. 159 H5
Périgueux France 66 E4
Perijá, Parque Nacional nat. park Venez. 176 D2
Perijá, Sierra de mts Venez. 176 D2
Peringat Malaysia 84 C1
Periyar India see Erode
Perkasie PA U.S.A. 165 H3
Perkat, Tanjung pt Sumatra Indon. 84 D3
Perlas, Archipiélago de las is Panama 166 [inset] K7
Perlas, Laguna de lag. Nicaragua 166 [inset] J6
Perlas, Punta de pt Nicaragua 166 [inset] J6
Perleberg Germany 63 L1
Perlis state Malaysia 84 C1
Perm' Russia 51 R4
Permas Russia 52 J4
Pernambuco Brazil see Recife
Pernambuco Plain sea feature S. Atlantic Ocean 184 G6
Pernatty Lagoon salt flat Australia 137 B6
Pernem India 106 B3
Pernik Bulg. 69 J3
Pernov Estonia see Pärnu
Perojpur Bangl. see Pirojpur
Peron Islands Australia 134 E3
Péronne France 62 C5
Perote Mex. 167 F5
Perpignan France 66 F5
Perranporth U.K. 59 B8
Perrégaux Alg. see Mohammadia
Perris CA U.S.A. 158 E5
Perros-Guirec France 66 C2
Perrot, Île i. Canada 165 I1
Perry FL U.S.A. 163 D6
Perry GA U.S.A. 163 D5
Perry MI U.S.A. 164 C2
Perry OK U.S.A. 161 D4
Perry Lake KS U.S.A. 160 E4
Perryton TX U.S.A. 161 C4
Perryville AK U.S.A. 148 H5
Perryville MO U.S.A. 160 F4
Perseverancia Bol. 176 F6
Pershore U.K. 59 E6
Persia country Asia see Iran
Persian Gulf Asia see The Gulf
Pertek Turkey 113 E3

►Perth Australia 135 A7
Capital of Western Australia. 4th most populous city in Oceania.

Perth Canada 165 G1
Perth U.K. 60 F4
Perth Amboy NJ U.S.A. 165 H3
Perth-Andover Canada 153 I5
Perth Basin sea feature Indian Ocean 185 P7
Pertominsk Russia 52 H2
Pertunmaa Fin. 55 O6
Pertusato, Capo c. Corsica France 66 I6
Peru atoll Kiribati see Beru

►Peru country S. America 176 D6
3rd largest and 5th most populous country in South America.

Peru IL U.S.A. 160 F3
Peru IN U.S.A. 164 B3
Peru NY U.S.A. 165 I1
Peru-Chile Trench sea feature S. Pacific Ocean 187 O6
Perugia Italy 68 E3
Peruru India 106 C3
Perusia Italy see Perugia
Péruwelz Belgium 62 D4
Pervomay Kyrg. 98 A4
Pervomaysk Russia 53 I5
Pervomays'k Ukr. 53 F6
Pervomayskiy Kazakh. 102 F1
Pervomayskiy Arkhangel'skaya Oblast' Russia see Novodvinsk
Pervomayskiy Tambovskaya Oblast' Russia 53 I5
Pervomays'kyy Ukr. 53 H6
Pervorechenskiy (abandoned) Russia 77 R3
Pervyy Brat, Gora hill Russia 90 F1
Pesaguan Kalimantan Indon. 85 E3
Pesaguan r. Indon. 85 E3
Pesaro Italy 68 E3
Pescadores is Taiwan see Penghu Qundao
Pescara Italy 68 F3
Pescara r. Italy 68 F3
Peschanokopskoye Russia 53 I7
Peschanoye Russia see Yashkul'
Peschanyy, Mys pt Kazakh. 113 H2
Pesé Panama 166 [inset] J8
Pesha r. Russia 52 J2
Peshawar Pak. 111 H3
Peshkopi Albania 69 I4
Peshtera Bulg. 69 K3
Peski Turkm. 111 F2
Peskovka Russia 52 L4
Pesnica Slovenia 68 F1
Pespire Hond. 166 [inset] I6
Pesqueira Mex. 166 C2
Pessac France 66 D4
Pessin Germany 63 M2
Pestovo Russia 52 G4
Pestravka Russia 53 K5
Petah Tiqwa Israel 107 B3
Petäjävesi Fin. 54 N5
Petak, Tanjung pt Halmahera Indon. 83 D2
Petaling Jaya Malaysia 87 C7
Petalion, Kolpos sea chan. Greece 69 K5
Petaluma CA U.S.A. 158 B2
Pétange Lux. 62 F5
Petangis Kalimantan Indon. 85 F3
Petatlán Mex. 168 D5
Petauke Zambia 123 D5
Petén Itzá, Lago l. Guat. 167 H5
Petenwell Lake WI U.S.A. 160 F2
Peterbell Canada 152 E4
Peterborough Australia 137 B7
Peterborough Canada 165 F1
Peterborough U.K. 59 G6
Peterborough NH U.S.A. 165 J2
Peterculter U.K. 60 G3
Peterhead U.K. 60 H3
Peter I Island Antarctica 188 K2
Peter I Øy i. Antarctica see Peter I Island
Peter Lake Canada 151 M2
Peterlee U.K. 58 F4
Petermann Bjerg nunatak Greenland 147 P2
Petermann Ranges mts Australia 135 E6
Peter Pond Lake Canada 151 I4
Peters, Lac l. Canada 153 H2
Petersberg Germany 63 J4
Petersburg AK U.S.A. 149 N4
Petersburg IL U.S.A. 160 F4
Petersburg IN U.S.A. 164 B4
Petersburg NY U.S.A. 165 I2
Petersburg VA U.S.A. 165 G5
Petersburg WV U.S.A. 164 F4
Petersfield U.K. 59 G7
Petershagen Germany 63 I2
Petersville AK U.S.A. 149 J3
Peter the Great Bay Russia see Petra Velikogo, Zaliv
Peth India 106 B2
Petilia Policastro Italy 68 G5
Petit Atlas mts Morocco see Anti-Atlas
Petitcodiac Canada 153 I5
Petitjean Morocco see Sidi Kacem
Petit Mécatina r. Canada 153 K4
Petit Mécatina, Île du i. Canada 153 K4
Petit Morin r. France 62 D6
Petitot r. Canada 150 F2
Petit St-Bernard, Col du pass France 66 H4
Petit Saut, Barrage du resr Fr. Guiana 177 H3
Peto Mex. 167 H4
Petoskey MI U.S.A. 162 C2
Petra tourist site Jordan 107 B4
Petra Velikogo, Zaliv b. Russia 90 C4
Petre, Point Canada 165 G2
Petrich Bulg. 69 J4
Petrified Forest National Park AZ U.S.A. 159 I4
Petrikau Poland see Piotrków Trybunalski
Petrikov Belarus see Pyetrykaw
Petrinja Croatia 68 G2
Petroaleksandrovsk Uzbek. see To'rtko'l
Petroglyphic Complexes tourist site Mongolia 102 G2
Petroglyphic Complexes of the Mongolian Altai tourist site Mongolia 88 F3
Petrograd Russia see St Petersburg
Petrohanski Prohod pass Bulg. 69 J3
Petrokov Poland see Piotrków Trybunalski
Petrolia Canada 164 D2
Petrolia CA U.S.A. 158 A1
Petrolina Brazil 177 J5
Petrolina de Goiás Brazil 179 A2
Petropavl Kazakh. see Petropavlovskoye
Petropavlovka Kazakh. 98 C3
Petropavlovka Russia 94 F1
Petropavlovsk Russia see Petropavlovsk-Kamchatskiy
Petropavlovsk-Kamchatskiy Russia 77 Q4
Petropavlovskoye Kazakh. 101 F1
Petrópolis Brazil 179 C3
Petroșani Romania 69 J2
Petrovsk Russia 53 J5
Petrovskoye Russia see Svetlograd
Petrovsk-Zabaykal'skiy Russia 95 G1
Petrozavodsk Russia 52 G3
Petrus Steyn S. Africa 125 I4
Petrusville S. Africa 124 G6
Petsamo Russia see Pechenga
Pettau Slovenia see Ptuj
Petten Neth. 62 E2
Pettigo U.K. 61 E3
Petukhovo Russia 76 H4
Petushki Russia 52 H5
Petzeck mt. Austria 57 N7
Peuetsagu, Gunung vol. Indon. 84 B1
Peureula Sumatra Indon. 84 B1
Pevek Russia 77 S3
Pêxung China 99 F6
Pey Ostān Iran 110 E3
Peza r. Russia 52 J2
Pezinok Slovakia 57 P6
Pezu Pak. 111 H3
Pfälzer Wald hills Germany 63 H5
Pforzheim Germany 63 I6
Pfungstadt Germany 63 I5
Phac Mo, Phu mt. Vietnam 86 C2
Phagameng S. Africa 125 I3
Phagwara India 104 C3
Phahameng S. Africa 125 H5
Phalaborwa S. Africa 125 J2
Phalodi India 104 C4
Phalsund India 104 B4
Phalta India 105 G5
Phaluai, Ko i. Thai. 87 B5
Phalut Peak India/Nepal 99 E8
Phan Thai. 86 B3
Phanat Nikhom Thai. 87 C4
Phangan, Ko i. Thai. 87 C5
Phang Hoei, San Khao mts Thai. 86 C3
Phangnga Thai. 87 B5
Phăng Xi Păng mt. Vietnam 86 C2
Phanom Dong Rak, Thiu Khao mts Cambodia/Thai. 87 D4
Phan Rang-Thap Cham Vietnam 87 E5
Phan Thiêt Vietnam 87 E5
Phapon Myanmar see Pyapon
Phat Diêm Vietnam 86 D2
Phatthalung Thai. 87 C6
Phawngpui India 105 H5
Phayam, Ko i. Thai. 87 B5
Phayao Thai. 86 B3
Phayuhakhiri Thai. 86 C4
Phek India 105 H4
Phelps Lake Canada 151 K3
Phen Thai. 86 C3
Phenix VA U.S.A. 165 F5
Phenix City AL U.S.A. 163 C5
Phet Buri Thai. 87 B4
Phetchabun Thai. 86 C3
Phiafai Laos 86 D4
Phichai Thai. 86 C3
Phichit Thai. 86 C3
Philadelphia Jordan see 'Ammān
Philadelphia Turkey see Alaşehir
Philadelphia MS U.S.A. 161 F5
Philadelphia NY U.S.A. 165 H1
Philadelphia PA U.S.A. 165 H4
Philip SD U.S.A. 160 C2
Philip Atoll Micronesia see Sorol
Philippeville Alg. see Skikda
Philippeville Belgium 62 E4
Philippi WV U.S.A. 164 E4
Philippi, Lake salt flat Australia 136 B5
Philippine Neth. 62 D3
Philippine Basin sea feature N. Pacific Ocean 186 E4
Philippines country Asia 82 C3
Philippine Sea N. Pacific Ocean 81 G3

►Philippine Trench sea feature N. Pacific Ocean 186 E4
3rd deepest trench in the world.

Philippolis S. Africa 125 G6
Philippopolis Bulg. see Plovdiv
Philippsburg Germany 63 I5
Philipsburg MT U.S.A. 156 E3
Philipsburg PA U.S.A. 165 F3
Philip Smith Mountains AK U.S.A. 149 J2
Philipstown S. Africa 124 G6
Phillip Island Australia 138 B7
Phillips ME U.S.A. 165 J1
Phillips WI U.S.A. 160 F2
Phillipsburg KS U.S.A. 160 D4
Phillips Range hills Australia 134 D4
Philmont NY U.S.A. 165 I2
Philomelium Turkey see Akşehir
Phiritona S. Africa 125 H4
Phitsanulok Thai. 86 C3

►Phnom Penh Cambodia 87 D5
Capital of Cambodia.

Phnum Pénh Cambodia see Phnom Penh
Pho, Laem pt Thai. 87 C6
Phoenicia NY U.S.A. 165 H2

►Phoenix AZ U.S.A. 157 E6
Capital of Arizona.

Phoenix Island Kiribati see Rawaki
Phoenix Islands Kiribati 133 I2
Phô Lu Vietnam 86 D2
Phon Thai. 86 C4
Phong Nha Vietnam 86 D3
Phôngsali Laos 86 C2
Phong Saly Laos see Phôngsali
Phong Thô Vietnam 86 C2
Phon Phisai Thai. 86 C3
Phônsavan Laos 86 C3
Phônsavan mt. Laos 86 C3
Phon Thong Thai. 86 C3
Phosphate Hill Australia 136 C4
Phrae Thai. 86 C3
Phra Nakhon Si Ayutthaya Thai. see Ayutthaya
Phrao Thai. 86 B3
Phra Saeng Thai. 87 B5
Phrom Phiram Thai. 86 C3
Phsar Réam Cambodia 87 C5
Phu Bai Vietnam 86 D3
Phuchong-Nayoi National Park Thai. 87 D4
Phu Cương Vietnam see Thu Dâu Một
Phuket Thai. 87 B6
Phuket, Ko i. Thai. 87 B6
Phu Khieo Wildlife Reserve nature res. Thai. 86 C3
Phulabani India see Phulbani
Phulbani India 106 E1
Phulchhari Ghat Bangl. see Fulchhari
Phulji Pak. 111 G5
Phu Lôc Soc Trăng Vietnam 87 D5
Phu Lôc Thưa Thiên-Huê Vietnam 86 D3
Phu Luang National Park Thai. 86 C3
Phu Ly Vietnam 86 D2
Phumiphon, Khuan Thai. 86 B3
Phu My Vietnam 87 E4
Phung Hiêp Vietnam 87 D5
Phươc Bưu Vietnam 87 D5
Phươc Hai Vietnam 87 D5
Phu Phan National Park Thai. 86 C3
Phu Quôc, Đao i. Vietnam 87 C5
Phu Quôc, Quân i. Vietnam see Phu Quôc, Đao
Phu Quy, Đao i. Vietnam 87 E5
Phu Tho Vietnam 86 D2
Phu Vinh Vietnam see Tra Vinh
Phyu Myanmar 86 B3
Piabung, Gunung mt. Indon. 85 F2
Piaca Brazil 177 I5
Piacenza Italy 68 C2
Piacouadie, Lac l. Canada 153 H4
Piagochioui r. Canada 152 F3
Piai, Tanjung pt Malaysia 84 C2
Pian r. Australia 138 D3
Pianguan China 95 G4
Pianosa, Isola i. Italy 68 D3
Piatra Neamț Romania 69 L1
Piave r. Italy 68 E2
Pibor Post South Sudan 121 G4
Pic r. Canada 152 D4
Picacho AZ U.S.A. 159 H5
Picachos, Cerro dos mt. Mex. 166 B2
Picardie admin. reg. France 62 C5
Picardie reg. France see Picardy
Picardy admin. reg. France see Picardie
Picardy reg. France 62 B5
Picauville France 59 F9
Picayune MS U.S.A. 161 F6
Piceance Creek r. CO U.S.A. 159 I1
Pich Mex. 167 H5
Pichácnic Mex. 166 D2
Pichanal Arg. 178 D2
Pichhor India 104 D4
Pichilemu Chile 178 B4
Pichilingue Mex. 166 C3
Pichucalco Mex. 167 G5
Pickens WV U.S.A. 164 E4
Pickering Canada 164 F2
Pickering U.K. 58 G4
Pickering, Vale of valley U.K. 58 G4
Pickle Lake Canada 147 I4
Pico Bonito, Parque Nacional nat. park Hond. 166 [inset] I6
Pico da Neblina, Parque Nacional do nat. park Brazil 176 E3
Pico de Orizaba, Parque Nacional nat. park Mex. 167 F5
Pico de Tancítaro, Parque Nacional nat. park Mex. 166 E5
Picos Brazil 177 J5
Picos de Europa, Parque Nacional de los nat. park Spain 67 D2
Pico Truncado Arg. 178 C7
Picton Australia 138 E5
Picton Canada 165 G2
Picton N.Z. 139 E5
Pictou Canada 153 J5
Picture Butte Canada 151 H5
Pidarak Pak. 111 F5
Pidurutalagala mt. Sri Lanka 106 D5
Piedade Brazil 179 B3
Piedra de Águila Arg. 178 B6
Piedras, Punta pt Arg. 178 E5
Piedras, Río de las r. Peru 176 E6
Piedras Blancas Point CA U.S.A. 158 C4
Piedras Negras Guat. 167 H5
Piedras Negras Coahuila Mex. 167 E2
Piedras Negras Veracruz Mex. 167 F5
Pie Island Canada 152 C4
Pieksämäki Fin. 54 O5
Pielavesi Fin. 54 O5
Pielinen l. Fin. 54 P5
Pieljekaise nationalpark nat. park Sweden 54 J3
Pienaarsrivier S. Africa 125 I3
Pieniński Park Narodowy nat. park Poland 57 R6
Pieninský národný park nat. park Slovakia 57 R6
Pierce NE U.S.A. 160 D3
Pierce Lake Canada 151 M4
Pierceland Canada 151 I4
Pierceton IN U.S.A. 164 C3
Pieria mts Greece 69 J4
Pierowall U.K. 60 G1
Pierpont OH U.S.A. 164 E3

▶Pierre SD U.S.A. 160 C2
Capital of South Dakota.

Pierrelatte France 66 G4
Pietermaritzburg S. Africa 125 J5
Pietersaari Fin. see Jakobstad
Pietersburg S. Africa see Polokwane
Pie Town NM U.S.A. 159 I4
Pietra Spada, Passo di pass Italy 68 G5
Piet Retief S. Africa see eMkhondo
Pietrosa mt. Romania 69 K1
Pigeon MI U.S.A. 164 D2
Pigeon Bay Canada 164 D3
Pigeon Lake Canada 150 H4
Piggott AR U.S.A. 161 F4
Pigg's Peak Swaziland 125 J3
Pigs, Bay of Cuba 163 D8
Piguicas mt. Mex. 167 F4
Pihij India 104 C5
Pihkva järv l. Estonia/Russia see Pskov, Lake
Pihlajavesi l. Fin. 54 P6
Pihlava Fin. 55 L6
Pihtipudas Fin. 54 N5
Piippola Fin. 54 N4
Piispajärvi Fin. 54 P4
Pijijiapan Mex. 167 G6
Pikalevo Russia 52 G4
Pike WV U.S.A. 164 E4
Pike Bay Canada 164 E1
Pikelot i. Micronesia 81 L5
Pikes Peak CO U.S.A. 156 G5
Piketon OH U.S.A. 164 D4
Pikeville KY U.S.A. 164 D5
Pikeville TN U.S.A. 162 C5
Pikinni atoll Marshall Is see Bikini
Pikmiktalik AK U.S.A. 148 G3
Pikou China 95 J4
Piła Poland 57 P4
Pila, Kyun i. Myanmar 87 B5
Pilanesberg National Park S. Africa 125 H3
Pilão Arcado Brazil 177 J5
Pilar Arg. 178 E4
Pilar Para. 178 E3
Pilar Phil. 82 D4
Pilar de Goiás Brazil 179 A1
Pilas i. Phil. 82 C5
Pilas Channel Phil. 82 C5
Pilaya r. Bol. 176 F8
Pilbara reg. Australia 134 B5
Pilcomayo r. Bol./Para. 176 F8
Pile Bay Village AK U.S.A. 148 I4
Piler India 106 C3
Pilgrim Springs AK U.S.A. 148 F2
Pili Luzon Phil. 82 C3
Pili, Cerro mt. Chile 178 C2
Pilibangan India 104 C3
Pilibhit India 104 D3
Pilipinas country Asia see Philippines
Pillau Russia see Baltiysk
Pillcopata Peru 176 D6
Pilliga Australia 138 D3
Pillsbury, Lake CA U.S.A. 158 B2
Pil'na Russia 52 J5
Pil'nya, Ozero l. Russia 52 M1
Pilões, Serra dos mts Brazil 179 B2
Pílos Greece see Pylos
Pilot Knob mt. ID U.S.A. 156 E3
Pilot Peak NV U.S.A. 158 E2
Pilot Point AK U.S.A. 148 H4
Pilot Station AK U.S.A. 148 G3
Pilottown LA U.S.A. 167 H2
Pilsen Czech Rep. see Plzeň
Piltene Latvia 55 L8
Pil'tun, Zaliv lag. Russia 90 F1
Pilu Pak. 111 H5
Pima AZ U.S.A. 159 I5
Pimenta Bueno Brazil 176 F6
Pimento IN U.S.A. 164 B4
Pimpalner India 106 B1
Pin r. India 104 D2
Pin r. Myanmar 86 A2
Pinahat India 104 D4
Pinaleno Mountains AZ U.S.A. 159 H5
Pinamalayan Mindoro Phil. 82 C3
Pinamar Arg. 178 E5
Pinang Malaysia see George Town
Pinang i. Malaysia 84 C1
Pinang state Malaysia 84 C1
Pinangah Sabah Malaysia 85 G1
Pınarbaşı Turkey 112 E3
Pinar del Río Cuba 169 H4
Pinarhisar Turkey 69 L4
Piñas Ecuador 176 C4
Pincher Creek Canada 150 H5
Pinckneyville IL U.S.A. 160 F4
Pinconning MI U.S.A. 164 D2
Pińczów Poland 57 R5
Pindaí Brazil 179 C1
Pindamonhangaba Brazil 179 B3
Pindar Australia 135 A7
Pindar r. India 99 B7
Pindaré r. Brazil 177 J4
Píndhos Óros mts Greece see Pindus Mountains
Pindos mts Greece see Pindus Mountains
Pindrei India 104 E5
Pindus Mountains Greece 69 I5
Pine watercourse Australia 137 C7
Pine r. MI U.S.A. 164 C1
Pine r. MI U.S.A. 164 C2
Pine Bluff AR U.S.A. 161 E5
Pine Bluffs WY U.S.A. 156 G4
Pine Creek Australia 134 E3
Pine Creek r. PA U.S.A. 165 G3
Pinecrest CA U.S.A. 158 C2
Pinedale NM U.S.A. 159 I4
Pinedale WY U.S.A. 156 F4
Pine Dock Canada 151 L5
Pine Falls Canada 151 L5
Pine Flat Lake CA U.S.A. 158 D3
Pinega Russia 52 I2
Pinega r. Russia 52 I2
Pinegrove Australia 135 A6
Pine Grove PA U.S.A. 165 G3
Pine Hills FL U.S.A. 163 D6
Pinehouse Lake Canada 151 J4
Pinehouse Lake l. Canada 151 J4
Pineimuta r. Canada 151 N4
Pineios r. Greece 69 J5
Pine Island Bay Antarctica 187 N10
Pine Island Glacier Antarctica 188 K1
Pine Islands FL U.S.A. 163 D7
Pine Islands FL U.S.A. 163 D7
Pine Knot KY U.S.A. 164 C5
Pineland TX U.S.A. 161 E6
Pine Mountain CA U.S.A. 158 C4
Pine Peak AZ U.S.A. 159 G4
Pine Point pt Canada 150 H2
Pine Point (abandoned) Canada 150 H2
Pineridge CA U.S.A. 158 D3
Pine Ridge SD U.S.A. 160 C3
Pinerolo Italy 68 B2
Pines, Akrotirio pt Greece 69 K4
Pines, Isle of i. Cuba see Juventud, Isla de la
Pines, Isle of i. New Caledonia see Pins, Île des
Pines, Lake o' the TX U.S.A. 167 G1
Pinetop AZ U.S.A. 159 I4
Pinetown S. Africa 125 J5
Pine Valley NY U.S.A. 165 G2
Pineville KY U.S.A. 164 D5
Pineville LA U.S.A. 167 G2
Pineville MO U.S.A. 161 E4
Pineville WV U.S.A. 164 E5
Ping, Mae Nam r. Thai. 86 C4
Ping'an China 94 E4
Ping'anyi China see Ping'an
Pingba China 96 E3
Pingbian China 96 D4
Ping Dao i. China 95 I5
Pingding China 95 H4
Pingdingbu China see Guyuan
Pingdingshan China 97 G1
Pingdong Taiwan 97 I4
Pingdu Jiangxi China see Anfu
Pingdu Shandong China 95 I4
Pinggang China 90 B4
Pinggu China 95 I3
Pinghe China 97 H3
Pinghu China see Pingtang
Pingjiang China 97 G2
Pingjin China 96 E2
Pingle China 97 F3
Pingli China 97 F1
Pingliang China 94 F5
Pinglu China 95 G5
Pingluo China 94 F4
Pingma China see Tiandong
Pingnan China 97 H3
Pingqiao China 97 G1
Pingquan China 95 I3
Pingshan Hebei China 95 H4
Pingshan Sichuan China 96 E2
Pingshan Yunnan China see Luquan
Pingshi China 97 G3
Pingshu China see Daicheng
Pingtan China 97 H3
Pingtan Dao i. China see Haitan Dao
Pingtang China 96 E3
P'ingtung Taiwan see Pingdong
Pingxi China see Yuping
Pingxiang Gansu China see Tongwei
Pingxiang Guangxi China 96 E4
Pingxiang Jiangxi China 97 G3
Pingyang Heilong. China 95 K1
Pingyang Zhejiang China 97 I3
Pingyao China 95 H4
Pingyi China 95 I5
Pingyin China 95 I4
Pingyu China 97 G1
Pingyuan Shandong China 95 I4
Pingyuan Yunnan China 96 D4
Pingzhai China see Liuzhi
Pinheiro Brazil 177 I4
Pinhoe U.K. 59 D8
Pini i. Indon. 84 B2
Piniós r. Greece see Pineios
Pinjin Australia 135 C7
Pink Mountain Canada 150 F3
Pinlaung Myanmar 86 B2
Pinlebu Myanmar 86 A1
Pinnacle hill Virginia/West Virginia U.S.A. 165 F4
Pinnacle Island AK U.S.A. 148 D3
Pinnacles National Monument nat. park CA U.S.A. 158 C3
Pinnau r. Germany 63 J1
Pinneberg Germany 63 J1
Pinnes, Akra pt Greece see Pines, Akrotirio
Pinoh r. Indon. 85 E3
Pinon Hills CA U.S.A. 158 E4
Pinos, Isla de i. Cuba see Juventud, Isla de la
Pinos, Mount CA U.S.A. 158 D4
Pinotepa Nacional Mex. 168 E5
Pinrang Celebes Indon. 83 A3
Pinrang Celebes Indon. 83 B3
Pins, Île des i. New Caledonia 133 G4
Pins, Pointe aux pt Canada 164 E2
Pinsk Belarus 55 O10
Pinta, Sierra hill AZ U.S.A. 159 G5
Pintada Creek watercourse NM U.S.A. 157 G6
Pintados Chile 178 C2
Pintasan Sabah Malaysia 85 G1
Pintura UT U.S.A. 159 G3
Pioche NV U.S.A. 159 F3
Piodi Dem. Rep. Congo 123 C4
Pioneer Mountains MT U.S.A. 156 E3
Pioner, Ostrov i. Russia 76 K2
Pionerskiy Kaliningradskaya Oblast' Russia 55 L9
Pionerskiy Khanty-Mansiyskiy Avtonomnyy Okrug-Yugra Russia 51 S3
Pionki Poland 57 R5
Piopio N.Z. 139 E4
Piopiotahi inlet N.Z. see Milford Sound
Piorini, Lago l. Brazil 176 F4
Piotrków Trybunalski Poland 57 Q5
Pipa Dingzi mt. China 90 C4
Pipar India 104 C4
Pipar Road India 104 C4
Piperi i. Greece 69 K5
Piper Peak NV U.S.A. 158 E3
Pipestone Canada 151 K5
Pipestone r. Canada 151 N4
Pipestone MN U.S.A. 160 D3
Pipli India 104 C3
Pipmuacan, Réservoir resr Canada 153 H4
Piqan China see Shanshan
Piqanlik China 98 C4
Piqua OH U.S.A. 164 C3
Piquiri r. Brazil 179 A4
Pira Benin 120 D4
Piracanjuba Brazil 179 A2
Piracicaba Brazil 179 B3
Piracicaba r. Brazil 179 C2
Piracuruca Brazil 177 J4
Piraeus Greece 69 J6
Piraí do Sul Brazil 179 A4
Piráievs Greece see Piraeus
Piraju Brazil 179 A3
Pirajuí Brazil 179 A3
Pirallahı Adası Azer. 113 H2
Piranhas Bahia Brazil 179 C1
Piranhas Goiás Brazil 177 H7
Piranhas r. Goiás Brazil 179 A2
Piranhas r. Rio Grande do Norte Brazil 177 K5
Pirapora Brazil 179 B2
Pirari Nepal 99 D8
Pirassununga Brazil 179 B3
Piraube, Lac l. Canada 153 H4
Pirawa India 104 D4
Pirenópolis Brazil 179 A1
Pires do Rio Brazil 179 A2
Pírgos Greece see Pyrgos
Pirin, Natsionalen Park nat. park Bulg. 69 J4
Pirineos mts Europe see Pyrenees
Piripiri Brazil 177 J4
Pirlerkondu Turkey see Taşkent
Pirmasens Germany 63 H5
Pirojpur Bangl. 105 G5
Pir Panjal Pass India 104 C2
Pir Panjal Range mts India/Pak. 111 I3
Pīr Shūrān, Selseleh-ye mts Iran 111 F4
Piru Seram Indon. 83 D3
Piru, Teluk b. Seram Indon. 83 D3
Piryatin Ukr. see Pyryatyn
Pīr Zādah Afgh. 111 G4
Pisa Italy 68 D3
Pisae Italy see Pisa
Pisagua Chile 176 D7
Pisang i. Moluccas Indon. 83 D3
Pisang, Kepulauan is Indon. 81 I7
Pisau, Tanjung pt Malaysia 85 G1
Pisaurum Italy see Pesaro
Pisco Peru 176 C6
Písek Czech Rep. 57 O6
Pisha China see Ningnan
Pishan China 99 B5
Pīshīn Iran 102 B6
Pishin Pak. 111 G4
Pīshīn Jān Afgh. 111 F3
Pishin Lora r. Pak. 111 G4
Pishpek Kyrg. see Bishkek
Pisidia reg. Turkey 112 C3
Pising Celebes Indon. 83 B4

▶Pissis, Cerro Arg. 178 C3
4th highest mountain in South America.

Pisté Mex. 167 H4
Pisticci Italy 68 G4
Pistoia Italy 68 D3
Pistoriae Italy see Pistoia
Pisuerga r. Spain 67 D3
Pita Guinea 120 B3
Pitaga Canada 153 I3
Pital Mex. 167 H5
Pitanga Brazil 179 A4
Pitangui Brazil 179 B2
Pitar India 104 B5
Pitarpunga Lake imp. l. Australia 138 A5
Pitcairn, Henderson, Ducie and Oeno Islands terr. S. Pacific Ocean see Pitcairn Islands
Pitcairn Island Pitcairn Is 187 L7

▶Pitcairn Islands terr. S. Pacific Ocean 187 L7
United Kingdom Overseas Territory.

Piteå Sweden 54 L4
Piteälven r. Sweden 54 L4
Pitelino Russia 53 I5
Piterka Russia 53 J6
Pitești Romania 69 K2
Pithoragarh India 104 E3
Pitihra India 104 D5
Pitiquito Mex. 166 B2
Pitkas Point AK U.S.A. 148 G3
Pitkyaranta Russia 52 F3
Pitlochry U.K. 60 F4
Pitong China see Pixian
Pitsane Siding Botswana 125 G3
Pitti i. India 106 B4
Pitt Island Canada 149 O5
Pitt Island N.Z. 133 I6
Pitt Islands Solomon Is see Vanikoro Islands
Pittsboro MS U.S.A. 161 F5
Pittsburg KS U.S.A. 161 E4
Pittsburg TX U.S.A. 161 E5
Pittsburgh PA U.S.A. 164 F3
Pittsfield MA U.S.A. 165 I2
Pittsfield ME U.S.A. 165 K1
Pittsfield VT U.S.A. 165 I2
Pittston PA U.S.A. 165 H3
Pittsworth Australia 138 E1
Pitz Lake Canada 151 L2
Piumhi Brazil 179 B3
Piura Peru 176 B5
Piute Mountains CA U.S.A. 159 F4
Piute Peak CA U.S.A. 158 D4
Piute Reservoir UT U.S.A. 159 G2
Piuthan Nepal 105 E3
Pivabiska r. Canada 152 E4
Pivka Slovenia 68 F2
Pixariá mt. Greece see Pyxaria
Pixian China 96 D2
Pixley CA U.S.A. 158 D4
Pixoyal Mex. 167 H5
Pizhanka Russia 52 K4
Pizhi Nigeria 120 D4
Pizhma Russia 52 J4
Pizhma r. Russia 52 K4
Pizhma r. Russia 52 L2
Pizhou China 95 I5
Pkulagalid Point Palau 82 [inset]
Pkulagasemieg pt Palau 82 [inset]
Pkulngril pt Palau 82 [inset]
Pkurengei pt Palau 82 [inset]
Placentia Canada 153 L5
Placentia Italy see Piacenza
Placentia Bay Canada 153 L5
Placer Masbate Phil. 82 C4
Placer Mindanao Phil. 82 D4
Placerville CA U.S.A. 158 C2
Placerville CO U.S.A. 159 I2
Placetas Cuba 163 E8
Plácido de Castro Brazil 176 E6
Plain Dealing LA U.S.A. 161 E5
Plainfield CT U.S.A. 165 J3
Plainfield IN U.S.A. 164 B4
Plainfield VT U.S.A. 165 I1
Plains KS U.S.A. 161 C4
Plains TX U.S.A. 161 C5
Plainview TX U.S.A. 161 C5
Plainville IN U.S.A. 164 B4
Plainville KS U.S.A. 160 D4
Plainwell MI U.S.A. 164 C2
Plaju Sumatra Indon. 84 D3
Plaka, Akra pt Greece see Plaka, Akrotirio
Plaka, Akrotirio pt Greece 69 L7
Plakoti, Cape Cyprus 107 B2
Plamondon Canada 151 H4
Plampang Sumbawa Indon. 85 G5
Planá Czech Rep. 63 M5
Plana Cays is Bahamas 163 F8
Planada CA U.S.A. 158 C3
Planaltina Brazil 179 B1
Plane r. Germany 63 M2
Plankinton SD U.S.A. 160 D3
Plano TX U.S.A. 161 D5
Planura Brazil 179 A3
Plaquemine LA U.S.A. 161 F6
Plasencia Spain 67 C3
Plaster City CA U.S.A. 159 F5
Plaster Rock Canada 153 I5
Plastun Russia 90 E3
Platani r. Sicily Italy 68 E6
Platberg mt. S. Africa 125 I5
Plateros Mex. 166 E4
Platina CA U.S.A. 158 B1
Platinum AK U.S.A. 148 G4
Plato Col. 176 D2
Platón Sánchez Mex. 167 F4
Platte r. NE U.S.A. 160 E3
Platte City MO U.S.A. 160 E4
Plattling Germany 63 M6
Plattsburgh NY U.S.A. 165 I1
Plattsmouth NE U.S.A. 160 E3
Plau am See Germany 63 M1
Plauen Germany 63 M4
Plauer See l. Germany 63 M1
Plavsk Russia 53 H5
Playa Azul Mex. 166 E5
Playa Noriega, Lago l. Mex. 157 F7
Playas Ecuador 176 B4
Playas Lake NM U.S.A. 159 I6
Plây Ku Vietnam 87 E4
Playón Mex. 166 C3
Pleasant, Lake AZ U.S.A. 159 G5
Pleasant Bay MA U.S.A. 165 K3
Pleasant Grove UT U.S.A. 159 H1
Pleasant Hill Lake OH U.S.A. 164 D3
Pleasanton TX U.S.A. 161 D6
Pleasant Point N.Z. 139 C7
Pleasantville NJ U.S.A. 165 H4
Pleasure Ridge Park KY U.S.A. 164 C4
Pleaux France 66 F4
Pledger Lake Canada 152 E4
Plei Doch Vietnam 87 D4
Pleihari Martapura, Suaka Margasatwa nature res. Kalimantan Indon. 85 F3
Pleihari Tanah, Suaka Margasatwa nature res. Kalimantan Indon. 85 F4
Plei Kân Vietnam 86 D4
Pleinfeld Germany 63 K5
Pleiße r. Germany 63 M3
Plenty watercourse Australia 136 B5
Plenty, Bay of g. N.Z. 139 F3
Plentywood MT U.S.A. 156 G2
Plesetsk Russia 52 I3
Pleshchentsy Belarus see Plyeshchanitsy
Plétipi, Lac l. Canada 153 H4
Plettenberg Germany 63 H3
Plettenberg Bay S. Africa 124 F8
Pleven Bulg. 69 K3
Plevna Bulg. see Pleven
Plieran r. Malaysia 85 F2
Pljevlja Montenegro 69 H3
Płock Poland 57 Q4
Pločno mt. Bos. & Herz. 68 G3
Plodovoye Russia 52 F3
Ploemeur France 66 C3
Ploești Romania see Ploiești
Ploiești Romania 69 L2
Plomb du Cantal mt. France 66 F4
Ploskoye Russia see Stanovoye
Płoty Poland 57 O4
Ploudalmézeau France 66 B2
Plouzané France 66 B2
Plovdiv Bulg. 69 K3
Plover Cove Reservoir H.K. China 97 [inset]
Plover Islands AK U.S.A. 148 I1
Plozk Poland see Płock
Plum PA U.S.A. 164 F3
Plumridge Lakes salt flat Australia 135 D7
Plung Lith. 55 L9
Plutarco Elías Calles, Presa resr Mex. 157 F7
Plutarco Elís Calles, Presa resr Mex. 166 C2
Pluto, Lac l. Canada 153 H3
Plyeshchanitsy Belarus 55 O9
Ply Huey Wati, Khao mt. Myanmar/Thai. 86 B3
Plymouth U.K. 59 C8
Plymouth CA U.S.A. 158 C2
Plymouth IN U.S.A. 164 B3
Plymouth MA U.S.A. 165 J3
Plymouth NC U.S.A. 162 E5
Plymouth NH U.S.A. 165 J2
Plymouth WI U.S.A. 164 B2

▶Plymouth (abandoned) Montserrat 169 L5
Capital of Montserrat, abandoned in 1997 owing to volcanic activity. Temporary capital established at Brades.

Plymouth Bay MA U.S.A. 165 J3
Plynlimon hill U.K. 59 D6
Plyussa Russia 55 P7
Plzeň Czech Rep. 57 N6
Pô Burkina Faso 120 C3
Po r. Italy 68 E2
Po, Tanjung pt Malaysia 85 E2
Poás, Volcán vol. Costa Rica 166 [inset] I7
Poat i. Indon. 83 B3
Pobeda Peak China/Kyrg. 98 C4
Pobedy, Pik mt. China/Kyrg. see Pobeda Peak
Pocahontas AR U.S.A. 161 F4
Pocatello ID U.S.A. 156 E4
Pochayiv Ukr. 53 E6
Pochep Russia 53 G5
Pochinki Russia 53 J5
Pochinok Russia 53 G5
Pochutla Mex. 168 E5
Pock, Gunung hill Malaysia 85 G1
Pocking Germany 57 N6
Pocklington U.K. 58 G5
Poções Brazil 179 C1
Pocomoke City MD U.S.A. 165 H4
Pocomoke Sound b. Maryland/Virginia U.S.A. 165 H5
Poconé Brazil 177 G7
Pocono Mountains hills PA U.S.A. 165 H3
Pocono Summit PA U.S.A. 165 H3
Poco Ranakah vol. Flores Indon. 83 B5
Poços de Caldas Brazil 179 B3
Podanur India 106 C4
Poddor'ye Russia 52 F4
Podgorenskiy Russia 53 H6

▶Podgorica Montenegro 69 H3
Capital of Montenegro.

Podgornoye Russia 76 J4
Podile India 106 C3
Podișul Transilvaniei plat. Romania see Transylvanian Basin
Podkamennaya Tunguska r. Russia 77 K3
Podocarpus, Parque Nacional nat. park Ecuador 176 C4
Podol'sk Russia 53 H5
Podporozh'ye Russia 52 G3
Podujevë Kosovo 69 I3
Podujevo Kosovo see Podujevë
Podz' Russia 52 K3
Poelela, Lagoa l. Moz. 125 L3
Poeppel Corner salt flat Australia 137 B5
Poetovio Slovenia see Ptuj
Pofadder S. Africa 124 D5
Pogar Russia 53 G5
Poggibonsi Italy 68 D3
Pogradec Albania 69 I4
Pogranichnyy Russia 90 C3
Poh Celebes Indon. 83 B3
Po Hai g. China see Bo Hai
Pohang S. Korea 91 C5
Pohnpei atoll Micronesia 186 G5
Pohri India 104 D4
Poi India 105 H4
Poiana Mare Romania 69 J3
Poigar Celebes Indon. 83 C2
Poindo China 99 E7
Poinsett, Cape Antarctica 188 F2
Point Arena CA U.S.A. 158 B2
Point au Fer Island LA U.S.A. 161 F6
Pointe à la Hache LA U.S.A. 161 F6
Pointe-à-Pitre Guadeloupe 169 L5
Pointe-Noire Congo 123 B4
Point Hope AK U.S.A. 148 F1
Point Lake Canada 150 H1
Point Lay AK U.S.A. 148 G1
Point of Rocks WY U.S.A. 156 F4
Point Pelee National Park Canada 164 D3
Point Pleasant NJ U.S.A. 165 H3
Point Pleasant WV U.S.A. 164 D4
Poitiers France 66 E3
Poitou reg. France 66 E3
Poix-de-Picardie France 62 B5
Pojuca r. Brazil 179 D1
Pokaran India 104 B4
Pokataroo Australia 138 D2
Pokcha Russia 51 R3
Pokhara Nepal 105 E3
Pokhran Landi Pak. 111 G5
Pokhvistnevo Russia 51 Q5
Pok Liu Chau i. H.K. China see Lamma Island
Poko Dem. Rep. Congo 122 C3
Poko Mountain hill AK U.S.A. 148 G1
Pokosnoye Russia 88 I1
P'ok'r Kovkas mts Asia see Lesser Caucasus
Pokrovka Primorskiy Kray Russia 90 C4
Pokrovka Zabaykal'skiy Kray Russia 90 A1
Pokrovsk Respublika Sakha (Yakutiya) Russia 77 N3
Pokrovsk Saratovskaya Oblast' Russia see Engel's
Pokrovskoye Russia 53 H7
Pokshen'ga r. Russia 52 J3
Pol India 104 C5
Pola Croatia see Pula
Pola Mindoro Phil. 82 C3
Polacca Wash watercourse AZ U.S.A. 159 H4
Pola de Siero Spain see La Pola Siero
Poland country Europe 50 J5
Poland NY U.S.A. 165 H2
Poland OH U.S.A. 164 E3
Polar Plateau Antarctica 188 A1
Polatlı Turkey 112 D3
Polatsk Belarus 55 P9
Polavaram India 106 D2
Polcirkeln Sweden 54 L3
Polee i. Papua Indon. 83 D3
Pol-e Fasā Iran 110 D4
Pol-e Khātūn Iran 111 F2
Pol-e Sefīd Iran 110 D2
Polessk Russia 55 L9
Poles'ye marsh Belarus/Ukr. see Pripet Marshes
Polewali Celebes Indon. 83 A3
Polgahawela Sri Lanka 106 D5
Poli China 95 I5
Poli Cyprus see Polis
Políaigos i. Greece see Polyaigos
Police Poland 57 O4
Policoro Italy 68 G4
Poligny France 66 G3
Políkastron Greece see Polykastro
Polillo i. Phil. 82 C3
Polillo Islands Phil. 82 C3
Polillo Strait Phil. 82 C3
Poliny Osipenko, imeni Russia 90 E1
Polis Cyprus 107 A2
Polis'ke (abandoned) Ukr. 53 F6
Polis'kyy Zapovidnyk nature res. Ukr. 53 F6
Politovo Russia 52 K2
Polýiros Greece see Polygyros
Polkowice Poland 57 P5
Pollachi India 106 C4
Pollard Islands HI U.S.A. see Gardner Pinnacles
Polle Germany 63 J3
Pollino, Monte mt. Italy 68 G5
Pollino, Parco Nazionale del nat. park Italy 68 G5
Polloc Harbour b. Mindanao Phil. 82 C5
Pollock Pines CA U.S.A. 158 C2
Pollock Reef Australia 135 C8
Polmak Norway 54 O1
Polnovat Russia 51 T3
Polo Fin. 54 P4
Poloat atoll Micronesia see Puluwat
Pologi Ukr. see Polohy
Polohy Ukr. 53 H7
Polokwane S. Africa 125 I2
Polokwane r. S. Africa 125 J2
Polomolok Mindanao Phil. 82 D5
Polonne Ukr. 53 E6
Polonnoye Ukr. see Polonne
Polotsk Belarus see Polatsk
Polperro U.K. 59 C8
Polska country Europe see Poland
Polson MT U.S.A. 156 E3
Polta r. Russia 52 I2
Poltava Ukr. 53 G6
Poltoratsk Turkm. see Aşgabat
Põltsamaa Estonia 55 N7
Polunochnoye Russia 51 S3
Põlva Estonia 55 O7
Polvadera NM U.S.A. 157 G6
Polvijärvi Fin. 54 P5
Polvoxal Mex. 167 H5
Polyaigos i. Greece 69 K6
Polyanovgrad Bulg. see Karnobat
Polyarnyy Russia 54 R2
Polyarnyy (abandoned) Russia 77 S3
Polyarnyye Zori Russia 54 R3
Polyarnyy Ural mts Russia 51 S2
Polygyros Greece 69 J4
Polykastro Greece 69 J4
Polynesia is Pacific Ocean 186 I6
Polynésie Française terr. S. Pacific Ocean see French Polynesia
Pom Indon. 81 J7
Pomarkku Fin. 55 M6
Pombal Pará Brazil 177 H4
Pombal Paraíba Brazil 177 K5
Pombal Port. 67 B4
Pomene Moz. 125 L2
Pomeranian Bay Poland 57 O3
Pomeroy S. Africa 125 J5
Pomeroy U.K. 61 F3
Pomeroy OH U.S.A. 164 D4
Pomeroy WA U.S.A. 156 D3
Pomezia Italy 68 E4
Pomfret S. Africa 124 F3
Pomona Belize 167 H5
Pomona Namibia 124 B4
Pomona CA U.S.A. 158 E4
Pomorie Bulg. 69 L3
Pomorskie, Pojezierze reg. Poland 57 O4
Pomorskiy Bereg coastal area Russia 52 G2
Pomorskiy Proliv sea chan. Russia 52 K1
Pomos Point Cyprus 107 A2
Pomo Tso l. China see Puma Yumco
Pomou, Akra pt Cyprus see Pomos Point

Pomozdino Russia 52 L3
Pompain China 99 F7
Pompano Beach FL U.S.A. 163 D7
Pompanua Celebes Indon. 83 B4
Pompei Italy 68 F4
Pompéia Brazil 179 A3
Pompey France 62 G6
Pompeyevka Russia 90 C2
Ponape atoll Micronesia see Pohnpei
Ponask Lake Canada 151 M4
Ponazyrevo Russia 52 J4
Ponca City OK U.S.A. 161 D4
Ponce Puerto Rico 169 K5
Ponce de Leon Bay FL U.S.A. 163 D7
Poncheville, Lac l. Canada 152 F4
Pondichéry India see Puducherry
Pond Inlet Canada 189 K2
Ponds Bay Canada see Pond Inlet
Poneloya Nicaragua 166 [inset] I6
Ponente, Riviera di coastal area Italy 68 B3
Poneto IN U.S.A. 164 C3
Ponferrada Spain 67 C2
Pongara, Pointe pt Gabon 122 A3
Pongaroa N.Z. 139 F5
Pongda China 99 F7
Pongo watercourse South Sudan 121 F4
Pongola r. S. Africa 125 K4
Pongolapoort Dam l. S. Africa 125 J4
Poniki, Gunung mt. Indon. 83 B2
Ponindilisa, Tanjung pt Indon. 83 B3
Ponnagyun Myanmar 86 A2
Ponnaiyar r. India 106 C4
Ponnampet India 106 B3
Ponnani India 106 B4
Ponnyadaung Range mts Myanmar 86 A2
Pono Moluccas Indon. 81 I8
Ponoka Canada 150 H4
Ponorogo Java Indon. 85 E4
Ponoy r. Russia 52 I2
Pons r. Canada 153 H2

▶Ponta Delgada Arquipélago dos Açores 184 G3
Capital of the Azores.

Ponta Grossa Brazil 179 A4
Pontal Brazil 179 A3
Pontalina Brazil 179 A2
Pont-à-Mousson France 62 G6
Ponta Porã Brazil 178 E2
Pontarfynach U.K. see Devil's Bridge
Pont-Audemer France 59 H9
Pontault-Combault France 62 C6
Pontax r. Canada 152 F4
Pontchartrain, Lake LA U.S.A. 161 F6
Pontcysyllte Aqueduct tourist site U.K. 59 D6
Pont d'Arc tourist site France 66 G4
Pont-de-Loup Belgium 62 E4
Ponte Alta do Tocantins Brazil 177 I6
Ponte de Sor Port. 67 B4
Ponte Firme Brazil 179 B2
Pontefract U.K. 58 F5
Ponteix Canada 151 J5
Ponteland U.K. 58 F3
Ponte Nova Brazil 179 C3
Pontes e Lacerda Brazil 177 G7
Pontevedra Spain 67 B2
Ponthierville Dem. Rep. Congo see Ubundu
Pontiac IL U.S.A. 160 F3
Pontiac MI U.S.A. 164 D2
Pontiae is Italy see Ponziane, Isole
Pontianak Kalimantan Indon. 85 E3
Pontine Islands is Italy see Ponziane, Isole
Pont-l'Abbé France 66 B3
Ponto de Santa Cruz Brazil 179 C1
Pontoise France 62 C5
Ponton watercourse Australia 135 C7
Ponton Canada 151 L4
Pontotoc MS U.S.A. 161 F5
Pont-Ste-Maxence France 62 C5
Pontypool U.K. 59 D7
Pontypridd U.K. 59 D7
Ponza, Isola di i. Italy 68 E4
Ponziane, Isole is Italy 68 E4
Poochera Australia 135 F8
Poole U.K. 59 F8
Poole KY U.S.A. 164 B5
Poolowanna Lake salt flat Australia 137 B5
Poona India see Pune
Pooncarie Australia 137 C7
Poonch India see Punch
Poopelloe Lake salt l. Australia 138 B3
Poopó, Lago de l. Bol. 176 E7
Poor Knights Islands N.Z. 139 E2
Poorman AK U.S.A. 148 I2
Popayán Col. 176 C3
Poperinge Belgium 62 C4
Popigay r. Russia 77 L2
Popiltah Australia 137 C7
Popilta Lake imp. l. Australia 137 C7
Poplar r. Canada 151 L4
Poplar MT U.S.A. 156 G2
Poplar Bluff MO U.S.A. 161 F4
Poplar Camp VA U.S.A. 164 E5
Poplarville MS U.S.A. 161 F6

▶Popocatépetl, Volcán vol. Mex. 168 E5
5th highest mountain in North America.

Popoh Java Indon. 85 E5
Popokabaka Dem. Rep. Congo 123 B4
Popondetta P.N.G. 81 L8
Popovichskaya Russia see Kalininskaya
Popovo Bulg. 69 L3
Popovo Polje plain Bos. & Herz. 68 G3
Poppberg hill Germany 63 L5
Poppenberg hill Germany 63 K3
Poprad Slovakia 57 R6
Poptún Guat. 167 H5
Poquoson VA U.S.A. 165 G5
Porali r. Pak. 111 G5
Porangahau N.Z. 139 F5
Porangatu Brazil 179 A1
Porbandar India 104 B5
Porcher Island Canada 149 O5
Porcos r. Brazil 179 B1
Porcupine r. Canada/U.S.A. 149 K2
Porcupine, Cape Canada 153 K3
Porcupine Abyssal Plain sea feature N. Atlantic Ocean 184 G2
Porcupine Gorge National Park Australia 136 D4
Porcupine Hills Canada 151 K4
Porcupine Mountains MI U.S.A. 160 F2
Poreč Croatia 68 E2
Porecatu Brazil 179 A3
Poretskoye Russia 53 J5
Porgyang China 99 C6
Pori Fin. 55 L6
Porirua N.Z. 139 E5
Porkhov Russia 55 P8
Porlamar Venez. 176 F1
Pormpuraaw Australia 136 C2
Pornic France 66 C3
Poro i. Phil. 82 D4
Poronaysk Russia 90 F2
Porong China 99 E7
Poros Greece 69 J6
Porosozero Russia 52 G3
Porpoise Bay Antarctica 188 G2
Porsangerfjorden sea chan. Norway 54 N1
Porsangerhalvøya pen. Norway 54 N1
Porsgrunn Norway 55 F7
Porsuk r. Turkey 69 N5
Portadown U.K. 61 F3
Portaferry U.K. 61 G3
Portage MI U.S.A. 164 C2
Portage PA U.S.A. 165 F3
Portage WI U.S.A. 160 F3
Portage Creek AK U.S.A. 148 H4
Portage Lakes OH U.S.A. 164 E3
Portage la Prairie Canada 151 L5
Portal ND U.S.A. 160 C1
Port Alberni Canada 150 E5
Port Albert Australia 138 C7
Portalegre Port. 67 C4
Portales NM U.S.A. 161 C5
Port-Alfred Canada see La Baie
Port Alfred S. Africa 125 H7
Port Alice Canada 150 E5
Port Allegany PA U.S.A. 165 F3
Port Allen LA U.S.A. 161 F6
Port Alma Australia 136 E4
Port Alsworth AK U.S.A. 148 I3
Port Angeles WA U.S.A. 156 C2
Port Antonio Jamaica 169 I5
Portarlington Ireland 61 E4
Port Arthur Australia 137 [inset]
Port Arthur China see Lüshunkou
Port Arthur TX U.S.A. 161 E6
Port Askaig U.K. 60 C5
Port Augusta Australia 137 B7

▶Port-au-Prince Haiti 169 J5
Capital of Haiti.

Port Austin MI U.S.A. 164 D1
Port aux Choix Canada 153 K4
Portavogie U.K. 61 G3
Port Beaufort S. Africa 124 E8
Port Blair India 87 A5
Port Bolster Canada 164 F1
Portbou Spain 67 H2
Port Brabant Canada see Tuktoyaktuk
Port Burwell Canada 164 E2
Port Campbell Australia 138 A7
Port Campbell National Park Australia 138 A7
Port Carling Canada 164 F1
Port-Cartier Canada 153 I4
Port Chalmers N.Z. 139 C7
Port Charlotte FL U.S.A. 163 D7
Port Clarence b. AK U.S.A. 148 F2
Port Clements Canada 149 N5
Port Clinton OH U.S.A. 164 D3
Port Credit Canada 164 F2
Port-de-Paix Haiti 169 J5
Port Dickson Malaysia 84 C2
Port Douglas Australia 136 D3
Port Edward Canada 149 O5
Port Edward S. Africa 125 J6
Porteira Brazil 177 G4
Porteirinha Brazil 179 C1
Portel Brazil 177 H4
Port Elgin Canada 164 E1
Port Elizabeth S. Africa 125 G7
Port Ellen U.K. 60 C5
Port Erin Isle of Man 58 C4
Porter Lake N.W.T. Canada 151 J2
Porter Lake Sask. Canada 151 J3
Porter Landing Canada 149 O4
Porterville S. Africa 124 D7
Porterville CA U.S.A. 158 D3
Port Étienne Mauritania see Nouâdhibou
Port Everglades FL U.S.A. see Fort Lauderdale
Port Fitzroy N.Z. 139 E3
Port Francqui Dem. Rep. Congo see Ilebo
Port-Gentil Gabon 122 A4
Port Gibson MS U.S.A. 167 H2
Port Glasgow U.K. 60 E5
Port Graham AK U.S.A. 149 J4
Port Harcourt Nigeria 120 D4
Port Harrison Canada see Inukjuak
Porthcawl U.K. 59 D7
Port Hedland Australia 134 B5
Port Heiden AK U.S.A. 148 H4
Port Heiden b. AK U.S.A. 148 H4
Port Henry NY U.S.A. 165 I1
Port Herald Malawi see Nsanje
Porthleven U.K. 59 B8
Porthmadog U.K. 59 C6
Port Hope Canada 165 F2
Port Hope Simpson Canada 153 L3
Port Hueneme CA U.S.A. 158 D4
Port Huron MI U.S.A. 164 D2
Portimão Port. 67 B5
Port Jackson Australia see Sydney
Port Jackson inlet Australia 138 E4
Port Keats Australia see Wadeye
Port Klang Malaysia see Pelabuhan Klang
Port Láirge Ireland see Waterford
Portland N.S.W. Australia 138 D4
Portland Vic. Australia 137 C8
Portland IN U.S.A. 164 C3
Portland ME U.S.A. 165 J2
Portland MI U.S.A. 164 C2
Portland OR U.S.A. 156 C3
Portland TN U.S.A. 164 B5
Portland, Isle of pen. U.K. 59 E8
Portland Bill hd U.K. see Bill of Portland
Portland Creek Pond l. Canada 153 K4
Portland Roads Australia 136 C2
Port-la-Nouvelle France 66 F5
Portlaoise Ireland 61 E4
Port Lavaca TX U.S.A. 161 D6
Portlaw Ireland 61 E5
Portlethen U.K. 60 G3
Port Lincoln Australia 137 A7
Port Lions AK U.S.A. 148 I4
Portlock AK U.S.A. 149 J4
Port Loko Sierra Leone 120 B4

▶Port Louis Mauritius 185 L7
Capital of Mauritius.

Port-Lyautrey Morocco see Kenitra
Port Macquarie Australia 138 F3
Portmadoc U.K. see Porthmadog
Port McNeill Canada 150 E5
Port-Menier Canada 153 I4
Port Moller AK U.S.A. 148 G5
Port Moller b. AK U.S.A. 148 G5

▶Port Moresby P.N.G. 81 L8
Capital of Papua New Guinea.

Portnaguran U.K. 60 C2
Portnahaven U.K. 60 C5
Port nan Giúran U.K. see Portnaguran
Port Neill Australia 137 B7
Portneuf r. Canada 153 H4
Port Nis U.K. see Port of Ness
Port Noarlunga Australia 137 B7
Port Nolloth S. Africa 124 C5
Port Norris NJ U.S.A. 165 H4
Port-Nouveau-Québec Canada see Kangiqsualujjuaq
Porto Port. see Oporto
Porto Acre Brazil 176 E5
Porto Alegre Brazil 179 A5
Porto Alexandre Angola see Tombua
Porto Amboim Angola 123 B5
Porto Amélia Moz. see Pemba
Porto Artur Brazil 177 G6
Porto Belo Brazil 179 A4
Portobelo Panama 166 [inset] K7
Portobelo, Parque Nacional nat. park Panama 166 [inset] K7
Port O'Brien AK U.S.A. 148 I4
Porto de Moz Brazil 177 H4
Porto dos Gaúchos Óbidos Brazil 177 G6
Porto Esperança Brazil 177 G7
Porto Esperidião Brazil 177 G7
Portoferraio Italy 68 D3
Port of Ness U.K. 60 C2
Porto Franco Brazil 177 I5

▶Port of Spain Trin. and Tob. 169 L6
Capital of Trinidad and Tobago.

Porto Grande Brazil 177 H3
Portogruaro Italy 68 E2
Porto Jofre Brazil 177 G7
Portola CA U.S.A. 158 C2
Portomaggiore Italy 68 D2
Porto Mendes Brazil 178 F2
Porto Murtinho Brazil 178 E2
Porto Nacional Brazil 177 I6

▶Porto-Novo Benin 120 D4
Capital of Benin.

Porto Novo Cape Verde 120 [inset]
Porto Primavera, Represa resr Brazil 178 F2
Port Orchard WA U.S.A. 156 C3
Port Orford OR U.S.A. 156 B4
Porto Rico Angola 123 B4
Porto Santo, Ilha de i. Madeira 120 B1
Porto Seguro Brazil 179 D2
Porto Tolle Italy 68 E2
Porto Torres Sardinia Italy 68 C4
Porto União Brazil 179 A4
Porto-Vecchio Corsica France 66 I6
Porto Velho Brazil 176 F5
Portoviejo Ecuador 176 B4
Porto Walter Brazil 176 D5
Portpatrick U.K. 60 D6
Port Perry Canada 165 F1
Port Phillip Bay Australia 138 B7
Port Pirie Australia 137 B7
Port Radium Canada see Echo Bay
Portreath U.K. 59 B8
Portree U.K. 60 C3
Port Rexton Canada 153 L4
Port Royal VA U.S.A. 165 G4
Port Royal Sound inlet SC U.S.A. 163 D5
Portrush U.K. 61 F2
Port Safaga Egypt see Būr Safājah
Port Safety AK U.S.A. 148 F2
Port Said Egypt 107 A4
Port St Joe FL U.S.A. 163 C6
Port St Mary Isle of Man 58 C4
Portsalon Ireland 61 E2
Port Sanilac MI U.S.A. 164 D2
Port Severn Canada 164 F1
Port Shepstone S. Africa 125 J6
Port Simpson Canada see Lax Kw'alaams
Portsmouth U.K. 59 F8
Portsmouth NH U.S.A. 165 J2
Portsmouth OH U.S.A. 164 D4
Portsmouth VA U.S.A. 165 G5
Portsoy U.K. 60 G3
Port Stanley Falkland Is see Stanley
Port Stephens b. Australia 138 F4
Portstewart U.K. 61 F2
Port St Lucie FL U.S.A. 163 D7
Port Sudan Sudan 108 E6
Port Sulphur LA U.S.A. 167 H2
Port Swettenham Malaysia see Pelabuhan Klang
Port Talbot U.K. 59 D7
Porttipahdan tekojärvi l. Fin. 54 O2
Port Townsend WA U.S.A. 156 C2
Portugal country Europe 67 C4
Portugália Angola see Chitato
Portuguese East Africa country Africa see Mozambique
Portuguese Guinea country Africa see Guinea-Bissau
Portuguese Timor country Asia see East Timor
Portuguese West Africa country Africa see Angola
Portumna Ireland 61 D4
Portus Herculis Monoeci country Europe see Monaco
Port-Vendres France 66 F5

▶Port Vila Vanuatu 133 G3
Capital of Vanuatu.

Portville NY U.S.A. 165 F2
Port-Vladimir Russia 54 R2
Port Waikato N.Z. 139 E3
Port Washington WI U.S.A. 164 B2
Port William U.K. 60 E6
Porvenir Bol. 176 E6
Porvenir Chile 178 B8
Porvoo Fin. 55 N6
Posada Spain 67 D2
Posada de Llanera Spain see Posada
Posadas Arg. 178 E3
Posen Poland see Poznań
Posen MI U.S.A. 164 D1
Poseyville IN U.S.A. 164 B4
Poshekhon'ye Russia 52 H4
Poshekon'ye-Volodarsk Russia see Poshekhon'ye
Poshteh-ye Chaqvīr hill Iran 110 E4
Posht-e Kūh mts Iran 110 B3
Posht-e Rūd va Zamīndāvar reg. Afgh. see Zamīndāwar
Posht Kūh hill Iran 110 C2
Posio Fin. 54 P3
Poskam China see Zepu
Poso Celebes Indon. 83 B3
Poso r. Indon. 83 B3
Poso, Danau l. Indon. 83 B3
Poso, Teluk b. Indon. 83 B3
Posof Turkey 113 F2
Possession Island Namibia 124 B4
Pößneck Germany 63 L4
Possum Kingdom Lake TX U.S.A. 167 F1
Post TX U.S.A. 161 C5
Postavy Belarus see Pastavy
Poste-de-la-Baleine Canada see Kuujjuarapik
Poste Weygand Alg. 120 D2
Postmasburg S. Africa 124 F5
Poston AZ U.S.A. 159 F4
Postville Canada 153 K3
Postville IA U.S.A. 152 C6
Postysheve Ukr. see Krasnoarmiys'k
Pota Flores Indon. 83 B5
Pótam Mex. 166 C3
Poté Brazil 179 C2
Poteau OK U.S.A. 161 E5
Potegaon India 106 D2
Potentia Italy see Potenza
Potenza Italy 68 F4
Poth TX U.S.A. 161 D6
Poti Georgia 113 F2
Potikal India 106 D2
Potiraguá Brazil 179 D1
Potiskum Nigeria 120 E3
Potlatch ID U.S.A. 156 D3
Pot Mountain ID U.S.A. 156 E3
Po Toi i. H.K. China 97 [inset]
Potomac r. Maryland/Virginia U.S.A. 165 G4
Potomana, Gunung mt. Indon. 83 C5
Potosí Bol. 176 E7
Potosi MO U.S.A. 160 F4
Potosi Mountain NV U.S.A. 159 F4
Pototan Panay Phil. 82 C4
Potrerillos Chile 178 C3
Potrerillos Hond. 166 [inset] I6
Potrero del Llano Mex. 166 D2
Potsdam Germany 63 N2
Potsdam NY U.S.A. 165 H1
Potter NE U.S.A. 160 C3
Potterne U.K. 59 E7
Potters Bar U.K. 59 G7
Potter Valley CA U.S.A. 158 B2
Pottstown PA U.S.A. 165 H3
Pottsville PA U.S.A. 165 G3
Pottuvil Sri Lanka 106 D5
Potwar reg. Pak. 111 I3
Pouch Cove Canada 153 L5
Poughkeepsie NY U.S.A. 165 I3
Poulin de Courval, Lac l. Canada 153 H4
Poulton-le-Fylde U.K. 58 E5
Pouso Alegre Brazil 179 B3
Poŭthĭsăt Cambodia 87 C4
Poŭthĭsăt, Stœng r. Cambodia 87 D4
Považská Bystrica Slovakia 57 Q6
Povenets Russia 52 G3
Poverty Bay N.Z. 139 F4
Poverty Point tourist site U.S.A. 161 F5
Povlen mt. Serbia 69 H2
Póvoa de Varzim Port. 67 B3
Povorino Russia 53 I6
Povorotnyy, Mys hd Russia 90 D4
Poway CA U.S.A. 158 E5
Powder r. MT U.S.A. 156 G3
Powder, South Fork r. WY U.S.A. 156 G4
Powder River WY U.S.A. 156 G4
Powell r. Tennessee/Virginia U.S.A. 164 D5
Powell, Lake resr UT U.S.A. 159 H3
Powell Lake Canada 150 E5
Powell Mountain NV U.S.A. 158 D2
Powell Point Bahamas 163 E7
Powell River Canada 150 E5
Powhatan AR U.S.A. 161 F4
Powhatan VA U.S.A. 165 G5
Powo China 96 C1
Pōwrize Turkm. 110 E2
Poxoréo Brazil 177 H7
Poyang China 97 H2
Poyang Hu l. China 97 H2
Poyan Reservoir Sing. 87 [inset]
Poyarkovo Russia 90 C2
Pōzak, Jahīl-e marsh Afgh. 111 F4
Pozantı Turkey 112 D3
Požarevac Serbia 69 I2
Poza Rica Mex. 168 E4
Pozdeyevka Russia 90 C2
Požega Croatia 68 G2
Požega Serbia 69 I3
Pozharskoye Russia 90 D3
Poznań Poland 57 P4
Pozoblanco Spain 67 D4
Pozo Colorado Para. 178 E2
Pozo Nuevo Mex. 166 C2
Pozsony Slovakia see Bratislava
Pozzuoli Italy 68 F4
Prabumulih Sumatra Indon. 84 D3
Prachatice Czech Rep. 57 O6
Prachi r. India 105 F6
Prachin Buri Thai. 87 C4
Prachuap Khiri Khan Thai. 87 B5
Prades France 66 F5
Prado Brazil 179 D2

▶Prague Czech Rep. 57 O5
Capital of the Czech Republic.

Praha Czech Rep. see Prague

▶Praia Cape Verde 120 [inset]
Capital of Cape Verde (Cabo Verde).

Praia do Bilene Moz. 125 K3
Prainha Brazil 177 H4
Prairie Australia 136 D4
Prairie r. MN U.S.A. 160 E2
Prairie Dog Town Fork r. TX U.S.A. 161 C5
Prairie du Chien WI U.S.A. 160 F3
Prairie River Canada 151 K4
Pram, Khao mt. Thai. 87 B5
Pran r. Thai. 87 C4
Pran Buri Thai. 87 B4
Prapat Sumatra Indon. 84 B2
Prasonisi, Akra pt Greece see Prasonisi, Akrotirio
Prasonisi, Akrotirio pt Greece 69 L7
Prata Brazil 179 A2
Prata r. Brazil 179 A2
Pratas Islands is China 82 B1
Prat de Llobregat Spain see El Prat de Llobregat
Prathes Thai country Asia see Thailand
Prato Italy 68 D3
Pratt KS U.S.A. 160 D4
Prattville AL U.S.A. 163 C5
Pravdinsk Russia 55 L9
Praya Lombok Indon. 85 G5
Preăh, Prêk r. Cambodia 87 D4
Preăh Vihéar Cambodia 87 D4
Preble NY U.S.A. 165 G2
Prechistoye Smolenskaya Oblast' Russia 53 G5
Prechistoye Yaroslavskaya Oblast' Russia 52 I4
Precipice National Park Australia 136 E5
Preeceville Canada 151 K5
Pregolya r. Russia 55 L9
Preiļi Latvia 55 O8
Prêk Kák Cambodia 87 D4
Prelate Canada 151 I5
Premer Australia 138 D3
Prémery France 66 F3
Premnitz Germany 63 M2
Prentiss MS U.S.A. 161 F6
Prenzlau Germany 57 N4
Preparis Island Cocos Is 80 A4
Preparis North Channel Cocos Is 80 A4
Preparis South Channel Cocos Is 80 A4
Přerov Czech Rep. 57 P6
Presa de la Amistad, Parque Natural nature res. Mex. 167 E2
Presa San Antonio Mex. 167 E3
Prescelly Mountains hills U.K. see Preseli, Mynydd
Prescott Canada 165 H1
Prescott AR U.S.A. 161 E5
Prescott AZ U.S.A. 159 G4
Prescott Valley AZ U.S.A. 159 G4
Preseli, Mynydd hills U.K. 59 C7
Preševo Serbia 69 I3
Presidencia Roque Sáenz Peña Arg. 178 D3
Presidente Dutra Brazil 177 J5
Presidente Hermes Brazil 176 F6
Presidente Manuel A Roxas Mindanao Phil. 82 C4
Presidente Olegário Brazil 179 B2
Presidente Prudente Brazil 179 A3
Presidente Venceslau Brazil 179 A3
Presidio TX U.S.A. 161 B6
Preslav Bulg. see Veliki Preslav
Prešov Slovakia 53 D6
Prespa, Lake Europe 69 I4
Prespansko Ezero l. Europe see Prespa, Lake
Prespës, Liqeni i l. Europe see Prespa, Lake
Prespon, Ethnikos Drymos nat. park Greece 69 I4
Presque Isle ME U.S.A. 162 G2
Presque Isle MI U.S.A. 164 D1
Pressburg Slovakia see Bratislava
Presteigne U.K. 59 D6
Preston U.K. 58 E5
Preston ID U.S.A. 156 F4
Preston MN U.S.A. 160 E3
Preston MO U.S.A. 160 E4
Preston, Cape Australia 134 B5
Prestonpans U.K. 60 G5
Prestonsburg KY U.S.A. 164 D5
Prestwick U.K. 60 E5
Preto r. Bahia Brazil 177 J6
Preto r. Bahia Brazil 179 D1
Preto r. Minas Gerais Brazil 179 B2

▶Pretoria S. Africa 125 I3
Official capital of South Africa.

Pretoria-Witwatersrand-Vereeniging prov. S. Africa see Gauteng
Pretzsch Germany 63 M3
Preussisch-Eylau Russia see Bagrationovsk
Preußisch Stargard Poland see Starogard Gdański
Preveza Greece 69 I5
Prewitt NM U.S.A. 159 I4
Prey Vêng Cambodia 87 D5
Priaral'skiy Karakum des. Kazakh. 102 B2
Priargunsk Russia 95 I1
Pribilof Islands AK U.S.A. 148 E4
Priboj Serbia 69 H3
Price r. Australia 134 E3
Price NC U.S.A. 164 F5
Price UT U.S.A. 159 H2
Price r. UT U.S.A. 159 H2
Price Island Canada 150 D4
Prichard AL U.S.A. 161 F6
Prichard WV U.S.A. 164 D4
Pridorozhnoye Russia see Khulkhuta
Priekule Latvia 55 L8
Priekuļi Latvia 55 N8
Priel'brus'ye, Natsional'nyy Park nat. park Russia 53 I8
Prienai Lith. 55 M9
Prieska S. Africa 124 F5
Prievidza Slovakia 57 Q6
Prignitz reg. Germany 63 M1
Prijedor Bos. & Herz. 68 G2
Prijepolje Serbia 69 H3
Prikaspiyskaya Nizmennost' lowland Kazakh./Russia see Caspian Lowland
Prilep Macedonia 69 I4
Priluki Ukr. see Pryluky
Přimda Czech Rep. 63 M5
Primero de Enero Cuba 163 E8
Primorsk Russia 55 P6
Primorsk Ukr. see Prymors'k
Primorskiy Kray admin. div. Russia 90 D3
Primorsko-Akhtarsk Russia 53 H7
Primo Tapia Mex. 166 A1
Primrose Lake Canada 151 I4
Prims r. Germany 62 G5
Prince Albert Canada 151 J4
Prince Albert S. Africa 124 F7
Prince Albert Mountains Antarctica 188 H1
Prince Albert National Park Canada 151 J4
Prince Albert Peninsula Canada 146 G2
Prince Albert Road S. Africa 124 E7
Prince Alfred, Cape Canada 146 F2
Prince Alfred Hamlet S. Africa 124 D7
Prince Charles Island Canada 147 K3
Prince Charles Mountains Antarctica 188 E2
Prince Edward Island prov. Canada 153 J5

▶Prince Edward Islands Indian Ocean 185 K9
Part of South Africa.

Prince Edward Point Canada 165 G2
Prince Frederick MD U.S.A. 165 G4
Prince George Canada 150 F4
Prince Harald Coast Antarctica 188 D2
Prince of Wales, Cape AK U.S.A. 148 E2
Prince of Wales Island Australia 136 C1
Prince of Wales Island Canada 147 I2
Prince of Wales Island AK U.S.A. 149 N5
Prince of Wales Strait Canada 146 G2
Prince Patrick Island Canada 146 G2
Prince Regent Inlet sea chan. Canada 147 I2
Prince Rupert Canada 149 O5
Princess Anne MD U.S.A. 165 H4
Princess Astrid Coast Antarctica 188 C2
Princess Charlotte Bay Australia 136 C2
Princess Elisabeth research station Antarctica 188 C2
Princess Elizabeth Land reg. Antarctica 188 E2
Princess Mary Lake Canada 151 L1
Princess Ragnhild Coast Antarctica 188 C2
Princess Royal Island Canada 150 D4
Princeton Canada 150 F5
Princeton CA U.S.A. 158 B2
Princeton IL U.S.A. 160 F3
Princeton IN U.S.A. 164 B4
Princeton MO U.S.A. 160 E3
Princeton NJ U.S.A. 165 H3
Princeton WV U.S.A. 164 E5
Prince William Sound b. AK U.S.A. 149 K3
Príncipe i. São Tomé and Príncipe 120 D4
Prindle, Mount AK U.S.A. 149 K2
Prineville OR U.S.A. 156 C3
Pring, Kaôh i. Cambodia 87 C5

Prins Harald Kyst coastal area Antarctica see Prince Harald Coast
Prinzapolka Nicaragua 166 [inset] J6
Priozersk Russia 55 Q6
Priozyorsk Russia see Priozersk
Pripet r. Belarus/Ukr. 53 F6 also spelt Pryp"yat' (Ukraine) or Prypyats' (Belarus)
Pripet Marshes Belarus/Ukr. 53 E6
Prirechnyy Russia 54 Q2

▶Prishtinë Kosovo 69 I3
Capital of Kosovo.

Priština Kosovo see Prishtinë
Pritzier Germany 63 L1
Pritzwalk Germany 63 M1
Privas France 66 G4
Privlaka Croatia 68 F2
Privolzhsk Russia 52 I4
Privolzhskaya Vozvyshennost' hills Russia 53 J6
Privolzhskiy Russia 53 J6
Privolzh'ye Russia 53 K5
Priyutnoye Russia 53 I7
Prizren Kosovo 69 I3
Probolinggo Java Indon. 85 F4
Probstzella Germany 63 L4
Probus U.K. 59 C8
Proddatur India 106 C3
Professor van Blommestein Meer resr Suriname 177 G3
Progreso Coahuila Mex. 167 E3
Progreso Hidalgo Mex. 167 F4
Progreso Yucatán Mex. 167 H4
Progress research station Antarctica 188 E2
Progress Russia 90 C2
Prokhladnyy Russia 113 G2
Prokop'yevsk Russia 88 F2
Prokuplje Serbia 69 I3
Proletarsk Russia 53 I7
Proletarskaya Russia see Proletarsk
Proletarskoye Vodokhranilishche l. Russia 53 I7
Prome Myanmar see Pyè
Promissão Brazil 179 A3
Promissão, Represa resr Brazil 179 A3
Prophet r. Canada 150 F3
Prophet River Canada 150 F3
Propriá Brazil 177 K6
Proskurov Ukr. see Khmel'nyts'kyy
Prosperidad Mindanao Phil. 82 D4
Prosser WA U.S.A. 156 D3
Protem S. Africa 124 E8
Provadia Bulg. 69 L3
Prøven Greenland see Kangersuatsiaq
Provence reg. France 66 G5
Providence KY U.S.A. 164 B5
Providence MD U.S.A. see Annapolis

▶Providence RI U.S.A. 165 J3
Capital of Rhode Island.

Providence, Cape N.Z. 139 A8
Providence, Cape AK U.S.A. 148 H4
Providencia, Isla de i. Caribbean Sea 169 H6
Provideniya Russia 148 D2
Provincetown MA U.S.A. 165 J2
Provo UT U.S.A. 159 H1
Provost Canada 151 I4
Prudentópolis Brazil 179 A4
Prudhoe Bay AK U.S.A. 149 J1
Prudhoe Bay AK U.S.A. 149 J1
Prüm Germany 62 G4
Prüm r. Germany 62 G5
Prunelli-di-Fiumorbo Corsica France 66 I5
Pruntytown WV U.S.A. 164 E4
Prusa Turkey see Bursa
Prushkov Poland see Pruszków
Pruszków Poland 57 R4
Prut r. Europe 53 F7
Prydz Bay Antarctica 188 E2
Pryluky Ukr. 53 G6
Prymors'k Ukr. 53 H7
Prymors'ke Ukr. see Sartana
Pryp"yat' r. Belarus/Ukr. 53 F6 see Pripet
Prypyats' r. Belarus/Ukr. 51 L5 see Pripet
Przemyśl Poland 53 D6
Przheval'sk Kyrg. see Karakol
Przheval'sk Pristany Kyrg. 98 B4
Psara i. Greece 69 K5
Pskov Russia 55 P8
Pskov, Lake Estonia/Russia 55 O7
Pskov Oblast admin. div. Russia see Pskovskaya Oblast'
Pskovskaya Oblast' admin. div. Russia 55 P8
Pskovskoye Ozero l. Estonia/Russia see Pskov, Lake
Ptolemaïda Greece 69 I4
Ptolemais Israel see 'Akko
Ptuj Slovenia 68 F1
Pu r. Indon. 84 C3
Pua Thai. 86 C3
Puaka hill Sing. 87 [inset]
Pu'an Guizhou China 96 E3
Pu'an Sichuan China 96 E2
Pucallpa Peru 176 D5
Pucheng Fujian China 97 H3
Pucheng Shaanxi China 95 G5
Puchezh Russia 52 I4
Pucio Point Panay Phil. 82 C4
Puck Poland 57 Q3
Pūdah Tal, Shēlah-ye watercourse Afgh. 111 F4
Pudai watercourse Afgh. see Pūdah Tal, Shēlah-ye
Pūdanū Iran 110 D3
Pudasjärvi Fin. 54 O4
Pudi Kalimantan Indon. 85 G3
Pudimoe S. Africa 124 G4
Pudong China 78 E4
Pudozh Russia 52 H3
Pudsey U.K. 58 F5
Pudu China see Suizhou
Puduchcheri India see Puducherry
Puducherry India 106 C4
Puducherry union terr. India 106 C4
Pudukkottai India 106 C4
Puebla Baja California Mex. 159 F5
Puebla Puebla Mex. 168 E5
Puebla state Mex. 167 F5
Puebla de Sanabria Spain 67 C2
Puebla de Zaragoza Mex. see Puebla
Pueblo CO U.S.A. 157 G5
Pueblo Nuevo Mex. 166 D4
Pueblo Nuevo Nicaragua 166 [inset] I6
Pueblo Viejo, Laguna de lag. Mex. 167 F4
Pueblo Yaqui Mex. 166 C3
Puelches Arg. 178 C5
Puelén Arg. 178 C5
Puente de Ixtla Mex. 167 F5
Puente Genil Spain 67 D5
Pu'er China see Ning'er
Puerco watercourse AZ U.S.A. 159 H4
Puerto Acosta Bol. 176 E7
Puerto Alegre Bol. 176 F6
Puerto Ángel Mex. 167 F6
Puerto Arista Mex. 167 G6
Puerto Armuelles Panama 166 [inset] J7
Puerto Ayacucho Venez. 176 E2
Puerto Bahía Negra Para. see Bahía Negra
Puerto Baquerizo Moreno Galápagos Ecuador 176 [inset]
Puerto Barrios Guat. 166 [inset] H6
Puerto Cabello Venez. 176 E1
Puerto Cabezas Nicaragua 166 [inset] J6
Puerto Cabo Gracias a Dios Nicaragua 166 [inset] J6
Puerto Carreño Col. 176 E2
Puerto Casado Para. 178 E2
Puerto Cavinas Bol. 176 E6
Puerto Coig (abandoned) Arg. 178 C8
Puerto Cortés Hond. 166 [inset] I6
Puerto Cortés Mex. 166 C3
Puerto de Lobos Mex. 166 B2
Puerto de Los Ángeles, Parque Natural nature res. Mex. 166 D4
Puerto de Morelos Mex. 167 I4
Puerto Deseado Arg. 178 C7
Puerto Escondido Mex. 168 E5
Puerto Francisco de Orellana Ecuador see Coca
Puerto Frey Bol. 176 F6
Puerto Génova Bol. 176 E6
Puerto Guarani Para. 178 E2
Puerto Heath Bol. 176 E6
Puerto Huitoto Col. 176 D3
Puerto Isabel Bol. 177 G7
Puerto Juáres Mex. 167 I4
Puerto Leguízamo Col. 176 D4
Puerto Lempira Hond. 166 [inset] J6
Puerto Libertad Mex. 166 B2
Puerto Limón Costa Rica 166 [inset] J7
Puertollano Spain 67 D4
Puerto Lobos Arg. 178 C6
Puerto Madero Mex. 167 G6
Puerto Madryn Arg. 178 C6
Puerto Magdalena Mex. 166 B3
Puerto Maldonado Peru 176 E6
Puerto Máncora Peru 176 B4
Puerto México Mex. see Coatzacoalcos
Puerto Montt Chile 178 B6
Puerto Morazán Nicaragua 166 [inset] I6
Puerto Natales Chile 178 B8
Puerto Nuevo Col. 176 E2
Puerto Peñasco Mex. 166 B2
Puerto Pirámides Arg. 178 D6
Puerto Plata Dom. Rep. 169 J5
Puerto Portillo Peru 176 D5
Puerto Prado Peru 176 D6
Puerto Princesa Palawan Phil. 82 B4
Puerto Princesa Subterranean River Natural Park Phil. 82 B4
Puerto Quepos Costa Rica 166 [inset] I7
Puerto Quetzal Guat. 166 H6
Puerto Real Mex. 167 H5
Puerto Rico Arg. 178 E3
Puerto Rico Bol. 176 E6

▶Puerto Rico terr. West Indies 169 K5
United States Commonwealth.

▶Puerto Rico Trench sea feature Caribbean Sea 184 D4
Deepest trench in the Atlantic Ocean.

Puerto Sandino Nicaragua 166 [inset] I6
Puerto San José Guat. 167 H6
Puerto San Julián Arg. 178 C7
Puerto Santa Cruz Arg. 178 C8
Puerto Santander Col. 176 D4
Puerto Sastre Para. 178 E2
Puerto Saucedo Bol. 176 F6
Puerto Somoza Nicaragua see Puerto Sandino
Puerto Suárez Bol. 177 G7
Puerto Supe Peru 176 C6
Puerto Vallarta Mex. 168 C4
Puerto Victoria Peru 176 D5
Puerto Visser Arg. 178 C7
Puerto Yartou Chile 178 B8
Puerto Ybapobó Para. 178 E2
Pugachev Russia 53 K5
Pugal India 104 C3
Puge China 96 D3
Puger Java Indon. 85 F5
Pūhāl-e Khamīr, Kūh-e mts Iran 110 D5
Puhiwaero c. N.Z. see South West Cape
Puigmal mt. France/Spain 66 F5
Pui O Wan b. H.K. China 97 [inset]
Pujada Bay Mindanao Phil. 82 D5
Puji Shaanxi China see Wugong
Puji Sichuan China see Puge
Pukaki, Lake N.Z. 139 C7
Pukapuka atoll Cook Is 133 J3
Pukaskwa National Park Canada 152 D4
Pukatawagan Canada 151 K4
Pukchin N. Korea 91 B4
Pukch'ŏng N. Korea 91 C4
Pukekohe N.Z. 139 E3
Puketeraki Range mts N.Z. 139 D6
Pukeuri Junction N.Z. 139 C7
Puksubaek-san mt. N. Korea 90 B4
Pula Croatia 68 E2
Pula Sardinia Italy 68 C5
Pulandian China 95 J4
Pulandian Wan b. China 95 J4
Pulangi r. Mindanao Phil. 82 D5
Pulangpisau Kalimantan Indon. 85 F3
Pulap atoll Micronesia 81 L5
Pulasi i. Indon. 83 B4
Pulaski NY U.S.A. 165 G2
Pulaski VA U.S.A. 164 E5
Pulaski WI U.S.A. 164 A1
Pulaukijang Sumatra Indon. 84 C3
Pulau Pinang state Malaysia see Pinang
Pulau Simeulue, Suaka Margasatwa nature res. Indon. 87 A7
Pul-e 'Alam Afgh. 111 H3
Pul-e Khumrī Afgh. 111 H3
Pulheim Germany 62 G3
Pulicat Lake inlet India 106 D3
Pulivendla India 106 C3
Pulkkila Fin. 54 N4
Pullman WA U.S.A. 156 D3
Pulog, Mount Luzon Phil. 82 C2
Pulozero Russia 54 R2
Púlpito, Punta pt Mex. 166 C3
Pulu China 99 C5
Pülümür Turkey 113 E3
Pulusuk atoll Micronesia 81 L5
Pulutan Celebes Indon. 83 C1
Puluwat atoll Micronesia 81 L5
Pulwama India 111 I3
Pumasillo, Cerro mt. Peru 176 D6
Puma Yumco l. China 99 E7
Pumiao China see Yongning
Puná, Isla i. Ecuador 176 B4
Punakha Bhutan 105 G4
Punch India 104 C2
Punchaw Canada 150 F4
Punda Maria S. Africa 125 J2
Pundri India 104 D3
Pune India 106 B2
P'ungsan N. Korea 90 C4
Puning China 97 H4
Punjab state India 104 C3
Punjab prov. Pak. 111 H4
Punmah Glacier China/Pak. 104 D2
Puno Peru 176 D7
Punta, Cerro de mt. Puerto Rico 169 K5
Punta Abreojos Mex. 157 E8
Punta Alta Arg. 178 D5
Punta Arenas Chile 178 B8
Punta del Este Uruguay 178 F5
Punta Delgada Arg. 178 D6
Punta Gorda Belize 166 [inset] H5
Punta Gorda Nicaragua 166 [inset] J7
Punta Gorda FL U.S.A. 163 D7
Punta Norte Arg. 178 D6
Punta Prieta Mex. 166 B2
Puntarenas Costa Rica 166 [inset] I7
Puntland area Somalia 122 E3
Punuk Islands AK U.S.A. 148 E3
Punxsutawney PA U.S.A. 165 F3
Puokio Fin. 54 O4
Puolanka Fin. 54 O4
Puqi China see Chibi
Pur r. Russia 76 I3
Puracé, Volcán de vol. Col. 176 C3
Purbalingga Java Indon. 85 E4
Purcell OK U.S.A. 161 D5
Purcell Mountain AK U.S.A. 148 H2
Purcell Mountains Canada 150 G5
Pur Co l. China 99 C6
Purgadala China 99 D6
Purgatoire r. CO U.S.A. 160 C4
Puri India 106 E2
Purmerend Neth. 62 E2
Purna r. Mahar. India 104 D5
Purna r. Mahar. India 106 C2
Purnea India see Purnia
Purnia India 105 F4
Purnululu National Park Australia 134 E4
Pursat Cambodia see Poŭthĭsăt
Puruandíro Mex. 167 E4
Purukcahu Kalimantan Indon. 85 F3
Puruliya India 105 F5

▶Purus r. Peru 176 F4
3rd longest river in South America.

Puruvesi l. Fin. 54 P6
Purvis MS U.S.A. 167 H2
Purwakarta Java Indon. 84 D4
Purwareja Java Indon. 85 E4
Purwodadi Java Indon. 85 E4
Purwokerto Java Indon. 85 E4
Puryŏng N. Korea 90 C4
Pusa India 99 D8
Pusa Sarawak Malaysia 85 E2
Pusad India 106 C2
Pusan S. Korea see Busan
Pusan Point Mindanao Phil. 82 D5
Pusatlı Dağı mt. Turkey 107 A1
Pushchino Russia 53 H5
Pushkin Russia 55 Q7
Pushkino Azer. see Biläsuvar
Pushkinskaya, Gora mt. Russia 90 F3
Pushkinskiye Gory Russia 55 P8
Pushma Russia 52 J3
Pushti-i-Rud reg. Afgh. see Zamīndāwar
Pūstīn Afgh. 111 F3
Pustoshka Russia 52 F4
Pusur r. Bangl. 105 G5
Putahow Lake Canada 151 K3
Putain Timor Indon. 83 C5
Putao Myanmar 86 B1
Puteoli Italy see Pozzuoli
Puteran i. Indon. 85 F4
Puthein Myanmar see Bassein
Putian China 97 H3
Puting China see De'an
Puting, Tanjung pt Indon. 85 E3
Putintsevo Kazakh. 98 D2
Putla Mex. 167 F5
Putlitz Germany 63 M1
Putna r. Romania 69 L2
Putney VT U.S.A. 165 I2
Putoi i. H.K. China see Po Toi
Putorana, Plato mts Russia 189 E2

▶Putrajaya Malaysia 84 C2
Joint capital (with Kuala Lumpur) of Malaysia.

Putre Chile 176 E7
Putsonderwater S. Africa 124 E5
Puttalam Sri Lanka 106 C4
Puttalam Lagoon Sri Lanka 106 C4
Puttelange-aux-Lacs France 62 G5
Putten Neth. 62 F2
Puttershoek Neth. 62 E3
Puttgarden Germany 57 M3
Putumayo r. Col. 176 D4 also known as Ica (Peru)
Putuo China 97 I2
Putusibau Kalimantan Indon. 85 F2
Puumala Fin. 55 P6
Pu'u'ula'ula mt. HI U.S.A. 157 [inset]
Pu'uwai HI U.S.A. 157 [inset]
Puvirnituq Canada 152 F1
Puxian China 95 G4
Puyallup WA U.S.A. 156 C3
Puyang China 95 H5
Puy de Sancy mt. France 66 F4
Puyehue, Parque Nacional nat. park Chile 178 B6
Puysegur Point N.Z. 139 A8
Puzla Russia 52 L3
Pweto Dem. Rep. Congo 123 C4
Pwinbyu Myanmar 86 A2
Pwllheli U.K. 59 C6
Pyal'ma Russia 52 G3
Pyalo Myanmar 86 A3
Pyamalaw r. Myanmar 86 A4
Pyandzh Tajik. see Panj
Pyaozero, Ozero l. Russia 54 Q3
Pyaozerskiy Russia 54 Q4
Pyapali India 106 C3
Pyapon Myanmar 86 A3
Pyasina r. Russia 76 J2
Pyatigorsk Russia 113 F1
Pyatikhatki Ukr. see P"yatykhatky
P"yatykhatky Ukr. 53 G6
Pyay Myanmar see Pyè
Pychas Russia 52 L4
Pyè Myanmar 86 A3
Pye, Mount hill N.Z. 139 B8
Pye Islands AK U.S.A. 149 J4
Pyeongchang S. Korea 91 C5
Pyeonghae S. Korea 91 C5
Pyeongtaek S. Korea 91 B5
Pyetrykaw Belarus 53 F5
Pygmalion Point India see Indira Point
Pyhäjoki Fin. 54 N4
Pyhäjoki r. Fin. 54 N4
Pyhäntä Fin. 54 O4
Pyhäsalmi Fin. 54 N5
Pyhäselkä l. Fin. 54 P5
Pyi Myanmar see Pyè
Pyin Myanmar see Pyè
Pyingaing Myanmar 86 A2
Pyinmana Myanmar 86 B3
Pyin-U-Lwin Myanmar 86 B2
Pyle U.K. 59 D7
Pyl'karamo Russia 76 J3
Pylos Greece 69 I6
Pymatuning Reservoir PA U.S.A. 164 E3
Pyŏktong N. Korea 90 B4
P'yŏnggang N. Korea 91 B5
P'yŏngsong N. Korea 91 B5

▶P'yŏngyang N. Korea 91 B5
Capital of North Korea.

Pyramid Hill Australia 138 B6
Pyramid Lake NV U.S.A. 158 D1
Pyramid Peak CO U.S.A. 159 J1
Pyramid Range mts NV U.S.A. 158 D2
Pyramids of Giza tourist site Egypt 112 C5
Pyrenees mts Europe 67 H2
Pyrénées mts Europe see Pyrenees
Pyrénées, Parc National des nat. park France/Spain 66 D5
Pyre Peak vol. AK U.S.A. 148 [inset] D5
Pyrgos Greece 69 I6
Pyryatyn Ukr. 53 G6
Pyrzyce Poland 57 O4
Pyshchug Russia 52 J4
Pytalovo Russia 55 O8
Pyxaria mt. Greece 69 J5

Qaa Lebanon 107 C2
Qaanaaq Greenland 147 L2
Qabātīyah West Bank 107 B3
Qabnag China 99 F7
Qabqa China see Gonghe
Qacentina Alg. see Constantine
Qacha's Nek Lesotho 125 I6
Qādērābād Iran 110 D4
Qadirpur Pak. 111 I4
Qādis Afgh. 111 F3
Qādisīyah, Sadd dam Iraq 113 F4
Qadisiyah Dam Iraq see Qādisīyah, Sadd
Qā'emābād Iran 111 F4
Qā'emshahr Iran 110 D2
Qā'en Iran 110 E3
Qagan China 95 I1
Qagan Nur Nei Mongol China 95 G4
Qagan Nur Nei Mongol China 95 H3
Qagan Nur Qinghai China 94 D4
Qagan Nur Xinjiang China 98 D4
Qagan Nur l. China 95 K2
Qagan Nur resr China 95 H3
Qagan Obo China 95 G2
Qagan Teg China 95 H3
Qagan Tohoi China 94 C5
Qagan Tungge China 98 C3
Qagan Us Nei Mongol China 89 K4
Qagan Us Qinghai China see Dulan
Qagan Us He r. China 94 D4
Qagbasêrag China 96 B2
Qagca China 96 C1
Qagcaka China 105 E2
Qagchêng China see Xiangcheng
Qahar Youyi Houqi China see Bayan Qagan
Qahar Youyi Qianqi China see Togrog Ul
Qahar Youyi Zhongqi China see Hobor
Qahremānshahr Iran see Kermānshāh
Qaidabad Pak. 111 H3
Qaidam He r. China 94 C4
Qaidam Pendi basin China 94 C4
Qaidam Shan mts China 94 C4
Qaidar China see Cêtar
Qainaqangma China 99 E6
Qaīṣār Afgh. 111 G3
Qaisar, Koh-i- mt. Afgh. see Qeyṣār, Kūh-e
Qakar China 99 C5
Qal'ah-ye Fārsī Afgh. 111 F3
Qal'ah-ye Now Afgh. 111 F3
Qal'ah-ye Rashīd Afgh. 111 G4
Qal'ah-ye Sang-e Takht Afgh. 111 G3
Qala-i-Kang Afgh. see Kang (abandoned)
Qalaikhumb Tajik. 111 H2
Qala Jamal Afgh. 111 F3
Qalāt Afgh. 111 G3
Qal'at al Ḥiṣn Syria 107 C2
Qal'at al Mu'aẓẓam Saudi Arabia 112 E6
Qal'at Bīshah Saudi Arabia 108 F5
Qal'at Dizah Iraq see Qeładize
Qal'at Muqaybirah, Jabal mt. Syria 107 D2
Qal'eh Dāgh mt. Iran 110 B2
Qal'eh-ye Shūrak well Iran 110 E3
Qalgar China 94 F4
Qalhāt Oman 110 E6
Qalīb Bāqūr well Iraq 113 G5
Qalluviartuuq, Lac l. Canada 152 G2
Qalyūb Egypt see Qalyūb
Qalyūb Egypt 112 C5
Qamalung China 94 D5
Qamanirjuaq Lake Canada 151 M2
Qamanittuaq Canada see Baker Lake
Qamashi Uzbek. 111 G2
Qamata S. Africa 125 H6
Qamdo China 96 C2
Qandahar Afgh. see Kandahār
Qandarānbāshī, Kūh-e mt. Iran 110 B2
Qandyaghash Kazakh. see Kandyagash
Qangdoi China 99 C6
Qangzê China 99 B7
Qapān-e Pā'īn Iran 110 D2
Qapqal China 98 C4
Qapshaghay Kazakh. see Kapshagay
Qapshaghay Bögeni resr Kazakh. see Kapshagay, Vodokhranilishche
Qaqortoq Greenland 147 N3
Qara Āghach r. Iran see Mand, Rūd-e
Qarabutaq Kazakh. see Karabutak
Qaraçala Azer. 110 C2
Qara Ertis r. China/Kazakh. see Ertix He
Qaraghandy Kazakh. see Karagandy
Qaraghayly Kazakh. see Karagayly
Qārah Egypt 112 B5
Qārah Saudi Arabia 113 F5
Qarah Bāgh Afgh. 111 H3
Qarah Tīkān Iran 111 F2
Qarah-ye Taray mt. Afgh. 111 G3
Qarak China 111 J2
Qaraqum des. Turkm. see Karakum Desert
Qarasu Azer. 113 H2
Qara Şū Chāy r. Syria/Turkey see Karasu
Qarataū Kazakh. see Karatau
Qarataū Zhotasy mts Kazakh. see Karatau, Khrebet
Qara Tikan Iran 110 C2
Qarazhal Kazakh. see Karazhal
Qardho Somalia 122 E3
Qareh Chāy r. Iran 110 C3
Qareh Sū r. Iran 110 B2
Qarhan China 94 C4
Qarkilik China see Ruoqiang
Qarn al Kabsh, Jabal mt. Egypt 112 D5
Qarnayn i. U.A.E. 110 D5
Qarnein i. U.A.E. see Qarnayn
Qarn el Kabsh, Gebel mt. Egypt see Qarn al Kabsh, Jabal
Qarnobcho'l cho'li plain Uzbek. 111 G2
Qarokŭl l. Tajik. 111 I2
Qarqan China see Qiemo
Qarqan He r. China 98 D5
Qarqaraly Kazakh. see Karkaraly
Qarqi Xinjiang China 98 C4
Qarqi Xinjiang China 98 D4
Qarshi Uzbek. 111 G2
Qarshi cho'li plain Uzbek. 111 G2
Qarshi chŭli plain Uzbek. see Qarshi cho'li
Qartaba Lebanon 107 B2
Qārūh, Jazīrat i. Kuwait 110 C4
Qārūn, Birkat l. Egypt 112 C5
Qârûn, Birket l. Egypt see Qārūn, Birkat
Qaryat al Gharab Iraq 113 G5
Qaryat al Ulyā Saudi Arabia 110 B5
Qasemābād Iran 110 E3
Qash Qā'ī reg. Iran 110 C4
Qasigiannguit Greenland 147 M3
Qasq China 95 G3
Qaṣr al Farāfirah Egypt 112 B6
Qaṣr al Kharānah Jordan 107 C4
Qaṣr al Khubbāz Iraq 113 F4
Qaṣr-e Shīrīn Iran 110 B3
Qaṣr Farâfra Egypt see Qaṣr al Farāfirah
Qassimiut Greenland 147 N3
Qaṭanā Syria 107 C3
Qatar country Asia 110 C5
Qaṭmah Syria 107 C1
Qaṭrūyeh Iran 110 D4
Qaṭṭāfī, Wādī al watercourse Jordan 107 C4
Qaṭṭâra, Râs esc. Egypt see Qaṭṭārah, Ra's
Qattara Depression Egypt 112 B5
Qaṭṭārah, Ra's esc. Egypt 112 B5
Qaṭṭīnah, Buḥayrat resr Syria 107 C2
Qax Azer. 113 G2
Qaxi China 98 C4
Qaynar Kazakh. see Kaynar
Qaysīyah, Qā' al imp. l. Jordan 107 C4
Qaysūm, Juzur is Egypt 112 D6
Qayū China 99 F7
Qayyārah Iraq 113 F4
Qazangöldağ mt. Armenia/Azer. 113 G3
Qazaq Shyghanaghy b. Kazakh. see Kazakhskiy Zaliv
Qazaqstan country Asia see Kazakhstan
Qazax Azer. 108 G1
Qazi Ahmad Pak. 111 H5
Qāẓī Deh Afgh. 111 H2
Qazvīn Iran 110 C2
Qedir China 98 D4
Qeh China 94 E3
Qeisûm, Gezâ'ir is Egypt see Qaysūm, Juzur
Qeisum Islands Egypt see Qaysūm, Juzur
Qeładize Iraq 113 G3
Qena Egypt see Qinā
Qeqertarsuaq Greenland 147 M3
Qeqertarsuaq i. Greenland 147 M3
Qeqertarsuatsiaat Greenland 147 M3
Qeqertarsuup Tunua b. Greenland 147 M3
Qeshm Iran 110 E5
Qeydār Iran 110 C2
Qeydū Iran 110 C3
Qeyṣar, Chāh-e well Iran 110 D4
Qeyṣār, Kūh-e mt. Afgh. 111 G3
Qezel Owzan, Rūdkhāneh-ye r. Iran 110 C2
Qeẓi'ot Israel 107 B4
Qian'an Hebei China 95 I4
Qian'an Jilin China 95 K2
Qiandao Hu resr China 97 H2
Qianfodong China 98 C4
Qian Gorlos China 90 B3
Qian He r. China 95 F5
Qianjiang Chongqing China 97 F2
Qianjiang Hubei China 97 G2
Qianjin Heilong. China 90 D3
Qianjin Jilin China 90 C3
Qianqihao China 95 J2
Qian Shan mts China 95 J3
Qianshangjie China 95 I4
Qianshanlaoba China 98 D3
Qianxi Guizhou China 96 E3
Qianxi Hebei China 95 I3
Qianxian China 95 G5
Qianyang China 95 F5
Qiaocheng China see Bozhou
Qiaocun China 95 H4
Qiaojia China 96 D3
Qiaoshan China see Huangling
Qiaotou China see Datong
Qiaowa China see Muli
Qiaowan China 94 D3
Qiaozhuang China see Qingchuan
Qibā' Saudi Arabia 113 G6
Qibing S. Africa 125 H5
Qichun China 97 G2
Qidong China 97 G3
Qidukou China 96 B1
Qiemo China 99 D5
Qihe China 95 I4
Qi He r. China 95 H5
Qijiang China 96 E2
Qijiaojing China 94 B3
Qikiqtarjuaq Canada 147 L3
Qiktim China 94 B3
Qila Ladgasht Pak. 111 F5
Qilaotu Shan mts China 95 I3
Qila Saifullah Pak. 111 H4
Qili China 98 F4
Qilian China 94 E4
Qilian Shan mt. China 94 D4
Qilian Shan mts China 94 D4
Qillak i. Greenland 147 O3
Qiman China 98 C4
Qiman Tag mts China 99 E5
Qimusseriarsuaq b. Greenland 147 L2
Qinā Egypt 108 D4
Qin'an China 94 F5
Qincheng Jiangxi China see Nanfeng
Qincheng Xinjiang China 94 C3
Qing'an China 90 B3
Qingcheng China 95 F4
Qingchuan China 96 E1
Qingdao China 95 J4
Qinggang China 90 B3
Qinggil China see Qinghe
Qinggilik China 99 D5
Qinggir China 98 E4
Qinghai prov. China 94 D4
Qinghai Hu salt l. China 94 E4
Qinghai Nanshan mts China 94 D4
Qinghe Hebei China 95 H4
Qinghe Heilong. China 90 C3
Qinghe Xinjiang China 94 B2
Qinghecheng China 90 B4
Qinghua China see Bo'ai
Qingjian China 95 G4
Qingjiang Jiangsu China see Huai'an
Qingjiang Jiangxi China see Zhangshu
Qing Jiang r. China 97 F2
Qingkou China see Ganyu
Qinglan China 97 F5
Qingliu China 97 H3

Qinglong China 95 I3
Qinglung China 99 E7
Qingpu China 97 I2
Qingquan China see Xishui
Qingshan China see Wudalianchi
Qingshizui China 94 E4
Qingshui Gansu China 94 D4
Qingshui Gansu China 94 F5
Qingshuihe Nei Mongol China 95 G4
Qingshuihe Qinghai China 96 C1
Qingshuihe Xinjiang China 98 C3
Qingshuihe Xinjiang China 98 D4
Qingshuipu China see Qingshui
Qingtian China 97 I2
Qingtongxia China 94 F4
Qingxian China 95 I4
Qingxu China 95 H4
Qingyang Anhui China 97 H2
Qingyang Gansu China see Qingcheng
Qingyang Gansu China 95 F5
Qingyang Jiangsu China see Sihong
Qingyuan Gansu China see Weiyuan
Qingyuan Guangdong China 97 G4
Qingyuan Guangxi China see Yizhou
Qingyuan Liaoning China 90 B4
Qingyuan Shanxi China see Qingxu
Qingyuan Zhejiang China 97 H3
Qingyun China 95 I4
Qingzang Gaoyuan plat. China see Tibet, Plateau of
Qingzhen China 96 E3
Qingzhou Hebei China see Qingxian
Qingzhou Shandong China 95 I4
Qinhuangdao China 95 I4
Qinjiang China see Shicheng
Qin Ling mts China 96 E1
Qinshui China 95 H5
Qinting China see Lianhua
Qinxian China 95 H4
Qinyang China 95 H5
Qinyuan China 95 H4
Qinzhou China 97 F4
Qionghai China 97 F5
Qiongjiexue China see Qonggyai
Qionglai China 96 D2
Qionglai Shan mts China 96 D2
Qiongxi China see Hongyuan
Qiongzhong China 97 F5
Qiongzhou Haixia strait China see Hainan Strait
Qiqian China 90 A1
Qiqihar China 95 J2
Qiqing China 94 D4
Qiquanhu China 98 E4
Qīr Iran 110 D4
Qira China 99 C5
Qirâîya, Wâdi watercourse Egypt see Qurayyah, Wādī
Qiryat Shemona Israel 107 B3
Qishan China 95 F5
Qishon, Naḥal r. Israel 107 B3
Qitab ash Shāmah vol. crater Saudi Arabia 107 C4
Qitai China 98 E4
Qitaihe China 90 C3
Qiubei China 96 E3
Qiujin China 97 G2
Qixia China 95 J4
Qixian Henan China 95 H5
Qixian Henan China 95 H5
Qixian Shanxi China 95 H4
Qixing He r. China 90 D3
Qiyang China 97 F3
Qiying China 94 F4
Qizhou Liedao i. China 97 F5
Qızılağac Körfäzi b. Azer. 110 C2
Qizil-Art, Aghbai pass Kyrg./Tajik. see Kyzylart Pass
Qizil Qal'ah Afgh. 111 H2
Qizilqum des. Kazakh./Uzbek. see Kyzylkum Desert
Qizilrabot Tajik. 111 I2
Qobād, Chāh-e well Iran 110 D3
Qobustan Azer. 113 H2
Qogir Feng mt. China/Pak. see K2
Qog UI China 95 I2
Qoigargoinba China 94 E5
Qoijê China 94 D4
Qolawat China 98 C4
Qol Tag mts China 98 E4
Qom Iran 110 C3
Qomdo China see Qumdo
Qomīsheh Iran see Shahreẕā
Qomolangma Feng mt. China/Nepal see Everest, Mount
Qomsheh Iran see Shahreẕā
Qonāq, Kūh-e hill Iran 110 C3
Qondūz Afgh. see Kunduz
Qonggyai China 99 E7
Qo'ng'irot Uzbek. 102 A3
Qongj China see Chuanjing
Qongkol China 98 D4
Qong Muztag mt. China 99 C6
Qongrat Uzbek. see Qo'ng'irot
Qonj China 94 D4
Qoornoq Greenland 147 M3
Qoqek China see Tacheng
Qo'qon Uzbek. 102 D3
Qorako'l Uzbek. 111 F2
Qorghalzhyn Kazakh. see Korgalzhyn
Qornet es Saouda mt. Lebanon 107 C2
Qorovulbozor Uzbek. 111 G2
Qorowulbozor Uzbek. see Qorovulbozor
Qorveh Iran 110 B3
Qo'shrabot Uzbek. 111 G1
Qostanay Kazakh. see Kostanay
Qoubaiyat Lebanon 107 C2
Qowowuyag mt. China/Nepal see Cho Oyu
Qozide Tajik. 111 H2
Quabbin Reservoir MA U.S.A. 165 I2
Quadra Island Canada 150 E5
Quadros, Lago dos l. Brazil 179 A5
Quail Mountains CA U.S.A. 158 E4
Quairading Australia 135 B8
Quakenbrück Germany 63 H2
Quakertown PA U.S.A. 165 H3
Quambatook Australia 138 A5
Quambone Australia 138 C3
Quamby Australia 136 C4
Quanah TX U.S.A. 161 D5
Quanbao Shan mt. China 95 G5
Quan Dao Hoang Sa is S. China Sea see Paracel Islands
Quan Dao Truong Sa is S. China Sea see Spratly Islands
Quang Ha Vietnam 86 D2
Quang Ngai Vietnam 86 E4
Quang Tri Vietnam 86 D3
Quan Hoa Vietnam 86 D2
Quan Long Vietnam see Ca Mau
Quannan China 97 G3
Quanshuigou China 99 B6
Quantock Hills U.K. 59 D7
Quanwan H.K. China see Tsuen Wan
Quanzhou Fujian China 97 H3
Quanzhou Guangxi China 97 F3
Qu'Appelle r. Canada 151 K5
Quaqtaq Canada 147 L3
Quarry Bay H.K. China 97 [inset]
Quartu Sant'Elena Sardinia Italy 68 C5
Quartzite Mountain NV U.S.A. 158 E3
Quartzsite AZ U.S.A. 159 F5
Quba Azer. 113 H2
Qūchān Iran 110 E2
Qudaym Syria 107 D2
Queanbeyan Australia 138 D5

▶Québec Canada 153 H5
Capital of Québec.

Québec prov. Canada 165 I1
Quebra Anzol r. Brazil 179 B2
Quedlinburg Germany 63 L3
Queen Adelaide Islands Chile see La Reina Adelaida, Archipiélago de
Queen Anne MD U.S.A. 165 H4
Queen Bess, Mount Canada 156 B2
Queen Charlotte Canada 149 N5
Queen Charlotte Islands Canada see Haida Gwaii
Queen Charlotte Sound sea chan. Canada 150 D5
Queen Charlotte Strait Canada 150 E5
Queen Creek AZ U.S.A. 159 H5
Queen Elizabeth Islands Canada 147 H2
Queen Elizabeth Land reg. Antarctica 188 L1
Queen Elizabeth National Park Uganda 122 C4
Queen Mary, Mount Canada 149 M3
Queen Mary Land reg. Antarctica 188 F2
Queen Maud Gulf Canada 147 H3
Queen Maud Land reg. Antarctica 188 C2
Queen Maud Mountains Antarctica 188 J1
Queenscliff Australia 138 B7
Queensland state Australia 138 B1
Queenstown Australia 137 [inset]
Queenstown Ireland see Cobh
Queenstown N.Z. 139 B7
Queenstown S. Africa 125 H6
Queenstown Sing. 87 [inset]
Que'er Shan mts China 96 C1
Queets WA U.S.A. 156 B3
Queimada, Ilha i. Brazil 177 H4
Quelimane Moz. 123 D5
Quelite Mex. 166 D4
Quellón Chile 178 B6
Quelpart Island S. Korea see Cheju-do
Quemado NM U.S.A. 159 I4
Quemoy i. Taiwan see Jinmen Dao
Que Que Zimbabwe see Kwekwe
Querétaro Mex. 168 D4
Querétaro state Mex. 167 F4
Querétaro de Arteaga Mex. see Querétaro
Querfurt Germany 63 L3
Querobabi Mex. 166 C2
Quesnel Canada 150 F4
Quesnel Lake Canada 150 F4
Quetta Pak. 111 G4
Quetzaltenango Guat. 167 H6
Queuco Chile 178 B5
Quezaltepeque El Salvador 167 H6
Quezon Palawan Phil. 82 B4

▶Quezon City Luzon Phil. 82 C3
Former capital of the Philippines.

Qufu China 95 I5
Quibala Angola 123 B5
Quibaxe Angola 123 B4
Quibdó Col. 176 C2
Quiberon France 66 C3
Quiçama, Parque Nacional do nat. park Angola 123 B4
Quiet Lake Canada 149 N3
Quilá Mex. 166 D3
Quilalí Nicaragua 166 [inset] I6
Quilengues Angola 123 B5
Quillabamba Peru 176 D6
Quillacollo Bol. 176 E7
Quillan France 66 F5
Quill Lakes Canada 151 J5
Quilmes Arg. 178 E4
Quilon India see Kollam
Quilpie Australia 138 B1
Quilpué Chile 178 B4
Quimbele Angola 123 B4
Quimilí Arg. 178 D3
Quimper France 66 B3
Quimperlé France 66 C3
Quinag hill U.K. 60 D2
Quinalasag i. Phil. 82 C3
Quincy CA U.S.A. 158 C2
Quincy FL U.S.A. 163 C6
Quincy IL U.S.A. 160 F4
Quincy IN U.S.A. 164 B4
Quincy MA U.S.A. 165 J2
Quincy MI U.S.A. 164 C3
Quincy OH U.S.A. 164 D3
Quines Arg. 178 C4
Quinga Moz. 123 E5
Quinhagak AK U.S.A. 148 G4
Quiniluban i. Phil. 82 C4
Quinn Canyon Range mts NV U.S.A. 159 F3
Quintana Roo state Mex. 167 H5
Quinto Spain 67 F3
Quionga Moz. 123 E5
Quiotepec Mex. 167 F5
Quipungo Angola 123 B5
Quiriguá tourist site Guat. 166 [inset] H6
Quirima Angola 123 B5
Quirimbas, Parque Nacional das nat. park Moz. 123 E5
Quirindi Australia 138 E3
Quirinópolis Brazil 179 A2
Quissanga Moz. 123 E5
Quitapa Angola 123 B5
Quitilipi Arg. 178 D3
Quitman GA U.S.A. 163 D6
Quitman MS U.S.A. 161 F5

▶Quito Ecuador 176 C4
Capital of Ecuador.

Quitovac Mex. 166 B2
Quixadá Brazil 177 K4
Quixeramobim Brazil 177 K5
Qujiang Guangdong China 97 G3
Qujiang Sichuan China see Quxian
Qujie China 97 F4
Qujing China 96 D3
Qulandy Kazakh. see Kulandy
Qulansiyah Yemen 109 H7
Qulbān Layyah well Iraq 110 B4
Qulho China 99 D7
Qulsary Kazakh. see Kul'sary
Qulyndy Zhazyghy plain Kazakh./Russia see Kulundinskaya Ravnina
Qulzum, Baḥr al Egypt see Suez Bay
Qumar He r. China 94 C5
Qumarheyan China 94 C5
Qumarlêb China 99 F6
Qumarrabdün China 96 B1
Qumbu S. Africa 125 I6
Qumdo China 99 F7
Qumigxung China 99 D7
Qumqo'rg'on Uzbek. 111 G2
Qumqŭrghon Uzbek. see Qumqo'rgo'n
Qumrha S. Africa 125 H7
Qumulangma mt. China/Nepal see Everest, Mount
Qunayfidhah, Nafūd des. Saudi Arabia 110 B5
Qunayy well Saudi Arabia 110 B6
Qundūz Afgh. see Kunduz
Qŭnghirot Uzbek. see Qo'ng'irot
Qu'ngoin He r. China 94 E5
Quntamari China 99 E6
Qu'nyido China 96 C2
Quoich r. Canada 151 M1
Quoich, Loch l. U.K. 60 D3
Quoile r. U.K. 61 G3
Quoin Point S. Africa 124 D8
Quoxo r. Botswana 124 G2
Qŭqon Uzbek. see Qo'qon
Qurama, Qatorkŭhi mts Asia see Kurama Range
Qurama tizmasi mts Asia see Kurama Range
Qurayyah, Wādī watercourse Egypt 107 B4
Qŭrghonteppa Tajik. 111 H2
Qusainka China 96 C2
Qusar Azer. 113 H2
Qushan China 96 E2
Qŭshrabot Uzbek. see Qo'shrabot
Qushtepe Iraq 113 F3
Qusmuryn Kazakh. see Kusmuryn
Qusum Xizang China 99 B6
Qusum Xizang China 99 F7
Quthing Lesotho see Moyeni
Quttinirpaaq National Park Canada 147 K1
Quwayq, Nahr r. Syria/Turkey 107 C2
Quwo China 95 G5
Quwu Shan mts China 94 F4
Quxian Sichuan China 96 E2
Quxian Zhejiang China see Quzhou
Qüxü China 99 E7
Quyang China see Jingzhou
Quy Châu Vietnam 86 D3
Quyghan Kazakh. see Kuygan
Quy Nhơn Vietnam 87 E4
Quyon Canada 165 G1
Qūyūn Eshek i. Iran 110 B2
Quzhou Hebei China 95 H4
Quzhou Zhejiang China 97 H2
Quzi China 95 F4
Qypshaq Köli salt l. Kazakh. see Azhibeksor, Ozero
Qyrghyz Zhotasy mts Kazakh./Kyrg. see Kirghiz Range
Qyteti Stalin Albania see Kuçovë
Qyzylorda Kazakh. see Kyzylorda
Qyzylqum des. Kazakh./Uzbek. see Kyzylkum Desert
Qyzyltū Kazakh. see Kishkenekol'
Qyzylzhar Kazakh. see Kyzylzhar

R

Raa Atoll Maldives see Maalhosmadulu Uthuruburi
Raab r. Austria 57 P7
Raab Hungary see Gyr
Raahe Fin. 54 N4
Rääkkylä Fin. 54 P5
Raalte Neth. 62 G2
Raanujärvi Fin. 54 N3
Raas i. Indon. 85 F4
Raasay i. U.K. 60 C3
Raasay, Sound of sea chan. U.K. 60 C3
Raba Sumbawa Indon. 85 G5
Rabang China 99 C6
Rabat Gozo Malta see Victoria
Rabat Malta 68 F7

▶Rabat Morocco 64 C5
Capital of Morocco.

Rabāṭak Afgh. 111 H2
Rabāṭ-e Jaldak Afgh. 111 G4
Rabaul P.N.G. 132 F2
Rabbath Ammon Jordan see 'Ammān
Rabbit r. Canada 149 P4
Rabbit Flat Australia 134 E5
Rabbitskin r. Canada 150 F2
Rabia Papua Indon. 83 D3
Rābigh Saudi Arabia 108 E5
Rabinal Guat. 167 H6
Rabnabad Islands Bangl. 105 G5
Râbniţa Moldova see Rîbniţa
Rabocheostrovsk Russia 52 G2
Racaka China 96 C2
Raccoon Cay i. Bahamas 163 F8
Race, Cape Canada 153 L5
Raceland LA U.S.A. 167 H2
Race Point MA U.S.A. 165 J2
Rachaïya Lebanon 107 B3
Rachal TX U.S.A. 161 D7
Racha Noi, Ko i. Thai. 84 B1
Rachaya Lebanon see Rachaïya
Racha Yai, Ko i. Thai. 84 B1
Rachel NV U.S.A. 159 F3
Rach Gia Vietnam 87 D5
Rach Gia, Vinh b. Vietnam 87 D5
Racibórz Poland 57 Q5
Racine WI U.S.A. 164 B2
Racine WV U.S.A. 164 E4
Rădăuţi Romania 53 E7
Radcliff KY U.S.A. 164 C5
Radde Russia 90 C2
Rádeyilikóé Canada see Fort Good Hope
Radford VA U.S.A. 164 E5
Radili Ko Canada see Fort Good Hope
Radisson Que. Canada 152 F3
Radisson Sask. Canada 151 J4
Radlinski, Mount Antarctica 188 K1
Radnevo Bulg. 69 K3
Radom Poland 57 R5
Radom Sudan 121 F4
Radomir Bulg. 69 J3
Radom National Park Sudan 121 F4
Radomsko Poland 57 Q5
Radoviš Macedonia 112 A2
Radstock U.K. 59 E7
Radstock, Cape Australia 135 F8
Radun' Belarus 55 N9
Radviliškis Lith. 55 M9
Radyvyliv Ukr. 53 E6
Rae Bareli India 104 E4
Raecreek r. Canada 149 M2
Rae-Edzo Canada see Behchokò
Rae Lakes Canada see Gamètì
Raeside, Lake salt flat Australia 135 C7
Raetihi N.Z. 139 E4
Rāf hill Saudi Arabia 113 E5
Rafaela Arg. 178 D4
Rafaḥ Gaza 107 B4
Rafaï Cent. Afr. Rep. 122 C3
Rafḥā' Saudi Arabia 113 F5
Rafiah Gaza see Rafaḥ
Rafsanjān Iran 110 D4
Raft r. Idaho/Nevada U.S.A. 156 E4
Raga South Sudan 121 F4
Ragang, Mount vol. Mindanao Phil. 82 D5
Ragay Gulf Luzon Phil. 82 C3
Rägelin Germany 63 M1
Ragged, Mount hill Australia 135 C8
Ragged Island Bahamas 163 F8
Rāgh Afgh. 111 H2
Rago Nasjonalpark nat. park Norway 54 J3
Ragösen Germany 63 M2
Ragueneau Canada 153 H4
Raguhn Germany 63 M3
Ragusa Croatia see Dubrovnik
Ragusa Sicily Italy 68 F6
Ragxi China 99 F7
Ra'gya China 94 E5
Raha Celebes Indon. 83 B4
Rahachow Belarus 53 F5
Rahad r. Sudan 108 D7
Rahaeng Thai. see Tak
Raḥbah, Manqa' imp. l. Syria 107 C3
Rahden Germany 63 I2
Rahimyar Khan Pak. 111 H4
Raḥmān, Chāh-e well Iran 111 E4
Rahovec Kosovo 69 I3
Rahuri India 106 B2
Rai, Hon i. Vietnam 87 D5
Raiatea i. Fr. Polynesia 187 J7
Raibu i. Indon. see Air
Raichur India 106 C2
Raiganj India 105 G4
Raigarh Chhattisgarh India 105 E5
Raigarh Odisha India 106 D2
Raijua i. Indon. 83 B5
Railroad City AK U.S.A. 148 H3
Railroad Pass NV U.S.A. 158 E2
Railroad Valley NV U.S.A. 159 F2
Raimangal r. Bangl. 105 G5
Raimbault, Lac l. Canada 153 H3
Rainbow Lake Canada 150 G3
Raine Island Australia 136 D1
Rainelle WV U.S.A. 164 E5
Raini r. Pak. 111 H4
Rainier, Mount vol. WA U.S.A. 156 C3
Rainis Celebes Indon. 83 C1
Rainy r. Canada/U.S.A. 151 M5
Rainy Lake Canada/U.S.A. 155 I2
Rainy River Canada 151 M5
Raipur Chhattisgarh India 105 E5
Raipur W. Bengal India 105 F5
Raisen India 104 D5
Raisio Fin. 55 M6
Raismes France 62 D4
Raitalai India 104 D5
Raivavae i. Fr. Polynesia 187 K7
Raiwind Pak. 111 I4
Raja i. Indon. 85 F4
Raja, Ujung pt Indon. 84 B2
Rajaampat, Kepulauan is Papua Indon. 83 D3
Rajabasa, Gunung vol. Indon. 84 D4
Rajahmundry India 106 D2
Raja-Jooseppi Fin. 54 P2
Rajang Sarawak Malaysia 85 E2
Rajang r. Malaysia 85 E2
Rajanpur Pak. 111 H4
Rajapalayam India 106 C4
Rajapur India 106 B2
Rajasthan state India 104 C4
Rajasthan Canal India 104 C3
Rajauri India see Rajouri
Rajbiraj town Nepal 105 F4
Rajevadi India 106 B2
Rajgarh India 104 D4
Rájijovsset Fin. see Raja-Jooseppi
Rajik Indon. 84 D3
Rajkot India 104 B5
Raj Mahal India 104 C4
Rajmahal Hills India 105 F4
Rajnandgaon India 104 E5
Rajouri India 104 C2
Rajpipla India 104 C5
Rajpur India 104 C5
Rajpura India 104 D3
Rajputana Agency state India see Rajasthan
Rajsamand India 104 C4
Rajshahi Bangl. 105 G4
Rājū Syria 107 C1
Rajula India 106 A1
Rajur India 106 C1
Rajura India 106 C2
Raka China 99 D7
Rakan, Ra's pt Qatar 110 C5
Rakaposhi mt. Pak. 104 C1
Raka Zangbo r. China see Dogxung Zangbo
Rakhiv Ukr. 53 E6
Rakhni Pak. 111 H4
Rakhni r. Pak. 111 H4
Rakhshan r. Pak. 111 F5
Rakit i. Indon. 85 E4
Rakit i. Indon. 85 G5
Rakitnoye Belgorodskaya Oblast' Russia 53 G6
Rakitnoye Primorskiy Kray Russia 90 D3
Rakiura i. N.Z. see Stewart Island
Rakiura National Park nat. park N.Z. 139 A8
Rakke Estonia 55 O7
Rakkestad Norway 55 G7
Rakmanovskie Klyuchi Kazakh. 98 D2
Rakovski Bulg. 69 K3
Rakushechnyy, Mys pt Kazakh. 113 H2
Rakvere Estonia 55 O7

▶Raleigh NC U.S.A. 162 E5
Capital of North Carolina.

Ralla Celebes Indon. 83 A4
Ralston PA U.S.A. 165 G3
Ram r. Canada 150 F2
Rama Nicaragua 166 [inset] I6
Ramagiri India 106 E2
Ramah NM U.S.A. 159 I4
Ramalho, Serra do hills Brazil 179 B1
Rāmallāh West Bank 107 B4
Ramanagaram India 106 C3
Ramanathapuram India 106 C4
Ramapo Deep sea feature N. Pacific Ocean 186 F3
Ramapur India 106 D1
Ramas, Cape India 106 B3
Ramatlabama S. Africa 125 G3
Rambhapur India 104 C5
Rambouillet France 62 B6
Rambutyo Island P.N.G. 81 L7
Ramciel South Sudan 121 G4
Rame Head hd Australia 138 D6
Rame Head hd U.K. 59 C8
Rameshki Russia 52 H4
Ramezān Kalak Iran 111 F5
Ramganga r. India 99 B8
Ramgarh Jharkhand India 105 F5
Ramgarh Rajasthan India 104 B4
Ramgarh Rajasthan India 104 C3
Ramgul reg. Afgh. 111 H3
Rāmhormoz Iran 110 C4
Ramingining Australia 134 F3
Ramitan Uzbek. see Romiton
Ramla Israel 107 B4
Ramlat Rabyānah des. Libya see Rebiana Sand Sea
Ramm, Jabal mts Jordan 107 B5
Ramnad India see Ramanathapuram
Râmnicu Sărat Romania 69 L2
Râmnicu Vâlcea Romania 69 K2
Ramon' Russia 53 H6
Ramona CA U.S.A. 158 E5
Ramos r. Mex. 161 B7
Ramos Arizpe Mex. 167 E3
Ramotswa Botswana 125 G3
Rampart AK U.S.A. 149 J2
Ramparts r. Canada 149 O2
Rampur Hima. Prad. India 99 B7
Rampur Uttar Prad. India 99 B7
Rampur Uttar Prad. India 104 D3
Rampur Boalia Bangl. see Rajshahi
Ramree Myanmar 86 A3
Ramree Island Myanmar 86 A3
Rāmsar Iran 110 C2
Ramsele Sweden 54 J5
Ramsey Isle of Man 58 C4
Ramsey U.K. 59 G6
Ramsey NJ U.S.A. 165 H3
Ramsey Bay Isle of Man 58 C4
Ramsey Island U.K. 59 B7
Ramsey Lake Canada 152 E5
Ramsgate U.K. 59 I7
Rāmshīr Iran 110 C4
Ramu Bangl. 105 H5
Ramusio, Lac l. Canada 153 J3
Ramygala Lith. 55 N9
Ranaghat India 105 G5
Ranai i. HI U.S.A. see Lāna'i
Rana Pratap Sagar resr India 104 C4
Ranapur India 104 C5
Ranasar India 104 B4
Ranau Sabah Malaysia 85 G1
Ranau, Danau l. Indon. 84 C4
Rancagua Chile 178 B4
Rancharia Brazil 179 A3
Rancheria Canada 149 O3
Rancheria r. Canada 149 O3
Ranchi India 105 F5
Rancho Grande Mex. 166 E4
Ranco, Lago l. Chile 178 B6
Rand Australia 138 C5
Randalstown U.K. 61 F3
Randers Denmark 55 G8
Randijaure l. Sweden 54 K3
Randolph ME U.S.A. 165 K1
Randolph UT U.S.A. 156 F4
Randolph VT U.S.A. 165 I2
Randsjö Sweden 54 H5
Råneå Sweden 54 M4
Ranérou Senegal 120 B3
Ranfurly N.Z. 139 C7
Ranga r. India 99 F8
Rangae Thai. 87 C6
Rangamati Bangl. 105 H5
Rangapara India 105 H4
Rangasa, Tanjung pt Indon. 83 A3
Rangeley Lake ME U.S.A. 165 J1
Rangely CO U.S.A. 159 I1
Ranger Lake Canada 152 E5
Ranggas, Ujung pt Indon. 83 A3
Rangiora N.Z. 139 D6
Rangitata r. N.Z. 139 C7
Rangitikei r. N.Z. 139 E5
Rangkasbitung Java Indon. 84 D4
Rangke China see Zamtang
Rangkŭl Tajik. 111 I2
Rangôn Myanmar see Rangoon

▶Rangoon Myanmar 86 B3
Former capital of Myanmar.

Rangoon r. Myanmar 86 B3
Rangpur Bangl. 105 G4
Rangsang i. Sumatra Indon. 84 C2
Rangse Myanmar 86 A1
Ranibennur India 106 B3
Raniganj India 105 F5
Ranipur Pak. 111 H5
Raniwara India 104 C4
Rānīyah/Ranye Iraq 113 G3
Rankin TX U.S.A. 161 C6
Rankin Inlet Canada 151 M2
Rankins Springs Australia 138 C4
Ranna Estonia 55 O7
Rannes Australia 136 E5
Rannoch, Loch U.K. 60 E4
Ranong Thai. 87 B5
Ranot Thai. 87 C6
Ranpur India 104 B5
Rānsa Iran 110 C3
Ransby Sweden 55 H6
Rantamarahio, Buttu mt. Indon. 83 B3
Rantasalmi Fin. 54 P5
Rantau Kalimantan Indon. 85 F3
Rantau i. Sumatra Indon. 84 C2
Rantaukampar Sumatra Indon. 84 C2
Rantaupanjang Kalimantan Indon. 85 F3
Rantaupanjang Kalimantan Indon. 85 G2
Rantauprapat Sumatra Indon. 84 B2
Rantaupulut Kalimantan Indon. 85 F3
Rantepang Celebes Indon. 83 A3
Rantoul IL U.S.A. 164 A3
Rantsila Fin. 54 N4
Ranua Fin. 54 O4
Ranyah, Wādī watercourse Saudi Arabia 108 F5
Rao Go mt. Laos/Vietnam 86 D3
Raohe China 90 D3
Raoui, Erg er des. Alg. 64 D6
Raoul Island Kermadec Is 133 I4
Rapa i. Fr. Polynesia 187 K7
Rapa-iti i. Fr. Polynesia see Rapa
Rapallo Italy 68 C2
Rapar India 104 B5
Raphoe Ireland 61 E3
Rapidan r. VA U.S.A. 165 G4
Rapid City SD U.S.A. 160 C2
Rapid River MI U.S.A. 162 C2
Rapla Estonia 55 N7
Rappang Celebes Indon. 83 A3
Rapti r. India 99 C8
Rapur Andhra Prad. India 106 C3
Rapur Gujarat India 104 B5
Rapurapu i. Phil. 82 D3
Raqqa Syria see Ar Raqqah
Raquette Lake NY U.S.A. 165 H2
Rara National Park Nepal 105 E3
Raritan Bay NJ U.S.A. 165 H3
Rarkan Pak. 111 H4
Raroia atoll Fr. Polynesia 187 K7
Rarotonga i. Cook Is 187 J7
Ras India 104 C4
Rasa i. Phil. 82 B4
Rasa, Punta pt Arg. 178 D6
Ra's al Ḥikmah Egypt 112 B5
Ras al Khaimah U.A.E. see Ra's al Khaymah
Ra's al Khaymah U.A.E. 110 D5
Ra's an Naqb Jordan 107 B4
Ras Dashen mt. Eth. see Ras Dejen

▶Ras Dejen mt. Eth. 122 D2
5th highest mountain in Africa.

Raseiniai Lith. 55 M9
Râs el Hikma Egypt see Ra's al Ḥikmah
Ra's Ghārib Egypt 112 D5
Rashaant Bayan-Ölgiy Mongolia see Delüün
Rashaant Dundgovĭ Mongolia see Öldziyt
Rashad Sudan 108 D7
Rashîd Egypt see Rashīd
Rashīd Egypt 112 C5
Rasht Iran 110 C2
Ras Koh mt. Pak. 111 G4
Raskoh mts Pak. 111 G4
Raso, Cabo c. Arg. 178 C6
Rason Lake salt flat Australia 135 D7
Rasony Belarus 55 P9
Raspberry Island AK U.S.A. 148 I4
Rasra India 105 E4
Rasshua, Ostrov i. Russia 89 S3
Rass Jebel Tunisia 68 D6
Rasskazovo Russia 53 I5
Rastatt Germany 63 I6
Rastede Germany 63 I1
Rastow Germany 63 L1
Rasūl watercourse Iran 110 D5
Rasul Pak. 111 I3
Ratae U.K. see Leicester
Ratai, Gunung mt. Indon. 84 D4
Rätan Sweden 54 I5
Ratanda S. Africa 125 I4
Ratangarh India 104 C3
Rätansbyn Sweden 54 I5
Rat Buri Thai. 87 B4
Rathangan Ireland 61 F4
Rathbun Lake IA U.S.A. 160 E3
Rathdowney Ireland 61 E5
Rathdrum Ireland 61 F5
Rathedaung Myanmar 86 A2
Rathenow Germany 63 M2
Rathfriland U.K. 61 F3
Rathkeale Ireland 61 D5
Rathlin Island U.K. 61 F2
Ratibor Poland see Racibórz
Ratingen Germany 62 G3
Ratisbon Germany see Regensburg
Rat Islands AK U.S.A. 148 [inset] B6
Ratiya India 104 C3
Rat Lake Canada 151 L3
Ratlam India 104 C5
Ratmanova, Ostrov i. Russia 148 E2
Ratnagiri India 106 B2
Ratnapura Sri Lanka 106 D5
Ratne Ukr. 53 E6
Ratno Ukr. see Ratne
Raton NM U.S.A. 157 G5
Rattray Head hd U.K. 60 H3
Rättvik Sweden 55 I6
Ratz, Mount Canada 149 N4
Ratzeburg Germany 63 K1
Rau i. Moluccas Indon. 83 D2
Raub Malaysia 84 C2
Rauðamýri Iceland 54 [inset 1]
Raudhatain Kuwait 110 B4
Rauenstein Germany 63 L4
Raufarhöfn Iceland 54 [inset 1]
Raukumara Range mts N.Z. 139 F4
Raul Soares Brazil 179 C3
Rauma Fin. 55 L6
Raupelyan Russia 148 E2
Raurkela India 105 F5
Rauschen Russia see Svetlogorsk
Rausu Japan 90 G3
Rautavaara Fin. 54 P5
Ravānsar Iran 110 B3
Rāvar Iran 110 E4
Ravat Kyrg. 111 H2
Ravels Belgium 62 E3
Ravena NY U.S.A. 165 I2
Ravenglass U.K. 58 D4
Ravenna Italy 68 E2
Ravenna NE U.S.A. 160 D3
Ravenna OH U.S.A. 164 E3
Ravensburg Germany 57 L7
Ravenshoe Australia 136 D3
Ravenswood Australia 136 D4
Ravi r. Pak. 111 H4
Ravnina Turkm. see Rawnina
Rawa Aopa Watumohai, Taman Nasional nat. park Indon. 83 B4
Rāwah Iraq 113 F4
Rawaki i. Kiribati 133 I2
Rawalpindi Pak. 111 I3
Rawalpindi Lake Canada 150 H1
Rawāndūz/Rewanduz Iraq 113 G3
Rawas r. Indon. 84 C3
Rawi, Ko i. Thai. 87 B6
Rawicz Poland 57 P5
Rawlinna Australia 135 D7
Rawlins WY U.S.A. 156 G4
Rawlinson Range hills Australia 135 E6
Rawnina Mary Turkm. 111 F2
Rawnina Mary Turkm. 111 F2
Rawson Arg. 178 C6
Rawu China 96 C2
Raxón, Cerro mt. Guat. 168 G5
Ray, Cape Canada 153 K5
Raya, Bukit mt. Kalimantan Indon. 85 E3
Raya, Bukit mt. Kalimantan Indon. 85 F3
Rayachoti India 106 C3
Rayadurg India 106 C3
Rayagada India 106 D2
Rayagarha India see Rayagada
Rayak Lebanon 107 C3
Raychikhinsk Russia 90 C2
Raydah Yemen 108 F6
Rayes Peak CA U.S.A. 158 D4
Rayevskiy Russia 51 Q5
Rayleigh U.K. 59 H7
Raymond NH U.S.A. 165 J2
Raymond Terrace Australia 138 E4
Raymondville TX U.S.A. 161 D7
Raymore Canada 151 J5
Ray Mountains AK U.S.A. 148 I2
Rayner Glacier Antarctica 188 D2
Rayones Mex. 167 E3
Rayong Thai. 87 C4
Raystown Lake PA U.S.A. 165 F3
Rayü China 99 F7
Raz, Pointe du pt France 66 B2
Razan Iran 110 C3
Rāzān Iran 110 C3
Razani Pak. 111 H3
Razāzah, Buḥayrat ar l. Iraq 113 F4
Razdan Armenia see Hrazdan
Razdel'naya Ukr. see Rozdil'na
Razdol'noye Russia 90 C4
Razeh Iran 110 C3
Razgrad Bulg. 69 L3
Razhêng Zangbo r. China 99 E7
Razim, Lacul lag. Romania 69 M2
Razisi China 96 D1
Razlog Bulg. 69 J4
Razmak Pak. 111 H3
Ré, Île de i. France 66 D3
Reading U.K. 59 G7
Reading MI U.S.A. 164 C3
Reading OH U.S.A. 164 C4
Reading PA U.S.A. 165 H3
Reagile S. Africa 125 H3
Realicó Arg. 178 D5
Réalmont France 66 F5
Reăng Kései Cambodia 87 C4
Reasi India 104 C2
Reata Mex. 167 E3
Reate Italy see Rieti
Rebais France 62 D6
Rebecca, Lake salt flat Australia 135 C7
Rebiana Sand Sea des. Libya 121 F2
Reboly Russia 54 Q5
Rebrikha Russia 88 E2
Rebun-tō i. Japan 90 F3
Recherche, Archipelago of the is Australia 135 C8
Rechitsa Belarus see Rechytsa
Rechna Doab lowland Pak. 111 I4
Rechytsa Belarus 53 F5
Recife Brazil 177 L5
Recife, Cape S. Africa 125 G8
Recklinghausen Germany 63 H3
Reconquista Arg. 178 E3
Recreo Arg. 178 C3
Rectorville KY U.S.A. 164 D4
Red r. Australia 136 C3
Red r. Canada 150 E3
Red r. Canada/U.S.A. 160 D1
Red r. LA U.S.A. 161 F6
Red r. TN U.S.A. 164 B5
Red r. Vietnam 86 D2
Redang i. Malaysia 84 C1
Red Bank NJ U.S.A. 165 H3
Red Bank TN U.S.A. 163 C5
Red Basin China see Sichuan Pendi
Red Bay Canada 153 K4
Red Bay Basque Whaling Station tourist site Canada 153 K4
Redberry Lake Canada 151 J4
Red Bluff CA U.S.A. 158 B1
Red Bluff Lake TX U.S.A. 161 C6
Red Butte mt. AZ U.S.A. 159 G4
Redcar U.K. 58 F4
Redcliff Canada 156 F2
Redcliffe, Mount hill Australia 135 C7
Red Cliffs Australia 137 C7
Red Cloud NE U.S.A. 160 D3
Red Deer Canada 150 H4
Red Deer r. Alba./Sask. Canada 151 I5
Red Deer r. Man./Sask. Canada 151 K4
Red Deer Lake Canada 151 K4
Reddersburg S. Africa 125 H5
Red Devil AK U.S.A. 148 H3
Redding CA U.S.A. 158 B1
Redditch U.K. 59 F6
Rede r. U.K. 58 E3
Redenção Brazil 177 H5
Redeyef Tunisia 68 C7
Redfield SD U.S.A. 160 D2
Red Granite Mountain Canada 149 M3
Red Hills KS U.S.A. 161 D4
Red Hook NY U.S.A. 165 I3
Red Idol Gorge China 99 E7
Red Indian Lake Canada 153 K4
Redkey IN U.S.A. 164 C3
Redkino Russia 52 H4
Redknife r. Canada 150 G2
Red Lake Canada 151 M5
Red Lake AZ U.S.A. 159 G4
Red Lake r. MN U.S.A. 160 D2
Red Lake Falls MN U.S.A. 151 L6
Red Lakes MN U.S.A. 160 E1
Redlands CA U.S.A. 158 E4
Red Lion PA U.S.A. 165 G4
Red Lodge MT U.S.A. 156 F3
Redmesa CO U.S.A. 159 I3
Redmond OR U.S.A. 156 C3
Redmond UT U.S.A. 159 H2
Red Oak IA U.S.A. 160 E3
Redonda Island Canada 150 E5
Redondo Port. 67 C4
Redondo Beach CA U.S.A. 158 D5
Redoubt Volcano AK U.S.A. 148 I3
Red Peak MT U.S.A. 156 E3
Red River, Mouths of the Vietnam 86 D2
Red Rock Canada 152 C4
Red Rock AZ U.S.A. 159 H5
Redrock NM U.S.A. 159 I5
Red Rock PA U.S.A. 165 G3
Redrock Lake Canada 150 H1
Red Sea Africa/Asia 108 D4
Redstone r. Canada 149 P2
Red Sucker Lake Canada 151 M4
Reduzum Neth. 62 F1
Redwater Canada 150 H4
Redway CA U.S.A. 158 B1
Red Wing MN U.S.A. 160 E2
Redwood City CA U.S.A. 158 B3
Redwood Falls MN U.S.A. 160 E2
Redwood National Park CA U.S.A. 156 B4
Redwood Valley CA U.S.A. 158 B2
Ree, Lough l. Ireland 61 E4
Reed KY U.S.A. 164 B5
Reed City MI U.S.A. 164 C2
Reedley CA U.S.A. 158 D3
Reedsport OR U.S.A. 156 B4
Reedsville OH U.S.A. 164 E4
Reedville VA U.S.A. 165 G5
Reedy WV U.S.A. 164 E4
Reedy Glacier Antarctica 188 J1
Reefton N.Z. 139 C6
Rees Germany 62 G3
Reese MI U.S.A. 164 D2
Reese r. NV U.S.A. 158 E1
Refahiye Turkey 112 E3
Refugio TX U.S.A. 161 D6
Rēgay Afgh. 111 G3
Regen Germany 63 N6
Regen r. Germany 63 M5
Regência Brazil 179 D2
Regensburg Germany 63 M5
Regenstauf Germany 63 M5
Reggane Alg. 120 D2
Reggio Calabria Italy see Reggio di Calabria
Reggio Emilia-Romagna Italy see Reggio nell'Emilia
Reggio di Calabria Italy 68 F5
Reggio Emilia Italy see Reggio nell'Emilia
Reggio nell'Emilia Italy 68 D2
Reghin Romania 69 K1

▶Regina Canada 151 J5
Capital of Saskatchewan.

Régina Fr. Guiana 177 H3
Rēgistān reg. Afgh. 111 G4
Registro Brazil 178 G2
Registro do Araguaia Brazil 179 A1
Regium Lepidum Italy see Reggio nell'Emilia
Regozero Russia 54 Q4
Rehau Germany 63 M4
Rehburg (Rehburg-Loccum) Germany 63 J2
Rehli India 104 D5
Rehoboth Namibia 124 C2
Rehoboth Bay DE U.S.A. 165 H4
Reḥovot Israel 107 B4
Reïbell Alg. see Ksar Chellala
Reibitz Germany 63 M3
Reichenbach im Vogtland Germany 63 M4
Reichshoffen France 63 H6
Reid Australia 135 E7
Reidh, Rubha pt U.K. 60 D3
Reidsville NC U.S.A. 162 E4
Reigate U.K. 59 G7
Reiley Peak AZ U.S.A. 159 H5
Reims France 62 E5
Reinbek Germany 63 K1
Reindeer r. Canada 151 K4
Reindeer Grazing Reserve nature res. Canada 149 O1
Reindeer Island Canada 151 L4
Reindeer Lake Canada 151 K3
Reine Norway 54 H3
Reinosa Spain 67 D2
Reinsfeld Germany 62 G5
Reipholsfjöll hill Iceland 54 [inset 1]
Reisaelva r. Norway 54 L2
Reisa Nasjonalpark nat. park Norway 54 M2
Reisjärvi Fin. 54 N5
Reitz S. Africa 125 I4
Rekapalle India 106 D2
Reken Germany 62 H3
Reliance Canada 151 I2
Relizane Alg. 67 G6
Rellano Mex. 166 D3
Rellingen Germany 63 J1
Remagen Germany 63 H4
Remarkable, Mount hill Australia 137 B7
Rembang Java Indon. 85 E4
Remedios Cuba 163 E8
Remedios, Punta pt El Salvador 167 H6
Remeshk Iran 110 E5
Remhoogte Pass Namibia 124 C2
Remi France see Reims
Remmel Mountain WA U.S.A. 156 C2
Rempang i. Sumatra Indon. 84 D2
Remscheid Germany 63 H3
Rena Norway 55 G6
Renaix Belgium see Ronse
Renam Myanmar 96 C3
Renapur India 106 C2
Renchinlhümbe Mongolia 94 D1
Rendsburg Germany 57 L3
René-Levasseur, Île i. Canada 153 H4
Renews Canada 153 L5
Renfrew Canada 165 G1
Renfrew U.K. 60 E5
Rengali Reservoir India 105 F5
Rengat Sumatra Indon. 84 C3
Rengo Chile 178 B4
Renhe China 97 G2
Ren He r. China 97 F1
Renhou China see Tangxian
Renhua China 97 G3
Reni Ukr. 69 M2
Renland reg. Greenland see Tuttut Nunaat
Rennell i. Solomon Is 133 G3
Rennerod Germany 63 I4
Rennes France 66 D2
Rennick Glacier Antarctica 188 H2
Rennie Canada 151 M5
Reno r. Italy 68 E2
Reno NV U.S.A. 158 D2
Renovo PA U.S.A. 165 G3
Renqiu China 95 I4
Rensselaer IN U.S.A. 164 B3
Renswoude Neth. 62 F2
Renton WA U.S.A. 156 C3
Réo Burkina Faso 120 C3
Reo Flores Indon. 83 B5
Repalle India 106 D2
Repetek Turkm. 111 F2
Repetek Döwlet Gorugy nature res. Turkm. 111 F2
Repolka Russia 55 P7
Repou, Tônle r. Laos 87 D4
Represa de Samuel resr Brazil 176 F5
Republic WA U.S.A. 156 D2
Republican r. NE U.S.A. 160 D4
Repulse Bay b. Australia 136 E4
Repulse Bay Canada 147 J3
Requena Peru 176 D5
Requena Spain 67 F4
Reşadiye Turkey 112 E2
Resag, Gunung mt. Indon. 84 D4
Reserva Brazil 179 A4
Reserva de la Biosfera Gran Desierto de Altar tourist site Mex. 168 B2
Reserve NM U.S.A. 159 I5
Reshi China 97 F2
Reshm Iran 110 D3
Reshteh-ye Alborz mts Iran see Elburz Mountains
Reshui China 94 E4
Resistencia Arg. 178 E3
Reşiţa Romania 69 I2
Resolute Canada 147 I2
Resolute Bay Canada see Resolute
Resolution Island Canada 147 L3
Resolution Island N.Z. 139 A7
Resplendor Brazil 179 C2
Restigouche r. Canada 153 I5
Resülayn Turkey see Ceylanpınar
Retalhuleu Guat. 167 H6
Retezat, Parcul Naţional nat. park Romania 69 J2
Retford U.K. 58 G5
Rethel France 62 E5
Rethem (Aller) Germany 63 J2
Réthimnon Greece see Rethymno
Rethymno Greece 69 K7
Retreat Australia 136 C5
Reuden Germany 63 M2

▶Réunion terr. Indian Ocean 185 L7
French Overseas Department.

Reus Spain 67 G3
Reusam, Pulau i. Indon. 84 B2
Reutlingen Germany 57 L6
Reval Estonia see Tallinn
Revda Russia 54 S3
Revel Estonia see Tallinn
Revel France 66 F5
Revelstoke Canada 150 G5
Revigny-sur-Ornain France 62 E6
Revillagigedo, Islas is Mex. 168 B5
Revillagigedo Island AK U.S.A. 149 O5
Revin France 62 E5
Revivim Israel 107 B4
Revolyutsii, Pik mt. Tajik. see Revolyutsiya, Qullai
Revolyutsiya, Qullai mt. Tajik. 111 I2
Rewa India 104 E4
Rewanduz Iraq see Rawāndūz/Rewanduz
Rewari India 104 D3
Rex AK U.S.A. 149 J2
Rexburg ID U.S.A. 156 F4
Rexton Canada 153 I5
Rey Iran 110 C3
Rey, Isla del i. Panama 166 [inset] K7
Reyābād Iran 110 D2
Reyes, Point CA U.S.A. 158 B2
Reyhanlı Turkey 107 C1
Reykir Iceland 54 [inset 1]
Reykjanes Ridge sea feature N. Atlantic Ocean 184 F2
Reykjanestá pt Iceland 54 [inset 1]

▶Reykjavík Iceland 54 [inset]
Capital of Iceland.

Reyneke, Ostrov i. Russia 90 E1
Reynoldsburg OH U.S.A. 164 D4
Reynolds Range mts Australia 134 F5
Reynosa Mex. 167 F3
Rezā Iran 110 D3
Reẓā'īyeh Iran see Urmia
Reẓā'īyeh, Daryācheh-ye salt l. Iran see Urmia, Lake
Rēzekne Latvia 55 O8
Rezvān Iran 111 F4
Rezvāndeh Iran see Rezvānshahr
Rezvānshahr Iran 110 C2
R. F. Magón Mex. see Ricardo Flores Magón
Rhaeadr Gwy U.K. see Rhayader
Rhayader U.K. 59 D6
Rheda-Wiedenbrück Germany 63 I3
Rhede Germany 62 G3
Rhegium Italy see Reggio di Calabria
Rheims France see Reims
Rhein r. Germany 63 G3 see Rhine
Rheine Germany 63 H2
Rheinland-Pfalz land Germany 63 H5
Rheinsberg Germany 63 M1
Rheinstetten Germany 63 I6
Rhemilès well Alg. 120 C2
Rhin r. Germany 63 I6 see Rhine
Rhine r. Germany 63 G3
also spelt Rhein (Germany) or Rhin (France)
Rhinebeck NY U.S.A. 165 I3
Rhinelander WI U.S.A. 160 F2
Rhineland-Palatinate land Germany see Rheinland-Pfalz
Rhinkanal canal Germany 63 M2
Rhinow Germany 63 M2
Rhiwabon U.K. see Ruabon
Rho Italy 68 C2
Rhode Island state U.S.A. 165 J3
Rhodes Greece 69 M6
Rhodes i. Greece 69 M6
Rhodesia country Africa see Zimbabwe
Rhodes Peak ID U.S.A. 156 E3
Rhodope Mountains Bulg./Greece 69 J4
Rhodus i. Greece see Rhodes
Rhône r. France/Switz. 66 G5
Rhum i. U.K. see Rum
Rhuthun U.K. see Ruthin
Rhydaman U.K. see Ammanford
Rhyl U.K. 58 D5
Riachão Brazil 177 I5
Riacho Brazil 179 C2
Riacho de Santana Brazil 179 C1
Riacho dos Machados Brazil 179 C1
Rialma Brazil 179 A1
Rialto CA U.S.A. 158 E4
Riam Kalimantan Indon. 85 E3
Riau prov. Indon. 84 C2
Riau, Kepulauan is Sumatra Indon. 84 D2
Ribadeo Spain 67 C2
Ribadesella/Ribeseya Spain 67 D2
Ribas do Rio Pardo Brazil 178 F2
Ribat-i-Shur waterhole Iran 110 E3
Ribáuè Moz. 123 D5
Ribble r. U.K. 58 E5
Ribblesdale valley U.K. 58 E4
Ribe Denmark 55 F9
Ribécourt-Dreslincourt France 62 C5
Ribeira r. Brazil 179 B4
Ribeirão Preto Brazil 179 B3
Ribemont France 62 D5
Ribérac France 66 E4
Riberalta Bol. 176 E6
Rîbniţa Moldova 53 F7
Ribnitz-Damgarten Germany 57 N3
Říčany Czech Rep. 57 O6
Ricardo Flores Magón Mex. 166 D2
Rice VA U.S.A. 165 F5
Rice Lake Canada 165 F1
Richard-Molard, Mont Africa 120 C4
Richards Bay S. Africa 125 K5
Richards Inlet Antarctica 188 H1
Richards Island Canada 149 N1
Richardson r. Canada 151 I3
Richardson AK U.S.A. 149 K2
Richardson TX U.S.A. 161 D5
Richardson Highway AK U.S.A. 149 K3
Richardson Island Canada 150 G1
Richardson Lakes ME U.S.A. 165 J1
Richardson Mountains Canada 149 N2
Richardson Mountains N.Z. 139 B7
Richfield UT U.S.A. 159 G2
Richfield Springs NY U.S.A. 165 H2
Richford NY U.S.A. 165 G2
Richford VT U.S.A. 165 I1
Richgrove CA U.S.A. 158 D4
Richland WA U.S.A. 156 D3
Richland Center WI U.S.A. 160 F3
Richmond N.S.W. Australia 138 E4
Richmond Qld Australia 136 C4
Richmond Canada 165 H1
Richmond N.Z. 139 D5
Richmond KwaZulu-Natal S. Africa 125 J5
Richmond N. Cape S. Africa 124 F6
Richmond U.K. 58 F4
Richmond CA U.S.A. 158 B3
Richmond IN U.S.A. 164 C4
Richmond KY U.S.A. 164 C5
Richmond MI U.S.A. 164 D2
Richmond MO U.S.A. 160 E4
Richmond TX U.S.A. 161 E6

▶Richmond VA U.S.A. 165 G5
Capital of Virginia.

Richmond Dale OH U.S.A. 164 D4
Richmond Hill GA U.S.A. 163 D6
Richmond Range hills Australia 138 F2
Richoi China 99 D7
Richvale CA U.S.A. 158 C2
Richwood WV U.S.A. 164 E4
Rico CO U.S.A. 159 I3
Ricomagus France see Riom
Riddell Nunataks Antarctica 188 E2
Ridder Kazakh. 98 C2
Rideau Lakes Canada 165 G1
Ridge r. Canada 152 D4
Ridgecrest CA U.S.A. 158 E4
Ridge Farm IL U.S.A. 164 B4
Ridgeland MS U.S.A. 161 F5
Ridgeland SC U.S.A. 163 D5
Ridgetop TN U.S.A. 164 B5
Ridgetown Canada 164 E2
Ridgeway OH U.S.A. 164 D3
Ridgeway VA U.S.A. 164 F5
Ridgway CO U.S.A. 159 J2
Ridgway PA U.S.A. 165 F3
Riding Mountain National Park Canada 151 K5
Riecito Venez. 176 E1
Riemst Belgium 62 F4
Riesa Germany 63 N3
Riesco, Isla i. Chile 178 B8
Riet watercourse S. Africa 124 E6
Rietavas Lith. 55 L9
Rietfontein S. Africa 124 E4
Rieti Italy 68 E3
Rifā'ī, Tall mt. Jordan/Syria 107 C3
Rifeng China see Lichuan
Rifle CO U.S.A. 159 J2
Rifstangi pt Iceland 54 [inset 1]
Rift Valley Lakes National Park Eth. see Abijatta-Shalla National Park

▶Rīga Latvia 55 N8
Capital of Latvia.

Riga, Gulf of Estonia/Latvia 55 M8
Rigain Pünco l. China 99 D6
Rīgas jūras līcis b. Estonia/Latvia see Riga, Gulf of
Rigby ID U.S.A. 156 F4
Rīgestān reg. Afgh. see Rēgistān
Rigolet Canada 153 K3
Rigside U.K. 60 F5
Riia laht b. Estonia/Latvia see Riga, Gulf of
Riihimäki Fin. 55 N6
Riiser-Larsen Ice Shelf Antarctica 188 B2
Riito Mex. 166 B1
Rijau Nigeria 120 D3
Rijeka Croatia 68 F2
Rikā, Wādī ar watercourse Saudi Arabia 110 B6
Rikitgaib Sumatra Indon. 84 B1
Rikor India 96 B2
Rikuchū-kaigan Kokuritsu-kōen Japan 91 F5
Rikuzen-takata Japan 91 F5
Rila mts Bulg. 69 J3
Rila China 99 D7
Riley OR U.S.A. 156 D4
Rileyville VA U.S.A. 165 F4
Rillieux-la-Pape France 66 G4
Rillito AZ U.S.A. 159 H5
Rimah, Wādī ar watercourse Saudi Arabia 108 F4
Rimau, Pulau i. Indon. 84 D3
Rimavská Sobota Slovakia 57 R6
Rimbey Canada 150 H4
Rimini Italy 68 E2
Rîmnicu Sărat Romania see Râmnicu Sărat
Rîmnicu Vîlcea Romania see Râmnicu Vâlcea
Rimo Glacier India 99 B6
Rimouski Canada 153 H4
Rimpar Germany 63 J5
Rimsdale, Loch l. U.K. 60 E2
Rinbung China 99 E7
Rinca i. Indon. 83 A5
Rincão Brazil 179 A3
Rincón de Romos Mex. 166 E4
Rind r. India 99 C8
Rindal Norway 54 F5
Rindü China 99 E7
Ringarooma Bay Australia 137 [inset]
Ringas India 104 C4
Ringe Germany 62 G2
Ringebu Norway 55 G6
Ringhkung Myanmar 86 B1
Ringkøbing Denmark 55 F8
Ringsend U.K. 61 F2
Ringsted Denmark 55 G9
Ringtor China 99 C7
Ringvassøya i. Norway 54 K2
Ringwood Australia 138 B6
Ringwood U.K. 59 F8
Rinjani, Gunung vol. Indon. 80 F8
Rinns Point U.K. 60 C5
Rinqênzê China 105 G3
Rinqin Xubco salt l. China 99 C7
Rinteln Germany 63 J2
Rinyirru (Lakefield) National Park Australia 136 D2
Río Abiseo, Parque Nacional nat. park Peru 176 C5
Rio Azul Brazil 179 A4
Riobamba Ecuador 176 C4
Rio Blanco CO U.S.A. 159 J2
Rio Bonito Brazil 179 C3
Rio Branco Brazil 176 E6
Rio Branco, Parque Nacional do nat. park Brazil 176 F3
Río Bravo, Parque Internacional del nat. park Mex. 166 E2
Rio Brilhante Brazil 178 F2
Rio Casca Brazil 179 C3
Rio Claro Brazil 179 B3
Río Colorado Arg. 178 D5
Río Cuarto Arg. 178 D4
Rio das Ostras Brazil 179 C3
Rio das Pedras Moz. 125 L2
Rio de Contas Brazil 179 C1

▶Rio de Janeiro Brazil 179 C3
Former capital of Brazil. 3rd most populous city in South America.

Rio de Janeiro state Brazil 179 C3
Río de Jesús Panama 166 [inset] J8

▶Río de la Plata-Paraná r. S. America 178 E4
2nd longest river in South America and 9th in the world.

Rio Dell CA U.S.A. 158 A1
Rio do Sul Brazil 179 A4
Río Frío Costa Rica 166 [inset] J7
Río Gallegos Arg. 178 C8
Río Grande Arg. 178 C8
Rio Grande Brazil 178 F4
Río Grande Mex. 161 C8
Rio Grande r. Mex./U.S.A. 157 G5
also known as Río Bravo del Norte
Rio Grande r. Mex./U.S.A. 167 D2
Rio Grande City TX U.S.A. 161 D7
Rio Grande do Sul state Brazil 179 A5
Rio Grande Rise sea feature S. Atlantic Ocean 184 F8
Riohacha Col. 176 D1
Río Hato Panama 166 [inset] J7
Río Hondo, Embalse resr Arg. 178 C3
Rioja Peru 176 C5
Río Lagartos Mex. 167 H4
Rio Largo Brazil 177 K5
Riom France 66 F4
Rio Manso, Represa do resr Brazil 177 G6
Río Mulatos Bol. 176 E7
Río Muni reg. Equat. Guinea 120 E4
Río Negro, Embalse del resr Uruguay 178 E4
Rioni r. Georgia 113 F2
Rio Novo Brazil 179 C3
Rio Pardo de Minas Brazil 179 C1
Río Plátano, Reserva Biósfera del nature res. Hond. 166 [inset] I6
Rio Preto Brazil 179 C3
Rio Preto, Serra do hills Brazil 179 B2
Rio Rancho NM U.S.A. 157 G6
Riosucio Col. 166 [inset] K8
Río Tigre Ecuador 176 C4
Río Tuba Palawan Phil. 82 B4

Riou Lake Canada 151 J3
Rio Verde Brazil 179 A2
Río Verde Quintana Roo Mex. 167 H5
Río Verde San Luis Potosí Mex. 167 F4
Rio Verde de Mato Grosso Brazil 177 H7
Rio Vista CA U.S.A. 158 C2
Ripky Ukr. 53 F6
Ripley England U.K. 58 F4
Ripley England U.K. 59 F5
Ripley NY U.S.A. 164 F2
Ripley OH U.S.A. 164 D4
Ripley WV U.S.A. 164 E4
Ripoll Spain 67 H2
Ripon U.K. 58 F4
Ripon CA U.S.A. 158 C3
Ripu India 105 G4
Risca U.K. 59 D7
Rishiri-tō i. Japan 90 F3
Rishon LeẔiyyon Israel 107 B4
Rīsh Pīsh Bālā Iran 111 F5
Rising Sun IN U.S.A. 164 C4
Rising Sun MD U.S.A. 165 G4
Risle r. France 59 H9
Risør Norway 55 F7
Rissa Norway 54 F5
Ristiina Fin. 55 O6
Ristijärvi Fin. 54 P4
Ristikent Russia 54 Q2
Risum China 99 B6
Ritan r. Indon. 85 F2
Ritang China 99 F7
Ritchie S. Africa 124 G5
Ritchie's Archipelago is India 87 A4
Ritch Island Canada 149 R2
Ritscher Upland mts Antarctica 188 B2
Ritsem Sweden 54 J3
Ritter, Mount CA U.S.A. 158 D3
Ritterhude Germany 63 I1
Rittō Japan 92 B3
Ritzville WA U.S.A. 156 D3
Riu, Laem pt Thai. 87 B5
Riva del Garda Italy 68 D2
Rivas Nicaragua 166 [inset] I7
Rivera Arg. 178 D5
Rivera Uruguay 178 E4
River Cess Liberia 120 C4
Riverhead NY U.S.A. 165 I3
Riverhurst Canada 151 J5
Riverina Australia 135 C7
Riverina reg. Australia 138 B5
Riversdale S. Africa 124 E8
Riverside S. Africa 125 I6
Riverside CA U.S.A. 158 E5
Rivers Inlet Canada 150 E5
Riversleigh Australia 136 B3
Riverton N.Z. 139 B8
Riverton VA U.S.A. 165 F4
Riverton WY U.S.A. 156 F4
Riverview Canada 153 I5
Rivesaltes France 66 F5
Riviera Beach FL U.S.A. 163 D7
Rivière-du-Loup Canada 153 H5
Rivière-Pentecôte Canada 153 I4
Rivière-Pigou Canada 153 I4
Rivne Ukr. 53 E6
Rivungo Angola 123 C5
Riwaka N.Z. 139 D5
Riwoqê China see **Racaka**

▶**Riyadh** Saudi Arabia 108 G5
Capital of Saudi Arabia.

Riyan India 111 I5
Riyue Shankou pass China 94 E4
Riza well Iran 110 D3
Rizal Luzon Phil. 82 C3
Rize Turkey 113 F2
Rizhao Shandong China 95 I5
Rizhao Shandong China see **Donggang**
Rizokarpaso Cyprus see **Rizokarpason**
Rizokarpason Cyprus 107 B2
Rīzū well Iran 110 E3
Rīzū'īyeh Iran 110 E4
Rjukan Norway 55 F7
Rjuvbrokkene mt. Norway 55 E7
Rkîz Mauritania 120 B3
Roa Norway 55 G6
Roachdale IN U.S.A. 164 B4
Roach Lake NV U.S.A. 159 F4
Roade U.K. 59 G6
Roads OH U.S.A. 164 D4

▶**Road Town** Virgin Is (U.K.) 169 L5
Capital of the British Virgin Islands.

Roan Norway 54 G4
Roan Fell hill U.K. 60 G5
Roan High Knob mt. TN U.S.A. 162 D4
Roanne France 66 G3
Roanoke IN U.S.A. 164 C3
Roanoke VA U.S.A. 164 F5
Roanoke r. NC U.S.A. 162 E4
Roanoke Rapids NC U.S.A. 162 E4
Roan Plateau UT U.S.A. 159 I2
Roaring Spring PA U.S.A. 165 F3
Roaringwater Bay Ireland 61 C6
Roatán Hond. 166 [inset] I5
Röbäck Sweden 54 L5
Robāṭ-e Posht-e Bādām Iran 110 D3
Robāṭ Karīm Iran 110 C3
Robāṭ Sang Iran 110 E3
Robāṭ Tork Iran 110 C3
Robb Canada 150 G4
Robbins Island Australia 137 [inset]
Robbinsville NC U.S.A. 163 D5
Robe Australia 137 B8
Robe r. Australia 134 A5
Robe r. Ireland 61 C4
Röbel/Müritz Germany 63 M1
Robe Noire, Lac de la l. Canada 153 J4
Robert-Bourassa, Réservoir resr Canada 152 F3
Robert Glacier Antarctica 188 D2
Robert Lee TX U.S.A. 161 C6
Roberts ID U.S.A. 156 E4
Roberts, Mount Australia 138 F2
Robertsburg WV U.S.A. 164 E4
Roberts Butte mt. Antarctica 188 H2
Roberts Creek Mountain NV U.S.A. 158 E2
Robertsfors Sweden 54 L4
Robertsganj India 105 E4
Robertson S. Africa 124 D7
Robertson, Lac l. Canada 153 K4
Robertson Bay Antarctica 188 H2
Robertson Island Antarctica 188 A2
Robertson Range hills Australia 135 C5
Robertsport Liberia 120 B4
Roberval Canada 153 G4
Robhanais, Rubha hd U.K. see **Butt of Lewis**
Robin Hood's Bay U.K. 58 G4
Robin's Nest hill H.K. China 97 [inset]
Robinson Canada 149 N3
Robinson IL U.S.A. 164 B4
Robinson Mountains AK U.S.A. 148 I4
Robinson Mountains AK U.S.A. 149 L3
Robinson Ranges hills Australia 135 B6
Robinson River Australia 136 B3
Robles Pass AZ U.S.A. 159 H5
Roblin Canada 151 K5
Robsart Canada 151 I5
Robson, Mount Canada 150 G4
Robstown TX U.S.A. 161 D7
Roby TX U.S.A. 161 C5
Roçadas Angola see **Xangongo**
Roca Partida, Punta pt Mex. 167 G5
Rocas Alijos is Mex. 166 B3
Rocha Uruguay 178 F4
Rochdale U.K. 58 E5
Rochechouart France 66 E4
Rochefort Belgium 62 F4
Rochefort France 66 D4
Rochefort, Lac l. Canada 153 G2
Rochegda Russia 52 I3
Rochester Australia 138 B6
Rochester U.K. 59 H7
Rochester IN U.S.A. 164 B3
Rochester MN U.S.A. 160 E2
Rochester NH U.S.A. 165 J2
Rochester NY U.S.A. 165 G2
Rochford U.K. 59 H7
Rochlitz Germany 63 M3
Roc'h Trévezel hill France 66 C2
Rock r. Y.T. Canada 149 M2
Rock r. Y.T. Canada 149 P3
Rockall i. N. Atlantic Ocean 50 D4
Rockall Bank sea feature N. Atlantic Ocean 184 G2
Rock Creek Canada 149 M2
Rock Creek OH U.S.A. 164 E3
Rock Creek r. MT U.S.A. 156 G2
Rockdale TX U.S.A. 161 D6
Rockefeller Plateau Antarctica 188 J1
Rockford AL U.S.A. 163 C5
Rockford IL U.S.A. 160 F3
Rockford MI U.S.A. 164 C2
Rockglen Canada 151 J5
Rockhampton Australia 136 E4
Rockhampton Downs Australia 134 F4
Rock Hill SC U.S.A. 163 D5
Rockingham Australia 135 A8
Rockingham NC U.S.A. 163 E5
Rockingham Bay Australia 136 D3
Rockinghorse Lake Canada 151 H1
Rock Island Canada 165 I1
Rock Island IL U.S.A. 160 F3
Rock Islands Southern Lagoon tourist site Palau 82 [inset]
Rock Lake ND U.S.A. 160 D1
Rockland MA U.S.A. 165 J2
Rockland ME U.S.A. 162 G2
Rocknest Lake Canada 150 H1
Rockport IN U.S.A. 164 B5
Rockport TX U.S.A. 161 D7
Rock Rapids IA U.S.A. 160 D3
Rock River WY U.S.A. 156 G4
Rock Sound Bahamas 163 E7
Rock Springs MT U.S.A. 156 G3
Rocksprings TX U.S.A. 161 C6
Rock Springs WY U.S.A. 156 F4
Rockstone Guyana 177 G2
Rockville CT U.S.A. 165 I3
Rockville IN U.S.A. 164 B4
Rockville MD U.S.A. 165 G4
Rockwell City IA U.S.A. 160 E3
Rockwood MI U.S.A. 164 D2
Rockwood PA U.S.A. 164 F4
Rockyford Canada 150 H5
Rocky Harbour Canada 153 K4
Rocky Hill OH U.S.A. 164 D4
Rocky Island Lake Canada 152 E5
Rocky Lane Canada 150 G3
Rocky Mount VA U.S.A. 164 F5
Rocky Mountain House Canada 150 H4
Rocky Mountain National Park CO U.S.A. 156 G4
Rocky Mountains Canada/U.S.A. 154 F3
Rocky Point pt AK U.S.A. 148 G2
Rocourt-St-Martin France 62 D5
Rocroi France 62 E5
Rødberg Norway 55 F6
Rødbyhavn Denmark 55 G9
Roddickton Canada 153 L4
Rodeio Brazil 179 A4
Rodel U.K. 60 C3
Roden Neth. 62 G1
Rödental Germany 63 L4
Rodeo Arg. 178 C4
Rodeo Mex. 166 D3
Rodeo NM U.S.A. 157 F7
Rodez France 66 F4
Ródhos i. Greece see **Rhodes**
Rodi i. Greece see **Rhodes**
Roding Germany 63 M5
Rodney, Cape AK U.S.A. 148 F2
Rodniki Russia 52 I4
Rodolfo Sánchez Toboada Mex. 166 A2
Rodopi Planina mts Bulg./Greece see **Rhodope Mountains**
Rodos Greece see **Rhodes**
Rodos i. Greece see **Rhodes**
Rodosto Turkey see **Tekirdağ**
Rodrigues Island Mauritius 185 M7
Roe r. U.K. 61 F2
Roebourne Australia 134 B5
Roebuck Bay Australia 134 C4
Roedtan S. Africa 125 I3
Roe Plains Australia 135 D7
Roermond Neth. 62 F3
Roeselare Belgium 62 D4
Roes Welcome Sound sea chan. Canada 147 J3
Rogachev Belarus see **Rahachow**
Rogätz Germany 63 L2
Rogers AR U.S.A. 161 E4
Rogers, Mount VA U.S.A. 164 E5
Rogers City MI U.S.A. 164 D1
Rogers Lake CA U.S.A. 158 E4
Rogerson ID U.S.A. 156 E4
Rogersville TN U.S.A. 164 D5
Roggan r. Canada 152 F3
Roggan, Lac l. Canada 152 F3
Roggeveen Basin sea feature S. Pacific Ocean 187 O8
Roggeveld plat. S. Africa 124 E7
Roggeveldberge esc. S. Africa 124 E7
Roghadal U.K. see **Rodel**
Rognan Norway 54 I3
Rögnitz r. Germany 63 K1
Rogue r. OR U.S.A. 156 B4
Roha India 106 B2
Rohnert Park CA U.S.A. 158 B2
Rohrbach in Oberösterreich Austria 57 N6
Rohrbach-lès-Bitche France 63 H5
Rohri Sangar Pak. 111 H5
Rohtak India 104 D3
Roi Et Thai. 86 C3
Roi Georges, Îles du is Fr. Polynesia 187 K6
Rois-Bheinn hill U.K. 60 D4
Roisel France 62 D5
Roja Latvia 55 M8
Rojas Arg. 178 D4
Rojo, Cabo c. Mex. 167 F4
Rokan r. Indon. 84 C2
Rokeby Australia 136 C2
Rokeby National Park Australia 136 C2
Rokiškis Lith. 55 N9
Roknäs Sweden 54 L4
Rokugō Japan 93 E3
Rokuriga-hara plain Japan 93 E2
Rokusei Japan 92 C2
Rokytne Ukr. 53 E6
Rola Co l. China 99 E6
Rolagang China 99 E6
Rola Kangri mt. China 99 E6
Rolândia Brazil 179 A3
Rolim de Moura Brazil 176 F6
Roll AZ U.S.A. 159 G5
Roll IN U.S.A. 164 C3
Rolla MO U.S.A. 160 F4
Rolla ND U.S.A. 160 D1
Rollag Norway 55 F6
Rolleston Australia 136 E5
Rolleville Bahamas 163 F8
Rolling Fork MS U.S.A. 161 F5
Rollins MT U.S.A. 156 E3
Roma Australia 137 E5
Roma Italy see **Rome**
Roma Lesotho 125 H5
Roma Sweden 55 K8
Roma TX U.S.A. 167 F3
Roma, Pulau i. Moluccas Indon. see **Romang, Pulau**
Romain, Cape SC U.S.A. 163 E5
Romaine r. Canada 153 J4
Roman Romania 69 L1
Română, Câmpia plain Romania 69 J2
Romanche Gap sea feature S. Atlantic Ocean 184 G6
Romanet, Lac l. Canada 153 I2
Romang, Pulau i. Moluccas Indon. 83 C4
Romania country Europe 69 K2
Roman-Kosh mt. Crimea 112 D1
Romano, Cape FL U.S.A. 163 D7
Romanovka Russia 89 K2
Romans-sur-Isère France 66 G4
Romanzof, Cape AK U.S.A. 148 F3
Romanzof Mountains AK U.S.A. 149 K1
Rombas France 62 G5
Romblon Phil. 82 C3
Romblon i. Phil. 82 C3
Romblon Pass Phil. 82 C3

▶**Rome** Italy 68 E4
Capital of Italy.

Rome GA U.S.A. 163 C5
Rome ME U.S.A. 165 K1
Rome NY U.S.A. 165 H2
Rome TN U.S.A. 164 B5
Rome City IN U.S.A. 164 C3
Romeo MI U.S.A. 164 D2
Romford U.K. 59 H7
Romilly-sur-Seine France 66 F2
Romiton Uzbek. 111 G2
Romney WV U.S.A. 165 F4
Romney Marsh reg. U.K. 59 H7
Romny Ukr. 53 G6
Rømø i. Denmark 55 F9
Romodanovo Russia 53 J5
Romorantin-Lanthenay France 66 E3
Rompin r. Malaysia 84 C2
Romsey U.K. 59 F8
Romu mt. Sumbawa Indon. 85 G5
Romulus MI U.S.A. 164 D2
Ron India 106 B3
Ron, Mui hd Vietnam 86 D3
Rona i. U.K. 60 D1
Ronas Hill hill U.K. 60 [inset]
Roncador, Serra do hills Brazil 177 H6
Roncador Reef Solomon Is 133 F2
Ronda Spain 67 D5
Ronda, Serranía de mts Spain 67 D5
Rondane Nasjonalpark nat. park Norway 55 F6
Rondon Brazil 178 F2
Rondonópolis Brazil 177 H7
Rondout Reservoir NY U.S.A. 165 H3
Rongcheng Anhui China see **Qingyang**
Rongcheng Guangxi China see **Rongxian**
Rongcheng Hubei China see **Jianli**
Rongcheng Shandong China 95 J4
Rongcheng Wan b. China 95 J4
Rong Chu r. China 99 E7
Rongelap atoll Marshall Is 186 H5
Rongjiang Guizhou China 97 F3
Rongjiang Jiangxi China see **Nankang**
Rongjiawan China see **Yueyang**
Rongklang Range mts Myanmar 86 A2
Rongmei China see **Hefeng**
Rongshui China 97 F3
Rongwo China see **Tongren**
Rongxian China 97 F4
Rongyul China 96 C2
Rongzhag China see **Danba**
Rönlap atoll Marshall Is see **Rongelap**
Rønne Denmark 55 I9
Ronneby Sweden 55 I8
Ronne Entrance strait Antarctica 188 L2
Ronne Ice Shelf Antarctica 188 L1
Ronnenberg Germany 63 J2
Ronse Belgium 62 D4
Roodeschool Neth. 62 G1
Rooke Island P.N.G. see **Umboi**
Roordahuizum Neth. see **Reduzum**
Roorkee India 104 D3
Roosendaal Neth. 62 E3
Roosevelt AZ U.S.A. 159 H5
Roosevelt UT U.S.A. 159 I1
Roosevelt, Mount Canada 150 E3
Roosevelt Sub-glacial Island Antarctica 188 I1
Root r. Canada 150 F2
Root r. MN U.S.A. 160 F3
Ropar India see **Rupnagar**
Roper r. Australia 136 A2
Roper Bar Australia 134 F3
Roquefort France 66 D4
Roraima, Mount Guyana 176 F2
Rorey Lake Canada 149 O2
Rori India 104 C3
Rori Indon. 81 J7
Røros Norway 54 G5
Rørvik Norway 54 G4
Rosa, Punta pt Mex. 166 C3
Rosales Mex. 166 D2
Rosalia WA U.S.A. 156 D3
Rosamond CA U.S.A. 158 D4
Rosamond Lake CA U.S.A. 158 D4
Rosamorada Mex. 166 D4
Rosario Arg. 178 D4
Rosário Brazil 177 J4
Rosario Baja California Mex. 166 B2
Rosario Coahuila Mex. 166 E3
Rosario Sinaloa Mex. 168 C4
Rosario Sonora Mex. 166 C3
Rosario Zacatecas Mex. 161 C7
Rosario Luzon Phil. 82 C2
Rosario Luzon Phil. 82 C3
Rosario Venez. 176 D1
Rosário do Sul Brazil 178 F4
Rosário Oeste Brazil 177 G6
Rosarito Baja California Mex. 166 A1
Rosarito Baja California Mex. 166 B2
Rosarito Baja California Sur Mex. 166 C3
Rosarno Italy 68 F5
Roscoe r. Canada 149 Q1
Roscoff France 66 C2
Roscommon Ireland 61 D4
Roscommon MI U.S.A. 164 C1
Roscrea Ireland 61 E5
Rose r. Australia 136 A2
Rose, Mount NV U.S.A. 158 D2
Rose Atoll American Samoa see **Rose Island**

▶**Roseau** Dominica 169 L5
Capital of Dominica.

Roseau MN U.S.A. 160 E1
Roseau r. MN U.S.A. 160 D1
Roseberth Australia 137 B5
Rose Blanche Canada 153 K5
Rosebud r. Canada 150 H5
Rosebud MT U.S.A. 156 G3
Roseburg OR U.S.A. 156 C4
Rose City MI U.S.A. 164 C1
Rosedale MS U.S.A. 161 F5
Rosedale Abbey U.K. 58 G4
Roseires Reservoir Sudan 108 D7
Rose Island atoll American Samoa 133 J3
Rosenberg TX U.S.A. 161 E6
Rosendal Norway 55 E7
Rosendal S. Africa 125 H5
Rosenheim Germany 57 N7
Rose Peak AZ U.S.A. 159 I5
Rose Point pt Canada 149 O5
Roseto degli Abruzzi Italy 68 F3
Rosetown Canada 151 J5
Rosetta Egypt see **Rashīd**
Rose Valley Canada 151 K4
Roseville CA U.S.A. 158 C2
Roseville MI U.S.A. 164 D2
Roseville OH U.S.A. 164 D4
Rosewood Australia 138 F1
Roshchino Russia 55 P6
Rosh Pinah Namibia 124 C4
Roshtkala Tajik. see **Roshtqal'a**
Roshtqal'a Tajik. 111 H2
Rosignano Marittimo Italy 68 D3
Roșiori de Vede Romania 69 K2
Roskilde Denmark 55 H9
Roskruge Mountains AZ U.S.A. 159 H5
Roslavl' Russia 53 G5
Roslyakovo Russia 54 R2
Roslyatino Russia 52 J4
Ross r. Canada 149 N3
Ross N.Z. 139 C6
Ross, Mount hill N.Z. 139 E5
Rossano Italy 68 G5
Rossan Point Ireland 61 D3
Ross Barnett Reservoir MS U.S.A. 161 F5
Ross Bay Junction Canada 153 I3
Rosscarbery Ireland 61 C6
Ross Dependency reg. Antarctica 188 I2
Rosseau, Lake Canada 164 F1
Rossel Island P.N.G. 136 F1
Ross Ice Shelf Antarctica 188 I1
Rossignol, Lac l. Canada 152 G3
Rössing Namibia 124 B2
Ross Island Antarctica 188 H1
Rossiyskaya Sovetskaya Federativnaya Sotsialisticheskaya Respublika country Asia/Europe see **Russia**
Rossland Canada 150 G5
Rosslare Ireland 61 F5
Rosslare Harbour Ireland 61 F5
Roßlau Germany 63 M3
Rosso Mauritania 120 B3
Ross-on-Wye U.K. 59 E7
Rossony Belarus see **Rasony**
Rossosh' Russia 53 H6
Ross River Canada 149 N3
Ross Sea Antarctica 188 H1
Roßtal Germany 63 K5
Røssvatnet l. Norway 54 I4
Rossville IL U.S.A. 164 B3
Roßwein Germany 63 N3
Rosswood Canada 150 D4
Rostāq Iran 110 D5
Rosthern Canada 151 J4
Rostock Germany 57 N3
Rostov Russia 52 H4
Rostov-na-Donu Russia 53 H7
Rostov-on-Don Russia see **Rostov-na-Donu**
Rosvik Sweden 54 L4
Roswell NM U.S.A. 157 G6
Rota i. N. Mariana Is 81 L4
Rot am See Germany 63 K5
Rotch Island Kiribati see **Tamana**
Rote i. Indon. 83 B5
Rotenburg (Wümme) Germany 63 J1
Roth Germany 63 L5
Rothaargebirge hills Germany 63 I4
Rothbury U.K. 58 F3
Rothenburg ob der Tauber Germany 63 K5
Rother r. U.K. 59 G8
Rothera research station Antarctica 188 L2
Rotherham U.K. 58 F5
Rothes U.K. 60 F3
Rothesay U.K. 60 D5
Rothwell U.K. 59 G6
Roti Indon. 83 B5
Roti i. Indon. see **Rote**
Roti, Selat sea chan. Indon. 83 B5
Roto Australia 138 B4
Rotomagus France see **Rouen**
Rotomanu N.Z. 139 C6
Rotondo, Monte mt. Corsica France 66 I5
Rotorua N.Z. 139 F4
Rotorua, Lake N.Z. 139 F4
Röttenbach Germany 63 L5
Rottendorf Germany 63 K5
Rottenmann Austria 57 O7
Rotterdam Neth. 62 E3
Rottleberode Germany 63 K3
Rottnest Island Australia 135 A8
Rottumeroog i. Neth. 62 G1
Rottweil Germany 57 L6
Rotuma i. Fiji 133 H3
Rotung India 96 B2
Rötviken Sweden 54 I5
Rötz Germany 63 M5
Roubaix France 62 D4
Rouen France 62 B5
Rough River Lake KY U.S.A. 164 B5
Roulers Belgium see **Roeselare**
Roumania country Europe see **Romania**
Roundeyed Lake Canada 153 H3
Round Hill hill U.K. 58 F4
Round Mountain Australia 138 F3
Round Rock AZ U.S.A. 159 I3
Round Rock TX U.S.A. 161 D6
Roundup MT U.S.A. 156 F3
Rousay i. U.K. 60 F1
Rouses Point NY U.S.A. 165 I1
Routh Bank sea feature Phil. see **Seahorse Shoal**
Rouxville S. Africa 125 H6
Rouyn-Noranda Canada 152 F4
Rouyuan China see **Huachi**
Rouyuanchengzi China see **Huachi**
Rovaniemi Fin. 54 N3
Roven'ki Russia 53 H6
Rovereto Italy 68 D2
Rôviĕng Cambodia 87 D4
Rovigo Italy 68 D2
Rovinj Croatia 68 E2
Rovno Ukr. see **Rivne**
Rovnoye Russia 53 J6
Rovuma r. Moz./Tanz. see **Ruvuma**
Rowena Australia 138 D2
Rowley Island Canada 147 K3
Rowley Shoals sea feature Australia 134 B4
Równe Ukr. see **Rivne**
Roxas Luzon Phil. 82 C2
Roxas Mindoro Phil. 82 C3
Roxas Palawan Phil. 82 B4
Roxas Panay Phil. 82 C4
Roxboro NC U.S.A. 162 E4
Roxburgh N.Z. 139 B7
Roxburgh Island Cook Is see **Rarotonga**
Roxby Downs Australia 137 B6
Roxo, Cabo c. Senegal 120 B3
Roy MT U.S.A. 156 F3
Roy NM U.S.A. 157 G5
Royal Canal Ireland 61 E4
Royal Chitwan National Park Nepal 105 F4
Royale, Île i. Canada see **Cape Breton Island**
Royale, Isle i. MI U.S.A. 160 F1
Royal Leamington Spa U.K. 59 F6
Royal Natal National Park S. Africa 125 I5
Royal National Park Australia 138 E5
Royal Oak MI U.S.A. 164 D2
Royal Sukla Phanta Wildlife Reserve Nepal 104 E3
Royal Tunbridge Wells U.K. 59 H7
Royal Wootton Bassett town U.K. 59 F7
Royan France 66 D4
Roye France 62 C5
Roy Hill Australia 134 B5
Royston U.K. 59 G6
Rozdil'na Ukr. 69 N1
Rozivka Ukr. 53 H7
Rtishchevo Russia 53 I5
Rua, Tanjung pt Sumba Indon. 83 A5
Ruabon U.K. 59 D6
Ruaha National Park Tanz. 123 D4
Ruahine Range mts N.Z. 139 F5
Ruanda country Africa see **Rwanda**
Ruang i. Indon. 83 C2

▶**Ruapehu, Mount** vol. N.Z. 139 E4
Highest active volcano in Oceania.

Ruapuke Island N.Z. 139 B8
Ruatoria N.Z. 139 G3
Ruba Belarus 53 F5

▶**Rub' al Khālī** des. Saudi Arabia 108 G6
Largest uninterrupted stretch of sand in the world.

Rubāṭ Māndêh r. Afgh. 111 F4
Rubaydā reg. Saudi Arabia 110 C5
Rubtsovsk Russia 102 F1
Ruby AK U.S.A. 148 I2
Ruby Dome mt. NV U.S.A. 159 F1
Ruby Mountains NV U.S.A. 159 F1
Rubys Inn UT U.S.A. 159 G3
Ruby Valley NV U.S.A. 159 F1
Rucheng China 97 G3
Ruckersville VA U.S.A. 165 F4
Rudall River National Park Australia 134 C5
Rudarpur India 105 E4
Ruda Śląska Poland 57 Q5
Rudauli India 105 E4
Rūdbār Iran 110 C2
Rudkøbing Denmark 55 G9
Rudnaya Pristan' Russia 90 D3
Rudnichnyy Russia 52 L4
Rudnik Ingichka Uzbek. see **Ingichka**
Rudnya Smolenskaya Oblast' Russia 53 F5
Rudnya Volgogradskaya Oblast' Russia 53 J6
Rudnyy Kazakh. 100 F1
Rudolf, Lake salt l. Eth./Kenya see **Turkana, Lake**

▶**Rudol'fa, Ostrov** i. Russia 76 G1
Most northerly point of Europe.

Rudolph Island Russia see **Rudol'fa, Ostrov**
Rudolstadt Germany 63 L4
Rudong China 97 I1
Rūdsar Iran 110 C2
Rue France 62 B4
Rufiji r. Tanz. 123 D4
Rufino Arg. 178 D4
Rufisque Senegal 120 B3
Rufrufua Indon. 81 I7
Rufunsa Zambia 123 C5
Rufus Lake Canada 149 O1
Rugao China 97 I1
Rugby U.K. 59 F6
Rugby ND U.S.A. 160 C1
Rugeley U.K. 59 F6
Rügen i. Germany 57 N3
Rugged Mountain Canada 150 E5
Rügland Germany 63 K5
Ruḥayyat al Ḥamr'ā' waterhole Saudi Arabia 110 B5
Ru He r. China 94 F5
Ruhengeri Rwanda 122 C4
Ruhnu i. Estonia 55 M8
Ruhr r. Germany 63 G3
Ruhuna National Park Sri Lanka see **Yala National Park**
Rui'an China 97 I3
Ruicheng China 97 F1
Ruijin China 97 G3
Ruili China 96 C3
Ruin Point Canada 151 P2
Ruipa Tanz. 123 D4
Ruiz Mex. 168 C4
Ruiz, Nevado del vol. Col. 176 C3
Rujaylah, Ḥarrat ar lava field Jordan 107 C3
Rūjiena Latvia 55 N8
Ruk is Micronesia see **Chuuk**
Rukanpur Pak. 111 I4
Rukumkot Nepal 105 E3
Rukuwa Celebes Indon. 83 C4
Rukwa, Lake Tanz. 123 D4
Rulin China see **Chengbu**
Rulong China see **Xinlong**
Rum i. U.K. 60 C4
Rum, Jebel mts Jordan see **Ramm, Jabal**
Ruma Serbia 69 H2
Rumāh Saudi Arabia 108 G4
Rumania country Europe see **Romania**
Rumbai Celebes Indon. 83 C2
Rumbek South Sudan 121 F4
Rumberpon i. Indon. 81 I7
Rum Cay i. Bahamas 163 F8
Rum Jungle (abandoned) Australia 134 E3
Rummānā hill Syria 107 D3
Rumphi Malawi 123 D5
Run i. Moluccas Indon. 83 D4

Runan China 97 G1
Runaway, Cape N.Z. 139 F3
Runcorn U.K. 58 E5
Rundu Namibia 123 B5
Runduma i. Indon. 83 C4
Rundvik Sweden 54 K5
Rũng, Kaôh i. Cambodia 87 C5
Rungan r. Indon. 85 F3
Rungwa Tanz. 123 D4
Rungwa r. Tanz. 123 D4
Runhe China 97 H1
Runing China see Runan
Runton Range hills Australia 135 C5
Ruokolahti Fin. 55 P6
Ruoqiang China 98 E5
Ruoqiang He r. China 98 E5
Ruo Shui watercourse China 94 E3
Rupa India 105 H4
Rupat i. Indon. 84 C2
Rupert r. Canada 152 F4
Rupert ID U.S.A. 156 E4
Rupert WV U.S.A. 164 E5
Rupert Bay Canada 152 F4
Rupert Coast Antarctica 188 J1
Rupert House Canada see Waskaganish
Rupnagar India 104 D3
Rupshu reg. India 104 D2
Ruqqād, Wādī ar watercourse Israel 107 B3
Rural Retreat VA U.S.A. 164 E5
Rusaddir N. Africa see Melilla
Rusape Zimbabwe 123 D5
Ruschuk Bulg. see Ruse
Ruse Bulg. 69 K3
Rusera India 105 F4
Rush KY U.S.A. 164 D4
Rushan China 95 J4
Rush Creek r. CO U.S.A. 160 C4
Rushden U.K. 59 G6
Rushinga Zimbabwe 123 D5
Rushville IL U.S.A. 160 F3
Rushville IN U.S.A. 164 C4
Rushville NE U.S.A. 160 C3
Rushworth Australia 138 B6
Rusk TX U.S.A. 161 E6
Russell Man. Canada 151 K5
Russell Ont. Canada 165 H1
Russell N.Z. 139 E2
Russell KS U.S.A. 160 D4
Russell PA U.S.A. 164 F3
Russell, Mount AK U.S.A. 149 J3
Russell Bay Antarctica 188 J2
Russell Lake Man. Canada 151 K3
Russell Lake N.W.T. Canada 150 H2
Russell Lake Sask. Canada 151 J3
Russell Range hills Australia 135 C8
Russell Springs KY U.S.A. 164 C5
Russellville AL U.S.A. 161 G5
Russellville AR U.S.A. 161 E5
Russellville KY U.S.A. 164 B5
Rüsselsheim Germany 63 I4

▶Russia country Asia/Europe 76 I3
Largest country in Europe and Asia and the world. Most populous country in Europe and 9th in the world.

Russian r. CA U.S.A. 158 B2
Russian Federation country Asia/Europe see Russia
Russian Mission AK U.S.A. 148 G3
Russian Mountains AK U.S.A. 148 H3
Russian Soviet Federal Socialist Republic country Asia/Europe see Russia
Russkaya Koshka, Kosa spit Russia 148 B2
Russkiy, Ostrov i. Russia 90 C4
Russkiy Kameshkir Russia 53 J5
Rustāq Afgh. 111 H2
Rustavi Georgia 113 G2
Rustburg VA U.S.A. 164 F5
Rustenburg S. Africa 125 H3
Ruston LA U.S.A. 161 E5
Ruta Moluccas Indon. 83 C3
Rutanzige, Lake Dem. Rep. Congo/Uganda see Edward, Lake
Ruteng Flores Indon. 83 B5
Ruth NV U.S.A. 159 F2
Rüthen Germany 63 I3
Rutherglen Australia 138 C6
Ruther Glen VA U.S.A. 165 G5
Ruthin U.K. 59 D5
Ruthiyai India 104 D4
Ruth Reservoir CA U.S.A. 158 B1
Rutka r. Russia 52 J4
Rutland VT U.S.A. 165 I2
Rutland Water resr U.K. 59 G6
Rutledge Lake Canada 151 I2
Rutog Xizang China 99 B6
Rutog Xizang China 99 D7
Rutog Xizang China 99 F7
Rutul Russia 113 G2
Ruukki Fin. 54 N4
Ruvuma r. Moz./Tanz. 123 E5 also known as Rovuma
Ruwayshid, Wādī watercourse Jordan 107 C3
Ruwayṭah, Wādī watercourse Jordan 107 C5
Ruweis U.A.E. 110 D5
Ruwenzori National Park Uganda see Queen Elizabeth National Park
Ruy Barbosa Brazil 179 C1
Rūy Dūāb Wuluswālī Afgh. 111 G3
Ruza Russia 52 H5
Ruzayevka Kazakh. 100 F1
Ruzayevka Russia 53 J5
Ruzhou China 95 H5
Ružomberok Slovakia 57 Q6
Rwanda country Africa 122 C4
Ryan, Loch b. U.K. 60 D5
Ryazan' Russia 53 H5
Ryazhsk Russia 53 I5
Rybachiy, Poluostrov pen. Russia 54 R2
Rybach'ye Kazakh. 98 C3
Rybach'ye Kyrg. see Balykchy
Rybinsk Russia 52 H4

▶Rybinskoye Vodokhranilishche resr Russia 52 H4
5th largest lake in Europe.

Rybnik Poland 57 Q5
Rybnitsa Moldova see Rîbnița
Rybnoye Russia 53 H5
Rybreka Russia 52 G3
Ryd Sweden 55 I8
Rydberg Peninsula Antarctica 188 L2
Ryde U.K. 59 F8
Rye U.K. 59 H8
Rye r. U.K. 58 G4
Rye Bay U.K. 59 H8
Ryegate MT U.S.A. 156 F3
Rye Patch Reservoir NV U.S.A. 158 D1
Rykovo Ukr. see Yenakiyeve
Ryl'sk Russia 53 G6
Rylstone Australia 138 D4
Ryn-Peski des. Kazakh. 51 P6
Ryōgami-san mt. Japan 93 E2
Ryōhaku-sanchi mts Japan 92 C3
Ryōkami Japan 93 E2
Ryōzen-zan mt. Japan 92 C3
Ryūga-dake mt. Japan 92 C3
Ryūgasaki Japan 93 G3
Ryukyu Islands Japan 91 B8
Ryūkyū-rettō is Japan see Ryukyu Islands
Ryukyu Trench sea feature N. Pacific Ocean 186 E4
Ryūō Japan 92 C3
Ryūsō-san mt. Japan 93 E3
Ryūyō Japan 93 D4
Rzeszów Poland 53 D6
Rzhaksa Russia 53 I5
Rzhev Russia 52 G4

Sa'ādah al Barṣā' pass Saudi Arabia 107 C5
Saal an der Donau Germany 63 L6
Saale r. Germany 63 L3
Saalfeld/Saale Germany 63 L4
Saanich Canada 150 F5
Saar land Germany see Saarland
Saar r. Germany 62 G5
Saarbrücken Germany 62 G5
Saaremaa i. Estonia 55 M7
Saarenkylä Fin. 54 N3
Saargau reg. Germany 62 G5
Saarijärvi Fin. 54 N5
Saari-Kämä Fin. 54 O3
Saarikoski Fin. 54 L2
Saaristomeren kansallispuisto nat. park Fin. see Skärgårdshavets nationalpark
Saarland land Germany 62 G5
Saarlouis Germany 62 G5
Saatlı Azer. 113 H3
Saatly Azer. see Saatlı
Sab'a Egypt see Saba'ah
Sabá Hond. 166 [inset] I6
Saba'ah Egypt 107 A4
Sab' Ābār Syria 107 C3
Šabac Serbia 69 H2
Sabadell Spain 67 H3
Sabae Japan 92 C3
Sabah state Malaysia 85 G1
Sabak Malaysia 84 C2
Sabalana i. Indon. 83 A4
Sabalana, Kepulauan is Indon. 83 A4
Sabalgarh India 99 B8
Sabana, Archipiélago de is Cuba 169 H4
Sabanagrande Hond. 166 [inset] I6
Sabang Celebes Indon. 83 A2
Sabang Celebes Indon. 83 B3
Sabang Sumatra Indon. 84 A1
Şabanözü Turkey 112 D2
Sabará Brazil 179 C2
Sabaru i. Indon. 83 A4
Sabasṭīyah West Bank 107 B3
Sab'atayn, Ramlat as des. Yemen 108 G6
Sabaudia Italy 68 E4
Sabaya Bol. 176 E7
Sabelo S. Africa 124 F6
Ṣabḥā Jordan 107 C3
Sabhā Libya 121 E2
Ṣabḥā' Saudi Arabia 110 B6
Sabhrai India 104 B5
Sabi r. India 104 D3
Sabi r. Moz./Zimbabwe see Save
Sabie Moz. 125 K3
Sabie r. Moz./S. Africa 125 K3
Sabie S. Africa 125 J3
Sabina OH U.S.A. 164 D4
Sabinal Mex. 166 D2
Sabinal, Cayo i. Cuba 163 E8
Sabinas Mex. 167 E3
Sabinas r. Mex. 161 C7
Sabinas Hidalgo Mex. 167 E3
Sabine r. Louisiana/Texas U.S.A. 161 E6
Sabine Lake Louisiana/Texas U.S.A. 161 E6
Sabine Pass TX U.S.A. 161 E6
Sabini, Monti mts Italy 68 E3
Sabirabad Azer. 113 H2
Sabkhat al Bardawīl Reserve nature res. Egypt see Lake Bardawil Reserve
Sablayan Mindoro Phil. 82 C3
Sable, Cape Canada 153 I6
Sable, Cape FL U.S.A. 163 D7
Sable, Lac du l. Canada 153 I3
Sable Island Canada 153 K6
Sable Island National Park Reserve nat. park Canada 153 K6
Sabon Kafi Niger 120 D3
Şabran Azer. 113 H2
Sabrina Coast Antarctica 188 F2
Sabtang i. Phil. 82 C1
Sabugal Port. 67 C3
Sabulu Celebes Indon. 83 B3
Sabunten i. Indon. 85 F4
Saburyū-yama mt. Japan 93 E2
Ṣabyā Saudi Arabia 108 F6
Sabzak, Kōtal-e Afgh. 111 F3
Sabzawar Afgh. see Shīndand
Sabzevār Iran 110 E2
Sabzvārān Iran see Jīroft
Sacalinul Mare, Insula i. Romania 69 M2
Sacaton AZ U.S.A. 159 H5
Sac City IA U.S.A. 160 E3
Săcele Romania 69 K2
Sacheon S. Korea 91 C6
Sachigo r. Canada 151 N4
Sachigo Lake Canada 151 M4
Sachin India 104 C5
Sach Pass India 104 D2
Sachsen land Germany 63 N3
Sachsen-Anhalt land Germany 63 L2
Sachsenheim Germany 63 J6
Sachs Harbour Canada 146 F2
Sacirsuyu r. Syria/Turkey see Sājūr, Nahr
Sackpfeife hill Germany 63 I4
Sackville Canada 153 I5
Saco ME U.S.A. 165 J2
Saco MT U.S.A. 156 G2
Sacol i. Phil. 82 C5
Sacramento Brazil 179 B2

▶Sacramento CA U.S.A. 158 C2
Capital of California.

Sacramento r. CA U.S.A. 158 C2
Sacramento Mountains NM U.S.A. 157 G6
Sacramento Valley CA U.S.A. 158 B1
Sacxán Mex. 167 H5
Sada S. Africa 125 H7
Sádaba Spain 67 F2
Sá da Bandeira Angola see Lubango
Ṣadad Syria 107 C2
Ṣa'dah Yemen 108 F6
Sadakphu mt. India/Nepal 105 G4
Sadang r. Indon. 83 A3
Sadao Thai. 87 C6
Saddat al Hindīyah Iraq 113 G4
Saddleback Mesa mt. NM U.S.A. 161 C5
Saddle Hill hill Australia 136 D2
Saddle Peak hill India 87 A4
Sadê China 96 D2
Sa Đec Vietnam 87 D5
Sadêng China 96 B2
Sadieville KY U.S.A. 164 C4
Sadīj watercourse Iran 110 E5
Sadiola Mali 120 B3
Sadiqabad Pak. 111 H4
Sad Ishtrāgh mt. Afgh./Pak. 111 I2
Sa'dīyah, Hawr as imp. l. Iraq 113 G4
Sa'diyyat i. U.A.E. 110 D5
Sado r. Port. 67 B4
Sadoga-shima i. Japan 91 E5
Sadong r. Malaysia 85 E2
Sadot Egypt see Sadūt (abandoned)
Sadovoye Russia 53 J7
Sa Dragonera i. Spain 67 H4
Sadras India 106 D3
Sadūt Egypt see Sadūt (abandoned)
Sadūt (abandoned) Egypt 107 B4
Sæby Denmark 55 G8
Saena Julia Italy see Siena
Safad Israel see Ẕefat
Şafāshahr Iran 110 D4
Safayal Maqūf well Iraq 113 G5
Safēd Khir, Kōh-e mts Afgh. 111 H2
Safēd Kōh mts Afgh./Pak. 111 H3
Safēd Kōh, Silsilah-ye mts Afgh. 111 F3
Saffānīyah, Ra's as pt Saudi Arabia 110 C4
Säffle Sweden 55 H7
Safford AZ U.S.A. 159 I5
Saffron Walden U.K. 59 H6
Safi Morocco 64 C5
Safīd, Chashmeh-ye spring Iran 110 E3
Safīdār, Kūh-e mt. Iran 110 D4
Safiras, Serra das mts Brazil 179 C2
Ṣāfītā Syria 107 C2
Safonovo Arkhangel'skaya Oblast' Russia 52 K2
Safonovo Smolenskaya Oblast' Russia 53 G5
Safranbolu Turkey 112 D2
Saga China 99 D7
Saga Japan 91 C6
Saga Kazakh. 102 B1
Sagaing Myanmar 86 A2
Sagamihara Japan 93 F3
Sagamiko Japan 93 F3
Sagami-nada g. Japan 93 F4
Sagami-wan b. Japan 93 F3
Sagamore PA U.S.A. 164 F3
Saganthit Kyun i. Myanmar 87 B4
Sagar Karnataka India 106 B3
Sagar Karnataka India 106 C2
Sagar Madh. Prad. India 104 D5
Sagara Japan 93 E4
Sagaredzho Georgia see Sagarejo
Sagarejo Georgia 113 G2
Sagar Island India 105 G5
Sagarmatha National Park Nepal 105 F4
Sagastyr Russia 77 N2
Sagavanirktok r. AK U.S.A. 149 J1
Sage WY U.S.A. 156 F4
Saggi, Har mt. Israel 107 B4
Sāghand Iran 110 D3
Sagigik Island AK U.S.A. 148 D6
Saginaw MI U.S.A. 164 D2
Saginaw Bay MI U.S.A. 164 D2
Saglek Bay Canada 153 J2
Saglouc Canada see Salluit
Sagly Russia 94 B1
Sagone, Golfe de b. Corsica France 66 I5
Sagres Port. 67 B5
Sagsay Gol watercourse Mongolia 94 D2
Sagthale India 104 C5
Sagu Indon. 83 B5
Saguache CO U.S.A. 157 G5
Sagua la Grande Cuba 169 H4
Saguaro Lake AZ U.S.A. 159 H5
Saguaro National Park AZ U.S.A. 159 H5
Saguenay r. Canada 153 H4
Saguling, Waduk resr Java Indon. 84 D4
Sagunt Spain see Sagunto
Sagunto Spain 67 F4
Saguntum Spain see Sagunto
Sagwon AK U.S.A. 149 J1
Sagzī Iran 110 D3
Sahabab India 99 B7
Sahagún Spain 67 D2
Sahand, Kūh-e mt. Iran 110 B2

▶Sahara des. Africa 120 D3
Largest desert in the world.

Ṣaḥara el Gharbîya des. Egypt see Western Desert
Ṣaḥara el Sharqîya des. Egypt see Eastern Desert
Saharan Atlas mts Alg. see Atlas Saharien
Saharanpur India 104 D3
Sahara Well Australia 134 C5
Saharsa India 105 F4
Sahaswan India 104 D3
Sahat, Kūh-e hill Iran 110 D3
Sahatwar India 105 F4
Şahbuz Azer. 113 G3
Sahdol India see Shahdol
Sahebganj India see Sahibganj
Sahebgunj India see Sahibganj
Saheira, Wâdi el watercourse Egypt see Suhaymī, Wādī as
Sahel reg. Africa 120 C3
Sahibganj India 105 F4
Sahiwal Pak. 111 I4
Sahlābād Iran 111 E3
Ṣaḥm Oman 110 E5
Ṣaḥneh Iran 110 B3
Ṣaḥrā al Ḥijārah reg. Iraq 113 G5
Sahu Halmahera Indon. 83 C2
Sahuaripa Mex. 166 C2
Sahuayo Mex. 168 D4
Sa Huynh Vietnam 87 E4
Sahyadri mts India see Western Ghats
Sahyadriparvat Range hills India 106 B1
Sai r. India 105 E4
Sai Buri Thai. 87 C6
Sai Buri, Mae Nam r. Thai. 84 C1
Saïda Alg. 67 G6
Saïda Lebanon see Sidon
Sa'īdābād Iran 110 E5
Sai Dao Tai, Khao mt. Thai. 87 C4
Saïdia Morocco 67 E6
Sa'īdīyeh Iran see Solṭānīyeh
Saidpur Bangl. 105 G4
Sai-gawa r. Japan 92 C2
Sai-gawa r. Japan 93 E2
Saiha India 105 H5
Saihan Tal China 95 H3
Saihan Toroi China 94 E3
Saijō Japan 91 D6
Saikai Kokuritsu-kōen Japan 91 C6
Saiki Japan 91 C6
Sai Kung H.K. China 97 [inset]
Sailana India 104 C5
Sailolof Papua Indon. 83 D3
Saimaa l. Fin. 55 P6
Saimbeyli Turkey 112 E3
Saindak Pak. 111 F4
St Abb's Head hd U.K. 60 G5
St Agnes U.K. 59 B8
St Agnes i. U.K. 59 A9
St Alban's Canada 153 L5
St Albans U.K. 59 G7
St Albans VT U.S.A. 165 I1
St Albans WV U.S.A. 164 E4
St Alban's Head hd U.K. see St Aldhelm's Head
St Albert Canada 150 H4
St Aldhelm's Head hd U.K. 59 E8
St-Amand-les-Eaux France 62 D4
St-Amand-Montrond France 66 F3
St-Amour France 66 G3
St-André, Cap pt Madag. see Vilanandro, Tanjona
St Andrews U.K. 60 G4
St Andrew Sound inlet GA U.S.A. 163 D6
St Anne IL U.S.A. 164 B3
St Ann's Bay Jamaica 169 I5
St Anthony Canada 153 L4
St Anthony ID U.S.A. 156 F4
St-Arnaud Alg. see El Eulma
St Arnaud Australia 138 A6
St Arnaud Range mts N.Z. 139 D6
St-Arnoult-en-Yvelines France 62 B6
St Asaph Bay Australia 83 D5
St-Augustin Canada 153 K4
St Augustin r. Canada 153 K4
St Augustine FL U.S.A. 163 D6
St Austell U.K. 59 C8
St-Avertin France 66 E3
St-Avold France 62 G5
St Barbe Canada 153 K4

▶St-Barthélemy i. West Indies 169 L5
French Overseas Collectivity.

St Bees U.K. 58 D4
St Bees Head hd U.K. 58 D4
St Bride's Bay U.K. 59 B7
St-Brieuc France 66 C2
St Catharines Canada 164 F2
St Catherines Island GA U.S.A. 163 D6
St Catherine's Point U.K. 59 F8
St-Céré France 66 E4
St-Chamond France 66 G4
St Charles ID U.S.A. 156 F4
St Charles MD U.S.A. 165 G4
St Charles MI U.S.A. 164 C2
St Charles MO U.S.A. 160 F4
St-Chély-d'Apcher France 66 F4
St Christopher and Nevis country West Indies see St Kitts and Nevis
St Clair r. Canada/U.S.A. 164 D2
St Clair, Lake Canada/U.S.A. 164 D2
St-Claude France 66 G3
St Clears U.K. 59 C7
St Cloud MN U.S.A. 160 E2
St Croix r. WI U.S.A. 152 B5
St Croix Falls WI U.S.A. 160 E2
St David AZ U.S.A. 159 H6
St David's Head hd U.K. 59 B7
St-Denis France 62 C6

▶St-Denis Réunion 185 L7
Capital of Réunion.

St-Denis-du-Sig Alg. see Sig
St-Dié-des-Vosges France 66 H2
St-Dizier France 62 E6
St-Domingue country West Indies see Haiti
Sainte Anne Canada 151 L5
Ste-Anne, Lac l. Canada 153 I4
St Elias, Cape AK U.S.A. 149 K4

▶St Elias, Mount AK U.S.A. 149 L3
4th highest mountain in North America.

St Elias Mountains Canada 149 L3
Ste-Marguerite r. Canada 153 I4
Ste-Marie, Cap c. Madag. see Vohimena, Tanjona
Sainte-Marie, Île i. Madag. see Boraha, Nosy
Ste-Maxime France 66 H5
Sainte Rose du Lac Canada 151 L5
Saintes France 66 D4
Sainte Thérèse, Lac l. Canada 150 F1
St-Étienne France 66 G4
St-Étienne-du-Rouvray France 62 B5
St-Fabien Canada 153 H4
St-Félicien Canada 153 G4
Saintfield U.K. 61 G3
St-Florent Corsica France 66 I5
St-Florent-sur-Cher France 66 F3
St-Flour France 66 F4
St Francis KS U.S.A. 160 C4
St Francis r. Arkansas/Missouri U.S.A. 161 F5
St Francis Isles Australia 135 F8
St Francisville LA U.S.A. 161 F6
St-François r. Canada 153 G5
St-François, Lac l. Canada 153 H5
St-Gaudens France 66 E5
St George Australia 138 D2
St George r. Australia 136 D3
St George AK U.S.A. 148 E4
St George SC U.S.A. 163 D5
St George UT U.S.A. 159 G3
St George, Point CA U.S.A. 156 B4
St George Island AK U.S.A. 148 E4
St George Range hills Australia 134 D4
St-Georges Canada 153 H5

▶St George's Grenada 169 L6
Capital of Grenada.

St George's Bay Nfld. and Lab. Canada 153 K4
St George's Bay N.S. Canada 153 J5
St George's Caye i. Belize 167 I5
St George's Channel Ireland/U.K. 61 F6
St George's Channel P.N.G. 132 F2
St George's Head hd Australia 138 E5
St Gotthard Hungary see Szentgotthárd
St Gotthard Pass Switz. 66 I3
St Govan's Head hd U.K. 59 C7
St Helen MI U.S.A. 164 C1
St Helena i. S. Atlantic Ocean 184 H7
St Helena CA U.S.A. 158 B2

▶St Helena, Ascension and Tristan da Cunha terr. S. Atlantic Ocean 184 H7
United Kingdom Overseas Territory.

St Helena Bay S. Africa 124 D7
St Helens Australia 137 [inset]
St Helens U.K. 58 E5
St Helens OR U.S.A. 156 C3
St Helens, Mount vol. WA U.S.A. 156 C3
St Helens Point Australia 137 [inset]

▶St Helier Channel Is 59 E9
Capital of Jersey.

Sainthiya India 105 F5
St-Hubert Belgium 62 F4
St-Hyacinthe Canada 153 G5
St Ignace MI U.S.A. 162 C2
St Ignace Island Canada 152 D4
St Ishmael U.K. 59 C7
St Ives England U.K. 59 B8
St Ives England U.K. 59 G6
St-Jacques, Cap Vietnam see Vung Tau
St-Jacques-de-Dupuy Canada 152 F4
St James MN U.S.A. 160 E3
St James MO U.S.A. 160 F4
St James, Cape Canada 149 O6
St-Jean r. Canada 153 I4
St-Jean, Lac l. Canada 153 G4
St-Jean-d'Acre Israel see 'Akko
St-Jean-d'Angély France 66 D4
St-Jean-de-Monts France 66 C3
St-Jean-sur-Richelieu Canada 165 I1
St-Jérôme Canada 152 G5
St Joe r. ID U.S.A. 156 D3
Saint John Canada 153 I5
St John KS U.S.A. 160 D4
St John r. ME U.S.A. 162 H2
St John, Cape Canada 153 L4
St John Bay Canada 153 K4
St John Island Canada 153 K4

▶St John's Antigua and Barbuda 169 L5
Capital of Antigua and Barbuda.

▶St John's Canada 153 L5
Capital of Newfoundland and Labrador.

St Johns AZ U.S.A. 159 I4
St Johns MI U.S.A. 164 C2
St Johns OH U.S.A. 164 C3
St Johns r. FL U.S.A. 163 D6
St Johnsbury VT U.S.A. 165 I1
St John's Chapel U.K. 58 E4
St Joseph IL U.S.A. 164 A3
St Joseph LA U.S.A. 161 F6
St Joseph MI U.S.A. 164 B2
St Joseph MO U.S.A. 160 E4
St Joseph r. MI U.S.A. 164 C3
St Joseph, Lake Canada 151 N5
St-Joseph-d'Alma Canada see Alma
St Joseph Island Canada 152 E5
St Joseph Island TX U.S.A. 167 F3
St-Junien France 66 E4
St Just U.K. 59 B8
St-Just-en-Chaussée France 62 C5
St Keverne U.K. 59 B8
St Kilda i. U.K. 50 E4
St Kilda is U.K. 56 C2
St Kitts and Nevis country West Indies 169 L5
St-Laurent inlet Canada see St Lawrence
St-Laurent, Golfe du g. Canada see St Lawrence, Gulf of
St-Laurent-du-Maroni Fr. Guiana 177 H2
St Lawrence Canada 153 L5
St Lawrence inlet Canada 153 H4
St Lawrence, Cape Canada 153 J5
St Lawrence, Gulf of Canada 153 J4
St Lawrence Island AK U.S.A. 148 E3
St Lawrence Islands National Park Canada 165 H1
St Lawrence Seaway sea chan. Canada/U.S.A. 165 H1
St-Léonard Canada 153 G5
St Leonard MD U.S.A. 165 G4
St Lewis r. Canada 153 K3
St-Lô France 66 D2
St-Louis Senegal 120 B3
St Louis MI U.S.A. 164 C2
St Louis MO U.S.A. 160 F4
St Louis r. MN U.S.A. 152 B5
St Lucia country West Indies 169 L6
St Lucia, Lake S. Africa 125 K5
St Lucia Estuary S. Africa 125 K5
St Luke's Island Myanmar see Zadetkale Kyun
St Magnus Bay U.K. 60 [inset]
St-Maixent-l'École France 66 D3
St-Malo France 66 C2
St-Malo, Golfe de g. France 66 C2
St-Marc Haiti 169 J5
St Maries ID U.S.A. 156 D3
St Marks S. Africa 125 H7
St Mark's S. Africa see Cofimvaba

▶St-Martin i. West Indies 169 L5
French Overseas Collectivity. The southern part of the island is the Dutch territory of Sint Maarten.

St-Martin terr. West Indies see Sint Maarten
St Martin, Cape S. Africa 124 C7
St Martin, Lake Canada 151 L5
St Martin's i. U.K. 59 A9
St Martin's Island Bangl. 86 A2
St Mary Peak Australia 137 B6
St Mary Reservoir Canada 150 H5
St Mary's Canada 164 E2
St Mary's U.K. 60 G2
St Mary's i. U.K. 59 A9
St Marys AK U.S.A. 148 G3
St Marys PA U.S.A. 165 F3
St Marys WV U.S.A. 164 E4
St Marys r. OH U.S.A. 164 C3
St Mary's, Cape Canada 153 L5
St Mary's Bay Canada 153 L5
St Marys City MD U.S.A. 165 G4
St Matthew Island AK U.S.A. 148 D3
St Matthews KY U.S.A. 164 C4
St Matthew's Island Myanmar see Zadetkyi Kyun
St Matthias Group is P.N.G. 81 L7
St-Maurice r. Canada 153 G5
St Mawes U.K. 59 B8
St-Médard-en-Jalles France 66 D4
St Meinrad IN U.S.A. 164 B4
St Michael AK U.S.A. 148 G3
St Michaels MD U.S.A. 165 G4
St Michael's Bay Canada 153 L3
St-Mihiel France 62 F6
St-Nazaire France 66 C3
St Neots U.K. 59 G6
St-Nicolas Belgium see Sint-Niklaas
St-Nicolas, Mont hill Lux. 62 G5
St-Nicolas-de-Port France 66 H2
St-Omer France 62 C4
Saintonge reg. France 66 D4
St-Pacôme Canada 153 H5
St-Palais France 66 D5
St Paris OH U.S.A. 164 D3
St-Pascal Canada 153 H5
St Paul r. Canada 153 K4
St-Paul atoll Fr. Polynesia see Hereheretue
St Paul AK U.S.A. 148 E4

▶St Paul MN U.S.A. 160 E2
Capital of Minnesota.

St Paul NE U.S.A. 160 D3
St-Paul, Île i. Indian Ocean 185 N8
St Paul Island AK U.S.A. 148 E4

St Peter and St Paul Rocks is N. Atlantic Ocean see São Pedro e São Paulo

▶St Peter Port Channel Is 59 E9
Capital of Guernsey.

St Peter's Canada 153 J5
St Peters Canada 153 J5
St Petersburg Russia 55 Q7
St Petersburg FL U.S.A. 163 D7
St-Pierre mt. France 66 G5

▶St-Pierre St Pierre and Miquelon 153 L5
Capital of St Pierre and Miquelon.

▶St Pierre and Miquelon terr. N. America 153 K5
French Territorial Collectivity.

St-Pierre-d'Oléron France 66 D4
St-Pierre-le-Moûtier France 66 F3
St-Pol-sur-Ternoise France 62 C4
St-Pourçain-sur-Sioule France 66 F3
St-Quentin France 62 D5
St Regis MT U.S.A. 156 E3
St Regis Falls NY U.S.A. 165 H1
St-Rémi Canada 165 I1
St-Saëns France 62 B5
St Sebastian Bay S. Africa 124 E8
St-Siméon Canada 153 H5
St Simons Island GA U.S.A. 163 D6
St Theresa Point Canada 151 M4
St Thomas Canada 164 E2
St-Trond Belgium see Sint-Truiden
St-Tropez France 66 H5
St-Tropez, Cap de c. France 66 H5
St-Vaast-la-Hougue France 59 F9
St-Valery-en-Caux France 59 H9
St-Véran France 66 H4
St Vincent MN U.S.A. 160 D1
St Vincent country West Indies see St Vincent and the Grenadines
St Vincent, Cape Australia 137 [inset]
St Vincent, Cape Port. see São Vicente, Cabo de
St Vincent, Gulf Australia 137 B7
St Vincent and the Grenadines country West Indies 169 L6
St Vincent Passage St Lucia/St Vincent 169 L6
St-Vith Belgium 62 G4
St Walburg Canada 151 I4
St Williams Canada 164 E2
St-Yrieix-la-Perche France 66 E4
Sain Us China 95 F3
Saioa mt. Spain 67 F2
Saipal mt. Nepal 104 E3
Saipan i. N. Mariana Is 81 L3
Saipan Palau 82 [inset]
Sai Pok Liu Hoi Hap H.K. China see West Lamma Channel
Saitama pref. Japan 93 E3
Saiteli Turkey see Kadınhanı
Saittanulkki hill Fin. 54 N3
Sai Yok National Park Thai. 87 B4
Sajam Indon. 81 I7
Sajama, Nevado mt. Bol. 176 E7
Sājir Saudi Arabia 110 B5
Sājūr, Nahr r. Syria/Turkey 107 D1
Sak watercourse S. Africa 124 E5
Sakado Japan 93 F3
Sakae Chiba Japan 93 G3
Sakae Nagano Japan 93 E2
Sakai Fukui Japan 92 C2
Sakai Gunma Japan 93 F2
Sakai Ibaraki Japan 93 F2
Sakai Nagano Japan 93 E2
Sakai Ōsaka Japan 92 B4
Sakaide Japan 91 D6
Sakaigawa Japan 93 E3
Sakākā Saudi Arabia 113 F5
Sakakawea, Lake ND U.S.A. 160 C2
Sakaki Japan 93 E2
Sakala i. Indon. 85 G4
Sakami Canada 152 G3
Sakami r. Canada 152 F3
Sakami-gawa r. Japan 93 F3
Sakami Lake Canada 152 F3
Sakar mts Bulg. 69 L4
Sakaraha Madag. 123 E6
Sak'art'velo country Asia see Georgia
Sakarya Turkey see Adapazarı
Sakarya r. Turkey 69 N4
Sakashita Japan 92 D3
Sakassou Côte d'Ivoire 120 C4
Sakata Japan 91 E5
Sakauchi Japan 92 C3
Sakchu N. Korea 91 B4
Saken Seyfullin Kazakh. 98 A2
Sakesar Pak. 111 I3
Sakhalin i. Russia 90 F2
Sakhalin Oblast admin. div. Russia see Sakhalinskaya Oblast'
Sakhalinskaya Oblast' admin. div. Russia 90 F2
Sakhalinskiy Zaliv b. Russia 90 F1
Sakhi India 104 C3
Sakhile S. Africa 125 I4
Şäki Azer. 113 G2
Saki Crimea see Saky
Saki Nigeria 120 D4
Šakiai Lith. 55 M9
Sakir mt. Pak. 111 G4
Sakishima-shotō is Japan 89 M8
Sakoli India 104 D5
Sakon Nakhon Thai. 86 D3
Sakrivier S. Africa 124 E6
Saku Japan 93 E2
Sakuho Japan 93 E2
Sakuma Japan 93 D3
Sakura Chiba Japan 93 G3
Sakura Tochigi Japan 93 F2
Sakuragawa Ibaraki Japan 93 G2
Sakuragawa Ibaraki Japan 93 G3
Sakura-gawa r. Japan 93 G2
Sakurai Japan 92 B4
Saku-shima i. Japan 92 D4
Saky Crimea 112 D1
Säkylä Fin. 55 M6
Sākzā'ī Afgh. 111 F3
Sal i. Cape Verde 120 [inset]
Sal r. Russia 53 I7
Sal, Punta pt Hond. 166 [inset] I6
Sala Sweden 55 J7
Salabangka, Kepulauan is Indon. 83 B3
Salaberry-de-Valleyfield Canada 165 H1
Salacgrīva Latvia 55 N8
Sala Consilina Italy 68 F4
Salada, Laguna salt l. Mex. 166 B1
Saladas Arg. 178 E3
Salado r. Buenos Aires Arg. 178 E5
Salado r. Santa Fe Arg. 178 D4
Salado r. Arg. 178 C5
Salado r. Mex. 167 F3
Salaga Ghana 120 C4
Salairskiy Kryazh ridge Russia 88 E2
Salajwe Botswana 124 G2
Şalālah Oman 109 H6
Salamá Guat. 167 H6
Salamá Hond. 166 [inset] I6
Salamanca Mex. 168 D4
Salamanca Spain 67 D3
Salamanca NY U.S.A. 165 F2
Salamanga Moz. 125 K4
Salamantica Spain see Salamanca
Salamat, Bahr r. Chad 121 E4
Salamban Kalimantan Indon. 85 F3
Salāmī Iran 111 E3
Salamina i. Greece 69 J6
Salamis tourist site Cyprus 107 A2
Salamís i. Greece see Salamina
Salamīyah Syria 107 C2
Salamonie r. IN U.S.A. 164 C3
Salamonie Lake IN U.S.A. 164 C3
Sālang, Tōnal-e Afgh. 111 H3
Salantai Lith. 55 L8
Salaqi China 95 G3
Salar de Pocitos Arg. 178 C2
Salari Pak. 111 G5
Salas Spain 67 C2
Salaspils Latvia 55 N8
Salatiga Java Indon. 85 E4
Salavan Laos 86 D4
Salawati i. Papua Indon. 83 D3
Salawin, Mae Nam r. China/Myanmar see Salween
Salay Mindanao Phil. 82 D4
Salaya India 104 B5
Sala y Gómez, Isla i. S. Pacific Ocean 187 M7
Salazar Angola see N'dalatando
Salbris France 66 F3
Salcha r. AK U.S.A. 149 K2
Šalčininkai Lith. 55 N9
Salcombe U.K. 59 D8
Saldae Alg. see Bejaïa
Saldaña Spain 67 D2
Saldanha S. Africa 124 C7
Saldanha Bay S. Africa 124 C7
Saldus Latvia 55 M8
Sale Australia 138 C7
Salea Celebes Indon. 83 B3
Saleh, Teluk b. Sumbawa Indon. 85 G5
Şāleḩābād Iran 110 C3
Salekhard Russia 76 H3
Salem India 106 C4
Salem AR U.S.A. 161 F4
Salem IL U.S.A. 160 F4
Salem IN U.S.A. 164 B4
Salem MA U.S.A. 165 J2
Salem MO U.S.A. 160 F4
Salem NJ U.S.A. 165 H4
Salem NY U.S.A. 165 I2
Salem OH U.S.A. 164 E3

▶Salem OR U.S.A. 156 C3
Capital of Oregon.

Salem SD U.S.A. 160 D3
Salem VA U.S.A. 164 E5
Salen Scotland U.K. 60 D4
Salen Scotland U.K. 60 D4
Salerno Italy 68 F4
Salerno, Golfo di g. Italy 68 F4
Salernum Italy see Salerno
Salford U.K. 58 E5
Salgótarján Hungary 57 Q6
Salgueiro Brazil 177 K5
Salibabu i. Indon. 83 C2
Salida CO U.S.A. 157 G5
Salies-de-Béarn France 66 D5
Şālīḩān Afgh. 111 F4
Salihli Turkey 69 M5
Salihorsk Belarus 55 O10
Salima Malawi 123 D5
Salimbatu Kalimantan Indon. 85 G2
Salina KS U.S.A. 160 D4
Salina UT U.S.A. 159 H2
Salina, Isola i. Italy 68 F5
Salina Cruz Mex. 168 E5
Salinas Brazil 179 C2
Salinas Ecuador 176 B4
Salinas Mex. 168 D4
Salinas r. Mex. 161 D7
Salinas CA U.S.A. 158 C3
Salinas r. CA U.S.A. 158 C3
Salinas, Cabo de c. Spain see Salines, Cap de ses
Salinas, Ponta das pt Angola 123 B5
Salinas Peak NM U.S.A. 157 G6
Saline MI U.S.A. 164 D2
Saline r. KS U.S.A. 160 D4
Salines, Cap de ses c. Spain 67 H4
Saline Valley depr. CA U.S.A. 158 E3
Salinópolis Brazil 177 I4
Salinosó Lachay, Punta pt Peru 176 C6
Salisbury U.K. 59 F7
Salisbury MD U.S.A. 165 H4
Salisbury NC U.S.A. 162 D5
Salisbury Zimbabwe see Harare
Salisbury, Mount AK U.S.A. 149 K1
Salisbury Plain U.K. 59 E7
Şalkhad Syria 107 C3
Salla Fin. 54 P3
Sallisaw OK U.S.A. 161 E5
Salluit Canada 189 K2
Sallum, Khalīj as b. Egypt 112 B5
Sallyana Nepal 105 E3
Salmās Iran 110 B2
Salmi Russia 52 F3
Salmo Canada 150 G5
Salmon ID U.S.A. 156 E3
Salmon r. ID U.S.A. 156 D3
Salmon Arm Canada 150 G5
Salmon Falls Creek r. Idaho/Nevada U.S.A. 156 E4
Salmon Fork r. Canada/U.S.A. 149 L2
Salmon Gums Australia 135 C8
Salmon Reservoir NY U.S.A. 165 H2
Salmon River Mountains ID U.S.A. 156 E3
Salmon Village AK U.S.A. 149 L2
Salmtal Germany 62 G5
Salo Fin. 55 M6
Salome AZ U.S.A. 159 G5
Salon India 104 E4
Salon-de-Provence France 66 G5
Salonga Nord, Parc National de la nat. park Dem. Rep. Congo 122 C4
Salonica Greece see Thessaloniki
Salonika Greece see Thessaloniki
Saloum Delta tourist site Senegal 120 B3
Salpausselkä reg. Fin. 55 N6
Salqīn Syria 107 C1
Salses, Étang de l. France see Leucate, Étang de
Sal'sk Russia 53 I7
Salsomaggiore Terme Italy 68 C2
Salt Jordan see As Salţ
Salt watercourse S. Africa 124 F7
Salt r. AZ U.S.A. 159 G5
Salta Arg. 178 C2
Saltaire U.K. 58 F5
Saltash U.K. 59 C8
Saltcoats U.K. 60 E5
Saltee Islands Ireland 61 F5
Saltfjellet-Svartisen Nasjonalpark nat. park Norway 54 I3
Saltfjorden sea chan. Norway 54 H3
Salt Flat TX U.S.A. 166 D2
Salt Fork Arkansas r. KS U.S.A. 161 D4
Salt Fork Lake OH U.S.A. 164 E3
Saltillo Mex. 167 E3
Salt Lake India 111 I5

▶Salt Lake City UT U.S.A. 159 H1
Capital of Utah.

Salt Lick KY U.S.A. 164 D4
Salto Brazil 179 B3
Salto Uruguay 178 E4
Salto da Divisa Brazil 179 D2
Salto de Agua Mex. 167 G5
Salto Grande Brazil 179 A3
Salton Sea salt l. CA U.S.A. 159 F5
Salto Santiago, Represa de resr Brazil 178 F3
Salt Range hills Pak. 111 I3
Salt River Canada 151 H2
Saluda VA U.S.A. 165 G5
Saluebesar i. Indon. 83 B3
Saluekecil i. Indon. 83 B3
Salue Timpaus, Selat sea chan. Indon. 83 B3
Sālūk, Kūh-e mt. Iran 110 E2
Salûm Egypt see As Sallūm
Salûm, Khalîg el b. Egypt see Sallum, Khalīj as
Salur India 106 D2
Saluzzo Italy 68 B2
Salvador Brazil 179 D1
Salvador country Central America see El Salvador
Salvador, Lake LA U.S.A. 161 F6
Salvaleón de Higüey Dom. Rep. see Higüey
Salvatierra Mex. 167 E4
Salvation Creek r. UT U.S.A. 159 H2
Salwah Saudi Arabia 122 F1
Salwah, Dawḩat b. Qatar/Saudi Arabia 110 C5
Salween r. China/Myanmar 96 C5
also known as Mae Nam Khong or Mae Nam Salawin or Nu Jiang (China) or Thanlwin (Myanmar)
Salyan Azer. 113 H3
Salyan Nepal see Sallyana
Sal'yany Azer. see Salyan
Salyersville KY U.S.A. 164 D5
Salzbrunn Namibia 124 C3
Salzburg Austria 57 N7
Salzgitter Germany 63 K2
Salzhausen Germany 63 K1
Salzkotten Germany 63 I3
Salzmünde Germany 63 L3
Salzwedel Germany 63 L2
Sam India 104 B4
Samae San, Ko i. Thai. 87 C4
Samagaltay Russia 94 C1
Samāh well Saudi Arabia 110 B4
Samaida Iran see Someydeh
Samaixung China 99 C6
Samak, Tanjung pt Indon. 84 D3
Samakhixai Laos see Attapu
Samal i. Phil. 82 D5
Samalanga Sumatra Indon. 84 B1
Samalantan Kalimantan Indon. 85 E2
Samalayuca Mex. 166 D2
Samales Group is Phil. 82 C5
Samalga Pass sea chan. AK U.S.A. 148 E5
Samalkot India 106 D2
Samālūţ Egypt 112 C5
Samâlûţ Egypt see Samālūţ
Samana Cay i. Bahamas 163 F8
Samanala mt. Sri Lanka see Adam's Peak
Samandağı Turkey 107 B1
Samangān Afgh. see Aībak
Samangān Iran 111 F3
Samani Japan 90 F4
Samanlı Dağları mts Turkey 69 M4
Samar Kazakh. see Samarskoye
Samar i. Phil. 82 D4
Samara Russia 53 K5
Samara r. Russia 51 Q5
Samarahan Sarawak Malaysia see Sri Aman
Samarga Russia 90 E3
Samarinda Kalimantan Indon. 85 G3
Samarka Russia 90 D3
Samarkand Uzbek. see Samarqand
Samarkand, Pik mt. Tajik. see Samarqand, Qullai
Samarobriva France see Amiens
Samarqand Uzbek. 111 G2
Samarqand, Qullai mt. Tajik. 111 H2
Sāmarrā' Iraq 113 F4
Samar Sea g. Phil. 82 D4
Samarskoye Kazakh. 102 F2
Samasata Pak. 111 H4
Samastipur India 105 F4
Samate Papua Indon. 83 D3
Şamaxı Azer. 113 H2
Samba India 104 C2
Samba r. Indon. 85 F3
Sambaliung mts Indon. 85 G2
Sambalpur India 105 E5
Sambar, Tanjung pt Indon. 85 E3
Sambas Kalimantan Indon. 85 E2
Sambat Ukr. see Kiev
Sambava Madag. 123 F5
Sambha India 105 G4
Sambhajinagar India see Aurangabad
Sambhal India 104 D3
Sambhar Lake India 104 C4
Sambiat Celebes Indon. 83 B3
Sambir Ukr. 53 D6
Sambit i. Indon. 85 G2
Sambito r. Brazil 177 J5
Samboja Kalimantan Indon. 85 G3
Sâmbor Cambodia 87 D4
Sambor Ukr. see Sambir
Samborombón, Bahía b. Arg. 178 E5
Sambre r. Belgium/France 62 E4
Sambre à l'Oise, Canal de la France 62 D5
Sambu Japan see Sanbu
Samcheok S. Korea 91 C5
Samch'ŏnp'o S. Korea see Sacheon
Same Tanz. 122 D4
Samegawa Japan 93 G1
Samer France 62 B4
Sami India 104 B5
Samia, Tanjung pt Indon. 83 B2
Samīrah Saudi Arabia 108 F4
Samīrum Iran see Īzad Khvāst
Samizu Japan 93 E2
Samjiyŏn N. Korea 90 C4
Şämkir Azer. 113 G2
Sam Neua Laos see Xam Nua
Samoa country S. Pacific Ocean 133 I3
Samoa Basin sea feature S. Pacific Ocean 186 I7
Samoa i Sisifo country S. Pacific Ocean see Samoa
Samobor Croatia 68 F2
Samoded Russia 52 I3
Samokov Bulg. 69 J3
Šamorín Slovakia 57 P6
Samos i. Greece 69 L6
Samosir i. Indon. 84 B2
Samothrace i. Greece see Samothraki
Samothraki i. Greece 69 K4
Samoylovka Russia 53 I6
Sampaga Celebes Indon. 83 A3
Sampang Java Indon. 85 F4
Sampit Kalimantan Indon. 85 F3
Sampit r. Indon. 85 F3
Sampit, Teluk b. Indon. 85 F3
Sampolawa Celebes Indon. 83 B4
Sâmraông Cambodia 87 C4
Sam Rayburn Reservoir TX U.S.A. 161 E6
Samrong Cambodia see Sâmraông
Samsang China 99 C7
Sam Sao, Phou mts Laos/Vietnam 86 C2
Samson AL U.S.A. 163 C6
Sâm Sơn Vietnam 86 D3
Samsun Turkey 112 E2
Samsy Kazakh. 98 B4
Samtī Afgh. 111 H2
Samui, Ko i. Thai. 87 C5
Samukawa Japan 93 F3
Samut Prakan Thai. 87 C4
Samut Sakhon Thai. 87 C4
Samut Songkhram Thai. 87 C4
Samyai China 99 E7
San Mali 120 C3
San, Phou mt. Laos 86 C3
San, Tônlé r. Cambodia 87 D4

▶Şan'ā' Yemen 108 F6
Capital of Yemen.

Sanaa Yemen see Şan'ā'
Sanada Japan 93 E2
SANAE IV research station Antarctica 188 B2
Sanage Japan 92 D3
San Agostín FL U.S.A. see St Augustine
San Agustin, Cape Mindanao Phil. 82 D5
San Agustin, Plains of NM U.S.A. 159 I5
San Agustín de Valle Fértil Arg. 178 C4
Sanak AK U.S.A. 148 G5
Sanak Island AK U.S.A. 148 G5
Sanana Moluccas Indon. 83 C3
Sanandaj Iran 110 B3
San Andreas CA U.S.A. 158 C2
San Andrés Guat. 167 H5
San Andres Phil. 82 D3
San Andrés, Isla de i. Caribbean Sea 169 H6
San Andres Mountains NM U.S.A. 157 G6
San Andrés Tuxtla Mex. 167 G5
San Angelo TX U.S.A. 161 C6
San Antonio Belize 167 H5
San Antonio Chile 178 B4
San Antonio Luzon Phil. 82 C3
San Antonio NM U.S.A. 157 G6
San Antonio TX U.S.A. 161 D6
San Antonio r. TX U.S.A. 161 D6
San Antonio, Cabo c. Cuba 169 H4
San Antonio Bay Palawan Phil. 82 B4
San Antonio del Mar Mex. 166 A2
San Antonio de Oriente Hond. 166 [inset] I6
San Antonio Oeste Arg. 178 D6
San Antonio Reservoir CA U.S.A. 158 C4
San Augustine TX U.S.A. 161 E6
San Bartolo Mex. 167 E4
San Benedetto del Tronto Italy 68 E3
San Benedicto, Isla i. Mex. 168 B5
San Benito Guat. 167 H5
San Benito TX U.S.A. 161 D7
San Benito r. CA U.S.A. 158 C3
San Benito Mountain CA U.S.A. 158 C3
San Bernardino CA U.S.A. 158 E4
San Bernardino Mountains CA U.S.A. 158 E4
San Bernardino Strait Phil. 82 D3
San Bernardo Chile 178 B4
San Bernardo Mex. 166 D3
San Blas Nayarit Mex. 166 D4
San Blas Sinaloa Mex. 166 C3
San Blas, Archipiélago de is Panama 166 [inset] K7
San Blas, Cape FL U.S.A. 163 C6
San Blas, Serranía de mts Panama 166 [inset] K7
San Borja Bol. 176 E6
Sanbornville NH U.S.A. 165 J2
Sanbu China see Kaiping
Sanbu Japan 93 G3
San Buenaventura Mex. 167 E3
San Carlos Chile 178 B5
San Carlos Equat. Guinea see Luba
San Carlos Coahuila Mex. 167 E2
San Carlos Tamaulipas Mex. 161 D7
San Carlos Nicaragua 166 [inset] I7
San Carlos Luzon Phil. 82 C3
San Carlos Negros Phil. 82 C4
San Carlos AZ U.S.A. 159 H5
San Carlos Venez. 176 E2
San Carlos de Bariloche Arg. 178 B6
San Carlos de Bolívar Arg. 178 D5
San Carlos Indian Reservation res. AZ U.S.A. 166 C1
San Carlos Lake AZ U.S.A. 159 H5
Sancha Gansu China 94 F5
Sancha Shanxi China 95 G4
Sanchahe China see Fuyu
Sancha He r. China 96 E3
Sanchakou Gansu China 94 D4
Sanchakou Xinjiang China 98 B5
Sanchi India 104 D5
San Chien Pau mt. Laos 86 C2
Sanchor India 104 B4
San Ciro de Acosta Mex. 167 F4
San Clemente CA U.S.A. 158 E5
San Clemente Island CA U.S.A. 158 D5
Sanclêr U.K. see St Clears
Sanco Point Mindanao Phil. 82 D4
San Cristóbal Arg. 178 D4
San Cristóbal i. Solomon Is see Makira
San Cristóbal Venez. 176 D2
San Cristóbal, Isla i. Galápagos Ecuador 176 [inset]
San Cristóbal, Volcán vol. Nicaragua 166 [inset] I6
San Cristóbal de las Casas Mex. 167 G5
Sancti Spíritus Cuba 169 I4
Sanda Japan 92 B4
Sandagou Russia 90 D4
Sandai Kalimantan Indon. 85 E3
Sanda Island U.K. 60 D5
Sandakan Sabah Malaysia 85 G1
Sandakan, Pelabuhan inlet Malaysia 85 G1
Sandakphu Peak India 99 E8
Sândăn Cambodia 87 D4
Sandane Norway 54 E6
Sandanski Bulg. 69 J4
Sandaohezi China see Shawan
Sandaré Mali 120 B3
Sandau (Elbe) Germany 63 M2
Sanday i. U.K. 60 G1
Sandbach U.K. 59 E5
Sandborn IN U.S.A. 164 B4
Sand Cay reef India 106 B4
Sandefjord Norway 55 G7
Sandercock Nunataks Antarctica 188 D2
Sanders AZ U.S.A. 159 I4
Sandersleben Germany 63 L3
Sanderson TX U.S.A. 161 C6
Sandfire Australia 134 C4
Sand Fork WV U.S.A. 164 E4
Sandgate Australia 138 F1
Sandhead U.K. 60 E6
Sand Hill r. MN U.S.A. 160 D2
Sand Hills NE U.S.A. 160 C3
Sandia Peru 176 E6
San Diego Mex. 166 D2
San Diego CA U.S.A. 158 E5
San Diego TX U.S.A. 161 D7
San Diego, Sierra mts Mex. 166 C2
Sandıklı Turkey 69 N5
Sandila India 104 E4
Sanding i. Indon. 84 C3
Sand Islands AK U.S.A. 148 F3
Sand Lake Canada 152 D5
Sand Lake l. Canada 151 M5
Sandnes Norway 55 D7
Sandnessjøen Norway 54 H3
Sandoa Dem. Rep. Congo 123 C4
Sandomierz Poland 53 D6
San Donà di Piave Italy 68 E2
Sandover watercourse Australia 136 B4
Sandovo Russia 52 H4
Sandoway Myanmar see Thandwe
Sandown U.K. 59 F8
Sandoy i. Faroe Is 54 [inset 2]
Sand Point AK U.S.A. 148 G5
Sandpoint ID U.S.A. 156 D2
Sandray i. U.K. 60 B4
Sandringham Australia 136 B5
Şandrul Mare, Vârful mt. Romania 69 L1
Sandsjö Sweden 55 I6
Sandspit Canada 149 O5
Sand Springs OK U.S.A. 161 D4
Sand Springs Salt Flat NV U.S.A. 158 D2
Sandstone Australia 135 B6
Sandstone MN U.S.A. 160 E2
Sandu Guizhou China 96 E3
Sandu Hunan China 97 G3
Sandur Faroe Is 54 [inset 2]
Sandusky MI U.S.A. 164 D2
Sandusky OH U.S.A. 164 D3
Sandveld mts S. Africa 124 D6
Sandverhaar Namibia 124 C4
Sandvika Akershus Norway 55 G7
Sandvika Nord-Trøndelag Norway 54 H5
Sandviken Sweden 55 J6
Sandwich Bay Canada 153 K3
Sandwich Island Vanuatu see Éfaté
Sandwich Islands is N. Pacific Ocean see Hawai'ian Islands
Sandwick U.K. 60 [inset]
Sandwip Bangl. 105 G5
Sandy UT U.S.A. 159 H1
Sandy r. ME U.S.A. 165 K1
Sandy Bay Canada 151 K4
Sandy Cape Qld Australia 136 F5
Sandy Cape Tas. Australia 137 [inset]
Sandy Hook KY U.S.A. 164 D4
Sandy Hook pt NJ U.S.A. 165 H3
Sandy Island Australia 134 C3
Sandykgachy Turkm. see Sandykgaçy
Sandykgaçy Turkm. 111 F2
Sandykly Gumy des. Turkm. 111 F2
Sandy Lake Alta Canada 150 H4
Sandy Lake Ont. Canada 151 M4
Sandy Lake l. Canada 151 M4
Sandy Springs GA U.S.A. 163 C5
San Estanislao Para. 178 E2
San Esteban, Isla i. Mex. 166 B2
San Felipe Chile 178 B4
San Felipe Baja California Mex. 166 B2
San Felipe Chihuahua Mex. 166 D3
San Felipe Guanajuato Mex. 167 E4
San Felipe Venez. 176 E1
San Felipe, Cayos de is Cuba 163 D8
San Felipe de Puerto Plata Dom. Rep. see Puerto Plata
San Fernando Chile 178 B4
San Fernando Baja California Mex. 166 B2
San Fernando Tamaulipas Mex. 167 F3
San Fernando watercourse Mex. 157 E7
San Fernando Luzon Phil. 82 C2
San Fernando Luzon Phil. 82 C3
San Fernando Spain 67 C5
San Fernando Trin. and Tob. 169 L6
San Fernando CA U.S.A. 158 D4
San Fernando de Apure Venez. 176 E2
San Fernando de Atabapo Venez. 176 E3
San Fernando de Monte Cristi Dom. Rep. see Monte Cristi
Sanford FL U.S.A. 163 D6
Sanford ME U.S.A. 165 J2
Sanford MI U.S.A. 164 C2
Sanford NC U.S.A. 162 E5
Sanford, Mount AK U.S.A. 149 K3
Sanford Lake MI U.S.A. 164 C2
San Francisco Arg. 178 D4
San Francisco Mex. 166 B2
San Francisco CA U.S.A. 158 B3
San Francisco, Cabo de c. Ecuador 176 B3
San Francisco, Passo de pass Arg./Chile 178 C3
San Francisco, Sierra mts Mex. 166 B3
San Francisco Bay inlet CA U.S.A. 158 B3
San Francisco del Oro Mex. 166 D3
San Francisco de Paula, Cabo c. Arg. 178 C7
San Francisco el Alto Mex. 167 F4
San Francisco Gotera El Salvador 166 [inset] H6
Sang, Loi mt. Myanmar 86 B2
San Gabriel, Punta pt Mex. 166 B2
San Gabriel Mountains CA U.S.A. 158 D4
Sangachaly Azer. see Sanqaçal
Sangaigerong Sumatra Indon. 84 D3
Sangameshwar India 106 B2
Sangamon r. IL U.S.A. 160 F3
Sangān, Kōh-e mt. Afgh. 111 G3
Sangan, Koh-i- mt. Afgh. see Sangān, Kōh-e
Sangar Russia 77 N3
Sangareddi India see Sangareddy
Sangareddy India 106 C2
Sangasanga Kalimantan Indon. 85 G3
Sanga Sanga i. Phil. 82 B5
San Gavino Monreale Sardinia Italy 68 C5
Sangay, Parque Nacional nat. park Ecuador 176 C4
Sangba China 99 F7
Sang Bar Afgh. 111 F3
Sangboy Islands Phil. 82 C5
Sangdankangsang Feng mt. China 99 E7
Sangeang i. Indon. 83 A5
Sangejing China 94 F3
Sangequanzi China 94 B3
Sanger CA U.S.A. 158 D3
Sangerfield NY U.S.A. 165 H2
Sangerhausen Germany 63 L3
Sang-e Surakh Iran 110 E2
Sanggar, Teluk b. Sumbawa Indon. 85 G5

Sanggarmai China 96 D1
Sanggau Kalimantan Indon. 85 E2
Sanggeluhang i. Indon. 83 C2
Sanggou Wan b. China 95 J4
San Giovanni in Fiore Italy 68 G5
Sangir India 104 C5
Sangir i. Indon. 83 C2
Sangir, Kepulauan is Indon. 83 C2
Sangiyn Dalay Mongolia see Erdenedalay
Sangiyn Dalay Nuur salt l. Mongolia 94 D1
Sangkapura Java Indon. 85 F4
Sangkarang, Kepulauan is Indon. 83 A4
Sangkulirang Kalimantan Indon. 85 G2
Sangkulirang, Teluk b. Indon. 85 G2
Sangli India 106 B2
Sangmai China see Dêrong
Sangmélima Cameroon 120 E4
Sangngagqoiling China 99 F7
Sango Zimbabwe 123 D6
Sangole India 106 B2
San Gorgonio Mountain CA U.S.A. 158 E4
Sangowo Moluccas Indon. 83 D2
Sangre de Cristo Range mts CO U.S.A. 157 G5
Sangri China 99 F7
Sangrur India 104 C3
Sangsang China 99 D7
Sangu r. Bangl. 105 G5
Sanguem India 106 B3
Sangutane r. Moz. 125 K3
Sangyuan China see Wuqiao
Sangzhi China 97 F2
Sanhe Guizhou China see Sandu
Sanhe Nei Mongol China 95 J1
San Hilario Mex. 166 C3
San Hipólito, Punta pt Mex. 166 B3
Sanhûr Egypt see Sanhūr
Sanhūr Egypt 112 C5
San Ignacio Belize 167 H5
San Ignacio Beni Bol. 176 E6
San Ignacio Santa Cruz Bol. 176 F7
San Ignacio Santa Cruz Bol. 176 F7
San Ignacio Baja California Mex. 166 B2
San Ignacio Baja California Sur Mex. 166 B3
San Ignacio Durango Mex. 161 C7
San Ignacio Sonora Mex. 166 C2
San Ignacio Para. 178 E3
San Ignacio, Laguna l. Mex. 166 B3
Sanikiluaq Canada 152 F2
San Ildefonso Peninsula Luzon Phil. 82 C2
Sanin-kaigan Kokuritsu-kōen nat. park Japan 92 A3
San Jacinto Masbate Phil. 82 C3
San Jacinto CA U.S.A. 158 E5
San Jacinto Peak CA U.S.A. 158 E5
San Javier Bol. 176 F7
Sanjiang Guangdong China see Liannan
Sanjiang Guangxi China 97 F3
Sanjiang Guizhou China see Jinping
Sanjiangkou China 95 J3
Sanjiaocheng China see Haiyan
Sanjiaoping China 97 F2
Sanjō Japan 91 E5
San Joaquin r. CA U.S.A. 158 C2
San Joaquin Valley CA U.S.A. 158 C3
Sanjoli India 104 C5
San Jon NM U.S.A. 161 C5
San Jorge, Golfo de g. Arg. 178 C7
San Jorge, Golfo de g. Spain see Sant Jordi, Golf de

▶San José Costa Rica 166 [inset] I7
Capital of Costa Rica.

San Jose Luzon Phil. 82 C3
San Jose Mindoro Phil. 82 C3
San Jose Mindoro Phil. 82 C3
San Jose CA U.S.A. 158 C3
San Jose NM U.S.A. 157 G6
San Jose watercourse NM U.S.A. 159 J4
San José, Isla i. Mex. 166 C3
San José de Amacuro Venez. 176 F2
San José de Bavicora Mex. 166 D2
San Jose de Buenavista Panay Phil. 82 C4
San José de Chiquitos Bol. 176 F7
San José de Comondú Mex. 166 C3
San José de Gracia Baja California Sur Mex. 166 B3
San José de Gracia Sinaloa Mex. 166 D3
San José de Gracia Sonora Mex. 166 C2
San José de la Brecha Mex. 166 C3
San José de las Lajas Cuba 163 D8
San José del Cabo Mex. 166 C4
San José del Guaviare Col. 176 D3
San José de Mayo Uruguay 178 E4
San José de Raíces Mex. 161 C7
Sanju China 99 B5
San Juan Arg. 178 C4
San Juan r. Costa Rica/Nicaragua 166 [inset] J7
San Juan mt. Cuba 163 D8
San Juan Chihuahua Mex. 166 D3
San Juan Coahuila Mex. 167 E3
San Juan r. Mex. 161 D7
San Juan Leyte Phil. 82 D4
San Juan Mindanao Phil. 82 D4

▶San Juan Puerto Rico 169 K5
Capital of Puerto Rico.

San Juan NM U.S.A. 159 J5
San Juan r. UT U.S.A. 159 H3
San Juan, Cabo c. Arg. 178 D8
San Juan, Cabo c. Equat. Guinea 120 D4
San Juan, Punta pt El Salvador 166 [inset] H6
San Juan Bautista Para. 178 E3
San Juan Bautista de las Misiones Para. see San Juan Bautista
San Juancito Hond. 166 [inset] I6
San Juan de Guadalupe Mex. 161 C7
San Juan del Norte Nicaragua 166 [inset] J7
San Juan del Norte, Bahía b. Nicaragua 166 [inset] J7
San Juan de los Morros Venez. 176 E2
San Juan del Río Durango Mex. 166 D3
San Juan del Río Querétaro Mex. 167 F4
San Juan del Sur Nicaragua 166 [inset] I7
San Juan Evangelista Mex. 167 G5
San Juanico, Punta pt Mex. 166 B3
San Juanito Mex. 166 D3
San Juanito, Isla i. Mex. 166 D4
San Juan Ixcoy Guat. 167 H6
San Juan Mountains CO U.S.A. 159 J3
San Juan y Martínez Cuba 163 D8
Sanju He watercourse China 99 B5
San Justo Arg. 178 D4
Sankari Drug India 106 C4
Sankh r. India 103 F7
Sankhu India 104 C3
Sankra Chhattisgarh India 106 D1
Sankra Rajasthan India 104 B4
Sankt Augustin Germany 63 H4
Sankt Gallen Switz. 66 I3
Sankt-Peterburg Russia see St Petersburg
Sankt Pölten Austria 57 O6
Sankt Veit an der Glan Austria 57 O7
Sankt Vith Belgium see St-Vith
Sankt Wendel Germany 63 H5
Sanku India 104 D2
San Lázaro, Cabo c. Mex. 166 B3
San Lázaro, Sierra de mts Mex. 166 C4
Şanlıurfa Turkey 112 E3
Şanlıurfa prov. Turkey 107 D1
San Lorenzo Arg. 178 D4
San Lorenzo Beni Bol. 176 E7
San Lorenzo Tarija Bol. 176 F8
San Lorenzo Ecuador 176 C3
San Lorenzo Hond. 166 [inset] I6
San Lorenzo Mex. 166 D2
San Lorenzo mt. Spain 67 E2
San Lorenzo, Isla i. Mex. 166 B2
San Lorenzo, Monte mt. Arg./Chile 178 B7
Sanlúcar de Barrameda Spain 67 C5
San Lucas Mex. 166 B3
San Lucas, Cabo c. Mex. 166 C4
San Lucas, Serranía de mts Col. 176 D2
San Luis Arg. 178 C4
San Luis Guat. 167 H5
San Luis Hond. 166 [inset] H6
San Luis Mex. 167 E5
San Luis AZ U.S.A. 159 F5
San Luis AZ U.S.A. 159 H5
San Luis CO U.S.A. 161 B4
San Luis, Isla i. Mex. 166 B2
San Luis de la Paz Mex. 167 E4
San Luis Gonzaga Mex. 166 C3
San Luisito Mex. 166 B2
San Luis Obispo CA U.S.A. 158 C4
San Luis Obispo Bay CA U.S.A. 158 C4
San Luis Potosí Mex. 168 D4
San Luis Potosí state Mex. 167 E4
San Luis Reservoir CA U.S.A. 158 C3
San Luis Río Colorado Mex. 166 B1
San Manuel Luzon Phil. 82 C2
San Manuel AZ U.S.A. 159 H5
San Marcial, Punta pt Mex. 166 C3
San Marcos Guat. 167 H6
San Marcos Mex. 167 F5
San Marcos TX U.S.A. 161 D6
San Marcos, Isla i. Mex. 166 B3
San Marcos de Colón Hond. 166 [inset] I6
San Marino country Europe 68 E3

▶San Marino San Marino 68 E3
Capital of San Marino.

San Martín research station Antarctica 188 L2
San Martín Catamarca Arg. 178 C3
San Martín Mendoza Arg. 178 C4
San Martín, Lago l. Arg./Chile 178 B7
San Martín, Volcán vol. Mex. 167 G5
San Martín de Bolaños Mex. 166 E4
San Martín de los Andes Arg. 178 B6
San Mateo CA U.S.A. 158 B3
San Mateo Mountains NM U.S.A. 159 J4
San Matías Bol. 177 G7
San Matías, Golfo g. Arg. 178 D6
Sanmen China 97 I2
Sanmen Wan b. China 97 I2
Sanmenxia China 95 G5
San Miguel El Salvador 166 [inset] H6
San Miguel Panama 166 [inset] K7
San Miguel Luzon Phil. 82 C3
San Miguel CA U.S.A. 158 C4
San Miguel r. CO U.S.A. 159 I2
San Miguel Bay Luzon Phil. 82 C3
San Miguel de Allende Mex. 167 E4
San Miguel de Cruces Mex. 166 D3
San Miguel de Horcasitas Mex. 166 C2
San Miguel de Huachi Bol. 176 E7
San Miguel de Tucumán Arg. 178 C3
San Miguel el Alto Mex. 166 E4
San Miguel Island CA U.S.A. 158 C4
San Miguel Islands Phil. 82 B5
San Miguelito Panama 166 [inset] K7
San Miguel Sola de Vega Mex. 167 F5
Sanming China 97 H3
Sanmu Japan 93 G3
Sannan Japan 92 B3
San Narciso Luzon Phil. 82 C3
Sanndraigh i. U.K. see Sandray
Sannicandro Garganico Italy 68 F4
San Nicolás Durango Mex. 161 B7
San Nicolás Guerrero Mex. 167 F5
San Nicolás Tamaulipas Mex. 161 D7
San Nicolas Luzon Phil. 82 C2
San Nicolas Island CA U.S.A. 158 D5
Sannieshof S. Africa 125 G4
Sanniquellie Liberia 120 C4
Sano Japan 93 F2
Sanok Poland 53 D6
San Pablo Bol. 176 E8
San Pablo Mex. 167 F4
San Pablo Luzon Phil. 82 C3
San Pablo de Manta Ecuador see Manta
San Pascual Phil. 82 C3
San Pedro Arg. 178 D2
San Pedro Belize 167 I5
San Pedro Bol. 176 F7
San Pedro Chile 178 C2
San-Pédro Côte d'Ivoire 120 C4
San Pedro Baja California Sur Mex. 166 C4
San Pedro Chihuahua Mex. 166 D2
San Pedro Para. see San Pedro de Ycuamandyyú
San Pedro watercourse AZ U.S.A. 159 H5
San Pedro, Punta pt Costa Rica 166 [inset] J7
San Pedro, Sierra de mts Spain 67 C4
San Pedro Carchá Guat. 167 H6
San Pedro Channel CA U.S.A. 158 D5
San Pedro de Arimena Col. 176 D3
San Pedro de Atacama Chile 178 C2
San Pedro de las Colonias Mex. 166 E3
San Pedro de Macorís Dom. Rep. 169 K5
San Pedro de Ycuamandyyú Para. 178 E2
San Pedro el Saucito Mex. 166 C2
San Pedro Martir, Parque Nacional nat. park Mex. 166 B2
San Pedro Sula Hond. 166 [inset] H6
San Pierre IN U.S.A. 164 B3
San Pietro, Isola di i. Sardinia Italy 68 C5
San Pitch r. UT U.S.A. 159 H2
Sanpu China 94 E4
Sanqaçal Azer. 113 H2
Sanquhar U.K. 60 F5
Sanquianga, Parque Nacional nat. park Col. 176 C3
San Quintín, Cabo c. Mex. 166 A2
San Rafael Arg. 178 C4
San Rafael CA U.S.A. 158 B3
San Rafael NM U.S.A. 159 J4
San Rafael r. UT U.S.A. 159 H2
San Rafael del Norte Nicaragua 166 [inset] I6
San Rafael Knob mt. UT U.S.A. 159 H2
San Rafael Mountains CA U.S.A. 158 C4
San Ramón Bol. 176 F6
Sanrao China 97 H3
Sanremo Italy 68 B3
San Roque Spain 67 B2
San Roque, Punta pt Mex. 166 B3
San Saba TX U.S.A. 161 D6
San Saba r. TX U.S.A. 167 F2
San Salvador i. Bahamas 163 F7

▶San Salvador El Salvador 167 H6
Capital of El Salvador.

San Salvador de Jujuy Arg. 178 C2
Sansanné-Mango Togo 120 D3
San Sebastián Arg. 178 C8
San Sebastián Spain 67 F2
San Sebastián de los Reyes Spain 67 E3
Sansepolcro Italy 68 E3
San Severo Italy 68 F4
San Simon AZ U.S.A. 159 I5
Sanski Most Bos. & Herz. 68 G2
Sansoral Islands Palau see Sonsorol Islands
Sansui China 97 F3
Sant Mongolia 94 E2
Santa r. Peru 176 C5
Santa Amelia Guat. 167 H5
Santa Ana Bol. 176 E7
Santa Ana El Salvador 167 H6
Santa Ana Mex. 166 C2
Santa Ana i. Solomon Is 133 G3
Santa Ana CA U.S.A. 158 E5
Santa Ana de Yacuma Bol. 176 E6
Santa Anita Mex. 166 C4
Santa Anna TX U.S.A. 161 D6
Santa Bárbara Brazil 179 C2
Santa Bárbara Cuba see La Demajagua
Santa Bárbara Hond. 166 [inset] H6
Santa Bárbara Mex. 166 D3
Santa Barbara CA U.S.A. 158 D4
Santa Bárbara, Ilha i. Brazil 179 D2
Santa Barbara Channel CA U.S.A. 158 C4
Santa Bárbara d'Oeste Brazil 179 B3
Santa Barbara Island CA U.S.A. 158 D5
Santa Catalina Panama 166 [inset] J7
Santa Catalina, Gulf of CA U.S.A. 158 E5
Santa Catalina, Isla i. Mex. 166 C3
Santa Catalina de Armada Spain 67 B2
Santa Catalina Island CA U.S.A. 158 D5
Santa Catarina state Brazil 179 A4
Santa Catarina Baja California Mex. 166 B2
Santa Catarina Nuevo León Mex. 167 E3
Santa Catarina, Ilha de i. Brazil 179 A4
Santa Clara Col. 176 E4
Santa Clara Cuba 169 I4
Santa Clara Mex. 166 D2
Santa Clara r. Mex. 166 D2
Santa Clara CA U.S.A. 158 C3
Santa Clara NM U.S.A. 159 I5
Santa Clara UT U.S.A. 159 G3
Santa Clarita CA U.S.A. 158 D4
Santa Clotilde Peru 176 D4
Santa Comba Angola see Waku-Kungo
Santa Croce, Capo c. Sicily Italy 68 F6
Santa Cruz Bol. 176 F7
Santa Cruz Brazil 177 K5
Santa Cruz Costa Rica 166 [inset] I7
Santa Cruz Mex. 166 C2
Santa Cruz Luzon Phil. 82 B3
Santa Cruz Luzon Phil. 82 C2
Santa Cruz Luzon Phil. 82 C3
Santa Cruz CA U.S.A. 158 B3
Santa Cruz watercourse AZ U.S.A. 159 G5
Santa Cruz, Isla i. Galápagos Ecuador 176 [inset]
Santa Cruz, Isla i. Mex. 166 C3
Santa Cruz Barillas Guat. 167 H6
Santa Cruz Cabrália Brazil 179 D2
Santa Cruz de Goiás Brazil 179 A2
Santa Cruz de la Palma Canary Is 120 B2
Santa Cruz del Sur Cuba 169 I4
Santa Cruz de Moya Spain 67 F4

▶Santa Cruz de Tenerife Canary Is 120 B2
Joint capital of the Canary Islands.

Santa Cruz de Yojoa Hond. 166 [inset] I6
Santa Cruz do Sul Brazil 178 F3
Santa Cruz Island CA U.S.A. 158 D4
Santa Cruz Islands Solomon Is 133 G3
Santa Elena, Bahía de b. Ecuador 176 B4
Santa Elena, Cabo c. Costa Rica 166 [inset] I7
Santa Elena, Punta pt Ecuador 176 B4
Santa Eudóxia Brazil 179 B3
Santa Eufemia, Golfo di g. Italy 68 G5
Santa Eulalia Mex. 167 E2
Santa Fe Arg. 178 D4
Santa Fe Cuba 163 D8
Santa Fe Panama 166 [inset] J7
Santa Fe Phil. 82 C3

▶Santa Fe NM U.S.A. 157 G6
Capital of New Mexico.

Santa Fé de Bogotá Col. see Bogotá
Santa Fé de Minas Brazil 179 B2
Santa Fé do Sul Brazil 179 A3
Santa Gertrudis Mex. 166 D3
Santa Helena Brazil 177 I4
Santa Helena de Goiás Brazil 179 A2
Santai Sichuan China 96 E2
Santai Xinjiang China 98 C3
Santai Xinjiang China 98 E3
Santai Yunnan China 96 D3
Santa Inês Brazil 177 I4
Santa Inés, Isla i. Chile 188 L3
Santa Isabel Arg. 178 C5
Santa Isabel Equat. Guinea see Malabo
Santa Isabel i. Solomon Is 133 F2
Santa Isabel, Sierra mts Mex. 166 B2
Santa Juliana Brazil 179 B2
Santalpur India 104 B5
Santa Lucia Guat. 167 H6
Santa Lucia Range mts CA U.S.A. 158 C3
Santa Margarita CA U.S.A. 158 C4
Santa Margarita, Isla i. Mex. 166 C3
Santa María Arg. 178 C3
Santa Maria Amazonas Brazil 177 G4
Santa Maria Distrito Federal Brazil 179 A1
Santa Maria Rio Grande do Sul Brazil 178 F3
Santa Maria Cape Verde 120 [inset]
Santa Maria Mex. 167 H5
Santa María r. Mex. 166 D2
Santa María Peru 176 D4
Santa Maria CA U.S.A. 158 C4
Santa Maria r. AZ U.S.A. 159 G4
Santa Maria, Cabo de c. Moz. 125 K4
Santa Maria, Cabo de c. Port. 67 C5
Santa Maria, Chapadão de hills Brazil 179 B1
Santa Maria, Serra de hills Brazil 179 B1
Santa Maria da Vitória Brazil 179 B1
Santa María de Cuevas Mex. 166 D3
Santa María del Oro Mex. 166 D3
Santa María del Río Mex. 167 E4
Santa Maria do Suaçuí Brazil 179 C2
Santa Maria Island Vanuatu 133 G3
Santa Maria Madalena Brazil 179 C3
Santa Maria Mountains AZ U.S.A. 159 G4
Santa Marta Col. 176 D1
Santa Marta, Cabo de c. Angola 123 B5
Santa Marta Grande, Cabo de c. Brazil 179 A5
Santa Martha, Cerro mt. Mex. 167 G5
Santa Maura i. Greece see Lefkada
Santa Monica CA U.S.A. 158 D4
Santa Monica, Pico mt. Mex. 157 E8
Santa Monica Bay CA U.S.A. 158 D5
Santan Kalimantan Indon. 85 G3
Santana Brazil 179 C1
Santana r. Brazil 179 A2
Santana do Araguaia Brazil 177 H5
Santander Spain 67 E2
Santa Nella CA U.S.A. 158 C3
Santanghu China 94 C2
Santanilla, Islas is Caribbean Sea see Cisne, Islas del
Santan Mountain hill AZ U.S.A. 159 H5
Sant'Antioco Sardinia Italy 68 C5
Sant'Antioco, Isola di i. Sardinia Italy 68 C5
Sant Antoni de Portmany Spain 67 G4
Santapilly India 106 D2
Santaquin UT U.S.A. 159 H2
Santa Quitéria Brazil 177 J4
Santarém Brazil 177 H4
Santarém Port. 67 B4
Santa Rita Mex. 167 E3
Santa Rosa Arg. 178 D5
Santa Rosa Brazil 178 F3
Santa Rosa Nuevo León Mex. 161 C7
Santa Rosa Quintana Roo Mex. 167 H5
Santa Rosa CA U.S.A. 158 B2
Santa Rosa NM U.S.A. 157 G6
Santa Rosa de Copán Hond. 166 [inset] H6
Santa Rosa de la Roca Bol. 176 F7
Santa Rosa do Purus Brazil 176 D5
Santa Rosa Island CA U.S.A. 158 C5
Santa Rosalía Mex. 166 B3
Santa Rosa Range mts NV U.S.A. 156 D4
Santa Rosa Wash watercourse AZ U.S.A. 159 G5
Santa Sylvina Arg. 178 D3
Santa Tecla El Salvador 167 H6
Santa Teresa Australia 135 F6
Santa Teresa r. Brazil 179 A1
Santa Teresa Nayarit Mex. 166 D4
Santa Teresa Tamaulipas Mex. 167 F3
Santa Vitória Brazil 179 A2
Santa Ynez r. CA U.S.A. 158 C4
Santa Ysabel i. Solomon Is see Santa Isabel
Santee CA U.S.A. 158 E5
Santee r. SC U.S.A. 163 E5
San Telmo Mex. 166 A2
Sant Francesc de Formentera Spain 67 G4
Santiago Brazil 178 F3
Santiago i. Cape Verde 120 [inset]

▶Santiago Chile 178 B4
Capital of Chile.

Santiago Dom. Rep. 169 J5
Santiago Mex. 166 C4
Santiago Panama 166 [inset] J7
Santiago Luzon Phil. 82 C2
Santiago, Cerro mt. Panama 166 [inset] J7
Santiago, Isla i. Galápagos Ecuador 176 [inset]
Santiago, Río Grande de r. Mex. 166 D4
Santiago Astata Mex. 167 G5
Santiago de Compostela Spain 67 B2
Santiago de Cuba Cuba 169 I4
Santiago del Estero Arg. 178 D3
Santiago de los Caballeros Dom. Rep. see Santiago
Santiago Ixcuintla Mex. 166 D4
Santiaguillo, Laguna de l. Mex. 161 B7
Santianna Point Canada 151 P2
Santigi Celebes Indon. 83 B2
Santiki, Tanjung pt Indon. 83 B2
Santipur India see Shantipur
Sant Jordi, Golf de g. Spain 67 G3
Santō Hyōgo Japan 92 A3
Santō Shiga Japan 92 C3
Santo Amaro Brazil 179 D1
Santo Amaro de Campos Brazil 179 C3
Santo Anastácio Brazil 179 A3
Santo André Brazil 179 B3
Santo Ângelo Brazil 178 F3

▶Santo Antão i. Cape Verde 120 [inset]
Most westerly point of Africa.

Santo Antônio Brazil 176 F4
Santo Antônio r. Brazil 179 C2
Santo Antônio São Tomé and Príncipe 120 D4
Santo Antônio, Cabo c. Brazil 179 D1
Santo Antônio da Platina Brazil 179 A3
Santo Antônio de Jesus Brazil 179 D1
Santo Antônio do Içá Brazil 176 E4
Santo Corazón Bol. 177 G7
Santo Domingo Cuba 163 D8

▶Santo Domingo Dom. Rep. 169 K5
Capital of the Dominican Republic.

Santo Domingo Guat. 167 H6
Santo Domingo Baja California Mex. 166 B2
Santo Domingo Baja California Sur Mex. 166 C3
Santo Domingo San Luis Potosí Mex. 167 E4
Santo Domingo Nicaragua 166 [inset] I6
Santo Domingo country West Indies see Dominican Republic
Santo Domingo de Guzmán Dom. Rep. see Santo Domingo
Santo Domingo Tehuantepec Mex. 167 G5
Santo Hipólito Brazil 179 B2
Santorini i. Greece 69 K6
Santos Brazil 179 B3
Santos Dumont Brazil 179 C3
Santos Luzardo, Parque Nacional nat. park Venez. 176 E2
Santos Plateau sea feature S. Atlantic Ocean 184 E7
Santo Tomás Mex. 157 E7
Santo Tomás Nicaragua 166 [inset] I6
Santo Tomás Peru 176 D6
Santo Tomé Arg. 178 E3
Sanup Plateau AZ U.S.A. 159 G3
San Valentín, Cerro mt. Chile 178 B7
San Vicente El Salvador 166 [inset] H6
San Vicente Mex. 166 A2
San Vicente Luzon Phil. 82 C2
San Vicente de Baracaldo Spain see Barakaldo
San Vicente de Cañete Peru 176 C6
San Vincenzo Italy 68 D3
San Vito, Capo c. Sicily Italy 68 E5
Sanwa Ibaraki Japan 93 F2
Sanwa Niigata Japan 93 E1
Sanwer India 104 C5
Sanya China 97 F5
Sanyuan China 95 G5
S. A. Nyýazow Adyndaky Turkm. 111 F2
Sanza Pombo Angola 123 B4
Sao, Phou mt. Laos 86 C3
São Bernardo do Campo Brazil 179 B3
São Borja Brazil 178 E3
São Carlos Brazil 179 B3
São Cristóvão Brazil 177 K6
São Domingos Brazil 179 B1
São Felipe, Serra de hills Brazil 179 B1
São Félix Brazil 179 D1
São Félix do Araguaia Brazil 177 H6
São Félix do Xingu Brazil 177 H5
São Fidélis Brazil 179 C3
São Francisco Brazil 179 B1

▶São Francisco r. Brazil 179 C1
5th longest river in South America.

São Francisco, Ilha de i. Brazil 179 A4
São Francisco de Paula Brazil 179 A5
São Francisco de Sales Brazil 179 A2
São Francisco do Sul Brazil 179 A4
São Gabriel Brazil 178 F4
São Gonçalo Brazil 179 C3
São Gonçalo do Abaeté Brazil 179 B2
São Gonçalo do Sapucaí Brazil 179 B3
São Gotardo Brazil 179 B2
São João, Ilhas de is Brazil 177 J4
São João da Barra Brazil 179 C3
São João da Boa Vista Brazil 179 B3
São João da Madeira Port. 67 B3
São João da Ponte Brazil 179 B1
São João del Rei Brazil 179 B3
São João do Paraíso Brazil 179 C1
São Joaquim Brazil 179 A5
São Joaquim da Barra Brazil 179 B3
São José Amazonas Brazil 176 E4
São José Santa Catarina Brazil 179 A4
São José do Rio Preto Brazil 179 A3
São José dos Campos Brazil 179 B3
São José dos Pinhais Brazil 179 A4
São Leopoldo Brazil 179 A5
São Lourenço Brazil 179 B3
São Lourenço r. Brazil 177 G7
São Luís Maranhão Brazil 177 J4
São Luís Pará Brazil 177 G4
São Luís de Montes Belos Brazil 179 A2
São Manuel Brazil 179 A3
São Marcos r. Brazil 179 B2
São Mateus Brazil 179 D2
São Mateus do Sul Brazil 179 A4
São Miguel i. Arquipélago dos Açores 184 G3
São Miguel r. Brazil 179 B2
São Miguel do Araguaia Brazil 179 A1
São Miguel do Tapuio Brazil 177 J5
Saône r. France 66 G4
Saoner India 104 D5
São Nicolau i. Cape Verde 120 [inset]

▶São Paulo Brazil 179 B3
Most populous city in South America and 7th in the world.

São Paulo state Brazil 179 A3
São Paulo de Olivença Brazil 176 E4
São Pedro da Aldeia Brazil 179 C3
São Pedro e São Paulo is N. Atlantic Ocean 184 G5
São Pires r. Brazil see Teles Pires
São Raimundo Nonato Brazil 177 J5
Saori Japan 92 C3
São Romão Amazonas Brazil 176 E5
São Romão Minas Gerais Brazil 179 B2
São Roque Brazil 179 B3
São Roque, Cabo de c. Brazil 177 K5
São Salvador Angola see M'banza Congo
São Salvador do Congo Angola see M'banza Congo
São Sebastião Brazil 179 B3
São Sebastião, Ilha do i. Brazil 179 B3
São Sebastião do Paraíso Brazil 179 B3
São Sebastião dos Poções Brazil 179 B1
São Simão Goiás Brazil 177 H7
São Simão São Paulo Brazil 179 B3
São Simão, Barragem de resr Brazil 179 A2
Sao-Siu Moluccas Indon. 83 C2
São Tiago i. Cape Verde see Santiago

▶São Tomé São Tomé and Príncipe 120 D4
Capital of São Tomé and Príncipe.

São Tomé i. São Tomé and Príncipe 120 D4
São Tomé, Cabo de c. Brazil 179 C3
São Tomé, Pico de mt. São Tomé and Príncipe 120 D4
São Tomé and Príncipe country Africa 120 D4
Saoura, Oued watercourse Alg. 64 D6
São Vicente Brazil 179 B3
São Vicente i. Cape Verde 120 [inset]
São Vicente, Cabo de c. Port. 67 B5
Sapako Sumatra Indon. 84 B3
Sapanca Turkey 69 N4
Saparua Moluccas Indon. 83 D3
Saparua i. Moluccas Indon. 83 D3
Sapaul India see Supaul
Sape, Selat sea chan. Indon. 83 A5
Sape, Teluk b. Sumbawa Indon. 85 G5
Şaphane Dağı mt. Turkey 69 N5
Sapo, Serranía del mts Panama 166 [inset] K8
Sapo National Park Liberia 120 C4
Sapouy Burkina Faso 120 C3
Sapozhok Russia 53 I5
Sappa Creek r. NE U.S.A. 160 D3
Sapporo Japan 90 F4
Sapudi i. Indon. 85 F4
Sapulpa OK U.S.A. 161 D4
Sapulu Java Indon. 85 F4
Sapulut Sabah Malaysia 85 G1
Sāqī Iran 110 E3
Saqqez Iran 110 B2
Sarā Iran 110 B2
Sarāb Iran 110 B2
Sara Buri Thai. 87 C4
Saradiya India 104 B5
Saragossa Spain see Zaragoza
Saragt Turkm. 111 F2
Saraguro Ecuador 176 C4
Sarahs Turkm. see Saragt
Sarai Sidhu Pak. 111 I4

▶Sarajevo Bos. & Herz. 68 H3
Capital of Bosnia and Herzegovina.

Sarakhs Iran 111 F2
Saraktash Russia 76 G4
Saraland AL U.S.A. 161 F6
Saramati mt. India/Myanmar 86 A1
Saran' Kazakh. 102 D2
Saran, Gunung mt. Indon. 85 E3
Saranac MI U.S.A. 164 C2

Saranac r. NY U.S.A. 165 I1
Saranac Lake NY U.S.A. 165 H1
Saranda Albania see Sarandë
Sarandë Albania 69 I5
Sarandib country Asia see Sri Lanka
Sarangani i. Phil. 82 D5
Sarangani Bay Mindanao Phil. 82 D5
Sarangani Islands Phil. 82 D5
Sarangani Strait Phil. 82 D5
Sarangpur India 104 D5
Saransk Russia 53 J5
Sara Peak Nigeria 120 D4
Saraphi Thai. 86 B3
Sarapul Russia 51 Q4
Sarāqib Syria 107 C2
Sarasota FL U.S.A. 163 D7
Saraswati r. India 111 H6
Sarata Ukr. 69 M1
Saratoga CA U.S.A. 158 B3
Saratoga WY U.S.A. 156 G4
Saratoga Springs NY U.S.A. 162 F3
Saratok Sarawak Malaysia 85 E2
Saratov Russia 53 J6
Saratovskoye Vodokhranilishche resr Russia 53 J5
Saratsina, Akrotirio pt Greece 69 K5
Sarāvān Iran 111 F5
Sarawak state Malaysia 85 E2
Saray Turkey 69 L4
Sarayköy Turkey 69 M6
Sarayönü Turkey 112 D3
Sarazm tourist site Tajik. 102 C4
Sarbāz Iran 109 J4
Sarbāz reg. Iran 111 F5
Sarbhang Bhutan 105 G4
Sar Bīsheh Iran 109 I3
Sarbulak China 94 B2
Sarda r. India/Nepal 99 C7
Sarda r. Nepal 105 E3
Sard Āb Afgh. 111 H2
Sardarshahr India 104 C3
Sardasht Iran 110 B2
Sardegna i. Sardinia Italy see Sardinia
Sardica Bulg. see Sofia
Sardinal Costa Rica 166 [inset] I7
Sardinia i. Sardinia Italy 68 C4
Sardis MS U.S.A. 161 F5
Sardis WV U.S.A. 164 E4
Sardis Lake resr MS U.S.A. 161 F5
Sar-e Būm Afgh. 111 G3
Sareks nationalpark nat. park Sweden 54 J3
Sarektjåkkå mt. Sweden 54 J3
Sarempaka, Gunung mt. Indon. 85 F3
Sar-e Pol-e Ẕahāb Iran 110 B3
Sar-e Pul Afgh. 111 G2
Sar Eskandar Iran see Hashtrūd
Sargasso Sea N. Atlantic Ocean 187 P4
Sargodha Pak. 111 I3
Sarh Chad 121 E4
Sarhad reg. Iran 111 F4
Sārī Iran 110 D2
Saria i. Greece 69 L7
Sar-i-Bum Afgh. see Sar-e Būm
Sáric Mex. 166 C2
Sarigan i. N. Mariana Is 81 L3
Sarigh Jilganang Kol salt l. China 104 D2
Sarıgöl Turkey 69 M5
Sarıkamış Turkey 113 F2
Sarikei Sarawak Malaysia 85 E2
Sarikül, Qatorkŭhi mts China/Tajik. see Sarykol Range
Sarila India 104 D4
Sarina Australia 136 E4
Sarıoğlan Kayseri Turkey 112 D3
Sarıoğlan Konya Turkey see Belören
Sariqamish Kuli salt l. Turkm./Uzbek. see Sarykamyshskoye Ozero
Sarita TX U.S.A. 161 D7
Sarıveliler Turkey 107 A1
Sariwŏn N. Korea 91 B5
Sarıyar Barajı resr Turkey 69 N5
Sarıyer Turkey 69 M4
Sarız Turkey 112 E3
Sark i. Channel Is 59 E9
Sark, Safrā' as esc. Saudi Arabia 108 F4
Sarkand Kazakh. 102 E2
Şarkikaraağaç Turkey 69 N5
Şarkışla Turkey 112 E3
Şarköy Turkey 69 L4
Sarlath Range mts Afgh./Pak. 111 G4
Sarmi Indon. 81 J7
Särna Sweden 55 H6
Sarneh Iran 110 B3
Sarnen Switz. 66 I3
Sarni India see Amla
Sarnia Canada 164 D2
Sarny Ukr. 53 E6
Saroako Celebes Indon. 83 B3
Sarōbī Afgh. 111 H3
Sarolangun Sumatra Indon. 84 C3
Saroma-ko l. Japan 90 F3
Saronikos Kolpos g. Greece 69 J6
Saros Körfezi b. Turkey 69 L4
Sarov Russia 53 I5
Sarpa, Ozero l. Russia 53 J6
Sarpan i. N. Mariana Is see Rota
Sar Passage Palau 82 [inset]
Sarpsborg Norway 55 G7
Sarqant Kazakh. see Sarkand
Sarre r. France 62 H5
Sarrebourg France 62 H6
Sarreguemines France 62 H5
Sarria Spain 67 C2
Sarry France 62 E6
Sartana Ukr. 53 H7
Sartanahu Pak. 111 H5
Sartène Corsica France 66 I6
Sarthe r. France 66 D3
Sartokay China 94 B2
Sartu China see Daqing
Saruna Pak. 111 G5
Sarupsar India 104 C3
Şärur Azer. 113 G3
Sarvābād Iran 110 B3
Sárvár Hungary 68 G1
Sarv-e Bālā Iran 110 D3
Sarwar India 104 C4
Saryarka plain Kazakh. 102 D1
Sar Yazd Iran 110 D4
Sary-Bulak Kyrg. 98 A4
Sarygamysh Köli salt l. Turkm./Uzbek. see Sarykamyshskoye Ozero
Sary-Ishikotrau, Peski des. Kazakh. see Saryyesik-Atyrau, Peski
Sary-Jaz r. Kyrg. 98 B4
Sarykamyshskoye Ozero salt l. Turkm./Uzbek. 113 J2
Sarykol Range mts China/Tajik. 111 I2
Sarykomey Kazakh. 98 A3
Saryozek Kazakh. 102 E3
Saryozen r. Kazakh./Russia 53 K6
Saryshagan Kazakh. 102 D2
Sarysu watercourse Kazakh. 102 C2
Sarytash Kazakh. 113 H1
Sary-Tash Kyrg. 111 I2
Sary-Ter, Gora mt. Kyrg. 98 B4
Saryýazy Suw Howdany resr Turkm. 111 F2
Saryyesik-Atyrau, Peski des. Kazakh. 102 E2
Saryzhal Kazakh. 98 B2
Saryzhaz Kazakh. 98 B4
Sarzha Kazakh. 113 H2
Sasak Sumatra Indon. 84 B2
Sasar, Tanjung pt Sumba Indon. 83 A5
Sasaram India 105 F4
Sasayama Japan 92 B3
Sasebo Japan 91 C6
Sashima Japan 93 F2
Saskatchewan prov. Canada 151 J4
Saskatchewan r. Canada 151 K4
Saskatoon Canada 151 J4
Saskylakh Russia 77 M2
Saslaya mt. Nicaragua 166 [inset] I6
Saslaya, Parque Nacional nat. park Nicaragua 166 [inset] I6
Sasoi r. India 104 B5
Sasolburg S. Africa 125 H4
Sasovo Russia 53 I5
Sass r. Canada 150 H2
Sassandra Côte d'Ivoire 120 C4
Sassari Sardinia Italy 68 C4
Sassenberg Germany 63 I3
Sassnitz Germany 57 N3
Sass Town Liberia 120 C4
Sasykkol', Ozero l. Kazakh. 102 F2
Sasykoli Russia 53 J7
Sasyqköl l. Kazakh. see Sasykkol', Ozero
Satahual i. Micronesia see Satawal
Sata-misaki c. Japan 91 C7
Satana India 106 B1
Satan Pass NM U.S.A. 159 I4
Satara India 106 B2
Satara S. Africa 125 J3
Satawal i. Micronesia 81 L5
Sätbaev Kazakh. see Satpayev
Satengar i. Indon. 85 G4
Satevó Mex. 166 D3
Satevó r. Mex. 157 G8
Satırlar Turkey see Yeşilova
Satkania Bangl. 105 H5
Satkhira Bangl. 105 G5
Satluj r. India/Pak. 104 B3
Satmala Range hills India 106 C2
Satna India 104 E4
Satomi Japan 93 G2
Satonda i. Indon. 85 G5
Satpayev Kazakh. 102 C2
Satpura Range mts India 104 C5
Satsuma-hantō pen. Japan 91 C7
Satsuma-Sendai Japan 91 C7
Sattahip Thai. 87 C4
Satte Japan 93 F2
Satteldorf Germany 63 K5
Satthwa Myanmar 86 A3
Satu Mare Romania 53 D7
Satun Thai. 87 C6
Satwas India 104 D5
Saubi i. Indon. 85 F4
Sauceda Mountains AZ U.S.A. 159 G5
Saucillo Mex. 166 D2
Sauda Norway 55 E7
Sauðárkrókur Iceland 54 [inset 1]

▶Saudi Arabia country Asia 108 F4
5th largest country in Asia.

Sauer r. France 63 I6
Saug r. Mindanao Phil. 82 D5
Saugatuck MI U.S.A. 164 B2
Saugeen r. Canada 164 E1
Sāūjbolāgh Iran see Mahābād
Sauk Center MN U.S.A. 160 E2
Saulieu France 66 G3
Saulnois reg. France 62 G6
Sault Sainte Marie Canada 152 D5
Sault Sainte Marie MI U.S.A. 162 C2
Saumalkol' Kazakh. 100 F1
Saumarez Reef Australia 136 F4
Saumlakki Moluccas Indon. 134 E2
Saumur France 66 D3
Saundatti India 106 B3
Saunders, Mount hill Australia 134 E3
Saunders Coast Antarctica 188 J1
Saurimo Angola 123 C4
Sausu Celebes Indon. 83 B3
Sautar Angola 123 B5
Sauvolles, Lac l. Canada 153 G3
Sauyr, Khrebet mts China/Kazakh. 98 D3
Sava r. Europe 68 I2
Savage River Australia 137 [inset]
Savai'i i. Samoa 133 I3
Savala r. Russia 53 I6
Savalou Benin 120 D4
Savānāt Iran see Estahbān
Savane r. Canada 153 H4
Savanna IL U.S.A. 160 F3
Savannah GA U.S.A. 163 D5
Savannah OH U.S.A. 164 D3
Savannah TN U.S.A. 161 F5
Savannah r. Georgia/S. Carolina U.S.A. 163 D5
Savannah Sound Bahamas 163 E7
Savannakhét Laos 86 D3
Savanna-la-Mar Jamaica 169 I5
Savant Lake Canada 152 C4
Savant Lake l. Canada 152 C4
Savanur India 106 B3
Sävar Sweden 54 L5
Savaştepe Turkey 69 L5
Savè Benin 120 D4
Save r. Moz./Zimbabwe 123 D6
Sāveh Iran 110 C3
Saverne France 63 H6
Saverne, Col de pass France 63 H6
Saviaho Fin. 54 P5
Savinskiy Russia 52 I3
Savitri r. India 106 B2
Savli India 104 C5
Savoie reg. France see Savoy
Savona Italy 68 C2
Savonlinna Fin. 54 P6
Savonranta Fin. 54 P5
Savoonga AK U.S.A. 148 E3
Savoy reg. France 66 H3
Şavşat Turkey 113 F2
Sävsjö Sweden 55 I8
Savu i. Indon. 83 B5
Savukoski Fin. 54 P3
Savur Turkey 113 F3
Savu Sea Indon. see Sawu, Laut
Savvo-Borzya Russia 95 I1
Saw Myanmar 86 A2
Sawahlunto Sumatra Indon. 84 C3
Sawai, Teluk b. Seram Indon. 83 D3
Sawai Madhopur India 104 D4
Sawan Kalimantan Indon. 85 F3
Sawan Myanmar 86 B1
Sawar India 104 C4
Sawatch Range mts CO U.S.A. 156 G5
Sawel Mountain hill U.K. 61 E3
Sawi, Ao b. Thai. 87 B5
Sawn Myanmar 86 B2
Sawtell Australia 138 F3
Sawtooth Mountain AK U.S.A. 149 J2
Sawtooth Range mts WA U.S.A. 156 C2
Sawu Indon. 83 B5
Sawu i. Indon. see Savu
Sawu, Laut sea Indon. 83 B5
Sawye Myanmar 86 B2
Sawyer MI U.S.A. 164 B3
Saxilby U.K. 58 G5
Saxman AK U.S.A. 149 O5
Saxmundham U.K. 59 I6
Saxnäs Sweden 54 I4
Saxony land Germany see Sachsen
Saxony-Anhalt land Germany see Sachsen-Anhalt
Saxton PA U.S.A. 165 F3
Say Niger 120 D3
Sayabouri Laos see Xaignabouli
Sayafi i. Moluccas Indon. 83 D2
Sayak Kazakh. 102 E2
Sayama Japan 93 F3
Sayang i. Papua Indon. 83 D2
Sayanogorsk Russia 88 G2
Sayano-Shushenskoye Vodokhranilishche resr Russia 88 G2
Sayansk Russia 88 I2
Sayaq Kazakh. see Sayak
Sayat Turkm. see Saýat
Saýat Turkm. 111 F2
Sayaxché Guat. 167 H5
Şaydā Lebanon see Sidon
Sāyen Iran 110 D4
Sayer Island Thai. see Similan, Ko
Sayghān Afgh. 111 G3
Sayhan Mongolia 94 E1
Sayhandulaan Mongolia 95 G2
Sayhan-Ovoo Mongolia 94 E2
Sayḥūt Yemen 108 H6
Sayingpan China 96 D3
Saykyn Kazakh. 51 P6
Saylac Somalia 121 H3
Saylan country Asia see Sri Lanka
Saylyugem, Khrebet mts Russia 98 E2
Saynshand Mongolia 95 G2
Sayn-Ust Mongolia see Höhmorĭt
Sayoa mt. Spain see Saioa
Sayot Turkm. see Saýat
Şayqal, Baḩr imp. l. Syria 107 C3
Sayqyn Kazakh. see Saykyn
Sayram Hu salt l. China 98 C3
Sayre OK U.S.A. 161 D5
Sayre PA U.S.A. 165 G3
Sayreville NJ U.S.A. 165 H3
Saysu China 94 C3
Sayula Jalisco Mex. 166 E5
Sayula Veracruz Mex. 168 F5
Sayyod Turkm. see Saýat
Sazdy Kazakh. 53 K7
Sazin Pak. 111 I3
Sbaa Alg. 64 D6
Sbeitla Tunisia 68 C7
Scaddan Australia 135 C8
Scafell Pike hill U.K. 58 D4
Scalasaig U.K. 60 C4
Scalea Italy 68 F5
Scalloway U.K. 60 [inset]
Scalpaigh, Eilean i. U.K. see Scalpay
Scalpay i. U.K. 60 C3
Scammon Bay AK U.S.A. 148 F3
Scapa Flow inlet U.K. 60 F2
Scarba i. U.K. 60 D4
Scarborough Canada 164 F2
Scarborough Trin. and Tob. 169 L6
Scarborough U.K. 58 G4
Scarborough Reef sea feature S. China Sea 80 F3
Scariff Island Ireland 61 B6
Scarp i. U.K. 60 B2
Scarpanto i. Greece see Karpathos
Scawfell Shoal sea feature S. China Sea 84 D1
Schaale r. Germany 63 K1
Schaalsee l. Germany 63 K1
Schaerbeek Belgium 62 E4
Schaffhausen Switz. 66 I3
Schafstädt Germany 63 L3
Schagen Neth. 62 E2
Schagerbrug Neth. 62 E2
Schakalskuppe Namibia 124 C4
Schärding Austria 57 N6
Scharendijke Neth. 62 D3
Scharteberg hill Germany 62 G4
Schaumburg IL U.S.A. 164 A2
Scheeßel Germany 63 J1
Schefferville Canada 153 I3
Scheibbs Austria 57 O6
Schelde r. Belgium see Scheldt
Scheldt r. Belgium 62 E3
Schell Creek Range mts NV U.S.A. 159 F2
Schellerten Germany 63 K2
Schellville CA U.S.A. 158 B2
Schenectady NY U.S.A. 165 I2
Schenefeld Germany 63 J1
Schermerhorn Neth. 62 E2
Schertz TX U.S.A. 161 D6
Schierling Germany 63 M6
Schiermonnikoog Neth. 62 G1
Schiermonnikoog i. Neth. 62 G1
Schiermonnikoog, Nationaal Park nat. park Neth. 62 G1
Schiffdorf Germany 63 I1
Schinnen Neth. 62 F4
Schio Italy 68 D2
Schkeuditz Germany 63 M3
Schleiden Germany 62 G4
Schleiz Germany 63 L4
Schleswig Germany 57 L3
Schleswig-Holstein land Germany 63 K1
Schleswig-Holsteinisches Wattenmeer, Nationalpark nat. park Germany 57 L3
Schleusingen Germany 63 K4
Schlitz Germany 63 J4
Schloß Holte-Stukenbrock Germany 63 I3
Schlüchtern Germany 63 J4
Schlüsselfeld Germany 63 K5
Schmalkalden Germany 63 K4
Schmallenberg Germany 63 I3
Schmidt Island Russia see Shmidta, Ostrov
Schmidt Peninsula Russia see Shmidta, Poluostrov
Schneeberg Germany 63 M4
Schneidemühl Poland see Piła
Schneidlingen Germany 63 L3
Schneverdingen Germany 63 J1
Schoharie NY U.S.A. 165 H2
Schönebeck Germany 63 M1
Schönebeck (Elbe) Germany 63 L2
Schönefeld airport Germany 63 N2
Schöningen Germany 63 K2
Schöntal Germany 63 J5
Schoolcraft MI U.S.A. 164 C2
Schoonhoven Neth. 62 E3
Schopfloch Germany 63 K5
Schöppenstedt Germany 63 K2
Schortens Germany 63 H1
Schouten Island Australia 137 [inset]
Schouten Islands P.N.G. 81 K7
Schrankogel mt. Austria 57 M7
Schreiber Canada 152 D4
Schroon Lake NY U.S.A. 165 I2
Schröttersburg Poland see Płock
Schulenburg TX U.S.A. 161 D6
Schuler Canada 151 I5
Schull Ireland 61 C6
Schultz Lake Canada 151 L1
Schüttorf Germany 63 H2
Schuyler NE U.S.A. 160 D3
Schuyler Lake NY U.S.A. 165 H2
Schuylkill Haven PA U.S.A. 165 G3
Schwabach Germany 63 L5
Schwäbische Alb mts Germany 57 L7
Schwäbisch Gmünd Germany 63 J6
Schwäbisch Hall Germany 63 J5
Schwaförden Germany 63 I2
Schwalm r. Germany 63 J3
Schwalmstadt-Ziegenhain Germany 63 J4
Schwandorf Germany 63 M5
Schwaner, Pegunungan mts Indon. 85 F3
Schwanewede Germany 63 I1
Schwarmstedt Germany 63 J2
Schwarze Elster r. Germany 63 M3
Schwarzenbek Germany 63 K1
Schwarzenberg/Erzgebirge Germany 63 M4
Schwarzer Mann hill Germany 62 G4
Schwarzrand mts Namibia 124 C3
Schwarzwald mts Germany see Black Forest
Schwatka, Mount AK U.S.A. 149 K2
Schwatka Mountains AK U.S.A. 148 H2
Schwaz Austria 57 M7
Schwebheim Germany 63 K5
Schwedt/Oder Germany 57 O4
Schwegenheim Germany 63 I5
Schweich Germany 62 G5
Schweinfurt Germany 63 K4
Schweinitz Germany 63 N3
Schweinrich Germany 63 M1
Schweiz country Europe see Switzerland
Schweizer-Reneke S. Africa 125 G4
Schwelm Germany 63 H3
Schwerin Germany 63 L1
Schweriner See l. Germany 63 L1
Schwetzingen Germany 63 I5
Schwyz Switz. 66 I3
Sciacca Sicily Italy 68 E6
Scicli Sicily Italy 68 F6
Science Hill KY U.S.A. 164 C5
Scilly, Île atoll Fr. Polynesia see Manuae
Scilly, Isles of U.K. 59 A9
Scioto r. OH U.S.A. 164 D4
Scipio UT U.S.A. 159 G2
Scobey MT U.S.A. 156 G2
Scodra Albania see Shkodër
Scofield Reservoir UT U.S.A. 159 H2
Scole U.K. 59 I6
Scone Australia 138 E4
Scone U.K. 60 F4
Scoresby Land reg. Greenland 147 P2
Scoresbysund Greenland see Ittoqqortoormiit
Scoresby Sund sea chan. Greenland see Kangertittivaq
Scorno, Punta dello pt Sardinia Italy see Caprara, Punta
Scorpion Bight b. Australia 135 D8
Scotia Ridge sea feature S. Atlantic Ocean 184 E9
Scotia Sea S. Atlantic Ocean 184 F9
Scotland Canada 164 E3
Scotland admin. div. U.K. 60 F3
Scotland MD U.S.A. 165 G4
Scotstown Canada 153 H5
Scott OH U.S.A. 164 C3
Scott, Cape Australia 134 E3
Scott, Cape Canada 150 D5
Scott, Mount hill OK U.S.A. 161 D5
Scott Base research station Antarctica 188 H1
Scottburgh S. Africa 125 J6
Scott City KS U.S.A. 160 C4
Scott Coast Antarctica 188 H1
Scott Glacier Antarctica 188 I1
Scott Island Antarctica 188 H2
Scott Islands Canada 150 D5
Scott Lake Canada 151 J3
Scott Mountains Antarctica 188 D2
Scott Reef Australia 134 C3
Scottsbluff NE U.S.A. 160 C3
Scottsboro AL U.S.A. 163 C5
Scottsburg IN U.S.A. 164 C4
Scottsville KY U.S.A. 164 B5
Scottsville VA U.S.A. 165 F5
Scourie U.K. 60 D2
Scousburgh U.K. 60 [inset]
Scrabster U.K. 60 F2
Scranton PA U.S.A. 165 H3
Scunthorpe U.K. 58 G5
Scuol Switz. 66 J3
Scupi Macedonia see Skopje
Scutari Albania see Shkodër
Scutari, Lake Albania/Montenegro 69 H3
Seaboard NC U.S.A. 165 G5
Seabrook, Lake salt flat Australia 135 B7
Seaford U.K. 59 H8
Seaforth Canada 164 E2
Seahorse Shoal sea feature Phil. 82 B4
Seal r. Canada 151 M3
Seal, Cape S. Africa 124 F8
Sea Lake Australia 137 C7
Seal Lake Canada 153 J3
Sealy TX U.S.A. 161 D6
Seaman OH U.S.A. 164 D4
Seaman Range mts NV U.S.A. 159 F3
Seamer U.K. 58 G4
Searchlight NV U.S.A. 159 F4
Searcy AR U.S.A. 161 F5
Searles Lake CA U.S.A. 158 E4
Seaside CA U.S.A. 157 C5
Seaside OR U.S.A. 156 C3
Seaside Park NJ U.S.A. 165 H4
Seattle WA U.S.A. 156 C3
Seattle, Mount Canada/U.S.A. 149 M3
Seaview Range mts Australia 136 D3
Seba Indon. 83 B5
Sébaco Nicaragua 166 [inset] I6
Sebago Lake ME U.S.A. 165 J2
Sebakung Kalimantan Indon. 85 G3
Sebangan, Teluk b. Indon. 85 F3
Sebangka i. Sumatra Indon. 84 D2
Sebastea Turkey see Sivas
Sebastian FL U.S.A. 163 D7
Sebastián Vizcaíno, Bahía b. Mex. 166 B2
Sebasticook r. ME U.S.A. 165 K1
Sebasticook Lake ME U.S.A. 165 K1
Sebastopol Crimea see Sevastopol'
Sebastopol CA U.S.A. 158 B2
Sebatik i. Indon. 85 G1
Sebauh Sarawak Malaysia 85 F2
Sebayan, Bukit mt. Indon. 85 E3
Sebba Burkina Faso 120 D3
Seben Turkey 69 N4
Sebenico Croatia see Šibenik
Sebeş Romania 69 J2
Sebesi i. Indon. 84 D4
Sebewaing MI U.S.A. 164 D2
Sebezh Russia 55 P8
Şebinkarahisar Turkey 112 E2
Seblat, Gunung mt. Indon. 84 C3
Sebree KY U.S.A. 164 B5
Sebring FL U.S.A. 163 D7
Sebrovo Russia 53 I6
Sebta N. Africa see Ceuta
Sebuku i. Indon. 85 G3
Sebuku r. Indon. 85 G1
Sebuku, Teluk b. Indon. 85 G2
Sebuku-Sembakung, Taman Nasional nat. park Kalimantan Indon. 85 G1
Sebuyau Sarawak Malaysia 85 E2
Sechelt Canada 150 F5
Sechenovo Russia 53 J5
Sechura Peru 176 B5
Sechura, Bahía de b. Peru 176 B5
Seckach Germany 63 J5
Second Mesa AZ U.S.A. 159 H4
Secretary Island N.Z. 139 A7
Secunda S. Africa 125 I4
Secunderabad India 106 C2
Sedalia MO U.S.A. 160 E4
Sedam India 106 C2
Sedan France 62 E5
Sedan KS U.S.A. 161 D4
Sedan Dip Australia 136 C3
Sedanka Island AK U.S.A. 148 F5
Seddon N.Z. 139 E5
Seddonville N.Z. 139 C5
Sederot Israel 107 B4
Sédhiou Gambia 120 B3
Sedlčany Czech Rep. 57 O6
Sedlets Poland see Siedlce
Sedom Israel 107 B4
Sedona AZ U.S.A. 159 H4
Sédrata Alg. 68 B6
Sedulang Kalimantan Indon. 85 G2
Šeduva Lith. 55 M9
Seedorf Germany 63 K1
Seehausen Germany 63 L2
Seehausen (Altmark) Germany 63 L2
Seeheim Namibia 124 C4
Seeheim-Jugenheim Germany 63 I5
Seela Pass Canada 149 M2
Seelig, Mount Antarctica 188 K1
Seelze Germany 63 J2
Seemandhra state India see Andhra Pradesh
Seenu Atoll Maldives see Addu Atholhu
Sées France 66 E2
Seesen Germany 63 K3
Seevetal Germany 63 K1
Sefare Botswana 125 H2
Seferihisar Turkey 69 L5
Sefīd, Kūh-e mt. Iran 110 C3
Sefīd Kūh mts Afgh. 111 G3
Sefīd Sang Iran 111 F3
Sefophe Botswana 125 H2
Segalstad Norway 55 G6
Segama r. Malaysia 85 G1
Segamat Malaysia 84 C2
Ségbana Benin 120 D3
Segeletz Germany 63 M2
Segeri Celebes Indon. 83 A4
Segezha Russia 52 G3
Segontia U.K. see Caernarfon
Segontium U.K. see Caernarfon
Segorbe Spain 67 F4
Ségou Mali 120 C3
Segovia r. Hond./Nicaragua see Coco
Segovia Spain 67 D3
Segozerskoye Vodokhranilishche resr Russia 52 G3
Seguam Island AK U.S.A. 148 D5
Seguam Pass sea chan. AK U.S.A. 148 [inset] D5
Séguédine Niger 120 E2
Séguéla Côte d'Ivoire 120 C4
Seguin TX U.S.A. 161 D6
Segula Island AK U.S.A. 148 [inset] B5
Segura r. Spain 67 F4
Segura, Sierra de mts Spain 67 E5
Sehithwa Botswana 123 C6
Sehlabathebe National Park Lesotho 125 I5
Seho i. Indon. 83 C3
Sehore India 104 D5
Sehwan Pak. 111 G5
Seibert CO U.S.A. 160 C4
Seignelay r. Canada 153 H4
Seika Japan 92 B4
Seikphyu Myanmar 86 A2
Seiland i. Norway 54 M1
Seille r. France 62 G5
Seinaiji Japan 92 D3
Seinäjoki Fin. 54 M5
Seine r. Canada 151 N5
Seine r. France 62 A5
Seine, Baie de b. France 66 D2
Seine, Val de valley France 66 F2
Seipinang Kalimantan Indon. 85 F3
Seistan reg. Iran see Sīstān
Seiwa Japan 92 C4
Sejaka Kalimantan Indon. 85 G3
Sejangkung Kalimantan Indon. 85 E2
Sejny Poland 55 M9
Sekadau Kalimantan Indon. 85 E2
Sekanak, Teluk b. Indon. 84 D3
Sekatak Bengara Kalimantan Indon. 85 G2
Sekayu Sumatra Indon. 84 C3
Seke China see Sêrtar
Seki Gifu Japan 92 C3
Seki Mie Japan 92 C4
Sekicau, Gunung vol. Indon. 84 D4
Sekidō-san hill Japan 92 C2
Sekigahara Japan 92 C3
Sekijō Japan 93 F2
Sekiyado Japan 93 F2
Sekoma Botswana 124 F3
Sekondi Ghana 120 C4
Sek'ot'a Eth. 122 D2
Sekura Kalimantan Indon. 85 E2
Şela Russia see Shali
Selagan r. Indon. 84 C3
Selakau Kalimantan Indon. 85 E2
Selama Malaysia 87 C6
Selangor state Malaysia 84 C2
Selaru i. Moluccas Indon. 83 D5
Selassi Indon. 81 I7
Selatan, Tanjung pt Indon. 85 F4
Selatpanjang Sumatra Indon. 84 C2
Selawik AK U.S.A. 148 G2
Selawik r. AK U.S.A. 148 G2
Selawik Lake AK U.S.A. 148 G2
Selawik National Wildlife Refuge nature res. AK U.S.A. 148 H2
Selayar, Pulau i. Indon. 83 B4
Selayar, Selat sea chan. Indon. 83 B4
Selb Germany 63 M4
Selbekken Norway 54 F5
Selbu Norway 54 G5
Selby U.K. 58 F5
Selby SD U.S.A. 160 C2
Selby, Lake AK U.S.A. 148 I2
Selbyville DE U.S.A. 165 H4
Selden KS U.S.A. 160 C4
Seldovia AK U.S.A. 149 J4
Sele Papua Indon. 83 D3
Sele, Selat sea chan. Papua Indon. 83 D3
Selebi-Phikwe Botswana 123 C6
Selebi-Pikwe Botswana see Selebi-Phikwe
Selemdzha r. Russia 90 C1
Selemdzhinsk Russia 90 C1
Selemdzhinskiy Khrebet mts Russia 90 D1

Selendi Turkey 69 M5
Selenduma Russia 94 F1

▶**Selenga** r. Mongolia/Russia 88 J2
Part of the Yenisey-Angara-Selenga, 3rd longest river in Asia.
Also known as Selenga Mörön.

Selenga r. Russia 94 G1
Selenge Bulgan Mongolia 94 E1
Selenge Hövsgöl Mongolia see **Ih-Uul**
Selenge prov. Mongolia 94 F1
Selenge Mörön r. Mongolia 94 F1
Sêlêpug China 99 C7
Seletar Sing. 87 [inset]
Seletar Reservoir Sing. 87 [inset]
Selety r. Kazakh. see **Silety**
Seletyteniz, Ozero salt l. Kazakh. see **Siletyteniz, Ozero**
Seleucia Turkey see **Silifke**
Seleucia Pieria Turkey see **Samandağı**
Selfridge ND U.S.A. 160 C2
Sel'gon Russia 90 D2
Sélibabi Mauritania 120 B3
Selibe-Phikwe Botswana see **Selebi-Phikwe**
Seligenstadt Germany 63 I4
Seliger, Ozero l. Russia 52 G4
Seligman AZ U.S.A. 159 G4
Selikhino Russia 90 E2
Selîma Oasis Sudan 108 C5
Selimbau Kalimantan Indon. 85 F2
Selimiye Turkey 69 L6
Selinsgrove PA U.S.A. 165 G3
Seliu i. Indon. 85 D3
Selizharovo Russia 52 G4
Seljord Norway 55 F7
Selkirk Canada 151 L5
Selkirk U.K. 60 G5
Selkirk Mountains Canada 150 G4
Sellafield U.K. 58 D4
Sellersburg IN U.S.A. 164 C4
Sellore Island Myanmar see **Saganthit Kyun**
Sells AZ U.S.A. 159 H6
Selm Germany 63 H3
Selma AL U.S.A. 163 C5
Selma CA U.S.A. 158 D3
Selmer TN U.S.A. 161 F5
Selong Lombok Indon. 85 G5
Selous, Mount Canada 149 N3
Selsey Bill hd U.K. 59 G8
Sel'tso Russia 53 G5
Selty Russia 52 L4
Selu i. Moluccas Indon. 134 E1
Seluan i. Indon. 85 D1
Selvas reg. Brazil 176 D5
Selvin IN U.S.A. 164 B4
Selway r. ID U.S.A. 156 E3
Selwyn Lake Canada 151 J2
Selwyn Mountains Canada 149 O2
Selwyn Range hills Australia 136 B4
Sël'yb Russia 52 K3
Selz r. Germany 63 I5
Semangka, Teluk b. Indon. 84 D4
Semarang Java Indon. 85 E4
Sematan Sarawak Malaysia 85 E2
Semau i. Indon. 83 B5
Semayang, Danau l. Indon. 85 G3
Sembakung r. Indon. 85 G2
Sembawang Sing. 87 [inset]
Sembé Congo 122 B3
Şemdinli Turkey 113 G3
Semendire Serbia see **Smederevo**
Semenivka Ukr. 53 G5
Semenov Russia 52 J4
Semenovka Ukr. see **Semenivka**
Semeru, Gunung vol. Indon. 84 F5
Semey Kazakh. 102 F1
Semidi Islands AK U.S.A. 148 H4
Semikarakorsk Russia 53 I7
Semiluki Russia 53 H6
Seminoe Reservoir WY U.S.A. 156 G4
Seminole TX U.S.A. 161 C5
Semipalatinsk Kazakh. see **Semey**
Semirara i. Phil. 82 C3
Semirara Islands Phil. 82 C4
Semīrom Iran 110 C4
Semitau Kalimantan Indon. 85 E2
Semiyarka Kazakh. 98 B2
Semizbuga Kazakh. 98 A2
Sem Kolodezy Crimea see **Lenine**
Semnān Iran 110 D3
Semnān va Dāmghaān reg. Iran 110 D3
Sêmnyi China 94 E4
Semois r. Belgium/France 62 E5
Semois, Vallée de la valley Belgium/France 62 E5
Semporna Sabah Malaysia 85 G1
Sempu i. Indon. 85 F5
Semyonovskoye Arkhangel'skaya Oblast' Russia see **Bereznik**
Semyonovskoye Kostromskaya Oblast' Russia see **Ostrovskoye**
Sena Bol. 176 E6
Senaja Sabah Malaysia 85 G1
Sena Madureira Brazil 176 E5
Senanga Zambia 123 C5
Senaning Kalimantan Indon. 85 E2
Sendai Japan 91 F5
Sêndo China 99 F7
Senduruhan Kalimantan Indon. 85 E3
Senebui, Tanjung pt Sumatra Indon. 84 C2
Seneca KS U.S.A. 160 D4
Seneca OR U.S.A. 156 D3
Seneca Lake NY U.S.A. 165 G2
Seneca Rocks WV U.S.A. 164 F4
Senecaville Lake OH U.S.A. 164 E4
Senegal country Africa 120 B3
Sénégal r. Mauritania/Senegal 120 B3
Seney MI U.S.A. 160 G2
Senftenberg Germany 57 O5
Senga Hill Zambia 123 D4
Sengar r. India 99 B8
Sengata Kalimantan Indon. 85 G2
Sêngdoi China 99 C7
Sengerema Tanz. 122 D4
Sengeyskiy, Ostrov i. Russia 52 K1
Sênggê Zangbo r. China 104 D2 see **Indus**
Sengilen, Khrebet mts Russia 94 C1
Sengiley Russia 53 K5
Sengirli, Mys pt Kazakh. see **Syngyrli, Mys**
Sengkang Celebes Indon. 83 B4
Sêngli Co l. China 99 D7
Senhor do Bonfim Brazil 177 J6
Senigallia Italy 68 E3
Senj Croatia 68 F2
Senja i. Norway 54 J2
Senjōga-dake mt. Japan 92 B4
Senjōga-dake mt. Japan 93 E3
Sen'kina Russia 52 K2
Şenköy Turkey 107 C1
Senlac S. Africa 124 F3
Senlin Shan mt. China 90 C4
Senlis France 62 C5
Sênmônoŭrôm Cambodia 87 D4
Sennan Japan 92 B4
Sennar Sudan 108 D7
Sennen U.K. 59 B8
Senneterre Canada 152 F4
Sennokura-yama mt. Japan 93 E2
Senqu r. Lesotho 125 H6
Sens France 66 F2
Sensuntepeque El Salvador 166 [inset] H6
Senta Serbia 69 I2
Senthal India 104 D3
Sentinel AZ U.S.A. 159 G5
Sentinel Peak Canada 150 F4
Sentispac Mex. 166 D4
Sentosa i. Sing. 87 [inset]
Sento Sé Brazil 177 J5
Senwabarwana S. Africa 125 I2
Senyiur Kalimantan Indon. 85 G2
Şenyurt Turkey 113 F3
Seocheon S. Korea 91 B5
Seo de Urgell Spain see **La Seu d'Urgell**
Seonath r. India 106 D1
Seongnam S. Korea 91 B5
Seoni India 104 D5
Seorak-san mt. S. Korea 91 C5
Seorak-san National Park S. Korea 91 C5
Seorinarayan India 105 E5
Seosan S. Korea 91 B5

▶**Seoul** S. Korea 91 B5
Capital of South Korea.

Sepanjang i. Indon. 85 F4
Separation Well Australia 134 C5
Sepasu Kalimantan Indon. 85 G2
Sepauk Kalimantan Indon. 85 E2
Sepik r. P.N.G. 81 K7
Sepinang Kalimantan Indon. 85 G2
Seping r. Malaysia 85 F2
Sep'o N. Korea 91 B5
Sepon India 105 H4
Seppa India 105 H4
Sept-Îles Canada 153 I4
Seputih r. Indon. 84 D4
Sequoia National Park CA U.S.A. 158 D3
Serafimovich Russia 53 I6
Sêraitang China see **Baima**
Seram i. Moluccas Indon. 83 D3
Seram, Laut sea Indon. 83 D3
Serang Java Indon. 84 D4
Serangoon Harbour b. Sing. 87 [inset]
Serapi, Gunung hill Indon. 87 E7
Serapong, Mount hill Sing. 87 [inset]
Serasan i. Indon. 85 E2
Serasan, Selat sea chan. Indon. 85 E2
Seraya i. Indon. 83 A5
Seraya i. Indon. 85 E2
Serbâl, Gebel mt. Egypt see **Sirbāl, Jabal**
Serbia country Europe 69 I3
Sêrbug Co l. China 99 E6
Sêrca China 99 F7
Serchhip India 105 H5
Serdar Turkm. 110 E2
Serdica Bulg. see **Sofia**
Serdo Eth. 122 E2
Serdoba r. Russia 53 J5
Serdobsk Russia 53 J5
Serdtse-Kamen', Mys c. Russia 148 E2
Serebryansk Kazakh. 102 F2
Seredka Russia 55 P7
Şereflikoçhisar Turkey 112 D3
Serekunda Gambia 120 B3
Seremban Malaysia 84 C2
Serengeti National Park Tanz. 122 D4
Serenje Zambia 123 D5
Serezha r. Russia 52 I5
Sergach Russia 52 J5
Sergelen Dornod Mongolia 95 H1
Sergelen Sühbaatar Mongolia see **Tüvshinshiree**
Sergeyevka Russia 90 B2
Sergiyev Posad Russia 52 H4
Sergo Ukr. see **Stakhanov**
Serh China 94 D4
Serhetabat Turkm. 111 F3
Seria Brunei 85 F1
Serian Sarawak Malaysia 85 E2
Seribu, Kepulauan is Indon. 84 D4
Serifos i. Greece 69 K6
Sérigny r. Canada 153 H3
Sérigny, Lac l. Canada 153 H3
Serik Turkey 112 C3
Serikbuya China 98 B5
Serikkembelo Seram Indon. 83 C3
Seringapatam Reef Australia 134 C3
Sêrkang China see **Nyainrong**
Sermata i. Moluccas Indon. 83 D5
Sermata, Kepulauan is Moluccas Indon. 83 D5
Sermersuaq glacier Greenland 147 M2
Sermilik inlet Greenland 147 O3
Sernovodsk Russia 53 K5
Sernur Russia 52 K4
Sernyy Zavod Turkm. see **Kükürtli**
Seronga Botswana 123 C5
Serov Russia 51 S4
Serowe Botswana 125 H2
Serpa Port. 67 C5
Serpa Pinto Angola see **Menongue**
Serpentine Hot Springs AK U.S.A. 148 F2
Serpentine Lakes salt flat Australia 135 E7
Serpukhov Russia 53 H5
Serra Brazil 179 C3
Serra Alta Brazil 179 A4
Serrachis r. Cyprus 107 A2
Serra da Bocaina, Parque Nacional da nat. park Brazil 179 B3
Serra da Canastra, Parque Nacional da nat. park Brazil 179 B3
Serra da Mesa, Represa resr Brazil 179 A1
Serra das Araras Brazil 179 B1
Serra do Divisor, Parque Nacional da nat. park Brazil 176 D5
Sérrai Greece see **Serres**
Serranía de la Neblina, Parque Nacional nat. park Venez. 176 E3
Serraria, Ilha i. Brazil see **Queimada, Ilha**
Serra Talhada Brazil 177 K5
Serre r. France 62 D5
Serres Greece 69 J4
Serrinha Brazil 177 K6
Serro Brazil 179 C2
Sers Tunisia 68 C6
Sertanópolis Brazil 179 A3
Sertãozinho Brazil 179 B3
Sêrtar China 96 D1
Sertavul Geçidi pass Turkey 107 A1
Sertolovo Russia 55 Q6
Serua vol. Moluccas Indon. 83 D4
Seruai Sumatra Indon. 84 B1
Serui Indon. 81 J7
Serule Botswana 123 C6
Seruna India 104 C3
Serutu i. Indon. 85 E3
Seruyan r. Indon. 85 F3
Serwaru Moluccas Indon. 83 C5
Sêrwolungwa China 94 C5
Sêrxü China 96 C1
Serykh Gusey, Ostrova is Russia 148 D2
Seryshevo Russia 90 C2
Sesayap Kalimantan Indon. 85 G2
Sesayap r. Indon. 85 G2
Seseganaga Lake Canada 152 C4
Sese Islands Uganda 122 D4
Sesel country Indian Ocean see **Seychelles**
Sesepe Moluccas Indon. 83 C3
Sesfontein Namibia 123 B5
Seshachalam Hills India 106 C3
Seshan Russia 148 E2
Sesheke Zambia 123 C5
Sesostris Bank sea feature India 106 A3
Sestri Levante Italy 68 C2
Sestroretsk Russia 55 P6
Set, Phou mt. Laos 86 D4
Sète France 66 F5
Sete Lagoas Brazil 179 B2
Setermoen Norway 54 K2
Setesdal valley Norway 55 E7
Seti r. Nepal 104 E3
Sétif Alg. 64 F4
Seto Japan 92 D3
Seto-naikai sea Japan 89 O6
Seto-naikai Kokuritsu-kōen Japan 91 D6
Setsan Myanmar 86 A3
Settat Morocco 64 C5
Settepani, Monte mt. Italy 68 C2
Settle U.K. 58 E4
Setúbal Port. 67 B4
Setúbal, Baía de b. Port. 67 B4
Seul, Lac l. Canada 151 M5
Seulimeum Sumatra Indon. 84 A1
Sevan Armenia 113 G2
Sevan, Lake Armenia 113 G2
Sevan, Ozero l. Armenia see **Sevan, Lake**
Sevana Lich l. Armenia see **Sevan, Lake**
Sevastopol' Crimea 112 D1
Seven Islands Canada see **Sept-Îles**
Seven Islands Bay Canada 153 J2
Sevenoaks U.K. 59 H7
Seventy Mile House Canada see **70 Mile House**
Sévérac-le-Château France 66 F4
Severn r. Australia 138 E2
Severn r. Canada 152 D3
Severn S. Africa 124 F4
Severn r. U.K. 59 E7
also known as Hafren
Severnaya Dvina r. Russia 52 I2
Severnaya Sos'va r. Russia 51 T3
Severnaya Zemlya is Russia 77 L1
Severn Lake Canada 151 N4
Severnoye Russia 51 Q5
Severnyy Nenetskiy Avtonomnyy Okrug Russia 52 K1
Severnyy Respublika Komi Russia 76 H3

▶**Severnyy, Ostrov** i. Russia 76 G2
4th largest island in Europe.

Severobaykal'sk Russia 89 J1
Severo-Baykal'skoye Nagor'ye mts Russia 77 M4
Severo-Chuyskiy Khrebet mts Russia 98 D2
Severodonetsk Ukr. see **Syeverodonets'k**
Severodvinsk Russia 52 H2
Severo-Kuril'sk Russia 77 Q4
Severomorsk Russia 54 R2
Severoonezhsk Russia 52 H3
Severo-Sibirskaya Nizmennost' lowland Russia see **North Siberian Lowland**
Severoural'sk Russia 51 R3
Severo-Yeniseyskiy Russia 76 K3
Severskaya Russia 112 E1
Severskiy Donets r. Russia/Ukr. see **Northern Donets**
Sevier UT U.S.A. 159 G2
Sevier r. UT U.S.A. 159 G2
Sevier Desert UT U.S.A. 159 G2
Sevier Lake UT U.S.A. 159 G2
Sevierville TN U.S.A. 162 D5
Sevilla Col. 176 C3
Sevilla Spain see **Seville**
Seville Spain 67 D5
Sevlyush Ukr. see **Vynohradiv**
Sêwa China 99 E6
Sewani India 104 C3
Seward AK U.S.A. 149 J3
Seward NE U.S.A. 160 D3
Seward Mountains Antarctica 188 L2
Seward Peninsula AK U.S.A. 148 F2
Sexi Spain see **Almuñécar**
Sexsmith Canada 150 G4
Sextín Mex. 166 D3
Sextín r. Mex. 166 D3
Seya Japan 93 F3
Seyakha Russia 189 F2
Seybaplaya Mex. 167 H5
Seychelles country Indian Ocean 185 L6
Seÿdi Turkm. 111 F2
Seydişehir Turkey 112 C3
Seyðisfjörður Iceland 54 [inset 1]
Seyhan Turkey see **Adana**
Seyhan r. Turkey 107 B1
Seyitgazi Turkey 69 N5
Seym r. Russia/Ukr. 53 G6
Seymchan Russia 77 Q3
Seymour Australia 138 B6
Seymour S. Africa 125 H7
Seymour IN U.S.A. 164 C4
Seymour TX U.S.A. 161 D5
Seymour Inlet Canada 150 E5
Seymour Range mts Australia 135 F6
Seypan i. N. Mariana Is see **Saipan**
Sézanne France 62 D6
Sfakia Greece see **Chora Sfakion**
Sfântu Gheorghe Romania 69 K2
Sfax Tunisia 68 D7
Sfikia, Limni resr Greece see **Sfikias, Limni**
Sfikias, Limni resr Greece 69 J4
Sfintu Gheorghe Romania see **Sfântu Gheorghe**
Sgiersch Poland see **Zgierz**
's-Graveland Neth. 62 F2
's-Gravenhage Neth. see **The Hague**
Sgurr Alasdair hill U.K. 60 C3
Sgurr Dhomhnuill hill U.K. 60 D4
Sgurr Mòr mt. U.K. 60 D3
Sgurr na Ciche mt. U.K. 60 D3
Shaanxi prov. China 95 G5
Shaartuz Tajik. see **Shahritus**
Shaban Pak. 111 G4
Shabani Zimbabwe see **Zvishavane**
Shabestar Iran 110 B2
Shabībī, Jabal ash mt. Jordan 107 B5
Shabla, Nos pt Bulg. 69 M3
Shabogamo Lake Canada 153 I3
Shabunda Dem. Rep. Congo 122 C4
Shache China 98 B5
Shacheng China see **Huailai**
Shackleton Coast Antarctica 188 H1
Shackleton Glacier Antarctica 188 I1
Shackleton Ice Shelf Antarctica 188 F2
Shackleton Range mts Antarctica 188 A1
Shadaogou China 97 F2
Shadaw Myanmar 86 B3
Shādegān Iran 110 C4
Shadihar Pak. 111 G4
Shady Cove OR U.S.A. 156 C4
Shady Spring WV U.S.A. 164 E5
Shadzud Tajik. 111 I2
Shafer, Lake IN U.S.A. 164 B3
Shafer Peak Antarctica 188 H2
Shafter CA U.S.A. 158 D4
Shaftesbury U.K. 59 E7
Shagamu r. Canada 152 D3
Shagan Kazakh. 98 B2
Shagan watercourse Kazakh. 98 B2
Shagedu China 95 G4
Shageluk AK U.S.A. 148 H3
Shaghyray Üstirti plat. Kazakh. see **Shagyray, Plato**
Shagonar Russia 102 H1
Shag Point N.Z. 139 C7
Shag Rocks is S. Georgia 178 H8
Shagyray, Plato plat. Kazakh. 102 A2
Shahabad Karnataka India 106 C2
Shahabad Rajasthan India 104 D4
Shahabad Uttar Prad. India 104 E4
Shāhābād Iran see **Eslāmābād-e Gharb**
Shah Alam Malaysia 84 C2
Shah Bandar Pak. 111 G5
Shahdād Iran 110 E4
Shahdol India 104 E5
Shahe Chongqing China 97 F2
Shahe Shandong China 95 I4
Shahe Shanxi China 95 H4
Shahejie China see **Jiujiang**
Shahepu China see **Linze**
Shahezhen Gansu China see **Linze**
Shahezhen Jiangxi China see **Jiujiang**
Shāh Fōlād mt. Afgh. 111 G3
Shahid, Ras pt Pak. 111 F5
Shāhīn Dezh Iran 110 B2
Shāh Ismā'īl Afgh. 111 G4
Shāh Jahān, Kūh-e mts Iran 110 E2
Shahjahanpur India 104 D4
Shāh Kūh mt. Iran 110 E4
Shahousuo China 95 J3
Shāhpūr Iran see **Salmās**
Shahrak Afgh. 111 G3
Shāhrakht Iran 111 F3
Shahr-e Bābak Iran 110 D4
Shahr-e Ghulghulah tourist site Afgh. 111 F4
Shahr-e Kord Iran 110 C3
Shahr-e Şafā Afgh. 111 G4
Shahreẓā Iran 110 C3
Shahrig Pak. 111 G4
Shahrisabz Uzbek. 111 G2
Shahr-i Sokhta tourist site Iran 111 F4
Shahriston Tajik. 111 H2
Shahritus Tajik. 111 H2
Shahr Sultan Pak. 111 H4
Shāhrūd Iran 110 D2
Shāhrūd, Rūdkhāneh-ye r. Iran 110 C2
Shāhrūd Bustām reg. Iran 110 D3
Shāh Savārān, Kūh-e mts Iran 110 E4
Shāh Taqī Iran see **Emām Taqī**
Shaighalu Pak. 111 H4
Shaikh Husain mt. Pak. 111 G4
Shaikhpura India see **Sheikhpura**
Shā'ir, Jabal mts Syria 107 C2
Sha'īra, Gebel mt. Egypt see **Sha'īrah, Jabal**
Sha'īrah, Jabal mt. Egypt 107 B5
Shaj'ah, Jabal hill Saudi Arabia 110 C5
Shajapur India 104 D5
Shajianzi China 90 B4
Shakaga-dake mt. Japan 92 B4
Shakaville S. Africa 125 J5
Shakh Tajik. see **Shoh**
Shakhbuz Azer. see **Şahbuz**
Shākhen Iran 111 E3
Shakhovskaya Russia 52 G4
Shakhrisabz Uzbek. see **Shahrisabz**
Shakhristan Tajik. see **Shahriston**
Shakhtinsk Kazakh. 102 D2
Shakhty Respublika Buryatiya Russia see **Gusinoozersk**
Shakhty Rostovskaya Oblast' Russia 53 I7
Shakhun'ya Russia 52 J4
Shaki Nigeria see **Saki**
Shakotan-hantō pen. Japan 90 F4
Shaktoolik AK U.S.A. 148 G2
Shalakusha Russia 52 I3
Shalang China 97 F4
Shali Russia 113 G2
Shaliangzi China 94 C4
Shaliuhe China see **Gangca**
Shalkar India 104 D3
Shalkar Kazakh. 102 A2
Shalkarteniz, Solonchak salt marsh Kazakh. 102 B2
Shalkodesu Kazakh. 98 B4
Shallow Bay Canada 149 M1
Shalqar Kazakh. see **Shalkar**
Shaluli Shan mts China 96 C2
Shaluni mt. India 105 I3
Shama r. Tanz. 123 D4
Shamāl Sīnā' governorate Egypt see **Shamāl Sīnā'**
Shamāl Sīnā' governorate Egypt 107 A4
Shāmat al Akbād des. Saudi Arabia 113 F5
Shamattawa Canada 151 N4
Shamattawa r. Canada 152 D3
Shambār Iran 110 C3
Shamgong Bhutan see **Zhemgang**
Shamīl Iran 110 E5
Shāmīyah des. Iraq/Syria 107 D2
Shamkhor Azer. see **Şämkir**
Shamrock TX U.S.A. 161 C5
Shancheng Fujian China see **Taining**
Shancheng Henan China 95 H5
Shancheng Shandong China see **Shanxian**
Shand Afgh. 111 F4
Shandan China 94 E4
Shandian He r. China 95 I3
Shandong prov. China 95 I4
Shandong Bandao pen. China 95 J4
Shandur Pass Pak. 111 I2
Shangchao China 97 F3
Shangcheng China 97 G2
Shang Chu r. China 99 E7
Shangchuan Dao i. China 97 G4
Shangdu Nei Mongol China 95 H3
Shangdu Nei Mongol China 95 I3
Shangganling China 90 C3

▶**Shanghai** China 97 I2
3rd most populous city in Asia and the world.

Shanghai mun. China 97 I2
Shanghe China 95 I4
Shangji China see **Xichuan**
Shangjie China see **Yangbi**
Shangjin China 97 F1
Shangkuli China 95 J1
Shangluo China 97 F1
Shangmei China see **Xinhua**
Shangnan China 97 F1
Shangpa China see **Fugong**
Shangpai China see **Feixi**
Shangpaihe China see **Feixi**
Shangqiu China 95 H5
Shangrao China 97 H2
Shangsanshilipu China 98 C3
Shangshui China 97 G1
Shangyou China 97 G3
Shangyou Shuiku resr China 98 C4
Shangyu China 97 I2
Shangzhi China 90 B3
Shangzhou China see **Shangluo**
Shanhaiguan China 95 I3
Shanhe Gansu China see **Zhengning**
Shanhe Heilong. China 90 B3
Shanhou He r. China 95 I5
Shankou Guangxi China 97 F4
Shankou Xinjiang China 94 C3
Shanlaragh Ireland 61 C6
Shannon airport Ireland 61 D5
Shannon est. Ireland 61 D5
Shannon r. Ireland 61 D5
Shannon, Mouth of the Ireland 61 C5
Shannon National Park Australia 135 B8
Shannon Ø i. Greenland 189 I1
Shan Plateau Myanmar 86 B2
Shanshan China 94 B3
Shanshanzhan China 94 B3
Shansi prov. China see **Shanxi**
Shan Teng hill H.K. China see **Victoria Peak**
Shantipur India 105 G5
Shantou China 97 H4
Shantung prov. China see **Shandong**
Shanwei China 97 G4
Shanxi prov. China 95 G4
Shanxian China 95 I5
Shanyang China 97 F1
Shanyin China 95 H4
Shaodong China 97 F3
Shaoguan China 97 G3
Shaowu China 97 H3
Shaoxing China 97 I2
Shaoyang China 97 F3
Shap U.K. 58 E4
Shapa China 97 F4
Shaping China see **Ebian**
Shapinsay i. U.K. 60 G1
Shapkina r. Russia 52 L2
Shapshal'skiy Khrebet mts Russia 98 E2
Shaqiuhe China 98 E3
Shaqrā' Saudi Arabia 108 G4
Shaquanzi China 98 C3
Shar Kazakh. 98 C2
Shār, Jabal mt. Saudi Arabia 112 D6
Sharaf well Iraq 113 F5
Sharalday Russia 95 F1
Sharan Jogizai Pak. 111 H4
Sharbulag Mongolia see **Dzavhan**
Shardara Kazakh. 102 C3
Shardara, Step' plain Kazakh. 102 C3
Sharga Govĭ-Altay Mongolia 94 C2
Sharga Hövsgöl Mongolia see **Tsagaan-Uul**
Shargīn Tsagaan Nuur salt l. Mongolia 94 C2
Sharhulsan Mongolia see **Mandal-Ovoo**
Shari r. Cameroon/Chad see **Chari**
Shārī, Buḩayrat imp. l. Iraq 113 G4
Shari-dake vol. Japan 90 G4
Sharīfah Syria 107 C2
Shariff Aguak Phil. 82 D5
Shārīmā Iran 110 E4
Sharjah U.A.E. 110 D5
Sharka-leb La pass China 99 E7
Sharkawshchyna Belarus 55 O9
Shark Bay Australia 135 A6
Shark Reef Australia 136 D2
Sharlyk Russia 51 Q5
Sharm ash Shaykh Egypt 112 D6
Sharm el Sheikh Egypt see **Sharm ash Shaykh**
Sharon PA U.S.A. 164 E3
Sharon Springs KS U.S.A. 160 C4
Sharpe Lake Canada 151 M4
Sharp Mountain Canada 149 M2
Sharp Peak hill H.K. China 97 [inset]
Sharqat Iraq see **Ash Sharqāț**
Sharqī, Jabal ash mts Lebanon/Syria 107 B3
Sharqiy Ustyurt Chink esc. Uzbek. 102 A3
Sharur Azer. see **Şärur**
Shar Us Gol r. Mongolia 94 D2
Shar'ya Russia 52 J4
Sharyn Kazakh. 98 B4
Sharyn r. Kazakh. 98 B4
Shashe r. Botswana/Zimbabwe 123 C6
Shashemenē Eth. 122 D3
Shashi China see **Jingzhou**
Shashubay Kazakh. 98 A3
Shasta CA U.S.A. 158 B1
Shasta, Mount vol. CA U.S.A. 156 C4
Shasta Lake CA U.S.A. 158 B1
Shatilki Belarus see **Svyetlahorsk**
Sha Tin H.K. China 97 [inset]
Shatki Russia 53 J5
Shaṭnat as Salmās, Wādī watercourse Syria 107 D2
Sha Tong Hau Shan H.K. China see **Bluff Island**
Shatoy Russia 113 G2
Shatsk Russia 53 I5
Shatsky Rise sea feature Pacific Ocean 186 G3
Shatt al Arab r. Iran/Iraq 113 H5
Shatura Russia 53 H5
Shaubak Jordan see **Ash Shawbak**
Shaunavon Canada 151 I5
Shaver Lake CA U.S.A. 158 D3
Shaviovik r. AK U.S.A. 149 K1
Shaw r. Australia 134 B5
Shawan China 98 D3
Shawangunk Mountains hills NY U.S.A. 165 H3
Shawano WI U.S.A. 164 A1
Shawano Lake WI U.S.A. 164 A1
Shawinigan Canada 153 G5
Shawnee OK U.S.A. 161 D5
Shawnee WY U.S.A. 156 G4
Shawneetown IL U.S.A. 160 F4
Shaxian China 97 H3
Shay Gap (abandoned) Australia 134 C5
Shaykh, Jabal ash mt. Lebanon/Syria see **Hermon, Mount**
Shaykh Miskīn Syria 107 C3
Shāzand Iran 110 C3
Shazaoyuan China 98 F5
Shchekino Russia 53 H5
Shchel'yayur Russia 52 L2
Shcherbakov Russia see **Rybinsk**
Shchigry Russia 53 H6
Shchors Ukr. 53 F6
Shchuchin Belarus see **Shchuchyn**
Shchuchyn Belarus 55 N10
Shebalino Russia 102 G1
Shebekino Russia 53 H6
Shebelē Wenz, Wabē r. Eth. 122 E3

▶**Shebelē Wenz, Wabē** r. Somalia 122 E3
5th longest river in Africa.

Sheboygan WI U.S.A. 164 B2
Shebshi Mountains Nigeria 120 E4
Shebunino Russia 90 F3
Shecheng China see **Shexian**
Shediac Canada 153 I5
Shedin Peak Canada 150 E4
Shedok Russia 113 F1

Sheelin, Lough l. Ireland 61 E4
Sheenjek r. AK U.S.A. 149 K2
Sheep Haven b. Ireland 61 E2
Sheepmoor S. Africa 125 J4
Sheep Mountain CO U.S.A. 159 J2
Sheep Peak NV U.S.A. 159 F3
Sheep's Head hd Ireland see Muntervary
Sheerness U.K. 59 H7
Sheet Harbour Canada 153 J5
Shefar'am Israel 107 B3
Sheffield N.Z. 139 D6
Sheffield U.K. 58 F5
Sheffield AL U.S.A. 163 C5
Sheffield PA U.S.A. 164 F3
Sheffield TX U.S.A. 161 C6
Sheffield Lake Canada 153 K4
Shēgē 'Alāqahdārī Afgh. 111 G4
Sheghnān Afgh. 111 H2
Shegmas Russia 52 K2
Shehong China 96 E2
Sheikh, Jebel esh mt. Lebanon/Syria see Hermon, Mount
Sheikhpura India 105 F4
Sheikhupura Pak. 111 I4
Shējā' ul Mulk Kêlay Afgh. 111 H4
Shekak r. Canada 152 D4
Shekār Āb Iran 110 D3
Shekhawati reg. India 111 I5
Shekhem West Bank see Nāblus
Shekhpura India see Sheikhpura
Sheki Azer. see Şäki
Shekka Ch'ün-Tao H.K. China see Soko Islands
Shek Kwu Chau i. H.K. China 97 [inset]
Shekou China 97 [inset]
Sheksna Russia 52 H4
Sheksninskoye Vodokhranilishche resr Russia 52 H4
Shek Uk Shan mt. H.K. China 97 [inset]
Shela China 99 F7
Shelagskiy, Mys pt Russia 77 S2
Shelbina MO U.S.A. 160 E4
Shelburn IN U.S.A. 164 B4
Shelburne N.S. Canada 153 I6
Shelburne Ont. Canada 164 E1
Shelburne Bay Australia 136 C1
Shelby MI U.S.A. 164 B2
Shelby MS U.S.A. 161 F5
Shelby MT U.S.A. 156 F2
Shelby NC U.S.A. 163 D5
Shelbyville IL U.S.A. 160 F4
Shelbyville IN U.S.A. 164 C4
Shelbyville KY U.S.A. 164 C4
Shelbyville TN U.S.A. 162 C5
Sheldon IA U.S.A. 160 E3
Sheldon IL U.S.A. 164 B3
Sheldrake Canada 153 I4
Shelek Kazakh. see Shilik
Shelikhova, Zaliv g. Russia 77 Q3
Shelikof Strait AK U.S.A. 148 I4
Shell WY U.S.A. 160 B2
Shellbrook Canada 151 J4
Shelley ID U.S.A. 156 E4
Shellharbour Australia 138 E5
Shell Lake Canada 151 J4
Shell Lake WI U.S.A. 160 F2
Shell Mountain CA U.S.A. 158 B1
Shelter Bay Canada see Port-Cartier
Shelter Island NY U.S.A. 165 I3
Shelter Point N.Z. 139 B8
Shelton WA U.S.A. 156 C3
Shemakha Azer. see Şamaxı
Shemonaikha Kazakh. 98 C2
Shemordan Russia 52 K4
Shenandoah IA U.S.A. 160 E3
Shenandoah PA U.S.A. 165 G3
Shenandoah Mountains Virginia/West Virginia U.S.A. 164 F4
Shenandoah National Park VA U.S.A. 165 F4
Shenchi China 95 H4
Shendam Nigeria 120 D4
Shending Shan hill China 90 D3
Shengel'dy Kazakh. 98 B3
Shengena mt. Tanz. 123 D4
Shengli China 97 G2
Shengli Daban pass China 98 D4
Shengli Feng mt. China/Kyrg. see Pobeda Peak
Shengli Qichang China 98 B4
Shengli Shibachang China 98 C4
Shengping China 90 B3
Shengrenjian China see Pinglu
Sheng Shan i. China 97 I2
Shengsi China 97 I2
Shengsi Liedao is China 97 I2
Shenjiamen China see Putuo
Shenkursk Russia 52 I3
Shenmu China 95 G4
Shennong Ding mt. China 97 F2
Shennongjia China 97 F2
Shenqiu China 97 G1
Shenshu China 90 C3
Shensi prov. China see Shaanxi
Shentala Russia 53 K5
Shenton, Mount hill Australia 135 C7
Shenxian Hebei China see Shenzhou
Shenxian Shandong China 95 H4
Shenyang China 95 J3
Shenzhen China 97 G4
Shenzhen Wan b. H.K. China see Deep Bay
Shenzhou China 95 H4
Sheopur India 104 D4
Shepetivka Ukr. 53 E6
Shepetovka Ukr. see Shepetivka
Shepherd Islands Vanuatu 133 G3
Shepherdsville KY U.S.A. 164 C5
Shepparton Australia 138 B6
Sheppey, Isle of i. U.K. 59 H7
Sheqi China 97 G1
Sherabad Uzbek. see Sherobod
Sherborne U.K. 59 E8
Sherbro Island Sierra Leone 120 B4
Sherbrooke Canada 153 H5
Sherburne NY U.S.A. 165 H2
Shercock Ireland 61 F4
Sherdyayak Kazakh. 98 C2
Shereiq Sudan 108 D6
Shergaon India 105 H4
Shergarh India 104 C4
Sheridan AR U.S.A. 161 E5
Sheridan WY U.S.A. 156 G3
Sheringham U.K. 59 I6
Sherlovaya Gora Russia 95 I1
Sherman TX U.S.A. 161 D5
Sherman Mountain NV U.S.A. 159 F1
Sherobod Uzbek. 111 G2
Sherpur Dhaka Bangl. 105 G4
Sherpur Rajshahi Bangl. 105 G4
Sherridon Canada 151 K4
's-Hertogenbosch Neth. 62 F3
Sherwood Forest reg. U.K. 59 F5
Sherwood Lake Canada 151 K2
Sheslay Canada 149 O4
Sheslay r. Canada 149 N4
Shethanei Lake Canada 151 L3
Shetland Islands is U.K. 60 [inset]
Shetpe Kazakh. 100 E2
Sheung Shui H.K. China 97 [inset]
Sheung Sze Mun sea chan. H.K. China 97 [inset]
Shevchenko Kazakh. see Aktau
Shevli r. Russia 90 D1
Shexian Anhui China 97 H2
Shexian Hebei China 95 H4
Sheyang China 97 I1
Sheyenne r. ND U.S.A. 160 D2
Shey Phoksundo National Park Nepal 105 E3
Sheyṭūr Iran 110 D4
Shezhin II Kazakh. 53 K6
Shiant Islands U.K. 60 C3
Shiashkotan, Ostrov i. Russia 77 Q5
Shibakawa Japan 93 E3
Shibām Yemen 108 G6
Shibandong Jing well China 94 C3
Shiban Jing well China 94 D3
Shibaocheng China 94 D4
Shibar, Kōtal-e Afgh. 111 H3
Shibata Japan 91 E5
Shibayama Japan 93 G3
Shibayama-gata l. Japan 92 C2
Shibazhan China 90 B1
Shibh Jazīrat Sīnā' pen. Egypt see Sinai
Shibīn al Kawm Egypt 112 C5
Shibîn el Kôm Egypt see Shibīn al Kawm
Shibirghān Afgh. 111 G2
Shibogama Lake Canada 152 C3
Shibotsu-jima i. Russia see Zelenyy, Ostrov
Shibukawa Japan 93 F2
Shibu-tōge pass Japan 93 E2
Shibutsu-san mt. Japan 93 F2
Shicheng Fujian China see Zhouning
Shicheng Jiangxi China 97 H3
Shicheng Dao i. China 95 J4
Shichimen-zan mt. Japan 93 E3
Shicun China see Xiangfen
Shidād al Mismā' hill Saudi Arabia 107 D4
Shidao China 95 J4
Shidao Wan b. China 95 J4
Shidian China 96 C3
Shidongsi China see Gaolan
Shiel, Loch l. U.K. 60 D4
Shield, Cape Australia 136 B2
Shīeli Kazakh. see Shiyeli
Shīf Iran 110 C4
Shifa, Jabal ash mts Saudi Arabia 112 D5
Shifang China 96 E2
Shiga Nagano Japan 93 D2
Shiga Shiga Japan 92 B3
Shiga pref. Japan 92 B3
Shigaraki Japan 92 C4
Shigatse China see Xigazê
Shigong China 98 F4
Shiguai China 95 G3
Shiguaigou China see Shiguai
Shiḥān mt. Jordan 107 B4
Shihezi China 98 D3
Shihkiachwang China see Shijiazhuang
Shijiao China see Fogang
Shijiazhuang China 95 H4
Shijiu Hu l. China 97 H2
Shijiusuo China see Rizhao
Shika Japan 92 C1
Shikag Lake Canada 152 C4
Shikar r. Pak. 111 F4
Shikarpur Pak. 111 H5
Shikengkong mt. China 97 G3
Shikhany Russia 53 J5
Shiki Japan 93 F3
Shikine-jima i. Japan 93 F4
Shikishima Japan 93 E3
Shikohabad India 104 D4
Shikoku i. Japan 91 D6
Shikoku-sanchi mts Japan 91 D6
Shikotan, Ostrov i. Russia 90 G4
Shikotan-tō i. Russia see Shikotan, Ostrov
Shikotsu-Tōya Kokuritsu-kōen Japan 90 F4
Shildon U.K. 58 F4
Shilega Russia 52 J2
Shilianghe Shuiku resr China 95 I5
Shiliguri India 105 G4
Shilik Kazakh. 102 E3
Shilik r. Kazakh. 98 B4
Shilin China 96 D3
Shilipu China 97 G2
Shiliu China see Changjiang
Shilla mt. India 104 D2
Shillelagh Ireland 61 F5
Shillo, Naḥal r. Israel 107 B3
Shillong India 105 G4
Shillong Peak mt. India 105 G4
Shilou China 95 G4
Shilovo Russia 53 I5
Shilüüstey Mongolia 94 D2
Shima Mie Japan 92 C4
Shima Mie Japan 92 C4
Shima spring Japan 93 E2
Shimada Japan 93 E4
Shimagahara Japan 92 C4
Shimamoto Japan 92 B4
Shimanovsk Russia 90 B1
Shimbiris mt. Somalia 122 E2
Shimen Gansu China 96 D1
Shimen Hunan China 97 F2
Shimen Yunnan China see Yunlong
Shimizu Fukui Japan 92 C2
Shimizu Shizuoka Japan 93 E3
Shimizu Shizuoka Japan 93 E3
Shimizu Wakayama Japan 92 B4
Shimla India 104 D3
Shimminato Japan see Shinminato
Shimo Japan 92 D2
Shimobe Japan 93 E3
Shimoda Japan 93 E4
Shimofusa Japan 93 G3
Shimoga India see Shivamogga
Shimoichi Japan 92 B4
Shimojō Japan 93 D3
Shimokita-hantō pen. Japan 90 F4
Shimokitayama Japan 92 B4
Shimoni Kenya 123 D4
Shimonita Japan 93 E2
Shimonoseki Japan 91 C6
Shimosuwa Japan 93 E2
Shimotsu Japan 92 B4
Shimotsuke Japan 93 F2
Shimotsuma Japan 93 F2
Shimoyama Japan 92 D3
Shimsk Russia 52 F4
Shin Japan 93 F2
Shin, Loch l. U.K. 60 E2
Shināfīyah Iraq see Ash Shanāfīyah
Shinan China see Xingye
Shinano Japan 93 E2
Shin'asahi Japan see Takashima
Shīndand Afgh. 111 F3
Shine-Ider Mongolia 94 D1
Shinejinst Mongolia 94 D2
Shingbwiyang Myanmar 86 B1
Shing-gai Myanmar 86 B1
Shinghshal Pass Pak. 111 I2
Shingletown CA U.S.A. 158 C1
Shingū Japan 91 E6
Shingwedzi S. Africa 125 J2
Shingwedzi r. S. Africa 125 J2
Shīnkaī Afgh. 111 G4
Shīnkay Ghar Afgh. 111 H3
Shinminato Japan 92 D2
Shinnston WV U.S.A. 164 E4
Shino-jima i. Japan 92 C4
Shinonoi Japan 93 E2
Shinsei Japan 92 C3
Shinshār Syria 107 C2
Shinshiro Japan 92 D4
Shinshūshin Japan 93 E2
Shintō Japan 93 E2
Shintone Japan 93 G3
Shinyanga Tanz. 122 D4
Shiobara Japan 93 F2
Shiocton WI U.S.A. 164 A1
Shiogama Japan 91 F5
Shiojiri Japan 93 D2
Shiomi-dake mt. Japan 93 E3
Shiono-misaki c. Japan 91 D6
Shioya Japan 93 F2
Shioya-zaki pt Japan 93 G1
Shiozawa Japan 93 E1
Shipai China 97 H2
Shiping China 96 D4
Shipki La China/India 99 B7
Shipman VA U.S.A. 165 F5
Shippegan Island Canada 153 I5
Shippensburg PA U.S.A. 165 G3
Shiprock NM U.S.A. 159 I3
Shiprock Peak NM U.S.A. 159 I3
Shipu Shaanxi China see Huanglong
Shipu Zhejiang China 97 I2
Shipunovo Russia 88 E2
Shiqi China see Zhongshan
Shiqian China 97 F3
Shiqiao China see Panyu
Shiquan China 97 F1
Shiquanhe Xizang China see Ali
Shiquanhe Xizang China see Gar
Shiquan He r. China see Indus
Shiquan Shuiku resr China 97 F1
Shira Russia 88 F2
Shīrābād Iran 110 C2
Shirahama Japan 93 F4
Shirai-san hill Japan 92 C4
Shirakawa Fukushima Japan 93 G1
Shirakawa Gifu Japan 92 C2
Shirakawa Gifu Japan 92 D3
Shirakawa-go and Gokayama tourist site Japan 91 E5
Shirake-mine mt. Japan 92 D2
Shirako Japan 93 G3
Shirakura-yama mt. Japan 92 D3
Shirama-yama hill Japan 92 B4
Shiramine Japan 92 C2
Shirane Japan 93 E3
Shirane-san mt. Japan 93 E2
Shirane-san mt. Japan 93 E3
Shirane-san vol. Japan 93 F2
Shirasawa Japan 93 F2
Shirase Coast Antarctica 188 J1
Shirase Glacier Antarctica 188 D2
Shīrāz Iran 110 D4
Shire r. Malawi 123 D5
Shireet Mongolia see Bayandelger
Shireza Pak. 111 G5
Shiriya-zaki c. Japan 90 F4
Shirkala reg. Kazakh. 102 A2
Shiroi Japan 93 G3
Shirokura-yama mt. Japan 93 D3
Shiroro Reservoir Nigeria 120 D3
Shirosato Japan 93 G2
Shirotori Japan 92 C3
Shirouma-dake mt. Japan 92 D2
Shiroyama Japan 93 F3
Shirpur India 104 C5
Shirten Holoy Gobi des. China 94 D3
Shīrvān Iran 110 E2
Shisanjianfang China 94 B3
Shisanzhan China 90 B2
Shishaldin Volcano AK U.S.A. 146 B4
Shisha Pangma mt. China see Xixabangma Feng
Shishmaref AK U.S.A. 148 F2
Shishmaref Inlet AK U.S.A. 148 F2
Shishou China 97 G2
Shisui Japan 93 G3
Shitan China 97 G3
Shitang China 97 I2
Shitanjing China 94 F4
Shitara Japan 92 D3
Shithāthah Iraq 113 F4
Shīū' Iran 110 D5
Shiv India 104 B4
Shivamogga India 106 B3
Shiveegovĭ Mongolia 95 G2
Shiveluch, Vulkan vol. Russia 77 R4
Shivpuri India 104 D4
Shivwits UT U.S.A. 159 G3
Shivwits Plateau AZ U.S.A. 159 G3
Shiwan China 95 G4
Shiwan Dashan mts China 96 E4
Shiwa N'gandu Zambia 123 D5
Shixing China 97 G3
Shiyan China 97 F1
Shiyeli Kazakh. 102 C3
Shizhong China 95 I5
Shizhu China 97 F2
Shizi Anhui China 97 H2
Shizi Gansu China 95 F5
Shizilu China see Junan
Shizong China 96 D3
Shizuishan China 94 F4
Shizuishanzhan China 94 F4
Shizuoka Japan 93 E4
Shizuoka pref. Japan 93 E4

▶Shkhara mt. Georgia/Russia 113 F2
3rd highest mountain in Europe.

Shklov Belarus see Shklow
Shklow Belarus 53 F5
Shkodër Albania 69 H3
Shkodra Albania see Shkodër
Shkodrës, Liqeni i l. Albania/Montenegro see Scutari, Lake
Shmidta, Ostrov i. Russia 76 K1
Shmidta, Poluostrov pen. Russia 90 F1
Shoal Lake Canada 151 K5
Shoals IN U.S.A. 164 B4
Shōbara Japan 91 D6
Shōgawa Japan 92 D2
Shō-gawa r. Japan 92 D2
Shoh Tajik. 111 H2
Shohi Pass Pak. see Tal Pass
Shokanbetsu-dake mt. Japan 90 F4
Shōkawa Japan 92 C2
Shokpar Kazakh. 98 A4
Sholakkorgan Kazakh. 102 C3
Sholapur India see Solapur
Sholaqqorghan Kazakh. see Sholakkorgan
Shomba r. Russia 54 R4
Shomvukovo Russia 52 K3
Shōmyō-gawa r. Japan 92 D2
Shona Ridge sea feature S. Atlantic Ocean 184 I9
Shonzhy Kazakh. 102 E3
Shor India 104 D2
Shōrābak reg. Afgh. 111 G4
Shorap Pak. 111 G5
Shorapur India 106 C2
Sho'rchi Uzbek. 111 G2
Shorewood IL U.S.A. 164 A3
Shorewood WI U.S.A. 164 B2
Shorkot Pak. 111 I4
Shorkozakhly, Solonchak salt flat Turkm. 113 J2
Shoshone CA U.S.A. 158 E4
Shoshone ID U.S.A. 156 E4
Shoshone r. WY U.S.A. 156 F3
Shoshone Mountains NV U.S.A. 158 E2
Shoshone Peak NV U.S.A. 158 E3
Shoshong Botswana 125 H2
Shoshoni WY U.S.A. 156 F4
Shostka Ukr. 53 G6
Shotoran, Chashmeh-ye well Iran 110 D3
Shotor Khūn Afgh. 111 G3
Shouguang China 95 I4
Shouyang China 95 H4
Shouyang Shan mt. China 97 F1
Shōwa Japan 93 F2
Showak Sudan 108 E7
Show Low AZ U.S.A. 159 H4
Shoyna Russia 52 J2
Shpola Ukr. 53 F6
Shqipëria country Europe see Albania
Shreve OH U.S.A. 164 D3
Shreveport LA U.S.A. 161 E5
Shrewsbury U.K. 59 E6
Shri Lanka country Asia see Sri Lanka
Shri Mohangarh India 104 B4
Shrirampur India 105 G5
Shu Kazakh. 102 D3
Shū r. Kazakh./Kyrg. see Shu
Shu r. Kazakh./Kyrg. 102 C3
Shū'ab, Ra's pt Yemen 109 H7
Shuajingsi China 96 D1
Shuangbai China 96 D3
Shuangcheng Fujian China see Zherong
Shuangcheng Heilong. China 90 B3
Shuanghe Hubei China 97 G2
Shuanghe Sichuan China 96 E2
Shuanghedagang China 90 C2
Shuanghu China 99 D6
Shuanghuyu China see Zizhou
Shuangjiang Guizhou China see Jiangkou
Shuangjiang Hunan China see Tongdao
Shuangjiang Yunnan China see Eshan
Shuangliao China 95 J3
Shuangliu China 96 D2
Shuangpai China 97 F3
Shuangshanzi China 95 I3
Shuangshipu China see Fengxian
Shuangxi China see Shunchang
Shuangyang China 90 B4
Shuangyashan China 90 C3
Shubarkudyk Kazakh. 102 A2
Shubayḥ well Saudi Arabia 107 D4
Shublik Mountains AK U.S.A. 149 K1
Shufu China 98 A5
Shugozero Russia 52 G4
Shu He r. China 95 I5
Shuiding China see Huocheng
Shuidong China see Dianbai
Shuiji China see Laixi
Shuijing China 96 E1
Shuijingkuang China 99 E6
Shuikou Guangxi China 96 E4
Shuikou Hunan China 97 F3
Shu-Ile, Gory mts Kazakh. 102 D3
Shuiluocheng China see Zhuanglang
Shuiquan China 94 F4
Shuiquanzi China 94 E4
Shuizhai China see Wuhua
Shuizhan China 99 E5
Shulakpachak Peak AK U.S.A. 148 I2
Shulan China 90 B3
Shule China 98 B5
Shulehe China 98 G4
Shule He r. China 94 C3
Shule Nanshan mts China 94 D4
Shulinzhao China 95 G3
Shulu China see Xinji
Shumagin Islands AK U.S.A. 148 G5
Shumba Zimbabwe 123 C5
Shumen Bulg. 69 L3
Shumerlya Russia 52 J5
Shumilina Belarus 53 F5
Shumyachi Russia 53 G5
Shūnan Japan 91 C6
Shunchang China 97 H3
Shuncheng China 90 A4
Shunde China 97 G4
Shungnak AK U.S.A. 148 H2
Shunyi China 95 I3
Shuoxian China see Shuozhou
Shuozhou China 95 H4
Shuqrah Yemen 108 G7
Shūr r. Iran 110 D4
Shūr r. Iran 111 F3
Shūr watercourse Iran 110 D5
Shur watercourse Iran 110 E3
Shūr, Chāh-e well Iran 110 D3
Shūr, Rūd-e watercourse Iran 110 E4
Shūr Āb watercourse Iran 110 D4
Shūrjestān Iran 110 D4
Shūrū Iran 111 F4
Shuryshkarskiy Sor, Ozero l. Russia 51 T2
Shūsh Iran 110 C3
Shusha Azer. see Şuşa
Shūshtar Iran 110 C3
Shutfah, Qalamat well Saudi Arabia 110 D6
Shuwayḥān Syria 107 D2
Shuwaysh, Tall ash hill Jordan 107 C4
Shuya Ivanovskaya Oblast' Russia 52 I4
Shuya Respublika Kareliya Russia 52 G3
Shuyak Island AK U.S.A. 148 I4
Shuyang China 95 I5
Shuyskoye Russia 52 I4
Shuẓāẓ, Jabal mt. Saudi Arabia 113 F6
Shwebo Myanmar 86 A2
Shwedwin Myanmar 86 A1
Shwegun Myanmar 86 B3
Shwegyin Myanmar 86 B3
Shweudaung mt. Myanmar 86 B2
Shyganak Kazakh. 102 D2
Shyghanaq Kazakh. see Shyganak
Shygys Konyrat Kazakh. 98 A3
Shymkent Kazakh. 102 C3
Shyngystau, Khrebet mts Kazakh. 102 E2
Shynkozha Kazakh. 98 C3
Shyok India 104 D2
Shyok r. India 99 B6
Shypuvate Ukr. 53 H6
Shyroke Ukr. 53 G7
Sia Moluccas Indon. 81 I8
Siabu Sumatra Indon. 84 B2
Siachen Glacier India 99 B6
Siahan Range mts Pak. 111 F5
Sīāh Cheshmeh Iran 110 B2
Siak r. Indon. 84 C2
Siak Sri Inderapura Sumatra Indon. 84 C2
Sialkot Pak. 111 I3
Siam country Asia see Thailand
Sian China see Xi'an
Sian Russia 90 B1
Siang r. India see Dihang
Siantan i. Indon. 84 D2
Siargao i. Phil. 82 D4
Siasi Phil. 82 C5
Siasi i. Phil. 82 C5
Siatlai Myanmar 86 A2
Siaton Negros Phil. 82 C4
Siau i. Indon. 83 C2
Šiauliai Lith. 55 M9
Siazan' Azer. see Siyäzän
Si Bai, Lam r. Thai. 86 D4
Sibasa S. Africa 125 J2
Sibati China see Xibet
Sibay i. Phil. 82 C4
Sibayi, Lake S. Africa 125 K4
Sibda China 96 C2
Šibenik Croatia 68 F3
Siberia reg. Russia 77 M3
Siberut i. Indon. 84 B3
Siberut, Selat sea chan. Indon. 84 B3
Siberut, Taman Nasional nat. park Indon. 84 B3
Sibi Pak. 111 G4
Sibidiri P.N.G. 81 K8
Sibigo Sumatra Indon. 84 A2
Sibiloi National Park Kenya 122 D3
Sibir' reg. Russia see Siberia
Sibiti Congo 122 B4
Sibiu Romania 69 K2
Sibley IA U.S.A. 160 E3
Siboa Celebes Indon. 83 B2
Sibolga Sumatra Indon. 84 B2
Siborongborong Sumatra Indon. 84 B2
Sibu Sarawak Malaysia 85 E2
Sibuco Mindanao Phil. 82 C5
Sibuco Bay Mindanao Phil. 82 C5
Sibuguey r. Mindanao Phil. 82 C5
Sibuguey Bay Mindanao Phil. 82 C5
Sibut Cent. Afr. Rep. 122 B3
Sibuti Sarawak Malaysia 85 F1
Sibutu i. Phil. 82 B5
Sibutu Passage Phil. 82 B5
Sibuyan i. Phil. 82 C3
Sibuyan Sea Phil. 82 C3
Sicamous Canada 150 G5
Sicapoo mt. Luzon Phil. 82 C2
Sicca Veneria Tunisia see Le Kef
Siccus watercourse Australia 137 B6
Sicheng Anhui China see Sixian
Sicheng Guangxi China see Lingyun
Sichon Thai. 87 B5
Sichuan prov. China 96 D2
Sichuan Pendi basin China 96 E2
Sicié, Cap c. France 66 G5
Sicilia i. Italy see Sicily
Sicilian Channel Italy/Tunisia 68 E6
Sicily i. Italy 68 F5
Sicuani Peru 176 D6
Sidangoli Halmahera Indon. 83 C2
Siddhapur India see Sidhpur
Siddipet India 106 C2
Sidenreng, Danau l. Indon. 83 A3
Sideros, Akra pt Greece see Sideros, Akrotirio
Sideros, Akrotirio pt Greece 69 L7
Sidesaviwa S. Africa 124 F7
Sidhauli India 104 E4
Sidhi India 105 E4
Sidhpur India 104 C5
Sidi Aïssa Alg. 67 H6
Sidi Ali Alg. 67 G5
Sīdī Barrānī Egypt 112 B5
Sidi Bel Abbès Alg. 67 F6
Sidi Bennour Morocco 64 C5
Sidi Bou Sa'īd Tunisia see Sidi Bouzid
Sidi Bouzid Tunisia 68 C7
Sidi el Barráni Egypt see Sīdī Barrānī
Sidi El Hani, Sebkhet de salt pan Tunisia 68 D7
Sidi Ifni Morocco 120 B2
Sidi Kacem Morocco 64 C5
Sidikalang Sumatra Indon. 84 B2
Sidi Khaled Alg. 64 E5
Sid Lake Canada 151 J2
Sidlaw Hills U.K. 60 F4
Sidley, Mount Antarctica 188 J1
Sidli India 105 G4
Sidmouth U.K. 59 D8
Sidney IA U.S.A. 160 E3
Sidney MT U.S.A. 156 G3
Sidney NE U.S.A. 160 C3
Sidney OH U.S.A. 164 C3
Sidney Lanier, Lake GA U.S.A. 163 D5
Sidoan Celebes Indon. 83 B2
Sidoan Celebes Indon. 83 B2
Sidoarjo Java Indon. 85 F4
Sidoktaya Myanmar 86 A2
Sidon Lebanon 107 B3
Sidr Egypt see Sudr
Siedlce Poland 53 D5
Sieg r. Germany 63 H4
Siegen Germany 63 I4
Siĕm Réab Cambodia 87 C4
Siem Reap Cambodia see Siĕm Réab
Si'en China see Huanjiang
Siena Italy 68 D3
Sieradz Poland 57 Q5
Si'erdingka China 99 F7
Sierra Blanca TX U.S.A. 157 G7
Sierra Colorada Arg. 178 C6
Sierra de Agalta, Parque Nacional nat. park Hond. 166 [inset] I6
Sierra Grande Arg. 178 C6
Sierra Leone country Africa 120 B4
Sierra Leone Basin sea feature N. Atlantic Ocean 184 G5
Sierra Leone Rise sea feature N. Atlantic Ocean 184 G5
Sierra Madre Mountains CA U.S.A. 158 C4
Sierra Mojada Mex. 166 E3
Sierra Nevada, Parque Nacional nat. park Venez. 176 D2
Sierra Nevada de Santa Marta, Parque Nacional nat. park Col. 176 D1
Sierraville CA U.S.A. 158 C2
Sierra Vista AZ U.S.A. 157 F7
Sierre Switz. 66 H3
Sievi Fin. 54 N5
Sifang Ling mts China 96 E4
Sifangtai China 90 B3
Sīfenī Eth. 122 E2
Sifnos i. Greece 69 K6
Sig Alg. 67 F6
Sigep, Tanjung pt Indon. 84 B3
Sigguup Nunaa pen. Greenland 147 M2
Sighetu Marmaţiei Romania 53 D7
Sighişoara Romania 69 K1
Siglap Sing. 87 [inset]
Sigli Sumatra Indon. 84 A1
Siglufjörður Iceland 54 [inset 1]
Sigma Panay Phil. 82 C4
Signal de Botrange hill Belgium 62 G4
Signal de la Ste-Baume mt. France 66 G5
Signal Peak AZ U.S.A. 159 F5
Signy research station Antarctica 188 A2
Signy-l'Abbaye France 62 E5
Sigoisooinan Sumatra Indon. 84 B3
Sigourney IA U.S.A. 160 E3
Sigri, Akra pt Greece see Saratsina, Akrotirio

Sigsbee Deep sea feature G. of Mexico 187 N4
Siguatepeque Hond. 167 I6
Sigüenza Spain 67 E3
Siguiri Guinea 120 C3
Sigulda Latvia 55 N8
Sigurd UT U.S.A. 159 H2
Sihanoukville Cambodia 87 C5
Sihaung Myauk Myanmar 86 A2
Sihawa India 106 D1
Sihong China 97 H1
Sihora India 104 E5
Sihou China see Changdao
Sihui China 97 G4
Siikajoki Fin. 54 N4
Siilinjärvi Fin. 54 O5
Siirt Turkey 113 F3
Sijawal Pak. 104 B4
Sijunjung Sumatra Indon. 84 C3
Sikaka Saudi Arabia see Sakākā
Sikakap Sumatra Indon. 84 C3
Sikandra Rao India 104 D4
Sikanni Chief Canada 150 F3
Sikanni Chief r. Canada 150 F3
Sikar India 104 C4
Sikaram mt. Afgh. 111 H3
Sikasso Mali 120 C3
Sikaw Myanmar 86 B2
Sikeli Celebes Indon. 83 B4
Sikeston MO U.S.A. 161 F4
Sikhote-Alin' mts Russia 90 D4
Sikhote-Alinskiy Zapovednik nature res. Russia 90 E3
Sikinos i. Greece 69 K6
Sikka India 104 B5
Sikkim state India 105 G4
Siknik Cape AK U.S.A. 148 E3
Siko i. Moluccas Indon. 83 C2
Siksjö Sweden 54 J4
Sikuaishi China 95 J4
Sikuati Sabah Malaysia 85 G1
Sil r. Spain 67 C2
Şila' i. Saudi Arabia 112 D6
Silago Leyte Phil. 82 D4
Šilal Lith. 55 M9
Si Lanna National Park Thai. 86 B3
Sila Point Samar Phil. 82 D3
Silas AL U.S.A. 161 F6
Silavatturai Sri Lanka 106 C4
Silawaih Agam vol. Indon. 84 A1
Silay Negros Phil. 82 C4
Silberberg hill Germany 63 J1
Silchar India 105 H4
Şile Turkey 69 M4
Sileru r. India 106 D2
Silesia reg. Czech Rep./Poland 57 P5
Silety r. Kazakh. 88 C2
Siletyteniz, Ozero salt l. Kazakh. 101 G1
Silghat India 105 H4
Siliana Tunisia 68 C6
Silifke Turkey 107 A1
Siliguri India see Shiliguri
Siling Co salt l. China 99 E7
Silipur India 104 D4
Silistra Bulg. 69 L2
Silistria Bulg. see Silistra
Silivri Turkey 69 M4
Siljan l. Sweden 55 I6
Silkeborg Denmark 55 F8
Sillajhuay mt. Chile 176 E7
Sillamäe Estonia 55 O7
Sille Turkey 112 D3
Silli India 105 F5
Sillod India 106 B1
Silobela S. Africa 125 J4
Silsbee TX U.S.A. 167 G2
Silsby Lake Canada 151 M4
Silt CO U.S.A. 159 J2
Siltaharju Fin. 54 O3
Siluas Kalimantan Indon. 85 E2
Silūp r. Iran 111 F5
Šilutė Lith. 55 L9
Silvan Turkey 113 F3
Silvânia Brazil 179 A2
Silvassa India 106 B1
Silver Bank Passage Turks and Caicos Is 169 J4
Silver Bay MN U.S.A. 160 F2
Silver City NM U.S.A. 159 I5
Silver City NV U.S.A. 158 D2
Silver City (abandoned) Canada 149 M3
Silver Côte d'Ivoire 120 C4
Silver Creek r. AZ U.S.A. 159 H4
Silver Lake OR U.S.A. 156 C4
Silver Lake l. CA U.S.A. 158 E4
Silvermine Mountains hills Ireland 61 D5
Silver Peak Range mts NV U.S.A. 158 E3
Silver Spring MD U.S.A. 165 G4
Silver Springs NV U.S.A. 158 D2
Silverthrone Mountain Canada 150 E5
Silvertip Mountain Canada 150 F5
Silverton U.K. 59 D8
Silverton CO U.S.A. 159 J3
Silverton TX U.S.A. 161 C5
Silvituc Mex. 167 H5
Sima China 99 E7
Simao China 96 D4
Simara i. Phil. 82 C3
Simard, Lac l. Canada 152 F5
Simaria India 105 F4
Simatang i. Indon. 83 B2
Simav Turkey 69 M5
Simav Dağları mts Turkey 69 M5
Simawat China 99 C5
Simba Dem. Rep. Congo 122 C3
Simbirsk Russia see Ul'yanovsk
Simcoe Canada 164 E2
Simcoe, Lake Canada 164 F1
Simdega India 106 E1
Simēn mts Eth. 122 D2
Simēn Mountains Eth. see Simēn
Simeonof Island AK U.S.A. 148 H5
Simeulue i. Indon. 84 B2
▶Simferopol' Crimea 112 D1
Capital of Crimea.
Simi i. Greece see Symi
Simikot Nepal 105 E3
Similan, Ko i. Thai. 87 B5
Simi Valley CA U.S.A. 158 D4
Simla India see Shimla
Simla CO U.S.A. 156 G5
Şimleu Silvaniei Romania 69 J1
Simlipal National Park India 105 F5
Simmerath Germany 62 G4
Simmern/Hunsrück Germany 63 H5
Simmesport LA U.S.A. 161 F6
Simms MT U.S.A. 156 F3
Simojärvi l. Fin. 54 O3
Simon Mex. 161 C7
Simonette r. Canada 150 G4
Simon Wash watercourse AZ U.S.A. 159 I5
Simoom Sound Canada 150 E5
Simoon Sound Canada see Simoom Sound
Simpang Sumatra Indon. 84 D3
Simpang Mangayau, Tanjung pt Malaysia 80 F5
Simpele Fin. 55 P6
Simplício Mendes Brazil 177 J5
Simplon Pass Switz. 66 I3
Simpson Canada 151 J5
Simpson MT U.S.A. 156 F2
Simpson Desert Australia 136 B5
Simpson Desert National Park Australia 136 B5
Simpson Desert Regional Reserve nature res. Australia 137 B5
Simpson Islands Canada 151 H2
Simpson Lake Canada 149 P1
Simpson Park Mountains NV U.S.A. 158 E2
Simpson Peninsula Canada 147 J3
Simrishamn Sweden 55 I9
Simuk i. Indon. 84 B3
Simulubek Sumatra Indon. 84 B3
Simunjan Sarawak Malaysia 85 E2
Simunul i. Phil. 82 B5
Simushir, Ostrov i. Russia 89 S3
Sina r. India 106 B2
Sinabang Sumatra Indon. 84 B2
Sinabung vol. Indon. 84 B2
Sinai pen. Egypt 107 A5
Sinai, Mont hill France 62 E5
Sinai al Janūbīya governorate Egypt see Janūb Sīnā'
Sinai ash Shamâlîya governorate Egypt see Shamāl Sīnā'
Si Nakarin, Ang Kep Nam Thai. 86 B4
Sinaloa state Mex. 157 F8
Sinalunga Italy 68 D3
Sinan China 97 F3
Sinancha Russia see Cheremshany
Sinbo Myanmar 86 B1
Sinbyubyin Myanmar 87 B4
Sinbyugyun Myanmar 86 A2
Sincan Turkey 112 E3
Sincelejo Col. 176 C2
Sinchu Taiwan see Taoyuan
Sinclair Mills Canada 150 F4
Sincora, Serra do hills Brazil 179 C1
Sind r. India 104 D4
Sind Pak. see Thul
Sind prov. Pak. see Sindh
Sinda Russia 90 E2
Sindañgan Mindanao Phil. 82 C4
Sindangan Bay Mindanao Phil. 82 C4
Sindangbarang Java Indon. 84 D4
Sindari India 104 B4
Sindeh, Teluk b. Flores Indon. 83 B5
Sindelfingen Germany 63 I6
Sindh prov. Pak. 111 H5
Sindhulimadi Nepal see Kamalamai
Sındırgı Turkey 69 M5
Sindor Russia 52 K3
Sindou Burkina Faso 120 C3
Sindri India 105 F5
Sind Sagar Doab lowland Pak. 111 H4
Sinel'nikovo Ukr. see Synel'nykove
Sines Port. 67 B5
Sines, Cabo de c. Port. 67 B5
Sinettä Fin. 54 N3
Sinfra Côte d'Ivoire 120 C4
Sing Myanmar 86 B2
Singa Sudan 108 D7
Singanallur India 106 C4
Singapore country Asia 84 C2
▶Singapore Sing. 87 [inset]
Capital of Singapore.
Singapore r. Sing. 87 [inset]
Singapore, Strait of Indon./Sing. 87 [inset]
Singapura country Asia see Singapore
Singapura Sing. see Singapore
Singapuru India 106 D2
Singaraja Bali Indon. 85 F5
Sing Buri Thai. 86 C4
Singgimtay China 98 E4
Singhampton Canada 164 E1
Singhana India 104 C3
Singida Tanz. 123 D4
Singidunum Serbia see Belgrade
Singim China see Singgimtay
Singkaling Hkamti Myanmar 86 A1
Singkarak Sumatra Indon. 84 C3
Singkawang Kalimantan Indon. 85 E2
Singkep i. Sumatra Indon. 84 D3
Singkil Sumatra Indon. 84 B2
Singkuang Sumatra Indon. 84 B2
Singleton Australia 138 E4
Singleton, Mount hill N.T. Australia 134 E5
Singleton, Mount hill W.A. Australia 135 B7
Singora Thai. see Songkhla
Sin'gosan N. Korea see Kosan
Singra India 105 G4
Singri India 105 H4
Singu Myanmar 96 B4
Singwara India 106 D1
Sin'gye N. Korea 91 B5
Sinhala country Asia see Sri Lanka
Sinhkung Myanmar 86 B1
Siniloan Luzon Phil. 82 C3
Sining China see Xining
Sinio, Gunung mt. Indon. 83 A3
Siniscola Sardinia Italy 68 C4
Sinj Croatia 68 G3
Sinjai Celebes Indon. 83 B4
Sinjār, Jabal mt. Iraq 113 F3
Sinkat Sudan 108 E6
Sinkiang aut. reg. China see Xinjiang Uygur Zizhiqu
Sinkiang Uighur Autonomous Region aut. reg. China see Xinjiang Uygur Zizhiqu
Sinmi-do i. N. Korea 91 B5
Sinn Germany 63 I4
Sinnamary Fr. Guiana 177 H2
Sinn Bishr, Gebel hill Egypt see Sinn Bishr, Jabal
Sinn Bishr, Jabal hill Egypt 107 A5
Sinneh Iran see Sanandaj
Sinoia Zimbabwe see Chinhoyi
Sinop Brazil 177 G6
Sinop Turkey 112 D2
Sinope Turkey see Sinop
Sinoquipe Mex. 166 C2
Sinp'a N. Korea see Kimjŏngsuk
Sinp'o N. Korea 91 C4
Sinsang N. Korea 91 B5
Sinsheim Germany 63 I5
Sintang Kalimantan Indon. 85 E2
Sint Eustatius mun. West Indies 169 L5
Sint-Laureins Belgium 62 D3
▶Sint Maarten terr. West Indies 169 L5
Self-governing Netherlands Territory. The northern part of the island is the French Overseas Collectivity of St-Martin.
Sint-Niklaas Belgium 62 E3
Sinton TX U.S.A. 161 D6
Sintra Port. 67 B4
Sint-Truiden Belgium 62 F4
Sinŭiju N. Korea 91 B4
Sinuk AK U.S.A. 148 F2
Sinzig Germany 63 H4
Siocon Mindanao Phil. 82 C5
Siófok Hungary 68 H1
Sioma Ngwezi National Park Zambia 123 C5
Sion Switz. 66 H3
Sion Mills U.K. 61 E3
Siorapaluk Greenland 147 K2
Sioux Center IA U.S.A. 155 H3
Sioux City IA U.S.A. 160 D3
Sioux Falls SD U.S.A. 160 D3
Sioux Lookout Canada 151 N5
Sipacate Guat. 167 H6
Sipadan, Pulau i. Sabah Malaysia 85 G1
Sipalay Negros Phil. 82 C4
Sipang, Tanjung pt Malaysia 85 E2
Siphaqeni S. Africa see Flagstaff
Siping China 90 B4
Sipitang Sabah Malaysia 85 F1
Sipiwesk Canada 151 L4
Sipiwesk Lake Canada 151 L4
Siple, Mount Antarctica 188 J2
Siple Coast Antarctica 188 I1
Siple Dome ice feature Antarctica 188 J1
Siple Island Antarctica 188 J2
Siponj Tajik. see Bartang
Sipsey r. AL U.S.A. 161 F5
Sipura i. Indon. 84 B3
Sipura, Selat sea chan. Indon. 84 B3
Siq, Wādī as watercourse Egypt 107 A5
Siquia r. Nicaragua 166 [inset] I6
Siquijor Phil. 82 C4
Siquijor i. Phil. 82 C4
Sir r. Pak. 111 H6
Sir, Dar"yoi r. Asia see Syrdar'ya
Sira India 106 C3
Sira r. Norway 55 E7
Şīr Abū Nu'āyr i. U.A.E. 110 D5
Siracusa Sicily Italy see Syracuse
Siraha Nepal see Sirha
Sirajganj Bangl. 105 G4
Sir Alexander, Mount Canada 150 F4
Şiran Turkey 113 E2
Sirbāl, Jabal mt. Egypt 112 D5
Şīr Banī Yās i. U.A.E. 110 D5
Sircilla India see Sirsilla
Sirdaryo r. Asia see Syrdar'ya
Sirdaryo Uzbek. 102 C3
Sir Edward Pellew Group is Australia 136 B2
Sireniki Russia 148 D2
Sirha Nepal 105 F4
Sirhān, Wādī an watercourse Saudi Arabia 112 E5
Sirḩān, Wādī as watercourse Jordan/Saudi Arabia 107 C4
Sirik, Tanjung pt Malaysia 85 E2
Siri Kit, Khuan Thai. 86 C3
Sirina i. Greece see Syrna
Sīrjā Iran 111 F5
Sir James MacBrien, Mount Canada 149 P3
Sīrjān Iran 110 D4
Sīrjān salt flat Iran 110 D4
Sirkazhi India 106 C4
Sirmilik National Park Canada 147 K2
Şırnak Turkey 113 F3
Sirohi India 104 C4
Sirombu Sumatra Indon. 84 B2
Sirong Celebes Indon. 83 B3
Sironj India 104 D4
Síros i. Greece see Syros
Sirpur India 106 C2
Sirr, Nafūd as des. Saudi Arabia 110 B5
Sirretta Peak CA U.S.A. 158 D4
Sīrrī, Jazīreh-ye i. Iran 110 D5
Sirsa India 104 C3
Sir Sandford, Mount Canada 150 G5
Sirsi Karnataka India 106 B3
Sirsi Madh. Prad. India 104 D4
Sirsi Uttar Prad. India 104 D3
Sirsilla India 106 C2
Sirte Libya 121 E1
Sirte, Gulf of Libya 121 E1
Sir Thomas, Mount hill Australia 135 E6
Siruguppa India 106 C3
Sirur India 106 B2
Şirvan Azer. 113 H3
Şirvan Turkey 113 F3
Sirvel India 106 C3
Širvintai Lith. see Širvintos
Širvintos Lith. 55 N9
Sīrwān r. Iraq 113 G4
Sir Wilfrid Laurier, Mount Canada 150 G4
Sis Turkey see Kozan
Sisak Croatia 68 G2
Sisaket Thai. 86 D4
Sisal Mex. 167 H4
Sischu Mountain AK U.S.A. 148 I2
Siscia Croatia see Sisak
Sishen S. Africa 124 F4
Sishilipu China 94 F5
Sishilisu China 95 G4
Sishuang Liedao is China 97 I3
Sisian Armenia 113 G3
Sisimiut Greenland 147 M3
Sisipuk Lake Canada 151 K4
Sisogúichic Mex. 166 D3
Sisŏphŏn Cambodia 87 C4
Sissano P.N.G. 81 K7
Sisseton SD U.S.A. 160 D2
Sīstān reg. Iran 111 F4
Sisteron France 66 G4
Sisters is India 87 A5
Sīt Iran 110 E5
Sitamarhi India 105 F4
Sitang China see Sinan
Sitangkai Phil. 82 B5
Sitapur India 104 E4
Siteia Greece 69 L7
Siteki Swaziland 125 J4
Site of Xanadu tourist site China 95 I3
Sithonia pen. Greece see Sithonias, Chersonisos
Sithonias, Chersonisos pen. Greece 69 J4
Sitía Greece see Siteia
Sitian China 94 C3
Sitidgi Lake Canada 149 N1
Sitila Moz. 125 L2
Siting China 96 E3
Sítio do Mato Brazil 179 C1
Sitka AK U.S.A. 149 N4
Sitka National Historical Park nat. park AK U.S.A. 149 N4
Sitkinak Island AK U.S.A. 148 I4
Sitkinak Strait AK U.S.A. 148 I4
Sitra oasis Egypt see Sitrah
Sitrah oasis Egypt 112 B5
Sittang r. Myanmar see Sittaung
Sittard Neth. 62 F4
Sittaung Myanmar 86 A1
Sittaung r. Myanmar 86 B3
Sittensen Germany 63 J1
Sittingbourne U.K. 59 H7
Sittoung r. Myanmar see Sittaung
Sittwe Myanmar 86 A2
Situbondo Java Indon. 85 F4
Siumpu i. Indon. 83 B4
Siuna Nicaragua 166 [inset] I6
Siuri India 105 F5
Sivaganga India 106 C4
Sivakasi India 106 C4
Sivaki Russia 90 B1
Sivan India see Siwan
Sivas Turkey 112 E3
Sivasagar India 105 H4
Sivaslı Turkey 69 M5
Siverek Turkey 113 E3
Siverskiy Russia 55 Q7
Sivers'kyy Donets' r. Russia/Ukr. see Northern Donets
Sivomaskinskiy Russia 51 S2
Sivrice Turkey 113 E3
Sivrihisar Turkey 69 N5
Sivukile S. Africa 125 I4
Sīwa Egypt see Sīwah
Siwa Celebes Indon. 83 B3
Sīwah Egypt 112 B5
Sīwah, Wāḩāt oasis Egypt 112 B5
Siwalik Range mts India/Nepal 104 D3
Siwan India 105 F4
Siwana India 104 C4
Siwa Oasis oasis Egypt see Sīwah, Wāḩāt
Sixian China 97 H1
Sixmilecross U.K. 61 E3
Sixtymile Canada 149 L2
Siyabuswa S. Africa 125 I3
Siyāh Band, Kōh-e mts Afgh. 111 F3
Siyāh Gird Afgh. 111 G2
Siyāh Kōh mts Afgh. 111 G3
Siyang China 95 I5
Siyäzän Azer. 113 H2
Siyitang China 95 G3
Sīyunī Iran 110 D3
Siziwang Qi China see Ulan Hua
Sjælland i. Denmark see Zealand
Sjenica Serbia 69 I3
Sjöbo Sweden 55 H9
Sjøvegan Norway 54 J2
Skadarsko Jezero, Nacionalni Park nat. park Montenegro 69 H3
Skadovs'k Ukr. 69 O1
Skaftafell Þjóðgarður nat. park Iceland 54 [inset 1]
Skaftárós r. mouth Iceland 54 [inset 1]
Skagafjörður inlet Iceland 54 [inset 1]
Skagen Denmark 55 G8
Skagerrak strait Denmark/Norway 55 F8
Skagit r. WA U.S.A. 156 C2
Skagway AK U.S.A. 149 N4
Skaidi Norway 54 N1
Skaland Norway 54 J2
Skalmodal Sweden 54 I4
Skanderborg Denmark 55 F8
Skaneateles Lake NY U.S.A. 165 G2
Skara Sweden 55 H7
Skardarsko Jezero l. Albania/Montenegro see Scutari, Lake
Skardu Pak. 104 C2
Skärgårdshavets nationalpark nat. park Fin. 55 L7
Skarnes Norway 55 G6
Skarżysko-Kamienna Poland 57 R5
Skaulo Sweden 54 L3
Skawina Poland 57 Q6
Skeena r. Canada 149 O5
Skeena Mountains Canada 149 O4
Skegness U.K. 58 H5
Skellefteå Sweden 54 L4
Skellefteälven r. Sweden 54 L4
Skelleftehamn Sweden 54 L4
Skelmersdale U.K. 58 E5
Skerries Ireland 61 F4
Ski Norway 55 G7
Skiathos i. Greece 69 J5
Skibbereen Ireland 61 C6
Skibotn Norway 54 L2
Skiddaw hill U.K. 58 D4
Skien Norway 55 F7
Skiermûntseach Neth. see Schiermonnikoog
Skiermûntseach i. Neth. see Schiermonnikoog
Skierniewice Poland 57 R5
Skikda Alg. 68 B6
Skipsea U.K. 58 G5
Skipton Australia 138 A6
Skipton U.K. 58 E5
Skirlaugh U.K. 58 G5
Skíros i. Greece see Skyros
Skive Denmark 55 F8
Skjern Denmark 55 F9
Skjolden Norway 55 E6
Skobelev Uzbek. see Farg'ona
Skobeleva, Pik mt. Kyrg. 111 I2
Skodje Norway 54 E5
Skoganvarri Norway 54 N2
Skokie IL U.S.A. 164 B2
Skomer Island U.K. 59 B7
Skopelos i. Greece 69 J5
Skopin Russia 53 H5
▶Skopje Macedonia 69 I4
Capital of Macedonia.
Skoplje Macedonia see Skopje
Skövde Sweden 55 H7
Skovorodino Russia 90 A1
Skowhegan ME U.S.A. 165 K1
Skrunda Latvia 55 M8
Skukum, Mount Canada 149 N3
Skukuza S. Africa 125 J3
Skull Valley AZ U.S.A. 159 G4
Skuodas Lith. 55 L8
Skurup Sweden 55 H9
Skutskär Sweden 55 J6
Skvyra Ukr. 53 F6
Skwentna r. AK U.S.A. 149 J3
Skye i. U.K. 60 C3
Skylge i. Neth. see Terschelling
Skyring, Seno b. Chile 178 B8
Skyros Greece 69 K5
Skyros i. Greece 69 K5
Skytrain Ice Rise Antarctica 188 L1
Slættaratindur hill Faroe Is 54 [inset 2]
Slagelse Denmark 55 G9
Slagnäs Sweden 54 K4
Slamet, Gunung vol. Indon. 85 E4
Slana AK U.S.A. 149 L3
Slane Ireland 61 F4
Slaney r. Ireland 61 F5
Slantsy Russia 55 P7
Slashers Reefs Australia 136 D3
Slatina Croatia 68 G2
Slatina Romania 69 K2
Slaty Fork WV U.S.A. 164 E4
Slava Russia 90 C1
Slave r. Canada 151 H2
Slave Coast Africa 120 D4
Slave Lake Canada 150 H4
Slave Point Canada 150 H2
Slavgorod Belarus see Slawharad
Slavgorod Russia 88 D2
Slavkovichi Russia 55 P8
Slavonska Požega Croatia see Požega
Slavonski Brod Croatia 68 H2
Slavuta Ukr. 53 E6
Slavutych Ukr. 53 F6
Slavyanka Russia 90 C4
Slavyansk Ukr. see Slov"yans'k
Slavyanskaya Russia see Slavyansk-na-Kubani
Slavyansk-na-Kubani Russia 112 E1
Slawharad Belarus 53 F5
Sławno Poland 57 P3
Slayton MN U.S.A. 160 E3
Sleaford U.K. 59 G5
Slea Head hd Ireland 61 B5
Sleat Neth. see Sloten
Sleat, Sound of sea chan. U.K. 60 D3
Sledge Island AK U.S.A. 148 F2
Sled Lake Canada 151 J4
Sleeper Islands Canada 152 F2
Sleeping Bear Dunes National Lakeshore nature res. MI U.S.A. 164 B1
Sleetmute AK U.S.A. 148 H3
Sleman Java Indon. 85 E4
Slick Rock CO U.S.A. 159 I2
Slidell LA U.S.A. 167 H2
Slide Mountain NY U.S.A. 165 H3
Slieve Bloom Mountains hills Ireland 61 E5
Slieve Car hill Ireland 61 C3
Slieve Donard hill U.K. 61 G3
Slieve Mish Mountains hills Ireland 61 B5
Slieve Snaght hill Ireland 61 E2
Sligachan U.K. 60 C3
Sligeach Ireland see Sligo
Sligo Ireland 61 D3
Sligo PA U.S.A. 164 F3
Sligo Bay Ireland 61 D3
Slinger WI U.S.A. 164 A2
Slippery Rock PA U.S.A. 164 E3
Slite Sweden 55 K8
Sliven Bulg. 69 L3
Sloan NV U.S.A. 159 F4
Sloat CA U.S.A. 158 C2
Sloboda Russia see Ezhva
Slobodchikovo Russia 52 K3
Slobodskoy Russia 52 K4
Slobozia Romania 69 L2
Slochteren Neth. 62 G1
Slonim Belarus 55 N10
Slootdorp Neth. 62 E2
Sloten Neth. 62 F2
Slough U.K. 59 G7
Slovakia country Europe 50 J6
Slovenia country Europe 68 F2
Slovenija country Europe see Slovenia
Slovenj Gradec Slovenia 68 F1
Slovensko country Europe see Slovakia
Slovenský raj, Národný park nat. park Slovakia 57 R6
Slov"yans'k Ukr. 53 H6
Słowiński Park Narodowy nat. park Poland 57 P3
Sluch r. Ukr. 53 E6
S'Lung, B'Nom mt. Vietnam 87 D5
Słupsk Poland 57 P3
Slussfors Sweden 54 J4
Slutsk Belarus 55 O10
Slyne Head hd Ireland 61 B4
Slyudyanka Russia 88 I2
Smăch, Kaôh i. Cambodia 87 C5
Small Point ME U.S.A. 165 K2
Smallwood Reservoir Canada 153 I3
Smalyavichy Belarus 55 P9
Smalyenskaya Wzvyshsha hills Belarus/Russia see Smolensko-Moskovskaya Vozvyshennost'
Smarhon' Belarus 55 O9
Smeaton Canada 151 J4
Smederevo Serbia 69 I2
Smederevska Palanka Serbia 69 I2
Smela Ukr. see Smila
Smethport PA U.S.A. 165 F3
Smidovich Russia 90 D2
Smila Ukr. 53 F6
Smilde Neth. 62 G2
Smiltene Latvia 55 N8
Smirnykh Russia 90 F2
Smith Canada 150 H4
Smith Arm b. Canada 149 Q2
Smith Bay AK U.S.A. 148 I1
Smith Center KS U.S.A. 160 D4
Smithers Canada 150 E4
Smithfield S. Africa 125 H6
Smithfield NC U.S.A. 162 E5
Smithfield UT U.S.A. 156 F4
Smith Glacier Antarctica 188 K1
Smith Island India 87 A4
Smith Island MD U.S.A. 165 G4
Smith Island VA U.S.A. 165 H5
Smith Mountain Lake VA U.S.A. 164 F5
Smith River Canada 149 P4
Smiths Falls Canada 165 G1
Smithton Australia 137 [inset]
Smithtown Australia 138 F3
Smithville OK U.S.A. 161 E5
Smithville WV U.S.A. 164 E4
Smoke Creek Desert NV U.S.A. 158 D1
Smoking Mountains Canada 149 P1
Smoky Bay Australia 135 F8
Smoky Cape Australia 138 F3
Smoky Falls Canada 152 E4
Smoky Hill r. KS U.S.A. 160 C4
Smoky Hills KS U.S.A. 154 H4
Smoky Hills KS U.S.A. 160 D4
Smoky Lake Canada 151 H4
Smoky Mountains ID U.S.A. 156 E4
Smøla i. Norway 54 E5
Smolenka Russia 53 K6
Smolensk Russia 53 G5
Smolensk-Moscow Upland hills Belarus/Russia see Smolensko-Moskovskaya Vozvyshennost'
Smolensko-Moskovskaya Vozvyshennost' hills Belarus/Russia 53 G5
Smolevichi Belarus see Smalyavichy
Smolyan Bulg. 69 K4
Smooth Rock Falls Canada 152 E4
Smoothrock Lake Canada 152 C4
Smoothstone Lake Canada 151 J4
Smørfjord Norway 54 N1
Smorgon' Belarus see Smarhon'
Smyley Island Antarctica 188 L2
Smyrna Turkey see İzmir
Smyrna DE U.S.A. 165 H4
Smyth Island atoll Marshall Is see Taongi
Snæfell mt. Iceland 54 [inset 1]
Snaefell hill Isle of Man 58 C4
Snag (abandoned) Canada 149 L3
Snake r. Canada 149 N2
Snake r. U.S.A. 156 D3
Snake Island Australia 138 C7
Snake Range mts NV U.S.A. 159 F2
Snake River Canada 150 F3
Snake River Plain ID U.S.A. 156 E4
Snare r. Canada 150 G2
Snare Lake Canada 151 J3
Snare Lakes Canada see Wekweètì
Snares Islands N.Z. 133 G6
Snåsa Norway 54 H4

Sneedville TN U.S.A. 164 D5
Sneek Neth. 62 F1
Sneem Ireland 61 C6
Sneeuberge mts S. Africa 124 G6
Snegamook Lake Canada 153 J3
Snegurovka Ukr. see Tetiyiv
Snelling CA U.S.A. 158 C3
Snettisham U.K. 59 H6
Snezhnogorsk Russia 76 J3
Snežnik mt. Slovenia 68 F2
Sniečkus Lith. see Visaginas
Snihurivka Ukr. 53 G7
Snits Neth. see Sneek
Snizort, Loch b. U.K. 60 C3
Snoqualmie Pass WA U.S.A. 156 C3
Snøtinden mt. Norway 54 H3
Snoul Cambodia see Snuŏl
Snover MI U.S.A. 164 D2
Snovsk Ukr. see Shchors
Snowbird Lake Canada 151 K2
Snowcap Mountain AK U.S.A. 148 I3
Snowcrest Mountain Canada 150 G5
Snowdon mt. U.K. 59 C5
Snowdonia National Park U.K. 59 D6
Snowdrift Canada see Łutselk'e
Snowdrift r. Canada 151 I2
Snowflake AZ U.S.A. 159 H4
Snow Hill MD U.S.A. 165 H4
Snow Lake Canada 151 K4
Snowville UT U.S.A. 156 E4
Snow Water Lake NV U.S.A. 159 F1
Snowy r. Australia 138 D6
Snowy Mountain NY U.S.A. 165 H2
Snowy Mountains Australia 138 C6
Snowy Peak AK U.S.A. 149 L2
Snowy River National Park Australia 138 D6
Snug Corner Bahamas 163 F8
Snug Harbour Nfld. and Lab. Canada 153 L3
Snug Harbour Ont. Canada 164 E1
Snuŏl Cambodia 87 D4
Snyder TX U.S.A. 161 C5
Soabuwe Seram Indon. 83 D3
Soalala Madag. 123 E5
Soalara Madag. 123 E6
Soan r. Pak. 111 H3
Soan-gundo is S. Korea 91 B6
Soanierana-Ivongo Madag. 123 E5
Soavinandriana Madag. 123 E5
Sobat r. South Sudan 108 D8
Sobatsubu-yama mt. Japan 93 E3
Sobger r. Indon. 81 K7
Sobinka Russia 52 I5
Sobradinho, Barragem de resr Brazil 177 J6
Sobral Brazil 177 J4
Sobue Japan 92 C3
Sochi Russia 113 E2
Society Islands Fr. Polynesia 187 J7
Socorro Brazil 179 B3
Socorro Col. 176 D2
Socorro NM U.S.A. 157 G6
Socorro, Isla i. Mex. 168 B5
Socotra i. Yemen 109 H7
Soc Trăng Vietnam 87 D5
Socuéllamos Spain 67 E4
Soda Lake CA U.S.A. 158 D4
Soda Lake CA U.S.A. 158 E4
Sodankylä Fin. 54 O3
Soda Plains China 99 B6
Soda Springs ID U.S.A. 156 F4
Sodegaura Japan 93 F3
Söderhamn Sweden 55 J6
Söderköping Sweden 55 J7
Södertälje Sweden 55 J7
Sodiri Sudan 108 C7
Sodo Eth. 122 D3
Södra Kvarken strait Fin./Sweden 55 K6
Sodus NY U.S.A. 165 G2
Soë Timor Indon. 83 C5
Soekarno, Puntjak mt. Indon. see Jaya, Puncak
Soerabaia Java Indon. see Surabaya
Soerendonk Neth. 62 F3
Soest Germany 63 I3
Soest Neth. 62 F2
Sofala Australia 138 D4

▶Sofia Bulg. 69 J3
Capital of Bulgaria.

Sofiya Bulg. see Sofia
Sofiyevka Ukr. see Vil'nyans'k
Sofiysk Khabarovskiy Kray Russia 90 D1
Sofiysk Khabarovskiy Kray Russia 90 E2
Sofporog Russia 54 Q4
Sofrana i. Greece 69 L6
Softa Kalesi tourist site Turkey 107 A1
Sōfu-gan i. Japan 91 F7
Sog China 99 F7
Soğanlı Dağları mts Turkey 113 F2
Sogat China 98 D4
Sogda Russia 90 D2
Sögel Germany 63 H2
Sogma China 99 C6
Sogmai China 99 B6
Søgne Norway 55 E7
Sognefjorden inlet Norway 55 D6
Sogod Leyte Phil. 82 D4
Sogod Bay Leyte Phil. 82 D4
Sog Qu r. China 99 F6
Sogruma China 96 D1
Söğüt Turkey 69 N4
Söğüt Dağı mts Turkey 69 M6
Soh Iran 110 C3
Sohâg Egypt see Sūhāj
Sohagpur India 104 D5
Soham U.K. 59 H6
Sohano P.N.G. 132 F2
Sohar Oman see Şuḩār
Sohawal India 104 E4
Sohela India 105 E5
Soheuksan-do i. S. Korea 91 B6
Sohng Gwe, Khao hill Myanmar/Thai. 87 B4
Sŏho-ri N. Korea 91 C4
Soignies Belgium 62 E4
Soila China 96 C2
Soini Fin. 54 N5
Soissons France 62 D5
Sojat India 104 C4
Sojat Road India 104 C4
Sojoton Point Negros Phil. 82 C4
Sok r. Russia 53 K5
Sŏka Japan 93 F3
Sokal' Ukr. 53 E6
Sokcho S. Korea 91 C5
Söke Turkey 69 L6
Sokhondo, Gora mt. Russia 95 G1
Sokhor, Gora mt. Russia 94 F1

▶Sokhumi Georgia 113 F2
Capital of Abkhazia.

Sokiryany Ukr. see Sokyryany
Sokodé Togo 120 D4
Soko Islands H.K. China 97 [inset]
Sokol Russia 52 I4
Sokolo Mali 120 C3
Sokolov Czech Rep. 63 M4
Sokoto Nigeria 120 D3
Sokoto r. Nigeria 120 D3
Sokyryany Ukr. 53 E6
Sola Cuba 163 E8
Sola i. Tonga see Ata
Solan India 104 D3
Solana Beach CA U.S.A. 158 E5
Solander Island N.Z. 139 A8
Solano Luzon Phil. 82 C2
Solapur India 106 B2
Soldotna AK U.S.A. 149 J3
Soledad CA U.S.A. 158 C3
Soledad de Doblado Mex. 167 F5
Soledade Brazil 178 F3
Solenoye Russia 53 I7
Solfjellsjøen Norway 54 H3
Solginskiy Russia 52 I3
Solhan Turkey 113 F3
Soligalich Russia 52 I4
Soligorsk Belarus see Salihorsk
Solihull U.K. 59 F6
Solikamsk Russia 51 R4
Sol'-Iletsk Russia 76 G4
Solimões r. S. America see Amazon
Solimón, Punta pt Mex. 167 I5
Solingen Germany 62 H3
Solitaire Namibia 124 B2
Sol-Karmala Russia see Severnoye
Şollar Azer. 113 H2
Sollefteå Sweden 54 J5
Söllichau Germany 63 M3
Solling hills Germany 63 J3
Sollstedt Germany 63 K3
Sollum, Gulf of Egypt see Sallum, Khalīj as
Solms Germany 63 I4
Solnechnogorsk Russia 52 H4
Solnechnyy Amurskaya Oblast' Russia 90 A1
Solnechnyy Khabarovskiy Kray Russia 90 E2
Solo r. Indon. 83 B3
Solo r. Indon. 85 F4
Solok Sumatra Indon. 84 C3
Sololá Guat. 167 H6
Solomon AK U.S.A. 148 F2
Solomon AZ U.S.A. 159 I5
Solomon, North Fork r. KS U.S.A. 160 D4

▶Solomon Islands country S. Pacific Ocean 133 G2
4th largest and 5th most populous country in Oceania.

Solomon Sea S. Pacific Ocean 132 F2
Solon China 95 J2
Solon ME U.S.A. 165 K1
Solon Springs WI U.S.A. 160 F2
Solor i. Indon. 83 B5
Solor, Kepulauan is Indon. 83 B5
Solothurn Switz. 66 H3
Solovetskiye Ostrova is Russia 52 G2
Solov'yevsk Mongolia 95 H1
Solov'yevsk Russia 90 B1
Šolta i. Croatia 68 G3
Solṭānābād Kermān Iran 110 E4
Solṭānābād Khorāsān-e Razavī Iran 111 E3
Solṭānābād Tehrān Iran 110 C3
Solṭānīyeh Iran 110 C2
Soltau Germany 63 J2
Sol'tsy Russia 52 F4
Solvay NY U.S.A. 165 G2
Sölvesborg Sweden 55 I8
Solway Firth est. U.K. 60 F6
Solwezi Zambia 123 C5
Soma Turkey 69 L5
Somain France 62 D4
Somalia country Africa 122 E3
Somali Basin sea feature Indian Ocean 185 L6
Somaliland disp. terr. Somalia 122 E3
Somali Republic country Africa see Somalia
Somba Celebes Indon. 83 A3
Sombang, Gunung mt. Indon. 85 G2
Sombo Angola 123 C4
Sombor Serbia 69 H2
Sombrerete Mex. 166 E4
Sombrero Channel India 87 A6
Sombrio, Lago do l. Brazil 179 A5
Somero Fin. 55 M6
Somerset KY U.S.A. 164 C5
Somerset MI U.S.A. 164 C2
Somerset OH U.S.A. 164 D4
Somerset PA U.S.A. 164 F4
Somerset, Lake Australia 138 F1
Somerset East S. Africa 125 G7
Somerset Island Canada 147 I2
Somerset Reservoir VT U.S.A. 165 I2
Somerset West S. Africa 124 D8
Somersworth NH U.S.A. 165 J2
Somerton AZ U.S.A. 159 F5
Somerville NJ U.S.A. 165 H3
Somerville TN U.S.A. 161 F5
Somerville Reservoir TX U.S.A. 167 F2
Someydeh Iran 110 B3
Somme r. France 62 B4
Somme, Canal de la France 62 C5
Sommen l. Sweden 55 I7
Sömmerda Germany 63 L3
Sommet, Lac du l. Canada 153 H3
Somnath India 104 B5
Somoniyon Tajik. 111 H2
Somotillo Nicaragua 166 [inset] I6
Somoto Nicaragua 166 [inset] I6
Somutu Myanmar 86 B1
Son r. India 105 F4
Soná Panama 166 [inset] J8
Sonag China see Zêkog
Sonapur India see Subarnapur
Sonar r. India 104 D4
Sŏnbong N. Korea 90 C4
Sŏnch'ŏn N. Korea 91 B5
Sønderborg Denmark 55 F9
Sondershausen Germany 63 K3
Søndre Strømfjord Greenland see Kangerlussuaq
Søndre Strømfjord inlet Greenland see Kangerlussuaq
Sondrio Italy 68 C1
Sonepat India see Sonipat
Sonepur India see Subarnapur
Song Sarawak Malaysia 85 F2
Song, Loi mt. Myanmar 86 B2
Songa Moluccas Indon. 83 C3
Songbai Hubei China see Shennongjia
Songbai Hunan China 97 G3
Songbu China 97 G2
Sông Câu Vietnam 87 E4
Songcheng China see Xiapu
Sông Đa, Hồ resr Vietnam 86 D2
Songea Tanz. 123 D5
Songhua Hu resr China 90 B4
Songhua Jiang r. Heilongjiang/Jilin China 90 D3
Songhua Jiang r. Jilin China 90 B3
Songjiachuan China see Wubu
Songjiang China 97 I2
Songjianghe China 90 B4
Sŏngjin N. Korea see Kimch'aek
Songkan China 96 E2
Songkhla Thai. 87 C6
Songköl l. Kyrg. 98 A4
Song Ling mts China 95 I3
Songlong Myanmar 86 B2
Songnim N. Korea 91 B5
Songo Angola 123 B4
Songo Moz. 123 D5
Songpan China 96 D1
Songshan Gansu China 94 E4
Songshan Guizhou China see Ziyun
Song Shan mt. China 95 H5
Songtao China 97 F2
Songxi China 97 H3
Songxian China 95 H5
Songyuan Fujian China see Songxi
Songyuan Jilin China 90 B3
Songzi China 97 F2
Sơn Hai Vietnam 87 E5
Soni Japan 92 C4
Sonid Youqi China see Saihan Tal
Sonid Zuoqi China see Mandalt
Sonipat India 104 D3
Sonkajärvi Fin. 54 O5
Sonkovo Russia 52 H4
Sơn La Vietnam 86 C2
Sonmiani Pak. 111 G5
Sonmiani Bay Pak. 111 G5
Sonneberg Germany 63 L4
Sono r. Minas Gerais Brazil 179 B2
Sono r. Tocantins Brazil 177 I5
Sonoma CA U.S.A. 158 B2
Sonoma Peak NV U.S.A. 158 E1
Sonora r. Mex. 166 C2
Sonora state Mex. 166 C2
Sonora CA U.S.A. 158 C3
Sonora KY U.S.A. 164 C5
Sonora TX U.S.A. 161 C6
Sonoran Desert AZ U.S.A. 159 G5
Sonoran Desert National Monument nat. park AZ U.S.A. 157 E6
Sonqor Iran 110 B3
Sonsogad mt. India 106 B3
Sonsonate El Salvador 167 H6
Sonsorol Islands Palau 81 I5
Sơn Tây Vietnam 86 D2
Sonwabile S. Africa 125 I6
Soochow China see Suzhou
Sooghmeghat AK U.S.A. 148 E3
Soomaaliya country Africa see Somalia
Sopi, Tanjung pt Moluccas Indon. 83 D2
Sopo watercourse South Sudan 121 F4
Sopot Bulg. 69 K3
Sopot Poland 57 Q3
Sop Prap Thai. 86 B3
Sopron Hungary 68 G1
Sopur India 104 C2
Soputan, Gunung vol. Indon. 83 C2
Sora Italy 68 E4
Sorab India 106 B3
Sorada India 106 E2
Söråker Sweden 54 J5
Sorel Canada 153 G5
Soreq, Naḥal r. Israel 107 B4
Sorgun Turkey 112 D3
Sorgun r. Turkey 107 B1
Soria Spain 67 E3
Sorikmarapi vol. Indon. 84 B2
Sorkh, Daqq-e salt flat Iran 110 D3
Sorkh, Kūh-e mts Iran 110 D3
Sorkhān Iran 110 E4
Sorkh Doz Afgh. 111 G4
Sorkheh Iran 110 D3
Sørli Norway 54 H4
Soro India 105 F5
Soroca Moldova 53 F6
Sorocaba Brazil 179 B3
Soroki Moldova see Soroca
Sorol atoll Micronesia 81 K5
Sorong Papua Indon. 83 D3
Soroti Uganda 122 D3
Sørøya i. Norway 54 M1
Sorraia r. Port. 67 B4
Sørreisa Norway 54 K2
Sorrento Italy 68 F4
Sorsele Sweden 54 J4
Sorsogon Luzon Phil. 82 D3
Sortavala Russia 54 Q6
Sortland Norway 54 I2
Sortopolovskaya Russia 52 K3
Sorvizhi Russia 52 K4
Sōsa Japan 93 G3
Sosenskiy Russia 53 G5
Soshanguve S. Africa 125 I3
Sosna r. Russia 53 H5
Sosneado mt. Arg. 178 C4
Sosnogorsk Russia 52 L3
Sosnovka Kyrg. 98 A4
Sosnovka Arkhangel'skaya Oblast' Russia 52 J3
Sosnovka Kaliningradskaya Oblast' Russia 51 K5
Sosnovka Murmanskaya Oblast' Russia 52 I2
Sosnovka Tambovskaya Oblast' Russia 53 I5
Sosnovo Russia 55 Q6
Sosnovo-Ozerskoye Russia 89 K2
Sosnovyy Russia 54 R4
Sosnovyy Bor Russia 55 P7
Sosnowiec Poland 57 Q5
Sosnowitz Poland see Sosnowiec
Sos'va Khanty-Mansiyskiy Avtonomnyy Okrug-Yugra Russia 51 S3
Sos'va Sverdlovskaya Oblast' Russia 51 S4
Sotang China 99 F7
Sotara, Volcán vol. Col. 176 C3
Sotkamo Fin. 54 P4
Soto la Marina Mex. 167 F4
Sotteville-lès-Rouen France 62 B5
Sotuta Mex. 167 H4
Souanké Congo 122 B3
Soubré Côte d'Ivoire 120 C4
Souderton PA U.S.A. 165 H3
Soufflenheim France 63 H6
Soufli Greece 69 L4
Soufrière St Lucia 169 L6
Soufrière vol. St Vincent 169 L6
Sougueur Alg. 67 G6
Souillac France 66 E4
Souilly France 62 F5
Souk Ahras Alg. 68 B6
Souk el Arbaâ du Rharb Morocco 64 C5
Sŏul S. Korea see Seoul
Soulac-sur-Mer France 66 D4
Soulom France 66 D5
Sounding Creek r. Canada 151 I4
Souni Cyprus 107 A2
Soûr Lebanon see Tyre
Sourdough AK U.S.A. 149 K3
Soure Brazil 177 I4
Sour el Ghozlane Alg. 67 H5
Souris Canada 151 K5
Souris r. Canada 151 L5
Souriya country Asia see Syria
Sousa Brazil 177 K5
Sousa Lara Angola see Bocoio
Sousse Tunisia 68 D7
Soustons France 66 D5

▶South Africa country Africa 124 F5
5th most populous country in Africa.

Southampton Canada 164 E1
Southampton U.K. 59 F8
Southampton NY U.S.A. 165 I3
Southampton, Cape Canada 147 J3
Southampton Island Canada 147 J3
South Andaman i. India 87 A5
South Anna r. VA U.S.A. 165 G5
South Anston U.K. 58 F5
South Aulatsivik Island Canada 153 J2
South Australia state Australia 132 D5
South Australian Basin sea feature Indian Ocean 185 P8
Southaven MS U.S.A. 161 F5
South Baldy mt. NM U.S.A. 157 G6
South Bank U.K. 58 F4
South Bass Island OH U.S.A. 164 D3
South Bend IN U.S.A. 164 B3
South Bend WA U.S.A. 156 C3
South Bluff pt Bahamas 163 F8
South Boston VA U.S.A. 165 F5
South Brook Canada 153 K4
South Cape pt HI U.S.A. see Ka Lae
South Carolina state U.S.A. 163 D5
South Charleston OH U.S.A. 164 D4
South Charleston WV U.S.A. 164 E4
South China Sea N. Pacific Ocean 80 F4
South Coast Town Australia see Gold Coast
South Dakota state U.S.A. 160 C2
South Downs hills U.K. 59 G8
South Downs National Park nat. park U.K. 59 G8
South East admin. dist. Botswana 125 G3
South East Cape Australia 137 [inset]
Southeast Cape AK U.S.A. 148 E3
Southeast Indian Ridge sea feature Indian Ocean 185 N8
South East Isles Australia 135 C8
Southeast Pacific Basin sea feature S. Pacific Ocean 187 M10
South East Point Australia 138 C7
Southend Canada 151 K3
Southend U.K. 60 D5
Southend-on-Sea U.K. 59 H7
Southern admin. dist. Botswana 124 G3
Southern Alps mts N.Z. 139 C6
Southern Cross Australia 135 B7
Southern Indian Lake Canada 151 L3
Southern Lau Group is Fiji 133 I3
Southern National Park South Sudan 121 F4
Southern Ocean 188 C2
Southern Pines NC U.S.A. 163 E5
Southern Rhodesia country Africa see Zimbabwe
Southern Uplands hills U.K. 60 E5
South Esk r. U.K. 60 F4
South Esk Tableland reg. Australia 134 D4
Southey Canada 151 J5
Southfield MI U.S.A. 164 D2
South Fiji Basin sea feature S. Pacific Ocean 186 H7
South Fork CA U.S.A. 158 B1
South Geomagnetic Pole (2015) Antarctica 188 F1
South Georgia i. S. Atlantic Ocean 178 I8

▶South Georgia and the South Sandwich Islands terr. S. Atlantic Ocean 178 I8
United Kingdom Overseas Territory

South Harris pen. U.K. 60 B3
South Haven MI U.S.A. 164 B2
South Henik Lake Canada 151 L2
South Hill VA U.S.A. 165 F5
South Honshu Ridge sea feature N. Pacific Ocean 186 F3
South Indian Lake Canada 151 L3

▶South Island N.Z. 139 D7
2nd largest island in Oceania.

South Islet reef Phil. 82 B4
South Junction Canada 151 M5
South Korea country Asia 91 B5
South Lake Tahoe CA U.S.A. 158 C2
South Luangwa National Park Zambia 123 D5
South Magnetic Pole (2015) Antarctica 188 G2
South Mills NC U.S.A. 165 G5
Southminster U.K. 59 H7
South Mountains hills PA U.S.A. 165 G4
South Naknek AK U.S.A. 148 H4
South New Berlin NY U.S.A. 165 H2
South Orkney Islands S. Atlantic Ocean 184 F10
South Ossetia disp. terr. Georgia 113 G2
South Paris ME U.S.A. 165 J1
South Platte r. CO U.S.A. 160 C3
South Point Bahamas 163 F8
South Pole Antarctica 188 C1
Southport Qld Australia 138 F1
Southport Tas. Australia 137 [inset]
Southport U.K. 58 D5
Southport NY U.S.A. 165 G2
South Portland ME U.S.A. 165 J2
South Ronaldsay i. U.K. 60 G2
South Royalton VT U.S.A. 165 I2
South Salt Lake UT U.S.A. 159 H1
South Sand Bluff pt S. Africa 125 J6
South Sandwich Islands is S. Atlantic Ocean 188 B3
South Sandwich Trench sea feature S. Atlantic Ocean 184 G9
South San Francisco CA U.S.A. 158 B3
South Saskatchewan r. Canada 151 J4
South Seal r. Canada 151 L3
South Shetland Islands Antarctica 188 A2
South Shetland Trough sea feature S. Atlantic Ocean 188 L2
South Shields U.K. 58 F3
South Sinai governorate Egypt see Janūb Sīnā'
South Solomon Trench sea feature S. Pacific Ocean 186 G6

▶South Sudan country Africa 121 G4
Gained independence from Sudan on 9 July 2011.

South Taranaki Bight b. N.Z. 139 E4
South Tasman Rise sea feature Southern Ocean 186 F9
South Tent mt. UT U.S.A. 159 H2
South Tons r. India 105 E4
South Twin Island Canada 152 F3
South Tyne r. U.K. 58 E4
South Uist i. U.K. 60 B3
South Wellesley Islands Australia 136 B3
South-West Africa country Africa see Namibia
South West Cape N.Z. 139 A8
Southwest Cape AK U.S.A. 148 E3
South West Entrance sea chan. P.N.G. 136 E1
Southwest Indian Ridge sea feature Indian Ocean 185 K8
South West National Park Australia 137 [inset]
Southwest Pacific Basin sea feature S. Pacific Ocean 186 I8
South-West Peru Ridge sea feature S. Pacific Ocean see Nazca Ridge
South West Rocks Australia 138 F3
South Whitley IN U.S.A. 164 C3
South Wichita r. TX U.S.A. 161 D5
South Windham ME U.S.A. 165 J2
Southwold U.K. 59 I6
Southwood National Park Australia 138 E1
Soutpansberg mts S. Africa 125 I2
Souttouf, Adrar mts W. Sahara 120 B2
Soverato Italy 68 G5
Sovereign Mountain AK U.S.A. 149 J3
Sovetsk Kaliningradskaya Oblast' Russia 55 L9
Sovetsk Kirovskaya Oblast' Russia 52 K4
Sovetskaya Gavan' Russia 90 F2
Sovetskiy Khanty-Mansiyskiy Avtonomnyy Okrug-Yugra Russia 51 S3
Sovetskiy Leningradskaya Oblast' Russia 55 P6
Sovetskiy Respublika Mariy El Russia 52 K4
Sovetskoye Chechenskaya Respublika Russia see Shatoy
Sovetskoye Stavropol'skiy Kray Russia see Zelenokumsk
Sovyets'kyy Crimea 112 D1
Sowa China 96 C2
Sōwa Japan 93 F2
Soweto S. Africa 125 H4
Şowma'eh Sarā Iran 110 C2
So'x Tajik. 111 H2
Sōya-kaikyō strait Japan/Russia see La Pérouse Strait
Sōya-misaki c. Japan 90 F3
Soyana r. Russia 52 I2
Soyma r. Russia 52 K2
Soyopa Mex. 157 F7
Sozh r. Europe 53 F6
Sozopol Bulg. 69 L3
Spa Belgium 62 F4

▶Spain country Europe 67 E3
4th largest country in Europe.

Spalato Croatia see Split
Spalatum Croatia see Split
Spalding U.K. 59 G6
Spanish Canada 152 E5
Spanish Fork UT U.S.A. 159 H1
Spanish Guinea country Africa see Equatorial Guinea
Spanish Netherlands country Europe see Belgium
Spanish Sahara disp. terr. Africa see Western Sahara
Spanish Town Jamaica 169 I5
Sparks NV U.S.A. 158 D2
Sparta Greece see Sparti
Sparta GA U.S.A. 163 D5
Sparta KY U.S.A. 164 C4
Sparta MI U.S.A. 164 C2
Sparta NC U.S.A. 164 E5
Sparta TN U.S.A. 162 C5
Spartanburg SC U.S.A. 163 D5
Sparti Greece 69 J6
Spartivento, Capo c. Italy 68 G6
Spas-Demensk Russia 53 G5
Spas-Klepiki Russia 53 I5
Spassk-Dal'niy Russia 90 D3
Spassk-Ryazanskiy Russia 53 I5
Spata (Eleftherios Venizelos) airport Greece 69 J6
Spatha, Akra pt Greece see Spatha, Akrotirio
Spatha, Akrotirio pt Greece 69 J7
Spearman TX U.S.A. 161 C4
Speedway IN U.S.A. 164 B4
Spence Bay Canada see Taloyoak
Spencer IA U.S.A. 160 E3
Spencer ID U.S.A. 156 E3
Spencer IN U.S.A. 164 B4
Spencer NE U.S.A. 160 D3
Spencer WV U.S.A. 164 E4
Spencer, Cape AK U.S.A. 149 M4
Spencer, Point pt AK U.S.A. 148 F2
Spencer Bay Namibia 124 B3
Spencer Gulf est. Australia 137 B7
Spencer Range hills Australia 134 E3
Spennymoor U.K. 58 F4
Sperrgebiet National Park nat. park Namibia 124 B4
Sperrin Mountains hills U.K. 61 E3
Sperryville VA U.S.A. 165 F4
Spessart reg. Germany 63 J5
Spétsai i. Greece see Spetses
Spetses i. Greece 69 J6
Spey r. U.K. 60 F3
Speyer Germany 63 I5
Spezand Pak. 111 G4
Spice Islands Indon. see Moluccas
Spijk Neth. 62 G1
Spijkenisse Neth. 62 E3
Spike Mountain AK U.S.A. 149 L2
Spilimbergo Italy 68 E1
Spilsby U.K. 58 H5
Spīn Bōldak Afgh. 111 G4
Spintangi Pak. 111 H4
Spirit Lake IA U.S.A. 160 E3
Spirit River Canada 150 G4
Spirovo Russia 52 G4
Spišská Nová Ves Slovakia 53 D6
Spiti r. India 104 D3

▶Spitsbergen i. Svalbard 76 C2
5th largest island in Europe.

Spittal an der Drau Austria 57 N7
Spitzbergen i. Svalbard see Spitsbergen
Split Croatia 68 G3
Split Lake Canada 151 L3
Split Lake l. Canada 151 L3
Spokane WA U.S.A. 156 D3
Spoletium Italy see Spoleto
Spoleto Italy 68 E3
Spóng Cambodia 87 D4
Spoon r. IL U.S.A. 160 F3
Spooner WI U.S.A. 160 F2
Spornitz Germany 63 L1
Spotsylvania VA U.S.A. 165 G4
Spotted Horse WY U.S.A. 156 G3
Spranger, Mount Canada 150 F4
Spratly Islands S. China Sea 80 E4
Spray OR U.S.A. 156 D3
Spree r. Germany 57 N4
Sprimont Belgium 62 F4
Springbok S. Africa 124 C5
Springdale Canada 153 L4
Springdale OH U.S.A. 164 C4

Springe Germany 63 J2
Springer NM U.S.A. 157 G5
Springerville AZ U.S.A. 159 I4
Springfield CO U.S.A. 160 C4

▶**Springfield** IL U.S.A. 160 F4
Capital of Illinois.

Springfield KY U.S.A. 164 C5
Springfield MA U.S.A. 165 I2
Springfield MO U.S.A. 161 E4
Springfield OH U.S.A. 164 D4
Springfield OR U.S.A. 156 C3
Springfield TN U.S.A. 164 B5
Springfield VT U.S.A. 165 I2
Springfield WV U.S.A. 165 F4
Springfontein S. Africa 125 G6
Spring Glen UT U.S.A. 159 H2
Spring Grove IL U.S.A. 164 A2
Springhill Canada 153 I5
Spring Hill FL U.S.A. 163 D6
Springhouse Canada 150 F5
Spring Mountains NV U.S.A. 159 F3
Springs Junction N.Z. 139 D6
Springsure Australia 136 E5
Spring Valley MN U.S.A. 160 E3
Spring Valley NY U.S.A. 165 H3
Springview NE U.S.A. 160 D3
Springville CA U.S.A. 158 D3
Springville NY U.S.A. 165 F2
Springville PA U.S.A. 165 H3
Springville UT U.S.A. 159 H1
Sprowston U.K. 59 I6
Spruce Grove Canada 150 H4
Spruce Knob mt. WV U.S.A. 162 E4
Spruce Mountain CO U.S.A. 159 I2
Spruce Mountain NV U.S.A. 159 F1
Spurn Head hd U.K. 58 H5
Spurr, Mount vol. AK U.S.A. 148 I3
Spuzzum Canada 150 F5
Squam Lake NH U.S.A. 165 J2
Square Lake ME U.S.A. 153 H5
Squaw Harbor AK U.S.A. 148 G5
Squillace, Golfo di g. Italy 68 G5
Squires, Mount hill Australia 135 D6
Sragen Java Indon. 85 E4
Srbija country Europe see Serbia
Srbinje Bos. & Herz. see Foča
Srê Âmběl Cambodia 87 C5
Srebrenica Bos. & Herz. 69 H2
Sredets Burgas Bulg. 69 L3
Sredets Sofia-Grad Bulg. see Sofia
Sredinnyy Khrebet mts Russia 77 Q4
Sredna Gora mts Bulg. 69 J3
Srednekolymsk Russia 77 Q3
Sredne-Russkaya Vozvyshennost' hills Russia see Central Russian Upland
Sredne-Sibirskoye Ploskogor'ye plat. Russia see Central Siberian Plateau
Sredneye Kuyto, Ozero l. Russia 54 Q4
Sredniy Ural mts Russia 51 R4
Srednyaya Akhtuba Russia 53 J6
Sreepur Bangl. see Sripur
Srê Khtum Cambodia 87 D4
Srê Noy Cambodia 87 D4
Sretensk Russia 89 L2
Sri Aman Sarawak Malaysia 85 E2
Sriharikota Island India 106 D3

▶**Sri Jayewardenepura Kotte** Sri Lanka 106 C5
Capital of Sri Lanka.

Srikakulam India 106 E2
Sri Kalahasti India 106 C3
Sri Lanka country Asia 106 D5
Srinagar India 104 C2
Sri Pada mt. Sri Lanka see Adam's Peak
Sripur Bangl. 105 G4
Srirangam India 106 C4
Sri Thep tourist site Thai. 86 C3
Srivardhan India 106 B2
Staaten r. Australia 136 C3
Staaten River National Park Australia 136 C3
Stabroek Guyana see Georgetown
Stade Germany 63 J1
Staden Belgium 62 D4
Stadskanaal Neth. 62 G2
Stadtallendorf Germany 63 J4
Stadthagen Germany 63 J2
Stadtilm Germany 63 L4
Stadtlohn Germany 62 G3
Stadtoldendorf Germany 63 J3
Stadtroda Germany 63 L4
Staffa i. U.K. 60 C4
Staffelberg hill Germany 63 L4
Stafford U.K. 59 E6
Stafford VA U.S.A. 165 G4
Stafford Creek Bahamas 163 E7
Stafford Springs CT U.S.A. 165 I3
Stagen Kalimantan Indon. 85 G3
Stagg Lake Canada 150 H2
Staicele Latvia 55 N8
Staines-upon-Thames U.K. 59 G7
Stakhanov Ukr. 53 H6
Stakhanovo Russia see Zhukovskiy
Stalbridge U.K. 59 E8
Stalham U.K. 59 I6
Stalin Bulg. see Varna
Stalinabad Tajik. see Dushanbe
Stalingrad Russia see Volgograd
Staliniri Georgia see Tskhinvali
Stalino Ukr. see Donets'k
Stalinogorsk Russia see Novomoskovsk
Stalinogród Poland see Katowice
Stalinsk Russia see Novokuznetsk
Stalowa Wola Poland 53 D6
Stamboliyski Bulg. 69 K3
Stamford Australia 136 C4
Stamford U.K. 59 G6
Stamford CT U.S.A. 165 I3
Stamford NY U.S.A. 165 H2
Stamford TX U.S.A. 167 F1
Stampalia i. Greece see Astypalaia
Stampriet Namibia 124 D3
Stamsund Norway 54 H2
Stanardsville VA U.S.A. 165 F4
Stanberry MO U.S.A. 160 E3
Stancomb-Wills Glacier Antarctica 188 B1
Standard Canada 150 H5
Standdaarbuiten Neth. 62 E3
Standerton S. Africa 125 I4
Standish MI U.S.A. 164 D2
Stanfield AZ U.S.A. 159 H5
Stanford KY U.S.A. 164 C5
Stanford MT U.S.A. 156 F3
Stanger S. Africa see KwaDukuza
Stanislaus r. CA U.S.A. 158 C3
Stanislav Ukr. see Ivano-Frankivs'k
Stanke Dimitrov Bulg. see Dupnitsa
Staňkov Czech Rep. 63 N5
Stanley Australia 137 [inset]
Stanley H.K. China 97 [inset]

▶**Stanley** Falkland Is 178 E8
Capital of the Falkland Islands (Islas Malvinas).

Stanley U.K. 58 F4
Stanley ID U.S.A. 156 E3
Stanley KY U.S.A. 164 B5
Stanley ND U.S.A. 160 C1
Stanley VA U.S.A. 165 F4
Stanley, Mount hill N.T. Australia 134 E5
Stanley, Mount hill Tas. Australia 137 [inset]
Stanley, Mount Dem. Rep. Congo/Uganda see Margherita Peak
Stanleyville Dem. Rep. Congo see Kisangani
Stann Creek Belize see Dangriga
Stannington U.K. 58 F3
Stanovoye Russia 53 H5
Stanovoye Nagor'ye mts Russia 89 L1
Stanovoy Khrebet mts Russia 77 N4
Stansmore Range hills Australia 134 E5
Stanthorpe Australia 138 E2
Stanton U.K. 59 H6
Stanton KY U.S.A. 164 D5
Stanton MI U.S.A. 164 C2
Stanton ND U.S.A. 160 C2
Stanton TX U.S.A. 161 C5
Stapleton NE U.S.A. 160 C3
Starachowice Poland 57 R5
Stara Planina mts Bulg./Serbia see Balkan Mountains
Staraya Russa Russia 52 F4
Stara Zagora Bulg. 69 K3
Starbuck Island Kiribati 187 J6
Star City IN U.S.A. 164 B3
Starcke National Park Australia 136 D2
Stargard in Pommern Poland see Stargard Szczeciński
Stargard Szczeciński Poland 57 O4
Staritsa Russia 52 G4
Starke FL U.S.A. 163 D6
Starkville MS U.S.A. 161 F5
Star Lake NY U.S.A. 165 H1
Starnberger See l. Germany 57 M7
Staroaleyskoye Russia 98 C2
Starobel'sk Ukr. see Starobil's'k
Starobil's'k Ukr. 53 H6
Starogard Gdański Poland 57 Q4
Starokonstantinov Ukr. see Starokostyantyniv
Starokostyantyniv Ukr. 53 E6
Starominskaya Russia 53 H7
Staroshcherbinovskaya Russia 53 H7
Star Peak NV U.S.A. 158 D1
Start Point U.K. 59 D8
Starve Island Kiribati see Starbuck Island
Staryya Darohi Belarus 53 F5
Staryye Dorogi Belarus see Staryya Darohi
Staryy Kayak Russia 77 L2
Staryy Oskol Russia 53 H6
Staßfurt Germany 63 L3
State College PA U.S.A. 165 G3
State Line MS U.S.A. 161 F6
Staten Island Arg. see Estados, Isla de los
Statenville GA U.S.A. 163 D6
Statesboro GA U.S.A. 163 D5
Statesville NC U.S.A. 162 D5
Statia mun. West Indies see Sint Eustatius
Station KY U.S.A. 164 C4
Station Nord Greenland 189 I1
Stauchitz Germany 63 N3
Staufenberg Germany 63 I4
Staunton VA U.S.A. 164 F4
Stavanger Norway 55 D7
Staveley U.K. 58 F5
Stavropol' Russia 113 F1
Stavropol Kray admin. div. Russia see Stavropol'skiy Kray
Stavropol'-na-Volge Russia see Tol'yatti
Stavropol'skaya Vozvyshennost' hills Russia 113 F1
Stavropol'skiy Kray admin. div. Russia 113 F1
Stayner Canada 164 E1
Stayton OR U.S.A. 156 C3
Steadville S. Africa 125 I5
Steamboat Springs CO U.S.A. 156 G4
Stearns KY U.S.A. 164 C5
Stebbins AK U.S.A. 148 G3
Steele Creek AK U.S.A. 149 L2
Steele Island Antarctica 188 L2
Steelville MO U.S.A. 160 F4
Steen r. Canada 150 G3
Steenderen Neth. 62 G2
Steenkampsberge mts S. Africa 125 J3
Steen River Canada 150 G3
Steens Mountain OR U.S.A. 156 D4
Steenstrup Gletscher glacier Greenland see Sermersuaq
Steenvoorde France 62 C4
Steenwijk Neth. 62 G2
Steese Highway AK U.S.A. 149 K2
Stefansson Island Canada 147 H2
Stegi Swaziland see Siteki
Steigerwald mts Germany 63 K5
Stein Germany 63 L5
Steinach Germany 63 L4
Steinaker Reservoir UT U.S.A. 159 I1
Steinbach Canada 151 L5
Steinfeld (Oldenburg) Germany 63 I2
Steinfurt Germany 63 H2
Steinhausen Namibia 123 B6
Steinheim Germany 63 J3
Steinkjer Norway 54 G4
Steinkopf S. Africa 124 C5
Steinsdalen Norway 54 G4
Stella S. Africa 124 G4
Stella Maris Bahamas 163 F8
Stellenbosch S. Africa 124 D7
Steller, Mount AK U.S.A. 149 L3
Stello, Monte mt. Corsica France 66 I5
Stelvio, Parco Nazionale dello nat. park Italy 68 D1
Stenay France 62 F5
Stendal Germany 63 L2
Stenhousemuir U.K. 60 F4
Stenungsund Sweden 55 G7
Steornabhagh U.K. see Stornoway
Stepanakert Azer. see Xankändi
Stephens, Cape N.Z. 139 D5
Stephens City VA U.S.A. 165 F4
Stephens Lake Canada 151 M3
Stephenville TX U.S.A. 161 D5
Stepnoy Kyrg. 98 A4
Stepnoy Russia see Elista
Stepnoye Russia 53 J6
Stepovak Bay AK U.S.A. 148 G5
Sterkfontein Dam resr S. Africa 125 I5
Sterkstroom S. Africa 125 H6
Sterlet Lake Canada 151 I1
Sterlibashevo Russia 51 R5
Sterling S. Africa 124 E6
Sterling CO U.S.A. 160 C3
Sterling IL U.S.A. 160 F3
Sterling MI U.S.A. 164 C1
Sterling UT U.S.A. 159 H2
Sterling City TX U.S.A. 161 C6
Sterling Heights MI U.S.A. 164 D2
Sterlitamak Russia 76 G4
Stettin Poland see Szczecin
Stettler Canada 151 H4
Steubenville KY U.S.A. 164 C5
Steubenville OH U.S.A. 164 E3
Stevenage U.K. 59 G7
Stevenson WA U.S.A. 156 C3
Stevenson Entrance sea chan. AK U.S.A. 148 I4
Stevenson Lake Canada 151 L4
Stevens Point WI U.S.A. 160 F2
Stevens Village AK U.S.A. 149 J2
Stevensville MI U.S.A. 164 B2
Stevensville PA U.S.A. 165 G3
Stevns Klint cliff Denmark 55 H9
Stewart Canada 149 O5
Stewart r. Canada 149 M3
Stewart, Isla i. Chile 178 B8
Stewart Crossing Canada 149 M3
Stewart Island N.Z. 139 A8
Stewart Islands Solomon Is 133 G2
Stewart Lake Canada 147 J3
Stewarton U.K. 60 E5
Stewarts Point CA U.S.A. 158 B2
Stewiacke Canada 153 J5
Steynsburg S. Africa 125 G6
Steyr Austria 57 O6
Steytlerville S. Africa 124 G7
Stiens Neth. 62 F1
Stif Alg. see Sétif
Stigler OK U.S.A. 161 E5
Stikine r. Canada 149 N4
Stikine Plateau Canada 149 O4
Stikine Ranges mts Canada 149 O4
Stikine Strait AK U.S.A. 150 C3
Stilbaai S. Africa 124 E8
Stiles WI U.S.A. 164 A1
Stillwater MN U.S.A. 160 E2
Stillwater OK U.S.A. 161 D4
Stillwater Range mts NV U.S.A. 158 D2
Stillwell IN U.S.A. 164 B3
Stilton U.K. 59 G6
Stilwell OK U.S.A. 161 E5
Stinnett TX U.S.A. 161 C5
Štip Macedonia 69 J4
Stirling Australia 134 F5
Stirling Canada 165 G1
Stirling U.K. 60 F4
Stirling Creek r. Australia 134 E4
Stirling Range National Park Australia 135 B8
Stittsville Canada 165 H1
Stjørdalshalsen Norway 54 G5
Stockbridge MI U.S.A. 164 C2
Stockerau Austria 57 P6
Stockheim Germany 63 L4

▶**Stockholm** Sweden 55 K7
Capital of Sweden.

Stockinbingal Australia 138 C5
Stockport U.K. 58 E5
Stockton CA U.S.A. 158 C3
Stockton KS U.S.A. 160 D4
Stockton MO U.S.A. 160 E4
Stockton UT U.S.A. 159 G1
Stockton Islands AK U.S.A. 149 K1
Stockton Lake MO U.S.A. 160 E4
Stockton-on-Tees U.K. 58 F4
Stockton Plateau TX U.S.A. 166 E2
Stockville NE U.S.A. 160 C3
Stod Czech Rep. 63 N5
Stœng Trêng Cambodia 87 D4
Stoer, Point of U.K. 60 D2
Stoke-on-Trent U.K. 59 E5
Stokesley U.K. 58 F4
Stokes Point Australia 137 [inset]
Stokes Range hills Australia 134 E4
Stokkseyri Iceland 54 [inset 1]
Stokkvågen Norway 54 H3
Stokmarknes Norway 54 I2
Stolac Bos. & Herz. 68 G3
Stolberg (Rheinland) Germany 62 G4
Stolboukha (abandoned) Kazakh. 98 D2
Stolbovoy Russia 189 G2
Stolbtsy Belarus see Stowbtsy
Stolin Belarus 55 O11
Stollberg Germany 63 M4
Stolp Poland see Słupsk
Stolzenau Germany 63 J2
Stone U.K. 59 E6
Stoneboro PA U.S.A. 164 E3
Stonecliffe Canada 152 F5
Stonecutters' Island pen. H.K. China 97 [inset]
Stonehaven U.K. 60 G4
Stonehenge Australia 136 C5
Stonehenge tourist site U.K. 59 F7
Stoner CO U.S.A. 159 I3
Stone Spheres of the Diquís tourist site Costa Rica 166 J7
Stonewall Canada 151 L5
Stonewall Jackson Lake WV U.S.A. 164 E4
Stony r. AK U.S.A. 148 H3
Stony Creek VA U.S.A. 165 G5
Stony Lake Canada 151 L3
Stony Point NY U.S.A. 165 G2
Stony Rapids Canada 151 J3
Stony River AK U.S.A. 146 C3
Stooping r. Canada 152 E3
Stora Lulevatten l. Sweden 54 K3
Stora Sjöfallets nationalpark nat. park Sweden 54 J3
Storavan l. Sweden 54 K4
Store Bælt sea chan. Denmark see Great Belt
Støren Norway 54 G5
Storfjordbotn Norway 54 O1
Storforshei Norway 54 I3
Storjord Norway 54 I3
Storkerson Peninsula Canada 147 H2
Storm Bay Australia 137 [inset]
Stormberg S. Africa 125 H6
Storm Lake IA U.S.A. 160 E3
Stornosa mt. Norway 54 E6
Stornoway U.K. 60 C2
Storozhevsk Russia 52 L3
Storozhynets' Ukr. 53 E6
Storrs CT U.S.A. 165 I3
Storseleby Sweden 54 J4
Storsjön l. Sweden 54 I5
Storskrymten mt. Norway 54 F5
Storslett Norway 54 L2
Stortemelk sea chan. Neth. 62 F1
Storuman Sweden 54 J4
Storuman l. Sweden 54 J4
Storvik Sweden 55 J6
Storvorde Denmark 55 G8
Storvreta Sweden 55 J7
Story WY U.S.A. 156 G3
Stotfold U.K. 59 G6
Stoughton Canada 151 K5
Stour r. England U.K. 59 F6
Stour r. England U.K. 59 F8
Stour r. England U.K. 59 I7
Stour r. England U.K. 59 I7
Stourbridge U.K. 59 E6
Stourport-on-Severn U.K. 59 E6
Stout Lake Canada 151 M4
Stowbtsy Belarus 55 O10
Stowe VT U.S.A. 165 I1
Stowmarket U.K. 59 H6
Stoyba Russia 90 C1
Strabane U.K. 61 E3
Stradbally Ireland 61 E4
Stradbroke U.K. 59 I6
Stradella Italy 68 C2
Strakonice Czech Rep. 57 N6
Stralsund Germany 57 N3
Strand S. Africa 124 D8
Stranda Norway 54 E5
Strangford U.K. 61 G3
Strangford Lough inlet U.K. 61 G3
Strangways r. Australia 134 F3
Stranraer U.K. 60 D6
Strasbourg France 66 H2
Strasburg VA U.S.A. 165 F4
Strasburg (Uckermark) Germany 63 N1
Strassburg France see Strasbourg
Stratford Australia 138 C6
Stratford Canada 164 E2
Stratford CA U.S.A. 158 D3
Stratford TX U.S.A. 161 C4
Stratford-upon-Avon U.K. 59 F6
Strathaven U.K. 60 E5
Strathmore Canada 150 H5
Strathmore r. U.K. 60 E2
Strathnaver Canada 150 F4
Strathroy Canada 164 E2
Strathspey valley U.K. 60 F3
Strathy U.K. 60 F2
Stratton U.K. 59 C8
Stratton ME U.S.A. 165 J1
Stratton Mountain VT U.S.A. 165 I2
Straubing Germany 63 M6
Straumnes pt Iceland 54 [inset 1]
Strawberry AZ U.S.A. 159 H4
Strawberry Mountain OR U.S.A. 156 D3
Strawberry Reservoir UT U.S.A. 159 H1
Streaky Bay Australia 135 F8
Streaky Bay b. Australia 135 F8
Streator IL U.S.A. 160 F3
Street U.K. 59 E7
Streetsboro OH U.S.A. 164 E3
Strehaia Romania 69 J2
Strehla Germany 63 N3
Streich Mound hill Australia 135 C7
Strelka Russia 77 Q3
Strel'na r. Russia 52 H2
Strenči Latvia 55 N8
Streymoy i. Faroe Is 54 [inset 2]
Stříbro Czech Rep. 63 M5
Strichen U.K. 60 G3
Strimonas r. Greece see Strymonas
Stroeder Arg. 178 D6
Strokestown Ireland 61 D4
Stroma, Island of U.K. 60 F2
Stromboli, Isola i. Italy 68 F5
Stromness S. Georgia 178 I8
Stromness U.K. 60 F2
Strömstad Sweden 55 G7
Strömsund Sweden 54 I5
Strongsville OH U.S.A. 164 E3
Stronsay i. U.K. 60 G1
Stroud Australia 138 E4
Stroud U.K. 59 E7
Stroud Road Australia 138 E4
Stroudsburg PA U.S.A. 165 H3
Struer Denmark 55 F8
Struga Macedonia 69 I4
Strugi-Krasnyye Russia 55 P7
Struis Bay S. Africa 124 E8
Strullendorf Germany 63 K5
Struma r. Bulg. 69 J4
also known as Strymonas (Greece)
Strumble Head hd U.K. 59 B6
Strumica Macedonia 69 J4
Struthers OH U.S.A. 164 E3
Stryama r. Bulg. 69 K3
Strydenburg S. Africa 124 F5
Strymonas r. Greece 69 J4
also known as Struma (Bulgaria)
Stryn Norway 54 E6
Stryy Ukr. 53 D6
Strzelecki, Mount hill Australia 134 F5
Strzelecki Regional Reserve nature res. Australia 137 B6
Stuart FL U.S.A. 163 D7
Stuart NE U.S.A. 160 D3
Stuart VA U.S.A. 164 E5
Stuart Island AK U.S.A. 148 G3
Stuart Lake Canada 150 E4
Stuart Range hills Australia 137 A6
Stuarts Draft VA U.S.A. 164 F4
Stuart Town Australia 138 D4
Stuchka Latvia see Aizkraukle
Stučka Latvia see Aizkraukle
Studholme Junction N.Z. 139 C7
Studsviken Sweden 54 K5
Study Butte TX U.S.A. 166 E2
Stukely, Lac l. Canada 165 I1
Stung Treng Cambodia see Stœng Trêng
Stupart r. Canada 151 M4
Stupino Russia 53 H5
Sturge Island Antarctica 188 H2
Sturgeon r. Ont. Canada 152 F5
Sturgeon r. Sask. Canada 151 J4
Sturgeon Bay b. Canada 151 L4
Sturgeon Bay WI U.S.A. 164 B1
Sturgeon Bay Canal lake channel WI U.S.A. 164 B1
Sturgeon Falls Canada 152 F5
Sturgeon Lake Ont. Canada 151 N5
Sturgeon Lake Ont. Canada 165 F1
Sturgis MI U.S.A. 164 C3
Sturgis SD U.S.A. 160 C2
Sturt, Mount hill Australia 137 C6
Sturt Creek watercourse Australia 134 D4
Sturt National Park Australia 137 C6
Sturt Stony Desert Australia 137 C6
Stutterheim S. Africa 125 H7
Stuttgart Germany 63 J6
Stuttgart AR U.S.A. 161 F5
Stuver, Mount AK U.S.A. 149 J1
Stykkishólmur Iceland 54 [inset 1]
Styr r. Belarus/Ukr. 53 E5
Suaçuí Grande r. Brazil 179 C2
Suai East Timor 83 C5
Suai Sarawak Malaysia 85 F2
Suakin Sudan 108 E6
Su'ao Taiwan 97 I3
Suaqui Grande Mex. 166 C2
Suau P.N.G. 136 E1
Subačius Lith. 55 N9
Subang Java Indon. 85 D4
Subankhata India 105 G4
Subansiri r. India 99 F8
Subarnapur India 106 D1
Sūbāshī Iran 110 C3
Subay reg. Saudi Arabia 110 B5
Şubayḩah Saudi Arabia 107 D4
Subei China 98 F5
Subi Besar i. Indon. 85 E2
Subi Kecil i. Indon. 85 E2
Sublette KS U.S.A. 161 C4
Sub Nur l. China 94 E3
Subotica Serbia 69 H1
Success, Lake CA U.S.A. 158 D3
Succiso, Alpe di mts Italy 68 D2
Suceava Romania 53 E7
Suchan Russia see Partizansk
Suck r. Ireland 61 D4
Suckling, Cape AK U.S.A. 149 L3
Suckling, Mount P.N.G. 136 E1
Suckow Germany 63 L1

▶**Sucre** Bol. 176 E7
Joint capital (with La Paz) of Bolivia.

Suczawa Romania see Suceava
Sud, Grand Récif du reef New Caledonia 133 G4
Suda Russia 52 H4
Sudak Crimea 112 D1

▶**Sudan** country Africa 121 F3
3rd largest country in Africa.

Suday Russia 52 I4
Sudayr reg. Saudi Arabia 110 B5
Sudbury Canada 152 E5
Sudbury U.K. 59 H6
Sudd swamp South Sudan 108 C8
Sude r. Germany 63 K1
Sudest Island P.N.G. see Tagula Island
Sudetenland mts Czech Rep./Poland see Sudety
Sudety mts Czech Rep./Poland 57 O5
Sudislavl' Russia 52 I4
Sudlersville MD U.S.A. 165 H4
Süd-Nord-Kanal canal Germany 62 H2
Sudogda Russia 52 I5
Sudr Egypt 107 A5
Suðuroy i. Faroe Is 54 [inset 2]
Sue watercourse South Sudan 121 F4
Sueca Spain 67 F4
Suez Egypt 107 A5
Suez, Gulf of Egypt 107 A5
Suez Bay Egypt 107 A5
Suez Canal Egypt 107 A4
Suffolk VA U.S.A. 165 G5
Sugarbush Hill hill WI U.S.A. 160 F2
Sugarloaf Mountain ME U.S.A. 165 J1
Sugarloaf Point Australia 138 F4
Suga-shima i. Japan 92 C4
Sugbuhan Point Phil. 82 D4
Süget China see Sogat
Sugi i. Sumatra Indon. 84 C2
Sugun China 98 B5
Sugut r. Malaysia 85 G1
Sugut, Tanjung pt Malaysia 85 G1
Suhai Hu l. China 98 F5
Suhai Obo China 94 F3
Suhait China 94 F4
Sūhāj Egypt 108 D4
Şuḩār Oman 110 E5
Suhaymī, Wādī as watercourse Egypt 107 A4
Sühbaatar Selenge Mongolia 94 F1
Sühbaatar Sühbaatar Mongolia 95 H2
Sühbaatar prov. Mongolia 95 H2
Suheli Par i. India 106 B4
Suhl Germany 63 K4
Suhlendorf Germany 63 K2
Suhul reg. Saudi Arabia 110 B6
Suhūl al Kidan plain Saudi Arabia 110 D6
Şuhut Turkey 69 N5
Sui Pak. 111 H4
Sui, Laem pt Thai. 87 B5
Suibin China 90 C3
Suid-Afrika country Africa see South Africa
Suide China 95 G4
Sui Dehar Pak. 111 H4
Suidzhikurmsy Turkm. see Madaw
Suifenhe China 90 C3
Suifu Japan 93 G2
Suigetsu-ko l. Japan 92 B3
Suigō-Tsukuba Kokutei-kōen park Japan 93 G2
Suihua China 90 B3
Suileng China 90 B3
Suining Hunan China 97 F3
Suining Jiangsu China 97 H1
Suining Sichuan China 96 E2
Suippes France 62 E5
Suir r. Ireland 61 E5
Suisse country Europe see Switzerland
Suita Japan 92 B4
Suixi China 97 H1
Suixian Henan China 95 H5
Suixian Hubei China see Suizhou
Suiyang Guizhou China 96 E3
Suiyang Henan China 95 H5
Suiza country Europe see Switzerland
Suizhong China 95 J3
Suizhou China 97 G2
Suj China 95 F3
Sujangarh India 104 C4
Sujawal Pak. 111 H5
Suk atoll Micronesia see Pulusuk
Sukabumi Java Indon. 84 D4
Sukadana Kalimantan Indon. 85 E3
Sukadana Sumatra Indon. 84 D4
Sukadana, Teluk b. Indon. 85 E3
Sukagawa Japan 91 F5
Sukanegara Java Indon. 84 D4
Sukaraja Kalimantan Indon. 85 E3
Sukaramai Kalimantan Indon. 85 E3
Sukarnapura Indon. see Jayapura
Sukarno, Puncak mt. Indon. see Jaya, Puncak
Sukau Sabah Malaysia 85 G1
Sukchŏn N. Korea 91 B5
Sukhinichi Russia 53 G5
Sukhona r. Russia 52 J3
Sukhothai Thai. 86 B3
Sukhumi Georgia see Sokhumi
Sukhum-Kale Georgia see Sokhumi
Sukkertoppen Greenland see Maniitsoq
Sukkozero Russia 52 G3
Sukkur Pak. 111 H5
Sukma India 106 D2
Sukpay Russia 90 E3
Sukpay r. Russia 90 E3
Sukri r. Rajasthan India 104 C4
Sukri r. Rajasthan India 104 C4
Suktel r. India 106 D1
Sukun i. Indon. 83 B5
Sula i. Norway 55 D6
Sula r. Russia 52 K2
Sula, Kepulauan is Indon. 83 C3
Sulabesi i. Indon. 83 C3
Sulaiman Range mts Pak. 111 H4
Sulak Russia 113 G2
Sülär Iran 110 C4
Sula Sgeir i. U.K. 60 C1
Sulasih, Gunung vol. Indon. 84 C3
Sulat i. Indon. 85 G5
Sulat Samar Phil. 82 D4
Sulatna Crossing AK U.S.A. 148 I2
Sulawesi i. Indon. see Celebes
Sulawesi Barat prov. Indon. 83 A3
Sulawesi Selatan prov. Indon. 83 A3
Sulawesi Tengah prov. Indon. 83 B3
Sulawesi Tenggara prov. Indon. 83 B4
Sulawesi Utara prov. Indon. 83 C2
Sulaymān Beg Iraq 113 G4
Sulayyimah Saudi Arabia 110 B6
Sulci Sardinia Italy see Sant'Antioco
Sulcis Sardinia Italy see Sant'Antioco
Suleman, Teluk b. Indon. 85 G2
Sule Skerry i. U.K. 60 E1
Sule Stack i. U.K. 60 E1
Suliki Sumatra Indon. 84 C3

Sulingen Germany **63** I2
Sulin Gol *r.* China **94** C4
Sulitjelma Norway **54** J3
Sulkava Fin. **54** P6
Sullana Peru **176** B4
Sullivan *IL* U.S.A. **160** F4
Sullivan *IN* U.S.A. **164** B4
Sullivan Bay Canada **150** E5
Sullivan Island Myanmar *see* **Lanbi Kyun**
Sullivan Lake Canada **151** I5
Sulmo Italy *see* **Sulmona**
Sulmona Italy **68** E3
Sulphur *LA* U.S.A. **161** E6
Sulphur *OK* U.S.A. **161** D5
Sulphur *r. TX* U.S.A. **161** E5
Sulphur Springs *TX* U.S.A. **161** E5
Sultan Canada **152** E5
Sultan, Koh-i- *mts* Pak. **111** F4
Sultanabad India *see* **Osmannagar**
Sultānābād Iran *see* **Ārāk**
Sultan Dağları *mts* Turkey **69** N5
Sultanıye Turkey *see* **Karapınar**
Sultanpur India **105** E4
Suluan *i.* Phil. **82** D4
Sulu Archipelago *is* Phil. **82** C5
Sulu Basin *sea feature* N. Pacific Ocean **186** E5
Suluke China **99** A5
Sülüklü Turkey **112** D3
Sülüktü Kyrg. **111** H2
Sulusaray Turkey **112** E3
Sulu Sea N. Pacific Ocean **80** F5
Suluvvaulik, Lac *l.* Canada **153** G2
Sulyukta Kyrg. *see* **Sülüktü**
Sulzbach-Rosenberg Germany **63** L5
Sulzberger Bay Antarctica **188** I1
Suma Japan **92** B4
Sumāil Oman **110** E6
Sumalata *Celebes* Indon. **83** B2
Sumampa Arg. **178** D3
Sumangat, Tanjung *pt* Malaysia **85** G1
Sumapaz, Parque Nacional *nat. park* Col. **176** D3
Sūmār Iran **110** B3
Sumatera *i.* Indon. *see* **Sumatra**
Sumatera Barat *prov.* Indon. **84** C3
Sumatera Selatan *prov.* Indon. **84** C3
Sumatera Utara *prov.* Indon. **84** B2

▶**Sumatra** *i.* Indon. **84** B2
2nd largest island in Asia and 6th in the world.

Šumava, Národní park *nat. park* Czech Rep. **57** N6
Sumayl/Sêmêl Iraq **113** F3
Sumba *i.* Indon. **83** B5
Sumba, Selat *sea chan.* Indon. **83** A5
Sumbar *r.* Turkm. **110** D2
Sumbawa *i.* Indon. **83** A5
Sumbawabesar *Sumbawa* Indon. **85** G5
Sumbawanga Tanz. **123** D4
Sumbe Angola **123** B5
Sumbing, Gunung *vol.* Indon. **84** C3
Sumbu National Park Zambia **123** D4
Sumburgh U.K. **60** [inset]
Sumburgh Head *hd* U.K. **60** [inset]
Sumdo *Sichuan* China **96** D2
Sumdo *Xinjiang* China **99** B6
Sumdum, Mount *AK* U.S.A. **149** N4
Sumedang *Java* Indon. **85** D4
Sumeih Sudan **108** C8
Sumenep *Java* Indon. **85** F4
Sumgait Azer. *see* **Sumqayıt**
Sumisu-jima *i.* Japan **89** Q6
Sümiyn Bulag Mongolia *see* **Gurvandzagal**
Summer Beaver Canada **152** C3
Summerford Canada **153** L4
Summer Island *MI* U.S.A. **162** C2
Summer Isles U.K. **60** D2
Summerland Canada **150** G5
Summersville *WV* U.S.A. **164** E4
Summit *AK* U.S.A. **149** J3
Summit Lake Canada **150** F4
Summit Lake *AK* U.S.A. **149** K3
Summit Mountain *NV* U.S.A. **158** E2
Summit Peak *CO* U.S.A. **157** G5
Sumnal China **99** B6
Sumner N.Z. **139** D6
Sumner, Lake N.Z. **139** D6
Sumon-dake *mt.* Japan **91** E5
Sumoto Japan **92** A4
Sumpangbinangae *Celebes* Indon. **83** A4
Šumperk Czech Rep. **57** P6
Sumpu Japan *see* **Shizuoka**
Sumqayıt Azer. **113** H2
Sumskiy Posad Russia **52** G2
Sumter *SC* U.S.A. **163** D5
Sumur India **104** D2
Sumxi China **99** C6
Sumy Ukr. **53** G6
Sumzom China **96** C2
Suna Russia **52** K4
Sunaj India **104** D4
Sunam India **104** C3
Sunamganj Bangl. **105** G4
Sunami Japan **92** C3
Sunan China **94** D4
Sunart, Loch *inlet* U.K. **60** D4
Şunaynah Oman **110** D6
Sunburst *MT* U.S.A. **156** F2
Sunbury Australia **138** B6
Sunbury *OH* U.S.A. **164** D3
Sunbury *PA* U.S.A. **165** G3
Suncheon S. Korea **91** B6
Sun City S. Africa **125** H3
Sun City *AZ* U.S.A. **159** G5
Sun City *CA* U.S.A. **158** E5
Sunda, Selat *str.* Indon. **84** D4
Sunda Kalapa *Java* Indon. *see* **Jakarta**
Sundance *WY* U.S.A. **156** G3
Sundarbans *coastal area* Bangl./India **105** G5
Sundarbans National Park Bangl./India **105** G5
Sundargarh India **105** F5
Sunda Shelf *sea feature* Indian Ocean **185** P5
Sunda Strait Indon. *see* **Sunda, Selat**
Sunda Trench *sea feature* Indian Ocean *see* **Java Trench**
Sunderland U.K. **58** F4
Sundern (Sauerland) Germany **63** I3
Sündiken Dağları *mts* Turkey **69** N5
Sundown National Park Australia **138** E2
Sundre Canada **150** H5
Sundridge Canada **152** F5
Sundsvall Sweden **54** J5
Sundukli, Peski *des.* Turkm. *see* **Sandykly Gumy**
Sundumbili S. Africa **125** J5
Sunduyka Russia **95** G1
Sungaiapit *Sumatra* Indon. **84** C2
Sungaiguntung *Sumatra* Indon. **84** C2
Sungaikabung *Sumatra* Indon. **84** C2
Sungaikakap *Kalimantan* Indon. **85** E3
Sungailiat *Sumatra* Indon. **84** D3
Sungaipenuh *Sumatra* Indon. **84** C3
Sungai Petani Malaysia **84** C1
Sungaipinyuh *Kalimantan* Indon. **85** E2
Sungaiselan Indon. **84** D3
Sungari *r.* China *see* **Songhua Jiang**
Sungei Seletar Reservoir Sing. **87** [inset]
Sungguminasa *Celebes* Indon. **83** A4
Sungkiang China *see* **Songjiang**
Sung Kong *i. H.K.* China **97** [inset]
Sungqu China *see* **Songpan**
Sungsang *Sumatra* Indon. **84** D3
Sungurlu Turkey **112** D2
Sunkar, Gora *mt.* Kazakh. **98** A3
Sun Kosi *r.* Nepal **105** F4
Sunman *IN* U.S.A. **164** C4
Sunndal Norway **55** E6
Sunndalsøra Norway **54** F5
Sunne Sweden **55** H7
Sunnyside *WA* U.S.A. **156** D3
Sunnyvale *CA* U.S.A. **158** B3
Suno-saki *pt* Japan **93** F4
Sun Prairie *WI* U.S.A. **160** F3
Sunset House Canada **150** G4
Sunset Peak *hill H.K.* China **97** [inset]
Suntar Russia **77** M3
Suntsar Pak. **111** F5
Sunwi-do *i.* N. Korea **91** B5
Sunwu China **90** B2
Sunyani Ghana **120** C4
Suolijärvet *l.* Fin. **54** P3
Suomi *country* Europe *see* **Finland**
Suomussalmi Fin. **54** P4
Suō-nada *b.* Japan **91** C6
Suonenjoki Fin. **54** O5
Suong *r.* Laos **86** C3
Suoyarvi Russia **52** G3
Suozhen China *see* **Huantai**
Supa India **106** B3
Supaul India **105** F4
Superior *AZ* U.S.A. **159** H5
Superior *MT* U.S.A. **156** E3
Superior *NE* U.S.A. **160** D3
Superior *WI* U.S.A. **160** E2
Superior, Laguna *lag.* Mex. **167** G5

▶**Superior, Lake** Canada/U.S.A. **155** J2
Largest lake in North America and 2nd in the world.

Suphan Buri Thai. **87** C4
Süphan Dağı *mt.* Turkey **113** F3
Supiori *i.* Indon. **81** J7
Suponevo Russia **53** G5
Support Force Glacier Antarctica **188** A1
Sūq ash Shuyūkh Iraq **113** G5
Suqian China **97** H1
Suquṭrá *i.* Yemen *see* **Socotra**
Şūr Oman **111** E6
Sur, Point *CA* U.S.A. **158** C3
Sur, Punta *pt* Arg. **178** E5
Sura *r.* Russia **53** J4
Şuraabad Azer. **113** H2
Surabaya *Java* Indon. **85** F4
Sūrak Iran **110** E5
Surakarta *Java* Indon. **85** E4
Suramana *Celebes* Indon. **83** A3
Sūrān Iran **111** F5
Şūrān Syria **107** C2
Surat Australia **138** D1
Surat India **104** C5
Suratgarh India **104** C3
Surat Thani Thai. **87** B5
Surazh Russia **53** G5
Surbiton Australia **136** D4
Surdulica Serbia **69** J3
Sûre *r.* Lux. **62** G5
Surendranagar India **104** B5
Suretka Costa Rica **166** [inset] J7
Surf *CA* U.S.A. **158** C4
Surgut Russia **76** I3
Suri India *see* **Siuri**
Suriapet India **106** C2
Surigao *Mindanao* Phil. **82** D4
Surigao Strait Phil. **82** D4
Surin Thai. **86** C4
Surinam *country* S. America *see* **Suriname**
Suriname *country* S. America **177** G3
Surin Nua, Ko *i.* Thai. **87** B5
Surkhet Nepal **105** E3
Surkhon Uzbek. *see* **Surxon**
Sürmene Turkey **113** F2
Surovikino Russia **53** I6
Surprise Canada **149** N4
Surprise Lake Canada **149** N4
Surrah, Nafūd as *des.* Saudi Arabia **110** A6
Surrey Canada **150** F5
Surry *VA* U.S.A. **165** G5
Surskoye Russia **53** J5
Surt Libya *see* **Sirte**
Surtsey *i.* Iceland **54** [inset 1]
Sūrū *Hormozgān* Iran **110** E5
Sūrū *Sīstān va Balūchestān* Iran **110** E5
Suruç Turkey **107** D1
Surud, Raas *pt* Somalia **122** E2
Surud Ad *mt.* Somalia *see* **Shimbiris**
Suruga-wan *b.* Japan **93** E4
Surulangun *Sumatra* Indon. **84** C3
Surup *Mindanao* Phil. **82** D5
Survey Pass *AK* U.S.A. **148** I2
Surwold Germany **63** H2
Surxon Uzbek. **111** G2
Suryapet India *see* **Suriapet**
Şuşa Azer. **113** G3
Susah Tunisia *see* **Sousse**
Susaki Japan **91** D6
Susan *VA* U.S.A. **165** G5
Süsangerd Iran **110** C4
Susanino Russia **90** F1
Susanville *CA* U.S.A. **158** C1
Suşehri Turkey **112** E2
Susitna *r. AK* U.S.A. **149** J3
Susitna, Mount *AK* U.S.A. **149** J3
Susitna Lake *AK* U.S.A. **149** K3
Suso Thai. **87** B6
Susobana-gawa *r.* Japan **93** E2
Susong China **97** H2
Susono Japan **93** E3
Susquehanna *PA* U.S.A. **165** H3
Susquehanna *r. PA* U.S.A. **165** G4
Susquehanna, West Branch *r. PA* U.S.A. **165** G3
Susques Arg. **178** C2
Sussex *VA* U.S.A. **165** G5
Susua *Celebes* Indon. **83** B3
Susul *Sabah* Malaysia **85** G1
Susuman Russia **77** P3
Susupu *Halmahera* Indon. **83** C2
Susurluk Turkey **69** M5
Sutak India **104** D2
Sutay Uul *mt.* Mongolia **94** C2
Sutherland Australia **138** E5
Sutherland S. Africa **124** E7
Sutherland *NE* U.S.A. **160** C3
Sutherland Range *hills* Australia **135** D6
Sutjeska, Nacionalni Park *nat. park* Bos. & Herz. **68** H3
Sutlej *r.* India/Pak. *see* **Satluj**
Sütlüce Turkey **107** A1
Sutter *CA* U.S.A. **158** C2
Sutterton U.K. **59** G6
Sutton Canada **165** I1
Sutton *r.* Canada **152** E3
Sutton U.K. **59** H6
Sutton *AK* U.S.A. **149** J3
Sutton *NE* U.S.A. **160** D3
Sutton *WV* U.S.A. **164** E4
Sutton Coldfield U.K. **59** F6
Sutton in Ashfield U.K. **59** F5
Sutton Lake Canada **152** D3
Sutton Lake *WV* U.S.A. **164** E4
Suttor *r.* Australia **136** D4
Suttsu Japan **90** F4
Sutwik Island *AK* U.S.A. **148** H4
Sutyr' *r.* Russia **90** D2
Suugaant Mongolia *see* **Gurvansayhan**
Suusamyr Kyrg. **98** A4

▶**Suva** Fiji **133** H3
Capital of Fiji.

Suvadiva Atoll Maldives *see* **Huvadhu Atholhu**
Suvalki Poland *see* **Suwałki**
Suvorov *atoll* Cook Is *see* **Suwarrow**
Suvorov Russia **53** H5
Suwa Japan **93** E2
Suwa-ko *l.* Japan **93** E2
Suwakong *Kalimantan* Indon. **85** F3
Suwałki Poland **53** D5
Suwannaphum Thai. **86** C4
Suwannee *r. FL* U.S.A. **163** D6
Suwanose-jima *i.* Japan **91** C7
Suwaran, Gunung *mt.* Indon. **85** G2
Suwarrow *atoll* Cook Is **133** J3
Suwaylih Jordan **107** B3
Suwayr *well* Saudi Arabia **113** F5
Suways, Khalīj as *g.* Egypt *see* **Suez, Gulf of**
Suways, Qanāt as *canal* Egypt *see* **Suez Canal**
Suweilih Jordan *see* **Suwaylih**
Suweis, Khalîg el *g.* Egypt *see* **Suez, Gulf of**
Suweis, Qanâ el *canal* Egypt *see* **Suez Canal**
Suwon S. Korea **91** B5
Suxik China **94** C4
Suykbulak Kazakh. **98** C2
Suyūl Ḥanīsh *i.* Yemen **108** F7
Suz, Mys *pt* Kazakh. **113** I2
Suzaka Japan **93** E2
Suzdal' Russia **52** I4
Suzhou *Anhui* China **97** H1
Suzhou *Gansu* China *see* **Jiuquan**
Suzhou *Jiangsu* China **97** I2
Suzi He *r.* China **90** B4
Suzuka Japan **92** C4
Suzuka-gawa *r.* Japan **92** C4
Suzuka Kokutei-kōen *park* Japan **92** C3
Suzuka-sanmyaku *mts* Japan **92** C4
Suzu-misaki *pt* Japan **91** E5
Sværholthalvøya *pen.* Norway **54** O1

▶**Svalbard** *terr.* Arctic Ocean **76** C2
Part of Norway.

Svappavaara Sweden **54** L3
Svartenhuk Halvø *pen.* Greenland *see* **Sigguup Nunaa**
Svatove Ukr. **53** H6
Svay Chék Cambodia **87** C4
Svay Riěng Cambodia **87** D5
Svecha Russia **52** J4
Sveg Sweden **55** I5
Sveķi Latvia **55** O8
Svelgen Norway **54** D6
Svellingen Norway **54** F5
Švenčionėliai Lith. **55** N9
Švenčionys Lith. **55** O9
Svendborg Denmark **55** G9
Svensbu Norway **54** K2
Svenstavik Sweden **54** I5
Sverdlovsk Russia *see* **Yekaterinburg**
Sverdlovs'k Ukr. **53** H6
Sverdrup Islands Canada **147** I2
Sverige *country* Europe *see* **Sweden**
Sveti Nikole Macedonia **69** I4
Svetlaya Russia **90** E3
Svetlogorsk Belarus *see* **Svyetlahorsk**
Svetlogorsk *Kaliningradskaya Oblast'* Russia **55** L9
Svetlogorsk *Krasnoyarskiy Kray* Russia **76** J3
Svetlograd Russia **113** F1
Svetlovodsk Ukr. *see* **Svitlovods'k**
Svetlyy *Kaliningradskaya Oblast'* Russia **55** L9
Svetlyy *Orenburgskaya Oblast'* Russia **102** B1
Svetlyy Yar Russia **53** J6
Svetogorsk Russia **55** P6
Svíahnúkar *vol.* Iceland **54** [inset 1]
Svilaja *mts* Croatia **68** G3
Svilengrad Bulg. **69** L4
Svinecea Mare, Vârful *mt.* Romania **69** J2
Svir Belarus **55** O9
Svir' *r.* Russia **52** G3
Svishtov Bulg. **69** K3
Svitava *r.* Czech Rep. **57** P6
Svitavy Czech Rep. **57** P6
Svitlovods'k Ukr. **53** G6
Sviyaga *r.* Russia **52** K5
Svizzer, Parc Naziunal Switz. **68** D1
Svizzera *country* Europe *see* **Switzerland**
Svobodnyy Russia **90** C2
Svolvær Norway **54** I2
Svrljiške Planine *mts* Serbia **69** J3
Svyatoy Nos, Mys *c.* Russia **52** K2
Svyetlahorsk Belarus **53** F5
Swadlincote U.K. **59** F6
Swaffham U.K. **59** H6
Swain Reefs Australia **136** F4
Swainsboro *GA* U.S.A. **163** D5
Swains Island *atoll* American Samoa **133** I3
Swakop *watercourse* Namibia **124** B2
Swakopmund Namibia **124** B2
Swale *r.* U.K. **58** F4
Swallow Islands Solomon Is **133** G3
Swamihalli India **106** C3
Swampy *r.* Canada **153** H2
Swan *r.* Australia **135** A7
Swan *r. Man./Sask.* Canada **151** K4
Swan *r. Ont.* Canada **152** E3
Swanage U.K. **59** F8
Swandale *WV* U.S.A. **164** E4
Swan Hill Australia **138** A5
Swan Hills Canada **150** H4
Swan Lake *B.C.* Canada **149** O5
Swan Lake *Man.* Canada **151** K4
Swanley U.K. **59** H7
Swanquarter *NC* U.S.A. **163** E5
Swan Reach Australia **137** B7
Swan River Canada **151** K4
Swansea U.K. **59** D7
Swansea Bay U.K. **59** D7
Swanton *CA* U.S.A. **158** B3
Swanton *VT* U.S.A. **165** I1
Swartbergpas *pass* S. Africa **124** F7
Swart Nossob *watercourse* Namibia *see* **Black Nossob**
Swartruggens S. Africa **125** H3
Swartz Creek *MI* U.S.A. **164** D2
Swasey Peak *UT* U.S.A. **159** G2
Swat Kohistan *reg.* Pak. **111** I3
Swatow China *see* **Shantou**
Swayzee *IN* U.S.A. **164** C3
Swaziland *country* Africa **125** J4

▶**Sweden** *country* Europe **54** I5
5th largest country in Europe.

Sweet Home *OR* U.S.A. **156** C3
Sweet Springs *WV* U.S.A. **164** E5
Sweetwater *TX* U.S.A. **161** C5
Sweetwater *r. WY* U.S.A. **156** G4
Swellendam S. Africa **124** E8
Świdnica Poland **57** P5
Świdwin Poland **57** O4
Świebodzin Poland **57** O4
Świecie Poland **57** Q4
Swift *r. AK* U.S.A. **148** H3
Swift Current Canada **151** J5
Swiftcurrent Creek *r.* Canada **151** J5
Swift Fork *r. AK* U.S.A. **148** I3
Swilly *r.* Ireland **61** E3
Swilly, Lough *inlet* Ireland **61** E2
Swindon U.K. **59** F7
Swinford Ireland **61** D4
Świnoujście Poland **57** O4
Swinton U.K. **60** G5
Swiss Confederation *country* Europe *see* **Switzerland**
Switzerland *country* Europe **66** I3
Swords Ireland **61** F4
Swords Range *hills* Australia **136** C4
Syamozero, Ozero *l.* Russia **52** G3
Syamzha Russia **52** I3
Syang Nepal **105** E3
Syas'troy Russia **52** G3
Sychevka Russia **52** G5
Sydenham *atoll* Kiribati *see* **Nonouti**

▶**Sydney** Australia **138** E4
Capital of New South Wales. Most populous city in Oceania.

Sydney Canada **153** J5
Sydney Island Kiribati *see* **Manra**
Sydney Lake Canada **151** M5
Sydney Mines Canada **153** J5
Syedra *tourist site* Turkey **107** A1
Syeverodonets'k Ukr. **53** H6
Syke Germany **63** I2
Sykesville *PA* U.S.A. **165** F3
Syktyvkar Russia **52** K3
Sylarna *mt.* Norway/Sweden **54** H5
Sylhet Bangl. **105** G4
Syloga Russia **52** I3
Sylt *i.* Germany **57** L3
Sylva *NC* U.S.A. **163** D5
Sylvania *GA* U.S.A. **163** D5
Sylvania *OH* U.S.A. **164** D3
Sylvan Lake Canada **150** H4
Sylvester *GA* U.S.A. **163** D6
Sylvester, Lake *salt flat* Australia **136** A3
Sylvia, Mount Canada **150** E3
Symerton *IL* U.S.A. **164** A3
Symi *i.* Greece **69** L6
Synel'nykove Ukr. **53** G6
Syngyrli, Mys *pt* Kazakh. **113** I2
Syntas Kazakh. **98** C2
Synya Russia **51** R2
Syowa *research station* Antarctica **188** D2
Syracusae *Sicily* Italy *see* **Syracuse**
Syracuse *Sicily* Italy **68** F6
Syracuse *KS* U.S.A. **160** C4
Syracuse *NY* U.S.A. **165** G2
Syrdar'ya *r.* Asia **102** C3
Syrdar'ya Uzbek. *see* **Sirdaryo**
Syrdaryinskiy Uzbek. *see* **Sirdaryo**
Syria *country* Asia **112** E4
Syriam Myanmar *see* **Thanlyin**
Syrian Desert Asia **112** E4
Syrna *i.* Greece **69** L6
Syros *i.* Greece **69** K6
Syrskiy Russia **53** H5
Sysmä Fin. **55** N6
Sysola *r.* Russia **52** K3
Syumsi Russia **52** K4
Syurkum Russia **90** F2
Syurkum, Mys *pt* Russia **90** F2
Syzran' Russia **53** K5
Szabadka Serbia *see* **Subotica**
Szczecin Poland **57** O4
Szczecinek Poland **57** P4
Szczytno Poland **57** R4
Szechwan *prov.* China *see* **Sichuan**
Szeged Hungary **69** I1
Székesfehérvár Hungary **68** H1
Szekszárd Hungary **68** H1
Szentes Hungary **69** I1
Szentgotthárd Hungary **68** G1
Szigetvár Hungary **68** G1
Szolnok Hungary **69** I1
Szombathely Hungary **68** G1
Sztálinváros Hungary *see* **Dunaújváros**

T

Taal, Lake *Luzon* Phil. **82** C3
Tabaco *Luzon* Phil. **82** C3
Tābah Saudi Arabia **108** F4
Tabajara Brazil **176** F5
Tabakhmela Georgia *see* **K'azreti**
Tabalo P.N.G. **81** L7
Tabanan *Bali* Indon. **85** F5
Tabang *Kalimantan* Indon. **85** G2
Tabang *r.* Indon. **85** F2
Ţabaqah *Ar Raqqah* Syria **107** D2
Ţabaqah *Ar Raqqah* Syria *see* **Ath Thawrah**
Tabar Islands P.N.G. **132** F2
Tabarka Tunisia **68** C6
Tabasco Mex. **166** E4
Tabasco *state* Mex. **167** G5
Ţabas-e Masīnā Iran **111** F3
Tabāsīn Iran **110** E4
Tābask, Kūh-e *mt.* Iran **110** C4
Tabatinga *Amazonas* Brazil **176** E4
Tabatinga *São Paulo* Brazil **179** A3
Tabatinga, Serra da *hills* Brazil **177** J6
T'abats'q'uri, T'ba *l.* Georgia **113** F2
Tabayama Japan **93** E3
Tabayin Myanmar **86** A2
Tabayoc, Mount *Luzon* Phil. **82** C2
Tabbita Australia **138** B5
Tabelbala Alg. **64** D6
Taber Canada **151** H5
Tabet, Nam *r.* Myanmar **86** B1
Tabin Wildlife Reserve *nature res.* Malaysia **85** G1
Tabir *r.* Indon. **84** C3
Tabiteuea *atoll* Kiribati **133** H2
Tabivere Estonia **55** O7
Tablas *i.* Phil. **82** C3
Tablas de Daimiel, Parque Nacional de las *nat. park* Spain **67** E4
Tablas Strait Phil. **82** C3
Table Cape N.Z. **139** F4
Table Mountain *AK* U.S.A. **149** L1
Table Mountain National Park S. Africa **124** D8
Table Point *Palawan* Phil. **82** B4
Tabligbo Togo **120** D4
Tábor Czech Rep. **57** O6
Tabora Tanz. **123** D4
Tabou Côte d'Ivoire **120** C4
Tabrīz Iran **110** B2
Tabuaeran *atoll* Kiribati **187** J5
Tabu He *r.* China **95** G3
Tabūk Saudi Arabia **112** E5
Tabulam Australia **138** F2
Tabulan *Celebes* Indon. **83** B3
Tabuyung *Sumatra* Indon. **84** B2
Tabwémasana, Mount Vanuatu **133** G3
Täby Sweden **55** K7
Tacalé Brazil **177** H3
Tacámbaro Mex. **167** E5
Tacaná, Volcán de *vol.* Mex. **167** G6
Tachakou China **98** D3
Tacheng China **98** C3
Tachie Canada **150** E4
Tachikawa Japan **93** F3
Tachov Czech Rep. **63** M5
Tacippi *Celebes* Indon. **83** B4
Tacloban *Leyte* Phil. **82** D4
Tacna Peru **176** D7
Tacna *AZ* U.S.A. **166** B1
Tacoma *WA* U.S.A. **156** C3
Taco Pozo Arg. **178** D3
Tacuarembó Uruguay **178** E4
Tacupeto Mex. **166** C2
Tadcaster U.K. **58** F5
Tademaït, Plateau du Alg. **64** E6
Tadenet Lake Canada **149** P1
Tadin New Caledonia **133** G4
Tadjikistan *country* Asia *see* **Tajikistan**
Tadjourah Djibouti **108** F7
Tadmur Syria **107** D2
Tado Japan **92** C3
Tadoule Lake Canada **151** L3
Tadoussac Canada **153** H4
Tadpatri India **106** C3
Tadwale India **106** C2
Tadzhikskaya S.S.R. *country* Asia *see* **Tajikistan**
Taean-haean National Park S. Korea **91** B5
Taebaek S. Korea **91** C5
Taedasa-do N. Korea **91** B5
Taedong-man *b.* N. Korea **91** B5
Taegu S. Korea *see* **Daegu**
Taehan-min'guk *country* Asia *see* **South Korea**
Taejŏn S. Korea *see* **Daejeon**
Taf *r.* U.K. **59** C7
Tafahi *i.* Tonga **133** I3
Tafalla Spain **67** F2
Tafeng China *see* **Lanshan**
Tafila Jordan *see* **Aţ Ţafilah**
Tafí Viejo Arg. **178** C3
Tafresh Iran **110** C3
Taft Iran **110** D4
Taft *CA* U.S.A. **158** D4
Taftān, Kūh-e *mt.* Iran **111** F4
Taftanāz Syria **107** C2
Tafwap India **87** A6
Taga Japan **92** C3
Tagagawik *r. AK* U.S.A. **148** H2
Taganrog Russia **53** H7
Taganrog, Gulf of Russia/Ukr. **53** H7
Taganrogskiy Zaliv *b.* Russia/Ukr. *see* **Taganrog, Gulf of**
Tagarev, Gora *mt.* Iran/Turkm. **110** E2
Tagarkaty, Pereval *pass* Tajik. **111** I2
Tagaung Myanmar **86** B2
Tagbilaran *Bohol* Phil. **82** C4
Tagchagpu Ri *mt.* China **99** C6
Tagdempt Alg. *see* **Tiaret**
Taghmon Ireland **61** F5
Tagish Canada **149** N3
Tagish Lake Canada **149** N4
Tagoloan *r. Mindanao* Phil. **82** D4
Tagtabazar Turkm. **111** F3
Taguchi-zaki *pt* Japan **92** B4
Tagudin *Luzon* Phil. **82** C2
Tagula P.N.G. **136** F1
Tagula Island P.N.G. **136** F1
Tagum *Mindanao* Phil. **82** D5
Tagus *r.* Port. **67** B4
also known as Tajo (Portugal) or Tejo (Spain)
Taha China **95** K2
Tahaetkun Mountain Canada **150** G5
Tahan, Gunung *mt.* Malaysia **84** C1
Tahanroz'ka Zatoka *b.* Russia/Ukr. *see* **Taganrog, Gulf of**
Tahara Japan **92** D4
Tahat, Mont *mt.* Alg. **120** D2
Tahaurawe *i. HI* U.S.A. *see* **Kaho'olawe**
Tahe China **90** B1
Taheke N.Z. **139** D2
Tahilt Mongolia *see* **Tsogt**
Tahiti *i.* Fr. Polynesia **187** K7
Tahlab, Dasht-i- *plain* Pak. **111** F4
Tahlequah *OK* U.S.A. **161** E5
Tahltan Canada **149** O4
Tahoe, Lake *CA* U.S.A. **158** C2
Tahoe Lake Canada **147** H3
Tahoe Vista *CA* U.S.A. **158** C2
Tahoka *TX* U.S.A. **161** C5
Tahoua Niger **120** D3
Tahrūd Iran **110** E4
Tahrūd *r.* Iran **110** E4
Tahtsa Peak Canada **150** E4
Tahulandang *i.* Indon. **83** C2
Tahuna *Celebes* Indon. **83** C2
Taï, Parc National de *nat. park* Côte d'Ivoire **120** C4
Tai'an *Liaoning* China **95** J3
Tai'an *Shandong* China **95** I4
Taibai *Gansu* China **95** G4
Taibai *Shaanxi* China **95** F5
Taibai Shan *mt.* China **96** E1

▶**Taibei** Taiwan **97** I3
Capital of Taiwan.

Taibus Qi China *see* **Baochang**
T'aichung Taiwan *see* **Taizhong**
Taidong Taiwan **97** I4
Taiei Japan **93** G3
Taigong China *see* **Taijiang**
Taigu China **95** H4
Taihang Shan *mts* China **95** H4
Taihang Shan *mts* China **95** H4
Taihape N.Z. **139** E4
Taihe *Jiangxi* China **97** G3
Taihe *Sichuan* China *see* **Shehong**
Taihezhen China *see* **Shehong**
Tai Ho Wan *H.K.* China **97** [inset]
Taihu China **97** H2
Tai Hu *l.* China **97** I2
Taihuai China **95** H4
Taijiang China **97** F3
Taikang *Heilong.* China *see* **Dorbod**
Taikang *Henan* China **95** H5

Taiki Japan 92 C4
Taiko-yama hill Japan 92 B3
Tailaco East Timor 83 C5
Tailai China 95 J2
Tai Lam Chung Shui Tong resr H.K. China 97 [inset]
Taileleo Sumatra Indon. 84 B3
Tailem Bend Australia 137 B7
Tai Long Wan b. H.K. China 97 [inset]
Tai Mo Shan hill H.K. China 97 [inset]
Tain U.K. 60 F2
Tainan Taiwan 97 I4
T'ainan Taiwan see Xinying
Tainaro, Akra pt Greece see Tainaro, Akrotirio
Tainaro, Akrotirio pt Greece 69 J6
Taining China 97 H3
Tai O H.K. China 97 [inset]
Taiobeiras Brazil 179 C1
Taipa Celebes Indon. 83 B3
Tai Pang Wan b. H.K. China see Mirs Bay
T'aipei Taiwan see Taibei
Taiping Guangdong China see Shixing
Taiping Guangxi China see Chongzuo
Taiping Guangxi China 97 F4
Taiping Malaysia 84 C1
Taipingchuan China 95 J2
Taiping Ding mt. China 95 I4
Taiping Ling mt. China 95 J2
Tai Po H.K. China 97 [inset]
Tai Po Hoi b. H.K. China see Tolo Harbour
Tai Poutini National Park N.Z. see Westland Tai Poutini National Park
Taiqian China 95 H5
Taira Japan 92 C2
Tairbeart U.K. see Tarbert
Tai Rom Yen National Park Thai. 87 B5
Tairuq Iran 110 B3
Tais Sumatra Indon. 84 C4
Tais P.N.G. 81 K8
Taishaku-san mt. Japan 93 F2
Taishan China 97 G4
Tai Shek Mo hill H.K. China 97 [inset]
Taishun China 97 H3
Tai Siu Mo To is H.K. China see The Brothers
Taissy France 62 E5
Taitaitanopo i. Indon. 84 C3
Taitao, Península de pen. Chile 178 B7
Taitapu N.Z. 139 D6
Tai To Yan mt. H.K. China 97 [inset]
Taitō-zaki pt Japan 93 G3
T'aitung Taiwan see Taidong
Tai Tung Shan hill H.K. China see Sunset Peak
Taivalkoski Fin. 54 P4
Taivaskero hill Fin. 54 N2
Taiwan country Asia 97 I4
T'aiwan Haihsia strait China/Taiwan see Taiwan Strait
Taiwan Haixia strait China/Taiwan see Taiwan Strait
Taiwan Shan mts Taiwan see Zhongyang Shanmo
Taiwan Strait China/Taiwan 97 H4
Taixian China see Jiangyan
Taixing China 97 I1
Taiyuan China 95 H4
Tai Yue Shan i. H.K. China see Lantau Island
Taiyue Shan mts China 95 G4
Taizhao China 99 F7
Taizhong Taiwan 97 I3
Taizhong Taiwan see Fengyuan
Taizhou Jiangsu China 97 H1
Taizhou Zhejiang China 97 I2
Taizhou Liedao i. China 97 I2
Taizhou Wan b. China 97 I2
Taizi He r. China 90 B4
Ta'izz Yemen 108 F7
Tājābād Iran 110 E4
Tajem, Gunung hill Indon. 85 D3
Tajerouine Tunisia 68 C7
Tajikistan country Asia 111 H2
Tajik National Park nat. park Tajik. 111 I2
Tajimi Japan 92 D3
Tajiri Japan 92 B4
Tajitos Mex. 166 B2
Tajjal Pak. 111 H5
Tajo r. Port. 67 C4 see Tagus
Tajrīsh Iran 110 C3
Tajumulco, Volcán de vol. Guat. 167 H6
Tak Thai. 86 B3
Taka Japan 92 A3
Takāb Iran 110 B2
Takabba Kenya 122 E3
Taka'Bonerate, Kepulauan atolls Indon. 83 B4
Taka Bonerate, Taman Nasional nat. park Indon. 83 B4
Takagi Japan 93 D3
Takahagi Japan 93 G2
Takahama Aichi Japan 92 C4
Takahama Fukui Japan 92 B3
Takahara-gawa r. Japan 92 D2
Takahashi Japan 91 D6
Takaishi Japan 92 B4
Takaiwa-misaki pt Japan 92 C1
Takamatsu Ishikawa Japan 92 C2
Takamatsu Kagawa Japan 91 D6
Takami-yama mt. Japan 92 C4
Takamori Japan 93 D3
Takane Gifu Japan 92 D2
Takane Yamanashi Japan 93 E3
Takanezawa Japan 93 F2
Takaoka Japan 92 D2
Takapuna N.Z. 139 E3
Takarazuka Japan 92 B4
Ta karpo China 105 G4
Takasago Japan 92 A4
Takasaki Japan 93 F2
Takashima Shiga Japan 92 C3
Takashima Shiga Japan 92 C3
Takashōzu-yama mt. Japan 92 C2
Takasu Japan 92 C3
Takasuma-yama mt. Japan 93 E2
Takasuzu-san hill Japan 93 G2
Takatō Japan 93 E3
Takatokwane Botswana 124 G3
Takatori Japan 92 B4
Takatshwaane Botswana 124 E2
Takatsuki Ōsaka Japan 92 B4
Takatsuki Shiga Japan 92 C3
Takatsuki-yama mt. Japan 91 D6
Takayama Gifu Japan 92 D2
Takayama Gunma Japan 93 E2
Tak Bai Thai. 87 C6
Takefu Japan see Echizen
Takengon Sumatra Indon. 84 B1
Takeno Japan 92 A3
Takeo Cambodia see Don Kêv
Takeshi Japan 93 E2
Take-shima i. N. Pacific Ocean see Liancourt Rocks
Tākestān Iran 110 C2
Taketoyo Japan 92 C4
Takhemaret Alg. 67 G6
Takhini Hotspring Canada 149 N3
Ta Khli Thai. 86 C4
Ta Khmau Cambodia 87 D5
Takhta-Bazar Turkm. see Tagtabazar
Takhtah Pul Afgh. 111 G4
Takht Apān, Kūh-e mt. Iran 110 C3
Takhteh Iran 110 D4
Takht-e Soleymān mt. Iran 110 C2
Takht-e Soleymān tourist site Iran 110 B2
Takht-i-Bahi tourist site Pak. 111 H3
Takht-i-Sulaiman mt. Pak. 111 H4
Taki Japan 92 C4
Takijuq Lake Canada see Napaktulik Lake
Takino Japan 92 A4
Takinoue Japan 90 F3
Takisung Kalimantan Indon. 85 F3
Takla Lake Canada 150 E4
Takla Landing Canada 150 E4
Takla Makan des. China see Taklimakan Desert
Taklimakan Desert China 98 C5
Taklimakan Shamo des. China see Taklimakan Desert
Tako Japan 93 G3
Takotna AK U.S.A. 148 H3
Takpa Shiri mt. China 99 F7
Takslesluk Lake AK U.S.A. 148 G3
Taku Canada 150 C3
Taku r. Canada/U.S.A. 149 N4
Takum Nigeria 120 D4
Takuu Islands P.N.G. 133 F2
Talab r. Iran/Pak. 111 F4
Talachyn Belarus 53 F5
Talaja India 104 C5
Talakan Amurskaya Oblast' Russia 90 C2
Talakan Khabarovskiy Kray Russia 90 D2
Talamanca, Cordillera de mts Costa Rica 166 [inset] J7
Talandzha Russia 90 C2
Talang, Gunung vol. Indon. 84 C3
Talangbatu Sumatra Indon. 84 D3
Talangbetutu Sumatra Indon. 84 D3
Talara Peru 176 B4
Talar-i-Band mts Pak. see Makran Coast Range
Talas Kyrg. 102 D3
Talas Ala-Too mts Kyrg. 102 D3
Talas Range mts Kyrg. see Talas Ala-Too
Talasskiy Alatau, Khrebet mts Kyrg. see Talas Ala-Too
Talatakoh i. Indon. 83 B3
Talaud, Kepulauan is Indon. 83 C1
Talavera de la Reina Spain 67 D4
Talawgyi Myanmar 86 B1
Talaya Russia 77 Q3
Talayan Mindanao Phil. 82 D5
Talbehat India 104 D4
Talbīsah Syria 107 C2
Talbot, Mount hill Australia 135 D6
Talbotton GA U.S.A. 163 C5
Talbragar r. Australia 138 D4
Talca Chile 178 B5
Talcahuano Chile 178 B5
Taldan Russia 90 B1
Taldom Russia 52 H4
Taldykorgan Kazakh. 102 E3
Taldy-Kurgan Kazakh. see Taldykorgan
Taldyqorghan Kazakh. see Taldykorgan
Taldy-Suu Kyrg. 98 B4
Talereh, Tanjung pt Indon. 83 A3
Tālesh Iran 110 C2
Talgar Kazakh. 98 B4
Talgar, Pik mt. Kazakh. 98 B4
Talgarth U.K. 59 D7
Talguppa India 106 B3
Talia Australia 137 A7
Taliabu i. Indon. 83 C3
Talibon Bohol Phil. 82 D4
Talikota India 106 C2
Talikud i. Phil. 82 D5
Talimardzhan Uzbek. see Tallimarjon
Talin Hiag China 95 K2
Taliparamba India 106 B3
Talisay Cebu Phil. 82 C4
Talisayan Kalimantan Indon. 85 G2
Talisayan Mindanao Phil. 82 D4
Taliş Dağları mts Azer./Iran 110 C2
Talisei i. Indon. 83 C2
Talitsa Russia 52 J4
Taliwang Sumbawa Indon. 85 G5
Talkeetna AK U.S.A. 149 J3
Talkeetna r. AK U.S.A. 149 J3
Talkeetna Mountains AK U.S.A. 149 J3
Talkh Āb Iran 110 E3
Tallacootra, Lake salt flat Australia 135 F7
Talladega AL U.S.A. 163 C5

▶Tallahassee FL U.S.A. 163 C6
Capital of Florida.

Tall al Aḥmar Syria 107 D1
Tallassee AL U.S.A. 167 I1
Tall Baydar Syria 113 F3
Tall-e Ḥalāl Iran 110 D4
Tallimarjon Uzbek. 111 G2

▶Tallinn Estonia 55 N7
Capital of Estonia.

Tall Kalakh Syria 107 C2
Tall Kayf Iraq 113 F3
Tallow Ireland 61 D5
Tallulah LA U.S.A. 161 F5
Tall 'Uwaynāt Iraq 113 F3
Tallymerjen Uzbek. see Tallimarjon
Talmont-St-Hilaire France 66 D3
Tal'ne Ukr. 53 F6
Tal'noye Ukr. see Tal'ne
Taloda India 104 C5
Talodi Sudan 108 D7
Taloga OK U.S.A. 161 D4
Talon, Lac l. Canada 153 I3
Ta-long Myanmar 86 B2
Talos Dome ice feature Antarctica 188 H2
Ta Loung San mt. Laos 86 C2
Talovaya Russia 53 I6
Taloyoak Canada 147 I3
Talpa Mex. 166 D4
Tal Pass Pak. 111 I3
Talshand Mongolia see Chandmanī
Talsi Latvia 55 M8
Tal Sīyāh Iran 111 F4
Taltal Chile 178 B3
Taltson r. Canada 151 H2
Talu China 99 F7
Talu Sumatra Indon. 84 B2
Taludaa Celebes Indon. 83 B2
Tāluqān Afgh. 111 H2
Taluti, Teluk b. Seram Indon. 83 D3
Talvik Norway 54 M1
Talwood Australia 138 D2
Talyshskiye Gory mts Azer./Iran see Taliş Dağları
Talyy Russia 52 L2
Tama Japan 93 F3
Tama Abu, Banjaran mts Malaysia 85 F2
Tamabo Range mts Malaysia see Tama Abu, Banjaran
Tama-gawa r. Japan 93 F3
Tamaki Japan 92 C4
Tamala Australia 135 A6
Tamala Russia 53 I5
Tamale Ghana 120 C4
Tamalung Kalimantan Indon. 85 F3
Tamamura Japan 93 F2
Tamana i. Kiribati 133 H2
Taman Nasional Sebangu nat. park Indon. 85 F3
Taman Negara National Park Malaysia 84 C1
Tamano Japan 91 D6
Tamanrasset Alg. 120 D2
Tamanthi Myanmar 86 A1
Tamaqua PA U.S.A. 165 H3
Tamar India 105 F5
Tamar Syria see Tadmur
Tamar r. U.K. 59 C8
Tamari Japan 93 G2
Tamar Qareh Qūzī Iran 110 D2
Tamarugal, Pampa de plain Chile 176 E7
Tamasane Botswana 125 H2
Tamatave Madag. see Toamasina
Tamatsukuri Japan 93 G2
Tamaulipas state Mex. 161 D7
Tamaulipas, Sierra de mts Mex. 167 F4
Tamazula Durango Mex. 166 D3
Tamazula Jalisco Mex. 166 E5
Tamazulápam Mex. 167 F5
Tamazunchale Mex. 167 F4
Tamba Japan see Kyōtanba
Tambacounda Senegal 120 B3
Tamba-kōchi plat. Japan see Tanba-kōchi
Tambalongang i. Indon. 83 B4
Tambang, Port b. Luzon Phil. 82 C3
Tambangmunjul Kalimantan Indon. 85 E3
Tambangsawah Sumatra Indon. 84 C3
Tambaqui Brazil 176 F5
Tambar Springs Australia 138 D3
Tambea Celebes Indon. 83 B4
Tambelan, Kepulauan is Indon. 84 D2
Tambelan Besar i. Indon. 85 D2
Tamberu Java Indon. 85 F4
Tambisan Sabah Malaysia 85 G1
Tambo r. Australia 138 C6
Tambohorano Madag. 123 E5
Tamboli Celebes Indon. 83 B3
Tambor Mex. 166 D3

▶Tambora, Gunung vol. Sumbawa Indon. 85 G5
Deadliest recorded volcanic eruption (1815).

Tamboritha mt. Australia 138 C6
Tambov Russia 53 I5
Tambovka Russia 90 C2
Tambu, Teluk b. Indon. 83 A2
Tambulanan, Bukit hill Malaysia 85 G1
Tambunan Sabah Malaysia 85 G1
Tambura South Sudan 121 F4
Tamburi Brazil 179 C1
Tambuyukon, Gunung mt. Malaysia 85 G1
Tâmchekkeț Mauritania 120 B3
Tamdybulak Uzbek. see Tomdibuloq
Tâmega r. Port. 67 B3
Tamenghest Alg. see Tamanrasset
Tamenglong India 105 H4
Tamerza Tunisia 68 B7
Tamgak, Adrar mt. Niger 120 D3
Tamgué, Massif du mt. Guinea 120 B3
Tamiahua Mex. 167 F4
Tamiahua, Laguna de lag. Mex. 168 E4
Tamiang r. Indon. 84 B1
Tamiang, Ujung pt Indon. 84 B1
Tamil Nadu state India 106 C4
Tamir Gol r. Mongolia 94 E2
Tamitsa Russia 52 H2
Ţâmîya Egypt see Ţāmīyah
Ţāmīyah Egypt 112 C5
Tamkuhi India 105 F4
Tam Ky Vietnam 86 E4
Tammarvi r. Canada 151 K1
Tammerfors Fin. see Tampere
Tammisaari Fin. see Ekenäs
Tampa FL U.S.A. 163 D7
Tampa Bay FL U.S.A. 163 D7
Tampang Sumatra Indon. 84 D4
Tampere Fin. 55 M6
Tampico Mex. 168 E4
Tampin Malaysia 84 C2
Tampines Sing. 87 [inset]
Tampo Celebes Indon. 83 B4
Tamsag Bulag China 94 E3
Tamsagbulag Mongolia 95 I2
Tamsweg Austria 57 N7
Tamu Myanmar 86 A1
Tamuín Mex. 167 F4
Tamworth Australia 138 E3
Tamworth U.K. 59 F6
Tan Kazakh. 98 B2
Tana r. Fin./Norway see Tenojoki
Tana r. Kenya 122 E4
Tana Madag. see Antananarivo
Tana r. AK U.S.A. 149 L3
Tana i. Vanuatu see Tanna
Tana, Lake Eth. 122 D2
Tanabe Japan 91 D6
Tanabi Brazil 179 A3
Tana Bru Norway 54 P1
Tanacross AK U.S.A. 149 L3
Tanadak Island AK U.S.A. 148 D5
Tanada Lake AK U.S.A. 150 A2
Tanafjorden inlet Norway 54 P1
Tanaga vol. AK U.S.A. 148 [inset] C6
Tanaga Island AK U.S.A. 148 [inset] C6
Tanaga Pass sea chan. AK U.S.A. 148 [inset] C6
Tanagura Japan 93 G1
Tanah, Tanjung pt Indon. 85 E4
T'ana Hāyk' l. Eth. see Tana, Lake
Tanahbala i. Indon. 84 B3
Tanahgrogot Kalimantan Indon. 85 G3
Tanahjampea i. Indon. 83 B4
Tanahmasa i. Indon. 84 B3
Tanahmerah Kalimantan Indon. 85 G2
Tanah Merah Malaysia 84 C1
Tanahputih Sumatra Indon. 84 C2
Tanah Rata Malaysia 84 C1
Tanakeke i. Indon. 83 A4
Tanami Australia 134 E4
Tanami Desert Australia 134 E4
Tân An Vietnam 87 D5
Tanana AK U.S.A. 148 I2
Tanana r. AK U.S.A. 148 I2
Tananarive Madag. see Antananarivo
Tanandava Madag. 123 E6
Tanauan Leyte Phil. 82 D4
Tanba Japan 92 B3
Tanba-kōchi plat. Japan 92 B3
Tanbu China 95 I5
Tancheng Fujian China see Pingtan
Tancheng Shandong China 95 I5
Tanch'ŏn N. Korea 91 C4
Tanda Côte d'Ivoire 120 C4
Tanda Uttar Prad. India 104 D3
Tanda Uttar Prad. India 105 E4
Tandag Mindanao Phil. 82 D4
Ţăndărei Romania 69 L2
Tandaué Angola 123 B5
Tandek Sabah Malaysia 85 G1
Tandi India 104 D2
Tandil Arg. 178 E5
Tando Adam Pak. 111 H5
Tando Allahyar Pak. 111 H5
Tando Bago Pak. 111 H5
Tandou Lake imp. l. Australia 137 C7
Tandragee U.K. 61 F3
Tandubatu i. Phil. 82 C5
Tandur India 106 C2
Tanduri Pak. 111 G4
Tanega-shima i. Japan 91 C7
Tanen Taunggyi mts Thai. 86 B3
Tanezrouft reg. Alg./Mali 120 C2
Ţanf, Jabal aţ hill Syria 107 D3
Tang, Kaôh i. Cambodia 87 C5
Tang, Ra's-e pt Iran 111 E5
Tanga Russia 95 G1
Tanga Tanz. 123 D4
Tangail Bangl. 105 G4
Tanga Islands P.N.G. 132 F2
Tanganyika country Africa see Tanzania

▶Tanganyika, Lake Africa 123 C4
Deepest and 2nd largest lake in Africa, and 6th largest in the world.

Tangará Brazil 179 A4
Tangasseri India 106 C4
Tangdan China 96 D3
Tangdê China 99 F7
Tangelī Iran 110 D2
Tanger Morocco see Tangier
Tangerang Java Indon. 84 D4
Tangerhütte Germany 63 L2
Tangermünde Germany 63 L2
Tang-e Sarkheh Iran 111 E5
Tanggarma China 94 D4
Tanggo China 99 E7
Tanggor China 96 D1
Tanggulashan China 94 C5
Tanggula Shan mt. China 99 E6
Tanggula Shan mts China 99 E6
Tanggula Shankou pass China 99 E6
Tangguo China 99 D7
Tanghai China 95 I4
Tanghe China 97 G1
Tangier Morocco 67 D6
Tangiers Morocco see Tangier
Tangkelemboko, Gunung mt. Indon. 83 B3
Tangkittebak, Gunung mt. Indon. 84 D4
Tang La pass China 99 E8
Tangla India 105 G4
Tanglag China 96 C1
Tanglin Sing. 87 [inset]
Tangmai China 99 F7
Tangnag China 94 E5
Tango Japan 92 B3
Tangorin Australia 136 D4
Tangra Yumco salt l. China 99 D7
Tangse Sumatra Indon. 84 A1
Tangshan Guizhou China see Shiqian
Tangshan Hebei China 95 I4
Tangte mt. Myanmar 86 B2
Tangtse India see Tanktse
Tangub Mindanao Phil. 82 C4
Tangwan China 97 F3
Tangwanghe China 90 C2
Tangxian China 95 H4
Tangyin China 95 H5
Tangyuan China 90 C3
Tangyung Tso salt l. China 105 F3
Tanhaçu Brazil 179 C1
Tanhua Fin. 54 O3
Tani Cambodia 87 D5
Taniantaweng Shan mts China 96 B2
Tanigawa-dake mt. Japan 93 E2
Tanigumi Japan 92 C3
Tanimbar, Kepulauan is Moluccas Indon. 134 E1
Taninthari Myanmar see Tenasserim
Tanintharyi Myanmar see Tenasserim
Taninthayi Myanmar see Tenasserim
Taniwel Seram Indon. 83 D3
Tanjah Morocco see Tangier
Tanjay Negros Phil. 82 C4
Tanjiajing China 94 E4
Tanjore India see Thanjavur
Tanjung Kalimantan Indon. 85 F3
Tanjung Sumatra Indon. 84 D3
Tanjungbalai Sumatra Indon. 84 B2
Tanjungbalai Sumatra Indon. 84 C2
Tanjungbaliha Moluccas Indon. 83 C3
Tanjungbatu Kalimantan Indon. 85 G2
Tanjungbatu Sumatra Indon. 84 C2
Tanjungbuayabuaya, Pulau i. Indon. 85 G2
Tanjungenim Sumatra Indon. 84 C3
Tanjunggaru Kalimantan Indon. 85 G3
Tanjungkarang-Telukbetung Sumatra Indon. see Bandar Lampung
Tanjungpandan Indon. 85 D3
Tanjungpinang Sumatra Indon. 84 D2
Tanjungpura Sumatra Indon. 84 B2
Tanjung Puting, Taman Nasional nat. park Indon. 85 F3
Tanjungraja Sumatra Indon. 84 D3
Tanjungredeb Kalimantan Indon. 85 G2
Tanjungsaleh i. Indon. 85 E3
Tanjungsatai Kalimantan Indon. 85 E3
Tanjungselor Kalimantan Indon. 85 G2
Tankhoy Russia 94 F1
Tankse India see Tanktse
Tanktse India 104 D2
Tankwa-Karoo National Park S. Africa 124 D7
Tanna i. Vanuatu 133 G3
Tannadice U.K. 60 G4
Tannan Japan 92 B3
Tännäs Sweden 54 H5
Tanner, Mount Canada 150 G5
Tannu-Ola, Khrebet mts Russia 94 B1
Tannu Tuva aut. rep. Russia see Tyva, Respublika
Tañon Strait Phil. 82 C4
Tanot India 104 B4
Tanout Niger 120 D3
Tanquian Mex. 167 F4
Tansen Nepal 105 E4
Tanshui Taiwan see Danshui
Tansyk Kazakh. 98 B3
Ţanţā Egypt 112 C5
Ţanţa Egypt see Ţanţā
Tan-Tan Morocco 120 B2
Tantō Japan 92 A3
Tantoyuca Mex. 167 F4
Tantu China 95 J2
Tanuku India 106 D2
Tanuma Japan 93 F2
Tanumbirini Australia 134 F4
Tanumshede Sweden 55 G7
Tanyurer r. Russia 148 A2
Tanzania country Africa 123 D4
Tanzawa-Ōyama Kokutei-kōen park Japan 93 F3
Tanzilla r. Canada 149 O4
Tao, Ko i. Thai. 87 B5
Tao'an China see Taonan
Taobh Tuath U.K. see Northton
Taocheng China see Daxin
Taocun China 95 J4
Tao'er He r. China 95 J2
Tao He r. China 94 E5
Taohong China see Longhui
Taohuajiang China see Taojiang
Taohuaping China see Longhui
Taojiang China 97 G2
Taolanaro Madag. see Tôlañaro
Taole China see Mataigou
Taonan China 95 J2
Taongi atoll Marshall Is 186 H5
Taos NM U.S.A. 157 G5
Taounate Morocco 64 D5
Taourirt Morocco 64 D5
Taoxi China 97 H3
Taoyang China see Lintao
Taoyuan China 97 F2
Taoyuan Taiwan 97 I3
Tapa Estonia 55 N7
Tapaan Passage Phil. 82 C5
Tapachula Mex. 167 G6
Tapah Malaysia 87 C6
Tapajós r. Brazil 177 H4
Tapaktuan Sumatra Indon. 84 B2
Tapalang Celebes Indon. 85 G3
Tapan Sumatra Indon. 84 C3
Tapanatepec Mex. 167 G5
Tapanuli, Teluk b. Indon. 84 B2
Tapat i. Moluccas Indon. 83 C3
Tapauá Brazil 176 F5
Tapauá r. Brazil 176 F5
Taperoá Brazil 179 D1
Tapiau Russia see Gvardeysk
Tapijulapa Mex. 167 G5
Tapinbini Kalimantan Indon. 85 E3
Tapis, Gunung mt. Malaysia 84 C1
Tapisuelas Mex. 166 C3
Taplejung Nepal 105 F4
Tap Mun Chau i. H.K. China 97 [inset]
Ta-pom Myanmar 86 B2
Tappahannock VA U.S.A. 165 G5
Tappal India 99 B7
Tappeh, Kūh-e hill Iran 110 C3
Taprobane country Asia see Sri Lanka
Tapti r. India 104 C5
Tapuae-o-Uenuku mt. N.Z. 139 D5
Tapul Phil. 82 C5
Tapul Group is Phil. 82 C5
Tapulonanjing mt. Indon. 84 B2
Tapung r. Indon. 84 C2
Tapurucuara Brazil 176 E4
Taputeouea atoll Kiribati see Tabiteuea
Taquara Brazil 179 A5
Taquari Brazil 179 A5
Taquarí r. Brazil 177 G7
Taquaritinga Brazil 179 A3
Tar r. Ireland 61 E5
Tara Australia 138 E1
Ţarābulus Lebanon see Tripoli
Ţarābulus Libya see Tripoli
Taragt Mongolia 94 E2
Tarahuwan India 104 E4
Tarai reg. India 105 G4
Tarakan Kalimantan Indon. 85 G2
Tarakan i. Indon. 85 G2
Tarākī reg. Afgh. 111 G3
Taraklı Turkey 69 N4
Taran, Mys pt Russia 55 K9
Tarana Australia 138 D4
Taranagar India 104 C3
Taranaki, Mount vol. N.Z. 139 E4
Tarancón Spain 67 E3
Tarangambadi India 106 C4
Tarangire National Park Tanz. 122 D4
Taranto Italy 68 G4
Taranto, Golfo di g. Italy 68 G4
Taranto, Gulf of Italy see Taranto, Golfo di
Tarapoto Peru 176 C5
Tarapur India 106 B2
Tararua Range mts N.Z. 139 E5
Tarascon-sur-Ariège France 66 E5
Tarasovskiy Russia 53 I6
Tarauacá Brazil 176 D5
Tarauacá r. Brazil 176 E5
Tarawera N.Z. 139 F4
Tarawera, Mount vol. N.Z. 139 F4
Taraz Kazakh. 102 D3
Tarazona Spain 67 F3
Tarazona de la Mancha Spain 67 F4
Tarbagatay Kazakh. 98 C3
Tarbagatay Russia 95 F1
Tarbagatay, Khrebet mts Kazakh. 102 F2
Tarbat Ness pt U.K. 60 F3
Tarbert Ireland 61 C5
Tarbert Scotland U.K. 60 C3
Tarbert Scotland U.K. 60 D5
Tarbes France 66 E5
Tarboro NC U.S.A. 162 E5
Tarcoola Australia 135 F7
Tarcoon Australia 138 C3
Tarcoonyinna watercourse Australia 135 F6
Tarcutta Australia 138 C5
Tardoki-Yangi, Gora mt. Russia 90 E2
Taree Australia 138 F3
Tarella Australia 137 C6
Tarentum Italy see Taranto
Ţarfā', Baţn aţ depr. Saudi Arabia 110 C6
Tarfaya Morocco 120 B2
Targa well Niger 120 D3
Targan China see Talin Hiag
Targhee Pass ID U.S.A. 156 F3
Targovishte Bulg. 69 L3
Târgoviște Romania 69 K2
Targuist Morocco 67 D6
Târgu Jiu Romania 69 J2
Târgu Mureș Romania 69 K1
Târgu Neamț Romania 69 L1
Târgu Secuiesc Romania 69 L1
Targyailing China 99 D7
Targyn Kazakh. 98 C2
Tari P.N.G. 81 K8
Tarian Gol China 95 G4
Tariat Mongolia 94 D1
Tarif U.A.E. 110 D5
Tarifa Spain 67 D5
Tarifa, Punta de pt Spain 67 D5
Tarigtig Point Luzon Phil. 82 C2
Tarija Bol. 176 F8
Tarikere India 106 B3
Tariku r. Indon. 81 J7
Tarim China 98 C4
Tarīm Yemen 108 G6
Tarim Basin China 98 C5
Tarime Tanz. 122 D4
Tarim He r. China 98 D4
Tarim Liuchang China 98 D4
Tarim Pendi basin China see Tarim Basin
Tarim Qichang China 98 D4
Tarīn Kōṭ Afgh. 111 G3
Taritatu r. Indon. 81 J7
Taritipan Sabah Malaysia see Tandek
Tarka r. S. Africa 125 G7
Tarkastad S. Africa 125 H7
Tarkio MO U.S.A. 160 E3
Tarko-Sale Russia 76 I3
Tarkwa Ghana 120 C4
Tarlac Luzon Phil. 82 C3
Tarlac r. Luzon Phil. 82 C2

Tarlag China 96 C1
Tarlauly Kazakh. 98 B3
Tarlo River National Park Australia 138 D5
Tarma Peru 176 C6
Tarmar China 99 E7
Tarmstedt Germany 63 J1
Tarn r. France 66 E4
Tärnaby Sweden 54 I4
Tarnak Röd r. Afgh. 111 G4
Târnăveni Romania 69 K1
Tarnobrzeg Poland 53 D6
Tarnogskiy Gorodok Russia 52 I3
Tarnopol Ukr. see Ternopil'
Tarnów Poland 53 D6
Tarnowitz Poland see Tarnowskie Góry
Tarnowskie Góry Poland 57 Q5
Taro Co salt l. China 99 D7
Tārom Iran 110 D4
Taroom Australia 137 E5
Tarō-san mt. Japan 93 F2
Taroudannt Morocco 64 C5
Tarpaulin Swamp Australia 136 B3
Ţarq Iran 110 C3
Tarqi China 95 J2
Tarquinia Italy 68 D3
Tarquinii Italy see Tarquinia
Tarrabool Lake salt flat Australia 136 A3
Tarraco Spain see Tarragona
Tarrafal Cape Verde 120 [inset]
Tarragona Spain 67 G3
Tårrajaur Sweden 54 K3
Tarran Hills hill Australia 138 C4
Tarrant Point Australia 136 B3
Tàrrega Spain 67 G3
Tarsus Turkey 107 B1
Tart China 99 F5
Tärtär Azer. 113 G2
Tartu Estonia 55 O7
Ţarţūs Syria 107 B2
Tarui Japan 92 C3
Tarumovka Russia 113 G1
Tarung Hka r. Myanmar 86 B1
Tarutao, Ko i. Thai. 87 B6
Tarutao National Park Thai. 87 B6
Tarutung Sumatra Indon. 84 B2
Tarvisium Italy see Treviso
Tarys-Arzhan Russia 94 D1
Ţarz Iran 110 E4
Tasai, Ko i. Thai. 87 B5
Tasaral Kazakh. 98 A3
Taschereau Canada 152 F4
Taseko Mountain Canada 150 F5
Tashauz Turkm. see Daşoguz
Tash-Bashat Kyrg. 98 B4
Tashi China 94 C3
Tashi Chho Bhutan see Thimphu
Tashigang Bhutan see Trashigang
Tashikuzuke Shan mts China 99 A5
Tashino Russia see Pervomaysk
Tashir Armenia 113 G2
Tashk, Daryācheh-ye l. Iran 110 D4
Tashkent Uzbek. see Toshkent
Tāshqurghān Afgh. see Khulm
Tashtagol Russia 88 F2
Tashtyp Russia 88 F2
Tasialujjuaq, Lac l. Canada 153 G2
Tasiat, Lac l. Canada 152 G2
Tasiilap Karra c. Greenland 147 O3
Tasiilaq Greenland 189 J2
Tasik Bakun resr Malaysia 85 F2
Tasikmalaya Java Indon. 85 E4
Tasīl Syria 107 B3
Tasiujaq Canada 153 H2
Tasiusaq Greenland 147 M2
Taskala Kazakh. 51 Q5
Taşkent Turkey 107 A1
Tasker Niger 120 E3
Taskesken Kazakh. 102 F2
Taşköprü Turkey 112 D2
Tasman Abyssal Plain sea feature Tasman Sea 186 G8
Tasman Basin sea feature Tasman Sea 186 G8
Tasman Bay N.Z. 139 D5

▶Tasmania state Australia 137 [inset]
4th largest island in Oceania.

Tasman Islands P.N.G. see Nukumanu Islands
Tasman Mountains N.Z. 139 D5
Tasman Peninsula Australia 137 [inset]
Tasman Sea S. Pacific Ocean 132 H6
Taşova Turkey 112 E2
Tassara Niger 120 D3
Tassialouc, Lac l. Canada 152 G2
Tassili n'Ajjer, Parc National de nat. park Alg. 120 D2
Tasty Kazakh. 102 C3
Taşucu Turkey 107 A1
Tas-Yuryakh Russia 77 M3
Tata Morocco 64 C6
Tataba Celebes Indon. 83 B3
Tatabánya Hungary 68 H1
Tatalin He r. China 99 F5
Tatamailau, Foho mt. East Timor 83 C5
Tataouine Tunisia 64 G5
Tatarbunary Ukr. 69 M2
Tatarsk Russia 76 I4
Tatarskiy Proliv strait Russia 90 F2
Tatar Strait Russia see Tatarskiy Proliv
Tatau Sarawak Malaysia 85 F2
Tate r. Australia 136 C3
Tatebayashi Japan 93 F2
Tateishi-misaki pt Japan 92 C3
Tateiwa Japan 93 F1
Tateshina Japan 93 E2
Tateshina-yama mt. Japan 93 E2
Tateyama Chiba Japan 93 F4
Tateyama Toyama Japan 92 D2
Tate-yama vol. Japan 92 D2
Tathlina Lake Canada 150 G2
Tathlīth Saudi Arabia 108 F6
Tathlīth, Wādī watercourse Saudi Arabia 108 F5
Tathra Australia 138 D6
Tatinnai Lake Canada 151 L2
Tatishchevo Russia 53 J6
Tatitlek AK U.S.A. 149 K3
Tatkon Myanmar 86 B2
Tatla Lake Canada 150 E5
Tatla Lake l. Canada 150 E5
Tatlayoko Lake Canada 150 E5
Tatnam, Cape Canada 151 N3
Tatra Mountains Poland/Slovakia 57 Q6
Tatrang China 99 D5
Tatry mts Poland/Slovakia see Tatra Mountains
Tatrzański Park Narodowy nat. park Poland 57 Q6
Tatshenshini r. Canada 149 M4
Tatshenshini-Alsek Provincial Wilderness Park Canada 150 B3
Tatsinskaya Russia 53 I6
Tatsuno Japan 93 D3
Tatsunokuchi Japan 92 C2
Tatsuruhama Japan 92 C1
Tatsuyama Japan 93 D4
Tatuí Brazil 179 B3
Tatuk Mountain Canada 150 E4
Tatum NM U.S.A. 161 C5
Tatvan Turkey 113 F3
Tau Norway 55 D7
Tauá Brazil 177 J5
Tauapeçaçu Brazil 176 F4
Taubaté Brazil 179 B3
Tauber r. Germany 63 J5
Tauberbischofsheim Germany 63 J5
Taucha Germany 63 M3
Taufstein hill Germany 63 J4
Taukum, Peski des. Kazakh. 102 D3
Taumarunui N.Z. 139 E4
Taumaturgo Brazil 176 D5
Taung S. Africa 124 G4
Taungdwingyi Myanmar 86 A2
Taunggyi Myanmar 86 B2
Taung-ngu Myanmar 86 B3
Taungnyo Range mts Myanmar 86 B3
Taungtha Myanmar 86 A2
Taungup Myanmar 96 B5
Taunton U.K. 59 D7
Taunton MA U.S.A. 165 J3
Taunus hills Germany 63 H4
Taupo N.Z. 139 F4
Taupo, Lake N.Z. 139 E4
Taurag Lith. 55 M9
Tauranga N.Z. 139 F3
Taurasia Italy see Turin
Taureau, Réservoir resr Canada 152 G5
Taurianova Italy 68 G5
Tauroa Point N.Z. 139 D2
Taurus Mountains Turkey 107 A1
Taute r. France 59 F9
Tauz Azer. see Tovuz
Tavas Turkey 69 M6
Tavastehus Fin. see Hämeenlinna
Tavayvaam r. Russia 148 B2
Taverham U.K. 59 I6
Taveuni i. Fiji 133 I3
Tavildara Tajik. 111 H2
Tavira Port. 67 C5
Tavistock Canada 164 E2
Tavistock U.K. 59 C8
Tavoy Myanmar see Dawei
Tavoy r. mouth Myanmar 87 B4
Tavoy Island Myanmar see Mali Kyun
Tavoy Point Myanmar 87 B4
Tavricheskoye Kazakh. 98 C2
Tavşanlı Turkey 69 M5
Taw r. U.K. 59 C7
Tawai, Bukit mt. Malaysia 85 G1
Tawakkul China 99 C5
Tawakoni, Lake TX U.S.A. 167 G1
Tawang India 105 G4
Tawaramoto Japan 92 B4
Tawas City MI U.S.A. 164 D1
Tawau Sabah Malaysia 85 G1
Tawau, Teluk b. Malaysia 85 G1
Tawè Myanmar see Dawei
Tawe r. U.K. 59 D7
Tawi r. India 99 A6
Ţawī Ḩafīr well U.A.E. 110 D5
Ţawī Murra well U.A.E. 110 D5
Tawi-Tawi i. Phil. 82 B5
Tawmaw Myanmar 86 B1
Tawu Taiwan see Dawu
Taxco Mex. 167 F5
Taxkorgan China 99 A5
Tay r. Canada 149 N3
Tay r. U.K. 60 F4
Tay, Firth of est. U.K. 60 F4
Tay, Lake salt flat Australia 135 C8
Tay, Loch l. U.K. 60 E4
Tayabas Bay Luzon Phil. 82 C3
Tayan Kalimantan Indon. 85 E2
Tayandu, Kepulauan is Moluccas Indon. 81 I8
Tāybād Iran 111 F3
Taybola Russia 54 R2
Taycheedah WI U.S.A. 164 A2
Taygan Mongolia see Delger
Tayinloan U.K. 60 D5
Taylor Canada 150 F3
Taylor AK U.S.A. 148 F2
Taylor MI U.S.A. 164 D2
Taylor NE U.S.A. 160 D3
Taylor TX U.S.A. 161 D6
Taylor, Mount NM U.S.A. 159 J4
Taylor Mountains AK U.S.A. 148 H3
Taylorsville KY U.S.A. 164 C4
Taylorville IL U.S.A. 160 F4
Taymā' Saudi Arabia 112 E6
Taymanī reg. Afgh. 111 F3
Taymura r. Russia 77 K3
Taymyr, Ozero l. Russia 77 L2
Taymyr, Poluostrov pen. Russia see Taymyr Peninsula
Taymyr Peninsula Russia 76 J2
Tây Ninh Vietnam 87 D5
Tayoltita Mex. 166 D3
Taypak Kazakh. 51 Q6
Taypaq Kazakh. see Taypak
Tayshet Russia 88 H1
Tayshir Mongolia 94 D2
Taytay Luzon Phil. 82 C3
Taytay Palawan Phil. 82 B4
Taytay Bay Palawan Phil. 82 B4
Taytay Point Leyte Phil. 82 D4
Tayu Java Indon. 85 E4
Tayuan China 90 B2
Taz r. Russia 76 I3
Taza Morocco 64 D5
Tāza Khurmātū Iraq 113 G4
Tazawa Japan 93 D2
Taze Myanmar 86 A2
Tazewell TN U.S.A. 164 D5
Tazewell VA U.S.A. 164 E5
Tazimina Lakes AK U.S.A. 148 I3
Tazin r. Canada 151 I2
Tazin Lake Canada 151 I3
Tāzirbū Libya 121 F2
Tazlina AK U.S.A. 149 K3
Tazlina Lake AK U.S.A. 149 K3
Tazmalt Alg. 67 I5
Tazovskaya Guba sea chan. Russia 76 I3
Tbessa Alg. see Tébessa

▶T'bilisi Georgia 113 G2
Capital of Georgia.

Tbilisskaya Russia 53 I7
Tchad country Africa see Chad
Tchamba Togo 120 D4
Tchibanga Gabon 122 B4
Tchigaï, Plateau du Niger 121 E2
Tchin-Tabaradene Niger 120 D3
Tcholliré Cameroon 121 E4
Tchula MS U.S.A. 161 F5
Tczew Poland 57 Q3
Té, Prêk r. Cambodia 87 D4
Teacapán Mex. 166 D4
Teague, Lake salt flat Australia 135 C6
Te Anau N.Z. 139 A7
Te Anau, Lake N.Z. 139 A7
Teapa Mex. 167 G5
Te Araroa N.Z. 139 G3
Teate Italy see Chieti
Te Awamutu N.Z. 139 E4
Teba Indon. 81 J7
Tébarat Niger 120 D3
Tebas Kalimantan Indon. 85 E2
Tebay U.K. 58 E4
Tebedu Sarawak Malaysia 85 E2
Tebesjuak Lake Canada 151 L2
Tébessa Alg. 68 C7
Tébessa, Monts de mts Alg. 68 C7
Tebingtinggi Sumatra Indon. 84 B2
Tebingtinggi Sumatra Indon. 84 C3
Tebo r. Indon. 84 C3
Tébourba Tunisia 68 C6
Téboursouk Tunisia 68 C6
T'ebulos Mta Georgia/Russia 113 G2
Tecalitlán Mex. 166 E5
Tecate Mex. 166 A1
Tece Turkey 107 B1
Techiman Ghana 120 C4
Tecka Arg. 178 B6
Tecklenburger Land reg. Germany 63 H2
Tecolutla Mex. 167 F4
Tecomán Mex. 166 E5
Tecoripa Mex. 166 C2
Técpan Mex. 168 D5
Tecuala Mex. 168 C4
Tecuci Romania 69 L2
Tecumseh MI U.S.A. 164 D3
Tecumseh NE U.S.A. 160 D3
Tedori-gawa r. Japan 92 C2
Tedzhen Turkm. see Tejen
Teec Nos Pos AZ U.S.A. 159 I3
Teel Mongolia see Öndör-Ulaan
Teeli Russia 98 E2
Tees r. U.K. 58 F4
Teeswater Canada 164 E1
Teet'lit Zhen Canada see Fort McPherson
Tefé r. Brazil 176 F4
Tefenni Turkey 69 M6
Tegal Java Indon. 85 E4
Tegel airport Germany 63 N2
Tegid, Llyn l. U.K. see Bala Lake
Tegineneng Sumatra Indon. 84 D4

▶Tegucigalpa Hond. 166 [inset] I6
Capital of Honduras.

Teguidda-n-Tessoumt Niger 120 D3
Tehachapi CA U.S.A. 158 D4
Tehachapi Mountains CA U.S.A. 158 D4
Tehachapi Pass CA U.S.A. 158 D4
Tehek Lake Canada 151 M1
Teheran Iran see Tehrān
Tehery Lake Canada 151 M1
Téhini Côte d'Ivoire 120 C4
Tehoru Seram Indon. 83 D3

▶Tehrān Iran 110 C3
Capital of Iran.

Tehri India see Tikamgarh
Tehuacán Mex. 168 E5
Tehuantepec, Gulf of g. Mex. 167 G6
Tehuantepec, Istmo de isthmus Mex. 168 F5
Tehuitzingo Mex. 167 F5
Teide, Pico del vol. Canary Is 120 B2
Teifi r. U.K. 59 C6
Teignmouth U.K. 59 D8
Teixeira de Freitas Brazil 179 D2
Teixeira de Sousa Angola see Luau
Teixeiras Brazil 179 C3
Teixeira Soares Brazil 179 A4
Tejakula Bali Indon. 85 F5
Tejen Turkm. 111 F2
Tejo r. Port. 67 B4 see Tagus
Tejon Pass CA U.S.A. 158 D4
Tejupan, Punta pt Mex. 166 E5
Tekapo, Lake N.Z. 139 C6
Tekari-dake mt. Japan 93 E3
Tekax Mex. 167 H4
Tekeli Kazakh. 102 E3
Tekes China 98 C4
Tekes Kazakh. 98 C4
Tekes He r. China 98 C4
Tekeze resr Eth. 122 D2
Tekiliktag mt. China 99 C5
Tekin Russia 90 D2
Tekirdağ Turkey 69 L4
Tekka India 106 D2
Tekkali India 106 E2
Teknaf Bangl. 105 H5
Tekong Kechil, Pulau i. Sing. 87 [inset]
Teku Celebes Indon. 83 B3
Te Kuiti N.Z. 139 E4
Tel r. India 106 D1
Tela Hond. 166 [inset] I6
Télagh Alg. 67 F6
Telan i. Sumatra Indon. 84 D2
Telanaipura Sumatra Indon. see Jambi
Telangana state India 106 C3
Telaquana Lake AK U.S.A. 148 I3
Telashi Hu salt l. China 99 F6
Tel Ashqelon tourist site Israel 107 B4
Télataï Mali 120 D3
Tel Aviv-Yafo Israel 107 B3
Telč Czech Rep. 57 O6
Telchac Puerto Mex. 167 H4
Telegapulang Kalimantan Indon. 85 F3
Telekhany Belarus see Tsyelyakhany
Telêmaco Borba Brazil 179 A4
Telen r. Indon. 85 G2
Teleorman r. Romania 69 K3
Telertheba, Djebel mt. Alg. 120 D2
Telescope Peak CA U.S.A. 158 E3
Teles Pires r. Brazil 177 G5
Telford U.K. 59 E6
Telgte Germany 63 H3
Telica, Volcán vol. Nicaragua 166 [inset] I6
Telida AK U.S.A. 148 I3
Télimélé Guinea 120 B3
Teljo, Jebel mt. Sudan 108 C7
Telkwa Canada 150 E4
Tell Atlas mts Alg. see Atlas Tellien
Tell City IN U.S.A. 164 B5
Teller AK U.S.A. 148 F2
Tell es Sultan West Bank see Jericho
Tellicherry India see Thalassery
Tellin Belgium 62 F4
Telloh Iraq 113 G5
Telluride CO U.S.A. 159 J3
Tel'mana, imeni Russia 90 D2
Telmen Mongolia 94 D1
Telmen Nuur salt l. Mongolia 94 D1
Tel'novskiy Russia 90 F2
Telo Sumatra Indon. 84 B3
Teloloapán Mex. 167 F5
Telo Martius France see Toulon
Telpoziz, Gora mt. Russia 51 R3
Telsen Arg. 178 C6
Telšiai Lith. 55 M9
Teltow Germany 63 N2
Teluk Anson Malaysia see Teluk Intan
Telukbajur Sumatra Indon. see Telukbayur
Telukbatang Kalimantan Indon. 85 E3
Telukbayur Sumatra Indon. 84 C3
Telukbetung Sumatra Indon. see Bandar Lampung
Teluk Cenderawasih, Taman Nasional Indon. 81 I7
Telukdalam Sumatra Indon. 84 B2
Teluk Intan Malaysia 84 C1
Telukkuantan Sumatra Indon. 84 C3
Telukmelano Kalimantan Indon. 85 E3
Teluknaga Java Indon. 84 D4
Telukpakedai Kalimantan Indon. 85 E3
Temagami Lake Canada 152 F5
Temaju i. Indon. 85 E2
Temanggung Java Indon. 85 E4
Temapache Mex. 167 F4
Têmarxung China 99 E6
Temax Mex. 167 H4
Temba S. Africa 125 I3
Tembagapura Indon. 81 J7
Tembenchi r. Russia 77 K3
Tembesi r. Indon. 84 C3
Tembilahan Sumatra Indon. 84 C3
Tembisa S. Africa 125 I4
Tembo Aluma Angola 123 B4
Teme r. U.K. 59 E6
Temecula CA U.S.A. 158 E5
Temenchula, Gora mt. Russia 94 D1
Temengor, Tasik resr Malaysia 84 C1
Temerluh Malaysia 84 C2
Temiang, Bukit mt. Malaysia 84 C1
Teminabuan Indon. 81 I7
Temirtau Kazakh. 102 D1
Témiscamie r. Canada 153 G4
Témiscamie, Lac l. Canada 153 G4
Témiscaming Canada 152 F5
Témiscamingue, Lac l. Canada 152 F5
Témiscouata, Lac l. Canada 153 H5
Temiyang i. Indon. 84 D2
Temmes Fin. 54 N4
Temnikov Russia 53 I5
Temora Australia 138 C5
Temósachic Mex. 166 D2
Tempe AZ U.S.A. 159 H5
Tempe, Danau l. Indon. 83 A4
Tempe Downs Australia 135 F6
Tempino Sumatra Indon. 84 C3
Temple MI U.S.A. 164 C1
Temple TX U.S.A. 161 D6
Temple Bar U.K. 59 C6
Temple Dera Pak. 111 H4
Templemore Ireland 61 E5
Templer Bank sea feature Phil. 82 B4
Temple Sowerby U.K. 58 E4
Templeton watercourse Australia 136 B4
Templin Germany 63 N1
Tempoal Mex. 167 F4
Tempué Angola 123 B5
Têmpung China 94 D4
Temryuk Russia 112 E1
Temryukskiy Zaliv b. Russia 53 H7
Temuco Chile 178 B5
Temuka N.Z. 139 C7
Temuli China see Butuo
Tena Ecuador 176 C4
Tenabo Mex. 167 H4
Tenabo, Mount NV U.S.A. 158 E1
Tenakee Springs AK U.S.A. 149 N4
Tenali India 106 D2
Tenango Mex. 167 F5
Tenasserim Myanmar 87 B4
Tenasserim r. Myanmar 87 B4
Tenbury Wells U.K. 59 E6
Tenby U.K. 59 C7
Tendaho Eth. 122 E2
Tende, Col de pass France/Italy 66 H4
Ten Degree Channel India 87 A5
Tendō Japan 91 F5
Tenedos i. Turkey see Bozcaada
Ténenkou Mali 120 C3
Ténéré reg. Niger 120 D2
Ténéré du Tafassâsset des. Niger 120 E2
Tenerife i. Canary Is 120 B2
Ténès Alg. 67 G5
Teng, Nam r. Myanmar 86 B3
Tengah, Kepulauan is Indon. 85 G4
Tengah, Sungai r. Sing. 87 [inset]
Tengahdai Flores Indon. 83 B5
Tengcheng China see Tengxian
Tengchong China 96 C3
Tengeh Reservoir Sing. 87 [inset]
Tenggarong Kalimantan Indon. 85 G3
Tengger Els China 94 F4
Tengger Shamo des. China 94 F4
Tenggul i. Malaysia 84 C1
Tengiz, Ozero salt l. Kazakh. 102 C1
Tengréla Côte d'Ivoire 120 C3
Ten'gushevo Russia 53 I5
Tengxian Guangxi China 97 F4
Tengxian Shandong China see Tengzhou
Tengzhou China 95 I5
Teni India see Theni
Teniente Jubany research station Antarctica see Carlini
Tenkawa Japan 92 B4
Tenke Dem. Rep. Congo 123 C5
Tenkeli Russia 77 P2
Tenkergynpil'gyn, Laguna lag. Russia 148 C1
Tenkodogo Burkina Faso 120 C3
Ten Mile Lake salt flat Australia 135 C6
Ten Mile Lake Canada 153 K4
Tennant Creek Australia 134 F4
Tennessee r. U.S.A. 161 F4
Tennessee state U.S.A. 164 C5
Tennessee Pass CO U.S.A. 156 G5
Tennevoll Norway 54 J2
Tennille FL U.S.A. 163 D6
Tenojoki r. Fin./Norway 54 P1
Tenom Sabah Malaysia 85 F1
Tenosique Mex. 167 H5
Tenpaku Japan 92 C3
Tenri Japan 92 B4
Tenryū Nagano Japan 93 D3
Tenryū Shizuoka Japan 93 D4
Tenryū-gawa r. Japan 93 D3
Tenryū-Okumikawa Kokutei-kōen park Japan 93 D3
Tenteno Celebes Indon. 83 B3
Tenterden U.K. 59 H7
Tenterfield Australia 138 F2
Ten Thousand Islands FL U.S.A. 163 D7
Tentolomatinan, Gunung mt. Indon. 83 B2
Tentudia mt. Spain 67 C4
Tentulia Bangl. see Tetulia
Teocelo Mex. 167 F5
Teodoro Sampaio Bahia Brazil 179 D1
Teodoro Sampaio São Paulo Brazil 178 F2
Teófilo Otoni Brazil 179 C2
Teomabal i. Phil. 82 C5
Teopisca Mex. 167 G5
Teotihuacán tourist site Mex. 167 F5
Tepa Moluccas Indon. 83 D4
Tepache Mex. 166 C2
Te Paki N.Z. 139 D2
Tepatitlán Mex. 168 D4
Tepehuanes Mex. 166 D3
Tepeji Mex. 167 F5
Tepeköy Turkey see Karakoçan
Tepelenë Albania 69 I4
Tepelmeme de Morelos Mex. 167 F5
Tepelská vrchovina hills Czech Rep. 63 M5
Tepequem, Serra mts Brazil 169 L8
Tepianlangsat Kalimantan Indon. 85 G2
Tepic Mex. 168 D4
Te Pirita N.Z. 139 C6
Teplá r. Czech Rep. 63 M4
Teplice Czech Rep. 57 N5
Teplogorka Russia 52 L3
Teploozersk Russia 90 C2
Teploye Russia 53 H5
Teploye Ozero Russia see Teploozersk
Tepoca, Cabo c. Mex. 157 E7
Tepopa, Punta pt Mex. 166 B2
Teq Teq Iraq 113 G4
Tequila Mex. 168 D4
Tequisistlán Mex. 167 G5
Tequisquiapan Mex. 167 F4
Ter r. Spain 67 H2
Téra Niger 120 D3
Teram Kangri mt. China 99 B6
Teramo Italy 68 E3
Terang Australia 138 A7
Ter Apel Neth. 62 H2
Terbang Selatan i. Moluccas Indon. 83 D4
Terbang Utara i. Moluccas Indon. 83 D4
Tercan Turkey 113 F3
Terebovlya Ukr. 53 E6
Tere-Khol' Russia 94 C1
Tere-Khol', Ozero l. Russia 94 D1
Terektinskiy Khrebet mts Russia 98 D2
Terekty Kazakh. 102 G2
Terengganu r. Malaysia 84 C1
Terengganu state Malaysia 84 C1
Terentang Kalimantan Indon. 85 E3
Terentang, Pulau i. Indon. 85 G3
Teresa Cristina Brazil 179 A4
Tereshka r. Russia 53 J6
Teresina Brazil 177 J5
Teresina de Goiás Brazil 179 B1
Teresita Col. 176 E3
Teresópolis Brazil 179 C3
Teressa Island India 87 A5
Terezinha Brazil 177 H3
Tergeste Italy see Trieste
Tergnier France 62 D5
Tergun Daba Shan mts China 94 C4
Tergüün Bogd Uul mt. Mongolia 102 J3
Terhiyn Tsagaan Nuur l. Mongolia 94 D1
Teriberka Russia 54 S2
Têring China 99 E7
Termas de Río Hondo Arg. 178 D3
Termez Uzbek. see Termiz
Termini Imerese Sicily Italy 68 E6
Términos, Laguna de lag. Mex. 167 H5
Termit and Tin Toumma National Nature and Cultural Reserve Niger 120 E3
Termit-Kaoboul Niger 120 E3
Termiz Uzbek. 111 G2
Termo CA U.S.A. 158 C1
Termoli Italy 68 F4
Termonde Belgium see Dendermonde
Tern r. U.K. 59 E6
Ternate Moluccas Indon. 83 C2
Ternate i. Moluccas Indon. 83 C2
Terneuzen Neth. 62 D3
Terney Russia 90 E3
Terni Italy 68 E3
Ternopil' Ukr. 53 E6
Ternopol' Ukr. see Ternopil'
Terpeniya, Mys c. Russia 90 G2
Terpeniya, Zaliv g. Russia 90 F2
Terra Alta WV U.S.A. 164 F4
Terra Bella CA U.S.A. 158 D4
Terrace Canada 150 D4
Terrace Bay Canada 152 D4
Terra Firma S. Africa 124 F3
Terråk Norway 54 H4
Terralba Sardinia Italy 68 C5
Terra Nova Bay Antarctica 188 H1
Terra Nova National Park Canada 153 L4
Terrazas Mex. 166 D2
Terre Adélie reg. Antarctica see Adélie Land
Terrebonne Bay LA U.S.A. 161 F6
Terre Haute IN U.S.A. 164 B4
Terrell TX U.S.A. 167 F1
Terre-Neuve prov. Canada see Newfoundland and Labrador
Terre-Neuve-et-Labrador prov. Canada see Newfoundland and Labrador
Terrero Mex. 166 D2
Terres Australes et Antarctiques Françaises terr. Indian Ocean see French Southern and Antarctic Lands
Terry MT U.S.A. 156 G3
Terschelling i. Neth. 62 F1
Terskey Ala-Too mts Kyrg. 98 B4
Terskiy Bereg coastal area Russia 52 H2
Tertenia Sardinia Italy 68 C5
Terter Azer. see Tärtär
Teruel Spain 67 F3
Tervola Fin. 54 N3
Tes Mongolia 94 C1
Tešanj Bos. & Herz. 68 G2
Teseney Eritrea 108 E6
Tesha r. Russia 53 I5
Teshekpuk Lake AK U.S.A. 148 I1
Teshio Japan 90 F3
Teshio-gawa r. Japan 90 F3
Tesiyn Gol r. Mongolia 94 C1
Teslin Canada 149 N3
Teslin r. Canada 149 N3
Teslin Lake Canada 149 N3
Tesouras r. Brazil 179 A1
Tessalit Mali 120 D2
Tessaoua Niger 120 D3
Tessolo Moz. 125 L1
Tesso Nilo, Taman Nasional tourist site Indon. 84 C5
Test r. U.K. 59 F8
Testour Tunisia 68 C6
Tetachuck Lake Canada 150 E4
Tetas, Punta pt Chile 178 B2
Tete Moz. 123 D5
Tetehosi Sumatra Indon. 84 B2
Te Teko N.Z. 139 F4
Teteriv r. Ukr. 53 F6
Teterow Germany 57 N4
Tetiyev Ukr. see Tetiyiv
Tetiyiv Ukr. 53 F6
Tetlin AK U.S.A. 149 L3
Tetlin Junction AK U.S.A. 149 L3
Tetlin Lake AK U.S.A. 149 L3
Tetlin National Wildlife Refuge nature res. AK U.S.A. 149 L3
Tetney U.K. 58 G5
Teton r. MT U.S.A. 156 F3
Tétouan Morocco 67 D6
Tetovo Macedonia 69 I3
Tetsyeh Mountain AK U.S.A. 149 K1
Tetuán Morocco see Tétouan
Tetulia Bangl. 105 G4
Tetulia sea chan. Bangl. 105 G5
Tetyukhe Russia see Dal'negorsk
Tetyukhe-Pristan' Russia see Rudnaya Pristan'
Tetyushi Russia 53 K5
Teuco r. Arg. 178 D2
Teufelsbach Namibia 124 C2
Teul de González Ortega Mex. 166 E4

Teun vol. Moluccas Indon. 83 D4
Teunom Sumatra Indon. 84 A1
Teunom r. Indon. 84 A1
Te Urewera National Park N.Z. 139 F4
Teutoburger Wald hills Germany 63 I2
Teuva Fin. 54 L5
Tevere r. Italy see Tiber
Teverya Israel see Tiberias
Teviot r. U.K. 60 G5
Te Waewae Bay N.Z. 139 A8
Tewah Kalimantan Indon. 85 F3
Te Waiponamu i. N.Z. see South Island
Tewane Botswana 125 H2
Tewantin Australia 137 F5
Teweh r. Indon. 85 F3
Tewkesbury U.K. 59 E7
Têwo Gansu China 94 E5
Têwo Sichuan China 94 E5
Texarkana AR U.S.A. 161 E5
Texarkana TX U.S.A. 161 E5
Texas Australia 138 E2
Texas state U.S.A. 161 D6
Texas City TX U.S.A. 167 G2
Texcoco Mex. 167 F5
Texel i. Neth. 62 E1
Texhoma OK U.S.A. 161 C4
Texoma, Lake Oklahoma/Texas U.S.A. 161 D5
Teyateyaneng Lesotho 125 H5
Teykovo Russia 52 I4
Teza r. Russia 52 I4
Teziutlán Mex. 167 F5
Tezpur India 105 H4
Tezu India 105 I4
Tha, Nâm r. Laos 86 C2
Thaa Atoll Maldives see Kolhumadulu
Tha-anne r. Canada 151 M2
Thabana-Ntlenyana mt. Lesotho 125 I5
Thaba Nchu S. Africa 125 H5
Thaba Putsoa mt. Lesotho 125 H5
Thaba-Tseka Lesotho 125 I5
Thabazimbi S. Africa 125 H3
Thab Lan National Park Thai. 87 C4
Tha Bo Laos 86 C3
Thabong S. Africa 125 H4
Thabyedaung Myanmar 96 C4
Thade r. Myanmar 86 A3
Thagyettaw Myanmar 87 B4
Tha Hin Thai. see Lop Buri
Thai Binh Vietnam 86 D2
Thailand country Asia 86 C4
Thailand, Gulf of Asia 87 C5
Thai Muang Thai. 87 B5
Thai Nguyên Vietnam 86 D2
Thaj Saudi Arabia 110 C5
Thakhèk Laos 86 D3
Thakurgaon Bangl. 105 G4
Thakurtola India 104 E5
Thal Germany 63 K4
Thala Tunisia 68 C7
Thalang Thai. 87 B5
Thalassery India 106 B4
Thal Desert Pak. 111 H4
Thale Germany 63 L3
Thaliparamba India see Taliparamba
Thallon Australia 138 D2
Thalo Pak. 111 G4
Thamaga Botswana 125 G3
Thamar, Jabal mt. Yemen 108 G7
Thamarīt Oman 109 H6
Thame r. U.K. 59 F7
Thames r. Ont. Canada 155 K3
Thames r. Ont. Canada 164 D2
Thames N.Z. 139 E3
Thames est. U.K. 59 H7
Thames r. U.K. 59 H7
Thamesford Canada 164 E2
Thana India see Thane
Thanatpin Myanmar 86 B3
Thandwe Myanmar 86 A3
Thane India 106 B2
Thanet, Isle of pen. U.K. 59 I7
Thangoo Australia 134 C4
Thangra India 104 D2
Thanh Hoa Vietnam 86 D3
Thanjavur India 106 C4
Than Kyun i. Myanmar 87 B5
Thanlwin r. China/Myanmar see Salween
Thanlyin Myanmar 86 B3
Thaolintoa Lake Canada 151 L2
Tha Pla Thai. 86 C3
Thap Put Thai. 87 B5
Thapsacus Syria see Dibsī
Thap Sakae Thai. 87 B5
Tharabwin Myanmar 87 B4
Tharad Gujarat India 104 B4
Tharad Gujarat India 104 B4
Thar Desert India/Pak. 111 H5
Thargomindah Australia 138 A1
Tharrawaw Myanmar 86 A3
Tharthār, Buḩayrat ath l. Iraq 113 F4
Tharwānīyyah U.A.E. 110 D6
Thasos i. Greece 69 K4
Thatcher AZ U.S.A. 159 I5
Thât Khê Vietnam 86 D2
Thaton Myanmar 86 B3
Thatta Pak. 111 G5
Thaungdut Myanmar 86 A1
Tha Uthen Thai. 86 D3
Thayawthadangyi Kyun i. Myanmar 87 B4
Thayetmyo Myanmar 86 A3
Thazi Magway Myanmar 86 A3
Thazi Mandalay Myanmar 105 I5
Thazzik Mountain AK U.S.A. 149 K2
The Aldermen Islands N.Z. 139 F3
Theba AZ U.S.A. 159 G5
The Bahamas country West Indies 163 E7
Thebes Greece see Thiva
The Bluff Bahamas 163 E7
The Broads nat. park U.K. 59 I6
The Brothers is H.K. China 97 [inset]
The Cheviot hill U.K. 58 E3
The Dalles OR U.S.A. 156 C3
Thedford NE U.S.A. 160 C3
The Entrance Australia 138 E4
The Faither stack U.K. 60 [inset]
The Fens reg. U.K. 59 G6
The Gambia country Africa 120 B3
Thegon Myanmar 86 A3
The Grampians mts Australia 137 C8
The Great Oasis oasis Egypt see Khārijah, Wāḩāt al
The Grenadines is St Vincent 169 L6
The Gulf Asia 110 C4

▶The Hague Neth. 62 E2
Seat of government of the Netherlands.

The Hunters Hills N.Z. 139 C7
Thekulthili Lake Canada 151 I2
The Lakes National Park Australia 138 C6
Thelon r. Canada 151 L1
The Lynd Junction Australia 136 D3
Themar Germany 63 K4
Thembalihle S. Africa 125 I4
The Minch sea chan. U.K. 60 C2
The Naze c. Norway see Lindesnes
The Needles stack U.K. 59 F8
Theni India 106 C4
Thenia Alg. 67 H5
Theniet El Had Alg. 67 H6
The North Sound sea chan. U.K. 60 G1
Theodore Australia 136 E5
Theodore Canada 151 K5
Theodore Roosevelt Lake AZ U.S.A. 159 H5
Theodore Roosevelt National Park ND U.S.A. 160 C2
Theodosia Crimea see Feodosiya
The Old Man of Coniston hill U.K. 58 D4
The Paps hill Ireland 61 C5
The Pas Canada 151 K4
The Pilot mt. Australia 138 D6
Thera i. Greece see Santorini
Thérain r. France 62 C5
Theresa NY U.S.A. 165 H1
Thermaïkos Kolpos g. Greece 69 J4
Thermopolis WY U.S.A. 156 F4
The Rock Australia 138 C5
Thérouanne France 62 C4
The Salt Lake salt flat Australia 137 C6

▶The Settlement Christmas I. 80 D9
Capital of Christmas Island.

The Sisters hill AK U.S.A. 148 G3
The Skaw spit Denmark see Grenen
The Skelligs is Ireland 61 B6
The Slot sea chan. Solomon Is see New Georgia Sound
The Solent strait U.K. 59 F8
Thessalon Canada 152 E5
Thessalonica Greece see Thessaloniki
Thessaloniki Greece 69 J4
The Storr hill U.K. 60 C3
Thet r. U.K. 59 H6
The Teeth mt. Palawan Phil. 82 B4
The Terraces hills Australia 135 C7
Thetford U.K. 59 H6
Thetford Mines Canada 153 H5
Thetkethaung r. Myanmar 86 A4
The Triangle mts Myanmar 86 B1
The Trossachs hills U.K. 60 E4
The Twins Australia 137 A6
Theva-i-Ra reef Fiji see Ceva-i-Ra

▶The Valley Anguilla 169 L5
Capital of Anguilla.

Thevenard Island Australia 134 A5
Thévenet, Lac l. Canada 153 H2
Theveste Alg. see Tébessa
The Wash b. U.K. 59 H6
The Weald reg. U.K. 59 H7
The Woodlands TX U.S.A. 161 E6
Thibodaux LA U.S.A. 161 F6
Thicket Portage Canada 151 L4
Thief River Falls MN U.S.A. 160 D1
Thiel Neth. see Tiel
Thiel Mountains Antarctica 188 K1
Thielsen, Mount OR U.S.A. 156 C4
Thielt Belgium see Tielt
Thiérache reg. France 62 D5
Thiers France 66 F4
Thiès Senegal 120 B3
Thika Kenya 122 D4
Thiladhunmathi Maldives 106 B5
Thimbu Bhutan see Thimphu

▶Thimphu Bhutan 105 G4
Capital of Bhutan.

Thionville France 62 G5
Thira i. Greece see Santorini
Thirsk U.K. 58 F4
Thirty Mile Lake Canada 151 L2
Thiruvananthapuram India 106 C4
Thiruvannamalai India see Tiruvannamalai
Thiruvarur India 106 C4
Thiruvattiyur India see Tiruvottiyur
Thisted Denmark 55 F8
Thistle Creek Canada 149 M3
Thistle Lake Canada 151 I1
Thityabin Myanmar 86 A2
Thiu Khao Luang Phrabang mts Laos/Thai. see Luang Phrabang, Thiu Khao
Thiva Greece 69 J5
Thívai Greece see Thiva
Thlewiaza r. Canada 151 M2
Thoa r. Canada 151 I2
Thô Chu, Đao i. Vietnam 87 C5
Thoen Thai. 96 C5
Thoeng Thai. 86 C3
Thohoyandou S. Africa 125 J2
Tholen Neth. 62 E3
Tholen i. Neth. 62 E3
Tholey Germany 62 H5
Thomas Hill Reservoir MO U.S.A. 160 E4
Thomas Hubbard, Cape Canada 147 I1
Thomaston CT U.S.A. 165 I3
Thomaston GA U.S.A. 163 C5
Thomastown Ireland 61 E5
Thomasville AL U.S.A. 163 C6
Thomasville GA U.S.A. 163 D6
Thommen Belgium 62 G4
Thompson Canada 151 L4
Thompson r. Canada 150 F5
Thompson UT U.S.A. 159 I2
Thompson r. MO U.S.A. 154 I4
Thompson Falls MT U.S.A. 156 E3
Thompson Peak NM U.S.A. 157 G6
Thompson's Falls Kenya see Nyahururu
Thompson Sound Canada 150 E5
Thomson GA U.S.A. 163 D5
Thon Buri Thai. 87 C4
Thonokied Lake Canada 151 I1
Thoothukudi India see Tuticorin
Thoreau NM U.S.A. 159 I4
Thorn Neth. 62 F3
Thorn Poland see Toruń
Thornaby-on-Tees U.K. 58 F4
Thornapple r. MI U.S.A. 164 C2
Thornbury U.K. 59 E7
Thorne U.K. 58 G5
Thorne NV U.S.A. 158 D2
Thornton r. Australia 136 B3
Thorold Canada 164 F2
Thorshavnfjella reg. Antarctica see Thorshavnheiane
Thorshavnheiane reg. Antarctica 188 C2
Thota-ea-Moli Lesotho 125 H5
Thôt Nôt Vietnam 87 D5
Thouars France 66 D3
Thoubal India 105 H4
Thourout Belgium see Torhout
Thousand Islands Canada/U.S.A. 165 G1
Thousand Lake Mountain UT U.S.A. 159 H2
Thousand Oaks CA U.S.A. 158 D4
Thousandsticks KY U.S.A. 164 D5
Thrace reg. Europe 69 L4
Thraki reg. Europe see Thrace
Thrakiko Pelagos sea Greece 69 K4
Three Gorges Reservoir resr China 97 F2
Three Hills Canada 150 H5
Three Hummock Island Australia 137 [inset]
Three Kings Islands N.Z. 139 D2
Three Oaks MI U.S.A. 164 B3
Three Pagodas Pass Myanmar/Thai. 86 B4
Three Points, Cape Ghana 120 C4
Three Rivers MI U.S.A. 164 C3
Three Rivers TX U.S.A. 167 F2
Three Sisters mt. OR U.S.A. 156 C3
Three Springs Australia 135 A7
Thrissur India 106 C4
Throckmorton TX U.S.A. 161 D5
Throssell, Lake salt flat Australia 135 D6
Throssel Range hills Australia 134 C5
Thrushton National Park Australia 138 C1
Thư Ba Vietnam 87 D5
Thubun Lakes Canada 151 I2
Thu Dâu Một Vietnam 87 D5
Thuddungra Australia 138 D5
Thu Đuc Vietnam 87 D5
Thuin Belgium 62 E4
Thul Pak. 111 H4
Thulaythāwāt Gharbī hill Syria 107 D2
Thule Greenland see Qaanaaq
Thule Air Base Greenland 189 K1
Thun Switz. 66 H3
Thunder Bay Canada 147 J5
Thunder Bay b. MI U.S.A. 164 D1
Thunder Creek r. Canada 151 J5
Thüngen Germany 63 J5
Thung Salaeng Luang National Park Thai. 86 C3
Thung Song Thai. 87 B5
Thung Wa Thai. 84 B1
Thung Yai Naresuan Wildlife Reserve nature res. Thai. 86 B4
Thüringen land Germany 63 K3
Thüringer Becken reg. Germany 63 L3
Thüringer Wald mts Germany 63 K4
Thuringia land Germany see Thüringen
Thuringian Forest mts Germany see Thüringer Wald
Thurles Ireland 61 E5
Thurn, Pass Austria 57 N7
Thursday Island Australia 136 C1
Thurso U.K. 60 F2
Thurso r. U.K. 60 F2
Thurston Island Antarctica 188 K2
Thurston Peninsula i. Antarctica see Thurston Island
Thüster Berg hill Germany 63 J2
Thuthukudi India see Tuticorin
Thwaite U.K. 58 E4
Thwaites Glacier Tongue Antarctica 188 K1
Thyatira Turkey see Akhisar
Thyborøn Denmark 55 F8
Thymerais reg. France 62 B6
Tiancang China 94 D3
Tianchang China 97 H1
Tiancheng Gansu China 94 D4
Tiancheng Hubei China see Chongyang
Tianchi Gansu China 95 F4
Tianchi Sichuan China see Lezhi
Tiandeng China 96 E4
Tiandong China 96 E4
Tianeti Georgia 113 G2
Tianfanjie China 97 H2
Tianguistengo Mex. 167 F4
Tianjin China 95 I4
Tianjin mun. China 95 I4
Tianjun China 94 D4
Tianlin China 96 E3
Tianma China see Changshan
Tianmen China 97 G2
Tianqiaoling China 90 C4
Tianquan China 96 D2
Tianshan China 95 J3
Tian Shan mts China/Kyrg. see Tien Shan
Tianshui Gansu China 94 F4
Tianshui Gansu China 94 F5
Tianshuihai China 99 B6
Tianshuijing China 98 F4
Tiantai China 97 I2
Tiantaiyong China 95 I3
Tiantang China see Yuexi
Tianyang China 96 E4
Tianyi China see Ningcheng
Tianzhen Shandong China see Gaoqing
Tianzhen Shanxi China 95 H3
Tianzhou China see Tianyang
Tianzhu Gansu China 94 E4
Tianzhu Guizhou China 97 F3
Tiaret Alg. 67 G6
Tiassalé Côte d'Ivoire 120 C4
Tibabar Sabah Malaysia see Tambunan
Tibagi Brazil 179 A4
Tibal, Wādī watercourse Iraq 113 F4
Tibati Cameroon 120 E4
Tibba Pak. 111 H4
Tibé, Pic de mt. Guinea 120 C4
Tiber r. Italy 68 E4
Tiberias Israel 107 B3
Tiberias, Lake Israel see Galilee, Sea of
Tiber Reservoir MT U.S.A. 156 F2
Tibesti mts Chad 121 E2
Tibet aut. reg. China see Xizang Zizhiqu
Tibet, Plateau of China 99 D6
Tibi India 111 I4
Tībīstī, Sarīr des. Libya 121 E2
Tibooburra Australia 137 C6
Tibrikot Nepal 105 E3
Tibro Sweden 55 I7
Tibur Italy see Tivoli
Tiburón, Isla i. Mex. 166 B2
Ticao i. Phil. 82 C3
Ticehurst U.K. 59 H7
Tichborne Canada 165 G1
Tichégami r. Canada 153 G4
Tîchît Mauritania 120 C3
Tîchît, Dahr hills Mauritania 120 C3
Tichla W. Sahara 120 B2
Ticinum Italy see Pavia
Ticonderoga NY U.S.A. 165 I2
Ticul Mex. 167 H4
Tidaholm Sweden 55 H7
Tiddim Myanmar 86 A2
Tiden India 87 A6
Tidjikja Mauritania 120 B3
Tidore i. Moluccas Indon. 83 C2
Tiechanggou China 98 D3
Tiefa China see Diaobingshan
Tiel Neth. 62 F3
Tieli China 90 B3
Tieling China 95 J3
Tielongtan China 99 B6
Tielt Belgium 62 D4
Tienen Belgium 62 E4
Tien Shan mts China/Kyrg. 88 D4
Tientsin China see Tianjin
Tientsin mun. China see Tianjin
Tiên Yên Vietnam 86 D2
Tierp Sweden 55 J6
Tierra Amarilla NM U.S.A. 157 G5
Tierra Blanca Mex. 167 F5
Tierra Colorada Mex. 167 F5

▶Tierra del Fuego, Isla Grande de i. Arg./Chile 178 C8
Largest island in South America.

Tierra del Fuego, Parque Nacional nat. park Arg. 178 C8
Tiétar r. Spain 67 D4
Tiétar, Valle del valley Spain 67 D3
Tietê r. Brazil 179 A3
Tieyon Australia 135 F6
Tiffin OH U.S.A. 164 D3
Tiflis Georgia see T'bilisi
Tifore i. Moluccas Indon. 83 C2
Tifton GA U.S.A. 163 D6
Tifu Buru Indon. 83 C3
Tiga i. Malaysia 85 F1
Tigalda Island AK U.S.A. 148 F5
Tigapuluh, Pegunungan mts Indon. 84 C3
Tiga Reservoir Nigeria 120 D3
Tigen Kazakh. 113 H1
Tīgh Āb Iran 111 F5
Tigheciului, Dealurile hills Moldova 69 M2
Tighina Moldova see Bender
Tigiretskiy Khrebet mts Kazakh./Russia 98 C2
Tigiria India 106 E1
Tignère Cameroon 120 E4
Tignish Canada 153 I5
Tigranocerta Turkey see Siirt
Tigre r. Venez. 176 F2
Tigre, Cerro del mt. Mex. 167 F4
Tigris r. Asia 113 G5
also known as Dicle (Turkey) or Nahr Dijlah (Iraq/Syria)
Tigrovaya Balka Zapovednik nature res. Tajik. 111 H2
Tiguidit, Falaise de esc. Niger 120 D3
Tīh, Gebel el plat. Egypt see Tīh, Jabal at
Tīh, Jabal at plat. Egypt 107 A5
Tihuatlán Mex. 167 F4
Tijuana Mex. 166 A1
Tikal tourist site Guat. 167 H5
Tikal, Parque Nacional nat. park Guat. 167 H5
Tikamgarh India 104 D4
Tikanlik China 98 D4
Tikchik Lakes AK U.S.A. 148 H4
Tikhoretsk Russia 53 I7
Tikhvin Russia 52 G4
Tikhvinskaya Gryada ridge Russia 52 G4
Tiki Basin sea feature S. Pacific Ocean 187 L7
Tikokino N.Z. 139 F4
Tikopia i. Solomon Is 133 G3
Tikrīt Iraq 113 F4
Tikse India 104 D2
Tikshozero, Ozero l. Russia 54 R3
Tiksi Russia 77 N2
Tila r. Nepal 99 C7
Tiladummati Atoll Maldives see Thiladhunmathi
Tilaiya Reservoir India 105 F4
Tilamuta Celebes Indon. 83 B2
Tilbeşar Ovasi plain Turkey 107 C1
Tilbooroo Australia 138 B1
Tilburg Neth. 62 F3
Tilbury Canada 164 D2
Tilbury U.K. 59 H7
Tilcara Arg. 178 C2
Tilcha Creek watercourse Australia 137 C6
Tilden TX U.S.A. 161 D6
Tilemsès Niger 120 D3
Tilemsi, Vallée du watercourse Mali 120 D3
Tilhar India 104 D4
Tilimsen Alg. see Tlemcen
Tilin Myanmar 86 A2
Tillabéri Niger 120 D3
Tillamook OR U.S.A. 156 C3
Tillanchong Island India 87 A5
Tillia Niger 120 D3
Tillicoultry U.K. 60 F4
Tillsonburg Canada 164 E2
Tillyfourie U.K. 60 G3
Tilonia India 111 I5
Tilos i. Greece 69 L6
Tilothu India 105 F4
Tilpa Australia 138 B3
Tilsit Russia see Sovetsk
Tilt r. U.K. 60 F4
Tilton IL U.S.A. 164 B3
Tilton NH U.S.A. 165 J2
Tilu, Bukit mt. Indon. 83 B3
Ţimā Egypt 108 D4
Timah, Bukit Sing. 87 [inset]
Timah, Bukit hill Sing. 87 [inset]
Timakara i. India 106 B4
Timanskiy Kryazh ridge Russia 52 K2
Timar Turkey 113 F3
Timaru N.Z. 139 C7
Timashëvsk Russia 53 H7
Timashevskaya Russia see Timashëvsk
Timbalier Bay LA U.S.A. 167 H2
Timbedgha Mauritania 120 C3
Timber Creek Australia 132 D3
Timber Mountain NV U.S.A. 158 E3
Timberville VA U.S.A. 165 F4
Timbuktu Mali 120 C3
Timbun Mata i. Malaysia 85 G1
Timétrine reg. Mali 120 C3
Timiaouine Alg. 120 D2
Timimoun Alg. 64 E6
Timirist, Râs pt Mauritania 120 B3
Timiskaming, Lake Canada see Témiscamingue, Lac
Timişoara Romania 69 I2
Timmins Canada 152 E4
Timms Hill hill WI U.S.A. 160 F2
Timon Brazil 177 J5
Timor i. Indon. 83 C5
Timor-Leste country Asia see East Timor
Timor Loro Sae country Asia see East Timor
Timor Sea Australia/Indon. 132 C3
Timor Timur country Asia see East Timor
Timpaus i. Indon. 83 C3
Timperley Range hills Australia 135 C6
Timrå Sweden 54 J5
Tīn, Ra's at pt Libya 112 A4
Ţīna, Khalīg el b. Egypt see Ţīnah, Khalīj aţ
Tīnah Syria 107 D1
Ţīnah, Khalīj aţ b. Egypt 107 A4
Tinambung Celebes Indon. 83 A3
Tin Can Bay Australia 137 F5
Tindivanam India 106 C3
Tindouf Alg. 64 C6
Ti-n-Essako Mali 120 D3
Tinggi i. Malaysia 84 D2
Tingha Australia 138 E2
Tingis Morocco see Tangier
Tingo María Peru 176 C5
Tingréla Côte d'Ivoire see Tengréla
Tingri China 99 D7
Tingsryd Sweden 55 I8
Tingvoll Norway 54 F5
Tingwall U.K. 60 F1
Tingzhou China see Changting
Tinharé, Ilha de i. Brazil 179 D1
Tinh Gia Vietnam 86 D3
Tinian i. N. Mariana Is 81 L4
Tini Heke is N.Z. see Snares Islands
Tinjar r. Malaysia 85 F1
Tinjil i. Indon. 84 D4
Tinnelvelly India see Tirunelveli
Tinogasta Arg. 178 C3
Tinompo Celebes Indon. 83 B2
Tinos Greece 69 K6
Tinos i. Greece 69 K6
Tinqueux France 62 D5
Tinrhert, Hamada de Alg. 120 D2
Tinsukia India 105 H4
Tintagel U.K. 59 C8
Ţînţâne Mauritania 120 B3
Tintina Arg. 178 D3
Tintinara Australia 137 C7
Tioga ND U.S.A. 160 C1
Tioman i. Malaysia 84 D2
Ti On, Nui mt. Vietnam 86 D4
Tionesta PA U.S.A. 164 F3
Tionesta Lake PA U.S.A. 164 F3
Tipasa Alg. 67 H5
Tiphsah Syria see Dibsī
Tipitapa Nicaragua 166 [inset] I6
Tipperary Ireland 61 D5
Tiptala Bhanjyang pass Nepal 99 D8
Tipton CA U.S.A. 158 D3
Tipton IA U.S.A. 160 F3
Tipton IN U.S.A. 164 B3
Tipton MO U.S.A. 160 E4
Tipton, Mount AZ U.S.A. 159 F4
Tiptop VA U.S.A. 164 E5
Tip Top Hill hill Canada 152 D4
Tiptree U.K. 59 H7
Tiptur India 106 C3
Tipturi India see Tiptur
Tiquisate Guat. 167 H6
Tiracambu, Serra do hills Brazil 177 I4
Tirah reg. Pak. 111 H3

▶Tirana Albania 69 H4
Capital of Albania.

Tiranë Albania see Tirana
Tirano Italy 68 D1
Tirari Desert Australia 137 B5

▶Tiraspol Moldova 69 M1
Capital of Transnistria.

Tiraz Mountains Namibia 124 C4
Tire Turkey 69 L5
Tirebolu Turkey 113 E2
Tiree i. U.K. 60 C4
Tîrgovişte Romania see Târgovişte
Tîrgu Jiu Romania see Târgu Jiu
Tîrgu Mureş Romania see Târgu Mureş
Tîrgu Neamţ Romania see Târgu Neamţ
Tîrgu Secuiesc Romania see Târgu Secuiesc
Tiri Pak. 111 G4
Tirich Mir mt. Pak. 111 H2
Tirlemont Belgium see Tienen
Tirna r. India 106 C2
Tîrnăveni Romania see Târnăveni
Tírnavos Greece see Tyrnavos
Tiros Brazil 179 B2
Tirourda, Col de pass Alg. 67 I5
Tir Pul Afgh. 111 F3
Tirreno, Mare sea France/Italy see Tyrrhenian Sea
Tirso r. Sardinia Italy 68 C5
Tirthahalli India 106 B3
Tiruchchendur India 106 C4
Tiruchchirappalli India 106 C4
Tiruchengodu India 106 C4
Tirunelveli India 106 C4
Tirupati India 106 C3
Tiruppattur Tamil Nadu India 106 C3
Tiruppattur Tamil Nadu India 106 C4
Tiruppur India 106 C4
Tiruttani India 106 C3
Tirutturaippundi India 106 C4
Tiruvallur India 106 C3
Tiruvannamalai India 106 C3
Tiruvottiyur India 106 D3
Tiru Well Australia 134 D5
Tisa r. Serbia 69 I2
also known as Tisza (Hungary), Tysa (Ukraine)
Tisdale Canada 151 J4
Tishomingo OK U.S.A. 161 D5
Tīsīyah Syria 107 C3
Tissemsilt Alg. 67 G6
Tista r. India 99 E8
Tisza r. Serbia see Tisa
Titabar India 99 F8
Titaluk r. AK U.S.A. 148 I1
Titalya Bangl. see Tetulia
Titan Dome ice feature Antarctica 188 H1
Titao Burkina Faso 120 C3
Tit-Ary Russia 77 N2
Titawin Morocco see Tétouan
Titicaca, Lago Bol./Peru see Titicaca, Lake

▶Titicaca, Lake Bol./Peru 176 E7
Largest lake in South America.

Titi Islands N.Z. 139 A8
Tititea mt. N.Z. see Aspiring, Mount
Titlagarh India 106 D1
Titograd Montenegro see Podgorica
Titova Mitrovica Kosovo see Mitrovicë
Titovo Užice Serbia see Užice
Titovo Velenje Slovenia see Velenje
Titov Veles Macedonia see Veles
Titov Vrbas Serbia see Vrbas
Ti Tree Australia 134 F5
Titu Romania 69 K2
Titusville FL U.S.A. 163 D6
Titusville PA U.S.A. 164 F3
Tiu Chung Chau i. H.K. China 97 [inset]
Tiumpain, Rubha an hd U.K. see Tiumpan Head
Tiumpan Head hd U.K. 60 C2
Tiva watercourse Kenya 122 D4
Tivari India 104 C4
Tiverton Canada 164 E1
Tiverton U.K. 59 D8
Tivoli Italy 68 E4
Ţīwī Oman 110 E6
Tiwi Aboriginal Land res. Australia 83 D5
Tiworo, Selat sea chan. Indon. 83 B4
Tixtla Mex. 167 F5
Ti-ywa Myanmar 87 B4
Tizimín Mex. 167 H4
Tizi Ouzou Alg. 67 I5
Tiznap He r. China 99 B5
Tiznit Morocco 120 C2
Tizoc Mex. 166 E3
Tiztoutine Morocco 67 E6
Tjaneni Swaziland 125 J3
Tjappsåive Sweden 54 K4
Tjeukemeer l. Neth. 62 F2
Tjirebon Java Indon. see Cirebon
Tjolotjo Zimbabwe see Tsholotsho
Tjorhom Norway 55 E7
Tkibuli Georgia see T'q'ibuli
Tlacotalpán Mex. 167 G5
Tlacotepec, Cerro mt. Mex. 167 E5
Tlahualilo Mex. 166 E3
Tlalnepantla Mex. 167 F5

Tlancualpican Mex. 167 F5
Tlapa Mex. 167 F5
Tlapacoyan Mex. 167 F5
Tlaxcala Mex. 168 E5
Tlaxcala *state* Mex. 167 F5
Tlaxco Mex. 167 F5
Tlaxiaco Mex. 167 F5
Tl'ell Canada 149 O5
Tlemcen Alg. 67 F6
Tlhakalatlou S. Africa 124 F5
Tlholong S. Africa 125 I5
Tlokweng Botswana 125 G3
Tlyarata Russia 113 G2
To *r.* Myanmar 86 B3
Toad *r.* Canada 150 E3
Toad River Canada 150 E3
Toagel Mlungui Palau 82 [inset]
Toamasina Madag. 123 E5
Toana *mts NV* U.S.A. 159 F1
Toano *VA* U.S.A. 165 G5
Toa Payoh Sing. 87 [inset]
Toba China 96 C2
Toba Japan 92 C4
Toba, Danau *l.* Indon. 84 B2
Toba, Lake Indon. *see* Toba, Danau
Toba and Kakar Ranges *mts* Pak. 111 G4
Toba Gargaji Pak. 111 I4
Tobago *i.* Trin. and Tob. 169 L6
Tobelo *Halmahera* Indon. 83 C2
Tobercurry Ireland 61 D3
Tobermorey Australia 136 B4
Tobermory Australia 138 A1
Tobermory Canada 164 E1
Tobermory U.K. 60 C4
Tobi *i.* Palau 81 I6
Tobias Fornier *Panay* Phil. 82 C4
Tobin, Lake *salt flat* Australia 134 D5
Tobin, Mount *NV* U.S.A. 158 E1
Tobin Lake Canada 151 K4
Tobin Lake *l.* Canada 151 K4
Tobishima Japan 92 C3
Tobi-shima *i.* Japan 91 E5
Tobli Liberia 120 C4
Toboali Indon. 84 D3
Tobol *r.* Kazakh./Russia *see* Tobyl
Tobol'sk Russia 76 H4
Toboso *Negros* Phil. 82 C4
Tobruk Libya *see* Tubruq
Tobseda Russia 52 L1
Tobyl *r.* Kazakh./Russia 100 F1
Tobysh *r.* Russia 52 K2
Tocache Nuevo Peru 176 C5
Tocantinópolis Brazil 177 I5
Tocantins *r.* Brazil 179 A1
Tocantins *state* Brazil 179 A1
Tocantinzinha *r.* Brazil 179 A1
Toccoa *GA* U.S.A. 163 D5
Tochi *r.* Pak. 111 H3
Tochigi Japan 93 F2
Tochigi *pref.* Japan 93 F2
Töcksfors Sweden 55 G7
Tocoa Hond. 166 [inset] I6
Tocopilla Chile 178 B2
Tocumwal Australia 138 B5
Tod, Mount Canada 150 G5
Toda Japan 93 F3
Todd *watercourse* Australia 136 A5
Todi Italy 68 E3
Todog China 98 C3
Todoga-saki *pt* Japan 91 F5
Todok China *see* Todog
Todos Santos Mex. 166 C4
Toe Head *hd* U.K. 60 B3
Tōei Japan 92 D3
Tofino Canada 150 E5
Toft U.K. 60 [inset]
Tofua *i.* Tonga 133 I3
Toga Japan 92 D2
Tōgane Japan 93 G3
Togatax China 99 C6
Togi Japan 92 C1
Togiak *AK* U.S.A. 148 G4
Togiak *r. AK* U.S.A. 148 G4
Togiak Bay *AK* U.S.A. 148 G4
Togiak Lake *AK* U.S.A. 148 H4
Togiak National Wildlife Refuge *nature res. AK* U.S.A. 148 G4
Togian *i.* Indon. 83 B3
Togian, Kepulauan *is* Indon. 83 B3
Togliatti Russia *see* Tol'yatti
Togo *country* Africa 120 D4
Tōgō Japan 92 D3
Tograsay He *r.* China 99 E5
Tögrög *Hovd* Mongolia *see* Manhan
Tögrög *Övörhangay* Mongolia 94 E2
Togrog Ul China 95 H3
Togtoh China 95 G3
Togton He *r.* China 99 F6
Togura Japan 93 E2
Tohatchi *NM* U.S.A. 159 I4
Tohenbatu *mt.* Malaysia 85 F2
Toholampi Fin. 54 N5
Tohom China 94 F3
Töhöm Mongolia *see* Mandah
Tohono O'Odham (Papago) Indian Reservation *res. AZ* U.S.A. 166 B1
Toi Japan 93 E4
Toiba China 99 E7
Toibalewe India 87 A5
Toide Japan 92 C2
Toijala Fin. 55 M6
Toili *Celebes* Indon. 83 B3
Toi-misaki *pt* Japan 91 C7
Tōin Japan 92 C3
Toineke *Timor* Indon. 83 C5
Toivakka Fin. 54 O5
Toiyabe Range *mts NV* U.S.A. 158 E2
Toja *Celebes* Indon. 83 B3
Tojikiston *country* Asia *see* Tajikistan
Tōjō Japan 92 B4
Tok *AK* U.S.A. 149 L3
Tōkai *Aichi* Japan 92 C3
Tōkai *Ibaraki* Japan 93 G2
Tokala, Gunung *mt.* Indon. 83 B3
Tōkamachi Japan 93 E1
Tokar Sudan 108 E6
Tokara-rettō *is* Japan 91 C7
Tokarevka Russia 53 I6
Tokat Turkey 112 E2
Tok-do *i.* N. Pacific Ocean *see* Liancourt Rocks

▶**Tokelau** *terr.* S. Pacific Ocean 133 I2
New Zealand Overseas Territory.

Toki Japan 92 D3
Tokigawa Japan 93 F2
Toki-gawa *r.* Japan 92 C3
Tokkuztara China *see* Gongliu
Toklat *AK* U.S.A. 149 J2
Toklat *r. AK* U.S.A. 149 J2
Tokmak Kyrg. *see* Tokmok
Tokmak Ukr. 53 G7
Tokmok Kyrg. 102 E3
Tokomaru Bay N.Z. 139 G4
Tokoname Japan 92 C4
Tokoroa N.Z. 139 E4
Tokorozawa Japan 93 F3
Tokoza S. Africa 125 I4
Toksook Bay *AK* U.S.A. 148 F3
Toksu China *see* Xinhe
Toksun China 98 E4
Tok-to *i.* N. Pacific Ocean *see* Liancourt Rocks
Toktogul Kyrg. 102 D3
Tokty Kazakh. 98 C3
Tokur Russia 90 D1
Tokushima Japan 91 D6
Tokuyama-ko *resr* Japan 92 C3

▶**Tōkyō** Japan 93 F3
Capital of Japan. Most populous city in Asia and the world.

Tōkyō *mun.* Japan 93 F3
Tōkyō-wan *b.* Japan 93 F3
Tokyrau *watercourse* Kazakh. 98 A3
Tolaga Bay N.Z. 139 G4
Tôlañaro Madag. 123 E6
Tolbo Mongolia 94 B1
Tolbukhin Bulg. *see* Dobrich
Tolbuzino Russia 90 B1
Tolé Panama 166 [inset] J7
Tole Bi Kazakh. 98 A4
Toledo Brazil 178 F2
Toledo Spain 67 D4
Toledo *IA* U.S.A. 160 E3
Toledo *OH* U.S.A. 164 D3
Toledo *OR* U.S.A. 156 C3
Toledo, Montes de *mts* Spain 67 D4
Toledo Bend Reservoir *Louisiana/Texas* U.S.A. 161 E6
Toletum Spain *see* Toledo
Toli China 98 C3
Toliara Madag. 123 E6
Tolitoli *Celebes* Indon. 83 B2
Tol'ka Russia 76 J3
Tolleson *AZ* U.S.A. 159 G5
Tolmachevo Russia 55 P7
Tolo Dem. Rep. Congo 122 B4
Toloa Creek Hond. 166 [inset] I6
Tolo Channel *H.K.* China 97 [inset]
Tolochin Belarus *see* Talachyn
Tolo Harbour *b. H.K.* China 97 [inset]
Tolonuu *i. Moluccas* Indon. 83 D2
Tolosa France *see* Toulouse
Tolosa Spain 67 E2
Tolovana *r. AK* U.S.A. 149 J2
Toluca Mex. 168 E5
Toluca de Lerdo Mex. *see* Toluca
Tol'yatti Russia 53 K5
Tom' *r.* Russia 90 B1
Tomaga-shima *i.* Japan 92 B4
Tomagashima-suidō *sea chan.* Japan 92 A4
Tomah *WI* U.S.A. 160 F3
Tomakomai Japan 90 F4
Tomales *CA* U.S.A. 158 B2
Tomali *Celebes* Indon. 81 G7
Tomamae Japan 90 F3
Tomani *Sabah* Malaysia 85 F1
Tomanivi *mt.* Fiji 133 H3
Tomar Brazil 176 F4
Tomar Port. 67 B4
Tomari Russia 90 F3
Tomarza Turkey 112 D3
Tomaszów Lubelski Poland 53 D6
Tomaszów Mazowiecki Poland 57 R5
Tomatin U.K. 60 F3
Tomatlán Mex. 168 C5
Tomazina Brazil 179 A3
Tombador, Serra do *hills* Brazil 177 G6
Tombigbee *r. AL* U.S.A. 163 C6
Tomboco Angola 123 B4
Tombouctou Mali *see* Timbuktu
Tombstone *AZ* U.S.A. 157 F7
Tombua Angola 123 B5
Tom Burke S. Africa 125 H2
Tomdibuloq Uzbek. 102 B3
Tome Moz. 125 L2
Tomea *i.* Indon. 83 B4
Tomelilla Sweden 55 H9
Tomelloso Spain 67 E4
Tomengi Kayrakty Kazakh. 98 A2
Tōmi Japan 93 E2
Tomi Romania *see* Constanţa
Tomika Japan 92 C3
Tomingley Australia 138 D4
Tomini, Teluk *g.* Indon. 83 B3
Tominian Mali 120 C3
Tomintoul U.K. 60 F3
Tomioka Japan 93 E2
Tomisato Japan 93 G3
Tomislavgrad Bos. & Herz. 68 G3
Tomiyama *Aichi* Japan 93 D3
Tomiyama *Chiba* Japan 93 F3
Tomizawa Japan *see* Nanbu
Tomkinson Ranges *mts* Australia 135 E6
Tømmerneset Norway 54 I3
Tommot Russia 77 N4
Tomo *r.* Col. 176 E2
Tomobe Japan *see* Kasama
Tomóchic Mex. 166 D2
Tomorlog China 99 E5
Tomort *mt.* China 94 C3
Tomortei China 95 H3
Tompira *Celebes* Indon. 83 B3
Tompkinsville *KY* U.S.A. 164 C5
Tompo *Celebes* Indon. 83 A3
Tom Price Australia 134 B5
Tomra China 99 D7
Tomsk Russia 76 J4
Toms River *NJ* U.S.A. 165 H4
Tomtabacken *hill* Sweden 55 I8
Tomtor Russia 77 P3
Tomur Feng *mt.* China/Kyrg. *see* Pobeda Peak
Tomuzlovka *r.* Russia 53 J7
Tom White, Mount *AK* U.S.A. 149 L3
Tonalá *Chiapas* Mex. 168 F5
Tonalá *Veracruz* Mex. 167 G5
Tonami Japan 92 C2
Tonantins Brazil 176 E4
Tonb-e Bozorg, Jazīreh-ye *i.* The Gulf 110 D5
Tonb-e Kūchek, Jazīreh-ye *i.* The Gulf 110 D5
Tonbridge U.K. 59 H7
Tondabayashi Japan 92 B4
Tondano *Celebes* Indon. 83 C2
Tønder Denmark 55 F9
Tondi India 106 C4
Tone *Gunma* Japan 93 F2
Tone *Ibaraki* Japan 93 G3
Tone *r.* U.K. 59 E7
Tone-gawa *r.* Japan 93 G3
Tonekābon Iran 110 C2
Toney Mountain Antarctica 188 K1
Tonga *country* S. Pacific Ocean 133 I4
Tongariro National Park N.Z. 139 E4
Tongatapu Group *is* Tonga 133 I4

▶**Tonga Trench** *sea feature* S. Pacific Ocean 186 I7
2nd deepest trench in the world.

Tongbai Shan *mts* China 97 G1
Tongcheng *Anhui* China 97 H2
Tongcheng *Shandong* China *see* Dong'e
T'ongch'ŏn N. Korea 91 B5
Tongchuan *Shaanxi* China 95 G5
Tongchuan *Sichuan* China *see* Santai
Tongdao China 97 F3
Tongde China 94 E5
Tongeren Belgium 62 F4
Tonggu China 97 G2
Tongguan China 95 G5
Tonggu Zui *pt* China 97 F5
Tonghai China 96 D3
Tonghe China 90 C3
Tonghua *Jilin* China 90 B4
Tonghua *Jilin* China 90 B4
Tongi Bangl. *see* Tungi
Tongjiang *Heilong.* China 90 D3
Tongjiang *Sichuan* China 96 E2
Tongking, Gulf of China/Vietnam 86 E2
Tongko *Celebes* Indon. 83 B3
Tonglau Myanmar 86 B2
Tongle China *see* Leye
Tongliang China 96 E2
Tongliao China 95 J3
Tongling China 97 H2
Tonglu China 97 H2
Tongo Australia 138 A3
Tongo Lake *salt flat* Australia 138 A3
Tongquil *i.* Phil. 82 C5
Tongren *Guizhou* China 97 F3
Tongren *Qinghai* China 94 E5
Tongres Belgium *see* Tongeren
Tongsa Bhutan *see* Trongsa
Tongshan China *see* Xuzhou
Tongta Myanmar 86 B2
Tongtian He *r. Qinghai* China 96 B1 *see* Yangtze
Tongtian He *r. Qinghai* China 99 G6
Tongue U.K. 60 E2
Tongue *r. MT* U.S.A. 156 G3
Tongue of the Ocean *sea chan.* Bahamas 163 E7
Tongwei China 94 F5
Tongxin China 94 F4
Tongyeong S. Korea 91 C6
Tongyu China 95 J2
Tongzhou China 95 I4
Tongzi China 96 E2
Tonhil Mongolia 94 C2
Tónichi Mex. 166 C2
Tonila Mex. 166 E5
Tonk India 104 C4
Tonki Cape *AK* U.S.A. 149 J4
Tonkin *reg.* Vietnam 86 D2
Tônlé Sab *l.* Cambodia *see* Tonle Sap

▶**Tonle Sap** *l.* Cambodia 87 C4
Largest lake in south-east Asia.

Tōno Japan 93 G1
Tonopah *AZ* U.S.A. 159 G5
Tonopah *NV* U.S.A. 158 E2
Tōnoshō Japan 93 G3
Tonosí Panama 166 [inset] J8
Tons *r.* India 99 B7
Tønsberg Norway 55 G7
Tonsina *AK* U.S.A. 149 K3
Tonstad Norway 55 E7
Tonto Creek *watercourse AZ* U.S.A. 159 H5
Tonūrjeh Iran 110 E3
Tonzang Myanmar 86 A2
Tonzi Myanmar 86 A1
Toobeah Australia 138 D2
Tooele *UT* U.S.A. 159 G1
Toogoolawah Australia 138 F1
Toolik *r. AK* U.S.A. 149 J1
Tooma *r.* Australia 138 D6
Toompine Australia 138 B1
Toora Australia 138 C7
Tooraweenah Australia 138 D3
Toorberg *mt.* S. Africa 124 G7
Toowoomba Australia 138 E1
Tooxin Somalia 122 F2
Tōp Afgh. 111 H3
Topagoruk *r. AK* U.S.A. 148 I1
Top Boğazı Geçidi *pass* Turkey 107 C1

▶**Topeka** *KS* U.S.A. 160 E4
Capital of Kansas.

Topia Mex. 166 D3
Toplana, Gunung *mt. Seram* Indon. 83 D3
Töplitz Germany 63 M2
Topoľčany Slovakia 57 Q6
Topolobampo Mex. 166 C3
Topolovgrad Bulg. 69 L3
Topozero, Ozero *l.* Russia 54 R4
Topsfield *ME* U.S.A. 162 H2
Torahime Japan 92 C3
Toranggekuduk China 94 B2
Torbalı Turkey 69 L5
Torbat-e Ḩeydarīyeh Iran 110 E3
Torbat-e Jām Iran 111 F3
Torbay Bay Australia 135 B8
Torbert, Mount *AK* U.S.A. 148 I3
Torbeyevo Russia 53 I5
Torch *r.* Canada 151 K4
Tordesillas Spain 67 D3
Tordesilos Spain 67 F3
Töre Sweden 54 M4
Torelló Spain 67 H2
Torenberg *hill* Neth. 62 F2
Toreo *Celebes* Indon. 83 B3
Toretam Kazakh. *see* Baykonyr
Torgau Germany 63 M3
Torgay Kazakh. 102 B2
Torghay Kazakh. *see* Torgay
Torgun *r.* Russia 53 J6
Torhout Belgium 62 D3
Torī Eth. 121 G4
Toride Japan 93 G3
Torigakubi-misaki *pt* Japan 93 E1
Torigoe Japan 92 C2
Torii-tōge *pass* Japan 93 D3
Torii-tōge *pass* Japan 93 E2
Torikabuto-yama *mt.* Japan 93 E2
Torino Italy *see* Turin
Tori-shima *i.* Japan 91 F7
Torit South Sudan 121 G4
Torkamānchāy Iran 110 B2
Tōr Kham Afgh. 111 H3
Torkovichi Russia 52 F4
Tornado Mountain Canada 150 H5
Torneå Fin. *see* Tornio
Torneälven *r.* Sweden 54 N4
Torneträsk *l.* Sweden 54 K2
Torngat, Monts *mts* Canada *see* Torngat Mountains
Torngat Mountains Canada 153 I2
Tornio Fin. 54 N4
Toro Spain 67 D3
Toro, Pico del *mt.* Mex. 161 C7
Torobuku *Celebes* Indon. 83 B4
Torom Russia 90 D1

▶**Toronto** Canada 164 F2
Capital of Ontario.

Toro Peak *CA* U.S.A. 158 E5
Toropets Russia 52 F4
Tororo Uganda 122 D3
Toros Dağları *mts* Turkey *see* Taurus Mountains
Torphins U.K. 60 G3
Torquay Australia 138 B7
Torquay U.K. 59 D8
Torrance *CA* U.S.A. 158 D5
Torrão Port. 67 B4
Torre *mt.* Port. 67 C3
Torreblanca Spain 67 G3
Torre Blanco, Cerro *mt.* Mex. 166 B1
Torrecerredo *mt.* Spain 67 D2
Torre del Greco Italy 68 F4
Torre de Moncorvo Port. 67 C3
Torrelavega Spain 67 D2
Torremolinos Spain 67 D5

▶**Torrens, Lake** *imp. l.* Australia 137 B6
2nd largest lake in Oceania.

Torrens Creek Australia 136 D4
Torrent Spain 67 F4
Torrente Spain *see* Torrent
Torreón Mex. 166 E3
Torres Brazil 179 A5
Torres Mex. 166 C2
Torres del Paine, Parque Nacional *nat. park* Chile 178 B8
Torres Islands Vanuatu 133 G3
Torres Novas Port. 67 B4
Torres Strait Australia 132 E2
Torres Vedras Port. 67 B4
Torrevieja Spain 67 F5
Torrey *UT* U.S.A. 159 H2
Torridge *r.* U.K. 59 C8
Torridon, Loch *b.* U.K. 60 D3
Torrijos Spain 67 D4
Torrington Australia 138 E2
Torrington *CT* U.S.A. 162 F3
Torrington *WY* U.S.A. 156 G4
Torsa Chhu *r.* Bhutan 99 E8
Torsby Sweden 55 H6

▶**Tórshavn** Faroe Is 54 [inset]
Capital of the Faroe Islands.

Tortilla Flat *AZ* U.S.A. 159 H5
To'rtko'l Uzbek. 102 B3
Törtköl Uzbek. *see* To'rtko'l
Tortolì *Sardinia* Italy 68 C5
Tortona Italy 68 C2
Tortosa Spain 67 G3
Tortuga, Laguna *l.* Mex. 167 F4
Tortuguero, Parque Nacional *nat. park* Costa Rica 166 [inset] J7
Tortum Turkey 113 F2
Toru-Aygyr Kyrg. 98 B4
Ţorūd Iran 110 D3
Torue *Celebes* Indon. 83 B3
Torugart, Pereval *pass* China/Kyrg. *see* Turugart Pass
Torul Turkey 113 E2
Toruń Poland 57 Q4
Tory Island Ireland 61 D2
Tory Sound *sea chan.* Ireland 61 D2
Torzhok Russia 52 G4
Torzī Afgh. 111 G4
Tosa Japan 91 D6
Tosbotn Norway 54 H4
Tosca S. Africa 124 F3
Tosca, Punta *pt* Mex. 166 C3
Toscano, Arcipelago *is* Italy 68 C3
Tosham India 104 C3
Tōshi-jima *i.* Japan 92 C4
To-shima *i.* Japan 93 F4
Tōshima-yama *mt.* Japan 91 F4

▶**Toshkent** Uzbek. 102 C3
Capital of Uzbekistan.

Tosno Russia 52 F4
Toson Hu *l.* China 94 D4
Tosontsengel *Dzavhan* Mongolia 94 D1
Tosontsengel *Hövsgöl* Mongolia 94 E1
Tostado Arg. 178 D3
Tostedt Germany 63 J1
Tosya Turkey 112 D2
Totapola *mt.* Sri Lanka 106 D5
Tôtes France 62 B5
Tot'ma Russia 52 I4
Totness Suriname 177 G2
Totolapan Mex. 167 F5
Totonicapán Guat. 167 H6
Totsuka Japan 93 F3
Totsukawa Japan 92 B4
Totsu-kawa *r.* Japan 92 B5
Totten Glacier Antarctica 188 F2
Tottenham Australia 138 C4
Totton U.K. 59 F8
Tottori Japan 91 D6
Touba Côte d'Ivoire 120 C4
Touba Senegal 120 B3
Toubkal, Jebel *mt.* Morocco 64 C5
Toubkal, Parc National du *nat. park* Morocco 64 C5
Touboro Cameroon 121 E4
Toudaohu China 94 F4
Tougan Burkina Faso 120 C3
Touggourt Alg. 64 F5
Tougué Guinea 120 B3
Touil Mauritania 120 B3
Toul France 62 F6
Touliu Taiwan *see* Douliu
Toulon France 66 G5
Toulon *IL* U.S.A. 160 F3
Toulouse France 66 E5
Toumodi Côte d'Ivoire 120 C4
Toupai China 97 F3
Tourane Vietnam *see* Đa Nāng
Tourcoing France 62 D4
Tourgis Lake Canada 151 J1
Tourlaville France 59 F9
Tournai Belgium 62 D4
Tournon-sur-Rhône France 66 G4
Tournus France 68 A1
Touros Brazil 177 K5
Tours France 66 E3
Tousside, Pic *mt.* Chad 121 E2
Toussoro, Mont *mt.* Cent. Afr. Rep. 122 C3
Toutai China 90 B3
Touwsrivier S. Africa 124 E7
Toužim Czech Rep. 63 M4
Töv *prov.* Mongolia 94 F2
Tovarkovo Russia 53 G5
Tovil'-Dora Tajik. *see* Tavildara
Tovuz Azer. 113 G2
Towada Japan 90 F4
Towak Mountain *hill AK* U.S.A. 148 F3
Towanda *PA* U.S.A. 165 G3
Towaoc *CO* U.S.A. 159 I3
Towari *Celebes* Indon. 83 B4
Towcester U.K. 59 G6
Tower Ireland 61 D6
Towner *ND* U.S.A. 160 C1
Townes Pass *CA* U.S.A. 158 E3
Townsend *MT* U.S.A. 156 F3
Townsend, Mount Australia 138 D6
Townshend Island Australia 136 E4
Townsville Australia 136 D3
Towori, Teluk *b.* Indon. 83 B3
Towot South Sudan 121 G4
Towson *MD* U.S.A. 165 G4
Towuti, Danau *l.* Indon. 83 B3
Towyn U.K. *see* Tywyn
Toxkan He *r.* China 98 C4
Toy *NV* U.S.A. 158 D1
Toyah *TX* U.S.A. 161 C6
Toyama Japan 92 D2
Toyama *pref.* Japan 92 D2
Toyama-wan *b.* Japan 92 D1
Toyêma China 94 E5
Toygunen Russia 148 D2
Toyoake Japan 92 D3
Toyoda Japan 93 D4
Toyohashi Japan 92 D4
Toyokawa Japan 92 D4
Toyo-kawa *r.* Japan 92 D4
Toyonaka Japan 92 B4
Toyone Japan 92 D3
Toyono *Nagano* Japan 93 E2
Toyono *Ōsaka* Japan 92 B4
Toyooka *Hyōgo* Japan 92 A3
Toyooka *Nagano* Japan 93 D3
Toyooka *Shizuoka* Japan 93 D4
Toyota Japan 92 D3
Toyoyama Japan 92 C3
Tozanlı Turkey *see* Almus
Tozê Kangri *mt.* China 99 C6
Tozeur Tunisia 64 F5
Tozi, Mount *AK* U.S.A. 149 J2
Tozitna *r. AK* U.S.A. 148 I2
T'q'ibuli Georgia 113 F2
Traben Germany 62 H5
Trâblous Lebanon *see* Tripoli
Trabotivište Macedonia 69 J4
Trabzon Turkey 113 E2
Tracy *CA* U.S.A. 158 C3
Tracy *MN* U.S.A. 160 E2
Trading *r.* Canada 152 C4
Traer *IA* U.S.A. 160 E3
Trafalgar *IN* U.S.A. 164 B4
Trafalgar, Cabo *c.* Spain 67 C5
Traffic Mountain Canada 149 O3
Trail Canada 150 G5
Tràille, Rubha na *pt* U.K. 60 D5
Traill Island Greenland *see* Traill Ø
Traill Ø *i.* Greenland 147 P2
Trainor Lake Canada 150 F2
Trajectum Neth. *see* Utrecht
Trakai Lith. 55 N9
Tra Khuc, Sông *r.* Vietnam 86 E4
Trakiya *reg.* Europe *see* Thrace
Trakt Russia 52 K3
Trakya *reg.* Europe *see* Thrace
Tralee Ireland 61 C5
Tralee Bay Ireland 61 C5
Trá Li Ireland *see* Tralee
Tramandaí Brazil 179 A5
Tramán Tepuí *mt.* Venez. 176 F2
Trá Mhór Ireland *see* Tramore
Trâm Kák Cambodia 87 D5
Tramore Ireland 61 E5
Tranås Sweden 55 I7
Trancas Arg. 178 C3
Trancoso Brazil 179 D2
Tranemo Sweden 55 H8
Tranent U.K. 60 G5
Trang Thai. 87 B6
Trangan *i. Moluccas* Indon. 134 F1
Trang An *tourist site* Vietnam 86 D2
Trangie Australia 138 C4
Trân Ninh, Cao Nguyên Laos 86 C3
Transantarctic Mountains Antarctica 188 H2
Trans Canada Highway Canada 151 H5
Transnistria *disp. terr.* Moldova 53 F7
Transylvanian Alps *mts* Romania 69 J2
Transylvanian Basin *plat.* Romania 69 K1
Trapani *Sicily* Italy 68 E5
Trapezus Turkey *see* Trabzon
Trapper Creek *AK* U.S.A. 149 J3
Trapper Peak *MT* U.S.A. 156 E3
Trappes France 62 C6
Traralgon Australia 138 C7
Trashigang Bhutan 105 G4
Trasimeno, Lago *l.* Italy 68 E3
Trasvase, Canal de Spain 67 E4
Trat Thai. 87 C4
Tratani *r.* Pak. 111 H4
Traunsee *l.* Austria 57 N7
Traunstein Germany 57 N7
Travaillant Lake Canada 149 O2
Travellers Lake *imp. l.* Australia 137 C7
Travers, Mount N.Z. 139 D6
Traverse City *MI* U.S.A. 164 C1
Traverse Peak *hill AK* U.S.A. 148 H2
Tra Vinh Vietnam 87 D5
Travis, Lake *TX* U.S.A. 167 F2
Travnik Bos. & Herz. 68 G2
Trbovlje Slovenia 68 F1
Tre, Hon *i.* Vietnam 87 E4
Treasury Islands Solomon Is 132 F2
Treat Island *AK* U.S.A. 148 H2
Trebbin Germany 63 N2
Trebević, Nacionalni Park *nat. park* Bos. & Herz. 68 H3
Třebíč Czech Rep. 57 O6
Trebinje Bos. & Herz. 68 H3
Trebišov Slovakia 53 D6
Trebizond Turkey *see* Trabzon
Trebnje Slovenia 68 F2
Trebur Germany 63 I5
Trece Martires Phil. 82 C3
Tree Island India 106 B4
Trefaldwyn U.K. *see* Montgomery
Treffurt Germany 63 K3
Treffynnon U.K. *see* Holywell
Tref-y-clawdd U.K. *see* Knighton
Trefynwy U.K. *see* Monmouth
Tregosse Islets and Reefs Australia 136 E3
Treinta y Tres Uruguay 178 F4
Trelew Arg. 178 C6
Trelleborg Sweden 55 H9
Trélon France 62 E4
Tremblant, Mont *hill* Canada 152 G5
Trembleur Lake Canada 150 E4
Tremiti, Isole *is* Italy 68 F3
Tremont *PA* U.S.A. 165 G3
Tremonton *UT* U.S.A. 156 E4
Tremp Spain 67 G2
Trenance U.K. 59 B8
Trenary *MI* U.S.A. 162 C2
Trenche *r.* Canada 153 G5
Trenčín Slovakia 57 Q6
Trendelburg Germany 63 J3
Trêng Cambodia 87 C4
Trenggalek *Java* Indon. 85 E5
Terengganu *state* Malaysia *see* Terengganu
Trenque Lauquén Arg. 178 D5
Trent Italy *see* Trento
Trent *r.* U.K. 59 G5
Trento Italy 68 D1
Trenton Canada 165 G1
Trenton *FL* U.S.A. 163 D6
Trenton *GA* U.S.A. 163 C5
Trenton *KY* U.S.A. 164 B5
Trenton *MO* U.S.A. 160 E3
Trenton *NC* U.S.A. 163 E5

Trenton NE U.S.A. 160 C3

▶**Trenton** NJ U.S.A. 165 H3
Capital of New Jersey.

Treorchy U.K. 59 D7
Trepassey Canada 153 L5
Tres Arroyos Arg. 178 D5
Tresco i. U.K. 59 A9
Três Corações Brazil 179 B3
Tres Esquinas Col. 176 C3
Tres Forcas, Cabo c. Morocco see Trois Fourches, Cap des
Três Lagoas Brazil 179 A3
Três Marias, Represa resr Brazil 179 B2
Tres Picachos, Sierra mts Mex. 157 G7
Tres Picos, Cerro mt. Arg. 178 D5
Tres Picos, Cerro mt. Mex. 167 G5
Três Pontas Brazil 179 B3
Tres Puntas, Cabo c. Arg. 178 C7
Três Rios Brazil 179 C3
Tres Zapotes tourist site Mex. 167 G5
Tretiy Severnyy Russia 51 S3
Tretten Norway 55 G6
Treuchtlingen Germany 63 K6
Treuenbrietzen Germany 63 M2
Treungen Norway 55 F7
Treves Germany see Trier
Treviglio Italy 68 C2
Treviso Italy 68 E2
Trevose Head hd U.K. 59 B8
Tri An, Hô resr Vietnam 87 D5
Triánda Greece see Trianta
Triangle VA U.S.A. 165 G4
Trianta Greece 69 M6
Tribal Areas admin. div. Pak. 111 H3
Tribune KS U.S.A. 160 C4
Tricase Italy 68 H5
Trichinopoly India see Tiruchchirappalli
Trichur India see Thrissur
Tricot France 62 C5
Trida Australia 138 B4
Tridentum Italy see Trento
Trier Germany 62 G5
Trieste Italy 68 E2
Trieste, Golfo di g. Europe see Trieste, Gulf of
Trieste, Gulf of Europe 68 E2
Triglav mt. Slovenia 68 E1
Triglavski narodni park nat. park Slovenia 68 E1
Trikala Greece 69 I5
Trikkala Greece see Trikala

▶**Trikora, Puncak** mt. Indon. 81 J7
2nd highest mountain in Oceania.

Trim Ireland 61 F4
Trincheras Mex. 166 C2
Trincomalee Sri Lanka 106 D4
Trindade Brazil 179 A2
Trindade, Ilha da i. S. Atlantic Ocean 184 G7
Trinidad Bol. 176 F6
Trinidad Cuba 169 I4
Trinidad i. Trin. and Tob. 169 L6
Trinidad Uruguay 178 E4
Trinidad CO U.S.A. 157 G5
Trinidad country West Indies see Trinidad and Tobago
Trinidad and Tobago country West Indies 169 L6
Trinity TX U.S.A. 161 E6
Trinity r. CA U.S.A. 158 B1
Trinity r. TX U.S.A. 161 E6
Trinity Bay Canada 153 L5
Trinity Islands AK U.S.A. 148 I4
Trinity Range mts NV U.S.A. 158 D1
Trinkat Island India 87 A5
Trionto, Capo c. Italy 68 G5
Tripa r. Indon. 84 B2
Tripkau Germany 63 L1
Tripoli Greece 69 J6
Tripoli Lebanon 107 B2

▶**Tripoli** Libya 121 E1
Capital of Libya.

Trípolis Greece see Tripoli
Tripolis Lebanon see Tripoli
Tripolitania reg. Libya 120 E1
Tripunittura India 106 C4
Tripura state India 105 G5

▶**Tristan da Cunha** i. S. Atlantic Ocean 184 H8
Part of St Helena, Ascension and Tristan da Cunha.

Trisul mt. India 104 D3
Triton Canada 153 L4
Triton Island atoll Paracel Is 80 E3
Trittau Germany 63 K1
Trittenheim Germany 62 G5
Trivandrum India see Thiruvananthapuram
Trivento Italy 68 F4
Trnava Slovakia 57 P6
Trobriand Islands P.N.G. 132 F2
Trochu Canada 150 H5
Trofors Norway 54 H4
Trogir Croatia 68 G3
Troia Italy 68 F4
Troisdorf Germany 63 H4
Trois Fourches, Cap des c. Morocco 67 E6
Trois-Ponts Belgium 62 F4
Trois-Rivières Canada 153 G5
Troitsko-Pechorsk Russia 51 R3
Troitskoye Altayskiy Kray Russia 88 E2
Troitskoye Khabarovskiy Kray Russia 90 E2
Troitskoye Respublika Kalmykiya-Khalm'g-Tangch Russia 53 J7
Troll research station Antarctica 188 C2
Trollhättan Sweden 55 H7
Trombetas r. Brazil 177 G4
Tromelin, Île i. Indian Ocean 185 L7
Tromelin Island Micronesia see Fais
Tromen, Volcán vol. Arg. 178 B5
Tromie r. U.K. 60 E3
Trompsburg S. Africa 125 G6
Tromsø Norway 54 K2
Trona CA U.S.A. 158 E4
Tronador, Monte mt. Arg. 178 B6
Trondheim Norway 54 G5
Trondheimsfjorden sea chan. Norway 54 F5
Trongsa Bhutan 105 G4
Trongsa Chhu r. Bhutan 99 E8
Troödos Mountains Cyprus 107 A2
Troon U.K. 60 E5
Tropeiros, Serra dos hills Brazil 179 B1
Tropic UT U.S.A. 159 G3
Tropic of Cancer 161 B8
Tropic of Capricorn 136 G4
Trosh Russia 52 L2
Trostan hill U.K. 61 F2
Trout r. B.C. Canada 150 E3
Trout r. N.W.T. Canada 150 G2
Trout Lake Alta Canada 150 H3
Trout Lake N.W.T. Canada 150 F2
Trout Lake l. N.W.T. Canada 150 F2
Trout Lake l. Ont. Canada 151 M5
Trout Peak WY U.S.A. 156 F3
Trout Run PA U.S.A. 165 G3
Trouville-sur-Mer France 59 H9
Trowbridge U.K. 59 E7
Troy tourist site Turkey 69 L5
Troy AL U.S.A. 163 C6
Troy KS U.S.A. 160 E4
Troy MI U.S.A. 164 D2
Troy MO U.S.A. 160 F4
Troy MT U.S.A. 156 E2
Troy NH U.S.A. 165 I2
Troy NY U.S.A. 165 I2
Troy OH U.S.A. 164 C3
Troy PA U.S.A. 165 G3
Troyan Bulg. 69 K3
Troyes France 66 G2
Troy Lake CA U.S.A. 158 E4
Troy Peak NV U.S.A. 159 F2
Trstenik Serbia 69 I3
Truc Giang Vietnam see Bên Tre
Trucial States country Asia see United Arab Emirates
Trud Russia 52 G4
Trufanova Russia 52 J2
Trujillo Hond. 166 [inset] I6
Trujillo Peru 176 C5
Trujillo Spain 67 D4
Trujillo Venez. 176 D2
Trujillo, Monte mt. Dom. Rep. see Duarte, Pico
Truk is Micronesia see Chuuk
Trulben Germany 63 H5
Trumbull, Mount AZ U.S.A. 159 G3
Trumon Sumatra Indon. 84 B2
Trundle Australia 138 C4
Trưng Hiệp Vietnam 86 D4
Trưng Khanh Vietnam 86 D2
Truong Sa is S. China Sea see Spratly Islands
Truro Canada 153 J5
Truro U.K. 59 B8
Trusan Sarawak Malaysia 85 F1
Trusan r. Malaysia 85 F1
Truskmore hill Ireland 61 D3
Trus Madi, Gunung mt. Malaysia 85 G1
Trutch Canada 150 F3
Truth or Consequences NM U.S.A. 157 G6
Trutnov Czech Rep. 57 O5
Truuli Peak AK U.S.A. 149 J4
Truva tourist site Turkey see Troy
Trypiti, Akra pt Greece see Trypiti, Akrotirio
Trypiti, Akrotirio pt Greece 69 K7
Trysil Norway 55 H6
Trzebiatów Poland 57 O3
Tsagaannuur Bayan-Ölgiy Mongolia 94 B1
Tsagaannuur Dornod Mongolia see Halhgol
Tsagaan-Olom Mongolia see Tayshir
Tsagaan-Ovoo Dornod Mongolia 95 H1
Tsagaan-Ovoo Övörhangay Mongolia see Nariynteel
Tsagaan-Uul Mongolia 94 D1
Tsagaan-Üür Mongolia 94 E1
Tsagan Aman Russia 53 J7
Tsagan Nur Russia 53 J7
Tsaidam Basin basin China see Qaidam Pendi
Tsaka La pass China/India 104 D2
Ts'alenjikha Georgia 113 F2
Tsaratanana, Massif du mts Madag. 123 E5
Tsarevo Bulg. 69 L3
Tsaris Mountains Namibia 124 C3
Tsaritsyn Russia see Volgograd
Tsast Uul mt. Mongolia 94 B1
Tsaukaib Namibia 124 B4
Tsavo East National Park Kenya 122 D4
Tsavo West National Park Africa 122 D3
Tseel Mongolia 94 C2
Tsefat Israel see Ẓefat
Tselinograd Kazakh. see Astana
Tsengel Bayan-Ölgiy Mongolia 94 B1
Tsengel Hövsgöl Mongolia see Tosontsengel
Tsenhermandal Mongolia 95 G2
Tsenogora Russia 52 J2
Tses Namibia 124 D3
Tsetseg Mongolia 94 C2
Tsetsegnuur Mongolia see Tsetseg
Tsetseng Botswana 124 F2
Tsetserleg Arhangay Mongolia 94 E1
Tsetserleg Arhangay Mongolia 94 E2
Tsetserleg Hövsgöl Mongolia 94 D1
Tshabong Botswana 124 F4
Tshad country Africa see Chad
Tshane Botswana 124 E3
Tshela Dem. Rep. Congo 123 B4
Tshibala Dem. Rep. Congo 123 C4
Tshikapa Dem. Rep. Congo 123 C4
Tshing S. Africa 125 H4
Tshipise S. Africa 125 J2
Tshitanzu Dem. Rep. Congo 123 C4
Tshofa Dem. Rep. Congo 123 C4
Tshokwane S. Africa 125 J3
Tsholotsho Zimbabwe 123 C5
Tshootsha Botswana 124 E2
Tshuapa r. Dem. Rep. Congo 121 F5
Tshwane S. Africa see Pretoria
Tsiigehtchic Canada 149 N2
Tsil'ma r. Russia 52 K2
Tsimlyansk Russia 53 I7
Tsimlyanskoye Vodokhranilishche resr Russia 53 I7
Tsimmermanovka Russia 90 E2
Tsinan China see Jinan
Tsineng S. Africa 124 F4
Tsinghai prov. China see Qinghai
Tsing Shan Wan H.K. China see Castle Peak Bay
Tsingtao China see Qingdao
Tsing Yi i. H.K. China 97 [inset]
Tsining China see Ulan Qab
Tsiombe Madag. 123 E6
Tsiroanomandidy Madag. 123 E5
Tsitsihar China see Qiqihar
Tsitsutl Peak Canada 150 E4
Tsivil'sk Russia 52 J5
Tskhaltubo Georgia see Ts'q'alt'ubo

▶**Tskhinvali** Georgia 113 F2
Capital of South Ossetia.

Tsna r. Russia 53 I5
Ts'nori Georgia 113 G2
Tsogt Mongolia 94 D2
Tsogt-Ovoo Mongolia 94 F2
Tsogttsetsiy Mongolia 94 F3
Tsokar Chumo l. India 104 D2
Tsolo S. Africa 125 I6
Tsomo S. Africa 125 H7
Tsona China see Cona
Ts'q'alt'ubo Georgia 113 F2
Tsu Japan 92 C4
Tsubata Japan 92 C2
Tsuchiura Japan 93 G2
Tsuchiyama Japan 92 C4
Tsuen Wan H.K. China 97 [inset]
Tsuga Japan 93 F2
Tsugarū-kaikyō strait Japan 90 F4
Tsugaru Strait Japan see Tsugarū-kaikyō
Tsuge Japan 92 B4
Tsugu Japan 92 D3
Tsukechi Japan 92 D3
Tsukigase Japan 92 C4
Tsukiyono Japan see Minakami
Tsukuba Japan 93 G2
Tsukubamirai Japan 93 G3
Tsukude Japan 92 D4
Tsukui Japan 93 F3
Tsumagoi Japan 93 E2
Tsumeb Namibia 123 B5
Tsumeki-zaki pt Japan 93 E4
Tsumis Park Namibia 124 C2
Tsumkwe Namibia 123 C5
Tsuna Japan see Awaji
Tsunan Japan 93 E1
Tsunega-misaki pt Japan 92 B3
Tsuru Japan 93 E3
Tsuruga Japan 92 C3
Tsuruga-wan b. Japan 92 B3
Tsurugi Japan 92 C2
Tsurugi-dake mt. Japan 92 D2
Tsurugi-san mt. Japan 91 D6
Tsurukhaytuy Russia see Priargunsk
Tsuruoka Japan 91 E5
Tsushima Aichi Japan 92 C3
Tsushima Nagasaki Japan 91 C6
Tsushima is Japan 91 C6
Tsushima-kaikyō strait Japan/S. Korea see Korea Strait
Tsuyama Japan 91 D6
Tswaane Botswana 124 E2
Tswaraganang S. Africa 125 G5
Tswelelang S. Africa 125 G4
Tsyelyakhany Belarus 55 N10
Tsypnavolok Russia 54 R2
Tsyurupyns'k Ukr. 69 O1
Tthedzeh Koe Canada see Wrigley
Tthenaagoo Canada see Nahanni Butte
Tu, Nam r. Myanmar 86 B2
Tua Dem. Rep. Congo 122 B4
Tua, Tanjung pt Indon. 84 D4
Tual Moluccas Indon. 81 I8
Tuam Ireland 61 D4
Tuamotu Archipelago is Fr. Polynesia see Tuamotu Islands
Tuamotu Islands Fr. Polynesia 187 K6
Tuân Giao Vietnam 86 C2
Tuangku i. Indon. 84 B2
Tuapse Russia 112 E1
Tuaran Sabah Malaysia 85 G1
Tuas Sing. 87 [inset]
Tuath, Loch a' b. U.K. 60 C2
Tuba City AZ U.S.A. 159 H3
Tubalai i. Moluccas Indon. 83 D3
Tuban Java Indon. 85 F4
Tubarão Brazil 179 A5
Tubarjal Saudi Arabia 107 D4
Tubau Sarawak Malaysia 85 F2
Tubbataha Reefs Phil. 82 B4
Tubigan i. Phil. 82 C5
Tübingen Germany 57 L6
Tubmanburg Liberia 120 B4
Tubod Mindanao Phil. 82 C4
Tubruq Libya 112 A4
Tubu r. Indon. 85 G2
Tubuai i. Fr. Polynesia 187 K7
Tubuai Islands Fr. Polynesia 187 J7
Tubutama Mex. 166 C2
Tucano Brazil 177 K6
Tucavaca Bol. 177 G7
Tüchen Germany 63 M1
Tuchheim Germany 63 M2
Tuchitua Canada 149 O3
Tuchodi r. Canada 150 F3
Tuckerton NJ U.S.A. 165 H4
Tucopia i. Solomon Is see Tikopia
Tucson AZ U.S.A. 159 H5
Tucson Mountains AZ U.S.A. 159 H5
Tuctuc r. Canada 153 I2
Tucumán Arg. see San Miguel de Tucumán
Tucumcari NM U.S.A. 161 C5
Tucupita Venez. 176 F2
Tucuruí Brazil 177 I4
Tucuruí, Represa de resr Brazil 177 I4
Tudela Spain 67 F2
Tuder Italy see Todi
Tüdevtey Mongolia 94 D1
Tudun Wada Nigeria 120 D3
Tuela r. Port. 67 C3
Tuen Mun H.K. China 97 [inset]
Tuensang India 105 H4
Tufts Abyssal Plain sea feature N. Pacific Ocean 187 K2
Tugidak Island AK U.S.A. 148 I4
Tuglung China 99 F7
Tuguan Maputi i. Indon. 83 A2
Tugubun Point Mindanao Phil. 82 D5
Tuguegarao Luzon Phil. 82 C2
Tugur Russia 90 E1
Tugyl Kazakh. 98 D3
Tuhemberua Sumatra Indon. 84 B2
Tujiabu China see Yongxiu
Tujuh, Kepulauan is Indon. 84 D3
Tujung Kalimantan Indon. 85 G2
Tukangbesi, Kepulauan is Indon. 83 B4
Tukarak Island Canada 152 F2
Ṭukhmān, Banī reg. Saudi Arabia 110 C6
Tŭkhtamish Tajik. 99 A5
Tukituki r. N.Z. 139 F4
Tuklung AK U.S.A. 148 H4
Tuktoyaktuk Canada 149 N1
Tuktut Nogait National Park Canada 149 Q1
Tuktuujaartuq Canada see Tuktoyaktuk
Tukums Latvia 55 M8
Tukung, Bukit mt. Indon. 85 E3
Tukuringra, Khrebet mts Russia 90 B1
Tukuyu Tanz. 123 D4
Tukzār Afgh. 111 G3
Tula Mex. 167 F4
Tula Russia 53 H5
Tulach Mhór Ireland see Tullamore
Tulagt Ar Gol r. China 99 F5
Tulai China 94 D4
Tulai Nanshan mts China 94 D4
Tulai Shan mts China 94 D4
Tūlak Afgh. 111 F3
Tulameen Canada 150 F5
Tula Mountains Antarctica 188 D2
Tulancingo Mex. 168 E4
Tulangbawang r. Indon. 84 D4
Tulare CA U.S.A. 158 D3
Tulare Lake Bed CA U.S.A. 158 D4
Tularosa NM U.S.A. 166 D1
Tularosa Mountains NM U.S.A. 159 I5
Tulasi mt. India 106 D2
Tulbagh S. Africa 124 D7
Tulcán Ecuador 176 C3
Tulcea Romania 69 M2
Tule r. TX U.S.A. 161 C5
Tuléar Madag. see Toliara
Tulehu Moluccas Indon. 83 D3
Tulemalu Lake Canada 151 L2
Tule Mod China 95 J2
Tulia TX U.S.A. 161 C5
Tulihe China 95 J1
Tulita Canada 149 P2
Tulkarem West Bank see Ṭūlkarm
Ṭūlkarm West Bank 107 B3
Tulla Ireland 61 D5
Tullahoma TN U.S.A. 162 C5
Tullamore Australia 138 C4
Tullamore Ireland 61 E4
Tulle France 66 E4
Tulleråsen Sweden 54 I5
Tullibigeal Australia 138 C4
Tullos LA U.S.A. 167 G2
Tullow Ireland 61 F5
Tully Australia 136 D3
Tully r. Australia 136 D3
Tully U.K. 61 E3
Tulos Russia 54 Q5
Tulqarem West Bank see Ṭūlkarm
Tulsa OK U.S.A. 161 E4
Tulsipur Nepal 105 E3
Tuluá Col. 176 C3
Tuluksak AK U.S.A. 148 G3
Tulūl al Ashāqif hills Jordan 107 C3
Tulum tourist site Mex. 167 I4
Tulun Russia 88 I2
Tulungagung Java Indon. 85 E5
Tulu-Tuloi, Serra hills Brazil 176 F3
Tulu Welel mt. Eth. 122 D3
Tuma r. Nicaragua 166 [inset] I6
Tuma Russia 53 I5
Tumaco Col. 176 C3
Tumahole S. Africa 125 H4
Tumain China 99 E6
Tumakuru India 106 C3
Tumannyy Russia 54 S2
Tumasik Sing. see Singapore
Tumba Dem. Rep. Congo 122 C4
Tumba Sweden 55 J7
Tumba, Lac l. Dem. Rep. Congo 122 B4
Tumbangmiri Kalimantan Indon. 85 F3
Tumbangsamba Kalimantan Indon. 85 F3
Tumbangsenamang Kalimantan Indon. 85 F3
Tumbangtiti Kalimantan Indon. 85 E3
Tumbarumba Australia 138 D5
Tumbes Peru 176 B4
Tumbiscatio Mex. 166 E5
Tumbler Ridge Canada 150 F4
Tumby Bay Australia 137 B7
Tumd Youqi China see Salaqi
Tumd Zuoqi China see Qasq
Tumen Jilin China 90 C4
Tumen Shaanxi China 97 F1
Tumereng Guyana 176 F2
Tumindao i. Phil. 82 B5
Tumiritinga Brazil 179 C2
Tumkur India see Tumakuru
Tummel r. U.K. 60 F4
Tummel, Loch l. U.K. 60 F4
Tumnin r. Russia 90 F2
Tump Pak. 111 F5
Tumpah Kalimantan Indon. 85 F3
Tumpat Malaysia 84 C1
Tumpôr, Phnum mt. Cambodia 87 C4
Tumpu, Gunung mt. Indon. 83 B3
Tumputiga, Gunung mt. Indon. 83 B3
Tumshuk Uzbek. 111 G2
Tumu Ghana 120 C3
Tumucumaque, Serra hills Brazil 177 G3
Tumudibandh India 106 D2
Tumut Australia 138 D5
Tumxuk China 98 C4
Tuna India 104 B5
Tuna Bay Mindanao Phil. 82 D5
Ṭunb al Kubrá i. The Gulf see Tonb-e Bozorg, Jazīreh-ye
Ṭunb aş Şughrá i. The Gulf see Tonb-e Küchek, Jazīreh-ye
Tunceli Turkey 113 E3
Tunchang China 97 F5
Tuncurry Australia 138 F4
Tundī imp. l. Afgh. 111 F3
Tunduru Tanz. 123 D5
Tunes Tunisia see Tunis
Tunga Nigeria 120 D4
Tungabhadra Reservoir India 106 C3
Tungawan Mindanao Phil. 82 C5
Tungi Bangl. 105 G5
Tungku Sabah Malaysia 85 G1
Tungla Nicaragua 166 [inset] I6
Tung Lung Island i. H.K. China 97 [inset]
Tungnaá r. Iceland 54 [inset 1]
Tungor Russia 90 F1
Tung Pok Liu Hoi Hap H.K. China see East Lamma Channel
Tung-sheng China see Dongsheng
Tungsten (abandoned) Canada 149 O3
Tungun, Bukit mt. Indon. 85 F2
Tung Wan b. H.K. China 97 [inset]
Tuni India 106 D2
Tūnī, Chāh-e well Iran 110 E3
Tunica MS U.S.A. 161 F5
Tūnis country Africa see Tunisia

▶**Tunis** Tunisia 68 D6
Capital of Tunisia.

Tunis, Golfe de g. Tunisia 68 D6
Tunisia country Africa 64 F5
Tunja Col. 176 D2
Tunkhannock PA U.S.A. 165 H3
Tunki Nicaragua 166 [inset] I6
Tunliu China 95 H4
Tunnsjøen l. Norway 54 H4
Tunstall U.K. 59 I6
Tuntsa Fin. 54 P3
Tuntsajoki r. Fin./Russia see Tuntsayoki
Tuntsayoki r. Fin./Russia 54 Q3 *also known as Tuntsajoki*
Tuntutuliak AK U.S.A. 148 G3
Tunulic r. Canada 153 I2
Tununak AK U.S.A. 148 F3
Tunungayualok Island Canada 153 J2
Tunxi China see Huangshan
Tuodian China see Shuangbai
Tuo He r. China 95 I5
Tuojiang China see Fenghuang
Tuŏl Khpós Cambodia 87 D5
Tuoniang Jiang r. China 96 E3
Tuoputiereke China see Jeminay
Tuotuoheyan China see Tanggulashan
Tüp Kyrg. 102 E3
Tupã Brazil 179 A3
Tupelo MS U.S.A. 161 F5
Tupik Russia 89 L2
Tupinambarama, Ilha i. Brazil 177 G4
Tupiraçaba Brazil 179 A1
Tupiza Bol. 176 E8
Tupper Canada 150 F4
Tupper Lake NY U.S.A. 165 H1
Tupper Lake l. NY U.S.A. 165 H1

▶**Tupungato, Cerro** mt. Arg./Chile 178 C4
5th highest mountain in South America.

Tuqayyid well Iraq 110 B4
Tuquan China 95 J2
Tuqu Wan b. China see Lingshui Wan
Tura China 99 D5
Tura India 105 G4
Tura Russia 77 L3
Turabah Saudi Arabia 108 F5
Turakina N.Z. 139 E5
Turan Russia 88 G2
Turana, Khrebet mts Russia 90 C2
Turan Lowland Asia 102 A4
Turan Oypaty lowland Asia see Turan Lowland
Turan Pesligi lowland Asia see Turan Lowland
Turanskaya Nizmennost' lowland Asia see Turan Lowland
Ṭurāq al 'Ilab hills Syria 107 D3
Turar Ryskulov Kazakh. 102 D3
Tura-Ryskulova Kazakh. see Turar Ryskulov
Ṭurayf Saudi Arabia 107 D4
Ṭurayf, Kutayfat vol. Saudi Arabia 107 D4
Turba Estonia 55 N7
Turbat Pak. 111 F5
Turbo Col. 176 C2
Turda Romania 69 J1
Tūreh Iran 110 C3
Turfan China see Turpan
Turfan Depression China see Turpan Pendi
Turgayskaya Dolina valley Kazakh. 102 B2
Türgen Uul mt. Mongolia 94 B1
Türgen Uul mts Mongolia 94 B1
Turgutlu Turkey 69 L5
Turhal Turkey 112 E2
Türi Estonia 55 N7
Turia r. Spain 67 F4
Turin Canada 151 H5
Turin Italy 68 B2
Turiy Rog Russia 90 C3

▶**Turkana, Lake** salt l. Eth./Kenya 122 D3
5th largest lake in Africa.

Turkestan Range mts Asia 111 G2
Turkey country Asia/Europe 112 D3
Turkey KY U.S.A. 164 D5
Turkey r. IA U.S.A. 160 F3
Turki Russia 53 I6
Turkish Republic of Northern Cyprus disp. terr. Asia see Northern Cyprus
Türkistan Kazakh. see Turkistan
Turkistan Kazakh. 102 C3
Turkistān, Silsilah-ye Band-e mts Afgh. 111 F3
Türkiye country Asia/Europe see Turkey
Türkmenabat Turkm. 111 F2
Türkmen Adasy i. Turkm. see Ogurjaly Adasy
Türkmen Aýlagy b. Turkm. 110 D2
Türkmen Aýlagy b. Turkm. see Türkmen Aýlagy
Türkmenbaşy Turkm. see Türkmenbaşy
Türkmenbaşy Turkm. 110 D1
Türkmenbaşy Aýlagy b. Turkm. 110 D2
Türkmenbaşy Aýlagy b. Turkm. see Türkmenbaşy Aýlagy
Türkmenbaşy Döwlet Gorugy nature res. Turkm. 110 D2
Türkmen Dağı mt. Turkey 69 N5
Turkmenistan country Asia 109 I2
Turkmeniya country Asia see Turkmenistan
Türkmenostan country Asia see Turkmenistan
Turkmenskaya S.S.R. country Asia see Turkmenistan
Türkoğlu Turkey 112 E3

▶**Turks and Caicos Islands** terr. West Indies 169 J4
United Kingdom Overseas Territory.

Turks Island Passage Turks and Caicos Is 163 G8
Turks Islands Turks and Caicos Is 169 J4
Turku Fin. 55 M6
Turkwel watercourse Kenya 122 D3
Turlock CA U.S.A. 158 C3
Turlock Lake CA U.S.A. 158 C3
Turmalina Brazil 179 C2
Turnagain r. Canada 150 E3
Turnagain, Cape N.Z. 139 F5
Turnberry U.K. 60 E5
Turnbull, Mount AZ U.S.A. 159 H5
Turneffe Islands atoll Belize 167 I5
Turner MI U.S.A. 164 D1
Turner Valley Canada 150 H5
Turnhout Belgium 62 E3
Turnor Lake Canada 151 I3
Türnovo Bulg. see Veliko Tarnovo
Turnu Măgurele Romania 69 K3
Turnu Severin Romania see Drobeta-Turnu Severin
Turon r. Australia 138 D4
Turones France see Tours
Turon pasttekisligi lowland Asia see Turan Lowland
Turovets Russia 52 I4
Turpan China 98 E4

▶**Turpan Pendi** depr. China 98 E4
Lowest point in northern Asia.

Turpan Zhan China 98 E4
Turquino, Pico mt. Cuba 169 I4
Turrialba Costa Rica 166 [inset] J7
Turriff U.K. 60 G3
Turris Libisonis Sardinia Italy see Porto Torres
Tursāq Iraq 113 G4
Turtle Island Fiji see Vatoa
Turtle Islands Phil. 82 B5
Turtle Lake Canada 151 I4
Turugart Pass China/Kyrg. 102 E3
Turugart Shankou pass China/Kyrg. see Turugart Pass
Turuvanur India 106 C3
Turvo r. Goiás Brazil 179 A2
Turvo r. São Paulo Brazil 179 A2
Tusayan AZ U.S.A. 159 G4
Tuscaloosa AL U.S.A. 163 C5
Tuscarawas r. OH U.S.A. 164 E3
Tuscarora Mountains hills PA U.S.A. 165 G3
Tuscola IL U.S.A. 160 F4
Tuscola TX U.S.A. 161 D5
Tuscumbia AL U.S.A. 163 C5
Tüshig Mongolia 94 F1
Tuskegee AL U.S.A. 163 C5
Tussey Mountains hills PA U.S.A. 165 F3
Tustin MI U.S.A. 164 C1
Tustumena Lake AK U.S.A. 149 J3
Tutak Turkey 113 F3
Tutayev Russia 52 H4
Tutera Spain see Tudela
Tuticorin India 106 C4
Tutoh r. Malaysia 85 F2
Tutong Brunei 85 F1

Tuttle Creek Reservoir *KS* U.S.A. **160** D4
Tuttlingen Germany **57** L7
Tuttut Nunaat *reg.* Greenland **147** P2
Tutuala East Timor **83** C5
Tutubu P.N.G. **136** E1
Tutubu Tanz. **123** D4
Tutuila *i.* American Samoa **133** I3
Tutume Botswana **123** C6
Tututalak Mountain *AK* U.S.A. **148** G2
Tututepec Mex. **167** F5
Tutwiler *MS* U.S.A. **161** F5
Tuul Gol *r.* Mongolia **94** F1
Tuun-bong *mt.* N. Korea **90** B4
Tuupovaara Fin. **54** Q5
Tuusniemi Fin. **54** P5
Tuva *aut. rep.* Russia *see* **Tyva, Respublika**
Tuvalu *country* S. Pacific Ocean **133** H2
Tuvinskaya A.S.S.R. *aut. rep.* Russia *see* **Tyva, Respublika**
Tüvshinshiree Mongolia **95** G2
Tuwau *r.* Indon. **85** G2
Tuwayq, Jabal *hills* Saudi Arabia **108** G4
Tuwayq, Jabal *mts* Saudi Arabia **108** G5
Ţuwayyil ash Shihāq *mt.* Jordan **107** C4
Tuwwal Saudi Arabia **108** E5
Tuxpan *Jalisco* Mex. **166** E5
Tuxpan *Nayarit* Mex. **166** D4
Tuxpan *Veracruz* Mex. **168** E4
Tuxtla Gutiérrez Mex. **167** G5
Tuya Lake Canada **149** O4
Tuyên Quang Vietnam **86** D2
Tuy Hoa Vietnam **87** E4
Tuyyk Kazakh. **98** B4
Tuz, Lake *salt l.* Turkey **112** D3
Tuz Gölü *salt l.* Turkey *see* **Tuz, Lake**
Tuzha Russia **52** J4
Tuz Khurmātū Iraq **113** G4
Tuzla Bos. & Herz. **68** H2
Tuzla Turkey **107** B1
Tuzla Gölü *lag.* Turkey **69** L4
Tuzlov *r.* Russia **53** I7
Tuzu *r.* Myanmar **86** A1
Tvedestrand Norway **55** F7
Tver' Russia **52** G4
Twain Harte *CA* U.S.A. **158** C2
Tweed Canada **165** G1
Tweed *r.* U.K. **60** G5
Tweed Heads Australia **138** F2
Tweedie Canada **151** I4
Tweefontein S. Africa **124** D7
Twee Rivier Namibia **124** D3
Twentekanaal *canal* Neth. **62** G2
Twentynine Palms *CA* U.S.A. **158** E4
Twin Bridges *CA* U.S.A. **158** C2
Twin Bridges *MT* U.S.A. **156** E3
Twin Buttes Reservoir *TX* U.S.A. **161** C6
Twin Falls Canada **153** I3
Twin Falls *ID* U.S.A. **156** E4
Twin Heads *hill* Australia **134** D5
Twin Hills *AK* U.S.A. **148** G4
Twin Mountain *AK* U.S.A. **148** H3
Twin Peak *CA* U.S.A. **158** C2
Twistringen Germany **63** I2
Twitchen Reservoir *CA* U.S.A. **158** C4
Twitya *r.* Canada **149** O2
Twizel N.Z. **139** C7
Twofold Bay Australia **138** D6
Two Harbors *MN* U.S.A. **160** F2
Two Hills Canada **151** I4
Two Rivers *WI* U.S.A. **164** B1
Tyan' Shan' *mts* China/Kyrg. *see* **Tien Shan**
Tyao *r.* India/Myanmar **96** B4
Tyatya, Vulkan *vol.* Russia **90** G3
Tydal Norway **54** G5
Tygart Valley *WV* U.S.A. **164** F4
Tygda Russia **90** B1
Tygda *r.* Russia **90** B1
Tyler *TX* U.S.A. **161** E5
Tylertown *MS* U.S.A. **161** F6
Tym' *r.* Russia **90** F2
Tymna, Laguna *lag.* Russia **148** B2
Tymovskoye Russia **90** F2
Tynda Russia **89** M1
Tyndall *SD* U.S.A. **160** D3
Tyndinskiy Russia *see* **Tynda**
Tyne *r.* U.K. **60** G4
Tynemouth U.K. **58** F3
Tyngekveyem *r.* Russia **148** B2
Tynset Norway **54** G5
Tyone *r. AK* U.S.A. **149** K3
Tyonek *AK* U.S.A. **149** J3
Tyoploozyorsk Russia *see* **Teploozersk**
Tyoploye Ozero Russia *see* **Teploozersk**
Tyr Lebanon *see* **Tyre**
Tyras Ukr. *see* **Bilhorod-Dnistrovs'kyy**
Tyre Lebanon **107** B3
Tyree, Mount Antarctica **188** L1
Tyrma Russia **90** D2
Tyrma *r.* Russia **90** C2
Tyrnävä Fin. **54** N4
Tyrnavos Greece **69** J5
Tyrnyauz Russia **113** F2
Tyrone *NM* U.S.A. **166** C1
Tyrone *PA* U.S.A. **165** F3
Tyrrell *r.* Australia **138** A5
Tyrrell, Lake *dry lake* Australia **137** C7
Tyrrell Lake Canada **151** J2
Tyrrhenian Sea France/Italy **68** D4
Tyrus Lebanon *see* **Tyre**
Tysa *r.* Serbia *see* **Tisa**
Tyukalinsk Russia **76** I4
Tyulen'i, Ostrova *is* Kazakh. **113** H1
Tyumen' Russia **76** H4
Tyup Kyrg. *see* **Tüp**
Tyuratam Kazakh. *see* **Baykonyr**
Tyva, Respublika *aut. rep.* Russia **94** D1
Tywi *r.* U.K. **59** C7
Tywyn U.K. **59** C6
Tzaneen S. Africa **125** J2
Tzia *i.* Greece **69** K6
Tzucacab Mex. **167** H4

Uaco Congo Angola *see* **Waku-Kungo**
Ualan *atoll* Micronesia *see* **Kosrae**
Uamanda Angola **123** C5
Uarc, Ras *c.* Morocco *see* **Trois Fourches, Cap des**
Uaroo Australia **135** A5
Uatumã *r.* Brazil **177** G4
Uauá Brazil **177** K5
Uaupés *r.* Brazil **176** E3
Uaxactún Guat. **167** H5
U'aylī, Wādī al *watercourse* Saudi Arabia **107** D4
U'aywij *well* Saudi Arabia **110** B4
U'aywij, Wādī al *watercourse* Saudi Arabia **113** F5
Ubá Brazil **179** C3
Ubaí Brazil **179** B2
Ubaitaba Brazil **179** D1
Ubangi *r.* Cent. Afr. Rep./Dem. Rep. Congo **122** B4
Ubangi-Shari *country* Africa *see* **Central African Republic**
Ubauro Pak. **111** H4
Ubayyiḍ, Wādī al *watercourse* Iraq/Saudi Arabia **113** F4
Ube Japan **91** C6
Úbeda Spain **67** E4
Uberaba Brazil **179** B2
Uberlândia Brazil **179** A2
Ubin, Pulau *i.* Sing. **87** [inset]
Ubiña, Peña *mt.* Spain **67** D2
Ubly *MI* U.S.A. **164** D2
Ubolratna, Ang Kep Nam Thai. **86** C3
Ubombo S. Africa **125** K4
Ubon Ratchathani Thai. **86** D4
Ubstadt-Weiher Germany **63** I5
Ubundu Dem. Rep. Congo **121** F5
Üçajy Turkm. **111** F2
Ucar Azer. **113** G2
Uçarı Turkey **107** A1
Ucayali *r.* Peru **176** D4
Uch Pak. **111** H4
Üchajy Turkm. *see* **Üçajy**
Üchān Iran **110** C2
Uchigō Japan **93** G1
Uchihara Japan **93** G2
Uchimura-gawa *r.* Japan **93** E2
Uchinada Japan **92** C2
Uchiura-wan *b.* Japan **90** F4
Uchiyama-tōge *pass* Japan **93** E2
Uchkeken Russia **113** F2
Uchkuduk Uzbek. *see* **Uchquduq**
Uchquduq Uzbek. **102** B3
Uchte Germany **63** I2
Uchte *r.* Germany **63** L2
Uchur *r.* Russia **77** O4
Uckermark *reg.* Germany **63** N1
Uckfield U.K. **59** H8
Ucluelet Canada **150** E5
Ucross *WY* U.S.A. **156** G3
Ud China **94** F4
Uda Japan **92** B4
Uda *r.* Russia **89** J2
Uda *r.* Russia **90** D1
Udachnoye Russia **53** J7
Udachnyy Russia **189** E2
Udagamandalam India **106** C4
Udaipur *Rajasthan* India **104** C4
Udaipur *Tripura* India **105** G5
Udanti *r.* India/Myanmar **105** E5
Uday *r.* Ukr. **53** G6
'Udaynān *well* Saudi Arabia **110** C6
Uddevalla Sweden **55** G7
Uddingston U.K. **60** E5
Uddjaure *l.* Sweden **54** J4
'Udeid, Khōr al *inlet* Qatar **110** C5
Uden Neth. **62** F3
Udgir India **106** C2
Udhagamandalam India *see* **Udagamandalam**
Udhampur India **104** C2
Udia-Milai *atoll* Marshall Is *see* **Bikini**
Udimskiy Russia **52** J3
Udine Italy **68** E1
Udit India **111** I5
Udjuktok Bay Canada **153** J3
Udmalaippettai India *see* **Udumalaippettai**
Udomlya Russia **52** G4
Udone-jima *i.* Japan **93** F4
Udon Thani Thai. **86** C3
Udskaya Guba *b.* Russia **77** O4
Udskoye Russia **90** D1
Udumalaippettai India **106** C4
Udupi India **106** B3
Udyl', Ozero *l.* Russia **90** E1
Udzhary Azer. *see* **Ucar**
Udzungwa Mountains National Park Tanz. **123** D4
Uéa *atoll* New Caledonia *see* **Ouvéa**
Uebonti *Celebes* Indon. **83** B3
Ueckermünde Germany **57** O4
Ueda Japan **93** E2
Uekuli *Celebes* Indon. **83** B3
Uele *r.* Dem. Rep. Congo **122** C3
Uelen Russia **148** E2
Uel'kal' Russia **148** C2
Uelzen Germany **63** K2
Ueno *Gunma* Japan **93** E2
Ueno *Mie* Japan *see* **Iga**
Uenohara Japan **93** F3
Uetersen Germany **63** J1
Uettingen Germany **63** J5
Uetze Germany **63** K2
Ufa Russia **51** R5
Ufa *r.* Russia **51** R5
Uffenheim Germany **63** K5
Uftyuga *r.* Russia **52** J3
Ugab *watercourse* Namibia **123** B6
Ugak Bay *AK* U.S.A. **148** I4
Ugalla *r.* Tanz. **123** D4
Uganda *country* Africa **122** D3
Uganik *AK* U.S.A. **148** I4
Ugashik *AK* U.S.A. **148** H4
Ugashik Bay *AK* U.S.A. **148** H4
Ugie S. Africa **125** I6
Ūgīnak Iran **111** F5
Uglegorsk Russia **90** F2
Uglich Russia **52** H4
Ugljan *i.* Croatia **68** F2
Uglovoye Russia **90** C2
Ugol'noye Russia **77** P3
Ugolnyy Russia *see* **Beringovskiy**
Ugol'nyye Kopi Russia **148** B2
Ugra Russia **53** G5
Ugtaaltsaydam Mongolia **94** F1
Uher Hudag China **95** G3
Uherské Hradiště Czech Rep. **57** P6
Úhlava *r.* Czech Rep. **63** N5
Uhrichsville *OH* U.S.A. **164** E3
Uibhist a' Deas *i.* U.K. *see* **South Uist**
Uibhist a' Tuath *i.* U.K. *see* **North Uist**
Uig U.K. **60** C3
Uíge Angola **123** B4
Uijeongbu S. Korea **91** B5
Ŭiju N. Korea **91** B4
Uimaharju Fin. **54** Q5
Uinta Mountains *UT* U.S.A. **159** H1
Uis Mine Namibia **123** B6
Uitenhage S. Africa **125** G7
Uithoorn Neth. **62** E2
Uithuizen Neth. **62** G1
Uivak, Cape Canada **153** J2
Ujhani India **104** D4
Uji Japan **92** B4
Uji-gawa *r.* Japan **92** B4
Uji-guntō *is* Japan **91** C7
Ujitawara Japan **92** B4
Ujiyamada Japan *see* **Ise**
Ujjain India **104** C5
Ujohbilang *Kalimantan* Indon. **85** F2
Ujung Kulon, Taman Nasional *nat. park* Indon. **84** D4
Ujung Pandang *Celebes* Indon. *see* **Makassar**
Újvidék Serbia *see* **Novi Sad**
Ukal Sagar *l.* India **104** C5
Ukata Nigeria **120** D3
'Ukayrishah *well* Saudi Arabia **110** B5
uKhahlamba-Drakensberg Park *nat. park* S. Africa **125** I5
Ukholovo Russia **53** I5
Ukhrul India **105** H4
Ukhta *Respublika Kareliya* Russia *see* **Kalevala**
Ukhta *Respublika Komi* Russia **52** L3
Ukiah *CA* U.S.A. **158** B2
Ukiah *OR* U.S.A. **156** D3
Ukkusiksalik National Park *nat. park* Canada **147** J3
Ukkusissat Greenland **147** M2
Ukmerge Lith. **55** N9

▶**Ukraine** *country* Europe **53** F6
2nd largest country in Europe.

Ukrainskaya S.S.R. *country* Europe *see* **Ukraine**
Ukrayina *country* Europe *see* **Ukraine**
Uku-jima *i.* Japan **91** C6
Ukwi Botswana **124** E2
Ukwi Pan *salt pan* Botswana **124** E2
Ul *r.* India **99** B7
Ulaanbaatar Mongolia *see* **Ulan Bator**
Ulaanbaatar *mun.* Mongolia **94** F2
Ulaanbadrah Mongolia **95** G3
Ulaan-Ereg Mongolia *see* **Bayanmönh**
Ulaangom Mongolia **94** C1
Ulaanhudag Mongolia *see* **Erdenesant**
Ulaan Nuur *salt l.* Mongolia **94** E2
Ulaan-Uul *Bayanhongor* Mongolia *see* **Öldziyt**
Ulaan-Uul *Dornogovĭ* Mongolia *see* **Erdene**
Ulak Island *AK* U.S.A. **148** [inset] C6
Ulan Australia **138** D4
Ulan *Nei Mongol* China **95** G4
Ulan *Qinghai* China **94** D4

▶**Ulan Bator** Mongolia **94** F2
Capital of Mongolia.

Ulanbel' Kazakh. **102** D3
Ulan Buh Shamo *des.* China **94** F3
Ulan Erge Russia **53** J7
Ulanhad China *see* **Chifeng**
Ulanhot China **95** J2
Ulan Hua China **95** G3
Ulan-Khol Russia **53** J7
Ulanlinggi China **98** D4
Ulan Mod China **94** F4
Ulan Qab China **95** H3
Ulan Suhai China **94** F3
Ulansuhai Nur *l.* China **95** G3
Ulan Tohoi China **94** E3
Ulan-Ude Russia **89** J2
Ulan Ul Hu *l.* China **99** E6
Ulaş Turkey **112** E3
Ulastai China **98** D4
Ulawa Island Solomon Is **133** G2
Ulayyah *reg.* Saudi Arabia **110** B6
Ul'banskiy Zaliv *b.* Russia **90** E1
Ul'bi Kazakh. **98** C2
Uldz Mongolia *see* **Norovlin**
Uldz Gol *r.* Mongolia **95** H1
Uleåborg Fin. *see* **Oulu**
Ulebsechel *i.* Palau *see* **Auluptagel**
Ulefoss Norway **55** F7
Ulekchin Russia **94** F1
Ülenurme Estonia **55** O7
Ulety Russia **95** H1
Ulgain Gol *r.* China **95** I2
Ulhasnagar India **106** B2
Uliastai China **95** I2
Uliastay Mongolia **94** D2
Uliatea *i.* Fr. Polynesia *see* **Raiatea**
Ulicoten Neth. **62** E3
Ulie *atoll* Micronesia *see* **Woleai**
Ulita *r.* Russia **54** R2
Ulithi *atoll* Micronesia **81** J4
Uljin S. Korea **91** C5
Ul'ken Aksu Kazakh. **98** B4
Ul'ken Boken Kazakh. **98** C2
Ul'ken Naryn Kazakh. **102** F2
Ul'ken Sulutor Kazakh. **98** A4
Ulladulla Australia **138** E5
Ullapool U.K. **60** D3
Ulla Ulla, Parque Nacional *nat. park* Bol. **176** E6
Ullava Fin. **54** M5
Ullersuaq *c.* Greenland **147** K2
Ulleung-do *i.* S. Korea **91** C5
Ullswater *l.* U.K. **58** E4
Ulm Germany **57** L6
Ulmarra Australia **138** F2
Ulmen Germany **62** G4
Uloowaranie, Lake *salt flat* Australia **137** B5
Ulricehamn Sweden **55** H8
Ulrum Neth. **62** G1
Ulsan S. Korea **91** C6
Ulsberg Norway **54** F5
Ulster *reg.* Ireland/U.K. **61** E3
Ulster *PA* U.S.A. **165** G3
Ulster Canal Ireland/U.K. **61** E3
Ultima Australia **138** A5
Ulu *Celebes* Indon. **83** C2
Ulúa *r.* Hond. **166** [inset] I6
Ulubat Gölü *l.* Turkey **69** M4
Ulubey Turkey **69** M5
Uluborlu Turkey **69** N5
Uludağ *mt.* Turkey **113** C2
Uludağ Milli Parkı *nat. park* Turkey **69** M4
Ulugqat China **98** A5
Ulu Kali, Gunung *mt.* Malaysia **84** C2
Ulukhaktok Canada **146** G2
Ulukışla Turkey **112** D3
Ulundi S. Africa **125** J5
Ulungur He *r.* China **98** D3
Ulungur Hu *l.* China **98** D3
Uluqsaqtuuq Canada *see* **Ulukhaktok**
Uluṟu *hill* Australia **135** E6
Uluṟu-Kata Tjuṯa National Park Australia **135** E6
Uluru National Park Australia *see* **Uluṟu-Kata Tjuṯa National Park**
Ulutau Kazakh. *see* **Ulytau**
Ulutau, Gory *mts* Kazakh. *see* **Ulytau, Gory**
Ulu Temburong National Park Brunei **85** F1
Uluyatır Turkey **107** C1
Ulva *i.* U.K. **60** C4
Ulvenhout Neth. **62** E3
Ulverston U.K. **58** D4
Ulvsjön Sweden **55** I6
Ül'yanov Kazakh. *see* **Botakara**
Ul'yanovsk Russia **53** K5
Ul'yanovskoye Kazakh. *see* **Botakara**
Ulyatuy Russia **95** I1
Ulysses *KS* U.S.A. **160** C4
Ulysses *KY* U.S.A. **164** D5
Ulytau Kazakh. **102** C2
Ulytau, Gory *mts* Kazakh. **102** C2
Ulyunkhan Russia **89** K2
Uma Russia **90** A1
Umal'ta (abandoned) Russia **90** D2
'Umān *country* Asia *see* **Oman**
Umán Mex. **167** H4
Uman' Ukr. **53** F6
Umarao Pak. **111** G4
'Umarī, Qā' al *salt pan* Jordan **107** C4
Umaria India **104** E5
Umarkhed India **106** C2
Umarkot India **106** D2
Umarkot *Punjab* Pak. **111** H4
Umarkot *Sindh* Pak. **111** H5
Umaroona, Lake *salt flat* Australia **137** B5
Umarpada India **104** C5
Umatilla *OR* U.S.A. **156** D3
Umayan *r. Mindanao* Phil. **82** D4
Umba Russia **52** G2
Umbagog Lake *NH* U.S.A. **165** J1
Umbeara Australia **135** F6
Umbele *i.* Indon. **83** B3
Umboi *i.* P.N.G. **81** L8
Umeå Sweden **54** L5
Umeälven *r.* Sweden **54** L5
Umera *Moluccas* Indon. **83** D3
Umfreville Lake Canada **151** M5
uMhlanga S. Africa **125** J5
Umiat *AK* U.S.A. **148** I1
Umi-gawa *r.* Japan **93** D1
Umiiviip Kangertiva *inlet* Greenland **147** N3
Umingmaktok Canada **189** L2
Umiujaq Canada **152** F2
Umkomaas S. Africa **125** J6
Umkumiute *AK* U.S.A. **148** F3
Umlaiteng India **105** H4
Umlazi S. Africa **125** J5
Umm ad Daraj, Jabal *mt.* Jordan **107** B3
Umm al 'Amad Syria **107** C2
Umm al Jamājim *well* Saudi Arabia **110** B5
Umm al Qaywayn U.A.E. **110** D5
Umm al Qaiwain U.A.E. *see* **Umm al Qaywayn**
Umm al Qulbān Saudi Arabia **113** F6
Umm ar Raqabah, Khabrat *imp. l.* Saudi Arabia **107** C5
Umm az Zumūl *well* Oman **110** D6
Umm Bāb Qatar **110** C5
Umm Bel Sudan **108** C7
Umm Keddada Sudan **108** C7
Umm Lajj Saudi Arabia **108** E4
Umm Nukhaylah *hill* Saudi Arabia **107** D5
Umm Qaşr Iraq **113** G5
Umm Quşūr *i.* Saudi Arabia **112** D6
Umm Ruwaba Sudan **108** D7
Umm Sa'ad Libya **112** B5
Umm Sa'id Qatar **110** C5
Umm Şalāl Muḥammad *town* Qatar **110** C5
Umm Shugeira Sudan **108** C7
Umm Wa'āl *hill* Saudi Arabia **107** D4
Umm Wazīr *well* Saudi Arabia **110** B6
Umnak Island *AK* U.S.A. **148** E5
Umnak Pass *sea chan. AK* U.S.A. **148** E5
Um Phang Wildlife Reserve *nature res.* Thai. **86** B4
Umpqua *r. OR* U.S.A. **156** B4
Umpulo Angola **123** B5
Umraniye Turkey **69** N5
Umred India **106** C1
Umri India **104** D4
Umtali Zimbabwe *see* **Mutare**
Umtata S. Africa *see* **Mthatha**
Umtentweni S. Africa **125** J6
Umuahia Nigeria **120** D4
Umuarama Brazil **178** F2
Umvuma Zimbabwe *see* **Mvuma**
Umzimkulu S. Africa **125** I6
Una *r.* Bos. & Herz./Croatia **68** G2
Una Brazil **179** D1
Una India **104** D3
'Unāb, Jabal al *hill* Jordan **107** C5
'Unāb, Wādī al *watercourse* Jordan **107** C4
Unaí Brazil **179** B2
Unakami Japan **93** G3
Unalakleet *AK* U.S.A. **148** G3
Unalakleet *r. AK* U.S.A. **148** G3
Unalaska *AK* U.S.A. **148** F5
Unalaska Island *AK* U.S.A. **148** F5
Unalga Island *AK* U.S.A. **148** F5
Unapool U.K. **60** D2
Unauna *i.* Indon. **83** B3
'Unayzah Saudi Arabia **108** F4
'Unayzah, Jabal *hill* Iraq **113** E4
Unazuki Japan **92** D2
Uncia Bol. **176** E7
Uncompahgre Peak *CO* U.S.A. **159** J2
Uncompahgre Plateau *CO* U.S.A. **159** I2
Undara National Park Australia **136** D3
Underberg S. Africa **125** I5
Underbool Australia **137** C7
Underwood *IN* U.S.A. **164** C4
Undu, Tanjung *pt Sumba* Indon. **83** B5
Undur *Seram* Indon. **83** D3
Unecha Russia **53** G5
Unga *AK* U.S.A. **148** G5
Unga Island *AK* U.S.A. **148** G5
Ungalik *AK* U.S.A. **148** G2
Ungalik *r. AK* U.S.A. **148** G2
Ungama Bay Kenya *see* **Ungwana Bay**
Ungarie Australia **138** C4
Ungava, Baie d' *b.* Canada *see* **Ungava Bay**
Ungava, Péninsule d' *pen.* Canada **152** G1
Ungava Bay Canada **153** I2
Ungava Peninsula Canada *see* **Ungava, Péninsule d'**
Ungeny Moldova *see* **Ungheni**
Ungheni Moldova **69** L1
Unguana Moz. **125** L2
Unguja *i.* Tanz. *see* **Zanzibar Island**
Unguz, Solonchakovyye Vpadiny *salt flat* Turkm. **110** E2
Üngüz Angyrsyndaky Garagum *des.* Turkm. **110** E1
Ungvár Ukr. *see* **Uzhhorod**
Ungwana Bay Kenya **122** E4
Uni Russia **52** K4
União Brazil **177** J4
União da Vitória Brazil **179** A4
União dos Palmares Brazil **177** K5
Uniara India **99** B8
Unimak Bight *b. AK* U.S.A. **148** F5
Unimak Island *AK* U.S.A. **148** F5
Unimak Pass *sea chan. AK* U.S.A. **148** F5
Unini *r.* Brazil **176** F4
Union *MO* U.S.A. **160** F4
Union *WV* U.S.A. **164** E5
Union, Mount *AZ* U.S.A. **159** G4
Union City *OH* U.S.A. **164** C3
Union City *PA* U.S.A. **164** F3
Union City *TN* U.S.A. **161** F4
Uniondale S. Africa **124** F7
Unión de Reyes Cuba **163** D8

▶**Union of Soviet Socialist Republics**
Divided in 1991 into 15 independent nations: Armenia, Azerbaijan, Belarus, Estonia, Georgia, Latvia, Kazakhstan, Kyrgyzstan, Lithuania, Moldova, Russia, Tajikistan, Turkmenistan, Ukraine and Uzbekistan.

Union Springs *AL* U.S.A. **163** C5
Uniontown *PA* U.S.A. **164** F4
Unionville *PA* U.S.A. **165** G3
United Arab Emirates *country* Asia **110** D6
United Arab Republic *country* Africa *see* **Egypt**

▶**United Kingdom** *country* Europe **56** G3
4th most populous country in Europe.

United Provinces *state* India *see* **Uttar Pradesh**

▶**United States of America** *country* N. America **154** F3
Most populous country in North America and 3rd most populous in the world. Also 2nd largest country in North America and 3rd in the world.

United States Range *mts* Canada **147** L1
Unity Canada **151** I4
Unjha India **104** C5
Unna Germany **63** H3
Unnao India **104** E4
Ŭnp'a N. Korea **91** B5
Unsan N. Korea **91** B4
Ŭnsan N. Korea **91** B5
Unst *i.* U.K. **60** [inset]
Unstrut *r.* Germany **63** L3
Untor, Ozero *l.* Russia **51** T3
Unuk *r.* Canada/U.S.A. **149** O4
Unuli Horog China **94** B5
Unzen-dake *vol.* Japan **91** C6
Unzha Russia **52** J4
Uozu Japan **92** D2
Upalco *UT* U.S.A. **159** H1
Upar Ghat *reg.* India **105** F5
Upemba, Lac *l.* Dem. Rep. Congo **123** C4
Upemba, Parc National de l' *nat. park* Dem. Rep. Congo **123** C4
Uperbada India **105** F5
Upernavik Greenland **147** M2
Upington S. Africa **124** E5
Upland *CA* U.S.A. **158** E4
Upleta India **104** B5
Upoloksha Russia **54** Q3
'Upolu *i.* Samoa **133** I3
Upper Arlington *OH* U.S.A. **164** D3
Upper Arrow Lake Canada **150** G5
Upper Chindwin Myanmar *see* **Mawlaik**
Upper Fraser Canada **150** F4
Upper Garry Lake Canada **151** K1
Upper Hutt N.Z. **139** E5
Upper Kalskag *AK* U.S.A. **148** G3
Upper Klamath Lake *OR* U.S.A. **156** C4
Upper Liard Canada **149** O3
Upper Lough Erne *l.* U.K. **61** E3
Upper Marlboro *MD* U.S.A. **165** G4
Upper Mazinaw Lake Canada **165** G1
Upper Missouri Breaks National Monument *nat. park MT* U.S.A. **160** A2
Upper Peirce Reservoir Sing. **87** [inset]
Upper Red Lake *MN* U.S.A. **160** E1
Upper Sandusky *OH* U.S.A. **164** D3
Upper Saranac Lake *NY* U.S.A. **165** H1
Upper Seal Lake Canada *see* **Iberville, Lac d'**
Upper Tunguska *r.* Russia *see* **Angara**
Upper Volta *country* Africa *see* **Burkina Faso**
Upper Yarra Reservoir Australia **138** B6
Uppinangadi India **106** B3
Uppsala Sweden **55** J7
Upright, Cape *AK* U.S.A. **148** D3
Upsala Canada **152** C4
Upshi India **104** D2
Upton *MA* U.S.A. **165** J2
'Uqayqah, Wādī *watercourse* Jordan **107** B4
'Uqayribāt Syria **107** C2
'Uqlat al 'Udhaybah *well* Iraq **113** G5
Uqturpan China *see* **Wushi**
Uracas *vol.* N. Mariana Is *see* **Farallon de Pajaros**
Urad Qianqi China *see* **Xishanzui**
Urad Zhongqi China *see* **Haliut**
Ūrāf Iran **110** E4
Uraga-suidō *sea chan.* Japan **93** F3
Uragawara Japan **93** E1
Urakawa Japan **90** F4
Ural *hill* Australia **138** C4
Ural *r.* Kazakh./Russia **100** E2
Uralla Australia **138** E3
Ural Mountains Russia **51** S2
Ural'sk Kazakh. **100** E1
Ural'skaya Oblast' *admin. div.* Kazakh. *see* **Zapadnyy Kazakhstan**
Ural'skiye Gory *mts* Russia *see* **Ural Mountains**
Ural'skiy Khrebet *mts* Russia *see* **Ural Mountains**
Urambo Tanz. **123** D4
Uran India **106** B2
Urana Australia **138** C5
Urana, Lake Australia **138** C5
Urandangi Australia **136** B4
Urandi Brazil **179** C1
Uranium City Canada **151** I3
Uranquinty Australia **138** C5
Uraricoera *r.* Brazil **176** F3
Urartu *country* Asia *see* **Armenia**
Ura-Tyube Tajik. *see* **Istaravshan**
Uravakonda India **106** C3
Uravan (abandoned) *CO* U.S.A. **159** I2
Urawa Japan **93** F3
Urayasu Japan **93** F3
'Urayf an Nāqah, Jabal *hill* Egypt **107** B4
Uray'irah Saudi Arabia **110** C5
'Urayq ad Duḥūl *des.* Saudi Arabia **110** B5
'Urayq Sāqān *des.* Saudi Arabia **110** B5
Urbana *IL* U.S.A. **160** F3
Urbana *OH* U.S.A. **164** D3
Urbino Italy **68** E3
Urbinum Italy *see* **Urbino**
Urbs Vetus Italy *see* **Orvieto**
Urdoma Russia **52** K3
Urd Tamir Gol *r.* Mongolia **94** E2
Urdyuzhskoye, Ozero *l.* Russia **52** K2
Ure *r.* U.K. **58** F4
Urek'i Georgia **113** F2
Ureliki Russia **148** D2
Uren' Russia **52** J4
Urengoy Russia **76** I3
Uréparapara *i.* Vanuatu **133** G3
Ures Mex. **166** C2
Ureshino Japan **92** C4
Urfa Turkey *see* **Şanlıurfa**
Urfa *prov.* Turkey *see* **Şanlıurfa**
Urga Mongolia *see* **Ulan Bator**
Urgal *r.* Russia **90** D2
Urganch Uzbek. **102** B3
Urgench Uzbek. *see* **Urganch**
Urgün-e Kalān Afgh. **111** H3
Ürgüp Turkey **112** D3
Urgut Uzbek. **111** G2
Urho China **98** D3
Urho Kekkosen kansallispuisto *nat. park* Fin. **54** O2

Urie r. U.K. 60 G3
Uril Russia 90 C2
Uripitijuata, Cerro mt. Mex. 166 E5
Urique Mex. 166 D3
Urisino Australia 138 A2
Urizura Japan 93 G2
Urjala Fin. 55 M6
Urk Neth. 62 F2
Urkan Russia 90 B1
Urkan r. Russia 90 B1
Urla Turkey 69 L5
Urlingford Ireland 61 E5
Urluk Russia 95 F1
Ūrmā aş Şughrá Syria 107 C1
Urmai China 99 D7
Urmia Iran 110 B2
Urmia, Lake salt l. Iran 110 B2
Urmston Road sea chan. H.K. China 97 [inset]
Uromi Nigeria 120 D4
Uroševac Kosovo see Ferizaj
Urosozero Russia 52 G3
Urru Co salt l. China 99 D7
Urt Mongolia see Gurvantes
Urt Moron China 99 F5
Urt Moron r. China 94 C4
Uruáchic Mex. 166 C3
Uruaçu Brazil 179 A1
Uruana Brazil 179 A1
Uruapan Baja California Mex. 157 D7
Uruapan Michoacán Mex. 168 D5
Urubamba r. Peru 176 D6
Urucará Brazil 177 G4
Urucu r. Brazil 176 F4
Uruçuca Brazil 179 D1
Uruçuí Brazil 177 J5
Uruçuí, Serra do hills Brazil 177 I5
Urucuia Brazil 179 B2
Urucurituba Brazil 177 G4
Urugi Japan 92 D3
Uruguai r. Arg./Uruguay see Uruguay
Uruguaiana Brazil 178 E3
Uruguay r. Arg./Uruguay 178 E4
also known as Uruguai
Uruguay country S. America 178 E4
Uruhe China 90 B2
Urukthapel i. Palau 82 [inset]
Urumchi China see Ürümqi
Ürümqi China 98 D4
Urundi country Africa see Burundi
Urup, Ostrov i. Russia 89 S3
Uru Pass China/Kyrg. 98 B4
Urusha Russia 90 A1
Urutaí Brazil 179 A2
Uruzgān Afgh. 111 G3
Uryupino Russia 89 M2
Uryupinsk Russia 53 I6
Urzhar Kazakh. 102 F2
Ürzhar Kazakh. see Urzhar
Urzhum Russia 52 K4
Urziceni Romania 69 L2
Usa Japan 91 C6
Usa r. Russia 52 M2
Uşak Turkey 69 M5
Usakos Namibia 124 B1
Usarp Mountains Antarctica 188 H2
Usborne, Mount hill Falkland Is 178 E8
Ushakova, Ostrov i. Russia 76 I1
Ushanovo Kazakh. 98 C2
Ushant i. France see Ouessant, Île d'
Usharal Kazakh. 102 F2
Üsharal Kazakh. see Usharal
Ush-Bel'dir Russia 88 H2
Ushibori Japan 93 G3
Ushiku Japan 93 G3
Ushimawashi-yama mt. Japan 92 B5
Ushkaniy Kryazh mts Russia 148 B2
Ushtobe Kazakh. 102 E2
Ush-Tyube Kazakh. see Ushtobe
Ushuaia Arg. 178 C8
Ushumun Russia 90 B1
Usingen Germany 63 I4
Usinsk Russia 51 R2
Usk U.K. 59 E7
Usk r. U.K. 59 E7
Uskhodni Belarus 55 O10
Uskoplje Bos. & Herz. see Gornji Vakuf
Üsküdar Turkey 69 M4
Uslar Germany 63 J3
Usman' Russia 53 H5
Usmanabad India see Osmanabad
Usmas ezers l. Latvia 55 M8
Usogorsk Russia 52 K3
Usol'ye-Sibirskoye Russia 88 I2
Uspenskoye Kazakh. 98 A2
Ussel France 66 F4
Ussuri r. China/Russia 90 D2
Ussuriysk Russia 90 C4
Ust'-Abakanskoye Russia see Abakan
Usta Muhammad Pak. 111 H4
Ust'-Balyk Russia see Nefteyugansk
Ust'-Donetskiy Russia 53 I7
Ust'-Dzheguta Russia 113 F1
Ust'-Dzhegutinskaya Russia see Ust'-Dzheguta
Ustica, Isola di i. Sicily Italy 68 E5
Ust'-Ilimsk Russia 77 L4
Ust'-Ilimskoye Vodokhranilishche resr Russia 77 L4
Ust'-Ilya Russia 95 H1
Ust'-Ilych Russia 51 R3
Ústí nad Labem Czech Rep. 57 O5
Ustinov Russia see Izhevsk
Üstirt plat. Kazakh./Uzbek. see Ustyurt Plateau
Ustka Poland 57 P3
Ust'-Kamchatsk Russia 77 R4
Ust'-Kamenogorsk Kazakh. 102 F2
Ust'-Kan Russia 98 D2
Ust'-Koksa Russia 98 D2
Ust'-Kulom Russia 52 L3
Ust'-Kut Russia 77 L4
Ust'-Kuyga Russia 77 O2
Ust'-Labinsk Russia 113 E1
Ust'-Labinskaya Russia see Ust'-Labinsk
Ust'-Lyzha Russia 52 M2
Ust'-Maya Russia 77 O3
Ust'-Nera Russia 77 P3
Ust'-Ocheya Russia 52 K3
Ust'-Olenek Russia 77 M2
Ust'-Omchug Russia 77 P3
Ust'-Ordynskiy Russia 88 I2
Ust'-Port Russia 76 J3
Ustrem Russia 51 T3
Ust'-Tsil'ma Russia 52 L2
Ust'-Uda Russia 88 I2
Ust'-Ulagan Russia 98 D2
Ust'-Umalta (abandoned) Russia 90 D2
Ust'-Undurga Russia 89 L2
Ust'-Ura Russia 52 J3
Ust'-Urgal Russia 90 D2
Ust'-Usa Russia 52 M2
Ust'-Vayen'ga Russia 52 I3
Ust'-Voya Russia 51 R3
Ust'-Vyyskaya Russia 52 J3
Ust'ya r. Russia 52 I3
Ust'ye Russia 52 H4
Ustyurt, Plato plat. Kazakh./Uzbek. see Ustyurt Plateau
Ustyurt Plateau Kazakh./Uzbek. 100 E2
Ustyurt Platosi plat. Kazakh./Uzbek. see Ustyurt Plateau
Ustyuzhna Russia 52 H4
Usu China 98 D3
Usu i. Indon. 83 B5
Usuda Japan 93 E2
Usulután El Salvador 166 [inset] H6
Usumacinta r. Guat./Mex. 167 G5
Usumbura Burundi see Bujumbura
Usun Apau, Dataran Tinggi plat. Malaysia 85 F2
Usvyaty Russia 52 F5
Utah state U.S.A. 156 F5
Utah Lake UT U.S.A. 159 H1
Utajärvi Fin. 54 O4
Utano Japan 92 B4
Utashinai Russia see Yuzhno-Kuril'sk
Utata Russia 94 E1
'Utaybah, Buḩayrat al imp. l. Syria 107 C3
Utena Lith. 55 N9
Uterlai India 104 B4
Uthai Thani Thai. 86 C4
Uthal Pak. 111 G5
'Uthmānīyah Syria 107 C2
uThukela r. S. Africa 125 J5
Utiariti Brazil 177 G6
Utica NY U.S.A. 165 H2
Utica OH U.S.A. 164 D3
Utiel Spain 67 F4
Utikuma Lake Canada 150 H4
Utila Hond. 166 [inset] I5
Utlwanang S. Africa 125 G4
Utopia AK U.S.A. 148 I2
Utrecht Neth. 62 F2
Utrecht S. Africa 125 J4
Utrera Spain 67 D5
Utsjoki Fin. 54 O2
Utsugi-dake mt. Japan 93 D3
Utsunomiya Japan 93 F2
Utta Russia 53 J7
Uttaradit Thai. 86 C3
Uttarakhand state India 104 D3
Uttaranchal state India see Uttarakhand
Uttarkashi India 104 D3
Uttar Kashi India see Uttarkashi
Uttar Pradesh state India 104 D4
Uttoxeter U.K. 59 F6
Uttranchal state India see Uttarakhand
Utu China see Miao'ergou
Utubulak China 98 D3
Utukok r. AK U.S.A. 148 G1
Utupua i. Solomon Is 133 G3
Uturuncu, Cerro mt. Bol. 176 E8
Uummannaq Fjord inlet Greenland 189 J2
Uummannarsuaq c. Greenland see Farewell, Cape
Uurainen Fin. 54 N5
Üüreg Nuur salt l. Mongolia 94 B1
Üür Gol r. Mongolia 94 E1
Uusikaarlepyy Fin. see Nykarleby
Uusikaupunki Fin. 55 L6
Uva Russia 52 L4
Uvalde TX U.S.A. 161 D6
Uvarovo Russia 53 I6
Uvéa atoll New Caledonia see Ouvéa
Uvinza Tanz. 123 D4
Uvs prov. Mongolia 94 C1
Uvs Nuur salt l. Mongolia 94 C1
Uwajima Japan 91 D6
'Uwayrid, Ḩarrat al lava field Saudi Arabia 108 E4
Uwaysiț well Saudi Arabia 107 D4
Uweinat, Jebel mt. Sudan 108 C5
Uwi i. Indon. 84 D2
Uxbridge Canada 164 F1
Uxbridge U.K. 59 G7
Uxin Ju China 95 G4
Uxin Qi China see Dabqig
Uxmal tourist site Mex. 167 H4
Uxxaktal China 98 D4
Uyak AK U.S.A. 148 I4
Uyaly Kazakh. 102 B3
Uyanga Mongolia 94 E2
Uyar Russia 88 G1
Üydzin Mongolia see Manlay
Uyo Nigeria 120 D4
Üyönch Mongolia 94 C2
Üyönch Gol r. China 94 B2
Uyu Chaung r. Myanmar 86 A1
Uyuni Bol. 176 E8
Uyuni, Salar de salt flat Bol. 176 E8
Uza r. Russia 53 J5
Uzbekiston country Asia 102 B3
Ŭzbekiston country Asia see Uzbekistan
Uzbekskaya S.S.R. country Asia see Uzbekistan
Uzbek S.S.R. country Asia see Uzbekistan
Uzboy Turkm. 110 D2
Uzen' Kazakh. see Kyzylsay
Uzhgorod Ukr. see Uzhhorod
Uzhhorod Ukr. 53 D6
Užhorod Ukr. see Uzhhorod
Užice Serbia 69 H3
Uzlovaya Russia 53 H5
Üzöngü Toosu mt. China/Kyrg. 98 B4
Üzümlü Turkey 69 M6
Uzun Uzbek. 111 H2
Uzunbulak China 98 D3
Uzun Bulak spring China 98 E4
Uzunköprü Turkey 69 L4
Uzynagash Almatinskaya Oblast' Kazakh. 98 B4
Uzynagash Almatinskaya Oblast' Kazakh. 98 B4
Uzynkair Kazakh. 102 B3

Vaajakoski Fin. 54 N5
Vaal r. S. Africa 125 F5
Vaala Fin. 54 O4
Vaalbos National Park S. Africa 124 G5
Vaal Dam S. Africa 125 I4
Vaalwater S. Africa 125 I3
Vaasa Fin. 54 L5
Vaavu Atoll Maldives see Felidhe Atholhu
Vác Hungary 57 Q7
Vacaria Brazil 179 A5
Vacaria, Campo da plain Brazil 179 A5
Vacaville CA U.S.A. 158 C2
Vachon r. Canada 153 H1
Vad Russia 52 J5
Vad r. Russia 53 I5
Vada India 106 B2
Vadakara India 106 B4
Vadla Norway 55 E7
Vadodara India 104 C5
Vadsø Norway 54 P1

▶Vaduz Liechtenstein 66 I3
Capital of Liechtenstein.

Værøy i. Norway 54 H3
Vaga r. Russia 52 I3
Vågåmo Norway 55 F6
Vaganski Vrh mt. Croatia 68 F2
Vágar i. Faroe Is 54 [inset 2]
Vagharshapat Armenia 113 G2
Vägsele Sweden 54 K4
Vágur Faroe Is 54 [inset 2]
Váh r. Slovakia 57 Q7
Vähäkyrö Fin. 54 M5

▶Vaiaku Tuvalu 133 H2
Capital of Tuvalu, on Funafuti atoll.

Vaida Estonia 55 N7
Vaiden MS U.S.A. 161 F5
Vail CO U.S.A. 154 F4
Vailly-sur-Aisne France 62 D5
Vaitupu i. Tuvalu 133 H2
Vajrakarur India see Kanur
Vakhsh Tajik. 111 H2
Vakhsh r. Tajik. 111 H2
Vakhshstroy Tajik. see Vakhsh
Vakīlābād Iran 110 E4
Valbo Sweden 55 J6
Valcheta Arg. 178 C6
Valdai Hills Russia see Valdayskaya Vozvyshennost'
Valday Russia 52 G4
Valdayskaya Vozvyshennost' hills Russia 52 G4
Valdecañas, Embalse de resr Spain 67 D4
Valdemārpils Latvia 55 M8
Valdemarsvik Sweden 55 J7
Valdepeñas Spain 67 E4
Val-de-Reuil France 62 B5
Valdés, Península pen. Arg. 178 D6
Valdez AK U.S.A. 149 K3
Valdivia Chile 178 B5
Val-d'Or Canada 152 F4
Valdosta GA U.S.A. 163 D6
Valdres valley Norway 55 F6
Vale Georgia 113 F2
Vale OR U.S.A. 156 D3
Valemount Canada 150 G4
Valença Bahia Brazil 179 D1
Valença Rio de Janeiro Brazil 179 C3
Valence France 66 G4
València Spain see Valencia
Valencia Spain 67 F4
Valencia reg. Spain 67 F4
Valencia Venez. 176 E1
Valencia, Golfo de g. Spain 67 G4
Valencia de Don Juan Spain 67 D2
Valencia Island Ireland 61 B6
Valenciennes France 62 D4
Valensole, Plateau de France 66 H5
Valentia Spain see Valencia
Valentin Russia 90 D4
Valentine NE U.S.A. 160 C3
Valentine TX U.S.A. 166 D2
Valenzuela Luzon Phil. 82 C3
Våler Norway 55 G6
Valera Venez. 176 D2
Vale Verde Brazil 179 D2
Val Grande, Parco Nazionale della nat. park Italy 68 C1
Valiyakara, Suheli India 106 B4
Valjevo Serbia 69 H2
Valka Latvia 55 O8
Valkeakoski Fin. 55 N6
Valkenswaard Neth. 62 F3
Valky Ukr. 53 G6
Valkyrie Dome ice feature Antarctica 188 D1
Valladolid Mex. 167 H4
Valladolid Spain 67 D3
Vallard, Lac l. Canada 153 H3
Valle Norway 55 E7
Vallecillos Mex. 167 F3
Vallecito Reservoir CO U.S.A. 159 J3
Valle de Banderas Mex. 166 D4
Valle de la Pascua Venez. 176 E2
Valle de Olivos Mex. 166 D3
Valle de Santiago Mex. 167 E4
Valle de Zaragoza Mex. 166 D3
Valledupar Col. 176 D1
Vallée-Jonction Canada 153 H5
Valle Fértil, Sierra de mts Arg. 178 C4
Valle Grande Bol. 176 F7
Valle Hermoso Mex. 167 F3
Vallejo CA U.S.A. 158 B2
Valle Nacional Mex. 167 F5
Vallenar Chile 178 B3
Valles Caldera National Preserve nat. park U.S.A. 157 G6

▶Valletta Malta 68 F7
Capital of Malta.

Valley r. Canada 151 L5
Valley U.K. 58 C5
Valley City ND U.S.A. 160 D2
Valley Head hd Luzon Phil. 82 C2
Valleyview Canada 150 G4
Valls Spain 67 G3
Val Marie Canada 151 J5
Valmiera Latvia 55 N8
Valmy NV U.S.A. 158 E1
Valnera mt. Spain 67 E2
Valognes France 59 F9
Valona Albania see Vlorë
Valozhyn Belarus 55 O9
Val-Paradis Canada 152 F4
Valparai India 106 C4
Valparaíso Chile 178 B4
Valparaíso Mex. 166 E4
Valparaiso FL U.S.A. 167 I2
Valparaiso IN U.S.A. 164 B3
Valpoi India 106 B3
Valréas France 66 G4
Vals, Tanjung c. Indon. 81 J8
Valsad India 106 B1
Valspan S. Africa 124 G4
Valtimo Fin. 54 P5
Valuyevka Russia 53 I7
Valuyki Russia 53 H6
Vammala Fin. 55 M6
Van Turkey 113 F3
Van, Lake salt l. Turkey 113 F3
Vanadzor Armenia 113 G2
Van Buren AR U.S.A. 161 E5
Van Buren MO U.S.A. 161 F4
Van Buren OH U.S.A. see Kettering
Vanceburg KY U.S.A. 164 D4
Vanch Tajik. see Vanj
Vancleve KY U.S.A. 164 D5
Vancouver Canada 150 F5
Vancouver WA U.S.A. 156 C3
Vancouver, Cape AK U.S.A. 148 F3
Vancouver, Mount Canada/U.S.A. 149 M3
Vancouver Island Canada 150 E5
Vanda Fin. see Vantaa
Vandalia IL U.S.A. 160 F4
Vandalia OH U.S.A. 164 C4
Vandekerckhove Lake Canada 151 K3
Vanderbijlpark S. Africa 125 H4
Vanderbilt MI U.S.A. 164 C1
Vandergrift PA U.S.A. 164 F3
Vanderhoof Canada 150 E4
Vanderkloof Dam resr S. Africa 124 G6
Vanderlin Island Australia 136 B2
Vanderwagen NM U.S.A. 159 I4
Van Diemen, Cape N.T. Australia 134 E2
Van Diemen, Cape Qld Australia 136 B3
Van Diemen Gulf Australia 134 F2
Vändra Estonia 55 N7
Väner, Lake Sweden see Vänern

▶Vänern l. Sweden 55 H7
4th largest lake in Europe.

Vänersborg Sweden 55 H7
Vangaindrano Madag. 123 E6
Van Gia Vietnam 87 E4
Van Gölü salt l. Turkey see Van, Lake
Van Horn TX U.S.A. 157 G7
Vanikoro Islands Solomon Is 133 G3
Vanimo P.N.G. 81 K7
Vanino Russia 90 F2
Vanivilasa Sagara resr India 106 C3
Vaniyambadi India 106 C3
Vanj Tajik. 111 H2
Vankarem Russia 148 D2
Vankarem r. Russia 148 C2
Vankarem, Laguna lag. Russia 148 D2
Vännäs Sweden 54 K5
Vannes France 66 C3
Vannes, Lac l. Canada 153 I3
Vannovka Kazakh. see Turar Ryskulov
Vannøya i. Norway 54 K1
Vanoise, Massif de la mts France 66 H4
Vanoise, Parc National de la nat. park France 66 H4
Van Rees, Pegunungan mts Indon. 81 J7
Vanrhynsdorp S. Africa 124 D6
Vansant VA U.S.A. 164 D5
Vansbro Sweden 55 I6
Vansittart Island Canada 147 J3
Van Starkenborgh Kanaal canal Neth. 62 G1
Vantaa Fin. 55 N6
Van Truer Tableland reg. Australia 135 C6
Vanua Lava i. Vanuatu 133 G3
Vanua Levu i. Fiji 133 H3
Vanuatu country S. Pacific Ocean 133 G3
Van Wert OH U.S.A. 164 C3
Van Wyksvlei S. Africa 124 E6
Van Wyksvlei Dam l. S. Africa 124 E6
Vân Yên Vietnam 86 D2
Van Zylsrus S. Africa 124 F4
Varadero Cuba 163 D8
Varahi India 104 B5
Varakļāni Latvia 55 O8
Varalé Côte d'Ivoire 120 C4
Varāmīn Iran 110 C3
Varanasi India 105 E4
Varandey Russia 52 M1
Varangerfjorden sea chan. Norway 54 P1
Varangerhalvøya pen. Norway 54 P1
Varaždin Croatia 68 G1
Varberg Sweden 55 H8
Vardar r. Macedonia 69 J4
Varde Denmark 55 F9
Vardenis Armenia 113 G2
Vardø Norway 54 Q1
Varel Germany 63 I1
Varna Lith. 55 N9
Varese Italy 68 C2
Varfolomeyevka Russia 90 D3
Vårgårda Sweden 55 H7
Varginha Brazil 179 B3
Varik Neth. 62 F3
Varillas Chile 178 B2
Varkaus Fin. 54 O5
Varna Bulg. 69 L3
Värnamo Sweden 55 I8
Värnäs Sweden 55 H6
Varnavino Russia 52 J4
Várnjárg pen. Norway see Varangerhalvøya
Varpaisjärvi Fin. 54 O5
Várpalota Hungary 68 H1
Varsh, Ozero l. Russia 52 J2
Varto Turkey 113 F3
Várzea da Palma Brazil 179 B2
Várzea Grande Brazil 177 G7
Vasa Fin. see Vaasa
Vasai India 106 B2
Vashka r. Russia 52 J2
Vasht Iran see Khāsh
Vasilkov Ukr. see Vasyl'kiv
Vasknarva Estonia 55 O7
Vaslui Romania 69 L1
Vassar MI U.S.A. 164 D2
Vas-Soproni-síkság hills Hungary 68 G1
Vastan Turkey see Gevaş
Västerås Sweden 55 J7
Västerdalälven r. Sweden 55 I6
Västerfjäll Sweden 54 J3
Västerhaninge Sweden 55 K7
Västervik Sweden 55 J8
Vasto Italy 68 F3
Vasyl'kiv Ukr. 53 F6
Vatan France 66 E3
Vaté i. Vanuatu see Éfaté
Vatersay i. U.K. 60 B4
Vathar India 106 B2
Vathí Greece see Vathy
Vathy Greece 69 L6

▶Vatican City Europe 68 E4
Independent papal state, the smallest country in the world.

Vaticano, Città del Europe see Vatican City
Vatnajökull ice cap Iceland 54 [inset 1]
Vatoa i. Fiji 133 I3
Vatra Dornei Romania 69 K1
Vätter, Lake Sweden see Vättern
Vättern l. Sweden 55 I7
Vaughn NM U.S.A. 157 G6
Vaupés r. Col. 176 E3
Vauquelin r. Canada 152 F3
Vauvert France 66 G5
Vauxhall Canada 151 H5
Vavatenina Madag. 123 E5
Vava'u Group is Tonga 133 I3
Vavitao i. Fr. Polynesia see Raivavae
Vavoua Côte d'Ivoire 120 C4
Vavozh Russia 52 K4
Vavuniya Sri Lanka 106 D4
Vawkavysk Belarus 55 N10
Växjö Sweden 55 I8
Vay, Đao i. Vietnam 87 C5
Vayenga Russia see Severomorsk
Vazante Brazil 179 B2
Vazáš Sweden see Vittangi
Veaikevárri Sweden see Svappavaara
Véal Rénh Cambodia 87 C5
Véal Vêng Cambodia 87 C4
Vecht r. Neth. 62 G2
also known as Vechte (Germany)
Vechta Germany 63 I2
Vechte r. Germany 63 G2
also known as Vecht (Netherlands)
Veckerhagen (Reinhardshagen) Germany 63 J3
Vedaranniyam India 106 C4
Vedasandur India 106 C4
Veddige Sweden 55 H8
Vedea r. Romania 69 K3
Veedersburg IN U.S.A. 164 B3
Veendam Neth. 62 G1
Veenendaal Neth. 62 F2
Vega i. Norway 54 G4
Vega TX U.S.A. 161 C5
Vega de Alatorre Mex. 167 F4
Vega Point pt AK U.S.A. 148 [inset] B6
Vegreville Canada 151 H4
Vehari Pak. 111 I4
Vehkalahti Fin. 55 O6
Vehowa Pak. 111 H4
Veinticinco de Mayo Buenos Aires Arg. see 25 de Mayo
Veinticinco de Mayo La Pampa Arg. see 25 de Mayo
Veirwaro Pak. 111 H5
Veitshöchheim Germany 63 J5
Vejle Denmark 55 F9
Vekil'bazar Turkm. see Wekilbazar
Velardena Mex. 166 D3
Velas, Cabo c. Costa Rica 166 [inset] I7
Velbert Germany 62 H3
Velbŭzhdki Prokhod pass Bulg./Macedonia 69 J3
Velddrif S. Africa 124 D7
Velebit mts Croatia 68 F2
Velen Germany 62 G3
Velenje Slovenia 68 F1
Veles Macedonia 69 I4
Vélez-Málaga Spain 67 D5
Vélez-Rubio Spain 67 E5
Velhas r. Brazil 179 B2
Velibaba Turkey see Aras
Velika Gorica Croatia 68 G2
Velika Plana Serbia 69 I2
Velikaya r. Russia 52 K4
Velikaya r. Russia 55 P8
Velikaya r. Russia 77 S3
Velikaya Kema Russia 90 E3
Veliki Preslav Bulg. 69 L3
Velikiye Luki Russia 52 F4
Velikiy Novgorod Russia 52 F4
Velikiy Ustyug Russia 52 J3
Velikonda Range hills India 106 C3
Veliko Tarnovo Bulg. 69 K3
Velikoye Russia 52 H4
Velikoye, Ozero l. Russia 53 I5
Veli Lošinj Croatia 68 F2
Velizh Russia 52 F5
Vella Lavella i. Solomon Is 133 F2
Vellar r. India 106 C4
Vellberg Germany 63 J5
Vellmar Germany 63 J3
Vellore India 106 C3
Velpke Germany 63 K2
Vel'sk Russia 52 I3
Velsuna Italy see Orvieto
Velten Germany 63 N2
Veluwezoom, Nationaal Park nat. park Neth. 62 F2
Velykyy Tokmak Ukr. see Tokmak
Vel'yu r. Russia 52 L3
Vemalwada India 106 C2
Vema Seamount sea feature S. Atlantic Ocean 184 I8
Vema Trench sea feature Indian Ocean 185 M6
Vempalle India 106 C3
Venado, Isla del i. Nicaragua 166 [inset] J7
Venado Tuerto Arg. 178 D4
Venafro Italy 68 F4
Vendinga Russia 52 J3
Vendôme France 66 E3
Venegas Mex. 161 C8
Venetia Italy see Venice
Venetie AK U.S.A. 149 K2
Venetie Landing AK U.S.A. 149 K2
Venev Russia 53 H5
Venezia Italy see Venice
Venezia, Golfo di g. Europe see Venice, Gulf of

▶Venezuela country S. America 176 E2
4th most populous country in South America.

Venezuela, Golfo de g. Venez. 176 D1
Venezuelan Basin sea feature S. Atlantic Ocean 184 D4
Vengurla India 106 B3
Veniaminof Volcano AK U.S.A. 146 C4
Venice Italy 68 E2
Venice FL U.S.A. 163 D7
Venice LA U.S.A. 167 H2
Venice, Gulf of Europe 68 E2
Vénissieux France 66 G4
Venkatapalem India 106 D2
Venkatapuram India 106 D2
Venlo Neth. 62 G3
Vennesla Norway 55 E7
Venray Neth. 62 F3
Venta r. Latvia/Lith. 55 M8
Venta Lith. 55 M8
Ventersburg S. Africa 125 H5
Ventersdorp S. Africa 125 H4
Venterstad S. Africa 125 G6
Ventnor U.K. 59 F8
Ventotene, Isola i. Italy 68 E4
Ventoux, Mont mt. France 66 G4
Ventspils Latvia 55 L8
Ventura CA U.S.A. 158 D4
Venus Bay Australia 138 B7
Venustiano Carranza Mex. 161 C7
Venustiano Carranza, Presa resr Mex. 167 E3
Vera Arg. 178 D3
Vera Spain 67 F5
Vera Cruz Brazil 179 A3
Veracruz Mex. 168 E5
Vera Cruz Mex. see Veracruz
Veracruz state Mex. 167 F4
Veraval India 104 B5
Verbania Italy 68 C2
Vercelli Italy 68 C2
Vercors reg. France 66 G4
Verdalsøra Norway 54 G5
Verde r. Goiás Brazil 179 A2
Verde r. Goiás/Minas Gerais Brazil 179 B2
Verde r. Minas Gerais Brazil 179 A2
Verde r. Minas Gerais Brazil 179 A2
Verde r. Mex. 166 D3
Verde r. AZ U.S.A. 159 H5
Verde Island Passage Phil. 82 C3
Verden (Aller) Germany 63 J2
Verde Pequeno r. Brazil 179 C1
Verdi NV U.S.A. 158 D2
Verdon r. France 66 G5
Verdun France 62 F5
Vereeniging S. Africa 125 H4
Vereshchagino Russia 51 Q4
Vergennes VT U.S.A. 165 I1
Véria Greece see Veroia
Verín Spain 67 C3
Veríssimo Brazil 179 A2
Verkhneberezovskiy Kazakh. 98 C2
Verkhneimbatsk Russia 76 J3
Verkhnekolvinsk Russia 52 M2
Verkhnespasskoye Russia 52 J4
Verkhnetulomskiy Russia 54 Q2

Verkhnetulomskoye Vodokhranilishche *res.* Russia **54** Q2
Verkhnevilyuysk Russia **77** N3
Verkhneye Kuyto, Ozero *l.* Russia **54** Q4
Verkhnezeysk Russia **89** N2
Verkhniy Shergol'dzhin Russia **95** G1
Verkhniy Ul'khun Russia **95** H1
Verkhniy Vyalozerskiy Russia **52** G2
Verkhnyaya Khava Russia **53** H6
Verkhnyaya Salda Russia **51** S4
Verkhnyaya Tunguska *r.* Russia *see* **Angara**
Verkhnyaya Tura Russia **51** R4
Verkhoshizhem'ye Russia **52** K4
Verkhovazh'ye Russia **52** I3
Verkhov'ye Russia **53** H5
Verkhoyansk Russia **77** O3
Verkhoyanskiy Khrebet *mts* Russia **77** N2
Verkhuba Kazakh. **98** C2
Vermand France **62** D5
Vermelho *r.* Brazil **179** A1
Vermilion Canada **151** I4
Vermilion Bay *LA* U.S.A. **161** F6
Vermilion Cliffs *AZ* U.S.A. **159** G3
Vermilion Cliffs *UT* U.S.A. **159** G3
Vermilion Cliffs National Monument *nat. park AZ* U.S.A. **159** H3
Vermilion Lake *MN* U.S.A. **160** E2
Vermillion *SD* U.S.A. **160** D3
Vermillion Bay Canada **151** M5
Vermont *state* U.S.A. **165** I1
Vernadsky *research station* Antarctica **188** L2
Vernal *UT* U.S.A. **159** I1
Verner Canada **152** E5
Verneuk Pan *salt pan* S. Africa **124** E5
Vernon Canada **150** G5
Vernon France **62** B5
Vernon *AL* U.S.A. **161** F5
Vernon *IN* U.S.A. **164** C4
Vernon *TX* U.S.A. **161** D5
Vernon *UT* U.S.A. **159** G1
Vernon Islands Australia **134** E3
Vernoye Russia **90** C2
Vernyy Kazakh. *see* **Almaty**
Vero Beach *FL* U.S.A. **163** D7
Veroia Greece **69** J4
Verona Italy **68** D2
Verona *VA* U.S.A. **164** F4
Versailles France **62** C6
Versailles *IN* U.S.A. **164** C4
Versailles *KY* U.S.A. **164** C4
Versailles *OH* U.S.A. **164** C3
Versec Serbia *see* **Vršac**
Versmold Germany **63** I2
Vert, Île *i.* Canada **153** H4
Vertou France **66** D3
Verulam S. Africa **125** J5
Verulamium U.K. *see* **St Albans**
Verviers Belgium **62** F4
Vervins France **62** D5
Verwood Canada **151** J5
Verzy France **62** E5
Vescovato *Corsica* France **66** I5
Vesele Ukr. **53** G7
Veselyy Russia **53** I7
Veselyy Yar Russia **90** D4
Veshenskaya Russia **53** I6
Vesle *r.* France **62** D5
Veslyana *r.* Russia **52** L3
Vesontio France *see* **Besançon**
Vesoul France **66** H3
Vessem Neth. **62** F3
Vesterålen *is* Norway **54** H2
Vesterålsfjorden *sea chan.* Norway **54** H2
Vestertana Norway **54** O1
Vestfjorddalen *valley* Norway **55** F7
Vestfjorden *sea chan.* Norway **54** H3
Véstia Brazil **179** A3
Vestmanna Faroe Is **54** [inset 2]
Vestmannaeyjar Iceland **54** [inset 1]
Vestmannaeyjar *is* Iceland **54** [inset 1]
Vestnes Norway **54** E5
Vesturhorn *hd* Iceland **54** [inset 1]
Vesuvio *vol.* Italy *see* **Vesuvius**
Vesuvius *vol.* Italy **68** F4
Ves'yegonsk Russia **52** H4
Veszprém Hungary **68** G1
Veteli Fin. **54** M5
Veteran Canada **151** I4
Vetlanda Sweden **55** I8
Vetluga Russia **52** J4
Vetluga *r.* Russia **52** J4
Vetluzhskiy *Kostromskaya Oblast'* Russia **52** J4
Vetluzhskiy *Nizhegorodskaya Oblast'* Russia **52** J4
Vettore, Monte *mt.* Italy **68** E3
Veurne Belgium **62** C3
Vevay *IN* U.S.A. **164** C4
Vevey Switz. **66** H3
Vexin Normand *reg.* France **62** B5
Veyo *UT* U.S.A. **159** G3
Vézère *r.* France **66** E4
Vezirköprü Turkey **112** D2
Viajas, Isla de las *i.* Peru **176** C6
Vialar Alg. *see* **Tissemsilt**
Viamão Brazil **179** A5
Viana *Espírito Santo* Brazil **179** C3
Viana *Maranhão* Brazil **177** J4
Viana do Castelo Port. **67** B3
Vianen Neth. **62** F3
Viangchan Laos *see* **Vientiane**
Viangphoukha Laos **86** C2
Viannos Greece **69** K7
Vianópolis Brazil **179** A2
Viareggio Italy **68** D3
Viborg Denmark **55** F8
Viborg Russia *see* **Vyborg**
Vibo Valentia Italy **68** G5
Vic Spain **67** H3
Vicam Mex. **166** C3
Vicecomodoro Marambio *research station* Antarctica *see* **Marambio**
Vicente, Point *CA* U.S.A. **158** D5
Vicente Guerrero Mex. **166** A2
Vicenza Italy **68** D2
Vich Spain *see* **Vic**
Vichada *r.* Col. **176** E3
Vichadero Uruguay **178** F4
Vichy France **66** F3
Vicksburg *AZ* U.S.A. **159** G5
Vicksburg *MS* U.S.A. **161** F5
Viçosa Brazil **179** C3
Victor, Mount Antarctica **188** D2
Victor Harbor Australia **137** B7
Victoria Arg. **178** D4
Victoria *r.* Australia **134** E3
Victoria *state* Australia **138** B6
▶**Victoria** Canada **150** F5
Capital of British Columbia.
Victoria Chile **178** B5
Victoria Malaysia *see* **Labuan**
Victoria Malta **68** F6
Victoria *Luzon* Phil. **82** C3
▶**Victoria** Seychelles **185** L6
Capital of the Seychelles.
Victoria *TX* U.S.A. **161** D6
Victoria *VA* U.S.A. **165** F5
Victoria *prov.* Zimbabwe *see* **Masvingo**
▶**Victoria, Lake** Africa **122** D4
Largest lake in Africa and 3rd in the world.
Victoria, Lake Australia **137** C7
Victoria, Mount Fiji *see* **Tomanivi**
Victoria, Mount Myanmar **86** A2
Victoria, Mount P.N.G. **81** L8
Victoria and Albert Mountains Canada **147** K2
Victoria Falls Zambia/Zimbabwe **123** C5
Victoria Harbour *sea chan. H.K.* China *see* **Hong Kong Harbour**
▶**Victoria Island** Canada **146** H2
3rd largest island in North America and 9th in the world.
Victoria Land *coastal area* Antarctica **188** H2
Victoria Peak Belize **168** G5
Victoria Peak *hill H.K.* China **97** [inset]
Victoria Range *mts* N.Z. **139** D6
Victoria River Downs Australia **134** E4
Victoriaville Canada **153** H5
Victoria West S. Africa **124** F6
Victorica Arg. **178** C5
Víctor Rosales Mex. **166** E4
Victorville *CA* U.S.A. **158** E4
Victory Downs Australia **135** F6
Vidalia *LA* U.S.A. **161** F6
Vidal Junction *CA* U.S.A. **159** F4
Videle Romania **69** K2
Vidisha India **104** D5
Vidlin U.K. **60** [inset]
Vidlitsa Russia **52** G3
Viechtach Germany **63** M5
Viedma Arg. **178** D6
Viedma, Lago *l.* Arg. **178** B7
Viejo, Cerro *mt.* Mex. **166** B2
Vielank Germany **63** L1
Vielsalm Belgium **62** F4
Vienenburg Germany **63** K3
▶**Vienna** Austria **57** P6
Capital of Austria.
Vienna *MO* U.S.A. **160** F4
Vienna *WV* U.S.A. **164** E4
Vienne France **66** G4
Vienne *r.* France **66** E3
▶**Vientiane** Laos **86** C3
Capital of Laos.
Vieques *i.* Puerto Rico **169** K5
Vieremä Fin. **54** O5
Viersen Germany **62** G3
Vierzon France **66** F3
Viesca Mex. **166** E3
Viesīte Latvia **55** N8
Vieste Italy **68** G4
Vietas Sweden **54** K3
Viêt Nam *country* Asia *see* **Vietnam**
Vietnam *country* Asia **86** D3
Viêt Quang Vietnam **86** D2
Viêt Tri Vietnam **86** D2
Vieux Comptoir, Lac du *l.* Canada **152** F3
Vieux-Fort Canada **153** K4
Vieux Poste, Pointe du *pt* Canada **153** J4
Vigan *Luzon* Phil. **82** C2
Vigevano Italy **68** C2
Vigia Brazil **177** I4
Vigía Chico Mex. **167** I5
Vignacourt France **62** C4
Vignemale *mt.* France **64** D3
Vignola Italy **68** D2
Vigo Spain **67** B2
Vihanti Fin. **54** N4
Vihti Fin. **55** N6
Viipuri Russia *see* **Vyborg**
Viitasaari Fin. **54** N5
Vijayadurg India **106** B2
Vijayanagaram India *see* **Vizianagaram**
Vijayapati India **106** C4
Vijayapura India **106** B2
Vijayawada India **106** D2
Vijayraghavgarh India **104** E5
Vík Iceland **54** [inset 1]
Vikajärvi Fin. **54** O3
Vikeke East Timor *see* **Viqueque**
Viking Canada **151** I4
Vikna *i.* Norway **54** G4
Vikøyri Norway **55** E6
Vila Vanuatu *see* **Port Vila**
Vila Alferes Chamusca Moz. *see* **Guija**
Vila Bela da Santíssima Trindade Brazil **176** G7
Vila Bittencourt Brazil **176** E4
Vila Bugaço Angola *see* **Camanongue**
Vila Cabral Moz. *see* **Lichinga**
Vila da Ponte Angola *see* **Kuvango**
Vila de Aljustrel Angola *see* **Cangamba**
Vila de Almoster Angola *see* **Chiange**
Vila de João Belo Moz. *see* **Xai-Xai**
Vila de María Arg. **178** D3
Vila de Trego Morais Moz. *see* **Chókwè**
Vila Fontes Moz. *see* **Caia**
Vila Franca de Xira Port. **67** B4
Vilagarcía de Arousa Spain **67** B2
Vila Gomes da Costa Moz. **125** K3
Vilalba Spain **67** C2
Vila Luísa Moz. *see* **Marracuene**
Vila Marechal Carmona Angola *see* **Uíge**
Vila Miranda Moz. *see* **Macaloge**
Vilanandro, Tanjona *pt* Madag. **123** E5
Vilanculos Moz. **125** L1
Vila Nova de Gaia Port. **67** B3
Vilanova i la Geltrú Spain **67** G3
Vila Pery Moz. *see* **Chimoio**
Vila Real Port. **67** C3
Vilar Formoso Port. **67** C3
Vila Salazar Angola *see* **N'dalatando**
Vila Salazar Zimbabwe *see* **Sango**
Vila Teixeira de Sousa Angola *see* **Luau**
Vila Velha Brazil **179** C3
Vilcabamba, Cordillera *mts* Peru **176** D6
Vil'cheka, Zemlya *i.* Russia **76** H1
Viled' *r.* Russia **52** J3
Vileyka Belarus *see* **Vilyeyka**
Vil'gort Russia **52** K3
Vilhelmina Sweden **54** J4
Vilhena Brazil **176** F6
Viliya *r.* Lith. *see* **Neris**
Viljandi Estonia **55** N7
Viljoenskroon S. Africa **125** H4
Vilkaviškis Lith. **55** M9
Vilkija Lith. **55** M9
Vil'kitskogo, Proliv *strait* Russia **77** K2
Vilkovo Ukr. *see* **Vylkove**
Villa Abecia Bol. **176** E8
Villa Ahumada Mex. **166** D2
Villa Ángela Arg. **178** D3
Villa Bella Bol. **176** E6
Villa Bens Morocco *see* **Tarfaya**
Villablino Spain **67** C2
Villacañas Spain **67** E4
Villach Austria **57** N7
Villacidro *Sardinia* Italy **68** C5
Villa Cisneros W. Sahara *see* **Dakhla**
Villa Comaltitlán Mex. **167** G6
Villa Coronado Mex. **166** D3
Villa de Álvarez Mex. **166** E5
Villa de Cos Mex. **166** E4
Villa de Guadalupe Mex. **167** H5
Villa de San Antonio Hond. **166** [inset] I6
Villa Dolores Arg. **178** C4
Villa Flores Mex. **167** G5
Villagarcía de Arosa Spain *see* **Vilagarcía de Arousa**
Villagrán Mex. **161** D7
Villaguay Arg. **178** E4
Villahermosa Mex. **167** G5
Villa Insurgentes Mex. **166** C3
Villajoyosa Spain *see* **Villajoyosa-La Vila Joiosa**
Villajoyosa-La Vila Joiosa Spain **67** F4
Villa La Venta Mex. **167** G5
Villaldama Mex. **167** E3
Villa Mainero Mex. **161** D7
Villa María Arg. **178** D4
Villa Montes Bol. **176** F8
Villa Nora S. Africa **125** I2
Villanueva Mex. **166** E4
Villanueva de la Serena Spain **67** D4
Villanueva de los Infantes Spain **67** E4
Villanueva-y-Geltrú Spain *see* **Vilanova i la Geltrú**
Villa Ocampo Arg. **178** E3
Villa Ocampo Mex. **166** D3
Villa Ojo de Agua Arg. **178** D3
Villa O. Pereyra Mex. *see* **Villa Orestes Pereyra**
Villa Orestes Pereyra Mex. **166** D3
Villaputzu *Sardinia* Italy **68** C5
Villa Regina Arg. **178** C5
Villarrica Para. **178** E3
Villarrica, Lago *l.* Chile **178** B5
Villarrica, Parque Nacional *nat. park* Chile **178** B5
Villarrobledo Spain **67** E4
Villas *NJ* U.S.A. **165** H4
Villasalazar Zimbabwe *see* **Sango**
Villa San Giovanni Italy **68** F5
Villa Sanjurjo Morocco *see* **Al Hoceima**
Villa Unión Arg. **178** C3
Villa Unión *Coahuila* Mex. **167** E2
Villa Unión *Durango* Mex. **161** B8
Villa Unión *Sinaloa* Mex. **168** C4
Villa Valeria Arg. **178** D4
Villavicencio Col. **176** D3
Villazon Bol. **176** E8
Villefranche-sur-Saône France **66** G4
Ville-Marie Canada *see* **Montréal**
Villena Spain **67** F4
Villeneuve-sur-Lot France **66** E4
Villeneuve-sur-Yonne France **66** F2
Ville Platte *LA* U.S.A. **167** G2
Villers-Cotterêts France **62** D5
Villers-sur-Mer France **59** G9
Villerupt France **62** F5
Villeurbanne France **66** G4
Villiers S. Africa **125** I4
Villingen Germany **57** L6
Villuppuram India *see* **Villupuram**
Villupuram India **106** C4
Vilna Canada **151** I4
Vilna Lith. *see* **Vilnius**
▶**Vilnius** Lith. **55** N9
Capital of Lithuania.
Vil'nyans'k Ukr. **53** G7
Vilppula Fin. **54** N5
Vils *r. Bayern* Germany **63** L5
Vils *r. Bayern* Germany **63** N6
Vilvoorde Belgium **62** E4
Vilyeyka Belarus **55** O9
Vilyuy *r.* Russia **77** N3
Vilyuyskoye Vodokhranilishche *resr* Russia **77** M3
Vimmerby Sweden **55** I8
Vimy France **62** C4
Vina *r.* Cameroon **121** E4
Vina *CA* U.S.A. **158** B2
Viña del Mar Chile **178** B4
Vinalhaven Island *ME* U.S.A. **162** G2
Vinaròs Spain **67** G3
Vinaroz Spain *see* **Vinaròs**
Vincelotte, Lac *l.* Canada **153** G3
Vincennes *IN* U.S.A. **164** B4
Vincennes Bay Antarctica **188** F2
Vinchina Arg. **178** C3
Vindelälven *r.* Sweden **54** K5
Vindeln Sweden **54** K4
Vindhya Range *hills* India **104** C5
Vindobona Austria *see* **Vienna**
Vine Grove *KY* U.S.A. **164** C5
Vineland *NJ* U.S.A. **165** H4
Vinh Vietnam **86** D3
Vinh Loc Vietnam **86** D2
Vinh Long Vietnam **87** D5
Vinh Thưc, Đao *i.* Vietnam **86** D2
Vinita *OK* U.S.A. **161** E4
Vinjhan India **104** B5
Vinland *i.* Canada *see* **Newfoundland**
Vinnitsa Ukr. *see* **Vinnytsya**
Vinnytsya Ukr. **53** F6
Vinogradov Ukr. *see* **Vynohradiv**
▶**Vinson, Mount** *mt.* Antarctica **188** L1
Highest mountain in Antarctica.
Vinstra Norway **55** F6
Vintar *Luzon* Phil. **82** C2
Vinton *IA* U.S.A. **160** E3
Vinukonda India **106** C2
Violeta Cuba *see* **Primero de Enero**
Vipperow Germany **63** M1
Viqueque East Timor **83** C5
Virac Phil. **82** D3
Viramgam India **104** C5
Virandozero Russia **52** H3
Viranşehir Turkey **113** E3
Virawah Pak. **111** H5
Virchow, Mount *hill* Australia **134** B5
Virdel India **104** C5
Virden Canada **151** K5
Virden *NM* U.S.A. **159** I5
Vire France **66** D2
Virei Angola **123** B5
Virgem da Lapa Brazil **179** C2
Virgilina *VA* U.S.A. **165** F5
Virgin *r. AZ* U.S.A. **159** F3
Virginia Ireland **61** E4
Virginia S. Africa **125** H5
Virginia *IL* U.S.A. **160** F4
Virginia *state* U.S.A. **164** F5
Virginia Beach *VA* U.S.A. **165** H5
Virginia City *MT* U.S.A. **156** F3
Virginia City *NV* U.S.A. **158** D2
Virginia Falls Canada **149** P3
▶**Virgin Islands (U.K.)** *terr.* West Indies **169** L5
United Kingdom Overseas Territory.
▶**Virgin Islands (U.S.A.)** *terr.* West Indies **169** L5
United States Unincorporated Territory.
Virgin Mountains *AZ* U.S.A. **159** F3
Virginópolis Brazil **179** C2
Virkkala Fin. **55** N6
Virôchey Cambodia **87** D4
Viroqua *WI* U.S.A. **160** F3
Virovitica Croatia **68** G2
Virrat Fin. **54** M5
Virton Belgium **62** F5
Virtsu Estonia **55** M7
Virudhunagar India **106** C4
Virudunagar India *see* **Virudhunagar**
Virunga, Parc National des *nat. park* Dem. Rep. Congo **122** C4
Vis *i.* Croatia **68** G3
Visaginas Lith. **55** O9
Visakhapatnam India *see* **Vishakhapatnam**
Visalia *CA* U.S.A. **158** D3
Visapur India **106** B2
Visayan Islands Phil. **82** D4
Visayan Sea Phil. **82** C4
Visbek Germany **63** I2
Visby Sweden **55** K8
Viscount Melville Sound *sea chan.* Canada **147** G2
Visé Belgium **62** F4
Viseu Brazil **177** I4
Viseu Port. **67** C3
Vishakhapatnam India **106** D2
Vishera *r.* Russia **51** R4
Vishera *r.* Russia **52** L3
Vishwanath India **96** B3
Viški Latvia **55** O8
Visnagar India **104** C5
Viso, Monte *mt.* Italy **68** B2
Visoko Bos. & Herz. **68** H3
Visp Switz. **66** H3
Visselhövede Germany **63** J2
Vista *CA* U.S.A. **158** E5
Vista Lake *CA* U.S.A. **158** D4
Vistonida, Limni *lag.* Greece **69** K4
Vistula *r.* Poland **57** Q3
Vitebsk Belarus *see* **Vitsyebsk**
Viterbo Italy **68** E3
Vitichi Bol. **176** E8
Vitigudino Spain **67** C3
Viti Levu *i.* Fiji **133** H3
Vitimskoye Ploskogor'ye *plat.* Russia **89** K2
Vitória Brazil **179** C3
Vitória da Conquista Brazil **179** C1
Vitoria-Gasteiz Spain **67** E2
Vitória Seamount *sea feature* S. Atlantic Ocean **184** F7
Vitré France **66** D2
Vitry-en-Artois France **62** C4
Vitry-le-François France **62** E6
Vitsyebsk Belarus **53** F5
Vittangi Sweden **54** L3
Vittel France **66** G2
Vittoria *Sicily* Italy **68** F6
Vittorio Veneto Italy **68** E2
Viveiro Spain **67** C2
Vivero Spain *see* **Viveiro**
Vivo S. Africa **125** I2
Vizagapatam India *see* **Vishakhapatnam**
Vizcaíno, Desierto de *des.* Mex. **166** B3
Vizcaíno, Sierra *mts* Mex. **166** B3
Vize Turkey **69** L4
Vize, Ostrov *i.* Russia **76** I2
Vizhas *r.* Russia **52** J2
Vizianagaram India **106** D2
Vizinga Russia **52** K3
Vlaardingen Neth. **62** E3
Vlădeasa, Vârful *mt.* Romania **69** J1
Vladikavkaz Russia **113** G2
Vladimir *Primorskiy Kray* Russia **90** D4
Vladimir *Vladimirskaya Oblast'* Russia **52** I4
Vladimiro-Aleksandrovskoye Russia **90** D4
Vladimir-Volynskiy Ukr. *see* **Volodymyr-Volyns'kyy**
Vladivostok Russia **90** C4
Vlakte S. Africa **125** I3
Vlasotince Serbia **69** J3
Vlas'yevo Russia **90** F1
Vlieland *i.* Neth. **62** E1
Vlissingen Neth. **62** D3
Vlora Albania *see* **Vlorë**
Vlorë Albania **69** H4
Vlotho Germany **63** I2
Vlotslavsk Poland *see* **Włocławek**
Vltava *r.* Czech Rep. **57** O5
Vobkent Uzbek. **111** G1
Vöcklabruck Austria **57** N6
Vodlozero, Ozero *l.* Russia **52** H3
Voe U.K. **60** [inset]
Voerendaal Neth. **62** F4
Vogelkop *pen.* Indon. *see* **Doberai, Jazirah**
Vogelsberg *hills* Germany **63** I4
Voghera Italy **68** C2
Vohburg an der Donau Germany **63** L6
Vohémar Madag. *see* **Iharaña**
Vohenstrauß Germany **63** M5
Vohibinany Madag. *see* **Ampasimanolotra**
Vohimarina Madag. *see* **Iharaña**
Vohimena, Tanjona *c.* Madag. **123** E6
Vohipeno Madag. **123** E6
Vöhl Germany **63** I3
Võhma Estonia **55** N7
Voinjama Liberia **120** C4
Vojens Denmark **55** F9
Vojvodina *prov.* Serbia **69** H2
Vokhma Russia **52** J4
Voknavolok Russia **54** Q4
Vokre, Hosséré *mt.* Cameroon **120** E4
Vol' *r.* Russia **52** L3
Volcán Barú, Parque Nacional *nat. park* Panama **166** [inset] J7
Volcano Bay Japan *see* **Uchiura-wan**
▶**Volcano Islands** Japan **81** K2
Part of Japan.
Volda Norway **54** E5
Vol'dino Russia **52** L3
Volendam Neth. **62** F2
Volga Russia **52** H4
▶**Volga** *r.* Russia **53** J7
Longest river in Europe.
Volga Upland *hills* Russia *see* **Privolzhskaya Vozvyshennost'**
Volgodonsk Russia **53** I7
Volgograd Russia **53** J6
Volgogradskoye Vodokhranilishche *resr* Russia **53** J6
Völkermarkt Austria **57** O7
Volkhov Russia **52** G4
Volkhov *r.* Russia **52** G3
Völklingen Germany **62** G5
Volkovysk Belarus *see* **Vawkavysk**
Volksrust S. Africa **125** I4
Vol'no-Nadezhdinskoye Russia **90** C4
Volnovakha Ukr. **53** H7
Vol'nyansk Ukr. *see* **Vil'nyans'k**
Volochanka Russia **76** K2
Volochisk Ukr. *see* **Volochys'k**
Volochys'k Ukr. **53** E6
Volodars'ke Ukr. **53** H7
Volodarskoye Kazakh. *see* **Saumalkol'**
Volodymyr-Volyns'kyy Ukr. **53** E6
Vologda Russia **52** H4
Volokolamsk Russia **52** G4
Volokovaya Russia **52** K2
Volos Greece **69** J5
Volosovo Russia **55** P7
Volot Russia **52** F4
Volovo Russia **53** H5
Volozhin Belarus *see* **Valozhyn**
Volsinii Italy *see* **Orvieto**
Vol'sk Russia **53** J5
▶**Volta, Lake** *resr* Ghana **120** D4
4th largest lake in Africa.
Volta Blanche *r.* Burkina Faso/Ghana *see* **White Volta**
Voltaire, Cape Australia **134** D3
Volta Redonda Brazil **179** B3
Vol'tevo Russia **52** J2
Volturno *r.* Italy **68** E4
Volubilis *tourist site* Morocco **64** C5
Volvi, Limni *l.* Greece **69** J4
Volzhsk Russia **52** K5
Volzhskiy *Samarskaya Oblast'* Russia **53** K5
Volzhskiy *Volgogradskaya Oblast'* Russia **53** J6
Vondanka Russia **52** J4
Von Frank Mountain *AK* U.S.A. **148** I3
Vontimitta India **106** C3
Vopnafjörður Iceland **54** [inset 1]
Vopnafjörður *b.* Iceland **54** [inset 1]
Vörå Fin. **54** M5
Voranava Belarus **55** N9
Voreies Sporades *is* Greece **69** J5
Voríai Sporádhes *is* Greece *see* **Voreies Sporades**
Voring Plateau *sea feature* N. Atlantic Ocean **184** I1
Vorjing *mt.* India **105** H3
Vorkuta Russia **76** H3
Vormsi *i.* Estonia **55** M7
Vorona *r.* Russia **53** I6
Voronezh Russia **53** H6
Voronezh *r.* Russia **53** H6
Voronov, Mys *pt* Russia **52** I2
Vorontsovo-Aleksandrovskoye Russia *see* **Zelenokumsk**
Voroshilov Russia *see* **Ussuriysk**
Voroshilovgrad Ukr. *see* **Luhans'k**
Voroshilovsk Russia *see* **Stavropol'**
Voroshilovsk Ukr. *see* **Alchevs'k**
Vorotynets Russia **52** J4
Vorozhba Ukr. **53** G6
Vorpommersche Boddenlandschaft, Nationalpark *nat. park* Germany **57** N3
Vorskla *r.* Russia **53** G6
Võrtsjärv *l.* Estonia **55** N7
Võru Estonia **55** O8
Vorukh Tajik. **111** H2
Vosburg S. Africa **124** F6
Vose' Tajik. **111** H2
Vosges *mts* France **66** H3
Voskresensk Russia **53** H5
Voskresenskoye Russia **52** H4
Voss Norway **55** E6
Vostochno-Sakhalinskiye Gory *mts* Russia **90** F2
Vostochno-Sibirskoye More *sea* Russia *see* **East Siberian Sea**
Vostochnyy *Kirovskaya Oblast'* Russia **52** L4
Vostochnyy *Sakhalinskaya Oblast'* Russia **90** F2
Vostochnyy Kazakhstan *admin. div.* Kazakh. **98** D2
Vostochnyy Sayan *mts* Russia **88** G2
▶**Vostok** *research station* Antarctica **188** F1
Lowest recorded screen temperature in the world.
Vostok *Primorskiy Kray* Russia **90** D3
Vostok *Sakhalinskaya Oblast'* Russia *see* **Neftegorsk (abandoned)**
Vostok Island Kiribati **187** J6
Vostroye Russia **52** J3
Votkinsk Russia **51** Q4
Votkinskoye Vodokhranilishche *resr* Russia **51** R4
Votuporanga Brazil **179** A3
Vouziers France **62** E5
Voves France **66** E2
Voyageurs National Park *MN* U.S.A. **160** E1
Voynitsa Russia **54** Q4
Vöyri Fin. *see* **Vörå**
Voyvozh Russia **52** L3
Vozhayel' Russia **52** K3
Vozhe, Ozero *l.* Russia **52** H3
Vozhega Russia **52** I3
Vozhgaly Russia **52** K4
Voznesens'k Ukr. **53** F7
Vozonin Trough *sea feature* Arctic Ocean **189** F1
Vozrozhdeniya Island *i.* Uzbek. **102** A3
Vozzhayevka Russia **90** C2
Vrangel' Russia **90** D4
Vrangelya, Mys *pt* Russia **90** E1
Vranje Serbia **69** I3
Vratnik *pass* Bulg. **69** L3
Vratsa Bulg. **69** J3
Vrbas Serbia **69** H2
Vrede S. Africa **125** I4
Vredefort S. Africa **125** H4
Vredenburg S. Africa **124** C7
Vredendal S. Africa **124** D6
Vresse-sur-Semois Belgium **62** E5
Vriddhachalam India **106** C4
Vries Neth. **62** G1
Vrigstad Sweden **55** I8
Vršac Serbia **69** I2
Vryburg S. Africa **124** G4
Vryheid S. Africa **125** J4
Vsevidof, Mount *vol. AK* U.S.A. **146** B4
Vsevolozhsk Russia **52** F3
Vu Ban Vietnam **86** D2
Vučitrn Kosovo *see* **Vushtrri**
Vukovar Croatia **69** H2
Vuktyl Russia **51** R3
Vukuzakhe S. Africa **125** I4
Vulcan Canada **150** H5
Vulcan Island P.N.G. *see* **Manam Island**
Vulcano, Isola *i.* Italy **68** F5

Vu Liêt Vietnam 86 D3
Vulkathunha-Gammon Ranges National Park Australia 137 B6
Vulture Mountains AZ U.S.A. 159 G5
Vung Tau Vietnam 87 D5
Vuntut National Park Canada 149 M1
Vuohijärvi Fin. 55 O6
Vuolijoki Fin. 54 O4
Vuollerim Sweden 54 L3
Vuostimo Fin. 54 O3
Vurnary Russia 52 J5
Vushtrri Kosovo 69 I3
Vvedenovka Russia 90 C2
Vyara India 104 C5
Vyarkhowye Belarus see Ruba
Vyatka Russia see Kirov
Vyatka r. Russia 52 K5
Vyatskiye Polyany Russia 52 K4
Vyazemskiy Russia 90 D3
Vyaz'ma Russia 53 G5
Vyazniki Russia 52 I4
Vyazovka Russia 53 J5
Vyborg Russia 55 P6
Vychegda r. Russia 52 J3
Vychegodskiy Russia 52 J3
Vydrino Russia 94 F1
Vyerkhnyadzvinsk Belarus 55 O9
Vyetryna Belarus 55 P9
Vygozero, Ozero l. Russia 52 G3
Vyksa Russia 53 I5
Vylkove Ukr. 69 M2
Vym' r. Russia 52 K3
Vynohradiv Ukr. 53 D6
Vypin Island India 106 C4
Vypolzovo Russia 52 G4
Vyritsa Russia 55 Q7
Vyrnwy, Lake U.K. 59 D6
Vyselki Russia 53 H7
Vysha Russia 53 I5
Vyshhorod Ukr. 53 F6
Vyshnevolotskaya Gryada ridge Russia 52 G4
Vyshniy-Volochek Russia 52 G4
Vyškov Czech Rep. 57 P6
Vysokaya Gora Russia 52 K5
Vysokogorniy Russia 90 E2
Vystupovychi Ukr. 53 F6
Vytegra Russia 52 H3
Vyya r. Russia 52 J3
Vyžuona r. Lith. 55 N9

Wa Ghana 120 C3
Waal r. Neth. 62 E3
Waalwijk Neth. 62 F3
Waat South Sudan 108 D8
Wabag P.N.G. 81 K8
Wabakimi Lake Canada 152 C4
Wabasca r. Canada 150 H3
Wabasca-Desmarais Canada 150 H4
Wabash IN U.S.A. 164 C3
Wabash r. IN U.S.A. 164 A5
Wabasha MN U.S.A. 160 E2
Wabassi r. Canada 152 D4
Wabatongushi Lake Canada 152 D4
Wabigoon Lake Canada 151 M5
Wabowden Canada 151 L4
Wabrah well Saudi Arabia 110 B5
Wabu China 97 H1
Wabuk Point Canada 152 D3
Wabush Canada 153 I3
Waccasassa Bay FL U.S.A. 163 D6
Wachi Japan 92 B3
Wächtersbach Germany 63 J4
Waco Canada 153 I4
Waco TX U.S.A. 161 D6
Waconda Lake KS U.S.A. 160 D4
Wada Japan 93 G3
Wada-misaki pt Japan 92 B4
Wada-tōge pass Japan 93 E2
Wadayama Japan see Asago
Wadbilliga National Park Australia 138 D6
Waddān Libya 65 H6
Waddell Dam AZ U.S.A. 159 G5
Waddeneilanden Neth. see West Frisian Islands
Waddenzee sea chan. Neth. 62 E2
Waddington, Mount Canada 150 E5
Waddinxveen Neth. 62 E2
Wadebridge U.K. 59 C8
Wadena Canada 151 K5
Wadena MN U.S.A. 160 E2
Wadern Germany 62 G5
Wadesville IN U.S.A. 164 B4
Wadeye Australia 134 E3
Wadgassen Germany 62 G5
Wadh Pak. 111 G5
Wadhwan India see Surendranagar
Wadi India 106 C2
Wādī as Sīr Jordan 107 B4
Wadi Halfa Sudan 108 D5
Wadi Howar National Park nat. park Sudan 122 C2
Wadi Rum tourist site Jordan 107 B5
Wadi Rum Protected Area tourist site Jordan 107 B5
Wad Madani Sudan 108 D7
Wad Rawa Sudan 108 D6
Wadsworth NV U.S.A. 158 D2
Wafangdian China 95 J4
Wafra Kuwait see Al Wafrah
Wagenfeld Germany 63 I2
Wagenhoff Germany 63 K2
Wagga Wagga Australia 138 C5
Wagner SD U.S.A. 160 D3
Wagoner OK U.S.A. 161 E4
Wagon Mound NM U.S.A. 157 G5
Wah Pak. 111 I3
Wahai Seram Indon. 83 D3
Wāḥāt Jālū Libya 121 F2
Wahemen, Lac l. Canada 153 H3
Wahiawā HI U.S.A. 157 [inset]
Wahlhausen Germany 63 J3
Wahpeton ND U.S.A. 160 D2
Wahran Alg. see Oran
Wah Wah Mountains UT U.S.A. 159 G2
Wai India 106 B2
Waialua HI U.S.A. 157 [inset]
Waiau N.Z. see Franz Josef Glacier
Waiau r. N.Z. 139 D6
Waiblingen Germany 63 J6
Waidhofen an der Ybbs Austria 57 O7
Waigama Papua Indon. 83 D3
Waigeo i. Papua Indon. 83 D3
Waiheke Island N.Z. 139 E3
Waikabubak Sumba Indon. 83 A5
Waikaia r. N.Z. 139 B7
Waikari N.Z. 139 D6
Waikerie Australia 137 B7
Waiklibang Flores Indon. 83 B5
Waikouaiti N.Z. 139 C7
Wailuku HI U.S.A. 157 [inset]
Waimangaroa N.Z. 139 C5
Waimarama N.Z. 139 F4
Waimate N.Z. 139 C7
Waimea HI U.S.A. 157 [inset]
Waimenda Celebes Indon. 83 B3
Wainganga r. India 106 C2
Waingapu Sumba Indon. 83 B5
Wainhouse Corner U.K. 59 C8
Waini Point Guyana 177 G2
Wainwright Canada 151 I4
Wainwright AK U.S.A. 148 H1
Waiouru N.Z. 139 E4
Waipahi N.Z. 139 B8
Waipaoa r. N.Z. 139 F4
Waipara N.Z. 139 D6
Waipawa N.Z. 139 F4
Waipukurau N.Z. 139 F4
Wairarapa, Lake N.Z. 139 E5
Wairau r. N.Z. 139 E5
Wairoa N.Z. 139 F4
Wairoa r. N.Z. 139 F4
Wairunu Flores Indon. 83 B5
Waisai Papua Indon. 83 D3
Waitahanui N.Z. 139 F4
Waitahuna N.Z. 139 B7
Waitakaruru N.Z. 139 E3
Waitaki r. N.Z. 139 C7
Waitangi N.Z. 133 I6
Waite River Australia 134 F5
Waiuku N.Z. 139 E3
Waiwera South N.Z. 139 B8
Waiya Seram Indon. 83 D3
Waiyang China 97 H3
Wajima Japan 91 E5
Wajir Kenya 122 E3
Waka Flores Indon. 83 B5
Waka, Tanjung pt Indon. 83 C3
Wakasa Japan 92 B3
Wakasa-wan b. Japan 92 B3
Wakasa-wan Kokutei-kōen park Japan 92 B3
Wakatipu, Lake N.Z. 139 B7
Wakatobi, Taman Nasional nat. park Indon. 83 B4
Wakaw Canada 151 J4
Wakayama Japan 92 B4
Wakayama pref. Japan 92 B5
Wake Atoll terr. N. Pacific Ocean see Wake Island
WaKeeney KS U.S.A. 160 D4
Wakefield N.Z. 139 D5
Wakefield U.K. 58 F5
Wakefield MI U.S.A. 160 F2
Wakefield RI U.S.A. 165 J3
Wakefield VA U.S.A. 165 G5

▶Wake Island terr. N. Pacific Ocean 186 H4
United States Unincorporated Territory.

Wakema Myanmar 86 A3
Wākhān reg. Afgh. 111 I2
Wakkanai Japan 90 F3
Wakkerstroom S. Africa 125 J4
Wakool Australia 138 B5
Wakool r. Australia 138 A5
Wakuach, Lac l. Canada 153 I3
Waku-Kungo Angola 123 B5
Wałbrzych Poland 57 P5
Walcha Australia 138 E3
Walcott WY U.S.A. 156 G4
Walcourt Belgium 62 E4
Wałcz Poland 57 P4
Waldburg Range mts Australia 135 B6
Walden NY U.S.A. 165 H3
Waldenbuch Germany 63 J6
Waldenburg Poland see Wałbrzych
Waldkraiburg Germany 57 N6
Waldo OH U.S.A. 164 D3
Waldoboro ME U.S.A. 165 K1
Waldorf MD U.S.A. 165 G4
Waldport OR U.S.A. 156 B3
Waldron AR U.S.A. 161 E5
Waldron, Cape Antarctica 188 F2
Walea, Selat sea chan. Indon. 83 B3
Waleabahi i. Indon. 83 B3
Waleakodi i. Indon. 83 B3
Walebing Australia 135 B7
Walêg China 96 D2
Wales admin. div. U.K. 59 D6
Wales AK U.S.A. 148 E2
Walgaon India 104 D5
Walgett Australia 138 D3
Walgreen Coast Antarctica 188 K1
Walhalla MI U.S.A. 164 B2
Walhalla ND U.S.A. 160 D1
Walikale Dem. Rep. Congo 121 F5
Walingai P.N.G. 81 L8
Walker r. Australia 136 A2
Walker watercourse Australia 135 F6
Walker MI U.S.A. 164 C2
Walker MN U.S.A. 160 E2
Walker r. NV U.S.A. 158 D2
Walker Bay S. Africa 124 D8
Walker Creek r. Australia 136 C3
Walker Lake Canada 151 L4
Walker Lake AK U.S.A. 148 I2
Walker Lake NV U.S.A. 158 D2
Walker Pass CA U.S.A. 158 D4
Walkersville MD U.S.A. 165 G4
Walkerton Canada 164 E1
Walkerton IN U.S.A. 164 B3
Wall, Mount hill Australia 134 B5
Wallaby Island Australia 136 C2
Wallace ID U.S.A. 156 D3
Wallace NC U.S.A. 163 E5
Wallace VA U.S.A. 164 D5
Wallaceburg Canada 164 D2
Wallal Downs Australia 134 C4
Wallangarra Australia 138 E2
Wallaroo Australia 137 B7
Wallasey U.K. 58 D5
Walla Walla Australia 138 C5
Walla Walla WA U.S.A. 156 D3
Walldürn Germany 63 J5
Wallekraal S. Africa 124 C6
Wallendbeen Australia 138 D5
Wallingford U.K. 59 F7
Wallis, Îles is Wallis and Futuna Is 133 I3

▶Wallis and Futuna Islands terr. S. Pacific Ocean 133 I3
French Overseas Collectivity.

Wallis et Futuna, Îles terr. S. Pacific Ocean see Wallis and Futuna Islands
Wallis Islands Wallis and Futuna Is see Wallis, Îles
Wallis Lake inlet Australia 138 F4
Wall of Genghis Khan tourist site Asia 95 H1
Wallonia, Major Mining Sites of tourist site Belgium 62 E4
Wallops Island VA U.S.A. 165 H5
Wallowa Mountains OR U.S.A. 156 D3
Walls U.K. 60 [inset]
Walls of Jerusalem National Park Australia 137 [inset]
Wallumbilla Australia 137 E5
Walmsley Lake Canada 151 I2
Walney, Isle of i. U.K. 58 D4
Walnut Creek CA U.S.A. 158 B3
Walnut Grove CA U.S.A. 158 C2
Walnut Ridge AR U.S.A. 161 F4
Walong India 105 I3
Walpole NH U.S.A. 165 I2
Walrus Island AK U.S.A. 148 E4
Walrus Islands AK U.S.A. 148 G4
Walsall U.K. 59 F6
Walsenburg CO U.S.A. 157 G5
Walsh CO U.S.A. 161 C4
Walsrode Germany 63 J2
Waltair India 106 D2
Walterboro SC U.S.A. 163 D5
Walters OK U.S.A. 161 D5
Walter's Range hills Australia 138 B2
Walthall MS U.S.A. 161 F5
Waltham MA U.S.A. 165 J2
Walton IN U.S.A. 164 B3
Walton KY U.S.A. 164 C4
Walton NY U.S.A. 165 H2
Walton WV U.S.A. 164 E4
Walvisbaai Namibia see Walvis Bay
Walvisbaai b. Namibia see Walvis Bay
Walvis Bay Namibia 124 B2
Walvis Bay b. Namibia 124 B2
Walvis Ridge sea feature S. Atlantic Ocean 184 H8
Wāmā Afgh. 111 H3
Wamba Équateur Dem. Rep. Congo 121 F5
Wamba Orientale Dem. Rep. Congo 122 C3
Wamba Nigeria 120 D4
Wamlana Buru Indon. 83 C3
Wampum PA U.S.A. 164 E3
Wampusirpi Hond. 166 [inset] I6
Wamsutter WY U.S.A. 156 G4
Wamulan Buru Indon. 83 C3
Wana Pak. 111 H3
Wanaaring Australia 138 B2
Wanaka N.Z. 139 B7
Wanaka, Lake N.Z. 139 B7
Wan'an China 97 G3
Wanapitei Lake Canada 152 E5
Wanasabari Celebes Indon. 83 B4
Wanbi Australia 137 C7
Wanbrow, Cape N.Z. 139 C7
Wanci Celebes Indon. 83 B4
Wanda Shan mts China 90 D3
Wandering River Canada 151 H4
Wandersleben Germany 63 K4
Wandlitz Germany 63 N2
Wando S. Korea 91 B6
Wandoan Australia 137 E5
Wanganui N.Z. 139 E4
Wanganui r. N.Z. 139 E4
Wangaratta Australia 138 C6
Wangcang China 96 E1
Wangcun China 95 J4
Wangda China see Zogang
Wangdain China 99 E7
Wangdu China 95 H4
Wangdue Phodrang Bhutan 105 G4
Wanggamet, Gunung mt. Sumba Indon. 83 B5
Wanggao China 97 F3
Wang Gaxun China 94 D4
Wanggezhuang China see Jiaonan
Wangguan China 96 E1
Wangiwangi i. Indon. 83 B4
Wangjiawan China 95 G4
Wangkibila Hond. 166 [inset] I6
Wangkui China 90 B3
Wangmo China 96 E3
Wangqing China 90 C4
Wangwu Shan mts China 97 F1
Wangying China see Huaiyin
Wanham Canada 150 G4
Wan Hsa-la Myanmar 86 B2
Wanie-Rukula Dem. Rep. Congo 122 C3
Wankaner India 104 B5
Wankie Zimbabwe see Hwange
Wanlaweyn Somalia 122 E3
Wanna Germany 63 I1
Wanna Lakes salt flat Australia 135 E7
Wannian China 97 H2
Wanning China 97 F5
Wanouchi Japan 92 C3
Wanroij Neth. 62 F3
Wanrong China 95 G5
Wanshan China 97 F3
Wanshan Qundao is China 97 G4
Wansheng China 96 E2
Wanshengchang China see Wansheng
Wantage U.K. 59 F7
Wanxian China see Wanzhou
Wanyuan China 97 F1
Wanzai China 97 G2
Wanze Belgium 62 F4
Wanzhou China 97 F2
Wapakoneta OH U.S.A. 164 C3
Wapawekka Lake Canada 151 J4
Wapello IA U.S.A. 160 F3
Wapikaimaski Lake Canada 152 C4
Wapikopa Lake Canada 152 C3
Wapiti r. Canada 150 G4
Wapotih Buru Indon. 83 C3
Wapusk National Park Canada 151 M3
Waqên China 96 D1
Waqf aṣ Ṣawwān, Jibāl hills Jordan 107 C4
War WV U.S.A. 164 E5
Wara Japan 92 D3
Warangal India 106 C2
Waranga Reservoir Australia 138 B6
Waratah Bay Australia 138 B7
Warbreccan Australia 136 C5
Warburg Germany 63 J3
Warburton Australia 135 D6
Warburton watercourse Australia 137 B5
Warburton Bay Canada 151 I2
Warche r. Belgium 62 F4
Ward, Mount N.Z. 139 B6
Warden S. Africa 125 I4
Wardenburg Germany 63 I1
Warder Eth. 122 E3
Wardha India 106 C1
Wardha r. India 106 C2
Ward Hill hill U.K. 60 F2
Ward Hunt, Cape P.N.G. 81 L8
Ware Canada 150 E3
Ware MA U.S.A. 165 I2
Wareham U.K. 59 E8
Waremme Belgium 62 F4
Waren (Müritz) Germany 63 M1
Warendorf Germany 63 H3
Warginburra Peninsula Australia 136 E4
Wargla Alg. see Ouargla
Warialda Australia 138 E2
Warin Chamrap Thai. 86 D4
Waring Mountains AK U.S.A. 148 G2
Warkum Neth. see Workum
Warkworth U.K. 58 F3
Warli China see Walêg
Warloy-Baillon France 62 C4
Warman Canada 151 J4
Warmbad Namibia 124 D5
Warmbad S. Africa see Bela-Bela
Warmbaths S. Africa see Bela-Bela
Warminster U.K. 59 E7
Warminster PA U.S.A. 165 H3
Warmond Neth. 62 E2
Warm Springs NV U.S.A. 158 E2
Warm Springs VA U.S.A. 164 F4
Warmwaterberg mts S. Africa 124 E7
Warner Canada 151 H5
Warner Lakes OR U.S.A. 156 D4
Warner Mountains CA U.S.A. 156 C4
Warnes Bol. 176 F7
Warning, Mount Australia 138 F2
Waronda India 106 C2
Warora India 106 C1
Warra Australia 138 E1
Warragamba Reservoir Australia 138 E5
Warragul Australia 138 B7
Warrambool r. Australia 138 C3
Warrandirinna, Lake salt flat Australia 137 B5
Warrandyte Australia 138 B6
Warrap South Sudan 108 C8
Warrawagine Australia 134 C5
Warrego r. Australia 138 B3
Warrego Range hills Australia 136 D5
Warren Australia 138 C3
Warren AR U.S.A. 161 E5
Warren MI U.S.A. 164 D2
Warren MN U.S.A. 160 D1
Warren OH U.S.A. 164 E3
Warren PA U.S.A. 164 F3
Warren Hastings Island Palau see Merir
Warren Island AK U.S.A. 150 C4
Warren Point pt Canada 149 N1
Warrenpoint U.K. 61 F3
Warrensburg MO U.S.A. 160 E4
Warrensburg NY U.S.A. 165 I2
Warrenton S. Africa 124 G5
Warrenton GA U.S.A. 163 D5
Warrenton MO U.S.A. 160 F4
Warrenton VA U.S.A. 165 G4
Warri Nigeria 120 D4
Warriners Creek watercourse Australia 137 B6
Warrington N.Z. 139 C7
Warrington U.K. 58 E5
Warrington FL U.S.A. 163 C6
Warrnambool Australia 137 C8
Warroad MN U.S.A. 160 E1
Warrumbungle National Park Australia 138 D3
Warsaj 'Alāqahdārī Afgh. 111 H2

▶Warsaw Poland 57 R4
Capital of Poland.

Warsaw IN U.S.A. 164 C3
Warsaw KY U.S.A. 164 C4
Warsaw MO U.S.A. 160 E4
Warsaw NY U.S.A. 165 F2
Warsaw VA U.S.A. 165 G5
Warshiikh Somalia 122 E3
Warstein Germany 63 I3
Warszawa Poland see Warsaw
Warta r. Poland 57 O4
Wartburg, Schloss tourist site Germany 63 K3
Waru Kalimantan Indon. 85 G3
Warwick Australia 138 F2
Warwick U.K. 59 F6
Warwick RI U.S.A. 165 J3
Warzhong China 96 D2
Wasaga Beach Canada 164 E1
Wasatch Range mts UT U.S.A. 156 F5
Wasbank S. Africa 125 J5
Wasco CA U.S.A. 158 D4
Washburn ND U.S.A. 160 C2
Washburn WI U.S.A. 160 F2
Wāshēr Afgh. 111 F3
Washiga-take mt. Japan 92 C3
Washim India 106 C1

▶Washington DC U.S.A. 165 G4
Capital of the United States of America.

Washington GA U.S.A. 163 D5
Washington IA U.S.A. 160 F3
Washington IN U.S.A. 164 B4
Washington MO U.S.A. 160 F4
Washington NC U.S.A. 162 E5
Washington NJ U.S.A. 165 H3
Washington PA U.S.A. 164 E3
Washington UT U.S.A. 159 G3
Washington state U.S.A. 156 C3
Washington, Cape Antarctica 188 H2
Washington, Mount NH U.S.A. 165 J1
Washington Court House OH U.S.A. 164 D4
Washington Island WI U.S.A. 162 C2
Washington Land reg. Greenland 147 L2
Washita r. OK U.S.A. 161 D5
Washpool National Park Australia 138 F2
Washtucna WA U.S.A. 156 D3
Washuk Pak. 111 G5
Wasi India 106 B2
Wasi' Saudi Arabia 110 B5
Wasi' well Saudi Arabia 110 C6
Wasiri Moluccas Indon. 83 C4
Wasisi Buru Indon. 83 C3
Waskaganish Canada 152 F4
Waskagheganish Canada see Waskaganish
Waskaiowaka Lake Canada 151 L3
Waskey, Mount AK U.S.A. 148 H4
Waspán Nicaragua 166 [inset] I6
Wassenaar Neth. 62 E2
Wasser Namibia 124 D4
Wasserkuppe hill Germany 63 J4
Wassertrüdingen Germany 63 K5
Wassuk Range mts NV U.S.A. 158 D2
Wasua P.N.G. 81 K8
Wasum P.N.G. 81 L8
Waswanipi r. Canada 152 F4
Waswanipi, Lac l. Canada 152 F4
Watam P.N.G. 81 K7
Watambayoli Celebes Indon. 83 B3
Watampone Celebes Indon. 83 B4
Watana, Mount AK U.S.A. 149 J3
Watansopeng Celebes Indon. 83 A4
Watapi Lake Canada 151 I4
Watarai Japan 92 C4
Watarase-gawa r. Japan 93 F2
Watarrka National Park Australia 135 E6
Watauchi Japan 93 E2
Watenstadt-Salzgitter Germany see Salzgitter
Waterbury CT U.S.A. 165 I3
Waterbury VT U.S.A. 165 I1
Waterbury Lake Canada 151 J3
Water Cays i. Bahamas 163 E8
Waterdown Canada 164 F2
Wateree r. SC U.S.A. 163 D5
Waterfall AK U.S.A. 149 N5
Waterford Ireland 61 E5
Waterford PA U.S.A. 164 F3
Waterford WI U.S.A. 164 A2
Waterford Harbour Ireland 61 F5
Watergrasshill Ireland 61 D5
Waterhen Lake Canada 151 L4
Waterloo Australia 134 E4
Waterloo Belgium 62 E4
Waterloo Ont. Canada 164 E2
Waterloo Que. Canada 165 I1
Waterloo IA U.S.A. 160 E3
Waterloo IL U.S.A. 160 F4
Waterloo NY U.S.A. 165 G2
Waterlooville U.K. 59 F8
Waterton Lakes National Park Canada 150 H5
Watertown NY U.S.A. 165 H2
Watertown SD U.S.A. 160 D2
Watertown WI U.S.A. 160 F3
Water Valley MS U.S.A. 161 F5
Waterville ME U.S.A. 165 K1
Waterville WA U.S.A. 156 C3
Watford Canada 164 E2
Watford U.K. 59 G7
Watford City ND U.S.A. 160 C2
Wathaman r. Canada 151 K3
Wathaman Lake Canada 151 K3
Watheroo National Park Australia 135 A7
Wathlingen Germany 63 K2
Watino Canada 150 G4
Watīr, Wādī watercourse Egypt 107 B5
Watkins Glen NY U.S.A. 165 G2
Watling Island Bahamas see San Salvador
Watmuri Moluccas Indon. 134 E1
Watonga OK U.S.A. 161 D5
Watowato, Bukit mt. Halmahera Indon. 83 D2
Watrous Canada 151 J5
Watrous NM U.S.A. 157 G6
Watseka IL U.S.A. 164 B3
Watsi Kengo Dem. Rep. Congo 121 F5
Watson r. Australia 136 C2
Watson Canada 151 J4
Watson Lake Canada 149 O3
Watsontown PA U.S.A. 165 G3
Watsonville CA U.S.A. 158 C3
Watten U.K. 60 F2
Watterson Lake Canada 151 L2
Watton U.K. 59 H6
Watts Bar Lake resr TN U.S.A. 162 C5
Wattsburg PA U.S.A. 164 F2
Watubela, Kepulauan is Moluccas Indon. 81 I7
Watuwila, Bukit mt. Indon. 83 B3
Wau P.N.G. 81 L8
Wau South Sudan 108 C8
Waubay Lake SD U.S.A. 160 D2
Wauchope N.S.W. Australia 138 F3
Wauchope N.T. Australia 134 F5
Waukara, Gunung mt. Indon. 83 A3
Waukaringa (abandoned) Australia 137 B7
Waukarlycarly, Lake salt flat Australia 134 C5
Waukegan IL U.S.A. 164 B2
Waukesha WI U.S.A. 164 A2
Waupaca WI U.S.A. 160 F2
Waupun WI U.S.A. 160 F3
Waurika OK U.S.A. 161 D5
Wausau WI U.S.A. 160 F2
Wausaukee WI U.S.A. 162 C2
Wauseon OH U.S.A. 164 C3
Wautoma WI U.S.A. 160 F2
Wave Hill Australia 134 E4
Waveney r. U.K. 59 I6
Waverly IA U.S.A. 160 E3
Waverly NY U.S.A. 165 G2
Waverly OH U.S.A. 164 D4
Waverly TN U.S.A. 162 C4
Waverly VA U.S.A. 165 G5
Wavre Belgium 62 E4
Waw Myanmar 86 B3
Wawa Canada 152 D5
Wawalalindu Celebes Indon. 83 B3
Wāw al Kabīr Libya 121 E2
Wawasee, Lake IN U.S.A. 164 C3
Wawo Celebes Indon. 83 B3
Wawotebi Celebes Indon. 83 B3
Waxahachie TX U.S.A. 161 D5
Waxü China 94 E5
Waxxari China 98 D5
Way, Lake salt flat Australia 135 C6
Wayabula Moluccas Indon. 83 D2
Wayag i. Papua Indon. 83 D2
Wayamli Halmahera Indon. 83 D2
Wayaobu China see Zichang
Waycross GA U.S.A. 163 D6
Wayhaya Moluccas Indon. 83 C3
Way Kambas, Taman Nasional nat. park Indon. 84 D4
Waykilo Moluccas Indon. 83 C3
Wayland KY U.S.A. 164 D5
Wayland MI U.S.A. 164 C2
Wayne NE U.S.A. 160 D3
Wayne WV U.S.A. 164 D4
Waynesboro GA U.S.A. 163 D5
Waynesboro MS U.S.A. 161 F6
Waynesboro TN U.S.A. 162 C5
Waynesboro VA U.S.A. 165 F4
Waynesburg PA U.S.A. 164 E4
Waynesville MO U.S.A. 160 E4
Waynesville NC U.S.A. 162 D5
Waynoka OK U.S.A. 161 D4
Waza, Parc National de nat. park Cameroon 121 E3
Wāzah Khwāh Afgh. see Mashōrêy
Wazirabad Pak. 111 I3
Wazuka Japan 92 B4
W du Niger, Parc National du nat. park Niger 120 D3
We, Pulau i. Indon. 84 A1
Weagamow Lake Canada 151 N4
Weam P.N.G. 81 K8
Wear r. U.K. 58 F4
Weare NH U.S.A. 165 J2
Weatherford TX U.S.A. 161 D5
Weaver Lake Canada 151 L4
Weaverville CA U.S.A. 156 C4
Webb, Mount hill Australia 134 E5
Webequie Canada 152 D3
Weber, Mount Canada 149 O5
Weber Basin sea feature Laut Banda 186 E6
Webster IN U.S.A. 164 C4
Webster MA U.S.A. 165 J2
Webster SD U.S.A. 160 D2
Webster City IA U.S.A. 160 E3
Webster Springs WV U.S.A. 164 E4
Wecho Lake Canada 150 H2
Weda Halmahera Indon. 83 C2
Weda, Teluk b. Halmahera Indon. 83 D2
Wedau P.N.G. 136 E1
Weddell Abyssal Plain sea feature Southern Ocean 188 A2
Weddell Island Falkland Is 178 D8
Weddell Sea Antarctica 188 A2
Wedderburn Australia 138 A6
Weddin Mountains National Park Australia 138 D4
Wedel Germany 63 J1
Wedge Mountain Canada 150 F5
Wedowee AL U.S.A. 163 C5
Weedville PA U.S.A. 165 F3
Weeim i. Papua Indon. 83 D3
Weenen S. Africa 125 J5
Weener Germany 63 H1
Weert Neth. 62 F3
Weethalle Australia 138 C4
Wee Waa Australia 138 D3

Wegberg Germany 62 G3
Węgorzewo Poland 57 R3
Weichang China 95 I3
Weida Germany 63 M4
Weidenberg Germany 63 L5
Weiden in der Oberpfalz Germany 63 M5
Weifang China 95 I4
Weihai China 95 J4
Wei He *r. Henan* China 95 H4
Wei He *r. Shaanxi* China 95 G5
Weihui China 95 H5
Weilburg Germany 63 I4
Weilmoringle Australia 138 C2
Weimar Germany 63 L4
Weinan China 95 G5
Weinheim Germany 63 I5
Weining China 96 E3
Weinsberg Germany 63 J5
Weipa Australia 136 C2
Weiqu China *see* **Chang'an**
Weir *r.* Australia 138 D2
Weirong China 94 F5
Weir River Canada 151 M3
Weirton *WV* U.S.A. 164 E3
Weiser *ID* U.S.A. 156 D3
Weishan *Shandong* China 95 I5
Weishan *Yunnan* China 96 D3
Weishan Hu *l.* China 95 I5
Weishi China 95 H5
Weiße Elster *r.* Germany 63 L3
Weißenburg in Bayern Germany 63 K5
Weißenfels Germany 63 L3
Weißkugel *mt.* Austria/Italy 57 M7
Weissrand Mountains Namibia 124 D3
Weiterstadt Germany 63 I5
Weitzel Lake Canada 151 J3
Weixi China 96 C3
Weixian China 95 H4
Weixin China 96 E3
Weiya China 94 C3
Weiyuan *Gansu* China 94 F5
Weiyuan *Qinghai* China *see* **Huzhu**
Weiyuan *Sichuan* China 96 E2
Weiyuan *Yunnan* China *see* **Jinggu**
Weiyuan Jiang *r.* China 96 D4
Weiz Austria 57 O7
Weizhou *Ningxia* China 94 F4
Weizhou *Sichuan* China *see* **Wenchuan**
Weizhou Dao *i.* China 97 F4
Weizi China 95 J3
Wejherowo Poland 57 Q3
Wekilbazar Turkm. 111 F2
Wekusko Canada 151 L4
Wekusko Lake Canada 151 L4
Wekweètì Canada 150 H1
Welatam Myanmar 86 B1
Welbourn Hill Australia 135 F6
Welch *WV* U.S.A. 164 E5
Weld *ME* U.S.A. 165 J1
Weldiya Eth. 122 D2
Welford National Park Australia 136 C5
Welk'īt'ē Eth. 122 D3
Welkom S. Africa 125 H4
Welland Canada 164 F2
Welland *r.* U.K. 59 G6
Welland Canal Canada 164 F2
Wellesley Canada 164 E2
Wellesley Islands Australia 136 B3
Wellesley Lake Canada 149 M3
Wellfleet *MA* U.S.A. 165 J3
Wellin Belgium 62 F4
Wellingborough U.K. 59 G6
Wellington Australia 138 D4
Wellington Canada 165 G2

▶**Wellington** N.Z. 139 E5
Capital of New Zealand.

Wellington S. Africa 124 D7
Wellington *England* U.K. 59 D8
Wellington *England* U.K. 59 E6
Wellington *CO* U.S.A. 156 G4
Wellington *IL* U.S.A. 164 B3
Wellington *KS* U.S.A. 161 D4
Wellington *NV* U.S.A. 158 D2
Wellington *OH* U.S.A. 164 D3
Wellington *TX* U.S.A. 161 C5
Wellington *UT* U.S.A. 159 H2
Wellington, Isla *i.* Chile 178 B7
Wellington Range *hills N.T.* Australia 134 F3
Wellington Range *hills W.A.* Australia 135 C6
Wells Canada 150 F4
Wells U.K. 59 E7
Wells *NV* U.S.A. 156 E4
Wells, Lake *salt flat* Australia 135 C6
Wellsboro *PA* U.S.A. 165 G3
Wellsburg *WV* U.S.A. 164 E3
Wellsford N.Z. 139 E3
Wells-next-the-Sea U.K. 59 H6
Wellston *MI* U.S.A. 164 C1
Wellsville *NY* U.S.A. 165 G2
Wellton *AZ* U.S.A. 159 F5
Wels Austria 57 O6
Welshpool U.K. 59 D6
Welsickendorf Germany 63 N3
Welwitschia Namibia *see* **Khorixas**
Welwyn Garden City U.K. 59 G7
Welzheim Germany 63 J6
Wem U.K. 59 E6
Wembesi S. Africa 125 I5
Wembley Canada 150 G4
Wemindji Canada 152 F3
Wenatchee *WA* U.S.A. 156 C3
Wenatchee Mountains *WA* U.S.A. 156 C3
Wenceslau Braz Brazil 179 A3
Wenchang China *see* **Zitong**
Wencheng China 97 F5
Wenchow China *see* **Wenzhou**
Wenchuan China 96 D2
Wendelstein Germany 63 L5
Wenden Germany 63 H4
Wenden Latvia *see* **Cēsis**
Wenden *AZ* U.S.A. 159 G5
Wendeng China 95 J4
Wendover *UT* U.S.A. 159 F1
Wenfeng China 94 F5
Weng'an China 96 E3
Wengda China 96 D2
Wengshui China 96 C2
Wengyuan China 97 G3
Wenhua China *see* **Weishan**
Wenlan China *see* **Mengzi**
Wenling China 97 I2
Wenlock *r.* Australia 136 C2
Wenping China *see* **Ludian**
Wenquan *Guizhou* China 96 E2
Wenquan *Henan* China *see* **Wenxian**
Wenquan *Hubei* China *see* **Yingshan**
Wenquan *Qinghai* China 94 D5

▶**Wenquan** *Qinghai* China 99 E6
Highest settlement in the world.

Wenquan *Xinjiang* China 98 C3
Wenshan China 96 E4
Wenshui China 96 E2
Wensu China 98 C4
Wensum *r.* U.K. 59 I6
Wentorf bei Hamburg Germany 63 K1
Wentworth Australia 137 C7
Wenxi China 97 F1
Wenxian *Gansu* China 96 E1
Wenxian *Henan* China 97 G1
Wenxing China *see* **Xiangyin**
Wenzhou China 97 I3
Wenzlow Germany 63 M2
Wepener S. Africa 125 H5
Wer India 104 D4
Werben (Elbe) Germany 63 L2
Werda Botswana 124 F3
Werdau Germany 63 M4
Werder (Havel) Germany 63 M2
Werdohl Germany 63 H3
Werinama *Seram* Indon. 83 D3
Werl Germany 63 H3
Wernberg-Köblitz Germany 63 M5
Werne Germany 63 H3
Wernecke Mountains Canada 149 M2
Wernigerode Germany 63 K3
Werra *r.* Germany 63 J3
Werris Creek Australia 138 E3
Wertheim Germany 63 J5
Wervik Belgium 62 D4
Werwaru *Moluccas* Indon. 83 D5
Wesel Germany 62 G3
Wesel-Datteln-Kanal *canal* Germany 62 G3
Wesenberg Germany 63 M1
Wesendorf Germany 63 K2
Weser *r.* Germany 63 I1
Weser *sea chan.* Germany 63 I1
Wesergebirge *hills* Germany 63 I2
Weslaco *TX* U.S.A. 161 D7
Weslemkoon Lake Canada 165 G1
Wesleyville Canada 153 L4
Wessel, Cape Australia 136 B1
Wessel Islands Australia 136 B1
Wesselsbron S. Africa 125 H4
Wesselton S. Africa 125 I4
Wessington Springs *SD* U.S.A. 160 D2
West *r.* Canada 149 P1
Westall, Point Australia 135 F8
West Allis *WI* U.S.A. 164 A2
West Antarctica *reg.* Antarctica 188 J1
West Australian Basin *sea feature* Indian Ocean 185 O7
West Bank *disp. terr.* Asia 107 B3
West Bay Canada 153 K3
West Bay *b. LA* U.S.A. 167 H2
West Bay *inlet FL* U.S.A. 163 C6
West Bend *WI* U.S.A. 164 A2
West Bengal *state* India 105 F5
West Branch *MI* U.S.A. 164 C1
West Bromwich U.K. 59 F6
Westbrook *ME* U.S.A. 165 J2
West Burke *VT* U.S.A. 165 J1
West Burra *i.* U.K. *see* **Burra**
Westbury U.K. 59 E7
West Caicos *i.* Turks and Caicos Is 163 F8
West Cape Howe Australia 135 B8
West Caroline Basin *sea feature* N. Pacific Ocean 186 F5
West Chester *PA* U.S.A. 165 H4
Westcliffe *CO* U.S.A. 157 G5
West Coast National Park S. Africa 124 D7
West End Bahamas 163 E7
Westerburg Germany 63 H4
Westerholt Germany 63 H1
Westerland Germany 57 L3
Westerlo Belgium 62 E3
Westerly *RI* U.S.A. 165 J3
Western *r.* Canada 151 J1
Western Australia *state* Australia 135 C6
Western Cape *prov.* S. Africa 124 E7
Western Desert Egypt 112 C6
Western Dvina *r.* Europe *see* **Zapadnaya Dvina**
Western Ghats *mts* India 106 B3
Western Lesser Sunda Islands *prov.* Indon. *see* **Nusa Tenggara Barat**
Western Port *b.* Australia 138 B7
Western Sahara *disp. terr.* Africa 120 B2
Western Samoa *country* S. Pacific Ocean *see* **Samoa**
Western Sayan Mountains *reg.* Russia *see* **Zapadnyy Sayan**
Westerschelde *est.* Neth. 62 D3
Westerstede Germany 63 H1
Westerville *OH* U.S.A. 164 D3
Westerwald *hills* Germany 63 H4
West Falkland *i.* Falkland Is 178 D8
West Fargo *ND* U.S.A. 160 D2
West Fayu *atoll* Micronesia 81 L5
Westfield *IN* U.S.A. 164 B3
Westfield *MA* U.S.A. 165 I2
Westfield *NY* U.S.A. 164 F2
Westfield *PA* U.S.A. 165 G3
West Frisian Islands Neth. 62 E1
Westgat *sea chan.* Neth. 62 G1
Westgate Australia 138 C1
West Glacier *MT* U.S.A. 156 E2
West Grand Lake *ME* U.S.A. 162 H2
West Hartford *CT* U.S.A. 165 I3
Westhausen Germany 63 K6
West Haven *CT* U.S.A. 165 I3
Westhill U.K. 60 G3
Westhope *ND* U.S.A. 160 C1
West Ice Shelf Antarctica 188 E2
West Indies *is* Caribbean Sea 169 J4
West Island India 87 A4
Westkapelle Neth. 62 D3
West Kazakhstan Oblast *admin. div.* Kazakh. *see* **Zapadnyy Kazakhstan**
West Kingston *RI* U.S.A. 165 J3
West Lafayette *IN* U.S.A. 164 B3
West Lamma Channel *H.K.* China 97 [inset]
Westland Australia 136 C4
Westland Tai Poutini National Park N.Z. 139 C6
Westleigh S. Africa 125 H4
Westleton U.K. 59 I6
West Liberty *KY* U.S.A. 164 D5
West Linton U.K. 60 F5
West Loch Roag *b.* U.K. 60 C2
Westlock Canada 150 H4
West Lorne Canada 164 E2
West Lunga National Park Zambia 123 C5
West MacDonnell National Park Australia 135 F5
West Malaysia *pen.* Malaysia *see* **Peninsular Malaysia**
Westmalle Belgium 62 E3
Westmar Australia 138 D1
West Mariana Basin *sea feature* N. Pacific Ocean 186 F4
West Memphis *AR* U.S.A. 161 F5
Westminster *MD* U.S.A. 165 G4
Westmoreland Australia 136 B3
Westmoreland *TN* U.S.A. 164 B5
Westmorland *CA* U.S.A. 159 F5
Weston *Sabah* Malaysia 85 F1
Weston *OH* U.S.A. 164 D3
Weston *WV* U.S.A. 164 E4
Weston-super-Mare U.K. 59 E7
West Palm Beach *FL* U.S.A. 163 D7
West Passage Palau *see* **Toagel Mlungui**
West Plains *MO* U.S.A. 161 F4
West Point *pt* Australia 137 [inset]
West Point *CA* U.S.A. 158 C2
West Point *KY* U.S.A. 164 C5
West Point *MS* U.S.A. 161 F5
West Point *NE* U.S.A. 160 D3
West Point *VA* U.S.A. 165 G5
West Point *mt. AK* U.S.A. 149 K2
West Point Lake *resr Alabama/Georgia* U.S.A. 163 C5
Westport Canada 165 G1
Westport Ireland 61 C4
Westport N.Z. 139 C5
Westport *CA* U.S.A. 158 B2
Westport *KY* U.S.A. 164 C4
Westport *NY* U.S.A. 165 I1
Westray Canada 151 K4
Westray *i.* U.K. 60 F1
Westray Firth *sea chan.* U.K. 60 F1
Westree Canada 152 E5
West Rutland *VT* U.S.A. 165 I2
West Salem *OH* U.S.A. 164 D3
West Siberian Plain Russia 76 J3
West-Skylge Neth. *see* **West-Terschelling**
West Stewartstown *NH* U.S.A. 165 J1
West-Terschelling Neth. 62 F1
West Topsham *VT* U.S.A. 165 I1
West Union *IA* U.S.A. 160 F3
West Union *IL* U.S.A. 164 B4
West Union *OH* U.S.A. 164 D4
West Union *WV* U.S.A. 164 E4
West Valley City *UT* U.S.A. 159 H1
Westville *IN* U.S.A. 164 B3
West Virginia *state* U.S.A. 164 E4
Westwood *CA* U.S.A. 158 C1
West Wyalong Australia 138 C4
West York *PA* U.S.A. 165 G4
Westzaan Neth. 62 E2
Wetan *i. Moluccas* Indon. 83 D4
Wetar *i. Moluccas* Indon. 83 C4
Wetar, Selat *sea chan.* Indon. 83 C5
Wetaskiwin Canada 150 H4
Wete Tanz. 123 D4
Wetter *r.* Germany 63 I4
Wettin Germany 63 L3
Wetumpka *AL* U.S.A. 163 C5
Wetwun Myanmar 86 B2
Wetzlar Germany 63 I4
Wevok *AK* U.S.A. 148 F1
Wewahitchka *FL* U.S.A. 163 C6
Wewak P.N.G. 81 K7
Wewoka *OK* U.S.A. 161 D5
Wexford Ireland 61 F5
Wexford Harbour *b.* Ireland 61 F5
Weyakwin Canada 151 J4
Weybridge U.K. 59 G7
Weyburn Canada 151 K5
Weyhe Germany 63 I2
Weymouth U.K. 59 E8
Weymouth *MA* U.S.A. 165 J2
Wezep Neth. 62 G2
Whakaari *i.* N.Z. 139 F3
Whakatane N.Z. 139 F3
Whalan Creek *r.* Australia 138 D2
Whale *r.* Canada *see* **Baleine, Rivière à la**
Whalsay *i.* U.K. 60 [inset]
Whampoa China *see* **Huangpu**
Whangamata N.Z. 139 E3
Whanganui National Park N.Z. 139 E4
Whangarei N.Z. 139 E2
Whapmagoostui Canada 152 F3
Wharfe *r.* U.K. 58 F5
Wharfedale *valley* U.K. 58 F4
Wharton *TX* U.S.A. 161 D6
Wharton Lake Canada 151 L1
Whatî Canada 149 R3
Wheatland *IN* U.S.A. 164 B4
Wheatland *WY* U.S.A. 156 G4
Wheaton *IL* U.S.A. 164 A3
Wheaton *MD* U.S.A. 165 G4
Wheaton *MN* U.S.A. 160 D2
Wheeler *TX* U.S.A. 161 C5
Wheeler Lake Canada 150 H2
Wheeler Lake *resr AL* U.S.A. 163 C5
Wheeler Peak *NM* U.S.A. 157 G5
Wheeler Peak *NV* U.S.A. 159 F2
Wheelersburg *OH* U.S.A. 164 D4
Wheeling *WV* U.S.A. 164 E3
Whernside *hill* U.K. 58 E4
Whinham, Mount Australia 135 E6
Whiskey Jack Lake Canada 151 K3
Whitburn U.K. 60 F5
Whitby Canada 165 F2
Whitby U.K. 58 G4
Whitchurch U.K. 59 E6
Whitchurch-Stouffville Canada 164 F2
White *r.* Canada 152 D4
White *r.* Canada/U.S.A. 149 M3
White *r. AR* U.S.A. 161 F5
White *r. CO* U.S.A. 159 I1
White *r. IN* U.S.A. 164 B4
White *r. MI* U.S.A. 164 B2
White *r. NV* U.S.A. 159 F3
White *r. SD* U.S.A. 160 D3
White *r. VT* U.S.A. 165 I2
White *watercourse AZ* U.S.A. 159 H5
White, Lake *salt flat* Australia 134 E5
White Bay Canada 153 K4
White Butte *mt. ND* U.S.A. 160 C2
White Canyon *UT* U.S.A. 159 H3
White Cloud *MI* U.S.A. 164 C2
Whitecourt Canada 150 H4
Whiteface Mountain *NY* U.S.A. 165 I1
Whitefield *NH* U.S.A. 165 J1
Whitefish *r.* Canada 149 P2
Whitefish *MT* U.S.A. 156 E2
Whitefish Bay *WI* U.S.A. 164 B1
Whitefish Lake Canada 151 J2
Whitefish Lake *AK* U.S.A. 148 I3
Whitefish Point *MI* U.S.A. 162 C2
Whitehall U.K. 60 G1
Whitehall *NY* U.S.A. 165 I2
Whitehall *WI* U.S.A. 160 F2
Whitehaven U.K. 58 D4
Whitehead U.K. 61 G3
White Hill *hill* Canada 153 J5
Whitehill U.K. 59 G7
White Hills *AK* U.S.A. 149 J1

▶**Whitehorse** Canada 149 N3
Capital of Yukon.

Whitehorse *NM* U.S.A. 159 J4
White Horse, Vale of *valley* U.K. 59 F7
White Horse Pass *NV* U.S.A. 159 F1
White House *TN* U.S.A. 164 B5
White Island Antarctica 188 D2
White Island N.Z. *see* **Whakaari**
White Lake *Ont.* Canada 152 D4
White Lake *Ont.* Canada 165 G1
White Lake *LA* U.S.A. 161 E6
White Lake *MI* U.S.A. 164 B2
Whitemark Australia 137 [inset]
White Mountain *AK* U.S.A. 148 G2
White Mountain Peak *CA* U.S.A. 158 D3
White Mountains *AK* U.S.A. 149 K2
White Mountains *NH* U.S.A. 165 J1
White Mountains National Park Australia 136 D4
Whitemouth Lake Canada 151 M5
Whitemud *r.* Canada 150 G3
White Nile *r.* Africa 108 D6
also known as Bahr el Abiad or Bahr el Jebel
White Nossob *watercourse* Namibia 124 D2
White Oak *KY* U.S.A. 164 D5
White Otter Lake Canada 151 N5
White Pass Canada/U.S.A. 149 N4
White Pine Range *mts NV* U.S.A. 159 F2
White Plains *NY* U.S.A. 165 I3
White River Canada 152 D4
Whiteriver *AZ* U.S.A. 159 I5
White River *SD* U.S.A. 160 C3
White River Valley *NV* U.S.A. 159 F2
White Rock Peak *NV* U.S.A. 159 F2
White Russia *country* Europe *see* **Belarus**
Whitesail Lake Canada 150 E4
White Salmon *WA* U.S.A. 156 C3
Whitesand *r.* Canada 150 H2
White Sands National Monument *nat. park NM* U.S.A. 157 G6
Whitesburg *KY* U.S.A. 164 D5
White Sea Russia 52 H2
Whitestone *r.* Canada 149 M2
White Stone *VA* U.S.A. 165 G5
White Sulphur Springs *MT* U.S.A. 156 F3
White Sulphur Springs *WV* U.S.A. 164 E5
Whitesville *WV* U.S.A. 164 E5
Whiteville *NC* U.S.A. 163 E5
White Volta *r.* Burkina Faso/Ghana 120 C4
also known as Nakambé or Nakanbe or Volta Blanche
Whitewater *CO* U.S.A. 159 I2
Whitewater Baldy *mt. NM* U.S.A. 159 I5
Whitewater Lake Canada 152 C4
Whitewood Australia 136 C4
Whitewood Canada 151 K5
Whitfield U.K. 59 I7
Whithorn U.K. 60 E6
Whitianga N.Z. 139 E3
Whitland U.K. 59 C7
Whitley Bay U.K. 58 F3
Whitmore Mountains Antarctica 188 K1
Whitney Canada 165 F1
Whitney, Lake *TX* U.S.A. 167 F2
Whitney, Mount *CA* U.S.A. 158 D3
Whitney Point *NY* U.S.A. 165 H2
Whitstable U.K. 59 I7
Whitsunday Group *is* Australia 136 E4
Whitsunday Island National Park Australia 136 E4
Whitsun Island Vanuatu *see* **Pentecost Island**
Whittemore *MI* U.S.A. 164 D1
Whittier *AK* U.S.A. 149 J3
Whittlesea Australia 138 B6
Whittlesey U.K. 59 G6
Whitton Australia 138 C5
Wholdaia Lake Canada 151 J2
Why *AZ* U.S.A. 159 G5
Whyalla Australia 137 B7
Wiang Sa Thai. 86 C3
Wiarton Canada 164 E1
Wibaux *MT* U.S.A. 156 G3
Wichelen Belgium 62 D3
Wichita *KS* U.S.A. 160 D4
Wichita *r. TX* U.S.A. 161 D5
Wichita Falls *TX* U.S.A. 161 D5
Wichita Mountains *OK* U.S.A. 161 D5
Wick U.K. 60 F2
Wick *r.* U.K. 60 F2
Wickenburg *AZ* U.S.A. 159 G5
Wickes *AR* U.S.A. 161 E5
Wickford U.K. 59 H7
Wickham *r.* Australia 134 E4
Wickham, Cape Australia 137 [inset]
Wickham, Mount *hill* Australia 134 E4
Wickliffe *KY* U.S.A. 161 F4
Wicklow Ireland 61 F5
Wicklow Head *hd* Ireland 61 G5
Wicklow Mountains Ireland 61 F5
Wicklow Mountains National Park Ireland 61 F4
Wide Bay *AK* U.S.A. 148 H4
Widerøe, Mount Antarctica 188 C2
Widerøefjellet *mt.* Antarctica *see* **Widerøe, Mount**
Widgeegoara *watercourse* Australia 138 B1
Widgiemooltha (abandoned) Australia 135 C7
Widi, Kepulauan *is Moluccas* Indon. 83 D3
Widnes U.K. 58 E5
Wi-do *i.* S. Korea 91 B6
Wied *r.* Germany 63 H4
Wiehengebirge *hills* Germany 63 I2
Wiehl Germany 63 H4
Wielkopolskie, Pojezierze *reg.* Poland 57 O4
Wielkopolski Park Narodowy *nat. park* Poland 57 P4
Wieluń Poland 57 Q5
Wien Austria *see* **Vienna**
Wiener Neustadt Austria 57 P7
Wien Lake *AK* U.S.A. 149 J2
Wierden Neth. 62 G2
Wieren Germany 63 K2
Wieringerwerf Neth. 62 F2
Wiesbaden Germany 63 I4
Wiesenfelden Germany 63 M5
Wiesentheid Germany 63 K5
Wiesloch Germany 63 I5
Wiesmoor Germany 63 H1
Wietze Germany 63 J2
Wietzendorf Germany 63 J2
Wieżyca *hill* Poland 57 Q3
Wigan U.K. 58 E5
Wiggins *MS* U.S.A. 161 F6
Wight, Isle of *i.* U.K. 59 F8
Wigierski Park Narodowy *nat. park* Poland 55 M9
Wignes Lake Canada 151 J2
Wigston U.K. 59 F6
Wigton U.K. 58 D4
Wigtown U.K. 60 E6
Wigtown Bay U.K. 60 E6
Wijchen Neth. 62 F3
Wijhe Neth. 62 G2
Wilberforce, Cape Australia 136 B1
Wilbur *WA* U.S.A. 156 D3
Wilburton *OK* U.S.A. 161 E5
Wilcannia Australia 138 A3
Wilcox *PA* U.S.A. 165 F3
Wilczek Land *i.* Russia *see* **Vil'cheka, Zemlya**
Wildberg Germany 63 M2
Wildcat Peak *NV* U.S.A. 158 E2
Wild Coast S. Africa 125 I6
Wildeshausen Germany 63 I2
Wild Horse Hill *mt. NE* U.S.A. 160 C3
Wildspitze *mt.* Austria 57 M7
Wildwood *FL* U.S.A. 163 D6
Wildwood *NJ* U.S.A. 165 H4
Wilge *r. Free State* S. Africa 125 I4
Wilge *r. Gauteng/Mpumalanga* S. Africa 125 I3
Wilgena Australia 135 F7

▶**Wilhelm, Mount** P.N.G. 81 L8
5th highest mountain in Oceania.

Wilhelm II Land *reg.* Antarctica *see* **Kaiser Wilhelm II Land**
Wilhelmina Gebergte *mts* Suriname 177 G3
Wilhelmina Kanaal *canal* Neth. 62 F3
Wilhelmshaven Germany 63 I1
Wilhelmshöhe, Bergpark *tourist site* Germany 63 J3
Wilhelmstal Namibia 124 C1
Wilkes-Barre *PA* U.S.A. 165 H3
Wilkesboro *NC* U.S.A. 162 D4
Wilkes Coast Antarctica 188 G2
Wilkes Land *reg.* Antarctica 188 G2
Wilkie Canada 151 I4
Wilkins Coast Antarctica 188 L2
Wilkins Ice Shelf Antarctica 188 L2
Wilkinson Lakes *salt flat* Australia 135 F7
Will, Mount Canada 149 O4
Willand U.K. 59 D8
Willandra Billabong *watercourse* Australia 138 B4
Willandra National Park Australia 138 B4
Willapa Bay *WA* U.S.A. 156 B3
Willard Mex. 166 C2
Willard *NM* U.S.A. 157 G6
Willard *OH* U.S.A. 164 D3
Willcox *AZ* U.S.A. 159 I5
Willcox Playa *salt flat AZ* U.S.A. 159 I5
Willebadessen Germany 63 J3
Willebroek Belgium 62 E3
Willemstad Curaçao 169 K6
Willeroo Australia 134 E3
Willette *TN* U.S.A. 164 C5
William, Mount Australia 137 C8
William Creek Australia 137 B6
William Lake Canada 151 L4
Williams *AZ* U.S.A. 159 G4
Williams *CA* U.S.A. 158 B2
Williamsburg *KY* U.S.A. 164 C5
Williamsburg *OH* U.S.A. 164 C4
Williamsburg *VA* U.S.A. 165 G5
Williams Lake Canada 150 F4
William Smith, Cap *c.* Canada 153 I1
Williamson *NY* U.S.A. 165 G2
Williamson *WV* U.S.A. 164 D5
Williamsport *IN* U.S.A. 164 B3
Williamsport *PA* U.S.A. 165 G3
Williamston *NC* U.S.A. 162 E5
Williamstown *KY* U.S.A. 164 C4
Williamstown *NJ* U.S.A. 165 H4
Willimantic *CT* U.S.A. 165 I3
Willis Group *atolls* Australia 136 E3
Williston S. Africa 124 E6
Williston *ND* U.S.A. 160 C1
Williston *SC* U.S.A. 163 D5
Williston Lake Canada 150 F4
Williton U.K. 59 D7
Willits *CA* U.S.A. 158 B2
Willmar *MN* U.S.A. 160 E2
Willoughby, Lake *VT* U.S.A. 165 I1
Willow *AK* U.S.A. 149 J3
Willow Beach *AZ* U.S.A. 159 F4
Willow Bunch Canada 151 J5
Willow Creek *AK* U.S.A. 149 K3
Willow Hill *PA* U.S.A. 165 G3
Willow Lake Canada 150 G2
Willowlake *r.* Canada 150 F2
Willowmore S. Africa 124 F7
Willowra Australia 134 F5
Willows *CA* U.S.A. 158 B2
Willow Springs *MO* U.S.A. 161 F4
Willowvale S. Africa 125 I7
Wills, Lake *salt flat* Australia 134 E5
Wilma *FL* U.S.A. 163 C6
Wilmington *DE* U.S.A. 165 H4
Wilmington *NC* U.S.A. 163 E5
Wilmington *OH* U.S.A. 164 D4
Wilmore *KY* U.S.A. 164 C5
Wilmslow U.K. 58 E5
Wilno Lith. *see* **Vilnius**
Wilnsdorf Germany 63 I4
Wilpattu National Park Sri Lanka 106 D4
Wilseder Berg *hill* Germany 63 J1
Wilson *watercourse* Australia 137 C5
Wilson *atoll* Micronesia *see* **Ifalik**
Wilson *KS* U.S.A. 160 D4
Wilson *NC* U.S.A. 162 E5
Wilson *NY* U.S.A. 165 F2
Wilson, Mount *CO* U.S.A. 159 J3
Wilson, Mount *NV* U.S.A. 159 F2
Wilson, Mount *OR* U.S.A. 156 C3
Wilsonia *CA* U.S.A. 158 D3
Wilson's Promontory *pen.* Australia 138 C7
Wilson's Promontory National Park Australia 138 C7
Wilsum Germany 62 G2
Wilton *r.* Australia 134 F3
Wilton *ME* U.S.A. 165 J1
Wiltz Lux. 62 F5
Wiluna Australia 135 C6
Wimereux France 62 B4
Wina *r.* Cameroon *see* **Vina**
Winamac *IN* U.S.A. 164 B3
Winbin *watercourse* Australia 137 D5
Winburg S. Africa 125 H5
Wincanton U.K. 59 E7
Winchester Canada 165 H1
Winchester U.K. 59 F7
Winchester *IN* U.S.A. 164 C3
Winchester *KY* U.S.A. 164 C5
Winchester *NH* U.S.A. 165 I2
Winchester *TN* U.S.A. 163 C5
Winchester *VA* U.S.A. 165 F4
Wind *r.* Canada 149 N2
Wind *r. WY* U.S.A. 156 F4
Windau Latvia *see* **Ventspils**
Windber *PA* U.S.A. 165 F3
Wind Cave National Park *SD* U.S.A. 160 C3
Windermere U.K. 58 E4
Windermere *l.* U.K. 58 E4
Windham *AK* U.S.A. 149 N4

▶**Windhoek** Namibia 124 C2
Capital of Namibia.

Windigo Lake Canada 151 N4
Windlestraw Law *hill* U.K. 60 G5
Wind Mountain *NM* U.S.A. 157 G6
Windom *MN* U.S.A. 160 E3
Windom Peak *CO* U.S.A. 159 J3
Windorah Australia 136 C5
Window Rock *AZ* U.S.A. 159 I4
Wind Point *WI* U.S.A. 164 B2
Wind River Range *mts WY* U.S.A. 156 F4
Windrush *r.* U.K. 59 F7
Windsbach Germany 63 K5
Windsor Australia 138 E4
Windsor *N.S.* Canada 153 I5
Windsor *Ont.* Canada 164 D2
Windsor U.K. 59 G7
Windsor *NC* U.S.A. 162 E4
Windsor *NY* U.S.A. 165 H2

Windsor VA U.S.A. 165 G5
Windsor VT U.S.A. 165 I2
Windsor Locks CT U.S.A. 165 I3
Windward Islands Caribbean Sea 169 L5
Windward Passage Cuba/Haiti 169 J5
Windy AK U.S.A. 146 D3
Windy Fork r. AK U.S.A. 148 I3
Winefred Lake Canada 151 I4
Winfield KS U.S.A. 161 D4
Winfield WV U.S.A. 164 E4
Wingate U.K. 58 F4
Wingen Australia 138 E3
Wingene Belgium 62 D3
Wingen-sur-Moder France 63 H6
Wingham Australia 138 F3
Wingham Canada 164 E2
Wini East Timor 83 C5
Winisk r. Canada 152 D3
Winisk (abandoned) Canada 152 D3
Winisk Lake Canada 152 D3
Winkana Myanmar 86 B4
Winkelman AZ U.S.A. 159 H5
Winkler Canada 151 L5
Winlock WA U.S.A. 156 C3
Winneba Ghana 120 C4
Winnebago, Lake WI U.S.A. 164 A1
Winnecke Creek watercourse Australia 134 E4
Winnemucca NV U.S.A. 158 E1
Winnemucca Lake NV U.S.A. 158 D1
Winner SD U.S.A. 160 C3
Winnett MT U.S.A. 156 F3
Winnfield LA U.S.A. 161 E6
Winnibigoshish, Lake MN U.S.A. 160 E2
Winnie TX U.S.A. 161 E6
Winning Australia 135 A5

▶Winnipeg Canada 151 L5
Capital of Manitoba.

Winnipeg r. Canada 151 L5
Winnipeg, Lake Canada 151 L5
Winnipegosis Canada 151 L5
Winnipegosis, Lake Canada 151 K4
Winnipesaukee, Lake NH U.S.A. 165 J2
Winnsboro LA U.S.A. 167 H1
Winona AZ U.S.A. 159 H4
Winona MN U.S.A. 160 F2
Winona MO U.S.A. 161 F4
Winona MS U.S.A. 161 F5
Winschoten Neth. 62 H1
Winsen (Aller) Germany 63 J2
Winsen (Luhe) Germany 63 K1
Winsford U.K. 58 E5
Winslow AZ U.S.A. 159 H4
Winslow ME U.S.A. 165 K1
Winsop, Tanjung pt Indon. 81 I7
Winsted CT U.S.A. 165 I3
Winston-Salem NC U.S.A. 162 D4
Winterberg Germany 63 I3
Winter Haven FL U.S.A. 163 D6
Winters CA U.S.A. 158 C2
Winters TX U.S.A. 161 D6
Wintersville OH U.S.A. 164 E3
Winterswijk Neth. 62 G3
Winterthur Switz. 66 I3
Winterton S. Africa 125 I5
Winthrop ME U.S.A. 165 K1
Winton Australia 136 C4
Winton N.Z. 139 B8
Winton NC U.S.A. 162 E4
Winwick U.K. 59 G6
Wiralaga Sumatra Indon. 84 D3
Wirral pen. U.K. 58 D5
Wirrulla Australia 137 A7
Wisbech U.K. 59 H6
Wiscasset ME U.S.A. 165 K1
Wisconsin r. WI U.S.A. 160 F3
Wisconsin state U.S.A. 164 A1
Wisconsin Rapids WI U.S.A. 160 F2
Wise VA U.S.A. 164 D5
Wiseman AK U.S.A. 149 J2
Wishaw U.K. 60 F5
Wishek ND U.S.A. 160 D2
Wisil Dabarow Somalia 122 E3
Wisła r. Poland see Vistula
Wismar Germany 57 M4
Wistaria Canada 150 E4
Witbank S. Africa see eMalahleni
Witbooisvlei Namibia 124 D3
Witham U.K. 59 H7
Witham r. U.K. 59 H6
Witherbee NY U.S.A. 165 I1
Withernsea U.K. 58 H5
Witherspoon, Mount AK U.S.A. 149 K3
Witjira National Park Australia 137 A5
Witmarsum Neth. 62 F1
Witney U.K. 59 F7
Witrivier S. Africa 125 J3
Witry-lès-Reims France 62 E5
Witteberg mts S. Africa 125 H6
Wittenberg Germany see Wittenberg, Lutherstadt
Wittenberg, Lutherstadt Germany 63 M3
Wittenberge Germany 63 L2
Wittenburg Germany 63 L1
Witti, Banjaran mts Malaysia 85 G1
Wittingen Germany 63 K2
Wittlich Germany 62 G5
Wittmund Germany 63 H1
Wittstock/Dosse Germany 63 M1
Witu Islands P.N.G. 81 L7
Witvlei Namibia 124 D2
Witzenhausen Germany 63 J3
Wivenhoe, Lake Australia 138 F1
Władysławowo Poland 57 Q3
Włocławek Poland 57 Q4
Wobkent Uzbek. see Vobkent
Wodonga Australia 138 C6
Wœrth France 63 H6
Woëvre, Plaine de la plain France 62 F5
Wohlthat Mountains Antarctica 188 C2
Woippy France 62 G5
Wōjjā atoll Marshall Is see Wotje
Wokam i. Moluccas Indon. 81 I8
Woken He r. China 90 C3
Wokha India 105 H4
Woking U.K. 59 G7
Wokingham watercourse Australia 136 C4
Wokingham U.K. 59 G7
Woko National Park Australia 138 E3
Wolcott IN U.S.A. 164 B3
Wolcott NY U.S.A. 165 G2
Woldegk Germany 63 N1
Wolea atoll Micronesia see Woleai
Woleai atoll Micronesia 81 K5
Wolf r. Canada 149 N3
Wolf r. TN U.S.A. 161 F5
Wolf r. WI U.S.A. 160 F2
Wolf Creek MT U.S.A. 156 E3
Wolf Creek OR U.S.A. 156 C4
Wolf Creek Mountain hill AK U.S.A. 148 G3
Wolf Creek Pass CO U.S.A. 157 G5
Wolfen Germany 63 M3
Wolfenbüttel Germany 63 K2
Wolfhagen Germany 63 J3
Wolf Lake Canada 149 O3
Wolf Mountain AK U.S.A. 148 I2
Wolf Point MT U.S.A. 156 G2
Wolfsberg Austria 57 O7
Wolfsburg Germany 63 K2
Wolfstein Germany 63 H5
Wolfville Canada 153 I5
Wolgast Germany 57 N3
Wolin Poland 57 O4
Wollaston Lake Canada 151 K3
Wollaston Lake l. Canada 151 K3
Wollaston Peninsula Canada 146 G3
Wollemi National Park Australia 138 E4
Wollongong Australia 138 E5
Wolmaransstad S. Africa 125 G4
Wolmirstedt Germany 63 L2
Wolong Natural Reserve nature res. China 96 D2
Wolowaru Flores Indon. 83 B5
Wolseley Australia 137 C8
Wolseley S. Africa 124 D7
Wolsey SD U.S.A. 160 D2
Wolsingham U.K. 58 F4
Wolvega Neth. 62 G2
Wolvegea Neth. see Wolvega
Wolverhampton U.K. 59 E6
Wolverine r. Canada 149 O1
Wolverine MI U.S.A. 164 C1
Wolya r. Indon. 84 A1
Womens Bay AK U.S.A. 148 I4
Wommelgem Belgium 62 E3
Womrather Höhe hill Germany 63 H5
Wonarah Australia 136 B3
Wondai Australia 137 E5
Wongalarroo Lake salt l. Australia 138 B3
Wongarbon Australia 138 D4
Wong Chuk Hang H.K. China 97 [inset]
Wong Leng hill H.K. China 97 [inset]
Wong Wan Chau H.K. China see Double Island
Wonju S. Korea 91 B5
Wonogiri Java Indon. 85 E4
Wonosari Java Indon. 85 E4
Wonosobo Java Indon. 85 E4
Wonowon Canada 150 F3
Wonreli Moluccas Indon. 83 C5
Wŏnsan N. Korea 91 B5
Wonthaggi Australia 138 B7
Wonyulgunna, Mount hill Australia 135 B6
Woocalla Australia 137 B6
Wood r. AK U.S.A. 149 J2
Wood, Mount Canada 149 L3
Woodbine GA U.S.A. 163 D6
Woodbine NJ U.S.A. 165 H4
Woodbridge U.K. 59 I6
Woodbridge VA U.S.A. 165 G4
Wood Buffalo National Park Canada 150 H3
Woodburn OR U.S.A. 156 C3
Woodbury NJ U.S.A. 165 H4
Woodbury TN U.S.A. 161 G5
Woodchopper Creek AK U.S.A. 149 L2
Wooded Bluff hd Australia 138 F2
Wood Lake Canada 151 K4
Woodlake CA U.S.A. 158 D3
Woodland CA U.S.A. 158 C2
Woodland PA U.S.A. 165 F3
Woodland WA U.S.A. 156 C3
Woodlands Sing. 87 [inset]
Woodlark Island P.N.G. 132 F2
Woodridge Canada 151 L5
Woodroffe watercourse Australia 136 B4
Woodroffe, Mount Australia 135 E6
Woodruff UT U.S.A. 156 F4
Woodruff WI U.S.A. 160 F2
Woods, Lake salt flat Australia 134 F4
Woods, Lake of the Canada/U.S.A. 155 I2
Woodsfield OH U.S.A. 164 E4
Woodside Australia 138 C7
Woodstock N.B. Canada 153 I5
Woodstock Ont. Canada 164 E2
Woodstock IL U.S.A. 160 F3
Woodstock VA U.S.A. 165 F4
Woodstock VT U.S.A. 165 I2
Woodsville NH U.S.A. 165 I1
Woodville Canada 165 F1
Woodville MS U.S.A. 161 F6
Woodville OH U.S.A. 164 D3
Woodville TX U.S.A. 161 E6
Woodward OK U.S.A. 161 D4
Woody CA U.S.A. 158 D4
Woody Island AK U.S.A. 148 I4
Wooler U.K. 58 E3
Woolgoolga Australia 138 F3
Wooli Australia 138 F2
Woollard, Mount Antarctica 188 K1
Woollett, Lac l. Canada 152 G4
Woolyeenyer Hill hill Australia 135 C8
Woomera Australia 137 B6
Woomera Prohibited Area Australia 135 F7
Woonsocket RI U.S.A. 165 J2
Woonsocket SD U.S.A. 160 D2
Woorabinda Australia 136 E5
Wooramel r. Australia 135 A6
Wooster OH U.S.A. 164 E3
Wootton Bassett town U.K. see Royal Wootton Bassett
Worbis Germany 63 K3
Worbody Point Australia 136 C2
Worcester S. Africa 124 D7
Worcester U.K. 59 E6
Worcester MA U.S.A. 165 J2
Worcester NY U.S.A. 165 H2
Wörgl Austria 57 N7
Workai i. Moluccas Indon. 81 I8
Workington U.K. 58 D4
Worksop U.K. 58 F5
Workum Neth. 62 F2
Worland WY U.S.A. 156 G3
Wörlitz Germany 63 M3
Wormerveer Neth. 62 E2
Worms Germany 63 I5
Worms Head hd U.K. 59 C7
Wortel Namibia 124 C2
Wörth am Rhein Germany 63 I5
Worthing U.K. 59 G8
Worthington IN U.S.A. 164 B4
Worthington MN U.S.A. 160 E3
Wosi Halmahera Indon. 83 C3
Wosu Celebes Indon. 83 B3
Wotje atoll Marshall Is 186 H5
Wotu Celebes Indon. 83 B3
Woudrichem Neth. 62 E3
Woustviller France 62 H5
Wowoni i. Indon. 83 B4
Wowoni, Selat sea chan. Indon. 83 B3
Wozrojdeniye oroli i. Uzbek. see Vozrozhdenya Island
Wrangel Island Russia 77 T2
Wrangell AK U.S.A. 149 N4
Wrangell, Cape AK U.S.A. 148 [inset] A5
Wrangell, Mount AK U.S.A. 149 K3
Wrangell Island AK U.S.A. 150 C3
Wrangell Mountains AK U.S.A. 148 H4
Wrangell-St Elias National Park and Preserve AK U.S.A. 149 L3
Wrath, Cape U.K. 60 D2
Wray CO U.S.A. 160 C3
Wreake r. U.K. 59 F6
Wreck Point S. Africa 124 C5
Wreck Reef Australia 136 F4
Wrecsam U.K. see Wrexham
Wrestedt Germany 63 K2
Wrexham U.K. 59 E5
Wrightmyo India 87 A5
Wrightson, Mount AZ U.S.A. 157 F7
Wrightwood CA U.S.A. 158 E4
Wrigley Canada 149 Q3
Wrigley KY U.S.A. 164 D4
Wrigley Gulf Antarctica 188 J2
Wrocław Poland 57 P5
Września Poland 57 P4
Wu'an Fujian China see Changtai
Wu'an Hebei China 95 H4
Wubin Australia 135 B7
Wubu China 95 G4
Wuchagou China 95 J2
Wuchang Heilong. China 90 B3
Wuchang Hubei China see Jiangxia
Wuchow China see Wuzhou
Wuchuan Guangdong China 97 F4
Wuchuan Guizhou China 96 E2
Wuchuan Nei Mongol China 95 G3
Wuda China see Ud
Wudalianchi China 90 B2
Wuḏām 'Alwā Oman 110 E6
Wudan China 95 I3
Wudang Shan mt. China 97 F1
Wudao China 95 J4
Wudaoliang China 94 C5
Wudi China 95 I4
Wuding China 96 D3
Wuding He r. China 95 G4
Wudinna Australia 135 F8
Wufeng Hubei China 97 F2
Wufeng Yunnan China see Zhenxiong
Wufo China 94 F4
Wugang China 97 F3
Wugong China 95 G5
Wuhai China 94 F4
Wuhan China 97 G2
Wuhe China 97 H1
Wuhu China 97 H2
Wuhua China 97 G4
Wuhubei China 97 H2
Wūjang China 99 B6
Wu Jiang r. China 96 E2
Wujin Jiangsu China see Changzhou
Wujin Sichuan China see Xinjin
Wukari Nigeria 120 D4
Wulang China 96 B2
Wulêswālī Bihsūd Afgh. 111 G3
Wuli China 94 C5
Wulian Feng mts China 96 D2
Wuliang Shan mts China 96 D3
Wuliaru i. Moluccas Indon. 134 E1
Wuli Jiang r. China 97 F4
Wulik r. AK U.S.A. 148 F2
Wuling Shan mts China 97 F2
Wulong China 96 E2
Wulongji China see Huaibin
Wulur Moluccas Indon. 83 D4
Wumatang China 99 E7
Wumeng Shan mts China 96 D3
Wuming China 97 F4
Wümme r. Germany 63 I1
Wundwin Myanmar 86 B2
Wuning China 97 G2
Wünnenberg Germany 63 I3
Wunnummin Lake Canada 147 J4
Wunsiedel Germany 63 M4
Wunstorf Germany 63 J2
Wupatki National Monument nat. park AZ U.S.A. 159 H4
Wuping China 97 H3
Wuppertal Germany 63 H3
Wuppertal S. Africa 124 D7
Wuqi China 95 G4
Wuqia China 98 A5
Wuqiang China 95 H4
Wuqiao China 95 I4
Wuqing China see Yangcun
Wuquan China see Wuyang
Wuranga Australia 135 B7
Wurno Nigeria 120 D3
Würzburg Germany 63 J5
Wurzen Germany 63 M3
Wushan Chongqing China 97 F2
Wushan Gansu China 94 F5
Wu Shan mts China 97 F2
Wushi Guangdong China 97 F4
Wushi Xinjiang China 98 B4
Wüstegarten hill Germany 63 J3
Wusuli Jiang r. China/Russia see Ussuri
Wutai Shanxi China 95 H4
Wutai Xinjiang China 98 C3
Wutai Shan mts China 95 H4
Wutonggou Gansu China 94 D3
Wutonggou Xinjiang China 98 E4
Wutongwozi Quan well China 94 C3
Wuvulu Island P.N.G. 81 K7
Wuwei China 94 E4
Wuxi Chongqing China 97 F2
Wuxi Hunan China 97 F2
Wuxi Hunan China see Qiyang
Wuxi Jiangsu China 97 I2
Wuxia China see Wushan
Wuxian China see Suzhou
Wuxiang China 95 H4
Wuxing China see Huzhou
Wuxu China 97 F4
Wuxuan China 97 F4
Wuxue China 97 G2
Wuyang Guizhou China see Zhenyuan
Wuyang Henan China 97 G1
Wuyang Shanxi China 95 H4
Wuyang Zhejiang China see Wuyi
Wuyi China 97 H2
Wuyiling China 90 C2
Wuyi Shan mts China 97 H3
Wuyuan Jiangxi China 97 H2
Wuyuan Nei Mongol China 95 G3
Wuyuan Zhejiang China see Haiyan
Wuyun China see Jinyun
Wuzhai China 95 G4
Wuzhi China 95 H5
Wuzhishan China 97 F5
Wuzhi Shan mts China 97 F5
Wuzhong China 94 F4
Wuzhou China 97 F4
Wyalkatchem Australia 135 B7
Wyalong Australia 138 C4
Wyandra Australia 138 B1
Wyangala Reservoir Australia 138 D4
Wyara, Lake salt flat Australia 138 B2
Wycheproof Australia 138 A6
Wylliesburg VA U.S.A. 165 F5
Wyloo Australia 134 B5
Wylye r. U.K. 59 F7
Wymondham U.K. 59 I6
Wymore NE U.S.A. 160 D3
Wynbring Australia 135 F7
Wyndham Australia 134 E3
Wyndham-Werribee Australia 138 B6
Wynne AR U.S.A. 161 F5
Wynyard Canada 151 J5
Wyola Lake salt flat Australia 135 E7
Wyoming MI U.S.A. 164 C2
Wyoming state U.S.A. 156 G4
Wyoming Peak WY U.S.A. 156 F4
Wyoming Range mts WY U.S.A. 156 F4
Wyong Australia 138 E4
Wyperfeld National Park Australia 137 C7
Wysox PA U.S.A. 165 G3
Wyszków Poland 57 R4
Wythall U.K. 59 F6
Wytheville VA U.S.A. 164 E5
Wytmarsum Neth. see Witmarsum

X

Xaafuun Somalia 122 F2

▶Xaafuun, Raas pt Somalia 108 H7
Most easterly point of Africa.

Xabyai China 99 G7
Xabyaisamba China 96 C2
Xaçmaz Azer. 113 H2
Xagjang China 99 F7
Xagnag China 99 C6
Xago China 99 E7
Xagquka China 99 F7
Xaidulla China 99 B5
Xaignabouli Laos 86 C3
Xaignabouri Laos see Xaignabouli
Xainza China 99 E7
Xaitongmoin China 99 E7
Xai-Xai Moz. 125 K3
Xakur China 98 B5
Xal, Cerro de hill Mex. 167 H4
Xalapa Mex. 168 E5
Xaltan Aşırımı Azer. 113 H2
Xaltianguis Mex. 167 F5
Xamba China 95 F3
Xambioá Brazil 177 I5
Xamgyi'nyilha China 96 C3
Xam Nua Laos 86 D2
Xá-Muteba Angola 123 B4
Xan r. Laos 86 C3
Xanagas Botswana 124 E2
Xangd China 94 E3
Xangda China see Nangqên
Xangdin Hural China 95 G3
Xangdoring China see Xungba
Xangongo Angola 123 B5
Xangzha China 99 F7
Xanh, Cu Lao i. Vietnam 87 E4
Xanica Mex. 167 F5

▶Xankändi Azer. 113 G3
Capital of Nagorno-Karabakh.

Xanthi Greece 69 K4
Xarag China 94 D4
Xarardheere Somalia 122 E3
Xarba La pass China 99 D7
Xar Burd China see Bayan Nurun
Xardong China 99 D7
Xar Hudag China 95 H2
Xar Moron r. China 95 J3
Xarru China 99 D7
Xarsingma China see Yadong
Xàtiva Spain 67 F4
Xavantes, Serra dos hills Brazil 177 I6
Xaxa China 99 C6
Xayar China 98 C4
Xazgat China 98 D3
Xcalak Mex. 167 I5
X-Can Mex. 167 I4
Xegil China 98 B4
Xekargol China 98 B5
Xékong Laos 86 D4
Xelva Spain see Chelva
Xenia OH U.S.A. 164 D4
Xênkyêr China 99 E7
Xero Potamos r. Cyprus see Xeros
Xeros r. Cyprus 107 A2
Xhora S. Africa see Elliotdale
Xia Awat China 98 B5
Xiabancheng China see Chengde
Xia Bazar China 98 B5
Xiabole Shan mt. China 90 B2
Xiachuan Dao i. China 97 G4
Xiacun China see Rushan
Xia Dawo China 94 D5
Xiadong China 94 C3
Xiaguan China see Dali
Xiaguanying China 94 F5
Xiahe China 94 E5
Xiajiang China see Xagjang
Xiajin China 95 I4
Xiamaya China 94 C3
Xiamen China 97 H3
Xi'an Ningxia China 94 F4
Xi'an Shaanxi China 95 G5
Xianfeng China 97 F2
Xiangcheng Henan China 95 H5
Xiangcheng Sichuan China 96 C2
Xiangcheng Yunnan China see Xiangyun
Xiangfan China see Xiangyang
Xiangfen China 95 G5
Xiangfeng China see Laifeng
Xianggang H.K. China see Hong Kong
Xianggang Tebie Xingzhengqu aut. reg. China see Hong Kong
Xiangkou China see Wulong
Xiangning China 95 G5
Xiangride China 94 D5
Xiangshan China see Menghai
Xiangshui China 95 I5
Xiangshuiba China 97 F3
Xiangtan China 97 G3
Xiangxiang China 97 G3
Xiangyang China 97 G1
Xiangyang Hu l. China 99 E6
Xiangyin China 97 G2
Xiangyun China 96 D3
Xianju China 97 I2
Xianning China 97 G2
Xiannümiao China see Jiangdu
Xianshui He r. China 96 D2
Xiantao China 97 G2
Xianxia Ling mts China 97 H3
Xianxian China 95 I4
Xianyang China 95 G5
Xiaoba China see Qingtongxia
Xiaocaohu China 102 G3
Xiaochang China 95 H3
Xiaodong China 97 F4
Xiaodongliang China 96 C1
Xiao'ergou China 95 J1
Xiaogan China 97 G2
Xiaogang China see Dongxiang
Xiaoguai China 98 D3
Xiaoguan China 95 F4
Xiaohaizi Shuiku resr China 98 B5
Xiao Hinggan Ling mts China 90 B2
Xiaojin Gansu China 95 F5
Xiaojin Sichuan China 96 D2
Xiaolangdi Shuiku resr China 95 H5
Xiaonanchuan China 94 C5
Xiao Qaidam China 99 F5
Xiaosanjiang China 97 G3
Xiaoshan China 97 I2
Xiao Shan mts China 95 G5
Xiaoshi China see Benxi
Xiao Surmang China 96 C1
Xiaotao China 97 H3
Xiaowutai Shan mt. China 95 H4
Xiaoxi China see Pinghe
Xiaoxian China 95 I5
Xiaoxiang Ling mts China 96 D2
Xiaoxita China see Yiling
Xiaoyi Henan China see Gongyi
Xiaoyi Shanxi China 95 G4
Xiaoyingpan China 98 C3
Xiapu China 97 I3
Xiaqiong China see Batang
Xiashan China see Zhanjiang
Xiasifen China 94 E4
Xiatil Mex. 167 H5
Xiaxian China 95 G5
Xiayang China see Yanling
Xiayingpan China see Liuzhi
Xiayukou China 97 F1
Xiazhen China see Weishan
Xiazhuang China see Linshu
Xibdê China 96 C2
Xibet China 98 E3
Xibing China 97 H3
Xibu China see Dongshan
Xichang China 96 D3
Xicheng China see Yangyuan
Xichou China 96 E4
Xichuan China 97 F1
Xide China 96 D2
Xidu China see Hengyang
Xiejiaji China see Qingyun
Xiema China 97 F2
Xiêng Lam Vietnam 86 D3
Xieyang Dao i. China 97 F4
Xifeng Gansu China see Qingyang
Xifeng Guizhou China 96 E3
Xifeng Liaoning China 90 B4
Xifengzhen China see Qingyang
Xigazê China 99 E7
Xihan Shui r. China 96 E1
Xihe China 94 F5
Xi He r. China 96 E2
Xihu China 98 F4
Xihua China 95 H5
Xihuachi China see Heshui
Xiji China 94 F5
Xi Jiang r. China 97 G4
Xijian Quan well China 94 D3
Xijir China 94 B5
Xijir Ulan Hu salt l. China 99 E6
Xijishui China 94 E4
Xil China 95 H3
Xilaotou Shan mt. China 95 J2
Xiliangzi China 98 F5
Xiliao He r. China 95 J3
Xiligou China see Ulan
Xilin China 96 E3
Xilin Gol China 94 F4
Xilinhot China 95 I3
Xilin Qagan Obo China see Qagan Obo
Ximiao China 94 E3
Xin China 95 G4
Xin'an Anhui China see Lai'an
Xin'an Guizhou China see Anlong
Xin'an Hebei China see Anxin
Xin'an Henan China 95 H5
Xinavane Moz. 125 K3
Xin Barag Youqi China see Altan Emel
Xin Barag Zuoqi China see Amgalang
Xin Bulag Jun China 95 I1
Xincai China 97 G1
Xinchang Jiangxi China see Yifeng
Xinchang Zhejiang China 97 I2
Xincheng Fujian China see Gutian
Xincheng Guangdong China see Xinxing
Xincheng Guangxi China 97 F3
Xincheng Shaanxi China 95 G4
Xincheng Shanxi China see Yuanqu
Xincheng Sichuan China see Zhaojue
Xinchengzi China 94 E4
Xinchepaizi China 98 D3
Xincun China see Dongchuan
Xincunjie China 95 I4
Xindi Guangxi China 97 F4
Xindi Hubei China see Honghu
Xindian China 95 K2
Xindu Guangxi China 97 F4
Xindu Sichuan China see Luhuo
Xindu Sichuan China 96 E2
Xinduqiao China 96 D2
Xinfeng Guangdong China 97 G3
Xinfeng Jiangxi China 97 G3
Xinfengjiang Shuiku resr China 97 G4
Xing'an Guangxi China 97 F3
Xingan China 97 G3
Xing'an Shaanxi China see Ankang
Xingang China 95 J4
Xingba China see Lhünzê
Xingcheng Hebei China see Qianxi
Xingcheng Liaoning China 95 J3
Xingdi China 98 D4
Xingguo Gansu China see Qin'an
Xingguo Hubei China see Yangxin
Xingguo Jiangxi China 97 G3
Xinghai China 94 D5
Xinghua China 97 H1
Xinghua Wan b. China 97 H3
Xingkai China 90 D3
Xingkai Hu l. China/Russia see Khanka, Lake
Xinglong Hebei China 95 I3
Xinglong Heilong. China 90 B2
Xinglong Heilong. China 90 B3
Xinglongzhen China 96 E1
Xingning Guangdong China 97 G3
Xingning Hunan China 97 G3
Xingou China 97 G2
Xingping China 95 G5
Xingqêngoin China 96 D2
Xingren Guizhou China 96 E3
Xingren Ningxia China 94 F4
Xingsagoinba China 94 E5
Xingshan Guizhou China see Majiang
Xingshan Hubei China 97 F2
Xingtai China 95 H4
Xingtang China 95 H4
Xingu r. Brazil 177 H4
Xingu, Parque Indígena do res. Brazil 177 H6
Xinguangwu China 95 H4
Xinguara Brazil 177 H5
Xingxian China 95 G4
Xingxingxia China 94 C3
Xingyang China 95 H5
Xingye China 97 F4
Xingyi China 96 E3
Xinhe Hebei China 95 H4
Xinhe Xinjiang China 98 C4
Xin Hot China 95 H3
Xinhua Guangdong China see Huadu
Xinhua Hunan China 97 F3
Xinhua Yunnan China see Qiaojia
Xinhua Yunnan China see Funing
Xinhuang China 97 F3
Xinhui Guangdong China 97 G4
Xinhui Nei Mongol China 95 I3
Xining China 94 E4
Xinji China 95 H4
Xinjian China 97 G2
Xinjiang China 95 G5

Xinjiang aut. reg. China see Xinjiang Uygur Zizhiqu
Xinjiangkou China see Songzi
Xinjiang Uygur Zizhiqu aut. reg. China 94 B3
Xinjie Nei Mongol China 95 G4
Xinjie Qinghai China 96 D1
Xinjie Yunnan China 96 C3
Xinjie Yunnan China 96 D4
Xinjin Liaoning China see Pulandian
Xinjin Sichuan China 96 D2
Xinjing China see Jingxi
Xinkai He r. China 95 J3
Xinkou China 89 K5
Xinling China see Badong
Xinlitun China 90 B2
Xinlong China 96 D2
Xinmi China 95 H5
Xinmin Heilong. China 90 B2
Xinmin Liaoning China 95 J3
Xinmin Shaanxi China 95 G4
Xinning Gansu China see Ningxian
Xinning Hunan China 97 F3
Xinning Jiangxi China see Wuning
Xinning Sichuan China see Kaijiang
Xinping China 96 D3
Xinqiao China 97 G1
Xinqing China 90 C2
Xinquan China 97 H3
Xinshan China see Anyuan
Xinshiba China see Ganluo
Xinsi China 96 E1
Xintai China 95 I5
Xintanpu China 97 G2
Xintian China 97 G3
Xinxian China see Xinzhou
Xinxiang China 95 H5
Xinxing China 97 G4
Xinyang Henan China see Pingqiao
Xinyang Henan China 97 G1
Xinyang Gang r. China 95 J5
Xinye China 97 G1
Xinyi Guangdong China 97 F4
Xinyi Jiangsu China 95 I5
Xinyi He r. China 95 I5
Xinying China 97 F5
Xinying Taiwan 97 I4
Xinyu China 97 G3
Xinyuan Qinghai China see Tianjun
Xinyuan Xinjiang China 98 C4
Xinzhangfang China 95 J1
Xinzheng China 95 H5
Xinzhou Guangxi China see Longlin
Xinzhou Hubei China 97 G2
Xinzhou Shanxi China 95 H4
Xinzhu Taiwan 97 I3
Xinzo de Limia Spain 67 C2
Xiongshan China see Zhenghe
Xiongshi China see Guixi
Xiongzhou China see Nanxiong
Xiping Henan China 97 F1
Xiping Henan China 97 G1
Xiqing Shan mts China 94 E5
Xiqu China 94 E4
Xique-Xique Brazil 177 J6
Xisa China see Xichou
Xishanzui China 95 G3
Xisha Qundao is S. China Sea see Paracel Islands
Xishuangbanna reg. China 96 D4
Xishuanghe China see Kenli
Xishui Guizhou China 96 E2
Xishui Hubei China 97 G2
Xi Taijnar Hu l. China 99 F5
Xitianmu Shan mt. China 97 H2
Xitieshan China 94 C4
Xiugu China see Jinxi
Xi Ujimqin Qi China see Bayan Ul
Xiuning China 97 H2
Xiushan Chongqing China 97 F2
Xiushan Yunnan China see Tonghai
Xiushui China 97 G2
Xiuwen China 96 E3
Xiuwu China 95 H5
Xiuyan Liaoning China 95 J3
Xiuyan Shaanxi China see Qingjian
Xiuying China 97 F4
Xiwanzi China see Chongli
Xiwol China 99 C5
Xiwu China 96 C1
Xixabangma Feng mt. China 99 D7
Xixia Henan China 97 F1
Xixia Ningxia China 94 F4
Xixian China 95 G4
Xixiang China 96 E1
Xixiu China see Anshun
Xixón Spain see Gijón/Xixón
Xiyang China 95 H4
Xiyang Dao i. China 97 I3
Xiyang Jiang r. China 96 E3
Xiying China 94 E4
Xiyuping Yu i. Taiwan 97 H4
Xizang aut. reg. China see Xizang Zizhiqu
Xizang Gaoyuan plat. China see Tibet, Plateau of
Xizang Zizhiqu aut. reg. China 105 G3
Xizhong Dao i. China 95 J4
Xobando China 99 F7
Xoi China see Qüxü
Xo'japiryox tog'i mt. Uzbek. 111 G2
Xo'jayli Uzbek. 102 A3
Xoka China 99 F7
Xorkol China 98 E5
Xortang China 99 D5
Xuancheng China 97 H2
Xuande Qundao is Paracel Is see Amphitrite Group
Xuan'en China 97 F2
Xuanhua China 95 H3
Xuân Lôc Vietnam 87 D5
Xuanwei China 96 E3
Xuanzhou China see Xuancheng
Xuchang China 97 G1
Xucheng China see Xuwen
Xuddur Somalia 122 E3
Xueba China 99 F7
Xuefeng China see Mingxi
Xuefeng Shan mts China 97 F3
Xuehua Shan hill China 95 G5
Xuejiawan China 95 G4
Xue Shan mts China 96 C3
Xue Shan mt. Taiwan 97 I3
Xugin Gol r. China 94 C5
Xugui Nei Mongol China 94 E3
Xugui Qinghai China 94 C5
Xuguit Qi China see Yakeshi
Xujiang China see Guangchang
Xulun Hobot Qagan Qi China see Ming'antu
Xulun Hoh Qi China see Shangdu
Xümatang China 96 C1
Xungba China 99 C6
Xungmai China 99 E7
Xung Qu r. China 99 F7
Xungru China 99 D7
Xunhe China 90 B2
Xun He r. China 90 C2
Xunhua China 94 E5
Xun Jiang r. China 97 F4
Xunwu China 97 G3
Xunxian China 95 H5
Xunyi China 95 G5
Xúquer, Riu r. Spain 67 F4
Xurgan China 94 C5
Xuru Co salt l. China 99 D7
Xushui China 95 H4
Xuwen China 80 E2
Xuyi China 97 H1
Xuyong China 96 E2
Xuzhou China 95 I5

Y

Ya'an China 96 D2
Yaba Moluccas Indon. 83 C3
Yabanabat Turkey see Kızılcahamam
Yabēlo Eth. 122 D3
Yablonovyy Khrebet mts Russia 95 G1
Yabrai China 94 E4
Yabrai Shan mts China 94 E4
Yabrīn reg. Saudi Arabia 110 C6
Yabu Hyōgo Japan 92 A3
Yabu Hyōgo Japan 92 A3
Yabuli China 90 C3
Yabuzukahon Japan 93 F2
Yacha China see Baisha
Yacheng China 97 F5
Yachi He r. China 96 E3
Yachimata Japan 93 G3
Yachiyo Chiba Japan 93 G3
Yachiyo Ibaraki Japan 93 F2
Yacuma r. Bol. 176 E6
Yadgir India 106 C2
Yadong China 99 E8
Yadrin Russia 52 J5
Yaeyama-rettō is Japan 89 M8
Yafa Israel see Tel Aviv-Yafo
Yagaba Ghana 120 C3
Yagan China 94 E3
Yağda Turkey see Erdemli
Yaghan Basin sea feature S. Atlantic Ocean 184 D9
Yagi Japan 92 B3
Yagkêng China 94 D4
Yagman Turkm. 110 D2
Yagmo China 99 D7
Yago Mex. 166 D4
Yagodnoye Russia 77 P3
Yagodnyy Russia 90 E2
Yagoua Cameroon 121 E3
Yagra China 99 C7
Yagradagzê Feng mt. China 94 C5
Yaguajay Cuba 163 E8
Yagul and Mitla, Prehistoric Caves of tourist site Mex. 167 F5
Yaha Thai. 87 C6
Yahagi-gawa r. Japan 92 C4
Yahk Canada 150 G5
Yahualica Mex. 168 D4
Yahyalı Turkey 65 L4
Yai Myanmar see Ye
Yai, Khao mt. Thai. 87 B4
Yairu Zangbo r. China 99 D7
Yaita Japan 93 F2
Yaizu Japan 93 E4
Yajiang China 96 D2
Yakacık Turkey 107 C1
Yakak, Cape AK U.S.A. 148 [inset] C6
Yakatograk China 98 D5
Yake-dake vol. Japan 92 D2
Yakeshi China 95 J1
Yakhab waterhole Iran 110 E3
Yakhchāl Afgh. 111 G4
Yakima WA U.S.A. 156 C3
Yakima r. WA U.S.A. 156 D3
Yakmach Pak. 111 F4
Yako Burkina Faso 120 C3
Yakovlevka Russia 90 D3
Yakuno Japan 92 A3
Yaku-shima i. Japan 91 C7
Yakutat AK U.S.A. 149 M4
Yakutat Bay AK U.S.A. 149 L4
Yakutsk Russia 77 N3
Yakymivka Ukr. 53 G7
Yala Thai. 87 C6
Yala National Park Sri Lanka 106 D5
Yalan Dünya Mağarası tourist site Turkey 107 A1
Yale Canada 150 F5
Yale MI U.S.A. 164 D2
Yalgoo Australia 135 B7
Yalkubul, Punta pt Mex. 167 H4
Yalleroi Australia 136 D5
Yaloké Cent. Afr. Rep. 122 B3
Yalova Turkey 69 M4
Yalta Crimea 112 D1
Yalu He r. China 95 J2
Yalu Jiang r. China/N. Korea 90 B4
Yalujiang Kou r. mouth China/N. Korea 91 B5
Yalvaç Turkey 69 N5
Yamada Chiba Japan 93 G3
Yamada Toyama Japan 92 D2
Yamagata Gifu Japan 92 C3
Yamagata Ibaraki Japan 93 G2
Yamagata Nagano Japan 93 D2
Yamagata Yamagata Japan 91 F5
Yamaguchi Nagano Japan 92 D3
Yamaguchi Yamaguchi Japan 91 C6
Yamakita Japan 93 F3
Yamal, Poluostrov pen. Russia see Yamal Peninsula
Yam-Alin', Khrebet mts Russia 90 D1
Yamal Peninsula Russia 76 H2
Yamanaka Japan 92 C2
Yamanakako Japan 93 E3
Yamanaka-ko l. Japan 93 E3
Yamanashi Japan 93 E3
Yamanashi pref. Japan 93 E3
Yamanie Falls National Park Australia 136 D3
Yamanouchi Japan 93 E2
Yamansu China 94 C3
Yamaoka Japan 92 D3
Yamarovka Russia 95 G1
Yamashiro Japan 92 B4
Yamato Gifu Japan 92 C3
Yamato Kanagawa Japan 93 F3
Yamato-Aogaki Kokutei-kōen park Japan 92 B4
Yamato-Kōriyama Japan 92 B4
Yamatotakada Japan 92 B4
Yamatsuri Japan 93 G2
Yamazoe Japan 92 C4
Yamba Australia 138 F2
Yamba Lake Canada 151 I1
Yambarran Range hills Australia 134 E3
Yambi, Mesa de hills Col. 176 D3
Yambio South Sudan 121 F4
Yambol Bulg. 69 L3
Yamdena i. Moluccas Indon. 134 E1
Yamethin Myanmar 86 B2

▶Yamin, Puncak mt. Indon. 81 J7
4th highest mountain in Oceania.

Yamizo-san mt. Japan 93 G2
Yamkanmardi India 106 B2
Yamkhad Syria see Aleppo
Yamm Russia 55 P7
Yamma Yamma, Lake salt flat Australia 137 C5

▶Yamoussoukro Côte d'Ivoire 120 C4
Capital of Côte d'Ivoire (Ivory Coast).

Yampa r. CO U.S.A. 159 I1
Yampil' Ukr. 53 F6
Yampol' Ukr. see Yampil'
Yamuna r. India 104 E4
Yamunanagar India 104 D3
Yamzho Yumco l. China 99 E7
Yana r. Russia 77 O2
Yanam India 106 D2
Yan'an China 95 G4
Yanaoca Peru 176 D6
Yanaon India see Yanam
Yanaul Russia 51 Q4
Yanbu' al Baḩr Saudi Arabia 108 E5
Yanceyville NC U.S.A. 162 E4
Yanchang China 95 G4
Yancheng Henan China 97 G1
Yancheng Jiangsu China 97 I1
Yancheng Shandong China see Qihe
Yanchep Australia 135 A7
Yanchi Ningxia China 95 F4
Yanchi Xinjiang China 94 C3
Yanchi Xinjiang China 98 D3
Yanchiwan China 98 F5
Yanchuan China 95 G4
Yanco Australia 138 C5
Yanco Creek r. Australia 138 B5
Yanco Glen Australia 137 C6
Yanda watercourse Australia 138 B3
Yandama Creek watercourse Australia 137 C6
Yandao China see Yingjing
Yandoon Myanmar 86 A3
Yandrakynnot Russia 148 D2
Yandun China 94 C3
Yanfolila Mali 120 C3
Ya'ngamdo Xizang China 99 F7
Ya'ngamdo Xizang China 99 F7
Yangbajain China 99 E7
Yangbi China 96 C3
Yangchang China 96 E3
Yangcheng Guangdong China see Yangshan
Yangcheng Shanxi China 95 H5
Yangchuan China see Suiyang
Yangchun China 97 F4
Yangcun Guangdong China 97 G4
Yangcun Tianjin China 95 I4
Yangdaxkak China 98 E5
Yangdok N. Korea 91 B5
Yanggao China 95 H3
Yanggu China 95 H4
Yanghe China see Yongning
Yang Hu l. China 99 D6
Yangi Davan pass China 99 B6
Yangi Nishon Uzbek. 111 G2
Yangī Qal'ah Afgh. 111 H2
Yangiqishloq Uzbek. 102 C3
Yangirabot Uzbek. 111 G1
Yangiyo'l Uzbek. 102 C3
Yangjiajiang China 97 G2
Yangjialing China 95 G4
Yangjiang China 97 F4
Yangkou China 95 I4
Yangming China see Heping
Yangôn Myanmar see Rangoon
Yangping China 97 F2
Yangquan China 95 H4
Yangquanqu China 95 G4
Yangshan China 97 G3
Yang Sin, Chư mt. Vietnam 87 E4
Yang Talat Thai. 86 C3
Yangtouyan China 96 D3
Yangtze r. Qinghai China see Tongtian He

▶Yangtze r. China 96 E2
Longest river in Asia and 3rd in the world. Also known as Chang Jiang or Jinsha Jiang or Tongtian He or Yangtze Kiang or Zhi Qu.

Yangtze Kiang r. China see Yangtze
Yanguan China 94 F5
Yangudi Rassa National Park Eth. 122 E2
Yangxi China 97 F4
Yangxian China 96 E1
Yangxin China 97 G2
Yangyang S. Korea 91 C5
Yangyuan China 95 H3
Yangzhou Jiangsu China 97 H1
Yangzhou Shaanxi China see Yangxian
Yanhe China 97 F2
Yanhu China 98 E4
Yanhuqu China 105 E2
Yanishpole Russia 52 G3
Yanis"yarvi, Ozero l. Russia 54 Q5
Yanji China 90 C4
Yanjiang China see Ziyang
Yanjin Henan China 95 H5
Yanjin Yunnan China 96 E2
Yanjing Sichuan China see Yanyuan
Yanjing Yunnan China see Yanjin
Yankari National Park Nigeria 120 E4
Yankton SD U.S.A. 160 D3
Yanling Henan China 95 H5
Yanling Hunan China 97 G3
Yanling Sichuan China see Weiyuan
Yannina Greece see Ioannina
Yano-Indigirskaya Nizmennost' lowland Russia 77 P2
Yanovski, Mount AK U.S.A. 149 N4
Yanqi China 98 D4
Yanqing China 95 H3
Yanrey r. Australia 135 A5
Yanshan Hebei China 95 I4
Yanshan Jiangxi China 97 H2
Yanshan Yunnan China 96 E4
Yan Shan mts China 95 I3
Yanshi China 95 H5
Yanshiping China 99 F6
Yanskiy Zaliv g. Russia 77 O2
Yantabulla Australia 138 B2
Yantai China 95 J4
Yanting China 96 E2
Yantongshan China 90 B4
Yantou China 97 I2
Yanwa China 96 C3
Yanweigang China 95 I5
Yany-Kurgan Kazakh. see Zhanakorgan
Yanyuan China 96 D3
Yanzhou China 95 I5
Yao Chad 121 E3
Yao Japan 92 B4
Yao'an China 96 D3
Yaodian China 95 G4
Yaodu China see Dongzhi
Yaojie China see Honggu
Yaoli China 97 H2
Yaoquanzi China 94 D4
Yaotsu Japan 92 D3

▶Yaoundé Cameroon 120 E4
Capital of Cameroon.

Yaoxian China see Yaozhou
Yaoxiaoling China 90 B2
Yao Yai, Ko i. Thai. 87 B6
Yaozhen China 95 G4
Yaozhou China 95 G5
Yap i. Micronesia 81 J5
Yapen i. Indon. 81 J7
Yappar r. Australia 136 C3
Yap Trench sea feature N. Pacific Ocean 186 F5
Yaqui r. Mex. 166 C3
Yar Russia 52 L4
Yaradzha Turkm. see Ýarajy
Ýarajy Turkm. 110 E2
Yaraka Australia 136 D5
Yarangüme Turkey see Tavas
Yaransk Russia 52 J4
Yardea Australia 137 A7
Yardımcı Burnu pt Turkey 69 N6
Yardımlı Azer. 113 H3
Yardoi China 99 E7
Yardymly Azer. see Yardımlı
Yare r. U.K. 59 I6
Yarega Russia 52 L3

▶Yaren Nauru 133 G2
Capital of Nauru.

Yarensk Russia 52 K3
Yariga-take mt. Japan 92 D2
Yarīm Yemen 108 F7
Yarımca Turkey see Körfez
Yarkand China see Shache
Yarkant China see Shache
Yarkant He r. China 99 B5
Yarker Canada 165 G1
Yarkhun r. Pak. 111 I2
Yarlêb China 99 D7
Yarlung Zangbo r. Xizang China 99 F7 see Dihang
Yarlung Zangbo r. Xizang Zizhiqu China 99 F7
Yarmouth Canada 153 I6
Yarmouth England U.K. 59 F8
Yarmouth England U.K. see Great Yarmouth
Yarmouth ME U.S.A. 165 J2
Yarmuk r. Asia 107 B3
Yarnell AZ U.S.A. 159 G4
Yaroslavl' Russia 52 H4
Yaroslavskiy Russia 90 D3
Yarra r. Australia 138 B6
Yarra Junction Australia 138 B6
Yarram Australia 138 C7
Yarraman Australia 138 E1
Yarrawonga Australia 138 B6
Yarra Yarra Lakes salt flat Australia 135 A7
Yarronvale Australia 138 B1
Yarrowmere Australia 136 D4
Yartö Tra La pass China 105 H3
Yartsevo Krasnoyarskiy Kray Russia 76 J3
Yartsevo Smolenskaya Oblast' Russia 53 G5
Yarumal Col. 176 C2
Yaruu Mongolia 94 D1
Yarwa China 96 C2
Yarzhong China 96 C2
Yaş Romania see Iaşi
Yasaka Kyōto Japan 92 B3
Yasaka Nagano Japan 93 D2
Yasato Japan 93 G2
Yasawa Group is Fiji 133 H3
Yashilkŭl l. Tajik. 111 I2
Yashiro Japan 93 E2
Yashkul' Russia 53 J7
Yasin Pak. 104 C1
Yasnogorsk Russia 53 H5
Yasnyy Russia 90 C1
Yasothon Thai. 86 D4
Yass Australia 138 D5
Yass r. Australia 138 D5
Yassı Burnu c. Cyprus see Plakoti, Cape
Yasu Japan 92 C3
Yāsūj Iran 110 C4
Yasuní, Parque Nacional nat. park Ecuador 176 C4
Yasuoka Japan 93 D3
Yasuzuka Japan 93 E1
Yatağan Turkey 69 M6
Yaté New Caledonia 133 G4
Yates r. Canada 150 H2
Yates Center KS U.S.A. 160 E4
Yathkyed Lake Canada 151 L2
Yatomi Japan 92 C3
Yatou China see Rongcheng
Yatsuga-take vol. Japan 93 E3
Yatsuga-take-Chūshin-kōgen Kokutei-kōen park Japan 93 E2
Yatsuo Japan 92 D2
Yatsushiro Japan 91 C6
Yaţţah West Bank 107 B4
Yatton U.K. 59 E7
Yauca Peru 176 D7
Yau Tong b. H.K. China 97 [inset]
Yauyupe Hond. 166 [inset] I6
Yavan Tajik. see Yovon
Yavarí r. Brazil/Peru 176 E4
Yávaros Mex. 166 C3
Yavatmal India 106 C1
Yavi Turkey 113 F3
Yaví, Cerro mt. Venez. 176 E2
Yavoriv Ukr. 53 D6
Yavuzlu Turkey 107 C1
Yawata Japan 92 B4
Yawatongguz He r. China 99 C5
Yawatongguzlangar China 99 C5
Yaw Chaung r. Myanmar 96 B4
Yaxchilan tourist site Guat. 167 H5
Yaxian China see Sanya
Yay Myanmar see Ye
Yayladağı Turkey 107 C2
Yazd Iran 110 D4
Yazdān Iran 111 F3
Yazd-e Khvāst Iran see Shāhīn Dezh
Yazıhan Turkey 112 E3
Yazoo r. MS U.S.A. 167 H1
Yazoo City MS U.S.A. 161 F5
Yazukami Japan 93 G2
Y Bala U.K. see Bala
Yding Skovhøj hill Denmark 57 L3
Ydra i. Greece 69 J6
Y Drenewydd U.K. see Newtown
Ye Myanmar 86 B4
Yea Australia 138 B6
Yealmpton U.K. 59 D8
Yebaishou China see Jianping
Yebawmi Myanmar 86 A1
Yebbi-Bou Chad 121 E2
Yecheng China 99 B5
Yécora Mex. 166 C2
Yedashe Myanmar 86 B3
Yedi Burun Başı pt Turkey 69 M6
Yeeda River Australia 134 C4
Yefremov Russia 53 H5
Yêgainnyin China see Henan
Yeghegnadzor Armenia 113 G3
Yegindybulak Kazakh. 98 B2
Yegindykol' Kazakh. 102 C1
Yegorlykskaya Russia 53 I7
Yegorova, Mys pt Russia 90 E3
Yegor'yevsk Russia 53 H5
Yei South Sudan 121 G4
Yei r. South Sudan 121 G4
Yeji China 97 G2
Yejiaji China see Yeji
Yekaterinburg Russia 76 H4
Yekaterinodar Russia see Krasnodar
Yekaterinoslav Ukr. see Dnipropetrovs'k
Yekaterinoslavka Russia 90 C2
Yekhegnadzor Armenia see Yeghegnadzor
Yekibastuz Kazakh. 102 E1
Ye Kyun i. Myanmar 86 A3
Yelabuga Khabarovskiy Kray Russia 90 D2
Yelabuga Respublika Tatarstan Russia 52 K5
Yelan' Russia 53 I6
Yelan' r. Russia 53 I6
Yelandur India 106 C3
Yelantsy Russia 88 J2
Yelarbon Australia 138 E2
Yelbarsli Turkm. 111 F2
Yelenovskiye Kar'yery Ukr. see Dokuchayevs'k
Yelets Russia 53 H5
Yeliguan China 94 E5
Yélimané Mali 120 B3
Yelizavetgrad Ukr. see Kirovohrad
Yelkhovka Russia 53 K5
Yell i. U.K. 60 [inset]
Yellabina Regional Reserve nature res. Australia 135 F7
Yellandu India 106 D2
Yellapur India 106 B3
Yellowhead Pass Canada 150 G4

▶Yellowknife Canada 150 H2
Capital of the Northwest Territories.

Yellowknife r. Canada 150 H2
Yellow Mountain hill Australia 138 C4

▶Yellow River r. China 95 I4
4th longest river in Asia and 7th in the world.

Yellow Sea N. Pacific Ocean 89 N5
Yellowstone r. MT U.S.A. 160 C2
Yellowstone Lake WY U.S.A. 156 F3
Yellowstone National Park U.S.A. 156 F3
Yell Sound strait U.K. 60 [inset]
Yeloten Turkm. see Ýolöten
Yelovo Russia 51 Q4
Yel'sk Belarus 53 F6
Yel'tay Kazakh. 98 C3
Yelucá mt. Nicaragua 166 [inset] I6
Yelva r. Russia 52 K3
Yema Nanshan mts China 94 C4
Yema Shan mts China 98 F5
Yematan Qinghai China 94 D4
Yematan Qinghai China 94 D5
Yemel' r. Kazakh. 98 C3
Yemen country Asia 108 G6
Yemetsk Russia 52 I3
Yemişenbükü Turkey see Taşova
Yemmiganur India see Emmiganuru
Yemtsa Russia 52 I3
Yemva Russia 52 K3
Yena Russia 54 Q3
Yenagoa Nigeria 120 D4
Yenakiyeve Ukr. 53 H6
Yenakiyevo Ukr. see Yenakiyeve
Yenangyat Myanmar 86 A2
Yenangyaung Myanmar 86 A2
Yenanma Myanmar 86 A3
Yenbek Kazakh. 98 B2
Yenda Australia 138 C5
Yêndum China see Zhag'yab
Yengisar Xinjiang China 98 B5
Yengisar Xinjiang China 98 D4
Yengisu China 98 D4
Yengo National Park Australia 138 E4
Yenice Turkey 69 L5
Yenidamlar Turkey see Demirtaş
Yenihan Turkey see Yıldızeli
Yenije-i-Vardar Greece see Giannitsa
Yenişehir Greece see Larisa
Yenişehir Turkey 69 M4

▶Yenisey r. Russia 76 J2
Part of the Yenisey-Angara-Selenga, 3rd longest river in Asia.

▶Yenisey-Angara-Selenga r. Russia 76 J2
3rd longest river in Asia and 6th in the world.

Yeniseysk Russia 76 K4
Yeniseyskaya Ravnina ridge Russia 76 K4
Yeniseyskiy Zaliv inlet Russia 189 F2
Yeniugou China 94 D4
Yeniugou Shisuzhan China 94 D5
Yeniyol Turkey see Borçka
Yên Minh Vietnam 86 D2
Yenotayevka Russia 53 J7
Yentna r. AK U.S.A. 149 J3
Yeola India 106 B1
Yeo Lake salt flat Australia 135 D6
Yeongil-man b. S. Korea 91 C6
Yeongju S. Korea 91 C5
Yeosu S. Korea 91 B6
Yeotmal India see Yavatmal
Yeoval Australia 138 D4
Yeovil U.K. 59 E8
Yeo Yeo r. Australia see Bland
Yepachi Mex. 166 C2
Yeppoon Australia 136 E4
Yeraliyev Kazakh. see Kuryk
Yerbabuena Mex. 167 E4
Yerbent Turkm. 110 E2
Yerbogachen Russia 77 L3
Yercaud India 106 C4

▶Yerevan Armenia 113 G2
Capital of Armenia.

Yereymentau Kazakh. 102 D1
Yergara India 106 C2
Yergeni hills Russia 53 J7
Yergoğu Romania see Giurgiu
Yeriho West Bank see Jericho
Yerilla Australia 135 C7
Yerington NV U.S.A. 158 D2
Yerköy Turkey 112 D3
Yerla r. India 106 B2
Yermak Kazakh. see Aksu
Yermakovo Russia 90 B1
Yermak Plateau sea feature Arctic Ocean 189 H1
Yermentau Kazakh. see Yereymentau
Yermo Mex. 166 D3
Yermo CA U.S.A. 158 E4
Yerofey Pavlovich Russia 90 A1
Yerres r. France 62 C6
Yërsha r. Russia 52 L2
Yershov Russia 53 K6

Yertsevo Russia 52 I3
Yeruḥam Israel 107 B4
Yerupaja mt. Peru 176 C6
Yerushalayim Israel/West Bank see Jerusalem
Yeruslan r. Russia 53 J6
Yesagyo Myanmar 86 A2
Yesan S. Korea 91 B5
Yesik Kazakh. 98 B4
Yesil' Kazakh. 100 F1
Yesil' r. Kazakh./Russia 102 D1
Yeşilhisar Turkey 112 D3
Yeşilırmak r. Turkey 112 E2
Yeşilova Burdur Turkey 69 M6
Yeşilova Yozgat Turkey see Sorgun
Yespe Kazakh. 98 A4
Yessentuki Russia 113 F1
Yessey Russia 77 L3
Yes Tor hill U.K. 59 C8
Yêtatang China see Baqên
Yetman Australia 138 E2
Ye-U Myanmar 86 A2
Yeu, Île d' i. France 66 C3
Yevdokimovskoye Russia see Krasnogvardeyskoye
Yevlakh Azer. see Yevlax
Yevlax Azer. 113 G2
Yevpatoriya Crimea 112 D1
Yevreyskaya Avtonomnaya Oblast' admin. div. Russia 90 D2
Yexian China see Laizhou
Yeyik China 99 C5
Yeysk Russia 53 H7
Yeyungou China 98 D4
Yezhou China see Jianshi
Yezhuga r. Russia 52 J2
Yezo i. Japan see Hokkaidō
Yezyaryshcha Belarus 52 F5
Y Fali U.K. see Valley
Y Fenni U.K. see Abergavenny
Y Fflint U.K. see Flint
Y Gelli Gandryll U.K. see Hay-on-Wye
Yialí i. Greece see Gyali
Yi'allaq, Gebel mt. Egypt see Yu'alliq, Jabal
Yialousa Cyprus see Aigialousa
Yi'an China 90 B3
Yianisádha i. Greece see Gianisada
Yiannitsá Greece see Giannitsa
Yibin Sichuan China 96 E2
Yibin Sichuan China 96 E2
Yibug Caka salt l. China 99 D6
Yichang China 97 F2
Yicheng Henan China see Zhumadian
Yicheng Hubei China 97 G2
Yicheng Shanxi China 95 G5
Yichuan Henan China 95 H5
Yichuan Shaanxi China 95 G5
Yichun Heilong. China 90 C3
Yichun Jiangxi China 97 G3
Yidu Hubei China see Zhicheng
Yidu Shandong China see Qingzhou
Yidun China 96 C2
Yifeng China 97 G2
Yiftaḥ Israel 107 B3
Yiggêtang China 94 D5
Yihatuoli China 94 D3
Yi He r. Henan China 95 H5
Yi He r. Shandong China 95 I5
Yihegaole China 95 H2
Yihuang China 97 H3
Yijun China 95 G5
Yilaha China 95 K1
Yilan China 90 C3
Yilan Taiwan 97 I3
Yıldız Dağları mts Turkey 69 L4
Yıldızeli Turkey 112 E3
Yilehuli Shan mts China 90 A2
Yiliang China 96 E3
Yiling China 97 F2
Yiliping China 99 F5
Yilong Heilong. China 90 B3
Yilong Sichuan China see Jincheng
Yilong Yunnan China see Shiping
Yilong Hu l. China 96 D4
Yimatu He r. China 95 I3
Yimianpo China 90 C3
Yimin He r. China 95 I1
Yinan China 95 I5
Yinbaing Myanmar 86 B3
Yincheng China see Dexing
Yinchuan China 94 F4
Yindarlgooda, Lake salt flat Australia 135 C7
Yingcheng China 97 G2
Yingde China 97 G3
Yinggehai China 97 F5
Yinggen China see Qiongzhong
Ying He r. China 97 H1
Yingjing China 96 D2
Yingkiong India 105 H3
Yingkou Liaoning China see Dashiqiao
Yingkou Liaoning China 95 J3
Yingpanshui China 94 F4
Yingshan China 97 G2
Yingtan China 97 H2
Yingtaoyuan China 95 H5
Yingxian China 95 H4
Yining Jiangxi China see Xiushui
Yining Xinjiang China 98 C4
Yining Xinjiang China 98 C4
Yinjiang China 97 F3
Yinkeng China 97 G3
Yinkengxu China see Yinkeng
Yinmabin Myanmar 86 A2
Yinnyein Myanmar 86 B3
Yin Shan mts China 95 G3
Yinxian China see Ningbo
Yi'ong Nongchang China 99 F7
Yi'ong Zangbo r. China 99 F7
Yipinglang China 96 D3
Yiquan China see Meitan
Yiran Co l. China 99 F6
Yirga Alem Eth. 122 D3
Yirol South Sudan 121 G4
Yirshi China 95 I2
Yirtkuq Bulak spring China 98 E4
Yirxie China see Yirshi
Yisa China see Honghe
Yishan Guangxi China see Yizhou
Yishan Jiangsu China see Guanyun
Yi Shan mt. China 95 I4
Yishui China 95 I5
Yishun Sing. 87 [inset]
Yíthion Greece see Gytheio
Yitiaoshan China see Jingtai
Yitong He r. China 90 B3
Yiwanquan China 94 C3
Yiwu Xinjiang China 94 C3
Yiwu Yunnan China 96 D4
Yiwulü Shan mts China 95 J3
Yixian China 95 J3
Yixing China 97 H2
Yiyang China 97 G2
Yiyuan China 95 I4
Yizheng China 97 H1
Yizhou Guangxi China 97 F3
Yizhou Liaoning China see Yixian
Yizra'el country Asia see Israel
Yläne Fin. 55 M6
Ylihärmä Fin. 54 M5
Yli-Ii Fin. 54 N4
Yli-Kärppä Fin. 54 N4
Ylikiiminki Fin. 54 O4
Yli-Kitka l. Fin. 54 P3
Ylistaro Fin. 54 M5
Ylitornio Fin. 54 M3
Ylivieska Fin. 54 N4
Ylöjärvi Fin. 55 M6
Ymer Ø i. Greenland 147 P2
Ynys Enlli i. U.K. see Bardsey Island
Ynys Môn i. U.K. see Anglesey
Yoakum TX U.S.A. 161 D6
Yoder IN U.S.A. 164 C3
Yodo-gawa r. Japan 92 B4
Yogan, Cerro mt. Chile 178 B8
Yogo Japan 92 C3
Yogyakarta Java Indon. 85 E4
Yogyakarta admin. dist. Indon. 85 E5
Yoho National Park Canada 150 G5
Yoigilanglêb He r. China 99 G6
Yojoa, Lago de l. Hond. 166 [inset] I6
Yōka Japan see Yabu
Yokadouma Cameroon 121 E4
Yokawa Japan 92 B4
Yokkaichi Japan 92 C4
Yoko Cameroon 120 E4
Yokohama Japan 93 F3
Yokokawa Japan 93 E2
Yokoshibahikari Japan 93 G3
Yokosuka Japan 93 F3
Yokote Japan 91 F5
Yokoze Japan 93 F3
Yola Nigeria 120 E4
Yolaina, Serranías de mts Nicaragua 166 [inset] I7
Yolo CA U.S.A. 158 C2
Yolombo Dem. Rep. Congo 122 C4
Ýolöten Turkm. 111 F2
Yoloxóchitl Mex. 167 F5
Yoluk Mex. 167 I4
Yom, Mae Nam r. Thai. 86 C4
Yomou Guinea 120 C4
Yomuka Indon. 81 J8
Yonaguni-jima i. Japan 97 I3
Yŏnan N. Korea 91 B5
Yonezawa Japan 91 F5
Yong'an Chongqing China see Fengjie
Yong'an Fujian China 97 H3
Yongbei China see Yongsheng
Yongchang China 94 E4
Yongcheng China 95 I5
Yongcong China 97 F3
Yongdeng China 94 E4
Yongding Fujian China 97 H3
Yongding Yunnan China see Fumin
Yongding Yunnan China see Yongren
Yongdinghe Ganqu r. China 95 I4
Yongfeng Jiangxi China 97 G3
Yongfeng Xinjiang China 98 D4
Yongfu China 97 F3
Yonghe China 95 G4
Yŏnghŭng N. Korea 91 B5
Yŏnghŭng-man b. N. Korea 91 B5
Yongjing Gansu China 94 E5
Yongjing Guizhou China see Xifeng
Yongkang Yunnan China 96 C3
Yongkang Zhejiang China 97 I2
Yongle China see Zhen'an
Yongnian China 95 H4
Yongning Guangxi China 97 F4
Yongning Jiangxi China see Tonggu
Yongning Ningxia China 94 F4
Yongning Sichuan China see Xuyong
Yongping China 96 C3
Yongqing China see Qingshui
Yongren China 96 D3
Yongsheng China 96 D3
Yongshou China 95 G5
Yongshun China 97 F2
Yongtai China 97 H3
Yongxi China see Nayong
Yongxin China 97 G3
Yongxing Hunan China 97 G3
Yongxing Shaanxi China 95 G4
Yongxiu China 97 G2
Yongyang China see Weng'an
Yongzhou China 97 F3
Yonkers NY U.S.A. 165 I3
Yopal Col. 176 D2
Yopurga China 98 B5
Yoquivo Mex. 166 D3
Yordu India 104 C2
Yorii Japan 93 F2
York Australia 135 B7
York Canada 164 F2
York U.K. 58 F5
York AL U.S.A. 161 F5
York NE U.S.A. 160 D3
York PA U.S.A. 165 G4
York, Cape Australia 136 C1
York, Kap c. Greenland see Innaanganeq
York, Vale of valley U.K. 58 F4
Yorke Peninsula Australia 137 B7
York Mountains AK U.S.A. 148 F2
Yorkshire Dales National Park U.K. 58 E4
Yorkshire Wolds hills U.K. 58 G5
Yorkton Canada 151 K5
Yorktown VA U.S.A. 165 G5
Yorkville IL U.S.A. 160 F3
Yoro Hond. 166 [inset] I6
Yōrō Japan 92 C3
Yoroi-zaki pt Japan 92 C4
Yoronga i. Moluccas Indon. 83 D3
Yöröö Gol r. Mongolia 94 F1
Yorosso Mali 120 C3
Yosano Japan 92 B3
Yosemite KY U.S.A. 164 C5
Yosemite National Park CA U.S.A. 158 D3
Yoshida Saitama Japan 93 F2
Yoshida Shizuoka Japan 93 E4
Yoshii Japan 93 E2
Yoshima Japan 93 G1
Yoshino Japan 92 B4
Yoshinodani Japan 92 C2
Yoshino-gawa r. Japan 92 B4
Yoshino-Kumano Kokuritsu-kōen nat. park Japan 92 C5
Yoshkar-Ola Russia 52 J4
Yösöndzüyl Mongolia 94 E2
Yos Sudarso i. Indon. see Dolok, Pulau
Yotsukaidō Japan 93 G3
Yotsukura Japan 93 G1
Yotvata Israel 107 B5
Youbou Canada 150 E5
Youdunzi China 99 E5
Youghal Ireland 61 E6
Young Australia 138 D5
Young AZ U.S.A. 159 H4
Younghusband, Lake salt flat Australia 137 B6
Younghusband Peninsula Australia 137 B7
Young Island Antarctica 188 H2
Youngstown Canada 151 I5
Youngstown OH U.S.A. 164 E3
Youshashan China 99 E5
You Shui r. China 97 F2
Youssoufia Morocco 64 C5
Youvarou Mali 120 C3
Youxi China 97 H3
Youxian China 97 G3
Youyang China 97 F2
Youyi China 90 C3
Youyi Feng mt. China/Russia 98 D2
Yovon Tajik. 111 H2
Yowah watercourse Australia 138 B2
Yozgat Turkey 112 D3
Ypres Belgium see Ieper
Yreka CA U.S.A. 156 C4
Yrghyz Kazakh. see Yrgyz
Yrgyz Kazakh. 102 B2
Yrgyz r. Kazakh. 102 B2
Yr Wyddfa mt. U.K. see Snowdon
Yser r. France 62 C4
also known as IJzer (Belgium)
Ysselsteyn Neth. 62 F3
Ystad Sweden 55 H9
Ystwyth r. U.K. 59 C6
Ysyk-Ata Kyrg. 98 A4
Ysyk-Köl Kyrg. see Balykchy
Ysyk-Köl admin. div. Kyrg. 98 B4

▶Ysyk-Köl salt l. Kyrg. 102 E3
5th largest lake in Asia.

Ythan r. U.K. 60 G3
Y Trallwng U.K. see Welshpool
Ytyk-Kyuyel' Russia 77 O3
Yu i. Moluccas Indon. 83 D3
Yu'alliq, Jabal mt. Egypt 107 A4
Yuan'an China 97 F2
Yuanbaoshan China 95 I3
Yuanbao Shan mt. China 97 F3
Yuanjiang Hunan China 97 G2
Yuanjiang Yunnan China 96 D4
Yuan Jiang r. Hunan China 97 F2
Yuan Jiang r. Yunnan China 96 D4
Yuanjiazhuang China see Foping
Yuanlin China 95 J1
Yuanling China 97 F2
Yuanma China see Yuanmou
Yuanmou China 96 D3
Yuanping China 95 H4
Yuanqu China 95 G5
Yuanquan China see Guazhou
Yuanshan China see Lianping
Yuanshanzi China 94 D4
Yuanyang China see Xinjie
Yuasa Japan 92 B4
Yub'ā i. Saudi Arabia 112 D6
Yuba City CA U.S.A. 158 C2
Yubei China 96 E2
Yuben' Tajik. 111 I2
Yucatán pen. Mex. 167 H5
Yucatán state Mex. 167 H4
Yucatan Channel Cuba/Mex. 167 I4
Yucca AZ U.S.A. 159 F4
Yucca Lake NV U.S.A. 158 E3
Yucca Valley CA U.S.A. 158 E4
Yucheng Henan China 95 H5
Yucheng Shandong China 95 I4
Yucheng Sichuan China see Ya'an
Yuci China see Jinzhong
Yudi Shan mt. China 90 A1
Yudu China 97 G3
Yuelai China see Huachuan
Yueliang Pao l. China 95 J2
Yuendumu Australia 134 E5
Yuen Long H.K. China 97 [inset]
Yueqing China 97 I2
Yuexi China 97 H2
Yueyang Hunan China 97 G2
Yueyang Hunan China 97 G2
Yueyang Sichuan China see Anyue
Yug r. Russia 52 J3
Yugan China 97 H2
Yugawara Japan 93 F3
Yugê China 99 F6
Yugorsk Russia 51 S3
Yuhang China 97 I2
Yuhu China see Eryuan
Yuhuan China 97 I2
Yuhuang Ding mt. China 95 I4
Yui Japan 93 E3
Yuin Australia 135 B6
Yu Jiang r. China 97 F4
Yukagirskoye Ploskogor'ye plat. Russia 77 Q3
Yukamenskoye Russia 52 L4
Yukarı Sakarya Ovaları plain Turkey 69 N5
Yukarısarıkaya Turkey 112 D3
Yūki Japan 93 F2
Yuki r. AK U.S.A. 148 H2
Yukon admin. div. Canada 149 N3

▶Yukon r. Canada/U.S.A. 148 F3
5th longest river in North America.

Yukon-Charley Rivers National Preserve nature res. AK U.S.A. 149 L2
Yukon Crossing (abandoned) Canada 149 M3
Yukon Delta AK U.S.A. 148 F3
Yukon Flats National Wildlife Refuge nature res. AK U.S.A. 149 K2
Yüksekova Turkey 113 G3
Yulara Australia 135 E6
Yule r. Australia 134 B5
Yuleba Australia 138 D1
Yulee FL U.S.A. 163 D6
Yuli China 98 D4
Yulin Guangxi China 97 F4
Yulin Shaanxi China 95 G4
Yulong Xueshan mt. China 96 D3
Yuma AZ U.S.A. 159 F5
Yuma CO U.S.A. 160 C3
Yuma Desert AZ U.S.A. 159 F5
Yumco China 99 D7
Yumen Gansu China 94 D3
Yumen Gansu China see Laojunmiao
Yumendong China 94 D4
Yumenguan China 98 F4
Yumenzhen China see Yumen
Yumin China 98 C3
Yumt Uul mt. Mongolia 94 D2
Yumurtalık Turkey 107 B1
Yuna Australia 135 A7
Yunak Turkey 112 C3
Yunan China 97 F4
Yunaska Island AK U.S.A. 148 E5
Yuncheng Shandong China 95 H5
Yuncheng Shanxi China 95 G5
Yundamindera Australia 135 C7
Yunfu China 97 G4
Yungas reg. Bol. 176 E7
Yungui Gaoyuan plat. China 96 D3
Yunhe Jiangsu China see Pizhou
Yunhe Yunnan China see Heqing
Yunhe Zhejiang China 97 H2
Yunjinghong China see Jinghong
Yunkai Dashan mts China 97 F4
Yünlin Taiwan see Douliu
Yunling China see Yunxiao
Yun Ling mts China 96 C3
Yunlong China 96 C3
Yunmeng China 97 G2
Yunmenling China see Junmenling
Yunnan prov. China 96 D3
Yunta Australia 137 B7
Yunt Dağı mt. Turkey 107 A1
Yunxi Hubei China 97 F1
Yunxi Sichuan China see Yanting
Yunxian Hubei China 97 F1
Yunxian Yunnan China 96 D3
Yunxiao China 97 H4
Yunyang Chongqing China 97 F2
Yunyang Henan China 97 G1
Yuping Guizhou China see Libo
Yuping Guizhou China 97 F3
Yuping Yunnan China see Pingbian
Yuqing China 96 E3
Yura Japan 92 B5
Yura-gawa r. Japan 92 B3
Yurayir National Park Australia 138 F2
Yurba Co l. China 99 D6
Yürekli Turkey 107 B1
Yurga Russia 76 J4
Yurihonjō Japan 91 F5
Yuriria Mex. 168 D4
Yurungkax He r. China 99 C5
Yur'ya Russia 52 K4
Yur'yakha r. Russia 52 L2
Yuryev Estonia see Tartu
Yur'yevets Russia 52 I4
Yur'yev-Pol'skiy Russia 52 H4
Yuscarán Hond. 166 [inset] I6
Yushan China 97 H2
Yu Shan mt. Taiwan 97 I4
Yushe China 95 H4
Yushino (abandoned) Russia 52 L1
Yushkozero Russia 54 R4
Yushu Jilin China 90 B3
Yushu Qinghai China 96 C1
Yushugou China 98 D4
Yushuwan China see Huaihua
Yusufeli Turkey 113 F2
Yus'va Russia 51 Q4
Yuta West Bank see Yaṭṭah
Yutai China 95 I5
Yutan China see Ningxiang
Yutian Hebei China 95 I4
Yutian Xinjiang China 99 C5
Yutiangao China 95 I3
Yūtō Japan 92 D4
Yuwang China 94 F4
Yuxi Guizhou China see Daozhen
Yuxi Hubei China 97 F2
Yuxi Yunnan China 96 D3
Yuxian Hebei China 95 H4
Yuxian Shanxi China 95 H4
Yuyangguan China 97 F2
Yuyao China 97 I2
Yuzawa Japan 91 F5
Yuzha Russia 52 I4
Yuzhno-Kamyshovyy Khrebet ridge Russia 90 F3
Yuzhno-Kuril'sk Russia 90 G3
Yuzhno-Muyskiy Khrebet mts Russia 89 K1
Yuzhno-Sakhalinsk Russia 90 F3
Yuzhno-Sukhokumsk Russia 113 G1
Yuzhnoukrayins'k Ukr. 53 F7
Yuzhnyy Russia see Adyk
Yuzhnyy, Ostrov i. Russia 76 G2
Yuzhnyy Altay, Khrebet mts Kazakh. 98 D2
Yuzhong China 94 F5
Yuzhou Chongqing China see Chongqing
Yuzhou Hebei China see Yuxian
Yuzhou Henan China 95 H5
Yuzovka Ukr. see Donets'k
Yuzuruha-yama hill Japan 92 A4
Yverdon-les-Bains Switz. 66 H3
Yvetot France 66 E2
Ywamun Myanmar 86 A2

Zaamin Uzbek. see Zomin
Zaandam Neth. 62 E2
Zaatari Jordan see Az Za'tarī4431084.99
Zab, Monts du mts Alg. 67 I6
Zabānābād Iran 110 E3
Zabaykal'sk Russia 95 I1
Zabaykal'skiy Kray admin. div. Russia 95 H1
Zabīd Yemen 108 F7
Zābolī Iran see Mehrestān
Zabqung China 99 D7
Zacapa Guat. 167 H6
Zacapu Mex. 167 E5
Zacatal Mex. 167 H5
Zacatecas Mex. 168 D4
Zacatecas state Mex. 161 C8
Zacatecoluca El Salvador 166 [inset] H6
Zacatepec Mex. 167 F5
Zacatlán Mex. 167 F5
Zacharo Greece 69 I6
Zacoalco Mex. 168 D4
Zacualpán Mex. 167 F5
Zacynthus i. Greece see Zakynthos
Zadar Croatia 68 F2
Zadetkale Kyun i. Myanmar 87 B5
Zadetkyi Kyun i. Myanmar 87 B5
Zadi Myanmar 87 B4
Zadoi China 99 F6
Zadonsk Russia 53 H5
Za'farâna Egypt see Za'farānah
Za'farānah Egypt 112 D5
Zafer Adaları is Cyprus see Kleides Islands
Zafer Burnu c. Cyprus see Apostolos Andreas, Cape
Zafora i. Greece see Sofrana
Zafra Spain 67 C4
Zagazig Egypt see Az Zaqāzīq
Zaghdeh well Iran 110 E3
Zaghouan Tunisia 68 D6
Zagorsk Russia see Sergiyev Posad

▶Zagreb Croatia 68 F2
Capital of Croatia.

Zagros, Kūhhā-ye mts Iran see Zagros Mountains
Zagros Mountains Iran 110 B3
Zagunao China see Lixian
Za'gya Zangbo r. China 99 E7
Zāhedān Iran 111 F4
Zahir Pir Pak. 111 H4
Zaḥlah Lebanon see Zahlé
Zahlé Lebanon 107 B3
Zähmet Turkm. 111 F2
Ẓahrān Saudi Arabia 108 F6
Zahrez Chergui salt pan Alg. 67 H6
Zahrez Rharbi salt pan Alg. 67 H6
Zainlha China see Xiaojin
Zainsk Russia 52 L5
Zaire country Africa see Congo, Democratic Republic of the
Zaïre r. Congo/Dem. Rep. Congo see Congo
Zaječar Serbia 69 J3
Zaka Zimbabwe 123 D6
Zakamensk Russia 94 E1
Zakataly Azer. see Zaqatala
Zakháro Greece see Zacharo
Zakhmet Turkm. see Zähmet
Zakhodnyaya Dzvina r. Europe see Zapadnaya Dvina
Zākhū/Zaxo Iraq 113 F3
Zákinthos i. Greece see Zakynthos
Zakopane Poland 57 Q6
Zakouma, Parc National de nat. park Chad 121 E3
Zakwaski, Mount Canada 150 F5
Zakynthos Greece 69 I6
Zakynthos i. Greece 69 I6
Zala China 99 F7
Zalaegerszeg Hungary 68 G1
Zalai-domsag hills Hungary 68 G1
Zalamea de la Serena Spain 67 D4
Zalantun China 95 J2
Zalari Russia 88 I2
Zalău Romania 69 J1
Zaleski OH U.S.A. 164 D4
Ẓalim Saudi Arabia 108 F5
Zalingei Sudan 121 F3
Ẓalmā, Jabal az mt. Saudi Arabia 108 E4
Zama Japan 93 F3
Zama City Canada 150 G3
Zambales Mountains Luzon Phil. 82 C3
Zambeze r. Africa 123 C5 see Zambezi

▶Zambezi r. Africa 123 C5
4th longest river in Africa.
Also known as Zambeze.

Zambezi Zambia 123 C5
Zambia country Africa 123 C5
Zamboanga Mindanao Phil. 82 C5
Zamboanga Peninsula Mindanao Phil. 82 C5
Zamboanguita Negros Phil. 82 C4
Zamfara watercourse Nigeria 120 D3
Zamīndāwar reg. Afgh. 111 F4
Zamkog China see Zamtang
Zamora Ecuador 176 C4
Zamora Spain 67 D3
Zamora de Hidalgo Mex. 168 D5
Zamość Poland 53 D6
Zamost'ye Poland see Zamość
Zamtang China 96 D1
Zamuro, Sierra del mts Venez. 176 F3
Zanaga Congo 122 B4
Zanatepec Mex. 167 G5
Zancle Sicily Italy see Messina
Zanda China 99 B7
Zandamela Moz. 125 L3
Zandvliet Belgium 62 E3
Zane Hills AK U.S.A. 148 H2
Zanesville OH U.S.A. 164 D4
Zangguy China 99 B5
Zangsêr Kangri mt. China 99 D6
Zangskar reg. India see Zanskar
Zangskar Mountains India see Zanskar Mountains
Zanhuang China 95 H4
Zanjān Iran 110 C2
Zanjān Rūd r. Iran 110 B2
Ẓannah, Jabal aẓ hill U.A.E. 110 D5
Zanskar r. India 99 B6
Zanskar reg. India 104 D2
Zanskar Mountains India 104 D2
Zante i. Greece see Zakynthos
Zanthus Australia 135 C7
Zanūghān Iran 110 E3
Zanzibar Tanz. 123 D4
Zanzibar Island Tanz. 123 D4
Zaosheng China 95 G5
Zaoshi Hubei China 97 G2
Zaoshi Hunan China 97 G3
Zaouatallaz Alg. 120 D2
Zaouet el Kahla Alg. see Bordj Omer Driss
Zaoyang China 97 G1
Zaoyangzhan China 97 G1
Zaoyuan China 98 D3
Zaozernyy Russia 77 K4
Zapadnaya Dvina r. Europe 52 F5
also known as Dvina or Zakhodnyaya Dzvina. English form Western Dvina
Zapadnaya Dvina Russia 52 G4
Zapadni Rodopi mts Bulg. 69 J4
Zapadno-Kazakhstanskaya Oblast' admin. div. Kazakh. see Zapadnyy Kazakhstan
Zapadno-Sakhalinskiye Gory mts Russia 90 F2
Zapadno-Sibirskaya Nizmennost' plain Russia see West Siberian Plain
Zapadno-Sibirskaya Ravnina plain Russia see West Siberian Plain
Zapadnyy Alamedin, Pik mt. Kyrg. 98 A4
Zapadnyy Chink Ustyurta esc. Kazakh. 113 I2
Zapadnyy Kazakhstan admin. div. Kazakh. 51 Q6
Zapadnyy Kil'din Russia 54 S2
Zapadnyy Sayan reg. Russia 88 F2
Zapata TX U.S.A. 161 D7
Zapata, Península de pen. Cuba 163 D8
Zapiga Chile 176 E7
Zapolyarnyy Russia 54 Q2
Zapol'ye Russia 52 H4
Zaporizhzhya Ukr. 53 G7
Zaporozh'ye Ukr. see Zaporizhzhya
Zapug China 99 C6
Zaqatala Azer. 113 G2
Zaqên China 99 F6
Za Qu r. China 96 C2
Zaqungngomar mt. China 99 E6
Zara China see Zari
Zara Croatia see Zadar
Zara Turkey 112 E3
Zarābād Iran 110 B2
Zarafshan Uzbek. see Zarafshon
Zarafshon Uzbek. 102 B3
Zarafshon, Qatorkŭhi mts Tajik. 111 G2
Zaragoza Mex. 167 E2
Zaragoza Spain 67 F3
Zaraḥ Sharan Afgh. 111 H3
Zarand Iran 110 E4
Zarang China 99 B7
Zaranikh Protected Area nature res. Egypt 107 B4
Zaranj Afgh. 111 F4
Zarasai Lith. 55 O9
Zárate Arg. 178 E4
Zaraysk Russia 53 H5
Zaraza Venez. 176 E2
Zarbdor Uzbek. 111 H1
Zärdab Azer. 53 J8
Zarechensk Russia 54 Q3
Zāreh Iran 110 C3
Zarembo Island AK U.S.A. 149 N4
Zargun mt. Pak. 111 G4
Zari China 99 E7
Zaria Nigeria 120 D3
Zarichne Ukr. 53 E6
Zarifête, Col des pass Alg. 67 F6
Zaring China 99 E7
Zarinsk Russia 88 E2
Zarmardān Afgh. 111 F3
Zarneh Iran 110 B3

Zărneşti Romania 69 K2
Zarqā' Jordan see Az Zarqā'
Zarqā', Nahr az r. Jordan 107 B3
Zarubino Russia 90 C4
Zaruga-dake mt. Japan 93 E3
Żary Poland 57 O5
Zarya Russia 53 H5
Zarzis Tunisia 64 G5
Zashchita Kazakh. 98 C2
Zasheyek Russia 54 Q3
Zaskar reg. India see Zanskar
Zaskar Range mts India see Zanskar Mountains
Zaslawye Belarus 55 O9
Zastron S. Africa 125 H6
Za'tarī, Wādī az watercourse Jordan 107 C3
Zaterechnyy Russia 53 J7
Zauche reg. Germany 63 M2
Zaunguzskiye Karakumy des. Turkm. see Üngüz Angyrsyndaky Garagum
Zautla Mex. 167 F5
Zavala Moz. 125 L3
Zavalla TX U.S.A. 161 E6
Zavetnoye Russia 53 I7
Zavety Il'icha Russia 90 F2
Zavidovići Bos. & Herz. 68 H2
Zavitaya Russia see Zavitinsk
Zavitinsk Russia 90 C2
Zavolzhsk Russia 52 I4
Zavolzh'ye Russia see Zavolzhsk
Závora, Ponta pt Moz. 125 L3
Zawa Qinghai China 94 E4
Zawa Xinjiang China 99 B5
Zawiercie Poland 57 Q5
Zawīlah Libya 121 E2
Zāwiyah, Jabal az hills Syria 107 C2
Zawr, Ra's az pt Saudi Arabia 113 H6
Zaxoi China 99 E7
Zaybāk Afgh. 104 B1
Zaydī, Wādī az watercourse Syria 107 C3
Zaysan Kazakh. 102 F2
Zaysan, Lake Kazakh. 102 F2
Zaysan, Ozero l. Kazakh. see Zaysan, Lake
Zayü China see Zhigang
Zayü Qu r. China/India 105 I3
Žďár nad Sázavou Czech Rep. 57 O6
Zdolbuniv Ukr. 53 E6
Zdolbunov Ukr. see Zdolbuniv
Zealand i. Denmark 55 G9
Zebulon KY U.S.A. 164 D5
Zedelgem Belgium 62 D3
Zeebrugge Belgium 62 D3
Zeeland MI U.S.A. 164 B2
Zeerust S. Africa 125 H3
Zefat Israel 107 B3
Zehdenick Germany 63 N2
Zeil, Mount Australia 135 F5
Zeil am Main Germany 63 K4
Zeist Neth. 62 F2
Zeitz Germany 63 M3
Zêkog China 94 E5
Zekti China 98 C4
Zela Turkey see Zile
Zelennik Russia 52 J3
Zelenoborsk Russia 51 S3
Zelenoborskiy Russia 54 R3
Zelenodol'sk Russia 52 K5
Zelenogorsk Russia 55 P6
Zelenograd Russia 52 H4
Zelenogradsk Russia 55 L9
Zelenokumsk Russia 113 F1
Zelentsovo Russia 52 J4
Zelenyy, Ostrov i. Russia 90 G4
Zelinggou China 94 D4
Zell am See Austria 57 N7
Zellingen Germany 63 J5
Zelzate Belgium 62 D3
Žemaitijos nacionalinis parkas nat. park Lith. 55 L8
Zêmdasam China 96 D1
Zemetchino Russia 53 I5
Zémio Cent. Afr. Rep. 122 C3
Zemmora Alg. 67 G6
Zempoaltépetl, Nudo de mt. Mex. 168 E5
Zengcheng China 97 G4
Zenica Bos. & Herz. 68 G2
Zenifim, Nahal watercourse Israel 107 B4
Zennor U.K. 59 B8
Zenta Serbia see Senta
Zenzach Alg. 67 H6
Zepu China 99 B5
Zerah, Gowd-e plain Afgh. 111 F4
Zeravshanskiy Khrebet mts Tajik. see Zarafshon, Qatorkŭhi
Zerbst/Anhalt Germany 63 M3
Zerenike Reserve nature res. Egypt see Zaranikh Protected Area
Zerf Germany 62 G5
Zernien Germany 63 K1
Zernitz Germany 63 M2
Zernograd Russia 53 I7
Zernovoy Russia see Zernograd
Zêsum China 99 E7
Zêtang China see Nêdong
Zetel Germany 63 H1
Zeulenroda Germany 63 L4
Zeven Germany 63 J1
Zevenaar Neth. 62 G3
Zevgari, Cape Cyprus 107 A2
Zeya Russia 90 B1
Zeya r. Russia 90 B2
Zeydar Iran 110 E2
Zeydī Iran 111 F5
Zeyskiy Zapovednik nature res. Russia 90 B1
Zeysko-Bureinskaya Vpadina depr. Russia 90 C2
Zeyskoye Vodokhranilishche resr Russia 90 B1
Zeytin Burnu c. Cyprus see Elaia, Cape
Zêzere r. Port. 67 B4
Zezhou China 95 H5
Zgharta Lebanon 107 B2
Zghorta Lebanon see Zgharta
Zgierz Poland 57 Q5
Zhabinka Belarus 55 N10
Zhaggo China see Luhuo
Zhaglag China 96 C1
Zhag'yab China 96 C2
Zhaksy Sarysu watercourse Kazakh. see Sarysu
Zhalanash Almatinskaya Oblast' Kazakh. 98 B4
Zhalanash Kostanayskaya Oblast' Kazakh. see Damdy
Zhalgyztobe Kazakh. 98 C2
Zhalpaktal Kazakh. 51 P6
Zhalpaqtal Kazakh. see Zhalpaktal
Zhaltyr Kazakh. 102 C1
Zhambyl Karagandinskaya Oblast' Kazakh. 102 D2
Zhambyl Zhambylskaya Oblast' Kazakh. see Taraz
Zhambylskaya Oblast' admin. div. Kazakh. 98 A3
Zhameuka Kazakh. 98 C3
Zhamo China see Bomi
Zhanakala Kazakh. 51 Q6
Zhana Kanay Kazakh. 98 C2
Zhanakazan Kazakh. 51 P6
Zhanakorgan Kazakh. 102 C3
Zhanang China 99 E7
Zhanaortalyk Kazakh. 98 A3
Zhanaozen Kazakh. 100 E2
Zhanatalan Kazakh. 98 B4
Zhanatas Kazakh. 102 C3
Zhanbei China 90 B2
Zhangaözen Kazakh. see Zhanaozen
Zhanga Qazan Kazakh. see Zhanakazan
Zhangaqorghan Kazakh. see Zhanakorgan
Zhangatas Kazakh. see Zhanatas
Zhangbang China 97 G2
Zhangbei China 95 H3
Zhangcheng China see Yongtai
Zhangcun China 97 H1
Zhangdian China see Zibo
Zhanggu China see Danba
Zhangguangcai Ling mts China 90 C3
Zhanggutai China 95 J3
Zhanghua Taiwan 97 I3
Zhangjiachuan China 94 F5
Zhangjiajie China 97 F2
Zhangjiakou China 95 H3
Zhangjiang China see Taoyuan
Zhangjiapan China see Jingbian
Zhangla China 96 D1
Zhangling China 90 A1
Zhanglou China 97 H1
Zhangping China 97 H3
Zhangqiang China 90 A4
Zhangqiao China 97 H1
Zhangqiu China 95 I4
Zhangshu China 97 G2
Zhangwu China 95 J3
Zhangxian China 94 F5
Zhangye China 94 E4
Zhangzhou China 97 H3
Zhangzi China 95 H4
Zhanhe China see Zhanbei
Zhanhua China 95 I4
Zhanibek Kazakh. 51 P6
Zhanjiang China 97 F4
Zhansugirov Kazakh. 98 B3
Zhao'an China 97 H4
Zhaodong China 90 B3
Zhaoge China see Qixian
Zhaojue China 96 D2
Zhaoliqiao China 97 G2
Zhaoping China 97 F3
Zhaoqing China 97 G4
Zhaoren China see Changwu
Zhaosu China 98 C4
Zhaosutai He r. China 95 J3
Zhaotong China 96 D3
Zhaoxian China 95 H4
Zhaoyang Hu l. China 95 I5
Zhaoyuan Heilong. China 90 B3
Zhaoyuan Shandong China 95 J4
Zhaozhou Hebei China see Zhaoxian
Zhaozhou Heilong. China 90 B3
Zharbulak Kazakh. 98 C3
Zhari Namco salt l. China 99 D7
Zharkamys Kazakh. 102 A2
Zharkent Kazakh. 102 F3
Zharkovskiy Russia 52 G5
Zharma Kazakh. 102 F2
Zharsuat (abandoned) Kazakh. 98 C3
Zharyk Kazakh. 98 C2
Zhashkiv Ukr. 53 F6
Zhashkov Ukr. see Zhashkiv
Zhaslyk Uzbek. see Jasliq
Zhaxi China see Weixin
Zhaxi Co salt l. China 99 D6
Zhaxigang Xizang China 99 B6
Zhaxigang Xizang China 99 E7
Zhaxizê China 96 C2
Zhaxizom China 99 D7
Zhayyq r. Kazakh./Russia see Ural
Zhdanov Ukr. see Mariupol'
Zhdanovsk Azer. see Beyläqan
Zhecheng China 95 H5
Zhedao China see Lianghe
Zhêhor China 96 D2
Zhejiang prov. China 97 I2
Zhekezhal Kazakh. 98 A2
Zhelaniya, Mys c. Russia 76 H2
Zheleznodorozhnyy Russia see Yemva
Zheleznodorozhnyy Uzbek. see Qo'ng'irot
Zheleznogorsk Russia 53 G5
Zhelou China see Ceheng
Zheltorangy Kazakh. 98 A3
Zheltyye Vody Ukr. see Zhovti Vody
Zhem Kazakh. see Emba
Zhem r. Kazakh. 102 A2
Zhemgang Bhutan 105 G4
Zhen'an China 97 F1
Zhenba China 96 E1
Zhengding China 95 H4
Zhenghe China 97 H3
Zhengjiakou China see Gucheng
Zhengjiatun China see Shuangliao
Zhengkou China see Gucheng
Zhenglan Qi China see Shangdu
Zhenglu China 94 E4
Zhengning China 95 G5
Zhengxiangbai Qi China see Ming'antu
Zhengyang China 97 G1
Zhengyangguan China 97 H1
Zhengzhou China 95 H5
Zhenhai China 97 I2
Zhenjiang China 97 H1
Zhenjiangguan China 96 D1
Zhenlai China 95 J2
Zhenning China 96 E3
Zhenping China 97 F2
Zhenwudong China see Ansai
Zhenxiong China 96 E3
Zhenyang China see Zhengyang
Zhenyuan Gansu China 95 F5
Zhenyuan Guizhou China 97 F3
Zherdevka Russia 53 I6
Zherong China 97 H3
Zheshart Russia 52 K3
Zhetysuskiy Alatau mts China/Kazakh. 102 E3
Zhêxam China 99 D7
Zhexi Shuiku resr China 97 F2
Zhezkazgan Kazakh. 102 C2
Zhezqazghan Kazakh. see Zhezkazgan
Zhicheng Hubei China 97 F2
Zhicheng Shandong China see Qingzhou
Zhicheng Zhejiang China see Changxing
Zhidan China 95 G4
Zhidoi China 99 F6
Zhifang China see Jiangxia
Zhigalovo Russia 88 J2
Zhigang China 96 C2
Zhigansk Russia 77 N3
Zhigong China see Yangxi
Zhigou China 95 I5
Zhigung China 99 E7
Zhijiang Hubei China 97 F2
Zhijiang Hunan China 86 E1
Zhijin China 96 E3
Zhiluo China 95 G5
Zhi Qu r. China see Yangtze
Zhishan China see Lingling
Zhitikara Kazakh. 100 F1
Zhitkovichi Belarus see Zhytkavichy
Zhitkur Russia 53 J6
Zhitomir Ukr. see Zhytomyr
Zhīvār Iran 110 B3
Zhiziluo China 96 C3
Zhlobin Belarus 53 F5
Zhmerinka Ukr. see Zhmerynka
Zhmerynka Ukr. 53 F6
Zhob Pak. 111 H4
Zhob r. Pak. 111 H3
Zholnuskau Kazakh. 98 C2
Zhong'an China see Fuyuan
Zhongba Guangdong China 97 G4
Zhongba Sichuan China see Jiangyou
Zhongba Xizang China 99 D7
Zhongduo China see Youyang
Zhongguo country Asia see China
Zhongguo Renmin Gongheguo country Asia see China
Zhonghe China see Xiushan
Zhongmou China 95 H5
Zhongning China 94 F4
Zhongping China see Huize
Zhongpu China 94 E4
Zhongshan research station Antarctica 188 E2
Zhongshan Guangdong China 97 G4
Zhongshan Guangxi China 97 F3
Zhongshan Guizhou China see Liupanshui
Zhongshu Yunnan China see Luxi
Zhongshu Yunnan China see Luliang
Zhongtai China see Lingtai
Zhongtiao Shan mts China 95 G5
Zhongwei China 94 F4
Zhongxin Guangdong China 97 G3
Zhongxin Yunnan China see Xamgyi'nyilha
Zhongxin Yunnan China see Huaping
Zhongxing Anhui China 97 H2
Zhongxing Jiangsu China see Siyang
Zhongxinzhan China 94 D5
Zhongyang China 95 G4
Zhongyang Shanmo mts Taiwan 97 I4
Zhongyaozhan China 90 B2
Zhongyicun China see Gucheng
Zhongyuan China 97 F5
Zhongzhai China 96 E1
Zhosaly Kazakh. 102 B2
Zhoucheng China 95 I5
Zhoujiajing China 94 E4
Zhoukou Henan China 97 G1
Zhoukou Sichuan China see Peng'an
Zhoukoudian tourist site China 95 H4
Zhouning China 97 H3
Zhoushan China 97 I2
Zhoushan Dao i. China 97 I2
Zhoushan Qundao is China 97 I2
Zhouzhi China 95 G5
Zhovti Vody Ukr. 53 G6
Zhuanghe China 95 J4
Zhuanglang China 94 F5
Zhubgyügoin China 96 C1
Zhucheng China 95 I5
Zhuchengzi China 90 B3
Zhudong Taiwan 97 I3
Zhugkyung China 94 D4
Zhugla China 99 F7
Zhugqu China 96 E1
Zhuhai China 97 G4
Zhuji China 97 I2
Zhujing China 97 I2
Zhukeng China 97 G4
Zhukovka Russia 53 G5
Zhukovskiy Russia 53 H5
Zhulong He r. China 95 H4
Zhumadian China 97 G1
Zhuokeji China 96 D2
Zhuolu China 95 H3
Zhuozhou China 95 I4
Zhuozi China 95 H3
Zhuozishan China see Zhuozi
Zhusandala, Step' plain Kazakh. 98 A3
Zhushan Hubei China 97 F1
Zhushan Hubei China see Xuan'en
Zhuxi China 97 F1
Zhuxiang China 97 H1
Zhuyang China see Dazhu
Zhuzhou Hunan China 97 G3
Zhuzhou Hunan China 97 G3
Zhydachiv Ukr. 53 E6
Zhympity Kazakh. 51 Q5
Zhytkavichy Belarus 55 O10
Zhytomyr Ukr. 53 F6
Zīā'ābād Iran 110 C3
Žiar nad Hronom Slovakia 57 Q6
Zibā salt pan Saudi Arabia 107 D4
Zibo China 95 I4
Zichang China 95 G4
Zicheng China see Zijin
Zicuirán Mex. 167 E5
Zidi Pak. 111 G5
Ziel, Mount Australia see Zeil, Mount
Zielona Góra Poland 57 O5
Ziemelkursas augstiene hills Latvia 55 M8
Zierenberg Germany 63 J3
Ziesar Germany 63 M2
Ziftá Egypt 112 C5
Zigê Tangco l. China 99 E6
Zīghan Libya 121 F2
Zigong China 96 E2
Ziguey Chad 121 E3
Ziguinchor Senegal 120 B3
Žīguri Latvia 55 O8
Zihuatanejo Mex. 168 D5
Zijin China 97 G4
Zijpenberg hill Neth. 62 G2
Ziketan China see Xinghai
Zile Turkey 112 D2
Žilina Slovakia 57 Q6
Zillah Libya 121 E2
Zima Russia 88 I2
Zimapán Mex. 167 F4
Zimatlán Mex. 167 F5
Zimba Zambia 123 C5
Zimbabwe country Africa 123 C5
Zimi Sierra Leone see Zimmi
Zimmerbude Russia see Svetlyy
Zimmi Sierra Leone 120 B4
Zimnicea Romania 69 K3
Zimniy Bereg coastal area Russia 52 H2
Zimovniki Russia 53 I7
Zimrīn Syria 107 B2
Zin Pak. 111 H4
Zin, Nahal watercourse Israel 107 B4
Zinave, Parque Nacional do nat. park Moz. 123 D6
Zinder Niger 120 D3
Zindo China 96 D2
Ziniaré Burkina Faso 120 C3
Zinjibār Yemen 108 G7
Zinoyevsk Ukr. see Kirovohrad
Zion IL U.S.A. 164 B2
Zion National Park UT U.S.A. 159 G3
Zionz Lake Canada 151 N5
Zippori Israel 107 B3
Zi Qu r. China 99 G6
Ziqudukou China 96 B1
Zirc Hungary 68 G1
Zirkel, Mount CO U.S.A. 156 G4
Zirkūh i. U.A.E. 110 D5
Zirndorf Germany 63 K5
Ziro India 105 H4
Zirreh Afgh. 111 F4
Zīr Rūd Iran 110 C4
Zi Shui r. China 89 K7
Zistersdorf Austria 57 P6
Zitácuaro Mex. 168 D5
Zitong China 96 E2
Zittau Germany 57 O5
Zitziana r. AK U.S.A. 149 J2
Zixi China 97 H3
Zixing China see Xingning
Ziyang Jiangxi China see Wuyuan
Ziyang Shaanxi China 97 F1
Ziyang Sichuan China 96 E2
Ziyaret Dağı hill Turkey 107 B1
Ziyuan China 97 F3
Ziyun China 96 E3
Ziz, Oued watercourse Morocco 64 D5
Zizhong China 96 E2
Zizhou China 95 G4
Zlatitsa Bulg. 69 K3
Zlatoustovsk Russia 90 D1
Zlín Czech Rep. 57 P6
Zmeinogorsk Russia 102 F1
Zmiyevka Russia 53 H5
Znamenka Kazakh. 98 B2
Znamenka Russia 53 I5
Znamenka Ukr. see Znam"yanka
Znam"yanka Ukr. 53 G6
Znojmo Czech Rep. 57 P6
Zoar S. Africa 124 E7
Zoco China 99 C6
Zoetermeer Neth. 62 E2
Zogainrawar China see Huashixia
Zogang China 96 C2
Zogqên China 96 C1
Zoidê Lhai China 99 E6
Zoigê China 96 D1
Zoji La pass India 104 C2
Zola S. Africa 125 H7
Zolder Belgium 62 F3
Zolochev Kharkivs'ka Oblast' Ukr. see Zolochiv
Zolochev L'vivs'ka Oblast' Ukr. see Zolochiv
Zolochiv Kharkivs'ka Oblast' Ukr. 53 G6
Zolochiv L'vivs'ka Oblast' Ukr. 53 E6
Zolotonosha Ukr. 53 G6
Zolotoye Russia 53 J6
Zolotoy Khrebet mts Russia 148 B2
Zolotukhino Russia 53 H5
▶Zomba Malawi 123 D5
Former capital of Malawi.
Zombor Serbia see Sombor
Zomin Uzbek. 111 H2
Zongjiafangzi China 94 D4
Zonguldak Turkey 69 N4
Zongxoi China 105 G3
Zongzhai China 94 D4
Zörbig Germany 63 M3
Zorgho Burkina Faso 120 C3
Zorgo Burkina Faso see Zorgho
Zorn r. France 63 I6
Żory Poland 57 Q5
Zossen Germany 63 N2
Zottegem Belgium 62 D4
Zouar Chad 121 E2
Zoucheng China 95 I5
Zouérat Mauritania 120 B2
Zoulang Nanshan mts China 94 D4
Zouping China 95 I4
Zousfana, Oued watercourse Alg. 64 D5
Zoushi China 97 F2
Zouxian China see Zoucheng
Zrenjanin Serbia 69 I2
Zschopau Germany 63 N4
Zschopau r. Germany 63 N3
Zschornewitz Germany 63 M3
Zuayyinī, Mishāsh az well Saudi Arabia 110 C5
Zubālah, Birkat waterhole Saudi Arabia 113 F5
Zubillaga Arg. 178 D5
Zubova Polyana Russia 53 I5
Zubtsov Russia 52 G4
Zuénoula Côte d'Ivoire 120 C4
Zug Switz. 66 I3
Zugdidi Georgia 113 F2
Zugspitze mt. Austria/Germany 57 M7
Zugu Nigeria 120 D3
Zuider Zee l. Neth. see IJsselmeer
Zuidhorn Neth. 62 G1
Zuid-Kennemerland, Nationaal Park nat. park Neth. 62 E2
Zuitai China see Kangxian
Zuitaizi China see Kangxian
Zuitou China see Taibai
Zújar r. Spain 67 D4
Zuli He r. China 94 F4
Zülpich Germany 62 G4
Zumba Ecuador 176 C4
Zumpango Mex. 167 F5
Zumpango del Río Mex. 167 F5
Zunheboto India 105 H4
Zunhua China 95 I3
Zuni NM U.S.A. 159 I4
Zuni watercourse Arizona/New Mexico U.S.A. 159 I4
Zuni Mountains NM U.S.A. 159 I4
Zun-Torey, Ozero l. Russia 95 H1
Zunyi Guizhou China 96 E3
Zunyi Guizhou China 96 E3
Zuo Jiang r. China/Vietnam 86 E2
Zuoquan China 95 H4
Zuoyun China 95 H4
Županja Croatia 68 H2
Zūrābād Iran 111 F3
Zürich Switz. 66 I3
Zurmat reg. Afgh. 111 H3
Zuru Nigeria 120 D3
Zurzuna Turkey see Çıldır
Zushi Japan 93 F3
Zutphen Neth. 62 G2
Zuwārah Libya 120 E1
Zuyevka Russia 52 K4
Zūzan Iran 111 E3
Zvishavane Zimbabwe 123 D6
Zvolen Slovakia 57 Q6
Zvornik Bos. & Herz. 69 H2
Zwedru Liberia 120 C4
Zweeloo Neth. 62 G2
Zweibrücken Germany 63 H5
Zweletemba S. Africa 124 D7
Zwelitsha S. Africa 125 H7
Zwethau Germany 63 N3
Zwettl Austria 57 O6
Zwickau Germany 63 M4
Zwochau Germany 63 M3
Zwolle Neth. 62 G2
Zwönitz Germany 63 M4
Zyablovo Russia 52 L4
Zygi Cyprus 107 A2
Zyryan Kazakh. see Zyryanovsk
Zyryanka Russia 77 Q3
Zyryanovsk Kazakh. 102 F2
Zyyi Cyprus see Zygi

Acknowledgements

Maps and data

Maps, design and origination by Collins Geo, HarperCollins Reference, Glasgow.
Illustrations created by HarperCollins Publishers unless otherwise stated.

General/Various themes: World Bank World Development Indicators
http://data.worldbank.org/data-catalog/world-development-indicators

Earthquake data (pp10–11): United States Geological Survey (USGS) National Earthquakes Information Center, Denver, USA.

Tropical Storms (pp12-13): National Oceanic and Atmospheric Administration (NOAA) National Hurricane Centre

Population map (pp16–17): 2005. Gridded Population of the World Version 3 (GPWv3). Palisades, NY: Socioeconomic Data and Applications Center (SEDAC), Columbia University. Available at: http://sedac.ciesn.columbia.edu/plue/gpw
http://www.ciesin.columbia.edu
United Nations Department of Economic and Social Affairs (UN DESA) World Population Prospects
http://esa.un.org/wpp/

Urbanization (pp18-19): United Nations Department of Economic and Social Affairs (UN DESA) World Urbanization Prospects http://esa.un.org/unpd/wup/

Communications (pp20-21): International Telecommunication Union (ITU), ICT ststistics
http://www.itu.int/en/ITU-D/Statistics/Pages/stat/default.aspx

Conflict (pp26-27): National Consortium for the Study of Terrorism and Responses to Terrorism (START). (2013). Global Terrorism Database (GTD).
http://www.start.umd.edu/gtd

Global Issues (pp28-29):International drugs trade - United Nations Office on Drugs and Crime (UNODC)
http://www.unodc.org/
HIV/AIDS - UNAIDS
http://www.unaids.org/

Environment (pp30-31): United Nations Environment Programme's World Conservation Monitoring Centre (UNEP-WCMC) http://unep-wcmc.org/ United Nations List of Protected Areas 2014

Coral reefs data (p31): World Resources Institute (WRI), Washington D.C., USA.

Desertification data (p31): U.S. Department of Agriculture Natural Resources Conservation Service.

Antarctica (p188): Antarctic Digital Database (versions1 and 2), ©Scientific Committee on Antarctic research (SCAR), Cambridge, UK.

Photographs and images

Page	Image	Credit
12–13	Hurricane Sandy	NASA Earth Observatory image by Robert Simmon with data courtesy of the NASA/NOAA GOES Project Science team
14–15	Cropland, Consuegra	Rick Barrentine / Corbis
	Tokyo	NASA Earth Observatory image courtesy Ron Beck, USGS Eros Data Center Satellite Systems Branch
	Mojave Desert	Keith Moore
	Larsen Ice Shelf	MODIS/NASA
16–17	Singapore	Wikipedia - Licenced under Creative Commons Attribution 1.0 Licence
	Kuna Indians	Danny Lehman / Corbis
18–19	Hong Kong	European Space Agency
24–25	London	QQ7/Shutterstock
	Malawi village	Magdanatka/Shutterstock
26–27	Refugee camp in Thailand	Liewluck/Shutterstock
28–29	Opium poppy	forbis/Shutterstock
	Ganga river, Varanasi	OlegD/Shutterstock
30–31	Deforestation, Itaipu	Images reproduced by kind permission of UNEP
	Aral Sea 1973, 1986, 2001	Images reproduced by kind permission of UNEP
	Aral Sea 2014	MODIS/NASA
	Great Barrier Reef	MODIS/NASA
32–33	Lake Chad	Images reproduced by kind permission of UNEP
	Tubarjal, Arabian Desert	Images reproduced by kind permission of UNEP
	Wax Lake Outlet	Landsat/NASA
	Athabasca Oil Sands	NASA/USGS
	Dubai	ASTER/NASA
34–35	Uluṟu (Ayers Rock)	GeoEye/Science Photo Library
36–37	Khor al Adaid	GeoEye/Science Photo Library
38–39	Taylor Valley	NASA image created by Jesse Allen, using data provided courtesy of NASA/GSFC/METI/ERSDAC/JAROS, and U.S./Japan ASTER Science Team.
40–41	Grand Coulee Dam	NASA image created by Jesse Allen, using Landsat data provided by the USGS
46–47	Iceland	MODIS/NASA
48–49	Bosporus	NASA/Johnson Space Center
72–73	Yangtze	MODIS/NASA
	Caspian Sea	MODIS/NASA
74–75	Timor	MODIS/NASA
	Beijing	GeoEye/Science Photo Library
116–117	Congo River	European Space Agency
	Lake Victoria	MODIS/NASA
118–119	Cape Town	esinel/Shutterstock
128–129	Heron Island	GeoEye/Science Photo Library
	Banks Peninsula	NASA
130–131	Noumea	NASA/Johnson Space Center
	Wellington	NASA/Johnson Space Center
142–143	Mississippi	ASTER/NASA
	Panama Canal	dazgee/Shutterstock
144–145	Mexicali	NASA
	The Bahamas	MODIS/NASA
172–173	Amazon / Rio Negro	NASA
	Tierra del Fuego	MODIS/NASA
174–175	Galapagos Islands	MODIS/NASA
	Falkland Islands	MODIS/NASA
180–181	Antarctica	Landsat Image Mosaic of Antarctica (LIMA) Project
182–183	Pacific Ocean globe	Anton Balazh/Shutterstock
	Atlantic Ocean globe	Anton Balazh/Shutterstock
	Indian Ocean globe	Anton Balazh/Shutterstock
	Antarctic Peninsula	MODIS/NASA

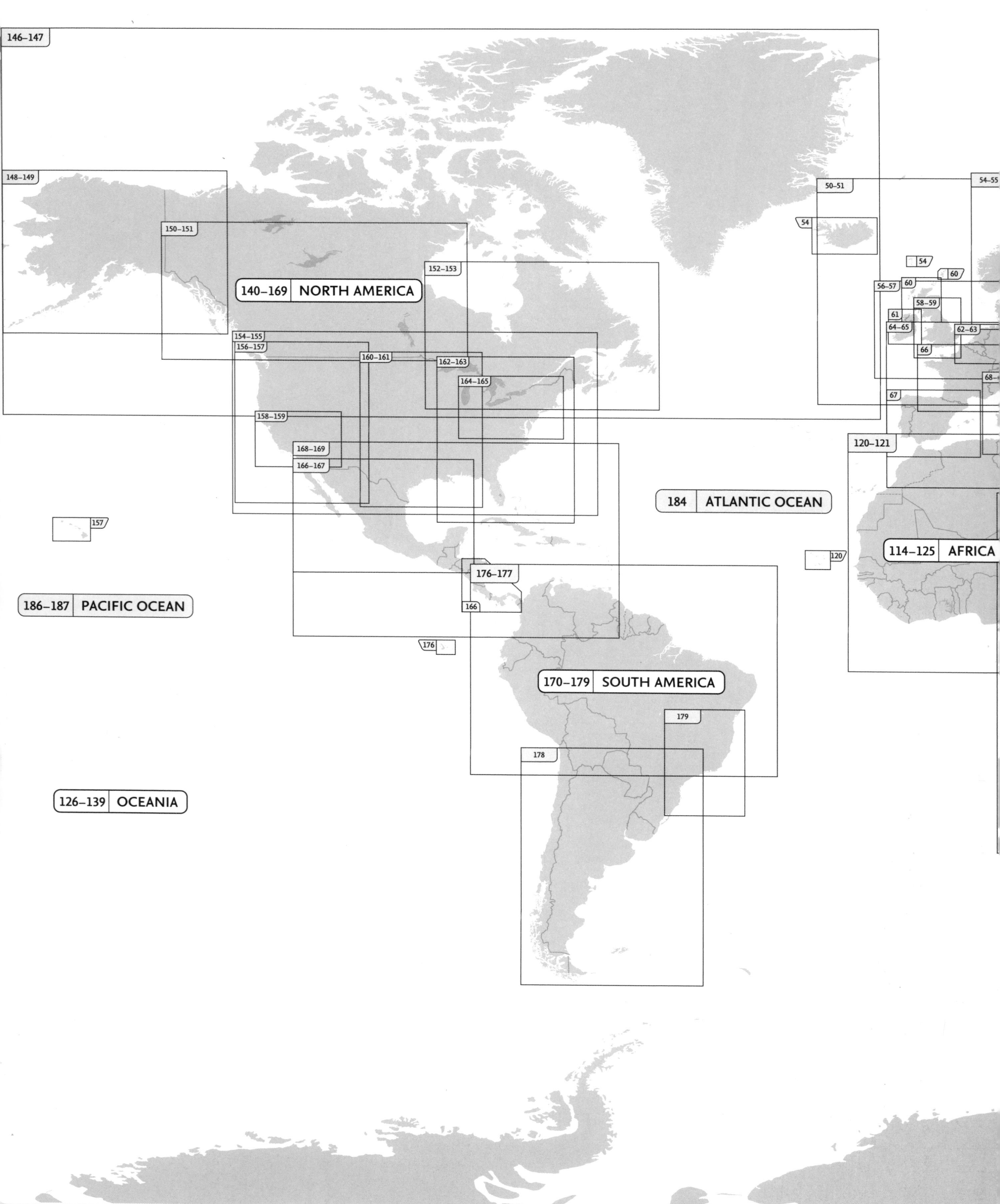

Find your map